English Pronouncing Dictionary

ENGLISH PHONETIC SYMBOLS AND SIGNS
(see also Introduction and Explanatory Notes)

The following consonant letters have their usual English sound values:

p, b, t, d, k, m, n, l, r, f, v, s, z, h, w

Key-words for the remaining English sounds are:

Vowels and Diphthongs

iː	bean	ɪ	pit	eɪ	bay
ɑː	barn	e	pet	aɪ	buy
ɔː	born	æ	pat	ɔɪ	boy
uː	boon	ʌ	putt	əu	no
ɜː	burn	ɒ	pot	au	now
		ʊ	put	ɪə	peer
		ə	another	eə	pair
				ʊə	poor

Note: ɔə also occurs as a variant of ɔː (as in 'four') or of ʊə (as in 'poor');

    * indicates a possible *r*-link before a following vowel.

Consonants

g	game	ŋ	long	ʃ	ship
tʃ	chain	θ	thin	ʒ	measure
dʒ	Jane	ð	then	j	yes

Note: x occurs as a variant for k in Scottish words (as in 'loch');
    subscript ˌ (as in ḷ, ṇ) indicates a syllabic consonant;
    a symbol in italic type indicates that the sound is often omitted.

Stress Accent

ˈ the following syllable carries primary (tonic) stress;
ˌ the following syllable carries secondary stress.

Everyman's ENGLISH PRONOUNCING DICTIONARY

CONTAINING OVER 59,000 WORDS
IN INTERNATIONAL PHONETIC
TRANSCRIPTION

Originally compiled by

DANIEL JONES
Late Professor of Phonetics in the University of London

EXTENSIVELY REVISED AND
EDITED BY

A. C. GIMSON
Late Professor of Phonetics in the University of London

FOURTEENTH EDITION

J. M. Dent & Sons Ltd
LONDON AND MELBOURNE

Printed and bound in Hong Kong by
Wing King Tong Company Limited
for
J. M. Dent & Sons Ltd
Aldine House, 33 Welbeck Street, London W1M 8LX
First published 1917
Reprinted 1919, 1921, 1922
Second Edition (revised, with Supplement) 1924
Third Edition (with revised Introduction) 1926
Reprinted 1927, 1928, 1930, 1931, 1932 (twice), 1934, 1935
Fourth Edition (revised, enlarged and reset) 1937
Fifth Edition 1940
Sixth Edition 1944
Seventh Edition (with Supplement) 1945
Eighth Edition 1947
Ninth Edition 1948
Tenth Edition 1949
Reprinted 1950, 1952, 1953, 1954 (twice), 1955
Eleventh Edition (completely revised, enlarged, brought
up to date and reset) 1956
Reprinted (with minor corrections) 1957
Reprinted (with minor corrections and
short supplement) 1958
Reprinted 1960
Twelfth Edition (revised, with new Supplement, and
with Glossary of Phonetic Terms) 1963
Reprinted (with corrections and
minor revisions by A. C. Gimson) 1964
Thirteenth Edition (revised, enlarged and reset),
© J. M. Dent & Sons Ltd, 1967
Reprinted (with corrections) 1969, 1972, 1974
Reprinted 1975
First paperback edition 1975
Fourteenth Edition (completely revised), © J. M. Dent &
Sons Ltd, 1977
Reprinted (with corrections) 1979, 1980, 1981, 1982, 1984
Reprinted 1986

Hardback ISBN: 0 460 03029 9

CONTENTS

Editor's Preface to the Fourteenth Edition   vii

INTRODUCTION
1.0 The Pronunciation Model   x
     1.5   The Sound Oppositions   xii
2.0 The Notation   xii
     2.2   Vowels and Diphthongs   xiii
     2.3   Consonants   xiii
3.0 Characteristics of the Model   xiv
     3.1   Vowels and Diphthongs   xiv
     3.5   Consonants   xviii
     3.17   Stress Accent   xxi
     3.23   Weak Forms   xxiii
     3.24   Syllable Division   xxiii

EXPLANATORY NOTES
  1 Simple Entries   xxiv
  2 Use of Commas   xxiv
  3 Use of [ ]   xxiv
  4 Rare or Old-fashioned Pronunciations   xxiv
  5 Use of Italic Symbols   xxiv
  6 Stress Accents ('), (,)   xxv
  7 Stress Accent in Derived Words   xxv
  8 Secondary Accent on /ɪə, ʊə/   xxv
  9 Variations of Stress Accent   xxv
 10 Variant Spellings   xxvi
 11 Proper Names Identical with Ordinary Words   xxvi
 12 Words Grouped under Head-words   xxvi
 13 Abbreviated Spellings   xxvii
 14 Linking /r/; Use of *   xxvii
 15 Syllabic Consonants   xxvii
 16 Strong and Weak Forms   xxvii

Contents

17 Syllable Division   xxviii
18 Foreign Sounds   xxviii
19 Extralinguistic Sounds   xxx
20 Summary of Conventional Signs   xxx
21 Abbreviations   xxx
22 English Phonetic Symbols and Signs   xxxi

SELECTED BOOK LIST   xxxii

DICTIONARY   1

EDITOR'S PREFACE TO THE
FOURTEENTH EDITION (1977)

In the thirteenth edition (1967), I introduced certain changes in the phonetic transcription as well as amendments to the pronunciations recorded, with the aim of reflecting more faithfully the current state of the style of speech on which the Dictionary had traditionally been based. Now, sixty years after the first appearance of the Dictionary, I have felt it necessary, while keeping the spirit of Daniel Jones's original work, to undertake a revision more thoroughgoing than that of any previous edition. As a result, the Introduction and most of the Explanatory Notes have been rewritten. The Glossary of Phonetic Terms, dating from 1963, has been omitted on the grounds that it has become to some extent out of date and that there are, for those interested in the more technical aspects of phonetic and phonological analysis, many textbooks which will supply their needs. Moreover, it is intended that the terminology employed in the introductory notes should be largely self-explanatory.

In addition, the definition of the speech model described has been modified. Although the traditional term 'received pronunciation' (RP) has been retained, I have thought it proper to widen its application (see Introduction, §§ 1.0–1.5). It seems no longer appropriate, at the end of the twentieth century, to define RP speakers in the strict social terms used by Daniel Jones in 1917 and in later editions of the Dictionary. The speech-style now recorded, while retaining its underlying South-Eastern English characteristics, is applicable to a wider sample of contemporary speakers, especially those of the middle generations. Such a model will be of particular relevance to foreign users of the Dictionary. As a result of this relaxation of definition, the ordering of pronunciation variants has been frequently been modified and certain new variants have been included.

I have also made changes in the phonetic symbolization of the vowels and diphthongs (see Introduction, §§ 2.0–2.2), with a view to underlining the essential qualitative differences between, for instance, the vowels of 'beat' and 'bit' or those of 'fool' and 'full', the traditional quantitative oppositions being often of lesser significance. The notation has also been simplified in three important respects: the syllable-division of recent editions is, with one exception, no longer shown in the phonetic transcription, the syllable boundaries (and the associated implications for pronunciation) being invariably evident from the orthography or the sense; the distinction between the falling diphthongs previously shown as 'iə, uə' and the rising diphthongs ('ĭə, ŭə') has been abandoned, the occurrence of either being predictable by a simple rule given in the introductory notes (see Introduction, § 3.4(h) and Explanatory Notes, § 8); and the symbolization 'ɛə' for the diphthong in 'there' has been simplified to 'eə'. It is of course possible to predict many other variants of sound and stress pattern by general rule, but I have felt it unwise to forsake further the principle that all possible pronunciation information should be immediately available at the point of entry in the Dictionary, without requiring constant recourse to rules of varying complexity in the Introduction.

Some 1032 new words (806 ordinary [1] words; 226 proper [2] names and abbreviations) have been added, and 208 deleted (143; 65), a net increase of 824 words. The present edition thus records the pronunciation of some 59,664 words, comprising:

Ordinary words	44,548
Proper names and abbreviations	15,116

Throughout the years of my editorship of the Dictionary, I have been much indebted to correspondents and colleagues in Britain and many other parts of the world for their suggestions and corrections. All such comments have been taken into account in the compilation of this new edition, although, since the size of the Dictionary requires that only a selection from the possible English vocabulary items can be included, a large proportion of the many thousand new entries suggested have had to be rejected, usually because they are of rare or over-technical usage or because they seem likely to have but an ephemeral existence. Nevertheless, the compiler of a dictionary such as this relies heavily on the comments of its users, and I will always be grateful to receive them.

---

[1] The number of 'ordinary' words is calculated as in previous editions, to include all head-words and those grouped under head-words with such terminations as '-ly, -ness, -er, -or, -ment'. Not included in the total (except when they occur as head-words with specific meanings) are plurals of nouns, similar forms without plural meaning (e.g. 'athletics'), comparatives and superlatives of adjectives, inflected forms of verbs, proper names of plural form grouped under the corresponding singular form (e.g. 'Ayre, -s'). Words of different meaning but the same pronunciation and spelling have a single entry (e.g. 'bear').

[2] 'Proper names' are defined as those entries written with a capital initial letter.

Of those who have helped me over the years, my especial gratitude is due to my colleague, Miss S. M. Ramsaran of University College, London, who gathered recorded material upon which the ordering of vowel variants in weak syllables has been largely based, who checked my revision of the entries and who helped in correcting the proofs; Mrs H. Wright and her colleagues of the BBC Pronunciation Unit who have been unstinting in giving me advice from their unique records; Mr Vincent Petti of Huddinge, Sweden, who has given me the benefit of his experience in lexicography as well as many suggestions concerning the addition and deletion of entries; Mr G. Walsh of Longman for many interesting discussions on problems of transcription; and Mr J. Windsor Lewis of the University of Leeds who has amassed invaluable information on the pronunciation usage of present-day BBC news-readers. I must thank, too, my colleagues in the Department of Phonetics and Linguistics, University College, London, who, with unfailing patience, have answered innumerable queries put to them at often inconvenient and unexpected moments.

1977   A. C. GIMSON

INTRODUCTION

1.0 The Pronunciation Model

1.1 In the first edition of this Dictionary (1917), Daniel Jones described the type of pronunciation recorded as 'that most usually heard in everyday speech in the families of Southern English persons whose menfolk have been educated at the great public boarding-schools'. Accordingly, he felt able to refer to his model as 'Public School Pronunciation' (PSP). In later editions, e.g. that of 1937, he added the remark that boys in boarding-schools tend to lose their markedly local peculiarities, whereas this is not the case for those in day-schools. He had by 1926, however, abandoned the term PSP in favour of 'received pronunciation' (RP). The type of speech he had in mind had for centuries been regarded as a kind of standard, having its base in the educated pronunciation of London and the Home Counties. Its use was not restricted to this region, however, being characteristic by the nineteenth century of upper-class speech throughout the country. Thus, though its base was a regional one, its occurrence was socially determined.

1.2 Such a definition of RP is hardly tenable today. Its regional base remains valid and it continues to have wide intelligibility throughout Britain (in a way that other regional forms do not)—one of the reasons why this type of pronunciation was originally adopted by the BBC for use by its news-readers. But in recent times, and especially in the last thirty years, the structure of British society has lost much of its earlier rigidity, so that it has become less easy to define a social class and, consequently, to correlate a certain type of pronunciation exclusively with one section of society. Because the whole population has, for nearly half a century, been exposed through broadcasting to RP in a way that was never the case before, it can safely be assumed that a much greater number of speakers, in more extensive layers of society, use RP or a style of pronunciation closely approximating to it. The result has been a certain dilution of the original concept of RP, a number of local variants formerly excluded by the definition having now to be admitted as of common and acceptable usage. Such an extended scope of usage is difficult to define. A specification in terms of a public boarding-school education is no longer valid, if only because the young are often influenced nowadays by other prestigious accents, e.g. Cockney or Mid-Atlantic, whatever their educational background. Nor can it be called simply 'educated' pronunciation, since not all educated speakers use it nor can all those who use it be safely described as 'educated'. If I have retained the traditional, though imprecise, term 'received pronunciation', it is because the label has such wide currency in books on present-day English and because it is a convenient name for an accent which remains generally acceptable and intelligible within Britain.

1.3 There are nevertheless two limiting factors which can be taken into account in defining the model. First, the pronunciation recorded in this Dictionary refers to usage current among speakers of the middle generations. Such a consideration is particularly relevant for foreign teachers and learners of English. So often, in general English dictionaries, the pronunciation given tends to be typical of the usage of an older generation, which must frequently be regarded as archaic or obsolescent. On the other hand, the speech of the young is likely at any time to be unstable, often reflecting transitory fashion. The extent to which new tendencies may be regarded as generally current among speakers of the middle generations has, in revising this Dictionary, been ascertained by consensus of opinion and by the analysis of recordings made by speakers of the relevant age groups, especially as regards certain crucial areas such as the type of vowel used in weak syllables (see Introduction, § 3.4(e)).

1.4 Secondly, certain bounds for the model are provided by the nature of the phonological system itself. Such constraints, apparently arbitrary, derive from the history of the model. They are concerned, in the first place, with the *number* of significantly oppositional sounds (phonemes) in the system. Thus, the model requires two significantly different vowels in pairs such as 'Sam' and 'psalm' or 'don' and 'dawn'. Next, the *incidence* of phonemes in words is generally determined (though there are a number of cases where alternatives exist). Thus, RP, in common with other accents, exploits the vowel opposition illustrated by the pair 'full, fool', the vowel of 'full' also occurring in the word 'book'; those accents which use the vowel of 'fool' in 'book' fall outside the definition. Or again, a feature of RP is that *r* is not pronounced before a following consonant or finally (except in the case of 'linking-*r*'—see

Introduction, § 3.13, and Explanatory Notes, § 14). Lastly, phonetic limits (i.e. concerning the specific quality of the sound) can be stated for the terms of the system. Thus, although RP and the local London accent oppose the diphthongs in 'bay' and 'buy', the qualitative realizations are different, the Cockney forms being sufficiently divergent to be unacceptable in RP.[1]

1.5 The following words illustrate the *sound oppositions* operating in the RP system:

(a) *Vowels*

5 *long*: be*a*n, b*ar*n, b*or*n, b*oo*n, b*ur*n

7 *short*: p*i*t, p*e*t, p*a*t, p*u*tt, p*o*t, p*u*t, an*o*th*er*

8 *diphthongs*: b*ay*, b*uy*, b*oy*, n*o*, n*ow*, p*eer*, p*air*, p*oor*

(b) *Consonants*

6 *plosives*: *p*in, *b*in, *t*in, *d*in, *c*ome, *g*um

2 *affricates*: *ch*ain, *J*ane

9 *fricatives*: *f*ine, *v*ine, *th*ink, *th*is, *s*eal, *z*eal, *sh*eep, mea*s*ure, *h*ow

3 *nasals*: su*m*, su*n*, su*ng*

1 *lateral*: *l*ight

3 *approximants* or *semi-vowels*: *r*ight, *w*et, *y*et

2.0 The Notation [2]

2.1 The notation remains basically phonemic (i.e. one symbol is assigned to each significant sound), but a major change in this edition of the Dictionary concerns the symbolization of the vowels and diphthongs. RP vowels have traditionally been classified in pairs of long and short, e.g. those of 'b*ea*t, b*i*t'; 'f*oo*l, f*u*ll'; 'c*augh*t, c*o*t'; 'c*ar*t, c*a*t'; 'f*orewor*d, f*or*ward'. Accordingly, the vowels in the pairs are often differentiated in phonetic notation only by the presence or absence of ':' (the length mark), e.g. /bi:t, bit/,[3] etc. In previous editions of this Dictionary, only in the case of the pair

---

[1] For more detail concerning the RP system and its phonetic specification, see A. C. Gimson, *Introduction to the Pronunciation of English* (Edward Arnold), 2nd ed., 1970.

[2] The alphabet is that of the International Phonetic Association. (See the *Principles of the International Phonetic Association*, obtainable through booksellers or from the Department of Phonetics and Linguistics, University College, London.)

[3] In this Introduction, the symbols and transcribed words in the text are enclosed in / /, following the linguistic convention of showing phonemic notation in this way. In the Dictionary entries, however, the transcribed forms follow the orthographic version unenclosed, variants being shown in [ ]. (See Explanatory Notes, §3.)

'cart, cat' has the additional qualitative distinction been shown as /kɑ:t, kæt/. I have thought it more realistic to show the differences of quality in all cases. Not only is the opposition of quality a strongly differentiating cue, but, in many cases, it is the only one of importance: thus, the so-called 'long' vowel in 'beat' is usually shorter than the so-called 'short' vowel in 'bid', and is only marginally (if at all) longer than the vowel in 'bit'. (See also Introduction, §§ 3.4 (a, b), for significant variations of vowel length.) It can reasonably be argued that to show features of both quality and quantity entails redundancy of notation, since either is predictable by rule from the other. The redundancy involved in the retention of the length mark (:) has, however, seemed justifiable both for the sake of greater explicitness in a large number of oppositions and also in order to provide an additional differentiating cue between /i/ and /ɪ/, /u/ and /ʊ/, which may be confused in small print. The short vowel symbols are also appropriate to denote one element of the diphthongs.

2.2 The RP *vowels and diphthongs* are now transcribed as follows:

bean	barn	born	boon	burn
i:	ɑ:	ɔ:	u:	ɜ:

pit	pet	pat	putt	pot	put	another
ɪ	e	æ	ʌ	ɒ	ʊ	ə	ə

bay	buy	boy	no	now	peer	pair	poor	(pour)
eɪ	aɪ	ɔɪ	əʊ	aʊ	ɪə	eə	ʊə	ɔə

Note: In addition to the changes mentioned in § 2.1, the former /ɛə/ as in 'pair' has been simplified to /eə/ (see § 3.4(f)).

2.3 The RP *consonants* are transcribed, as in previous editions, as follows:

pin	bin	tin	din	come	gum	chain	Jane
p	b	t	d	k	g	tʃ	dʒ

fine	vine	think	this	seal	zeal	sheep	measure	how
f	v	θ	ð	s	z	ʃ	ʒ	h

sum	sun	sung	light	right	wet	yet
m	n	ŋ	l	r	w	j

2.4 The symbols used for *primary and secondary stress accent* (ˈ and ˌ) remain unchanged, but the conventions attached to them have been somewhat modified (see Introduction, § 3.17 et seq., and Explanatory Notes, §§ 6–9).

2.5   The sign for syllable division (-) has generally been omitted in this edition. Formerly, 'toe-strap' was transcribed as /'təu-stræp/ compared with 'toastrack' /'təust-ræk/. The situation of the syllable division (juncture) has implications for the duration and quality of the sounds involved: thus, in 'toe-strap' /əʊ/ is relatively long and /r/ is considerably devoiced (i.e. the vocal folds do not vibrate throughout most of the sound), whereas in 'toastrack' /əʊ/ is much reduced in length and there may be little devoicing of /r/. However, such divisions and their implications for pronunciation are generally evident from the orthography and from the meaningful segmentation (morpheme boundaries) of the word (see Introduction, § 3.24, for the special case of /t-ʃ/).

3.0   Characteristics of the Model

The following notes deal with topics of particular relevance to the interpretation of the Dictionary entries. For fuller information, readers are referred to the works recommended in the Selected Book List (p. xxxiii).

3.1   Vowels and Diphthongs

The phonetic (qualitative) characteristics may be described in terms of the conventional Cardinal Vowel diagram. This diagram, used in a simplified version in Figs. 1–3, was originally constructed by plotting the highest points of raising of the tongue during the production of vowel sounds.[1] The eight primary cardinal vowels (the relationship of which is shown by the numbers on Figs. 1–3) occupy the extreme peripheral positions, their qualities approximating to the following language values: 1—French 'si'; 2—French 'thé'; 3—French 'même'; 4—French 'la'; 5—French 'pas'; 6—German 'Sonne'; 7—French 'beau'; 8—French 'doux'. Essentially, the area assigned to an RP vowel or to the direction of movement shown for a diphthong on the diagram can be said to denote their auditory relationships with the cardinal vowels and with other English vowels.

---

[1] For more details concerning the selection of the cardinal vowels, readers are referred in particular to those works by Daniel Jones and A. C. Gimson in the Selected Book List (p. xxxiii). Recordings of the cardinal vowels, made by Daniel Jones, are obtainable from the Linguaphone Institute (nos. ENG 252–3).

3.2 *Vowels*

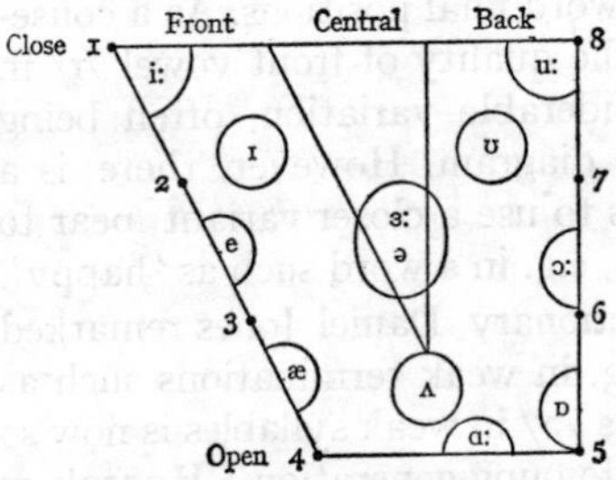

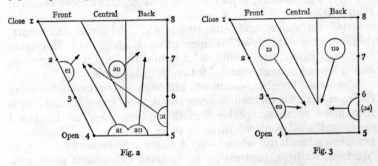

Fig. 1

3.3 *Diphthongs*

Fig. 2

Fig. 3

3.4

(a) The length of long vowels and diphthongs is very much reduced when they occur in syllables closed by the consonants /p, t, k, tʃ, f, θ, s, ʃ/. Thus, /iː/ in 'beat' has only about half the length of /iː/ in 'bead' or 'bee'; similarly, /eɪ/ in 'place' is much reduced in length compared with /eɪ/ in 'plays' or 'play'. In these cases, vowel duration provides a significant cue to meaning.

(b) The vowel /æ/, classified as a short vowel, is nevertheless generally lengthened by RP speakers before /b, d, g, dʒ, m, n/. Thus, /æ/ in 'bag' is considerably longer than /æ/ in 'back'.

(c) /ɜː/∼/ə/. These two vowels are only rarely in opposition, e.g. 'foreword' *v.* 'forward' (/ə/ occurring essentially only in weak syllables), nor do they differ in quality to the extent of, for instance, /iː/ and /ɪ/. However, /ə/ can be either more open than /ɜː/, e.g. in a final position as in 'China', or closer, e.g. adjacent to /k/, /g/ or /ŋ/ as in 'long ago'.

(d) The short vowels /ɪ, æ, ɒ, ʊ/ differ noticeably in quality from the long vowels traditionally paired with them (cf. their positions on Fig. 1). /e, æ, ʌ, ɒ/ do not occur in word final positions. As a consequence of this lack of oppositions, the quality of front vowel /ɪ/ in such a position is capable of considerable variation, often being lowered more than is shown in the diagram. However, there is a tendency among young RP speakers to use a closer variant, near to the quality of /iː/, in a final position, e.g. in a word such as 'happy'.

(e) In previous editions of the Dictionary, Daniel Jones remarked on the varying use of /ɪ/ or /ə/, e.g. in weak terminations such as '-less' and '-ness'. The trend towards /ə/ in weak syllables is now so firmly established among middle and young generation RP speakers that a number of changes in the ordering of pronunciation forms have been made in the present edition, particularly in the following cases:

'-ity', e.g. 'quality, capacity': /-ətɪ/ is generally more common than /-ɪtɪ/.

'-ate' (in nouns and adjectives), e.g. 'deliberate, fortunate, delicate, chocolate': /-ət/ is more common than /-ɪt/. In certain cases, e.g. 'magistrate, candidate', a form with /-eɪt/ is also common, and in a word such as 'nitrate' is the dominant form.

'-ess', e.g. 'hopeless, goodness': although /-ɪs/ remains the more common form for the middle generations, /-əs/ gains ground and is introduced as an acceptable variant. A form /-es/ is also heard occasionally in words of three or more syllables, e.g. 'happiness, penniless'. Similarly, when '-ess' denotes a feminine form, e.g. in 'duchess, waitress, mistress', /-ɪs/ remains a dominant pronunciation, with /-əs/ as an increasingly frequent variant; /-es/ is dominant in, for instance, 'heiress, hostess'.

'-et', e.g. 'sonnet, carpet, bonnet': is predominantly with /-ɪt/; /-ɪt/ is generally used after /k, g, tʃ, dʒ/, e.g. 'pocket, target, hatchet, budget'. However, in the endings '-let, -ret', e.g. 'bracelet, scarlet, toilet, claret, garret', /-ət/ is either dominant or a common variant.

'-ily', e.g. 'easily, happily, worthily': /-əlɪ/ gains ground, especially after /r/, e.g. 'angrily, primarily, extraordinarily', when it is the dominant form, and in certain words such as 'family'.

'-ace', e.g. 'palace, necklace, preface, populace': /ɪ/ and /ə/ are alternatives, with an increasing tendency to /ə/.

'-es, -ed', e.g. 'horses, waited': the /-ɪz, -ɪd/ forms remain dominant in RP, even among the young, despite the influence of the alternative /-əz, -əd/ characteristic of other types of English. The pairs 'boxes, boxers' and 'chatted, chattered' therefore retain the distinction based on /ɪ/ in the weak syllable of the first member of the pair and /ə/ in the second word.

In all other cases of weak terminations, /ɪ/ is retained as the vowel of first choice, though readers will note a number of cases where /ə/ has been introduced as a variant.

(f) The transcription /ɛə/, e.g. in 'there, pair', has been replaced by /eə/ for the sake of simplicity, with the convention that the first part of the diphthong is more open than the short vowel of 'pen', except when /eə/ results from the elision of /ɪ/ in the sequence /eɪə/, in which case /e/ may retain the closer quality typical of the first element of the diphthong /eɪ/.

(g) It is to be noted that, whenever the sequences /eɪ, aɪ, ɔɪ, əʊ, aʊ/ + /ə/ occur, the medial /ɪ/ or /ʊ/ may be elided, e.g. in 'player, fire, employer, slower, power'. This is especially true of /aɪ, aʊ/ + /ə/, which are sometimes reduced to a long open vowel, e.g. 'power' /pɑː/. However, the full disyllabic forms have been retained in the Dictionary entries, with the understanding that the reduced forms are common. The only case where /ɑː/ is recorded is that of 'our' which, being so often weak, is particularly liable to reduction.

(h) The treatment of /ɪə, ʊə/ has been simplified. In the most recent editions of the Dictionary, Daniel Jones introduced the distinction between falling diphthongs, where the prominence falls on the first element, e.g. in 'here, poor' (transcribed with /ɪə, ʊə/), and rising diphthongs in weak syllables, where the prominence is on the second element or where there may be said to be a syllable division between the two elements, e.g. in 'period, easier, genius, influence, rescuer' (transcribed with /ĭə, ŭə/). Although the phonetic distinction is real, I have thought it convenient to avoid the explicit notation of the rising diphthongs by the application of a general rule. Thus, all unstressed syllables containing /ɪə, ʊə/ are taken to have the pronunciation with a rising diphthong or with the variants /jə, wə/ or /ɪ-ə, ʊ-ə/. There are, however, a certain number of cases (some 60 for /ɪə/ and 100 for /ʊə/), previously carrying no stress in the Dictionary, where the falling diphthongs are used, e.g. 'reindeer, Shakespeare, contour, sinecure'. In these cases, the secondary stress sign ˌ has been used exceptionally to denote the necessity for a falling diphthongal pronunciation, e.g. /ˈreɪnˌdɪə, ˈʃeɪkˌspɪə, ˈkɒnˌtʊə, ˈsɪnɪˌkjʊə/. (See also Explanatory Notes, § 8.)

(i) The falling diphthong /ʊə/ is increasingly replaced by /ɔː/ or /ɔə/. Thus, the most common form of 'sure' has /ɔː/, with a similar, though less conclusive, tendency being true for 'poor, moor, tour' and their derivatives. Rare words, such as 'gourd, dour', tend to retain /ʊə/ without a common /ɔː/ variant. The sequences /-jʊə/ are also strongly maintained, e.g. 'pure, cure, sewer', though in some cases with /ɔ:, əɛ/ variants. In addition, /ʊə/ is generally kept in derived forms such as 'fewer, doer' and also 'jewel, duel', where an alternative pronunciation with /u:ə/ is common.

(j) The form /ɔə/ is retained as a variant for /ɔ:/ in such words as 'pour, score' and for /ʊə/ (or /ɔ:/) in 'poor, sure'. Some RP speakers still use /ɔə/ to distinguish, for instance, 'pour' from 'paw' (/pɔə, pɔ:/), but this usage seems to be becoming increasingly rare. On the other hand, I have abandoned the variant /ɜ:/ for /ʊə, ɔ:/ or /ɔə/, e.g. in 'sure, pure, cure', which I introduced in the 1967 edition and which now seems to me too idiosyncratic to warrant inclusion.

(k) Some forms, such as /geəl/ for 'girl', I have deleted as archaic. Others, such as the use of /ɔ:/ in 'broth, cloth, cost, cross, cough, frost, froth, loss, off, often, soft, trough', have been retained but characterized as 'old-fashioned', while the /ɔ:/ variant in 'gone' has been deleted. I have also indicated the increasing dominance of /su:-/ over /sju:-/ in words like 'superstitious, suit'.

3.5 Consonants

3.6 The following table shows the system and general phonetic specification of the RP consonants:

TABLE OF ENGLISH CONSONANTS

	Bilabial	Labio-Dental	Dental	Alveolar	Post-Alveolar	Palato-Alveolar	Palatal	Velar	Glottal
Plosive	p b			t d				k g	
Affricate						tʃ dʒ			
Fricative		f v	θ ð	s z		ʃ ʒ		(x)	h
Nasal	m			n				ŋ	
Lateral				l					
Approximant or Semi-vowel	w						r	j	

Note: Where consonants appear in pairs, the one on the left is fortis (voiceless, i.e. typically without vibration of the vocal folds) and that on the right is lenis (often voiced, i.e. with vocal fold vibration, but always weaker in articulation than the fortis member of the pair). The presence of /x/ in ( ) denotes that the sound is optional.

3.7 It is to be noted that certain consonants have a restricted distribution. Thus, /ʒ/ occurs typically only in word medial positions; /ŋ/ occurs only in syllable final positions; /h, w, r, j/ occur only before a vowel.

3.8 /p, t, k/ are typically accompanied by aspiration (i.e. an interval of breath before the following vowel onset), especially when initial in a stressed syllable. Thus, 'pin' is distinguished from 'bin' very largely by the aspiration accompanying /p/. However, in the stressed syllable-initial sequences /sp-, st-, sk-/, /p, t, k/ lack such aspiration. Within a word, therefore, the situation of the stress accent in relation to such sequences will denote presence or absence of aspiration, e.g. the notation /əˈspaɪə/ for 'aspire' indicates that the /p/ is not aspirated. I have in many cases, including the word 'aspire' (formerly transcribed as /əsˈpaɪə/), found it necessary to shift the stress accent given in previous editions in order to denote or preclude aspiration of the plosive. Sometimes, such phonetic considerations over-ride traditional (etymological) syllable divisions, e.g. 'discover' transcribed as /dɪˈskʌvə/, whereas 'discolour' is retained as /dɪsˈkʌlə/. The criterion determining the separation of /s/ from /p, t, k/ appears to be the presence of an 'intuitively transparent morpheme boundary'[1] (i.e. a separation based on clearly felt sense units). There are, however, cases where usage regarding syllable division and the consequent presence or absence of aspiration cannot be easily determined, e.g. 'distasteful', where practice varies between speakers and according to the style of utterance.

3.9 Final syllabic /n/ is to be understood following /t, d, f, v, s, z, ʃ, ʒ/ as in 'cotton, sudden, often, oven, listen, dozen, ocean, vision'; in other sequences, e.g. 'open, broken', an intervening /ə/ is commonly heard. More freedom of choice as to the presence or absence of an /ə/ is recorded in the case of proper names, and also in such long words as 'metropolitan' where the sequence /-tən/ is frequently heard (see also Explanatory Notes, § 15).

---

[1] The term is used by Niels Davidsen-Nielsen, to whom I am much indebted for advice; see his article 'Syllabification in English words with medial *sp*, *st*, *sk*', *Journal of Phonetics*, vol. 2, no. 1 (1974).

3.10 Final syllabic /l/ is similarly to be understood following /p, b, t, d, k, g, f, v, θ, s, z, ʃ, m, n/ as in 'apple, trouble, cattle, medal, buckle, struggle, trifle, oval, Ethel, castle, hazel, bushel, camel, final', other sequences, e.g. in 'satchel, oral', often having an intervening /ə/ (see also Explanatory Notes, § 15).

3.11 The phoneme /l/ must be understood to have the following important allophones (i.e. variants predictable from their environment or their position in the word): a 'clear' /l/ (with a front vowel resonance) before a vowel or /j/, e.g. in 'leaf, million'; a 'dark' /l/ (with a back vowel resonance) finally, before a consonant and as a syllabic sound, e.g. in 'feel, help, middle'; and a partially or wholly voiceless /l/ (with little or no vibration of the vocal folds) following stressed /p, k/, e.g. 'please, clean'.

3.12 The phonemes /r, j, w/ are similarly devoiced following stressed /p, t, k/, e.g. in 'cry, pure, tune, cure, twist, quick'. In the case of /r/, some speakers use a 'one-tap' consonant, instead of the more usual frictionless approximant, when the sound occurs between vowels, e.g. in 'very, sorry, hurry'.

3.13 Many words ending in /-ə, -ɪə, -eə, -ʊə, -ɛə, -ɑ:, -ɔ:/, with an 'r' in the spelling, usually have a link with /r/ when followed by a word beginning with a vowel, particularly within a close-knit sense-group, e.g. 'father and mother, here and there, pair of, poor old, far off, pour out'. This potential link in connected speech is shown by *, e.g. 'father' /ˈfɑːðə*/. (Some speakers tend not to use such a link after the weak ending /-rə/, although the condition of an 'r' in the spelling exists, e.g. 'error of (judgment)' may be said as /ˈerə əv -/ rather than /ˈerər əv -/ or /ˈerɽ əv -/.) By analogy, it is common for an /r/ link to be used when there is no 'r' in the spelling—an 'intrusive' /r/, e.g. in connected speech, 'China/r/ and Japan'; within a word, 'draw/r/ing'. Although this usage has been common in South-Eastern England for at least two centuries, it can be regarded as optional and is not specifically indicated in the Dictionary entries (see also Explanatory Notes, § 14).

3.14 The sound /x/ is optional and is used only in the pronunciation of Scottish English words, e.g. 'loch' /lɒk/ or /lɒx/, 'Buchan' /ˈbʌkən/ or /ˈbʌxən/.

3.15 The pronunciation with /hw/ in the case of many words

having 'wh' in the spelling, e.g. 'which, white, when', etc., must be regarded as increasingly rare among RP speakers. It is, however, retained as a variant because it may still be heard from some speakers, especially in more formal styles of speech.

3.16 The following features of consonant clusters are to be noted:

(a) It is to be understood that when a plosive is followed by another plosive or affricate, e.g. 'act' /ækt/, 'object' /əb'dʒekt/, the first plosive has no audible release. Similarly, there may be no audible release for plosives in final positions, e.g. in 'sit, bid'. Such features are not marked in the notation. (For the use of glottal closure with or in place of /p, t, k/ in certain positions, see the handbooks on English pronunciation recommended in the Selected Book List, p. xxxiii.)

(b) Certain consonants, especially /n/, may or may not assimilate to an adjacent consonant. Such variants within a word, depending on the style of utterance and on the habits of particular speakers, are only occasionally shown in the Dictionary. Thus, 'inconvenient' is given with both /ˌɪnk-/ and /ˌɪŋk-/. Often, assimilation within a word will depend upon the extent to which the word is felt as a compound, e.g. 'income' is treated as a simple word with the common form /'ɪŋk-/, whereas in 'incoming' the separateness of the elements is more strongly felt, resulting in a most frequent form with /'ɪnˌk-/. It should also be noted that in normal discourse isolate word final /n/ and /t, d, s, z/ are particularly liable to assimilation with the initial consonant of a following word, e.g. 'one more' /n → m/, 'that boy' /t → p/, 'this shop' /s → ʃ/, etc.

3.17 Stress Accent

3.18 Primary Stress

English polysyllabic words contain one or more syllables which are more prominent than their neighbours. This salience of syllables is achieved not only by stress (energy of articulation) but also by factors relating to pitch, length and inherent quality. In the Dictionary, the stress-marking takes into account both stress and pitch. Thus, the sign ' placed before a syllable, e.g. 'above' /ə'bʌv/, indicates that the syllable has primary (tonic) stress, with a potential associated pitch movement. When a word is said in isolation, the pitch change (tone) is likely to be falling; but when the word occurs within connected speech the type of movement will depend upon the overall intonation of the utterance, the possibilities varying between falling, rising, combinations of fall and rise, or level.[1]

3.19 *Secondary Stress*

When more than one syllable in a word is stressed, stresses other than the primary must be regarded as secondary. These are marked with ˌ placed before the syllable, e.g. 'conversation' /ˌkɒnvə'seɪʃn/. Such secondary stresses may occur before the primary (pre-tonic), as in the example given, or following the primary (post-tonic). In the Dictionary, post-tonic secondary stresses are shown only in the case of polysyllabic second elements of compounds, e.g. 'season-ticket' /'siːzn ˌtɪkɪt/ (see Introduction, § 3.4(h), for the exceptional cases of /ɪə, ʊə/). Pre-tonic secondary stress may also have pitch prominence, especially when the syllable in question is strongly meaningful. Thus, in the word 'unprepared' /ˌʌnprɪ'peəd/, the syllable /ˌʌn-/ may have high or low pitch or even a pitch movement, but, unless some special contrastive meaning is intended, it remains subsidiary in prominence to /-'peəd/. The sign ˌ must therefore be taken to subsume subsidiary pitch variation. (In former editions, a word such as 'unprepared' was given the variants /ˌʌnprɪ'peəd/ and /'ʌnprɪ'peəd/, referring essentially to the pitch of the first syllable. The conventions attaching to the present system of stress-marking embrace the variants previously shown.)

3.20 A difficulty arises when it is a question of a possible secondary stress on a syllable immediately preceding the primary stress, e.g. in many words with the prefix 'un-' /ʌn-/. The decision in these cases is based as far as possible on the criterion of potential separability or contrastiveness, e.g. 'un-' in 'uncouth' is not separably meaningful and thus carries no secondary stress, whereas the prefix of 'uncork' would always seem to attract a secondary stress associated with meaning. In the majority of cases, however, usage may vary as to the presence or absence of secondary stress. In these cases, the alternatives are shown, e.g. 'uncertain' as either /ʌn'sɜːtn/ or /ˌʌn'sɜːtn/, the choice depending not only upon the significance placed on the negative weight of this particular prefix but also, when embedded in an extended utterance, on the preceding stress pattern.

3.21 It frequently happens that words carrying secondary and primary stress (especially compound adjectives) have a stress pattern in the citation or predicative forms which changes when

[1] For works on English intonation, see Selected Book List, p. xxxiii.

used attributively or within the general stress pattern of the context. Thus, 'afternoon' has the citation pattern /ˌ--'-/ which changes to /'---/ when followed by stressed 'tea'; similarly, 'good-looking' /ˌ-'--/ may change to /'-ˌ--/ when followed by stressed 'man'. Such variants are noted in the entries when relevant.

3.22　There is one exceptional case where the rule of only one sign ' per word has been relaxed. Many long polysyllabic words or compounds have two secondary stresses preceding the primary, e.g. 'cross-examination, decontamination, mispronunciation, intercontinental', etc. Of the two secondary stresses, the first is the stronger (while remaining subsidiary to the primary). It would have been possible to state a simple rule governing these cases, but, in order to be more explicit in the entries, I have chosen to use ' for the first secondary, e.g. 'cross-examination' /'krɒsɪgˌzæmɪ'neɪʃn/ with the convention that the first sign ' is subsidiary to the second '.

3.23　*Weak Forms*
A pronouncing dictionary is obliged, if it is not to enter into exhaustive complications, to record primarily the citation forms of words. Such a practice is nevertheless misleading as regards those words (grammatical items such as pronouns, conjunctions, prepositions, etc.) which invariably have a different pronunciation when unstressed in connected speech. An analysis of their occurrence in connected speech indicates clearly that the weakened form is overwhelmingly the most frequent. If I have persisted with the convention of previous editions, i.e. recording the pronunciation of, for example, 'and' as /ænd/ with variants /ənd, nd, ən, n/, it must be emphasized that the strong forms are typical only of the citation pronunciation and of the rarer stressed (contrastive) instances to be found in normal discourse.

3.24　*Syllable Division*
I have generally abandoned the use of - to show syllable division for the reasons given in Introduction, § 2.5. However, the mark has been retained in one case, viz. to signify the distinction between /tʃ/, e.g. in 'satchel' /'sætʃəl/ and the sequence /t/ + /ʃ/, e.g. in 'nutshell' /'nʌt-ʃel/, the /ʃ/ of the latter example being longer than the /ʃ/ element of the affricate in the first. This distinguishing mark is used in some 20 cases, e.g. 'courtship, pot-shot, Wiltshire', etc. In some other cases, e.g. 'profit-sharing' /'prɒfɪtˌʃeərɪŋ/, the syllable division is indicated by the post-tonic secondary stress mark.

EXPLANATORY NOTES

The following notes explain how the entries are to be interpreted, within the conventions stated in the Introduction.

1. Simple Entries
A simple entry such as

    celluloid ˈseljʊlɔɪd

is to be taken to mean that, in the type of pronunciation referred to in the Introduction, §§ 1.1–5, and in a normal colloquial style of speech, the word **celluloid** is generally pronounced /ˈseljʊlɔɪd/, the decision being the result of the editor's observations.

2. The Use of Commas
An entry, for which two or more pronunciations are separated by commas, e.g.

    controversy ˈkɒntrəvɜːsɪ, kənˈtrɒvəsɪ

indicates that the two pronunciations appear to be equally common. Similarly, the entry

    Batho ˈbæθəʊ, ˈbeɪθəʊ

means that some people with this name pronounce /ˈbæθəʊ/, others /ˈbeɪθəʊ/.

3. The Use of [ ]
When variants are enclosed in [ ] as in

    dinastic dɪˈnæstɪk [daɪˈn-]

it is to be understood that there occur two or more pronunciations of the word, but that it has been judged that the forms enclosed in [ ], although widely used, are somewhat less common than the unenclosed form.

In an entry such as

    professional prəˈfeʃənl [prʊˈf-, -ʃnəl, -ʃn̩l, -ʃnl̩, -ʃənəl]

the last four variants denote different realizations of the final two syllables having little significance beyond that of individual choice or of style of speech.

When variants are given for different elements of the word, e.g.

    Australia ɒˈstreɪljə [ɔːˈs-, -lɪə]

the entry signifies that four possible forms occur: /ɒˈstreɪljə, ɒˈstreɪlɪə, ɔːˈstreɪljə, ɔːˈstreɪlɪə/.

4. Rare or Old-fashioned Pronunciations
Some pronunciations are characterized as *rarely* or *old-fashioned*. This comment is to be taken to mean either that the form in question is judged to have a relatively low frequency of occurrence or that it is a conservative form characteristic of the older generations, e.g.

    Persia ˈpɜːʃə [*rarely* ˈpɜːʒə]

    loss lɒs [*old-fashioned* lɔːs]

5. The Use of Italic Symbols
Many entries include pronunciations which contain an italic symbol, e.g.

    notation nəʊˈteɪʃn̩; **contempt** kənˈtempt; **strawberry** ˈstrɔːbərɪ; **conference** ˈkɒnfərəns; **territory** ˈterɪtərɪ; **regiment** ˈredʒɪmənt; **Tibetan** tɪˈbetən; **engine** ˈendʒɪn.

The italicized symbol indicates that the sound is commonly omitted, the form with the sound elided being often characteristic of normal, familiar speech. Thus, the same speaker may use different pronunciations on different occasions.

In the case of potential elision of the medial vowel in a three-vowel sequence, e.g.

player 'pleɪə*

note should be taken of the comments in Introduction, §§ 3.4(f), (g).

6. Stress Accents ('), (ˌ)

Three degrees of stress accent are shown (see also Introduction, §§ 3.17–22):

  (i) Primary (tonic) stress accent: ' placed before the syllable, e.g. **above** əˈbʌv; **under** ˈʌndə*; **afterwards** ˈɑːftəwədz.

  (ii) Pre-tonic secondary stress accent: ˌ placed before the syllable, e.g. **conversation** ˌkɒnvəˈseɪʃn; **undo** ˌʌnˈduː; **consideration** kənˌsɪdəˈreɪʃn. *Note:* When more than one secondary stress precedes the primary, the first secondary is shown as ', e.g. **cross-examination** ˈkrɒsɪgˌzæmɪ-ˈneɪʃn (see Introduction, § 3.22).

  (iii) Post-tonic secondary stress accent: ˌ placed before the syllable, but used only in the polysyllabic second element of compounds, e.g. **season-ticket** ˈsiːznˌtɪkɪt (see Introduction, § 3.19).

  (iv) Weak syllables: unmarked.

7. Stress Accent in Derived Words

  (i) When the head-word is a monosyllable, and a termination for forming a derived word adds another syllable, it is to be understood that the derived word retains a primary stress on the root-syllable, e.g. in the entry

  nine, -s, -fold naɪn, -z, -fəʊld

  where **ninefold** has a primary stress on the first syllable.

  (ii) In cases such as

  ewe, -s ; -lamb/s juː, -z; -ˈlæm/z

  it is to be understood that the form **ewe-lamb** is pronounced with two stressed syllables: /ˌjuːˈlæm/.

  (iii) When a head-word is a compound of which the second separable element is a weak syllable, and a termination for forming a derived word adds yet another syllable, it is to be understood that the derived word has secondary stress on the first syllable of the second element, e.g. the entry

  greenhou|se, -ses ˈgriːnhaʊ|s, -zɪz

  implies that **greenhouses** is pronounced /ˈgriːnˌhaʊzɪz/.

  Exceptions to this rule are shown, e.g. the entry

  tea-cup, -s ; ful/s ˈtiːkʌp, -s; -ˌfʊl/z

  where the secondary stress is applied to **-ful** /ˈtiːkʌpˌfʊl/.

8. Secondary Accent on /ɪə, ʊə/ (see also Introduction, § 3.4(h))

The convention adopted in the Dictionary is that /ɪə, ʊə/ are to be taken as falling diphthongs (i.e. with the prominence associated with the first element) when carrying primary or secondary accent. In a weak syllable, the diphthongs are rising or are realized as /jə, wə/ or are to be treated as disyllabic sequences, e.g. the entry **easier** is to be interpreted as having alternative pronunciations with /-zɪə*/ (rising diphthong), /-zjə*/, /-zɪ-ə*/ (disyllabic).

In some cases, where /ɪə, ʊə/ are falling but have not previously carried a stress mark, the secondary stress sign has been used exceptionally to indicate that they are falling, e.g.

reindeer ˈreɪnˌdɪə*; **contour** ˈkɒnˌtʊə*

9. Variations of Stress Accent (see also Introduction, § 3.21)

Variations in the stressing of the citation form resulting from the general stress pattern of the context (e.g. in the attributive use of adjectives) are shown usually by representing the syllables of the word in question by hyphens, e.g. the entry

    Waterloo ˌwɔːtəˈluː: [ˈ---]

is to be taken to mean that **Waterloo** before, for instance, **Road** or **Bridge** is likely to have the stress pattern /ˈ---/.

10. Variant Spellings

Square brackets [ ] are also used to show variant orthographic forms of the head-word, without implication as to the frequency of such forms, e.g. **organization** [-isa-].

Where a spelling variant involves the presence or absence of a single letter, that letter is enclosed, when convenient, in round brackets ( ), e.g. **Ham(m)ond.**

When such variants would be widely separated in alphabetic order, such a device is not generally employed, e.g. **coloration** and **colouration** are shown separately.

11. Proper Names Identical with Ordinary Words

When a proper name is identical with an ordinary word in spelling and pronunciation, the fact is indicated by placing a capital letter in ( ) after the ordinary spelling of the word, e.g.

    hay (H.) heɪ

When two proper names exist, one of which is identical in spelling and pronunciation with the singular and the other with the plural of an ordinary word, the one bracketed capital letter placed after the singular form is to be understood to apply also to the name having the plural form, e.g.

    gibbon (G.), -s ˈgɪbən, -z

implies that the proper names **Gibbon** and **Gibbons** are pronounced /ˈgɪbən/ and /ˈgɪbənz/.

Where, however, a name of plural form has a pronunciation different from that of the plural ordinary word, it is given a separate entry, e.g.

    gillie (G.), -s ˈgɪlɪ, -z
    Gillies ˈgɪlɪs

12. Words Grouped under Head-words

The pronunciations of all plurals of nouns are shown under the singulars; all comparatives and superlatives of adjectives and inflected forms of verbs are given under the simple words from which they are derived. Likewise nouns formed from other words by means of the terminations **-er, -ing, -ment, -or** or **-ness,** and adverbs formed by adding the termination **-ly,** will as a rule be found under the words from which they may be considered to be derived. Thus, **talker, meeting** (noun), **annulment** will be found under **talk, meet, annul.**

Other derivatives are also grouped under simple words, when no difficulty in finding them is caused thereby. Thus, **refractive** will be found under **refract, motherhood** and **motherless** under **mother.**

The derived forms of words are not as a rule written out in full, but the terminations to be added are each preceded by a hyphen and divided by a comma, or sometimes by a semicolon, from what preceded. Thus the entry

    afford, -s, -ing, -ed əˈfɔːd, -z, -ɪŋ, -ɪd

is to be taken to mean that in RP the words **afford, affords, affording, afforded** are pronounced /əˈfɔːd, əˈfɔːdz, əˈfɔːdɪŋ, əˈfɔːdɪd/.

When the final part of the spelling of a head-word is not repeated before adding a termination, the part to be repeated is marked off by a vertical line | (see, for instance, **addendum, fade**). The same device is employed when the final part undergoes some alteration in pronunciation, though not in spelling, in an inflected form (see, for instance, **house, nocturnal,** where | precedes the **-se** and the **-al**).

Words not grammatically connected (especially proper names) are often similarly grouped together, with or without the use of the mark |, where no difficulty in finding the words is caused thereby. Thus the entry

Ruther|ford, -glen 'rʌðəfəd, -glen

is to be taken to mean that in RP **Rutherford** is pronounced /'rʌðəfəd/ and **Rutherglen** /'rʌðəglen/.

The mark / is often used to indicate derivatives of words grouped under a head-word. Thus the entry

elegan|ce, -t/ly 'elɪgən|s, -t/lɪ

is to be taken to mean that in RP the words **elegance, elegant, elegantly** are pronounced /'elɪgəns, 'elɪgənt, 'elɪgəntlɪ/.

When one or more derived words are grouped under a head-word as explained above, and a variant of the head-word is given, that variant is to be taken to apply to all the derived words in so far as this may be possible. Thus it is to be understood from the entry

Galt, -on gɔːlt [gɒlt], -ən

that **Galton** as well as **Galt** is subject to the variant pronunciation with /ɒ/.

13. Abbreviated Spellings
A certain number of common abbreviations, e.g. **Bros., Chas., cwt., E.C., q.v., V.I.P.,** are included and arranged in alphabetical order according to the letters composing them.

14. Linking /r/; Use of * (see also Introduction, § 3.13)
The sign * following final /-ə, -ɪə, -eə, -ʊə, -ɔə, -ɑː, -ɔː/ indicates a potential /r/ link (the spelling containing a letter 'r') before another word beginning with a vowel, especially within the same sense-group, e.g. **here** hɪə*, indicating that an /r/ link is normally used in such a phrase as **here and there**; similarly, **later** 'leɪtə*, which is likely to have an /r/ link in **later on.**

An 'intrusive' linking /r/ in other cases (with the above vowel endings but without the orthographic 'r') is frequently used by analogy but is not indicated in the Dictionary. Thus, intrusive /r/ sounds are commonly heard especially after /-ə, -ɪə/, e.g. **China**/r/ **and Japan, the idea**/r/ **of it,** or after /-ɑː/ in such a phrase as **Shah**/r/ **of Persia.** Native listeners tend to tolerate less easily an intrusive /r/ after /ɔː/, e.g. in phrases such as **law**/r/ **and order, I saw**/r/ **it.**

15. Syllabic Consonants (see also Introduction, §§ 3.9–10)
The fact that a consonant is syllabic (i.e. functions as a syllable without an accompanying vowel) is marked, by placing ˌ under the symbol, only where there might be ambiguity. Thus, the notation /'trævl̩/ for **travel** implies unambiguously that the /l/ is syllabic, whereas in the derived form **travelling** it is important to distinguish a three-syllable form /'trævl̩ɪŋ/ from the alternative two-syllable form /'trævlɪŋ/. Syllabic /ŋ/ is also common, e.g. to distinguish the forms /'bʌtn̩ɪŋ/ and /'bʌtnɪŋ/ for **buttoning.** /r/ is used less frequently, e.g. to show the alternatives /'memərɪ, 'memr̩ɪ, 'memrɪ/ for **memory.**

16. Strong and Weak Forms (see also Introduction, § 3.23)
The terms 'strong' and 'weak' refer to the alternative pronunciations possible for grammatical items in connected speech, the strong form being appropriate generally only when the items carry stress.[1] The citation form is obviously stressed and is given first in the Dictionary, but it must be noted that the weak form has a higher frequency of occurrence in connected speech.

---

[1] For more information concerning those cases where such items have a strong form, even when relatively unstressed, see my *Introduction to the Pronunciation of English,* op. cit., or other books given in the Selected Book List (p. xxxiii).

17. Syllable Division (see also Introduction, §§ 2.5, 3.24)
The hyphen, placed between symbols, indicates a point of syllable division, and is used only to distinguish the close-knit affricate /tʃ/ from the sequence /t/+ /ʃ/, e.g. **satchel** /'sætʃəl/ as opposed to **nutshell** /'nʌt-ʃel/

18. Foreign Sounds
(i) A number of foreign words and proper names are included in the Dictionary. Many such personal and place names have an accepted anglicized form. Other entries, especially ordinary words and phrases, may be anglicized to a varying extent by English speakers or may be said with a pronunciation identical to or approximating to the foreign pronunciation. Where there is no single established English form, the foreign pronunciation is enclosed in ( ). The languages thus treated include French, German, Italian, Spanish, Russian, Hindi, North Welsh and, more occasionally, Scottish English, Hungarian and Afrikaans. The transcription of such foreign words inevitably involves the introduction of a number of non-English phonetic symbols (listed below) or the use of symbols employed for English but with different values. For the precise phonetic values to be assigned to symbols used for foreign words, readers are recommended to refer to textbooks and pronouncing dictionaries concerned with specific languages, of which the following are a selection:

French: L. E. Armstrong, *The Phonetics of French* (Bell, London); P. A. D. MacCarthy, *The Pronunciation of French* (Oxford University Press); A. Martinet and H. Walter, *Dictionnaire de la Prononciation Française dans son Usage Réel* (France Expansion).
German: P. A. D. MacCarthy, *The Pronunciation of German* (Oxford University Press); C. and P. Martens, *Phonetik der deutschen Sprache* (München); Duden: *Aussprachewörterbuch*, 1975.
Italian: P. Fiorelli, *Corso di pronunzia italiana* (Padova) and *Dizionario d'ortografia e di pronunzia* (Torino).
Spanish: W. Stirling, *The Pronunciation of Spanish* (Cambridge University Press); T. Navarro Tomás, *Manual de pronunciación española* (New York).
Russian: D. Jones and D. Ward, *The Phonetics of Russian* (Cambridge University Press); B. A. Lapidus and S. V. Shevtsova, *A Russian-English Dictionary* (Moscow).
Hindi: A. H. Harley, *Colloquial Hindustani* (Kegan Paul); R. McGregor, *An Outline of Hindi Grammar* (Oxford University Press).
Welsh: J. Morris Jones, *A Welsh Grammar* (Oxford University Press).

Brief information concerning the phonetic characteristics of these languages may also be found in *The Principles of the International Phonetic Association* (obtainable through booksellers or from the Secretary of the International Phonetic Association, University College, London, WC1E 6BT).
(ii) *Notes on the notation of foreign words*
No stress is marked in the transcription of French and Hindi, since these languages make no use of lexically significant word-stress. It is to be understood that there is a certain increase of stress on the final syllables of polysyllabic French words, but that stress for special intensity may be applied to other syllables. Similarly, no particular stress is associated with any syllables of Hindi words, though there is generally prominence by length on /i, e, a, o, u/ and on /əy, əw/.

For German, the short, more open /i, u/ vowels are denoted simply by 'i, u', without the length mark ':' appropriate for the long, closer vowels.

For Spanish, /b, d, g/ are commonly to be interpreted as having frictionless continuant values, except when they follow a nasal consonant or when /d/ follows /l/, in which case they have plosive values. Thus, they have frictionless continuant values in the Spanish renderings of **Oviedo** /o'bjedo/ or **Guadalquivir** /gwadalki'bir/, but /d/ has a plosive value in **Santander** /santan'der/ or **Calderon** /kalde'ron/.

For Russian, the transcription is phonemic, except that the retracted variety of /i/ (a type of unrounded /u/ used after 'hard' consonants) is shown with 'ɨ', and the 'obscured' variety of /a/ (used in all unstressed positions except pretonic ones, and in initial positions when two unstressed syllables follow) is shown with 'ə'. Thus, **Kuibyshev** /'kujbɨʃɨf/ and **Ladoga** /'ladəgə/; /a/ is, however, used in **Onega** /a'njegə/, where the first vowel, though unstressed, is pre-tonic; also in the first syllable of **Vladivostok** /vladjiva'stok/, where the first syllable is followed by two weak syllables. The affricates and palatalized ('soft') consonants are represented digraphically, i.e. /ts, tʃ, pj, dj/, etc.

For Hindi, the transcription follows 'World Orthography', except that IPA 'ɟ' and 'j' replace 'j' and consonantal 'y'. It should be noted that Hindi /a/ is close to English RP /ɑ:/ in quality; /i, e, o, u/ have approximately cardinal values nos. 1, 2, 7, 8 (see Introduction, § 3.1). The open varieties of /i, u/ are represented by 'y, w'. /ə/ is an obscure central vowel, resembling the more open quality of RP /ə/ when final. /əy, əw/ are only slightly diphthongal. /v/ is similar to English /v/ but without friction.

For Scottish, the open variety of /i/ is written with 'ɪ', though it may have a quality similar to that of RP /ɪ/, e.g. **Lerwick** /'lɛrwɪk/. /e, a, ɔ, o/ have approximately cardinal values nos. 2, 4, 6, 7, while /ɛ/ is similar to RP /e/. For Welsh, 'ɨ' denotes a central unrounded close vowel. /gw/ preceding /l/ or /r/ in Welsh words denotes a lip-rounded /g/; thus, **Gwrych** /gwrɨ:x/ constitutes a single syllable. /hr/ indicates a voiceless /r/.

(iii) *Additional Symbols used for Foreign Sounds*

The additional symbols used in phonetic transcriptions of foreign or other unusual pronunciations are as follows:

ţ   'retroflex' /t/.

ḍ   'retroflex' /d/.

c   Hindi sound resembling English sound of **ch** (/tʃ/).

ɟ   Hindi sound resembling English sound of **j** (/dʒ/).

ɲ   French 'n mouillé' (sound of **gn** as in **signe**).

ɳ   'retroflex' /n/ (occurs only in Sanskrit words; it is used by Indian scholars, but ordinary Hindi speakers replace it by /n/).

ļ   voiceless /l/.

ŗ   'retroflex' /r/.

ɹ   'post-alveolar fricative', as in **draw;** also used to denote 'retroflex continuants', as in American pronunciation of **fur.**

ʎ   Italian sound of **gl** in **gli.**

ṛ   voiceless /r/.

ɸ   bi-labial /f/.

ṣ   'retroflex' /s/ (occurs only in Sanskrit words; it is used by Indian scholars, but ordinary Hindi speakers replace it by /ʃ/ or /s/.

ç   the sound of **ch** in German **ich.**

x   the sound of **ch** in Scottish **loch**, German **ach.**

ɣ   voiced consonant corresponding to /x/.

ɥ   the sound of **u** in French **nuit.**

ɛ   the sound of **ê** in French **même.**

y   normally the sound of **u** in French **lune.** For special use of /y/ in Hindi see above.

ø the sound of **eu** in French **peu**.

œ the sound of **eu** in French **neuf**.

~ nasalization.

ɛ̃ the sound of **in** in French **vin**.

æ̃ nasalized /æ/ in English version of French /ɛ̃/.

ã a nasalized /a/.

ɑ̃ the sound of **an** in French **blanc**.

ɔ̃ the sound of **on** in French **bon**.

œ̃ the sound of **un** in French **brun**.

ɨ the North Welsh sound of **u** in **Llandudno** (/ɬanˈdɨdno/), Russian sound of ы. Also used to denote ordinary 'open' /i/ in transcriptions of Scottish pronunciation.

ɯ 'unrounded' /u/, a vowel resembling the Russian /ɨ/ (sound of ы).

ɐ an 'open' variety of /ə/, as in Portuguese **para**.

ǂ alveolar or dental click (often used for English **tut**).

ʖ lateral click (the sound used for urging on a horse).

19. Extralinguistic Sounds

Some sounds, e.g. interjections and hesitation noises, are commonly used in English but fall outside the normal sound system. An attempt is made to represent such extralinguistic sounds by the use of the following symbols:

ẙ French /y/ but without voice.

ə̃ nasalized /ə/.

ʌː a lengthened vowel similar in quality to RP /ʌ/.

m̥ voiceless /m/.

n̥ voiceless /n/.

20. Summary of Conventional Signs

[ ] encloses alternative pronunciations (Explanatory Notes, § 3). Also alternative spellings (Explanatory Notes, § 10).

( ) encloses alternative spellings (Explanatory Notes, §§ 10, 11). Also foreign pronunciations (Explanatory Notes, § 18).

| marks off the part of word repeated in derivatives or other words grouped under a head-word (Explanatory Notes, § 12).

‑‑ (in association with ' or ˌ) denotes syllables (Explanatory Notes, § 9).

21. Abbreviations

abbrev.	means	abbreviation
accus.	„	accusative
adj.	„	adjective
adv.	„	adverb
auxil.	„	auxiliary
compar.	„	comparative
conj.	„	conjunction
cp.	„	compare
demonstr.	„	demonstrative
E.	„	East

esp.	means	especially
fem.	„	feminine, female
freq.	„	frequent, frequently
Heb.	„	Hebrew
Hung.	„	Hungarian
interj.	„	interjection
IPA	„	International Phonetic Association
N.	„	North
opp.	„	as opposed to
p.	„	past
partic.	„	participle
plur.	„	plural
Port.	„	Portuguese
prep.	„	preposition
pres.	„	present
pron.	„	pronoun
RP	„	Received Southern English Pronunciation (see §§ 1.0–1.5 in the Introduction)
s.	„	substantive (noun)
S.	„	South
sing.	„	singular
v.	„	verb
W.	„	West
WO	„	'World Orthography'
zoolog.	„	zoological

22. English Phonetic Symbols and Signs (see also Introduction and Explanatory Notes)

The following consonant letters have their usual English sound values:

p, b, t, d, k, m, n, l, r, f, v, s, z, h, w

Key-words for the remaining English sounds are:

Vowels and Diphthongs

iː	bean	ɪ	pit	eɪ	bay
ɑː	barn	e	pet	aɪ	buy
ɔː	born	æ	pat	ɔɪ	boy
uː	boon	ʌ	putt	əʊ	no
ɜː	burn	ɒ	pot	aʊ	now
		ʊ	put	ɪə	peer
		ə	another	eə	pair
				ʊə	poor

Note : eə also occurs as a variant of ɔː (as in 'four') or of ʊə (as in 'poor');
* indicates a possible *r*-link before a following vowel.

Consonants

g	game	ŋ	long	ʃ	ship
tʃ	chain	θ	thin	ʒ	measure
dʒ	Jane	ð	then	j	yes

Note : x occurs as a variant for k in Scottish words (as in 'loch');
subscript ˌ (as in l̩, ŋ̍) indicates a syllabic consonant;
a symbol in italic type indicates that the sound is often omitted.

Stress Accent
ˈ the following syllable carries primary (tonic) stress;
ˌ the following syllable carries secondary stress.

SELECTED BOOK LIST

The following books on British English pronunciation are recommended as a selection of works amplifying the information given in the introductory sections of this Dictionary.

G. F. Arnold, *Stress in English Words* (North Holland Publishing Co.), 1957.

C. Barber, *Linguistic Change in Present-Day English* (Oliver Boyd), 1957.

D. Crystal, *Prosodic Systems and Intonation in English* (Cambridge University Press), 1969.

A. C. Gimson, *Introduction to the Pronunciation of English* (Edward Arnold), 3rd ed., 1980.

—, *A Practical Course of English Pronunciation* (Edward Arnold), 1975.

M. A. K. Halliday, *Intonation and Grammar in British English* (Mouton), 1967.

International Phonetic Association, *The Principles*, 1949.

Daniel Jones, *An Outline of English Phonetics* (Cambridge University Press), 9th ed., 1975.

—, *The Pronunciation of English* (Cambridge University Press), definitive ed., 1972.

R. Kingdon, *Groundwork of English Intonation* (Longman), 1958.

—, *Groundwork of English Stress* (Longman), 1958.

J. Windsor Lewis, *A Concise Pronouncing Dictionary of British and American English* (Oxford University Press), 1972.

P. A. D. MacCarthy, *English Pronunciation* (Heffer), 4th ed., 1952.

G. E. Pointon, *BBC Pronouncing Dictionary of British Names* (Oxford University Press), 2nd ed., 1983.

J. D. O'Connor, *Better English Pronunciation* (Cambridge University Press), 1967.

— and G. F. Arnold, *Intonation of Colloquial English* (Longman), 2nd ed., 1973.

J. T. Pring, *Colloquial English Pronunciation* (Longman), 1959

B. Strang, *A History of English* (Methner), 1970.

I. C. Ward, *The Phonetics of English* (Cambridge University Press), definitive ed., 1975.

H. C. Wyld, *A History of Modern Colloquial English* (Blackwell), 1936.

A

A (*the letter*), -**'s** eɪ, -z
a (*indefinite article*) eɪ (*strong form*), ə (*weak form*)
aardvark, -s 'ɑːdvɑːk, -s
Aaron, -s 'eərən, -z
aback ə'bæk
Abaco (*in Bahamas*) 'æbəkəʊ
abacus, -es 'æbəkəs, -ɪz
Abadan (*in Iran*) ˌæbə'dɑːn [-'dæn]
Abaddon ə'bædən
abaft ə'bɑːft
abandon (*s.*) ə'bændən (abɑ̃dɔ̃)
abandon (*v.*), -s, -ing, -ed/ly, -ment ə'bændən, -z, -ɪŋ, -d/lɪ, -mənt
abas|e, -es, -ing, -ed, -ement ə'beɪs, -ɪz, -ɪŋ, -t, -mənt
abash, -es, -ing, -ed ə'bæʃ, -ɪz, -ɪŋ, -t
abatab|le, -ly ə'beɪtəb|l, -lɪ
abat|e, -es, -ing, -ed, -ement/s ə'beɪt, -s, -ɪŋ, -ɪd, -mənt/s
abatis (*sing.*) 'æbətɪs [-tiː]
abatis (*plur.*) 'æbəti:z
abatises (*plur.*) 'æbətɪsɪz
abattis, -es ə'bætɪs, -ɪz
abattoir, -s 'æbətwɑ:* [-twɔ:*], -z
Abba 'æbə
abbac|y, -ies 'æbəs|ɪ, -ɪz
Abbas 'æbəs [-bæs]
abbé, -s 'æbeɪ (abe), -z
abbess, -es 'æbes [-bɪs], -ɪz
abbey (A.), -s 'æbɪ, -z
abbot (A.), -s 'æbət, -s
Abbotsford 'æbətsfəd
abbotship, -s 'æbət-ʃɪp, -s
Abbott 'æbət
abbreviat|e, -es, -ing, -ed, -or/s ə'bri:-vɪeɪt [vjeɪt], -s, -ɪŋ, -ɪd, -ə*/z
abbreviation, -s əˌbri:vɪ'eɪʃn, -z
abbreviatory ə'bri:vjətərɪ [-teɪr-, -vɪeɪt-]
abc, -'s ˌeɪbiː'si:, -z
Abdera æb'dɪərə
abdicant, -s 'æbdɪkənt, -s
abdicat|e, -es, -ing, -ed 'æbdɪkeɪt, -s, -ɪŋ, -ɪd
abdication, -s ˌæbdɪ'keɪʃn, -z
Abdiel 'æbdɪəl [-djəl]

abdomen, -s 'æbdəmen [æb'dəʊmen, -mɪn, -mən], -z
abdomin|al, -ally æb'dɒmɪn|l [əb-], -əlɪ
abduct, -s, -ing, -ed, -or/s æb'dʌkt [əb-], -s, -ɪŋ, -ɪd, -ə*/z
abduction, -s æb'dʌkʃn [əb-], -z
Abdulla, -s æb'dʌlə [əb-], -z
Abdy 'æbdɪ
Abe eɪb
abeam ə'bi:m
abecedarian ˌeɪbi:si:'deərɪən
A Becket ə'bekɪt
abed ə'bed
Abednego ˌæbed'ni:gəʊ [ə'bednɪgəʊ]
Abel (*biblical name, English name*) 'eɪbəl, (*foreign name*) 'ɑ:bəl
Abelard 'æbɪlɑ:d ['æbə-]
Abell 'eɪbəl
Abelmeholah ˌeɪbəlmɪ'həʊlə [-mə'h-]
Aberavon ˌæbə'rævən [-bɔ:'r-] (*Welsh* aber'avon)
Aberbrothock ˌæbə'brɒθək [-bɔ:'b-]
    Note.—This place-name has to be pronounced ˌæbəbrə'θɒk [-bɔ:b-] *in Southey's 'Inchcape Rock'.*
Abercorn 'æbəkɔ:n
Abercrombie [-by] 'æbəkrʌmbɪ [-krɒm-, ˌ--'--]
Aberdare ˌæbə'deə* (*Welsh* aber'da:r)
Aberdeen, -shire ˌæbə'di:n, -ʃə* [-ˌʃɪə*]
aberdevine, -s ˌæbədə'vaɪn, -z
Aberdonian, -s ˌæbə'dəʊnjən [-nɪən], -z
Aberdour ˌæbə'daʊə*
Aberdovey ˌæbə'dʌvɪ (*Welsh* aber'dəvi)
Abergavenny (*family name*) ˌæbə'genɪ, (*place*) ˌæbəgə'venɪ (*Welsh* aber-ga'veni)
Abergele ˌæbə'gelɪ (*Welsh* aber'gele)
Abernethy ˌæbə'neθɪ [*in the S. also* -'ni:θɪ]
aberran|ce, -cy, -t æ'berən|s [ə'b-], -sɪ, -t
aberrat|e, -es, -ing, -ed 'æbəreɪt [-ber-], -s, -ɪŋ, -ɪd
aberration, -s ˌæbə'reɪʃn [-be'r-], -z
Abersychan ˌæbə'sɪkən (*Welsh* aber-'səxan)
Abert 'eɪbɜ:t

1

Abertillery ˌæbətɪ'leərɪ (*Welsh* abertə'leri)

Aberystwyth ˌæbə'rɪstwɪθ (*Welsh* aber'əstuiθ)

abet, -s, -ting, -ted, -tor/s, -ment ə'bet, -s, -ɪŋ, -ɪd, -ə*/z, -mənt

abeyance ə'beɪəns

abhor, -s, -ring, -red, -rer/s əb'hɔ:*, -z, -rɪŋ, -d, -rə*/z

abhorren|ce, -t əb'hɒrən|s, -t

Abia (*biblical name*) ə'baɪə, (*city*) 'æbɪə

Abiathar ə'baɪəθə*

Abib 'eɪbɪb ['ɑ:bɪb]

abid|e, -es, -ing, abode ə'baɪd, -z, -ɪŋ, ə'bəʊd

abies 'æbɪi:z ['eɪb-]

abigail, -s 'æbɪgeɪl, -z

Abigail 'æbɪgeɪl [*with some Jews* ˌæbɪ'geɪl]

Abijah ə'baɪdʒə

Abilene (*in Syria*) ˌæbɪ'li:nɪ, (*in U.S.A.*) 'æbɪli:n

abilit|y, -ies ə'bɪlət|ɪ [-lɪt-], -ɪz

Abi|melech, -nadab ə'bɪ|mələk, -nədæb

Abingdon 'æbɪŋdən

Abinger 'æbɪndʒə*

ab initio ˌæbɪ'nɪʃɪəʊ [-'nɪtɪəʊ, -'nɪsɪəʊ]

Abinoam ə'bɪnəʊæm [*with some Jews* ˌæbɪ'nəʊəm]

abiogenesis ˌeɪbaɪəʊ'dʒenɪsɪs [-nəsɪs]

Abishai æ'bɪʃeraɪ [ə'b-, 'æbɪʃaɪ, ˌɑ:bɪ-'ʃeraɪ]

abject, -ly, -ness 'æbdʒekt, -lɪ, -nɪs [-nəs]

abjection æb'dʒekʃn

abjudicat|e, -es, -ing, -ed æb'dʒu:dɪ-keɪt [əb-], -s, -ɪŋ, -ɪd

abjuration, -s ˌæbdʒʊə'reɪʃn, [-dʒɔə'r-, -dʒɔ:'r-], -z

abjur|e, -es, -ing, -ed, -er/s əb'dʒʊə* [æb-, -'dʒɔə*, -'dʒɔ:*], -z, -rɪŋ, -d, -rə*/z

ablation æb'leɪʃn [əb-]

ablatival ˌæblə'taɪvl

ablative (*s. adj.*), **-s** 'æblətɪv, -z

ablaut, -s 'æblaʊt ('aplaut), -s

ablaze ə'bleɪz

ab|le, -ler, -lest, -ly 'eɪb|l, -lə*, -lɪst, -lɪ

able-bodied ˌeɪbl'bɒdɪd ['eɪbl,b-]

ablution, -s ə'blu:ʃn, -z

abnegat|e, -es, -ing, -ed 'æbnɪgeɪt [-neg-], -s, -ɪŋ, -ɪd

abnegation, -s ˌæbnɪ'geɪʃn [-'neg-], -z

Abner 'æbnə*

abnorm|al, -ally æb'nɔ:m|l [əb-, ˌæb'n-], -əlɪ

abnormalit|y, -ies ˌæbnɔ:'mælət|ɪ [-lɪt-], -ɪz

abnormit|y, -ies æb'nɔ:mət|ɪ [əb-, -mɪt-], -ɪz

aboard ə'bɔ:d [-'bɒəd]

abode (*s. v.*), **-s** ə'bəʊd, -z

abolish, -es, -ing, -ed, -er/s ə'bɒlɪʃ, -ɪz, -ɪŋ, -t, -ə*/z

abolition, -s ˌæbəʊ'lɪʃn [-bʊ'l-], -z

abolitioni|sm, -st/s ˌæbəʊ'lɪʃənɪ|zəm [-bʊ'l-, -ʃnɪ-], -st/s

abominab|le, -ly, -leness ə'bɒmɪnəb|l, -lɪ, -lnɪs [-nəs]

abominat|e, -es, -ing, -ed ə'bɒmɪneɪt, -s, -ɪŋ, -ɪd

abomination, -s ə,bɒmɪ'neɪʃn, -z

aborigin|al, -ally ˌæbə'rɪdʒən|l [-bɒ'r-, -dʒɪn-], -əlɪ

aborigines ˌæbə'rɪdʒəni:z [-bɒ'r-, -dʒɪ-]

abort, -s, -ing, -ed ə'bɔ:t, -s, -ɪŋ, -ɪd

abortion, -s, -ist/s ə'bɔ:ʃn, -z, -ɪst/s

abortive, -ly, -ness ə'bɔ:tɪv, -lɪ, -nɪs [-nəs]

Aboukir, -s ˌæbu:'kɪə* [ˌɑ:b-, -bʊ-]

abound, -s, -ing, -ed ə'baʊnd, -z, -ɪŋ, -ɪd

about ə'baʊt

above ə'bʌv

above-board ə,bʌv'bɔ:d [-'bɒəd, -'--]

above-mentioned ə,bʌv'menʃnd [*when attributive also* -'-,--]

abovo ˌæb'əʊvəʊ

abracadabra, -s ˌæbrəkə'dæbrə, -z

abrad|e, -es, -ing, -ed ə'breɪd, -z, -ɪŋ, -ɪd

Abraham 'eɪbrəhæm [-həm, *as a biblical name freq. also* 'ɑ:b-]

Abrahams 'eɪbrəhæmz

Abram 'eɪbrəm [-ræm, *as a biblical name freq. also* 'ɑ:b-]

abranchi|al, -ate æ'bræŋkɪ|əl, -eɪt [ə'br-]

abrasion, -s ə'breɪʒn, -z

abrasive ə'breɪsɪv

abraxus ə'bræksəs

abreac|t, -ts, -ting, -ted, -tion ˌæbrɪ'æk|t, -ts, -tɪŋ, -tɪd, -ʃn

abreast ə'brest

abridg|e, -es, -ing, -ed, -(e)ment/s ə'brɪdʒ, -ɪz, -ɪŋ, -d, -mənt/s

abroad ə'brɔ:d

abrogat|e, -es, -ing, -ed 'æbrəʊgeɪt [-rʊg-], -s, -ɪŋ, -ɪd

abrogation, -s ˌæbrəʊ'geɪʃn [-rʊ'g-], -z

A'Brook ə'brʊk

abrupt, -est, -ly, -ness ə'brʌpt, -ɪst, -lɪ, -nɪs [-nəs]

Abruzzi ə'brʊtsi: [-sɪ]

Absalom 'æbsələm

abscess, -es 'æbsɪs [-ses], -ɪz

absciss|a, -ae, -as æb'sɪs|ə [əb-], -i:, -əz
abscission, -s æb'sɪʒn [-sɪʃn], -z
abscond, -s, -ing, -ed əb'skɒnd [æb-], -z, -ɪŋ, -ɪd
absence, -s 'æbsəns, -ɪz
absent (adj.), -ly 'æbsənt, -lɪ
absent (v.), -s, -ing, -ed æb'sent [əb-], -s, -ɪŋ, -ɪd
absentee, -s, -ism ˌæbsən'ti: [-sen-], -z -ɪzəm
absent-minded, -ly, -ness ˌæbsənt-'maɪndɪd [also '--,--, when attributive], -lɪ, -nɪs [-nəs]
absinth 'æbsɪnθ
absolute, -st, -ness 'æbsəlu:t [-slu:-, -lju:t], -ɪst, -nɪs [-nəs]
absolutely 'æbsəlu:tlɪ [-slu:-, -lju:-, also ˌ--'--]
Note.—Some people use the form '---- meaning 'completely' and ˌ--'-- meaning 'certainly'.
absolution, -s ˌæbsə'lu:ʃn [-'lju:-], -z
absoluti|sm, -st/s 'æbsəlu:tɪ|zəm [-lju:-], -st/s
absolv|e, -es, -ing, -ed, -er/s əb'zɒlv, -z, -ɪŋ, -d, -ə*/z
absorb, -s, -ing/ly, -ed, -edly; -able; -ent/ly əb'sɔ:b [əb'zɔ:b], -z, -ɪŋ/lɪ, -d, -ɪdlɪ; -əbl; -ənt/lɪ
absorption əb'sɔ:pʃn [əb'zɔ:-]
absorptive əb'sɔ:ptɪv [əb'zɔ:-]
abstain, -s, -ing, -ed, -er/s əb'steɪn [æb-], -z, -ɪŋ, -d, -ə*/z
abstemious, -ly, -ness æb'sti:mjəs [əb-, -mɪəs], -lɪ, -nɪs [-nəs]
abstention, -s əb'stenʃn [æb-], -z
abstergent (s. adj.), -s əb'stɜ:dʒənt, -s
abstinen|ce, -t 'æbstɪnən|s, -t
abstract (s. adj.), -s, -ly, -ness 'æbs-trækt, -s, -lɪ [-'--], -nɪs [-nəs, -'--]
abstract (v.), -s, -ing, -ed/ly, -edness æb'strækt [əb-], -s, -ɪŋ, -ɪd/lɪ, -ɪdnɪs [-nəs]
abstraction, -s æb'strækʃn [əb-], -z
abstruse, -ly, -ness æb'stru:s [əb-], -lɪ, -nɪs [-nəs]
absurd, -est, -ly, -ness; -ity, -ities əb'sɜ:d, -ɪst, -lɪ, -nɪs [-nəs]; -ətɪ [-ɪtɪ], -ətɪz [-ɪtɪz]
Abu 'ɑ:bu:
Abukir ˌæbu:'kɪə* [ˌɑ:b-, -bʊ-]
abundan|ce, -t/ly ə'bʌndən|s, -t/lɪ
Abury 'eɪbərɪ
abuse (s.), -s ə'bju:s, -ɪz
abus|e (v.), -es, -ing, -ed, -er/s ə'bju:z, -ɪz, -ɪŋ, -d, -ə*/z
abusive, -ly, -ness ə'bju:sɪv, -lɪ, -nɪs [-nəs]

abut, -s, -ting, -ted, -ment/s; -tal ə'bʌt, -s, -ɪŋ, -ɪd, -mənt/s; -l
abutilon, -s ə'bju:tɪlən, -z
Abydos ə'baɪdɒs
abysm, -s ə'bɪzəm, -z
abysm|al, -ally ə'bɪzm|l, -əlɪ
abyss, -es ə'bɪs, -ɪz
Abyssinia, -n/s ˌæbɪ'sɪnjə [-bə's-, -nɪə], -n/z
acacia, -s ə'keɪʃə [-'keɪsjə], -z
academic, -al, -ally ˌækə'demɪk, -l, -əlɪ
academician, -s əˌkædə'mɪʃn [-de'm-, -dɪ'm-], -z
academ|y, -ies ə'kædəm|ɪ, -ɪz
Acadia, -n/s ə'keɪdjə [-dɪə], -n/z
acajou, -s 'ækəʒu:, -z
acanth|us, -i, -uses, -ine ə'kænθ|əs, -aɪ, -əsɪz, -aɪn
acatalectic æˌkætə'lektɪk [əˌk-]
acatalepsy æ'kætəlepsɪ [ə'k-]
acataleptic æˌkætə'leptɪk [əˌk-]
Accad 'ækæd
Accadia, -n/s ə'keɪdjə [-dɪə], -n/z
acced|e, -es, -ing, -ed, -er/s æk'si:d [ək-], -z, -ɪŋ, -ɪd, -ə*/z
accelerando ækˌselə'rændəʊ [ək-, əˌtʃel-]
accelerat|e, -es, -ing, -ed ək'seləreɪt [æk-], -s, -ɪŋ, -ɪd
acceleration, -s əkˌselə'reɪʃn [æk-], -z
accelerative ək'selərətɪv [æk-, -reɪt-]
accelerator, -s ək'seləreɪtə* [æk-], -z
accent (s.), -s 'æksənt [-sent], -s
accent (v.), -s, -ing, -ed æk'sent [ək-], -s, -ɪŋ, -ɪd
accentual, -ly æk'sentjʊəl [ək-, -tjwəl, -tjʊl, -tʃʊəl], -ɪ
accentuat|e, -es, -ing, -ed æk'sentjʊeɪt [ək-, -tʃʊeɪt], -s, -ɪŋ, -ɪd
accentuation, -s ækˌsentjʊ'eɪʃn [-ək-, -tʃʊ-], -z
accept, -s, -ing, -ed, -er/s, -or/s ək'sept [æk-], -s, -ɪŋ, -ɪd, -ə*/z, -ə*/z
acceptability əkˌseptə'bɪlətɪ [æk-, -lɪt-]
acceptab|le, -ly, -leness ək'septəb|l [æk-], -lɪ, -lnɪs [-nəs]
acceptan|ce, -ces, -cy, -t/s ək'septən|s [æk-], -sɪz, -sɪ, -t/s
acceptation, -s ˌæksep'teɪʃn, -z
access 'ækses
accessar|y (s. adj.), -ies ək'sesər|ɪ [æk-], -ɪz
accessibility əkˌsesə'bɪlətɪ [æk-, -sɪ'b-, -lɪt-]
accessible ək'sesəbl [æk-, -sɪb-]
accession, -s æk'seʃn [ək-], -z
accessit, -s æk'sesɪt [ək-], -s
accessor|y (s. adj.), -ies ək'sesər|ɪ [æk-], -ɪz

3

acciaccatura ə‚tʃækə'tʊərə
accidence 'æksɪdəns
accident, -s 'æksɪdənt, -s
accident|al, -ally ‚æksɪ'dent|l, -əlɪ [-l̩ɪ]
acclaim, -s, -ing, -ed ə'kleɪm, -z, -ɪŋ, -d
acclamation, -s ‚æklə'meɪʃn, -z
acclamatory ə'klæmətərɪ
acclimatation ə‚klaɪmə'teɪʃn
acclimation ‚æklaɪ'meɪʃn
acclimatization [-isa-] ə‚klaɪmətaɪ'zeɪʃn [-tɪ'z-]
acclimatiz|e [-is|e], -es, -ing, -ed ə'klaɪmətaɪz, -ɪz, -ɪŋ, -d
acclivit|y, -ies ə'klɪvət|ɪ [æ'k-, -vɪ-], -ɪz
accolade, -s 'ækəʊleɪd [-lɑːd, ‚--'-], -z
accommodat|e, -es, -ing/ly, -ed, -or/s; -ive/ly ə'kɒmədeɪt, -s, -ɪŋ/lɪ, -ɪd, -ə*/z; -ɪv/lɪ
accommodation, -s ə‚kɒmə'deɪʃn, -z
accompaniment, -s ə'kʌmpənɪmənt, -s
accompanist, -s ə'kʌmpənɪst, -s
accompan|y, -ies, -ying, -ied, -ier/s; -yist/s ə'kʌmpən|ɪ, -ɪz, -ɪɪŋ, -ɪd, -ɪə*/z; -ɪɪst/s
accomplice, -s ə'kʌmplɪs [-'kɒm-], -ɪz
accomplish, -es, -ing, -ed, -ment/s ə'kʌmplɪʃ [-'kɒm-], -ɪz, -ɪŋ, -t, -mənt/s
accord (s. v.), -s, -ing, -ed ə'kɔːd, -z -ɪŋ, -ɪd
accordan|ce, -t ə'kɔːdən|s, -t
according, -ly ə'kɔːdɪŋ, -lɪ
accordion, -s ə'kɔːdjən [-dɪən], -z
accost, -s, -ing, -ed ə'kɒst, -s, -ɪŋ, -ɪd
accouchement, -s ə'kuːʃmɑ̃ːŋ [-mɔ̃ː-, -mɒŋ] (akuʃmɑ̃)
accoucheur, -s ‚æku:'ʃɜː* [ə'ku:ʃɜ:*] (akuʃœːr), -z
accoucheuse, -s ‚æku:'ʃɜːz (akuʃøːz), -z
account (s. v.), -s, -ing, -ed ə'kaʊnt, -s, -ɪŋ, -ɪd
accountability ə‚kaʊntə'bɪlətɪ [-lɪt-]
accountab|le, -ly, -leness ə'kaʊntəb|l, -lɪ, -lnɪs [-nəs]
accountan|cy, -t/s ə'kaʊntən|sɪ, -t/s
account-book, -s ə'kaʊntbʊk, -s
accou|tre, -tres, -tring, -tred; -trement/s ə'ku:|tə*, -təz, -tərɪŋ [-trɪŋ], -təd; -təmənt/s [-trəmənt/s]
Accra (in Ghana) ə'krɑ: [æ'k-]
accredit, -s, -ing, -ed ə'kredɪt, -s, -ɪŋ, -ɪd
accretion, -s ə'kri:ʃn [ə'k-], -z
accretive æ'kri:tɪv [ə'k-]
Accrington 'ækrɪŋtən
accru|e, -es, -ing, -ed ə'kru:, -z, -ɪŋ [ə'krʊɪŋ], -d

accumulat|e, -es, -ing, -ed, -or/s ə'kju:mjʊleɪt [-mjəl-], -s, -ɪŋ, -ɪd, -ə*/z
accumulation, -s ə‚kju:mjʊ'leɪʃn [-mjə'l-], -z
accumulative ə'kju:mjʊlətɪv [-mjəl-, -leɪt-]
accuracy 'ækjʊrəsɪ [-kjər-, -rɪsɪ]
accur|ate, -ately, -ateness 'ækjʊr|ət [-kjər-, -rɪt], -ətlɪ [-ɪtlɪ], -ətnɪs [-ɪtnɪs, -nəs]
accursed, -ly ə'kɜːsɪd, -lɪ
accusal, -s ə'kju:zl, -z
accusation, -s ‚ækju:'zeɪʃn [-kjʊ-], -z
accusatival ə‚kju:zə'taɪvl
accusative (s. adj.), -s ə'kju:zətɪv, -z
accusatory ə'kju:zətərɪ
accus|e, -es, -ing, -ed, -er/s ə'kju:z, -ɪz, -ɪŋ, -d, -ə*/z
accustom, -s, -ing, -ed/ness ə'kʌstəm, -z, -ɪŋ, -d/nɪs [-nəs]
ace, -s eɪs, -ɪz
Aceldama ə'keldəmə [ə'sel-]
acerbity ə'sɜːbətɪ [-bɪ-]
Acestes ə'sesti:z
acetate 'æsɪteɪt [-tɪt]
acetic ə'si:tɪk [æ's-, -'set-]
aceti|fy, -fies, -fying, -fied ə'setɪ|faɪ [æ's-], -faɪz, -faɪɪŋ, -faɪd
acetone 'æsɪtəʊn
acet|ose, -ous 'æsɪtəʊs, -əs
acetyl 'æsɪtɪl
acetylene ə'setɪli:n [æ's-, -təl-]
Achaea, -n/s ə'ki:ə [-'kɪə], -n/z
Achaia ə'kaɪə
Achates ə'keɪti:z
ach|e (s.v.) (pain), -es, -ing, -ed, -er/s eɪk, -s, -ɪŋ, -t, -ə*/z
ache (letter H), -s eɪtʃ, -ɪz
Achernar (star) 'eɪkənɑ:*
Acheron 'ækərɒn [-rən]
Acheson 'ætʃɪsn
achiev|e, -es, -ing, -ed, -ement/s; -able ə'tʃi:v, -z, -ɪŋ, -d, -mənt/s; -əbl
Achil(l) 'ækɪl
Achilles ə'kɪli:z
Achille Serre ‚æʃɪl'seə* [-ʃi:l-]
Achin ə'tʃi:n
Achish 'eɪkɪʃ
Achonry 'ækənrɪ
Achray ə'kreɪ [ə'xreɪ]
achromatic, -ally ‚ækrəʊ'mætɪk [-krʊ'm-], -əlɪ
achromatism ə'krəʊmətɪzəm [æ'k-, eɪ'k-]
achromatiz|e [-is|e], -es, -ing, -ed ə'krəʊmətaɪz [æ'k-], -ɪz, -ɪŋ, -d

4

acid (s. adj.), -s, -est, -ly, -ness 'æsɪd, -z, -ɪst, -lɪ, -nɪs [-nəs]

acidi|fy, -fies, -fying, -fied ə'sɪdɪ|faɪ [æ's-], -faɪz, -faɪɪŋ, -faɪd

acidity ə'sɪdɪtɪ [æ's-, -ɪtɪ]

acidiz|e [-is|e], -es, -ing, -ed 'æsɪdaɪz, -ɪz, -ɪŋ, -d

acidosis ,æsɪ'dəʊsɪs

acidulat|e, -es, -ing, -ed ə'sɪdjʊleɪt [æ's-], -s, -ɪŋ, -ɪd

acidulous ə'sɪdjʊləs [æ's-]

Acis 'eɪsɪs

ack æk

ack-ack ,æk'æk

Ackerman(n) 'ækəmən [-mæn]

acknowledg|e, -es, -ing, -ed, -(e)ment/s; -eable ək'nɒlɪdʒ [æk-], -ɪz, -ɪŋ, -d, -mənt/s; -əbl
Note.—There is also a rare form -'nəʊl-.

Ackroyd 'ækrɔɪd

Acland 'æklənd

acme, -s 'ækmɪ, -z

acne 'æknɪ

Acol (road in London, system of bridge playing) 'ækəl

acolyte, -s 'ækəʊlaɪt, -s

Acomb 'eɪkəm

aconite, -s 'ækənaɪt, -s

acorn, -s; -shell/s 'eɪkɔːn, -z; -ʃel/z

acotyledon, -s ,ə,kɒtɪ'liːdən [ə,k-, ,eɪkɒt-], -z

acoustic, -ally, -s ə'kuːstɪk [old-fashioned -'kaʊs-], -əlɪ, -s

acquaint, -s, -ing, -ed; -ance/s ə'kweɪnt, -s, -ɪŋ, -ɪd; -əns/ɪz

acquaintanceship, -s ə'kweɪntənʃɪp [-nsʃ-, -nʃʃ-], -s

acquest, -s æ'kwest [ə'k-], -s

acquiesc|e, -es, -ing, -ed; -ence, -ent ,ækwɪ'es, -ɪz, -ɪŋ, -t; -ns, -nt

acquir|e, -es, -ing, -ed, -ement/s; -able ə'kwaɪə*, -z, -rɪŋ, -d, -mənt/s; -rəbl

acquisition, -s ,ækwɪ'zɪʃn, -z

acquisitive, -ness ə'kwɪzɪtɪv [æ'k-, -zət-], -nɪs [-nəs]

acquit, -s, -ting, -ted; -tal/s ə'kwɪt, -s, -ɪŋ, -ɪd; -l/z

acre (A.), -s; -age/s 'eɪkə*, -z; -rɪdʒ/ɪz

acrid, -ly, -ness 'ækrɪd, -lɪ, -nɪs [-nəs]

acridity æ'krɪdətɪ [ə'k-, -dɪ-]

acrimonious, -ly, -ness ,ækrɪ'məʊnjəs [-nɪəs], -lɪ, -nɪs [-nəs]

acrimon|y, -ies 'ækrɪmən|ɪ, ɪz

acritude 'ækrɪtjuːd

acrobat, -s; -ism 'ækrəbæt, -s; -ɪzəm

acrobatic, -s, -ally ,ækrəʊ'bætɪk, -s, -əlɪ

acronym, -s 'ækrəʊnɪm, -z

acrophobia ,ækrəʊ'fəʊbjə [-bɪə]

acropolis, -es ə'krɒpəlɪs [-plɪs], -ɪz

across ə'krɒs [old-fashioned -'krɔːs]

acrostic, -s ə'krɒstɪk, -s

Acrux (star) 'eɪkrʌks

acrylic ə'krɪlɪk [æ'k-]

act (s. v.), -s, -ing, -ed, -or/s ækt, -s, -ɪŋ, -ɪd, -ə*/z

acta 'æktə

A.C.T.H. ,eɪsiːtiː'eɪtʃ [ækθ]

actinic æk'tɪnɪk

actinium æk'tɪnɪəm [-njəm]

action, -s 'ækʃn, -z

actionable 'ækʃɲəbl [-ʃnəb-, -ʃənəb-]

Actium 'æktɪəm [-tjəm]

activable 'æktɪvəbl

activat|e, -es, -ing, -ed 'æktɪveɪt, -s, -ɪŋ, -ɪd

active, -ly, -ness 'æktɪv, -lɪ, -nɪs [-nəs]

activist, -s 'æktɪvɪst, -s

activit|y, -ies æk'tɪvət|ɪ [-vɪ-], -ɪz

Acton 'æktən

actor, -s 'æktə*, -z

actress, -es 'æktrɪs [-trəs, -tres], -ɪz

actual, -ly 'æktʃʊəl [-tjwəl, -tjʊl, -tjʊəl, -tʃwəl, -tʃʊl], -ɪ

actualit|y, -ies ,æktʃʊ'ælət|ɪ [-tjʊ-, -lɪ-], -ɪz

actualiz|e [-is|e], -es, -ing, -ed 'æktʃʊəlaɪz [-tjwəl-, -tjʊəl-, -tʃwəl-], -ɪz, -ɪŋ, -d

actuarial ,æktjʊ'eərɪəl [-tʃʊ-]

actuar|y, -ies 'æktjʊər|ɪ [-tjwər-, -tʃʊər-, -tʃwər-], -ɪz

actuate, -es, -ing, -ed 'æktjʊeɪt [-tʃʊ-], -s, -ɪŋ, -ɪd

actuation, -s ,æktjʊ'eɪʃn [-tʃʊ-], -z

acuity ə'kjuːətɪ [-'kjʊ-, -ɪtɪ]

acumen 'ækjʊmen [ə'kjuːmen]

acute, -r, -st, -ly, -ness ə'kjuːt, -ə*, -ɪst, -lɪ, -nɪs [-nəs]

A.D. ,eɪ'diː [,ænəʊ'dɒmɪnaɪ]

ad æd

Ada 'eɪdə

adage, -s 'ædɪdʒ, -ɪz

adagio, -s ə'dɑːdʒɪəʊ [-dʒjəʊ], -z

Adair ə'deə*

Adalbert 'ædəlbɜːt

Adam 'ædəm

adamant 'ædəmənt

adamantine ,ædə'mæntaɪn

adamite (A.), -s 'ædəmaɪt, -s

Adams 'ædəmz

Adamson 'ædəmsn

Adamthwaite 'ædəmθweɪt

adapt, -s, -ing, -ed, -er/s ə'dæpt, -s, -ɪŋ, -ɪd, -ə*/z

adaptability ə,dæptə'bɪlətɪ [-lɪt-]

adaptable, -ness ə'dæptəbl, -nıs [-nəs]
adaptation, -s ˌædæp'teıʃn [-dəp-], -z
Adar 'eıda:*
Adare ə'deə*
Adastral ə'dæstrəl
Adcock 'ædkɒk
add, -s, -ing, -ed æd, -z, -ıŋ, -ıd
addend|um, -a ə'dend|əm [æ'd-], -ə
adder, -s; -'s-tongue, -wort 'ædə*, -z;
-ztʌŋ, -wɜːt
addict (s.), -s 'ædıkt, -s
addict (v.), -s, -ing, -ed/ness ə'dıkt, -s,
-ıŋ, -ıd/nıs [-nəs]
addiction, -s ə'dıkʃn, -z
Addington 'ædıŋtən
Addis Ababa ˌædıs'æbəbə [-'ɑːb-]
Addiscombe 'ædıskəm
Addison 'ædısn
addition, -s ə'dıʃn, -z
addi|tional, -tionally ə'dı|ʃnəl [-ʃnəl,
-ʃŋl, -ʃnl, -ʃnəl], -ʃŋəlı [-ʃnəlı, -ʃŋlı,
-ʃnlı, -ʃnəlı]
additive, -s 'ædıtıv [-də-], -z
add|le (adj. v.), -les, -ling, -led 'æd|l, -lz,
-lıŋ [-lıŋ], -ld
addle|headed, -pated 'ædl|ˌhedıd,
-ˌpeıtıd [ˌ--'--]
Addlestone 'ædlstən
address (s. v.), -es, -ing, -ed ə'dres, -ız,
-ıŋ, -t
addressee, -s ˌædre'siː, -z
addressograph, -s ə'dresəʊgrɑːf [-græf],
-s
adduc|e, -es, -ing, -ed, -er/s; -ible
ə'djuːs [æ'd-], -ız, -ıŋ, -t, -ə*/z; -əbl
[-ıbl]
Adeane ə'diːn
Adel (in West Yorkshire) 'ædl
Adela (English name) 'ædılə, (foreign
name) ə'deılə
Adelaide (in Australia) 'ædəleıd [-dıl-,
-lıd]. (Christian name, road in
London) 'ædələıd [-dıl-]
Note. — The pronunciation in Australia is with -leıd.
Adelina ˌædı'liːnə [-də'l-]
Adeline 'ædıliːn [-dəl-, -laın]
Adelphi ə'delfı
Aden (in the Yemen) 'eıdn, (in Grampian Region) 'ædn
adenoid, -s 'ædınɔıd [-dən-], -z
adenoidal ˌædı'nɔıdl [-də'n-]
adept (s.), -s 'ædept [ə'dept, æ'd-,
rarely 'eıdept], -s
adept (adj.) 'ædept [ə'd-, æ'd-]
adequacy 'ædıkwəsı
adequate, -ly, -ness 'ædıkwət [-ıt], -lı
[-ıtlı], -nıs [-nəs]

adher|e, -es, -ing, -ed, -er/s əd'hıə*
[æd-], -z, -rıŋ, -d, -rə*/z
adheren|ce, -t/s əd'hıərən|s [æd-], -t/s
adhesion, -s əd'hiːʒn [æd-], -z
adhesive, -ly, -ness əd'hiːsıv [æd-,
-'hiːzıv], -lı, -nıs [-nəs]
ad hoc ˌæd'hɒk [-'həʊk]
Adie 'eıdı
adieu, -s ə'djuː, -z
ad infinitum ˌæd ınfı'naıtəm
adipocere ˌædıpəʊ'sıə*
adipose 'ædıpəʊs
Adirondack, -s ˌædı'rɒndæk, -s
adit, -s 'ædıt, -s
adjacen|cy, -t/ly ə'dʒeısən|sı, -t/lı
adjectiv|al, -ally ˌædʒek'taıv|l [-dʒık-,
-dʒək-], -əlı
adjective, -s 'ædʒıktıv [-dʒəkt-,
-dʒekt-], -z
adjoin, -s, -ing, -ed ə'dʒɔın, -z, -ıŋ, -d
adjourn, -s, -ing, -ed, -ment/s ə'dʒɜːn,
-z, -ıŋ, -d, -mənt/s
adjudg|e, -es, -ing, -ed, -ment/s
ə'dʒʌdʒ [æ'dʒ-], -ız, -ıŋ, -d, -mənt/s
adjudicat|e, -es, -ing, -ed, -or/s ə'dʒuː-
dıkeıt, -s, -ıŋ, -ıd, -ə*/z
adjudication, -s əˌdʒuːdı'keıʃn, -z
adjunct, -s, -ly 'ædʒʌŋkt, -s, -lı
[ə'dʒʌŋktlı]
adjuration, -s ˌædʒʊə'reıʃn, -z
adjuratory ə'dʒʊərətərı
adjur|e, -es, -ing, -ed ə'dʒʊə*, -z, -rıŋ,
-d
adjus|t, -ts, -ting, -ted, -table, -tment/s
ə'dʒʌs|t, -ts, -tıŋ, -tıd, -təbl,
-tmənt/s
adjutage 'ædʒʊtıdʒ [ə'dʒuːt-]
adjutan|cy, -t/s 'ædʒʊtən|sı [-dʒət-],
-t/s
Adlai 'ædleı
Adler 'ædlə*, 'ɑːdlə*
ad lib. ˌæd'lıb
ad-man 'ædmæn
admass 'ædmæs
admeasur|e, -es, -ing, -ed, -ement/s
æd'meʒə* [əd-], -z, -rıŋ, -d, -mənt/s
administ|er, -ers, -ering, -ered əd-
'mınıst|ə*, -əz, -ərıŋ, -əd
administr|able, -ant/s əd'mınıstr|əbl,
-ənt/s
administration, -s əd ˌmını'streıʃn, -z
administrative əd'mınıstrətıv [-treıt-]
administrator, -s, -ship/s əd'mınıs-
treıtə*, -z, -ʃıp/s
administratri|x, -xes, -ces əd'mınıs-
treıtrı|ks, -ksız, -siːz
admirab|le, -ly, -leness 'ædmərəb|l, -lı,
-lnıs [-nəs]

admiral, -s 'ædmərəl, -z
admiralt|y, -ies 'ædmərəlt|ɪ, -ɪz
admiration ˌædmə'reɪʃn [-mɪ'r-]
admir|e, -es, -ing/ly, -ed, -er/s
  əd'maɪə*, -z, -rɪŋ/lɪ, -d, -rə*/z
admissibility ədˌmɪsə'bɪlətɪ [-sɪ'b-, -lɪt-]
admissible əd'mɪsəbl [-sɪb-]
admission, -s əd'mɪʃn, -z
admit, -s, -ting, -ted/ly; -tance/s
  əd'mɪt, -s, -ɪŋ, -ɪd/lɪ; -əns/ɪz
admix, -es, -ing, -ed; -ture/s æd'mɪks
  [əd-], -ɪz, -ɪŋ, -t; -tʃə*/z
admonish, -es, -ing, -ed, -ment/s
  əd'mɒnɪʃ, -ɪz, -ɪŋ, -t, -mənt/s
admonition, -s ˌædməʊ'nɪʃn, -z
admonitory əd'mɒnɪtərɪ [æd-]
ad nauseam ˌæd 'nɔːzɪæm
ado ə'duː
adobe, -s ə'dəʊbɪ [ə'dəʊb], -z
adolescen|ce, -t/s ˌædəʊ'lesn|s, -t/s
Adolf (English name) 'ædɒlf, (German
  name) 'aːdɒlf ['æd-] ('aːdɒlf)
Adolphus ə'dɒlfəs
Adonais ˌædəʊ'neɪɪs
Adonijah ˌædəʊ'naɪdʒə
Adonis ə'dəʊnɪs
adopt, -s, -ing, -ed; -ive ə'dɒpt, -s, -ɪŋ,
  -ɪd; -ɪv
adoption, -s ə'dɒpʃn, -z
adorab|le, -ly, -leness ə'dɔːrəb|l, -lɪ,
  -lnɪs [-nəs]
adoration, -s ˌædə'reɪʃn [-dɔː'r-], -z
ador|e, -es, -ing/ly, -ed, -er/s ə'dɔː*
  [-'dɔə*], -z, -rɪŋ/lɪ, -d, -rə*/z
adorn, -s, -ing, -ed, -ment/s ə'dɔːn,
  -z, -ɪŋ, -d, -mənt/s
adrenal ə'driːnl
adrenalin ə'drenəlɪn
Adria, -n 'eɪdrɪə, -n
Adrianople ˌeɪdrɪə'nəʊpl [ˌæd-]
Adriatic ˌeɪdrɪ'ætɪk [ˌæd-]
adrift ə'drɪft
adroit, -est, -ly, -ness ə'drɔɪt, -ɪst, -lɪ,
  -nɪs [-nəs]
adsorb, -s, -ing, -ed æd'sɔːb [əd-], -z,
  -ɪŋ, -d
adsum 'ædsʌm [-sʊm, -səm]
adulation, -s ˌædjʊ'leɪʃn, -z
adulatory 'ædjʊleɪtərɪ [-lət-, ͵--'--]
Adullam, -ite/s ə'dʌləm, -aɪt/s
adult (s. adj.), -s 'ædʌlt [ə'dʌlt], -s
adulterat|e, -es, -ing, -ed, -or/s
  ə'dʌltəreɪt, -s, -ɪŋ, -ɪd, -ə*/z
adulteration, -s əˌdʌltə'reɪʃn, -z
adulter|er/s, -ess/es ə'dʌltər|ə*/z,
  -ɪs/ɪz [-es/ɪz]
adulterous, -ly ə'dʌltərəs, -lɪ
adulter|y, -ies ə'dʌltər|ɪ, -ɪz

adumbrat|e, -es, -ing, -ed 'ædʌmbreɪt
  [-dəm-], -s, -ɪŋ, -ɪd
adumbration, -s ˌædʌm'breɪʃn [-dəm-],
  -z
ad valorem ˌædvə'lɔːrem [-væ'l-, -rəm]
advanc|e (s. adj. v.), -es, -ing, -ed,
  -ment/s əd'vɑːns, -ɪz, -ɪŋ, -t,
  -mənt/s
advantage, -s əd'vɑːntɪdʒ, -ɪz
advantageous, -ly, -ness ˌædvən-
  'teɪdʒəs [-vɑː-, -væn-], -lɪ, -nɪs
  [-nəs]
adven|e, -es, -ing, -ed æd'viːn [əd-], -z,
  -ɪŋ, -d
advent (A.), -s 'ædvənt [-vent], -s
adventitious, -ly ˌædven'tɪʃəs [-vən-], -lɪ
advent|ure (s. v.), -ures, -uring, -ured,
  -urer/s, -uress/es əd'ventʃ|ə*, -əz,
  -ərɪŋ, -əd, -ərə*/z, -ərɪs [-res] /ɪz
adventuresome əd'ventʃəsəm
adventurous, -ly, -ness əd'ventʃərəs,
  -lɪ, -nɪs [-nəs]
adverb, -s 'ædvɜːb, -z
adverbial, -ly əd'vɜːbjəl [æd-, -bɪəl], -ɪ
adversar|y, -ies 'ædvəsər|ɪ, -ɪz
adversative əd'vɜːsətɪv [æd-]
adverse, -ly 'ædvɜːs, -lɪ [æd'vɜːslɪ]
adversit|y, -ies əd'vɜːsət|ɪ [-ɪt|ɪ], -ɪz
advert (advertisement), -s 'ædvɜːt, -s
advert (v.), -s, -ing, -ed əd'vɜːt [æd-], -s,
  -ɪŋ, -ɪd
adverten|ce, -cy, -t/ly əd'vɜːtən|s, -sɪ,
  -t/lɪ
advertis|e, -es, -ing, -ed, -er/s 'ædvə-
  taɪz, -ɪz, -ɪŋ, -d, -ə*/z
advertisement, -s əd'vɜːtɪsmənt
  [-tɪzm-], -s
advice, -s əd'vaɪs, -ɪz
advisability ədˌvaɪzə'bɪlətɪ [-lɪt-]
advisab|le, -ly, -leness əd'vaɪzəb|l, -lɪ,
  -lnɪs [-nəs]
advis|e, -es, -ing, -ed, -edly, -edness,
  -er/s, -or/s; -ory əd'vaɪz, -ɪz, -ɪŋ,
  -d, -ɪdlɪ, -ɪdnɪs [-nəs], -ə*/z, -ə*/z;
  -ərɪ
advocacy 'ædvəkəsɪ [-vʊk-]
advocate (s.), -s 'ædvəkət [-vʊk-,
  -keɪt, -kɪt], -s
advocat|e (v.), -es, -ing, -ed, -or/s
  'ædvəkeɪt [-vʊk-], -s, -ɪŋ, -ɪd, -ə*/z
advocation ˌædvə'keɪʃn [-vʊ'k-]
advowson, -s əd'vaʊzn, -z
Adye 'eɪdɪ
adynamic ˌædaɪ'næmɪk [-dɪ'n-]
adz|e (s. v.), -es, -ing, -ed ædz, -ɪz, -ɪŋ,
  -d
Aeacus 'iːəkəs
Aeaea iː'iːə

7

aedile, -s; -ship/s 'i:daɪl, -z; -ʃɪp/s
Aeetes i:'i:ti:z
Aegean i:'dʒi:ən [ɪ'dʒ-, -ɪən]
Aegeus 'i:dʒju:s [-dʒjəs, -dʒɪəs]
Aegina i:'dʒaɪnə [ɪ'dʒ-]
aegis 'i:dʒɪs
aegrotat, -s i:'grəʊtæt [ɪ'g-, 'i:grəʊt-], -s
Aelfric 'ælfrɪk
Aemilius i:'mɪləs [ɪ'm-, -ljəs]
Aeneas i:'ni:æs [ɪ'n-, 'i:nɪæs]
Aeneid, -s 'i:nɪɪd [-njɪd], -z
Aeneus 'i:nju:s ['i:njəs, -nɪəs]
Aeolia, -n/s i:'əʊljə ['ɪ'əʊ-, -lɪə], -n/z
Aeolic i:'ɒlɪk [ɪ'ɒ-]
Aeolus 'i:əʊləs ['ɪəʊ-]
aeon, -s 'i:ən ['i:ɒn], -z
aerat|e, -es, -ing, -ed, -or/s 'eɪəreɪt, -s, -ɪŋ, -ɪd, -ə*/z
aeration eɪə'reɪʃn
aerial (s. adj.), -s, -ly 'eɪərɪəl, -z, -ɪ
aerie, -s 'eərɪ ['ɪərɪ], -z
aeri|fy, -fies, -fying, -fied 'eərɪ|faɪ, -faɪz, -faɪɪŋ, -faɪd
aero 'eərəʊ
aerobatic|s ˌeərəʊ'bætɪk|s
aerodrome, -s 'eərədrəʊm, -z
aerodynamic, -s ˌeərəʊdaɪ'næmɪk [-dɪ'n-], -s
aerodyne, -s 'eərəʊdaɪn, -z
aerogram, -s 'eəgrəʊgræm, -z
aerolite, -s 'eərəʊlaɪt, -s
aerolith, -s 'eərəʊlɪθ, -s
aerological ˌeərəʊ'lɒdʒɪkl
aerolog|ist/s, -y eə'rɒlədʒ|ɪst/s, -ɪ
aeronaut, -s 'eərənɔ:t, -s
aeronautic, -al, -s ˌeərə'nɔ:tɪk, -l, -s
aerophone, -s 'eərəfəʊn, -z
aeroplane, -s 'eərəpleɪn, -z
aerosol, -s 'eərəʊsɒl, -z
aerospace 'eərəʊspeɪs
aerostat, -s 'eərəʊstæt, -s
aertex 'eəteks
aeruginous ɪə'ru:dʒɪnəs
aer|y (s.) (= aerie), -ies, 'eər|ɪ ['ɪər|ɪ], -ɪz
aery (adj.) 'eərɪ
Aeschines 'i:skɪni:z
Aeschylus 'i:skɪləs
Aesculapius ˌi:skjʊ'leɪpjəs [-pɪəs]
Aesop 'i:sɒp
aesthete, -s 'i:sθi:t ['es-], -s
aesthetic, -al, -ally, -s i:s'θetɪk [ɪs-, es-], -l, -əlɪ, -s
aesthetici|sm, -st/s i:s'θetɪsɪ|zəm [ɪs-, es-], -st/s
aestival i:'staɪvl
Aethelstan 'æθəlstən
aether 'i:θə*

aetiology ˌi:tɪ'ɒlədʒɪ
Aetna 'etnə
afar ə'fɑ:*
afeard ə'fɪəd
affability ˌæfə'bɪlɪtɪ [-lɪt-]
affab|le, -ly, -leness 'æfəb|l, -lɪ, -lnɪs [-nəs]
affair, -s ə'feə*, -z
affect, -s, -ing/ly, -ed/ly, -edness ə'fekt, -s, -ɪŋ/lɪ, -ɪd/lɪ, -ɪdnɪs [-nəs]
affectation, -s ˌæfek'teɪʃn [-fɪk-], -z
affection, -s ə'fekʃn, -z
affectionate, -ly, -ness ə'fekʃnət [-ʃnət, -ʃənət, -nɪt], -lɪ, -nɪs [-nəs]
affective ə'fektɪv [æ'f-]
afferent 'æfərənt
affettuoso ə,fetjʊ'əʊzəʊ [æ,f-, -tʊ-]
affianc|e, -es, -ing, -ed ə'faɪəns, -ɪz, -ɪŋ, -t
affidavit, -s ˌæfɪ'deɪvɪt, -s
affiliat|e, -es, -ing, -ed ə'fɪlɪeɪt, -s, -ɪŋ, -ɪd
affiliation, -s ə,fɪlɪ'eɪʃn, -z
affinit|y, -ies ə'fɪnɪt|ɪ [-ɪt|ɪ], -ɪz
affirm, -s, -ing, -ed; -able ə'fɜ:m, -z, -ɪŋ, -d; -əbl
affirmation, -s ˌæfə'meɪʃn, -z
affirmative, -ly ə'fɜ:mətɪv, -lɪ
affirmatory ə'fɜ:mətərɪ
affix (s.), -es 'æfɪks, -ɪz
affix (v.), -es, -ing, -ed ə'fɪks [æ'f-], -ɪz, -ɪŋ, -t
afflatus ə'fleɪtəs
afflict, -s, -ing, -ed; -ive ə'flɪkt, -s, -ɪŋ, -ɪd; -ɪv
affliction, -s ə'flɪkʃn, -z
affluen|ce, -t/s, -tly 'æflʊən|s [-flwən-], -t/s, -tlɪ
afflux, -es 'æflʌks, -ɪz
afford, -s, -ing, -ed ə'fɔ:d, -z, -ɪŋ, -ɪd
afforest, -s, -ing, -ed æ'fɒrɪst [ə'f-], -s, -ɪŋ, -ɪd
afforestation, -s æ,fɒrɪ'steɪʃn [ə,f-, -re's-], -z
affranchis|e, -es, -ing, -ed ə'fræntʃaɪz [æ'f-], -ɪz, -ɪŋ, -d
affray, -s ə'freɪ, -z
affricate (s. adj.), -s 'æfrɪkət [-kɪt, -keɪt], -s
affricated 'æfrɪkeɪtɪd
affrication ˌæfrɪ'keɪʃn
affricative (s. adj.), -s æ'frɪkətɪv [ə'f-], -z
affright, -s, -ing, -ed/ly ə'fraɪt, -s, -ɪŋ, -ɪd/lɪ
affront (s. v.), -s, -ing, -ed ə'frʌnt, -s, -ɪŋ, -ɪd
Afghan, -s 'æfgæn, -z

Afghanistan æf'gænɪstæn [-tən, -stɑːn, æf͵gænɪ'stæn, æf͵gænɪ'stɑːn]
aficionado ə͵fɪsjə'nɑːdəʊ (afɪθjo'nado)
afield ə'fiːld
afire ə'faɪə*
aflame ə'fleɪm
afloat ə'fləʊt
afoot ə'fʊt
afore, -said, -thought, -time ə'fɔː* [-'fɔə*], -sed, -θɔːt, -taɪm
aforementioned ə͵fɔː'menʃənd [-͵fɔə-] (also -'-,-- when attributive)
a fortiori 'eɪ͵fɔːtɪ'ɔːraɪ [-͵fɔː-͵rɪ, 'ɑː͵fɔːtɪ'ɔːriː]
afraid ə'freɪd
afreet, -s 'æfriːt, -s
afresh ə'freʃ
Afric 'æfrɪk
Africa, -n/s 'æfrɪkə, -n/z
Africander, -s ͵æfrɪ'kændə*, -z
Africanus ͵æfrɪ'kɑːnəs [-'keɪn-]
Afridi, -s æ'friːdɪ [ə'f-], -z
Afrikaans ͵æfrɪ'kɑːns
Afrikaner, -s ͵æfrɪ'kɑːnə*, -z
afrit, -s 'æfriːt, -s
Afro-Asian, -s ͵æfrəʊ'eɪʃn [-'eɪʒn], -z
aft ɑːft
after 'ɑːftə*
after-birth, -s 'ɑːftəbɜːθ, -s
after-care 'ɑːftəkeə*
after-crop, -s 'ɑːftəkrɒp, -s
afterglow, -s 'ɑːftəgləʊ, -z
after-guard, -s 'ɑːftəgɑːd, -z
aftermath, -s 'ɑːftəmæθ [-mɑːθ], -s
afternoon, -s ͵ɑːftə'nuːn [attributively 'ɑːftənuːn], -z
after-piece, -s 'ɑːftəpiːs, -ɪz
after-shave 'ɑːftəʃeɪv
afterthought, -s 'ɑːftəθɔːt, -s
afterward, -s 'ɑːftəwəd, -z
Aga 'ɑːgə
Agag 'eɪgæg
again, -st ə'gen [-'geɪn], -st
Agamemnon ͵ægə'memnən [-nəʊn, -nɒn]
agape (s.), **-s** 'ægəpi: [-pɪ, -peɪ], -z
agape (adj. adv.) ə'geɪp
agapemone ͵ægə'piːmənɪ [-'pem-]
Agar 'eɪgɑː*, 'eɪgə*
agaric (s.), **-s** 'ægərɪk [ə'gærɪk], -s
agaric (adj.) æ'gærɪk [ə'g-]
Agassiz (town in British Columbia) ͵ægə'si:
Agassizhorn ə'gæsɪhɔːn
agate (stone), **-s** 'ægət [-gɪt], -s
Agate (surname) 'eɪgət, 'ægət
Agatha 'ægəθə
Agathocles ə'gæθəʊkliːz

agave, -s ə'geɪvɪ ['ægeɪv], -z
agaze ə'geɪz
age (s. v.), **-s, -ing, -d** (p. tense and partic.) eɪdʒ, -ɪz, -ɪŋ, -d
aged (adj.) (old) 'eɪdʒɪd, (of the age of) eɪdʒd
agedness 'eɪdʒɪdnɪs [-nəs]
ageless 'eɪdʒlɪs [-ləs]
agelong 'eɪdʒlɒŋ
agenc|y, -ies 'eɪdʒəns|ɪ, -ɪz
agend|a, -s ə'dʒendə, -z
agene 'eɪdʒiːn
Agenor ə'dʒiːnɔː*
agent, -s 'eɪdʒənt, -s
agent provocateur 'æʒɑ̃ːŋ prə͵vɒkə'tɜː* [-ɒŋ-] (aʒɑ̃ provokatœːr)
Ager 'eɪdʒə*
Agesilaus ə͵dʒesɪ'leɪəs
Aggie 'ægɪ
agglomerate (s. adj.), **-s** ə'glɒmərət [-rɪt, -reɪt], -s
agglomerat|e (v.), **-es, -ing, -ed** ə'glɒməreɪt, -s, -ɪŋ, -ɪd
agglomeration, -s ə͵glɒmə'reɪʃn, -z
agglutinate (adj.) ə'gluːtɪnət [-nɪt, -neɪt]
agglutinat|e (v.), **-es, -ing, -ed** ə'gluː-tɪneɪt, -s, -ɪŋ, -ɪd
agglutination, -s ə͵gluːtɪ'neɪʃn, -z
agglutinative ə'gluːtɪnətɪv [-neɪt-]
aggrandiz|e [-is|e], **-es, -ing, -ed** ə'grændaɪz ['ægrəndaɪz], -ɪz, -ɪŋ, -d
aggrandizement [-ise-] ə'grændɪzmənt
aggravat|e, -es, -ing/ly, -ed 'ægrəveɪt, -s, -ɪŋ/lɪ, -ɪd
aggravation, -s ͵ægrə'veɪʃn, -z
aggregate (s. adj.), **-s** 'ægrɪgət [-gɪt, -geɪt], -s
aggregat|e (v.), **-es, -ing, -ed** 'ægrɪgeɪt, -s, -ɪŋ, -ɪd
aggregation, -s ͵ægrɪ'geɪʃn, -z
aggress, -es, -ing, -ed, -or/s ə'gres [æ'g-], -ɪz, -ɪŋ, -t, -ə*/z
aggression, -s ə'greʃn [æ'g-], -z
aggressive, -ly, -ness ə'gresɪv [æ'g-], -lɪ, -nɪs [-nəs]
aggriev|e, -es, -ing, -ed ə'griːv, -z, -ɪŋ, -d
Aggy 'ægɪ
aghast ə'gɑːst
agile, -st, -ly, -ness 'ædʒaɪl, -ɪst, -lɪ, -nɪs [-nəs]
agility ə'dʒɪlətɪ [-ɪtɪ]
Agincourt 'ædʒɪnkɔːt
agiotage 'ædʒətɪdʒ
agitat|e, -es, -ing, -ed, -or/s 'ædʒɪteɪt, -s, -ɪŋ, -ɪd, -ə*/z
agitation, -s ͵ædʒɪ'teɪʃn, -z

9

agitato ˌædʒɪˈtɑːtəʊ
Aglaia æˈglaɪə
aglow əˈgləʊ
agnail, -s ˈægneɪl, -z
agnate ˈægneɪt
agnation ægˈneɪʃn
Agnes ˈægnɪs
Agnew ˈægnjuː
agnomen, -s ægˈnəʊmen [ˌægˈn-], -z
agnostic, -s ægˈnɒstɪk [əg-], -s
agnosticism ægˈnɒstɪsɪzəm [əg-]
Agnus Dei, -s ˌɑːgnʊsˈdeɪi: [ˌɑːnjəs-, ˌægnəsˈdiːaɪ], -z
ago əˈgəʊ
agog əˈgɒg
agone əˈgɒn
Agonistes ˌægəʊˈnɪstiːz
agonistic, -ally, -s ˌægəʊˈnɪstɪk, -əlɪ, -s
agoniz|e [-is|e], -es, -ing/ly, -ed ˈægənaɪz, -ɪz, -ɪŋ/lɪ, -d
agon|y, -ies ˈægən|ɪ, -ɪz
agor|a, -ae, -as ˈægər|ə [-gɑː-], -iː, -əz
agoraphobia, ˌægərəˈfəʊbjə [-bɪə]
agouti, -s əˈguːtɪ, -z
Agra ˈɑːgrə
agrarian, -s, -ism əˈgreərɪən [eɪˈg-], -z, -ɪzəm
agree, -s, -ing, -d əˈgriː, -z, -ɪŋ, -d
agreeab|le, -ly, -leness əˈgriːəb|l, -lɪ, -lnɪs [-nəs]
agreement, -s əˈgriːmənt, -s
agrestic əˈgrestɪk [æˈg-]
Agricola əˈgrɪkəʊlə
agricultur|al, -alist/s ˌægrɪˈkʌltʃər|əl [-tʃʊr-], -əlɪst/s
agriculture ˈægrɪkʌltʃə*
agriculturist, -s ˌægrɪˈkʌltʃərɪst, -s
agrimony ˈægrɪmənɪ
Agrippa əˈgrɪpə
agronomics ˌægrəˈnɒmɪks
agronomy əˈgrɒnəmɪ
aground əˈgraʊnd
ague, -s ˈeɪgjuː, -z
Aguecheek ˈeɪgjuːtʃiːk
Agutter əˈgʌtə*, ˈægətə*
ah ɑ
aha ɑːˈhɑ: [əˈh-]
Ahab ˈeɪhæb
Ahasuerus əˌhæzjʊˈrərəs [eɪˌhæz-, esp. by Jews]
Ahaz ˈeɪhæz
Ahaziah ˌeɪhəˈzaɪə
ahead əˈhed
aheap əˈhiːp
ahem mˈm̩m [m̩m, hm]
A'Hern ˈeɪhɜːn
Aherne əˈhɜːn
Ahijah əˈhaɪdʒə

Ahimelech əˈhɪmələk
Ahithophel əˈhɪθəʊfel
Ahmed ˈɑːmed
ahoy əˈhɔɪ
ahungered əˈhʌŋgəd
Ai ˈeɪaɪ [rarely eɪ, aɪ]
aid (s. v.), -s, -ing, -ed, -er/s eɪd, -z, -ɪŋ, -ɪd, -ə*/z
Aïda aɪˈiːdə
aide-de-camp, -s ˌeɪddəˈkɑ̃ːŋ [-ˈkɔ̃ːŋ, -ˈkɒŋ] (eddəkã), -z
aides-de-camp ˌeɪdzdəˈkɑ̃ːŋ [-kɔ̃ːŋ, -ˈkɒŋ] (eddəkã)
aigrette, -s ˈeɪgret [eɪˈgret], -s
aiguille, -s ˈeɪgwiːl [-wiː] (egɥiːj, ɛg-), -z
Aik|en, -in ˈeɪk|ɪn, -ɪn
ail, -s, -ing, -ed, -ment/s eɪl, -z, -ɪŋ, -d, -mənt/s
Aileen ˈeɪliːn
aileron, -s ˈeɪlərɒn, -z
Ailesbury ˈeɪlzbərɪ
Ailsa ˈeɪlsə
aim (s. v.), -s, -ing, -ed eɪm, -z, -ɪŋ, -d
aimless, -ly, -ness ˈeɪmlɪs [-ləs], -lɪ, -nɪs [-nəs]
Ainger ˈeɪndʒə*
Ainsl|ey, -ie ˈeɪnzl|ɪ, -ɪ
Ainsworth ˈeɪnzwɜːθ [-wəθ]
ain't eɪnt
Ainu, -s ˈaɪnuː, -z
air (s. v.), -s, -ing/s, -ed eə*, -z, -rɪŋ/z, -d
air-arm, -s ˈeərɑːm, -z
air-base, -s ˈeəbeɪs, -ɪz
air-ba|th, -ths ˈeəbɑː|θ [ˌeəˈb-], -ðz
air-bladder, -s ˈeəˌblædə*, -z
airborne ˈeəbɔːn [-bɔən]
air-brake, -s ˈeəbreɪk, -s
air-brick, -s ˈeəbrɪk, -s
air-carrier, -s ˈeəˌkærɪə*, -z
air-cell, -s ˈeəsel, -z
air-chamber, -s ˈeəˌtʃeɪmbə*, -z
air-condi|tion, -tions, -tioning, -tioned ˈeəkənˌdɪʃn, -ʃnz, -ʃənɪŋ [-ʃnɪŋ, -ʃnɪŋ], -ʃnd
air-cooled ˈeəkuːld
aircraft ˈeəkrɑːft
aircraft|man, -men ˈeəkrɑːft|mən, -mən
aircraft|woman, -women ˈeəkrɑːft|ˌwʊmən, -wɪmɪn
air-cushion, -s ˈeəˌkʊʃn [ˌeəˈk-, -ʃm], -z
Aird eəd
airdrome, -s ˈeədrəʊm, -z
Airedale, -s ˈeədeɪl, -z
air-engine, -s ˈeərˌendʒɪn [ˈeəˌen-], -z
Airey ˈeərɪ
airfield, -s ˈeəfiːld, -z
airgraph, -s ˈeəgrɑːf [-græf], -s

air-gun, -s 'eəgʌn, -z
air-hole, -s 'eəhəul, -z
air-hostess, -es 'eə,həustɪs [-stes], -ɪz
airless 'eəlɪs [-ləs]
air-letter, -s 'eə,letə*, -z
Airlie 'eəlɪ
air-lift, -s 'eəlɪft, -s
airline, -s 'eəlaɪn, -z
air-lock, -s 'eəlɒk, -s
air-mail, -s 'eəmeɪl, -z
air|man, -men 'eə|mən [-mæn], -men [-mən]
air-minded 'eə,maɪndɪd
air-plane, -s 'eəpleɪn, -z
air-pocket, -s 'eə,pɒkɪt, -s
airport, -s 'eəpɔːt, -s
air-pump, -s 'eəpʌmp, -s
air-raid, -s 'eəreɪd, -z
air-route, -s 'eəruːt, -s
air-shaft, -s 'eəʃɑːft, -s
airship, -s 'eəʃɪp, -s
air-sick 'eəsɪk
air-sickness 'eə,sɪknɪs [-nəs]
air-space 'eəspeɪs
air-strip, -s 'eəstrɪp, -s
air-terminal, -s 'eə,tɜːmɪnl, -z
airtight 'eətaɪt
airway, -s 'eəweɪ, -z
airworth|y, -iness 'eə,wɜː'ð|ɪ, -ɪnɪs [-məs]
air|y (A.), -ier, -iest, -ily, -iness 'eər|ɪ, -ɪə*, -ɪɪst, -ɪlɪ, -ɪnɪs [-məs], -əlɪ [-ɪlɪ]
Aisgill 'eɪsgɪl
Aislaby (in North Yorkshire) 'eɪzləbɪ [locally 'eɪzlbɪ]
aisle, -s, -d aɪl, -z, -d
aitch (letter H), -es eɪtʃ, -ɪz
aitchbone, -s 'eɪtʃbəun, -z
Aitchison 'eɪtʃɪsn
Aith eɪθ
Aitken 'eɪtkɪn [-kən], 'eɪk-
Aix eɪks (eks)
Aix-la-Chapelle ,eɪkslɑː'ʃæ'pel [-'ʃə'p-] (ɛkslaʃapɛl)
Aix-les-Bains ,eɪksleɪ'bæ̃ŋ [-'bæŋ] (ɛkslebɛ̃)
Ajaccio ə'jætʃɪəu [ə'dʒæsɪəu]
ajar ə'dʒɑː*
Ajax, -es 'eɪdʒæks, -ɪz
ajutage 'ædʒutɪdʒ [ə'dʒuːt-]
Akaba 'ækəbə
Akbar 'ækbɑː* ['ʌkbə*] (Hindi əkbər)
Akenside 'eɪkənsaɪd [-kɪn-]
Akerman 'ækəmən
Akers 'eɪkəz
akimbo ə'kɪmbəu
akin ə'kɪn
Akkad 'ækæd

Akond of Swat (former title of the Wali of Swat territory in Pakistan) ə,kuːndəv'swɒt, (fancy name in poem by Edward Lear) ,ækəndəv'swɒt
Akron 'ækrɒn [-rən]
Akroyd 'ækrɔɪd
Al æl
à la ɑːlɑː (ala)
Alabama ,ælə'bæmə [-'bɑːmə]
alabaster 'æləbɑːstə* [-bæs-]
Alabaster 'æləbɑːstə*
à la carte ,ɑːlɑː'kɑːt [,ælɑː-, ,ælə-] (alakart)
alack ə'læk
alackaday ə'lækədeɪ [-,-'-]
alacrity ə'lækrətɪ [-krɪtɪ]
Aladdin ə'lædɪn
Alamein 'æləmeɪn
à la mode ,ɑːlɑː'məud [,ælə'mɒd] (alamɔd)
Alan 'ælən
Aland 'ɑːlənd ['ɔːl-]
aland (adv.) ə'lænd
alar 'eɪlə*
Alaric 'ælərɪk
alarm (s. v.), -s, -ing/ly, -ed ; -ist/s ə'lɑːm, -z, -ɪŋ/lɪ, -d ; -ɪst/s
alarm-clock, -s ə'lɑːmklɒk, -s
alarum, -s ə'leərəm [-'lɑːr-, -'lær-], -z
alas ə'læs [-'lɑːs]
Alaska ə'læskə
Alastair 'æləstə*
Alastor ə'læstɔː* [æ'l-]
alate (winged) 'eɪleɪt
alb, -s ælb, -z
Alba 'ælbə
Alban 'ɔːlbən ['ɒl-]
Albani æl'bɑːnɪ
Albania, -n/s æl'beɪnjə [ɔːl-, -nɪə], -n/z
Albano æl'bɑːnəu
Albany (in London) 'ɔːlbənɪ ['ɒl-, 'æl-], (in Australia) 'æl-, (in U.S.A.) 'ɔːl- ['ɒl-]
albatross, -es 'ælbətrɒs, -ɪz
albeit ɔːl'biːɪt
Albemarle 'ælbəmɑːl [-bɪm-]
Alberic 'ælbərɪk
albert (A.), -s 'ælbət, -s
Alberta æl'bɜːtə
albescent æl'besənt
Albigenses ,ælbɪ'gensiːz [-'dʒensiːz]
Albin 'ælbɪn
albinism 'ælbɪnɪzəm
albino, -s æl'biːnəu, -z
Albion 'ælbjən [-brən]
Albrecht 'ælbrekt ('albrɛçt)
Albright 'ɔːlbraɪt ['ɒl-]

Albrighton 'ɔːbraɪtn ['ɔːlb-, 'ɒlb-]
Albrow 'ɔːlbraʊ
albugineous ˌælbjuː'dʒɪnɪəs [-bjʊ-, -njəs]
Albula 'ælbjʊlə
album, -s 'ælbəm, -z
albumen 'ælbjʊmɪn [æl'bjuːmɪn, -men, -mən]
albumin 'ælbjʊmɪn [æl'bjuːmɪn]
albumin|oid/s, -ous æl'bjuːmɪn|ɔɪd/z, -əs
albuminuria ˌælbjuːmɪ'njʊərɪə [-bjʊ-]
alburnum, -s æl'bɜːnəm, -z
Albury (surname, town in Australia) 'ɔːlbərɪ ['ɒl-]
Alcaeus æl'siːəs [-'sɪəs]
alcaic, -s æl'keɪɪk, -s
Alcatraz ˌælkə'træz
Alcazar (Spanish palace) ˌælkə'zɑː, (al'kaθar), (music hall) æl'kæzə*
Alcester 'ɔːlstə* ['ɒl-]
Alcestis æl'sestɪs
alchemic, -al æl'kemɪk, -l
alchem|ist/s, -y 'ælkɪm|ɪst/s [-kəm-], -ɪ
Alcibiades ˌælsɪ'baɪədiːz
Alcides æl'saɪdiːz
Alcinous æl'sɪnəʊəs
Alcmene ælk'miːniː [-nɪ]
Alcock 'ælkɒk, 'ɔːlkɒk ['ɒl-]
alcohol, -s, -ism 'ælkəhɒl, -z, -ɪzəm
alcoholic, ˌælkə'hɒlɪk
alcoholomet|er/s, -ry ˌælkəhɒ'lɒmɪt|ə*/z [-mət|ə*/z], -rɪ
Alcoran ˌælkɒ'rɑːn [-kɔː'r-, -kə'r-]
Alcorn 'ɔːlkɔːn ['ɒl-]
Alcott 'ɔːlkɒt ['ɒl-]
alcove, -s, -d 'ælkəʊv, -z, -d
alcuin 'ælkwɪn
Alcyone æl'saɪənɪ
Aldborough (in North Yorkshire) 'ɔːldbərə ['ɒl-, locally 'ɔːbrə]
Aldbury 'ɔːldbərɪ ['ɒl-]
Aldebaran æl'debərən [-ræn]
Aldeburgh 'ɔːldbərə ['ɒl-]
aldehyde, -s 'ældɪhaɪd, -z
Alden 'ɔːldən ['ɒl-]
Aldenham 'ɔːldnəm ['ɒl-, -dnəm]
alder (A.), -s 'ɔːldə* ['ɒl-], -z
alder|man (A.), -men, -manly 'ɔːldəmən ['ɒl-], -mən, -mənlɪ
aldermanic ˌɔːldə'mænɪk [ˌɒl-]
aldern 'ɔːldən ['ɒl-, -dɜːn]
Alderney 'ɔːldənɪ ['ɒl-]
Aldersgate 'ɔːldəzgeɪt ['ɒl-, -gɪt]
Aldershot 'ɔːldəʃɒt ['ɒl-]
Alderwasley ˌældəwɒz'liː
Aldgate 'ɔːldɡɪt ['ɒl-, -geɪt]
Aldine 'ɔːldaɪn ['ɒl-, -diːn]

Aldis 'ɔːldɪs ['ɒl-]
Aldous 'ɔːldəs ['ɒl-], 'ældəs
Aldred 'ɔːldrɪd ['ɒl-, -dred]
Aldrich 'ɔːldrɪtʃ ['ɒl-, -ɪdʒ]
Aldridge 'ɔːldrɪdʒ ['ɒl-]
Aldsworth 'ɔːldzwəθ ['ɒl-, -wɜːθ]
Aldus 'ɔːldəs ['ɒl-, 'æl-]
Aldwych 'ɔːldwɪtʃ ['ɒl-]
ale (A.), -s eɪl, -z
aleatory 'eɪlɪətərɪ [-ljə-]
Alec(k) 'ælɪk [-lek]
alehou|se, -ses 'eɪlhaʊ|s, -zɪz
Alemannic ˌælɪ'mænɪk [-le'm-]
alembic, -s ə'lembɪk, -s
Aleppo ə'lepəʊ
alert (s. adj.), -s, -est, -ly, -ness ə'lɜːt, -s, -ɪst, -lɪ, -nɪs [-nəs]
Alessandria ˌælɪ'sændrɪə [-le's-, -'sɑːn-]
Alethea ˌælə'θɪə
Aletsch 'ælɪtʃ ['ɑːl-, -letʃ]
Aleutian ə'luːʃjən [-'ljuː-, -ʃɪən, -ʃn]
A-level, -s 'eɪˌlevl, -z
alewi|fe, -ves 'eɪlwaɪ|f, -vz
Alexand|er, -ra, -ria, -rian/s ˌælɪg'zɑːn-d|ə* [-leg-, -'zæn-, -k's-], -rə, -rɪə, -rɪən/z
Alexandrina ˌælɪgzɑː'n'driːnə [-leg-, -zæn-, -ks-]
alexandrine, -s ˌælɪg'zændraɪn [-leg-, -'zɑːn-, -k's-], -z
alexia eɪ'leksɪə [-sjə]
Alexis ə'leksɪs
alfalfa æl'fælfə
Alfonso æl'fɒnzəʊ [-nsəʊ]
Alford 'ɔːlfəd ['ɒl-]
Alfred 'ælfrɪd
Alfreda æl'friːdə
Alfredian æl'friːdjən [-drən]
Alfree 'ɔːlfrɪ ['ɒl-]
alfresco æl'freskəʊ
Alfreton 'ɔːlfrɪtən ['ɒl-]
Alfric 'ælfrɪk
Alfriston (in Sussex) ɔːl'frɪstən ['---, ɒl-, 'æl-]
al|ga, -gae 'æl|gə, -dʒiː [-giː]
algebra, -s 'ældʒɪbrə [-dʒə-], -z
algebraic, -al, -ally ˌældʒɪ'breɪk [-dʒə-], -l, -əlɪ
algebraist, -s ˌældʒɪ'breɪst [-dʒe-, '----], -s
Algeciras ˌældʒɪ'sɪərəs [-dʒə's-, -dʒe's-, -'saɪər-]
Alger 'ældʒə*
Algeria, -n/s æl'dʒɪərɪə, -n/z
Algernon 'ældʒənən
Algiers æl'dʒɪəz [rarely '-ˌ-]
Algoa æl'gəʊə
Algol 'ælgɒl

12

Algonquin æl'gɒŋkwɪn [-kɪn]
algorithm, -s 'ælgərɪðm, -z
algorithmic ˌælgə'rɪðmɪk
Algy 'ældʒɪ
Alhambra æl'hæmbrə [əl-]
alhambresque ˌælhæm'bresk
alias, -es 'eɪlɪæs [-ljæs, -lɪəs, -ljəs], -ɪz
Ali Baba ˌælɪ'bɑːbə [ˌɑːl-, 'bɑːbɑː]
alibi, -s 'ælɪbaɪ, -z
Alicant 'ælɪkænt
Alicante, -s ˌælɪ'kæntɪ, -z
Alice 'ælɪs
Alicia ə'lɪʃɪə [-ʃjə, -ʃə]
Alick 'ælɪk
alien (s. adj. v.), -s, -ing, -ed; -able, -age
  'eɪljən [-lɪən], -z, -ɪŋ, -d; -əbl, -ɪdʒ
Aliena ˌælɪ'iːnə
alienat|e, -es, -ing, -ed, -or/s 'eɪljəneɪt
  [-lɪən-], -s, -ɪŋ, -ɪd, -ə*/z
alienation, -s ˌeɪljə'neɪʃn [-lɪə'n-], -z
alienee, -s ˌeɪljə'niː [ˌeɪlɪə-], -z
alieni|sm, -st/s 'eɪljənɪ|zm [-lɪən-],
  -st/s
alight (adj. v.), -s, -ing, -ed ə'laɪt, -s,
  -ɪŋ, -ɪd
align, -s, -ing, -ed, -ment/s ə'laɪn, -z,
  -ɪŋ, -d, -mənt/s
alike ə'laɪk
aliment, -s 'ælɪmənt, -s
aliment|al, -ary ˌælɪ'ment|l, -ərɪ
alimentation ˌælɪmen'teɪʃn
alimon|y, -ies 'ælɪmən|ɪ, -ɪz
alin|e, -es, -ing, -ed ə'laɪn, -z, -ɪŋ, -d
Aline æ'liːn [ə'l-], 'æli:n
alineation, -s ə,lɪnɪ'eɪʃn, -z
Alington 'ælɪŋtən
Ali Pasha ˌɑːlɪ'pɑːʃə [ˌæl-, -'pæʃə,
  rarely -pə'ʃɑː]
aliqu|ant, -ot 'ælɪkw|ənt, -ɒt
Alison 'ælɪsn
Alist|air, -er 'ælɪst|ə*, -ə*
alive ə'laɪv
alizarin ə'lɪzərɪn
alkahest 'ælkəhest
alkalescen|ce, -cy, -t ˌælkə'lesn|s, -sɪ, -t
alkali, -(e)s 'ælkəlaɪ, -z
alkali|fy, -fies, -fying, -fied 'ælkəlɪ|faɪ
  [æl'kæl-], -faɪz, -faɪŋ, -faɪd
alkaline 'ælkəlaɪn
alkalinity ˌælkə'lɪnətɪ [-ɪtɪ]
alkaloid, -s, -al 'ælkələɪd, -z, -l
Alkoran ˌælkɒ'rɑːn [-kɔː'r-, -kə'r-]
all ɔːl
Allah 'ælə [-lɑː]
Allahabad ˌæləhə'bɑːd [-'bæd] (Hindi
  allahabad)
Allan 'ælən
Allan-a-Dale ˌælənə'deɪl

Allandale 'æləndeɪl
Allard 'ælɑːd [-ləd]
Allardice 'ælədaɪs
allay, -s, -ing, -ed ə'leɪ, -z, -ɪŋ, -d
Allbright 'ɔːlbraɪt ['ɒl-]
Allbutt 'ɔːlbət ['ɒl-]
Allchin 'ɔːlʃɪn ['ɒl-]
Allcorn 'ɔːlkɔːn ['ɒl-]
Allcroft 'ɔːlkrɒft ['ɒl-]
allegation, -s ˌælɪ'geɪʃn [-le'g-], -z
alleg|e, -es, -ing, -ed ə'ledʒ, -ɪz, -ɪŋ, -d
Alleghany 'ælɪgenɪ
Allegheny 'ælɪgenɪ
allegian|ce, -t ə'liːdʒən|s, -t
allegoric, -al, -ally ˌælɪ'gɒrɪk [-lə'g-,
  -le'g-], -l, -əlɪ
allegorist, -s 'ælɪgərɪst [-ləg-, -leg-], -s
allegoriz|e [-is|e], -es, -ing, -ed 'ælɪ-
  gəraɪz [-ləg-, -leg-], -ɪz, -ɪŋ, -d
allegor|y, -ies 'ælɪgər|ɪ [-ləg-, -leg-], -ɪz
allegretto, -s ˌælɪ'gretəʊ [-le'g-], -z
allegro, -s ə'leɪgrəʊ [æ'l-, -'leg-, rarely
  'ælɪgrəʊ], -z
Allegwash 'ælɪgwɒʃ
Allein(e) 'ælɪn
alleluia (A.), -s ˌælɪ'luːjə, -z
allemande, -s 'ælmɑ̃ːnd [-mɔ̃ːnd,
  -mɑːnd, -mɒnd] (almɑ̃ːd), -z
Allen 'ælən [-lɪn]
Allenby 'ælənbɪ
Allendale 'ælɪndeɪl [-lən-]
Allentown 'ælɪntaʊn [-lən-]
allergic ə'lɜːdʒɪk
allerg|y, -ies 'ælədʒ|ɪ, -ɪz
Allerton 'ælətən
alleviat|e, -es, -ing, -ed, -or/s ə'liːvɪeɪt,
  [-vjeɪt], -s, -ɪŋ, -ɪd, -ə*/z
alleviation ə,liːvɪ'eɪʃn
alley, -s 'ælɪ, -z
Alleyn (founder of Dulwich College),
  'ælɪn
Alleyne æ'liːn, 'ælɪn, 'æleɪn
Alleynian, -s ə'leɪnjən [æ'l-, -nɪən], -z
All-Fools'-Day, -s ˌɔːl'fuːlzdeɪ, -z
all-fours ˌɔːl'fɔːz [-'fɔəz]
Allfrey 'ɔːlfrɪ ['ɒl-]
all-hail ˌɔːl'heɪl
All-Hallows ˌɔːl'hæləʊz
Allhusen æl'hjuːzn
alliance, -s ə'laɪəns, -ɪz
Allies 'ælaɪz [ə'laɪz]
alligator, -s 'ælɪgeɪtə*, -z
all-in ˌɔːl'ɪn ['-- when attributive]
allineation, -s ə,lɪnɪ'eɪʃn [æ,l-], -z
Allingham 'ælɪŋəm
Allison 'ælɪsn
alliterat|e, -es, -ing, -ed ə'lɪtəreɪt [æ'l-],
  -s, -ɪŋ, -ɪd

13

alliteration, -s ə‚lɪtə'reɪʃn [æ‚l-], -z
alliterative ə'lɪtərətɪv [æ'l-, -reɪt-]
Allman 'ɔːlmən
Alloa 'æləʊə
Allobroges ə'lɒbrədʒiːz [æ'l-, -brəʊdz-, ‚ælə'brəʊdz-]
allocat|e, -es, -ing, -ed 'æləʊkeɪt, -s, -ɪŋ, -ɪd
allocation, -s ‚æləʊ'keɪʃn, -z
allochrone, -s 'æləʊkrəʊn, -z
allocution, -s ‚æləʊ'kjuːʃn, -z
allodi|al/s, -um ə'ləʊdj|əl/z [-dɪ|-], -əm
allomorph, -s 'æləʊmɔːf, -s
Allon 'ælən
allopath, -s 'æləʊpæθ, -s
allopathic ‚æləʊ'pæθɪk
allopath|ist/s, -y ə'lɒpəθ|ɪst/s [æ'l-], -ɪ
allophone, -s 'æləʊfəʊn, -z
allophonic ‚æləʊ'fɒnɪk
allot, -s, -ting, -ted, -ment/s ə'lɒt, -s, -ɪŋ, -ɪd, -mənt/s
allotone, -s 'æləʊtəʊn, -z
allotropic ‚æləʊ'trɒpɪk
allotropy æ'lɒtrəpɪ [ə'l-]
all-out 'ɔːl'aʊt ['-- when attributive]
allow, -s, -ing, -ed ə'laʊ, -z, -ɪŋ, -d
allowab|le, -ly, -leness ə'laʊəb|l, -lɪ, -lnɪs [-nəs]
allowanc|e (s. v.), -es, -ing, -ed ə'laʊəns, -ɪz, -ɪŋ, -t
Alloway 'æləweɪ ['æləʊeɪ]
alloy (mixture of metals), -s 'ælɔɪ [ə'lɔɪ], -z, (figurative sense) ə'lɔɪ
alloy (v.), -s, -ing, -ed ə'lɔɪ, -z, -ɪŋ, -d
Allpress 'ɔːlpres
all-round, -er/s ‚ɔːl'raʊnd ['-- when attributive], -ə*/z
All-Saints'-Day, -s ‚ɔːl'seɪntsdeɪ, -z
Allsop(p) 'ɔːlsɒp ['ɒl-, -səp]
All-Souls'-Day, -s ‚ɔːl'səʊlzdeɪ, -z
allspice 'ɔːlspaɪs
Allt (surname) ɔːlt
allud|e, -es, -ing, -ed ə'luːd [-'ljuːd], -z, -ɪŋ, -ɪd
allur|e, -es, -ing/ly, -ed, -ement/s ə'ljʊə* [-'lʊə*, -'ljʊə*, -'ljɔ:*], -z, -rɪŋ/lɪ, -d, -mənt/s
allusion, -s ə'luːʒn [-'ljuː-], -z
allusive, -ly, -ness ə'luːsɪv [-'lju:-], -lɪ, -nɪs [-nəs]
alluvi|al, -on/s, -um/s, -a ə'luːvj|əl [-'lju:-, -vɪ|əl], -ən/z, -əm/z, -ə
Allworth 'ɔːlwəθ [-wɜ:θ]
Allworthy 'ɔːl‚wɜ:ðɪ
all|y (party to alliance), -ies 'ælaɪ [ə'laɪ], -z
all|y (marble), -ies 'æl|ɪ, -ɪz

all|y (v.), -ies, -ying, -ied ə'l|aɪ [æ'l-, 'ælaɪ], -aɪz, -aɪɪŋ, -aɪd [bɪd]
Note.—allied is generally pronounced 'ælaɪd when attributive.
Ally 'ælɪ
Alma 'ælmə
Almack 'ɔːlmæk ['ɒl-]
almagest, -s 'ælmədʒest, -s
Alma Mater, -s ‚ælmə'mɑːtə* [-'meɪtə*, -z
almanac(k), -s 'ɔːlmənæk ['ɒl-], -s
Almanzor æl'mænzɔ:* [-zə*]
Alma-Tadema ‚ælmə'tædəmə
Almeria, -s ‚ælmə'rɪə, -z
Almesbury 'ɑːmzbərɪ
almight|y (A.), -ily, -iness ɔːl'maɪt|ɪ, -ɪlɪ [-əlɪ], -ɪnɪs [-nəs]
almner, -s 'ɑːmnə*, -z
almoi(g)n 'ælmɔɪn
Almon 'ælmən
almond (A.), -s 'ɑːmənd, -z
Almondbury (in West Yorkshire) 'ælmənd‚bərɪ, ['ɑː‚mənd-, 'ɔː‚mbərɪ, 'eɪm‚bərɪ]
Almondsbury 'ɑːməndzbərɪ
almoner, -s 'ɑːmənə* ['ælm-], -z
almonr|y, -ies 'ɑːmənr|ɪ ['ælm-], -ɪz
almost 'ɔːlməʊst ['ɒl-, -məst]
Almroth 'ælmrəʊθ
alms ɑːmz
almsgiv|er/s, -ing 'ɑːmz‚gɪv|ə*/z, -ɪŋ
almshou|se, -ses 'ɑːmzhaʊ|s, -zɪz
Alne (in North Yorkshire, Warwickshire) ɔːn
Alnmouth 'ælnmaʊθ
Alnwick 'ænɪk
aloe, -s 'æləʊ, -z
aloft ə'lɒft
alone, -ness ə'ləʊn, -nɪs [-nəs]
along, -side ə'lɒŋ, (-,-) -'saɪd
aloof, -ness ə'luːf, -nɪs [-nəs]
Alor Star ‚æloː'stɑː*
aloud ə'laʊd
Aloysius ‚æləʊ'ɪʃəs [-'ɪsɪəs]
alp (A.), -s ælp, -s
alpaca, -s æl'pækə, -z
alpenrose, -s 'ælpənrəʊz [-pɪn-], -ɪz
alpenstock, -s 'ælpɪnstɒk [-pən-], -s
Alperton 'ælpətən
alpestrian æl'pestrɪən
alpha, -s 'ælfə, -z
alphabet, -s 'ælfəbɪt [-bet], -s
alphabetic, -al, -ally ‚ælfə'betɪk, -l, -əlɪ
Alphaeus æl'fiːəs [-'frəs]
Alphonso æl'fɒnzəʊ [-nsəʊ]
alpine 'ælpaɪn
alpinist, -s 'ælpɪnɪst, -s

14

already ɔːl'redɪ [ɒl-, *also* '-,-- *when followed by a stress*]
Alresford [*locally* 'ɔːlsfəd]
Alsace æl'sæs [-l'zæs, '--] (alzas)
Alsager (*in Cheshire*) 'ɔːlsɪdʒə* [-sədʒ-], ɔːl'seɪdʒə
Alsa|tia, -tian/s æl'seɪ|ʃjə [-ʃɪə, -ʃə], -ʃjən/z [-ʃɪən/z, -ʃn/z]
also 'ɔːlsəʊ ['ɒl-]
Alsop(p) 'ɔːlsɒp ['ɒl-, -səp]
Alston 'ɔːlstən ['ɒl-]
alt ælt
Altai æl'teraɪ [-'taɪ]
Altaic æl'teɪɪk
Altair æl'teə* ['ælteə*]
altar, -s 'ɔːltə* ['ɒl-], -z
altar|-cloth, -cloths 'ɔːltə|klɒθ ['ɒl-, *old-fashioned* -klɔːθ], -klɒθs [*old-fashioned* -klɔːðz, -klɔːθs]
altar-piece, -s 'ɔːltəpiːs ['ɒl-], -ɪz
altar-rail, -s 'ɔːltəreɪl ['ɒl-], -z
altazimuth, -s ælt'æzɪməθ, -s
alt|er, -ers, -ering, -ered; -erable; -erant/s 'ɔːlt|ə* ['ɒl-], -əz, -ərɪŋ, -əd; -ərəbl; -ərənt/s
alteration, -s ,ɔːltə'reɪʃn [,ɒl-], -z
alterative 'ɔːltərətɪv ['ɒl-, -reɪt-]
altercat|e, -es, -ing, -ed 'ɔːltəkeɪt ['ɒl-], -s, -ɪŋ, -ɪd
altercation, -s ,ɔːltə'keɪʃn [,ɒl-]
alter ego ,æltər'egəʊ [-tə'eg-, -'iːg-]
alternance, -s ɔːl'tɜːnəns [ɒl-, *rarely* æl-], -ɪz
alternant, -s ɔːl'tɜːnənt [ɒl-, *rarely* æl-], -s
alternate (*adj.*), -ly, -ness ɔːl'tɜːnət [ɒl-, *rarely* æl-, -nɪt], -lɪ, -nɪs [-nəs]
alternat|e (*v.*), -es, -ing, -ed 'ɔːltəneɪt ['ɒl-, *rarely* 'æl-], -s, -ɪŋ, -ɪd
alternation, -s ,ɔːltə'neɪʃn [,ɒl-, *rarely* ,æl-], -z
alternative (*s. adj.*), -s, -ly ɔːl'tɜːnətɪv [ɒl-, *rarely* æl-], -z, -lɪ
Althorp 'ɔːlθɔːp ['ɒl-], 'ɔːltrəp ['ɒl-]
although ɔːl'ðəʊ [ɒl-]
altimeter, s 'æltɪmiːtə* ['ɔːl-], -z
altimetry æl'tɪmɪtrɪ [*rarely* ɔːl-, ɒl-, -mətrɪ]
altissimo æl'tɪsɪməʊ
altitude, -s 'æltɪtjuːd, -z
alto, -s 'æltəʊ [*rarely* 'ɑːl-], -z
altogether ,ɔːltə'geðə* [,ɒl-, -tʊ'g-, *also sometimes* '--,-- *when attributive*]
Alton 'ɔːltən ['ɒl-]
Altona (*in Germany*) 'æltəʊnə, ('alto:na:), (*in U.S.A.*) æl'təʊnə
alto-relievo ,æltəʊrɪ'liːvəʊ
alto-rilievo ,æltəʊrɪlɪ'eɪvəʊ

Altrincham 'ɔːltrɪŋəm ['ɒl-]
altrui|sm, -st/s 'æltrʊɪ|zəm, -st/s
altruistic, -ally ,æltrʊ'ɪstɪk, -əlɪ
alum (A.), -s 'æləm, -z
alumina ə'ljuːmɪnə [æ'l-, -'luː-]
aluminium ,æljʊ'mɪnjəm [-nɪəm]
aluminous ə'ljuːmɪnəs [æ'l-, -'luː-]
alumn|a, -ae ə'lʌmn|ə, -iː
alumn|us, -i ə'lʌmn|əs, -aɪ
Alva 'ælvə
Alvar 'ælvɑː* [-və*]
Alvary 'ælvərɪ
Alvechurch 'ɔːlvtʃɜːtʃ
alveolar, -s æl'vɪələ* [,ælvɪ'əʊlə*, 'ælvɪələ*], -z
alveole, -s 'ælvɪəʊl, -z
alveol|us, -i æl'vɪəl|əs [,ælvɪ'əʊl-, 'ælvɪəl-], -aɪ [-iː]
Alverstone 'ɔːlvəstən ['ɒl-]
Alvescot 'ælvɪskɒt [-kət, *locally* 'ɔːlskət]
Alveston (*in Avon*) 'ælvɪstən
alway 'ɔːlweɪ
always 'ɔːlweɪz [-wəz, -wɪz]
Alwyn 'ælwɪn
alyssum 'ælɪsəm
a.m. ,eɪ'em
am, æm (*strong form*), əm, m (*weak forms*)
Amabel 'æməbel
Amadis 'æmədɪs
amadou 'æməduː
amain ə'meɪn
Amalek 'æmələk
Amalekite, -s ə'mælikaɪt, -s
Amalfi ə'mælfɪ [æ'm-]
amalgam, -s ə'mælgəm, -z
amalgamation, -s ə,mælgə'meɪʃn, -z
Aman 'æmən
Amanda ə'mændə
amandine ə'mændaɪn
Amantia ə'mænʃɪə [-ʃjə]
amanuens|is, -es ə,mænjʊ'ens|ɪs, -iːz
Amara ə'mɑːrə
amaranth, -s 'æmərænθ, -s
amaranthine ,æmə'rænθaɪn
amaryllis (A.), -es ,æmə'rɪlɪs, -ɪz
Amasa 'æməsə [ə'meɪsə]
Amasis ə'meɪsɪs
amass, -es, -ing, -ed ə'mæs, -ɪz, -ɪŋ, -t
Amata ə'meɪtə
amateur, -s 'æmətə* [-tɜː*, -tjʊə*, -tjɔə*, -tjɔː*, -tʃə*, ,æmə'tɜː*], -z
amateurish, -ly, -ness ,æmə'tɜːrɪʃ [-'tjʊər-, -'tjɔər-, -'tjɔː-r-, 'æmət-, -tʃə-], -lɪ, -nɪs [-nəs]
amateurism 'æmətərɪzəm [-tɜː-, -tjə-, -tjʊə-, -tjɔə-, -tjɔː-, -tʃə-]

15

Amati, -s ə'mɑːtɪ [æ'm-], -z
amative, -ness 'æmətɪv, -nɪs [-nəs]
amatol 'æmətɒl
amatory 'æmətərɪ
amaurosis ˌæmɔː'rəʊsɪs
Amaury ə'mɔːrɪ
amaz|e, -es, -ing/ly, -ed, -edly, -edness, -ement/s ə'meɪz, -ɪz, -ɪŋ/lɪ, -d, -ɪdlɪ, -ɪdnɪs [-nəs], -mənt/s
Amaziah ˌæmə'zaɪə
amazon (A.), -s 'æməzən, -z
amazonian, ˌæmə'zəʊnjən [-nɪən]
ambage, -s 'æmbɪdʒ, æm'beɪdʒiːz ['æmbɪdʒɪz]
ambassador, -s æm'bæsədə* [-sɪd-], -z
ambassadorial æmˌbæsə'dɔːrɪəl [ˌæmb-, -sɪ'd-]
ambassadress, -es æm'bæsədrɪs [-sɪd-, -dres], -ɪz
ambe, -s 'æmbɪ, -z
amber 'æmbə*
ambergris 'æmbəgriːs [-grɪs]
ambidexter, -s ˌæmbɪ'dekstə*, -z
ambidexterity ˌæmbɪdek'sterətɪ [-rtɪ]
ambidextrous ˌæmbɪ'dekstrəs
ambience, -s 'æmbɪəns [-bjəns], -ɪz
ambient 'æmbɪənt [-bjənt]
ambiguit|y, -ies ˌæmbɪ'gjuːɪt|ɪ [-'gjʊɪ-, -ət|ɪ], -ɪz
ambiguous, -ly, -ness æm'bɪgjʊəs [-gjwəs], -lɪ, -nɪs [-nəs]
Ambiorix æm'baɪərɪks
ambit, -s 'æmbɪt, -s
ambition, -s æm'bɪʃn, -z
ambitious, -ly, -ness æm'bɪʃəs, -lɪ, -nɪs [-nəs]
ambivalen|ce,   -t ˌæmbɪ'veɪlən|s [æm'bɪvələns], -t [æm'bɪvələnt]
amb|le, -les, -ling, -led, -ler/s 'æmb|l, -lz, -lɪŋ [-lɪŋ], -ld, -lə*/z [-lə*/z]
Ambler 'æmblə*
Ambleside 'æmblsaɪd
amboyna (A.) æm'bɔɪnə
Ambree 'æmbrɪ
Ambrose 'æmbrəʊz [-əʊs]
ambrosia, -l, -lly, -n æm'brəʊzjə [-zɪə, -ʒjə, -ʒɪə], -l, -lɪ, -n
ambr|y, -ies 'æmbr|ɪ, -ɪz
ambs-ace 'eɪmzeɪs ['æm-]
ambulance, -s 'æmbjʊləns, -ɪz
ambulant 'æmbjʊlənt
ambulat|e, -es, -ing, -ed 'æmbjʊleɪt, -s, -ɪŋ, -ɪd
ambulation, -s ˌæmbjʊ'leɪʃn, -z
ambulator|y (s. adj.), -ies 'æmbjʊlə-tər|ɪ [-leɪt-, ˌæmbjʊ'leɪt-], -ɪz
ambuscad|e (s. v.), -es, -ing, -ed ˌæmbəs'keɪd, -z, -ɪŋ, -ɪd

ambush (s. v.), -es, -ing, -ed 'æmbʊʃ, -ɪz, -ɪŋ, -t
Amelia ə'miːljə [-lɪə]
ameliorat|e, -es, -ing, -ed ə'miːljəreɪt [-lɪər-, -lɪɔːr-, -ljɔːr-], -s, -ɪŋ, -ɪd
amelioration, -s əˌmiːljə'reɪʃn [-lɪə'r-, -lɪɔː'r-, -ljɔː'r-], -z
ameliorative ə'miːljərətɪv [-lɪər-, -lɪɔːr-, -ljɔːr-, -reɪt-]
amen, -s ˌɑː'men, ˌeɪ'men, -z
amenability əˌmiːnə'bɪlətɪ [-lɪt-]
amenab|le, -ly, -leness ə'miːnəb|l, -lɪ, -lnɪs [-nəs]
Amen Corner ˌeɪmen 'kɔːnə*
amen|d, -ds, -ding, -ded, -dment/s ə'men|d, -dz, -dɪŋ, -dɪd, -dmənt/s
Amen House ˌeɪmen 'haʊs
amenit|y, -ies ə'miːnət|ɪ[-'men-, -ɪt|ɪ], -ɪz
amerc|e, -es, -ing, -ed, -ement/s ə'mɜːs, -ɪz, -ɪŋ, -t, -mənt/s
America, -n/s ə'merɪkə, -n/z
Americana əˌmerɪ'kɑːnə
americanism, -s ə'merɪkənɪzəm, -z
americanization [-isa-] əˌmerɪkənaɪ-'zeɪʃn [-nɪ'z-]
americaniz|e [-is|e], -es, -ing, -ed ə'merɪkənaɪz, -ɪz, -ɪŋ, -d
americium ˌæmə'rɪsɪəm [-sjəm, -ʃɪəm, -ʃjəm]
Amerindian, -s ˌæmər'ɪndjən [-dɪən], -z
Amersham 'æməʃəm
Amery 'eɪmərɪ
Ames, -bury eɪmz, -bərɪ
amethyst, -s 'æmɪθɪst [-məθ-, -meθ-], -s
amethystine ˌæmɪ'θɪstaɪn [-mə'θ-, -me'θ-]
Amharic æm'hærɪk
Amherst 'æməst, 'æmhɜːst
amiability ˌeɪmjə'bɪlətɪ [-mɪə-, -lɪt-]
amiab|le, -ly, -leness 'eɪmjəb|l [-mɪə-], -lɪ, -lnɪs [-nəs]
Amias 'eɪmɪəs [-mjəs]
amicability ˌæmɪkə'bɪlətɪ [-lɪt-]
amicab|le, -ly, -leness 'æmɪkəb|l, -lɪ, -lnɪs [-nəs]
amice, -s 'æmɪs, -ɪz
Amice 'eɪmɪs
amid ə'mɪd
Amidas 'æmɪdæs
amide, -s 'æmaɪd, -z
amidships ə'mɪdʃɪps
amidst ə'mɪdst [-rtst]
Amiel 'æmɪəl ['eɪm-, -mjəl]
Amiens (French city) 'æmjæ̃ːŋ [-mɪæ̃ːŋ, -mɪæŋ, -mɪənz, -mjənz] (amjɛ̃), (Shakespearian character) 'æmɪənz [-mjənz], (street in Dublin) 'eɪmjənz [-mɪənz]

Amies 'eɪmɪz
amir, -s ə'mɪə* [æ'm-, 'æˌmɪə*], -z
Amis 'eɪmɪs
amiss ə'mɪs
amity 'æmətɪ [-ɪtɪ]
Amlwch 'æmlʊk [-lʊx] (Welsh 'amlux)
Amman ə'mɑːn
ammeter, -s 'æmɪtə* [-mətə*], -z
Ammon 'æmən [-mɒn]
ammonia ə'məʊnjə [-nɪə]
ammoniac ə'məʊnɪæk [-njæk]
ammoniacal ˌæməʊ'naɪəkl
ammoniated ə'məʊnɪeɪtɪd [-njeɪ-]
ammonite (A.), -s 'æmənaɪt, -s
ammonium ə'məʊnjəm [-nɪəm]
ammunition ˌæmjʊ'nɪʃn
amnesia æm'niːzjə [-zɪə, -ʒjə, -ʒə]
amnest|y, -ies 'æmnɪst|ɪ[-nəs-, -nes-], -ɪz
Amnon 'æmnɒn
amoeb|a, -ae, -as, -ic ə'miːb|ə, -iː, -əz, -ɪk
amok ə'mɒk ['ɑːməʊ]
  Note.—'ɑːməʊ is the pronunciation
  used in Malaya.
among, -st ə'mʌŋ, -st [ə'mʌŋkst]
amontillado (A.) əˌmɒntɪ'lɑːdəʊ [-ɪ'ljɑː-]
Amoore 'eɪˌmʊə*
amoral ˌeɪ'mɒrəl [ə'm-, æ'm-]
amorist, -s 'æmərɪst, -s
Amorite, -s 'æməraɪt, -s
amorous, -ly, -ness 'æmərəs, -lɪ, -nɪs [-nəs]
amorpha, -s ə'mɔːfə, -z
amorph|ism, -ous ə'mɔːf|ɪzəm, -əs
amortization [-isa-], -s əˌmɔːtɪ'zeɪʃn, [ˌæmɔːt-, ˌæmət-, -taɪ-], -z
amortiz|e, -es, -ing, -ed ə'mɔːtaɪz [-tɪz], -ɪz, -ɪŋ, -d
Amory 'eɪmərɪ
Amos 'eɪmɒs
amount (s. v.), -s, -ing, -ed ə'maʊnt, -s, -ɪŋ, -ɪd
amour, -s ə'mʊə* [æ'm-], -z
amour-propre ˌæmʊə'prɒprə [-'prɒpə*] (amurprɔpr)
Amoy ə'mɔɪ
amp, -s æmp, -s
ampelopsis ˌæmpɪ'lɒpsɪs
ampère [-pere], -s 'æmpeə*, -z
Ampère 'æmpeə* (ɑ̃pɛːr)
ampersand, -s 'æmpəsænd, -z
amphibi|a, -an/s, -ous æm'fɪbɪ|ə [-bjə], -ən/z, -əs
amphibole (mineral) 'æmfɪbəʊl
amphibole (net), -s æm'fɪbəlɪ, -z
amphibology ˌæmfɪ'bɒlədʒɪ
amphibol|y, -ies æm'fɪbəl|ɪ, -ɪz

amphibrach, -s 'æmfɪbræk, -s
Amphictyon, -s æm'fɪktɪən [-tjən], -z
amphictyonic æmˌfɪktɪ'ɒnɪk
Amphimedon æm'fɪmɪdən [-dəʊn]
Amphion æm'faɪən
Amphipolis æm'fɪpəlɪs
amphiscian, -s æm'fɪʃɪən [-ʃjən], -z
amphitheatre, -s 'æmfɪˌθɪətə* [-θɪˌetə*], -z
Amphitrite 'æmfɪtraɪtɪ
Amphitryon æm'fɪtrɪən
amphor|a, ae, -as 'æmfər|ə, -iː, -əz
amphoric æm'fɒrɪk
amp|le, -ler, -lest, -ly, -leness 'æmp|l, -lə*, -lɪst, -lɪ, -lnɪs [-nəs]
amplification, -s ˌæmplɪfɪ'keɪʃn, -z
amplificatory 'æmplɪfɪkeɪtərɪ [ˌ---'---]
ampli|fy, -fies, -fying, -fied, -fier/s 'æmplɪ|faɪ, -faɪz, -faɪɪŋ, -faɪd, -faɪə*/z
amplitude, -s 'æmplɪtjuːd, -z
ampoule, -s 'æmpuːl, -z
Ampthill 'æmpθɪl
ampull|a, -ae æm'pʊl|ə, -iː
amputat|e, -es, -ing, -ed 'æmpjʊteɪt, -s, -ɪŋ, -ɪd
amputation, -s ˌæmpjʊ'teɪʃn, -z
Amram 'æmræm
Amritsar æm'rɪtsə* (Hindi əmrytsər)
Amsterdam ˌæmstə'dæm [-mps-, '--ˌ-]
amuck ə'mʌk
amulet, -s 'æmjʊlɪt [-let, -lət], -s
Amulree ˌæməl'riː
Amundsen 'ɑːmʊndsən [-mən-]
Amur ə'mʊə* [æ'm-, 'æˌmʊə*]
amus|e, -es, -ing/ly, -ingness, -ed, -ement/s ə'mjuːz, -ɪz, -ɪŋ/lɪ, -ɪŋnɪs [-nəs], -d, -mənt/s
Amy 'eɪmɪ
Amyas 'eɪmjəs [-mɪəs]
amygdaloid ə'mɪgdələɪd [æ'm-]
amyl 'æmɪl
amytal 'æmɪtæl
an æn (strong form), ən, n (weak forms)
ana 'ɑːnə
anabapti|sm, -st/s ˌænə'bæptɪ|zəm, -st/s
anabaptistic ˌænəbæp'tɪstɪk
anabas|is, -es ə'næbəs|ɪs, -iːz
anabolism ə'næbəʊlɪzəm
anachorism, -s ə'nækərɪzəm, -z
anachron|ism/s, -ous/ly ə'nækrən|ɪzəm/z, -əs/lɪ
anachronistic əˌnækrə'nɪstɪk [-krɒ'n-]
anacoluth|on, -a ˌænəkəʊ'luːθ|ɒn [-næk-, -'ljuː-, -θ|ən], -ə
anaconda, -s ˌænə'kɒndə, -z
Anacreon ə'nækrɪən
anacrus|is, -es ˌænə'kruːs|ɪs, -iːz

Anadin 'ænədɪn
anaemia ə'niːmjə [æ'n-, -mɪə]
anaemic ə'niːmɪk [æ'n-]
anaesthesia ˌænɪs'θiːzjə [-niːs-, -nəs-, -zɪə, -ʒjə, -ʒɪə, -ʒə]
anaesthetic, -s, -ally ˌænɪs'θetɪk [-niːs-, -nəs-], -s, -əlɪ
anaesthetist, -s æ'niːsθətɪst [ə'n-, -θɪt-], -s
anaesthetiz|e [-is|e], -es, -ing, -ed æ'niːsθətaɪz [ə'n-, -θɪt-], -ɪz, -ɪŋ, -d
anagogic, -s, -al, -ally ˌænə'gɒdʒɪk, -s, -l, -əlɪ
anagogy 'ænəgɒdʒɪ [-gɒgɪ, -gəʊdʒɪ]
anagram, -s 'ænəgræm, -z
anagrammatic, -al, -ally ˌænəgrə'mætɪk, -l, -əlɪ
Anak 'eɪnæk [rarely 'ænæk]
Anakim 'ænəkɪm [rarely ə'nɑːkɪm]
anal 'eɪnl
analects 'ænəlekts
analgesia ˌænæl'dʒiːzjə [-iːzɪə, -iːsjə, -iːsɪə]
analgesic ˌænæl'dʒiːsɪk [-'dʒesɪk]
analogic, -al, -ally ˌænə'lɒdʒɪk, -l, -əlɪ
analogist, -s ə'nælədʒɪst, -s
analogous, -ly, -ness ə'næləgəs, -lɪ, -nɪs [-nəs]
analogue, -s 'ænələg, -z
analog|y, -ies ə'nælədʒ|ɪ, -ɪz
analphabetic, -al, -ally ˌænælfə'betɪk, -l, -əlɪ
analysable 'ænəlaɪzəbl
analys|e, -es, -ing, -ed 'ænəlaɪz, -ɪz, -ɪŋ, -d
analys|is, -es ə'næləs|ɪs [-lɪs-], -iːz
analyst, -s 'ænəlɪst, -s
analytic, -s, -al, -ally ˌænə'lɪtɪk, -s, -l, -əlɪ
anamorphosis ˌænə'mɔːfəsɪs
anana, -s (plur.) ə'nɑːnə, -z
ananas (sing.), -es ə'nɑːnəs, -ɪz
Ananias ˌænə'naɪəs
anapaest, -s 'ænəpiːst [-pest], -s
anapaestic ˌænə'piːstɪk [-'pest-]
anaphora, -s ə'næfərə, -z
anaphoric ˌænə'fɒrɪk
anarch, -s 'ænɑːk, -s
anarchic, -al, -ally æ'nɑːkɪk [ə'n-], -l, -əlɪ
anarch|ism, -ist/s, -y 'ænək|ɪzəm, -ɪst/s, -ɪ
Anastasia (English Christian name) ˌænə'steɪzjə [-zɪə], (foreign name) ˌænə'stɑːz-
anastigmat, -s ə'næstɪgmæt [æ'n-], -s
anastomosis ˌænəstə'məʊsɪs [ˌænæs-]
anastrophe, -s ə'næstrəfɪ [æ'n-], -z

anathema, -s ə'næθəmə [-θɪm-], -z
anathematization [-isa-], -s əˌnæθə-mətaɪ'zeɪʃn [-θɪm-, -tɪ'z-], -z
anathematiz|e [-is|e], -es, -ing, -ed ə'næθəmətaɪz [-θɪm-], -ɪz, -ɪŋ, -d
Anatolia, -n/s ˌænə'təʊljə [-lɪə], -n/z
anatomic, -al, -ally ˌænə'tɒmɪk, -l, -əlɪ
anatomist, -s ə'nætəmɪst, -s
anatomiz|e [-is|e], -es, -ing, -ed ə'nætə-maɪz, -ɪz, -ɪŋ, -d
anatom|y, -ies ə'nætəm|ɪ, -ɪz
Anaxagoras ˌænæk'sægɒræs [-rəs]
ancestor, -s 'ænsestə* [-sɪs-, -səs-], -z
ancestral æn'sestrəl
ancestress, -es 'ænsestrɪs [-sɪs-, -səs-, -tres, -trəs], -ɪz
ancestr|y, -ies 'ænsestr|ɪ [-sɪs-, -səs-], -ɪz
Anchises æn'kaɪsiːz [æn'k-]
Ancholme 'æŋkhəʊm
anchor (s. v.), -s, -ing, -ed 'æŋkə* [-z, -rɪŋ, -d
anchorage, -s 'æŋkərɪdʒ, -ɪz
anchoress, -es 'æŋkərɪs [-res], -ɪz
anchoret, -s 'æŋkərət [-rɪt], -s
anchorhold, -s 'æŋkəhəʊld, -z
anchorite, -s 'æŋkəraɪt [-kɒr-], -s
anchov|y, -ies 'æntʃəv|ɪ [æn'tʃəʊv-], -ɪz
anchylosis ˌæŋkaɪ'ləʊsɪs [ˌæŋk-]
ancient, -est, -ly, -s 'eɪnʃənt, -ɪst, -lɪ, -s
ancillary æn'sɪlərɪ
ancipit|al, -ous æn'sɪpɪt|l, -əs
Ancren Riwle ˌæŋkrɪn'rɪʊlɪ [-kren-, -krən-, -lə]
ancress, -es 'æŋkrɪs [-kres], -ɪz
Ancyra æn'saɪərə
and ænd (strong form), ənd, ən, nd, n, m, ŋ (weak forms)
    Note.—The form m only occurs next to p or b, and the form ŋ only occurs next to k or g.
Andalusia ˌændə'luːzjə [-uːzɪə, -uːʒjə, -uːʒɪə, -uːsjə, -uːsɪə, -uːʃjə, -uːʃɪə]
Andaman 'ændəmæn [-mən]
andante, -s æn'dæntɪ, -z
andantino ˌændæn'tiːnəʊ
Ander|sen, -son 'ændə|sn, -sn
Andes 'ændiːz
andiron, -s 'ændaɪən, -z
Andorra æn'dɔːrə [-'dɒrə]
Andover 'ændəʊvə*
Andow (surname) 'ændaʊ
Andrade (English surname) 'ændreɪd
Andrassy æn'dræsɪ
Andreas 'ændrɪæs [-ɪəs]
Andrew 'ændruː
Andrewatha (Cornish family) æn-'druːθə, (Plymouth family) æn-'druːəθə, ˌændruː'ɒθə

Andrews 'ændru:z
Andria 'ændrɪə
Androcles 'ændrəʊkli:z
Androclus æn'drɒkləs
androgynous æn'drɒdʒɪnəs
android, -s 'ændrɔɪd, -z
Androm|ache, -eda æn'drɒm|əkɪ, -ɪdə
Andronicus (Byzantine emperors and
other figures in ancient history)
ˌændrə'naɪkəs [æn'drɒnɪkəs], (in
Shakespeare's Titus Andronicus)
æn'drɒnɪkəs
Andros 'ændrɒs
anecdotal ˌænek'dəʊtl [-nɪk-]
anecdote, -s 'ænɪkdəʊt [-nek-], -s
anecdotic, -al, -ally ˌænek'dɒtɪk [-nɪk-],
-l, -əlɪ
anechoic ˌænɪ'kəʊɪk
Anelay (surname) 'eɪnlɪ
anelectric, -s ˌænɪ'lektrɪk, -s
anelectrode, -s ˌænɪ'lektrəʊd, -z
anemomet|er/s, -ry ˌænɪ'mɒmɪt|ə*/z
[-mət|ə*/z], -rɪ
anemometric ˌænɪməʊ'metrɪk
anemone, -s ə'nemənɪ, -z
anemoscope, -s ə'neməskəʊp, -s
anent ə'nent
aneroid, -s 'ænərɔɪd [-nɪr-], -z
aneurin 'ænjʊərɪn
Aneurin ə'naɪərɪn (Welsh a'nəirin)
aneurism, -s 'ænjʊərɪzəm, -z
anew ə'nju:
anfractuosity ˌænfræktjʊ'ɒsətɪ [-ɪtɪ]
Angear 'æn‚gɪə*
angel (A.), -s 'eɪndʒəl, -z
Angela 'ændʒələ [-dʒɪl-]
Angeles 'ændʒɪli:z ['æŋgɪl-, -əl-, -‚lɪz,
-lɪs]
angelic, -al, -ally æn'dʒelɪk, -l, -əlɪ
angelica (A.) æn'dʒelɪkə
Angelina ˌændʒɪ'li:nə [-dʒe'l-, -dʒə'l-]
Angelo 'ændʒɪləʊ [-ələʊ]
angelus, -es 'ændʒɪləs [-dʒəl-], -ɪz
anger (s. v.), -s, -ing, -ed 'æŋgə*, -z
-rɪŋ, -d
Angevin 'ændʒɪvɪn [-əvɪn]
Angier 'æn‚dʒɪə*
angina, -s æn'dʒaɪnə, -z
ang|le (s. v.) (A.), -les, -ling, -led, -ler/s
'æŋg|l, -lz, -lɪŋ, -ld, -lə*/z
angledozer, -s 'æŋgl‚dəʊzə*, -z
Angle|sea, -sey 'æŋgl|sɪ [-si:], -sɪ
[-si:]
Anglia, -n/s 'æŋglɪə [-gljə], -n/z
Anglic|an/s, -anism 'æŋglɪk|ən/z,
-ənɪzəm
anglice 'æŋglɪsɪ
anglici|sm/s, -st/s 'æŋglɪsɪ|zəm/z, -st/s

anglicization [-isa-] ˌæŋglɪsaɪ'zeɪʃn
[-sɪ'z-]
angliciz|e [-is|e], -es, -ing, -ed 'æŋglɪ-
saɪz, -ɪz, -ɪŋ, -d
Anglo-French ˌæŋgləʊ'frentʃ
anglomania ˌæŋgləʊ'meɪnjə [-nɪə]
Anglo-Norman ˌæŋgləʊ'nɔ:mən
anglophile, -s 'æŋgləʊfaɪl, -z
anglophobe, -s 'æŋgləʊfəʊb, -z
anglophobia ˌæŋgləʊ'fəʊbjə [-bɪə]
Anglo-Saxon, -s ˌæŋgləʊ'sæksən, -z
Anglo-Saxondom ˌæŋgləʊ'sæksəndəm
Anglo-Saxonism, -s ˌæŋgləʊ'sæk-
sənɪzəm [-sn̩ɪ-], -z
Angmering 'æŋmərɪŋ
Angola æn'gəʊlə
Angora (old form of Ankara in Turkey)
'æŋgərə [æŋ'gɔ:rə]
Angora (cat, rabbit, cloth), -s æŋ'gɔ:rə,-z
Angostura ˌæŋgə'stjʊərə [-gɒ's-,
-'stjɔərə, -'stjɔ:rə, -'stʊərə, -'stɔərə,
-'stɔ:rə]
angr|y, -ier, -iest, -ily, -iness 'æŋgr|ɪ,
-ɪə*, -ɪɪst, -əlɪ [-ɪlɪ], -ɪnɪs [-ɪnəs]
angst æŋst (aŋst)
angstrom, -s 'æŋstrəm, -z
anguine 'æŋgwɪn
anguish, -ed 'æŋgwɪʃ, -t
angular 'æŋgjʊlə*
angularit|y, -ies ˌæŋgjʊ'lærət|ɪ [-ɪt|ɪ], -ɪz
angulate 'æŋgjʊlɪt [-lɪt, -lət]
angulated 'æŋgjʊleɪtɪd
Angus 'æŋgəs
Angustura ˌæŋgə'stjʊərə [-'stjɔərə,
-'stjɔ:rə, -'stʊərə, -'stɔərə, -'stɔ:rə]
anharmonic ˌænhɑ:'mɒnɪk
anhungered ən'hʌŋgəd
anhydr|ide/s, -ite, -ous æn'haɪdr|aɪd/z,
-aɪt, -əs
anil 'ænɪl
anile 'eɪnaɪl ['æn-]
aniline 'ænɪli:n [-lɪn, rarely -laɪn]
anility æ'nɪlətɪ [ə'n-, -ɪtɪ]
animadversion, -s ˌænɪmæd'vɜ:ʃn
[-məd-], -z
animadvert, -s, -ing, -ed ˌænɪmæd'vɜ:t
[-məd-], -s, -ɪŋ, -ɪd
animal, -s 'ænɪml [-nəm-], -z
animalcular ˌænɪ'mælkjʊlə*
animalcule, -s ˌænɪ'mælkju:l, -z
animalism 'ænɪməlɪzəm [-mlɪ-]
animate (adj.) 'ænɪmət [-mɪt, -meɪt]
animat|e (v.), -es, -ing, -ed/ly, -or/s
'ænɪmeɪt, -s, -ɪŋ, -ɪd/lɪ, -ə*/z
animation ˌænɪ'meɪʃn
animism 'ænɪmɪzəm
animosit|y, -ies ˌænɪ'mɒsət|ɪ [-ɪt|ɪ], -ɪz
animus 'ænɪməs

19

anion, -s 'ænaɪən, -z
anise 'ænɪs
aniseed 'ænɪsiːd
anisette ˌænɪ'zet [-'set]
Anita ə'niːtə
Anjou ɑ̃ːɲˈʒuː [-ɒŋ-] (ɑ̃ʒu)
Ankara (in Turkey) 'æŋkərə
anker, -s 'æŋkə*, -z
ankh, -s æŋk, -s
ankle, -s 'æŋkl, -z
anklet, -s 'æŋklɪt [-lət], -s
Ann æn
anna (A.), -s 'ænə, -z
Annabel 'ænəbel
Annabella ˌænə'belə
Annagh æ'nɑː ['ænɑː]
Annakin 'ænəkɪn
annalist, -s 'ænəlɪst, -s
annals 'ænlz
Annaly 'ænəlɪ
Annam æn'æm ['ænæm]
Annamese ˌænə'miːz
Annan, -dale 'ænən, -deɪl
Annapolis ə'næpəlɪs [æ'n-]
Annas 'ænæs [-nəs]
annatto ə'nætəʊ [æ'n-]
Anne æn
anneal, -s, -ing, -ed ə'niːl, -z, -ɪŋ, -d
Annesley 'ænzlɪ
annex (s.), -es 'æneks, -ɪz
annex (v.), -es, -ing, -ed, -ment/s
ə'neks [æ'n-], -ɪz, -ɪŋ, -t, -mənt/s
annexation, -s ˌænek'seɪʃn, -z
annexe, -s 'æneks, -ɪz
Annie 'ænɪ
annihilat|e, -es, -ing, -ed, -or/s ə'naɪə-
leɪt [-'naɪl-, rarely 'ænɪel-], -s, -ɪŋ,
-ɪd, -ə*/z
annihilation, -s ə,naɪə'leɪʃn [-,naɪ'l-,
rarely ˌænɪə'l-], -z
Anning 'ænɪŋ
Anniston 'ænɪstən
anniversar|y, -ies ˌænɪ'vɜːsər|ɪ, -ɪz
Anno Domini ˌænəʊ'dɒmɪnaɪ
annotat|e, -es, -ing, -ed, -or/s 'ænəʊ-
teɪt, -s, -ɪŋ, -ɪd, -ə*/z
annotation, -s ˌænəʊ'teɪʃn, -z
announc|e, -es, -ing, -ed, -er/s,
-ement/s ə'naʊns, -ɪz, -ɪŋ, -t, -ə*/z,
-mənt/s
annoy, -s, -ing/ly, -ed; -ance/s ə'nɔɪ,
-z, -ɪŋ/lɪ, -d; -əns/ɪz
annual (s. adj.), -s, -ly 'ænjʊəl [-njwəl,
-njʊl], -z, -ɪ
annuit|y, -ies, -ant/s ə'njuːɪt|ɪ [-'njʊ-,
-ət|ɪ], -ɪz, -ənt/s
annul, -s, -ling, -led, -ment/s ə'nʌl, -z,
-ɪŋ, -d, -mənt/s

annul|ar, -ate, -ated 'ænjʊl|ə*, -eɪt [-ɪt],
-eɪtɪd
annulet, -s 'ænjʊlet [-lɪt, -lət], -s
annunciat|e, -es, -ing, -ed ə'nʌnsɪeɪt
[-nʃɪeɪt, -nsɪeɪt, -nsjeɪt], -s, -ɪŋ, -ɪd
annunciation (A.), -s ə,nʌnsɪ'eɪʃn, -z
anode, -s 'ænəʊd, -z
anodyne, -s 'ænəʊdaɪn, -z
anoint, -s, -ing, -ed, -ment/s ə'nɔɪnt,
-s, -ɪŋ, -ɪd, -mənt/s
anomalous, -ly ə'nɒmələs, -lɪ
anomal|y, -ies ə'nɒməl|ɪ, -ɪz
anon ə'nɒn
anonym, -s 'ænənɪm [-nɒn-], -z
anonymity ˌænə'nɪmɪtɪ [-nɒ'n-, -rtɪ]
anonymous, -ly ə'nɒnɪməs, -lɪ
anopheles ə'nɒfɪliːz [-fəl-]
anorak, -s 'ænəræk, -s
anorexia ˌænə'reksɪə [-ksjə]
another ə'nʌðə*
Anouilh 'ænuːiː [-uːɪ] (anuːj)
Anrias 'ænrɪæs
Anselm 'ænselm
anserine 'ænsəraɪn
An|sley, -son 'æn|zlɪ, -sn
Ansonia æn'səʊnjə [-nɪə]
Ansted 'ænsted [-tɪd]
Anster 'ænstə*
Anstey 'ænstɪ
Anstruther 'ænstrʌðə*
answ|er (s. v.), -ers, -ering, -ered,
-erer/s 'ɑːns|ə*, -əz, -ərɪŋ, -əd,
-ərə*/z
answerab|le, -ly 'ɑːnsərəb|l, -lɪ
ant, -s ænt, -s
antacid (s. adj.), -s ˌænt'æsɪd ['ænt,æ-],
-z
Antaeus æn'tiːəs [-'tɪəs]
antagoni|sm/s, -st/s æn'tægənɪ|zəm/z,
-st/s
antagonistic, -ally æn,tægə'nɪstɪk
[ˌ---'--], -əlɪ
antagoniz|e [-is|e], -es, -ing, -ed
æn'tægənaɪz, -ɪz, -ɪŋ, -d
Antananarivo 'æntə,nænə'riːvəʊ
Antarctic æn'tɑːktɪk [æn't-, '-,--]
Antares æn'teəriːz
ant-bear, -s 'æntbeə*, -z
ant-eater, -s 'ænt,iːtə*, -z
anteceden|ce, -t/ly, -ts ˌæntɪ'siːdən|s
['æntɪ,s-], -t/lɪ, -ts
antechamber, -s 'æntɪ,tʃeɪmbə*, -z
antechapel, -s 'æntɪ,tʃæpl, -z
antedat|e, -es, -ing, -ed ˌæntɪ'deɪt ['---],
-s, -ɪŋ, -ɪd
antediluvi|an/s, -al/ly ˌæntɪdɪ'luː-
vj|ən/z [-daɪ'l-, -'lju:-, -vɪ|ə-], -əl/ɪ
antelope, -s 'æntɪləʊp, -s

antemeridian ˌæntɪməˈrɪdɪən [-djən]
antenatal ˌæntɪˈneɪtl
antenn|a, -ae, -al, -ary ænˈten|ə, -iː, -l,
-ərɪ
Antenor ænˈtiːnɔː*
antenuptial ˌæntɪˈnʌpʃl [-tʃəl]
antepenult, -s ˌæntɪpɪˈnʌlt [-peˈn-,
-pəˈn-], -s
antepenultimate, -s ˌæntɪpɪˈnʌltɪmət
[-peˈn-, -pəˈn-, -mɪt], -s
anteprandial ˌæntɪˈprændjəl [-dɪəl]
anterior, -ly, -ness ænˈtɪərɪə*, -lɪ, -nɪs
[-nəs]
anteroom, -s ˈæntɪrʊm [-ruːm], -z
Anthaea ænˈθɪə [-ˈθiːə, ˈænθɪə, ˈænθjə]
ant-heap, -s ˈænthiːp, -s
antheli|on/s, -a ænˈθiːlɪj|ən/z [-lɪ|ə-], -ə
anthelix, -es ænˈθiːlɪks [ˈænθɪlɪks], -ɪz
anthem, -s ˈænθəm [-θem], -z
anther, -s ˈænθə*, -z
anthill, -s ˈænthɪl, -z
anthological ˌænθəˈlɒdʒɪkl [-θəʊˈl-]
antholog|y, -ies, -ist/s ænˈθɒləldʒ|ɪ, -ɪz,
-ɪst/s
Anthon ˈænθən
Anthony ˈæntənɪ, ˈænθənɪ
anthracic ænˈθræsɪk
anthracite ˈænθrəsaɪt
anthracitic ˌænθrəˈsɪtɪk
anthrax ˈænθræks
anthropocentric ˌænθrəʊpəʊˈsentrɪk
anthropoid (s. adj.), -s ˈænθrəʊpɔɪd
[ænˈθrəʊpɔɪd], -z
anthropoidal ˌænθrəʊˈpɔɪdl
anthropologic|al, -ally ˌænθrəpəˈlɒdʒ-
ɪk|l [-θrəʊp-], -əlɪ
anthropolog|ist/s, -y ˌænθrəˈpɒlədʒ|-
ɪst/s [-θrəʊˈp-], -ɪ
anthropometric ˌænθrəʊpəʊˈmetrɪk
anthropometry ˌænθrəˈpɒmɪtrɪ[-θrəʊˈp-,
-mətrɪ, ˈænθrəʊpəʊmetrɪ]
anthropomorph|ic, -ism, -ist/s, -ous
ˌænθrəpəʊˈmɔːf|ɪk [-θrəʊp-], -ɪzəm,
-ɪst/s, -əs
anthropophagi ˌænθrəʊˈpɒfəgaɪ
[-fədʒaɪ]
anthropopha|gous, -gy ˌænθrəʊˈpɒ-
fə|gəs, -dʒɪ
anthroposoph|ist/s, -y ˌænθrəʊˈpɒsəf|-
ɪst/s, -ɪ
anti- ˈæntɪ-
Note.—Numerous compounds may be
formed by prefixing anti- to other
words. Those not entered below have
double stress.
anti-aircraft ˌæntɪˈeəkrɑːft
antibilious ˌæntɪˈbɪljəs [-lɪəs]
antibiotic (s. adj.), -s ˌæntɪbaɪˈɒtɪk, -s

antibod|y, -ies ˈæntɪˌbɒd|ɪ, -ɪz
antic, -s ˈæntɪk, -s
anticatholic, -s ˌæntɪˈkæθəlɪk [-ˈkɑːθ-,
-θlɪk], -s
Antichrist, -s ˈæntɪkraɪst, -s
antichristian, -s (opposing Christianity)
ˌæntɪˈkrɪstjən [-tɪən, -tʃən], (pertaining to Antichrist) ˈæntɪˌk-, -z
anticipant, -s ænˈtɪsɪpənt, -s
anticipat|e, -es, -ing, -ed; -ive/ly
ænˈtɪsɪpeɪt, -s, -ɪŋ, -ɪd; -ɪv/lɪ
anticipation, -s ænˌtɪsɪˈpeɪʃn [ˌæntɪ-],
-z
anticipator|y, -ily ænˈtɪsɪpeɪtər|ɪ [-pət-],
-əlɪ [-ɪlɪ]
anticiz|e [-is|e], -es, -ing, -ed ˈæntɪsaɪz,
-ɪz, -ɪŋ, -d
anticlerical ˌæntɪˈklerɪkl
anticlimax, -es ˌæntɪˈklaɪmæks [in contrast ˈæntɪˌklaɪmæks], -ɪz
anticyclone, -s ˌæntɪˈsaɪkləʊn [ˈæntɪˌs-],
-z
anticyclonic ˌæntɪsaɪˈklɒnɪk
anti-dazzle ˌæntɪˈdæzl
anti-depressant, -s ˌæntɪdɪˈpresnt, -s
antidotal ˈæntɪdəʊtl [ˌæntɪˈd-]
antidote, -s ˈæntɪdəʊt, -s
antifebrile ˌæntɪˈfiːbraɪl [-ˈfeb-]
anti-freeze ˈæntɪfriːz [ˌ--ˈ-]
Antigon|e, -us ænˈtɪgən|ɪ, -əs
Antigua ænˈtiːgə
anti|helix, -helixes, -helices ˌæntɪ|ˈhiː-
lɪks, -ˈhiːlɪksɪz, -ˈhiːlɪsiːz [-helɪsiːz]
antihistamine ˌæntɪˈhɪstəmɪn [-miːn]
anti-icer, -s ˌæntɪˈaɪsə*, -z
Antilles ænˈtɪliːz
antilog|y, -ies ænˈtɪlədʒ|ɪ, -ɪz
antimacassar, -s ˌæntɪməˈkæsə*, -z
Antimachus ænˈtɪməkəs
antimonarchical ˌæntɪmɒˈnɑːkɪkl
[-məˈn-]
antimonarchist, -s ˌæntɪˈmɒnəkɪst, -s
antimonial, -s ˌæntɪˈməʊnjəl [-nɪəl], -z
antimonic ˌæntɪˈmɒnɪk
antimony ˈæntɪmənɪ
anti-national ˌæntɪˈnæʃənl [-ʃnəl, -ʃn̩l,
-ʃn̩], -ʃənəl]
antinomic, -al, -ally ˌæntɪˈnɒmɪk, -l, -əlɪ
antinom|y, -ies ænˈtɪnəm|ɪ, -ɪz
Antinous ænˈtɪnəʊəs
Antioch ˈæntɪɒk [-tjɒk]
Antiochian, -s ˌæntɪˈəʊkjən [-kɪən], -z
Antiochus ænˈtaɪəkəs
Antioquia ˌæntɪɒˈkiːə [-ɪə]
Antipas ˈæntɪpæs
Antipater ænˈtɪpətə*
antipathetic ˌæntɪpəˈθetɪk [-,--ˈ--]
antipath|y, -ies ænˈtɪpəθ|ɪ, -ɪz

21

anti-personnel ˌæntɪpɜːsəˈnel [-snˈel]
antiphlogistic ˌæntɪfləʊˈdʒɪstɪk
antiphlogistine ˌæntɪfləʊˈdʒɪstiːn
[-flɒˈdʒ-, -tɪn]
antiphon, -s ˈæntɪfən [-fɒn], -z
antiphon|al/s, -er/s æn'trɪfən|l/z, -ə*/z
antiphonic, -al, -ally ˌæntɪˈfɒnɪk, -l, -əlɪ
antiphon|y, -ies æn'tɪfən|ɪ, -ɪz
antipodal æn'tɪpədl
antipodean æn,tɪpəˈdiːən [ˌæntɪp-,
-pəʊˈd-, -'dɪən]
antipodes æn'tɪpədiːz
antipope, -s ˈæntɪpəʊp, -s
antipyretic, -s ˌæntɪpaɪˈretɪk [-paɪəˈr-,
-pɪˈr-], -s
antipyrin ˌæntɪˈpaɪərɪn
antiquarian, -s -ism ˌæntɪˈkweərɪən, -z,
-ɪzəm
antiquar|y, -ies ˈæntɪkwər|ɪ, -ɪz
antiquate (adj.) ˈæntɪkwɪt [-kweɪt]
antiquated ˈæntɪkweɪtɪd
antique (s. adj.), -s, -ly, -ness æn'tiːk,
-s, -lɪ, -nɪs [-nəs]
antiquit|y, -ies æn'tɪkwət|ɪ [-kwɪt|ɪ], -ɪz
antirrhinum, -s ˌæntɪˈraɪnəm [-təˈr-], -z
antiscorbutic, -s ˌæntɪskɔːˈbjuːtɪk, -s
anti-semitic ˌæntɪsɪˈmɪtɪk [-sə-]
anti-semitism ˌæntɪˈsemɪtɪzəm [-mət-]
antiseptic (s. adj.), -s, -ally ˌæntɪˈseptɪk,
-s, -əlɪ
antisocial ˌæntɪˈsəʊʃl
antisocialist, -s ˌæntɪˈsəʊʃəlɪst [-ʃlɪ-], -s
antistrophe, -s æn'tɪstrəfɪ, -z
antistrophic ˌæntɪˈstrɒfɪk
anti-tank ˌæntɪˈtæŋk
antithes|is, -es æn'tɪθɪs|ɪs [-θəs-], -iːz
antithetic, -ally ˌæntɪˈθetɪk, -əlɪ
antitoxi|c, -n/s ˌæntɪˈtɒksɪ|k, -n/z
anti-trade, -s ˌæntɪˈtreɪd, -z
antiviral ˌæntɪˈvaɪrəl
anti-vivisection, -ist/s ˈæntɪ,vɪvɪˈsekʃn,
-ɪst/s
antler, -s, -ed ˈæntlə*, -z, -d
ant-lion, -s ˈænt,laɪən, -z
Antoinette ˌæntwɑːˈnet [ˌɑːn-, -twəˈn-]
(ãtwanɛt)
Antonia æn'təʊnjə [-nɪə]
Antonine, -s ˈæntənaɪn, -z
Antoninus ˌæntəʊˈnaɪnəs
Antonio æn'təʊnɪəʊ [-njəʊ]
Antonius æn'təʊnjəs [-nɪəs]
Antony ˈæntənɪ
antonym, -s ˈæntəʊnɪm, -z
antonymy æn'tɒnɪmɪ [-nəmɪ]
Antrim ˈæntrɪm
Antrobus ˈæntrəʊbəs
antr|um, -ums, -a ˈæntr|əm, -əmz, -ə
antrycide ˈæntrɪsaɪd

Antwerp ˈæntwɜːp
anus, -es ˈeɪnəs, -ɪz
anvil, -s ˈænvɪl, -z
Anwick ˈænɪk
anxiet|y, -ies æŋˈzaɪət|ɪ [-ŋgˈz-], -ɪz
anxious, -ly, -ness ˈæŋkʃəs, -lɪ, -nɪs
[-nəs]
any ˈenɪ (normal form), ənɪ (occasional
weak form), ŋɪ (occasional weak form
after t or d)
anybody ˈenɪ,bɒdɪ [-bədɪ]
anyhow ˈenɪhaʊ
anyone ˈenɪwʌn [-wən]
anything ˈenɪθɪŋ
anyway ˈenɪweɪ
anywhere ˈenɪweə* [-hweə*]
anywise ˈenɪwaɪz
Anzac, -s ˈænzæk, -s
Aonia, -n/s eɪˈəʊnjə [-nɪə-], -n/z
aorist, -s ˈeərɪst [ˈerər-], -s
aort|a/s, -al, -ic eɪˈɔːt|ə/z, -l, -ɪk
Aosta ɑːˈɒstə
apace əˈpeɪs
Apache (American Indian), -s əˈpætʃɪ, -
-z
apache (ruffian), -s əˈpæʃ [æˈp-, -ˈpɑːʃ]
(apaʃ), -ɪz
apart, -ness əˈpɑːt, -nɪs [-nəs]
apartheid əˈpɑːtheɪt [-eɪd, -aɪt] (Afrikaans aˈpartheɪt)
apartment, -s əˈpɑːtmənt, -s
apathetic, -al, -ally ˌæpəˈθetɪk, -l, -əlɪ
apath|y, -ies ˈæpəθ|ɪ, -ɪz
ap|e (s. v.), -es, -ing, -ed eɪp, -s, -ɪŋ, -t
apehood ˈeɪphʊd
Apelles əˈpeliːz
Apennines ˈæpɪnaɪnz [-pen-]
aperçu, -s ˌæpɜːˈsjuː [-ˈsuː] (apɛrsy), -z
aperient, -s əˈpɪərɪənt, -s
aperitive, -s əˈperətɪv [-rɪt-], -z
aperture, -s ˈæpə,tjʊə* [-,tʃʊə*, -tʃə*],
-z
aper|y, -ies ˈeɪpər|ɪ, -ɪz
apex, -es, -apices ˈeɪpeks, -ɪz, ˈeɪpɪsiːz
[ˈæpɪsiːz]
aphasia əˈfeɪzjə [æˈf-, eɪˈf-, -zɪə, -ʒjə,
-ʒɪə, -ʒə]
aphasic əˈfeɪzɪk
apheli|on, -a æˈfiːlj|ən [-lɪ|ən], -ə
apheresis æˈfɪərɪsɪs [-rəs-]
aphesis ˈæfɪsɪs [-fəs-]
aphid ˈeɪfɪd
aphidian, -s eɪˈfɪdɪən [æˈf-, -djən], -z
aph|is, -ides, -ises ˈeɪf|ɪs [ˈæf-], -ɪdiːz,
-ɪsɪz
aphonia eɪˈfəʊnjə [æˈf-, əˈf-, -nɪə]
aphonic eɪˈfɒnɪk [æˈf-, əˈf-]
aphony ˈæfənɪ

aphori|sm/s, -st/s 'æfərɪ|zəm/z [-fɒr-],
-st/s

aphoristic, -ally ˌæfə'rɪstɪk [-fɒ'r-], -əlɪ

aphoriz|e [-is|e], -es, -ing, -ed, -er/s
'æfəraɪz [-fɒr-], -ɪz, -ɪŋ, -d, -ə*/z

aphrodis|iac/s, -ian ˌæfrəʊ'dɪz|ræk/s,
-ɪən [-jən]

Aphrodite ˌæfrəʊ'daɪtɪ

aphtha 'æfθə

apian 'eɪpjən [-pɪən]

apiarian, -s ˌeɪpɪ'eərɪən, -z

apiar|y, -ies, -ist/s 'eɪpjər|ɪ [-pɪər-], -ɪz,
-ɪst/s

apic|al, -ally 'æpɪk|l ['eɪp-], -əlɪ

apices (plur. of apex) 'eɪpɪsi:z ['æp-]

apiculture 'eɪpɪkʌltʃə*

apiece ə'pi:s

apis (bee) 'eɪpɪs

Apis 'ɑ:pɪs ['eɪpɪs]

apish, -ly, -ness 'eɪpɪʃ, -lɪ, -nɪs [-nəs]

aplomb ə'plɒm ['æplɔ̃:ŋ, -plɔ̃:m] (aplɔ̃)

apocalyp|se/s (A.), -st/s, -t/s ə'pɒkə-
lɪp|s/ɪz, -st/s, -t/s

apocalypti|c, -st/s əˌpɒkə'lɪptɪ|k, -st/s

apocopate (adj.) ə'pɒkəʊpɪt [-pət,
-peɪt]

apocopat|e (v.), -es, -ing, -ed ə'pɒkəʊ-
peɪt, -s, -ɪŋ, -ɪd

apocopation, -s əˌpɒkəʊ'peɪʃn, -z

apocope, -s ə'pɒkəʊpɪ, -z

apocryph|a/s, -al ə'pɒkrɪf|ə/z, -l

apodeictic, -al, -ally ˌæpəʊ'daɪktɪk, -l,
-əlɪ

apodos|is, -es ə'pɒdəʊs|ɪs, -i:z

apogee, -s 'æpəʊdʒi:, -z

Apollinaris əˌpɒlɪ'neərɪs [-'nɑ:r-]

Apollo ə'pɒləʊ

Apollodorus əˌpɒlə'dɔ:rəs

Apolloni|a, -an, -us ˌæpə'ləʊnj|ə [-pɒ'l-,
-nɪ|ə], -ən, -əs

Apollos ə'pɒlɒs

Apollyon ə'pɒljən [-lɪən]

apologetic, -al, -ally, -s əˌpɒlə'dʒetɪk,
-l, -əlɪ, -s

apologist, -s ə'pɒlədʒɪst, -s

apologiz|e [-is|e], -es, -ing, -ed, -er/s
ə'pɒlədʒaɪz, -ɪz, -ɪŋ, -d, -ə*/z

apologue, -s 'æpəlɒg [-pəʊl-, -ləʊg], -z

apolog|y, -ies ə'pɒlədʒ|ɪ, -ɪz

apophthegm, -s 'æpəʊθem, -z

apoplectic, -al, -ally ˌæpəʊ'plektɪk, -l,
-əlɪ

apoplex|y, -ies 'æpəʊpleks|ɪ, -ɪz

aposiopes|is, -es ˌæpəʊsaɪəʊ'pi:s|ɪs,
əˌpɒsɪəʊ'pi:sɪs, -i:z

apostas|y, -ies ə'pɒstəs|ɪ, -ɪz

apostate, -s ə'pɒsteɪt [-tɪt, -tət], -s

apostatic, -al ˌæpəʊ'stætɪk, -l

apostatiz|e [-is|e], -es, -ing, -ed
ə'pɒstətaɪz, -ɪz, -ɪŋ, -d

a posteriori 'eɪpɒsˌterɪ'ɔ:raɪ [-ˌtɪər-,
'ɑ:pɒsˌterɪ'ɔ:ri:]

apostigmat, -s 'æpəʊstɪgmæt, -s

apostil, -s ə'pɒstɪl, -z

apostle, -s, -ship ə'pɒsl, -z, -ʃɪp

apostolate, -s ə'pɒstəʊlət [-lɪt, -leɪt], -s

apostolic, -al, -ally ˌæpə'stɒlɪk, -l, -əlɪ

apostolicism ˌæpə'stɒlɪsɪzəm

apostrophe, -s ə'pɒstrəfɪ, -z

apostrophiz|e [-is|e], -es, -ing, -ed
ə'pɒstrəfaɪz, -ɪz, -ɪŋ, -d

apothecar|y, -ies ə'pɒθəkər|ɪ [-θɪk-], -ɪz

apotheos|is, -es əˌpɒθɪ'əʊs|ɪs [ˌæpəʊθ-],
-i:z

apotheosiz|e [-is|e], -es, -ing, -ed
ə'pɒθɪəʊsaɪz [-θɪəs-, ˌæpəʊ'θɪəʊsaɪz],
-ɪz, -ɪŋ, -d

appal, -s, -ling/ly, -led ə'pɔ:l, -z, -ɪŋ/lɪ,
-d

Appalachian ˌæpə'leɪtʃjən [-tʃɪən]

appanage, -s 'æpənɪdʒ, -ɪz

apparatus, -es æpə'reɪtəs, -ɪz

apparatus (alternative plur. of apparatus) ˌæpə'reɪtəs

appar|el (s. v.), -els, -elling, -elled
ə'pær|əl, -əlz, -əlɪŋ [-lɪŋ], -əld

apparent, -ly, -ness ə'pærənt [-'peər-],
-lɪ, -nɪs [-nəs]

apparition, -s ˌæpə'rɪʃn, -z

apparitor, -s ə'pærɪtɔ:* [-tə*], -z

appassionata (Beethoven sonata)
əˌpæsjə'nɑ:tə [-sɪə-]

appeal (s. v.), -s, -ing/ly, -ingness, -ed,
-er/s ə'pi:l, -z, -ɪŋ/lɪ, -ɪŋnɪs [-nəs], -d,
-ə*/z

appear, -s, -ing, -ed, -er/s; -ance/s
ə'pɪə*, -z, -ɪŋ, -d, -rə*/z; -rəns/ɪz

appeas|e, -es, -ing/ly, -ed; -able
ə'pi:z, -ɪz, -ɪŋ/lɪ, -d; -əbl

appellant, -s ə'pelənt, -s

appellate ə'pelət [æ'p-, -leɪt, -lɪt]

appellation, -s ˌæpə'leɪʃn [-pɪ'l-, -pe'l-],
-z

appellative, -ly, -ness ə'pelətɪv [æ'p-],
-lɪ, -nɪs [-nəs]

append, -s, -ing, -ed; -age/s ə'pend, -z,
-ɪŋ, -ɪd; -ɪdʒ/ɪz

appendectomy ˌæpen'dektəmɪ

appendicitis əˌpendɪ'saɪtɪs [-də-]

append|ix, -ixes, -ices ə'pend|ɪks, -ɪksɪz,
-ɪsi:z

apperception ˌæpə'sepʃn

appertain, -s, -ing, -ed ˌæpə'teɪn, -z, -ɪŋ,
-d

appertinent ə'pə:tɪnənt [æ'p-]

appeten|ce, -cy, -t 'æpɪtən|s, -sɪ, -t

23

appetite, -s ˈæpɪtaɪt, -s
appetiz|e, -es, -ing/ly, -ed, -er/s
ˈæpɪtaɪz, -ɪz, -ɪŋ/lɪ, -d, -ə*/z
Appi|an, -us ˈæpɪ|ən [-pj|-], -əs
applaud, -s, -ing/ly, -ed, -er/s əˈplɔːd,
-z, -ɪŋ/lɪ, -ɪd, -ə*/z
applause əˈplɔːz
apple, -s; -blight ˈæpl, -z; -blaɪt
apple-blossom ˈæpl͵blɒsəm
Appleby ˈæplbɪ
apple-cart ˈæplkɑːt
Appledore ˈæpldɔː* [-dɔə*]
Appleford ˈæplfəd
Applegate ˈæplgeɪt [-gɪt]
apple|-pie/s, -sauce ͵æpl|ˈpaɪ/z, -ˈsɔːs
Appleton ˈæpltən
apple-tree, -s ˈæpltriː, -z
appliable, -ness əˈplaɪəbl, -nɪs [-nəs]
appliance, -s əˈplaɪəns, -ɪz
applicability ͵æplɪkəˈbɪlətɪ [ə͵plɪk-, -lɪt-]
applicab|le, -ly, -leness ˈæplɪkəb|l
[əˈplɪk-], -lɪ, -lnɪs [-nəs]
applicant, -s ˈæplɪkənt, -s
applicate ˈæplɪkət [-kɪt, -keɪt]
application, -s ͵æplɪˈkeɪʃn, -z
appliqué, -s æˈpliːkeɪ [əˈp-] (aplike),
-z
appl|y, -ies, -ying, -ied əˈpl|aɪ, -aɪz,
-aɪɪŋ, -aɪd
appoggiatura, -s ə͵pɒdʒəˈtʊərə [-dʒjə-,
-dʒɪə-, -ˈtjʊər-, -ˈtjɔːr-, -ˈtjɔːr-], -z
appoint, -s, -ing, -ed, -ment/s əˈpɔɪnt,
-s, -ɪŋ, -ɪd, -mənt/s
appointee, -s, əpɔɪnˈtiː: [͵æpɔɪnˈt-], -z
apport, -s, -ing, -ed əˈpɔːt, -s, -ɪŋ, -ɪd
apporti|on, -ons, -oning, -oned, -on-
ment/s əˈpɔːʃ|n, -ənz, -ŋɪŋ [-nɪŋ,
-ənɪŋ], -nd, -nmənt/s
appos|e, -es, -ing, -ed æˈpəʊz, -ɪz, -ɪŋ, -d
apposite, -ly, -ness ˈæpəʊzɪt, -lɪ, -nɪs
[-nəs]
apposition, -s ͵æpəʊˈzɪʃn [-pʊˈz-], -z
appositional ͵æpəʊˈzɪʃənl [-pʊˈz-, -ʃnəl,
-ʃn̩l, -ʃn̩l, -ʃənəl]
apprais|e, -es, -ing, -ed, -er/s, -ement/s;
-able, -al/s əˈpreɪz, -ɪz, -ɪŋ, -d, -ə*/z,
-mənt/s; -əbl, -l/z
appreciab|le, -ly, əˈpriːʃəb|l [-ʃjəb-,
-ʃɪəb-], -lɪ
appreciat|e, -es, -ing/ly, -ed, -or/s
əˈpriːʃɪeɪt [-ʃjeɪt, -iːsɪeɪt, -iːsjeɪt], -s,
-ɪŋ/lɪ, -ɪd, -ə*/z
appreciation, -s ə͵priːʃɪˈeɪʃn [-iːsɪ-], -z
appreciative, -ly, -ness əˈpriːʃjətɪv
[-ʃɪət-, -ʃɪert-], -lɪ, -nɪs [-nəs]
appreciatory əˈpriːʃjətərɪ [-ʃɪət-, -ʃɪert-]
apprehend, -s, -ing, -ed ͵æprɪˈhend, -z,
-ɪŋ, -ɪd

apprehensibility ˈæprɪ͵hensɪˈbɪlətɪ
[-sə-ˈb-, -lɪt-]
apprehensible ͵æprɪˈhensəbl [-sɪb-]
apprehension, -s ͵æprɪˈhenʃn, -z
apprehensive, -ly, -ness ͵æprɪˈhensɪv,
-lɪ, -nɪs [-nəs]
apprentic|e (s. v.), -es, -ing, -ed
əˈprentɪs, -ɪz, -ɪŋ, -t
apprenticeship, -s əˈprentɪʃɪp [-tɪsʃɪp,
-tɪʃʃɪp], -s
appris|e, -es, -ing, -ed əˈpraɪz, -ɪz, -ɪŋ,
-d
appriz|e, -es, -ing, -ed, -er/s əˈpraɪz,
-ɪz, -ɪŋ, -d, -ə*/z
appro ˈæprəʊ
approach (s. v.), -es, -ing, -ed; -able
əˈprəʊtʃ, -ɪz, -ɪŋ, -t; -əbl
approachability ə͵prəʊtʃəˈbɪlətɪ [-lɪt-]
approbat|e, -es, -ing, -ed; -ive ˈæprəʊ-
beɪt [-prʊb-], -s, -ɪŋ, -ɪd; -ɪv
approbation, -s ͵æprəʊˈbeɪʃn [-prʊˈb-],
-z
approbatory ͵æprəʊˈbeɪtərɪ
appro|priate (adj.), -priately, -priateness
əˈprəʊ|prɪət [-prɪt], -prɪətlɪ [-prɪtlɪ],
-prɪətnɪs [-prɪt-, -nəs]
appropriat|e (v.), -es, -ing, -ed, -or/s
əˈprəʊprɪeɪt, -s, -ɪŋ, -ɪd, -ə*/z
appropriation, -s ə͵prəʊprɪˈeɪʃn, -z
approv|e, -es, -ing/ly, -ed, -er/s; -able,
-al/s əˈpruːv, -z, -ɪŋ/lɪ, -d, -ə*/z;
-əbl, -l/z
approximant, -s əˈprɒksɪmənt, -s
approximate (adj.), -ly əˈprɒksɪmət
[-mɪt], -lɪ [-mɪtlɪ]
approximat|e (v.), -es, -ing, -ed əˈprɒks-
ɪmeɪt, -s, -ɪŋ, -ɪd
approximation, -s ə͵prɒksɪˈmeɪʃn, -z
approximative əˈprɒksɪmətɪv
appui æˈpwiː [əˈp-] (apɥi)
Appuldurcombe ͵æpldəˈkuːm
appulse, -s æˈpʌls [əˈpʌls, ˈæpʌls], -ɪz
appurtenan|ce, -ces, -t əˈpɜːtɪnən|s
[-tən-, -tnə-], -sɪz, -t
apricot, -s ˈeɪprɪkɒt, -s
April, -s ˈeɪprəl [-rɪl], -z
a priori ͵eɪpraɪˈɔːraɪ [͵ɑːpriːˈɔːriː:, -ˈrɪˈɔː:-]
apriority ͵eɪpraɪˈɒrətɪ [-rɪt]
apron, -s, -ed ˈeɪprən, -z, -d
apron-string, -s ˈeɪprənstrɪŋ, -z
apropos ˈæprəpəʊ [͵--ˈ-]
apse, -s æps, -ɪz
apsidal ˈæpsɪdl
apsis, apsides ˈæpsɪs, æpˈsaɪdiːz [ˈæp-
sɪdiːz]
Apsley ˈæpslɪ
apt, -er, -est, -ly, -ness æpt, -ə*, -ɪst,
-lɪ, -nɪs [-nəs]

apter|al, -ous 'æptər|əl, -əs
apteryges æp'terɪdʒi:z
apteryx, -es 'æptərɪks, -ɪz
aptitude, -s 'æptɪtju:d, -z
Apulia, -n/s ə'pju:ljə [-lɪə], -n/z
apyretic ˌæpaɪ'retɪk [-paɪə'r-, -pɪ'r-]
aqua-fortis ˌækwə'fɔ:tɪs
aqua-lung, -s 'ækwəlʌŋ, -z
aquamarine, -s ˌækwəmə'ri:n, -z
aqua-plane, -s 'ækwəpleɪn, -z
aqua-regia ˌækwə'ri:dʒə [-dʒɪə]
aquarell|e, -es; -ist/s ˌækwə'rel, -z; -ɪst/s
aquarist, -s 'ækwərɪst, -s
aquari|um, -ums, -a ə'kweərɪ|əm, -əmz, -ə
Aquari|us, -an/s ə'kweərɪ|əs, -ən/z
aquatic (s. adj.), -s ə'kwætɪk [-'kwɒt-], -s
aquatint, -s 'ækwətɪnt, -s
aquavit 'ækwəvɪt [-vi:t]
aqua-vitae ˌækwə'vaɪti: [-tɪ]
aqueduct, -s 'ækwɪdʌkt [-kwəd-], -s
aqueous, -ly 'eɪkwɪəs ['æk-], -lɪ
Aquila 'ækwɪlə [as constellation also ə'kwɪlə]
aquilegia, -s ˌækwɪ'li:dʒə [-dʒɪə], -z
aquiline 'ækwɪlaɪn
Aquinas ə'kwaɪnæs [æ'k-, -nəs]
Aquitaine ˌækwɪ'teɪn
Aquitania ˌækwɪ'teɪnjə [-nɪə]
Arab, -s 'ærəb, -z
Arabella ˌærə'belə
arabesque, -s, -d ˌærə'besk, -s, -t
Arabia, -n/s ə'reɪbə [-bɪə], -n/z
Arabic (of Arabia) 'ærəbɪk, (name of ship) 'ærəbɪk [ə'ræb-]
arabis 'ærəbɪs
arable 'ærəbl ['eər-]
Araby 'ærəbɪ
Arachne ə'ræknɪ
arachnid, -a, -s ə'ræknɪd, -ə, -z
arachnologist, -s ˌæræk'nɒlədʒɪst [-rək-], -s
Aragon 'ærəgən
aragonite ə'rægənaɪt
Aral 'ɑ:rəl ['eər-]
Aram (biblical name) 'eəræm [-rəm], (surname) 'eərəm
Aramai|c, -sm ˌærə'meɪ|k, -zəm
Aramean, -s ˌærə'mi:ən [-'mɪən], -s
Aramite, -s 'ærəmaɪt ['eəræm-, -rəm-], -s
Aran 'ærən
Ararat 'ærəræt
Araucania ˌærɔ:'keɪnjə [-nɪə]
araucaria, -s ˌærɔ:'keərɪə, -z
Arber 'ɑ:bə*

Arberry 'ɑ:bərɪ
arbiter, -s 'ɑ:bɪtə*, -z
arbitrage (arbitration) 'ɑ:bɪtrɪdʒ
arbitrage (of stocks, etc.) ˌɑ:bɪ'trɑ:ʒ ['ɑ:bɪtrɪdʒ]
arbitrament, -s ɑ:'bɪtrəmənt [-trɪm-], -s
arbitrar|y, -ily, -iness 'ɑ:bɪtrər|ɪ, -əlɪ [-ɪlɪ], -ɪnɪs [-ɪnəs]
arbitrat|e, -es, -ing, -ed, -or/s 'ɑ:bɪtreɪt, -s, -ɪŋ, -ɪd, -ə*/z
arbitration, -s ˌɑ:bɪ'treɪʃn, -z
arbitress, -es 'ɑ:bɪtrɪs [-tres], -ɪz
Arblay 'ɑ:bleɪ
arbor (tree) 'ɑ:bɔ:* [-bə*]
arbor (axle, arbour), -s 'ɑ:bə*, -z
Arbor 'ɑ:bə*
arboraceous ˌɑ:bə'reɪʃəs [-bɔ:'r-]
arbore|al, -ous ɑ:'bɔ:rɪ|əl, -əs
arborescen|ce, -t ˌɑ:bə'resn|s [-bɔ:'r-], -t
arboretum, -s ˌɑ:bə'ri:təm [-bɔ:'r-], -z
arboriculture 'ɑ:bərɪkʌltʃə* [-bɔ:r-]
arbor-vitae, -s ˌɑ:bə'vaɪtɪ [-ti:], -z
arbour, -s 'ɑ:bə*, -z
Arbroath ɑ:'brəʊθ
Arbuthnot(t) ɑ:'bʌθnət [ə'b-]
arbutus, -es ɑ:'bju:təs, -ɪz
arc (A.), -s ɑ:k, -s
arcade, -s ɑ:'keɪd, -z
Arcadia, -n/s ɑ:'keɪdjə [-dɪə], -n/z
arcan|um, -a ɑ:'keɪn|əm, -ə
arch (s. v.), -es, -ing, -ed ɑ:tʃ, -ɪz, -ɪŋ, -t
arch (adj.), -est, -ly, -ness ɑ:tʃ, -ɪst, -lɪ, -nɪs [-nəs]
archaean ɑ:'ki:ən [-'kɪən]
archaeologic|al, -ally ˌɑ:kɪə'lɒdʒɪk|l [-kjə-], -əlɪ
archaeolog|ist/s, -y ˌɑ:kɪ'ɒlədʒ|ɪst/s, -ɪ
archaeopteryx, -es ˌɑ:kɪ'ɒptərɪks, -ɪz
archaic, -ally ɑ:'keɪk, -əlɪ
archaism, -s ɑ:'keɪzəm, -z
archangel, -s 'ɑ:k,eɪndʒəl [ˌɑ:k'eɪn-], -z
Archangel 'ɑ:k,eɪndʒəl [ˌɑ:k'eɪn-]
archbishop, -s ˌɑ:tʃ'bɪʃəp [also '-,--according to sentence-stress], -s
archbishopric, -s ˌɑ:tʃ'bɪʃəprɪk, -s
Arch|bold, -dale 'ɑ:tʃ|bəʊld, -deɪl
archdeacon, -s ˌɑ:tʃ'di:kən [also '-,--according to sentence-stress]
archdeaconr|y, -ies ˌɑ:tʃ'di:kənr|ɪ, -ɪz
archdiocese, -s ˌɑ:tʃ'daɪəsɪs [-si:s], -ɪz
archducal ˌɑ:tʃ'dju:kl
archduchess, -es ˌɑ:tʃ'dʌtʃɪs, -ɪz
archduch|y, -ies ˌɑ:tʃ'dʌtʃ|ɪ, -ɪz
archduke, -s ˌɑ:tʃ'dju:k ['--], -s
archdukedom, -s ˌɑ:tʃ'dju:kdəm, -z
Archelaus ˌɑ:kɪ'leɪəs

25

arch-enem|y, -ies ˌɑːtʃ'enɪm|ɪ [-nəm-], -ɪz

archer (A.), -s 'ɑːtʃə*, -z

archeress, -es 'ɑːtʃərɪs [-res], -ɪz

archery 'ɑːtʃərɪ

archetype, -s 'ɑːkɪtaɪp, -s

arch-fiend (A.), -s ˌɑːtʃ'fiːnd, -z

arch-heretic, -s ˌɑːtʃ'herətɪk [-rɪt-], -s

Archibald 'ɑːtʃɪbɔːld [-bəld]

archidiaconal ˌɑːkɪdaɪ'ækənl [-dɪ'æk-, -kn̩l]

Archie 'ɑːtʃɪ

archiepiscop|acy, -al, -ate ˌɑːkɪ'pɪskəp|əsɪ [-kɪe'p-], -l, -ɪt [-ət, -eɪt]

Archilochus ɑː'kɪləkəs

Archimage 'ɑːkɪmeɪdʒ

archimandrite, -s ˌɑːkɪ'mændraɪt, -s

archimedean ˌɑːkɪ'miːdjən [-dɪən, ˌɑːkɪmi'diːən, -mɪ-, -'dɪən]

Archimedes ˌɑːkɪ'miːdiːz

archipelago, -(e)s ˌɑːkɪ'pelɪgəʊ [-ləg-], -z

archiphoneme, -s 'ɑːkɪˌfəʊniːm, -z

architect, -s 'ɑːkɪtekt, -s

architectonic ˌɑːkɪtek'tɒnɪk

architec|tural, -turally ˌɑːkɪ'tek|tʃərəl [-tʃʊrəl], -tʃərəlɪ [-tʃərlɪ, -tʃʊrəlɪ]

architecture 'ɑːkɪtektʃə*

architrave, -s, -d 'ɑːkɪtreɪv, -z, -d

archival ɑː'kaɪvl

archive, -s 'ɑːkaɪv, -z

archivist, -s 'ɑːkɪvɪst, -s

archon, -s 'ɑːkən [-kɒn], -z

arch-prelate, -s ˌɑːtʃ'prelət [-lɪt], -s

arch-priest, -s ˌɑːtʃ'priːst, -s

arch-traitor, -s ˌɑːtʃ'treɪtə*, -z

archway (A.), -s 'ɑːtʃweɪ, -z

archwise 'ɑːtʃwaɪz

Archyll 'ɑːkɪl

Archytas ɑː'kaɪtæs [-təs]

Arcite 'ɑːsaɪt

Arcot ɑː'kɒt

arctic 'ɑːktɪk

Arcturus ɑːk'tjʊərəs [-'tjɔər-, -'tjɔːr-]

arcuate 'ɑːkjʊɪt [-kjʊeɪt, -kjʊət]

arcuated 'ɑːkjʊeɪtɪd

Arcy 'ɑːsɪ

Ardagh 'ɑːdə [-dɑː]

Ardee ɑː'diː

Arden 'ɑːdn

arden|cy, -t/ly 'ɑːdən|sɪ, -t/lɪ

Ardennes ɑː'den [-'denz] (ardɛn)

Ardilaun ˌɑːdɪ'lɔːn

Arding 'ɑːdɪŋ

Ardingly (in West Sussex) 'ɑːdɪŋlaɪ [ˌ--'-]

Ardlamont ɑːd'læmənt

Ard|leigh, -ley 'ɑːd|lɪ, -lɪ

Ardoch 'ɑːdɒk [-ɒx]

ardour 'ɑːdə*

Ardrishaig ɑː'drɪʃɪg

Ardrossan ɑː'drɒsən

Arduin 'ɑːdwɪn

arduous, -ly, -ness 'ɑːdjʊəs [-djwəs], -lɪ, -nɪs [-nəs]

Ardwick 'ɑːdwɪk

are (surface measure), -s ɑː*, -z

are (from be) ɑː* (strong form), ə* (weak form), r (occasional weak form before vowels)

area, -s 'eərɪə, -z

areca, -s 'ærɪkə [æ'riːkə, ə'riːkə], -z

arena, -s ə'riːnə, -z

Arendt 'ærənt ['ɑːr-]

aren't ɑːnt

areol|a, -as, -ae æ'rɪəʊl|ə [ə'r-], -əz, -iː

areomet|er/s, -ry ˌærɪ'ɒmɪt|ə*/z [ˌeər-, -mət|ə*/z], -rɪ

Areopagite, -s ˌærɪ'ɒpəgaɪt [-ədʒaɪt], -s

areopagitic, -a ˌærɪɒpə'dʒɪtɪk, -ə

Areopagus ˌærɪ'ɒpəgəs

Arequipa ˌærɪ'kiːpə [-re'k-] (are'kipa)

Ares 'eəriːz

arête, -s æ'reɪt [ə'r-, -'ret] (arɛːt), -s

Arete ə'riːtɪ [æ'r-, -tɪ]

Arethusa ˌærɪ'θjuːzə [-re'θ-, -'θuːzə]

Argalus 'ɑːgələs

argand (A.), -s 'ɑːgænd [-gənd], -z

argent 'ɑːdʒənt

argentiferous ˌɑːdʒən'tɪfərəs [-dʒen't-]

Argentina ˌɑːdʒən'tiːnə [-dʒen't-]

argentine 'ɑːdʒəntaɪn

Argentine 'ɑːdʒəntaɪn [-tiːn]

argil 'ɑːdʒɪl

argillaceous ˌɑːdʒɪ'leɪʃəs

Argive, -s 'ɑːgaɪv, -z

Argo 'ɑːgəʊ

argol 'ɑːgɒl

Argolis 'ɑːgəlɪs

argon 'ɑːgɒn [-gən]

Argonaut, -s 'ɑːgənɔːt, -s

Argonautic ˌɑːgə'nɔːtɪk

Argos 'ɑːgɒs

argos|y, -ies 'ɑːgəs|ɪ, -ɪz

argot, -s 'ɑːgəʊ (argo), -z

arg|ue, -ues, -uing, -ued, -uer/s; -uable 'ɑːg|juː, -juːz, -jʊɪŋ [-jwɪŋ], -juːd, -jʊə*/z [-jwə*/z]; -jʊəbl [-jwəbl]

argument, -s 'ɑːgjʊmənt, -s

argumental ˌɑːgjʊ'mentl

argumentation, -s ˌɑːgjʊmen'teɪʃn [-mən't-], -z

argumentative, -ly, -ness ˌɑːgjʊ'mentətɪv, -lɪ, -nɪs [-nəs]

argus (A.), -es 'ɑːgəs, -ɪz

Argyle ɑː'gaɪl

Argyll ɑːˈgaɪl [*attributively also* '--]
Argyllshire ɑːˈgaɪlʃə* [-ˌʃɪə*]
aria, -s ˈɑːrɪə, -z
Ariadne ˌærɪˈædnɪ
Arian, -s, -ism ˈeərɪən, -z, -ɪzəm
arianiz|e [-is|e]. -es, -ing, -ed ˈeərɪən-
aɪz, -ɪz, -ɪŋ, -d
arid, -ly, -ness ˈærɪd, -lɪ, -nɪs [-nəs]
aridity æˈrɪdɪtɪ [əˈr-, -dɪtɪ]
ariel (A.), -s ˈeərɪəl, -z
Aries (*constellation*) ˈeəriːz [ˈeərɪːz,
ˈærɪːz]
arietta, -s ˌærɪˈetə, -z
aright əˈraɪt
Arimathaea ˌærɪməˈθɪə [-ˈθiːə]
Arion əˈraɪən [æˈr-]
arioso ˌɑːrɪˈəʊzəʊ [ˌær-]
Ariosto ˌærɪˈɒstəʊ
aris|e, -es, -ing, arose, arisen əˈraɪz,
-ɪz, -ɪŋ, əˈrəʊz, əˈrɪzn
Ariss ˈeərɪs
Aristaeus ˌærɪˈstiːəs [-ˈstɪəs]
Aristarch ˈærɪstɑːk
Aristarchus ˌærɪˈstɑːkəs
Aristides ˌærɪˈstaɪdiːz
aristocrac|y, -ies ˌærɪˈstɒkrəs|ɪ, -ɪz
aristocrat, -s ˈærɪstəkræt [æˈrɪs-, əˈrɪs-],
-s
aristocratic, -al, -ally ˌærɪstəˈkrætɪk,
-l, -əlɪ
aristocratism ˌærɪˈstɒkrətɪzəm
Aristogiton ˌærɪstəʊˈdʒaɪtn
Aristophanes ˌærɪˈstɒfəniːz [-fɲiːz]
aristophanic ˌærɪstəʊˈfænɪk [-tɒˈf-]
aristotelian, -s ˌærɪstəʊˈtiːljən [-təʊˈt-,
-lɪən], -z
Aristotle ˈærɪstɒtl
Aristoxenus ˌærɪˈstɒksɪnəs [-sən-]
arithmetic (*s.*), -s əˈrɪθmətɪk [-mɪt-], -s
arithmetic (*adj.*), -al, -ally ˌærɪθ-
ˈmetɪk, -l, -əlɪ
arithmetician, -s əˌrɪθməˈtɪʃn [ˌærɪθ-,
-mɪˈt-], -z
Arius ˈeərɪəs [əˈraɪəs]
Arizona ˌærɪˈzəʊnə
ark (A.), -s ɑːk, -s
Arkansas (*state, city, river*) ˈɑːkənsɔː
[əˈkænzəs]
Note.—*The most usual pronunciation
in U.S.A. appears to be* (ˈɑːkənsɔː),
but (ɑːˈkænzəs) *is also in use locally.*
Ark|low, -wright ˈɑːk|ləʊ, -raɪt
Arlberg ˈɑːlbɜːg
Arlington ˈɑːlɪŋtən
arm (*s. v.*), -s, -ing, -ed ɑːm, -z, -ɪŋ, -d
armada (A.), -s ɑːˈmɑːdə [*old-fashioned*
-ˈmeɪd-], -z
Armadale ˈɑːmədeɪl

armadillo, -s ˌɑːməˈdɪləʊ, -z
Armageddon ˌɑːməˈgedn
Armagh ɑːˈmɑː
armament, -s ˈɑːməmənt, -s
armature, -s ˈɑːməˌtjʊə* [-ˌtʃʊə*,
-tʃə*], -z
armchair, -s ˌɑːmˈtʃeə* [*also* '--, *esp.
when followed by a stress*], -z
Armenia, -n/s ɑːˈmiːnjə [-nɪə], -n/z
Armes ɑːmz
Armfield ˈɑːmfiːld
armful, -s ˈɑːmfʊl, -z
armhole, -s ˈɑːmhəʊl, -z
armiger (A.), -s ˈɑːmɪdʒə*, -z
arm-in-arm ˌɑːmɪnˈɑːm
Arminian, -s ɑːˈmɪnɪən [-njən], -z
Armistead ˈɑːmɪsted [-tɪd]
armistice, -s ˈɑːmɪstɪs, -ɪz
Armitage ˈɑːmɪtɪdʒ
armless ˈɑːmlɪs [-ləs]
armlet, -s ˈɑːmlɪt [-lət], -s
armorial ɑːˈmɔːrɪəl
Armoric ɑːˈmɒrɪk
Armorica, -n/s ɑːˈmɒrɪkə, -n/z
armor|y, -ies = armour-
armour (A.), -s ˈɑːmə*, -z
armour-bearer, -s ˈɑːməˌbeərə*, -z
armourer, -s ˈɑːmərə*, -z
armour-plat|e, -es, -ing, -ed ˈɑːməpleɪt
[ˌɑːməˈp-], -s, -ɪŋ, -ɪd
armour|y, -ies ˈɑːmər|ɪ, -ɪz
armpit, -s ˈɑːmpɪt, -s
Armstead ˈɑːmsted [-stɪd]
Armstrong ˈɑːmstrɒŋ
arm|y, -ies ˈɑːm|ɪ, -ɪz
army-corps (*sing.*) ˈɑːmɪkɔː*, (*plur.*)
-kɔːz
Arnald ˈɑːnəld
Arne ɑːn
Arnhem ˈɑːnəm, ˈɑːnhem
arnica ˈɑːnɪkə
Arno ˈɑːnəʊ
Arnold, -son ˈɑːnəld, -sn
Arnot(t) ˈɑːnət [-nɒt]
Arolla əˈrɒlə
aroma, -s əˈrəʊmə, -z
aromatic (*s. adj.*), -s ˌærəʊˈmætɪk, -s
arose (*from* arise) əˈrəʊz
around əˈraʊnd
arous|e, -es, -ing, -ed; -al/s əˈraʊz, -ɪz,
-ɪŋ, -d; -l/z
arpeggio, -s ɑːˈpedʒɪəʊ, -z
arquebus, -es ˈɑːkwɪbəs, -ɪz
arquebusier, -s ˌɑːkwɪbəˈsɪə*, -z
arrack ˈærək
arrah ˈærə
arraign, -s, -ing, -ed, -er/s, -ment/s
əˈreɪn, -z, -ɪŋ, -d, -ə*/z, -mənt/s

27

Arran 'ærən
arran|ge, -es, -ing, -ed, -ement/s
ə'reɪn*d*ʒ, -ɪz, -ɪŋ, -d, -mənt/s
arrant, -ly 'ærənt, -lɪ
arras, -es 'ærəs, -ɪz
Arras (*French town*) 'ærəs (arɑ:s)
array (*s. v.*), -s, -ing, -ed ə'reɪ, -z, -ɪŋ, -d
arrear, -s, -age ə'rɪə*, -z, -rɪdʒ
arrest (*s. v.*), -s, -ing, -ed, -ment/s;
   -able ə'rest, -s, -ɪŋ, -ɪd, -mənt/s; -əbl
arrestation, -s ˌære'steɪʃn, -z
Arrian 'ærɪən
arrière-ban, -s ˌærɪeə'bæn, -z
'Arriet 'ærɪət
arris, -es 'ærɪs, -ɪz
arriv|e, -es, -ing, -ed; -al/s ə'raɪv, -z,
   -ɪŋ, -d; -l/z
arrogan|ce, -cy, -t/ly 'ærəgən|s [-rʊg-],
   -sɪ, -t/lɪ
arrogat|e, -es, -ing, -ed 'ærəʊgeɪt
   [-rʊg-], -s, -ɪŋ, -ɪd
arrogation, -s ˌærəʊ'geɪʃn [-rʊ'g-], -z
arrow, -s 'ærəʊ, -z
arrow-head, -s 'ærəʊhed, -z
Arrowpoint 'ærəʊpɔɪnt
arrowroot 'ærəʊruːt
Arrowsmith 'ærəʊsmɪθ
arrowy 'ærəʊɪ
'Arry, -ish 'ærɪ, -ɪʃ
Ars ɑːz
arse, -s ɑːs, -ɪz
arsenal, -s 'ɑːsənl [-sn̩l, -snl, -smnl], -z
arsenate, -s 'ɑːsənɪt [-sɪn-, -snɪt, -snɪt,
   -ət, -eɪt], -s
arsenic (*s.*) 'ɑːsnɪk
arsenic (*adj.*), -al ɑː'senɪk, -l
arsenious ɑː'siːnjəs [-nɪəs]
arsenite, -s 'ɑːsənaɪt [-sɪn-]
ars|is, -es 'ɑːs|ɪs, -iːz
arson 'ɑːsn
art (*s.*), -s ɑːt, -s
art (*from* be) ɑːt (*normal form*), ət
   (*occasional weak form*)
Artaxerxes ˌɑːtəg'zɜːksiːz ['ɑːt-,
   -ək'sɜː-, -ə'zɜː-]
artefact, -s 'ɑːtɪfækt, -s
Artegal 'ɑːtɪgəl
Artemis 'ɑːtɪmɪs [-təm-]
Artemus 'ɑːtɪməs
arterial ɑː'tɪərɪəl
arterio-sclerosis ɑːˌtɪərɪəʊsklɪə'rəʊsɪs
   [-sklɪə'r-, -sklɪ'r-, -sklə'r-]
arteritis ˌɑːtə'raɪtɪs
arter|y, -ies 'ɑːtər|ɪ, -ɪz
artesian ɑː'tiːzjən [-zɪən, -ʒən, -ʒɪən,
   -ʒn]
art|ful, -fully, -fulness 'ɑːt|fʊl, -fʊlɪ
   [-fəlɪ], -fʊlnɪs [-nəs]

28

arthritic (*s. adj.*), -s ɑː'θrɪtɪk, -s
arthritis ɑː'θraɪtɪs
Arthur 'ɑːθə*
Arthurian ɑː'θjʊərɪən [-jɔər-, -jɔːr-]
artichoke, -s 'ɑːtɪtʃəʊk, -s
artic|le (*s. v.*), -les, -ling, -led 'ɑːtɪk|l,
   -lz, -lɪŋ, -ld
articular ɑː'tɪkjʊlə*
articulate (*adj.*), -ly, -ness ɑː'tɪkjʊlət
   [-lɪt], -lɪ, -nɪs [-nəs]
articulat|e (*v.*), -es, -ing, -ed, -or/s
   ɑː'tɪkjʊleɪt, -s, -ɪŋ, -ɪd, -ə*/z
articulation, -s ɑːˌtɪkjʊ'leɪʃn, -z
articulatory ɑː'tɪkjʊlətərɪ [-leɪt-,
   ɑːˌtɪkjʊ'leɪtərɪ]
artifact, -s 'ɑːtɪfækt, -s
artifice, -s 'ɑːtɪfɪs, -ɪz
artificer, -s ɑː'tɪfɪsə* ['----], -z
artifici|al, -ally, -alness ˌɑːtɪ'fɪʃ|l, -əlɪ
   [-ʃɪ], -lnɪs [-nəs]
   Note.—When used attributively, some-
   times 'ɑːtɪfɪʃl (*esp. in the expression*
   artificial silk).
artificialit|y, -ies ˌɑːtɪfɪʃɪ'ælət|ɪ [-ɪt|ɪ],
   -ɪz
artificializ|e [-is|e], -es, -ing, -ed
   ˌɑːtɪ'fɪʃəlaɪz [-ʃlaɪz], -ɪz, -ɪŋ, -d
artiller|y, -ies, -ist/s ɑː'tɪlər|ɪ, -ɪz, -ɪst/s
artillery-|man, -men ɑː'tɪlərɪ|mən
   [-mæn], -mən [-men]
artisan, -s ˌɑːtɪ'zæn ['---], -z
artist, -s 'ɑːtɪst, -s
artiste, -s ɑː'tiːst (artist), -s
artistic, -al, -ally ɑː'tɪstɪk, -l, -əlɪ
artistry 'ɑːtɪstrɪ
artless, -ly, -ness 'ɑːtlɪs [-ləs], -lɪ, -nɪs
   [-nəs]
art-school, -s 'ɑːtskuːl, -z
arts|man, -men 'ɑːts|mæn, -men
arty 'ɑːtɪ
arum, -s 'eərəm, -z
Arun 'ærən
Arundel 'ærəndl
Arundell 'ærəndel [-dl]
Aryan, -s, -ism 'eərɪən ['ɑːr-], -z, -ɪzəm
arytenoid (*s. adj.*), -s ˌærɪ'tiːnɔɪd
   [-rə't-], -z
as (*s.*), (*coin*), -es æs, -ɪz
as (*conj.*), æz (*strong form*), əz, z (*weak
   forms*)
Asa (*biblical name*) 'eɪsə ['ɑːsə], (*as
   modern Christian name*) 'eɪzə
asafoetida ˌæsə'fetɪdə [-'fiːt-]
Asaph 'æsəf
asbest|ic, -os, -ous æz'best|ɪk [əz-, æs-,
   əs-], -ɒs [-əs], -əs
Ascalon 'æskəlɒn [-lən]
Ascanius æ'skeɪnjəs [-nɪəs]

ascend, -s, -ing, -ed ə'send [æ's-], -z, -ɪŋ, -ɪd-

ascendan|ce, -cy, -t ə'sendən|s [æ's-], -sɪ, -t

ascen:den|ce, -cy, -t ə'sendən|s [æ's-], -sɪ, -t

ascension (A.), -s ə'senʃn, -z

ascensional ə'senʃənl [-ʃnəl, -ʃn̩l, -ʃnl, -ʃənəl]

Ascension-day, -s ə'senʃndeɪ, -z

ascent, -s ə'sent [æ's-], -s

ascertain, -s, -ing, -ed, -ment; -able ˌæsə'teɪn, -z, -ɪŋ, -d, -mənt; -əbl

ascetic (s. adj.), -al, -ally, -s ə'setɪk [æ's-], -l, -əlɪ, -s

asceticism ə'setɪsɪzəm [æ's-]

Ascham 'æskəm

ascian, -s 'æʃɪən [-ʃjən], -z

asclepiad, -s æ'skliːpɪæd [-pjæd, -pɪəd, -pjəd], -z

ascorbic ə'skɔːbɪk [æ's-]

Ascot, -s 'æskət, -s

ascrib|e, -es, -ing, -ed; -able ə'skraɪb, -z, -ɪŋ, -d; -əbl

ascription ə'skrɪpʃn [æs-]

asdic, -s 'æzdɪk, -s

asepsis æ'sepsɪs [eɪ's-, ə's-]

aseptic (s. adj.), -s æ'septɪk [eɪ's-, ə's-], -s

asexual eɪ'seksjʊəl [æ's-, ə's-, -ksjwəl, -ksjʊl, -kʃʊəl, -kʃwəl, -kʃʊl]

Asgard 'æsgaːd

Asgill 'æsgɪl

ash (A.), -es æʃ, -ɪz

Asham 'æʃəm

asham|ed, -edly, -edness ə'ʃeɪm|d, -ɪdlɪ, -ɪdnɪs [-nəs]

Ashanti, -s ə'ʃæntɪ, -z

Ashbee 'æʃbɪ

Ashbourne 'æʃbɔːn [-bɔən, -buən, -bɜːn]

Ashburne 'æʃbɜːn

Ashbur|nham, ton 'æʃbɜː|nəm, -tn

Ash|bury, -by 'æʃ|bərɪ, -bɪ

Ashby - de - la - Zouch ˌæʃbɪdələː'zuːʃ [-delə-]

Ashcombe 'æʃkəm

Ashdod 'æʃdɒd

Ashdown 'æʃdaʊn

Ashe æʃ

ashen 'æʃn

Asher 'æʃə*

asher|y, -ies 'æʃər|ɪ, ɪz

Ash|field, -ford 'æʃ|fiːld, -fəd

ash-heap, -s 'æʃhiːp, -s

Ashkelon 'æʃkɪlən [-kəl-, -lɒn]

Ashland 'æʃlənd

ashlar 'æʃlə*

Ash|ley, -mole 'æʃ|lɪ, -məʊl

Ashmolean æʃ'məʊljən [-lɪən]

Ashmore 'æʃmɔː* [-mɔə*]

Ashopton 'æʃəptən

ashore ə'ʃɔː* [-'ʃɔə*]

Ashover 'æʃəʊvə*

ash-pan, -s 'æʃpæn, -z

Ashtaroth 'æʃtərɒθ

Ashton 'æʃtən

Ashtoreth 'æʃtəreθ [-tɒr-]

ash-tray, -s 'æʃtreɪ, -z

Ash-Wednesday, -s ˌæʃ'wenzdɪ [-'wednz-, -deɪ], -z

Ash|well, -worth 'æʃ|wəl [-wel], -wɜːθ

ash|y, -ier, -iest, -iness 'æʃ|ɪ, -ɪə*, -ɪɪst, -ɪnɪs [-ɪnəs]

Asia 'eɪʃə ['eɪʒə]

Asian, -s 'eɪʃn ['eɪʃjən, 'eɪʃɪən, 'eɪsɪən, 'eɪʒən, 'eɪʒn, rarely 'eɪzɪən, 'eɪzjən], -z

Asiatic, -s ˌeɪʃɪ'ætɪk [ˌeɪsɪ-, ˌeɪʒɪ-], -s

aside (s. adv.), -s ə'saɪd, -z

asinine 'æsɪnaɪn

asininit|y, -ies ˌæsɪ'nɪnət|ɪ [-ɪt|ɪ], -ɪz

ask (s.) (newt), -s æsk, -s

ask (v.), -s, -ing, -ed aːsk, -s, -ɪŋ, -t [also aːst in familiar speech]

askance ə'skæns [-'kaːns]

askant ə'skænt

Aske æsk

Askelon 'æskɪlən [-kəl-, -lɒn]

askew ə'skjuː

Askew 'æskjuː

Ask|rigg, -with 'æsk|rɪg, -wɪθ

aslant ə'slaːnt

asleep ə'sliːp

Asmodeus æs'məʊdjəs [-dɪəs]

Note.—The name must be pronounced ˌæsməʊ'diːəs *in Milton's ' Paradise Lost', iv, 168.*

Asoka ə'səʊkə [ə'ʃəʊ-] (*Hindi* əʃoka)

asp, -s æsp [aːsp], -s

asparagus ə'spærəgəs

Aspasia æ'speɪʒjə [-ʒɪə, -zjə, -zɪə]

aspect, -s 'æspekt, -s

aspectable æ'spektəbl

aspen, -s 'æspən ['aːs-, -pen, -pɪn], -z

asper 'æspə*

asperg|e, -es, -ing, -ed ə'spɜːdʒ [æ's-], -ɪz, -ɪŋ, -d

asperges (*religious service*) æ'spɜːdʒiːz [ə's-]

aspergill, -s 'æspədʒɪl, -z

asperit|y, -ies æ'sperət|ɪ [ə'sp-, -ɪt|ɪ], -ɪz

aspers|e, -es, -ing, -ed ə'spɜːs [æ's-], -ɪz -ɪŋ, -t

aspersion, -s ə'spɜː|ʃn [æ's-], -z

asphalt (s.), -s 'æsfælt, -s

asphalt (v.), -s, -ing, -ed 'æsfælt
  [æs'fælt], -s, -ɪŋ, -ɪd
asphaltic æs'fæltɪk
asphodel, -s 'æsfədel [-fɒd-], -z
asphyxia æs'fɪksɪə [əs-, -sjə]
asphyxiat|e, -es, -ing, -ed, -or/s əs-
  'fɪksɪeɪt [æs-], -s, -ɪŋ, -ɪd, -ə*/z
asphyxiation, -s əs,fɪksɪ'eɪʃn [æs-], -z
asphyx|y, -ies æs'fɪks|ɪ, -ɪz
aspic 'æspɪk
aspidistra, -s ,æspɪ'dɪstrə, -z
Aspinall 'æspɪnl [-nɔːl]
Aspinwall 'æspɪnwɔːl
aspirant, -s ə'spaɪərənt ['æspɪrənt], -s
aspirate (s. adj.), -s 'æspərət [-rɪt], -s
aspirat|e (v.), -es, -ing, -ed, -or/s
  'æspəreɪt [-pɪr-], -s, -ɪŋ, -ɪd, -ə*/z
aspiration, -s ,æspə'reɪʃn [-pɪ'r-], -z
aspir|e, -es, -ing/ly, -ingness, -ed, -er/s
  ə'spaɪə*, -z, -rɪŋ/lɪ, -rɪŋnɪs [-nəs], -d,
  -rə*/z
aspirin, -s 'æspərɪn [-pɪr-], -z
aspirine, -s 'æspəriːn [-pɪr-], -z
asplenium, -s æ'spliːnjəm [ə's-, -nɪəm],
  -z
Asquith 'æskwɪθ
ass, -es æs [ɑːs, esp. as term of con-
  tempt], -ɪz
assagai, -s 'æsəgaɪ, -z
assai æ'saɪ
assail, -s, -ing, -ed; -able, -ant/s ə'seɪl,
  -z, -ɪŋ, -d; -əbl, -ənt/s
Assam æ'sæm ['æsæm]
Assamese ,æsə'miːz [-sæ'm-]
assassin, -s ə'sæsɪn, -z
assassinat|e, -es, -ing, -ed, -or/s
  ə'sæsɪneɪt [-sən-, -sneɪt], -s, -ɪŋ, -ɪd,
  -ə*/z
assassination, -s ə,sæsɪ'neɪʃn [-sə'n-], -z
assault (s. v.), -s, -ing, -ed, -er/s
  ə'sɔːlt [-'sɒlt], -s, -ɪŋ, -ɪd, -ə*/z
assay (s. v.), -s, -ing, -ed, -er/s ə'seɪ
  [æ's-], -z, -ɪŋ, -d, -ə*/z
Assaye æ'seɪ
assay-master, -s ə'seɪ,mɑːstə* [æ's-,
  'æseɪ-], -z
assay-office ə'seɪ,ɒfɪs [æ's-, 'æseɪ-]
Assche æʃ
assegai, -s 'æsɪgaɪ, -z
assemblage, -s ə'semblɪdʒ, -ɪz
assemb|le, -les, -ling, -led ə'semb|l, -lz,
  -lɪŋ, -ld
assembl|y, -ies ə'sembl|ɪ, -ɪz
assembly-room, -s ə'semblɪruːm [-ruːm],
  -z
assent (s. v.), -s, -ing/ly, -ed ə'sent
  [æ's-], -s, -ɪŋ/lɪ, -ɪd
Asser 'æsə*

assert, -s, -ing, -ed, -er/s, or/s; -able
  ə'sɜːt, -s, -ɪŋ, -ɪd, -ə*/z, -ə*/z; -əbl
assertion, -s ə'sɜːʃn, -z
assertive, -ly, -ness ə'sɜːtɪv, -lɪ, -nɪs
  [-nəs]
assess, -es, -ing, -ed, -or/s, -ment/s;
  -able ə'ses, -ɪz, -ɪŋ, -t, -ə*/z, -mənt/s;
  -əbl
asset, -s 'æset [-sɪt], -s
assever, -s, -ing, -ed æ'sevə* [ə's-], -z,
  -rɪŋ, -d
asseverat|e, -es, -ing/ly, -ed ə'sevəreɪt
  [æ's-], -s, -ɪŋ/lɪ, -ɪd
asseveration, -s ə,sevə'reɪʃn [æ,s-], -z
Assheton 'æʃtən
assibilated ə'sɪbɪleɪtɪd [æ's-, -bəl-]
assibilation, -s ə,sɪbɪ'leɪʃn [æ,s-, -bə'l-],
  -z
assiduit|y, -ies ,æsɪ'djuːət|ɪ [-'djʊ-,
  -ɪt|ɪ], -ɪz
assiduous, -ly, -ness ə'sɪdjʊəs [-djwəs],
  -lɪ, -nɪs [-nəs]
assign (s. v.), -s, -ing, -ed, -er/s,
  -ment/s; -able ə'saɪn, -z, -ɪŋ, -d,
  -ə*/z, -mənt/s; -əbl
assignat, -s ,æsɪn'jɑː (asiɲa), -z ['æsɪg-
  -næt, -s]
assignation, -s ,æsɪg'neɪʃn, -z
assignee, -s ,æsɪ'niː [-saɪ'n-], -z
assimilat|e, -es, -ing, -ed ə'sɪmɪleɪt
  [-məl-], -s, -ɪŋ, -ɪd
assimilation, -s ə,sɪmɪ'leɪʃn [-mə'l-], -z
assimilative ə'sɪmɪleɪtɪv [-məl-, -lert-]
assimilatory ə'sɪmɪlətərɪ [-məl-, ə,sɪmɪ-
  'leɪtərɪ, -mə'l-]
Assiniboine ə'sɪnɪbɔɪn
Assisi ə'siːzɪ [æ's-]
assist, -s, -ing, -ed, -er/s ə'sɪst, -s, -ɪŋ,
  -ɪd, -ə*/z
assistan|ce/s, -t/s ə'sɪstən|s/ɪz, -t/s
Assiut æ'sjuːt
assiz|e, -es, -er/s ə'saɪz, -ɪz, -ə*/z
associable ə'səʊʃjəbl [-ʃɪə-, -ʃə-, -sjə-,
  -sɪə-]
associate (s.), -s ə'səʊʃɪət [-ʃɪt, -ʃjət,
  -ʃjɪt, -sɪt, -sjɪt, -sjət, -sɪət, -ʃɪeɪt,
  -ʃjeɪt], -s
associat|e (v.), -es, -ing, -ed ə'səʊʃɪeɪt
  [-əʊsɪ-, -əʊsj-, -ʃjeɪt], -s, -ɪŋ, -ɪd
association, -s ə,səʊsɪ'eɪʃn [-əʊʃɪ-], -z
associative ə'səʊʃjətɪv [-ʃɪət-, -ʃɪeɪt-,
  -ʃjeɪt-, -əʊsɪət-, -əʊsɪeɪt-, -əʊsɪət-,
  -əʊsjeɪt-]
assoilzie (s. v.), -s, -ing, -d ə'sɔɪljɪ [-lɪ],
  -z, -ɪŋ, -d
assonan|ce/s, -t 'æsəʊnən|s/ɪz [-sɒə-], -t
assonat|e, -es, -ing, -ed 'æsəʊneɪt,
  -s, -ɪŋ, -ɪd

30

assort, -s, -ing, -ed, -ment/s ə'sɔːt, -s, -ɪŋ, -ɪd, -mənt/s

Assouan ˌæsuː'æn [-'ɑːn, 'æsuæn, -ɑːn, esp. when attributive, as in Assouan dam]

assuag|e, -es, -ing, -ed, -ement ə'sweɪdʒ, -ɪz, -ɪŋ, -d, -mənt

assum|e, -es, -ing/ly, -ed, -edly; -able, -ably ə'sjuːm [-'suːm], -z, -ɪŋ/lɪ, -d, -ɪdlɪ; -əbl, -əblɪ

assumpsit ə'sʌmpsɪt

assumption (A.), -s ə'sʌmpʃn, -z

assumptive ə'sʌmptɪv

assur|e, -es, -ing, -ed, -edly, -edness, -er/s; -ance/s ə'ʃuə* [-'ʃɔə*, -'ʃɔː*], -z, -rɪŋ, -d, -rɪdlɪ, -dnɪs [-rɪdnɪs, -nəs], -rə*/z; -rəns/ɪz

Assynt 'æsɪnt

Assyria, -n/s ə'sɪrɪə, -n/z

assyriolog|ist/s, -y əˌsɪrɪ'ɒlədʒ|ɪst/s, -ɪ

Astarte æ'stɑːtɪ

Astbury 'æstbərɪ

aster, -s 'æstə* [rarely 'ɑːs-], -z

asterisk, -s 'æstərɪsk, -s

asterism, -s 'æstərɪzəm, -z

astern ə'stɜːn

asteroid, -s 'æstərɔɪd, -z

asthenia æs'θiːnjə [-nɪə, rarely ˌæsθɪ'naɪə]

asthenic, -al æs'θenɪk, -l

asthma 'æsmə [rarely 'æsθm-, 'æstm-]

asthmatic, -al, -ally, -s æs'mætɪk [rarely æsθ'm-, æst'm-, əs-], -l, -əlɪ, -s

Asti 'æsti: [-tɪ]

astigmatic ˌæstɪg'mætɪk

astigmatism æ'stɪgmətɪzəm [ə's-]

astir ə'stɜː*

Astle 'æsl, æstl

Astley 'æstlɪ

Aston 'æstən

astonish, -es, -ing/ly, -ed/ly, -ment ə'stɒnɪʃ, -ɪz, -ɪŋ/lɪ, -t/lɪ, -mənt

Astor 'æstə*, 'æstɔː*

Astoria æ'stɔːrɪə [ə's-]

astound, -s, -ing, -ed ə'staund, -z, -ɪŋ, -ɪd

astraddle ə'strædl

astragal, -s 'æstrəgəl, -z

astrakhan (A.) ˌæstrə'kæn

astr|al, -ally 'æstr|əl, -əlɪ

astray ə'streɪ

astride ə'straɪd

astring|e, -es, -ing, -ed ə'strɪndʒ, -ɪz, -ɪŋ, -d

astringen|cy, -t/s, -tly ə'strɪndʒən|sɪ, -t/s, -tlɪ

astrolabe, -s 'æstrəuleɪb, -z

astrologer, -s ə'strɒlədʒə*, -z

astrologic, -al, -ally ˌæstrə'lɒdʒɪk, -l, -əlɪ

astrology ə'strɒlədʒɪ

astromet|er/s, -ry æ'strɒmɪt|ə*/z [-mət|ə*/z] -rɪ

astronaut, -s 'æstrənɔːt, -s

astronomer, -s ə'strɒnəmə*, -z

astronomic, -al, -ally ˌæstrə'nɒmɪk, -l, -əlɪ

astronom|y, -ies ə'strɒnəm|ɪ, -ɪz

Astrophel 'æstrəufel

astrophysics ˌæstrəu'fɪzɪks

Asturias æ'stuərɪæs [-'stjuər, -'stjɔər-, -'stjɔːr-, -rɪəs]

astute, -r, -st, -ly, -ness ə'stjuːt [æ's-], -ə*, -ɪst, -lɪ, -nɪs [-nəs]

Astyanax ə'staɪənæks [æ's-]

Asuncion əˌsunsɪ'əun [-'ɒn]

asunder ə'sʌndə*

Aswan æs'wɑːn

asylum, -s ə'saɪləm, -z

asymmetric, -al, -ally ˌæsɪ'metrɪk [ˌeɪsɪ'm-], -l, -əlɪ

asymmetry æ'sɪmətrɪ [ˌæ'sɪm-, ˌeɪ'sɪm-, -mɪ-]

asymptote, -s 'æsɪmptəut, -s

asymptotic, -al, -ally ˌæsɪmp'tɒtɪk, -l, -əlɪ

asyndet|on, -a æ'sɪndɪt|ən [ə's-], -ə

At (member of A.T.S.), -s æt, -s

at (prep.) æt (strong form), ət (weak form)

Atalanta ˌætə'læntə

Atall 'ætɔːl

Ataturk 'ætətɜːk [ˌ‚-'-]

atavism 'ætəvɪzəm

atavistic ˌætə'vɪstɪk

ataxia ə'tæksɪə [æ't-, eɪ't-]

atax|y, -ies ə'tæks|ɪ, -ɪz

Atbara æt'bɑːrə

Atcheen ə'tʃiːn

Atchison 'ætʃɪsn, 'eɪtʃɪsn

Ate (s.) 'ɑːtɪ ['eɪtɪ]

ate (from eat) et [eɪt]

atelier, -s 'ætəlɪeɪ ['ætel-, æ'tel-, -ljeɪ] (atəlje), -z

Atfield 'ætfiːld

Athabasca ˌæθə'bæskə

Athaliah ˌæθə'laɪə

Athanase 'æθəneɪz

Athanasian ˌæθə'neɪʃn [-θɪ'eɪ-, -ʃjən, -ʃɪən, -sjən, -sɪən]

Athanasius ˌæθə'neɪʃəs [-θɪ'eɪ-, -ʃjəs, -ʃɪəs, -sjəs, -sɪəs]

Athawes (surname) 'æθɔːz

athei|sm, -st/s 'eɪθɪɪ|zəm [-θjɪ|-], -st/s

atheistic, -al, -ally ˌeɪθɪ'ɪstɪk, -l, -əlɪ

31

atheling (**A.**), **-s** 'æθəlɪŋ [-θɪl-], **-z**
Athelney 'æθəlnɪ
Athelstan 'æθəlstən (*Old English* 'æðəlstɑːn)
Athena ə'θiːnə
Athenaeum, **-s** ˌæθɪ'niːəm [-'nɪəm], **-z**
Athene ə'θiːniː [-nɪ]
Athenian, **-s** ə'θiːnjən [-nɪən], **-z**
Athenry ˌæθɪn'raɪ [-θən-]
Athens 'æθɪnz
Atherley 'æθəlɪ
Ather|ston, **-ton** 'æθə|stən, **-tən**
athirst ə'θɜːst
athlete, **-s** 'æθliːt, **-s**
athletic, **-al, -ally, -s** æθ'letɪk [əθ-], **-l**, **-əlɪ, -s**
athleticism æθ'letɪsɪzəm [əθ-]
Athlone æθ'ləʊn [*also* '-- *when attributive, as in* the Athlone Press]
Athlumney æθ'lʌmnɪ
Athole 'æθəl
Atholl 'æθəl
at home, **-s** ət'həʊm [ə'təʊm], **-z**
Athos 'æθɒs ['eɪθ-]
athwart ə'θwɔːt
Athy ə'θaɪ
Atkin|s, **-son** 'ætkɪn|z, **-sn**
Atlanta ət'læntə [æt'læn-, ə'tlæn-]
atlantean ˌætlæn'tiːən [-lən-, -'tɪən, ət'læntɪən, æt'læntɪən, ət'læntjən, æt'læntjən, ə'tlænt-]
Atlantes (*statues*) ət'læntiːz [æt'læn-, ə'tlæn-], (*in Ariosto's 'Orlando Furioso'*) ət'læntes [æt-]
Atlantic ət'læntɪk [ə'tlæn-]
Atlantis ət'læntɪs [æt'læn-, ə'tlæn-]
atlas, **-es** 'ætləs, **-ɪz**
Atlas 'ætləs [-læs]
atmometer, **-s** æt'mɒmɪtə* [-mətə*], **-z**
atmosphere, **-s** 'ætməˌsfɪə*, **-z**
atmospheric, **-al, -ally, -s** ˌætməs'ferɪk, **-l**, **-əlɪ, -s**
atoll, **-s** 'ætɒl [ə'tɒl], **-z**
atom, **-s** 'ætəm, **-z**
atomic ə'tɒmɪk
atomistic ˌætəʊ'mɪstɪk
atomization [-isa-] ˌætəʊmaɪ'zeɪʃn
atomiz|e [-is|e], **-es, -ing, -ed, -er/s** 'ætəʊmaɪz, **-ɪz, -ɪŋ, -d, -ə*/z**
atonal eɪ'təʊnl [æ't-, ə't-]
aton|e, **-es, -ing/ly, -ed, -er/s, -ment/s** ə'təʊn, **-z, -ɪŋ/lɪ, -d, -ə*/z, -mənt/s**
atonic (*s. adj.*), **-s** æ'tɒnɪk [ə't-, eɪ't-], **-s**
atony 'ætənɪ
atrabilious ˌætrə'bɪljəs [-lɪəs]
Atreus 'eɪtrɪuːs [-truːs, -trjuːs, -trɪəs]
atri|um, **-a** 'ɑːtrɪ|əm ['eɪt-], **-ə**

atrocious, **-ly, -ness** ə'trəʊʃəs, **-lɪ, -nɪs [-nəs]**
atrocit|y, **-ies** ə'trɒsət|ɪ [-ɪt|ɪ], **-ɪz**
atrophic æ'trɒfɪk [ə't-]
atroph|y (*s. v.*), **-ies, -ying, -ied** 'ætrəf|ɪ [-trʊf-], **-ɪz, -ɪŋ, -ɪd**
atropine 'ætrəpɪn [-trʊp-, -piːn]
Atropos 'ætrəpɒs [-trʊp-]
attach, **-es, -ing, -ed, -ment/s; -able** ə'tætʃ, **-ɪz, -ɪŋ, -t, -mənt/s; -əbl**
attaché, **-s** ə'tæʃeɪ [æ't-] (ataʃe), **-z**
attaché-case, **-s** ə'tæʃɪkeɪs [-ʃeɪ-], **-ɪz**
attack (*s. v.*), **-s, -ing, -ed, -er/s** ə'tæk, **-s, -ɪŋ, -t, -ə*/z**
attain, **-s, -ing, -ed, -ment/s; -able** ə'teɪn, **-z, -ɪŋ, -d, -mənt/s; -əbl**
attainability əˌteɪnə'bɪlətɪ [-lɪt-]
attainder, **-s** ə'teɪndə*, **-z**
attaint (*s. v.*), **-s, -ing, -ed** ə'teɪnt, **-s, -ɪŋ, -ɪd**
attar 'ætə*
attemper, **-s, -ing, -ed** ə'tempə* [æ't-], **-z, -rɪŋ, -d**
attempt (*s. v.*), **-s, -ing, -ed, -er/s; -able** ə'tem*p*t, **-s, -ɪŋ, -ɪd, -ə*/z; -əbl**
Attenborough 'ætnbrə [-bərə, -bʌrə]
attend, **-s, -ing, -ed, -er/s; -ance/s, -ant** ə'tend, **-z, -ɪŋ, -ɪd, -ə*/z; -əns/ɪz, -ənt/s**
attention, **-s** ə'tenʃn, **-z**
attentive, **-ly, -ness** ə'tentɪv, **-lɪ, -nɪs [-nəs]**
attenuate (*adj.*) ə'tenjʊɪt [-njʊət, -njʊeɪt]
attenuat|e (*v.*), **-es, -ing, -ed** ə'tenjʊeɪt, **-s, -ɪŋ, -ɪd**
attenuation, **-s** əˌtenjʊ'eɪʃn, **-z**
attenuator, **-s** ə'tenjʊeɪtə*, **-z**
Atter|bury, **-cliffe** 'ætə|bərɪ, **-klɪf**
attest (*s. v.*), **-s, -ing, -ed, -or/s; -able** ə'test, **-s, -ɪŋ, -ɪd, -ə*/z; -əbl**
attestation, **-s** ˌæte'steɪʃn, **-z**
Attfield 'ætfiːld
attic, **-s** 'ætɪk, **-s**
Attica 'ætɪkə
atticism, **-s** 'ætɪsɪzəm, **-z**
atticiz|e [-is|e], **-es, -ing, -ed** 'ætɪsaɪz, **-ɪz, -ɪŋ, -d**
Attila 'ætɪlə
attir|e (*s. v.*), **-es, -ing, -ed, -ement** ə'taɪə*, **-z, -rɪŋ, -d, -mənt**
attitude, **-s** 'ætɪtjuːd, **-z**
attitudinal ˌætɪ'tjuːdɪnl
attitudinarian, **-s** ˌætɪtjuːdɪ'neərɪən, **-z**
attitudiniz|e [-is|e], **-es, -ing, -ed, -er/s** ˌætɪ'tjuːdɪnaɪz, **-ɪz, -ɪŋ, -d, -ə*/z**
Attleborough 'ætlbrə [-bərə, -bʌrə]
Attlee 'ætlɪ

Attock ə'tɒk (*Hindi* əṭək)

attorn, -s, -ing, -ed ə'tɜːn, -z, -ɪŋ, -d

attorney, -s; -ship/s ə'tɜːnɪ, -z; -ʃɪp/s

attorney-general ə‚tɜːnɪ'dʒenrəl

attract, -s, -ing/ly, -ed, -or/s; -able ə'trækt, -s, -ɪŋ/lɪ, -ɪd, -ə*/z; -əbl

attractability ə‚træktə'bɪlətɪ [-lɪt-]

attraction, -s ə'trækʃn, -z

attractive, -ly, -ness ə'træktɪv, -lɪ, -nɪs [-nəs]

attrahent ə'trerənt ['ætrəhənt, 'ætrənt]

attributable ə'trɪbjʊtəbl

attribute (s.), -s 'ætrɪbjuːt, -s

attrib|ute (v.), -utes, -uting, -uted ə'trɪb|juːt, -juːts, -jʊtɪŋ, -jʊtɪd

attribution, -s ‚ætrɪ'bjuːʃn, -z

attributive, -ly ə'trɪbjʊtɪv, -lɪ

Attride 'ætraɪd

attrition ə'trɪʃn [æ't-]

attun|e, -es, -ing, -ed ə'tjuːn [æ't-], -z, -ɪŋ, -d

Attwood 'ætwʊd

At|water, -wood 'æt|‚wɔːtə*, -wʊd

atypical ‚eɪ'tɪpɪkl

aubade, -s əʊ'bɑːd, -z

auberge, -s əʊ'beəʒ ['əʊb-] (oberʒ), -ɪz

aubergine, -s 'əʊbəʒiːn [-dʒiːn, ‚əʊbə-'ʒiːn, ‚əʊbə'dʒiːn, ‚əʊbeə'ʒiːn] (oberʒin), -z

Aubrey 'ɔːbrɪ

aubrietia, -s ɔː'briːʃjə [-ʃɪə, -ʃə], -z

auburn (A.) 'ɔːbən [-bɜːn]

Aucher 'ɔːkə*

Auchindachie ‚ɔːkɪn'dækɪ [‚ɔːxɪn'dæxɪ] (*Scottish* ‚ɔxɪn'daxi)

Auchinleck ‚ɔːkɪn'lek ['---, ‚ɔːx-] (*Scottish* ‚ɔxɪn'lek)

Auchmuty ɔːk'mjuːtɪ

Auchtermuchty ‚ɔːktə'mʌktɪ [‚ɒktə-, ‚ɔːxtə'mʌxtɪ, ‚ɒxtə-] (*Scottish* ‚ɔxtər-'mʌxti)

Auckland 'ɔːklənd

aucti|on (s. v.), -ons, -oning, -oned 'ɔːkʃ|n ['ɒk-], -nz, -ənɪŋ [-ṇɪŋ], -nd

auctionary 'ɔːkʃənərɪ ['ɒk-, -ʃṇə-]

auctioneer, -s ‚ɔːkʃə'nɪə* [‚ɒk-, -ʃṇ'ɪə*], -z

audacious, -ly, -ness ɔː'deɪʃəs, -lɪ, -nɪs [-nəs]

audacit|y, -ies ɔː'dæsət|ɪ [-ɪt|ɪ], -ɪz

Auden 'ɔːdn [-dən]

Audi 'aʊdɪ ['ɔːdɪ]

audibility ‚ɔːdɪ'bɪlətɪ [-də'b-, -lɪt-]

audib|le, -ly, -leness 'ɔːdəb|l [-dɪb-], -lɪ, -lnɪs [-nəs]

audience, -s 'ɔːdjəns [-dɪəns], -ɪz

audiometer, -s ‚ɔːdɪ'ɒmɪtə* [-mətə*], -z

audiometry ‚ɔːdɪ'ɒmɪtrɪ [-mətrɪ]

audio-typ|ing, -ist/s 'ɔːdɪəʊ‚taɪp|ɪŋ ['ɔːdjəʊ-], -ɪst/s

audio-visual ‚ɔːdɪəʊ'vɪzjʊəl [-ʒʊəl, -ʒwəl, -zjwəl, -zjəl, -ʒʊl, -ʒl]

audiphone, -s 'ɔːdɪfəʊn, -z

audit (s. v.), -s, -ing, -ed, -or/s 'ɔːdɪt, -s, -ɪŋ, -ɪd, -ə*/z

audition, -s ɔː'dɪʃn, -z

auditorium, -s ‚ɔːdɪ'tɔːrɪəm, -z

auditorship, -s 'ɔːdɪtəʃɪp, -s

auditor|y (s. adj.), -ies ɔː'dɪtər|ɪ, -ɪz

Aud|ley, -rey 'ɔːd|lɪ, -rɪ

au fait ‚əʊ 'feɪ (o fɛ)

Augean ɔː'dʒiːən [-'dʒɪən]

Augeas ɔː'dʒiːæs ['ɔːdʒɪæs]

Augener (*music publisher*) 'aʊɡənə*

auger, -s 'ɔːɡə*, -z

Aughrim 'ɔːɡrɪm

aught ɔːt

augment (s.), -s 'ɔːɡmənt, -s

augment (v.), -s, -ing, -ed; -able ɔːɡ'ment, -s, -ɪŋ, -ɪd; -əbl

augmentation, -s ‚ɔːɡmen'teɪʃn [-mən-], -z

augmentative ɔːɡ'mentətɪv

au gratin ‚əʊ 'ɡrætæ̃ŋ [-tæŋ, -tæn] (o ɡratɛ̃)

augur (s. v.), -s, -ing, -ed 'ɔːɡə*, -z, -rɪŋ, -d

augural 'ɔːɡjʊrəl

augur|y, -ies 'ɔːɡjʊr|ɪ [-jər-], -ɪz

August (s.), -s 'ɔːɡəst, -s

august (adj.), -est, -ly, -ness ɔː'ɡʌst, -ɪst, -lɪ, -nɪs [-nəs]

August|a, -an ɔː'ɡʌst|ə [ə'ɡ-], -ən

Augustine (*Saint*) ɔː'ɡʌstɪn [ə'ɡ-, *rarely* 'ɔːɡəstɪn]

Augustinian ‚ɔːɡə'stɪnɪən [-njən]

Augustus ɔː'ɡʌstəs [ə'ɡ-]

auk, -s ɔːk, -s

aul|a, -ae 'ɔːl|ə ['aʊlə], -iː [-laɪ, -leɪ]

auld lang syne ‚ɔːldlæŋ'saɪn

Ault ɔːlt

aumbr|y, -ies 'ɔːmbr|ɪ, -ɪz

Aumonier əʊ'mɒnɪeɪ [-'məʊn-, -njeɪ] (omɔnje)

Aungier (*street in Dublin*) 'eɪndʒə*

aunt, -s; -ie/s ɑːnt, -s; -ɪ/z

au pair ‚əʊ 'peə* (o pɛːr)

aura, -s 'ɔːrə, -z

aur|al, -ally 'ɔːr|əl, -əlɪ

aurate, -s 'ɔːreɪt [-rɪt], -s

aureate 'ɔːrɪɪt [-reɪt, -rət]

Aureli|a, -an, -us ɔː'riːlj|ə [-lɪ|ə], -ən, -əs

aureola -s ɔː'rɪəʊlə, -z

aureole, -s 'ɔːrɪəʊl, -z

aureomycin ‚ɔːrɪəʊ'maɪsɪn

33

au revoir ‚əʊ rə'vwɑ:* [rɪ-] (o rəvwɑ:r)
auric 'ɔ:rɪk
auricle, -s 'ɔ:rɪkl, -z
auricula, -s ə'rɪkjʊlə [ɔ:'r-, ʊ'r-, -jələ], -z
auricular, -ly ɔ:'rɪkjʊlə*, -lɪ
auricul|ate, -ated ɔ:'rɪkjʊl|ət [ʊ'r-, -ɪt, -eɪt], -eɪtɪd
auriferous ɔ:'rɪfərəs
Auriga ɔ:'raɪgə
Aurignacian ‚ɔ:rɪg'neɪʃn [-ʃjən, -ʃɪən]
aurist, -s 'ɔ:rɪst, -s
aurochs, -es 'ɔ:rɒks, -ɪz
auror|a (A.), -as, -al ɔ:'rɔ:r|ə [ə'r-], -əz, -əl
auscultat|e, -es, -ing, -ed 'ɔ:skəlteɪt ['ɒs-, -kʌl-], -s, -ɪŋ, -ɪd
auscultation, -s ‚ɔ:skəl'teɪʃn [‚ɒs-, -kʌl-], -z
auscultator, -s 'ɔ:skəlteɪtə* ['ɒs-, -kʌl-], -z
auspice, -s 'ɔ:spɪs ['ɒs-], -ɪz
auspicious, -ly, -ness ɔ:'spɪʃəs [ɒ's-], -lɪ, -nɪs
Aussie, -s 'ɒzɪ ['ɒsɪ], -z
Austell 'ɔ:stəl ['ɒs-, local Cornish pronunciation 'ɔ:sl]
Austen 'ɒstɪn ['ɔ:s-]
Auster 'ɔ:stə*
austere, -r, -st, -ly, -ness ɒ'stɪə* [ɔ:'s-], -rə*, -rɪst, -lɪ, -nɪs [-nəs]
austerit|y, -ies ɒ'sterət|ɪ [ɔ:'s-, -ɪt|ɪ], -ɪz
Austerlitz 'ɔ:stəlɪts
Austin, -s 'ɒstɪn ['ɔ:s-], -z
austral 'ɔ:strəl
Australasia ‚ɒstrə'leɪʒə [‚ɔ:s-, -ʒɪə, -ʒə, -zjə, -zɪə, -ʃjə, -ʃɪə, -ʃə]
Australasian, -s ‚ɒstrə'leɪʒn [‚ɔ:s-, -ʒɪən, -zjən, -zɪən, -ʃjən, -ʃɪən, -ʃn], -z
Australia, -n/s ɒ'streɪljə [ɔ:'s-, -lɪə], -n/z
Austria, -n/s 'ɒstrɪə ['ɔ:s-], -n/z
Austro|-German, -Hungarian ‚ɒstrəʊ|-'dʒɜ:mən [‚ɔ:s-], -hʌŋ'geərɪən
authentic, -al, -ally ɔ:'θentɪk, -l, -əlɪ
authenticat|e, -es, -ing, -ed ɔ:'θentɪkeɪt, -s, -ɪŋ, -ɪd
authentication, -s ɔ:‚θentɪ'keɪʃn, -z
authenticit|y, -ies ‚ɔ:θen'tɪsət|ɪ [-θən-, -ɪt|ɪ], -ɪz
author, -s; -ess/es 'ɔ:θə*, -z; -rɪs/ɪz [-res/ɪz]
authoritarianism ɔ:‚θɒrɪ'teərɪənɪzəm [-‚θɒrə-, -rjə-]
authoritative, -ly, -ness ɔ:'θɒrɪtətɪv [ɒ'θ-, ə'θ-, -'θɒrə-, -teɪt-], -lɪ, -nɪs [-nəs]

authorit|y, -ies ɔ:'θɒrət|ɪ [ɒ'θ-, ə'θ-, -ɪt|ɪ], -ɪz
authorization [-isa-], -s ‚ɔ:θəraɪ'zeɪʃn [-rɪ'z-], -z
authoriz|e [-is|e], -es, -ing, -ed; -able 'ɔ:θəraɪz, -ɪz, -ɪŋ, -d; -əbl
authorship 'ɔ:θəʃɪp
autism 'ɔ:tɪzm
autistic ɔ:'tɪstɪk
autobahn, -s 'ɔ:təbɑːn ['aʊt-], -z
autobiograph|er/s, -y, -ies ‚ɔ:təʊbaɪ-'ɒgrəf|ə*/z [-bɪ'ɒg-], -ɪ, -ɪz
autobiographic, -al, -ally 'ɔ:təʊ‚baɪəʊ-'græfɪk, -l, -əlɪ
auto-car, -s 'ɔ:təʊkɑː*, -z
autochthon, -s ɔ:'tɒkθən ['ɔ:tək-, -θɒn], -z
autochthonous ɔ:'tɒkθənəs [-θɒs]
autocrac|y, ies ɔ:'tɒkrəs|ɪ, -ɪz
autocrat, -s 'ɔ:təʊkræt, -s
autocratic, -al, -ally ‚ɔ:təʊ'krætɪk, -l, -əlɪ
auto-da-fé, -s ‚ɔ:təʊdɑː'feɪ [‚aʊt-], -z
autogiro [-gyro], -s ‚ɔ:təʊ'dʒaɪərəʊ, -z
autograph, -s 'ɔ:təgrɑːf [-græf], -s
autographic, -al, -ally ‚ɔ:təʊ'græfɪk, -l, -əlɪ
autography ɔ:'tɒgrəfɪ
autogyro, -s ‚ɔ:təʊ'dʒaɪərəʊ, -z
Autolycus ɔ:'tɒlɪkəs
automat 'ɔ:təʊmæt
automatic, -al, -ally ‚ɔ:tə'mætɪk, -l, -əlɪ
automation ‚ɔ:tə'meɪʃn
automati|sm, -st/s ɔ:'tɒmətɪ|zəm, -st/s
automat|on, -ons, -a ɔ:'tɒmət|ən, -ənz, -ə
automobile, -s 'ɔ:təməʊbi:l [-tʊm-, -mʊb-, ‚—'-, ‚ɔ:təʊ'məʊbi:l, -tʊ'm-]
autonomic ‚ɔ:təʊ'nɒmɪk
autonom|ous, -y, -ies ɔ:'tɒnəm|əs, -ɪ, -ɪz
autonym, -s 'ɔ:tənɪm, -z
auto-pilot, -s 'ɔ:təʊ‚paɪlət, -s
autops|y, -ies 'ɔ:təps|ɪ [-tɒp-, ɔ:'tɒpsɪ], -ɪz
auto-suggestion ‚ɔ:təʊsə'dʒestʃən [-eʃtʃən]
autotyp|e (s. v.), -es, -ing, -ed 'ɔ:təʊtaɪp, -s, -ɪŋ, -t
autotypography ‚ɔ:təʊtaɪ'pɒgrəfɪ
autumn, -s 'ɔ:təm, -z
autumn|al, -ally ɔ:'tʌmn|əl [-l], -əlɪ
Auvergne əʊ'veən [-'vɜ:n] (ovɛrn, ɔv-)
auxiliar|y (s. adj.), -ies ɔ:g'zɪljər|ɪ [ɔ:k'sɪl-, ɒg'zɪl-, ɒk'sɪl-, -lɪər-], -ɪz
Ava 'ɑ:və, 'eɪvə
avail (s. v.), -s, -ing/ly, -ed ə'veɪl, -z, -ɪŋ/lɪ, -d

availability ə,veɪlə'bɪlətɪ [-lɪt-]

availab|le, -ly, -leness ə'veɪləb|l, -lɪ, -lnɪs [-nəs]

avalanche, -s 'ævəla:nʃ [-la:ntʃ, -lɔ:ntʃ], -ɪz

Avalon 'ævəlɒn

avant-courier, -s ˌævɑ̃:ŋ'kʊrɪə* [-vɔ̃:ŋ'k-, -vɑ:ŋ'k-, -vɒŋ'k-, -vɔ:ŋ-, -vənt'k-], -z

avant-garde ˌævɑ̃:ŋ'gɑ:d [-vɔ̃:ŋ, -vɔ:ŋ, -vɑ:ŋ, -vɒŋ, -vəŋ] (avã gard)

avarice 'ævərɪs

avaricious, -ly, -ness ˌævə'rɪʃəs, -lɪ, -nɪs [-nəs]

avast ə'vɑ:st

avatar, -s ˌævə'tɑ:* ['---] (Hindi əwtar), -z

avaunt ə'vɔ:nt

ave (prayer), -s 'ɑ:vɪ, -z

Avebury 'eɪvbərɪ

Aveling 'eɪvlɪŋ

Ave Maria (prayer), -s ˌɑ:vɪmɑ'rɪə [-'ri:ə], -z

Ave Maria Lane 'ɑ:vɪmɑˌrɪə'leɪn [formerly 'eɪvɪməˌraɪə'leɪn]

aveng|e, -es, -ing, -ed, -er/s; -eful ə'vendʒ, -ɪz, -ɪŋ, -d, -ə*/z; -fʊl

avengeress, -es ə'vendʒərɪs [-res], -ɪz

avenue, -s 'ævənju: [-vɪn-], -z

aver, -s, -ring, -red, -ment/s ə'vɜ:*, -z, -rɪŋ, -d, -mənt/s

averag|e (s. adj. v.), -es, -ing, -ed 'ævərɪdʒ, -ɪz, -ɪŋ, -d

averruncat|e, -es, -ing, -ed ˌævə'rʌŋkeɪt [-vɪ'r-, -ve'r-], -s, -ɪŋ, -ɪd

averruncator, -s ˌævə'rʌŋkeɪtə* [-vɪ'r-, -ve'r-], -z

averse, -ly, -ness ə'vɜ:s, -lɪ, -nɪs [-nəs]

aversion, -s ə'vɜ:ʃn, -z

avert, -s, -ing, -ed; -ible ə'vɜ:t, -s, -ɪŋ, -ɪd; -əbl [-ɪbl]

avertin ə'vɜ:tɪn

Avery 'eɪvərɪ

Avesta ə'vestə

aviar|ist/s, -y, -ies 'eɪvjər|ɪst/s [-vɪə-], -ɪ, -ɪz

aviation ˌeɪvɪ'eɪʃn

aviator, -s 'eɪvɪeɪtə* [-vjeɪ-], -z

Avice (fem. name) 'eɪvɪs

Avicenna ˌævɪ'senə

aviculture 'eɪvɪkʌltʃə*

avid 'ævɪd

avidity ə'vɪdətɪ [æ'v-, -ɪtɪ]

Aviemore ˌævɪ'mɔ:* [-'mɔə*, '---]

Avilion æ'vɪlɪən [-ljən]

aviso, -s ə'vaɪzəʊ [-'vi:z-], -z

Avoca ə'vəʊkə

avocado, -s ˌævəʊ'kɑ:dəʊ, -z

avocation, -s ˌævəʊ'keɪʃn, -z

avocet, -s 'ævəʊset, -s

Avoch ɔ:k [ɔ:x] (Scottish ɒx)

avoid, -s, -ing, -ed; -able, -ance/s ə'vɔɪd, -z, -ɪŋ, -ɪd; -əbl, -əns/ɪz

avoirdupois ˌævədə'pɔɪz

Avon (in Avon, etc.) 'eɪvən, (in Devon) 'ævən, (in the Grampian Region) ɑ:n

Avondale 'eɪvəndeɪl

Avonmouth 'eɪvənmaʊθ [-məθ]

Avory 'eɪvərɪ

avouch, -es, -ing, -ed ə'vaʊtʃ, -ɪz, -ɪŋ, -t

avow (s. v.), -s, -ing, -ed, -edly; -al/s ə'vaʊ, -z, -ɪŋ, -d, -ɪdlɪ; -əl/z

avuncular ə'vʌŋkjʊlə*

await, -s, -ing, -ed ə'weɪt, -s, -ɪŋ, -ɪd

awak|e (adj. v.), -es, -ing, -ed, awoke ə'weɪk, -s, -ɪŋ, -t, ə'wəʊk

awak|en, -ens, -ening, -ened, -enment/s ə'weɪk|ən, -ənz, -nɪŋ [-ŋɪŋ, -ənɪŋ], -ənd, -ənmənt/s

awakening (s.), -s ə'weɪknɪŋ, -z

award (s. v.), -s, -ing, -ed; -able ə'wɔ:d, -z, -ɪŋ, -ɪd; -əbl

aware, -ness ə'weə*, -nɪs [-nəs]

awash ə'wɒʃ

away ə'weɪ

aw|e (s. v.), (A.), -es, -ing, -ed ɔ:, -z, -ɪŋ, -d

awe-inspiring 'ɔ:ɪnˌspaɪərɪŋ

aweless, -ness 'ɔ:lɪs [-ləs], -nɪs [-nəs]

awesome, -ness 'ɔ:səm, -nɪs [-nəs]

awe-stricken 'ɔ:ˌstrɪkən

awe-struck 'ɔ:strʌk

awful, -ness (terrible) 'ɔ:fʊl [-fl], -nɪs [-nəs], (great, considerable) 'ɔ:fl

awfully (terribly) 'ɔ:fʊlɪ, (very) 'ɔ:flɪ

awhile ə'waɪl [ə'hw-]

awkward, -est, -ly, -ness, -ish 'ɔ:kwəd, -ɪst, -lɪ, -nɪs [-nəs], -ɪʃ

awl, -s ɔ:l, -z

awn, -s -ed ɔ:n, -z, -d

awning, -s 'ɔ:nɪŋ, -z

awoke (from awake) ə'wəʊk

awry ə'raɪ

axe, -s æks, -ɪz

axes (plur. of axis) 'æksi:z

Axholm(e) 'ækshəʊm [-səm]

axial, -ly 'æksɪəl [-sjəl], -ɪ

axil, -s 'æksɪl, -z

axill|a, -ae; -ar, -ary æk'sɪl|ə, -i:; -ə*, -ərɪ

axiom, -s 'æksɪəm [-sjəm], -z

axiomatic, -al, -ally ˌæksɪəʊ'mætɪk [-sjəʊ'm-], -l, -əlɪ

ax|is, -es 'æks|ɪs, -i:z

axle, -s, -d 'æksl, -z, -d

35

axle-tree, -s 'æksltri:, -z
Axminster, -s 'æksmɪnstə*, -z
axolotl, -s ˌæksə'lɒtl, -z
ay (yes), -es aɪ, -z
ayah, -s 'aɪə ['ɑːjə], -z
aye (ever), eɪ
aye (yes), -s aɪ, -z
aye-aye (animal), -s 'aɪaɪ, -z
Ayer, -s eə*, -z
Ayerst 'aɪəst, 'erəst
Aylesbury 'eɪlzbərɪ
Aylesford 'eɪlzfəd [-lsf-]
Ayliffe 'eɪlɪf
Ayling 'eɪlɪŋ
Aylmer 'eɪlmə*
Aylsham 'eɪlʃəm
Aylward 'eɪlwəd
Aylwin 'eɪlwɪn
Aymer 'eɪmə*
Ayot 'eɪət
Ayr, -shire eə*, -ʃə* [-ˌʃɪə*]
Ayre, -s eə*, -z
Ayrton 'eətn

Ayscough 'æskə, 'æskjuː, 'eɪskəf
Ayscue 'eɪskjuː
Ayt|on, -oun 'eɪt|n, -n
azalea, -s ə'zeɪljə [-lɪə], -z
Azariah ˌæzə'raɪə .
Azaziel ə'zeɪzjəl [-zɪəl]
azimuth, -s 'æzɪməθ, -s
azoic ə'zəʊɪk [æ'z-]
Azores ə'zɔːz [-'zɒɛz]

> Note.—It is customary to pronounce
> ə'zɔːrɪz (or ə'zɪɒɛz or-rez) in
> reciting Tennyson's poem 'The
> Revenge'.

azote ə'zəʊt [æ'z-, 'æzəʊt]
azotic ə'zɒtɪk [æ'z-]
Azov 'ɑːzɒv
Azrael 'æzreɪəl [-reɪl, -rɪəl]
Aztec, -s 'æztek, -s
azure 'æʒə* ['eɪʒ-, -ˌʒjʊə*, -ˌʒʊə*, -ʒjə*, -ˌzjʊə*]
azur|ine/s, -ite 'æʒʊr|aɪn/z ['æʒər-, 'æˌʒʊər-, 'æʒjʊr-, 'æˌʒjʊər-, 'æzjʊr-, 'æˌzjʊər-], -aɪt

B

B (*the letter*), **-'s** bi:, -z
ba (*note in Tonic Sol-fa*), **-s** beɪ, -z
B.A. (British Airways, Bachelor of Arts) ˌbiːˈeɪ
baa (*s. v.*), **-s, -ing, -ed** bɑː, -z, -ɪŋ, -d
Baal ˈbeɪəl [ˈbeɪæl, *Jewish pronunciation* bɑːl]
baa-lamb, **-s** ˈbɑːlæm, -z
Baalim ˈbeɪəlɪm [*Jewish pronunciation* ˈbɑːlɪm]
Baal Schem ˌbɑːlˈʃem
baas, **-es** bɑːs, -ɪz
Babbage ˈbæbɪdʒ
babb|le, **-les, -ling, -led, -ler/s, -lement/s** ˈbæb|l, -lz, -lɪŋ [-lɪŋ], -ld, -lə*/z [-lə*/z], -lmənt/s
Babcock ˈbæbkɒk
babe, **-s** beɪb, -z
babel (B.), **-s** ˈbeɪbl, -z
Bab-el-Mandeb ˌbæbelˈmændeb
Babington ˈbæbɪŋtən
Baboo (B.), **-s** ˈbɑːbuː, -z
baboon, **-s** bəˈbuːn, -z
babooner|y, **-ies** bəˈbuːnər|ɪ, -ɪz
babu (B.), **-s** ˈbɑːbuː, -z
bab|y (B.), **-ies** ˈbeɪb|ɪ, -ɪz
baby-farmer, **-s** ˈbeɪbɪˌfɑːmə*, -z
babyhood ˈbeɪbɪhʊd
babyish, **-ly, -ness** ˈbeɪbɪɪʃ [-bjɪʃ], -lɪ, -nɪs [-nəs]
Babylon ˈbæbɪlən
Babylonia, **-n/s** ˌbæbɪˈləʊnjə [-nɪə], -n/z
baby-sitt|er/s, **-ing** ˈbeɪbɪˌsɪt|ə*/z, -ɪŋ
baccalaureate, **-s** ˌbækəˈlɔːrɪət [-rɪɪt], -s
baccara(t) ˈbækərɑː [ˌbækəˈr-]
Bacchae ˈbæki:
bacchanal, **-s** ˈbækənl [-næl], -z
bacchanalia, **-n/s** ˌbækəˈneɪljə [-lɪə], -nz
bacchant, **-s** ˈbækənt, -s
bacchante, **-s** bəˈkæntɪ, -z [bəˈkænt, -s]
bacchic ˈbækɪk
Bacchus ˈbækəs
Bacchylides bæˈkɪlɪdiːz [bəˈk-]
baccy ˈbækɪ
Bach (*English surname*) beɪtʃ, bætʃ, (*German composer*) bɑːx [bɑːk](bax)
Bache beɪtʃ
bachelor (B.), **-s; -hood, -ship** ˈbætʃələ* [-tʃɪl-, -tʃlə*], -z; -hʊd, -ʃɪp

bacill|us, **-i, -ary** bəˈsɪl|əs, -aɪ, -ərɪ
back (*s. v. adv.*) (B.), **-s, -ing, -ed, -er/s** bæk, -s, -ɪŋ, -t, -ə*/z
backache, **-s** ˈbækeɪk, -s
back-bencher, **-s** ˌbækˈbentʃə*, -z
backbit|e, **-es, -ing, backbit, backbitten** ˈbækbaɪt, -s, -ɪŋ, ˈbækbɪt, ˈbækˌbɪtn
backbiter, **-s** ˈbækˌbaɪtə*, -z
backboard, **-s** ˈbækbɔːd [-bɔəd], -z
backbone, **-s** ˈbækbəʊn, -z
backchat ˈbæktʃæt
backdat|e, **-es, -ing, -ed** ˌbækˈdeɪt, -s, -ɪŋ, -ɪd
back-door, **-s** ˌbækˈdɔː* [ˈ-dɔə*], -z
backfir|e, **-es, -ing, -ed** ˌbækˈfaɪə* [ˈ--], -z, -rɪŋ, -d
backgammon bækˈgæmən [ˈbækˌg-]
background, **-s** ˈbækgraʊnd, -z
back-hair ˌbækˈheə*
back-hand, **-s, -ed, -er/s** ˈbækhænd [ˌbækˈh-], -z, -ɪd, -ə*/z
Backhouse ˈbækhaʊs
backing (s.), **-s** ˈbækɪŋ, -z
backlash ˈbæklæʃ
backless ˈbæklɪs [-ləs]
backlog, **-s** ˈbæklɒg, -z
back-pedal, **-s, -ling, -led** ˌbækˈpedl, -lz, -lɪŋ [-lɪŋ], -ld
back-room ˌbækˈruːm [-ˈrʊm, ˈ--]
backsheesh [-shish] ˈbækʃiːʃ [ˌ-ˈ-]
backside, **-s** ˌbækˈsaɪd [ˈbæksaɪd], -z
backslid|e, **-es, -ing, backslid, backslider/s** ˌbækˈslaɪd [ˈ--], -z, -ɪŋ, ˌbækˈslɪd, ˌbækˈslaɪdə* [ˈ-,--]/z
backstairs ˌbækˈsteəz [ˈ--]
backstay, **-s** ˈbæksteɪ, -z
backstitch, **-es** ˈbækstɪtʃ, -ɪz
backstrap, **-s** ˈbækstræp, -s
backward, **-s, -ly, -ness** ˈbækwəd, -z, -lɪ, -nɪs [-nəs]
backwash, **-es** ˈbækwɒʃ, -ɪz
backwater, **-s** ˈbækˌwɔːtə*, -z
backwoods, **-man, -men** ˈbækwʊdz, -mən, -mən
back-yard, **-s** ˌbækˈjɑːd, -z
bacon ˈbeɪkən [-kŋ]
Bacon ˈbeɪkən [-kn]
Baconian, **-s** beɪˈkəʊnjən [bəˈk-, -nɪən], -z

37

bacteriological ˌbækˌtɪərɪəˈlɒdʒɪkl [ˌ---ˈ---]

bacteriolog|ist/s, -y bækˌtɪərɪˈɒlədʒ|-ɪst/s [ˌbæktɪərɪˈɒ-], -ɪ

bacteri|um, -a, -al bækˈtɪərɪ|əm, -ə, -əl

Bactria, -n/s ˈbæktrɪə, -n/z

Bacup ˈbeɪkəp

bad; bad|ly, -ness bæd; ˈbæd|lɪ, -nɪs [-nəs]

Badajoz ˈbædəhɒz (badaˈxoθ)

Badam, -s ˈbædəm, -z

Baddeley ˈbædəlɪ, ˈbædlɪ

baddish ˈbædɪʃ

bade (from bid) bæd [beɪd]

Badel bəˈdel

Badely ˈbædlɪ

Baden (in Germany) ˈbɑːdn

Baden-Powell ˌbeɪdnˈpəʊəl [-ˈpəʊl, -ˈpəʊel, -ˈpəʊəl]

Bader (Scottish surname) ˈbɑːdə*, ˈbeɪdə*

badg|e (s. v.), -es, -ing, -ed bædʒ, -ɪz, -ɪŋ, -d

badger (s. v.) (B.), -s, -ing, -ed ˈbædʒə*, -z, -rɪŋ, -d

badger-baiting ˈbædʒəˌbeɪtɪŋ

badger-dog, -s ˈbædʒədɒg, -z

Badham, ˈbædəm

badinage ˈbædɪnɑːʒ [ˌ--ˈ-] (badinaːʒ)

badminton (B.) ˈbædmɪntən

Baeda ˈbiːdə

Baedeker, -s ˈbeɪdɪkə* [-dek-], -z

Baffin ˈbæfɪn

baff|le (s. v.), -les, -ling, -led, -ler/s ˈbæf|l, -lz, -lɪŋ [-lɪŋ], -ld, -lə*/z [-lə*/z]

baffleboard, -s ˈbæflbɔːd [-bɔəd], -z

bag (s.), -s bæg, -z

bag (v.), -s, -ging, -ged bæg, -z, -ɪŋ, -d

bagatelle, -s; -board/s ˌbægəˈtel, -z; -bɔːd/z [-bɔəd/z]

Bagdad (in Iraq) ˌbægˈdæd [ˈ--], (in Tasmania, Florida) ˈbægdæd

Bagehot ˈbædʒət

baggage, -s ˈbægɪdʒ, -ɪz

baggage|man, -men ˈbægɪdʒ|mæn [-mən], -men [-mən]

Baggallay ˈbægəlɪ

bagg|y, -ier, -iest, -ily, -iness ˈbæg|ɪ, -ɪə*, -ɪɪst, -ɪlɪ, -ɪnɪs [-nəs]

Baghdad ˌbægˈdæd [ˈ--]

Bagnall ˈbægnəl [-nl, -nɔːl]

Bagnell ˈbægnəl [-nl]

bagnio, -s ˈbɑːnjəʊ [-nɪəʊ], -z

Bagot ˈbægət

bagpipe, -s, -r/s ˈbægpaɪp, -s, -ə*/z

Bagrie ˈbægrɪ

Bagsh|aw(e), -ot ˈbægʃ|ɔː, -ɒt

Bagworthy (in Devon) ˈbædʒərɪ

bah bɑː

bahadur, -s bəˈhɑːdə*, -z

Bahama, -s bəˈhɑːmə, -z

Bahia bəˈhiːə [-ˈhɪə]

Bahrein (-rain), -i bɑːˈreɪn, -ɪ

Baiae ˈbaɪiː

baignoire, -s ˈbeɪnwɑː* [-wɔː*], -z

bail (s. v.), -s, -ing, -ed, -er/s; -able beɪl, -z, -ɪŋ, -d, -ə*/z; -əbl

bail-bond, -s ˈbeɪlbɒnd [ˌbeɪlˈb-], -z

bailee, -s ˌbeɪˈliː, -z

Bailey ˈbeɪlɪ

Bailhache ˈbeɪlhæʃ

bailie (B.), -s ˈbeɪlɪ, -z

bailiff, -s ˈbeɪlɪf, -s

bailiwick, -s ˈbeɪlɪwɪk, -s

Baillieu ˈbeɪljuː

bailment, -s ˈbeɪlmənt, -s

Baily ˈbeɪlɪ

Bain, -es beɪn, -z

Bainbridge ˈbeɪmbrɪdʒ [ˈbeɪmb-]

Baird beəd

bairn, -s beən, -z

bait (s. v.), -s, -ing, -ed beɪt, -s, -ɪŋ, -ɪd

baize, -s beɪz, -ɪz

bak|e, -es, -ing, -ed, -er/s beɪk, -s, -ɪŋ, -t, -ə*/z

bakehou|se, -ses ˈbeɪkhaʊ|s, -zɪz

bakelite ˈbeɪkəlaɪt

Baker ˈbeɪkə*

Bakerloo ˌbeɪkəˈluː

baker|y, -ies ˈbeɪkər|ɪ, -ɪz

baking-powder ˈbeɪkɪŋˌpaʊdə*

baksheesh ˈbækʃiːʃ [ˌ-ˈ-]

Bala (in Wales) ˈbælə (Welsh ˈbala)

balaam (B.), -s ˈbeɪlæm [-ləm], -z

balaclava (B.), -s ˌbæləˈklɑːvə, -z

Balakirev bəˈlækɪrev [-ˈlɑːk-] (baˈlakirjif)

balalaika, -s ˌbæləˈlaɪkə, -z

balanc|e (s. v.), -es, -ing, -ed ˈbæləns, -ɪz, -ɪŋ, -t

balance-sheet, -s ˈbælənsʃiːt [-nʃʃiːt, -nʃiːt], -s

Balbriggan bælˈbrɪgən

Balbus ˈbælbəs

Balcarres bælˈkærɪs

Balchin ˈbɔːltʃɪn [ˈbɒl-]

balcon|y, -ies ˈbælkən|ɪ, -ɪz

bald, -er, -est, -ly, -ness bɔːld, -ə*, -ɪst, -lɪ, -nɪs [-nəs]

baldachin, -s ˈbɔːldəkɪn, -z

balderdash ˈbɔːldədæʃ

bald-head, -s ˈbɔːldhed, -z

bald-headed ˌbɔːldˈhedɪd [also ˈbɔːldˌh- when attributive]

Baldock ˈbɔːldɒk

38

baldric, -s 'bɔːldrɪk, -s
Baldry 'bɔːldrɪ
Baldwin 'bɔːldwɪn
ball|e (s. v.), -es, -ing, -ed beɪl, -z, -ɪŋ, -d
Bâle (in Switzerland) bɑːl
Balean (surname) 'bælɪn
Balearic ˌbælɪ'ærɪk
baleen, -s bə'liːn [bæ'l-], -z
bale|ful, -fully, -fulness 'beɪl|fʊl, -fʊlɪ
[-fəlɪ], -fʊlnɪs [-nəs]
baler, -s 'beɪlə*, -z
Balfour 'bælfə* [-fɔː*, -ˌfʊə*, -fɔə*]
Balgony bæl'gəʊnɪ
Balguy 'bɔːlgɪ
Balham 'bæləm
Baliol 'beɪljəl [-lɪəl]
balk (s. v.), -s, -ing, -ed bɔːk [bɔːlk], -s,
-ɪŋ, -t
Balkan, -s 'bɔːlkən ['bɒl-], -z
ball (B.), -s bɔːl, -z
ballad, -s 'bæləd, -z
ballade, -s bæ'lɑːd (balad), -z
Ballan|tine, -tyne 'bælən|taɪn, -taɪn
Ballarat, ˌbælə'ræt ['---]
Ballard 'bæləd, -lɑːd
ballast, -s 'bæləst, -s
Ballater 'bælətə*
ball-bearing, -s ˌbɔːl'beərɪŋ, -z
ball-cock, -s 'bɔːlkɒk, -s
Balleine (surname in Channel Islands)
bæ'len
ballerina, -s ˌbælə'riːnə, -z
ballet, -s 'bæleɪ [-lɪ], -z
ballet-dancer, -s 'bælɪˌdɑːnsə* [-leɪˌd-],
-z
ballet-girl, -s 'bælɪgɜːl [-leɪg-], -z
balletomane, -s 'bælɪtəʊmeɪn [-let-], -z
Balliol 'beɪljəl [-lɪəl]
ballistic, -s bə'lɪstɪk, -s
balloon, -s, -ist/s bə'luːn, -z, -ɪst/s
ballot (s. v.), -s, -ing, -ed; -age 'bælət,
-s, -ɪŋ, -ɪd; -ɪdʒ
ballot-box, -es 'bælətbɒks, -ɪz
ball-point, -s, -ed 'bɔːlpɔɪnt, -s, -ɪd
ball-proof 'bɔːlpruːf
ball-room, -s 'bɔːlrʊm [-ruːm], -z
bally 'bælɪ
Bally|castle, -mena, -money ˌbælɪ|-
'kɑːsl, -'miːnə, -'mʌnɪ
ballyhoo ˌbælɪ'huː
ballyrag, -s, -ging, -ged 'bælɪræg, -z,
-ɪŋ, -d
balm, -s bɑːm, -z
Balm(e) bɑːm
Balmoral bæl'mɒrəl
balm|y, -ier, -iest, -ily, -iness 'bɑːm|ɪ,
-ɪə* [-jə*], -ɪɪst [-jɪst], -ɪlɪ [-əlɪ],
-ɪnɪs [-ɪnəs]

Balniel bæl'niːl
Balogh 'bælɒg
baloney bə'ləʊnɪ
balsa 'bɒlsə ['bɔː-]
balsam, -s 'bɔːlsəm ['bɒl-], -z
balsamic bɔːl'sæmɪk [bæl-, bɒl-]
Balta (in Ukraine) 'bæltə
Balthazar (in Shakespeare) ˌbælθə'zɑː*
['---], (otherwise) bæl'θæzə*
Baltic 'bɔːltɪk ['bɒl-]
baltimore (B.), -s 'bɔːltɪmɔː* ['bɒlt-,
-mɔə*], -z
Baluchistan bə'luːtʃɪstɑːn [-tæn, -ˌ--'-]
baluster, -s, -ed 'bæləstə*, -z, -d
balustrade, -s, ˌbælə'streɪd, -z
Baly 'beɪlɪ
Balzac 'bælzæk (balzak)
bamboo, -s bæm'buː, -z
bambooz|le, -les, -ling, -led bæm'buːz|l,
-lz, -lɪŋ [-lɪŋ], -ld
Bamborough 'bæmbərə
Bam|field, -ford 'bæm|fiːld, -fəd
bamfooz|le, -les, -ling, -led bæm'fuːz|l,
-lz, -lɪŋ [-lɪŋ], -ld
Bamfyld 'bæmfiːld
ban (s. v.), -s, -ning, -ned bæn, -z, -ɪŋ,
-d
banal bə'nɑːl [bæ'n-, 'beɪnl]
Banal 'bænəl [-nl]
banalit|y, -ies bə'nælət|ɪ [bæ'n-, -ɪt|ɪ],
-ɪz
banana, -s bə'nɑːnə, -z
Banaras bə'nɑːrəs (Hindi bənərəs)
Banbury 'bænbərɪ ['bæmbərɪ]
Banchory 'bæŋkərɪ
banco 'bæŋkəʊ
Bancroft 'bænkrɒft ['bæŋk-]
band (s.), -s bænd, -z
band (v.), -s, -ing, -ed bænd, -z, -ɪŋ,
-ɪd
bandag|e (s. v.), -es, -ing, -ed 'bændɪdʒ,
-ɪz, -ɪŋ, -d
bandana, -s bæn'dænə [-'dɑːnə], -z
bandanna, -s bæn'dænə, -z
bandbox, -es 'bændbɒks, -ɪz
bandeau, -x 'bændəʊ, -z
banderole, -s 'bændərəʊl, -z
bandicoot, -s 'bændɪkuːt, -s
bandit, -s 'bændɪt, -s
banditti bæn'dɪtɪ [-tiː]
bandmaster, -s 'bændˌmɑːstə*, -z
bandog, -s 'bændɒg, -z
bandoleer [-lier], -s ˌbændəʊ'lɪə*, -z
bandoline 'bændəʊliːn
bands|man, -men 'bændz|mən, -mən
[-men]
bandstand, -s 'bændstænd ['bænstænd],
-z

band|y (*adj. v.*), -ier, -iest; -ies, -ying,
-ied 'bænd|ɪ, -ɪə* [-jə*], -ɪɪst [-jɪst];
-ɪz, -ɪɪŋ [-jɪŋ], -ɪd
bandy-legged 'bændɪlegd [,--'-]
bane, -s beɪn, -z
bane|ful, -fully, -fulness 'beɪn|fʊl, -fʊlɪ
[-fəlɪ], -fʊlnɪs [-nəs]
Banff, -shire bæmf [bænf], -ʃə* [-,ʃɪə*]
Banfield 'bænfiːld
bang (*s. v.*), -s, -ing, -ed bæŋ, -z, -ɪŋ,
-d
Bangalore ,bæŋgə'lɔː* [-'lɔə*]
Banger 'beɪndʒə*
Bangkok ,bæŋ'kɒk ['--]
Bangladesh ,bæŋglə'deʃ [-'deɪʃ]
bangle, -s, -d 'bæŋgl, -z, -d
Bangor (*in Wales*) 'bæŋgə* (*Welsh*
'baŋgor), (*in U.S.A.*) 'bæŋgɔː*
Banham 'bænəm
banian, -s 'bænɪən [-njən, -nɪæn,
-njæn], -z
banish, -es, -ing, -ed, -ment/s 'bænɪʃ,
-ɪz, -ɪŋ, -t, -mənt/s
banister, -s 'bænɪstə*, -z
banjo, -s 'bændʒəʊ [-'-], -z
bank (*s. v.*), -s, -ing, -ed, -er/s bæŋk, -s,
-ɪŋ, -t [bæŋt], -ə*/z
Bankes bæŋks
bank-holiday, -s ,bæŋk'hɒlɪdɪ [-lɪd-,
-deɪ], -z
bank-note, -s 'bæŋknəʊt, -s
bank-rate, -s 'bæŋkreɪt, -s
bankrupt, -s 'bæŋkrʌpt [-rəpt], -s
bankruptc|y, -ies 'bæŋkrəp*s|ɪ [-krʌp-],
-ɪz
Banks bæŋks
banksia, -s 'bæŋksɪə [-sjə], -z
Bannatyne 'bænətaɪn
banner (B.), -s 'bænə*, -z
Bannerman 'bænəmən
Banning 'bænɪŋ
Bannister 'bænɪstə*
bannock, -s 'bænək, -s
Bannockburn 'bænəkbɜːn
banns bænz
banquet (*s. v.*), -s, -ing, -ed 'bæŋkwɪt,
-s, -ɪŋ, -ɪd
banqueting-hall, -s 'bæŋkwɪtɪŋhɔːl, -z
banquette, -s bæŋ'ket, -s
Banquo 'bæŋkwəʊ
banshee, -s bæn'ʃiː ['--], -z
bant, -s, -ing, -ed bænt, -s, -ɪŋ, -ɪd
bantam (B.), -s 'bæntəm, -z
banter (*s. v.*), -s, -ing, -ed 'bæntə*, -z,
-rɪŋ, -d
Banting 'bæntɪŋ
bantling, -s 'bæntlɪŋ, -z
Bantry 'bæntrɪ

Bantu ,bæn'tuː: [,bɑːn't-, *also* '--
according to sentence-stress]
banyan, -s 'bænɪən [-njən, -nɪæn,
-njæn], -z
baobab, -s 'beɪəʊbæb, -z
baptism, -s 'bæptɪzəm, -z
baptism|al, -ally bæp'tɪzm|l, -əlɪ
baptist, -s 'bæptɪst, -s
baptister|y, -ies 'bæptɪstər|ɪ, -ɪz
baptistr|y, -ies 'bæptɪstr|ɪ, -ɪz
baptiz|e, -es, -ing, -ed bæp'taɪz, -ɪz, -ɪŋ,
-d
bar (*s. v. prep.*), -s, -ring, -red bɑː*, -z,
-rɪŋ, -d
Barabbas bə'ræbəs
Barak 'beəræk [-rək]
Barat 'bærət
barb (*s. v.*), -s, -ing, -ed bɑːb, -z, -ɪŋ, -d
Barbad|os, -ian bɑː'beɪd|ɒs [-əs,
-əʊz], -ɪən [-jən]
Barbara 'bɑːbərə
barbarian, -s bɑː'beərɪən, -z
barbaric bɑː'bærɪk
barbarism, -s 'bɑːbərɪzəm, -z
barbarit|y, -ies bɑː'bærət|ɪ [-ɪt|ɪ], -ɪz
barbariz|e [-ise], -es, -ing, -ed 'bɑːbə-
raɪz, -ɪz, -ɪŋ, -d
Barbarossa ,bɑːbə'rɒsə
barbarous, -ly, -ness 'bɑːbərəs, -lɪ, -nɪs
[-nəs]
Barbary 'bɑːbərɪ
barbate 'bɑːbeɪt [-bɪt]
barbated 'bɑːbeɪtɪd [bɑː'beɪtɪd]
barbecu|e (*s. v.*), -es, -ing, -ed 'bɑːbɪkjuː:,
-z, -ɪŋ [-kjʊɪŋ], -d
barber (B.), -s 'bɑːbə*, -z
barberr|y, -ies 'bɑːbər|ɪ, -ɪz
barbette, -s bɑː'bet, -s
barbican (B.), -s bɑː'bɪkən, -z
Barbirolli ,bɑːbɪ'rɒlɪ
barbitone, -s 'bɑːbɪtəʊn, -z
barbiturate, -s bɑː'bɪtjʊrət [-rɪt, -reɪt],
-s
barbituric ,bɑːbɪ'tjʊərɪk [-'tjɔər-,
-'tjɔːr-, ,bɑː'bɪtjʊrɪk]
Barbour 'bɑːbə*
Barca 'bɑːkə
barcarolle, -s 'bɑːkərəʊl [-rɒl, ,--'-], -z
Barcelona ,bɑːsɪ'ləʊnə [-sə'l-]
Barclay 'bɑːklɪ [-leɪ]
Barcroft 'bɑːkrɒft
bard (B.), -s, -ic bɑːd, -z, -ɪk
Bardell bɑː'del, 'bɑːdəl [-del, -dl]
*Note.—In 'Pickwick' generally pro-
nounced* bɑː'del.
bardolatry bɑː'dɒlətrɪ
Bard|olph, -sley 'bɑːd|ɒlf, -zlɪ
Bardswell 'bɑːdzwəl [-wel]

Bardwell 'bɑ:dwəl [-wel]
bare (adj.), -r, -st, -ly, -ness beə*, -rə*, -rɪst, -lɪ, -nɪs [-nəs]
bare (archaic p. tense of bear) beə*
bareback, -ed 'beəbæk, -t
Barebones 'beəbəʊnz
barefac|ed, -edly, -edness 'beəfeɪs|t, -tlɪ [-ɪdlɪ], -tnɪs [-tnəs]
barefoot 'beəfʊt
barefooted ,beə'fʊtɪd ['-,--]
bare-headed ,beə'hedɪd ['-,--]
Bareilly bə'reɪlɪ (Hindi bərylli)
bare-legged ,beə'legd ['beəlegd, -'legɪd]
bare-necked ,beə'nekt ['-,--]
Barfield 'bɑ:fi:ld
bargain (s. v.), -s, -ing, -ed, -er/s 'bɑ:gɪn, -z, -ɪŋ, -d, -ə*/z
barge, -s bɑ:dʒ, -ɪz
bargee, -s bɑ:'dʒi: [,bɑ:'dʒi:], -z
barge|man, -men 'bɑ:dʒ|mən [-mæn], -mən [-men]
bargepole, -s 'bɑ:dʒpəʊl, -z
Barger 'bɑ:dʒə*
Bargery 'bɑ:dʒərɪ
Bargh bɑ:dʒ, bɑ:f
Bargrave 'bɑ:greɪv
Barham (surname) 'bærəm, 'bɑ:rəm, (in Kent) 'bærəm
Baring 'beərɪŋ, 'bærɪŋ
baritone, -s 'bærɪtəʊn, -z
barium 'beərɪəm
Barjesus 'bɑ:,dʒi:zəs
bark (s. v.), -s, -ing, -ed, -er/s bɑ:k, -s, -ɪŋ, -t, -ə*/z
Barker 'bɑ:kə*
Barkston 'bɑ:kstən
barley 'bɑ:lɪ
barleycorn (B.), -s 'bɑ:lɪkɔ:n, -z
barley-sugar 'bɑ:lɪ,ʃʊgə* [,--'--]
barley-water 'bɑ:lɪ,wɔ:tə*
Barlow(e) 'bɑ:ləʊ
barm bɑ:m
barmaid, -s 'bɑ:meɪd, -z
bar|man, -men 'bɑ:|mən [-mæn], -mən [-men]
Barmby 'bɑ:mbɪ
Barmecide 'bɑ:mɪsaɪd
Barmouth 'bɑ:məθ
barm|y, -ier, -iest 'bɑ:m|ɪ, -ɪə*, -ɪɪst
barn, -s bɑ:n, -z
Barnab|as, -y 'bɑ:nəb|əs [-æs], -ɪ
barnacle, -s 'bɑ:nəkl, -z
Barnard 'bɑ:nəd
Barnardiston ,bɑ:nə'dɪstən
Barnardo bɑ:'nɑ:dəʊ [bə'n-]
Barnby 'bɑ:nbɪ
barn-door (s.), -s ,bɑ:n'dɔ:* ['-'dɔə*], -z
Barnea 'bɑ:nɪə [bɑ:'nɪə]

Barnes bɑ:nz
Barnet(t) 'bɑ:nɪt
Barney 'bɑ:nɪ
Barnham 'bɑ:nəm
Barnicott 'bɑ:nɪkət [-kɒt]
Barnoldswick (in Lancashire) bɑ:-'nəʊldzwɪk
Barnsley 'bɑ:nzlɪ
Barnstaple 'bɑ:nstəpl [locally -əbl]
barnstormer, -s 'bɑ:n,stɔ:mə*, -z
Barnum 'bɑ:nəm
Baroda bə'rəʊdə (Gujarati vəḍodra)
barograph, -s 'bærəʊgrɑ:f [-græf], -s
Barolong (Botswana tribe) ,bɑ:rəʊ'ləʊŋ [,bær-, -'lɒŋ]
baromet|er/s, -ry bə'rɒmɪt|ə*/z [-mət|ə*/z], -rɪ
barometric, -al, -ally ,bærəʊ'metrɪk, -l, -əlɪ
baron (B.), -s 'bærən, -z
baron|age/s, -ess/es 'bærən|ɪdʒ/ɪz [-rɪ̩-], -ɪs/ɪz [-es/ɪz]
baronet, -s 'bærənɪt [-rɪt, -et], -s
baronetage, -s 'bærənɪtɪdʒ [-rɪ̩-], -ɪz
baronetc|y, -ies 'bærənɪts|ɪ [-rɪ̩-, -et-], -ɪz
baronial bə'rəʊnjəl [-nɪəl]
baron|y, -ies 'bærən|ɪ [-rɪ̩-], -ɪz
baroque bə'rɒk [-'rəʊk]
barouche, -s bə'ru:ʃ [bæ'r-], -ɪz
barque, -s bɑ:k, -s
Barr bɑ:*
barrack (s. v.), -s, -ing, -ed 'bærək, -s, -ɪŋ, -t
Barraclough 'bærəklʌf
barracuda ,bærə'kju:də [-'ku:də]
barrage, -s 'bærɑ:ʒ [bæ'rɑ:ʒ, -rɑ:dʒ], -ɪz
barratry 'bærətrɪ
Barrat(t) 'bærət
barrel, -s 'bærəl, -z
barrel-organ, -s 'bærəl,ɔ:gən, -z
barr|en, -enest, -enly, -enness 'bær|ən, -ənɪst [-ɪ̩st], -ənlɪ, -ənnɪs [-ənnəs]
Barrett 'bærət [-ret, -rɪt]
barricad|e (s. v.), -es, -ing, -ed ,bærɪ'keɪd [-rə'k-], -z, -ɪŋ, -ɪd
Barrie 'bærɪ
barrier (B.), -s 'bærɪə*, -z
barring 'bɑ:rɪŋ
Barrington 'bærɪŋtən
barrister, -s 'bærɪstə*, -z
barrister-at-law, barristers-at-law ,bærɪstərət'lɔ:, ,bærɪstəzət'lɔ:
barristerial ,bærɪ'stɪərɪəl
Barron 'bærən
barrow (B.), -s 'bærəʊ, -z
Barrow-in-Furness ,bærəʊɪn'fɜ:nɪs [-nes]

41

Barry 'bærɪ
Barrymore 'bærɪmɔ:* [-mɔə*]
bart. (B.), barts bɑ:t, -s
Bartelot 'bɑ:tɪlət [-lɒt]
bar-tender, -s 'bɑ:ˌtendə*, -z
barter (B.) (s. v.), -s, -ing, -ed 'bɑːtə*,
  -z, -rɪŋ, -d
Bartholomew bɑː'θɒləmju: [bə'θ-]
Bartimeus [-maeus] ˌbɑːtɪ'miːəs
  [-'mɪəs]
Bartle 'bɑːtl
Bartlett 'bɑːtlɪt
Bartók 'bɑːtɒk
Bartolozzi ˌbɑːtə'lɒtsɪ
Barton 'bɑːtn
Bart's bɑːts
Baruch (biblical name) 'bɑːrʊk ['beər-,
  -rək], (modern surname) bə'ruːk
Barugh (surname, place in South
  Yorkshire) bɑːf
Barum 'beərəm
Barwick 'bærɪk
barysphere, -s 'bærɪˌsfɪə*, -z
barytone, -s = barit-
basal 'beɪsl
basalt 'bæsɔːlt ['bæsəlt, bə'sɔːlt, bə'sɒlt]
basaltic bə'sɔːltɪk [-'sɒl-]
basan 'bæzən
Basan 'beɪsæn
bascule, -s 'bæskjuːl, -z
bas|e (s. adj. v.), -es; -er, -est, -ely,
  -eness; -ing, -ed beɪs, -ɪz; -ə*, -ɪst,
  -lɪ, -nɪs [-nəs]; -ɪŋ, -d; -t
base-ball 'beɪsbɔːl
base-born 'beɪsbɔːn
basecourt, -s 'beɪskɔːt [-kɔət], -s
Baseden 'beɪzdən
baseless, -ly, -ness 'beɪslɪs [-ləs], -lɪ,
  -nɪs [-nəs]
basement, -s 'beɪsmənt -s
bases (from base) 'beɪsɪz, (plur. of basis)
  'beɪsiːz
Basford (in Nottinghamshire) 'beɪsfəd,
  (in Staffordshire) 'bæsfəd
bash, -es, -ing, -ed bæʃ, -ɪz, -ɪŋ, -t
Basham (surname) 'bæʃəm
Bashan 'beɪʃæn
Bashford 'bæʃfəd
bash|ful, -fullest, -fully, -fulness 'bæʃ|-
  fʊl, -fʊlɪst [-fəlɪst, -flɪst], -fʊlɪ [-fəlɪ,
  -flɪ], -fʊlnɪs [-nəs]
basic (B.), -ally 'beɪsɪk, -əlɪ
basil (B.), bæzl [-zɪl]
basilica, -s, -n bə'zɪlɪkə [-'sɪl-], -z, -n
basilisk, -s 'bæzɪlɪsk [-z|ɪ-], -s
basin, -s 'beɪsn, -z
Basingstoke 'beɪzɪŋstəʊk
bas|is, -es 'beɪs|ɪs, -iːz

bask, -s, -ing, -ed bɑːsk, -s, -ɪŋ, -t
Basker (surname) 'bɑːskə*
Baskervill(e) 'bæskəvɪl
basket, -s -ful/s 'bɑːskɪt, -s, -fʊl/z
basket-ball, 'bɑːskɪtbɔːl
basket-work 'bɑːskɪtwɜːk
Basle bɑːl
basque (B.), -s bæsk [bɑːsk], -s
Basra(h) 'bæzrə ['bʌzrə, 'bæsrə]
bas-relief, -s 'bæsrɪˌliːf ['bɑːr-, 'bɑːsr-,
  ˌ--'-], -s
bass (fish, fibre, beer) (B.) bæs
bass (in music), -es beɪs, -ɪz
Bassanio bə'sɑːnɪəʊ [bæ's-, -njəʊ]
basset, -s 'bæsɪt, -s
basset-horn, -s 'bæsɪthɔːn [ˌ--'-], -z
Basset(t) 'bæsɪt
bassinet(te), -s ˌbæsɪ'net, -s
basso, -s 'bæsəʊ, -z
bassoon, -s, -ist/s bə'suːn [bə'zuːn], -z,
  -ɪst/s
bass-wood 'bæswʊd
bast bæst
Bastable 'bæstəbl
bastard, -s, -y 'bɑːstəd ['bæs-], -z, -ɪ
bastardiz|e [-is|e], -es, -ing, -ed 'bæst|-
  ədaɪz ['bɑːs-], -ɪz, -ɪŋ, -d
bast|e, -es, -ing, -ed beɪst, -s, -ɪŋ, -ɪd
bastille (B.), -s bæ'stiːl (bɑstiːj), -z
bastinad|o (s. v.), -oes, -oing, -oed
  ˌbæstɪ'neɪd|əʊ [-'nɑːd-], -əʊz, -əʊɪŋ,
  -əʊd
bastion, -s, -ed 'bæstɪən [-tjən], -z, -d
Basuto, -s bə'suːtəʊ [bə'zuː-], -z
Basutoland bə'suːtəʊlænd [bə'zuː-]
bat (s. v.), -s, -ting, -ted bæt, -s, -ɪŋ, -ɪd
Batavia bə'teɪvjə [-vɪə]
Batavier ˌbætə'vɪə*
batch, -es bætʃ, -ɪz
Batchel|ar, -or 'bætʃəl|ə* [-tʃɪl-], -ə*
bat|e (B.), -es, -ing, -ed beɪt, -s, -ɪŋ, -ɪd
Bate|man, -s, -son 'beɪt|mən, -s, -sən
Batey 'beɪtɪ
ba|th (s.) (B.), -ths bɑː|θ, -ðz
bath (v.), -s, -ing, -ed bɑːθ, -s, -ɪŋ, -t
bath-brick, -s 'bɑːθbrɪk, -s
bath-chair, -s bɑː'tʃeə*, -z
bath|e (s. v.), -es, -ing, -ed, -er/s beɪð,
  -z, -ɪŋ, -d, -ə*/z
bathetic bə'θetɪk [bæ-]
Batho 'bæθəʊ, 'beɪθəʊ
bat-horse, -s 'bæthɔːs, -ɪz
bathos 'beɪθɒs
bathrobe, -s 'bɑːθrəʊb, -z
bathroom, -s 'bɑːθrʊm [-ruːm], -z
Bathsheba bæθ'ʃiːbə ['bæθʃɪbə]
bath-stone 'bɑːθstəʊn
Bathurst 'bæθɜːst [-θəst]

42

bathyscaphe, -s 'bæθɪskæf, -s
bathysphere, -s 'bæθɪˌsfɪə*, -z
batik 'bætɪk
batiste bæ'tiːst [bə't-] (batist)
bat|man (military), -men 'bæt|mən, -mən
batman (oriental weight), -s 'bætmən, -z
baton, -s 'bætən [-tɒn, -tɔ̃ːŋ] (batɔ̃), -z
Baton Rouge ˌbætən'ruːʒ
batrachian, -s bə'treɪkjən [-kɪən], -z
bats bæts
bats|man, men 'bæts|mən, -mən
battalion, -s bə'tæljən, -z
battels 'bætlz
batt|en (s. v.), -ens, -ening, -ened 'bæt|n, -nz, -nɪŋ [-nɪŋ], -nd
Battenberg 'bætnbɜːg
batter (s. v.), -s, -ing, -ed 'bætə*, -z, -rɪŋ, -d
battering-ram, -s 'bætərɪŋræm, -z
Battersby 'bætəzbɪ
Battersea 'bætəsɪ
batter|y, -ies 'bætər|ɪ, -ɪz
batting (s.) 'bætɪŋ
Battishill 'bætɪʃɪl [-ʃl]
batt|le (s. v.) (B.), -les, -ling, -led 'bæt|l, -lz, -lɪŋ [-lɪŋ], -ld
battle-axe, -s 'bætlæks, -ɪz
battle-cruiser, -s 'bætlˌkruːzə*, -z
battle-cr|y, -ies 'bætlkr|aɪ, -aɪz
battledore [-door], -s 'bætldɔː* [-dɔə*], -z
battle-dress, -es 'bætldres, -ɪz
battlefield, -s 'bætlfiːld, -z
battle-ground, -s 'bætlgraʊnd, -z
battlement, -s, -ed 'bætlmənt, -s, -ɪd
battle-royal, -s 'bætl'rɔɪəl, -s
battleship, -s 'bætlʃɪp, -s
battue, -s bæ'tuː [-'tjuː, '--] (baty), -z
Battye 'bætɪ
Batum bɑː'tuːm
Baty 'bertɪ
bauble, -s 'bɔːbl, -z
Baucis 'bɔːsɪs
Bauer 'baʊə*
Baugh bɔː
Baughan bɔːn
Baughurst 'bɔːghɜːst
baulk (s. v.), -s, -ing, -ed bɔːk [bɔːlk], -s, -ɪŋ, -t
bauxite 'bɔːksaɪt
Bavaria, -n/s bə'veərɪə, -n/z
bawbee, -s ˌbɔː'biː, -z
Baugh bɔː
bawd, -s; -ry, -y bɔːd, -z; -rɪ, -ɪ
bawdy-hou|se, -ses 'bɔːdɪhaʊ|s, -zɪz
bawl, -s, -ing, -ed, -er/s bɔːl, -z, -ɪŋ, -d, -ə*/z

Bax bæks
Baxandall 'bæksəndɔːl
Baxter 'bækstə*
bay (s. adj. v.) (B.), -s, -ing, -ed, beɪ, -z, -ɪŋ, -d
bayard (B.) (horse), -s 'berəd, -z
Bayard (surname) 'beɪɑːd
Bayard (airship), -s beɪ'ɑːd ['beɪɑːd, 'berəd] (baja:r), -z
Bayeux baɪ'jɜː [baɪ'ɜː, old-fashioned beɪ'juː] (bajø)
bay-lea|f, -ves 'beɪliː|f, -vz
Bayl(e)y 'beɪlɪ
Bayliss 'beɪlɪs
Baynes beɪnz
bayonet, -s 'beɪənɪt [-nət, -net], -s
Bayreuth 'baɪrɔɪt ['-'-] (bai'rɔyt)
bay-rum ˌbeɪ'rʌm
bay-salt ˌbeɪ'sɔːlt [-'sɒlt]
Bayswater 'beɪzˌwɔːtə*
bay-tree, -s 'beɪtriː, -z
bay-window, -s ˌbeɪ'wɪndəʊ, -z
bazaar, -s bə'zɑː*, -z
Bazalgette 'bæzəldʒɪt [-dʒet]
bazooka, -s bə'zuːkə, -z
B.B.C. ˌbiːbiː'siː
B.C. ˌbiː'siː
B.C.G. ˌbiːsiː'dʒiː
bdellium 'delɪəm [-ljəm]
be; being, been biː: (strong form), bɪ (weak form); 'biːɪŋ, biːn [bɪn]
Beacall 'biːkɔːl
beach (s. v.) (B.), -es, -ing, -ed biːtʃ, -ɪz, -ɪŋ, -t
beachcomber (B.), -s 'biːtʃˌkəʊmə*, -z
beachhead, -s 'biːtʃhed, -z
beach-la-mar ˌbiːtʃlə'mɑː*
beachwear 'biːtʃweə*
beachy (B.) 'biːtʃɪ
beacon, -s 'biːkən, -z
Beaconsfield (place in Buckinghamshire) 'bekənzfiːld, (title of Benjamin Disraeli) 'biːk-
bead, -s, -ing/s, -ed, -er/s biːd, -z, -ɪŋ/z, -ɪd, -ə*/z
beadle (B.), -s 'biːdl, -z
Beadnall 'biːdnəl [-nl]
Beadon 'biːdn
bead|y, -ier, -iest, -iness 'biːd|ɪ, -ɪə*, -ɪɪst, -ɪnɪs [-məs]
beagle, -s 'biːgl, -z
beak, -s, -ed biːk, -s, -t
beaker, -s 'biːkə*, -z
Beal(e) biːl
beam (s. v.), -s, -ing, -ed biːm, -z, -ɪŋ, -d
beam-ends ˌbiːm'endz ['--]
beam-engine, -s 'biːmˌendʒɪn, -z

43

Beaminster 'bemɪnstə* [*locally also* 'bemɪstə*]
Note.—'biːm- *is sometimes heard from people unfamiliar with the place.*
Beamish 'biːmɪʃ
beam|y, -ily, -iness 'biːm|ɪ, -ɪlɪ [-əlɪ], -ɪnɪs [-ɪnəs]
bean, -s biːn, -z
beanfeast, -s, -er/s 'biːnfiːst, -s, -ə*/z
beano, -s 'biːnəʊ, -z
beanstalk, -s 'biːnstɔːk, -s
bear (*s. v.*), **-s, -ing, bore, born(e), bearer/s** beə*, -z, -rɪŋ, bɔː* [beə*], bɔːn, 'beərə*/z
bearab|le, -ly, -leness 'beərəb|l, -lɪ, -lnɪs [-lnəs]
bear-baiting 'beə,beɪtɪŋ
beard (**B.**), **-s, -ed** bɪəd, -z, -ɪd
Beard|er, -sley 'bɪəd|ə*, -zlɪ
beardless 'bɪədlɪs [-ləs]
Beare bɪə*
bear-garden, -s 'beə,gɑːdn, -z
bearing (*s.*), **-s** 'beərɪŋ, -z
bearing-rein, -s 'beərɪŋreɪn, -z
bearish, -ly, -ness 'beərɪʃ, -lɪ, -nɪs [-nəs]
Bearsden (*in Scotland*) beəz'den
bearskin, -s 'beəskɪn, -z
Bearsted 'bɜːsted, 'beəsted
Beasley 'biːzlɪ
beast, -s biːst, -s
beastl|y, -ier, -iest, -iness 'biːstl|ɪ, -ɪə* [-jə*], -ɪɪst [-jɪst], -ɪnɪs [-ɪnəs]
beat (*s. v.*), **-s, -ing/s, -en** biːt, -s, -ɪŋ/z, -n
beatific, -al, -ally ‚biːə'tɪfɪk [bɪə't-], -l, -əlɪ
beatification, -s biː‚ætɪfɪ'keɪʃn [bɪ‚æ-], -z
beati|fy, -fies, -fying, -fied bi:'ætɪ|faɪ [bɪ'æ-], -faɪz, -faɪɪŋ, -faɪd
beatitude, -s bi:'ætɪtjuːd [bɪ'æ-], -z
beatnik, -s 'biːtnɪk, -s
Beatri|ce, -x 'brətrɪ|s, -ks
Beatt|ie, -y 'biːt|ɪ, -ɪ
beau, -s bəʊ, -z
Beauchamp 'biːtʃəm
Beau|clerc, -clerk 'bəʊ|kleə*, -kleə*
Beaufort 'bəʊfət [-fɔːt]
Beaufoy 'bəʊfɔɪ
Beaujolais 'bəʊʒəleɪ [-ʒɒ-] (boʒɔlɛ)
Beaulieu (*in Hampshire*) 'bjuːlɪ
Beaumaris bəʊ'mærɪs [bjuː'm-] (*Welsh* biu'maris)
Beaumont 'bəʊmənt [-mɒnt]
Beaune bəʊn
beauteous, -ly, -ness 'bjuːtjəs [-tɪəs], -lɪ, -nɪs [-nəs]

44

beautician, -s bjuː'tɪʃn, -z
beautiful 'bjuːtəfʊl [-tɪf-]
beautifully 'bjuːtəflɪ [-tɪf-, -fʊlɪ, -fəlɪ]
beauti|fy, -fies, -fying, -fied, -fier/s 'bjuːtɪ|faɪ, -faɪz, -faɪɪŋ, -faɪd, -faɪə*/z
beaut|y, -ies 'bjuːt|ɪ, -ɪz
beauty-parlour, -s 'bjuːtɪpɑːlə*, -z
beauty-sleep 'bjuːtɪsliːp
beauty-spot, -s 'bjuːtɪspɒt, -s
Beav|an, -en 'bev|ən, -ən
beaver (**B.**), **-s** 'biːvə*, -z
Beaverbrook 'biːvəbrʊk
beaver|y, -ies 'biːvər|ɪ, -ɪz
Beavis 'biːvɪs
Beavon 'bevən
Beaworthy 'biː‚wɜːðɪ
Beazley 'biːzlɪ
becalm, -s, -ing, -ed bɪ'kɑːm [bə'k-], -z, -ɪŋ, -d
became (*from* **become**) bɪ'keɪm [bə'k-]
because bɪ'kɒz [bə'kɒz, bɪkəz, *rarely* bɪ'kɔːz, *colloquially also* kɒz, kəz]
Beccles 'beklz
Becher 'biːtʃə*
Bechstein, -s 'bekstaɪn, -z
Bechuana, -s, -land ‚betʃʊ'ɑːnə [be'tʃwɑː-], -z, -lænd
beck (**B.**), **-s** bek, -s
Becke bek
Beckenham 'bekənəm [-knəm, -knəm]
Becket(t) 'bekɪt
Beckles 'beklz
Beckley 'beklɪ
beck|on, -ons, -oning, -oned 'bek|ən, -əns, -nɪŋ [-ənɪŋ, -nɪŋ], -ənd
Beck|ton, -with 'bek|tən, -wɪθ
Becky 'bekɪ
becloud, -s, -ing, -ed bɪ'klaʊd [bə'k-], -z, -ɪŋ, -ɪd
becom|e, -es, -ing/ly, -ingness, became bɪ'kʌm [bə'k-], -z, -ɪŋ/lɪ, -ɪŋnɪs [-nəs], bɪ'keɪm [bə'k-]
Becontree 'bekəntri:
bed (*s. v.*), **-s, -ding, -ded** bed, -z, -ɪŋ, -ɪd
bedad bɪ'dæd [bə'd-]
Bedale (*North Yorkshire*) 'biːdl, 'biːdeɪl
Bedales 'biːdeɪlz
bedaub, -s, -ing, -ed bɪ'dɔːb [bə'd-], -z, -ɪŋ, -d
bedazz|le, -les, -ling, -led bɪ'dæz|l [bə-], -lz, -lɪŋ [-l̩ŋ], -ld
bedchamber, -s 'bed‚tʃeɪmbə*, -z
bedclothes 'bedkləʊðz [*old-fashioned* -kləʊz]
bedder, -s 'bedə*, -z
Beddgelert beð'gelət [-lɜːt] (*Welsh* be:ð'gelert)
bedding (*s.*) 'bedɪŋ

Beddoes 'bedəuz
Bede bi:d
bedeck, -s, -ing, -ed bɪ'dek [bə'd-], -s, -ɪŋ, -t
Bedel 'bi:dl, bɪ'del [bə'd-]
bedel(l), -s be'del [bɪ'd-, bə'd-], -z
bedev|il, -ils, -lling, -lled bɪ'dev|l [bə-], -lz, -lɪŋ [-lɪŋ], -ld
bedevilment bɪ'devlmənt [bə-]
bed|ew, -ews, -ewing, -ewed bɪ'd|ju: [bə'd-], -ju:z, -ju:ɪŋ [-jʊɪŋ], -ju:d
bedfellow, -s 'bed,feləʊ, -z
Bedford, -shire 'bedfəd, -ʃə* [-,ʃɪə*]
bedim, -s, -ming, -med bɪ'dɪm [bə'd-], -z, -ɪŋ, -d
Bedivere 'bedɪ,vɪə*
bediz|en, -ens, -ening, -ened bɪ'daɪz|n [bə'd-, -'dɪz-], -enz, -nɪŋ, -nd
bedjacket, -s 'bed,dʒækɪt, -s
Bedlam 'bedləm
Bedlamite, -s 'bedləmaɪt, -s
bedlinen 'bed,lɪnɪn
bedmaker, -s 'bed,meɪkə*, -z
Bedouin, -s 'bedʊɪn, -z
bedpan, -s 'bedpæn, -z
bedplate, -s 'bedpleɪt, -s
bedpost, -s 'bedpəʊst, -s
bedragg|le, -les, -ling, -led bɪ'dræg|l [bə'd-], -lz, -lɪŋ [-lɪŋ], -ld
bed-ridden 'bed,rɪdn
bedrock, -s ,bed'rɒk ['bedrɒk], -s
bedroom, -s 'bedrʊm [-ru:m], -z
Bedruthan bɪ'drʌðən [bə'd-]
Beds. bedz
bedside 'bedsaɪd
bedsitter, -s ,bed'sɪtə* ['-,--], -z
bed-sore, -s 'bedsɔ:*, [-sɔə*], -z
bedspread, -s 'bedspred, -z
bedstead, -s 'bedsted [-stɪd], -z
bedstraw, -s 'bedstrɔ:, -z
bedtime 'bedtaɪm
Bedwell 'bedwəl [-wel]
bee (B.), -s bi:, -z
Beeby 'bi:bɪ
beech (B.), -es bi:tʃ, -ɪz
Beecham 'bi:tʃəm
Beecher 'bi:tʃə*
Beeching 'bi:tʃɪŋ
beechnut, -s 'bi:tʃnʌt, -s
bee-eater, -s 'bi:,i:tə*, -z
bee|f, -ves bi:|f, -vz
beefburger, -s 'bi:f,bɜ:gə*, -z
beefeater, -s 'bi:f,i:tə*, -z
beefsteak, -s ,bi:f'steɪk [also '-- when attributive], -s
beef-tea ,bi:f'ti:
beef|y, -ier, -iest, -ily, -iness 'bi:f|ɪ, -ɪə*, -ɪɪst, -ɪlɪ [-əlɪ], -ɪnɪs [-məs]

bee-hive, -s 'bi:haɪv, -z
bee-line, -s 'bi:laɪn [,bi:'laɪn], -z
Beelzebub bi:'elzɪbʌb [bɪ'el-]
been (from be) bi:n [bɪn]
beer (B.), -s bɪə*, -z
Beerbohm 'bɪəbəʊm
beer-hou|se, -ses 'bɪəhaʊ|s, -zɪz
beer-money 'bɪə,mʌnɪ
Beersheba bɪə'ʃi:bə ['bɪəʃɪbə]
beer|y, -ier, -iest, -ily, -iness 'bɪər|ɪ, -ɪə*, -ɪɪst, -əlɪ [-ɪlɪ], -ɪnɪs [-məs]
Beesl(e)y 'bi:zlɪ
bee-sting, -s 'bi:stɪŋ, -z
beestings 'bi:stɪŋz
beeswax 'bi:zwæks
beeswing 'bi:zwɪŋ
beet, -s bi:t, -s
Beetham 'bi:θəm
Beethoven (composer) 'beɪthəʊvn, (London street) 'bi:thəʊvn
beet|le (s. v.), -les, -ling, -led 'bi:t|l, -lz, -lɪŋ [-lɪŋ], -ld
Beeton 'bi:tn
beetroot, -s 'bi:tru:t, -s
beeves (plur. of beef) bi:vz
be|fall, -falls, -falling, -fell, -fallen bɪ'fɔ:l [bə-], -'fɔ:lz, -fɔ:lɪŋ, -'fel, -'fɔ:lən
befit, -s, -ting/ly, -ted bɪ'fɪt [bə'f-], -s, -ɪŋ/lɪ, -ɪd
before bɪ'fɔ:* [bə'f-, -'fɔə*]
beforehand bɪ'fɔ:hænd [bə'f-, -'fɔəh-]
before - mentioned bɪ'fɔ:,menʃnd [-'fɔə,m-, -,-'--]
beforetime bɪ'fɔ:taɪm [bə'f-, -'fɔət-]
befoul, -s, -ing, -ed bɪ'faʊl [bə'f-], -z, -ɪŋ, -d
befriend, -s, -ing, -ed bɪ'frend [bə'f-], -z -ɪŋ, -ɪd
beg, -s, -ging, -ged beg, -z, -ɪŋ, -d
begad bɪ'gæd [bə'g-]
began (from begin) bɪ'gæn [bə'g-]
be|get, -gets, -getting, -gat, -gotten bɪ|'get [bə|-], -'gets, -'getɪŋ, -'gæt, -'gɒtn
beggar, -s 'begə*, -z
beggar|ly, -iness 'begəl|ɪ, -ɪnɪs [-məs]
beggar-my-neighbour ,begəmɪ'neɪbə*
beggary 'begərɪ
Beggs begz
be|gin, -gins, -ginning/s, -gan, -gun, -ginner/s bɪ|'gɪn [bə|-], -'gɪnz, -'gɪnɪŋ/z, -'gæn, -'gʌn, -'gɪnə*/z
begone bɪ'gɒn [bə'g-]
begonia, -s bɪ'gəʊnjə [bə'g-, -nɪə], -z
begorra bɪ'gɒrə [bə'g-]
begot, -ten (from beget) bɪ'gɒt [bə'g-], -n

begrim|e, -es, -ing, -ed bɪˈgraɪm [bəˈg-], -z, -ɪŋ, -d

begrudge, -es, -ing, -ed bɪˈgrʌdʒ [bəˈg-], -ɪz, -ɪŋ, -d

beguil|e, -es, -ing, -ed bɪˈgaɪl [bəˈg-], -z, -ɪŋ, -d

Begum, -s ˈbeɪgəm [old-fashioned ˈbiːg-], -z

begun (from begin) bɪˈgʌn [bəˈg-]

behalf bɪˈhɑːf [bəˈh-]

Behar (surname) ˈbiːhɑ*, (former spelling of Bihar, q.v.) bɪˈhɑː*

behav|e, -es, -ing, -ed bɪˈheɪv [bəˈh-], -z, -ɪŋ, -d

behaviour, -s bɪˈheɪvjə* [bəˈh-], -z

behaviouri|sm, -st/s bɪˈheɪvjərɪ|zəm [bəˈh-], -st/s

behead, -s, -ing, -ed bɪˈhed [bəˈh-], -z, -ɪŋ, -ɪd

beheld (from behold) bɪˈheld [bəˈh-]

behemoth (B.) bɪˈhiːmɒθ [ˈbiːhɪməʊθ]

behest, -s bɪˈhest [bəˈh-], -s

behind, -hand bɪˈhaɪnd [bəˈh-], -hænd

be|hold, -holds, -holding, -held, -holder/s bɪˈhəʊld [bə-], -ˈhəʊldz, -ˈhəʊldɪŋ, -ˈheld, -ˈhəʊldə*/z

beholden bɪˈhəʊldən [bəˈh-]

behoof bɪˈhuːf [bəˈh-]

behov|e, -es, -ing, -ed bɪˈhəʊv [bəˈh-], -z, -ɪŋ, -d

Behrens (English name), ˈbeərənz

beige beɪʒ [beɪdʒ]

being (s.), -s ˈbiːɪŋ, -z

being (from be) ˈbiːɪŋ

Beira ˈbaɪərə (Port. ˈbeɪrə)

Beirut ˌbeɪˈruːt

Beit baɪt

Beith biːθ

bejan, -s ˈbiːdʒən, -z

bejewel, -s, -led, bejewelling bɪˈdʒuːəl [-ˈdʒʊəl, -ˈdʒuːl, -ˈdʒuːɪl, -ˈdʒʊɪl], -z, -d, bɪˈdʒuːəlɪŋ [bɪˈdʒʊəlɪŋ, bɪˈdʒuːɪlɪŋ, -ˈdʒʊɪlɪŋ]

bel, -s bel, -z

belab|our, -ours, -ouring, -oured bɪˈleɪb|ə* [bəˈl-], -əz, -ərɪŋ, -əd

belated, -ly, -ness bɪˈleɪtɪd [bəˈl-], -lɪ, -nɪs [-nəs]

belaud, -s, -ing, -ed bɪˈlɔːd [bəˈl-], -z, -ɪŋ, -ɪd

Belaugh ˈbiːlɔː

belay, -s, -ing, -ed bɪˈleɪ [bəˈl-], -z, -ɪŋ, -d

belch, -es, -ing, -ed, -er/s beltʃ [belʃ], -ɪz, -ɪŋ, -t, -ə*/z

Belcher ˈbeltʃə*, ˈbelʃə*

beldam(e), -s ˈbeldəm, -z

beleaguer, -s, -ing, -ed, -er/s bɪˈliːgə* [bəˈl-], -z, -rɪŋ, -d, -rə*/z

belemnite, -s ˈbeləmnaɪt, -s

Belfast ˌbelˈfɑːst [also ˈ--, esp. when attributive]

belfr|y, -ies ˈbelfr|ɪ, -ɪz

Belg|ian/s, -ic ˈbeldʒ|ən/z, -ɪk

Belgium ˈbeldʒəm

Belgrade ˌbelˈgreɪd

Belgrave ˈbelgreɪv

Belgravia, -n belˈgreɪvjə [-vɪə], -n

Belial ˈbiːljəl [-lɪəl]

bel|ie, -ies, -ying, -ied bɪˈl|aɪ [bəˈl-], -aɪz, -aɪɪŋ, -aɪd

belief, -s bɪˈliːf [bəˈl-], -s

believ|e, -es, -ing/ly, -ed, -er/s; -able bɪˈliːv [bəˈl-], -z, -ɪŋ/lɪ, -d, -ə*/z; -əbl

belike bɪˈlaɪk [bəˈl-]

Belinda bɪˈlɪndə [beˈl-, bəˈl-]

Belisha bɪˈliːʃə [beˈl-, bəˈl-]

belitt|le, -les, -ling, -led bɪˈlɪt|l [bəˈl-], -lz, -lɪŋ, [-lɪŋ], -ld

Belize beˈliːz [bəˈl-]

bell (s. v.) (B.), -s, -ing, -ed bel, -z, -ɪŋ, -d

Bella ˈbelə

belladonna ˌbeləˈdɒnə

Bellamy ˈbeləmɪ

Bellatrix (star) ˈbelətrɪks [beˈleɪtrɪks, bəˈleɪt-]

bell-buoy, -s ˈbelbɔɪ, -z

belle (B.), -s bel, -z

Belleisle beˈliːl

Belle Isle ˌbelˈaɪl

Bellerophon bəˈlerəfn [bɪˈl-]

belles lettres ˌbelˈletrə [-ˈleɪə*] (belletr̩)

Bellevue ˌbelˈvjuː [ˈbelvjuː]

Bellew ˈbelju:

bell-founder, -s ˈbelˌfaʊndə*, -z

bell-glass, -es ˈbelglɑːs, -ɪz

bell-hanger, -s ˈbelˌhæŋə*, -z

bellicose, -ly ˈbelɪkəʊs, -lɪ

bellicosity ˌbelɪˈkɒsətɪ [-ɪtɪ]

belligerency bɪˈlɪdʒərənsɪ [beˈl-, bəˈl-, -dʒrən-]

belligerent, -s bɪˈlɪdʒərənt [beˈl-, bəˈl-, -dʒrənt], -s

Bellingham (in Northumberland) ˈbelɪndʒəm, (surname) ˈbelɪndʒəm, ˈbelɪŋəm, (S. London) ˈbelɪŋəm

bell|man, men ˈbel|mən [-mæn], -mən [-men]

bell-metal ˈbelˌmetl

Belloc ˈbelɒk

Bellot beˈlɒt

bellow, -s, -ing, -ed ˈbeləʊ, -z, -ɪŋ, -d

bellows (s.) ˈbeləʊz

Bellows ˈbeləʊz

bell-ringer, -s ˈbelˌrɪŋə*, -z

bell-rope, -s 'belrəʊp, -s
bell-shaped 'belʃeɪpt
bell-tent, -s 'beltent, -s
bell-tower, -s 'bel,taʊə*, -z
bell-wether, -s 'bel,weðə*, -z
bell|y (s. v.), -ies, -ying, -ied 'bel|ɪ, -ɪz, -ɪŋ, -ɪd
belly-ache, -s 'belɪeɪk, -s
belly-band, -s 'belɪbænd, -z
bellyful, -s 'belɪfʊl, -z
Belmont 'belmɒnt [-mənt]
Beloe 'biːləʊ
belong, -s, -ing/s, -ed bɪ'lɒŋ [bə'l-], -z, -ɪŋ/z, -d
beloved (used predicatively) bɪ'lʌvd [bə'l-], (used attributively or as noun) bɪ'lʌvd [bə'l-, -vɪd]
below bɪ'ləʊ [bə'l-]
Belsh|am, -aw 'belʃ|əm, -ɔː
Belshazzar bel'ʃæzə*
Belsize 'belsaɪz
Belstead 'belstɪd [-sted]
belt (B.), -s, -ed belt, -s, -ɪd
Belteshazzar ,beltɪ'ʃæzə*
belting, -s 'beltɪŋ, -z
Beltingham (in Northumberland) 'beltɪndʒəm
Belton 'beltən
Beluchistan bə'luːtʃɪstɑːn [bə'l-, bɪ'l-, -tæn, -,-'-]
belvedere (B.), -s 'belvɪ,dɪə* [-və-,belvɪ'd-], -z
Belvoir (castle) 'biːvə*, (in names of streets, etc.) 'belvwɔː* [-vɔɪə*, -vɔə*, -vɔː*]
bema, -s, -ta 'biːmə, -z, -tə
Beman 'biːmən
Bembridge 'bembrɪdʒ
Bemerton 'bemətən
bemoan, -s, -ing, -ed bɪ'məʊn [bə'm-], -z, -ɪŋ, -d
bemus|e, -es, -ing, -ed bɪ'mjuːz [bə'm-], -ɪz, -ɪŋ, -d
Ben ben
Benares (old form of Banaras, q.v.) bɪ'nɑːrɪz [be'n-, bə'n-]
Benbow 'benbəʊ
bench, -es bentʃ, -ɪz
bencher, -s 'bentʃə*, -z
bend (s. v.), -s, -ing, -ed, bent bend, -z, -ɪŋ, -ɪd, bent
beneath bɪ'niːθ [bə'n-]
Benedicite, -s ,benɪ'daɪsɪtɪ [,bene'diːtʃɪtɪ, -ətɪ], -z
Benedick, -s 'benɪdɪk, -s
Benedict 'benɪdɪkt, 'benɪt
benedictine (liqueur), -s ,benɪ'dɪktiːn, -z

Benedictine (monk), -s ,benɪ'dɪktɪn [-taɪn], -z
Note.—Members of the Order pronounce -tɪn.
benediction, -s ,benɪ'dɪkʃn, -z
Benedictus, -es ,benɪ'dɪktəs [,bene'dɪktʊs], -ɪz
benefaction, -s ,benɪ'fækʃn ['benɪf-], -z
benefactor, -s 'benɪfæktə* [,benɪ'f-], -z
benefactress, -es 'benɪfæktrɪs [,benɪ'f-, -tres], -ɪz
benefic bɪ'nefɪk
benefice, -s, -d 'benɪfɪs, -ɪz, -t
beneficen|ce, -t/ly bɪ'nefɪsn|s [bə'n-], -t/lɪ
benefici|al, -ally, -alness ,benɪ'fɪʃ|l, -əlɪ, -lnɪs [-nəs]
beneficiar|y, -ies ,benɪ'fɪʃər|ɪ [-ʃɪə-, -ʃjə-], -ɪz
benefit (s. v.), -s, -ing, -ed 'benɪfɪt, -s, -ɪŋ, -ɪd
Benelux 'benɪlʌks
Benenden 'benəndən
Bene't 'benɪt
Benet 'benɪt
Benét (American surname) be'neɪ
benevolen|ce, -t/ly bɪ'nevələn|s [bə'n-, -vl̩]-, -vʊl-], -t/lɪ
Bengal ,beŋ'gɔːl [,ben'g-, occasionally also '-- when followed by a stress]
Bengali, -s beŋ'gɔːlɪ [ben'g-], -z
bengal-light, -s ,beŋgɔːl'laɪt [,beng-], -s
Benge (surname) bendʒ
Benger (food) 'bendʒə* ['beŋgə*]
Benham 'benəm
Benians 'benɪənz [-njənz]
benighted bɪ'naɪtɪd [bə'n-]
benign, -est, -ly bɪ'naɪn [bə'n-], -ɪst, -lɪ
benignan|cy, -t/ly bɪ'nɪgnən|sɪ [bə'n-], -t/lɪ
benignity bɪ'nɪgnətɪ [bə'n-, -ɪtɪ]
Benin be'nɪn [bɪ'n-, bə'n-]
benison, -s 'benɪzn [-ɪsn], -z
Benis(s)on 'benɪsn
Benjamin 'bendʒəmɪn [-mən]
Benjamite, -s 'bendʒəmaɪt, -s
Bennet(t) 'benɪt
Bennette be'net [bə'n-]
Ben Nevis ,ben'nevɪs
Bennington 'benɪŋtən
Benoliel ,benə'lɪəl [-'liːl]
Bensham (near Newcastle) 'benʃəm
Bensley 'benzlɪ
Benson 'bensn
bent (s.), -s bent, -s
bent (from bend) bent
Benten 'bentən
Bentham 'bentəm [-nθəm]

47

Bentinck (*surname*) 'bentɪŋk, *old-fashioned* 'bentɪk, (*as name of street*) 'bentɪŋk

Bentley, -s 'bentlɪ, -z

Benton 'bentən

benumb, -s, -ing, -ed bɪ'nʌm [bə'n-], -z, -ɪŋ, -d

benzedrine 'benzədriːn [-drɪn]

benzene 'benziːn [-'-]

benzine 'benziːn [-'-]

benzoic ben'zəʊɪk ['benzəʊɪk]

benzoin 'benzəʊɪn

benzol 'benzɒl

benzoline 'benzəʊliːn

Beowulf 'beɪəʊwʊlf

bequea|th, -ths, -thing, -thed bɪ'kwiː|ð [bə'k-, -iː|θ], -ðz [-θs], -ðɪŋ, -ðd [-θt]

bequest, -s bɪ'kwest [bə'k-], -s

berat|e, -es, -ing, -ed bɪ'reɪt [bə-], -s, -ɪŋ, -ɪd

Berber, -s 'bɜːbə*, -z

berceuse beə'sɜːz (bɛrsøːz)

Bere bɪə*

Berea bə'rɪə [bɪ'r-]

bereav|e, -es, -ing, -ed, bereft bɪ'riːv [bə'r-], -z, -ɪŋ, -d, bɪ'reft [bə'r-]

bereavement, -s bɪ'riːvmənt [bə'r-], -s

bereft (*from* bereave) bɪ'reft [bə'r-]

Berengaria ˌberɪŋ'geərɪə [-reŋ-, -rəŋ-]

Berenice (*in ancient Egypt, etc.*) ˌberɪ'naɪsɪ: [-sɪ], (*opera by Handel*) ˌberɪ'niːtʃɪ

Beresford 'berɪzfəd [-ɪsf-]

beret, -s 'bereɪ ['berɪ], -z ['berɪt, -s]

berg, -s bɜːɡ, -z

bergamot, -s 'bɜːɡəmɒt [-mət], -s

Bergen 'bɜːɡən ['beəɡ-]

Berger (*English surname*) 'bɜːdʒə*

beriberi ˌberɪ'berɪ

Bering 'berɪŋ ['bɪər-, 'beər-]

Berkeleian bɑː'kliːən [-'klɪən]

Berkeley (*in England*) 'bɑːklɪ [*rarely* 'bɜːk-], (*in U.S.A.*) 'bɜːklɪ

berkelium 'bɜːklɪəm

Berkhamsted [-mpstead] 'bɜːkəmpstɪd [-sted, *less commonly* 'bɑːk-]

Note.—*The usual pronunciation is* 'bɜːk-, *but the form* 'bɑːk- *is used by some residents.*

Berks. bɑːks [*rarely* bɜːks]

Berkshire 'bɑːkʃə* [-ˌʃɪə*, *rarely* 'bɜːk-]

Berlin (*in Germany*) bɜː'lɪn [*occasionally also* '-- *when attributive*], (*surname*) 'bɜːlɪn, bɜː'lɪn, (*town in U.S.A.*) 'bɜːlɪn

Berlioz (*composer*) 'beəlɪəʊz ['bɜːl-] (bɛrljoːz)

Berlitz 'bɜːlɪts [-'-]

Bermondsey 'bɜːməndzɪ

Bermuda, -s bə'mjuːdə, -z

Bernard (*Christian name*) 'bɜːnəd, (*surname*) bɜː'nɑːd, 'bɜːnəd

Bern(e) bɜːn [beən]

Berners 'bɜːnəz

Bernese ˌbɜː'niːz [*also* '-- *when attributive*]

Bernice (*biblical name*) bɜː'naɪsɪ: [-sɪ], (*modern Christian name*) 'bɜːnɪs, (*surname*) 'bɜːnɪs, bɜː'niːs

Bernstein 'bɜːnstaɪn, -stiːn

Berowne bə'rəʊn

Berridge 'berɪdʒ

berr|y (B.), -ies 'ber|ɪ, -ɪz

bersaglieri ˌbeəsɑːlɪ'eərɪ: [-rɪ] (bersaʎʎeːri)

berserk, -s -er/s bə'sɜːk [bɜː-], -s, -ə*/z

berth (*s.*), -s bɜːθ, -s [bɜːðz]

berth (*v.*), -s, -ing, -ed bɜːθ, -s, -ɪŋ, -t

Bertha 'bɜːθə

Berthold 'bɜːθəʊld

Bertie (*Christian name*) 'bɜːtɪ, (*surname*) 'bɑːtɪ, 'bɜːtɪ

Bertram 'bɜːtrəm

Berwick, -shire 'berɪk, -ʃə* [-ˌʃɪə*]

beryl (B.), -s 'berɪl, -z

beryllium be'rɪljəm [bə'r-, -lɪəm]

Besant 'besənt, 'bezənt, bɪ'zænt [bə'z-]

beseech, -es, -ing/ly, besought bɪ'siːtʃ [bə's-], -ɪz, -ɪŋ/lɪ, bɪ'sɔːt [bə's-]

beseem, -s, -ing, -ed bɪ'siːm [bə's-], -z, -ɪŋ, -d

beset, -s -ting bɪ'set [bə's-], -s, -ɪŋ

beshrew bɪ'ʃru: [bə'ʃ-]

beside, -s bɪ'saɪd [bə's-], -z

besieg|e, -es, -ing, -ed, -er/s bɪ'siːdʒ [bə's-], -ɪz, -ɪŋ, -d, -ə*/z

Besley 'bezlɪ

besmear, -s, -ing, -ed bɪ'smɪə* [bə's-], -z, -rɪŋ, -d

besmirch, -es, -ing, -ed bɪ'smɜːtʃ [bə's-], -ɪz, -ɪŋ, -t

besom, -s 'biːzəm ['bɪz-], -z

besotted, -ly, -ness bɪ'sɒtɪd [bə's-], -lɪ, -nɪs [-nəs]

besought (*from* beseech) bɪ'sɔːt [bə's-]

bespang|le, -les, -ling, -led bɪ'spæŋg|l [bə's-], -lz, -lɪŋ [-lɪŋ], -ld

bespatter, -s, -ing, -ed bɪ'spætə* [bə's-], -z, -rɪŋ, -d

bespeak, -s, -ing, bespoke, bespoken bɪ'spiːk [bə's-], -s, -ɪŋ, bɪ'spəʊk [bə's-], bɪ'spəʊkən [bə's-]

bespectacled bɪ'spektəkld [-tɪk-]

besprink|le, -les, -ling, -led bɪ'sprɪŋk|l [bə's-], -lz, -lɪŋ [-lɪŋ], -ld

Bess bes

Bessarabia ˌbesəˈreɪbjə [-bɪə]
Bessborough ˈbezbrə
Bessemer ˈbesɪmə* [-səmə*]
Besses o' th' Barn ˌbesɪzəðˈbɑːn
Bessie ˈbesɪ
best (adj. adv. v.) (B.), -s, -ing, -ed best, -s, -ɪŋ, -ɪd
bestial, -ly, -ism ˈbestjəl [-tɪəl], -ɪ, -ɪzəm
bestialit|y, -ies ˌbestɪˈælət|ɪ [-ɪt|ɪ], -ɪz
bestiar|y, -ies ˈbestɪər|ɪ [-tjə-], -ɪz
bestir, -s, -ring, -red bɪˈstɜː* [bə's-], -z, -rɪŋ, -d
best|ow, -ows, -owing, -owed bɪˈst|əʊ [bə's-], -əʊz, -əʊɪŋ, -əʊd
bestowal, -s bɪˈstəʊəl [bə's-], -z
bestrid|e, -es, -ing, bestrode, bestridden bɪˈstraɪd [bə's-], -z, -ɪŋ, bɪˈstrəʊd [bə's-], bɪˈstrɪdn [bə's-]
Beswick ˈbezɪk
bet (s. v.) (B.), -s, -ting, -ted, -tor/s bet, -s, -ɪŋ, -ɪd, -ə*/z
beta, -s ˈbiːtə, -z
be|take, -takes, -taking, -took, -taken bɪˈteɪk [bə-], -ˈteɪks, -ˈteɪkɪŋ, -ˈtʊk, -ˈteɪkən
betel, -nut/s ˈbiːtl, -nʌt/s
Betelgeuse ˌbiːtlˈɜːz [ˌbet-, ˈbetldʒuːz]
bête noire, -s ˌbeɪtˈnwɑː* [ˌbet-] (beːtnwaːr), -z
Bethany ˈbeθənɪ [-θnɪ]
Bethel ˈbeθl [beˈθel]
    Note.—When used to denote a non-conformist chapel, the pronunciation is ˈbeθl.
Bethesda beˈθezdə [bɪˈθ-, bəˈθ-]
bethink, -s, -ing, bethought bɪˈθɪŋk [bəˈθ-], -s, -ɪŋ, bɪˈθɔːt [bəˈθ-]
Bethlehem ˈbeθlɪhem [-lɪəm, -ljəm]
Bethnal ˈbeθnəl
Bethphage ˈbeθfədʒɪ
Bethsaida beθˈseɪdə [-ˈsaɪdə]
Bethune (surname) ˈbiːtn, (in names of streets, etc.) beˈθjuːn [bɪˈθ-, bəˈθ-]
Béthune (French town) beˈθjuːn [bɪˈθ-, bəˈθ-, -ˈtjuːn, -ˈtuːn] (betyn)
betide bɪˈtaɪd [bəˈt-]
betimes bɪˈtaɪmz [bəˈt-]
Betjeman ˈbetʃəmən [-tjə-]
betok|en, -ens, -ening, -ened bɪˈtəʊk|ən [bəˈt-], -ənz, -nɪŋ [-ənɪŋ], -ənd
betony ˈbetənɪ
betook (from betake) bɪˈtʊk [bəˈt-]
betray, -s, -ing, -ed, -er/s bɪˈtreɪ [bəˈt-], -z, -ɪŋ, -d, -ə*/z [-ˈtreə*/z]
betrayal, -s bɪˈtreɪəl [bəˈt-, -ˈtreɪl], -z
betro|th, -ths, -thing, -thed bɪˈtrəʊ|ð [bə't-, əʊ|θ], -ðz [-θs], -ðɪŋ, -ðd [-θt]

betrothal, -s bɪˈtrəʊðl [bə't-], -z
Betsy ˈbetsɪ
Betteley ˈbetəlɪ
better (s. adj. v.), -s, -ing, -ed ˈbetə*, -z, -rɪŋ, -d
betterment ˈbetəmənt
betting, -s ˈbetɪŋ, -z
Bettws ˈbetəs (Welsh ˈbetus)
Bettws-y-Coed ˌbetəsɪˈkɔɪd [-tʊsɪ-, -təɪ-, -ˈkəʊɪd] (Welsh ˈbetusəˈkoɪd)
Betty ˈbetɪ
between bɪˈtwiːn [bəˈt-]
betweentimes bɪˈtwiːntaɪmz [bəˈt-]
betwixt bɪˈtwɪkst [bəˈt-]
Beulah ˈbjuːlə
Beurle bəːl
beurré (pear), -s ˈbjʊərɪ, -z
Beuthin ˈbjuːθɪn
Bevan ˈbevən
bev|el (s. v.), -els, -elling, -elled ˈbev|l, -lz, -lɪŋ [-əlɪŋ], -ld
Beven ˈbevən
beverage, -s ˈbevərɪdʒ, -ɪz
Beveridge ˈbevərɪdʒ
Beverley ˈbevəlɪ
Beves ˈbiːvɪs
Bevin ˈbevɪn
Bevis ˈbiːvɪs, ˈbevɪs
bev|y, -ies ˈbev|ɪ, -ɪz
bewail, -s, -ing, -ed bɪˈweɪl [bə'w-], -z, -ɪŋ, -d
beware bɪˈweə* [bə'w-]
Bewick(e) ˈbjuːɪk [ˈbjʊɪk]
bewild|er, -ers, -ering/ly, -ered, -erment/s bɪˈwɪld|ə* [bə'w-], -əz, -ərɪŋ/lɪ, -əd, -əmənt/s
bewitch, -es, -ing/ly, -ed, -ment/s bɪˈwɪtʃ [bə'w-], -ɪz, -ɪŋ/lɪ, -t, -mənt/s
Bewley ˈbjuːlɪ
bewrayeth bɪˈrenθ [bə'r-]
Bexhill ˌbeksˈhɪl
Bexley ˈbekslɪ
Bey, -s beɪ, -z
beyond bɪˈjɒnd [bɪˈɒnd]
Beyrout(h) (former spelling of Beirut) ˌbeɪˈruːt
Beyts beɪts
bezant, -s ˈbezənt, -s
bezel, -s ˈbezl, -z
bezique bɪˈziːk [beˈz-, bəˈz-]
bheest|y, -ies ˈbiːst|ɪ, -ɪz
Biarritz ˌbɪəˈrɪts [ˈ--] (bjarits)
bias (s. v.), -(s)es, -(s)ing, -(s)ed ˈbaɪəs, -ɪz, -ɪŋ, -t
biax|al, -ial ˌbaɪˈæks|l -rəl [-jəl]
bib, -s bɪb, -z
Bibby ˈbɪbɪ
Bible, -s ˈbaɪbl, -z

biblic|al, -ally 'bɪblɪk|l, -əlɪ
bibliograph|er/s, -y, -ies ˌbɪblɪ'ɒ-grəf|ə*/z, -ɪ, -ɪz
bibliolat|er/s, -ry ˌbɪblɪ'ɒlət|ə*/z, -rɪ
bibliomania ˌbɪblɪəʊ'meɪnjə [-nɪə]
bibliomaniac, -s ˌbɪblɪəʊ'meɪnɪæk [-njæk], -s
bibliophile, -s 'bɪblɪəʊfaɪl [-ljəf-], -z
bibulous 'bɪbjʊləs
bicarbonate, -s baɪ'kɑ:bənɪt [ˌbaɪ'k--bnɪt, -bnɪt, -eɪt, -ət], -s
bice baɪs
Bice 'bi:tʃɪ
bicentenar|y (s. adj.), -ies ˌbaɪsen'ti:-nər|ɪ [-'ten-, baɪ'sentɪn-], -ɪz
bicentennial ˌbaɪsen'tenjəl [-nɪəl]
biceps, -es 'baɪseps, -ɪz
Bicester 'bɪstə*
bichloride ˌbaɪ'klɔ:raɪd
bichromate ˌbaɪ'krəʊmeɪt [-mɪt]
bicker, -s, -ing/s, -ed, -er/s 'bɪkə*, -z, -rɪŋ/z, -d, -rə*/z
Bickerstaff 'bɪkəstɑ:f
Bickersteth 'bɪkəsteθ [-stɪθ]
Bickerton 'bɪkətən
Bickford 'bɪkfəd
Bick|leigh, -ley 'bɪk|lɪ, -lɪ
Bicknell 'bɪknəl
bicuspid, -s ˌbaɪ'kʌspɪd [bɪ'k-], -z
bicyc|le (s. v.), -les, -ling, -led 'baɪsɪk|l [-səkl], -lz, -lɪŋ, -ld
bicyclist, -s 'baɪsɪklɪst [-sək-], -s
bid (s.), -s bɪd, -z
bid (v.) (at auction), -s, -ding, -der/s bɪd, -z, -ɪŋ, -ə*/z
bid (v.) (command), -s, -ding, bade, bidden bɪd, -z, -ɪŋ, bæd [beɪd], 'bɪdn
Bidder 'bɪdə*
Biddle 'bɪdl
Biddulph 'bɪdʌlf [-dəlf]
bid|e (B.), -es, -ing, -ed baɪd, -z, -ɪŋ, -ɪd
Bideford 'bɪdɪfəd
Biden 'baɪdn
bidet, -s 'bi:deɪ, -z (bidɛ)
biennial, -ly baɪ'enɪəl [-njəl], -ɪ
bier, -s bɪə*, -z
biff (s. v.), -s, -ing, -ed bɪf, -s, -ɪŋ, -t
bifocal (s. adj.), -s ˌbaɪ'fəʊkl, -z
bifurcat|e, -es, -ing, -ed 'baɪfəkeɪt [-fɜ:-], -s, -ɪŋ, -ɪd
bifurcation, -s ˌbaɪfə'keɪʃn [-fɜ:-], -z
big, -ger, -gest, -ness bɪg, -ə*, -ɪst, -nɪs [-nəs]
bigamist, -s 'bɪgəmɪst, -s
bigamous, -ly 'bɪgəməs, -lɪ
bigam|y, -ies 'bɪgəm|ɪ, -ɪz
Bigelow 'bɪgɪləʊ [-gəl-]
Bigge bɪg

biggish 'bɪgɪʃ
Big|gs, -ham bɪg|z, -əm
bight, -s baɪt, -s
Bignell 'bɪgnəl
Bigod 'baɪgɒd
bigot, -s, -ed; -ry 'bɪgət, -s, -ɪd; -rɪ
bigraph, -s 'baɪgrɑ:f [-græf], -s
bigwig, -s 'bɪgwɪg, -z
Bihar bɪ'hɑ:* (Hindi. byhar)
bijou, -s 'bi:ʒu:, -z
bik|e (s. v.), -es, -ing, -ed baɪk, -s, -ɪŋ, -t
bikini (B.), -s bɪ'ki:nɪ, -z
bilabial (s. adj.), -s ˌbaɪ'leɪbjəl [-bɪəl], -z
bilater|al, -ally ˌbaɪ'lætər|əl, -əlɪ
Bilbao bɪl'bɑ:əʊ [-'berəʊ]
bilberr|y, -ies 'bɪlbər|ɪ, -ɪz
Bilborough 'bɪlbərə
Bilbrough 'bɪlbrə
bile baɪl
bilg|e (s. v.), -es, -ing, -ed bɪldʒ, -ɪz, -ɪŋ, -d
bilge-pump, -s 'bɪldʒpʌmp, -s
bilge-water 'bɪldʒˌwɔ:tə*
bilgy 'bɪldʒɪ
biliary 'bɪljərɪ [-lɪər-]
bilingual, -ism baɪ'lɪŋgwəl [ˌbaɪ'l-], -ɪzəm
bilious, -ly, -ness 'bɪljəs [-lɪəs], -lɪ, -nɪs [-nəs]
biliteral ˌbaɪ'lɪtərəl
bilk, -s, -ing, -ed bɪlk, -s, -ɪŋ, -t
bill (B.), -s bɪl, -z
Billerica 'bɪlrɪkə
Billericay ˌbɪlə'rɪkɪ
billet (s. v.), -s, -ing, -ed 'bɪlɪt, -s, -ɪŋ, -ɪd
billet-doux (sing.) ˌbɪleɪ'du: [-lɪ'd-], (plur.) -z
bill-hook, -s 'bɪlhʊk, -s
billiard, -s; -ball/s, -cue/s, -marker/s, -room/s, -table/s 'bɪljəd, -z; -bɔ:l/z, -kju:/z, -ˌmɑ:kə*/z, -rʊm/z [-ru:m/z], -ˌteɪbl/z
Billing, -s, -hurst 'bɪlɪŋ, -z, -hɜ:st
Billingsgate 'bɪlɪŋzgɪt [-geɪt]
Billington 'bɪlɪŋtən
billion, -s, -th/s 'bɪljən, -z, -θ/s
bill-of-fare, -s ˌbɪləv'feə* [-lə'feə*], -z
bill|ow, -ows, -owy 'bɪl|əʊ, -əʊz, -əʊɪ
bill-poster, -s 'bɪlˌpəʊstə*, -s
bill-stick|er/s, -ing 'bɪlˌstɪk|ə*/z, -ɪŋ
bill|y (B.), -ies 'bɪl|ɪ, -ɪz
billycock, -s 'bɪlɪkɒk, -s
billy-goat, -s 'bɪlɪgəʊt, -s
Bilston(e) 'bɪlstən
Bilton 'bɪltən
bimestrial ˌbaɪ'mestrɪəl

bimetalli|sm, -st/s ˌbaɪˈmetəlɪ|zəm [-tǀ-], -st/s

bi-monthl|y, -ies ˌbaɪˈmʌnθl|ɪ, -ɪz

bin, -s bɪn, -z

binary ˈbaɪnərɪ

binaural ˌbaɪnˈɔːrəl [bɪn-]

bind (s. v.), -s, -ing, bound, binder/s baɪnd, -z, -ɪŋ, baʊnd, ˈbaɪndə*/z

bindweed ˈbaɪndwiːd

Binegar ˈbɪnɪgə*

binge, -s bɪndʒ, -ɪz

Bing|ham, -ley ˈbɪŋ|əm, -lɪ

bingo ˈbɪŋgəʊ

Bink(e)s bɪŋks

binnacle, -s ˈbɪnəkl, -z

Binn|ey, -ie ˈbɪn|ɪ, -ɪ

Binns bɪnz

binocle, -s ˈbɪnɒkl [ˈbaɪn-, -nəkl], -z

binocular (s.), -s bɪˈnɒkjʊlə* [ˌbaɪˈn-, -kjəl-], -z

binocular (adj.) ˌbaɪˈnɒkjʊlə* [bɪˈn-, -kjəl-]

binomial ˌbaɪˈnəʊmjəl [-mɪəl]

Binste(a)d ˈbɪnstɪd [-sted]

Binyon ˈbɪnjən

biochemist, -s, -ry ˌbaɪəʊˈkemɪst, -s, -rɪ

biogenesis ˌbaɪəʊˈdʒenɪsɪs [-nəsɪs]

biograph, -s ˈbaɪəʊgrɑːf [-græf], -s

biographer, -s baɪˈɒgrəfə* [bɪˈɒ-], -z

biographic, -al, -ally ˌbaɪəʊˈgræfɪk [ˌbɪəʊˈg-, brəˈg-], -l, -əlɪ

biograph|y, -ies baɪˈɒgrəf|ɪ [bɪˈɒ-], -ɪz

biologic, -al, -ally ˌbaɪəʊˈlɒdʒɪk, -l, -əlɪ

biolog|ist/s, -y baɪˈɒlədʒ|ɪst/s, -ɪ

biometric/s, -al ˌbaɪəʊˈmetrɪk/s, -l

biometry baɪˈɒmɪtrɪ [-mətrɪ]

biophysic|s, -al ˌbaɪəʊˈfɪzɪk|s, -l

bioscope, -s ˈbaɪəskəʊp, -s

biosphere, -s ˈbaɪəʊˌsfɪə*, -z

biparous ˈbɪpərəs

bipartisan ˌbaɪpɑːtɪˈzæn |ˌ-ˈ---|

bipartite ˌbaɪˈpɑːtaɪt [ˈbaɪˌpɑːtaɪt]

biped, -s ˈbaɪped, -z

bipedal ˈbaɪˌpedl

biplane, -s ˈbaɪpleɪn, -s

biquadratic (s. adj.), -s ˌbaɪkwɒˈdrætɪk [-kwəˈd-], -s

birch (s. v.) (B.), -es, -ing, -ed bɜːtʃ, -ɪz, -ɪŋ, -t

birchen ˈbɜːtʃən

Birchenough ˈbɜːtʃɪnʌf

bird (B.), -s bɜːd, -z

bird-cage ˈbɜːdkeɪdʒ, -ɪz

bird-call, -s ˈbɜːdkɔːl, -z

bird-fancier, -s ˈbɜːdˌfænsɪə* [-sjə*], -z

birdie, -s ˈbɜːdɪ, -z

bird-lime ˈbɜːdlaɪm

bird-nest, -s, -ing, -ed ˈbɜːdnest, -s, -ɪŋ, -ɪd

birdseed ˈbɜːdsiːd

bird's-eye (s. adj.), -s ˈbɜːdzaɪ, -z

Birdseye ˈbɜːdzaɪ

bird's-nest (s. v.), -s, -ing, -ed ˈbɜːdznest, -s, -ɪŋ, -ɪd

bireme, -s ˈbaɪriːm [ˈbaɪər-], -z

biretta, -s bɪˈretə, -z

Birkbeck (surname) ˈbɜːbek, ˈbɜːkbek, (college in London) ˈbɜːkbek

Birkenhead (in Merseyside) ˈbɜːkənhed [locally ˌbɜːkənˈhed], (Earl) ˈbɜːkənhed

Birkett ˈbɜːkɪt

Birley ˈbɜːlɪ

Birling ˈbɜːlɪŋ

Birmingham ˈbɜːmɪŋəm

Birnam ˈbɜːnəm

biro, -s ˈbaɪərəʊ, -z

Biron (modern surname) ˈbaɪərən
Note.—bɪˈruːn in 'Love's Labour's Lost'.

Birrell ˈbɪrəl

birth, -s bɜːθ, -s

birth-control ˈbɜːθkən.trəʊl

birthday, -s ˈbɜːθdeɪ [-dɪ], -z

birthmark, -s ˈbɜːθmɑːk, -s

birthplace, -s ˈbɜːθpleɪs, -ɪz

birth-rate, -s ˈbɜːθreɪt, -s

birthright, -s ˈbɜːθraɪt, -s

Birtwistle ˈbɜːt.wɪsl

bis bɪs

Biscay ˈbɪskeɪ [-kɪ]

biscuit, -s ˈbɪskɪt, -s

bisect, -s, -ing, -ed, -or/s baɪˈsekt, -s, -ɪŋ, -ɪd, -ə*/z

bisection, -s baɪˈsekʃn, -z

bisexual ˌbaɪˈseksjʊəl [-ksjwəl, -ksjʊl, -kʃjʊəl, -kʃwəl, -kʃʊl]

bishop (B.), -s; -ric/s ˈbɪʃəp, -s; -rɪk/s

Bishopsgate ˈbɪʃəpsgeɪt [-gɪt]

Bishopst|oke, -on ˈbɪʃəpstǀəʊk, -ən

Bishop's Stortford ˌbɪʃəpsˈstɔːfəd [-ɔːtf-]

Bisley, -s ˈbɪzlɪ, -z

Bismarck ˈbɪzmɑːk (ˈbismark)

bismuth ˈbɪzməθ

bison, -s ˈbaɪsn, -z

Bispham (surname) ˈbɪsfəm, ˈbɪspəm, (place) ˈbɪspəm

bisque, -s bɪsk, -s

Bisseker ˈbɪsɪkə*

Bissell ˈbɪsl

bissextile, -s bɪˈsekstaɪl, -z

bistour|y, -ies ˈbɪstʊr|ɪ [-tər-], -ɪz

bistre ˈbɪstə*

bistro(t), -s ˈbiːstrəʊ, -z (bistro)

bisulph|ate, -ite ˌbaɪˈsʌlf|eɪt [-ɪt], -aɪt
bisurated ˈbɪsjʊəreɪtɪd
bit, -s bɪt, -s
bit (from bite) bɪt
bitch, -es bɪtʃ, -ɪz
bit|e (s. v.), -es, -ing, bit, bitten,
    biter/s baɪt, -s, -ɪŋ, bɪt, ˈbɪtn,
    ˈbaɪtə*/z
Bithell bɪˈθel, ˈbɪθəl
Bithynia bɪˈθɪnɪə [baɪˈθ-, -njə]
bitter, -er, -est, -ly, -ness ˈbɪtə*, -rə*,
    -rɪst, -lɪ, -nɪs [-nəs]
bittern, -s ˈbɪtən [-tɜːn], -z
bitters ˈbɪtəz
bittersweet ˈbɪtəswiːt [ˌ--ˈ-]
bitumen, -s ˈbɪtjʊmɪn [-men, -mən,
    bɪˈtjuːm-], -z
bituminous bɪˈtjuːmɪnəs
bivalen|ce, -t ˈbaɪˌveɪlən|s [ˌbaɪˈv-], -t
bivalve, -s ˈbaɪvælv, -z
bivouac (s. v.), -s, -king, -ked ˈbɪvʊæk
    [-vwæk], -s, -ɪŋ, -t
bi-weekl|y (s. adv.), -ies ˌbaɪˈwiːkl|ɪ,
    -ɪz
bizarre bɪˈzɑː* (bizaːr)
Bizet ˈbiːzeɪ (bizɛ)
blab, -s, -bing, -bed, -ber/s blæb, -z,
    -ɪŋ, -d, -ə*/z
Blachford ˈblæʃfəd
black (s. adj. v.) (B.), -s; -er, -est, -ish,
    -ly, -ness; -ing, -ed blæk, -s; -ə*, -ɪst,
    -ɪʃ, -lɪ, -nɪs [-nəs]; -ɪŋ, -t
blackamoor, -s ˈblækəˌmʊə* [-mɔə*,
    -mɔː*], -z
blackball (v.), -s, -ing, -ed ˈblækbɔːl, -z,
    -ɪŋ, -d
blackbeetle, -s ˌblækˈbiːtl, -z
blackberr|y, -ies ˈblækbər|ɪ [-ˌber-], -ɪz
blackberrying ˈblækˌberɪŋ [-bər-]
blackbird, -s ˈblækbɜːd, -z
blackboard, -s ˈblækbɔːd [-bɔəd], -z
Blackburn(e) ˈblækbɜːn
blackcap, -s ˈblækkæp, -s
black-cattle ˌblækˈkætl
blackcock, -s ˈblækkɒk, -s
black-currant, -s ˌblækˈkʌrənt, -s
black-draught ˌblækˈdrɑːft
black|en, -ens, -ening, -ened ˈblæk|ən,
    -ənz, -ṇɪŋ [-ənɪŋ, -nɪŋ], -ənd
Blackett ˈblækɪt
black-eye, -s ˌblækˈaɪ, -z
black-eyed ˈblækaɪd [ˌ-ˈ-]
Blackford ˈblækfəd
Blackfriars ˌblækˈfraɪəz [ˈ--, esp. when
    attributive]
blackgame ˈblækgeɪm
blackguard, -s, -ly ˈblægɑːd, -z, -lɪ
blackhead, -s ˈblækhed, -z

Blackheath ˌblækˈhiːθ [also ˈ--, accord-
    ing to sentence-stress]
Blackie ˈblækɪ, in the N. also ˈbleɪkɪ
blacking (s.), -s ˈblækɪŋ, -z
blacklead (s. v.), -s, -ing, -ed ˌblækˈled,
    -z, -ɪŋ, -ɪd
blackleg, -s ˈblækleg, -z
black-letter ˌblækˈletə* [ˈblækˌl-]
Blackley (Manchester) ˈbleɪklɪ, (sur-
    name) ˈblæklɪ
black-list (s. v.), -s, -ing, -ed ˈblæklɪst,
    -s, -ɪŋ, -ɪd
blackmail (s. v.), -s, -ing, -ed, -er/s
    ˈblækmeɪl, -z, -ɪŋ, -d, -ə*/z
Blackman ˈblækmən
Blackmoor ˈblækˌmʊə* [-mɔə*, -mɔː*]
Blackmore ˈblækmɔː* [-mɔə*]
black-out, -s ˈblækaʊt, -s
Blackpool ˈblækpuːl   ·
Blackpudlian, -s ˌblækˈpʌdlɪən [-ljən], -z
Blackrock ˈblækrɒk
black-rod, -s ˌblækˈrɒd, -z
blacksmith, -s ˈblæksmɪθ, -s
Blackston(e) ˈblækstən
blackthorn, -s ˈblækθɔːn, -z
Blackwall ˈblækwɔːl
blackwater (B.) ˈblækˌwɔːtə*
Blackwell ˈblækwəl [-wel]
Blackwood (surname) ˈblækwʊd, (place
    in Gwent) ˌblækˈwʊd
bladder, -s ˈblædə*, -z
bladderwort, -s ˈblædəwɜːt, -s
blade, -s bleɪd, -z
blade-bone, -s ˈbleɪdbəʊn, -z
blaeberr|y, -ies ˈbleɪbər|ɪ, -ɪz
Blagrave ˈblægreɪv
Blagrove ˈbleɪgrəʊv
blah-blah ˌblɑːˈblɑː
Blaikie ˈbleɪkɪ
Blaikley ˈbleɪklɪ
blain, -s bleɪn, -z
Blair bleə*
Blair Atholl ˌbleərˈæθl
Blairgowrie ˌbleəˈgaʊərɪ
Blake, -ney bleɪk, -nɪ
Blakiston ˈblækɪstən, ˈbleɪk-
blamab|le, -ly, -leness ˈbleɪməb|l, -lɪ,
    -lnɪs [-lnəs]
blam|e (s. v.), -es, -ing, -ed bleɪm, -z,
    -ɪŋ, -d
blameless, -ly, -ness ˈbleɪmlɪs [-ləs], -lɪ,
    -nɪs [-nəs]
blameworth|y, -iness ˈbleɪmˌwɜːð|ɪ,
    -ɪnɪs [-ɪnəs]
Blamires bləˈmaɪəz
Blanc (Mont) blɑ̃ːŋ [blɔ̃ːŋ, blɑːŋ, blɒŋ]
    (blɑ̃)
blanch, -es, -ing, -ed blɑːntʃ, -ɪz, -ɪŋ, -t

Blanchard 'blæntʃəd [-tʃɑ:d]
Blanche blɑ:ntʃ
blancmange, -s blə'mɒnʒ [-'mɔ̃:nʒ, -'mɔ:nʒ, -'mɑ:nʒ], -ɪz
blanco 'blæŋkəʊ
bland (B.), -er, -est, -ly, -ness blænd, -ə*, -ɪst, -lɪ, -nɪs ['blænnɪs, -nəs]
Blandford 'blændfəd
blandish, -es, -ing, -ed, -ment/s 'blændɪʃ, -ɪz, -ɪŋ, -t, -mənt/s
Blandy 'blændɪ
blank (s. adj. v.), -s; -er, -est, -ly, -ness; -ing, -ed blæŋk, -s; -ə*, -ɪst, -lɪ, -nɪs [-nəs]; -ɪŋ, -t
blanket (s. v.), -s, -ing, -ed 'blæŋkɪt, -s, -ɪŋ, -ɪd
Blankley 'blæŋklɪ
blank-verse ,blæŋk'vɜ:s
Blantyre blæn'taɪə* (in Malawi '—)
blar|e (s. v.), -es, -ing, -ed bleə*, -z, -rɪŋ, -d
blarney (B.) 'blɑ:nɪ
blasé 'blɑ:zeɪ (blaze)
blasphem|e, -es, -ing/ly, -ed, -er/s blæs'fi:m [blɑ:s-], -z, -ɪŋ/lɪ, -d, -ə*/z
blasphemous, -ly 'blæsfəməs ['blɑ:s-, -fɪm-, -fm̩-], -lɪ
blasphem|y, -ies 'blæsfəm|ɪ ['blɑ:s-, -fɪm-, -fm̩-], -ɪz
blast (s. v.), -s, -ing, -ed blɑ:st, -s, -ɪŋ, -ɪd
blast-furnace, -s 'blɑ:st,fɜ:nɪs [-nəs, ,-'--], -ɪz
blastoderm, -s 'blæstəʊdə:m, -z
blast-pipe, -s 'blɑ:stpaɪp, -s
blatan|cy, -t/ly 'bleɪtən|sɪ, -t/lɪ
Blatchford 'blætʃfəd
blather, -s, -ing, -ed 'blæðə*, -z, -rɪŋ, -d
Blawith (in Cumbria) 'blɑ:ɪθ, (road at Harrow) 'bleɪwɪθ
Blaydes bleɪdz
blaz|e (s. v.), -es, -ing, -ed bleɪz, -ɪz, -ɪŋ, -d
blazer, -s 'bleɪzə*, -z
Blazes 'bleɪzɪz
Blazey 'bleɪzɪ
blaz|on, -ons, -oning, -oned 'bleɪz|n [in original heraldic sense also 'blæz-], -nz, -n̩ɪŋ [-ənɪŋ, -nɪŋ], -nd
bleach, -es, -ing, -ed bli:tʃ, -ɪz, -ɪŋ, -t
bleaching-powder 'bli:tʃɪŋ,paʊdə*
bleak, -er, -est, -ly, -ness bli:k, -ə*, -ɪst, -lɪ, -nɪs [-nəs]
blear, -eyed blɪə*, -raɪd [,-'-]
blear|y, -ier, -iest, -ily, -iness 'blɪər|ɪ, -ɪə*, -ɪɪst, -əlɪ [-ɪlɪ], -ɪnɪs [-ɪnəs]
bleat (s. v.), -s, -ing, -ed bli:t, -s, -ɪŋ, -ɪd

bleb, -s bleb, -z
bled bled
Bledisloe 'bledɪsləʊ
bleed, -s, -ing, bled bli:d, -z, -ɪŋ, bled
blemish (s. v.), -es, -ing, -ed 'blemɪʃ, -ɪz, -ɪŋ, -t
blench, -es, -ing, -ed blentʃ, -ɪz, -ɪŋ, -t
Blencowe blen'kəʊ
blend (s. v.), -s, -ing, -ed, -er/s blend, -z, -ɪŋ, -ɪd, -ə*/z
blende blend
Blenheim 'blenɪm [-nəm]
Blenkinsop 'bleŋkɪnsɒp
Blennerhassett ,blenə'hæsɪt
Blériot, -s 'blerɪəʊ ['blɪər-] (blerjo), -z
bless, -es, -ing, -ed (p. tense, p. partic.), blest bles, -ɪz, -ɪŋ, -t, blest
blessed (adj.), -ly, -ness 'blesɪd, -lɪ, -nɪs [-nəs]
blessing (s.), -s 'blesɪŋ, -z
blest (from bless) blest
Bletchley 'bletʃlɪ
bleth|er, -ers, -ering, -ered 'bleð|ə*, -əz, -ərɪŋ, -əd
blew (from blow) blu:
Blew|ett, -itt 'blu:|ɪt ['bluɪt], -ɪt
Bligh blaɪ
blight (s. v.), -s, -ing, -ed blaɪt, -s, -ɪŋ, -ɪd
blighter, -s 'blaɪtə*, -z
Blighty 'blaɪtɪ
blimey 'blaɪmɪ
blimp, -s blɪmp, -s
blind (s. adj. v.), -er, -est, -ly, -ness; -s, -ing, -ed blaɪnd, -ə*, -ɪst, -lɪ, -nɪs ['blaɪnnɪs, -nəs]; -z, -ɪŋ, -ɪd
blindfold (adj. v.), -s, -ing, -ed 'blaɪndfəʊld, -z, -ɪŋ, -ɪd
blindman's-buff ,blaɪndmænz'bʌf
blindworm, -s 'blaɪndwɜ:m, -z
blink (s. v.), -s, -ing, -ed blɪŋk, -s, -ɪŋ, -t [blɪŋt]
blinker, -s 'blɪŋkə*, -z
bliss (B.) blɪs
Blissett 'blɪsɪt
bliss|ful, -fully, -fulness 'blɪs|fʊl, -fʊlɪ [-fəlɪ], -fʊlnɪs [-nəs]
blist|er (s. v.), -ers, -ering, -ered 'blɪst|ə*, -əz, -ərɪŋ, -əd
blithe, -r, -st, -ly, -ness blaɪð, -ə*, -ɪst, -lɪ, -nɪs [-nəs]
blith|er (v.), -ers, -ering, -ered, -erer/s 'blɪð|ə*, -əz, -ərɪŋ, -əd, -ərə*/z
blithesome, -ly, -ness 'blaɪðsəm, -lɪ, -nɪs [-nəs]
blitz (s. v.), -es, -ing, -ed blɪts, -ɪz, -ɪŋ, -t
blitzkrieg, -s 'blɪtskri:g, -z
blizzard, -s 'blɪzəd, -z

bloat, -s, -ing, -ed/ness bləʊt, -s, -ɪŋ, -ɪd/nɪs [-nəs]

bloater, -s 'bləʊtə*, -z

blob, -s blɒb, -z

bloc, -s blɒk, -s

block (s. v.) (B.), -s, -ing, -ed, -er/s blɒk, -s, -ɪŋ, -t, -ə*/z

blockad|e (s. v.), -es, -ing, -ed, -er/s blɒ'keɪd [blə'k-], -z, -ɪŋ, -ɪd, -ə*/z

blockbuster, -s 'blɒkbʌstə*, -z

blockhead, -s 'blɒkhed, -z

blockhou|se, -ses 'blɒkhaʊ|s, -zɪz

Bloemfontein 'bluːmfɒntem [-fɒn-]

Blois blwɑ: [surname blɔɪs] (blwa, blwɑ)

bloke, -s bləʊk, -s

Blom (surname) blɒm

Blomefield 'bluːmfiːld

Blomfield 'blɒmfiːld, 'blʊm-, 'blʌm-, 'bluː:m-

blond(e), -s blɒnd, -z

Blondel(l) 'blʌndl, 'blɒndl, blɒn'del

Blondin (French tight-rope walker) 'blɒndɪn (blɔ̃dɛ̃)

blood, -s blʌd, -z

bloodcurdling 'blʌd,kɜːdlɪŋ

blood-donor, -s 'blʌd,dəʊnə*, -z

blood-group, -s 'blʌdgruːp, -s

blood-guiltiness 'blʌd,gɪltɪnɪs [-nəs]

bloodheat 'blʌdhiːt

blood-horse, -s 'blʌdhɔːs, -ɪz

bloodhound, -s 'blʌdhaʊnd, -z

bloodless, -ly, -ness 'blʌdlɪs [-ləs], -lɪ, -nɪs [-nəs]

blood-money 'blʌd,mʌnɪ

bloodpoisoning 'blʌd,pɔɪzn̩ɪŋ [-znɪŋ]

blood-pressure 'blʌd,preʃə*

blood-red ,blʌd'red [also '-- when attributive]

blood-relation, -s ,blʌdrɪ'leɪʃn ['--,--], -z

blood|shed, -shot 'blʌd|ʃed, -ʃɒt

bloodstain, -s, -ed 'blʌdsteɪn, -z, -d

blood-stone, -s 'blʌdstəʊn, -z

blood-sucker, -s 'blʌd,sʌkə*, -z

bloodthirst|y, -ier, -iest, -ily, -iness 'blʌd,θɜːst|ɪ, -ɪə* [-jə*], -ɪɪst [-jɪst], -ɪlɪ [-əlɪ], -ɪnɪs [-məs]

blood-vessel, -s 'blʌd,vesl, -z

blood|y, -ier, -iest, -ily, -iness 'blʌd|ɪ, -ɪə*, -ɪɪst, -ɪlɪ [-əlɪ], -ɪnɪs [-məs]

bloom (s. v.), -s, -ing, -ed bluːm, -z, -ɪŋ, -d

bloomer (B.), -s 'bluːmə*, -z

Bloomfield 'bluːmfiːld

Bloomsbury 'bluːmzbərɪ

Blore blɔ:* [bloə*]

blossom (s. v.) (B.), -s, -ing, -ed 'blɒsəm, -z, -ɪŋ, -d

blot (s. v.), -s, -ting, -ted blɒt, -s, -ɪŋ, -ɪd

blotch (s. v.), -es, -ing, -ed blɒtʃ, -ɪz, -ɪŋ, -t

blotch|y, -ier, -iest, -ily, -iness 'blɒtʃ|ɪ, -ɪə*, -ɪɪst, -ɪlɪ [-əlɪ], -ɪnɪs [-məs]

blotter, -s 'blɒtə*, -z

blotting-paper, -s 'blɒtɪŋ,peɪpə*, -z

blotto 'blɒtəʊ

Blougram 'bləʊgrəm ['blaʊ-]

Bloundelle 'blʌndl

Blount blʌnt

blouse, -s blaʊz, -ɪz

blow (s. v.) (B.), -s, -ing, blew, blow|n, -ed, -er/s bləʊ, -z, -ɪŋ, bluː, bləʊ|n, -d, -ə*/z

blow-fl|y, -ies 'bləʊfl|aɪ, -aɪz

blow-hole, -s 'bləʊhəʊl, -z

blow-lamp, -s 'bləʊlæmp, -s

blown (from blow) bləʊn

blow-out, -s 'bləʊaʊt, -s

blowpipe, -s 'bləʊpaɪp, -s

blow|y, -ier, -iest, -ily, -iness 'bləʊ|ɪ, -ɪə*, -ɪɪst, -ɪlɪ [-əlɪ], -ɪnɪs [-məs]

blowz|y, -ier, -iest, -iness 'blaʊz|ɪ, -ɪə*, -ɪɪst, -ɪnɪs [-məs]

Blox(h)am 'blɒksəm

blub, -s, -bing, -bed blʌb, -z, -ɪŋ, -d

blubber (s. v.), -s, -ing, -ed, -er/s 'blʌbə*, -z, -rɪŋ, -d, -rə*/z

bludg|eon (s. v.), -eons, -eoning, -eoned 'blʌdʒ|ən, -ənz, -n̩ɪŋ [-ənɪŋ], -ənd

blue (s. adj. v.), -s; -r, -st; -ing, -d bluː, -z; -ə* [bluə*], -ɪst ['bluɪst]; -ɪŋ ['bluːɪŋ], -d

Bluebeard 'bluː,bɪəd

bluebell, -s 'bluː:bel, -z

blueberr|y, -ies 'bluːbər|ɪ, -ɪz [-,ber|ɪ, -ɪz]

blue-black ,bluː'blæk ['--]

blue-blooded ,bluː'blʌdɪd ['-,--]

blue-book, -s 'bluːbʊk, -s

bluebottle, -s 'bluː,bɒtl, -z

blue-coat, -s 'bluː:kəʊt, -s

blue-devils ,bluː'devlz

blue-jacket, -s 'bluː,dʒækɪt, -s

blue-john 'bluːdʒɒn

blue-light, -s ,bluː'laɪt, -s

blueness 'bluːnɪs [-nəs]

blue-penc|il, -ils, -illing, -illed ,bluː'pens|l, -lz, -l̩ɪŋ [-əlɪŋ], -ld

blue-pill, -s ,bluː'pɪl, -z

blue-print, -s 'bluːprɪnt, -s

bluestocking, -s 'bluː,stɒkɪŋ, -z

Bluett 'bluːɪt ['bluɪt]

bluey 'bluːɪ ['bluɪ]

bluff (s. adj. v.), -s; -er, -est, -ly, -ness; -ing, -ed blʌf, -s; -ə*, -ɪst, -lɪ, -nɪs [-nəs]; -ɪŋ, -t

bluish 'bluːɪʃ ['bluɪʃ]
Blundell 'blʌndl
blund|er (s. v.), -ers, -ering, -ered,
-erer/s 'blʌnd|ə*, -əz, -ərɪŋ, -əd,
-ərə*/z
blunderbuss, -es 'blʌndəbʌs, -ɪz
Blunn blʌn
blunt (adj. v.) (B.), -er, -est, -ly, -ness;
-s, -ing, -ed blʌnt, -ə*, -ɪst, -lɪ, -nɪs
[-nəs]; -s, -ɪŋ, -ɪd
blur, -s, -ring, -red blɜː*, -z, -rɪŋ, -d
blurb, -s blɜːb, -z
blurt, -s, -ing, -ed blɜːt, -s, -ɪŋ, -ɪd
blush (s. v.), -es, -ing/ly, -ed, -er/s
blʌʃ, -ɪz, -ɪŋ/lɪ, -t, -ə*/z
blust|er, -ers, -ering/ly, -ered, -erer/s
'blʌst|ə*, -əz, -ərɪŋ/lɪ, -əd, -ərə*/z
Bly blaɪ
Blyth blaɪ, blaɪθ, blaɪð
Blythborough 'blaɪbərə
Blythe blaɪð
Blyton 'blaɪtn
boa, -s 'bəʊə [bɔə, bɔː], -z
Boadicea ˌbəʊədɪ'sɪə
Boag bəʊg
Boanas 'bəʊnəs
Boanerges ˌbəʊə'nɜːdʒiːz
boar, -s bɔː* [bɔə*], -z
board (s. v.), -s, -ing, -ed, -er/s bɔːd
[bɔəd], -z, -ɪŋ, -ɪd, -ə*/z
boarding-hou|se, -ses 'bɔːdɪŋhaʊ|s
['bɔəd-], -zɪz
boarding-school, -s 'bɔːdɪŋskuːl
['bɔəd-], -z
boardroom, -s 'bɔːdrʊm [-ruːm], -z
board-school, -s 'bɔːdskuːl ['bɔəd-], -z
board-wages ˌbɔːd'weɪdʒɪz [ˌbɔəd-]
boar-hound, -s 'bɔːhaʊnd ['bɔəh-], -z
boarish 'bɔːrɪʃ ['bɔər-]
Boas 'bəʊæz, 'bəʊəz
Boase bəʊz
boast (s. v.), -s, -ing, -ed, -er/s bəʊst, -s,
-ɪŋ, -ɪd, -ə*/z
boast|ful, -fully, -fulness 'bəʊst|fʊl,
-fʊlɪ [-fəlɪ], -fʊlnɪs [-nəs]
boat, -s; -er/s bəʊt, -s; -ə*/z
boat-hook, -s 'bəʊthʊk, -s
boat-hou|se, -ses 'bəʊthaʊ|s, -zɪz
boating 'bəʊtɪŋ
boat|man, -men 'bəʊt|mən, -mən
boat-race, -s 'bəʊtreɪs, -ɪz
boatswain, -s 'bəʊsn ['bəʊtsweɪn], -z
Boaz 'bəʊæz
bob (s. v.) (B.), -s, -bing, -bed bɒb, -z,
-ɪŋ, -d
bobbin, -s 'bɒbɪn, -z
bobbish, -ly, -ness 'bɒbɪʃ, -lɪ, -nɪs
[-nəs]

bobb|y (B.), -ies 'bɒb|ɪ, -ɪz
bobbysox, -er/s 'bɒbɪsɒks, -ə*/z
bobolink, -s 'bɒbəlɪŋk [-bəʊl-], -s
bobsleigh, -s 'bɒbsleɪ, -z
bobstay, -s 'bɒbsteɪ, -z
bobtail, -s 'bɒbteɪl, -z
bob-wig, -s ˌbɒb'wɪg ['bɒbwɪg], -z
Boccaccio bɒ'kɑːtʃɪəʊ [bə'k-, -'kætʃ-,
-tʃjəʊ] (bo'kattʃo)
Bochaton 'bɒkətən
Bockett 'bɒkɪt
Bodd|ington, -y 'bɒd|ɪŋtən, -ɪ
bod|e (B.), -es, -ing, -ed bəʊd, -z, -ɪŋ,
-ɪd
bodega (B.), -s bəʊ'diːgə, -z
Bodey 'bəʊdɪ
Bodiam 'bəʊdjəm [-dɪəm]
bodice, -s 'bɒdɪs, -ɪz
Bodie 'bəʊdɪ
Bodilly bə'dɪlɪ [bɒ'd-, bəʊ'd-]
bodily 'bɒdɪlɪ [-əlɪ]
bodkin (B.), -s 'bɒdkɪn, -z
Bodleian bɒd'liːən [-'lɪən, 'bɒdlɪən,
esp. when attributive]
Bod|ley, -min 'bɒd|lɪ, -mɪn
bod|y, -ies 'bɒd|ɪ, -ɪz
bodyguard, -s 'bɒdɪgɑːd, -z
body-snatcher, -s 'bɒdɪˌsnætʃə*, -z
Boeing 'bəʊɪŋ
Boeo|tia, -tian/s bɪ'əʊ|ʃjə [-ʃɪə, -ʃə],
-ʃjən/z [-ʃɪən/z, -ʃn/z]
Boer, -s 'bəʊə* [bɔə*, bɔː*, bʊə*], -z
Boethius bəʊ'iːθjəs [-θɪəs]
boffin (B.), -s 'bɒfɪn, -z
Bofors 'bəʊfəz
bog, -s bɒg, -z
bogey, -s 'bəʊgɪ, -z
bogey|man, -men 'bəʊgɪ|mæn, -men
bogg|le, -les, -ling, -led, -ler/s 'bɒg|l,
-lz, -lɪŋ [-lɪŋ], -ld, -lə*/z [-lə*/z]
bogg|y, -ier, -iest, -iness 'bɒg|ɪ, -ɪə*,
-ɪɪst, -ɪnɪs [-ɪnəs]
bogie, -s 'bəʊgɪ, -z
bogie-engine, -s 'bəʊgɪˌendʒɪn, -z
bogie-wheel, -s 'bəʊgɪwiːl [-ɪhw-], -z
Bognor 'bɒgnə*
bog-oak ˌbɒg'əʊk
Bogotá (in Colombia) ˌbɒgəʊ'tɑː
[ˌbəʊg-]
Bogota (in New Jersey) bə'gəʊtə
bogus 'bəʊgəs
bog|y, -ies 'bəʊg|ɪ, -ɪz
bohea bəʊ'hiː
Bohemia, -n/s bəʊ'hiːmjə [-mɪə], -n/z
Bohn bəʊn
Bohun 'bəʊən, buːn
Note.—buːn in Shaw's 'You never
can tell'.

55

boil (s. v.), **-s, -ing, -ed, -er/s** bɔɪl, -z, -ɪŋ, -d, -ə*/z

boiling-point, **-s** 'bɔɪlɪŋpɔɪnt, -s

Bois bɔɪs

Boisragon 'bɒrəgən

boisterous, **-ly, -ness** 'bɔɪstərəs, -lɪ, -nɪs [-nəs]

Boivie (English surname) 'bɛɪvɪ

Bojador ˌbɒhə'dɔː* [ˌbɒxə-]

Bokhara bəʊ'kɑːrə

Bolander 'bəʊlændə*

bolas, **-es** 'bəʊləs, -ɪz

bold, **-er, -est, -ly, -ness** bəʊld, -ə*, -ɪst, -lɪ, -nɪs [-nəs]

bold-faced 'bəʊldfeɪst

Boldre 'bəʊldə*

bole, **-s** bəʊl, -z

bolero, **-s** (dance) bə'leərəʊ [bɒ'l-, -'lɪə-], (garment) 'bɒlərəʊ, -z

Boleyn 'bʊlɪn [bʊ'lɪn, bʊ'liːn]

Bolingbroke 'bɒlɪŋbrʊk [old-fashioned 'bʊl-]

Bolinger 'bəʊlɪndʒə* ['bɒl-]

Bolitho bə'laɪθəʊ [bɒ'l-]

Bolivar (S. American general) bɒ'liːvɑː* (bo'libar), (places in U.S.A.) 'bɒlɪvə* [-vɑː*]

Bolivia, **-n/s** bə'lɪvɪə [bɒ'l-, -vjə], -n/z

boll, **-s, -ed** bəʊl [bɒl], -z, -d

bollard, **-s** 'bɒləd [-lɑːd], -z

Bolling 'bəʊlɪŋ

Bollinger (in U.S.A.) 'bɒlɪndʒə*

bolo, **-s** 'bəʊləʊ, -z

Bologna bə'ləʊnjə (bo'loɲɲa)

bolometer, **-s** bəʊ'lɒmɪtə* [-mətə*], -z

boloney bə'ləʊnɪ

Bolshevi|k/s, **-st/s, -sm** 'bɒlʃɪvɪ|k/s [-ʃəv-, -ʃev-], -st/s, -zəm

bolshie, **-s** 'bɒlʃɪ, -z

Bolshoy bɒl'ʃɔɪ ['--]

bolshy 'bɒlʃɪ, -z

Bolsover (surname, street in London) 'bɒlsəvə* [-səʊvə*], (in Derbyshire) 'bəʊlzəʊvə*

bolst|er (s. v.), **-ers, -ering, -ered** 'bəʊlst|ə*, -əz, -ərɪŋ, -əd

bolt (s. v.) (B.), **-s, -ing, -ed** bəʊlt, -s, -ɪŋ, -ɪd

bolter (B.), **-s** 'bəʊltə*, -z

Bolton 'bəʊltən

bolt-upright ˌbəʊlt'ʌprɪaɪt

bolus, **-es** 'bəʊləs, -ɪz

bomb (s. v.), **-s, -ing, -ed** bɒm, -z, -ɪŋ, -d

bombard (s.), **-s** 'bɒmbɑːd, -z

bombard (v.), **-s, -ing, -ed, -ment/s** bɒm'bɑːd [bəm-], -z, -ɪŋ, -ɪd, -mənt/s

bombardier, **-s** ˌbɒmbə'dɪə* [ˌbʌm-, -bɑː'd-], -z

bombardon, **-s** bɒm'bɑːdn, -z

bombasine 'bɒmbəsiːn [-əziːn, ˌ--'-]

bombast 'bɒmbæst

bombastic bɒm'bæstɪk

Bombay ˌbɒm'beɪ [also 'bɒmbeɪ when attributive]

bombe, **-s** bɔ̃ːmb [bɒmb] (bɔ̃ːb), -z

bomber, **-s** 'bɒmə*, -z

bomb-proof 'bɒmpruːf

bombshell, **-s** 'bɒmʃel, -z

Bompas 'bʌmpəs

bon bɒn (bɔ̃)

bona fid|e, **-es** ˌbəʊnə'faɪd|ɪ, -iːz [-ɪz]

bonanza, **-s** bəʊ'nænzə, -z

Bonapart|e, **-ist/s** 'bəʊnəpɑːt, -ɪst/s

Bonar 'bɒnə*

bon-bon, **-s** 'bɒnbɒn ['bɒmbɒn, 'bɒmbɒŋ, bɔ̃ːmbɔ̃ːŋ] (bɔ̃bɔ̃), -z

Bonchurch 'bɒntʃəːtʃ

bond (s. v.) (B.), **-s, -ing, -ed; -age** bɒnd, -z, -ɪŋ, -ɪd; -ɪdʒ

bond-holder, **-s** 'bɒnd.həʊldə*, -z

bondmaid, **-s** 'bɒndmeɪd, -z

bond|man, **-men** 'bɒnd|mən, -mən [-men]

bonds|man, **-men** 'bɒndz|mən, -mən [-men]

bonds|woman, **-women** 'bɒndz|-ˌwʊmən, -ˌwɪmɪn

bond|woman, **-women** 'bɒnd|ˌwʊmən, -ˌwɪmɪn

bon|e (s. v.), **-es, -ing, -ed** bəʊn, -z, -ɪŋ, -d

bone-ash 'bəʊnæʃ

Bonella bəʊ'nelə

bone-meal 'bəʊnmiːl

bone-setter, **-s** 'bəʊnˌsetə*, -z

bone-shaker, **-s** 'bəʊnˌʃeɪkə*, -z

Bo'ness ˌbəʊ'nes

bonfire, **-s** 'bɒnˌfaɪə*, -z

Bonham 'bɒnəm

bonhomie 'bɒnɒmɪ [-nəm-, -mɪ]

Boniface 'bɒnɪfeɪs

Bonn bɒn

bonne-bouche, **-s** ˌbɒn'buːʃ (bɔnbuʃ), -ɪz

Bonner 'bɒnə*

bonnet (s. v.), **-s, -ing, -ed** 'bɒnɪt, -s, -ɪŋ, -ɪd

Bonnett 'bɒnɪt

bonn|y, **-ier, -iest, -ily, -iness** 'bɒn|ɪ, -ɪə*, -ɪɪst, -ɪlɪ [-əlɪ], -ɪnɪs [-ɪnəs]

bonsai 'bɒnsaɪ

Bonsor 'bɒnsə*

Bonthron 'bɒnθrən

bonus, **-es** 'bəʊnəs, -ɪz

bon|y, **-ier, -iest, -iness** 'bəʊn|ɪ, -ɪə* [-jə*], -ɪɪst [-jɪst], -ɪnɪs [-ɪnəs]

Bonython bə'naɪθən [bɒ'n-]

bonze, -s bɒnz, -ɪz

boo (v. interj.), -s, -ing, -ed, -er/s buː, -z, -ɪŋ, -d, -ə*/z

boob|y, -ies, -yish 'buːb|ɪ, -ɪz, -ɪʃ [-jɪʃ]

booby-prize, -s 'buːbɪpraɪz, -ɪz

booby-trap, -s 'buːbɪtræp, -s

boodle (B.) 'buːdl

Boog bʊɡ

boogie-woogie 'buːɡɪˌwuːɡɪ [ˌ,--'--]

book (s. v.), -s, -ing, -ed, -er/s bʊk, -s, -ɪŋ, -t, -ə*/z

bookable 'bʊkəbl

bookbind|er/s, -ing 'bʊkˌbaɪnd|ə*/z, -ɪŋ

bookcase, -s 'bʊkkeɪs [rarely 'bʊkeɪs], -ɪz

book-club, -s 'bʊkklʌb, -z

book-debt, -s 'bʊkdet, -s

Booker 'bʊkə*

bookie, -s 'bʊkɪ, -z

booking, -s 'bʊkɪŋ, -z

booking-office, -s 'bʊkɪŋˌɒfɪs, -ɪz

bookish, -ly, -ness 'bʊkɪʃ, -lɪ, -nɪs [-nəs]

book-keep|er/s, -ing 'bʊkˌkiːp|ə*/z, -ɪŋ

bookland 'bʊklænd

book-learning 'bʊkˌlɜːnɪŋ

booklet, -s 'bʊklɪt [-lət], -s

book-mak|er/s, -ing 'bʊkˌmeɪk|ə*/z, -ɪŋ

book|man, men 'bʊk|mən, -mən

book-mark, -s 'bʊkmɑːk, -s

book-muslin 'bʊkˌmʌzlɪn

bookplate, -s 'bʊkpleɪt, -s

book-post 'bʊkpəʊst

book-sell|er/s, -ing 'bʊkˌsel|ə*/z, -ɪŋ

book-shel|f, -ves 'bʊkʃel|f, -vz

book-shop, -s 'bʊkʃɒp, -s

book-stall, -s 'bʊkstɔːl, -z

bookstand, -s 'bʊkstænd, -z

bookwork 'bʊkwɜːk

bookworm, -s 'bʊkwɜːm, -z

boom (s. v.), -s, -ing, -ed buːm, -z, -ɪŋ, -d

boomerang, -s 'buːməræŋ, -z

boon, -s buːn, -z

Boon(e) buːn

boor, -s bʊə*, -z

Boord bɔːd

boorish, -ly, -ness 'bʊərɪʃ ['bɔːr-], -lɪ, -nɪs [-nəs]

Boosey 'buːzɪ

boost (s. v.), -s, -ing, -ed, -er/s buːst, -s, -ɪŋ, -ɪd, -ə*/z

boot (s. v.) (B.), -s, -ing, -ed buːt, -s, -ɪŋ, -ɪd

bootblack, -s 'buːtblæk, -s

bootee, -s 'buːtiː [ˌ,-'-], -z

Boötes bəʊ'əʊtiːz

booth (B.), -s buːð, -z

Boothby 'buːðbɪ

Boothe buːð

bootjack, -s 'buːtdʒæk, -s

bootlace, -s 'buːtleɪs, -ɪz

Bootle 'buːtl

bootlegg|er/s, -ing 'buːtˌleɡ|ə*/z, -ɪŋ

bootless, -ly, -ness 'buːtlɪs [-ləs], -lɪ, -nɪs [-nəs]

boots (hotel servant) (sing.) buːts, (plur.) buːts ['buːtsɪz]

Boots buːts

boot-tree, -s 'buːttriː, -z

booty 'buːtɪ

booz|e, -es, -ing, -ed, -er/s buːz, -ɪz, -ɪŋ, -d, -ə*/z

booz|y, -ier, -iest 'buːz|ɪ, -ɪə* [-jə*], -ɪɪst [-jɪst]

Bo-peep ˌbəʊ'piːp

boracic bə'ræsɪk [bɒ'r-]

borage 'bɒrɪdʒ ['bʌr-]

borate, -s 'bɔːreɪt [-rɪt], -s

borax 'bɔːræks

Bord bɔːd

Bordeaux bɔː'dəʊ (bordo)

bord|er (s. v.), -ers, -ering, -ered, -erer/s 'bɔːd|ə*, -əz, -ərɪŋ, -əd, -ərə*/z

borderland, -s 'bɔːdəlænd, -z

borderline, -s 'bɔːdəlaɪn, -z

bordure, -s 'bɔːˌdjʊə* [-djə*], -z

bor|e (s. v.), -es, -ing, -ed, -er/s bɔː* [bɔə*], -z, -rɪŋ, -d, -rə*/z

borealis ˌbɔːrɪ'eɪlɪs [ˌbɒrɪ-]

Boreas 'bɒrɪæs ['bɔː-]

boredom 'bɔːdəm ['bɔəd-]

Boreham 'bɔːrəm ['bɔər-]

Borgia 'bɔːdʒjə [-dʒɪə, -dʒə]

boric 'bɔːrɪk ['bɒrɪk]

Boris 'bɒrɪs

Borland 'bɔːlənd

born (from bear, bring forth) bɔːn

borne (from bear, carry) bɔːn

Borneo 'bɔːnɪəʊ

boron 'bɔːrɒn [-rən]

borough, -s 'bʌrə, -z

borough-English ˌbʌrə'ɪŋɡlɪʃ

borough-reeve, -s ˌbʌrə'riːv, -z

borrow (B.), -s, -ing, -ed, -er/s 'bɒrəʊ, -z, -ɪŋ, -d, -ə*/z

Borrowdale 'bɒrəʊdeɪl

Borstal 'bɔːstl

borstch bɔːstʃ [-ʃtʃ]

Borthwick 'bɔːθwɪk

Borwick 'bɒrɪk

borzoi, -s 'bɔːzɔɪ, -z

Bosanquet 'bəʊznket [-kɪt]

boscage, -s 'bɒskɪdʒ, -ɪz

Boscastle 'bɒs₁kɑːsl
Boscawen bɒs'kəʊən [-'kəʊɪn, -'kɔːɪn]
bosh bɒʃ
Bosham (in West Sussex) 'bɒzəm ['bɒsəm]
 Note.—A new pronunciation 'bɒʃəm is now heard.
Bosher 'bəʊʒə*
Bosinney bɒ'sɪnɪ [bə's-]
bosky 'bɒskɪ
Bosnia, -n/s 'bɒznɪə [-njə], -n/z
bosom, -s 'bʊzəm, -z
Bosphorus 'bɒsfərəs ['bɒspə-]
Bosporus 'bɒspərəs
boss (s. v.) (B.), -es, -ing, -ed bɒs, -ɪz, -ɪŋ, -t
boss-eyed 'bɒsaɪd [₁-'-]
Bossiney bɒ'sɪnɪ [bə's-]
boss|y, -ier, -iest, -ily, -iness 'bɒs|ɪ, -ɪə*, -ɪɪst, -ɪlɪ [-əlɪ], -ɪnɪs [-ɪnəs]
Bostock 'bɒstɒk
Boston 'bɒstən
Bostonian, -s bɒ'stəʊnjən [-nɪən], -z
bo'sun, -s 'bəʊsn, -z
Boswell 'bɒzwəl [-wel]
Bosworth 'bɒzwəθ [-wɜːθ]
botanic, -al, -ally bə'tænɪk [bɒ't-], -l, -əlɪ
botanist, -s 'bɒtənɪst [-tnɪ-], -s
botaniz|e [-is|e], -es, -ing, -ed 'bɒtənaɪz [-tnaɪz], -ɪz, -ɪŋ, -d
botany 'bɒtənɪ [-tnɪ]
botch (s. v.), -es, -ing, -ed, -er/s bɒtʃ, -ɪz, -ɪŋ, -t, -ə*/z
both bəʊθ
Botha 'bəʊtə
Botham 'bɒðəm
both|er (s. v.), -ers, -ering, -ered 'bɒð|ə*, -əz, -ərɪŋ, -əd
botheration ₁bɒðə'reɪʃn
bothersome 'bɒðəsəm
Bothnia 'bɒθnɪə [-njə]
Bothwell 'bɒθwəl [-ɒðw-, -wel]
both|y, -ies 'bɒθ|ɪ, -ɪz
Botolph 'bɒtɒlf [-təlf]
Botswana bɒ'tswɑːnə [bə-]
Botticelli, -s ₁bɒtɪ'tʃelɪ, -z
bottine, -s bɒ'tiːn, -z
bott|le (s. v.), -les, -ling, -led, -ler/s 'bɒt|l, -lz, -lɪŋ [-lɪŋ], -ld, -lə*/z [-lə*/z]
bottle-green 'bɒtlgriːn [₁bɒtl'g-]
bottleneck, -s 'bɒtlnek, -s
bottle-nose, -s, -d 'bɒtlnəʊz, -ɪz, -d
bottle-wash|er/s, -ing 'bɒtl₁wɒʃ|ə*/z, -ɪŋ
bottom (s. v.) (B.), -s, -ing, -ed 'bɒtəm, -z, -ɪŋ, -d

Bottome (surname) bə'təʊm
bottomless 'bɒtəmlɪs [-ləs, -les]
Bottomley 'bɒtəmlɪ
bottomry 'bɒtəmrɪ
botulism 'bɒtjʊlɪzəm
Boucicault 'buːsɪkəʊ
Boudicca bəʊ'dɪkə [buː-]
boudoir, -s 'buːdwɑː* [-wɔː*], -z
bouffe buːf
Bougainville 'buːɡənvɪl
bougainvillea, -s ₁buːɡən'vɪlɪə [-ɡeɪn-, -ljə], -z
bough, -s baʊ, -z
Boughey 'bəʊɪ
bought (from buy) bɔːt
Boughton 'bɔːtn, 'baʊtn
bougie, -s 'buːʒiː, -z
bouillabaisse 'buːjəbes [-beɪs, ₁--'-] (bujabɛs)
bouillon 'buːjɔ̃ŋ (bujɔ̃)
Boulby 'bəʊlbɪ
boulder, -s 'bəʊldə*, -z
boulevard, -s 'buːlvɑː* [-lɪv-, -ləv-, -vɑːd] (bulvaːr)
Boulger 'bəʊldʒə*
Boulogne bʊ'lɔɪn [bə'l-, -'ləʊn] (bulɔɲ)
Boult bəʊlt
Boulter 'bəʊltə*
Boulton 'bəʊltən
Bouly 'buːlɪ, 'baʊlɪ
Boumphrey 'bʌmfrɪ
bounc|e (s. v.), -es, -ing, -ed, -er/s baʊns, -ɪz, -ɪŋ, -t, -ə*/z
Bouncer 'baʊnsə*
bound (s. v.), -s, -ing, -ed baʊnd, -z, -ɪŋ, -ɪd
bound (from bind) baʊnd
boundar|y, -ies 'baʊndər|ɪ, -ɪz
bounden 'baʊndən
bounder, -s 'baʊndə*, -z
boundless, -ly, -ness 'baʊndlɪs [-ləs], -lɪ, -nɪs [-nəs]
bounteous, -ly, -ness 'baʊntɪəs [-tjəs], -lɪ, -nɪs [-nəs]
bounti|ful, -fully, -fulness 'baʊntɪ|fʊl, -fʊlɪ [-fəlɪ], -fʊlnɪs [-nəs]
bount|y, -ies 'baʊnt|ɪ, -ɪz
bouquet, -s bʊ'keɪ [buː-, 'buːkeɪ, 'bʊ-, bəʊ'keɪ], -z
Bourbon, -s 'bʊəbən [-bɒn] (burbɔ̃), -z
bourbon (drink) 'bɜːbən ['bʊə-, -bɒn]
Bourchier English surname) 'baʊtʃə*
Bourdillon (English surname) bə'dɪljən, bɔː'dɪljən [bəʊ'd-], bɔː'dɪlən [bəʊ'd-]
bourdon, -s 'bʊədn ['bɔːd-, 'bɔːd-], -z
bourgeois (middle class) 'bʊəʒwɑː (burʒwa)

bourgeois (*printing type*) bə:'dʒɔɪs

bourgeoisie ˌbʊəʒwɑːˈziː [-ʒwəˈz-] (burʒwazi)

Bourke bɜːk

bourn(e), -s bʊən [bɔːn, bɔːn], -z

Bourne bʊən [bɔːn, bɔːn], *as surname also* bɜːn

Bournemouth 'bɔːnməθ ['bɔən-, 'bʊən-, *rarely* -maʊθ]

Bournville 'bɔːnvɪl ['bɔən-, 'bʊən-]

bourrée, -s 'bʊreɪ (bure), -z

bourse, -s bʊəs, -ɪz

bous|e (*drink*), -es, -ing, -ed buːz [baʊz], -ɪz, -ɪŋ, -d

bous|e (*nautical term*), -es, -ing, -ed baʊz, -ɪz, -ɪŋ, -d

Bousfield 'baʊsfiːld

boustrophedon ˌbaʊstrəˈfiːdən

bout, -s baʊt, -s

boutique, -s buːˈtiːk, -s (butik)

bouts-rimés ˌbuːˈriːmeɪ [-eɪz] (burime)

Bouverie 'buːvərɪ

Bovey (*place*) 'bʌvɪ, (*surname*) 'buːvɪ, 'bəʊvɪ, 'bʌvɪ

Bovill 'bəʊvɪl

bovine 'bəʊvaɪn

Bovingdon (*in Hertfordshire*) 'bʌvɪŋdən ['bɒv-]
   Note.—Locally 'bʌv-.

bovril 'bɒvrəl [-rɪl]

bow (*s.*) (*bending, fore end of ship*), -s baʊ, -z

bow (*s.*) (*for shooting, etc., knot*) (B.), -s bəʊ, -z

bow (*v.*) (*bend*), -s, -ing, -ed baʊ, -z, -ɪŋ, -d

bow (*v.*) (*in playing the violin, etc.*), -s, -ing/s, -ed bəʊ, -z, -ɪŋ/z, -d

Bowater (*surname*) 'bəʊˌwɔːtə*, 'baʊətə*

Bowden 'bəʊdn, 'baʊdn

Bowdler 'baʊdlə*

bowdlerization [-isa-] ˌbaʊdlərarˈzeɪʃn

bowdleriz|e [-is|e], -es, -ing, -ed 'baʊdləraɪz, -ɪz, -ɪŋ, -d

Bowdoin 'bəʊdn

bowel, -s 'baʊəl [-el, baʊl], -z

Bowen 'bəʊɪn

bower (B.), -s 'baʊə*, -z

Bowering 'baʊərɪŋ

bowery (B.) 'baʊərɪ

Bowes, -Lyon bəʊz, -'laɪən

Bowie (*Scottish surname*) 'baʊɪ

bowie-kni|fe, -ves 'bəʊɪnaɪ|f [ˌ--'-], -vz

Bowker 'baʊkə*

bow-knot, -s 'bəʊnɒt [ˌbəʊ'n-], -s

bowl (*s. v.*), -s, -ing, -ed, -er/s bəʊl, -z, -ɪŋ, -d, -ə*/z

Bowland 'bəʊlənd

bow-legged 'bəʊlegd [-ˌlegɪd, ˌ-'-(-)]

bowler (B.), -s 'bəʊlə*, -z

Bowles bəʊlz

bowline, -s 'bəʊlɪn, -z

Bowling 'bəʊlɪŋ

bowling-green, -s 'bəʊlɪŋgriːn, -z

Bowlker 'bəʊkə*

bow|man (B.), -men 'bəʊ|mən, -mən [-men]

Bowmer 'bəʊmə*

Bown baʊn

Bowness bəʊ'nes [ˌbəʊ'nes]

Bowra 'baʊrə ['baʊərə]

Bowring 'baʊrɪŋ ['baʊər-]

Bowron 'baʊrən ['baʊər-]

bowshot, -s 'bəʊʃɒt, -s

bowsprit, -s 'bəʊsprɪt, -s

bowstring, -s 'bəʊstrɪŋ, -z

Bowtell bəʊ'tel

bow-tie, -s ˌbəʊ'taɪ ['--], -z

bow-window, -s ˌbəʊ'wɪndəʊ, -z

bow-wow, -s (*interj.*) ˌbaʊ'waʊ, (*s., dog*) 'baʊwaʊ, -z

Bowyer 'bəʊjə*

box (*s. v.*) (B.), -es, -ing, -ed, -er/s bɒks, -ɪz, -ɪŋ, -t, -ə*/z

box-bed, -s ˌbɒks'bed ['bɒksb-], -z

box-cloth 'bɒksklɒθ [*old-fashioned* -klɔ:θ]

boxer (B.), -s 'bɒksə*, -z

Boxing-day, -s 'bɒksɪŋdeɪ, -z

boxing-glove, -s 'bɒksɪŋglʌv, -z

boxing-match, -es 'bɒksɪŋmætʃ, -ɪz

Boxmoor 'bɒksˌmʊə* [-mɔə*, -mɔ:*, *also locally* -'-]

box-office, -s 'bɒksˌɒfɪs, -ɪz

box-room, -s 'bɒksrʊm [-ruːm], -z

boxwood 'bɒkswʊd

boy, -s bɔɪ, -z

Boyce bɔɪs

boycott (*s. v.*) (B.), -s, -ing, -ed, -er/s 'bɔɪkɒt [-kət], -s, -ɪŋ, -ɪd, -ə*/z

Boyd bɔɪd

Boyet (*Shakespearian character*) bɔɪ'et ['--]

boyhood, -s 'bɔɪhʊd, -z

boyish, -ly, -ness 'bɔɪʃ, -lɪ, -nɪs [-nəs]

Boy|le, -ne bɔɪ|l, -n

Boyton 'bɔɪtn

Boz bɒz [*rarely* bəʊz]
   Note.—This pen-name of Charles Dickens was originally pronounced bəʊz, but this pronunciation is not often heard now.

Bozman 'bɒzmən

bra, -s brɑː, -z

Brabant brə'bænt

Brabantio (*Shakespearian character*) brə'bæntɪəʊ [-nʃɪəʊ, -nʃjəʊ]
Brabazon 'bræbəzn
Brabourne (*place*) 'breɪbɔːn [-bəən], (*family name*) 'breɪbən, -bɔːn [-bəən]
brac|e (*s. v.*) (B.), -es, -ing, -ed breɪs, -ɪz, -ɪŋ, -t
bracelet, -s 'breɪslɪt [-lət], -s
brach, -es brætʃ, -ɪz
Bracher 'brertʃə*
brachial 'breɪkjəl [-kɪəl]
brachycephalic ,brækɪke'fælɪk [-kɪkɪ'f-, -kɪse'f-, -kɪsɪ'f-]
brack, -s bræk, -s
bracken 'brækən
Brackenbury 'brækənbərɪ
bracket (*s. v.*), -s, -ing, -ed 'brækɪt, -s, -ɪŋ, -ɪd
brackish, -ness 'brækɪʃ, -nɪs [-nəs]
Bracknell 'bræknəl [-nl]
brad, -s bræd, -z
bradawl, -s 'brædɔːl, -z
Bradbury 'brædbərɪ
Braddon 'brædn
Braden breɪdn
Brad|field, -ford 'bræd|fiːld, -fəd
Bradgate 'brædgɪt [-geɪt]
Brading 'breɪdɪŋ
Bradlaugh 'brædlɔː
Brad|law, -ley, -shaw 'bræd|lɔː, -lɪ, -ʃɔː
Bradwardine 'brædwədiːn
Brady 'breɪdɪ
brae, -s breɪ, -z
Braemar breɪ'mɑː* (*also* '— *when attributive*)
Braeriach ,breɪə'rɪək [-əx]
brag, -s, -ging/ly, -ged bræg, -z, -ɪŋ/lɪ, -d
Bragg bræg
braggadocio, -s ,brægə'dəʊtʃɪəʊ [-tʃjəʊ], -z
braggart, -s 'brægət [-gɑːt], -s
Braham 'breɪəm
Brahan brɔːn, brɑːn
Brahe (*Danish astronomer*) 'brɑːə ['brɑːhə, 'brɑːɪ, 'brɑːhɪ]
brahma (B.), -s 'brɑːmə, -z
Brahman, -s, -ism 'brɑːmən, -z, -ɪzəm
Brahmaputra ,brɑːmə'puːtrə (*Hindi* brəhməpwtra)
Brahmin, -s, -ism 'brɑːmɪn, -z, -ɪzəm
brahminical brɑː'mɪnɪkl
Brahms brɑːmz (brɑːms)
braid (*s. v.*) (B.), -s, -ing, -ed breɪd, -z, -ɪŋ, -ɪd
brail, -s breɪl, -z
Braille (*writing for the blind*) breɪl
Brailsford 'breɪlsfəd

brain (B.), -s breɪn, -z
brain|-fag, -fever 'breɪn|fæg, -,fiːvə*
brainless, -ness 'breɪnlɪs [-ləs], -nɪs [-nəs]
brainsick 'breɪnsɪk
brainstorm, -s 'breɪnstɔːm, -z
Braintree 'breɪntri: [*locally* -trɪ]
brainwash, -es, -ing, -ed 'breɪnwɒʃ, -ɪz, -ɪŋ, -t
brainwave, -s 'breɪnweɪv, -z
brain|y, -ier, -iest 'breɪn|ɪ, -ɪə* [-jə*], -ɪɪst [-jɪst]
brais|e, -es, -ing, -ed breɪz, -ɪz, -ɪŋ, -d
Braithwaite 'breɪθweɪt
brake, (*s.*), -s breɪk, -s
Brakenridge 'brækənrɪdʒ
brake-van, -s 'breɪkvæn, -z
Bralsford 'brælsfəd
Bramah 'brɑːmə
Bramall 'brɑːmɔːl
bramble, -s; -bush/es 'bræmbl, -z; -bʊʃ/ɪz
brambly 'bræmblɪ
Bramley, -s 'bræmlɪ, -z
Brampton 'bræmptən
Bramwell 'bræmwəl [-wel]
bran bræn
brancard, -s 'bræŋkəd [-kɑːd], -z
branch (*s. v.*) (B.), -es, -ing, -ed brɑːntʃ, -ɪz, -ɪŋ, -t
bran|chia, -chiae 'bræŋ|kɪə, -kriː
branchiate 'bræŋkɪeɪt [-kɪt, -kɪət]
brand (*s. v.*) (B.), -s, -ing, -ed brænd, -z, -ɪŋ, -ɪd
Brandenburg 'brændənbɜːg
branding-iron, -s 'brændɪŋ,aɪən, -z
brandish, -es, -ing, -ed 'brændɪʃ, -ɪz, -ɪŋ, -t
brand-new ,brænd'nju: ['—]
Brandon 'brændən
Brandram 'brændrəm
brand|y, -ies, -ied 'brænd|ɪ, -ɪz, -ɪd
brandy-snap, -s 'brændɪsnæp, -s
brank, -s bræŋk, -s
Branksome 'bræŋksəm
bran-mash ,bræn'mæʃ
bran-pie, -s ,bræn'paɪ, -z
Branson 'brænsn
Branston 'brænstən
brant, -s brænt, -s
Brant (*surname*) brɑːnt
brant|-goose, -geese ,brænt|'guːs, -'giːs
Braque brɑːk [bræk]
Brasenose 'breɪznəʊz
brash (*s. adj.*), -es bræʃ, -ɪz
brasier, -s 'breɪzjə* [-zɪə*, -ʒjə*, -ʒɪə*, -ʒə*], -z
Brasilia brə'zɪljə

brass, -es brɑːs, -ız

brassard, -s 'bræsɑːd [bræ'sɑːd], -z

brass-band, -s ˌbrɑːs'bænd, -z

brasserie, -s 'bræsərɪ, -z

Brassey 'bræsɪ

brass-founder, -s 'brɑːsˌfaʊndə*, -z

brass-hat, -s ˌbrɑːs'hæt ['--], -s

brassière, -s 'bræsɪə* [-sjə*, -sɪeə*, 'bræzɪə*, -zjə*], -z

brass|y [-|ie] (golf club), -ies 'brɑːs|ɪ, -ɪz

brass|y (adj.), -ier, -iest 'brɑːs|ɪ, -ɪə*, -ɪɪst

Brasted 'breɪstɪd ['bræ-]

brat, -s bræt, -s

Bratislava ˌbrætɪ'slɑːvə

bratt|le, -les, -ling, -led 'bræt|l, -lz, -lɪŋ [-lɪŋ], -ld

Brattleboro 'brætlbərə

Braughing 'bræfɪŋ

Braun (English surname) brɔːn

bravado, -(e)s brə'vɑːdəʊ, -z

brav|e (adj. v.), -er, -est, -ely; -es, -ing, -ed breɪv, -ə*, -ɪst, -lɪ; -z, -ɪŋ, -d

braver|y, -ies 'breɪvər|ɪ, -ɪz

Bravington 'brævɪŋtən

bravo (s. interj.), -(e)s ˌbrɑː'vəʊ [brɑː'v-], -z

bravura brə'vʊərə [-'vjʊər-]

brawl (s. v.), -s, -ing, -ed, -er/s brɔːl, -z, -ɪŋ, -d, -ə*/z

brawn brɔːn

Brawne brɔːn

brawn|y, -ier, -iest, -iness 'brɔːn|ɪ, -ɪə* [-jə*], -ɪɪst [-jɪst], -ɪnɪs [-ɪnəs]

Braxton 'brækstən

braxy 'bræksɪ

bray (s. v.), (B.), -s, -ing, -ed breɪ, -z, -ɪŋ, -d

Brayley 'breɪlɪ

braz|e, -es, -ing, -ed breɪz, -ɪz, -ɪŋ, -d

brazen, -ly, -ness 'breɪzn, -lɪ, -nɪs [-nəs]

brazen-faced 'breɪznfeɪst [ˌ--'-]

brazier, -s 'breɪzjə* [-zɪə*, -ʒjə*, -ʒɪə, -ʒə*], -z

Brazier (surname) 'breɪzə*

Brazil (country) brə'zɪl, (English surname) 'bræzɪl [-zl]

Brazilian, -s brə'zɪljən [-lɪən], -z

Brazil-nut, -s brə'zɪlnʌt, -s

breach (s. v.), -es, -ing, -ed briːtʃ, -ɪz, -ɪŋ, -t

bread, -s bred, -z

Breadalbane (Earl) brə'dɔːlbən, (place) brə'dælbən [-'dɔːl-]

bread-basket, -s 'bredˌbɑːskɪt, -s

breadcrumb, -s 'bredkrʌm, -z

bread-fruit 'bredfruːt

bread-stuff, -s 'bredstʌf, -s

breadth, -s bredθ [bretθ], -s

breadth|ways, -wise 'bredθ|weɪz ['bretθ-], -waɪz

bread-winner, -s 'bredˌwɪnə*, -z

break (s. v.), -s, -ing, broke, broken breɪk, -s, -ɪŋ, brəʊk, 'brəʊkən

breakable, -s 'breɪkəbl, -z

breakage, -s 'breɪkɪdʒ, -ɪz

break-away, -s 'breɪkəweɪ [ˌ--'-], -z

breakdown, -s 'breɪkdaʊn, -z

breaker, -s 'breɪkə*, -z

breakfast (s. v.), -s, -ing, -ed 'brekfəst, -s, -ɪŋ, -ɪd

breakfast-set, -s 'brekfəstset, -s

break-neck 'breɪknek

Breakspear 'breɪkˌspɪə*

break-through, -s 'breɪkθruː [ˌ-'-], -z

break-up, -s ˌbreɪk'ʌp ['breɪkʌp], -s

breakwater, -s 'breɪkˌwɔːtə*, -z

bream (B.), -s briːm, -z

Breamore 'bremə*

breast (s. v.), -s, -ing, -ed brest, -s, -ɪŋ, -ɪd

breast-bone, -s 'brestbəʊn, -z

breast|-deep, -high ˌbrest|'diːp, -'haɪ

breast-plate, -s 'brestpleɪt, -s

breastsummer, -s 'bresəmə*, -z

breastwork, -s 'brestwɜːk, -s

breath, -s breθ, -s

breathalys|e, -es, -ed, -ing, -er/s 'breθəlaɪz, -ɪz, -d, -ɪŋ, -ə*/z

breath|e, -es, -ing, -ed briːð, -z, -ɪŋ, -d

breathed (phonetic term) breθt [briːðd]

breather, -s 'briːðə*, -z

breath-group, -s 'breθgruːp, -s

breathiness 'breθɪnɪs [-nəs]

breathing-space, -s 'briːðɪŋspeɪs, -ɪz

breathless, -ly, -ness 'breθlɪs [-ləs], -lɪ, -nɪs [-nəs]

breath|y, -ier, -iest 'breθ|ɪ, -ɪə*, -ɪɪst

Brebner 'brebnə*

Brechin (in Scotland) 'briːkɪn ['briːxɪn]

Breckenridge [-kin-] 'breknrɪdʒ

Brecknock, -shire 'breknɒk [-nək], -ʃə* [-ˌʃɪə*]

Brecon 'brekən

bred (from breed) bred

Bredon 'briːdən

bree briː

breech (s.) (of a gun, etc.), -es, -ed briːtʃ, -ɪz, -t

breeches (garment) 'brɪtʃɪz

breeching, -s 'brɪtʃɪŋ, -z

breech-loader, -s 'briːtʃˌləʊdə*, -z

breed (s. v.), -s, -ing, bred briːd, -z, -ɪŋ, bred

breeder, -s 'briːdə*, -z

breeder-reactor, -s 'bri:dəri:ˌæktə* [-rɪˌækt-], -z

breeks bri:ks

breeze, -s bri:z, -ɪz

breez|y, -ier, -iest, -ily, -iness 'bri:z|ɪ, -ɪə* [-jə*], -ɪɪst [-jɪst], -ɪlɪ [-əlɪ], -ɪnɪs [-ɪnəs]

Breingan 'brɪŋən

Bremen 'breɪmən ('bre:mən)

Brennan 'brenən

Brent brent

Brentford 'brentfəd

brent|-goose, -geese ˌbrent|'gu:s, -'gi:s

Brer brɜ:* [breə*]

Brereton 'brɪətn

Breslau (now Wrocław) 'brezlau ('brɛslau)

Brest brest

brethren (archaic plur. of brother) 'breðrən [-rɪn]

Breton, -s 'bretən (brətɔ̃), -z

Bret(t) bret

Brettagh 'bretə

Bretwalda bret'wɔ:ldə ['bret,w-, -ɒl-]

Breughel (Flemish artist) 'brɔɪgəl ['brɜ:g-, 'bru:g-]

breve, -s bri:v, -z

brevet (s. v.), -s, -ing, -ed 'brevɪt, -s, -ɪŋ, -ɪd

breviar|y, -ies 'bri:vjər|ɪ [-vɪə-], -ɪz

breviate, -s 'bri:vɪɪt [-vjɪt, -ət], -s

brevier brə'vɪə* [brɪ'v-]

brevity 'brevətɪ [-ɪtɪ]

brew (s. v.) (B.), -s, -ing, -ed, -er/s bru:, -z, -ɪŋ ['bruɪŋ], -d, -ə*/z [bruə*/z]

Brewer 'bru:ə* [bruə]

brewer|y, -ies 'bruər|ɪ ['bru:ər-], -ɪz

Brewster 'bru:stə*

Brian 'braɪən

briar, -s 'braɪə*, -z

Briareus braɪ'eərɪəs

Briault 'bri:əu

brib|e (s. v.), -es, -ing, -ed, -er/s braɪb, -z, -ɪŋ, -d, -ə*/z

briber|y, -ies 'braɪbər|ɪ, -ɪz

bric-à-brac 'brɪkəbræk

Brice braɪs

brick, -s brɪk, -s

brickbat, -s 'brɪkbæt, -s

brick-dust 'brɪkdʌst

brick-field, -s 'brɪkfi:ld, -z

brick-kiln, -s 'brɪkkɪln [-kɪl], -z
   Note.—The pronunciation -kɪl *is
   used chiefly by those concerned with
   the working of kilns.*

bricklayer, -s 'brɪkˌleɪə*, -z

bricklaying 'brɪkˌleɪŋ

brickmak|er/s, -ing 'brɪkˌmeɪk|ə*/z, -ɪŋ

brickwork 'brɪkwɜ:k

bridal 'braɪdl

bride, -s braɪd, -z

bride-chamber, -s 'braɪdˌtʃeɪmbə*, -z

bridegroom, -s 'braɪdgrʊm [-gru:m], -z

bridesmaid, -s 'braɪdzmeɪd, -z

brides|man, -men 'braɪdz|mən, -mən [-men]

Bridewell 'braɪdwəl [-wel]

bridg|e (s. v.) (B.), -es, -ing, -ed brɪdʒ, -ɪz, -ɪŋ, -d

bridgehead, -s 'brɪdʒhed, -z

Bridgenorth 'brɪdʒnɔ:θ

Bridger 'brɪdʒə*

Bridgerule 'brɪdʒru:l

Bridges 'brɪdʒɪz

Bridget 'brɪdʒɪt

Bridgetown 'brɪdʒtaʊn

Bridgewater 'brɪdʒˌwɔ:tə*

Bridgnorth 'brɪdʒnɔ:θ

Bridgwater 'brɪdʒˌwɔ:tə*

bridie (B.), -s 'braɪdɪ, -z

brid|le (s. v.), -les, -ling, -led 'braɪd|l, -lz, -lɪŋ [-lɪŋ], -ld

bridle-pa|th, -ths 'braɪdlpɑ:|θ, -ðz

Bridlington 'brɪdlɪŋtən

bridoon, -s brɪ'du:n, -z

Bridport 'brɪdpɔ:t

Bridson 'braɪdsn

brief (s. adj. v.), -s, -er, -est, -ly, -ness; -ing, -ed bri:f, -s, -ə*, -ɪst, -lɪ, -nɪs [-nəs]; -ɪŋ, -t

briefcas|e, -es 'bri:fkeɪs, -ɪz

briefless 'bri:flɪs [-ləs]

brier, -s 'braɪə*, -z

Brierley 'braɪəlɪ

brig, -s brɪg, -z

brigade, -s brɪ'geɪd, -z

brigadier, -s ˌbrɪgə'dɪə* [attributively also '-ˌ-], -z

brigadier-general, -s 'brɪgəˌdɪə-'dʒenərəl, -z

brigand, -s, -age 'brɪgənd, -z, -ɪdʒ

brigantine, -s 'brɪgəntaɪn [-ti:n], -z

Brigg, -s brɪg, -z

Brigham 'brɪgəm

bright (B.), -er, -est, -ly, -ness braɪt, -ə*, -ɪst, -lɪ, -nɪs [-nəs]

bright|en, -ens, -ening, -ened 'braɪt|n, -nz, -nɪŋ [-ɪŋ], -nd

Brightlingsea 'braɪtlɪŋsi:

Brighton 'braɪtn

Brigid 'brɪdʒɪd

Brigstock(e) 'brɪgstɒk

brill (B.), -s brɪl, -z

brillian|ce, -cy 'brɪljən|s, -sɪ

brilliant (s. adj.), -s, -ly, -ness 'brɪljənt, -s, -lɪ, -nɪs [-nəs]

brilliantine ˌbrɪljən'ti:n ['—]
brim (s. v.), -s, -ming, -med brɪm, -z, -ɪŋ, -d
brimful ˌbrɪm'fʊl ['—]
brimstone 'brɪmstən
Brind brɪnd
Brindisi 'brɪndɪzɪ [-zi:]
brindle (B.), -s, -d 'brɪndl, -z, -d
brine braɪn
bring, -s, -ing, brought, bringer/s brɪŋ, -z, -ɪŋ, brɔ:t, 'brɪŋə*/z
brink, -s brɪŋk, -s
brinkmanship 'brɪŋkmənʃɪp
Brinsley 'brɪnzlɪ
Brinsmead, -s 'brɪnzmi:d, -z
brin|y, iness 'braɪn|ɪ, -ɪnɪs [-məs]
bri-nylon ˌbraɪ'naɪlən [-lɒn]
brio 'bri:əʊ ['brɪəʊ]
brioche, -s bri:'ɒʃ ['—, brɪ-, -əʊʃ] (brɪɔ̃ʃ), -ɪz
briquette, -s brɪ'ket, -s
Brisbane 'brɪzbən [-beɪn]
Note.—'brɪzbən is the pronunciation in Australia.
brisk, -er, -est, -ly, -ness brɪsk, -ə*, -ɪst, -lɪ, -nɪs [-nəs]
brisket, -s 'brɪskɪt, -s
brist|le (s. v.), -les, -ling, -led 'brɪs|l, -lz, -lɪŋ [-lɪŋ], -ld
brist|ly, -liness 'brɪs|lɪ [-lɪ], -lɪnɪs [-lɪnɪs, -nəs]
Bristol 'brɪstl
Bristow(e) 'brɪstəʊ
Britain 'brɪtn [-tən]
Britannia brɪ'tænjə
Britannic, -a brɪ'tænɪk, -ə
briticism, -s 'brɪtɪsɪzəm, -z
British, -er/s 'brɪtɪʃ, -ə*/z
britishism, -s 'brɪtɪʃɪzəm, -z
Briton, -s 'brɪtn [-tən], -z
Brittain (surname) brɪ'teɪn, 'brɪtn [-tən]
Brittany 'brɪtənɪ [-tnɪ]
Britten 'brɪtn [-tən]
britt|le, -ler, -lest, -leness 'brɪt|l, -lə*, -lɪst, -lnɪs [-nəs]
Britton 'brɪtən
Brixton 'brɪkstən
Brno 'bə:nəʊ, brə'nəʊ
broach, -es, -ing, -ed brəʊtʃ, -ɪz, -ɪŋ, -t
broad, -er, -est, -ly, -ness brɔ:d, -ə*, -ɪst, -lɪ, -nɪs [-nəs]
Broad, -s brɔ:d, -z
broad-arrow, -s ˌbrɔ:d'ærəʊ, -z
Broadbent 'brɔ:dbent
broadbrimmed ˌbrɔ:d'brɪmd [also '— when attributive]

broadcast (s. adj. v.), -s, -ing, -er/s 'brɔ:dkɑ:st, -s, -ɪŋ, -ə*/z
broadcloth 'brɔ:dklɒθ [old-fashioned -klɔ:θ]
broad|en, -ens, -ening, -ened 'brɔ:d|n, -nz, -nɪŋ [-nɪŋ], -nd
broad-gauge 'brɔ:dgeɪdʒ
Broadhurst 'brɔ:dhə:st
broadloom 'brɔ:dlu:m
broad-minded ˌbrɔ:d'maɪndɪd ['-ˌ—]
broad-mindedness ˌbrɔ:d'maɪndɪdnɪs [-nəs]
Broadmoor 'brɔ:dˌmʊə* [-mɔə*, -mɔ:*]
broadsheet, -s 'brɔ:dʃi:t, -s
broadside, -s 'brɔ:dsaɪd, -z
Broadstairs 'brɔ:dsteəz
broadsword, -s 'brɔ:dsɔ:d [-sɔəd], -z
Broad|way, -wood/s 'brɔ:d|weɪ, -wʊd/z
Brobdingnag 'brɒbdɪŋnæg
Brobdingnagian, -s ˌbrɒbdɪŋ'nægɪən, -z
brocade, -s, -d brəʊ'keɪd [brʊ'k-], -z, -ɪd
brocard, -s 'brəʊkəd [-kɑ:d], -z
broc(c)oli 'brɒkəlɪ [also -laɪ, esp. in country districts]
brochure, -s 'brəʊʃə* [-ˌʃjʊə*, -ˌʃʊə*, brɒ'ʃjʊə*, brɒ'ʃʊə*, brə'ʃʊə*], -z
brock (B.), -s brɒk, -s
Brocken 'brɒkən
Brockenhurst 'brɒkənhə:st
Brocklehurst 'brɒklhə:st
Brock|ley, -man 'brɒk|lɪ, -mən
Brockwell 'brɒkwəl
Brod(e)rick 'brɒdrɪk
Brodie 'brəʊdɪ
brogue, -s brəʊg, -z
broil (s. v.), -s, -ing, -ed brɔɪl, -z, -ɪŋ, -d
brok|e (v.), -es, -ing, -ed brəʊk, -s, -ɪŋ, -t
broke (from break), -n/ly brəʊk, -ən/lɪ
Broke brʊk
broken-down ˌbrəʊkən'daʊn [also '— when attributive]
broken-hearted ˌbrəʊkən'hɑ:tɪd ['—ˌ— when attributive]
broken-winded ˌbrəʊkən'wɪndɪd
broker, -s; -age, -y 'brəʊkə*, -z; -rɪdʒ, -rɪ
broll|y, -ies 'brɒl|ɪ, -ɪz
Bromage 'brʌmɪdʒ
bromate, -s 'brəʊmeɪt [-mɪt], -s
brome (grass), -s brəʊm [rarely bru:m], -z
Brome (surname) bru:m
Bromham 'brɒməm
bromic 'brəʊmɪk
bromide, -s 'brəʊmaɪd, -z
bromine 'brəʊmi:n [-mɪn]

Bromley 'brɒmlɪ ['brʌm-]
Brompton 'brɒmptən ['brʌm-]
Bromsgrove 'brɒmzgrəʊv ['brʌm-]
Bromwich (*in* **Castle Bromwich**, *district of Birmingham*) 'brɒmɪdʒ ['brʌm-, -ɪtʃ], (*in* **West Bromwich**, *West Midlands*) 'brɒmɪdʒ ['brʌm-, -ɪtʃ], (*surname*) 'brʌmɪdʒ
bron|chia, -chiae 'brɒŋ|kɪə [-kjə], -kɪi: [-kji:]
bronchial 'brɒŋkjəl [-kɪəl]
bronchitic brɒŋ'kɪtɪk [brɒn'k-]
bronchitis brɒŋ'kaɪtɪs [brɒn'k-]
broncho-pneumonia ˌbrɒŋkəʊnjuː-'məʊnjə [-njʊ'm-, -nɪə]
bronch|us, -i 'brɒŋk|əs, -aɪ
bronco, -s 'brɒŋkəʊ, -z
Brontë 'brɒntɪ [-teɪ]
brontosaur|us, -uses, -i ˌbrɒntə'sɔːr|əs -əsɪz, -aɪ
Bronx brɒŋks
bronz|e (s. v.), -es, -ing, -ed; -y brɒnz, -ɪz, -ɪŋ, -d; -ɪ
brooch, -es brəʊtʃ, -ɪz
brood (s. v.), -s, -ing, -ed bruːd, -z, -ɪŋ, -ɪd
brood|y, -ily, -iness 'bruːd|ɪ, -ɪlɪ [-əlɪ], -ɪnɪs [-ɪnəs]
brook (s. v.), -s, -ing, -ed brʊk, -s, -ɪŋ, -t
Brook(e), -s brʊk, -s
Brookfield 'brʊkfiːld
Brookland, -s 'brʊklənd, -z
brooklet, -s 'brʊklɪt [-lət], -s
Brookline 'brʊklaɪn
Brooklyn 'brʊklɪn
Brooksmith 'brʊksmɪθ
Brookwood 'brʊkwʊd
broom (*shrub*), -s bruːm [brʊm], -z
broom (*for sweeping*), -s bruːm [brʊm], -z
Note.—*Some people pronounce* bruːm *normally, but* -brʊm *when the word occurs unstressed as the second element of a compound.*
Broom(e) bruːm
Broomfield 'bruːmfiːld [brʊm-]
broomstick, -s 'bruː:mstɪk ['brʊm-], -s
Bros. 'brʌðəz [*sometimes facetiously* brɒs, brɒz]
Brosnahan 'brɒznəhən ['brɒs-]
broth, -s brɒθ [*old-fashioned* brɔːθ, *and in compounds*], brɒθs [brɔːðz, brɔːθs]
brothel, -s 'brɒθl, -z
brother, -s 'brʌðə*, -z
brotherhood, -s 'brʌðəhʊd, -z
broth|er-in-law, -ers-in-law 'brʌð|ərɪn-lɔː, -əzɪnlɔː-
brotherl|y, -iness 'brʌðəl|ɪ, -ɪnɪs [-ɪnəs]

Brough brʌf
brougham, -s 'bruːəm [brʊəm, *old-fashioned* bruːm], -z
Brougham brʊm [bruːm], 'bruːəm, 'brəʊəm
Note.—*The present baron pronounces* brʊm.
Brougham and Vaux ˌbruːmən'vɔːks
brought (*from* bring) brɔːt
Broughton (*in* *Northamptonshire*) 'brɔːtn, (*all others in England*) 'brɔːtn
Broughty 'brɔːtɪ
brow, -s braʊ, -z
browbeat, -s, -ing, -en 'braʊbiːt, -s, -ɪŋ, -n
brown (s. adj. v.) (**B.**), -s; -er, -est, -ness; -ing, -ed braʊn, -z; -ə*, -ɪst, -nɪs [-nəs]; -ɪŋ, -d
Browne braʊn
brownie, -s 'braʊnɪ, -z
browning (**B.**) 'braʊnɪŋ
brownish 'braʊnɪʃ
Brownrigg 'braʊnrɪg
Brownsmith 'braʊnsmɪθ
brows|e, -es, -ing, -ed braʊz, -ɪz, -ɪŋ, -d
Browse braʊz
Bruce, -smith bruːs, -smɪθ
Bruckner 'brʊknə*
Bruges bruːʒ (bry:ʒ)
bruin (**B.**), -s 'bruːɪn ['brʊɪn], -z
bruis|e (s. v.), -es, -ing, -ed, -er/s bruːz, -ɪz, -ɪŋ, -d, -ə*/z
bruit (s. v.), -s, -ing, -ed bruːt, -s, -ɪŋ,-ɪd
brume bruːm
Brummagem 'brʌmədʒəm
Brunei 'bruːnaɪ
Brunel brʊ'nel [bruː'n-]
brunette, -s bruː'net [brʊ'n-] (brynɛt), -s
Brünnhilde brʊn'hɪldə ['brʊn,h-] (bryn'hildə)
Brunswick 'brʌnzwɪk
brunt brʌnt
Brunton 'brʌntən
brush (s. v.), -es, -ing, -ed brʌʃ, -ɪz, -ɪŋ, -t
brushwood 'brʌʃwʊd
brusque, -ly, -ness brʊsk [bruː:sk, brʌsk] (brysk), -lɪ, -nɪs [-nəs]
Brussels 'brʌslz
Brussels-sprouts ˌbrʌsl'spraʊts
brut|al, -ally 'bruː:t|l, -əlɪ [-lɪ]
brutalit|y, -ies bruː'tælət|ɪ [brʊ't-, -ɪt|ɪ], -ɪz
brutaliz|e [-is|e], -es, -ing, -ed 'bruː:tə-laɪz [-tlaɪz], -ɪz, -ɪŋ, -d
brute, -s bruː:t, -s

brutish, -ly, -ness 'bruːtɪʃ, -lɪ, -nɪs [-nəs]
Brutnell 'bruːtnel [-nəl]
Bruton 'bruːtən
Brutus 'bruːtəs
Bryan, -s, -t 'braɪən, -z, -t
Bryce braɪs
Brydson 'braɪdsn
Bryers 'braɪəz
Brynmawr (in Wales) brɪn'mauə* (Welsh brɪn'maur)
Bryn Mawr (in U.S.A.) brɪn'mɔː*
Brynmor 'brɪnmɔː* (Welsh 'brɪnmor)
bryony 'braɪənɪ
Bryson 'braɪsn
bubb|le (s. v.), -les, -ling, -led 'bʌb|l, -lz, -lɪŋ [-lɪŋ], -ld
bubble-and-squeak ˌbʌbl̩ən'skwiːk
bubble-gum 'bʌblgʌm
bubbly 'bʌblɪ [-lɪ]
bubo, -es 'bjuːbəʊ, -z
bubonic bju:'bɒnɪk [bjʊ-]
buccal 'bʌkəl
buccaneer, -s ˌbʌkə'nɪə*, -z
Buccleuch bə'kluː
Bucephalus bju:'sefələs [bjʊ-]
Buchan 'bʌkən ['bʌxən]
Buchanan bju:'kænən [bjʊ-]
Bucharest ˌbjuːkə'rest [ˌbuː-, '---]
Buchel 'bjuːʃl
buck (s. v.) (B.), -s, -ing, -ed bʌk, -s, -ɪŋ, -t
buckboard, -s 'bʌkbɔːd [-bɔəd], -z
bucket, -s 'bʌkɪt, -s
bucketful, -s 'bʌkɪtfʊl, -z
buckhorn 'bʌkhɔːn
buckhound, -s 'bʊkhaʊnd, -z
Buckhurst 'bʌkhəːst ['bʌkəːst]
Buckingham, -shire 'bʌkɪŋəm, -ʃə* [-ˌʃɪə*]
Buckland 'bʌklənd
buck|le (s. v.) (B.), -les, -ling, -led 'bʌk|l, -lz, -lɪŋ [-lɪŋ], -ld
buckler, -s 'bʌklə*, -z
Buckley 'bʌklɪ
Buckmaster 'bʌkˌmɑːstə*
Buckn|all, -ell 'bʌkn|ɔːl [-l], -əl [-l]
Bucknill 'bʌknɪl
buck-passing 'bʌkˌpɑːsɪŋ
buckram, -s 'bʌkrəm, -z
Bucks. bʌks
buckshee ˌbʌk'ʃi: ['--]
buckshot 'bʌkʃɒt
buckskin, -s, 'bʌkskɪn, -z
Buckston 'bʌkstən
buckwheat 'bʌkwiːt [-khw-]
bucolic, -al, -ally bju:'kɒlɪk [bjʊ-], -l, -əlɪ

bud (s. v.), -s, -ding, -ded bʌd, -z, -ɪŋ, -ɪd
Budapest ˌbjuːdə'pest [ˌbuː-]
Budd bʌd
Buddha 'bʊdə (Hindi bwddha)
buddhi|c, -sm, -st/s 'bʊdɪ|k, -zəm, -st/s
buddleia, -s 'bʌdlɪə, -z
Bude bjuːd
budg|e (B.), -es, -ing, -ed bʌdʒ, -ɪz, -ɪŋ, -d
budgerigar, -s 'bʌdʒərɪgɑː*, -z
budget (s. v.), -s, -ing, -ed, -ary 'bʌdʒɪt, -s, -ɪŋ, -ɪd, -ərɪ
Budleigh 'bʌdlɪ
Buenos Aires ˌbwenəs'aɪərɪz [ˌbuɪn-, ˌbəʊɪn-, ˌbəʊn-, -nə'zaɪərɪz, -nə'zeərɪz, -rɪs, -nə'zeəz] (ˌbwenos-'aires)
Buesst bjuːst
buff bʌf
buffalo, -es 'bʌfələʊ [-f|əʊ], -z
buffer, -s 'bʌfə*, -z
buffet (s.) (blow, sideboard), -s 'bʌfɪt, -s
buffet (s.) (refreshment), -s 'bʊfeɪ (byfɛ)
buffet (v.) (strike), -s, -ing, -ed 'bʌfɪt, -s, -ɪŋ, -ɪd
buffo, -s 'bʊfəʊ, -z
buffoon, -s bə'fuːn [bʌ'f-], -z
buffooner|y, -ies bə'fuːnər|ɪ [bʌ'f-], -ɪz
Buffs bʌfs
bug, -s bʌg, -z
Bug (river) buːg [bʌg]
bugaboo, -s 'bʌgəbuː, -z
Buganda bu'gændə
bugbear, -s 'bʌgbeə*, -z
bugger (s. v.), -s, -ing, -ed; -y 'bʌgə*, -z, -rɪŋ, -d; -rɪ
Buggs (surname) bju:gz, bʌgz
bugg|y, -ies 'bʌg|ɪ, -ɪz
bugle (B.), -s 'bju:gl, -z
bugler, -s 'bjuːglə*, -z
bugloss 'bjuːglɒs
buhl buːl
Buick, -s 'bjuːɪk ['bjʊɪk], -s
build, -s, -ing, built, builder/s bɪld, -z, -ɪŋ, bɪlt, 'bɪldə*/z
build-up, -s 'bɪldʌp [ˌ-'-], -s
Builth bɪlθ
Buist bjuːst
Bulawayo ˌbʊlə'weɪəʊ [-'waɪəʊ]
bulb, -s bʌlb, -z
bulbaceous bʌl'beɪʃəs
bulbous 'bʌlbəs
bulbul, -s 'bʊlbʊl, -z
Bulgar, -s 'bʌlgɑː*, -z
Bulgaria, -n/s bʌl'geərɪə, -n/z
bulg|e (s. v.), -es, -ing, -ed bʌldʒ, -ɪz, -ɪŋ, -d

65

bulg|y, -iness 'bʌldʒ|ɪ, -ɪnɪs [-ɪnəs]
bulk (s. v.), -s, -ing, -ed bʌlk, -s, -ɪŋ, -t
bulkhead, -s 'bʌlkhed, -z
bulk|y, -ier, -iest, -ily, -iness 'bʌlk|ɪ, -ɪə* [-jə*], -ɪɪst [-jɪst], -ɪlɪ [-əlɪ], -ɪnɪs [-ɪnəs]
bull (s. v.) (B.), -s, -ing, -ed bʊl, -z, -ɪŋ, -d
bullace, -s 'bʊlɪs, -ɪz
Bullard 'bʊlɑːd
bull-baiting 'bʊl,beɪtɪŋ
bull-cal|f, -ves ˌbʊl'kɑː|f ['bʊlkɑː|f], -vz
bulldog, -s 'bʊldɒg, -z
bulldoz|e, -es, -ing, -ed, -er/s 'bʊldəʊz, -ɪz, -ɪŋ, -d, -ə*/z
Bulleid 'bʊliːd
Bull|en, -er 'bʊl|ɪn [-ən], -ə*
bullet, -s 'bʊlɪt, -s
bulletin, -s 'bʊlɪtɪn [-lət-], -z
bullet-proof 'bʊlɪtpruːf
bullfight, -s 'bʊlfaɪt, -s
bullfinch, -es 'bʊlfɪntʃ, -ɪz
bull-frog, -s 'bʊlfrɒg, -z
bullion, -ist/s 'bʊljən [-lɪən], -ɪst/s
bullish 'bʊlɪʃ
bullock (B.), -s 'bʊlək, -s
Bullokar 'bʊləkɑː* [-lɒk-, -kə]
Bullough 'bʊləʊ
bull-ring, -s 'bʊlrɪŋ, -z
bull's-eye, -s 'bʊlzaɪ, -z
bull-terrier, -s ˌbʊl'terɪə* [-rjə*], -z
bull|y (s. v.), -ies, -ying, -ied 'bʊl|ɪ, -ɪz, -ɪɪŋ, -ɪd
Bulmer 'bʊlmə*
bulrush, -es 'bʊlrʌʃ, -ɪz
Bulstrode 'bʊlstrəʊd, 'bʌl-
Bultitude 'bʊltɪtjuːd
bulwark, -s 'bʊlwək [-wɜːk], -s
Bulwer 'bʊlwə*
bum, -s bʌm, -z
bumble-bee, -s 'bʌmblbiː, -z
bumblepuppy 'bʌmbl,pʌpɪ
bumboat, -s 'bʌmbəʊt, -s
bumkin, -s 'bʌmkɪn [-mpk-], -z
bummaree, -s ˌbʌmə'riː ['---], -z
bummel 'bʊml ['bʌm-]
bump (s. v.), -s, -ing, -ed bʌmp, -s, -ɪŋ, -t [bʌmt]
bumper, -s 'bʌmpə*, -z
bumpkin, -s 'bʌmpkɪn, -z
bumptious, -ly, -ness 'bʌmpʃəs, -lɪ, -nɪs [-nəs]
Bumpus 'bʌmpəs
bump|y, -ier, -iest, -iness 'bʌmp|ɪ, -ɪə* [-jə*], -ɪɪst [-jɪst], -ɪnɪs [-ɪnəs]
bun, -s bʌn, -z

bunch (s. v.) (B.), -es, -ing, -ed bʌntʃ, -ɪz, -ɪŋ, -t
buncombe (B.) 'bʌŋkəm
bund|le (s. v.), -les, -ling, -led 'bʌnd|l, -lz, -lɪŋ [-lɪŋ], -ld
bung (s. v.), -s, -ing, -ed bʌŋ, -z, -ɪŋ, -d
bungaloid 'bʌŋgəlɔɪd
bungalow, -s 'bʌŋgələʊ [-g]əʊ], -z
Bungay 'bʌŋgɪ
Bunge 'bʌŋɪ
bung|le (s. v.), -les, -ling, -led, -ler/s 'bʌŋg|l, -lz, -lɪŋ [-lɪŋ], -ld, -lə*/z [-lə*/z]
bunion, -s 'bʌnjən, -z
bunk (s. v.), -s, -ing, -ed bʌŋk, -s, -ɪŋ, -t [bʌŋt]
bunker (s. v.) (B.), -s, -ing, -ed 'bʌŋkə*, -z, -rɪŋ, -d
bunkum 'bʌŋkəm
Bunnett 'bʌnɪt
bunn|y, -ies 'bʌn|ɪ, -ɪz
Bunsen 'bʊnsn ['bʌn-]
bunsen burner, -s ˌbʌnsn'bɜːnə*, -z
bunt, -s bʌnt, -s
bunting (B.), -s 'bʌntɪŋ, -z
buntline, -s 'bʌntlaɪn, -z
Bunyan 'bʌnjən
buoy (s. v.), -s, -ing, -ed bɔɪ, -z, -ɪŋ, -d
buoyan|cy, -t/ly 'bɔɪən|sɪ, -t/lɪ
bur, -s bɜː*, -z
Burbage 'bɜːbɪdʒ
Burberr|y, -ies 'bɜːbər|ɪ, -ɪz
Burbey 'bɜːbɪ
burb|le, -les, -ling, -led 'bɜːb|l, -lz, -lɪŋ [-lɪŋ], -ld
Burbury 'bɜːbərɪ
Burch, -ell bɜːtʃ, -əl
burd|en (s. v.) (B.), -ens, -ening, -ened 'bɜːd|n, -nz, -nɪŋ [-nɪŋ], -nd
burdensome 'bɜːdnsəm
Burdett bɜː'det [bə-]
Burdett-Coutts ˌbɜːdet'kuːts [bɜːˌdet-'kuːts, bə-]
burdock, -s 'bɜːdɒk, -s
Burdon 'bɜːdn
bureau, -s 'bjʊərəʊ [bjʊə'rəʊ], -z
bureaucrac|y, -ies bjʊə'rɒkrəs|ɪ [bjə'r-, -'rəʊk-], -ɪz
bureaucrat, -s 'bjʊərəʊkræt, -s
bureaucratic ˌbjʊərəʊ'krætɪk
burette, -s bjʊə'ret, -s
Burford 'bɜːfəd
burg, -s bɜːg, -z
Burgclere 'bɜːkleə*
Burge, -s bɜːdʒ, -ɪz
burgee, -s 'bɜːdʒiː, -z
burge|on (s. v.), -ons, -oning, -oned 'bɜːdʒ|ən, -ənz, -ənɪŋ [-ŋɪŋ], -ənd

burgess (**B.**), -es 'bɜːdʒɪs [-dʒes], -ɪz
burgh, -s 'bʌrə, -z
Burgh bɜːg, (*Baron*) 'bʌrə, (*Heath, in Surrey*) 'bʌrə, (*in Lincolnshire*) 'bʌrə, (*in Suffolk*) bɜːg ['bʌrə], (*Burgh-by-Sands*) brʌf
Burghclere 'bɜːkleə*
burgher, -s 'bɜːgə*, -z
Burghersh 'bɜːgəʃ
Burghley 'bɜːlɪ
Burgin 'bɜːgɪn, 'bɜːdʒɪn
burglar, -s 'bɜːglə*, -z
burglarious, -ly bɜː'gleərɪəs, -lɪ
burglar|y, -ies 'bɜːglər|ɪ, -ɪz
burg|le, -les, -ling, -led 'bɜːg|l, -lz, -lɪŋ [-lɪŋ], -ld
burgomaster, -s 'bɜːgəʊˌmɑːstə*, -z
Burgoyne 'bɜːgɔɪn, bɜː'gɔɪn
burgund|y (**B.**), -ies 'bɜːgənd|ɪ, -ɪz
burial, -s; -ground/s, -place/s 'berɪəl, -z; -graʊnd/z, -pleɪs/ɪz
burin, -s 'bjʊərɪn, -z
burk|e (**B.**), -es, -ing, -ed bɜːk, -s, -ɪŋ, -t
burlap 'bɜːlæp
Burleigh 'bɜːlɪ
burlesqu|e (*s. v.*), -es, -ing, -ed bɜː'lesk, -s, -ɪŋ, -t
Burley 'bɜːlɪ
Burlington 'bɜːlɪŋtən
burl|y (**B.**), -ier, -iest, -iness 'bɜːl|ɪ, -ɪə* [-jə*], -ɪɪst [-jɪst], -ɪnɪs [-ɪnəs]
Burma 'bɜːmə
Burman, -s 'bɜːmən, -z
Burmese ˌbɜː'miːz
burn (*s. v.*), -s, -ing, -ed, burnt bɜːn, -z, -ɪŋ, -d, bɜːnt
Burnaby 'bɜːnəbɪ
Burnand bɜː'nænd [bə-]
Burne-Jones bɜːn, -'dʒəʊnz
burner, -s 'bɜːnə*. -z
burnet (**B.**), -s 'bɜːnɪt, -s
Burnett bɜː'net [bə-], 'bɜːnɪt
Burney 'bɜːnɪ
Burnham 'bɜːnəm
burning|-glass, -glasses 'bɜːnɪŋ|glɑːs, -ˌglɑːsɪz
burnish, -es, -ing, -ed, -er/s 'bɜːnɪʃ, -ɪz, -ɪŋ, -t, -ə*/z
Burnley 'bɜːnlɪ
burnous, -es bɜː'nuːs, -ɪz
burnouse, -s bɜː'nuːz, -ɪz
Burns bɜːnz
Burnside 'bɜːnsaɪd
burnt (*from* burn) bɜːnt
Burntisland bɜːnt'aɪlənd
burr (**B.**), -s bɜː*, -z
Burrell 'bʌrəl

Burrough(e)s 'bʌrəʊz
burr|ow (*s. v.*), -ows, -owing, -owed 'bʌr|əʊ, -əʊz, -əʊɪŋ, -əʊd
Burrows 'bʌrəʊz
bursar, -s 'bɜːsə*, -z
bursarship, -s 'bɜːsəʃɪp, -s
bursar|y, -ies 'bɜːsər|ɪ, -ɪz
Burslem 'bɜːzləm*
burst (*s. v.*), -s, -ing bɜːst, -s, -ɪŋ
Burt bɜːt
Burtchaell 'bɜːtʃəl
burthen, -s 'bɜːðn, -z
Burton 'bɜːtn
Burundi bʊ'rʊndɪ
bur|y, -ies, -ying, -ied 'ber|ɪ, -ɪz, -ɪŋ, -ɪd
Bury (*place*) 'berɪ, (*surname*) 'bjʊərɪ, 'berɪ
burying-ground, -s 'berɪŋgraʊnd, -z
burying-place, -s 'berɪŋpleɪs, -ɪz
bus, -es bʌs, -ɪz
busb|y, -ies 'bʌzb|ɪ, -ɪz
bus-conductor, -s 'bʌskənˌdʌktə*, -z
bush (*s. v.*) (**B.**), -es, -ing, -ed bʊʃ, -ɪz, -ɪŋ, -t
bushel, -s 'bʊʃl, -z
Bushell 'bʊʃl
Bushey 'bʊʃɪ
Bushire bju:'ʃaɪə* [bjʊ-, bu:-]
bush|man (**B.**), -men 'bʊʃ|mən, -mən [-men]
Bushmills 'bʊʃmɪlz
Bushnell 'bʊʃnəl
bushranger, -s 'bʊʃˌreɪndʒə*, -z
bush|y (**B.**), -ily, -iness 'bʊʃ|ɪ, -ɪlɪ [-əlɪ], -ɪnɪs [-ɪnəs]
business (*profession, etc.*), -es 'bɪznɪs [-nɪs], -ɪz
business-like 'bɪznɪslaɪk
business-man, -men 'bɪznɪsmæn [-mən], -men [-mən]
busk (*s. v.*) (**B.**), -s, -ing, -ed bʌsk, -s, -ɪŋ, -t
buskin, -s, -ed 'bʌskɪn, -z, -d
bus|-man, -men 'bʌs|mən [-mæn], -mən [-men]
Busoni bju:'səʊnɪ [bjʊ-, bʊ-, bu:-, -'zəʊ-]
buss (*s. v.*) (**B.**), -es, -ing, -ed bʌs, -ɪz, -ɪŋ, -t
bus-stop, -s 'bʌsstɒp, -s
bust (*s.*), -s bʌst, -s
bust (*s. v.*) (*burst*), -s, -ing bʌst, -s, -ɪŋ
bustard, -s 'bʌstəd, -z
buster (**B.**), -s 'bʌstə*, -z
bust|le (*s. v.*), -les, -ling, -led 'bʌs|l, -lz, -lɪŋ [-lɪŋ], -ld

67

Busvine 'bʌzvaɪn
bus|y, -ier, -iest, -ily 'bɪz|ɪ, -ɪə*, -ɪɪst, -ɪlɪ [-ɪlɪ]
busybod|y, -ies 'bɪzɪ,bɒd|ɪ, -ɪz
busyness (state of being busy) 'bɪzɪnɪs [-nəs]
Buszard 'bʌzəd
but bʌt (strong form), bət (weak form)
butane 'bjuːteɪn
butcher (s. v.) (B.), -s, -ing, -ed 'butʃə*, -z, -ɪŋ, -d
butcher|y, -ies 'butʃər|ɪ, -ɪz
Bute bjuːt
butler (B.), -s 'bʌtlə*, -z
butler|age; -y, -ies 'bʌtlər|ɪdʒ; -ɪ, -ɪz
Butlin 'bʌtlɪn
butt (s. v.) (B.), -s, -ing, -ed bʌt, -s, -ɪŋ, -ɪd
Buttar bə'tɑː*
butt-end, -s ,bʌt'end ['bʌtend], -z
butter, -s 'bʌtə*, -z
butter-boat, -s 'bʌtəbəut, -s
buttercup, -s 'bʌtəkʌp, -s
butter-dish, -es 'bʌtədɪʃ, -ɪz
Butterfield 'bʌtəfiːld
butter-fingers 'bʌtə,fɪŋgəz
butterfl|y, -ies 'bʌtəfl|aɪ, -aɪz
Butterick 'bʌtərɪk
butter-kni|fe, -ves 'bʌtənaɪ|f, -vz
Butter|leigh, -ley 'bʌtə|lɪ, -lɪ
buttermilk 'bʌtəmɪlk
butternut, -s 'bʌtənʌt, -s
butterscotch 'bʌtəskɒtʃ [,bʌtə's-]
Butterwick 'bʌtərɪk, 'bʌtəwɪk
Butterworth 'bʌtəwəθ [-wɜːθ]
butter|y (s. adj.), -ies 'bʌtər|ɪ, -ɪz
buttery-hatch, -es ,bʌtərɪ'hætʃ, -ɪz
buttock, -s 'bʌtək, -s
butt|on (s. v.) (B.), -ons, -oning, -oned 'bʌt|n, -nz, -nɪŋ [-nɪŋ], -nd
button-hol|e (s. v.), -es, -ing, -ed 'bʌtn-həul, -z, -ɪŋ, -d
button-hook, -s 'bʌtnhuk, -s
buttress, -es 'bʌtrɪs [-rəs], -ɪz
butyric bju:'tɪrɪk [bjʊ't-]
buxom, -ness 'bʌksəm, -nɪs [-nəs]
Buxton 'bʌkstən

buy, -s, -ing, bought baɪ, -z, -ɪŋ, bɔːt
buyable 'baɪəbl
buyer, -s 'baɪə*, -z
Buzfuz 'bʌzfʌz
buzz (s. v.), -es, -ing, -ed, -er/s bʌz, -ɪz, -ɪŋ, -d, -ə*/z
buzzard, -s 'bʌzəd, -z
by baɪ (normal form), bɪ, bə (occasional weak forms)
by-and-by ,baɪənd'baɪ [-əm'b-]
Byard 'baɪəd
Byas(s) 'baɪəs
bye, -s baɪ, -z
bye-bye (sleep), -s 'baɪbaɪ, -z
bye-bye (goodbye) ,baɪ'baɪ
bye-law, -s 'baɪlɔː, -z
by-election, -s 'baɪɪ,lekʃn, -z
Byends 'baɪendz
Byers 'baɪəz
Byfleet 'baɪfliːt
bygone, -s 'baɪgɒn, -z
by-law, -s 'baɪlɔː, -z
Byles baɪlz
Byng bɪŋ
Bynoe 'baɪnəu
by-pass, -es 'baɪpɑːs, -ɪz
by-pa|th, -ths 'baɪpɑː|θ, -ðz
by-play 'baɪpleɪ
by-product, -s 'baɪ,prɒdʌkt [-dəkt], -s
Byrd bɜːd
byre, -s 'baɪə*, -z
Byrne bɜːn
by-road, -s 'baɪrəud, -z
Byron 'baɪərən
Byronic, -ally baɪ'rɒnɪk [,baɪə'r-], -əlɪ
Bysshe bɪʃ
byssus 'bɪsəs
bystander, -s 'baɪ,stændə*, -z
by-street, -s 'baɪstriːt, -s
Bythesea 'bɪðəsi:
by|way/s, -word/s 'baɪ|weɪ/z, -wɜːd/z
Byzantian bɪ'zæntɪən [baɪ'z-, -ntjən, -nʃɪən, -nʃjən]
Byzantine bɪ'zæntaɪn [baɪ'z-, 'bɪzən-taɪn, -tiːn]
Byzantium bɪ'zæntɪəm [baɪ'z-, -ntjəm, -nʃɪəm, -nʃjəm]

68

C

C (*the letter*), -'s si:, -z
cab, -s kæb, -z
cabal, -s kə'bæl, -z
Cabala kə'bɑ:lə [kæ'b-]
cabalistic, -al, -ally ˌkæbə'lıstık, -l, -əlı
cabaret, -s 'kæbərei, -z
cabbage, -s 'kæbıdʒ, -ız
cabbage-rose, -s 'kæbıdʒrəuz, -ız
Cabbala kə'bɑ:lə [kæ'b-]
cabbalistic, -al, -ally ˌkæbə'lıstık, -l, -əlı
cabb|y, -ies 'kæb|ı, -ız
Cabell 'kæbəl
caber, -s 'keıbə*, -z
cabin, -s; -boy/s 'kæbın, -z; -bɔı/z
cabinet, -s; -maker/s 'kæbınıt [-bn̩ıt, -ət], -s; -ˌmeıkə*/z
cab|le (*s. v.*), -les, -ling, -led 'keıb|l, -lz, -lıŋ [-lıŋ], -ld
cablegram, -s 'keıblgræm, -z
cab|man, -men 'kæb|mən, -mən [-men]
caboodle kə'bu:dl
caboose, -s kə'bu:s, -ız
cabot, -s 'kæbəu, -z
Cabot 'kæbət
cabotage 'kæbətɑ:ʒ [-tıdʒ]
cabriole ˌkæbrı'əul
cab|-stand/s, -tout/s 'kæb|stænd/z, -taut/s
cacao kə'kɑ:əu [-'kereu]
cachalot, -s 'kæʃəlɒt, -s
cache, -s kæʃ, -ız
cachet, -s 'kæʃeı (kaʃɛ), -z
cachinnat|e, -es, -ing, -ed 'kækıneıt, -s, -ıŋ, -ıd
cachinnation ˌkækı'neıʃn
cachou, -s 'kæʃu: [kæ'ʃu:, kə-], -z
cachucha, -s kə'tʃu:tʃə, -z
cacique, -s kæ'si:k [kɑ's-], -s
cack|le (*s. v.*), -les, -ling, -led, -ler/s 'kæk|l, -lz, -lıŋ [-lıŋ], -ld, -lə*/z [-lə*/z]
cacodyl 'kækəudaıl [-dıl]
cacoepy 'kækəuepı
cacographic ˌkækəu'græfık
cacography kæ'kɒgrəfı [kə'k-]
cacology kæ'kɒlədʒı [kə'k-]
cacophonic, -al, -ally ˌkækəu'fɒnık, -l, -əlı

cacophonous kæ'kɒfənəs [kə'k-]
cacophon|y, -ies kæ'kɒfən|ı [kə'k-], -ız
cactus, -es, cacti 'kæktəs, -ız, 'kæktaı
cacuminal (*s. adj.*), -s kæ'kju:mınl [kə'k-], -z
cad, -s kæd, -z
cadastral kə'dæstrəl
cadaver, -s kə'deıvə* [-'dɑ:-], -z
cadaveric kə'dævərık
cadaverous, -ness kə'dævərəs, -nıs [-nəs]
Cad|bury, -by 'kæd|bərı, -bı
Caddell kə'del
caddice 'kædıs
caddie, -s 'kædı, -z
caddis; -fly, -flies 'kædıs; -flaı, -flaız
caddish, -ly, -ness 'kædıʃ, -lı, -nıs [-nəs]
cadd|y, -ies 'kæd|ı, -ız
cade (C.), -s keıd, -z
Cadell 'kædl, kə'del
caden|ce/s, -cy 'keıdən|s/ız, -sı
cadenza, -s kə'denzə, -z
Cader Idris ˌkædər'ıdrıs [-də'ı-]
cadet, -s kə'det, -s
cadet-corps (*sing.*) kə'detkɔ:*, (*plur.*) -z
cadetship, -s kə'det-ʃıp, -s
cadg|e, -es, -ing, -ed, -er/s kædʒ, -ız, -ıŋ, -d, -ə*/z
cadi, -s 'kɑ:dı ['keıdı], -z
Cadillac, -s 'kædılæk ['kædlæk], -s
Cadiz (*in Spain*) kə'dız ['keıdız] ('kadiθ), (*in Philippines*) 'kɑ:di:s, (*in U.S.A.*) 'kædız, 'keıdız
Cadman 'kædmən
Cadmean kæd'mi:ən [-'mıən]
cadmium 'kædmıəm [-mjəm]
Cadmus 'kædməs
Cadogan kə'dʌgən
cadre, -s 'kɑ:də* ['kɑ:drə, 'kædrı], 'kɑ:dəz ['kædrız]
caduce|us, -i kə'dju:sj|əs [-sı|əs, -ʃj|əs, -ʃı|əs], -aı
caec|um, -a 'si:k|əm, -ə
Caedmon 'kædmən
Caen (*French town*) kɑ̃:ŋ [kɔ̃:ŋ] (kɑ̃)
Caen (*in Caen stone*) keın
Caerleon kɑ:'li:ən [kə'l-, -'lıən]
Caernarvon, -shire kə'nɑ:vən, -ʃə* [-ˌʃıə*]

69

Caerphilly kɑː'fɪlɪ [keə'f-, kə'f-] (*Welsh* kar'fili, kair'fili)

Caesar, -s 'siːzə*, -z

Caesarea ˌsiːzə'rɪə

Caesarean (*of Caesarea*) ˌsiːzə'rɪən

caesarean (*of Caesar*) siː'zeərɪən [sɪ'z-]

caesium 'siːzjəm [-zɪəm]

caesura, -s siː'zjʊərə [sɪ'z-, -'zjɔər-, -'zjɔːr-, -'ʒj-], -z

café, -s 'kæfeɪ ['kæfɪ] (kafe), -z

café chantant, -s ˌkæfeɪ'ʃɑːntɑːɲ [-'ʃɔ̃ːn-tɔ̃ːŋ, -'ʃɑːntɑːŋ, -'ʃɒntɒŋ] (kafe-ʃɑ̃tɑ̃), -z

cafeteria, -s ˌkæfɪ'tɪərɪə [-fə't-], -z

caffeine 'kæfiːn [-fiːn, -feɪn]

cag|e (*s. v.*), -es, -ing, -ed keɪdʒ, -ɪz, -ɪŋ, -d

cageling, -s 'keɪdʒlɪŋ, -z

Cagliari kæ'ljɑːrɪ [ˌkælɪ'ɑː-] ('kaʎʎari)

Cagliostro kæ'ljɒstrəʊ [ˌkælɪ'ɒ-]

Cahan (*surname*) kɑːn

Cahill 'kɑːhɪl, 'keɪhɪl

Caiaphas 'kaɪəfæs [-fəs]

Caillard (*English name*) 'keɪləd

Cain(e) keɪn

Cainite, -s 'keɪnaɪt, -s

caique, -s kaɪ'iːk [kɑː'iːk], -s

Cairene 'kaɪəriːn

cairn, -s keən, -z

cairngorm (C.), -s ˌkeən'gɔːm ['--], -z

Cairns keənz

Cairo (*in Egypt*) 'kaɪərəʊ, (*in U.S.A.*) 'keərəʊ

caisson, -s kə'suːn ['keɪsən], -z
  Note.—Engineers pronounce kə'suːn.

Caithness 'keɪθnes [-nəs, ˌkeɪθ'nes]

caitiff, -s 'keɪtɪf, -s

Caius (*Roman name, character in Shakespeare's 'Merry Wives'*) 'kaɪəs, 'keɪəs, (*Cambridge College*) kiːz

cajol|e, -es, -ing, -ed, -er/s kə'dʒəʊl, -z -ɪŋ, -d, -ə*/z

cajoler|y, -ies kə'dʒəʊlər|ɪ, -ɪz

Cajun 'keɪdʒən

cak|e (*s. v.*), -es, -ing, -ed; -y keɪk, -s, -ɪŋ, -t; -ɪ

cakewalk, -s 'keɪkwɔːk, -s

Calabar ˌkælə'bɑː* ['kæləb-]

calabash, -es 'kæləbæʃ, -ɪz

Calabria, -n/s kə'læbrɪə [-'lɑːb-, *old-fashioned* -'leɪb-], -n/z

Calais 'kæleɪ ['kælɪ, *old-fashioned* 'kælɪs] (kalɛ)

calamine 'kæləmaɪn

calamitous, -ly, -ness kə'læmɪtəs, -lɪ, -nɪs [-nəs]

calamit|y, -ies kə'læmət|ɪ [-ɪt|ɪ], -ɪz

calamus 'kæləməs

calcareous, -ness kæl'keərɪəs, -nɪs [-nəs]

calceolaria, -s ˌkælsɪə'leərɪə [-sjə'l-], -z

calces (*plur. of* calx) 'kælsiːz

calciferous kæl'sɪfərəs

calcification ˌkælsɪfɪ'keɪʃn

calci|fy, -fies, -fying, -fied 'kælsɪ|faɪ, -faɪz, -faɪɪŋ, -faɪd

calcimine 'kælsɪmaɪn

calcination ˌkælsɪ'neɪʃn

calcin|e, -es, -ing, -ed 'kælsaɪn, -z, -ɪŋ, -d

calcite 'kælsaɪt

calcium 'kælsɪəm [-sjəm]

Calcot (*near Reading*) 'kælkət

Calcott 'kɔːlkət ['kɒl-]

calculable 'kælkjʊləbl [-kjəl-]

calculat|e, -es, -ing, -ed, -or/s 'kælkjʊleɪt [-kjəl-], -s, -ɪŋ, -ɪd, -ə*/z

calculation, -s ˌkælkjʊ'leɪʃn [-kjə'l-], -z

calculative 'kælkjʊlətɪv [-kjəl-, -leɪtɪv]

calcul|us, -uses, -i 'kælkjʊl|əs [-kjəl-], -əsɪz, -aɪ

Calcutt (*surname*) 'kælkʌt

Calcutta kæl'kʌtə

Caldcleugh 'kɑːldklʌf

Caldecote (*in Hertfordshire*) 'kɔːldɪkət

Caldecott 'kɔːldəkət ['kɒl-, -dɪk-]

Calder 'kɔːldə* ['kɒl-]

Calderara ˌkældə'rɑːrə

Calderon (*English name*) 'kɔːldərən ['kɒl-, 'kæl-], (*Spanish name*) ˌkældə'rɒn (kalde'ron)

caldron, -s 'kɔːldrən ['kɒl-], -z

Caldwell 'kɔːldwəl ['kɒl-, -wel]

Caleb 'keɪleb

Caledon 'kælɪdən

Caledonia, -n/s ˌkælɪ'dəʊnjə [-nɪə], -n/z

calefaction ˌkælɪ'fækʃn

calefactor|y, -ies ˌkælɪ'fæktər|ɪ, -ɪz

calendar, -s 'kælɪndə* [-lən-], -z

calend|er (*s. v.*), -ers, -ering, -ered 'kælɪnd|ə* [-lən-], -əz, -ərɪŋ, -əd

calends 'kælɪndz [-lendz, -ləndz]

calenture, -s 'kælən,tjʊə* [-,tʃʊə*, -tʃə*], -z

cal|f, -ves kɑː|f, -vz

calf's-foot (*jelly*) 'kɑːvzfʊt ['kɑːfsfʊt]

calf-skin 'kɑːfskɪn

Calgary 'kælgərɪ

Calhoun kæl'həʊn, kə'huːn

Caliban 'kælɪbæn [-bən]

calibrat|e, -es, -ing, -ed 'kælɪbreɪt [-ləb-], -s, -ɪŋ, -ɪd

calibration ˌkælɪ'breɪʃn [-lə'b-]

calibre, -s 'kælɪbə* [kə'liːbə*], -z

calicle, -s 'kælɪkl, -z

calico, -(e)s 'kælɪkəʊ, -z

70

Calicut 'kælɪkət
calif = caliph
California, -n/s ˌkælɪ'fɔːnjə [-nɪə], -n/z
Caligula kə'lɪgjʊlə
calipash 'kælɪpæʃ
calipee 'kælɪpiː [ˌkælɪ'piː]
caliper, -s 'kælɪpə*, -z
caliph, -s 'kælɪf ['keɪl-, 'kɑːl-], -s
caliphate, -s 'kælɪfeɪt [-fɪt, -fət], -s
Calippus kə'lɪpəs
calisthenic, -s ˌkælɪs'θenɪk, -s
calk (s. v.), -s, -ing, -ed kɔːk, -s, -ɪŋ, -t
calkin, -s 'kælkɪn ['kɔːkɪn], -z
call (s. v.), -s, -ing, -ed, -er/s kɔːl, -z,
   -ɪŋ, -d, -ə*/z
Callaghan 'kæləhæn [-hæn], 'kæləgən
Callander 'kæləndə*
call-boy, -s 'kɔːlbɔɪ, -z
Callcott 'kɔːlkət ['kɒl-]
Callender 'kæləndə* [-lən-]
Caller 'kælə*
Callicrates kə'lɪkrətiːz [kæ'l-]
Callie 'kɔːlɪ
calligraph|er/s, -ist/s, -y kə'lɪgrəf|ə*/z
   [kæ'l-], -ɪst/s, -ɪ
calligraphic, -al, -ally ˌkælɪ'græfɪk, -l,
   -əlɪ
calling (s.), -s 'kɔːlɪŋ, -z
Calliope kə'laɪəpɪ [kæ'l-]
calliper, -s 'kælɪpə*, -z
Callirrhoe kæ'lɪrəʊɪ: [kə'l-, -əʊɪ]
Callisthenes kæ'lɪsθənɪz [kə'l-]
callisthenic, -s ˌkælɪs'θenɪk, -s
Callistratus kæ'lɪstrətəs [kə'l-]
call-office, -s 'kɔːlˌpfɪs, -ɪz
callosit|y, -ies kæ'lɒsət|ɪ [kə'l-, -ɪt|ɪ], -ɪz
callous, -ly, -ness 'kæləs, -lɪ, -nɪs [-nəs]
call|ow (C.), -ower, -owest 'kæl|əʊ,
   -əʊə*, -əʊɪst
calm (s. adj. v.), -s; -er, -est, -ly, -ness;
   -ing, -ed kɑːm, -z; -ə*, -ɪst, -lɪ, -nɪs
   [-nəs]; -ɪŋ, -d
calmative, -s 'kælmətɪv ['kɑːm-], -z
Calne kɑːn
calomel 'kæləʊmel
calor 'kælə*
caloric kə'lɒrɪk ['kælərɪk]
calorie, -s 'kælərɪ, -z
calorific ˌkælə'rɪfɪk [-lɔː'r-, -lɒ'r-]
calorification ˌkəˌlɒrɪfɪ'keɪʃn [ˌkælər-,
   ˌkælɔː-r-, ˌkælɒr-]
calorimet|er/s, -ry ˌkælə'rɪmɪt|ə*/z
   [-lɔː'r-, -lɒ'r-, -mət|ə*], -rɪ
calotte, -s kə'lɒt, -s
caloyer, -s 'kælɔɪə*, -z
Calpurnia kæl'pɜːnjə [-nɪə]
calque, -s kælk, -s
Calshot (in Hampshire) 'kælʃɒt

Calthorpe (district in Birmingham)
   'kælθɔːp, (surname) 'kɔːlθɔːp ['kɒl-],
   'kælθɔːp
Calton (Edinburgh) 'kɔːltən, (Glasgow)
   'kɑːltən
caltrop, -s 'kæltrəp, -s
calumet, -s 'kæljʊmet, -s
calumniat|e, -es, -ing, -ed, -or/s
   kə'lʌmnɪeɪt [-njert], -s, -ɪŋ, -ɪd, -ə*/z
calumniation, -s kəˌlʌmnɪ'eɪʃn, -z
column|y, -ies 'kæləmn|ɪ, -ɪz
calvar|y (C.), -ies 'kælvər|ɪ, -ɪz
calv|e, -es, -ing, -ed kɑːv, -z, -ɪŋ, -d
Calverley (surname) 'kælvəlɪ, (place in
   West Yorkshire) 'kɑːvəlɪ ['kɔːvəlɪ]
Calvert 'kælvɜːt [-vət], 'kɔːlvət
calves'-foot 'kɑːvzfʊt
Calvin, -ism, -ist/s 'kælvɪn, -ɪzəm, -ɪst/s
calvinistic, -al, -ally ˌkælvɪ'nɪstɪk, -l,
   -əlɪ
cal|x, -ces, -xes kæl|ks, -siːz, -ksɪz
calycle, -s 'kælɪkl, -z
Calydon 'kælɪdən
caly|x, -ces, -xes 'keɪlɪ|ks ['kæl-], -siːz,
   -ksɪz
cam (C.), -s kæm, -z
Camalodunum ˌkæmələʊ'djuːnəm
camaraderie ˌkæmə'rɑːdərɪ [-'ræd-, -rɪ]
camarilla, -s ˌkæmə'rɪlə, -z
camber, -s 'kæmbə*, -z
Camberley 'kæmbəlɪ [-bli]
Camberwell 'kæmbəwəl [-wel]
Cambodia, -n kæm'bəʊdjə [-dɪə], -n
Camborne 'kæmbɔːn [-bən]
Cambria, -n/s 'kæmbrɪə, -n/z
cambric 'keɪmbrɪk
Cambridge 'keɪmbrɪdʒ
Cambridgeshire 'keɪmbrɪdʒʃə*
   [-brɪdʒˌʃɪə*, -brɪd,ʃɪə*, -brɪdʃə*]
Cambs. kæmbz
Cambyses kæm'baɪsiːz
Camden 'kæmdən
came (from come) keɪm
camel, -s 'kæml, -z
cameleer, -s ˌkæmɪ'lɪə* [-mə'l-], -z
Camelford 'kæmlfəd
camellia, -s kə'miːljə [-'mel-, -lɪə]
camel|man, -men 'kæml|mæn [-mən],
   -men [-mən]
camelopard, -s (giraffe) 'kæmɪləpɑːd
   [kə'meləpɑːd, -ləʊp-], (facetiously
   applied to a person) ˌkæml'lepəd, -z
Camelot 'kæmɪlɒt [-məl-]
Camembert 'kæməmbeə* (kamɑ̃bɛːr)
cameo, -s 'kæmɪəʊ, -z
camera, -s 'kæmərə, -z
camera|-man, -men 'kæmərə|mæn
   [-mən], -men

71

Cameron 'kæmərən
Cameronian, -s ˌkæmə'rəʊnjən [-nɪən], -z
Cameroon, -s 'kæməru:n [ˌkæmə'r-], -z
cami-knickers ˌkæmɪ'nɪkəz ['--ˌ--]
Camilla kə'mɪlə
camisole, -s 'kæmɪsəʊl, -z
Camlachie (Glasgow) kæm'lækɪ [-'læxɪ]
camomile 'kæməʊmaɪl
camouflag|e (s. v.), -es, -ing, -ed 'kæmʊflɑ:ʒ [-məf-, -ɑ:dʒ], -ɪz, -ɪŋ, -d
Camoys kə'mɔɪz
camp (s. v.), -s, -ing, -ed kæmp, -s, -ɪŋ, -t [kæmt]
Campagna kæm'pɑ:njə (kam'paɲɲa)
campaign (s. v.), -s, -ing, -ed, -er/s kæm'peɪn, -z, -ɪŋ, -d, -ə*/z
campanile, -s ˌkæmpə'ni:lɪ, -z
campanolog|ist/s, -y ˌkæmpə'nɒlədʒ|ɪst/s, -ɪ
campanula, -s kəm'pænjʊlə [-njələ], -z
camp-bed, -s ˌkæmp'bed, -z
Campbell, -s 'kæmbl, -z
Campbellite, -s 'kæmbəlaɪt [-blaɪt], -s
Campden 'kæmpdən
Campeachy kæm'pi:tʃɪ
Camperdown 'kæmpədaʊn
camp-follower, -s 'kæmpˌfɒləʊə*, -z
camphor, -s, -ated 'kæmfə*, -z, -reɪtɪd
camphoric kæm'fɒrɪk
campion (C.) 'kæmpjən [-pɪən]
camp-stool, -s 'kæmpstu:l, -z
campus, -es 'kæmpəs, -ɪz
cam-wood 'kæmwʊd
can (s.), -s kæn, -z
can (auxil. v.) kæn (strong form), kən, kn, kŋ (weak forms)
    Note.—The form kŋ occurs only before words beginning with k or g.
can (v.) (put in cans), -s, -ning, -ned kæn, -z, -ɪŋ, -d
Cana 'keɪnə
Canaan 'keɪnən [-njən, -nɪən, Jewish pronunciation kə'neɪən]
Canaanite, -s 'keɪnənaɪt [-njən-, -nɪən-, Jewish pronunciation kə'neɪənaɪt], -s
Canada 'kænədə
Canadian, -s kə'neɪdjən [-dɪən], -z
canal, -s kə'næl, -z
canalization [-isa-] ˌkænəlaɪ'zeɪʃn [-nlaɪ-, -lɪ'z-]
canaliz|e [-is|e], -es, -ing, -ed 'kænəlaɪz [-nlaɪ-], -ɪz, -ɪŋ, -d
Cananite, -s 'kænənaɪt ['keɪn-], -s
canapé, -s 'kænəpeɪ, -z
canard, -s kæ'nɑ:d [kə'nɑ:d, 'kænɑ:d] (kana:r), -z
Canarese ˌkænə'ri:z

canar|y (C.), -ies kə'neər|ɪ, -ɪz
canasta kə'næstə
canaster, -s kə'næstə*, -z
Canberra 'kænbərə ['kæm-]
canc|el, -els, -elling, -elled 'kæns|l, -lz, -əlɪŋ [-lɪŋ, -lɪŋ], -ld
cancellation, -s ˌkænsə'leɪʃn [-se'leɪ-, -sɪ'leɪ-, -s|'eɪ-], -z
cancer, -s 'kænsə*, -z
Cancer (constellation) 'kænsə*
cancerous 'kænsərəs
Candace kæn'deɪsɪ
candelabr|a, -as, -um, ˌkændɪ'lɑ:br|ə [-də'l-, -'læb-, -'leɪb-], -əz, -əm
Candia 'kændɪə [-djə]
candid, -ly, -ness 'kændɪd, -lɪ, -nɪs [-nəs]
Candida 'kændɪdə
candidate, -s 'kændɪdət [-deɪt, -dɪt], -s
candidature, -s 'kændɪdətʃə* [-dɪtʃ-, -dertʃ-, -ˌtʃʊə*, -ˌtjʊə*], -z
candied 'kændɪd
candle, -s 'kændl, -z
candle-light 'kændllaɪt
Candlemas 'kændlməs [-mæs]
candlepower, -s 'kændlˌpaʊə*, -z
candlestick, -s 'kændlstɪk, -s
candour 'kændə*
cand|y (s. v.) (C.), -ies, -ying, -ied 'kænd|ɪ, -ɪz, -ɪŋ [-jɪŋ], -ɪd
candy-floss 'kændɪflɒs
candytuft 'kændɪtʌft
cane (C.), -s keɪn, -z
Canford 'kænfəd
canicular kə'nɪkjʊlə* [kæ'n-]
canine (adj.) (in zoology and general use) 'keɪnaɪn ['kæn-]
canine (s. adj.) (in dentistry), -s 'kæɪnaɪn ['keɪn-], -z
Canis (constellation) 'keɪnɪs
canister, -s 'kænɪstə*, -z
canker (s. v.), -s, -ing, -ed 'kæŋkə*, -z, -rɪŋ, -d
cankerous 'kæŋkərəs
canna, -s 'kænə, -z
cannabis 'kænəbɪs
Cannan 'kænən
canner|y, -ies 'kænər|ɪ, -ɪz
cannibal, -s 'kænɪbl, -z
cannibalism 'kænɪbəlɪzəm [-bl̩-]
cannibalistic ˌkænɪbə'lɪstɪk
cannibaliz|e [-is|e], -es, -ing, -ed 'kænɪbəlaɪz [-blaɪz], -ɪz, -ɪŋ, -d
cannikin, -s 'kænɪkɪn, -z
Cann|ing, -ock 'kæn|ɪŋ, -ək
cannon (C.), -s 'kænən, -z
cannonad|e (s. v.), -es, -ing, -ed ˌkænə'neɪd, -z, -ɪŋ, -ɪd
cannon-ball, -s 'kænənbɔ:l, -z

cannoneer, -s ˌkænəˈnɪə*, -z
cannon-proof ˈkænənpruːf
cannonry ˈkænənrɪ
cannon-shot, -s ˈkænənʃɒt, -s
cannot ˈkænɒt [-nət]
  Note.—This word is usually con-
    tracted to kɑːnt. See **can't.**
cannula, -s ˈkænjʊlə, -z
cann|y, -ier, -iest, -ily, -iness ˈkæn|ɪ,
  -ɪə*, -ɪɪst, -ɪlɪ [-əlɪ], -ɪnɪs [-ɪnəs]
canoe (s. v.), -s, -ing, -d kəˈnuː, -z, -ɪŋ
  [kəˈnʊɪŋ], -d
canon, -s ˈkænən, -z
cañon, -s ˈkænjən, -z
canoness, -es ˈkænənɪs [-nes], -ɪz
canonic, -al/s, -ally kəˈnɒnɪk, -l/z, -əlɪ
canonization [-isa-], -s ˌkænənaɪˈzeɪʃn
  [-nɪˈz-], -z
canoniz|e [-is|e], -es, -ing, -ed ˈkænə-
  naɪz, -ɪz, -ɪŋ, -d
canon|ry, -ies ˈkænənr|ɪ, -ɪz
Canopus kəˈnəʊpəs
canop|y, -ies ˈkænəp|ɪ, -ɪz
canst (archaic form from can) kænst
  (strong form), kənst (weak form)
cant (s. v.) (C.), -s, -ing, -ed, -er/s
  kænt, -s, -ɪŋ, -ɪd, -ə*/z
can't kɑːnt
Cantab. ˈkæntæb
cantabile kænˈtɑːbɪlɪ
Cantabrian kænˈteɪbrɪən
Cantabrigian,   -s   ˌkæntəˈbrɪdʒɪən
  [-dʒjən], -z
cantaloup, -s ˈkæntəluːp, -s
cantankerous, -ly, -ness kænˈtæŋkərəs
  [kən-], -lɪ, -nɪs [-nəs]
cantata, -s kænˈtɑːtə [kən-], -z
cantatrice, -s ˈkæntətriːs, -ɪz
canteen, -s kænˈtiːn, -z
cant|er (s. v.), -ers, -ering, -ered
  ˈkænt|ə*, -əz, -ərɪŋ, -əd
Canterbury ˈkæntəbərɪ [-berɪ]
cantharides kænˈθærɪdiːz [kən-]
canticle, -s ˈkæntɪkl, -z
cantilever, -s ˈkæntɪliːvə*, -z
Cantire kænˈtaɪə*
Cantling ˈkæntlɪŋ
canto, -s ˈkæntəʊ, -z
canton (Swiss state) ˈkæntɒn [-'-], (in
  heraldry) ˈkæntən, -z
Canton (in China) ˌkænˈtɒn, (in Wales,
  surname) ˈkæntən
canton (v.) (divide into portions or
  districts), -s, -ing, -ed kænˈtɒn, -z,
  -ɪŋ, -d
canton (v.) (quarter soldiers), -s, -ing,
  -ed; -ment/s kænˈtuːn [kən-], -z, -ɪŋ,
  -d; -mənt/s

cantonal ˈkæntənl [kænˈtɒnl]
Cantonese ˌkæntəˈniːz [-tɒˈn-]
cantor, -s ˈkæntɔː*, -z
cantoris kænˈtɔːrɪs
Cantuar. ˈkæntjʊɑ:*
Cantuarian ˌkæntjʊˈeərɪən
Canute kəˈnjuːt
canvas, -es ˈkænvəs, -ɪz
canvas-back, -s ˈkænvəsbæk, -s
canvass (s. v.), -es, -ing, -ed, -er/s
  ˈkænvəs, -ɪz, -ɪŋ, -t, -ə*/z
Canvey ˈkænvɪ
canyon, -s ˈkænjən [-nɪən], -z
canzone, -s kænˈtsəʊnɪ [-nˈzəʊ-], -z
canzonet, -s ˌkænzəʊˈnet, -s
caoutchouc ˈkaʊtʃʊk [-tʃuːk, -tʃuː]
cap (s. v.), -s, -ping, -ped kæp, -s, -ɪŋ, -t
capabilit|y, -ies ˌkeɪpəˈbɪlət|ɪ [-lɪt-], -ɪz
capab|le, -ly, -leness ˈkeɪpəb|l, -lɪ, -lnɪs
  [-nəs]
capacious, -ly, -ness kəˈpeɪʃəs, -lɪ, -nɪs
  [-nəs]
capacitat|e, -es, -ing, -ed kəˈpæsɪteɪt, -s,
  -ɪŋ, -ɪd
capacit|y, -ies kəˈpæsət|ɪ [-ɪt|ɪ], -ɪz
cap-à-pie ˌkæpəˈpiː
caparis|on (s. v.), -ons, -oning, -oned
  kəˈpærɪs|n, -nz, -ṇɪŋ, -nd
cape (C.), -s keɪp, -s
Capel (in Surrey) ˈkeɪpl, (in Wales)
  ˈkæpl (Welsh ˈkapel)
Capel Curig ˌkæplˈkɪrɪg   (Welsh
  ˌkapelˈkerig, -ˈkɪrig)
Capell ˈkeɪpəl
capel(l)et, -s ˈkæpəlet [-ɪt], -s
cap|er (s. v.), -ers, -ering, -ered, -erer/s
  ˈkeɪp|ə*, -əz, -ərɪŋ, -əd, -ərə*/z
caper (capercailzie), -s ˈkæpə*, -z
capercailzie [-caillie], -s ˌkæpəˈkeɪlɪ
  [-ljɪ, -lzɪ], -z
Capernaum kəˈpɜːnjəm [-nɪəm]
Cape Town [Capetown] ˈkeɪptaʊn [ˌ-ˈ-]
capias, -es ˈkeɪpɪæs [-pjæs, -pjəs, -pɪəs],
  -ɪz
capillaire ˌkæpɪˈleə*
capillarity ˌkæpɪˈlærətɪ [-rɪt-]
capillary kəˈpɪlərɪ
capit|al (s. adj.), -als, -ally ˈkæpɪt|l, -lz,
  -lɪ [-lɪ]
capitali|sm,   -st/s   ˈkæpɪtəl|zəm
  [kəˈpɪt-, kæˈpɪt-, -tlɪ-], -st/s
capitalization [-isa-], -s ˌkæpɪtəlaɪˈzeɪ-
  ʃn [kæˌp-, kə,p-, -tlaɪ-], -z
capitaliz|e [-is|e], -es, -ing, -ed ˈkæpɪtə-
  laɪz [kæˈp-, kəˈpɪ-, -tlaɪz], -ɪz, -ɪŋ, -d
capitation, -s ˌkæpɪˈteɪʃn, -z
capitol (C.), -s ˈkæpɪtl, -z
capitolian ˌkæpɪˈtəʊljən [-lɪən]

73

capitoline kə'pɪtəʊlaɪn
capitular (s. adj.), -s kə'pɪtjʊlə*, -z
capitular|y, -ies kə'pɪtjʊlər|ɪ, -ɪz
capitulat|e, -es, -ing, -ed kə'pɪtjʊleɪt,
  -s, -ɪŋ, -ɪd
capitulation kə,pɪtjʊ'leɪʃn, -z
capivi kə'paɪvi
capon, -s 'keɪpən, -z
caporal (cigarette), -s ,kæpə'rɑːl, -z
capot (s. v.), -s, -ting, -ted kə'pɒt, -s,
  -ɪŋ, -ɪd
capote, -s kə'pəʊt, -s
Cappado|cia, -cian/s ,kæpə'dəʊ|sjə
  [-sɪə, -ʃjə, -ʃɪə, -ʃə], -sjən/z [-sɪən/z,
  -ʃjən/z, -ʃɪən/z, -ʃn/z]
Capper 'kæpə*
Capri 'kæpri: ['kɑːp-, -prɪ] ('ka:pri)
capric 'kæprɪk
capriccio, -s kə'prɪtʃɪəʊ [-tʃjəʊ], -z
capriccioso kə,prɪtʃɪ'əʊzəʊ [-'əʊsəʊ]
caprice, -s kə'pri:s, -ɪz
capricious, -ly, -ness kə'prɪʃəs, -lɪ, -nɪs
  [-nəs]
Capricorn (constellation), -us 'kæprɪk-
  ɔ:n, ,kæprɪ'kɔ:nəs
capriol|e (s. v.), -es, -ing, -ed 'kæprɪəʊl,
  -z, -ɪŋ, -d
Capron 'keɪprən
capsicum 'kæpsɪkəm
capsiz|e, -es, -ing, -ed kæp'saɪz, -ɪz,
  -ɪŋ, -d
capstan, -s 'kæpstən, -z
capsular 'kæpsjʊlə*
capsule, -s 'kæpsju:l, -z
captain, -s 'kæptɪn, -z
captainc|y, -ies 'kæptɪns|ɪ, [-tən-], -ɪz
caption, -s 'kæpʃn, -z
captious, -ly, -ness 'kæpʃəs, -lɪ, -nɪs
  [-nəs]
captivat|e, -es, -ing, -ed 'kæptɪveɪt, -s,
  -ɪŋ, -ɪd
captive, -s 'kæptɪv, -z
captivit|y, -ies kæp'tɪvət|ɪ [-ɪt|ɪ], -ɪz
captor, -s 'kæptə* [-tɔ:*], -z
capt|ure (s. v.), -ures, -uring, -ured
  'kæptʃ|ə*, -əz, -ərɪŋ, -əd
Capua (Italian town) 'kæpjʊə ['kɑːpʊə]
  ('ka:pua)
capuche, -s kə'pu:ʃ, -ɪz
capuchin, -s 'kæpjʊʃɪn [-tʃɪn], -z
Capulet 'kæpjʊlet [-lət, -lɪt]
car, -s kɑː*, -z
carabineer, -s ,kærəbɪ'nɪə*, -z
caracal, -s 'kærəkæl, -z
Caracas kə'rækəs [-'rɑːk-]
caracole, -s 'kærəkəʊl, -z
Caractacus kə'ræktəkəs
Caradoc kə'rædək

carafe, -s kə'ræf [-'rɑːf], -s
caramel, -s 'kærəmel, -z
carapace, -s 'kærəpeɪs, -ɪz
carat, -s 'kærət, -s
Caratacus ,kærə'tɑːkəs
caravan, -s 'kærəvæn [,kærə'v-], -z
caravanserai, -s ,kærə'vænsəraɪ [-reɪ,
  -rɪ], -z
caravanser|y, -ies ,kærə'vænsər|ɪ, -ɪz
caraway, -s 'kærəweɪ, -z
caraway-seed, -s 'kærəweɪsi:d, -z
Carbery 'kɑːbərɪ
carbide, -s 'kɑːbaɪd, -z
carbine, -s 'kɑːbaɪn, -z
carbineer, -s ,kɑːbɪ'nɪə*, -z
carbohydrate, -s ,kɑːbəʊ'haɪdreɪt [-rɪt],
  -s
carbolic kɑː'bɒlɪk [kə'b-]
carbon, -s (substance) 'kɑːbən [-bɒn,
  -bn], (in typewriting, photography,
  etc.) 'kɑːbən [-bn], -z
carbonaceous ,kɑːbəʊ'neɪʃəs
carbonate, -s 'kɑːbənɪt [-bɲɪt, -ət,
  -eɪt], -s
carbonated 'kɑːbəneɪtɪd
carbonic kɑː'bɒnɪk
carboniferous ,kɑːbə'nɪfərəs
carbonization [-isa-] ,kɑːbənaɪ'zeɪʃn
  [-bɲaɪ-]
carboniz|e [-is|e], -es, -ing, -ed 'kɑː-
  bənaɪz, -ɪz, -ɪŋ, -d
carborundum ,kɑːbə'rʌndəm
carboy, -s 'kɑːbɔɪ, -z
carbuncle, -s 'kɑːbʌŋkl, -z
carburet (s. v.), -s, -ting, -ted 'kɑːbjʊret
  [-bər-, ,--'-], -s, -ɪŋ, -ɪd
carburett|er/s, -or/s ,kɑːbjʊ'ret|ə*/z
  [-bər-, '-----], -ə*/z
carcase, -s 'kɑːkəs, -ɪz
carcass, -es 'kɑːkəs, -ɪz
Carchemish 'kɑːkɪmɪʃ [-kəm-]
carcinoma, -s ,kɑːsɪ'nəʊmə, -z
card (s. v.), -s, -ing, -ed kɑːd, -z, -ɪŋ, -ɪd
cardamom [-mum] 'kɑːdəməm
cardboard 'kɑːdbɔːd [-bɔəd]
card-case, -s 'kɑːdkeɪs, -ɪz
Cardew 'kɑːdju:
cardiac 'kɑːdɪæk [-djæk]
cardiacal kɑː'daɪəkl
Cardiff 'kɑːdɪf
cardigan, -s 'kɑːdɪgən, -z
Cardigan, -shire 'kɑːdɪgən, -ʃə* [-,ʃɪə*]
cardinal (s. adj.), -s; -ship/s 'kɑːdɪnl
  [-dɲl, -dnl], -z; -ʃɪp/s
cardioid, -s 'kɑːdɪɔɪd, -z
cardiolog|ist/s, -y ,kɑːdɪ'ɒlədʒ|ɪst/s, -ɪ
cardiometer, -s ,kɑːdɪ'ɒmɪtə* [-mətə*],
  -z

card-sharper, -s 'kɑːdˌʃɑːpə*, -z
card-table, -s 'kɑːdˌteɪbl, -z
Card|well, -y 'kɑːd|wəl [-wel], -ɪ
car|e (s. v.), -es, -ing, -ed keə*, -z, -rɪŋ, -d
careen, -s, -ing, -ed kə'riːn, -z, -ɪŋ, -d
career (s. v.), -s, -ing, -ed kə'rɪə*, -z, -rɪŋ, -d
careerist, -s kə'rɪərɪst, -s
care|ful, -fullest, -fully, -fulness 'keə-fʊl, -flɪst [-flɪst, -fəlɪst, -fʊlɪst], -flɪ [-flɪ, -fəlɪ, -fʊlɪ], -fʊlnɪs [-nəs]
careless, -ly, -ness 'keəlɪs [-ləs], -lɪ, -nɪs [-nəs]
caress (s. v.), -es, -ing, -ed kə'res, -ɪz, -ɪŋ, -t
caret, -s 'kærət, -s
caretaker, -s 'keəˌteɪkə*, -z
Carew kə'ruː, 'keərɪ, see also Pole Carew
careworn 'keəwɔːn
Carey 'keərɪ
Carfax 'kɑːfæks
car-ferr|y, -ies 'kɑːˌfer|ɪ, -ɪz
Cargill 'kɑːgɪl, kɑː'gɪl
cargo, -es 'kɑːgəʊ, -z
Caria 'keərɪə
Carib, -s 'kærɪb, -z
Caribbean ˌkærɪ'biːən [-'brən, kə'rɪb-rən]
Caribbees 'kærɪbiːz
caribou (C.), -s 'kærɪbuː, -z
caricatur|e (s. v.), -es, -ing, -ed 'kærɪkə-ˌtjʊə* [-tjɔː*, -tjɔə*, -ˌtʃʊə*, ˌ---'-], -z, -rɪŋ, -d
caricaturist, -s 'kærɪkəˌtjʊərɪst [-tjɔː-, -tjɔə-, -tjə-, -ˌtʃʊə-, -tʃə-, ˌ---'-], -s
caries 'keəriːz
carillon, -s 'kærɪljən [-lɒn, kə'rɪljən], -z
Carinthia kə'rɪnθɪə [-θjə]
carious 'keərɪəs
Carisbrooke 'kærɪsbrʊk [-ɪzb-]
Carl kɑːl
Carleton 'kɑːltən
Carlile kɑː'laɪl
Carlisle kɑː'laɪl [locally '--]
Carlist, -s 'kɑːlɪst, -s
Carlos 'kɑːlɒs
Carlovingian ˌkɑːləʊ'vɪndʒɪən [-dʒən, -dʒən]
Carlow 'kɑːləʊ
Carlsbad (K-) 'kɑːlzbæd
Carlsruhe (K-) 'kɑːlzˌruːə [-ˌrʊə]
Carlton 'kɑːltən
Carluke kɑː'luːk
Carlyle kɑː'laɪl [ˌkɑː'laɪl]
Carlyon kɑː'laɪən
car|man, -men 'kɑː|mən, -mən [-men]

Carmarthen, -shire kə'mɑːðn, -ʃə* [-ˌʃɪə*]
Carmel 'kɑːmel [-məl]
Carmelite, -s 'kɑːmɪlaɪt [-məl-, -mel-], -s
Carmen 'kɑːmen
Carmichael kɑː'maɪkl
carminative (s. adj.), -s 'kɑːmɪnətɪv, -z
carmine 'kɑːmaɪn
Carnaby 'kɑːnəbɪ
Carnac 'kɑːnæk
carnage 'kɑːnɪdʒ
Carnaghan 'kɑːnəgən
carn|al, -ally 'kɑːn|l, -əlɪ
carnality kɑː'nælətɪ [-ɪtɪ]
Carnarvon, old spelling of Caernarvon, q.v.
Carnatic kɑː'nætɪk
carnation, -s kɑː'neɪʃn, -z
Carnegie kɑː'negɪ, -'neɪgɪ, -'niːgɪ
carnelian, -s kə'niːljən [kɑː'n-, -lɪən], -z
Carnforth 'kɑːnfɔːθ
carnival, -s 'kɑːnɪvl, -z
carnivore, -s 'kɑːnɪvɔː* [-vɔə*], -z
carnivorous kɑː'nɪvərəs
Carnochan 'kɑːnəkən [kɑː'nɒ-, -xən]
Carnwath kɑːn'wɒθ, 'kɑːnwɒθ
car|ol (s. v.) (C.), -ols, -olling, -olled 'kær|əl, -əlz, -əlɪŋ [-lɪŋ], -əld
Carolina ˌkærə'laɪnə
Caroline 'kærəlaɪn [-rlaɪn], less freq. -rəlɪn [-rlɪn]
carolus (C.), -es 'kærələs [-rləs], -ɪz
Carothers kə'rʌðəz
carotid, -s kə'rɒtɪd, -z
carous|e (s. v.), -es, -ing, -ed; -al/s kə'raʊz, -ɪz, -ɪŋ, -d; -l/z
car(r)ousel ˌkæruː'zel [-rʊ'z-]
carp (s. v.), -s, -ing, -ed, -er/s kɑːp, -s, -ɪŋ, -t, -ə*/z
car-park, -s 'kɑːpɑːk, -s
Carpathian, -s kɑː'peɪθjən [-θɪən, -ðjən, -ðɪən], -z
carpel, -s 'kɑːpel, -z
Carpentaria ˌkɑːpən'teərɪə [-pen't-]
carpent|er (s. v.) (C.), -ers, -ering, -ered 'kɑːpənt|ə* [-pɪn-, -pn-], -əz, -ərɪŋ], -əd
carpentry 'kɑːpəntrɪ [-pɪn-, -pn-]
carpet (s. v.), -s, -ing, -ed 'kɑːpɪt, -s, -ɪŋ, -ɪd
carpet-bag, -s 'kɑːpɪtbæg, -z
carpet-beat|er/s, -ing 'kɑːpɪtˌbiːt|ə*/z, -ɪŋ
carpet-broom, -s 'kɑːpɪtbrʊm [-bruːm], -z
carpet-sweeper, -s 'kɑːpɪtˌswiːpə*, -z
Carpmael 'kɑːpmeɪl
Carr kɑː*

75

carrag(h)een 'kærəgi:n
Carrara kə'rɑ:rə
carraway, -s 'kærəweɪ, -z
Carrhae 'kæri:
carriage, -s 'kærɪdʒ, -ɪz
carriage-drive, -s 'kærɪdʒdraɪv, -z
carriage-horse, -s 'kærɪdʒhɔ:s, -ɪz
carriage-way 'kærɪdʒweɪ
carrick (C.) 'kærɪk
Carrickfergus ˌkærɪk'fɜ:gəs
carrier-bag, -s 'kærɪəbæg, -z
Carrington 'kærɪŋtən
carrioca ˌkærɪ'əʊkə
carrion; -crow/s 'kærɪən; (ˌ--) -'krəʊ/z
Carrodus 'kærədəs
Carroll 'kærəl
carrot, -s, -y 'kærət, -s, -ɪ
Carruthers kə'rʌðəz
carr|y, -ies, -ying, -ied, -ier/s 'kær|ɪ,
-ɪz, -ɪŋ, -ɪd, -ɪə*/z
carry-cot, -s 'kærɪkɒt, -s
carryings-on ˌkærɪɪŋz'ɒn
Carshalton kə'ʃɔ:ltən [kɑ:'ʃ-, old-
fashioned local pronunciations keɪs-
'hɔ:ltən, keɪs'hɔ:tn, keɪ'ʃɔ:tn]
Carson 'kɑ:sn
Carstairs 'kɑ:steəz
cart (s. v.) (C.), -s, -ing, -ed, -er/s;
-age kɑ:t, -s, -ɪŋ, -ɪd, -ə*/z; -ɪdʒ
Carta 'kɑ:tə
Cartagena ˌkɑ:tə'dʒi:nə
carte (C.) kɑ:t
carte blanche ˌkɑ:t'blɑ̃:nʃ [-'blɔ̃:nʃ,
-'blɑ:nʃ, -'blɔ:nʃ] (kartblɑ̃:ʃ)
carte-de-visite, -s ˌkɑ:tdəvi:'zi:t [-vɪ'z-]
(kartdəvizit), -s
cartel, -s (business combine) kɑ:'tel,
(other senses) kɑ:'tel ['kɑ:tl], -z
Carter 'kɑ:tə*
Carteret (surname) 'kɑ:təret [-rɪt],
(American place name) ˌkɑ:tə'ret
Cartesian kɑ:'ti:zjən [-zɪən, -ʒjən,
-ʒɪən, -ʒn]
Carthage 'kɑ:θɪdʒ
Carthaginian, -s ˌkɑ:θə'dʒɪnɪən [-njən],
-z
cart-horse, -s 'kɑ:thɔ:s, -ɪz
Carthusian, -s kɑ:'θju:zjən [-'θu:-,
-zɪən], -z
cartilage, -s 'kɑ:tɪlɪdʒ [-təl-], -ɪz
cartilaginous ˌkɑ:tɪ'lædʒɪnəs [-tə'l-,
-dʒnəs]
cart-load, -s 'kɑ:tləʊd, -z
Cartmel(e) 'kɑ:tmel
cartograph|y, -er/s kɑ:'tɒgrəf|ɪ, -ə*/z
cartomancy 'kɑ:təʊmænsɪ
carton, -s 'kɑ:tən [-tn], -z
cartoon, -s, -ist/s kɑ:'tu:n, -z, -ɪst/s

cartouche, -s kɑ:'tu:ʃ, -ɪz
cartridge, -s 'kɑ:trɪdʒ, -ɪz
cartridge-paper 'kɑ:trɪdʒˌpeɪpə*
cart-track, -s 'kɑ:ttræk, -s
cart-wheel, -s 'kɑ:twi:l [-thw-], -z
cartwright (C.), -s 'kɑ:traɪt, -s
caruncle, -s 'kærəŋkl [kə'rʌŋkl], -z
Carus 'keərəs
Caruso kə'ru:zəʊ [-'ru:səʊ]
Caruthers kə'rʌðəz
car|ve, -es, -ing, -ed, -er/s (C.) kɑ:v, -z,
-ɪŋ, -d, -ə*/z
carving-kni|fe, -ves 'kɑ:vɪŋnaɪ|f, -vz
Carwardine 'kɑ:wədi:n
Cary 'keərɪ
caryatid, -s, -es ˌkærɪ'ætɪd, -z, -i:z
Caryll 'kærɪl [-rəl]
Carysfort 'kærɪsfɔ:t
Casabianca ˌkæsəbɪ'æŋkə [-æzə-, -'bjæ-]
Casablanca ˌkæsə'blæŋkə
Casanova ˌkæzə'nəʊvə [ˌkæsə-]
cascade, -s kæ'skeɪd, -z
cascara, -s kæ'skɑ:rə [kə's-], -z
cascarilla ˌkæskə'rɪlə
cas|e (s. v.) (C.), -es, -ing, -ed keɪs, -ɪz,
-ɪŋ, -t
case-ending, -s 'keɪsˌendɪŋ, -z
case-hardened 'keɪsˌhɑ:dnd
casein 'keɪsɪːn [-sɪn]
case-kni|fe, -ves 'keɪsnaɪ|f, -vz
case-law 'keɪslɔ:
casemate, -s 'keɪsmeɪt, -s
casement, -s 'keɪsmənt [old-fashioned
'keɪzm-], -s
Casement 'keɪsmənt
casern, -s kə'zɜ:n, -z
case-shot 'keɪsʃɒt ['keɪʃʃɒt]
case-worm, -s 'keɪswɜ:m, -z
Casey 'keɪsɪ
cash (s. v.), -es, -ing, -ed kæʃ, -ɪz, -ɪŋ, -t
cash-account, -s ˌkæʃə'kaʊnt ['--ˌ-], -s
cash-book, -s 'kæʃbʊk, -s
cash-box, -es 'kæʃbɒks, -ɪz
cashew, -s kæ'ʃu: [kə'ʃ-, 'kæʃu:], -z
cashier (s.), -s kæ'ʃɪə*, -z
cashier (v.), -s, -ing, -ed, -er/s kə'ʃɪə*
[kæ'ʃ-], -z, -ɪŋ, -d, -ə*/z
cashmere (C.), -s kæʃ'mɪə* [also '-ˌ-
when attributive], -z
casing (s.), -s 'keɪsɪŋ, -z
casino, -s kə'si:nəʊ [kə'zi:-], -z
cask (s. v.), -s, -ing, -ed kɑ:sk, -s, -ɪŋ, -t
casket, -s 'kɑ:skɪt, -s
Caslon 'kæzlən
Caspar 'kæspə* [-pɑ:*]
Caspian 'kæspɪən [-pjən]
casque, -s kæsk, -s
Cassandra kə'sændrə

cassation, -s kæ'seɪʃn [kə's-], -z
cassava kə'sɑːvə
Cassel(l) 'kæsl
casserole, -s 'kæsərəʊl, -z
cassette, -s kæ'set [kə-], -s
cassia 'kæsɪə [-sjə]
Cassidy 'kæsɪdɪ [-sədɪ]
Cassill(l)is 'kæslz ['kɑːs-]
Cassio 'kæsɪəʊ
Cassiopeia ˌkæsɪəʊ'piːə [-'pɪə, *as name of constellation also* ˌkæsɪ'əʊpjə, -'əʊpɪə]
Cassius 'kæsɪəs [-sjəs]
Cassivelaunus ˌkæsɪvɪ'lɔːnəs
cassock, -s, -ed 'kæsək, -s, -t
cassowar|y, -ies 'kæsəweər|ɪ [-wər-], -ɪz
cast (*s. v.*), -s, -ing kɑːst, -s, -ɪŋ
Castalia, -n/s kæ'steɪljə [-lɪə], -n/z
castanet, -s ˌkæstə'net, -s
castaway, -s 'kɑːstəweɪ, -z
caste, -s kɑːst, -s
castellated 'kæstəleɪtɪd [-tɪl-, -tel-]
Castelnau (*road in S.W. London*) 'kɑːslnɔː [-nəʊ]
caster, -s 'kɑːstə*, -z
castigat|e, -es, -ing, -ed, -or/s 'kæstɪgeɪt, -s, -ɪŋ, -ɪd, -ə*/z
castigation, -s ˌkæstɪ'geɪʃn, -z
Castile kæ'stiːl
Castilian, -s kæ'stɪlɪən [kə-, -ljən], -z
casting (*s.*), -s 'kɑːstɪŋ, -z
casting-net, -s 'kɑːstɪŋnet, -s
casting-vote, -s ˌkɑːstɪŋ'vəʊt ['---], -s
cast-iron ˌkɑːst'aɪən [*also* 'kɑːstˌaɪən *when attributive*]
castle, -s 'kɑːsl, -z
Castlebar ˌkɑːsl'bɑː*
Castlenau (*engineering firm*) 'kɑːslnɔː
Castlerea(gh) 'kɑːslreɪ
Castleton 'kɑːsltən
cast-off, -s ˌkɑːst'ɒf [*old-fashioned* 'ɔːf, *also* '--], -s
castor (C.), -s 'kɑːstə*, -z
castor-oil ˌkɑːstər'ɔɪl [-tə'ɔɪl]
castrametation ˌkæstrəme'teɪʃn [-mɪ't-]
castrat|e, -es, -ing, -ed kæ'streɪt ['kæstreɪt], -s, -ɪŋ, -ɪd
castration, -s kæ'streɪʃn, -z
castrat|o, -i kæ'strɑːt|əʊ, -iː
Castro 'kæstrəʊ
casual, -ly 'kæʒjʊəl [-ʒjwəl, -ʒjʊl, -ʒʊəl, -ʒwəl, -ʒʊl, -ʒjʊəl, -ʒjwəl, -ʒjʊl], -ɪ
casualt|y, -ies 'kæʒjʊəlt|ɪ [-ʒjwəl-, -ʒjʊl-, -ʒʊəl-, -ʒwəl-, -ʒʊl-, -ʒjʊəl-, -ʒjwəl-, -ʒjʊl-], -ɪz
casuist, -s, -ry 'kæzjʊɪst ['kæʒjʊ-, 'kæʒʊ-], -s, -rɪ

casuistic, -al ˌkæzjʊ'ɪstɪk [ˌkæʒjʊ-, ˌkæʒʊ-], -l
casus belli ˌkɑːsʊs'beliː: [ˌkeɪsəs'belaɪ]
Caswell 'kæzwəl [-wel]
cat, -s kæt, -s
cataclysm, -s 'kætəklɪzəm, -z
catacomb, -s 'kætəkuːm [-kəʊm], -z
catafalque, -s 'kætəfælk, -s
Catalan, -s 'kætələn [-læn], -z
catalectic ˌkætə'lektɪk
cataleps|y, -ies 'kætəleps|ɪ, -ɪz
cataleptic ˌkætə'leptɪk
catalogu|e (*s. v.*), -es, -ing, -ed 'kætəlɒg, -z, -ɪŋ, -d
Catalonia, -n/s ˌkætə'ləʊnjə [-nɪə], -n/z
catalpa, -s kə'tælpə, -z
catalysis kə'tælɪsɪs [-ləs-]
catalyst, -s 'kætəlɪst, -s
catalytic ˌkætə'lɪtɪk
catamaran, -s ˌkætəmə'ræn, -z
Catania kə'teɪnjə [-nɪə]
cataplasm, -s 'kætəplæzəm, -z
catapult, -s 'kætəpʌlt, -s
cataract, -s 'kætərækt, -s
catarrh, -s, -al kə'tɑː* [kæ't-], -z, -rəl
catasta, -s kə'tæstə, -z
catastas|is, -es kə'tæstəs|ɪs, -iːz
catastrophe, -s kə'tæstrəfɪ, -z
catastrophic ˌkætə'strɒfɪk
catawba (C.) kə'tɔːbə
catbird, -s 'kætbɜːd, -z
catboat, -s 'kætbəʊt, -s
catcall, -s 'kætkɔːl, -z
catch (*s. v.*), -es, -ing, caught, catcher/s kætʃ, -ɪz, -ɪŋ, kɔːt, 'kætʃə*/z
catching (*adj.*) 'kætʃɪŋ
catchpenn|y, -ies 'kætʃˌpen|ɪ, -ɪz
catchpole, -s 'kætʃpəʊl, -z
catchpoll, -s 'kætʃpəʊl, -z
catchword, -s 'kætʃwɜːd, -z
catch|y, -iness 'kætʃ|ɪ, -ɪnɪs [-ɪnəs]
Catcott 'kætkət
catechetic, -al, -ally ˌkætɪ'ketɪk [-te'k-, -tək-], -l, -əlɪ
catechi|sm/s, -st/s 'kætɪkɪ|zəm/z [-tək-], -st/s
catechiz|e [-is|e], -es, -ing, -ed, -er/s 'kætɪkaɪz [-tək-], -ɪz, -ɪŋ, -d, -ə*/z
catechu 'kætɪtʃuː [-tə-]
catechumen, -s ˌkætɪ'kjuːmen [-tə'k-, -mɪn], -z
categoric|al, -ally ˌkætɪ'gɒrɪk|l [-te'g-, -tə'g-], -əlɪ
categoriz|e [-is|e], -es, -ing, -ed 'kætɪgəraɪz [-teg-, -təg-], -ɪz, -ɪŋ, -d
categor|y, -ies 'kætɪgər|ɪ [-teg-, -təg-], -ɪz
catena, -s kə'tiːnə, -z

catenar|y, -ies kə'ti:nər|ı, -ız
catenat|e, -es, -ing, -ed 'kætɪneɪt [-tən-],
-s, -ıŋ, -ɪd
catenation, -s ˌkætɪ'neɪʃn [-tə'n-], -z
cateniz|e [-is|e], -es, -ing, -ed 'kætɪnaɪz
[-tən-], -ız, -ıŋ, -d
cat|er (C.), -ers, -ering, -ered, -erer/s
'keɪt|ə*, -əz, -ərıŋ, -əd, -ərə*/z
cater-cousin, -s 'keɪtəˌkʌzn, -z
Caterham 'kertərəm
Caterina ˌkætə'ri:nə
caterpillar, -s 'kætəpɪlə*, -z
caterwaul (s. v.), -s, -ing, -ed 'kætəwɔ:l,
-z, -ıŋ, -d
Catesby 'kertsbɪ
cat-eyed 'kætaɪd
catfish, -es 'kætfɪʃ, -ız
Catford 'kætfəd
catgut 'kætgʌt [-gət]
Catharine 'kæθərɪn
cathari|sm, -st|s 'kæθərɪ|zəm, -st/s
catharsis kə'θɑ:sɪs [kæ'θ-]
cathartic, -s kə'θɑ:tɪk [kæ'θ-], -s
Cathay kæ'θeɪ [kə'θ-]
Cathcart 'kæθkət [-kɑ:t], kæθ'kɑ:t
[kəθ-]
cathead, -s 'kæthed, -z
cathedra, -s kə'θi:drə [-'θed-], -z
cathedra (in phrase ex cathedra)
kə'θi:drə [kæ'tedrɑ:, kæ'θed-,
kə'ted-, kə'θed-]
cathedral, -s kə'θi:drəl, -z
Cather 'kæðə*
Catherine 'kæθərɪn
catherine-wheel, -s 'kæθərɪnwi:l
[-nhw-], -z
catheter, -s 'kæθɪtə* [-θet-], -z
cathetometer, -s ˌkæθɪ'tɒmɪtə* [-θə't-,
-mətə*], -z
cathode, -s 'kæθəʊd, -z
cat-hole, -s 'kæthəʊl, -z
catholic (C.), -s 'kæθəlɪk [-θ]ɪk, -θlɪk,
rarely 'kɑ:θ-], -s
catholicism kə'θɒlɪsɪzəm
catholicity ˌkæθəʊ'lɪsɪtɪ [-ɪtɪ]
catholiciz|e [-is|e], -es, -ing, -ed kə'θɒ-
lɪsaɪz, -ız, -ıŋ, -d
Catiline 'kætɪlaɪn [-təl-]
cation, -s 'kætaɪən, -z
catkin, -s 'kætkɪn, -z
catlike 'kætlaɪk
catmint 'kætmɪnt
Cato 'kertəʊ
cat-o'-nine-tails ˌkætə'naɪnteɪlz
Cator 'kertə*
Catriona kə'trɪɒnə [kæ't-, -'tri:nə,
rarely ˌkætrɪ'əʊnə]
cat's-cradle 'kæts̩kreɪdl [ˌ-'--]

cat's-eye, -s 'kætsaɪ, -z
cat's-meat 'kætsmi:t
cat's-paw, -s 'kætspɔ:, -z
catsup, -s 'kætsəp ['kætʃəp, 'ketʃəp], -s
Cattanach 'kætənæk [-nɑ:x]
Cattegat 'kætɪgæt
Cattell kæ'tel [kə't-]
Cattermole 'kætəməʊl
cattish 'kætɪʃ
cattle 'kætl
cattle-pen, -s 'kætlpen, -z
cattle-show, -s 'kætlʃəʊ, -z
cattle-truck, -s 'kætltrʌk, -s
catt|y, -ier, -iest, -ily, -iness 'kæt|ı, -ɪə*,
-ɪɪst, -ɪlɪ [-əlɪ], -ɪnɪs [-ınəs]
Catullus kə'tʌləs
Caucasia kɔ:'keɪzjə [-zɪə, -ʒjə, -ʒɪə, -ʒə]
Caucasian, -s kɔ:'keɪzjən [-eɪzɪən,
-eɪʒjən, -eɪʒɪən, -eɪʒn], -z
Caucasus 'kɔ:kəsəs
caucus, -es 'kɔ:kəs, -ız
caudal 'kɔ:dl
caudillo, -s kaʊ'dɪləʊ [-'dɪljəʊ], -z
Caudine 'kɔ:daɪn
caudle (C.) 'kɔ:dl
caught (from catch) kɔ:t
caul, -s kɔ:l, -z
cauldron, -s 'kɔ:ldrən ['kɒl-], -z
cauliflower, -s 'kɒlɪˌflaʊə*, -z
caulk, -s, -ing, -ed kɔ:k, -s, -ıŋ, -t
caulker, -s 'kɔ:kə*, -z
caus|al, -ally 'kɔ:z|l, -əlɪ [-l̩ɪ]
causality kɔ:'zælɪtɪ [-ɪtɪ]
causation kɔ:'zeɪʃn
causative, -ly 'kɔ:zətɪv, -lɪ
caus|e (s. v.), -es, -ing, -ed kɔ:z, -ız, -ıŋ,
-d
cause célèbre ˌkəʊz se'lebrə [-leɪbrə]
(ko:z selɛbr)
causeless, -ly 'kɔ:zlɪs [-ləs], -lɪ
causerie, -s 'kəʊzəri: [-rɪ] (kozri), -z
causeway, -s 'kɔ:zweɪ, -z
caustic, -al, -ally 'kɔ:stɪk ['kɒs-], -l,
-əlɪ
causticity kɔ:'stɪsɪtɪ [kɒ's-, -ɪtɪ]
cauterization [-isa-], -s ˌkɔ:təraɪ'zeɪʃn
[-rɪ'z-], -z
cauteriz|e [-is|e], -es, -ing, -ed 'kɔ:təraɪz,
-ız, -ıŋ, -d
cauter|y, -ies 'kɔ:tər|ı, -ız
cauti|on (s. v.), -ons, -oning, -oned,
-oner/s 'kɔ:ʃ|n, -nz, -nıŋ [-ənıŋ,
-nıŋ], -nd, -nə*/z [-ənə*/z, -nə*/z]
cautionary 'kɔ:ʃnərɪ [-ʃənə-, -ʃnə-]
caution-money 'kɔ:ʃnˌmʌnɪ
cautious, -ly, -ness 'kɔ:ʃəs, -lɪ, -nɪs
[-nəs]
cavalcade, -s ˌkævl'keɪd, -z

cavalier, -s ˌkævəˈlɪə*, -z
Cavalleria Rusticana kəˌvæləˈriːə-
ˌrʊstɪˈkɑːnə [ˌkævəl-, -ˈrɪə]
cavalr|y, -ies ˈkævlr|ɪ, -ɪz
cavalry|man, -men ˈkævlrɪ|mən
[-mæn], -mən [-men]
Cavan ˈkævən
Cavanagh ˈkævənə
Cavanaugh ˈkævənɔː
cavatina, -s ˌkævəˈtiːnə, -z
cav|e (s. v.) (C.), -es, -ing, -ed keɪv, -z,
-ɪŋ, -d
cave (beware) ˈkeɪvɪ
caveat, -s ˈkævɪæt [ˈkeɪv-], -s
cave-dweller, -s ˈkeɪvˌdweləˈ*, -z
Cavell ˈkævl, kəˈvel
Note.—The family of Nurse Edith
Cavell pronounces ˈkævl.
cave|man, -men ˈkeɪv|mæn, -men
Cavendish ˈkævəndɪʃ
cavern, -s, -ous ˈkævən [-vɜːn], -z, -əs
Caversham ˈkævəʃəm
caviar(e) ˈkævɪɑː* [ˌkævɪˈɑː*]
cavil (s. v.), -s, -ling, -led, -ler/s ˈkævɪl
[-vl], -z, -ɪŋ, -d, -əˈ*/z
cavillation, -s ˌkævɪˈleɪʃn [-vəl-], -z
cavit|y, -ies ˈkævət|ɪ [-ɪt|ɪ], -ɪz
cavort, -s, -ing, -ed kəˈvɔːt, -s, -ɪŋ, -ɪd
cav|y, -ies ˈkeɪv|ɪ, -ɪz
caw, -s, -ing, -ed kɔː, -z, -ɪŋ, -d
Caw|dor, -ley ˈkɔː|dəˈ*, -lɪ
Cawnpore (old spelling of Kanpur)
kɔːnˈpɔː* [-ˈpɔə*] (Hindi kanpwr)
Cawse kɔːz
Caxton ˈkækstən
cayenne (C.) keɪˈen [but ˈkeɪen in
Cayenne pepper]
Cayley ˈkeɪlɪ
cayman (C.), -s ˈkeɪmən, -z
Cearns keənz
ceas|e, -es, -ing, -ed siːs, -ɪz, -ɪŋ, -t
cease-fire ˌsiːsˈfaɪə* [ˈ—]
ceaseless, -ly, -ness ˈsiːslɪs [-ləs], -lɪ,
-nɪs [-nəs]
Cecil (Christian name, surname) ˈsesl
[-sɪl], ˈsɪsl [-sɪl]
Note.—The family name of the Marquess of Exeter and that of the
Marquess of Salisbury is ˈsɪsl [-sɪl].
Cecile (Christian name) ˈsesɪl [-sl],
ˈsesiːl
Cecilia sɪˈsɪljə [səˈs-, -ˈsiː-, -lɪə]
Cecily ˈsɪsɪlɪ [-əlɪ], ˈsesɪlɪ [-əlɪ]
cedar, -s ˈsiːdəˈ*, -z
ced|e, -es, -ing, -ed siːd, -z, -ɪŋ, -ɪd
cedilla, -s sɪˈdɪlə [sə-], -z
Cedric ˈsiːdrɪk, ˈsedrɪk
ceil, -s, -ing, -ed siːl, -z, -ɪŋ, -d

ceilidh, -s ˈkeɪlɪ, -z
ceiling (s.), -s ˈsiːlɪŋ, -z
celadon ˈseládʊn [-dən]
celandine, -s ˈseləndaɪn, -z
celanese ˌseləˈniːz
Celebes seˈliːbɪz [sɪˈl-]
celebrant, -s ˈselɪbrənt, -s
celebrat|e, -es, -ing, -ed, -or/s ˈselɪbreɪt,
-s, -ɪŋ, -ɪd, -əˈ*/z
celebration, -s ˌselɪˈbreɪʃn, -z
celebratory ˈselɪbrətərɪ [-breɪt-, ˌselɪ-
ˈbreɪtərɪ]
celebrit|y, -ies sɪˈlebrət|ɪ [səˈl-, -ɪt|ɪ], -ɪz
celeriac sɪˈlerɪæk [səˈl-, ˈselərɪæk]
celerity sɪˈlerɪtɪ [səˈl-, -ɪtɪ]
celery ˈselərɪ
celeste, -s sɪˈlest [səˈl-], -s
celestial (C.), -ly sɪˈlestjəl [səˈl-, -tɪəl],
-ɪ
celestine (mineral) ˈselɪstaɪn
Celestine, -s ˈselɪstaɪn [-ləs-, sɪˈlestaɪn,
sɪˈlestɪn, səˈl-], -z
Celia ˈsiːljə [-lɪə]
celibacy ˈselɪbəsɪ
celibatarian, -s ˌselɪbəˈteərɪən, -z
celibate, -s ˈselɪbət [-bɪt], -s
cell, -s sel, -z
cellar, -s; -age, -er/s ˈseləˈ*, -z; -ɪdʒ,
-rəˈ*/z
cellaret, -s ˌseləˈret [ˈseləret], -s
cellarist, -s ˈselərɪst, -s
cellar|man, -men seləˈ|mən [-mæn],
-mən [-men]
cellist, -s ˈtʃelɪst, -s
cello, -s ˈtʃeləʊ, -z
cellophane ˈseləʊfeɪn
cellular ˈseljʊləˈ*
cellule, -s ˈseljuːl, -z
celluloid ˈseljʊlɔɪd
cellulose ˈseljʊləʊs
Celsius ˈselsjəs [-sɪəs]
celt, -s selt, -s
Celt, -s (as generally used) kelt [rarely
selt], (member of football team) selt, -s
Celtic (as generally used) ˈkeltɪk [rarely
ˈseltɪk], (in names of football team)
ˈseltɪk, (for Sea) ˈkeltɪk
Cely ˈsiːlɪ
cembalo, -s ˈtʃembələʊ, -z
cement (s. v.), -s, -ing, -ed sɪˈment
[səˈm-], -s, -ɪŋ, -ɪd
cementation, -s ˌsiːmenˈteɪʃn, -z
cementium sɪˈmenʃjəm [-ʃɪəm]
cemeter|y, -ies ˈsemɪtr|ɪ [-ətr|ɪ], -ɪz
Cenci (poem by Shelley) ˈtʃentʃɪ
Cenis səˈniː [seˈn-] (səni)
cenobite, -s ˈsiːnəʊbaɪt, -s
cenotaph, -s ˈsenəʊtɑːf [-tæf], -s

cens|e, -es, -ing, -ed sens, -ɪz, -ɪŋ, -t
censer, -s 'sensə*, -z
cens|or (s. v.), -ors, -oring, -ored
'sens|ə*, -əz, -ərɪŋ, -əd
censorial, -ly sen'sɔːrɪəl, -ɪ
censorian sen'sɔːrɪən
censorious, -ly, -ness sen'sɔːrɪəs, -lɪ,
-nɪs [-nəs]
censorship, -s 'sensəʃɪp, -s
censurable 'senʃərəbl
censur|e (s. v.), -es, -ing, -ed 'senʃə*, -z,
-rɪŋ, -d
census, -es 'sensəs, -ɪz
census-paper, -s 'sensəsˌpeɪpə*, -z
cent, -s sent, -s
centage 'sentɪdʒ
cental, -s 'sentl, -z
centaur, -s 'sentɔː*, -z
centaur|y, -ies 'sentɔːr|ɪ, -ɪz
centenarian, -s ˌsentɪ'neərɪən, -z
centenar|y, -ies sen'tiːnər|ɪ [-'ten-,
'sentɪnər|ɪ], -ɪz
centennial sen'tenjəl [-nɪəl]
center (s. v.), -s, -ing, -ed 'sentə*, -z,
-rɪŋ, -d
centesim|al, -ally sen'tesɪm|l, -əlɪ
centigrade 'sentɪgreɪd
centigramme, -s 'sentɪgræm, -z
centilitre, -s 'sentɪˌliːtə*, -z
centime, -s 'sɒntiːm ['sãːn-, 'sɔ̃ːnt-,
'sɑːnt-, 'sɔːnt-] (sãtim), -z
centimetre, -s 'sentɪˌmiːtə*, -z
centipede, -s 'sentɪpiːd, -z
centner, -s 'sentnə* ('tsɛntnər), -z
cento, -s 'sentəʊ, -z
centr|al, -ally 'sentr|əl, -əlɪ
centrality sen'trælətɪ [-ɪtɪ]
centralization [-isa-] ˌsentrəlaɪ'zeɪʃn
[-trlaɪ'z-, -trəlɪ'z-, -trlɪ'z-]
centraliz|e [-is|e], -es, -ing, -ed, 'sentrə-
laɪz [-trl-], -ɪz, -ɪŋ, -d
cent|re (s. v.), -res, -ring, -red 'sent|ə*,
-əz, -ərɪŋ, -əd
centre-bit, -s 'sentəbɪt, -s
centre-piece, -s 'sentəpiːs, -ɪz
centric, -al, -ally 'sentrɪk, -l, -əlɪ
centrifugal sen'trɪfjʊgl ['sentrɪfjuːg-,
ˌsentrɪ'fjuːg-]
centripetal sen'trɪpɪtl ['sentrɪpiːt-,
ˌsentrɪ'piːt-]
centr|um, -a 'sentr|əm, -ə
centumvir, -s sen'tʌmvɜː* [ken'tʊm-,
-və*], -z
centumvirate, -s sen'tʌmvɪrət [-vər-,
-ɪt], -s
centuple 'sentjʊpl
centurion, -s sen'tjʊərɪən [-'tjɔər-,
-'tjɔː-, -'tʃʊər-], -z

centur|y, -ies 'sentʃʊr|ɪ [-tjʊr-, -tʃər-,
'senʃər-], -ɪz
cephalic ke'fælɪk [kɪ'f-, se'f-, sɪ'f-]
Note.—Members of the medical profession usually pronounce ke'f- or
kɪ'f-.
cephalopod, -s 'sefələʊpɒd, -z
cephalopoda ˌsefə'lɒpədə
Cephas 'siːfæs
Cepheid, -s 'siːfɪɪd, -z
Cepheus 'siːfjuːs [-fjəs, -frəs]
ceramic, -s sɪ'ræmɪk [se'r-, sə'r-, kɪ'r-,
ke'r-, kə'r-], -s (experts tend to use
the forms with k-)
cerastes sɪ'ræstiːz [se'r-, sə'r-]
cerate, -s 'sɪərɪt [-reɪt, -rət], -s
Cerberus 'sɜːbərəs
cerca|ria, -riae sɜː'keə|rɪə, -rɪiː
cer|e (s. v.), -es, -ing, -ed sɪə*, -z, -rɪŋ,
-d
cereal, -s 'sɪərɪəl, -z
cerebell|um, -ums, -a ˌserɪ'bel|əm,
-əmz, -ə
cerebos 'serɪbɒs
cerebral (s. adj.), -s 'serɪbrəl, -z
cerebration ˌserɪ'breɪʃn
cerebr|um, -a 'serɪbr|əm, -ə
cere|-cloth, -cloths 'sɪə|klɒθ [old-
fashioned -klɔːθ], -klɒθs [-klɔːðz,
-klɔːθs]
cerement, -s 'sɪəmənt, -s
ceremonial (s. adj.), -s, -ly; -ism
ˌserɪ'məʊnjəl [-rə'm-, -nɪəl], -z, -ɪ;
-ɪzəm
ceremonious, -ly, -ness ˌserɪ'məʊnjəs
[-rə'm-, -nɪəs], -lɪ, -nɪs [-nəs]
ceremon|y, -ies 'serɪmən|ɪ [-rəm-], -ɪz
cereous 'sɪərɪəs
Ceres 'sɪəriːz
cerif [ser-], -s 'serɪf, -s
cerise sə'riːz [sɪ'r-, -'riːs]
ceroplastic ˌsɪərəʊ'plæstɪk [-'plɑːs-]
certain, -ly 'sɜːtn [-tən, -tɪn], -lɪ
certaint|y, -ies 'sɜːtnt|ɪ [-tən-, -tɪn-], -ɪz
certes 'sɜːtɪz [sɜːts]
certifiabl|e, -ly ˌsɜːtɪ'faɪəb|l, -lɪ
certificate (s.), -es sə'tɪfɪkət [sɜː't-, -kɪt],
-s
certificat|e (v.), -es, -ing, -ed sə'tɪfɪkeɪt
[sɜː't-], -s, -ɪŋ, -ɪd [sə'tɪfɪkətɪd,
-kɪt-]
certification, -s (act of certifying) ˌsɜːtɪfɪ'keɪʃn, (providing with a certificate)
ˌsɜːtɪfɪ'keɪʃn [sə,t-], -z
certificatory sə'tɪfɪkətərɪ [sɜː't-, -keɪt-]
certi|fy, -fies, -fying, -fied, -fier/s 'sɜː-
tɪ|faɪ, -faɪz, -faɪɪŋ, -faɪd, -faɪə*/z
certiorari, -s ˌsɜːtɪɔː'reəraɪ [-tɪə'r-], -z

certitude 'sə:tɪtjuːd
cerulean sɪ'ruːljən [sɪə'r-, -lɪən]
cerumen sɪ'ruːmen
ceruse 'sɪərʊːs [sɪ'ruːs, sə'r-]
Cervantes sə:'væntɪz [-tiːz]
cervical sə:'vaɪkl [sə'v-, 'sə:vɪkl]
cervine 'sə:vaɪn
cervi|x, -ces, -xes 'sə:vɪ|ks, -siːz, -ksɪz
César 'seɪzɑ:* [-zə*] (seza:r)
Cesarewitch (Russian prince) sɪ'zɑ:rə-
    vɪtʃ [-rɪv-], (race) sɪ'zærəwɪtʃ [-'zɑ:r-,
    -rɪw-]
Cesario si:'zɑ:rɪəʊ [-'zær-]
cess, -es ses, -ɪz
cessation, -s se'seɪʃn, -z
cession, -s 'seʃn, -z
cessionar|y, -ies 'seʃənər|ɪ [-ʃnər-], -ɪz
cesspit, -s 'sespɪt, -s
cesspool, -s 'sespuːl, -z
Cestrian 'sestrɪən
cestui que trust, -s ˌsetɪkɪ'trʌst, -s
cestui que vie, -s ˌsetɪkɪ'viː, -z
cestuis que trust ˌsetɪzkɪ'trʌst
cestuis que vie ˌsetɪzkɪ'viː
cest|us, -i 'sest|əs, -aɪ
ceta|cea, -cean/s sɪ'teɪ|ʃjə [se't-, -ʃɪə,
    -ʃə, -sjə, -sɪə], -ʃjən/z [-ʃɪən/z, -ʃn/z,
    -sjən/z, -sɪən/z]
cetaceous sɪ'teɪʃjəs [se't-, -ʃɪəs, -ʃəs,
    -sjəs, -sɪəs]
cetane 'siːteɪn
Cetewayo ketʃ'waɪʊ [ˌketɪ'waɪʊ,
    -'wɑːjəʊ, old-fashioned ˌsetɪ'weɪʊ]
    (Zulu ȝetʃ'waːjo)
Cet(t)inje tse'tɪnjɪ [se't-]
Ceuta 'sjuːtə
Cévennes sɪ'ven [sə'v-, -enz] (sevɛn)
Ceylon sɪ'lɒn
Ceylonese ˌselə'niːz [ˌsiː-]
Ceyx 'siːɪks
Cézanne seɪ'zæn [sɪ-, se-] (sezan)
cf. kəm'peə* [kən'fɔ:*, ˌsiː'ef]
Chablis 'ʃæbliː [-blɪ] (ʃabli)
chaconne, -s ʃə'kɒn [ʃæ'k-] (ʃakɔn), -z
Chad tʃæd
Chadwick 'tʃædwɪk
chaf|e, -es, -ing, -ed tʃeɪf, -s, -ɪŋ, -t
chafer, -s 'tʃeɪfə*, -z
chaff (s. v.), -s, -ing/ly, -ed, -er/s tʃɑːf
    [tʃæf], -s, -ɪŋ/lɪ, -t, -ə*/z
chaff-cutter, -s 'tʃɑːfˌkʌtə*, -z
chaffer (v.), -s, -ing, -ed 'tʃæfə*, -z,
    -rɪŋ, -d
Chaffey 'tʃeɪfɪ
chaffinch, -es 'tʃæfɪntʃ, -ɪz
chaff|y, -iness 'tʃɑːf|ɪ, -ɪnɪs [-ɪnəs]
chafing-dish, -es 'tʃeɪfɪŋdɪʃ, -ɪz
chagrin (s.) 'ʃægrɪn

chagrin (v.), -s, -ing, -ed 'ʃægrɪn
    [ʃə'griːn], -z, -ɪŋ, -d
Chaim haɪm (Heb. 'xajim, xa'jiːm)
chain (s. v.), -s, -ing, -ed tʃeɪn, -z, -ɪŋ, -d
chain-armour ˌtʃeɪn'ɑːmə* ['-ˌ--]
chain-bridge, -s ˌtʃeɪn'brɪdʒ ['--], -ɪz
chain-gang, -s 'tʃeɪngæŋ, -z
chainless 'tʃeɪnlɪs [-ləs]
chain-mail ˌtʃeɪn'meɪl ['--]
chainstitch 'tʃeɪnstɪtʃ
chain-stores 'tʃeɪnstɔ:z [-stɔəz]
chainwork 'tʃeɪnwə:k
chair (s. v.), -s, -ing, -ed tʃeə*, -z, -rɪŋ,
    -d
chair-bed, -s 'tʃeəbed [ˌ-'-], -z
chair|man, -men 'tʃeə|mən, -mən
chairmanship, -s 'tʃeəmənʃɪp, -s
chaise, -s ʃeɪz, -ɪz
chaise-longue ˌʃeɪz'lɔ̃:ŋg [ˌʃez-, -'lɒŋg]
    (ʃɛ:zlɔ̃:g)
Chalcedon 'kælsɪdən [-dn, -dɒn]
chalcedony kæl'sedənɪ
chalcedonyx, -es ˌkælsɪ'dɒnɪks, -ɪz
Chalcis 'kælsɪs
chalcography kæl'kɒgrəfɪ
Chaldaic kæl'deɪɪk
Chaldea, -n/s kæl'diːə [-'dɪə], -n/z
Chaldee, -s kæl'diː, -z
chaldron, -s 'tʃɔːldrən, -z
chalet, -s 'ʃæleɪ ['ʃælɪ] (ʃalɛ), -z
Chalfont (in Buckinghamshire)
    'tʃælfənt [-fɒnt] [old-fashioned
    'tʃɑ:fənt]
Chaliapin ˌʃælɪ'ɑːpɪn (ʃa'ljapjin)
chalice, -s, -d 'tʃælɪs, -ɪz, -t
chalk (s. v.) (C.), -s, -ing, -ed tʃɔːk, -s,
    -ɪŋ, -t
Chalkis 'kælkɪs
chalk-pit, -s 'tʃɔːkpɪt, -s
chalk-stone, -s 'tʃɔːkstəʊn, -z
chalk|y, -ier, -iest, -ily, -iness 'tʃɔːk|ɪ,
    -ɪə* [-jə*], -ɪɪst [-jɪst], -ɪlɪ [-əlɪ],
    -ɪnɪs [-ɪnəs]
Challen 'tʃælɪn
challeng|e (s. v.), -es, -ing, -ed, -er/s
    'tʃælɪndʒ [-əndʒ], -ɪz, -ɪŋ, -d, -ə*/z
Challenor 'tʃælɪnə*
challis 'ʃælɪs ['tʃælɪ]
Challoner 'tʃælənə*
Chalmers 'tʃɑːməz
Chaloner 'tʃælənə*
chalybeate kə'lɪbɪət [kæ'l-, -bjət, -ɪt]
Cham kæm
chamade, -s ʃə'mɑːd, -z
chamber, -s, -ed 'tʃeɪmbə*, -z, -d
Chamberlain 'tʃeɪmbəlɪn [-blɪn, -lən],
    -bələɪn
chamberlain, -s 'tʃeɪmbəlɪn [-blɪn], -z

chamberlainship, -s 'tʃeɪmbəlɪnʃɪp [-blɪn-], -s

chamber-maid, -s 'tʃeɪmbəmeɪd, -z

Chambers 'tʃeɪmbəz

chameleon, -s kə'miːljən [-lɪən], -s

chamfer, -s 'tʃæmfə* ['ʃæm-], -z

chamois (sing.) 'ʃæmwɑ: [-wɔ:] [in chamois leather usually 'ʃæmɪ], (plur.) -z

Chamonix 'ʃæmənɪ [-niː]

champ, -s, -ing, -ed tʃæmp, -s, -ɪŋ, -t [tʃæmt]

champagne, -s ˌʃæm'peɪn [also '— when attributive], -z

champaign, -s 'tʃæmpeɪn, -z

champerty 'tʃæmpəːtɪ [-pət-]

champignon, -s tʃæm'pɪnjən (ʃãpiɲɔ̃), -z

champion (s. adj. v.) (C.), -s, -ing, -ed; -ship/s 'tʃæmpjən, -z, -ɪŋ, -d; -ʃɪp/s

Champs Elysées ˌʃãːnze'liːzeɪ [ˌʃɒnz-, ˌʃɔ̃:nz-, ˌʃɔ:nz-] (ʃãzelize)

chanc|e (s. v.), -es, -ing, -ed tʃɑːns, -ɪz, -ɪŋ, -t

chancel, -s 'tʃɑːnsl, -z

chanceller|y, -ies 'tʃɑːnsələr|ɪ [-slə-, -əlrɪ], -ɪz

chancellor (C.), -s; -ship/s 'tʃɑːnsələ* [-slə*, -slə*, -sɪlə*], -z; -ʃɪp/s

chancer|y (C.), -ies 'tʃɑːnsər|ɪ, -ɪz

chancre 'ʃæŋkə*

chanc|y, -ier, -iest 'tʃɑːns|ɪ, -ɪə [-jə], -ɪɪst [-jɪst]

chandelier, -s ˌʃændə'lɪə* [-dɪ'l-], -z

chandler (C.), -s 'tʃɑːndlə*, -z

Chandos 'ʃændɒs, 'tʃændɒs
Note.—Lord Chandos pronounces 'ʃæn-. Chandos Street in London is generally pronounced with 'tʃ-.

chang|e (s. v.), -es, -ing, -ed, -er/s tʃeɪndʒ, -ɪz, -ɪŋ, -d, -ə*/z

changeability ˌtʃeɪndʒə'bɪlətɪ [-lɪt-]

changeab|le, -ly, -leness 'tʃeɪndʒəb|l, -lɪ, -lnɪs [-nəs]

changeless 'tʃeɪndʒlɪs [-ləs]

changeling, -s 'tʃeɪndʒlɪŋ, -z

chann|el (s. v.), -els, -elling, -elled 'tʃæn|l, -lz, -lɪŋ [-əlɪŋ], -ld

Channell 'tʃænl

Channing 'tʃænɪŋ

Channon 'ʃænən, 'ʃænən

chant (s. v.) (C.), -s, -ing, -ed, -er/s tʃɑːnt, -s, -ɪŋ, -ɪd, -ə*/z

Chanter 'tʃɑːntə*

chanterelle, -s ˌtʃæntə'rel, -z

chanticleer, -s ˌtʃæntɪ'klɪə* [ˌtʃɑːnt-, ˌʃæn-, -, ˌʃɑːn-, '———], -z

Chantilly ʃæn'tɪlɪ [ʃã:n't-, ʃɔ̃:n't-, ʃɑːn't-, ʃɒn't-] (ʃãtiji)

Chantrey 'tʃɑːntrɪ

chantr|y, -ies 'tʃɑːntr|ɪ, -ɪz

chant|y, -ies 'tʃɑːnt|ɪ, -ɪz

chaos 'keɪɒs

chaotic keɪ'ɒtɪk

chap (s. v.), -s, -ping, -ped tʃæp, -s, -ɪŋ, -t

chap-book, -s 'tʃæpbʊk, -s

chape, -s tʃeɪp, -s

chapel, -s 'tʃæpl, -z

Chapel - en - le - Frith ˌtʃæplənlə'frɪθ [-plen-]

chapelr|y, -ies 'tʃæplr|ɪ, -ɪz

chaperon (s. v.), -s, -ing, -ed; -age 'ʃæpərəʊn, -z, -ɪŋ, -d; -ɪdʒ

chapfallen 'tʃæpˌfɔ:lən

chaplain, -s 'tʃæplɪn, -z

chaplainc|y, -ies 'tʃæplɪns|ɪ [-lən-], -ɪz

chaplet, -s 'tʃæplɪt [-lət, -let], -s

Chap|lin, -man 'tʃæp|lɪn, -mən

Chapp|ell, -le 'tʃæp|l, -l

chapter, -s 'tʃæptə*, -z

chapter-hou|se, -ses 'tʃæptəhaʊ|s, -zɪz

char (s. v.), -s, -ring, -red tʃɑ:*, -z, -rɪŋ, -d

char-à-banc, -s 'ʃærəbæŋ [-bã:ŋ, -bɔ̃:ŋ, -bɒŋ] (ʃarabã, as if French), -z

character, -s 'kærəktə* [-rɪk-], -z

characteristic, -s, -al, -ally ˌkærək-tə'rɪstɪk [-rɪk-], -s, -al, -əlɪ

characterization [-isa-], -s ˌkærəktəraɪ-'zeɪʃn [-rɪk-, -rɪ'z-], -z

characteriz|e [-is|e], -es, -ing, -ed 'kærəktəraɪz [-rɪk-], -ɪz, -ɪŋ, -d

charade, -s ʃə'rɑːd, -z

charcoal 'tʃɑːkəʊl

Chard tʃɑːd

char|e, -es, -ing, -ed tʃeə*, -z, -rɪŋ, -d

charg|e (s. v.), -es, -ing, -ed tʃɑːdʒ, -ɪz, -ɪŋ, -d

chargeab|le, -ly, -leness 'tʃɑːdʒəb|l, -lɪ, -lnɪs [-nəs]

chargé(s) d'affaires (sing.) ˌʃɑːˌʒeɪ-dæ'feə* [-də'f-] (ʃarʒedafɛːr), (plur.) -z

charger, -s 'tʃɑːdʒə*, -z

Charig 'tʃærɪg

Charing Cross ˌtʃærɪŋ'krɒs [ˌtʃeər-, old-fashioned -'krɔːs]

chariot, -s 'tʃærɪət, -s

charioteer, -s ˌtʃærɪə'tɪə*, -z

charisma kə'rɪzmə

charismatic ˌkærɪz'mætɪk

charitab|le, -ly, -leness 'tʃærətəb|l [-rɪt-], -lɪ, -lnɪs [-nəs]

charit|y, -ies 'tʃærət|ɪ [-ɪt|ɪ], -ɪz

charivari, -s ˌʃɑːrɪ'vɑːrɪ, -z

charivaria ˌʃɑːrɪ'vɑːrɪə

charlad|y, -ies 'tʃɑːˌleɪd|ɪ, -ɪz

charlatan, -s ʃɑːlətən [-tæn], -z

charlatan|ism/s, -ry ʃɑːlətən|ɪzəm/z [-tn̩|-], -rɪ

Charlecote 'tʃɑːlkəʊt

Charlemagne 'ʃɑːləmeɪn [ˌ--'-, -'maɪn] (ʃarləmaɲ)

Charlemont 'tʃɑːlɪmənt ['tʃɑːlm-]

Charles tʃɑːlz

Charleston 'tʃɑːlstən

Charlestown 'tʃɑːlztaʊn

Charlesworth 'tʃɑːlzwɜːθ [-wəθ]

Charl|ey, -ie 'tʃɑːl|ɪ, -ɪ

charlock 'tʃɑːlɒk

charlotte (C.), -s 'ʃɑːlət, -s

Charlottenburg ʃɑːˈlɒtnbɜːg

Charlton 'tʃɑːltən

charm (s. v.), -s, -ing/ly, -ed, -er/s tʃɑːm, -z, -ɪŋ/lɪ, -d, -ə*/z

Charmian 'tʃɑːmjən ['ʃɑː-, -mɪən]

charnel 'tʃɑːnl

charnel-hou|se, -ses 'tʃɑːnlhaʊ|s, -zɪz

Charnock 'tʃɑːnɒk [-nək]

Charon 'keərən [-rɒn]

Charrington 'tʃærɪŋtən

chart, -s tʃɑːt, -s

chart|er (s. v.), -ers, -ering, -ered, -erer/s 'tʃɑːt|ə*, -əz, -ərɪŋ, -əd, -ərə*/z

Charterhouse 'tʃɑːtəhaʊs

Charteris 'tʃɑːtəz, tʃɑːˈtərɪs

charter-part|y, -ies 'tʃɑːˌtəˌpɑːt|ɪ, -ɪz

charti|sm, -st/s 'tʃɑːtɪ|zəm, -st/s

Chartreuse, -s ʃɑːˈtrɜːz (ʃartrø:z), -ɪz

char|woman, -women 'tʃɑːˌ|wʊmən, -ˌwɪmɪn

char|y, -ier, -iest, -ily, -iness 'tʃeər|ɪ, -ɪə*, -ɪɪst, -əlɪ [-ɪlɪ], -ɪnɪs [-ɪnəs]

Charybdis kəˈrɪbdɪs

Chas. tʃɑːlz [rarely tʃæs]

chas|e (s. v.) (C.), -es, -ing, -ed, -er/s tʃeɪs, -ɪz, -ɪŋ, -t, -ə*/z

chasm, -s 'kæzəm, -z

chasmy 'kæzmɪ [-zəmɪ]

chassé, -s 'ʃæseɪ (ʃase), -z

chasseur, -s ʃæˈsɜː* (ʃasœːr), -z

chassis (sing.) 'ʃæsɪ [-siː], (plur.) 'ʃæsɪz [-siːz]

chaste, -ly, -ness tʃeɪst, -lɪ, -nɪs [-nəs]

chast|en, -ens, -ening, -ened 'tʃeɪs|n, -nz, -nɪŋ [-nɪŋ], -nd

chastis|e, -es, -ing, -ed, -er/s tʃæˈstaɪz, -ɪz, -ɪŋ, -d, -ə*/z

chastisement, -s 'tʃæstɪzmənt [tʃæ-ˈstaɪzmənt], -s

chastity 'tʃæstətɪ [-ɪtɪ]

Chastney 'tʃæsnɪ

chasuble, -s 'tʃæzjʊbl, -z

chat (s. v.), -s, -ting, -ted tʃæt, -s, -ɪŋ, -ɪd

Chataway 'tʃætəweɪ

château, -x 'ʃætəʊ (ʃato), -z

chatelain(e), -s 'ʃætəleɪn [-tɪl-], -z

Chater 'tʃeɪtə*

Chatham 'tʃætəm

Chatsworth 'tʃætswɜːθ [-wəθ]

chattel, -s 'tʃætl, -z

Chatter, -s, -ing, -ed, -er/s 'tʃætə*, -z, -rɪŋ, -d, -rə*/z

chatterbox, -es 'tʃætəbɒks, -ɪz

Chatteris 'tʃætərɪs

Chatterton 'tʃætətən

chatto 'tʃætəʊ

chatt|y, -ier, -iest, -ily, -iness 'tʃæt|ɪ, -ɪə*, -ɪɪst, -ɪlɪ [-əlɪ], -ɪnɪs [-ɪnəs]

Chaucer 'tʃɔːsə*

Chaucerian tʃɔːˈsɪərɪən

chaudron, -s 'tʃɔːdrən, -z

chauffer, -s 'tʃɔːfə*, -z

chauffeur, -s 'ʃəʊfə* [ʃəʊˈfɜː*], -z

Chauncey 'tʃɔːnsɪ

chauvini|sm, -st/s 'ʃəʊvɪnɪ|zəm [-vən-], -st/s

chaw, -s, -ing, -ed tʃɔː, -z, -ɪŋ, -d

Chawner 'tʃɔːnə*

Chaworth 'tʃɑːwɜːθ [-wəθ]

Chaytor 'tʃeɪtə*

cheap, -er, -est, -ly, -ness tʃiːp, -ə*, -ɪst, -lɪ, -nɪs [-nəs]

cheap|en, -ens, -ening, -ened 'tʃiːp|ən, -ənz, -ɲɪŋ [-nɪŋ], -ənd

cheap-jack, -s 'tʃiːpdʒæk, -s

Cheapside ˌtʃiːpˈsaɪd ['tʃiːpsaɪd]

cheat (s. v.), -s, -ing, -ed tʃiːt, -s, -ɪŋ, -ɪd

Cheatham 'tʃiːtəm

check (s. v. interj.), -s, -ing, -ed tʃek, -s, -ɪŋ, -t

checkers 'tʃekəz

checkmat|e (s. v. interj.), -es, -ing, -ed 'tʃekmeɪt [tʃek'm-], -s, -ɪŋ, -ɪd

check-rein, -s 'tʃekreɪn [ˌtʃek'r-], -z

check-weigher, -s 'tʃekˌweɪə*, -z

Cheddar 'tʃedə*

cheek (s. v.), -s, -ing, -ed tʃiːk, -s, -ɪŋ, -t

cheekbone, -s 'tʃiːkbəʊn, -z

Cheeke tʃiːk

cheek|y, -ier, -iest, -ily, -iness 'tʃiːk|ɪ, -ɪə* [-jə*], -ɪɪst [-jɪst], -ɪlɪ [-əlɪ], -ɪnɪs [-ɪnəs]

cheep, -s, -ing, -ed tʃiːp, -s, -ɪŋ, -t

cheer (s. v.), -s, -ing, -ed tʃɪə*, -z, -rɪŋ, -d

cheer|ful, -fully, -fulness 'tʃɪə|fʊl, -fʊlɪ [-fəlɪ], -fʊlnɪs [-nəs]

cheerio ˌtʃɪərɪ'əʊ

83

cheerless, -ly, -ness 'tʃɪəlɪs [-ləs], -lɪ, -nɪs [-nəs]

cheer|y, -ier, -iest, -ily, -iness 'tʃɪər|ɪ, -ɪə*, -ɪɪst, -əlɪ [-ɪlɪ], -ɪnɪs [-ɪnəs]

Cheeryble 'tʃɪərɪbl

cheese, -s tʃiːz, -ɪz

cheeseburger, -s 'tʃiːz,bɜːɡə*, -z

cheesecake, -s 'tʃiːzkeɪk, -s

Cheeseman 'tʃiːzmən

cheesemonger, -s 'tʃiːz,mʌŋɡə*, -z

cheese-paring 'tʃiːz,peərɪŋ

Cheesewright 'tʃezraɪt

chees|y, -iness 'tʃiːz|ɪ, -ɪnɪs [-ɪnəs]

cheetah, -s 'tʃiːtə, -z

Cheetham 'tʃiːtəm

chef, -s ʃef, -s

chef-d'œuvre, -s ˌʃeɪ'dɜːvrə [-və*] (ʃedœ:vr), -z

cheiromancy 'kaɪərəʊmænsɪ

Cheke tʃiːk

chel|a (claw), -ae 'kiːl|ə, -iː

chela (disciple), -s 'tʃeɪlə ['tʃiːlə], -z

Chelmsford 'tʃelmsfəd [old-fashioned local pronunciation 'tʃem-, 'tʃɒm-]

Chelsea 'tʃelsɪ

Cheltenham 'tʃeltnəm [-tnəm]

chemic, -al, -ally, -als 'kemɪk, -l, -əlɪ, -lz

chemise, -s ʃə'miːz [ʃɪ'm-], -ɪz

chemisette, -s ˌʃemi:'zet [-mɪ'z-], -s

chemist, -s, -ry 'kemɪst, -s, -rɪ [-məstrɪ]

Chemnitz 'kemnɪts

Chemosh 'kiːmɒʃ

Chenevix 'ʃenɪvɪks [-nəv-], 'tʃen-

Cheney 'tʃiːnɪ, 'tʃeɪnɪ

Chenies (in Buckinghamshire) 'tʃeɪnɪz ['tʃiːn-], (street in London) 'tʃiːnɪz

chenille ʃə'niːl

Cheops 'kiːɒps

Chepstow 'tʃepstəʊ

cheque, -s tʃek, -s

cheque-book, -s 'tʃekbʊk, -s

chequer (s. v.), -s, -ing, -ed 'tʃekə*, -z, -rɪŋ, -d

Chequers 'tʃekəz

cherish, -es, -ing, -ed 'tʃerɪʃ, -ɪz, -ɪŋ, -t

Cherith 'kɪərɪθ ['ker-]

Cherokee ˌtʃerə'kiː ['---]

cheroot, -s ʃə'ruːt [ʃɪ'r-], -s

cherr|y, -ies 'tʃer|ɪ, -ɪz

cherry-brand|y, -ies ˌtʃerɪ'brænd|ɪ, -ɪz

cherry-pie, -s ˌtʃerɪ'paɪ, -z

cherry-stone, -s 'tʃerɪstəʊn, -z

Chersonese 'kɜːsəniːs, -niːz

Chertsey 'tʃɜːtsɪ

cherub, -s 'tʃerəb, -z

cherubic tʃe'ruːbɪk [tʃɪ'r-, tʃə'r-]

cherubim 'tʃerəbɪm [-rʊb-]

Cherubini ˌkerʊ'biːniː [-rə'b-, -nɪ]

chervil 'tʃɜːvɪl

Cherwell (river, Lord) 'tʃɑːwəl

Chesapeake 'tʃesəpiːk

Chesebro(ugh) 'tʃiːzbrə

Chesham 'tʃeʃəm [-fʃəm old-fashioned local pronunciation 'tʃesəm]

Cheshire 'tʃeʃə* [-ˌʃɪə*]

Cheshunt 'tʃesnt

Chesney 'tʃesnɪ, 'tʃeznɪ

chess tʃes

chessboard, -s 'tʃesbɔːd [-bɒd], -z

chess|-man, -men 'tʃes|mæn, -men

chest, -s, -ed tʃest, -s, -ɪd

Chester 'tʃestə*

chesterfield (C.), -s 'tʃestəfiːld, -z

Chester-le-Street ˌtʃestəlɪ'striːt

Chesterton 'tʃestətən [-tn]

chest-note, -s 'tʃestnəʊt, -s

chestnut, -s 'tʃesnʌt [-stn-, -nət], -s

Chetham 'tʃetəm

Chet|wode, -wynd 'tʃet|wʊd, -wɪnd

cheval-glass, -es ʃə'vælglɑːs, -ɪz

chevalier, -s ˌʃevə'lɪə*, -z

Chevalier (surname) ʃə'væljeɪ [ʃɪ'v-]

Chevening (in Kent) 'tʃiːvnɪŋ

Chevenix 'ʃevɪnɪks [-vən-]

cheveril 'ʃevərɪl [-rəl]

Cheves tʃiːvz

Cheviot (hills, sheep) 'tʃevɪət [-vjət, also 'tʃɪv-, 'tʃiːv- mostly by people accustomed to Scottish pronunciation], (cloth) 'tʃevɪət [-vjət]

Chevis 'tʃevɪs

Chevrolet 'ʃevrəʊleɪ [ˌ--'-]

chevron, -s 'ʃevrən, -z

chev|y (s. v.) (C.), -ies, -ying, -ied 'tʃev|ɪ, -ɪz, -ɪɪŋ, -ɪd

chew, -s, -ing, -ed tʃuː, -z, -ɪŋ ['tʃuɪŋ], -d

chewing-gum 'tʃuːɪŋɡʌm ['tʃuɪŋ-]

Cheyenne ʃaɪ'æn [-'en]

Cheylesmore 'tʃaɪlzmɔ:* [-mɔə*], 'tʃɪl-, 'tʃeɪl-

Cheyne 'tʃeɪnɪ, tʃeɪn

Note.—In Cheyne Walk some say 'tʃeɪnɪ and others tʃeɪn.

Cheyney 'tʃeɪnɪ

chianti (C.) kɪ'æntɪ

chiaroscuro kɪˌɑːrə'skuərəʊ [-rɒ's-, -'skjʊə-]

chic ʃiːk [ʃɪk]

Chicago ʃɪ'kɑːɡəʊ [tʃɪ-, also -'kɔːɡəʊ in imitation of one American pronunciation]

chican|e (s. v.), -es, -ing, -ed, -er/s ʃɪ'keɪn [tʃɪ-], -z, -ɪŋ, -d, -ə*/z

chicaner|y, -ies ʃɪ'keɪnər|ɪ, -ɪz

Chichele 'tʃɪtʃɪlɪ
Chichester 'tʃɪtʃɪstə*
chi-chi 'ʃi:ʃi:
chick (C.), -s tʃɪk, -s
chickabidd|y, -ies 'tʃɪkə,bɪd|ɪ, -ɪz
chicken, -s 'tʃɪkɪn, -z
chicken-feed 'tʃɪkɪnfi:d
chicken-hearted 'tʃɪkɪn,hɑ:tɪd [,--'--]
chicken-pox 'tʃɪkɪnpɒks
chickweed 'tʃɪkwi:d
chicory 'tʃɪkərɪ
Chiddingly (in East Sussex) ,tʃɪdɪŋ'laɪ ['---]
chid|e, -es, -ing, chid tʃaɪd, -z, -ɪŋ, tʃɪd
chief (s. adj.), -s, -ly tʃi:f, -s, -lɪ
chieftain, -s 'tʃi:ftən [-tɪn], -z
chieftanc|y, -ies 'tʃi:ftəns|ɪ [-tɪn-], -ɪz
Chiene ʃi:n
chiff-chaff, -s 'tʃɪf-tʃæf, -s
chiffon, -s 'ʃɪfɒn, -z
chiffonier, -s ,ʃɪfə'nɪə*, -z
chignon, -s 'ʃi:njɔ̃:ŋ [-njɒŋ, old-fashioned ʃɪ'nɒn], -z
chihuahua (dog), -s tʃɪ'wɑ:wə [-wɑ:], -z
chilblain, -s 'tʃɪlbleɪn, -z
child (C.), -ren tʃaɪld, 'tʃɪldrən ['tʃʊldr-, 'tʃɪldr-]
child|bed, -birth 'tʃaɪld|bed, -bɜ:θ
Childe tʃaɪld
Childermas 'tʃɪldəmæs [-məs]
Childers 'tʃɪldəz
childhood 'tʃaɪldhʊd
childish, -ly, -ness 'tʃaɪldɪʃ, -lɪ, -nɪs [-nəs]
child|less, -like 'tʃaɪld|lɪs [-ləs], -laɪk
Chile [-ili] 'tʃɪlɪ
Chilean, -s 'tʃɪlɪən [-ljən], -z
chiliad, -s 'kɪlɪæd ['kaɪl-, -ljæd], -z
chilia|sm, -st/s 'kɪlɪæ|zəm, -st/s
chill (s. adj. v.), -s, -ing, -ed, -ness tʃɪl, -z, -ɪŋ, -d, -nɪs [-nəs]
chilli, -s 'tʃɪlɪ, -z
Chillingham (in Northumberland) 'tʃɪlɪŋəm
Chillingworth 'tʃɪlɪŋwɜ:θ [-wəθ]
Chillon 'ʃi:lɔ̃:ŋ ['ʃi:ʃɔ̃:ŋ, -ɔ:ŋ, old-fashioned 'ʃɪlən, 'ʃɪlɒn, ʃɪ'lɒn] (ʃijɔ̃)
Note.—In reading Byron's 'Castle of Chillon' it is usual to pronounce 'ʃɪlən or 'ʃɪlɒn.
chill|y, -ier, -iest, -iness 'tʃɪl|ɪ, -ɪə*, -ɪɪst, -ɪnɪs [-nəs]
Chiltern 'tʃɪltən
Chilton 'tʃɪltən
Chimborazo ,tʃɪmbə'rɑ:zəʊ [-bɒ'r-]
chim|e (s. v.), -es, -ing, -ed, -er/s tʃaɪm, -z, -ɪŋ, -d, -ə*/z
chimera, -s kaɪ'mɪərə [kɪ'm-], -z

chimere, -s tʃɪ'mɪə* [ʃɪ-], -z
chimeric, -al, -ally kaɪ'merɪk [kɪ'm-], -l, -əlɪ
chimney, -s 'tʃɪmnɪ, -z
chimney-corner, -s 'tʃɪmnɪ,kɔ:nə*, -z
chimney-piece, -s 'tʃɪmnɪpi:s, -ɪz
chimney-pot, -s 'tʃɪmnɪpɒt, -s
chimney-stack, -s 'tʃɪmnɪstæk, -s
chimney-sweep, -s 'tʃɪmnɪswi:p, -s
chimney-sweeper, -s 'tʃɪmnɪ,swi:pə*, -z
chimpanzee, -s ,tʃɪmpən'zi: [-pæn-], -z
chin, -s tʃɪn, -z
China (C.), 'tʃaɪnə
china-clay ,tʃaɪnə'kleɪ
China|man, -men 'tʃaɪnə|mən, -mən
chinchilla, -s tʃɪn'tʃɪlə, -z
Chindau tʃɪn'daʊ ['--]
chin-deep ,tʃɪn'di:p
Chindit 'tʃɪndɪt
chin|e (s. v.), -es, -ing, -ed tʃaɪn, -z, -ɪŋ, -d
Chinee, -s tʃaɪ'ni:, -z
Chinese ,tʃaɪ'ni:z [also '-- according to sentence-stress]
Chingford 'tʃɪŋfəd
chink, -s tʃɪŋk, -s
Chinnereth 'tʃɪnərəθ
Chinnock 'tʃɪnək
Chinnor 'tʃɪnə*
Chinook tʃɪ'nʊk
chintz, -es tʃɪnts, -ɪz
Chios 'kaɪɒs
chip (s. v.), -s, -ping, -ped tʃɪp, -s, -ɪŋ, -t
chipmuck, -s 'tʃɪpmʌk, -s
chipmunk, -s 'tʃɪpmʌŋk, -s
chipolata, -s ,tʃɪpə'lɑ:tə, -z
Chipp, -endale, -enham tʃɪp, -əndeɪl, -nəm [-ənem]
Chippewa, -s 'tʃɪpɪwɑ: [-wə], -z
Chipping 'tʃɪpɪŋ
chipp|y, -ier, -iest, -iness 'tʃɪp|ɪ, -ɪə*, -ɪɪst, -ɪnɪs [-nəs]
chirograph, -s 'kaɪərəʊgrɑ:f ['kaɪr-, -græf], -s
chirographer, -s ,kaɪə'rɒgrəfə* [kaɪ'r-], -z
chirographic ,kaɪərəʊ'græfɪk [,kaɪr-]
chirograph|ist/s, -y ,kaɪə'rɒgrəf|ɪst/s [kaɪ'r-], -ɪ
Chirol 'tʃɪrəl
chiromancer, -s 'kaɪərəʊmænsə*, -z
chiromancy 'kaɪərəʊmænsɪ ['kaɪr-]
Chiron (centaur) 'kaɪərən ['kaɪr-]
chiropod|ist/s, -y kɪ'rɒpəd|ɪst/s [ʃɪ'r-, tʃɪ'r-, old-fashioned ,kaɪə'r-], -ɪ
chirp (s. v.), -s, -ing, -ed; -y, -ier, -iest, -ily, -iness tʃɜ:p, -s, -ɪŋ, -t; -ɪ, -ɪə* [-jə*], -ɪɪst [-jɪst], -ɪlɪ [-əlɪ], -ɪnɪs [-ɪnəs]

Chirrol 'tʃɪrəl

chirrup (s. v.), -s, -ing, -ed 'tʃɪrəp, -s, -ɪŋ, -t

chis|el (s. v.), -els, -elling, -elled 'tʃɪz|l, -lz, -lɪŋ [-lŋ], -ld

Chisholm 'tʃɪzəm

Chislehurst 'tʃɪzlhɜːst

Chiswick 'tʃɪzɪk

chit, -s tʃɪt, -s

chit-chat 'tʃɪttʃæt

chitin 'kaɪtɪn

Chittenden 'tʃɪtndən

Chitty 'tʃɪtɪ

chivalric 'ʃɪvlrɪk [old-fashioned 'tʃɪv-]

chivalrous, -ly, -ness 'ʃɪvlrəs [old-fashioned 'tʃɪv-], -lɪ, -nɪs [-nəs]

chivalry 'ʃɪvlrɪ [old-fashioned 'tʃɪv-]

chive, -s tʃaɪv, -z

Chivers 'tʃɪvəz

chiv|y (s. v.), -ies, -ying, -ied 'tʃɪv|ɪ, -ɪz, -ɪŋ, -ɪd

Chladni 'klædnɪ

chlamy|s, -des 'klæmɪ|s ['kleɪm-], -diːz

Chloe 'kləʊɪ

chloral 'klɔːrəl

chlorate, -s 'klɔːreɪt [-rɪt], -s

chloric 'klɔːrɪk ['klɒr-]

chloride, -s 'klɔːraɪd, -z

chlorinat|e, -es, -ing, -ed 'klɔːrɪneɪt ['klɒr-], -s, -ɪŋ, -ɪd

chlorine 'klɔːriːn

Chloris 'klɔːrɪs ['klɒr-]

chlorite, -s 'klɔːraɪt, -s

chlorodyne 'klɒrədaɪn ['klɔːr-]

chloroform (s. v.), -s, -ing, -ed 'klɒrəfɔːm ['klɔːr-], -z, -ɪŋ, -d

chloromycetin ˌklɔːrəʊmaɪ'siːtɪn [ˌklɒr-]

chlorophyll 'klɒrəfɪl ['klɔːr-]

chlorous 'klɔːrəs

Choate tʃəʊt

chock, -s; -full tʃɒk, -s; -'fʊl

chock-a-block ˌtʃɒkə'blɒk

chocolate, -s 'tʃɒkələt [-lɪt], -s

choice (s. adj.), -s, -r, -st, -ly, -ness tʃɔɪs, -ɪz, -ə*, -ɪst, -lɪ, -nɪs [-nəs]

choir, -s 'kwaɪə*, -z

choirboy, -s 'kwaɪəbɔɪ, -z

choir-organ, -s 'kwaɪərˌɔːgən, ['kwaɪəˌɔː-], -z

choir-screen, -s 'kwaɪəskriːn, -z

chok|e, -es, -ing, -ed tʃəʊk, -s, -ɪŋ, -t

choke-damp 'tʃəʊkdæmp

chok|y, -ier, -iest, -iness 'tʃəʊk|ɪ, -ɪə*, [-jə*], -ɪɪst [-jɪst], -ɪnɪs [-nəs]

Cholderton (near Salisbury) 'tʃəʊldətən [-tn]

choler 'kɒlə*

cholera 'kɒlərə

choleraic ˌkɒlə'reɪɪk

choleric 'kɒlərɪk [kɒ'lerɪk]

cholesterol kə'lestərɒl [kɒ-, -tɪər-, -rəl]

choliamb, -s 'kəʊlɪæmb, -z

choliambic ˌkəʊlɪ'æmbɪk

Cholmeley 'tʃʌmlɪ

Cholmondeley 'tʃʌmlɪ

Cholsey 'tʃəʊlzɪ

Chomley 'tʃʌmlɪ

Chomolhari ˌtʃɒmɒl'hʌrɪ [ˌtʃəʊməl'haːrɪ]

Chomolungma ˌtʃəʊməʊ'lʊŋmaː

choos|e, -es, -ing, chose, chosen, chooser/s tʃuːz, -ɪz, -ɪŋ, tʃəʊz, 'tʃəʊzn, 'tʃuːzə*/z

choos|y, -ier, -iest, -iness 'tʃuːz|ɪ, -ɪə* [-jə*], -ɪɪst [-jɪst], -ɪnɪs [-nəs]

chop (s. v.), -s, -ping, -ped tʃɒp, -s, -ɪŋ, -t

chop-hou|se, -ses 'tʃɒphaʊ|s, -zɪz

Chopin 'ʃɒpæ:ŋ ['ʃəʊp-, -pæŋ] (ʃɔpɛ̃)

chopper, -s 'tʃɒpə*, -z

chopp|y, -ier, -iest, -ily, -iness 'tʃɒp|ɪ, -ɪə*, -ɪɪst, -ɪlɪ [-əlɪ], -ɪnɪs [-ɪnəs]

chop-stick, -s 'tʃɒpstɪk, -s

chop-suey ˌtʃɒp'suːɪ [-'sjuːɪ, -'sʊɪ]

chor|al, -ally 'kɔːr|əl ['kɒr-], -əlɪ

chorale, -s kɒ'rɑːl [kə'r-, kɔː'r-, -'rɑːl], -z

Chorazin kɒ'reɪzɪn [kə'r-]

chord, -s kɔːd, -z

chore, -s tʃɔː* [tʃəə*], -z

chorea kɒ'rɪə [kɔː'r-]

choreg|us, -i kɒ'riːg|əs [kɔː'r-, kə'r-], -aɪ

choreographer, -s ˌkɒrɪ'ɒgrəfə* [ˌkɔːr-], -z

choreographic ˌkɒrɪə'græfɪk [ˌkɔːr-, -rɪəʊ'g-]

choreography ˌkɒrɪ'ɒgrəfɪ [ˌkɔːr-]

choriamb, -s 'kɒrɪæmb ['kɔːr-], -z

choriambic ˌkɒrɪ'æmbɪk [ˌkɔːr-]

choric 'kɒrɪk

chorister, -s 'kɒrɪstə*, -z

Chorley 'tʃɔːlɪ

chort|le, -les, -ling, -led 'tʃɔːt|l, -lz, -lɪŋ [-lŋ], -ld

chorus (s. v.), -es, -ing, -ed 'kɔːrəs, -ɪz, -ɪŋ, -t

chose (legal term), ʃəʊz

chose (from choose), -n tʃəʊz, -n

Chosen ˌtʃəʊ'sen

Chou-en-Lai ˌtʃəʊen'laɪ

chough, -s tʃʌf, -s

chouse, -s tʃaʊs, -ɪz

choux (pastry) ʃuː

chow, -s tʃaʊ, -z

chow-chow, -s ˌtʃaʊ'tʃaʊ ['--], -z

chowder, -s 'tʃaʊdə*, -z

Chowles tʃəʊlz
chrestomath|y, -ies kreˈstɒməθ|ɪ, -ɪz
chrism ˈkrɪzəm
chrisom, -s ˈkrɪzəm, -z
Christ, -s kraɪst, -s
Christabel ˈkrɪstəbel [-bəl]
Christchurch ˈkraɪstʃɜːtʃ
Christ-cross-row, -s ˌkrɪskrɒsˈrəʊ
  [old-fashioned -krɔːs-], -z
Christdom ˈkraɪstdəm
christ|en, -ens, -ening, -ened ˈkrɪs|n,
  -nz, -nɪŋ [-nɪŋ], -nd
Christendom ˈkrɪsndəm
christening, -s ˈkrɪsnɪŋ [-nɪŋ], -z
Christi (in Corpus Christi) ˈkrɪstɪ
Christian, -s ˈkrɪstjən [-tɪən, -tʃən], -z
Christiana ˌkrɪstɪˈɑːnə
Christiania ˌkrɪstɪˈɑːnjə [-nɪə]
Christianism ˈkrɪstjənɪzəm [-tɪən-,
  -tʃən-, -tʃn̩-]
Christianity ˌkrɪstɪˈænɪtɪ [krɪˈstjæn-,
  -ɪtɪ]
christianiz|e [-is|e], -es, -ing, -ed
  ˈkrɪstjənaɪz [-tɪən-, -tʃən-, -tʃn̩-], -ɪz,
  -ɪŋ, -d
christianly ˈkrɪstjənlɪ [-tɪən-, -tʃən-]
Christian name, -s ˈkrɪstjənneɪm
  [-tʃən-], -z
Christie ˈkrɪstɪ
Christina krɪˈstiːnə
Christine ˈkrɪstiːn, krɪˈstiːn
Christlike ˈkraɪstlaɪk
Christliness ˈkraɪstlɪnɪs [-nəs]
Christmas, -es ˈkrɪsməs [-stm-], -ɪz
Christmas-box, -es ˈkrɪsməsbɒks
  [-stm-], -ɪz
Christmas-card, -s ˈkrɪsməskɑːd
  [-stm-], -z
Christmas-tree, -s ˈkrɪsməstriː [-stm-], -z
Christminster ˈkrɪstmɪnstə*
Christopher ˈkrɪstəfə*
Christopherson krɪˈstɒfəsn
Christy ˈkrɪstɪ
chromate, -s ˈkrəʊmeɪt [-mɪt], -s
chromatic, -ally krəʊˈmætɪk, -əlɪ
chrome krəʊm
chromic ˈkrəʊmɪk
chromite, -s ˈkrəʊmaɪt, -s
chromium ˈkrəʊmjəm [-mɪəm]
chromium-plated ˌkrəʊmjəmˈpleɪtɪd
  [-mɪəm-, ˈ--,--]
chromium-plating ˌkrəʊmjəmˈpleɪtɪŋ
  [-mɪəm-, ˈ--,--]
chromolithograph, -s ˌkrəʊməʊˈlɪθəʊ-
  grɑːf [-græf], -s
chromolithography ˌkrəʊməʊlɪˈθɒɡrəfɪ
chromosome, -s ˈkrəʊməsəʊm, -z
chromosphere, -s ˈkrəʊməˌsfɪə*, -z

chromotype ˈkrəʊməʊtaɪp
chroneme, -s ˈkrəʊniːm, -z
chronemic krəʊˈniːmɪk
chronic, -al, -ally ˈkrɒnɪk, -l, -əlɪ
chronic|le (s. v.), -les, -ling, -led, -ler/s
  ˈkrɒnɪk|l, -lz, -lɪŋ, -ld, -lə*/z
chronogram, -s ˈkrɒnəʊɡræm, -z
chronograph, -s ˈkrɒnəʊɡrɑːf [-græf], -s
chronologic, -al, -ally ˌkrɒnəˈlɒdʒɪk,
  -l, -əlɪ
chronolog|ist/s, -y, -ies krəˈnɒlədʒ|-
  ɪst/s [krɒˈn-], -ɪ, -ɪz
chronomet|er/s, -ry krəˈnɒmɪt|ə*/z
  [-mət|ə*], -rɪ
chronometric, -al, -ally ˌkrɒnəʊˈmetrɪk
  -l, -əlɪ
chronopher, -s ˈkrɒnəfə*, -z
chrysalis, -es, chrysalides ˈkrɪsəlɪs [-sɪl-,
  -sl-], -ɪz, krɪˈsælɪdiːz
chrysanthemum, -s krɪˈsænθəməm
  [-ɪˈzæ-, -θɪm-], -z
chryselephantine ˌkrɪselɪˈfæntaɪn
Chrysler, -s ˈkraɪzlə*, -z
chrysolite, -s ˈkrɪsəʊlaɪt, -s
chrysoprase, -s ˈkrɪsəʊpreɪz, -ɪz
chrysoprasus, -es krɪˈsɒprəsəs, -ɪz
Chrysostom ˈkrɪsəstəm
chub, -s tʃʌb, -z
Chubb tʃʌb
chubb|y, -ier, -iest, -ily, -iness ˈtʃʌb|ɪ,
  -ɪə*, -ɪɪst, -ɪlɪ [-əlɪ], -ɪnɪs [-məs]
chuck (s. v.), -s, -ing, -ed tʃʌk, -s, -ɪŋ, -t
chucker-out, chuckers-out ˌtʃʌkərˈaʊt
  [-əˈaʊt], ˌtʃʌkəzˈaʊt
chuck|le (s. v.), -les, -ling, -led ˈtʃʌk|l,
  -lz, -lɪŋ [-lɪŋ], -ld
Chudleigh ˈtʃʌdlɪ
chuff, -s tʃʌf, -s
Chuffey ˈtʃʌfɪ
chukker, -s ˈtʃʌkə*, -z
chum (s. v.), -s, -ming, -med tʃʌm, -z,
  -ɪŋ, -d
Chumalhari ˌtʃʊməlˈhʌrɪ [-ˈhɑːrɪ]
Chumbi ˈtʃʊmbɪ
chumm|y, -ier, -iest, -ily, -iness ˈtʃʌm|ɪ,
  -ɪə*, -ɪɪst, -ɪlɪ [-əlɪ], -ɪnɪs [-məs]
chump, -s tʃʌmp, -s
Chungking ˌtʃʊŋˈkɪŋ [ˌtʃʌŋ-]
chunk, -s tʃʌŋk, -s
Chunnel ˈtʃʌnl
church, -es tʃɜːtʃ, -ɪz
Churchdown (near Gloucester) ˈtʃɜːtʃ-
  daʊn
  Note.—There was until recently a
  local pronunciation ˈtʃəʊzn, which
  is preserved as the name of a hill
  near by, which is now written
  Chosen.

church-goer, -s 'tʃɜːtʃˌɡəʊə*, -z
Churchill 'tʃɜːtʃɪl
churching, -s 'tʃɜːtʃɪŋ, -z
church|man (C.), -men 'tʃɜːtʃ|mən,
-mən
church-rate, -s 'tʃɜːtʃreɪt, -s
churchwarden, -s ˌtʃɜːtʃ'wɔːdn, -z
church|y, -ier, -iest, -ily, -iness 'tʃɜːtʃ|ɪ,
-ɪə*, -ɪɪst, -ɪlɪ [-əlɪ], -ɪnɪs [-ɪnəs]
churchyard, -s ˌtʃɜːtʃ'jɑːd [also '--
according to sentence-stress], -z
Note.—Some people always pronounce '--.
Churchyard (surname) 'tʃɜːtʃəd
churl, -s tʃɜːl, -z
churlish, -ly, -ness 'tʃɜːlɪʃ, -lɪ, -nɪs
[-nəs]
churn (s. v.), -s, -ing, -ed tʃɜːn, -z, -ɪŋ, -d
Churton 'tʃɜːtn
chute, -s ʃuːt, -s
Chute tʃuːt
Chuter 'tʃuːtə*
chutney [-nee], -s 'tʃʌtnɪ, -z
Chuzzlewit 'tʃʌzlwɪt
chyle kaɪl
chyme kaɪm
Cibber 'sɪbə*
cibori|um/s, -a sɪ'bɔːrɪ|əm/z, -ə
cicada, -s sɪ'kɑːdə [-'keɪd-], -z
cicala, -s sɪ'kɑːlə, -z
cicatrice, -s 'sɪkətrɪs, -ɪz
cicatrices (Latin plur. of cicatrix)
ˌsɪkə'traɪsiːz
cicatrix 'sɪkətrɪks
cicatriz|e [-is|e], -es, -ing, -ed 'sɪkətraɪz,
-ɪz, -ɪŋ, -d
Cicely 'sɪsɪlɪ [-əlɪ]
Cicero 'sɪsərəʊ
cicerone, -s ˌtʃɪtʃə'rəʊnɪ [ˌsɪsə'r-], -z
Ciceronian ˌsɪsə'rəʊnjən [-nɪən]
cicisbe|o, -i ˌtʃɪtʃɪz'beɪ|əʊ, -iː
C.I.D. ˌsiːaɪ'diː
cider, -s 'saɪdə*, -z
cider-cup, -s 'saɪdəkʌp [ˌsaɪdə'k-], -s
cigar, -s sɪ'gɑː*, -z
cigarette, -s ˌsɪgə'ret, -s
cigarette-holder, -s ˌsɪgə'ret,həʊldə*, -z
cigar-shaped sɪ'gɑːʃeɪpt
cilia 'sɪlɪə [-ljə]
ciliary 'sɪlɪərɪ [-ljə-]
cilice, -s 'sɪlɪs, -ɪz
Cilicia saɪ'lɪʃɪə [sɪ'l-, -ʃjə, -sɪə, -sjə]
cill, -s sɪl, -z
Cilla 'sɪlə
Cimabue ˌtʃɪmə'buːɪ [ˌtʃiːm-, -'buːeɪ,
-'buɪ, -'bueɪ]
Cimmer|ian, -ii sɪ'mɪər|ɪən, -ɪaɪ
cinch, -es sɪntʃ, -ɪz

cinchona, -s sɪŋ'kəʊnə, -z
Cincinnati ˌsɪnsɪ'nætɪ [-'nɑːtɪ]
cincture, -s 'sɪŋktʃə* [-ˌtʃʊə*], -z
cinder, -s 'sɪndə*, -z
Cinderella ˌsɪndə'relə
cinder-pa|th, -ths 'sɪndəpɑː|θ, -ðz
cinder-sifter, -s 'sɪndəˌsɪftə*, -z
cinder-track, -s 'sɪndətræk, -s
cinecamera, -s 'sɪnɪˌkæmərə [ˌ--'---], -z
cinema, -s 'sɪnəmə [-nɪ-, -mɑː], -z
cinemascope, -s 'sɪnəməskəʊp [-nɪm-],
-s
cinematic ˌsɪnɪ'mætɪk [ˌsɪnə-]
cinematograph, -s ˌsɪnə'mætəɡrɑːf
[-nɪ'm-, -græf], -s
cinematographic ˌsɪnəmætə'ɡræfɪk
[-nɪˌm-]
cinematography ˌsɪnəmə'tɒɡrəfɪ [-nɪ-]
cine-projector, -s 'sɪnɪprəˌdʒektə*, -z
cinerama ˌsɪnə'rɑːmə [-nɪ-]
cineraria, -s ˌsɪnə'reərɪə, -z
cinerarium, -s ˌsɪnə'reərɪəm, -z
cinerary 'sɪnərərɪ
cineration ˌsɪnə'reɪʃn
Cingalese ˌsɪŋɡə'liːz
cinnabar 'sɪnəbɑː*
cinnamon 'sɪnəmən
cinque (C.) sɪŋk
cinquefoil 'sɪŋkfɔɪl
Cinque Ports 'sɪŋkpɔːts
cinzano sɪn'zɑːnəʊ [tʃɪn'z-]
ciph|er (s. v.), -ers, -ering, -ered 'saɪf|ə*,
-əz, -ərɪŋ, -əd
cipher-key, -s 'saɪfəkiː, -z
Cipriani ˌsɪprɪ'ɑːnɪ
circa 'sɜːkə
Circassia, -n/s sɜː'kæsɪə [-sjə, -ʃɪə, -ʃjə],
-n/z
Circe 'sɜːsɪ
circ|le (s. v.), -les, -ling, -led 'sɜːk|l, -lz,
-lɪŋ [-lɪŋ], -ld
circlet, -s 'sɜːklɪt [-lət], -s
circuit, -s 'sɜːkɪt, -s
circuitous, -ly, -ness sə'kjuːɪtəs [sɜː-,
-'kjʊɪ-], -lɪ, -nɪs [-nəs]
circular (s. adj.), -s 'sɜːkjʊlə* [-kjəl-], -z
circulariz|e [-is|e], -es, -ing, -ed
'sɜːkjʊləraɪz [-kjəl-], -ɪz, -ɪŋ, -d
circulat|e, -es, -ing, -ed, -or/s 'sɜːkjʊ-
leɪt [-kjəl-], -s, -ɪŋ, -ɪd, -ə*/z
circulation, -s ˌsɜːkjʊ'leɪʃn [-kjə'l-], -z
circulatory ˌsɜːkjʊ'leɪtərɪ ['sɜːkjʊlətərɪ]
circumambient ˌsɜːkəm'æmbɪənt
[-bjənt]
circumambulat|e, -es, -ing, -ed ˌsɜːk-
əm'æmbjʊleɪt, -s, -ɪŋ, -d
circumcis|e, -es, -ing, -ed 'sɜːkəmsaɪz,
-ɪz, -ɪŋ, -d

circumcision, -s ˌsɜːkəmˈsɪʒn, -z
circumference, -s səˈkʌmfərəns, -ɪz
circumferential səˌkʌmfəˈrenʃl
circumflex, -es ˈsɜːkəmfleks, -ɪz
circumlocution, -s ˌsɜːkəmləˈkjuːʃn, -z
circumlocutory ˌsɜːkəmˈlɒkjutərɪ
 [-ləˈkjuːtərɪ]
circumnavigat|e, -es, -ing, -ed, -or/s
 ˌsɜːkəmˈnævɪgeɪt, -s, -ɪŋ, -ɪd, -ə*/z
circumnavigation, -s ˈsɜːkəmˌnævɪ-
 ˈgeɪʃn, -z
circumpolar ˌsɜːkəmˈpəʊlə*
circumscrib|e, -es, -ing, -ed ˈsɜːkəm-
 skraɪb [ˌsɜːkəmˈskraɪb], -z, -ɪŋ, -d
circumscription, -s ˌsɜːkəmˈskrɪpʃn, -z
circumspect, -ly, -ness ˈsɜːkəmspekt,
 -lɪ, -nɪs [-nəs]
circumspection ˌsɜːkəmˈspekʃn
circumstance, -s, -d ˈsɜːkəmstəns
 [-stæns, -stɑːns], -ɪz, -t
circumstanti|al, -ally ˌsɜːkəmˈstænʃl,
 -əlɪ
circumstantiality ˈsɜːkəmˌstænʃɪˈælətɪ
 [-ɪtɪ]
circumstantiat|e, -es, -ing, -ed ˌsɜːkəm-
 ˈstænʃɪeɪt [-ʃjeɪt], -s, -ɪŋ, -ɪd
circumvallation, -s ˌsɜːkəmvəˈleɪʃn
 [-væˈl-], -z
circumvent, -s, -ing, -ed ˌsɜːkəmˈvent,
 -s, -ɪŋ, -ɪd
circumvention, -s ˌsɜːkəmˈvenʃn, -z
circus, -es ˈsɜːkəs, -ɪz
Cirencester ˈsaɪərənsestə* [ˈsɪsɪtə*,
 ˈsɪsɪstə*]
 Note.—The pronunciation most
 usually heard in the town is
 ˈsaɪərənsestə* (or -stər with the
 dialectal retroflex r). An older
 pronunciation ˈsɪzɪtər may still be
 heard in the country around.
Ciriax ˈsɪrɪæks
cirque, -s sɜːk [sɪək], -s
cirrhosis sɪˈrəʊsɪs
cirro-cumulus ˌsɪrəʊˈkuːmjʊləs [-mjəl-]
cirro-stratus ˌsɪrəʊˈstrɑːtəs [-ˈstreɪt-]
cirrous ˈsɪrəs
cirrus ˈsɪrəs
Cisalpine sɪsˈælpaɪn
Cissie ˈsɪsɪ
cissoid, -s ˈsɪsɔɪd, -z
Cissy ˈsɪsɪ
cist, -s sɪst, -s
Cistercian, -s sɪˈstɜːʃjən [-ʃɪən, -ʃn], -z
cistern, -s ˈsɪstən, -z
cistus, -es ˈsɪstəs, -ɪz
citadel, -s ˈsɪtədəl [-tɪd-, -del], -z
citation, -s saɪˈteɪʃn [sɪˈt-], -z
citatory ˈsaɪtətərɪ [ˈsɪt-, saɪˈteɪtərɪ]

cit|e, -es, -ing, -ed saɪt, -s, -ɪŋ, -ɪd
cithar|a, -ae ˈsɪθər|ə, -iː
cither, -s ˈsɪθə*, -z
cithern, -s ˈsɪθən [-θɜːn, ˈsɪðən], -z
citizen, -s; -ship ˈsɪtɪzn, -z; -ʃɪp
citole, -s sɪˈtəʊl, -z
citrate, -s ˈsɪtreɪt [ˈsaɪt-, -trɪt], -s
citrated ˈsɪtreɪtɪd [ˈsaɪt-]
citric ˈsɪtrɪk
Citrine sɪˈtriːn
Citroën, -s ˈsɪtrəʊən [sɪˈt-, -əʊɪn, -əʊen]
 (sitrɔen), -z
citron, -s ˈsɪtrən, -z
citr|ous, -us ˈsɪtr|əs, -əs
cittern, -s ˈsɪtɜːn [-tən], -z
cit|y, -ies ˈsɪt|ɪ, -ɪz
civet, -s ˈsɪvɪt, -s
civic, -s ˈsɪvɪk, -s
civ|il, -illy ˈsɪv|l [ˈsɪv|ɪl], -əlɪ [-ɪlɪ]
civilian, -s sɪˈvɪljən [-lɪən], -z
civilit|y, -ies sɪˈvɪlət|ɪ [-ɪt|ɪ], -ɪz
civilizable [-isa-] ˈsɪvɪlaɪzəbl
civilization [-isa-], -s ˌsɪvɪlaɪˈzeɪʃn
 [-vəlaɪˈz-, -vlaɪˈz-, -vɪlɪˈz-, -vlɪˈz-], -z
civiliz|e [-is|e], -es, -ing, -ed ˈsɪvɪlaɪz
 [-vəl-, -vl-], -ɪz, -ɪŋ, -d
civv|y, -ies ˈsɪv|ɪ, -ɪz
clack (s. v.), -s, -ing, -ed klæk, -s, -ɪŋ, -t
Clackmannan klækˈmænən
clack-valve, -s ˈklækvælv, -z
Clacton ˈklæktən
clad (from clothe) klæd
claim (s. v.), -s, -ing, -ed kleɪm, -z, -ɪŋ,
 -d
claimant, -s ˈkleɪmənt, -s
claimer, -s ˈkleɪmə*, -z
clairaudien|ce, -t kleərˈɔːdjən|s [-dɪə-],
 -t
clairvoyan|ce, -cy, -t/s, -te/s kleə-
 ˈvɔɪən|s, -sɪ, -t/s, -t/s
clam, -s klæm, -z
clamant ˈkleɪmənt
clamb|er, -ers, -ering, -ered ˈklæmb|ə*,
 -əz, -ərɪŋ, -əd
clamm|y, -ier, -iest, -ily, -iness ˈklæm|ɪ,
 -ɪə*, -ɪɪst, -ɪlɪ [-əlɪ], -ɪnɪs [-ɪnəs]
clamorous, -ly, -ness ˈklæmərəs, -lɪ,
 -nɪs [-nəs]
clamour (s. v.), -s, -ing, -ed ˈklæmə*, -z,
 -rɪŋ, -d
clamp (s. v.), -s, -ing, -ed klæmp, -s, -ɪŋ,
 -t [klæmt]
clan, -s klæn, -z
clandestine, -ly klænˈdestɪn [-taɪn,
 ˈ---], -lɪ
clang (s. v.), -s, -ing, -ed klæŋ, -z, -ɪŋ, -d
clanger, -s ˈklæŋə*, -z
clangorous, -ly ˈklæŋgərəs [-ŋə-], -lɪ

clangour 'klæŋgə* [-ŋə*]

clank (s. v.), -s, -ing, -ed klæŋk, -s, -ɪŋ, -t [klæŋt]

Clanmaurice klæn'mɒrɪs

Clanmorris klæn'mɒrɪs

clannish, -ly, -ness 'klænɪʃ, -lɪ, -nɪs [-nəs]

Clanricarde klæn'rɪkəd ['klæn,rɪkəd]

  Note.—The second pronunc:ation may often be heard from residents in the neighbourhood of Clanricarde Gardens, London.

clanship 'klænʃɪp

clans|man, -men 'klænz|mən, -mən

clap (s. v.), -s, -ping, -ped klæp, -s, -ɪŋ, -t

clapboard, -s 'klæpbɔːd [-bəd], -z

Clapham 'klæpəm [-pm]

clapper, -s 'klæpə*, -z

Clapton 'klæptən

clap-trap 'klæptræp

claque, -s klæk, -s

Clara 'kleərə

clarabella (C.), -s ,klærə'belə, -z

Clare kleə*

Claremont 'kleəmɒnt [-mənt]

Clarence 'klærəns

Clarenc(i)eux 'klærənsu: [-sju:]

clarendon (C.) 'klærəndən

claret, -s 'klærət [-ɪt], -s

claret-cup 'klærətkʌp [,klærət'k-, -rɪt-]

Clarges (street) 'klɑːdʒɪz

Claridge, -'s 'klærɪdʒ, -ɪz

clarification ,klærɪfɪ'keɪʃn

clari|fy, -fies, -fying, -fied, -fier/s 'klærɪ|faɪ, -faɪz, -faɪɪŋ, -faɪd, -faɪə*/z

Clarina klə'raɪnə

clarinet, -s ,klærɪ'net [-rə-], -s

clarinettist, -s ,klærɪ'netɪst [-rə-], -s

clarion, -s 'klærɪən, -z

Clarissa klə'rɪsə

clarity 'klærɪtɪ [-ɪtɪ]

Clark(e) klɑːk

clarkia, -s 'klɑːkjə [-kɪə], -z

Clarkson 'klɑːksn

clash (s. v.), -es, -ing, -ed klæʃ, -ɪz, -ɪŋ, -t

clasp (s. v.), -s, -ing, -ed klɑːsp, -s, -ɪŋ, -t

clasp-kni|fe, -ves 'klɑːspnaɪ|f, -vz

class (s. v.), -es, -ing, -ed klɑːs, -ɪz, -ɪŋ, -t

Classen 'klæsn

classic, -s, -al, -ally, -alness 'klæsɪk, -s, -l, -əlɪ, -əlnɪs [-nəs]

classicism, -s 'klæsɪsɪzəm, -z

classicist, -s 'klæsɪsɪst, -s

classifiable 'klæsɪfaɪəbl [,--'---]

classification, -s ,klæsɪfɪ'keɪʃn, -z

classificatory ,klæsɪfɪ'keɪtərɪ ['klæsɪfɪ-kətərɪ]

classi|fy, -fies, -fying, -fied, -fier/s 'klæsɪ|faɪ, -faɪz, -faɪɪŋ, -faɪd, -faɪə*/z

class|man, -men 'klɑːs|mæn [-mən], -men [-mən]

classroom, -s 'klɑːsrʊm [-ruːm], -z

class|y, -ier, -iest, -iness 'klɑːs|ɪ, -ɪə* [-jə*], -ɪɪst [-jɪst], -ɪnɪs [-ɪnəs]

clatter (s. v.), -s, -ing, -ed 'klætə*, -z, -rɪŋ, -d

Claud(e) klɔːd

Claudia, -n 'klɔːdjə [-dɪə], -n

Claudius 'klɔːdjəs [-dɪəs]

clause, -s klɔːz, -ɪz

claustral 'klɔːstrəl

claustrophob|ia, -ic ,klɔːstrə'fəʊb|jə [-bɪə], -ɪk

clave (archaic p. of cleave) kleɪv

clavecin, -s 'klævɪsɪn, -z

Claverhouse 'kleɪvəhaʊs

clavichord, -s 'klævɪkɔːd, -z

clavicle, -s 'klævɪkl, -z

clavicular klə'vɪkjʊlə* [klæ'v-]

clavier (keyboard), -s 'klævɪə* [-vjə*], -z

clavier (instrument), -s klə'vɪə* ['klævɪə*, 'klævjə*], -z

claw (s. v.), -s, -ing, -ed klɔː, -z, -ɪŋ, -d

Claxton 'klækstən

clay (C.), -s kleɪ, -z

clayey 'kleɪɪ

Clayhanger 'kleɪ,hæŋə*

claymore, -s 'kleɪmɔː:* [-mɔə*], -z

Clayton 'kleɪtn

clean (s. adj. v.), -s; -er, -est, -ly (adv.), -ness; -ing, -ed, -er/s kliːn, -z; -ə*, -ɪst, -lɪ, -nɪs [-nəs]; -ɪŋ, -d, -ə*/z

clean-cut ,kliːn'kʌt [also '-- when attributive]

clean|ly (adj.), -ier, -iest, -iness 'klenl|ɪ, -ɪə* [-jə*], -ɪɪst [-jɪst], -ɪnɪs [-ɪnəs]

cleans|e, -es, -ing, -ed, -er/s; -able klenz, -ɪz, -ɪŋ, -d, -ə*/z; -əbl

clean-up, -s ,kliːn'ʌp ['--], -s

clear (adj. v.), (C.), -er, -est, -ly, -ness; -s, -ing, -ed klɪə*, -rə*, -rɪst, -lɪ, -nɪs [-nəs]; -z, -rɪŋ, -d

clearage 'klɪərɪdʒ

clearance, -s 'klɪərəns, -ɪz

clear-cut ,klɪə'kʌt [also '-- when attributive]

clear-headed ,klɪə'hedɪd [also '-,-- when attributive]

clearing-hou|se, -ses 'klɪərɪŋhaʊ|s, -zɪz

clear-sighted ,klɪə'saɪtɪd [also '-,-- when attributive]

clear-sighted|ly, -ness ˌklɪə'saɪtɪd|lɪ, -nɪs [-nəs]

clearstor|y, -ies 'klɪəstər|ɪ [-stɔ:r-], -ɪz

clearway, -s 'klɪəweɪ, -z

cleat, -s kli:t, -s

Cleather 'kleðə*

cleavage, -s 'kli:vɪdʒ, -ɪz

cleav|e, -es, -ing, -ed, clove, cleft, cloven kli:v, -z, -ɪŋ, -d, kləʊv, kleft, 'kləʊvn

cleaver (C.), -s 'kli:və*, -z

cleek (s. v.), -s, -ing, -ed kli:k, -s, -ɪŋ, -t

Cleethorpe, -s 'kli:θɔ:p, -s

clef, -s klef, -s

cleft (s.), -s kleft, -s

cleft (from cleave) kleft

cleg -s kleg, -z

Clegg kleg

Cleishbotham 'kli:ʃbɒðəm

clematis 'klemətɪs [klɪ'meɪtɪs, klə-'meɪt-, kle'meɪt-]

Clemence 'klemɪns

clemen|cy, -t/ly 'klemən|sɪ, -t/lɪ

Clemens 'klemənz

Clement, -s 'klemənt, -s

Clementi klɪ'mentɪ [klə'm-]

Clementina ˌklemən'ti:nə

clementine (C.), -s 'kleməntaɪn [-ti:n], -z

clench, -es, -ing, -ed klentʃ, -ɪz, -ɪŋ, -t

Clendenin klen'denɪn

Cleo 'klɪəʊ ['kli:-, 'klerəʊ]

Cleobury (in Norfolk) 'klɪbərɪ ['kleb-]

Cleopatra klɪə'pætrə [ˌklɪəʊ'p-, -'pɑ:t-]

clepsydr|a, -ae 'klepsɪdr|ə [klep's-], -i:

clerestor|y, -ies 'klɪəstər|ɪ [-stɔ:r-], -ɪz

clergy 'klɜ:dʒɪ

clergy|man, -men 'klɜ:dʒɪ|mən, -mən

cleric (s. adj.), -s, -al/s, -ally 'klerɪk, -s, -l/z, -əlɪ

clerihew (C.) 'klerɪhju:

clerk (C.), -s klɑ:k, -s

Clerke klɑ:k

Clerkenwell 'klɑ:kənwel [-wəl]

clerkship, -s 'klɑ:kʃɪp, -s

Clermont (towns in Ireland, village in Norfolk) 'kleəmɒnt [-mənt], (in U.S.A.) 'kleəmɒnt, 'klɜ:mɒnt

Clery 'klɪərɪ

Clevedon 'kli:vdən

Cleveland 'kli:vlənd

clever, -er, -est, -ly, -ness, -ish 'klevə*, -rə*, -rɪst, -lɪ, -nɪs [-nəs], -rɪʃ

Cleverdon 'klevədən

Cleves kli:vz

clew (s. v.), -s, -ing, -ed klu:, -z, -ɪŋ ['kluɪŋ], -d

cliché, -s 'kli:ʃeɪ (kliʃe), -z

click (s. v.), -s, -ing, -ed klɪk, -s, -ɪŋ, -t

client, -s 'klaɪənt, -s

clientèle, -s ˌkli:ɑ:n'tel [-ɔ̃:n't-, -ɑ:n't-, -ɒn't-, -'teɪl] (kliɑ̃tɛl), -z

cliff, -s klɪf, -s

Cliff(e) klɪf

cliff-hanger, -s 'klɪf,hæŋə*, -z

Clifford 'klɪfəd

cliffy 'klɪfɪ

clift, -s klɪft, -s

Clifton 'klɪftən

climacteric, -s klaɪ'mæktərɪk [ˌklaɪmæk'terɪk], -s

climacterical ˌklaɪmæk'terɪkl

climactic, -al, -ally klaɪ'mæktɪk, -l, -əlɪ

climate, -s 'klaɪmɪt [-mət], -s

climatic, -al, -ally klaɪ'mætɪk, -l, -əlɪ

climatolog|ist/s, -y ˌklaɪmə'tɒlədʒ|ɪst/s, -ɪ

climax, -es 'klaɪmæks, -ɪz

climb (s. v.), -s, -ing, -ed, -er/s klaɪm, -z, -ɪŋ, -d, -ə*/z

clime, -s klaɪm, -z

clinch (C.), -es, -ing, -ed, -er/s klɪntʃ, -ɪz, -ɪŋ, -t, -ə*/z

cline, -s klaɪn, -z

cling, -s, -ing, clung klɪŋ, -z, -ɪŋ, klʌŋ

clingy 'klɪŋɪ

clinic, -s, -al, -ally 'klɪnɪk, -s, -l, -əlɪ

clink (s. v.), -s, -ing, -ed klɪŋk, -s, -ɪŋ, -t [klɪŋt]

clinker, -s 'klɪŋkə*, -z

clinomet|er/s, -ry klaɪ'nɒmɪt|ə*/z [klɪ'n-, -mət|ə*/z], -rɪ

clinometric ˌklaɪnəʊ'metrɪk

Clinton 'klɪntən

Clio 'klaɪəʊ

clip, -s, -ping, -ped klɪp, -s, -ɪŋ, -t

clipper, -s 'klɪpə*, -z

clippie, -s 'klɪpɪ, -z

clipping (s. adj.), -s 'klɪpɪŋ, -z

clique, -s kli:k, -s

cliquish 'kli:kɪʃ

cliqu|y, -ier, -iest, -iness 'kli:k|ɪ, -ɪə* [-jə*], -ɪɪst [-jɪst], -ɪnɪs [-ɪnəs]

Clissold 'klɪsəld [-səʊld]

Clitheroe 'klɪðərəʊ

clitoris 'klɪtərɪs ['klaɪ-]

Clive klaɪv

Cliveden (in Berkshire) 'klɪvdən ['kli:v-]

cloac|a/s, -ae kləʊ'eɪk|ə/z, -i:

cloacal kləʊ'eɪkl

cloak (s. v.) (C.), -s, -ing, -ed kləʊk, -s, -ɪŋ, -t

cloak-room, -s 'kləʊkrʊm [-ru:m], -z

Cloan kləʊn

cloche, -s kləʊʃ [klɒʃ], -ɪz

91

clock, -s klɒk, -s
clock-face, -s 'klɒkfeɪs, -ɪz
clock-maker, -s 'klɒk,meɪkə*, -z
clock|wise, -work 'klɒk|waɪz, -wɜːk
clod, -s, -dy klɒd, -z, -ɪ
clodhopp|er/s, -ing 'klɒd,hɒp|ə*/z, -ɪŋ
Cloete kləʊ'iːtɪ, 'kluːtɪ
clog (s. v.), -s, -ging, -ged klɒg, -z, -ɪŋ, -d
clogg|y, -ier, -iest, -ily, -iness 'klɒg|ɪ, -ɪə*, -ɪɪst, -ɪlɪ [-əlɪ], -ɪnɪs [-ɪnəs]
Clogher 'klɒhə* ['klɒxə*], 'klɔːə*, klɔː* [klɔə*]
cloist|er (s. v.), -ers, -ering, -ered 'klɔɪst|ə*, -əz, -ərɪŋ, -əd
cloistral 'klɔɪstrəl
Clonbrock klɒn'brɒk
Clonmel klɒn'mel ['klɒnmel]
Cloomber 'kluːmbə*
close (s.) (enclosure, yard), -s kləʊs, -ɪz
close (s.) (end), -s kləʊz, -ɪz
Close kləʊs
close (adj.), -r, -st, -ly, -ness kləʊs, -ə*, -ɪst, -lɪ, -nɪs [-nəs]
clos|e (v.), -es, -ing, -ed -er/s kləʊz, -ɪz, -ɪŋ, -d, -ə*/z
close-fisted ˌkləʊs'fɪstɪd ['--- when attributive]
close-grained ˌkləʊs'greɪnd ['-- when attributive]
close-hauled ˌkləʊs'hɔːld
close-season, -s 'kləʊs,siːzn, -z
closet (s. v.), -s, -ing, -ed 'klɒzɪt, -s, -ɪŋ, -ɪd
close-time, -s 'kləʊstaɪm, -z
close-up (picture), -s 'kləʊsʌp [ˌ-'-], -s
closure, -s 'kləʊʒə*, -z
clot (s. v.), -s, -ting, -ted klɒt, -s, -ɪŋ, -ɪd
Cloten 'kləʊtn
cloth, -s klɒθ [old-fashioned klɔːθ, and in compounds], klɒθs [klɔːðz, klɔːθs] Note.— The plur. forms klɔːðz, klɔːθs are only used by those who pronounce klɔːθ in the sing.
cloth|e, -es, -ing, -ed, clad kləʊð, -z, -ɪŋ, -d, klæd
clothes (s.) kləʊðz [sometimes kləʊz]
clothes-basket,   -s   'kləʊðz,bɑːskɪt [sometimes 'kləʊz-], -s
clothes-brush, -es 'kləʊðzbrʌʃ [sometimes 'kləʊz-], -ɪz
clothes-horse, -s 'kləʊðzhɔːs [sometimes 'kləʊz-], -ɪz
clothes-line, -s 'kləʊðzlaɪn [sometimes 'kləʊz-], -z
clothes-peg, -s 'kləʊðzpeg [sometimes 'kləʊz-], -z
clothier, -s 'kləʊðɪə* [-ðjə*], -z

clothing (s.) 'kləʊðɪŋ
Clotho 'kləʊθəʊ
cloth-yard, -s ˌklɒθ'jɑːd [ˌklɔːθ-, also '-- when followed by a stress], -z
cloud (s. v.), -s, -ing, -ed klaʊd, -z, -ɪŋ, -ɪd
cloudberr|y, -ies 'klaʊd,ber|ɪ [-bər|ɪ], -ɪz
cloud-burst, -s 'klaʊdbɜːst, -s
cloud-capt 'klaʊdkæpt
Cloudesley 'klaʊdzlɪ
cloudless, -ly, -ness 'klaʊdlɪs [-ləs], -lɪ, -nɪs [-nəs]
cloud|y, -ier, -iest, -ily, -iness 'klaʊd|ɪ, -ɪə* [-jə*], -ɪɪst [-jɪst], -ɪlɪ [-əlɪ], -ɪnɪs [-nəs]
clough, -s klʌf, -s
Clough klʌf, kluː
Clouston 'kluːstən, 'klaʊstən
clout (s. v.), -s, -ing, -ed klaʊt, -s, -ɪŋ, -ɪd
clove (s.), -s kləʊv, -z
clove (from cleave), -n kləʊv, -n
Clovelly klə'velɪ
cloven-footed ˌkləʊvn'fʊtɪd ['--,--]
clover, -s 'kləʊvə*, -z
Clovis 'kləʊvɪs
Clow (surname) kləʊ
Clowes (in Norfolk) kluːz, (surname) klaʊz, kluːz
clown, -s klaʊn, -z
clownish, -ly, -ness 'klaʊnɪʃ, -lɪ, -nɪs [-nəs]
cloy, -s, -ing, -ed klɔɪ, -z, -ɪŋ, -d
club (s. v.), -s, -bing, -bed klʌb, -z, -ɪŋ, -d
clubbable 'klʌbəbl
club-f|oot, -eet ˌklʌb'f|ʊt ['--], -iːt
club-footed ˌklʌb'fʊtɪd ['-,--]
club-hou|se, ses 'klʌbhaʊ|s [ˌ-'-], -zɪz
clubland 'klʌblænd
club-law ˌklʌb'lɔː: ['--]
club|man, -men 'klʌb|mən [-mæn], -mən [-men]
club-moss, -es ˌklʌb'mɒs ['--], -ɪz
club-room, -s 'klʌbrʊm [-ruːm], -z
club-shaped 'klʌbʃeɪpt
cluck (s. v.), -s, -ing, -ed klʌk, -s, -ɪŋ, -t
clue, -s kluː, -z
clump (s. v.), -s, -ing, -ed klʌmp, -s, -ɪŋ, -t [klʌmt]
clumpy 'klʌmpɪ
clums|y, -ier, -iest, -ily, -iness 'klʌmz|ɪ, -ɪə* [-jə*], -ɪɪst [-jɪst], -ɪlɪ [-əlɪ], -ɪnɪs [-ɪnəs]
clunch klʌntʃ
clung (from cling) klʌŋ
Cluse kluːz, kluːs

clust|er (s. v.), -ers, -ering, -ered
'klʌst|ə*, -əz, -ərɪŋ, -əd

clutch (s. v.), -es, -ing, -ed klʌtʃ, -ɪz,
-ɪŋ, -t

clutter, -s, -ing, -ed 'klʌtə*, -z, -rɪŋ, -d

Clutterbuck 'klʌtəbʌk

Clutton 'klʌtn

Clwyd 'kluːɪd (Welsh kluɪd)

Clyde, -bank klaɪd, -bæŋk

Clymene 'klɪmɪnɪ [-mənɪ]

clyp|eus, -ei 'klɪp|ɪəs, -ɪaɪ

clyster, -s 'klɪstə*, -z

Clytemnestra ˌklaɪtɪm'nestrə [-tiːm-,
-tem-]

Clytie (nymph in Greek mythology)
'klɪtɪ: ['klaɪtɪ:], (modern Christian
name, chignon) 'klaɪtɪ [-tiː]

Cnidus 'naɪdəs ['kn-]

Cnut kə'njuːt

Co. kəʊ ['kʌmpənɪ]

coach (s. v.), -es, -ing, -ed kəʊtʃ, -ɪz, -ɪŋ,
-t

coach-horse, -s 'kəʊtʃhɔːs, -ɪz

coach|man, -men 'kəʊtʃ|mən, -mən

coac|tion, -tive kəʊ'æk|ʃn, -tɪv

coadjacent ˌkəʊə'dʒeɪsnt

coadjutor, -s kəʊ'ædʒʊtə* [-dʒət-], -z

co-administrator, -s ˌkəʊəd'mɪnɪs-
treɪtə*, -z

coagulat|e, -es, -ing, -ed kəʊ'ægjʊleɪt,
-s, -ɪŋ, -ɪd

coagulation, -s kəʊˌægjʊ'leɪʃn, -z

coal (s. v.), -s, -ing, -ed kəʊl, -z, -ɪŋ, -d

coal-bed, -s 'kəʊlbed, -z

coal-black ˌkəʊl'blæk ['-- when attri-
butive]

coal-bunker, -s 'kəʊlˌbʌŋkə*, -z

coalesc|e, -es, -ing, -ed ˌkəʊə'les, -ɪz,
-ɪŋ, -t

coalescen|ce, -t ˌkəʊə'lesn|s, -t

coal-field, -s 'kəʊlfiːld, -z

coal-gas 'kəʊlgæs [ˌ-'-]

coal-heaver, -s 'kəʊlˌhiːvə*, -z

coal-hole, -s 'kəʊlhəʊl, -z

coal-hou|se, -ses 'kəʊlhaʊ|s, -zɪz

coaling-station, -s 'kəʊlɪŋˌsteɪʃn, -z

coalite 'kəʊlaɪt

coalition, -s ˌkəʊə'lɪʃn, -z

coal|man, -men 'kəʊl|mæn [-mən],
-men [-mən]

coal-measure, -s 'kəʊlˌmeʒə*, -z

coal-mine, -s 'kəʊlmaɪn, -z

coal-owner, -s 'kəʊlˌəʊnə*, -z

coal-pit, -s 'kəʊlpɪt, -s

coal-scuttle, -s 'kəʊlˌskʌtl, -z

coal-tar ˌkəʊl'tɑː* ['--, esp. when
attributive]

coal-tit, -s 'kəʊltɪt, -s

coarse, -r, -st, -ly, -ness kɔːs [kɔəs],
-ə*, -ɪst, -lɪ, -nɪs [-nəs]

coarse-grained 'kɔːsgreɪnd ['kɔəs-]

coars|en, -ens, -ening, -ened 'kɔːs|n
['kɔəs-], -nz, -ɳɪŋ [-nɪŋ], -nd

coast (s. v.), -s, -ing, -ed kəʊst, -s, -ɪŋ,
-ɪd

coaster, -s 'kəʊstə*, -z

coast-guard, -s 'kəʊstgɑːd, -z

coast-line, -s 'kəʊstlaɪn, -z

coastwise 'kəʊstwaɪz

coat (s. v.), -s, -ing, -ed kəʊt, -s, -ɪŋ, -ɪd

Coatbridge 'kəʊtbrɪdʒ

coatee, -s 'kəʊti: [ˌkəʊ'tiː], -z

Coat(e)s kəʊts

coat-hanger, -s 'kəʊtˌhæŋə*, -z

coating, -s 'kəʊtɪŋ, -z

coat-of-arms, coats-of-arms ˌkəʊtəv-
'ɑːmz, ˌkəʊtsəv'ɑːmz

coax (s. v.), -es, -ing/ly, -ed, -er/s
kəʊks, -ɪz, -ɪŋ/lɪ, -t, -ə*/z

co-axial ˌkəʊ'æksɪəl [-sjəl]

cob, -s kɒb, -z

cobalt kəʊ'bɔːlt [-'bɒlt, 'kəʊbɔːlt]

Cobb, -ett kɒb, -ɪt

cobb|le (s. v.), -les, -ling, -led, -ler/s
'kɒb|l, -lz, -lɪŋ [-lɪŋ], -ld, -lə*/z

cobbler's-wax 'kɒbləzwæks

cobble-stone, -s 'kɒblstəʊn, -s

Cobbold 'kɒbəʊld [-bld]

Cobden 'kɒbdən

Cobh kəʊv

Cobham 'kɒbəm

Coblenz (K-) kəʊ'blents ['kəʊblents]

cob-nut, -s 'kɒbnʌt, -s

cobra, -s 'kəʊbrə ['kɒ-], -z

Coburg (K-), -s 'kəʊbɜːg, -z

cobweb, -s 'kɒbweb, -z

coca 'kəʊkə

coca-cola ˌkəʊkə'kəʊlə

cocaine kəʊ'keɪn [kɒ'k-]

cocciferous kɒk'sɪfərəs

coc|cus, -ci 'kɒk|əs, -aɪ ['kɒksaɪ]

coccyx, -es 'kɒksɪks, -ɪz

Cochin (in India) 'kəʊtʃɪn [ˌkəʊ'tʃɪn]

Cochin-China ˌkɒtʃɪn'tʃaɪnə

cochineal 'kɒtʃɪniːl [ˌ--'-]

cochl|ea, -eas, -eae 'kɒkl|ɪə, -ɪəz, -riː:

Cochran 'kɒkrən

Cochrane 'kɒkrən [-rɪn]

cock (s. v.), -s, -ing, -ed kɒk, -s, -ɪŋ, -t

cockade, -s kɒ'keɪd, -z

cock-a-doodle-doo ˌkɒkəduːdl'duː

cock-a-hoop ˌkɒkə'huːp ['---]

Cockaigne kɒ'keɪn [kə'k-]

cockalorum, -s ˌkɒkə'lɔːrəm, -z

cockatoo, -s ˌkɒkə'tuː, -z

cockatrice, -s 'kɒkətraɪs [-trɪs], -ɪz

93

Cockburn 'kəʊbɜːn [-bən]
cockchafer, -s 'kɒk,tʃeɪfə*, -z
Cockcroft 'kəʊkkrɒft, 'kɒkkrɒft
cock-cr|ow, -owing 'kɒkkr|əʊ, -əʊɪŋ
Cocke (*place*) kɒk, (*surname*) kəʊk, kɒk
Cockell 'kɒkl
cocker (C.), -s 'kɒkə*, -z
cockerel, -s 'kɒkərəl, -z
Cockerell 'kɒkərəl
Cockermouth 'kɒkəməθ [-maʊθ]
　Note.—*Locally* -məθ.
cock-eye, -d 'kɒkaɪ, -d [ˌ-'-]
cock-fight, -s, -ing 'kɒkfaɪt, -s, -ɪŋ
Cockfosters ˌkɒk'fɒstəz
cock-horse, -s ˌkɒk'hɔːs ['--, *also* -'-
　when preceded by a stress], -ɪz
cock|le (*s. v.*) (C.), -les, -ling, -led
　'kɒk|l, -lz, -lɪŋ [-lɪŋ], -ld
cockleshell, -s 'kɒklʃel, -z
cockney (C.), -s 'kɒknɪ, -z
cockneyism, -s 'kɒknɪɪzəm [-njɪz-], -z
cock-pit, -s 'kɒkpɪt, -s
cockroach, -es 'kɒkrəʊtʃ, -ɪz
Cockroft 'kəʊkrɒft ['kɒk-]
cockscomb, -s 'kɒkskəʊm, -z
Cocksedge 'kɒksɪdʒ [-sedʒ], 'kɒsɪdʒ,
　'kəʊsɪdʒ
Cockshott 'kɒkʃɒt
cock-sh|y, -ies 'kɒkʃ|aɪ, -aɪz
Cockspur 'kɒkspɜː* [-pə*]
cock-sure ˌkɒk'ʃʊə* [-'ʃɔə*, -'ʃɔː*]
cocktail, -s 'kɒkteɪl, -z
Cockwood (*in Devon*) 'kɒkwʊd
　Note.—*There exists also a local pro-*
　nunciation 'kɒkʊd.
cock|y, -ier, -iest, -ily, -iness 'kɒk|ɪ,
　-ɪə*, -ɪɪst, -ɪlɪ [-əlɪ], -ɪnɪs [-ɪnəs]
cocky-leeky ˌkɒkɪ'liːkɪ
Cocles 'kɒkliːz
coco, -s 'kəʊkəʊ, -z
cocoa, -s 'kəʊkəʊ, -z
coco(a)nut, -s 'kəʊkənʌt, -s
cocoon, -s kə'kuːn [kɒ'k-], -z
cocotte, -s kɒ'kɒt [kəʊ-], -s
Cocytus kəʊ'saɪtəs
cod, -s kɒd, -z
Coddington 'kɒdɪŋtən
codd|le, -les, -ling, -led 'kɒd|l, -lz, -lɪŋ
　[-lɪŋ], -ld
code, -s kəʊd, -z
codeine 'kəʊdiːn [-diːn]
cod|ex, -exes, -ices 'kəʊd|eks, -eksɪz,
　-ɪsiːz ['kɒdɪsiːz]
cod-fish|er/s, -ing 'kɒd,fɪʃ|ə*/z, -ɪŋ
cod-fisher|y, -ies 'kɒd,fɪʃər|ɪ, -ɪz
codger, -s 'kɒdʒə*, -z
codicil, -s 'kɒdɪsɪl, -z
codicillary ˌkɒdɪ'sɪlərɪ

Codicote 'kəʊdɪkəʊt
codification, -s ˌkəʊdɪfɪ'keɪʃn [ˌkɒd-], -z
codi|fy, -fies, -fying, -fied 'kəʊdɪ|faɪ
　['kɒd-], -faɪz, -faɪɪŋ, -faɪd
codling, -s 'kɒdlɪŋ, -z
cod-liver-oil ,kɒdlɪvər'ɔɪl [-'və-]
codpiec|e, -es 'kɒdpiːs, -ɪz
Codrington 'kɒdrɪŋtən
Cody 'kəʊdɪ
Coe kəʊ
co-ed ˌkəʊ'ed
coeducation ˌkəʊedjuː'keɪʃn [-djʊ-,
　-dʒuː-, -dʒʊ-]
coeducational ˌkəʊedjuː'keɪʃənl [-djʊ-,
　-dʒuː-, -dʒʊ-, -ʃnəl, -ʃn̩l, -ʃn̩l,
　-ʃnəl]
coefficient, -s ˌkəʊɪ'fɪʃnt, -s
coelacanth, -s 'siːləkænθ, -s
Coelesyria ˌsiːlɪ'sɪrɪə
coemption kəʊ'empʃn
coenobite, -s 'siːnəʊbaɪt, -s
coequ|al, -ally kəʊ'iːkw|əl, -əlɪ
coequality ˌkəʊiː'kwɒlətɪ [ˌkəʊɪ-, -ɪtɪ]
coerc|e, -es, -ing, -ed kəʊ'ɜːs, -ɪz, -ɪŋ, -t
coercib|le, -ly kəʊ'ɜːsɪb|l [-səb-], -lɪ
coercion kəʊ'ɜːʃn
coercionist, -s kəʊ'ɜːʃnɪst [-ʃənɪst], -s
coercive, -ly kəʊ'ɜːsɪv, -lɪ
co-eternal ˌkəʊɪ'tɜːnl [-iː't-]
Cœur de Lion ˌkɜːdə'liːɔ̃ːŋ [-'liːɒŋ]
　(kœrdəljɔ̃)
coeval kəʊ'iːvl
co-executor, -s ˌkəʊɪg'zekjʊtə* [-eg-,
　-kjət-], -z
co-exist, -s, -ing, -ed ˌkəʊɪg'zɪst [-eg-],
　-s, -ɪŋ, -ɪd
co-existen|ce, -t ˌkəʊɪg'zɪstən|s [-eg-], -t
co-extend, -s, -ing, -ed ˌkəʊɪk'stend
　[-ek-], -z, -ɪŋ, -ɪd
co-extension, -s ˌkəʊɪk'stenʃn [-ek-], -z
co-extensive ˌkəʊɪk'stensɪv [-ek-]
coffee, -s 'kɒfɪ, -z
coffee-bar, -s 'kɒfɪbɑː*, -z
coffee-bean, -s 'kɒfɪbiːn, -z
coffee-cup, -s 'kɒfɪkʌp, -s
coffee-hou|se, -ses 'kɒfɪhaʊ|s, -zɪz
coffee-mill, -s 'kɒfɪmɪl, -z
coffee-pot, -s 'kɒfɪpɒt, -s
coffee-room, -s 'kɒfɪrʊm [-ruːm], -z
coffer, -s 'kɒfə*, -z
coffin (*s. v.*) (C.), -s, -ing, -ed 'kɒfɪn, -z,
　-ɪŋ, -d
cog (*s. v.*), -s, -ging, -ged kɒg, -z, -ɪŋ, -d
cogen|ce, -cy, -t/ly 'kəʊdʒən|s, -sɪ, -t/lɪ
Coggeshall (*in Essex*) 'kɒgɪʃl, (*sur-*
　name) 'kɒgzɔːl
Coggin 'kɒgɪn
Coghill 'kɒgɪl [-hɪl]

cogitat|e, -es, -ing, -ed, -or/s 'kɒdʒɪteɪt, -s, -ɪŋ, -ɪd, -ə*/z

cogitation, -s ˌkɒdʒɪ'teɪʃn, -z

cogitative 'kɒdʒɪtətɪv [-teɪt-]

cognac, -s 'kɒnjæk ['kəʊn-] (kɔɲak), -s

cognate (s. adj.), -s 'kɒgneɪt [-'-], -s

cognation kɒg'neɪʃn

cognition, -s kɒg'nɪʃn, -z

cognitive 'kɒgnɪtɪv

cognizable [-isa-] 'kɒgnɪzəbl ['kɒn-]

cognizan|ce [-isa-], -ces, -t 'kɒgnɪzən|s ['kɒn-], -sɪz, -t

cogniz|e [-is|e], -es, -ing, -ed kɒg'naɪz ['--], -ɪz, -ɪŋ, -d

cognomen, -s kɒg'nəʊmen, -z

cognominal kɒg'nɒmɪnl [-'nɒm-]

cognoscent|e, -i ˌkɒnjəʊ'ʃent|ɪ [ˌkɒnəʊ-, ˌkɒgnəʊ-], -i: [-ɪ]

cognovit, -s kɒg'nəʊvɪt, -s

cogwheel, -s 'kɒgwi:l [-ghw-], -z

cohabit, -s, -ing, -ed kəʊ'hæbɪt, -s, -ɪŋ, -ɪd

cohabitant, -s kəʊ'hæbɪtənt, -s

cohabitation ˌkəʊhæbɪ'teɪʃn [kəʊˌhæ-]

co-heir, -s ˌkəʊ'eə* ['--], -z

co-heiress, -es ˌkəʊ'eərɪs [-res], -ɪz

Cohen 'kəʊɪn

coher|e, -es, -ing, -ed kəʊ'hɪə*, -z, -rɪŋ, -d

coheren|ce, -cy, -t/ly kəʊ'hɪərən|s, -sɪ, -t/lɪ

cohesion kəʊ'hi:ʒn

cohesive, -ly, -ness kəʊ'hi:sɪv, -lɪ, -nɪs [-nəs]

Cohn kəʊn

Cohorn 'kəʊhɔ:n

cohort, -s 'kəʊhɔ:t, -s

coif (s. v.), -s, -ing, -ed kɔɪf, -s, -ɪŋ, -t

coiffé, -s, -ing, -d 'kwɑ:feɪ ['kwæf-, 'kwɒf-] (kwafe), -z, -ɪŋ, -d

coiffeur, -s kwɑ:'fɜ:* [kwæ'f-, kwɒ'f-] (kwafœ:r), -z

coiffure, -s kwɑ:'fjʊə* [kwæ'f-, kwɒ'f-] (kwafy:r), -z

coign, -s kɔɪn, -z

coil (s. v.), -s, -ing, -ed kɔɪl, -z, -ɪŋ, -d

Coimbra kəʊ'ɪmbrə

coin (s. v.), -s, -ing, -ed, -er/s kɔɪn, -z, -ɪŋ, -d, -ə*/z

coinage, -s 'kɔɪnɪdʒ, -ɪz

coincid|e, -es, -ing, -ed ˌkəʊɪn'saɪd, -z, -ɪŋ, -ɪd

coinciden|ce, -ces, -t/ly kəʊ'ɪnsɪdən|s, -sɪz, -t/lɪ

coincident|al, -ally kəʊˌɪnsɪ'dent|l [ˌkəʊɪn-], -əlɪ

co-inheritor, -s ˌkəʊɪn'herɪtə*, -z

coir 'kɔɪə*

coition kəʊ'ɪʃn

coitus 'kəʊɪtəs

coke kəʊk

Coke kəʊk, kʊk

Note.—Members of the Essex family pronounce kʊk. So also the family name of the Earl of Leicester.

Coker 'kəʊkə*

col, -s kɒl, -z

Col. 'kɜ:nl

cola 'kəʊlə

colander, -s 'kʌləndə* ['kɒl-], -z

Colby 'kəʊlbɪ

Colchester 'kəʊltʃɪstə*

colchicum 'kɒltʃɪkəm [-lkɪ-]

Colchis 'kɒlkɪs

Colcleugh 'kəʊklklu:

Colclough 'kəʊklɪ, 'kɒlklʌf, 'kəʊlklʌf

cold (s. adj.), -s, -er, -est, -ly, -ness kəʊld, -z, -ə*, -ɪst, -lɪ, -nɪs [-nəs]

cold-blooded, -ly, -ness ˌkəʊld'blʌdɪd ['-ˌ-- *when attributive*], -lɪ, -nɪs [-nəs]

cold-cream ˌkəʊld'kri:m

cold-hearted ˌkəʊld'hɑ:tɪd ['-ˌ--]

coldish 'kəʊldɪʃ

cold-shoulder, -s, -ing, -ed ˌkəʊld-'ʃəʊldə*, -z, -rɪŋ, -d

cold-storage ˌkəʊld'stɔ:rɪdʒ

Coldstream 'kəʊldstri:m

cole (C.), -s kəʊl, -z

Colebrook(e) 'kəʊlbrʊk

Coleby 'kəʊlbɪ

Coleclough 'kəʊlklaʊ

Coleford 'kəʊlfəd

Coleman 'kəʊlmən

Colenso kə'lenzəʊ

coleopter|a, -al ˌkɒlɪ'ɒptər|ə, -əl

Coleraine kəʊl'reɪn

Coleridge 'kəʊlərɪdʒ

Coles kəʊlz

coleslaw 'kəʊlslɔ:

Colet 'kɒlɪt

cole-tit, -s 'kəʊltɪt, -s

Colgate 'kəʊlgeɪt ['kɒl-, -gɪt]

colic 'kɒlɪk

Colin, -dale 'kɒlɪn, -deɪl

Coling 'kəʊlɪŋ

Coliseum ˌkɒlɪ'sɪəm [-lə-, -'si:əm]

colitis kɒ'laɪtɪs [kəʊ'l-]

collaborat|e, -es, -ing, -ed, -or/s kə'læbəreɪt [kɒ'l-], -s, -ɪŋ, -ɪd, -ə*/z

collaboration, -s kəˌlæbə'reɪʃn [kɒˌl-], -z

collage, -s kɒ'lɑ:ʒ, -ɪz

collaps|e (s. v.), -es, -ing, -ed kə'læps, -ɪz, -ɪŋ, -t

collapsible kə'læpsəbl [-sɪb-]

collar (s. v.), -s, -ing, -ed 'kɒlə*, -z, -rɪŋ, -d

collar-bone, -s ˈkɒləbəʊn, -z
Collard ˈkɒləd
Collas ˈkɒləs
collat|e, -es, -ing, -ed, -or/s kɒˈleɪt
[kəˈl-], -s, -ɪŋ, -ɪd, -ə*/z
collater|al/s, -ally kɒˈlætər|əl/z [kəˈl-],
-əlɪ
collation, -s kɒˈleɪʃn [kəˈl-], -z
colleague, -s ˈkɒliːg, -z
collect (s.), -s ˈkɒlekt [-lɪkt], -s
collect (v.), -s, -ing, -ed, -er/s kəˈlekt,
-s, -ɪŋ, -ɪd, -ə*/z
collectanea ˌkɒlekˈtɑːnjə [-ˈteɪn-, -nɪə]
collected (adj.), -ly, -ness kəˈlektɪd, -lɪ,
-nɪs [-nəs]
collection, -s kəˈlekʃn, -z
collective, -ly kəˈlektɪv, -lɪ
collectivi|sm, -st/s kəˈlektɪvɪ|zəm, -st/s
collector, -s kəˈlektə*, -z
colleen, -s ˈkɒliːn [in Ireland kɒˈliːn],
-z
college, -s; -r/s ˈkɒlɪdʒ, -ɪz; -ə*/z
collegian, -s kəˈliːdʒjən [kɒˈl-, -dʒɪən],
-z
collegiate kəˈliːdʒɪət [kɒˈl-, -dʒjət,
-dʒɪt, -dʒɪt]
Collen ˈkɒlɪn
Colles ˈkɒlɪs
collet (C.), -s ˈkɒlɪt, -s
collid|e, -es, -ing, -ed kəˈlaɪd, -z, -ɪŋ, -ɪd
collie (C.), -s ˈkɒlɪ, -z
collier (C.), -s ˈkɒlɪə* [-ljə*], -z
collier|y, -ies ˈkɒljər|ɪ, -ɪz
collimat|e, -es, -ing, -ed ˈkɒlɪmeɪt, -s,
-ɪŋ, -ɪd
collimation ˌkɒlɪˈmeɪʃn
collimator, -s ˈkɒlɪmeɪtə*, -z
collinear kɒˈlɪnjə* [kəˈl-, -nɪə*]
Collingham ˈkɒlɪŋəm
Collingwood ˈkɒlɪŋwʊd
Collin|s, -son ˈkɒlɪn|z, -sn
Collis ˈkɒlɪs
collision, -s kəˈlɪʒn, -z
collocat|e, -es, -ing, -ed ˈkɒləʊkeɪt, -s,
-ɪŋ, -ɪd
collocation, -s ˌkɒləʊˈkeɪʃn, -z
collodion kəˈləʊdjən [-dɪən]
colloid, -s ˈkɒlɔɪd, -z
collop, -s ˈkɒləp, -s
colloquial, -ly, -ism/s kəˈləʊkwɪəl
[-kwjəl], -ɪ, -ɪzəm/z
colloquium kəˈləʊkwɪəm
colloqu|y, -ies ˈkɒləkw|ɪ, -ɪz
collotype, -s ˈkɒləʊtaɪp, -s
Colls kɒlz
collud|e, -es, -ing, -ed, -er/s kəˈluːd
[kɒˈl-, -ˈljuːd], -z, -ɪŋ, -ɪd, -ə*/z
collusion, -s kəˈluːʒn [-ˈljuː-], -z

collusive, -ly kəˈluːsɪv [-ˈljuː-], -lɪ
Collyns ˈkɒlɪnz
collywobbles ˈkɒlɪˌwɒblz
Colman ˈkəʊlmən
Colmekill ˈkəʊlmkɪl
Colnaghi kɒlˈnɑːgɪ
Colnbrook ˈkəʊlnbrʊk [ˈkəʊn-]
Colne kəʊn, kəʊln
Colney ˈkəʊnɪ
Cologne kəˈləʊn
Colombia, -n/s kəˈlɒmbɪə [-ˈlʌm-, -bjə],
-n/z
Colombo kəˈlʌmbəʊ [-ˈlɒm-]
colon (punctuation mark), -s ˈkəʊlən
[-lɒn], -z
colon (intestine), -s ˈkəʊlən [-lɒn], -z
Colon kɒlɒn
colonel, -s; -cy, -cies, -ship/s ˈkɜːnl, -z;
-sɪ, -sɪz, -ʃɪp/s
colonial (s. adj.), -s kəˈləʊnjəl [-nɪəl], -z
colonist, -s ˈkɒlənɪst, -s
colonization [-isa-] ˌkɒlənaɪˈzeɪʃn
[-nɪˈz-]
coloniz|e [-is|e], -es, -ing, -ed, -er/s
ˈkɒlənaɪz, -ɪz, -ɪŋ, -d, -ə*/z
colonnade, -s ˌkɒləˈneɪd, -z
Colonus kəˈləʊnəs
colon|y, -ies ˈkɒlən|ɪ [-lŋ|ɪ], -ɪz
colophon, -s ˈkɒləfən [-fɒn], -z
Colorado ˌkɒləˈrɑːdəʊ
coloration ˌkʌləˈreɪʃn
coloratura ˌkɒlərəˈtʊərə [-ˈtjʊər-]
colorific ˌkɒləˈrɪfɪk
colossal kəˈlɒsl
Colosseum ˌkɒləˈsɪəm [-ˈsiːəm]
Colossian, -s kəˈlɒʃn [-ɒsɪən, -ɒsjən,
-ɒʃɪən, -ɒʃjən], -z
coloss|us, -i kəˈlɒs|əs, -aɪ
colour (s. v.), -s, -ing, -ed ˈkʌlə*, -z,
-rɪŋ, -d
colourab|le, -ly ˈkʌlərəb|l, -lɪ
colouration ˌkʌləˈreɪʃn
colour-bar, -s ˈkʌləbɑː*, -z
colour-blin|d, -dness ˈkʌləblaɪn|d
[ˌkʌləˈb-], -dnɪs [-nəs]
colour|ful, -less ˈkʌlə|fʊl, -lɪs [-ləs]
colour|man, -men ˈkʌlə|mən [-mæn],
-mən [-men]
colour-proc|ess, -esses ˈkʌləˌprəʊs|es
[rarely -ˌprɒs-], -esɪz [-ɪsɪz]
colour-sergeant, -s ˈkʌləˌsɑːdʒənt, -s
colporteur, -s ˈkɒlˌpɔːtə* [ˌkɒlpɔːˈtɜː*],
-z
Colquhoun kəˈhuːn
Cols. ˈkɜːnlz
Colson ˈkəʊlsn
Colston ˈkəʊlstən
colt, -s kəʊlt, -s

coltsfoot, -s 'kəʊltsfʊt, -s
coluber, -s 'kɒljʊbə*, -z
colubrine 'kɒljʊbraɪn
Columba kə'lʌmbə
columbarium, -s ,kɒləm'beərɪəm, -z
Columbia, -n/s kə'lʌmbɪə [-bjə], -n/z
columbine, -s 'kɒləmbaɪn, -z
Columbus kə'lʌmbəs
column, -s, -ed 'kɒləm, -z, -d
column|al, -ar kə'lʌmn|l, -ə*
columnist, -s 'kɒləmnɪst [-əmɪst], -s
colure, -s kə'ljʊə*, -z
Colwyn 'kɒlwɪn
Colyton 'kɒlɪtn
colza 'kɒlzə
coma (deep sleep), -s 'kəʊmə, -z
com|a (tuft), -as, -ae 'kəʊm|ə, -əz, -iː
Coma Berenices 'kəʊmə ,berɪ'naɪsiːz
comatose 'kəʊmətəʊs
comb (s. v.), -s, -ing/s, -ed kəʊm, -z, -ɪŋ/z, -d
comb|at (s. v.), -ats, -ating, -ated 'kɒmb|æt ['kʌm-, -ət], -æts [-əts], -ətɪŋ, -ətɪd
combatant, -s 'kɒmbətənt ['kʌm-], -s
combative, -ly, -ness 'kɒmbətɪv ['kʌm-], -lɪ, -nɪs [-nəs]
combe (C.), -s kuːm, -z
comber (combing machine), -s 'kəʊmə*, -z
comber (fish) (C.), -s 'kɒmbə*, -z
combination, -s; -room/s ,kɒmbɪ'neɪʃn, -z; -rʊm/z [-ruːm/z]
combinative 'kɒmbɪnətɪv [-nert-]
combinatory 'kɒmbɪnətərɪ [,kɒmbɪ'nertərɪ]
combine (s.), -s 'kɒmbaɪn [kəm'baɪn], -z
combin|e (v.), -es, -ing, -ed kəm'baɪn, -z, -ɪŋ, -d
combust kəm'bʌst
combustibility kəm,bʌstə'bɪlətɪ [-tɪ'b-, -lɪt-]
combustible, -ness kəm'bʌstəbl [-tɪb-], -nɪs [-nəs]
combustion, -s kəm'bʌstʃən, -z
com|e, -es, -ing, came kʌm, -z, -ɪŋ, keɪm
come-at-able ,kʌm'ætəbl
come-back, -s 'kʌmbæk, -s
comedian, -s kə'miːdjən [-dɪən], -z
comédienne, -s kə,meɪdɪ'en [,kɒm-, kə,miːd-] (kɔmedjɛn), -z
come-down, -s 'kʌmdaʊn [,-'-], -z
comed|y, -ies 'kɒmɪd|ɪ [-mədɪ], -ɪz
comel|y, -ier, -iest, -iness 'kʌml|ɪ, -ɪə* [-jə*], -ɪɪst [-jɪst], -ɪnɪs [-ɪnəs]
Comenius kə'meɪnjəs [kɒ'm-, -nɪəs]
comestible, -s kə'mestɪbl [-əbl], -z

comet, -s; -ary 'kɒmɪt, -s; -ərɪ
comfit, -s 'kʌmfɪt ['kɒm-], -s
comfort (s. v.), -s, -ing, -ed, -er/s 'kʌmfət, -s, -ɪŋ, -ɪd, -ə*/z
comfortab|le, -ly 'kʌmfətəb|l, -lɪ
comforter (scarf), -s 'kʌmfətə*, -z
comfortless 'kʌmfətlɪs [-ləs]
comfrey 'kʌmfrɪ
comf|y, -ier, -iest, -ily, -iness 'kʌmf|ɪ -ɪə* [-jə*], -ɪɪst [-jɪst], -ɪlɪ [-əlɪ], -ɪnɪs [-ɪnəs]
comic, -al, -ally, -alness 'kɒmɪk, -əl, -əlɪ, -əlnɪs [-nəs]
Comin 'kʌmɪn
Cominform 'kɒmɪnfɔːm [,--'-]
Comintern 'kɒmɪntɜːn [,--'-]
comity 'kɒmɪtɪ
comma, -s 'kɒmə, -z
Commager 'kɒmədʒə*
command (s. v.), -s, -ing/ly, -ed, -er/s kə'mɑːnd, -z, -ɪŋ/lɪ, -ɪd, -ə*/z
commandant, -s ,kɒmən'dænt [-'dɑːnt, '---], -s
commandantship, -s ,kɒmən'dænt-ʃɪp [-'dɑːnt-], -s
commandeer, -s, -ing, -ed ,kɒmən'dɪə*, -z, -rɪŋ, -d
commander-in-chief, commanders-in-chief kə,mɑːndərɪn'tʃiːf [-dəɪn-], kə,mɑːndəzɪn'tʃiːf
commandership, -s kə'mɑːndəʃɪp, -s
commandment, -s kə'mɑːndmənt, -s
commando, -(e)s kə'mɑːndəʊ, -z
comme-il-faut ,kɒmiːl'fəʊ (kɔmilfo)
commemorat|e, -es, -ing, -ed, -or/s kə'meməreɪt [-mʊr-], -s, -ɪŋ, -ɪd, -ə*/z
commemoration, -s kə,memə'reɪʃn [-mʊr-], -z
commemorative kə'memərətɪv [-mʊr-, -reɪt-]
commenc|e, -es, -ing, -ed, -ement/s kə'mens, -ɪz, -ɪŋ, -t, -mənt/s
commend, -s, -ing, -ed kə'mend, -z, -ɪŋ, -ɪd
commendab|le, -ly, -leness kə'mend-əb|l, -lɪ, -lnɪs [-nəs]
commendation, -s ,kɒmen'deɪʃn [-mən-], -z
commendatory kɒ'mendətərɪ [kə'm-]
commensurability kə,menʃərə'bɪlətɪ [-sjər-, -sjʊr-, -ʃʊr-, -lɪt-]
commensurab|le, -ly, -leness kə'men-ʃərəb|l [-sjʊr-, -sjər-, -sjʊr-], -lɪ, -lnɪs [-nəs]
commensurate, -ly, -ness kə'menʃərət [-ʃʊr-, -sjər-, -sjʊr-, -rɪt], -lɪ, -nɪs [-nəs]

comment (s.), -s ˈkɒment, -s
comment (v.), -s, -ing, -ed ˈkɒment [-mənt, *rarely* kɒˈment, kəˈment], -s, -ɪŋ, -ɪd
commentar|y, -ies ˈkɒməntər|ɪ, -ɪz
commentator, -s ˈkɒmenteɪtə* [-mən-], -z
commerce ˈkɒmɜːs
commerci|al, -ally kəˈmɜːʃ|l, -əlɪ [-|ɪ]
commercialese kə,mɜːʃəˈliːz [-ʃ|ˈiːz]
commerciali|sm, -st/s kəˈmɜːʃəlɪ|zəm [-ʃɪ-], -st/s
commerciality kə,mɜːʃɪˈælətɪ [-ɪtɪ]
commercializ|e [-is|e], -es, -ing, -ed kəˈmɜːʃəlaɪz [-ʃaɪz], -ɪz, -ɪŋ, -d
comminat|e, -es, -ing, -ed ˈkɒmɪneɪt, -s, -ɪŋ, -ɪd
commination, -s ,kɒmɪˈneɪʃn, -z
comminatory ˈkɒmɪnətərɪ [-neɪt-]
comming|le, -les, -ling, -led kɒˈmɪŋg|l [kəʊˈm-], -lz, -lɪŋ [-lɪŋ], -ld
comminut|e, -es, -ing, -ed ˈkɒmɪnjuːt, -s, -ɪŋ, -ɪd
comminution ,kɒmɪˈnjuːʃn
commiserat|e, -es, -ing, -ed kəˈmɪzəreɪt [kɒˈm-], -s, -ɪŋ, -ɪd
commiseration kə,mɪzəˈreɪʃn [kɒ,m-]
commissar, -s ,kɒmɪˈsɑː* [ˈ—-], -z
commissarial ,kɒmɪˈseərɪəl
commissariat ,kɒmɪˈseərɪət [-ˈsær-, -rɪæt]
commissar|y, -ies ˈkɒmɪsər|ɪ [kəˈmɪs-], -ɪz
commissi|on (s. v.), -ons, -oning, -oned, -oner/s kəˈmɪʃ|n, -nz, -nɪŋ [-ənɪŋ], -nd, -nə*/z [-ənə*/z, -nə*/z]
commission-agent, -s kəˈmɪʃn,eɪdʒənt -s
commissionaire, -s kə,mɪʃəˈneə* [-ʃnˈeə*, -sjəˈneə*], -z
commissure, -s ˈkɒmɪ,sjʊə* [-ɪ,ʃʊə*], -z
commit, -s, -ting, -ted, -ter/s, -ment/s kəˈmɪt, -s, -ɪŋ, -ɪd, -ə*/z, -mənt/s
committal, -s kəˈmɪtl, -z
committee (*council*), -s kəˈmɪtɪ, -z
committee (*one committed*), -s ,kɒmɪˈtiː, -z
committor, -s ,kɒmɪˈtɔː*, -z
commix, -es, -ing, -ed kɒˈmɪks, -ɪz, -ɪŋ, -t
commode, -s kəˈməʊd, -z
commodious, -ly, -ness kəˈməʊdjəs [-dɪəs], -lɪ, -nɪs [-nəs]
commodit|y, -ies kəˈmɒdət|ɪ [-ɪt|ɪ], -ɪz
commodore, -s ˈkɒmədɔː* [-dɔə*], -z
common (s. adj.), -s; -er, -est, -ly, -ness ˈkɒmən, -z; -ə*, -ɪst, -lɪ, -nɪs [-nəs]
commonage ˈkɒmənɪdʒ

commonalt|y, -ies ˈkɒmən|t|ɪ [-nəl-], -ɪz
Commondale ˈkɒməndeɪl
commoner, -s ˈkɒmənə*, -z
common law ˈkɒmənlɔː
commonplace (s. adj.), -s ˈkɒmənpleɪs, -ɪz
common-room, -s ˈkɒmənrʊm [-ruːm], -z
commons (C.) ˈkɒmənz
commonwealth, -s ˈkɒmənwelθ, -s
commotion, -s kəˈməʊʃn, -z
communal ˈkɒmjʊnl [kəˈmjuːnl]
commune (s.), -s ˈkɒmjuːn, -z
commun|e (v.), -es, -ing, -ed kəˈmjuːn [ˈkɒmjuːn], -z, -ɪŋ [ˈkɒmjʊnɪŋ], -d
communicab|le, -ly, -leness kəˈmjuːnɪ-kəb|l [-ˈmjʊn-], -lɪ, -lnɪs [-nəs]
communicant, -s kəˈmjuːnɪkənt [-ˈmjʊn-], -s
communicat|e, -es, -ing, -ed, -or/s kəˈmjuːnɪkeɪt [-ˈmjʊn-], -s, -ɪŋ, -ɪd, -ə*/z
communication, -s kə,mjuːnɪˈkeɪʃn [-,mjʊn-], -z
communicative, -ness kəˈmjuːnɪkətɪv [-ˈmjʊn-, -keɪt-], -nɪs [-nəs]
communion, -s kəˈmjuːnjən [-nɪən], -z
communiqué, -s kəˈmjuːnɪkeɪ [kɒˈm-, -ˈmjʊn-] (komynike), -z
communi|sm, -st/s ˈkɒmjʊnɪ|zəm [-mjuːn-, -mjən-], -st/s
communit|y, -ies kəˈmjuːnət|ɪ [-rt|ɪ], -ɪz
commutability kə,mjuːtəˈbɪlətɪ [-lɪt-]
commutable kəˈmjuːtəbl
commutation, -s ,kɒmjuːˈteɪʃn [-mjʊ-], -z
commutative, -ly kəˈmjuːtətɪv [ˈkɒm- juːteɪtɪv, -mjʊ-], -lɪ
commutator, -s ˈkɒmjuːteɪtə* [-mjʊ-], -z
commut|e, -es, -ing, -ed, -er/s kəˈmjuːt [kɒˈm-], -s, -ɪŋ, -ɪd, -ə*/z
Como ˈkəʊməʊ
Comont ˈkəʊmɒnt
Comorin ˈkɒmərɪn
comose ˈkəʊməʊs
compact (s.), -s ˈkɒmpækt, -s
compact (adj. v.), -er, -est, -ly, -ness; -s, -ing, -ed kəmˈpækt, -ə*, -ɪst, -lɪ, -nɪs [-nəs]; -s, -ɪŋ, -ɪd
companion, -s, -ship kəmˈpænjən, -z, -ʃɪp
companionable, -ness kəmˈpænjənəbl, -nɪs [-nəs]
companionate kəmˈpænjənɪt [-nət]
companion-way, -s kəmˈpænjənweɪ, -z
compan|y, -ies ˈkʌmpən|ɪ, -ɪz

comparability ˌkɒmpərə'bɪlətɪ [-lɪt-]
comparab|le, -ly, -leness 'kɒmpərəb|l, -lɪ, -lnɪs [-nəs]
comparative (s. adj.), -s, -ly kəm-'pærətɪv, -z, -lɪ
compar|e (s. v.), -es, -ing, -ed kəm'peə*, -z, -rɪŋ, -d
comparison, -s kəm'pærɪsn, -z
compartment, -s kəm'pɑ:tmənt, -s
compartmentalization [-isa-] 'kɒm-pɑ:tˌmentlaɪ'zeɪʃn [-]ɪz-]
compartmentaliz|e [-is|e], -es, -ing, -ed ˌkɒmpɑ:t'mentlaɪz, -ɪz, -ɪŋ, -d
compass (s. v.), -es, -ing, -ed 'kʌmpəs, -ɪz, -ɪŋ, -t
compassion kəm'pæʃn
compassionate, -ly, -ness kəm'pæʃənət [-ʃṇət, -ʃnət, -ɪt], -lɪ, -nɪs [-nəs]
compatibility kəmˌpætə'bɪlətɪ [-tɪ'b-, -lɪt-]
compatib|le, -ly, -leness kəm'pætəb|l [-tɪb-], -lɪ, -lnɪs [-nəs]
compatriot, -s kəm'pætrɪət [kɒm-], -s
compeer, -s kɒm'pɪə* ['kɒm,pɪə*], -z
compel, -s, -ling, -led; -lable kəm'pel, -z, -ɪŋ, -d; -əbl
compendious, -ly, -ness kəm'pendɪəs [-djəs], -lɪ, -nɪs [-nəs]
compendium, -s kəm'pendɪəm [-djəm], -z
compensat|e, -es, -ing, -ed 'kɒmpen-seɪt [-pən-], -s, -ɪŋ, -ɪd
compensation, -s ˌkɒmpen'seɪʃn [-pən-], -z
compensative kəm'pensətɪv ['kɒmpen-seɪt-, 'kɒmpənseɪt-]
compensatory kəm'pensətərɪ ['kɒm-penseɪtərɪ, 'kɒmpənseɪtərɪ, ˌkɒm-pən'seɪtərɪ]
comper|e (s. v.), -es, -ing, -ed 'kɒmpeə*, -z, -rɪŋ, -d
compet|e, -es, -ing, -ed kəm'pi:t, -s, -ɪŋ, -ɪd
competen|ce, -cy, -t/ly 'kɒmpɪtən|s [-pət-], -sɪ, -t/lɪ
competition, -s ˌkɒmpɪ'tɪʃn [-pə't-], -z
competitive kəm'petətɪv [-tɪt-]
competitor, -s kəm'petɪtə* [-tətə*], -z
compilation, -s ˌkɒmpɪ'leɪʃn [-paɪ'l-], -z
compil|e, -es, -ing, -ed, -er/s kəm'paɪl, -z, -ɪŋ, -d, -ə*/z
complacen|ce, -cy, -t/ly kəm'pleɪsn|s, -sɪ, -t/lɪ
complain, -s, -ing, -ed, -er/s kəm'pleɪn, -z, -ɪŋ, -d, -ə*/z
complainant, -s kəm'pleɪnənt, -s
complaint, -s kəm'pleɪnt, -s
complaisan|ce, -t/ly kəm'pleɪzən|s, -t/lɪ

complement (s.), -s 'kɒmplɪmənt, -s
complement (v.), -s, -ing, -ed 'kɒm-plɪment [ˌkɒmplɪ'ment], -s, -ɪŋ, -ɪd
complement|al, -ary ˌkɒmplɪ'ment|l, -ərɪ
complet|e (adj. v.), -est, -ely, -eness; -es, -ing, -ed kəm'pli:t, -ɪst, -lɪ, -nɪs [-nəs]; -s, -ɪŋ, -ɪd
completion kəm'pli:ʃn
complex (s. adj.), -es 'kɒmpleks, -ɪz
complexion, -s, -ed kəm'plekʃn, -z, -d
complexit|y, -ies kəm'pleksət|ɪ [kɒm-, -ɪt|ɪ], -ɪz
complian|ce, -ces, -t/ly kəm'plaɪən|s, -sɪz, -t/lɪ
complicat|e, -es, -ing, -ed 'kɒmplɪkeɪt, -s, -ɪŋ, -ɪd
complication, -s ˌkɒmplɪ'keɪʃn, -z
complicity kəm'plɪsətɪ [kɒm-, -ɪtɪ]
compliment (s.), -s 'kɒmplɪmənt, -s
compliment (v.), -s, -ing, -ed 'kɒmplɪ-ment [ˌkɒmplɪ'ment], -s, -ɪŋ, -ɪd
complimentar|y (s. adj.), -ies ˌkɒm-plɪ'mentər|ɪ, -ɪz
complin, -s 'kɒmplɪn, -z
compline, -s 'kɒmplɪn [-laɪn], -z
compl|y, -ies, -ying, -ied kəm'pl|aɪ, -aɪz, -aɪɪŋ, -aɪd
compo 'kɒmpəʊ
component, -s kəm'pəʊnənt, -s
comport, -s, -ing, -ed, -ment kəm'pɔ:t, -s, -ɪŋ, -ɪd, -mənt
compos|e, -es, -ing, -ed, -er/s kəm'pəʊz, -ɪz, -ɪŋ, -d, -ə*/z
compos|ed (adj.), -edly, -edness kəm-'pəʊz|d, -ɪdlɪ, -ɪdnɪs [-nəs]
composite, -ly, -ness 'kɒmpəzɪt [-sɪt, -zaɪt, -saɪt], -lɪ, -nɪs [-nəs]
composition, -s ˌkɒmpə'zɪʃn, -z
compositor, -s kəm'pɒzɪtə*, -z
compost, -s 'kɒmpɒst, -s
composure kəm'pəʊʒə*
compote, -s 'kɒmpɒt [-pəʊt] (kɔ̃pɒt), -s
compound (s. adj.), -s 'kɒmpaʊnd, -z
compound (v.), -s, -ing, -ed kəm'paʊnd [kɒm-], -z, -ɪŋ, -ɪd
comprehend, -s, -ing, -ed ˌkɒmprɪ-'hend, -z, -ɪŋ, -ɪd
comprehensibility 'kɒmprɪˌhensə'bɪlətɪ [-sɪ'b-, -lɪt-]
comprehensib|le, -ly, -leness ˌkɒmprɪ-'hensəb|l [-sɪb-], -lɪ, -lnɪs [-nəs]
comprehension ˌkɒmprɪ'henʃn
comprehensive, -ly, -ness ˌkɒmprɪ'hen-sɪv, -lɪ, -nɪs [-nəs]
compress (s.), -es 'kɒmpres, -ɪz
compress (v.), -es, -ing, -ed, -or/s kəm'pres, -ɪz, -ɪŋ, -t, -ə*/z

compressibility kəm,presə'bɪlətɪ [-sɪ'b-, -lɪt-]

compressible, -ness kəm'presəbl [-sɪb-], -nɪs [-nəs]

compression, -s kəm'preʃn, -z

compressive kəm'presɪv

compris|e (s. v.), -es, -ing, -ed; -able kəm-'praɪz, -ɪz, -ɪŋ, -d; -əbl

compromis|e (s. v.), -es, -ing, -ed, -er/s 'kɒmprəmaɪz [-prʊm-], -ɪz, -ɪŋ, -d, -ə*/z

comptometer, -s kɒmp'tɒmɪtə* [-mətə*], -z

Compton 'kɒmptən, 'kʌm-
Note.—As surname more often 'kʌm-; as place-name more often 'kɒm-; London street generally 'kɒm-.

comptroller, -s kən'trəʊlə*, -z

compulsion kəm'pʌlʃn

compulsor|y, -ily kəm'pʌlsər|ɪ, -əlɪ [-ɪlɪ]

compunction kəm'pʌŋkʃn

compunctious kəm'pʌŋkʃəs

compurgation ,kɒmpə:'geɪʃn

compurgator, -s 'kɒmpə:geɪtə*, -z

computable kəm'pju:təbl ['kɒmpjut-əbl]

computation, -s ,kɒmpju:'teɪʃn [-pjʊ-], -z

computator, -s 'kɒmpju:teɪtə* [-pjʊ-], -z

comput|e, -es, -ing, -ed, -er/s kəm'pju:t, -s, -ɪŋ, -ɪd, -ə*/z

computerization [-isa-] kəm,pju:təraɪ-'zeɪʃn [-rɪz-]

computeriz|e [-is|e], -es, -ing, -ed kəm'pju:təraɪz, -ɪz, -ɪŋ, -d

computist, -s kəm'pju:tɪst, -s

comrade, -s, -ship 'kɒmreɪd ['kɒmrɪd, 'kʌmrɪd], -z, -ʃɪp

Comte kɔ̃:nt [kɔ:nt] (kɔ̃:t)

comti|sm, -st/s 'kɔ̃:ntɪ|zəm ['kɔ:nt-], -st/s

Comus 'kəʊməs

Comyn 'kʌmɪn

con (s. v.), -s, -ning, -ned kɒn, -z, -ɪŋ, -d

Conan (personal name) 'kəʊnən, 'kɒnən, (place in Scotland) 'kɒnən
Note.—The members of the family of Sir Arthur Conan Doyle pronounce 'kəʊnən.

Conant 'kɒnənt

conation kəʊ'neɪʃn

conative 'kəʊnətɪv

concatenat|e, -es, -ing, -ed kɒn'kætɪneɪt [kən-], -s, -ɪŋ, -ɪd

concatenation, -s kɒn,kætɪ'neɪʃn [kən-, ,kɒnkæt-], -z

concave ,kɒn'keɪv ['kɒnkeɪv, 'kɒŋk-, kɒn'k-]
Note.—The form kɒn'keɪv is not used attributively.

concavit|y, -ies kɒn'kævət|ɪ [kən-, -ɪt|ɪ], -ɪz

conceal, -s, -ing, -ed, -ment/s; -able kən'si:l, -z, -ɪŋ, -d, -mənt/s; -əbl

conced|e, -es, -ing, -ed kən'si:d, -z, -ɪŋ, -ɪd

conceit, -s kən'si:t, -s

conceited, -ly, -ness kən'si:tɪd, -lɪ, -nɪs [-nəs]

conceivab|le, -ly, -leness kən'si:vəb|l, -lɪ, -lnɪs [-nəs]

conceiv|e, -es, -ing, -ed kən'si:v, -z, -ɪŋ, -d

concent kən'sent [kɒn-]

concentrat|e, -es, -ing, -ed (s. v.), 'kɒn-səntreɪt [-sɪn-, -sen-], -s, -ɪŋ, -ɪd

concentration, -s ,kɒnsən'treɪʃn [-sɪn-, -sen-], -z

concentrative 'kɒnsəntreɪtɪv [-sɪn-, -sen-]

concent|re, -res, -ring, -ering, -red kɒn'sent|ə*, -əz, -rɪŋ, -ərɪŋ, -əd

concentric, -ally kɒn'sentrɪk [kən-], -əlɪ

concept, -s 'kɒnsept, -s

conception, -s kən'sepʃn, -z

conceptual kən'septjʊəl [-tjwəl, -tʃʊəl]

concern (s. v.), -s, -ing, -ed, -ment/s kən'sɜ:n, -z, -ɪŋ, -d, -mənt/s

concern|ed (adj.), -edly, -edness kən-'sɜ:n|d, -ɪdlɪ, -ɪdnɪs [-nəs]

concert (s.) (musical entertainment), -s 'kɒnsət, -s

concert (C.) (union), -s 'kɒnsɜ:t [-sət], -s

concert (v.), -s, -ing, -ed kən'sɜ:t, -s, -ɪŋ, -ɪd

concertante ,kɒntʃə'tæntɪ [-tʃeə-, -teɪ]

concertina, -s ,kɒnsə'ti:nə, -z

concerto, -s kən'tʃeətəʊ [-'tʃɜ:t-], -z

concession, -s kən'seʃn, -z

concessionaire, -s kən,seʃə'neə* [-ʃn'eə*], -z

concessionary kən'seʃnərɪ [-ʃənə-]

concessive kən'sesɪv

conch, -s kɒntʃ, -ɪz [kɒŋk, -s]

concha, -s 'kɒŋkə, -z

conchoid, -s 'kɒŋkɔɪd, -z

concholog|ist/s, -y kɒŋ'kɒlədʒ|ɪst/s [kɒn'k], -ɪ

concierge, -s ,kɔ̃:nsɪ'eəʒ [,kɒ:ns-, ,kɒns-, '---] (kɔ̃sjɛrʒ), -ɪz

conciliat|e, -es, -ing, -ed, -or/s kən-'sɪlɪeɪt, -s, -ɪŋ, -ɪd, -ə*/z

conciliation kən,sɪlɪ'eɪʃn

conciliative kən'sɪlɪətɪv [-ljət-, -lɪeɪt-]
conciliatory kən'sɪlɪətərɪ [-ljə-, -lɪeɪtərɪ]
concise, -r, -st, -ly, -ness kən'saɪs, -ə*, -ɪst, -lɪ, -nɪs [-nəs]
concision, -s kən'sɪʒn, -z
conclave, -s 'kɒnkleɪv ['kɒŋk-], -z
conclud|e, -es, -ing, -ed kən'klu:d [kəŋ'k-], -z, -ɪŋ, -ɪd
conclusion, -s kən'klu:ʒn [kəŋ'k-], -z
conclusive, -ly, -ness kən'klu:sɪv [kəŋ'k-], -lɪ, -nɪs [-nəs]
concoct, -s, -ing, -ed, -er/s kən'kɒkt [kəŋ'k-], -s, -ɪŋ, -ɪd, -ə*/z
concoction, -s kən'kɒkʃn [kəŋ'k-], -z
concomitan|ce, -cy, -t/ly kən'kɒmɪtən|s, -sɪ, -t/lɪ
concord (s.), -s 'kɒŋkɔ:d ['kɒnk-], -z
concord (v.), -s, -ing, -ed kən'kɔ:d [kəŋ'k-], -z, -ɪŋ, -ɪd
concordan|ce, -ces, -t/ly kən'kɔ:dən|s [kəŋ'k-], -sɪz, -t/lɪ
concordat, -s kɒn'kɔ:dæt [kən'k-, kəŋ'k-], -s
concourse, -s 'kɒŋkɔ:s ['kɒnk-, -kɔəs], -ɪz
concrete (s. adj.) 'kɒnkri:t ['kɒŋk-]
concret|e (v.) (cover with concrete), -es, -ing, -ed 'kɒnkri:t ['kɒŋk-], -s, -ɪŋ, -ɪd
concret|e (v.) (coalesce, cause to coalesce), -es, -ing, -ed kən'kri:t [kəŋ'k-], -s, -ɪŋ, -ɪd
concrete|ly, -ness 'kɒnkri:t|lɪ ['kɒŋk-, kɒn'k-], -nɪs [-nəs]
concretion, -s kən'kri:ʃn [kəŋ-, kɒn-], -z
concretiz|e [-is|e], -es, -ing, -ed 'kɒnkri:taɪz ['kɒŋk-, -krɪ-], -ɪz, -ɪŋ, -d
concubinage kɒn'kju:bɪnɪdʒ [kən-]
concubine, -s 'kɒŋkjubaɪn ['kɒnk-], -z
concupiscen|ce, -t kən'kju:pɪsən|s [ˌkɒnkju:'p-, -kjʊ-], -t
concur, -s, -ring, -red kən'kɜ:* [kəŋ'k-], -z, -rɪŋ, -d
concurren|ce, -cy, -t/ly kən'kʌrən|s [kəŋ'k-], -sɪ, -t/lɪ
concuss, -es, -ing, -ed kən'kʌs [kəŋ'k-], -ɪz, -ɪŋ, -t
concussion, -s kən'kʌʃn [kəŋ'k-], -z
concyclic kɒn'saɪklɪk [kən-]
condemn, -s, -ing, -ed; -able kən'dem, -z, -ɪŋ, -d; -nəbl
condemnation, -s ˌkɒndem'neɪʃn [-dəm-], -z
condemnatory kən'demnətərɪ [ˌkɒndem'neɪtərɪ, -dəm-]
condensation, -s ˌkɒnden'seɪʃn [-dən-], -z

condens|e, -es, -ing, -ed; -able kən'dens, -ɪz, -ɪŋ, -t; -əbl
condenser, -s kən'densə*, -z
condescend, -s, -ing, -ed ˌkɒndɪ'send, -z, -ɪŋ, -ɪd
condescension ˌkɒndɪ'senʃn
condign, -ly, -ness kən'daɪn, -lɪ, -nɪs [-nəs]
condiment, -s 'kɒndɪmənt, -s
conditi|on (s. v.), -ons, -oning, -oned kən'dɪʃ|n, -nz, -ɲ̩ŋ [-ənɪŋ, -nɪŋ], -nd
condi|tional, -tionally kən'dɪ|ʃənl [-ʃnəl, -ʃn̩l, -ʃn̩l, -ʃənəl], -ʃnəlɪ [-ʃnəlɪ, -ʃn̩lɪ, -ʃn̩lɪ, -ʃənəlɪ]
condol|e, -es, -ing, -ed, -ement/s kən'dəʊl, -z, -ɪŋ, -d, -mənt/s
condolence, -s kən'dəʊləns ['kɒndələns], -ɪz
condolent kən'dəʊlənt
condom, -s 'kɒndəm [-dɒm], -z
condominium, -s ˌkɒndə'mɪnɪəm [-njəm], -z
condonation, -s ˌkɒndəʊ'neɪʃn, -z
condon|e, -es, -ing, -ed kən'dəʊn, -z, -ɪŋ, -d
condor, -s 'kɒndɔ:* [-də*], -z
conduc|e, -es, -ing, -ed, -ement/s kən'dju:s, -ɪz, -ɪŋ, -t, -mənt/s
conducive, -ly, -ness kən'dju:sɪv, -lɪ, -nɪs [-nəs]
conduct (s.), -s 'kɒndʌkt [-dəkt], -s
conduct (v.), -s, -ing, -ed, -or/s kən'dʌkt, -s, -ɪŋ, -ɪd, -ə*/z
conductibility kənˌdʌktɪ'bɪlətɪ [-tə'b-, -lɪt-]
conductible kən'dʌktəbl [-tɪb-]
conduction kən'dʌkʃn
conductive kən'dʌktɪv
conductivity ˌkɒndʌk'tɪvətɪ [-dək-, -ɪtɪ]
conductress, -es kən'dʌktrɪs [-tres, -trəs], -ɪz
conduit, -s 'kɒndɪt [old-fashioned 'kʌndɪt, as an electrical term also 'kɒndjʊɪt and 'kɒndwɪt], -s
Conduit (Street) 'kɒndɪt ['kʌn-]
Condy 'kɒndɪ
condyle, -s 'kɒndɪl [-daɪl], -z
cone, -s kəʊn, -z
coney (C.), -s 'kəʊnɪ, -z
confab, -s 'kɒnfæb [kɒn'fæb], -z
confabulat|e, -es, -ing, -ed kən'fæbjʊleɪt [kɒn-], -s, -ɪŋ, -ɪd
confabulation, -s kənˌfæbjʊ'leɪʃn [kɒn-], -z
confect (s.), -s 'kɒnfekt, -s
confect (v.), -s, -ing, -ed kən'fekt, -s, -ɪŋ, -ɪd

101

confecti|on (*s. v.*), -ons, -oning, -oned, -oner/s kən'fekʃ|n, -nz, -ŋɪŋ [-ənɪŋ], -nd, -nə-*/z [-ŋə*/z, -ənə*/z]

confectionery kən'fekʃnərɪ [-ʃənərɪ, -ʃnərɪ, -ʃənrɪ]

confederac|y, -ies kən'fedərəs|ɪ, -ɪz

confederate (*s. adj.*), -s kən'fedərət [-rɪt], -s

confederat|e (*v.*), -es, -ing, -ed kən'fedəreɪt, -s, -ɪŋ, -ɪd

confederation, -s kən,fedə'reɪʃn, -z

confer, -s, -ring, -red; -able kən'fɜ:*, -z, -ɪŋ, -d; -rəbl

conference, -s 'kɒnfərəns, -ɪz

confess, -es, -ing, -ed, -edly, -or/s kən'fes, -ɪz, -ɪŋ, -t, -ɪdlɪ, -ə*/z

Note.—Some Catholics pronounce confessor *as* 'kɒnfesə* *or* 'kɒn-fesɔ:*.

confession, -s kən'feʃn, -z

confessional, -s kən'feʃənl [-ʃnəl, -ʃŋl, -ʃnl, -ʃənəl], -z

confetti kən'fetɪ [kɒn-]

confidant(e), -s ,kɒnfɪ'dænt ['kɒnfɪdænt], -s

confid|e, -es, -ing/ly, -ed, -er/s kən'faɪd, -z, -ɪŋ/lɪ, -ɪd, -ə*/z

confiden|ce, -ces, -t/ly 'kɒnfɪdən|s, -sɪz, -t/lɪ

confidenti|al, -ally ,kɒnfɪ'denʃ|l, -əlɪ

configuration, -s kən,fɪgjʊ'reɪʃn [,kɒnfɪg-, -gjʊə'r-, -gjə'r-, -gə'r-], -z

confine (*s.*) 'kɒnfaɪn, -z

confin|e (*v.*), -es, -ing, -ed, -ement/s kən'faɪn, -z, -ɪŋ, -d, -mənt/s

confirm, -s, -ing, -ed, -er/s kən'fɜ:m, -z, -ɪŋ, -d, -ə*/z

confirmation, -s ,kɒnfə'meɪʃn [-fm̩'eɪ-], -z

confirmat|ive, -ory kən'fɜ:mət|ɪv, -ərɪ

confiscable kɒn'fɪskəbl [kən-]

confiscat|e, -es, -ing, -ed, -or/s 'kɒn-fɪskeɪt, -s, -ɪŋ, -ɪd, -ə*/z

confiscation, -s ,kɒnfɪ'skeɪʃn, -z

confiscatory kən'fɪskətərɪ [kɒn'f-, 'kɒnfɪskeɪtərɪ, ͵--'---]

confiserie, -s kɒn'fi:zərɪ [-rɪ], -z

confiteor, -s kɒn'fɪtɪɔ:* [kɒn-], -z

conflagration, -s ,kɒnflə'greɪʃn, -z

conflat|e, -es, -ing, -ed kən'fleɪt [kɒn-], -s, -ɪŋ, -ɪd

conflation kən'fleɪʃn [kɒn-]

conflict (*s.*), -s 'kɒnflɪkt, -s

conflict (*v.*), -s, -ing, -ed kən'flɪkt, -s, -ɪŋ, -ɪd

confluen|ce, -ces, -t/ly, -t/s 'kɒn-fluən|s [-flwən-], -sɪz, -t/lɪ, -t/s

conform, -s, -ing, -ed, -er/s kən'fɔ:m, -z, -ɪŋ, -d, -ə*/z

conformability kən,fɔ:mə'bɪlətɪ [-lɪt-]

conformab|le, -ly kən'fɔ:məb|l, -lɪ

conformation, -s ,kɒnfɔ:'meɪʃn [-fə'm-], -z

conformist, -s kən'fɔ:mɪst, -s

conformit|y, -ies kən'fɔ:mət|ɪ [-ɪt|ɪ], -ɪz

confound, -s, -ing, -ed/ly kən'faʊnd [*as oath also* ,kɒn'faʊnd], -z, -ɪŋ, -ɪd/lɪ

confraternit|y, -ies ,kɒnfrə'tɜ:nət|ɪ [-ɪt|ɪ], -ɪz

confrère, -s 'kɒnfreə* [kɔ̃frɛ:r], -z

confront, -s, -ing, -ed kən'frʌnt, -s, -ɪŋ, -ɪd

confrontation, -s ,kɒnfrʌn'teɪʃn [-frən-], -z

Confucian, -s kən'fju:ʃjən, [-ʃɪən, -ʃn], -z

Confuciani|sm, -st/s kən'fju:ʃjənɪ|zəm [-ʃɪənɪ-, -ʃənɪ-, -ʃnɪ-], -st/s

Confucius kən'fju:ʃjəs [-ʃɪəs, -ʃəs]

confus|e, -es, -ing, -ed, -edly, -edness kən'fju:z, -ɪz, -ɪŋ, -d, -ɪdlɪ, -ɪdnɪs [-nəs]

confusion, -s kən'fju:ʒn, -z

confutable kən'fju:təbl

confutation, -s ,kɒnfju:'teɪʃn [-fjʊ't-], -z

confut|e, -es, -ing, -ed kən'fju:t, -s, -ɪŋ, -ɪd

conga, -s 'kɒŋgə, -z

congé, -s 'kɔ̃:nʒeɪ ['kɒ:nʒ-, 'kɒnʒ-] (kɔ̃ʒe), -z

congeal, -s, -ing, -ed; -able kən'dʒi:l, -z, -ɪŋ, -d; -əbl

congee, -s 'kɒndʒi:, -z

congelation ,kɒndʒɪ'leɪʃn

congener, -s 'kɒndʒɪnə* [kən'dʒi:n-], -z

congenial, -ly kən'dʒi:njəl [-nɪəl], -ɪ

congeniality kən,dʒi:nɪ'ælətɪ [-ɪtɪ]

congenit|al, -ally kən'dʒenɪt|l [kɒn-], -əlɪ [-lɪ]

conger, -s 'kɒŋgə*, -z

conger-eel, -s ,kɒŋgər'i:l [-gə'i:l], -z

congeries kɒn'dʒɪəri:z [-'dʒɪərɪz, -'dʒɪərɪɪ:z, -'dʒerɪi:z, 'kɒndʒəriz]

congest, -s, -ing, -ed; -ive kən'dʒest, -s, -ɪŋ, -ɪd; -ɪv

congestion, -s kən'dʒestʃən [-eʃtʃ-], -z

Congleton 'kɒŋgltən

conglobat|e (*adj. v.*), -es, -ing, -ed 'kɒŋgləʊbeɪt ['kɒŋg-], -s, -ɪŋ, -ɪd

conglobation ,kɒŋgləʊ'beɪʃn [,kɒŋg-]

conglomerate (*s. adj.*), -s kən'glɒmərət [kəŋ-, kɒn-, -rɪt], -s

conglomerat|e (*v.*), -es, -ing, -ed kən'glɒməreɪt [kəŋ-, kɒn-], -s, -ɪŋ, -ɪd

conglomeration, -s kən,glɒmə'reɪʃn [kəŋ-, kɒn,glɒm-, ,kɒŋglɒm-, ,kɒŋglɒm-], -z
Congo 'kɒŋgəʊ
Congolese ,kɒŋgəʊ'li:z
congratulat|e, -es, -ing, -ed, -or/s kən'grætjʊleɪt [kən'g-, -tʃʊl-, -tʃəl-], -s, -ɪŋ, -ɪd, -ə*/z
congratulation, -s kən,grætjʊ'leɪʃn [kəŋ,g-, -tʃʊ'l-, -tʃə'l-], -z
congratulatory kən'grætjʊlətərɪ [kəŋ'g-, -tʃʊl-, -tʃəl-, -leɪtərɪ]
congregat|e, -es, -ing, -ed 'kɒŋgrɪgeɪt, -s, -ɪŋ, -ɪd
congregation, -s ,kɒŋgrɪ'geɪʃn, -z
congregational ,kɒŋgrɪ'geɪʃənl [-ʃnəl, -ʃn̩l, -ʃn̩l, -ʃənəl]
congregationali|sm, -st/s ,kɒŋgrɪ'geɪʃnəlɪ|zəm [-ʃnəlɪ-, -ʃn̩lɪ-, -ʃn̩lɪ-, -ʃənəlɪ-], -st/s
Congresbury 'kɒŋzbrɪ, 'ku:mzbərɪ
congress, -es 'kɒŋgres, -ɪz
congressional kən'greʃənl [kɒŋ-, -ʃnəl, -ʃn̩l, -ʃn̩l, -ʃənəl]
congress|man, -men 'kɒŋgres|mən, -mən [-men]
Congreve 'kɒŋgri:v
congruen|ce/s, -cy, -cies, -t/ly 'kɒŋgrʊən|s/ɪz [-grwən-], -sɪ, -sɪz, -t/lɪ
congruit|y, -ies kɒŋ'gru:ət|ɪ [kən-, kəŋ-, -'grʊ-, -ɪt|ɪ], -ɪz
congruous, -ly, -ness 'kɒŋgrʊəs [-grwəs], -lɪ, -nɪs [-nəs]
conic, -s, -al, -ally, -alness 'kɒnɪk, -s, -l, -əlɪ, -lnɪs [-nəs]
conifer, -s 'kɒnɪfə* ['kəʊn-], -z
coniferous kəʊ'nɪfərəs [kɒ-]
coniform 'kəʊnɪfɔ:m
Coningham 'kʌnɪŋəm
Conisbee 'kɒnɪsbɪ
Conisbrough 'kɒnɪsbrə, 'kʌn-
Coniston 'kɒnɪstən
conjecturable kən'dʒektʃərəbl
conjectur|al, -ally kən'dʒektʃər|əl [-tʃʊr-], -əlɪ
conject|ure (s. v.), -ures, -uring, -ured kən'dʒektʃ|ə*, -əz, -ərɪŋ, -əd
conjoin, -s, -ing, -ed kən'dʒɔɪn [kɒn-]-z, -ɪŋ, -d
conjoint, -ly 'kɒndʒɔɪnt [,kɒn'dʒ-, kən'dʒ-], -lɪ
conjug|al, -ally 'kɒndʒʊg|l [-dʒəg-], -əlɪ
conjugality ,kɒndʒʊ'gælətɪ [-ɪtɪ]
conjugate (s. adj), -s 'kɒndʒʊgɪt [dʒəg-, -geɪt], -s
conjugat|e (v.), -es, -ing, -ed 'kɒndʒʊgeɪt [-dʒəg-], -s, -ɪŋ, -ɪd

conjugation, -s ,kɒndʒʊ'geɪʃn [-dʒə'g-], -z
conjunct, -ly kən'dʒʌŋkt [,kɒn'dʒ-, 'kɒndʒ-], -lɪ
conjunction, -s kən'dʒʌŋkʃn, -z
conjunctiva ,kɒndʒʌŋk'taɪvə
conjunctive, -ly kən'dʒʌŋktɪv, -lɪ
conjunctivitis kən,dʒʌŋktɪ'vaɪtɪs
conjuncture, -s kən'dʒʌŋktʃə*, -z
conjuration, -s ,kɒndʒʊə'reɪʃn, -z
conjur|e (charge solemnly), -es, -ing, -ed kən'dʒʊə*, -z, -rɪŋ, -d
conj|ure (invoke a spirit, do things as if by magic), -ures, -uring, -ured, -urer/s, -uror/s 'kʌndʒ|ə*, -əz, -ərɪŋ, -əd, -ərə*/z, -ərə*/z
conk, -s kɒŋk, -s
conker, -s 'kɒŋkə*, -z
Conn. (1) = Connecticut, (2) = Connaught
Connally 'kɒnəlɪ
connate 'kɒneɪt
Connaught 'kɒnɔ:t
connect, -s, -ing, -ed/ly kə'nekt, -s, -ɪŋ, -ɪd/lɪ
connectible kə'nektəbl [-tɪb-]
Connecticut kə'netɪkət
connection, -s kə'nekʃn, -z
connective (s. adj.), -s, -ly kə'nektɪv, -z, -lɪ
Connemara ,kɒnɪ'mɑ:rə
connexion, -s kə'nekʃn, -z
Connie 'kɒnɪ
conning-tower, -s 'kɒnɪŋ,taʊə*, -z
connivance kə'naɪvəns
conniv|e, -es, -ing, -ed kə'naɪv, -z, -ɪŋ, -d
connoisseur, -s ,kɒnə'sɜ:* [,kɒnɪ-, -'sʊə*, -'sjʊə*], -z
Connolly 'kɒnəlɪ
Connor 'kɒnə*
connotat|e, -es, -ing, -ed 'kɒnəʊteɪt, -s, -ɪŋ, -ɪd
connotation, -s ,kɒnəʊ'teɪʃn, -z
connotative 'kɒnəʊteɪtɪv [kə'nəʊtətɪv]
connot|e, -es, -ing, -ed kɒ'nəʊt [kə'n-], -s, -ɪŋ, -ɪd
connubial, -ly kə'nju:bjəl [kɒ'n-, -bɪəl], -ɪ
connubiality kə,nju:bɪ'ælətɪ [kɒ,n-, -ɪtɪ]
conoid, -s 'kəʊnɔɪd, -z
conoidal kəʊ'nɔɪdl
Conolly 'kɒnəlɪ
conqu|er, -ers, -ering, -ered, -eror/s; -erable 'kɒŋk|ə*, -əz, -ərɪŋ, -əd, -ərə*/z; -ərəbl
conquest (C.), -s 'kɒŋkwest, -s

103

conquistador, -s kɒnˈkwɪstədɔː*
[kɒŋˈk-, -ˌ-ˈ-], -z
Conrad ˈkɒnræd
consanguine kɒnˈsæŋgwɪn
consanguin|eous, -ity ˌkɒnsæŋˈgwɪn|ɪəs,
-ətɪ [-ɪtɪ]
conscience, -s ˈkɒnʃəns, -ɪz
conscientious, -ly, -ness ˌkɒnʃɪˈenʃəs
[kɒnˈʃjen-], -lɪ, -nɪs [-nəs]
conscionab|le, -ly, -leness ˈkɒnʃ[nəb|l
[-ʃnə-, -ʃənə-], -lɪ, -lnɪs [-nəs]
conscious, -ly, -ness ˈkɒnʃəs, -lɪ, -nɪs
[-nəs]
conscrib|e, -es, -ing, -ed kənˈskraɪb, -z,
-ɪŋ, -d
conscript (s.), -s ˈkɒnskrɪpt, -s
conscript (v.), -s, -ing, -ed kənˈskrɪpt,
-s, -ɪŋ, -ɪd
conscription, -s kənˈskrɪpʃn, -z
consecrat|e, -es, -ing, -ed, -or/s ˈkɒnsɪ-
kreɪt, -s, -ɪŋ, -ɪd, -ə*/z
consecration, -s ˌkɒnsɪˈkreɪʃn, -z
consecutive, -ly, -ness kənˈsekjʊtɪv, -lɪ,
-nɪs [-nəs]
consensus kənˈsensəs [kɒn-]
consent (s. v.), -s, -ing, -ed kənˈsent, -s,
-ɪŋ, -ɪd
consequen|ce/s, -t/ly ˈkɒnsɪkwən|s/ɪz,
-t/lɪ
consequenti|al, -ally ˌkɒnsɪˈkwenʃ|l,
-əlɪ
conservable kənˈsɜːvəbl
conservanc|y, -ies kənˈsɜːvəns|ɪ, -ɪz
conservation ˌkɒnsəˈveɪʃn
conservatism kənˈsɜːvətɪzm
conservative, -s, -ly, -ness kənˈsɜːvətɪv,
-z, -lɪ, -nɪs [-nəs]
conservatoire, -s kənˈsɜːvətwɑː* [kɒn-,
-ˈseəv-, -twɔː*], -z
conservator (preserver), -s ˈkɒnsəveɪtə*,
-z
conservator (official guardian), -s kən-
ˈsɜːvətə*, -z
conservator|y, -ies kənˈsɜːvətr|ɪ, -ɪz
conserve (s.), -s kənˈsɜːv [ˈkɒnsɜːv], -z
conserv|e (v.), -es, -ing, -ed kənˈsɜːv, -z,
-ɪŋ, -d
consid|er, -ers, -ering, -ered kənˈsɪd|ə*,
-əz, -ərɪŋ, -əd
considerab|le, -ly, -leness kənˈsɪdər-
əb|l, -lɪ, -lnɪs [-nəs]
considerate, -ly, -ness kənˈsɪdərət [-ɪt],
-lɪ, -nɪs [-nəs]
consideration, -s kənˌsɪdəˈreɪʃn, -z
consign, -s, -ing, -ed, -er/s, -ment/s;
-able kənˈsaɪn, -z, -ɪŋ, -d, -ə*/z,
-mənt/s; -əbl
consignation ˌkɒnsaɪˈneɪʃn

consignee, -s ˌkɒnsaɪˈniː [-sɪˈniː], -z
consist, -s, -ing, -ed kənˈsɪst, -s, -ɪŋ, -ɪd
consisten|ce, -cy, -cies, -t/ly kən-
ˈsɪstən|s, -sɪ, -sɪz, -t/lɪ
consistorial ˌkɒnsɪˈstɔːrɪəl
consistor|y, -ies kənˈsɪstər|ɪ, -ɪz
consolable kənˈsəʊləbl
consolation, -s ˌkɒnsəˈleɪʃn [-sḷˈeɪʃ-,
-səʊ-], -z
consolatory kənˈsɒlətərɪ [-ˈsəʊl-]
console (s.), -s ˈkɒnsəʊl, -z
consol|e (v.), -es, -ing, -ed, -er/s kən-
ˈsəʊl, -z, -ɪŋ, -d, -ə*/z
consolidat|e, -es, -ing, -ed, -or/s; -ive
kənˈsɒlɪdeɪt, -s, -ɪŋ, -ɪd, -ə*/z; -ɪv
consolidation, -s kənˌsɒlɪˈdeɪʃn, -z
consols ˈkɒnsəlz [-sɒlz]
consommé kənˈsɒmeɪ [ˈkɒnsɒmeɪ]
(kɔ̃sɔme)
consonance, -s ˈkɒnsənəns [-sn̩ə-,
-snə-], -ɪz
consonant (s. adj.), -s, -ly ˈkɒnsənənt
[-sn̩ə-, -snə-], -s, -lɪ
consonant|al, -ally ˌkɒnsəˈnænt|l
[-sn̩ˈæ-], -əlɪ
consort (s.), -s ˈkɒnsɔːt, -s
consort (v.), -s, -ing, -ed kənˈsɔːt
[kɒnˈs-], -s, -ɪŋ, -ɪd
consortium, -s kənˈsɔːtjəm [-trəm], -z
conspectus, -es kənˈspektəs, -ɪz
conspicuous, -ly, -ness kənˈspɪkjʊəs
[-kjwəs], -lɪ, -nɪs [-nəs]
conspirac|y, -ies kənˈspɪrəs|ɪ, -ɪz
conspirator, -s kənˈspɪrətə* [-rɪt-], -z
conspiratorial kənˌspɪrəˈtɔːrɪəl
[ˌkɒnsp-, -rjəl]
conspir|e, -es, -ing, -ed, -er/s kən-
ˈspaɪə*, -z, -rɪŋ, -d, -rə*/z
constable, -s ˈkʌnstəbl [ˈkɒn-], -z
Constable (surname) ˈkʌnstəbl, in Scotland ˈkɒn-
constabular|y, -ies kənˈstæbjʊlər|ɪ, -ɪz
Constance ˈkɒnstəns
constancy ˈkɒnstənsɪ
constant (s. adj.), -s, -ly, -ness ˈkɒn-
stənt, -s, -lɪ, -nɪs [-nəs]
Constantine ˈkɒnstəntaɪn
Constantinople ˌkɒnstæntɪˈnəʊpl
constellation, -s ˌkɒnstəˈleɪʃn [-te'l-,
-tɪˈl-], -z
consternat|e, -es, -ing, -ed ˈkɒnstəneɪt,
-s, -ɪŋ, -ɪd
consternation ˌkɒnstəˈneɪʃn
constipat|e, -es, -ing, -ed ˈkɒnstɪpeɪt, -s,
-ɪŋ, -ɪd
constipation ˌkɒnstɪˈpeɪʃn
constituen|cy, -cies, -t/s kənˈstɪtjʊən|sɪ
[-tjwən-], -sɪz, -t/s

constitut|e, -es, -ing, -ed 'kɒnstɪtjuːt,
-s, -ɪŋ, -ɪd

constitution, -s ˌkɒnstɪ'tjuːʃn, -z

constitu|tional, -tionally ˌkɒnstɪ'tjuː|-
ʃənl [-ʃnəl, -ʃṇl, -ʃnl, -ʃənəl], -ʃṇəlɪ
[-ʃnəlɪ, -ʃṇlɪ, -ʃnlɪ, -ʃənəlɪ]

constitutionali|sm, -st|s ˌkɒnstɪ'tjuː-
ʃṇəlɪ|zəm [-ʃnəlɪ-, -ʃṇlɪ-, -ʃnlɪ-,
-ʃənəlɪ-], -st/s

constitutionaliz|e [-is|e], -es, -ing, -ed
ˌkɒnstɪ'tjuːʃṇəlaɪz [-ʃnəl-, -ʃṇl-,
-ʃnl-, -ʃənəl-], -ɪz, -ɪŋ, -d

constitutive 'kɒnstɪtjuːtɪv [kən'stɪtjuː-,
-tjʊt-]

constrain, -s, -ing, -ed, -edly; -able
kən'streɪn, -z, -ɪŋ, -d, -ɪdlɪ; -əbl

constraint, -s kən'streɪnt, -s

constrict, -s, -ing, -ed, -or/s; -ive kən-
'strɪkt, -s, -ɪŋ, -ɪd, -ə*/z; -ɪv

constriction, -s kən'strɪkʃn, -z

construct, -s, -ing, -ed, -or/s kən-
'strʌkt, -s, -ɪŋ, -ɪd, -ə*/z

construction, -s kən'strʌkʃn, -z

construc|tional, -tionally kən'strʌk|ʃənl
[-ʃnəl, -ʃṇl, -ʃnl, -ʃənəl], -ʃṇəlɪ [-ʃnəlɪ,
-ʃṇlɪ, -ʃnlɪ, -ʃənəlɪ]

constructive, -ly, -ness kən'strʌktɪv, -lɪ,
-nɪs [-nəs]

constr|ue (s. v.), -ues, -uing, -ued
kən'str|uː [:['kɒnst-], -uːz, -uːɪŋ [-ʊɪŋ],
-uːd

consubstanti|al, -ally ˌkɒnsəb'stænʃ|l
[-bz't-], -əlɪ [-lɪ]

consubstantiat|e, -es, -ing, -ed ˌkɒn-
səb'stænʃɪeɪt [-bz't-, -ʃjeɪt], -s, -ɪŋ,
-ɪd

consubstantiation 'kɒnsəbˌstænʃɪ'eɪʃn
[-bzˌt-, -nsɪ-]

consul, -s; -ship/s 'kɒnsəl, -z; -ʃɪp/s

consular 'kɒnsjʊlə* [-sjəl-]

consulate, -s 'kɒnsjʊlət [-sjəl-, -lɪt], -s

consult, -s, -ing, -ed kən'sʌlt, -s, -ɪŋ, -ɪd

consultant, -s kən'sʌltənt, -s

consultation, -s ˌkɒnsəl'teɪʃn [-sʌl-], -z

consultative kən'sʌltətɪv

consultatory kən'sʌltətərɪ [ˌkɒnsəl-
'teɪtərɪ]

consultee, -s ˌkɒnsʌl'tiː [-səl-], -z

consumable, -s kən'sjuːməbl [-'suː-], -z

consum|e, -es, -ing, -ed, -er/s kən-
'sjuːm [-'suːm], -z, -ɪŋ, -d, -ə*/z

consummate (adj.), -ly kən'sʌmɪt
[-mət], -lɪ

consummat|e (v.), -es, -ing, -ed, -or/s
'kɒnsəmeɪt [-sʌm-, -sjʊ-], -s, -ɪŋ, -ɪd,
-ə*/z

consummation, -s ˌkɒnsə'meɪʃn
[-sʌ'm-, -sjʊ-], -z

consummative 'kɒnsəmeɪtɪv [-sʌm-,
-sjʊ-, kən'sʌmətɪv]

consumption kən'sʌmpʃn

consumptive (s. adj.), -s, -ly, -ness
kən'sʌmptɪv, -z, -lɪ, -nɪs [-nəs]

contact (s.), -s 'kɒntækt, -s

contact (v.), -s, -ing, -ed 'kɒntækt
[kɒn'tækt, kən'tækt], -s, -ɪŋ, -ɪd

contagion, -s kən'teɪdʒən [-dʒjən,
-dʒɪən], -z

contagious, -ly, -ness kən'teɪdʒəs, -lɪ,
-nɪs [-nəs]

contain, -s, -ing, -ed, -er/s; -able
kən'teɪn, -z, -ɪŋ, -d, -ə*/z; -əbl

contaminat|e, -es, -ing, -ed, -er/s kən-
'tæmɪneɪt, -s, -ɪŋ, -ɪd, -ə*/z

contamination, -s kənˌtæmɪ'neɪʃn, -z

contaminative kən'tæmɪneɪtɪv [-neɪt-]

contango, -s kən'tæŋgəʊ [kɒn-], -z

contemn, -s, -ing, -ed, -er/s kən'tem,
-z, -ɪŋ, -d, -ə*/z [-nə*/z]

contemplat|e, -es, -ing, -ed, -or/s 'kɒn-
templeɪt [-təm-], -s, -ɪŋ, -ɪd, -ə*/z

contemplation, -s ˌkɒntem'pleɪʃn
[-təm-], -z

contemplative (pensive), -ly, -ness 'kɒn-
templeɪtɪv [-təm-, kən'templət-], -lɪ,
-nɪs [-nəs]

contemplative (of religious orders)
kən'templətɪv

contemporaneity kənˌtempərə'niːətɪ
[kɒn-, -'niːɪtɪ, -'nɪə-, -'nɪɪ-, -'neɪətɪ,
-'neɪtɪ]

contemporaneous, -ly, -ness kənˌtem-
pə'reɪnjəs [kɒn-, -nɪəs], -lɪ, -nɪs
[-nəs]

contemporar|y (s. adj.), -ies, -ily kən-
'tempərər|ɪ, -ɪz, -əlɪ [-ɪlɪ]

contempt kən'tempt

contemptibility kənˌtemptə'bɪlətɪ
[-tɪ'b-, -lɪt-]

contemptib|le, -ly, -leness kən'tempt-
təb|l [-tɪb-], -lɪ, -lnɪs [-nəs]

contemptuous, -ly, -ness kən'temp-
tjʊəs [-tjwəs], -lɪ, -nɪs [-nəs]

contend, -s, -ing, -ed, -er/s kən'tend,
-z, -ɪŋ, -ɪd, -ə*/z

content (s.) (what is contained) 'kɒntent,
(contentment) kən'tent

content (adj. v.), -s, -ing, -ed/ly,
-edness, -ment kən'tent, -s, -ɪŋ,
-ɪd/lɪ, -ɪdnɪs [-nəs], -mənt

contention, -s kən'tenʃn, -z

contentious, -ly, -ness kən'tenʃəs, -lɪ,
-nɪs [-nəs]

contents (s.) 'kɒntents [kən't-]
Note.—Always 'kɒntents in contents-
bill.

105

contermin|al, -ous kɒn'tɜ:mɪn|l [kən-],
-əs

contest (s.), -s 'kɒntest, -s

contest (v.), -s, -ing, -ed; -able kən-
'test, -s, -ɪŋ, -ɪd; -əbl

contestant, -s kən'testənt, -s

contestation, -s ˌkɒntes'teɪʃn, -z

context, -s 'kɒntekst, -s

contextual, -ly kɒn'tekstjʊəl [kən-,
-tjwəl, -tjʊl, -tʃʊəl, -tʃwəl, -tʃʊl], -ɪ

contiguity ˌkɒntɪ'gju:ətɪ [-'gjʊ-, -ɪtɪ]

contiguous, -ly, -ness kən'tɪgjʊəs
[kɒn-, -gjwəs], -lɪ, -nɪs [-nəs]

continen|ce, -cy 'kɒntɪnən|s, -sɪ

continent (s. adj.), -s, -ly 'kɒntɪnənt, -s,
-lɪ

continental ˌkɒntɪ'nentl

contingen|ce, -cy, -cies kən'tɪndʒən|s,
-sɪ, -sɪz

contingent (s. adj.), -s, -ly kən'tɪndʒənt,
-s, -lɪ

continual, -ly kən'tɪnjʊəl [-njwəl,
-njʊl], -ɪ

continuan|ce, -t/s kən'tɪnjʊən|s
[-njwən-], -t/s

continuation, -s kənˌtɪnjʊ'eɪʃn, -z

continuative kən'tɪnjʊətɪv [-njwət-]

continuator, -s kən'tɪnjʊeɪtə*, -z

contin|ue, -ues, -uing, -ued, -uer/s
kən'tɪn|ju: [-njʊ], -ju:z [-njʊz], -jʊɪŋ
[-jwɪŋ], -ju:d [-jʊd], -jʊə*/z
[-jwə*/z]

continuity ˌkɒntɪ'nju:ətɪ [-'njʊ-, -ɪtɪ]

continuo kən'tɪnjʊəʊ [-nʊəʊ]

continuous, -ly, -ness kən'tɪnjʊəs
[-njwəs], -lɪ, -nɪs [-nəs]

continu|um, -a kən'tɪnjʊ|əm [-njw|əm],
-ə

conto, -s 'kɒntəʊ, -z

contoid, -s 'kɒntɔɪd, -z

contort, -s, -ing, -ed kən'tɔ:t, -s, -ɪŋ,
-ɪd

contortion, -s kən'tɔ:ʃn, -z

contortionist, -s kən'tɔ:ʃnɪst [-ʃənɪ-], -s

contour (s. v.), -s, -ing, -ed 'kɒnˌtʊə*,
-z, -rɪŋ, -d

contra 'kɒntrə

contraband; -ist/s 'kɒntrəbænd; -ɪst/s

contrabass, -es ˌkɒntrə'beɪs ['---], -ɪz

contraception ˌkɒntrə'sepʃn

contraceptive, -s ˌkɒntrə'septɪv, -z

contract (s.), -s 'kɒntrækt, -s

contract (v.), -s, -ing, -ed, -or/s; -ive
kən'trækt, -s, -ɪŋ, -ɪd, -ə*/z; -ɪv

contractibility kənˌtræktə'bɪlətɪ [-tɪ'b-,
-lɪt-]

contractib|le, -ly, -leness kən'træktəb|l
[-trɪb-], -lɪ, -lnɪs [-nəs]

contractile kən'træktaɪl

contraction, -s kən'trækʃn, -z

contractual kən'træktʃʊəl [-tjʊəl,
-tjwəl, -tjʊl, -tʃwəl, -tʃʊl]

contradict, -s, -ing, -ed ˌkɒntrə'dɪkt, -s,
-ɪŋ, -ɪd

contradiction, -s ˌkɒntrə'dɪkʃn, -z

contradictor|y, -ily, -ness ˌkɒntrə-
'dɪktər|ɪ, -ɪlɪ [-əlɪ], -nɪs [-nəs]

contradistinc|tion, -tive ˌkɒntrədɪ-
'stɪŋk|ʃn, -tɪv

contradistinguish, -es, -ing, -ed ˌkɒn-
trədɪ'stɪŋgwɪʃ, -ɪz, -ɪŋ, -t

contralto, -s kən'træltəʊ [-'trɑ:l-], -z

contraposition ˌkɒntrəpə'zɪʃn [-pʊ'z-]

contraption, -s kən'træpʃn, -z

contrapuntal ˌkɒntrə'pʌntl

contrapuntist, -s 'kɒntrəpʌntɪst, -s

contrariant, -s kən'treərɪənt, -s

contrariety ˌkɒntrə'raɪətɪ [-aɪtɪ]

contrari|ness, -wise 'kɒntrərɪ|nɪs [kən-
'treərɪ-, -nəs], -waɪz

contrar|y, -ies, -ily 'kɒntrər|ɪ [also
kən'treər- in sense of 'obstinate'],
-ɪz, -əlɪ [-ɪlɪ]

contrast (s.), -s 'kɒntrɑ:st, -s

contrast (v.), -s, -ing, -ed kən'trɑ:st,
-s, -ɪŋ, -ɪd

contrastive kən'trɑ:stɪv

contraven|e, -es, -ing, -ed ˌkɒntrə'vi:n,
-z, -ɪŋ, -d

contravention, -s ˌkɒntrə'venʃn, -z

contretemps (sing.) 'kɔ̃:ntrətɑ̃:ŋ
['kɔ:nt-, 'kɒnt-, -tɔ̃:ŋ, -tɑːŋ, -tɒŋ]
(kɔ̃trətɑ̃), (plur.) -z

contrib|ute, -utes, -uting, -uted, -utor/s
kən'trɪb|ju:t ['kɒntrɪbju:t], -ju:ts,
-jʊtɪŋ, -jʊtɪd, -jʊtə*/z

contribution, -s ˌkɒntrɪ'bju:ʃn, -z

contribut|ive, -ory kən'trɪbjʊt|ɪv, -ərɪ

contrite, -ly, -ness 'kɒntraɪt, -lɪ, -nɪs
[-nəs]

contrition kən'trɪʃn

contrivance, -s kən'traɪvns, -ɪz

contriv|e, -es, -ing, -ed, -er/s kən'traɪv,
-z, -ɪŋ, -d, -ə*/z

control (s.), -s kən'trəʊl [in machinery
also 'kɒntrəʊl], -z

control (v.), -s, -ling, -led, -ler/s; -lable
kən'trəʊl, -z, -ɪŋ, -d, -ə*/z; -əbl

controversi|al, -ally ˌkɒntrə'vɜ:ʃ|l
[-trʊ'v-], -əlɪ [-lɪ]

controversialist, -s ˌkɒntrə'vɜ:ʃəlɪst
[-trʊ'v-, -ʃlɪ-], -s

controvers|y, -ies 'kɒntrəvɜ:s|ɪ [-trʊv-,
-vəs-], kən'trɒvəs|ɪ, -ɪz

controvert, -s, -ing, -ed 'kɒntrəvɜ:t
['kɒntrʊv-, ˌ--'-], -s, -ɪŋ, -ɪd

controvertib|le, -ly ˌkɒntrəˈvɜːtəb|l [ˌkɒntrʊˈv-, -tɪb-, ˈ----], -lɪ

contumacious, -ly, -ness ˌkɒntjuː-ˈmeɪʃəs [-tjʊ-], -lɪ, -nɪs [-nəs]

contumacity ˌkɒntjuːˈmæsətɪ [-tjʊ-, -ɪtɪ]

contumacy ˈkɒntjʊməsɪ

contumelious, -ly, -ness ˌkɒntjuːˈmiː-ljəs [-tjʊ-, -lɪəs], -lɪ, -nɪs [-nəs]

contumel|y, -ies ˈkɒntjuːml|ɪ [-tjʊ-, ˈkɒntjʊmɪlɪ, -əlɪ, *rarely* kənˈtjuːmɪl|ɪ], -ɪz

contus|e, -es, -ing, -ed kənˈtjuːz, -ɪz, -ɪŋ, -d

contusion, -s kənˈtjuːʒn, -z

conundrum, -s kəˈnʌndrəm, -z

conurbation, -s ˌkɒnɜːˈbeɪʃn [-nəˈb-], -z

convalesc|e, -es, -ing, -ed ˌkɒnvəˈles, -ɪz, -ɪŋ, -t

convalescen|ce, -t/s ˌkɒnvəˈlesn|s, -t/s

convection kənˈvekʃn

convector, -s kənˈvektə*, -z

convenance, -s ˈkɔ̃ːnvɑ̃ːns [ˈkɔ̃ːŋv-, ˈkɔːnv-, ˈkɒnv-, -vɪn-, -nɔ̃ːns, -nɑːns] (kɔ̃vnɑ̃ːs), -ɪz

conven|e, -es, -ing, -ed, -er/s kənˈviːn, -z, -ɪŋ, -d, -ə*/z

convenien|ce/s, -t/ly kənˈviːnjən|s/ɪz [-nɪən-], -t/lɪ

convent, -s ˈkɒnvənt [-vent], -s

conventicle, -s kənˈventɪkl, -z

convention, -s kənˈvenʃn, -z

conven|tional, -tionally kənˈven|ʃənl [-ʃnəl, -ʃn̩l, -ʃnl, -ʃənəl], -ʃnəlɪ [-ʃnəlɪ, -ʃn̩lɪ, -ʃnlɪ, -ʃənəlɪ]

conventionali|sm, -st/s kənˈvenʃnəlɪ|-zəm [-ʃnəl-, -ʃn̩l-, -ʃnl-, -ʃənəl-], -st/s

conventionalit|y, -ies kənˌvenʃəˈnælət|ɪ [-ʃn̩ˈæl-, -ɪt|ɪ], -ɪz

conventionaliz|e [-is|e], -es, -ing, -ed kənˈvenʃnəlaɪz [-ʃnəl-, -ʃn̩l-, -ʃnl-, -ʃənəl-], -ɪz, -ɪŋ, -d

conventual, -s kənˈventjʊəl [-tjwəl, -tjʊl, -tʃʊəl, -tʃwəl, -tʃʊl], -z

converg|e, -es, -ing, -ed kənˈvɜːdʒ [kɒn-], -ɪz, -ɪŋ, -d

convergen|ce, -cy, -t/ly kənˈvɜːdʒən|s [kɒn-], -sɪ, -t/lɪ

conversable kənˈvɜːsəbl

conversan|ce, -cy kənˈvɜːsən|s [ˈkɒnvəs-], -sɪ

conversant, -ly kənˈvɜːsənt [ˈkɒnvəs-], -lɪ

conversation, -s ˌkɒnvəˈseɪʃn, -z

conversa|tional, -tionally ˌkɒnvəˈseɪ|ʃənl [-ʃnəl, -ʃn̩l, -ʃnl, -ʃənəl], -ʃnəlɪ [-ʃnəlɪ, -ʃn̩lɪ, -ʃnlɪ, -ʃənəlɪ]

conversationalist, -s ˌkɒnvəˈseɪʃnəlɪst [-ʃnəl-, -ʃn̩l-, -ʃnl-, -ʃənəl-], -s

conversazione, -s ˌkɒnvəsætsɪˈəʊnɪ, -z

converse (*s. adj.*), **-s, -ly** ˈkɒnvɜːs, -ɪz, -lɪ [ˌkɒnˈvɜːslɪ]

convers|e (*v.*), **-es, -ing, -ed** kənˈvɜːs, -ɪz, -ɪŋ, -t

conversion, -s kənˈvɜːʃn, -z

convert (*s.*), **-s** ˈkɒnvɜːt, -s

convert (*v.*), **-s, -ing, -ed, -er/s** kənˈvɜːt, -s, -ɪŋ, -ɪd, -ə*/z

convertibility kənˌvɜːtəˈbɪlətɪ [-tɪˈb-, -lɪt-]

convertib|le, -ly kənˈvɜːtəb|l [-tɪb-], -lɪ

convex, -ly kɒnˈveks [ˈkɒnv-], -lɪ
Note.—The form kɒnˈveks *is not used attributively.*

convexit|y, -ies kɒnˈveksət|ɪ [kən-, -ɪt|ɪ], -ɪz

convey, -s, -ing, -ed, -er/s; -able kənˈveɪ, -z, -ɪŋ, -d, -ə*/z [-ˈveə*/z]; -əbl [-ˈveəbl]

conveyance, -s kənˈveɪəns, -ɪz

conveyanc|er/s, -ing kənˈveɪəns|ə*/z, -ɪŋ

convict (*s.*), **-s** ˈkɒnvɪkt, -s

convict (*v.*), **-s, -ing, -ed** kənˈvɪkt, -s, -ɪŋ, -ɪd

conviction, -s kənˈvɪkʃn, -z

convinc|e, -es, -ing/ly, -ed kənˈvɪns, -ɪz, -ɪŋ/lɪ, -t

convincible kənˈvɪnsəbl [-sɪb-]

convivial, -ly kənˈvɪvɪəl [-vjəl], -ɪ

conviviality kənˌvɪvɪˈælətɪ [-ɪtɪ]

convocation, -s ˌkɒnvəʊˈkeɪʃn, -z

convok|e, -es, -ing, -ed kənˈvəʊk, -s, -ɪŋ, -t

convolute, -d ˈkɒnvəluːt [-ljuːt], -ɪd

convolution, -s ˌkɒnvəˈluːʃn [-ˈljuː-], -z

convolv|e, -es, -ing, -ed kənˈvɒlv, -z, -ɪŋ, -d

convolvul|us, -i, -uses kənˈvɒlvjʊl|əs [-vjəl-], -aɪ, -əsɪz

convoy (*s. v.*), **-s, -ing, -ed** ˈkɒnvɔɪ, -z, -ɪŋ, -d

convuls|e, -es, -ing, -ed kənˈvʌls, -ɪz, -ɪŋ, -t

convulsion, -s kənˈvʌlʃn, -z

convulsionary kənˈvʌlʃnərɪ [-ʃənə-]

convulsive, -ly, -ness kənˈvʌlsɪv, -lɪ, -nɪs [-nəs]

Conway ˈkɒnweɪ

con|y, -ies ˈkəʊn|ɪ, -ɪz

Conybeare ˈkɒnɪˌbɪə*, ˈkʌn-

Conyngham ˈkʌnɪŋəm

coo (*s. v.*), **-es, -ing, -ed** kuː, -z, -ɪŋ, -d

Cooch kuːtʃ

cooee (s. v.), -s, -ing, -d 'ku:ɪ ['ku-, -i:], -z, -ɪŋ, -d

cook (s. v.), -s, -ing, -ed kʊk, -s, -ɪŋ, -t

Cook(e) kʊk

cookery; -book/s 'kʊkərɪ; -bʊk/s

cook-hou|se, -ses 'kʊkhaʊ|s, -zɪz

cookie, -s 'kʊkɪ, -z

cook-room, -s 'kʊkrʊm [-ru:m], -z

cook-shop, -s 'kʊkʃɒp, -s

cool (s. adj. v.), -er, -est, -ly, -ness; -s, -ing, -ed, -er/s ku:l, -ə*, -ɪst, -lɪ [-l-], -nɪs [-nəs]; -z, -ɪŋ, -d, -ə*/z

coolant, -s 'ku:lənt, -s

cool-headed ,ku:l'hedɪd ['-,-- when attributive]

Coolidge 'ku:lɪdʒ

coolie, -s 'ku:lɪ, -z

Cooling 'ku:lɪŋ

coom, -s ku:m, -z

coomb, -s ku:m, -z

Coomb(e) ku:m

Coomber 'ku:mbə*

Coombes ku:mz

coon, -s; -song/s ku:n, -z; -sɒŋ/z

coop (s. v.), -s, -ing, -ed ku:p, -s, -ɪŋ, -t

co-op, -s 'kəʊɒp, -s

cooper (s. v.) (C.), -s, -ing, -ed 'ku:pə*, -z, -ɪŋ, -d

cooperage, -s 'ku:pərɪdʒ, -ɪz

co-operat|e, -es, -ing, -ed, -or/s kəʊ-'ɒpəreɪt, -s, -ɪŋ, -ɪd, -ə*/z

co-operation, -s kəʊ,ɒpə'reɪʃn [,---'--], -z

co-operative (s. adj.), -s kəʊ'ɒpərətɪv, -z

coopery 'ku:pərɪ

Coopman 'ku:pmən

co-opt, -s, -ing, -ed kəʊ'ɒpt, -s, -ɪŋ, -ɪd

co-optation ,kəʊɒp'teɪʃn

co-option kəʊ'ɒpʃn

co-ordinate (s. adj.), -s, -ly, -ness kəʊ'ɔ:dnət [-dɪnət, -dənət, -nɪt], -s, -lɪ, -nɪs [-nəs]

co-ordinat|e (v.), -es, -ing, -ed kəʊ'ɔ:-dɪneɪt [-dn̩eɪt], -s, -ɪŋ, -ɪd

co-ordination kəʊ,ɔ:dɪ'neɪʃn [-dn̩'eɪ-]

co-ordinative kəʊ'ɔ:dɪnətɪv [-dnət-, -dɪneɪt-]

coot, -s ku:t, -s

Coote ku:t

co-ownership ,kəʊ'əʊnəʃɪp

cop (s. v.), -s, -ping, -ped kɒp, -s, -ɪŋ, -t

copaiba kɒ'paɪbə [kəʊ'p-]

copal 'kəʊpəl [kəʊ'pæl]

coparcener, -s ,kəʊ'pɑ:sənə* [-sɪn-], -z

copartner, -s; -ship/s ,kəʊ'pɑ:tnə*, -z; -ʃɪp/s

cop|le (s. v.) (C.), -es, -ing, -ed kəʊp, -s, -ɪŋ, -t

copeck, -s 'kəʊpek ['kɒp-], -s

Copeland 'kəʊplənd

Copenhagen ,kəʊpn'heɪgən [-pən-]

coper, -s 'kəʊpə*, -z

Copernic|an, -us kəʊ'pɜ:nɪk|ən, -əs

Cophetua kəʊ'fetjʊə [-tjwə]

coping (s.), -s 'kəʊpɪŋ, -z

coping-stone, -s 'kəʊpɪŋstəʊn, -z

copious, -ly, -ness 'kəʊpjəs [-pɪəs], -lɪ, -nɪs [-nəs]

Copland 'kɒplənd, 'kəʊplənd

Copleston 'kɒplstən

Copley 'kɒplɪ

Copp kɒp

Copped kɒpt

copper (s. v.), -s, -ing, -ed 'kɒpə*, -z, -rɪŋ, -d

copperas 'kɒpərəs

copper-bottomed ,kɒpə'bɒtəmd [also 'kɒpə,b- when attributive]

Copperfield 'kɒpəfi:ld

copper-plate 'kɒpəpleɪt [,--'-]

copper-smith, -s 'kɒpəsmɪθ, -s

coppery 'kɒpərɪ

coppice, -s 'kɒpɪs, -ɪz

copra 'kɒprə

copse, -s kɒps, -ɪz

Copt, -s kɒpt, -s

Copthall 'kɒptɔ:l [-thɔ:l]

Coptic 'kɒptɪk

copul|a, -ae, -as 'kɒpjʊl|ə, -i:, -əz

copulat|e, -es, -ing, -ed 'kɒpjʊleɪt, -s, -ɪŋ, -ɪd

copulation, -s ,kɒpjʊ'leɪʃn, -z

copulative 'kɒpjʊlətɪv [-leɪt-]

cop|y (s. v.), -ies, -ying, -ied, -ier/s 'kɒp|ɪ, -ɪz, -ɪɪŋ, -ɪd, -ɪə*/z

copy-book, -s 'kɒpɪbʊk, -s

copyhold, -s, -er/s 'kɒpɪhəʊld, -z, -ə*/z

copyist, -s 'kɒpɪɪst, -s

copyright (s. v.), -s, -ing, -ed 'kɒpɪraɪt, -s, -ɪŋ, -ɪd

coquet (s. v.), -s, -ting, -ted kɒ'ket [kəʊ'k-], -s, -ɪŋ, -ɪd

coquetr|y, -ies 'kɒkɪtr|ɪ ['kəʊk-, -ətr], -ɪz

coquette (s.), -s kɒ'ket [kəʊ'k-], -s

coquettish, -ly, -ness kɒ'ketɪʃ [kəʊ'k-], -lɪ, -nɪs [-nəs]

cor, -s kɔ:*, -z

Cora 'kɔ:rə

cor(s) anglais ,kɔ:r 'ɑ̃:ŋglèɪ [-'ɒŋg-]

coracle, -s 'kɒrəkl, -z

coral, -s 'kɒrəl, -z

corallaceous ,kɒrə'leɪʃəs

corall|ine, -ite 'kɒrəl|aɪn [-rl-], -aɪt

coral-reef, -s ˈkɒrəlriːf, -s
Coram ˈkɔːrəm
coranto, -s kɒˈræntəʊ [kəˈr-], -z
corban ˈkɔːbæn
corbel, -s ˈkɔːbəl, -z
Corbett ˈkɔːbɪt [-bet, -bət]
Corbishley ˈkɔːbɪʃlɪ
Corbyn ˈkɔːbɪn
Corcoran ˈkɔːkərən
Corcyra kɔːˈsaɪərə
cord (s. v.), -s, -ing, -ed; -age kɔːd, -z,
  -ɪŋ, -ɪd; -ɪdʒ
Cordelia kɔːˈdiːljə [-lɪə]
cordelier (C.), -s ˌkɔːdɪˈlɪə*, -z
cordial (s. adj.), -s, -ly ˈkɔːdjəl [-dɪəl],
  -z, -ɪ
cordialit|y, -ies ˌkɔːdɪˈælətɪ [-ɪtɪ], -ɪz
cordillera (C.), ˌkɔːdɪˈljeərə [-ˈleərə]
cording (s.) ˈkɔːdɪŋ
cordite ˈkɔːdaɪt
cor|don (s. v.), -dons, -doning, -doned
  ˈkɔː|dn [-dən], -dnz [-dənz], -dnɪŋ
  [-dənɪŋ], -dnd [-dənd]
cordon bleu ˌkɔːdɔ̃ːmˈblɜː [-dɒn]
  (kɔrdɔ̃ blø)
Cordova, -n/s ˈkɔːdəvə, -n/z
corduroy, -s ˈkɔːdərɔɪ [-djʊr-, ˌ--ˈ-], -z
cordwainer, -s ˈkɔːdˌweɪnə*, -z
cor|e (s. v.), -es, -ing, -ed, -er/s kɔː*
  [kɔə*], -z, -rɪŋ, -d, -rə*/z
co-regent, -s ˌkəʊˈriːdʒənt, -s
co-religionist, -s ˌkəʊrɪˈlɪdʒənɪst [-rə-,
  -dʒn-], -s
Corelli kɒˈrelɪ [kɒˈr-]
co-respondent, -s ˌkəʊrɪˈspɒndənt
  [ˈkəʊrɪˌsp-], -s
corf, -s kɔːf, -s
Corfe kɔːf
Corfu kɔːˈfuː [-ˈfjuː]
corgi (dog), -s ˈkɔːgɪ, -z
coriaceous ˌkɒrɪˈeɪʃəs
coriander, -s ˌkɒrɪˈændə*, -z
Corin ˈkɒrɪn
Corinth ˈkɒrɪnθ
Corinthian, -s kəˈrɪnθɪən [kʊˈr-, -θjən],
  -z
Coriolanus ˌkɒrɪəʊˈleɪnəs
Corioles kəˈraɪəliːz [kɒˈr-]
cork (s. v.), (C.), -s, -ing, -ed; -age
  kɔːk, -s, -ɪŋ, -t; -ɪdʒ
corker (C.), -s ˈkɔːkə*, -z
Corkran ˈkɔːkrən
cork-screw (s. v.), -s, -ing, -ed ˈkɔːk-
  skruː, -z, -ɪŋ [-ˌskrʊɪŋ], -d
corky ˈkɔːkɪ
corm, -s kɔːm, -z
Cormac (king in Irish mythology)
  ˈkɔːmæk [ˈkɔːm-]

Cormack ˈkɔːmæk
cormorant, -s ˈkɔːmərənt, -s
corn (s. v.), -s, -ing, -ed kɔːn, -z, -ɪŋ, -d
Cornbury ˈkɔːnbərɪ
corn-chandler, -s ˈkɔːnˌtʃɑːndlə*, -z
corn-crake, -s ˈkɔːnkreɪk, -s
cornea, -s, -l ˈkɔːnɪə, -z, -l
Corneille kɔːˈneɪ [-ˈneɪl] (kɔrnɛːj)
Cornelia kɔːˈniːljə [-lɪə]
cornelian, -s kɔːˈniːljən [kəˈn-, -lɪən], -z
Cornelius kɔːˈniːljəs [-lɪəs]
Cornell kɔːˈnel [also ˈkɔːnel when
  attributive]
Cornemuse ˈkɔːnəmjuːz [-nɪ-]
corner (s. v.), -s, -ing, -ed ˈkɔːnə*, -z,
  -rɪŋ, -d
corner-stone, -s ˈkɔːnəstəʊn, -z
corner-wise ˈkɔːnəwaɪz
cornet, -s ˈkɔːnɪt, -s
corn-field, -s ˈkɔːnfiːld, -z
cornflour ˈkɔːnflaʊə*
corn-flower, -s ˈkɔːnflaʊə*, -z
Cornhill ˌkɔːnˈhɪl [also ˈ-- according to
  sentence-stress]
cornice, -s ˈkɔːnɪs, -ɪz
Cornish, -man, -men ˈkɔːnɪʃ, -mən,
  -mən [-men]
cornopean, -s kəˈnəʊpjən [kɔːˈn-,
  -pɪən], -z
cornucopia, -s ˌkɔːnjʊˈkəʊpjə [-pɪə], -z
Cornwall ˈkɔːnwəl [rarely -wɔːl]
Cornwallis kɔːnˈwɒlɪs
corolla, -s kəˈrɒlə, -z
corollar|y, -ies kəˈrɒlər|ɪ, -ɪz
Coromandel ˌkɒrəʊˈmændl
coron|a, -ae, -as kəˈrəʊn|ə, -iː, -əz
Corona (fem. name) ˈkɒrənə
coronach (C.), -s ˈkɒrənək [-nəx,
  -næk], -s
coronal (s.), -s ˈkɒrənl, -z
coronal (adj.) (pertaining to the sun's
  corona) kəˈrəʊnl, (medical, botanical
  and phonetic senses) ˈkɒrənl
  [kəˈrəʊnl]
coronary ˈkɒrənərɪ
coronation, -s ˌkɒrəˈneɪʃn [-rɪˈeɪ-], -z
Coronel ˈkɒrənel
coroner, -s ˈkɒrənə* [-rɪnə*], -z
coronet, -s ˈkɒrənɪt [-rɪnɪt, -net, -nət],
  -s
coronis, -es kəˈrəʊnɪs, -ɪz
corpor|al (s. adj.), -als, -ally ˈkɔːpər|əl,
  -əlz, -əlɪ
corporality ˌkɔːpəˈrælətɪ [-ɪtɪ]
corporate, -ly, -ness ˈkɔːpərət [-rɪt], -lɪ,
  -nɪs [-nəs]
corporation, -s ˌkɔːpəˈreɪʃn, -z
corporator, -s ˈkɔːpəreɪtə*, -z

corporeal, -ly kɔː'pɔːrɪəl, -ɪ
corps (sing.) kɔː*, (plur.) kɔːz
corps de ballet ˌkɔːdə'bæleɪ [-lɪ] (kɔːrdəbalɛ)
corps diplomatique 'kɔːˌdɪpləmæ'tiːk (kɔːrdiplɔmatik)
corpse, -s kɔːps, -ɪz
corpulen|ce, -cy, -t 'kɔːpjulən|s, -sɪ, -t
corp|us, -era 'kɔːp|əs, -ərə
Corpus Christi ˌkɔːpəs'krɪstɪ
corpuscle, -s 'kɔːpʌsl [kɔː'pʌsl], -z
corpuscular kɔː'pʌskjulə*
corpuscule, -s kɔː'pʌskjuːl [-skjul], -z
corral, -s kɔː'rɑːl, -z
correct (adj. v.), -est, -ly, -ness; -s, -ing, -ed, -or/s kə'rekt, -ɪst, -lɪ, -nɪs [-nəs]; -s, -ɪŋ, -ɪd, -ə*/z
correction, -s kə'rekʃn, -z
correctional kə'rekʃənl [-ʃnəl, -ʃn̩l, -ʃnl, -ʃənəl]
correctitude kə'rektɪtjuːd
corrective, -s kə'rektɪv, -z
correlat|e, -es, -ing, -ed 'kɒrəleɪt [-rɪl-], -s, -ɪŋ, -ɪd
correlation, -s ˌkɒrə'leɪʃn [-rɪ'l-], -z
correlative, -ly, -ness kɒ'relətɪv [kə'r-, -'reɪt-], -lɪ, -nɪs [-nəs]
correspond, -s, -ing/ly, -ed ˌkɒrɪ'spɒnd [-rə's-], -z, -ɪŋ/lɪ, -ɪd
corresponden|ce/s, -t/s, -tly ˌkɒrɪ'spɒndən|s/ɪz [-rə's-], -t/s, -tlɪ
corridor, -s; -train/s 'kɒrɪdɔː* [-də*], -z; -treɪn/z
Corrie 'kɒrɪ
Corrientes ˌkɒrɪ'entes
corrigend|um, -a ˌkɒrɪ'dʒend|əm [-ɪ'gen-], -ə
corrigible 'kɒrɪdʒəbl [-dʒɪb-]
corroborant, -s kə'rɒbərənt, -s
corroborat|e, -es, -ing, -ed, -or/s kə'rɒbəreɪt, -s, -ɪŋ, -ɪd, -ə*/z
corroboration, -s kəˌrɒbə'reɪʃn, -z
corroborative kə'rɒbərətɪv [-bəreɪt-]
corroboratory kə'rɒbərətərɪ
corroboree, -s kə'rɒbərɪ [kɒ'r-, -riː], -z
corrod|e, -es, -ing, -ed kə'rəud, -z, -ɪŋ, -ɪd
corrodible kə'rəudəbl [-dɪb-]
corrosion, -s kə'rəuʒn, -z
corrosive (s. adj.), -s, -ly, -ness kə'rəusɪv [-əuzɪv], -z, -lɪ, -nɪs [-nəs]
corrugat|e, -es, -ing, -ed 'kɒrugeɪt [-rəg-], -s, -ɪŋ, -ɪd
corrugation, -s ˌkɒru'geɪʃn [-rə'g-], -z
corrupt (adj. v.), -est, -ly, -ness; -s, -ing, -ed, -er/s kə'rʌpt, -ɪst, -lɪ, -nɪs [-nəs]; -s, -ɪŋ, -ɪd, -ə*/z

corruptibility kəˌrʌptə'bɪlətɪ [-tɪ'b-, -lɪt-]
corruptib|le, -ly, -leness kə'rʌptəb|l [-tɪb-], -lɪ, -lnɪs [-nəs]
corruption, -s kə'rʌpʃn, -z
corruptive kə'rʌptɪv
corsage, -s kɔː'sɑːʒ ['kɔːsɑːʒ] (kɔrsaːʒ), -ɪz
corsair, -s 'kɔːseə*, -z
corse, -s kɔːs, -ɪz
corselet, -s 'kɔːslɪt [-lət], -s
corset, -s 'kɔːsɪt, -s
Corsica, -n/s 'kɔːsɪkə, -n/z
corslet, -s 'kɔːslɪt [-lət], -s
cortège, -s kɔː'teɪʒ (kɔrtɛːʒ), -ɪz
Cortes 'kɔːtes [-tez] ('kortes)
cort|ex, -ices 'kɔːt|eks, -ɪsiːz
cortical 'kɔːtɪkl
cortisone 'kɔːtɪzəun
corundum kə'rʌndəm
Corunna kɒ'rʌnə [kə'r-]
coruscat|e, -es, -ing, -ed 'kɒrəskeɪt, -s, -ɪŋ, -ɪd
coruscation, -s ˌkɒrə'skeɪʃn, -z
corvée, -s 'kɔːveɪ (kɔrve), -z
corvette, -s kɔː'vet, -s
Corwen 'kɔːwɪn [-wen]
corybant, -s, corybantes 'kɒrɪbænt, -s, ˌkɒrɪ'bænti:z
corybantic ˌkɒrɪ'bæntɪk
Corydon 'kɒrɪdən [-dɒn]
corymb 'kɒrɪmb
coryphae|us, -i ˌkɒrɪ'fi:|əs, -aɪ
coryphée 'kɒrɪfeɪ
Coryton 'kɒrɪtən
cos (C.) kɒs
cosaque, -s kɒ'zɑːk [kə'z-], -s
cosec 'kəusek
cosecant, -s ˌkəu'si:kənt, -s
Cosgrave 'kɒzgreɪv
cosh (instrument), -es kɒʃ, -ɪz
cosh (mathematical term) kɒʃ
Cosham (in Hampshire) 'kɒsəm
cosher (feast, pamper), -s, -ing, -ed 'kɒʃə*, -z, -rɪŋ, -d
cosher (=kosher) 'kəuʃə* ['kɒʃ-]
    Note.—The Jewish pronunciation is with əu.
co-signator|y, -ies 'kəu'sɪgnətər|ɪ, -ɪz
cosine, -s 'kəusaɪn, -z
cos-lettuce, -s ˌkɒs'letɪs ['kɒsˌl-, -təs], -ɪz
cosmetic (s. adj.), -s, -al, -ally kɒz'metɪk, -s, -l, -əlɪ
cosmic, -al, -ally 'kɒzmɪk, -l, -əlɪ
cosmi|sm, -st/s 'kɒzmɪ|zəm, -st/s
cosmogonic, -al, -ally ˌkɒzməu'gɒnɪk, -l, -əlɪ

cosmogon|ist/s, -y kɒz'mɒgən|ɪst/s, -ɪ
cosmograph|er/s, -y kɒz'mɒgrəf|ə*/z, -ɪ
cosmographic, -al, -ally ˌkɒzməʊ'græfɪk -l, -əlɪ
cosmological ˌkɒzməʊ'lɒdʒɪkl
cosmolog|ist/s, -y kɒz'mɒlədʒ|ɪst/s, -ɪ
cosmonaut, -s 'kɒzmənɔːt, -s
cosmopolitan (s. adj.), -s ˌkɒzmə-'pɒlɪtən, -z
cosmopolitanism ˌkɒzmə'pɒlɪtənɪzəm [-tʊɪ-]
cosmopolite, -s kɒz'mɒpəlaɪt, -s
cosmos 'kɒzmɒs
Cossack, -s 'kɒsæk, -s
cosset (s. v.), -s, -ing, -ed 'kɒsɪt, -s, -ɪŋ, -ɪd
cost (s. v.), -s, -ing kɒst [old-fashioned kɔːst], -s, -ɪŋ
Costa 'kɒstə
Costain kɒ'steɪn
costal 'kɒstl
costard (apple), -s 'kʌstəd ['kɒs-], -z
Costard (Shakespearian character) 'kɒstəd [-tɑːd]
Costa Rica, -n/s ˌkɒstə'riːkə, -n/z
Costello (surname) kɒ'steləʊ [kə's-], 'kɒstələʊ
coster, -s; -monger/s 'kɒstə*, -z; -ˌmʌŋgə*/z
costive, -ly, -ness 'kɒstɪv, -lɪ, -nɪs [-nəs]
costl|y, -ier, -iest, -iness 'kɒstl|ɪ [old-fashioned 'kɔːs-], -ɪə* [-jə*], -ɪɪst [-jɪst], -ɪnɪs [-məs]
costmary 'kɒstmeərɪ
costume (s.), -s 'kɒstjuːm [kɒ'stjuːm], -z
costum|e (v.), -es, -ing, -ed 'kɒstjuːm [-'-], -z, -ɪŋ, -d
costumier, -s kɒ'stjuːmɪə* [-mjə*], -z
Cosway, -s 'kɒzweɪ, -z
cos|y (s. adj.), -ies; -ier, -iest, -ily, -iness 'kəʊz|ɪ, -ɪz; -ɪə* [-jə*], -ɪɪst [-jɪst], -ɪlɪ [-əlɪ], -ɪnɪs [-məs]
cot, -s kɒt, -s
cot (mathematical term) kɒt
cotangent, -s ˌkəʊ'tændʒənt ['kəʊˌt-], -s
cot|e (s. v.), -es, -ing, -ed kəʊt, -s, -ɪŋ, -ɪd
co-tenant, -s ˌkəʊ'tenənt, -s
coterie, -s 'kəʊtərɪ, -z
coterminous ˌkəʊ'tɜːmɪnəs
Cotgrave 'kɒtgreɪv
cotill(i)on, -s kə'tɪljən [kɒ't-], -z
Coton 'kəʊtn
cotoneaster, -s kəˌtəʊnɪ'æstə* [kɒˌt-], -z

Cotopaxi ˌkɒtəʊ'pæksɪ
co-trustee, -s ˌkəʊtrʌs'tiː, -z
Cotswold, -s 'kɒtswəʊld [-wəld], -z
Cotsworth 'kɒtzwɜːθ [-wəθ]
cottage, -s; -r/s 'kɒtɪdʒ; -ɪz; -ə*/z
Cottam 'kɒtəm
Cottenham 'kɒtnəm ['kɒtnəm]
cotter (C.), -s 'kɒtə*, -z
Cotterell 'kɒtrəl
Cottesloe 'kɒtsləʊ
Cottian 'kɒtɪən [-tjən]
Cottingham 'kɒtŋəm
cott|on (s. v.) (C.), -ons, -oning, -oned 'kɒt|n, -nz, -nɪŋ, -nd
cotton-grass 'kɒtngrɑːs
cotton-plant, -s 'kɒtnplɑːnt, -s
cotton-seed 'kɒtnsiːd
cotton-spinner, -s 'kɒtnˌspɪnə*, -z
cotton-tail, -s 'kɒtnteɪl, -z
cotton-wool ˌkɒtn'wʊl
cottony 'kɒtnɪ [-tənɪ]
cotyledon/s, -onous ˌkɒtɪ'liːd|ən/z, -ənəs [-ŋəs]
couch (s. v.), -es, -ing, -ed kaʊtʃ, -ɪz, -ɪŋ, -t
couch (grass) kuːtʃ, kaʊtʃ
Couch kuːtʃ
couchant 'kaʊtʃənt
couchée, -s 'kuːʃeɪ (kuʃe), -z
couchette, -s kuː'ʃet, -s
Coué, -ism 'kuːeɪ, -ɪzəm
cougar, -s 'kuːgə*, -z
cough (s. v.), -s, -ing, -ed, -er/s kɒf [old-fashioned kɔːf, and in compounds] -s, -ɪŋ, -t, -ə*/z
Coughlan 'kɒglən, 'kɒklən ['kɒxlən]
Coughlin 'kɒglɪn, 'kɒklɪn ['kɒxlɪn]
could (from can) kʊd (strong form), kəd (weak form)
couldn't 'kʊdnt
coulisse, -s kuː'liːs [kʊ'l-], -ɪz
couloir, -s 'kuːlwɑː* [-wɔː*], -z
coulomb, -s 'kuːlɒm, -z
Coulsdon (in Greater London) 'kəʊlzdən, 'kuː-l-
Note.—'kəʊl- is the traditional local pronunciation. People unfamiliar with the place generally pronounce 'kuː-l-, as also do new residents in the district.
Coulson 'kəʊlsn, 'kuːlsn
coulter, -s 'kəʊltə*, -z
Coulton 'kəʊltən
council, -s 'kaʊnsl [-sɪl], -z
council-chamber, -s 'kaʊnslˌtʃeɪmbə* [-sɪl-], -z
councillor, -s 'kaʊnsələ* [-sɪlə*, -slə*, -slə*], -z

111

couns|el (s. v.), -els, -elling, -elled,
-ellor/s 'kaʊns|l, -lz, -lɪŋ [-əlɪŋ, -lɪŋ],
-ld, -lə*/z [-ələ*/z, -lə*/z]
count (s. v.), -s, -ing, -ed kaʊnt, -s, -ɪŋ,
-ɪd
count-down 'kaʊntdaʊn
countenanc|e (s. v.), -es, -ing, -ed
'kaʊntənəns [-tɪ-], -ɪz, -ɪŋ, -t
counter (s. adj. v. adv.), -s, -ing, -ed
'kaʊntə*, -z, -rɪŋ, -d
counteract, -s, -ing, -ed ˌkaʊntə'rækt,
[-tər'ækt], -s, -ɪŋ, -ɪd
counteraction (counteracting), -s ˌkaʊntə'rækʃn [-tər'æk-], -z
counter-action (action by way of reply),
-s 'kaʊntərˌækʃn [-tə ˌæk-], -z
counteractive, -ly ˌkaʊntə'ræktɪv
[-tər'æk-], -lɪ
counter-attack, -s 'kaʊntərəˌtæk
[-təə,tæk], -s
counter-attraction, -s 'kaʊntərəˌtræk-
ʃn [-təə,træk-], -z
counterbalance (s.), -s 'kaʊntəˌbæləns,
-ɪz
counterbalanc|e (v.), -es, -ing, -ed
ˌkaʊntə'bæləns, -ɪz, -ɪŋ, -t
counterblast, -s 'kaʊntəblɑːst, -s
counter-blow, -s 'kaʊntəbləʊ, -z
counter-charg|e (s. v.), -es, -ing, -ed
'kaʊntətʃɑːdʒ, -ɪz, -ɪŋ, -d
counter-claim (s. v.), -s, -ing, -ed
'kaʊntəkleɪm, -z, -ɪŋ, -d
counter-clockwise ˌkaʊntə'klɒkwaɪz
['--,-- when in contrast with clockwise]
counter-espionage ˌkaʊntər'espjənɑːʒ
[-tə'e, ,----'-, -nɪdʒ]
counterfeit (s. v.), -s, -ing, -ed 'kaʊntə-
fɪt [-fiːt], -s, -ɪŋ, -ɪd
counterfoil, -s 'kaʊntəfɔɪl, -z
counter-intelligence 'kaʊntərɪnˌtelɪ-
dʒəns [-təm-, ,----'---]
countermand (s. v.), -s, -ing, -ed
ˌkaʊntə'mɑːnd ['kaʊntəm-], -z, -ɪŋ,
-ɪd
counter-move, -s 'kaʊntəmuːv, -z
counterpane, -s 'kaʊntəpeɪn [-pɪn], -z
counterpart, -s 'kaʊntəpɑːt, -s
counter-plot, -s 'kaʊntəplɒt, -s
counterpoint 'kaʊntəpɔɪnt
counterpois|e (s. v.), -es, -ing, -ed
'kaʊntəpɔɪz, -ɪz, -ɪŋ, -d
counter-revolution, -s 'kaʊntərevəˌluː-
ʃn [-v],uː-, -vəˌlju:-, ,----'--], -z
counterscarp, -s 'kaʊntəskɑːp, -s
countersign (s.), -s 'kaʊntəsaɪn, -z
countersign (v.), -s, -ing, -ed 'kaʊntəsaɪn [ˌkaʊntə's-], -z, -ɪŋ, -d
counterstroke, -s 'kaʊntəstrəʊk, -s

counter-tenor, -s ˌkaʊntə'tenə* ['--ˌ--],
-z
countervail, -s, -ing, -ed 'kaʊntəveɪl
[ˌ--'-], -z, -ɪŋ, -d
countess, -es 'kaʊntɪs [-tes], -ɪz
counting-hou|se, -ses 'kaʊntɪŋhaʊ|s,
-zɪz
countless 'kaʊntlɪs [-ləs]
countrified 'kʌntrɪfaɪd
countr|y, -ies 'kʌntr|ɪ, -ɪz
country-folk, -s 'kʌntrɪfəʊk, -s
country-hou|se, -ses ˌkʌntrɪ'haʊ|s, -zɪz
country|man, -men 'kʌntrɪ|mən, -mən
country-seat, -s ˌkʌntrɪ'siːt, -s
country-side 'kʌntrɪsaɪd [ˌ--'-]
country|woman, -women 'kʌntrɪ|-
ˌwʊmən, -ˌwɪmɪn
count|y, -ies 'kaʊnt|ɪ, -ɪz
coup, -s kuː, -z
coup d'état, -s ˌkuː'deɪ'tɑː: [-de't-]
(kudeta), -z
coupé, -s 'kuːpeɪ (kupe), -z
Couper 'kuːpə*
Coupland 'kuːplənd
coup|le (s. v.), -les, -ling, -led 'kʌp|l,
-lz, -lɪŋ [-lɪŋ], -ld
coupler, -s 'kʌplə*, -z
couplet, -s 'kʌplɪt [-lət], -s
coupling (s.), -s 'kʌplɪŋ, -z
coupon, -s 'kuːpɒn [rarely -pɔ̃:ŋ, -poːŋ,
-pɒŋ] (kupɔ̃), -z
courage (C.) 'kʌrɪdʒ
courageous, -ly, -ness kə'reɪdʒəs, -lɪ,
-nɪs [-nəs]
courant (newspaper), -s kʊ'rænt, -s
courante, -s kʊ'rɑ̃:nt [-'rɔ̃:nt, -'rɑːnt,
-'rænt] (kurɑ̃:t), -s
courgette, -s ˌkʊə'ʒet [kɔ:-], -s
courier, -s 'kʊrɪə* ['kʌ-], -z
Courland 'kʊələnd [-lænd]
cours|e (s. v.), -es, -ing, -ed, -er/s kɔːs
[kɔəs], -ɪz, -ɪŋ, -t, -ə*/z
court (s. v.), -s, -ing, -ed kɔːt [kɔət], -s,
-ɪŋ, -ɪd
Courtauld 'kɔːtəʊld, 'kɔːtəʊ
court-card, -s 'kɔːtkɑːd ['kɔət-], -z
court-dress, -es 'kɔːt'dres [ˌkɔət-], -ɪz
Courtenay 'kɔːtnɪ ['kɔət-]
courteous, -ly, -ness 'kɜːtjəs ['kɔːt-,
'kɔət-, -tɪəs], -lɪ, -nɪs [-nəs]
courtesan, -s ˌkɔːtɪ'zæn [ˌkɔət-, ˌkʊə-,
'---]
courtes|y, -ies 'kɜːtɪs|ɪ ['kɔːt-, 'kɔət-,
-təs-], -ɪz
court-guide, -s 'kɔːtgaɪd ['kɔət-], -z
Courthope 'kɔːtəp ['kɔət-], -thəʊp
court-hou|se, -ses 'kɔːthaʊ|s ['kɔət-],
-zɪz

Courtice 'kɔːtɪs

courtier, -s 'kɔːtjə* ['kɔət-, -tɪə*], -z

courtl|y, -ier, -iest, -iness 'kɔːtl|ɪ
['kɔət-], -ɪə* [-jə*], -ɪɪst [-jɪst], -ɪnɪs
[-ɪnəs]

court-marti|al (s. v.), -als, -alling, -alled
ˌkɔːt'mɑːʃ|l [ˌkɔət-], -lz, -lɪŋ [-əlɪŋ],
-ld

Courtneidge 'kɔːtnɪdʒ ['kɔət-]

Courtney 'kɔːtnɪ ['kɔət-]

court-plaster ˌkɔːt'plɑːstə* ['kɔət-, '-,--]

courtship, -s 'kɔːt-ʃɪp ['kɔət-], -s

courts-martial ˌkɔːts'mɑːʃl [ˌkɔəts-]

courtyard, -s 'kɔːtjɑːd ['kɔət-], -z

cousin, -s 'kʌzn, -z

Cousins 'kʌznz

Coutts kuːts

coutur|e, -ier/s kuː'tjʊə* [kʊ-], -rɪeɪ
[-rɪə*]/z

Couzens 'kʌznz

cove (C.), -s, kəʊv, -z

coven, -s 'kʌvn, -z

covenant (s. v.), -s, -ing, -ed, -er/s
'kʌvənənt [-vɪn-, -vn̩-], -s, -ɪŋ, -ɪd,
-ə*/z

Covent 'kɒvənt [old-fashioned 'kʌv-]

Coventry 'kɒvəntrɪ [rarely 'kʌv-]

cov|er (s. v.), -ers, -ering/s, -ered, -erage
'kʌv|ə*, -əz, -ərɪŋ/z, -əd, -ərɪdʒ

Coverack 'kɒvəræk [locally also -rək]

covercharg|e, -es 'kʌvətʃɑːdʒ, -ɪz

Coverdale 'kʌvədeɪl

coverlet, -s 'kʌvəlɪt [-lət], -s

Coverley 'kʌvəlɪ

Covernton 'kʌvəntən

cover-point, -s ˌkʌvə'pɔɪnt ['kʌvəp-], -s

covert (s.) (shelter, cloth), -s 'kʌvə*, -z
['kʌvət, -s]
Note.—See also wing-covert.

covert (adj.), -ly 'kʌvət, -lɪ

covert-coat, -s ˌkʌvət'kəʊt ['---, less
freq. 'kʌvəkəʊt], -s

coverture 'kʌvəˌtjʊə* [-ˌtʃʊə*]

covet, -s, -ing, -ed 'kʌvɪt [-vət], -s, -ɪŋ,
-ɪd

covetous, -ly, -ness 'kʌvɪtəs [-vət-], -lɪ,
-nɪs [-nəs]

covey (of birds), -s 'kʌvɪ, -z

covey (familiar diminutive of cove), -s
'kəʊvɪ, -z

Covington 'kʌvɪŋtən

cow (s. v.), -s, -ing, -ed kaʊ, -z, -ɪŋ, -d

Cowal 'kaʊəl

Cowan 'kaʊən

coward (C.), -s 'kaʊəd, -z

cowardice 'kaʊədɪs

cowardl|y, -iness 'kaʊədl|ɪ, -ɪnɪs [-ɪnəs]

cowbane 'kaʊbeɪn

cowboy, -s 'kaʊbɔɪ, -z

cow-catcher, -s 'kaʊˌkætʃə*, -z

Cowden (in Kent) 'kaʊden [kaʊ'den]

Cowdenbeath ˌkaʊdn'biːθ

Cowdray 'kaʊdreɪ [attributively also
-drɪ]

Cowdrey 'kaʊdrɪ

Cowen 'kaʊɪn ['kaʊən], 'kəʊɪn ['kəʊən]

cower, -s, -ing -ed 'kaʊə*, -z, -rɪŋ, -d

Cowes kaʊz

cowherd, -s 'kaʊhɜːd, -z

cowhide 'kaʊhaɪd

cow-hou|se, -ses 'kaʊhaʊ|s, -zɪz

Cowie 'kaʊɪ

cowl, -s kaʊl, -z

Cowley 'kaʊlɪ

cowlike 'kaʊlaɪk

Cowper 'kaʊpə*, 'kuːpə*
Note.—The poet called himself
'kuːpə*. 'kuːpə* is also the pronunciation in Cowper Powys
(ˌkuːpə* 'pəʊɪs) and Cowper-Black.

cow-pox 'kaʊpɒks

cow-puncher, -s 'kaʊˌpʌntʃə*, -z

cowr|ie [r|y], -ies 'kaʊr|ɪ ['kaʊər-], -ɪz

cowshed, -s 'kaʊʃed, -z

cowslip, -s 'kaʊslɪp, -s

Cowt|an, -on 'kaʊt|n, -n

cox (C.), -es kɒks, -ɪz

coxcomb, -s 'kɒkskəʊm, -z

coxswain, -s 'kɒksweɪn [nautical pronunciation 'kɒksn], -z

Coxtie 'kɒkstɪ

cox|y, -ier, -iest, -iness 'kɒks|ɪ, -ɪə*,
-ɪɪst, -ɪnɪs [-ɪnəs]

coy, -er, -est, -ly, -ness kɔɪ, -ə*, -ɪst, -lɪ,
-nɪs [-nəs]

coyish, -ly, -ness 'kɔɪʃ, -lɪ, -nɪs [-nəs]

coyote, -s 'kɔɪəʊt [kɔɪ'əʊt], -s [kɔɪ'əʊtɪ,
-z]

coypu, -s 'kɔɪpuː [-pjuː], -z

Coysh kɔɪʃ

coz kʌz

coz|en, -ens, -ening, -ened, -ener/s
'kʌz|n, -nz, -n̩ɪŋ, -nd, -nə*/z

Cozens 'kʌznz

crab, -s kræb, -z

crab-apple, -s 'kræbˌæpl, -z

Crabbe kræb

crabbed, -ly, -ness 'kræbɪd, -lɪ, -nɪs
[-nəs]

crabtree (C.), -s 'kræbtriː, -z

crack (s. v.), -s, -ing, -ed kræk, -s, -ɪŋ, -t

crack-brain, -ed 'krækbreɪn, -d

Crackenthorpe 'krækənθɔːp

cracker, -s 'krækə*, -z

crack|le, -les, -ling, -led 'kræk|l, -lz, -lɪŋ
[-lɪŋ], -ld

113

crackling (s.) 'kræklɪŋ

crackly 'kræklɪ ['kræklɪ]

cracknel, -s 'kræknl [-nəl], -z

Cracknell 'kræknl [-nəl]

cracks|man, -men 'kræks|mən, -mən

Cracow 'krækəʊ ['krɑːk-, -kaʊ]

crad|le (s. v.), -les, -ling, -led 'kreɪd|l, -lz, -lɪŋ [-lɪŋ], -ld

cradlesnatch, -ing, -er/s 'kreɪdlsnætʃ, -ɪŋ, -ə*/z

Cradley 'kreɪdlɪ

craft, -s krɑːft, -s

crafts|man, -men, -manship 'krɑːfts|mən, -mən, -mənʃɪp

craft|y, -ier, -iest, -ily, -iness 'krɑːft|ɪ, -ɪə* [-jə*], -ɪɪst [-jɪst], -ɪlɪ [-əlɪ], -ɪnɪs [-ɪnəs]

crag, -s kræg, -z

Cragg kræg

cragg|y, -ier, -iest, -ily, -iness 'kræg|ɪ, -ɪə*, -ɪɪst, -ɪlɪ [-əlɪ], -ɪnɪs [-ɪnəs]

crags|man, -men 'krægz|mən, -mən [-men]

Craig, -ie kreɪg, -ɪ

Craigavon (Viscount) kreɪg'ævən

Craigenputtock ˌkreɪgən'pʌtək

Craik kreɪk

crak|e (s. v.), -es, -ing, -ed kreɪk, -s, -ɪŋ, -t

cram (s. v.), -s, -ming, -med, -mer/s kræm, -z, -ɪŋ, -d, -ə*/z

crambo 'kræmbəʊ

Cramer 'krɑːmə*

cram-full ˌkræm'fʊl [also '-- when followed by a stress]

Cramlington 'kræmlɪŋtən

cramoisy 'kræmɔɪzɪ

cramp (s. v.) (C.), -s, -ing, -ed kræmp, -s, -ɪŋ, -t [kræmt]

cramp-iron, -s 'kræmp,aɪən, -z

crampon, -s 'kræmpən, -z

Crampton 'kræmptən

cran, -s kræn, -z

cranage 'kreɪnɪdʒ

Cranage (surname) 'krænɪdʒ

cranberr|y, -ies 'krænbər|ɪ, -ɪz

Cranborne 'krænbɔːn [-bɔən]

Cranbourn(e) 'krænbɔːn [-bɔən, -ˌbʊən]

Cranbrook 'krænbrʊk

cran|e (s. v.) (C.), -es, -ing, -ed kreɪn, -z, -ɪŋ, -d

Cranford 'krænfəd

cranial 'kreɪnjəl [-nɪəl]

craniolog|ist/s, -y ˌkreɪnɪ'ɒlədʒ|ɪst/s, -ɪ

crani|um, -ums, -a 'kreɪnj|əm [-nɪ|əm], -əmz, -ə

crank, -s kræŋk, -s

Crankshaw 'kræŋkʃɔː

crank|y, -ier, -iest, -ily, -iness 'kræŋk|ɪ, -ɪə* [-jə*], -ɪɪst [-jɪst], -ɪlɪ [-əlɪ], -ɪnɪs [-ɪnəs]

Cran|leigh, -ley, -mer 'kræn|lɪ, -lɪ, -mə*

crann|y, -ies, -ied 'kræn|ɪ, -ɪz, -ɪd

Cran|ston, -worth 'kræn|stən, -wɜːθ [-wəθ]

crape, -s kreɪp, -s

crapulen|ce, -t/ly 'kræpjʊlən|s, -t/lɪ

crapulous 'kræpjʊləs

crash (s. v.), -es, -ing, -ed kræʃ, -ɪz, -ɪŋ, -t

Crashaw 'kræʃɔː

crash-div|e (s. v.), -es, -ing, -ed 'kræʃdaɪv, -z, -ɪŋ, -d

crash-helmet, -s 'kræʃˌhelmɪt, -s

crash-land, -s, -ing, -ed 'kræʃlænd [ˌ-'-], -z, -ɪŋ, -ɪd

crasis 'kreɪsɪs

crass, -er, -est, -ly, -ness kræs, -ə*, -ɪst, -lɪ, -nɪs [-nəs]

crassitude 'kræsɪtjuːd

cratch, -es krætʃ, -ɪz

Cratchit 'krætʃɪt

crate, -s kreɪt, -s

crater, -s 'kreɪtə*, -z

Crathie 'kræθɪ

cravat, -s, -ted krə'væt, -s, -ɪd

crav|e, -es, -ing/s, -ed, -er/s kreɪv, -z, -ɪŋ/z, -d, -ə*/z

craven (C.), -s 'kreɪvən, -z

craw, -s krɔː, -z

Crawcour 'krɔːkə*

crawfish, -es 'krɔːfɪʃ, -ɪz

Crawford 'krɔːfəd

crawl (s. v.), -s, -ing, -ed, -er/s krɔːl, -z, -ɪŋ, -d, -ə*/z

Crawley 'krɔːlɪ

crawl|y, -ier, -iest, -iness 'krɔː|lɪ, -ɪə* [-jə*], -ɪɪst [-jɪst], -ɪnɪs [-ɪnəs]

crayfish, -es 'kreɪfɪʃ, -ɪz

crayon, -s 'kreɪən ['kreɪɒn], -z

craze, -s, -d kreɪz, -ɪz, -d

craz|y, -ier, -iest, -ily, -iness 'kreɪz|ɪ, -ɪə* [-jə*], -ɪɪst [-jɪst], -ɪlɪ [-əlɪ], -ɪnɪs [-ɪnəs]

Creagh kreɪ

Creaghan 'kriːgən

creak (s. v.), -s, -ing, -ed kriːk, -s, -ɪŋ, -t

creak|y, -ier, -iest, -ily, -iness 'kriːk|ɪ, -ɪə* [-jə*], -ɪɪst [-jɪst], -ɪlɪ [-əlɪ], -ɪnɪs [-ɪnəs]

cream, -s kriːm, -z

cream-cheese, -s ˌkriːm'tʃiːz, -ɪz

cream-coloured 'kriːmˌkʌləd

creamer|y, -ies 'kriːmər|ɪ, -ɪz

cream-laid ˌkriːm'leɪd

cream-wove ˌkriːm'wəʊv

cream|y, -ier, -iest, -ily, -iness 'kri:m|ɪ, -ɪə* [-jə*], -ɪɪst [-jɪst], -ɪlɪ [-əlɪ], -ɪnɪs [-məs]

creas|e (s. v.), -es, -ing, -ed kri:s, -ɪz, -ɪŋ, -t

Creas(e)y 'kri:sɪ

creasy (adj.) 'kri:sɪ

creat|e, -es, -ing, -ed kri:'eɪt [krɪ-], -s, -ɪŋ, -ɪd

creation (C.), -s kri:'eɪʃn [krɪ-], -z

creationi|sm, -st/s kri:'eɪʃɳɪ|zəm [krɪ-, -ʃənɪ-], -st/s

creative, -ly, -ness kri:'eɪtɪv [krɪ-], -lɪ, -nɪs [-nəs]

creativity ,kri:eɪ'tɪvətɪ [,krɪ-, -ɪtɪ]

creator (C.), -s, kri:'eɪtə* [krɪ-], -z

creature, -s 'kri:tʃə*, -z

crèche, -s kreɪʃ, -ɪz

Crécy 'kresɪ

credence 'kri:dəns

credential, -s krɪ'denʃl, -z

credibility ,kredɪ'bɪlətɪ [-də'b-, -ɪt-]

credib|le, -ly, -leness 'kredəb|l [-dɪb-], -lɪ, -lnɪs [-nəs]

credit (s. v.), -s, -ing, -ed, -or/s 'kredɪt, -s, -ɪŋ, -ɪd, -ə*/z

creditab|le, -ly, -leness 'kredɪtəb|l, -lɪ, -lnɪs [-nəs]

Crediton 'kredɪtn

credo, -s 'kri:dəʊ ['kreɪd-], -z

credulity krɪ'dju:lətɪ [krə'd-, kre'd-, -ɪtɪ]

credulous, -ly, -ness 'kredjʊləs, -lɪ, -nɪs [-nəs]

creed (C.), -s kri:d, -z

creek, -s kri:k, -s

creel, -s kri:l, -z

creep, -s, -ing, crept kri:p, -s, -ɪŋ, krept

creeper, -s 'kri:pə*, -z

creep|y, -ier, -iest, -ily, -iness 'kri:p|ɪ, -ɪə* [-jə*], -ɪɪst [-jɪst], -ɪlɪ [-əlɪ], -ɪnɪs [-məs]

Crees kri:s, kri:z

creese, -s kri:s, -ɪz

Creighton 'kraɪtn

cremat|e, -es, -ing, -ed, -or/s krɪ'meɪt [krə'm-], -s, -ɪŋ, -ɪd, -ə*/z

cremation, -s krɪ'meɪʃn [krə'm-], -z

crematori|al, -um/s, -a ,kremə'tɔ:rɪ|əl, -əm/z, -ə

cremator|y, -ies 'kremətər|ɪ, -ɪz

crème - de - menthe ,kreɪmdə'mɑ:nt [-'mɔ:nt, -'mɒnt] (krɛːmdəmã:t)

Cremona krɪ'məʊnə [krə'm-]

crenate 'kri:neɪt

crenel(l)at|e, -es, -ing, -ed 'krenəleɪt [-nɪl-], -s, -ɪŋ, -ɪd

crenel(l)ation, -s ,krenə'leɪʃən [-nɪ'l-], -z

Creole, -s 'kri:əʊl ['krɪəʊl], -z

Creolian kri:'əʊljən [krɪ-, -lɪən]

creosote 'krɪəsəʊt ['kri:əs-]

crêpe, -s kreɪp, -s

crêpe de chine ,kreɪpdə'ʃi:n (krɛpdə-ʃin)

crepitat|e, -es, -ing, -ed 'krepɪteɪt, -s, -ɪŋ, -ɪd

crepitation, -s ,krepɪ'teɪʃn, -z

crépon 'krepɔ̃:ŋ ['kreɪp-, -pɔːŋ, -pɒn] (krepɔ̃)

crept (from creep) krept

crepuscular krɪ'pʌskjʊlə* [kre'p-]

crepuscule 'krepəskju:l

Crerar 'krɪərə*

crescendo, -s krɪ'ʃendəʊ [krə'ʃ-], -z

crescent (moon, shape), -s 'kresnt [-eznt], -s

crescent (growing, when applied to objects other than the moon) 'kresnt

Crespigny (surname) 'krepɪnɪ, 'krepnɪ, 'krespɪnɪ, (in London streets) kre'spi:nɪ

cress, -es kres, -ɪz

Cressida 'kresɪdə

Cresswell 'krezwəl, -esw-

Cressy 'kresɪ

crest (s. v.), -s, -ing, -ed krest, -s, -ɪŋ, -ɪd

crestfallen 'krest,fɔ:lən

Creswick 'krezɪk

cretaceous krɪ'teɪʃəs [kre't-, -ʃjəs, -ʃɪəs]

Cretan, -s 'kri:tn, -z

Crete kri:t

Cretic, -s 'kri:tɪk, -s

cretin, -s 'kretɪn ['kri:t-], -z

cretinism 'kretɪnɪzəm ['kri:t-]

cretonne, -s 'kretɒn [kre'tɒn], -z

Creusa krɪ'u:zə [krɪ'ju:-]

crevasse, -s, -d krɪ'væs [krə'v-], -ɪz, -t

crevice, -s 'krevɪs, -ɪz

crew, -s kru:, -z

crew (from crow) kru:

crew-cut 'kru:kʌt

Crewe kru:

crewel, -s 'kru:əl ['krʊɪl, -ʊəl], -z

Crewkerne 'kru:kə:n ['krʊkən, rarely kru:'kə:n]

Crianlarich ,krɪən'lærɪk [-ɪx]

crib (s. v.), -s, -bing, -bed, -ber|s krɪb, -z, -ɪŋ, -d, -ə*/z

cribbage 'krɪbɪdʒ

cribbage - board, -s 'krɪbɪdʒbɔːd [-bəəd], -z

Criccieth 'krɪkɪeθ [-kɪəθ, -kjəθ] (Welsh 'krikjeθ)

115

Crichel 'krɪtʃəl
Crichton 'kraɪtn
crick (s. v.), -s, -ing, -ed krɪk, -s, -ɪŋ, -t
cricket, -s, -er/s 'krɪkɪt, -s, -ə*/z
cricket-match, -es 'krɪkɪtmætʃ, -ɪz
cricklite 'krɪklaɪt
cricoid 'kraɪkɔɪd
cried (from cry) kraɪd
Crieff kri:f
crier, -s 'kraɪə*, -z
cries (from cry) kraɪz
crime, -s kraɪm, -z
Crimea, -n kraɪ'mɪə [krɪ'm-], -n
crimin|al/s, -ally 'krɪmɪn|l/z [-mən-], -əlɪ
criminality ˌkrɪmɪ'nælətɪ [-mə'n-, -ɪtɪ]
criminat|e, -es, -ing, -ed 'krɪmɪneɪt [-mən-], -s, -ɪŋ, -ɪd
crimination, -s ˌkrɪmɪ'neɪʃn [-mə'n-], -z
criminolog|ist/s, -y ˌkrɪmɪ'nɒlədʒ|ɪst/s [-mə'n-], -ɪ
crimp (adj. v.), -s, -ing, -ed krɪmp, -s, -ɪŋ, -t [krɪmt]
crimplene 'krɪmpli:n
crims|on (s. v. adj.), -ons, -oning, -oned 'krɪmz|n, -nz, -ŋɪŋ [-nɪŋ], -nd
crinal 'kraɪnl
cring|e (s. v.), -es, -ing, -ed, -er/s krɪndʒ, -ɪz, -ɪŋ, -d, -ə*/z
crink|le, -les, -ling, -led 'krɪŋk|l, -lz, -lɪŋ [-lŋ], -ld
crinkly 'krɪŋklɪ
crinoid, -s 'kraɪnɔɪd ['krɪn-], -z
crinoline (s.), -s 'krɪnəli:n [-lɪn, ˌkrɪnə-'li:n], -z
crinoline (adj.) 'krɪnəlɪn
Crippen 'krɪpɪn [-pən]
cripp|le (s. v.), -les, -ling, -led 'krɪp|l, -lz, -lɪŋ [-lŋ], -ld
Cripplegate 'krɪplgeɪt [-gɪt]
Crisfield 'krɪsfi:ld
cris|is, -es 'kraɪs|ɪs, -i:z
crisp (C.), -er, -est, -ly, -ness krɪsp, -ə*, -ɪst, -lɪ, -nɪs [-nəs]
crisp-bread 'krɪspbred
Crispin 'krɪspɪn
criss-cross 'krɪskrɒs [old-fashioned -krɔ:s]
criteri|on (C.), -ons, -a kraɪ'tɪərɪ|ən, -ənz, -ə
critic, -s; -al, -ally, -alness 'krɪtɪk, -s; -l, -əlɪ, -lnɪs [-nəs]
criticism, -s 'krɪtɪsɪzəm, -z
criticizable [-isa-] 'krɪtɪsaɪzəbl [ˌkrɪtɪ's-]
criticiz|e [-is|e], -es, -ing, -ed 'krɪtɪsaɪz, -ɪz, -ɪŋ, -d
critique, -s krɪ'ti:k, -s
Crittenden 'krɪtndən

croak (s. v.), -s, -ing/s, -ed, -er/s krəʊk, -s, -ɪŋ/z, -t, -ə*/z
croak|y, -ier, -iest, -ily, -iness 'krəʊk|ɪ, -ɪə* [-jə*], -ɪɪst [-jɪst], -ɪlɪ [-əlɪ], -ɪnɪs [-ɪnəs]
Croat, -s 'krəʊæt [-ət], -s
Croatia krəʊ'eɪʃjə [-ʃɪə, -ʃə]
Croatian, -s krəʊ'eɪʃjən [-ʃɪən, -ʃn], -z
crochet (s. v.), -s, -ing, -ed 'krəʊʃeɪ [-ʃɪ], -z, -ɪŋ, -d
crochet-hook, -s 'krəʊʃɪhʊk [-ʃeɪh-], -s
crock, -s krɒk, -s
Crocker 'krɒkə*
crockery 'krɒkərɪ
crocket, -s 'krɒkɪt, -s
Crockett 'krɒkɪt
crocodile, -s 'krɒkədaɪl, -z
crocus, -es 'krəʊkəs, -ɪz
Croesus 'kri:səs
croft (C.), -s krɒft, -s
crofter, -s 'krɒftə*, -z
croissant, -s 'krwɑ:sã:ŋ [-sɒŋ, -sõ:ŋ], -z (krwɑsã)
Croker 'krəʊkə*
Cro-Magnon krəʊ'mænjõ:ŋ (krɔmaɲõ)
Cromarty 'krɒmətɪ
Crombie 'krɒmbɪ, 'krʌm-
Crome krəʊm
Cromer 'krəʊmə*
cromlech, -s 'krɒmlek, -s
Crommelin 'krʌmlɪn, 'krɒm-
Crompton 'krʌmptən, 'krɒm-
Cromwell 'krɒmwəl ['krʌm-, -wel]
Cromwellian krɒm'welɪən [krʌm-, -ljən]
crone, -s krəʊn, -z
Cronin 'krəʊnɪn
cron|y, -ies 'krəʊn|ɪ, -ɪz
crook (s. v.) (C.), -s, -ing, -ed (p. partic.) krʊk, -s, -ɪŋ, -t
Crookback 'krʊkbæk
crook-backed 'krʊkbækt
Crooke, -s krʊk, -s
crooked (adj.) (not straight), -er, -est, -ly, -ness 'krʊkɪd, -ə*, -ɪst, -lɪ, -nɪs [-nəs]
crooked (adj.) (having a crook) krʊkt
Croome kru:m
croon (s. v.), -s, -ing, -ed, -er/s kru:n, -z, -ɪŋ, -d, -ə*/z
crop (s. v.), -s, -ping, -ped krɒp, -s, -ɪŋ, -t
cropper, -s 'krɒpə*, -z
croquet (s. v.), -s, -ing, -ed 'krəʊkeɪ [-kɪ], -z, -ɪŋ, -d
croquette, -s krɒ'ket [krəʊ-], -s
crore, -s krɔ:* [krɔə*], -z
Crosby 'krɒzbɪ, 'krɒsbɪ

116

Crosfield 'krɒsfi:ld [old-fashioned 'krɔ:s-]
Croshaw 'krɒʃɔ:
crosier, -s 'krəʊʒə*, -z
Crosier 'krəʊʒjə* [-zɪə*], 'krəʊʒə*
cross (s. adj. v.) (C.), -es; -er, -est, -ly, -ness; -ing, -ed krɒs [old-fashioned krɔ:s, and in compounds], -ɪz; -ə*, -ɪst, -lɪ, -nɪs [-nəs]; -ɪŋ, -t
cross-action, -s 'krɒs,ækʃn ['krɔ:s-], -z
cross-bar, -s 'krɒsbɑ:* ['krɔ:s-], -z
cross-beam, -s 'krɒsbi:m ['krɔ:s-], -z
cross-bench, -es 'krɒsbentʃ ['krɔ:s-], -ɪz
cross-bencher, -s ,krɒs'bentʃə* [,krɔ:s-, '-,--], -z
crossbill, -s 'krɒsbɪl ['krɔ:s-], -z
crossbones 'krɒsbəʊnz ['krɔ:s-]
crossbow, -s 'krɒsbəʊ ['krɔ:s-], -z
crossbred 'krɒsbred ['krɔ:s-]
crossbreed, -s 'krɒsbri:d ['krɔ:s-], -z
cross-bun, -s ,krɒs'bʌn [,krɔ:s-], -z
cross-country ,krɒs'kʌntrɪ [,krɔ:s-, '-,-- when followed by a stress]
crosscut, -s 'krɒskʌt ['krɔ:s-], -s
crosse, -s krɒs, -ɪz
Crosse krɒs [krɔ:s]
cross-examination, -s 'krɒsɪg,zæmɪ-'neɪʃn ['krɔ:s-, -eg-], -z
cross-examin|e, -es, -ing, -ed, -er/s ,krɒsɪg'zæmɪn [,krɔ:s-, -eg-], -z, -ɪŋ, -d, -ə*/z
cross|-eyed, -grained 'krɒs|aɪd ['krɔ:s-, ,-'-], -greɪnd
cross-fire 'krɒs,faɪə* ['krɔ:s-]
crossing (s.), -s 'krɒsɪŋ ['krɔ:s-], -z
crossing-sweeper, -s 'krɒsɪŋ,swi:pə* ['krɔ:s-], -z
cross-jack, -s 'krɒsdʒæk ['krɔ:s-], -s
cross-legged 'krɒslegd ['krɔ:s-, ,-'-]
Cross|ley, -man 'krɒs|lɪ ['krɔ:s-], -mən
crosspatch, -es 'krɒspætʃ ['krɔ:s-], -ɪz
cross-purpose, -s ,krɒs'pɜ:pəs [,krɔ:s-], -ɪz
cross-questi|on, -ons, -oning, -oned ,krɒs'kwestʃ|ən [,krɔ:s-, -eʃtʃ-], -ənz, -ənɪŋ [-ŋɪŋ], -ənd
cross-reference, -s ,krɒs'refərəns [,krɔ:s-], -ɪz
cross-road, -s 'krɒsrəʊd ['krɔ:s-], -z
cross-row, -s 'krɒsrəʊ ['krɔ:s-], -z
cross-section, -s ,krɒs'sekʃn [,krɔ:s-], -z
cross-stitch 'krɒsstɪtʃ ['krɔ:s-]
crossway, -s 'krɒsweɪ ['krɔ:s-], -z
cross-wise 'krɒswaɪz ['krɔ:swaɪz]
cross-word, -s 'krɒswɜ:d ['krɔ:swɜ:d], -z
Crosthwaite 'krɒsθweɪt ['krɔ:s-]
crotal|um, -a 'krɒtəl|əm, -ə

crotch (C.), -es krɒtʃ, -ɪz
crotchet, -s, -y, -iness 'krɒtʃɪt, -s, -ɪ, -ɪnɪs [-ɪnəs]
croton (C.), 'krəʊtən
crouch (C.), -es, -ing, -ed krautʃ, -ɪz, -ɪŋ, -t (village in Kent kru:tʃ)
croup, -s kru:p, -s
croupier, -s 'kru:pɪə* [-pjə*, -pɪeɪ] (krupje), -z
crow (s. v.), -s, -ing, -ed, crew krəʊ, -z, -ɪŋ, -d, kru:
crowbar, -s 'krəʊbɑ:*, -z
crowd (s. v.), -s, -ing, -ed kraud, -z, -ɪŋ, -ɪd
Crowe krəʊ
crow-foot 'krəʊfʊt
Crow|hurst, -land, -ley 'krəʊ|hɜ:st, -lənd, -lɪ
crown (s. v.), -s, -ing, -ed kraun, -z, -ɪŋ, -d
Crowndale 'kraundeɪl
crown-glass ,kraun'glɑ:s [in contrast '--]
crown-land, -s ,kraun'lænd [in contrast '--], -z
crown-prince, -s ,kraun'prɪns [also '-- when attributive], -ɪz
crow-quill, -s 'krəʊkwɪl, -z
crow's|-foot, -feet 'krəʊz|fʊt, -fi:t
crow's-nest, -s 'krəʊznest, -s
Crowte kraut
Crowther 'krauðə*
Croyd|en, -on 'krɔɪd|n, -n
crozier, -s 'krəʊʒə*, -z
Crozier 'krəʊʒjə* [-zɪə*], 'krəʊʒə*
crucial 'kru:ʃl [-ʃɪəl, -ʃjəl]
crucible, -s 'kru:sɪbl [-əbl], -z
crucifix, -es 'kru:sɪfɪks, -ɪz
crucifixion (C.), -s ,kru:sɪ'fɪkʃn, -z
cruciform 'kru:sɪfɔ:m
cruci|fy, -fies, -fying, -fied, -fier/s 'kru:sɪ|faɪ, -faɪz, -faɪɪŋ, -faɪd, -faɪə*/z
crude, -r, -st, -ly, -ness kru:d, -ə*, -ɪst, -lɪ, -nɪs [-nəs]
Cruden 'kru:dn [-dən]
crudit|y, -ies 'kru:dɪt|ɪ [-ət|ɪ], -ɪz
cruel, -ness kruəl ['kru:əl, 'kruɪl, 'kru:ɪl, kru:l], -nɪs [-nəs]
cruel|ler, -lest, -ly 'kruəl|ə* ['kru:l-, 'kruɪl-, 'kru:əl-], -ɪst, -ɪ
cruelt|y, -ies 'kruəlt|ɪ ['kru:əl-, 'kruɪl-, 'kruɪl-, 'kru:l-], -ɪz
cruet, -s; -stand/s 'kru:ɪt ['kruɪt], -s; -stænd/z
Crui(c)kshank 'krʊkʃæŋk
cruis|e (s. v.), -es, -ing, -ed, -er/s kru:z, -ɪz, -ɪŋ, -d, -ə*/z

117

crumb (s. v.), -s, -ing, -ed krʌm, -z, -ɪŋ,
-d

crumb-brush, -es 'krʌmbrʌʃ, -ɪz

crumb|le, -les, -ling, -led 'krʌmb|l, -lz,
-lɪŋ, -ld

crumby 'krʌmɪ

Crummock 'krʌmək

crummy 'krʌmɪ

crump, -s, -ing, -ed krʌmp, -s, -ɪŋ, -t
[krʌmt]

crumpet, -s 'krʌmpɪt, -s

crump|le, -les, -ling, -led 'krʌmp|l, -lz,
-lɪŋ [-lɪŋ], -ld

crunch, -es, -ing, -ed krʌntʃ, -ɪz, -ɪŋ,
-t

crupper, -s 'krʌpə*, -z

crusade, -s, -er/s kru:'seɪd, -z, -ə*/z

cruse, -s kru:z, -ɪz

crush (s. v.), -es, -ing, -ed, -er/s krʌʃ,
-ɪz, -ɪŋ, -t, -ə*/z

crush-hat, -s ˌkrʌʃ'hæt, -s

crush-room, -s 'krʌʃrʊm [-ru:m], -z

Crusoe 'kru:səʊ ['kru:zəʊ]

crust, -s krʌst, -s

crusta|cea, -cean/s, -ceous krʌ'steɪ|ʃjə
[-ʃɪə, -ʃə], -ʃjən/z [-ʃɪən/z, -ʃn/z],
-ʃjəs [-ʃɪəs, -ʃəs]

crustate 'krʌsteɪt

crustated krʌ'steɪtɪd

crustation, -s krʌ'steɪʃn, -z

crusted 'krʌstɪd

crust|y, -ier, -iest, -ily, -iness 'krʌst|ɪ,
-ɪə* [-jə*], -ɪɪst [-jɪst], -ɪlɪ [-əlɪ], -ɪnɪs
[-ɪnəs]

crutch, -es, -ed krʌtʃ, -ɪz, -t

Crutched   Friars   ˌkrʌtʃɪd'fraɪəz
[ˌkrʌtʃt-]

Cruttwell 'krʌtwəl

crux, -es krʌks, -ɪz

cr|y (s. v.), -ies, -ying, -ied, -ier/s kr|aɪ,
-aɪz, -aɪɪŋ, -aɪd, -aɪə*/z

cry-bab|y, -ies 'kraɪˌbeɪb|ɪ, -ɪz

crypt, -s krɪpt, -s

cryptic, -al, -ally 'krɪptɪk, -l, -əlɪ

crypto, -s 'krɪptəʊ, -z

cryptogam, -s 'krɪptəʊgæm, -z

cryptogram, -s 'krɪptəʊgræm, -z

cryptograph, -s 'krɪptəʊgrɑ:f [-græf], -s

cryptograph|er/s, -y krɪp'tɒgrəf|ə*/z,
-ɪ

cryptology krɪp'tɒlədʒɪ

Crysell 'kraɪsl

crystal, -s 'krɪstl, -z

crystal-gaz|er/s, -ing 'krɪstlˌgeɪz|ə*/z,
-ɪŋ

crystalline 'krɪstəlaɪn [-tlaɪn]

crystallizable [-isa-] 'krɪstəlaɪzəbl
[-tlaɪ-]

crystallization [-isa-], -s ˌkrɪstəlaɪ-
'zeɪʃn [-tlaɪ-], -z

crystalliz|e [-is|e], -es, -ing, -ed 'krɪs-
təlaɪz [-tlaɪz], -ɪz, -ɪŋ, -d

crystallograph|er/s, -y ˌkrɪstə'lɒgrə-
f|ə*/z, -ɪ

crystalloid, -s 'krɪstəlɔɪd, -z

C-spring, -s 'si:sprɪŋ, -z

cub (s. v.), -s, -bing, -bed kʌb, -z, -ɪŋ,
-d

Cuba, -n/s 'kju:bə, -n/z

cubage 'kju:bɪdʒ

cubbish 'kʌbɪʃ

cubb|y, -ies 'kʌb|ɪ, -ɪz

cubby-hole, -s 'kʌbɪhəʊl, -z

cub|e (s. v.), -es, -ing, -ed kju:b, -z,
-ɪŋ, -d

cubic, -al, -ally 'kju:bɪk, -l, -əlɪ

cubicle, -s 'kju:bɪkl, -z

cub|ism, -ist/s 'kju:b|ɪzəm, -ɪst/s

cubistic kju:'bɪstɪk

cubit, -s, -al 'kju:bɪt, -s, -l

Cubitt 'kju:bɪt

cuboid, -s 'kju:bɔɪd, -z

Cuchulinn 'ku:kʊlɪn ['ku:xʊ-]

Cuckfield 'kʊkfi:ld

cucking-stool, -s 'kʌkɪŋstu:l, -z

Cuckmere 'kʊk.mɪə*

cuckold (s. v.), -s, -ing, -ed 'kʌkəʊld
[-kəld], -z, -ɪŋ, -ɪd

cuck|oo (s. v.), -oos, -ooing, -ooed
'kʊk|u:, -u:z, -u:ɪŋ [-ʊɪŋ], -u:d

cuckoo (interj.) ˌkʊ'ku: ['kʊku:]

cuckoo-clock, -s 'kʊku:klɒk, -s

cuckoo-flower, -s 'kʊku:ˌflaʊə*, -z

cuckoo-pint, -s 'kʊku:pɪnt, -s

cuckoo-spit, -s 'kʊku:spɪt, -s

cucumber, -s 'kju:kʌmbə* ['kjʊkʌm-,
'kju:kəm-], -z

cud, -s kʌd, -z

Cudahy 'kʌdəhɪ

cudd|le (s. v.), -les, -ling, -led 'kʌd|l, -lz,
-lɪŋ [-lɪŋ], -ld

cudd|y, -ies 'kʌd|ɪ, -ɪz

cudg|el (s. v.), -els, -elling, -elled
'kʌdʒ|əl, -əlz, -lɪŋ [-əlɪŋ], -əld

Cudworth 'kʌdwəθ [-wɜ:θ]

cue, -s kju:, -z

Cufa 'kju:fə

cuff (s. v.), -s, -ing, -ed kʌf, -s, -ɪŋ, -t

Cuffe kʌf

Cuffley 'kʌflɪ

Cufic 'kju:fɪk

cui bono ˌkwi:'bɒnəʊ [ˌku:ɪ'bɒnəʊ,
ˌku:ɪ'bəʊnəʊ]

cuirass, -es kwɪ'ræs, -ɪz

cuirassier, -s ˌkwɪrə'sɪə*, -z

cuisine kwi:'zi:n [kwɪ'z-] (kɥizin)

cuisse, -s kwɪs, -ɪz
cul-de-sac, -s ˌkʊldəˈsæk, ˈkʌldəsæk (kyldəsak, *pronounced as if French*), -s
Note.—The actual French pronunciation is kydsak *or* kytsak.
Culebra kuːˈlebrə [kʊˈl-]
Culham ˈkʌləm
culinary ˈkʌlɪnərɪ [*old-fashioned* ˈkjuːl-]
cull, -s, -ing, -ed kʌl, -z, -ɪŋ, -d
Cull|en, -ey ˈkʌl|ɪn, -ɪ
cullender, -s ˈkʌlɪndə* [-lən-], -z
Cullinan ˈkʌlɪnən [-næn]
Cullinnan kʌˈlɪnən [kəˈl-]
Culloden kəˈlɒdn [kʌˈl-, -ˈləʊdn]
Cullompton kəˈlʌmptən
culm, -s kʌlm, -z
Culme kʌlm
culminat|e, -es, -ing, -ed ˈkʌlmɪneɪt, -s, -ɪŋ, -ɪd
culmination, -s ˌkʌlmɪˈneɪʃn, -z
culotte, -s kjuːˈlɒt [kjʊˈl-] (kylɔt), -s
culpability ˌkʌlpəˈbɪlətɪ [-lɪt-]
culpab|le, -ly, -leness ˈkʌlpəb|l, -lɪ, -lnɪs [-nəs]
culprit, -s ˈkʌlprɪt, -s
Culross (*place in Scotland*) ˈkuːrɒs [-rəs], (*Scottish surname*) ˈkuːrɒs [-rəs], (*English surname*) ˈkʌlrɒs, (*street in London*) ˈkʌlrɒs [kʌlˈrɒs]
cult, -s kʌlt, -s
Culter (*in Scotland*) ˈkuːtə*
cultivable ˈkʌltɪvəbl
cultivat|e, -es, -ing, -ed, -or/s; -able ˈkʌltɪveɪt, -s, -ɪŋ, -ɪd, -ə*/z; -əbl
cultivation ˌkʌltɪˈveɪʃn
Cults kʌlts
cultur|able, -al ˈkʌltʃər|əbl [-tʃʊr-], -əl
culture, -s, -d ˈkʌltʃə*, -z, -d
culver, -s ˈkʌlvə*, -z
culverin, -s ˈkʌlvərɪn, -z
culvert, -s; -age ˈkʌlvət, -s; -ɪdʒ
Culzean (*in Strathclyde*) kəˈleɪn
cum kʌm
cumbent ˈkʌmbənt
cumb|er, -ers, -ering, -ered, -erer/s ˈkʌmb|ə*, -əz, -ərɪŋ, -əd, -ərə*/z
Cumberland ˈkʌmbələnd [-blənd]
cumbersome, -ly, -ness ˈkʌmbəsəm, -lɪ, -nɪs [-nəs]
Cumbria, -n/s ˈkʌmbrɪə, -n/z
cumbrous, -ly, -ness ˈkʌmbrəs, -lɪ, -nɪs [-nəs]
cumin ˈkʌmɪn
cummerbund, -s ˈkʌməbʌnd, -z
cummin ˈkʌmɪn
Cumming, -s ˈkʌmɪŋ, -z
Cummuskey (*surname*) ˈkʌmskɪ

Cumnor ˈkʌmnə*
cumulate (*adj.*) ˈkjuːmjʊlət [-mjəl-, -lɪt, -leɪt]
cumulat|e (*v.*), -es, -ing, -ed ˈkjuːmjʊleɪt [-mjəl-], -s, -ɪŋ, -ɪd
cumulation, -s ˌkjuːmjʊˈleɪʃn [-mjəˈl-], -z
cumulative, -ly, -ness ˈkjuːmjʊlətɪv [-mjəl-, -leɪt-], -lɪ, -nɪs [-nəs]
cumulus ˈkjuːmjʊləs [-mjəl-]
Cunard, -er/s kjuːˈnɑːd [*also* ˈ— *when attributive*], -ə*/z
cunctation, -s kʌŋkˈteɪʃn, -z
cunctator, -s kʌŋkˈteɪtə*, -z
Cund|all, -ell ˈkʌnd|l, -l
cuneiform ˈkjuːnɪfɔːm [-njɪf-, -nɪf-]
cuniform ˈkjuːnɪfɔːm
Cunliffe ˈkʌnlɪf
cunning (*s. adj.*), -est, -ly, -ness ˈkʌnɪŋ, -ɪst, -lɪ, -nɪs
Cunningham ˈkʌnɪŋəm
cup (*s. v.*), -s, -ping, -ped kʌp, -s, -ɪŋ, -t
Cupar ˈkuːpə*
cup-bearer, -s ˈkʌpˌbeərə*, -z
cupboard, -s ˈkʌbəd, -z
cupboard-love ˈkʌbədlʌv [ˌkʌbədˈl-]
cupful, -s ˈkʌpfʊl, -z
cupid (C.), -s ˈkjuːpɪd, -z
cupidity kjuːˈpɪdətɪ [kjʊ-, -ɪtɪ]
cupola, -s ˈkjuːpələ, -z
cupping-glass, -es ˈkʌpɪŋglɑːs, -ɪz
cupr|eous, -ic, -ous ˈkjuːpr|ɪəs, -ɪk, -əs
cupriferous kjuːˈprɪfərəs [kjʊ-]
cur, -s kɜː*, -z
curability ˌkjʊərəˈbɪlətɪ [ˌkjɔər- ˌkjɔːr-, -lɪt-]
curable ˈkjʊərəbl [ˈkjɔər-, ˈkjɔːr-]
curaç|ao (C.), -oa (C.) ˌkjʊərəˈs|əʊ [ˌkjɔər-, ˌkjɔːr-], -əʊə
curaç|y, -ies ˈkjʊərəs|ɪ [ˈkjɔər-, ˈkjɔːr-], -ɪz
Curan ˈkʌrən
curare kjʊˈrɑːrɪ [ˌkjʊəˈr-]
curate, -s ˈkjʊərət [ˈkjɔər-, ˈkjɔːr-, -rɪt], -s
curative ˈkjʊərətɪv [ˈkjɔər-, ˈkjɔːr-]
curator, -s; -ship/s ˌkjʊəˈreɪtə* [kjʊˈr-, kjɔəˈr-, kjɔːˈr-], -z; -ʃɪp/s
curb (*s. v.*), -s, -ing, -ed kɜːb, -z, -ɪŋ, -d
curbstone, -s ˈkɜːbstəʊn, -z
curd, -s kɜːd, -z
curd|le, -les, -ling, -led ˈkɜːd|l, -lz, -lɪŋ [-lɪŋ], -ld
curd|y, -ier, -iest, -iness ˈkɜːd|ɪ, -ɪə* [-jə*], -ɪɪst [-jɪst], -ɪnɪs [-ɪnəs]
cur|e (*s. v.*), -es, -ing, -ed, -er/s kjʊə* [kjɔə*, kjɔː*], -z, -rɪŋ, -d, -rə*/z
curfew, -s ˈkɜːfjuː, -z

cu|ria, -riae 'kjʊə|rɪə ['kjɔər-, 'kjɔːr-, 'kʊər-], -rɪː ['kʊərɪaɪ]

curie, -s 'kjʊərɪ, -z

curio, -s 'kjʊərɪoʊ ['kjɔər-, 'kjɔːr-], -z

curiosit|y, -ies ˌkjʊərɪ'ɒsət|ɪ [ˌkjɔər-, ˌkjɔːr-, -ɪt|ɪ], -ɪz

curious, -ly, -ness 'kjʊərɪəs ['kjɔər-, 'kjɔːr-], -lɪ, -nɪs [-nəs]

curium 'kjʊərɪəm

curl (s. v.), -s, -ing, -ed, -er/s kɜːl, -z, -ɪŋ, -d, -ə*/z

curlew, -s 'kɜːlju: [-luː], -z

curling (s.) 'kɜːlɪŋ

curling-iron, -s 'kɜːlɪŋ,aɪən, -z

curling-stone, -s 'kɜːlɪŋstəʊn, -z

curling-tongs 'kɜːlɪŋtɒŋz

curl|y, -ier, -iest 'kɜːl|ɪ, -ɪə* [-jə*], -ɪɪst [-jɪst]

curmudgeon, -s kɜː'mʌdʒən [kə'm-], -z

curr, -s, -ing, -ed kɜː*, -z, -ɪŋ, -d

curragh (C.), -s 'kʌrə, -z

Curran 'kʌrən

currant, -s 'kʌrənt, -s

currenc|y, -ies 'kʌrəns|ɪ, -ɪz

current (s. adj.), -s, -ly, -ness 'kʌrənt, -s, -lɪ, -nɪs [-nəs]

Currer 'kʌrə*

curricul|um, -a, -ar kə'rɪkjʊl|əm [-kjəl-], -ə, -ə*

Currie 'kʌrɪ

currish, -ly, -ness 'kɜːrɪʃ, -lɪ, -nɪs [-nəs]

curr|y (s. v.) (C.), -ies, -ying, -ied, -ier/s 'kʌr|ɪ, -ɪz, -ɪŋ, -ɪd, -ɪə*/z

curry-powder 'kʌrɪ,paʊdə*

curs|e (s. v.), -es, -ing, -ed kɜːs, -ɪz, -ɪŋ, -t

cursed (adj.), -ly, -ness 'kɜːsɪd, -lɪ, -nɪs [-nəs]

cursive, -ly, -ness 'kɜːsɪv, -lɪ, -nɪs [-nəs]

Cursor Mundi ˌkɜːsɔː'mʊndiː [-'mʌndaɪ]

cursor|y, -ily, -iness 'kɜːsər|ɪ, -əlɪ [-ɪlɪ], -ɪnɪs [-ɪnəs]

cursus 'kɜːsəs

curt, -er, -est, -ly, -ness kɜːt, -ə*, -ɪst, -lɪ, -nɪs [-nəs]

curtail, -s, -ing, -ed, -ment/s kɜː'teɪl, -z, -ɪŋ, -d, -mənt/s

curtain, -s, -ed 'kɜːtn [-tən, -tɪn], -z, -d

curtain-raiser, -s 'kɜːtn,reɪzə*, -z

curtesy 'kɜːtɪsɪ [-təsɪ]

Curti|ce, -s(s) 'kɜːtɪ|s, -s

curtsey (s. v.), -s, -ing, -ed 'kɜːtsɪ, -z, -ɪŋ [-jɪŋ], -d

curts|y (s. v.), -ies, -ying, -ied 'kɜːts|ɪ, -ɪz, -ɪŋ [-jɪŋ], -ɪd

curvaceous kɜː'veɪʃəs

curvation, -s kɜː'veɪʃn, -z

curvature, -s 'kɜːvətjə* [-,tʃʊə*, -,tjʊə*], -z

curv|e (s. v.), -es, -ing, -ed kɜːv, -z, -ɪŋ, -d

curvet (s. v.), -s, -(t)ing, -(t)ed kɜː'vet, -s, -ɪŋ, -ɪd

curviline|al, -ar ˌkɜːvɪ'lɪnɪ|əl [-njəl], -ə*

curvital 'kɜːvɪtl

Curwen 'kɜːwɪn [-wən]

Curzon 'kɜːzn

Cusack 'kjuːsæk, 'kjuːzək

cushat, -s 'kʌʃət [-ʃæt], -s

Cushing 'kʊʃɪŋ

cushi|on (s. v.), -ons, -oning, -oned 'kʊʃ|n [-ɪn], -nz [-ɪnz], -nɪŋ [-ənɪŋ, -ɪnɪŋ], -nd [-ɪnd]

Cushny 'kʌʃnɪ

cushy 'kʊʃɪ

Cusins 'kjuːzɪnz

cusp, -s kʌsp, -s

cuspidor, -s 'kʌspɪdɔː*, -z

cuss, -es kʌs, -ɪz

cussed, -ly, -ness 'kʌsɪd, -lɪ, -nɪs [-nəs]

Custance 'kʌstəns

custard, -s 'kʌstəd, -z

custard-apple, -s 'kʌstəd,æpl, -z

custodial kʌ'stəʊdjəl [-dɪəl]

custodian, -s kʌ'stəʊdjən [-dɪən], -z

custody 'kʌstədɪ

custom, -s 'kʌstəm, -z

customar|y, -ily, -iness 'kʌstəmər|ɪ, -əlɪ [-ɪlɪ], -ɪnɪs [-ɪnəs]

customer, -s 'kʌstəmə*, -z

custom-hou|se, -ses 'kʌstəmhaʊ|s, -zɪz

custos, custodes 'kʌstɒs, kʌ'stəʊdiːz

cut (s. v.), -s, -ting, -ter/s kʌt, -s, -ɪŋ, -ə*/z

cutaneous kjuː'teɪnjəs [kjʊ-, -nɪəs]

cut-away 'kʌtəweɪ

Cutch kʌtʃ (Hindi kəch)

cutcherr|y, -ies kʌ'tʃer|ɪ [kə'tʃ-], -ɪz

cute, -r, -st, -ly, -ness kjuːt, -ə*, -ɪst, -lɪ, -nɪs [-nəs]

Cutforth 'kʌtfɔːθ

Cuthbert, -son 'kʌθbət, -sn

cuticle, -s 'kjuːtɪkl

cuticular kjuː'tɪkjʊlə* [kjʊ-]

cutis 'kjuːtɪs

cutlass, -es 'kʌtləs, -ɪz

cutler, -s, -y 'kʌtlə*, -z, -rɪ

cutlet, -s 'kʌtlɪt [-lət], -s

cut-off, -s 'kʌtɒf [old-fashioned -ɔːf], -s

cut-out, -s 'kʌtaʊt, -s

Cuttell kə'tel

cutter, -s 'kʌtə*, -z

cut-throat, -s 'kʌtθrəʊt, -s

cutting (s.), -s 'kʌtɪŋ, -z

cuttle (C.), -s ; -bone 'kʌtl, -z; -bəʊn
cuttle-fish, -es 'kʌtlfɪʃ, -ɪz
cutt|y, -ies 'kʌt|ɪ, -ɪz
cutwater, -s 'kʌt,wɔ:tə*, -z
cuvette, -s kju:'vet (kyvɛt), -s
Cuvier 'kju:vɪeɪ ['ku:-] (kyvje)
Cuxhaven 'kʊks,hɑ:vn (kuks'ha:fən)
Cuyp, -s kaɪp, -s
cwm, -s ku:m [kʊm] (Welsh kum), -z
cwt., cwts. 'hʌndrədweɪt [-drɪd-], -s
cyanate 'saɪəneɪt
cyanic saɪ'ænɪk
cyanide, -s 'saɪənaɪd, -z
cyanogen saɪ'ænədʒɪn [-dʒen]
cybernetic, -s ,saɪbə'netɪk [-bə:'n-], -s
Cyclades 'sɪklədi:z
cyclamate, -s 'saɪkləmeɪt ['sɪk-], -s
cyclamen, -s 'sɪkləmən [-klɪm-], -z
cyc|le (s. v.), -les, -ling, -led 'saɪk|l, -lz, -lɪŋ, -ld
cyclic, -al, -ally 'saɪklɪk ['sɪk-], -l, -əlɪ
cyclist, -s 'saɪklɪst, -s
cyclograph, -s 'saɪkləʊgrɑ:f [-græf], -s
cycloid, -s 'saɪklɔɪd, -z
cycloidal saɪ'klɔɪdl
cyclometer, -s saɪ'klɒmɪtə* [-mətə*], -z
cyclone, -s 'saɪkləʊn, -z
cyclonic saɪ'klɒnɪk
cyclopaed|ia [-ped-], -ias, -ic ,saɪkləʊ-'pi:d|jə [-d|ɪə], -jəz [-ɪəz], -ɪk
cyclopean saɪ'kləʊpjən [-pɪən, ,saɪkləʊ-'pi:ən]
cyclops, cyclopes 'saɪklɒps, saɪ'kləʊpi:z
cyclorama, -s ,saɪklə'rɑ:mə, -z
cyclostyl|e (s. v.), -es, -ing, -ed 'saɪkləʊ-staɪl, -z, -ɪŋ, -d
cyclotron, -s 'saɪklətrɒn, -z
cyder, -s 'saɪdə*, -z
cygnet, -s 'sɪgnɪt [-nət], -s
Cygnus 'sɪgnəs
cylinder, -s 'sɪlɪndə*, -z
cylindric, -al, -ally sɪ'lɪndrɪk, -l, -əlɪ
cylindriform sɪ'lɪndrɪfɔ:m
cylindroid, -s 'sɪlɪndrɔɪd [sɪ'l-], -z
cyli|x, -ces 'saɪlɪ|ks, -si:z
cyma, -s, -ta 'saɪmə, -z, -tə
cymar, -s sɪ'mɑ:*, -z
cymbal, -s 'sɪmbl, -z

cymbalo, -s 'sɪmbələʊ, -z
Cymbeline 'sɪmbɪli:n [-bəl-]
cyme, -s saɪm, -z
Cymr|ic, -y 'kɪmr|ɪk, -ɪ
Cynewulf 'kɪnɪwʊlf ['kɪnə-]
cynic (s. adj.), -s, -al, -ally 'sɪnɪk, -s, -l, -əlɪ
cynicism, -s 'sɪnɪsɪzəm, -z
cynocephalic ,saɪnəʊse'fælɪk [-ke'f-]
cynocephalous ,saɪnəʊ'sefələs [-'kef-]
cynosure, -s 'sɪnə,zjʊə* ['saɪn-, -ə,ʒjʊə*, -ə,ʒʊə*, -ə,sjʊə*, -ə,ʃʊə*], -z
Cynthi|a, -us 'sɪnθɪ|ə [-θj|ə], -əs
cyph|er (s. v.), -ers, -ering, -ered 'saɪf|ə*, -əz, -ərɪŋ, -əd
cy près ,si:'preɪ
cypress, -es 'saɪprəs [-prɪs], -ɪz
Cyprian, -s 'sɪprɪən, -z
Cypriot, -s 'sɪprɪət [-rɪɒt], -s
Cypriote, -s 'sɪprɪəʊt, -s
Cyprus 'saɪprəs
Cyrenaica ,saɪəreɪə'neɪkə [-rɪ'n-, -'naɪkə]
Cyrene saɪ'ri:nɪ [,saɪə'r-]
Cyrenian saɪ'ri:njən [,saɪə'r-, sɪ'r-, -nɪən]
Cyrenius saɪ'ri:njəs [,saɪə'r-, -nɪəs]
Cyril 'sɪrəl [-rɪl]
Cyrille 'sɪrɪl, sɪ'ri:l
Cyrillic sɪ'rɪlɪk
Cyrus 'saɪərəs
cyst, -s, -ic, -oid sɪst, -s, -ɪk, -ɔɪd
cystitis sɪs'taɪtɪs
Cythera sɪ'θɪərə
Cytherean ,sɪθə'ri:ən [-'rɪən]
cytology saɪ'tɒlədʒɪ
czar (C.), -s zɑ:*, -z
czardas, -es 'tʃɑ:dæʃ ['zɑ:dæs, -dəs], -ɪz
czarevitch (C.), -es 'zɑ:rəvɪtʃ [-rɪv-], -ɪz
czarevna (C.), -s zɑ:'revnə, -z
czarina, -s zɑ:'ri:nə, -z
czarist, -s 'zɑ:rɪst, -s
Czech, -s tʃek, -s
Czechoslovak, -s ,tʃekəʊ'sləʊvæk, -s
Czechoslovakia, -n ,tʃekəʊsləʊ'vækɪə [-'vækjə, -'vɑ:kɪə, -'vɑ:kjə], -n
Czerny 'tʃɜ:nɪ ['zɜ:-]

D

D (*the letter*), **-'s** di:, -z

dab (*s. v.*), **-s, -bing, -bed, -ber/s** dæb, -z, -ɪŋ, -d, -ə*/z

dabb|le, -les, -ling, -led, -ler/s 'dæb|l, -lz, -lɪŋ [-lɪŋ], -ld, -lə*/z [-lə*/z]

dabchick, -s 'dæbtʃɪk, -s

da capo dɑ:'kɑ:pəʊ

dace deɪs

dachshund, -s 'dækshʊnd, -z

Da|cia, -cian/s 'deɪ|sjə [-sɪə, -ʃjə, -ʃɪə, -ʃə], -sjən/z [-sɪən/z, -ʃjən/z, -ʃɪən/z, -ʃn/z]

dacoit, -s, -age də'kɔɪt, -s, -ɪdʒ

Dacre, -s 'deɪkə*, -z

dacron 'dækrɒn ['deɪ-]

dactyl, -s 'dæktɪl, -z

dactylic dæk'tɪlɪk

dactylogram, -s dæk'tɪləʊɡræm ['----], -z

dactylography ˌdæktɪ'lɒɡrəfɪ

dad, -s dæd, -z

Dadaism 'dɑ:dəɪzəm

Daddo 'dædəʊ

dadd|y, -ies 'dæd|ɪ, -ɪz

daddy-long-legs ˌdædɪ'lɒŋleɡz

dado, -s 'deɪdəʊ, -z

Daedalus 'di:dələs

daemon, -s 'di:mən, -z

daemonic di:'mɒnɪk [dɪ-]

D'Aeth deɪθ

daffadowndill|y, -ies ˌdæfədaʊn'dɪl|ɪ, -ɪz

daffodil, -s 'dæfədɪl, -z

daft, -er, -est, -ly, -ness dɑ:ft, -ə*, -ɪst, -lɪ, -nɪs [-nəs]

dag, -s dæg, -z

dagger, -s 'dægə*, -z

Daggett 'dæɡɪt

dago, -(e)s 'deɪɡəʊ, -z

dagoba, -s 'dɑ:ɡəbə, -z

Dagobert 'dæɡəʊbə:t

Dagon 'deɪɡɒn [-ɡən]

Dagonet 'dæɡənət [-nɪt]

daguerr(e)otype, -s də'ɡerəʊtaɪp, -s

D'Aguilar 'dæɡwɪlə*

dahlia, -s 'deɪljə [-ɪə], -z

Dahomey də'həʊmɪ

Dai daɪ

Daiches (*surname*) 'deɪʃɪz, 'deɪtʃɪz

Dáil Eireann ˌdaɪl'eərən [ˌdɔɪl-, *rarely* ˌdɑ:l-, ˌdɔ:l-]

dail|y (*s. adj. adv.*), **-ies** 'deɪl|ɪ, -ɪz

Daimler (*car*), **-s** 'deɪmlə*, -z

Dain, -es deɪn, -z

Daintree 'deɪntrɪ [-trɪ]

daint|y (*s. adj.*), **-ies; -ier, -iest, -ily, -iness** 'deɪnt|ɪ, -ɪz; -ɪə* [-jə*], -ɪɪst [-jɪst], -ɪlɪ [-əlɪ], -ɪnɪs [-ɪnəs]

Dairen daɪ'ren

dair|y, -ies 'deər|ɪ, -ɪz

dairy-farm, -s 'deərɪfɑ:m, -z

dairymaid, -s 'deərɪmeɪd, -z

dairy|man, -men 'deərɪ|mən [-mæn], -mən [-men]

dais, -es 'deɪɪs [deɪs], -ɪz

dais|y (**D.**), **-ies** 'deɪz|ɪ, -ɪz

daisy-chain, -s 'deɪzɪtʃeɪn, -z

Dakar 'dækə*, 'dækɑ:*

Dakota, -s də'kəʊtə, -z

Dalai Lama, -s ˌdælaɪ'lɑ:mə [ˌdɑ:laɪ-, dəˌlaɪ-], -z

Dalbeattie dæl'bi:tɪ

Dalbiac 'dɔ:lbɪæk

Dalby 'dɔ:lbɪ, 'dælbɪ

Daldy 'dældɪ

dale (**D.**), **-s** deɪl, -z

dales|man, -men 'deɪlz|mən [-mæn], -mən [-men]

Dalgleish dæl'ɡli:ʃ

Dalhousie dæl'haʊzɪ

Dalila də'laɪlə

Dalkeith dæl'ki:θ

Dalkey (*suburb of Dublin*) 'dɔ:kɪ

Dallam 'dæləm

Dallas 'dæləs

dalliance 'dælɪəns [-ljəns]

dall|y, -ies, -ying, -ied, -ier/s 'dæl|ɪ, -ɪz, -ɪŋ, -ɪd, -ɪə*/z

Dalmanutha ˌdælmə'nu:θə [-'nju:-]

Dalma|tia, -tian/s dæl'meɪ|ʃjə [-ʃɪə, -ʃə], -ʃjən/z [-ʃɪən/z, -ʃn/z]

Dalmeny dæl'menɪ

Dalnaspidal ˌdælnə'spɪdl

Dalny 'dælnɪ

Dalry dæl'raɪ

Dalrymple dæl'rɪmpl [dəl'r-], 'dælrɪmpl
Note.—*The family name of the Earl of Stair is* dæl'r- [dəl'r-].

Dalston 'dɔːlstən ['dɒl-]
Dalton 'dɔːltən ['dɒl-]
Dalua dæ'luːə [də'l-]
Dalwhinnie dæl'wɪnɪ [-'hw-]
Daly 'deɪlɪ
Dalyell 'dæljəl, di:'el
Dalzell dæl'zeɫ, di:'el
Dalziel 'dælzɪəl [-zjəl], 'dæljəl [-lɪəl], di:'el
Note.—The form di:'el is chiefly used in Scotland.
dam (s. v.), -s, -ming, -med dæm, -z, -ɪŋ, -d
damag|e (s. v.), -es, -ing, -ed 'dæmɪdʒ, -ɪz, -ɪŋ, -d
Damaraland də'mɑːrələænd ['dæmərə-]
Damaris 'dæmərɪs
damascene, -s 'dæməsiːn [ˌdæmə's-], -z
Damascus də'mɑːskəs [-'mæs-]
damask, -s 'dæməsk, -s
dame, -s deɪm, -z
Damien 'deɪmjən [-mɪən]
damn, -s, -ing, -ed dæm, -z, -ɪŋ, -d
damnab|le, -ly, -leness 'dæmnəb|l, -lɪ, -lnɪs [-nəs]
damnation, -s dæm'neɪʃn, -z
damnatory 'dæmnətərɪ
damni|fy, -fies, -fying, -fied 'dæmnɪ|faɪ, -faɪz, -faɪɪŋ, -faɪd
Damocles 'dæməkliːz
Damon 'deɪmən [-mɒn]
damosel, -s 'dæməʊzel, -z
damp (s. adj. v.), -er, -est, -ly, -ness, -ish; -s, -ing, -ed dæmp, -ə*, -ɪst, -lɪ, -nɪs [-nəs], -ɪʃ; -s, -ɪŋ, -t [dæmt]
damp-course, -s 'dæmpkɔːs [-kɔəs], -ɪz
damp|en, -ens, -ening, -ened 'dæmp|ən, -ənz, -nɪŋ [-ənɪŋ], bne- [ɪŋ]
damper, -s 'dæmpə*, -z
Dampier 'dæmpjə* [-pɪə*, -ˌpɪə*]
damp-proof 'dæmppruːf
damsel, -s 'dæmzl, -z
damson, -s 'dæmzən, -z
dan (D.), -s dæn, -z
Dana (personal name) (in U.S.A.) 'deɪnə, (in Canada) 'dænə
Danaë 'dæneri: [-niː]
Danakil ˌdænə'kiːl
Danbury 'dænbərɪ
Danby 'dænbɪ
danc|e (s. v.), -es, -ing, -ed, -er/s dɑːns, -ɪz, -ɪŋ, -t, -ə*/z
Dance dɑːns, dæns
dance-music dɑːns,mjuːzɪk
Dancer (surname) 'dɑːnsə*
dancing-girl, -s 'dɑːnsɪŋgɜːl, -z
dancing-master, -s 'dɑːnsɪŋˌmɑːstə*, -z

dancing-mistress, -es 'dɑːnsɪŋˌmɪstrɪs [-əs], -ɪz
Danckwerts 'dæŋkwəːts
dandelion, -s 'dændɪlaɪən, -z
dandiacal dæn'daɪəkl
dandi|fy, -fies, -fying, -fied 'dændɪ|faɪ, -faɪz, -faɪɪŋ, -faɪd
dand|le, -les, -ling, -led 'dænd|l, -lz, -lɪŋ [-lɪŋ], -ld
dandr|iff, -uff 'dændr|ɪf, -ʌf [-əf]
dand|y, -ies; -yish, -yism 'dænd|ɪ, -ɪz; -ɪʃ [-jɪʃ], -ɪɪzəm
Dane, -s deɪn, -z
danegeld 'deɪngeld
Dane|lagh, -law 'deɪn|lɔː, -lɔː
danger, -s 'deɪndʒə*, -z
Dangerfield 'deɪndʒəfiːld
dangerous, -ly, -ness 'deɪndʒərəs, -lɪ, -nɪs [-nəs]
danger-signal, -s 'deɪndʒəˌsɪgnl [-nəl], -z
dang|le (D.), -les, -ling, -led, -ler/s 'dæŋg|l, -lz, -lɪŋ [-lɪŋ], -ld, -lə*/z [-ɭə*/z]
Daniel(l), -s 'dænjəl, -z
Danish 'deɪnɪʃ
Danite, -s 'dænaɪt, -s
dank, -er, -est, -ly, -ness dæŋk, -ə*, -ɪst, -lɪ, -nɪs [-nəs]
Dannatt 'dænət
Dannemora ˌdænɪ'mɔːrə
Dannreuther 'dænrɔɪtə*
danseuse, -s dɑːn'sɜːz [dɑ̃ːn's-, dɔ̃ːn's-] (dɑ̃søːz), -ɪz
Dansville 'dænzvɪl
Dante 'dæntɪ ['dɑːn-, -teɪ]
Dantzic 'dæntsɪk
Danube 'dænjuːb
Danubian dæ'njuːbjən [də'n-, -bɪən]
Dan|vers, -ville 'dæn|vəz, -vɪl
Danzig 'dæntsɪg [-ɪk] ('dantsiç)
Daphn|e, -is 'dæfn|ɪ, -ɪs
dapper (D.), -est 'dæpə*, -rɪst
dappled 'dæpld
dapple-grey ˌdæpl'greɪ
darbies 'dɑːbɪz
Darbishire 'dɑːbɪʃə* [-ˌʃɪə*]
Darby 'dɑːbɪ
D'Arcy, Darcy 'dɑːsɪ
Dardanelles ˌdɑːdə'nelz [-dn̩'elz]
Dardani|a, -us dɑː'deɪnjə [-nɪ|ə], -əs
Dardanus 'dɑːdənəs
dar|e (D.), -es, -ing, -ed, durst deə*, -z, -rɪŋ, -d, dɜːst
dare-devil, -s 'deə,devl, -z
daren't deənt
Darenth 'dærənθ
Dares 'deəriːz

123

daresay ˌdeə'seɪ [also '-- according to
    sentence-stress]
Daresbury (Baron) 'dɑ:zbərɪ
Dar-es-Salaam ˌdɑ:ressə'lɑːm
Darfield 'dɑ:fiːld
Darfur 'dɑ:fə* [dɑ:'fɜ:*]
Dargue dɑːg
Darien 'deərɪən, 'dær-
daring (adj.), -ly 'deərɪŋ, -lɪ
Darius də'raɪəs
Darjeeling dɑ:'dʒiːlɪŋ
dark, -er, -est, -ly, -ness dɑːk, -ə*, -ɪst,
    -lɪ, -nɪs [-nəs]
dark|en, -ens, -ening, -ened 'dɑːk|ən,
    -ənz, -nɪŋ [-ŋ, -ənɪŋ], -ənd
dark-haired ˌdɑːk'heəd ['-- when attri-
    butive]
darkish 'dɑːkɪʃ
darkling 'dɑːklɪŋ
dark-room, -s 'dɑːkrʊm [-ruːm], -z
dark-skinned 'dɑːkskɪnd [also ˌ-'- when
    not attributive]
darksome 'dɑːksəm
dark|y, -ies 'dɑːk|ɪ, -ɪz
Darlaston 'dɑːləstən
Darley 'dɑːlɪ
darling (D.), -s 'dɑːlɪŋ, -z
Darlington 'dɑːlɪŋtən
Darmady (surname) dɑː'meɪdɪ
Darmstadt 'dɑːmstæt ('darmʃtat)
darn (s. v.), -s, -ing, -ed dɑːn, -z, -ɪŋ,
    -d
darnel 'dɑːnl
darning-needle, -s 'dɑːnɪŋˌniːdl, -z
Darnley 'dɑːnlɪ
Darracq 'dærək
Darrell 'dærəl
Darsie 'dɑːsɪ
dart (s. v.) (D.), -s, -ing, -ed dɑːt, -s, -ɪŋ,
    -ɪd
darter, -s 'dɑːtə*, -z
Dartford 'dɑːtfəd
Dartie 'dɑːtɪ
Dartle 'dɑːtl
Dartmoor 'dɑːtˌmʊə* [-mɔə*, -mɔː*]
Dartmouth 'dɑːtməθ
Darton 'dɑːtn
Darwen 'dɑːwɪn
Darwin, -ism 'dɑːwɪn, -ɪzəm
Darwinian dɑː'wɪnɪən [-njən]
Daryll 'dærɪl
Dasent 'deɪsənt
dash (s. v.) (D.), -es, -ing, -ed, -er/s
    dæʃ, -ɪz, -ɪŋ, -t, -ə*/z
dash-board, -s 'dæʃbɔːd [-bɔəd], -z
dashing (adj.), -ly 'dæʃɪŋ, -lɪ
Dashwood 'dæʃwʊd
dastard, -s 'dæstəd ['dɑːs-], -z

dastardl|y (adj.), -iness 'dæstədl|ɪ
    ['dɑːs-], -ɪnɪs [-ɪnəs]
data (plur. of datum) 'deɪtə ['dɑːtə]
datar|y, -ies 'deɪtər|ɪ, -ɪz
Datchˌery, -et 'dætʃ|ərɪ, -ɪt
dat|e (s. v.), -es, -ing, -ed deɪt, -s, -ɪŋ, -ɪd
date-palm, -s 'deɪtpɑːm, -z
date-tree, -s 'deɪttriː, -z
Dathan 'deɪθæn [-θən]
datival də'taɪvl [deɪ't-]
dative (s. adj.), -s 'deɪtɪv, -z
Datsun 'dætsən [-tsʊn]
dat|um, -a 'deɪt|əm ['dɑːt-], -ə
daub (s. v.), -s, -ing, -ed, -er/s dɔːb,
    -z, -ɪŋ, -d, -ə*/z
Daubeney 'dɔːbənɪ
Daudet 'dəʊdeɪ (dodɛ)
daughter, -s 'dɔːtə*, -z
daughter-in-law, daughters-in-law
    'dɔːtərɪnlɔː [-təɪn-], 'dɔːtəzɪnlɔː
daughterl|y, -iness 'dɔːtəl|ɪ, -ɪnɪs [-ɪnəs]
Daukes dɔːks
Daulis 'dɔːlɪs
Daun dɔːn
daunt (D.), -s, -ing, -ed dɔːnt, -s, -ɪŋ, -ɪd
dauntless, -ly, -ness 'dɔːntlɪs [-ləs], -lɪ,
    -nɪs [-nəs]
dauphin (D.), -s 'dɔːfɪn, -z
Dauphine 'dɔːfɪn [-fiːn]
Dauphiné 'dəʊfɪneɪ [-nɪ] (dofine)
dauphiness (D.), -es 'dɔːfɪnɪs [-nes], -ɪz
Davenant 'dævɪnənt
davenport (D.), -s 'dævnpɔːt [-vmp-], -s
Daventry 'dævəntrɪ [old-fashioned local
    pronunciation 'deɪntrɪ]
Davey 'deɪvɪ
David, -s 'deɪvɪd, -z
Davidge 'dævɪdʒ
Davidson 'deɪvɪdsn
Davies 'deɪvɪs
Davis 'deɪvɪs
Davison 'deɪvɪsn
davit, -s 'dævɪt, -s
Davos 'dɑːvɒs [-vəʊs, dɑː'vəʊs]
dav|y (D.), -ies 'deɪv|ɪ, -ɪz
davy-lamp, -s 'deɪvɪlæmp [ˌ--'-], -s
daw (D.), -s dɔː, -z
dawd|le, -les, -ling, -led, -ler/s 'dɔːd|l,
    -lz, -lɪŋ [-lɪŋ], -ld, -lə*/z [-lə*/z]
Dawdon 'dɔːdn
Dawe, -s dɔː, -z
Dawk|es, -ins 'dɔːk|s, -ɪnz
Dawl|ey, -ish 'dɔːl|ɪ, -ɪʃ
dawn (s. v.) (D.), -s, -ing, -ed dɔːn, -z,
    -ɪŋ, -d
Dawson 'dɔːsn
day (D.), -s deɪ, -z
day-boarder, -s 'deɪˌbɔːdə* [-ˌbɔəd-], -z

day-book, -s 'deɪbʊk, -s
day-boy, -s 'deɪbɔɪ, -z
daybreak, -s 'deɪbreɪk, -s
day-dream, -s 'deɪdriːm, -z
day-labour, -er/s 'deɪ,leɪbə* [,deɪ'l-],
  -rə*/z
Daylesford 'deɪlzfəd [-lsf-]
daylight 'deɪlaɪt
daylight-saving 'deɪlaɪt,seɪvɪŋ [,--'--]
day-lil|y, -ies 'deɪ,lɪl|ɪ [,deɪ'l-], -ɪz
day-nurser|y, -ies 'deɪ,nɜːsər|ɪ [,-'---],
  -ɪz
day-school, -s 'deɪskuːl, -z
dayspring 'deɪsprɪŋ
day-star, -s 'deɪstɑː*, -z
day-time 'deɪtaɪm
Dayton 'deɪtn
Daytona deɪ'təʊnə
daywork 'deɪwɜːk
daz|e, -es, -ing, -ed, -edly deɪz, -ɪz, -ɪŋ,
  -d, -ɪdlɪ
dazz|le, -les, -ling/ly, -led 'dæz|l, -lz,
  -lɪŋ/lɪ [-lɪŋ/lɪ], -ld
D-day 'diːdeɪ
D.D.T. ,diːdiː'tiː
de (note in Tonic Sol-fa), -s diː, -z
deacon (D.), -s 'diːkən, -z
deaconess, -es 'diːkənɪs [-knɪs, -es], -ɪz
deacon|hood, -ry, -ries, -ship/s 'diːkən|-
  hʊd, -rɪ, -rɪz, -ʃɪp/s
dead ded
dead-alive ,dedə'laɪv
dead-beat ,ded'biːt
dead-drunk ,ded'drʌŋk
dead|en, -ens, -ening, -ened 'ded|n,
  -nz, -nɪŋ [-nɪŋ], -nd
dead-eye (D.), -s 'dedaɪ, -z
deadhead, -s 'dedhed, -z
dead-heat, -s ,ded'hiːt ['--], -s
dead-letter, -s ,ded'letə*, -z
deadline, -s 'dedlaɪn, -z
deadlock, -s 'dedlɒk, -s
deadl|y, -ier, -iest, -iness 'dedl|ɪ, -ɪə*
  [-jə*], -ɪɪst [-jɪst], -ɪnɪs [-nəs]
dead-march, -es ,ded'mɑːtʃ, -ɪz
dead-nettle, -s ,ded'netl ['-,--], -z
dead-pan ,ded'pæn ['--]
dead-reckoning, -s ,ded'rekənɪŋ [-kənɪŋ],
  -z
dead-set, -s ,ded'set ['--], -s
dead-wall, -s ,ded'wɔːl, -z
dead-water, -s 'ded,wɔːtə*, -z
dead-weight, -s 'dedweɪt [,-'-], -s
deaf, -er, -est, -ly, -ness def, -ə*, -ɪst,
  -lɪ, -nɪs [-nəs]
deaf-aid, -s 'defeɪd, -z
deaf|en, -ens, -ening, -ened 'def|n, -nz,
  -nɪŋ [-nɪŋ], -nd

deaf-mute, -s ,def'mjuːt, -s
Deakin 'diːkɪn
deal (s. v.) (D.), -s, -ing/s, dealt,
  dealer/s diːl, -z, -ɪŋ/z, delt, 'diːlə*/z
Dealtry (surname) 'dɔːltrɪ, 'dɪəltrɪ,
  (road in London) 'deltrɪ
dean, -s ; -ship/s diːn, -z; -ʃɪp/s
Dean(e) diːn
deaner|y, -ies 'diːnər|ɪ, -ɪz
Deans diːnz
dear (s. adj. interj.), -s; -er, -est, -ly,
  -ness dɪə*, -z; -rə*, -rɪst, -lɪ, -nɪs
  [-nəs]
Dearmer 'dɪəmə*
dearth (D.), -s dɜːθ, -s
dear|y, -ies 'dɪər|ɪ, -ɪz
Dease diːs
death, -s deθ, -s
Death (surname) deɪθ, deθ, diːθ, diː'æθ
  [dɪ'æθ]
deathbed, -s 'deθbed, -z
death-bell, -s 'deθbel, -z
death-blow, -s 'deθbləʊ, -z
death-dut|y, -ies 'deθ,djuːt|ɪ, -ɪz
death|less, -like 'deθ|lɪs [-ləs], -laɪk
death|ly, -lier, -liest, -liness 'deθ|lɪ, -lɪə*
  [-ljə*], -lɪst [-ljɪst], -lɪnɪs [-nəs]
death-mask, -s 'deθmɑːsk, -s
death-rate, -s 'deθreɪt, -s
death-rattle, -s 'deθ,rætl, -z
death's-head, -s 'deθshed, -z
death-trap, -s 'deθtræp, -s
death-warrant, -s 'deθ,wɒrənt, -s
death-watch 'deθwɒtʃ
débâcle, -s deɪ'bɑːkl [de'b-, dɪ'b-], -z
debar, -s, -ring, -red dɪ'bɑː*, -z, -rɪŋ,
  -d
debark, -s, -ing, -ed dɪ'bɑːk, -s, -ɪŋ, -t
debarkation, -s ,diːbɑː'keɪʃn, -z
debas|e, -es, -ing/ly, -ed, -ement
  dɪ'beɪs, -ɪz, -ɪŋ/lɪ, -t, -mənt
debatab|le, -ly dɪ'beɪtəb|l, -lɪ
debat|e (s. v.), -es, -ing, -ed, -er/s
  dɪ'beɪt, -s, -ɪŋ, -ɪd, -ə*/z
De Bathe də'bɑːθ
debauch (s. v.), -es, -ing, -ed, -er/s
  dɪ'bɔːtʃ, -ɪz, -ɪŋ, -t, -ə*/z
debauchee, -s ,debɔː'tʃiː [-ɔː'ʃiː], -z
debaucher|y, -ies dɪ'bɔːtʃər|ɪ, -ɪz
Debbitch 'debɪtʃ
Debeney 'debənɪ
Debenham 'debənəm [-bnəm, -bn̩əm]
debenture, -s dɪ'bentʃə* [də'b-], -z
debile 'diːbaɪl
debilitat|e, -es, -ing, -ed dɪ'bɪlɪteɪt
  [-lət-], -s, -ɪŋ, -ɪd
debilitation dɪ,bɪlɪ'teɪʃn [-lə't-]
debility dɪ'bɪlətɪ [-ɪtɪ]

125

debit (s. v.), -s, -ing, -ed 'debɪt, -s, -ɪŋ, -ɪd
De Blaquiere də'blækɪə*
debonair, -ly, -ness ˌdebə'neə* [-ɒɒ'n-],
  -lɪ, -nɪs [-nəs]
Deborah 'debərə
debouch, -es, -ing, -ed, -ment dɪ'baʊtʃ
  [-'buːʃ], -ɪz, -ɪŋ, -t, -mənt
De Bourgh də'bɔːg
De Bow də'bəʊ
Debrett də'bret [dɪ'b-]
debris 'deɪbriː ['deb-, -brɪ]
debt, -s det, -s
debtor, -s 'detə*, -z
debunk, -s, -ing, -ed ˌdiː'bʌŋk, -s, -ɪŋ,
  -t [-'bʌŋt]
De Bunsen də'bʌnsn
De Burgh də'bɔːg
Debussy də'buːsi: [-'buːs-, -'bjuːs-, -sɪ]
  (dəbysi)
début, -s 'deɪbuː ['deb-, -bjuː, -'-]
  (deby), -z
débutant, -s 'debjuːtã:ŋ ['deɪb-, -bjʊ-,
  -tɑːŋ, -tɔːŋ, -tɒŋ] (debytã), -z
débutante, -s 'debjuːtɑːnt ['deɪb-,
  -bjʊ-, -tænt, -tã:nt, -tɒnt] (debytã:t),
  -s
decachord, -s 'dekəkɔːd, -z
decade, -s 'dekeɪd [-kəd, -kɪd, dɪ'keɪd,
  de'keɪd], -z
decaden|ce, -cy, -t 'dekədən|s [dɪ'keɪd-,
  de'keɪd-], -sɪ, -t
decagon, -s 'dekəgən, -z
decagram(me), -s 'dekəgræm, -z
decalcification 'diːˌkælsɪfɪ'keɪʃn
decalci|fy, -fies, -fying, -fied ˌdiː'kælsɪ|-
  faɪ, -faɪz, -faɪɪŋ, -faɪd
decalitre, -s 'dekəˌliːtə*, -z
decalogue, -s 'dekəlɒg, -z
Decameron dɪ'kæmərən [de'k-]
decametre, -s 'dekəˌmiːtə*, -z
decamp, -s, -ing, -ed dɪ'kæmp [ˌdiː-], -s,
  -ɪŋ, -t [dɪ'kæmt]
decanal dɪ'keɪnl [de'k-]
decani dɪ'keɪnaɪ [de'k-]
decant, -s, -ing, -ed dɪ'kænt [ˌdiː-], -s,
  -ɪŋ, -ɪd
decantation, -s ˌdiːkæn'teɪʃn, -z
decanter, -s dɪ'kæntə*, -z
decapitat|e, -es, -ing, -ed dɪ'kæpɪteɪt
  [ˌdiː'k-], -s, -ɪŋ, -ɪd
decapitation, -s dɪˌkæpɪ'teɪʃn [diːˌk-], -z
decapod, -s 'dekəpɒd, -z
Decapolis dɪ'kæpəlɪs [de'k-]
decarbonization [-isa-] diːˌkɑːbənaɪ-
  'zeɪʃn ['diːˌkɑːbənaɪ'z-, -bənɪ'z-,
  -bɲaɪ'z-, -bɲɪ'z-]
decarboniz|e [-is|e], -es, -ing, -ed ˌdiː-
  'kɑːbənaɪz [-bɲaɪz], -ɪz, -ɪŋ, -d

decarburiz|e [-is|e], -es, -ing, -ed
  ˌdiː'kɑːbjʊəraɪz, -ɪz, -ɪŋ, -d
decasyllabic ˌdekəsɪ'læbɪk
decasyllable, -s 'dekəsɪləbl, -z
decathlon, -s dɪ'kæθlɒn [de-, -lən], -z
decay (s. v.), -s, -ing, -ed dɪ'keɪ, -z, -ɪŋ,
  -d
Decca 'dekə
Deccan 'dekən [-kæn] (Hindi dəkhən)
deceas|e (s. v.), -es, -ing, -ed dɪ'siːs, -ɪz,
  -ɪŋ, -t
deceit, -s dɪ'siːt, -s
deceit|ful, -fully, -fulness dɪ'siːt|fʊl,
  -fʊlɪ [-fəlɪ], -fʊlnɪs [-nəs]
deceivable, -ness dɪ'siːvəbl, -nɪs [-nəs]
deceiv|e, -es, -ing, -ed, -er/s dɪ'siːv, -z,
  -ɪŋ, -d, -ə*/z
decelerat|e, -es, -ing, -ed ˌdiː'seləreɪt,
  -s, -ɪŋ, -ɪd
deceleration, -s 'diːˌselə'reɪʃn [-ˌ--'--],
  -z
December, -s dɪ'sembə* [diː's-], -z
decemvir, -s dɪ'semvə* [-vɜː*], -z
decemvirate, -s dɪ'semvɪrət [-vər-, -rɪt],
  -s
decen|cy, -cies, -t/ly 'diːsn|sɪ, -sɪz,
  -t/lɪ
decennial dɪ'senjəl [de's-, diː's-, -nɪəl]
decentralization [-isa-] diːˌsentrəlaɪ-
  'zeɪʃn ['diːˌsentrəlaɪ'z-, -trʃaɪ'z-,
  -trəlɪ'z-, -tr̩lɪ'z-]
decentraliz|e [-is|e], -es, -ing, -ed
  ˌdiː'sentrəlaɪz, -ɪz, -ɪŋ, -d
deception, -s dɪ'sepʃn, -z
deceptive, -ly, -ness dɪ'septɪv, -lɪ, -nɪs
  [-nəs]
decibel, -s 'desɪbel [-bəl, -bl], -z
decid|e, -es, -ing, -ed/ly, -er/s dɪ'saɪd,
  -z, -ɪŋ, -ɪd/lɪ, -ə*/z
deciduous, -ly, -ness dɪ'sɪdjʊəs [-djwəs],
  -lɪ, -nɪs [-nəs]
Decies 'diːʃɪz
decigram(me), -s 'desɪgræm, -z
decilitre, -s 'desɪˌliːtə*, -z
decillion, -s dɪ'sɪljən [diː's-], -z
decim|al, -als, -ally 'desɪm|l [-səm-],
  -lz, -əlɪ
decimaliz|e [-is|e], -es, -ing, -ed 'desɪ-
  məlaɪz [-səm-], -ɪz, -ɪŋ, -d
decimalization [-isation] ˌdesɪmələr-
  'zeɪʃn [-səm-, -mʃaɪ-, -ɪ'zeɪ-]
decimat|e, -es, -ing, -ed, -or/s 'desɪ-
  meɪt, -s, -ɪŋ, -ɪd, -ə*/z
decimation ˌdesɪ'meɪʃn
decimetre, -s 'desɪˌmiːtə*, -z
deciph|er, -ers, -ering, -ered dɪ'saɪf|ə*,
  -əz, -ərɪŋ, -əd
decipherable dɪ'saɪfərəbl

decision, -s dɪ'sɪʒn, -z
decisive, -ly, -ness dɪ'saɪsɪv [-aɪzɪv], -lɪ, -nɪs [-nəs]
Decius 'di:ʃjəs [-ʃɪəs, -sjəs, -sɪəs, 'dekɪəs, 'desɪəs]
deck (s. v.), -s, -ing, -ed, -er/s dek, -s, -ɪŋ, -t, -ə*/z
deck-cabin, -s ˌdek'kæbɪn [also '-ˌ-- for contrast], -z
deck-chair, -s 'dektʃeə* [ˌ-'-], -z
deck-hand, -s 'dekhænd, -z
deck-hou|se, -ses 'dekhaʊ|s, -zɪz
deckle, -s 'dekl, -z
deckle-edge, -d ˌdekl'edʒ ['dekɭedʒ], -d
deck-passenger, -s 'dekˌpæsɪndʒə*, [-sən-], -z
declaim, -s, -ing, -ed, -er/s; -ant/s dɪ'kleɪm, -z, -ɪŋ, -d, -ə*/z; -ənt/s
declamation, -s ˌdeklə'meɪʃn, -z
declamatory dɪ'klæmətərɪ
declarable dɪ'kleərəbl
declaration, -s ˌdeklə'reɪʃn, -z
declarat|ive/ly, -ory dɪ'klærət|ɪv/lɪ [-'kleər-], -ərɪ
declar|e, -es, -ing, -ed, -er/s dɪ'kleə*, -z, -rɪŋ, -d, -rə*/z
declass, -es, -ing, -ed ˌdi:'klɑ:s [-'-], -ɪz, -ɪŋ, -t
declension, -s dɪ'klenʃn, -z
declination, -s ˌdeklɪ'neɪʃn, -z
declin|e (s. v.), -es, -ing, -ed; -able dɪ'klaɪn, -z, -ɪŋ, -d; -əbl
declinometer, -s ˌdeklɪ'nɒmɪtə* [-mətə*], -z
declivitous, -ly, -ness dɪ'klɪvɪtəs, -lɪ, -nɪs [-nəs]
declivit|y, -ies dɪ'klɪvət|ɪ [-rt|ɪ], -ɪz
declutch, -es, -ing, -ed ˌdi:'klʌtʃ ['di:klʌtʃ], -ɪz, -ɪŋ, -t
decoct, -s, -ing, -ed dɪ'kɒkt, -s, -ɪŋ, -ɪd
decoction, -s dɪ'kɒkʃn, -z
decod|e, -es, -ing, -ed ˌdi:'kəʊd, -z, -ɪŋ, -ɪd
décolletage ˌdeɪkɒl'tɑ:ʒ [-'--] (dekɔlta:ʒ)
décolleté(e) deɪ'kɒlteɪ [de'k-, dɪ'k-] (dekɔlte)
decolo(u)rization [-isa-] di:ˌkʌləraɪ-'zeɪʃn ['di:ˌk-]
decolo(u)riz|e [-is|e], -es, -ing, -ed di:'kʌləraɪz, -ɪz, -ɪŋ, -d
decompos|e, -es, -ing, -ed; -able ˌdi:kəm'pəʊz, -ɪz, -ɪŋ, -d; -əbl
decomposition, -s ˌdi:kɒmpə'zɪʃn, -z
decompound, -s, -ing, -ed ˌdi:kəm-'paʊnd, -z, -ɪŋ, -ɪd
decompress, -es, -ing, -ed, -er/s ˌdi:kəm'pres, -ɪz, -ɪŋ, -t, -ə*/z

decompression ˌdi:kəm'preʃn
deconsecrat|e, -es, -ing, -ed ˌdi:'kɒn-sɪkreɪt, -s, -ɪŋ, -ɪd
deconsecration, -s 'di:ˌkɒnsɪ'kreɪʃn, -z
decontaminat|e, -es, -ing, -ed ˌdi:kən-'tæmɪneɪt, -s, -ɪŋ, -ɪd
decontamination 'di:kənˌtæmɪ'neɪʃn
decontrol (s. v.), -s, -ling, -led ˌdi:kən-'trəʊl, -z, -ɪŋ, -d
decor, -s 'deɪkɔ:* ['dekɔ:*, dɪ'kɔ:*], -z
decorat|e, -es, -ing, -ed, -or/s 'dekəreɪt, -s, -ɪŋ, -ɪd, -ə*/z
decoration, -s ˌdekə'reɪʃn, -z
decorative, -ly, -ness 'dekərətɪv, -lɪ, -nɪs [-nəs]
decorous, -ly, -ness 'dekərəs [old-fashioned and poetical dɪ'kɔ:rəs], -lɪ, -nɪs [-nəs]
decorum dɪ'kɔ:rəm
De Courcy də'kʊəsɪ [-'kɔəs-, -'kɔ:s-], də'kɜ:sɪ
decoy (v.), -s, -ing, -ed dɪ'kɔɪ, -z, -ɪŋ, -d
decoy (s.), -s 'di:kɔɪ [dɪ'kɔɪ], -z
decoy-duck, -s dɪ'kɔɪdʌk [ˌdɪˌkɔɪ'd-], -s
decrease (s.), -s 'di:kri:s [di:'kri:s, dɪ'k-], -ɪz
decreas|e (v.), -es, -ing/ly, -ed di:'kri:s [dɪ'k-, 'di:k-], -ɪz, -ɪŋ/lɪ, -t
decree (s. v.), -s, -ing, -d dɪ'kri:, -z, -ɪŋ, -d
decree nisi dɪˌkri:'naɪsaɪ [-sɪ]
decrement, -s 'dekrɪmənt, -s
decrepit, -est, -ness; -ude dɪ'krepɪt, -ɪst, -nɪs [-nəs]; -ju:d
decrepitation, -s dɪˌkrepɪ'teɪʃn, -z
decrescendo, -s ˌdi:krɪ'ʃendəʊ, -z
De Crespigny də'krepɪnɪ, də'krespɪnɪ
decrial, -s dɪ'kraɪəl, -z
decr|y, -ies, -ying, -ied, -ier/s dɪ'kr|aɪ, -aɪz, -aɪɪŋ, -aɪd, -aɪə*/z
decumben|ce, -cy, -t/ly dɪ'kʌmbən|s, -sɪ, -t/lɪ
decup|le (s. adj. v.), -les, -ling, -led 'dekjʊp|l, -lz, -lɪŋ, -ld
Dedan, -ite/s 'di:dən, -aɪt/s
Deddes 'dedɪs
Deddington 'dedɪŋtən
Dedham 'dedəm
dedicat|e, -es, -ing, -ed, -or/s 'dedɪkeɪt, -s, -ɪŋ, -ɪd, -ə*/z
dedicatee, -s ˌdedɪkə'ti:, -z
dedication, -s ˌdedɪ'keɪʃn, -z
dedicatory 'dedɪkətərɪ [-keɪtrɪ, ˌdedɪ-'keɪtərɪ]
de Dion, -s də'di:ən [-'dɪ-, -'di:ɔ̃ːɳ, -'di:ɒŋ, -'di:ɒn] (dədjɔ̃), -z
Ded|lock, -man 'ded|lɒk, -mən

127

deduc|e, -es, -ing, -ed dɪ'dju:s, -ɪz, -ɪŋ, -t

deducibility dɪˌdju:sə'bɪlətɪ [-sɪ'b-, -lɪt-]
deducible dɪ'dju:səbl [-sɪb-]
deduct, -s, -ing, -ed ; -ive/ly dɪ'dʌkt, -s, -ɪŋ, -ɪd ; -ɪv/lɪ
deduction, -s dɪ'dʌkʃn, -z
Dee di:
deed, -s di:d, -z
Deedes di:dz
Deek(e)s di:ks
deem, -s, -ing, -ed di:m, -z, -ɪŋ, -d
Deems di:mz
deemster, -s 'di:mstə*, -z
deep (s. adj.), -s, -er, -est, -ly, -ness di:p, -s, -ə*, -ɪst, -lɪ, -nɪs [-nəs]
deep-drawn ˌdi:p'drɔ:n ['-- when attributive]
deep|en, -ens, -ening, -ened 'di:p|ən, -ənz, -ṇɪŋ [-ənɪŋ, -nɪŋ], -ənd
deep-freeze ˌdi:p'fri:z
deep-laid ˌdi:p'leɪd [also '-- when attributive]
deep-mouthed ˌdi:p'mavðd [-'mavθt, '-- when attributive]
deep-rooted ˌdi:p'ru:tɪd [also '-ˌ-- when attributive]
deep-sea ˌdi:p'si: [also '-- when attributive]
deep-seated ˌdi:p'si:tɪd [also '-ˌ-- when attributive]
deer dɪə*
Deerfield 'dɪəfi:ld
deer-forest, -s 'dɪəˌfɒrɪst, -s
deer-hound, -s 'dɪəhavnd, -z
deer-park, -s 'dɪəpɑ:k, -s
deer-skin 'dɪəskɪn
deer-stalk|ing, -er/s 'dɪəˌstɔ:k|ɪŋ, -ə*/z
de-escalat|e, -es, -ing, -ed ˌdi:'eskəleɪt, -s, -ɪŋ, -ɪd
de-escalation ˌdi:eskə'leɪʃn [-ˌ--'--]
defac|e, -es, -ing, -ed, -er/s, -ement/s dɪ'feɪs, -ɪz, -ɪŋ, -t, -ə*/z, -mənt/s
de facto di:'fæktəʊ [deɪ'f-]
defalcat|e, -es, -ing, -ed 'di:fælkeɪt [di:'fæl-, rarely 'di:fɔ:l-], -s, -ɪŋ, -ɪd
defalcation, -s ˌdi:fæl'keɪʃn [-fɔ:l-], -z
defalcator, -s 'di:fælkeɪtə* [-fɔ:l-], -z
defamation, -s ˌdefə'meɪʃn [ˌdi:fə'm-], -z
defamatory dɪ'fæmətərɪ
defam|e, -es, -ing, -ed, -er/s dɪ'feɪm, -z, -ɪŋ, -d, -ə*/z
default (s. v.), -s, -ing, -ed, -er/s dɪ'fɔ:lt [-'fɒlt], -s, -ɪŋ, -ɪd, -ə*/z
defeasance dɪ'fi:zns
defeasib|le, -ly, -leness dɪ'fi:zəb|l [-zɪb-], -lɪ, -lnɪs [-nəs]

defeat (s. v.), -s, -ing, -ed dɪ'fi:t, -s, -ɪŋ, -ɪd
defeati|sm, -st/s dɪ'fi:tɪ|zəm, -st/s
defect (s.), -s 'di:fekt [dɪ'fekt], -s
defect (v.), -s, -ing, -ed, -or/s dɪ'fekt, -s, -ɪŋ, -ɪd, -ə*/z
defection, -s dɪ'fekʃn, -z
defective, -ly, -ness dɪ'fektɪv, -lɪ, -nɪs [-nəs]
defence, -s dɪ'fens, -ɪz
defenceless, -ly, -ness dɪ'fenslɪs [-ləs, -les], -lɪ, -nɪs [-nəs]
defend, -s, -ing, -ed, -er/s dɪ'fend, -z, -ɪŋ, -ɪd, -ə*/z
defendant, -s dɪ'fendənt, -s
defensibility dɪˌfensɪ'bɪlətɪ [-sə'b-, -lɪt-]
defensib|le, -ly dɪ'fensəb|l [-sɪb-], -lɪ
defensive, -ly, -ness dɪ'fensɪv, -lɪ, -nɪs [-nəs]
defer, -s, -ring, -red, -rer/s dɪ'fɜ:*, -z, -rɪŋ, -d, -rə*/z
deferen|ce, -t 'defərən|s, -t
deferenti|al, -ally ˌdefə'renʃ|l, -əlɪ
defian|ce, -t/ly, -tness dɪ'faɪən|s, -t/lɪ, -tnɪs [-nəs]
deficien|cy, -cies, -t/ly dɪ'fɪʃn|sɪ, -sɪz, -t/lɪ
deficit, -s 'defɪsɪt ['di:f-, -fəs-, dɪ'fɪsɪt], -s
defilad|e (s. v.), -es, -ing, -ed ˌdefɪ'leɪd, -z, -ɪŋ, -ɪd
defile (s.), -s 'di:faɪl [dɪ'faɪl, di:'f-], -z
defil|e (v.), -es, -ing, -ed, -er/s, -ement dɪ'faɪl, -z, -ɪŋ, -d, -ə*/z, -mənt
definable dɪ'faɪnəbl
defin|e, -es, -ing, -ed, -er/s dɪ'faɪn, -z, -ɪŋ, -d, -ə*/z
definite, -ly, -ness 'defɪnɪt [-fṇɪt, -fnɪt, -ət], -lɪ, -nɪs [-nəs]
definition, -s ˌdefɪ'nɪʃn [-fṇ'ɪʃ-], -z
definitive, -ly, -ness dɪ'fɪnɪtɪv [de'f-, -ətɪv], -lɪ, -nɪs
deflagrat|e, -es, -ing, -ed, -or/s 'defləgreɪt ['di:f-], -s, -ɪŋ, -ɪd, -ə*/z
deflagration, -s ˌdeflə'greɪʃn [ˌdi:f-], -z
deflat|e, -es, -ing, -ed dɪ'fleɪt [ˌdi:'f-], -s, -ɪŋ, -ɪd
deflation, -ary dɪ'fleɪʃn [ˌdi:'f-], -ərɪ
deflect, -s, -ing, -ed, -or/s dɪ'flekt, -s, -ɪŋ, -ɪd, -ə*/z
deflection [-exion], -s dɪ'flekʃn, -z
defloration, -s ˌdi:flɔ:'reɪʃn [ˌdef-], -z
deflower, -s, -ing, -ed ˌdi:'flaʊə* [dɪ'f-], -z, -rɪŋ, -d
Defoe dɪ'fəʊ [də'f-]
defoliat|e, -es, -ing, -ed ˌdi:'fəʊlɪeɪt, -s, -ɪŋ, -ɪd
defoliation ˌdi:fəʊlɪ'eɪʃn [-ˌ--'--]

De Forest dəˈfɒrɪst
deforest, -s, -ing, -ed ˌdiːˈfɒrɪst, -s, -ɪŋ, -ɪd
deforestation diːˌfɒrɪˈsteɪʃn [ˈ-ˌ--ˈ--]
deform, -s, -ing, -ed, -er/s dɪˈfɔːm, -z, -ɪŋ, -d, -ə*/z
deformation, -s ˌdiːfɔːˈmeɪʃn, -z
deformit|y, -ies dɪˈfɔːmət|ɪ [-ɪt|ɪ], -ɪz
defraud, -s, -ing, -ed, -er/s dɪˈfrɔːd, -z, -ɪŋ, -ɪd, -ə*/z
defray, -s, -ing, -ed, -er/s, -ment dɪˈfreɪ, -z, -ɪŋ, -d, -ə*/z, -mənt
defrayal, -s dɪˈfreɪəl, -z
De Freitas dəˈfreɪtəs
defrock, -s, -ing, -ed ˌdiːˈfrɒk, -s, -ɪŋ, -t
de-frost, -s, -ing, -ed ˌdiːˈfrɒst [old-fashioned -ˈfrɔːst], -s, -ɪŋ, -ɪd
deft, -er, -est, -ly, -ness deft, -ə*, -ɪst, -lɪ, -nɪs [-nəs]
defunct (s. adj.), -s dɪˈfʌŋkt, -s
defus|e, -es, -ing, -ed ˌdiːˈfjuːz, -ɪz, -ɪŋ, -d
def|y, -ies, -ying, -ied, -ier/s dɪˈf|aɪ, -aɪz, -aɪɪŋ, -aɪd, -aɪə*/z
Degas (s.) [ˈdeɪɡɑː] (dəɡɑ)
De Gaulle dəˈɡəʊl (dəɡo:l)
degauss, -es, -ing, -ed ˌdiːˈɡaʊs, -ɪz, -ɪŋ, -t
degeneracy dɪˈdʒenərəsɪ
degenerate (adj.), -ly, -ness dɪˈdʒenərət [-rɪt], -lɪ, -nɪs [-nəs]
degenerat|e (v.), -es, -ing, -ed dɪˈdʒenəreɪt, -s, -ɪŋ, -ɪd
degeneration dɪˌdʒenəˈreɪʃn
degenerative dɪˈdʒenərətɪv [-nəreɪt-]
deglutinat|e, -es, -ing, -ed dɪˈgluːtɪneɪt, -s, -ɪŋ, -ɪd
deglutition ˌdiːgluːˈtɪʃn
degradation, -s ˌdegrəˈdeɪʃn, -z
degrad|e, -es, -ing/ly, -ed dɪˈɡreɪd, -z, -ɪŋ/lɪ, -ɪd
degree, -s dɪˈgriː, -z
dehisc|e, -es, -ing, -ed; -ence, -ent dɪˈhɪs [diːˈh-], -ɪz, -ɪŋ, -t; -ns, -nt
Dehra Dun ˌdeɪrəˈduːn (Hindi dehra-dun)
dehumaniz|e [-is|e], -es, -ing, -ed ˌdiːˈhjuːmənaɪz, -ɪz, -ɪŋ, -d
dehydrat|e, -es, -ing, -ed ˌdiːˈhaɪdreɪt, -s, -ɪŋ, -ɪd
dehydration ˌdiːhaɪˈdreɪʃn
dehypnotiz|e [-is|e], -es, -ing, -ed ˌdiːˈhɪpnətaɪz, -ɪz, -ɪŋ, -d
de-ic|e, -es, -ing, -ed, -er/s ˌdiːˈaɪs, -ɪz, -ɪŋ, -t, -ə*/z
deicide, -s ˈdiːɪsaɪd [ˈdeɪɪs-], -z
deictic ˈdaɪktɪk

deification, -s ˌdiːɪfɪˈkeɪʃn [ˌdeɪɪf-], -z
dei|fy, -fies, -fying, -fied ˈdiːɪ|faɪ [ˈdeɪɪ-], -faɪz, -faɪɪŋ, -faɪd
Deighton (surname) ˈdaɪtn, ˈdeɪtn, (place in North Yorkshire) ˈdiːtn
deign, -s, -ing, -ed deɪn, -z, -ɪŋ, -d
deipnosophist, -s daɪpˈnɒsəfɪst, -s
Deirdre ˈdɪədrɪ [-dreɪ]
dei|sm, -st/s ˈdiːɪ|zəm [ˈdeɪɪ-], -st/s
deistic, -al diːˈɪstɪk [deɪˈɪ-], -l
deit|y (D.), -ies ˈdiːɪt|ɪ [ˈdiːət-, ˈdɪət-, ˈdeɪt-, ˈdeɪət-], -ɪz
deject, -s, -ing, -ed/ly, -edness dɪˈdʒekt, -s, -ɪŋ, -ɪd/lɪ, -ɪdnɪs [-nəs]
dejection dɪˈdʒekʃn
déjeuner, -s ˈdeɪʒəneɪ [-ʒɜː-] (deʒøne, -ʒœne), -z
de jure diːˈdʒʊərɪ [ˌdeɪˈjʊərɪ]
Dekker ˈdekə*
de la Bère (English surname) ˌdeləˈbɪə*
Delagoa ˌdeləˈɡəʊə [also ˈdeləg- in Delagoa Bay]
delaine dəˈleɪn [dɪˈl-]
Delamain ˈdeləmeɪn
De la Mare ˌdeləˈmeə*
Delamere ˈdeləˌmɪə*
De Lancey dəˈlɑːnsɪ
Deland ˈdiːlənd
Delan|e, -y dəˈleɪn [dɪˈl-], -ɪ
De la Pasture dəˈlæpətʃə* [-ˌtjʊə*, -tʃə*]
De la Poer ˌdeləˈpʊə* [-ˈpɔə*, -ˈpɔː*]
De la Pole ˌdeləˈpəʊl
De la Rue ˈdeləru: [ˌdeləˈr-]
De Laszlo dəˈlæsləʊ
de la Torre (English surname) ˌdeləˈtɔː*
Delaware ˈdeləweə*
De la Warr ˈdeləweə*
delay (s. v.), -s, -ing, -ed, -er/s dɪˈleɪ, -z, -ɪŋ, -d, -ə*/z
del credere ˌdelˈkredərɪ
dele ˈdiːlɪ [-lɪ]
delectab|le, -ly, -leness dɪˈlektəb|l, -lɪ, -lnɪs [-nəs]
delectation ˌdiːlekˈteɪʃn
delegac|y, -ies ˈdelɪɡəs|ɪ, -ɪz
delegate (s.), -s ˈdelɪɡət [-ɡeɪt, -ɡɪt], -s
delegat|e (v.), -es, -ing, -ed ˈdelɪɡeɪt, -s, -ɪŋ, -ɪd
delegation, -s ˌdelɪˈɡeɪʃn, -z
delend|um, -a dɪˈlend|əm [diː-l-], -ə
delet|e, -es, -ing, -ed dɪˈliːt [diː-l-], -s, -ɪŋ, -ɪd
deleterious, -ly, -ness ˌdelɪˈtɪərɪəs [dɪl-, ˌdiːl-], -lɪ, -nɪs [-nəs]
deletion, -s dɪˈliːʃn [diː-l-], -z
delf delf

Delft, -ware delft, -weə*
Delham 'deləm
Delhi 'delɪ
Delia, -n/s 'di:ljə [-lɪə], -n/z
deliber|ate (adj.), -ately, -ateness dɪ-
'lɪbər|ət [-ɪt], -ətlɪ [-ɪtlɪ], -ətnɪs [-ɪt-,
-nəs]
deliberat|e (v.), -es, -ing, -ed, -or/s
dɪ'lɪbəreɪt, -s, -ɪŋ, -ɪd, -ə*/z
deliberation, -s dɪˌlɪbə'reɪʃn, -z
deliberative, -ly dɪ'lɪbərətɪv, -lɪ
delicac|y, -ies 'delɪkəs|ɪ, -ɪz
delicate, -ly, -ness 'delɪkət [-kɪt], -lɪ,
-nɪs [-nəs]
delicatessen, -s ˌdelɪkə'tesn, -z
delicious, -ly, -ness dɪ'lɪʃəs, -lɪ, -nɪs
[-nəs]
delict, -s 'di:lɪkt, -s
delight (s. v.), -s, -ing, -ed/ly dɪ'laɪt, -s,
-ɪŋ, -ɪd/lɪ
delight|ful, -fully, -fulness dɪ'laɪt|fʊl,
-fəlɪ·[-fʊlɪ], -fʊlnɪs [-nəs]
delightsome dɪ'laɪtsəm
Delilah dɪ'laɪlə
delimit, -s, -ing, -ed di:'lɪmɪt [dɪ'l-], -s,
-ɪŋ, -ɪd
delimitation, -s dɪˌlɪmɪ'teɪʃn [ˌdi:-
lɪmɪ't-], -z
delineat|e, -es, -ing, -ed, -or/s dɪ-
'lɪnɪeɪt, -s, -ɪŋ, -ɪd, -ə*/z
delineation, -s dɪˌlɪnɪ'eɪʃn, -z
delinquen|cy, -cies, -t/s dɪ'lɪŋkwən|sɪ,
-sɪz, -t/s
deliquesc|e, -es, -ing, -ed ˌdelɪ'kwes, -ɪz,
-ɪŋ, -t
deliquescen|ce, -t ˌdelɪ'kwesn|s, -t
delirious, -ly, -ness dɪ'lɪrɪəs [-'lɪər-], -lɪ,
-nɪs [-nəs]
delirium, -tremens dɪ'lɪrɪəm [-'lɪər-],
-'tri:menz
De l'Isle (English name) də'laɪl
Delisle (French name) də'li:l (dəlil)
Delius 'di:ljəs [-lɪəs]
deliv|er, -ers, -ering, -ered, -erer/s
dɪ'lɪv|ə*, -əz, -ərɪŋ, -əd, -ərə*/z
deliverance, -s dɪ'lɪvərəns, -ɪz
deliver|y, -ies dɪ'lɪvər|ɪ, -ɪz
dell, -s del, -z
Delmar 'delmɑ:*, del'mɑ:*
Delos 'di:lɒs
de-lou|se, -ses, -sing, -sed ˌdi:'laʊ|s [-z],
-sɪz [-zɪz], -sɪŋ [-zɪŋ], -st [-zd]
Delphi (in Greece) 'delfaɪ [-fɪ], (city in
U.S.A.) 'delfaɪ
Delph|ian, -ic 'delf|ɪən [-jən], -ɪk
delphinium, -s del'fɪnɪəm [-njəm], -z
delta, -s 'deltə, -z
deltoid 'deltɔɪd

delud|e, -es, -ing, -ed, -er/s dɪ'lu:d
[-'lju:d], -z, -ɪŋ, -ɪd, -ə*/z
deluge (s. v.), -es, -ing, -ed 'delju:dʒ
[-ljʊdʒ], -ɪz, -ɪŋ, -d
delusion, -s dɪ'lu:ʒn [-'lju:-], -z
delusive, -ly, -ness dɪ'lu:sɪv [-'lju:-], -lɪ,
-nɪs [-nəs]
delusory dɪ'lu:sərɪ [-'lju:-, -u:zərɪ]
de luxe də'lʊks [dɪ-, -'lu:ks, -'lʌks]
delv|e, -es, -ing, -ed, -er/s delv, -z, -ɪŋ,
-d, -ə*/z
Delville 'delvɪl
demagnetization [-isa-], -s 'di:ˌmæg-
nɪtaɪ'zeɪʃn [di:ˌm-, -nət-], -z
demagnetiz|e [-is|e], -es, -ing, -ed
ˌdi:'mægnɪtaɪz [di:'m-, -nət-], -ɪz,
-ɪŋ, -d
demagogic, -al ˌdemə'gɒgɪk [-'gɒdʒɪk],
-l
demagogue, -s 'deməgɒg, -z
demagogy 'deməgɒgɪ [-gɒdʒɪ]
demand (s. v.), -s, -ing, -ed dɪ'mɑ:nd,
-z, -ɪŋ, -ɪd
Demant dɪ'mænt [də'm-]
demarcat|e, -es, -ing, -ed 'di:mɑ:keɪt,
-s, -ɪŋ, -ɪd
demarcation ˌdi:mɑ:'keɪʃn
demarcative di:'mɑ:kətɪv
démarche, -s 'deɪmɑ:ʃ [-'-'-], -ɪz
Demas 'di:mæs
dematerializ|e [-is|e], -es, -ing, -ed
ˌdi:mə'tɪərɪəlaɪz, -ɪz, -ɪŋ, -d
De Mauley də'mɔ:lɪ
demean, -s, -ing, -ed; -our/s dɪ'mi:n,
-z, -ɪŋ, -ɪd; -ə*/z
dement, -s, -ing, -ed dɪ'ment, -s, -ɪŋ, -ɪd
dementia dɪ'menʃɪə [-ʃjə, -ʃə]
Demerara (district in Guyana) ˌdemə-
'rɑ:rə, (sugar from there) ˌdemə'reərə
demerit, -s di:'merɪt ['di:ˌm-], -s
demesne, -s dɪ'meɪn [də'm-, -'mi:n], -z
Demeter dɪ'mi:tə*
Demetrius dɪ'mi:trɪəs
demigod, -s 'demɪgɒd, -z
demijohn, -s 'demɪdʒɒn, -z
demilitariz|e [-is|e], -es, -ing, -ed
ˌdi:'mɪlɪtəraɪz, -ɪz, -ɪŋ, -d
demilitarization [-isa-] 'di:ˌmɪlɪtəraɪ-
'zeɪʃn [di:ˌm-, -rɪ'z-]
demi-monde ˌdemɪ'mɔ̃:nd [-'mɔ:nd,
-'mɒnd, '---] (dəmimɔ̃:d)
demis|e (s. v.), -es, -ing, -ed dɪ'maɪz, -ɪz,
-ɪŋ, -d
demi-semiquaver, -s 'demɪsemɪˌkweɪ-
və*, -z
demission, -s dɪ'mɪʃn, -z
de-mist, -s, -ing, -ed, -er*/s ˌdi:'mɪst,
-s, -ɪŋ, -ɪd, -ə*/z

demiurge, -s ˈdiːmɪɜːdʒ [ˈdem-], -ɪz
demivolt, -s ˈdemɪvɒlt, -s
demo, -s ˈdeməʊ, -z
demob, -s, -bing, -bed ˌdiːˈmɒb, -z, -ɪŋ, -d
demobilization [-isa-], -s ˈdiːˌməʊbɪlaɪˈzeɪʃn [dɪˌməʊbɪlaɪˈz-, -lɪˈz-, -bəl-, -bl̩-], -z
demobiliz|e [-is|e], -es, -ing, -ed diː-ˈməʊbɪlaɪz [dɪˈm-, ˈdiːm-, -bəl-, -bl̩aɪz], -ɪz, -ɪŋ, -d
democracy, -ies dɪˈmɒkrəs|ɪ, -ɪz
democrat, -s ˈdeməkræt [-mʊk-], -s
democratic, -al, -ally ˌdeməˈkrætɪk [-mʊˈk-], -l, -əlɪ
democratization [-isa-] dɪˌmɒkrətaɪˈzeɪʃn [-tɪˈz-]
democratiz|e [-is|e], -es, -ing, -ed dɪˈmɒkrətaɪz, -ɪz, -ɪŋ, -d
Democritus dɪˈmɒkrɪtəs
demogorgon, -s ˌdiːməʊˈgɔːgən, -z
demography diːˈmɒgrəfɪ
Demoivre dəˈmɔɪvə* [dɪˈm-]
De Moleyns ˈdeməliːnz [-mʊl-]
demolish, -es, -ing, -ed, -er/s dɪˈmɒlɪʃ, -ɪz, -ɪŋ, -t, -ə*/z
demolition, -s ˌdeməˈlɪʃn [ˌdiːm-, -mʊˈl-], -z
demon, -s ˈdiːmən, -z
demonetization [-isa-] diːˌmʌnɪtaɪˈzeɪʃn [-ˌmɒn-, -tɪˈz-]
demonetiz|e [-is|e], -es, -ing, -ed ˌdiːˈmʌnɪtaɪz [dɪˈm-, -ˈmɒn-], -ɪz, -ɪŋ, -d
demoniac (s. adj.), -s dɪˈməʊnɪæk [-njæk], -s
demoniac|al, -ally ˌdiːməʊˈnaɪək|l [-mʊˈn-], -əlɪ
demonic diːˈmɒnɪk [dɪˈm-]
demoni|sm, -st/s ˈdiːmənɪ|zəm, -st/s
demonology ˌdiːməˈnɒlədʒɪ
demonstrability ˌdemənstrəˈbɪlətɪ [dɪˌmɒns-, -lɪt-]
demonstrab|le, -ly ˈdemənstrəb|l [dɪˈmɒn-], -lɪ
demonstrat|e, -es, -ing, -ed, -or/s ˈdemənstreɪt, -s, -ɪŋ, -ɪd, -ə*/z
demonstration, -s ˌdemənˈstreɪʃn, -z
demonstrative (s. adj.), -s, -ly, -ness dɪˈmɒnstrətɪv, -z, -lɪ, -nɪs [-nəs]
demoralization [-isa-] dɪˌmɒrəlaɪˈzeɪʃn [-rˈlaɪˈz-, -rəlɪˈz-, -rˈlɪˈz-]
demoraliz|e [-is|e], -es, -ing, -ed dɪ-ˈmɒrəlaɪz [-rˈlaɪz], -ɪz, -ɪŋ, -d
De Morgan dəˈmɔːgən
de mortuis ˌdeɪˈmɔːtjʊɪs [ˌdiː-, -tuːɪs]
Demos ˈdiːmɒs
Demosthenes dɪˈmɒsθəniːz [dəˈm-, -θɪn-]

demot|e, -es, -ing, -ed ˌdiːˈməʊt [dɪ-], -s, -ɪŋ, -ɪd
demotic diːˈmɒtɪk [dɪ-]
demotion ˌdiːˈməʊʃn [dɪ-]
Dempster ˈdempstə*
demur (s. v.), -s, -ring, -red dɪˈmɜː*, -z, -rɪŋ, -d
demure, -r, -st, -ly, -ness dɪˈmjʊə* [-ˈmjɔə*, -ˈmjɔː*], -rə*, -rɪst, -lɪ, -nɪs [-nəs]
demurrage dɪˈmʌrɪdʒ
demurrer (one who demurs), -s dɪˈmɜːrə*, -z
demurrer (objection on ground of irrelevance), -s dɪˈmʌrə*, -z
Demuth dəˈmuːθ
dem|y, -ies dɪˈm|aɪ [də'm-], -aɪz
demyship, -s dɪˈmaɪʃɪp [dəˈm-], -s
den, -s den, -z
dena|rius, -rii dɪˈneə|rɪəs, -rɪaɪ [de-ˈnɑːrɪəs, deˈnɑːriː]
denary ˈdiːnərɪ
denationalization [-isa-] ˈdiːˌnæʃnəlaɪˈzeɪʃn [-ʃnəl-, -ʃn̩l-, -ʃnl-, -ʃənəl-, -lɪˈz-]
denationaliz|e [-is|e], -es, -ing, -ed ˌdiːˈnæʃnəlaɪz [-ʃnəl-, -ʃn̩l-, -ʃnl-, -ʃənəl-], -ɪz, -ɪŋ, -d
denaturalization [-isa-] ˈdiːˌnætʃrəlaɪˈzeɪʃn [-tʃʊr-, -tʃər-, -lɪˈz-]
denaturaliz|e [-is|e], -es, -ing, -ed ˌdiːˈnætʃrəlaɪz [-tʃʊr-, -tʃər-], -ɪz, -ɪŋ, -d
Denbigh, -shire ˈdenbɪ, -ʃə* [-ˌʃɪə*]
Denby ˈdenbɪ
dendrology denˈdrɒlədʒɪ
dene (D.), -s diːn, -z
Deneb ˈdeneb
Denebola dɪˈnebələ [deˈn-, dəˈn-]
dengue ˈdeŋgɪ
Denham ˈdenəm
Denholm(e) ˈdenəm
Denia, -s ˈdiːnjə [-nɪə], -z
deniable dɪˈnaɪəbl
denial, -s dɪˈnaɪəl, -z
denier (coin), -s dɪˈnɪə* [ˈdenɪə*], -z
denier (thickness of yarn) ˈdenɪə* [ˈdenjə*, -nɪeɪ] (dənje)
denier (one who denies), -s dɪˈnaɪə*, -z
denigrat|e, -es, -ing, -ed ˈdenɪgreɪt, -s, -ɪŋ, -ɪd
denigration ˌdenɪˈgreɪʃn
denim, -s ˈdenɪm, -z
Denis ˈdenɪs
Denise dəˈniːz [deˈn-]
Denison ˈdenɪsn
denizen, -s ˈdenɪzn, -z
Denman ˈdenmən
Denmark ˈdenmɑːk

Dennehy—depose

Dennehy 'denəhɪ, -hi:
Dennis 'denɪs
Denny, -s 'denɪ, -s
denominat|e, -es, -ing, -ed dɪ'nɒmɪneɪt, -s, -ɪŋ, -ɪd
denomination, -s dɪ,nɒmɪ'neɪʃn, -z
denominational dɪ,nɒmɪ'neɪʃənl [-ʃnəl, -ʃn̩l, -ʃn̩l, -ʃənəl]
denominationalism dɪ,nɒmɪ'neɪʃn̩əl-ɪzəm [-ʃnəl-, -ʃn̩l-, -ʃn̩l-, -ʃənəl-]
denominative dɪ'nɒmɪnətɪv
denominator, -s dɪ'nɒmɪneɪtə*, -z
denotation, -s ,di:nəʊ'teɪʃn, -z
denot|e, -es, -ing, -ed dɪ'nəʊt, -s, -ɪŋ, -ɪd
dénouement, -s deɪ'nu:mɑ̃:ŋ [-mɑ:ŋ, -mɔ̃:ŋ, -mɒŋ] (denumɑ̃), -z
denounc|e, -es, -ing, -ed, -er/s, -ement/s dɪ'naʊns, -ɪz, -ɪŋ, -t, -ə*/z, -mənt/s
de novo ,di:'nəʊvəʊ [,deɪ-]
dense, -r, -st, -ly, -ness dens, -ə*, -ɪst, -lɪ, -nɪs [-nəs]
densit|y, -ies 'densət|ɪ [-ɪt|ɪ], -ɪz
dent (s. v.) (D.), -s, -ing, -ed dent, -s, -ɪŋ, -ɪd
dental (s. adj.), -s 'dentl, -z
dentaliz|e [-is|e], -es, -ing, -ed 'dentə-laɪz [-nt̩l-], -ɪz, -ɪŋ, -d
dentate 'dentert
dentated 'dentertɪd [den't-]
denticle, -s 'dentɪkl, -z
dentifrice, -s 'dentɪfrɪs, -ɪz
dentil, -s 'dentɪl, -z
dentilingual (s. adj.), -s ,dentɪ'lɪŋgwəl, -z
dentine 'denti:n
dentist, -s, -ry 'dentɪst, -s, -rɪ
dentition den'tɪʃn
Denton 'dentən
denture, -s 'dentʃə*, -z
denudation, -s ,di:nju:'deɪʃn [-nju-], -z
denud|e, -es, -ing, -ed dɪ'nju:d, -z, -ɪŋ, -ɪd
denunciat|e, -es, -ing, -ed, -or/s dɪ'nʌnsɪeɪt [-nsjeɪt, -nʃɪeɪt, -nʃjeɪt], -s, -ɪŋ, -ɪd, -ə*/z
denunciation, -s dɪ,nʌnsɪ'eɪʃn, -z
denunciatory dɪ'nʌnsɪətərɪ [-nʃɪə-, -nsjə-, -nʃjə-, dɪ'nʌnsɪeɪtərɪ, dɪ-'nʌnʃɪeɪtərɪ]
Denver 'denvə*
den|y, -ies, -ying, -ied, -ier/s dɪ'n|aɪ, -aɪz, -aɪɪŋ, -aɪd, -aɪə*/z
Denys 'denɪs
Denyse də'ni:z [de'n-]
Denzil 'denzɪl
deodand, -s 'dɪəʊdænd, -z

deodar, -s 'dɪəʊdɑ:*, -z
deodara, -s ,dɪə'dɑ:rə [dɪəʊ'd-, -'deərə], -z
deodorant, -s di:'əʊdərənt [dɪ'əʊ-], -s
deodorization [-isa-], -s di:,əʊdərai-'zeɪʃn [dɪ,əʊ-, -rɪ'z-], -z
deodoriz|e [-is|e], -es, -ing, -ed, -er/s di:'əʊdəraɪz [dɪ'əʊ-], -ɪz, -ɪŋ, -d, -ə*/z
deoxidization [-isa-], -s di:,ɒksɪdaɪ-'zeɪʃn ['di:,ɒ-], -z
deoxidiz|e [-is|e], -es, -ing, -ed, -er/s di:'ɒksɪdaɪz [,di:'ɒ-, -ɪz, -ɪŋ, -d, -ə*/z
depart, -s, -ing, -ed dɪ'pɑ:t, -s, -ɪŋ, -ɪd
department, -s dɪ'pɑ:tmənt, -s
departmental ,di:pɑ:t'mentl
departure, -s dɪ'pɑ:tʃə*, -z
depast|ure, -ures, -uring, -ured di:-'pɑ:stʃ|ə*, -əz, -ərɪŋ, -əd
depauperiz|e [-is|e], -es, -ing, -ed ,di:'pɔ:pəraɪz, -ɪz, -ɪŋ, -d
depend, -s, -ing, -ed dɪ'pend, -z, -ɪŋ, -ɪd
dependable, -ness dɪ'pendəbl, -nɪs [-nəs]
dependant, -s dɪ'pendənt, -s
dependen|ce, -cy, -cies, -t/s, -tly dɪ-'pendən|s, -sɪ, -sɪz, -t/s, -tlɪ
Depere dɪ'pɪə* [də'p-]
Depew dɪ'pju: [də'p-]
depict, -s, -ing, -ed dɪ'pɪkt, -s, -ɪŋ, -ɪd
depiction dɪ'pɪkʃn
depilat|e, -es, -ing, -ed 'depɪleɪt, -s, -ɪŋ, -ɪd
depilatory dɪ'pɪlətərɪ [de'p-]
deplet|e, -es, -ing, -ed dɪ'pli:t [di:'p-], -s, -ɪŋ, -ɪd
depletion, -s dɪ'pli:ʃn [di:'p-], -z
deplet|ive, -ory dɪ'pli:t|ɪv [di:'p-], -ərɪ
deplorab|le, -ly, -leness dɪ'plɔ:rəb|l [-'plɔər-], -lɪ, -lnɪs [-nəs]
deplor|e, -es, -ing, -ed dɪ'plɔ:* [-'plɔə*], -z, -rɪŋ, -d
deploy, -s, -ing, -ed; -ment dɪ'plɔɪ, -z, -ɪŋ, -d; -mənt
depolarization [-isa-] 'di:,pəʊləraɪ'zeɪʃn [-rɪ'z-]
depolariz|e [-is|e], -es, -ing, -ed ,di:-'pəʊləraɪz, -ɪz, -ɪŋ, -d
deponent (s. adj.), -s dɪ'pəʊnənt, -s
depopulat|e, -es, -ing, -ed, -or/s ,di:-'pɒpjʊleɪt, -s, -ɪŋ, -ɪd, -ə*/z
depopulation di:,pɒpjʊ'leɪʃn ['-,--'--]
deport, -s, -ing, -ed dɪ'pɔ:t, -s, -ɪŋ, -ɪd
deportation, -s ,di:pɔ:'teɪʃn, -z
deportment dɪ'pɔ:tmənt
deposal, -s dɪ'pəʊzl, -z
depos|e, -es, -ing, -ed dɪ'pəʊz, -ɪz, -ɪŋ, -d

deposit (s. v.), -s, -ing, -ed, -or/s dɪ-
'pɒzɪt, -s, -ɪŋ, -ɪd, -ə*/z
depositar|y, -ies dɪ'pɒzɪtər|ɪ, -ɪz
deposition, -s ˌdepə'zɪʃn [ˌdi:p-, -pʊ'z-],
-z
depositor|y, -ies dɪ'pɒzɪtər|ɪ, -ɪz
depot, -s 'depəʊ, -z
depravation ˌdeprə'veɪʃn
deprav|e, -es, -ing, -ed, -edly, -edness
dɪ'preɪv, -z, -ɪŋ, -d, -dlɪ [-ɪdlɪ], -dnɪs
[-ɪdnɪs, -nəs]
depravity dɪ'prævətɪ [-ɪtɪ]
deprecat|e, -es, -ing/ly, -ed, -or/s
'deprɪkeɪt [-prə-], -s, -ɪŋ/lɪ, -ɪd,
-ə*/z
deprecation, -s ˌdeprɪ'keɪʃn [-prə-], -z
deprecatory 'deprɪkətərɪ [-prə-, -keɪt-]
depreciat|e, -es, -ing/ly, -ed, -or/s
dɪ'pri:ʃɪeɪt [-ʃɪeɪt, -sɪeɪt, -sjeɪt], -s,
-ɪŋ/lɪ, -ɪd, -ə*/z
depreciation dɪˌpri:ʃɪ'eɪʃn [-sɪ'eɪ-]
depreciatory dɪ'pri:ʃjətərɪ [-ʃɪət-, -ʃət-,
-ʃɪeɪtərɪ]
depredat|e, -es, -ing, -ed, -or/s 'de-
prɪdeɪt [-prəd-], -s, -ɪŋ, -ɪd, -ə*/z
depredation, -s ˌdeprɪ'deɪʃn [-prə'd-], -z
depredatory dɪ'predətərɪ
depress, -es, -ing/ly, -ed, -or/s dɪ'pres,
-ɪz, -ɪŋ/lɪ, -t, -ə*/z
depression, -s dɪ'preʃn, -z
depressive dɪ'presɪv
depressurization [-isation] di:ˌpreʃəraɪ-
'zeɪʃn ['-ˌ---'--, -ərɪ'z-]
depressuriz|e [-is|e], -es, -ing, -ed
ˌdi:'preʃəraɪz, -ɪz, -ɪŋ, -d
deprivation, -s ˌdeprɪ'veɪʃn [ˌdi:-
praɪ'v-], -z
depriv|e, -es, -ing, -ed dɪ'praɪv, -z, -ɪŋ,
-d
Deptford 'detfəd ['depfəd]
depth, -s depθ, -s
depth-charge, -s 'depθtʃɑ:dʒ, -ɪz
deputation, -s ˌdepjʊ'teɪʃn [-pju:-], -z
deput|e, -es, -ing, -ed dɪ'pju:t, -s, -ɪŋ,
-ɪd
deputiz|e [-is|e], -es, -ing, -ed 'de-
pjʊtaɪz, -ɪz, -ɪŋ, -d
deput|y, -ies 'depjʊt|ɪ, -ɪz
De Quincey də'kwɪnsɪ
derail, -s, -ing, -ed, -ment/s dɪ'reɪl
[ˌdi:'r-], -z, -ɪŋ, -d, -mənt/s
derang|e, -es, -ing, -ed, -ement/s
dɪ'reɪndʒ [də'r-], -ɪz, -ɪŋ, -d, -mənt/s
derat|e, -es, -ing, -ed ˌdi:'reɪt, -s, -ɪŋ,
-ɪd
de-ra|tion, -tions, -tioning, -tioned
ˌdi:'ræ|ʃn, -ʃnz, -ʃənɪŋ [-ʃn̩ɪŋ, -ʃnɪŋ],
-ʃnd

Derbe 'dɜ:bɪ
Derby, -shire 'dɑ:bɪ, -ʃə* [-ˌʃɪə*]
Note.—The form 'dɜ:bɪ is also heard,
mainly from dialectal speakers.
Dereham 'dɪərəm
Derek 'derɪk
derelict (s. adj.), -s 'derɪlɪkt [-rəl-], -s
dereliction ˌderɪ'lɪkʃn [-rə'l-]
derequisi|tion, -tions, -tioning, -tioned
'di:ˌrekwɪ'zɪ|ʃn, -ʃnz, -ʃənɪŋ [-ʃn̩ɪŋ,
-ʃnɪŋ], -ʃnd
D'Eresby 'dɪəzbɪ
De Reszke də'reskɪ
Derg(h) dɜ:g
Derham 'derəm
derid|e, -es, -ing/ly, -ed, -er/s dɪ'raɪd
[də'r-], -z, -ɪŋ/lɪ, -ɪd, -ə*/z
de rigueur dərɪ'gɜ:* (dərigœ:r)
Dering 'dɪərɪŋ
derision dɪ'rɪʒn [də'r-]
derisive, -ly, -ness dɪ'raɪsɪv [də'r-,
-'raɪzɪv, -'rɪzɪv], -lɪ, -nɪs [-nəs]
derisory dɪ'raɪsərɪ [də'r-, -'raɪzərɪ]
derivation, -s ˌderɪ'veɪʃn, -z
derivative (s. adj.), -s, -ly dɪ'rɪvətɪv
[də'r-], -z, -lɪ
deriv|e, -es, -ing, -ed; -able dɪ'raɪv
[də'r-], -z, -ɪŋ, -d; -əbl
d'Erlanger (English surname) 'deə-
lɑ̃:nʒeɪ [-lɔ̃:n-, -lɑ:n-]
derm, -al dɜ:m, -l
dermatitis ˌdɜ:mə'taɪtɪs
dermatolog|ist/s, -y ˌdɜ:mə'tɒlədʒ|ɪst/s,
-ɪ
derogat|e, -es, -ing, -ed 'derəʊgeɪt, -s,
-ɪŋ, -ɪd
derogation ˌderəʊ'geɪʃn
derogator|y, -ily, -iness dɪ'rɒgətər|ɪ
[də'r-], -əlɪ [-ɪlɪ], -ɪnɪs [-məs]
De Rohan də'rəʊən
Deronda də'rɒndə [dɪ'r-]
De Ros də'ru:s
derrick (D.), -s 'derɪk, -s
derring-do ˌderɪŋ'du:
derringer (D.), -s 'derɪndʒə*, -z
Derry 'derɪ
De Rutzen də'rʌtsn
derv dɜ:v
Derviche 'dɜ:vɪtʃ
dervish (D.), -es 'dɜ:vɪʃ, -ɪz
Derwent (river) 'dɜ:wənt [-went, -wɪnt],
'dɑ:w-
Derwentwater 'dɜ:wəntˌwɔ:tə* [-went-,
-wɪnt-]
De Salis də'sælɪs [dɪ's-], -'sɑ:lɪs
Desart 'dezət
de Satgé də'sætdʒeɪ
Desbarres deɪ'bɑ:*

Desborough 'dezbrə

descal|e, -es, -ing, -ed ˌdiː'skeɪl, -z, -ɪŋ, -d

descant (s.), -s 'deskænt, -s

descant (v.), -s, -ing, -ed dɪ'skænt [des'-], -s, -ɪŋ, -ɪd

Descartes deɪ'kɑːt ['deɪkɑːt] (dekart)

descend, -s, -ing, -ed dɪ'send, -z, -ɪŋ, -ɪd

descendant (s. adj.), -s dɪ'sendənt, -s

descendent dɪ'sendənt

descent, -s dɪ'sent, -s

describ|e, -es, -ing, -ed, -er/s; -able dɪ'skraɪb, -z, -ɪŋ, -d, -ə*/z; -əbl

description, -s dɪ'skrɪpʃn, -z

descriptive, -ly, -ness dɪ'skrɪptɪv, -lɪ, -nɪs [-nəs]

descr|y, -ies, -ying, -ied dɪ'skr|aɪ, -aɪz, -aɪɪŋ, -aɪd

Desdemona ˌdezdɪ'məʊnə

desecrat|e, -es, -ing, -ed, -or/s 'desɪkreɪt, -s, -ɪŋ, -ɪd, -ə*/z

desecration, -s ˌdesɪ'kreɪʃn, -z

desegregat|e, -es, -ing, -ed ˌdiː'segrɪgeɪt [-grə-], -s, -ɪŋ, -ɪd

desegregation ˌdiːsegrɪ'geɪʃn [-grə-]

de Selincourt də'selɪnkɔːt [-lɪŋk-]

desensitiz|e [-is|e], -es, -ing, -ed ˌdiː-'sensɪtaɪz, -ɪz, -ɪŋ, -d

desert (s.) (what is deserved), -s dɪ'zɜːt, -s

desert (s. adj.) (wilderness, desolate), -s 'dezət, -s

desert (v.), -s, -ing, -ed, -er/s dɪ'zɜːt, -s, -ɪŋ, -ɪd, -ə*/z

desertion, -s dɪ'zɜːʃn, -z

deserv|e, -es, -ing/ly, -ed, -edly dɪ'zɜːv, -z, -ɪŋ/lɪ, -d, -ɪdlɪ

deshabille 'dezæbiːl [-zəb-]

déshabillé ˌdeɪzæ'biːeɪ [ˌdez-, -zə'b-, -'biːleɪ] (dezabije)

desiccat|e, -es, -ing, -ed 'desɪkeɪt, -s, -ɪŋ, -ɪd

desiccation ˌdesɪ'keɪʃn

desiccative de'sɪkətɪv [dɪ's-, 'desɪkətɪv]

desiderat|e, -es, -ing, -ed dɪ'zɪdəreɪt [dɪ'sɪ-], -s, -ɪŋ, -ɪd

desideration, -s dɪˌzɪdə'reɪʃn [dɪˌsɪ-], -z

desiderative dɪ'zɪdərətɪv [dɪ'sɪ-]

desiderat|um, -a dɪˌzɪdə'reɪt|əm [dɪˌsɪ-, -'rɑːt-], -ə

design (s. v.), -s, -ing, -ed, -edly, -er/s; -able dɪ'zaɪn, -z, -ɪŋ, -d, -ɪdlɪ, -ə*/z; -əbl

designate (adj.) 'dezɪgneɪt [-nɪt, -nət]

designat|e (v.), -es, -ing, -ed, -or/s 'dezɪgneɪt, -s, -ɪŋ, -ɪd, -ə*/z

designation, -s ˌdezɪg'neɪʃn, -z

desilveriz|e [-is|e], -es, -ing, -ed ˌdiː-'sɪlvəraɪz, -ɪz, -ɪŋ, -d

desinence, -s 'desɪnəns, -ɪz

desirability dɪˌzaɪərə'bɪlətɪ [-lɪt-]

desirab|le, -ly, -leness dɪ'zaɪərəb|l, -lɪ, -lnɪs [-nəs]

desir|e (s. v.), -es, -ing, -ed, -er/s dɪ'zaɪə*, -z, -ɪŋ, -d, -rə*/z

Désirée (English name) deɪ'zɪəreɪ [de'z-]

desirous, -ly dɪ'zaɪərəs, -lɪ

desist, -s, -ing, -ed dɪ'zɪst [dɪ'sɪst], -s, -ɪŋ, -ɪd

desistance dɪ'zɪstəns [dɪ'sɪs-]

desk, -s desk, -s

Deslys deɪ'liːs

Des Moines (in U.S.A.) dɪ'mɔɪn [-'mɔɪnz]

Desmond 'dezmənd

desolate (adj.), -ly, -ness 'desələt [-s]-, -ɪt], -lɪ, -nɪs [-nəs]

desolat|e (v.), -es, -ing, -ed, -or/s 'desəleɪt, -s, -ɪŋ, -ɪd, -ə*/z

desolation, -s ˌdesə'leɪʃn, -z

despair (s. v.), -s, -ing/ly, -ed dɪ'speə*, -z, -rɪŋ/lɪ, -d

Despard 'despəd [-pɑːd]

despatch (s. v.), -es, -ing, -ed, -er/s dɪ'spætʃ, -ɪz, -ɪŋ, -ɪd, -ə*/z

despatch-boat, -s dɪ'spætʃbəʊt, -s

despatch-box, -es dɪ'spætʃbɒks, -ɪz

despatch-rider, -s dɪ'spætʃˌraɪdə*, -z

desperado, -es ˌdespə'rɑːdəʊ [-'reɪd-], -z

desperate, -ly, -ness 'despərət [-rɪt], -lɪ, -nɪs [-nəs]

desperation ˌdespə'reɪʃn

despicability ˌdespɪkə'bɪlətɪ [dɪˌspɪk-, -lɪt-]

despicab|le, -ly, -leness 'despɪkəb|l [dɪ'spɪk-], -lɪ, -lnɪs [-nəs]

despis|e, -es, -ing, -ed, -er/s dɪ'spaɪz, -ɪz, -ɪŋ, -d, -ə*/z

despite, -ful, -fully dɪ'spaɪt, -fʊl, -fʊlɪ [-fəlɪ]

despoil, -s, -ing, -ed, -er/s dɪ'spɔɪl, -z, -ɪŋ, -d, -ə*/z

despond (D.), -s, -ing/ly, -ed dɪ'spɒnd, -z, -ɪŋ/lɪ, -ɪd

desponden|ce, -cy, -t/ly dɪ'spɒndən|s, -sɪ, -t/lɪ

despot, -s 'despɒt [-pət], -s

despotic, -al, -ally, -alness de'spɒtɪk [dɪ's-], -l, -əlɪ, -əlnɪs [-nəs]

despotism, -s 'despətɪzəm, -z

dessert, -s dɪ'zɜːt, -s

dessert-kni|fe, -ves dɪ'zɜːtnaɪ|f, -vz

dessert-service, -s dɪ'zɜːtˌsɜːvɪs, -ɪz

dessert-spoon, -s dɪ'zɜːtspuːn, -z

destination, -s ˌdestɪ'neɪʃn, -z

destin|e, -es, -ing, -ed 'destɪn, -z, -ɪŋ, -d
destin|y, -ies 'destɪn|ɪ [-ən|ɪ], -ɪz
destitute, -ly, -ness 'destɪtjuːt, -lɪ, -nɪs [-nəs]
destitution ˌdestɪ'tjuːʃn
destroy, -s, -ing, -ed, -er/s dɪ'strɔɪ, -z, -ɪŋ, -d, -ə*/z
destructibility dɪˌstrʌktɪ'bɪlətɪ [-tə'b-, -lɪt-]
destructible dɪ'strʌktəbl [-tɪb-]
destruction, -s dɪ'strʌkʃn, -z
destructive, -ly, -ness dɪ'strʌktɪv, -lɪ, -nɪs [-nəs]
destructor, -s dɪ'strʌktə*, -z
desuetude dɪ'sjuːɪtjuːd [-'sjʊɪ-, 'deswɪtjuːd, 'diːswɪ-]
desultor|y, -ily, -iness 'desəltər|ɪ, -əlɪ [-ɪlɪ] -nɪs [-nəs]
Desvaux 'deɪvəʊ, deɪ'vəʊ, də'vəʊ
Des Vœux deɪ'vɜː
detach, -es, -ing, -ed, -edly, -ment/s; -able dɪ'tætʃ, -ɪz, -ɪŋ, -t, -tlɪ [-ɪdlɪ], -mənt/s; -əbl
detail (s. v.), -s, -ing, -ed 'diːteɪl [dɪ'teɪl], -z, -ɪŋ, -d
detain, -s, -ing, -ed, -er/s dɪ'teɪn, -z, -ɪŋ, -d, -ə*/z
detainee, -s ˌdiːteɪ'niː [dɪteɪ'niː], -z
detainer (legal term) dɪ'teɪnə*
detect, -s, -ing, -ed, -or/s; -able dɪ'tekt, -s, -ɪŋ, -ɪd, -ə*/z; -əbl
detection, -s dɪ'tekʃn, -z
detective (s. adj.), -s dɪ'tektɪv, -z
detent, -s dɪ'tent, -s
détente deɪ'tɑ̃ːnt [-ɑːnt, -ɔ̃ːnt, -ɒnt] (detɑ̃ːt)
detention, -s dɪ'tenʃn, -z
deter, -s, -ring, -red dɪ'tɜː*, -z, -rɪŋ, -d
Deterding 'detədɪŋ
detergent (s. adj.), -s dɪ'tɜːdʒənt, -s
deteriorat|e, -es, -ing, -ed dɪ'tɪərɪəreɪt, -s, -ɪŋ, -ɪd
deterioration dɪˌtɪərɪə'reɪʃn
determinable dɪ'tɜːmɪnəbl
determinant (s. adj.), -s dɪ'tɜːmɪnənt, -s
determinate, -ly, -ness dɪ'tɜːmɪnət [-ɪt], -lɪ, -nɪs [-nəs]
determination, -s dɪˌtɜːmɪ'neɪʃn, -z
determinative dɪ'tɜːmɪnətɪv
determin|e, -es, -ing, -ed/ly dɪ'tɜːmɪn, -z, -ɪŋ, -d/lɪ
determini|sm, -st/s dɪ'tɜːmɪnɪ|zəm, -st/s
deterrent (s. adj.), -s dɪ'terənt, -s
detest, -s, -ing, -ed dɪ'test, -s, -ɪŋ, -ɪd
detestab|le, -ly, -leness dɪ'testəb|l, -lɪ, -lnɪs [-nəs]
detestation ˌdiːte'steɪʃn [dɪte'st-]

dethron|e, -es, -ing, -ed, -ement dɪ'θrəʊn [ˌdiː-], -z, -ɪŋ, -d, -mənt
Detmold (surname) 'detməʊld, (German town) 'detməʊld ('dɛtmolt)
detonat|e, -es, -ing, -ed, -or/s 'detəneɪt ['diːt-], -s, -ɪŋ, -ɪd, -ə*/z
detonation, -s ˌdetə'neɪʃn [ˌdiːt-], -z
détour, -s 'diːˌtʊə* ['deɪ-, deɪ'tʊə*, dɪ't-] (detuːr), -z
detract, -s, -ing/ly, -ed, -or/s dɪ'trækt, -s, -ɪŋ/lɪ, -ɪd, -ə*/z
detraction, -s dɪ'trækʃn, -z
detract|ive, -ory dɪ'trækt|ɪv, -ərɪ
detrain, -s, -ing, -ed ˌdiː'treɪn, -z, -ɪŋ, -d
de Trey də'treɪ
detriment, -s 'detrɪmənt, -s
detrimental ˌdetrɪ'mentl
detrition dɪ'trɪʃn
detritus dɪ'traɪtəs
Detroit də'trɔɪt [dɪ't-]
de trop də'trəʊ (dətro)
detruncat|e, -es, -ing, -ed ˌdiː'trʌŋkeɪt ['---], -s, -ɪŋ, -ɪd
detruncation, -s ˌdiːtrʌŋ'keɪʃn, -z
Dettol 'detɒl [-təl]
Deucalion djuː'keɪljən [djʊ-, -lɪən]
deuce, -s djuːs, -ɪz
deuc|ed, -edly djuːs|t ['djuːs|ɪd], -ɪdlɪ
deuterium djuː'tɪərɪəm [djʊ-]
deuteronomic ˌdjuːtərə'nɒmɪk
Deuteronomy ˌdjuːtə'rɒnəmɪ ['djuːtərənəmɪ]
deutzia, -s 'djuːtsjə ['dɔɪts-, -sɪə], -z
deva, -s 'deɪvə ['diːvə] (Hindi deva), -z
de Valera dəvə'leərə [ˌdev-]
devaluation, -s ˌdiːvælju'eɪʃn [dɪ-, -ˌ--'--], -z
deval|ue, -ues, -uing, -ued ˌdiː'væl|juː [-jʊ], -juːz [-jʊz], -jʊɪŋ [-jwɪŋ], -juːd [-jʊd]
Devanagari ˌdeɪvə'nɑːgərɪ [ˌdev-]
Devant də'vænt [dɪ'v-]
devastat|e, -es, -ing, -ed 'devəsteɪt, -s, -ɪŋ, -ɪd
devastation, -s ˌdevə'steɪʃn, -z
develop, -s, -ing, -ed, -er/s, -ment/s; -able dɪ'veləp [də'v-], -s, -ɪŋ, -t, -ə*/z, -mənt/s; -əbl
Devenish 'devnɪʃ [-vənɪʃ]
Deventer 'devəntə*
Deventhaugh 'devənθɔː
De Vere də'vɪə* [dɪ'v-]
Devereux 'devəruː, -ruːks
Deveron 'devərən
Devers (surname) 'diːvəz, 'devəz
Deverson 'devəsn
De Vesci də'vesɪ
deviant, -s 'diːvjənt [-vɪənt], -s

135

deviat|e, -es, -ing, -ed, -or/s 'di:vɪeɪt
[-vjeɪt], -s, -ɪŋ, -ɪd, -ə*/z
deviation, -s ˌdi:vɪˈeɪʃn, -z
deviation|ism, -ist/s ˌdi:vɪˈeɪʃən|ɪzəm
[-ʃn̩], -ɪst/s
device, -s dɪˈvaɪs, -ɪz
dev|il (s. v.), -ils, -illing, -illed 'dev|l,
-lz, -lɪŋ [-lɪŋ], -ld
devil-fish, -es 'devlfɪʃ, -ɪz
devilish, -ly, -ness 'dev|ɪʃ [-vlɪʃ], -lɪ,
-nɪs [-nəs]
devil-may-care ˌdevlmeɪˈkeə*
devilment, -s 'devlmənt, -s
devilr|y, -ies 'devlr|ɪ, -ɪz
devil-worship, -per/s 'devlˌwɜːʃɪp,
-ə*/z
Devine dəˈvaɪn [dɪˈv-]
devious, -ly, -ness 'di:vjəs [-vɪəs], -lɪ,
-nɪs [-nəs]
devis|e, -es, -ing, -ed, -er/s; -able
dɪˈvaɪz, -ɪz, -ɪŋ, -d, -ə*/z; -əbl
devisee, -s ˌdevɪˈzi: [dɪvaɪˈzi:], -z
devisor, -s ˌdevɪˈzɔ:* [dɪvaɪˈzɔ:*,
dɪˈvaɪzɔ:*], -z
devitalization [-isa-] di:ˌvaɪtəlaɪˈzeɪʃn
['di:ˌvaɪ-, -tlaɪ-]
devitaliz|e [-is|e], -es, -ing, -ed ˌdi:-
'vaɪtəlaɪz [-tlaɪ-], -ɪz, -ɪŋ, -d
Devizes dɪˈvaɪzɪz
devocalization [-isa-], -s di:ˌvəʊkəlaɪ-
'zeɪʃn ['di:ˌvəʊkəlaɪˈz-, -klaɪ-], -z
devocaliz|e [-is|e], -es, -ing, -ed ˌdi:-
'vəʊkəlaɪz [-klaɪz], -ɪz, -ɪŋ, -d
devoic|e, -es, -ing, -ed ˌdi:ˈvɔɪs, -ɪz, -ɪŋ,
-t
devoid dɪˈvɔɪd
devolution, -s ˌdi:vəˈlu:ʃn [ˌdev-,
-vl̩'u:-, -vəˈlju:-], -z
devolv|e, -es, -ing, -ed dɪˈvɒlv, -z, -ɪŋ,
-d
Devon, -shire 'devn, -ʃə* [-ˌʃɪə*]
Devonian, -s deˈvəʊnjən [dɪˈv-, -nɪən],
-z
Devonport 'devnpɔ:t [-vmp-]
devot|e, -es, -ing, -ed/ly, -edness
dɪˈvəʊt, -s, -ɪŋ, -ɪd/lɪ, -ɪdnɪs [-nəs]
devotee, -s ˌdevəʊˈti:, -z
devotion, -s dɪˈvəʊʃn, -z
devo|tional, -tionally dɪˈvəʊ|ʃnəl [-ʃnəl,
-ʃn̩l, -ʃnl, -ʃənəl], -ʃnəlɪ [-ʃnəl, -ʃn̩lɪ,
-ʃn̩ɪ, -ʃənəlɪ]
devour, -s, -ing, -ed, -er/s dɪˈvaʊə*, -z,
-rɪŋ, -d, -rə*/z
devout, -er, -est, -ly, -ness dɪˈvaʊt, -ə*,
-ɪst, -lɪ, -nɪs [-nəs]
dew, -s dju:, -z
dewan, -s dɪˈwɑ:n, -z
Dewar 'dju:ə* [djʊə]

dewberr|y, -ies 'dju:ber|ɪ [-bər-], -ɪz
dew-claw, -s 'dju:klɔ:, -z
dew-drop, -s 'dju:drɒp, -s
D'Ewes dju:z
De Wet dəˈvet [dəˈwet]
Dewey 'dju:ɪ ['djʊɪ]
De Wiart (English name) dəˈwaɪət
dewlap, -s 'dju:læp, -s
dew-point, -s 'dju:pɔɪnt, -s
dew-pond, -s 'dju:pɒnd, -z
Dewsbury 'dju:zbərɪ
dew|y, -ness 'dju:|ɪ ['djʊ|ɪ], -ɪnɪs [-ɪnəs]
dexter (D.) 'dekstə*
dexterity dekˈsterətɪ [-rɪtɪ]
dexterous, -ly, -ness 'dekstərəs, -lɪ, -nɪs
[-nəs]
dextrose 'dekstrəʊs
D'Eyncourt 'deɪnkɔ:t [-kɔ:t]
De Zoete dəˈzu:t
dhobi, -(e)s 'dəʊbɪ (Hindi dhobi), -z
dhoti, -(e)s 'dəʊtɪ, -z
dhow, -s daʊ, -z
diabetes ˌdaɪəˈbi:ti:z [-ɪz]
diabetic, -s ˌdaɪəˈbetɪk [-ˈbi:t-], -s
diabolic, -al, -ally ˌdaɪəˈbɒlɪk, -l, -əlɪ
diabolism daɪˈæbəlɪzəm
diaboliz|e [-is|e], -es, -ing, -ed daɪ-
'æbəlaɪz, -ɪz, -ɪŋ, -d
diabolo dɪˈɑ:bələʊ [-ˈæb-]
diachronic ˌdaɪəˈkrɒnɪk
diaconal daɪˈækənl
diaconate, -s daɪˈækəneɪt [-nɪt, -nət], -s
diacritic (s. adj.), -s, -al ˌdaɪəˈkrɪtɪk, -s,
-l
diadem, -s 'daɪədem [-dəm], -z
diaeres|is, -es daɪˈɪərɪs|ɪs [daɪˈer-, -rəs-],
-i:z
Diaghilev dɪˈægɪlef
diagnos|e, -es, -ing, -ed 'daɪəgnəʊz
[ˌdaɪəgˈn-], -ɪz, -ɪŋ, -d
diagnos|is, -es ˌdaɪəgˈnəʊs|ɪs, -i:z
diagnostic (s. adj.), -s ˌdaɪəgˈnɒstɪk, -s
diagon|al (s. adj.), -als, -ally daɪˈægən|l,
-lz, -əlɪ [-l̩ɪ]
diagram, -s 'daɪəgræm, -z
diagrammatic, -al, -ally ˌdaɪəgrə-
'mætɪk, -l, -əlɪ
dial (s. v.), -s, -ling, -led 'daɪəl, -z,
'daɪəlɪŋ, 'daɪəld
dialect, -s 'daɪəlekt, -s
dialectal ˌdaɪəˈlektl
dialectic, -s, -al, -ally ˌdaɪəˈlektɪk, -s,
-l, -əlɪ
dialectician, -s ˌdaɪəlekˈtɪʃn, -z
dialectolog|ist/s, -y ˌdaɪəlekˈtɒlədʒ|-
ɪst/s, -ɪ
diallage (figure of speech) daɪˈæləgɪ
[-lədʒɪ]

diallage (*mineral*) 'daɪəlɪdʒ
dialogi|sm, -st/s daɪ'æləʤɪ|zəm, -st/s
dialogue, -s 'daɪəlɒg, -z
dial-plate, -s 'daɪəlpleɪt, -s
dialys|is, -es daɪ'ælɪs|ɪs [-ləs-], -iːz
diamagnetic (*s. adj.*), -s, -ally ,daɪəmæg-
  'netɪk [-məg-], -s, -əlɪ
diamagnetism ,daɪə'mægnɪtɪzəm [-nət-]
diamanté də'mɒnteɪ [daɪə-]
diameter, -s daɪ'æmɪtə* [-mət-], -z
diametr|al, -ally daɪ'æmɪtr|əl, -əlɪ
diametric|al, -ally ,daɪə'metrɪk|l, -əlɪ
  [-|ɪ]
diamond, -s 'daɪəmənd, -z
diamond-field, -s 'daɪəməndfiːld, -z
Diana daɪ'ænə
dianthus, -es daɪ'ænθəs, -ɪz
diapason, -s ,daɪə'peɪsn [-'peɪzn], -z
diaper, -s 'daɪəpə*, -z
diaphanous daɪ'æfənəs
diaphone, -s 'daɪəfəʊn, -z
diaphonic ,daɪə'fɒnɪk
diaphragm, -s 'daɪəfræm [-frəm], -z
diaphragmatic ,daɪəfræg'mætɪk [-frəg-]
diapositive, -s ,daɪə'pɒzɪtɪv [-zət-], -z
diarch|y, -ies 'daɪɑːk|ɪ, -ɪz
diarist, -s 'daɪərɪst, -s
diarrhoea ,daɪə'rɪə
diar|y, -ies 'daɪər|ɪ, -ɪz
Diaspora daɪ'æspərə
diastase 'daɪəsteɪs
diastole, -s daɪ'æstəl|ɪ, -z
diastolic ,daɪə'stɒlɪk
diatherm|ic, -ous ,daɪə'θɜːm|ɪk, -əs
diatom, -s 'daɪətəm [-tɒm], -z
diatonic, -ally ,daɪə'tɒnɪk, -əlɪ
diatribe, -s 'daɪətraɪb, -z
diazepam daɪ'æzɪpæm
dib (*s. v.*), -s, -bing, -bed, -ber/s dɪb, -z,
  -ɪŋ, -d, -ə*/z
Dibb dɪb
dibb|le (*s. v.*), -les, -ling, -led, -ler/s
  'dɪb|l, -lz, -lɪŋ [-lɪŋ], -ld, -lə*/z
  [-lə*/z]
Dibdin 'dɪbdɪn
dicast, -s 'dɪkæst, -s
dice (*plur.* of die) daɪs
dic|e (*v.*), -es, -ing, -ed daɪs, -ɪz, -ɪŋ, -t
dice-box, -es 'daɪsbɒks, -ɪz
dicey (D.) 'daɪsɪ
dichloride, -s daɪ'klɔːraɪd, -z
dichotom|y, -ies daɪ'kɒtəm|ɪ [dɪ-], -ɪz
Dick dɪk
dickens (D.) 'dɪkɪnz
Dickensian dɪ'kenzɪən [-'kens- -jən]
Dicker 'dɪkə*
dickey, -s 'dɪkɪ, -z
Dickins 'dɪkɪnz

Dickinson 'dɪkɪnsn
Dicksee 'dɪksi: [-sɪ]
Dickson 'dɪksn
dick|y (D.), -ies 'dɪk|ɪ, -ɪz
dickybird, -s 'dɪkɪbɜːd, -z
dicotyledon, -s ,daɪkɒtɪ'liːdən [-tə'l-],
  -z
dictaphone, -s 'dɪktəfəʊn, -z
dictate (s.), -s 'dɪkteɪt, -s
dictat|e (v.), -es, -ing, -ed, -or/s dɪk-
  'teɪt, -s, -ɪŋ, -ɪd, -ə*/z
dictation, -s dɪk'teɪʃn, -z
dictatorial, -ly ,dɪktə'tɔːrɪəl, -ɪ
dictatorship, -s dɪk'teɪtəʃɪp, -s
diction 'dɪkʃn
dictionar|y, -ies 'dɪkʃənr|ɪ [-ʃənər-], -ɪz
dict|um, -a, -ums 'dɪkt|əm, -ə, -əmz
did (*from* do) dɪd
Didache 'dɪdəkɪ [-kɪ]
didactic, -al, -ally dɪ'dæktɪk [daɪ'd-], -l,
  -əlɪ
didacticism dɪ'dæktɪsɪzəm [daɪ'd-]
didapper, -s 'daɪdæpə*, -z
Didcot 'dɪdkət
didd|le, -les, -ling, -led, -ler/s 'dɪd|l, -lz,
  -lɪŋ [-lɪŋ], -ld, -lə*/z [-lə*/z]
Diderot 'diːdərəʊ (didro)
didn't 'dɪdnt [*also* 'dɪdn *when not final*]
Dido 'daɪdəʊ
Didymus 'dɪdɪməs
die (s.) (*stamp*), -s daɪ, -z
die (s.) (*cube*), dice daɪ, daɪs
die (v.), -s, dying, died daɪ, -z, -ɪŋ, -d
dielectric (*s. adj.*), -s ,daɪə'lektrɪk, -s
Dieppe di:'ep [dɪ'ep] (djɛp)
dies (*from* die) daɪz
Diesel, -s 'di:zl, -z
die-sink, -er/s, -ing, 'daɪsɪŋk, -ə*/z, -ɪŋ
dies irae ,di:eɪz'ɪəraɪ [,di:ez-, ,di:es-,
  -'ɪəreɪ, *old-fashioned* ,daɪɪz'aɪəri:]
dies|is, -es 'daɪɪs|ɪs [daɪəs-], -iːz
dies non, -s ,daɪi:z'nɒn, -z
diet (s. v.), -s, -ing, -ed 'daɪət, -s, -ɪŋ, -ɪd
dietar|y (s. adj.), -ies 'daɪətər|ɪ [-daɪt-],
  -ɪz
dietetic (s. adj.), -s, -al, -ally ,daɪə'tetɪk
  [,daɪɪt-], -s, -l, -əlɪ
dietitian [-ician], -s ,daɪə'tɪʃn
  [,daɪɪt-], -z
differ, -s, -ing, -ed 'dɪfə*, -z, -rɪŋ, -d
differen|ce, -ces, -t/ly 'dɪfrən|s
  [-fərən-], -sɪz, -t/lɪ
differenti|al, -als, -ally ,dɪfə'renʃ|l, -lz,
  -əlɪ
differentiat|e, -es, -ing, -ed ,dɪfə'ren-
  ʃɪeɪt [-ʃjeɪt], -s, -ɪŋ, -ɪd
differentiation, -s ,dɪfərenʃɪ'eɪʃn [-nsɪ-],
  -z

137

difficult 'dɪfɪkəlt [-fək-]
difficult|y, -ies 'dɪfɪkəlt|ɪ [-fək-], -ɪz
diffiden|ce, -t/ly 'dɪfɪdən|s, -t/lɪ
diffract, -s, -ing, -ed dɪ'frækt, -s, -ɪŋ, -ɪd
diffraction dɪ'frækʃn
diffuse (adj.), -ly, -ness dɪ'fju:s, -lɪ, -nɪs [-nəs]
diffus|e (v.), -es, -ing, -ed, -edly, -edness, -er/s dɪ'fju:z, -ɪz, -ɪŋ, -d, -ɪdlɪ, -ɪdnɪs [-nəs], -ə*/z
diffusibility dɪ,fju:zə'bɪlətɪ [-zɪ'b-, -lɪt-]
diffusible dɪ'fju:zəbl [-zɪb-]
diffusion dɪ'fju:ʒn
diffusive, -ly, -ness dɪ'fju:sɪv, -lɪ, -nɪs [-nəs]
dig (s. v.), -s, -ging, -ged, dug dɪg, -z, -ɪŋ, -d, dʌg
dig. (in phrase infra dig.) dɪg
digamma, -s daɪ'gæmə ['daɪgæmə], -z
Digby 'dɪgbɪ
digest (s.), -s 'daɪdʒest, -s
digest (v.), -s, -ing, -ed dɪ'dʒest [daɪ'dʒ-], -s, -ɪŋ, -ɪd
digestibility dɪ,dʒestə'bɪlətɪ [daɪ,dʒ-, -tɪ'b-, -lɪt-]
digestible dɪ'dʒestəbl [daɪ'dʒ-, -tɪb-]
digestion, -s dɪ'dʒestʃən [daɪ'dʒ-, -eʃtʃ-], -z
digestive (s. adj.), -s, -ly, -ness dɪ'dʒes-tɪv [daɪ'dʒ-], -z, -lɪ, -nɪs [-nəs]
digger, -s 'dɪgə*, -z
Digges dɪgz
diggings 'dɪgɪŋz
Diggle, -s 'dɪgl, -z
Diggory 'dɪgərɪ
dight daɪt
Dighton 'daɪtn
digit, -s; -al/s 'dɪdʒɪt, -s; -l/z
digitali|n, -s ,dɪdʒɪ'teɪlɪ|n, -s
digni|fy, -fies, -fying, -fied 'dɪgnɪ|faɪ, -faɪz, -faɪɪŋ, -faɪd
dignitar|y, -ies 'dɪgnɪtər|ɪ, -ɪz
dignit|y, -ies 'dɪgnət|ɪ [-ɪt|ɪ], -ɪz
digraph, -s 'daɪgrɑ:f [-græf], -s
digress, -es, -ing, -ed daɪ'gres [dɪ'g-], -ɪz, -ɪŋ, -t
digression, -s daɪ'greʃn [dɪ'g-], -z
digressive, -ly, -ness daɪ'gresɪv [dɪ'g-], -lɪ, -nɪs [-nəs]
digs (lodgings) dɪgz
Dijon 'di:ʒɔ̃:ŋ [-ʒɒŋ, -ʒɒn] (diʒɔ̃)
dik|e (s. v.), -es, -ing, -ed daɪk, -s, -ɪŋ, -t
diktat 'dɪktɑ:t [-tæt]
dilapidat|e, -es, -ing, -ed dɪ'læpɪdeɪt, -s, -ɪŋ, -ɪd
dilapidation, -s dɪ,læpɪ'deɪʃn, -z
dilatability daɪ,leɪtə'bɪlətɪ [dɪ,l-, -'bɪlɪt-]
dilatation, -s ,daɪleɪ'teɪʃn [-lət-], -z

dilat|e, -es, -ing, -ed, -er/s; -able daɪ'leɪt [dɪ'l-], -s, -ɪŋ, -ɪd, -ə*/z; -əbl
dilation, -s daɪ'leɪʃn [dɪ'l-], -z
dilator|y, -ily, -iness 'dɪlətər|ɪ, -əlɪ [-ɪlɪ], -ɪnɪs [-nəs]
dilemma, -s dɪ'lemə [daɪ'l-], -z
dilettante, -s ,dɪlɪ'tæntɪ, -z
dilettantism ,dɪlɪ'tæntɪzəm
diligence 'dɪlɪdʒəns
diligent, -ly 'dɪlɪdʒənt, -lɪ
Dilke, -s dɪlk, -s
dill (D.), -s dɪl, -z
Dillon 'dɪlən
Dillwyn (English surname) 'dɪlɪn, 'dɪlwɪn
dilly-dall|y, -ies, -ying, -ied 'dɪlɪdæl|ɪ, -ɪz, -ɪɪŋ, -ɪd
diluent (s. adj.), -s 'dɪljʊənt [-ljwənt], -s
dilut|e (adj. v.), -eness; -es, -ing, -ed daɪ'lju:t [dɪ'l-, -'lu:t], -nɪs [-nəs]; -s, -ɪŋ, -ɪd
dilutee, -s ,daɪlju:'ti: [-lu:'t-], -z
dilution, -s daɪ'lu:ʃn [dɪ'l-, -'lju:-], -z
diluvia|l, -n daɪ'lu:vjə|l [dɪ'l-, -'lju:-, -vɪə-], -n
diluvi|um, -a daɪ'lu:vj|əm [dɪ'l-, -'lju:-, -vɪ|əm], -ə
Dilwyn 'dɪlwɪn (Welsh 'dilwɪn)
Dilys 'dɪlɪs (Welsh 'dilɪs)
dim (adj. v.), -mer, -mest, -ly, -ness; -s, -ming, -med dɪm, -ə*, -ɪst, -lɪ, -nɪs [-nəs]; -z, -ɪŋ, -d
Diman 'daɪmən
dime, -s daɪm, -z
dimension, -s dɪ'menʃn [daɪ'm-], -z
dimensional dɪ'menʃənl [daɪ'm-, -ʃnəl, ʃn̩l, -ʃnl, -ʃənəl]
dimeter, -s 'dɪmɪtə* [-mə-], -z
dimidiate (adj.) dɪ'mɪdɪət [-djət, -ɪt]
dimidiat|e (v.), -es, -ing, -ed dɪ'mɪdɪeɪt, -s, -ɪŋ, -ɪd
dimidiation dɪ,mɪdɪ'eɪʃn
diminish, -es, -ing, -ed; -able dɪ'mɪnɪʃ, -ɪz, -ɪŋ, -t; -əbl
diminuendo, -s dɪ,mɪnjʊ'endəʊ, -z
diminution, -s ,dɪmɪ'nju:ʃn, -z
diminutive, -ly, -ness dɪ'mɪnjʊtɪv, -lɪ, -nɪs [-nəs]
dimity 'dɪmɪtɪ [-ətɪ]
Dimmesdale 'dɪmzdeɪl
dimmish 'dɪmɪʃ
dim-out, -s 'dɪmaʊt, -s
dimp|le (s. v.), -les, -ling, -led 'dɪmp|l, -lz, -lɪŋ [-lɪŋ], -ld
dimply 'dɪmplɪ
Dimsdale 'dɪmzdeɪl
din (s. v.), -s, -ning, -ned dɪn, -z, -ɪŋ, -d
Dinah 'daɪnə

138

dinar, -s (*monetary unit in Yugoslavia*) 'di:nɑ:*, (*in Iran, Iraq, Jordan*) 'di:nɑ:* [di:'nɑ:*], -z
Dindigul 'dɪndɪgəl
din|e, -es, -ing, -ed, -er/s daɪn, -z, -ɪŋ, -d, -ə*/z
Dinely (*surname*) 'dɪnlɪ
ding, -s, -ing, -ed dɪŋ, -z, -ɪŋ, -d
dingdong ˌdɪŋ'dɒŋ [*also* '-- *according to sentence-stress*]
dingey, -s 'dɪŋgɪ [-ŋɪ], -z
dingh|y, -ies 'dɪŋg|ɪ [-ŋ|ɪ], -ɪz
dingle (D.), -s 'dɪŋgl, -z
Dingley 'dɪŋlɪ
dingo, -s 'dɪŋgəʊ, -z
Dingwall 'dɪŋwɔ:l [-wəl]
ding|y (*adj.*) (*dirty, drab*), **-ier, -iest, -ily, -iness** 'dɪn*dʒ*|ɪ, -ɪə* [-jə*], -ɪɪst [-jɪst], -ɪlɪ [-əlɪ], -ɪnɪs [-nəs]
dining-car, -s 'daɪnɪŋkɑ:*, -z
dining-room, -s 'daɪnɪŋrʊm [-ru:m], -z
dining-table, -s 'daɪnɪŋˌteɪbl, -z
dink|y, -ier, -iest, -iness 'dɪŋk|ɪ, -ɪə* [-jə*], -ɪɪst [-jɪst], -ɪnɪs [-nəs]
Dinmont 'dɪnmɒnt [-mənt]
Dinneford 'dɪnɪfəd
dinner, -s 'dɪnə*, -z
dinner-bell, -s 'dɪnəbel, -z
dinner-hour, -s 'dɪnərˌaʊə* ['dɪnəˌaʊə*], -z
dinner-jacket, -s 'dɪnəˌdʒækɪt, -s
dinner-part|y, -ies 'dɪnəˌpɑ:t|ɪ, -ɪz
dinner-plate, -s 'dɪnəpleɪt, -s
dinner-service, -s 'dɪnəˌsɜ:vɪs, -ɪz
dinner-set, -s 'dɪnəset, -s
dinner-table, -s 'dɪnəˌteɪbl, -z
dinner-time, -s 'dɪnətaɪm, -z
dinner-wagon, -s 'dɪnəˌwægən, -z
Dinocrates daɪ'nɒkrəti:z
Dinorah dɪ'nɔ:rə
dinosaur, -s 'daɪnəʊsɔ:*, -z
dinosaur|us, -i ˌdaɪnə'sɔ:r|əs, -aɪ
dinotheri|um, -a ˌdaɪnəʊ'θɪərɪ|əm, -ə
dint dɪnt
Dinwiddie dɪn'wɪdɪ
diocesan daɪ'ɒsɪsn [-səs-]
diocese, -s 'daɪəsɪs [-si:s, -si:z], -ɪz
Diocles 'daɪəkli:z
Diocletian ˌdaɪə'kli:ʃjən [-ʃɪən, -ʃn]
diode, -s 'daɪəʊd, -z
Diodorus ˌdaɪə'dɔ:rəs
Diogenes daɪ'ɒdʒmi:z [-dʒən-]
Diomed 'daɪəmed
Diomede 'daɪəmi:d
Diomedes ˌdaɪə'mi:di:z
Dion (*Greek*) 'daɪən, (*French*) 'di:ən ['di:ɔ̃:ŋ, 'di:ɒŋ, 'di:ɒn] (djɔ̃), (*in* D. Boucicault) 'daɪən

Dionysia, -n ˌdaɪə'nɪzɪə [-zjə, -ʒɪə, -ʒjə, -sɪə, -sjə], -n
Dionysius ˌdaɪə'nɪsɪəs [-sjəs]
Dionysus ˌdaɪə'naɪsəs
diopter, -s daɪ'ɒptə*, -z
dioptric daɪ'ɒptrɪk
Dior 'dɪɔ:* [dɪ'ɔ:*] (djɔ:r)
diorama, -s ˌdaɪə'rɑ:mə, -z
dioramic ˌdaɪə'ræmɪk
Diosy dɪ'əʊsɪ
dioxide, -s daɪ'ɒksaɪd [ˌdaɪ'ɒ-], -z
dip (*s. v.*), **-s, -ping, -ped, -per/s** dɪp, -s, -ɪŋ, -t, -ə*/z
diphtheria dɪf'θɪərɪə [dɪp'θ-]
diphthong, -s 'dɪfθɒŋ ['dɪpθ-], -z
diphthong|al, -ally dɪf'θɒŋg|l [dɪp'θ--ɒŋ|l], -əlɪ
diphthongization [-isa-], -s ˌdɪfθɒŋgaɪ'zeɪʃn [ˌdɪpθ-, -ɒŋgaɪ-], -z
diphthongiz|e [-is|e], -es, -ing, -ed 'dɪfθɒŋgaɪz ['dɪpθ-, -ɒŋaɪ-], -ɪz, -ɪŋ, -d
diplodoc|us, -uses, -i dɪ'plɒdək|əs, -əsɪz, -aɪ
diploma, -s dɪ'pləʊmə, -z
diplomacy dɪ'pləʊməsɪ
diplomat, -s 'dɪpləmæt [-plʊm-], -s
diplomatic (*s. adj.*), **-s, -al, -ally** ˌdɪplə'mætɪk [-plʊ'm-], -s, -l, -əlɪ
diplomatist, -s dɪ'pləʊmətɪst, -s
diplomatiz|e [-is|e], -es, -ing, -ed dɪ'pləʊmətaɪz, -ɪz, -ɪŋ, -d
dipole, -s 'daɪpəʊl, -z
dipper, -s 'dɪpə*, -z
Diprose 'dɪprəʊz
dipsomania ˌdɪpsəʊ'meɪnjə [-nɪə]
dipsomaniac (*s. adj.*), **-s** ˌdɪpsəʊ'meɪnɪæk [-njæk], -s
dipter|a, -al, -ous 'dɪptər|ə, -əl, -əs
diptych, -s 'dɪptɪk, -s
dire, -r, -st, -ness 'daɪə*, -rə*, -rɪst, -nɪs [-nəs]
direct (*adj. v.*), **-est, -ness; -s, -ing, -ed, -or/s** dɪ'rekt [də'r-, daɪ'r-, *occasionally* 'daɪrekt *when attributive adj.*], -ɪst, -nɪs [-nəs]; -s, -ɪŋ, -ɪd, -ə*/z
direction, -s dɪ'rekʃn [də'r-, daɪ'r-], -z
directional dɪ'rekʃənl [də'r-, daɪ'r-, -ʃnəl, -ʃn̩l, -ʃnl, -ʃənəl]
directive (*s. adj.*), **-s** dɪ'rektɪv [də'r-, daɪ'r-], -z
directly dɪ'rektlɪ [də'r-, daɪ'r-, 'dreklɪ]
Note.—The form 'drekl̩ı is not used in the sense of 'in a straight manner'; it is, however, freq. in the sense of 'at once', and still more freq. in the sense of 'as soon as'.
directorate, -s dɪ'rektərət [də'r-, daɪ'r-, -ɪt], -s

139

directorship, -s dɪˈrektəʃɪp [dəˈr-, daɪˈr-], -s

director|y, -ies dɪˈrektər|ɪ [dəˈr-, daɪˈr-], -ɪz

dire|ful, -fully, -fulness ˈdaɪə|fʊl, -fʊlɪ [-fəlɪ], -fʊlnɪs [-nəs]

dirge, -s dɜːdʒ, -ɪz

dirigible (s. adj.), -s ˈdɪrɪdʒəbl [-dʒɪb-, dɪˈrɪdʒ-], -z

dirk (D.), -s dɜːk, -s

dirndl [-dle], -s ˈdɜːndl, -z

dirt dɜːt

dirt-cheap ˌdɜːtˈtʃiːp

dirt-track, -s ˈdɜːtˈtræk, -s

dirt|y (adj. v.), -ier, -iest, -ily, -iness; -ies, -ying, -ied ˈdɜːt|ɪ, -ɪə* [-jə*], -ɪɪst [-jɪst], -ɪlɪ [-əlɪ], -ɪnɪs [-ɪnəs]; -ɪz, -ɪɪŋ [-jɪŋ], -ɪd

Dis dɪs

disabilit|y, -ies ˌdɪsəˈbɪlət|ɪ [ˌdɪzə-, -lɪt-], -ɪz

disab|le, -les, -ling, -led, -lement dɪsˈeɪb|l [dɪˈzeɪ-], -lz, -lɪŋ [-lɪŋ], -ld, -lmənt

disabus|e, -es, -ing, -ed ˌdɪsəˈbjuːz, -ɪz, -ɪŋ, -d

disaccustom, -s, -ing, -ed ˌdɪsəˈkʌstəm, -z, -ɪŋ, -d

disadvantage, -s ˌdɪsədˈvɑːntɪdʒ, -ɪz

disadvantageous, -ly, -ness ˌdɪsædvɑːnˈteɪdʒəs [ˈdɪsˌædvɑːnˈt-, -vən-], -lɪ, -nɪs [-nəs]

disaffect, -s, -ing, -ed/ly, -edness ˌdɪsəˈfekt, -s, -ɪŋ, -ɪd/lɪ, -ɪdnɪs [-nəs]

disaffection ˌdɪsəˈfekʃn

disagree, -s, -ing, -d, -ment/s ˌdɪsəˈgriː, -z, -ɪŋ, -d, -mənt/s

disagreeab|le, -ly, -leness, -les ˌdɪsəˈgrɪəb|l, -lɪ, -lnɪs [-nəs], -lz

disallow, -s, -ing, -ed ˌdɪsəˈlaʊ, -z, -ɪŋ, -d

disallow|able, -ance ˌdɪsəˈlaʊ|əbl, -əns

disappear, -s, -ing, -ed ˌdɪsəˈpɪə*, -z, -rɪŋ, -d

disappearance, -s ˌdɪsəˈpɪərəns, -ɪz

disappoint, -s, -ing, -ed, -ment/s ˌdɪsəˈpɔɪnt, -s, -ɪŋ, -ɪd, -mənt/s

disapprobation ˌdɪsæprəʊˈbeɪʃn [ˈdɪsˌæprəʊˈb-, -prʊˈb-]

disapproval ˌdɪsəˈpruːvl

disapprov|e, -es, -ing/ly, -ed ˌdɪsəˈpruːv, -z, -ɪŋ/lɪ, -d

disarm, -s, -ing, -ed dɪsˈɑːm [dɪˈzɑːm], -z, -ɪŋ, -d

disarmament dɪsˈɑːməmənt [dɪˈzɑːm-]

disarrang|e, -es, -ing, -ed ˌdɪsəˈreɪndʒ, -ɪz, -ɪŋ, -d

disarrangement, -s ˌdɪsəˈreɪndʒmənt, -s

disarray (s. v.), -s, -ing, -ed ˌdɪsəˈreɪ, -z, -ɪŋ, -d

disarticulat|e, -es, -ing, -ed ˌdɪsɑːˈtɪkjʊleɪt, -s, -ɪŋ, -ɪd

disarticulation ˈdɪsɑːˌtɪkjʊˈleɪʃn

disaster, -s dɪˈzɑːstə*, -z

disastrous, -ly, -ness dɪˈzɑːstrəs, -lɪ, -nɪs [-nəs]

disavow, -s, -ing, -ed, -al ˌdɪsəˈvaʊ, -z, -ɪŋ, -d, -əl

disband, -s, -ing, -ed, -ment dɪsˈbænd, -z, -ɪŋ, -ɪd, -mənt [dɪsˈbænmənt]

disbar, -s, -ring, -red dɪsˈbɑː*, -z, -rɪŋ, -d

disbark, -s, -ing, -ed dɪsˈbɑːk, -s, -ɪŋ, -t

disbelief ˌdɪsbɪˈliːf [-bə-, ˈ---]

disbeliev|e, -es, -ing, -ed, -er/s ˌdɪsbɪˈliːv [-bə-], -z, -ɪŋ, -d, -ə*/z

disburs|e, -es, -ing, -ed, -ement/s dɪsˈbɜːs, -ɪz, -ɪŋ, -t, -mənt/s

disc, -s dɪsk, -s

discard (s.), -s ˈdɪskɑːd [dɪˈskɑːd], -z

discard (v.), -s, -ing, -ed dɪˈskɑːd, -z, -ɪŋ, -ɪd

discern, -s, -ing, -ed, -er/s, -ment dɪˈsɜːn [dɪˈzɜːn], -z, -ɪŋ, -d, -ə*/z, -mənt

discernib|le, -ly, -leness dɪˈsɜːnəb|l [dɪˈzɜː-, -nɪb-], -lɪ, -lnɪs [-nəs]

discharge (s.), -s dɪsˈtʃɑːdʒ [ˈdɪstʃɑːdʒ], -ɪz

discharg|e (v.), -es, -ing, -ed, -er/s dɪsˈtʃɑːdʒ, -ɪz, -ɪŋ, -d, -ə*/z

disciple, -s; -ship dɪˈsaɪpl, -z; -ʃɪp

disciplinarian, -s ˌdɪsɪplɪˈneərɪən [-səp-], -z

disciplinary ˈdɪsɪplɪnərɪ [ˌ--ˈ---, -sə-, ˌdɪsɪˈplaɪ-]

disciplin|e (s. v.), -es, -ing, -ed ˈdɪsɪplɪn [-səp-], -z, -ɪŋ, -d

disc-jockey, -s ˈdɪskˌdʒɒkɪ, -z

disclaim, -s, -ing, -ed, -er/s dɪsˈkleɪm, -z, -ɪŋ, -d, -ə*/z

disclaimer (denial), -s dɪsˈkleɪmə*, -z

disclos|e, -es, -ing, -ed dɪsˈkləʊz, -ɪz, -ɪŋ, -d

disclosure, -s dɪsˈkləʊʒə*, -z

discobol|us, -i dɪˈskɒbəl|əs [-bl|-], -aɪ

discolo(u)ration, -s dɪsˌkʌləˈreɪʃn [ˌdɪsk-], -z

discolour, -s, -ing, -ed dɪsˈkʌlə*, -z, -rɪŋ, -d

discomfit, -s, -ing, -ed dɪsˈkʌmfɪt, -s, -ɪŋ, -ɪd

discomfiture dɪsˈkʌmfɪtʃə* [-fə-]

discomfort (s. v.), -s, -ing, -ed dɪsˈkʌmfət, -s, -ɪŋ, -ɪd

discompos|e, -es, -ing, -ed ˌdɪskəm-
'pəʊz, -ɪz, -ɪŋ, -d
discomposure ˌdɪskəm'pəʊʒə*
disconcert, -s, -ing, -ed ˌdɪskən'sɜːt, -s,
-ɪŋ, -ɪd
disconnect, -s, -ing, -ed ˌdɪskə'nekt, -s,
-ɪŋ, -ɪd
disconnection ˌdɪskə'nekʃn
disconsolate, -ly, -ness dɪs'kɒnsəlɪt
[-lɪt], -lɪ, -nɪs [-nəs]
discontent, -ed, -edly, -edness ˌdɪskən'tent, -ɪd, -ɪdlɪ, -ɪdnɪs [-nəs]
discontinuance ˌdɪskən'tɪnjʊəns
[-njwəns]
discontin|ue, -ues, -uing, -ued ˌdɪskən-
'tɪn|juː [-jʊ], -juːz [-jʊz], -jʊɪŋ
[-jwɪŋ], -juːd [-jʊd]
discontinuit|y, -ies ˌdɪskɒntɪ'njuːət|ɪ
[-'njʊ-, -ɪt|ɪ, -ˌ--'---], -ɪz
discontinuous, -ly ˌdɪskən'tɪnjʊəs
[-njwəs], -lɪ
discord (s.), -s 'dɪskɔːd, -z
discord (v.), -s, -ing, -ed dɪ'skɔːd, -z, -ɪŋ,
-ɪd
discordan|ce, -cy, -t/ly dɪ'skɔːdən|s,
-sɪ, -t/lɪ
discothèque, -s 'dɪskəʊtek [-teɪk], -s
(diskɔtɛk)
discount (s.), -s 'dɪskaʊnt, -s
discount (v.), -s, -ing, -ed, -er/s 'dɪskaʊnt, dɪ'skaʊnt, -s, -ɪŋ, -ɪd, -ə*/z
discountenanc|e, -es, -ing, -ed
dɪ'skaʊntɪnəns [-tən-], -ɪz, -ɪŋ, -t
discourag|e, -es, -ing/ly, -ed, -ement/s
dɪ'skʌrɪdʒ, -ɪz, -ɪŋ/lɪ, -d, -mənt/s
discourse (s.), -s 'dɪskɔːs [dɪ'skɔːs,
-ɔəs], -ɪz
discours|e (v.), -es, -ing, -ed, -er/s
dɪ'skɔːs [-'kɔəs], -ɪz, -ɪŋ, -t, -ə*/z
discourteous, -ly, -ness dɪs'kɜːtjəs
[-'kɔːt-, -'kɔət-, -trəs], -lɪ, -nɪs [-nəs]
discourtesy dɪs'kɜːtɪsɪ [-'kɔːt-, -'kɔət-,
-təsɪ]
discov|er, -ers, -ering, -ered, -erer/s
dɪ'skʌv|ə*, -əz, -ərɪŋ, -əd, -ərə*/z
discoverable dɪ'skʌvərəbl
discovert dɪs'kʌvət
discover|y, -ies dɪ'skʌvər|ɪ, -ɪz
discredit, -s, -ing, -ed dɪs'kredɪt
[ˌdɪs'k-], -s, -ɪŋ, -ɪd
discreditab|le, -ly, -leness dɪs'kredɪt-
əb|l, -lɪ, -lnɪs [-nəs]
discreet, -est, -ly, -ness dɪ'skriːt, -ɪst,
-lɪ, -nɪs [-nəs]
discrepan|cy, -cies, -t dɪ'skrepən|sɪ,
-sɪz, -t
discrete, -ly, -ness dɪ'skriːt [also '--
when attributive], -lɪ, -nɪs [-nəs]

discretion, -s dɪ'skreʃn, -z
discre|tional, -tionally dɪ'skre|ʃənl
[-ʃnəl, -ʃn̩l, -ʃn̩l, -ʃənəl], -ʃnəlɪ
[-ʃnəlɪ, -ʃn̩lɪ, -ʃn̩lɪ, -ʃənəlɪ]
discretionar|y, -ily dɪ'skreʃn̩ər|ɪ
[-ʃənər-], -əlɪ [-ɪlɪ]
discriminate (adj.), -ly dɪ'skrɪmɪnət
[-ɪt], -lɪ
discriminat|e (v.), -es, -ing/ly, -ed dɪ-
'skrɪmɪneɪt, -s, -ɪŋ/lɪ, -ɪd
discrimination, -s dɪˌskrɪmɪ'neɪʃn, -z
discriminative, -ly dɪ'skrɪmɪnətɪv
[-neɪt-], -lɪ
discriminatory dɪ'skrɪmɪnətərɪ [dɪ-
ˌskrɪmɪ'neɪtərɪ]
discursion, -s dɪ'skɜːʃn, -z
discursive, -ly, -ness dɪ'skɜːsɪv, -lɪ, -nɪs
[-nəs]
discursory dɪ'skɜːsərɪ
disc|us, -i 'dɪsk|əs, -aɪ
discuss, -es, -ing, -ed; -able dɪ'skʌs, -ɪz,
-ɪŋ, -t; -əbl
discussion, -s dɪ'skʌʃn, -z
disdain (s. v.), -s, -ing, -ed dɪs'deɪn
[dɪz'd-], -z, -ɪŋ, -d
disdain|ful, -fully, -fulness dɪs'deɪn|fʊl
[dɪz'd-], -fʊlɪ [-fəlɪ], -fʊlnɪs [-nəs]
disease, -s, -d dɪ'ziːz, -ɪz, -d
disembark, -s, -ing, -ed ˌdɪsɪm'bɑːk
[-sem-], -s, -ɪŋ, -t
disembarkation, -s ˌdɪsembɑː'keɪʃn
[-sɪm-], -z
disembarkment, -s ˌdɪsɪm'bɑːkmənt
[-sem-], -s
disembarrass, -es, -ing, -ed ˌdɪsɪm-
'bærəs [-sem-], -ɪz, -ɪŋ, -t
disembarrassment, -s ˌdɪsɪm'bærəsmənt
[-sem-], -s
disembod|y, -ies, -ying, -ied ˌdɪsɪm-
'bɒd|ɪ [-sem-], -ɪz, -ɪŋ [-jɪŋ], -ɪd
disemb|owel, -owels, -owelling, -owelled
ˌdɪsɪm'b|aʊəl [-sem-, -aʊl], -aʊəlz,
-aʊəlɪŋ, -aʊəld [-aʊld]
disenchant, -s, -ing, -ed ˌdɪsɪn'tʃɑːnt
[-sen-], -s, -ɪŋ, -ɪd
disenchantment, -s ˌdɪsɪn'tʃɑːntmənt
[-sen-], -s
disencumb|er, -ers, -ering, -ered ˌdɪsɪn-
'kʌmb|ə* [-sen-], -əz, -ərɪŋ, -əd
disendow, -s, -ing, -ed ˌdɪsɪn'daʊ
[-sen-], -z, -ɪŋ, -d
disendowment ˌdɪsɪn'daʊmənt [-sen-]
disenfranchis|e, -es, -ing, -ed ˌdɪsɪn-
'fræntʃaɪz [-sen-], -ɪz, -ɪŋ, -d
disenfranchisement ˌdɪsɪn'fræntʃɪzmənt
[-sen-]
disengag|e, -es, -ing, -ed ˌdɪsɪn'geɪdʒ
[-sɪŋ'g-, -sen'g-], -ɪz, -ɪŋ, -d

141

disentail (*s. v.*), **-s, -ing, -ed** ˌdɪsɪn'teɪl [-sen-], -z, -ɪŋ, -d

disentang|le, -les, -ling, -led ˌdɪsɪn-'tæŋg|l [-sen-], -lz, -lɪŋ, [-lɪŋ], -ld

disentanglement ˌdɪsɪn'tæŋglmənt [-sen-]

disentit|le, -les, -ling, -led ˌdɪsɪn'taɪt|l [-sen-], -lz, -lɪŋ [-lɪŋ], -ld

disequilibrium ˌdɪsekwɪ'lɪbrɪəm

disestablish, -es, -ing, -ed ˌdɪsɪ'stæblɪʃ [-ses-], -ɪz, -ɪŋ, -t

disestablishment ˌdɪsɪ'stæblɪʃmənt [-ses-]

disfavour ˌdɪs'feɪvə* [dɪs'f-]

disfiguration, -s dɪsˌfɪgjʊə'reɪʃn [ˌdɪsf-, -gjə-], -z

disfigur|e, -es, -ing, -ed, -ement/s dɪs-'fɪgə*, -z, -rɪŋ, -d, -mənt/s

disfranchis|e, -es, -ing, -ed ˌdɪs'fræn-tʃaɪz [dɪs'f-], -ɪz, -ɪŋ, -d

disfranchisement dɪs'fræntʃɪzmənt

disgorg|e, -es, -ing, -ed dɪs'ɡɔːdʒ, -ɪz, -ɪŋ, -d

disgrac|e (*s. v.*), -es, -ing, -ed dɪs'ɡreɪs [dɪz-], -ɪz, -ɪŋ, -t

disgrace|ful, -fully, -fulness dɪs'ɡreɪs|-fʊl [dɪz-], -fʊlɪ [-fəlɪ], -fʊlnɪs [-nəs]

disgruntled dɪs'ɡrʌntld

disguis|e (*s. v.*), -es, -ing, -ed, -er/s dɪs'ɡaɪz [dɪz-], -ɪz, -ɪŋ, -d, -ə*/z

disgust (*s. v.*), -s, -ing/ly, -ed dɪs'ɡʌst [dɪz-], -s, -ɪŋ/lɪ, -ɪd

dish (*s. v.*), -es, -ing, -ed dɪʃ, -ɪz, -ɪŋ, -t

dishabille ˌdɪsæ'biːl [-sə'b-]

disharmony ˌdɪs'hɑːmənɪ

dish|cloth, -cloths 'dɪʃ|klɒθ [*old-fashioned* -klɔːθ], -klɒθs [-klɔːðz, -klɔːθs]

dish-cover, -s 'dɪʃˌkʌvə*, -z

disheart|en, -ens, -ening, -ened dɪs-'hɑːt|n, -nz, -nɪŋ [-ŋɪŋ], -nd

disherison dɪs'herɪzn [-ɪsn]

dishev|el, -els, -elling, -elled dɪ'ʃev|l, -lz, -lɪŋ [-lɪŋ], -ld

dishful, -s 'dɪʃfʊl, -z

dishonest, -ly dɪs'ɒnɪst [dɪ'zɒ-], -lɪ

dishonest|y, -ies dɪs'ɒnɪst|ɪ [dɪ'zɒ-, -əst|ɪ], -ɪz

dishonour (*s. v.*), -s, -ing, -ed, -er/s dɪs'ɒnə* [dɪ'zɒ-], -z, -rɪŋ, -d, -rə*/z

dishonourab|le, -ly, -leness dɪs'ɒnərəb|l [dɪ'zɒ-], -lɪ, -lnɪs [-nəs]

dishors|e, -es, -ing, -ed dɪs'hɔːs, -ɪz, -ɪŋ,-t

dishwasher, -s 'dɪʃˌwɒʃə*, -z

dish-water 'dɪʃˌwɔːtə*

disillusi|on (*s. v.*), -ons, -oning, -oned, -onment/s ˌdɪsɪ'luːʒ|n [-'ljuː-], -nz, -ŋɪŋ [-ənɪŋ], -nd, -nmənt/s

disinclination ˌdɪsɪnklɪ'neɪʃn [-ŋk-, -ntl-, -lə'n-]

disinclin|e, -es, -ing, -ed ˌdɪsɪn'klaɪn [-ŋ'kl-, -ɪn'tl-], -z, -ɪŋ, -d

disinfect, -s, -ing, -ed ˌdɪsɪn'fekt, -s, -ɪŋ, -ɪd

disinfectant (*s. adj.*), -s ˌdɪsɪn'fektənt, -s

disinfection, -s ˌdɪsɪn'fekʃn, -z

disinfestation ˌdɪsɪnfe'steɪʃn

disinflation ˌdɪsɪn'fleɪʃn

disingenuous, -ly, -ness ˌdɪsɪn'dʒen-jʊəs [-njwəs], -lɪ, -nɪs [-nəs]

disinherit, -s, -ing, -ed ˌdɪsɪn'herɪt, -s, -ɪŋ, -ɪd

disinheritance ˌdɪsɪn'herɪtəns

disintegrable dɪs'ɪntɪɡrəbl

disintegrat|e, -es, -ing, -ed, -or/s dɪs-'ɪntɪɡreɪt, -s, -ɪŋ, -ɪd, -ə*/z

disintegration, -s dɪsˌɪntɪ'ɡreɪʃn [ˌdɪsɪn-], -z

disinter, -s, -ring, -red ˌdɪsɪn'tɜː*, -z, -rɪŋ, -d

disinterested, -ly, -ness dɪs'ɪntrəstɪd [ˌdɪs'ɪn-, -'ɪntərest-, -'ɪntrɪst-], -lɪ, -nɪs [-nəs]

disinterment, -s ˌdɪsɪn'tɜːmənt -s

disjoin, -s, -ing, -ed dɪs'dʒɔɪn, -z, -ɪŋ, -d

disjoint, -s, -ing, -ed/ly, -edness dɪs-'dʒɔɪnt, -s, -ɪŋ, -ɪd/lɪ, -ɪdnɪs [-nəs]

disjunct dɪs'dʒʌŋkt ['—]

disjunction, -s dɪs'dʒʌŋkʃn, -z

disjunctive, -ly dɪs'dʒʌŋktɪv [ˌdɪs'dʒ-], -lɪ

disk, -s dɪsk, -z

dislik|e (*s. v.*), -es, -ing, -ed dɪs'laɪk, -s, -ɪŋ, -t
Note.—*The stress* '— *is, however, used in the expression* likes and dislikes.

dislocat|e, -es, -ing, -ed 'dɪsləʊkeɪt, -s, -ɪŋ, -ɪd

dislocation, -s ˌdɪsləʊ'keɪʃn, -z

dislodg|e, -es, -ing, -ed, -(e)ment dɪs-'lɒdʒ, -ɪz, -ɪŋ, -d, -mənt

disloy|al, -ally, -alty ˌdɪs'lɔɪ|əl [dɪs'l-], -əlɪ, -əltɪ

dism|al, -ally, -alness 'dɪzm|əl, -əlɪ, -əlnɪs [-nəs]

dismant|le, -les, -ling, -led dɪs'mænt|l, -lz, -lɪŋ, -ld

dismast, -s, -ing, -ed ˌdɪs'mɑːst, -s, -ɪŋ, -ɪd

dismay (*s. v.*), -s, -ing, -ed dɪs'meɪ [dɪz'm-], -z, -ɪŋ, -d

dismember, -s, -ing, -ed, -ment dɪs-'membə*, -z, -rɪŋ, -d, -mənt

dismiss, -es, -ing, -ed dɪs'mɪs, -ɪz, -ɪŋ, -t

dismissal, -s dɪs'mɪsl, -z

dismount, -s, -ing, -ed ˌdɪsˈmaʊnt [dɪsˈm-], -s, -ɪŋ, -ɪd

Disney ˈdɪznɪ

disobedien|ce, -t/ly ˌdɪsəˈbiːdjən|s [-dɪən-], -t/lɪ

disobey, -s, -ing, -ed ˌdɪsəˈbeɪ, -z, -ɪŋ, -d

disoblig|e, -es, -ing/ly, -ingness, -ed ˌdɪsəˈblaɪdʒ, -ɪz, -ɪŋ/lɪ, -ɪŋnɪs [-nəs], -d

disord|er (s. v.), -ers, -ering, -ered dɪsˈɔːd|ə* [dɪˈzɔː-], -əz, -ərɪŋ, -əd

disorder|ly, -liness dɪsˈɔːdə|lɪ [dɪˈzɔː-], -lɪnɪs [-nəs]

disorganization [-isa-] dɪsˌɔːgənaɪˈzeɪʃn [dɪˌzɔː-, ˌdɪsɔː-, -gnaɪˈz-, -gənɪˈz-, -gn ɪˈz-]

disorganiz|e [-is|e], -es, -ing, -ed dɪsˈɔːgənaɪz [dɪˈzɔː-, ˌdɪsˈɔː-, -gnaɪz],-ɪz, -ɪŋ, -d

disorientat|e, -es, -ing, -ed dɪsˈɔːrɪenteɪt [ˌdɪs-, -ˈɒr-, -rjə-, -rɪə-], -s, -ɪŋ, -ɪd

disorientation dɪsˌɔːrɪenˈteɪʃn [ˌ----ˈ-, -ɒr-, -rjə-, -rɪə-]

disown, -s, -ing, -ed dɪsˈəʊn [ˌdɪsˈəʊn], -z, -ɪŋ, -d

disparag|e, -es, -ing/ly, -ed, -er/s, -ement dɪˈspærɪdʒ, -ɪz, -ɪŋ/lɪ, -d, -ə*/z, -mənt

disparate (s. adj.), -s ˈdɪspərət [-rɪt, -reɪt], -s

disparity dɪˈspærətɪ [-rɪtɪ]

dispassionate, -ly, -ness dɪˈspæʃnət [-ʃənət, -ʃnət, -rɪt], -lɪ, -nɪs [-nəs]

dispatch (s. v.), -es, -ing, -ed, -er/s dɪˈspætʃ, -ɪz, -ɪŋ, -t, -ə*/z

dispatch-boat, -s dɪˈspætʃbəʊt, -s

dispatch-box, -es dɪˈspætʃbɒks, -ɪz

dispatch-rider, -s dɪˈspætʃˌraɪdə*, -z

dispel, -s, -ling, -led dɪˈspel, -z, -ɪŋ, -d

dispensable dɪˈspensəbl

dispensar|y, -ies dɪˈspensər|ɪ, -ɪz

dispensation, -s ˌdɪspenˈseɪʃn [-pən-], -z

dispensator|y (s. adj.), -ies dɪˈspensə-tər|ɪ, -ɪz

dispens|e, -es, -ing, -ed, -er/s dɪˈspens, -ɪz, -ɪŋ, -t, -ə*/z

dispeop|le, -les, -ling, -led ˌdɪsˈpiːp|l, -lz, -lɪŋ [-lɪŋ], -ld

dispersal, -s dɪˈspɜːsl, -z

dispers|e, -es, -ing, -ed, -er/s dɪˈspɜːs, -ɪz, -ɪŋ, -t, -ə*/z

dispersion, -s dɪˈspɜːʃn, -z

dispersive dɪˈspɜːsɪv

dispirit, -s, -ing, -ed/ly, -edness dɪˈspɪrɪt, -s, -ɪŋ, -ɪd/lɪ, -ɪdnɪs [-nəs]

displac|e, -es, -ing, -ed, -ement/s dɪsˈpleɪs, -ɪz, -ɪŋ, -t [also ˈdɪspleɪst when attributive], -mənt/s

display (s. v.), -s, -ing, -ed, -er/s dɪˈspleɪ, -z, -ɪŋ, -d, -ə*/z

displeas|e, -es, -ing/ly, -ingness, -ed dɪsˈpliːz, -ɪz, -ɪŋ/lɪ, -ɪŋnɪs [-nəs], -d

displeasure dɪsˈpleʒə*

disport, -s -ing, -ed dɪˈspɔːt, -s, -ɪŋ, -ɪd

dispos|e, -es, -ing, -ed, -er/s; -able, -al|s dɪˈspəʊz, -ɪz, -ɪŋ, -d, -ə*/z; -əbl, -l/z

disposition, -s ˌdɪspəˈzɪʃn [-pʊˈz-], -z

dispossess, -es, -ing, -ed ˌdɪspəˈzes [-pʊˈz-], -ɪz, -ɪŋ, -t

disproof ˌdɪsˈpruːf [-ˈ-]

disproportion, -ed ˌdɪsprəˈpɔːʃn [-prʊˈp-] -d [ˈ-ˌ-]

dispropor|tional, -tionally ˌdɪsprəˈpɔː|-ʃənl [-prʊˈp-, -ʃnəl, -ʃn̩l, -ʃnl, -ʃənel], -ʃnəlɪ [-ʃnəlɪ, -ʃn̩lɪ, -ʃnlɪ, -ʃənəlɪ]

disproportionate, -ly, -ness ˌdɪsprə-ˈpɔːʃnət [-prʊˈp-, -ʃnət, -ʃənət; -nɪt], -lɪ, -nɪs [-nəs]

disproval dɪsˈpruːvl [ˌdɪsˈp-]

disprov|e, -es, -ing, -ed dɪsˈpruːv [ˌdɪsˈp-], -z, -ɪŋ, -d

disputable dɪˈspjuːtəbl [ˈdɪspjʊtəbl]

disputableness dɪˈspjuːtəblnɪs [-nəs]

disputant (s. adj.), -s dɪˈspjuːtənt [ˈdɪspjʊtənt], -s

disputation, -s ˌdɪspjuːˈteɪʃn [-pjʊ-], -z

disputatious, -ly, -ness ˌdɪspjuːˈteɪʃəs [-pjʊ-], -lɪ, -nɪs [-nəs]

disputative dɪˈspjuːtətɪv

disput|e (s. v.), -es, -ing, -ed, -er/s dɪ-ˈspjuːt, -s, -ɪŋ, -ɪd, -ə*/z Note.—The stress pattern ˈ-- is increasingly used for the noun.

disqualification, -s dɪsˌkwɒlɪfɪˈkeɪʃn [ˌdɪsk-], -z

disquali|fy, -fies, -fying, -fied dɪs-ˈkwɒlɪfaɪ [ˌdɪsˈk-], -faɪz, -faɪɪŋ, -faɪd

disquiet (s. v.), -s, -ing, -ed dɪsˈkwaɪət, -s, -ɪŋ, -ɪd

disquietude dɪsˈkwaɪətjuːd [-ˈkwaɪt-]

disquisition, -s ˌdɪskwɪˈzɪʃn, -z

disquisitional ˌdɪskwɪˈzɪʃənl [-ʃnəl, -ʃn̩l, -ʃnl, -ʃənəl]

disquisitive dɪˈskwɪzɪtɪv

Disraeli dɪsˈreɪlɪ [dɪz-]

disregard (s. v.), -s, -ing, -ed ˌdɪsrɪˈgɑːd [-rəˈg-], -z, -ɪŋ, -ɪd

disregard|ful, -fully ˌdɪsrɪˈgɑːd|fʊl [-rəˈg-], -fʊlɪ [-fəlɪ]

disrepair ˌdɪsrɪˈpeə* [-rəˈp-]

disreputability dɪsˌrepjʊtəˈbɪlətɪ [-lɪt-]

disreputab|le, -ly, -leness dɪsˈrepjʊ-təb|l [-pjət-], -lɪ, -lnɪs [-nəs]

disrepute ˌdɪsrɪˈpjuːt [-rəˈp-]

disrespect ˌdɪsrɪˈspekt [-rəˈs-]

143

disrespect|ful, -fully, -fulness ˌdɪs-rɪ'spekt|fʊl [-rə's-], -fʊlɪ [-fəlɪ], -fʊlnɪs [-nəs]

disrob|e, -es, -ing, -ed ˌdɪs'rəʊb [dɪs'r-], -z, -ɪŋ, -d

disrupt, -s, -ing, -ed dɪs'rʌpt, -s, -ɪŋ, -ɪd

disruption, -s dɪs'rʌpʃn, -z

disruptive dɪs'rʌptɪv

Diss dɪs

dissatisfaction 'dɪsˌsætɪs'fækʃn [ˌdɪs-sæt-]

dissatisfactor|y, -ily, -iness 'dɪsˌsætɪs-'fæktər|ɪ [ˌdɪssæt-], -əlɪ [-ɪlɪ], -ɪnɪs [-nəs]

dissatis|fy, -fies, -fying, -fied ˌdɪs'sætɪs|-faɪ [dɪs's-], -faɪz, -faɪɪŋ, -faɪd

dissect, -s, -ing, -ed, -or/s; -ible dɪ'sekt, -s, -ɪŋ, -ɪd, -ə*/z; -əbl [-ɪbl]

dissecting-room, -s dɪ'sektɪŋrʊm [-ruːm], -z

dissection, -s dɪ'sekʃn, -z

disseis|e, -es, -ing, -ed; -in/s ˌdɪs'siːz, -ɪz, -ɪŋ, -d; -ɪn/z

dissemblance, -s dɪ'sembləns, -ɪz

dissemb|le, -les, -ling, -led, -ler/s dɪ'semb|l, -lz, -lɪŋ, -ld, -lə*/z

disseminat|e, -es, -ing, -ed, -or/s dɪ-'semɪneɪt, -s, -ɪŋ, -ɪd, -ə*/z

dissemination dɪˌsemɪ'neɪʃn

dissension, -s dɪ'senʃn, -z

dissent (s. v.), -s, -ing, -ed, -er/s dɪ'sent, -s, -ɪŋ, -ɪd, -ə*/z

dissentient, -s dɪ'senʃɪənt [-ʃjənt, -ʃənt], -s

dissertation, -s ˌdɪsə'teɪʃn, -z

disservice, -s ˌdɪs'sɜːvɪs [dɪs's-], -ɪz

dissev|er, -ers, -ering, -ered, -erment; -erance dɪs'sev|ə*, -əz, -ərɪŋ, -əd, -əmənt; -ərəns

dissiden|ce, -t/s 'dɪsɪdən|s, -t/s

dissimilar, -ly ˌdɪ'sɪmɪlə* [ˌdɪs's-, dɪ-'sɪm-], -lɪ

dissimilarit|y, -ies ˌdɪsɪmɪ'lærət|ɪ [ˌdɪss-, -mə-, -ɪt|ɪ], -ɪz

dissimilat|e, -es, -ing, -ed dɪ'sɪmɪleɪt [ˌdɪ's-, -mə-], -s, -ɪŋ, -ɪd

dissimilation, -s ˌdɪsɪmɪ'leɪʃn [dɪˌs-, -mə-], -z

dissimilitude ˌdɪsɪ'mɪlɪtjuːd [ˌdɪss-]

dissimulat|e, -es, -ing, -ed, -or/s dɪ-'sɪmjʊleɪt, -s, -ɪŋ, -ɪd, -ə*/z

dissimulation, -s dɪˌsɪmjʊ'leɪʃn, -z

dissipat|e, -es, -ing, -ed; -ive 'dɪsɪpeɪt, -s, -ɪŋ, -ɪd; -ɪv

dissipation, -s ˌdɪsɪ'peɪʃn, -z

dissociable (separable) dɪ'səʊʃjəbl [-ʃɪəbl], (unsociable) dɪ'səʊʃəbl

dissociat|e, -es, -ing, -ed dɪ'səʊʃɪeɪt [-əʊʃjeɪt, -əʊsɪeɪt, -əʊsjeɪt], -s, -ɪŋ, -ɪd

dissociation dɪˌsəʊsɪ'eɪʃn [ˌdɪs-, -əʊʃɪ-]

dissolubility dɪˌsɒljʊ'bɪlətɪ [-lɪt-]

dissolub|le, -ly, -leness dɪ'sɒljʊb|l, -lɪ, -lnɪs [-nəs]

dissolute (s. adj.), -s, -ly, -ness 'dɪsəluːt [-ljuːt], -s, -lɪ, -nɪs [-nəs]

dissolution, -s ˌdɪsə'luːʃn [-'ljuː-], -z

dissolvability dɪˌzɒlvə'bɪlətɪ [-lɪt-]

dissolv|e, -es, -ing, -ed; -able dɪ'zɒlv, -z, -ɪŋ, -d; -əbl

dissolvent (s. adj.), -s dɪ'zɒlvənt [dɪ'sɒ-], -s

dissonan|ce, -ces, -t/ly 'dɪsənən|s [-sn̩-], -sɪz, -t/lɪ

dissuad|e, -es, -ing, -ed dɪ'sweɪd, -z, -ɪŋ, -ɪd

dissuasion dɪ'sweɪʒn

dissuasive, -ly, -ness dɪ'sweɪsɪv; -lɪ, -nɪs [-nəs]

dissyll- = disyll-

dissymmetric ˌdɪsɪ'metrɪk [ˌdɪssɪ'm-]

dissymmetry ˌdɪ'sɪmɪtrɪ [ˌdɪs's-, dɪs's-, -mətrɪ]

distaff, -s 'dɪstɑːf, -s

distan|ce (s. v.), -es, -ing, -ed 'dɪstəns, -ɪz, -ɪŋ, -t

distant, -ly 'dɪstənt, -lɪ

distaste, -s ˌdɪs'teɪst [dɪs't-], -s

distaste|ful, -fully, -fulness dɪs'teɪst|-fʊl [ˌdɪs't-], -fʊlɪ [-fəlɪ], -fʊlnɪs [-nəs]

distemp|er (s. v.), -ers, -ering, -ered dɪ'stemp|ə*, -əz, -ərɪŋ, -əd

distend, -s, -ing, -ed dɪ'stend, -z, -ɪŋ, -ɪd

distensible dɪ'stensəbl [-sɪb-]

distension dɪ'stenʃn

distich, -s, -ous 'dɪstɪk, -s, -əs

distil, -s, -ling, -led, -ler/s dɪ'stɪl, -z, -ɪŋ, -d, -ə*/z

distillate, -s 'dɪstɪlət [-leɪt, -lɪt], -s

distillation, -s ˌdɪstɪ'leɪʃn, -z

distillatory dɪ'stɪlətərɪ

distiller|y, -ies dɪ'stɪlər|ɪ, -ɪz

disti|nct, -nctest, -nctly, -nctness dɪ-'stɪ|ŋkt, -ŋktɪst, -ŋktlɪ [-ŋklɪ], -ŋktnɪs [-ŋknɪs, -nəs]

distinction, -s dɪ'stɪŋkʃn, -z

distinctive, -ly, -ness dɪ'stɪŋktɪv, -lɪ, -nɪs [-nəs]

distinguish, -es, -ing, -ed; -able, -ably dɪ'stɪŋgwɪʃ, -ɪz, -ɪŋ, -t; -əbl, -əblɪ

distoma, -s 'dɪstəʊmə, -z

distort, -s, -ing, -ed dɪ'stɔːt, -s, -ɪŋ, -ɪd

distortion, -s dɪ'stɔːʃn, -z

distract, -s, -ing, -ed/ly, -edness dɪ-'strækt, -s, -ɪŋ, -ɪd/lɪ, -ɪdnɪs [-nəs]

distraction, -s dɪ'strækʃn, -z

distrain, -s, -ing, -ed, -er/s; -able dɪ-
  'streɪn, -z, -ɪŋ, -d, -ə*/z; -əbl
distrainee, -s ˌdɪstreɪ'niː, -z
distrainor, -s ˌdɪstreɪ'nɔː*, -z
distraint, -s dɪ'streɪnt, -s
distrait, -e dɪ'streɪ ['dɪstreɪ] (distrɛ), -t
distraught dɪ'strɔːt
distress (s. v.), -es, -ing/ly, -ed dɪ'stres,
  -ɪz, -ɪŋ/lɪ, -t
distress|ful, -fully dɪ'stres|fʊl, -fʊlɪ
  [-fəlɪ]
distributable dɪ'strɪbjʊtəbl
distribut|e, -es, -ing, -ed, -or/s dɪ-
  'strɪbjuːt ['dɪstrɪbjuːt], -s, dɪ'strɪbjʊtɪŋ ['dɪstrɪbjuːtɪŋ], dɪ'strɪbjʊtɪd
  ['dɪstrɪbjuːtɪd], dɪ'strɪbjʊtə*/z ['dɪs-
  trɪbjuːtə*/z]
distribution, -s ˌdɪstrɪ'bjuːʃn, -z
distributive, -ly dɪ'strɪbjʊtɪv, -lɪ
district, -s 'dɪstrɪkt, -s
distringas dɪ'strɪŋgæs [-gəs]
distrust (s. v.), -s, -ing, -ed dɪs'trʌst
  [ˌdɪs't-], -s, -ɪŋ, -ɪd
distrust|ful, -fully, -fulness dɪs'trʌst|-
  fʊl [ˌdɪs't-] -fʊlɪ [-fəlɪ], -fʊlnɪs [-nəs]
disturb, -s, -ing, -ed, -er/s dɪ'stɜːb, -z,
  -ɪŋ, -d, -ə*/z
disturbance, -s dɪ'stɜːbəns, -ɪz
distyle, -s 'dɪstaɪl ['daɪstaɪl], -z
disulphate, -s daɪ'sʌlfeɪt [-fɪt], -s
disulphide, -s daɪ'sʌlfaɪd, -z
disunion, -s ˌdɪs'juːnjən [dɪs'j-, -nɪən],
  -z
disunit|e, -es, -ing, -ed ˌdɪsju:'naɪt
  [-jʊ'n-], -s, -ɪŋ, -ɪd
disuse (s.) ˌdɪs'juːs [dɪs'j-]
disus|e (v.), -es, -ing, -ed ˌdɪs'juːz
  [dɪs'j-], -ɪz, -ɪŋ, -d [also 'dɪsjuːzd
  when attributive]
disyllabic ˌdɪsɪ'læbɪk [ˌdaɪ-, '--,--]
disyllable, -s dɪ'sɪləbl [ˌdɪ's-, 'daɪˌs-], -z
ditch (s. v.), -es, -ing, -ed, -er/s dɪtʃ, -ɪz,
  -ɪŋ, -t, -ə*/z
Ditchling 'dɪtʃlɪŋ
ditch-water 'dɪtʃˌwɔːtə*
dither, -s, -ing, -ed 'dɪðə*, -z, -rɪŋ, -d
dithyramb, -s 'dɪθɪræmb, -z
dithyramb|us, -i, -ic/s ˌdɪθɪ'ræmb|əs,
  -aɪ, -ɪk/s
ditto, -s 'dɪtəʊ, -z
Ditton 'dɪtn
ditt|y, -ies 'dɪt|ɪ, -ɪz
diuretic (s. adj.), -s ˌdaɪjʊə'retɪk, -s
diurn|al (s. adj.), -als, -ally daɪ'ɜːn|l, -lz,
  -əlɪ
diva, -s 'diːvə, -z
divagat|e, -es, -ing, -ed 'daɪvəgeɪt, -s,
  -ɪŋ, -ɪd

divagation, -s ˌdaɪvə'geɪʃn, -z
divalent 'daɪˌveɪlənt [ˌdaɪ'v-]
divan, -s dɪ'væn [daɪ'v-, 'daɪvæn], -z
divaricat|e, -es, -ing, -ed daɪ'værɪkeɪt
  [dɪ'v-], -s, -ɪŋ, -ɪd
divarication, -s daɪˌværɪ'keɪʃn [dɪˌv-], -z
div|e (s. v.), -es, -ing, -ed, -er/s daɪv, -z,
  -ɪŋ, -d, -ə*/z
dive-bomb, -s, -ing, -ed, -er/s 'daɪv-
  bɒm, -z, -ɪŋ, -d, -ə*/z
Diver 'daɪvə*
diverg|e, -es, -ing, -ed daɪ'vɜːdʒ [dɪ'v-],
  -ɪz, -ɪŋ, -d
divergen|ce, -ces, -cy, -cies, -t/ly
  daɪ'vɜːdʒən|s [dɪ'v-], -sɪz, -sɪ, -sɪz,
  -t/lɪ
divers (adj.) 'daɪvəz [-ɜːz]
diverse, -ly daɪ'vɜːs ['daɪvɜːs], -lɪ
diversification, -s daɪˌvɜːsɪfɪ'keɪʃn [dɪ-],
  -z
diversi|fy, -fies, -fying, -fied daɪ'vɜːsɪ|-
  faɪ [dɪ-], -faɪz, -faɪɪŋ, -faɪd
diversion, -s, -ary, -ist daɪ'vɜːʃn
  [dɪ'v-], -z, -ərɪ, -ɪst
diversit|y, -ies daɪ'vɜːsət|ɪ [dɪ'v-, -ɪt|ɪ],
  -ɪz
divert, -s, -ing/ly, -ed daɪ'vɜːt [dɪ'v-],
  -s, -ɪŋ/lɪ, -ɪd
divertimento dɪˌvɜːtɪ'mentəʊ [-ˌveə-]
divertissement ˌdiːveə'tiːsmãː ŋ [-və-,
  -vɜː-, -mɒŋ, -mɔ̃ː ŋ] (divɛrtismã)
Dives (rich man) 'daɪviːz, (surname)
  daɪvz
divest, -s, -ing, -ed daɪ'vest [dɪ'v-], -s,
  -ɪŋ, -ɪd
divestiture daɪ'vestɪtʃə* [dɪ'v-]
divid|e (s. v.), -es, -ing, -ed/ly, -er/s;
  -able dɪ'vaɪd, -z, -ɪŋ, -ɪd/lɪ, -ə*/z;
  -əbl
dividend, -s 'dɪvɪdend [-dənd], -z
dividend-warrant, -s 'dɪvɪdendˌwɒrənt
  [-dənd-], -s
divination, -s ˌdɪvɪ'neɪʃn, -z
divine (s. adj.), -s, -r, -st, -ly, -ness
  dɪ'vaɪn, -z, -ə*, -ɪst, -lɪ, -nɪs [-nəs]
divin|e (v.), -es, -ing, -ed, -er/s dɪ'vaɪn,
  -z, -ɪŋ, -d, -ə*/z
diving-bell, -s 'daɪvɪŋbel, -z
diving-dress, -es 'daɪvɪŋdres, -ɪz
diving-rod, -s dɪ'vaɪnɪŋrɒd, -z
divinit|y, -ies dɪ'vɪnət|ɪ [-ɪt|ɪ], -ɪz
divisibility dɪˌvɪzɪ'bɪlətɪ [-zə'b-, -lɪt-]
divisib|le, -ly dɪ'vɪzəb|l [-zɪb-], -lɪ
division, -s dɪ'vɪʒn, -z
divisional dɪ'vɪʒənl [-ʒn̩l, -ʒnl]
divisive, -ly, -ness dɪ'vaɪsɪv, -lɪ, -nɪs
  [-nəs]
divisor, -s dɪ'vaɪzə*, -z

145

divorc|e (s. v.), -es, -ing, -ed, -er/s, -ement dɪˈvɔːs, -ɪz, -ɪŋ, -t, -əˈ/z, -mənt

divorcée, -s dɪˌvɔːˈsiː: [ˌ--ˈ-, -ˈ--, dɪˈvɔːˈseɪ] (divorse), -z

divot, -s ˈdɪvət, -s

divulg|e, -es, -ing, -ed daɪˈvʌldʒ [dɪˈv-], -ɪz, -ɪŋ, -d

divulsion, -s daɪˈvʌlʃn [dɪˈv-], -z

diwan, -s dɪˈwɑːn, -z

Dix dɪks

Dixey ˈdɪksɪ

Dixie ˈdɪksɪ

Dixon ˈdɪksn

Dixwell ˈdɪkswəl [-wel]

diz|en, -ens, -ening, -ened ˈdaɪz|n, -nz, -nɪŋ, -nd

dizz|y (adj. v.), -ier, -iest, -ily, -iness; -ies, -ying, -ied ˈdɪz|ɪ, -ɪə*, -ɪst, -ɪlɪ [-əlɪ], -ɪnɪs [-ɪnəs]; -ɪz, -ɪŋ, -ɪd

Djakarta [Ja-] dʒəˈkɑːtə

Djibouti dʒɪˈbuːtɪ

djinn dʒɪn

Dnie|per, -ster ˈdni:|pə*, -stə*

do (s.) (musical note), -s dəʊ, -z

do (s.) (swindle, entertainment), -s duː, -z

do. ˈdɪtəʊ

do (v.); dost; doth; doeth; does; doing, did, done, doer/s duː (strong form), dʊ (weak form, also alternative strong form before vowels), də, d (weak forms); dʌst (strong form), dəst (weak form); dʌθ (strong form), dəθ (weak form); ˈduːθ [ˈdʊɪθ]; dʌz (strong form), dəz, dz (weak forms); ˈduːɪŋ [ˈdʊɪŋ], dɪd, dʌn, ˈduːə*/z [dʊə*/z]

Doane dəʊn

Dobb, -s dɒb, -z

dobbin (D.), -s ˈdɒbɪn, -z

Dobell dəʊˈbel

Dobie ˈdəʊbɪ

Dobrée ˈdəʊbreɪ

Dobson ˈdɒbsn

docent, -s dəʊˈsent [ˈdəʊsənt], -s

Docet|ism, -ist/s dəʊˈsiːt|ɪzəm, -ɪst/s

docile ˈdəʊsaɪl [ˈdɒs-]

docility dəʊˈsɪlətɪ [-ɪtɪ]

dock (s. v.), -s, -ing, -ed, -er/s; -age dɒk, -s, -ɪŋ, -t, -ə*/z; -ɪdʒ

Docker ˈdɒkə*

docket (s. v.), -s, -ing, -ed ˈdɒkɪt, -s, -ɪŋ, -ɪd

dock-land ˈdɒklænd

dockyard, -s ˈdɒkjɑːd, -z

doct|or (s. v.), -ors, -oring, -ored; -orate/s, -orship/s ˈdɒkt|ə*, -əz, -ərɪŋ, -əd; -ərɪt/s [-ərət/s], -əʃɪp/s

doctrinaire, -s ˌdɒktrɪˈneə*, -z

doctrin|al, -ally dɒkˈtraɪn|l [ˈdɒktrɪn-], -əlɪ

doctrinarian, -s ˌdɒktrɪˈneərɪən, -z

doctrine, -s ˈdɒktrɪn, -z

document (s.), -s ˈdɒkjʊmənt, -s

document (v.), -s, -ing, -ed ˈdɒkjʊment, -s, -ɪŋ, -ɪd

documental ˌdɒkjʊˈmentl

documentar|y (s. adj.), -ies ˌdɒkjʊˈmentər|ɪ, -ɪz

documentation ˌdɒkjʊmenˈteɪʃn [-mən-]

Docwra ˈdɒkrə

Dod(d), -s dɒd, -z

dodder (s. v.), -s, -ing, -ed ˈdɒdə*, -z, -rɪŋ, -d

Doddington ˈdɒdɪŋtən

Doddridge ˈdɒdrɪdʒ

dodecagon, -s dəʊˈdekəgən, -z

dodecahedr|on, -ons, -a; -al ˌdəʊdekəˈhedr|ən [-dɪk-, -ˈhiːd-, ˈ---,--], -ənz, -ə; -l

Dodecanese ˌdəʊdɪkəˈniːz [-dek-]

dodg|e (s. v.) (D.), -es, -ing, -ed, -er/s dɒdʒ, -ɪz, -ɪŋ, -d, -ə*/z

Dodgson ˈdɒdʒsn

Dodington ˈdɒdɪŋtən

dodo (D.), -s ˈdəʊdəʊ, -z

Dodona dəʊˈdəʊnə

Dodsley ˈdɒdzlɪ

Dodson ˈdɒdsn

Dodwell ˈdɒdwəl [-wel]

doe (D.), -s dəʊ, -z

Doeg ˈdəʊeg

doer, -s ˈduːə* [dʊə*], -z

does (from do) dʌz (strong form), dəz, dz (weak forms)

doeskin, -s ˈdəʊskɪn, -z

doesn't ˈdʌznt [also ˈdʌzn when not final]

doeth (from do) ˈduːɪθ [ˈdʊɪθ]

doff, -s, -ing, -ed, -er/s dɒf, -s, -ɪŋ, -t, -ə*/z

Dofort ˈdəʊfɜːt

dog (s. v.), -ging, -ged (p. tense, p. partic.) dɒg, -z, -ɪŋ, -d

dog-bane ˈdɒgbeɪn

Dogberry ˈdɒgberɪ [-bərɪ]

dog-biscuit, -s ˈdɒgˌbɪskɪt, -s

dog-cart, -s ˈdɒgkɑːt, -s

dog-collar, -s ˈdɒgˌkɒlə*, -z

dog-days ˈdɒgdeɪz

doge, -s dəʊdʒ, -ɪz

dog-ear (s. v.), -s, -ing, -ed ˈdɒgˌɪə*, -z, -rɪŋ, -d

dog-faced ˈdɒgfeɪst

dog-fancier, -s ˈdɒgˌfænsɪə* [-sjə*], -z

146

dog-fight, -s 'dɒgfaɪt, -s
dog-fish, -es 'dɒgfɪʃ, -ɪz
dogged (adj.), -ly, -ness 'dɒgɪd, -lɪ, -nɪs [-nəs]
dogger (D.), -s 'dɒgə*, -z
doggerel 'dɒgərəl [-rɪl]
Doggett 'dɒgɪt
doggish, -ly, -ness 'dɒgɪʃ, -lɪ, -nɪs [-nəs]
doggo 'dɒgəʊ
doggrel 'dɒgrəl
dogg|y (s. adj.), -ies 'dɒg|ɪ, -ɪz
dog-headed 'dɒg,hedɪd
dog-kennel, -s 'dɒg,kenl, -z
dog-Latin ,dɒg'lætɪn ['-,--]
dogma, -s 'dɒgmə, -z
dogmatic (s. adj.), -s, -al, -ally dɒg'mætɪk, -s, -l, -əlɪ
dogmati|sm, -st/s 'dɒgmətɪ|zəm, -st/s
dogmatiz|e [-is|e], -es, -ing, -ed, -er/s 'dɒgmətaɪz, -ɪz, -ɪŋ, -d, -ə*/z
do-gooder, -s ,du:'gʊdə*, -z
dog-rose, -s 'dɒgrəʊz, -ɪz
dog's-ear (s. v.), -s, -ing, -ed 'dɒgz,ɪə*, -z, -rɪŋ, -d
dog-skin 'dɒgskɪn
dog-star 'dɒgstɑː*
dog-tired ,dɒg'taɪəd
dog|-tooth, -teeth 'dɒg|tuːθ, -tiːθ
dog-watch, -es 'dɒgwɒtʃ, -ɪz
dogwood 'dɒgwʊd
doh (note in Tonic Sol-fa), -s dəʊ, -z
Doherty 'dəʊətɪ, dəʊ'hɜːtɪ, 'dɒhətɪ ['dɒxə-]
Dohnanyi dɒk'nɑːnjɪ [dɒx'n-, -njɪ]
Dohoo 'duːhuː
doil|y, -ies 'dɔɪl|ɪ, -ɪz
doing, -s 'duːɪŋ ['dʊɪŋ], -z
doit, -s dɔɪt, -s
do-it-yourself ,duːɪtjɔː'self [,dʊɪt-]
dolce 'dɒltʃɪ ['dəʊl-] ('doltʃe)
doldrum, -s 'dɒldrəm, -z
dol|e (s. v.), -es, -ing, -ed dəʊl, -z, -ɪŋ, -d
dole|ful, -fully, -fulness 'dəʊl|fʊl, -fʊlɪ [-fəlɪ], -fʊlnɪs [-nəs]
dolerite 'dɒləraɪt
Dolgellau [Dolgelley] dɒl'geθlaɪ [-'gelaɪ, -lɪ] (Welsh dol'geɫa, -ɫaɪ)
dolichocephalic ,dɒlɪkəʊse'fælɪk [-sɪ'f-, -ke'f-, -kɪ'f-]
doll, -s dɒl, -z
dollar (D.), -s 'dɒlə*, -z
Dollond 'dɒlənd
dollop, -s 'dɒləp, -s
doll's-hou|se, -ses 'dɒlzhaʊ|s, -zɪz
doll|y (D.), -ies 'dɒl|ɪ, -ɪz
dolman, -s 'dɒlmən, -z
dolmen, -s 'dɒlmen, -z

dolomite (D.), -s 'dɒləmaɪt, -s
dolor 'dɒlə* ['dəʊ-]
dolorous, -ly, -ness 'dɒlərəs, -lɪ, -nɪs [-nəs]
dolour 'dɒlə* ['dəʊ-]
dolphin, -s 'dɒlfɪn, -z
dolt, -s dəʊlt, -s
doltish, -ly, -ness 'dəʊltɪʃ, -lɪ, -nɪs [-nəs]
Dolton 'dəʊltən
domain, -s dəʊ'meɪn, -z
Dombey 'dɒmbɪ
dome, -s, -d dəʊm, -z, -d
Domesday 'duːmzdeɪ
domestic (s. adj.), -s, -ally dəʊ'mestɪk, -s, -əlɪ
domesticat|e, -es, -ing, -ed dəʊ'mestɪkeɪt, -s, -ɪŋ, -ɪd
domestication dəʊ,mestɪ'keɪʃn
domesticity ,dəʊme'stɪsɪtɪ [,dɒm-, -rtɪ]
domett (material) dəʊ'met
Domett (surname) 'dɒmɪt
domicil|e (s. v.), -es, -ing, -ed 'dɒmɪsaɪl ['dəʊ-, -sɪl], -z, -ɪŋ, -d
domiciliary ,dɒmɪ'sɪljərɪ [-lɪərɪ]
dominant (s. adj.), -s, -ly 'dɒmɪnənt, -s, -lɪ
dominat|e, -es, -ing, -ed, -or/s 'dɒmɪneɪt, -s, -ɪŋ, -ɪd, -ə*/z
domination, -s ,dɒmɪ'neɪʃn, -z
domineer, -s, -ing, -ed ,dɒmɪ'nɪə*, -z, -rɪŋ, -d
Domingo dəʊ'mɪŋgəʊ [dɒ'm-]
Dominic 'dɒmɪnɪk
Dominica (in the Leeward Islands) ,dɒmɪ'niːkə [də'mɪnɪkə]
dominical də'mɪnɪkl [dɒ'm-]
Dominican (republic, religious order), -s də'mɪnɪkən [dɒ'm-], (of Dominica) ,dɒmɪ'niːkən, -z
dominie, -s 'dɒmɪnɪ, -z
dominion, -s də'mɪnjən [-nɪən], -z
domino, -es 'dɒmɪnəʊ, -z
Domitian dəʊ'mɪʃɪən [dɒ'm-, -ʃjən, -ʃn]
Domvil(l)e 'dʌmvɪl
don (s. v.) (D.), -s, -ning, -ned dɒn, -z, -ɪŋ, -d
dona(h), -s 'dəʊnə, -z
Donaghadee ,dɒnəkə'diː [-nəxə-]
Donalbain 'dɒnlbeɪn
Donald, -son 'dɒnld, -sn
Donat 'dəʊnæt
donat|e, -es, -ing, -ed dəʊ'neɪt, -s, -ɪŋ, -ɪd
Donatello ,dɒnə'teləʊ
donation, -s dəʊ'neɪʃn, -z
Donatist, -s 'dəʊnətɪst, -s

147

donative, -s 'dəʊnətɪv, -z
donator, -s dəʊ'neɪtə*, -z
donatory 'dəʊnətərɪ ['dɒn-, dəʊ'neɪ-]
Donatus dəʊ'neɪtəs
Don Carlos ˌdɒn'kɑːlɒs
Doncaster 'dɒŋkəstə*
done (from do) dʌn
Done dəʊn
donee, -s dəʊ'niː, -z
Donegal (place) 'dɒnɪɡɔːl ['dʌn-, ˌ--'-]
   Note.—ˌdʌnɪ'ɡɔːl appears to be the
   most usual pronunciation in
   Ireland.
Donegall (Marquess) 'dɒnɪɡɔːl
Donelson 'dɒnlsn
Doneraile 'dʌnəreɪl
Donetz dɒ'nets (da'njets)
donga, -s 'dɒŋɡə, -z
Dongan 'dɒŋɡən
Dönges (South African surname)
   'dɜːnjes
Don Giovanni ˌdɒndʒɪəʊ'vɑːnɪ [-'vænɪ]
   (dondʒo'vanni)
Dongola 'dɒŋɡələ
Donington 'dʌnɪŋtən
Doniphan 'dɒnɪfən
Donizetti ˌdɒnɪ'zetɪ [-ɪ'dze-] (doni-
   'dzetti)
donjon, -s 'dɒndʒən ['dʌn-], -z
Don Juan ˌdɒn'dʒuːən [-'dʒʊən]
donkey, -s 'dɒŋkɪ, -z
donkey-engine, -s 'dɒŋkɪˌendʒɪn, -z
donna, -s 'dɒnə, -z
Donnan 'dɒnən
Donne dʌn, dɒn
Donnington 'dɒnɪŋtən
donnish 'dɒnɪʃ
Donnithorne 'dɒnɪθɔːn
Donnybrook 'dɒnɪbrʊk
Dono(g)hue 'dʌnəhuː, 'dɒn- [-hjuː]
Donohoe 'dʌnəhuː, 'dɒn-
donor, -s 'dəʊnə* [-nɔː*], -z
do-nothing, -s 'duːˌnʌθɪŋ, -z
Donough 'dɒnəʊ
Donoughmore 'dʌnəmɔː* [-məɔ*]
Donovan 'dɒnəvən
Don Pasquale ˌdɒnpæs'kwɑːlɪ
Don Quixote ˌdɒn'kwɪksət [-səʊt,
   -sɒt, ˌdɒnkɪ'həʊtɪ, -teɪ]
donship, -s 'dɒnʃɪp, -s
don't dəʊnt [also dəʊn when not final,
   also dəʊmp before the sounds p, b, m,
   and dəʊŋk before k, g]
   Note.—Weak forms dən, dn may
   sometimes be heard in the expression
   I don't know, and a weak form dəm
   in the expression I don't mind.
Doo duː

dood|le (s. v.), -les, -ling, -led 'duːd|l,
   -lz, -lɪŋ [-lɪŋ], -ld
doodlebug, -s 'duːdlbʌg, -z
doom (s. v.), -s, -ing, -ed duːm, -z, -ɪŋ,
   -d
Doomsday 'duːmzdeɪ
Doon(e) duːn
door, -s dɔː* [dɔə*], -z
door-bell, -s 'dɔːbel ['dɔə-], -z
door-keeper, -s 'dɔːˌkiːpə* ['dɔə-], -z
door-knocker, -s 'dɔːˌnɒkə* ['dɔə-], -z
Doorly 'dʊəlɪ
door-mat, -s 'dɔːmæt ['dɔə-], -s
door-nail, -s 'dɔːneɪl ['dɔə-], -z
door-plate, -s 'dɔːpleɪt ['dɔə-], -s
door-post, -s 'dɔːpəʊst ['dɔə-], -s
doorstep, -s 'dɔːstep ['dɔə-], -s
doorway, -s 'dɔːweɪ ['dɔə-], -z
dop|e (s. v.), -es, -ing, -ed, -er/s dəʊp,
   -s, -ɪŋ, -t, -ə*/z
doppelganger 'dɒplˌgæŋə*
Dora 'dɔːrə
dorado, -s də'rɑːdəʊ [dɒ'r-], -z
Doran 'dɔːrən
Dorando də'rændəʊ [dɒ'r-]
Dorcas 'dɔːkəs [-kæs]
Dorchester 'dɔːtʃɪstə*
Dore dɔː* [dɔə*]
Doreen dɔː'riːn [dɒ'r-, də'r-, 'dɔːriːn]
Dorian (s. adj.), -s 'dɔːrɪən, -z
Doric 'dɒrɪk
Doricism, -s 'dɒrɪsɪzəm, -z
Doris (modern Christian name) 'dɒrɪs,
   (district and fem. name in Greek
   history) 'dɔːrɪs
Dorking 'dɔːkɪŋ
dorman|cy, -t 'dɔːmən|sɪ, -t
dormer-window, -s ˌdɔːmə'wɪndəʊ, -z
dormie 'dɔːmɪ
dormitor|y, -ies 'dɔːmɪtr|ɪ [-mətr|ɪ], -ɪz
dor|mouse, -mice 'dɔː|maʊs, -maɪs
dormy 'dɔːmɪ
Dornoch 'dɔːnɒk [-nək, -nɒx, -nəx]
Dornton 'dɔːntən
Dorothea ˌdɒrə'θɪə
Dorothy 'dɒrəθɪ
Dorr dɔː*
Dorrien 'dɒrɪən
Dorriforth 'dɒrɪfɔːθ
Dorrit 'dɒrɪt
dors|al, -ally 'dɔːs|l, -əlɪ
Dors|et, -etshire 'dɔːs|ɪt, -ɪt-ʃə* [-ɪtˌʃɪə*]
dor|y, -ies 'dɔːr|ɪ, -ɪz
dosage, -s 'dəʊsɪdʒ, -ɪz
dos|e (s. v.), -es, -ing, -ed dəʊs, -ɪz, -ɪŋ,
   -t
Dos Passos ˌdɒs'pæsɒs
doss, -es dɒs, -ɪz

148

dossal, -s 'dɒsl, -z

doss-hou|se, -ses 'dɒshaʊ|s, -zɪz

dossier, -s 'dɒsɪeɪ (dosje), -z

dost (from do) dʌst (strong form), dəst (weak form)

Dostoievski ˌdɒstɔɪ'efskɪ

dot (s. v.), -s, -ting, -ted dɒt, -s, -ɪŋ, -ɪd

dotage 'dəʊtɪdʒ

dotard, -s 'dəʊtəd, -z

dot|e, -es, -ing/ly, -ed, -er/s dəʊt, -s, -ɪŋ/lɪ, -ɪd, -ə*/z

doth (from do) dʌθ (strong form), dəθ (weak form)

Dothan 'dəʊðæn [-θən]

Dotheboys Hall ˌduːðəbɔɪz'cɔːl

dott(e)rel, -s 'dɒtrəl, -z

dottle, -s 'dɒtl, -z

dott|y, -ier, -iest, -ily, -iness 'dɒt|ɪ, -ɪə*, -ɪɪst, -ɪlɪ [-əlɪ], -ɪnɪs [-ɪnəs]

Douai (French town) 'duːeɪ (dwe), (school near Reading) 'daʊeɪ ['daʊɪ], (version of Bible) 'daʊeɪ ['daʊɪ, 'duːeɪ]

douane, -s duː'ɑːn [dʊ'ɑːn], -z

doub|le (s. adj. v.), -ly, -leness; -les, -ling, -led 'dʌb|l, -lɪ, -lnɪs [-nəs]; -lz, -lɪŋ [-lɪŋ], -ld

double-barrelled 'dʌbl̩bærəld [ˌ--'--]

double-bass, -es ˌdʌbl̩'beɪs, -ɪz

double-bedded 'dʌbl̩bedɪd [ˌ--'--]

Doublebois 'dʌblbɔɪz

double-breasted ˌdʌbl̩'brestɪd ['--ˌ--]

double-cross, -es, -ing, -ed ˌdʌbl̩'krɒs [old-fashioned -'krɔːs], -ɪz, -ɪŋ, -t

Doubleday 'dʌbldeɪ

double-deal|er/s, -ing ˌdʌbl̩'diːl|ə*/z ['--ˌ--], -ɪŋ

double-decked ˌdʌbldekt

double-decker, -s ˌdʌbl̩'dekə* ['--ˌ--], -z

double-dyed ˌdʌbl̩'daɪd [also '--- when attributive]

double-edged ˌdʌbl̩'edʒd ['---]

double entendre ˌduːbl̩ɑ̃ːn'tɑ̃ːndrə [-ɔ̃ːnˌtɔ̃ːndrə, -ɑːn'tɑːndrə, -ɒn'tɒndrə] (dublɑ̃tɑ̃ːdr, pronounced as if French)

double-entry ˌdʌbl̩'entrɪ

double-faced ˌdʌblfeɪst

double-first, -s ˌdʌbl̩'fɜːst, -s

double-headed 'dʌbl̩hedɪd

double-locked ˌdʌbl̩'lɒkt

double-minded ˌdʌbl̩'maɪndɪd ['--ˌ--]

double-quick ˌdʌbl̩'kwɪk

double-stopping, -s ˌdʌbl̩'stɒpɪŋ, -z

double-stout ˌdʌbl̩'staʊt

doublet, -s 'dʌblɪt [-lət], -s

double-tongued ˌdʌbl̩'tʌŋd ['---]

doubloon, -s dʌ'bluːn, -z

doubt (s. v.), -s, -ing/ly, -ed, -er/s daʊt, -s, -ɪŋ/lɪ, -ɪd, -ə*/z

doubt|ful, -fullest, -fully, -fulness 'daʊt|fʊl, -fʊlɪst [-fəlɪst], -fʊlɪ [-fəlɪ], -fʊlnɪs [-nəs]

Doubting 'daʊtɪŋ

doubtless, -ly 'daʊtlɪs [-ləs], -lɪ

douch|e (s. v.), -es, -ing, -ed duːʃ, -ɪz, -ɪŋ, -t

Doudney 'daʊdnɪ, 'duːdnɪ, 'djuːdnɪ

Dougal(l) 'duːgəl

Dougan 'duːgən

dough dəʊ

Dougherty 'dəʊətɪ

doughfaced 'dəʊfeɪst

dough-nut, -s 'dəʊnʌt, -s

dought|y (D.), -ier, -iest, -ily, -iness 'daʊt|ɪ, -ɪə* [-jə*], -ɪɪst, [-jɪst], -ɪlɪ [-əlɪ], -ɪnɪs [-nəs]

dough|y, -ily, -iness 'dəʊ|ɪ, -ɪlɪ, -ɪnɪs [-nəs]

Douglas(s) 'dʌgləs

Douie 'daʊɪ ['duːɪ], 'daʊɪ

douloureux (in tic d.) ˌduːlə'rɜː [-luː'r-, -lʊ'r-]

Doulton 'dəʊltən

dour dʊə*

Douro 'dʊərəʊ

Dousabel 'duːsəbel

dous|e, -es, -ing, -ed daʊs, -ɪz, -ɪŋ, -t

Doust daʊst

Dousterswivel 'duːstəswɪvl

dove, -s dʌv, -z

Dove (surname, tributary of River Trent), dʌv

dove-colour, -ed 'dʌvˌkʌlə*, -d

dove-cot, -s 'dʌvkɒt, -s

dovecote, -s 'dʌvkəʊt [-kɒt], -s

Dovedale 'dʌvdeɪl

dove-like 'dʌvlaɪk

Dover 'dəʊvə*

dovetail (s. v.), -s, -ing, -ed 'dʌvteɪl, -z, -ɪŋ, -d

Dovey (in Wales) 'dʌvɪ (Welsh 'dəvi)

Dow daʊ

dowager, -s 'daʊədʒə* ['daʊɪdʒ-], -z

Dowden 'daʊdn

dow|dy (s. adj.), -ies, -ier, -iest, -ily, -iness 'daʊd|ɪ, -ɪz, -ɪə* [-jə*], -ɪɪst [-jɪst], -ɪlɪ [-əlɪ], -ɪnɪs [-ɪnəs]

dowel (s. v.), -s, -ling, -led 'daʊəl ['daʊel], -z, -ɪŋ, -d

Dowell 'daʊəl [-ɪl, -el]

dower, -s; -less 'daʊə*, -z; -lɪs [-ləs]

Dowgate 'daʊgɪt [-geɪt]

Dowie 'daʊɪ

Dow Jones ˌdaʊ'dʒəʊnz

149

Dowland 'daʊlənd

dowlas (D.) 'daʊləs

Dowle daʊl

Dowler 'daʊlə*

down (s. adj. v. adv. prep. interj.), -s, -ing, -ed daʊn, -z, -ɪŋ, -d

Down, -shire daʊn, -ʃə* [-ˌʃɪə*]

down-bed, -s ˌdaʊn'bed [in contrast '--], -z

downcast 'daʊnkɑ:st [ˌ-'-]

down-draught, -s 'daʊndrɑ:ft, -s

Downe, -s daʊn, -z

Downey 'daʊnɪ

downfall, -s 'daʊnfɔ:l, -z

Downham 'daʊnəm

down-hearted ˌdaʊn'hɑ:tɪd

downhill ˌdaʊn'hɪl [also '-- according to sentence-stress]

Downing 'daʊnɪŋ

downland (D.) 'daʊnlænd

Downpatrick daʊn'pætrɪk

downpour, -s 'daʊnpɔ:* [-pɔə*], -z

down-quilt, -s ˌdaʊn'kwɪlt [in contrast '--], -s

downright, -ness 'daʊnraɪt, -nɪs [-nəs]

downrush, -es 'daʊnrʌʃ, -ɪz

Downs daʊnz

Downside 'daʊnsaɪd

down-sitting ˌdaʊn'sɪtɪŋ ['daʊnˌs-]

downstairs ˌdaʊn'steəz [also '-- according to sentence-stress]

downstream ˌdaʊn'stri:m [in contrast '--]

Downton 'daʊntən

downtrodden 'daʊnˌtrɒdn

downward, -s 'daʊnwəd, -z

down|y, -ier, -iest 'daʊn|ɪ, -ɪə* [-jə*], -ɪɪst [-jɪst]

dowr|y, -ies 'daʊər|ɪ ['daʊr-], -ɪz

dowsabel (D.), -s 'du:səbel ['daʊs-], -z

dows|e, -es, -ing, -ed, -er/s daʊz [daʊs], -ɪz, 'daʊzɪŋ ['daʊsɪŋ], daʊzd [daʊst], 'daʊzə*/z ['daʊsə*/z]

Dowse daʊs

dowsing-rod, -s 'daʊzɪŋrɒd ['daʊsɪŋ-], -z

Dowson 'daʊsn

Dowton 'daʊtn

doxolog|y, -ies dɒk'sɒlədʒ|ɪ, -ɪz

doyen, -s 'dɔɪən ['dɔɪen, 'dwaɪæ̃ŋ (dwajɛ̃), -z

Doyle dɔɪl

doyley, -s 'dɔɪlɪ, -z

D'Oyl(e)y 'dɔɪlɪ

doz|e (s. v.), -es, -ing, -ed, -er/s dəʊz, -ɪz, -ɪŋ, -d, -ə*/z

dozen, -s, -th 'dʌzn, -z, -θ

doz|y, -ier, -iest, -ily, -iness 'dəʊz|ɪ, -ɪə* [-jə*], -ɪɪst [-jɪst], -ɪlɪ [-əlɪ], -ɪnɪs [-ɪnəs]

Dr. 'dɒktə*, 'detə*

drab (s. adj.), -s dræb, -z

drabb|le, -les, -ling, -led 'dræb|l, -lz, -lɪŋ [-lɪŋ], -ld

dracaena, -s drə'si:nə, -z

Drachenfels 'drækənfelz [-fels] ('draxənfels)

drachm, -s dræm, -z

drachm|a, -as, -ae 'drækm|ə, -əz, -i:

Draco (Greek legislator) 'dreɪkəʊ, (English surname) 'drɑ:kəʊ

Draconian drə'kəʊnjən [dreɪ'k-, -nɪən]

Dracula 'drækjʊlə

draff dræf [drɑ:f]

draft (s. v.), -s, -ing, -ed, -er/s drɑ:ft, -s, -ɪŋ, -ɪd, -ə*/z

drafts|man, -men, -manship 'drɑ:fts|mən, -mən [-men], -mənʃɪp

drag (s. v.), -s, -ging, -ged dræg, -z, -ɪŋ, -d

Drage dreɪdʒ

dragg|le, -les, -ling, -led 'dræg|l, -lz, -lɪŋ [-lɪŋ], -ld

draggle-tail, -s, -ed 'dræglteɪl, -z, -d

drag-net, -s 'drægnet, -s

drago|man, -mans, -men 'drægəʊ|mən [-mæn], -mənz [-mænz], -mən [men]

dragon, -s 'drægən, -z

dragonet, -s 'drægənɪt [-net], -s

dragon-fl|y, -ies 'drægənfl|aɪ, -aɪz

dragon|ish, -like 'drægən|ɪʃ [-gn̩|-], -laɪk

dragonnade, -s ˌdrægə'neɪd, -z

dragon's-blood 'drægənzblʌd

dragoon, -s drə'gu:n, -z

drain (s. v.), -s, -ing, -ed, -er/s; -able, -age dreɪn, -z, -ɪŋ, -d, -ə*/z; -əbl, -ɪdʒ

draining-board, -s 'dreɪnɪŋbɔ:d [-bɔəd], -z

drain-pipe, -s 'dreɪnpaɪp, -s

drake (D.), -s dreɪk, -s

dram (s. v.), -s, -ming, -med dræm, -z, -ɪŋ, -d

drama, -s 'drɑ:mə, -z

dramatic, -al, -ally, -s drə'mætɪk, -l, -əlɪ, -s

dramatis personae ˌdrɑ:mətɪspɜ:'səʊnaɪ [ˌdræmətɪspə:'səʊni:]

dramatist, -s 'dræmətɪst, -s

dramatization [-isa-], -s ˌdræmətaɪ'zeɪʃn [-tɪ'z-], -z

dramatiz|e [-is|e], -es, -ing, -ed; -able 'dræmətaɪz, -ɪz, -ɪŋ, -d; -əbl

dramaturge, -s 'dræmətɜ:dʒ, -ɪz

dramaturgic ˌdræmə'tɜ:dʒɪk

drambuie dræm'bju:ɪ [-'bjʊɪ]
drank (from drink) dræŋk
drap|e, -es, -ing, -ed dreɪp, -s, -ɪŋ, -t
draper (D.), -s 'dreɪpə*, -z
draper|y, -ies 'dreɪpər|ɪ, -ɪz
Drapier 'dreɪpɪə* [-pjə*]
drastic, -ally 'dræstɪk ['drɑ:s-], -əlɪ
drat dræt
draught, -s drɑ:ft, -s
draught-board, -s 'drɑ:ftbɔ:d [-bɔəd], -z
draught-horse, -s 'drɑ:fthɔ:s, -ɪz
draught-net, -s 'drɑ:ftnet, -s
draughts|man (person who draws), -men 'drɑ:fts|mən, -mən
draughts|man (piece used in game of draughts), -men 'drɑ:fts|mæn [-mən], -men [-mən]
draught|y, -ier, -iest, -ily, -iness 'drɑ:ft|ɪ, -ɪə* [-jə*], -ɪɪst [-jɪst], -ɪlɪ [-əlɪ], -ɪnɪs [-ɪnəs]
Dravidian, -s drə'vɪdɪən [-djən], -z
draw (s. v.), -s, -ing, drew, drawn; drawable drɔ:, -z, -ɪŋ, dru:, drɔ:n; 'drɔ:əbl
drawback, -s 'drɔ:bæk, -s
drawbridge, -s 'drɔ:brɪdʒ, -ɪz
Drawcansir 'drɔ:kænsə*
drawee, -s drɔ:'i:, -z
drawer (person who draws), -s 'drɔ:ə* [drɔə*], -z
drawer (sliding box), -s drɔ:* [drɔə*], -z
drawers (garment) drɔ:z [drɔəz]
drawing-board, -s 'drɔ:ɪŋbɔ:d [-bɔəd], -z
drawing-kni|fe, -ves 'drɔ:ɪŋnaɪ|f, -vz
drawing-master, -s 'drɔ:ɪŋ,mɑ:stə*, -z
drawing-pen, -s 'drɔ:ɪŋpen, -z
drawing-pencil, -s 'drɔ:ɪŋ,pensl, -z
drawing-pin, -s 'drɔ:ɪŋpɪn, -z
drawing-room, -s (room for drawing) 'drɔ:ɪŋrʊm [-ru:m], (reception room) 'drɔ:ɪŋrʊm ['drɔm-, -ru:m]
drawing-table, -s 'drɔ:ɪŋ,teɪbl, -z
drawl (s. v.), -s, -ing, -ed, -er/s drɔ:l, -z, -ɪŋ, -d, -ə*/z
drawn (from draw) drɔ:n
draw-well, -s 'drɔ:wel, -z
Drax dræks
dray, -s dreɪ, -z
dray|man, -men 'dreɪ|mən [-mæn], -mən [-men]
Drayton 'dreɪtn
dread (s. v.), -s, -ing, -ed dred, -z, -ɪŋ, -ɪd
dread|ful, -fully, -fulness 'dred|fʊl, -fʊlɪ [-fəlɪ], -fʊlnɪs [-nəs]
dreadnought (D.), -s 'drednɔ:t, -s

dream (s. v.), -s, -ing/ly, -ed, -t, -er/s dri:m, -z, -ɪŋ/lɪ, dremt [drempt, rarely dri:md], dremt [-mpt], 'dri:mə*/z
dreamland 'dri:mlænd
dreamless, -ly 'dri:mlɪs [-ləs], -lɪ
dream|y, -ier, -iest, -ily, -iness 'dri:m|ɪ, -ɪə* [-jə*], -ɪɪst [-jɪst], -ɪlɪ [-əlɪ], -ɪnɪs [-ɪnəs]
drear drɪə*
drear|y, -ier, -iest, -ily, -iness, -isome 'drɪər|ɪ, -ɪə*, -ɪɪst, -əlɪ [-ɪlɪ], -ɪnɪs [-ɪnəs], -ɪsəm
dredg|e (s. v.), -es, -ing, -ed, -er/s dredʒ, -ɪz, -ɪŋ, -d, -ə*/z
dregg|y, -ily, -iness 'dreg|ɪ, -ɪlɪ [-əlɪ], -ɪnɪs [-ɪnəs]
dregs dregz
drench (s. v.), -es, -ing, -ed, -er/s drentʃ, -ɪz, -ɪŋ, -t, -ə*/z
Dresden 'drezdən ('dre:sdən)
dress (s. v.), -es, -ing, -ed, -er/s dres, -ɪz, -ɪŋ, -t, -ə*/z
dressage 'dresɑ:ʒ [-ɑ:dʒ]
dress-circle, -s ,dres'sɜ:kl ['-,--], -z
dress-coat, -s ,dres'kəʊt, -s
dresser (piece of furniture), -s 'dresə*, -z
dressing-case, -s 'dresɪŋkeɪs, -ɪz
dressing-gown, -s 'dresɪŋgaʊn, -z
dressing-jacket, -s 'dresɪŋ,dʒækɪt, -s
dressing-room, -s 'dresɪŋrʊm [-ru:m], -z
dressing-table, -s 'dresɪŋ,teɪbl, -z
dressmak|er/s, -ing 'dres,meɪk|ə*/z, -ɪŋ
dress-suit, -s ,dres'su:t [-'sju:t], -s
dress|y, -ier, -iest, -ily, -iness 'dres|ɪ, -ɪə*, -ɪɪst, -ɪlɪ [-əlɪ], -ɪnɪs [-ɪnəs]
drew (from draw) dru:
Drew, -s dru:, -z
Dreyfus 'dreɪfəs, 'draɪf-
dribb|le (s. v.), -les, -ling, -led, -ler/s 'drɪb|l, -lz, -lɪŋ, [-lɪŋ], -ld, -lə*/z [-lə*/z]
driblet, -s 'drɪblɪt [-lət], -s
dried (from dry v.) draɪd
drier (s. adj.), -s 'draɪə*, -z
dries (from dry v.) draɪz
driest 'draɪɪst
Driffield 'drɪfi:ld
drift (s. v.), -s, -ing, -ed drɪft, -s, -ɪŋ, -ɪd
drift-ice 'drɪftaɪs
driftless 'drɪftlɪs [-ləs]
drift-wood 'drɪftwʊd
drifty 'drɪftɪ
drill (s. v.), -s, -ing, -ed drɪl, -z, -ɪŋ, -d
drill-sergeant, -s 'drɪl,sɑ:dʒənt, -s
drily (= dryly) 'draɪlɪ

151

drink (s. v.), -s, -ing, drank, drunk,
 drinker/s drɪŋk, -s, -ɪŋ, dræŋk,
 drʌŋk, 'drɪŋkə*/z
drinkable 'drɪŋkəbl
drinking-bout, -s 'drɪŋkɪŋbaʊt, -s
drinking-fountain, -s 'drɪŋkɪŋ,faʊntɪn
 [-tən], -z
drinking-horn, -s 'drɪŋkɪŋhɔːn, -z
drinking-song, -s 'drɪŋkɪŋsɒŋ, -z
drinking-water 'drɪŋkɪŋ,wɔːtə*
drink-offering, -s 'drɪŋk,ɒfərɪŋ, -z
Drinkwater 'drɪŋk,wɔːtə*
drip (s. v.), -s, -ping/s, -ped, -per/s drɪp,
 -s, -ɪŋ/z, -t, -ə*/z
drip-dry ,drɪp'draɪ
dripping (melted fat) 'drɪpɪŋ
dripping-pan, -s 'drɪpɪŋpæn, -z
drip-stone, -s 'drɪpstəʊn, -z
drivable 'draɪvəbl
driv|e (s. v.), -es, -ing, drove, driven,
 driver/s draɪv, -z, -ɪŋ, drəʊv, 'drɪvn,
 'draɪvə*/z
driv|el (s. v.), -els, -elling, -elled,
 -eller/s 'drɪv|l, -lz, -lɪŋ [-lɪŋ], -ld,
 -lə*/z [-lə*/z]
Driver 'draɪvə*
driving-belt, -s 'draɪvɪŋbelt, -s
driving-iron, -s 'draɪvɪŋ,aɪən, -z
driving-licenc|e, -es 'draɪvɪŋ,laɪsns, -ɪz
driving-wheel, -s 'draɪvɪŋwiːl [-ŋhw-],
 -z
drizz|le (s. v.), -les, -ling, -led 'drɪz|l,
 -lz, -lɪŋ [-lɪŋ], -ld
drizzly 'drɪzlɪ [-zlɪ]
Droeshout 'druːʃaʊt
Drogheda (place) 'drɒɪdə ['drɔːɪdə,
 'drɔːədə, 'drɒhədə], (Earl) 'drɒɪdə
drogher, -s 'drəʊgə*, -z
Droitwich 'drɔɪtwɪtʃ [rarely 'drɔɪtɪtʃ]
droll, -er, -est, -y drəʊl, -ə*, -ɪst, -lɪ
 ['drəʊlɪ]
droller|y, -ies 'drəʊlər|ɪ, -ɪz
dromedar|y, -ies 'drɒmədər|ɪ ['drʌm-,
 -mɪd-], -ɪz
Dromio 'drəʊmɪəʊ [-mjəʊ]
Dromore 'drəʊmɔː* [-mɔə*]
dron|e (s. v.), -es, -ing, -ed drəʊn, -z,
 -ɪŋ, -d
Dronfield 'drɒnfiːld
droop, -s, -ing/ly, -ed druːp, -s, -ɪŋ/lɪ,
 -t
drop (s. v.), -s, -ping/s, -ped, -per/s
 drɒp, -s, -ɪŋ/z, -t, -ə*/z
drop-curtain, -s 'drɒp,kɜːtn [-tən, -tɪn],
 -z
drop-kick, -s 'drɒpkɪk, -s
drop-out, -s 'drɒpaʊt, -s
drop-scene, -s 'drɒpsiːn, -z

dropsic|al, -ally, -alness 'drɒpsɪk|l, -əlɪ,
 -lnɪs [-nəs]
dropsy 'drɒpsɪ
Dros drɒs
drosera 'drɒsərə
droshk|y, -ies 'drɒʃk|ɪ, -ɪz
drosometer, -s drɒ'sɒmɪtə* [-mətə*], -z
dross, -y drɒs, -ɪ
drought, -s, -y draʊt, -s, -ɪ
drove (s.), -s drəʊv, -z
drove (from drive) drəʊv
drover, -s 'drəʊvə*, -z
drow, -s draʊ, -z
Drower, 'draʊə*
drown, -s, -ing, -ed draʊn, -z, -ɪŋ, -d
drows|e (s. v.), -es, -ing, -ed draʊz, -ɪz,
 -ɪŋ, -d
drows|y, -ier, -iest, -ily, -iness 'draʊz|ɪ,
 -ɪə* [-jə*], -ɪɪst [-jɪst], -ɪlɪ [-əlɪ], -ɪnɪs
 [-nəs]
Drs. 'dɒktəz
drub, -s, -bing, -bed drʌb, -z, -ɪŋ, -d
Druce druːs
Drucker 'drʊkə*
drudg|e (s. v.), -es, -ing/ly, -ed drʌdʒ,
 -ɪz, -ɪŋ/lɪ, -d
drudgery 'drʌdʒərɪ
drug (s. v.), -s, -ging, -ged drʌg, -z, -ɪŋ,
 -d
drugget, -s 'drʌgɪt, -s
druggist, -s 'drʌgɪst, -s
druid, -s, -ess/es, -ism 'druːɪd ['drʊɪd],
 -z, -ɪs/ɪz [-es/ɪz], -ɪzəm
druidic, -al druː'ɪdɪk [drʊ-], -l
drum (s. v.), -s, -ming, -med, -mer/s
 drʌm, -z, -ɪŋ, -d, -ə*/z
Drumclog drʌm'klɒg
drum-fire 'drʌm,faɪə*
drumhead, -s 'drʌmhed, -z
drum-major, -s ,drʌm'meɪdʒə*, -z
Drummond 'drʌmənd
drumstick, -s 'drʌmstɪk, -s
drunk (s. adj.), -s drʌŋk, -s
drunk (from drink) drʌŋk
drunkard, -s 'drʌŋkəd, -z
drunken, -ly, -ness 'drʌŋkən, -lɪ, -nɪs
 [-nəs]
drupe, -s druːp, -s
Drury 'drʊərɪ
druse (geological term), -s druːz, -ɪz
Druse (surname) druːz, druːs
Druse (member of sect in Syria), -s
 druːz, -ɪz
Drusilla druː'sɪlə [drʊ-]
dr|y (adj. v.), -ier, -iest, -yly, -yness;
 -ies, -ying, -ied, -ier/s dr|aɪ, -aɪə*,
 -aɪɪst, -aɪlɪ, -aɪnɪs [-nəs]; -aɪz, -aɪɪŋ,
 -aɪd, -aɪə*/z

152

dryad, -s 'draɪəd ['draɪæd], -z
Dryasdust 'draɪəzdʌst
dry-bob, -s 'draɪbɒb, -z
Dryburgh 'draɪbərə
dry-clean, -s, -ing, -ed, -er/s ˌdraɪ'kliːn,
-z, -ɪŋ, -d, -ə*/z
Dryden 'draɪdn
dry-dock (s. v.), -s, -ing, -ed ˌdraɪ'dɒk
['--], -s, -ɪŋ, -t
Dryfesdale 'draɪfsdeɪl
Dryhurst 'draɪhɜːst
drying (from dry v.) 'draɪɪŋ
dryly 'draɪlɪ
dry-measure 'draɪˌmeʒə*
dryness 'draɪnɪs [-nəs]
dry-nurs|e (s. v.), -es, -ing, -ed ˌdraɪ-
'nɜːs, -ɪz, -ɪŋ, -t
dry-plate, -s ˌdraɪ'pleɪt ['--], -s
dry-point 'draɪpɔɪnt
dry-rot ˌdraɪ'rɒt
drysalter, s 'draɪˌsɔːltə* [-ˌsɒl-], -z
drysalter|y, -ies 'draɪˌsɔːltər|ɪ [-ˌsɒl-],
-ɪz
Drysdale 'draɪzdeɪl
dryshod ˌdraɪ'ʃɒd ['--]
dual 'djuːəl [djʊəl]
duali|sm, -st/s 'djuːəlɪ|zəm ['djʊəl-],
-st/s
dualistic ˌdjuːə'lɪstɪk [ˌdjʊə'l-]
dualit|y, -ies djuː'ælət|ɪ [djʊ'æ-, -ɪt|ɪ],
-ɪz
Duane duː'eɪn [dʊ'eɪn]
dub (s. v.), -s, -bing, -bed dʌb, -z, -ɪŋ,
-d
dubbin 'dʌbɪn
Dubhe 'dʊbeɪ
dubiety djuː'baɪətɪ [djʊ-, -aɪtɪ]
dubious, -ly, -ness 'djuːbjəs [-bɪəs], -lɪ,
-nɪs [-nəs]
dubitat|e, -es, -ing, -ed 'djuːbɪteɪt, -s,
-ɪŋ, -ɪd
dubitation, -s ˌdjuːbɪ'teɪʃn [djʊbɪ't-], -z
dubitative, -ly 'djuːbɪtətɪv [-teɪt-], -lɪ
Dublin 'dʌblɪn
Du Buisson (English name) 'djuːbɪsn
duc|al, -ally 'djuːk|l, -əlɪ
Du Cane djʊ'keɪn [djuː'k-]
ducat, -s 'dʌkət, -s
duce, -s 'duːtʃɪ, -z
Duchesne (English name) djuː'ʃeɪn,
duː'ʃeɪn
duchess, -es 'dʌtʃɪs [-es], -ɪz
duch|y, -ies 'dʌtʃ|ɪ, -ɪz
Ducie 'djuːsɪ
duck (s. v.), -s, -ing, -ed dʌk, -s, -ɪŋ, -t
duck-bill, -s 'dʌkbɪl, -z
duck-board, -s 'dʌkbɔːd [-bɔəd], -z
duckling, -s 'dʌklɪŋ, -z

duck-pond, -s 'dʌkpɒnd, -z
duck's-egg, -s 'dʌkseg, -z
duck-shot 'dʌkʃɒt
duckweed 'dʌkwiːd
Duckworth 'dʌkwəθ [-wɜːθ]
duck|y, -ies 'dʌk|ɪ, -ɪz
Du Croz (English surname) djʊ'krəʊ
[dju:'k-]
duct, -s dʌkt, -s
ductile 'dʌktaɪl
ductility dʌk'tɪlətɪ [-rtɪ]
ductless 'dʌktlɪs [-ləs]
dud, -s dʌd, -z
Duddell dʌ'del, djuː'del [djʊ-]
Duddeston 'dʌdɪstən
Duddington 'dʌdɪŋtən
Duddon 'dʌdn
dude, -s djuːd, -z
Dudeney (surname) 'duːdnɪ, 'djuːdnɪ
dudgeon, -s 'dʌdʒən, -z
Dudhope 'dʌdəp
Dudley 'dʌdlɪ
dudu 'duːduː
due (s. adj.), -s djuː, -z
duel (s. v.), -s, -ling, -led, -ler/s; -list/s
'djuːəl [djʊəl, -ɪl], -z, -ɪŋ, -d, -ə*/z;
-ɪst/s
duenna, -s djuː'enə [djʊ'e-], -z
Duer 'djuːə*
duet, -s djuː'et [djʊ'e-], -s
duettino, -s ˌdjuːe'tiːnəʊ [ˌdjʊe-] -z
duettist, -s djuː'etɪst [djʊ'e-], -s
duetto, -s djuː'etəʊ [djʊ'e-], -z
Duff dʌf
duffel 'dʌfl
duffer, -s 'dʌfə*, -z
Dufferin 'dʌfərɪn
Duffield 'dʌfiːld
duffle-coat, -s 'dʌflkəʊt, -s
Duffy 'dʌfɪ
dug (s.), -s dʌg, -z
dug (from dig) dʌg
Dugald 'duːgəld
Dugan 'duːgən
Dugdale 'dʌgdeɪl
dugong, -s 'duːgɒŋ ['djuː-], -z
dug-out (s.), -s 'dʌgaʊt, -s
dug-out (adj.) ˌdʌg'aʊt
Duguid 'djuːgɪd, 'duːgɪd
duiker, -s 'daɪkə*, -z
duke (D.), -s djuːk, -s
dukedom, -s 'djuːkdəm, -z
duker|y, -ies 'djuːkər|ɪ, -ɪz
Dukinfield 'dʌkɪnfiːld
dulcamara ˌdʌlkə'mɑːrə [-'meər-]
Dulce (Christian name) 'dʌlsɪ
dulcet 'dʌlsɪt
Dulcie 'dʌlsɪ

153

dulci|fy, -fies, -fying, -fied 'dʌlsɪ|faɪ, -faɪz, -faɪɪŋ, -faɪd

dulcimer, -s 'dʌlsɪmə*, -z

Dulcinea ˌdʌlsɪ'nɪə [dʌl'sɪnɪə]

dulia dju:'laɪə

dull (adj. v.), -er, -est, -y, -ness; -s, -ing, -ed dʌl, -ə*, -ɪst, -ɪ [-lɪ], -nɪs [-nəs]; -z, -ɪŋ, -d

dullard, -s 'dʌləd, -z

dull|-brained, -eyed 'dʌl|breɪnd, -aɪd

Dulles 'dʌlɪs [-ləs]

dullish 'dʌlɪʃ

dulness (=dullness) 'dʌlnɪs [-nəs]

Duluth dju:'lu:θ [dʊ'l-]

Dulwich 'dʌlɪdʒ [-ɪtʃ]

duly 'dju:lɪ

Duma 'du:mə ['dju:-]

Dumain dju:'meɪn [djʊ-]

Dumaresq du:'merɪk [dʊ-]

Dumas 'dju:mɑ: ['du:-] (dymɑ)

Du Maurier (English surname) dju:-'mɔ:rɪeɪ [dʊ-, du:-, -'rɪɒr-]

Dumayne dju:'meɪn [djʊ'm-]

dumb (adj. v.), -ly, -ness; -s, -ing, -ed dʌm, -lɪ, -nɪs [-nəs]; -z, -ɪŋ, -d

Dumbarton dʌm'bɑ:tn

dumb-bell, -s 'dʌmbel, -z

dumbfound, -s, -ing, -ed, -er/s dʌm-'faʊnd, -z, -ɪŋ, -ɪd, -ə*/z

Dumbiedikes 'dʌmbɪdaɪks

dumb-show, -s 'dʌmʃəʊ [ˌ-'-], -z

dumb-waiter, -s ˌdʌm'weɪtə*, -z

dumdum, -s 'dʌmdʌm, -z

Dumfries, -shire dʌm'fri:s [dəm-], -ʃə* [-ˌʃɪə*, dʌm'fri:ʃʃə*]

dumm|y (s. adj.), -ies 'dʌm|ɪ, -ɪz

Dumnorix 'dʌmnərɪks

dump, -s, -ing, -ed dʌmp, -s, -ɪŋ, -t [dʌmt]

Dumphreys 'dʌmfrɪz

dumpish, -ly, -ness 'dʌmpɪʃ, -lɪ, -nɪs [-nəs]

dumpling, -s 'dʌmplɪŋ, -z

dumps dʌmps

dump|y, -ier, -iest 'dʌmp|ɪ, -ɪə* [-jə*], -ɪɪst [-jɪst]

Dumville 'dʌmvɪl

dun (s. adj. v.), -s, -ning, -ned dʌn, -z, -ɪŋ, -d

Dunalley dʌ'nælɪ

Dunbar (place, surname) dʌn'bɑ:*, 'dʌnbɑ:*
  Note.—In Scotland always -'-.

Dunblane dʌn'bleɪn

Duncan 'dʌŋkən ['dʌŋk-]

Duncannon dʌn'kænən [dʌŋ'k-]

Duncansby 'dʌŋkənzbɪ ['dʌŋk-]

dunce, -s dʌns, -ɪz

Dunciad 'dʌnsɪæd

Duncombe 'dʌŋkəm ['dʌŋk-]

Dundalk dʌn'dɔ:k [-'dɔ:lk, also '—
  when attributive]

Dundas dʌn'dæs, 'dʌndæs

Dundee dʌn'di: [ˌdʌn'd-, also 'dʌnd-
  when attributive]

dunderhead, -s 'dʌndəhed, -z

Dundonald dʌn'dɒnld

dundrear|y (D.), -ies dʌn'drɪər|ɪ, -ɪz

Dundrennan dʌn'drenən

Dundrum dʌn'drʌm ['dʌndrəm]

dune, -s dju:n, -z

Dunedin (in New Zealand) dʌ'ni:dɪn [-dn]

Dunell dju'nel [dju:'n-]

Dunfermline dʌn'fɜ:mlɪn [dʌm'f-]

dung dʌŋ

Dungannon dʌn'gænən [dʌŋ'g-]

dungaree, -s ˌdʌŋgə'ri:, -z

Dungarvan dʌn'gɑ:vən [dʌŋ'g-]

Dungeness ˌdʌndʒɪ'nes, dʌndʒ'nes [-dʒə-]

dungeon, -s 'dʌndʒən, -z

dung-hill, -s 'dʌŋhɪl, -z

Dunglison 'dʌŋglɪsn

dungy 'dʌŋɪ

Dunhill 'dʌnhɪl

Dunholme 'dʌnəm

Dunkeld dʌn'keld [dʌŋ'k-]

Dunker, -s 'dʌŋkə*, -z

Dunkirk dʌn'kɜ:k [ˌdʌn'kɜ:k, dʌŋ'k-, ˌdʌŋ'k-]

Dun Laoghaire dʌn'lɪərɪ [less usually -'leərə]

Dunlap 'dʌnləp [-læp]

dunlin, -s 'dʌnlɪn, -z

Dunlop (surname) 'dʌnlɒp, dʌn'lɒp

Dunlop (tyre), -s 'dʌnlɒp, -s

Dunmail dʌn'meɪl

Dunmore dʌn'mɔ:* [-'mɒə*], attributively also '—, as in D. Road

Dunmow 'dʌnməʊ

Dunn(e) dʌn

Dunning 'dʌnɪŋ

dunnock, -s 'dʌnək, -s

Dunnottar dʌ'nɒtə* [də'n-]

Dunraven dʌn'reɪvn

Dunrobin dʌn'rɒbɪn

Dunsany dʌn'seɪnɪ

Dunse dʌns

Dunsinane (in Tayside) dʌn'sɪnən
  Note.—This name has to be pro-
  nounced 'dʌnsɪneɪn in Shakespeare's
  'Macbeth'.

Dunstable 'dʌnstəbl

Dunstaffnage dʌn'stæfnɪdʒ [-'stɑ:f-]

Dunst|an, -er, -on 'dʌnst|ən, -ə*, -ən

154

Dunton 'dʌntən

duo, -s 'dju:əʊ ['djʊəʊ], -z

duodecennial ˌdju:əʊdɪ'senjəl [ˌdjʊəʊ-, -nɪəl]

duodecimal, -s ˌdju:əʊ'desɪml [ˌdjʊəʊ-, djʊə'd-, -səm-], -z

duodecimo, -s ˌdju:əʊ'desɪməʊ [ˌdjʊəʊ-], -z

duodenal ˌdju:əʊ'di:nl [ˌdjʊəʊ-]

duodenary ˌdju:əʊ'di:nərɪ [ˌdjʊəʊ-]

duoden|um, -ums, -a ˌdju:əʊ'di:n|əm [ˌdjʊəʊ-], -əmz, -ə

duologue, -s 'djʊəlɒg ['dju:-ə-], -z

Duparcq (surname) du:'pɑːk [dju:-]

dup|le (s. v.), -es, -ing, -ed dju:p, -s, -ɪŋ, -t

dupery 'dju:pərɪ

Du Plat dju:'plɑ

duple 'dju:pl

Dupleix (governor in India) dju:'pleɪks (dyplɛks), (historian) dju:'pleɪ (dyplɛ)

duplex 'dju:pleks

duplicate (s. adj.), -s 'dju:plɪkət [-ɪt], -s

duplicat|e (v.), -es, -ing, -ed, -or/s 'dju:-plɪkeɪt, -s, -ɪŋ, -ɪd, -ə*/z

duplication, -s ˌdju:plɪ'keɪʃn, -z

duplicature, -s 'dju:plɪkeɪtʃə* ['dju:plɪkə,tjʊə*], -z

duplicity dju:'plɪsətɪ [djʊ-, -ɪtɪ]

dupl|y, -ies dju:'pl|aɪ [djʊ-], -aɪz

Dupont (American surname) 'dju:pɒnt

Duquesne (French naval commander) dju:'keɪn [djʊ-] (dykɛːn), (place in U.S.A.) dju:'keɪn [djʊ-, du:'k-]

durability ˌdjʊərə'bɪlətɪ [ˌdjɔər-, ˌdjɔːr-, -ɪt-]

durab|le, -ly, -leness 'djʊərəb|l ['djɔər-, 'djɔːr-], -lɪ, -lnɪs [-nəs]

dural 'djʊərəl ['djɔə-, 'djɔː-]

duralumin djʊə'ræljʊmɪn [djɔə'r-, djɔː'r-]

duramen djʊə'reɪmen

durance 'djʊərəns

Durand djʊə'rænd

Durant djʊ'rɑːnt, djʊ'rænt

duration, -s djʊə'reɪʃn [djɔə'r-, djɔː'r-], -z

durative 'djʊərətɪv ['djɔər-, 'djɔːr-]

Durban 'dɜːbən

durbar, -s 'dɜːbɑː*, -z

Durbin 'dɜːbɪn

Durden 'dɜːdn

durdle, -s 'dɜːdl, -z

Durell djʊə'rel

Dürer, -s 'djʊərə* ('dy:rər), -z

duress djʊə'res ['djʊəres, 'djʊərɪs]

Durham 'dʌrəm

during 'djʊərɪŋ ['djɔər-, 'djɔːr-, 'dʒʊər-, 'dʒɔːr-]

Durlacher də'lækə*

Durnford 'dɜːnfəd

Durran dʌ'ræn [də'r-]

Durrant 'dʌrənt

Durrell 'dʌrəl

durst (from dare), -n't dɜːst, 'dɜːsnt

Durward 'dɜːwəd

Duse 'du:zɪ

dusk (s. adj. v.), -s, -ing, -ed dʌsk, -s, -ɪŋ, -t

dusk|y, -ier, -iest, -ily, -iness 'dʌsk|ɪ, -ɪə* [-jə*], -ɪɪst [-jɪst], -ɪlɪ [-əlɪ], -ɪnɪs [-ɪnəs]

dust (s. v.), -s, -ing, -ed dʌst, -s, -ɪŋ, -ɪd

dustbin, -s 'dʌstbɪn, -z

dust-cart, -s 'dʌstkɑːt, -s

dust-coat, -s 'dʌstkəʊt, -s

dust-colour, -ed 'dʌstˌkʌlə*, -d

duster, -s 'dʌstə*, -z

dusthole, -s 'dʌsthəʊl, -z

dust-jacket, -s 'dʌstˌdʒækɪt, -s

dust|man, -men 'dʌst|mən, -men

dust-pan, -s 'dʌstpæn, -z

dustproof 'dʌstpru:f

dust|y, -ier, -iest, -ily, -iness 'dʌst|ɪ, -ɪə* [-jə*], -ɪɪst [-jɪst], -ɪlɪ [-əlɪ], -ɪnɪs [-ɪnəs]

Dutch, -man, -men dʌtʃ, -mən, -men

Dutch|woman, -women 'dʌtʃ|ˌwʊmən, -ˌwɪmɪn

duteous, -ly, -ness 'dju:tjəs [-tɪəs], -lɪ, -nɪs [-nəs]

Duthie 'dʌθɪ

Duthoit də'θɔɪt

dutiable 'dju:tjəbl [-tɪəb-]

duti|ful, -fully, -fulness 'dju:tɪ|fʊl, -fʊlɪ [-fəlɪ], -fʊlnɪs [-nəs]

Dutton 'dʌtn

dut|y, -ies 'dju:t|ɪ, -ɪz

duty-free ˌdju:tɪ'fri:

duumvir, -s dju:'ʌmvə* [djʊ'ʌ-, 'dju:əmv-, du:'ʊm-], -z

duumvirate, -s dju:'ʌmvɪrət [djʊ'ʌ-, -vər-, -rɪt], -s

duumviri (alternative plur. of duumvir) du:'ʊmvɪriː [dju:'ʌmvɪraɪ, djʊ'ʌ-, -vər-]

Duveen dju:'vi:n [djʊ-]

duvet, -s 'dju:veɪ, -z

dux, -es dʌks, -ɪz

Duxbury 'dʌksbərɪ

D.V. (deo volente) ˌdi:'vi:

Dvorak [-řák] 'dvɔːʒɑːk [-ɔːrɑːk, -æk]

dwale dweɪl

dwarf (s. v.), -s, -ing, -ed dwɔːf, -s, -ɪŋ, -t

155

dwarfish, -ly, -ness 'dwɔːfɪʃ, -lɪ, -nɪs [-nəs]

dwell, -s, -ing/s, dwelt, dweller/s dwel, -z, -ɪŋ/z, dwelt, 'dwelə*/z

dwelling-hou|se, -ses 'dwelɪŋhaʊ|s, -zɪz

dwelling-place, -s 'dwelɪŋpleɪs, -ɪz

Dwight dwaɪt

Dwina 'dviːnə ['dwiː-] (dvji'na)

dwind|le, -les, -ling, -led 'dwɪnd|l, -lz, -lɪŋ [-l̩ŋ], -ld

dyad, -s 'daɪæd ['daɪəd], -z

Dyak, -s 'daɪæk ['daɪək], -s

dyarch|y, -ies 'daɪɑːk|ɪ, -ɪz

Dyce daɪs

Dyche daɪtʃ

dye (s. v.), -s, -ing, -d, -r/s daɪ, -z, -ɪŋ, -d, 'daɪə*/z

Dyer 'daɪə*

dyestuff, -s 'daɪstʌf, -s

dye-wood 'daɪwʊd

dye-works 'daɪwɜːks

Dyfed 'dʌvɪd (Welsh 'dəved)

Dyffryn 'dʌfrɪn (Welsh 'dəfrin)

dying (from die v.) 'daɪɪŋ

dyk|e (s. v.), -es, -ing, -ed daɪk, -s, -ɪŋ, -t

Dyke, -s daɪk, -s

Dylan 'dɪlən (Welsh 'dəlan)

Dym|ock, -oke 'dɪm|ək, -ək

Dymon|d, -t 'daɪmən|d, -t

dynameter, -s daɪ'næmɪtə* [dɪ'n-, -mətə*], -z

dynamic, -al, -ally, -s daɪ'næmɪk [dɪ'n-], -l, -əlɪ, -s

dynamism 'daɪnəmɪzəm

dynamit|e (s. v.), -es, -ing, -ed, -er/s 'daɪnəmaɪt, -s, -ɪŋ, -ɪd, -ə*/z

dynamo, -s 'daɪnəməʊ, -z

dynamometer, -s ˌdaɪnə'mɒmɪtə* [-mətə*], -z

dynamometric, -al ˌdaɪnəməʊ'metrɪk, -l

dynast, -s 'dɪnəst ['dɪnæst, 'daɪnəst, 'daɪnæst], -s

dynastic dɪ'næstɪk [daɪ'n-]

dynast|y, -ies 'dɪnəst|ɪ ['daɪn-], -ɪz

dynatron, -s 'daɪnətrɒn, -z

dyne, -s daɪn, -s

Dynevor 'dɪnɪvə*

Dysart 'daɪsət [-sɑːt, -zɑːt]

dysarthria dɪs'ɑːθrɪə

dyscrasia dɪs'kreɪzjə [-zɪə, -ʒjə, -ʒɪə, -ʒə]

dysenteric ˌdɪsn'terɪk [-sən-, -sen-]

dysentery 'dɪsntrɪ [-sən-]

dyslalia dɪs'leɪlɪə [-ljə]

dyslexia dɪs'leksɪə [-ksjə]

Dyson 'daɪsn

dyspepsia dɪs'pepsɪə [-sjə]

dyspeptic (s. adj.), -s dɪs'peptɪk, -s

dyspnoea dɪs'pniːə [-'pnɪə]

dysuria dɪs'jʊərɪə [-rjə]

dziggetai, -s 'dzɪgɪtaɪ, -z

E

E (*the letter*), -'s i:, -z
each i:tʃ
Ead|ie, -y 'i:d|ɪ, -ɪ
eager, -ly, -ness 'i:gə*, -lɪ, -nɪs [-nəs]
eagle, -s 'i:gl, -z
eagle-eyed ˌi:gl'aɪd ['i:glaɪd]
Eaglefield 'i:glfi:ld
Eaglehawk 'i:glhɔ:k
eagle-owl, -s ˌi:gl'aʊl [*in contrast* '---], -z
eaglet, -s 'i:glɪt [-lət], -s
eagre, -s 'eɪgə* ['i:gə*], -z
Ealing 'i:lɪŋ
Eames i:mz, eɪmz
Eamon 'eɪmən
ear, -s ɪə*, -z
ear-ache 'ɪəreɪk
Eardley 'ɜ:dlɪ
ear-drum, -s 'ɪədrʌm, -z
eared ɪəd
earl, -s; -dom/s ɜ:l, -z; -dəm/z
Earl(e) ɜ:l
earl-marshal, -s ˌɜ:l'mɑ:ʃl, -z
Earl's Court ˌɜ:lz'kɔ:t
earl|y, -ier, -iest, -iness 'ɜ:l|ɪ, -ɪə*
[-jə*], -ɪɪst [-jɪst], -ɪnɪs [-ɪnəs]
earmark (*s. v.*), -s, -ing, -ed 'ɪəmɑ:k, -s, -ɪŋ, -t
earn (E.), -s, -ing, -ed ɜ:n, -z, -ɪŋ, -d [ɜ:nt]
earnest (*s. adj.*), -s, -ly, -ness 'ɜ:nɪst, -s, -lɪ, -nɪs [-nəs]
earnest-money, -s 'ɜ:nɪstˌmʌnɪ, -z
earnings 'ɜ:nɪŋz
Earp ɜ:p
earphone, -s 'ɪəfəʊn, -z
earring, -s 'ɪərɪŋ, -s
Earsdon 'ɪəzdən
earshot 'ɪəʃɒt
earth (*s.*), -s ɜ:θ, -s [ɜ:ðz]
earth (*v.*), -s, -ing, -ed ɜ:θ, -s, -ɪŋ, -t
earth-board, -s 'ɜ:θbɔ:d [-bɒəd], -z
earth-born 'ɜ:θbɔ:n
earthbound 'ɜ:θbaʊnd
earth-bred 'ɜ:θbred
earth-closet, -s 'ɜ:θˌklɒzɪt, -s
earthen, -ware 'ɜ:θn, -weə*
earthiness 'ɜ:θɪnɪs [-nəs]
earthl|y, -ier, -iest, -iness 'ɜ:θl|ɪ, -ɪə*
[-jə*], -ɪɪst [-jɪst], -ɪnɪs [-ɪnəs]

earthly-minded, -ness ˌɜ:θlɪ'maɪndɪd
['ɜ:θlɪˌm-], -nɪs [-nəs]
earthquake, -s 'ɜ:θkweɪk, -s
earthward 'ɜ:θwəd
earthwork, -s 'ɜ:θwɜ:k, -s
earthworm, -s 'ɜ:θwɜ:m, -z
earthy 'ɜ:θɪ
ear-trumpet, -s 'ɪəˌtrʌmpɪt, -s
ear-wax 'ɪəwæks
earwig, -s 'ɪəwɪg, -z
ear-witness, -es ˌɪə'wɪtnɪs ['-ˌ--, -nəs], -ɪz
Easdale 'i:zdeɪl
eas|e (*s. v.*), -es, -ing, -ed i:z, -ɪz, -ɪŋ, -d
Easebourne 'i:zbɔ:n [-bɔən]
easel, -s 'i:zl, -z
easement, -s 'i:zmənt, -s
Easingwold 'i:zɪŋwəʊld
east (E.) i:st
Eastbourne 'i:stbɔ:n [-bɔən]
Eastcheap 'i:stʃi:p
East-end, -er/s ˌi:st'end, -ə*/z
Easter, -s 'i:stə*, -z
Easter-day, -s ˌi:stə'deɪ ['---], -z
easterly 'i:stəlɪ
eastern, -most 'i:stən [-tn], -məʊst [-məst]
East Ham ˌi:st'hæm
Eastham 'i:sthəm
Easthampton ˌi:st'hæmptən
easting 'i:stɪŋ
Eastlake 'i:stleɪk
Eastleigh 'i:stli: [ˌi:st'li:]
Eastman 'i:stmən
east-north-east ˌi:stnɔ:θ'i:st [*in nautical usage* -nɔ:r'i:st]
Easton 'i:stən
Eastport 'i:stpɔ:t
east-south-east ˌi:stsaʊθ'i:st [*in nautical usage also* -saʊ'i:st]
eastward, -ly, -s 'i:stwəd, -lɪ, -z
Eastwood 'i:stwʊd
eas|y, -ier, -iest, -ily, -iness 'i:z|ɪ, -ɪə*
[-jə*], -ɪɪst [-jɪst], -ɪlɪ [-əlɪ], -ɪnɪs [-ɪnəs]
easy-chair, -s ˌi:zɪ'tʃeə* ['--ˌ-], -z
easygoing 'i:zɪˌgəʊɪŋ [ˌ--'--]
eat (*pres. tense*), -s, -ing, ate, eat|en, -er/s; -able/s i:t, -s, -ɪŋ, et [eɪt], 'i:t|n, -ə*/z; -əbl/z

157

eating-hou|se, -ses 'iːtɪŋhaʊ|s, -zɪz
Eaton 'iːtn
eau-de-Cologne ˌəʊdəkə'ləʊn [-dɪk-]
eau-de-vie ˌəʊdə'viː (odvi)
eau-forte, eaux-fortes ˌəʊ'fɔːt (ofort), -s
eave, -s (E.) iːv, -z
eavesdrop, -s, -ping, -ped, -per/s
  'iːvzdrɒp, -s, -ɪŋ, -t, -ə*/z
Ebal 'iːbæl [-bəl]
ebb (s. v.), -s, -ing, -ed eb, -z, -ɪŋ, -d
Ebbsfleet 'ebzfliːt
ebb-tide, -s ˌeb'taɪd ['--], -z
Ebbw 'ebu: (Welsh 'ebu)
Ebel e'bel, 'iːbl
Ebenezer ˌebɪ'niːzə* [-bə-]
Ebionite, -s 'iːbjənaɪt [-bɪən-], -s
E-boat, -s 'iːbəʊt, -s
ebon, -ite 'ebən, -aɪt
ebony 'ebənɪ
Eboracum iː'bɒrəkəm [ɪ'b-]
ebriate 'iːbrɪət [-ɪt]
ebriety iː'braɪətɪ [ɪ'b-, -ɪtɪ]
Ebrington 'ebrɪŋtən
Ebro 'iːbrəʊ ['eb-] ('ebro)
ebullien|ce, -cy, -t ɪ'bʌljən|s [-'bʊl-,
  -lɪən-], -sɪ, -t
ebullition, -s ˌebə'lɪʃn [-bʊ'l-], -z
Ebury 'iːbərɪ
E.C. ˌiː'siː
écarté eɪ'kɑːteɪ (ekarte)
Ecbatana ek'bætənə [ˌekbə'tɑːnə]
Ecce Homo ˌeksɪ'həʊməʊ [ˌekeɪ-,
  -'hɒməʊ]
eccentric (s. adj), -s, -al, -ally ɪk'sentrɪk [ek-], -s, -l, -əlɪ
eccentricit|y, -ies ˌeksen'trɪsət|ɪ [-sən-,
  -ɪt|ɪ], -ɪz
Ecclefechan ˌekl'fekən [-'fexən]
Eccles, -field 'eklz, -fiːld
eccles|ia, -iast/s ɪ'kliːz|jə [-ɪə], -ɪæst/s
Ecclesiastes ɪˌkliːzɪ'æstiːz [-ɪ'ɑːs-]
ecclesiastic (s. adj.), -s, -al, -ally
  ɪˌkliːzɪ'æstɪk [-ɪ'ɑːs-], -s, -l, -əlɪ
ecclesiasticism ɪˌkliːzɪ'æstɪsɪzəm
  [-ɪ'ɑːs-]
Ecclesiasticus ɪˌkliːzɪ'æstɪkəs [-ɪ'ɑːs-]
Eccleston 'eklstən
echelon, -s, -ned 'eʃəlɒn ['eɪʃ-], -z, -d
echidn|a, -ae e'kɪdn|ə [ɪ'k-], -iː
echin|us, -i e'kaɪn|əs [ɪ'k-], -aɪ
echo (s. v.), -es, -ing, -ed 'ekəʊ, -z, -ɪŋ,
  -d
echoic e'kəʊɪk [ɪ'k-]
Echuca ɪ'tʃuːkə
Eckersl(e)y 'ekəzlɪ
Eck|ert, -ford 'ek|ət, -fəd
éclair, -s eɪ'kleə* [ɪ'k-, 'eɪkleə*], -z
eclampsia ɪ'klæmpsɪə [e'k-, -sjə]

éclat, -s 'eɪklɑː [-'-] (ekla), -z
eclectic (s. adj.), -s, -al, -ally e'klektɪk
  [ɪ'klek-, iː'klek-], -s, -l, -əlɪ
eclecticism e'klektɪsɪzəm [ɪ'klek-,
  iː'klek-]
eclips|e (s. v.), -es, -ing, -ed ɪ'klɪps, -ɪz,
  -ɪŋ, -t
ecliptic, -s ɪ'klɪptɪk, -s
eclogue, -s 'eklɒg, -z
ecological ˌiːkə'lɒdʒɪkl [ˌek-]
ecolog|y, -ist/s iː'kɒləd|ʒ|ɪ [ɪ'k-, e'k-],
  -ɪst/s
economic, -al, -ally, -s ˌiːkə'nɒmɪk
  [ˌek-], -l, -əlɪ, -s
economist, -s ɪ'kɒnəmɪst [iː'k-], -s
economiz|e [-is|e], -es, -ing, -ed, -er/s
  ɪ'kɒnəmaɪz [iː'k-], -ɪz, -ɪŋ, -d, -ə*/z
econom|y, -ies ɪ'kɒnəm|ɪ [iː'k-], -ɪz
ecru 'eɪkru: (e'kru:]
ecstas|y, -ies 'ekstəs|ɪ, -ɪz
ecstatic, -al, -ally ɪk'stætɪk [ek-], -l,
  -əlɪ
ectoplasm 'ektəʊplæzəm
Ecuador 'ekwədɔ:* [ˌ-'-]
ecumenic, -al ˌiːkju:'menɪk [ˌek-,-kjʊ-],
  -l
ecumeni|sm, -st/s iː'kju:mənɪ|zəm
  [ɪ'kju:-], -st/s
eczema 'eksɪmə [-səm-]
eczematous ek'semətəs [ek'zem-, rarely
  ek'si:m-, ek'zi:m-]
edacious ɪ'deɪʃəs [iː'd-, e'd-]
Edam (cheese) 'iːdæm
Edda, -s 'edə, -z
Eddington 'edɪŋtən
edd|y (s. v.) (E.), -ies, -ying, -ied 'ed|ɪ,
  -ɪz, -ɪɪŋ, -ɪd
Eddystone 'edɪstən
Ede iːd
edelweiss 'eɪdlvaɪs
Eden, -bridge 'iːdn, -brɪdʒ
Edenfield (in Greater Manchester)
  'iːdnfiːld
Edessa ɪ'desə
Edgar 'edgə*
Edgbaston 'edʒbəstən
Edgcumbe 'edʒkəm [-kuːm]
edg|e (s. v.) (E.), -es, -ing, -ed edʒ, -ɪz,
  -ɪŋ, -d
Edgecomb(e) 'edʒkəm
Edgecote 'edʒkəʊt [-kət]
Edgehill (name of a hill) ˌedʒ'hɪl, (sur-
  name) 'edʒhɪl
edgeless 'edʒlɪs [-ləs]
Edgerton 'edʒətən
edge|ways, -wise 'edʒ|weɪz, -waɪz
Edgeworth 'edʒwɜːθ [-wəθ]
edging, -s 'edʒɪŋ, -z

Edgington 'edʒɪŋtən
Edgley 'edʒlɪ
Edgware (town) 'edʒweə*, (Road) 'edʒ-weə* [-wə*]
edgy 'edʒɪ
edibility ˌedɪ'bɪlətɪ [-də'b-, -lɪt-]
edible (s. adj.), -s, -ness 'edɪbl [-dəb-], -z, -nɪs [-nəs]
edict, -s 'i:dɪkt, -s
Edie 'i:dɪ
edification ˌedɪfɪ'keɪʃn
edifice, -s 'edɪfɪs, -ɪz
edi|fy, -fies, -fying, -fied 'edɪ|faɪ, -faɪz, -faɪŋ, -faɪd
edile, -s 'i:daɪl, -z
Edina ɪ'daɪnə [e'd-]
Edinburgh 'edɪnbərə ['edn-, -bʌrə]
Edington 'edɪŋtən
Edison 'edɪsn
Ediss 'i:dɪs, 'edɪs
edit, -s, -ing, -ed, -or/s 'edɪt, -s, -ɪŋ, -ɪd, -ə*/z
Edith 'i:dɪθ
edition, -s ɪ'dɪʃn, -z
editorial (s. adj.), -s, -ly ˌedɪ'tɔ:rɪəl, -z, -ɪ
editorship, -s 'edɪtəʃɪp, -s
Edmond, -s 'edmənd, -z
Edmonton 'edməntən
Edmund, -s 'edmənd, -z
Edna 'ednə
Edom, -ite/s 'i:dəm, -aɪt/s
Edridge 'edrɪdʒ
Edsall 'edsl
educability ˌedjʊkə'bɪlətɪ [-lɪt-]
educable 'edjʊkəbl
educat|e, -es, -ing, -ed, -or/s 'edju:keɪt [-dʒu:-, -djʊ-, -dʒʊ-], -s, -ɪŋ, -ɪd, -ə*/z
education ˌedju:'keɪʃn [-dʒu:-, -djʊ-, -dʒʊ-]
educa|tional, -tionally ˌedju:'keɪ|ʃənl [-dʒu:-, -djʊ-, -dʒʊ-, -ʃnəl, -ʃn̩l, -ʃn̩, -ʃənəl], -ʃŋəlɪ [-ʃnəlɪ, -ʃn̩lɪ, -ʃn̩lɪ, -ʃənəlɪ]
educationalist, -s ˌedju:'keɪʃn̩əlɪst [-dʒu:-, -djʊ-, -dʒʊ-, -ʃnəl-, -ʃn̩l-, -ʃn̩-, -ʃənəl-], -s
educationist, -s ˌedju:'keɪʃn̩ɪst [-dʒu:-, -djʊ-, -dʒʊ-, -ʃnɪst, -ʃənɪst], -s
educative 'edju:kətɪv [-dʒu:-, -djʊ-, -dʒʊ-, -keɪt-]
educ|e, -es, -ing, -ed i:'dju:s [ɪ'd-], -ɪz, -ɪŋ, -t
eduction, -s i:'dʌkʃn [ɪ'd-], -z
Edward, -(e)s 'edwəd, -z
Edwardian (s. adj.), -s ed'wɔ:djən [-dɪən], -z

Edwin, -stowe 'edwɪn, -stəʊ
eel, -s i:l, -z
e'en i:n
e'er eə*
eer|ie, -y, -ily, -iness 'ɪər|ɪ, -ɪ, -əlɪ [-ɪlɪ], -ɪnɪs [-ɪnəs]
effac|e, -es, -ing, -ed, -ement; -eable ɪ'feɪs [e'f-], -ɪz, -ɪŋ, -t, -mənt; -əbl
effect (s. v.), -s, -ing, -ed ɪ'fekt, -s, -ɪŋ, -ɪd
effective, -s, -ly, -ness ɪ'fektɪv, -z, -lɪ, -nɪs [-nəs]
effectual, -ly ɪ'fektʃʊəl [-tʃwəl, -tʃʊl, -tjʊəl, -tjwəl, -tjʊl], -ɪ
effectuality ɪˌfektjʊ'ælətɪ [-tʃʊ-, -rɪt-]
effectuat|e, -es, -ing, -ed ɪ'fektjʊeɪt [-tʃʊ-], -s, -ɪŋ, -ɪd
effeminacy ɪ'femɪnəsɪ [e'f-]
effeminate (adj.), -ly, -ness ɪ'femɪnət [e'f-, -nɪt], -lɪ, -nɪs [-nəs]
effeminat|e (v.), -es, -ing, -ed ɪ'femɪneɪt [e'f-], -s, -ɪŋ, -ɪd
Effendi e'fendɪ
efferent 'efərənt
effervesc|e, -es, -ing, -ed; -ence, -ent ˌefə'ves, -ɪz, -ɪŋ, -t; -ns, -nt
effete ɪ'fi:t [e'f-]
efficacious, -ly, -ness efɪ'keɪʃəs, -lɪ, -nɪs [-nəs]
efficacity ˌefɪ'kæsətɪ [-rɪt-]
efficacy 'efɪkəsɪ
efficien|cy, -t/ly ɪ'fɪʃən|sɪ, -t/lɪ
Effie 'efɪ
effig|y, -ies 'efɪdʒ|ɪ [-fədʒ|ɪ], -ɪz
Effingham 'efɪŋəm
effloresc|e, -es, -ing, -ed; -ence, -ent ˌeflɔ:'res [-flɒ'r-, -flə'r-], -ɪz, -ɪŋ, -t; -ns, -nt
effluen|ce, -t/s 'eflʊən|s [-flwən-], -t/s
effluvium ɪ'flu:vjəm [e'f-, -vɪəm]
efflux, -es 'eflʌks, -ɪz
effort, -s; -less 'efət, -s; -lɪs [-ləs]
effronter|y, -ies ɪ'frʌntər|ɪ [e'f-], -ɪz
effulg|e, -es, -ing, -ed ɪ'fʌldʒ [e'f-], -ɪz, -ɪŋ, -d
effulgen|ce, -t/ly ɪ'fʌldʒən|s [e'f-], -t/lɪ
effuse (adj.) ɪ'fju:s [e'f-]
effus|e (v.), -es, -ing, -ed ɪ'fju:z [e'f-], -ɪz, -ɪŋ, -d
effusion, -s ɪ'fju:ʒn [e'f-], -z
effusive, -ly, -ness ɪ'fju:sɪv [e'f-], -lɪ, -nɪs [-nəs]
Efik 'efɪk
eft, -s eft, -s
e.g. ˌi:'dʒi: [ˌfərɪg'zɑ:mpl]
egad i:'gæd
egalitarian, -ism ɪˌgælɪ'teərɪən, -ɪzəm
Egan 'i:gən

159

Egbert ˈegbəːt [-bət]

Egeria iːˈdʒɪərɪə [ɪˈdʒ-]

Egerton ˈedʒətən

Egeus (in Greek mythology) ˈiːdʒjuːs, (Shakespearian character) iːˈdʒiːəs [ɪˈdʒ-]

egg (s. v.), -s, -ing, -ed, -er/s eg, -z, -ɪŋ, -d, -ə*/z

egg-cup, -s ˈegkʌp, -s

Eggle|ton, -ston ˈegl|tən, -stən

egg-plant, -s ˈegplɑːnt, -s

egg-shaped ˈegʃeɪpt

eggshell, -s ˈegʃel, -z

egg-spoon, -s ˈegspuːn, -z

Egham ˈegəm

Eglamore ˈegləmɔː* [-mɔə*]

eglantine (E.) ˈegləntaɪn

Eglingham (in Northumberland) ˈeglɪndʒəm

Eglinton ˈeglɪntən

Eglon ˈeglɒn

Egmont ˈegmɒnt [-mənt]

ego, -s ˈegəʊ [ˈiːg-], -z

egocentric ˌegəʊˈsentrɪk [ˌiːg-]

egoi|sm, -st/s ˈegəʊɪ|zəm, -st/s

egoistic, -al, -ally ˌegəʊˈɪstɪk [ˌiːg-], -l, -əlɪ

Egon ˈegən [-gɒn]

egoti|sm, -st/s ˈegəʊtɪ|zəm [ˈiːg-], -st/s

egotistic, -al, -ally ˌegəʊˈtɪstɪk [ˌiːg-], -l, -əlɪ

egotiz|e [-is|e], -es, -ing, -ed ˈegəʊtaɪz [ˈiːg-], -ɪz, -ɪŋ, -d

egregious, -ly, -ness ɪˈgriːdʒəs [-dʒəs, -dʒɪəs], -lɪ, -nɪs [-nəs]

Egremont (in Merseyside, Cumbria) ˈegrəmənt [-grɪm-, -mɒnt]

egress, -es ˈiːgres, -ɪz

egression, -s iːˈgreʃn [ɪˈg-], -z

egressive iːˈgresɪv [ɪˈg-]

egret, -s ˈiːgret [ˈeg-, -ət, -ɪt], -s

Egton ˈegtən

Egypt ˈiːdʒɪpt

Egyptian, -s ɪˈdʒɪpʃn, -z

egyptolog|ist/s, -y ˌiːdʒɪpˈtɒlədʒ|ɪst/s, -ɪ

eh eɪ

eider, -s ˈaɪdə*, -z

eiderdown, -s ˈaɪdədaʊn, -z

eider-duck, -s ˈaɪdəˈdʌk [in contrast ˈ---], -s

eidograph, -s ˈaɪdəʊgrɑːf [-græf], -s

eidol|on, -ons, -a aɪˈdəʊl|ɒn, -ɒnz, -ə

Eifel ˈaɪfl

Eiffel Tower, -s ˌaɪflˈtaʊə*, -z

Eiger ˈaɪgə*

eight, -s eɪt, -s

eighteen, -s, -th/s ˌeɪˈtiːn [also ˈ--, according to sentence-stress], -z, -θ/s

eightfold ˈeɪtfəʊld

eighth, -s, -ly eɪtθ, -s, -lɪ

eightieth, -s ˈeɪtɪɪθ [-tjɪθ, -tɪəθ, -tjəθ], -s

eightish ˈeɪtɪʃ

eight|pence, -penny ˈeɪt|pəns, -pənɪ (see note under penny)

eight|y, -ies ˈeɪt|ɪ, -ɪz
　Note.—In the N. of England often ˈeɪttɪ.

Eilean (near Inverness) ˈiːlən

Eileen ˈaɪliːn

Eiloart ˈaɪləʊɑːt

Einstein ˈaɪnstaɪn

Eire ˈeərə

Eirene aɪˈriːnɪ [ˌaɪəˈr-]

eirenicon, -s aɪˈriːnɪkɒn [ˌaɪəˈr-, -ˈren-], -z

Eisenhower ˈaɪznˌhaʊə*

eisteddfod, -s [-au] aɪsˈteðvɒd [-vəd] (Welsh əisˈteðvod), -z [-aɪ] (-ai̯)

either ˈaɪðə* [ˈiːðə*]

ejaculat|e, -es, -ing, -ed ɪˈdʒækjʊleɪt, -s, -ɪŋ, -ɪd

ejaculation, -s ɪˌdʒækjʊˈleɪʃn, -z

ejaculative ɪˈdʒækjʊlətɪv [-leɪt-]

ejaculatory ɪˈdʒækjʊlətərɪ [-leɪtərɪ]

eject (s.), -s ˈiːdʒekt, -s

eject (v.), -s, -ing, -ed, -or/s; -ment/s ɪˈdʒekt [iːˈdʒ-], -s, -ɪŋ, -ɪd, -ə*/z; -mənt/s

ejection, -s ɪˈdʒekʃn [iːˈdʒ-], -z

ejective, -s ɪˈdʒektɪv [iːˈdʒ-], -z

ek|e (v. adv.), -es, -ing, -ed iːk, -s, -ɪŋ, -t

Ekron ˈekrɒn

elabor|ate (adj.), -ately, -ateness ɪˈlæbər|ət [-ɪt], -ətlɪ [-ɪtlɪ], -ətnɪs [-ɪt-, -nəs]

elaborat|e (v.), -es, -ing, -ed, -or/s ɪˈlæbəreɪt, -s, -ɪŋ, -ɪd, -ə*/z

elaboration, -s ɪˌlæbəˈreɪʃn, -z

elaborative ɪˈlæbərətɪv [-reɪt-]

Elah ˈiːlə

Elaine eˈleɪn [ɪˈl-]

Elam, -ite/s ˈiːləm, -aɪt/s

élan eɪˈlɑ̃ːŋ [-ˈlɔ̃ːŋ] (elɑ̃)

eland (E.), -s ˈiːlənd, -zˈ

elaps|e, -es, -ing, -ed ɪˈlæps, -ɪz, -ɪŋ, -t

elastic (s. adj.), -s, -ally ɪˈlæstɪk [-ˈlɑː-], -s, -əlɪ

elasticity ˌelæˈstɪsətɪ [ɪl-, ˌiːl-, -ləˈs-, -lɑːˈs-, -ɪtɪ]

Elastoplast ɪˈlæstəʊplɑːst [iːˈl-, eˈl-, -plæst]

elat|e (adj. v.), -es, -ing, -ed/ly ɪˈleɪt, -s, -ɪŋ, -ɪd/lɪ

elation ɪˈleɪʃn

Elba 'elbə
Elbe elb
elbow (s. v.), -s, -ing, -ed 'elbəʊ, -z, -ɪŋ, -d
elbow-grease 'elbəʊgri:s
elbow-room 'elbəʊrʊm [-ru:m]
Elcho 'elkəʊ
elder (s. adj.), -s 'eldə*, -z
elder-berr|y, -ies 'eldə,ber|ɪ ['eldəbər-], -ɪz
elderl|y, -iness 'eldəl|ɪ, -mɪs [-ɪnəs]
elder-wine ,eldə'waɪn ['---]
eldest 'eldɪst
Eldon 'eldən
El Dorado ,eldə'rɑ:dəʊ [-dɒ'r-]
Eldred 'eldrɪd [-red]
Eldridge 'eldrɪdʒ
Eleanor 'elmə* [-lən-]
Eleanora ,elɪə'nɔ:rə [-ljə-]
Eleazar ,elɪ'eɪzə*
elecampane, -s ,elɪkæm'peɪn, -z
elect (s. adj. v.), -s, -ing, -ed, -or/s; -ive/ly ɪ'lekt, -s, -ɪŋ, -ɪd, -ə*/z; -ɪv/lɪ
election, -s ɪ'lekʃn, -z
electioneer, -s, -ing, -ed, -er/s ɪ,lekʃə'nɪə* [-ʃn'ɪə*], -z, -rɪŋ, -d, -rə*/z
electoral ɪ'lektərəl
electorate, -s ɪ'lektərət [-ɪt], -s
Electra ɪ'lektrə
electric, -al, -ally ɪ'lektrɪk [ə'lek-], -l, -əlɪ
electrician, -s ,ɪlek'trɪʃn [,elek-, ,i:lek-, ,elɪk-], -z
electricity ,ɪlek'trɪsətɪ [,elek-, ,i:lek-, ,elɪk-, -'trɪzə-, -'trɪzɪ-, -'trɪsɪ-]
electrification, -s ɪ,lektrɪfɪ'keɪʃn, -z
electri|fy, -fies, -fying, -fied; -fiable ɪ'lektrɪ|faɪ, -faɪz, -faɪɪŋ, -faɪd; -faɪəbl
electro-biology ɪ,lektrəʊbaɪ'ɒlədʒɪ
electrocardio|gram/s, -graph/s ɪ,lektrəʊ'kɑ:dɪəʊ|græm/z [-djəʊ-], -grɑ:f/s [-græf/s]
electro-chemistry ɪ,lektrəʊ'kemɪstrɪ [-məstrɪ]
electrocut|e, -es, -ing, -ed ɪ'lektrəkju:t, -s, -ɪŋ, -ɪd
electrocution, -s ɪ,lektrə'kju:ʃn, -z
electrode, -s ɪ'lektrəʊd, -z
electro-dynamic, -s ɪ,lektrəʊdaɪ'næmɪk [dɪ'n-], -s
electro-kinetics ɪ,lektrəʊkaɪ'netɪks
electrolier, -s ɪ,lektrəʊ'lɪə*, -z
electrolys|e, -es, -ing, -ed ɪ'lektrəʊlaɪz, -ɪz, -ɪŋ, -d
electrolys|is, -es ,ɪlek'trɒlɪs|ɪs [,el-, ,i:l-, -ləs-], -i:z
electrolyte, -s ɪ'lektrəʊlaɪt, -s
electrolytic ɪ,lektrəʊ'lɪtɪk

electro-magnet, -s, -ism ɪ,lektrəʊ'mægnɪt [ɪ'lektrəʊ,m-], -s, -ɪzəm
electro-magnetic ɪ,lektrəʊmæg'netɪk [-məg-]
electrometer, -s ɪlek'trɒmɪtə* [,el-, ,i:l-, -mətə*], -z
electromotive ɪ,lektrəʊ'məʊtɪv
electro-motor, -s ɪ,lektrəʊ'məʊtə* [ɪ'lektrəʊ,m-], -z
electron, -s ɪ'lektrɒn, -z
electronic, -s ,ɪlek'trɒnɪk [,el-, ,i:l-], -s
electrophone, -s ɪ'lektrəfəʊn, -z
electrophorus, -es ,ɪlek'trɒfərəs [,el-, ,i:l-], -ɪz
electroplat|e (s. v.), -es, -ing, -ed, -er/s ɪ'lektrəʊpleɪt [ɪ,lektrəʊ'p-], -s, -ɪŋ, -ɪd, -ə*/z
electro-polar ɪ,lektrəʊ'pəʊlə*
electro-positive ɪ,lektrəʊ'pɒzətɪv [-zɪt-]
electroscope, -s ɪ'lektrəskəʊp, -s
electrostatic, -s ɪ,lektrəʊ'stætɪk, -s
electro-therapeutic, -s ɪ,lektrəʊθerə-'pju:tɪk, -s
electro-therapy ɪ,lektrəʊ'θerəpɪ
electro-thermal ɪ,lektrəʊ'θɜ:ml
electrotype, -s ɪ'lektrəʊtaɪp, -s
electrum ɪ'lektrəm
electuar|y, -ies ɪ'lektjʊər|ɪ [-tjwər-], -ɪz
eleemosynary ,elɪi:'mɒsɪnərɪ [,eli:'m-, ,elɪ'm-, -'mɒzɪ-]
elegan|ce, -t/ly 'elɪgən|s, -t/lɪ
elegiac (s. adj.), -s, -al ,elɪ'dʒaɪək, -s, -l
elegist, -s 'elɪdʒɪst [-lədʒ-], -s
elegit ɪ'li:dʒɪt [e'l-]
elegiz|e [-is|e], -es, -ing, -ed 'elɪdʒaɪz [-lədʒ-], -ɪz, -ɪŋ, -d
eleg|y, -ies 'elɪdʒ|ɪ [-lədʒ-], -ɪz
element, -s 'elɪmənt [-ləm-], -s
element|al (s. adj.), -als, -ally ,elɪ-'ment|l [-lə'm-], -lz, -əlɪ
elementar|y, -ily, -iness ,elɪ'mentər|ɪ [-lə'm-] -əlɪ [-ɪlɪ], -ɪnɪs [-ɪnəs]
elemi 'elɪmɪ
elenchus ɪ'leŋkəs
Eleonora ,elɪə'nɔ:rə [-ljə-]
elephant, -s 'elɪfənt [-ləf-], -s
elephantiasis ,elɪfən'taɪəsɪs [-ləf-, -fæn-]
elephantine ,elɪ'fæntaɪn [-lə'f-]
Eleusinian ,elju:'sɪnɪən [-ljʊ-, -njən]
Eleusis e'lju:sɪs [ɪ'l-]
elevat|e, -es, -ing, -ed, -or/s; -ory 'elɪveɪt, -s, -ɪŋ, -ɪd, -ə*/z; -ərɪ
elevation, -s ,elɪ'veɪʃn, -z
eleven, -s, -th/s ɪ'levn, -z, -θ/s
elevenish ɪ'levnɪʃ
eleven|pence, -penny ɪ'levn|pəns [-vm|p-], -pənɪ (see note under penny)

161

elevenses ɪ'levnzɪz
el|f, -ves el|f, -vz
elfin (s. adj.)ˑ -s 'elfɪn, -z
elfish 'elfɪʃ
elf|-land, -lock/s 'elf|lænd, -lɒk/s
Elfrida el'fri:də
Elgar 'elgə* [-gɑː*]
Elgie 'eldʒɪ, 'elgɪ
Elgin 'elgɪn
Elham (in Kent) 'i:ləm
Eli 'i:laɪ
Elia 'i:ljə [-lɪə]
Eliab ɪ'laɪæb [e'l-, -'laɪəb]
Eliakim ɪ'laɪəkɪm [e'l-]
Elias ɪ'laɪəs [e'l-, -aɪæs]
Eliashow e'laɪəʃoʊ
Elibank 'elɪbæŋk
elicit, -s, -ing, -ed ɪ'lɪsɪt [e'l-], -s, -ɪŋ, -ɪd
elicitation ɪ,lɪsɪ'teɪʃn [e,l-]
elid|e, -es, -ing, -ed; -able ɪ'laɪd, -z, -ɪŋ, -ɪd; -əbl
Elie 'i:lɪ
Eliezer ,elɪ'i:zə*
eligibility ,elɪdʒə'bɪlətɪ [-dʒɪ'b-, -lɪt-]
eligib|le, -ly, -leness 'elɪdʒəb|l [-dʒɪb-], -lɪ, -lnɪs [-nəs]
Elihu ɪ'laɪhju: [e'l-]
Elijah ɪ'laɪdʒə
Eliman 'elɪmən
Elimelech ɪ'lɪmələk [e'l-]
eliminat|e, -es, -ing, -ed ɪ'lɪmɪneɪt [e'l-, -mən-], -s, -ɪŋ, -ɪd
elimination, -s, ɪ,lɪmɪ'neɪʃn [e,l-, -mə'n-], -z
Elinor 'elmə*
Eliot(t) 'eljət [-lɪət]
Eliphaz 'elɪfæz
Elis 'i:lɪs
Elisabeth ɪ'lɪzəbəθ
Elisha (prophet) ɪ'laɪʃə, (place in Northumberland) e'lɪʃə
elision, -s ɪ'lɪʒn, -z
Elissa ɪ'lɪsə
élite eɪ'li:t (elit)
éliti|st, -sm eɪ'li:tɪ|st, -zəm
elixir, -s ɪ'lɪksə* [e'l-], -z
Eliza ɪ'laɪzə
Elizabeth ɪ'lɪzəbəθ
Elizabethan, -s ɪ,lɪzə'bi:θn, -z
Elizabethian, -s ɪ,lɪzə'bi:θjən [-θɪən], -z
elk, -s elk, -s
Elkanah el'kɑːnə [-'keɪn-]
Elkhart 'elkhɑːt
Elkin 'elkɪn
Elkington 'elkɪŋtən
Elkins 'elkɪnz
ell, -s el, -z

Ella 'elə
Ellaline 'eləli:n
Ellam 'eləm
Elland, -un 'elənd, -ən
Ellangowan ,elən'gaʊən
Ellen, -borough 'elɪn, -bərə
Ellery 'elərɪ
Ellesmere 'elz,mɪə*
Ellet 'elɪt
Ellice 'elɪs
Ellicott 'elɪkət [-kɒt]
Elliman 'elɪmən
Ellingham (in Northumberland) 'elɪndʒəm, (surname) 'elɪŋəm
Elliot(t), -son 'eljət [-lɪət], -sn
ellipse, -s ɪ'lɪps, -ɪz
ellips|is, -es ɪ'lɪps|ɪs, -i:z
ellipsoid, -s ɪ'lɪpsɔɪd, -z
ellipsoidal ,elɪp'sɔɪdl [ɪlɪp's-]
elliptic, -al, -ally ɪ'lɪptɪk, -l, -əlɪ
ellipticity ,elɪp'tɪsətɪ [,ɪlɪp't-, -ɪtɪ]
Ellis, -on, -ton 'elɪs, -n, -tən
Ellsworth 'elzwɜ:θ [-wəθ]
Ellwood 'elwʊd
elm (E.), -s elm, -z
Elmes elmz
Elmhurst 'elmhɜ:st
Elmina el'mi:nə
Elmo 'elməʊ
Elmore 'elmɔ:* [-mɔə*]
Elmsley 'elmzlɪ
Elmwood 'elmwʊd
elocution ,elə'kju:ʃn
elocutionary ,elə'kju:ʃnərɪ [-ʃənərɪ, -ʃnərɪ]
elocutionist, -s ,elə'kju:ʃnɪst [-ʃənɪst, -ʃnɪst], -s
Elohim e'ləʊhɪm
Eloi i:'ləʊaɪ ['i:ləʊaɪ, 'i:lɔɪ]
Eloisa ,eləʊ'i:zə [-'i:sə]
elongat|e, -es, -ing, -ed i:'lɒŋgeɪt, -s, -ɪŋ, -ɪd
elongation, -s ,i:lɒŋ'geɪʃn, -z
elop|e, -es, -ing, -ed, -ement/s ɪ'ləʊp, -s, -ɪŋ, -t, -mənt/s
eloquen|ce, -t/ly 'eləkwən|s, -t/lɪ
Elphin, -ston(e) 'elfɪn, -stən
Elsa (English name) 'elsə, (German name) 'elzə ('elza:)
else, -'s els, -ɪz
elsewhere ,els'weə* [-s'hw-]
Elsie 'elsɪ
Elsinore ,elsɪ'nɔ:* [-'nɔə*, '---]
Note.—The stressing ,--'- has to be used in Shakespeare's 'Hamlet'.
Elsmere 'elz,mɪə*
Elspeth 'elspəθ [-peθ]
Elstree 'elstri: ['elz-, -trɪ]

Elswick 'elsɪk, 'elzɪk, 'elzwɪk
Note.—**Elswick** *in Tyne and Wear is locally* 'elsɪk *or* 'elzɪk.

Elsworthy 'elzˌwɜːðɪ
Eltham (*in Kent*) 'eltəm
Elton 'eltən
elucidat|e, -es, -ing, -ed, -or/s
ɪ'luːsɪdeɪt [-'ljuː-], -s, -ɪŋ, -ɪd, -ə*/z
elucidation, -s ɪˌluːsɪ'deɪʃn [-ˌljuː-], -z
elucidative ɪ'luːsɪdeɪtɪv [-'ljuː-, -dət-]
elucidatory ɪ'luːsɪdeɪtərɪ [-'ljuː-]
elud|e, -es, -ing, -ed ɪ'luːd [-'ljuːd], -z,
-ɪŋ, -ɪd
elusion, -s ɪ'luːʒn [-'ljuː-], -z
elusive, -ly, -ness ɪ'luːsɪv [-'ljuː-], -lɪ,
-nɪs [-nəs]
elusory ɪ'luːsərɪ [-'ljuː-]
elvan 'elvən
Elvedon (*in Suffolk*) 'elvdən ['eldən]
elver, -s 'elvə*, -z
elves (*plur. of* elf) elvz
Elv|ey, -in 'elv|ɪ, -ɪn
Elvira el'vaɪərə, el'vɪərə
elvish 'elvɪʃ
Elwes 'elwɪz [-wez]
Ely 'iːlɪ
Elyot 'eljət [-lət]
Elysi|an, -um ɪ'lɪzɪ|ən [-zj|-], -əm
elzevir (E.) 'elzɪˌvɪə* [-zəˌv-]
em, -s em, -z
'em (*weak form of* them) əm [m]
emaciat|e, -es, -ing, -ed ɪ'meɪʃɪeɪt [e'm-,
-'meɪʃjeɪt, -'meɪsɪeɪt, -'meɪsjeɪt,
-'mæsɪeɪt], -s, -ɪŋ, -ɪd
emaciation ɪˌmeɪsɪ'eɪʃn [eˌm-, -ˌmeɪʃɪ-,
-ˌmæsɪ-]
emanat|e, -es, -ing, -ed; -ive 'eməneɪt
[*rarely* 'iːm-], -s, -ɪŋ, -ɪd; -ɪv
emanation, -s ˌemə'neɪʃn [*rarely*
ˌiːm-], -z
emancipat|e, -es, -ing, -ed, -or/s
ɪ'mænsɪpeɪt [e'm-], -s, -ɪŋ, -ɪd, -ə*/z
emancipation, -s ɪˌmænsɪ'peɪʃn [eˌm-],
-z
Emanuel ɪ'mænjʊəl [e'm-, -njwəl,
-njʊel]
emasculate (*adj.*) ɪ'mæskjʊlɪt [-lət]
emasculat|e (*v.*), -es, -ing, -ed, -or/s
ɪ'mæskjʊleɪt, -s, -ɪŋ, -ɪd, -ə*/z
emasculation, -s ɪˌmæskjʊ'leɪʃn, -z
Emaus 'emɑːs
embalm, -s, -ing, -ed, -er/s, -ment/s
ɪm'bɑːm [em-], -z, -ɪŋ, -d, -ə*/z,
-mənt/s
embank, -s, -ing, -ed, -ment/s ɪm-
'bæŋk [em-], -s, -ɪŋ, -t [-'bæŋt],
-mənt/s
embarcation, -s ˌembɑː'keɪʃn, -z

embargo (*s.*), -s em'bɑːgəʊ [ɪm-], -z
embargo (*v.*), -es, -ing, -ed em'bɑːgəʊ
[ɪm-], -z, -ɪŋ, -d
embark, -s, -ing, -ed ɪm'bɑːk [em-], -s,
-ɪŋ, -t
embarkation, -s ˌembɑː'keɪʃn, -z
embarrass, -es, -ing, -ed, -ment/s ɪm-
'bærəs [em-], -ɪz, -ɪŋ, -t, -mənt/s
embass|y, -ies 'embəs|ɪ, -ɪz
embatt|le, -les, -ling, -led ɪm'bæt|l
[em-], -lz, -lɪŋ [-lɪŋ], -ld
embay, -s, -ing, -ed ɪm'beɪ [em-], -z, -ɪŋ,
-d
embed, -s, -ding, -ded, -ment ɪm'bed
[em-], -z, -ɪŋ, -ɪd, -mənt
embellish, -es, -ing, -ed, -er/s, -ment/s
ɪm'belɪʃ, -ɪz, -ɪŋ, -t, -ə*/z, -mənt/s
ember, -s 'embə*, -z
Ember|-day/s, -week/s 'embəˌdeɪ/z,
-ˌwiːk/s
embezz|le, -les, -ling, -led, -ler/s,
-lement/s ɪm'bez|l [em-], -lz, -lɪŋ
[-lɪŋ], -ld, -lə*/z [-lə*/z], -lmənt/s
embitter, -s, -ing, -ed, -er/s, -ment
ɪm'bɪtə* [em-], -z, -rɪŋ, -d, -rə*/z,
-mənt
emblaz|on, -ons, -oning, -oned,
-onment/s; -onry ɪm'bleɪz|n [em-],
-nz, -nɪŋ [-nɪŋ], -nd, -nmənt/s; -nrɪ
emblem, -s 'embləm [-lem, -lɪm], -z
emblematic, -al, -ally ˌemblɪ'mætɪk
[-lə'm-], -l, -əlɪ
emblematiz|e [-is|e], -es, -ing, -ed
em'blemətaɪz ['emblem-], -ɪz, -ɪŋ, -d
emblement, -s 'emblmənt, -s
embod|y, -ies, -ying, -ied, -iment/s
ɪm'bɒd|ɪ [em-], -ɪz, -ɪɪŋ, -ɪd, -ɪmənt/s
embold|en, -ens, -ening, -ened ɪm-
'bəʊld|ən [em-], -ənz, -ənɪŋ [-nɪŋ],
-ənd
embolism, -s 'embəlɪzəm, -z
embonpoint,ɔ:mbɔ̃:m'pwæ̃:ŋ [ˌɒmbɒm-,
-'pwɑː:ŋ, -'pwɒŋ, -'pwæ̃ŋ] (ãbõpwɛ̃)
embosom, -s, -ing, -ed ɪm'bʊzəm
[em-], -z, -ɪŋ, -d
emboss, -es, -ing, -ed, -er/s, -ment/s
ɪm'bɒs [em-], -ɪz, -ɪŋ, -t, -ə*/z,
-mənt/s
embouchure, -s ˌɒmbʊ'ʃʊə* [ˌɑːm-,
-'ʃjʊə*, '--,-] (ãbuʃyːr), -z
emb|owel, -owels, -owelling, -owelled
ɪm'b|aʊəl [em-, -aʊl], -aʊəlz, -aʊəlɪŋ,
-aʊəld [-aʊld]
embower, -s, -ing, -ed ɪm'baʊə* [em-],
-z, -rɪŋ, -d
embrac|e (*s. v.*), -es, -ing, -ed, -er/s,
-ement ɪm'breɪs [em-], -ɪz, -ɪŋ, -t,
-ə*/z, -mənt

163

embranchment, -s ɪmˈbrɑ:ntʃmənt
[em-], -s
embrasure, -s ɪmˈbreɪʒə* [em-, -ˌʒʊə,
-ˌʒʊə*], -z
embrocat|e, -es, -ing, -ed ˈembrəʊkeɪt,
-s, -ɪŋ, -ɪd
embrocation, -s ˌembrəʊˈkeɪʃn, -z
embroglio, -s emˈbrəʊljəʊ [ɪm-, -lɪəʊ],
-z
embroid|er, -ers, -ering, -ered, -erer/s
ɪmˈbrɔɪd|ə* [em-], -əz, -ərɪŋ, -əd,
-ərə*/z
embroider|y, -ies ɪmˈbrɔɪdər|ɪ [em-],
-ɪz
embroil, -s, -ing, -ed, -ment/s ɪmˈbrɔɪl
[em-], -z, -ɪŋ, -d, -mənt/s
embryo, -s ˈembrɪəʊ, -z
embryolog|ist/s, -y ˌembrɪˈɒlədʒ|ɪst/s,
-ɪ
embry|on, -ons, -a ˈembrɪ|ɒn [-ən],
-ɒnz [-ənz], -ə
embryonic ˌembrɪˈɒnɪk
Embury ˈembərɪ
Emeer, -s eˈmɪə* [ɪˈm-, ˈeˌmɪə*], -z
Emeline ˈemɪli:n
emend, -s, -ing, -ed; -able iˈmend
[ɪˈm-], -z, -ɪŋ, -ɪd; -əbl
emendat|e, -es, -ing, -ed, -or/s ˈi:men-
deɪt, -s, -ɪŋ, -ɪd, -ə*/z
emendation, -s ˌi:menˈdeɪʃn, -z
emendatory iˈmendətərɪ [ɪˈm-]
emerald, -s ˈemərəld [ˈemrəld], -z
emerg|e, -es, -ing, -ed ɪˈmɜ:dʒ, -ɪz, -ɪŋ,
-d
emergen|ce, -t/ly iˈmɜ:dʒən|s [ɪˈm-],
-t/lɪ
emergenc|y, -ies ɪˈmɜ:dʒəns|ɪ, -ɪz
emeritus iˈmerɪtəs [ɪˈm-]
emerod, -s ˈemərɒd, -z
emersion, -s i:ˈmɜ:ʃn [ɪˈm-], -z
Emerson ˈeməsn
emery (E.), -paper/s, -powder, -wheel/s
ˈemərɪ, -ˌpeɪpə*/z, -ˌpaʊdə*, -wi:l/z
[-hw-]
emetic (s. adj.), -s, -al, -ally ɪˈmetɪk, -s,
-l, -əlɪ
émeute, -s eɪˈmɜ:t (emø:t), -s
emigrant (s. adj.), -s ˈemɪgrənt, -s
emigrate, -es, -ing, -ed, -or/s
ˈemɪgreɪt, -s, -ɪŋ, -ɪd, -ə*/z
emigration, -s ˌemɪˈgreɪʃn, -z
emigratory ˈemɪgrətərɪ [-greɪt-]
émigré, -s ˈemɪgreɪ, -z
Emilia ɪˈmɪlɪə [-ljə]
Emily ˈemɪlɪ [-məlɪ]
eminen|ce, -ces, -cy, -t/ly ˈemɪnən|s,
-sɪz, -sɪ, -t/lɪ
Emir, -s eˈmɪə* [ɪˈm-, ˈeˌmɪə*], -z

emirate, -s eˈmɪərət [ɪˈm-, ˈeˌmɪər-,
-rɪt, -reɪt], -s
emissar|y (s. adj.), -ies ˈemɪsər|ɪ, -ɪz
emission -s ɪˈmɪʃn [i:ˈm-], -z
emissive ɪˈmɪsɪv [i:ˈm-]
emit, -s, -ting, -ted, -ter/s ɪˈmɪt [i:ˈm-],
-s, -ɪŋ, -ɪd, -ə*/z
emitter-valve, -s ɪˈmɪtəvælv [i:ˈm-], -z
Emley ˈemlɪ
Emma ˈemə
Emmanuel (biblical name) ɪˈmænjʊəl
[eˈm, -jwəl, -jʊəl], (Cambridge college)
ɪˈmænjʊəl [-njʊl]
Emmaus eˈmeɪəs
Emmeline ˈemɪli:n
emmet (E.), -s ˈemɪt, -s
Emm|ie, -y ˈem|ɪ, -ɪ
emollient (s. adj.), -s ɪˈmɒlɪənt [eˈm-,
-ljənt], -s
emolument, -s ɪˈmɒljʊmənt [eˈm-], -s
Emory ˈemərɪ
emotion, -s; -less ɪˈməʊʃn, -z; -lɪs
[-ləs]
emo|tional, -tionally ɪˈməʊ|ʃnəl [-ʃnəl,
-ʃn̩l, -ʃnl, -ʃənəl], -ʃnəlɪ [-ʃnəlɪ, -ʃn̩lɪ,
-ʃnlɪ, -ʃənəlɪ]
emotionalism ɪˈməʊʃnəlɪzəm [-ʃnəl-,
-ʃn̩l-, -ʃnl-, -ʃənəl-]
emotive ɪˈməʊtɪv
empan|el, -els, -elling, -elled,
-elment/s ɪmˈpæn|l [em-], -lz, -lɪŋ,
-ld, -lmənt/s
empathy ˈempəθɪ
Empedocles emˈpedəʊkli:z
emperor, -s ˈempərə*, -z
emphasis ˈemfəsɪs
emphasiz|e [-is|e], -es, -ing, -ed ˈem-
fəsaɪz, -ɪz, -ɪŋ, -d
emphatic, -al, -ally, -alness ɪmˈfætɪk
[em-], -l, -əlɪ, -lnɪs [-nəs]
emphysema, -s ˌemfɪˈsi:mə, -z
empire, -s ˈempaɪə*, -z
empiric (s. adj.), -s, -al, -ally emˈpɪrɪk
[ɪm-], -s, -l, -əlɪ
empirici|sm, -st/s emˈpɪrɪsɪ|zəm [ɪm-],
-st/s
emplacement, -s ɪmˈpleɪsmənt [em-],
-s
employ (s. v.), -s, -ing, -ed, -er/s,
-ment/s; -able ɪmˈplɔɪ [em-], -z, -ɪŋ,
-d, -ə*/z, -mənt/s; -əbl
employé, -s ɒmˈplɔɪeɪ [ɔ̃:m-] (ăplwaje),
-z
employee, -s ˌemplɔɪˈi: [emˈplɔi:, ɪm-
ˈplɔɪi:], -z
emporium, -s emˈpɔ:rɪəm, -z
empower, -s, -ing, -ed ɪmˈpaʊə* [em-],
-z, -ɪŋ, -d

empress, -es 'emprıs [-rəs], -ız
Empson 'empsn
emption 'empʃn
empt|y (s. adj. v.), -ier, -iest, -ily,
-iness; -ies, -ying, -ied 'emptı|ı, -ıə*
[-jə*], -ııst [-jıst], -ılı [-əlı], -ınıs
[-ınəs]; -ız, -ııŋ [-jıŋ], -ıd
empty-handed ,emptı'hændıd
empyema ,empaı'i:mə
empyrea|l, -n ,empaı'ri:ə|l[-pı'r-, -'rıə|l,
em'pırıə-], -n
Emsworth 'emzwəθ [-wɜ:θ]
emu, -s 'i:mju:, -z
emulat|e, -es, -ing, -ed, -or/s 'emjʊleıt,
-s, -ıŋ, -ıd, -ə*/z
emulation ,emjʊ'leıʃn
emulative 'emjʊlətıv [-leıt-]
emulous, -ly 'emjʊləs, -lı
emulsi|fy, -fies, -fying, -fied ı'mʌlsı|faı,
-faız, -faııŋ, -faıd
emulsion, -s ı'mʌlʃn, -z
emunctor|y (s. adj.), -ies ı'mʌŋktər|ı,
-ız
enab|le, -les, -ling, -led ı'neıb|l [e'n-],
-lz, -lıŋ [-lıŋ], -ld
enact, -s, -ing, -ed, -or/s, -ment/s;
-ive ı'nækt [e'n-], -s, -ıŋ, -ıd, -ə*/z,
-mənt/s; -ıv
enam|el (s. v.), -els, -elling, -elled,
-eller/s, -ellist/s ı'næm|l, -lz, -lıŋ
[-əlıŋ], -ld, -lə*/z [-ələ*/z], -lıst/s
[-əlıst/s]
enamour, -s, -ing, -ed ı'næmə* [e'n-],
-z, -rıŋ, -d
Encaenia en'si:njə [-nıə]
encag|e, -es, -ing, -ed ın'keıdʒ [ıŋ-,
en-], -ız, -ıŋ, -d
encamp, -s, -ing, -ed, -ment/s ın'kæmp
[ıŋ-, en-], -s, -ıŋ, -t [-'kæmt], -mənt/s
encas|e, -es, -ing, -ed, -ement/s ın'keıs
[ıŋ-, en-], -ız, -ıŋ, -t, -mənt/s
encaustic (s. adj.), -s, -ally en'kɔ:stık,
-s, -əlı
enceinte (s. adj.), -s ɑ̃:ŋ'sæ̃:nt
[ɑ̃:n'sæ̃:nt, ɔ̃:ŋ'sæ̃:nt, ɔ̃:n'sæ̃:nt,
ɑ:n'sænt, ɒn'sænt] (ɑ̃sɛ̃:t), -s
Enceladus en'selədəs
encephalic ,enkə'fælık [,enkı'f-, eŋk-,
,ense'f-, ,ensı'f-]
encephalitis ,enkefə'laıtıs [,enkıf-,
en,kef-, eŋ,k-, ,ensef-, en,sef-]
encephalogram, -s en'sefələʊgræm
[ın's-, en'k-, eŋ'k-, ın'k-, ıŋ'k-], -z
encephalograph, -s en'sefələʊgra:f
[ın's-, en'k-, eŋ'k-, ın'k-, ıŋ'k-,
-græf], -s
enchain, -s, -ing, -ed, -ment ın'tʃeın
[en-], -z, -ıŋ, -d, -mənt

enchant, -s, -ing, -ed, -er/s, -ress/es,
-ment/s ın'tʃɑ:nt [en-], -s, -ıŋ, -ıd,
-ə*/z, -rıs/ız, -mənt/s
enchiridion, -s ,enkaıə'rıdıən [,eŋk-,
-dıɒn], -z
encirc|le, -les, -ling, -led, -lement/s
ın'sɜ:k|l [en-], -lz, -lıŋ, -ld, -lmənt/s
Encke 'eŋkə
enclasp, -s, -ing, -ed ın'klɑ:sp [ıŋ-,
en-], -s, -ıŋ, -t
enclave, -s 'enkleıv ['eŋ-, -'-], -z
enclitic (s. adj.), -s, -ally ın'klıtık [ıŋ-,
en-], -s, -əlı
enclos|e, -es, -ing, -ed, -er/s ın'kləʊz
[ıŋ-, en-], -ız, -ıŋ, -d, -ə*/z
enclosure, -s ın'kləʊʒə* [ıŋ-, en-], -z
encod|e, -es, -ing, -ed en'kəʊd [,en-,
eŋ-], -z, -ıŋ, -ıd
encom|iast/s, -ium/s en'kəʊm|ıæst/s
[eŋ-], -jəm/z [-ıəm/z]
encompass, -es, -ing, -ed ın'kʌmpəs
[ıŋ-, en-], -ız, -ıŋ, -t
encore (s. v.), -es, -ing, -ed ɒŋ'kɔ:*
[-'kɔə*, '--], -z, -rıŋ, -d
encore (interj.) ɒŋ'kɔ:* [-'kɔə*]
encount|er (s. v.), -ers, -ering, -ered ın-
'kaʊnt|ə* [ıŋ-, en-], -əz, -ərıŋ, -əd
encourag|e, -es, -ing/ly, -ed, -er/s,
-ement/s ın'kʌrıdʒ [ıŋ-, en-], -ız,
-ıŋ/lı, -d, -ə*/z, -mənt/s
encroach, -es, -ing/ly, -ed, -er/s,
-ment/s ın'krəʊtʃ [ıŋ-, en-], -ız,
-ıŋ/lı, -t, -ə*/z, -mənt/s
encrust, -s, -ing, -ed ın'krʌst [ıŋ-, en-],
-s, -ıŋ, -ıd
encumb|er, -ers, -ering, -ered ın'kʌm-
b|ə* [ıŋ-, en-], -əz, -ərıŋ, -əd
encumbrance, -s ın'kʌmbrəns [ıŋ-, en-],
-ız
encyclic, -s, -al/s en'sıklık [ın-], -s,
-l/z
encyclop(a)edia, -s, -n en,saıkləʊ'pi:djə
[ın,saık-, ,ensaık-, -klʊ'p-, -dıə], -z,
-n
encyclop(a)edic, -al en,saıkləʊ'pi:dık
[ın,saık-, ,ensaık-, -klʊ'p-], -l
encyclop(a)edi|sm, -st/s en,saıkləʊ'pi:-
dı|zəm [ın,saık-, ,ensaık-, -klʊ'p-],
-st/s
end (s. v.), -s, -ing, -ed end, -z, -ıŋ, -ıd
endang|er, -ers, -ering, -ered, -erer/s,
-erment ın'deındʒ|ə* [en-], -əz, -ərıŋ,
-əd, -ərə*/z, -əmənt
endear, -s, -ing, -ed, -ment ın'dıə*
[en-], -z, -rıŋ, -d, -mənt
endeav|our (s. v.), -ours, -ouring, -oured
ın'dev|ə*, -əz, -ərıŋ, -əd
Endell 'endl

165

endemic (s. adj.), -s, -al, -ally, en-
'demɪk, -s, -l, -əlɪ
Enderby 'endəbɪ
endermic, -al, -ally en'dɜ:mɪk, -l, -əlɪ
Endicott 'endɪkət [-kɒt]
ending (s.), -s 'endɪŋ, -z
endive, -s 'endɪv, -z
endless, -ly, -ness 'endlɪs [-ləs], -lɪ, -nɪs
[-nəs]
endlong 'endlɒŋ
endmost 'endməʊst
endocrine 'endəʊkraɪn
endogamy n'dɒgəmɪ
Endor 'endɔ:*
endors|e, -es, -ing, -ed, -er/s, -ement/s
ɪn'dɔ:s [en-], -ɪz, -ɪŋ, -t, -ə*/z,
-mənt/s
endorsee, -s ˌendɔ:'si:, -z
endow, -s, -ing, -ed, -ment/s ɪn'daʊ
[en-], -z, -ɪŋ, -d, -mənt/s
endower, -s ɪn'daʊə* [en-], -z
end-product, -s 'endˌprɒdʌkt [-dəkt,
ˌ'-'-], -s
endu|e, -es, -ing, -ed ɪn'dju: [en-], -z,
-ɪŋ [-'djʊɪŋ], -d
endurab|le, -ly, -leness ɪn'djʊərəb|l
[en-, -'djɔər-, -'djɔ:r-], -lɪ, -lnɪs [-nəs]
endur|e, -es, -ing, -ed, -er/s; -ance
ɪn'djʊə* [en-, -'djɔə*, -'djɔ:*], -z,
-ɪŋ, -d, -rə*/z; -rəns
end|ways, -wise 'end|weɪz, -waɪz
Endymion en'dɪmɪən [-mjən]
Eneas i:'ni:æs [ɪ'n-, 'i:nɪæs]
Eneid 'i:nɪɪd [-njɪd]
enema, -s 'enɪmə ['enə-, ɪ'ni:mə], -z
enem|y, -ies 'enəm|ɪ [-nɪm-], -ɪz
energetic, -al, -ally ˌenə'dʒetɪk, -l,
-əlɪ
energiz|e [-is|e], -es, -ing, -ed, -er/s
'enədʒaɪz, -ɪz, -ɪŋ, -d, -ə*/z
energumen, -s ˌenɜ:'gju:men, -z
energ|y, -ies 'enədʒ|ɪ, -ɪz
enervat|e, -es, -ing, -ed 'enɜ:veɪt
[-nəv-], -s, -ɪŋ, -ɪd
enervation ˌenɜ:'veɪʃn [-nə'v-]
enfeeb|le, -les, -ling, -led, -lement ɪn-
'fi:b|l [en-], -lz, -lɪŋ [-lɪŋ], -ld, -lmənt
enfeoff, -s, -ing, -ed, -ment/s ɪn'fef
[en-, -'fi:f], -s, -ɪŋ, -t, -mənt/s
Enfield 'enfi:ld
enfilad|e (s. v.), -es, -ing, -ed ˌenfɪ'leɪd,
-z, -ɪŋ, -ɪd
enfold, -s, -ing, -ed, -ment ɪn'fəʊld
[en-], -z, -ɪŋ, -ɪd, -mənt
enforc|e, -es, -ing, -ed, -edly, -ement
ɪn'fɔ:s [en-], -ɪz, -ɪŋ, -t, -ɪdlɪ, -mənt
enfranchis|e, -es, -ing, -ed ɪn'fræntʃaɪz
[en-], -ɪz, -ɪŋ, -d

enfranchisement, -s ɪn'fræntʃɪzmənt
[en-], -s
Engadine 'eŋgədi:n
engag|e, -es, -ing/ly, -ed, -er/s,
-ement/s ɪn'geɪdʒ [ɪŋ-, en-], -ɪz,
-ɪŋ/lɪ, -d, -ə*/z, -mənt/s
Engedi en'gi:dɪ [eŋ'g-, -'geð-]
engend|er, -ers, -ering, -ered ɪn'dʒen-
d|ə* [en-], -əz, -ərɪŋ, -əd
engin|e (s. v.), -es, -ing, -ed; -ery
'endʒɪn, -z, -ɪŋ, -d; -ərɪ
engine-driver, -s 'endʒɪnˌdraɪvə*, -z
engineer (s. v.), -s, -ing, -ed ˌen-
dʒɪ'nɪə* [-dʒə-], -z, -rɪŋ, -d
engird, -s, -ing, -ed ɪn'gɜ:d [ɪŋ-, en-],
-z, -ɪŋ, -ɪd
Eng|land, -er/s 'ɪŋglənd [-ŋl-, rarely
'eŋ-], -ə*/z
Engledow 'eŋgldaʊ
Engle|field, -wood 'eŋgl|fi:ld, -wʊd
English 'ɪŋglɪʃ [-ŋl-, rarely 'eŋ-]
english, -es, -ing, -ed 'ɪŋglɪʃ [-ŋl-,
rarely 'eŋ-], -ɪz, -ɪŋ, -t
English|man, -men 'ɪŋglɪʃ|mən [-ŋl-,
rarely 'eŋ-], -mən [-men]
Englishry 'ɪŋglɪʃrɪ [-ŋl-, rarely 'eŋ-]
English|woman, -women 'ɪŋglɪʃ|-
ˌwʊmən [-ŋl-, rarely 'eŋ-], -ˌwɪmɪn
engraft, -s, -ing, -ed, -ment ɪn'grɑ:ft
[ɪŋ-, en-], -s, -ɪŋ, -ɪd, -mənt
engrailed ɪn'greɪld [ɪŋ-, en-]
engrain, -s, -ing, -ed ɪn'greɪn [ɪŋ-, en-],
-z, -ɪŋ, -d
engrav|e, -es, -ing/s, -ed, -er/s; -ery
ɪn'greɪv [ɪŋ-, en-], -z, -ɪŋ/z, -d, -ə*/z;
-ərɪ
engross, -es, -ing, -ed, -er/s, -ment/s
ɪn'grəʊs [ɪŋ-, en-], -ɪz, -ɪŋ, -t, -ə*/z,
-mənt/s
engulf, -s, -ing, -ed, -ment ɪn'gʌlf [ɪŋ-,
en-], -s, -ɪŋ, -t, -mənt
enhan|ce, -es, -ing, -ed, -ement/s ɪn-
'hɑ:ns [en-, -'hæns], -ɪz, -ɪŋ, -t,
-mənt/s
enharmonic, -al, -ally ˌenhɑ:'mɒnɪk,
-l, -əlɪ
Enid 'i:nɪd
enigma, -s ɪ'nɪgmə ['e'n-], -z
enigmatic, -al, -ally ˌenɪg'mætɪk, -l,
-əlɪ
enigmatist, -s ɪ'nɪgmətɪst ['e'n-], -s
enigmatiz|e [-is|e], -es, -ing, -ed
ɪ'nɪgmətaɪz ['e'n-], -ɪz, -ɪŋ, -d
Enim 'i:nɪm
enjambment, -s ɪn'dʒæmmənt [en-],
-s
enjoin, -s, -ing, -ed, -er/s ɪn'dʒɔɪn
[en-], -z, -ɪŋ, -d, -ə*/z

enjoy, -s, -ing, -ed, -er/s, -ment/s
ɪn'dʒɔɪ [en-], -z, -ɪŋ, -d, -ə*/z,
-mənt/s

enjoyab|le, -ly, -leness ɪn'dʒɔɪəb|l [en-],
-lɪ, -lnɪs [-nəs]

enkind|le, -les, -ling, -led ɪn'kɪnd|l
[en-], -lz, -lɪŋ, -ld

enlac|e, -es, -ing, -ed, -ement/s ɪn'leɪs
[en-], -ɪz, -ɪŋ, -t, -mənt/s

enlarg|e, -es, -ing, -ed, -er/s, -ement/s
ɪn'lɑːdʒ [en-], -ɪz, -ɪŋ, -d, -ə*/z,
-mənt/s

enlight|en, -ens, -ening, -ened,
-enment ɪn'laɪt|n [en-], -nz, -ɪ̃ɪŋ
[-nɪŋ], -nd, -nmənt

enlist, -s, -ing, -ed, -ment/s ɪn'lɪst [en-],
-s, -ɪŋ, -ɪd, -mənt/s

enliv|en, -ens, -ening, -ened, -ener/s
ɪn'laɪv|n [en-], -nz, -ɪ̃ɪŋ [-nɪŋ], -nd,
-nə*/z [-nə*/z]

en masse ɑ̃:ŋ'mæs [ɔ̃:ŋ-, ɑ:ŋ-, ɒŋ-]
(ãmas)

enmesh, -es, -ing, -ed ɪn'meʃ [en-], -ɪz,
-ɪŋ, -t

enmit|y, -ies 'enmət|ɪ [-mɪt|-], -ɪz

Ennis 'enɪs

Enniscorthy ,enɪs'kɔ:θɪ

Enniskillen ,enɪs'kɪlən [-lɪn]

Ennius 'enɪəs [-njəs]

ennob|le, -les, -ling, -led, -lement
ɪ'nəʊb|l [e'n-], -lz, -lɪŋ, -ld, -lmənt

ennui ɑ̃:'nwi: [ɔ̃:'n-, ɑ:'n-, ɒ'n-, '--]
(ãnɥi)

Eno, -'s 'i:nəʊ, -z

Enoch 'i:nɒk

enormit|y, -ies ɪ'nɔ:mət|ɪ [-ɪt|ɪ], -ɪz

enormous, -ly, -ness ɪ'nɔ:məs, -lɪ, -nɪs
[-nəs]

Enos 'i:nɒs

enough ɪ'nʌf [ə'nʌf, n̩'ʌf]

enounc|e, -es, -ing, -ed i:'naʊns [ɪ'n-],
-ɪz, -ɪŋ, -t

enow ɪ'naʊ

en passant ɑ̃:m'pæsɑ̃:ŋ [ɔ̃:m'pæsɔ̃:ŋ,
ɑ:m'pæsɑ:ŋ, ɒm'pæsɒŋ, -'pɑ:s-, ,—'-']
(ãpasã)

enquir|e, -es, -ing, -ed, -er/s ɪn'kwaɪə*
[ɪŋ-, en-], -z, -rɪŋ, -d, -rə*/z

enquir|y, -ies ɪn'kwaɪər|ɪ [ɪŋ-, en-], -ɪz

enrag|e, -es, -ing, -ed ɪn'reɪdʒ [en-], -ɪz,
-ɪŋ, -d

enrapt ɪn'ræpt [en-]

enrapt|ure, -ures, -uring, -ured ɪn'ræp-
tʃ|ə* [en-], -əz, -ərɪŋ, -əd

enregist|er, -ers, -ering, -ered ɪn-
'redʒɪst|ə* [en-], -əz, -ərɪŋ, -əd

enrich, -es, -ing, -ed, -ment ɪn'rɪtʃ
[en-], -ɪz, -ɪŋ, -t, -mənt

enrob|e, -es, -ing, -ed ɪn'rəʊb [en-], -z,
-ɪŋ, -d

enrol, -s, -ling, -led, -ment/s ɪn'rəʊl
[en-], -z, -ɪŋ, -d, -mənt/s

en route ɑ̃:n'ru:t [ɔ̃:n'r-, ɑ:n'r-, ɒn'r-]
(ãrut)

en|s, -tia en|z, -ʃɪə [-ʃjə, -tɪə, -tjə]

ensample, -s en'sɑ:mpl, -z

ensanguined ɪn'sæŋgwɪnd [en-]

ensconc|e, -es, -ing, -ed ɪn'skɒns [en-],
-ɪz, -ɪŋ, -t

ensemble, -s ɑ̃:n'sɑ̃:mbl [ɔ̃:n'sɔ̃:mbl,
ɑ:n'sɑ:mbl, ɒn'sɒmbl] (ãsã:bl), -z

enshrin|e, -es, -ing, -ed, -ement ɪn-
'ʃraɪn [en-], -z, -ɪŋ, -d, -mənt

enshroud, -s, -ing, -ed ɪn'ʃraʊd [en-],
-z, -ɪŋ, -ɪd

ensign (flag), -s 'ensaɪn [in the navy
'ensn], -z

ensign (officer), -s; -cy, -cies, -ship/s
'ensaɪn, -z; -sɪ, -sɪz, -ʃɪp/s

ensign (v.), -s, -ing, -ed en'saɪn [ɪn-], -z,
-ɪŋ, -d

ensilage 'ensɪlɪdʒ

enslav|e, -es, -ing, -ed, -er/s, -ement
ɪn'sleɪv [en-], -z, -ɪŋ, -d, -ə*/z, -ement

ensnar|e, -es, -ing, -ed, -er/s ɪn'sneə*
[en-], -z, -rɪŋ, -d, -rə*/z

ensoul, -s, -ing, -ed ɪn'səʊl [en-], -z, -ɪŋ,
-d

ensu|e, -es, -ing, -ed ɪn'sju: [en-, -'su:],
-z, -ɪŋ [-'sjʊɪŋ, -'sʊɪŋ], -d

ensur|e, -es, -ing, -ed ɪn'ʃʊə* [en-,
-'ʃɔə*, -'ʃɔ:*], -z, -rɪŋ, -d

entablature, -s en'tæblətʃə* [ɪn-, -blɪtʃ-,
-,tʃʊə*, -,tjʊə*], -z

entail (s. v.), -s, -ing, -ed, -er/s, -ment
ɪn'teɪl [en-], -z, -ɪŋ, -d, -ə*/z, -mənt

entang|le, -les, -ling, -led, -lement/s
ɪn'tæŋg|l [en-], -lz, -lɪŋ, -ld, -lmənt/s

entente, -s ɑ̃:n'tɑ̃:nt [ɔ̃:n'tɔ̃:nt,
ɑ:n'tɑ:nt, ɒn'tɒnt] (ãtã:t), -s

ent|er, -ers, -ering, -ered, -erer/s
'ent|ə*, -əz, -ərɪŋ, -əd, -ərə*/z

enteric en'terɪk

enteritis ,entə'raɪtɪs

enterology ,entə'rɒlədʒɪ

enterotomy ,entə'rɒtəmɪ

enterpris|e, -es, -ing/ly 'entəpraɪz, -ɪz,
-ɪŋ/lɪ

entertain, -s, -ing/ly, -ed, -er/s,
-ment/s ,entə'teɪn, ·-ɪŋ, -ɪŋ/lɪ, -d,
-ə*/z, -mənt/s

enthral, -s, -ling, -led, -ment ɪn'θrɔ:l
[en-], -z, -ɪn, -d, -mənt

enthrall = enthral

enthron|e, -es, -ing, -ed, -ement/s
ɪn'θrəʊn [en-], -z, -ɪŋ, -d, -mənt/s

167

enthus|e, -es, -ing, -ed ɪn'θjuːz [en-], -ɪz, -ɪŋ, -d

enthusia|sm, -st/s ɪn'θjuːzɪæ|zəm [en-, -'θuː:-, -zjæ-], -st/s

enthusiastic, -al, -ally ɪn,θjuːzɪ'æstɪk [en-, -,θuː:-, -ɪ'ɑ:s-], -l, -əlɪ

entia (plur. of ens) 'enʃɪə [-ʃjə, -tɪə, -tjə]

entic|e, -es, -ing/ly, -ed, -er/s, -ement/s ɪn'taɪs [en-], -ɪz, -ɪŋ/lɪ, -t, -ə*/z, -mənt/s

entire, -ly, -ness ɪn'taɪə* [en-], -lɪ, -nɪs [-nəs]

entiret|y, -ies ɪn'taɪət|ɪ [en-, ɪn'taɪərə-t|ɪ], -ɪz

entit|le, -les, -ling, -led ɪn'taɪt|l [en-], -lz, -lɪŋ [-lɪŋ], -ld

entit|y, -ies 'entət|ɪ [-ɪt|ɪ], -ɪz

entomb, -s, -ing, -ed, -ment/s ɪn'tuːm [en-], -z, -ɪŋ, -d, -mənt/s

entomologic|al, -ally ,entəmə'lɒdʒɪk|l [-təʊməʊ'l], -əlɪ

entomolog|ist/s, -y ,entəʊ'mɒlədʒ|ɪst/s, -ɪ

entomologiz|e [-is|e], -es, -ing, -ed ,entəʊ'mɒlədʒaɪz, -ɪz, -ɪŋ, -d

entourage, -s ,ɒntʊ'rɑːʒ [,ɔ̃:nt-, ,ɑ̃:nt-, ,ɑ:nt-, 'ɒn,tʊə'r-] (ãtuːraːʒ), -ɪz

entr'acte, -s 'ɒntrækt [ɒn'trækt, ɔ̃:n't-, ɑ̃:nt-, ɑ:n't-] (ãtrakt), -s

entrails 'entreɪlz

entrain, -s, -ing, -ed ɪn'treɪn [en-], -z, -ɪŋ, -d

entramm|el, -els, -elling, -elled ɪn-'træm|l [en-], -lz, -lɪŋ [-əlɪŋ], -ld

entrance (s.) (entry, place of entry, etc.), -s 'entrəns, -ɪz

entranc|e (v.) (put in state of trance, delight), -es, -ing/ly, -ed, -ement/s ɪn'trɑːns [en-], -ɪz, -ɪŋ/lɪ, -t, -mənt/s

entrant (s. adj.), -s 'entrənt, -s

entrap, -s, -ping, -ped, -per/s, -ment ɪn'træp [en-], -s, -ɪŋ, -t, -ə*/z, -mənt

entreat, -s, -ing/ly, -ed, -ment ɪn'triːt [en-], -s, -ɪŋ/lɪ, -ɪd, -mənt

entreaty, -ies ɪn'triːt|ɪ [en-], -ɪz

entrecôte, -s 'ɒntrəkəʊt ['ɔ̃:nt-, 'ɑ̃:nt-, 'ɑ:nt-] (ãtrəkoːt), -s

entrée, -s 'ɒntreɪ ['ɔ̃:nt-, 'ɑ̃:nt-, 'ɑ:nt-] (ãtre), -z

entremets (sing.) 'ɒntrəmeɪ ['ɔ̃:nt-, 'ɑ̃:nt-, 'ɑ:nt-] (ãtrəme), (plur.) -z

entrench, -es, -ing, -ed, -ment/s ɪn-'trentʃ [en-], -ɪz, -ɪŋ, -t, -mənt/s

entrenching-tool, -s ɪn'trentʃɪŋtuːl [en-] -z

entrepôt, -s 'ɒntrəpəʊ ['ɔ̃:nt-, 'ɑ̃:nt-, 'ɑ:nt-] (ãtrəpo), -z

entrepreneu|r, -rs, -rial ,ɒntrəprə'nə:* [,ɔ̃:n-, ,ɑ̃:n-, ,ɑ:n-, -pre'n-] (ãtrə-prənœ:r), -z, -rɪəl

entresol, -s 'ɒntrəsɒl ['ɔ̃:n-, 'ɑ̃:n-, 'ɑ:n-] (ãtrəsɔl), -z

entropy 'entrəpɪ

entrust, -s, -ing, -ed ɪn'trʌst [en-], -s, -ɪŋ, -ɪd

entr|y, -ies 'entr|ɪ, -ɪz

entwin|e, -es, -ing, -ed ɪn'twaɪn [en-], -z, -ɪŋ, -d

entwist, -s, -ing, -ed ɪn'twɪst [en-], -s, -ɪŋ, -ɪd

enumerable ɪ'njuːmərəbl [iː'n-]

enumerat|e, -es, -ing, -ed, -or/s ɪ'njuː-məreɪt, -s, -ɪŋ, -ɪd, -ə*/z

enumeration, -s ɪ,njuːmə'reɪʃn, -z

enumerative ɪ'njuːmərətɪv [-reɪt-]

enunciable ɪ'nʌnʃɪəbl [-nʃjə-, -nsɪə-, -nsjə-]

enunciat|e, -es, -ing, -ed, -or/s ɪ'nʌn-sɪeɪt [-nsjeɪt, -nʃɪeɪt, -nʃjeɪt], -s, -ɪŋ, -ɪd, -ə*/z

enunciation, -s ɪ,nʌnsɪ'eɪʃn, -z

enunciative ɪ'nʌnʃɪətɪv [-nʃjət- -nsɪət-, -nsjət-, -nʃɪeɪt-, -ʃjeɪt-, -nsɪeɪt-, -nsjeɪt-]

enur|e, -es, -ing, -ed ɪ'njʊə* [en-], -z, -ɪŋ, -d

enuresis ,enjʊə'riːsɪs

envelop, -s, -ing, -ed, -ment/s ɪn-'veləp [en-], -s, -ɪŋ, -t, -mənt/s

envelope, -s 'envələʊp ['ɒn-, -vɪl-], -s

envenom, -s, -ing, -ed ɪn'venəm [en-], -z, -ɪŋ, -d

enviab|le, -ly, -leness 'envɪəb|l [-vjə-], -lɪ, -lnɪs [-nəs]

envious, -ly, -ness 'envɪəs [-vjəs], -lɪ, -nɪs [-nəs]

envir|on (v.), -ons, -oning, -oned, -onment/s ɪn'vaɪər|ən [en-], -ənz, -ənɪŋ [-ŋɪŋ], -ənd, -ənmənt/s

environmental ɪn,vaɪərən'mentl [en-]

environs (s.) ɪn'vaɪərənz ['envɪrənz, en'vaɪər-]

envisag|e, -es, -ing, -ed ɪn'vɪzɪdʒ [en-], -ɪz, -ɪŋ, -d

envoy, -s 'envɔɪ, -z

env|y (s. v.), -ies, -ying, -ied, -ier/s 'env|ɪ, -ɪz, -ɪŋ [-jɪŋ], -ɪd, -ɪə*/z [-jə*/z]

enwrap, -s, -ping, -ped ɪn'ræp [en-], -s, -ɪŋ, -t

enwreath|e, -es, -ing, -ed ɪn'riːð [en-], -z, -ɪŋ, -d

enzyme, -s 'enzaɪm, -z

eocene 'iːəʊsiːn ['ɪəʊ-]

Eochaidh 'jɒkeɪ ['jɒxeɪ]

Eoli- = Aeoli-

168

eolith, -s 'i:əʊlɪθ, -s
Eothen (title of book by Kinglake)
i:'əʊθen [ɪ'əʊ-, 'i:əʊθen, 'ɪəʊ-, -θn]
epact, -s 'i:pækt, -s
Epaminondas e,pæmɪ'nɒndæs [ɪ,p-]
eparch, -s; -y, -ies 'epɑ:k, -s; -ɪ, -ɪz
epaulement, -s e'pɔ:lmənt [ɪ'p-], -s
epaulet, -s 'epɒʊlet [-pɔ:l-, ,epə'let], -s
epenthes|is, -es e'penθɪs|ɪs [-θəs|-], -i:z
epenthetic ,epen'θetɪk
epergne, -s ɪ'pɜ:n [e'peən], -z
epexegesis e,peksɪ'dʒi:sɪs
epexegetic, -al, -ally e,peksɪ'dʒetɪk, -l,
-əlɪ
ephah, -s 'i:fə, -z
ephemer|a, -as, -al ɪ'femər|ə [e'f-,
-'fi:m-], -əz, -əl
ephemeralit|y, -ies ɪ,femə'rælət|ɪ
[e,f-, -,fi:m-, -ɪt|ɪ], -ɪz
ephemeris, ephemerides ɪ'femərɪs [e'f-,
-'fi:m-], ,efɪ'merɪdi:z
ephemeron, -s ɪ'femərɒn [e'f-, -'fi:m-,
-rən], -z
ephemerous ɪ'femərəs [e'f-, -'fi:m-]
Ephesian, -s ɪ'fi:ʒjən [-i:ʒɪən, -i:ʒn,
-i:zjən, -i:zɪən], -z
Ephesus 'efɪsəs [-fə-]
ephod, -s 'i:fɒd ['ef-], -z
Ephraim 'i:frenm [-,frɪəm]
Ephrata 'efrətə
Ephron 'efrɒn ['i:f-]
epiblast, -s 'epɪblæst, -s
epic (s. adj.), -s 'epɪk, -s
epicene (s. adj.), -s 'episi:n, -z
epicentre, -s 'episentə*, -z
Epicharmus ,epɪ'kɑ:məs
epici|sm, -st/s 'episɪ|zəm, -st/s
Epictetus ,epɪk'ti:təs
epicure, -s 'epɪ,kjʊə* [-kjɔə*, -kjɔ:*], -z
Epicurean, -s ,epɪkjʊə'ri:ən [-kjɔə'r-,
-kjɔ:'r-, -'rɪən], -z
epicurism 'epɪkjʊərɪzəm [-kjɔər-,
-kjɔ:r-]
Epicurus ,epɪ'kjʊərəs [-'kjɔər-, -'kjɔ:r-]
epicycle, -s 'episaɪkl, -z
epicyclic ,epɪ'saɪklɪk [-'sɪk-]
epicycloid, -s ,epɪ'saɪklɔɪd, -z
Epidaurus ,epɪ'dɔ:rəs
epidemic (s. adj.), -s, -al, -ally ,epɪ-
'demɪk, -s, -l, -əlɪ
epiderm|al, -ic, -is, -oid ,epɪ'dɜ:m|l, -ɪk,
-ɪs, -ɔɪd
epidiascope, -s ,epɪ'daɪəskəʊp, -s
epigene 'epɪdʒi:n
epigenesis ,epɪ'dʒenəsɪs [-ɪsɪs]
epiglott|al, -ic ,epɪ'glɒt|l ['epɪ,g-], -ɪk
epiglottis, -es ,epɪ'glɒtɪs ['epɪ,g-], -ɪz
epigone, -s 'epɪgəʊn, -z

Epigoni e'pɪgənaɪ [-ni:]
epigram, -s 'epɪgræm, -z
epigrammatic, -al, -ally ,epɪgrə'mætɪk,
-l, -əlɪ
epigrammatist, -s ,epɪ'græmətɪst, -s
epigrammatiz|e [-is|e], -es, -ing, -ed
,epɪ'græmətaɪz, -ɪz, -ɪŋ, -d
epigraph, -s 'epɪgrɑ:f [-græf], -s
epigrapher, -s e'pɪgrəfə* [ɪ'p-], -z
epigraphic ,epɪ'græfɪk
epigraph|ist/s, -y e'pɪgrəf|ɪst/s [ɪ'p-], -ɪ
epilepsy 'epɪlepsɪ
epileptic (s. adj.), -s, -al ,epɪ'leptɪk, -s,
-l
epilogic ,epɪ'lɒdʒɪk
epilogiz|e [-is|e], -es, -ing, -ed e'pɪləʊ-
dʒaɪz [ɪ'p-], -ɪz, -ɪŋ, -d
epilogue, -s 'epɪlɒg, -z
Epimenides ,epɪ'menɪdi:z
Epinal 'epɪnl (epinal)
epiphan|y (E.), -ies ɪ'pɪfən|ɪ [e'p-, -fn|ɪ],
-ɪz
Epipsychidion ,epɪsaɪ'kɪdɪɒn [-ɪpsaɪ-,
-dɪən]
Epirus e'paɪrəs [ɪ'p-]
episcopac|y, -ies ɪ'pɪskəpəs|ɪ [e'p-], -ɪz
episcop|al, -ally ɪ'pɪskəp|l [e'p-], -əlɪ
episcopalian (s. adj.), -s, -ism ɪ,pɪskəʊ-
'peɪljən [e,p-, -lɪən], -z, -ɪzəm
episcopate, -s ɪ'pɪskəʊpət [e'p-, -pɪt,
-peɪt], -s
episcope, -s 'episkəʊp, -s
episcopiz|e [-is|e], -es, -ing, -ed ɪ'pɪs-
kəʊpaɪz [e'p-], -ɪz, -ɪŋ, -d
episode, -s 'episəʊd, -z
episodic, -al, -ally ,epɪ'sɒdɪk, -l, -əlɪ
epistemology e,pɪsti:'mɒlədʒɪ [ɪ,p-, -tɪ-,
-tə-]
epistle, -s ɪ'pɪsl, -z
epistler, -s ɪ'pɪs#lə*, -z
epistolary ɪ'pɪstələrɪ [e'p-, -tlərɪ]
epistoler, -s ɪ'pɪstələ* [e'p-], -z
epistoliz|e [-is|e], -es, -ing, -ed ɪ'pɪs-
təlaɪz [e'p-], -ɪz, -ɪŋ, -d
epistyle, -s 'epɪstaɪl, -z
epitaph, -s 'epɪtɑ:f [-tæf], -s
epithalami|um, -a, -ums ,epɪθə'leɪ-
mj|əm [-mɪ|-], -ə, -əmz
epithelium, -s ,epɪ'θi:ljəm [-lɪəm], -z
epithet, -s 'epɪθet [-θɪt], -s
epithetic ,epɪ'θetɪk
epitome, -s ɪ'pɪtəmɪ [e'p-], -z
epitomic, -al ,epɪ'tɒmɪk, -l
epitomist, -s ɪ'pɪtəmɪst [e'p-], -s
epitomiz|e [-is|e], -es, -ing, -ed, -er/s
ɪ'pɪtəmaɪz [e'p-], -ɪz, -ɪŋ, -d, -ə*/z
epoch, -s 'i:pɒk [rarely 'ep-], -s
epochal 'epɒkl [i:'pɒk-]

169

epoch-making 'iːpɒk͵meɪkɪŋ
epode, -s 'epəʊd, -z
eponym, -s 'epəʊnɪm, -z
eponymous ɪ'pɒnɪməs [e'p-]
epopee, -s 'epəʊpiː, -z
epos, -es 'epɒs, -ɪz
Epping 'epɪŋ
Epps eps
epsilon, -s ep'saɪlən [-lɒn, *rarely* 'epsɪlən], -z
Epsom 'epsəm
Epstein (*sculptor*) 'epstaɪn
Epworth 'epwɜːθ [-wəθ]
equability ͵ekwə'bɪlətɪ [͵iːk-, -ɪtɪ]
equab|le, -ly, -leness 'ekwəb|l ['iːk-], -lɪ, -lnɪs [-nəs]
equ|al (*s. adj. v.*), -ally, -alness; -als, -alling, -alled 'iːkw|əl, -əlɪ, -əlnɪs [-nəs]; -əlz, -əlɪŋ, -əld
equalit|y, -ies iː'kwɒlət|ɪ [ɪ'k-, -ɪt|ɪ], -ɪz
equalization [-isa-], -s ͵iːkwəlaɪ'zeɪʃn [-lɪ'z-], -z
equaliz|e [-is|e], -es, -ing, -ed 'iːkwəlaɪz, -ɪz, -ɪŋ, -d
equanimity ͵ekwə'nɪmətɪ [͵iːk-, -ɪtɪ]
equanimous, -ly, -ness iː'kwænɪməs [ɪ'k-, e'k-], -lɪ, -nɪs [-nəs]
equat|e, -es, -ing, -ed ɪ'kweɪt [iː'k-], -s, -ɪŋ, -ɪd
equation, -s ɪ'kweɪʒn [-eɪʃn], -z
equator, -s ɪ'kweɪtə*, -z
equatorial (*s. adj.*), -s, -ly ͵ekwə'tɔːrɪəl [͵iːk-], -z, -ɪ
equerr|y, -ies 'ekwər|ɪ, ɪ'kwer|ɪ, -ɪz
Note.—The pronunciation at court is ɪ'kwerɪ.
equestrian (*s. adj.*), -s, -ism ɪ'kwestrɪən [e'k-], -z, -ɪzəm
equestrienne, -s ɪ͵kwestrɪ'en [e͵k-], -z
equiangular ͵iːkwɪ'æŋgjʊlə*
equidistant, -ly ͵iːkwɪ'dɪstənt, -lɪ
equilateral ͵iːkwɪ'lætərəl
equilibrat|e, -es, -ing, -ed ͵iːkwɪ-'laɪbreɪt [-'lɪb-, iː'kwɪlɪb-, ɪ'k-], -s, -ɪŋ, -ɪd
equilibration ͵iːkwɪlaɪ'breɪʃn [͵iːkwɪ-lɪ'b-, iː͵kwɪlɪ'b-, ɪ͵k-]
equilibrist, -s iː'kwɪlɪbrɪst [ɪ'k-, ͵iːkwɪ-'lɪbrɪst], -s
equilibrium ͵iːkwɪ'lɪbrɪəm [͵ekw-]
equimultiple, -s ͵iːkwɪ'mʌltɪpl, -z
equine 'ekwaɪn ['iːk-]
equinoctial (*s. adj.*), -s ͵iːkwɪ'nɒkʃl [͵ek-], -z
equinox, -es 'iːkwɪnɒks ['ek-], -ɪz
equip, -s, -ping, -ped, -ment/s ɪ'kwɪp, -s, -ɪŋ, -t, -mənt/s
equipage, -s 'ekwɪpɪdʒ, -ɪz

equipois|e (*s. v.*), -es, -ing, -ed 'ekwɪ-pɔɪz ['iːk-], -ɪz, -ɪŋ, -d
equitab|le, -ly, -leness 'ekwɪtəb|l, -lɪ, -lnɪs [-nəs]
equitation ͵ekwɪ'teɪʃn
equit|y, -ies 'ekwət|ɪ [-ɪt|ɪ], -ɪz
equivalen|ce, -t/s, -tly ɪ'kwɪvələn|s [-v|ə-], -t/s, -tlɪ
equivoc|al, -ally, -alness ɪ'kwɪvək|l [-vʊk-], -əlɪ, -lnɪs [-nəs]
equivocat|e, -es, -ing, -ed, -or/s ɪ'kwɪvəkeɪt [-vʊk-], -s, -ɪŋ, -ɪd, -ə*/z
equivocation, -s ɪ͵kwɪvə'keɪʃn [-vʊ'k-], -z
equivoke [-voque], -s 'ekwɪvəʊk, -s
Equuleus e'kwʊlɪəs
er (*interj.*) ʌː, ɜː
era, -s 'ɪərə, -z
eradiat|e, -es, -ing, -ed ɪ'reɪdɪeɪt [iː'r-, -dʲert], -s, -ɪŋ, -ɪd
eradiation ɪ͵reɪdɪ'eɪʃn [iː͵r-]
eradicable ɪ'rædɪkəbl
eradicat|e, -es, -ing, -ed ɪ'rædɪkeɪt, -s, -ɪŋ, -ɪd
eradication ɪ͵rædɪ'keɪʃn
eradicative ɪ'rædɪkətɪv [-keɪt-]
Erard, -s 'erɑːd (erɑːr), -z
eras|e, -es, -ing, -ed, -er/s, -ement -able ɪ'reɪz, -ɪz, -ɪŋ, -d, -ə*/z, -mənt; -əbl
erasion, -s ɪ'reɪʒn, -z
Erasmian, -s, -ism ɪ'ræzmɪən [e'r-, -mjən], -z, -ɪzəm
Erasmus ɪ'ræzməs [e'r-]
Erastian, -s, -ism ɪ'ræstɪən [e'r-, -tjən], -z, -ɪzəm
Erastus ɪ'ræstəs [e'r-]
erasure, -s ɪ'reɪʒə*, -z
Erath ɪ'rɑːθ [e'r-]
Erdington 'ɜːdɪŋtən
ere eə*
Erebus 'erɪbəs
Erec 'ɪərek
Erechtheum ͵erek'θiːəm [-'θɪəm]
Erechtheus ɪ'rekθjuːs [e'r-, -θɪəs, -θjəs]
erect (*adj. v.*), -ly, -ness; -s, -ing, -ed; -ile ɪ'rekt, -lɪ, -nɪs [-nəs]; -s, -ɪŋ, -ɪd; -aɪl
erection, -s ɪ'rekʃn, -z
eremite, -s 'erɪmaɪt, -s
eremitic, -al ͵erɪ'mɪtɪk, -l
Eretria, -n/s ɪ'retrɪə [e'r-], -n/z
erewhile eə'waɪl [-'hw-]
Erewhon 'erɪwɒn [-wən, -ɪhw-]
erg, -s ɜːg, -z
ergo 'ɜːgəʊ
ergon, -s 'ɜːgɒn, -z
ergonic, -s, -ally ɜː'gɒnɪk, -s, -əlɪ

ergonomics ˌɜːgəʊˈnɒmɪks
ergosterol ɜːˈgɒstərɒl [-stɪər-]
ergot, -ism ˈɜːgət [-gɒt], -ɪzəm
eric (E.), -s ˈerɪk, -s
erica (E.) ˈerɪkə
ericaceous ˌerɪˈkeɪʃəs
Erie ˈɪərɪ
Erin ˈɪərɪn
Eris ˈerɪs
eristic, -s eˈrɪstɪk, -s
Erith ˈɪərɪθ
Eritrea, -n/s ˌerɪˈtreɪə [-ˈtrɪə], -n/z
Erle ɜːl
erl-king, -s ˈɜːlkɪŋ [ˌɜːlˈkɪŋ], -z
Erlynne ˈɜːlɪn
ermine, -s, -d ˈɜːmɪn, -z, -d
erne (E.), -s ɜːn, -z
Ernest ˈɜːnɪst
Ernle ˈɜːnlɪ
erod|e, -es, -ing, -ed ɪˈrəʊd [eˈr-], -z, -ɪŋ, -ɪd
erogenous ɪˈrɒdʒɪnəs [eˈr-, -dʒə-]
Eroica |eˈrəʊɪkə [ɪˈr-]
Eros ˈɪərɒs [ˈerɒs, also ˈerəʊz]
erosion, -s ɪˈrəʊʒn [eˈr-], -z
erosive ɪˈrəʊsɪv [eˈr-]
erotic (s. adj.), -s ɪˈrɒtɪk [eˈr-], -s
erotica ɪˈrɒtɪkə [eˈr-]
eroticism ɪˈrɒtɪsɪzəm [eˈr-]
err, -s, -ing, -ed ɜː:*, -z, -rɪŋ, -d
errand, -s ˈerənd, -z
errand-boy, -s ˈerəndbɔɪ, -z
errant, -ly, -ry ˈerənt, -lɪ, -rɪ
erratic, -al, -ally ɪˈrætɪk [eˈr-], -l, -əlɪ
errat|um, -a eˈrɑːt|əm [ɪˈr-, -ˈreɪt|-], -ə
Erroll ˈerəl
erroneous, -ly, -ness ɪˈrəʊnjəs [eˈr-, -nɪəs], -lɪ, -nɪs [-nəs]
error, -s ˈerə*, -z
ersatz ˈeəzæts [ˈɜːsɑːts] (ɛrˈzats)
Erse ɜːs
Erskine ˈɜːskɪn
erst ɜːst
erstwhile ˈɜːstwaɪl [-thw-]
erubescen|ce, -cy, -t ˌeruːˈbesn|s [-rʊ-], -sɪ, -t
eruct, -s, -ing, -ed ɪˈrʌkt [iːˈr-], -s, -ɪŋ, -ɪd
eructat|e, -es, -ing, -ed ɪˈrʌkteɪt [iːˈr-], -s, -ɪŋ, -ɪd
eructation, -s ˌiːrʌkˈteɪʃn, -z
erudite, -ly, -ness ˈeruːdaɪt [-rʊ-, -rjuː-, -rjʊ-], -lɪ, -nɪs [-nəs]
erudition ˌeruːˈdɪʃn [-rʊ-, -rjuː-, -rjʊ-]
erupt, -s, -ing, -ed ɪˈrʌpt [eˈr-], -s, -ɪŋ, -ɪd
eruption, -s ɪˈrʌpʃn [eˈr-], -z
eruptive, -ly, -ness ɪˈrʌptɪv [eˈr-], -lɪ, -nɪs [-nəs]

Ervine ˈɜːvɪn
erysipelas ˌerɪˈsɪpɪləs [-pəl-, -lɪs]
erythema ˌerɪˈθiːmə
Eryx ˈerɪks
Erzerum ˈeəzəruːm
Esau ˈiːsɔː
escalad|e (s. v.), -es, -ing, -ed ˌeskəˈleɪd [ˈ---], -z, -ɪŋ, -ɪd
escalat|e, -es, -ing, -ed ˈeskəleɪt, -s, -ɪŋ, -ɪd
escalation ˌeskəˈleɪʃn
escalator, -s ˈeskəleɪtə*, -z
escallop, -ed ɪˈskɒləp [eˈs-], -t
escapade, -s ˌeskəˈpeɪd [ˈ---], -z
escap|e (s. v.), -es, -ing, -ed, -ement/s ɪˈskeɪp [eˈs-], -s, -ɪŋ, -t, -mənt/s
escapi|sm, -st/s ɪˈskeɪpɪ|zəm [eˈs-], -st/s
escapologist, -s ˌeskeɪˈpɒlədʒɪst [-skə'p-], -s
escarp (s. v.), -s, -ing, -ed, -ment/s ɪˈskɑːp [eˈs-], -s, -ɪŋ, -t, -mənt/s
eschalot, -s ˈeʃəlɒt [ˌeʃəˈl-], -s
eschar, -s ˈeskɑː*, -z
escharotic (s. adj.), -s ˌeskəˈrɒtɪk, -s
eschatological ˌeskətəˈlɒdʒɪkl [-kæt-]
eschatolog|ist/s, -y ˌeskəˈtɒlədʒ|ɪst/s, -ɪ
escheat (s. v.), -s, -ing, -ed ɪsˈtʃiːt [es-], -s, -ɪŋ, -ɪd
eschew, -s, -ing, -ed ɪsˈtʃuː [es-], -z, -ɪŋ [-ˈtʃʊɪŋ], -d
eschscholtzia, -s ɪsˈkɒlʃə [ɪsˈkɒltʃə, esˈkɒltsɪə, esˈkɒltsjə, eˈʃɒltsɪə, eˈʃɒltsjə], -z
Escombe ˈeskəm
Escorial ˌeskɒrɪˈɑːl [eˈskɔːrɪəl]
escort (s.), -s ˈeskɔːt, -s
escort (v.), -s, -ing, -ed ɪˈskɔːt [eˈs-], -s, -ɪŋ, -ɪd
Escow ˈeskəʊ
escritoire, -s ˌeskriːˈtwɑː* [-krɪ-, -ˈtwɔː:*, ˈ---] (əskritwaːr), -z
escudo, -s eˈskuːdəʊ, -z
esculent (s. adj.), -s ˈeskjʊlənt, -s
Escurial eˈskjʊərɪəl
escutcheon, -s ɪˈskʌtʃ ən [eˈs-], -z
Esdaile ˈezdeɪl
Esdraelon ˌezdreɪˈiːlɒn [-drəˈiː-]
Esdras ˈezdræs [-rəs]
Esher ˈiːʃə*
Esias ɪˈzaɪəs [eˈz-, -æs]
Esk esk
Eskimo, -s ˈeskɪməʊ, -z
Esmé ˈezmɪ
Esmeralda ˌezməˈrældə
Esmond(e) ˈezmənd
esophageal iːˌsɒfəˈdʒiːəl [ɪˈsɒf-, -ˈdʒɪəl]
esopha|gus, -gi iːˈsɒfə|gəs [ɪˈs-], -gaɪ [-dʒaɪ]

171

esoteric, -al, -ally ˌesəʊˈterɪk [ˌiːs-], -l, -əlɪ

espalier (s. v.), -s, -ing, -ed ɪˈspæljə* [eˈs-, -lɪə*], -z, -rɪŋ, -d

esparto eˈspɑːtəʊ

especi|al, -ally ɪˈspeʃɪl [eˈs-], -əlɪ [-lɪ]

Esperant|ist/s, -o ˌespəˈrænt|ɪst/s [-peˈr-, -ˈrɑːn-], -əʊ

Espeut eˈspjuːt

espial ɪˈspaɪəl [eˈs-]

espionage ˌespɪəˈnɑːʒ [ˌespjəˈnɑːʒ, ˈesprənɪdʒ, ˈesprənɑːdʒ, eˈspaɪənɪdʒ, ɪˈspaɪənɪdʒ] (espjɔnɑːʒ, pronounced as French espionnage)

esplanade, -s ˌespləˈneɪd [-ˈnɑːd, rarely ˈesplənɑːd], -z

Esplanade (in Western Australia) ˈesplənɑːd

espous|e, -es, -ing, -ed, -er/s; -al/s ɪˈspaʊz [eˈs-], -ɪz, -ɪŋ, -d, -ə*/z; -l/z

espressivo ˌespreˈsiːvəʊ

espresso eˈspresəʊ [ɪˈs-]

esprit ˈespriː: (espri)

esprit-de-corps ˌespriːdəˈkɔː* (esprid-kɔːr)

esp|y, -ies, -ying, -ied ɪˈsp|aɪ [eˈs-], -aɪz, -aɪɪŋ, -aɪd

Espy ˈespɪ

Esq. ɪˈskwaɪə* [eˈs-]

Esquiline ˈeskwɪlaɪn

Esquimalt eˈskwaɪmɔːlt

Esquimau, -x ˈeskɪməʊ, -z

esquire, -s ɪˈskwaɪə* [eˈs-], -z

ess, -es es, -ɪz

essay (s.), -s; -ist/s ˈeseɪ [-sɪ], -z; -ɪst/s

essay (v.), -s, -ing, -ed, -er/s eˈseɪ [ˈeseɪ], -z, -ɪŋ, -d, -ə*/z

esse ˈesɪ

Essen ˈesn

essence, -s ˈesns, -ɪz

Essene, -s ˈesiːn [eˈsiːn], -z

essenti|al, -als, -ally, -alness ɪˈsenʃ|l [eˈs-], -lz, -əlɪ [-lɪ], -lnɪs [-nəs]

essentiality ɪˌsenʃɪˈælətɪ [eˌs-, -ɪtɪ]

Essex ˈesɪks

establish, -es, -ing, -ed, -er/s, -ment/s ɪˈstæblɪʃ [eˈs-], -ɪz, -ɪŋ, -t, -ə*/z, -mənt/s

estate, -s ɪˈsteɪt [eˈs-], -s

estate-car, -s ɪˈsteɪtkɑː* [eˈs-], -z

Estcourt ˈestkɔːt

Este ˈestɪ

esteem (s. v.), -s, -ing, -ed ɪˈstiːm [eˈs-], -z, -ɪŋ, -d

Estey ˈestɪ

Esther ˈestə* [ˈesθə*], esp. in the N.

esthet- = aesthet-

Esthonia, -n/s eˈstəʊnjə [esˈθəʊ-, -nɪə], -n/z

estimab|le, -ly, -leness ˈestɪməb|l, -lɪ, -lnɪs [-nəs]

estimate (s.), -s ˈestɪmət [-mɪt, -meɪt], -s

estimat|e (v.), -es, -ing, -ed, -or/s ˈestɪmeɪt, -s, -ɪŋ, -ɪd, -ə*/z

estimation ˌestɪˈmeɪʃn

estiv- = aestiv-

Estmere ˈest,mɪə*

Estonia, -n/s eˈstəʊnjə [-nɪə], -n/z

estop, -s, -ping, -ped; -page, -pel/s ɪˈstɒp [eˈs-], -s, -ɪŋ, -t; -ɪdʒ, -l/z

estrade, -s eˈstrɑːd, -z

estrang|e, -es, -ing, -ed, -edness, -ement/s ɪˈstreɪndʒ [eˈs-], -ɪz, -ɪŋ, -d, -ɪdnɪs [-nəs], -mənt/s

estreat (s. v.), -s, -ing, -ed ɪˈstriːt [eˈs-], -s, -ɪŋ, -ɪd

estuar|y, -ies ˈestjʊər|ɪ [-tjwər-, -ˌtjʊər-, -tʃʊər-, -tʃwər-, -ˌtʃʊər-, -tjʊr-, -tʃʊr-], -ɪz

esurien|ce, -cy, -t ɪˈsjʊərɪən|s, -sɪ, -t

eta ˈiːtə

etacism ˈeɪtəsɪzəm

Etah ˈiːtə

Etain ˈeteɪn

Etamin ˈetəmɪn

etc. ɪtˈsetərə [et-, ət-]

etcetera, -s ɪtˈsetərə [et-, ət-], -z

etch, -es, -ing/s, -ed, -er/s etʃ, -ɪz, -ɪŋ/z, -t, -ə*/z

etern|al, -ally iːˈtɜːn|l [ɪˈt-], -əlɪ [-lɪ]

eternaliz|e [-is|e], -es, -ing, -ed iːˈtɜːnəlaɪz [ɪˈt-, -nlaɪz], -ɪz, -ɪŋ, -d

eternit|y, -ies iːˈtɜːnət|ɪ [ɪˈt-, -ɪt|ɪ], -ɪz

eterniz|e [-is|e], -es, -ing, -ed iːˈtɜːnaɪz [ɪˈt-], -ɪz, -ɪŋ, -d

Etesian ɪˈtiːʒjən [-ʒɪən, -ʒn]

Eteson ˈiːtsn

Ethbaal eθˈbeɪəl [usual Jewish pronunciation eθˈbɑːl]

Ethel, -bald, -bert ˈeθl, -bɔːld, -bɜːt

Ethelberta ˌeθlˈbɜːtə [ˈ--,--]

Ethelburga ˌeθlˈbɜːgə [ˈ--,--]

Ethel|red, -wulf ˈeθl|red, -wʊlf

ether, -s ˈiːθə*, -z

ethereal, -ly iːˈθɪərɪəl [ɪˈθ-], -ɪ

etherealiz|e [-is|e], -es, -ing, -ed iːˈθɪərɪəlaɪz [ɪˈθ-], -ɪz, -ɪŋ, -d

Etherege ˈeθərɪdʒ

etheric, -s -ally iːˈθerɪk [ɪˈθ-], -s, -əlɪ

Etherington ˈeðərɪŋtən

etheriz|e [-is|e], -es, -ing, -ed ˈiːθəraɪz, -ɪz, -ɪŋ, -d

ethic (s. adj.), -s, -al, -ally ˈeθɪk, -s, -l, -əlɪ

Ethiop, -s 'iːθɪɒp [-θjɒp], -s
Ethiopia, -n/s ˌiːθɪˈəʊpjə [-pɪə], -n/z
Ethiopic ˌiːθɪˈɒpɪk [-ˈəʊp-]
ethnic, -al, -ally 'eθnɪk, -l, -əlɪ
ethnographer, -s eθ'nɒgrəfə*, -z
ethnographic ˌeθnəʊˈgræfɪk
ethnography eθ'nɒgrəfɪ
ethnologic, -al, -ally ˌeθnəʊˈlɒdʒɪk, -l, -əlɪ
ethnolog|ist/s, -y eθ'nɒlədʒ|ɪst/s, -ɪ
ethologic, -al i:θəʊˈlɒdʒɪk, -l
etholog|ist/s, -y iːˈθɒlədʒ|ɪst/s [ɪˈθ-], -ɪ
ethos 'iːθɒs
ethyl (commercial and general pronunciation) 'eθɪl, (chemists' pronunciation) 'iːθaɪl
ethylene 'eθɪliːn
etiolat|e, -es, -ing, -ed 'iːtɪəʊleɪt [-tɪəl-], -s, -ɪŋ, -ɪd
etiolog|ist/s, -y ˌiːtɪˈɒlədʒ|ɪst/s, -ɪ
etiquette 'etɪket [-kət, ˌetɪˈket]
Etna 'etnə
Eton 'iːtn
Etonian, -s iːˈtəʊnjən [ɪˈt-, -nɪən], -z
Etruria, -n/s ɪˈtrʊərɪə, -n/z
Etruscan, -s ɪˈtrʌskən, -z
Ettrick 'etrɪk
Etty 'etɪ
étude(s) eɪˈtjuːd ['--] (etyd)
etui, -s e'twiː, -z
etymologic, -al, -ally ˌetɪməˈlɒdʒɪk, -l, -əlɪ
etymolog|ist/s, -y, -ies ˌetɪˈmɒlədʒ|-ɪst/s, -ɪ, -ɪz
etymologiz|e [-is|e], -es, -ing, -ed ˌetɪˈmɒlədʒaɪz, -ɪz, -ɪŋ, -d
etymon, -s 'etɪmɒn, -z
Euboea juːˈbɪə [jʊˈb-, -ˈbiːə]
eucalyptus, -es ˌjuːkəˈlɪptəs [jʊk-], -ɪz
Eucharist, -s 'juːkərɪst, -s
eucharistic, -al, -ally ˌjuːkəˈrɪstɪk [jʊk-], -l, -əlɪ
euchre (s. v.), -s, -ing, -d 'juːkə*, -z, -rɪŋ, -d
Euclid, -s 'juːklɪd, -z
Euclidean juːˈklɪdɪən [jʊˈk-, -djən]
eud(a)emoni|sm, -st/s juːˈdiːmənɪ|zəm [jʊˈd-], -st/s
eudiometer, -s ˌjuːdɪˈɒmɪtə* [jʊd-, -mətə*], -z
Eudocia juːˈdəʊʃjə [jʊˈd-, -ʃɪə, -sjə, -sɪə]
Eudora juːˈdɔːrə [jʊˈd-]
Eudoxia juːˈdɒksɪə [jʊˈd-, -sjə]
Eudoxus juːˈdɒksəs [jʊˈd-]
Eugen (English name) 'juːdʒen [-dʒɪn, -dʒən], (German name) 'ɔɪgən (ɔyˈge:n)

Eugene (English name) juːˈʒeɪn, 'juːdʒiːn, juːˈdʒiːn
Eugene Onegin ˌjuːdʒiːn ɒˈnjeɪgɪn (jivˈgenji aˈnjegin)
Eugénia juːˈdʒiːnjə [jʊˈdʒ-, -ˈdʒeɪ-, -nɪə]
eugenic, -s juːˈdʒenɪk [jʊˈdʒ-], -s
Eugénie (as English name) juːˈʒeɪnɪ, juːˈʒiːnɪ, juːˈdʒiːnɪ
Eugenius juːˈdʒiːnjəs [jʊˈdʒ-, -ˈdʒeɪ-, -nɪəs]
Eulalia juːˈleɪljə [jʊˈl-, -lɪə]
Euler (English name) 'juːlə*, (German name) 'ɔɪlə* (ˈɔylər)
eulogist, -s 'juːlədʒɪst, -s
eulogistic, -al, -ally ˌjuːləˈdʒɪstɪk, -l -əlɪ
eulogium, -s juːˈləʊdʒjəm [jʊˈl-, -dʒɪəm], -z
eulogiz|e [-is|e], -es, -ing, -ed 'juːlə-dʒaɪz, -ɪz, -ɪŋ, -d
eulog|y, -ies 'juːlədʒ|ɪ, -ɪz
Eumenides juːˈmenɪdiːz [jʊˈm-]
Eunice (modern Christian name) 'juːnɪs, (biblical name) juːˈnaɪsɪ [jʊˈn-]
eunuch, -s, -ism 'juːnək, -s, -ɪzəm
euonymus, -es juːˈɒnɪməs [jʊˈɒ-], -ɪz
eupepsia juːˈpepsɪə [-sjə]
eupeptic juːˈpeptɪk
Euphemia juːˈfiːmjə [jʊˈf-, -mɪə]
euphemism, -s 'juːfɪmɪzəm [-fə-], -z
euphemistic, -al, -ally ˌjuːfɪˈmɪstɪk [-fə-], -l, -əlɪ
euphemiz|e [-is|e], -es, -ing, -ed 'juːfɪ-maɪz [-fə-], -ɪz, -ɪŋ, -d
euphonic, -al, -ally juːˈfɒnɪk [jʊˈf-], -l, -əlɪ
euphonious, -ly juːˈfəʊnjəs [jʊˈf-, -nɪəs], -lɪ
euphonium, -s juːˈfəʊnjəm [jʊˈf-, -nɪəm], -z
euphoniz|e [-is|e], -es, -ing, -ed 'juː-fənaɪz [-fəʊn-, -fɒn-], -ɪz, -ɪŋ, -d
euphony 'juːfənɪ [-fʊn-]
euphoria juːˈfɔːrɪə [jʊˈf-]
euphoric juːˈfɒrɪk [jʊ-]
euphrasy 'juːfrəsɪ
Euphrates juːˈfreɪtiːz [jʊˈf-]
Euphronius juːˈfrəʊnjəs [jʊˈf-, -nɪəs]
Euphrosyne juːˈfrɒzɪnɪ [jʊˈf-]
Euphues juːˈfjuːiːz [-fjʊiːz]
euphui|sm/s, -st/s 'juːfjuːɪ|zəm/z [-fjʊɪ-], -st/s
euphuistic ˌjuːfjuːˈɪstɪk [-fjʊˈɪ-]
Eurasian, -s jʊəˈreɪʒjən [jɔːˈr-, jɔːˈr-, -eɪʒɪən, -eɪʒn, -eɪʃn], -z
Euratom jʊəˈrætəm
eureka jʊəˈriːkə

173

eurhythm|ic/s, -y juːˈrɪðm|ɪk/s [jʊˈr-, ˌjʊəˈr-, -ˈrɪθm-], -ɪ
Euripides jʊəˈrɪpidiːz
Euripus jʊəˈraɪpəs
Europa jʊəˈrəʊpə
Europe ˈjʊərəp [ˈjɔːr-]
European, -s ˌjʊərəˈpiːən [ˌjɔːr-, -ˈpɪən], -z
europeaniz|e [-is|e], -es, -ing, -ed ˌjʊərəˈpiːənaɪz [ˌjɔːr-, -ˈpɪən-], -ɪz, -ɪŋ, -d
Eurovision ˈjʊərəʊˌvɪʒn
Eurus ˈjʊərəs
Eurydice jʊəˈrɪdɪsiː [-sɪ]
Eurylochus jʊəˈrɪləkəs
Eusebian, -s juːˈsiːbjən [jʊˈs-, -bɪən], -z
Eusebius juːˈsiːbjəs [jʊˈs-, -bɪəs]
Euskarian, -s juːˈskeərɪən, -z
Eustace ˈjuːstəs [-tɪs]
Eustachian juːˈsteɪʃjən [-ʃɪən, -ʃn, rarely -ˈsteɪkjən, -ˈsteɪkɪən]
Eustachius juːˈsteɪkjəs [-kɪəs]
Eustis ˈjuːstɪs
Euston ˈjuːstən
Eutaw ˈjuːtɔː
Euterpe juːˈtɜːpɪ [jʊˈt-]
euthanasia ˌjuːθəˈneɪzjə [-eɪzɪə, -eɪʒjə, -eɪʒɪə, -eɪʒə]
Eutropius juːˈtrəʊpjəs [jʊˈt-, -pɪəs]
Euxine ˈjuːksaɪn
Eva ˈiːvə
evacuant (s. adj.), -s ɪˈvækjʊənt [iːˈv-, -kjwənt], -s
evacuat|e, -es, -ing, -ed, -or/s ɪˈvækjʊeɪt [iːˈv-], -s, -ɪŋ, -ɪd, -ə*/z
evacuation, -s ɪˌvækjʊˈeɪʃn [iːˌv-], -z
evacuee, -s ɪˌvækjuːˈiː [iːˌv-, -kjuˈiː], -z
evad|e, -es, -ing, -ed, -er/s ɪˈveɪd, -z, -ɪŋ, -ɪd, -ə*/z
evaluat|e, -es, -ing, -ed ɪˈvæljʊeɪt, -s, -ɪŋ, -ɪd
evaluation, -s ɪˌvæljʊˈeɪʃn, -z
Evan ˈevən
Evander ɪˈvændə*
evanesc|e, -es, -ing, -ed ˌiːvəˈnes [ˌev-], -ɪz, -ɪŋ, -t
evanescen|ce, -t/ly ˌiːvəˈnesn|s [ˌev-], -t/lɪ
evangel, -s ɪˈvændʒel [-dʒəl], -z
evangelic (s. adj.), -s, -al/s, -ally, -alism ˌiːvænˈdʒelɪk [ˌev-, -vən-], -s, -l/z, -əlɪ, -əlɪzəm [-]ɪz-]
Evangeline ɪˈvændʒɪliːn [-dʒəl-, -dʒl-]
evangelist, -s ɪˈvændʒəlɪst [-dʒɪl-, -dʒl-], -s
evangelistic ɪˌvændʒəˈlɪstɪk [-dʒɪˈl-, -dʒl̩ˈɪstɪk]

evangelization [-isa-] ɪˌvændʒəlaɪˈzeɪʃn [-dʒɪl-, -dʒl]-, -lɪˈz-]
evangeliz|e [-is|e], -es, -ing, -ed ɪˈvændʒəlaɪz [-dʒɪl-, -dʒl]-], -ɪz, -ɪŋ, -d
Evans ˈevənz
Evanson ˈevənsn
Evanston ˈevənstən
Evansville ˈevənzvɪl
evaporable ɪˈvæpərəbl
evaporat|e, -es, -ing, -ed, -or/s ɪˈvæpəreɪt, -s, -ɪŋ, -ɪd, -ə*/z
evaporation, -s ɪˌvæpəˈreɪʃn, -z
evasion, -s ɪˈveɪʒn, -z
evasive, -ly, -ness ɪˈveɪsɪv, -lɪ, -nɪs [-nəs]
eve (E.), -s, iːv, -z
Evele(i)gh ˈiːvlɪ
Evelina ˌevɪˈliːnə
Eveline ˈiːvlɪn, ˈevlɪn, ˈevɪliːn
Evelyn ˈiːvlɪn, ˈevlɪn
ev|en (s. adj. v. adv.), -enly, -enness; -ens, -ening, -ened ˈiːv|n, -nlɪ, -nnɪs [-nəs]; -nz, -nɪŋ [-ənɪŋ], -nd
Evenden ˈevəndən
evening (s.) (close of day), -s ˈiːvnɪŋ, -z
Evens ˈevənz
evensong, -s ˈiːvnsɒŋ, -z
event, -s; -ful ɪˈvent, -s; -fʊl [-fəl]
eventide, -s ˈiːvntaɪd, -z
eventual, -ly ɪˈventʃʊəl [-tjwəl, -tjuəl, -tʃwəl, -tjʊl, -tʃʊl], -ɪ
eventualit|y, -ies ɪˌventʃʊˈælət|ɪ [-tjʊ-, -ɪt|ɪ], -ɪz
eventuat|e, -es, -ing, -ed ɪˈventʃʊeɪt [-tjʊeɪt], -s, -ɪŋ, -ɪd
ever ˈevə*
Ever|ard, -est, -ett ˈevər|ɑːd, -ɪst, -ɪt
evergreen (s. adj.), -s ˈevəgriːn, -z
Everitt ˈevərɪt
everlasting, -ly, -ness ˌevəˈlɑːstɪŋ, -lɪ, -nɪs [-nəs]
evermore ˌevəˈmɔː* [-ˈmɒə*, also sometimes ˈ—— when followed by a stress]
Evers ˈevəz
Evershed ˈevəʃed
eversion ɪˈvɜːʃn [iːˈv-]
Eversley ˈevəzlɪ
evert, -s, -ing, -ed ɪˈvɜːt [iːˈv-], -s, -ɪŋ, -ɪd
Everton ˈevətən
every, -body ˈevrɪ, -ˌbɒdɪ [-bədɪ]
everyday (adj.) ˈevrɪdeɪ [ˌ—ˈ—ˈ]
Everyman ˈevrɪmæn
everyone ˈevrɪwʌn
everything ˈevrɪθɪŋ
everywhere ˈevrɪweə* [-ɪhw-]
Evesham ˈiːvʃəm [locally also ˈiːvɪʃəm]

Evett, -s 'evɪt, -s
evict, -s, -ing, -ed ɪ'vɪkt [iː'v-], -s, -ɪŋ, -ɪd
eviction, -s ɪ'vɪkʃn [iː'v-], -z
evidenc|e (s. v.), -es, -ing, -ed 'evɪdəns, -ɪz, -ɪŋ, -t
evident, -ly 'evɪdənt, -lɪ
evidenti|al, -ally ˌevɪ'denʃ|l, -əlɪ
evidentiary ˌevɪ'denʃərɪ
ev|il (s. adj.), -ils, -illy 'iːv|l [-ɪl], -lz [-ɪlz], -əlɪ [-ɪlɪ]
evil-doer, -s ˌiːvl'duːə* [ˌiːvɪl-, -'dʊə*, '-ˌ--], -z
evil-eye, -s, -d ˌiːvl̩'aɪ [ˌiːvɪl'aɪ], -z, -d
evil-minded, -ness ˌiːvl'maɪndɪd [ˌiːvɪl-, '-ˌ--], -nɪs [-nəs]
evil-speaking ˌiːvl'spiːkɪŋ [ˌiːvɪl-]
evinc|e, -es, -ing, -ed; -ive ɪ'vɪns, -ɪz, -ɪŋ, -t; -ɪv
evincib|le, -ly ɪ'vɪnsəb|l [-sɪb-], -lɪ
evirat|e, -es, -ing, -ed 'iː'vɪreɪt ['ev-], -s, -ɪŋ, -ɪd
eviscerat|e, -es, -ing, -ed ɪ'vɪsəreɪt [iː'v-], -s, -ɪŋ, -ɪd
evisceration ɪˌvɪsə'reɪʃn [iː'v-]
evocat|e, -es, -ing, -ed 'evəʊkeɪt ['iː'v-], -s, -ɪŋ, -ɪd
evocation, -s ˌevəʊ'keɪʃn [ˌiː'v-], -z
evocative ɪ'vɒkətɪv
evok|e, -es, -ing, -ed ɪ'vəʊk [iː'v-], -s, -ɪŋ, -t
evolute, -s 'iːvəluːt ['ev-, -ljuːt], -s
evolution, -s ˌiːvə'luːʃn [ˌev-, -'ljuː-], -z
evolutional ˌiːvə'luːʃənl [ˌev-, -'ljuː-, -ʃnəl, -ʃn̩l, -ʃnl, -ʃənəl]
evolutionary ˌiːvə'luːʃnərɪ [ˌev-, -'ljuː-, -ʃn̩rɪ, -ʃənərɪ]
evolutioni|sm, -st/s ˌiːvə'luːʃənɪ|zəm [ˌev-, -'ljuː-, -ʃn̩r-], -st/s
evolv|e, -es, -ing, -ed; -able ɪ'vɒlv [iː'v-], -z, -ɪŋ, -d; -əbl
Evors 'iːvɔːz
evulsion, -s ɪ'vʌlʃn [iː'v-], -z
Ewart 'juːət, jʊət
Ewbank 'juːbæŋk
ewe, -s; -lamb/s juː, -z; -læm/z
Ewell 'juːəl, jʊəl
Ewen 'juːɪn, 'jʊɪn [-ən]
ewe-neck, -s 'juːnek, -s
ewer, -s 'juːə* [jʊə*], -z
Ewing 'juːɪŋ, 'jʊɪŋ
ex eks
exacerbat|e, -es, -ing, -ed ek'sæsəbeɪt [ɪg'zæs-], -s, -ɪŋ, -ɪd
exacerbation, -s ek,sæsə'beɪʃn [ɪg,zæs-], -z

exact (adj. v.), -er, -est, -ly, -ness; -s, -ing, -ed, -er/s, -or/s ɪg'zækt [eg-], -ə*, -ɪst, -lɪ [ɪg'zæklɪ, 'gzæklɪ], -nɪs [-nəs] [ɪg'zæknɪs, -nəs]; -s, -ɪŋ, -ɪd, -ə*/z, -ə*/z
exaction, -s ɪg'zækʃn [eg-], -z
exactitude ɪg'zæktɪtjuːd [eg-]
exaggerat|e, -es, -ing, -ed, -or/s ɪg-'zædʒəreɪt [eg-], -s, -ɪŋ, -ɪd, -ə*/z
exaggeration, -s ɪg,zædʒə'reɪʃn [eg-], -z
exaggerative ɪg'zædʒərətɪv [eg-, -reɪt-]
exalt, -s, -ing, -ed/ly, -edness ɪg'zɔːlt [eg-, -'zɒlt], -s, -ɪŋ, -ɪd/lɪ, -ɪdnɪs [-nəs]
exaltation, -s ˌegzɔːl'teɪʃn [ˌeks-, -ɒl-], -z
exam, -s ɪg'zæm [eg-], -z
examen, -s eg'zeɪmen, -z
examination, -s ɪg,zæmɪ'neɪʃn [eg-], -z
examin|e, -es, -ing, -ed, -er/s ɪg'zæmɪn [eg-], -z, -ɪŋ, -d, -ə*/z
examinee, -s ɪg,zæmɪ'niː [eg-], -z
examp|le (s. v.), -les, -ling, -led ɪg-'zɑːmp|l [eg-], -lz, -lɪŋ, -ld
exarch, -s; -ate/s 'eksɑːk, -s; -eɪt/s
exasperat|e, -es, -ing, -ed, -or/s ɪg-'zæspəreɪt [eg-, -'zɑːs-], -s, -ɪŋ, -ɪd, -ə*/z
exasperation ɪg,zæspə'reɪʃn [eg-, -,zɑːs-]
Excalibur eks'kælɪbə*
ex cathedra ˌekskə'θiːdrə
excavat|e, -es, -ing, -ed, -or/s 'ekskəveɪt, -s, -ɪŋ, -ɪd, -ə*/z
excavation, -s ˌekskə'veɪʃn, -z
exceed, -s, -ing, -ed ɪk'siːd [ek-], -z, -ɪŋ, -ɪd
exceeding (adj.), -ly ɪk'siːdɪŋ [ek-], -lɪ
excel, -s, -ling, -led ɪk'sel [ek-], -z, -ɪŋ, -d
excellen|ce, -ces, -cy, -cies, -t/ly 'eksələn|s, -sɪz, -sɪ, -sɪz, -t/lɪ
excelsior ek'selsɪɔː* [ɪk-, -sɪə*, -sjə*]
except (v. prep. conj.), -s, -ing, -ed ɪk'sept [ek-], -s, -ɪŋ, -ɪd
exception, -s ɪk'sepʃn [ek-], -z
exceptionab|le, -ly, -leness ɪk'sepʃnəb|l [ek-, -ʃnə-, -ʃənə-], -lɪ, -lnɪs [-nəs]
excep|tional, -tionally ɪk'sepʃənl [ek-, -ʃnəl, -ʃn̩l, -ʃnl, -ʃənəl], -ʃn̩əlɪ [-ʃnəlɪ, -ʃn̩lɪ, -ʃnlɪ, -ʃənəlɪ]
excerpt (s.), -s 'eksəːpt [ɪk'səːpt, ek's-], -s
excerpt (v.), -s, -ing, -ed ek'səːpt [ɪk-], -s, -ɪŋ, -ɪd
excerption, -s ek'səːpʃn [ɪk-], -z
excess (s. v.), -es, -ing, -ed ɪk'ses [ek-] (also 'ekses when noun is used attributively), -ɪz, -ɪŋ, -t

175

excessive, -ly, -ness ɪk'sesɪv [ek-], -lɪ, -nɪs [-nəs]

exchang|e (s. v.), -es, -ing, -ed, -er/s; -eable ɪks't∫eɪndʒ [eks-], -ɪz, -ɪŋ, -d, -ə*/z; -əbl

exchangeability ɪks,t∫eɪndʒə'bɪlətɪ [eks-, -lɪt-]

exchangee, -s ,ekst∫eɪn'dʒi: [ɪks,t∫-], -z

exchequer, -s ɪks't∫ekə* [eks-], -z

excisable ek'saɪzəbl [ɪk-]

excise (s.) (tax), -man, -men 'eksaɪz [ɪk's-, ek'saɪz], -mæn, -men

excis|e (v.) (cut out), -es, -ing, -ed ek'saɪz [ɪk-], -ɪz, -ɪŋ, -d

excision, -s ek'sɪʒn [ɪk-], -z

excitability ɪk,saɪtə'bɪlətɪ [ek-, -lɪt-]

excitant, -s 'eksɪtənt [ɪk'saɪtənt], -s

excitation, -s ,eksɪ'teɪ∫n, -z

excitat|ive, -ory ek'saɪtət|ɪv [ɪk-], -ərɪ

excit|e, -es, -ing, -ed, -er/s, -ement/s; -able/ness ɪk'saɪt [ek-], -s, -ɪŋ, -ɪd, -ə*/z, -mənt/s; -əbl/nɪs [-nəs]

exclaim, -s, -ing, -ed ɪk'skleɪm [ek's-], -z, -ɪŋ, -d

exclamation, -s ,eksklə'meɪ∫n, -z

exclamatory ek'sklæmətərɪ [ɪk's-]

exclud|e, -es, -ing, -ed ɪk'sklu:d [ek's-], -z, -ɪŋ, -ɪd

exclusion, -s ɪk'sklu:ʒn [ek's-], -z

exclusionist, -s ɪk'sklu:ʒənɪst [ek's-, -ʒnɪst], -s

exclusive, -ly, -ness ɪk'sklu:sɪv [ek's-], -lɪ, -nɪs [-nəs]

excogitat|e, -es, -ing, -ed eks'kɒdʒɪteɪt [ɪks-], -s, -ɪŋ, -ɪd

excogitation, -s eks,kɒdʒɪ'teɪ∫n [ɪks,kɒdʒ-, ,ekskɒdʒ-], -z

excommunicat|e, -es, -ing, -ed ,ekskə-'mju:nɪkeɪt, -s, -ɪŋ, -ɪd

excommunication, -s 'ekskə,mju:nɪ-'keɪ∫n [-,mjʊn-], -z

excoriat|e, -es, -ing, -ed eks'kɔ:rɪeɪt [ɪks-, -'kɒr-], -s, -ɪŋ, -ɪd

excoriation, -s eks,kɔ:rɪ'eɪ∫n [ɪks-, -,kɒr-], -z

excrement, -s 'ekskrɪmənt [-krəm-], -s

excremental ,ekskrɪ'mentl [-krə'm-]

excrementitious ,ekskrɪmen'tɪ∫əs [-krəm-]

excrescen|ce, -ces, -t ɪk'skresn|s [ek's-], -sɪz, -t

excret|e, -es, -ing, -ed; -ive, -ory ek'skri:t [ɪk's-], -s, -ɪŋ, -ɪd; -ɪv, -ərɪ

excretion, -s ek'skri:∫n [ɪk's-], -z

excret|um, -a ɪk'skri:t|əm [ek's-], -ə

excruciat|e, -es, -ing/ly, -ed ɪk'skru:-∫ɪeɪt [ek's-, -∫jeɪt], -s, -ɪŋ/lɪ, -ɪd

excruciation ɪk,skru:∫ɪ'eɪ∫n [ek,s-, -u:sɪ-]

exculpat|e, -es, -ing, -ed 'ekskʌlpeɪt, -s, -ɪŋ, -ɪd

exculpation ,ekskʌl'peɪ∫n

exculpatory eks'kʌlpətərɪ ['ekskʌl-peɪtərɪ]

excurs|e, -es, -ing, -ed ɪk'skɜ:s [ek's-], -ɪz, -ɪŋ, -t

excursion, -s ɪk'skɜ:∫n [ek's-], -z

excursionist, -s ɪk'skɜ:∫nɪst [ek's-, -∫ənɪst], -s

excursioniz|e [-is|e], -es, -ing, -ed ɪk'skɜ:∫naɪz [ek's-, -∫ənaɪz], -ɪz, -ɪŋ, -d

excursive, -ly, -ness ek'skɜ:sɪv [ɪk's-], -lɪ, -nɪs [-nəs]

excursus, -es ek'skɜ:səs [ɪk's-], -ɪz

excusab|le, -ly, -leness ɪk'skju:zəb|l [ek's-], -lɪ, -lnɪs [-nəs]

excusatory ɪk'skju:zətərɪ [ek's-]

excuse (s.), -s ɪk'skju:s [ek's-], -ɪz

excus|e (v.), -es, -ing, -ed ɪk'skju:z [ek's-], -ɪz, -ɪŋ, -d

Exe eks

exeat, -s 'eksɪæt [-sjæt], -s

execrab|le, -ly, -leness 'eksɪkrəb|l, -lɪ, -lnɪs [-nəs]

execrat|e, -es, -ing, -ed 'eksɪkreɪt, -s, -ɪŋ, -ɪd

execration, -s ,eksɪ'kreɪ∫n, -z

execrat|ive, -ively, -ory 'eksɪkreɪt|ɪv, -ɪvlɪ, -ərɪ

executant, -s ɪg'zekjʊtənt ['eg-], -s

execut|e, -es, -ing, -ed, -er/s; -able 'eksɪkju:t, -s, -ɪŋ, -ɪd, -ə*/z; -əbl

execution, -s ,eksɪ'kju:∫n, -z

executioner, -s ,eksɪ'kju:∫nə* [-∫nə*, -∫ənə*], -z

executive (s. adj.), -s, -ly ɪg'zekjʊtɪv [eg-], -z, -lɪ

executor, -s; -ship/s ɪg'zekjʊtə* [eg-], -z; -∫ɪp/s

executory ɪg'zekjʊtərɪ [eg-]

executrix, -es ɪg'zekjʊtrɪks [eg-], -ɪz

exegesis ,eksɪ'dʒi:sɪs

exegetic, -al, -ally, -s ,eksɪ'dʒetɪk, -l, -əlɪ, -s

Exell 'eksl

exemplar, -s ɪg'zemplə* [eg-, -la:*], -z

exemplarity ,egzem'plærətɪ [-rɪtɪ]

exemplar|y, -ily, -iness ɪg'zemplər|ɪ [eg-], -əlɪ [-ɪlɪ], -ɪnɪs [-nəs]

exemplification, -s ɪg,zemplɪfɪ'keɪ∫n [eg-], -z

exempli|fy, -fies, -fying, -fied ɪg'zem-plɪ|faɪ [eg-], -faɪz, -faɪɪŋ, -faɪd

exempt (*adj. v.*), **-s, -ing, -ed** ɪɡˈzempt
[eg-], -s, -ɪŋ, -ɪd

exemption, -s ɪɡˈzempʃn [eg-], -z

exequatur, -s ˌeksɪˈkweɪtə*, -z

exequies ˈeksɪkwɪz

exercis|e (*s. v.*), **-es, -ing, -ed, -er/s**
ˈeksəsaɪz, -ɪz, -ɪŋ, -d, -ə*/z

exercitation eɡˌzɜːsɪˈteɪʃn [ɪɡ-]

exergue, -s ekˈsɜːɡ [ˈeksɜːɡ], -z

exert, -s, -ing, -ed; -ive ɪɡˈzɜːt [eg-], -s,
-ɪŋ, -ɪd; -ɪv

exertion, -s ɪɡˈzɜːʃn [eg-], -z

exes ˈeksɪz

Exeter ˈeksɪtə* [-sətə*]

exeunt ˈeksɪʌnt [-sjʌnt, -sɪʊnt, -sɪənt,
-sjənt]

exfoliat|e, -es, -ing, -ed eksˈfəʊlɪeɪt
[-ljeɪt], -s, -ɪŋ, -ɪd

exfoliation, -s eksˌfəʊlɪˈeɪʃn [ˌeksfəʊ-],
-z

exhalant eksˈheɪlənt [eɡˈzeɪ-]

exhalation, -s ˌekshəˈleɪʃn [ˌeɡzəˈl-],
-z

exhal|e, -es, -ing, -ed eksˈheɪl [eɡˈzeɪl],
-z, -ɪŋ, -d

exhaust (*s. v.*), **-s, -ing, -ed, -er/s; -ible,
-less** ɪɡˈzɔːst [eg-], -s, -ɪŋ, -ɪd, -ə*/z;
-əbl [-ɪbl], -lɪs [-ləs]

exhaustion ɪɡˈzɔːstʃən [eg-]

exhaustive, -ly, -ness ɪɡˈzɔːstɪv [eg-],
-lɪ, -nɪs [-nəs]

exhaust-pipe, -s ɪɡˈzɔːstpaɪp [eg-], -s

exhibit (*s.*), **-s** ɪɡˈzɪbɪt [eɡˈzɪb-, ˈeɡzɪb-],
-s

exhibit (*u.*), **-s, -ing, -ed, -or/s; -ive,
-ory** ɪɡˈzɪbɪt [eg-], -s, -ɪŋ, -ɪd, -ə*/z;
-ɪv, -ərɪ

exhibitioner, -s ˌeksɪˈbɪʃn, -z

exhibitioner, -s ˌeksɪˈbɪʃnə* [-ʃənə*,
-ʃnə*], -z

exhibitionism ˌeksɪˈbɪʃnɪzəm [-ʃənɪ-]

exhilarant, -s ɪɡˈzɪlərənt [eɡˈz-, ekˈs-],
-s

exhilarat|e, -es, -ing, -ed ɪɡˈzɪləreɪt
[eɡˈz-, ekˈs-], -s, -ɪŋ, -ɪd

exhilaration ɪɡˌzɪləˈreɪʃn [eɡˌz-, ekˌs-]

exhilarative ɪɡˈzɪlərətɪv [eɡˈz-, ekˈs-,
-reɪt-]

exhort, -s, -ing, -ed ɪɡˈzɔːt [eg-], -s, -ɪŋ,
-ɪd

exhortation, -s ˌeɡzɔːˈteɪʃn [ˌeksɔː-],
-z

exhortat|ive, -ory ɪɡˈzɔːtətɪv [eg-], -ərɪ

exhumation, -s ˌekshjuːˈmeɪʃn, -z

exhum|e, -es, -ing, -ed, -er/s eks-
ˈhjuːm [ɪɡˈzjuːm], -z, -ɪŋ, -d, -ə*/z

exigen|ce, -ces -t ˈeksɪdʒən|s [ˈeɡzɪ-],
-sɪz, -t

exigenc|y, -ies ˈeksɪdʒəns|ɪ [ˈeɡzɪdʒ-,
ɪɡˈzɪdʒ-, eɡˈzɪdʒ-, ekˈsɪdʒ-], -ɪz
Note.—The form ɪɡˈzɪdʒənsɪ *is increasingly common.*

exiguity ˌeksɪˈɡjuːətɪ [-ˈɡjʊɪ-, -ɪtɪ]

exiguous, -ness eɡˈzɪɡjʊəs [ɪɡˈz-, ekˈs-,
-ɡjwəs], -nɪs [-nəs]

exil|e (*s. v.*), **-es, -ing, -ed** ˈeksaɪl
[ˈeɡz-], -z, -ɪŋ, -d

exilic eɡˈzɪlɪk [ekˈs-]

exility eɡˈzɪlətɪ [ekˈs-, -ɪtɪ]

exist, -s, -ing, -ed ɪɡˈzɪst [eg-], -s, -ɪŋ,
-ɪd

existen|ce, -ces, -t ɪɡˈzɪstən|s [eg-],
-sɪz, -t

existential ˌeɡzɪˈstenʃl

existentiali|sm, -st/s ˌeɡzɪˈstenʃəɪr|zəm
[-ʃɪ-], -st/s

exit, -s ˈeksɪt [ˈeɡzɪt], -s

ex-libris eksˈlaɪbrɪs [-ˈlɪb-]

Exmoor ˈeksˌmʊə* [-mɔə*, -mɔː*]

Exmouth (*in Devon*) ˈeksmaʊθ [-məθ],
(*in Australia*) ˈeksmaʊθ
*Note.—Both pronunciations are heard
locally at Exmouth in Devon.*

exode, -s ˈeksəʊd, -z

exodus (E.), -es ˈeksədəs, -ɪz

ex officio ˌeksəˈfɪʃɪəʊ [-sɒˈf-, -ʃjəʊ,
-ɪsɪəʊ, -ɪsjəʊ]

exogam|ous, -y ekˈsɒɡəm|əs, -ɪ

exon, -s ˈeksɒn, -z

exonerat|e, -es, -ing, -ed ɪɡˈzɒnəreɪt
[eg-], -s, -ɪŋ, -ɪd

exoneration ɪɡˌzɒnəˈreɪʃn [eg-]

exonerative ɪɡˈzɒnərətɪv [eg-, -reɪt-]

exorbitan|ce, -cy, -t/ly ɪɡˈzɔːbɪtən|s
[eg-], -sɪ, -t/lɪ

exorcis|e, -es, -ing, -ed ˈeksɔːsaɪz [ˈeɡz-,
-səsaɪz], -ɪz, -ɪŋ, -d

exorci|sm, -st/s ˈeksɔːsɪ|zəm [ˈeɡz-,
-səsɪ|zəm], -st/s

exordium, -s ekˈsɔːdjəm [eɡˈz-, -dɪəm], -z

exoteric (*s. adj.*), **-s, -al, -ally** ˌeksəʊ-
ˈterɪk, -s, -l, -əlɪ

exotic (*s. adj.*), **-s** ɪɡˈzɒtɪk [ekˈs-, eɡˈz-],
-s

expand, -s, -ing, -ed, -er/s ɪkˈspænd
[ekˈs-], -z, -ɪŋ, -ɪd, -ə*/z

expanse, -s ɪkˈspæns [ekˈs-], -ɪz

expansibility ɪkˌspænsəˈbɪlətɪ [ekˌsp-,
-sɪˈb-, -lɪt-]

expansib|le, -ly, -leness ɪkˈspænsəb|l
[ekˈs-, -sɪb-], -lɪ, -lnɪs [-nəs]

expansile ɪkˈspænsaɪl [ekˈs-]

expansion, -s ɪkˈspænʃn [ekˈs-], -z

expansioni|sm, -st/s ɪkˈspænʃənɪ|zəm
[ekˈs-, -ʃn̩-], -st/s

expansive, -ly, -ness ɪk'spænsɪv [ek's-],
-lɪ, -nɪs [-nəs]

ex parte ˌeks'pɑːtɪ

expatiat|e, -es, -ing, -ed ek'speɪʃɪeɪt
[ɪk's-, -ʃjeɪt], -s, -ɪŋ, -ɪd

expatiation, -s ek,speɪʃɪ'eɪʃn [ɪk,s-], -z

expatiat|ive, -ory ek'speɪʃjət|ɪv [ɪk's-,
-ʃɪət-, -ʃɪeɪt-], -ərɪ

expatriate (s. adj.), -s eks'pætrɪət [ɪks-,
-'peɪt-, -ɪɪt, -ɪeɪt], -s

expatriat|e (v), -es, -ing, -ed eks'pætrɪeɪt
[ɪks-, -'peɪt-], -s, -ɪŋ, -ɪd

expatriation eks,pætrɪ'eɪʃn [ɪks,pæt-,
-,peɪt-, ,ekspeɪt-, ,ekspæt-]

expect, -s, -ing, -ed, -er/s ɪk'spekt
[ek's-], -s, -ɪŋ, -ɪd, -ə*/z

expectan|ce, -cy, -cies, -t/ly ɪk'spek-
tən|s [ek's-], -sɪ, -sɪz, -t/lɪ

expectation, -s ˌekspek'teɪʃn, -z

expectorant (s. adj.), -s ek'spektərənt
[ɪk's-], -s

expectorat|e, -es, -ing, -ed ek'spektəreɪt
[ɪk's-], -s, -ɪŋ, -ɪd

expectoration ek,spektə'reɪʃn [ɪk,s-]

expedien|ce, -cy, -t/s, -tly ɪk'spiːdjən|s
[ek's-, -dɪən-], -sɪ, -t/s, -tlɪ

expedit|e, -es, -ing, -ed 'ekspɪdaɪt
[-pəd-, -ped-], -s, -ɪŋ, -ɪd

expedition, -s ˌekspɪ'dɪʃn [-pə'd-], -z

expeditionary ˌekspɪ'dɪʃənərɪ [-pə'd-]

expeditious, -ly, -ness ˌekspɪ'dɪʃəs
[-pə'd-], -lɪ, -nɪs [-nəs]

expel, -s, -ling, -led; -lable ɪk'spel
[ek's-], -z, -ɪŋ, -d; -əbl

expend, -s, -ing, -ed ɪk'spend [ek's-], -z,
-ɪŋ, -ɪd

expendable (s. adj.), -s ɪk'spendəbl
[ek's-], -z

expenditure, -s ɪk'spendɪtʃə* [ek's-], -z

expense, -s ɪk'spens [ek's-], -ɪz

expensive, -ly, -ness ɪk'spensɪv [ek's-],
-lɪ, -nɪs [-nəs]

experienc|e (s. v.), -es, -ing, -ed ɪk'spɪə-
rɪəns [ek's-], -ɪz, -ɪŋ, -t

experiment (s.), -s ɪk'sperɪmənt [ek's-],
-s

experiment (v.), -s, -ing, -ed ɪk'sperɪ-
ment [ek's-], -s, -ɪŋ, -ɪd

experiment|al, -ally ek,sperɪ'ment|l
[ɪk,sper-, ,eksper-], -əlɪ [-lɪ]

experimentali|sm, -st/s ek,sperɪ'men-
təlɪ|zəm [ɪk,sper-, ,eksper-, -t|ɪ-],
-st/s

experimentaliz|e [-is|e], -es, -ing, -ed
ek,sperɪ'mentəlaɪz [ɪk,sper-,
,eksper-, -t|aɪ-], -ɪz, -ɪŋ, -d

experimentation, -s ek,sperɪmen'teɪʃn
[ɪk,s-], -z

expert (s.), -s 'ekspəːt, -s

expert (adj.), -est, -ly, -ness 'ekspəːt
[also ek'spəːt, ɪk'spəːt, when not
attributive], -ɪst, -lɪ, -nɪs [-nəs]

expertise ,ekspəː'tiːz [-pə't-]

expiable 'ekspɪəbl [-pjə-]

expiat|e, -es, -ing, -ed, -or/s 'ekspɪeɪt
[-pjeɪt], -s, -ɪŋ, -ɪd, -ə*/z

expiation, -s ,ekspɪ'eɪʃn, -z

expiatory 'ekspɪətərɪ [-pjət-, -pɪeɪt-]

expiration, -s ,ekspɪ'reɪʃn [-pə'r-,
-paɪə'r-], -z

expiratory ɪk'spaɪərətərɪ [ek's-]

expir|e, -es, -ing, -ed ɪk'spaɪə* [ek's-],
-z, -rɪŋ, -d

expiry ɪk'spaɪərɪ [ek's-]

explain, -s, -ing, -ed, -er/s; -able
ɪk'spleɪn [ek's-], -z, -ɪŋ, -d, -ə*/z;
-əbl

explanation, -s ,eksplə'neɪʃn, -z

explanator|y, -ily, -iness ɪk'splænətər|ɪ
[ek's-, -nɪt-], -əlɪ [-ɪlɪ], -mɪs [-məs]

expletive (s. adj.), -s, -ly ek'spliːtɪv
[ɪk's-], -z, -lɪ

explicable ɪk'splɪkəbl ['eksplɪkəbl]
*Note.—The form with the stress on the
second syllable has generally super-
seded that with the stress on the
first.*

explicat|e, -es, -ing, -ed 'eksplɪkeɪt, -s,
-ɪŋ, -ɪd

explication, -s ,eksplɪ'keɪʃn, -z

explicative ek'splɪkətɪv [ɪk's-, 'eksplɪ-
keɪtɪv]

explicatory ek'splɪkətərɪ [ɪk's-, 'eksplɪ-
keɪtərɪ, ,eksplɪ'keɪt-]

explicit, -ly, -ness ɪk'splɪsɪt [ek's-], -lɪ,
-nɪs [-nəs]

explod|e, -es, -ing, -ed, -er/s ɪk'spləud
[ek's-], -z, -ɪŋ, -ɪd, -ə*/z

exploit (s.), -s 'eksplɔɪt, -s

exploit (v.), -s, -ing, -ed ɪk'splɔɪt [ek's-],
-s, -ɪŋ, -ɪd

exploitation ,eksplɔɪ'teɪʃn

exploration, -s ,eksplə'reɪʃn [-plɔː'r-], -z

explorat|ive, -ory ek'splɒrət|ɪv [ɪk's-,
-'plɔːr-, -'plɔər-], -ərɪ

explor|e, -es, -ing, -ed, -er/s ɪk'splɔː*
[ek's-, -'plɔə*], -z, -rɪŋ, -d, -rə*/z

explosion, -s ɪk'spləuʒn [ek's-], -z

explosive (s. adj.), -s, -ly, -ness ɪk's-
pləusɪv [ek's-, -əuzɪv], -z, -lɪ, -nɪs
[-nəs]

exponent, -s ek'spəunənt [ɪk's-], -s

exponential ,ekspəu'nenʃl

export (s.), -s 'ekspɔːt, -s

export (v.), -s, -ing, -ed, -er/s ek'spɔːt
[ɪk's-, 'ekspɔːt], -s, -ɪŋ, -ɪd, -ə*/z

exportable ek'spɔ:təbl [ɪk's-]
exportation ˌekspɔ:'teɪʃn
exposal, -s ɪk'spəʊzl [ek's-], -z
expos|e, -es, -ing, -ed, -edness, -er/s ɪk'spəʊz [ek's-], -ɪz, -ɪŋ, -d, -dnɪs [-nəs], -ə*/z
exposé, -s ek'spəʊzeɪ (ɛkspoze), -z
exposition, -s ˌekspəʊ'zɪʃn [-pʊ'z-], -z
expositive ek'spɒzɪtɪv [ɪk's-, -zət-]
exposit|or/s, -ory ek'spɒzɪt|ə*/z [ɪk's-], -ərɪ
expostulat|e, -es, -ing, -ed, -or/s ɪk'spɒstjʊleɪt [ek's-, -tʃʊ-], -s, -ɪŋ, -ɪd, -ə*/z
expostulation, -s ɪkˌspɒstjʊ'leɪʃn [ek's-, -tʃʊ-], -z
expostulative ɪk'spɒstjʊlətɪv [ek's-, -tʃʊ-, -leɪt-]
expostulatory ɪk'spɒstjʊlətərɪ [ek's-, -tʃʊ-, -leɪtərɪ]
exposure, -s ɪk'spəʊʒə* [ek's-], -z
expound, -s, -ing, -ed, -er/s ɪk'spaʊnd [ek's-], -z, -ɪŋ, -ɪd, -ə*/z
express (s. adj. v.), -es; -ly, -ness; -ing, -ed ɪk'spres [ek's-, 'ekspres attributively], -ɪz; -lɪ, -nɪs [-nəs]; -ɪŋ, -t
expressible ɪk'spresəbl [ek's-, -sɪb-]
expression, -s ɪk'spreʃn [ek's-], -z
expressional ɪk'spreʃənl [ek's-, -ʃn̩, -ʃnl]
expression|ism, -ist/s ɪk'spreʃŋ|ɪzəm [ek's-, -ʃən-], -ɪst/s
expressionistic ɪkˌspreʃə'nɪstɪk [ekˌs-, -ʃŋ'ɪs-]
expressionless ɪk'spreʃnlɪs [ek's-, -ləs]
expressive, -ly, -ness ɪk'spresɪv [ek's-], -lɪ, -nɪs [-nəs]
express|man, -men ɪk'spres|mæn [ek's-], -men
expropriat|e, -es, -ing, -ed, -or/s eks'prəʊprɪeɪt, -s, -ɪŋ, -ɪd, -ə*/z
expropriation, -s eksˌprəʊprɪ'eɪʃn [ˌeksprəʊ-], -z
expugn, -s, -ing, -ed eks'pju:n [ɪks-], -z, -ɪŋ, -d
expugnable eks'pʌgnəbl [ɪks-]
expulsion, -s ɪk'spʌlʃn [ek's-], -z
expulsive ɪk'spʌlsɪv [ek's-]
expung|e, -es, -ing, -ed ek'spʌndʒ [ɪk's-], -ɪz, -ɪŋ, -d
expurgat|e, -es, -ing, -ed, -or/s 'ekspɜ:geɪt [-pəg-], -s, -ɪŋ, -ɪd, -ə*/z
expurgation, -s ˌekspɜ:'geɪʃn [-spə'g-], -z
expurgatorial ekˌspɜ:gə'tɔ:rɪəl [ˌekspɜ:-]
expurgatory ek'spɜ:gətərɪ

exquisite, -ly, -ness 'ekskwɪzɪt [ek-'skwɪzɪt, ɪk'skwɪzɪt], -lɪ, -nɪs [-nəs]
Note.—The forms ek'skwɪzɪt and ɪk'skwɪzɪt are becoming very common.
exscind, -s, -ing, -ed ek'sɪnd [ɪk-], -z, -ɪŋ, -ɪd
exsect, -s, -ing, -ed ek'sekt [ɪk-], -s, -ɪŋ, -ɪd
exsection, -s ek'sekʃn [ɪk-], -z
ex-service ˌeks'sɜ:vɪs ['eksˌsɜ:vɪs]
exsiccat|e, -es, -ing, -ed, -or/s 'eksɪkeɪt ['ekssɪ-], -s, -ɪŋ, -ɪd, -ə*/z
exsiccation ˌeksɪ'keɪʃn [ˌekssɪ-]
extant ek'stænt [ɪk'st-, 'ekstənt]
extemporaneous, -ly, -ness ekˌstempə'reɪnjəs [ˌekstem-, -pʊ'r-, -nɪəs], -lɪ, -nɪs [-nəs]
extemporary ɪk'stempərərɪ [ek's-]
extempore ek'stempərɪ [ɪk's-]
extemporization [-isa-], -s ekˌstempəraɪ'zeɪʃn [ɪkˌs-, -pʊr-], -z
extemporiz|e [-is|e], -es, -ing, -ed, -er/s ɪk'stempəraɪz [ek's-, -pʊr-], -ɪz, -ɪŋ, -d, -ə*/z
extend, -s, -ing, -ed ɪk'stend [ek's-], -z, -ɪŋ, -ɪd
extensibility ɪkˌstensə'bɪlətɪ [ekˌs-, -sɪ'b-, -lɪt-]
extensible ɪk'stensəbl [ek's-, -sɪb-]
extensile ek'stensaɪl [ɪk's-]
extension, -s ɪk'stenʃn [ek's-], -z
extensive, -ly, -ness ɪk'stensɪv [ek's-], -lɪ, -nɪs [-nəs]
extensor, -s ɪk'stensə* [ek's-], -z
extent, -s ɪk'stent [ek's-], -s
extenuat|e, -es, -ing/ly, -ed ek'stenjʊeɪt [ɪk's-], -s, -ɪŋ/lɪ, -ɪd
extenuation, -s ekˌstenjʊ'eɪʃn [ɪk's-], -z
extenuative ek'stenjʊətɪv [ɪk's-, -jwət-, -jʊeɪt-]
extenuatory ek'stenjʊətərɪ [ɪk's-, -jwət-, -jʊeɪt-]
exterior (s. adj.), -s, -ly ek'stɪərɪə* [ɪk'st-], -z, -lɪ
exteriority ekˌstɪərɪ'ɒrətɪ [ˌekstɪə-, ɪkˌst-, -rɪt-]
exterioriz|e [-is|e], -es, -ing, -ed ek'stɪərɪəraɪz [ɪk's-], -ɪz, -ɪŋ, -d
exterminable ek'stɜ:mɪnəbl [ɪk's-]
exterminat|e, -es, -ing, -ed, -or/s ɪk'stɜ:mɪneɪt [ek's-], -s, -ɪŋ, -ɪd, -ə*/z
extermination, -s ɪkˌstɜ:mɪ'neɪʃn [ekˌs-], -z
exterminative ɪk'stɜ:mɪnətɪv [ek's-, -neɪt-]
exterminatory ɪk'stɜ:mɪnətərɪ [ek's-, -neɪt-]

extern (s. adj.), -s ek'stɜ:n, -z
extern|al (s. adj.), -als, -ally ek'stɜ:n|l
['ekst-, ɪk'st-], -]z, -əlɪ [-lɪ]
Note.—The form 'ekstɜ:nl is chiefly
used attributively, or when the word
is in contrast with **internal**.
externali|sm, -st/s ek'stɜ:nəlɪ|zəm
[-nlɪ-, ɪk'st-], -st/s
externality ˌekstɜ:'nælətɪ [-ɪtɪ]
externalization [-isa-] ek,stɜ:nəlaɪ'zeɪʃn
[ɪk,st-, -n]aɪ-]
externaliz|e [-is|e], -es, -ing, -ed ek-
'stɜ:nəlaɪz [ɪk'st-, -n]aɪz], -ɪz, -ɪŋ, -d
exterritorial 'eks,terɪ'tɔ:rɪəl
extinct ɪk'stɪŋkt [ek's-]
extinction, -s ɪk'stɪŋkʃn [ek's-], -z
extinctive ɪk'stɪŋktɪv [ek's-]
extinguish, -es, -ing, -ed, -er/s, -ment;
-able ɪk'stɪŋgwɪʃ [ek's-], -ɪz, -ɪŋ, -t,
-ə*/z, -mənt; -əbl
extirpat|e, -es, -ing, -ed, -or/s 'eks-
tɜ:peɪt [-təp-], -s, -ɪŋ, -ɪd, -ə*/z
extirpation, -s ˌekstɜ:'peɪʃn [-tə'p-], -z
extol, -s, -ling, -led ɪk'stəʊl [ek's-,
-'tɒl], -z, -ɪŋ, -d
Exton 'ekstən
extort, -s, -ing, -ed, -er/s ɪk'stɔ:t [ek's-],
-s, -ɪŋ, -ɪd, -ə*/z
extortion, -s ɪk'stɔ:ʃn [ek's-], -z
extortionate, -ly ɪk'stɔ:ʃnət [ek's-,
-ʃənət, -ʃnət, -nɪt], -lɪ
extortioner, -s ɪk'stɔ:ʃnə* [ek's-, -ʃənə*,
-ʃnə*], -z
extra (s. adj. adv.), -s 'ekstrə, -z
extract (s.), -s 'ekstrækt, -s
extract (v.), -s, -ing, -ed, -or/s; -able,
-ive ɪk'strækt [ek's-], -s, -ɪŋ, -ɪd,
-ə*/z; -əbl, -ɪv
extraction, -s ɪk'strækʃn [ek's-], -z
extra-curricular ˌekstrəkə'rɪkjələ*
[-kjʊ-]
extradit|e, -es, -ing, -ed; -able 'ekstrə-
daɪt, -s, -ɪŋ, -ɪd; -əbl
extradition, -s ˌekstrə'dɪʃn, -z
extrados, -es eks'treɪdɒs, -ɪz
extrajudici|al, -ally ˌekstrədʒu:'dɪʃ|l
[-dʒʊ-], -əlɪ [-lɪ]
extra-marital ˌekstrə'mærɪtl
extramural ˌekstrə'mjʊərəl [-'mjɔ:ər-,
-'mjɔ:r-]
extraneous, -ly ek'streɪnjəs [-nɪəs], -lɪ
extraordinar|y, -ily, -iness ɪk'strɔ:dnr|ɪ
[ek'strɔ:-, ˌekstrə'ɔ:-, -dɪnər|ɪ,
-dənər|ɪ], -əlɪ [-ɪlɪ], -ɪnɪs [-ɪnəs]
extrapolat|e, -es, -ing, -ed ek'stræpəʊ-
leɪt [ɪk's-], -s, -ɪŋ, -ɪd
extrasensory ˌekstrə'sensərɪ
extraterritorial 'ekstrə,terɪ'tɔ:rɪəl

extravagan|ce, -ces, -t/ly ɪk'strævəgən|s
[ek's-, -vɪg-], -sɪz, -t/lɪ
extravaganza, -s ek,strævə'gænzə
[ɪk,strævə-, ˌekstræv-], -z
extravasat|e, -es, -ing, -ed ek'strævə-
seɪt [ɪk's-], -s, -ɪŋ, -ɪd
extravasation, -s ek,strævə'seɪʃn
[ˌekstræv-], -z
extreme (s. adj.), -s, -st, -ly, -ness
ɪk'stri:m [ek's-], -z, -ɪst, -lɪ, -nɪs
[-nəs]
Note.—Some Catholics pronounce
'ekstri:m in **extreme unction**.
extremi|sm, -st/s ɪk'stri:mɪ|zəm [ek's-],
-st/s
extremit|y, -ies ɪk'stremət|ɪ [ek's-,
-ɪt|ɪ], -ɪz
extricable 'ekstrɪkəbl
extricat|e, -es, -ing, -ed 'ekstrɪkeɪt, -s,
-ɪŋ, -ɪd
extrication ˌekstrɪ'keɪʃn
extrinsic, -al, -ally ek'strɪnsɪk, -l, -əlɪ
extroversion ˌekstrəʊ'vɜ:ʃn
extrovert, -s 'ekstrəʊvɜ:t, -s
extrud|e, -s, -ing, -ed ek'stru:d [ɪk's-],
-z, -ɪŋ, -ɪd
extrusion, -s ek'stru:ʒn [ɪk's-], -z
extrus|ive, -ory ek'stru:s|ɪv [ɪk's-],
-ərɪ
exuberan|ce, -cy, -t/ly ɪg'zju:bərən|s
[eg-, -'zu:-], -sɪ, -t/lɪ
exuberat|e, -es, -ing, -ed ɪg'zju:bəreɪt
[eg-, -'zu:-], -s, -ɪŋ, -ɪd
exudation, -s ˌeksju:'deɪʃn [ˌegz-], -z
exud|e, -es, -ing, -ed ɪg'zju:d [eg'z-,
ek's-], -z, -ɪŋ, -ɪd
exult, -s, -ing/ly, -ed ɪg'zʌlt [eg-], -s,
-ɪŋ/lɪ, -ɪd
exultan|ce, -cy, -t/ly ɪg'zʌltən|s [eg-],
-sɪ, -t/lɪ
exultation ˌegzʌl'teɪʃn [ˌeks-, -əl-]
exuviae ɪg'zju:vɪi: [eg-, -'zu:-]
exuvial ɪg'zju:vjəl [eg-, -'zu:-, -vɪəl]
exuviat|e, -es, -ing, -ed ɪg'zju:vɪeɪt
[eg-, -'zu:-, -vjeɪt], -s, -ɪŋ, -ɪd
exuviation ɪg,zju:vɪ'eɪʃn [eg-, -,zu:-]
ex voto ˌeks'vəʊtəʊ
Eyam 'i:əm
eyas, -es 'aɪəs, -ɪz
Eyck aɪk
eye (s. v.), -s, -ing, -d aɪ, -z, -ɪŋ, -d
Eye (place) aɪ
eye-ball, -s 'aɪbɔ:l, -z
eye-bath, -s 'aɪbɑ:θ, -s
eyebright 'aɪbraɪt
eyebrow, -s 'aɪbraʊ, -z
eyeglass, -es 'aɪglɑ:s, -ɪz
eye-hole, -s 'aɪhəʊl, -z

eyelash, -es 'aɪlæʃ, -ɪz
eyeless 'aɪlɪs [-ləs]
eyelet, -s 'aɪlɪt [-lət], -s
eye-lid, -s 'aɪlɪd, -z
eyemark, -s 'aɪmɑːk, -s
Eyemouth 'aɪməθ
eye-opener, -s 'aɪˌəʊpnə* [-pn̩ə*], -z
eye-piece, -s 'aɪpiːs, -ɪz
eye-rhyme, -s 'aɪraɪm, -z
eye-shadow 'aɪˌʃædəʊ
eyeshot 'aɪʃɒt
eyesight, -s 'aɪsaɪt, -s
eyesore, -s 'aɪsɔː* [-sɔə*], -z
eye-strain 'aɪstreɪn
eye|-tooth, -teeth 'aɪ|tuːθ, -tiːθ
eyewash 'aɪwɒʃ
eye-water 'aɪˌwɔːtə*

eye-witness, -es ˌaɪ'wɪtnɪs ['-ˌ--, -nəs], -ɪz
Eyles aɪlz
Eynsford 'eɪnsfəd
Eynsham (in Oxfordshire) 'eɪnʃəm [locally 'ensəm]
eyot, -s eɪt ['eɪət], -s
  Note.—The local pronunciation in the Thames valley is eɪt.
eyre (E.) eə*
eyr|ie, -y, -ies 'aɪər|ɪ ['ɪər-, 'eər-], -ɪ, -ɪz
Eyton (in Salop) 'aɪtn, (in Hereford and Worcester) 'eɪtn, (surname) 'aɪtn, 'iːtn
Ezekiel ɪ'ziːkjəl [-kɪəl]
Eziongeber ˌiːzɪɒn'giːbə* [-zɪən-, -zjən-]
Ezra 'ezrə

F

F (*the letter*), -'s ef, -s
fa (*musical note*), -s fɑː, -z
Fabel 'feɪbəl
Faber (*English name*) 'feɪbə*, (*German name*) 'fɑːbə* ('fɑːbər)
Fabian, -s 'feɪbjən [-bɪən], -z
Fa|bius, -bii 'feɪ|bjəs [-bɪəs], -bɪaɪ
fable, -s -d 'feɪbl, -z, -d
fabric, -s 'fæbrɪk, -s
fabricat|e, -es, -ing, -ed, -or/s 'fæbrɪkeɪt, -s, -ɪŋ, -ɪd, -ə*/z
fabrication, -s ˌfæbrɪ'keɪʃn, -z
Fabricius fə'brɪʃɪəs [-ʃjəs, -ʃəs]
fabulist, -s 'fæbjʊlɪst, -s
fabulous, -ly, -ness 'fæbjʊləs, -lɪ, -nɪs [-bjə-, -nəs]
Fabyan 'feɪbjən [-bɪən]
façade, -s fə'sɑːd [fæ'sɑː-], -z
fac|e (*s. v.*), -es, -ing, -ed feɪs, -ɪz, -ɪŋ, -t
face-ache 'feɪseɪk
face-lifting 'feɪsˌlɪftɪŋ
facer, -s 'feɪsə*, -z
facet, -s, -ed 'fæsɪt ['feɪs-, -set], -s, -ɪd
facetiae fə'siːʃɪi [-'ʃjiː]
facetious, -ly, -ness fə'siːʃəs, -lɪ, -nɪs [-nəs]
facia, -s 'feɪʃə, -z
faci|al, -ally 'feɪʃ|l [-ʃjəl, -ʃɪ|əl], -əlɪ
facile 'fæsaɪl [-sɪl]
facilitat|e, -es, -ing, -ed fə'sɪlɪteɪt [-lət-], -s, -ɪŋ, -ɪd
facilitation fəˌsɪlɪ'teɪʃn [-lə't-]
facilit|y, -ies fə'sɪlət|ɪ [-lɪt-], -ɪz
facing (*s.*), -s 'feɪsɪŋ, -z
facsimile, -s fæk'sɪmɪlɪ [-əlɪ], -z
fact, -s fækt, -s
fact-finding 'fæktˌfaɪndɪŋ
faction, -s 'fækʃn, -z
factional 'fækʃənl [-ʃn̩l, -ʃnl]
factious, -ly, -ness 'fækʃəs, -lɪ, -nɪs [-nəs]
factitious, -ly, -ness fæk'tɪʃəs, -lɪ, -nɪs [-nəs]
factitive 'fæktɪtɪv
factor, -s; -age 'fæktə*, -z; -rɪdʒ
factorial fæk'ɔːrɪəl
factor|y, -ies 'fæktər|ɪ, -ɪz
factotum, -s fæk'təʊtəm, -z

factual 'fæktʃʊəl [-tʃwəl, -tʃʊl, -tjʊəl, -tjwəl, -tjʊl]
facul|a, -ae 'fækjʊl|ə, -iː
facultative 'fækltətɪv [-teɪt-]
facult|y, -ies 'fæklt|ɪ, -ɪz
fad, -s fæd, -z
Faddiley 'fædɪlɪ
faddi|sh, -sm, -st/s 'fædɪ|ʃ, -zəm, -st/s
Faddle 'fædl
fadd|y, -ier, -iest, -ily, -iness 'fæd|ɪ, -ɪə*, -ɪɪst, -ɪlɪ [-əlɪ], -ɪnɪs [-ɪnəs]
fad|e, -es, -ing, -ed feɪd, -z, -ɪŋ, -ɪd
Fadladeen ˌfædlə'diːn
faeces 'fiːsiːz
Faed feɪd
faerie [-ry] (F.) 'feɪərɪ
Faeroe, -s 'feərəʊ, -z
Faeroese ˌfeərəʊ'iːz
Fafner 'fɑːfnə* ['fæf-] ('fɑːfnər)
fag (*s. v.*), -s, -ging, -ged fæg, -z, -ɪŋ, -d
Fagan 'feɪgən
fag-end, -s ˌfæg'end ['--], -z
Fagg(e) fæg
Faggetter 'fægɪtə*
faggot, -s 'fægət, -s
Fagin 'feɪgɪn
fag-master, -s 'fægˌmɑːstə*, -z
fagott|ist/s, -o/s, -i fə'gɒt|ɪst/s, -əʊ/z, -iː
fah (*note in Tonic Sol-fa*), -s fɑː, -z
Fah|ey, -ie 'feɪ|ɪ, -ɪ
Fahrenheit 'færənhaɪt ['fɑːr-]
Fahy 'fɑːɪ
faience faɪ'ãːns [feɪ-, -'ɔ̃ːns, -'ɑːns] (fajɑ̃ːs)
fail (*s. v.*), -s, -ing/s, -ed feɪl, -z, -ɪŋ/z, -d
faille (*silk material*) feɪl
Failsworth 'feɪlzwɜːθ [-wəθ]
failure, -s 'feɪljə*, -z
fain feɪn
Fainall 'feɪnɔːl
faint (*s. adj. v.*), -s, -ly, -ness; -ing, -ed feɪnt, -s, -lɪ, -nɪs [-nəs]; -ɪŋ, -ɪd
faint-heart, -s 'feɪnthɑːt, -s
faint-hearted, -ly, -ness ˌfeɪnt'hɑːtɪd ['-ˌ--], -lɪ, -nɪs [-nəs]
faintish 'feɪntɪʃ
Fainwell 'feɪnwel [-wəl]

fair (s. adj. adv.) (F.), -s, -er, -est, -ly,
  -ness feə*, -z, -rə*, -rɪst, -lɪ, -nɪs
  [-nəs]
Fairbairn, -s 'feəbeən, -z
Fairbank, -s 'feəbæŋk, -s
Fairbeard 'feə,brəd
Fairbrother 'feə,brʌðə*
Fairburn 'feəbə:n
Fairbury 'feəbərɪ
Fairchild 'feətʃaɪld
Fairclough 'feəklʌf
fair-do ,feə'du:
fair-faced ,feə'feɪst
Fairfax 'feəfæks
Fairfield 'feəfi:ld
Fairford 'feəfəd
fair-haired ,feə'heəd ['--, esp. when
  attributive]
Fairhaven 'feə,heɪvn
Fairholme 'feəhəum
Fairholt 'feəhəult
fairish 'feərɪʃ
Fairlegh 'feəlɪ
Fairleigh 'feəlɪ, -li:
Fairlight 'feəlaɪt
Fairman 'feəmən
fair-minded ,feə'maɪndɪd ['-,--]
Fairmont 'feəmənt [-mɒnt]
Fairmount 'feəmaʊnt
Fairport 'feəpɔ:t
Fairscribe 'feəskraɪb
Fairservice 'feə,sə:vɪs
fair-spoken ,feə'spəukən ['-,--]
Fairview 'feəvju:
fairway, -s 'feəweɪ, -z
fair-weather 'feə,weðə*
Fairweather 'feə,weðə*
fair|y (s. adj.), -ies 'feər|ɪ, -ɪz
fairy|land, -like 'feərɪ|lænd, -laɪk
fairy-ring, -s ,feərɪ'rɪŋ ['---], -z
fairy-tale, -s 'feərɪteɪl, -z
fait accompli ,feɪtə'kɒmpli: [,fet-,
  -'kɔ̃:m-, ,---'-] (fetakɔ̃pli)
faith (F.), -s feɪθ, -s
faith|ful (F.), -fully, -fulness 'feɪθ|fʊl,
  -fʊlɪ [-fəlɪ], -fʊlnɪs [-nəs]
Faithfull 'feɪθfʊl
faith-heal|er/s, -ing 'feɪθ,hi:l|ə*/z, -ɪŋ
faithless, -ly, -ness 'feɪθlɪs [-ləs], -lɪ,
  -nɪs [-nəs]
Faithorne 'feɪθɔ:n
fak|e (s. v.), -es, -ing, -ed, -er/s feɪk, -s,
  -ɪŋ, -t, -ə*/z
Fakenham 'feɪknəm [-knəm]
Fakes feɪks
fakir, -s; -ism 'feɪ,kɪə* ['fæ-, 'fɑ:-,
  fə'kɪə*], -z; -rɪzəm
Fal fæl

fa-la, -s fɑ:'lɑ:, -z
Falaba ,fælə'bɑ:
falcate, -d 'fælkeɪt, -ɪd
falchion, -s 'fɔ:ltʃən, -z
falcon, -s, -er/s 'fɔ:lkən ['fɒlk-, 'fɔ:k-],
  -z, -ə*/z
  Note.—'fɔ:k- is the usual pronuncia-
  tion among those who practise the
  sport of falconry.
Falconbridge 'fɔ:kənbrɪdʒ ['fɔ:lk-,
  'fɒlk-]
Falconer 'fɔ:knə*, 'fɔ:lkənə* ['fɒlk-]
falconry 'fɔ:lkənrɪ ['fɒlk-, 'fɔ:k-] (see
  note to falcon)
Falcy 'fælsɪ, 'fɔ:lsɪ
Falder 'fɔ:ldə* ['fɒl-]
falderal, -s ,fældə'ræl ['---], -z
faldstool, -s 'fɔ:ldstu:l, -z
Falerii fæ'lɪərɪaɪ [fæ'l-, -ri:]
Falernian fə'lə:njən [-nɪən]
Falk fɔ:k
Falkenbridge 'fɔ:kənbrɪdʒ ['fɔ:lk-,
  'fɒlk-]
Falkirk 'fɔ:lkə:k ['fɒlk-]
Falkland (Viscount) 'fɔ:klənd, (place in
  Scotland) 'fɔ:lklənd ['fɒlk-], (islands)
  'fɔ:lklənd ['fɒlk-, 'fɔ:k-]
Falkner 'fɔ:knə*
fall (s. v.), -s, -ing, fell, fallen fɔ:l, -z,
  -ɪŋ, fel, 'fɔ:lən
fallacious, -ly, -ness fə'leɪʃəs, -lɪ, -nɪs
  [-nəs]
fallac|y, -ies 'fæləs|ɪ, -ɪz
fal-lal, -s ,fæ'læl [,fæl'læl], -z
Faller 'fælə*
fallibility ,fæləbɪlətɪ [-lɪ'b-, -lɪt-]
fallib|le, -ly, -leness 'fæləb|l [-lɪb-], -lɪ,
  -nɪs [-nəs]
Fallod|en, -on 'fæləʊd|ən, -ən
Fallopian fə'ləʊpɪən [fæ-, -pjən]
fall-out 'fɔ:laʊt
fallow (s. adj. v.), -s, -ness; -ing, -ed
  'fæləʊ, -z, -nɪs [-nəs]; -ɪŋ, -d
fallow-deer 'fæləʊ,dɪə* [,fæləʊ'd-]
Fallowfield 'fæləʊfi:ld
Fallows 'fæləʊz
Falmouth 'fælməθ
false, -r, -st, -ly, -ness fɔ:ls [fɒls], -ə*,
  -ɪst, -lɪ, -nɪs [-nəs]
falsehood, -s 'fɔ:lshʊd ['fɒls-, -sʊd], -z
falsetto, -s fɔ:l'setəʊ [fɒl-], -z
Falshaw 'fɔ:lʃɔ: ['fɒl-]
falsification, -s ,fɔ:lsɪfɪ'keɪʃn [,fɒls-], -z
falsi|fy -fies, -fying, -fied, -fier/s
  'fɔ:lsɪ|faɪ ['fɒls-], -faɪz, -faɪɪŋ, -faɪd,
  -faɪə*/z
falsit|y, -ies 'fɔ:lsət|ɪ ['fɒls-, -ɪt|ɪ], -ɪz
Falstaff 'fɔ:lstɑ:f ['fɒl-]

Falstaffian fɔ:l'stɑ:fjən [fɒl-, -fɪən]
falt|er (s. v.), **-ers, -ering/ly, -ered, -erer/s** 'fɔ:lt|ə* ['fɒl-], -əz, -ərɪŋ/lɪ, -əd, -ərə*/z
Famagusta ˌfæmə'gʊstə [ˌfɑ:m-]
fame, -d feɪm, -d
familiar (s. adj.), **-s, -ly** fə'mɪljə* [-lɪə*], -z, -lɪ
familiarit|y, -ies fəˌmɪlɪ'ærət|ɪ [-ɪt|ɪ], -ɪz
familiariz|e [-is|e], **-es, -ing, -ed** fə'mɪljəraɪz [-lɪər-], -ɪz, -ɪŋ, -d
famil|y, -ies 'fæməl|ɪ [-mɪl-], -ɪz
famine, -s 'fæmɪn, -z
famish, -es, -ing, -ed 'fæmɪʃ, -ɪz, -ɪŋ, -t
famous, -ly, -ness 'feɪməs, -lɪ, -nɪs [-nəs]
fan (s. v.) (**F.**), **-s, -ning, -ned** fæn, -z, -ɪŋ, -d
fanatic (s. adj.), **-s, -al, -ally** fə'nætɪk [fn̩'æ-], -s, -l, -əlɪ
fanaticism fə'nætɪsɪzəm [fn̩'æ-]
fanaticiz|e [-is|e], **-es, -ing, -ed** fə'nætɪsaɪz [fn̩'æ-], -ɪz, -ɪŋ, -d
fanci|ful, -fully, -fulness 'fænsɪ|fʊl, -fʊlɪ [-fəlɪ], -fʊlnɪs [-nəs]
Fancourt 'fænkɔːt
fanc|y (s. adj. v.), **-ies, -ying, -ied, -er/s** 'fæns|ɪ, -ɪz, -ɪŋ [-jɪŋ], -ɪd, -ɪə*/z [-jə*/z]
fancy-ball, -s ˌfænsɪ'bɔːl, -z
fancy-dress, -es ˌfænsɪ'dres [also '-- when attributive], -ɪz
fancy-free ˌfænsɪ'fri:
fancy-work 'fænsɪwɜːk
fandango, -s fæn'dæŋgəʊ, -z
fane (**F.**), **-s** feɪn, -z
Faneuil 'fænl
fanfare, -s 'fænfeə*, -z
fanfaronade, -s ˌfænfærə'nɑːd [-'neɪd], -z
fang (**F.**), **-s, -ed; -less** fæŋ, -z, -d; -lɪs [-ləs]
Faning 'feɪnɪŋ
fanlight, -s 'fænlaɪt, -s
fanner, -s 'fænə*, -z
Fann|ick, -ing, -y 'fæn|ɪk, -ɪŋ, -ɪ
Fanshawe 'fænʃɔː
fantail, -s 'fænteɪl, -z
fantasia, -s fæn'teɪzjə [-'tɑ:z-, -zɪə, ˌfæntə'zɪə, ˌfæntə'sɪə], -z
fantastic, -al, -ally, -alness fæn'tæstɪk [fən-], -l, -əlɪ, -lnɪs [-nəs]
fantas|y, -ies 'fæntəs|ɪ [-əz|ɪ], -ɪz
fantod, -s 'fæntɒd, -z
far fɑ:*
farad, -s 'færəd, -z
Faraday 'færədɪ [-deɪ]
far-away (adj.) 'fɑ:rəweɪ [ˌ--'-]

farce, -s fɑ:s, -ɪz
farceur, -s fɑ:'sɜ:*, -z
farcic|al, -ally 'fɑ:sɪk|l, -əlɪ
farcy 'fɑ:sɪ
fardel, -s 'fɑ:dl, -z
Fardel 'fɑ:del
far|e (s. v.), **-es, -ing, -ed** feə*, -z, -rɪŋ, -d
Farebrother 'feəˌbrʌðə*
Fareham 'feərəm
farewell, -s ˌfeə'wel ['-- according to sentence-stress], -z
Farewell 'feəwel [-wəl]
far-famed ˌfɑ:'feɪmd [also '-- when attributive]
far-fetched ˌfɑ:'fetʃt [also '-- when attributive]
far-flung ˌfɑ:'flʌŋ [also '-- when attributive]
Farg|o, -us 'fɑ:g|əʊ, -əs
Faribault 'færɪbəʊ
farina fə'raɪnə
Farina fə'ri:nə
farinaceous ˌfærɪ'neɪʃəs
Faring|don, -ton 'færɪŋ|dən, -tən
farinose 'færɪnəʊs
Farjeon 'fɑ:dʒən
Far|leigh, -ley 'fɑ:|lɪ, -lɪ
farm (s. v.), **-s, -ing, -ed, -er/s** fɑ:m, -z, -ɪŋ, -d, -ə*/z
Farm|an, -er 'fɑ:m|ən, -ə*
farmhou|se, -ses 'fɑ:mhaʊ|s, -zɪz
Farmington 'fɑ:mɪŋtən
farmland 'fɑ:mlænd [-lənd]
farmstead, -s 'fɑ:msted, -z
farmyard, -s 'fɑ:mjɑ:d [ˌ-'-], -z
Farnaby 'fɑ:nəbɪ
Farnborough 'fɑ:nbərə
Farn(e) fɑ:n
Farn|ham, -worth 'fɑ:n|əm, -wɜ:θ
faro 'feərəʊ
Faroe 'feərəʊ
faroese ˌfeərəʊ'i:z
farouche fə'ru:ʃ [fɑ:'r-, fæ'r-]
Farquhar 'fɑ:kwə*, 'fɑ:kə*
Farquharson 'fɑ:kəsn, 'fɑ:kwəsn
Farr fɑ:*
farrago, -(e)s fə'rɑ:gəʊ [-'reɪg-], -z
Farragut 'færəgət
Farr|ant, -ar 'fær|ənt, -ə*
Farr|en, -er 'fær|ən, -ə*
far-reaching ˌfɑ:'ri:tʃɪŋ [also '-,-- when attributive]
farrier, -s; -y, -ies 'færɪə*, -z; -rɪ, -rɪz
Farring|don, -ford, -ton 'færɪŋ|dən, -fəd, -tən
farrow (s. v.) (**F.**), **-s, -ing, -ed** 'færəʊ, -z, -ɪŋ, -d

far-seeing ˌfɑːˈsiːɪŋ [ˈ-ˌ--]
far-sighted, -ness ˌfɑːˈsaɪtɪd, -nɪs [-nəs]
Farsley ˈfɑːzlɪ
farth|er, -est ˈfɑːð|ə*, -ɪst
farthing, -s ˈfɑːðɪŋ, -z
farthingale, -s ˈfɑːðɪŋɡeɪl, -z
Farwell ˈfɑːwel [-wəl]
fasces ˈfæsiːz
fascia, -s (name-board, instrument
  board, belt on a planet) ˈfeɪʃə [-ʃjə,
  -ʃɪə], (strip of stone, wood, etc., in
  architecture) ˈfeɪʃə [-ʃjə, -ʃɪə], also
  when referring to classical architecture ˈfeɪsjə], (medical term) ˈfæʃɪə
  [-ʃjə, -ʃə], -z
fasciated ˈfæʃɪeɪtɪd
fascicle, -s ˈfæsɪkl, -z
fascicule, -s ˈfæsɪkjuːl, -z
fascinat|e, -es, -ing/ly, -ed, -or/s ˈfæsɪ-
  neɪt, -s, -ɪŋ/lɪ, -ɪd, -ə*/z
fascination, -s ˌfæsɪˈneɪʃn, -z
fascine, -s fæˈsiːn [fəˈs-], -z
fascism ˈfæʃɪzəm
Fascist, -s ˈfæʃɪst, -s
Fascisti fæˈʃɪstiː [fəˈʃ-]
fash, -es, -ing, -ed fæʃ, -ɪz, -ɪŋ, -t
fashi|on (s. v.), -ons, -oning, -oned,
  -oner/s ˈfæʃ|n, -nz, -ŋɪŋ [-ənɪŋ],
  -nd, -nə*/z [-ənə*/z]
fashionab|le, -ly, -leness ˈfæʃnəb|l
  [-ˌfnə-], -lɪ, -lnɪs [-nəs]
fashion-plate, -s ˈfæʃnpleɪt, -s
Fasolt ˈfɑːzɒlt (ˈfɑːzɔlt)
fast (s. adj. v. adv.), -s, -er, -est, -ness;
  -ing, -ed, -er/s fɑːst, -s, -ə*, -ɪst,
  -nɪs [-nəs]; -ɪŋ, -ɪd, -ə*/z
fast-day, -s ˈfɑːstdeɪ, -z
fast|en, -ens, -ening, -ened ˈfɑːs|n, -nz,
  -nɪŋ [-ŋɪŋ], -nd
fastener, -s ˈfɑːsnə*, -z
fastening (s.) (contrivance for fastening),
  -s ˈfɑːsnɪŋ, -z
fasti (F.) ˈfæstiː [-taɪ]
fastidious, -ly, -ness fəˈstɪdɪəs [fæˈs-,
  -djəs], -lɪ, -nɪs [-nəs]
fastness, -es ˈfɑːstnɪs [-nəs], -ɪz
Fastnet ˈfɑːstnet [-nɪt]
fat (s. adj.), -ter, -test, -ness, -ted fæt,
  -ə*, -ɪst, -nɪs [-nəs], -ɪd
fat|al, -ally ˈfeɪt|l, -əlɪ [-tlɪ]
fatali|sm, -st/s ˈfeɪtəlɪ|zəm [-tlɪ-], -st/s
fatalistic ˌfeɪtəˈlɪstɪk [-tlˈɪ-]
fatalit|y, -ies fəˈtælət|ɪ [feɪˈt-, -ɪt|ɪ], -ɪz
fate (F.), -s, -ed feɪt, -s, -ɪd
fateful ˈfeɪtful
fathead, -s ˈfæthed, -z
fath|er (s. v.), -ers, -ering, -ered
  ˈfɑːð|ə*, -əz, -ərɪŋ, -əd

fatherhood ˈfɑːðəhʊd
father - in - law,   fathers - in - law
  ˈfɑːðərɪnlɔː [-ðəɪn-], ˈfɑːðəzɪnlɔː
fatherland, -s ˈfɑːðəlænd, -z
fatherless ˈfɑːðəlɪs [-ləs, -les]
fatherl|y, -iness ˈfɑːðəl|ɪ, -ɪnɪs [-məs]
fathom (s. v.), -s, -ing, -ed; -able, -less
  ˈfæðəm, -z, -ɪŋ, -d; -əbl, -lɪs [-ləs]
fathom-line, -s ˈfæðəmlaɪn, -z
fatigu|e (s. v.), -es, -ing/ly, -ed fəˈtiːɡ,
  -z, -ɪŋ/lɪ, -d
Fatima ˈfætɪmə
fatling, -s ˈfætlɪŋ, -z
fatt|en, -ens, -ening, -ened, -ener/s
  ˈfæt|n, -nz, -ŋɪŋ [-nɪŋ], -nd, -nə*/z
fattish ˈfætɪʃ
fatt|y (s. adj.), -ies, -ier, -iest, -iness
  ˈfæt|ɪ, -ɪz, -ɪə*, -ɪɪst, -ɪnɪs [-məs]
fatuity fəˈtjuːətɪ [fæˈt-, -ˈtjʊ-, -ɪtɪ]
fatuous, -ly, -ness ˈfætjʊəs [-tjwəs], -lɪ,
  -nɪs [-nəs]
faubourg, -s ˈfəʊˌbʊəɡ [-bɜːɡ] (fobuːr), -z
faucal ˈfɔːkl
fauces ˈfɔːsiːz
faucet, -s ˈfɔːsɪt, -s
Fauc|ett, -it ˈfɔːs|ɪt, -ɪt
Faudel ˈfɔːdl
faugh pφ: [fɔː]
  Note.—This φ is often accompanied
  by vibration of the lips.
Faulconbridge ˈfɔːkənbrɪdʒ [ˈfɔːlk-]
Faulds fəʊldz, fɔːldz
Faulhorn ˈfaʊlhɔːn
Faulk fɔːk
Faulkes fɔːks, fɔːlks
Faulkland ˈfɔːklənd [ˈfɔːlk-]
Faulkner ˈfɔːknə*
Faulks fəʊks
fault, -s fɔːlt [fɒlt], -s
faultfind|er/s,   -ing ˈfɔːltˌfaɪnd|ə*/z
  [ˈfɒlt-], -ɪŋ
faultless, -ly, -ness ˈfɔːltlɪs [ˈfɒlt-, -ləs],
  -lɪ, -nɪs [-nəs]
fault|y, -ier, -iest, -ily, -iness ˈfɔːlt|ɪ
  [ˈfɒlt-], -ɪə* [-jə*], -ɪɪst [-jɪst], -ɪlɪ
  [-əlɪ], -ɪnɪs [-məs]
faun, -s fɔːn, -z
fauna ˈfɔːnə
Faunch fɔːntʃ
Fauntleroy ˈfɔːntlərɔɪ [ˈfɒnt-]
Faust faʊst
Faustina fɔːˈstiːnə
Faustus ˈfɔːstəs
fauteuil, -s ˈfəʊtɜːɪ [fəʊˈtɜːɪ, -ɜːl]
  (fotœːj), -z
Faux fəʊ, fɔːks
faux pas (sing.) ˌfəʊˈpɑː, (plur.)
  ˌfəʊˈpɑːz

185

Favel (*surname*) 'fervəl
Faversham 'fævəʃəm
Favoni|an, -us fə'vəʊnj|ən [fer'v-, -nɪ|ən], -əs
fav|our (*s. v.*), -ours, -ouring, -oured, -ourer/s 'ferv|ə*, -əz, -ərɪŋ, -əd, -ərə*/z
favourab|le, -ly, -leness 'fervərəb|l, -lɪ, -lnɪs [-nəs]
favourit|e, -es; -ism 'fervərɪt, -s; -ɪzəm
favourless 'fervəlɪs [-ləs]
Fawcett 'fɔːsɪt, 'fɒsɪt
Fawkes fɔːks
Fawkner 'fɔːknə*
Fawley 'fɔːlɪ
fawn (*s. adj. v.*), -s, -ing/ly, -ed, -er/s fɔːn, -z, -ɪŋ/lɪ, -d, -ə*/z
Fawssett 'fɔːsɪt
fay (F.), -s fer, -z
Fayette fer'et
Fayette City ˌferet'sɪtɪ
Fayetteville 'feretvɪl
Faygate 'fergert
Faza(c)kerley fə'zækəlɪ
F.B.I. ˌefbiː'aɪ
fe (*name of note in Tonic Sol-fa*), -('s fiː, -z
fe (*syllable used in Tonic Sol-fa for counting a short note off the beat*) *generally* fɪ, *but the first* fe *in the sequence* ta fe tay fe *is sometimes sounded as* fə. See ta.
Feaist fiːst
fealty 'fiːəltɪ
fear (*s. v.*), -s, -ing, -ed fɪə*, -z, -rɪŋ, -d
Fearenside 'fɜːnsaɪd, 'fɪərənsaɪd
fear|ful, -fully, -fulness 'fɪə|fʊl, -fəlɪ [-fʊlɪ], -fʊlnɪs [-nəs]
Feargus 'fɜːgəs
fearless, -ly, -ness 'fɪəlɪs [-ləs], -lɪ, -nɪs [-nəs]
Fearn(e) fɜːn
Fearnside 'fɜːnsaɪd
Fearon 'fɪərən
fearsome, -ly, -ness 'fɪəsəm, -lɪ, -nɪs [-nəs]
feasibility ˌfiːzə'bɪlətɪ [-zɪ'b-, -lɪt-]
feasib|le, -ly, -leness 'fiːzəb|l [-zɪb-], -lɪ, -lnɪs [-nəs]
feast (*s. v.*), -s, -ing, -ed, -er/s fiːst, -s, -ɪŋ, -ɪd, -ə*/z
feat, -s fiːt, -s
feather (*s. v.*), -s, -ing, -ed feðə*, -z, -rɪŋ, -d
feather-bed, -s 'feðəbed [ˌ--'-], -z
feather-brain, -s, -ed 'feðəbreɪn, -z, -d
feather-edge, -s 'feðəredʒ ['feðəedʒ, ˌ--'-], -ɪz

feather-head, -s 'feðəhed, -z
featherstitch (*s. v.*), -es, -ing, -ed 'feðəstɪtʃ, -ɪz, -ɪŋ, -t
Featherston 'feðəstən
Featherstone 'feðəstən [-stəʊn]
Featherstonehaugh 'feðəstənhɔː, 'fænʃɔː ['festənhɔː, 'frəstənhɔː]
featherweight, -s 'feðəweɪt, -s
feather|y, -iness 'feðər|ɪ, -ɪnɪs [-nəs]
Featley 'fiːtlɪ
featly 'fiːtlɪ
featur|e (*s. v.*), -es, -ing, -ed; -eless 'fiːtʃə*, -z, -rɪŋ, -d; -lɪs [-ləs]
febrifuge, -s 'febrɪfjuːdʒ, -ɪz
febrile 'fiːbraɪl
February 'februərɪ [-rər-, -rʊr-, -'feb-jʊərɪ]
fecit 'fiːsɪt ['ferkɪt]
Feckenham 'fekŋəm [-kənəm]
feckless, -ly, -ness 'feklɪs [-ləs], -lɪ, -nɪs [-nəs]
feculen|ce, -t 'fekjʊlən|s, -t
fecund 'fiːkənd ['fek-, -kʌnd]
fecundat|e, -es, -ing, -ed 'fiːkəndert ['fek-, -kʌn-], -s, -ɪŋ, -ɪd
fecundation ˌfiːkən'deɪʃn [ˌfek-, -kʌn-]
fecundity fɪ'kʌndətɪ [fiː'k-, fe'k-, -ɪtɪ]
fed (*from* feed) fed
federal 'fedərəl
federali|sm, -st/s 'fedərəlɪ|zəm, -st/s
federate (*s. adj.*), -s 'fedərət [-rɪt, -rert], -s
federat|e (*v.*), -es, -ing, -ed 'fedərert, -s, -ɪŋ, -ɪd
federation, -s ˌfedə'reɪʃn, -z
federative 'fedərətɪv [-rert-]
fed-up ˌfed'ʌp
fee (*s. v.*), -s, -ing, -d fiː, -z, -ɪŋ, -d
feeb|le, -ler, -lest, -ly, -leness 'fiːb|l, -lə*, -lɪst, -lɪ, -lnɪs [-nəs]
feeble-minded, -ness ˌfiːbl'maɪndɪd ['--,--], -nɪs [-nəs]
feed (*s. v.*), -s, -ing, fed, feeder/s fiːd, -z, -ɪŋ, fed, 'fiːdə*/z
feed-back 'fiːdbæk
feeding-bottle, -s 'fiːdɪŋˌbɒtl, -z
feeding-cup, -s 'fiːdɪŋkʌp, -s
feed-pipe, -s 'fiːdpaɪp, -s
feed-tank, -s 'fiːdtæŋk, -s
fee-fo-fum 'fiːˌfəʊ'fʌm
Feeheny 'fiːnɪ, 'frənɪ
feel (*s. v.*), -s, -ing, felt fiːl, -z, -ɪŋ, felt
feeler, -s 'fiːlə*, -z
feeling (*s. adj.*), -s, -ly 'fiːlɪŋ, -z, -lɪ
fee-simple, -s ˌfiː'sɪmpl, -z
feet (*plur. of* foot) fiːt
fee-tail ˌfiː'teɪl

feign, -s, -ing, -ed, -edly, -edness feɪn,
-z, -ɪŋ, -d, -ɪdlɪ, -ɪdnɪs [-nəs]
Feilden 'fiːldən
Feilding 'fiːldɪŋ
Feiling 'faɪlɪŋ
Feiller 'faɪlə*
feint (s. v.), -s, -ing, -ed feɪnt, -s, -ɪŋ, -ɪd
Feiron 'fɪərən
Feisal 'faɪsl ['feɪs-]
Feist fiːst
feldspar 'feldspɑː* ['felspɑː*]
Felicia fə'lɪsɪə [fe'l-, fɪ'l-, -sjə, -ʃɪə,
-ʃjə]
felicitat|e, -es, -ing, -ed fə'lɪsɪteɪt [fe'l-,
fɪ'l-], -s, -ɪŋ, -ɪd
felicitation, -s fə,lɪsɪ'teɪʃn [fe,l-, fɪ,l-], -z
felicitous, -ly, -ness fə'lɪsɪtəs [fe'l-, fɪ'l-],
-lɪ, -nɪs [-nəs]
felicity (F.) fə'lɪsɪtɪ [fe'l-, fɪ'l-, -ɪtɪ]
feline (s. adj.), -s 'fiːlaɪn, -z
felinity fɪ'lɪnɪtɪ [fiː'l-, fə'l-, -ɪtɪ]
Felix, -stowe 'fiːlɪks, -təʊ
Felkin 'felkɪn
fell (s. adj. v.) (F.), -s, -ing, -ed, -er/s
fel, -z, -ɪŋ, -d, -ə*/z
fell (from fall) fel
fellah, -s -een 'felə, -z, -hiːn [,felə'hiːn]
Felling 'felɪŋ
felloe, -s 'feləʊ, -z
fellow, -s 'feləʊ [colloquially also 'felə
in sense of ' person'], -z
fellow|-citizen/s, -creature/s ,feləʊ|-
'sɪtɪzn/z, -'kriːtʃə*/z
Fellowes 'feləʊz
fellow-feeling ,feləʊ'fiːlɪŋ
fellow|-man, -men ,feləʊ|'mæn, -'men
Fellows 'feləʊz
fellowship, -s 'feləʊʃɪp, -s
fellow-traveller, -s ,feləʊ'trævələ*
[-vlə*], -z
Felltham 'felθəm
fell|y, -ies 'fel|ɪ, -ɪz
felo de se ,fiːləʊdiː'siː [,fe-, -'seɪ]
felon, -s 'felən, -z
felonious, -ly, -ness fə'ləʊnjəs [fe'l-,
fɪ'l-, -nɪəs], -lɪ, -nɪs [-nəs]
felon|y, -ies 'felən|ɪ, -ɪz
Felpham 'felpəm
felspar 'felspɑː*
Felste(a)d 'felstɪd [-ted]
felt (s.), -s felt, -s
felt (from feel) felt
Feltham (place) 'feltəm, (personal
name) 'felθəm
felting, -s 'feltɪŋ, -z
Felton 'feltən
felucca, -s fe'lʌkə [fɪ'l-], -z
female (s. adj.), -s 'fiːmeɪl, -z

feme, -s fiːm, -z
feminine, -ly, -ness 'femɪnɪn [-mənɪm],
-lɪ, -nɪs [-nəs]
femininit|y, -ies ,femɪ'nɪnɪt|ɪ [-mə'n-,
-ɪt|ɪ], -ɪz
femini|sm, -st/s 'femɪnɪ|zəm [-mən-],
-st/s
feminiz|e [-is|e], -es, -ing, -ed 'femɪnaɪz
[-mən-] -ɪz, -ɪŋ, -d
femora (alternative plur. of femur)
'femərə ['fiːm-]
femoral 'femərəl
femur, -s 'fiːmə*, -z
fen, -s (F.) fen, -z
fenc|e (s. v.), -es, -ing, -ed, -er/s;
-eless fens, -ɪz, -ɪŋ, -t, -ə*/z; -lɪs [-ləs]
Fenchurch 'fentʃɜːtʃ
fend, -s, -ing, -ed fend, -z, -ɪŋ, -ɪd
fender, -s 'fendə*, -z
Fenella fɪ'nelə [fə'n-]
fenestr|a, -al fɪ'nestr|ə [fə'n-], -əl
fenestrat|e, -es, -ing, -ed fɪ'nestreɪt
[fə-], -s, -ɪŋ, -ɪd
fenestration, -s ,fenɪ'streɪʃn [-nə's-], -z
Fenham 'fenəm
Fenian, -s; -ism 'fiːnjən [-nɪən], -z;
-ɪzəm
Fenimore 'fenɪmɔː* [-mɔə*]
Fenn fen
fennel 'fenl
Fennell 'fenl
Fennessy 'fenɪsɪ [-nəs-]
Fennimore 'fenɪmɔː* [-mɔə*]
fenny (F.) 'fenɪ
Fenton 'fentən
Fenwick (English surname) 'fenɪk
[-wɪk] (American surname) 'fenwɪk,
(places in Great Britain) 'fenɪk
Feodor 'fiːəʊdɔː* ['fɪ-]
Feodora ,fiːəʊ'dɔːrə [,fɪ-]
feoff (v.), -s, -ing, -ed, -er/s, -ment/s
fef [fiːf], -s, -ɪŋ, -t, -ə*/z, -mənt/s
feoffee, -s fe'fiː [fiː'fiː], -z
feoffor, -s fe'fɔː* [fiː'fɔː*], -z
feral 'fɪərəl ['fer-]
Feramors 'ferəmɔːz
Ferdinand 'fɜːdɪnænd [-dnənd]
feretor|y, -ies 'ferɪtər|ɪ, -ɪz
Fergus, -(s)on 'fɜːgəs, -n
ferial 'fɪərɪəl ['fer-]
ferine 'fɪəraɪn
Feringhee, -s fə'rɪŋgɪ, -z
Fermanagh fə'mænə [fɑː-]
ferment (s.), -s 'fɜːment, -s
ferment (v.), -s, -ing, -ed; -able
fə'ment [fɑː-], -s, -ɪŋ, -ɪd; -əbl
fermentation, -s ,fɜːmen'teɪʃn [-mən-],
-z

187

fermentative, -ly, -ness fə'mentətɪv, -lɪ, -nɪs [-nəs]

Fermor 'fɜːmɔː*

Fermoy (near Cork) fɜː'mɔɪ, (street in London) 'fɜːmɔɪ

fern (F.), -s fɜːn, -z

Fernandez (Spanish navigator) fɜː'nændez [fə'n-], see also Juan F.

ferner|y, -ies 'fɜːnər|ɪ, -ɪz

Fernhough 'fɜːnhəʊ

Fernihough [-nyh-] 'fɜːnɪhʌf, -həʊ

ferny 'fɜːnɪ

ferocious, -ly, -ness fə'rəʊʃəs [fɪ'r-, fe'r-], -lɪ, -nɪs [-nəs]

ferocity fə'rɒsətɪ [fɪ'r-, fe'r-, -ɪtɪ]

Ferrand 'ferənd

Ferranti fə'ræntɪ [fɪ-, fe-]

Ferrar 'ferə*

ferrel (F.), -s 'ferəl, -z

ferreous 'ferɪəs

Ferrer, -s 'ferə*, -z

ferret (s. v.) (F.), -s, -ing, -ed 'ferɪt [-rət], -s, -ɪŋ, -ɪd

ferric 'ferɪk

Ferrier 'ferɪə*

Ferris, -burg 'ferɪs, -bɜːg

ferro-concrete ˌferəʊ'kɒŋkriːt [-'kɒnk-]

ferrotype, -s 'ferəʊtaɪp, -s

ferrous 'ferəs

ferruginous fe'ruːdʒɪnəs [fə'r-]

ferrule, -s 'feruːl [-rəl], -z

Note.—'ferəl *is the pronunciation used by those connected with the umbrella trade.*

ferr|y (s. v.) (F.), -ies, -ying, -ied 'fer|ɪ, -ɪz, -ɪɪŋ, -ɪd

ferry-boat, -s 'ferɪbəʊt, -s

ferry|man, -men 'ferɪ|mən [-mæn], -mən [-men]

fertile, -ly 'fɜːtaɪl, -lɪ

fertility fə'tɪlətɪ [-ɪtɪ]

fertilization [-isa-] ˌfɜːtɪlaɪ'zeɪʃn [-təl-, -lɪ'z-]

fertiliz|e [-is|e], -es, -ing, -ed, -er/s 'fɜːtɪlaɪz [-təl-], -ɪz, -ɪŋ, -d, -ə*/z

ferule, -s 'feruːl, -z

ferven|cy, -t/ly, -tness 'fɜːvən|sɪ, -t/lɪ, -tnɪs [-nəs]

fervid, -ly, -ness 'fɜːvɪd, -lɪ, -nɪs [-nəs]

fervour 'fɜːvə*

fescue, -s 'feskjuː, -z

fesse, -s fes, -ɪz

Fessenden 'fesndən

fest|al, -ally 'fest|l, -əlɪ

fest|er (s. v.), -ers, -ering, -ered 'fest|ə*, -əz, -ərɪŋ, -əd

Festiniog fe'stɪnɪɒg (Welsh fes'tinjog)

festival, -s 'festəvl [-tɪv-], -z

festive, -ly, -ness 'festɪv, -lɪ, -nɪs [-nəs]

festivit|y, -ies fe'stɪvət|ɪ [-ɪt|ɪ], -ɪz

festoon (s. v.), -s, -ing, -ed fe'stuːn, -z, -ɪŋ, -d

Festus 'festəs

fetch (s. v.), -es, -ing, -ed, -er/s fetʃ, -ɪz, -t, -ə*/z

fête, -s; -day/s feɪt, -s; -deɪ/z

fetid, -ly, -ness 'fetɪd ['fiːtɪd], -lɪ, -nɪs [-nəs]

fetish, -es; -ism 'fiːtɪʃ ['fetɪʃ], -ɪz; -ɪzəm

fetlock, -s, -ed 'fetlɒk, -s, -t

fetter (s. v.) (F.), -s, -ing, -ed 'fetə*, -z, -rɪŋ, -d

Fettes (place) 'fetɪs, (surname) 'fetɪs, 'fetɪz

Fettesian, -s fe'tiːzjən [-zɪən], -z

fett|le (s. v.), -les, -ling, -led 'fet|l, -lz, -lɪŋ, -ld

feu (s. v.), -s, -ing, -ed fjuː, -z, -ɪŋ ['fjʊɪŋ], -d

feud, -s; -al fjuːd, -z; -l

feudali|sm, -st/s 'fjuːdəlɪ|zəm [-dlɪ-], -st/s

feudality fjuː'dælətɪ [-rtɪ]

feudalization [-isa-] ˌfjuːdəlaɪ'zeɪʃn [-dlaɪ'z-, -dəlɪ'z-, -dlɪ'z-]

feudaliz|e [-is|e], -es, -ing, -ed 'fjuːdəlaɪz [-dlaɪz], -ɪz, -ɪŋ, -d

feudatory 'fjuːdətərɪ

feuilleton, -s 'fɜːrtɔ̃ːŋ ['fɜːlt-, -tɒŋ] (fœjtɔ̃), -z

fever, -s, -ed 'fiːvə*, -z, -d

fever-heat 'fiːvəhiːt

feverish, -ly, -ness 'fiːvərɪʃ, -lɪ, -nɪs [-nəs]

Feversham 'fevəʃəm

few, -er, -est, -ness fjuː, -ə* [fjʊə*], -ɪst ['fjʊɪst], -nɪs [-nəs]

fey feɪ

fez (F.), -es fez, -ɪz

Fezzan fe'zɑːn ['fezæn]

Ffitch fɪtʃ

Ffolliot 'fɒljət [-lɪət]

Ffoulkes fəʊks, fəʊlks, fauks, fuːks

Ffrangcon 'fræŋkən

fiancé(e), -s fɪ'ɑ̃ːŋseɪ [fɪ'ɔ̃ːŋs-, fɪ'ɑːns-, fɪ'ɒns-, fɪ'ɒŋs-] (fjɑ̃se), -z

fiasco, -s fɪ'æskəʊ, -z

fiat (decree), -s 'faɪæt ['faɪət], -s

Fiat (car), -s fɪɒt ['fiːæt], -s

fib (s. v.), -s, -bing, -bed, -ber/s fɪb, -z, -ɪŋ, -d, -ə*/z

fibre, -s, -d; -less 'faɪbə*, -z, -d; -lɪs [-ləs]

fibreglass 'faɪbəglɑːs

fibriform 'faɪbrɪfɔːm

fibr|il/s, -in 'faɪbr|ɪl/z, -ɪn
fibrositis ˌfaɪbrəʊ'saɪtɪs
fibrous, -ly, -ness 'faɪbrəs, -lɪ, -nɪs [-nəs]
fibul|a, -as, -ae 'fɪbjʊl|ə, -əz, -i:
fichu, -s 'fi:ʃu: ['ˈfɪʃ-, -ʃju:] (fiʃy), -z
fick|le, -ler, -lest, -leness 'fɪk|l, -lə*, -lɪst, -lnɪs [-nəs]
fiction, -s 'fɪkʃn, z
fictional 'fɪkʃənl [-ʃnəl, -ʃn̩l, -ʃn̩l, -ʃənəl]
fictionist, -s 'fɪkʃənɪst [-ʃnɪst], -s
fictitious, -ly, -ness fɪk'tɪʃəs, -lɪ, -nɪs [-nəs]
fictive 'fɪktɪv
fid, -s fɪd, -z
fidd|le (s. v.), -les, -ling, -led, -ler/s 'fɪd|l, -lz, -lɪŋ [-lɪŋ], -ld, -lə*/z [-lə*/z]
fiddle-bow, -s 'fɪdlbəʊ, -z
fiddle-case, -s 'fɪdlkeɪs, -ɪz
fiddle-de-dee ˌfɪdldɪ'di:
fiddle-fadd|le (s. v. interj.), -les, -ling, -led 'fɪdlˌfæd|l, -lz, -lɪŋ, -ld
fiddlestick, -s 'fɪdlstɪk, -s
Fidele fɪ'di:lɪ
Fidelia fɪ'di:ljə [-lɪə]
Fidelio (opera) fɪ'deɪlɪəʊ [-ljəʊ]
fidelity fɪ'delətɪ [faɪ'd-, -ɪtɪ]
fidget (s. v.), -s, -ing, -ed 'fɪdʒɪt, -s, -ɪŋ, -ɪd
fidget|y, -ier, -iest, -ily, -iness 'fɪdʒɪt|ɪ [-ət|ɪ], -ɪə*, -ɪɪst, -ɪlɪ [-əlɪ], -ɪnɪs [-ɪnəs]
Fido 'faɪdəʊ
fiducial, -ly fɪ'dju:ʃjəl [-u:ʃɪəl, -u:sjəl, -u:sɪəl], -ɪ
fiduciar|y, -ies fɪ'dju:ʃjər|ɪ [-u:ʃɪə-, -u:ʃə-, -u:sjə-, -u:sɪə-], -ɪz
fie faɪ
fief, -s fi:f, -s
field (s. v.) (F.), -s, -ing, -ed, -er/s fi:ld, -z, -ɪŋ, -ɪd, -ə*/z
field-day, -s 'fi:lddeɪ, -z
Field|en, -er 'fi:ld|ən, -ə*
fieldfare, -s 'fi:ldfeə*, -z
field-glass, -es 'fi:ldglɑ:s, -ɪz
field-grey ˌfi:ld'greɪ
field-gun, -s 'fi:ldgʌn, -z
field-hospital, -s ˌfi:ld'hɒspɪtl, -z
field-ice 'fi:ldaɪs
Fielding 'fi:ldɪŋ
field-marshal, -s ˌfi:ld'mɑːʃl ['-,--],ˌ-,-z
field|-mouse, -mice 'fi:ld|maʊs, -maɪs
field-officer, -s 'fi:ldˌɒfɪsə*, -z
fields|man, -men 'fi:ldz|mən, -mən [-men]
field-telegraph, -s ˌfi:ld'telɪgrɑ:f [-græf], -s

field-telephone, -s ˌfi:ld'telɪfəʊn, -z
field-work, -s 'fi:ldwɜːk, -s
Fieller 'faɪlə*
fiend (F.), -s fi:nd, -z
fiendish, -ly, -ness 'fi:ndɪʃ, -lɪ, -nɪs [-nəs]
Fiennes faɪnz
fierce, -r, -st, -ly, -ness fɪəs, -ə*, -ɪst, -lɪ, -nɪs [-nəs]
fier|y, -ily, -iness 'faɪər|ɪ, -əlɪ [-ɪlɪ] -ɪnɪs [-nəs]
fif|e (s. v.), -es, -ing, -ed, -er/s faɪf, -s, -ɪŋ, -t, -ə*/z
Fife, -shire faɪf, -ʃə* [-ˌʃɪə*]
fife-major, -s ˌfaɪf'meɪdʒə*, -z
Fifield 'faɪfi:ld
fifteen, -s, -th/s fɪf'ti:n [also 'fɪft-, fɪf't- according to sentence-stress], -z, -θ/s
fifth, -s, -ly fɪfθ [-ftθ], -s, -lɪ
fift|y, -ies, -ieth/s, -yfold 'fɪft|ɪ, -ɪz, -ɪɪθ/s [-jɪθ/s, -ɪə0/s, -jəθ/s], -ɪfəʊld
fifty-fifty ˌfɪftɪ'fɪftɪ
fig (s. v.), -s, -ging, -ged fɪg, -z, -ɪŋ, -d
Figaro 'fɪgərəʊ (figaro)
Figg, -is fɪg, -ɪs
fight (s. v.), -s, -ing, fought, fighter/s faɪt, -s, -ɪŋ, fɔ:t, 'faɪtə*/z
fighting-cock, -s 'faɪtɪŋkɒk, -s
fig-lea|f, -ves 'fɪgli:|f, -vz
figment, -s 'fɪgmənt, -s
fig-tree, -s 'fɪgtri:, -z
figurability ˌfɪgjʊərə'bɪlətɪ [-gər-, -lɪt-]
figurable 'fɪgjʊərəbl [-gər-]
figurant, -s 'fɪgjʊərənt, -s
figurante (French fem. of figurant), -s ˌfɪgjʊ'rɑːnt ['-'rɔ̃:nt, -'rɑ:nt] (figyrɑ̃:t), -s
figurant|e (Italian form of figurant), -i ˌfɪgjʊ'rænt|ɪ, -i:
figuration, -s ˌfɪgjʊ'reɪʃn [-gjə-, -gə-], -z
figurative, -ly, -ness 'fɪgjʊrətɪv [-gjər-, -gər-], -lɪ, -nɪs [-nəs]
figur|e (s. v.), -es, -ing, -ed 'fɪgə*, -z, -rɪŋ, -d
figure-head, -s 'fɪgəhed, -z
figurine, -s 'fɪgjʊri:n [ˌ--'-], -z
Fiji ˌfi:'dʒi: ['--]
Fijian, -s ˌfi:'dʒi:ən, -z
filacer, -s 'fɪləsə*, -z
filament, -s 'fɪləmənt, -s
filamentous ˌfɪlə'mentəs
filature, -s 'fɪlətʃə* [-ˌtjʊə*, -tjə*, -ˌtʃʊə*], -z
filbert, -s 'fɪlbət, -s
filch, -es, -ing, -ed, -er/s fɪltʃ, -ɪz, -ɪŋ, -t, -ə*/z

Fildes faɪldz
fill|e (s. v.), -es, -ing, -ed faɪl, -z, -ɪŋ, -d
filemot 'fɪlɪmɒt
Filey 'faɪlɪ
filial, -ly, -ness 'fɪljəl [-lɪəl], -ɪ, -nɪs [-nəs]
filiation ˌfɪlɪ'eɪʃn
filibeg, -s 'fɪlɪbeg, -z
filibust|er (s. v.), -ers, -ering, -ered 'fɪlɪbʌst|ə*, -əz, -ərɪŋ, -əd
filigr|ane, -ee 'fɪlɪgr|eɪn, -iː
filings 'faɪlɪŋz
Filioque ˌfiːlɪ'əʊkwɪ [ˌfaɪl-, -fɪl-]
Filipino, -s ˌfɪlɪ'piːnəʊ [-lə'p-], -z
Filkin, -s 'fɪlkɪn, -z
fill (s. v.), -s, -ing/s, -ed, -er/s fɪl, -z, -ɪŋ/z, -d, -ə*/z
fillet (s. v.), -s, -ing, -ed 'fɪlɪt, -s, -ɪŋ, -ɪd
fillip (s. v.), -s, -ing, -ed 'fɪlɪp, -s, -ɪŋ, -t
Fillmore 'fɪlmɔ:* [-mɔə*]
fill|y, -ies 'fɪl|ɪ, -ɪz
film, -s fɪlm, -z
film-actor, -s 'fɪlmˌæktə*, -z
filmland 'fɪlmlænd
film-star, -s 'fɪlmstɑ:*, -z
film|y, -ier, -iest, -ily, -iness 'fɪlm|ɪ, -ɪə* [-jə*], -ɪɪst [-jɪst], -ɪlɪ [-əlɪ], -ɪnɪs [-ɪnəs]
Filon (surname) 'faɪlən
filt|er (s. v.), -ers, -ering, -ered 'fɪlt|ə*, -əz, -ərɪŋ, -əd
filter-paper, -s 'fɪltəˌpeɪpə*, -z
filter-tip, -s 'fɪltətɪp, -s
filth fɪlθ
filth|y, -ier, -iest, -ily, -iness 'fɪlθ|ɪ, -ɪə* [-jə*], -ɪɪst [-jɪst], -ɪlɪ [-əlɪ], -ɪnɪs [-ɪnəs]
filtrate (s.), -s 'fɪltreɪt [-rɪt], -s
filtrat|e (v.), -es, -ing, -ed 'fɪltreɪt, -s, -ɪŋ, -ɪd
filtration, -s fɪl'treɪʃn, -z
fin, -s fɪn, -z
finable 'faɪnəbl
fin|al, -ally 'faɪn|l, -əlɪ [-lɪ]
finale, -s fɪ'nɑ:lɪ, -z
finalist, -s 'faɪnəlɪst [-nlɪst], -s
finality faɪ'nælətɪ [-ɪtɪ]
finaliz|e [-is|e], -es, -ing, -ed 'faɪnəlaɪz [-nlaɪz], -ɪz, -ɪŋ, -d
financ|e (s. v.), -es, -ing, -ed faɪ'næns [fɪ'n-, 'faɪnæns], -ɪz, -ɪŋ, -t
financi|al, -ally faɪ'nænʃ|l [fɪ'n-], -əlɪ
financier (s.), -s faɪ'nænsɪə* [fɪ'n-, -sjə*], -z
finch (F.), -es fɪntʃ, -ɪz
Finchale (Priory in Durham) 'fɪŋkl
Finchampsted (in Berkshire) 'fɪntʃəmsted [-tɪd]

Finchley 'fɪntʃlɪ
find (s. v.), -s, -ing/s, found, finder/s faɪnd, -z, -ɪŋ/z, faʊnd, 'faɪndə*/z
Findlater 'fɪndlətə* [-leɪtə*]
Findlay 'fɪndleɪ [-lɪ]
fin|e (s. adj. v.), -es; -er, -est, -ely, -eness; -ing, -ed faɪn, -z; -ə*, -ɪst, -lɪ, -nɪs [-nəs]; -ɪŋ, -d
fine-draw, -s, -ing, -n, fine-drew ˌfaɪn'drɔ: ['--], -z, -ɪŋ, -n, ˌfaɪn'dru: ['--]
finery 'faɪnərɪ
fine-spun ˌfaɪn'spʌn ['--]
finess|e (s. v.), -es, -ing, -ed fɪ'nes, -ɪz, -ɪŋ, -t
Fingal (place) 'fɪŋgəl
Fingall (Lord) fɪŋ'gɔ:l
fing|er (s. v.), -ers, -ering/s, -ered 'fɪŋg|ə*, -əz, -ərɪŋ/z, -əd
finger-alphabet, -s 'fɪŋgərˌælfəbɪt [-gəˌæl-, -bet], -s
finger-board, -s 'fɪŋgəbɔ:d [-bɔəd], -z
finger-bowl, -s 'fɪŋgəbəʊl, -z
finger-breadth, -s 'fɪŋgəbredθ [-bretθ], -s
finger-glass, -es 'fɪŋgəglɑ:s, -ɪz
finger-mark, -s 'fɪŋgəmɑ:k, -s
finger-nail, -s 'fɪŋgəneɪl, -z
finger-plate, -s 'fɪŋgəpleɪt, -s
finger-post, -s 'fɪŋgəpəʊst, -s
finger-print, -s 'fɪŋgəprɪnt, -s
finger-stall, -s 'fɪŋgəstɔ:l, -z
Fingest (in Buckinghamshire) 'fɪndʒɪst
finial, -s 'faɪnɪəl ['fɪn-], -z
finic|al, -ally, -alness 'fɪnɪk|l, -əlɪ, -lnɪs [-nəs]
finicking 'fɪnɪkɪŋ
finick|y, -ier, -iest, -ily, -iness 'fɪnɪk|ɪ, -ɪə*, -ɪɪst, -ɪlɪ [-əlɪ], -ɪnɪs [-nəs]
finikin 'fɪnɪkɪn
finis 'fɪnɪs ['fi:nɪs, 'faɪnɪs]
finish (s. v.), -es, -ing, -ed, -er/s 'fɪnɪʃ, -ɪz, -ɪŋ, -t, -ə*/z
Finisterre ˌfɪnɪ'steə* ['---]
finite, -ly, -ness 'faɪnaɪt, -lɪ, -nɪs [-nəs]
finitude 'faɪnɪtjuː d
Finlaison 'fɪnlɪsn
Finland, -er/s 'fɪnlənd, -ə*/z
Finlay 'fɪnleɪ [-lɪ]
Finlayson 'fɪnlɪsn
Finley 'fɪnlɪ
Finn, -s fɪn, -z
Finnan 'fɪnən
Finney 'fɪnɪ
Finn|ic, -ish 'fɪn|ɪk, -ɪʃ
Finnon 'fɪnən
Finno-Ugrian ˌfɪnəʊ'juːgrɪən
finny 'fɪnɪ
Finsbury 'fɪnzbərɪ

Finsteraarhorn ˌfɪnstər'ɑːhɔːn
Finzean 'fɪŋən
Finzi 'fɪnzɪ
Fiona fɪ'əʊnə
fiord, -s fjɔːd [fɪ'ɔːd], -z
fiorin 'faɪərɪn
fir, -s fɜː:*, -z
Firbank 'fɜːbæŋk
fir|e (s. v.), -es, -ing, -ed, -er/s 'faɪə*,
  -z, -rɪŋ, -d, -rə*/z
fire-alarm, -s 'faɪərəˌlɑːm ['faɪəˌl-], -z
fire-arm, -s 'faɪərɑːm ['faɪəˌɑːm], -z
fireball, -s 'faɪəbɔːl, -z
fire-balloon, -s 'faɪəbəˌluːn, -z
fire-bomb, -s 'faɪəbɒm, -z
fire-box, -es 'faɪəbɒks, -ɪz
firebrand, -s 'faɪəbrænd, -z
fire-brick, -s 'faɪəbrɪk, -s
fire-brigade, -s 'faɪəbrɪˌɡeɪd, -z
fireclay 'faɪəkleɪ
fire-control, -s 'faɪəkən,trəʊl, -z
firecrest, -s 'faɪəkrest, -s
firedamp 'faɪədæmp
fire-dance, -s 'faɪədɑːns, -ɪz
fire-drill, -s 'faɪədrɪl, -z
fire-eat|er/s,   -ing   'faɪərˌiːt|ə*/z
  ['faɪəˌiːt-], -ɪŋ
fire-engine, -s 'faɪərˌendʒɪn ['faɪəˌen-],
  -z
fire-escape, -s 'faɪərɪˌskeɪp ['faɪəɪˌs-], -s
fire-extinguisher, -s 'faɪərɪkˌstɪŋgwɪʃə*
  ['faɪəɪkˌs-, -ekˌs-], -z
fire-fight|er/s, -ing 'faɪəˌfaɪt|ə*/z, -ɪŋ
firefl|y, -ies 'faɪəflaɪ, -aɪz
fire-guard, -s 'faɪəɡɑːd, -z
fire-hose, -s 'faɪəhəʊz, -ɪz
fire-insurance,   -s   'faɪərɪnˌʃʊərəns
  ['faɪəɪn-, -ˌɔə-, -ˌʃɔːr-], -ɪz
fire-iron, -s 'faɪərˌaɪən ['faɪəˌaɪən], -z
fire-light, -er/s 'faɪəlaɪt, -ə*/z
firelock, -s 'faɪəlɒk, -s
fire|man, -men 'faɪə|mən, -mən [-men]
fireplace, -s 'faɪəpleɪs, -ɪz
fire-plug, -s 'faɪəplʌg, -z
fire-power 'faɪəˌpaʊə*
fireproof 'faɪəpruːf
fire-screen, -s 'faɪəskriːn, -z
fire-ship, -s 'faɪəʃɪp, -s
fireside, -s 'faɪəsaɪd, -z
fire-stick, -s 'faɪəstɪk, -s
firestone 'faɪəstəʊn
fire-trap, -s 'faɪətræp, -s
fire-watch, -es, -ing, -ed, -er/s 'faɪə-
  wɒtʃ, -ɪz, -ɪŋ, -t, -ə*/z
fire-water 'faɪəˌwɔːtə*
firewood 'faɪəwʊd
fireworks 'faɪəwɜːks
fire-worship, -per/s 'faɪəˌwɜːʃɪp, -ə*/z

firing, -line/s, -party, -parties, -point/s,
  -squad/s 'faɪərɪŋ, -laɪn/z, -ˌpɑːtɪ,
  -ˌpɑːtɪz, -pɔɪnt/s, -skwɒd/z
firkin, -s 'fɜːkɪn, -z
firm (s. adj.), -s, -er, -est, -ly, -ness
  fɜːm, -z, -ə*, -ɪst, -lɪ, -nɪs [-nəs]
firmament, -s 'fɜːməmənt, -s
firman, -s fɜː'mɑːn ['fɜːmɑːn, 'fɜːmən],
  -z
firr|y, -iness 'fɜːr|ɪ, -ɪnɪs [-ɪnəs]
Firsby 'fɜːzbɪ
first, -ly fɜːst, -lɪ
firstborn 'fɜːstbɔːn
first-class ˌfɜːst'klɑːs [also '— when
  attributive]
first-fruit, -s 'fɜːstfruːt, -s
first-hand ˌfɜːst'hænd [also '— when
  attributive]
firstling, -s 'fɜːstlɪŋ, -z
firstly 'fɜːstlɪ
first-rate ˌfɜːst'reɪt [also '— when
  attributive]
firth (F.), -s fɜːθ, -s
fisc fɪsk
fiscal (s. adj.), -s 'fɪskl, -z
fish (s. v.) (F.), -es, -ing, -ed, -er/s fɪʃ,
  -ɪz, -ɪŋ, -t, -ə*/z
fish-ball, -s 'fɪʃbɔːl, -z
fishbone, -s 'fɪʃbəʊn, -z
fish-cake, -s 'fɪʃkeɪk, -s
fish-carver, -s 'fɪʃˌkɑːvə*, -z
fisher (F.), -s 'fɪʃə*, -z
fisher|man, -men 'fɪʃə|mən, -mən
  [-men]
fisher|y, -ies 'fɪʃər|ɪ, -ɪz
Fishguard 'fɪʃɡɑːd
fish-hook, -s 'fɪʃhʊk ['fɪʃʊk], -s
fishing-rod, -s 'fɪʃɪŋrɒd, -z
fishing-tackle 'fɪʃɪŋˌtækl
Fishkill 'fɪʃkɪl
fish-kni|fe, -ves 'fɪʃnaɪ|f, -vz
fishmonger, -s 'fɪʃˌmʌŋɡə*, -z
fishplate, -s 'fɪʃpleɪt, -s
fishpond, -s 'fɪʃpɒnd, -z
fish-sauce ˌfɪʃ'sɔːs
fish-slice, -s 'fɪʃslaɪs, -ɪz
fish-strainer, -s 'fɪʃˌstreɪnə*, -z
fishtail 'fɪʃteɪl
fish-torpedo, -es 'fɪʃtɔːˌpiːdəʊ, -z
Fishwick 'fɪʃwɪk
fishwi|fe, -ves 'fɪʃwaɪ|f, -vz
fish|woman,   -women   'fɪʃ|ˌwʊmən,
  -ˌwɪmɪn
fish|y, -ier, -iest, -ily, -iness 'fɪʃ|ɪ, -ɪə*,
  -ɪɪst, -ɪlɪ [-əlɪ], -ɪnɪs [-ɪnəs]
Fisk(e) fɪsk
Fison 'faɪsn
fissile 'fɪsaɪl

191

fission 'fɪʃn
fissionable 'fɪʃnəbl [-fənəbl]
fissiparous fɪ'sɪpərəs
fissure, -s, -d 'fɪʃə* [-,ʃʊə*], -z, -d
fist, -s; -ic, -ical fɪst, -s; -ɪk, -ɪkl
fisticuff, -s 'fɪstɪkʌf, -s
fistul|a, -as, -ar, -ous 'fɪstjʊl|ə, -əz, -ə*, -əs
fit (s. adj. v.), -s, -ter, -test, -ly, -ness; -ting/ly, -ted, -ter/s fɪt, -s, -ə*, -ɪst, -lɪ, -nɪs [-nəs]; -ɪŋ/lɪ, -ɪd, -ə*/z
fitch (F.), -es fɪtʃ, -ɪz
Fitchburg 'fɪtʃbɜ:g
fitchew, -s 'fɪtʃu:, -z
fit|ful, -fully, -fulness 'fɪt|fʊl, -fʊlɪ [-fəlɪ], -fʊlnɪs [-nəs]
fitment, -s 'fɪtmənt, -s
fitting-out ,fɪtɪŋ'aʊt
fitting-room, -s 'fɪtɪŋrʊm [-ru:m], -z
fitting-shop, -s 'fɪtɪŋʃɒp, -s
Fitzalan fɪts'ælən
Fitzcharles fɪts'tʃɑːlz
Fitzclarence fɪts'klærəns
Fitzdottrel fɪts'dɒtrəl
Fitzgeorge fɪts'dʒɔːdʒ
Fitzgerald fɪts'dʒerəld
Fitzgibbon fɪts'gɪbən
Fitzhardinge fɪts'hɑːdɪŋ
Fitzharris fɪts'hærɪs
Fitzherbert fɪts'hɜːbət
Fitzhugh fɪts'hjuː
Fitzjames fɪts'dʒeɪmz [in James Fitz-james often 'fɪtsdʒ-]
Fitzjohn (surname) fɪts'dʒɒn
Fitzjohn's Avenue ,fɪtsdʒɒnz'ævənjuː [-vɪn-]
Fitzmaurice fɪts'mɒrɪs
Fitzpatrick fɪts'pætrɪk
Fitzroy (surname) fɪts'rɔɪ, (square and street in London) 'fɪtsrɔɪ
Fitzsimmons fɪts'sɪmənz
Fitzstephen fɪts'stiːvn
Fitzurse fɪts'ɜːs
Fitzwalter fɪts'wɔːltə* [-'wɒl-]
Fitzwilliam fɪts'wɪljəm
Fitzwygram fɪts'waɪgrəm
five, -s -fold faɪv, -z, -fəʊld
five-ish 'faɪvɪʃ
fivepen|ce, -ny 'faɪfpən|s ['faɪvp-], -ɪ (see note under penny)
five-ply 'faɪvplaɪ [,-'-]
fiver, -s 'faɪvə*, -z
fix (s. v.), -es, -ing, -ed, -edly, -edness, -er/s; -able, -ative fɪks, -ɪz, -ɪŋ, -t, -ɪdlɪ, -ɪdnɪs [-nəs], -ə*/z; -əbl, -ətɪv
fixation fɪk'seɪʃn
fixity 'fɪksətɪ [-ɪtɪ]
fixture, -s 'fɪkstʃə*, -z

fizz (s. v.), -es, -ing, -ed, -er/s fɪz, -ɪz, -ɪŋ, -d, -ə*/z
fizz|le (s. v.), -les, -ling, -led 'fɪz|l, -lz, -lɪŋ [-lɪŋ], -ld
fizz|y, -ier, -iest, -iness 'fɪz|ɪ, -ɪə*, -ɪɪst, -ɪnɪs [-ɪnəs]
fjord, -s fjɔːd, -z
flab flæb
flabbergast, -s, -ing, -ed 'flæbəgɑːst, -s, -ɪŋ, -ɪd
flabb|y, -ier, -iest, -ily, -iness 'flæb|ɪ, -ɪə*, -ɪɪst, -ɪlɪ [-əlɪ], -ɪnɪs [-ɪnəs]
flaccid, -ly, -ness 'flæksɪd, -lɪ, -nɪs [-nəs]
flaccidity flæk'sɪdətɪ [-ɪtɪ]
Flaccus 'flækəs
Fladgate 'flædgɪt [-geɪt]
flag (s. v.), -s, -ging, -ged flæg, -z, -ɪŋ, -d
flag-captain, -s ,flæg'kæptɪn [',-,-], -z
flag-day, -s 'flægdeɪ, -z
flagellant, -s 'flædʒələnt [-dʒɪ-, flə'dʒel-, flæ'dʒel-], -s
flagellat|e, -es, -ing, -ed, -or/s 'flædʒə-leɪt [-dʒɪl-, -dʒel-], -s, -ɪŋ, -ɪd, -ə*/z
flagellation, -s ,flædʒə'leɪʃn [-dʒɪ'l-, -dʒe'l-], -z
flagell|um, -a flə'dʒel|əm [flæ'dʒ-], -ə
flageolet, -s ,flædʒəʊ'let ['---], -s
Flagg flæg
flaggy 'flægɪ
flagitious, -ly, -ness flə'dʒɪʃəs, -lɪ, -nɪs [-nəs]
flag-lieutenan|t, -ts, -cy, -cies ,flæglef-'tenən|t [-ləf't-], -ts, -sɪ, -sɪz (see note under lieutenancy)
flag-officer, -s 'flæg,ɒfɪsə*, -z
flagon, -s 'flægən, -z
flagpole, -s 'flægpəʊl, -z
flagran|cy, -t/ly 'fleɪgrən|sɪ, -t/lɪ
flag|-ship/s, -staff/s 'flæg|ʃɪp/s, -stɑːf/s
flagstone, -s 'flægstəʊn, -z
flag-wagging 'flæg,wægɪŋ
flag-waving 'flæg,weɪvɪŋ
Flaherty 'fleətɪ, 'flɑːhətɪ, 'flæhətɪ
flail (s. v.), -s, -ing, -ed fleɪl, -z, -ɪŋ, -d
flair, -s fleə*, -z
flak flæk
flak|e (s. v.), -es, -ing, -ed fleɪk, -s, -ɪŋ, -t
flake-white ,fleɪk'waɪt [-'hw-, in contrast '--]
flak|y, -ily, -iness 'fleɪk|ɪ, -ɪlɪ [-əlɪ], -ɪnɪs [-ɪnəs]
flam, -s flæm, -z
Flambard 'flæmbɑːd [-bəd]
flambeau (F.), -s 'flæmbəʊ, -z
Flamborough 'flæmbərə
flamboyant flæm'bɔɪənt

flam|e (s. v.), -es, -ing, -ed fleɪm, -z, -ɪŋ, -d

flame-colour, -ed 'fleɪmˌkʌlə*, -d

flamen, -s 'fleɪmen, -z

flamenco flə'meŋkəʊ

flamingo, -(e)s flə'mɪŋgəʊ [flæ'm-], -z

Flaminius flə'mɪnɪəs [flæ'm-, -njəs]

Flammock 'flæmək

Flamstead 'flæmstɪd [-sted]

Flamsteed 'flæmsti:d

flamy 'fleɪmɪ

flan, -s flæn, -z

Flanders 'flɑ:ndəz

flange, -s, -d flændʒ, -ɪz, -d

flank (s. v.), -s, -ing, -ed, -er/s flæŋk, -s, -ɪŋ, -t [flæŋt], -ə*/z

flannel, -s, -led 'flænl, -z, -d

flannelette ˌflænl̩'et [-nə'let]

flannelly 'flænl̩ɪ

flap (s. v.), -s, -ping, -ped flæp, -s, -ɪŋ, -t

flapdoodle 'flæpˌdu:dl

flapjack, -s 'flæpdʒæk, -s

flapper, -s 'flæpə*, -z

flar|e (s. v.), -es, -ing/ly, -ed fleə*, -z, -rɪŋ/lɪ, -d

flare-pa|th, -ths 'fleəpɑ:|θ, -ðz

flare-up, -s ˌfleə'rʌp ['--], -s

flash (s. adj. v.) (F.), -es, -ing, -ed flæʃ, -ɪz, -ɪŋ, -t

flashback, -s 'flæʃbæk, -s

flash-card, -s 'flæʃkɑ:d, -z

flashlight, -s 'flæʃlaɪt, -s

flash-point, -s 'flæʃpɔɪnt, -s

flash|y, -ier, -iest, -ily, -iness 'flæʃ|ɪ, -ɪə*, -ɪɪst, -ɪlɪ [-əlɪ], -ɪnɪs [-ɪnəs]

flask, -s flɑ:sk, -s

flasket, -s 'flɑ:skɪt, -s

flat (s. adj.), -s, -ter, -test, -ly, -ness flæt, -s, -ə*, -ɪst, -lɪ, -nɪs [-nəs]

Flatbush 'flætbʊʃ

flatfish, -es 'flætfɪʃ, -ɪz

flatfoot 'flætfʊt

flat-footed ˌflæt'fʊtɪd ['-ˌ--]

flathead, -s 'flæthed, -z

flat-iron, -s 'flætˌaɪən, -z

Flatland 'flætlænd

flatlet, -s 'flætlɪt [-lət], -s

flatt|en, -ens, -ening, -ened 'flæt|n̩, -nz, -n̩ɪŋ [-nɪŋ], -nd

flatter, -s, -ing/ly, -ed, -er/s 'flætə*, -z, -rɪŋ/lɪ, -d, -rə*/z

flatter|y, -ies 'flætər|ɪ, -ɪz

flattish 'flætɪʃ

flatulen|ce, -cy, -t/ly 'flætjʊlən|s [-tʃʊ-], -sɪ, -t/lɪ

flatus, -es 'fleɪtəs, -ɪz

flat|ways, -wise 'flæt|weɪz, -waɪz

flaunt, -s, -ing/ly, -ed, -er/s flɔ:nt, -s, -ɪŋ/lɪ, -ɪd, -ə*/z

flautist, -s 'flɔ:tɪst, -s

Flavel 'flævəl

Flavell flə'vel, 'fleɪvəl

Flavi|a, -an, -us 'fleɪvjə [-vɪ|ə], -ən, -əs

flavorous 'fleɪvərəs

flav|our (s. v.), -ours, -ouring/s, -oured; -ourless 'fleɪv|ə*, -əz, -ərɪŋ/z, -əd; -əlɪs [-ləs]

flaw (s. v.), -s, -ing, -ed flɔ:, -z, -ɪŋ, -d

flawless, -ly, -ness 'flɔ:lɪs [-ləs], -lɪ, -nɪs [-nəs]

flax, -en flæks, -ən

Flaxman 'flæksmən

flaxy 'flæksɪ

flay, -s, -ing, -ed, -er/s fleɪ, -z, -ɪŋ, -d, -ə*/z

flea, -s fli:, -z

fleabane 'fli:beɪn

flea-bite, -s 'fli:baɪt, -s

fleam, -s fli:m, -z

Fleance 'fli:əns [flɪəns]

Fleay fleɪ

flèche, -s fleɪʃ, -ɪz

fleck (s. v.), -s, -ing, -ed flek, -s, -ɪŋ, -t

Flecknoe 'fleknəʊ

flection, -s 'flekʃn, -z

flectional 'flekʃənl [-ʃn̩l, -ʃn̩l, -ʃənəl]

fled (from flee) fled

fledg|e, -es, -ing, -ed; -(e)ling/s fledʒ, -ɪz, -ɪŋ, -d; -lɪŋ/z

flee, -s, -ing, fled, fleer/s fli:, -z, -ɪŋ, fled, 'fli:ə*/z

fleec|e (s. v.), -es, -ing, -ed, -er/s; -y, -iness fli:s, -ɪz, -ɪŋ, -t, -ə*/z; -ɪ, -ɪnɪs [-ɪnəs]

Fleeming 'flemɪŋ

fleer (sneer) (s. v.), -s, -ing, -ed flɪə*, -z, -rɪŋ, -d

fleet (s. adj. v.) (F.), -s; -er, -est, -ly, -ness; -ing/ly, -ed fli:t, -s; -ə*, -ɪst, -lɪ, -nɪs [-nəs]; -ɪŋ/lɪ, -ɪd

Fleet Street 'fli:tstri:t

Fleetwood 'fli:twʊd

Fleming, -s, -ton 'flemɪŋ, -z, -tən

Flemish 'flemɪʃ

Flemming 'flemɪŋ

flens|e, -es, -ing, -ed flenz, -ɪz, -ɪŋ, -d

flesh (s. v.), -es, -ing/s, -ed fleʃ, -ɪz, -ɪŋ/z, -t

flesh-colour, -ed 'fleʃˌkʌlə*, -d

flesh-eat|er/s, -ing 'fleʃˌi:t|ə*/z, -ɪŋ

flesh-hook, -s 'fleʃhʊk ['fleʃʊk], -s

fleshless 'fleʃlɪs [-ləs]

fleshl|y, -iness 'fleʃl|ɪ, -ɪnɪs [-ɪnəs]

flesh-pot, -s 'fleʃpɒt, -s

193

flesh-tint 'fleʃtɪnt
flesh-wound, -s 'fleʃwuːnd, -z
flesh|y, -iness 'fleʃ|ɪ, -ɪnɪs [-məs]
fletcher (F.), -s 'fletʃə*, -z
Flete fliːt
fleur-de-lis ˌflɜːdə'liː [-'liːs] (flœrdəlis)
Fleur de Lis (place in Gwent), ˌflɜːdə'liː
flew (from fly v.) fluː
flex (s. v.), -es, -ing, -ed fleks, -ɪz, -ɪŋ, -t
flexibility ˌfleksə'bɪlɪtɪ [-sɪ'b-, -lɪt-]
flexib|le, -ly, -leness 'fleksəb|l [-sɪb-], -lɪ, -lnɪs [-nəs]
flexion, -s 'flekʃn, -z
flexor, -s 'fleksə*, -z
flexure, -s 'flekʃə*, -z
flibbertigibbet, -s ˌflɪbətɪ'dʒɪbɪt, -s
flick (s. v.), -s, -ing, -ed flɪk, -s, -ɪŋ, -t
flicker (s. v.), -s, -ing, -ed 'flɪkə*, -z, -rɪŋ, -d
flick-kni|fe, -ves 'flɪknaɪ|f, -vz
flier, -s 'flaɪə*, -z
flight (F.), -s flaɪt, -s
flight-deck, -s 'flaɪtdek, -s
flight-path, -s 'flaɪtpɑːθ, -s [-pɑːðz]
flight|y, -ier, -iest, -ily, -iness 'flaɪt|ɪ, -ɪə* [-jə*], -ɪɪst [-jɪst], -ɪlɪ [-əlɪ], -ɪnɪs [-məs]
flim-flam, -s 'flɪmflæm, -z
Flimnap 'flɪmnæp
flims|y, -ier, -iest, -ily, -iness 'flɪmz|ɪ, -ɪə* [-jə*], -ɪɪst [-jɪst], -ɪlɪ [-əlɪ], -ɪnɪs [-məs]
flinch, -es, -ing/ly, -ed, -er/s flɪntʃ, -ɪz, -ɪŋ/lɪ, -t, -ə*/z
flinders (F.) 'flɪndəz
fling (s. v.), -s, -ing, flung flɪŋ, -z, -ɪŋ, flʌŋ
flint (F.), -s flɪnt, -s
flint-glass ˌflɪnt'glɑːs ['—]
flint-lock, -s 'flɪntlɒk, -s
Flintshire 'flɪnt-ʃə* [-ˌʃɪə*]
flintstone 'flɪntstəʊn
Flintwinch 'flɪntwɪntʃ
flint|y, -ier, -iest, -ily, -iness 'flɪnt|ɪ, -ɪə* [-jə*], -ɪɪst [-jɪst], -ɪlɪ [-əlɪ], -ɪnɪs [-məs]
flip (s. v.), -s, -ping, -ped flɪp, -s, -ɪŋ, -t
flip-flap (s. adv.), -s 'flɪpflæp, -s
flippan|cy, -t/ly, -tness 'flɪpən|sɪ, -t/lɪ, -tnɪs [-nəs]
flipper, -s 'flɪpə*, -z
flirt (s. v.), -s, -ing/ly, -ed flɜːt, -s, -ɪŋ/lɪ, -ɪd
flirtation, -s flɜː'teɪʃn, -z
flirtatious flɜː'teɪʃəs
flirty 'flɜːtɪ
flit, -s, -ting, -ted flɪt, -s, -ɪŋ, -ɪd
flitch (F.), -es flɪtʃ, -ɪz

194

Flite flaɪt
flitter, -s, -ing, -ed 'flɪtə*, -z, -rɪŋ, -d
flitter-mouse, -mice 'flɪtə|maʊs, -maɪs
Flixton 'flɪkstən
float (s. v.), -s, -ing, -ed, -er/s; -able, -age fləʊt, -s, -ɪŋ, -ɪd, -ə*/z; -əbl, -ɪdʒ
floatation fləʊ'teɪʃn
floating|-bridge/s, -dock/s ˌfləʊtɪŋ|-'brɪdʒ/ɪz, -'dɒk/s
float-stone, -s 'fləʊtstəʊn, -z
floccule, -s 'flɒkjuːl, -z
flocculent 'flɒkjʊlənt
flock (s. v.), -s, -ing, -ed; -y flɒk, -s, -ɪŋ, -t; -ɪ
Flockton 'flɒktən
Flodden 'flɒdn
floe, -s fləʊ, -z
flog, -s, -ging/s, -ged flɒg, -z, -ɪŋ/z, -d
flood (s. v.) (F.), -s, -ing, -ed; -gate/s flʌd, -z, -ɪŋ, -ɪd; -geɪt/s
floodlight (s. v.), -s, -ing, floodlit 'flʌdlaɪt, -s, -ɪŋ, 'flʌdlɪt
floodtide 'flʌdtaɪd
Flook flʊk
floor (s. v.), -s, -ing, -ed, -er/s flɔː* [flɔə*], -z, -rɪŋ, -d, -rə*/z
floor|-cloth, -cloths 'flɔː|klɒθ ['flɔə|-, old-fashioned -klɔːθ], -klɒθs [-klɔːðz, -klɔːθs]
flop (s. v. adv. interj.), -s, -ping, -ped, -per/s flɒp, -s, -ɪŋ, -t, -ə*/z
flopp|y, -ier, -iest, -ily, -iness 'flɒp|ɪ, -ɪə*, -ɪɪst, -ɪlɪ [-əlɪ], -ɪnɪs [-məs]
flora (F.) 'flɔːrə
floral 'flɔːrəl ['flɒr-]
Floren|ce, -tine 'flɒrən|s, -taɪn
Flores 'flɔːrɪz
florescen|ce, -t flɔː'resn|s [flɒ'r-, flə'r-], -t
floret, -s 'flɔːrɪt [-ret], -s
Florian 'flɔːrən
floriat|e, -es, -ing, -ed 'flɔːrɪeɪt, -s, -ɪŋ, -ɪd
floricultur|al, -ist/s ˌflɔːrɪ'kʌltʃər|əl [ˌflɒr-, -tʃʊr-], -ɪst/s
floriculture 'flɔːrɪkʌltʃə* ['flɒr-]
florid, -est, -ly, -ness 'flɒrɪd, -ɪst, -lɪ, -nɪs [-nəs]
Florida 'flɒrɪdə
floriferous flɔː'rɪfərəs [flɒ'r-]
Florimel 'flɒrɪmel
florin, -s 'flɒrɪn, -z
Florinda flɔː'rɪndə [flɒ'r-, flə'r-]
Florio 'flɔːrɪəʊ
florist, -s 'flɒrɪst, -s
Florizel 'flɒrɪzel
Florrie 'flɒrɪ

floruit 'flɔːrʊɪt [-rjʊɪt]
Florus 'flɔːrəs
floss (F.), -y flɒs, -ɪ
Flossie 'flɒsɪ
floss-silk ˌflɒs'sɪlk
flotation, -s fləʊ'teɪʃn, -z
flotilla, -s flə'tɪlə, -z
flotsam 'flɒtsəm
Floud flʌd
flounc|e (s. v.), -es, -ing, -ed flaʊns, -ɪz, -ɪŋ, -t
found|er (s. v.), -ers, -ering, -ered 'flaʊnd|ə*, -əz, -ərɪŋ, -əd
flour (s. v.), -s, -ing, -ed 'flaʊə*, -z, -ɪŋ, -d
flourish (s. v.), -es, -ing/ly, -ed 'flʌrɪʃ, -ɪz, -ɪŋ/lɪ, -t
flour-mill, -s 'flaʊəmɪl, -z
floury 'flaʊərɪ
flout (s. v.), -s, -ing/ly, -ed flaʊt, -s, -ɪŋ/lɪ, -ɪd
fl|ow (s. v.), -ows, -owing/ly, -owing-ness, -owed fl|əʊ, -əʊz, -əʊɪŋ/lɪ, -əʊɪŋnɪs [-nəs], -əʊd
flower (s. v.) (F.), -s, -ing, -ed, -er/s 'flaʊə*, -z, -ɪŋ, -d, -rə*/z
flower-bearing 'flaʊəˌbeərɪŋ
flower|-bed/s, -bud/s 'flaʊə|bed/z, -bʌd/z
floweret, -s 'flaʊərɪt [-ret], -s
flower|-garden/s, -girl/s, -head/s 'flaʊə|ˌgɑːdn/z, -gɜːl/z, -hed/z
flowerless 'flaʊəlɪs [-ləs]
flower|-pot/s, -service/s, -stalk/s 'flaʊə|pɒt/s, -ˌsɜːvɪs/ɪz, -stɔːk/s
flowery 'flaʊərɪ
flown (from fly) fləʊn
Floy|d, -er flɔɪ|d, -ə*
'flu fluː
fluctuat|e, -es, -ing, -ed 'flʌktjʊeɪt [-tʃʊeɪt], -s, -ɪŋ, -ɪd
fluctuation, -s ˌflʌktjʊ'eɪʃn [-tʃʊ-], -z
Flud|d, -yer flʌd, -jə*
flue, -s fluː, -z
Fluellen fluː'elɪn [flʊ'e-]
fluen|cy, -t/ly, -tness 'fluːən|sɪ ['flʊən-], -t/lɪ, -tnɪs [-nəs]
flue-pipe, -s 'fluːpaɪp, -s
flue-work 'fluːwɜːk
fluff (s. v.), -s, -ing, -ed; -y, -ier, -iest, -iness flʌf, -s, -ɪŋ, -t; -ɪ, -ɪə*, -ɪɪst, -ɪnɪs [-nəs]
fluid (s. adj.), -s 'fluːɪd ['flʊɪd], -z
fluidity fluː'ɪdətɪ [flʊ'ɪ-, -ɪtɪ]
fluk|e (s. v.), -es, -ing, -ed, -er/s; -y, -ier, -iest, -iness fluːk, -s, -ɪŋ, -t, -ə*/z; -ɪ, -ɪə* [-jə*], -ɪɪst [-jɪst], -ɪnɪs [-ɪnəs]

flummery 'flʌmərɪ
flummox, -es, -ing, -ed 'flʌməks, -ɪz, -ɪŋ, -t
flump (s. v.), -s, -ing, -ed flʌmp, -s, -ɪŋ, -t [flʌmt]
flung (from fling) flʌŋ
flunkey, -s; -ism 'flʌŋkɪ, -z; -ɪzəm
fluor 'fluːɔː* ['flʊɔː*, 'fluːə*, flʊə*]
fluorescen|ce, -t ˌflʊə'resn|s [ˌfluːə'r-, ˌfluːɔː'r-, ˌflʊɔː-, ˌfluːɒ'r-, ˌflʊɒ-], -t
fluoric fluː'ɒrɪk
fluoridat|e, -es, -ing, -ed 'flʊərɪdeɪt ['flɔːr-], -s, -ɪŋ, -ɪd
fluoridation ˌflʊərɪ'deɪʃn [ˌflɔːr-, -raɪ-]
fluoride 'flʊəraɪd ['flɔːr-]
fluoridization [-isa-] ˌflʊərɪdaɪ'zeɪʃn [ˌflɔː-, -raɪd-, -dɪ-]
fluoridiz|e [-is|e-], -es, -ing, -ed 'flʊərɪdaɪz ['flɔː-] -ɪz, -ɪŋ, -d
fluor|ine, -ite 'flʊər|iːn ['fluː:ər-], -aɪt
fluor-spar 'flʊəspɑː* ['fluːə-, 'fluːɔː-]
flurr|y (s. v.), -ies, -ying, -ied 'flʌr|ɪ, -ɪz, -ɪɪŋ, -ɪd
flush (s. v.), -es, -ing, -ed flʌʃ, -ɪz, -ɪŋ, -t
flushing (F.), -s 'flʌʃɪŋ, -z
flust|er (s. v.), -ers, -ering, -ered 'flʌst|ə*, -əz, -ərɪŋ, -əd
flut|e (s. v.) (F.), -es, -ing, -ed; -ist/s; -y, -ier, -iest, -iness fluːt, -s, -ɪŋ, -ɪd; -ɪst/s; -ɪ, -ɪə* [-jə*], -ɪɪst [-jɪst], -ɪnɪs [-ɪnəs]
flutter (s. v.) (F.), -s, -ing, -ed, -er/s 'flʌtə*, -z, -ɪŋ, -d, -rə*/z
fluvial 'fluːvjəl [-vɪəl]
flux, -es flʌks, -ɪz
fluxion, -s 'flʌkʃn, -z
fluxional 'flʌkʃənl [-ʃn̩], -ʃn̩l]
fl|y (s. v.) (all senses) (F.), -ies, -ying, flew, flown, flier/s fl|aɪ, -aɪz, -aɪɪŋ, fluː, fləʊn, 'flaɪə*/z
flyable 'flaɪəbl
fly-blow, -s, -n 'flaɪbləʊ, -z, -n
fly-bomb, -s 'flaɪbɒm, -z
fly-button, -s 'flaɪbʌtn, -z
fly-by-night 'flaɪbaɪnaɪt
fly|-catcher/s, -fishing 'flaɪ|ˌkætʃə*/z, -ˌfɪʃɪŋ
flyer, -s 'flaɪə*, -z
flying|-man, -men 'flaɪɪŋ|mæn, -men
flying-officer, -s 'flaɪɪŋˌɒfɪsə*, -z
fly-lea|f, -ves 'flaɪliː|f, -vz
fly-line, -s 'flaɪlaɪn, -z
Flyn|n, -t flɪn, -t
flyover, -s 'flaɪˌəʊvə*, -z
fly-paper, -s 'flaɪˌpeɪpə*, -z
fly-sheet, -s 'flaɪʃiːt, -s
fly-swatter, -s 'flaɪˌswɒtə*, -z
flyway, -s 'flaɪweɪ, -z

flywheel, -s 'flaıwi:l [-hwi:l], -z
Foakes fəʊks
foal (s. v.), -s, -ing, -ed fəʊl, -z, -ıŋ, -d
foam (s. v.), -s, -ing, -ed; -y, -iness
    fəʊm, -z, -ıŋ, -d; -ı, -ınıs [-nəs]
Foard fɔ:d [fɔəd]
fob (s. v.), -s, -bing, -bed fɒb, -z, -ıŋ, -d
focal 'fəʊkl
Fochabers 'fɒkəbəz ['fɒxə-]
Focke (surname) fɒk
fo'c'sle, -s 'fəʊksl, -z
fo|cus (s.), -ci 'fəʊ|kəs, -saı [-ki:]
focus (v.), -ses, -sing, -sed 'fəʊkəs, -ız,
    -ıŋ, -t
fodder 'fɒdə*
foe, -s fəʊ, -z
foe|man, -men 'fəʊ|mən, -mən [-men]
foetal 'fi:tl
foetid, -ly, -ness 'fi:tıd, -lı, -nıs [-nəs]
foetus, -es 'fi:təs, -ız
fog (s. v.), -s, -ging, -ged fɒg, -z, -ıŋ, -d
fog-bank, -s 'fɒgbæŋk, -s
fog-bound 'fɒgbaʊnd
Fogerty 'fəʊgətı
fogey, -s, -ish, -ism 'fəʊgı, -z, -ıʃ, -ızəm
Fogg fɒg
fogg|y, -ier, -iest, -ily, -iness 'fɒg|ı,
    -ıə*, -ııst, -ılı [-əlı], -ınıs [-ınəs]
fog-horn, -s 'fɒghɔ:n, -z
fogram, -s 'fəʊgræm, -z
fog-signal, -s 'fɒg,sıgnl̩ [-nəl], -z
fog|y, -ies 'fəʊg|ı, -ız
fogyi|sh, -sm 'fəʊgıı|ʃ, -zəm
foible, -s 'fɔıbl, -z
foil (s. v.), -s, -ing, -ed fɔıl, -z, -ıŋ, -d
foison, -s 'fɔızn, -z
foist, -s, -ing, -ed fɔıst, -s, -ıŋ, -ıd
Foker 'fəʊkə*
fold (s. v.), -s, -ing, -ed, -er/s fəʊld, -z,
    -ıŋ, -ıd, -ə*/z
Foley 'fəʊlı
Folgate 'fɒlgıt [-geıt]
Folger 'fəʊldʒə*
foliage 'fəʊlııdʒ [-ljıdʒ]
foliate (adj.) 'fəʊlıət [-lıt, -ljıt, -lıeıt,
    -ljeıt]
foliat|e (v.), -es, -ing, -ed 'fəʊlıeıt
    [-ljeıt], -s, -ıŋ, -ıd
foliation, -s ,fəʊlı'eıʃn, -z
folio, -s 'fəʊlıəʊ [-ljəʊ], -z
Foliot 'fɒlıət [-ljət]
Foljambe 'fʊldʒəm
folk, -s fəʊk, -s
folk-dance, -s 'fəʊkdɑ:ns, -ız
Folkes fəʊlks
Folkestone 'fəʊkstən
folklore 'fəʊklɔ:* [-lɔə*]
folklorist, -s 'fəʊk,lɔ:rıst, -s

folk-song, -s 'fəʊksɒŋ, -z
folk-tale, -s 'fəʊkteıl, -z
Foll|ow, -ett 'fɒl|ın [-ən], -ıt
Follick 'fɒlık
follicle, -s 'fɒlıkl, -z
Folliott 'fɒlıət [-ljət]
foll|ow (s. v.), -ows, -owing/s, -owed,
    -ower/s 'fɒl|əʊ, -əʊz, -əʊıŋ/z, -əʊd,
    -əʊə*/z
follow-my-leader ,fɒləʊmı'li:də*
follow-on, -s ,fɒləʊ'ɒn, -z
follow-through, -s ,fɒləʊ'θru:, -z
foll|y, -ies (F.) 'fɒl|ı, -ız
Fomalhaut 'fəʊmələʊt ['fɒməlhɔ:t]
foment, -s, -ing, -ed, -er/s fəʊ'ment,
    -s, -ıŋ, -ıd, -ə*/z
fomentation, -s ,fəʊmen'teıʃn [-mən-],
    -z
fond, -er, -est, -ly, -ness fɒnd, -ə*, -ıst,
    -lı, -nıs ['fɒnnıs, -nəs]
fond|le, -les, -ling, -led, -ler/s 'fɒnd|l,
    -lz, -lıŋ, -ld, -lə*/z
font, -s -al fɒnt, -s, -l
Fontenoy 'fɒntənɔı [-tın-]
Fonteyn fɒn'teın
Fonthill 'fɒnthıl
Foochow ,fu:'tʃaʊ
food, -s; -less fu:d, -z, -lıs [-ləs]
food-stuff, -s 'fu:dstʌf, -s
fool (s. v.), -s, -ing, -ed fu:l, -z, -ıŋ, -d
fooler|y, -ies 'fu:lər|ı, -ız
fool-hard|y, -iest, -ily, -iness 'fu:l-
    ,hɑ:d|ı, -ııst [-jıst], -ılı [-əlı], -ınıs
    [-ınəs]
foolish, -ly, -ness 'fu:lıʃ, -lı, -nıs [-nəs]
fool-proof 'fu:lpru:f
foolscap (cap), -s 'fu:lzkæp, -s
foolscap (paper size) 'fu:lskæp [-lzk-]
f|oot (s.), -eet f|ʊt, -i:t
foot (v.), -s, -ing, -ed fʊt, -s, -ıŋ, -ıd
football, -s, -er/s 'fʊtbɔ:l, -z, -ə*/z
foot-ba|th, -ths 'fʊtbɑ:|θ, -ðz
footboard, -s 'fʊtbɔ:d [-bəəd], -z
foot-bridge, -s 'fʊtbrıdʒ, -ız
Foote fʊt
footer 'fʊtə*
foot|-fall/s, -guard/s 'fʊt|fɔ:l/z,
    -gɑ:d/z
foot-fault (s. v.), -s, -ing, -ed 'fʊtfɔ:lt
    [-fɒlt], -s, -ıŋ, -ıd
foothill, -s 'fʊthıl, -z
foothold, -s 'fʊthəʊld, -z
footing (s.), -s 'fʊtıŋ, -z
foot|le, -les, -ling, -led 'fu:t|l, -lz, -lıŋ,
    -ld
foot-light, -s 'fʊtlaıt, -s
foot|man, -men 'fʊt|mən, -mən
footmark, -s 'fʊtmɑ:k, -s

footnote, -s 'fʊtnəʊt, -s
footpad, -s 'fʊtpæd, -z
foot-passenger, -s 'fʊt͵pæsɪndʒə* [-əndʒə*], -z
footpa|th, -ths 'fʊtpɑːθ, -ðz
footplate, -s 'fʊtpleɪt, -s
foot-pound, -s 'fʊtpaʊnd, -z
foot-print, -s 'fʊtprɪnt, -s
foot-pump, -s 'fʊtpʌmp, -s
foot-race, -s 'fʊtreɪs, -ɪz
foot-rule, -s 'fʊtruːl, -z
Foots Cray ͵fʊts'kreɪ
foot-soldier, -s 'fʊt͵səʊldʒə* [rarely -djə*], -z
footsore 'fʊtsɔː* [-sɔə*]
footstep, -s 'fʊtstep, -s
footstool, -s 'fʊtstuːl, -z
foot-warmer, -s 'fʊt͵wɔːmə*, -z
footwear 'fʊtweə*
fooz|le (s. v.) (F.), -les, -ling, -led, -ler/s 'fuːz|l, -lz, -lɪŋ [-lɪŋ], -ld, -lə*/z [-lə*/z]
fop, -s fɒp, -s
fopper|y, -ies 'fɒpər|ɪ, -ɪz
Foppington 'fɒpɪŋtən
foppish, -ly, -ness 'fɒpɪʃ, -lɪ, -nɪs [-nəs]
for (prep. conj.) fɔː* (strong form), fɒr (occasional strong form before vowels), fə* (weak form), f (alternative weak form before consonants), fr (alternative weak form before vowels).
forag|e (s. v.), -es, -ing, -ed, -er/s 'fɒrɪdʒ, -ɪz, -ɪŋ, -d, -ə*/z
forasmuch fərəz'mʌtʃ [͵fɔːr-, ͵fɒr-]
foray (s. v.), -s, -ing, -ed 'fɒreɪ, -z, -ɪŋ, -d
forbade (from forbid) fə'bæd [fɔː'b-, -'beɪd]
forbear (s.) (ancestor), -s 'fɔːbeə*, -z
forbear (v.), -s, -ing/ly, forbore, forborne fɔː'beə*, -z, -rɪŋ/lɪ, fɔː'bɔː* [-'bɔə*], fɔː'bɔːn
forbearance fɔː'beərəns
Forbes fɔːbz, 'fɔːbɪs
forbid, -s, -ding/ly, forbade, forbidden fə'bɪd [fɔː'b-], -z, -ɪŋ/lɪ, fə'bæd [fɔː'b-, -'beɪd], fə'bɪdn [fɔː'b-]
forbore (from forbear) fɔː'bɔː* [-'bɔə*]
forc|e (s. v.) (F.), -es, -ing, -ed, -edly, -edness, -er/s fɔːs, -ɪz, -ɪŋ, -t, -ɪdlɪ, -ɪdnɪs [-nəs], -ə*/z
force|ful, -fully, -fulness 'fɔːs|fʊl, -fʊlɪ [-fəlɪ], -fʊlnɪs [-nəs]
force majeure ͵fɔːs mæ'ʒɜː* (fɔrs maʒœːr)
force-meat 'fɔːsmiːt
forceps, -es 'fɔːseps [-sɪps], -ɪz
force-pump, -s 'fɔːspʌmp, -s

forcer, -s 'fɔːsə*, -z
forcib|le, -ly, -leness 'fɔːsəb|l [-sɪb-], -lɪ, -lnɪs [-nəs]
forcing-pit, -s 'fɔːsɪŋpɪt, -s
ford (s. v.), (F.), -s, -ing, -ed; -able fɔːd, -z, -ɪŋ, -ɪd; -əbl
Fordcombe 'fɔːdkəm
Ford|e, -er, -ham, -ingbridge fɔːd, -ə*, -əm, -ɪŋbrɪdʒ
fordone fɔː'dʌn
Fordoun 'fɔːdən [-dn]
Fordyce 'fɔːdaɪs
fore fɔː* [fɔə*]
forearm (s.), -s 'fɔːrɑːm ['fɔərɑːm, 'fɔːɑːm, 'fɔəɑːm], -z
forearm (v.), -s, -ing, -ed fɔːr'ɑːm [fɔər'ɑːm, fɔː'ɑːm, fɔə'ɑːm, ͵-'-], -z, -ɪŋ, -d
forebod|e, -es, -ing/ly, -ed, -er/s fɔː'bəʊd [fə'b-], -z, -ɪŋ/lɪ, -ɪd, -ə*/z
foreboding (s.), -s fɔː'bəʊdɪŋ [fə'b-], -z
forecabin, -s 'fɔː͵kæbɪn ['fɔə͵k-], -z
forecast (s.), -s 'fɔːkɑːst ['fɔə-], -s
forecast (v.), -s, -ing, -ed, -er/s 'fɔːkɑːst ['fɔəkɑːst, fɔː'kɑːst, fɔə'kɑːst], -s, -ɪŋ, -ɪd, -ə*/z
forecastle, -s 'fəʊksl, -z
foreclos|e, -es, -ing, -ed fɔː'kləʊz, -ɪz, -ɪŋ, -d
foreclosure, -s fɔː'kləʊʒə*, -z
forecourt, -s 'fɔːkɔːt ['fɔə-], -s
foredoom, -s, -ing, -ed fɔː'duːm, -z, -ɪŋ, -d
fore-end, -s 'fɔːrend ['fɔərend, 'fɔːend, 'fɔəend], -z
fore|father/s, -finger/s 'fɔː|͵fɑːðə*/z ['fɔə|-], -͵fɪŋgə*/z
fore|-foot, -feet -fʊt ['fɔə-], -fiːt
forefront 'fɔːfrʌnt ['fɔə-]
fore|go, -goes, -going, -went, -gone, -goer/s fɔː|'gəʊ, -'gəʊz, -'gəʊɪŋ, -'went, -'gɒn [as adjective '--], -'gəʊə*/z
foreground, -s 'fɔːgraʊnd ['fɔəg-], -z
forehand 'fɔːhænd ['fɔə-]
forehead, -s 'fɒrɪd [-red, 'fɔːhed, 'fɔəhed], -z
foreign, -er/s 'fɒrən [-rɪn], -ə*/z
forejudg|e, -es, -ing, -ed fɔː'dʒʌdʒ, -ɪz, -ɪŋ, -d
fore|know, -knows, -knowing, -knew, -known fɔː|'nəʊ, -'nəʊz, -'nəʊɪŋ, -'njuː, -'nəʊn
foreknowledge ͵fɔː'nɒlɪdʒ [fɔː'n-]
forel 'fɒrəl
foreland (F.), -s 'fɔːlənd ['fɔəl-], -z
foreleg, -s 'fɔːleg ['fɔəl-], -z
forelock, -s 'fɔːlɒk ['fɔə-], -s

fore|man (**F.**), **-men** 'fɔː|mən ['fɔə-], -mən

foremast, **-s** 'fɔːmɑːst ['fɔə-, *nautical pronunciation* -məst], -s

foremost 'fɔːməust ['fɔə-, -məst]

forenoon, **-s** 'fɔːnuːn ['fɔə-, -'-], -z

forensic fə'rensɪk [fɒ'r-]

fore-ordain, **-s**, **-ing**, **-ed** ˌfɔːrɔː'deɪn [ˌfɔə-], -z, -ɪŋ, -d

forepart, **-s** 'fɔːpɑːt ['fɔə-], -s

fore|run, **-runs**, **running**, **-ran** fɔː|'rʌn [fɔə-], -'rʌnz, -'rʌnɪŋ, -'ræn

forerunner, **-s** 'fɔːˌrʌnə* ['fɔə-, ˌ-'--], -z

foresail, **-s** 'fɔːseɪl ['fɔə-, *nautical pronunciation* -sl], -z

fore|see, **-sees**, **-seeing**, **-saw**, **-seen** fɔː|'siː [fɔə-], -'siːz, -'siːɪŋ, -'sɔː, -'siːn

foreshad|ow, **-ows**, **-owing**, **-owed**, **-ower/s** fɔː'ʃæd|əʊ [fɔə-], -əʊz, -əʊɪŋ, -əʊd, -əʊə*/z

foreshore, **-s** 'fɔːʃɔː* ['fɔː'ʃɔə*, 'fɔəʃɔə*], -z

foreshort|en, **-ens**, **-ening**, **-ened** fɔː-'ʃɔːt|n [fɔə-], -nz, -n̩ɪŋ [-nɪŋ], -nd

foreshow, **-s**, **-ing**, **-ed**, **-n** fɔː'ʃəʊ [fɔə-], -z, -ɪŋ, -d, -n

foresight, **-s** 'fɔːsaɪt ['fɔəsaɪt], -s

foreskin, **-s** 'fɔːskɪn ['fɔəskɪn], -z

forest (**F.**), **-s** 'fɒrɪst, -s

forestall, **-s** **-ing**, **-ed**, **-er/s** fɔː'stɔːl [fɔə-], -z, -ɪŋ, -d, -ə*/z

forester (**F.**), **-s** 'fɒrɪstə* [-rəstə*], -z

forest-land 'fɒrɪstlænd

forestry 'fɒrɪstrɪ [-rəstrɪ]

foretaste (*s.*), **-s** 'fɔːteɪst ['fɔə-], -s

foretast|e (*v.*), **-es**, **-ing**, **-ed** fɔː'teɪst [fɔə-], -s, -ɪŋ, -ɪd

fore|tell, **-tells**, **-telling**, **-told**, **-teller/s** fɔː|'tel [fɔə-], -'telz, -'telɪŋ, -'təʊld, -'telə*/z

forethought 'fɔːθɔːt ['fɔəθɔːt]

foretop, **-s**; **-mast/s** 'fɔːtɒp ['fɔːt-, *nautical pronunciation* -təp], -s; -mɑːst/s

fore-topsail, **-s** 'fɔːtɒpseɪl ['fɔət-, *nautical pronunciation* -sl], -z

forever fə'revə*

forewarn, **-s**, **-ing**, **-ed** fɔː'wɔːn [fɔə-], -z, -ɪŋ, -d

forewent (*from* forego) fɔː'went [fɔə-]

fore|woman, **-women** 'fɔː|ˌwʊmən ['fɔə-], -ˌwɪmɪn

foreword, **-s** 'fɔːwɜːd ['fɔə-], -z

Forfar 'fɔːfə* ['fɔːfɑː*]

forfeit (*s. v.*), **-s**, **-ing**, **-ed**, **-er/s**; **-able** 'fɔːfɪt, -s, -ɪŋ, -ɪd, -ə*/z; -əbl

forfeiture, **-s** 'fɔːfɪtʃə*, -z

forfend, **-s**, **-ing**, **-ed** fɔː'fend, -z, -ɪŋ, -ɪd

forgather, **-s**, **-ing**, **-ed** fɔː'gæðə*, -z, -rɪŋ, -d

forg|e (*s. v.*), **-es**, **-ing**, **-ed**, **-er/s** fɔːdʒ, -ɪz, -ɪŋ, -d, -ə*/z

forger|y, **-ies** 'fɔːdʒər|ɪ, -ɪz

for|get, **-gets**, **-getting**, **-got**, **-gotten** fə|'get, -'gets, -'getɪŋ, -'gɒt, -'gɒtn

forget|ful, **-fully**, **-fulness** fə'get|fʊl, -fʊlɪ [-fəlɪ], -fʊlnɪs [-nəs]

forget-me-not, **-s** fə'getmɪnɒt, -s

forgiv|e, **-es**, **-ing**, **forgave**, **forgiv|en**; **-able**, **-eness** fə'gɪv, -z, -ɪŋ, fə'geɪv, fə'gɪv|n; -əbl, -nɪs [-nəs]

for|go, **-goes**, **-going**, **-went**, **-gone** fɔː|'gəʊ, -'gəʊz, -'gəʊɪŋ, -'went, -'gɒn

forgot (*from* forget) fə'gɒt

Forington 'fɒrɪŋtən

fork (*s. v.*), **-s**, **-ing**, **-ed** fɔːk, -s, -ɪŋ, -t

fork|y, **-iness** 'fɔːk|ɪ, -ɪnɪs [-ɪnəs]

forlorn, **-ness** fə'lɔːn, -nɪs [-nəs]

form (*s. v.*), **-s**, **-ing**, **-ed**, **-er/s** fɔːm, -z, -ɪŋ, -d, -ə*/z

form|al, **-ally** 'fɔːm|l, -əlɪ

formaldehyde fɔː'mældɪhaɪd

formalin 'fɔːməlɪn

formali|sm, **-st/s** 'fɔːməlɪ|zəm [-m|ɪ-], -st/s

formalit|y, **-ies** fɔː'mælət|ɪ [-ɪt|ɪ], -ɪz

Forman 'fɔːmən

formant, **-s** 'fɔːmənt, -s

format, **-s** 'fɔːmæt, -s [-mɑː, -z]

formation, **-s** fɔː'meɪʃn, -z

formative 'fɔːmətɪv

forme, **-s** fɔːm, -z

former (*adj.*), **-ly** 'fɔːmə*, -lɪ

formic 'fɔːmɪk

formica fɔː'maɪkə [fə'm-]

formidab|le, **-ly**, **-leness** 'fɔːmɪdəb|l fɔː'mɪd-, fə'm-], -lɪ, -lnɪs [-nəs]

Formidable (*name of ship*) fɔː'mɪdəbl ['fɔː'mɪd-]

formless, **-ness** 'fɔːmlɪs [-əs], -nɪs [-nəs]

Formorian, **-s** fɔː'mɔːrɪən, -z

Formos|a, **-an/s** fɔː'məʊs|ə [-əʊz|ə], -n/z

Formosus fɔː'məʊsəs

formul|a, **-ae**, **-as** 'fɔːmjʊl|ə [-jəl-], -iː, -əz

formular|y, **-ies** 'fɔːmjʊlər|ɪ [-jəl-], -ɪz

formulat|e, **-es**, **-ing**, **-ed** 'fɔːmjʊleɪt [-jəl-], -s, -ɪŋ, -ɪd

formulation, **-s** ˌfɔːmjʊ'leɪʃn [-jə'l-], -z

Forn|ax, **-ey** 'fɔːn|æks, -ɪ

fornicat|e, -es, -ing, -ed, -or/s 'fɔːnɪ-keɪt, -s, -ɪŋ, -ɪd, -ə*/z
fornication ˌfɔːnɪ'keɪʃn
forrader 'fɒrədə*
Forres 'fɒrɪs
Forrest, -er 'fɒrɪst, -ə*
for|sake, -sakes, -saking, -sook, -saken fə|'seɪk [fɔː's-], -'seɪks, -'seɪkɪŋ, -'sʊk, -'seɪkən
Forshaw 'fɔːʃɔː
forsooth fə'suːθ [fɔː's-]
Forster 'fɔːstə*
forswear, -s, -ing, forswore, forsworn fɔː'sweə*, -z, -rɪŋ, fɔː'swɔː:* [-ɔə*], fɔː'swɔːn
Forsyte, -ism 'fɔːsaɪt, -ɪzəm
Forsyth fɔː'saɪθ
forsythia, -s fɔː'saɪθjə [fə's-, -θɪə], -z
fort, -s fɔːt, -s
fortalice, -s 'fɔːtəlɪs, -ɪz
forte (strong point), -s 'fɔːteɪ [-tɪ, fɔːt], -z [fɔːts]
forte (in music), -s 'fɔːtɪ, -z
Fortescue 'fɔːtɪskjuː
Forteviot fɔː'tiːvjət [-vɪət]
forth (F.) fɔːθ
forthcoming ˌfɔːθ'kʌmɪŋ [also '-ˌ— when attributive]
forthwith ˌfɔːθ'wɪθ [-'wɪð]
Forties (area in the North Sea) 'fɔːtɪz
fortieth, -s 'fɔːtɪɪθ [-tjɪθ, -tɪəθ, -tjəθ], -s
fortification, -s ˌfɔːtɪfɪ'keɪʃn, -z
forti|fy, -fies, -fying, -fied, -fier/s; -fiable 'fɔːtɪ|faɪ, -faɪz, -faɪɪŋ, -faɪd, -faɪə*/z; -faɪəbl
Fortinbras 'fɔːtɪnbræs
fort|is (phonetic term), -es 'fɔːt|ɪs, -iːz [-eɪz]
fortissimo, -s fɔː'tɪsɪməʊ, -z
fortitude 'fɔːtɪtjuːd
fortnight, -s 'fɔːtnaɪt, -s
fortnightl|y (F.), -ies 'fɔːtˌnaɪtl|ɪ [ˌ-'--], -ɪz
Fortnum 'fɔːtnəm
Fortran 'fɔːtræn
fortress, -es 'fɔːtrɪs [-trəs], -ɪz
fortuitous, -ly, -ness fɔː'tjuːɪtəs [-'tjʊɪ-, -ətəs], -lɪ, -nɪs [-nəs]
fortuit|y, -ies fɔː'tjuːɪt|ɪ [-'tjʊɪ-, -ət|ɪ], -ɪz
fortun|ate, -ately, -ateness 'fɔːtʃn|ət, [-tʃn|ət, -tʃən|ət, -ɪt], -ətlɪ [-ɪtlɪ], -ətnɪs [-ɪt-, -nəs]
Fortunatus ˌfɔːtjuː'neɪtəs [-tjʊ-]
fortune, -s; -less 'fɔːtʃuːn [-tʃən, -tjuːn], -z; -lɪs [-ləs]
Fortune (surname) 'fɔːtjuːn

fortune|-hunter/s, -teller/s 'fɔːtʃ ʃən|-ˌhʌntə*/z [-tʃuːn, -tjuːn], -ˌtelə*/z
fort|y, -ies, -ieth/s, -yfold 'fɔːt|ɪ, -ɪz, -ɪːθ/s [-jɪθ/s, -ɪəθ/s, -jəθ/s], -ɪfəʊld
forum, -s 'fɔːrəm, -z
forward (s. adj. v. interj.), -s, -ly, -ness, -er, -est; -ing, -ed, -er/s [in nautical use 'fɒrəd], -z, -lɪ, -nɪs [-nəs], -ə*, -ɪst; -ɪŋ, -ɪd, -ə*/z
forwent (from forgo) fɔː'went
Fos|bery, -broke, -bury 'fɒz|bərɪ, -brʊk, -bərɪ
Foss fɒs
fosse, -s fɒs, -ɪz
fossil, -s 'fɒsl [-sɪl], -z
fossiliferous ˌfɒsɪ'lɪfərəs
fossilization [-isa-] ˌfɒsɪlaɪ'zeɪʃn [-səl-, -lɪ'z-]
fossiliz|e [-is|e], -es, -ing, -ed 'fɒsɪlaɪz [-səl-], -ɪz, -ɪŋ, -d
fost|er (s. v.) (F.), -ers, -ering, -ered, -erer/s; -erage 'fɒst|ə*, -əz, -ərɪŋ, -əd, -ərə*/z; -ərɪdʒ
foster|-brother/s, -child, -children, -father/s, -mother/s, -sister/s 'fɒstə|ˌbrʌðə*/z, -tʃaɪld, -ˌtʃɪldrən [-ˌtʃʊld-], -ˌfɑːðə*/z, -ˌmʌðə*/z, -ˌsɪstə*/z
fother, -s 'fɒðə*, -z
Fothergill 'fɒðəgɪl
Fothering|ay, -ham 'fɒðərɪŋ|geɪ, -əm
Fouberts 'fuːbɜːts
fought (from fight) fɔːt
foul (s. adj. v.), -s; -er, -est, -ly, -ness, -ing, -ed faʊl, -z; -ə*, -ɪst, -lɪ ['faʊlɪ], -nɪs [-nəs]; -ɪŋ, -d
foulard 'fuːlɑː*
Foulden 'fəʊldən
Foulds fəʊldz
Foulerton 'fʊlətən
Foulger 'fuːldʒə*, 'fuːlgə*
Foulis faʊlz
Foulkes fəʊks, faʊks
foul-mouthed 'faʊlmaʊðd [ˌ-'-]
foulness 'faʊlnɪs [-nəs]
Foulness ˌfaʊl'nes [also '-- according to sentence-stress]
foul-play ˌfaʊl'pleɪ
Foulsham (in Norfolk) 'fəʊlʃəm
foul-spoken 'faʊlˌspəʊkən [ˌ-'--]
found, -s, -ing, -ed, -er/s faʊnd, -z, -ɪŋ, -ɪd, -ə*/z
found (from find) faʊnd
foundation, -s faʊn'deɪʃn, -z
foundationer, -s faʊn'deɪʃnə* [-ʃənə*, -ʃnə*], -z
found|er, -ers, -ering, -ered 'faʊnd|ə*, -əz, -ərɪŋ, -əd

199

foundling (F.), **-s** 'faʊndlɪŋ, -z
foundress, -es 'faʊndrɪs [-res], -ɪz
foundr|y, -ies 'faʊndr|ɪ, -ɪz
fount (*fountain, source*), **-s** faʊnt, -s
fount (*of type*), **-s** faʊnt [fɒnt], -s
Note.—Those connected with the printing trade generally pronounce fɒnt.
fountain (F.), **-s** 'faʊntɪn [-tən], -z
fountain-head, -s ˌfaʊntɪn'hed [-tən-, '‑‑‑], -z
fountain-pen, -s 'faʊntɪnpen [-tən-], -z
four, -s, -th/s, -thly fɔː* [fɔə*], -z, -θ/s, -θlɪ
four-cornered ˌfɔː'kɔːnəd [ˌfɔə-, *also* '‑,‑‑ *when attributive*]
four-dimensional ˌfɔːdɪ'menʃənl [ˌfɔə-, -daɪ'm-, -ʃnəl, -ʃn̩l, -ʃnl̩, -ʃənəl]
fourfold 'fɔːˌfəʊld ['fɔə-]
four-footed ˌfɔː'fʊtɪd [ˌfɔə-, *also* '‑,‑‑ *when attributive*]
Fourier 'fʊrɪeɪ ['fʊrɪə*] (furje)
four-in-hand, -s ˌfɔːrɪn'hænd [ˌfɔərɪn-, ˌfɔːɪn-], -z
fourish 'fɔːrɪʃ ['fɔər-]
four-legged 'fɔːlegd ['fɔə-, ˌfɔː'legɪd]
fourpence 'fɔːpəns
fourpenny 'fɔːpənɪ [-pn̩ɪ, -pnɪ] (*see note under* **penny**)
four-ply 'fɔːplaɪ ['fɔə-, ˌ‑'‑]
four-poster, -s ˌfɔː'pəʊstə* [ˌfɔə-], -z
fourscore ˌfɔː'skɔː* [ˌfɔə'skɔə*, *also* 'fɔːskɔː*, 'fɔəskɔə* *when immediately followed by a stress*]
four-sidedness ˌfɔː'saɪdɪdnɪs [ˌfɔə's-, -nəs]
foursome, -s 'fɔːsəm ['fɔə-], -z
foursquare ˌfɔː'skweə* [ˌfɔə'skweə*, '‑‑]
fourteen, -s, -th/s ˌfɔː'tiːn [ˌfɔə-, *also* '‑‑, -'‑ *according to sentence-stress*], -z, -θ/s
fourth, -s -ly fɔːθ [fɔəθ], -s, -lɪ
four-wheeler, -s ˌfɔː'wiːlə* [ˌfɔə-, -'hw‑], -z
Fowey fɔɪ ['fəʊɪ]
Fowke faʊk, fəʊk
Fowkes fəʊks
fowl (s. v.), **-s, -ing, -ed, -er/s** faʊl, -z, -ɪŋ, -d, -ə*/z
Fowler 'faʊlə*
Fowles faʊlz
fowl-hou|se, -ses 'faʊlhaʊ|s, -zɪz
fowling/-net/s, -piece/s 'faʊlɪŋ|net/s, -piːs/ɪz
fowl-run, -s 'faʊlrʌn, -z
Fownes faʊnz

fox (s. v.) (F.), **-es, -ing, -ed** fɒks, -ɪz, -ɪŋ, -t
Foxboro' 'fɒksbərə
fox-brush, -es 'fɒksbrʌʃ, -ɪz
Foxcroft 'fɒkskrɒft
Foxfield 'fɒksfiːld
foxglove, -s 'fɒksglʌv, -z
foxhole, -s 'fɒkshəʊl, -z
foxhound, -s 'fɒkshaʊnd, -z
foxhunt, -s 'fɒkshʌnt, -s
foxterrier, -s ˌfɒks'terɪə*, -z
foxtrot, -s 'fɒkstrɒt, -s
Foxwell 'fɒkswəl [-wel]
fox|y, -ier, -iest, -ily, -iness 'fɒks|ɪ, -ɪə* [-jə*], -ɪɪst [-jɪst], -ɪlɪ [-əlɪ], -ɪnɪs [-ɪnəs]
foyer, -s 'fɔɪeɪ (fwaje), -z
Foyers 'fɔɪəz
Foyle fɔɪl
fracas (*sing.*) 'frækɑː, (*plur.*) -z
Frackville 'frækvɪl
fraction, -s 'frækʃn, -z
fractional 'frækʃənl [-ʃnəl, -ʃn̩l, -ʃnl̩, -ʃənəl]
fractious, -ly, -ness 'frækʃəs, -lɪ, -nɪs [-nəs]
frac|ture (s. v.), **-tures, -turing, -tured** 'fræk|tʃə*, -tʃəz, -tʃərɪŋ, -tʃəd
Fradin 'freɪdɪn
fragile, -ly, -ness 'frædʒaɪl [*rarely* -dʒɪl], -lɪ, -nɪs [-nəs]
fragility frə'dʒɪlətɪ [fræ'dʒ-, -ɪtɪ]
fragment (s.), **-s** 'frægmənt, -s
fragment (v.), **-s, -ing, -ed** fræg'ment, -s, -ɪŋ, -ɪd
fragmental fræg'mentl
fragmentar|y, -ily, -iness 'frægmən-tər|ɪ [fræg'mentər|ɪ], -əlɪ [-ɪlɪ], -ɪnɪs [-ɪnəs]
fragmentation ˌfrægmen'teɪʃn [-mən-]
fragran|ce, -cy, -t/ly, -tness 'freɪgrən|s, -sɪ, -t/lɪ, -tnɪs [-nəs]
frail, -er, -est, -ly, -ness freɪl, -ə*, -ɪst, -lɪ, -nɪs [-nəs]
frailt|y, -ies 'freɪlt|ɪ, -ɪz
Fram fræm
fram|e (s. v.), **-es, -ing, -ed, -er/s** freɪm, -z, -ɪŋ, -d, -ə*/z
frame-up, -s 'freɪmʌp, -s
framework, -s 'freɪmwɜːk, -s
Framingham 'freɪmɪŋəm
Framlingham 'fræmlɪŋəm
Frampton 'fræmptən
franc, -s fræŋk, -s
France frɑːns
Frances 'frɑːnsɪs
Francesca fræn'seskə, fræn'tʃeskə
franchise, -s 'fræntʃaɪz, -ɪz

franchisee, -s ˌfræntʃaɪˈziː, -z
Francie ˈfrɑːnsɪ
Francillon frænˈsɪlən
Francis ˈfrɑːnsɪs
Franciscan, -s frænˈsɪskən, -z
Francisco (personal name) frænˈsɪskəʊ, (in San Francisco) frənˈsɪskəʊ
Franck frɑ̃ːŋk [frɑːŋk, fræŋk] (frɑ̃ːk)
Franco-German ˌfræŋkəʊˈdʒɜːmən
francolin, -s ˈfræŋkəʊlɪn, -z
Franconia, -n fræŋˈkəʊnjə [-nɪə], -n
francophile, -s ˈfræŋkəʊfaɪl, -z
francophobe, -s ˈfræŋkəʊfəʊb, -z
frangibility ˌfrændʒɪˈbɪlətɪ [-dʒəˈb-, -lɪt-]
frangible, -ness ˈfrændʒɪbl [-dʒəb-], -nɪs [-nəs]
frank (adj. v.), -er, -est, -ly, -ness; -s, -ing, -ed fræŋk, -ə*, -ɪst, -lɪ, -nɪs [-nəs]; -s, -ɪŋ, -t [fræŋt]
Frank, -s fræŋk, -s
Frankau (English surname) ˈfræŋkəʊ
Frankenstein ˈfræŋkənstaɪn
Frankfort (-furt) ˈfræŋkfət [-fɔːt]
frankfurter, -s ˈfræŋkfɜːtə*, -z
frankincense ˈfræŋkɪnˌsens
Frankish ˈfræŋkɪʃ
Frankland ˈfræŋklənd
franklin (F.), -s ˈfræŋklɪn, -z
Franklyn ˈfræŋklɪn
frantic, -ally, -ness ˈfræntɪk, -əlɪ, -nɪs [-nəs]
Franz frænts
frap, -s, -ping, -ped fræp, -s, -ɪŋ, -t
frappé ˈfræpeɪ (frape)
Frascati fræˈskɑːtɪ
Fraser, -burgh ˈfreɪzə*, -bərə* [-bʌrə]
fratern|al, -ally frəˈtɜːn|l, -əlɪ
fraternit|y, -ies frəˈtɜːnət|ɪ [-ɪt|ɪ], -ɪz
fraternization [-isa-] ˌfrætənaɪˈzeɪʃn [-nɪˈz-]
fraterniz|e [-is|e], -es, -ing, -ed, -er/s ˈfrætənaɪz, -ɪz, -ɪŋ, -d, -ə*/z
fratricidal ˌfrætrɪˈsaɪdl [ˌfreɪt-]
fratricide, -s ˈfrætrɪsaɪd [ˈfreɪt-], -z
Fratton ˈfrætn
fraud, -s frɔːd, -z
fraudulen|ce, -t/ly ˈfrɔːdjʊlən|s, -t/lɪ
fraught frɔːt
fray (s. v.), -s, -ing, -ed freɪ, -z, -ɪŋ, -d
Frazer ˈfreɪzə*
frazil ˈfreɪzɪl
frazz|le (s. v.), -les, -ling, -led ˈfræz|l, -lz, -lɪŋ [-lɪŋ], -ld
freak, -s friːk, -s
Freake friːk
freakish, -ly, -ness ˈfriːkɪʃ, -lɪ, -nɪs [-nəs]

freak|y, -ier, -iest, -ily, -iness ˈfriːk|ɪ, -ɪə* [-jə*], -ɪɪst [-jɪst], -ɪlɪ [-əlɪ], -ɪnɪs [-ɪnəs]
Frean friːn
freck|le (s. v.), -les, -ling, -led ˈfrek|l, -lz, -lɪŋ [-lɪŋ], -ld
freckly ˈfreklɪ [-lɪ]
Frecknall ˈfreknɔːl [-nl̩]
Fred, -die, -dy fred, -ɪ, -ɪ
Frederic(k) ˈfredrɪk
Frederica ˌfredəˈriːkə
free (adj. v.), -r, -st, -ly; -s, -ing, -d, -r/s friː, -ə* [frɪə*], -ɪst, -lɪ; -z, -ɪŋ, -d, -ə*/z [frɪə*/z]
freebooter, -s ˈfriːˌbuːtə*, -z
free-born ˌfriːˈbɔːn [ˈ--, esp. when attributive]
freed|man, -men ˈfriːd|mæn [-mən], -men [-mən]
freedom, -s ˈfriːdəm, -z
free-for-all ˈfriːfərˌɔːl [ˌ--ˈ-]
free-hand (adj.) ˈfriːhænd
free-hearted, -ly, -ness ˌfriːˈhɑːtɪd, -lɪ, -nɪs [-nəs]
freehold, -s; -er/s ˈfriːhəʊld [ˈfriːəʊld], -z; -ə*/z
free-lance, -s ˈfriːlɑːns [ˌ-ˈ-], -ɪz
Freeling ˈfriːlɪŋ
free|man (of a city), -men ˈfriː|mən, -mən, (opposed to slave) ˈfriː|mæn [-mən], -men [-mən]
Freeman ˈfriːmən
freemason, -s ˈfriːˌmeɪsn, -z
freemasonry ˈfriːˌmeɪsnrɪ [ˌfriːˈm-]
Freeport ˈfriːpɔːt
freesia, -s ˈfriːzjə [-zɪə, -ʒjə, -ʒɪə, -ʒə], -z
free-spoken ˌfriːˈspəʊkən [ˈ-ˌ--]
freestone ˈfriːstəʊn
freethinker, -s ˌfriːˈθɪŋkə*, -z
Freetown ˈfriːtaʊn
free-trade, -er/s ˌfriːˈtreɪd, -ə*/z
free-wheel (s. v.), -s, -ing, -ed ˌfriːˈwiːl [-ˈhw-, ˈ--], -z, -ɪŋ, -d
freewill ˌfriːˈwɪl [also ˈ-- according to sentence-stress]
freez|e, -es, -ing, froze, frozen, freezer/s friːz, -ɪz, -ɪŋ, frəʊz, ˈfrəʊzn, ˈfriːzə*/z
freezing-machine, -s ˈfriːzɪŋməˌʃiːn, -z
freezing-mixture ˈfriːzɪŋˌmɪkstʃə*
freezing-point ˈfriːzɪŋpɔɪnt
Freiburg ˈfraɪbəːg
freight (s. v.), -s, -ing, -ed, -er/s; -age freɪt, -s, -ɪŋ, -ɪd, -ə*/z; -ɪdʒ
Fremantle ˈfriːmæntl
fremitus ˈfremɪtəs
Fremont frɪˈmɒnt
French frentʃ

frenchi|fy, -fies, -fying, -fied 'frent∫ı|-
faı, -faız, -faııŋ, -faıd
French|man, -men 'frent∫|mən, -mən
french-polish (s. v.), -es, -ing, -ed, -er/s
‚frent∫'pɒlı∫, -ız, -ıŋ, -t, -ə*/z
French|woman, -women 'frent∫|-
‚wʊmən, -‚wımın
french|y, -ily, -iness 'frent∫ı|ı, -əlı
[-ılı], -ınıs [-ınəs]
frenetic frə'netık [frı-, fre-]
frenz|y, -ies, -ied/ly 'frenz|ı, -ız, -ıd/lı
frequen|ce, -cy, -cies 'fri:kwən|s, -sı,
-sız
frequent (adj.), -ly, -ness 'fri:kwənt, -lı,
-nıs [-nəs]
frequent (v.), -s, -ing, -ed, -er/s frı-
'kwent [fri:'k-], -s, -ıŋ, -ıd, -ə*/z
frequentation ‚fri:kwen'teı∫n
frequentative (s. adj.), -s frı'kwentətıv,
-z
Frere frıə*
fresco, -(e)s 'freskəʊ, -z
fresh, -er, -est, -ly, -ness fre∫, -ə*, -ıst,
-lı, -nıs [-nəs]
fresh|en, -ens, -ening, -ened 'fre∫|n,
-nz, -ŋıŋ [-nıŋ], -nd
fresher (s.), -s 'fre∫ə*, -z
freshet, -s 'fre∫ıt, -s
fresh|man, -men 'fre∫|mən, -mən
freshwater (F.) 'fre∫‚wɔ:tə*
Fresno 'freznəʊ
fret (s. v.), -s, -ting, -ted, -ter/s fret,
-s, -ıŋ, -ıd, -ə*/z
fret|ful, -fully, -fulness 'fret|fʊl, -fʊlı
[-fəlı], -fʊlnıs [-nəs]
fret|saw/s, -work 'fret|sɔ:/z, -wɜ:k
Freud, -ian frɔıd, -jən [-ıən]
Frey (English surname) freı
Freyberg 'fraıbə:g
Freyer frıə*, 'fraıə*
friability ‚fraıə'bılətı [-lıt-]
friable, -ness 'fraıəbl, -nıs [-nəs]
friar, -s 'fraıə*, -z
friar|y, -ies 'fraıər|ı, -ız
fribb|le (s. v.), -les, -ling, -led, -ler/s
'frıb|l, -lz, -lıŋ [-lıŋ], -ld, -lə*/z
[-lə*/z]
fricandeau, -x 'frıkəndəʊ [-kɑ:n-]
(frikãdo), -z
fricassee (s.), -s 'frıkəsi: [‚--'-], -z
fricassee (v.), -s, -ing, -d ‚frıkə'si: ['---],
-z, -ıŋ, -d
fricative (s. adj.), -s 'frıkətıv, -z
friction, -s; -less 'frık∫n, -z; -lıs [-ləs,
-les]
frictional 'frık∫ənl [-∫nl, -∫nl, -∫ənəl]
Friday, -s 'fraıdı [-deı], -z
fridge, -s frıdʒ, -ız

fried (from fry) fraıd
friend, -s frend, -z
friendless, -ness 'frendlıs [-ləs], -nıs
[-nəs]
friendl|y, -ier, -iest, -iness 'frendl|ı,
-ıə* [-jə*], -ııst [-jıst], -ınıs [-ınəs]
Friendl|y, -ies 'frendl|ı, -ız
friendship, -s 'frend∫ıp, -s
Friern 'fraıən
fries (from fry) fraız
Fries fri:s [fri:z]
Friesian 'fri:zjən [-zıən, -ʒən, -ʒıən,
-ʒən]
Friesic 'fri:zık
Friesland, -er/s 'fri:zlənd [-lænd], -ə*/z
frieze (F.), -s fri:z, -ız
frigate, -s 'frıgıt [-gət], -s
fright (s. v.), -s, -ing, -ed fraıt, -s, -ıŋ,
-ıd
fright|en, -ens, -ening, -ened 'fraıt|n,
-nz, -nıŋ [-ŋıŋ], -nd
fright|ful, -fully, -fulness 'fraıt|fʊl, -flı
[-fəlı, -fʊlı], -fʊlnıs [-nəs]
frigid, -ly, -ness 'frıdʒıd, -lı, -nıs [-nəs]
frigidity frı'dʒıdətı [-ıtı]
Friis fri:s
frill (s. v.), -s, -ing, -ed frıl, -z, -ıŋ, -d
frill|y, -ier, -iest 'frıl|ı, -ıə*, -ııst
Frimley 'frımlı
fring|e (s. v.), -es, -ing, -ed; -eless, -y
frındʒ, -ız, -ıŋ, -d; -lıs [-ləs], -ı
fripper|y, -ies 'frıpər|ı, -ız
frisette, -s frı'zet, -s
Frisian, -s 'frızıən [-zjən, -ʒıən, -ʒjən,
-ʒən], -z
frisk (s. v.), -s, -ing, -ed, -er/s frısk,
-s, -ıŋ, -t, -ə*/z
frisket, -s 'frıskıt, -s
frisk|y, -ier, -iest, -ily, -ness 'frısk|ı,
-ıə* [-jə*], -ııst [-jıst], -ılı [-əlı], -ınıs
[-ınəs]
Friswell 'frızwəl [-wel]
frit (s. v.), -s, -ting, -ted frıt, -s, -ıŋ, -ıd
frith (F.), -s frıθ, -s
Frithsden (near Berkhamsted) 'fri:zdən
['frız-, 'frıθsdən]
fritillar|y, -ies frı'tılər|ı, -ız
fritter (s. v.), -s, -ing, -ed 'frıtə*, -z,
-rıŋ, -d
Fritton 'frıtn
Fritz frıts
friv|ol, -ols, -ol(l)ing, -ol(l)ed 'frıv|l,
-lz, -lıŋ [-əlıŋ], -ld
frivolit|y, -ies frı'vɒlət|ı [-ıt|ı], -ız
frivolous, -ly, -ness 'frıvələs [-vləs], -lı,
-nıs [-nəs]
Frizell frı'zel
frizette, -s frı'zet, -s

Frizinghall 'fraɪzɪŋhɔːl
Frizington 'frɪzɪŋtən
friz(z), -es, -ing, -ed frɪz, -ɪz, -ɪŋ, -d
frizz|le, -les, -ling, -led 'frɪz|l, -lz, -lɪŋ [-lɪŋ], -ld
frizzl|y, -iness 'frɪzl|ɪ [-zl|ɪ], -ɪnɪs [-məs]
frizz|y, -ier, -iest, -iness 'frɪz|ɪ, -ɪə*, -ɪɪst, -ɪnɪs [-məs]
fro frəʊ
Frobisher 'frəʊbɪʃə*
frock, -s frɒk, -s
frock-coat, -s, -ed ˌfrɒk'kəʊt [also '-- when followed by a stress], -s, -ɪd
Froebel 'frəʊbl ['frɜːbl] ('frøːbəl)
frog, -s frɒg, -z
frogg|y (s. adj.), -ies 'frɒg|ɪ, -ɪz
frog|man, -men 'frɒg|mən, -mən
frog-march, -es, -ing, -ed 'frɒgmɑːtʃ, -ɪz, -ɪŋ, -t
Frogmore 'frɒgmɔː* [-mɔə*]
frolic (s. v.), -s, -king, -ked 'frɒlɪk, -s, -ɪŋ, -t
frolicsome, -ness 'frɒlɪksəm, -nɪs [-nəs]
from frɒm (strong form), frəm, frm (weak forms)
Frome (in Somerset) fruːm
frond, -s frɒnd, -z
front (s. adj. v.), -s, -ing, -ed frʌnt, -s, -ɪŋ, -ɪd
frontage, -s 'frʌntɪdʒ, -ɪz
frontal (s.), -s 'frʌntl ['frɒn-], -z
frontal (adj.) 'frʌntl
frontier, -s 'frʌnˌtɪə* ['frɒn-, -tɪə*, -tjə*], -z
frontispiece, -s 'frʌntɪspiːs ['frɒn-], -ɪz
front|less, -let/s 'frʌnt|lɪs [-ləs, -les], -lɪt/s [-lət/s]
frost (s. v.) (F.), -s, -ing, -ed frɒst [old-fashioned frɔːst, and in compounds], -s, -ɪŋ, -ɪd
frost|bite/s, -bitten, -bound 'frɒst|baɪt/s ['frɔː-st-], -ˌbɪtn, -baʊnd
frostwork 'frɒstwɜːk ['frɔːst-]
frost|y, -ier, -iest, -ily, -iness 'frɒst|ɪ ['frɔː-st-], -ɪə* [-jə*], -ɪɪst [-jɪst], -ɪlɪ [-əlɪ], -ɪnɪs [-məs]
froth (s. v.), -s, -ing, -ed frɒθ [old-fashioned frɔːθ], -s, -ɪŋ, -t
Frothingham 'frɒðɪŋəm
froth|y, -ier, -iest, -ily, -iness 'frɒθ|ɪ ['frɔː-θ|ɪ], -ɪə*, -ɪɪst, -ɪlɪ [-əlɪ], -ɪnɪs [-məs]
Froud fruːd, fraʊd
Froude fruːd
frou-frou 'fruːfruː
froward, -ly, -ness 'frəʊəd, -lɪ, -nɪs [-nəs]
Frowde fruːd, fraʊd

frown (s. v.), -s, -ing/ly, -ed fraʊn, -z, -ɪŋ/lɪ, -d
frowst (s. v.), -s, -ing, -ed; -y, -iness fraʊst, -s, -ɪŋ, -ɪd; -ɪ, -ɪnɪs [-məs]
frowz|y, -iness 'fraʊz|ɪ, -ɪnɪs [-məs]
froze, -n (from freeze) frəʊz, -n
fructiferous frʌk'tɪfərəs
fructification ˌfrʌktɪfɪ'keɪʃn
fructi|fy, -fies, -fying, -fied 'frʌktɪ|faɪ, -faɪz, -faɪɪŋ, -faɪd
frug|al, -ally, -alness 'fruːg|l, -əlɪ, -lnɪs [-nəs]
frugality fruː'gælətɪ [frʊ'g-, -ɪtɪ]
fruit (s. v.), -s, -ing, -ed; -age fruːt, -s, -ɪŋ, -ɪd; -ɪdʒ
fruitarian, -s fruː'teərɪən, -z
fruiterer, -s 'fruːtərə*, -z
fruit|ful, -fully, -fulness 'fruːt|fʊl, -fʊlɪ [-fəlɪ], -fʊlnɪs [-nəs]
fruition fruː'ɪʃn [frʊ'ɪ-]
fruitless, -ly, -ness 'fruːtlɪs [-ləs], -lɪ, -nɪs [-nəs]
fruit-machine, -s 'fruːtməˌʃiːn, -z
fruit|y, -ier, -iest, -iness 'fruːt|ɪ, -ɪə*, -ɪɪst, -ɪnɪs [-məs]
frumenty 'fruːməntɪ
frump, -s; -ish frʌmp, -s; -ɪʃ
frustrat|e, -es, -ing, -ed frʌ'streɪt ['frʌstreɪt], -s, -ɪŋ, -ɪd
frustration frʌ'streɪʃn
frust|um, -a, -ums 'frʌst|əm, -ə, -əmz
fr|y (s. v.) (F.), -ies, -ying, -ied fr|aɪ, -aɪz, -aɪɪŋ, -aɪd
Frye fraɪ
Fuad 'fuːæd ['fʊæd]
fuchsia, -s 'fjuːʃə, -z
fuchsine 'fuːksiːn
fu|cus, -ci 'fjuː|kəs, -saɪ
fudd|le (s. v.), -les, -ling, -led, -ler/s 'fʌd|l, -lz, -lɪŋ, -ld, -lə*/z
fudg|e (s. v.), -es, -ing, -ed fʌdʒ, -ɪz, -ɪŋ, -d
Fudge fjuːdʒ, fʌdʒ
Fuehrer, -s 'fjʊərə* ['fjɔə-, 'fjɔː-], -z
fuel, -s fjʊəl ['fjuːəl, fjuːl], -z
fug, -s fʌg, -z
fugacious, -ly, -ness fjuː'geɪʃəs [fjʊ'g-], -lɪ, -nɪs [-nəs]
fugacity fjuː'gæsətɪ [fjʊ'g-, -ɪtɪ]
fugal 'fjuːgl
fugg|y, -ier, -iest, -iness 'fʌg|ɪ, -ɪə*, -ɪɪst, -ɪnɪs [-məs]
fugitive (s. adj.), -s, -ly, -ness 'fjuːdʒɪtɪv [-dʒət-], -z, -lɪ, -nɪs [-nəs]
fugle|man, -men 'fjuːglmæn [-mən], -men [-mən]
fugue, -s fjuːg, -z
Fulcher 'fʊltʃə*

fulcr|um, -a, -ums 'fʌlkr|əm ['fʊl-], -ə, -əmz

fulfil, -s, -ling, -led, -ler/s, -ment fʊl'fıl, -z, -ıŋ, -d, -ə*/z, -mənt

Fulford 'fʊlfəd

fulgent, -ly 'fʌldʒənt, -lı

fulgurat|e, -es, -ing, -ed 'fʌlgjʊəreıt, -s, -ıŋ, -ıd

Fulham 'fʊləm

fuliginous, -ly fju:'lıdʒınəs, -lı

Fulke fʊlk

full, -er, -est, -y, -ness fʊl, -ə*, -ıst, -ı, -nıs [-nəs]

full-back, -s 'fʊlbæk [ˌ-'-], -s

full-blooded ˌfʊl'blʌdıd [also '-ˌ-- when attributive]

full-blown ˌfʊl'bləʊn [also '-- when attributive]

full-bodied ˌfʊl'bɒdıd [also '-ˌ- when attributive]

fuller (F.), -s 'fʊlə*, -z

Fullerton 'fʊlətn

full-face ˌfʊl'feıs ['--]

full-fledged ˌfʊl'fledʒd [also '-- when attributive]

full-grown ˌfʊl'grəʊn [also '-- when attributive]

full-length ˌfʊl'leŋkθ [also '-- when attributive]

fulmar, -s 'fʊlmə* [-mɑ:*], -z

Fulmer (in Buckinghamshire) 'fʊlmə*

fulminat|e, -es, -ing, -ed 'fʌlmıneıt, -s, -ıŋ, -ıd

fulmination, -s ˌfʌlmı'neıʃn, -z

fulness 'fʊlnıs [-nəs]

fulsome, -ly, -ness 'fʊlsəm, -lı, -nıs [-nəs]

Fulton 'fʊltən

Fulvia 'fʌlvıə [-vjə]

fulvous 'fʌlvəs

Fulwood 'fʊlwʊd

fumb|le, -les, -ling, -led, -ler/s 'fʌmb|l, -lz, -lıŋ, -ld, -lə*/z

fum|e (s. v.), -es, -ing, -ed fju:m, -z, -ıŋ, -d

fumigat|e, -es, -ing, -ed, -or/s 'fju:mıgeıt, -s, -ıŋ, -ıd, -ə*/z

fumigation, -s ˌfju:mı'geıʃn, -z

fun fʌn

funambulist, -s fju:'næmbjʊlıst [fjʊ'n-], -s

Funchal fʊn'ʃɑ:l

functi|on (s. v.), -ons, -oning, -oned 'fʌŋkʃ|n, -nz, -nıŋ [-ənıŋ], -nd

functionalism 'fʌŋkʃnəlızəm [-ʃn̩-, -ʃənlı-, -ʃənəl-]

functionar|y, -ies 'fʌŋkʃnər|ı [-ʃənər-, -ʃnər-], -ız

fund (s. v.), -s, -ing, -ed fʌnd, -z, -ıŋ, -ıd

fundament, -s 'fʌndəmənt, -s

fundament|al (s. adj.), -als, -ally ˌfʌndə'ment|l, -lz, -əlı [-lı]

fundamentali|sm, -st/s ˌfʌndə'mentəlı|zəm [-tlı-], -st/s

fundamentality ˌfʌndəmen'tælətı [-ıtı]

fund-holder, -s 'fʌndˌhəʊldə*, -z

fundless 'fʌndlıs [-ləs, -les]

Fundy 'fʌndı

funeral, -s 'fju:nərəl, -z

funereal fju:'nıərıəl [fjʊ'n-]

funfair, -s 'fʌnfeə*, -z

fungible (s. adj.), -s 'fʌndʒıbl [-dʒəbl], -z

fungicide, -s 'fʌndʒısaıd ['fʌŋgı-], -z

fung|us, -i, -uses; -oid, -ous, -usy 'fʌŋg|əs, -aı ['fʌndʒı, 'fʌndʒaı], -əsız; -ɔıd, -əs, -əsı

funicle, -s 'fju:nıkl, -z

funicular (s. adj.), -s fju:'nıkjʊlə* [fjʊ'n-, fə'nık-, fn̩'ık-, -kjəl-], -z

funicul|us, -i fju:'nıkjʊl|əs [fjʊ'n-, -kjəl-], -aı

funk (s. v.) (F.), -s, -ing, -ed fʌŋk, -s, -ıŋ, -t [fʌŋt]

funkia, -s 'fʌŋkjə [-kıə], -z

funk|y, -ier, -iest, -ily, -iness 'fʌŋk|ı, -ıə* [-jə*], -ııst [-jıst], -ılı [-əlı], -ınıs [-nəs]

funnel, -s 'fʌnl, -z

funn|y, -ier, -iest, -ily, -iness 'fʌn|ı, -ıə*, -ııst, -ılı [-əlı], -ınıs [-nəs]

funnybone, -s 'fʌnıbəʊn, -z

fur (s. v.), -s, -ring, -red fɜ:*, -z, -rıŋ, -d

Furbear 'fɜ:beə*

furbelow, -s 'fɜ:bıləʊ, -z

furbish, -es, -ing, -ed 'fɜ:bıʃ, -ız, -ıŋ, -t

furcate (adj.) 'fɜ:keıt [-kıt, -kət]

furcat|e (v.), -es, -ing, -ed 'fɜ:keıt [fɜ:'k-], -s, -ıŋ, -ıd

furcation, -s fɜ:'keıʃn, -z

furibund 'fjʊərıbʌnd ['fjɔər-, 'fjɔ:r-, -bənd]

furioso (F.) ˌfjʊərı'əʊzəʊ [ˌfjɔər-, ˌfjɔ:r-, -'əʊsəʊ]

furious, -ly, -ness 'fjʊərıəs ['fjɔər-, 'fjɔ:r-], -lı, -nıs [-nəs]

furl, -s, -ing, -ed fɜ:l, -z, -ıŋ, -d

furlong, -s 'fɜ:lɒŋ, -z

furlough, -s 'fɜ:ləʊ, -z

furnace, -s 'fɜ:nıs [-nəs], -ız

Furneaux 'fɜ:nəʊ

Furness 'fɜ:nıs [-nes]

Furneux (in Hertfordshire) 'fɜ:nıks [-nu:, -nəʊ]

Note.—'fɜ:nıks is the more usual local pronunciation.

furnish, -es, -ing, -ed, -er/s 'fɜːnɪʃ, -ɪz, -ɪŋ, -t, -ə*/z
furniture 'fɜːnɪtʃə*
Furnival(l) 'fɜːnɪvəl
furore (admiration, craze), -s fjʊə'rɔːrɪ ['fjʊərɔː*], -z
furore (musical term) fʊ'rɔːrɪ
furrier (s.), -s 'fʌrɪə*, -z
furrier|y, -ies 'fʌrɪər|ɪ, -ɪz
furr|ow (s. v.), -ows, -owing, -owed; -owy 'fʌr|əʊ, -əʊz, -əʊɪŋ, -əʊd; -əʊɪ
furr|y, -ier, -iest, -iness 'fɜːr|ɪ [rarely 'fʌr-], -ɪə*, -ɪɪst, -ɪnɪs [-nəs]
furth|er (adj. v. adv.), -ers, -ering, -ered, -erer/s 'fɜːð|ə*, -əz, -ərɪŋ, -əd, -ərə*/z
furtherance 'fɜːðərəns
furthermore ,fɜːðə'mɔː* [-'mɔːə*]
furthermost 'fɜːðəməʊst
furthest 'fɜːðɪst
furtive, -ly, -ness 'fɜːtɪv, -lɪ, -nɪs [-nəs]
furuncle, -s 'fjʊərʌŋkl, -z
fur|y (F.), -ies 'fjʊər|ɪ ['fjɔər-, 'fjɔːr-], -ɪz
furze; -bush/es fɜːz; -bʊʃ/ɪz
Fusbos 'fʌzbɒs
fuscous 'fʌskəs
fus|e (s. v.), -es, -ing, -ed fjuːz, -ɪz, -ɪŋ, -d
fusee, -s fjuː'ziː, -z
fuselage, -s 'fjuːzɪlɑːʒ [-zə-, -lɪdʒ], -ɪz
fusel-oil ,fjuːzl'ɔɪl ['---]
fusibility ,fjuːzə'bɪlətɪ [-zɪ'b-, -lɪt-]
fusible 'fjuːzəbl [-zɪb-]
fusil, -s 'fjuːzɪl, -z

fusile 'fjuːsaɪl [-uːzaɪl]
fusilier, -s ,fjuːzɪ'lɪə* [-zə'lɪə*, -zl'ɪə*], -z
fusillade, -s ,fjuːzɪ'leɪd [-zə'l-], -z
fusion, -s 'fjuːʒn, -z
fuss (s. v.), -es, -ing, -ed, -er/s fʌs, -ɪz, -ɪŋ, -t, -ə*/z
fuss|y, -ier, -iest, -ily, -iness 'fʌs|ɪ, -ɪə*, -ɪɪst, -ɪlɪ [-əlɪ], -ɪnɪs [-ɪnəs]
fustian 'fʌstɪən [-tjən]
fustic 'fʌstɪk
fustigat|e, -es, -ing, -ed 'fʌstɪɡeɪt, -s, -ɪŋ, -ɪd
fustigation, -s ,fʌstɪ'ɡeɪʃn, -z
fust|y, -ier, -iest, -ily, -iness 'fʌst|ɪ, -ɪə* [-jə*], -ɪɪst [-jɪst], -ɪlɪ [-əlɪ], -ɪnɪs [-nəs]
futile, -ly, -ness 'fjuːtaɪl, -lɪ, -nɪs [-nəs]
futilit|y, -ies fjuː'tɪlət|ɪ [fjʊ't-, -ɪt|ɪ], -ɪz
futtock, -s 'fʌtək, -s
future (s. adj.), -s 'fjuːtʃə*, -z
futurist, -s 'fjuːtʃərɪst [-tʃʊr-], -s
futuristic ,fjuːtʃə'rɪstɪk [-tʃʊ'r-, -tjə-, -tjʊ-]
futurit|y, -ies fjuː'tjʊərət|ɪ [fjʊ'tj-, -'tjɔər-, -'tjɔːr-, -ɪt|ɪ], -ɪz
fuzz (s. v.), -es, -ing, -ed fʌz, -ɪz, -ɪŋ, -d
fuzzball, -s 'fʌzbɔːl, -z
fuzzbuzz, -es 'fʌzbʌz, -ɪz
fuzz|y, -ier, -iest, -ily, -iness 'fʌz|ɪ, -ɪə*, -ɪɪst, -ɪlɪ [-əlɪ], -ɪnɪs [-nəs]
Fyf(f)e faɪf
Fyfield 'faɪfiːld
Fyne, -s faɪn, -z
Fyson 'faɪsn

G

G (*the letter*), **-'s** dʒi:, -z

gab (*s. v.*), **-s, -bing, -bed** gæb, -z, -ɪŋ, -d

Gabbatha 'gæbəθə

Gabbitas 'gæbɪtæs

gabb|le, **-les, -ling, -led, -ler/s** 'gæb|l, -lz, -lɪŋ [-lɪŋ], -ld, -lə*/z [-lə*/z]

gaberdine, **-s** ˌgæbədi:n [ˌ-'-], -z

gaberlunzie, **-s** ˌgæbə'lʌnzɪ ['gæbəl-, -njɪ], -z

Gabii 'gæbɪɪ: [-bɪaɪ]

gabion, **-s** 'geɪbjən [-brən], -z

gable, **-s, -d** 'geɪbl, -z, -d

gablet, **-s** 'geɪblɪt [-lət], -s

gable-window, **-s** ˌgeɪbl'wɪndəu, -z

Gabon gæ'bɒŋ [gə-, 'gæbɔ̃ːŋ]

Gabonese ˌgæbɒ'ni:z [-bə-]

Gaboon gə'bu:n

Gabriel 'geɪbrɪəl

gab|y, **-ies** 'geɪb|ɪ, -ɪz

Gaby 'gɑ:bɪ

Gacrux (*star*) 'geɪkrʌks

gad (*s. v. interj.*) (G.), **-s, -ding, -ded** gæd, -z, -ɪŋ, -ɪd

gadabout, **-s** 'gædəbaut, -s

Gadara 'gædərə

Gadarene, **-s** ˌgædə'ri:n ['---], -z

Gaddesden 'gædzdən

Gade (*English river*) geɪd, (*Danish composer*) 'gɑ:də

Gades 'geɪdi:z

gadfl|y, **-ies** 'gædfl|aɪ, -aɪz

gadget, **-s, -ry** 'gædʒɪt, -s, -rɪ

Gadhel, **-s** 'gædel, -z

Gadhelic gæ'delɪk [gə'd-]

Gadite, **-s** 'gædaɪt, -s

gadroon, **-s** gə'dru:n, -z

Gads|by, **-den, -hill** 'gædz|bɪ, -dən, -hɪl

gadwall, **-s** 'gædwɔ:l, -z

gadzooks ˌgæd'zu:ks

Gael, **-s** geɪl, -z

Gaelic 'geɪlɪk ['gælɪk]

Gaetulia gi:'tju:ljə [dʒi:-, -lɪə]

gaff (*s. v.*), **-s, -ing, -ed** gæf, -s, -ɪŋ, -t

gaffe, **-s** gæf, -s

gaffer, **-s** 'gæfə*, -z

Gaffney 'gæfnɪ

gag (*s. v.*), **-s, -ging, -ged** gæg, -z, -ɪŋ, -d

gaga (*s. adj.*), **-s** 'gɑ:gɑ: ['gæ-], -z

gag|e (*s. v.*) (G.), **-es, -ing, -ed** geɪdʒ, -ɪz, -ɪŋ, -d

gaggle, **-s** 'gægl, -z

gaiet|y (G.), **-ies** 'geɪət|ɪ ['geɪt-], -ɪz

gaily 'geɪlɪ

gain (*s. v.*), **-s, -ing/s, -ed, -er/s; -able, -less** geɪn, -z, -ɪŋ/z, -d, -ə*/z; -əbl, -lɪs [-ləs]

Gaines geɪnz

gain|ful, **-fully, -fulness** 'geɪn|fʊl, -fʊlɪ [-fəlɪ], -fʊlnɪs [-nəs]

gain|say, **-says, -saying, -sayed, -said, -sayer/s** ˌgeɪn|'seɪ, -'seɪz, -'seɪɪŋ, -'seɪd, -'seɪd [-'sed], -'seə*/z

Gainsborough, **-s** 'geɪnzbərə, -z

Gairdner 'geədnə*, 'gɑ:d-

Gairloch 'geəlɒk [-lɒx]

Gaisberg 'gaɪzbə:g

Gaisford 'geɪsfəd

gait, **-s** geɪt, -s

gaiter, **-s** 'geɪtə*, -z

Gaitskell 'geɪtskəl [-kɪl]

Gaius 'gaɪəs

gala, **-s** 'gɑːlə ['geɪl-], -z

Gala (*river*) 'gɑ:lə

galactic gə'læktɪk

Galahad 'gæləhæd

Galan (*surname*) 'geɪlən

galantine, **-s** 'gælənti:n [ˌ-'-], -z

Galapagos gə'læpəgəs [-gɒs]

Galapas 'gæləpæs

Galashiels ˌgælə'ʃi:lz

Galata 'gælətə

Galatea ˌgælə'tɪə

Galatia gə'leɪʃjə [-ʃɪə, -ʃə]

Galatian, **-s** gə'leɪʃjən [-ʃɪən, -ʃn], -z

galax|y, **-ies** 'gæləks|ɪ, -ɪz

Galba 'gælbə

galbanum 'gælbənəm

Galbraith gæl'breɪθ

gale (G.), **-s** geɪl, -z

Galen 'geɪlɪn [-lən]

galena (G.) gə'li:nə

galenic, **-al** gə'lenɪk [geɪ'l-], -

Galerius gə'lɪərɪəs

Galesburg 'geɪlzbə:g

Galicia, **-n** gə'lɪʃɪə [-ʃjə, -sɪə, -sjə], -n

Galilean, **-s** ˌgælɪ'li:ən [-'lɪən], -z

Galilee 'gælɪli:

206

Galileo ˌgælɪˈleɪəʊ [-ˈliːəʊ]
galingale ˈgælɪŋgeɪl
Galion ˈgælɪən [-ljən]
galipot ˈgælɪpɒt
gall (s. v.), -s, -ing, -ed gɔːl, -z, -ɪŋ, -d
Gallagher ˈgæləhə* [-əxə*]
Gallaher ˈgæləhə*
gallant (s.), -s ˈgælənt [rarely gəˈlænt],
  -s
gallant (adj.) (brave), -ly, -ness
  ˈgælənt, -lɪ, -nɪs [-nəs]
gallant (adj.) (amorous), -ly, -ness
  ˈgælənt [gəˈlænt], -lɪ, -nɪs [-nəs]
gallantry ˈgæləntrɪ
Gallatin ˈgælətɪn
gall-bladder, -s ˈgɔːlˌblædə*, -z
galleon, -s ˈgælɪən [-ljən], -z
galler|y, -ies, -ied ˈgælər|ɪ, -ɪz, -ɪd
galley, -s ˈgælɪ, -z
galley-proof, -s ˈgælɪpruːf, -s
galley-slave, -s ˈgælɪsleɪv, -z
gall-fl|y, -ies ˈgɔːlfl|aɪ, -aɪz
Gallia ˈgælɪə
galliambic (s. adj.), -s ˌgælɪˈæmbɪk, -s
galliard, -s ˈgæljɑːd [-lɪɑːd], -z
gallic (G.) ˈgælɪk
Gallican (s. adj.), -s ˈgælɪkən, -z
gallice ˈgælɪsiː [-sɪ]
gallicism, -s ˈgælɪsɪzəm, -z
galliciz|e [-is|e], -es, -ing, -ed ˈgælɪsaɪz,
  -ɪz, -ɪŋ, -d
gallinaceous ˌgælɪˈneɪʃəs [-ʃjəs, -ʃɪəs]
Gallio ˈgælɪəʊ
galliot, -s ˈgælɪət, -s
Gallipoli gəˈlɪpəlɪ
Gallipolis (in U.S.A) ˌgælɪpəˈliːs
gallipot ˈgælɪpɒt, -s
gallivant, -s, -ing, -ed ˌgælɪˈvænt [ˈ---],
  -s, -ɪŋ, -ɪd
gall-nut, -s ˈgɔːlnʌt, -s
gallon, -s ˈgælən, -z
galloon gəˈluːn
gallop (s. v.), -s, -ing, -ed, -er/s ˈgæləp,
  -s, -ɪŋ, -t, -ə*/z
gallopade, -s ˌgæləˈpeɪd, -z
Gallovidian (s. adj.), -s ˌgæləʊˈvɪdɪən
  [-djən], -z
galloway (G.), -s ˈgæləweɪ [-lʊw-], -z
gallows ˈgæləʊz
gallows-bird, -s ˈgæləʊzbɜːd, -z
gall-stone, -s ˈgɔːlstəʊn, -z
Gallup ˈgæləp
Gallus ˈgæləs
galop, -s ˈgæləp [gæˈlɒp], -s
galore gəˈlɔː* [-ˈlɔə*]
galosh, -es gəˈlɒʃ, -ɪz
Galpin ˈgælpɪn
Galsham ˈgɔːlsəm [ˈgɒl-]

Galsworthy ˈgɔːlzwɜːðɪ, ˈgæl-
  Note.—John Galsworthy, the author,
  is commonly called ˈgɔːlzwɜːðɪ.
Galt, -on gɔːlt [gɒlt], -ən
galumph, -s, -ing, -ed gəˈlʌmf, -s, -ɪŋ, -t
Galvani gælˈvɑːnɪ
galvanic gælˈvænɪk
galvanism ˈgælvənɪzəm [-vɪn-]
galvaniz|e [-is|e], -es, -ing, -ed, -er/s
  ˈgælvənaɪz [-vɪnaɪz], -ɪz, -ɪŋ, -d, -ə*/z
galvanometer, -s ˌgælvəˈnɒmɪtə*
  [-vɪˈn-, -mətə*], -z
Galvestone ˈgælvɪstən
Galway ˈgɔːlweɪ
Gama ˈgɑːmə
Gamage, -'s ˈgæmɪdʒ, -ɪz
Gamaliel gəˈmeɪljəl [-lɪəl, in Jewish
  usage also gəˈmɑːlɪəl, ˌgæməˈliːəl]
gamba, -s ˈgæmbə, -z
gambado (jump), -(e)s gæmˈbeɪdəʊ
  [-ˈbɑːd-], -z
gambadoes (leggings) gæmˈbeɪdəʊz
Gambetta gæmˈbetə
Gambia ˈgæmbɪə [-bjə]
gambier (substance used in dyeing)
  ˈgæmˌbɪə*
Gambier (surname) ˈgæmˌbɪə* [-bɪə*,
  -bjə*]
gambist, -s ˈgæmbɪst, -s
gambit, -s ˈgæmbɪt, -s
gamb|le (s. v.) (G.), -les, -ling, -led,
  -ler/s ˈgæmb|l, -lz, -lɪŋ, -ld, -lə*/z
gambling-hou|se, -ses ˈgæmblɪŋhaʊ|s,
  -zɪz
gamboge gæmˈbuːʒ
gamb|ol (s. v.), -ols, -olling, -olled
  ˈgæmb|l, -lz, -lɪŋ [-əlɪŋ], -ld
gam|e (s. adj. v.), -es; -er, -est, -ely,
  -eness; -ing, -ed geɪm, -z; -ə*, -ɪst,
  -lɪ, -nɪs [-nəs]; -ɪŋ, -d
game|-bag/s,   -cock/s,   -keeper/s,
  -law/s,   -licence/s   ˈgeɪm|bæg/z,
  -kɒk/s, -ˌkiːpə*/z, -lɔː/z, -ˌlaɪsns/ɪz
Game|lyn, -lin ˈgæmɪlɪn [-mlɪn]
games|-master/s, -mistress/es ˈgeɪmz|-
  ˌmɑːstə*/z, -ˌmɪstrɪs/ɪz [-trəs/ɪz]
gamester, -s ˈgeɪmstə*, -z
gaming|-house,   -houses,   -table/s
  ˈgeɪmɪŋ|haʊs, -ˌhaʊzɪz, -ˌteɪbl/z
gamma, -s ˈgæmə, -z
Gammell ˈgæməl
gammer, -s ˈgæmə*, -z
gammon (s. v.), -s, -ing, -ed ˈgæmən, -z,
  -ɪŋ, -d
gamp (G.), -s gæmp, -s
gamut, -s ˈgæmət, -s
gam|y, -ier, -iest, -iness ˈgeɪm|ɪ, -ɪə*
  [-jə*], -ɪɪst [-jɪst], -ɪnɪs [-ɪnəs]

207

gander, -s 'gændə*, -z
Gandercleugh 'gændəklu:, -klu:x
Gandhi 'gændi: ['gɑ:n-, -dɪ] (Hindi
gãdhi)
Gandhi|ism, -ite/s 'gændɪ|ɪzəm, -aɪt/s
gang, -s; -er/s gæŋ, -z; -ə*/z
Ganges 'gændʒi:z
gangli|on, -a, -ons 'gæŋglɪ|ən, -ə, -ənz
gangren|e (s. v.), -es, -ing, -ed 'gæŋ-
gri:n, -z, -ɪŋ, -d
gangrenous 'gæŋgrɪnəs
gangster, -s 'gæŋstə* [-ŋks-], -z
gangway, -s 'gæŋweɪ, -z
Gannel 'gænl
gannet, -s 'gænɪt, -s
Gannett 'gænɪt
gan(n)ister 'gænɪstə*
Gannon 'gænən
ganoid 'gænɔɪd
gantr|y, -ies 'gæntr|ɪ, -ɪz
Ganymede 'gænɪmi:d
gaol (s. v.), -s, -ing, -ed, -er/s dʒeɪl, -z,
-ɪŋ, -d, -ə*/z
gaolbird, -s 'dʒeɪlbɜ:d, -z
gap, -s gæp, -s
gap|e (s. v.), -es, -ing, -ed, -er/s geɪp,
-s, -ɪŋ, -t, -ə*/z
garag|e (s. v.), -es, -ing, -ed 'gærɑ:dʒ
[-ɪdʒ, -rɑ:ʒ, occasionally gə'rɑ:dʒ,
-ɑ:ʒ], -ɪz, -ɪŋ, -d
garb, -s, -ed gɑ:b, -z, -d
garbage 'gɑ:bɪdʒ
garb|le, -les, -ling, -led 'gɑ:b|l, -lz, -lɪŋ
[-lɪŋ], -ld
Garbutt 'gɑ:bət
Garcia (English surname) 'gɑ:ʃjə [-ʃɪə],
'gɑ:sjə [-sɪə]
gard|en (s. v.) (G.), -ens, -ening, -ened,
-ener/s 'gɑ:d|n, -nz, -nɪŋ, -nd, -nə*/z
gardenia, -s gɑ:'di:njə [gə'd-, -nɪə],
-z
garden-part|y, -ies 'gɑ:dn,pɑ:t|ɪ, -ɪz
Gard(i)ner 'gɑ:dnə*
garefowl, -s 'geəfaʊl, -z
Gareth 'gæreθ [-rəθ, -rɪθ] (Welsh
'gareθ)
Garfield 'gɑ:fi:ld
garfish 'gɑ:fɪʃ
garganey, -s 'gɑ:gənɪ, -z
Gargantua gɑ:'gæntjʊə [-tjwə]
gargantuan gɑ:'gæntjʊən [-tjwən]
Gargery 'gɑ:dʒərɪ
garg|le (s. v.), -les, -ling/s, -led 'gɑ:g|l,
-lz, -lɪŋ/z, -ld
gargoyle, -s 'gɑ:gɔɪl, -z
Garibaldi ,gærɪ'bɔ:ldɪ [-'bæl-]
Garioch (district in Scotland, surname)
'gærɪɒk [-ɒx]

garish, -ly, -ness 'geərɪʃ ['gær-], -lɪ, -nɪs
[-nəs]
garland (G.), -s 'gɑ:lənd, -z
garlic, -ky 'gɑ:lɪk, -ɪ
Garlick 'gɑ:lɪk
garment, -s, -ed 'gɑ:mənt, -s, -ɪd
garner (s. v.), -s, -ing, -ed 'gɑ:nə*, -z,
-rɪŋ, -d
garnet, -s 'gɑ:nɪt, -s
Garn|et(t), -ham 'gɑ:n|ɪt, -əm
garnish (s. v.), -es, -ing, -ed, -ment/s
'gɑ:nɪʃ, -ɪz, -ɪŋ, -t, -mənt/s
garnishee (s. v.), -s, -ing, -d ,gɑ:nɪ'ʃi:,
-z, -ɪŋ, -d
garniture 'gɑ:nɪtʃə*
Garr|ard, -att 'gær|əd, -ət
Garraway 'gærəweɪ
garret, -s 'gærət [-rɪt], -s
Garr|et(t), -ick 'gær|ət [-ɪt], -ɪk
Garrioch (district in Scotland) 'gɪərɪ,
(surname) 'gærɪək [-əx]
garris|on (s. v.) (G.), -ons, -oning, -oned
'gærɪs|n, -nz, -nɪŋ [-ənɪŋ], -nd
Garr|od, -o(u)ld 'gær|əd, -əld
garrot, -s 'gærət, -s
garrott|e (s. v.), -es, -ing, -ed, -er/s
gə'rɒt, -s, -ɪŋ, -ɪd, -ə*/z
garrulity gæ'ru:lətɪ [gə'r-, -'rju:-, -ɪtɪ]
garrulous, -ly, -ness 'gærələs [-rʊl-,
-rjʊl-], -lɪ, -nɪs [-nəs]
Garston 'gɑ:stən
garter (s. v.), -s, -ing, -ed 'gɑ:tə*, -z,
-rɪŋ, -d
garth (G.), -s gɑ:θ, -s
Garwood 'gɑ:wʊd
gas (s.), -es gæs, -ɪz
gas (v.), -ses, -sing, -sed gæs, -ɪz, -ɪŋ, -t
gas|-bag/s, -bracket/s, -burner/s 'gæs|-
bæg/z, -,brækɪt/s, -,bɜ:nə*/z
Gascoigne 'gæskɔɪn
Gascon, -s 'gæskən, -z
gasconnad|e (s. v.), -es, -ing, -ed ,gæs-
kə'neɪd, -z, -ɪŋ, -ɪd
Gascony 'gæskənɪ
Gascoyne 'gæskɔɪn
Gaselee 'geɪzli: [-lɪ]
gaselier, -s ,gæsə'lɪə*, -z
gas-engine, -s 'gæs,endʒɪn, -z
gaseous, -ness 'gæsjəs ['geɪ-, -sɪəs,
-zjəs, -zɪəs, -ʃjəs, -ʃɪəs], -nɪs [-nəs]
gas-fire, -s 'gæs,faɪə* [,-'-'-], -z
gas|-fitter/s, -fixture/s 'gæs|,fɪtə*/z,
-,fɪkstʃə*/z
gash (s. v.), -es, -ing, -ed gæʃ, -ɪz, -ɪŋ, -t
gas-helmet, -s 'gæs,helmɪt, -s
gasi|fy, -fies, -fying, -fied 'gæsɪ|faɪ
['geɪzɪ-], -faɪz, -faɪɪŋ, -faɪd
gas-jet, -s 'gæsdʒet, -s

Gaskell 'gæskəl [-kel]
gasket, -s 'gæskɪt, -s
gaskin (G.), -s 'gæskɪn, -z
gas-light 'gæslaɪt
gas-main -s 'gæsmeɪn, -z
gas|-man, -men 'gæs|mæn, -men
gas|-mantle/s, -mask/s 'gæs|ˌmæntl/z, -mɑːsk/s
gas-meter, -s 'gæsˌmiːtə*, -z
gasolene [-line] 'gæsəʊliːn
gasometer, -s gæ'sɒmɪtə* [gə'sɒ-, gə'zɒ-, -mətə*], -z
gasp (s. v.), -s, -ing, -ed gɑːsp, -s, -ɪŋ, -t
gas|-pipe/s, -ring/s 'gæs|paɪp/s, -rɪŋ/z
gas-stove, -s 'gæsstəʊv [ˌ-'-], -z
gass|y, -ier, -iest, -iness 'gæs|ɪ, -ɪə*, -ɪɪst, -ɪnɪs [-ɪnəs]
gasteropod, -s 'gæstərəpɒd, -z
gastric 'gæstrɪk
gastritis gæ'straɪtɪs
gastronome, -s 'gæstrənəʊm, -z
gastronomic, -al ˌgæstrə'nɒmɪk, -l
gastronom|ist/s, -y gæ'strɒnəm|ɪst/s, -ɪ
gasworks 'gæswɜːks
Gatacre 'gætəkə*
gat|e (s. v.), -es, -ing, -ed geɪt, -s, -ɪŋ, -ɪd
gâteau, -x[-s] 'gætəʊ, -z (gɑto)
gatecrash, -es, -ing, -ed, -er/s 'geɪtkræʃ, -ɪz, -ɪŋ, -t, -ə*/z
gate|-fine/s, -keeper/s 'geɪt|faɪn/z, -ˌkiːpə*/z
gate-legged 'geɪtlegd
gateless 'geɪtlɪs [-ləs]
gate|-money, -post/s 'geɪt|ˌmʌnɪ, -pəʊst/s
Gatenby 'geɪtnbɪ
Gater 'geɪtə*
Gates geɪts
Gateshead 'geɪtshed
gateway, -s 'geɪtweɪ, -z
Gath gæθ
gath|er (s. v.), -ers, -ering/s, -ered, -erer/s 'gæð|ə*, -əz, -ərɪŋ/z, -əd, -ərə*/z
Gathorne 'geɪθɔːn
Gat|ley, -ling 'gæt|lɪ, -lɪŋ
Gatty 'gætɪ
Gatwick 'gætwɪk
gauche gəʊʃ
gaucherie, -s 'gəʊʃərɪ: [-rɪ], -z
gaucho, -s 'gaʊtʃəʊ ['gɔːtʃ-], -z
gaud, -s gɔːd, -z
Gauden 'gɔːdn
gaud|y, -ier, -iest, -ily, -iness 'gɔːd|ɪ, -ɪə* [-jə*], -ɪɪst [-jɪst], -ɪlɪ [-əlɪ], -ɪnɪs [-ɪnəs]

gaug|e (s. v.), -es, -ing, -ed, -er/s; -eable geɪdʒ, -ɪz, -ɪŋ, -d, -ə*/z; -əbl
Gaul, -s, -ish gɔːl, -z, -ɪʃ
gauleiter, -s 'gaʊlaɪtə*, -z
Gauloise(s) (cigarette) 'gəʊlwɑːz [-'-] (golwaːz)
gaum (s. v.), -s, -ing, -ed gɔːm, -z, -ɪŋ, -d
Gaumont 'gəʊmɒnt [-mənt]
gaunt (G.), -er, -est, -ly, -ness gɔːnt, -ə*, -ɪst, -lɪ, -nɪs [-nəs]
gauntlet (G.), -s, -ed 'gɔːntlɪt [-lət], -s, -ɪd
Gauntlett 'gɔːntlɪt, 'gɑːn-
Gauss gaʊs
gauz|e, -es; -y, -iness gɔːz, -ɪz; -ɪ, -ɪnɪs [-ɪnəs]
gave (from give) geɪv
gavel, -s 'gævl, -z
gavelkind 'gævlkaɪnd [-kɪnd]
Gaveston 'gævɪstən
Gavey 'geɪvɪ
Gavin 'gævɪn
gavotte, -s gə'vɒt, -s
Gawain 'gɑːweɪn ['gæw-]
Gawith (surname) 'geɪwɪθ
gawk, -s gɔːk, -s
gawk|y, -ier, -iest, -iness 'gɔːk|ɪ, -ɪə*, -ɪɪst, -ɪnɪs [-ɪnəs]
gay (G.), -er, -est, gaily, gayness geɪ, -ə* [geə*], -ɪst, 'geɪlɪ, 'geɪnɪs [-nəs]
Gayn|ham, -or 'geɪn|əm, -ə*
Gaza (in Israel, formerly in Egypt) 'gɑːzə [in biblical use also 'geɪzə]
Gaza (Greek scholar) 'gɑːzə
gaz|e (s. v.), -es, -ing, -ed, -er/s geɪz, -ɪz, -ɪŋ, -d, -ə*/z
gazebo, -s gə'ziːbəʊ, -z
gazelle, -s gə'zel, -z
gazett|e (s. v.), -es, -ing, -ed gə'zet, -s, -ɪŋ, -ɪd
gazetteer, -s ˌgæzə'tɪə* [-zɪ't-], -z
gazogene 'gæzəʊdʒiːn
gazump, -s, -ing, -ed gə'zʌmp, -s, -ɪŋ, -t [-'zʌmt]
Geall giːl
gear (s. v.), -s, -ing, -ed gɪə*, -z, -rɪŋ, -d
gear|-box/es, -case/s 'gɪə|bɒks/ɪz, -keɪs/ɪz
Geare gɪə*
Geary 'gɪərɪ
Gebal 'giːbəl [-bæl]
Gebir 'dʒiːˌbɪə*
gecko, -s 'gekəʊ, -z
Geb ged
Geddes 'gedɪs
gee (s. v.) (G.), -s, -ing -d dʒiː, -z, -ɪŋ, -d
geegee, -s 'dʒiːdʒiː, -z

209

Geelong dʒɪ'lɒŋ [dʒə'l-]
Geering 'gɪərɪŋ
geese (*plur. of* goose) giːs
Geeson 'dʒiːsn, 'giːsn
gee-up 'dʒiːʌp
geezer, -s 'giːzə*, -z
Gehazi gɪ'heɪzaɪ [geˈh-, gəˈh-, -ˈheɪzɪ, -ˈhɑːzɪ]
Gehenna gɪ'henə [gəˈh-]
Geierstein 'gaɪəstaɪn
Geiger 'gaɪgə*
Geikie 'giːkɪ
geisha, -s 'geɪʃə, -z
gelatine ˌdʒelə'tiːn ['—]
gelatiniz|e [-is|e], -es, -ing, -ed dʒə'læ-tɪnaɪz [dʒe'l-, dʒɪ'l-, -tən-], -ɪz, -ɪŋ, -d
gelatinous dʒə'lætɪnəs [dʒe'l-, dʒɪ'l-, -tən-]
geld (*adj. v.*), -s, -ing, -ed geld, -z, -ɪŋ, -ɪd
gelding (*s.*), -s 'geldɪŋ, -z
gelid, -ly, -ness 'dʒelɪd, -lɪ, -nɪs [-nəs]
gelignite 'dʒelɪgnaɪt
Gell gel, dʒel
Gell|an, -er 'gel|ən, -ə*
Gellatl(e)y 'gelətlɪ, geˈlætlɪ
gem, -s dʒem, -z
Gemara ge'mɑːrə [gɪ'm-]
geminat|e, -es, -ing, -ed 'dʒemɪneɪt, -s, -ɪŋ, -ɪd
gemination ˌdʒemɪ'neɪʃn
Gemini (*constellation*) 'dʒemɪnaɪ [-niː, -nɪ], (*aircraft*) 'dʒemɪnɪ
Gemistus dʒe'mɪstəs [dʒɪ'm-]
Gemmi 'gemɪ
gemmiferous dʒe'mɪfərəs
gemot, -s gɪ'məʊt [gə'm-], -s
gemsbok, -s 'gemzbɒk, -s
gemshorn, -s 'gemzhɔːn, -z
gen dʒen
gendarme, -s 'ʒɑ̃ːndɑːm ['ʒɔ̃ːnd-, 'ʒɑːnd-, 'ʒɒnd-] [ʒɑ̃darm], -z
gender (*s. v.*), -s, -ing, -ed 'dʒendə*, -z, -rɪŋ, -d
gene (G.), -s dʒiːn, -z
genealogic|al, -ally ˌdʒiːnjə'lɒdʒɪk|l [ˌdʒen-, -nɪə-], -əlɪ
genealog|ist/s, -y, -ies ˌdʒiːnɪ'æləter|dʒ|-ɪst/s [ˌdʒen-], -ɪ, -ɪz
genera (*plur. of* genus) 'dʒenərə
gener|al (*s. adj.*), -als, -ally 'dʒenər|əl, -əlz, -əlɪ
generalissimo, -s ˌdʒenərə'lɪsɪməʊ, -z
generalit|y, -ies ˌdʒenə'rælət|ɪ [-rɪt|ɪ], -ɪz
generalization [-isa-], -s ˌdʒenərə-laɪ'zeɪʃn [-lɪ'z-], -z
generaliz|e [-is|e-], -es, -ing, -ed ; -able 'dʒenərəlaɪz, -ɪz, -ɪŋ, -d; -əbl

generalship 'dʒenərəlʃɪp
generat|e, -es, -ing, -ed, -or/s 'dʒenə-reɪt, -s, -ɪŋ, -ɪd, -ə*/z
generation, -s ˌdʒenə'reɪʃn, -z
generative 'dʒenərətɪv [-reɪt-]
generator, -s 'dʒenəreɪtə*, -z
generatri|x, -ces 'dʒenəreɪtrɪ|ks, -siːz
generic, -ally dʒɪ'nerɪk [dʒə'n-, dʒe'n-], -əlɪ
generosity ˌdʒenə'rɒsətɪ [-rɪt-]
generous, -ly, -ness 'dʒenərəs, -lɪ, -nɪs [-nəs]
genesis 'dʒenɪsɪs [-nəsɪs]
Genesis (*book of the Bible*) 'dʒenɪsɪs [-nəsɪs, *old-fashioned* -sɪz]
Genesius dʒɪ'niːsjəs [dʒe'n-, dʒə'n-, -sɪəs]
Genesta dʒɪ'nestə [dʒe'n-, dʒə'n-]
genet, -s 'dʒenɪt, -s
genetic, -s, -ally dʒɪ'netɪk [dʒe'n-, dʒə'n-], -s, -əlɪ
geneticist, -s dʒɪ'netɪsɪst [dʒe-, dʒə-], -s
Geneva, -n/s dʒɪ'niːvə [dʒə'n-], -n/z
Genevieve (*in Coleridge's poem 'Love'*) ˌdʒenə'viːv, 'dʒenɪviːv [-nəv-]
Geneviève (*Saint*) ˌʒenvɪ'eɪv (ʒənvjɛːv)
Genghis Khan ˌdʒeŋgɪs 'kɑːn [-gɪz-]
genial (*amiable*), -ly, -ness 'dʒiːnjəl [-nɪəl], -ɪ, -nɪs [-nəs]
genial (*of the chin*) dʒɪ'naɪəl
geniality ˌdʒiːnɪ'ælətɪ [-rɪt-]
genie, -s 'dʒiːnɪ, -z
genista, -s dʒɪ'nɪstə [dʒe'n-, dʒə'n-], -s
genital, -s 'dʒenɪtl, -z
genitival ˌdʒenɪ'taɪvl
genitive, -s 'dʒenɪtɪv [-nət-], -z
ge|nius, -nii, -niuses 'dʒiː|njəs [-nɪəs], -nɪaɪ, -njəsɪz [-nɪəsɪz]
Gennesare|t, -th gɪ'nezərɪ|t [ge'n-, gə'n-, -re|t], -θ
Genoa 'dʒenəʊə [dʒə'nəʊə]
genocide 'dʒenəʊsaɪd
Genoese ˌdʒenəʊ'iːz [*also* 'dʒenəʊiːz *when attributive*]
genre 'ʒɑ̃ːŋrə ['ʒɔ̃ːŋrə, 'ʒɑːŋrə, 'ʒɒŋrə] (ʒɑ̃ːr)
gen|s, -tes dʒen|z, -tiːz
Genseric 'gensərɪk ['dʒen-]
Gensing 'genzɪŋ [-nsɪŋ]
gent, -s dʒent, -s
genteel, -ly, -ness dʒen'tiːl [dʒən-], -lɪ, -nɪs [-nəs]
gentes (*plur. of* gens) 'dʒentiːz
gentian, -s 'dʒenʃɪən [-ʃjən, -ʃn], -z
gentile (G.), -s 'dʒentaɪl, -z
gentility dʒen'tɪlətɪ [dʒən-, -rɪt-]
gent|le, -ler, -lest, -ly, -leness 'dʒent|l, -lə*, -lɪst, -lɪ, -lnɪs [-nəs]

gentlefolk, -s 'dʒentlfəuk, -s
gentle|man, -men 'dʒentl|mən, -mən
[-men]
gentle|man-at-arms, -men-at-arms
ˌdʒentl|mənət'ɑːmz, -mənət'ɑːmz
[-men-]
gentlemanlike 'dʒentlmənlaɪk
gentleman|y, -iness 'dʒentlmənl|ɪ, -ɪnɪs
[-ɪnəs]
gentle|woman,-women 'dʒentl|ˌwʊmən,
-ˌwɪmɪn
gentry (G.) 'dʒentrɪ
genuflect, -s, -ing, -ed 'dʒenjuːflekt
[-njʊ-], -s, -ɪŋ, -ɪd
genuflection, -s ˌdʒenjuː'flekʃn [-njʊ-],
-z
genuine, -ly, -ness 'dʒenjʊɪn, -lɪ, -nɪs
[-nəs]
gen|us, -era 'dʒiːn|əs ['dʒen|əs],
'dʒenərə
Geo. dʒɒːdʒ
geocentric, -al, -ally ˌdʒiːəʊ'sentrɪk
[ˌdʒɪ-], -l, -əlɪ
geode, -s 'dʒiːəʊd ['dʒɪ-], -z
geodesic, -al ˌdʒiːəʊ'desɪk [ˌdʒɪ-,
-'diːs-], -l
geodesy dʒiː'ɒdɪsɪ [dʒɪ-, -dəsɪ]
Geoffr(e)y 'dʒefrɪ
Geoghegan 'geɪgən, 'gəʊgən
geographer, -s dʒɪ'ɒgrəfə*, -z
geographic, -al, -ally dʒɪə'græfɪk
[dʒiːəʊ'g-], -l, -əlɪ
geograph|y, -ies dʒɪ'ɒgrəf|ɪ ['dʒɒɒg-], -ɪz
geologic, -al, -ally dʒɪəʊ'lɒdʒɪk, -l, -əlɪ
geolog|ist/s, -y dʒɪ'ɒlədʒ|ɪst/s, -ɪ
geologiz|e [-is|e], -es, -ing, -ed dʒɪ'ɒlə-
dʒaɪz, -ɪz, -ɪŋ, -d
geomancy 'dʒiːəʊmænsɪ
geometer, -s dʒɪ'ɒmɪtə* [-mətə*], -z
geometric, -al, -ally ˌdʒiːəʊ'metrɪk, -l,
-əlɪ
geometrician, -s ˌdʒiːəʊmə'trɪʃn
[dʒɪ,ɒm-, -mɪ't-], -z
geometr|y, -ies dʒɪ'ɒmɪtr|ɪ ['dʒɒm-,
-mɪtr|ɪ], -ɪz
geophysic|al, -s ˌdʒiːəʊ'fɪzɪk|l [ˌdʒɪ-], -z
Geordie 'dʒɒːdɪ
George, -s dʒɒːdʒ, -ɪz
georgette dʒɒː'dʒet
Georgia, -n/s 'dʒɒːdʒjə [-dʒɪə], -n/z
Georgiana ˌdʒɒːdʒɪ'ɑːnə
georgic (G.), -s 'dʒɒːdʒɪk, -s
Georgina dʒɒː'dʒiːnə
Geraint 'geraɪnt
Gerald 'dʒerəld
Geraldine 'dʒerəldiːn, -daɪn
Note.—'dʒerəldaɪn in Coleridge's
'Christabel'.

geranium, -s dʒɪ'reɪnjəm [dʒəˈr-,
-nɪəm], -z
Gerard (English name) 'dʒerɑːd
['dʒerəd], dʒe'rɑːd [dʒəˈrɑːd]
Gérard (French name) dʒe'rɑːd (ʒera:r)
gerfalcon, -s 'dʒɜːˌfɔːlkən [-ˌfɔːkən],
-z
Note.—Those who practise the sport
of falconry pronounce -ˌfɔːk-.
Gergesene, -s 'gɜːgɪsiːn [-gəs-, -ges-,
ˌ--'-], -z
geriatric, -s ˌdʒerɪ'ætrɪk, -s
geriatrician, -s ˌdʒerɪə'trɪʃn, -z
geriatry 'dʒerɪətrɪ [-ætrɪ]
Gerizim ge'raɪzɪm [gəˈr-, -'riːzɪm, 'gerɪ-
-zɪm]
germ, -s dʒɜːm, -z
Germain (street) 'dʒɜːmən [-meɪn]
German, -s 'dʒɜːmən, -z
germander dʒɜː'mændə* [dʒəˈm-]
germane dʒɜː'meɪn ['--]
Germanic dʒɜː'mænɪk [dʒəˈm-]
germani|sm/s, -st/s 'dʒɜːmənɪ|zəm/z,
-st/s
germanization [-isa-] ˌdʒɜːmənaɪ'zeɪʃn
germaniz|e [-is|e], -es, -ing, -ed
'dʒɜːmənaɪz, -ɪz, -ɪŋ, -d
Germany 'dʒɜːmənɪ
germicide, -s 'dʒɜːmɪsaɪd, -z
germinal 'dʒɜːmɪnl
germinat|e, -es, -ing, -ed 'dʒɜːmɪneɪt,
-s, -ɪŋ, -ɪd
germination, -s ˌdʒɜːmɪ'neɪʃn, -z
Gerontius gə'rɒntɪəs [gɪ'r-, ge'r-,
-ntjəs, -nʃɪəs, -nʃjəs, -nʃəs]
gerontolog|ist/s, -y ˌdʒerɒn'tɒlədʒ|ɪst/s
[ˌger-, -rən-], -ɪ
Gerrans 'gerənz
Gerrard 'dʒerəd [-rɑːd], dʒe'rɑːd
[dʒəˈrɑːd]
Gerrard's Cross ˌdʒerədz'krɒs [-rɑːdz-,
old-fashioned -'krɔːs]
Gerry 'gerɪ, 'dʒerɪ
gerrymand|er (s. v.), -ers, -ering, -ered
'dʒerɪmænd|ə* [rarely 'ge-], -əz,
-ərɪŋ, -əd
Gershwin 'gɜːʃwɪn
Gert|ie, -y 'gɜːt|ɪ, -ɪ
Gertrude 'gɜːtruːd
gerund, -s 'dʒerənd [-rʌnd], -z
gerundive, -s dʒɪ'rʌndɪv [dʒeˈr-,
dʒəˈr-], -z
Gervase 'dʒɜːvəs
Geryon 'gerɪən
gesso 'dʒesəʊ
gest, -s dʒest, -s
gestalt gə'ʃtɑːlt [-'ʃtælt]
Gestapo ge'stɑːpəʊ

211

gestat|e, -es, -ing, -ed dʒe'steɪt, -s, -ɪŋ, -ɪd

gestation dʒe'steɪʃn

gestatorial ,dʒestə'tɔːrɪəl

gesticulat|e, -es, -ing, -ed, -or/s dʒe'stɪkjʊleɪt, -s, -ɪŋ, -ɪd, -ə*/z

gesticulation, -s dʒe,stɪkjʊ'leɪʃn, -z

gesticulatory dʒe'stɪkjʊlətərɪ [-leɪt-]

gesture, -s 'dʒestʃə*, -z

get, -s, -ting, got get, -s, -ɪŋ, gɒt

Getae 'geɪtaɪ ['dʒiːtiː]

get-at-able get'ætəbl

get-away, -s 'getəweɪ, -z

Gethin 'geθɪn

Gethsemane geθ'semənɪ

get-rich-quick ,getrɪtʃ'kwɪk

Getty 'getɪ

Gettysburg 'getɪzbəːg

get-up, -s 'getʌp [,get'ʌp], -s

geum, -s 'dʒiːəm [dʒɪəm], -z

gewgaw, -s 'gjuːgɔː, -z

geyser (hot spring), -s 'gaɪzə* ['giːz-], -z Note.—In New Zealand the pronunciation is always 'gaɪzə*.

geyser (apparatus for heating water), -s 'giːzə* [in New Zealand 'gaɪzə*], -z

Ghana 'gɑːnə

Ghanaian, -s gɑː'neɪən, -z

ghastl|y, -ier, -iest, -iness 'gɑːstl|ɪ, -ɪə* [-jə*], -ɪst [-jɪst], -ɪnɪs [-ɪnəs]

Ghat, -s gɔːt, -s

ghee giː

Ghent gent

gherkin, -s 'gəːkɪn, -z

ghetto, -s 'getəʊ, -z

Ghibelline, -s 'gɪbɪlaɪn, -z

ghost, -s; -like gəʊst, -s; -laɪk

ghostl|y, -iness 'gəʊstl|ɪ, -ɪnɪs [-ɪnəs]

ghost-writer, -s 'gəʊst,raɪtə*, -z

ghoul, -s; -ish guːl [gaʊl], -z; -ɪʃ

Ghurka, -s 'gəːkə ['gʊək-], -z

G.I., -'s ,dʒiː'aɪ [attributively '--], -z

giant, -s; -like 'dʒaɪənt, -s; -laɪk

giantess, -es 'dʒaɪəntes [-tɪs, dʒaɪən'tes], -ɪz

Giaour 'dʒaʊə*

Gibb gɪb

gibber, -s, -ing, -ed 'dʒɪbə*, -z, -rɪŋ, -d

gibberish 'dʒɪbərɪʃ ['gɪb-]

gibbet (s. v.), -s, -ing, -ed 'dʒɪbɪt, -s, -ɪŋ, -ɪd

Gibbie 'dʒɪbɪ

gibbon (G.), -s 'gɪbən, -z

gibbosity gɪ'bɒsɪtɪ [-ɪtɪ]

gibbous, -ly, -ness 'gɪbəs, -lɪ, -nɪs [-nəs]

Gibbs gɪbz

gib|e (s. v.), -es, -ing/ly, -ed, -er/s dʒaɪb, -z, -ɪŋ/lɪ, -d, -ə*/z

Gibeah 'gɪbɪə

Gibeon 'gɪbɪən

giblet, -s 'dʒɪblɪt [-lət], -s

Giblett 'gɪblɪt

Gibraltar dʒɪ'brɔːltə* [-rɒl-]

Gibraltarian, -s ,dʒɪbrɔːl'teərɪən [-rɒl-], -z

Gibson 'gɪbsn

gibus, -es 'dʒaɪbəs ['dʒɪb-], -ɪz

Gick dʒɪk

Gide ʒiːd (ʒid)

Gidding, -s 'gɪdɪŋ, -z

gidd|y (G.), -ier, -iest, -ily, -iness 'gɪd|ɪ, -ɪə*, -ɪst, -ɪlɪ [-əlɪ], -ɪnɪs [-ɪnəs]

giddy-headed 'gɪdɪ,hedɪd

Gidea 'gɪdɪə

Gideon 'gɪdɪən

Gielgud (English name) 'giːlgʊd

Gieve giːv

Giffard 'dʒɪfəd

Giffen 'gɪfɪn, 'dʒɪfɪn

Gifford (place near Haddington) 'gɪfəd, (surname) 'gɪfəd, 'dʒɪfəd

gift, -s, -ed gɪft, -s, -ɪd

gig, -s gɪg, -z

giga- 'gɪgə- ['gaɪgə-]

Gigadibs 'gɪgədɪbz

gigant|ean, -esque ,dʒaɪgæn't|iːən [-ɪən], -esk

gigantic, -ally dʒaɪ'gæntɪk, -əlɪ

gigg|le (s. v.), -les, -ling, -led, -ler/s 'gɪg|l, -lz, -lɪŋ [-lɪŋ], -ld, -lə*/z [-lə*/z]

Gight (in Scotland) gɪkt [gɪxt]

Gigli 'dʒiːlɪ [-ljiː]

Giglio 'dʒiːlɪəʊ [-ljəʊ]

gigolo, -s 'ʒɪgələʊ ['dʒɪ-] -z

gigot, -s 'dʒɪgət, -s

gigue, -s ʒiːg [ʒɪg], -z

Gihon 'gaɪhɒn [in Jewish usage sometimes 'giːhəʊn]

gila (monster lizard), -s 'hiːlə, -z

Gilbert 'gɪlbət

Gilbertian gɪl'bəːtjən [-tɪən]

Gilbey 'gɪlbɪ

Gilboa gɪl'bəʊə

Gilchrist 'gɪlkrɪst

gild, -s, -ing, -ed, gilt, gilder/s gɪld, -z, -ɪŋ, -ɪd, gɪlt, 'gɪldə*/z

Gilder, -sleeve, -some 'gɪldə*, -sliːv, -səm

Gilding 'gɪldɪŋ

Gildredge 'gɪldrɪdʒ [-redʒ]

Gilead 'gɪlɪæd

Giles dʒaɪlz

Gilfil 'gɪlfɪl

Gilfillan gɪl'fɪlən

Gilford 'gɪlfəd

212

Gilgal 'gɪlgæl [-gɔːl, *rarely* gɪl'gɔːl]
Gilham 'gɪləm
Gilheney (*surname*) gɪ'liːnɪ
Gilheny gɪl'hiːnɪ
Gilkes dʒɪlks
gill (*respiratory organ, ravine*), -s gɪl, -z
gill (*measure*), -s dʒɪl, -z
Gill gɪl
    Note.—But dʒɪl in Jack and Gill (*now
    more usually written* Jack and Jill).
Gillam 'gɪləm
Gillard gɪ'lɑːd, 'gɪlɑːd, 'gɪləd
Gillen 'gɪlən
Gilleney (*surname*) 'gɪlənɪ
Gillespie gɪ'lespɪ
Gillett 'gɪlɪt, 'gɪlət, gɪ'let, dʒɪ'let
Gillette (*surname, razor*), -s dʒɪ'let, -s
Gilley 'gɪlɪ
Gilliam 'gɪlɪəm
Gillian 'dʒɪlɪən [-ljən], 'gɪl-
Gilliat 'gɪlɪət [-ljət]
Gillick 'gɪlɪk
gillie (G.), -s 'gɪlɪ, -z
Gillies 'gɪlɪs
Gilling, -s 'gɪlɪŋ, -z
Gillingham (*in Kent*) 'dʒɪlɪŋəm, (*in
    Dorset and Norfolk*) 'gɪl-, (*surname*)
    'gɪl-, 'dʒɪl-
Gillison 'gɪlɪsn
Gillmore 'gɪlmɔː* [-mɔə*]
Gillott 'dʒɪlət, 'gɪlət
Gill|ow, -ray 'gɪl|əʊ, -reɪ
Gills gɪlz
Gillson 'dʒɪlsn
gillyflower, -s 'dʒɪlɪˌflaʊə*, -z
Gil|man, -mer, -more 'gɪl|mən, -mə*,
    -mɔː* [-mɔə*]
Gilmour 'gɪlmə* [-mɔː*, -mɔə*]
Gilpatrick gɪl'pætrɪk
Gilpin 'gɪlpɪn
Gilroy 'gɪlrɔɪ
Gilson 'dʒɪlsn, 'gɪlsn
gilt (*s.*) gɪlt
gilt-edged ˌgɪlt'edʒd [*also* '-- *when
    attributive*]
Gilwhite 'gɪlwaɪt ['gɪlhw-]
gimbal, -s 'dʒɪmbəl, -z
gimb|le, -les, -ling, -led 'gɪmb|l, -lz,
    -lɪŋ, -ld
Gimblett 'gɪmblɪt
gimcrack, -s 'dʒɪmkræk, -s
gimlet, -s 'gɪmlɪt [-lət], -s
gimmick, -s 'gɪmɪk, -s
gimp gɪmp
Gimson 'gɪmsn, 'dʒɪmsn
gin (*s.*) (*all senses*), -s dʒɪn, -z
Ginevra dʒɪ'nevrə
Gingell 'gɪndʒəl

ginger, -s 'dʒɪndʒə*, -z
ginger-ale ˌdʒɪndʒər'eɪl [-dʒə'eɪl]
gingerbeer, -s ˌdʒɪndʒə'bɪə*, -z
gingerbeer-bottle, -s ˌdʒɪndʒə'bɪəˌbɒtl,
    -z
gingerbread, -s 'dʒɪndʒəbred, -z
gingerly 'dʒɪndʒəlɪ
ginger-wine ˌdʒɪndʒə'waɪn
ginger|y, -iness 'dʒɪndʒər|ɪ, -ɪnɪs [-ɪnəs]
gingham, -s 'gɪŋəm, -z
gingival dʒɪn'dʒaɪvl
gingivitis ˌdʒɪndʒɪ'vaɪtɪs
gingko, -s 'gɪŋkəʊ, -z
Ginkel(l) 'gɪŋkəl
Ginn gɪn
gin-palace, -s 'dʒɪnˌpælɪs [-əs], -ɪz
Ginsberg 'gɪnzbɜːg
ginseng 'dʒɪnseŋ
gin-shop, -s 'dʒɪnʃɒp, -s
gin-sling, -s ˌdʒɪn'slɪŋ, -z
Giovanni ˌdʒɪəʊ'vɑːnɪ [dʒəʊ'v-, -'vænɪ]
    (dʒo'vanni)
gip (*gipsy*), -s dʒɪp, -s
gip (*to clean fish*), -s, -ping, -ped gɪp, -s,
    -ɪŋ, -t
Gippsland 'gɪpslænd
gips|y, -ies 'dʒɪps|ɪ, -ɪz
giraffe, -s dʒɪ'rɑːf [dʒə-, -'ræf], -s
Giralda dʒɪ'rældə
girandole, -s 'dʒɪrəndəʊl, -z
gird (*s. v.*), -s, -ing, -ed, girt gɜːd, -z, -ɪŋ,
    -ɪd, gɜːt
girder, -s 'gɜːdə*, -z
gird|le (*s. v.*), -les, -ling, -led 'gɜːd|l, -lz,
    -lɪŋ [-lɪŋ], -ld
Girdlestone 'gɜːdlstən
Girgashite, -s 'gɜːgəʃaɪt, -s
Girgasite, -s 'gɜːgəsaɪt, -s
girl, -s; -hood; -ish/ly, -ishness gɜːl,
    -z; -hʊd; -ɪʃ/lɪ, -ɪʃnɪs [-nəs]
Giro 'dʒaɪrəʊ
Girondist, -s dʒɪ'rɒndɪst, -s
girt (*s.*), -s gɜːt, -s
girt (*from* gird) gɜːt
girth, -s gɜːθ, -s
Girtin 'gɜːtɪn
Girton 'gɜːtn
Girtonian, -s gɜː'təʊnjən [-nɪən], -z
Gisbourne 'gɪzbɔːn [-bɔən]
Gissing 'gɪsɪŋ
gist, -s dʒɪst, -s
Gita 'giːtə (*Hindi* gita)
Gitane(s) (*cigarette*) ʒiː'tɑːn (ʒitan)
gittern, -s 'gɪtɜːn, -z
Giuseppe dʒuː'sepɪ [dʒʊ's-] (dʒu'seppe)
giv|e, -es, -ing, gave, giv|en, -er/s gɪv,
    -z, -ɪŋ, geɪv, 'gɪv|n, -ə*/z
give-and-take ˌgɪvən'teɪk

213

Givenchy gɪ' venᵗʃɪ (ʒivã̃ʃi)

Gizeh 'giːzeɪ [-zə]

gizzard, -s 'gɪzəd, -z

glacé 'glæseɪ

glacial 'gleɪsjəl [-sɪəl, -ʃjəl, -ʃɪəl, -ʃl, 'glæsɪəl, 'glæsjəl]

glaciation ˌglæsɪ'eɪʃn [ˌgleɪs-]

glacier, -s 'glæsjə* ['gleɪs-, -sɪə*], -z

glacis (sing.) 'glæsɪs ['glæsɪ], (plur.) 'glæsɪz

glacises (alternative plur. of glacis) 'glæsɪsɪz

glad (adj.); glad|der, -dest, -ly, -ness glæd; 'glæd|ə*, -ɪst, -lɪ, -nɪs [-nəs]

glad (v.), -s, -ding, -ded glæd, -z, -ɪŋ, -ɪd

gladd|en, -ens, -ening, -ened 'glæd|n, -nz, -nɪŋ [-nɪŋ], -nd

glade, -s gleɪd, -z

gladiator, -s 'glædɪeɪtə*, -z

gladiatorial ˌglædɪə'tɔːrɪəl [-djə-]

gladiole, -s 'glædɪəʊl, -z

gladiol|us, -i 'glædɪ'əʊl|əs ['glædɪəʊl-, 'glædɪəl-, rarely glə'daɪəl-], -aɪ

gladsome, -ly, -ness 'glædsəm, -lɪ, -nɪs [-nəs]

gladstone (G.), -s 'glædstən, -z

Gladstonian glæd'stəʊnjən [-nɪən]

Glad|win, -ys 'glæd|wɪn, -ɪs

glagolitic ˌglægəʊ'lɪtɪk

glair, -eous, -y gleə*, -rɪəs, -rɪ

Glaisdale (in North Yorkshire) 'gleɪz-deɪl [locally -dl]

Glaisher 'gleɪʃə*

glaive, -s gleɪv, -z

Glamis glɑːmz

Glamorgan, -shire glə'mɔːgən, -ʃə [-ˌʃɪə*]

glamorous, -ly 'glæmərəs, -lɪ

glamour 'glæmə*

glanc|e (s. v.), -es, -ing/ly, -ed glɑːns, -ɪz, -ɪŋ/lɪ, -t

gland, -s glænd, -z

glander|s, -ed 'glændə|z ['glɑːn-], -d

glandiferous glæn'dɪfərəs

glandul|ar, -ous 'glændjʊl|ə* [-dʒələ*], -əs

glandule, -s 'glændjuːl, -z

Glanvill(e) 'glænvɪl

Glapthorne 'glæpθɔːn

glar|e (s. v.), -es, -ing/ly, -ingness, -ed gleə*, -z, -rɪŋ/lɪ, -rɪŋnɪs [-nəs], -d

Glarus 'glɑːrəs

Glasgow 'glɑːsgəʊ ['glɑːzg-, 'glɑːsk-, 'glæsg-, 'glæzg-, 'glæsk-]

glasier (G.), -s 'gleɪzjə* [-zɪə*, -ʒjə*, -ʒɪə*, -ʒə*], -z

Glasneven glɑːs'nevən

glass, -es glɑːs, -ɪz

glass-blow|er/s, -ing 'glɑːsˌbləʊ|ə*/z, -ɪŋ

Glasscock (surname) 'glɑːskɒk, -kəʊ

glass-cutter, -s 'glɑːsˌkʌtə*, -z

glassful, -s 'glɑːsfʊl, -z

glass-hou|se, -ses 'glɑːshaʊ|s, -zɪz

glass-paper 'glɑːsˌpeɪpə*

glassware 'glɑːsweə*

glass-work, -s 'glɑːswɜːk, -s

glasswort 'glɑːswɜːt

glass|y, -ier, -iest, -ily, -iness 'glɑːs|ɪ, -ɪə* [-jə*], -ɪɪst [-jɪst], -ɪlɪ [-əlɪ], -ɪnɪs [-ɪnəs]

Glastonbury 'glæstənbərɪ ['glæsn-, 'glɑːs-]

Glaswegian, -s glæs'wiːdʒjən [glɑːs-, glæz-, glɑːz-, -dʒɪən, -dʒən], -z

glaucoma, -tous glɔː'kəʊmə, -təs

glaucous 'glɔːkəs

Glave gleɪv

glaz|e (s. v.), -es, -ing, -ed, -er/s gleɪz, -ɪz, -ɪŋ, -d, -ə*/z

Glazebrook 'gleɪzbrʊk

glazier, -s 'gleɪzjə* [-zɪə, -ʒjə*, -ʒɪə* -ʒə*], -z

Glazunov 'glæzuːnɒf [-zʊ-, -nɒv] (gləzu'nof)

gleam (s. v.), -s, -ing, -ed; -y gliːm, -z, -ɪŋ, -d; -ɪ

glean, -s, -ing/s, -ed, -er/s gliːn, -z, -ɪŋ/z, -d, -ə*/z

glebe, -s gliːb, -z

glee, -s gliː, -z

glee|ful, -fully, -fulness 'gliː|fʊl, -fʊlɪ [-fəlɪ], -fʊlnɪs [-nəs]

glee|man, -men 'gliː|mən [-mæn], -mən [-men]

glee-singer, -s 'gliːˌsɪŋə*, -z

Glegg gleg

Gleichen (English surname) 'glaɪkən

Glemsford 'glemsfəd

glen (G.), -s glen, -z

Glenallan glen'ælən

Glenalmond glen'ɑːmənd

Glenavon (in Northern Ireland) glen-'ævən

Glenavy (in Northern Ireland) glen-'eɪvɪ

Glencairn glen'keən

Glencoe glen'kəʊ

Glendale glen'deɪl, 'glendeɪl

Glendin(n)ing glen'dɪnɪŋ

Glendower glen'daʊə*

Glenelg glen'elg

Glenfinnan glen'fɪnən

glengarr|y (G.), -ies glen'gær|ɪ, -ɪz

Glenlivet glen'lɪvɪt

Glenmore glen'mɔː* [-'mɔə*]

Glenrothes glen'rɒθɪs
Glenwood 'glenwʊd
glib, -ber, -best, -ly, -ness glɪb, -ə*, -ɪst, -lɪ, -nɪs [-nəs]
glid|e (*s. v.*), **-es, -ing/ly, -ed, -er/s** glaɪd, -z, -ɪŋ/lɪ, -ɪd, -ə*/z
glimmer (*s. v.*), **-s, -ing/s, -ingly, -ed** 'glɪmə*, -z, -rɪŋ/z, -rɪŋlɪ, -d
glimps|e (*s. v.*), **-es, -ing, -ed** glɪmʃps, -ɪz, -ɪŋ, -t
glint, -s, -ing, -ed glɪnt, -s, -ɪŋ, -ɪd
glissad|e (*s. v.*), **-es, -ing, -ed** glɪ'sɑːd [-'seɪd], -z, -ɪŋ, -ɪd
Glisson 'glɪsn
glist|en, -ens, -ening, -ened 'glɪs|n, -nz, -nɪŋ [-nɪŋ], -nd
glitt|er (*s. v.*), **-ers, -ering/ly, -ered** 'glɪt|ə*, -əz, -ərɪŋ/lɪ, -əd
Gloag (*surname*) gləʊg
gloaming 'gləʊmɪŋ
gloat, -s, -ing, -ed gləʊt, -s, -ɪŋ, -ɪd
global 'gləʊbl
globe, -s gləʊb, -z
globe-trott|er/s, -ing 'gləʊb,trɒt|ə*/z, -ɪŋ
globose 'gləʊbəʊs [gləʊ'b-]
globosity gləʊ'bɒsətɪ [-ɪtɪ]
globous 'gləʊbəs
globular, -ly 'glɒbjʊlə*, -lɪ
globule, -s 'glɒbjuːl, -z
glockenspiel, -s 'glɒkənspiːl, -z
gloom (*s. v.*), **-s, -ing, -ed** gluːm, -z, -ɪŋ, -d
gloom|y, -ier, -iest, -ily, -iness 'gluːm|ɪ, -ɪə* [-jə*], -ɪɪst [-jɪst], -ɪlɪ [-əlɪ], -ɪnɪs [-ɪnəs]
Gloria, -s 'glɔːrɪə, -z
Gloriana ˌglɔːrɪ'ɑːnə
glorification ˌglɔːrɪfɪ'keɪʃn
glori|fy, -fies, -fying, -fied, -fier/s 'glɔːrɪ|faɪ, -faɪz, -faɪɪŋ, -faɪd, -faɪə*/z
glorious, -ly, -ness 'glɔːrɪəs, -lɪ, -nɪs [-nəs]
glor|y (*s. v.*), **-ies, -ying, -ied** 'glɔːr|ɪ, -ɪz, -ɪɪŋ, -ɪd
glory-hole, -s 'glɔːrɪhəʊl, -z
Glos. glɒs
gloss (*s. v.*), **-es, -ing, -ed, -er/s** glɒs, -ɪz, -ɪŋ, -t, -ə*/z
glossarial glɒ'seərɪəl
glossar|ist/s, -y, -ies 'glɒsər|ɪst/s, -ɪ, -ɪz
glossematic, -s ˌglɒsɪ'mætɪk, -s
glossic 'glɒsɪk
glossograph|er/s, -y glɒ'sɒgrəf|ə*/z, -ɪ
glossological ˌglɒsəʊ'lɒdʒɪkl
glossolog|ist/s, -y glɒ'sɒlədʒ|ɪst/s, -ɪ
Glossop 'glɒsəp

gloss|y, -ier, -iest, -ily, -iness 'glɒs|ɪ, -ɪə*, -ɪɪst, -ɪlɪ [-əlɪ], -ɪnɪs [-ɪnəs]
Gloster 'glɒstə*
glottal 'glɒtl [*rarely* 'gləʊtl]
glottalic glɒ'tælɪk [glə-]
glottic 'glɒtɪk
glottis, -es 'glɒtɪs, -ɪz
glottology glɒ'tɒlədʒɪ
Gloucester, -shire 'glɒstə* [*old-fashioned* 'glɔːs-], -ʃə* [-ˌʃɪə*]
glove, -s, -d glʌv, -z, -d
glove-fight, -s 'glʌvfaɪt, -s
glover (G.), -s 'glʌvə*, -z
glove-stretcher, -s 'glʌv,stretʃə*, -z
gl|ow (*s. v.*), **-ows, -owing/ly, -owed** gl|əʊ, -əʊz, -əʊɪŋ/lɪ, -əʊd
glower, -s, -ing, -ed 'glaʊə*, -z, -rɪŋ, -d
glow-worm, -s 'gləʊwɜːm, -z
gloxinia, -s glɒk'sɪnjə [-nɪə], -z
gloz|e (*s. v.*), **-es, -ing, -ed** gləʊz, -ɪz, -ɪŋ, -d
Glubbdubbdrib ˌglʌbdʌb'drɪb
Gluck glʊk, gluːk
glucose 'gluːkəʊs [-əʊz]
glu|e (*s. v.*), **-es, -ing, -ed, -er/s** gluː:, -z, -ɪŋ ['glʊɪŋ], -d, -ə*/z [gluə*/z]
glue-pot, -s 'gluː:pɒt, -s
gluey, -ness 'gluː:ɪ ['glʊɪ], -nɪs [-nəs]
gluish 'gluː:ɪʃ ['glʊɪʃ]
glum, -mer, -mest, -ly, -ness glʌm, -ə*, -ɪst, -lɪ, -nɪs [-nəs]
glut (*s. v.*), **-s, -ting, -ted** glʌt, -s, -ɪŋ, -ɪd
glut|en, -in 'gluː:t|ən [-|ɪn, -|n], -ɪn
glutinous, -ly, -ness 'gluː:tɪnəs [-tən-], -lɪ, -nɪs [-nəs]
glutton, -s 'glʌtn, -z
gluttoniz|e [-is|e], -es, -ing, -ed 'glʌtŋ-aɪz [-tənaɪz], -ɪz, -ɪŋ, -d
gluttonous, -ly 'glʌtŋəs [-tənəs], -lɪ
gluttony 'glʌtŋɪ [-tənɪ]
glycerine 'glɪsəriːn [ˌglɪsə'riːn, 'glɪsərɪn]
glycerol 'glɪsərɒl
glycogen 'glɪkəʊdʒen ['glaɪk-]
glycol 'glaɪkɒl ['glɪk-, -kl]
Glyn glɪn
Glynde (*in East Sussex*) glaɪnd
Glyndebourne 'glaɪndbɔːn [-bəən]
Glynis 'glɪnɪs
Glynne glɪn
glyph, -s glɪf, -s
glyptic 'glɪptɪk
glyptography glɪp'tɒgrəfɪ
G|-man, -men 'dʒiː:|mæn, -men
gnaphalium næ'feɪljəm [nə'f-, -lɪəm]
gnar, -s, -ring, -red nɑː:*, -z, -rɪŋ, -d
gnarl, -s, -ed nɑːl, -z, -d
gnash, -es, -ing, -ed næʃ, -ɪz, -ɪŋ, -t

215

gnat, -s næt, -s
gnathic 'næθɪk
gnaw, -s, -ing, -ed, -er/s nɔː, -z, -ɪŋ, -d, -ə*/z
gneiss naɪs [gn-]
gnome (goblin), -s nəʊm, -z
gnome (maxim), -s 'nəʊmiː, -z
gnomic, -al 'nəʊmɪk, -l
gnomish 'nəʊmɪʃ
gnomon, -s 'nəʊmɒn [-mən], -z
gnomonic, -al, -ally nəʊ'mɒnɪk, -l, -əlɪ
gnos|is, -es 'nəʊs|ɪs, -iːz
Gnossall (near Stafford) 'nəʊsl
gnostic (s. adj.), -s 'nɒstɪk, -s
gnosticism 'nɒstɪsɪzəm
gnu, -s nuː [njuː], -z
go (s. v.), -es, -ing, went, gone, goer/s gəʊ, -z, -ɪŋ, went, gɒn, 'gəʊə*/z
Goa 'gəʊə
Goad gəʊd, 'gəʊəd
goad (s. v.), -s, -ing, -ed gəʊd, -z, -ɪŋ, -ɪd
go-ahead 'gəʊəhed [,--'-]
goal, -s; -keeper/s, -post/s gəʊl, -z; -,kiːpə*/z, -pəʊst/s
Goanese ,gəʊə'niːz
goat, -s gəʊt, -s
goatee, -s gəʊ'tiː: [also '-- in goatee beard], -z
goat-herd, -s 'gəʊthɜːd, -z
Goathland 'gəʊθlənd
goatish 'gəʊtɪʃ
goat's-beard, -s 'gəʊts,bɪəd, -z
goat-sucker, -s 'gəʊt,sʌkə*, -z
gob, -s gɒb, -z
gobang gəʊ'bæŋ ['gəʊb-]
gobbet, -s 'gɒbɪt, -s
gobb|le, -les, -ling, -led, -ler/s 'gɒb|l, -lz, -lɪŋ [-lɪŋ], -ld, -lə*/z [-lə*/z]
Gobbo 'gɒbəʊ
Gobelin 'gəʊbəlɪn ['gɒbəlɪn] (gɔblɛ̃)
go-between, -s 'gəʊbɪ,twiːn [-bə-], -z
Gobi 'gəʊbi
goblet, -s 'gɒblɪt [-lət], -s
goblin, -s 'gɒblɪn, -z
gob|y, -ies 'gəʊb|ɪ, -ɪz
go-by 'gəʊbaɪ
go-cart, -s 'gəʊkɑːt, -s
god, -s gɒd, -z
God gɒd
Godalming 'gɒdlmɪŋ
god|child, -children 'gɒd|tʃaɪld, -,tʃɪldrən [-,tʃʊldrən, -,tʃldrən]
Goddard 'gɒdəd, -dɑːd
god-daughter, -s 'gɒd,dɔːtə*, -z
goddess, -es 'gɒdɪs [-des], -ɪz
Goderich 'gəʊdrɪtʃ
godetia, -s gəʊ'diːʃə [-ʃjə, -ʃɪə], -z
godfather, -s 'gɒd,fɑːðə*, -z

god-fearing 'gɒd,fɪərɪŋ
god-forsaken 'gɒdfə,seɪkən
God|free, -frey 'gɒd|frɪ, -frɪ
god-given 'gɒd,gɪvn
godhead (G.), -s 'gɒdhed, -z
Godiva gəʊ'daɪvə
Godkin 'gɒdkɪn
godless, -ly, -ness 'gɒdlɪs [-ləs, -les], -lɪ, -nɪs [-nəs]
godlike 'gɒdlaɪk
god|ly, -ier, -iest, -iness 'gɒdl|ɪ, -ɪə* [-jə*], -ɪɪst [-jɪst], -ɪnɪs [-ɪnəs]
Godman (surname) 'gɒdmən
God-man (Christ) ,gɒd'mæn ['--]
Godmanchester 'gɒdmən,tʃestə*
godmother, -s 'gɒd,mʌðə*, -z
Godolphin gə'dɒlfɪn
godown, -s 'gəʊdaʊn, -z
godparent, -s 'gɒd,peərənt, -s
God's-acre, -s 'gɒdz,eɪkə*, -z
godsend, -s 'gɒdsend, -z
godson, -s 'gɒdsʌn, -z
god-speed ,gɒd'spiːd
godward (G.) 'gɒdwəd
Godwin 'gɒdwɪn
godwit, -s 'gɒdwɪt, -s
Goethe 'gɜːtə [-tɪ] ('gøːtə)
Goff(e) gɒf
goffer, -s, -ing, -ed 'gəʊfə*, -z, -rɪŋ, -d
Gog, -s gɒg, -z
Gogarty 'gəʊgətɪ
gogg|le (s. v.), -les, -ling, -led 'gɒg|l, -lz, -lɪŋ [-lɪŋ], -ld
goggle-eyed 'gɒglaɪd
Gogmagog 'gɒgməgɒg
Gogo 'gəʊgəʊ
going|s, -s-on 'gəʊɪŋ|z, -z-'ɒn
goitre, -s, -d 'gɔɪtə*, -z, -d
goitrous 'gɔɪtrəs
Golby 'gəʊlbɪ
Golconda gɒl'kɒndə
gold gəʊld
gold-beater, -s 'gəʊld,biːtə*, -z
goldcrest, -s 'gəʊldkrest, -s
gold-digger, -s 'gəʊld,dɪgə*, -z
gold-dust 'gəʊlddʌst [,gəʊld'd-]
golden 'gəʊldən
goldeneye, -s 'gəʊldənaɪ, -z
goldfield, -s 'gəʊldfiːld, -z
goldfinch, -es 'gəʊldfɪntʃ, -ɪz
goldfish, -es 'gəʊldfɪʃ, -ɪz
goldilocks (G.) 'gəʊldɪlɒks
Golding 'gəʊldɪŋ
gold-lace ,gəʊld'leɪs
gold-leaf 'gəʊldliːf [,-'-]
gold-mine, -s 'gəʊldmaɪn, -z
Goldsborough 'gəʊldzbərə

216

Goldschmidt (*English name*) 'gəʊldʃmɪt
goldsmith (G.), -s 'gəʊldsmɪθ, -s
goldstick, -s 'gəʊldstɪk, -s
gold-wire ˌgəʊld'waɪə*
golf (*s. v.*), -s, -ing, -ed, -er/s gɒlf [*sometimes by players* gɒf], -s, -ɪŋ, -t, -ə*/z
golf|-club/s, -links 'gɒlf|klʌb/z [*sometimes by players* 'gɒf-], -lɪŋks
Golgotha 'gɒlgəθə
Goliath gəʊ'laɪəθ
Golightly (*surname*) gəʊ'laɪtlɪ
Gollancz gə'lænts, gɒ'lænts, 'gɒlənts ['gɒlæŋks, gɒ'læŋks]
golliwog, -s 'gɒlɪwɒg, -z
golly 'gɒlɪ
golosh, -es gə'lɒʃ, -ɪz
Golton 'gɒltən
Gomar, -ist/s 'gəʊmə*, -rɪst/s
Gomersal (*in West Yorkshire*) 'gɒməsəl
Gomes 'gəʊmez
Gomme gɒm
Gomorrah gə'mɒrə
Gomshall (*in Surrey*) 'gʌmʃl ['gɒm-]
gonad, -s 'gəʊnæd, -z
Gondibert 'gɒndɪbɜːt
gondola, -s 'gɒndələ, -z
gondolier, -s ˌgɒndə'lɪə*, -z
gone (*from* go) gɒn
Goneril 'gɒnərɪl
gonfalon, -s 'gɒnfələn, -z
gong, -s gɒŋ, -z
Gonin 'gəʊnɪn
goniometer, -s ˌgəʊnɪ'ɒmɪtə* [-mətə*], -z
gonorrhea ˌgɒnə'rɪə
Gonville 'gɒnvɪl
Gooch guːtʃ
good (*s. adj.*) (G.), -s, -ness gʊd, -z, -nɪs [-nəs]
good (*interj.*) gʊd
Good|ale, -all, -body 'gʊd|eɪl, -ɔːl, -ˌbɒdɪ
good-bye (*s.*), -s ˌgʊd'baɪ, -z
good-bye (*interj.*) ˌgʊd'baɪ
Goodchild 'gʊdtʃaɪld
good day ˌgʊd'deɪ
Goode gʊd
Goodell gʊ'del
Good|enough, -eve 'gʊd|ɪnʌf, -iːv
good evening ˌgʊd'iːvnɪŋ
Goodfellow 'gʊdˌfeləʊ
good-for-nothing (*s. adj.*), -s 'gʊdfə-ˌnʌθɪŋ [-fŋˌʌθɪŋ, -f,nʌθɪŋ], -z
Goodge gʊdʒ [guːdʒ]
Goodhart 'gʊdhɑːt
good-hearted ˌgʊd'hɑːtɪd ['-ˌ-- *when attributive*]

good-humoured, -ly ˌgʊd'hjuːməd [*old-fashioned* -'juː, '-ˌ-- *when attributive*], -lɪ
goodish 'gʊdɪʃ
Goodliffe 'gʊdlɪf
good-looking ˌgʊd'lʊkɪŋ [*also* '-ˌ-- *according to sentence-stress*]
good|ly, -ier, -iest, -iness 'gʊdl|ɪ, -ɪə* [-jə*], -ɪɪst [-jɪst], -ɪnɪs [-ɪnəs]
good|man, -men 'gʊd|mæn, -men
Goodman 'gʊdmən
good morning ˌgʊd'mɔːnɪŋ
good morrow ˌgʊd'mɒrəʊ
good-natured, -ly ˌgʊd'neɪtʃəd ['-ˌ-- *when attributive*], -lɪ
goodness 'gʊdnɪs [-nəs]
good night ˌgʊd'naɪt
Good|rich, -sir, -son 'gʊd|rɪtʃ, -sə*, -sn
goods-train, -s 'gʊdztreɪn, -z
good-tempered, -ly ˌgʊd'tempəd ['-ˌ-- *when attributive*], -lɪ
goodwi|fe, -ves 'gʊdwaɪ|f, -vz
goodwill, -s ˌgʊd'wɪl, -z
Good|win, -wood 'gʊd|wɪn, -wʊd
good|y (G.), -ier, -iest, -ily, -iness 'gʊd|ɪ, -ɪə*, -ɪɪst, -ɪlɪ [-əlɪ], -ɪnɪs [-nəs]
Good|year, -yer 'gʊd|jɜː* [-jə*, -ˌjɪə*], -jə*
goof|y, -ier, -iest, -ily, -iness 'guːf|ɪ, -ɪə*, -ɪɪst, -ɪlɪ [-əlɪ], -ɪnɪs [-ɪnəs]
Googe gʊdʒ [guːdʒ]
Googie 'guːgɪ
googly 'guːglɪ
Goole guːl
goon, -s guːn, -z
Goonhilly 'guːnˌhɪlɪ
goop|y, -ier, -iest, -ily, -iness 'guːp|ɪ, -ɪə*, -ɪɪst, -ɪlɪ [-əlɪ], -ɪnɪs [-ɪnəs]
goosander, -s guː'sændə*, -z
g|oose (*bird*), -eese g|uːs, -iːs
goose (*tailor's iron*), -s guːs, -ɪz
gooseberr|y, -ies; -y-fool 'gʊzbər|ɪ, -ɪz; (ˌgʊzbr) -ɪ'fuːl
goose|-flesh, -grass 'guːs|fleʃ, -grɑːs
goose-note, -s 'guːsnəʊt, -s
goose-quill, -s 'guːskwɪl, -z
goose-step 'guːsstep
goosey, -s 'guːsɪ, -z
gopher, -s 'gəʊfə*, -z
Gophir 'gəʊfə*
Gorboduc 'gɔːbədʌk
Gordi|an, -um 'gɔːdj|ən [-dɪ|ən], -əm
Gordon 'gɔːdn
Gordonstoun 'gɔːdənstən
gor|e (*s. v.*) (G.), -es, -ing, -ed gɔː* [gɔə*], -z, -rɪŋ, -d
Gorell 'gɒrəl

217

gorg|e (s. v.), -es, -ing, -ed gɔːdʒ, -ɪz, -ɪŋ, -d

gorgeous, -ly, -ness 'gɔːdʒəs, -lɪ, -nɪs [-nəs]

Gorges 'gɔːdʒɪz

gorget, -s 'gɔːdʒɪt, -s

Gorgie 'gɔːgɪ

Gorgon, -s 'gɔːgən, -z

Gorgonzola, -s ˌgɔːgənˈzəʊlə, -z

Gorham 'gɔːrəm

gorilla, -s gəˈrɪlə [gʊ'r-], -z

Goring 'gɔːrɪŋ

Gorizia gɒˈrɪtsɪə [gəˈr-]

Gorleston 'gɔːlstən

gormandiz|e [-is|e], -es, -ing, -ed, -er/s 'gɔːməndaɪz, -ɪz, -ɪŋ, -d, -ə*/z

Gornergrat 'gɔːnəgræt

Goronwy gəˈrɒnwɪ (Welsh goˈronui)

Gorringe 'gɒrɪndʒ

gorse gɔːs

Gorst gɔːst

Gorton 'gɔːtn

gor|y, -ier, -iest, -ily, -iness 'gɔːr|ɪ, -ɪə*, -ɪɪst, -əlɪ [-ɪlɪ], -ɪnɪs [-ɪnəs]

gos, -es gɒs, -ɪz

Goschen 'gəʊʃn

gosh gɒʃ

goshawk, -s 'gɒshɔːk, -s

Goshen 'gəʊʃn

gosling (G.), -s 'gɒzlɪŋ, -z

go-slow ˌgəʊˈsləʊ

gospel (G.), -s 'gɒspl [-pel], -z

gospeller, -s 'gɒspələ*, -z

Gosport 'gɒspɔːt

gossamer 'gɒsəmə*

Gosschalk 'gɒstʃɔːk

Goss(e) gɒs

gossip (s. v.), -s, -ing, -ed; -y 'gɒsɪp, -s, -ɪŋ, -t; -ɪ

got (from get) gɒt

Göteborg 'gɜːtəbɔːg (Swedish jøːtə-ˈbɔrj)

Goth, -s gɒθ, -s

Gotha (in Germany) 'gəʊθə ['gəʊtə] ('goːtaː), (old-fashioned English spelling of Göta in Sweden) 'gəʊtə

Gotham (in Nottinghamshire) 'gəʊtəm, (in New York) 'gəʊθəm, 'gɒθəm

Gothenburg 'gɒθənbɜːg ['gɒtn-]

Gothic 'gɒθɪk

gothicism, -s 'gɒθɪsɪzəm, -z

gothiciz|e [-is|e], -es, -ing, -ed 'gɒθɪsaɪz, -ɪz, -ɪŋ, -d

Gothland 'gɒθlənd

gotten (from get) 'gɒtn

gouache gʊˈɑːʃ [gwɑː'ʃ] (gwaʃ)

Gouda (Dutch town, cheese) 'gaʊdə

Goudie 'gaʊdɪ

goug|e (s. v.), -es, -ing, -ed gaʊdʒ [gu:dʒ], -ɪz, -ɪŋ, -d

Gough gɒf

goulash, -es 'gu:læʃ [-lɑː'ʃ], -ɪz

Goulburn (place-name) 'gəʊlbɜːn, (surname) 'gu:lbɜːn

Gould gu:ld

Goulden 'gu:ldən

Goulding 'gu:ldɪŋ

Gounod 'gu:nəʊ (guno)

gourd, -s gʊəd, -z

Gourl|ay, -ey 'gʊəl|ɪ, -ɪ

gourmand, -s 'gʊəmənd (gurmɑ̃), -z

gourmet, -s 'gʊəmeɪ (gurmɛ), -z

gout, -y, -ily, -iness gaʊt, -ɪ, -ɪlɪ [-əlɪ], -ɪnɪs [-ɪnəs]

Govan 'gʌvən

Gover 'gəʊvə*

govern, -s, -ing, -ed; -able, -ance, -ess/es 'gʌvn, -z, -ɪŋ ['gʌvnɪŋ], -d; -əbl ['gʌvnəbl], -əns ['gʌvnəns], -ɪs/ɪz ['gʌvnɪs/ɪz]

government, -s 'gʌvnmənt [-vɪmmənt, -vənmənt, -vəmənt], -s

governmental ˌgʌvnˈmentl

governor, -s 'gʌvənə* [-vn̩ə*, -vnə*], -z

governor-general, -s ˌgʌvənəˈdʒenərəl [-vn̩ə-, -vnə-], -z

governorship, -s 'gʌvənəʃɪp [-vn̩ə-, -vnə-], -s

Govey 'gəʊvɪ

Govier 'gəʊvɪə*

Gow gaʊ

Gowan 'gaʊən

Gowen 'gaʊən ['gaʊɪn]

Gower 'gaʊə*, gɔː* [gɔə*]

  Note.—'gaʊə* is used in Gower Street and for the place in Wales. gɔː* [gɔə*] is the family name of the Duke of Sutherland; this pronunciation is also used in Leveson-Gower (q.v.).

Gowing 'gaʊɪŋ

gowk, -s gaʊk, -s

gown, -s, -ed gaʊn, -z, -d

gowns|man, -men 'gaʊnz|mən, -mən [-men]

Gowrie 'gaʊərɪ

Gozo 'gəʊzəʊ

G.P., -s ˌdʒiːˈpiː, -z

grab (s. v.), -s, -bing, -bed, -ber/s græb, -z, -ɪŋ, -d, -ə*/z

grabb|le, -les, -ling, -led 'græb|l, -lz, -lɪŋ [-lɪŋ], -ld

Grabham 'græbəm

Gracch|us, -i 'græk|əs, -iː [-aɪ]

grac|e (s. v.) (G.), -es, -ing, -ed greɪs, -ɪz, -ɪŋ, -t

Gracechurch 'greɪstʃəːtʃ

grace|ful, -fully, -fulness 'greɪs|fʊl,
-fʊlɪ [-fəlɪ], -fʊlnɪs [-nəs]

graceless, -ly, -ness 'greɪslɪs [-ləs], -lɪ,
-nɪs [-nəs]

grace-note, -s 'greɪsnəʊt, -s

Gracie 'greɪsɪ

gracious, -ly, -ness 'greɪʃəs, -lɪ, -nɪs
[-nəs]

grackle, -s 'grækl, -z

gradat|e, -es, -ing, -ed grə'deɪt, -s, -ɪŋ,
-ɪd

gradation, -s grə'deɪʃn, -z

gradational grə'deɪʃənl [-ʃn̩l, -ʃnl,
-ʃənəl]

grad|e (s. v.), -es, -ing, -ed greɪd, -z, -ɪŋ,
-ɪd

Gradgrind 'grædgraɪnd

gradient, -s 'greɪdjənt [-dɪənt], -s

gradin, -s 'greɪdɪn, -z

gradual (s. adj.), -s, -ly 'grædʒʊəl
[-dʒwəl, -dʒʊl, -djʊəl, -djwəl, -djʊl],
-z, -ɪ

graduate (s.), -s 'grædʒʊət [-djʊət,
-djʊɪt, -djʊeɪt, -dʒʊɪt], -s

graduat|e (v.), -es, -ing, -ed 'grædjʊeɪt
[-dʒʊeɪt], -s, -ɪŋ, -ɪd

graduation, -s ˌgrædjʊ'eɪʃn [-dʒʊ-], -z

graduator, -s 'grædjʊeɪtə*, -z

gradus, -es 'grædəs ['greɪd-], -ɪz

Grady 'greɪdɪ

Graeme greɪm, 'greɪəm

graffiti grə'fiːtɪ [græ-]

graft (s. v.), -s, -ing, -ed, -er/s grɑːft,
-s, -ɪŋ, -ɪd, -ə*/z

Grafton 'grɑːftən

Graham(e) 'greɪəm

Grahamston 'greɪəmstən

Grahamstown 'greɪəmztaun

grail (G.), -s greɪl, -z

grain (s. v.), -s, -ing, -ed, -er/s; -y
greɪn, -z, -ɪŋ, -d, -ə*/z; -ɪ

Grainger 'greɪndʒə*

gram, -s græm, -z

gramercy grə'məːsɪ

graminaceous ˌgræmɪ'neɪʃəs [ˌgreɪm-]

gramineous grə'mɪnɪəs [græ'm-, greɪ-,
-njəs]

graminivorous ˌgræmɪ'nɪvərəs

grammalogue, -s 'græməlɒg, -z

grammar, -s 'græmə*, -z

grammar-school, -s 'græməskuːl, -z

grammarian, -s grə'meərɪən, -z

grammatic, -al, -ally grə'mætɪk, -l, -əlɪ

grammaticiz|e [-is|e], -es, -ing, -ed
grə'mætɪsaɪz, -ɪz, -ɪŋ, -d

gramme, -s græm, -z

gramophone, -s 'græməfəʊn, -z

Grampian, -s 'græmpjən [-pɪən], -z

grampus, -es 'græmpəs, -ɪz

Granada grə'nɑːdə (gra'nada)

granar|y, -ies 'grænər|ɪ, -ɪz

Granbury 'grænbərɪ

Granby 'grænbɪ

grand; grand|er, -est, -ly, -ness grænd;
'grænd|ə*, -ɪst, -lɪ, -nɪs ['grænnɪs,
-nəs]

grandam, -s 'grændæm, -z

grand-aunt, -s 'grændɑːnt, -s

grand|child, -children 'grænd|tʃaɪld,
-ˌtʃɪldrən [-ˌtʃʊldrən, -ˌtʃɪldrən]

granddad, -s 'grændæd [-ndd-], -z

granddaughter, -s 'grænˌdɔːtə*
[-ndˌd-], -z

grand-duchess, -es ˌgrænd'dʌtʃɪs [also
'grændˌd-, esp. when followed by a
stress], -ɪz

grand-duke, -s ˌgrænd'djuːk [also
'grænndd-, esp. when followed by a
stress], -s

grandee, -s græn'diː, -z

grandeur 'grændʒə* [-ˌdjʊə*, -djə*]

grandfather, -s 'grænd,fɑːðə*, -z

Grandgent 'grændʒent [-dʒənt]

grandiloquen|ce, -t/ly græn'dɪləkwən|s
[-lʊk-], -t/lɪ

grandiose, -ly 'grændɪəʊs [-djəʊs,
-dɪəʊz, -djəʊz], -lɪ

grandiosity ˌgrændɪ'ɒsɪtɪ [-ɪtɪ]

Grandison 'grændɪsn

grandma, -s 'grænmɑː, -z

grandmamma, -s 'grænmə,mɑː, -z

grandmother, -s 'græn,mʌðə* [-nd,m-],
-z

grand-nephew, -s 'græn,nevju: [-nd,n-,
-,nefju:, ˌ-'--], -z

grand-niece, -s 'grænni:s [-ndn-, ˌ-'-],
-ɪz

grandpa, -s 'grænpɑː, -z

grandpapa, -s 'grænpə,pɑː, -z

grandparent, -s 'græn,peərənt [-nd,p-],
-s

grandsire, -s 'græn,saɪə* [-nd,s-], -z

grandson, -s 'grænsʌn [-nds-], -z

grand-stand, -s 'grændstænd, -z

grand-uncle, -s 'grænd,ʌŋkl, -z

grange (G.), -s greɪndʒ, -ɪz

Grangemouth 'greɪndʒməθ [-maʊθ]

granger (G.), -s 'greɪndʒə*, -z

grangeriz|e [-is|e], -es, -ing, -ed 'greɪn-
dʒəraɪz, -ɪz, -ɪŋ, -d

Grange|town, -ville 'greɪndʒ|taʊn, -vɪl

granite (G.), -s 'grænɪt, -s

granitic græ'nɪtɪk

grann|y, -ies 'græn|ɪ, -ɪz

granolithic ˌgrænəʊ'lɪθɪk

219

grant (s. v.) (G.), -s, -ing, -ed grɑːnt, -s, -ɪŋ, -ɪd

grantee, -s grɑːnˈtiː, -z

Grantham (in Lincolnshire) 'grænθəm [rarely 'græntəm], (surname) 'grænθəm

Grantie 'grɑːntɪ

Granton 'grɑːntən ['græn-]

grantor, -s grɑːnˈtɔː*, -z

Grantown 'græntaʊn

granular, -y 'grænjʊlə* [-njəl-], -rɪ

granulat|e, -es, -ing, -ed 'grænjʊleɪt [-njəl-], -s, -ɪŋ, -ɪd

granulation, -s ˌgrænjʊ'leɪʃn [-njə'l-], -z

granule, -s 'grænjuːl, -z

granul|ite, -ous 'grænjʊl|aɪt [-njəl-], -əs

Granville 'grænvɪl

grape (G.), -s greɪp, -s

grape-cure, -s 'greɪpˌkjʊə* [-kjɔə*, -kjɔː*], -z

grape-fruit, -s 'greɪpfruːt, -s

grape-shot 'greɪpʃɒt

grape|-stone/s, -sugar, -vine/s 'greɪp|stəʊn/z, -ˌʃʊgə*, -vaɪn/z

graph, -s græf [grɑːf], -s

graphic (G.), -s, -al, -ally 'græfɪk, -s, -l, -əlɪ

graphite 'græfaɪt ['greɪf-]

graphology græˈfɒlədʒɪ

graphometer, -s græˈfɒmɪtə* [-mətə*], -z

grapnel, -s 'græpnl, -z

grapp|le, -les, -ling, -led, -ler/s 'græp|l, -lz, -lɪŋ [-lɪŋ], -ld, -lə*/z [-lə*/z]

grappling-iron, -s 'græp|lɪŋˌaɪən [-plɪŋ-], -z

grapy 'greɪpɪ

Grasmere 'grɑːsˌmɪə*

grasp (s. v.), -s, -ing/ly, -ed, -er/s grɑːsp, -s, -ɪŋ/lɪ, -t, -ə*/z

grass (s. v.), -es, -ing, -ed grɑːs, -ɪz, -ɪŋ, -t

grass-cutter, -s 'grɑːsˌkʌtə*, -z

grass-green ˌgrɑːs'griːn ['grɑːsg-]

grasshopper, -s 'grɑːsˌhɒpə*, -z

grass-land 'grɑːslænd [-lənd]

grass-plot, -s ˌgrɑːs'plɒt ['--], -s

grass-root (adj.), -s (s.) ˌgrɑːs'ruːt ['— when attributive], -s

grass-wid|ow/s, -ower/s ˌgrɑːs'wɪd|əʊ/z, -əʊə*/z

grass|y, -ier, -iest 'grɑːs|ɪ, -ɪə* [-jə*], -ɪɪst [-jɪst]

grata (in persona grata) 'grɑːtə [old-fashioned 'greɪtə]

grat|e (s. v.), -es, -ing/ly, -ed, -er/s greɪt, -s, -ɪŋ/lɪ, -ɪd, -ə*/z

grate|ful, -fully, -fulness 'greɪt|fʊl, -fʊlɪ [-fəlɪ], -fʊlnɪs [-nəs]

Gratian 'greɪʃjən [-ʃɪən]

Gratiano (Shakespearian character) ˌgræʃɪ'ɑːnəʊ [ˌgrɑː-]

gratification, -s ˌgrætɪfɪ'keɪʃn, -z

grati|fy, -fies, -fying, -fied, -fier/s 'grætɪ|faɪ, -faɪz, -faɪɪŋ, -faɪd, -faɪə*/z

gratin 'grætæŋ [-tæn] (gratẽ)

grating (s.), -s 'greɪtɪŋ, -z

Gratiot (in U.S.A.) 'græʃɪət [-ʃjət, 'greɪʃ-]

gratis 'greɪtɪs ['grɑːtɪs, 'grætɪs]

gratitude 'grætɪtjuːd

Grattan 'grætn

gratuitous, -ly, -ness grə'tjuːɪtəs [-'tjʊɪ-], -lɪ, -nɪs [-nəs]

gratuit|y, -ies grə'tjuːət|ɪ [-'tjʊə-, -ɪt|ɪ], -ɪz

gravam|en, -ina grə'veɪm|en, -ɪnə

grave (accent above a letter) grɑːv

grav|e (s. adj. v.) (other senses), -es; -er, -est, -ely, -eness; -ing, -ed, -en, -er/s greɪv, -z; -ə*, -ɪst, -lɪ, -nɪs [-nəs]; -ɪŋ, -d, -n, -ə*/z

grave|-clothes, -digger/s 'greɪv|kləʊðz [old-fashioned -kləʊz], -ˌdɪgə*/z

grav|el (s. v.), -els, -elling, -elled, -elly 'græv|l, -lz, -lɪŋ [-əlɪŋ], -ld, -lɪ [-əlɪ]

gravel|-pit/s, -walk/s 'grævl|pɪt/s (ˌgrævl)-'wɔːk/s

graven (from grave v.) 'greɪvn

Graves (surname) greɪvz, (wine) grɑːv

Gravesend ˌgreɪvz'end [-v'zend]

grave|-stone/s, -yard/s 'greɪv|stəʊn/z, -jɑːd/z

graving-dock, -s 'greɪvɪŋdɒk, -s

gravitas 'grævɪtæs

gravitat|e, -es, -ing, -ed 'grævɪteɪt, -s, -ɪŋ, -ɪd

gravitation ˌgrævɪ'teɪʃn

gravity 'grævətɪ [-ɪtɪ]

gravure grə'vjʊə* [-'vjɔə*, -'vjɔː*]

grav|y, -ies 'greɪv|ɪ, -ɪz

gravy-spoon, -s 'greɪvɪspuːn, -z

gray (s. adj.) (G.), -s, -er, -est, -ness greɪ, -z, -ə* [greə*], -ɪst, 'greɪnɪs [-nəs]

graybeard, -s 'greɪˌbɪəd, -z

gray-eyed 'greɪaɪd [ˌ-'- when not attributive]

gray-haired ˌgreɪ'heəd ['— when attributive]

gray-headed ˌgreɪ'hedɪd ['-ˌ-- when attributive]

grayish 'greɪʃ

grayling, -s 'greɪlɪŋ, -z

Grayson 'greɪsn

graystone 'greɪstəʊn

graz|e, -es, -ing, -ed greɪz, -ɪz, -ɪŋ, -d

grazier, -s 'greɪzjə* [-zɪə*, -ʒjə*, -ʒɪə*, -ʒə*], -z

grease (s.), -s griːs, -ɪz

greas|e (v.), -es, -ing, -ed, -er/s griːz [griːs], -ɪz ['griːsɪz], -ɪŋ ['griːsɪŋ], griːzd [griːst], -ə*/z

grease-box, -es 'griːsbɒks, -ɪz

grease-paint 'griːspeɪnt

grease-trap, -s 'griːstræp, -s

greas|y, -ier, -iest, -ily, -iness 'griːz|ɪ ['griːs|ɪ], -ɪə* [-jə*], -ɪɪst [-jɪst], -ɪlɪ [-əlɪ], -ɪnɪs [-ɪnəs]

Note.—Some people use the forms 'griːsɪ and 'griːzɪ with a difference of meaning, 'griːsɪ having reference merely to the presence of grease and 'griːzɪ having reference to slipperiness caused by grease.

great, -er, -est, -ly, -ness greɪt, -ə*, -ɪst, -lɪ, -nɪs [-nəs]

great-aunt, -s ˌgreɪt'ɑːnt ['--], -s

great-coat, -s 'greɪtkəʊt, -s

great-grand|child, -children ˌgreɪt-'græn|tʃaɪld, -ˌtʃɪldrən [-ˌtʃʊldrən, -ˌtʃldrən]

great-granddaughter, -s ˌgreɪt'græn-ˌdɔːtə* [-nd,d-], -z

great-grandfather, -s ˌgreɪt'grænd-ˌfɑːðə*, -z

great-grandmother, -s ˌgreɪt'græn-ˌmʌðə* [-nd,m-], -z

great-grandparent, -s ˌgreɪt'grænd-ˌpeərənt, -s

great-grandson, -s ˌgreɪt'grænsʌn [-nds-], -z

Greatham (in Durham) 'griːtəm, (in Northamptonshire and West Sussex) 'gretəm

Greathead 'greɪthed

Greatheart 'greɪthɑːt

great-hearted ˌgreɪt'hɑːtɪd [also '-ˌ--, esp. when attributive]

Greatorex 'greɪtəreks

greats greɪts

great-uncle, -s ˌgreɪt'ʌŋkl ['-ˌ--], -z

greaves griːvz

Greaves griːvz, greɪvz

grebe, -s griːb, -z

Grecian, -s 'griːʃn, -z

Grec|ism, -ize 'griːs|ɪzm, -aɪz

Greco-Roman ˌgrekəʊ'rəʊmən [ˌgriːk-]

Greece griːs

greed, -y, -ier, -iest, -ily, -iness griːd, -ɪ, -ɪə* [-jə*], -ɪɪst [-jɪst], -ɪlɪ [-əlɪ], -ɪnɪs [-ɪnəs]

Greek, -s griːk, -s

Greel(e)y 'griːlɪ

green (s. adj. v.), -s; -er, -est, -ly, -ness; -ing, -ed griːn, -z; -ə*, -ɪst, -lɪ, -nɪs [-nəs]; -ɪŋ, -d

Green(e) griːn

Greenall 'griːnɔːl

Greenaway 'griːnəweɪ

greenery 'griːnərɪ

green-eyed 'griːnaɪd [ˌ-'- when not attributive]

Greenfield 'griːnfiːld

greenfinch, -es 'griːnfɪntʃ, -ɪz

greenfly 'griːnflaɪ

Greenford 'griːnfəd

greengage, -s 'griːngeɪdʒ ['griːŋg-, also -'-, according to sentence-stress], -ɪz

greengrocer, -s 'griːnˌgrəʊsə* [-iːŋ,g-], -z

Greenhalgh 'griːnhælʒ, -hældʒ, -hɔː

Green|haulgh, -hill 'griːn|hɔː, -hɪl

Greenhithe 'griːnhaɪð

greenhou|se, -ses 'griːnhaʊ|s, -zɪz

greenish (G.), -ness 'griːnɪʃ, -nɪs [-nəs]

Greenland (country), -er/s 'griːnlənd [-lænd], -ə*/z

Greenland (surname) 'griːnlənd

Greenleaf 'griːnliːf

Greenock 'griːnək ['grɪn-, 'gren-]

Greenore griː'nɔː* [-'nɔə*]

Greenough 'griːnəʊ

Green|point, -port 'griːn|pɔɪnt, -pɔːt

green-room, -s 'griːnrʊm [-ruːm], -z

greensand 'griːnsænd

greenshank, -s 'griːnʃæŋk, -s

Greenslade 'griːnsleɪd

Greensleeves 'griːnsliːvz

greenstone 'griːnstəʊn

greensward 'griːnswɔːd

Green|ville, -well 'griːn|vɪl, -wəl [-wel]

Greenwich 'grɪnɪdʒ ['gren-, -ɪtʃ]

greenwood (G.), -s 'griːnwʊd, -z

greeny 'griːnɪ

greet (G.), -s, -ing/s, -ed griːt, -s, -ɪŋ/z, -ɪd

Greetland 'griːtlənd

Greg(g) greg

gregarious, -ly, -ness grɪ'geərɪəs [grə'g-, gre'g-], -lɪ, -nɪs [-nəs]

Gregorian, -s grɪ'gɔːrɪən [grə'g-, gre'g-], -z

Gregory, -powder 'gregərɪ, -ˌpaʊdə*

Greig greg

gremlin, -s 'gremlɪn, -z

Grenada gre'neɪdə [grə'n-]

grenade, -s grɪ'neɪd [gre'n-, grə'n-], -z

grenadier (G.), -s ˌgrenə'dɪə*, -z

grenadin, -s 'grenədɪn, -z

221

grenadine ˌgrenə'di:n ['grenədi:n]
Grenadines ˌgrenə'di:nz
Grendel 'grendl
Gren|fell, -ville 'gren|fel [-fl], -vɪl
Gresham 'greʃəm
Gres|ley, -well 'grez|lɪ, -wəl
Greta (English name) 'gri:tə, 'gretə, 'greɪtə
Gretel (German name) 'gretl ('gre:təl)
Gretna 'gretnə
Greuze, -s grɜ:z (grø:z), -ɪz
Greville 'grevɪl [-vl]
grew (from grow) (G.) gru:
grey (s. adj.) (G.), -s, -er, -est, -ness greɪ, -z, -ə* [greə*], -ɪst, 'greɪnɪs [-nəs]
greybeard, -s 'greɪˌbɪəd, -z
greycoat (G.), -s 'greɪkəʊt, -s
grey-eyed 'greɪaɪd [ˌ-'- when not attributive]
grey-haired ˌgreɪ'heəd ['-- when attributive]
grey-headed ˌgreɪ'hedɪd ['-ˌ-- when attributive]
greyhound, -s 'greɪhaʊnd, -z
greyish 'greɪʃ
Grey|lock, son 'greɪ|lɒk, -sn
Gribble 'grɪbl
Grice graɪs
grid, -s grɪd, -z
griddle, -s 'grɪdl, -z
gridiron, -s 'grɪdˌaɪən, -z
Gridley 'grɪdlɪ
grief, -s gri:f, -z
Grieg (Norwegian composer) gri:g
Grierson 'grɪəsn
grievance, -s 'gri:vns, -ɪz
griev|e, -es, -ing, -ed, -er/s gri:v, -z, -ɪŋ, -d, -ə*/z
grievous, -ly, -ness 'gri:vəs, -lɪ, -nɪs [-nəs]
griffin (G.), -s 'grɪfɪn, -z
Griffith, -s 'grɪfɪθ, -s
grig, -s grɪg, -z
Grigg, -s grɪg, -z
Grildrig 'grɪldrɪg
grill (s. v.), -s, -ing, -ed, -er/s grɪl, -z, -ɪŋ, -d, -ə*/z
grillage, -s 'grɪlɪdʒ, -ɪz
grille, -s grɪl, -z
grill-room, -s 'grɪlrʊm [-ru:m], -z
grilse grɪls
grim, -mer, -mest, -ly, -ness grɪm, -ə*, -ɪst, -lɪ, -nɪs [-nəs]
grimac|e (s. v.), -es, -ing, -ed grɪ'meɪs ['grɪməs], -ɪz, -ɪŋ, -t
Grimald 'grɪməld
grimalkin, -s grɪ'mælkɪn, -z

grim|e (s. v.), -es, -ing, -ed graɪm, -z, -ɪŋ, -d
Grimes graɪmz
Grimm grɪm
Grimond 'grɪmənd
Grimsby 'grɪmzbɪ
Grimsel 'grɪmzl
Grim|shaw, -wig 'grɪm|ʃɔ:, -wɪg
grim|y, -ier, -iest, -ily, -iness 'graɪm|ɪ, -ɪə* [-jə*], -ɪɪst [-jɪst], -ɪlɪ [-əlɪ], -ɪnɪs [-məs]
grin (s. v.), -s, -ning, -ned grɪn, -z, -ɪŋ, -d
grind (s. v.), -s, -ing, ground, grinder/s graɪnd, -z, -ɪŋ, graʊnd, 'graɪndə*/z
Grindal 'grɪndəl
Grindelwald 'grɪndlvɑ:ld
grindery 'graɪndərɪ
Grindon 'grɪndən
grindstone, -s 'graɪndstəʊn, -z
Grinnell grɪ'nel
Grinstead 'grɪnstɪd [-sted]
grip (s. v.), -s, -ping, -ped grɪp, -s, -ɪŋ, -t
grip|e (s. v.), -es, -ing, -ed graɪp, -s, -ɪŋ, -t
gripes (s.) graɪps
grippe grɪp [gri:p] (grip)
gripsack, -s 'grɪpsæk, -s
grisaille grɪ'zeɪl [gri:'zaɪ, grɪ-, -'zaɪl] (grizɑ:j)
Griscom 'grɪskəm
Griselda grɪ'zeldə
grisette, -s gri:'zet, -s
Grisewood 'graɪzwʊd
griskin 'grɪskɪn
grisl|y, -ier, -iest, -iness 'grɪzl|ɪ, -ɪə*, -ɪɪst, -ɪnɪs [-ɪnəs]
Grisons 'gri:zɔ̃:ŋ [-zɔ:ŋ, -zɒŋ] (grizɔ̃)
grist grɪst
gristle 'grɪsl
gristly 'grɪslɪ [-slɪ]
Griswold 'grɪzwəʊld
grit, -s; -stone grɪt, -s; -stəʊn
Gritton 'grɪtn
gritt|y, -ier, -iest, -ily, -iness 'grɪt|ɪ, -ɪə*, -ɪɪst, -ɪlɪ [-əlɪ], -ɪnɪs [-məs]
Grizel grɪ'zel
grizzle, -d 'grɪzl, -d
grizzl|y (s. adj.), -ies 'grɪzl|ɪ, -ɪz
groan (s. v.), -s, -ing/s, -ed grəʊn, -z, -ɪŋ/z, -d
groat (coin), -s grəʊt, -s
groats (grain) grəʊts
Grobian, -s 'grəʊbjən [-bɪən], -z
grocer, -s 'grəʊsə*, -z
grocer|y, -ies 'grəʊsər|ɪ, -ɪz
Grocott 'grɒkət

Grocyn 'grəʊsɪn
grog grɒg
grogg|y, -ier, -iest, -ily, -iness 'grɒg|ɪ, -ɪə*, -ɪıst, -ɪlı [-əlı], -ınıs [-ınəs]
program 'grɒgræm
grog-shop, -s 'grɒgʃɒp, -s
groin, -s grɔɪn, -z
gromwell 'grɒmwəl [-wel]
Grongar 'grɒŋgə*
groom (s. v.), -s, -ing, -ed gruːm [grʊm], -z, -ɪŋ, -d
grooms|man, -men 'gruːmz|mən, ['grʊmz-] -mən [-men]
groov|e (s. v.), -es, -ing, -ed gruːv, -z, -ɪŋ, -d
groov|y, -ier, -iest, -iness 'gruːv|ɪ, -ɪə* [-jə*], -ɪıst [-jıst], -ınıs [-ınəs]
grop|e, -es, -ing/ly, -ed, -er/s grəʊp, -s, -ɪŋ/lı, -t, -ə*/z
Grosart 'grəʊzɑːt
grosbeak, -s 'grəʊsbiːk ['grɒs-, 'grəʊz-], -s
groschen 'grəʊʃn ['grɒʃ-]
Grose grəʊs, grəʊz
Grosmont (in North Yorkshire) 'grəʊmənt [-mɒnt, locally also 'grəʊsmənt], (in Gwent) 'grɒsmənt
gross (s. adj.), -er, -est, -ly, -ness grəʊs, -ə*, -ıst, -lı, -nıs [-nəs]
Gross (surname) grɒs, grəʊs
Grossmith 'grəʊsmɪθ
Grosvenor 'grəʊvnə*
Grote grəʊt
grotesque, -ly, -ness grəʊ'tesk, -lı, -nıs [-nəs]
grotto, -s 'grɒtəʊ, -z
ground (s. v.) (all senses), -s, -ing, -ed, -er/s graʊnd, -z, -ɪŋ, -ɪd, -ə*/z
ground (from grind) graʊnd
groundage 'graʊndɪdʒ
ground-ash ˌgraʊnd'æʃ
ground-bass, -es ˌgraʊnd'beıs, -ız
ground-floor, -s ˌgraʊnd'flɔː* [-'flɔə*, also '--, esp. when attributive], -z
ground-hog, -s ˌgraʊnd'hɒg ['--], -z
ground-ivy 'graʊndˌaɪvɪ [ˌ-'--]
groundless, -ly, -ness 'graʊndlɪs [-ləs], -lı, -nıs [-nəs]
groundling, -s 'graʊndlɪŋ, -z
ground|-man, -men 'graʊnd|mæn [-mən], -men [-mən]
ground-nut, -s 'graʊndnʌt, -s
ground-plan, -s ˌgraʊnd'plæn ['--], -z
ground-rent, -s 'graʊndrent, -s
groundsel 'graʊnsl
grounds|man, -men 'graʊndz|mən [-mæn], -mən [-men]
ground-swell, -s 'graʊndswel, -z

groundwork 'graʊndwɜːk
group (s. v.), -s, -ing/s, -ed gruːp, -s, -ɪŋ/z, -t
grous|e (s. v.) (G.), -es, -ing, -ed, -er/s graʊs, -ız, -ɪŋ, -t, -ə*/z
grove (G.), -s grəʊv, -z
grov|el, -els, -elling, -elled, -eller/s 'grɒv|l ['grʌv-], -lz, -lɪŋ [-lıŋ], -ld, -lə*/z [-lə*/z]
Grover 'grəʊvə*
gr|ow, -ows, -owing, grew, gr|own, -ower/s gr|əʊ, -əʊz, -əʊɪŋ, gruː, gr|əʊn, -əʊə*/z
growl (s. v.), -s, -ing, -ed, -er/s graʊl, -z, -ɪŋ, -d, -ə*/z
grown-up (s.), -s 'grəʊnʌp [ˌgrəʊn'ʌp], -s
grown-up (adj.), ˌgrəʊn'ʌp ['--]
growth, -s grəʊθ, -s
groyne, -s grɔɪn, -z
grub (s. v.), -s, -bing, -bed, -ber/s grʌb, -z, -ɪŋ, -d, -ə*/z
grubb|y, -ier, -iest, -iness 'grʌb|ɪ, -ɪə*, -ıst, -ınıs [-ınəs]
grudg|e (s. v.), -es, -ing/ly, -ed grʌdʒ, -ız, -ɪŋ/lı, -d
gruel grʊəl ['gruːəl]
gruelling (s. adj.), -s 'grʊəlɪŋ ['gruːəl-], -z
Gruenther (American surname) 'grʌnθə*
gruesome, -ly, -ness gruːsəm, -lı, -nıs [-nəs]
gruff, -er, -est, -ly, -ness grʌf, -ə*, -ıst, -lı, -nıs [-nəs]
grumb|le, -les, -ling, -led, -ler/s 'grʌmb|l, -lz, -lıŋ, -ld, -lə*/z
grump|y, -ier, -iest, -ily, -iness 'grʌmp|ɪ, -ɪə* [-jə*], -ıst [-jıst], -ılı [-əlı], -ınıs [-ınəs]
Grundig 'grʊndɪg
Grundtvig (English surname) 'grʊntvɪg
Grundy 'grʌndɪ
grunt (s. v.), -s, -ing, -ed, -er/s grʌnt, -s, -ɪŋ, -ɪd, -ə*/z
Gruyère 'gruːjeə* [-jə*] (gryjɛːr)
gryphon, -s 'grɪfn, -z
Guadalquivir ˌgwɑːdl'kwɪvə* [ˌgwɑː-dəlkı'vɪə*] (gwadalkı'bir)
Guadeloupe ˌgwɑːdə'luːp
Guaira 'gwaɪərə
guano, -s 'gwɑːnəʊ [gjuː'ɑːnəʊ, gjʊ'ɑː], -z
Guarani, -s ˌgwɑːrə'niː, -z
guarantee (s. v.), -s, -ing, -d ˌgærən'tiː, -z, -ɪŋ, -d
guarantor, -s ˌgærən'tɔː* [gə'ræntɔː*], -z

223

guarant|y, -ies 'gærənt|ɪ, -ɪz

guard (s. v.) (G.), -s, -ing, -ed/ly, -edness gɑːd, -z, -ɪŋ, -ɪd/lɪ, -ɪdnɪs [-nəs]

guardian (G.), -s; -ship 'gɑːdjən [-dɪən], -z; -ʃɪp

guardrail, -s 'gɑːdreɪl, -z

guard-room, -s 'gɑːdrʊm [-ruːm], -z

guard-ship, -s 'gɑːdʃɪp, -s

guards|man, -men 'gɑːdz|mən [-mæn], -mən [-men]

Guarner|i, -ius/es gwɑːˈnɪər|ɪ, -ɪəs/ɪz

Guatemala, -n/s ˌgwætɪˈmɑːlə [ˌgwɑːt-, -tə-], -n/z

guava, -s 'gwɑːvə, -z

Guayaquil ˌgwaɪəˈkiːl [-ˈkɪl]

Guayra (old-fashioned spelling of Guaira) 'gwaɪərə

Gubbins 'gʌbɪnz

gudgeon, -s 'gʌdʒən, -z

Gudrun 'gʊdruːn [gʊˈd-]

Gue gju:

Guedalla gwɪˈdælə [gweˈd-, gwəˈd-]

guelder-rose, -s ˌgeldəˈrəʊz, -ɪz

Guelph gwelf

guerdon, -s 'gɜːdən, -z

guerilla gəˈrɪlə [gjə-]

guernsey (G.), -s 'gɜːnzɪ, -z

guerrilla, -s gəˈrɪlə [gjə-], -z

guess (s. v.), -es, -ing, -ed, -er/s; -able, -work ges, -ɪz, -ɪŋ, -t, -ə*/z; -əbl, -wɜːk

guest (G.), -s gest, -s

guest-chamber, -s 'gestˌtʃeɪmbə*, -z

guest-hou|se, -ses 'gesthaʊ|s, -zɪz

guest-night, -s 'gestnaɪt, -s

guest-room, -s 'gestrʊm [-ruːm], -z

guest-towel, -s 'gestˌtaʊəl [-taʊl], -z

guffaw (s. v.), -s, -ing, -ed gʌ'fɔː [gə'f-], -z, -ɪŋ, -d

Guggenheim 'gʊgənhaɪm ['guː-]

Guggisberg (English surname) 'gʌgɪsbɜːg

Guiana gaɪˈænə [old-fashioned British pronunciation gɪˈɑːnə]

Guianese ˌgaɪəˈniːz

guid|e (s. v.), -es, -ing, -ed; -ance gaɪd, -z, -ɪŋ, -ɪd; -ns

guide-book, -s 'gaɪdbʊk, -s

guide-post, -s 'gaɪdpəʊst, -s

guide-rail, -s 'gaɪdreɪl, -z

guide-rope, -s 'gaɪdrəʊp, -s

Guido 'gwiːdəʊ

guidon, -s 'gaɪdən, -z

guild, -s gɪld, -z

Guildenstern 'gɪldənstɜːn

guilder, -s 'gɪldə*, -z

Guildford 'gɪlfəd

guildhall (G.), -s ˌgɪldˈhɔːl [also '--, esp. when attributive], -z

Guilding 'gɪldɪŋ

guile gaɪl

guile|ful, -fully, -fulness 'gaɪl|fʊl, -fʊlɪ [-fəlɪ], -fʊlnɪs [-nəs]

guileless, -ly, -ness 'gaɪllɪs [-ləs], -lɪ, -nɪs [-nəs]

Guilford 'gɪlfəd

Guillamore 'gɪləmɔː* [-mɔː*]

Guillebaud (English surname) 'giːlbəʊ, 'gɪlɪbəʊ

guillemot, -s 'gɪlɪmɒt, -s

Guillim 'gwɪlɪm

guillotin|e (s. v.), -es, -ing, -ed ˌgɪləˈtiːn ['gɪlət-], -z, -ɪŋ, -d

Note.—Some people use '--- for the noun and ˌ--'- for the verb.

guilt, -y, -ier, -iest, -ily, -iness gɪlt, -ɪ, -ɪə* [-jə*], -ɪɪst [-jɪst], -ɪlɪ [-əlɪ], -ɪnɪs [-nəs]

guiltless, -ly, -ness 'gɪltlɪs [-ləs], -lɪ, -nɪs [-nəs]

guinea (G.), -s 'gɪnɪ, -z

guinea|-corn, -fowl/s, -pig/s 'gɪnɪ|kɔːn, -faʊl/z, -pɪg/z

Guinevere 'gwɪnɪˌvɪə* ['gɪn-]

Guinness 'gɪnɪs, gɪˈnes

Note.—The beer is called 'gɪnɪs.

Guisborough (in Cleveland) 'gɪzbərə

guise, -s gaɪz, -ɪz

Guise giːz [gwiːz] (gɥiːz, giːz)

Guiseley 'gaɪzlɪ

guitar, -s gɪˈtɑː*, -z

guitarist, -s gɪˈtɑːrɪst, -s

Guiver 'gaɪvə*

Gujarat ˌguːdʒəˈrɑːt [ˌgʊdʒ-] (Hindi gwɪrat)

Gujarati ˌguːdʒəˈrɑːtɪ [ˌgʊdʒ-] (Hindi gwɪrati)

Gulbenkian gʊlˈbeŋkɪən [-kjən]

gulch (s. v.), -es gʌlʃ, -ɪz

gulden, -s 'gʊldən ['guː-l-], -z

gules gjuːlz

gulf, -s; -y gʌlf, -s; -ɪ

gull (s. v.) (G.), -s, -ing, -ed gʌl, -z, -ɪŋ, -d

gull-catcher, -s 'gʌlˌkætʃə*, -z

guller|y, -ies 'gʌlər|ɪ, -ɪz

gullet, -s 'gʌlɪt [-lət], -s

gullibility ˌgʌləˈbɪlətɪ [-lɪˈb-, -lɪt-]

gullible 'gʌləbl [-lɪb-]

Gulliver 'gʌlɪvə*

gull|y (G.), -ies 'gʌl|ɪ, -ɪz

gulp (s. v.), -s, -ing, -ed gʌlp, -s, -ɪŋ, -t

gum (s. v.) (all senses), -s, -ming, -med, -mer/s gʌm, -z, -ɪŋ, -d, -ə*/z

gumboil, -s 'gʌmbɔɪl, -z

Gummere 'gʌmərɪ
Gummidge 'gʌmɪdʒ
gumm|y (s. adj.), -ies, -ier, -iest, -iness
'gʌm|ɪ, -ɪz, -ɪə*, -ɪɪst, -ɪnɪs [-ɪnəs]
gumption 'gʌmpʃn
gum-tree, -s 'gʌmtri:, -z
gun (s. v.), -s, -ning, -ned, -ner/s gʌn,
-z, -ɪŋ, -d, -ə*/z
gun|-barrel/s, -boat/s, -carriage/s,
-case/s, -cotton 'gʌn|ˌbærəl/z,
-bəʊt/s, -ˌkærɪdʒ/ɪz, -keɪs/ɪz, -ˌkɒtn
Gunby Hadath ˌgʌnbɪ'hædəθ
gun-drill 'gʌndrɪl
gun-fire 'gʌnˌfaɪə*
gun|man, -men 'gʌn|mən [-mæn],
-mən [-men]
gun-metal 'gʌnˌmetl
gunnel, -s 'gʌnl, -z
Gunner 'gʌnə*
Gunnersbury 'gʌnəzbərɪ
gunnery 'gʌnərɪ
Gunning 'gʌnɪŋ
Gunnison 'gʌnɪsn
gunny 'gʌnɪ
gunpowder 'gʌnˌpaʊdə*
gun-room, -s 'gʌnrʊm [-ru:m], -z
gun-runn|er/s, -ing 'gʌnˌrʌn|ə*/z, -ɪŋ
gunshot, -s 'gʌnʃɒt, -s
gunsmith, -s 'gʌnsmɪθ, -s
gun-stock, -s 'gʌnstɒk, -s
Gunt|er, -ram 'gʌnt|ə*, -rəm
gunwale, -s 'gʌnl, -z
Gupta 'gʊptə (Hindi gwptə)
gurg|le (s. v.), -les, -ling, -led 'gɜ:g|l,
-lz, -lɪŋ, -ld
Gurkha, -s 'gɜ:kə ['gʊək-], -z
Gurley 'gɜ:lɪ
Gurnall 'gɜ:nl
gurnard (G.), -s 'gɜ:nəd, -z
gurnet, -s 'gɜ:nɪt, -s
Gur|ney, -ton 'gɜ:|nɪ, -tn
guru, -s 'gʊru: ['gu:r-, 'gʊər-] (Hindi
gwru), -z
Gus gʌs
gush (s. v.), -es, -ing/ly, -ed, -er/s gʌʃ,
-ɪz, -ɪŋ/lɪ, -t, -ə*/z
Gushington 'gʌʃɪŋtən
gusset, -s 'gʌsɪt, -s
Guss|ie, -y 'gʌs|ɪ, -ɪ
gust, -s gʌst, -s
gustation gʌ'steɪʃn
gustatory 'gʌstətərɪ [gʌ'steɪtərɪ]
Gustavus gʊ'stɑ:vəs [gʌ's-]
gusto 'gʌstəʊ
gust|y, -ier, -iest, -ily, -iness 'gʌst|ɪ,
-ɪə* [-jə*], -ɪɪst [-jɪst], -ɪlɪ [-əlɪ],
-ɪnɪs [-ɪnəs]
gut (s. v.), -s, -ting, -ted gʌt, -s, -ɪŋ, -ɪd

Gutenberg 'gu:tnbɜ:g
Guthrie 'gʌθrɪ
gutta-percha ˌgʌtə'pɜ:tʃə
gutter (s. v.), -s, -ing, -ed 'gʌtə*, -z,
-rɪŋ, -d
guttersnipe, -s 'gʌtəsnaɪp, -s
guttur|al (s. adj.), -als, -ally 'gʌtər|əl,
-əlz, -əlɪ
guy (G.), -s gaɪ, -z
Guyana gaɪ'ænə
Guyda (Christian name) 'gaɪdə
Guy Fawkes ˌgaɪ'fɔ:ks ['--]
Guysborough 'gaɪzbərə
Guzman (character in Kingsley's 'West-
ward Ho!') 'gʌzmən ['gʊzm-, 'gʊθ-
mɑ:n]
guzz|le, -les, -ling, -led, -ler/s 'gʌz|l,
-lz, -lɪŋ [-lɪŋ], -ld, -lə*/z [-lə*/z]
Gwalia 'gwɑ:ljə [-lɪə]
Gwalior 'gwɑ:lɔ:* [-ljɔ:*] (Hindi
gvaljər)
Gwatkin 'gwɒtkɪn
Gwen gwen
Gwendo|len, -line, -lyn 'gwendə|lɪn, -lɪn
[-li:n], -lɪn
Gwent gwent
Gwinear 'gwɪnɪə*
Gwinnett gwɪ'net
Gwladys 'glædɪs (Welsh 'gwladis)
Gwrych gʊ'ri:k [-'ri:x] (Welsh gwri:x)
Gwydyr 'gwɪdɪə* [-də*] (Welsh 'gwɪdir)
Gwynedd 'gwɪnəð
gwyniad, -s 'gwɪnɪæd, -z
Gwyn(ne) gwɪn
gyb|e, -es, -ing, -ed dʒaɪb, -z, -ɪŋ, -d
Gye dʒaɪ, gaɪ
Gyges 'gaɪdʒi:z
Gyle (surname) gaɪl
gym dʒɪm
gymkhana, -s dʒɪm'kɑ:nə, -z
gymnasium, -s dʒɪm'neɪzjəm [-zɪəm],
-z
gymnast, -s 'dʒɪmnæst, -s
gymnastic, -s, -al, -ally dʒɪm'næstɪk, -s,
-l, -əlɪ
gymnosophist, -s dʒɪm'nɒsəfɪst, -s
Gympie 'gɪmpɪ
gynaecological ˌgaɪnɪkə'lɒdʒɪkl [-ni:k-,
-nək-]
gynaecolog|ist/s, -y ˌgaɪnɪ'kɒlədʒ|-
ɪst/s [-ni:'k-, -nə'k-], -ɪ
Gyngell 'gɪndʒəl
gyp, -s dʒɪp, -s
Gyp (nickname) dʒɪp, (French authoress)
ʒɪp (ʒip)
gyps|eous, -ous 'dʒɪps|ɪəs [-jəs], -əs
gypsophila, -s dʒɪp'sɒfɪlə, -z
gypsum 'dʒɪpsəm

225

gyps|y, -ies 'dʒɪps|ɪ, -ɪz
gyrate (adj.) 'dʒaɪəreɪt ['dʒaɪəreɪt, -tər]
gyrat|e (v.), -es, -ing, -ed ,dʒaɪə'reɪt, -s, bɪ-ɪŋ, -ɪd
gyration, -s ,dʒaɪə'reɪʃn, -z
gyratory 'dʒaɪərətərɪ [,dʒaɪə'reɪtərɪ]
gyr|e (s. v.), -es, -ing, -ed 'dʒaɪə*, -z, -rɪŋ, -d
gyrodine, -s 'dʒaɪərəʊdaɪn, -z

gyromancy 'dʒaɪərəʊmænsɪ
gyron, -s 'dʒaɪərən [-rɒn], -z
gyroscope, -s 'dʒaɪərəskəʊp ['gaɪə], -s
gyroscopic ,dʒaɪərə'skɒpɪk [,gaɪə-]
gyrosin, -s 'dʒaɪərəʊzɪn, -z
gyrostat, -s 'dʒaɪərəʊstæt ['gaɪə], -s
gyrostatic, -s ,dʒaɪərəʊ'stætɪk [,gaɪə-], -s
gyv|e, -es, -ing, -ed dʒaɪv, -z, -ɪŋ, -d

H

H (*the letter*), -'s eɪtʃ, -ɪz
ha hɑ:
Haakon 'hɔ:kɒn ['hɑ:k-, -kən]
Haarlem 'hɑ:ləm [-lem]
Habakkuk 'hæbəkək [-kʌk, hə'bækək]
Habberton 'hæbətən
habeas corpus ˌheɪbjəs'kɔ:pəs [-bɪəs-, -bɪæs-]
habendum hə'bendəm [hæ'b-]
haberdasher, -s, -y 'hæbədæʃə*, -z, -ɪɪ
habergeon, -s 'hæbədʒən, -z
Habershon 'hæbəʃn
habiliment, -s hə'bɪlɪmənt [hæ'b-, *also occasionally* ə'b- *when not initial*], -s
habilitat|e, -es, -ing, -ed, -or/s hə'bɪlɪtert [hæ'b-, -lə-], -s, -ɪɪ, -ɪd, -ə*/z
habilitation həˌbɪlɪ'teɪʃn [hæˌb-, -lə-]
Habington 'hæbɪɪtən
habit (*s. v.*), -s, -ing, -ed 'hæbɪt, -s, -ɪɪ, -ɪd
habitab|le, -ly, -leness 'hæbɪtəb|l, -lɪ, -lnɪs [-nəs]
habitant (*inhabitant*), -s 'hæbɪtənt, -s
habitant (*Canadian*), -s 'hæbɪtɔ̃:ŋ ['æb-, -tɒŋ] (abitã), -z
habitat, -s 'hæbɪtæt, -s
habitation, -s ˌhæbɪ'teɪʃn, -z
habitual, -ly hə'bɪtjʊəl [hæ'b-, -tjwəl, -tjʊl, -tʊəl, -tʃwəl, -tʃʊl], -ɪ
habituat|e, -es, -ing, -ed hə'bɪtjʊeɪt [hæ'b-, -tʃʊeɪt], -s, -ɪɪ, -ɪd
habitude, -s 'hæbɪtju:d, -z
habitué, -s hə'bɪtjʊeɪ [hæ'b-, *also occasionally* ə'b- *when not initial*] (abitɥe), -z
Habsburg 'hæpsbɔ:g
hachures hæ'ʃjʊə* [-'ʃʊə*]
hacienda, -s ˌhæsɪ'endə, -z
hack (*s. v.*) (H.), -s, -ing, -ed, -er/s hæk, -s, -ɪɪ, -t, -ə*/z
hackberr|y, -ies 'hækber|ɪ [-bər|ɪ], -ɪz
hacker|y, -ies 'hækər|ɪ, -ɪz
Hackett 'hækɪt
hack|le (*s. v.*), -les, -ling, -led 'hæk|l, -lz, -lɪɪ [-lɪɪ], -ld
hackney (*s. v.*) (H.), -s, -ing, -ed 'hæknɪ, -z, -ɪɪ ['hæknjɪɪ], -d
hacksaw, -s 'hæksɔ:, -z
hackwork 'hækwɜ:k

had (*from* have) hæd (*strong form*), həd, əd, d (*weak forms*)
Hadad 'heɪdæd
Hadadezer ˌhædə'di:zə*
Hadar (*star*) 'heɪdɑ:*
Hadath 'hædəθ
Haddington 'hædɪɪtən
haddock (H.), -s 'hædək, -s
Haddon 'hædn
had|e, -es, -ing, -ed heɪd, -z, -ɪɪ, -ɪd
Haden 'heɪdn
Hades 'heɪdi:z
Hadfield 'hædfi:ld
hadji, -s 'hædʒi:, -z
Had|leigh, -ley, -low 'hæd|lɪ, -lɪ, -ləʊ
hadn't 'hædnt [*also* 'hædn *when not final*]
Hadow 'hædəʊ
Hadrian 'heɪdrɪən
hadst hædst (*strong form*), hədst, ədst (*weak forms*)
Hadubrand 'hædʊbrænd
haemal 'hi:ml
haematite 'hemətaɪt ['hi:m-]
haemoglobin ˌhi:məʊ'gləʊbɪn
haemophilia ˌhi:məʊ'fɪlɪə
haemorrhage, -s 'hemərɪdʒ, -ɪz
haemorrhoid, -s 'hemərɔɪd, -z
Haes (*English surname*) heɪz
haft, -s hɑ:ft, -s
hag, -s hæg, -s
Hagar (*biblical name*) 'heɪgɑ:* [-gə*], (*modern personal name*) 'heɪgə*
Hagarene, -s 'hægəri:n [ˌ--'-, ˌheɪgɑ:-'ri:n], -z
hagberr|y, -ies 'hægber|ɪ [-bər|ɪ], -ɪz
Hagerstown 'heɪgəztaʊn
Haggai 'hægeɪaɪ [-gɪaɪ, -gaɪ, hæ'geɪaɪ]
haggard (H.), -est 'hægəd, -ɪst
Hagger, -ston 'hægə*, -stən
haggis, -es 'hægɪs, -ɪz
haggish, -ly, -ness 'hægɪʃ, -lɪ, -nɪs [-nəs]
hagg|le, -les, -ling, -led, -ler/s 'hæg|l, -lz, -lɪɪ [-lɪɪ], -ld, -lə*/z [-lə*/z]
hagio|grapher/s, -graphy ˌhægɪ'ɒ|grəfə*/z, -grəfɪ
hagiolatry ˌhægɪ'ɒlətrɪ
hagiolog|ist/s, -y ˌhægɪ'ɒlədʒ|ɪst/s, -ɪ

227

hagioscope, -s 'hægrəskəʊp [-gjəs-], -s
hag-seed 'hægsi:d
Hague heɪg
hag-weed 'hægwi:d
ha-ha (interj.) hɑː'hɑː: ['--]
ha-ha (sunken fence), -s 'hɑːhɑː:, -z
Haidarabad 'haɪdərəbæd [ˌhaɪdərə'b-ˌ],
  (Hindi həydərabad)
Haidee haɪ'di:
Haifa 'haɪfə
Haig heɪg
Haigh heɪg, heɪ
hail (s. v. interj.), -s, -ing, -ed; -y heɪl,
  -z, -ɪŋ, -d; -ɪ
Hailes heɪlz
Haile Selassie ˌhaɪlɪsɪ'læsɪ [-sə'l-]
Haileybury 'heɪlɪbərɪ
hail-fellow, -s 'heɪl,feləʊ, -z
hail-fellow-well-met 'heɪl,feləʊ,wel-
  'met
Hailsham 'heɪlʃəm
hailstone, -s 'heɪlstəʊn, -z
hailstorm, -s 'heɪlstɔ:m, -z
Hainan ˌhaɪ'næn
Hainault (forest) 'heɪnɔ:t [-nɔ:lt, -nɒlt]
Hainhault 'heɪnɔ:lt
hair, -s heə*, -z
hair-breadth, -s 'heəbredθ [-bretθ], -s
hairbrush, -es 'heəbrʌʃ, -ɪz
haircloth 'heəklɒθ [old-fashioned -klɔ:θ]
haircut, -s 'heəkʌt, -s
haircutt|er/s, -ing 'heə,kʌt|ə*/z, -ɪŋ
hair-do, -s 'heədu:, -z
hairdresser, -s 'heə,dresə*, -z
hair-dye, -s 'heədaɪ, -z
hairgrass 'heəgrɑ:s
hairless 'heəlɪs [-ləs]
hair-line, -s 'heəlaɪn, -z
hair-net, -s 'heənet, -s
hair-oil, -s 'heərɔɪl ['heəɔɪl]
hairpin, -s 'heəpɪn, -z
hair's-breadth, -s 'heəzbredθ [-bretθ],
  -s
hair-shirt, -s heə'ʃɜ:t ['--], -s
hair-slide, -s 'heəslaɪd, -z
hair-space, -s 'heəspeɪs, -ɪz
hair-splitting 'heə,splɪtɪŋ
hair-spring, -s 'heəsprɪŋ, -z
hair-stroke, -s 'heəstrəʊk, -s
hair|y, -ier, -iest, -ily, -iness 'heər|ɪ,
  -ɪə*, -ɪɪst, -əlɪ [-ɪlɪ], -ɪnɪs [-ɪnəs]
Haiti 'heɪtɪ
Haitian, -s 'heɪʃjən [-ʃɪən, -ʃn, 'heɪtjən,
  -tɪən], -z
hake, -s heɪk, -s
Hakluyt 'hæklu:t
Hakodate ˌhækəʊ'dɑ:tɪ
Hal hæl

halation, -s hə'leɪʃn [hæ'l-], -z
halberd, -s 'hælbɜːd ['hɔ:l-, -bəd], -z
halberdier, -s ˌhælbə'dɪə*, -z
halcyon, -s 'hælsɪən [-sjən], -z
Halcyone hæl'saɪənɪ
Hald|ane, -on 'hɔ:ld|eɪn ['hɒl-], -ən
hal|e (adj. v.) (H.), -er, -est; -es, -ing,
  -ed heɪl, -ə*, -ɪst; -z, -ɪŋ, -d
Hales, -worth heɪlz, -wɜ:θ
hal|f, -ves hɑː|f, -vz

  Note 1.—Words not entered below
  which are formed by prefixing half-
  to a partic. have double stress, e.g.
  half-done ˌhɑ:f'dʌn, half-ashamed
  ˌhɑ:fə'ʃeɪmd, half-dressed ˌhɑ:f-
  'drest.

  Note 2.—Half past, in half past ten,
  half past eleven, etc., is pronounced ˌhɑ:pɑ:s(t) by some:
  ˌhɑ:pəs 'ten, ˌhɑ:pəst ɪ'levn, etc.

half a crown ˌhɑ:fə'kraʊn [also '--
  according to sentence-stress]
half a dozen ˌhɑ:fə'dʌzn [also '-ˌ--
  according to sentence-stress]
half and half ˌhɑ:fənd'hɑ:f
half-back, -s ˌhɑ:f'bæk ['--], -s
half-baked ˌhɑ:f'beɪkt ['--]
half-binding 'hɑ:f,baɪndɪŋ
half-blood 'hɑ:fblʌd
half-bound ˌhɑ:f'baʊnd ['--]
half-bred 'hɑ:fbred
half|-breed/s, -brother/s, -caste/s
  'hɑ:f|bri:d/z, -,brʌðə*/z, -kɑ:st/s
half-crown, -s ˌhɑ:f'kraʊn, -z
half-dozen, -s ˌhɑ:f'dʌzn [also '-ˌ--
  according to sentence-stress], -z
half-hardy ˌhɑ:f'hɑ:dɪ [also '-ˌ-- when
  attributive]
half-hearted ˌhɑ:f'hɑ:tɪd ['-ˌ--, esp.
  when attributive]
half-hearted|ly, -ness ˌhɑ:f'hɑ:tɪd|lɪ,
  -nɪs [-nəs]
half-holiday, -s ˌhɑ:f'hɒlədɪ [-lɪd-,
  -deɪ], -z
half-hose ˌhɑ:f'həʊz ['--]
half-hour, -s ˌhɑ:f'aʊə* [also '--
  according to sentence-stress], -z
half-hourly ˌhɑ:f'aʊəlɪ
half-length, -s ˌhɑ:f'leŋθ [-ŋkθ, '--], -s
half-mast ˌhɑ:f'mɑ:st
half-measure, -s ˌhɑ:f'meʒə* ['-ˌ--], -z
half-moon, -s ˌhɑ:f'mu:n, -z
half-mourning ˌhɑ:f'mɔ:nɪŋ [-'mɔən-]
half-nelson ˌhɑ:f'nelsn
Halford 'hɔ:lfəd ['hɒl-], 'hæl-
half-pay ˌhɑ:f'peɪ
halfpence 'heɪpəns (see note under
  penny)

halfpenn|y, -ies; -yworth/s 'heɪpn|ɪ
[-pn̩|ɪ, -pən|ɪ], -ɪz; -ɪwɜ:θ/s [-wəθ/s,
'heɪpə̆θ/s] (see note under penny)
Halfpenny 'hɑ:fpenɪ [-pənɪ]
half-plate, -s 'hɑ:fpleɪt, -s
half-price ˌhɑ:f'praɪs [also '-- according
to sentence-stress]
half-seas-over ˌhɑ:fsi:z'əʊvə*
half-shift, -s ˌhɑ:f'ʃɪft ['--], -s
half-sister, -s 'hɑ:fˌsɪstə*, -z
half-size ˌhɑ:f'saɪz [also '-- when
attributive]
half-sovereign, -s ˌhɑ:f'sɒvrɪn, -z
half-tide ˌhɑ:f'taɪd ['--]
half-time, -r/s ˌhɑ:f'taɪm, -ə*/z
half-tint, -s 'hɑ:ftɪnt, -s
half-tone, -s 'hɑ:ftəʊn, -z
half-tru|th, -ths 'hɑ:ftru:|θ, -ðz
half-volley, -s ˌhɑ:f'vɒlɪ, -z
half-way ˌhɑ:f'weɪ [also '-- according to
sentence-stress]
half-witted ˌhɑ:f'wɪtɪd [also '-,-- when
attributive]
half-year, -s ˌhɑ:f'jɜ:* [-'jɪə*], -z
half-yearly ˌhɑ:f'jɜ:lɪ [-'jɪəlɪ]
Haliburton 'hælɪbɜ:tn
halibut 'hælɪbət [-bʌt]
Halicarnassus ˌhælɪkɑ:'næsəs
halidom 'hælɪdəm
Halidon 'hælɪdən
Halifax 'hælɪfæks
halitosis ˌhælɪ'təʊsɪs
Halkett 'hɔ:lkɪt, 'hælkɪt, 'hækɪt
hall (H.), -s hɔ:l, -z
Hallam 'hæləm
Hallé 'hæleɪ [-lɪ]
hallelujah (H.), -s ˌhælɪ'lu:jə, -z
Haller 'hælə*
Halley 'hælɪ
halliard = halyard
Halli|day, -well 'hælɪ|deɪ, -wəl [-wel]
hall-mark (s. v.), -s, -ing, -ed 'hɔ:l-
mɑ:k [ˌ-'-], -s, -ɪŋ, -t
hallo(a) hə'ləʊ [hæ'ləʊ]
halloo (s. v. interj.), -s, -ing, -ed hə'lu:
[hæ'l-], -z, -ɪŋ, -d
hall|ow, -ows, -owing, -owed 'hæl|əʊ,
-əʊz, -əʊɪŋ, -əʊd
Hallowe'en ˌhæləʊ'i:n
Hallowmas, -es 'hæləʊmæs [-məs], -ɪz
Hallows 'hæləʊz
hall-stand, -s 'hɔ:lstænd, -z
hallucination, -s həˌlu:sɪ'neɪʃn [-ˌlju:-],
-z
hallucinatory həˈlu:sɪnətərɪ [-'lju:-,
həˌlu:sɪ'neɪtərɪ]
halm, -s hɑ:m, -z
halma 'hælmə

halo (s.), -(e)s 'heɪləʊ, -z
hall|o (v.), -oes, -oing, -oed 'heɪl|əʊ,
-əʊz, -əʊɪŋ, -əʊd
Halpine 'hælpɪn
Hals (Dutch artist), -es hæls [hælz],
-ɪz
Halsbury 'hɔ:lzbərɪ ['hɒl-]
Halsey 'hɔ:lsɪ, 'hɔ:lzɪ, 'hælzɪ
Halstead 'hɔ:lsted ['hɒl-, -stɪd], 'hæl-
halt (s. adj. v.), -s, -ing/ly, -ed hɔ:lt
[hɒlt], -s, -ɪŋ/lɪ, -ɪd
halter, -s 'hɔ:ltə* ['hɒl-], -z
halv|e, -es, -ing, -ed hɑ:v, -z, -ɪŋ, -d
halves (plur. of half) hɑ:vz
halyard, -s 'hæljəd, -z
Halys 'heɪlɪs
ham (H.), -s hæm, -z
hamadryad, -s ˌhæmə'draɪəd [-'draɪæd],
-z
Haman (biblical name) 'heɪmæn [-mən],
(modern surname) 'heɪmən
Hamar 'heɪmɑ:*
Hamath 'heɪmæθ
Hamble, -den, -don, -ton 'hæmbl, -dən,
-dən, -tən
Hamblin 'hæmblɪn
Hambourg 'hæmbɜ:g [-,bʊəg]
Hambro 'hæmbrə [-brəʊ]
Hamburg 'hæmbɜ:g
hamburger, -s 'hæmbɜ:gə*, -z
hamburg(h), -s 'hæmbɜːə, -z
Hamelin 'hæmɪlɪn
Hamerton 'hæmətən
ham-fisted ˌhæm'fɪstɪd
ham-handed 'hæmˌhændɪd [ˌ-'--]
Hamilcar hæ'mɪlkɑ:* [hə'm-, 'hæmɪl-]
Hamilton 'hæmɪltən [-məl-, -mɪl-]
Hamiltonian ˌhæmɪl'təʊnjən [-məl-,
-mɪl-, -nɪən]
Hamish 'heɪmɪʃ
Hamite, -s 'hæmaɪt, -s
Hamitic hæ'mɪtɪk [hə'm-]
hamlet (H.), -s 'hæmlɪt [-lət], -s
Haml|ey, -in 'hæml|ɪ, -ɪn
hammam, -s 'hæmæm [-məm,
hə'mɑ:m, 'hʌmæm], -z
hammer (s. v.) (H.), -s, -ing, -ed
'hæmə*, -z, -rɪŋ, -d
hammer-blow, -s 'hæməbləʊ, -z
Hammerfest 'hæməfest
hammer-head, -s 'hæməhed, -z
Hammersmith 'hæməsmɪθ
hammock, -s 'hæmək, -s
Ham(m)ond 'hæmənd
Hammurabi ˌhæmʊ'rɑ:bɪ
Hampden 'hæmpdən, 'hæmdən
hamper (s. v.), -s, -ing, -ed 'hæmpə*, -z,
-rɪŋ, -d

229

Hampshire 'hæmpʃə* [-ˌʃɪə*]

Hamp|stead, -ton 'hæmp|stɪd [-sted], -tən

Hamshaw 'hæmʃɔ:

hamster, -s 'hæmstə*, -z

hamstring (s. v.), -s, -ing, -ed, hamstrung 'hæmstrɪŋ, -z, -ɪŋ, -d, 'hæmstrʌŋ

hamza, -s 'hæmzə, -z

Han (Chinese dynasty) hæn

Hanan 'hænən

Hananiah ˌhænə'naɪə

Hanbury 'hænbərɪ

Hancock 'hænkɒk ['hæŋ-]

hand (s. v.) (H.), -s; hand|ing, -ed, -er/s hænd, -z; 'hænd|ɪŋ, -ɪd, -ə*/z

hand|-bag/s, -barrow/s, -bell/s, -bill/s, -book/s, -cart/s 'hænd|bæg/z, -ˌbærəʊ/z, -bel/z, -bɪl/z, -bʊk/s, -kɑ:t/s

Handcock 'hændkɒk

handcuff (s. v.), -s, -ing, -ed 'hændkʌf ['hæŋk-], -s, -ɪŋ, -t

Handel 'hændl

Handelian hæn'di:ljən [-lɪən]

handful, -s hændfʊl, -z

hand-glass, -es 'hændglɑ:s, -ɪz

hand-grenade, -s 'hændgrəˌneɪd [-grɪˌn-, -greˌn-], -z

handgrip, -s 'hændgrɪp, -s

handhold, -s 'hændhəʊld, -z

handicap (s. v.), -s, -ping, -ped, -per/s 'hændɪkæp, -s, -ɪŋ, -t, -ə*/z

handi|craft/s, -work 'hændɪ|krɑ:ft/s, -wɜ:k

handkerchief, -s 'hæŋkətʃɪf [-tʃəf], -s

Note.—There exists also a pronunciation 'hæŋkətʃi:f with a plur. -tʃi:fs or -tʃi:vz.

hand|le (s. v.), -les, -ling, -led, -ler/s 'hænd|l, -lz, -lɪŋ [-lɪŋ], -ld, -lə*/z [-lə*/z]

handle-bar, -s 'hændlbɑ:*, -z

handless 'hændlɪs [-ləs]

Handley 'hændlɪ

hand|-line/s, -loom/s 'hænd|laɪn/z, -lu:m/z

hand-made ˌhænd'meɪd [also '— when attributive]

hand-maid, -s, -en/s 'hændmeɪd, -z, -n/z

hand-out, -s 'hændaʊt, -s

hand-rail, -s 'hændreɪl, -z

Hands hændz

hand-screen, -s 'hændskri:n, -z

handsel = hansel

handshake, -s 'hændʃeɪk, -s

handsome, -r, -st, -ly, -ness 'hænsəm [-ntsəm], -ə*, -ɪst, -lɪ, -nɪs [-nəs]

handwork 'hændwɜ:k

hand-worked ˌhænd'wɜ:kt ['—]

handwriting, -s 'hændˌraɪtɪŋ, -z

hand|y, -ier, -iest, -ily, -iness 'hænd|ɪ, -ɪə* [-jə*], -ɪɪst [-jɪst], -ɪlɪ [-əlɪ], -ɪnɪs [-ɪnəs]

handy-man, -men 'hændɪmæn [-mən], -men

hang, -s, -ing/s, -ed, hung, hanger/s hæŋ, -z, -ɪŋ/z, -d, hʌŋ, 'hæŋə*/z

hangar, -s 'hæŋə* [-ŋgə*], -z

hang-dog (s. adj.), -s 'hæŋdɒg, -z

Hanger 'hæŋə*

hanger-on, hangers-on ˌhæŋər'ɒn, ˌhæŋəz'ɒn

hang|man, -men 'hæŋ|mən, -mən

hang-nail, -s 'hæŋneɪl, -z

hang-over, -s 'hæŋˌəʊvə*, -z

hank, -s hæŋk, -s

hank|er, -ers, -ering, -ered 'hæŋk|ə*, -əz, -ərɪŋ, -əd

Hankow ˌhæn'kaʊ [ˌhæŋ'k-]

hank|y, -ies 'hæŋk|ɪ, -ɪz

hanky-panky ˌhæŋkɪ'pæŋkɪ ['—ˌ—]

Hanley 'hænlɪ

Hannah 'hænə

Hann|ay, -en 'hæn|eɪ, -ən

Hannibal 'hænɪbl

Hannington 'hænɪŋtən

Hanoi hæ'nɔɪ

Hanover 'hænəʊvə* (ha'no:fər)

Hanoverian, -s ˌhænəʊ'vɪərɪən, -z

Hansa 'hænsə [-nzə]

Hansard 'hænsɑ:d [-səd]

Hanse, -s hæns, -ɪz

Hanseatic ˌhænsɪ'ætɪk [-nzt-]

hans|el, -els, -elling, -elled 'hæns|l, -lz, -əlɪŋ [-lɪŋ], -ld

Hänsel (German name) 'hænsl ('hɛnzəl)

Hans|ell, -on 'hæns|l, -n

hansom (H.), -s; -cab/s 'hænsəm, -z; -kæb/z

Hants hænts

Han|way, -well 'hæn|weɪ, -wəl [-wel]

hap (s. v.), -s, -ping, -ped hæp, -s, -ɪŋ, -t

haphazard ˌhæp'hæzəd

hapless, -ly, -ness 'hæplɪs [-ləs], -lɪ, -nɪs [-nəs]

haply 'hæplɪ

hap'orth, -s 'heɪpəθ, -s

happ|en, -ens, -ening/s -ened 'hæp|ən, -ənz, -nɪŋ/z [-ənɪŋ/z, -nɪŋ/z], -ənd

Happisburgh (in Norfolk) 'heɪzbərə

happ|y, -ier, -iest, -ily, -iness 'hæp|ɪ, -ɪə*, -ɪɪst, -ɪlɪ [-əlɪ], -ɪnɪs [-ɪnəs]

happy-go-lucky ˌhæpɪgəʊˈlʌkɪ ['—ˌ—]
Hapsburg 'hæpsbɜ:g
hara-kiri ˌhærəˈkɪrɪ
harangu|e (s. v.), -es, -ing, -ed, -er/s
hə'ræŋ, -z, -ɪŋ, -d, -ə*/z
harass, -es, -ing, -ed, -er/s, -ment
'hærəs, -ɪz, -ɪŋ, -t, -ə*/z, -mənt
Harben 'hɑ:bən
Harberton 'hɑ:bətən
harbinger, -s 'hɑ:bɪndʒə*, -z
Harborough 'hɑ:bərə
harb|our (s. v.), -ours, -ouring, -oured,
-ourer/s; -ourage, -ourless 'hɑ:b|ə*,
-əz, -ərɪŋ, -əd, -ərə*/z; -ərɪdʒ, -əlɪs
[-ləs]
harbour-master, -s 'hɑ:bəˌmɑ:stə*, -z
Harcourt 'hɑ:kət [-kɔ:t]
hard (H.), -er, -est, -ly, -ness hɑ:d, -ə*,
-ɪst, -lɪ, -nɪs [-nəs]
hardbake (s.) 'hɑ:dbeɪk
hard-baked ˌhɑ:d'beɪkt ['—]
hard-bitten ˌhɑ:d'bɪtn ['—]
hardboard 'hɑ:dbɔ:d [-bɔəd]
hard-boiled ˌhɑ:d'bɔɪld ['— when attri-
butive]
Hardcastle 'hɑ:dˌkɑ:sl
hard-earned ˌhɑ:d'ɜ:nd [also '— when
attributive]
hard|en (H.), -ens, -ening, -ened
'hɑ:d|n, -nz, -nɪŋ [-nɪŋ], -nd
hard-featured ˌhɑ:d'fi:tʃəd ['-ˌ—]
hard-fought ˌhɑ:d'fɔ:t ['—]
hard-grained ˌhɑ:d'greɪnd ['—]
hard-headed ˌhɑ:d'hedɪd [also '-ˌ—
according to sentence-stress]
hard-hearted, -ly, -ness ˌhɑ:d'hɑ:tɪd
[also '-ˌ— according to sentence-stress],
-lɪ, -nɪs
Hardicanute 'hɑ:dɪkənju:t [ˌhɑ:dɪkə'n-]
hardihood 'hɑ:dɪhʊd
Harding(e) 'hɑ:dɪŋ
hard|ish, -ly 'hɑ:d|ɪʃ, -lɪ
Hardres hɑ:dz
Hardress 'hɑ:dres [-drɪs]
hardship, -s 'hɑ:dʃɪp, -s
hard-up ˌhɑ:d'ʌp
hardware 'hɑ:dweə*
Hardwick(e) 'hɑ:dwɪk
hardwood 'hɑ:dwʊd
hard|y (H.), -ier, -iest, -ily, -iness,
-ihood 'hɑ:d|ɪ, -ɪə* [-jə*], -ɪɪst [-jɪst],
-ɪlɪ [-əlɪ], -ɪnɪs [-ɪnəs], -ɪhʊd
hare (H.), -s; -bell/s, -brained heə*,
-z; -bel/z, -breɪnd
harelip, -s -ped ˌheə'lɪp ['-—], -s, -t
harem, -s 'hɑ:ri:m [-rem, hə'ri:m,
hɑ:'ri:m, 'heərəm], -z
Harenc (surname) 'hærɒŋ

hare's-foot 'heəzfʊt
Harewood 'hɑ:wʊd, 'heəwʊd
  Note.—The Earl of Harewood pronounces 'hɑ:wʊd, and his house is
  called ˌhɑ:wʊd 'haʊs. The village
  in West Yorkshire is now generally pronounced 'heəwʊd, though
  'hɑ:wʊd may sometimes be heard
  from very old people there. Other
  people with the surname Harewood
  pronounce 'heəwʊd.
Har|ford, -graves 'hɑ:|fəd, -greɪvz
Hargreaves 'hɑ:gri:vz, -greɪvz
haricot, -s 'hærɪkəʊ, -z
Haringey 'hærɪŋgeɪ
Harington 'hærɪŋtən
hark (v. interj.), -s, -ing, -ed hɑ:k, -s,
-ɪŋ, -t
Harlaw 'hɑ:lɔ: [hɑ:'lɔ:]
Harlech 'hɑ:lek [-lex]
Harleian hɑ:'li:ən [-'lɪən, 'hɑ:lɪən, esp.
when attributive]
Harlem 'hɑ:ləm [-lem]
harlequin, -s 'hɑ:lɪkwɪn [-lək-], -z
harlequinade, -s ˌhɑ:lɪkwɪ'neɪd [-lək-],
-z
Harlesden 'hɑ:lzdən
Harley 'hɑ:lɪ
Harlock 'hɑ:lɒk
harlot, -s, -ry 'hɑ:lət, -s, -rɪ
Harlow(e) 'hɑ:ləʊ
harm (s. v.), -s, -ing, -ed hɑ:m, -z, -ɪŋ,
-d
Harman 'hɑ:mən
Harmer 'hɑ:mə*
harm|ful, -fully, -fulness 'hɑ:m|fʊl,
-fʊlɪ [-fəlɪ], -fʊlnɪs [-nəs]
harmless, -ly, -ness 'hɑ:mlɪs [-ləs], -lɪ,
-nɪs [-nəs]
Harmonia hɑ:'məʊnjə [-nɪə]
harmonic (s. adj.), -s, -al, -ally
hɑ:'mɒnɪk, -s, -l, -əlɪ
harmonic|a/s, -on/s hɑ:'mɒnɪk|ə/z,
-ən/z
harmonious, -ly, -ness hɑ:'məʊnjəs
[-nɪəs], -lɪ, -nɪs [-nəs]
harmonist, -s 'hɑ:mənɪst, -s
harmonium, -s hɑ:'məʊnjəm [-nɪəm],
-z
harmonization [-isa-], -s ˌhɑ:mənaɪ-
'zeɪʃn, -z
harmoniz|e [-is|e], -es, -ing, -ed, -er/s
'hɑ:mənaɪz, -ɪz, -ɪŋ, -d, -ə*/z
harmon|y, -ies 'hɑ:mən|ɪ, -ɪz
Harmsworth 'hɑ:mzwəθ [-wɜ:θ]
Harnack 'hɑ:næk
harness (s. v.) (H.), -es, -ing, -ed, -er/s
'hɑ:nɪs, -ɪz, -ɪŋ, -t, -ə*/z

Harold 'hærəld

Harosheth 'hærəʊʃeθ

harp (s. v.), -s, -ing, -ed, -er/s hɑ:p, -s, -ɪŋ, -t, -ə*/z

Harpenden 'hɑ:pəndən

Harper 'hɑ:pə*

Harpham 'hɑ:pəm

harpist, -s 'hɑ:pɪst, -s

Harpocration ˌhɑ:pəʊ'kreɪʃən [-ʃɪən]

harpoon (s. v.), -s, -ing, -ed, -er/s hɑ:'pu:n, -z, -ɪŋ, -d, -ə*/z

harpsichord, -s 'hɑ:psɪkɔ:d, -z

harp|y, -ies 'hɑ:p|ɪ, -ɪz

harquebus, -es 'hɑ:kwɪbəs, -ɪz

Harraden 'hærədən [-den]

Harrap 'hærəp

harridan, -s 'hærɪdən, -z

Harrie 'hærɪ

harrier, -s 'hærɪə*, -z

Harr|ies, -iet 'hær|ɪs, -ɪət

Harri|man, -ngton 'hærɪ|mən, -ŋtən

Harriot 'hærɪət

Harris, -on 'hærɪs, -n

Harrisson 'hærɪsn

Harrod, -s 'hærəd, -z

Harrogate 'hærəʊgɪt [-geɪt, -gət]

Harrop 'hærəp

Harrovian, -s hə'rəʊvjən [hæ'r-, -vɪən], -z

harr|ow (s. v.) (H.), -ows, -owing/ly, -owed 'hær|əʊ, -əʊz, -əʊɪŋ/lɪ, -əʊd

Harrowby 'hærəʊbɪ

harr|y (H.), -ies, -ying, -ied 'hær|ɪ, -ɪz, -ɪŋ, -ɪd

Harsant 'hɑ:sənt

harsh, -er, -est, -ly, -ness hɑ:ʃ, -ə*, -ɪst, -lɪ, -nɪs [-nəs]

hart (H.), -s hɑ:t, -s

Harte hɑ:t

hartebeest, -s 'hɑ:tɪbi:st, -s

Hartford 'hɑ:tfəd

Harthan (surname) 'hɑ:ðən, 'hɑ:θən

Hartington 'hɑ:tɪŋtən

Hartland 'hɑ:tlənd

Hartlepool 'hɑ:tlɪpu:l

Hartley 'hɑ:tlɪ

harts|horn (H.), -tongue/s 'hɑ:ts|hɔ:n, -tʌŋ/z

Hartz hɑ:ts

harum-scarum ˌheərəm'skeərəm

Harun-al-Raschid hæˌru:nælræ'ʃi:d [hɑ:ˌr-, ˌ—'—-, -'ræʃɪd]

haruspex, haruspices hə'rʌspeks ['hærə-speks], hə'rʌspɪsi:z

Harvard 'hɑ:vəd [-vɑ:d]

Harverson 'hɑ:vəsn

harvest (s. v.), -s, -ing, -ed, -er/s 'hɑ:vɪst, -s, -ɪŋ, -ɪd, -ə*/z

harvest-bug, -s 'hɑ:vɪstbʌg, -z

harvest-festival, -s ˌhɑ:vɪst'festəvl [-trv-], -z

harvest-home ˌhɑ:vɪst'həʊm

harvest|-man, -men; -moon/s 'hɑ:vɪst|-mæn, -men; -'mu:n/z

Harvey 'hɑ:vɪ

Harwich 'hærɪdʒ [rarely -ɪtʃ]

Harwood 'hɑ:wʊd

Harz hɑ:ts

has (from have) hæz (strong form), həz, əz, z, s (weak forms)

Note.—In the auxil. verb, the form z is used only after words ending in a voiced sound other than z or ʒ; s is used only after words ending in a voiceless consonant other than s or ʃ.

Hasdrubal 'hæzdrʊbl [-bæl]

Haselden 'hæzldən

Hasemer 'heɪzmə*

hash (s. v.), -es, -ing, -ed, -er/s hæʃ, -ɪz, -ɪŋ, -t, -ə*/z

hashish 'hæʃi:ʃ [-ʃɪʃ]

Haslam 'hæzləm

Haslemere 'heɪzlˌmɪə*

haslet 'heɪzlɪt [-lət]

Haslett 'heɪzlɪt [-lət], 'hæzlɪt

Haslingden 'hæzlɪŋdən

Hasluck 'hæzlʌk [-lək]

hasn't 'hæznt [also 'hæzn when not final]

hasp (s. v.), -s, -ing, -ed hɑ:sp [hæsp], -s, -ɪŋ, -t

Hassall 'hæsl

Hassan (district in India) 'hʌsən ['hæs-], (Arabic name) hə'sɑ:n ['hæsən, 'hʌsən]

hassock (H.), -s 'hæsək, -s

hast (from have) (H.) hæst (strong form), həst, əst, st (weak forms)

hast|e (s. v.), -es, -ing, -ed heɪst, -s, -ɪŋ, -ɪd

hast|en, -ens, -ening, -ened 'heɪs|n, -nz, -nɪŋ [-ŋɪŋ], -nd

Hastings 'heɪstɪŋz

hast|y, -ier, -iest, -ily, -iness 'heɪst|ɪ, -ɪə* [-jə*], -ɪɪst [-jɪst], -ɪlɪ [-əlɪ], -ɪnɪs [-məs]

hasty-pudding 'heɪstɪˌpʊdɪŋ

hat, -s hæt, -s

hat-band, -s 'hætbænd, -z

hat-box, -es 'hætbɒks, -ɪz

hat-brush, -es 'hætbrʌʃ, -ɪz

hatch (s. v.) (H.), -es, -ing, -ed hætʃ, -ɪz, -ɪŋ, -t

hatchet, -s 'hætʃɪt, -s

hatchment, -s 'hætʃmənt, -s

hatchway (H.), -s 'hætʃweɪ, -z

hat|e (s. v.), -es, -ing, -ed, -er/s heɪt, -s, -ɪŋ, -ɪd, -ə*/z

hate|ful, -fully, -fulness 'heɪt|fʊl, -fʊlɪ [-fəlɪ], -fʊlnɪs [-nəs]

Hatfield 'hætfiːld

hath (from have) hæθ (strong form), həθ, əθ (weak forms)

Hathaway 'hæθəweɪ

Hather|ell, -leigh, -ley 'hæðə|rəl, -lɪ [-liː], -lɪ

Hathersage 'hæðəsɪdʒ [-sedʒ]

Hatherton 'hæðətən

Hathorn(e) 'hɔːθɔːn

Hathway 'hæθweɪ

hatless 'hætlɪs [-ləs, -les]

hat-peg, -s 'hætpeg, -z

hat-pin, -s 'hætpɪn, -z

hat-rack, -s 'hætræk, -s

hatred 'heɪtrɪd

hat-stand, -s 'hætstænd, -z

hatter, -s 'hætə*, -z

Hatteras 'hætərəs

Hatt|o, -on 'hæt|əʊ, -n

hauberk, -s 'hɔːbɜːk, -s

haugh, -s hɔː, -z

Haughton 'hɔːtn

haught|y, -ier, -iest, -ily, -iness 'hɔːt|ɪ, -ɪə* [-jə*], -ɪɪst [-jɪst], -ɪlɪ [-əlɪ], -ɪnɪs [-məs]

haul (s. v.), -s, -ing, -ed; -age hɔːl, -z, -ɪŋ, -d; -ɪdʒ

haulier, -s 'hɔːljə* [-lɪə*], -z

haulm, -s hɔːm, -z

haunch, -es hɔːntʃ, -ɪz

haunt (s. v.), -s, -ing, -ed hɔːnt, -s, -ɪŋ, -ɪd

Hausa, -s 'haʊsə ['haʊzə], -z

hautboy, -s 'əʊbɔɪ ['həʊ-], -z

haute (couture) əʊt

hauteur əʊ'tɜː* ['əʊtɜː*] (otœːr)

Havana, -s hə'vænə, -z

Havant 'hævənt

Havard 'hævɑːd [-vəd]

have (one who has), -s hæv, -z

have (v.); hast; has; having; had hæv (strong form), həv, əv, v (weak forms); hæst (strong form), həst, əst, st (weak forms); hæz (strong form), həz, əz, z, s (weak forms); 'hævɪŋ; hæd (strong form), həd, əd, d (weak forms)

Note.—In the auxil. verb, the weak form z is used only after voiced sounds other than z and ʒ. The weak form s is used only after voiceless consonants other than s and ʃ.

Havell 'hævəl

Havelo(c)k 'hævlɒk [-lək]

haven, -s 'heɪvn, -z

have-not, -s 'hævnɒt, -s

haven't 'hævnt [also 'hævn when not final]

haver (v.) (talk nonsense), -s, -ing, -ed 'heɪvə*, -z, -rɪŋ, -d

Haverford, -west 'hævəfəd, -'west

Havergal 'hævəgəl

Haverhill 'heɪvərɪl

haversack, -s 'hævəsæk, -s

Haverstock 'hævəstɒk

Havil|ah, -and 'hævɪl|ə, -ənd

havoc 'hævək

Havre 'hɑːvrə [-və*]

haw (s. v.), -s, -ing, -ed hɔː, -z, -ɪŋ, -d

Hawaii hə'waɪi: [hɑː'w-, -'wɑːiː]

Hawaiian hə'waɪən [hɑː'w-, -'waɪjən]

Haward 'heɪwəd, 'hɔːd, hɔːd

Hawarden (in Clwyd) 'hɑːdn ['hɔːdn], (Viscount) 'heɪˌwɔːdn, (town in U.S.A.) 'heɪˌwɑːdn

Haweis 'hɔːɪs

Hawes hɔːz

hawfinch, -es 'hɔːfɪntʃ, -ɪz

haw-haw (s.), -s 'hɔːhɔː, -z (interj.) ˌhɔː'hɔː

Hawick 'hɔːɪk [hɔɪk]

hawk (s. v.), -s, -ing, -ed, -er/s hɔːk, -s, -ɪŋ, -t, -ə*/z

Hawke, -s hɔːk, -s

hawk-eyed 'hɔːkaɪd

Hawkins 'hɔːkɪnz

hawkish 'hɔːkɪʃ

Hawksley 'hɔːkslɪ

hawkweed 'hɔːkwiːd

Hawkwood 'hɔːkwʊd

Hawley 'hɔːlɪ

Haworth 'hɔːɔːθ, 'hɔːwəθ [-wɜːθ], 'haʊəθ

hawse, -s; -hole/s, -pipe/s hɔːz, -ɪz; -həʊl/z, -paɪp/s

hawser, -s 'hɔːzə*, -z

hawthorn, -s 'hɔːθɔːn, -z

Hawthornden 'hɔːθɔːndən

Hawthorne 'hɔːθɔːn

hay (H.) heɪ

hay-box, -es 'heɪbɒks, -ɪz

hay-cart, -s 'heɪkɑːt, -s

haycock, -s 'heɪkɒk, -s

Haycock 'heɪkɒk

Hayd|en, -on 'heɪd|n, -n

Haydn (English surname) 'heɪdn, (Austrian composer) 'haɪdn

Hayes, -ford heɪz, -fəd

hay-fever 'heɪˌfiːvə* [ˌ-'--]

hay-field, -s 'heɪfiːld, -z

hay-fork, -s 'heɪfɔːk, -s

Hayhurst 'haɪəst, 'heɪhɜːst

233

Hayles heɪlz
hay-loft 'heɪlɒft, -s
hay-mak|er/s, -ing 'heɪˌmeɪk|ə*/z, -ɪŋ
Haymarket 'heɪˌmɑːkɪt
Haynes heɪnz
hayrick, -s 'heɪrɪk, -s
Hays heɪz
haystack, -s 'heɪstæk, -s
Hayt|er, -or 'heɪt|ə*, -ə*
hayward (H.), -s 'heɪwəd, -z
Hazael 'hæzeɪel ['heɪz-, -zeɪəl, hæ'z-,
    hə'z-]
hazard (s. v.) (H.), -s, -ing, -ed 'hæzəd,
    -z, -ɪŋ, -ɪd
hazardous, -ly, -ness 'hæzədəs, -lɪ, -nɪs
    [-nəs]
haz|e (s. v.), -es, -ing, -ed heɪz, -ɪz, -ɪŋ,
    -d
hazel, -s; -nut/s 'heɪzl, -z; -nʌt/s
Hazelhurst 'heɪzlhɜːst
Hazen 'heɪzn
Hazledean 'heɪzldiːn
hazlerigg 'heɪzlrɪg
Hazlett 'heɪzlɪt [-lət], 'hæzlɪt [-lət]
Hazlitt 'heɪzlɪt, 'hæzlɪt
    Note.—William Hazlitt, the essayist,
    called himself 'heɪzlɪt, and the
    present members of his family pro-
    nounce the name thus. He is, how-
    ever, commonly referred to as
    'hæzlɪt. In the Hazlitt Gallery in
    London the pronunciation is
    'hæzlɪt.
Hazor 'heɪzɔː*
haz|y, -ier, -iest, -ily, -iness 'heɪz|ɪ, -ɪə*
    [-jə*], -ɪɪst [-jɪst], -ɪlɪ [-əlɪ], -ɪnɪs
    [-ɪnəs]
H-bomb, -s 'eɪtʃbɒm, -z
he hiː (normal form), iː, hɪ, ɪ (freq. weak
    forms)
head (s. v.) (H.), -s, -ing, -ed hed, -z,
    -ɪŋ, -ɪd
headach|e, -es, -y 'hedeɪk, -s, -ɪ
headband, -s 'hedbænd, -z
head|-cloth, -cloths 'hed|klɒθ [old-
    fashioned -klɔːθ], -klɒθs [-klɔːðz,
    -klɔːθs]
head-dress, -es 'heddres, -ɪz
header, -s 'hedə*, -z
head-first ˌhed'fɜːst
head-gear, -s 'hedˌgɪə*, -z
head-hunt|er/s, -ing 'hedˌhʌnt|ə*/z,
    -ɪŋ
heading, -s 'hedɪŋ, -z
Headingl(e)y 'hedɪŋlɪ
Headlam 'hedləm
headland, -s 'hedlənd, -z
headless 'hedlɪs [-ləs]

head-light, -s 'hedlaɪt, -s
headline, -s 'hedlaɪn, -z
headlong 'hedlɒŋ [ˌ-'-]
head|man, -men (of group of workers)
    ˌhed|'mæn ['hedmæn], -'men ['--],
    (of tribe) 'hed|mæn [-mən], -men
    [-mən]
head|-master/s, -mistress/es ˌhed|-
    'mɑːstə*/z, -'mɪstrɪs [-trəs]/ɪz
head-note, -s 'hednəʊt, -s
head-on ˌhed'ɒn ['--]
headphone, -s 'hedfəʊn, -z
headpiece, -s 'hedpiːs, -ɪz
headquarters ˌhed'kwɔːtəz   [also
    'hed,k- according to sentence-stress]
head-rest, -s 'hedrest, -s
head-room 'hedrʊm [-ruːm]
headship, -s 'hedʃɪp, -s
heads|man, -men 'hedz|mən, -mən
headstone (H.), -s 'hedstəʊn, -z
headstrong 'hedstrɒŋ
head-water, -s 'hedˌwɔːtə*, -z
headway, -s 'hedweɪ, -z
head-wind, -s 'hedwɪnd, -z
head-word, -s 'hedwɜːd, -z
head-work 'hedwɜːk
head|y, -ier, -iest, -ily, -iness 'hed|ɪ, -ɪə*,
    -ɪɪst, -ɪlɪ [-əlɪ], -ɪnɪs [-nəs]
Heagerty 'hegətɪ
heal (H.), -s, -ing, -ed, -er/s hiːl, -z, -ɪŋ,
    -d, -ə*/z
Healey 'hiːlɪ
health, -s helθ, -s
health|ful, -fully, -fulness 'helθ|fʊl,
    -fʊlɪ [-fəlɪ], -fʊlnɪs [-nəs]
health-giving 'helθˌgɪvɪŋ
health|y, -ier, -iest, -ily, -iness 'helθ|ɪ,
    -ɪə* [-jə*], -ɪɪst [-jɪst], -ɪlɪ [-əlɪ], -ɪnɪs
    [-nəs]
Healy 'hiːlɪ
Heanor (near Derby) 'hiːnə*
heap (s. v.), -s, -ing, -ed hiːp, -s, -ɪŋ, -t
hear, -s, -ing/s, heard, hearer/s hɪə*,
    -z, -ɪŋ/z, hɜːd, 'hɪərə*/z
heard (from hear) (H.) hɜːd
hear hear ˌhɪə'hɪə*
heark|en, -ens, -ening, -ened 'hɑːk|ən,
    -ənz, -nɪŋ [-ənɪŋ, -ənɪŋ], -ənd
Hearn(e) hɜːn
hearsay 'hɪəseɪ
hearse, -s hɜːs, -ɪz
hearse|-cloth, -cloths 'hɜːs|klɒθ [old-
    fashioned -klɔːθ], -klɒθs [-klɔːðz,
    -klɔːθs]
Hearsey 'hɜːsɪ
Hearst hɜːst
heart, -s hɑːt, -s
heartache 'hɑːteɪk

234

heart-beat, -s 'hɑ:tbi:t, -s
heart-blood 'hɑ:tblʌd
heartbreak, -ing 'hɑ:tbreɪk, -ɪŋ
heart-broken 'hɑ:t,brəʊkən
heartburn, -ing/s 'hɑ:tbɜ:n, -ɪŋ/z
heart|en, -ens, -ening, -ened 'hɑ:t|n,
 -nz, -nɪŋ [-nɪŋ], -nd
heartfelt 'hɑ:tfelt
hearth, -s; -brush/es, -rug/s, -stone/s
 hɑ:θ, -s; -brʌʃ/ɪz, -rʌg/z, -stəʊn/z
heartless, -ly, -ness 'hɑ:tlɪs [-ləs], -lɪ,
 -nɪs [-nəs]
heart-rending 'hɑ:t,rendɪŋ
heart-searching, -s 'hɑ:t,sɜ:tʃɪŋ, -z
heart's-ease 'hɑ:t-i:z
heart-shaped 'hɑ:t-ʃeɪpt
heart-sick, -ness 'hɑ:tsɪk, -nɪs [-nəs]
heartsore 'hɑ:tsɔ:* [-sɔə*]
heart-string, -s 'hɑ:tstrɪŋ, -z
heart|y, -ier, -iest, -ily, -iness 'hɑ:t|ɪ,
 -ɪə* [-jə*], -ɪɪst [-jɪst], -ɪlɪ [-əlɪ], -ɪnɪs
 [-ɪnəs]
heat (s. v.), -s, -ing, -ed, -er/s hi:t, -s,
 -ɪŋ, -ɪd, -ə*/z
heath (H.), -s hi:θ, -s
Heathcoat 'hi:θkəʊt
Heathcote 'heθkət, 'hi:θkət
heathen (s. adj.), -s, -dom 'hi:ðn, -z,
 -dəm
heathenish, -ly, -ness 'hi:ðənɪʃ [-ðŋɪʃ],
 -lɪ, -nɪs [-nəs]
heathenism 'hi:ðənɪzəm [-ðŋɪ-]
heatheniz|e [-is|e], -es, -ing, -ed
 'hi:ðənaɪz [-ðŋaɪz], -ɪz, -ɪŋ, -d
heather (H.), -s, -y 'heðə*, -z, -rɪ
heather-bell, -s 'heðəbel, -z
Heath|field, -man 'hi:θ|fi:ld, -mən
heath|y, -ier, -iest 'hi:θ|ɪ, -ɪə* [-jə*],
 -ɪɪst [-jɪst]
Heaton 'hi:tn
heat-spot, -s 'hi:tspɒt, -s
heat-stroke, -s 'hi:tstrəʊk, -s
heat-wave, -s 'hi:tweɪv, -z
heav|e (s. v.), -es, -ing, -ed, hove,
 heaver/s hi:v, -z, -ɪŋ, -d, həʊv,
 'hi:və*/z
heaven, -s; -born 'hevn, -z; -bɔ:n
heavenl|y, -iness 'hevnl|ɪ, -ɪnɪs [-ɪnəs]
heavenward, -s 'hevnwəd, -z
Heaviside 'hevɪsaɪd
heav|y, -ier, -iest, -ily, -iness 'hev|ɪ,
 -ɪə* [-jə*], -ɪɪst [-jɪst], -ɪlɪ [-əlɪ], -ɪnɪs
 [-ɪnəs]
heavy-handed ,hevɪ'hændɪd ['--,--]
heavy-hearted ,hevɪ'hɑ:tɪd ['--,--]
heavy-laden ,hevɪ'leɪdn [also '--,-- when
 attributive]
heavy-weight, -s 'hevɪweɪt, -s

Heazell 'hi:zəl
Hebden 'hebdən
hebdomad|al, -ary heb'dɒməd|l, -ərɪ
Hebe 'hi:bi: [-bɪ]
Heber 'hi:bə*
Heberden 'hebədən
Hebraic, -al, -ally hi:'breɪk [hɪ-,
 he'b-], -l, -əlɪ
Hebrai|sm/s, -st/s 'hi:breɪ|zəm/z,
 -st/s
hebraiz|e [-is|e], -es, -ing, -ed
 'hi:breɪaɪz, -ɪz, -ɪŋ, -d
Hebrew, -s 'hi:bru:, -z
Hebrides 'hebrɪdi:z [-brəd-]
Hebron (biblical place-name) 'hebrɒn
 ['hi:b-], (modern surname) 'hebrən
 [-rɒn]
Hecate 'hekətɪ [-ti:, in Shakespeare
 sometimes 'hekət]
hecatomb, -s 'hekətu:m [-təʊm, -təm],
 -z
heck|le, -les, -ling, -led, -ler/s 'hek|l,
 -lz, -lɪŋ [-lɪŋ], -ld, -lə*/z [-lə*/z]
Hecla 'heklə
hectare, -s 'hektɑ:* [-teə*] (ɛktɑ:r),
 -z
hectic 'hektɪk
hectogramme, -s 'hektəʊgræm, -z
hectograph (s. v.), -s, -ing, -ed 'hektəʊ-
 grɑ:f [-græf], -s, -ɪŋ, -t
hectographic ,hektəʊ'græfɪk
hectolitre, -s 'hektəʊ,li:tə*, -z
hectometre, -s 'hektəʊ,mi:tə*, -z
hector (s. v.) (H.), -s, -ing, -ed 'hektə*,
 -z, -rɪŋ, -d
Hecuba 'hekjʊbə
Hecyra 'hekɪrə
hedera 'hedərə
Hedgcock 'hedʒkɒk
hedg|e (s. v.), -es, -ing, -ed, -er/s hedʒ,
 -ɪz, -ɪŋ, -d, -ə*/z
hedgehog, -s 'hedʒhɒg, -z
hedgehop, -s, -ping, -ped 'hedʒhɒp, -s,
 -ɪŋ, -t
Hedgeley 'hedʒlɪ
Hedger, -ley 'hedʒə*, -lɪ
hedgerow, -s 'hedʒrəʊ, -z
Hedges 'hedʒɪz
hedge-sparrow, -s 'hedʒ,spærəʊ [,-'--],
 -z
Hedley 'hedlɪ
hedoni|sm, -st/s 'hi:dəʊnɪ|zəm, -st/s
hedonistic ,hi:də'nɪstɪk
heed (s. v.), -s, -ing, -ed hi:d, -z, -ɪŋ, -ɪd
heed|ful, -fully, -fulness 'hi:d|fʊl, -fʊlɪ
 [-fəlɪ], -fʊlnɪs [-nəs]
heedless, -ly, -ness 'hi:dlɪs [-ləs], -lɪ,
 -nɪs [-nəs]

235

heehaw (s. v. interj.), -s, -ing, -ed ˌhiːˈhɔː: [ˈ--], -z, -ɪŋ, -d

heel (s. v.), -s, -ing, -ed hiːl, -z, -ɪŋ, -d

Heelas ˈhiːləs

Heep hiːp

Heffer ˈhefə*

heft|y, -ier, -iest, -ily, -iness ˈheft|ɪ, -ɪə* [-jə*], -ɪɪst [-jɪst], -ɪlɪ [-əlɪ], -ɪnɪs [-ɪnəs]

Hegarty ˈhegətɪ

Hegel ˈheɪgl (ˈheːgəl)

Hegelian herˈgiːljən [heˈg-, hɪˈg-, -lɪən]

hegemony hɪˈgemənɪ [hiː-, ˈhedʒɪm-, ˈhegɪm-]

Hegira ˈhedʒɪrə [hɪˈdʒaɪərə, heˈdʒaɪərə]

he-goat, -s ˈhiːgəʊt, -s

Heidelberg ˈhaɪdlbəːg

Heidsieck ˈhaɪdsiːk [-sɪk]

heifer, -s ˈhefə*, -z

heigh her

heigh-ho ˌherˈhəʊ

Heigho ˈherəʊ, ˈharəʊ

height, -s haɪt, -s

height|en, -ens, -ening, -ened ˈhaɪt|n, -nz, -nɪŋ [-nɪŋ], -nd

Heighton ˈhertn

Highway ˈharwer

Heinekey ˈhaɪnɪkɪ

Heinemann ˈhaɪnəmən [-mæn]

heinous, -ly, -ness ˈhemǝs, -lɪ, -nɪs [-nǝs]

Heinz haɪnts, haɪnz

heir, -s; -dom, -less eə*, -z; -dəm, -lɪs [-ləs, -les]

heir-apparent, heirs-apparent ˌeərə-ˈpærənt [ˌeəˈp-, -ˈpeər-], ˌeəzə-ˈp-

heir-at-law, heirs-at-law ˌeərətˈlɔː: [ˌeəst-], ˌeəzətˈlɔː

heiress, -es ˈeərɪs [-res, eəˈres], -ɪz

heirloom, -s ˈeəluːm, -z

heirship ˈeəʃɪp

Hekla ˈheklə

held (from hold) held

Helen ˈhelɪn [-lən]

Helena ˈhelɪnə, heˈliːnə [-lənə, hɪˈl-, həˈl-]
Note.—ˈhelɪnə, ˈhelənə are the more usual pronunciations, except in the name of the island St. Helena (q.v.).

Helensburgh ˈhelɪnzbərə [-bʌrə]

Helenus ˈhelɪnəs

heliac ˈhiːlɪæk

heliac|al, -ally hiːˈlaɪək|l [hɪ-, heˈl-], -əlɪ

Heliades heˈlaɪədiːz

helianth|us, -i, -uses ˌhiːlɪˈænθ|əs [ˌhel-], -aɪ, -əsɪz

helical ˈhelɪkl

Helicon ˈhelɪkən [-kɒn]

helicopter, -s ˈhelɪkɒptə*, -z

Heligoland ˈhelɪgəʊlænd

heliocentric, -al, -ally ˌhiːlɪəʊˈsentrɪk [-ljəʊ-], -l, -əlɪ

Heliogabalus ˌhiːlɪəʊˈgæbələs [-ljəʊ-]

heliogram, -s ˈhiːlɪəʊgræm [-ljəʊg-], -z

heliograph, -s ˈhiːlɪəʊgrɑːf [-ljəʊg-, -græf], -s

heliograph|er/s, -y ˌhiːlɪˈɒgrəf|ə*/z, -ɪ [-ljəʊˈg-], -l

heliographic, -al ˌhiːlɪəʊˈgræfɪk [-ljəʊˈg-], -l

heliogravure, -s ˌhiːlɪəʊgrəˈvjʊə*, -z

heliometer, -s ˌhiːlɪˈɒmɪtə* [-mətə*], -z

Heliopolis ˌhiːlɪˈɒpəlɪs

Helios ˈhiːlɪɒs

helioscope, -s ˈhiːlɪəskəʊp [-lɪɒs-], -s

heliostat, -s ˈhiːlɪəʊstæt [-ljəʊs-], -s

heliotrope, -s ˈheljətrəʊp [-lɪə-, ˈhiːl-], -s

helium ˈhiːlɪəm [-lɪəm]

heli|x, -xes, helices ˈhiːlɪ|ks, -ksɪz, ˈhelɪsiːz [ˈhiːl-]

hell (H.), -s hel, -z

he'll (= he will) hiːl

Hellas ˈheləs

hellebore, -s ˈhelɪbɔː* [-bɔə*]

Hellene, -s ˈheliːn, -z

Hellenic heˈliːnɪk

helleni|sm/s -st/s ˈhelɪnɪ|zəm/z, -st/s

hellenistic, -al, -ally ˌhelɪˈnɪstɪk, -l, -əlɪ

helleniz|e [-is|e], -es, -ing, -ed ˈhelɪnaɪz, -ɪz, -ɪŋ, -d

Heller ˈhelə*

Hellespont ˈhelɪspɒnt

hell-fire ˌhelˈfaɪə* [ˈ-,--]

hell-gate, -s ˌhelˈgeɪt, -s

hell-hound, -s ˈhelhaʊnd, -z

Hellingly (in East Sussex) ˈhelɪŋlaɪ

hellish, -ly, -ness ˈhelɪʃ, -lɪ, -nɪs [-nəs]

hello həˈləʊ [he-]

hellward ˈhelwəd

helm, -s helm, -z

helmet, -s -ed ˈhelmɪt, -s, -ɪd

Helmholtz ˈhelmhəʊlts (ˈhelmhɔlts)

helminth, -s ˈhelmɪnθ, -s

Helmsley (in North Yorkshire) ˈhelmzlɪ [locally ˈhemz-]

helms-man, -men ˈhelmz|mən, -mən [-men]

helot, -s; -age, -ism, -ry ˈhelət, -s; -ɪdʒ, -ɪzəm, -rɪ

help (s. v.), -s, -ing, -ed, -er/s help, -s, -ɪŋ, -t, -ə*/z

help|ful, -fully, -fulness ˈhelp|fʊl, -fʊlɪ [-fəlɪ], -fʊlnɪs [-nəs]

helpless, -ly, -ness ˈhelplɪs [-ləs], -lɪ, -nɪs [-nəs]

helpmate, -s 'helpmeɪt, -s
helpmeet, -s 'helpmiːt, -s
Helps helps
Helsingfors 'helsɪŋfɔːz
Helsinki 'helsɪŋkɪ [-'--]
Helston(e) 'helstən
helter-skelter ,heltə'skeltə*
helve, -s helv, -z
Helvellyn hel'velɪn
Helvetia, -n/s hel'viːʃjə [-ʃɪə], -n/z
Helvetic hel'vetɪk
Helvetius hel'viːʃjəs [-ʃɪəs] (ɛlvɛsjys)
Hely 'hiːlɪ
hem (s. v.), -s, -ming, -med hem, -z, -ɪŋ, -d
hem (interj.) m̩m [hm]
hemal 'hiːməl [-ml]
he|-man, -men 'hiː|mæn, -men
Hemans 'hemənz
hematite 'hemətaɪt
Hemel Hempstead ,heml'hempstɪd
hemicycle, -s 'hemɪ,saɪkl, -z
Heming 'hemɪŋ
hemisphere, -s 'hemɪ,sfɪə*, -z
hemispheric, -al ,hemɪ'sferɪk, -l
hemistich, -s 'hemɪstɪk, -s
hemline, -s 'hemlaɪn, -z
hemlock, -s 'hemlɒk, -s
hemoglobin ,hiːməʊ'gləʊbɪn
hemorrhage, -s 'hemərɪdʒ, -ɪz
hemorrhoid, -s 'hemərɔɪd, -z
hemp, -en; -seed hemp, -ən; -siːd
Hemp(e)l 'hempl
hem-stitch (s. v.), -es, -ing, -ed 'hemstɪtʃ, -ɪz, -ɪŋ, -t
Hemy 'hemɪ
hen, -s; -bane hen, -z; -beɪn
hence hens
hence|forth, -forward ,hens|'fɔːθ, -'fɔːwəd
hench|man, -men 'hentʃ|mən, -mən
hen-coop, -s 'henkuːp, -s
hendecagon, -s hen'dekəgən, -z
hendecasyllabic, -s ,hendekəsɪ'læbɪk, -s
hendecasyllable, -s 'hendekə,sɪləbl, -z
Henderson 'hendəsn
hendiadys hen'daɪədɪs
Hendon 'hendən
Heneage 'henɪdʒ
Hengist 'hengɪst
Henley 'henlɪ
Henlopen hen'ləʊpən
henna 'henə
henner|y, -ies 'henər|ɪ, -ɪz
Henness(e)y 'henɪsɪ [-nəs-]
Henniker 'henɪkə*
Henning 'henɪŋ
henpeck, -s, -ing, -ed 'henpek, -s, -ɪŋ, -t

Henrietta ,henrɪ'etə
Henriques (English surname) hen'riːkɪz
hen-roost, -s 'henruːst, -s
Henry 'henrɪ
Hensen 'hensn
Hens|ley, -low(e) 'henz|lɪ, -ləʊ
Henson 'hensn
Henty 'hentɪ
hepatic hɪ'pætɪk [he'p-]
hepatica, -s hɪ'pætɪkə [he'p-], -z
hepatite 'hepətaɪt
hepatitis ,hepə'taɪtɪs
Hepburn 'hebɜːn ['hepb-, -bən]
Hephaestus hɪ'fiːstəs [he'f-]
Hephzibah 'hefsɪbə ['heps-]
heptachord, -s 'heptəkɔːd, -z
heptad, -s 'heptæd, -z
heptaglot 'heptəglɒt
heptagon, -s 'heptəgən, -z
heptagonal hep'tægənl
heptahedr|on, -ons, -a; -al ,heptə'he-dr|ən [-'hiːd-, 'heptə,h-], -ənz, -ə; -l
heptameron hep'tæmərən
heptarch, -s; -y, -ies 'heptɑːk, -s; -ɪ, -ɪz
Heptateuch 'heptətjuːk
Hepworth 'hepwɜːθ [-wəθ]
her hɜː* (normal form), ɜː*, hə*, ə* (freq. weak forms)
Heraclean ,herə'kliːən [-'klɪən]
Heracles 'herəkliːz ['hɪər-]
Heraclitus ,herə'klaɪtəs
herald (s. v.), -s, -ing, -ed; -ry 'herəld, -z, -ɪŋ, -ɪd; -rɪ
heraldic, -ally he'rældɪk [hɪ'r-, hə'r-], -əlɪ
Herapath (surname) 'herəpɑːθ
Herat he'ræt [hɪ'r-, hə'r-, -'rɑːt]
herb, -s; -age hɜːb, -z; -ɪdʒ
herbaceous hɜː'beɪʃəs [hə'b-]
herbal 'hɜːbl
herbalist, -s 'hɜːbəlɪst [-blɪst], -s
herbarium, -s hɜː'beərɪəm, -z
Herbert 'hɜːbət
herbivorous hɜː'bɪvərəs [hə'b-]
herborist, -s 'hɜːbərɪst, -s
herboriz|e -is|e, -es, -ing, -ed 'hɜː-bəraɪz, -ɪz, -ɪŋ, -d
Herculaneum ,hɜːkjʊ'leɪnjəm [-nɪəm]
herculean ,hɜːkjʊ'liːən [-'lɪən, hɜː-'kjuːljən, -'kjuːlɪən]
Hercules 'hɜːkjʊliːz
herd (s. v.) (H.), -s, -ing, -ed hɜːd, -z, -ɪŋ, -ɪd
Herdener 'hɜːdənə* [-dɪn-]
herd-instinct ,hɜːd'ɪnstɪŋkt ['-,--]
herds|man, -men 'hɜːdz|mən, -mən
here hɪə*

237

hereabouts 'hɪərə,baʊts [,—'-]
hereafter ,hɪər'ɑ:ftə*
hereby ,hɪə'baɪ [*also* '— *according to sentence-stress*]
hereditable hɪ'redɪtəbl [he'r-, hə'r-]
hereditament, -s ,herɪ'dɪtəmənt [-rə'd-, -tɪm-], -s
hereditar|y, -ily, -iness hɪ'redɪtər|ɪ [he'r-, hə'r-], -əlɪ [-ɪlɪ], -ɪnɪs [-məs]
heredity hɪ'redətɪ [he'r-, hə'r-, -ɪtɪ]
Hereford, -shire 'herɪfəd, -ʃə* [-,ʃɪə*]
herein ,hɪər'ɪn
hereinafter ,hɪərɪn'ɑ:ftə*
hereof ,hɪər'ɒv [-'ɒf]
hereon ,hɪər'ɒn
Herero, -s 'hɪərərəʊ [he'rɪərəʊ, hə'rɪərəʊ], -z
heresiarch, -s he'ri:zɪɑ:k, -s
heres|y, -ies 'herəs|ɪ [-rɪs-], -ɪz
heretic (*s. adj.*), -s 'herətɪk [-rɪt-], -s
heretic|al, -ly hɪ'retɪk|l [he'r-], -əlɪ
hereto ,hə'tu:
hеr▮▮▮▮▮▮ ▮▮▮▮▮▮▮▮▮▮ ▮ ▮▮▮▮*▮
h▮▮▮▮▮▮▮▮▮▮
hereunto ,hɪərʌn'tu:
hereupon ,hɪərə'pɒn
Hereward 'herɪwəd
herewith ,hɪə'wɪð [-'wɪθ]
Herford 'hɜ:fəd, 'hɑ:fəd
heriot, -s 'herɪət, -s
herit|able, -age/s, -or/s 'herɪt|əbl, -ɪdʒ/ɪz, -ə*/z
Herkomer, -s 'hɜ:kəmə*, -z
Herlichy 'hɜ:lɪkɪ
Herlihy 'hɜ:lɪhɪ
Herman 'hɜ:mən
hermaphrodite, -s hɜ:'mæfrədaɪt [-frʊd-], -s
Hermes 'hɜ:mi:z
hermetic, -al, -ally hɜ:'metɪk, -l, -əlɪ
Hermia 'hɜ:mjə [-mɪə]
Hermione hɜ:'maɪənɪ [hə'm-]
hermit, -s 'hɜ:mɪt, -s
hermitage (H.), -s 'hɜ:mɪtɪdʒ, -ɪz
hermit-crab, -s 'hɜ:mɪtkræb [,—'-], -z
hermitical 'hɜ:mɪtɪkl
Hermocrates hɜ:'mɒkrəti:z
Hermogenes hɜ:'mɒdʒɪni:z [-dʒən-]
Hermon 'hɜ:mən
hern, -s hɜ:n, -z
Herne hɜ:n
hernia, -l 'hɜ:njə [-nɪə], -l
hero (H.), -es 'hɪərəʊ, -z
Herod 'herəd
Herodian, -s he'rəʊdjən [hɪ'r-, hə'r-, -dɪən], -z
Herodias he'rəʊdɪæs [hɪ'r-, hə'r-]
Herodotus he'rɒdətəs [hɪ'r-, hə'r-]

heroic, -s, -al, -ally hɪ'rəʊɪk [he'r-, hə'r-], -s, -l, -əlɪ
heroin 'herəʊɪn
heroi|ne, -nes, -sm 'herəʊɪ|n, -nz, -zəm
heron (▮▮▮▮; -ry, -ries 'herən, -z; -rɪ, -rɪz
▮▮ro-worship 'hɪərəʊ,wɜ:ʃɪp
herpes 'hɜ:pi:z
Herr (*German title*) heə* (hɛr)
Herr|ick, -ies 'her|ɪk, -ɪs
herring (H.), -s; -bone/s, -pond/s 'herɪŋ, -z; -bəʊn/z, -pɒnd/s
Herrnhuter, -s 'heən,hu:tə* ['heərən-], -z
hers hɜ:z
Hersant 'hɜ:snt
Herschel(l) 'hɜ:ʃl
herself hɜ:'self [hə's-, *also* ɜ:'s-, ə's- *when not initial*]
Herstmonceux ,hɜ:stmən'sju: [-mɒn-, -'su:]
Hertford (*in England*), -shire 'hɑ:fəd ['hɑ:tf-], -ʃə* [-,ʃɪə*]
Hertford (*in U.S.A.*) 'hɜ:tfəd
Herts. hɑ:ts [hɜ:ts]
Hertslet 'hɜ:tslɪt
Hertz, -ian hɜ:ts [heə-], -ɪən [-jən]
Hervey 'hɑ:vɪ, 'hɜ:vɪ
Herzegovina ,heətsəgəʊ'vi:nə [,hɜ:ts-]
Herzog (*English surname*) 'hɜ:tsɒg
he's (= he is *or* he has) hi:z (*strong form*), hɪz, ɪz (*occasional weak forms*)
Hesba 'hezbə
Heseltine 'hesltaɪn
Hesiod 'hi:sɪɒd ['hes-, -jəd, -rəd]
hesitan|ce, -cy, -t/ly 'hezɪtən|s, -sɪ, -t/lɪ
hesitat|e, -es, -ing/ly, -ed 'hezɪteɪt, -s, -ɪŋ/lɪ, -ɪd
hesitation, -s ,hezɪ'teɪʃn, -z
Hesketh 'heskɪθ [-keθ, -kəθ]
Hesper 'hespə*
Hesperian he'spɪərɪən
Hesperides he'sperɪdi:z
Hesperus 'hespərəs
Hess|e, -en 'hes|ɪ ['hesə, hes], -n
hessian (H.), -s 'hesɪən [-sjən], -z
Hester 'hestə*
Hesychius he'sɪkɪəs
heteroclite (*s. adj.*), -s 'hetərəʊklaɪt, -s
heterodox, -y 'hetərəʊdɒks, -ɪ
heterodyne 'hetərəʊdaɪn
heterogeneity ,hetərəʊdʒɪ'ni:ɪtɪ [-dʒə'n-, -'ni:ɪtɪ, -'nɪətɪ]
heterogeneous, -ly, -ness ,hetərəʊ'dʒi:njəs [-'dʒen-, -nɪəs], -lɪ, -nɪs [-nəs]
heterogenesis ,hetərəʊ'dʒenɪsɪs [-'dʒenəsɪs]
heteronym|ous, -y ,hetə'rɒnɪm|əs, -ɪ

hetero-sexual ˌhetərəʊ'seksjʊəl [-sjwəl,
    -sjʊl, -ʃʊəl, -ʃwəl, -ʃʊl]
Hetherington 'heðərɪŋtən
Hetton-le-Hole ˌhetnlɪ'həʊl
Hetty 'hetɪ
Heugh (place) hjuːf, (surname) hjuː
heuristic hjʊə'rɪstɪk
Hever 'hiːvə*
hew, -s, -ing, -ed, -n, -er/s hjuː, -z, -ɪŋ
    ['hjuɪŋ], -d, -n, -ə*/z [hjʊə*/z]
Hew|ard, -art, -etson, -ett, -itt 'hjuː|əd
    [hjʊəd], -ət, -ɪtsn, -ɪt, -ɪt
Hewke hjuːk
Hew|lett, -son 'hjuː|lɪt, -sn
hexachord, -s 'heksəkɔːd, -z
hexagon, -s 'heksəgən, -z
hexagon|al, -ally hek'sægən|l, -əlɪ
hexahedr|on, -ons, -a; -al ˌheksə'he-
    dr|ən [-'hiːd-], 'heksə,h-], -ənz, -ə; -əl
Hexam 'heksəm
hexameter, -s hek'sæmɪtə* [-mətə*],
    -z
Hexateuch 'heksətjuːk
Hexham 'heksəm
hey heɪ
Heycock 'heɪkɒk
heyday 'heɪdeɪ
Heyno 'heɪnəʊ
Heysham 'hiːʃəm
Heytesbury 'heɪtsbərɪ
Heywood 'heɪwʊd
Hezekiah ˌhezɪ'kaɪə
Hezlewood 'hezlwʊd
hi haɪ
hiatus, -es haɪ'eɪtəs, -ɪz
Hiawatha ˌhaɪə'wɒθə
Hibbert 'hɪbət [-bɜːt]
hibernal haɪ'bɜːnl
hibernat|e, -es, -ing, -ed 'haɪbəneɪt, -s,
    -ɪŋ, -ɪd
hibernation, -s ˌhaɪbə'neɪʃn, -z
Hibernia haɪ'bɜːnjə [-nɪə]
Hibernian (s. adj.), -s (as ordinarily
    used) haɪ'bɜːnjən [-nɪən], (in name of
    football club) hɪ'bɜːnjən [-nɪən], -z
Hibernicism, -s haɪ'bɜːnɪsɪzəm, -z
hibiscus hɪ'bɪskəs
hiccup [-ough] (s. v.), -s, -ing, -ed
    'hɪkʌp, -s, -ɪŋ, -t
Hichens 'hɪtʃɪnz
Hickinbotham 'hɪkɪnbɒtəm
hickory (H.) 'hɪkərɪ
Hick|s, -son hɪk|s, -sn
hid (from hide) hɪd
hidalgo, -s hɪ'dælgəʊ, -z
hide (s.), -s haɪd, -z
hid|e (conceal), -es, -ing/s, hid, hidden
    haɪd, -z, -ɪŋ/z, hɪd, 'hɪdn

hid|e (beat), -es, -ing/s, -ed haɪd, -z,
    -ɪŋ/z, -ɪd
hidebound 'haɪdbaʊnd
hideous, -ly, -ness 'hɪdɪəs [-djəs], -lɪ,
    -nɪs [-nəs]
hiding-place, -s 'haɪdɪŋpleɪs, -ɪz
hie, -s, -ing, -d haɪ, -z, -ɪŋ, -d
Hierapolis ˌhaɪə'ræpəlɪs [-pʊl-]
hierarch, -s 'haɪərɑːk, -s
hierarchal ˌhaɪə'rɑːkl
hierarchic, -al, -ally ˌhaɪə'rɑːkɪk, -l, -əlɪ
hierarch|y, -ies 'haɪərɑːk|ɪ, -ɪz
hieratic ˌhaɪə'rætɪk
hieroglyph, -s ˌhaɪərəʊglɪf, -s
hieroglyphic (s. adj.), -s, -al, -ally
    ˌhaɪərəʊ'glɪfɪk, -s, -l, -əlɪ
Hieronymus ˌhaɪə'rɒnɪməs
hierophant, -s ˌhaɪərəʊfænt, -s
hi-fi ˌhaɪ'faɪ ['--]
Higginbotham 'hɪgɪnbɒtəm
Higgin|s, -son 'hɪgɪn|z, -sn
higg|le, -les, -ling, -led, -ler/s 'hɪg|l, -lz,
    -lɪŋ [-lɪŋ], -ld, -lə*/z [-lə*/z]
higgledy-piggledy ˌhɪgldɪ'pɪgldɪ
high, -er, -est haɪ, 'haɪə*, 'haɪɪst
Higham, -s 'haɪəm, -z
highborn 'haɪbɔːn
highbrow (s. adj.), -s 'haɪbraʊ, -z
high-chair, -s 'haɪtʃeə* [ˌ-'-], -z
high-church, -man, -men ˌhaɪ'tʃɜːtʃ,
    -mən, -mən [-men]
high-day, -s 'haɪdeɪ, -z
high-falut|in, -ing ˌhaɪfə'luːt|ɪn, -ɪŋ
highflier (-flyer), -s ˌhaɪ'flaɪə*, -z
highflown 'haɪfləʊn [ˌ-'-]
Highflyer 'haɪˌflaɪə*
high-frequency ˌhaɪ'friːkwənsɪ
Highgate 'haɪgɪt [-geɪt]
high-handed ˌhaɪ'hændɪd [also '-ˌ—
    when attributive]
highland (H.), -s; -er/s 'haɪlənd, -z;
    -ə*/z
high-level ˌhaɪ'levl [also '-ˌ— when
    attributive]
highlight (s. v.), -s, -ing, -ed 'haɪlaɪt, -s,
    -ɪŋ, -ɪd
highly (in a high manner, very) 'haɪlɪ
highly-strung ˌhaɪlɪ'strʌŋ
high-minded ˌhaɪ'maɪndɪd [also '-ˌ—
    according to sentence-stress]
high-mindedness ˌhaɪ'maɪndɪdnɪs [-nəs]
high-necked ˌhaɪ'nekt [also '— when
    attributive]
highness (quality of being high) 'haɪnɪs
    [-nəs]
Highness (title), -es 'haɪnɪs [-nəs], -ɪz
high-pitched ˌhaɪ'pɪtʃt [also '— when
    attributive]

high-pressure ˌhaɪˈpreʃə* [*also* '-,– *when attributive*]

high-priced ˌhaɪˈpraɪst [*also* '– *when attributive*]

high-priest, -s, -hood ˌhaɪˈpriːst, -s, -hʊd

high-principled ˌhaɪˈprɪnsəpld [-sɪp-]

high-rank|er/s, -ing 'haɪˌræŋk|ə*/z [ˌ-'--], -ɪŋ

high-road, -s 'haɪrəʊd, -z

high-school, -s 'haɪskuːl, -z

high-sounding 'haɪˌsaʊndɪŋ [*also* ˌ-'-- *when not attributive*]

high-spirited ˌhaɪˈspɪrɪtɪd

high-stepper, -s ˌhaɪˈstepə* ['-ˌ--], -z

high-stepping 'haɪˌstepɪŋ

High Street 'haɪstriːt

Highton 'haɪtn

high-toned ˌhaɪˈtəʊnd ['--]

high-up, -s 'haɪʌp [ˌ-'-], -s

high-water ˌhaɪˈwɔːtə*

high-water-mark, -s ˌhaɪˈwɔːtəmɑːk, -s

highway, -s 'haɪweɪ, -z

highway-code ˌhaɪweɪˈkəʊd ['--ˌ-]

highway|man, -men 'haɪweɪ|mən, -mən

hijack (*s. v.*), -s, -ing, -ed, -er/s 'haɪdʒæk, -s, -ɪŋ, -t, -ə*/z

hik|e, -es, -ing, -ed, -er/s haɪk, -s, -ɪŋ, -t, -ə*/z

Hilaire (*Belloc*) 'hɪleə* [-'-]

hilarious, -ly, -ness hɪˈleərɪəs, -lɪ, -nɪs [-nəs]

hilarity hɪˈlærətɪ [-ɪtɪ]

Hilary 'hɪlərɪ

Hilda 'hɪldə

Hildebrand 'hɪldəbrænd

Hildegard(e) 'hɪldəgɑːd

hill (H.), -s hɪl, -z

Hillary 'hɪlərɪ

Hillborn 'hɪlbɔːn

Hillel 'hɪlel [-ləl]

hill-folk 'hɪlfəʊk

Hillhead hɪlˈhed ['--]

Note.—The pronunciation in Scotland is with -'-.

Hilliard 'hɪlɪəd [-ljəd, -lɪɑːd, -ljɑːd]

Hillingdon 'hɪlɪŋdən

hill|man, -men 'hɪl|mæn, -men

Hillman, -s 'hɪlmən -z

hillock, -s 'hɪlək, -s

Hillsboro 'hɪlzbərə [-bʌrə]

Note.—The local pronunciation in U.S.A. is with -ˌbʌrəʊ.

Hillsborough 'hɪlzbərə

hill-side, -s hɪlˈsaɪd ['--], -z

Hillside ˌhɪlˈsaɪd ['--]

hill-top ˌhɪlˈtɒp ['--], -s

Hilltop (*name of road*) 'hɪltɒp

hill|y, -ier, -iest, -iness 'hɪl|ɪ, -ɪə*, -ɪɪst, -ɪnɪs [-nəs]

Hillyard 'hɪljəd [-jɑːd]

hilt, -s, -ed hɪlt, -s, -ɪd

Hilton 'hɪltən

hilum, -s 'haɪləm, -z

Hilversum 'hɪlvəsum [-səm]

him hɪm (*normal form*), ɪm (*freq. weak form*)

Himalaya, -s, -n ˌhɪmə'leɪə [*rarely* hɪˈmɑːləjə, hɪˈmɑːljə, hɪˈmɑːljə], (*Hindi* hɪmaləjə), -z, -n

himself hɪmˈself [*also* ɪm- *when not initial*]

Himyaritic ˌhɪmjəˈrɪtɪk [-mɪə-]

Hinchcliffe 'hɪntʃklɪf

Hinchliffe 'hɪntʃlɪf

Hinckley 'hɪŋklɪ

hind (s. adj.) (H.), -s haɪnd, -z

Hinde haɪnd

Hindemith 'hɪndəmɪt [-mɪθ]

hinder (adj.), -most 'haɪndə*, -məʊst

hind|er (v.), -ers, -ering, -ered, -erer/s 'hɪnd|ə*, -əz, -ərɪŋ, -əd, -ərə*/z

Hinderwell 'hɪndəwel [-wəl]

Hindi 'hɪndi: (*Hindi* hɪndi)

Hindle 'hɪndl

Hindley (*surname*) 'haɪndlɪ, 'hɪndlɪ, (*town in Greater Manchester*) 'hɪndlɪ

Hindlip 'hɪndlɪp

hindmost 'haɪndməʊst

hind-quarters ˌhaɪndˈkwɔːtəz ['-ˌ--]

hindrance, -s 'hɪndrəns, -ɪz

hindsight 'haɪndsaɪt

Hindu [-doo], -s ˌhɪnˈduː [*also* 'hɪnduː *when attributive*], -z

Hinduism 'hɪnduːɪzəm [-dʊɪzəm, -'---]

Hindu-Kush ˌhɪnduːˈkuːʃ [-'kʊʃ]

Hindustan ˌhɪnduːˈstɑːn [-ˈstæn]

Hindustani ˌhɪnduːˈstɑːnɪ [-ˈstænɪ]

hing|e (s. v.), -es, -ing, -ed hɪndʒ, -ɪz, -ɪŋ, -d

Hingston 'hɪŋkstən

Hinkson 'hɪŋksn

hint (s. v.), -s, -ing, -ed hɪnt, -s, -ɪŋ, -ɪd

hinterland 'hɪntəlænd

Hinton 'hɪntən

Hiorns 'haɪənz

hip (s. v.), -s, -ping, -ped hɪp, -s, -ɪŋ, -t

hip-ba|th, -ths 'hɪpbɑː|θ, -ðz

hip-bone, -s 'hɪpbəʊn, -z

hip-joint, -s 'hɪpdʒɔɪnt, -s

Hipparchus hɪˈpɑːkəs

hipped hɪpt

hippety-hop, -pety ˌhɪpətɪˈhɒp, -ətɪ

Hippias 'hɪpɪæs

hippie, -s 'hɪpɪ, -z

hippish 'hɪpɪʃ

hippo, -s 'hɪpəʊ, -z
Hippocrates hɪ'pɒkrəti:z
hippocratic ˌhɪpəʊ'krætɪk
Hippocrene ˌhɪpəʊ'kri:ni: [-'kri:nɪ, *also in poetry* 'hɪpəʊkri:n]
Hippodamia ˌhɪpəʊdə'maɪə
hippodrome (H.), -s 'hɪpədrəʊm, -z
Hippolyt|a, -e, -us hɪ'pɒlɪt|ə, -i:, -əs
hippopotam|us, -uses, -i ˌhɪpə'pɒtəm|əs, -əsɪz, -aɪ
Hiram (*biblical name*) 'haɪərəm [-ræm], (*modern personal name*) 'haɪərəm, (*town in U.S.A.*) 'haɪərəm
hircine 'hɜ:saɪn
Hird hɜ:d
hir|e (*s. v.*), -es, -ing, -ed, -er/s; -eling/s 'haɪə*, -z, -rɪŋ, -d, -rə*/z; -lɪŋ/z
Hiroshima hɪ'rɒʃɪmə [ˌhɪrɒ'ʃi:mə]
Hirst hɜ:st
hirsute 'hɜ:sju:t
his hɪz (*normal form*), ɪz (*freq. weak form*)
hispanic hɪ'spænɪk
hispanist, -s 'hɪspənɪst [-pæn-], -s
hiss (*s. v.*), -es, -ing, -ed, -er/s hɪs, -ɪz, -ɪŋ, -t, -ə*/z
hist s:t [hɪst]
histamine 'hɪstəmi:n [-mɪn]
histologic|al, -ally ˌhɪstə'lɒdʒɪk|l, -əlɪ
histolog|ist/s, -y hɪ'stɒlədʒ|ɪst/s, -ɪ
historian, -s hɪ'stɔ:rɪən [*also occasionally* ɪs- *when not initial, with* ən *as preceding indefinite article*], -z
historic, -al, -ally hɪ'stɒrɪk [*also occasionally* ɪs- *when not initial, with* ən *as preceding indefinite article*], -l, -əlɪ
historiograph|er/s, -y ˌhɪstɔ:rɪ-'ɒgrəf|ə*/z [hɪˌstɔ:r-, ˌhɪstɒr-, hɪˌstɒr-], -ɪ
histor|y, -ies 'hɪstər|ɪ, -ɪz
Histriomastix ˌhɪstrɪəʊ'mæstɪks
histrionic, -al, -ally ˌhɪstrɪ'ɒnɪk, -l, -əlɪ
histrionism 'hɪstrɪənɪzəm
hit (*s. v.*), -s, -ting, -ter/s hɪt, -s, -ɪŋ, -ə*/z
hitch (*s. v.*), -es, -ing, -ed hɪtʃ, -ɪz, -ɪŋ, -t
Hitch|cock, -ens 'hɪtʃ|kɒk, -ɪnz
hitch-hik|e, -es, -ing, -ed, -er/s 'hɪtʃhaɪk, -s, -ɪŋ, -t, -ə*/z
Hitchin, -s 'hɪtʃɪn, -z
hither (H.) 'hɪðə*
hitherto ˌhɪðə'tu: [*also* '— *according to sentence-stress*]
Hitler (*German name*) 'hɪtlə* ('hitlər)
Hitlerian hɪt'lɪərɪən
Hitlerite, -s 'hɪtləraɪt, -s
Hittite, -s 'hɪtaɪt, -s

hiv|e (*s. v.*), -es, -ing, -ed haɪv, -z, -ɪŋ, -d
hives (*disease*) haɪvz
Hivite, -s 'haɪvaɪt, -s
ho həʊ
Hoadl(e)y 'həʊdlɪ
Hoangho ˌhəʊæŋ'həʊ
hoar (H.) hɔ:* [hɔə*]
hoard (*s. v.*), -s, -ing, -ed, -er/s hɔ:d [hɔəd], -z, -ɪŋ, -ɪd, -ə*/z
hoarding (*s.*), -s 'hɔ:dɪŋ ['hɔəd-], -z
Hoare hɔ:* [hɔə*]
hoar-frost, -s ˌhɔ:'frɒst [ˌhɔə'f-, *old-fashioned* -'frɔ:st, '—], -s
hoarse, -r, -st, -ly, -ness hɔ:s [hɔəs], -ə*, -ɪst, -lɪ, -nɪs [-nəs]
hoar|y, -ier, -iest, -ily, -iness 'hɔ:r|ɪ ['hɔər-], -ɪə*, -ɪɪst, -əlɪ [-ɪlɪ], -ɪnɪs [-ɪnəs]
hoax (*s. v.*), -es, -ing, -ed, -er/s həʊks, -ɪz, -ɪŋ, -t, -ə*/z
hob, -s hɒb, -z
Hobart 'həʊbɑ:t
hobbadehoy, -s ˌhɒbədɪ'hɔɪ, -z
Hobbema, -s 'hɒbɪmə, -z
Hobbes hɒbz
hobb|le (*s. v.*), -les, -ling, -led, -ler/s 'hɒb|l, -lz, -lɪŋ [-lɪŋ], -ld, -lə*/z [-lə*/z]
hobbledehoy, -s ˌhɒbldɪ'hɔɪ, -z
Hobbs hɒbz
hobb|y, -ies 'hɒb|ɪ, -ɪz
hobby-horse, -s 'hɒbɪhɔ:s, -ɪz
Hobday 'hɒbdeɪ
hobgoblin, -s 'hɒbgɒblɪn [ˌ-'—'], -z
Hobhouse 'hɒbhaʊs
hobnail, -s, -ed 'hɒbneɪl, -z, -d
hobnob (*s. v.*), -s, -bing, -bed 'hɒbnɒb [ˌ-'—'], -z, -ɪŋ, -d
hobo, -s 'həʊbəʊ, -z
Hoboken 'həʊbəʊkən [-bək-]
Hobson 'hɒbsn
Hoby 'həʊbɪ
Hoccleve 'hɒkli:v
hochheimer 'hɒkhaɪmə* ['hɒxh-]
hock, -s hɒk, -s
hockey 'hɒkɪ
hockey-stick, -s 'hɒkɪstɪk, -s
Hock|in, -ing 'hɒk|ɪn, -ɪŋ
hocus-pocus ˌhəʊkəs'pəʊkəs
hod, -s hɒd, -z
Hodd|er, -esdon 'hɒd|ə*, -zdən
hodge (H.), -s hɒdʒ, -ɪz
hodge-podge 'hɒdʒpɒdʒ
Hodg|es, -kin/son 'hɒdʒ|ɪz, -kɪn/sn
Hodgson 'hɒdʒsn, *in N. of England also* 'hɒdʒən
hod|man, -men 'hɒd|mən, -mən [-men]
hodograph, -s 'hɒdəʊgrɑ:f [-græf], -s

hodometer, -s hɒˈdɒmɪtə* [-mətə*], -z
Hodson ˈhɒdsn
hoe (s. v.), -s, -ing, -d, -r/s həʊ, -z, -ɪŋ, -d, -ə*/z
Hoe həʊ
Hoey hɔɪ, ˈhəʊɪ
hog, -s hɒg, -z
Hogan ˈhəʊgən
Hogarth ˈhəʊgɑːθ
Hogarthian həʊˈgɑːθjən [-θɪən]
Hogben ˈhɒgbən [-ben]
Hogg hɒg
hogger|y, -ies ˈhɒgər|ɪ, -ɪz
hogget (H.), -s ˈhɒgɪt, -s
hoggish, -ly, -ness ˈhɒgɪʃ, -lɪ, -nɪs [-nəs]
hogmanay ˈhɒgməneɪ [ˌ—ˈ-]
hogshead, -s ˈhɒgzhed, -z
Hogue həʊg
Hohenlinden ˌhəʊənˈlɪndən
Hohenzollern, -s ˌhəʊənˈzɒlən [ˌhəʊm-] (ˌho:ənˈtsɔlern), -z
hoik, -s, -ing, -ed hɔɪk, -s, -ɪŋ, -t
hoi polloi ˌhɔɪˈpɒlɔɪ [ˌ—ˈ-]
hoist (s. v.), -s, -ing, -ed hɔɪst, -s, -ɪŋ, -ɪd
hoity-toity ˌhɔɪtɪˈtɔɪtɪ
hok(e)y-pok(e)y ˌhəʊkɪˈpəʊkɪ
hokum ˈhəʊkəm
Holbech ˈhəʊlbiːtʃ
Holbeck ˈhɒlbek
Holbein, -s ˈhɒlbaɪn, -z
Holborn (in London) ˈhəʊbən [ˈhəʊlb-]
Holbrook(e) ˈhəʊlbrʊk, ˈhɒl-
Holburn (near Aberdeen) ˈhɒlˈbɜːn [ˈhəʊl-]
Holcroft ˈhəʊlkrɒft
hold (s. v.), -s, -ing, held, holder/s həʊld, -z, -ɪŋ, held, ˈhəʊldə*/z
hold-all, -s ˈhəʊldɔːl, -z
Holden ˈhəʊldən
Holder ˈhəʊldə*
Holdfast, -s ˈhəʊldfɑːst, -s
holding (s.), -s ˈhəʊldɪŋ, -z
Holdsworth ˈhəʊldzwɜːθ [-wəθ]
hold-up, -s ˈhəʊldʌp, -s
hol|e (s. v.) (H.), -es, -ing, -ed həʊl, -z, -ɪŋ, -d
hole-and-corner ˌhəʊlənd'kɔːnə*
Holford ˈhəʊlfəd
holiday, -s ˈhɒlədɪ [-lɪd-, -deɪ], -z
Holiday ˈhɒlɪdeɪ
holiday-maker, -s ˈhɒlədɪˌmeɪkə* [-lɪd-, -deɪ-], -z
Holies ˈhəʊlɪz
Holifield ˈhɒlɪfiːld
Holinshed ˈhɒlɪnʃed
holism ˈhɒlɪzm [ˈhəʊ-]

Holkam ˈhəʊkəm
holland (H.), -s ˈhɒlənd, -z
hollandaise ˌhɒlənˈdeɪz [also ˈ— when attributive]
Hollander, -s ˈhɒləndə*, -z
hollands ˈhɒləndz
Holles ˈhɒlɪs
Hollingsworth ˈhɒlɪŋzwɜːθ [-wəθ]
Hollins ˈhɒlɪnz
holl|o, -oes, -oing, -oed ˈhɒl|əʊ, -əʊz, -əʊɪŋ, -əʊd
Hollom ˈhɒləm
holl|ow (s. adj. v.), -ows; -ower, -owest, -owly, -owness; -owing, -owed ˈhɒl|əʊ, -əʊz; -əʊə*, -əʊɪst, -əʊlɪ, -əʊnɪs [-nəs]; -əʊɪŋ, -əʊd
Holloway ˈhɒləweɪ [-lʊw-]
hollow-eyed ˈhɒləʊaɪd [ˌ—ˈ-]
holl|y (H.), -ies ˈhɒl|ɪ, -ɪz
hollyhock, -s ˈhɒlɪhɒk, -s
Hollywood ˈhɒlɪwʊd
holm (H.), -s həʊm, -z
Holman ˈhəʊlmən
Holmby ˈhəʊmbɪ
Holmer ˈhəʊlmə*
Holmes, -dale həʊmz, -deɪl
holm-oak, -s ˌhəʊmˈəʊk [ˈ—], -s
holocaust, -s ˈhɒləkɔːst, -s
Holofernes ˌhɒləʊˈfɜːniːz
hologram, -s ˈhɒləʊgræm, -z
holograph, -s ˈhɒləʊgrɑːf [-græf], -s
holography hɒˈlɒgrəfɪ
holpen (archaic p. partic. of help) ˈhəʊlpən, ˈhɒlpən
Holroyd ˈhɒlrɔɪd
Holst (Gustav Holst, musical composer) həʊlst
Holstein ˈhɒlstaɪn
holster, -s, -ed ˈhəʊlstə*, -z, -d
holt (H.), -s həʊlt, -s
Holtby ˈhəʊltbɪ
Holtham (surname) ˈhəʊlθəm, ˈhɒlθəm, ˈhəʊθəm
holus-bolus ˌhəʊləsˈbəʊləs
hol|y (H.), -ier, -iest, -iness ˈhəʊl|ɪ, -ɪə* [-jə*], -ɪɪst [-jɪst], -ɪnɪs [-nəs]
Holycross ˈhəʊlɪkrɒs [old-fashioned -krɔːs]
Holyhead ˈhɒlɪhed
Holyoake ˈhəʊlɪəʊk
Holyrood ˈhɒlɪruːd
holyston|e (s. v.), -es, -ing, -ed ˈhəʊlɪstəʊn, -z, -ɪŋ, -d
Holy-week ˈhəʊlɪwiːk
Holywell ˈhɒlɪwəl [-wel]
homage; -r/s ˈhɒmɪdʒ; -ə*/z
homburg (H.), -s ˈhɒmbɜːg, -z
home (s. adv.), -s həʊm, -z

242

Home həʊm, hju:m
Note.—hju:m *in* **Milne-Home,
Douglas-Home,** *and the* **Earl of
Home.**
home-bred ˌhəʊm'bred [*also* '— *when
attributive*]
home-brewed ˌhəʊm'bru:d [*also* '—
when attributive]
home-coming, -s 'həʊmˌkʌmɪŋ, -z
home-grown ˌhəʊm'grəʊn [*also* '—
when attributive]
homeland (H.), -s 'həʊmlænd, -z
homeless, -ness 'həʊmlɪs [-ləs], -nɪs
[-nəs]
homelike 'həʊmlaɪk
homel|y, -ier, -iest, -iness 'həʊml|ɪ, -ɪə*,
-ɪɪst, -ɪnɪs [-məs]
home-made ˌhəʊm'meɪd [*also* '— *when
attributive*]
Homer 'həʊmə*
Homeric (*relating to Homer*) həʊ'merɪk,
(*name of ship*) 'həʊmərɪk
Homerton 'hɒmətən
homesick, -ness 'həʊmsɪk, -nɪs [-nəs]
homespun, -s 'həʊmspʌn, -z
homestead, -s 'həʊmsted [-stɪd], -z
home-thrust, -s ˌhəʊm'θrʌst, -s
homeward, -s 'həʊmwəd, -z
homework 'həʊmwɜ:k
Homfray 'hʌmfrɪ
homicidal ˌhɒmɪ'saɪdl ['——, *esp. when
attributive*]
homicide, -s 'hɒmɪsaɪd, -z
Homildon 'hɒmɪldən
homil|y, -ies 'hɒmɪl|ɪ [-əl|ɪ], -ɪz
hominoid, -s 'hɒmɪnɔɪd, -z
hominy 'hɒmɪnɪ [-mənɪ]
homo 'həʊməʊ
homoeopath, -s 'həʊmjəʊpæθ ['hɒm-,
-mɪəp-], -s
homoeopathic, -al, -ally ˌhəʊmjəʊ-
'pæθɪk [ˌhɒm-, -mɪəʊ'p-], -l, -əlɪ
homoeopath|ist/s, -y ˌhəʊmɪ'ɒpəθ|ɪst/s
[ˌhɒm-], -ɪ
homogeneity ˌhɒməʊdʒe'ni:ɪtɪ [ˌhəʊm-,
-dʒə'n-, -dʒɪ'n-, -'ni:ɪtɪ, -'nɪeɪtɪ
homogeneous, -ly, -ness ˌhɒməʊ'dʒi:-
njəs [ˌhəʊm-, -'dʒen-, -nɪəs], -lɪ, -nɪs
[-nəs]
homogenize, -d hɒ'mɒdʒənaɪz [hə-], -d
homograph, -s 'hɒməʊgrɑːf [-græf], -s
homographic ˌhɒməʊ'græfɪk [ˌhəʊm-]
homologous hɒ'mɒləgəs [hə-'m-]
homologue, -s 'hɒmələg, -z
homology hɒ'mɒlədʒɪ [həʊ'm-]
homonym, -s 'hɒməʊnɪm, -z
homonymous, -ly hɒ'mɒnɪməs
[həʊ'm-], -lɪ

homonymy hɒ'mɒnɪmɪ [həʊ'm-,
-nəmɪ]
homophone, -s 'hɒməʊfəʊn, -z
homophon|ous, -y hɒ'mɒfən|əs
[həʊ'm-], -ɪ
homorganic ˌhɒmɔː'gænɪk [ˌhəʊ-]
homosexual, -ist/s ˌhɒməʊ'seksjʊəl
[ˌhəʊm-, -ksjwəl, -ksjʊl, -kʃʊəl,
-kʃwəl, -kʃʊl], -ɪst/s
homosexuality ˌhɒməʊseksjʊ'ælətɪ
['həʊm-, -kʃʊ-, -ɪtɪ]
hon. (H.) (*son of a peer, etc.*) 'ɒnərəbl,
(*without salary*) 'ɒnərərɪ
Honda 'hɒndə
Hondur|as, -an/s hɒn'djʊər|əs [-r|æs],
-ən/z
hon|e (*s. v.*) (H.), -es, -ing, -ed həʊn,
-z, -ɪŋ, -d
honest, -ly; -y 'ɒnɪst, -lɪ; -ɪ ['ɒnəstɪ]
honey, -ed 'hʌnɪ, -d
honey-bag, -s 'hʌnɪbæg, -z
honey-bee, -s 'hʌnɪbiː, -z
Honeybourne 'hʌnɪbɔːn [-bəən,
-ˌbʊən]
honeycomb (H.), -s, -ed 'hʌnɪkəʊm, -z,
-d
honeydew 'hʌnɪdjuː
honey-guide, -s 'hʌnɪgaɪd, -z
honeymoon, -s 'hʌnɪmuːn, -z
honeysucker, -s 'hʌnɪˌsʌkə*, -z
honeysuckle, -s 'hʌnɪsʌkl, -z
Hong Kong ˌhɒŋ'kɒŋ
Honiton 'hɒnɪtn [*locally* 'hʌn-]
Honolulu ˌhɒnə'luːlu:
Honor 'ɒnə*
honorarium, -s ˌɒnə'reərɪəm [-'rɑːr-],
-z
honorary 'ɒnərərɪ
honorific (*s. adj.*), -s ˌɒnə'rɪfɪk, -s
Honorius hɒ'nɔːrɪəs [hɒ'n-]
honour (*s. v.*), -s, -ing, -ed 'ɒnə*, -z,
-rɪŋ, -d
honourab|le, -ly, -leness 'ɒnərəb|l, -lɪ,
-lnɪs [-nəs]
honours|-man, -men 'ɒnəz|mæn, -men
Honyman 'hʌnɪmən
hood (*s. v.*) (H.), -s, -ing, -ed; -less
hʊd, -z, -ɪŋ, -ɪd; -lɪs [-ləs]
hoodlum, -s 'huːdləm, -z
hoodwink, -s -ing, -ed 'hʊdwɪŋk, -s,
-ɪŋ, -t [-wɪŋt]
hoo|f (*s.*), -fs, -ves huː|f, -fs, -vz
hoof (*v.*), -s, -ing, -ed huːf, -s, -ɪŋ, -t
Hoog(h)ly 'huːglɪ
hook (*s. v.*) (H.), -s, -ing, -ed, -er/s
hʊk, -s, -ɪŋ, -t, -ə*/z
hookah, -s 'hʊkə [-kɑː], -z
Hooke, -r hʊk, -ə*

243

hook-nosed 'hʊknəʊzd
hook-up, -s 'hʊkʌp, -s
Hooley 'huːlɪ
hooligan (H.), -s 'huːlɪgən, -z
hoop (s. v.), -s, -ing, -ed huːp, -s, -ɪŋ, -t
hooper (H.), -s 'huːpə*, -z
hooping-cough 'huːpɪŋkɒf [old-fashioned -kɔːf]
hoop-la 'huːplɑː ['hʊp-]
hoopoe, -s 'huːpuː:, -z
hooray hʊ'reɪ
hoot (s. v.), -s, -ing, -ed huːt, -s, -ɪŋ, -ɪd
hooter, -s 'huːtə*, -z
hoover (s. v.) (H.), -s, -ing, -ed 'huːvə*, -z, -rɪŋ, -d
hooves (from hoof) huːvz
hop (s. v.), -s, -ping, -ped, -per/s hɒp, -s, -ɪŋ, -t, -ə*/z
Hopcraft 'hɒpkrɑːft
hop|e (s. v.) (H.), -es, -ing, -ed həʊp, -s, -ɪŋ, -t
hope|ful (H.), -fully, -fulness 'həʊp|-fʊl, -fʊlɪ [-fəlɪ], -fʊlnɪs [-nəs]
hopeless, -ly, -ness 'həʊplɪs [-ləs], -lɪ, -nɪs [-nəs]
Hopetoun 'həʊptən, -taʊn
hop-field, -s 'hɒpfiːld, -z
Hopkin|s, -son 'hɒpkɪn|z, -sn
hoplite, -s 'hɒplaɪt, -s
hop-manure 'hɒpmə,njʊə* [-,njɔː*]
Hop-o'-my-thumb ,hɒpəmɪ'θʌm ['----]
hop-pick|er/s, -ing 'hɒp,pɪk|ə*/z, -ɪŋ
Hoppner, -s 'hɒpnə*, -z
hopscotch 'hɒpskɒtʃ
Hopton 'hɒptən
hop-vine, -s 'hɒpvaɪn, -z
Hor hɔː*
Horace 'hɒrəs [-rɪs]
Horatian hə'reɪʃjən [hɒ'r-, -ʃɪən, -ʃn]
Horatio hə'reɪʃɪəʊ [hɒ'r-, -ʃjəʊ]
Hora|tius, -tii hə'reɪ|ʃjəs [hɒ'r-, -ʃɪəs, -ʃəs], -ʃɪaɪ
Horbury 'hɔːbərɪ
horde, -s hɔːd, -z
Horeb 'hɔːreb
horehound 'hɔːhaʊnd ['hɒəh-]
horizon, -s hə'raɪzn [hʊ'r-, also occasionally ə'r-, ʊ'r- when not initial, with ən as preceding indefinite article], -z
horizont|al, -ally ,hɒrɪ'zɒnt|l, -əlɪ [-lɪ]
Horlick 'hɔːlɪk
hormone, -s 'hɔːməʊn, -z
horn (H.), -s hɔːn, -z
hornbeam, -s 'hɔːnbiːm, -z
hornbill, -s 'hɔːnbɪl, -z
hornblende 'hɔːnblend
hornbook, -s 'hɔːnbʊk, -s

Horncastle 'hɔːn,kɑːsl
Horne hɔːn
horned (poppy) 'hɔːnɪd [-nd], (of cattle, birds, etc.) hɔːnd, (poetically, as in horned moon) 'hɔːnɪd
-horned -hɔːnd
Hornell hɔː'nel
Horner 'hɔːnə*
hornet, -s 'hɔːnɪt, -s
Horniman 'hɔːnɪmən
hornpipe, -s 'hɔːnpaɪp, -s
Hornsey 'hɔːnzɪ
hornwork, -s 'hɔːnwɜːk, -s
horn|y, -ier, -iest, -iness 'hɔːn|ɪ, -ɪə* [-jə*], -ɪɪst [-jɪst], -ɪnɪs [-ɪnəs]
horny-handed 'hɔːnɪ,hændɪd [,--'--]
horography hɒ'rɒgrəfɪ [hɔː'r-]
horologe, -s 'hɒrəlɒdʒ ['hɔːr-, -ləʊdʒ], -ɪz
horolog|er/s, -ist/s, -y hɒ'rɒlədʒ|ə*/z [hɔː'r-], -ɪst/s, -ɪ
horological ,hɒrə'lɒdʒɪkl [,hɔːr-]
horoscope, -s 'hɒrəskəʊp, -s
horoscopic ,hɒrə'skɒpɪk
horoscop|ist/s, -y hɒ'rɒskəp|ɪst/s [hə'r-], -ɪ
Horowitz 'hɒrəvɪts
horrib|le, -ly, -leness 'hɒrəb|l [-rɪb-], -lɪ, -lnɪs [-nəs]
horrid, -er, -est, -ly, -ness 'hɒrɪd, -ə*, -ɪst, -lɪ, -nɪs [-nəs]
horrific hɒ'rɪfɪk [hə-]
horri|fy, -fies, -fying, -fied 'hɒrɪ|faɪ, -faɪz, -faɪɪŋ, -faɪd
Horrocks, -es 'hɒrəks, -ɪz
horror, -s 'hɒrə*, -z
horror|-stricken, -struck 'hɒrə|,strɪkən, -strʌk
Horsa 'hɔːsə
hors de combat ,hɔːdə'kɔ̃ːmbɑː [-'kɔːm-, -'kɒm-] (ɔrdəkɔ̃ba)
hors-d'œuvre, -s ɔː'dɜːvrə [hɔː'd-, ,-'-] (ɔrdœːvr), -z
horse, -s, -d hɔːs, -ɪz, -t
horseback 'hɔːsbæk
horse-block, -s 'hɔːsblɒk, -s
horse-box, -es 'hɔːsbɒks, -ɪz
horsebreaker, -s 'hɔːs,breɪkə*, -z
horse-bus, -es 'hɔːsbʌs, -ɪz
horse-chestnut, -s ,hɔːs'tʃesnʌt [-nət, -stn-], -s
horse|-cloth, -cloths 'hɔːs|klɒθ [old-fashioned -klɔːθ], -klɒθs [-klɔːðz, -klɒːθs]
horse-dealer, -s 'hɔːs,diːlə*, -z
horse-doctor, -s 'hɔːs,dɒktə*, -z
horseflesh 'hɔːsfleʃ
horsefl|y, -ies 'hɔːsfl|aɪ, -aɪz

Horse-guard, -s 'hɔːsgɑːd [ˌ-'-], -z
horse|-hair, -laugh/s 'hɔːs|heə*, -lɑːf/s
horse|man (H.), -men; -manship
'hɔːs|mən, -mən [-men]; -mənʃɪp
horse-marine, -s 'hɔːsməˌriːn, -z
horseplay 'hɔːspleɪ
horse-pond, -s 'hɔːspɒnd, -z
horse-power 'hɔːsˌpaʊə*
horse-rac|e, -es, -ing 'hɔːsreɪs, -ɪz, -ɪŋ
horse-radish, -es 'hɔːsˌrædɪʃ [ˌ-'--], -ɪz
horse-sense 'hɔːssens
horse-shoe, -s 'hɔːʃʃuː ['hɔːsʃuː], -z
horse-show, -s 'hɔːʃʃəʊ ['hɔːs-], -z
horse-train|er/s, -ing 'hɔːsˌtreɪn|ə*/z, -ɪŋ
horse-truck, -s 'hɔːstrʌk, -s
horse-whip (s. v.), -s, -ping, -ped 'hɔːswɪp ['hɔːshw-], -s, -ɪŋ, -t
horse|-woman, -women 'hɔːs|ˌwʊmən, -ˌwɪmɪn
Horsfall 'hɔːsfɔːl
Horsham 'hɔːʃəm
Horsley (surname, place-name) 'hɔːzlɪ, 'hɔːslɪ
Horsmonden (in Kent) ˌhɔːsmən'den [old-fashioned local pronunciation ˌhɔːsn'den]
hors|y, -ier, -iest, -ily, -iness 'hɔːs|ɪ, -ɪə* [-jə*], -ɪɪst [-jɪst], -ɪlɪ [-əlɪ], -ɪnɪs [-ɪnəs]
hortat|ive, -ory 'hɔːtət|ɪv, -ərɪ
Hortensi|a, -us hɔː'tensɪ|ə [-nsj|ə,-nʃɪ|ə, -nʃj|ə], -əs
horticultur|al, -ist/s ˌhɔːtɪ'kʌltʃər|əl [-tʃʊr-], -ɪst/s
horticulture 'hɔːtɪkʌltʃə*
Horton 'hɔːtn
Horwich 'hɒrɪtʃ
Hosack 'hɒsək
hosanna, -s həʊ'zænə, -z
hose, -s həʊz, -ɪz
Hosea həʊ'zɪə
hose-pipe, -s 'həʊzpaɪp, -s
hosier, -s, -y 'həʊzɪə [-zjə*, -ʒə*, -ʒjə*, -ʒɪə*], -z, -rɪ
Hosier (surname) 'həʊzjə* [-zɪə*]
Hosmer 'hɒzmə*
hospice, -s 'hɒspɪs, -ɪz
hospitab|le, -ly, -leness 'hɒspɪtəb|l [hɒ'spɪt-, həs-], -lɪ, -lnɪs [-nəs]
hospital, -s 'hɒspɪtl, -z
hospitalit|y, -ies ˌhɒspɪ'tælət|ɪ [-ɪt|ɪ], -ɪz
hospital(l)er, -s 'hɒspɪtlə* [-tələ*], -z
host (H.), -s həʊst, -s
hostage, -s 'hɒstɪdʒ, -ɪz
hostel, -s; -ry, -ries 'hɒstl, -z; -rɪ, -rɪz
hosteller, -s 'hɒstələ*, -z
hostess, -es 'həʊstɪs [-tes], -ɪz

hostile, -ly 'hɒstaɪl, -lɪ
hostilit|y, -ies hɒ'stɪlət|ɪ [-lɪt-], -ɪz
hostler, -s 'ɒslə*, -z
hot (adj. v.), -ter, -test, -ly, -ness; -s, -ting, -ted hɒt, -ə*, -ɪst, -lɪ, -nɪs [-nəs]; -s, -ɪŋ, -ɪd
hotbed, -s 'hɒtbed, -z
hot-blooded ˌhɒt'blʌdɪd ['-ˌ--]
Hotchkiss 'hɒtʃkɪs
hotch|pot, -potch 'hɒtʃ|pɒt, -pɒtʃ
hot-dog, -s ˌhɒt'dɒg, -z
hotel, -s həʊ'tel [əʊ't-], -z
Note.—Some use the form əʊ'tel always; others use it occasionally when the word is not initial, with ən as preceding indefinite article.
hotelier, -s həʊ'telɪeɪ [-lɪə*], -z
Hotham (surname) 'hʌðəm
hothead, -s 'hɒthed, -z
hot-headed ˌhɒt'hedɪd ['-ˌ--]
hothou|se, -ses 'hɒthaʊ|s, -zɪz
hotpot, -s 'hɒtpɒt, -s
hotspur (H.), -s 'hɒtspɜː* [-spə*], -z
Hottentot, -s 'hɒtntɒt, -s
hot-water-bottle, -s ˌhɒt'wɔːtəˌbɒtl, -z
Houdini huː'diːnɪ
hough (s. v.), -s, -ing, -ed hɒk, -s, -ɪŋ, -t
Hough hʌf, hɒf
Houghall (in Durham) 'hɒfl
Hougham (in Kent) 'hʌfəm
Houghton 'hɔːtn, 'haʊtn, 'həʊtn
Note.—'hɔːtn, 'haʊtn seem more usual when the word is a surname.
Houghton-le-Spring ˌhəʊtnlɪ'sprɪŋ [ˌhaʊtn-]
Houltby 'həʊltbɪ
hound (s. v.), -s, -ing, -ed haʊnd, -z, -ɪŋ, -ɪd
Houndsditch 'haʊndzdɪtʃ
Hounslow 'haʊnzləʊ
hour, -s, -ly 'aʊə*, -z, -lɪ
hourglass, -es 'aʊəglɑːs, -ɪz
hour-hand, -s 'aʊəhænd, -z
houri, -s 'hʊərɪ, -z
hou|se (s.) (H.), -ses haʊ|s, -zɪz
hous|e (v.), -es, -ing, -ed haʊz, -ɪz, -ɪŋ, -d
house|-agent/s, -boat/s 'haʊs|ˌeɪdʒ-ənt/s, -bəʊt/s
house-break|er/s, -ing 'haʊsˌbreɪk|ə*/z, -ɪŋ
house-dog, -s 'haʊsdɒg, -z
house-dut|y, -ies 'haʊsˌdjuːt|ɪ, -ɪz
house-fl|y, -ies 'haʊsfl|aɪ, -aɪz
houseful, -s 'haʊsfʊl, -z
household, -s; -er/s 'haʊshəʊld, -z; -ə*/z

housekeep|er/s, -ing 'haʊsˌkiːp|ə*/z, -ɪŋ

Housel 'haʊzl

house-leek, -s 'haʊsliːk, -s

houseless 'haʊslɪs [-ləs]

housemaid, -s 'haʊsmeɪd, -z

house|man, -men 'haʊsmən [-mæn], -mən [-men]

housemaster, -s 'haʊsˌmɑːstə*, -z

house-parlourmaid, -s ˌhaʊsˈpɑːləmeɪd, -z

house-part|y, -ies 'haʊsˌpɑːt|ɪ, -ɪz

house-physician, -s 'haʊsfɪˌzɪʃn [-fə-], -z

house-room 'haʊsrʊm [-ruːm]

house-surgeon, -s 'haʊsˌsɜːdʒən, -z

house-to-house ˌhaʊstəˈhaʊs

housetop, -s 'haʊstɒp, -s

house-warming, -s 'haʊsˌwɔːmɪŋ, -z

housewi|fe (woman), -ves 'haʊswaɪ|f, -vz

housewi|fe (needle-case), -fes, -ves 'hʌzɪ|f, -fs, -vz

housewifely 'haʊsˌwaɪflɪ

housewifery 'haʊswɪfərɪ ['hʌzɪfrɪ]

house-work 'haʊswɜːk

Housman 'haʊsmən

Houston (English surname) 'huːstən, 'haʊs-, (Scottish surname) 'huːstən, (city in U.S.A.) 'hjuːstən

Houyhnhnm, -s 'hʊɪhnəm [hʊ'ɪhnəm], -z

hove (from heave) (H.) həʊv

hov|el (s. v.), -els, -elling, -elled, -eller/s 'hɒv|l ['hʌv-], -lz, -lɪŋ [-əlɪŋ], -ld, -lə*/z [-ələ*/z]

Hovell (surname) 'həʊvl, 'hɒvl, həʊ'vel

Hovenden 'hɒvndən

hov|er, -ers, -ering, -ered 'hɒv|ə* ['hʌv-], -əz, -ərɪŋ, -əd

hovercraft 'hɒvəkrɑːft

hover-fl|y, -ies 'hɒvəfl|aɪ, -aɪz

Hovis 'həʊvɪs

how (H.) haʊ

Howard 'haʊəd

howbeit ˌhaʊ'biːɪt

howdah, -s 'haʊdə, -z

how do you do ˌhaʊdjʊ'duː [-djə'd-, -dɪ'd-, -dʒʊ'd-, -dʒə'd-]

howdy-do, -s ˌhaʊdɪ'duː, -z

Howe haʊ

Howell, -s 'haʊəl, -z

however haʊ'evə*

Note.—Variants 'haʊevə*, 'haʊevə* are used by some people when the meaning is 'however that may be'.

Howick 'haʊɪk

How|ie, -itt 'haʊ|ɪ, -ɪt

howitzer, -s 'haʊɪtsə*, -z

howl (s. v.), -s, -ing, -ed haʊl, -z, -ɪŋ, -d

howler, -s 'haʊlə*, -z

Howley 'haʊlɪ

Howorth 'haʊəθ

Howse haʊz

howsoever ˌhaʊsəʊ'evə*

Howson 'haʊsn

Howth (near Dublin) həʊθ

Hoxton 'hɒkstən

hoy (s. interj.) (H.), -s hɔɪ, -z

hoyden (H.), -s 'hɔɪdn, -z

Hoylake 'hɔɪleɪk

hub, -s hʌb, -z

Huback 'hjuːbæk

Hubback 'hʌbæk, -bək

Hubbard 'hʌbəd

hubble-bubble, -s 'hʌblˌbʌbl, -z

hubbub, -s 'hʌbʌb [-bəb], -z

hubb|y, -ies 'hʌb|ɪ, -ɪz

hub-cap, -s 'hʌbkæp, -s

Hubert 'hjuːbət [-bəːt]

huckaback, -s 'hʌkəbæk, -s

huckleberr|y (H.), -ies 'hʌklbər|ɪ [-ˌber|ɪ], -ɪz

Hucknall 'hʌknəl

huckster, -s 'hʌkstə*, -z

Huddersfield 'hʌdəzfiːld

hudd|le (s. v.), -les, -ling, -led 'hʌd|l, -lz, -lɪŋ [-lɪŋ], -ld

Hud(d)leston 'hʌdlstən

Hudibras 'hjuːdɪbræs

Hud|nott, -son 'hʌd|nɒt, -sn

hue, -s hjuː, -z

hue and cry ˌhjuː:ən'kraɪ [-ən'k-]

Hueffer 'hefə*

huff (s. v.), -s, -ing, -ed hʌf, -s, -ɪŋ, -t

huffish, -ly, -ness 'hʌfɪʃ, -lɪ, -nɪs [-nəs]

huff|y, -ier, -iest, -ily, -iness 'hʌf|ɪ, -ɪə*, -ɪɪst, -ɪlɪ [-əlɪ], -ɪnɪs [-ɪnəs]

hug (s. v.), -s, -ging, -ged hʌg, -z, -ɪŋ, -d

Hugall 'hjuːgəl

huge, -r, -st, -ly, -ness hjuːdʒ, -ə*, -ɪst, -lɪ, -nɪs [-nəs]

Hugesson 'hjuːgɪsn

hugger-mugger 'hʌgəˌmʌgə*

Huggin, -s 'hʌgɪn, -z

Hugh, -es hjuː, -z

Hughenden 'hjuːəndən ['hjuən-]

Hugo (English name) 'hjuːgəʊ

Hugon 'hjuːgən [-gɒn]

Hugue|not, -nots 'hjuːgə|nɒt [-nəʊ-], -nɒts [-nəʊz]

Huish 'hjuːɪʃ ['hjʊɪʃ]

Hulbert 'hʌlbət

hulk, -s, -ing, hʌlk, -s, -ɪŋ

hull (s. v.) (H.), -s, -ing, -ed hʌl, -z, -ɪŋ, -d

hullabaloo, -s ˌhʌləbə'luː, -z

Hullah 'hʌlə
hullo hə'ləʊ [hʌ'l-]
Hulme hju:m, hu:m
Hulse hʌls
Hulsean hʌl'si:ən [-'sɪən]
hum (s. v.), -s, -ming, -med hʌm, -z,
-ɪŋ, -d
human, -ly 'hju:mən, -lɪ
humane, -r, -st, -ly, -ness hju:'meɪn
[hjʊ-], -ə*, -ɪst, -lɪ, -nɪs [-nəs]
humani|sm, -st/s 'hju:mənɪ|zəm, -st/s
humanistic ˌhju:mə'nɪstɪk
humanitarian, -s, -ism hju:ˌmænɪ-
'teərɪən [hjʊ-, ˌhju:mæn-], -z, -ɪzəm
humanit|y, -ies hju:'mænət|ɪ [hjʊ-,
-ɪt|ɪ], -ɪz
humanization [-isa-] ˌhju:mənaɪ'zeɪʃn
humaniz|e [-is|e], -es, -ing, -ed 'hju:-
mənaɪz, -ɪz, -ɪŋ, -d
humankind ˌhju:mən'kaɪnd
Humber, -s, -side 'hʌmbə*, -z, -saɪd
Humbert 'hʌmbət [-bə:t]
humb|le (adj. v.), -ler, -lest, -ly, -leness;
-les, -ling, -led 'hʌmb|l, -lə*, -lɪst, -lɪ,
-lnɪs [-nəs]; -lz, -lɪŋ, -ld
humble-bee, -s 'hʌmblbi:, -z
humble-pie ˌhʌmbl'paɪ
Humboldt 'hʌmbəʊlt ['hʊm-] ('hum-
bolt)
humbug (s. v.), -s, -ging, -ged 'hʌmbʌg,
-z, -ɪŋ, -d
humdrum 'hʌmdrʌm
Hume hju:m
humer|us, -i, -al 'hju:mər|əs, -aɪ, -əl
Humian 'hju:mjən [-mɪən]
humid, -ness 'hju:mɪd, -nɪs [-nəs]
humidity hju:'mɪdətɪ [hjʊ-, -ɪtɪ]
humiliat|e, -es, -ing, -ed hju:'mɪlɪeɪt
[hjʊ-], -s, -ɪŋ, -ɪd
humiliation, -s hju:ˌmɪlɪ'eɪʃn [hjʊ-,
ˌhju:mɪl-], -z
humility hju:'mɪlətɪ [hjʊ-, -lɪt-]
humming-bird, -s 'hʌmɪŋbɜ:d, -z
humming-top, -s 'hʌmɪŋtɒp, -s
hummock, -s, -ed; -y 'hʌmək, -s, -t; -ɪ
humor|al, -alism, -alist/s 'hju:mər|əl,
-əlɪzəm, -əlɪst/s
humoresque, -s ˌhju:mə'resk, -s
humorist, -s 'hju:mərɪst [old-fashioned
'ju:-], -s
humoristic ˌhju:mə'rɪstɪk [old-fashioned
ˌju:-]
humorous, -ly, -ness 'hju:mərəs [old-
fashioned 'ju:-], -lɪ, -nɪs [-nəs]
humour (s. v.), -s, -ing, -ed 'hju:mə*
[old-fashioned 'ju:-], -z, -rɪŋ, -d
humoursome, -ly, -ness 'hju:məsəm
[old-fashioned 'ju:-], -lɪ, -nɪs [-nəs]

hump (s. v.), -s, -ing, -ed hʌmp, -s, -ɪŋ,
-t [hʌmt]
humpback, -s, -ed 'hʌmpbæk, -s, -t
humph, m̩m, m̩m̩m̩, mm̩m̩, hə̃h [hʌmf]
Humphery 'hʌmfrɪ
Humphr(e)y, -s 'hʌmfrɪ, -z
Humphry-dumpty ˌhʌmpftɪ'dʌmpftɪ
hump|y, -ier, -iest, -iness 'hʌmp|ɪ, -ɪə*
[-jə*], -ɪɪst [-jɪst], -ɪnɪs [-ɪnəs]
humus 'hju:məs
Hun, -s hʌn, -z
hunch (s. v.), -es, -ing, -ed hʌntʃ, -ɪz,
-ɪŋ, -t
hunchback, -s, -ed 'hʌntʃbæk, -s, -t
hundred, -s 'hʌndrəd [-drɪd], -z
hundredfold 'hʌndrədfəʊld [-drɪd-]
hundredth, -s 'hʌndrədθ [-drɪdθ, -drətθ,
-drɪtθ], -s
hundredweight, -s 'hʌndrədweɪt
[-drɪd-], -s
hung (from hang) hʌŋ
Hungarian, -s hʌŋ'geərɪən, -z
Hungary 'hʌŋgərɪ
hunger (s. v.), -s, -ing, -ed, -er/s 'hʌŋ-
gə*, -z, -rɪŋ, -d, -rə*/z
Hungerford 'hʌŋgəfəd
hunger-strik|e (s. v.), -es, -ing, hunger-
struck, hunger-striker/s 'hʌŋgə-
straɪk, -s, -ɪŋ, 'hʌŋgəstrʌk, 'hʌŋgə-
ˌstraɪkə*/z
hungr|y, -ier, -iest, -ily, -iness 'hʌŋ-
gr|ɪ, -ɪə*, -ɪɪst, -əlɪ [-ɪlɪ], -ɪnɪs [-ɪnəs]
hunk, -s hʌŋk, -s
Hunn|ic, -ish 'hʌn|ɪk, -ɪʃ
Hunslet 'hʌnslɪt
Hunstanton hʌn'stæntən [locally
'hʌnstən]
Hunsworth 'hʌnzwəθ [-wɜ:θ]
hunt (s. v.) (H.), -s, -ing, -ed, -er/s
hʌnt, -s, -ɪŋ, -ɪd, -ə*/z
Hunter 'hʌntə*
Hunterian hʌn'tɪərɪən
hunting-box, -es 'hʌntɪŋbɒks, -ɪz
hunting-cap, -s 'hʌntɪŋkæp, -s
hunting-crop, -s 'hʌntɪŋkrɒp, -s
Huntingdon, -shire 'hʌntɪŋdən, -ʃə*
[-ˌʃɪə*]
Huntingdonian, -s ˌhʌntɪŋ'dəʊnjən
[-nɪən], -z
hunting-field, -s 'hʌntɪŋfi:ld, -z
Huntingford 'hʌntɪŋfəd
hunting-ground, -s 'hʌntɪŋgraʊnd, -z
hunting-horn, -s 'hʌntɪŋhɔ:n, -z
hunting-kni|fe, -ves 'hʌntɪŋnaɪ|f, -vz
hunting-song, -s 'hʌntɪŋsɒŋ, -z
Huntington 'hʌntɪŋtən
Huntl(e)y 'hʌntlɪ
Hunton 'hʌntən

247

huntress, -es 'hʌntrɪs [-trəs, -tres], -ɪz
Hunts. hʌnts
hunts|man, -men, -manship 'hʌnts|-
mən, -mən [-men], -mənʃɪp
Hunyadi 'hʊnjɑːdɪ ['hʌnj-, -'--]
Hurd hɜːd
hurd|le (s. v.), -les, -ling, -led 'hɜːd|l,
-lz, -lɪŋ [-lɪŋ], -ld
hurdle-race, -s 'hɜːdlreɪs, -ɪz
hurdy-gurd|y, -ies 'hɜːdɪˌgɜːd|ɪ, -ɪz
Hurford 'hɜːfəd
hurl (s. v.), -s, -ing, -ed, -er/s hɜːl, -z,
-ɪŋ, -d, -ə*/z
hurley (H.), -s 'hɜːlɪ, -z
Hurlingham 'hɜːlɪŋəm
Hurlstone 'hɜːlstən
hurly-burly 'hɜːlɪˌbɜːlɪ
Huron 'hjʊərən
hurrah (s. v.), -s, -ing, -ed hʊ'rɑː, -z,
-ɪŋ, -d
hurrah (interj.) hʊ'rɑː
hurray (s.), -s hʊ'reɪ, -z
hurray (interj.) hʊ'reɪ
hurricane, -s 'hʌrɪkən [-kɪn, -keɪn], -z
hurr|y (s. v.), -ies, -ying, -ied/ly, -ier/s
'hʌr|ɪ, -ɪz, -ɪŋ, -ɪd/lɪ, -ɪə*/z
hurry-scurry ˌhʌrɪ'skʌrɪ
hurst, -s hɜːst, -s
Hurstmonceux ˌhɜːstmən'sjuː [-mɒn-,
-'suː]
Hurstpierpoint ˌhɜːstpɪə'pɔɪnt
hurt (s. v.) (H.), -s, -ing hɜːt, -s, -ɪŋ
hurt|ful, -fully, -fulness 'hɜːt|fʊl, -fʊlɪ
[-fəlɪ], -fʊlnɪs [-nəs]
hurtle, -les, -ling, -led 'hɜːt|l, -lz, -lɪŋ,
-ld
husband (s. v.), -s, -ing, -ed 'hʌzbənd,
-z, -ɪŋ, -ɪd
husbandly 'hʌzbəndlɪ
husband|man, -men 'hʌzbənd|mən,
-mən [-men]
husbandry 'hʌzbəndrɪ
hush (s. v.), -es, -ing, -ed hʌʃ, -ɪz, -ɪŋ, -t
hush (interj.) ʃ; [hʌʃ]
hushaby 'hʌʃəbaɪ
Hushai 'hjuːʃeɪaɪ ['huː-, -ʃaɪ]
hush-hush ˌhʌʃ'hʌʃ ['--]
hush-money 'hʌʃˌmʌnɪ
husk, -s hʌsk, -s
Huskisson 'hʌskɪsn
husk|y, -ier, -iest, -ily, -iness 'hʌsk|ɪ,
-ɪə* [-jə*], -ɪɪst [-jɪst], -ɪlɪ [-əlɪ],
-ɪnɪs [-ɪnəs]
hussar, -s hʊ'zɑː*, -z
Hussey 'hʌsɪ
Hussite, -s 'hʌsaɪt, -s
huss|y, -ies 'hʌs|ɪ ['hʌz|ɪ], -ɪz
Hussy 'hʌsɪ

hustings 'hʌstɪŋz
hust|le, -les, -ling, -led, -ler/s 'hʌs|l,
-lz, -lɪŋ [-lɪŋ], -ld, -lə*/z [-lə*/z]
hut, -s hʌt, -s
hutch, -es hʌtʃ, -ɪz
Hutch|eson, -ings 'hʌtʃ|ɪsn, -ɪŋz
Hutchinson 'hʌtʃɪnsn
Hutchinsonian, -s ˌhʌtʃɪn'səʊnjən
[-nɪən], -z
Hutchison 'hʌtʃɪsn
Huth, -waite huːθ, -weɪt
hutment, -s 'hʌtmənt, -s
Hutton 'hʌtn
Hux|ley, -table 'hʌks|lɪ, -təbl
Huygens 'haɪgənz
huzza (s. interj.), -s hʊ'zɑː [hʌ'z-], -z
Hwang-ho ˌhwæŋ'həʊ
hyacinth (H.), -s 'haɪəsɪnθ, -s
hyacinthine ˌhaɪə'sɪnθaɪn
Hyades 'haɪədiːz
hyaena, -s haɪ'iːnə, -z
hyal|ine, -ite, -oid 'haɪəl|ɪn [-iːn, -aɪn],
-aɪt, -ɔɪc
Hyam, -son 'haɪəm, -sn
hybrid, -s; -ism 'haɪbrɪd, -z; -ɪzəm
hybridity haɪ'brɪdətɪ [-ɪtɪ]
hybridization [-isa-] ˌhaɪbrɪdaɪ'zeɪʃn
hybridiz|e [-is|e], -es, -ing, -ed, -er/s
'haɪbrɪdaɪz, -ɪz, -ɪŋ, -d, -ə*/z
Hydaspes haɪ'dæspiːz
Hyde haɪd
Hyde Park ˌhaɪd'pɑːk ['haɪdp- according to sentence-stress]
Hyderabad 'haɪdərəbæd [ˌhaɪdərə'b-]
(Hindi həydərabad)
hydra, -s 'haɪdrə, -z
Hydrabad 'haɪdrəbæd [ˌhaɪdrə'b-]
hydrangea, -s haɪ'dreɪndʒə [-dʒjə,
-dʒɪə], -z
hydrant, -s 'haɪdrənt, -s
hydrargyrum haɪ'drɑːdʒɪrəm
hydrate, -s 'haɪdreɪt [-rɪt], -s
hydraulic, -s haɪ'drɔːlɪk [-'drɒl-], -s
hydro, -s 'haɪdrəʊ, -z
hydrocarbon, -s ˌhaɪdrəʊ'kɑːbən
[-bɒn], -z
hydrocephalus ˌhaɪdrəʊ'sefələs [ˌhaɪ-,
-'kef-]
hydrochloric ˌhaɪdrəʊ'klɒrɪk [-'klɔːr-,
also '--ˌ-- according to sentence-stress]
hydrodynamic, -al, -ally, -s ˌhaɪdrəʊ-
daɪ'næmɪk [-dɪ'n-], -l, -əlɪ, -s
hydrofoil, -s 'haɪdrəʊfɔɪl, -z
hydrogen 'haɪdrədʒən [-drɪdʒən,
-drədʒɪn]
hydrogenous haɪ'drɒdʒɪnəs [-dʒən-]
hydrograph|er/s, -y haɪ'drɒgrəf|ə*/z,
-ɪ

hydrographic, -al, -ally ˌhaɪdrəʊ-
ˈgræfɪk, -l, -əlɪ
hydro|logy, -lysis haɪˈdrɒ|lədʒɪ, -lɪsɪs
[-ləsɪs]
hydromechanics ˌhaɪdrəʊmɪˈkænɪks
[-mə'k-]
hydrometer, -s haɪˈdrɒmɪtə* [-mətə*],
-z
hydrometric, -al, -ally ˌhaɪdrəʊˈmetrɪk,
-l, -əlɪ
hydrometry haɪˈdrɒmɪtrɪ [-mətrɪ]
hydropathic (s. adj.), -s, -al, -ally ˌhaɪ-
drəʊˈpæθɪk, -s, -l, -əlɪ
hydropath|ist/s, -y haɪˈdrɒpəθ|ɪst/s, -ɪ
hydrophobia ˌhaɪdrəʊˈfəʊbjə [-bɪə]
hydrophobic ˌhaɪdrəʊˈfəʊbɪk [-ˈfɒb-]
hydropic haɪˈdrɒpɪk
hydroplane, -s ˈhaɪdrəʊpleɪn, -z
hydropsy ˈhaɪdrɒpsɪ
hydroquinone ˌhaɪdrəʊkwɪˈnəʊn
[-ˈkwaɪnəʊn, haɪˈdrɒkɪnəʊn]
hydroscope, -s ˈhaɪdrəskəʊp, -s
hydrostat, -s ˈhaɪdrəʊstæt, -s
hydrostatic, -al, -ally, -s ˌhaɪdrəʊ-
ˈstætɪk, -l, -əlɪ, -s
hydrosulphuric ˌhaɪdrəʊsʌlˈfjʊərɪk
[-ˈfjɔər-, -ˈfjɔːr]
hydrous ˈhaɪdrəs
hydrox|ide/s, -yl haɪˈdrɒks|aɪd/z, -ɪl
hyena, -s haɪˈiːnə, -z
Hygeia haɪˈdʒiːə [-ˈdʒɪə]
hygiene ˈhaɪdʒiːn
hygienic, -ally haɪˈdʒiːnɪk, -əlɪ
hygromet|er/s, -ry haɪˈgrɒmɪt|ə*
[-mət|ə*]/z, -rɪ
hygrometric, -al, -ally ˌhaɪgrəʊˈmetrɪk,
-l, -əlɪ
hygroscope, -s ˈhaɪgrəskəʊp, -s
Hyksos ˈhɪksɒs
Hylas ˈhaɪlæs
Hylton ˈhɪltən
Hyman ˈhaɪmən
hymen (H.), -s ˈhaɪmen, -z
hymene|al, -an ˌhaɪmeˈniː|əl [-məˈn-,
-ˈnɪəl], -ən
Hymettus haɪˈmetəs
hymn (s. v.), -s, -ing, -ed hɪm, -z, -ɪŋ,
-d
hymnal, -s ˈhɪmnəl, -z
hymnar|y, -ies ˈhɪmnər|ɪ, -ɪz
hymn-book, -s ˈhɪmbʊk, -s
hymnic ˈhɪmnɪk
hymnody ˈhɪmnəʊdɪ
hymnolog|ist/s, -y hɪmˈnɒlədʒ|ɪst/s, -ɪ
Hyndley ˈhaɪndlɪ
Hyndman ˈhaɪndmən
hyoid ˈhaɪɔɪd
hyoscine ˈhaɪəʊsiːn

hypallage haɪˈpælədʒi: [-gɪ, -lədʒɪ]
Hypatia haɪˈpeɪʃjə [-ʃɪə, -ʃə]
hyperacute, -ness ˌhaɪpərəˈkjuːt, -nɪs
[-nəs]
hyperbol|a, -ae, -as haɪˈpɜːbəl|ə, -iː, -əz
hyperbole, -s haɪˈpɜːbəlɪ, -z
hyperbolic, -al, -ally ˌhaɪpəˈbɒlɪk, -l,
-əlɪ
hyperboli|sm, -st/s haɪˈpɜːbəlɪ|zəm,
-st/s
hyperboliz|e [-is|e], -es, -ing, -ed haɪ-
ˈpɜːbəlaɪz, -ɪz, -ɪŋ, -d
hyperboloid, -s haɪˈpɜːbəlɔɪd, -z
hyperborean, -s ˌhaɪpəbɔːˈriːən [-pɜː-,
-ˈrɪən, -bɒˈriːən, -bɒˈrɪən, -ˈbɔːrɪən]
hypercritic|al, -ally ˌhaɪpəˈkrɪtɪk|l, -əlɪ
hypercriticism ˌhaɪpəˈkrɪtɪsɪzəm
hypercriticiz|e [-is|e], -es, -ing, -ed
ˌhaɪpəˈkrɪtɪsaɪz, -ɪz, -ɪŋ, -d
Hyperides ˌhaɪpəˈraɪdiː:z, haɪˈperɪdiː:z
Hyperion haɪˈpɪərɪən [-ˈper-]
hypersensitive ˌhaɪpəˈsensətɪv [-sɪtɪv]
hyper-space ˌhaɪpəˈspeɪs
hypertension ˌhaɪpəˈtenʃn [-pɜː-]
hypertroph|y, -ied haɪˈpɜːtrəʊf|ɪ, -ɪd
hyph|en (s. v.), -ens, -ening, -ened
ˈhaɪf|n, -nz, -nɪŋ [-ənɪŋ], -nd
hyphenat|e, -es, -ing, -ed ˈhaɪfəneɪt
[-fn-, -fɪn-], -s, -ɪŋ, -ɪd
hypnosis hɪpˈnəʊsɪs
hypnotic hɪpˈnɒtɪk
hypnoti|sm, -st/s ˈhɪpnətɪ|zəm, -st/s
hypnotization [-isa-] ˌhɪpnətaɪˈzeɪʃn
hypnotiz|e [-is|e], -es, -ing, -ed, -er/s
ˈhɪpnətaɪz, -ɪz, -ɪŋ, -d, -ə*/z
hypo ˈhaɪpəʊ
hypocaust, -s ˈhaɪpəʊkɔːst, -s
hypochond|ria, -riac/s ˌhaɪpəʊˈkɒnd|rɪə
[ˌhɪp-], -rɪæk/s
hypochondriacal ˌhaɪpəʊkɒnˈdraɪəkl
[ˌhɪp-, -kən-]
hypochondriasis ˌhaɪpəʊkɒnˈdraɪəsɪs
[ˌhɪp-, -kən-]
hypocris|y, -ies hɪˈpɒkrəs|ɪ [-krɪs-], -ɪz
hypocrite, -s ˈhɪpəkrɪt [-pʊk-], -s
hypocritic|al, -ally ˌhɪpəʊˈkrɪtɪk|l,
-əlɪ
hypocycloid, -s ˌhaɪpəʊˈsaɪklɔɪd, -z
hypoderm|a, -ic ˌhaɪpəʊˈdɜːm|ə, -ɪk
hypophosphate, -s ˌhaɪpəʊˈfɒsfeɪt [-fɪt],
-s
hypostasis haɪˈpɒstəsɪs
hypostatiz|e [-is|e], -es, -ing, -ed
haɪˈpɒstətaɪz, -ɪz, -ɪŋ, -d
hypostyle ˈhaɪpəʊstaɪl
hyposulphite ˌhaɪpəʊˈsʌlfaɪt
hypotax|is, -es ˌhaɪpəʊˈtæks|ɪs [ˈ--ˌ--],
-iː:z

hypotension ˌhaɪpəʊˈtenʃn

hypotenuse, -s haɪˈpɒtənjuːz [-njuːs, -tnj-, -tnᵢ-, -tᵢn-], -ɪz

hypothecat|e, -es, -ing, -ed haɪˈpɒθɪkeɪt [-θə-], -s, -ɪŋ, -ɪd bi-, -ɪn-

hypothecation, -s haɪˌpɒθɪˈkeɪʃn [-θə-], -z

hypothermia ˌhaɪpəʊˈθɜːmɪə [-mjə]

hypothes|is, -es haɪˈpɒθɪs|ɪs [-θəs-], -iːz

hypothetic, -al, -ally ˌhaɪpəʊˈθetɪk, -l, -əlɪ

hypsomet|er/s, -ry hɪpˈsɒmɪt|ə* [-mət|ə*]/z, -rɪ

hyrax, -es ˈhaɪəræks, -ɪz

Hyslop ˈhɪzləp

hyson (H.), ˈhaɪsn

hyssop ˈhɪsəp

hysteria hɪˈstɪərɪə

hysteric, -s, -al, -ally hɪˈsterɪk, -s, -l, -əlɪ

hysteron-proteron ˌhɪstərɒnˈprɒtərɒn [-ˈprəʊ-]

hythe (H.), -s haɪð, -z

Hywel ˈhaʊəl

I

I (*the letter, pron.*), **-'s** aɪ, -z
Iacchus ɪˈækəs [aɪˈæk-]
Iachimo ɪˈækɪməʊ [aɪˈæk-]
Iago ɪˈɑːgəʊ
Iain ɪən [ˈiːən]
iamb, -s ˈaɪæmb, -z
iamb|ic/s, -us/es aɪˈæmb|ɪk/s, -əs/ɪz
Ian ɪən [ˈiːən]
I'Anson ˈaɪənsn
Ianthe aɪˈænθɪ
Iason ˈaɪəsn
iatrogenic aɪˌætrəʊˈdʒenɪk [ˌ—ˈ—]
Ibadan (*in Nigeria*) ɪˈbædən
Ibbertson ˈɪbətsn [-bɑːt-]
Ibbetson ˈɪbɪtsn [-bət-]
Iberia, -n/s aɪˈbɪərɪə, -n/z
Iberus aɪˈbɪərəs
ibex, -es ˈaɪbeks, -ɪz
ibidem ɪˈbaɪdem [ˈɪbɪdem]
ibis, -es ˈaɪbɪs, -ɪz
Ibrahim ˈɪbrəhiːm [ˌɪbrəˈhiːm]
Ibrox ˈaɪbrɒks
Ibsen ˈɪbsn
Icaria, -n ɪˈkeərɪə [aɪˈk-], -n
Icarus ˈɪkərəs [ˈaɪk-]
ic|e (*s. v.*), **-es, -ing, -ed** aɪs, -ɪz, -ɪŋ, -t
ice-axe, -s ˈaɪsæks, -ɪz
iceberg, -s ˈaɪsbɜːg, -z
ice-boat, -s ˈaɪsbəʊt, -s
icebound ˈaɪsbaʊnd
ice-breaker, -s ˈaɪsˌbreɪkə*, -z
ice-cap, -s ˈaɪskæp, -s
ice-cream, -s ˌaɪsˈkriːm [*attributively* ˈ—], -z
icedrome, -s ˈaɪsdrəʊm, -z
icefall, -s ˈaɪsfɔːl, -z
ice|-field/s, -floe/s ˈaɪs|fiːld/z, -fləʊ/z
ice-hockey ˈaɪsˌhɒkɪ
ice-hou|se, -ses ˈaɪshaʊ|s, -zɪz
Iceland ˈaɪslənd
Icelander, -s ˈaɪsləndə* [-lændə*], -z
Icelandic aɪsˈlændɪk
ice|-man, -men ˈaɪs|mæn [-mən], -men [-mən]
ice-pack, -s ˈaɪspæk, -s
ice-pail, -s ˈaɪspeɪl, -z
ice-spar ˌaɪsˈspɑː* [ˈ—]
Ichabod ˈɪkəbɒd [ˈɪxə-]
ichneumon, -s ɪkˈnjuːmən, -z

ichnography ɪkˈnɒgrəfɪ
ichor ˈaɪkɔː*
ichthyolog|ist/s, -y ˌɪkθɪˈɒlədʒ|ɪst/s, -ɪ
ichthyosaur|us, -i, -uses ˌɪkθɪəˈsɔːr|əs [-θjə's-, -θɪəʊ-], -aɪ, -əsɪz
icicle, -s ˈaɪsɪkl, -z
icing (*s.*) ˈaɪsɪŋ
Icknield ˈɪkniːld
Ickornshaw ˈɪkɔːnʃɔː
Icolmkill ˌiːkɒlmˈkɪl
icon, -s ˈaɪkɒn [-kən], -z
iconic aɪˈkɒnɪk
Iconium aɪˈkəʊnjəm [-nɪəm]
iconocla|sm, -st/s aɪˈkɒnəʊklæ|zəm, -st/s
iconoclastic aɪˌkɒnəʊˈklæstɪk
iconograph|er/s, -y ˌaɪkɒˈnɒgrəf|ə*/z [-kə'n-], -ɪ
iconoscope, -s aɪˈkɒnəskəʊp, -s
icosahedr|on, -ons, -a; -al ˌaɪkəsə-ˈhedr|ən [-kɒs-, -ˈhiːd-, ˈ—-,—], -ənz, -ə; -əl
ictus, -es ˈɪktəs, -ɪz
ic|y, -ier, -iest, -ily, -iness ˈaɪs|ɪ, -ɪə* [-jə*], -ɪɪst [-jɪst], -ɪlɪ [-əlɪ], -ɪnɪs [-məs]
id ɪd
I'd (= **I would, I should,** *or* **I had**) aɪd
Ida ˈaɪdə
Idaho ˈaɪdəhəʊ
Idalia, -n aɪˈdeɪljə [-lɪə], -n
Iddesleigh ˈɪdzlɪ
Ide (*in Devon*) iːd
idea, -s aɪˈdɪə, -z
    Note.—The pronunciation ˈaɪdɪə *is also sometimes heard, esp. when a stress immediately follows.*
ideal (*s.*), **-s** aɪˈdɪəl [-ˈdiːəl, -ˈdiːl], -z
ideal (*adj.*) aɪˈdɪəl [-ˈdiːəl, -ˈdiːl, ˈ—, *esp. when attributive*]
ideal|ism, -ist/s aɪˈdɪəl|ɪzəm [aɪˈdiːəl-, ˈaɪdjəl-, ˈaɪdɪəl-], -ɪst/s
idealistic aɪˌdɪəˈlɪstɪk [aɪˌdiːəˈl-, ˌaɪdjəˈl-, ˌaɪdɪəˈl-]
ideality ˌaɪdɪˈælətɪ [-ɪtɪ]
idealization [-isa-], **-s** aɪˌdɪəlaɪˈzeɪʃn [-ˌdiːəl-, -lɪˈz-, ˌ—ˈ—], -z
idealiz|e [-is|e], **-es, -ing, -ed** aɪˈdɪəlaɪz [-ˈdiːəl-], -ɪz, -ɪŋ, -d

251

ideally aɪ'dɪəlɪ [-'di:əlɪ]
idem 'aɪdem ['ɪdem]
Iden 'aɪdn
identic|al, -ally, -alness aɪ'dentɪk|l [ɪ'd-], -əlɪ, -lnɪs [-nəs]
identification, -s aɪ,dentɪfɪ'keɪʃn [ɪ,d-], -z
identi|fy, -fies, -fying, -fied, -fier/s; -fiable aɪ'dentɪ|faɪ [ɪ'd-], -faɪz, -faɪɪŋ, -faɪd, -faɪə*/z; -faɪəbl [-,--'---]
identit|y, -ies aɪ'dentət|ɪ [ɪ'd-, -ɪt|ɪ], -ɪz
ideogram, -s 'ɪdɪəʊɡræm ['aɪd-], -z
ideograph, -s 'ɪdɪəʊɡrɑ:f ['aɪd-, -ɡræf], -s
ideographic, -al, -ally ,ɪdɪəʊ'ɡræfɪk [,aɪd-], -l, -əlɪ
ideography ,ɪdɪ'ɒɡrəfɪ [,aɪd-]
ideological ,aɪdɪə'lɒdʒɪkl [,ɪd-]
ideolog|ist/s, -y, -ies ,aɪdɪ'ɒlədʒ|ɪst/s [,ɪd-], -ɪ, -ɪz
Ides aɪdz
idioc|y, -ies 'ɪdɪəs|ɪ ['ɪdjəs-], -ɪz
idiolect, -s 'ɪdɪəʊlekt, -s
idiom, -s 'ɪdɪəm ['ɪdjəm], -z
idiomatic, -al, -ally ,ɪdɪə'mætɪk [,ɪdjəʊ'm-, ,ɪdɪʊ'm-, ,ɪdjʊ'm-], -l, -əlɪ
idiosyncras|y, -ies ,ɪdɪə'sɪŋkrəs|ɪ [-djə's-, -dɪʊ's-, -djʊ's-, -dɪəʊ's-, -djəʊ's-], -ɪz
idiosyncratic, -ally ,ɪdɪəsɪŋ'krætɪk [,ɪdɪəʊ-, ,ɪdjəʊ-], -əlɪ
idiot, -s 'ɪdɪət ['ɪdjət], -s
idiotic, -al, -ally ,ɪdɪ'ɒtɪk, -l, -əlɪ
idiotism, -s 'ɪdɪətɪzəm ['ɪdjət-], -z
Idist, -s 'i:dɪst, -s
id|le (adj. v.), **-ly, -leness; -les, -ling, -led, -ler/s** 'aɪd|l, -lɪ, -lnɪs [-nəs]; -lz, -lɪŋ, -ld, -lə*/z
Ido 'i:dəʊ
idol, -s 'aɪdl, -z
idolater, -s aɪ'dɒlətə*, -z
idolatress, -es aɪ'dɒlətrɪs [-trəs, -tres], -ɪz
idolatrous, -ly aɪ'dɒlətrəs, -lɪ
idolatr|y, -ies aɪ'dɒlətr|ɪ, -ɪz
idoli|sm, -st/s 'aɪdəlɪ|zəm [-d|ɪ-], -st/s
idolization [-isa-] ,aɪdəlaɪ'zeɪʃn [-d|aɪ-]
idoliz|e [-is|e], -es, -ing, -ed, -er/s 'aɪdəlaɪz [-d|-], -ɪz, -ɪŋ, -d, -ə*/z
Idomeneus aɪ'dɒmɪnju:s [ɪ'd-]
Idris 'ɪdrɪs ['aɪdrɪs]
Idumea ,aɪdju:'mi:ə [,ɪd-, -djʊm-, -'mɪə]
idyll, -s 'ɪdɪl ['aɪd-], -z
idyllic aɪ'dɪlɪk [ɪ'd-]
idyllist, -s 'aɪdɪlɪst, -s
i.e. ,aɪ'i: [,ðæt'ɪz]

if ɪf
Ife (surname) aɪf, (town in Nigeria) 'i:feɪ
Iffley 'ɪflɪ
Ifor 'aɪvə*
Iggulden 'ɪɡldən
Ightham 'aɪtəm
igloo, -s 'ɪɡlu:, -z
Igna|tian, -tius ɪɡ'neɪ|ʃjən [-ʃɪən, -ʃn], -ʃjəs [-ʃɪəs, -ʃəs]
igneous 'ɪɡnɪəs [-njəs]
ignis-fatuus ,ɪɡnɪs'fætjʊəs [-tjwəs]
ignit|e, -es, -ing, -ed; -able ɪɡ'naɪt, -s, -ɪŋ, -ɪd; -əbl
ignition ɪɡ'nɪʃn
ignobility ,ɪɡnəʊ'bɪlətɪ [-ɪtɪ]
ignob|le, -ly, -leness ɪɡ'nəʊb|l, -lɪ, -lnɪs [-nəs]
ignominious, -ly, -ness ,ɪɡnəʊ'mɪnɪəs [-njəs], -lɪ, -nɪs [-nəs]
ignominy 'ɪɡnəmɪnɪ [-nɒm-, -mən-]
ignoramus, -es ,ɪɡnə'reɪməs [-nʊ'r-], -ɪz
ignoran|ce, -t/ly 'ɪɡnərən|s [-nʊr-], -t/lɪ
ignor|e, -es, -ing, -ed ɪɡ'nɔ:* [-'nɔə*], -z, -rɪŋ, -d
Igoe (surname) 'aɪɡəʊ
Igor 'i:ɡɔ:*
iguana, -s ɪ'ɡwɑ:nə [,ɪɡjʊ'ɑ:nə], -z
iguanodon, -s ɪ'ɡwɑ:nədɒn [,ɪɡjʊ'ɑ:-, -dən], -z
ike (I.), -s aɪk, -s
Ikey 'aɪkɪ
ikon, -s 'aɪkɒn [-kən], -z
Ilchester 'ɪltʃɪstə*
ilex, -es 'aɪleks, -ɪz
Ilford 'ɪlfəd
Ilfracombe 'ɪlfrəku:m [,ɪlfrə'k-]
iliac 'ɪlɪæk
Iliad 'ɪlɪəd ['ɪljəd, 'ɪlɪæd, 'ɪljæd]
Iliffe 'aɪlɪf
ili|um, -a 'ɪlɪ|əm ['ɪlj|əm], -ə
Ilium 'aɪlɪəm ['ɪl-, -ljəm]
ilk ɪlk
Ilkestone 'ɪlkɪstən [-kəs-]
Ilkley 'ɪlklɪ
ill, -ness/es ɪl, -nɪs [-nəs]/ɪz
I'll (= I will) aɪl
ill-advised ,ɪləd'vaɪzd
illative ɪ'leɪtɪv
ill-boding ,ɪl'bəʊdɪŋ
ill-bred ,ɪl'bred [also '-- when attributive]
ill-breeding ,ɪl'bri:dɪŋ
ill-conditioned ,ɪlkən'dɪʃnd [also '--,-- when attributive]
illeg|al, -ally ɪ'li:ɡ|l [,ɪ'l-], -əlɪ
illegalit|y, -ies ,ɪli:'ɡælət|ɪ [-lɪ'ɡ-, -ɪt|ɪ], -ɪz

252

illegibility ɪˌledʒɪ'bɪlətɪ [ˌ---'---, -dʒə'b- -lɪt-]

illegib|le, -ly, -leness ɪ'ledʒəb|l [ˌɪ'l-, -dʒɪb-], -lɪ, -lnɪs [-nəs]

illegitimacy ˌɪlɪ'dʒɪtɪməsɪ [-lə'dʒ-, -təm-]

illegitimate, -ly ˌɪlɪ'dʒɪtɪmət [-lə'dʒ-, -təm-, -mɪt], -lɪ

ill-fated ˌɪl'feɪtɪd

ill-favoured, -ly, -ness ˌɪl'feɪvəd [also '-ˌ-- when attributive], -lɪ, -nɪs [-nəs]

ill-feeling ˌɪl'fiːlɪŋ

ill-gotten ˌɪl'gɒtn [also '-ˌ-- when attributive]

illiber|al, -ally ɪ'lɪbər|əl [ˌɪ'l-], -əlɪ

illiberality ɪˌlɪbə'rælətɪ [ˌɪlɪbə'r-, -ɪtɪ]

illicit, -ly, -ness ɪ'lɪsɪt [ˌɪ'l-], -lɪ, -nɪs [-nəs]

illimitab|le, -ly, -leness ɪ'lɪmɪtəb|l [ˌɪ'l-], -lɪ, -lnɪs [-nəs]

Illingworth 'ɪlɪŋwəθ [-wɜː:θ]

Illinois ˌɪlɪ'nɔɪ [rarely -'nɔɪz]

illiteracy ɪ'lɪtərəsɪ [ˌɪ'l-]

illiterate (s. adj.), **-s, -ly, -ness** ɪ'lɪtərət [ˌɪ'l-, -rɪt], -s, -lɪ, -nɪs [-nəs]

ill-judged ˌɪl'dʒʌdʒd [also '-- when attributive]

ill-looking 'ɪl,lʊkɪŋ

ill-mannered ˌɪl'mænəd

ill-nature ˌɪl'neɪtʃə*

ill-natured, -ly ˌɪl'neɪtʃəd [also '-ˌ-- when attributive], -lɪ

illness, -es 'ɪlnɪs [-nəs], -ɪz

Illogan ɪ'ləʊgən, ɪ'lʌgən

illogic|al, -ally, -alness ɪ'lɒdʒɪk|l [ˌɪ'l-], -əlɪ, -lnɪs [-nəs]

illogicalit|y, -ies ˌɪlɒdʒɪ'kælət|ɪ [ˌɪˌl-, -ɪt|ɪ], -ɪz

ill-omened ˌɪl'əʊmend [-mənd, -mɪnd]

ill-starred ˌɪl'stɑːd [also '-- when attributive]

ill-tempered ˌɪl'tempəd [also '-ˌ-- when attributive]

ill-timed ˌɪl'taɪmd [also '-- when attributive]

ill-treat, -s, -ing, -ed, -ment ˌɪl'triːt [ɪl't-], -s, -ɪŋ, -ɪd, -mənt

illum|e, -es, -ing, -ed ɪ'ljuːm [ɪ'luːm], -z, -ɪŋ, -d

illuminat|e, -es, -ing, -ed, -or/s ɪ'ljuː- mɪneɪt [ɪ'luː-], -s, -ɪŋ, -ɪd, -ə*/z

Illuminati ɪˌluːmɪ'nɑːtiː [old-fashioned -'neɪtaɪ]

illumination, -s ɪˌljuːmɪ'neɪʃn [ɪˌluː-], -z

illuminative ɪ'ljuːmɪnətɪv [ɪ'luː-, -neɪt-]

illumin|e, -es, -ing, -ed ɪ'ljuːmɪn [ɪ'luː-], -z, -ɪŋ, -d

ill-usage ˌɪl'juːzɪdʒ [-'juːs-]

ill-used ˌɪl'juːzd [also '-- according to sentence-stress]

illusion, -s ɪ'luːʒn [ɪ'ljuː-], -z

illusioni|sm, -st/s ɪ'luːʒənɪ|zəm [ɪ'ljuː-, -ʒn̩-], -st/s

illusive, -ly, -ness ɪ'luːsɪv [ɪ'ljuː-], -lɪ, -nɪs [-nəs]

illusor|y, -ily, -iness ɪ'luːsər|ɪ [ɪ'ljuː-, -uːzərɪ], -əlɪ [-ɪlɪ], -ɪnɪs [-ɪnəs]

illustrat|e, -es, -ing, -ed, -or/s 'ɪləs- treɪt, -s, -ɪŋ, -ɪd, -ə*/z

illustration, -s ˌɪlə'streɪʃn, -z

illustrative, -ly 'ɪləstrətɪv [-streɪt-, rarely ɪ'lʌstrətɪv], -lɪ

illustrious, -ly, -ness ɪ'lʌstrɪəs, -lɪ, -nɪs [-nəs]

ill-will ˌɪl'wɪl

ill-wisher, -s ˌɪl'wɪʃə* ['-ˌ--], -z

Illyria, -n/s ɪ'lɪrɪə, -n/z

Illyricum ɪ'lɪrɪkəm

Ilminster 'ɪlmɪnstə*

I'm (= **I am**) aɪm

imag|e (s. v.) (**I.**), **-es, -ing, -ed** 'ɪmɪdʒ, -ɪz, -ɪŋ, -d

imagery 'ɪmɪdʒərɪ

image-worship 'ɪmɪdʒˌwɜːʃɪp

imaginab|le, -ly, -leness ɪ'mædʒɪnəb|l [-dʒən-], -lɪ, -lnɪs [-nəs]

imaginar|y, -ily, -iness ɪ'mædʒɪnər|ɪ [-dʒənər-], -əlɪ [-ɪlɪ], -ɪnɪs [-ɪnəs]

imagination, -s ɪˌmædʒɪ'neɪʃn [-dʒə'n-], -z

imaginative, -ly, -ness ɪ'mædʒɪnətɪv [-dʒən-], -lɪ, -nɪs [-nəs]

imagin|e, -es, -ing/s, -ed, -er/s ɪ'mæ- dʒɪn [-dʒən], -z, -ɪŋ/z, -d, -ə*/z

imago, -s, imagines (plur. of **imago**) ɪ'meɪgəʊ [ɪ'mɑːg-], -z, ɪ'meɪdʒɪniːz [ɪ'mɑːgɪniːz]

imam, -s ɪ'mɑːm, -z

imbalance ˌɪm'bæləns

imbecile, -s 'ɪmbɪsiːl [-bəs-, -saɪl], -z

imbecilit|y, -ies ˌɪmbɪ'sɪlət|ɪ [-bə's-, -ɪt|ɪ], -ɪz

imbib|e, -es, -ing, -ed, -er/s ɪm'baɪb, -z, -ɪŋ, -d, -ə*/z

imbroglio, -s ɪm'brəʊlɪəʊ [-ljəʊ], -z

imbru|e, -es, -ing, -ed ɪm'bruː, -z, -ɪŋ [ɪm'bruɪŋ], -d

imbu|e, -es, -ing, -ed ɪm'bjuː, -z, -ɪŋ [ɪm'bjʊɪŋ], -d

Imeson 'aɪmɪsn

imitability ˌɪmɪtə'bɪlətɪ [-lɪt-]

imitable 'ɪmɪtəbl

imitat|e, -es, -ing, -ed, -or/s 'ɪmɪteɪt, -s, -ɪŋ, -ɪd, -ə*/z

imitation, -s ˌɪmɪ'teɪʃn, -z

253

imitative, -ly, -ness 'ımıtətıv [-teıt-], -lı, -nıs [-nəs]

immaculate, -ly, -ness ı'mækjʊlət [-lıt], -lı, -nıs [-nəs]

immanen|ce, -t 'ımənən|s, -t

Immanuel ı'mænjʊəl [-njwəl, -njʊl]

immaterial, -ly ˌımə'tıərıəl, -ı

immateriali|sm, -st/s ˌımə'tıərıəlı|zəm, -st/s

immateriality 'ımə,tıərı'ælətı [-ıtı]

immaterializ|e [-is|e], -es, -ing, -ed ˌımə'tıərıəlaız, -ız, -ıŋ, -d

immature, -ly, -ness ˌımə'tjʊə* [-'tjɔə*, -'tjɔ:*, -'tʃʊə*, -'tʃɔ:*], -lı, -nıs [-nəs]

immaturity ˌımə'tjʊərətı [-'tjɔər-, -'tjɔ:r-, -'tʃʊər-, -'tʃɔ:r-, -ıtı]

immeasurable ı'meʒərəbl [ˌı'm-]

immeasurab|ly, -leness ı'meʒərəb|lı, -lnıs [-nəs]

immediacy ı'mi:djəsı [-dɪəsı]

immediate, -ly ı'mi:djət [-dʒət, -dıət, -dıt, -djıt], -lı

immemorial, -ly ˌımı'mɔ:rıəl [-mə'm-], -lı

immense, -ly, -ness ı'mens, -lı, -nıs [-nəs]

immensit|y, -ies ı'mensət|ı [-ıt|ı], -ız

immers|e, -es, -ing, -ed ı'mɜ:s, -ız, -ıŋ, -t

immersion, -s ı'mɜ:ʃn, -z

immersion-heater, -s ı'mɜ:ʃn,hi:tə*, -z

immigrant, -s 'ımıgrənt, -s

immigrat|e, -es, -ing, -ed 'ımıgreıt, -s, -ıŋ, -ıd

immigration, -s ˌımı'greıʃn, -z

imminen|ce, -t/ly 'ımınən|s, -t/lı

immobile ı'məʊbaıl [-bi:l]

immobility ˌıməʊ'bılətı [-lıt-]

immobilization [-isa-] ı,məʊbılaı'zeıʃn [-bəl-, -lı'z-]

immobiliz|e [-is|e], -es, -ing, -ed ı'məʊbılaız [-bəl-], -ız, -ıŋ, -d

immoderate, -ness ı'mɒdərət [ˌı'm-, -rıt], -nıs [-nəs]

immoderately ı'mɒdərətlı [-rıt-]

immoderation ı,mɒdə'reıʃn

immodest, -ly ı'mɒdıst [ˌı'm-], -lı

immodesty ı'mɒdıstı [ˌı'm-, -dəst-]

immolat|e, -es, -ing, -ed, -or/s 'ıməʊleıt, -s, -ıŋ, -ıd, -ə*/z

immolation, -s ˌıməʊ'leıʃn, -z

immor|al, -ally ı'mɒr|əl [ˌı'm-], -əlı [-lı]

immoralit|y, -ies ˌımə'rælət|ı [-mɒ'r-, -ıt|ı], -ız

immort|al (s. adj.), -als, -ally ı'mɔ:t|l [ˌı'm-], -lz, -əlı [-lı]

immortality ˌımɔ:'tælətı [-ıtı]

immortaliz|e [-is|e], -es, -ing, -ed ı'mɔ:təlaız [-tʃaız], -ız, -ıŋ, -d

immortelle, -s ˌımɔ:'tel, -z

immovability ı,mu:və'bılətı [ˌımu:v-, -lıt-]

immovab|le, -leness ı'mu:vəb|l [ˌı'm-], -lnıs [-nəs]

immovably ı'mu:vəblı

immune ı'mju:n

immunit|y, -ies ı'mju:nət|ı [-ıt|ı], -ız

immunization [-isa-] ˌımju:naı'zeıʃn [-mjʊn-, -nı'z-]

immuniz|e [-is|e], -es, -ing, -ed 'ımju:naız [-mjʊn-], -ız, -ıŋ, -d

immunolog|y, -ist/s ˌımju:n'ɒlədʒ|ı [-mjʊn-], -ıst/s

immur|e, -es, -ing, -ed, -ement ı'mjʊə* [-'mjɔə*, -'mjɔ:*], -z, -rıŋ, -d, -mənt

immutability ı,mju:tə'bılətı ['ı,m-, -lıt-]

immutab|le, -ly, -leness ı'mju:təb|l, -lı, -lnıs [-nəs]

Imogen 'ıməʊdʒən [-dʒen]

imp (s. v.), -s, -ing, -ed ımp, -s, -ıŋ, -t [ımt]

impact (s.), -s 'ımpækt, -s

impact (v.), -s, -ing, -ed ım'pækt, -s, -ıŋ, -ıd

impair, -s, -ing, -ed ım'peə*, -z, -rıŋ, -d

impairment ım'peəmənt

impal|e, -es, -ing, -ed, -ement ım'peıl, -z, -ıŋ, -d, -mənt

impalpab|le, -ly ım'pælpəb|l [ˌım'p-], -lı

imparisyllabic 'ım,pærısı'læbık [-rəs-]

impart, -s, -ing, -ed ım'pɑ:t, -s, -ıŋ, -ıd

impartation ˌımpɑ:'teıʃn

imparti|al, -ally, -alness ım'pɑ:ʃ|l [ˌım'p-], -əlı, -lnıs [-nəs]

impartiality 'ım,pɑ:ʃı'ælətı [ˌımpɑ:-, ım,pɑ:-, -ıtı]

impassability 'ım,pɑ:sə'bılətı [-lıt-]

impassable ım'pɑ:səbl [ˌım'p-]

impasse, -s æm'pɑ:s ['--] (ɛ̃pɑ:s), -ız

impassible ım'pæsəbl [-sıbl]

impassioned ım'pæʃnd

impassive, -ly, -ness ım'pæsıv, -lı, -nıs [-nəs]

impassivity ˌımpæ'sıvətı [-ıtı]

impatien|ce, -t/ly ım'peıʃn|s, -t/lı

impeach, -es, -ing, -ed, -er/s, -ment/s; -able ım'pi:tʃ, -ız, -ıŋ, -t, -ə*/z, -mənt/s; -əbl

impeccability ım,pekə'bılətı [ˌımpek-, -lıt-]

impeccable ım'pekəbl

impecunious, -ness ˌımpı'kju:njəs [-nıəs], -nıs [-nəs]

impedance ım'pi:dəns

imped|e, -es, -ing, -ed ɪm'piːd, -z, -ɪŋ, -ɪd

impediment, -s ɪm'pedɪmənt, -s

impedimenta ɪm,pedɪ'mentə [,ɪmped-]

impel, -s, -ling, -led, -ler/s; -lent ɪm'pel, -z, -ɪŋ, -d, -ə*/z; -ənt

impend, -s, -ing, -ed ɪm'pend, -z, -ɪŋ, -ɪd

impenetrability ɪm,penɪtrə'bɪlətɪ ['ɪm,p-, -lɪt-]

impenetrab|le, -ly, -leness ɪm'penɪtrəb|l, -lɪ, -lnɪs [-nəs]

impeniten|ce, -t/ly ɪm'penɪtən|s [,ɪm'p-], -t/lɪ

imperative (s. adj.), -s, -ly, -ness ɪm'perətɪv, -z, -lɪ, -nɪs [-nəs]

imperator, -s ,ɪmpə'rɑːtɔː* [-'reɪtɔː*, -tə*], -z

imperatorial ɪm,perə'tɔːrɪəl [,ɪmper-]

imperceptibility 'ɪmpə,septə'bɪlətɪ [-tɪ'b-, -lɪt-]

imperceptib|le, -ly, -leness ,ɪmpə-'septəb|l [-tɪb-], -lɪ, -lnɪs [-nəs]

imperfect (s. adj.), -s, -ly, -ness ɪm-'pɜːfɪkt [,ɪm'p-], -s, -lɪ, -nɪs

imperfection, -s ,ɪmpə'fekʃn, -z

imperforate ɪm'pɜːfərət [,ɪm'p-, -rɪt]

imperial (s. adj.), -s, -ly ɪm'pɪərɪəl, -z, -ɪ

imperiali|sm -st/s ɪm'pɪərɪəlɪ|zəm, -st/s

imper|il, -ils, -illing, -illed ɪm'per|əl [-ɪl], -əlz [-ɪlz], -əlɪŋ [-ɪlɪŋ, -lɪŋ], -əld [-ɪld]

imperious, -ly, -ness ɪm'pɪərɪəs, -lɪ, -nɪs [-nəs]

imperishability ɪm,perɪʃə'bɪlətɪ ['ɪm,p-, -lɪt-]

imperishab|le, -ly, -leness ɪm'perɪʃəb|l [,ɪm'p-], -lɪ, -lnɪs [-nəs]

impermeability ɪm,pɜːmjə'bɪlətɪ ['ɪm,p-, -mɪə-, -lɪt-]

impermeable, -ly, -leness ɪm'pɜːmjəb|l [,ɪm'p-, -mɪə-], -lɪ, -lnɪs [-nəs]

impers|onal, -onally ɪm'pɜːs|n̩l [,ɪm'p-, -n̩l, -ənl], -nəlɪ [-nəlɪ, -n̩lɪ, -n̩lɪ, -ən̩lɪ]

impersonality ɪm,pɜːsə'nælətɪ ['ɪm,p-, -sn̩'æ-, -ɪtɪ]

impersonat|e, -es, -ing, -ed, -or/s ɪm-'pɜːsəneɪt [-sn̩ert], -s, -ɪŋ, -ɪd, -ə*/z

impersonation, -s ɪm,pɜːsə'neɪʃn [-sn̩'eɪ-], -z

impertinen|ce (insolence, etc.), -t/ly ɪm'pɜːtɪnən|s [-tn̩ən-], -t/lɪ

impertinen|ce (irrelevance, etc.), -t/ly ɪm'pɜːtɪnən|s [,ɪm'p-], -t/lɪ

imperturbability 'ɪmpə,tɜːbə'bɪlətɪ [-lɪt-]

imperturbab|le, -ly, -leness ,ɪmpə-'tɜːbəb|l, -lɪ, -lnɪs [-nəs]

impervious, -ly, -ness ɪm'pɜːvjəs [,ɪm'p-, -vɪəs], -lɪ, -nɪs [-nəs]

impetigo ,ɪmpɪ'taɪgəʊ [-pə't-, -pe't-]

impetuosity ɪm,petjʊ'ɒsətɪ [-ɪtɪ]

impetuous, -ly, -ness ɪm'petjʊəs [-tjwəs], -lɪ, -nɪs [-nəs]

impetus 'ɪmpɪtəs [-pət-]

Impey 'ɪmpɪ

impiet|y, -ies ɪm'paɪət|ɪ [,ɪm'p-, -aɪt-], -ɪz

imping|e, -es, -ing, -ed, -ement/s ɪm-'pɪndʒ, -ɪz, -ɪŋ, -d, -mənt/s

impious, -ly, -ness 'ɪmpɪəs [-pjəs], -lɪ, -nɪs [-nəs]

impish, -ly, -ness 'ɪmpɪʃ, -lɪ, -nɪs [-nəs]

implacability ɪm,plækə'bɪlətɪ ['ɪm,plæk-, -,pleɪk-, -lɪt-]

implacab|le, -ly, -leness ɪm'plækəb|l [-'pleɪk-], -lɪ, -lnɪs [-nəs]

implant (s.), -s 'ɪmplɑːnt, -s

implant (v.), -s, -ing, -ed, -er/s ɪm-'plɑːnt, -s, -ɪŋ, -ɪd, -ə*/z

implantation ,ɪmplɑːn'teɪʃn [-plæn-]

implement (s.), -s 'ɪmplɪmənt [-plə-], -s

implement (v.), -s, -ing, -ed 'ɪmplɪment [-plə-], -s, -ɪŋ, -ɪd

implementation ,ɪmplɪmen'teɪʃn [-plə-]

implicate (s.) 'ɪmplɪkət [-kɪt, -keɪt]

implicat|e (v.), -es, -ing, -ed 'ɪmplɪkeɪt, -s, -ɪŋ, -ɪd

implication, -s ,ɪmplɪ'keɪʃn, -z

implicative, -ly ɪm'plɪkətɪv ['ɪmplɪkeɪtɪv], -lɪ

implicit, -ly, -ness ɪm'plɪsɪt, -lɪ, -nɪs [-nəs]

implod|e, -es, -ing, -ed ɪm'pləʊd, -z, -ɪŋ, -ɪd

implor|e, -es, -ing/ly, -ed, -er/s ɪm-'plɔː* [-'plɔə*], -z, -rɪŋ/lɪ, -d, -rə*/z

implosion, -s ɪm'pləʊʒn, -z

implosive (s. adj.), -s ɪm'pləʊsɪv [,ɪm'p-, -əʊzɪ-], -z

impl|y, -ies, -ying, -ied, -iedly ɪm'pl|aɪ, -aɪz, -aɪɪŋ, -aɪd, -aɪdlɪ

impolicy ɪm'pɒləsɪ [,ɪm'p-, -lɪs-]

impolite, -ly, -ness ,ɪmpə'laɪt [-pəʊ'l-, -pʊ'l-], -lɪ, -nɪs [-nəs]

impolitic ɪm'pɒlətɪk [,ɪm'p-, -lɪt-]

imponderable (s. adj.), -s ɪm'pɒndərəbl, -z

import (s.), -s, 'ɪmpɔːt, -s

import (v.), -s, -ing, -ed, -er/s ɪm'pɔːt [rarely 'ɪmpɔːt], -s, -ɪŋ, -ɪd, -ə*/z

importable ɪm'pɔːtəbl

importan|ce, -t/ly ɪm'pɔːtn̩|s, -t/lɪ

importation, -s ˌimpɔː'teiʃn, -z

importunate, -ly, -ness im'pɔːtjunət [-tʃu-, -tʃə-, -nit], -li, -nis [-nəs]

importun|e, -es, -ing, -ed im'pɔːtju:n [-tʃu:n, ˌimpɔː'tju:n], -z, im'pɔːtjunin [-tʃunin, ˌimpɔː'tju:nin], im'pɔːtju:nd [-tʃu:nd, ˌimpɔː'tju:nd]

importunit|y, -ies ˌimpɔː'tju:nət|i [-it|i], -iz

impos|e, -es, -ing, -ed, -er/s; -able im'pəuz, -iz, -in, -d, -ə*/z; -əbl

imposing (adj.), -ly, -ness im'pəuzin, -li -nis [-nəs]

imposition, -s ˌimpə'ziʃn [-pu'z-], -z

impossibilit|y, -ies im,pɒsə'bilət|i [ˌimpɒs-, -si'b-, -lit-], -iz

impossib|le, -ly im'pɒsəb|l [-sib-], -li

impost, -s 'impəust, -s

impos|tor/s, -ture/s im'pɒs|tə*/z -tʃə*/z

impoten|ce, -cy, -t/ly 'impətən|s[-put-], -si, -t/li

impound, -s, -ing, -ed im'paund, -z, -in, -id

impoverish, -es, -ing, -ed, -ment im-'pɒvəriʃ, -iz, -in, -t, -mənt

impracticability, -ies im,præktikə-'bilət|i ['im,præktikə'b-, -lit-], -iz

impracticab|le, -ly, -leness im'præktik-əb|l [ˌim'p-], -li, -lnis [-nəs]

imprecat|e, -es, -ing, -ed, -or/s 'im-prikeit, -s, -in, -id, -ə*/z

imprecation, -s ˌimpri'keiʃn, -z

imprecatory 'imprikeitəri [im'prekə-təri]

impregn, -s, -ing, -ed im'pri:n, -z, -in, -d

impregnability im,pregnə'bilət|i [-lit-]

impregnab|le, -ly im'pregnəb|l, -li

impregnate (adj.) im'pregnit [-nət, -neit]

impregnat|e (v.), -es, -ing, -ed 'im-pregneit [im'pregneit], -s, -in, -id

impregnation, -s ˌimpreg'neiʃn, -z

impresario, -s ˌimpri'sɑːriəu [-prə's-, -pre's-, -'zɑː-], -z

impress (s.), -es 'impres, -iz

impress (v.), -es, -ing, -ed im'pres, -iz, -in, -t

impressibility im,presi'bilət|i [-sə'b-, -lit-]

impressib|le, -ly, -leness im'presəb|l [-sib-], -li, -lnis [-nəs]

impression, -s im'preʃn, -z

impressionability im,preʃnə'bilət|i [-ʃənə-, -ʃnə-, -lit-]

impressionable im'preʃnəbl [-ʃənə-, -ʃnə-]

impressioni|sm, -st/s im'preʃn̩i|zəm [-ʃni-], -st/s

impressionistic im,preʃə'nistik [-ʃn̩'i-]

impressive, -ly, -ness im'presiv, -li, -nis [-nəs]

impressment, -s im'presmənt, -s

imprest, -s 'imprest, -s

imprimatur, -s ˌimpri'meitə* [-prai'm-, -'mɑːtə*, -ˌtuə*], -z

imprimis im'praimis

imprint (s.), -s 'imprint, -s

imprint (v.), -s, -ing, -ed im'print, -s, -in, -id

impris|on, -ons, -oning, -oned, -onment/s im'priz|n, -nz, -n̩in, -nd, -nmənt/s

improbabilit|y, -ies im,prɒbə'bilət|i ['im,prɒbə'b-, -lit-], -iz

improbab|le, -ly im'prɒbəb|l [ˌim'p-], -li

improbity im'prəubəti [ˌim'p-, -'prɒb-, -iti]

impromptu, -s im'prɒmptju:, -z

improper, -ly im'prɒpə* [ˌim'p-], -li

impropriat|e, -es, -ing, -ed, -or/s im-'prəuprieit, -s, -in, -id, -ə*/z

impropriation, -s im,prəupri'eiʃn, -z

impropriet|y, -ies ˌimprə'praiət|i [-pru'p-], -iz

improvability im,pru:və'bilət|i [-lit-]

improvab|le, -ly, -leness im'pru:vəb|l, -li, -lnis [-nəs]

improv|e, -es, -ing, -ed, -er/s, -ement/s im'pru:v, -z, -in, -d, -ə*/z, -mənt/s

improviden|ce, -t/ly im'prɒvidən|s, -t/li

improvisation, -s ˌimprəvai'zeiʃn [-prɒv-, ˌimprɒvi'z-], -z

improvis|e, -es, -ing, -ed, -er/s 'im-prəvaiz [-prɒv-], -iz, -in, -d, -ə*/z

impruden|ce, -t/ly im'pru:dən|s [ˌim'p-], -t/li

impuden|ce, -t/ly 'impjudən|s, -t/li

impugn, -s, -ing, -ed, -er/s im'pju:n, -z, -in, -d, -ə/*z

impuissan|ce, -t im'pju:isn|s [-'pjuɪ-], -t

impulse, -s 'impʌls, -iz

impulsion, -s im'pʌlʃn, -z

impulsive, -ly, -ness im'pʌlsiv, -li, -nis [-nəs]

impunity im'pju:nəti [-iti]

impur|e, -ely, -eness; -ity, -ities im'pjuə* [ˌim'p-, -'pjɔə*, -'pjɔ:*], -li, -nis [-nəs]; -rəti [-riti], -rətiz [-ritiz]

imputability im,pju:tə'bilət|i [ˌimpju:t-, -lit-]

imputation, -s ˌɪmpjuː'teɪʃn [-pjʊ-], -z
imput|e, -es, -ing, -ed, -er/s; -able
 ɪm'pjuːt, -s, -ɪŋ, -ɪd, -ə*/z; -əbl
Imr|ay, -e, -ie 'ɪmr|eɪ, -ɪ, -ɪ
in ɪn
Ina 'aɪnə
inability ˌɪnə'bɪlətɪ [-lɪt-]
inaccessibility 'ɪnækˌsesə'bɪlətɪ [-nək-,
 -sɪ'b-, -lɪt-]
inaccessib|le, -ly, -leness ˌɪnæk'sesəb|l
 [-nək-, -sɪb-], -lɪ, -lnɪs [-nəs]
inaccurac|y, -ies ɪn'ækjʊrəs|ɪ [ˌɪn'æ-,
 -kjər-, -rɪs-], -ɪz
inaccur|ate, -ately ɪn'ækjʊr|ət [ˌɪn'æ-,
 -kjər-, -rɪt], -ətlɪ [-ɪtlɪ]
inaction ɪn'ækʃn [ˌɪn'æ-]
inactive, -ly ɪn'æktɪv [ˌɪn'æ-], -lɪ
inactivity ˌɪnæk'tɪvətɪ [-ɪtɪ]
inadequacy ɪn'ædɪkwəsɪ [ˌɪn'æ-]
inadequate, -ly, -ness ɪn'ædɪkwət
 [ˌɪn'æ-, -kwɪt], -lɪ, -nɪs [-nəs]
inadmissibility 'ɪnədˌmɪsə'bɪlətɪ [-sɪ'b-,
 -lɪt-]
inadmissib|le, -ly ˌɪnəd'mɪsəb|l [-sɪb-],
 -lɪ
inadverten|ce, -cy, -t/ly ˌɪnəd'vɜː-
 tən|s, -sɪ, -t/lɪ
inadvisable ˌɪnəd'vaɪzəbl
inalienability ɪnˌeɪljənə'bɪlətɪ ['ɪnˌeɪ-,
 -lɪən-, -lɪt-]
inalienable ɪn'eɪljənəbl [ˌɪn'eɪ-, -lɪən-]
inalienab|ly, -leness ɪn'eɪljənəb|lɪ
 [-lɪən-], -lnɪs [-nəs]
inamorata, -s ɪnˌæmə'rɑːtə [ˌɪnæ-,
 -mɒ'r-], -z
inane, -ly, -ness ɪ'neɪn, -lɪ, -nɪs [-nəs]
inanimate, -ly, -ness ɪn'ænɪmət [ˌɪn'æ-,
 -mɪt], -lɪ, -nɪs [-nəs]
inanition ˌɪnə'nɪʃn [-næ'n-]
inanit|y, -ies ɪ'nænət|ɪ [-'nem-, -ɪt|ɪ],
 -ɪz
inappeasable ˌɪnə'piːzəbl
inapplicability 'ɪnˌæplɪkə'bɪlətɪ ['ɪn-
 əˌplɪk-, -lɪt-]
inapplicable, -ness ɪn'æplɪkəbl [ˌɪn'æ-,
 ˌɪnə'plɪk-], -nɪs [-nəs]
inapposite, -ly ɪn'æpəzɪt [ˌɪn'æ-, -pʊz-],
 -lɪ
inappreciab|le, -ly ˌɪnə'priː:ʃəb|l [-ʃə-,
 -ʃɪə-], -lɪ
inapproachab|le, -ly ˌɪnə'prəʊtʃəb|l
 -lɪ
inappropri|ate, -ately, -ateness ˌɪnə-
 'prəʊprɪ|ət [-prɪ|ɪt], -ətlɪ [-ɪtlɪ], -ətnɪs
 [-ɪt-, -nəs]
inapt, -ly, -ness ɪn'æpt [ˌɪn'æpt], -lɪ,
 -nɪs [-nəs]
inaptitude ɪn'æptɪtjuːd [ˌɪn'æ-]

inarticulate, -ly, -ness ˌɪnɑː'tɪkjʊlət
 [-lɪt], -lɪ, -nɪs [-nəs]
inartistic, -al, -ally ˌɪnɑː'tɪstɪk, -l, -əlɪ
inasmuch ˌɪnəz'mʌtʃ
inattention ˌɪnə'tenʃn
inattentive, -ly, -ness ˌɪnə'tentɪv,
 -lɪ, -nɪs [-nəs]
inaudibility ɪnˌɔːdə'bɪlətɪ ['ɪnˌɔːdə'b-,
 -dɪ'b-, -lɪt-]
inaudib|le, -ly, -leness ɪn'ɔːdəb|l [ˌɪn'ɔː-,
 -dɪb-], -lɪ, -lnɪs [-nəs]
inaugural ɪ'nɔːgjʊrəl [-gjər-]
inaugurat|e, -es, -ing, -ed, -or/s ɪ'nɔː-
 gjʊreɪt [-gjər-], -s, -ɪŋ, -ɪd, -ə*/z
inauguration, -s ɪˌnɔːgjʊ'reɪʃn [-gjə'r-],
 -z
inauspicious, -ly, -ness ˌɪnɔː'spɪʃəs,
 [-nɒ's-], -lɪ, -nɪs
inborn ˌɪn'bɔːn [also 'ɪnb- when attribu-
 tive]
inbreath|e, -es, -ing, -ed ˌɪn'briːð, -z,
 -ɪŋ, -d [also 'ɪnbriːð when attribu-
 tive]
inbreed, -s, -ing, inbred ˌɪn'briːd, -z,
 -ɪŋ, ˌɪn'bred [also 'ɪnbred when
 attributive]
Inca, -s 'ɪŋkə, -z
incalculability ɪnˌkælkjʊlə'bɪlətɪ ['ɪn-
 ˌkælkjʊlə'b-, (')ɪŋˌk-, -kjəl-, -lɪt-]
incalculable, -ness ɪn'kælkjʊləbl [ˌɪn'k-,
 (ˌ)ɪŋ'k-, -kjəl-], -nɪs [-nəs]
incalculably ɪn'kælkjʊləblɪ [ɪŋ'k-,
 -kjəl-]
in camera ˌɪn'kæmərə [ˌɪŋ-]
incandescen|ce -t ˌɪnkæn'desn|s [ˌɪŋk-,
 -kən-], -t
incantation, -s ˌɪnkæn'teɪʃn [ˌɪŋk-], -z
incapabilit|y, -ies ɪnˌkeɪpə'bɪlət|ɪ
 ['ɪnˌkeɪpə'b-, (')ɪŋˌk-, -lɪt-], -ɪz
incapable, -ness ɪn'keɪpəbl [ˌɪn'k-,
 (ˌ)ɪŋ'k-], -nɪs [-nəs]
incapacitat|e, -es, -ing, -ed ˌɪnkə'pæsɪ-
 teɪt [ˌɪŋk-, -sət-], -s, -ɪŋ, -ɪd
incapacitation 'ɪnkəˌpæsɪ'teɪʃn ['ɪŋk-,
 -sə't-]
incapacit|y, -ies ˌɪnkə'pæsət|ɪ [ˌɪŋk-,
 -ɪt|ɪ], -ɪz
incarcerat|e, -es, -ing, -ed ɪn'kɑːsəreɪt
 [ɪŋ'k-], -s, -ɪŋ, -ɪd
incarceration, -s ɪnˌkɑːsə'reɪʃn [ˌɪnkɑː-,
 ɪŋˌk-, ˌɪŋk-], -z
incarnadine ɪn'kɑːnədaɪn [ɪŋ'k-]
incarnate (adj.) ɪn'kɑːneɪt [ɪŋ'k-, -nɪt]
incarnat|e (v.), -es, -ing, -ed 'ɪnkɑːneɪt
 [ɪn'kɑːneɪt, 'ɪŋk-, ɪŋ'k-], -s, -ɪŋ, -ɪd
incarnation (I.), -s ˌɪnkɑː'neɪʃn [ˌɪŋk-],
 -z
incaution ɪn'kɔːʃn [ˌɪn'k-, (ˌ)ɪŋ'k-]

257

incautious, -ly, -ness ɪnˈkɔːʃəs [ˌɪnˈk-, (ˌ)ɪŋ-], -lɪ, -nɪs [-nəs]

Ince ɪns

incendiar|ism, -y, -ies ɪnˈsendjər|ɪzəm [-dɪə-], -ɪ, -ɪz

incense (s.) ˈɪnsens

incens|e (v.) (enrage), **-es, -ing, -ed** ɪnˈsens, -ɪz, -ɪŋ, -t

incens|e (v.) (burn incense), **-es, -ing, -ed** ˈɪnsens, -ɪz, -ɪŋ, -t

incentive, -s ɪnˈsentɪv, -z

incept, -s, -ing, -ed, -or/s; -ive ɪnˈsept, -s, -ɪŋ, -ɪd, -ə*/z; -ɪv

inception, -s ɪnˈsepʃn, -z

incertitude ɪnˈsɜːtɪtjuːd [ˌɪnˈs-]

incessant, -ly ɪnˈsesnt, -lɪ

incest ˈɪnsest

incestuous, -ly, -ness ɪnˈsestjʊəs [-tjwəs], -lɪ, -nɪs [-nəs]

inch (s. v.) (**I.**), **-es, -ing, -ed** ɪntʃ, -ɪz, -ɪŋ, -t

Inch|bald, -cape, -colm, -iquin, -keith ˈɪntʃ|bɔːld, -keɪp, -kəm, -ɪkwɪn, -kiːθ

inchoate (adj.), **-ly** ˈɪŋkəʊeɪt [ˈɪŋk-, -kəʊɪt, -ˈ--], -lɪ

inchoat|e (v.), **-es, -ing, -ed** ˈɪŋkəʊeɪt [ˈɪŋk-], -s, -ɪŋ, -ɪd

inchoation ˌɪŋkəʊˈeɪʃn [ˌɪŋk-]

inchoative ˌɪŋkəʊertɪv [ˈɪŋk-, ɪnˈkəʊə-tɪv, ɪŋˈkəʊətɪv]

Inchrye ɪntʃˈraɪ

inciden|ce, -t/s ˈɪnsɪdən|s, -t/s

incident|al, -ally, -alness ˌɪnsɪˈdent|l, -lɪ [-əlɪ], -lnɪs [-nəs]

incinerat|e, -es, -ing, -ed, -or/s ɪnˈsɪnəreɪt, -s, -ɪŋ, -ɪd, -ə*/z

incineration ɪnˌsɪnəˈreɪʃn

incipien|ce, -cy, -t/ly ɪnˈsɪpɪən|s [-pjən-], -sɪ, -t/lɪ

incis|e, -es, -ing, -ed, -or/s ɪnˈsaɪz, -ɪz, -ɪŋ, -d, -ə*/z

incision, -s ɪnˈsɪʒn, -z

incisive, -ly, -ness ɪnˈsaɪsɪv, -lɪ, -nɪs [-nəs]

incitation, -s ˌɪnsaɪˈteɪʃn [-sɪˈt-], -z

incit|e, -es, -ing/ly, -ed, -er/s, -ement/s ɪnˈsaɪt, -s, -ɪŋ/lɪ, -ɪd, -ə*/z, -mənt/s

incivilit|y, -ies ˌɪnsɪˈvɪlət|ɪ [-ɪt|ɪ], -ɪz

Incledon ˈɪŋkldən

inclemen|cy, -t/ly ɪnˈklemən|sɪ [ˌɪnˈk-, (ˌ)ɪŋˈk-], -t/lɪ

inclination, -s ˌɪnklɪˈneɪʃn [ˌɪŋkl-, -ləˈn-], -z

incline (s.), **-s** ɪnˈklaɪn [ɪŋˈkl-, ˈɪnklaɪn, ˈɪŋklaɪn], -z

inclin|e (v.), **-es, -ing, -ed; -able** ɪnˈklaɪn [ɪŋˈkl-], -z, -ɪŋ, -d; -əbl

inclos|e, -es, -ing, -ed ɪnˈkləʊz [ɪŋˈkl-], -ɪz, -ɪŋ, -d

inclosure, -s ɪnˈkləʊʒə* [ɪŋˈkl-], -z

includ|e, -es, -ing, -ed ɪnˈkluːd [ɪŋˈkl-], -z, -ɪŋ, -ɪd

inclusion, -s ɪnˈkluːʒn [ɪŋˈkl-], -z

inclusive, -ly ɪnˈkluːsɪv [ɪŋˈkl-, ˌ-ˈ--], -lɪ

incog. ɪnˈkɒg [ˌɪnˈk-, ɪŋˈk-, ˌɪŋˈk-]

incognito (s. adj. adv.), **-s** ɪnˈkɒgnɪtəʊ [ɪŋˈk-, ˌɪnkɒgˈniːtəʊ], -z

incoheren|ce -t/ly ˌɪnkəʊˈhɪərən|s [ˌɪŋk-], -t/lɪ

incombustibility ˈɪnkəmˌbʌstəˈbɪlətɪ [ˈɪŋk-, -tɪˈb-, -lɪt-]

incombustible, -ness ˌɪnkəmˈbʌstəbl [ˌɪŋk-, -tɪb-], -nɪs [-nəs]

income, -s ˈɪŋkʌm [ˈɪnk-, -kəm], -z

incomer, -s ˈɪnˌkʌmə*, -z

income-tax, -es ˈɪnkəmtæks [ˈɪŋk-, -kʌm-], -ɪz

incoming (s. adj.), **-s** ˈɪnˌkʌmɪŋ, -z

incommensurability ˌɪnkəˌmenʃərə-ˈbɪlətɪ [ˈɪŋk-, -ʃʊr-, -lɪt-]

incommensurab|le (s. adj.), **-les, -ly, -leness** ˌɪnkəˈmenʃərəb|l [ˌɪŋk-, -ʃʊr-], -lz, -lɪ, -lnɪs [-nəs]

incommensurate, -ly, -ness ˌɪnkəˈmenʃərət [ˌɪŋk-, -ʃʊr-, -rɪt], -lɪ, -nɪs [-nəs]

incommod|e, -es, -ing, -ed ˌɪnkəˈməʊd [ˌɪŋk-], -z, -ɪŋ, -ɪd

incommodious, -ness ˌɪnkəˈməʊdjəs [ˌɪŋk-, -dɪəs], -lɪ, -nɪs [-nəs]

incommunicab|le, -ly, -leness ˌɪn-kəˈmjuːnɪkəb|l [ˌɪŋk-, -ˈmjʊn-], -lɪ, -lnɪs [-nəs]

incommunicado ˌɪnkəmjuːnɪˈkɑːdəʊ [ˌɪŋk-, -mjʊnɪ-, ˈ--,--ˈ--]

incommutab|le, -ly, -leness ˌɪnkəˈmjuː-təb|l [ˌɪŋk-], -lɪ, -lnɪs [-nəs]

incomparability ɪnˌkɒmpərəˈbɪlətɪ [ɪŋˌk-, -lɪt-]

incomparab|le, -ly, -leness ɪnˈkɒmpər-əb|l [ɪŋˈk-], -lɪ, -lnɪs [-nəs]

incompatibility ˈɪnkəmˌpætəˈbɪlətɪ [ˈɪŋk-, -tɪˈb-, -lɪt-]

incompatib|le, -ly, -leness ˌɪnkəm-ˈpætəb|l [ˌɪŋk-, -tɪb-], -lɪ, -lnɪs [-nəs]

incompeten|ce, -cy, -t/ly ɪnˈkɒmpɪ-tən|s [ˌɪnˈk-, (ˌ)ɪŋˈk-], -sɪ, -t/lɪ

incomplete, -ly, -ness ˌɪnkəmˈpliːt [ˌɪŋk-], -lɪ, -nɪs [-nəs]

incompletion ˌɪnkəmˈpliːʃn [ˌɪŋk]

incomprehensibility ɪnˌkɒmprɪhensə-ˈbɪlətɪ [ˈɪnˌkɒmprɪhensəˈb-, ɪŋˌk-, ˈɪŋˌk-, -sɪˈb-, -lɪt-]

incomprehensib|le, -ly, -leness ɪnˌkɒm-prɪˈhensəb|l [ˈɪnˌkɒmprɪˈh-, ɪŋˌk-, ˈɪŋˌk-, -sɪb-], -lɪ, -lnɪs [-nəs]

incompressibility ˈɪnkəmˌpresəˈbɪlətɪ [ˈɪŋk-, -sɪˈb-, -lɪt-]
incompressible, -ness ˌɪnkəmˈpresəbl [ˌɪŋk-, -sɪb-], -nɪs [-nəs]
incomputable ˌɪnkəmˈpju:təbl [ˌɪŋkəmˈp-, ɪnˈkɒmpjutəbl, ˌɪnˈkɒmpjʊt-, ɪŋˈkɒmpjʊt-]
inconceivability ˈɪnkənˌsi:vəˈbɪlətɪ [ˈɪŋk-, -lɪt-]
inconceivable, -ness ˌɪnkənˈsi:vəbl [ˌɪŋk-, -nɪs [-nəs]
inconceivably ˌɪnkənˈsi:vəblɪ [ˌɪŋk-]
inconclusive, -ly, -ness ˌɪnkənˈklu:sɪv [ˌɪŋk-, -kəŋˈk-], -lɪ, -nɪs [-nəs]
incongruit|y, -ies ɪnkɒŋˈgru:ət|ɪ [ˌɪŋk-, -ˈgrʊ-, -ɪt|ɪ], -ɪz
incongruous, -ly, -nes ɪnˈkɒŋgrʊəs [ɪŋˈk-, -grwəs], -lɪ, -nɪs [-nəs]
inconsequen|ce, -ces, -t/ly ɪnˈkɒnsɪkwən|s [ɪŋˈk-], -sɪz, -t/lɪ
inconsequential ˌɪnkɒnsɪˈkwenʃl [ˌɪŋk-, -ˌ--ˈ--]
inconsiderab|le, -ly, -leness ˌɪnkənˈsɪdərəb|l [ˌɪŋk-], -lɪ, -lnɪs [-nəs]
inconsiderate, -ly, -ness ˌɪnkənˈsɪdərət [ˌɪŋk-, -rɪt], -lɪ, -nɪs [-nəs]
inconsideration ˈɪnkənˌsɪdəˈreɪʃn [ˈɪŋk-]
inconsisten|cy, -cies, -t/ly ˌɪnkənˈsɪstən|sɪ [ˌɪŋk-], -sɪz, -t/lɪ
inconsolab|le, -ly, -leness ˌɪnkənˈsəʊləb|l [ˌɪŋk-], -lɪ, -lnɪs [-nəs]
inconspicuous, -ly, -ness ˌɪnkənˈspɪkjʊəs [ˌɪŋk-, -kjwəs], -lɪ, -nɪs [-nəs]
inconstan|cy, -t/ly ɪnˈkɒnstən|sɪ [ˌɪnˈk-, ɪŋˈk-, ˌɪŋˈk-], -t/lɪ
incontestability ˈɪnkənˌtestəˈbɪlətɪ [ˈɪŋk-, -lɪt-]
incontestab|le, -ly ˌɪnkənˈtestəb|l [ˌɪŋk-], -lɪ
incontinen|ce, -t/ly ɪnˈkɒntɪnən|s [ˌɪnˈk-, ɪŋˈk-, ˌɪŋˈk-], -t/lɪ
incontrollab|le, -ly ˌɪnkənˈtrəʊləb|l [ˌɪŋk-], -lɪ
incontrovertibility ɪnˌkɒntrəvɜːtəˈbɪlətɪ [ˈɪnˌkɒntrəvɜːtəˈb-, ɪŋˌk-, ˈɪŋˌk-, -trʊv-, -tɪˈb-, -lɪt-]
incontrovertib|le, -ly ˌɪnkɒntrəˈvɜːtəb|l [ˌɪŋk-, -trʊv-, -tɪb-, -ˌ--ˈ---, -ˈ----], -lɪ
inconvenienc|e (s. v.), -es, -ing, -ed ˌɪnkənˈvi:njəns [ˌɪŋk-, -nɪəns], -ɪz, -ɪŋ, -t
inconvenient, -ly ˌɪnkənˈvi:njənt [ˌɪŋk-, -nɪənt], -lɪ
inconvertibility ˈɪnkənˌvɜːtəˈbɪlətɪ [ˈɪŋk-, -tɪˈb-, -lɪt-]
inconvertib|le, -ly ˌɪnkənˈvɜːtəb|l [ˌɪŋk-, -tɪb-], -lɪ

incorporate (adj.) ɪnˈkɔːpərət [ɪŋˈk-, -rɪt]
incorporat|e (v.), -es, -ing, -ed ɪnˈkɔːpəreɪt [ɪŋˈk-], -s, -ɪŋ, -ɪd
incorporation, -s ɪnˌkɔːpəˈreɪʃn [ɪŋˌk-], -z
incorporeal, -ly ˌɪnkɔːˈpɔːrɪəl [ˌɪŋk-], -ɪ
incorrect, -ly, -ness ˌɪnkəˈrekt [ˌɪŋk-], -lɪ, -nɪs [-nəs]
incorrigibility ɪnˌkɒrɪdʒəˈbɪlətɪ [ɪŋˌk-, -dʒɪˈb-, -lɪt-]
incorrigib|le, -ly, -leness ɪnˈkɒrɪdʒəb|l [ɪŋˈk-, -dʒɪb-], -lɪ, -lnɪs [-nəs]
incorruptibility ˈɪnkəˌrʌptəˈbɪlətɪ [ˈɪŋk-, -tɪˈb-, -lɪt-]
incorruptib|le, -ly, -leness ˌɪnkəˈrʌptəb|l [ˌɪŋk-, -tɪb-], -lɪ, -lnɪs [-nəs]
incorruption (when contrasted with corruption, as is usually the case) ˈɪnkəˌrʌpʃn [ˈɪŋk-, (when not so contrasted) ˌɪnkəˈr- [ˌɪŋk-]
increase (s.), -s ˈɪnkri:s [ˈɪŋkri:s, ɪnˈkri:s, ɪŋˈkri:s], -ɪz
increas|e (v.), -es, -ing/ly, -ed ɪnˈkri:s [ɪŋˈk-, ˈɪnkri:s, ˈɪŋkri:s], -ɪz, -ɪŋ/lɪ, -t
incredibility ɪnˌkredɪˈbɪlətɪ [ɪŋˌk,-dəˈb-, -lɪt-]
incredib|le, -ly, -leness ɪnˈkredəb|l [ɪŋˈk-, -dɪb-], -lɪ, -lnɪs [-nəs]
incredulity ˌɪnkrɪˈdju:lətɪ [ˌɪŋkrɪˈd-, -kreˈd-, -krəˈd-, -ɪtɪ]
incredulous, -ly, -ness ɪnˈkredjʊləs [ɪŋˈk-], -lɪ, -nɪs [-nəs]
increment, -s ˈɪnkrɪmənt [ˈɪŋk-, -krə-], -s
incremental ˌɪnkrɪˈmentl [ˌɪŋk-, -krə-]
incriminat|e, -es, -ing, -ed ɪnˈkrɪmɪneɪt [ɪŋˈk-], -s, -ɪŋ, -ɪd
incrimination ɪnˌkrɪmɪˈneɪʃn
incriminatory ɪnˈkrɪmɪnətərɪ [ɪŋˈk-, -neɪtərɪ]
incrust, -s, -ing, -ed ɪnˈkrʌst [ɪŋˈk-], -s, -ɪŋ, -ɪd
incrustation, -s ˌɪnkrʌsˈteɪʃn [ˌɪŋk-], -z
incubat|e, -es, -ing, -ed, -or/s; -ive, -ory ˈɪnkjʊbeɪt [ˈɪŋk-], -s, -ɪŋ, -ɪd, -ə*/z; -ɪv, -ərɪ
incubation ˌɪnkjʊˈbeɪʃn [ˌɪŋk-]
incubus, -es ˈɪŋkjʊbəs [ˈɪnk-], -ɪz
inculcat|e, -es, -ing, -ed, -or/s ˈɪnkʌlkeɪt [ˈɪŋk-, -kəl-, ɪnˈkʌlkeɪt, ɪŋˈkʌl-], -s, -ɪŋ, -ɪd, -ə*/z
inculcation ˌɪnkʌlˈkeɪʃn [ˌɪŋk-]
inculpat|e, -es, -ing, -ed ˈɪnkʌlpeɪt [ˈɪŋk-, ɪnˈkʌlpeɪt, ɪŋˈk-], -s, -ɪŋ, -ɪd
inculpation ˌɪnkʌlˈpeɪʃn [ˌɪŋk-]
inculpatory ɪnˈkʌlpətərɪ [ɪŋˈk-, ˈɪnkʌlpeɪtərɪ, ˈɪŋkʌlpeɪtərɪ]

incumben|cy, -cies, -t/s, -tly ɪn'kʌmbən|sɪ [ɪŋ'k-], -sɪz, -t/s, -tlɪ

incunabula ˌɪnkjuː'næbjʊlə [ˌɪŋk-, -kjʊ'n-]

incur, -s, -ring, -red ɪn'kɜː:* [ɪŋ'k-], -z, -rɪŋ, -d

incurability ɪnˌkjʊərə'bɪlətɪ ['ɪnˌkjʊərə'b-, ɪŋˌk-, 'ɪŋˌk-, -jɔər-, -jɔ:r-, -lɪt-]

incurable, -ness ɪn'kjʊərəbl [ˌɪn'k-, ɪŋ'k-, ˌɪŋ'k-, -'kjɔər-, -'kjɔ:r-, -nɪs [-nəs]

incurious ɪn'kjʊərɪəs [ˌɪn'k-, ɪŋ'k-, ˌɪŋ'k-, -'kjɔər-, -'kjɔ:r-]

incursion, -s ɪn'kɜː:ʃn [ɪŋ'k-, -'kɜ:ʒn], -z

incursive ɪn'kɜ:sɪv [ɪŋ'k-]

incurvat|e, -es, -ing, -ed 'ɪnkɜːveɪt ['ɪŋk-], -s, -ɪŋ, -ɪd

incurvation ˌɪnkɜː'veɪʃn [ˌɪŋk-]

incurv|e, -es, -ing, -ed ˌɪn'kɜ:v [ɪn'k-, ɪŋ'k-], -z, -ɪŋ, -d [also 'ɪnkɜ:vd, 'ɪŋkɜ:vd, esp. when attributive]

incus|e (s. adj. v.), -es, -ing, -ed ɪn'kju:z [ɪŋ'k-], -ɪz, -ɪŋ, -d

Ind (surname) ɪnd, (India) ɪnd [aɪnd]

Indaur ɪn'dɔ:* (Hindi) yndəwr

indebted, -ness ɪn'detɪd, -nɪs [-nəs]

indecen|cy, -cies, -t/ly ɪn'di:sn|sɪ [ˌɪn'd-], -sɪz, -t/lɪ

indecipherable ˌɪndɪ'saɪfərəbl

indecision ˌɪndɪ'sɪʒn

indecisive, -ly, -ness ˌɪndɪ'saɪsɪv -lɪ, -nɪs [-nəs]

indeclinable (s. adj.), -s ˌɪndɪ'klaɪnəbl, -z

indecomposable 'ɪnˌdi:kəm'pəʊzəbl

indecorous, -ly, -ness ɪn'dekərəs [ˌɪn'd-], -lɪ, -nɪs [-nəs]

indecorum ˌɪndɪ'kɔ:rəm

indeed (adv) ɪn'di:d, (interj.) ɪn'di:d

indefatigable, -ness ˌɪndɪ'fætɪgəbl, -nɪs [-nəs]

indefatigably ˌɪndɪ'fætɪgəblɪ

indefeasibility 'ɪndɪˌfi:zə'bɪlətɪ [-zɪ'b-, -lɪt-]

indefeasible ˌɪndɪ'fi:zəbl [-zɪb-]

indefeasibly ˌɪndɪ'fi:zəblɪ [-zɪb-]

indefensibility 'ɪndɪˌfensə'bɪlətɪ [-sɪ'b-, -lɪt-]

indefensible ˌɪndɪ'fensəbl [-sɪb-]

indefensibly ˌɪndɪ'fensəblɪ [-sɪb-]

indefinable ˌɪndɪ'faɪnəbl

indefinably ˌɪndɪ'faɪnəblɪ

indefinite, -ly, -ness ɪn'defɪnət [ˌɪn'd-, -fənət, -fnət, -fnət, -ɪt], -lɪ, -nɪs [-nəs]

indelibility ɪnˌdelɪ'bɪlətɪ ['ɪnˌdelɪ'b-, -lə'b-, -lɪt-]

indelible ɪn'deləbl [ˌɪn'd-, -lɪb-]

indelibly ɪn'deləblɪ [-lɪb-]

indelicac|y, -ies ɪn'delɪkəs|ɪ [ˌɪn'd-], -ɪz

indelicate, -ly ɪn'delɪkət [ˌɪn'd-, -kɪt], -lɪ

indemnification, -s ɪnˌdemnɪfɪ'keɪʃn, -z

indemni|fy, -fies, -fying, -fied ɪn'demnɪ|faɪ, -faɪz, -faɪɪŋ, -faɪd

indemnit|y, -ies ɪn'demnət|ɪ [-ɪt|ɪ], -ɪz

indemonstrable ɪn'demənstrəbl [ˌɪn'd-, ˌɪndɪ'mɒns-]

indent (s.), -s 'ɪndent [-'-], -s

indent (v.), -s, -ing, -ed ɪn'dent, -s, -ɪŋ, -ɪd

indentation, -s ˌɪnden'teɪʃn, -z

indenture, -s ɪn'dentʃə*, -z

independen|ce, -cy ˌɪndɪ'pendən|s, -sɪ

independent (s. adj.), -s, -ly ˌɪndɪ'pendənt, -s, -lɪ

Inderwick 'ɪndəwɪk [-də:-]

indescribable ˌɪndɪ'skraɪbəbl

indescribably ˌɪndɪ'skraɪbəblɪ

indestructibility 'ɪndɪˌstrʌktə'bɪlətɪ [-tɪ'b-, -lɪt-]

indestructible, -ness ˌɪndɪ'strʌktəbl [-tɪb-], -nɪs [-nəs]

indestructibly ˌɪndɪ'strʌktəblɪ [-tɪb-]

indeterminable, -ness ˌɪndɪ'tɜ:mɪnəbl, -nɪs [-nəs]

indeterminacy ˌɪndɪ'tɜ:mɪnəsɪ

indeterminate, -ly, -ness ˌɪndɪ'tɜ:mɪnət [-nɪt], -lɪ, -nɪs [-nəs]

indetermination 'ɪndɪˌtɜ:mɪ'neɪʃn

ind|ex, -exes, -ices 'ɪnd|eks, -eksɪz, -ɪsi:z

India, -n/s 'ɪndjə [-dɪə], -n/z

Indiana ˌɪndɪ'ænə [-'ɑ:n-]

Indianapolis ˌɪndɪə'næpəlɪs [-djə-, -pʊl-]

india-rubber, -s ˌɪndjə'rʌbə* [-dʒə-, also '--,--, according to sentence-stress], -z

indicat|e, -es, -ing, -ed, -or/s 'ɪndɪkeɪt, -s, -ɪŋ, -ɪd, -ə*/z

indication, -s ˌɪndɪ'keɪʃn, -z

indicative (s. adj.) (in grammar), -s, -ly ɪn'dɪkətɪv, -z, -lɪ

indicative (adj.) (pointing out), -ly ɪn'dɪkətɪv ['ɪndɪkeɪtɪv], -lɪ

indicatory ɪn'dɪkətərɪ ['ɪndɪkeɪtərɪ]

indict, -s, -ing, -ed, -er/s, -ment/s; -able ɪn'daɪt, -s, -ɪŋ, -ɪd, -ə*/z, -mənt/s; -əbl

indiction, -s ɪn'dɪkʃn, -z

Indies 'ɪndɪz

indifferen|ce, -cy, -t/ly ɪn'dɪfrən|s [-fərən-], -sɪ, -t/lɪ

indigen|ce, -t/ly 'ɪndɪdʒən|s, -t/lɪ

indigene, -s 'ɪndɪdʒi:n, -z

indigenous ɪn'dɪdʒɪnəs [-dʒŋəs, -dʒənəs]
indigestibility 'ɪndɪˌdʒestə'bɪlətɪ [-tɪ'b-, -lɪt-]
indigestible, -ness ˌɪndɪ'dʒestəbl [-tɪb-], -nɪs [-nəs]
indigestion ˌɪndɪ'dʒestʃən [-eʃtʃ-]
indignant, -ly ɪn'dɪgnənt, -lɪ
indignation ˌɪndɪg'neɪʃn
indignit|y, -ies ɪn'dɪgnət|ɪ [-ɪt|ɪ], -ɪz
indigo, -s 'ɪndɪgəʊ, -z
indirect, -ly, -ness ˌɪndɪ'rekt [-daɪ'r-, -də'r-], -lɪ, -nɪs [-nəs]
indiscernible ˌɪndɪ'sɜːnəbl [-dɪ'zɜː-, -nɪb-]
indisciplin|e, -able ɪn'dɪsɪplɪn [ˌɪn'd-, -səp-], -əbl
indiscreet, -ly, -ness ˌɪndɪ'skriːt, -lɪ, -nɪs [-nəs]
indiscretion, -s ˌɪndɪ'skreʃn, -z
indiscriminate, -ly ˌɪndɪ'skrɪmɪnət [-mən-, -nɪt], -lɪ
indiscrimination 'ɪndɪˌskrɪmɪ'neɪʃn [-mə'n-]
indispensability 'ɪndɪˌspensə'bɪlətɪ [-lɪt-]
indispensable, -ness ˌɪndɪ'spensəbl, -nɪs [-nəs]
indispos|e, -es, -ing, -ed ˌɪndɪ'spəʊz, -ɪz, -ɪŋ, -d
indisposition, -s ˌɪndɪspə'zɪʃn ['ɪn-ˌdɪspə'z-, -pʊ'z-], -z
indisputability ˌɪndɪspjuːtə'bɪlətɪ [ɪn-ˌdɪspjʊtə'b-, -lɪt-]
indisputable, -ness ˌɪndɪ'spjuːtəbl [ɪn'dɪspjʊtəbl], -nɪs [-nəs]
indisputably ˌɪndɪ'spjuːtəblɪ [ɪn'dɪs-pjʊt-]
indissociable ˌɪndɪ'səʊʃjəbl [-ʃɪə-, -ʃə-]
indissolubility 'ɪndɪˌsɒljʊ'bɪlətɪ [-lɪt-]
indissoluble, -ness ˌɪndɪ'sɒljʊbl [ɪn'dɪsəl-], -nɪs [-nəs]
indissolubly ˌɪndɪ'sɒljʊblɪ [ɪn'dɪsəl-]
indistinct, -ly, -ness ˌɪndɪ'stɪŋkt -lɪ, -nɪs [-nəs]
indistinctive, -ly, -ness ˌɪndɪ'stɪŋktɪv, -lɪ, -nɪs [-nəs]
indistinguishab|le, -ly, -leness ˌɪndɪ-'stɪŋgwɪʃəb|l, -lɪ, -lnɪs [-nəs]
indit|e, -es, -ing, -ed, -er/s ɪn'daɪt, -s, -ɪŋ, -ɪd, -ə*/z
individual (s. adj.), -s, -ly ˌɪndɪ'vɪdjʊəl [-djwəl, -djʊl, -dʒʊəl, -dʒwəl, -dʒʊl], -z, -ɪ
individuali|sm, -st/s ˌɪndɪ'vɪdjʊəlɪ|zəm [-djwəl-, -djʊl-, -dʒʊəl-, -dʒwəl-, -dʒʊl-] -st/s
individualistic 'ɪndɪˌvɪdjʊə'lɪstɪk [-djwə'l-, -djʊ'l-, -dʒʊə'l-, -dʒwə'l-, -dʒʊ'l-]

individualit|y, -ies 'ɪndɪˌvɪdjʊ'ælət|ɪ [-ˌvɪdʒʊ-, -ɪt|ɪ], -ɪz
individualization [-isa-] 'ɪndɪˌvɪdjʊəlaɪ-'zeɪʃn [-djwəl-, -djʊl-, -dʒʊəl-, -dʒwəl-, -dʒʊl-, -lɪ'z-]
individualiz|e [-is|e], -es, -ing, -ed ˌɪn-dɪ'vɪdjʊəlaɪz [-djwəl-, -djʊl-, -dʒʊəl-, -dʒwəl-, -dʒʊl-], -ɪz, -ɪŋ, -d
individu|um, -ums, -a ˌɪndɪ'vɪdjʊ|əm [-djw|əm], -əmz, -ə
indivisibility 'ɪndɪˌvɪzɪ'bɪlətɪ [-zə'b-, -lɪt-]
indivisib|le, -ly, -leness ˌɪndɪ'vɪzəb|l [-zɪb-], -lɪ, -lnɪs [-nəs]
Indo-China ˌɪndəʊ'tʃaɪnə
Indo-Chinese ˌɪndəʊtʃaɪ'niːz
indocile ɪn'dəʊsaɪl [ˌɪn'd-, -'dɒs-]
indocility ˌɪndəʊ'sɪlɪtɪ [-lətɪ]
indoctrinat|e, -es, -ing, -ed ɪn'dɒk-trɪneɪt, -s, -ɪŋ, -ɪd
indoctrination ɪnˌdɒktrɪ'neɪʃn
Indo-European, -s 'ɪndəʊˌjʊərə'piːən [-ˌjɔːr-, -ˌjɔːr-, -'prən], -z
Indo-Germanic ˌɪndəʊdʒə'mænɪk [-dʒɜː-]
indolen|ce, -t/ly 'ɪndələn|s [-dʊl-], -t/lɪ
indomitab|le, -ly ɪn'dɒmɪtəb|l, -lɪ
Indone|sia, -sian/s ˌɪndəʊ'niː|zjə [-zɪə, -ʒə, -sjə, -sɪə, -ʃə], -zjən/z [-zɪən/z, -ʒn/z, -sjən/z, -sɪən/z, -ʃn/z]
indoor 'ɪndɔː* [-dəə*]
indoors ˌɪn'dɔːz [-'dəəz, also ɪn'd- when preceded by a stress]
Indore (former spelling of Indaur, q.v.) ɪn'dɔː* [-'dəə*]
indors|e, -es, -ing, -ed, -ement/s ɪn'dɔːs, -ɪz, -ɪŋ, -t, -mənt/s
Indra 'ɪndrə
indraught, -s 'ɪndrɑːft, -s
indrawn ˌɪn'drɔːn ['ɪndrɔːn when attributive]
indubitable, -ness ɪn'djuːbɪtəbl, -nɪs [-nəs]
indubitably ɪn'djuːbɪtəblɪ
induc|e, -es, -ing, -ed, -er/s, -ement/s ɪn'djuːs, -ɪz, -ɪŋ, -t, -ə*/z, -mənt/s
induct, -s, -ing, -ed, -or/s ɪn'dʌkt, -s, -ɪŋ, -ɪd, -ə*/z
inductile ɪn'dʌktaɪl [ˌɪn'd-]
inductility ˌɪndʌk'tɪlətɪ [-lɪt-]
induction, -s ɪn'dʌkʃn, -z
induction-coil, -s ɪn'dʌkʃnkɔɪl, -z
inductive, -ly ɪn'dʌktɪv, -lɪ
indulg|e, -es, -ing, -ed, -er/s ɪn'dʌldʒ, -ɪz, -ɪŋ, -d, -ə*/z
indulgen|ce, -ces, -t/ly ɪn'dʌldʒən|s, -sɪz, -t/lɪ

261

indurat|e, -es, -ing, -ed ˈɪndjʊəreɪt [-jʊr-], -s, -ɪŋ, -ɪd
Indus ˈɪndəs
industrial, -ly ɪnˈdʌstrɪəl, -ɪ
industriali|sm, -st/s ɪnˈdʌstrɪəlɪ|zəm, -st/s
industrialization ɪnˌdʌstrɪəlaɪˈzeɪʃn [-lɪˈz-]
industrializ|e, -es, -ing, -ed ɪnˈdʌstrɪəlaɪz, -ɪz, -ɪŋ, -d
industrious, -ly ɪnˈdʌstrɪəs, -lɪ
industr|y, -ies ˈɪndəstr|ɪ, -ɪz
indwel|l, -ls, -ling, -t ˌɪnˈdwel [-ˈ-], -z, -ɪŋ, -t
indweller, -s ˈɪnˌdwelə*, -z
inebriate (s. adj.), **-s** ɪˈniːbrɪət [-brɪɪt, -brɪeɪt], -s
inebriat|e (v.), **-es, -ing, -ed** ɪˈniːbrɪeɪt, -s, -ɪŋ, -ɪd
inebriation ɪˌniːbrɪˈeɪʃn
inebriety ˌɪniːˈbraɪətɪ [-nɪˈb-]
inedible ɪnˈedɪbl [ˌɪnˈe-, -dəb-]
inedited ɪnˈedɪtɪd [ˌɪnˈe-]
ineducable ɪnˈedjʊkəbl [-dʒʊ-]
ineffab|le, -ly, -leness ɪnˈefəb|l, -lɪ, -lnɪs [-nəs]
ineffaceable ˌɪnɪˈfeɪsəbl
ineffaceably ˌɪnɪˈfeɪsəblɪ
ineffective, -ly ˌɪnɪˈfektɪv, -lɪ
ineffectual, -ly, -ness ˌɪnɪˈfektʃʊəl [-tʃwəl, -tʃʊl, -tjʊəl, -tjwəl, -tjʊl], -ɪ, -nɪs [-nəs]
inefficacious, -ly ˌɪnefɪˈkeɪʃəs, -lɪ
inefficacy ɪnˈefɪkəsɪ [ˌɪnˈe-]
inefficien|cy, -t/ly ˌɪnɪˈfɪʃn|sɪ, -t/lɪ
inelastic ˌɪnɪˈlæstɪk [-ˈlɑːs-]
inelasticity ˌɪnɪlæsˈtɪsətɪ [ˌɪniːˈlæsˈt-, -lɑːs-, -rtɪ]
inelegan|ce, -t/ly ɪnˈelɪgən|s [ˌɪnˈe-], -t/lɪ
ineligibility ɪnˌelɪdʒəˈbɪlətɪ [ˈɪnˌelɪdʒəˈb-, -dʒɪˈb-, -lɪt-]
ineligib|le, -ly ɪnˈelɪdʒəb|l [ˌɪnˈe-, -dʒɪb-], -lɪ
ineluctable ˌɪnɪˈlʌktəbl
inept, -ly, -ness ɪˈnept [ɪnˈept], -lɪ, -nɪs [-nəs]
ineptitude ɪˈneptɪtjuːd [ɪnˈep-]
inequalit|y, -ies ˌɪnɪˈkwɒlət|ɪ [-niː-, -ɪt|ɪ], -ɪz
inequitab|le, -ly ɪnˈekwɪtəb|l [ˌɪnˈe-], -lɪ
inequit|y, -ies ɪnˈekwət|ɪ [ˌɪnˈe-, -ɪt|ɪ], -ɪz
ineradicable ˌɪnɪˈrædɪkəbl
ineradicably ˌɪnɪˈrædɪkəblɪ
inert, -ly, -ness ɪˈnɜːt, -lɪ, -nɪs [-nəs]
inertia ɪˈnɜːʃjə [-ʃɪə, -ʃə]

inescapable ˌɪnɪˈskeɪpəbl
inessential ˌɪnɪˈsenʃl
inestimable ɪnˈestɪməbl [ˌɪnˈe-]
inestimably ɪnˈestɪməblɪ
inevitability ɪnˌevɪtəˈbɪlətɪ [ɪˌne-, -lɪt-]
inevitable, -ness ɪnˈevɪtəbl [ˌɪnˈe-, ɪˈne-], -nɪs [-nəs]
inevitably ɪnˈevɪtəblɪ [ɪˈne-]
inexact, -ly, -ness ˌɪnɪgˈzækt [-eg-], -lɪ, -nɪs [-nəs]
inexactitude, -s ˌɪnɪgˈzæktɪtjuːd [-eg-], -z
inexcusable, -ness ˌɪnɪkˈskjuːzəbl [-ek-], -nɪs [-nəs]
inexcusably ˌɪnɪkˈskjuːzəblɪ [-ek-]
inexhaustibility ˈɪnɪgˌzɔːstəˈbɪlətɪ [-eg-, -tɪˈb-, -rtɪ]
inexhaustible ˌɪnɪgˈzɔːstəbl [-eg-, -tɪb-]
inexhaustibly ˌɪnɪgˈzɔːstəblɪ [-eg-, -tɪb-]
inexorability ɪnˌeksərəˈbɪlətɪ [-lɪt-]
inexorab|le, -ly, -leness ɪnˈeksərəb|l, -lɪ, -lnɪs [-nəs]
inexpedien|cy, -t/ly ˌɪnɪkˈspiːdjən|sɪ [-ek-, -dɪən-], -t/lɪ
inexpensive ˌɪnɪkˈspensɪv [-ek-]
inexperience, -d ˌɪnɪkˈspɪərɪəns [-ek-], -t
inexpert, -ness ɪnˈekspɜːt [ˌɪn-, ˌɪnekˈsp-, -nɪkˈsp-], -nɪs [-nəs]
inexpiable, -ness ɪnˈekspɪəbl [ˌɪnˈe-, -pjə-], -nɪs [-nəs]
inexplicability ɪnˌeksplɪkəˈbɪlətɪ [ˈɪnˌeksplɪkəˈb-, ˈɪnɪkˌsplɪkəˈb-, ˈɪnekˌsplɪkəˈb-, -lɪt-]
inexplicable, -ness ˌɪnɪkˈsplɪkəbl [ɪnˈeksplɪkəbl], -nɪs [-nəs]
inexplicably ˌɪnɪkˈsplɪkəblɪ [ɪnˈeksplɪkəblɪ]
inexplicit ˌɪnɪkˈsplɪsɪt [-ek-]
inexplorable ˌɪnɪkˈsplɔːrəbl [-ek-]
inexpressible ˌɪnɪkˈspresəbl [-ek-, -sɪb-]
inexpressibly ˌɪnɪkˈspresəblɪ [-ek-, -sɪb-]
inexpressive, -ness ˌɪnɪkˈspresɪv [-ek-], -nɪs [-nəs]
inexpugnable ˌɪnɪkˈspʌgnəbl [-ek-]
inextensible ˌɪnɪkˈstensəbl [-ek-, -sɪb-]
inextinguishable ˌɪnɪkˈstɪŋgwɪʃəbl [-ek-]
inextinguishably ˌɪnɪkˈstɪŋgwɪʃəblɪ [-ek-]
inextricable ɪnˈekstrɪkəbl [ˌɪnɪkˈstrɪk-, ˌɪnekˈstrɪk-]
inextricably ɪnˈekstrɪkəblɪ [ˌɪnɪkˈstrɪk-, ˌɪnekˈstrɪk-]
Inez ˈiːnez
infallibility ɪnˌfæləˈbɪlətɪ [-lɪˈb-, -lɪt-]
infallib|le, -ly ɪnˈfæləb|l [-lɪb-], -lɪ
infamous, -ly, -ness ˈɪnfəməs [-fɪməs], -lɪ, -nɪs [-nəs]

infamy 'ɪnfəmɪ [-fɪ̥ɪ]
infancy 'ɪnfənsɪ
infant, -s 'ɪnfənt, -s
infanta, -s ɪn'fæntə, -z
infante, -s ɪn'fæntɪ, -z
infanticide, -s ɪn'fæntɪsaɪd, -z
infant|ile, -ine 'ɪnfənt|aɪl, -aɪn
infantry, -man, -men 'ɪnfəntrɪ, -mən
  [-mæn], -mən [-men]
infatuat|e, -es, -ing, -ed ɪn'fætjʊeɪt
  [-'fætʃʊ-], -s, -ɪŋ, -ɪd
infatuation, -s ɪnˌfætjʊ'eɪʃn [-ˌfætʃʊ-],
  -z
infect, -s, -ing, -ed ɪn'fekt, -s, -ɪŋ, -ɪd
infection, -s ɪn'fekʃn, -z
infectious, -ly, -ness ɪn'fekʃəs, -lɪ, -nɪs
  [-nəs]
infecundity ˌɪnfɪ'kʌndətɪ [-fiː'k-, -fe'k-,
  -ɪtɪ]
infelicit|ous, -y ˌɪnfɪ'lɪsɪt|əs [-fe'l-,
  -sət|əs], -ɪ
infer, -s, -ring, -red; -able ɪn'fɜː*, -z,
  -rɪŋ, -d; -rəbl
inference, -s 'ɪnfərəns, -ɪz
inferenti|al, -ally ˌɪnfə'renʃ|l, -əlɪ
inferior (s. adj.), -s ɪn'fɪərɪə* [ˌɪn'f-],
  -z
inferiority ɪnˌfɪərɪ'ɒrətɪ [ˌɪnfɪərɪ'ɒ-, -ɪtɪ]
infern|al (s. adj.), -als, -ally ɪn'fɜːn|l,
  -lz, -əlɪ [-lɪ]
inferno, -s ɪn'fɜːnəʊ, -z
Inferno ɪn'fɜːnəʊ [-'feən-]
infertile ɪn'fɜːtaɪl [ˌɪn'f-]
infest, -s, -ing, -ed ɪn'fest, -s, -ɪŋ, -ɪd
infestation ˌɪnfe'steɪʃn
infidel, -s 'ɪnfɪdəl [-del], -z
infidelit|y, -ies ˌɪnfɪ'delət|ɪ [-faɪ'd-,
  -ɪt|ɪ], -ɪz
infiltrat|e, -es, -ing, -ed 'ɪnfɪltreɪt [-'--],
  -s, -ɪŋ, -ɪd
infiltration, -s ˌɪnfɪl'treɪʃn, -z
in fine ˌɪn'faɪnɪ [-'fiːn-]
infinite (in non-technical sense), -ly,
  -ness 'ɪnfɪnət [-fɪ̥ət, -ɪt], -lɪ, -nɪs
  [-nəs]
  Note.—In church music it is custom-
  ary to pronounce this word 'ɪnfɪnaɪt
  or 'ɪnfaɪnaɪt, but these forms are
  not heard in ordinary speech.
infinite (technical senses in mathematics
  and grammar, opposed to finite)
  'ɪnfɪnət [-fɪ̥ət, -ɪt, 'ɪnˌfaɪnaɪt]
infinitesim|al, -ally ˌɪnfɪnɪ'tesɪm|l,
  [-nə't-], -əlɪ
infinitival ɪnˌfɪnɪ'taɪvl [ˌɪnfɪnɪ't-]
infinitive, -s, -ly ɪn'fɪnətɪv [-nɪt-], -z, -lɪ
infinitude, -s ɪn'fɪnɪtjuːd, -z
infinit|y, -ies ɪn'fɪnət|ɪ [-ɪt|ɪ], -ɪz

infirm, -ly ɪn'fɜːm [ˌɪn'fɜːm], -lɪ
infirmar|y, -ies ɪn'fɜːmər|ɪ [-mr|ɪ], -ɪz
infirmit|y, -ies ɪn'fɜːmət|ɪ [-ɪt|ɪ], -ɪz
infix (s.), -es 'ɪnfɪks, -ɪz
infix (v.), -es, -ing, -ed ɪn'fɪks, -ɪz, -ɪŋ,
  -t
inflam|e, -es, -ing, -ed ɪn'fleɪm, -z, -ɪŋ,
  -d
inflammability ɪnˌflæmə'bɪlətɪ [-lɪt-]
inflammable, -ness ɪn'flæməbl, -nɪs
  [-nəs]
inflammation, -s ˌɪnflə'meɪʃn, -z
inflammatory ɪn'flæmətərɪ
inflat|e, -es, -ing, -ed, -or/s ɪn'fleɪt, -s,
  -ɪŋ, -ɪd, -ə*/z
inflation, -s ɪn'fleɪʃn, -z
inflationary ɪn'fleɪʃnərɪ [-ʃnərɪ, -ʃn̩rɪ,
  -ʃənərɪ]
inflect, -s, -ing, -ed ɪn'flekt, -s, -ɪŋ, -ɪd
inflection, -s ɪn'flekʃn, -z
inflectional ɪn'flekʃənl [-ʃnəl, -ʃn̩l, -ʃnl,
  -ʃənəl]
inflective ɪn'flektɪv
inflexibility ɪnˌfleksə'bɪlətɪ ['ɪnˌfleksə'b-, -sɪ'b-, -lɪt-]
inflexib|le, -ly, -leness ɪn'fleksəb|l
  [-sɪb-], -lɪ, -lnɪs [-nəs]
inflexion, -s ɪn'flekʃn, -z
inflexional ɪn'flekʃənl [-ʃnəl, -ʃn̩l, -ʃnl,
  -ʃənəl]
inflict, -s, -ing, -ed ɪn'flɪkt, -s, -ɪŋ, -ɪd
infliction, -s ɪn'flɪkʃn, -z
inflow, -s 'ɪnfləʊ, -z
influenc|e (s. v.), -es, -ing, -ed 'ɪnflʊəns
  [-flwəns], -ɪz, -ɪŋ, -t
influent, -s 'ɪnflʊənt [-flwənt], -s
influenti|al, -ally ˌɪnflʊ'enʃ|l, -əlɪ
influenza ˌɪnflʊ'enzə
influx, -es 'ɪnflʌks, -ɪz
influxion ɪn'flʌkʃn
inform, -s, -ing, -ed, -er/s ɪn'fɔːm, -z,
  -ɪŋ, -d, -ə*/z
inform|al, -ally ɪn'fɔːm|l [ˌɪn'f-], -əlɪ
informalit|y, -ies ˌɪnfɔː'mælət|ɪ [-ɪt|ɪ], -ɪz
informant, -s ɪn'fɔːmənt, -s
information, -s ˌɪnfə'meɪʃn [-fɔː'm-], -z
informat|ive, -ory ɪn'fɔːmət|ɪv, -ərɪ
infra 'ɪnfrə
infract, -s, -ing, -ed ɪn'frækt, -s, -ɪŋ, -ɪd
infraction, -s ɪn'frækʃn, -z
infralapsarian, -s ˌɪnfrəlæp'seərɪən, -z
infrangibility ɪnˌfrændʒɪ'bɪlətɪ ['ɪn-
  ˌfrændʒɪ'b-, -dʒɒ'b-, -lɪt-]
infrangible ɪn'frændʒɪbl [ˌɪn'f-, -dʒəb-]
infra-red ˌɪnfrə'red
infra-structure, -s 'ɪnfrəˌstrʌktʃə*, -z
infrequen|cy, -t ɪn'friːkwən|sɪ [ˌɪn'f-], -t
infrequently ɪn'friːkwəntlɪ

263

infring|e, -es, -ing, -ed, -er/s, -ement/s
ɪnˈfrɪndʒ, -ɪz, -ɪŋ, -d, -ə*/z, -mənt/s

infuriat|e, -es, -ing, -ed ɪnˈfjʊərɪeɪt
[-ˈfjɔər-, -ˈfjɔ:r-], -s, -ɪŋ, -ɪd

infus|e, -es, -ing, -ed, -er/s ɪnˈfju:z, -ɪz,
-ɪŋ, -d, -ə*/z

infusible (capable of being infused)
ɪnˈfju:zəbl [-zɪb-]

infusible (not fusible) ɪnˈfju:zəbl [ˌɪnˈf-,
-zɪb-]

infusion, -s ɪnˈfju:ʒn, -z

infusoria, -l, -n ˌɪnfju:ˈzɔ:rɪə [-ˈsɔ:-], -l,
-n

infusory ɪnˈfju:zərɪ [-u:sə-]

Ingall ˈɪŋgɔ:l

Ingatestone ˈɪŋgeɪtstəʊn [ˈɪŋg-]

ingathering, -s ˈɪn,gæðərɪŋ, -z

Inge ɪŋ, ɪndʒ

Ingelow ˈɪndʒɪləʊ

ingenious, -ly, -ness ɪnˈdʒi:njəs [-nɪəs],
-lɪ, -nɪs [-nəs]

ingénue, -s ˈæ̃nʒeɪnju: [ˈæŋʒ-, ˌ-ˈ-]
(ɛ̃ʒeny), -z

ingenuity ˌɪndʒɪˈnju:ɪtɪ [-dʒəˈn-, -ˈnjʊ-,
-ɪtɪ]

ingenuous, -ly, -ness ɪnˈdʒenjʊəs
[-njwəs], -lɪ, -nɪs [-nəs]

Ingersoll, -s ˈɪŋgəsɒl, -z

Ingestre ˈɪŋgestrɪ

Ingham ˈɪŋəm

ingle (I.), -s ˈɪŋgl, -z

Ingle|borough, -by ˈɪŋgl|bərə, -bɪ

ingle-nook, -s ˈɪŋglnʊk, -s

Inglewood ˈɪŋglwʊd

Inglis ˈɪŋglz, ˈɪŋglɪs

inglorious, -ly, -ness ɪnˈglɔ:rɪəs [ˌɪnˈg-,
ɪŋˈg-, ˌɪŋˈg-], -lɪ, -nɪs [-nəs]

ingoing ˈɪn,gəʊɪŋ

Ingold ˈɪŋgəʊld

Ingoldsby ˈɪŋgəldzbɪ

ingot, -s ˈɪŋgət [-gɒt], -s

Ingpen ˈɪŋpen

Ingraham ˈɪŋgrəhəm [-græm]

ingrain, -ed ˌɪnˈgreɪn [also ˈ-ˈ- according
to sentence-stress], -d

Ingram ˈɪŋgrəm

ingrate, -s ɪnˈgreɪt, -s

ingratiat|e, -es, -ing, -ed ɪnˈgreɪʃɪeɪt
[-ʃjert], -s, -ɪŋ, -ɪd

ingratitude ɪnˈgrætɪtju:d [ˌɪnˈg-, ɪŋˈg-,
ˌɪŋˈg-]

Ingrebourne ˈɪŋgrɪbɔ:n [-bɔən]

ingredient, -s ɪnˈgri:djənt [ɪŋˈg-,
-dɪənt], -s

ingress ˈɪngres [ˈɪŋg-]

ingressive ɪnˈgresɪv

in|growing, -growth ˈɪn|,grəʊɪŋ, -grəʊθ

inguinal ˈɪŋgwɪnl

inhabit, -s, -ing, -ed, -er/s; -able,
-ant/s ɪnˈhæbɪt, -s, -ɪŋ, -ɪd, -ə*/z;
-əbl, -ənt/s

inhabitation ɪn,hæbɪˈteɪʃn

inhalation, -s ˌɪnhəˈleɪʃn, -z

inhal|e, -es, -ing, -ed, -er/s ɪnˈheɪl, -z,
-ɪŋ, -d, -ə*/z

inharmonious, -ly, -ness ˌɪnhɑ:ˈməʊnjəs
[-nɪəs], -lɪ, -nɪs [-nəs]

inher|e, -es, -ing, -ed ɪnˈhɪə*, -z, -ɪŋ,
-d

inheren|ce, -cy, -t/ly ɪnˈhɪərən|s
[-ˈher-], -sɪ, -t/lɪ

inherit, -s, -ing, -ed, -or/s; -able,
-ance/s ɪnˈherɪt, -s, -ɪŋ, -ɪd, -ə*/z;
-əbl, -əns/ɪz

inheritrix, -es ɪnˈherɪtrɪks, -ɪz

inhibit, -s, -ing, -ed; -ory ɪn hɪbɪt, -s,
-ɪŋ, -ɪd; -ərɪ

inhibition, -s ˌɪnhɪˈbɪʃn, -z

inhospitab|le, -ly, -leness ɪnˈhɒsprtəb|l
[ˌɪnˈh-, ˌɪnhɒˈsp-], -lɪ, -lnɪs [-nəs]

inhospitality ɪn,hɒspɪˈtælətɪ [-ɪtɪ]

inhuman, -ly ɪnˈhju:mən [ˌɪnˈh-], -lɪ

inhumane, -ly ˌɪnhju:ˈmeɪn [-hjʊ-], -lɪ

inhumanit|y, -ies ˌɪnhju:ˈmænət|ɪ
[-hjʊ-, -ɪt|ɪ], -ɪz

inhumation, -s ˌɪnhju:ˈmeɪʃn [-hjʊ-], -z

inhum|e, -es, -ing, -ed ɪnˈhju:m, -z, -ɪŋ,
-d

Inigo ˈɪnɪgəʊ

inimic|al, -ally ɪˈnɪmɪk|l, -əlɪ

inimitability ɪ,nɪmɪtəˈbɪlətɪ [-ɪt-]

inimitab|le, -ly, -leness ɪˈnɪmɪtəb|l, -lɪ,
-lnɪs [-nəs]

iniquitous, -ly ɪˈnɪkwɪtəs, -lɪ

iniquit|y, -ies ɪˈnɪkwət|ɪ [-ɪt|ɪ], -ɪz

initi|al (s. adj. v.), -als, -ally; -al(l)ing,
-al(l)ed ɪˈnɪʃ|l, -lz, -əlɪ [-lɪ]; -əlɪŋ
[-lɪŋ], -ld

initiate (s.), -s ɪˈnɪʃɪət [-ʃjət, -ʃɪeɪt,
-ʃjeɪt, -ʃɪɪt, -ʃjɪt], -s

initiat|e (v.), -es, -ing, -ed, -or/s
ɪˈnɪʃɪeɪt [-ʃjeɪt], -s, -ɪŋ, -ɪd, -ə*/z

initiation, -s ɪ,nɪʃɪˈeɪʃn, -z

initiative ɪˈnɪʃɪətɪv [-ʃjət-, -ʃət-]

initiatory ɪˈnɪʃɪətərɪ [-ʃjət-, -ʃɪeɪtərɪ]

initio (in ab initio) ɪˈnɪʃɪəʊ [-ˈnɪtɪəʊ,
-ˈnɪsɪ-]

inject, -s, -ing, -ed, -or/s ɪnˈdʒekt, -s,
-ɪŋ, -ɪd, -ə*/z

injection, -s ɪnˈdʒekʃn, -z

injudicious, -ly, -ness ˌɪndʒu:ˈdɪʃəs
[-dʒʊ-], -lɪ, -nɪs [-nəs]

injunction, -s ɪnˈdʒʌŋkʃn, -z

injurant, -s ˈɪndʒʊərənt [-dʒər-], -s

inj|ure, -ures, -uring, -ured, -urer/s
ˈɪndʒ|ə*, -əz, -ərɪŋ, -əd, -ərə*/z

injurious, -ly, -ness ɪn'dʒʊərɪəs [-'dʒɔər-, -'dʒɔːr-], -lɪ, -nɪs [-nəs]

injur|y, -ies 'ɪndʒər|ɪ, -ɪz

injustice ɪn'dʒʌstɪs [ˌɪn'dʒ-]

ink (s. v.), -s, -ing, -ed, -er/s ɪŋk, -s, -ɪŋ, -t [ɪŋt], -ə*/z

ink-bottle, -s 'ɪŋk.bɒtl, -z

Inkerman 'ɪŋkəmən

ink-horn, -s 'ɪŋkhɔːn, -z

inking-roller, -s 'ɪŋkɪŋˌrəʊlə*, -z

inkling, -s 'ɪŋklɪŋ, -z

ink-pot, -s 'ɪŋkpɒt, -s

ink-stain, -s 'ɪŋksteɪn, -z

inkstand, -s 'ɪŋkstænd, -z

ink|y, -ier, -iest, -iness 'ɪŋk|ɪ, -ɪə* [-jə*], -ɪɪst [-jɪst], -ɪnɪs [-məs]

inland (s. adj.), -s 'ɪnlənd [-lænd], -z

inland (adv.) ɪn'lænd [ˌ-'-]

inlander, -s 'ɪnləndə*, -z

inlay (s.) 'ɪnleɪ

inlay (v.), -s, -ing, inlaid ˌɪn'leɪ, -z, -ɪŋ, ˌɪn'leɪd [also 'ɪnleɪd when attributive]

inlet, -s 'ɪnlet [-lɪt, -lət], -s

inly 'ɪnlɪ

Inman 'ɪnmən

inmate, -s 'ɪnmeɪt, -s

inmost 'ɪnməʊst [-məst]

inn, -s ɪn, -z

innate, -ly, -ness ˌɪ'neɪt ['--], -lɪ, -nɪs [-nəs]

innavigable ɪ'nævɪgəbl [ˌɪn'næ-]

inner, -most 'ɪnə*, -məʊst

innervat|e, -es, -ing, -ed 'ɪnɜːveɪt [ɪ'nɜːv-], -s, -ɪŋ, -ɪd

innervation ˌɪnɜː'veɪʃn

Innes(s) 'ɪnɪs

innings, -es 'ɪnɪŋz, -ɪz

Innisfail ˌɪnɪs'feɪl

Innisfree ˌɪnɪs'friː

innkeeper, -s 'ɪnˌkiːpə*, -z

innocen|ce, -cy 'ɪnəsən|s [-nʊs-], -sɪ

innocent (s. adj.) (I.), -s, -ly 'ɪnəsnt [-nʊs-, -nəʊs-], -s, -lɪ

innocuous, -ly, -ness ɪ'nɒkjʊəs [-kjwəs], -lɪ, -nɪs [-nəs]

innominate ɪ'nɒmɪnət [-nɪt, -neɪt]

Innous 'ɪnəs

innovat|e, -es, -ing, -ed, -or/s 'ɪnəʊveɪt, -s, -ɪŋ, -ɪd, -ə*/z

innovation, -s ˌɪnəʊ'veɪʃn, -z

innoxious, -ly, -ness ɪ'nɒkʃəs, -lɪ, -nɪs [-nəs]

Innsbruck 'ɪnzbrʊk (insbruk)

innuendo, -es ˌɪnjuː'endəʊ [-njʊ-], -z

innumerability ɪˌnjuːmərə'bɪlətɪ [-lɪt-]

innumerab|le, -ly, -leness ɪ'njuːmərəb|l, -lɪ, -lnɪs [-nəs]

innutriti|on, -ous ˌɪnjuː'trɪʃ|n [-njʊ-], -əs

inobservan|ce, -t ˌɪnəb'zɜːvən|s, -t

inoccupation 'ɪnˌɒkjʊ'peɪʃn

inoculat|e, -es, -ing, -ed, -or/s ɪ'nɒkjʊleɪt, -s, -ɪŋ, -ɪd, -ə*/z

inoculation, -s ɪˌnɒkjʊ'leɪʃn, -z

inodorous ɪn'əʊdərəs [ˌɪn'əʊ-]

inoffensive, -ly, -ness ˌɪnə'fensɪv [-nʊ'f-], -lɪ, -nɪs [-nəs]

inofficious ˌɪnə'fɪʃəs [-nʊ'f-]

inoperable ɪn'ɒpərəbl

inoperative ɪn'ɒpərətɪv [ˌɪn'ɒ-]

inopportune, -ly ɪn'ɒpətjuːn [ˌɪn'ɒpət-, ˌɪnɒpə't-], -lɪ

inordinate, -ly, -ness ɪ'nɔːdɪnət [-dnət, -ɪt], -lɪ, -nɪs [-nəs]

inorganic, -ally ˌɪnɔː'gænɪk, -əlɪ

inosculat|e, -es, -ing, -ed ɪ'nɒskjʊleɪt, -s, -ɪŋ, -ɪd

inosculation ɪˌnɒskjʊ'leɪʃn

in-patient, -s 'ɪnˌpeɪʃnt, -s

input, -s 'ɪnpʊt ['ɪm-], -s

inquest, -s 'ɪnkwest ['ɪŋk-], -s

inquietude ɪn'kwaɪətjuːd [ɪŋ'k-, -aɪt-]

inquir|e, -es, -ing/ly, -ed, -er/s ɪn'kwaɪə* [ɪŋ'k-], -z, -rɪŋ/lɪ, -d, -rə*/z

inquir|y, -ies ɪn'kwaɪər|ɪ [ɪŋ'k-], -ɪz

inquisition (I.), -s ˌɪnkwɪ'zɪʃn [ˌɪŋk-], -z

inquisitional ˌɪnkwɪ'zɪʃənl [ˌɪŋk-, -ʃnəl, -ʃŋl, -ʃnl, -ʃənəl]

inquisitive, -ly, -ness ɪn'kwɪzətɪv [ɪŋ'k-, -zɪt-], -lɪ, -nɪs [-nəs]

inquisitor, -s ɪn'kwɪzɪtə* [ɪŋ'k-], -z

inquisitorial, -ly ɪnˌkwɪzɪ'tɔːrɪəl [ɪŋˌk-, ˌɪnkwɪzɪ't-, ˌɪŋkwɪzɪ't-], -ɪ

inroad, -s 'ɪnrəʊd, -z

inrush, -es 'ɪnrʌʃ, -ɪz

insalubr|ious, -ity ˌɪnsə'luːbr|ɪəs [-'ljuː-], -ətɪ [-ɪtɪ]

insane, -ly, -ness ɪn'seɪn, -lɪ, -nɪs [-nəs]

insanitar|y, -ily, -iness ɪn'sænɪtər|ɪ [ˌɪn's-, -nət-], -əlɪ [-ɪlɪ], -ɪnɪs [-məs]

insanity ɪn'sænətɪ [-ɪtɪ]

insatiability ɪnˌseɪʃjə'bɪlətɪ [-ʃɪə-, -ʃə-, -lɪt-]

insatiable, -ness ɪn'seɪʃjəbl [-ʃɪə-, -ʃə-], -nɪs [-nəs]

insatiate ɪn'seɪʃɪət [-ʃət, -ʃɪt, -ʃɪt]

inscrib|e, -es, -ing, -ed, -er/s ɪn'skraɪb, -z, -ɪŋ, -d, -ə*/z

inscription, -s ɪn'skrɪpʃn, -z

inscrutability ɪnˌskruːtə'bɪlətɪ [ˌɪnskruː-, -lɪt-]

inscrutab|le, -ly, -leness ɪn'skruːtəb|l, -lɪ, -lnɪs [-nəs]

insect, -s 'ɪnsekt, -s

insectarium, -s ˌɪnsek'teərɪəm, -z

insecticide, -s ɪn'sektɪsaɪd, -z

insectivorous ˌɪnsek'tɪvərəs

insecur|e, -ely, -ity ˌɪnsɪ'kjʊə* [-'kjɔə*, -'kjɔ:*], -lɪ, -rətɪ [-rɪtɪ]

inseminat|e, -es, -ing, -ed ɪn'semɪneɪt, -s, -ɪŋ, -ɪd

insemination ɪnˌsemɪ'neɪʃn [ˌɪnsem-]

insensate, -ly, -ness ɪn'senseɪt [-sət, -sɪt], -lɪ, -nɪs [-nəs]

insensibility ɪnˌsensə'bɪlətɪ [ˌɪnsen-, -sɪ'b-, -lɪt-]

insensib|le, -ly, -leness ɪn'sensəb|l [-sɪb-], -lɪ, -lnɪs [-nəs]

insensitive, -ness ɪn'sensətɪv [ˌɪn's-, -sɪt-], -nɪs [-nəs]

inseparability ɪnˌsepərə'bɪlətɪ ['ɪn-ˌsepərə'b-, -lɪt-]

inseparable ɪn'sepərəbl [ˌɪn's-]

inseparab|ly, -leness ɪn'sepərəb|lɪ, -lnɪs [-nəs]

insert (s.), -s 'ɪnsɜ:t, -s

insert (v.), -s, -ing, -ed ɪn'sɜ:t, -s, -ɪŋ, -ɪd

insertion, -s ɪn'sɜ:ʃn, -z

inset (s.), -s 'ɪnset, -s

inset (v.), -s, -ting ˌɪn'set, -s, -ɪŋ

inseverable ɪn'sevərəbl [ˌɪn's-]

inshore ˌɪn'ʃɔ:* [-'ʃɔə*, also 'ɪnʃ- according to sentence-stress]

inside (s. adj. adv. prep.), -s ˌɪn'saɪd [also 'ɪns-, ɪn's- according to sentence-stress], -z

insider, -s ˌɪn'saɪdə* [also ɪn's- when preceded by a stress], -z

insidious, -ly, -ness ɪn'sɪdɪəs [-djəs], -lɪ, -nɪs [-nəs]

insight 'ɪnsaɪt

insignia ɪn'sɪgnɪə [-njə]

insignifican|ce, -cy, -t/ly ˌɪnsɪg'nɪfɪkən|s, -sɪ, -t/lɪ

insincere, -ly ˌɪnsɪn'sɪə* [-sn's-], -lɪ

insincerit|y, -ies ˌɪnsɪn'serət|ɪ [-sn's-, -ɪt|ɪ], -ɪz

insinuat|e, -es, -ing/ly, -ed, -or/s ɪn-'sɪnjʊeɪt, -s, -ɪŋ/lɪ, -ɪd, -ə*/z

insinuation, -s ɪnˌsɪnjʊ'eɪʃn, -z

insipid, -ly, -ness ɪn'sɪpɪd, -lɪ, -nɪs [-nəs]

insipidity ˌɪnsɪ'pɪdətɪ [-rɪtɪ]

insipien|ce, -t ɪn'sɪpɪən|s [-pjə-], -t

insist, -s, -ing, -ed ɪn'sɪst, -s, -ɪŋ, -ɪd

insisten|ce, -cy, -t/ly ɪn'sɪstən|s, -sɪ, -t/lɪ

Inskip 'ɪnskɪp

insobriety ˌɪnsəʊ'braɪətɪ [-aɪtɪ]

insolation ˌɪnsəʊ'leɪʃn

insolen|ce, -t/ly 'ɪnsələn|s [-sʊl-], -t/lɪ

insolubility ɪnˌsɒljʊ'bɪlətɪ ['ɪnˌsɒljʊ'b-, -lɪt-]

insoluble, -ness ɪn'sɒljʊbl [ˌɪn's-], -nɪs [-nəs]

insolvable ɪn'sɒlvəbl [ˌɪn's-]

insolven|cy, -t ɪn'sɒlvən|sɪ [ˌɪn's-], -t

insomnia ɪn'sɒmnɪə [-njə]

insomuch ˌɪnsəʊ'mʌtʃ

insouciance ɪn'su:sjəns [-sɪəns] (ɛ̃susjɑ̃:s)

insouciant ɪn'su:sjənt [-sɪənt] (ɛ̃susjɑ̃)

inspect, -s, -ing, -ed, -or/s ɪn'spekt, -s, -ɪŋ, -ɪd, -ə*/z

inspection, -s ɪn'spekʃn, -z

inspectorate, -s ɪn'spektərət [-rɪt], -s

inspectorship, -s ɪn'spektəʃɪp, -s

inspectress, -es ɪn'spektrɪs [-trəs], -ɪz

inspiration, -s ˌɪnspə'reɪʃn [-spɪ'r-], -z

inspirational ˌɪnspə'reɪʃənl [-spɪ'r-, -ʃnəl, -ʃnḷ, -ʃn̩l, -ʃənəl]

inspirator, -s 'ɪnspəreɪtə* [-spɪr-], -z

inspiratory ɪn'spaɪərətərɪ

inspir|e, -es, -ing/ly, -ed, -er/s ɪn-'spaɪə*, -z, -rɪŋ/lɪ, -d, -rə*/z

inspirit, -s, -ing, -ed ɪn'spɪrɪt, -s, -ɪŋ, -ɪd

inspissate ɪn'spɪseɪt

inst. ɪnst, 'ɪnstənt

instability ˌɪnstə'bɪlətɪ [-lɪt-]

install, -s, -ing, -ed ɪn'stɔ:l, -z, -ɪŋ, -d

installation, -s ˌɪnstə'leɪʃn [-stɔ:'l-], -z

instalment, -s ɪn'stɔ:lmənt, -s

instanc|e (s. v.), -es, -ing, -ed 'ɪnstəns, -ɪz, -ɪŋ, -t

instant (s. adj.), -s, -ly 'ɪnstənt, -s, -lɪ

instantaneous, -ly, -ness ˌɪnstən'teɪnjəs [-nɪəs], -lɪ, -nɪs [-nəs]

instanter ɪn'stæntə*

instead ɪn'sted

instep, -s 'ɪnstep, -s

instigat|e, -es, -ing, -ed, -or/s 'ɪnstɪgeɪt, -s, -ɪŋ, -ɪd, -ə*/z

instigation, -s ˌɪnstɪ'geɪʃn, -z

instil, -s, -ling, -led, -ment ɪn'stɪl, -z, -ɪŋ, -d, -mənt

instillation, -s ˌɪnstɪ'leɪʃn

instinct (s.), -s 'ɪnstɪŋkt, -s

instinct (adj.) ɪn'stɪŋkt

instinctive, -ly ɪn'stɪŋktɪv, -lɪ

institut|e (s. v.), -es, -ing, -ed, -or/s 'ɪnstɪtjuːt, -s, -ɪŋ, -ɪd, -ə*/z

institution, -s ˌɪnstɪ'tjuːʃn, -z

institutional ˌɪnstɪ'tjuːʃənl [-ʃnəl, -ʃṇl, -ʃn̩l, -ʃənəl]

instruct, -s, -ing, -ed, -or/s, -ress/es ɪn'strʌkt, -s, -ɪŋ, -ɪd, -ə*/z, -rɪs/ɪz

instruction, -s ɪn'strʌkʃn, -z

instructional ɪn'strʌkʃənl [-ʃnəl, -ʃṇl, -ʃn̩l, -ʃənəl]

instructive, -ly, -ness ɪnˈstrʌktɪv, -lɪ, -nɪs [-nəs]

instrument, -s ˈɪnstrʊmənt [-trəm-], -s

instrument|al, -ally; -alist/s ˌɪnstrʊˈment|l [-trəˈm-], -əlɪ [-l̩ɪ]; -əlɪst/s [-lɪst/s]

instrumentality ˌɪnstrʊmenˈtælətɪ [-trəm-, -mən-, -rtɪ]

instrumentation ˌɪnstrʊmenˈteɪʃn [-trəm-, -mən-]

insubordinate ˌɪnsəˈbɔːdn̩ət [-dənət, -dɪnət, -ɪt]

insubordination ˈɪnsəˌbɔːdɪˈneɪʃn [-dəˈn-]

insubstantial ˌɪnsəbˈstænʃl [-bzˈt-]

insufferable ɪnˈsʌfərəbl

insufferably ɪnˈsʌfərəblɪ

insufficien|cy, -t/ly ˌɪnsəˈfɪʃn|sɪ, -t/lɪ

insular, -ly, -ism ˈɪnsjʊlə* [-sjəl-], -lɪ, -rɪzəm

insularity ˌɪnsjʊˈlærətɪ [-sjəˈl-, -rtɪ]

insulat|e, -es, -ing, -ed, -or/s ˈɪnsjʊleɪt [-sjəl-], -s, -ɪŋ, -ɪd, -ə*/z

insulation ˌɪnsjʊˈleɪʃn [-sjəˈl-]

insulin ˈɪnsjʊlɪn

insult (s.), -s ˈɪnsʌlt, -s

insult (v.), -s, -ing/ly, -ed, -er/s ɪnˈsʌlt, -s, -ɪŋ/lɪ, -ɪd, -ə*/z

insuperability ɪnˌsjuːpərəˈbɪlətɪ [ˈɪn-ˌsjuːpərəˈb-, -suː-, -lɪt-]

insuperable ɪnˈsjuːpərəbl [ˌɪnˈs-, -ˈsuː-]

insuperably ɪnˈsjuːpərəblɪ [-ˈsuː-]

insupportable, -ness ˌɪnsəˈpɔːtəbl, -nɪs [-nəs]

insupportably ˌɪnsəˈpɔːtəblɪ

insuppressible ˌɪnsəˈpresəbl [-sɪb-]

insur|e, -es, -ing, -ed, -er/s; -able, -ance/s ɪnˈʃʊə* [-ˈʃɔə*, -ˈʃɔː*], -z, -rɪŋ, -d, -rə*/z; -rəbl, -rəns/ɪz

insurgent, -s ɪnˈsɜːdʒənt, -s

insurmountability ˈɪnsəˌmaʊntəˈbɪlətɪ [-lɪt-]

insurmountable ˌɪnsəˈmaʊntəbl

insurrection, -s ˌɪnsəˈrekʃn, -z

insurrectional ˌɪnsəˈrekʃənl [-ʃnəl, -ʃn̩l, -ʃn̩l̩, -ʃənəl]

insurrectionar|y (s. adj.), -ies ˌɪnsəˈrekʃnər|ɪ [-ʃnə-, -ʃənə-], -ɪz

insurrectioni|sm, -st/s ˌɪnsəˈrekʃn̩ɪ|zəm [-ʃənɪ-], -st/s

insusceptibility ˈɪnsəˌseptəˈbɪlətɪ [-tɪˈb-, -lɪt-]

insusceptible ˌɪnsəˈseptəbl [-tɪb-]

intact, -ness ɪnˈtækt [ˌɪnˈt-], -nɪs [-nəs]

intaglio, -s ɪnˈtɑːliəʊ [-ˈtæl-, -ljəʊ], -z

intake ˈɪnteɪk

intangibility ɪnˌtændʒəˈbɪlətɪ [ˈɪnˌtændʒəˈb-, -dʒɪˈb-, -lɪt-]

intangible, -ness ɪnˈtændʒəbl [ˌɪnˈt-, -dʒɪb-], -nɪs [-nəs]

intangibly ɪnˈtændʒəblɪ [-dʒɪb-]

integer, -s ˈɪntɪdʒə*, -z

integral (s.), -s ˈɪntɪgrəl, -z

integral (adj.), -ly ˈɪntɪgrəl [ɪnˈtegrəl], -ɪ
Note.—As a mathematical term always ˈɪntɪgrəl.

integrat|e, -es, -ing, -ed ˈɪntɪgreɪt, -s, -ɪŋ, -ɪd

integration, -s ˌɪntɪˈgreɪʃn, -z

integrity ɪnˈtegrətɪ [-rtɪ]

integument, -s ɪnˈtegjʊmənt, -s

intellect, -s ˈɪntəlekt [-tɪl-], -s

intellection ˌɪntəˈlekʃn [-tɪˈl-]

intellective ˌɪntəˈlektɪv [-tɪˈl-]

intellectual, -ly ˌɪntəˈlektjʊəl [-tɪˈl-, -tjwəl, -tjʊl, -tʃʊəl, -tʃwəl, -tʃʊl], -ɪ

intellectuali|sm, -st/s ˌɪntəˈlektjʊəlɪ|zəm [-tɪˈl-, -tjwəl-, -tjʊl-, -tʃʊəl-, -tʃwəl-, -tʃʊl-], -st/s

intellectuality ˈɪntəˌlektjʊˈælətɪ [-tɪˌl-, -tʃʊ-, -rtɪ]

intellectualiz|e [-is|e], -es, -ing, -ed ˌɪntəˈlektjʊəlaɪz [-tɪˈl-, -tjwəl-, -tjʊl-, -tʃʊəl-, -tʃwəl-, -tʃʊl-], -ɪz, -ɪŋ, -d

intelligen|ce, -ces, -t/ly, -cer/s ɪnˈtelɪdʒən|s, -sɪz, -t/lɪ, -sə*/z

intelligentsia ɪnˌtelɪˈdʒentsɪə [ˌɪnte-lɪˈdʒ-, -ˈgen-, -tsjə]

intelligibility ɪnˌtelɪdʒəˈbɪlətɪ [-dʒɪˈb-, -lɪt-]

intelligib|le, -ly, -leness ɪnˈtelɪdʒəb|l [-dʒɪb-], -lɪ, -lnɪs [-nəs]

intemperance ɪnˈtempərəns [ˌɪnˈt-]

intemperate, -ly, -ness ɪnˈtempərət [ˌɪnˈt-, -rɪt], -lɪ, -nɪs [-nəs]

intend, -s, -ing, -ed ɪnˈtend, -z, -ɪŋ, -ɪd

intendan|ce, -cy, -t/s ɪnˈtendən|s, -sɪ, -t/s

intense, -r, -st, -ly, -ness ɪnˈtens, -ə*, -ɪst, -lɪ, -nɪs [-nəs]

intensification, -s ɪnˌtensɪfɪˈkeɪʃn, -z

intensi|fy, -fies, -fying, -fied, -fier/s ɪnˈtensɪ|faɪ, -faɪz, -faɪɪŋ, -faɪd, -faɪə*/z

intension ɪnˈtenʃn

intensit|y, -ies ɪnˈtensət|ɪ [-srt-], -ɪz

intensive, -ly, -ness ɪnˈtensɪv, -lɪ, -nɪs [-nəs]

intent (s. adj.), -s, -er, -est, -ly, -ness ɪnˈtent, -s, -ə*, -ɪst, -lɪ, -nɪs [-nəs]

intention, -s, -ed ɪnˈtenʃn, -z, -d

inten|tional, -tionally ɪnˈten|ʃənl [-ʃnəl, -ʃn̩l̩, -ʃn̩l, -ʃənəl], -ʃnəlɪ [-ʃnəlɪ, -ʃn̩lɪ, -ʃn̩lɪ, -ʃənəlɪ]

inter (v.), -s, -ring, -red ɪnˈtɜː*, -z, -rɪŋ, -d

inter (*Latin prep.*, *in such phrases as* inter alia, inter se) 'ɪntə*

interact (*s.*), -s 'ɪntərækt, -s

interact (*v.*), -s, -ing, -ed ˌɪntər'ækt [-tə'ækt], -s, -ɪŋ, -ɪd

interaction ˌɪntər'ækʃn [-tə'æ-]

interactive ˌɪntər'æktɪv [-tə'æ-]

interblend, -s, -ing, -ed ˌɪntə'blend, -z, -ɪŋ, -ɪd

inter|breed, -breeds, -breeding, -bred ˌɪntə'briːd, -'briːdz, -'briːdɪŋ, -'bred

intercalary ɪn'tɜːkələrɪ [ˌɪntə'kælərɪ]

intercalat|e, -es, -ing, -ed ɪn'tɜːkəlert, -s, -ɪŋ, -ɪd

intercalation, -s m,tɜːkə'leɪʃn, -z

interced|e, -es, -ing, -ed, -er/s ˌɪntə-'siːd, -z, -ɪŋ, -ɪd, -ə*/z

intercept (*s.*), -s 'ɪntəsept, -s

intercept (*v.*), -s, -ing, -ed, -er/s ˌɪntə-'sept, -s, -ɪŋ, -ɪd, -ə*/z

interception, -s ˌɪntə'sepʃn, -z

interceptive ˌɪntə'septɪv

interceptor, -s ˌɪntə'septə*, -z

intercession, -s ˌɪntə'seʃn, -z

intercessional ˌɪntə'seʃənl [-ʃnəl, -ʃn̩l, -ʃn̩l, -ʃənəl]

intercessor, -s ˌɪntə'sesə* ['ɪntəsesə*], -z

intercessory ˌɪntə'sesərɪ

interchange (*s.*), -s ˌɪntə'tʃeɪndʒ ['ɪntətʃ-], -ɪz

interchang|e (*v.*), -es, -ing, -ed ˌɪntə-'tʃeɪndʒ, -ɪz, -ɪŋ, -d

interchangeability 'ɪntəˌtʃeɪndʒə'bɪlətɪ [-lɪt-]

interchangeable, -ness ˌɪntə'tʃeɪndʒ-əbl, -nɪs [-nəs]

interchangeably ˌɪntə'tʃeɪndʒəblɪ

intercollegiate ˌɪntəkə'liːdʒɪət [-kɒ'l-, -dʒət, -dʒɪət, -dʒɪɪt, -dʒjɪt]

intercolonial ˌɪntəkə'ləʊnjəl [-nɪəl]

intercommunicat|e, -es, -ing, -ed ˌɪntəkə'mjuːnɪkeɪt [-'mjʊn-], -s, -ɪŋ, -ɪd

intercommunication 'ɪntəkəˌmjuːnɪ-'keɪʃn [-ˌmjʊn-]

intercommunion ˌɪntəkə'mjuːnjən [-nɪən]

intercommunity ˌɪntəkə'mjuːnətɪ [-ɪtɪ]

interconnect, -s, -ing, -ed ˌɪntəkə'nekt, -s, -ɪŋ, -ɪd

interconnection, -s ˌɪntəkə'nekʃn, -z

intercontinental 'ɪntəˌkɒntɪ'nentl

intercostal ˌɪntə'kɒstl

intercourse 'ɪntəkɔːs [-kɔəs]

intercurren|ce, -t ˌɪntə'kʌrən|s, -t

interdental ˌɪntə'dentl

interdependen|ce, -t ˌɪntədɪ'pendən|s, -t

interdict (*s.*), -s 'ɪntədɪkt, -s

interdict (*v.*), -s, -ing, -ed ˌɪntə'dɪkt, -s, -ɪŋ, -ɪd

interdiction, -s ˌɪntə'dɪkʃn, -z

interest (*s. v*), -s, -ing, -ed/ly'ɪntrəst [-tərest, -trɪst], -s, -ɪŋ, -ɪd/lɪ

interesting (*adj.*), -ly 'ɪntrəstɪŋ [-tərest-trɪst-, ˌɪntə'restɪŋ], -lɪ

interfer|e, -es, -ing, -ed, -er/s; -ence/s ˌɪntə'fɪə*, -z, -rɪŋ, -d, -rə*/z; -rəns/ɪz

interfus|e, -es, -ing, -ed ˌɪntə'fjuːz, -ɪz, -ɪŋ, -d

interfusion ˌɪntə'fjuːʒn

interglacial ˌɪntə'gleɪsjəl [-sɪəl, -ʃjəl, -ʃɪəl, -ʃl, -'glæsɪəl, -'glæsjəl]

interim 'ɪntərɪm

interior (*s. adj.*), -s, -ly ɪn'tɪərɪə*, -z, -lɪ

interject, -s, -ing, -ed, -or/s ˌɪntə-'dʒekt, -s, -ɪŋ, -ɪd, -ə*/z

interjection, -s ˌɪntə'dʒekʃn, -z

interjec|tional, -tionally ˌɪntə'dʒek|-ʃənl [-ʃnəl, -ʃn̩l, -ʃn̩l, -ʃənəl], -ʃn̩lɪ [-ʃnəlɪ, -ʃn̩lɪ, -ʃn̩lɪ, -ʃənəlɪ]

interknit, -s, -ting, -ted ˌɪntə'nɪt, -s, -ɪŋ, -ɪd

interlac|e, -es, -ing, -ed, -ement ˌɪntə-'leɪs, -ɪz, -ɪŋ, -t, -mənt

Interlaken 'ɪntəlɑːkən

interlard, -s, -ing, -ed ˌɪntə'lɑːd, -z, -ɪŋ, -ɪd

interlea|f, -ves 'ɪntəliː|f, -vz

interleav|e, -es, -ing, -ed ˌɪntə'liːv, -z, -ɪŋ, -d

interlin|e, -es, -ing, -ed ˌɪntə'laɪn, -z, -ɪŋ, -d

interlinear ˌɪntə'lɪnɪə* [-njə*]

interlineation, -s 'ɪntəˌlɪnɪ'eɪʃn, -z

interlink, -s, -ing, -ed ˌɪntə'lɪŋk, -s, -ɪŋ, -t [-'lɪŋt]

interlock, -s, -ing, -ed ˌɪntə'lɒk, -s, -ɪŋ, -t

interlocution, -s ˌɪntələʊ'kjuːʃn [-lɒ'k-], -z

interlocutor, -s, -y ˌɪntə'lɒkjʊtə*, -z, -rɪ

interlop|e, -es, -ing, -ed ˌɪntə'ləʊp, -s, -ɪŋ, -t

interloper, -s 'ɪntələʊpə* [ˌɪntə'l-], -z

interlude, -s 'ɪntəluːd [-ljuːd], -z

intermarriage, -s ˌɪntə'mærɪdʒ, -ɪz

intermarr|y, -ies, -ying, -ied ˌɪntə-'mær|ɪ, -ɪz, -ɪŋ, -ɪd

intermedd|le, -les, -ling, -led, -ler/s ˌɪntə'med|l, -lz, -lɪŋ [-lɪŋ], -ld, -lə*/z [-lə*/z]

intermediar|y, -ies ˌɪntə'miːdjər|ɪ [-dɪər-], -ɪz

intermediate (*s. adj.*), -s, -ly ˌɪntə-'miːdjət [-dɪət, -djɪt, -dɪɪt], -s, -lɪ

interment, -s ɪn'tɜ:mənt, -s
intermezzo, -s ˌɪntə'metsəʊ [-'medzəʊ]
(inter'meddzo), -z
interminable ɪn'tɜ:mɪnəbl [ˌɪn't-]
interminab|ly, -leness ɪn'tɜ:mɪnəb|lɪ,
-lnɪs [-nəs]
interming|le, -les, -ling, -led ˌɪntə-
'mɪŋg|l, -lz, -lɪŋ, -ld
intermission ˌɪntə'mɪʃn
intermit, -s, -ting/ly, -ted; -tent/ly ˌɪntə'mɪt, -s, -ɪŋ/lɪ, -ɪd; -ənt/lɪ
intermix, -es, -ing, -ed ˌɪntə'mɪks, -ɪz,
-ɪŋ, -t
intermixture, -s ˌɪntə'mɪkstʃə*, -z
intern (s.), -s 'ɪntɜ:n [-'-], -z
intern (v.), -s, -ing, -ed, -ment/s
ɪn'tɜ:n, -z, -ɪŋ, -d, -mənt/s
intern|al, -ally ɪn'tɜ:n|l [ˌɪn't-], -əlɪ [-lɪ]
interna|tional, -tionally ˌɪntə'næʃ|ənl
[-ʃnəl, -ʃnl, -ʃnl, -ʃənəl], -ʃnəlɪ [-ʃnəlɪ,
-ʃnlɪ, -ʃnlɪ, -ʃənəlɪ]
Internationale ˌɪntənæʃə'nɑːl [-ʃɪə'n-,
-ʃjə'n-]
internationali|sm, -st/s ˌɪntə'næʃnəl-
ɪ|zəm [-ʃnəl-, -ʃnl-, -ʃnl-, -ʃənəl-],
-st/s
internationalization [-isa-] 'ɪntəˌnæʃ-
nəlaɪ'zeɪʃn [-ʃnəl-, -ʃnl-, -ʃnl-, -ʃənəl-,
-lɪ'z-]
internationaliz|e [-is|e], -es, -ing, -ed
ˌɪntə'næʃnəlaɪz [-ʃnəl-, -ʃnl-, -ʃnl-,
-ʃənəl-], -ɪz, -ɪŋ, -d
internecine ˌɪntə'niːsaɪn [-tə:'n-]
internee, -s ˌɪntɜ:'niː, -z
interoceanic 'ɪntərˌəʊʃɪ'ænɪk [-tə,əʊ-]
interpellant, -s ˌɪntə'pelənt, -s
interpellat|e, -es, -ing, -ed ɪn'tɜ:pelert
[-pəl-, -pɪl-], -s, -ɪŋ, -ɪd
interpellation, -s ɪnˌtɜ:pe'leɪʃn [-pə'l-,
-pɪ'l-], -z
interpenetrat|e, -es, -ing, -ed ˌɪntə-
'penɪtreɪt, -s, -ɪŋ, -ɪd
interpenetration 'ɪntəˌpenɪ'treɪʃn
interplanetary ˌɪntə'plænɪtərɪ [-nət-]
interplay ˌɪntə'pleɪ ['---]
interpolat|e, -es, -ing, -ed, -or/s ɪn-
'tɜ:pəʊleɪt [-pʊl-], -s, -ɪŋ, -ɪd, -ə*/z
interpolation, -s ɪnˌtɜ:pəʊ'leɪʃn [-pʊ'l-],
-z
interposal, -s ˌɪntə'pəʊzl, -z
interpos|e, -es, -ing, -ed, -er/s ˌɪntə-
'pəʊz, -ɪz, -ɪŋ, -d, -ə*/z
interposition, -s ɪnˌtɜ:pə'zɪʃn [ˌɪntə-,
-pʊ'z-], -z
interpret, -s, -ing, -ed, -er/s; -able
ɪn'tɜ:prɪt, -s, -ɪŋ, -ɪd, -ə*/z; -əbl
interpretation, -s ɪnˌtɜ:prɪ'teɪʃn
[-prə't-], -z

interpretative, -ly ɪn'tɜ:prɪtətɪv [-prət-,
-tert-], -lɪ
interracial ˌɪntə'reɪʃjəl [-ʃrəl-, -ʃl]
interregnum, -s ˌɪntə'regnəm, -z
interrelation, -s ˌɪntərɪ'leɪʃn, -z
interrogat|e, -es, -ing, -ed, -or/s ɪn-
'terəʊgert [-rʊg-], -s, -ɪŋ, -ɪd, -ə*/z
interrogation, -s ɪnˌterəʊ'geɪʃn [-rʊ'g-],
-z
interrogative (s. adj.), -s, -ly ˌɪntə'rɒgətɪv, -z, -lɪ
interrogator|y (s. adj.), -ies ˌɪntə'rɒgə-
tər|ɪ, -ɪz
interrupt, -s, -ing, -ed, -er/s ˌɪntə'rʌpt,
-s, -ɪŋ, -ɪd, -ə*/z
interruption, -s ˌɪntə'rʌpʃn, -z
intersect, -s, -ing, -ed, -or/s ˌɪntə'sekt,
-s, -ɪŋ, -ɪd, -ə*/z
intersection, -s ˌɪntə'sekʃn, -z
interspac|e (s. v.), -es, -ing, -ed ˌɪntə-
'speɪs, -ɪz, -ɪŋ, -t
interspers|e, -es, -ing, -ed ˌɪntə'spɜ:s,
-ɪz, -ɪŋ, -t
interspersion ˌɪntə'spɜ:ʃn
interstellar ˌɪntə'stelə* [also 'ɪntəˌs-
when attributive]
interstice, -s ɪn'tɜ:stɪs, -ɪz
intertribal ˌɪntə'traɪbl
intertwin|e, -es, -ing, -ed ˌɪntə'twaɪn,
-z, -ɪŋ, -d
intertwist, -s, -ing, -ed ˌɪntə'twɪst, -s,
-ɪŋ, -ɪd
interval, -s 'ɪntəvl, -z
interven|e, -es, -ing, -ed, -er/s ˌɪntə-
'viːn, -z, -ɪŋ, -d, -ə*/z
intervention, -s ˌɪntə'venʃn, -z
interview (s. v.), -s, -ing, -ed, -er/s
'ɪntəvjuː, -z, -ɪŋ [-vjuɪŋ], -d, -ə*/z
[-,vjʊə*/z]
intervocalic ˌɪntəvəʊ'kælɪk [-vʊ'k-]
interweav|e, -es, -ing, -ed, interwove, -n
ˌɪntə'wiːv, -z, -ɪŋ, -d, ˌɪntə'wəʊv, -n
intestac|y, -ies ɪn'testəs|ɪ, -ɪz
intestate (s. adj.), -s ɪn'testert [-tɪt,
-ət], -s
intestinal ɪn'testɪnl [ˌɪntes'taɪnl]
intestine (s. adj.), -s ɪn'testɪn, -z
intimac|y, -ies 'ɪntɪməs|ɪ, -ɪz
intimate (s. adj.), -s, -ly 'ɪntɪmət [-ɪt],
-s, -lɪ
intimat|e (v.), -es, -ing, -ed 'ɪntɪmert, -s,
-ɪŋ, -ɪd
intimation, -s ˌɪntɪ'meɪʃn, -z
intimidat|e, -es, -ing, -ed, -or/s ɪn'tɪ-
mɪdert, -s, -ɪŋ, -ɪd, -ə*/z
intimidation ɪnˌtɪmɪ'deɪʃn
intimity ɪn'tɪmətɪ [-ɪtɪ]
intituled ɪn'tɪtjuːld

269

into 'ɪntʊ ['ɪntu:], 'ɪntə
Note.—The variant 'ɪntu: *occurs chiefly at the ends of sentences. The form* 'ɪntə *is used only before words beginning with a consonant.*

intolerab|le, -ly, -leness ɪn'tɒlərəb|l, -lɪ, -lnɪs [-nəs]

intoleran|ce, -t/ly ɪn'tɒlərən|s [,ɪn't-], -t/lɪ

intonat|e, -es, -ing, -ed 'ɪntəʊneɪt, -s, -ɪŋ, -ɪd

intonation, -s ,ɪntəʊ'neɪʃn, -z

intonational ,ɪntəʊ'neɪʃənl [-ʃnəl, -ʃn̩l, -ʃn̩l, -ʃənəl]

inton|e, -es, -ing, -ed, -er/s ɪn'təʊn, -z, -ɪŋ, -d, -ə*/z

intoxicant (*s. adj.*), **-s** ɪn'tɒksɪkənt, -s

intoxicat|e, -es, -ing, -ed ɪn'tɒksɪkeɪt, -s, -ɪŋ, -ɪd

intoxication ɪn,tɒksɪ'keɪʃn

intractability ɪn,træktə'bɪlətɪ ['ɪn,trækt-, -lɪt-]

intractab|le, -ly, -leness ɪn'træktəb|l, -lɪ, -lnɪs [-nəs]

intrados, -es ɪn'treɪdɒs, -ɪz

intramural ,ɪntrə'mjʊərəl [-'mjɔər-, -'mjɔːr-]

intransigen|t, -ce ɪn'trænsɪdʒən|t [-'trɑː-nsɪ-, -'trænzɪ-, -'trɑː-nzɪ-], -s

intransitive, -ly ɪn'trænsɪtɪv [,ɪn't-, -'trɑː-ns-], -lɪ

intravenous ,ɪntrə'viːnəs

in-tray, -s 'ɪntreɪ, -z

intrench, -es, -ing, -ed, -ment/s ɪn-'trentʃ, -ɪz, -ɪŋ, -t, -mənt/s

intrepid, -ly ɪn'trepɪd, -lɪ

intrepidity ,ɪntrɪ'pɪdətɪ [-tre'p-, -rtɪ]

intricac|y, -ies 'ɪntrɪkəs|ɪ [ɪn'trɪk-], -ɪz

intricate, -ly, -ness 'ɪntrɪkət [ɪn'trɪk-, -kɪt], -lɪ, -nɪs [-nəs]

intrigu|e (*s. v.*), **-es, -ing, -ed, -er/s** ɪn-'triːg [*also* '- *for noun*], -z, -ɪŋ, -d, -ə*/z

intrinsic, -ally ɪn'trɪnsɪk [-nzɪk], -əlɪ

introduc|e, -es, -ing, -ed, -er/s ,ɪn-trə'djuːs [-trʊ'd-], -ɪz, -ɪŋ, -t, -ə*/z

introduction, -s ,ɪntrə'dʌkʃn [-trʊ'd-], -z

introduct|ive, -ory, -orily ,ɪntrə'dʌk-t|ɪv [-trʊ'd-], -ərɪ, -ərəlɪ [-ɪlɪ]

introit, -s 'ɪntrɔɪt ['ɪntrəʊɪt, ɪn'trəʊɪt], -s

intromission ,ɪntrəʊ'mɪʃn

intromit, -s, -ting, -ted ,ɪntrəʊ'mɪt, -s, -ɪŋ, -ɪd

introspect, -s, -ing, -ed ,ɪntrəʊ'spekt, -s, -ɪŋ, -ɪd

introspection ,ɪntrəʊ'spekʃn

introspective ,ɪntrəʊ'spektɪv

introversion ,ɪntrəʊ'vɜːʃn

introvert (*s.*), **-s** 'ɪntrəʊvɜːt, -s

introvert (*v.*), **-s, -ing, -ed** ,ɪntrəʊ'vɜːt, -s, -ɪŋ, -ɪd

intrud|e, -es, -ing, -ed, -er/s ɪn'truːd, -z, -ɪŋ, -ɪd, -ə*/z

intrusion, -s ɪn'truːʒn, -z

intrusive, -ly, -ness ɪn'truːsɪv, -lɪ, -nɪs [-nəs]

intuit, -s, -ing, -ed ɪn'tjuːɪt [-'tjʊɪt, 'ɪntjuːɪt, -tjʊɪt], -s, ɪn'tjuːɪtɪŋ [-'tjʊɪtɪŋ], ɪn'tjuːɪtɪd [-'tjʊɪtɪd]

intuition ,ɪntjuː'ɪʃn [-tjʊ'ɪ-]

intuitional ,ɪntjuː'ɪʃənl [-tjʊ'ɪ-, -ʃnəl, -ʃn̩l, -ʃn̩l, -ʃənəl]

intuitive, -ly, -ness ɪn'tjuːɪtɪv [-'tjʊɪ-, -'tjʊə-], -lɪ, -nɪs [-nəs]

intumescen|ce, -t ,ɪntjuː'mesn|s [-tjʊ-], -t

inundat|e, -es, -ing, -ed 'ɪnʌndeɪt [-nən-], -s, -ɪŋ, -ɪd

inundation, -s ,ɪnʌn'deɪʃn [-nən-], -z

inur|e, -es, -ing, -ed, -ement ɪ'njʊə* [-jɔə*, -jɔː*], -z, -ɪŋ, -d, -mənt

inutility ,ɪnjuː'tɪlətɪ [-jʊ't-, -rtɪ]

invad|e, -es, -ing, -ed, -er/s ɪn'veɪd, -z, -ɪŋ, -ɪd, -ə*/z

invalid (*s. adj.*) (*infirm through illness, etc.*), **-s** 'ɪnvəlɪd [-liːd], -z

invalid (*adj.*) (*not valid*) ɪn'vælɪd [,ɪn'v-]

invalid (*v.*), **-s, -ing, -ed** 'ɪnvəliːd [,--'-], -z, -ɪŋ, -ɪd

invalidat|e, -es, -ing, -ed ɪn'vælɪdeɪt, -s, -ɪŋ, -ɪd

invalidation ɪn,vælɪ'deɪʃn

invalidity ,ɪnvə'lɪdətɪ [-rtɪ]

invaluable ɪn'væljʊəbl [-ljwəb-, -ljʊb-]

invar ɪn'vɑː*

invariability ɪn,veərɪə'bɪlətɪ ['ɪn,veə-rɪə'b-, -lɪt-]

invariable ɪn'veərɪəbl [,ɪn'v-]

invariab|ly, -leness ɪn'veərɪəb|lɪ, -lnɪs [-nəs]

invasion, -s ɪn'veɪʒn, -z

invasive ɪn'veɪsɪv

invective, -s ɪn'vektɪv, -z

inveigh, -s, -ing, -ed ɪn'veɪ, -z, -ɪŋ, -d

inveig|le, -les, -ling, -led, -lement/s ɪn'veɪg|l, [-'viːg-], -lz, -lɪŋ [-lɪŋ], -ld, -lmənt/s

invent, -s, -ing, -ed, -er/s, -or/s ɪn'vent, -s, -ɪŋ, -ɪd, -ə*/z, -ə*/z

invention, -s ɪn'venʃn, -z

inventive, -ly, -ness ɪn'ventɪv, -lɪ, -nɪs [-nəs]

inventor|y, -ies 'ɪnvəntr|ɪ, -ɪz

Inver|ary, -arity ˌɪnvəˈr|eərɪ [-eərə], -ærətɪ [-ɪtɪ]

Invercargill (in Scotland) ˌɪnvəkɑːˈgɪl [-ˈkɑːgɪl], (in New Zealand) ˌɪnvəˈkɑː-gɪl

Invergordon ˌɪnvəˈgɔːdn

Inverkeithing ˌɪnvəˈkiːðɪŋ

Inverlochy ˌɪnvəˈlɒkɪ [-ˈlɒxɪ]

inverness (I.), -es ˌɪnvəˈnes [ˈ— when attributive], -ɪz

Inverness-shire ˌɪnvəˈnesʃə* [-ˈnesˌʃɪə*, -ˈneʃˌʃɪə*, -ˈneʃʃə*]

inverse (s. adj.), -s, -ly ˌɪnˈvɜːs [ɪnˈv-, also ˈ— when attributive], -ɪz, -lɪ

inversion, -s ɪnˈvɜːʃn, -z

invert (s. adj.), -s ˈɪnvɜːt, -s

invert (v.), -s, -ing, -ed ɪnˈvɜːt, -s, -ɪŋ, -ɪd

invertebrata ɪnˌvɜːtɪˈbrɑːtə [-ˈbreɪtə, ˈɪnˌvɜːtɪˈb-]

invertebrate, -s ɪnˈvɜːtɪbrət [ˌɪnˈv-, -brɪt, -breɪt], -s

Inverurie ˌɪnvəˈrʊərɪ

invest, -s, -ing, -ed, -or/s ɪnˈvest, -s, -ɪŋ, -ɪd, -ə*/z

investigat|e, -es, -ing, -ed, -or/s; -ive, -ory ɪnˈvestɪgeɪt, -s, -ɪŋ, -ɪd, -ə*/z; -ɪv, -ərɪ

investigation, -s ɪnˌvestɪˈgeɪʃn, -z

investiture, -s ɪnˈvestɪtʃə* [-ˌtjʊə*], -z

investment, -s ɪnˈvestmənt, -s

inveteracy ɪnˈvetərəsɪ

inveterate, -ly, -ness ɪnˈvetərət [-rɪt], -lɪ, -nɪs [-nəs]

invidious, -ly, -ness ɪnˈvɪdɪəs [-djəs], -lɪ, -nɪs [-nəs]

invigilat|e, -es, -ing, -ed, -or/s ɪnˈvɪdʒɪlert, -s, -ɪŋ, -ɪd, -ə*/z

invigilation, -s ɪnˌvɪdʒɪˈleɪʃn, -z

invigorat|e, -es, -ing, -ed, -or/s ɪn-ˈvɪgəreɪt, -s, -ɪŋ, -ɪd, -ə*/z

invigoration ɪnˌvɪgəˈreɪʃn

invincibility ɪnˌvɪnsɪˈbɪlətɪ [-sə'b-, -ɪrt-]

invincib|le, -ly, -leness ɪnˈvɪnsəb|l [-sɪb-], -lɪ, -lnɪs [-nəs]

inviolability ɪnˌvaɪələˈbɪlətɪ [ˈɪnˌvaɪəl-ə'b-, -ɪrt-]

inviolab|le, -ly, -leness ɪnˈvaɪələb|l, -lɪ, -lnɪs [-nəs]

inviolate, -ly, -ness ɪnˈvaɪələt [-lɪt, -leɪt], -lɪ, -nɪs

invisibility ɪnˌvɪzəˈbɪlətɪ [ˈɪnˌvɪzə'b-, -zɪ'b-, -ɪrt-]

invisible ɪnˈvɪzəbl [ˌɪnˈv-, -zɪb-]

invisib|ly, -leness ɪnˈvɪzəb|lɪ [-zɪb-], -lnɪs [-nəs]

invitation, -s ˌɪnvɪˈteɪʃn, -z

invit|e, -es, -ing/ly, -ingness, -ed, -er/s ɪnˈvaɪt, -s, -ɪŋ/lɪ, -ɪŋnɪs [-nəs], -ɪd, -ə*/z

invocate, -s, -ing, -ed ˈɪnvəʊkeɪt, -s, -ɪŋ, -ɪd

invocation, -s ˌɪnvəʊˈkeɪʃn [-vʊ'k-], -z

invoic|e (s. v.), -es, -ing, -ed ˈɪnvɔɪs, -ɪz, -ɪŋ, -t

invok|e, -es, -ing, -ed ɪnˈvəʊk, -s, -ɪŋ, -t

involucre, -s ˈɪnvəluːkə* [-lju:-], -z

involuntar|y, -ily, -iness ɪnˈvɒləntər|ɪ [ˌɪnˈv-, -ɒlnt-], -əlɪ [-ɪlɪ], -mɪs [-nəs]

involute, -s, -d ˈɪnvəluːt [-lju:t], -s, -ɪd

involution, -s ˌɪnvəˈluːʃn [-ˈlju:-], -z

involv|e, -es, -ing, -ed ɪnˈvɒlv, -z, -ɪŋ, -d

involvement ɪnˈvɒlvmənt

invulnerability ɪnˌvʌlnərəˈbɪlətɪ [ˈɪn-ˌvʌlnərə'b-, -ɪrt-]

invulnerable ɪnˈvʌlnərəbl [ˌɪnˈv-]

invulnerab|ly, -leness ɪnˈvʌlnərəb|lɪ, -lnɪs [-nəs]

inward, -s, -ly, -ness ˈɪnwəd, -z, -lɪ, -nɪs [-nəs]

Inwards ˈɪnwədz

inweav|e, -es, -ing, -ed, inwove, -n ˌɪnˈwiːv, -z, -ɪŋ, -d, ˌɪnˈwəʊv, -n

Inwood ˈɪnwʊd

inwrought ˌɪnˈrɔːt [also ˈɪnr- when attributive]

io (I.), -s ˈaɪəʊ, -z

iodate, -s, -d ˈaɪəʊdeɪt, -s, -ɪd

iodic aɪˈɒdɪk

iodide, -s ˈaɪəʊdaɪd, -z

iodine ˈaɪəʊdiːn [ˈaɪədaɪn]

iodiz|e (-is|e), -es, -ing, -ed ˈaɪəʊdaɪz, -ɪz, -ɪŋ, -d

iodoform aɪˈɒdəfɔːm ˈaɪə-

Iolanthe ˌaɪəʊˈlænθɪ

Iolcus ɪˈɒlkəs [aɪˈɒl-]

iolite ˈaɪəʊlaɪt

Iolo (Welsh Christian name) ˈjəʊləʊ (Welsh ˈjolo)

ion (I.), -s ˈaɪən [ˈaɪɒn], -z

Iona aɪˈəʊnə

Ionesco jɒˈneskəʊ [ˌɪɒ-, -skuː]

Ionia, -n/s aɪˈəʊnjə [-nɪə], -n/z

Ionic aɪˈɒnɪk

ionization [-isa-] ˌaɪənaɪˈzeɪʃn

ioniz|e (-is|e), -es, -ing, -ed ˈaɪənaɪz, -ɪz, -ɪŋ, -d

ionosphere, -s aɪˈɒnəˌsfɪə*, -z

iota, -s; -cism/s aɪˈəʊtə, -z; -sɪzəm/z

I O U, -s ˌaɪəʊˈjuː, -z

Iowa ˈaɪəʊə [ˈaɪəwə]

IPA ˌaɪpiːˈeɪ

ipecacuanha ˌɪpɪkækjʊˈænə [ˈɪpɪ-ˌkækjʊˈæ-, -ˈɑːnə]

271

Iphicrates ɪ'fɪkrəti:z

Iphigenia ɪ,fɪdʒɪ'naɪə [,ɪfɪdʒ-]

Ipoh 'i:pəʊ

ipso facto ,ɪpsəʊ'fæktəʊ

Ipswich 'ɪpswɪtʃ

Iquique ɪ'ki:kɪ

Ira 'aɪərə

Irak, -i/s ɪ'rɑːk, -ɪ/z

Iran ɪ'rɑːn [,ɪə'rɑːn]

Iranian, -s ɪ'reɪnjən [aɪ'r-, ,aɪə'r-, -nɪən], -z

Iraq, -i/s ɪ'rɑːk, -ɪ/z

irascibility ɪ,ræsə'bɪlətɪ [aɪə,r-, -sɪ'b-, -lɪt-]

irascib|le, -ly, -leness ɪ'ræsəb|l [,aɪə'r-, -sɪb|l], -lɪ, -lnɪs [-nəs]

irate aɪ'reɪt [,aɪə'r-]

Irawadi ,ɪrə'wɒdɪ

ire 'aɪə*

Ire|dale, -dell 'aɪə|deɪl, -del

ire|ful, -fully, -fulness 'aɪə|fʊl, -fʊlɪ [-fəlɪ], -fʊlnɪs [-nəs]

Ireland 'aɪələnd

Iremonger 'aɪə,mʌŋgə*

Irene aɪ'ri:nɪ [,aɪə'r-], in modern use also 'aɪri:n ['aɪər-]

irenic, -al aɪ'ri:nɪk [,aɪə'r-, -'ren-], -l

irenicon, -s aɪ'ri:nɪkən [,aɪə'r-, -'ren-, -kɒn], z

Ireton 'aɪətn

irian (pertaining to the iris) 'aɪərɪən

Irian (New Guinea) 'ɪrɪən

iridescen|ce, -t ,ɪrɪ'desn|s, -t

iridium aɪ'rɪdɪəm [,aɪə'r-, ɪ'rɪd-, -djəm]

Irion 'ɪrɪən

iris (I.), -es 'aɪərɪs, -ɪz

Irish; -ism/s 'aɪərɪʃ; -ɪzəm/z

Irish|man, -men 'aɪərɪʃ|mən, -mən [-men]

Irishry 'aɪərɪʃrɪ

Irish|woman, -women 'aɪərɪʃ|,wʊmən, -,wɪmɪn

irk, -s, -ing, -ed ɜːk, -s, -ɪŋ, -t

irksome, -ly, -ness 'ɜːksəm, -lɪ, -nɪs [-nəs]

Irkutsk ɜː'kʊtsk [ɪə'k-] (ir'kutsk)

iron (s. v.) (I.), -s, -ing, -ed 'aɪən, -z, -ɪŋ, -d

ironbound 'aɪənbaʊnd

ironclad, -s 'aɪənklæd, -z

iron-found|er/s, -ry, -ries 'aɪən,faʊnd|ə*/z, -rɪ, -rɪz

irongray [-grey] ,aɪən'greɪ [also '-- when attributive]

ironic, -al, -ally aɪ'rɒnɪk [,aɪə'r-], -l, -əlɪ

ironing-board, -s 'aɪənɪŋbɔːd [-bɔəd], -z

ironmonger, -s 'aɪən,mʌŋgə*, -z

ironmongery 'aɪən,mʌŋgərɪ

ironmould 'aɪənməʊld

ironside (I.), -s 'aɪənsaɪd, -z

iron-stone 'aɪənstəʊn

Ironton 'aɪəntən

ironware 'aɪənweə*

ironwood (I.) 'aɪənwʊd

ironwork, -s 'aɪənwɜːk, -s

iron|y (s.) (sarcasm, etc.), -ies 'aɪərən|ɪ [-rɪ|-], -ɪz

irony (adj.) (like iron) 'aɪənɪ

Iroquoian ,ɪrəʊ'kwɔɪən

Iroquois (sing.) 'ɪrəkwɔɪ [-kwɔɪz], (plur.) 'ɪrəkwɔɪz

irradian|ce, -cy, -t ɪ'reɪdjən|s [-dɪən-], -sɪ, -t

irradiat|e, -es, -ing, -ed ɪ'reɪdɪeɪt, -s, -ɪŋ, -ɪd

irradiation, -s ɪ,reɪdɪ'eɪʃn [,ɪreɪ-], -z

irra|tional, -tionally ɪ'ræ|ʃənl [,ɪ'r-, -ʃnəl, -ʃn̩l, -ʃn̩l, -ʃənəl], -ʃnəlɪ [-ʃnəlɪ, -ʃnl̩ɪ, -ʃn̩lɪ, -ʃənəlɪ]

irrationality ɪ,ræʃə'nælətɪ ['ɪ,ræʃə'n-, -ʃn̩'æ-, -ɪtɪ]

irrebuttable ,ɪrɪ'bʌtəbl

irreceptive ,ɪrɪ'septɪv

irreclaimable ,ɪrɪ'kleɪməbl

irreclaimably ,ɪrɪ'kleɪməblɪ

irrecognizable [-isa-] ɪ'rekəgnaɪzəbl ['ɪ,rekəg'n-]

irreconcilability ɪ,rekənsaɪlə'bɪlətɪ ['ɪ,rekənsaɪlə'b-, -lɪt-]

irreconcilable, -ness ɪ'rekənsaɪləbl ['ɪ,rekən's-], -nɪs [-nəs]

irreconcilably ɪ'rekənsaɪləblɪ [,ɪrekən's-]

irrecoverable, -ness ,ɪrɪ'kʌvərəbl, -nɪs [-nəs]

irrecoverably ,ɪrɪ'kʌvərəblɪ

irredeemable, -ness ,ɪrɪ'di:məbl, -nɪs [-nəs]

irredeemably ,ɪrɪ'di:məblɪ

irredenti|sm, -st/s ,ɪrɪ'dentɪ|zəm, -st/s

irreducible, -ness ,ɪrɪ'dju:səbl [-sɪb-], -nɪs [-nəs]

irreducibly ,ɪrɪ'dju:səblɪ [-sɪb-]

irreformable ,ɪrɪ'fɔːməbl

irrefragability ɪ,refrəgə'bɪlətɪ [-lɪt-]

irrefragab|le, -ly, -leness ɪ'refrəgəb|l, -lɪ, -lnɪs [-nəs]

irrefutability ɪ,refjʊtə'bɪlətɪ ['ɪ,refjʊtə'b-, ,ɪrɪ,fjuːtə'b-, -lɪt-]

irrefutable ɪ'refjʊtəbl [,ɪrɪ'fjuːt-]

irrefutably ɪ'refjʊtəblɪ [,ɪrɪ'fjuːt-]

irregular, -ly ɪ'regjʊlə* [-gjəl-], -lɪ

irregularit|y, -ies ɪ,regjʊ'lærət|ɪ ['ɪ,regjʊ'l-, -gjə'l-, -rɪt|ɪ], -ɪz

irrelevan|ce, -cy, -cies, -t/ly ɪ'reləvən|s [-lɪv-], -sɪ, -sɪz, -t/lɪ

irreligion ˌɪrɪˈlɪdʒən [-rəˈl-]
irreligious, -ly, -ness ˌɪrɪˈlɪdʒəs [-rəˈl-], -lɪ, -nɪs [-nəs]
irremediable ˌɪrɪˈmiːdjəbl [-dɪə-]
irremediably ˌɪrɪˈmiːdjəblɪ [-dɪə-]
irremovability ˈɪrɪˌmuːvəˈbɪlətɪ [-lɪt-]
irremovable ˌɪrɪˈmuːvəbl
irrepairable ˌɪrɪˈpɛərəbl
irreparability ɪˌrepərəˈbɪlətɪ [ˈɪˌrepərəˈb-, -lɪt-]
irreparable, -ness ɪˈrepərəbl, -nɪs [-nəs]
irreparably ɪˈrepərəblɪ
irrepatriable ˌɪrɪˈpætrɪəbl
irreplaceable ˌɪrɪˈpleɪsəbl
irrepressible, -ness ˌɪrɪˈpresəbl [-sɪb-], -nɪs [-nəs]
irrepressibly ˌɪrɪˈpresəblɪ [-sɪb-]
irreproachability ˈɪrɪˌprəʊtʃəˈbɪlətɪ [-lɪt-]
irreproachable, -ness ˌɪrɪˈprəʊtʃəbl, -nɪs [-nəs]
irreproachably ˌɪrɪˈprəʊtʃəblɪ
irresistibility ˈɪrɪˌzɪstəˈbɪlətɪ [-tɪˈb-, -lɪt-]
irresistible, -ness ˌɪrɪˈzɪstəbl [-tɪb-], -nɪs [-nəs]
irresistibly ˌɪrɪˈzɪstəblɪ [-tɪb-]
irresoluble ɪˈrezəljʊbl
irresolute, -ly, -ness ɪˈrezəluːt [ˌɪˈr-, -zljuːt, -zəljuːt], -lɪ, -nɪs [-nəs]
irresolution ɪˌrezəˈluːʃn [-zl]uː-, -zəˈlju:-]
irresolvability ˈɪrɪˌzɒlvəˈbɪlətɪ [-lɪt-]
irresolvable, -ness ˌɪrɪˈzɒlvəbl, -nɪs [-nəs]
irrespective, -ly ˌɪrɪˈspektɪv, -lɪ
irresponsibility ˈɪrɪˌspɒnsəˈbɪlətɪ [-sɪˈb-, -lɪt-]
irresponsib|le, -ly ˌɪrɪˈspɒnsəb|l [-sɪb-], -lɪ
irresponsive, -ly, -ness ˌɪrɪˈspɒnsɪv, -lɪ, -nɪs [-nəs]
irrestrainable ˌɪrɪˈstreɪnəbl
irretentive ˌɪrɪˈtentɪv
irretrievability ˈɪrɪˌtriːvəˈbɪlətɪ [-lɪt-]
irretrievable ˌɪrɪˈtriːvəbl
irretrievably ˌɪrɪˈtriːvəblɪ
irreveren|ce, -t/ly ɪˈrevərən|s [ˌɪˈr-, -t/lɪ
irreversibility ˈɪrɪˌvəːsəˈbɪlətɪ [-sɪˈb-, -lɪt-]
irreversible, -ness ˌɪrɪˈvəːsəbl [-sɪb-], -nɪs [-nəs]
irrevocability ɪˌrevəkəˈbɪlətɪ [-vʊk-, -lɪt-]
irrevocable ɪˈrevəkəbl [-vʊk-], (when applied to letters of credit) ˌɪrɪˈvəʊkəbl
irrevocably ɪˈrevəkəblɪ [-vʊk-]

irrigable ˈɪrɪgəbl
irrigat|e, -es, -ing, -ed, -or/s ˈɪrɪgeɪt, -s, -ɪŋ, -ɪd, -ə*/z
irrigation, -s ˌɪrɪˈgeɪʃn, -z
irritability ˌɪrɪtəˈbɪlətɪ [-lɪt-]
irritab|le, -ly, -leness ˈɪrɪtəb|l, -lɪ, -lnɪs [-nəs]
irritant (s. adj.), -s ˈɪrɪtənt, -s
irritat|e, -es, -ing/ly, -ed; -ive ˈɪrɪteɪt, -s, -ɪŋ/lɪ, -ɪd; -ɪv
irritation, -s ˌɪrɪˈteɪʃn, -z
irruption, -s ɪˈrʌpʃn, -z
irruptive, -ly ɪˈrʌptɪv, -lɪ
Irv|ine, -ing ˈɜːv|ɪn [-vaɪn], -ɪŋ
Irving|ism, -ite/s ˈɜːvɪŋ|ɪzəm, -aɪt/s
Irwin ˈɜːwɪn
is (from be) ɪz (strong form), z, s (weak forms)
    Note.—z is used only when the preceding word ends in a vowel or a voiced consonant other than z or ʒ. s is used only when the preceding word ends in a voiceless consonant other than s or ʃ.
Isaac, -s ˈaɪzək, -s
Isabel ˈɪzəbel
Isabella ˌɪzəˈbelə
Isaiah aɪˈzaɪə [old-fashioned -ˈzerə]
Isambard ˈɪzəmbɑːd
Isard ˈɪzɑːd
Iscariot ɪˈskærɪət
Ischia ˈɪskɪə [-kjə]
Iseult iːˈzuːlt [ɪˈz-, -ˈsuːlt]
Isham (surname) ˈaɪʃəm
Ishbosheth ˈɪʃbəʃeθ [-bɒʃ-, ɪʃˈbɒʃeθ, ɪʃˈbəʊʃeθ]
Isherwood ˈɪʃəwʊd
Ishmael ˈɪʃmeɪəl [-ˌmɪəl, -mɪəl]
Ishmaelit|e, -es, -ish ˈɪʃˌmɪəlaɪt [-mɪəl-, -mjəl-, -merəl-, -məl-], -s, -ɪʃ
Ishtar ˈɪʃtɑː*
Isidore ˈɪzɪdɔː* [-zə-, -dɔə*]
Isidorian ˌɪzɪˈdɔːrɪən [-zəˈd-]
isinglass ˈaɪzɪŋglɑːs
Isis ˈaɪsɪs
Isla ˈaɪlə
Islam ˈɪzlɑːm [-læm, -ləm, ɪzˈlɑːm, ɪsˈl-]
islamic ɪzˈlæmɪk [ɪsˈl-]
Islam|ism, -ite/s ˈɪzləm|ɪzəm, -aɪt/s
island, -s, -er/s ˈaɪlənd, -z, -ə*/z
Islay ˈaɪleɪ [locally ˈaɪlə]
isle, -s aɪl, -z
islet, -s ˈaɪlɪt [-lət, -let], -s
Isleworth ˈaɪzlwəθ [-wɜːθ]
Islington ˈɪzlɪŋtən
Islip (archbishop) ˈɪzlɪp, (in Oxfordshire) ˈaɪslɪp
ism, -s ˈɪzəm, -z

273

Ismail ˌɪzmɑːˈiːl [ˌɪsmɑː-, ˈɪzmaɪl, ˈɪzmeɪl]
Ismailia ˌɪzmaɪˈliːə [ˌɪsmaɪ-, -ˈlɪə]
Ismay ˈɪzmeɪ
isn't ˈɪznt [*also occasionally* ˈɪzn *when not final*]
isobar, -s ˈaɪsəʊbɑːˈ*, -z
Isobel ˈɪzəbel [-zəʊb-]
isochromatic ˌaɪsəʊkrəʊˈmætɪk
isochron|al, -ism, -ous aɪˈsɒkrən|l, -ɪzəm, -əs
Isocrates aɪˈsɒkrətiːz
isogloss, -es ˈaɪsəʊglɒs, -ɪz
isolate (s.), -s ˈaɪsəʊleɪt [-lət], -s
isolat|e (v.), -es, -ing, -ed ˈaɪsəleɪt [*rarely* ˈaɪzəl-], -s, -ɪŋ, -ɪd
isolation ˌaɪsəˈleɪʃn
isolationi|sm, -st/s ˌaɪsəˈleɪʃɪ|zəm, -st/s
isolative ˈaɪsələtɪv [-səleɪt-]
Isolda ɪˈzɒldə
Isolde ɪˈzɒldə (iːˈzɒldə)
isomeric ˌaɪsəʊˈmerɪk
isomer|ism, -ous aɪˈsɒmər|ɪzəm, -əs
isometric, -al, -ally ˌaɪsəʊˈmetrɪk, -l, -əlɪ
isomorph|ic, -ism, -ous ˌaɪsəʊˈmɔːf|ɪk, -ɪzəm, -əs
isophone, -s ˈaɪsəʊfəʊn, -z
isosceles aɪˈsɒsɪliːz [-səl-, -s|-]
isotherm, -s ˈaɪsəʊθɜːm, -z
isothermal ˌaɪsəʊˈθɜːml
isotope, -s ˈaɪsəʊtəʊp, -s
isotopic ˌaɪsəʊˈtɒpɪk
isotype, -s ˈaɪsəʊtaɪp, -s
Ispahan ˌɪspəˈhɑːn [-ˈhæn]
Israel ˈɪzreɪəl [-ˌrəl, -rɪəl, in formal reading also -reɪel]
Israeli, -s ɪzˈreɪlɪ, -z
Israelit|e, -es, -ish ˈɪz,rɪəlaɪt [-rɪəl-, -rəl-, -reɪəl-], -s, -ɪʃ
Issachar ˈɪsəkəˈ [-kɑːˈ]
iss|ue (s. v.), -ues, -uing, -ued, -uer/s; -uable, -uance ˈɪʃ|uː [ˈɪsj|uː, ˈɪʃj|uː], -uːz, -uːɪŋ [-ʊɪŋ], -uːd, -uːəˈ* [-ʊə*]/z; -uːəbl [-ʊəbl], -uːəns [-ʊəns]
Istanbul ˌɪstænˈbuːl [-tɑːn-, -ˈbʊl]
isthmian (I.) ˈɪsθmɪən [-stm-, -sm-, -mjən]
isthmus, -es ˈɪsməs [-sθm-, -stm-], -ɪz
istle ˈɪstlɪ
Istria ˈɪstrɪə
it ɪt
itacism ˈiːtəsɪzəm
Italian (s. adj.), -s ɪˈtæljən, -z
italianate ɪˈtæljəneɪt [-nət, -nɪt]

italianism, -s ɪˈtæljənɪzəm, -z
italianiz|e [-is|e], -es, -ing, -ed ɪˈtæljən-aɪz, -ɪz, -ɪŋ, -d
italic (I.), -s ɪˈtælɪk, -s
italicization [-isa-] ɪˌtælɪsaɪˈzeɪʃn
italiciz|e [-is|e], -es, -ing, -ed ɪˈtælɪsaɪz, -ɪz, -ɪŋ, -d
Italy ˈɪtəlɪ [ˈɪtl̩ɪ]
itch (s. v.), -es, -ing, -ed ɪtʃ, -ɪz, -ɪŋ, -t
Itchen ˈɪtʃɪn
itch|y, -iness ˈɪtʃ|ɪ, -mɪs [-məs]
item, -s ˈaɪtəm [-tem, -tɪm], -z
itemiz|e [-is|e], -es, -ing, -ed ˈaɪtəmaɪz, -ɪz, -ɪŋ, -d
iterat|e, -es, -ing, -ed ˈɪtəreɪt, -s, -ɪŋ, -ɪd
iteration ˌɪtəˈreɪʃn
iterative ˈɪtərətɪv [-reɪt-]
Ithaca ˈɪθəkə
Ithamar ˈɪθəmɑːˈ* [-məˈ*]
Ithuriel ɪˈθjʊərɪəl
itineran|cy, -t/s ɪˈtɪnərən|sɪ [aɪˈt-], -t/s
itinerar|y, -ies aɪˈtɪnərərɪ [ɪˈt-], -ɪz
itinerat|e, -es, -ing, -ed ɪˈtɪnəreɪt [aɪˈt-], -s, -ɪŋ, -ɪd
its ɪts
it's (= it is) ɪts
itself ɪtˈself
Iuca aɪˈjuːkə
Ivan ˈaɪvən
Ivanhoe ˈaɪvənhəʊ
Ivanoff ɪˈvɑːnəf [iːˈv-, -nɒf] (iˈvanəf)
Ivatt, -s ˈaɪvət [-væt], -s
I've (= I have) aɪv
Iveagh ˈaɪvə
Ivens ˈaɪvənz
Iver ˈaɪvəˈ*
Ives (surname, and towns St. Ives in Cornwall and Cambridgeshire) aɪvz, (in Stevenson's 'St. Ives') iːvz
Ivey ˈaɪvɪ
Ivimey ˈaɪvɪmɪ
Ivone ˈaɪvən
Ivor ˈaɪvəˈ*
ivor|y (s. adj.) (I.), -ies ˈaɪvər|ɪ, -ɪz
ivory-black ˌaɪvərɪˈblæk
iv|y (I.), -ies, -ied ˈaɪv|ɪ, -ɪz, -ɪd
Ivybridge ˈaɪvɪbrɪdʒ
ixia, -s ˈɪksɪə [-sjə], -z
Ixion ɪkˈsaɪən
Iza ˈaɪzə
Izaby (surname) ˈɪzəbɪ
Izal ˈaɪzəl
izard, -s ˈɪzəd, -z
Izard ˈaɪzɑːd, ˈaɪzəd, ˈɪzəd
Izod ˈaɪzɒd
Izzard ˈɪzəd

J

J (*the letter*), **-'s** dʒeɪ, -z

jab (*s. v.*), **-s, -bing, -bed** dʒæb, -z, -ɪŋ, -d

jabber (*s. v.*), **-s, -ing, -ed, -er/s** 'dʒæbə*, -z, -ɪŋ, -d, -rə*/z

Jabberwock, -y 'dʒæbəwɒk, -ɪ

Jabesh-gilead ˌdʒeɪbeʃ'gɪlræd [-lɪəd, -ljəd]

Jabez 'dʒeɪbez [-bɪz]

Jabin 'dʒeɪbɪn

jabiru, -s 'dʒæbɪruː, -z

jaborandi ˌdʒæbə'rændɪ [-bɔː'r-]

jabot, -s 'ʒæbəʊ (ʒabo), -z

jacaranda ˌdʒækə'rændə

Jachin 'dʒeɪkɪn

jacinth, -s 'dʒæsɪnθ ['dʒeɪs-], -s

jack (**J.**), **-s** dʒæk, -s

jackal, -s 'dʒækɔːl [-kəl], -z

jackanapes, -es 'dʒækəneɪps, -ɪz

jackass, -es 'dʒækæs [-kɑːs], -ɪz

Note.— 'dʒækæs *is more usual for the animal and bird, but* 'dʒækɑːs *is commoner when the word is used colloquially as a term of contempt.*

jack-boot, -s 'dʒækbuːt [ˌdʒæk'b-], -s

jackdaw, -s 'dʒækdɔː, -z

jacket, -s, -ed 'dʒækɪt, -s, -ɪd

jack-in-office, jacks-in-office 'dʒækɪnˌɒfɪs, 'dʒæksɪnˌɒfɪs

jack-in-the-box, -es 'dʒækɪnðəbɒks, -ɪz

jack-in-the-green, -s 'dʒækɪnðəgriːn [ˌdʒækɪnðə'g-], -z

jack-kni|fe, -ves 'dʒæknaɪ|f, -vz

Jackman 'dʒækmən

jack-of-all-trades ˌdʒækəv'ɔːltreɪdz

jack-o'-lantern, -s 'dʒækəʊˌlæntən [ˌ-'--], -z

jack-plane, -s 'dʒækpleɪn, -z

jackpot, -s 'dʒækpɒt, -s

jack-pudding, -s ˌdʒæk'pʊdɪŋ, -z

Jackson 'dʒæksn

jack-tar, -s ˌdʒæk'tɑː* ['--], -z

Jacob 'dʒeɪkəb

Jacobean ˌdʒækəʊ'biːən [-'bɪən]

Jacobi dʒə'kəʊbɪ

jacobian (**J.**), **-s** dʒə'kəʊbjən [-bɪən], -z

Jacobin, -s, -ism 'dʒækəʊbɪn [-kʊb-], -z, -ɪzəm

Jacobit|e, -es, -ism 'dʒækəʊbaɪt [-kʊb-], -s, -ɪzəm

Jacob|s, -son 'dʒeɪkəb|z, -sn

Jacob's-ladder, -s ˌdʒeɪkəbz'lædə*, -z

jacobus (**J.**), **-es** dʒə'kəʊbəs, -ɪz

Jacoby dʒə'kəʊbɪ, 'dʒækəbɪ [-kʊb-]

Jacomb 'dʒeɪkəm

Jacqueline 'dʒækliːn ['ʒæ-, -kəlɪn]

Jacques dʒeɪks

jactitation ˌdʒæktɪ'teɪʃn

jad|e (*s. v.*), **-es, -ing, -ed** dʒeɪd, -z, -ɪŋ, -ɪd

jaeger (**J.**), **-s** 'jeɪgə*, -z

Jael 'dʒeɪəl [dʒeɪl, 'dʒeɪel]

Jaffa, -s 'dʒæfə, -z

jag (*s. v.*), **-s, -ging, -ged** dʒæg, -z, -ɪŋ, -d

Jagan (*Guyanese politician*) 'dʒægən

Jaggard 'dʒægəd

jagged (*adj.*), **-ly, -ness** 'dʒægɪd, -lɪ, -nɪs [-nəs]

jagger (**J.**), **-s** 'dʒægə*, -z

jagg|y, -ier, -iest, -iness 'dʒæg|ɪ, -ɪə*, -ɪɪst, -ɪnɪs [-ɪnəs]

Jago 'dʒeɪgəʊ

jaguar (**J.**), **-s** 'dʒægjʊə* [-gwə*], -z

Jah dʒɑː: [jɑː]

Jahaz 'dʒeɪhæz

Jahveh 'jɑːveɪ [ˌjɑː'veɪ, 'dʒɑːveɪ, 'jɑːvə]

jail, -s dʒeɪl, -z

jailbird, -s 'dʒeɪlbɜːd, -z

jailer, -s 'dʒeɪlə*, -z

Jaipur ˌdʒaɪ'pʊə* [-'pʊə*, -'pɔː*] (*Hindi*, ɟəypwr)

Jairus dʒeɪ'aɪərəs ['dʒaɪərəs]

Jalalabad dʒə,lɑːlə'bɑːd [-'bæd] (*Hindi* ɟəlalabad)

jalap 'dʒæləp

jalop|y, -ies dʒə'lɒp|ɪ, -ɪz

jalousie, -s 'ʒæluːziː [-lʊz-, ˌʒælu:'z-, -lʊ'z-], -z

jam (*s.*), **-s** dʒæm, -z

jam (*v.*) (*wedge, spread with jam*), **-s, -ming, -med** dʒæm, -z, -ɪŋ, -d

Jam (*Indian title*), **-s** dʒɑːm (*Hindi* ɟam), -z

Jamaica, -n/s dʒə'meɪkə, -n/z

jamb, -s dʒæm, -z

jamboree, -s ˌdʒæmbə'riː ['--], -z

James dʒeɪmz

275

Jameson (*surname*) 'dʒeɪmsn, 'dʒɪm-, 'dʒem-, -mɪsn
James's 'dʒeɪmzɪz
Jamia 'dʒʌmɪə ['dʒæm-] (*Hindi* ɟəmya)
Jamieson (*surname*) 'dʒeɪmɪsn, 'dʒæm-, 'dʒem-, 'dʒɪm-
jam-jar, -s 'dʒæmdʒɑ:*, -z
jamm|y, -ier, -iest, -iness 'dʒæm|ɪ, -ɪə*, -ɪɪst, -ɪnɪs [-ɪnəs]
jam-pot, -s 'dʒæmpɒt, -s
Jamrach 'dʒæmræk
Jamy 'dʒeɪmɪ
Jan dʒæn
Jane dʒeɪn
Janeiro dʒə'nɪərəʊ
Janet 'dʒænɪt
jang|le, -les, -ling, -led, -ler/s 'dʒæŋg|l, -lz, -lɪŋ [-lɪŋ], -ld, -lə*/z [-lə*/z]
Janiculum dʒæ'nɪkjʊləm [dʒə'n-]
janissar|y, -ies 'dʒænɪsər|ɪ, -ɪz
janitor, -s 'dʒænɪtə*, -z
Jan(n)ette dʒə'net
Jansen 'dʒænsn
Janseni|sm, -st/s 'dʒænsn̩ɪ|zm [-sənɪ-], -st/s
Jantzen 'jæntsən ['dʒæn-]
Januarius ˌdʒænjʊ'eərɪəs
Januar|y, -ies 'dʒænjʊər|ɪ [-ˌnjʊər-, -njwər-, -njʊr-], -ɪz
Janus 'dʒeɪnəs
Jap, -s dʒæp, -s
japan (*s. v.*) (J.), -s, -ning, -ned, -ner/s dʒə'pæn, -z, -ɪŋ, -d, -ə*/z
Japanese ˌdʒæpə'niːz [-pŋ'iːz]
jap|e (*s. v.*), -es, -ing, -ed dʒeɪp, -s, -ɪŋ, -t
Japhet 'dʒeɪfet
Japhetic dʒeɪ'fetɪk [dʒə'f-]
japonica, -s dʒə'pɒnɪkə, -z
Jaques dʒeɪks, dʒæks, (*Shakespearian character*) 'dʒeɪkwɪz
jar (*s. v.*), -s, -ring/ly, -red dʒɑ:*, -z, -rɪŋ/lɪ, -d
Jardine 'dʒɑ:diːn
jardinière, -s ˌʒɑ:dɪ'njeə* [-mɪ'eə*] (ʒardɪnjɛːr), -z
jarful, -s 'dʒɑ:fʊl, -z
jargon, -s 'dʒɑ:gən, -z
jargonelle, -s ˌdʒɑ:gə'nel, -z
Jar|ley, -man 'dʒɑ:|lɪ, -mən
Jarr|att, -ett 'dʒær|ət, -ət [-ɪt]
Jarr|old, -ow 'dʒær|əld, -əʊ
jarvey, -s 'dʒɑ:vɪ, -z
Jarv|ie, -is 'dʒɑ:v|ɪ, -ɪs
Jas. dʒeɪmz [dʒæs]
jasey, -s 'dʒeɪzɪ, -z
Jasher 'dʒæʃə*
jasmine (J.) 'dʒæsmɪn [-æzm-]

Jason 'dʒeɪsn
jasper (J.), -s 'dʒæspə* [*rarely* 'dʒɑ:s-], -z
Jassy 'dʒæsɪ
jaundice, -d 'dʒɔ:ndɪs [*rarely* 'dʒɑ:n-], -t
jaunt (*s. v.*), -s, -ing, -ed dʒɔ:nt, -s, -ɪŋ, -ɪd
jaunt|y, -ier, -iest, -ily, -iness 'dʒɔ:nt|ɪ, -ɪə* [-jə*], -ɪɪst [-jɪst], -ɪlɪ [-əlɪ], -ɪnɪs [-ɪnəs]
Java 'dʒɑ:və
Javan (*of Java*) 'dʒɑ:vən, (*biblical name*) 'dʒeɪvæn
Javanese ˌdʒɑ:və'niːz [*also* '— *when attributive*]
javelin (*spear*), -s 'dʒævlɪn [-vəlɪn], (J.) (*car, aeroplane*) 'dʒævələn ['dʒævlɪn], -z
jaw (*s. v.*), -s, -ing, -ed dʒɔ:, -z, -ɪŋ, -d
jaw-bone, -s 'dʒɔ:bəʊn, -z
jaw-break|er/s, -ing 'dʒɔ:ˌbreɪk|ə*/z, -ɪŋ
Jaxartes dʒæk'sɑːtiːz
jay (J.), -s dʒeɪ, -z
jazz dʒæz
jazz-band, -s 'dʒæzbænd, -z
Jeaffreson 'dʒefəsn
Jeakes dʒeɪks
jealous, -ly, -ness 'dʒeləs, -lɪ, -nɪs [-nəs]
jealous|y, -ies 'dʒeləs|ɪ, -ɪz
Jeames dʒiːmz
jean (*cotton fabric*) dʒeɪn
Jean dʒiːn
Jeaner 'dʒenə*
Jeanette dʒɪ'net [dʒə'n-]
jeans (*trousers*) (J.) dʒiːnz
Jebb dʒeb
Jebus 'dʒiːbəs
Jebusite, -s 'dʒebjʊzaɪt [-bjuːz-], -s
Jedburgh 'dʒedbərə
Jeddah 'dʒedə
Jedediah ˌdʒedɪ'daɪə
jeep, -s dʒiːp, -s
jeer (*s. v.*), -s, -ing/ly, -ed, -er/s dʒɪə*, -z, -rɪŋ/lɪ, -d, -rə*/z
Jefferies 'dʒefrɪz
Jefferson 'dʒefəsn
Jeffery 'dʒefrɪ
Jeffrey, -s 'dʒefrɪ, -z
Jehoahaz dʒɪ'həʊəhæz [dʒə'h-]
Jehoash dʒɪ'həʊæʃ [dʒə'h-]
Jehoiachin dʒɪ'hɔɪəkɪn [dʒə'h-]
Jehoiada dʒɪ'hɔɪədə [dʒə'h-]
Jehoiakim dʒɪ'hɔɪəkɪm [dʒə'h-]
Jehonadab dʒɪ'hɒnədæb [dʒə'h-]
Jehoram dʒɪ'hɔ:rəm [dʒə'h-, -ræm]
Jehoshaphat dʒɪ'hɒʃəfæt [dʒə'h-]
Jehovah dʒɪ'həʊvə [dʒə'h-]

jehu (**J.**), **-s** 'dʒiːhjuː, -z

jejune, **-ly**, **-ness** dʒɪ'dʒuːn, -lɪ, -nɪs [-nəs]

jejunum, **-s** dʒɪ'dʒuːnəm, -z

Jekyll (*surname*) 'dʒiːkɪl, 'dʒekɪl [-kəl]
Note.—In Jekyll and Hyde *freq. pronounced* 'dʒekɪl.

Jelf dʒelf

jell, **-s**, **-ing**, **-ed** dʒel, -z, -ɪŋ, -d

Jellicoe 'dʒelɪkəʊ

jell|y (*s. v.*), **-ies**, **-ying**, **-ied** 'dʒel|ɪ, -ɪz, -ɪŋ [-jɪŋ], -ɪd

jelly-bag, **-s** 'dʒelɪbæg, -z

Jellyby 'dʒelɪbɪ

jelly-fish, **-es** 'dʒelɪfɪʃ, -ɪz

jellygraph (*s. v.*), **-s**, **-ing**, **-ed** 'dʒelɪgrɑːf [-græf], -s, -ɪŋ, -t

Jemima dʒɪ'maɪmə [dʒə'm-]

jemm|y, **-ies** 'dʒem|ɪ, -ɪz

Jena 'jeɪnə ('jeːnaː)

Jenkin, **-s**, **-son** 'dʒeŋkɪn ['dʒenk-], -z, -sn

Jenner 'dʒenə*

jennet, **-s** 'dʒenɪt, -s

Jennifer 'dʒenɪfə*

Jennings 'dʒenɪŋz

jenn|y (*in machinery*), **-ies** 'dʒen|ɪ, -ɪz

jenn|y (*in billiards*), **-ies** 'dʒɪn|ɪ ['dʒen-], -ɪz

Jenny 'dʒenɪ, 'dʒɪnɪ

Jensen (*car*), **-s** 'dʒensn, -z

jeopardiz|e [-is|e], **-es**, **-ing**, **-ed** 'dʒepədaɪz, -ɪz, -ɪŋ, -d

jeopardy 'dʒepədɪ

Jephthah 'dʒefθə

jerboa, **-s** dʒɜː'bəʊə, -z

jeremiad, **-s** ,dʒerɪ'maɪəd [-'maɪæd], -z

Jeremiah ,dʒerɪ'maɪə [-rə'm-]

Jeremy 'dʒerɪmɪ [-rəmɪ]

Jericho 'dʒerɪkəʊ

jerk (*s. v.*), **-s**, **-ing**, **-ed** dʒɜːk, -s, -ɪŋ, -t

jerkin, **-s** 'dʒɜːkɪn, -z

jerk|y, **-ier**, **-iest**, **-ily**, **-iness** 'dʒɜːk|ɪ, -ɪə* [-jə*], -ɪɪst [-jɪst], -ɪlɪ [-əlɪ], -ɪnɪs [-ɪnəs]

Jermyn 'dʒɜːmɪn

jeroboam (**J.**), **-s** ,dʒerə'bəʊəm, -z

Jerome (*Saint*) dʒə'rəʊm [dʒe'r-, dʒɪ'r-, *rarely* 'dʒerəm], (*surname*) dʒə'rəʊm [dʒe'r-, dʒɪ'r-], 'dʒerəm
Note.—Jerome K. *Jerome, the author, pronounced* dʒə'rəʊm.

Jerram 'dʒerəm

Jerrold 'dʒerəld

jerr|y (**J.**), **-ies** 'dʒer|ɪ, -ɪz

jerry-build|er/s, **-ing** 'dʒerɪˌbɪld|ə*/z, -ɪŋ

jerry-built 'dʒerɪbɪlt

jersey (**J.**), **-s** 'dʒɜːzɪ, -z

Jerubbaal ,dʒerəb'beɪəl [*Jewish pronunciation* ,dʒerə'bɑːl]

Jerusalem dʒə'ruːsələm [dʒɪ'r-, -lem]

Jervaulx (*in Yorkshire*) 'dʒɜːvəʊ ['dʒɑː'vəʊ]

Jervis 'dʒɑːvɪs, 'dʒɜːvɪs

Jervois 'dʒɜːvɪs

Jespersen 'jespəsn

jess (*s. v.*) (**J.**), **-es**, **-ing**, **-ed** dʒes, -ɪz, -ɪŋ, -t

jessamine (**J.**) 'dʒesəmɪn

Jess|e, **-el**, **-ica**, **-ie**, **-op** 'dʒes|ɪ, -l, -ɪkə, -ɪ, -əp

jest (*s. v.*), **-s**, **-ing/ly**, **-ed**, **-er/s** dʒest, -s, -ɪŋ/lɪ, -ɪd, -ə*/z

Jeston 'dʒestən

Jesu 'dʒiːzjuː

Jesuit, **-s**, **-ism** 'dʒezjʊɪt [-zʊɪt, -ʒʊɪt], -s, -ɪzəm

jesuitic, **-al**, **-ally** ,dʒezjʊ'ɪtɪk [-zʊ'ɪt-, -ʒʊ'ɪt-], -l, -əlɪ

Jesus 'dʒiːzəs

jet (*s. v.*), **-s**, **-ting**, **-ted** dʒet, -s, -ɪŋ, -ɪd

jet-black ,dʒet'blæk ['-- *when attributive*]

Jethro 'dʒeθrəʊ

jetsam 'dʒetsəm [-sæm]

jettis|on (*s. v.*), **-ons**, **-oning**, **-oned** 'dʒetɪs|n [-tɪz|n], -nz, -nɪŋ [-ənɪŋ], -nd

jett|y (*s. adj.*), **-ies** 'dʒet|ɪ, -ɪz

jeu, **-s** ʒɜː (ʒø), -z

Jeune dʒuːn

Jevons 'dʒevənz

Jew, **-s** dʒuː, -z

jewel (*s. v.*) (**J.**), **-s**, **-led**, **jewelling** 'dʒuːəl [dʒʊəl, dʒuːl], -z, -d, 'dʒuːəlɪŋ ['dʒʊəlɪŋ]

jewel-box, **-es** 'dʒuːəlbɒks ['dʒʊəl-, 'dʒuːl-], -ɪz

jewel-case, **-s** 'dʒuːəlkeɪs ['dʒʊəl-'dʒuːl-], -ɪz

jeweller, **-s** 'dʒuːələ* ['dʒʊələ*], -z

jewellery 'dʒuːəlrɪ ['dʒʊəl-, 'dʒuːl-]

Jewess, **-es** 'dʒuːɪs ['dʒʊɪs, 'dʒuːes, 'dʒʊes], -ɪz

Jewin 'dʒuːɪn, 'dʒʊɪn

Jewish, **-ly**, **-ness** 'dʒuːɪʃ ['dʒʊɪʃ], -lɪ, -nɪs [-nəs]

Jewry 'dʒʊərɪ

Jewsbury 'dʒuːzbərɪ

jew's-harp, **-s** ,dʒuːz'hɑːp, -s

Jeyes dʒeɪz

jezail dʒe'zeɪl

Jezebel 'dʒezəbl [-zɪb-, -bel]

Jezreel dʒez'riːl

jib (*s. v.*), **-s**, **-bing**, **-bed** dʒɪb, -z, -ɪŋ, -d

jib-boom, **-s** ,dʒɪb'buːm, -s

jib|e (s. v.), -es, -ing, -ed dʒaɪb, -z, -ɪŋ, -d
jiff|y, -ies 'dʒɪf|ɪ, -ɪz
jig (s. v.), -s, -ging, -ged dʒɪg, -z, -ɪŋ, -d
jigger, -s 'dʒɪgə*, -z
jiggered 'dʒɪgəd
jiggery-pokery ˌdʒɪgərɪ'pəʊkərɪ
jigg|le (v.), -les, -ling, -led 'dʒɪg|l, -lz, -lɪŋ [-lɪŋ], -ld
jigot, -s 'dʒɪgət, -s
jigsaw, -s 'dʒɪgsɔ:, -z
Jill dʒɪl
jilt (s. v.), -s, -ing, -ed dʒɪlt, -s, -ɪŋ, -ɪd
Jim, -my dʒɪm, -ɪ
jimjams 'dʒɪmdʒæmz
jimp, -s dʒɪmp, -s
jing|le (s. v.) (J.), -les, -ling, -led 'dʒɪŋg|l, -lz, -lɪŋ, -ld
jingo (J.), -es 'dʒɪŋgəʊ, -z
jingoism 'dʒɪŋgəʊɪzəm
jink, -s dʒɪŋk, -s
jinn, -s dʒɪn, -z
jinnee, -s dʒɪ'ni:, -z
jinrick|sha/s, -shaw/s ˌdʒɪn'rɪk|ʃə/z, -ʃɔ:/z
jitterbug (s.v.), -s, -ging, -ged 'dʒɪtəbʌg, -z, -ɪŋ, -d
jitters 'dʒɪtəz
jitter|y, -iness 'dʒɪtər|ɪ, -ɪnɪs [-məs]
jiujitsu dʒju:'dʒɪtsu: [dʒu:-]
jiv|e (s. v.), -es, -ing, -ed dʒaɪv, -z, -ɪŋ, -d
jo, -es dʒəʊ, -z
Joab 'dʒəʊæb
Joachim (violinist) 'jəʊəkɪm ('jo:axim)
Joan dʒəʊn
Joanna dʒəʊ'ænə
Joash 'dʒəʊæʃ
job (s. v.), -s, -bing, -bed, -ber/s; -bery dʒɒb, -z, -ɪŋ, -d, -ə*/z; -ərɪ
Job dʒəʊb
jobation dʒəʊ'beɪʃn
jobmaster, -s 'dʒɒbˌmɑ:stə*, -z
Jobson 'dʒɒbsn, 'dʒəʊbsn
Jocasta dʒəʊ'kæstə
Jocelyn 'dʒɒslɪn
Jochebed 'dʒɒkəbed
Jock dʒɒk
jockey (s. v.), -s, -ing, -ed; -ship 'dʒɒkɪ, -z, -ɪŋ, -d; -ʃɪp
Jockey Club 'dʒɒkɪklʌb
jocose, -ly, -ness dʒəʊ'kəʊs, -lɪ, -nɪs [-nəs]
jocosity dʒəʊ'kɒsətɪ [-ɪtɪ]
jocular, -ly 'dʒɒkjʊlə* [-kjə-], -lɪ
jocularity ˌdʒɒkjʊ'lærətɪ [-kjə-, -ɪtɪ]
jocund, -ly, -ness 'dʒɒkənd ['dʒəʊk-, -kʌnd], -lɪ, -nɪs [-nəs]
jocundity dʒəʊ'kʌndətɪ [dʒɒ'k-, -ɪtɪ]
jod, -s jɒd, -z

jod|el, -els, -elling, -elled 'jəʊd|l ['jɒd-], -lz, -lɪŋ [-əlɪŋ], -ld
jodhpurs 'dʒɒdpəz [-pɜ:z, -ˌpʊəz]
Jodrell 'dʒɒdrəl
Joe dʒəʊ
Joel 'dʒəʊel ['dʒəʊəl, dʒəʊl]
Joey 'dʒəʊɪ
jog (s. v.), -s, -ging, -ged, -ger/s dʒɒg, -z, -ɪŋ, -d, -ə*/z
jogg|le (s. v.), -les, -ling, -led 'dʒɒg|l, -lz, -lɪŋ [-lɪŋ], -ld
jog-trot 'dʒɒgtrɒt [ˌ-'-]
johannes (coin), -es dʒəʊ'ænɪs, -ɪz
Johannes (personal name) jəʊ'hænɪs
Johannesburg dʒəʊ'hænɪsbɜ:g [-ɪzb-, -nəs-, -nəz-]
Note.—There exists also a local pronunciation dʒə'hɒnɪsbɜ:g, which is used by many English-speaking South Africans.
Johannine dʒəʊ'hænaɪn
Johannisburger jəʊ'hænɪsbɜ:gə*
John dʒɒn
john-dor|y, -ies ˌdʒɒn'dɔ:r|ɪ, -ɪz
Johnes dʒəʊnz, dʒɒnz
Johnian, -s 'dʒəʊnjən [-nɪən], -z
johnn|y (J.), -ies 'dʒɒn|ɪ, -ɪz
John o' Groat's ˌdʒɒnə'grəʊts
John|s, -son dʒɒn|z, -sn
Johnsonese ˌdʒɒnsə'ni:z [-sn̩'i:z]
Johnsonian dʒɒn'səʊnjən [-nɪən]
Johnston(e) 'dʒɒnstən, 'dʒɒnsn
Johore dʒəʊ'hɔ:*
join (s. v.), -s, -ing, -ed, -er/s; -ery dʒɔɪn, -z, -ɪŋ, -d, -ə*/z; -ərɪ
joint (s. adj. v.), -s, -ly; -ing, -ed, -er/s dʒɔɪnt, -s, -lɪ; -ɪŋ, -ɪd, -ə*/z
joint-stock 'dʒɔɪntstɒk
joint-tenan|cy, -cies, -t/s ˌdʒɔɪnt-'tenən|sɪ, -sɪz, -t/s
jointure, -s 'dʒɔɪntʃə*, -z
joist, -s dʒɔɪst, -s
jok|e (s. v.), -es, -ing/ly, -ed, -er/s dʒəʊk, -s, -ɪŋ/lɪ, -t, -ə*/z
Jolland 'dʒɒlənd
Jolliffe 'dʒɒlɪf
jollification, -s ˌdʒɒlɪfɪ'keɪʃn, -z
jolli|fy, -fies, -fying, -fied 'dʒɒlɪ|faɪ, -faɪz, -faɪŋ, -faɪd
jollit|y, -ies 'dʒɒlət|ɪ [-ɪt|ɪ], -ɪz
joll|y (J.), -ier, -iest, -ily, -iness 'dʒɒl|ɪ, -ɪə*, -ɪɪst, -ɪlɪ [-əlɪ], -ɪnɪs [-məs]
jollyboat, -s 'dʒɒlɪbəʊt, -s
jolt (s. v.), -s, -ing/ly, -ed dʒəʊlt, -s, -ɪŋ/lɪ, -ɪd
jolt|y, -ier, -iest, -ily, -iness 'dʒəʊlt|ɪ, -ɪə* [-jə*], -ɪɪst [-jɪst], -ɪlɪ [-əlɪ], -ɪnɪs [-məs]

278

Jolyon 'dʒɒuljən ['dʒɒl-]
Jon dʒɒn
Jonadab 'dʒɒnədæb
Jonah 'dʒɒunə
Jonas 'dʒɒunəs [-næs]
Jonathan 'dʒɒnəθən
Jones dʒɒunz
jongleur, -s ʒɔ̃ː'ŋ'glə:* [ʒɔ:ŋ-, ʒɒŋ-] (ʒɔ̃-
   glœ:r), -z
jonquil, -s 'dʒɒŋkwɪl, -z
Jonson 'dʒɒnsn
Joppa 'dʒɒpə
Jopson 'dʒɒpsn
Joram 'dʒɔːrəm [-ræm]
Jordan, -s 'dʒɔːdn, -z
jorum, -s 'dʒɔːrəm, -z
joseph (J.), 'dʒəuzɪf [-zəf], -s
Josephine 'dʒəuzɪfiːn [-zəf-]
Josephus dʒəu'siːfəs
Josh dʒɒʃ
Joshua 'dʒɒʃwə [-ʃuə, -ʃjuə, -ʃjwə]
Josiah dʒəu'saɪə [-'zaɪə]
Josias dʒəu'saɪəs [-'zaɪəs]
joss, -es dʒɒs, -ɪz
joss-hou|se, -ses 'dʒɒshəu|s, -zɪz
joss-stick, -s 'dʒɒsstɪk, -s
Jost jəust
jost|le, -les, -ling, -led 'dʒɒs|l, -lz, -lɪŋ
   [-lɪŋ], -ld
jot (s. v.), -s, -ting/s, -ted dʒɒt, -s,
   -ɪŋ/z, -ɪd
jotation, -s jəu'teɪʃn, -z
joule, -s dʒuːl [dʒaul], -z
Joule (English surname) dʒuːl, dʒəul,
   dʒaul
journal, -s 'dʒɜːnl, -z
journalese ,dʒɜːnə'liːz [-nl'iːz]
journali|sm, -st/s 'dʒɜːnəlɪ|zəm [-nlɪ-],
   -st/s
journalistic ,dʒɜːnə'lɪstɪk [-nl'ɪ-]
journaliz|e [-is|e], -es, -ing, -ed
   'dʒɜːnəlaɪz [-nlaɪz], -ɪz, -ɪŋ, -d
journ|ey (s. v.), -eys, -eying/s, -eyed
   'dʒɜːn|ɪ, -ɪz, -ɪŋ/z [-jɪŋ/z], -ɪd
journey|man, -men 'dʒɜːnɪ|mən, -mən
joust, -s dʒaust [dʒuːst], -s
Jove dʒəuv
jovial, -ly, -ness 'dʒəuvjəl [-vɪəl], -ɪ,
   -nɪs [-nəs]
joviality ,dʒəuvɪ'ælətɪ [-ɪtɪ]
Jowett 'dʒauɪt, 'dʒəuɪt
   Note.—'dʒauɪt appears to be the
   commoner pronunciation.
Jowitt 'dʒauɪt, 'dʒəuɪt
jowl, -s dʒaul, -z
joy (s. v.) (J.), -s, -ing, -ed dʒɔɪ, -z, -ɪŋ,
   -d
Joyce dʒɔɪs

joy|ful, -fullest, -fully, -fulness 'dʒɔɪ|-
   ful, -fulɪst [-fəlɪst], -fulɪ [-fəlɪ],
   -fulnɪs [-nəs]
joyless, -ly, -ness 'dʒɔɪlɪs [-ləs], -lɪ, -nɪs
   [-nəs]
joyous, -ly, -ness 'dʒɔɪəs, -lɪ, -nɪs
   [-nəs]
joy-ride, -s 'dʒɔɪraɪd, -z
joy-stick, -s 'dʒɔɪstɪk, -s
jr. 'dʒuː'njə* [-nɪə*]
Juan 'dʒuːən [dʒuən, hwɑːn] (xwan)
Juan Fernandez (island) ,dʒuːən-
   fə'nændez [,dʒuən-]
Juanita (as English Christian name)
   dʒuə'niːtə [,dʒuːə'n-], also hwə'niːtə
   (approximation to the Spanish pronunciation xwa'nita)
Jubal 'dʒuːbəl [-bæl]
jubilant, -ly 'dʒuːbɪlənt, -lɪ
Jubilate (s.), -s ,dʒuːbɪ'lɑːtɪ [,juːbɪ'lɑːtɪ,
   old-fashioned ,dʒuːbɪ'leɪtɪ], -z
jubilat|e (v.), -es, -ing, -ed 'dʒuːbɪleɪt,
   -s, -ɪŋ, -ɪd
jubilation, -s ,dʒuːbɪ'leɪʃn, -z
jubilee, -s 'dʒuːbɪli: [-lɪ, ,dʒuːbɪ'li:], -z
Judaea, -n/s dʒuː'dɪə [dʒu-, -'diːə],
   -n/z
Judaeo- dʒuː'diːəu- [dʒu'd-] (following
   element also stressed)
Juda(h) 'dʒuːdə
Judaic, -al, -ally dʒuː'deɪk [dʒu'd-],
   -l, -əlɪ
Judai|sm, -st/s 'dʒuːdeɪɪ|zəm, -st/s
judaiz|e [-is|e], -es, -ing, -ed, -er/s
   'dʒuːderaɪz, -ɪz, -ɪŋ, -d, -ə*/z
Judas, -es 'dʒuːdəs, -ɪz
Judd dʒʌd
Jude dʒuːd
Judea, -n/s dʒuː'dɪə [dʒu-, -'diːə], -n/z
judg|e (s. v.) (J.), -es, -ing, -ed dʒʌdʒ,
   -ɪz, -ɪŋ, -d
judg(e)ment, -s ; -day/s, -hall/s, -seat/s
   'dʒʌdʒmənt, -s; -deɪ/z, -hɔːl/z,
   -siːt/s
judgeship, -s 'dʒʌdʒʃɪp [-dʃʃɪp, -dʃɪp],
   -s
judicature 'dʒuːdɪkətʃə* [dʒuː'dɪk-,
   dʒu'd-, -,tjuə*]
judi|cial, -cially dʒuː'dɪ|ʃl [dʒu'd-],
   -ʃlɪ [-ʃlɪ]
judiciary dʒuː'dɪʃɪərɪ [dʒu'd-, -ʃjə-,
   -ʃə-]
judicious, -ly, -ness dʒuː'dɪʃəs [dʒu'd-],
   -lɪ, -nɪs [-nəs]
Judith 'dʒuːdɪθ
judo 'dʒuːdəu
Judson 'dʒʌdsn
Judy 'dʒuːdɪ

jug (s. v.), -s, -ging, -ged dʒʌg, -z, -ɪŋ, -d

jugful, -s 'dʒʌgfʊl, -z

juggernaut (J), -s 'dʒʌgənɔːt, -s

juggins (J.), -es 'dʒʌgɪnz, -ɪz

jugg|le (s. v.), -les, -ling, -led, -ler/s 'dʒʌg|l, -lz, -lɪŋ [-lɪŋ], -ld, -lə*/z [-lə*/z]

jugglery 'dʒʌglərɪ

Jugoslav, -s ˌjuːgəʊ'slɑːv [-'slæv, also 'juːgəʊsl-, esp. when attributive], -z

Jugoslavia, -n ˌjuːgəʊ'slɑːvjə [-vɪə], -n

jugular 'dʒʌgjʊlə* [-gjə-, rarely 'dʒuːg-]

Jugurtha dʒʊ'gɜːθə [juː-]

juice, -s; -less dʒuːs, -ɪz; -lɪs [-les, -ləs]

juic|y, -ier, -iest, -ily, -iness 'dʒuːs|ɪ, -ɪə* [-jə*], -ɪɪst [-jɪst], -ɪlɪ [-əlɪ], -ɪnɪs [-ɪnəs]

jujitsu dʒuː'dʒɪtsuː

jujube, -s 'dʒuːdʒuːb, -z

juke-box, -es 'dʒuːkbɒks, -ɪz

Jukes dʒuːks

julep, -s 'dʒuːlep [-lɪp], -s

Julia, -n 'dʒuːljə [-lɪə], -n

Juliana ˌdʒuːlɪ'ɑːnə, -'ænə

julienne ˌdʒuːlɪ'en [ˌʒuː-] (ʒyljɛn)

Juliet 'dʒuːljət [-lɪət, -ljet]

Julius 'dʒuːljəs [-lɪəs]

Jul|y, -ies dʒuː'l|aɪ [dʒʊ'laɪ], -aɪz

Julyan 'dʒuːljən

jumb|le (s. v.), -les, -ling, -led; -le-sale/s 'dʒʌmb|l, -lz, -lɪŋ, -ld; -lseɪl/z

Jumbl|y, -ies 'dʒʌmbl|ɪ, -ɪz

jumbo (J.), -s 'dʒʌmbəʊ, -z

Jumna 'dʒʌmnə (Hindi ʤəmnə)

jump (s. v.), -s, -ing, -ed, -er/s dʒʌmp, -s, -ɪŋ, -t [dʒʌmt], -ə*/z

jun. 'dʒuː'njə* [-nɪə*]

junction, -s 'dʒʌŋkʃn, -z

juncture, -s 'dʒʌŋktʃə*, -z

June, -s dʒuːn, -z

Jungfrau 'jʊŋfraʊ

jungle, -s 'dʒʌŋgl, -z

jungle-fowl, -s 'dʒʌŋglfaʊl, -z

jungly 'dʒʌŋglɪ

junior, -s 'dʒuːnjə* [-nɪə*], -z

juniority ˌdʒuːnɪ'ɒrɪtɪ [-rɪtɪ]

juniper, -s 'dʒuːnɪpə* ['dʒʊn-], -z

Junius 'dʒuːnjəs [-nɪəs]

junk, -s dʒʌŋk, -s

junker (J.), -s 'jʊŋkə*, -z

junket, -s, -ing 'dʒʌŋkɪt, -s, -ɪŋ

junkie, -s 'dʒʌŋkɪ, -z

Juno 'dʒuːnəʊ

Junoesque ˌdʒuːnəʊ'esk

Junonian dʒuː'nəʊnjən [dʒʊ'n-, -nɪən]

junt|a/s, -o/s 'dʒʌnt|ə/z ['dʒʊ-], -əʊ/z

jupe, -s ʒuːp (ʒyp), -s

Jupiter 'dʒuːpɪtə* ['dʒʊp-]

jupon, -s 'ʒuːpɒn ['dʒuː-, -pɔ̃ːŋ, -pɒŋ] (ʒypɔ̃), -z

Jura 'dʒʊərə

jurat, -s 'dʒʊəræt, -s

juridic|al, -ally ˌdʒʊə'rɪdɪk|l [dʒʊ'r-], -əlɪ

jurisconsult, -s 'dʒʊərɪskən,sʌlt, -s

jurisdiction, -s ˌdʒʊərɪs'dɪkʃn, -z

jurisdictional ˌdʒʊərɪs'dɪkʃənl [-ʃnəl, -ʃn̩l, -ʃnl, -ʃənəl]

jurisprudence ˌdʒʊərɪs'pruːdəns ['--,-]

jurist, -s 'dʒʊərɪst, -s

juror, -s 'dʒʊərə*, -z

jur|y, -ies 'dʒʊər|ɪ, -ɪz

jury-box, -es 'dʒʊərɪbɒks, -ɪz

jury|man, -men 'dʒʊərɪ|mən, -mən [-men]

jury-mast, -s 'dʒʊərɪmɑːst [nautical pronunciation -məst], -s

jus dʒʌs

just (adj.) (J.), -er, -est, -ly, -ness dʒʌst, -ə*, -ɪst, -lɪ, -nɪs [-nəs]

just (adv.) dʒʌst [rarely dʒest], with some dʒəst even when stressed

justice, -s 'dʒʌstɪs, -ɪz

justiciable dʒʌ'stɪʃɪəbl [-ʃjə-, -ʃə-]

justiciar, -s dʒʌ'stɪʃɪɑː* [-ɪsɪ-], -z

justiciar|y, -ies dʒʌ'stɪʃɪər|ɪ [-ɪʃjə-, -ɪʃə-, -ɪsɪə-, -ɪsjə-], -ɪz

justifiab|le, -ly, -leness 'dʒʌstɪfaɪəb|l [ˌdʒʌstɪ'f-], -lɪ, -lnɪs [-nəs]

justification, -s ˌdʒʌstɪfɪ'keɪʃn, -z

justificat|ive, -ory 'dʒʌstɪfɪkeɪt|ɪv [-kət-], -ərɪ

justi|fy, -fies, -fying, -fied, -fier/s 'dʒʌstɪ|faɪ, -faɪz, -faɪɪŋ, -faɪd, -faɪə*/z

Justin 'dʒʌstɪn

Justinian dʒʌ'stɪnɪən [-njən]

Justus 'dʒʌstəs

jut, -s, -ting, -ted dʒʌt, -s, -ɪŋ, -ɪd

Juta (surname) 'dʒuːtə

jute (J.), -s dʒuːt, -s

Jutland 'dʒʌtlənd

Juvenal 'dʒuːvənl [-vnl]

juvenescen|ce, -t ˌdʒuːvə'nesn|s [-vɪ'n-], -t

juvenile (s. adj.), -s 'dʒuːvənaɪl [-vɪn-], -z

juvenility ˌdʒuːvə'nɪlɪtɪ [-vɪ'n-, -rɪtɪ]

juxtapos|e, -es, -ing, -ed ˌdʒʌkstə'pəʊz ['---], -ɪz, -ɪŋ, -d

juxtaposition, -s ˌdʒʌkstəpə'zɪʃn [-pʊ'z-], -z

juxtapositional ˌdʒʌkstəpə'zɪʃənl [-pʊ'z-, -ʃnəl, -ʃn̩l, -ʃnl, -ʃənəl]

K

K (the letter), -'s keɪ, -z
Kaaba 'kɑːbə ['kɑːəbɑː]
Kabaka, -s kə'bɑːkə, -z
Kab(b)ala kə'bɑːlə [kæ'b-]
Kabul 'kɑːbl ['kɔː-, -bʊl]
Kabyle, -s kə'baɪl [kæ'b-, 'kæbiːl], -z
Kabylia kæ'bɪlɪə [kə'b-, -ljə]
Kadesh 'keɪdeʃ
Kadesh-barnea ˌkeɪdeʃbɑː'nɪə [-'bɑː-nɪə]
Kadmonite, -s 'kædmənaɪt [-mɒn-], -s
Kaffir, -s 'kæfə*, -z
Kafka 'kæfkə
Kahn kɑːn
kailyard, -s 'keɪljɑːd, -z
Kaiser, -s 'kaɪzə*, -z
kakemono, -s ˌkækɪ'məʊnəʊ, -z
Kalat kə'lɑːt
kale keɪl
kaleidoscope, -s kə'laɪdəskəʊp, -s
kaleidoscopic kəˌlaɪdə'skɒpɪk
Kalends 'kælendz [-lɪndz, -ləndz]
Kalgoorlie kæl'gʊəlɪ
Kaliningrad kə'liːnɪngrɑːd [-græd]
Kalundborg 'kælənbɔːg
kam|a, -ic 'kɑːm|ə, -ɪk
Kamel 'kæml
Kamerun 'kæməruːn [ˌ--'-]
Kampala kæm'pɑːlə
Kampong kæm'pɒŋ
kana (Japanese syllabic writing) 'kɑːnə
Kanarese ˌkænə'riːz
Kandahar ˌkændə'hɑː*
Kandy 'kændɪ
Kane keɪn
kangaroo, -s ˌkæŋgə'ruː [sometimes in
   Australia '--], -z
Kanpur (Cawnpore) kɑːn'pʊə* (Hindi
   kanpwr)
Kansas 'kænzəs [-nsəs]
Kant kænt
Kantian 'kæntɪən [-tjən]
Kanti|sm, -st/s 'kæntɪ|zəm, -st/s
kaolin 'keɪəlɪn
kapok 'keɪpɒk
kappa 'kæpə
Karachi kə'rɑːtʃɪ (Hindi kəraci)
karate kə'rɑːtɪ [kæ'r-]
Karen, -s kə'ren, -z, (girl's name)
   'kɑːrən, 'kærən

Karl kɑːl
Karlsbad 'kɑːlzbæd ('karlsbaːt)
karm|a, -ik 'kɑːm|ə, -ɪk
   Note.—Some theosophists pronounce
   'kɜːmə, 'kɜːmɪk, thus distinguish-
   ing these words from kama, kamic.
   'kɜːmə is an attempt at the Hindi
   pronunciation kərma.
Karnak 'kɑːnæk
karroo, -s kə'ruː, -z
Kars kɑːz
Kashgar 'kæʃgɑː*
Kashmir ˌkæʃ'mɪə* [also '— when
   attributive]
Kaspar 'kæspə* [-pɑː*]
Katakana ˌkætə'kɑːnə
Kate keɪt
Kater 'keɪtə*
Katharina ˌkæθə'riːnə
Katharine 'kæθərɪn
Katherine 'kæθərɪn
Kathie 'kæθɪ
Kathleen 'kæθliːn
Katie 'keɪtɪ
Katin (surname) 'keɪtɪn
Katisha 'kætɪʃɑː [-ʃə]
Katmandu ˌkætmæn'duː [ˌkɑːtmɑːn-]
   (Hindi kaθmɑ̃du)
Katrine 'kætrɪn
Kattegat ˌkætɪ'gæt ['—]
Katty 'kætɪ
katydid, -s 'keɪtɪdɪd, -z
Kaunda kɑː'ʊndə [kɑːˈuːn-]
Kavanagh 'kævənə, kə'vænə
   Note.—In Ireland always 'kævənə.
Kay keɪ
kayak, -s 'kaɪæk, -s
Kaye, -s keɪ, -z
kea (parrot), -s 'kerə, -z
Kean(e) kiːn
Kearn(e)y 'kɜːnɪ, 'kɑːnɪ
Kearsarge 'kɪəsɑːdʒ
Kearsley 'kɪəzlɪ [locally 'kɜːzlɪ]
Kearsney (in Kent) 'kɜːznɪ
Kearton 'kɪətn, 'kɜːtn
Keary 'kɪərɪ
Keating(e) 'kiːtɪŋ
Keats kiːts
Keble 'kiːbl

281

Kedah (*in Malaya*) 'kedə
Kedar 'ki:dɑ:* [-də*]
Kedesh 'ki:deʃ
kedg|e (*s. v.*), -es, -ing, -ed kedʒ, -ɪz, -ɪŋ, -d
kedgeree, -s ˌkedʒə'ri: ['---], -z
Kedleston 'kedlstən
Kedron 'kedrɒn ['ki:d-]
Keeble 'ki:bl
keel (*s. v.*), -s, -ing, -ed ki:l, -z, -ɪŋ, -d
keelhaul, -s, -ing, -ed 'ki:lhɔ:l, -z, -ɪŋ, -d
keelson, -s 'kelsn ['ki:l-], -z
keen, -er, -est, -ly, -ness ki:n, -ə*, -ɪst, -lɪ, -nɪs [-nəs]
Keen(e) ki:n
keep (*s. v.*), -s, -ing, kept, keeper/s ki:p, -s, -ɪŋ, kept, 'ki:pə*/z
keepsake, -s 'ki:pseɪk, -s
Kefauver 'ki:ˌfɔ:və* [-ˌfəʊvə*]
keg, -s keg, -z
Kegan 'ki:gən
Kehoe kjəʊ, 'ki:əʊ, 'kɪəʊ
Keig ki:g
Keighley (*place in West Yorkshire*) 'ki:θlɪ, (*surname*) 'ki:θlɪ, 'ki:lɪ, 'kaɪlɪ
Keightley 'ki:tlɪ, 'kaɪtlɪ
Keigwin 'kegwɪn
Keiller 'ki:lə*
Keir kɪə*
Keith ki:θ
Kekewich 'kekwɪtʃ [-wɪdʒ], 'kekɪwɪtʃ
Kelantan ke'læntən [kə'l-]
Kelat kɪ'læt
Kelland 'kelənd
Kellas 'kelæs
Kell(e)y 'kelɪ
Kellogg 'kelɒg
kelp kelp
kelpie, -s 'kelpɪ, -z
Kelsey 'kelsɪ, 'kelzɪ
Kelso 'kelsəʊ
kelson, -s 'kelsn, -z
Kelt, -s, -ic kelt, -s, -ɪk
Kelvin 'kelvɪn
Kelway 'kelwɪ, -weɪ
Kemal (*Pasha*) ke'mɑ:l [kə'm-]
Kemble 'kembl
kemp (K.) kemp
Kempenfelt 'kempənfelt
Kempis 'kempɪs
ken (*s. v.*) (K.), -s, -ning, -ned ken, -z, -ɪŋ, -d
Kend|al(l), -rick 'kend|l, -rɪk
Kenealy kɪ'ni:lɪ [kə'n-, ke'n-]
Kenelm 'kenelm
Kenilworth 'kenəlwɜ:θ [-nɪl-, -wəθ]
Kenite, -s 'ki:naɪt, -s
Kenmare ken'meə*

Kenmore 'kenmɔ:* [-mɔə*]
Kennaird ke'neəd [kə'n-]
Kennan 'kenən
Kennard ke'nɑ:d [kə'n-]
Kennedy 'kenɪdɪ [-nədɪ]
kenn|el (K.) (*s. v.*), -els, -elling, -elled 'ken|l, -lz, -ɪŋ, -ld
Kennerley 'kenəlɪ
Kenn|et, -eth, -ey 'ken|ɪt, -ɪθ, -ɪ
Kenn|icot, -ington 'ken|ɪkət, -ɪŋtən
Kennish 'kenɪʃ
Kenny 'kenɪ
Kenrick 'kenrɪk
Kensal 'kensl
Kensington 'kenzɪŋtən
Kensit 'kenzɪt [-nsɪt]
Kent, -s, -ish kent, -s, -ɪʃ
Kentucky ken'tʌkɪ
Kenwood 'kenwʊd
Kenya 'kenjə ['ki:n-]
Note.—*Both pronunciations are heard locally.*
Kenyatta ken'jætə
Kenyon 'kenjən [-nɪən]
Keogh kjəʊ, 'ki:əʊ, 'kɪəʊ
Kepler 'keplə*
Keppel 'kepəl
kept (*from* keep) kept
Ker kɑ:*, keə*, kɜ:* (*in Scotland* kɛr)
Kerala (*in S. India*) 'kerələ
Kerans 'kerənz
keratin 'kerətɪn
keratitis ˌkerə'taɪtɪs
kerb, -s kɜ:b, -z
kerbstone, -s 'kɜ:bstəʊn, -z
kerchief, -s, -ed 'kɜ:tʃɪf, -s, -t
Kerenhappuch ˌkɪəren'hæpʊk [ˌker-, -rən-, -pək]
Kergenwen kə'genwən
Kerguelen 'kɜ:gɪlɪn [-gəl-]
Kerioth 'kɪərɪɒθ ['ker-]
Kerith 'kɪərɪθ ['ker-]
kermes 'kɜ:mɪz [-mi:z]
Kermit 'kɜ:mɪt
kern (*s. v.*), -s, -ing, -ed kɜ:n, -z, -ɪŋ, -d
Kernahan 'kɜ:nəhən [-nɪən]
kernel, -s 'kɜ:nl, -z
kerosene 'kerəsi:n [*also* ˌ--'-, *when not attributive*]
Kerr kɑ:*, kɜ:*
Kerry 'kerɪ
Kerse kɜ:s
kersey (K.), -s; -mere 'kɜ:zɪ, -z; -ˌmɪə*
Kesteven 'kestɪvən, ke'sti:vən [-'stɪv-]
kestrel, -s 'kestrəl, -z
Keswick 'kezɪk
ketch (K.), -es ketʃ, -ɪz
ketchup, -s 'ketʃəp, -s

Kettering 'ketərɪŋ
kettle (K.), -s 'ketl, -z
kettledrum, -s 'ketldrʌm, -z
Keturah ke'tjʊərə [kɪ't-, kə'tʊərə]
Keux kju:
Kevin 'kevɪn
Kew kju:
key (s. v.) (K.), -s, -ing, -ed ki:, -z, -ɪŋ, -d
keyboard, -s 'ki:bɔːd [-bɔəd], -z
Keyes ki:z, kaɪz
key-hole, -s 'ki:həʊl, -z
Keymour 'ki:mə*
Keyne ki:n
Keynes (surname, place near Swindon) keɪnz
key-note, -s 'ki:nəʊt [ˌki:'nəʊt], -s
key-ring, -s 'ki:rɪŋ, -z
Keyser 'ki:zə*, 'kaɪzə*
keystone, -s 'ki:stəʊn, -z
Keyte (surname) ki:t
Kezia kɪ'zaɪə [ke'z-]
khaki, -s 'kɑːkɪ [-ki:], -z
Khalif, -s kɑː'li:f [kə'li:f, 'kɑːlɪf], -s
Khalifa, -s kɑː'li:fə [kə'l-], -z
Khan kɑːn
Khanpur kɑːn'pʊə* ['--] (Hindi khanpwr)
Khart(o)um kɑː'tu:m
Khatmandu, incorrect spelling of Katmandu, q.v.
Khayyam kaɪ'ɑːm [kaɪ'jɑːm]
khedival kɪ'diːvl [ke'd-, kə'd-]
Khedive, -s kɪ'diːv [ke'd-, kə'd-], -z
khedivial kɪ'diːvjəl [ke'd-, kə'd-, -vɪəl]
Khelat (former spelling of Kalat) kə'lɑːt [kɪ'l-, ke'l-]
Khmer kmeə*
Khyber 'kaɪbə*
Kia Ora ˌkɪə'ɔːrə
kibbutz, -im ki:'bu:ts [kɪ'b-], -ɪm
kibe, -s kaɪb, -z
kibosh 'kaɪbɒʃ
kick (s. v.), -s, -ing, -ed, -er/s kɪk, -s, -ɪŋ, -t, -ə*/z
kick-off, -s ˌkɪk'ɒf [old-fashioned -'ɔːf, '--], -s
kickshaw, -s 'kɪkʃɔː, -z
kid (s. v.), -s, -ding, -ded kɪd, -z, -ɪŋ, -ɪd
Kidd kɪd
Kidderminster 'kɪdəmɪnstə*
kiddle (K.), -s 'kɪdl, -z
kidd|y, -ies 'kɪd|ɪ, -ɪz
kid-glove (adj.) 'kɪdglʌv [ˌ-'-]
kidling, -s 'kɪdlɪŋ, -z
kidnap, -s, -ping, -ped, -per/s 'kɪdnæp, -s, -ɪŋ, -t, -ə*/z
kidney, -s; -bean/s 'kɪdnɪ, -z; -'bi:n/z

Kidron 'kaɪdrɒn ['kɪd-]
Kieff 'ki:ef ('kijif)
Kiel ki:l
kier (K.), -s kɪə*, -z
Kiev 'ki:ev [-ef] ('kijif)
Kikuyu kɪ'ku:ju:
Kilbowie kɪl'bəʊɪ
Kilburn 'kɪlbən [-bə:n]
Kilchurn kɪl'hɜːn [-'xɜːn]
Kildale 'kɪldeɪl
Kildare kɪl'deə*
kilderkin, -s 'kɪldəkɪn, -z
Kilham 'kɪləm
Kilimanjaro ˌkɪlɪmən'dʒɑːrəʊ
Kilkenny kɪl'kenɪ
kill (s. v.), -s, -ing, -ed, -er/s kɪl, -z, -ɪŋ, -d, -ə*/z
Killaloe ˌkɪlə'lu:
Killarney kɪ'lɑːnɪ
Killearn kɪ'lɜːn
Killick 'kɪlɪk
Killiecrankie ˌkɪlɪ'kræŋkɪ
Killigrew 'kɪlɪgru:
Killin kɪ'lɪn
killjoy, -s 'kɪldʒɔɪ, -z
Killwick 'kɪlwɪk
Kilmacolm ˌkɪlmə'kəʊm
Kilmainham kɪl'meɪnəm
Kilmansegg 'kɪlmənseg
Kilmarnock kɪl'mɑːnək [-nɒk]
kiln, -s kɪln [kɪl], -z
  Note.—The pronunciation kɪl appears to be used only by those concerned with the working of kilns.
kilo, -s 'ki:ləʊ, -z
kilocycle, -s 'kɪləʊˌsaɪkl, -z
kilogramme, -s 'kɪləʊgræm, -z
kilolitre, -s 'kɪləʊˌli:tə*, -z
kilometre [-meter], -s 'kɪləʊˌmi:tə* [kɪ'lɒmɪtə*, -mətə*], -z
kiloton, -s 'kɪləʊtʌn, -z
kilowatt, -s 'kɪləʊwɒt, -s
Kilpatrick kɪl'pætrɪk
Kilrush kɪl'rʌʃ
Kilsyth kɪl'saɪθ
kilt (s. v.), -s, -ing, -ed kɪlt, -s, -ɪŋ, -ɪd
Kilwarden kɪl'wɔːdn
Kim kɪm
Kimb|all, -erley 'kɪmb|l, -əlɪ
Kimbolton kɪm'bəʊltən
Kimmeridge 'kɪmərɪdʒ
Kimmins 'kɪmɪnz
kimono, -s kɪ'məʊnəʊ, -z
kin kɪn
kinaesthetic ˌkaɪni:s'θetɪk [ˌkɪn-, -nɪs-]
Kincardine kɪn'kɑːdɪn [kɪŋ'k-, -dn]
Kinchinjunga ˌkɪntʃɪn'dʒʌŋgə
kincob 'kɪŋkəb

283

kind (s. adj.), -s, -er, -est, -ly, -ness/es
kaɪnd, -z, -ə*, -ɪst, -lɪ, -nɪs ['kaɪnnɪs,
-nəs]/ɪz
kindergarten, -s 'kɪndə,gɑ:tn, -z
kind-hearted, -ly, -ness ,kaɪnd'hɑ:tɪd
[also '-,-- when attributive], -lɪ, -nɪs
[-nəs]
kind|le, -les, -ling, -led, -ler/s 'kɪnd|l,
-lz, -lɪŋ [-lŋ], -ld, -lə*/z [-lə*/z]
kindl|y, -ier, -iest, -iness 'kaɪndl|ɪ, -ɪə*
[-jə*], -ɪɪst [-jɪst], -ɪnɪs [-məs]
kindred 'kɪndrɪd
kine kaɪn
kinema, -s 'kɪnɪmə [-nəmə], -z
kinematic, -al, -s ,kɪnɪ'mætɪk [,kaɪn-,
-nə'm-], -l, -s
kinematograph, -s ,kɪnɪ'mætəʊgrɑ:f
[,kaɪn-, -nə'm-, -græf], -s
kinesis kaɪ'ni:sɪs [kɪ'n-]
kinesthetic ,kaɪni:s'θetɪk [,kɪn-, -nɪs-]
kinetic (s. adj.), -s kaɪ'netɪk [kɪ'n-], -s
king (K.), -s kɪŋ, -z
king-at-arms, kings-at-arms ,kɪŋət-
'ɑ:mz, ,kɪŋzət'ɑ:mz
kingcraft 'kɪŋkrɑ:ft
kingcup, -s 'kɪŋkʌp, -s
kingdom (K.), -s 'kɪŋdəm, -z
Kingdon 'kɪŋdən
kingfisher, -s 'kɪŋ,fɪʃə*, -z
King|horn, -lake 'kɪŋ|hɔ:n, -leɪk
kingless 'kɪŋlɪs [-les, -ləs]
kinglet, -s 'kɪŋlɪt [-lət], -s
kinglike 'kɪŋlaɪk
kingl|y, -ier, -iest, -iness 'kɪŋl|ɪ, -ɪə*
[-jə*], -ɪɪst [-jɪst], -ɪnɪs [-məs]
king-maker (K.), -s 'kɪŋ,meɪkə*, -z
kingpin, -s 'kɪŋpɪn [,-'-], -z
King's Bench ,kɪŋz'bentʃ
Kings|borough, -bury, -cote 'kɪŋz|-
bərə, -bərɪ, -kət [-kəʊt]
King's Counsel ,kɪŋz'kaʊnsl
kingship 'kɪŋʃɪp
Kingsley 'kɪŋzlɪ
Kings|man (member of King's College),
-men 'kɪŋz|mən [-mæn], -mən [-men]
Kingston(e) 'kɪŋstən [-ŋks-]
Kingstown 'kɪŋstən [-ŋks-, 'kɪŋztaʊn]
Kingsway 'kɪŋzweɪ
Kingussie kɪŋ'ju:sɪ
kink (s. v.), -s, -ing, -ed kɪŋk, -s, -ɪŋ, -t
[kɪŋt]
kinkajou, -s 'kɪŋkədʒu:, -z
kinless 'kɪnlɪs [-les, -ləs]
Kinn|aird, -ear, -oull kɪ'n|eəd, -ɪə*, -u:l
kino 'ki:nəʊ
Kinross kɪn'rɒs
Kinsale kɪn'seɪl
kinsfolk 'kɪnzfəʊk

kinship 'kɪnʃɪp
kins|man, -men 'kɪnz|mən, -mən
[-men]
kins|woman, -women 'kɪnz|,wʊmən,
-,wɪmɪn
Kintore kɪn'tɔ:* [-'tɔə*]
Kintyre kɪn'taɪə*
Kinvig 'kɪnvɪg
kiosk, -s 'ki:ɒsk ['kiɒsk, kjɒsk,
kɪ'ɒsk], -s
kip, -s kɪp, -s
Kipling 'kɪplɪŋ
kipper (s. v.), -s, -ing, -ed 'kɪpə*, -z,
-rɪŋ, -d
Kirby 'kɜ:bɪ
Kircaldie (surname) kɜ:'kɔ:ldɪ
Kirghiz 'kɜ:gɪz
Kirjathjearim ,kɜ:dʒæθ'dʒɪərɪm
[,kɪrɪæθ-, -dʒɪ'ɑ:rɪm]
Note.—The pronunciation ,kɜ:dʒæθ-
is usual in the Church of England.
,kɪrɪæθ- is a form used by some Jews.
kirk, -s kɜ:k, -s
Kirk(e) kɜ:k
Kirkby (surname) 'kɜ:bɪ, 'kɜ:kbɪ,
(place) 'kɜ:bɪ
Kirkcaldy (place) kɜ:'kɔ:dɪ [-'kɔ:ldɪ],
(surname) kɜ:'kɔ:dɪ
Note.—The forms kɜ:'kædɪ and
kɜ:'kɑ:dɪ may be heard occa-
sionally. They are probably imita-
tions of a local Scottish pronuncia-
tion kər'kadɪ.
Kirkcudbright kɜ:'ku:brɪ [kə'k-]
Kirk|dale, -ham 'kɜ:k|deɪl, -əm
Kirkland 'kɜ:klənd
Kirkman 'kɜ:kmən
Kirkness kɜ:k'nes
Kirkpatrick kɜ:k'pætrɪk
Kirkstall (in West Yorkshire) 'kɜ:kstɔ:l
Kirkwall 'kɜ:kwɔ:l
Kirriemuir ,kɪrɪ'mjʊə* [-'mjɔə*,
-'mjɔ:*]
kirsch, -wasser kɪəʃ, -,vɑ:sə* [-,væsə*]
kirtle, -s 'kɜ:tl, -z
Kishon 'kaɪʃɒn [with some Jews 'ki:ʃɒn]
kismet 'kɪsmet ['kɪzmet]
kiss (s. v.), -es, -ing, -ed kɪs, -ɪz, -ɪŋ, -t
kissing-crust, -s 'kɪsɪŋkrʌst, -s
Kissinger 'kɪsɪndʒə* [-ɪŋə*]
kit, -s kɪt, -s
kit-bag, -s 'kɪtbæg, -z
kitcat (K.), -s 'kɪtkæt, -s
kitchen (K.), -s 'kɪtʃɪn [-tʃən], -z
kitchener (K.), -s 'kɪtʃɪnə* [-tʃən-], -z
kitchenette, -s ,kɪtʃɪ'net, -s
kitchen-garden, -s ,kɪtʃɪn'gɑ:dn ['--,--,
-tʃən-], -z

kitchen-maid, -s ˈkɪtʃɪnmeɪd [-tʃən-], -z
kitchen-midden, -s ˌkɪtʃɪnˈmɪdn [-tʃən-], -nz
Kitch|in, -ing ˈkɪtʃ|ɪn, -ɪŋ
kite, -s; -flying kaɪt, -s; -ˌflaɪŋ
kite-balloon, -s ˈkaɪtbəˌluːn, -z
kith kɪθ
Kitson ˈkɪtsn
kitten, -s ˈkɪtn, -z
kittenish ˈkɪtnɪʃ
kittiwake, -s ˈkɪtɪweɪk, -s
kittle ˈkɪtl
Kitto ˈkɪtəʊ
Kittredge ˈkɪtrɪdʒ
Kitts kɪts
Kittson ˈkɪtsn
Kitty ˈkɪtɪ
kiwi, -s ˈkiːwiː [-wɪ], -z
Klaipeda ˈklaɪpɪdə [-pedə
klaxon, -s ˈklæksn, -z
Kleenex ˈkliːneks
kleptoma|nia, -niac/s ˌkleptəʊˈmeɪ|njə
[-nɪə], -nɪæk/s [-njæk/s]
Klondike ˈklɒndaɪk
Kluge (English name) kluːdʒ
knack, -s næk, -s
knacker, -s ˈnækə*, -z
knacker|y, -ies ˈnækər|ɪ, -ɪz
knag, -s; -gy næg, -z; -ɪ
knap, -s, -ping, -ped, -per/s næp, -s, -ɪŋ,
-t, -ə*/z
knapsack, -s ˈnæpsæk, -s
knar, -s nɑː*, -z
Knaresborough ˈneəzbərə
knave, -s neɪv, -z
knaver|y, -ies ˈneɪvər|ɪ, -ɪz
knavish, -ly, -ness ˈneɪvɪʃ, -lɪ, -nɪs
[-nəs]
knead, -s, -ing, -ed, -er/s niːd, -z, -ɪŋ,
-ɪd, -ə*/z
kneading-trough, -s ˈniːdɪŋtrɒf, -s
Note.—Some bakers pronounce -traʊ
(plur. -traʊz).
knee (s. v.), -s, -ing, -d niː, -z, -ɪŋ, -d
knee-breeches ˈniːˌbrɪtʃɪz
knee-cap, -s ˈniːkæp, -s
knee-deep ˌniːˈdiːp [ˈ--]
knee-joint, -s ˈniːdʒɔɪnt, -s
kneel, -s, -ing, -ed, knelt niːl, -z, -ɪŋ, -d,
ˌnelt
knell (s. v.), -s, -ing, -ed nel, -z, -ɪŋ, -d
Kneller, -s ˈnelə*, -z
knelt (from kneel) nelt
Knesset ˈkneset
knew (from know) njuː
knickerbocker (K.), -s ˈnɪkəbɒkə*, -z
knickers ˈnɪkəz
knick-knack, -s; -ery ˈnɪknæk, -s; -ərɪ

kni|fe (s.), -ves naɪ|f, -vz
knif|e (v.), -es, -ing, -ed naɪf, -s, -ɪŋ, -t
knife-board, -s ˈnaɪfbɔːd [-bɔəd], -z
knife-edge, -s, -d ˈnaɪfedʒ, -ɪz, -d
knife-grind|er/s, -ing ˈnaɪfˌɡraɪnd|ə*/z,
-ɪŋ
knife-rest, -s ˈnaɪfrest, -s
knife-tray, -s ˈnaɪftreɪ, -z
knight (s. v.) (K.), -s, -ing, -ed naɪt, -s,
-ɪŋ, -ɪd
knightage ˈnaɪtɪdʒ
knight-bachelor,   knights-bachelor
ˌnaɪtˈbætʃələ* [-tʃɪlə*], ˌnaɪts'b-
knight-errant,   knights-errant   ˌnaɪt-
ˈerənt, ˌnaɪtsˈerənt
knighthood, -s ˈnaɪthʊd, -z
knightl|y, -ier, -iest, -iness ˈnaɪtl|ɪ, -ɪə*
[jə*], -ɪɪst [-jɪst], -ɪnɪs [-ɪnəs]
Knighton ˈnaɪtn
Knightsbridge ˈnaɪtsbrɪdʒ
knight-service ˈnaɪtˌsɜːvɪs
knit, -s, -ting, -ted, -ter/s nɪt, -s, -ɪŋ,
-ɪd, -ə*/z
knitting-machine, -s ˈnɪtɪŋməˌʃiːn, -z
knitting-needle, -s ˈnɪtɪŋˌniːdl, -z
knitwear ˈnɪtweə*
knob, -s nɒb, -z
knobbly ˈnɒbl|ɪ [-blɪ]
knobb|y, -ier, -iest, -iness ˈnɒb|ɪ, -ɪə*,
-ɪɪst, -ɪnɪs [-ɪnəs]
knock (s. v.), -s, -ing/s, -ed, -er/s nɒk,
-s, -ɪŋ/z, -t, -ə*/z
knockabout, -s ˈnɒkəbaʊt, -s
Knockbreda nɒkˈbriːdə
knock-down, ˌnɒkˈdaʊn [ˈ--]
knock-kneed, ˌnɒkˈniːd [ˈ--]
knock-out, -s ˈnɒkaʊt, -s
knock-up, -s ˌnɒkˈʌp, -s
knoll, -s nəʊl, -z
Knoll|es, -ys nəʊl|z, -z
knop, -s nɒp, -s
Knossos ˈknɒʊsɒs [ˈknɒs-, -əs]
knot (s. v.), -s, -ting, -ted nɒt, -s, -ɪŋ, -ɪd
knot-grass ˈnɒtɡrɑːs
knott|y, -ier, -iest, -ily, -iness ˈnɒt|ɪ,
-ɪə*, -ɪɪst, -ɪlɪ [-əlɪ], -ɪnɪs [-ɪnəs]
knout (s. v.), -s, -ing, -ed naʊt, -s, -ɪŋ,
-ɪd
know (s. v.), -s, -ing, knew, know|n,
-er/s; -able nəʊ, -z, -ɪŋ, njuː, nəʊ|n,
-ə*/z; -əbl
know-how ˈnəʊhaʊ
knowing (adj.), -ly, -ness ˈnəʊɪŋ, -lɪ,
-nɪs [-nəs]
knowledge, -s ˈnɒlɪdʒ, -ɪz
Knowles nəʊlz
know-nothing, -s ˈnəʊˌnʌθɪŋ, -z
Knox nɒks

knuck|le (s. v.), -les, -ling, -led 'nʌk|l, -lz, -lɪŋ [-lɪŋ], -ld
knuckle-bone, -s 'nʌklbəʊn, -z
knuckleduster, -s 'nʌkl,dʌstə*, -z
knuckle-joint, -s 'nʌkldʒɔɪnt, -s
knur(r), -s nɜ:*, -z
Knutsford 'nʌtsfəd
Knyvett 'nɪvɪt
koala, -s kəʊ'ɑ:lə, -z
Kobe 'kəʊbɪ
kobold, -s 'kɒbəʊld ['kəʊb-, -bld], -z
kodak, -s 'kəʊdæk, -s
Kodály 'kəʊdaɪ [-'-]
Kohathite, -s 'kəʊəθaɪt ['kəʊhə-], -s
Koh-i-noor 'kəʊɪ,nʊə* [-nɔə*, -nɔ:*, ,--'-]
kohl kəʊl
kohl-rabi ,kəʊl'rɑ:bɪ
koine 'kɔɪnɪ
kola (K.) 'kəʊlə
Kolaba kə'lɑ:bə [kɒ'l-]
Kolnai (surname) 'kɒlnaɪ
Kongo 'kɒŋgəʊ
Königsberg 'kɜ:nɪgzbeəg [-bɜ:g] ('kø:niçsberk, -berç)
Konrad 'kɒnræd
koodoo, -s 'ku:du:, -z
kookaburra, -s 'kʊkə,bʌrə, -z
kopeck, -s 'kəʊpek ['kɒp-], -s
kopje, -s 'kɒpɪ, -z
Kops kɒps
Korah 'kɔ:rə
Koran kɒ'rɑ:n [kɔ:'r-, kʊ'r-, kə'r-]
koranic kɒ'rænɪk [kɔ:'r-, kʊ'r-, kə'r-]
Korea, -n/s kə'rɪə [kɒ'r-, kɔ:'r-], -n/z
Koreish 'kɔ:raɪʃ
kosher 'kəʊʃə* [occasionally 'kɒʃə* by non-Jews]
kotow (s. v.), -s, -ing, -ed ,kəʊ'taʊ, -z, -ɪŋ, -d
Kough kjəʊ, kəʊ
koumiss 'ku:mɪs
Kowloon ,kaʊ'lu:n
kowtow, -s, -ing, -ed ,kaʊ'taʊ, -z, -ɪŋ, -d
kraal, -s krɑ:l [krɔ:l], -z
  Note.—Usually pronounced krɑ:l in England, but krɔ:l in South Africa.
krait, -s kraɪt, -s
Krakatoa ,krækə'təʊə
kraken, -s 'krɑ:kən, -z

kremlin (K.), -s 'kremlɪn, -z
Kresge 'kresgɪ
kreutzer (K.), -s 'krɔɪtsə*, -z
kris, -es kri:s, -ɪz
Krishna 'krɪʃnə
krone, -s 'krəʊnə, -z
Kronin 'krəʊnɪn
Krons(h)tadt 'krɒnʃtæt
Kruger 'kru:gə*
Krupp krʊp [krʌp]
Kuala Kangsar ,kwɑ:lə'kʌŋsə* [,kwɒl-, -'kæŋ-]
Kuala Lumpur ,kwɑ:lə'lʊm,pʊə* [,kwɒl-, -'lʌm-, -pə*]
Kublai Khan ,kʊblaɪ'kɑ:n
kudos 'kju:dɒs
Kuibyshev 'kwɪbɪʃev [-ʃef] ('kujbɪʃiʃ)
Ku-Klux-Klan ,kju:klʌks'klæn
kultur kʊl'tʊə* (kul'tu:r)
Kumasi ku:'mæsɪ [kʊ'm-]
kümmel 'kʊməl ['kɪm-] ('kymәl)
Kuomintang ,kwəʊmɪn'tæŋ
Kup (surname) kʌp
Kurath (American surname) 'kjʊəræθ
Kurd, -s kɜ:d, -z
Kurdistan ,kɜ:dɪ'stɑ:n [-'stæn]
Kuril, -s kʊ'ri:l, -z
Kurile (old spelling of Kuril), -s kʊ'ri:l, -z
kursaal, -s 'kʊəzɑ:l ['kʊəsɑ:l, 'kɜ:sɑ:l], -z
Kuwait kʊ'weɪt
Kuyper 'kaɪpə*
Kwantung ,kwæn'tʌŋ
Kwoyu ,kwəʊ'ju:
Kyd kɪd
Kyffin 'kʌfɪn
kyle (K.), -s kaɪl, -z
kylin, -s 'kaɪlɪn, -z
Kyllachy 'kaɪləkɪ [-əxɪ]
kyloe, -s 'kaɪləʊ, -z
kymo|graph, -s, -gram/s 'kaɪməʊ|grɑ:f [-græf], -s, -græm/z
kymographic ,kaɪməʊ'græfɪk
Kynance 'kaɪnæns
Kynaston 'kɪnəstən
Kyoto 'kjəʊtəʊ [kɪ'əʊtəʊ]
kyrie, -s 'kɪəri:eɪ ['kɪərɪɪ, 'kɪrɪɪ, rarely 'kaɪərɪ]
Kyrle kɜ:l
Kythe 'kaɪθɪ

L

L (*the letter*), -'s el, -z
la (*musical note*), -s ɑ:, -z
la (*meaningless syllable used for singing a melody*) lɑ: (*length of vowel is determined by the note sung*)
la (*interj.*) lɔ:
laager, -s 'lɑ:gə*, -z
Laban 'leɪbən [-bæn]
lab|el, -els, -elling, -elled 'leɪb|l, -lz, -lɪŋ [-lɪŋ], -ld
labial (*s. adj.*), -s, -ly 'leɪbjəl [-bɪəl], -z, -ɪ
labialization [-isa-] ˌleɪbɪəlaɪ'zeɪʃn [-bjəl-, -lɪ'z-]
labializ|e [-is|e], -es, -ing, -ed 'leɪbɪəlaɪz [-bjəl-], -ɪz, -ɪŋ, -d
Labienus ˌlæbɪ'i:nəs
labile 'leɪbaɪl
labiodental (*s. adj.*), -s ˌleɪbɪəʊ'dentl [-bjəʊ-], -z
laborator|y, -ies lə'bɒrətər|ɪ ['læbərə-], -ɪz
laborious, -ly, -ness lə'bɔ:rɪəs, -lɪ, -nɪs [-nəs]
Labouchere ˌlæbu:'ʃeə* ['læbu:ʃeə*, -bʊ-]
lab|our, -ours, -ouring, -oured, -ourer/s 'leɪb|ə*, -əz, -ərɪŋ, -əd, -ərə*/z
labourite, -s 'leɪbəraɪt, -s
labour-saving 'leɪbəˌseɪvɪŋ
Labrador 'læbrədɔ:*
Labuan lə'bu:ən [-'bʊən, 'læbjʊən]
laburnum, -s lə'bə:nəm, -z
labyrinth, -s 'læbərɪnθ [-bɪr-], -s
labyrinth|ian, -ine ˌlæbə'rɪnθ|ɪən [-bɪ'r-, -jən], -aɪn
lac, -s læk, -s
Laccadive, -s 'lækədɪv, -z
lac|e (*s. v.*), -es, -ing, -ed leɪs, -ɪz, -ɪŋ, -t
Lacedaemon ˌlæsɪ'di:mən
Lacedaemonian, -s ˌlæsɪdɪ'məʊnjən [-nɪən], -z
lacerat|e (*v.*), -es, -ing, -ed 'læsəreɪt, -s, -ɪŋ, -ɪd
laceration, -s ˌlæsə'reɪʃn, -z
Lacert|a (*constellation*), -ae lə'sə:t|ə, -i:
Lacey 'leɪsɪ
laches 'leɪtʃɪz ['lætʃɪz]
Lachesis 'lækɪsɪs

Lachish 'leɪkɪʃ
Lachlan 'læklən, 'lɒklən
lachrymal 'lækrɪml
lachrymatory 'lækrɪmətərɪ [-meɪtərɪ, ˌlækrɪ'meɪtərɪ]
lachrymose, -ly 'lækrɪməʊs, -lɪ
lack (*s. v.*), -s, -ing, -ed læk, -s, -ɪŋ, -t
lackadaisical ˌlækə'deɪzɪkl
lackaday 'lækədeɪ [ˌ-'-']
lackey (*s. v.*), -s, -ing, -ed 'lækɪ, -z, -ɪŋ, -d
lack-lustre 'lækˌlʌstə*
Lacon 'leɪkən
Laconia, -n/s lə'kəʊnjə [-nɪə], -n/z
laconic (L.), -al, -ally lə'kɒnɪk, -l, -əlɪ
lacquer (*s. v.*), -s, -ing, -ed, -er/s 'lækə*, -z, -rɪŋ, -d, -rə*/z
lacquey (*s. v.*), -s, -ing, -ed 'lækɪ, -z, -ɪŋ, -d
lacrosse lə'krɒs [lɑ:'k-]
lactat|e, -es, -ing, -ed 'læ: kteɪt, -s, -ɪŋ, -ɪd
lactation læk'teɪʃn
lacteal 'læktɪəl [-tjəl]
lactic 'læktɪk
lactometer, -s læk'tɒmɪtə* [-mətə*], -z
lacun|a, -ae, -as lə'kju:n|ə [læ'k-], -i:, -əz
lacustrine lə'kʌstraɪn [læ'k-, -trɪn]
Lacy 'leɪsɪ
lad, -s læd, -z
Ladakh (*in Kashmir*) lə'dɑ:k [*old-fashioned* lə'dɔ:k]
Ladbroke 'lædbrʊk
ladder, -s 'lædə*, -z
laddie, -s 'lædɪ, -z
lad|le, -es, -ing, -ed, -en leɪd, -z, -ɪŋ, -ɪd, -n
Ladefoged (*English surname*) 'lædɪfəʊgɪd
ladida(h) ˌlɑ:dɪ'dɑ:
ladies'|-man, -men 'leɪdɪz|mæn, -men
Ladislaus 'lædɪslɔ:s
Ladislaw 'lædɪslɔ:
lad|le, -les, -ling, -led 'leɪd|l, -lz, -lɪŋ [-lɪŋ], -ld
ladleful, -s 'leɪdlfʊl, -z
Ladoga 'lædəʊgə ['lɑ:d-, *old-fashioned* lə'dəʊgə] ('ladəgə)

ladrone (*Scottish term of reproach*), -s 'lædrən, -z

ladrone (*highwayman in Spain, etc.*), -s lə'drəʊn, -z

Ladrone (*Islands*) lə'drəʊn

lad|y (L.), -ies 'leɪd|ɪ, -ɪz

ladybird, -s 'leɪdɪbɜːd, -z

lady-chapel, -s 'leɪdɪ,tʃæpl, -z

Ladyday, -s 'leɪdɪdeɪ, -z

lady-help, -s 'leɪdɪ'help, -s

lady - in - waiting, ladies - in - waiting ˌleɪdɪɪn'weɪtɪŋ [-djɪn-], ˌleɪdɪzɪn-'weɪtɪŋ

lady-killer, -s 'leɪdɪ,kɪlə*, -z

lady|like, -love/s, -ship/s 'leɪdɪ|laɪk, -lʌv/z, -ʃɪp/s

lady's-maid, -s 'leɪdɪzmeɪd, -z

Ladysmith 'leɪdɪsmɪθ

Laertes leɪ'ɜːtiːz

Laestrygones liːs'traɪɡəniːz

Laetitia lɪ'tɪʃɪə [liː't-, -ʃjə, -ʃə]

Lafayette (*French name*) ˌlɑːfaɪ'et (lafajɛt), (*in U.S.A.*) ˌlɑːfeɪ'et

Lafcadio læf'kɑːdɪəʊ

Laffan 'læfən, lə'fæn

Laf(f)itte lɑː'fiːt [læ'f-, lə'f-] (lafit)

lag (*s. v.*), -s, -ging, -ged, -ger/s læg, -z, -ɪŋ, -d, -ə*/z

lager (*beer*), -s 'lɑːɡə*, -z

Lager (*English surname*) 'leɪɡə*

laggard, -s 'læɡəd, -z

lagoon, -s lə'ɡuːn, -z

Lagos 'leɪɡɒs

lah (*note in Tonic Sol-fa*), -s lɑː, -z

Lahore lə'hɔː* [lɑː'h-, -'hɔə*]

laic, -al 'leɪɪk, -l

laid (*from* lay) leɪd

Laidlaw 'leɪdlɔː

lain (*from* lie) leɪn

Laing læŋ, leɪŋ

lair, -s leə*, -z

laird (L.), -s; -ship leəd, -z; -ʃɪp

laissez-faire ˌleɪseɪ'feə* (lɛsefɛːr)

laity 'leɪətɪ ['leɪɪtɪ]

Laius 'laɪəs ['leɪəs]

lake (L.), -s leɪk, -s

Lakeland 'leɪklænd [-lənd]

lakeside (L.) 'leɪksaɪd

lakh, -s lɑːk [læk] (*Hindi* lakh)

lak|y, -ier, -iest 'leɪk|ɪ, -ɪə*, -ɪɪst

Lalage 'læləɡɪ [-ɡɪ, -ədʒɪ]

L'Allegro læ'leɪɡrəʊ [-'leɡ-]

lam, -s, -ming, -med læm, -z, -ɪŋ, -d

lama (L.), -s 'lɑːmə, -z

lamaser|y, -ies 'lɑːməsər|ɪ ['læməs-, lə'mæs-], -ɪz

lamb (*s. v.*) (L.), -s, -ing, -ed læm, -z, -ɪŋ, -d

lambast|e, -es, -ing, -ed læm'beɪst, -s, -ɪŋ, -ɪd

lambda, -s 'læmdə, -z

lambdacism, -s 'læmdəsɪzəm, -z

lamben|cy, -t 'læmbən|sɪ, -t

Lambert 'læmbət

Lambeth 'læmbəθ

lambkin, -s 'læmkɪn [-mpk-], -z

lamblike 'læmlaɪk

lambrequin, -s 'læmbəkɪn [-brək-], -z

Lambretta læm'bretə

lambskin 'læmskɪn

lamb's-wool 'læmzwʊl

Lambton 'læmtən [-mpt-]

lam|e (*adj. v.*), -er, -est, -ely, -ness; -es, -ing, -ed leɪm, -ə*, -ɪst, -lɪ, -nɪs [-nəs]; -z, -ɪŋ, -d

Lamech 'leɪmek ['lɑːmek, 'lɑːmex]

lamell|a, -ae, -ar lə'mel|ə, -iː, -ə*

lament (*s. v.*), -s, -ing, -ed lə'ment, -s, -ɪŋ, -ɪd

lamentab|le, -ly 'læməntəb|l [-mm-, lə'mentəbl], -lɪ

lamentation, -s (L.) ˌlæmen'teɪʃn [-mən-, -mɪn-], -z

lamin|a, -ae, -as, -ar 'læmɪn|ə, -iː, -əz, -ə*

laminat|e, -es, -ing, -ed 'læmɪneɪt, -s, -ɪŋ, -ɪd

Lamington (*Baron*) 'læmɪŋtən

Lammas, -tide 'læməs, -taɪd

lammergeier, -s 'læməɡaɪə*, -z

Lammermoor 'læmə,mʊə* [-mɔə*, -mɔː*, ˌ--'-]

Lamond 'læmənd

Lamont 'læmənt, (*in U.S.A.*) lə'mɒnt

lamp, -s læmp, -s

lampas (*silk material*) 'læmpəs

lampas (*swelling in horse's mouth*) 'læmpəz

lampblack 'læmpblæk [ˌlæmp'b-]

Lampet 'læmprt

Lampeter 'læmprtə*

Lampetie læm'petriː

lampion, -s 'læmprən [-pjən], -z

lamplight, -er/s 'læmplaɪt, -ə*/z

Lamplough 'læmplu:, -lʌf

Lamplugh 'læmplu:

lamp-oil 'læmpɔɪl

lampoon (*s. v.*), -s, -ing, -ed, -er/s læm'pu:n, -z, -ɪŋ, -d, -ə*/z

lamp-post, -s 'læmppəʊst, -s

lamprey, -s 'læmprɪ, -z

lamp-shade, -s 'læmpʃeɪd, -z

Lampson 'læmpsn

Lanagan 'lænəɡən

Lanark, -shire 'lænək [-nɑːk], -ʃə* [-,ʃɪə*]

Lancashire 'læŋkəʃə* [-kɪʃ-, -ˌʃɪə]
Lancaster 'læŋkəstə* [-kɪs-]
Lancasterian, -s ˌlæŋkæ'stɪərɪən [-kə's-], -z
Lancastrian, -s læŋ'kæstrɪən, -z
lan|ce (s. v.) (L.), -es, -ing, -ed lɑ:ns, -ɪz, -ɪŋ, -t
lance-corporal, -s ˌlɑ:ns'kɔ:pərəl ['-ˌ---], -z
Lancelot 'lɑ:nslət [-lɒt]
lancer, -s 'lɑ:nsə*, -z
lancet (L.), -s 'lɑ:nsɪt, -s
Lancing 'lɑ:nsɪŋ
Lancs. læŋks
land (s. v.), -s, -ing, -ed lænd, -z, -ɪŋ, -ɪd
landau, -s 'lændɔ:, -z
land-breeze, -s 'lændbri:z, -ɪz
Lander 'lændə*
land-force, -s 'lændfɔ:s, -ɪz
landgrabb|er/s, -ing 'lændˌgræb|ə*/z, -ɪŋ
landgrave, -s 'lændgreɪv, -z
landgravine, -s 'lændgrəvi:n, -z
landholder, -s 'lændˌhəʊldə*, -z
landing (s.), -s; -net/s, -place/s, -stage/s 'lændɪŋ, -z; -net/s, -pleɪs/ɪz, -steɪdʒ/ɪz
landlad|y, -ies 'lænˌleɪd|ɪ [-ndˌl-], -ɪz
landless 'lændlɪs [-ləs]
landlocked 'lændlɒkt
landlord, -s, -ism 'lænlɔ:d [-ndl-], -z, -ɪzəm
land-lubber, -s 'lændˌlʌbə*, -z
landmark, -s 'lændmɑ:k, -s
land-mine, -s 'lændmaɪn, -z
Land|on, -or 'lænd|ən, -ɔ:* [-ə*]
land-own|er/s, -ing 'lændˌəʊn|ə*/z, -ɪŋ
landrail, -s 'lændreɪl, -z
land-rover, -s 'lændˌrəʊvə*, -z
landscape, -s 'lænskeɪp [-nds-, old-fashioned -skɪp], -s
landscaper, -s 'lænˌskeɪpə* [-ndˌs-], -z
Landseer, -s 'lænˌsɪə* [-nds-, -sjə*], -z
Land's End ˌlændz'end
land|slide/s, -skip/s 'lænd|slaɪd/z, -slɪp/s
lands|man, -men 'lændz|mən, -mən
land-tax, -es 'lændtæks, -ɪz
land|ward, -wind/s 'lænd|wəd, -wɪnd/z
landwehr 'lændveə*
lane (L.), -s leɪn, -z
Lanfranc 'lænfræŋk
Lang læŋ
Lang|baine, -bourne, -dale 'læŋ|beɪn, -bɔ:n [-bɔən], -deɪl
Langbarugh 'læŋbɑ:f
Lang|ham, -holm 'læŋ|əm, -əm

Langhorne 'læŋhɔ:n
Lang|land, -ley 'læŋ|lənd, -lɪ
Langmere 'læŋˌmɪə*
Lang|ridge, -rish(e) 'læŋg|rɪdʒ, -rɪʃ
Langside ˌlæŋ'saɪd ['læŋsaɪd]
lang-syne ˌlæŋ'saɪn
Lang|ton, -try 'læŋ|tən, -trɪ
language, -s 'læŋgwɪdʒ, -ɪz
languid, -ly, -ness 'læŋgwɪd, -lɪ, -nɪs [-nəs]
languish (L.), -es, -ing/ly, -ed, -ment 'læŋgwɪʃ, -ɪz, -ɪŋ/lɪ, -t, -mənt
languor, -ous 'læŋgə*, -rəs
Lanigan 'lænɪgən
lank, -er, -est, -ly, -ness læŋk, -ə*, -ɪst, -lɪ, -nɪs [-nəs]
Lankester 'læŋkɪstə* [-kəs-]
lank|y, -ier, -iest, -ily, -iness 'læŋk|ɪ, -ɪə* [-jə*], -ɪɪst [-jɪst], -ɪlɪ [-əlɪ], -ɪnɪs [-ɪnəs]
lanoline 'lænəʊli:n [-lɪn]
Lansbury 'lænzbərɪ
Lansdown(e) 'lænzdaʊn
Lansing (in U.S.A.) 'lænsɪŋ
lantern, -s 'læntən, -z
lanyard, -s 'lænjəd [-jɑ:d], -z
Laocoön leɪ'ɒkəʊʊn [-əʊən]
Laodamia ˌleɪəʊdə'maɪə
Laodicea, -n/s ˌleɪəʊdɪ'sɪə, -n/z
Laoighis (Irish county = Leix) li:ʃ
Laoighise (Irish town) 'li:ʃə
Laomedon leɪ'ɒmɪdən
Laos 'lɑ:ɒs [laʊs, laʊz]
Laotian 'laʊʃɪən [-ʃjən]
Lao-tsze ˌlɑ:əʊ'tseɪ [ˌlaʊ-, -'tsi:]
lap (s. v.), -s, -ping, -ped, -per/s læp, -s, -ɪŋ, -t, -ə*/z
La Paz lɑ:'pæz (la'pas)
lap-dog, -s 'læpdɒg, -z
lapel, -s lə'pel [læ'pel], -z
lapful, -s 'læpfʊl, -z
lapidar|y (s. adj.), -ies 'læpɪdər|ɪ, -ɪz
lapis lazuli ˌlæpɪs'læzjʊlaɪ
Lapithae 'læpɪθi:
Lapland 'læplænd
Laplander, -s 'læplændə* [-lən-], -z
Lapp, -s, -ish læp, -s, -ɪʃ
lappet, -s, -ed 'læpɪt, -s, -ɪd
laps|e (s. v.), -es, -ing, -ed læps, -ɪz, -ɪŋ, -t
lapsus linguae ˌlæpsəs'lɪŋgwaɪ [old-fashioned -gwi:]
Laput|a, -an/s lə'pju:t|ə, -ən/z
lapwing, -s 'læpwɪŋ, -z
lar, lares lɑ:*, 'leəri:z ['lɑ:reɪz]
Larbert 'lɑ:bət
larboard 'lɑ:bəd [-bɔ:d, -bɔəd]
larcenous, -ly 'lɑ:sənəs [-sɪn-, -sn̩-], -lɪ

289

larcen|y, -ies 'lɑ:sən|ɪ [-sn|ɪ, -sn̩|ɪ], -ɪz
larch, -es lɑ:tʃ, -ɪz
lard (s. v.), -s, -ing, -ed lɑːd, -z, -ɪŋ, -ɪd
larder, -s 'lɑːdə*, -z
lares 'leəriːz ['lɑːreɪz]
largactil lɑːˈɡæktɪl
large, -r, -st, -ly, -ness lɑːdʒ, -ə*, -ɪst, -lɪ, -nɪs [-nəs]
large-hearted, -ness ˌlɑːdʒˈhɑːtɪd ['-ˌ--], -nɪs [-nəs]
large-minded, -ness ˌlɑːdʒˈmaɪndɪd ['-ˌ--], -nɪs [-nəs]
Largen 'lɑːdʒən
largess, -es lɑːˈdʒes [-ˈʒes, 'lɑː-, -dʒɪs], -ɪz
larghetto (s. adv.), -s lɑːˈɡetəʊ, -z
largish 'lɑːdʒɪʃ
largo (s. adv.), -s 'lɑːɡəʊ, -z
lariat (s. v.), -s, -ing, -ed 'læriət, -s, -ɪŋ, -ɪd
lark (s. v.), -s, -ing, -ed lɑːk, -s, -ɪŋ, -t
Larkin, -s 'lɑːkɪn, -z
larkspur, -s 'lɑːkspə:* [-spə*], -z
lark|y, -ier, -iest, -iness 'lɑːk|ɪ, -ɪə* [-jə*], -ɪɪst [-jɪst], -mɪs [-ɪnəs]
Larmor 'lɑːmɔ:*
larrikin, -s 'lærɪkɪn, -z
Lars Porsena ˌlɑːzˈpɔːsɪnə
larum, -s 'lærəm, -z
larv|a, -ae, -al 'lɑːv|ə, -iː, -l
laryngal ləˈrɪŋɡl [læˈr-, leəˈr-]
laryngeal ˌlærɪnˈdʒiːəl [ˌleərɪnˈdʒ-, -ˈdʒɪəl, ləˈrɪndʒɪəl, ləˈrɪndʒɪəl]
laryngectom|y, -ies ˌlærɪnˈdʒektəm|ɪ [ˌleər-, -ŋˈɡek-], -ɪz
laryngitis ˌlærɪnˈdʒaɪtɪs [ˌleər-]
laryngolog|ist/s, -y ˌlærɪŋˈɡɒlədʒ|ɪst/s [ˌleər-], -ɪ
laryngoscope, -s ləˈrɪŋɡəskəʊp [læˈr-, leəˈr-, 'lærɪŋɡ-, 'leərɪŋɡ-], -s
laryngoscopic ləˌrɪŋɡəˈskɒpɪk [læˌr-, leəˌr-, ˌlærɪŋɡ-, ˌleərɪŋɡ-]
laryngoscop|ist/s, -y ˌlærɪŋˈɡɒskəp|-ɪst/s [ˌleər-], -ɪ
larynx, -es 'lærɪŋks ['leər-], -ɪz
Lascar, -s 'læskə*, -z
Lascelles 'læslz
lascivious, -ly, -ness ləˈsɪvɪəs [-vjəs], -lɪ, -nɪs [-nəs]
laser, -s 'leɪzə*, -z
lash (s. v.), -es, -ing/s, -ed, -er/s læʃ, -ɪz, -ɪŋ/z, -t, -ə*/z
Lasham (in Hampshire) 'læʃəm (locally 'læsəm)
Las Palmas ˌlæsˈpælməs
lass, -es læs, -ɪz
Lassell læˈsel [ləˈs-]
lassie, -s 'læsɪ, -z

lassitude 'læsɪtjuːd
lasso (s.), -s læˈsuː [ləˈs-, 'læsəʊ], -z
lass|o (v.), -oes, -oing, -oed læˈs|uː [ləˈs-], -uːz, -uːɪŋ [-ʊɪŋ], -uːd ['læs|əʊ, -əʊz, -əʊɪŋ, -əʊd]
last (s. adj. v.), -s, -ly, -ing/ly, -ed lɑːst, -s, -lɪ, -ɪŋ/lɪ, -ɪd
Las Vegas ˌlæsˈveɪɡəs [ˌlɑːs-]
Latakia ˌlætəˈkɪə [-ˈkiːə]
latch (s. v.), -es, -ing, -ed lætʃ, -ɪz, -ɪŋ, -t
latchet, -s 'lætʃɪt, -s
latchkey, -s 'lætʃkiː, -z
late, -r, -st, -ly, -ness leɪt, -ə*, -ɪst, -lɪ, -nɪs [-nəs]
lateen ləˈtiːn
laten|cy, -t/ly 'leɪtən|sɪ, -t/lɪ
later|al (s. v.), -als, -ally 'lætər|əl, -əlz, -əlɪ
Lateran 'lætərən
latex 'leɪteks
lath, -s lɑːθ, -s [lɑːðz]
Latham 'leɪθəm, 'leɪðəm
  Note.—Generally 'leɪθəm in S. of England; always 'leɪðəm in N.
Lathbury 'læθbərɪ
lathe, -s leɪð, -z
lather (s. v.), -s, -ing, -ed 'lɑːðə* ['læð-], -z, -rɪŋ, -d
Lathom 'leɪθəm, 'leɪðəm
Lathrop 'leɪθrəp
lathy 'lɑːθɪ
Latimer 'lætɪmə*
Latin 'lætɪn
latini|sm/s, -st/s 'lætɪnɪ|zəm/z, -st/s
latinity ləˈtɪnətɪ [læˈt-, -ɪtɪ]
latiniz|e [-is|e], -es, -ing, -ed 'lætɪnaɪz, -ɪz, -ɪŋ, -d
Latinus ləˈtaɪnəs
latish 'leɪtɪʃ
latitude, -s 'lætɪtjuːd, -z
latitudinal ˌlætɪˈtjuːdɪnl
latitudinarian, -s, -ism ˌlætɪtjuːdɪ-ˈneərɪən, -z, -ɪzəm
Latium 'leɪʃjəm [-ʃɪəm]
latria ləˈtraɪə
latrine, -s ləˈtriːn, -z
latter, -ly 'lætə*, -lɪ
lattice, -s, -d 'lætɪs, -ɪz, -t
lattice-work 'lætɪswɜːk
Latvia, -n/s 'lætvɪə [-vjə], -n/z
laud (s. v.) (L.), -s, -ing, -ed lɔːd, -z, -ɪŋ, -ɪd
laudab|le, -ly, -leness 'lɔːdəb|l, -lɪ, -lnɪs [-nəs]
laudanum 'lɒdnəm ['lɔː-, -dən-]
laudatory 'lɔːdətərɪ
Lauder, -dale 'lɔːdə*, -deɪl

laugh (s. v.), -s, -ing/ly, -ed, -er/s lɑːf,
-s, -ɪŋ/lɪ, -t, -əˈ/z

laughab|le, -ly, -leness 'lɑːfəb|l, -lɪ,
-lnɪs [-nəs]

laughing-gas 'lɑːfɪŋgæs [ˌ--ˈ-]

laughing-stock, -s 'lɑːfɪŋstɒk, -s

Laughland 'lɒklənd [in Scotland
'lɒxlənd]

Laughlin 'lɒklɪn ['lɒxlɪn], 'lɒflɪn,
'lɑːflɪn

laughter 'lɑːftəˈ

Laughton 'lɔːtn

launce, -s lɑːns, -ɪz

Launce lɑːns, lɔːns

Launcelot 'lɑːnslət [-əlɒt], 'lɔːns-

Launceston (in Cornwall) 'lɔːnstən
[locally 'lɑː-], (in Tasmania)
'lɔːnsəstən [locally 'lɒnsəstn]

launch (s. v.), -es, -ing, -ed lɔːntʃ
[rarely lɑːntʃ], -ɪz, -ɪŋ, -t

laund|er, -ers, -ering, -ered 'lɔːnd|əˈ
[rarely 'lɑː-], -əz, -ərɪŋ, -əd

laundress, -es 'lɔːndrɪs [rarely 'lɑːn-,
-dres], -ɪz

laund(e)ret(te), -s ˌlɔːndəˈret [lɔːnˈdret],
-s

laundr|y, -ies 'lɔːndr|ɪ [rarely 'lɑːn-], -ɪz

laundry-|maid/s, -man, -men 'lɔːndrɪ|-
meɪd/z [rarely 'lɑːn-], -mən [-mæn],
-mən [-men]

Laundy 'lɔːndɪ

Laura 'lɔːrə

laureate (s. adj.), -s, -ship/s 'lɔːrɪət
['lɒr-, -rɪɪt], -s, -ʃɪp/s

laureat|e (v.), -es, -ing, -ed 'lɔːrɪeɪt
['lɒr-], -s, -ɪŋ, -ɪd

laurel, -s, -led 'lɒrəl, -z, -d

Laurence 'lɒrəns

Laurie 'lɔːrɪ, 'lɒrɪ

Laurier (English name) 'lɒrɪəˈ,
(Canadian) 'lɒrɪeɪ, 'lɒrɪəˈ

Lauriston 'lɒrɪstən

laurustinus, -es ˌlɒrəˈstaɪnəs, -ɪz

Lausanne ləʊˈzæn (lozan, lozan)

Lauterbrunnen 'laʊtəbrʊnən

lava 'lɑːvə

lavabo, -s (ritual) ləˈveɪbəʊ, (basin)
ləˈveɪbəʊ ['lævəbəʊ], -z

lavage, -s læˈvɑːʒ [-ɑːdʒ], -ɪz

Lavater lɑːˈvɑːtəˈ ['lɑːvɑːtəˈ]

lavator|y, -ies 'lævətəˈɪ, -ɪz

lav|e, -es, -ing, -ed leɪv, -z, -ɪŋ, -d

lavender 'lævəndəˈ [-vɪn-]

Lavengro ləˈvɛŋɡrəʊ

laver (L.), -s 'leɪvəˈ [river 'lɑːvəˈ], -z

Lavery 'leɪvərɪ, 'læv-

Lavington 'lævɪŋtən

Lavinia, -n ləˈvɪnɪə [-njə], -n

lavish (adj. v.), -ly, -ness; -es, -ing, -ed
'lævɪʃ, -lɪ, -nɪs [-nəs]; -ɪz, -ɪŋ, -t

law (L.), -s lɔː, -z

law|-abiding, -book/s 'lɔː|əˌbaɪdɪŋ,
-bʊk/s

law-break|er/s, -ing 'lɔːˌbreɪk|əˈ/z, -ɪŋ

Law|es, -ford lɔː|z, -fəd

law|ful, -fully, -fulness 'lɔː|fʊl, -fʊlɪ
[-fəlɪ], -fʊlnɪs [-nəs]

law-giv|er/s, -ing 'lɔːˌgɪv|əˈ/z, -ɪŋ

lawks lɔːks

lawless (L.), -ly, -ness 'lɔːlɪs [-ləs], -lɪ,
-nɪs [-nəs]

law|-list/s, -lord/s 'lɔː|lɪst/s, -lɔːd/z

law-mak|er/s, -ing 'lɔːˌmeɪk|əˈ/z, -ɪŋ

lawn, -s lɔːn, -z

lawn-mower, -s 'lɔːnˌməʊəˈ, -z

lawn-tennis ˌlɔːnˈtenɪs

Lawr|ance, -ence 'lɒr|əns [rarely 'lɔːr-],
-əns

Lawrenson 'lɒrənsn

Lawson 'lɔːsn

law-suit, -s 'lɔːsuːt [-sjuːt], -s

Lawton 'lɔːtn

lawyer, -s 'lɔːjəˈ ['lɔɪəˈ], -z

lax, -er, -est, -ly, -ness læks, -əˈ, -ɪst,
-lɪ, -nɪs [-nəs]

laxative (s. adj.), -s 'læksətɪv, -z

laxity 'læksətɪ [-ɪtɪ]

lay (s. adj. v.), -s, -ing, laid leɪ, -z, -ɪŋ,
leɪd

layabout, -s 'leɪəˌbaʊt, -s

Layamon 'laɪəmən [-mɒn] (Middle
English 'lɑːʒəmən)

Layard leəd

lay-brother, -s ˌleɪˈbrʌðəˈ ['-ˌ--], -z

lay-by, -s 'leɪbaɪ, -z

Laycock 'leɪkɒk

layer (s.) (one who lays), -s 'leɪəˈ, -z

layer (s.) (stratum, of plants), -s 'leɪəˈ,
-z

layer (v.), -s, -ing, -ed 'leɪəˈ, -z, -rɪŋ, -d

layette, -s leɪˈet, -s

lay-figure, -s ˌleɪˈfɪɡəˈ, -z

ˌlay|man, -men 'leɪ|mən, -mən

lay-out, -s 'leɪaʊt, -s

lay-reader, -s ˌleɪˈriːdəˈ ['-ˌ--], -z

Layton 'leɪtn

lazar, -s 'læzəˈ, -z

lazaretto, -s ˌlæzəˈretəʊ, -z

Lazarus 'læzərəs

laz|e, -es, -ing, -ed leɪz, -ɪz, -ɪŋ, -d

Lazenby 'leɪznbɪ

lazul|i, -ite 'læzjʊl|aɪ, -aɪt

laz|y, -ier, -iest, -ily, -iness 'leɪz|ɪ, -ɪəˈ
[-jəˈ], -ɪst [-jɪst], -ɪlɪ [-əlɪ], -ɪnɪs
[-ɪnəs]

lazy-bones 'leɪzɪˌbəʊnz

lb., lbs., paʊnd, paʊndz
le (*note in Tonic Sol-fa*), **-s** liː, -z
lea (L.), -s liː, -z
leach (*s. v.*) **(L.), -es, -ing, -ed** liːtʃ, -ɪz, -ɪŋ, -t
Leachman 'liːtʃmən
Leacock 'liːkɒk
lead (*s. v.*) (*metal*), **-s, -ing, -ed** led, -z, -ɪŋ, -ɪd
lead (*s. v.*) (*to conduct, etc.*), **-s, -ing, led** liːd, -z, -ɪŋ, led
Lead (*surname*) liːd
leaden 'ledn
Leadenhall 'lednhɔːl
leader, -s; -ship 'liːdə*, -z; -ʃɪp
leaderette, -s ˌliːdə'ret, -s
lead-in, -s ˌliːd'ɪn, -z
leading-rein, -s 'liːdɪŋreɪn, -z
leading-strings 'liːdɪŋstrɪŋz
lead-off, -s ˌliːd'ɒf [*old-fashioned* -'ɔːf], -s
lead-pencil, -s ˌled'pensl [-sɪl], -z
leads (*s.*) (*roofing*) ledz
leady (*like lead*) 'ledɪ
lea|f (*s.*), **-ves** liː|f, -vz
leaf (*v.*), **-s, -ing, -ed** liːf, -s, -ɪŋ, -t
leafless 'liːflɪs [-ləs]
leaflet, -s 'liːflɪt [-lət], -s
leaf-mould 'liːfməʊld
leaf|y, -ier, -iest, -iness 'liːf|ɪ, -ɪə* [-jə*], -ɪɪst [-jɪst], -ɪnɪs [-məs]
leagu|e (*s. v.*), **-es, -ing, -ed** liːg, -z, -ɪŋ, -d
leaguer (L.), -s 'liːgə*, -z
Leah lɪə
Leahy 'liːhɪ ['liːɪ]
leak (*s. v.*), **-s, -ing, -ed; -age/s** liːk, -s, -ɪŋ, -t; -ɪdʒ/ɪz
Leake liːk
Leakey 'liːkɪ
leak|y, -ier, -iest, -iness 'liːk|ɪ, -ɪə* [-jə*], -ɪɪst [-jɪst], -ɪnɪs [-mənəs]
leal liːl
Leamington 'lemɪŋtən
lean (*s. adj. v.*), **-er, -est, -ly, -ness; -s, -ing, -ed, leant** liːn, -ə*, -ɪst, -lɪ, -nɪs [-nəs]; -z, -ɪŋ, lent [liːnd], lent
Leander liː'ændə* [lɪ'æ-]
lean-to, -s 'liːntuː [ˌ-'-], -z
leap (*s. v.*), **-s, -ing, -ed, leapt** liːp, -s, -ɪŋ, lept [liːpt], lept
leaper, -s 'liːpə*, -z
leap-frog (*s. v.*), **-s, -ging, -ged** 'liːpfrɒg, -z, -ɪŋ, -d
leap-year, -s 'liːpjɜː* [-ˌjɪə*], -z
Lear lɪə*
learn, -s, -ing, -ed, -t, -er/s lɜːn, -z, -ɪŋ, -t [-d], -t, -ə*/z

learned (*adj.*), **-ly, -ness** 'lɜːnɪd, -lɪ, -nɪs [-nəs]
Learney (*in Grampian*) 'leənɪ
leas|e (*s. v.*), **-es, -ing, -ed** liːs, -ɪz, -ɪŋ, -t
leasehold (*s. adj.*), **-s; -er/s** 'liːshəʊld, -z; -ə*/z
lease-lend (*s. v.*), **-lends, -lending, -lent** ˌliːs'lend, -'lendz, -'lendɪŋ, -'lent
leash (*s. v.*), **-es, -ing, -ed** liːʃ, -ɪz, -ɪŋ, -t
leasing (*telling lies*) 'liːsɪŋ
least, -ways, -wise liːst, -weɪz, -waɪz
leat, -s liːt, -s
Leatham 'liːθəm
Leathart 'liːθɑːt
leather (*s. v.*), **-s, -ing, -ed** 'leðə*, -z, -ɪŋ, -d
leatherette ˌleðə'ret
Leatherhead 'leðəhed
leathern 'leðən
leath|ery, -eriness 'leð|ərɪ, -ərɪnɪs [-nəs]
Leathes liːðz
leave (*s.*), **-s** liːv, -z [*formerly, in the army also* liːf, -s]
leav|e (*v.*), **-es, -ing/s, left** liːv, -z, -ɪŋ/z, left
leaved liːvd
leav|en, -ens, -ening, -ened 'lev|n, -nz, -nɪŋ [-nɪn], -nd
Leavenworth 'levnwɜːθ [-wəθ]
leaves (*plur. of leaf*) liːvz
Leavis 'liːvɪs
Leavitt 'levɪt
Lebanese ˌlebə'niːz
Lebanon 'lebənən
Le Beau lə'bəʊ
Leburn 'liːbɜːn
lecher, -s 'letʃə*, -z
lecherous, -ly, -ness 'letʃərəs, -lɪ, -nɪs [-nəs]
lechery 'letʃərɪ
Lechlade 'letʃleɪd
Lechmere 'leʃˌmɪə*, 'letʃ-
Leckhampton 'lek,hæmptən
Lecky 'lekɪ
Leconfield 'lekənfiːld
lectern, -s 'lektɜːn [-tən], -z
lection, -s 'lekʃn, -z
lectionar|y, -ies 'lekʃnərɪ [-ʃənər-, -ʃnər-], -ɪz
lector, -s 'lektɔː*, -z
lect|ure (*s. v.*), **-ures, -uring, -ured, -urer/s; -ureship/s** 'lektʃ|ə*, -əz, -ərɪŋ, -əd, -ərə*/z; -əʃɪp/s
led (*from* **lead** liːd) led
Leda 'liːdə
Ledbury 'ledbərɪ
ledge, -s ledʒ, -ɪz
ledger, -s 'ledʒə*, -z
ledger-line, -s 'ledʒəlaɪn, -z

Ledi 'ledɪ
Lediard 'ledɪəd [-dɪɑːd, -djəd]
Ledward 'ledwəd
Ledyard 'ledjəd
lee (L.), -s liː, -z
leech (L.), -es liːtʃ, -ɪz
Leeds liːdz
leek (L.), -s liːk, -s
leer (s. v.), -s, -ing/ly, -ed lɪə*, -z, -rɪŋ/lɪ, -d
Lees liːz
leet, -s liːt, -s
leetle 'liːtl
leeward 'liːwəd [nautical pronunciation 'luːəd, luəd, 'ljuːəd, ljuəd]
Leeward (Islands) 'liːwəd
leeway 'liːweɪ
Lefanu (Le Fanu) 'lefənjuː [-fæn-], lə'fɑːnuː
Lefevre lə'fiːvə*, lə'feɪvə*, lə'fɛːvrə (as in French)
    Note.—lə'fiːvə* in Sterne's 'Sentimental Journey'.
Lefroy lə'frɔɪ
left left
left-hand (adj.) 'lefthænd [ˌ-'-]
left-hand|ed, -edness, -er/s ˌleft-'hænd|ɪd, -ɪdnɪs [-nəs], -ə*/z
leftist, -s 'leftɪst, -s
left-off, -s ˌleft'ɒf [old-fashioned -'ɔːf, also '-- when attributive], -s
leftward, -s 'leftwəd, -z
leg (s. v.), -s, -ging, -ged leg, -z, -ɪŋ, -d
legac|y, -ies 'legəs|ɪ, -ɪz
leg|al, -ally 'liːg|l, -əlɪ
legali|sm, -st/s 'liːgəlɪ|zəm [-glɪ-], -st/s
legality liː'gælətɪ [lɪ'g-, -ɪtɪ]
legalization [-isa-] ˌliːgəlaɪ'zeɪʃn [-glaɪ-]
legaliz|e [-is|e], -es, -ing, -ed 'liːgəlaɪz [-glaɪz], -ɪz, -ɪŋ, -d
legate, -s 'legɪt [-gət, -geɪt], -s
legatee, -s ˌlegə'tiː, -z
legatine 'legətaɪn
legation, -s lɪ'geɪʃn [le'g-], -z
legatissimo ˌlegɑː'tɪsɪməʊ [-gə't-]
legato lə'gɑːtəʊ [lɪ'g-]
leg-bail, -s ˌleg'beɪl ['-- when in contrast with off-bail], -z
leg-bye, -s ˌleg'baɪ ['-- when in contrast with off-bye], -z
legend, -s 'ledʒənd, -z
legendary 'ledʒəndərɪ [-dɪn-]
Leger 'ledʒə*, see also St. Leger
legerdemain ˌledʒədə'meɪn
Leggatt 'legət
Legge leg
-legged -legd [-'legɪd]
Leggett, -er 'legɪt, -ə*

legging, -s 'legɪŋ, -z
leggy 'legɪ
Legh liː
leghorn (fowl), -s le'gɔːn [lɪ'g-, lə'g-], -z
leghorn (straw hat), -s 'leghɔːn [le'gɔːn, lɪ'gɔːn, lə'gɔːn], -z
Leghorn (place) ˌleg'hɔːn [also '-- according to sentence-stress]
legibility ˌledʒɪ'bɪlətɪ [-dʒə'b-, -lɪt-]
legib|le, -ly, -leness 'ledʒəb|l [-dʒɪb-], -lɪ, -lnɪs [-nəs]
legion (L.), -s 'liːdʒən, -z
legionar|y (s. adj.), -ies 'liːdʒənər|ɪ [-dʒnə-], -ɪz
legislat|e, -es, -ing, -ed, -or/s 'ledʒɪsleɪt, -s, -ɪŋ, -ɪd, -ə*/z
legislation ˌledʒɪs'leɪʃn
legislative 'ledʒɪslətɪv [-leɪt-]
legislature, -s 'ledʒɪsleɪtʃə* [-lətʃə*, -ˌtjuə*, -ˌtʃuə*], -z
legist, -s 'liːdʒɪst, -s
legitimacy lɪ'dʒɪtɪməsɪ [lə-, -təm-]
legitimate (adj.), -ly, -ness lɪ'dʒɪtɪmət [lə-, -təm-, -mɪt], -lɪ, -nɪs [-nəs]
legitimat|e (v.), -es, -ing, -ed lɪ'dʒɪtɪmeɪt [lə-, -təm-], -s, -ɪŋ, -ɪd
legitimation lɪˌdʒɪtɪ'meɪʃn [lə-, -tə'm-]
legitimatiz|e [-is|e], -es, -ing, -ed lɪ'dʒɪtɪmətaɪz [lə-, -təm-], -ɪz, -ɪŋ, -d
legitimist, -s lɪ'dʒɪtɪmɪst [lə-, -təm-], -s
legitimiz|e [-is|e], -es, -ing, -ed lɪ'dʒɪtɪmaɪz [lə-, -təm-], -ɪz, -ɪŋ, -d
leg-pull, -s, -ing, -ed 'legpʊl, -z, -ɪŋ, -d
Legros (English surname) lə'grəʊ
legume, -s 'legjuːm, -z
leguminous le'gjuːmɪnəs [lɪ'g-]
Le Havre lə'hɑːvrə (lə ɑːvr)
Lehigh 'liːhaɪ
Lehmann 'leɪmən
lei 'leɪiː
Leicester, -shire 'lestə*, -ʃə* [-ˌʃɪə*]
Leics. (always said in full) 'lestəʃə* [-ˌʃɪə*]
Leiden (Dutch city) 'laɪdn
Leigh (surname) liː
Leigh (place-name) liː, laɪ
    Note.—The places in Essex and Greater Manchester are liː; those in Surrey, Kent and Dorset are laɪ.
Leighton 'leɪtn
Leila 'liːlə
Leinster (Irish province) 'lenstə*, (Duke of) 'lɪnstə*, (square in London) 'lenstə*
Leipzig 'laɪpzɪg ('laɪptsɪç)
Leishman 'liːʃmən, 'lɪʃ-
leister, -s 'liːstə*, -z
Leister 'lestə*

293

Leiston (*in Suffolk*) 'leɪstən
leisure, -d, -ly, -liness 'leʒə*, -d, -lɪ, -lɪnɪs [-nəs]
Leitch liːtʃ
Leith liːθ
leitmotif, -s 'laɪtməʊˌtiːf [ˌ—'-], -s
Leitrim 'liːtrɪm
Leix (*Irish county*) liːʃ
Le Lacheur lə'læʃə*
Leland 'liːlənd
Lelean lə'liːn
Lely (*portraitist*) 'liːlɪ ['lɪlɪ]
leman, -s 'lemən, -z
Leman (*lake*) 'lemən ['liːmən, lɪ'mæn, lə'mæn, lə'mɑːŋ], (*surname*) 'lemən, 'liːmən, (*street in London*) 'lemən [*formerly* lɪ'mæn]
Le Marchant lə'mɑːtʃənt
Lemare lə'meə*
Le May lə'meɪ
Lemberg 'lembɜːg
Lemesurier lə'meʒərə*
lemma, -s 'lemə, -z
lemming, -s 'lemɪŋ, -z
Lemnos 'lemnɒs
Lemoine lə'mɔɪn
lemon (L.), -s 'lemən, -z
lemonade, -s ˌlemə'neɪd, -z
lemon-coloured 'lemənˌkʌləd
lemon-drop, -s 'leməndrɒp, -s
lemon-juice 'leməndʒuːs
lemon-squash, -es ˌlemən'skwɒʃ, -ɪz
lemon-squeezer, -s 'lemənˌskwiːzə*, -z
lemon-yellow ˌlemən'jeləʊ
Lemuel 'lemjʊəl [-jʊel]
lemur, -s 'liːmə*, -z
Lena (*personal name*) 'liːnə, (*Siberian river*) 'lemə ('ljenə)
lend, -s, -ing, lent, lender/s lend, -z, -ɪŋ, lent, 'lendə*/z
lending-librar|y, -ies 'lendɪŋˌlaɪbrər|ɪ [-brɪ|-], -ɪz
Le Neve lə'niːv
length, -s leŋθ [-ŋkθ], -s
length|en, -ens, -ening, -ened 'leŋθ|ən [-ŋkθ-], -ənz, -ənɪŋ [-ŋɪŋ, -nɪŋ], -ənd
length|ways, -wise 'leŋθ|weɪz [-ŋkθ-], -waɪz
length|y, -ier, -iest, -ily, -iness 'leŋθ|ɪ [-ŋkθ-], -ɪə* [-jə*], -ɪɪst [-jɪst], -ɪlɪ [-əlɪ], -ɪnɪs [-ɪnəs]
lenien|ce, -cy, -t/ly 'liːnjən|s [-nɪən-], -sɪ, -t/lɪ
Lenin 'lenɪn ['lenɪn] ('ljenjin)
Leningrad 'lenɪŋgræd [-grɑːd] (ljinjin-'grat)
lenis, lenes 'leɪnɪs ['liːnɪs], 'leɪneɪz ['liːniːz]

lenitive (*s. adj.*), -s 'lenɪtɪv, -z
lenity 'lenətɪ ['liːnɪ-, -rɪtɪ]
Lennox 'lenəks
leno (L.) 'liːnəʊ
Lenoir (*surname*) lə'nwɑː*, (*town in U.S.A.*) lə'nɔː*
Lenore lə'nɔː* [lɪ'n-, -'nɔə*]
Lenox 'lenəks
lens, -es lenz, -ɪz
lent (*from* lend) lent
Lent, -en lent, -ən
Lenthall (*surname*) 'lentɔːl, (*place in Yorkshire*) 'lenθɔːl [-θəl]
lenticular len'tɪkjʊlə*
lentil, -s 'lentɪl [-tl], -z
lento 'lentəʊ
Lentulus 'lentjʊləs
Leo (*constellation, name of popes*) 'liːəʊ ['lɪəʊ]
Leofric 'leɪəʊfrɪk
Leominster 'lemstə* ['lemɪnstə*]
Leon 'liːən [lɪən]
Léon (*as English name*) 'leɪɒn ['leɪən]
Leonard, -s 'lenəd, -z
Leonardo, -s ˌliːəʊ'nɑːdəʊ [ˌlɪəʊ-], -z
Leonid, -s 'liːəʊnɪd ['lɪəʊ-], -z
Leonidas liː'ɒnɪdæs [lɪ'ɒ-]
leonine 'liːəʊnaɪn ['lɪəʊ-]
Leonora ˌliːə'nɔːrə [ˌlɪə-, ljə-]
Leontes liː'ɒntiːz [lɪ'ɒ-]
leopard, -s; -ess/es 'lepəd, -z; -ɪs [-es]/ɪz
Leopold 'lɪəpəʊld
leotard, -s 'liːəʊtɑːd ['lɪəʊ-], -z
Lepanto lɪ'pæntəʊ
Le Patourel lə'pætʊrəl [-tər-]
Lepel lə'pel
leper, -s 'lepə*, -z
lepidoptera ˌlepɪ'dɒptərə
Lepidus 'lepɪdəs
Le Play lə'pleɪ
Le Poer lə'pɔː* [-'pɔə*]
Lepontine lɪ'pɒntaɪn [le'p-]
Leporis 'lepərɪs
leprechaun, -s 'leprəkɔːn [-prɪkɔːn, -prəhɔːn, -prɪhɔːn], -z
leprosy 'leprəsɪ
leprous, -ly, -ness 'leprəs, -lɪ, -nɪs [-nəs]
Lepsius 'lepsɪəs [-sjəs]
lept|on, -a 'lept|ɒn [-t|ən], -ə
Lepus (*constellation*) 'liːpəs ['lep-]
Le Queux lə'kjuː
Lereculey ˌlerɪ'kjuːlɪ
Lermontoff 'leəmɒntɒf ['leəməntəf] ('ljerməntəf)
Lerwick 'lɜːwɪk [*locally* 'lɛrwɪk]
Lesbia, -n 'lezbɪə [-bjə], -n
Lesbos 'lezbɒs

Le Seelleur lə'seɪlə*

lèse-majesté ˌleɪz'mæʒesteɪ [-'mædʒ-, -ʒɪs-, -ʒəs-] (lɛːzmaʒeste)

lese-majesty ˌliːz'mædʒɪstɪ [-dʒəs-]

lesion, -s 'liːʒn, -z

Leslie, -ley 'lezlɪ, in U.S.A. 'leslɪ

Lesmahagow ˌlesmə'heɪgəʊ

Lesotho lə'suːtu: [-'səʊ-, -təʊ]

less, -er les, -ə*

lessee, -s le'siː: [ˌle'siː:], -z

less|en, -ens, -ening, -ened 'les|n, -nz, -n̩ŋ [-nɪŋ], -nd

Lesseps le'seps ['leseps]

Lessing 'lesɪŋ

lesson, -s 'lesn, -z

lessor, -s le'sɔː:* [ˌle'sɔː:*], -z

lest lest

Lestrade le'streɪd, -'strɑːd

L'Estrange lə'streɪndʒ [le's-]

let (s. v.), -s, -ting let, -s, -ɪŋ

Letchworth 'letʃwəθ [-wɑː:θ]

let-down, -s 'letdaʊn [-'-], -z

Lethaby 'leθəbɪ

lethal 'liːθl

lethargic, -al, -ally, -alness le'θɑːdʒɪk [lɪ'θ-, lə'θ-], -l, -əlɪ, -lnɪs [-nəs]

lethargy 'leθədʒɪ

Lethe 'liːθiː [-θɪ]

Letheby 'leθəbɪ

Lethem 'leθəm

Letitia lɪ'tɪʃɪə [lə-, -ʃjə, -ʃə]

Lett, -s let, -s

letter (s. v.), -s, -ing, -ed 'letə*, -z, -rɪŋ, -d

letter-balance, -s 'letəˌbæləns, -ɪz

letter-box, -es 'letəbɒks, -ɪz

letter-card, -s 'letəkɑːd, -z

letter-case, -s 'letəkeɪs, -ɪz

letter-perfect ˌletə'pɜːfɪkt

letterpress 'letəpres

letter-weight, -s 'letəweɪt, -s

letter-writer, -s 'letəˌraɪtə*, -z

Lettic 'letɪk

Lettice 'letɪs

Lettish 'letɪʃ

Lettonian, -s le'təʊnjən [-nɪən], -z

Letts lets

lettuce, -s 'letɪs [-təs], -ɪz

Letty 'letɪ

Leuchars (place in Scotland) 'luːkəz ['ljuː:-, -uːxəz] (Scottish 'luxərz), (southern surname) 'luːʃɑːz ['ljuː:-]

leucocyte, -s 'ljuːkəʊsaɪt ['luː:-], -s

leucopathy lju:'kɒpəθɪ [luː:-]

leucotomy lju:'kɒtəmɪ [luː:-]

Leuctra 'ljuːktrə

leukaemia lju:'kiːmɪə [ljʊ-, luː:-, lʊ-, lə-, -mjə]

Levant (s.) (E. Mediterranean, leather) lɪ'vænt [lə'v-]

levant (adj.) (opp. couchant) 'levənt

levant (v.) (abscond), -s, -ing, -ed lɪ'vænt [lə'v-], -s, -ɪŋ, -ɪd

levanter (L.), -s lɪ'væntə* [lə'v-], -z

Levantine 'levəntaɪn [-vn-, -tiːn]

levee (royal reception), -s 'levɪ [-veɪ], -z

levee (embankment), -s 'levɪ [lə'viː:], -z

lev|el (s. adj. v.), -els, -elness; -elling, -elled, -eller/s 'lev|l, -lz, -lnɪs [-nəs]; -lɪŋ [-əlɪŋ], -ld, -lə*/z [-ələ*/z]

level-crossing, -s ˌlevl'krɒsɪŋ [old-fashioned -'krɔːs-], -z

level-headed ˌlevl'hedɪd [also '--ˌ-- when attributive]

Leven (loch) 'liːvən, (Earl of) 'liːvən, (surname) 'levən, 'liːvən

lev|er (s. v.) (L.), -ers, -ering, -ered; -erage 'liːv|ə*, -əz, -ərɪŋ, -əd; -ərɪdʒ

leveret, -s 'levərɪt [-rət], -s

Leverett 'levərɪt

Leverhulme 'liːvəhjuːm

Leverkes (surname) 'levəkəs

Leveson (surname) 'levɪsn

Leveson-Gower ˌluːsn'gɔː:* [ˌljuː:-, -'gəʊ*]

Levett 'levɪt

Levey 'liːvɪ, 'levɪ

Levi 'liːvaɪ

leviable 'levɪəbl

leviathan (L.), -s lɪ'vaɪəθn [lə'v-], -z

Levin 'levɪn

Levine lə'viːn

levirate 'liːvɪrɪt [-rət]

Levis (in Quebec) 'levɪ

levitat|e, -es, -ing, -ed 'levɪteɪt, -s, -ɪŋ, -ɪd

levitation, -s ˌlevɪ'teɪʃn, -z

Levite, -s 'liːvaɪt, -s

levitic, -al, -ally lɪ'vɪtɪk, -l, -əlɪ

Leviticus lɪ'vɪtɪkəs [lə-]

levit|y, -ies 'levət|ɪ [-ɪt|ɪ], -ɪz

lev|y (s. v.), -ies, -ying, -ied, -ier/s 'lev|ɪ, -ɪz, -ɪŋ [-jɪŋ], -ɪd, -ɪə*/z [-jə*/z]

Levy (surname) 'liːvɪ, 'levɪ, (American town) 'liːvaɪ

lewd, -er, -est, -ly, -ness ljuːd [luː:d], -ə*, -ɪst, -lɪ, -nɪs [-nəs]

Lew|es, -in 'luː:|ɪs ['lʊɪs, 'ljuː:-, 'ljʊɪs], -ɪn

lewis (L.), -es 'luː:ɪs ['lʊɪs, 'ljuː:ɪs, 'ljʊɪs], -ɪz

Lewisham 'luː:ɪʃəm ['lʊɪ-, 'ljuː:ɪ-, 'ljʊɪ-]

Lewison 'luː:ɪsn ['lʊɪ-, 'ljuː:ɪ-, 'ljʊɪ-]

Lewsey 'ljuː:sɪ

lexic|al, -ally 'leksɪk|l, -əlɪ

lexicograph|er/s, -y ˌleksɪ'kɒgrəf|ə*/z, -ɪ

lexicographic, -al ˌleksɪkəʊ'græfɪk, -l

lexicon, -s 'leksɪkən, -z

Lexington 'leksɪŋtən

ley (land under grass) leɪ

Ley liː

Leybourne (in Kent) 'leɪbɔːn [-bʊən]

Leyburn (in North Yorkshire) 'leɪbɜːn

Leycester 'lestə*

Leyden (old-fashioned spelling of Leiden, q.v.)

Leyden jar, -s ˌleɪdn'dʒɑː*, -z

Leyland 'leɪlənd

Leys liːz

Leyshon 'leɪʃn

Leyton 'leɪtn

Lhasa 'lɑːsə ['læs-]

Lhuyd lɔɪd

li (Chinese measure of length) liː

liabilit|y, -ies ˌlaɪə'bɪlət|ɪ [-lɪt-], -ɪz

liable, -ness 'laɪəbl, -nɪs [-nəs]

liaison, -s liː'eɪzɔ̃ːŋ [lɪ'eɪ-, -zɒn, -zən] (ljezɔ̃), -z
Note.—In military use always -zən.

liais|e, -es, -ing, -ed lɪ'eɪz, -ɪz, -ɪŋ, -d

Liam lɪəm

liana lɪ'ɑːnə

liar, -s 'laɪə*, -z

lias 'laɪəs

liassic laɪ'æsɪk

Libanus 'lɪbənəs

libat|e, -es, -ing, -ed laɪ'beɪt, -s, -ɪŋ, bɪ-

libation, -s laɪ'beɪʃn [lɪ'b-], -z

lib|el, -els, -elling, -elled, -eller/s 'laɪb|l, -lz, -lɪŋ [-əlɪŋ], -ld, -lə*/z [-ələ*/z]

libellous, -ly 'laɪb|əs [-bələs], -lɪ

Liber 'laɪbə*

liber|al (s. adj.), -als, -ally 'lɪbər|əl, -əlz, -əlɪ

liberalism 'lɪbərəlɪzm

liberality ˌlɪbə'rælətɪ [-ɪtɪ]

liberaliz|e [-is|e], -es, -ing, -ed 'lɪbərəl-aɪz, -ɪz, -ɪŋ, -d

liberat|e, -es, -ing, -ed, -or/s 'lɪbəreɪt, -s, -ɪŋ, -ɪd-, -ə*/z

liberation ˌlɪbə'reɪʃn

Liberia, -n/s laɪ'bɪərɪə, -n/z

libertin|age, -ism 'lɪbətɪn|ɪdʒ, -ɪzəm

libertine, -s 'lɪbətiːn [-tɪn, -taɪn], -z

Liberton 'lɪbətn

libert|y (L.), -ies 'lɪbət|ɪ, -ɪz

libidinous, -ly, -ness lɪ'bɪdɪnəs, -lɪ, -nɪs [-nəs]

libido lɪ'biːdəʊ [-'baɪd-, 'lɪbɪdəʊ]

libr|a (pound), -ae 'laɪbr|ə, -iː ['liːbr|ə, -eɪ, -aɪ]

Libra (constellation) 'laɪbrə ['liːb-, 'lɪb-]

librarian, -s; -ship laɪ'breərɪən, -z; -ʃɪp

librar|y, -ies 'laɪbrər|ɪ [-brɪr|ɪ], -ɪz

libration, -s laɪ'breɪʃn, -z

librett|o, -os, -i lɪ'bret|əʊ, -əʊz, -ɪ [-iː]

librettist, -s lɪ'bretɪst, -s

Libya, -n/s 'lɪbɪə [-bjə], -n/z

lice (plur. of louse) laɪs

licence, -s, -d 'laɪsəns, -ɪz, -t

licens|e, -es, -ing, -ed, -er/s 'laɪsəns, -ɪz, -ɪŋ, -t, -ə*/z

licensee, -s ˌlaɪsən'siː, -z

licentiate, -s laɪ'senʃɪət [lɪ's-, -ʃət, -ʃɪt, -ʃɪt, -ʃət], -s

licentious, -ly, -ness laɪ'senʃəs, -lɪ, -nɪs [-nəs]

lichen, -s, -ed 'laɪkən [-kɪn, -ken, 'lɪtʃɪn], -z, -d

lichenous 'laɪkənəs ['lɪtʃ-, -kɪn-]

Lichfield 'lɪtʃfiːld

lichgate, -s 'lɪtʃgeɪt, -s

Licini|an, -us laɪ'sɪnɪ|ən [lɪ's-, nj|-], -əs

licit 'lɪsɪt

lick (s. v.) (L.), -s, -ing/s, -ed, -er/s lɪk, -s, -ɪŋ/z, -t, -ə*/z

licorice 'lɪkərɪs

lictor, -s 'lɪktə* [-tɔː*], -z

lid, -s lɪd, -z

Liddell 'lɪdl, lɪ'del

Lidd|esdale, -on 'lɪd|zdeɪl, -n

Lidell lɪ'del

Lidgate (place near Newmarket) 'lɪdgeɪt [-gɪt]

Lido, -s 'liːdəʊ, -z

lie (s. v.) (falsehood, etc.), lies, lying/ly, lied, liar/s laɪ, laɪz, 'laɪɪŋ/lɪ, laɪd, 'laɪə*/z

lie (v.) (recline, etc.), lies, lying, lay, lain, lier/s laɪ, laɪz, 'laɪɪŋ, leɪ, leɪn, 'laɪə*/z

lie-abed, -s 'laɪəbed, -z

Liebig 'liːbɪg

Liechtenstein 'lɪktənstaɪn ['lɪx-, 'liː-]

lief, -er liːf, -ə*

liege, -s liːdʒ, -ɪz

Liège lɪ'eɪʒ (ljɛːʒ)

liege|man, -men 'liːdʒmæn [-mən], -men [-mən]

lien, -s lɪən ['liːən], -z

lieu ljuː [luː]

lieutenanc|y, -ies lef'tenənsɪ [ləf-], -ɪz
Note.—Until recently, the forms with lef't-, ləf't- were used in the Army, whereas in the Navy alternative forms with lə't-, le't-, luː't- were current.

lieutenant, -s lef'tenənt [ləf-], -s (*see note under* lieutenancy)

lieutenant-colonel, -s lef,tenənt'kɜ:nl [ləf-], -z

lieutenant-commander, -s lef,tenənt-kə'mɑ:ndə* [ləf't-], -z (*see note under* lieutenancy)

lieutenant-general, -s lef,tenənt-'dʒenərəl [ləf-], -z

lieutenant-governor, -s lef,tenənt-'gʌvənə* [ləf-, -vnə*, -vnə*], -z

li|fe, -ves laɪ|f, -vz

life-assurance, -s 'laɪfə,ʃʊərəns [-,ʃɔər-, -,ʃɔ:r-], -ɪz

life|-belt/s, -blood 'laɪf|belt/s, -blʌd

life-boat, -s 'laɪfbəʊt, -s

life-buoy, -s 'laɪfbɔɪ, -z

life-estate, -s ,laɪfɪ'steɪt ['--,-], -s

life-giving 'laɪf,gɪvɪŋ

life-guard, -s 'laɪfgɑ:d, -z

life-interest, -s ,laɪf'ɪntrɪst [-'ɪntərest], -s

life-jacket, -s 'laɪf,dʒækɪt, -s

lifeless, -ly, -ness 'laɪflɪs [-ləs], -lɪ, -nɪs [-nəs]

lifelike 'laɪflaɪk

life-line, -s 'laɪflaɪn, -z

lifelong 'laɪflɒŋ [,-'-]

life-preserver, -s 'laɪfprɪ,zɜ:və*, -z

life-rent, -s 'laɪfrent, -s

life-saving 'laɪf,seɪvɪŋ

life-sentence, -s 'laɪf,sentəns [,-'--], -ɪz

life-size ,laɪf'saɪz [*also* '-- *according to sentence-stress*]

life-tenan|cy, -cies, -t/s ,laɪf'tenən|sɪ, -sɪz, -t/s

lifetime, -s 'laɪftaɪm, -z

life-work, -s ,laɪf'wɜ:k ['--], -s

Liff|ey, -ord 'lɪf|ɪ, -əd

lift (*s. v.*), -s, -ing, -ed, -er/s lɪft, -s, -ɪŋ, -ɪd, -ə*/z

lift-boy, -s 'lɪftbɔɪ, -z

lift|-man, -men 'lɪft|mæn, -men

lift-off 'lɪftɒf [*old-fashioned* -ɔ:f]

ligament, -s 'lɪgəmənt, -s

ligament|al, -ous ,lɪgə'ment|l, -əs

ligature, -s, -d 'lɪgə,tʃʊə* [-tʃə*, -,tjʊə*], -z, -d

liger, -s 'laɪgə*, -z

Ligertwood 'lɪdʒətwʊd [-dʒɜ:t-]

light (*s. adj. v.*), -s; -er, -est, -ly, -ness; -ing, -ed, lit laɪt, -s; -ə*, -ɪst, -lɪ, -nɪs [-nəs]; -ɪŋ, -ɪd, lɪt

light|en, -ens, -ening, -ened 'laɪt|n, -nz, -nɪŋ [-nɪŋ], -nd

lighter, -s 'laɪtə*, -z

lighterage 'laɪtərɪdʒ

lighter|man, -men 'laɪtə|mən, -mən

light-fingered 'laɪt,fɪŋgəd [,-'--]

lightfoot (L.) 'laɪtfʊt

light-handed 'laɪt,hændɪd [,-'--]

light-headed, -ly, -ness ,laɪt'hedɪd [*also* '-,-- *when attributive*], -lɪ, -nɪs [-nəs]

light-hearted, -ly, -ness ,laɪt'hɑ:tɪd [*also* '-,-- *when attributive*], -lɪ, -nɪs [-nəs]

light-horse|man, -men ,laɪt'hɔ:s|mən, -mən

lighthou|se, -ses 'laɪthaʊ|s, -zɪz

lighthousekeeper, -s 'laɪthaʊs,ki:pə*, -z

lightminded, -ly, -ness ,laɪt'maɪndɪd [*also* '-,-- *when attributive*], -lɪ, -nɪs [-nəs]

lightning, -s 'laɪtnɪŋ, -z

lightning-conductor, -s 'laɪtnɪŋkən-,dʌktə*, -z

lightship, -s 'laɪt-ʃɪp, -s

lightsome, -ly, -ness 'laɪtsəm, -lɪ, -nɪs [-nəs]

light-spirited ,laɪt'spɪrɪtɪd [-'spɪrət-]

light-wave, -s 'laɪtweɪv, -z

light-weight, -s 'laɪtweɪt, -s

ligneous 'lɪgnɪəs [-njəs]

lignite 'lɪgnaɪt

lignum 'lɪgnəm

Liguria, -n/s lɪ'gjʊərɪə [-'gjɔər-, -'gjɔ:r-], -n/z

likable 'laɪkəbl

lik|e (*s. adj. v.*), -es, -ing, -ed laɪk, -s, -ɪŋ, -t

likel|y, -ier, -iest, -iness, -ihood 'laɪkl|ɪ, -ɪə* [-jə*], -ɪɪst [-jɪst], -ɪnɪs [-ɪnəs], -ɪhʊd

likeminded ,laɪk'maɪndɪd ['-,--]

lik|en, -ens, -ening, -ened 'laɪk|ən, -ənz, -nɪŋ [-nɪŋ, -ənɪŋ], -ənd

likeness, -es 'laɪknɪs [-nəs], -ɪz

likewise 'laɪkwaɪz

liking, -s 'laɪkɪŋ, -z

lilac, -s 'laɪlək, -s

liliaceous ,lɪlɪ'eɪʃəs

Lilia|n, -s 'lɪlɪə|n [-ljə-], -s

Lilith 'lɪlɪθ

Lill|a, -ey 'lɪl|ə, -ɪ

Lilliput 'lɪlɪpʌt [-pʊt, -pət]

lilliputian (L.), -s ,lɪlɪ'pju:ʃjən [-ʃrən, -ʃn], -z

Lilly, -white 'lɪlɪ, -waɪt [-hwaɪt]

lilt (*s. v.*), -s, -ing, -ed lɪlt, -s, -ɪŋ, -ɪd

lil|y (L.), -ies 'lɪl|ɪ, -ɪz

lily-white ,lɪlɪ'waɪt [-ɪ'hw-], '--- *when attributive*]

Lima (*in Peru*) 'li:mə [*old-fashioned* 'laɪmə] (*in U.S.A.*) 'laɪmə

limb, -s, -ed lɪm, -z, -d

limber (*s. adj.*), -s 'lɪmbə*, -z

297

limbo (**L.**) 'lımbəʊ
lim|e (s. v.), **-es, -ing, -ed** laım, -z, -ıŋ, -d
Limehouse 'laımhaʊs
lime-juice 'laımdʒu:s
limekiln, **-s** 'laımkıln [-kıl], -z
lime-light, **-s** 'laımlaıt, -s
limen 'laımen
limerick (**L.**), **-s** 'lımərık, -s
lime|stone, **-tree/s** 'laım|stəʊn, -tri:/z
limewash (s. v.), **-es, -ing, -ed** 'laımwɒʃ,
   -ız, -ıŋ, -t
limewater 'laım,wɔ:tə*
liminal 'lımınl
limit (s. v.), **-s, -ing, -ed/ness; -able**
   'lımıt, -s, -ıŋ, -ıd/nıs [-nəs]; -əbl
limitation, **-s** ,lımı'teıʃn, -z
limitless 'lımıtlıs [-ləs]
limitrophe 'lımıtrəʊf
limn, **-s, -ing, -ed, -er/s** lım, -z, -ıŋ
   [-nıŋ], -d, -nə*/z
Limoges lı'məʊʒ (limɔ:ʒ)
limousine, **-s** 'lımu:zi:n [-mʊz-, -məz-,
   ,--'-], -z
limp (s. adj. v.), **-s; -er, -est, -ly, -ness;
   -ing/ly, -ed** lımp, -s; -ə*, -ıst, -lı,
   -nıs [-nəs]; -ıŋ/lı, -t [lımt]
limpet, **-s** 'lımpıt, -s
limpid, **-est, -ly, -ness** 'lımpıd, -ıst, -lı,
   -nıs [-nəs]
limpidity lım'pıdətı [-ıtı]
Limpopo lım'pəʊpəʊ
limy 'laımı
Linacre 'lınəkə*
linage, **-s** 'laınıdʒ, -ız
linchpin, **-s** 'lınʃ/pın, -z
Lincoln, **-shire** 'lıŋkən, -ʃə* [-,ʃıə*]
Lincs. lıŋks
Lind lınd
Lindbergh 'lındbɜ:g
linden (**L.**), **-s** 'lındən, -z
Lindisfarne 'lındısfɑ:n
Lindley 'lındlı
Lindon 'lındən
Lind|say, **-sey** 'lınd|zı, -zı
lin|e (s. v.) (**L.**), **-es, -ing, -ed** laın, -z,
   -ıŋ, -d
lineage, **-s** 'lınııdʒ [-njıdʒ], -ız
lineal, **-ly** 'lınıəl [-njəl], -ı
lineament, **-s** 'lınıəmənt [-njə-], -s
linear, **-ly** 'lınıə* [-njə*], -lı
lineation, **-s** ,lını'eıʃn, -z
line-engraving,   **-s**   'laının,greıvıŋ
   [-ıŋ,g-], -z
linen, **-s** 'lının, -z
linen-draper, **-s, -y** 'lının,dreıpə*, -z, -rı
liner, **-s** 'laınə*, -z
lines|man, **-men** 'laınz|mən, -mən
   [-men]

ling (**L.**), **-s** lıŋ, -z
Ling|ay, **-en** 'lıŋg|ı, -ən
ling|er, **-ers, -ering/ly, -ered, -erer/s**
   'lıŋg|ə*, -əz, -ərıŋ/lı, -əd, -ərə*/z
lingerie 'læ:nʒəri: ['læŋg-, -rı] (lɛ̃ʒri)
lingo, **-s** 'lıŋgəʊ, -z
lingua franca ,lıŋgwə'fræŋkə
lingu|al (s. adj.), **-als, -ally** 'lıŋgw|əl,
   -əlz, -əlı
linguaphone (**L.**) 'lıŋgwəfəʊn
linguist, **-s** 'lıŋgwıst, -s
linguistic, **-s, -al, -ally** lıŋ'gwıstık, -s, -l,
   -əlı
linguistician, **-s** ,lıŋgwı'stıʃn, -z
linguo-dental ,lıŋgwəʊ'dentl
liniment, **-s** 'lınımənt [-nəm-], -s
lining (s.), **-s** 'laınıŋ, -z
link (s. v.), **-s, -ing, -ed** lıŋk, -s, -ıŋ, -t
   [lıŋt]
Linklater 'lıŋk,leıtə*
links (s.) lıŋks
Linley 'lınlı
Linlithgow lın'lıθgəʊ
Linlithgowshire lın'lıθgəʊ ʃə* [-,ʃıə*]
Linnae|an [-ne|-], **-us** lı'ni:|ən [-'nıən],
   -əs
linnet (**L.**), **-s** 'lınıt, -s
lino, **-s** 'laınəʊ, -z
lino-cut, **-s** 'laınəʊkʌt, -s
linoleum, **-s** lı'nəʊljəm [-lıəm], -z
linotype, **-s** 'laınəʊtaıp, -s
linseed, **-oil** 'lınsi:d, -'ɔıl
linsey, **-woolsey** 'lınzı, -'wʊlzı
lint lınt
lintel, **-s** 'lıntl, -z
Linthwaite 'lınθweıt
Lint|on, **-ot(t)** 'lınt|ən, -ɒt
lion, **-s; -ess/es** 'laıən, -z; -es/ız
   [-ıs/ız, laıə'nes/ız]
Lionel 'laıənl
Lion-heart 'laıənhɑ:t
lion-hearted 'laıən,hɑ:tıd
lion-hunter, **-s** 'laıən,hʌntə*, -z
lioniz|e [-is|e], **-es, -ing, -ed** 'laıənaız,
   -ız, -ıŋ, -d
lion-like 'laıənlaık
lion-tamer, **-s** 'laıən,teımə*, -z
lip (s. v.), **-s, -ping, -ped** lıp, -s, -ıŋ,
   -t
Lipari 'lıpərı ('li:pari)
lipogram, **-s** 'lıpəʊgræm, -z
Lippincott 'lıpıŋkət [-kɒt]
lip-reading 'lıp,ri:dıŋ
lip-salve, **-s** 'lıpsælv [-sɑ:lv], -z
Lipscomb(e) 'lıpskəm
lip-service 'lıp,sɜ:vıs
lip-stick, **-s** 'lıpstık, -s
Lipton 'lıptən

liquefaction ˌlɪkwɪˈfækʃn

lique|fy, -fies, -fying, -fied, -fier/s;
-fiable ˈlɪkwɪ|faɪ, -faɪz, -faɪɪŋ, -faɪd,
-faɪə*/z; -faɪəbl

liqueur, -s; -glass/es lɪˈkjʊə* [-ˈkjɔɛ*,
-ˈkjɔː*, -ˈkjɜː*, -ˈkɜː*], -z; -glɑːs/ɪz

liquid (s. adj.), -s, -est, -ly, -ness
ˈlɪkwɪd, -z, -ɪst, -lɪ, -nɪs [-nəs]

liquidat|e, -es, -ing, -ed, -or/s ˈlɪkwɪ-
deɪt, -s, -ɪŋ, -ɪd, -ə*/z

liquidation, -s ˌlɪkwɪˈdeɪʃn, -z

liquidity lɪˈkwɪdətɪ [-ɪtɪ]

liquor (s. v.), -s, -ing, -ed ˈlɪkə*, -z, -rɪŋ,
-d

liquorice ˈlɪkərɪs

lir|a, -as, -e ˈlɪər|ə, -əz, -ɪ

Lisa ˈliːzə, ˈlaɪzə

Lisb|et, -eth ˈlɪzb|ɪt [-et, -ət], -əθ [-əθ,
-ɪθ]

Lis|bon, -burn ˈlɪz|bən, -bɜːn

Liskeard lɪsˈkɑːd

lisle (thread) laɪl

Lisle laɪl, liːl
    Note.—Baron Lisle pronounces laɪl.

Lismore (in Scotland and Ireland)
lɪzˈmɔː* [-ˈmɔə*], (in Australia)
ˈlɪzmɔː* [-ˈmɔə*]

lisp (s. v.), -s, -ing/ly, -ed, -er/s lɪsp, -s,
-ɪŋ/lɪ, -t, -ə*/z

lissome, -ness ˈlɪsəm, -nɪs [-nəs]

Lisson ˈlɪsn

list (s. v.), -s, -ing, -ed lɪst, -s, -ɪŋ, -ɪd

list|en, -ens, -ening, -ened, -ener/s
ˈlɪs|n, -nz, -nɪŋ [-nɪŋ], -nd, -nə*/z
[-nə*/z]

Lister ˈlɪstə*

listerine ˈlɪstəriːn

listless, -ly, -ness ˈlɪstlɪs [-ləs], -lɪ, -nɪs
[-nəs]

Liston ˈlɪstən

Listowel lɪˈstəʊəl

Liszt lɪst

lit (from light) lɪt

litan|y, -ies ˈlɪtən|ɪ [-tn̩|ɪ], -ɪz

Litchfield ˈlɪtʃfiːld

literacy ˈlɪtərəsɪ

liter|al, -ally, -alness ˈlɪtər|əl, -əlɪ,
-əlnɪs [-nəs]

literali|sm, -st/s ˈlɪtərəlɪ|zəm, -st/s

literality ˌlɪtəˈrælətɪ [-ɪtɪ]

literar|y, -ily, -iness ˈlɪtərər|ɪ [-tr̩r|ɪ],
-əlɪ [-ɪlɪ], -mɪs [-ɪnəs]

literate (s. adj.), -s ˈlɪtərət [-rɪt], -s

literati ˌlɪtəˈrɑːtiː [old-fashioned -ˈreɪtaɪ]

literatim ˌlɪtəˈrɑːtɪm [-ˈreɪtɪm]

literature, -s ˈlɪtərətʃə* [-rɪtʃə*,
-ˌtjʊə*], -z

litharge ˈlɪθɑːdʒ

lithe, -r, -st, -ly, -ness laɪð, -ə*, -ɪst, -lɪ,
-nɪs [-nəs]

Litheby ˈlɪðɪbɪ [-ðəb-]

lither (supple) ˈlɪðə*

lithesome, -ness ˈlaɪðsəm, -nɪs [-nəs]

Lithgow ˈlɪθgəʊ

lithia ˈlɪθɪə [-θjə]

lithic ˈlɪθɪk

lithium ˈlɪθɪəm [-θjəm]

litho, -s ˈlaɪθəʊ, -z

lithochromatic, -s ˌlɪθəʊkrəʊˈmætɪk, -s

lithograph (s. v.), -s, -ing, -ed ˈlɪθəʊ-
grɑːf [-græf], -s, -ɪŋ, -t
    Note.—In printers' usage ˈlaɪθ-. *So
    also with derived words* (**litho**-
    grapher, *etc.*).

lithographer, -s lɪˈθɒgrəfə*, -z

lithographic, -al, -ally ˌlɪθəʊˈgræfɪk,
-l, -əlɪ

lithography lɪˈθɒgrəfɪ

lithoprint (s. v.), -s, -ing, -ed ˈlɪθəʊ-
prɪnt, -s, -ɪŋ, -ɪd

lithosphere, -s ˈlɪθəʊˌsfɪə*, -z

lithotyp|e (s. v.), -es, -ing, -ed, -er/s
ˈlɪθəʊtaɪp, -s, -ɪŋ, -t, -ə*/z

Lithuania, -n/s ˌlɪθjuːˈeɪnjə [-θjʊˈeɪ-,
-θuː-, -θʊˈeɪ-, -nɪə], -n/z

litigant, -s ˈlɪtɪgənt, -s

litigat|e, -es, -ing, -ed ˈlɪtɪgeɪt, -s, -ɪŋ,
-ɪd

litigation, -s ˌlɪtɪˈgeɪʃn, -z

litigious, -ly, -ness lɪˈtɪdʒəs, -lɪ, -nɪs
[-nəs]

litmus ˈlɪtməs

litotes ˈlaɪtəʊtiːz

litre, -s ˈliːtə*, -z

Littel lɪˈtel

litter (s. v.), -s, -ing, -ed ˈlɪtə*, -z, -rɪŋ, -d

litt|le (L.), -ler, -lest, -leness ˈlɪt|l, -lə*,
-lɪst, -lnɪs [-nəs]

Littlechild ˈlɪtltʃaɪld

little-englander, -s ˌlɪtlˈɪŋgləndə*
[rarely -ˈeŋg-], -z

little-go, -es ˈlɪtlgəʊ, -z

Littlehampton ˈlɪtlˌhæmptən [ˌ--ˈ--]

Littlejohn ˈlɪtldʒɒn

Littler ˈlɪtlə*

Littleton ˈlɪtltən

Litton ˈlɪtn

littoral, -s ˈlɪtərəl, -z

liturgic, -al, -ally lɪˈtɜːdʒɪk, -l, -əlɪ

liturgist, -s ˈlɪtədʒɪst [-tɜː-], -s

liturg|y, -ies ˈlɪtədʒ|ɪ [-tɜː-], -ɪz

livable ˈlɪvəbl

live (adj.) laɪv

liv|e (v.), -es, -ing, -ed, -er/s lɪv, -z, -ɪŋ,
-d, -ə*/z

live-circuit, -s ˈlaɪvˈsɜːkɪt, -s

299

livelihood, -s 'laɪvlɪhʊd, -z
livelong 'lɪvlɒŋ ['laɪv-]
livel|y, -ier, -iest, -iness 'laɪvl|ɪ, -ɪə* [-jə*], -ɪɪst [-jɪst], -ɪnɪs [-ɪnəs]
liv|en, -ens, -ening, -ened 'laɪv|n [-ən], -nz [-ənz], -ŋɪŋ [-nɪŋ, -ənɪŋ], -nd [-ənd]
Livens 'lɪvənz
liver, -s, -ish 'lɪvə*, -z, -rɪʃ
live-rail, -s ‚laɪv'reɪl, -z
Livermore 'lɪvəmɔː* [-mɔə*]
Liverpool 'lɪvəpuːl
Liverpudlian (s. adj.), -s ‚lɪvə'pʌdlɪən [-ljən], -z
liver|y, -ies, -ied 'lɪvər|ɪ, -ɪz, -ɪd
livery|man, -men 'lɪvərɪ|mən, -mən [-men]
livery-stable, -s 'lɪvərɪˌsteɪbl, -z
lives (plur. of life) laɪvz, (from live v.) lɪvz
Livesey 'lɪvsɪ, 'lɪvzɪ
live-stock 'laɪvstɒk
Livia 'lɪvɪə [-vjə]
livid, -est, -ly, -ness 'lɪvɪd, -ɪst, -lɪ, -nɪs [-nəs]
lividity lɪ'vɪdɪtɪ [-ɪtɪ]
living (s.), -s 'lɪvɪŋ, -z
living-room, -s 'lɪvɪŋrʊm [-ruːm], -z
living-space 'lɪvɪŋspeɪs
Livingston(e) 'lɪvɪŋstən
Livonia, -n/s lɪ'vəʊnjə [-nɪə], -n/z
Livy 'lɪvɪ
lixiviat|e, -es, -ing, -ed lɪk'sɪvɪeɪt, -s, -ɪŋ, -ɪd
Liza 'laɪzə
lizard (L.), -s 'lɪzəd, -z
Lizzie 'lɪzɪ
llama (L.), -s 'lɑːmə, -z
Llanberis læn'berɪs [θlæn-] (Welsh l̯an'berɪs)
Llandaff 'lændəf (Welsh l̯an'daːv)
Llandilo læn'daɪləʊ [θlæn-] (Welsh l̯an'dəɪlo)
Llandovery læn'dʌvərɪ [θlæn-] (Welsh l̯an'dəvrɪ)
Llandrindod Wells læn‚drɪndɒd'welz [θlæn-] (Welsh l̯an‚drɪndod'wels)
Llandudno læn'dɪdnəʊ [θlæn-, -'dʌd-] (Welsh l̯an'dɪdno)
Llanelly læ'neθlɪ [lə'n-, θlæn-, θlə'n-] (Welsh l̯an'eθli)
Llanfair 'lænfeə* ['θlæn-, -nvaɪə*] (Welsh l̯anvair)
Llanfairfechan ‚lænfeə'fekən [‚θlæn-, -nvaɪə've-, -exən] (Welsh l̯anvair-'vexan)
Llangattock læn'gætək [θlæn-] (Welsh l̯an'gatok)

Llangollen læn'gɒθlən [θlæn-, -'gɒθlen] (Welsh l̯an'gol̯en)
Llanrwst læn'ruːst [θlæn-] (Welsh l̯an'ruːst)
Llanuwchllyn læ'njuːklɪn [θlæ'n-, -uːxlɪn] (Welsh l̯an'iuxl̯ɪn)
Llewellyn (English name) luː'elɪn [lʊ'e-] (Welsh name) luː'elɪn [θlu-, lʊ'e-, θlʊ'e-] (Welsh l̯e'welɪn)
Llewelyn luː'elɪn [θlu-, lʊ'e-, θlʊ'e-] (Welsh l̯welɪn, l̯e'welɪn)
Lloyd lɔɪd
Llywelyn lə'welɪn [θlə-] (Welsh l̯ə'welɪn)
lo ləʊ
load (s. v.), -s, -ing, -ed ləʊd, -z, -ɪŋ, -ɪd
load-shedding 'ləʊdˌʃedɪŋ
loadstone, -s 'ləʊdstəʊn, -z
loa|f (s.), -ves ləʊ|f, -vz
loaf (v.), -s, -ing, -ed, -er/s ləʊf, -s, -ɪŋ, -t, -ə*/z
loaf-sugar 'ləʊfˌʃʊgə*
loam ləʊm
loam|y, -ier, -iest, -iness 'ləʊm|ɪ, -ɪə* [-jə*], -ɪɪst [-jɪst], -ɪnɪs [-ɪnəs]
loan (s. v.), -s, -ing, -ed ləʊn, -z, -ɪŋ, -d
loan-collection, -s 'ləʊnkəˌlekʃn, -z
loan-office, -s 'ləʊnˌɒfɪs, -ɪz
loanword, -s 'ləʊnwɜːd, -z
loath (adj.), -ness ləʊθ, -nɪs [-nəs]
loath|e (v.), -es, -ing/ly, -ed ləʊð, -z, -ɪŋ/lɪ, -d
loathl|y, -iness 'ləʊðl|ɪ, -ɪnɪs [-ɪnəs]
loathsome, -ly, -ness 'ləʊðsəm ['ləʊθs-], -lɪ, -nɪs [-nəs]
loaves (plur. of loaf) ləʊvz
lob (s. v.) (L.), -s, -bing, -bed, -ber/s lɒb, -z, -ɪŋ, -d, -ə*/z
lobb|y (s. v.), -ies, -ying, -ied 'lɒb|ɪ, -ɪz, -ɪŋ [-jɪŋ], -ɪd
lobe, -s, -d ləʊb, -z, -d
lobelia, -s ləʊ'biːljə [-lɪə], -z
lobotomy ləʊ'bɒtəmɪ
lobster, -s 'lɒbstə*, -z
lobular 'lɒbjʊlə*
lobule, -s 'lɒbjuːl, -z
loc|al, -als, -ally 'ləʊk|l, -lz, -əlɪ [-lɪ]
locale, -s ləʊ'kɑːl, -z
locali|sm, -st/s 'ləʊkəlɪ|zəm [-kl̩ɪ-], -st/s
localit|y, -ies ləʊ'kælət|ɪ [-ɪt|ɪ], -ɪz
localization [-isa-] ‚ləʊkəlaɪ'zeɪʃn [-klaɪ'z-, -kəlɪ'z-, -kl̩ɪ'z-]
localiz|e [-is|e], -es, -ing, -ed 'ləʊkəlaɪz [-kl̩aɪz], -ɪz, -ɪŋ, -d
Locarno ləʊ'kɑːnəʊ [lɒ'k-] (lo'karno)
locat|e, -es, -ing, -ed ləʊ'keɪt, -s, -ɪŋ, -ɪd
location, -s ləʊ'keɪʃn, -z

locative (s. adj.), -s 'lɒkətɪv, -z
loc. cit. ,lɒk'sɪt [,lɒkəʊsɪ'tɑ:təʊ, old-fashioned ,ləʊkəʊsɪ'teɪtəʊ]
loch (L.), -s lɒk [lɒx], -s
Lochaber lɒ'kɑ:bə* [-'kæb-, lɒ'x-]
Lochhead 'lɒkhed [in Scotland lɒx'hɛd]
Lochiel lɒ'ki:l [lɒ'xi:l]
Lochinvar ,lɒkɪn'vɑ:* [,lɒxɪn-]
Lochleven lɒk'li:vən [lɒx-]
Lochnagar ,lɒknə'gɑ:* [,lɒxn-]
lock (s. v.) (L.), -s, -ing, -ed lɒk, -s, -ɪŋ, -t
Locke lɒk
locker (L.), -s 'lɒkə*, -z
Lockerbie 'lɒkəbɪ
locket, -s 'lɒkɪt, -s
lockgate, -s ,lɒk'geɪt ['--], -s
Lockhart 'lɒkət, 'lɒkhɑ:t
    Note.—The Bruce-Lockhart family pronounce 'lɒkət (or in the Scottish manner 'lɒkərt).
Lockie 'lɒkɪ
lock-jaw 'lɒkdʒɔ:
lock-keeper, -s 'lɒk,ki:pə*, -z
lockout, -s 'lɒkaʊt, -s
Locksley 'lɒkslɪ
locksmith, -s 'lɒksmɪθ, -s
lockstitch, -es 'lɒkstɪtʃ, -ɪz
lock-up, -s 'lɒkʌp, -s
Lock|wood, -yer 'lɒk|wʊd, -jə*
locomotion ,ləʊkə'məʊʃn
locomotive (s. adj.), -s 'ləʊkə,məʊtɪv [,ləʊkə'm-], -z
locomotor (s.), -s 'ləʊkə,məʊtə*, -z
locomotor (adj.) ,ləʊkə'məʊtə* ['--,--]
locoum, -s 'ləʊkəm [-kʊm]
Locria, -n/s 'ləʊkrɪə, -n/z
Locris 'ləʊkrɪs
locum, -s 'ləʊkəm, -z
locum-tenens ,ləʊkəm'ti:nenz [-'ten-]
locus, loci 'ləʊkəs ['lɒkəs], 'ləʊsaɪ ['ləʊkaɪ, 'lɒki:]
locust, -s 'ləʊkəst, -s
locution, -s ləʊ'kju:ʃn [lɒ'k-], -z
locutor|y, -ies 'lɒkjʊtər|ɪ, -ɪz
lode, -s; -star/s, -stone/s ləʊd, -z; -stɑ:*/z, -stəʊn/z
lodge (s. v.) (L.), -es, -ing/s, -ed, -er/s lɒdʒ, -ɪz, -ɪŋ/z, -d, -ə*/z
lodg(e)ment, -s 'lɒdʒmənt, -s
lodging-hou|se, -ses 'lɒdʒɪŋhaʊ|s, -zɪz
Lodore ləʊ'dɔ:* [-'dɔə*]
Lodovico ,lɒdəʊ'vi:kəʊ
Lodowick 'lɒdəwɪk [-dəʊɪk]
Loe lu:
Loeb lɜ:b [ləʊb]
loess 'ləʊɪs [lɜ:s]
Loewe (English surname) 'ləʊɪ

Lofoten ləʊ'fəʊtən ['ləʊ,fəʊtən]
loft (s. v.), -s, -ing, -ed, -er/s lɒft, -s, -ɪŋ, -ɪd, -ə*/z
Lofthouse 'lɒftəs [-thaus]
Loftus 'lɒftəs
loft|y, -ier, -iest, -ily, -iness 'lɒft|ɪ, -ɪə* [-jə*], -ɪɪst [-jɪst], -ɪlɪ [-əlɪ], -ɪnɪs [-ɪnəs]
log, -s lɒg, -z
Logan (personal name) 'ləʊgən
logan (L.) (rocking-stone), -s 'lɒgən, -z
loganberr|y, -ies 'ləʊgənbər|ɪ [-,ber-], -ɪz
logarithm, -s 'lɒgərɪðəm [-ɪθəm], -z
logarithmic, -al, -ally ,lɒgə'rɪðmɪk [-ɪθm-], -l, -əlɪ
log-book, -s 'lɒgbʊk, -s
log-cabin, -s 'lɒg,kæbɪn, -z
loggerhead, -s 'lɒgəhed, -z
loggia, -s 'lɒʊdʒə ['lɒ-, -dʒɪə, -dʒjə], -z
logging 'lɒgɪŋ
Logia 'lɒgɪə
logic, -al, -ally 'lɒdʒɪk, -l, -əlɪ
logician, -s ləʊ'dʒɪʃn [lɒ'dʒ-], -z
Logie 'ləʊgɪ
logistic, -al, -s ləʊ'dʒɪstɪk [lɒ'dʒ-], -l, -s
logogram, -s 'lɒgəʊgræm, -z
logograph, -s 'lɒgəʊgrɑ:f [-græf], -s
logomach|ist/s, -y, -ies lɒ'gɒmək|ɪst/s, -ɪ, -ɪz
logopaedic, -s ,lɒgəʊ'pi:dɪk, -s
Log|os, -oi 'lɒg|ɒs, -ɔɪ
logotype, -s 'lɒgəʊtaɪp, -s
log-roll, -s, -ing, -ed, -er/s 'lɒgrəʊl, -z, -ɪŋ, -d, -ə*/z
Logue ləʊg
log-wood 'lɒgwʊd
Lohengrin 'ləʊɪŋgrɪn ['ləʊən-, -ŋg-] ('lo:əngri:n)
loin, -s lɔɪn, -z
loin|-cloth, -cloths 'lɔɪn|klɒθ [old-fashioned -klɔ:θ], -klɒθs [-klɔ:ðz, -klɔ:θs]
Lois 'ləʊɪs
loit|er, -ers, -ering, -ered, -erer/s 'lɔɪt|ə*, -əz, -ərɪŋ, -əd, -ərə*/z
loll, -s, -ing, -ed, -er/s lɒl, -z, -ɪŋ, -d, -ə*/z
Lollard, -s 'lɒləd [-lɑ:d], -z
lollipop, -s 'lɒlɪpɒp, -s
lollop, -s, -ing, -ed 'lɒləp, -s, -ɪŋ, -t
Lomax 'ləʊmæks [-məks]
Lombard, -s 'lɒmbəd [-bɑ:d, old-fashioned 'lʌmbəd], -z
Lombardic lɒm'bɑ:dɪk
Lombardy 'lɒmbədɪ [old-fashioned 'lʌm-]
Lomond 'ləʊmənd

Londesborough ˈlɒnzbərə

London, -er/s, -ism/s ˈlʌndən, -ə*/z, -ɪzəm/z

Londonderry (place) ˌlʌndənˈderɪ [also ˈ—,—]

Londonderry (Lord) ˈlʌndənderɪ [-derɪ]

lone ləʊn

lonel|y, -ier, -iest, -iness ˈləʊnl|ɪ, -ɪə* [-jə*], -ɪɪst [-jɪst], -ɪnɪs [-nəs]

lonesome, -ly, -ness ˈləʊnsəm, -lɪ, -nɪs [-nəs]

long (s. adj.) (L.), -s, -er, -est lɒŋ, -z, -gə*, -gɪst

long (v.), -s, -ing/ly, -ed, -er/s lɒŋ, -z, -ɪŋ/lɪ, -d, -ə*/z

longboat, -s ˈlɒŋbəʊt, -s

long-bow (L.), -s ˈlɒŋbəʊ, -z

long-drawn ˌlɒŋˈdrɔːn [also ˈ— when attributive]

long-drawn-out ˌlɒŋdrɔːnˈaʊt

longeron, -s ˈlɒndʒərən, -z

longeval lɒnˈdʒiːvl

longevity lɒnˈdʒevətɪ [-ɪtɪ]

Longfellow ˈlɒŋˌfeləʊ

Longford ˈlɒŋfəd

longhand ˈlɒŋhænd

long-headed ˌlɒŋˈhedɪd [ˈ—,—, esp. when attributive]

longing (s.), -s ˈlɒŋɪŋ, -z

Longinus lɒnˈdʒaɪnəs [lɒŋˈgiːnəs]

longish ˈlɒŋɪʃ

longitude, -s ˈlɒndʒɪtjuːd [-ŋgɪ-], -z

longitudin|al, -ally ˌlɒndʒɪˈtjuːdɪn|l [-ŋgɪ-], -əlɪ [-lɪ]

Longland ˈlɒŋlənd

Longleat ˈlɒŋliːt

long-leg|ged, -s ˈlɒŋleg|d [-ˌleg|ɪd, ˌ—ˈ-(-)], -z

long-lived ˌlɒŋˈlɪvd [also ˈ— when attributive]

Longman, -s ˈlɒŋmən, -z

long-off, -s ˌlɒŋˈɒf [old-fashioned -ˈɔːf], -s

long-on, -s ˌlɒŋˈɒn, -z

long-range ˌlɒŋˈreɪndʒ [also ˈ— when attributive]

Longridge ˈlɒŋgrɪdʒ

Long|sdon, -shanks ˈlɒŋ|zdən, -ʃæŋks

long-shore, -man, -men ˈlɒŋˈʃɔː* [-ʃəə*], -mən, -mən [-men]

long-sighted, -ness ˌlɒŋˈsaɪtɪd [ˈ—,—], -nɪs [-nəs]

Longstaff ˈlɒŋstɑːf

long-stop, -s ˈlɒŋstɒp, -s

long-suffering ˌlɒŋˈsʌfərɪŋ [ˈ—,—]

long-tailed ˈlɒŋteɪld

Longton ˈlɒŋtən

Longus ˈlɒŋgəs

long|ways, -wise ˈlɒŋ|weɪz, -waɪz

long-winded, -ness ˌlɒŋˈwɪndɪd, -nɪs [-nəs]

Lonsdale ˈlɒnzdeɪl

loo (s. v.) (L.), -es, -ing, -ed luː, -z, -ɪŋ, -d

loob|y, -ies ˈluːb|ɪ, -ɪz

Looe luː

loofah, -s ˈluːfə [-fɑː], -z

look (s. v.), -s, -ing, -ed, -er/s lʊk, -s, -ɪŋ, -t, -ə*/z

looker - on, lookers - on ˌlʊkərˈɒn, ˌlʊkəzˈɒn

looking-glass, -es ˈlʊkɪŋglɑːs, -ɪz

look-out ˈlʊkaʊt

loom, -s, -ing, -ed luːm, -z, -ɪŋ, -d

loon, -s luːn, -z

loon|y, -ies ˈluːn|ɪ, -ɪz

loop (s. v.), -s, -ing, -ed luːp, -s, -ɪŋ, -t

loophole, -s, -d ˈluːphəʊl, -z, -d

Loos (battlefield) ləʊs [luːs]

loos|e (s. adj. v.), -es; -er, -est, -ely, -eness; -ing, -ed luːs, -ɪz; -ə*, -ɪst, -lɪ, -nɪs [-nəs], -ɪŋ, -t

loos|en, -ens, -ening, -ened ˈluːs|n, -nz, -nɪŋ [-nɪŋ], -nd

loot (s. v.), -s, -ing, -ed, -er/s luːt, -s, -ɪŋ, -ɪd, -ə*/z

lop (s. v.), -s, -ping, -ped, -per/s lɒp, -s, -ɪŋ, -t, -ə*/z

lop|e (s. v.), -es, -ing, -ed ləʊp, -s, -ɪŋ, -t

lop-eared ˈlɒpˌɪəd

Lopez ˈləʊpez

lopping (s.), -s ˈlɒpɪŋ, -z

lop-sided, -ness ˌlɒpˈsaɪdɪd, -nɪs [-nəs]

loquacious, -ly, -ness ləʊˈkweɪʃəs [lɒˈk-], -lɪ, -nɪs [-nəs]

loquacity ləʊˈkwæsətɪ [lɒˈk-, -ɪtɪ]

lor lɔː*

Loraine lɒˈreɪn [ləˈr-]

Loram ˈlɔːrəm

lorcha, -s ˈlɔːtʃə, -z

lord (s. v.) (L.), -s, -ing, -ed lɔːd, -z, -ɪŋ, -ɪd

Note.—Lawyers addressing a judge in court sometimes pronounce my lord as mɪˈlʌd instead of the normal mɪˈlɔːd.

lordling, -s ˈlɔːdlɪŋ, -z

lord|ly, -ier, -iest, -iness ˈlɔːdl|ɪ, -ɪə* [-jə*], -ɪɪst [-jɪst], -ɪnɪs [-nəs]

Lord's-day, -s ˈlɔːdzdeɪ, -z

lordship (L.), -s ˈlɔːdʃɪp, -s

lore lɔː* [ləʊ*]

Loreburn ˈlɔːbɜːn [ˈ-bəb-]

Lorelei ˈlɔːrəlaɪ [ˈlɒr-] (loːrəˈlai)

Lorenzo lɒˈrenzəʊ [ləˈr-]

Loretto (school) ləˈretəʊ [lɔːˈr-]
lorgnette, -s lɔːˈnjet (lɔrɲet), -s
Lorie ˈlɒrɪ
lorimer (L.), -s ˈlɒrɪmə*, -z
loris, -es ˈlɔːrɪs, -ɪz
lorn lɔːn
Lorna ˈlɔːnə
Lorne lɔːn
Lorraine lɒˈreɪn [ləˈr-]
lorr|y, -ies ˈlɒr|ɪ, -ɪz
lor|y, -ies ˈlɔːr|ɪ, -ɪz
losable ˈluːzəbl
Los Angeles lɒsˈændʒɪliːz [-ˈæŋgɪ-, -dʒəl-, -lɪz, -lɪs]
los|e, -es, -ing, lost, loser/s luːz, -ɪz, -ɪŋ, lɒst [old-fashioned lɔːst], ˈluːzə*/z
loss, -es lɒs [old-fashioned lɔːs, and in compounds], -ɪz
loss-leader, -s ˌlɒsˈliːdə*, -z
lost (from lose) lɒst [lɔːst]
Lostwithiel lɒstˈwɪθɪəl [-θjəl]
lot (s. v.) (L.), -s, -ting, -ted lɒt, -s, -ɪŋ, -ɪd
loth ləʊθ
Lothair ləʊˈθeə*
Lothario ləʊˈθɑːrɪəʊ [-ˈθeər-]
Lothbury ˈləʊθbərɪ [ˈlɒθ-]
Lothian ˈləʊðjən [-ðɪən]
lotion, -s ˈləʊʃn, -z
lotter|y, -ies ˈlɒtər|ɪ, -ɪz
Lottie ˈlɒtɪ
lotto ˈlɒtəʊ
lotus, -es; -eater/s ˈləʊtəs, -ɪz; -ˌiːtə*/z
Lou luː
loud, -er, -est, -ly, -ness laʊd, -ə*, -ɪst, -lɪ, -nɪs [-nəs]
loud-hailer, -s ˌlaʊdˈheɪlə*, -z
Loud|on, -oun ˈlaʊd|n, -n
loud-speaker, -s ˌlaʊdˈspiːkə*, -z
Loudwater ˈlaʊdˌwɔːtə*
lough (lake), -s lɒk [lɒx], -s
Lough (surname) lʌf
Loughborough ˈlʌfbərə
Loughlin ˈlɒklɪn
Loughman ˈlʌfmən
Loughrea lɒkˈreɪ [lɒxˈr-]
Loughton ˈlaʊtn
Louie ˈluːɪ [ˈlʊɪ]
louis ˈluːɪ [ˈlʊɪ], (plur.) -z
Louis (English name) ˈluːɪ, ˈlʊɪ, ˈluːɪs, ˈlʊɪs, (French name) ˈluːɪ, ˈluːiː, ˈlʊɪ, ˈlʊiː (lwi)
Louisa luːˈiːzə [lʊˈiː-]
Louisburg ˈluːɪsbɜːg [ˈlʊɪs-]
louis-d'or, -s ˌluːɪˈdɔː* [ˌlʊɪ-], -z
Louise (English name) luːˈiːz [lʊˈiːz]
Louisiana luːˌiːzɪˈænə [lʊˌiː-, -ˈɑːnə]
Louisville ˈluːɪvɪl [ˈlʊɪ-]

loung|e (s. v.), -es, -ing, -ed, -er/s laʊndʒ, -ɪz, -ɪŋ, -d, -ə*/z
lounge-lizard, -s ˈlaʊndʒˌlɪzəd, -z
Lounsbury ˈlaʊnzbərɪ
lour (s. v.), -s, -ing, -ed ˈlaʊə*, -z, -rɪŋ, -d
Lourdes lʊəd (lurd)
Lourenço Marques ləˌrensəʊˈmɑːk
louse (s.), lice laʊs, laɪs
lous|e (v.), -es, -ing, -ed laʊz [laʊs], -ɪz, -ɪŋ, -d [laʊst]
lous|y, -ier, -iest, -ily, -iness ˈlaʊz|ɪ, -ɪə* [-jə*], -ɪɪst [-jɪst], -ɪlɪ [-əlɪ], -ɪnɪs [-məs]
lout (s. v.), -s, -ing, -ed laʊt, -s, -ɪŋ, -ɪd
Louth (in Ireland) laʊð, (in Lincoln-shire) laʊθ
loutish, -ly, -ness ˈlaʊtɪʃ, -lɪ, -nɪs [-nəs]
Louvain ˈluːvæ:ŋ [-veɪn, -væŋ] (luvẽ)
louver, -s ˈluːvə*, -z
Louvre ˈluːvrə [ˈluːvə*] (luːvr)
lovable, -ness ˈlʌvəbl, -nɪs [-nəs]
Lovat ˈlʌvət
lov|e (s. v.) (L.), -es, -ing/ly, -ed, -er/s lʌv, -z, -ɪŋ/lɪ, -d, -ə*/z
loveable, -ness ˈlʌvəbl, -nɪs [-nəs]
love-affair, -s ˈlʌvəˌfeə*, -z
lovebird, -s ˈlʌvbɜːd, -z
love|-child, -children ˈlʌv|tʃaɪld, -ˌtʃɪldrən [-ˌtʃʊldrən]
Loveday ˈlʌvdeɪ
love-feast, -s ˈlʌvfiːst, -s
Lovejoy ˈlʌvdʒɔɪ
love-knot, -s ˈlʌvnɒt, -s
Lovel(l) ˈlʌvl
Lovelace ˈlʌvleɪs
loveless ˈlʌvlɪs [-ləs]
love-letter, -s ˈlʌvˌletə*, -z
Lovell ˈlʌvl
lovelorn ˈlʌvlɔːn
lovel|y (s. adj.), -ies, -ier, -iest, -iness ˈlʌvl|ɪ, -ɪz, -ɪə* [-jə*], -ɪɪst [-jɪst], -ɪnɪs [-məs]
love-making ˈlʌvˌmeɪkɪŋ
love-match, -es ˈlʌvmætʃ, -ɪz
love-potion, -s ˈlʌvˌpəʊʃn, -z
lovesick ˈlʌvsɪk
love-song, -s ˈlʌvsɒŋ, -z
love-stor|y, -ies ˈlʌvˌstɔːr|ɪ, -ɪz
Lovett ˈlʌvɪt
Loveys ˈlʌvɪs
Lovibond ˈlʌvɪbɒnd
Lovick ˈlʌvɪk
loving-cup, -s ˈlʌvɪŋkʌp [ˌ-ˈ-], -s
loving-kindness, -es ˌlʌvɪŋˈkaɪndnɪs [-nəs], -ɪz
low (adj. v. adv.) (L.), -er, -est, -ness; -s, -ing, -ed ləʊ, -ə*, -ɪst, ˈləʊnɪs [-nəs]; -z, -ɪŋ, -d

303

low-born ˌləʊˈbɔːn [*also* '– *when attributive*]

low-bred ˌləʊˈbred [*also* '– *when attributive*]

low-brow 'ləʊbraʊ

low-church, -man, -men ˌləʊˈtʃɜːtʃ, -mən, -mən

low-down (*s. adj.*) 'ləʊdaʊn

Lowe ləʊ

Lowein (*surname*) 'ləʊɪn

Lowell 'ləʊəl ['ləʊel]

lower (*compar. of* low) 'ləʊə*

lower (*v.*) (*cause to descend*), -s, -ing, -ed 'ləʊə*, -z, -rɪŋ, -d

lower (*v.*) (*look threatening*), -s, -ing/ly, -ed 'laʊə*, -z, -rɪŋ/lɪ, -d

lower-case 'ləʊəkeɪs [ˌ–'-]

lowermost 'ləʊəməʊst [-məst]

Lowery 'laʊərɪ

Lowes ləʊz

Lowestoft 'ləʊstɒft ['ləʊɪs-, -təft, *locally* 'ləʊstəf]

Lowick 'ləʊɪk

Lowis 'laʊɪs

lowland (L.), -s, -er/s 'ləʊlənd, -z, -ə*/z

low-life ˌləʊˈlaɪf ['--]

lowl|y, -ier, -iest, -iness 'ləʊl|ɪ, -ɪə* [-jə*], -ɪɪst [-jɪst], -ɪnɪs [-ɪnəs]

low-lying ˌləʊˈlaɪɪŋ ['-,-- *when attributive*]

Lowndes laʊndz

low-necked ˌləʊˈnekt [*also* '– *when attributive*]

Lowood 'ləʊwʊd

low-pressure ˌləʊˈpreʃə* [*also* '-,-- *when attributive*]

Lowries 'laʊərɪz ['laʊr-]

Lowry 'laʊərɪ ['laʊrɪ]

Lowsley 'ləʊzlɪ

Lowson 'ləʊsn, 'laʊsn

low-spirited, -ly, -ness ˌləʊˈspɪrɪtɪd [-rət-], -lɪ, -nɪs [-nəs]

Lowth laʊθ

Lowther 'laʊðə*

Lowton 'ləʊtn

Lowville (*in U.S.A.*) 'laʊvɪl

Loxley 'lɒkslɪ

loy|al, -ally 'lɔɪ|əl, -əlɪ

loyalist, -s 'lɔɪəlɪst, -s

loyalt|y, -ies 'lɔɪəlt|ɪ, -ɪz

Loyd lɔɪd

Loyola lɔɪˈəʊlə ['lɔɪələ, 'lɔɪəʊlə]

lozenge, -s; -shaped 'lɒzɪndʒ [-zəndʒ], -ɪz; -ʃeɪpt

L. S. D. ˌeles'diː

Ltd. 'lɪmɪtɪd

lubber, -s 'lʌbə*, -z

lubberly 'lʌbəlɪ

Lubbock 'lʌbək

Lübeck 'luːbek ['ljuː-] ('lyːbɛk)

Lubin 'luːbɪn

lubricant, -s 'luːbrɪkənt ['ljuː-], -s

lubricat|e, -es, -ing, -ed, -or/s 'luːbrɪkeɪt ['ljuː-], -s, -ɪŋ, -ɪd, -ə*/z

lubrication, -s ˌluːbrɪ'keɪʃn [ˌljuː-], -z

lubricity luː'brɪsətɪ [ljuː-, -ɪtɪ]

Lucan 'luːkən ['ljuː-]

Lucania luː'keɪnjə [ljuː-, -nɪə]

lucarne, -s luː'kɑːn [ljuː-], -z

Lucas 'luːkəs ['ljuː-]

lucen|cy, -t 'luːsn|sɪ ['ljuː-], -t

Lucentio luː'senʃɪəʊ [ljuː-]

lucern(e) luː'sɜːn [ljuː's-, lʊ's-, 'luːsɜːn]

Lucerne luː'sɜːn [ljuː's-, lʊ's-]

Lucia 'luːsjə [-sɪə]

Lucian 'luːsjən [-sɪən, -ʃjən, -ʃɪən]

Luciana ˌluːsɪ'ɑːnə

Lucianus ˌluːsɪ'ɑːnəs [ˌljuː-, -sɪ'eɪn-]

lucid, -est, -ly, -ness 'luːsɪd ['ljuː-], -ɪst, -lɪ, -nɪs [-nəs]

lucidity luː'sɪdətɪ [ljuː-, -ɪtɪ]

Lucie 'luːsɪ ['ljuː-]

lucifer, -s 'luːsɪfə* ['ljuː-], -z

Lucilius luː'sɪlɪəs [-ljəs]

Lucina luː'saɪnə [ljuː-, luː'kiː-]

Lucius 'luːsjəs [-sɪəs, -ʃjəs, -ʃɪəs]

luck, -s lʌk, -s

luckless, -ly, -ness 'lʌklɪs [-ləs], -lɪ, -nɪs [-nəs]

Lucknow 'lʌknaʊ [ˌlʌk'n-] (*Hindi* ləkhnəw)

luck|y, -ier, -iest, -ily, -iness 'lʌk|ɪ, -ɪə*, -ɪɪst, -ɪlɪ [-əlɪ], -ɪnɪs [-ɪnəs]

Lucock 'lʌkɒk

lucrative, -ly 'luːkrətɪv ['ljuː-], -lɪ

lucre 'luːkə* ['ljuː-]

Lucrece luː'kriːs [ljuː-]

Lucreti|a, -us luː'kriːʃj|ə [lju:'k-, lʊ'k-, ljʊ'k-, -ʃɪ|ə, -ʃj|ə], -əs

lucubrat|e, -es, -ing, -ed 'luːkjuːbreɪt ['ljuː-, -kjʊ-], -s, -ɪŋ, -ɪd

lucubration, -s ˌluːkjuː'breɪʃn [ˌljuː-, -kjʊ-], -z

Lucullian luː'kʌlɪən [ljuː'k-, lʊ'k-, ljʊ'k-, -ljən]

Lucullus luː'kʌləs [ljuː'k-, lʊ'k-, ljʊ'k-]

Lucy 'luːsɪ

Lud lʌd

Ludgate 'lʌdgɪt [-geɪt, -gət]

ludicrous, -ly, -ness 'luːdɪkrəs ['ljuː-], -lɪ, -nɪs [-nəs]

Ludlow 'lʌdləʊ

ludo 'luːdəʊ

Ludovic 'luːdəvɪk

luff (s. v.) (L.), -s, -ing, -ed lʌf, -s, -ɪŋ, -t
lug (s. v.), -s, -ging, -ged lʌg, -z, -ɪŋ, -d
Lugano lu:ˈgɑ:nəʊ [lʊˈg-, ləˈg-] (luˈga:no)
Lugard lu:ˈgɑ:d
luggage ˈlʌgɪdʒ
lugger, -s ˈlʌgə*, -z
lugsail, -s ˈlʌgseɪl [nautical pronunciation -sl], -z
lugubrious, -ly, -ness lu:ˈgu:brɪəs [lju:ˈg-, lʊˈg-, ləˈg- -ˈgju:-], -lɪ, -nɪs [-nəs]
lug-worm, -s ˈlʌgwɜ:m, -z
Luia ˈlu:jə [ˈlu:ɪə]
Luke lu:k [lju:k]
lukewarm, -ly, -ness ˈlu:kwɔ:m [ˈlju:k-, ˌ-ˈ-], -lɪ, -nɪs [-nəs]
lull (s. v.), -s, -ing, -ed lʌl, -z, -ɪŋ, -d
lullab|y, -ies ˈlʌləb|aɪ, -aɪz
lumbago lʌmˈbeɪgəʊ
lumbar ˈlʌmbə*
lumb|er (s. v.), -ers, -ering, -ered -erer/s ˈlʌmb|ə*, -əz, -ərɪŋ, -əd, -ərə*/z
lumber-room, -s ˈlʌmbərʊm [-ru:m], -z
luminar|y, -ies ˈlu:mɪnər|ɪ [ˈlju:-], -ɪz
luminiferous ˌlu:mɪˈnɪfərəs [ˌlju:-]
luminosity ˌlu:mɪˈnɒsɪtɪ [ˌlju:-, -ɪtɪ]
luminous, -ly, -ness ˈlu:mɪnəs [ˈlju:-], -lɪ, -nɪs [-nəs]
Lumley ˈlʌmlɪ
lummy ˈlʌmɪ
lump (s. v.), -s, -ing, -ed lʌmp, -s, -ɪŋ, -t [lʌmt]
Lumphanan lʌmˈfænən
lumpish, -ly, -ness ˈlʌmpɪʃ, -lɪ, -nɪs [-nəs]
lump|y, -ier, -iest, -iness ˈlʌmp|ɪ, -ɪə* [-jə*], -ɪɪst [-jɪst], -ɪnɪs [-ɪnəs]
lunacy ˈlu:nəsɪ [ˈlju:-]
lunar ˈlu:nə* [ˈlju:-]
lunate ˈlu:neɪt [ˈlju:-, -nɪt]
lunated ˈlu:neɪtɪd [ˈlju:-]
lunatic (s. adj.), -s ˈlu:nətɪk, -s
lunation, -s lu:ˈneɪʃn [lju:ˈn-, lʊˈn-, ljʊˈn-], -z
Luncarty ˈlʌŋkətɪ
lunch (s. v.), -es, -ing, -ed lʌntʃ, -ɪz, -ɪŋ, -t
luncheon, -s ˈlʌntʃən, -z
Lund lʊnd
Lundy ˈlʌndɪ
lune, -s lu:n [lju:n], -z
lunette, -s lu:ˈnet [lju:ˈn-, lʊˈn-, ljʊˈn-], -s
lung, -s lʌŋ, -z
lung|e (s. v.), -es, -ing, -ed lʌndʒ, -ɪz, -ɪŋ, -d

lunged (furnished with lungs) lʌŋd, (from lunge) lʌndʒd
lung-fish, -es ˈlʌŋfɪʃ, -ɪz
lunul|a, -ae ˈlu:njʊl|ə [ˈlju:-], -i:
lunule, -s ˈlu:nju:l [ˈlju:-], -z
Lupercal ˈlu:pəkæl [ˈlju:-, -pɜ:-]
Lupercalia ˌlu:pəˈkeɪljə [ˌlju:-, -pɜ:ˈk-, -lɪə]
lupin(e) (flower), -s ˈlu:pɪn [ˈlju:-], -z
lupine (adj.) (wolfish) ˈlu:paɪn [ˈlju:-]
lupulin ˈlu:pjʊlɪn [ˈlju:-]
lupus ˈlu:pəs [ˈlju:-]
lurch (s. v.), -es, -ing, -ed lɜ:tʃ, -ɪz, -ɪŋ, -t
lur|e (s. v.), -es, -ing, -ed ljʊə* [lʊə*, ljɔə*, ljɔ:*], -z, -rɪŋ, -d
lurid, -ly, -ness ˈljʊərɪd [ˈlʊər-, ˈljɔər-, ˈljɔ:r-], -lɪ, -nɪs [-nəs]
lurk, -s, -ing, -ed, -er/s lɜ:k, -s, -ɪŋ, -t, -ə*/z
lurking-place, -s ˈlɜ:kɪŋpleɪs, -ɪz
Lusaka lu:ˈsɑ:kə [lʊˈs-]
Lusa|tia, -tian/s lu:ˈseɪ|ʃjə [-ʃɪə, -ʃə], -ʃjən/z [-ʃɪən/z, -ʃn/z]
luscious, -ly, -ness ˈlʌʃəs, -lɪ, -nɪs [-nəs]
lush (L.) lʌʃ
Lushington ˈlʌʃɪŋtən
Lusiad, -s ˈlu:sɪæd [ˈlju:-], -z
Lusitania ˌlu:sɪˈteɪnjə [ˌlju:-, -nɪə]
lust (s. v.), -s, -ing, -ed lʌst, -s, -ɪŋ, -ɪd
lust|ful, -fully, -fulness ˈlʌst|fʊl, -fʊlɪ [-fəlɪ], -fʊlnɪs [-nəs]
lustration, -s lʌˈstreɪʃn, -z
lustre, -s; -less ˈlʌstə*, -z; -lɪs [-ləs]
lustrel ˈlʌstrəl
lustrous, -ly, -ness ˈlʌstrəs, -lɪ, -nɪs [-nəs]
lustr|um, -ums, -a ˈlʌstr|əm, -əmz, -ə
lust|y, -ier, -iest, -ily, -iness ˈlʌst|ɪ, -ɪə* [-jə*], -ɪɪst [-jɪst], -ɪlɪ [-əlɪ], -ɪnɪs [-ɪnəs]
lute, -s; -string/s lu:t [lju:t], -s; -strɪŋ/z
lutenist [-ta-], -s ˈlu:tənɪst [ˈlju:-, -tʊɪst], -s
Luth|er, -eran/s, -eranism, -erism ˈlu:θ|ə* [ˈlju:-], -ərən/z, -ərənɪzəm, -ərɪzəm
Lutine (bell at Lloyd's) lu:ˈti:n
lutist, -s ˈlu:tɪst [ˈlju:-], -s
Luton ˈlu:tn
Lutterworth ˈlʌtəwəθ [-wɜ:θ]
Luttrell ˈlʌtrəl
Lutwyche ˈlʌtwɪtʃ
Lutyens (English surname) ˈlʌtʃənz [-tjənz]

305

lux lʌks
luxe lʊks [luːks, lʌks] (lyks)
Luxemb(o)urg 'lʌksəmbɜːg
Luxor 'lʌksɔː*
Luxulyan lʌk'sɪljən [-'sʌl-, -lɪən]
luxurian|ce, -t/ly lʌg'zjʊərɪən|s
[ləg'zj-, lʌk'sj-, lək'sj-, -jɔːr-, -jɔːr-, lʌg'ʒʊə-, ləg'ʒ-], -t/lɪ
luxuriat|e, -es, -ing, -ed lʌg'zjʊərɪeɪt [ləg'zj-, lʌk'sj-, lək'sj-, -jɔːr-, -jɔːr-, lʌg'ʒʊə-, ləg'ʒ-], -s, -ɪŋ, -ɪd
luxurious, -ly, -ness lʌg'zjʊərɪəs [ləg'zj-, lʌk'sj-, lək'sj-, -jɔːr-, -jɔːr-, lʌg'ʒʊə-, ləg'ʒ-], -lɪ, -nɪs
luxur|y, -ies 'lʌkʃər|ɪ [-kʃʊr-], -ɪz
Luzon luː'zɒn
Lyall 'laɪəl
lycée, -s 'liːseɪ (lise), -z
Lycett 'laɪsɪt [-set]
lyceum (L.), -s laɪ'sɪəm [-'siːəm], -z
lychee, -s ˌlaɪ'tʃiː ['—, 'lɪtʃiː, 'liː-], -z
lychgate, -s 'lɪtʃgeɪt, -s
lychnis 'lɪknɪs
Lycia, -n/s 'lɪsɪə [-sjə, -ʃɪə, -ʃjə], -n/z
Lycidas 'lɪsɪdæs
Lycoming laɪ'kɒmɪŋ
lycopodium, -s ˌlaɪkə'pəʊdjəm [-dɪəm], -z
Lycurgus laɪ'kɜːgəs
Lydall 'laɪdl
Lydd lɪd
lyddite 'lɪdaɪt
Lydekker laɪ'dekə*
Lydgate (fifteenth-century poet) 'lɪdgeɪt [-gɪt], (lane in Sheffield) 'lɪdʒɪt
Lydia, -n/s 'lɪdɪə [-djə], -n/z
Lydon 'laɪdn
lye (L.) laɪ
Lyell 'laɪəl
Lyghe laɪ
Lygon 'lɪgən
lying (from lie), -ly 'laɪɪŋ, -lɪ
lying-in ˌlaɪɪŋ'ɪn ['— when attributive]

Lyly 'lɪlɪ
Lyme Regis ˌlaɪm'riːdʒɪs
Lymington 'lɪmɪŋtən
Lympany (surname) 'lɪmpənɪ
lymph, -s; -ous lɪmf, -s; -əs
lymphatic, -s lɪm'fætɪk, -s
Lympne lɪm
Lynam 'laɪnəm
lynch (L.), -es, -ing, -ed; -law lɪntʃ, -ɪz, -ɪŋ, -t; -lɔː
Lynd|hurst, -on 'lɪnd|hɜːst, -ən
Lynmouth 'lɪnməθ
Lynn lɪn
Lynton 'lɪntən
lynx, -es lɪŋks, -ɪz
lynx-eyed 'lɪŋksaɪd
Lyon (surname) 'laɪən
Lyonesse ˌlaɪə'nes [ˌlaɪɒ'n-]
Lyons (English surname) 'laɪənz, (French city) 'laɪənz, 'liːɔ̃ŋ (or as French ljɔ̃)
Lyr|a (constellation), -ae 'laɪər|ə, -iː
lyrate 'laɪərɪt [-reɪt, -rət]
lyre, -s; -bird/s 'laɪə*, -z; -bɜːd/z
lyric (L.), -s, -al, -ally 'lɪrɪk, -s, -l, -əlɪ
lyricism 'lɪrɪsɪzəm
lyrist (player on the lyre), -s 'laɪərɪst ['lɪr-], -s
lyrist (lyric poet), -s 'lɪrɪst, -s
Lysaght 'laɪsət, 'laɪsaːt
Lysander laɪ'sændə*
Lysias 'lɪsɪæs
Lysicrates laɪ'sɪkrətiːz
Lysippus laɪ'sɪpəs
Lysistrata laɪ'sɪstrətə
lysol 'laɪsɒl
Lystra 'lɪstrə
Lyte laɪt
Lytham 'lɪðəm
Lythe laɪð
Lyttelton 'lɪtltən
Lytton 'lɪtn
Lyveden 'lɪvdən

M

M (*the letter*), -'s em, -z
ma (*mother*), -s mɑː, -z
ma (*note in Tonic Sol-fa*), -s mɔː, -z
ma'am mæm [mɑːm, məm, m]
    Note.—mɑːm, or alternatively mæm,
    is used in addressing members of
    the royal family.
Maas (*English surname*) mɑːz, (*river in
    Holland*) mɑːs
Mab mæb
Mabel 'meɪbl
Mablethorpe 'meɪblθɔːp
Mabley 'mæblɪ
Mabs mæbz
Mac mæk
macabre mə'kɑːbrə [mæˈk-, -bə*]
macadam mə'kædəm
MacAdam mə'kædəm, mək'ædəm
macadamization [-isa-] mə,kædəmaɪ-
    'zeɪʃn
macadamiz|e [-is|e], -es, -ing, -ed
    mə'kædəmaɪz, -ɪz, -ɪŋ, -d
MacAdoo ,mækə'duː, 'mækədu:
Macalister mə'kælɪstə*
McAll mə'kɔːl
McAllister mə'kælɪstə*
McAloren ,mækə'lɔːrən
McAlpine mə'kælpɪn, mə'kælpaɪn
Macan mə'kæn
MacAnnaly ,mækə'nælɪ
Macao mə'kaʊ
McAra mə'kɑːrə
macaroni ,mækə'rəʊnɪ
macaroon, -s ,mækə'ruːn ['--- *when
    attributive*], -z
MacArthur mə'kɑːθə*, mək'ɑːθə*
macassar (M.); -oil mə'kæsə*; -r'ɔɪl
    [-ə'ɔɪl]
Macaulay mə'kɔːlɪ
M(a)cAvoy 'mækəvɔɪ
macaw, -s mə'kɔː, -z
Mc|Bain, -Bean mək|'beɪn, -'beɪn
Macbeth mək'beθ [mæk-]
    Note.—In Scotland always mək-.
McBride mək'braɪd
Maccabees 'mækəbiːz
Maccabeus ,mækə'biːəs [-'bɪəs]
McCall [MacC-] mə'kɔːl
McCallie mə'kɔːlɪ

McCallum [MacC-] mə'kæləm
McCann mə'kæn
MacCarthy mə'kɑːθɪ
McClellan mə'klelən
Macclesfield 'mæklzfiːld [-lsf-]
McClintock mə'klɪntək [-tɒk]
McClure [M'Clure] mə'klʊə*
McConochie mə'kɒnəkɪ [-əxɪ]
McCormick mə'kɔːmɪk
McCorquodale mə'kɔːkədeɪl
Mc|Crae, -Crea mə|'kreɪ, -'kreɪ
McCulloch mə'kʌlək [-ləx]
MacCumhail mə'kuːl
MacCunn mə'kʌn
MacDaire mək'dɑːrə
MacDonald [Macd-] mək'dɒnəld [mæk-]
McDonald mək'dɒnəld
MacDonnell [Macd-] ,mækdə'nel, (*in
    Ireland*) mək'dɒnl
McDonough mək'dʌnə
MacDougal [Macd-] mək'duːgl [mæk-]
McDougall mək'duːgl
McDowell mək'daʊəl [-el]
MacDuff mək'dʌf [mæk-]
    Note.—In Scotland always mək-.
mace, -s meɪs, -ɪz
McEachran mə'kekrən [-exr-]
Macedon 'mæsɪdən
Macedonia, -n/s ,mæsɪ'dəʊnjə [-nɪə],
    -n/z
McElderry 'mæklderɪ
McEldowney 'mækldaʊnɪ
MacElwain mə'kelweɪn, mək'el-, 'mækl-
    weɪn
McElwin mə'kelwɪn, mək'el-
macerat|e, -es, -ing, -ed 'mæsəreɪt, -s,
    -ɪŋ, -ɪd
McErlain 'mækələɪn
McEwen mə'kjuːən [-ɪn]
McFadzean mək'fædʒən
MacFarlane mək'fɑːlɪn [-lən]
Macfarren mək'fær ən
Macfie mək'fiː [mæk-]
McGahey mə'gæhɪ [-'gæxɪ], mə'geɪɪ
McGee mə'giː
MacGillicuddy (*Reeks*) mə'gɪlɪkʌdɪ,
    (*family name*) 'mæglɪkʌdɪ
McGillivray mə'gɪlɪvrɪ [-'gɪlv-, -'glɪv-,
    -reɪ]

307

McGowan məˈgaʊən
McGrath məˈgrɑː
McGregor məˈgregə*
MacGregor [Macg-, MˈG-] məˈgregə*
mach mɑːk [mæk, mɒk]
Machen ˈmeɪtʃən [-tʃɪn], ˈmækɪn
machete, -s məˈtʃetɪ [-ˈtʃeɪtɪ], -z
Machiavelli ˌmækɪəˈvelɪ [-kjə-]
machiavellian ˌmækɪəˈvelɪən [-kjə-, -ljən]
machicolat|e, -es, -ing, -ed mæˈtʃɪkəʊleɪt [məˈtʃ-], -s, -ɪŋ, -ɪd
Machin ˈmeɪtʃɪn
machinat|e, -es, -ing, -ed, -or/s ˈmækɪneɪt [ˈmæʃ-], -s, -ɪŋ, -ɪd, -ə*/z
machination, -s ˌmækɪˈneɪʃn [ˌmæʃ-], -z
machin|e (s. v.), -es, -ing, -ed; -e-gun/s məˈʃiːn, -z, -ɪŋ, -d; -gʌn/z
machine-made məˈʃiːnmeɪd
machinery məˈʃiːnərɪ
machine-tool, -s məˈʃiːntuːl, -z
machinist, -s məˈʃiːnɪst, -s
McIlrath ˈmæklrɑːθ
MacIlwain ˈmæklweɪn
MacIlwraith [McI-] ˈmæklreɪθ
Macindoe ˈmækɪnduː
MacInn|es, -is məˈkɪn|ɪs, -ɪs
McIntosh ˈmækɪntɒʃ
MacIntyre ˈmækɪntaɪə*
Macirone ˌmætʃɪˈrəʊnɪ
MacIvor məˈkiːvə*, məˈkaɪvə*
Mack mæk
Mackay məˈkaɪ, məˈkeɪ
   Note.—məˈkeɪ mainly in U.S.A.
McKeag məˈkiːg
McKee məˈkiː
McKenna məˈkenə
Mackenzie məˈkenzɪ
mackerel, -s ˈmækrəl, -z
Mackerras məˈkerəs
McKichan məˈkɪkən [-ˈkɪxən]
Mackie ˈmækɪ
McKie məˈkaɪ, məˈkiː
Mackin ˈmækɪn
Mackin|lay, -ley məˈkɪn|lɪ, -lɪ
McKinley məˈkɪnlɪ
mackintosh (M.), -es ˈmækɪntɒʃ, -ɪz
Mackmurdo mækˈmɜːdəʊ [mæk-]
Mackowie [MacK-] məˈkaʊɪ
MacLachlan məˈklɒklən [-ˈklɒxlən], məˈklæklən [-ˈklæxlən]
MacLaglan məkˈlæglən
M(a)cl|aren, -aurin məˈkl|ærən, -ɔːrɪn
McLaughlin məˈklɒklɪn [-ɒxlɪn]
McˈLay məˈkleɪ
Macl|ean(e) (surname), -ear məˈkl|eɪn [-ˈkl|iːn], -ɪə*
McLean məˈkleɪn

MacLehose ˈmæklhəʊz
Macleod məˈklaʊd
McLeod məˈklaʊd
MacLiammoir məkˈlɪəmɔː*
Maclise məˈkliːs
Macmahon məkˈmɑːən
MacManus məkˈmænəs, -ˈmɑːnəs, -ˈmeɪnəs
McMaster məkˈmɑːstə*
Macmillan məkˈmɪlən [mæk-]
Macmorran məkˈmɒrən [mæk-]
MacNab məkˈnæb
Macnaghten [McN-] məkˈnɔːtn
Macnamara ˌmæknəˈmɑːrə
MacNaught, -on məkˈnɔːt [mæk-], -n
MacNeice məkˈniːs
Mâcon (in France, wine) ˈmɑːkɔ̃ːŋ [ˈmæ-, -kɒn, -kən] (makɔ̃)
Macon (in U.S.A.) ˈmeɪkən
Maconchy məˈkɒŋkɪ
Maconochie məˈkɒnəkɪ [-əxɪ]
MacOuart məˈkjuːət [-ˈkjʊət]
McOutra məˈkuːtrə
Macpelah mækˈpiːlə
MacPherson [Macph-] məkˈfɜːsn [mæk-]
Macquarie məˈkwɒrɪ
Macquoid məˈkwɔɪd
Macready məˈkriːdɪ
macrocosm, -s ˈmækrəʊkɒzəm, -z
macron, -s ˈmækrɒn, -z
Macrow məˈkrəʊ
McShea məkˈʃeɪ
MacSwiney məkˈswiːnɪ [mæk-]
MacTavish məkˈtævɪʃ
macul|a, -ae ˈmækjʊl|ə, -iː
McVeagh məkˈveɪ
McVean məkˈveɪn
McVit(t)ie məkˈvɪtɪ
mad; mad|der, -dest, -ly, -ness mæd; ˈmæd|ə*, -ɪst, -lɪ, -nɪs [-nəs]
Madagascar ˌmædəˈgæskə*
madam ˈmædəm
madame (M.) ˈmædəm
Madan ˈmædən, ˈmeɪdn
madcap, -s ˈmædkæp, -s
Maddalo ˈmædələʊ
madd|en (M.), -ens, -ening, -ened ˈmæd|n, -nz, -ŋɪŋ [-nɪŋ], -nd
madder (plant, colour), -s ˈmædə*, -z
madding ˈmædɪŋ
Maddox ˈmædəks
made (from make) meɪd
Madeira, -s məˈdɪərə, -z
Madeleine (English name) ˈmædlɪn [-dəlɪn, -eɪn]
Madeley (in Salop) ˈmeɪdlɪ
mademoiselle, -s ˌmædəm(w)əˈzel [ˌmæmwəˈzel] (madmwazɛl), -z

Madge mædʒ
madhou|se, -ses 'mædhaʊ|s, -zɪz
Madingley 'mædɪŋlɪ
Madison 'mædɪsn
mad|man, -men 'mæd|mən, -mən
  [-men]
Madoc 'mædək
Madonna, -s mə'dɒnə, -z
Madras mə'drɑːs [-'dræs]
madrepore, -s ˌmædrɪ'pɔː* [-'pɔə*], -z
Madrid mə'drɪd
madrigal, -s 'mædrɪgl, -z
madrigalist, -s 'mædrɪgəlɪst, -s
Madura (in S. India) 'mædjʊrə [-dʒʊ-,
  -dʊ-]
Maecenas miːˈsiːnæs [mɪ'-, maɪ's-,
  -nəs]
maelstrom 'meɪlstrɒm [-strəʊm]
maenad, -s 'miːnæd, -z
maestoso ˌmɑːe'stəʊzəʊ [maɪ's-, -əʊsəʊ]
maestro, -s mɑː'estrəʊ ['maɪstrəʊ], -z
Maeterlinck 'meɪtəlɪŋk ['mɑːt-]
Mae West, -s ˌmeɪ'west, -s
Mafeking 'mæfɪkɪŋ [-fə-]
maffick, -s, -ing, -ed 'mæfɪk, -s, -ɪŋ, -t
mafia 'mæfɪə ['mɑː-, -fjə]
mag (M.), -s mæg, -z
Magan 'meɪgən, mə'gæn
magazine, -s ˌmægə'ziːn [rarely '---], -z
  Note.—The stressing '--- is usual in
  the N. of England, but uncommon
  in the S.
Magdala 'mægdələ
magdalen, -s 'mægdəlɪn, -z
Magdalen (biblical name, modern Christian name, Canadian islands) 'mægdəlɪn, (Oxford college and street)
  'mɔːdlɪn
Magdalene (biblical name) ˌmægdə'liːnɪ
  ['mægdəliːn, -lɪn], (modern Christian
  name) 'mægdəlɪn, (Cambridge college
  and street) 'mɔːdlɪn
Magdalenian ˌmægdə'liːnjən [-nɪən]
Magdeburg 'mægdəbɜːg [-dɪb-] ('mak-
  dəburk, -burç)
mage, -s meɪdʒ, -ɪz
Magee mə'giː
Magellan mə'gelən
magenta (M.) mə'dʒentə
Maggersfontein 'mɑːgəz,fɒnteɪn ['---,-]
Maggie 'mægɪ
Maggiore ˌmædʒɪ'ɔːrɪ [mæ'dʒɔːrɪ,
  mə'dʒɔːrɪ] (mad'dʒɔːre)
maggot, -s, -y 'mægət, -s, -ɪ
Maghull (near Liverpool) mə'gʌl
Magi 'meɪdʒaɪ [-gaɪ]
magic (s. adj.), -al, -ally 'mædʒɪk, -l,
  -əlɪ

magician, -s mə'dʒɪʃn, -z
magic-lantern, -s ˌmædʒɪk'læntən, -z
magilp mə'gɪlp
Maginot 'mæzɪnəʊ ['mædʒɪ-] (maʒino)
magisterial, -ly ˌmædʒɪ'stɪərɪəl, -ɪ
magistrac|y, -ies 'mædʒɪstrəs|ɪ, -ɪz
magistral mə'dʒɪstrəl [mæ'dʒ-]
magistrate, -s 'mædʒɪstreɪt [-trɪt,
  -strət], -s
magistrature, -s 'mædʒɪstrəˌtjʊə*
  [-,tʃʊə*, -tʃə*], -z
Magna Carta ˌmægnə'kɑːtə
magnanimity ˌmægnə'nɪmətɪ [-rɪtɪ]
magnanimous, -ly mæg'nænɪməs
  [məg-], -lɪ
magnate, -s 'mægneɪt [-nɪt], -s
magnesia (substance) mæg'niːʃə [məg-,
  -ʃjə, -ʃɪə, -zjə, -zɪə, -ʒə]
Magnesia (city) mæg'niːzjə [-zɪə, -ʒjə,
  -ʒɪə, -ʃjə, -ʃɪə]
magnesium mæg'niːzjəm [məg-, -zɪəm,
  -sjəm, -sɪəm, -ʃjəm, -ʃɪəm]
magnet, -s 'mægnɪt, -s
magnetic, -al, -ally mæg'netɪk [məg-],
  -l, -əlɪ
magnetism 'mægnɪtɪzəm [-nət-]
magnetiz|e [-is|e], -es, -ing, -ed, -er/s
  'mægnɪtaɪz [-nət-], -ɪz, -ɪŋ, -d, -ə*/z
magneto, -s mæg'niːtəʊ [məg-], -z
magnetron, -s 'mægnɪtrɒn, -z
Magnificat, -s mæg'nɪfɪkæt [məg-], -s
magnification, -s ˌmægnɪfɪ'keɪʃn, -z
magnificen|ce, -t/ly mæg'nɪfɪsn|s
  [məg-], -t/lɪ
magnifico, -s mæg'nɪfɪkəʊ, -z
magni|fy, -fies, -fying, -fied, -fier/s;
  -fiable 'mægnɪ|faɪ, -faɪz, -faɪɪŋ, -faɪd,
  -faɪə*/z; -faɪəbl
magniloquen|ce, -t mæg'nɪləʊkwən|s, -t
magnitude, -s 'mægnɪtjuːd, -z
magnolia, -s mæg'nəʊljə [məg-, -lɪə], -z
magnum, -s 'mægnəm, -z
magnum bonum, -s ˌmægnəm'bəʊnəm
  [-'bɒn-], -z
magnum opus ˌmægnəm'əʊpəs [-'ɒpəs]
Magnus 'mægnəs
Magog 'meɪgɒg
magpie, -s 'mægpaɪ, -z
Magrath mə'grɑː
Magruder mə'gruːdə*
Maguiness mə'gɪnɪs [-nəs]
Maguire mə'gwaɪə*
Ma|gus, -gi 'meɪ|gəs, -dʒaɪ [-gaɪ]
Magyar 'mægjɑː* [-gɪɑː*], -z
Mahaffy mə'hæfɪ
Mahan mə'hæn, mɑːn
Mahanaim ˌmeɪə'neɪɪm [usual Jewish
  pronunciation ˌmɑːhɑː'nɑːɪm]

309

Mahany 'mɑːnɪ
maharajah, -s ˌmɑːhəˈrɑːdʒə (*Hindi* məharaɟa), -z
maharanee, -s ˌmɑːhəˈrɑːniː (*Hindi* məharani), -z
mahatma, -s məˈhɑːtmə [-ˈhæt-] (*Hindi* məhatma), -z
Mahdi, -s 'mɑːdiː [-dɪ], -z
mah-jong(g) mɑːˈdʒɒŋ
Mahler 'mɑːlə*
mahl-stick, -s 'mɔːlstɪk, -s
Mahmud mɑːˈmuːd
mahogany məˈhɒgənɪ [-gn̩ɪ]
Mahomet (*prophet*) məˈhɒmɪt ['merə-met, 'merəmɪt], (*English surname*) 'merəmet [-mɪt]
Mahometan, -s məˈhɒmɪtən, -z
Mahommed məˈhɒmɪd [-med]
Mahommedan, -s məˈhɒmɪdən, -z
Mahon mɑːn, məˈhuːn, məˈhəʊn
Mahon(e)y 'mɑːənɪ ['mɑːnɪ]
mahout, -s məˈhaʊt, -s
Mahratta, -s məˈrætə, -z
maia 'maɪə
maid, -s meɪd, -z
Maida 'meɪdə
maidan (M.), -s maɪˈdɑːn, -z
maiden (*s. adj.*), -s, -ly; -hair/s 'meɪdn̩, -z, -lɪ; -heə*/z
Maidenhead 'meɪdnhed
maidenhood 'meɪdnhʊd
maiden-name, -s 'meɪdnneɪm, -z
maid-servant, -s 'meɪdˌsɜːvənt, -s
Maidstone 'meɪdstən [-stəʊn]
maieutic maɪˈjuːtɪk [maɪˈj-]
mail (*s. v.*), -s, -ing, -ed meɪl, -z, -ɪŋ, -d
mail-bag, -s 'meɪlbæg, -z
mail-cart, -s 'meɪlkɑːt, -s
mail-coach, -es 'meɪlkəʊtʃ, -ɪz
Maillard (*surname*) 'meɪləd
mail-order 'meɪlˌɔːdə*
mail-train, -s 'meɪltreɪn, -z
maim, -s, -ing, -ed meɪm, -z, -ɪŋ, -d
main (*s. adj.*), -s, -ly meɪn, -z, -lɪ
Main (*German river*) maɪn [meɪn]
mainbrace, -s 'meɪnbreɪs, -ɪz
Maine meɪn
mainland 'meɪnlənd [-lænd]
mainmast, -s 'meɪnmɑːst [*nautical pronunciation* -məst], -s
mainsail, -s 'meɪnseɪl [*nautical pronunciation* -sl̩], -z
mainspring, -s 'meɪnsprɪŋ, -z
mainstay, -s 'meɪnsteɪ, -z
mainstream 'meɪnstriːm [ˌ-'-]
maintain, -s, -ing, -ed, -er/s; -able meɪnˈteɪn [mən-, men-], -z, -ɪŋ, -d, -ə*/z; -əbl

maintenance 'meɪntənəns [-tɪn-, -tɲəns, -tnəns]
Mainwaring 'mænərɪŋ, (*in Wales* 'meɪn-wərɪŋ)
Mainz maɪnts
Mais meɪz
Maisie 'meɪzɪ
maison(n)ette, -s ˌmeɪzəˈnet, -s
Maitland 'meɪtlənd
maitre(s) d'hôtel ˌmetrədəʊˈtel [ˌmeɪt-] (mɛːtrə dotɛl)
maize meɪz
Majendie 'mædʒəndɪ
majestic (M.), -al, -ally məˈdʒestɪk, -l, -əlɪ
majest|y (M.), -ies 'mædʒəst|ɪ [-dʒɪs-], -ɪz
majolica məˈjɒlɪkə [məˈdʒɒl-]
major (*s. adj. v.*) (M.), -s, -ing, -ed 'meɪdʒə*, -z, -rɪŋ, -d
Majorca məˈdʒɔːkə [məˈjɔː-]
major-domo, -s ˌmeɪdʒəˈdəʊməʊ, -z
major-general, -s ˌmeɪdʒəˈdʒenərəl, -z
majorit|y, -ies məˈdʒɒrət|ɪ [-rɪt|-], -ɪz
Majuba məˈdʒuːbə
majuscule, -s 'mædʒəskjuːl, -z
mak|e (*s. v.*), -es, -ing, made, mak|er, -ers meɪk, -s, -ɪŋ, meɪd, 'meɪk|ə*, -əz
make-believe 'meɪkbɪˌliːv [-bəˌl-]
Makeham 'meɪkəm
Makepeace 'meɪkpiːs
Makerere məˈkerərɪ
makeshift, -s 'meɪkʃɪft, -s
make-up, -s 'meɪkʌp, -s
makeweight, -s 'meɪkweɪt, -s
Makins 'meɪkɪnz
Makower məˈkaʊə*
Malabar ˌmæləˈbɑː* [*also* 'mæləb- *when attributive*]
Malacca məˈlækə
Malachi 'mæləkaɪ
malachite 'mæləkaɪt
maladjusted ˌmæləˈdʒʌstɪd [*also* '--ˌ-- *when attributive*]
maladjustment, -s ˌmæləˈdʒʌstmənt, -s
maladministration 'mælədˌmɪnɪˈstreɪʃn̩
maladroit, -ly, -ness ˌmæləˈdrɔɪt ['---], -lɪ, -nɪs [-nəs]
malad|y, -ies 'mæləd|ɪ, -ɪz
mala fide ˌmeɪləˈfaɪdɪ [ˌmæləˈfɪdɪ, -ˈfɪdeɪ]
Malaga 'mæləgə
Malagasy ˌmæləˈgæsɪ
malaise mæˈleɪz
Malan (*English surname*) 'mælən, (*South African name*) məˈlæn, məˈlɑːn
Malaprop 'mæləprɒp
malapropism, -s 'mæləprɒpɪzəm, -z

malapropos ˌmæl'æprəpəʊ [ˌ---'-]
malaria, -l, -n mə'leərɪə, -l, -n
Malawi, -an mə'lɑ:wɪ, -ən
Malay (s. adj.), -s mə'leɪ, -z
Malaya, -n/s mə'leɪə, -n/z
Malayalam ˌmælɪ'ɑ:ləm [-leɪ'ɑ:-, -lə'jɑ:-]
Malaysia mə'leɪzɪə [-zjə, -ʒɪə, -ʒə]
Malchus 'mælkəs
Malcolm 'mælkəm
malcontent, -s 'mælkən,tent, -s
Malden 'mɔ:ldən ['mɒl-]
Maldive, -s 'mɔ:ldɪv ['mɒl-], -z
Maldivian, -s mɔ:l'dɪvɪən [mɒl-, -vjən], -z
Maldon 'mɔ:ldən ['mɒl-]
male, -s meɪl, -z
malediction, -s ˌmælɪ'dɪkʃn, -z
maledictory ˌmælɪ'dɪktərɪ
malefaction, -s ˌmælɪ'fækʃn, -z
malefactor, -s 'mælɪfæktə*, -z
malefic mə'lefɪk
maleficent mə'lefɪsnt [mæ'l-]
Malet 'mælɪt
malevolen|ce, -t/ly mə'levələn|s [mæ'l-, -vlə-], -t/lɪ
malfeasance mæl'fi:zns
Malfi 'mælfɪ
malformation, -s ˌmælfɔ:'meɪʃn [-fə'm-], -z
malfunction (s. v.), -s, -ing, -ed ˌmæl'fʌŋkʃn, -z, -ɪŋ, -d
Mali 'mɑ:lɪ
malic 'mælɪk ['meɪl-]
malice 'mælɪs
malicious, -ly, -ness mə'lɪʃəs, -lɪ, -nɪs [-nəs]
malign (adj. v.), -ly; -s, -ing, -ed, -er/s mə'laɪn, -lɪ; -z, -ɪŋ, -d, -ə*/z
malignan|cy, -t/ly mə'lɪgnən|sɪ, -t/lɪ
malignity mə'lɪgnətɪ [-ɪtɪ]
Malin (region of sea) 'mælɪn
Malines mæ'li:n (malin)
malinger, -s, -ing, -ed, -er/s mə'lɪŋgə*, -z, -rɪŋ, -d, -rə*/z
Malins 'meɪlɪnz
malkin, -s 'mɔ:kɪn ['mɔ:lk-], -z
Malkin 'mælkɪn
mall, -s mɔ:l, -z
Mall (in The Mall, Chiswick Mall) mæl, (in Pall Mall) mæl [mel]
mallard, -s 'mælɑ:d [-ləd], -z
malleability ˌmælɪə'bɪlətɪ [-ljə'b-, -lə'b-, -lɪt-]
malleable, -ness 'mælɪəbl [-ljə-, -lə-], -nɪs [-nəs]
mallet (M.), -s 'mælɪt [-lət], -s
Malling (in Kent) 'mɔ:lɪŋ
Mallorca mə'ljɔ:kə [mə'lɔ:-]

Mallory 'mælərɪ
mallow (M.), -s 'mæləʊ, -z
Malmaison, -s ˌmæl'meɪzɔ̃:ŋ [-zɒn] (malmɛzɔ̃)
Malmesbury 'mɑ:mzbərɪ
malmsey (M.) 'mɑ:mzɪ
malnutrition ˌmælnju:'trɪʃn [-njʊ-]
malodorant (s. adj.), -s mæl'əʊdərənt, -s
malodorous mæl'əʊdərəs
Malone mə'ləʊn
Malory 'mælərɪ
Malpas (near Truro) 'məʊpəs, (in Cheshire) 'mɔ:lpəs ['mɔ:pəs, 'mælpəs]
Malplaquet 'mælpləkeɪ
malpractice, -s ˌmæl'præktɪs, -ɪz
malt (s. v.), -s, -ing, -ed mɔ:lt [mɒlt], -s, -ɪŋ, -ɪd
Malta 'mɔ:ltə ['mɒl-]
Maltese ˌmɔ:l'ti:z [ˌmɒl-, also '-- according to sentence-stress]
Malthus 'mælθəs
Malthusian, -s, -ism mæl'θju:zjən [-'θu:-, -zɪən], -z, -ɪzəm
Malton (in North Yorkshire) 'mɔ:ltən ['mɒl-]
Maltravers mæl'trævəz
maltreat, -s, -ing, -ed, -ment ˌmæl'tri:t, -s, -ɪŋ, -ɪd, -mənt
maltster, -s 'mɔ:ltstə* ['mɒl-], -z
Malvern 'mɔ:lvən ['mɒl-, -vɜ:n, locally also 'mɔ:vən]
malversation ˌmælvɜ:'seɪʃn
Malvolio mæl'vəʊljəʊ [-lɪəʊ]
Malyon 'mæljən [-lɪən]
Mameluke, -s 'mæmɪlu:k [-lju:k], -s
Mamie 'meɪmɪ
Mamilius mə'mɪlɪəs [mæ'm-, -ljəs]
mamma (mother), -s mə'mɑ:, -z
mamm|a (milk-secreting organ), -ae 'mæm|ə, -i:
mammal, -s 'mæml, -z
mammalia, -n mæ'meɪljə [mə'm-, -lɪə], -n
mammaliferous ˌmæmə'lɪfərəs
mammary 'mæmərɪ
mammon (M.) 'mæmən
mammoth, -s 'mæməθ, -s
mamm|y, -ies 'mæm|ɪ, -ɪz
man (s.) (M.), men mæn, men
man (v.), -s, -ning, -ned mæn, -z, -ɪŋ, -d
manac|le, -les, -ling, -led 'mænək|l, -lz, -lɪŋ, -ld
manag|e, -es, -ing, -ed, -ement/s 'mænɪdʒ, -ɪz, -ɪŋ, -d, -mənt/s
manageability ˌmænɪdʒə'bɪlətɪ [-nədʒ-, -lɪt-]
manageab|le, -ly, -leness 'mænɪdʒəb|l [-nədʒ-], -lɪ, -lnɪs [-nəs]

311

manager, -s 'mænɪdʒə* [-nədʒ-], -z
manageress, -es ˌmænɪdʒə'res [-nədʒ-, 'mænɪdʒəres], -ɪz
managerial ˌmænə'dʒɪərɪəl
Manasseh mə'næsɪ [-sə]
Manasses mə'næsɪz [-si:z]
man-at-arms, men-at-arms mænət-'ɑːmz, ˌmenət'ɑːmz
manatee (M.), -s ˌmænə'tiː, -z
Manchester 'mæntʃɪstə* [-tʃestə*, -tʃəstə*]
Manchu, -s ˌmæn'tʃuː: [also 'mæntʃuː when attributive], -z
Manchukuo ˌmæntʃuː'kwəu
Manchuria, -n/s mæn'tʃuərɪə [-'tʃɔːr-, -'tʃɔːr-], -n/z
manciple, -s 'mænsɪpl, -z
Mancunian, -s mæŋ'kjuːnjən [-nɪən], -z
Mandalay ˌmændə'leɪ
mandamus, -es mæn'deɪməs, -ɪz
mandarin, -s 'mændərɪn, -z
mandate (s.), -s 'mændeɪt [-dɪt], -s
mandat|e (v.), -es, -ing, -ed 'mændeɪt [-'-], -s, -ɪŋ, -ɪd
mandator|y (s. adj.), -ies 'mændeɪtər|ɪ [mæn'deɪtər|ɪ], -ɪz
Mander (surname) 'mɑːndə*, 'mændə*
Mandeville 'mændəvɪl [-dɪv-]
mandible, -s 'mændɪbl [-dəbl], -z
mandolin, -s 'mændəlɪn, -z
mandoline, -s ˌmændə'liːn ['mændəli:n, 'mændəlɪn], -z
mandragora mæn'drægərə [mən-]
mandrake, -s 'mændreɪk, -s
mandrill, -s 'mændrɪl, -z
mane, -s, -d meɪn, -z, -d
man-eater, -s 'mænˌiːtə*, -z
manège, -s mæ'neɪʒ ['mæneɪʒ], -ɪz
manes (ghosts) (M.) 'mɑːneɪz ['meɪniːz]
manet 'mænet [old-fashioned 'meɪnet]
Manfred 'mænfred [-frɪd]
man|ful, -fully, -fulness 'mæn|fʊl, -fʊlɪ [-fəlɪ], -fʊlnɪs [-nəs]
manganese 'mæŋgənɪːz [ˌ-'-]
manganic mæŋ'gænɪk
mange meɪndʒ
mangel-wurzel, -s 'mæŋgl,wɜːzl [ˌ-'--], -z
manger, -s 'meɪndʒə*, -z
mang|le, -les, -ling, -led 'mæŋg|l, -lz, -lɪŋ [-lɪŋ], -ld
mango, -es 'mæŋgəu, -z
mangold, -s 'mæŋgəld, -z
mangosteen, -s 'mæŋgəusti:n, -z
mangrove, -s 'mæŋgrəuv, -z
mang|y, -ier, -iest, -ily, -iness 'meɪndʒ|ɪ, -ɪə* [-jə*], -ɪɪst [-jɪst], -ɪlɪ [-əlɪ], -ɪnɪs [-ɪnəs]

man-hand|le, -les, -ling, -led 'mæn-ˌhænd|l [ˌ-'--], -lz, -lɪŋ [-ḷɪŋ], -ld
Manhattan mæn'hætn
manhole, -s 'mænhəul, -z
manhood (M.) 'mænhʊd
mania, -s 'meɪnjə [-nɪə], -z
maniac, -s 'meɪnɪæk [-njæk], -s
maniac|al, -ally mə'naɪək|l, -əlɪ
manic-depressive ˌmænɪkdɪ'presɪv
Manichean, -s ˌmænɪ'ki:ən [-'kɪən], -z
manicur|e (s. v.), -es, -ing, -ed; -ist/s 'mænɪˌkjuə* [-kjɔə*, -kjɔ:*,] -z, -rɪŋ, -d; -rɪst/s
manifest (s. adj. v.), -ly; -s, -ing, -ed 'mænɪfest, -lɪ; -s, -ɪŋ, -ɪd
manifestation, -s ˌmænɪfe'steɪʃn [-fə's-], -z
manifesto, -s ˌmænɪ'festəu, -z
manifold, -ness 'mænɪfəuld [rarely 'men-], -nɪs [-nəs]
manikin, -s 'mænɪkɪn, z
manil(l)a (M.), -s mə'nɪlə, -z
manioc 'mænɪɒk
maniple, -s 'mænɪpl, -z
manipulat|e, -es, -ing, -ed, -or/s mə'nɪpjuleɪt [-pjəl-], -s, -ɪŋ, -ɪd, -ə*/z
manipulation, -s mə,nɪpjuˈleɪʃn [-pjə'l-], -z
manipulative mə'nɪpjulətɪv [-pjəl-]
Manitoba ˌmænɪ'təubə
mankind (in general) mæn'kaɪnd, (when opp. womankind) 'mænkaɪnd
Manley 'mænlɪ
manlike 'mænlaɪk
Manlius 'mænlɪəs [-ljəs]
man|ly, -lier, -liest, -liness 'mæn|lɪ, -lɪə* [-ljə*], -lɪɪst [-ljɪst], -lɪnɪs [-ɪnəs]
Mann mæn
manna 'mænə
mannequin, -s 'mænɪkɪn, -z
manner, -s, -ed; -ism/s 'mænə*, -z, -d; -rɪzəm/z
manner|ly, -liness 'mænə|lɪ, -lɪnɪs [-ɪnəs]
Manners 'mænəz
Mannheim 'mænhaɪm ('manhaim)
mannikin, -s 'mænɪkɪn, -z
Manning 'mænɪŋ
mannish 'mænɪʃ
Manns mænz
manny 'mænɪ
Manoah mə'nəuə
manœuvrability məˌnuː'vrə'bɪlətɪ [-vər-, -lɪt-]
manœuvrable mə'nuː'vrəbl [-vər-]
manœuv|re, -res, -ring, -red, -rer/s mə'nuː'v|ə*, -əz, -ərɪŋ, -əd, -ərə*/z

man-of-war, men-of-war ˌmænəvˈwɔː*, ˌmenəvˈwɔː*
manometer, -s məˈnɒmɪtə* [-mətə*], -z
manometric ˌmænəʊˈmetrɪk
manor, -s ˈmænə*, -z
manor-hou|se, -ses ˈmænəhaʊ|s, -zɪz
manorial məˈnɔːrɪəl [mæˈn-]
manostat, -s ˈmænəʊstæt, -s
manpower ˈmænˌpaʊə*
manqué ˈmɑ̃ːŋkeɪ [ˈmɒŋ-] (mãke)
Manresa (town in Spain) mænˈreɪsə [-ˈreɪzə] (manˈresa), (in names of streets, etc.) mænˈriːzə [-ˈriːsə]
Mansa ˈmænsə
manse, -s mæns, -ɪz
Mansel(l) ˈmænsl
Mansergh ˈmænsə*
Mansfield ˈmænsfiːld
mansion (M.), -s ˈmænʃn, -z
mansion-hou|se (M.), -ses ˈmænʃn-haʊ|s, -zɪz
manslaughter ˈmænˌslɔːtə*
man-slayer, -s ˈmænˌsleɪə*, -z
mansuetude ˈmænswɪtjuːd
mantel, -s ˈmæntl, -z
mantel-board, -s ˈmæntlbɔːd [-bɔəd], -z
mantelpiece, -s ˈmæntlpiːs, -ɪz
mantelshel|f, -ves ˈmæntlʃel|f, -vz
mantilla, -s mænˈtɪlə, -z
Mantinea ˌmæntɪˈnɪə [-ˈniːə]
mantis, -es ˈmæntɪs, -ɪz
mant|le, -les, -ling, -led ˈmænt|l, -lz, -lɪŋ [-l̩ɪŋ], -ld
mantra, -s ˈmæntrə, -z
mantramistic ˌmæntrəˈmɪstɪk
mantrap, -s ˈmæntræp, -s
mantua (M.), -s ˈmæntjʊə [-tjwə, ˈmæntʊə], -z
manual (s. adj.), -s, -ly ˈmænjʊəl [-njwəl, -njʊl], -z, -ɪ
Manuel ˈmænjʊel [-njʊəl, -njwəl]
manufactor|y, -ies ˌmænjʊˈfæktər|ɪ, -ɪz
manufact|ure (s. v.), -ures, -uring, -ured, -urer/s ˌmænjʊˈfæktʃ|ə*, -əz, -ərɪŋ, -əd, -ərə*/z
manumission, -s ˌmænjʊˈmɪʃn, -z
manumit, -s, -ting, -ted ˌmænjʊˈmɪt, -s, -ɪŋ, -ɪd
manur|e (s. v.), -es, -ing, -ed məˈnjʊə* [-ˈnjʊə*, -ˈnjɔː*], -z, -rɪŋ, -d
manuscript, -s ˈmænjʊskrɪpt [-njəs-], -s
Manutius məˈnjuːʃjəs [-ʃɪəs, -ʃəs]
Manwaring ˈmænərɪŋ
Manx, -man, -men mæŋks, -mən [-mæn], -mən [-men]
many ˈmenɪ
manysided ˌmenɪˈsaɪdɪd [also ˈ--ˌ-- when attributive]

manysidedness ˌmenɪˈsaɪdɪdnɪs [-nəs]
manzanilla ˌmænzəˈnɪlə [-ɪljə]
mao|ist/s, -ism ˈmaʊ|ɪst/s, -ɪzəm
Maori, -s ˈmaʊrɪ [ˈmɑːər-], -z
Mao Tse-tung ˌmaʊtseˈtʊŋ
map (s. v.), -s, -ping, -ped mæp, -s, -ɪŋ, -t
maple (M.), -s ˈmeɪpl, -z
Mapother ˈmeɪpɒðə*
Mappin ˈmæpɪn
maquillage ˌmækiːˈɑːʒ [-kɪˈɑːʒ] (makijaːʒ)
maquis ˈmækiː [ˈmɑːk-] (maki)
mar (M.), -s, -ring, -red mɑː*, -z, -rɪŋ, -d
marabou, -s ˈmærəbuː, -z
maraschino (M.) ˌmærəˈskiːnəʊ
Marathi, -s məˈrɑːtɪ (Hindi məraṭhi), -z
Marathon ˈmærəθn
maraud, -s, -ing, -ed, -er/s məˈrɔːd, -z, -ɪŋ, -ɪd, -ə*/z
Marazion ˌmærəˈzaɪən
marble, -s, -d ˈmɑːbl, -z, -d
Marburg (German town) ˈmɑːˌbʊəg [-bɜːg] (ˈmarburk, -burç)
marcasite ˈmɑːkəsaɪt
Marcel(le) mɑːˈsel [also ˈ-- when attributive]
Marcella mɑːˈselə
Marcellus mɑːˈseləs
march (s. v.) (M.), -es, -ing, -ed mɑːtʃ, -ɪz, -ɪŋ, -t
Marchant ˈmɑːtʃənt
Marchbank, -s ˈmɑːtʃbæŋk, -s
Marchesi mɑːˈkeɪzɪ
marchioness, -es ˈmɑːʃənɪs [ˌmɑːʃəˈnes], -ɪz
Marchmont ˈmɑːtʃmənt
marchpane ˈmɑːtʃpeɪn
Marcia ˈmɑːsjə [-sɪə]
Marco ˈmɑːkəʊ
Marconi mɑːˈkəʊnɪ
marconigram, -s mɑːˈkəʊnɪgræm, -z
Marcus ˈmɑːkəs
Marden (in Kent) ˈmɑːdən [old-fashioned mɑːˈden]
mare, -s meə*, -z
Marengo məˈreŋgəʊ
mare's-nest, -s ˈmeəznest, -s
mare's-tail, -s ˈmeəzteɪl, -z
Margaret ˈmɑːgərɪt
margarine ˌmɑːdʒəˈriːn [ˌmɑːgə-, ˈ---]
Margarita ˌmɑːgəˈriːtə
Margate ˈmɑːgɪt [locally -geɪt]
marge mɑːdʒ
Margerison mɑːˈdʒerɪsn, ˈmɑːdʒərɪsn
Margery ˈmɑːdʒərɪ
Margetson ˈmɑːdʒɪtsn, ˈmɑːgɪtsn

Margetts 'mɑ:gɪts

margin, -s 'mɑ:dʒɪn, -z

margin|al, -ally 'mɑ:dʒɪn|l, -əlɪ

marginalia ˌmɑ:dʒɪ'neɪljə [-lɪə]

Margoliouth 'mɑ:gəlju:θ

Margot 'mɑ:gəʊ

margrave (M.), -s 'mɑ:greɪv, -z

margravine, -s 'mɑ:grəvi:n, -z

marguerite (M.), -s ˌmɑ:gə'ri:t -s,

Margulies 'mɑ:gʊlɪs

Marham (in Norfolk) 'mærəm ['mɑ:r-]
Note.—The pronunciation of the local
residents is 'mærəm.

Marhamchurch 'mærəmtʃɜ:tʃ

Maria (English name) mə'raɪə, mə'rɪə,
(Latin name) mə'ri:ə [-'rɪə]

Marian 'meərɪən, 'mær-

Mariana (English name) ˌmeərɪ'ænə
[ˌmær-], -'ɑ:nə, (Spanish historian)
ˌmɑ:rɪ'ɑ:nə (mari'ana)

Marie (Christian name) 'mɑ:rɪ [-ri:],
mə'ri:, (biscuits) 'mɑ:rɪ [-ri:]

Marienbad mə'ri:ənbɑ:d [-'rɪən-, mɑ:'r-]
(mɑ:'ri:ənbɑ:t)

marigold (M.), -s 'mærɪgəʊld, -z

marihuana (-juana) ˌmærɪ'hwɑ:nə,
-'jwɑ:nə, -ju'ɑ:nə, -'dʒwɑ:nə
[-dʒʊ'ɑ:nə]

Marilyn 'mærɪlɪn

marina (M.), -s mə'ri:nə, -z

marinade ˌmærɪ'neɪd

marine (s. adj.), -s mə'ri:n, -z

mariner, -s 'mærɪnə* [-rən-], -z

mariolatry ˌmeərɪ'ɒlətrɪ [ˌmær-]

Marion 'mærɪən, 'meər-

marionette, -s ˌmærɪə'net, -s

Marischal (college at Aberdeen) 'mɑ:ʃl

marish (s. adj.) (marsh, marshy), -es
'mærɪʃ, -ɪz

marish (adj.) (like a mare) 'meərɪʃ

Marishes 'mærɪʃɪz

marital 'mærɪtl [mə'raɪtl]

maritime (M.) 'mærɪtaɪm

Marius 'meərɪəs, 'mærɪəs

marj [marge] mɑ:dʒ

marjoram 'mɑ:dʒərəm

Marjoribanks 'mɑ:tʃbæŋks, 'mɑ:ʃb-

Marjor|ie, -y 'mɑ:dʒər|ɪ, -ɪ

mark (s. v.) (M.), -s, -ing/s, -ed, -edly,
-er/s 'mɑ:k, -s, -ɪŋ/z, -t, -ɪdlɪ, -ə*/z

Markby 'mɑ:kbɪ

market (s. v.) (M.), -s, -ing, -ed; -able
'mɑ:kɪt, -s, -ɪŋ, -ɪd; -əbl

marketability ˌmɑ:kɪtə'bɪlətɪ [-ɪtɪ]

market-day, -s 'mɑ:kɪtdeɪ, -z

marketeer, -s ˌmɑ:kə'tɪə*, -z

market-garden, -s 'mɑ:kɪtˌgɑ:dn [ˌ--'--],
-z

market-place, -s 'mɑ:kɪtpleɪs, -ɪz

market-price, -s ˌmɑ:kɪt'praɪs, -ɪz

market-town, -s 'mɑ:kɪttaʊn, -z

Markham 'mɑ:kəm

Marks mɑ:ks

marks|man, -men 'mɑ:ks|mən, -mən
[-men]

marksmanship 'mɑ:ksmənʃɪp

marl mɑ:l

Marlborough 'mɔ:lbərə ['mɑ:l-]
Note.—'mɔ:lbərə is the usual pronunciation of the name of the town
in Wiltshire and of the family name.
'mɑ:l- is not infrequently heard in
names of London streets. 'mɑ:l- is
also the form used for the name of
the town in U.S.A. and the district
in New Zealand.

Marlene (English name) 'mɑ:li:n,
mɑ:'li:n, (German name) mɑ:'leɪnə
(mar'le:nə)

Marler 'mɑ:lə*

Marl|ey, -ing 'mɑ:l|ɪ, -ɪŋ

Marlow(e) 'mɑ:ləʊ

Marmaduke 'mɑ:mədju:k

marmalade, -s 'mɑ:məleɪd [-mḷeɪd], -z

Marmion 'mɑ:mjən [-mɪən]

marmite 'mɑ:maɪt [-mi:t]

Marmora 'mɑ:mərə

marmoset, -s 'mɑ:məʊzet, -s

marmot, -s 'mɑ:mət, -s

Marne mɑ:n

Marner 'mɑ:nə*

marocain 'mærəkem

maroon (s. v.), -s, -ing, -ed mə'ru:n, -z,
-ɪŋ, -d

Marquand 'mɑ:kwənd

marque mɑ:k

marquee, -s mɑ:'ki:, -z

Marquesas mɑ:'keɪsæs [-eɪzæs, -əs]

marquess [-quis], -es 'mɑ:kwɪs, -ɪz

marquessate, -s 'mɑ:kwɪsət [-ɪt], -s

marquet(e)ry 'mɑ:kɪtrɪ [-ətrɪ]

marquisate, -s 'mɑ:kwɪzət [-ɪt], -s

Marrakesh ˌmærə'keʃ [mə'rækeʃ]

marram 'mærəm

marriage, -s; -able 'mærɪdʒ, -ɪz; -əbl

marrow, -s, -y 'mærəʊ, -z, -ɪ

marrowbone, -s 'mærəʊbəʊn, -z

marrowfat, -s 'mærəʊfæt, -s

marr|y (v. interj.), -ies, -ying, -ied
'mær|ɪ, -ɪz, -ɪɪŋ, -ɪd

Marryat 'mærɪət

Mars mɑ:z

Marsala mɑ:'sɑ:lə

Marsden 'mɑ:zdən

Marseillaise ˌmɑ:seɪ'jeɪz [-seɪ'eɪz, -sə-
'leɪz, -sḷ'eɪz] (marsɛjɛ:z)

Marseilles mɑ:'seɪlz [-'seɪ]
marsh (M.), -es mɑ:ʃ, -ɪz
marsh|al (s. v.), -als, -alling, -alled
'mɑ:ʃ|l, -lz, -lɪŋ [-əlɪŋ], -ld
Marshall 'mɑ:ʃl
marshalsea (M.) 'mɑ:ʃlsi: [-sɪ]
marsh|y, -ier, -iest, -iness 'mɑ:ʃ|ɪ, -ɪə*
[-jə*], -ɪɪst [-jɪst], -ɪnɪs [-ɪnəs]
Marsland 'mɑ:zlənd
Marston 'mɑ:stən
marsupial (s. adj.), -s mɑ:'sju:pjəl
[-'su:-, -pɪəl], -z
mart, -s mɑ:t, -s
martel(l) mɑ:'tel
martello mɑ:'teləʊ
marten, -s 'mɑ:tɪn, -z
Martha 'mɑ:θə
marti|al (M.), -ally 'mɑ:ʃ|l, -əlɪ
Martian, -s 'mɑ:ʃjən [-ʃɪən, -ʃn], -z
martin (M.), -s 'mɑ:tɪn, -z
Martineau 'mɑ:tɪnəʊ
martinet, -s ,mɑ:tɪ'net, -s
martini (M.), -s mɑ:'ti:nɪ, -z
Martinique ,mɑ:tɪ'ni:k
Martinmas 'mɑ:tɪnməs [-mæs]
martyr (s. v.) (M.), -s, -ing, -ed 'mɑ:tə*,
-z, -rɪŋ, -d
martyrdom, -s 'mɑ:tədəm, -z
martyriz|e [-is|e], -es, -ing, -ed 'mɑ:-
təraɪz [-tɪr-], -ɪz, -ɪŋ, -d
marv|el (s. v.), -els, -elling, -elled
'mɑ:v|l, -lz, -lɪŋ [-əlɪŋ], -ld
Marvell 'mɑ:vl
marvellous, -ly, -ness 'mɑ:vələs, -lɪ,
-nɪs [-nəs]
Marx mɑ:ks
marxian 'mɑ:ksjən [-ɪən]
marxi|sm, -st/s 'mɑ:ksɪ|zəm, -st/s
Mary 'meərɪ
Maryborough 'meərɪbərə [-bʌrə]
Maryculter ,meərɪ'ku:tə*
Maryland 'meərɪlænd [-lənd, also 'merɪ-
lənd in imitation of American pro-
nunciation]
Marylebone (road, district (without St.))
'mærələbən [-bəʊn, 'mærəbən, 'mærɪ-
bən, 'mɑ:lɪbən]
Mary-le-Bone (preceded by St. as in the
expressions Church of, Borough of
St. M.) ,meərɪlə'bəʊn
Maryport 'meərɪpɔ:t
Marzials 'mɑ:zjəlz [-zɪəlz]
marzipan ,mɑ:zɪ'pæn ['---]
Masai (African people, language)
'mɑ:saɪ
Masaryk 'mæsərɪk ['mæz-]
Mascagni mæ'skɑ:nji: [-njɪ]
mascara mæ'skɑ:rə

mascot, -s 'mæskət [-skɒt], -s
masculine (s. adj.), -s 'mæskjʊlɪn
['mɑ:s-, -kjə-], -z
masculinity ,mæskjʊ'lɪnətɪ [,mɑ:s-,
-kjə-, -ɪtɪ]
Masefield 'meɪsfi:ld ['meɪz-]
maser, -s 'meɪzə*, -z
mash (s. v.) (M.), -es, -ing, -ed mæʃ,
-ɪz, -ɪŋ, -t
Masham (in North Yorkshire) 'mæsəm,
(surname) 'mæsəm, 'mæʃəm
masher, -s 'mæʃə*, -z
mash|ie [-sh|y], -ies 'mæʃ|ɪ, -ɪz
Mashona, -land mə'ʃɒnə [old-fashioned
-'ʃəʊn-], -lænd
Masie 'meɪzɪ
mask (s. v.), -s, -ing, -ed mɑ:sk, -s, -ɪŋ,
-t
Maskell 'mæskl ['mɑ:s-]
Maskelyne 'mæskɪlɪn [-kəl-]
Maslin 'mæzlɪn
masochi|sm, -st/s 'mæsəʊkɪ|zəm, -st/s
masochistic ,mæsəʊ'kɪstɪk
mason (M.), -s 'meɪsn, -z
masonic mə'sɒnɪk
masonry 'meɪsnrɪ
masque, -s mɑ:sk [mæsk], -s
masquerad|e (s. v.), -es, -ing, -ed, -er/s
,mæskə'reɪd [,mɑ:s-], -z, -ɪŋ, -ɪd,
-ə*/z
mass (s.) (quantity of matter), -es mæs,
-ɪz
mass (s.) (celebration of Eucharist) (M.),
-es mæs [mɑ:s], -ɪz
mass (v.), -es, -ing, -ed mæs, -ɪz, -ɪŋ,
-t
Massachusetts ,mæsə'tʃu:sɪts [-səts]
massac|re (s. v.), -res, -ring, -red
'mæsək|ə* [-sɪk-], -əz, -ərɪŋ [-ərɪŋ]
massag|e (s. v.), -es, -ing, -ed 'mæsɑ:ʒ
[-ɑ:dʒ], -ɪz, -ɪŋ, -d
mass-book, -s 'mæsbʊk ['mɑ:s-], -s
Massenet 'mæsəneɪ (masnɛ)
masseur, -s mæ'sɜ:* (masœ:r), -z
masseuse, -s mæ'sɜ:z (masø:z), -ɪz
massif, -s 'mæsi:f [-'-], -s
Massinger 'mæsɪndʒə*
massive, -ly, -ness 'mæsɪv, -lɪ, -nɪs
[-nəs]
mass-meeting, -s ,mæs'mi:tɪŋ ['-,--], -z
Masson 'mæsn
Massowa mə'səʊə
mass-produc|e (v.), -es, -ing, -ed 'mæs-
prə,dju:s [-prʊ,d-, ,-'-], -ɪz, -ɪŋ, -t
mass-production ,mæsprə'dʌk|ʃn
[-prʊ'd-, ,--,--]
mass|y, -iness 'mæs|ɪ, -ɪnɪs [-ɪnəs]
mast (all senses), -s mɑ:st, -s

315

mast|er (*s. v.*), **-ers, -ering, -ered**
  'mɑːst|ə*, -əz, -ərɪŋ, -əd
master|ful, -fully, -fulness 'mɑːstə|fʊl,
  -fʊlɪ [-fəlɪ], -fʊlnɪs [-nəs]
master-hand, -s 'mɑːstəhænd, -z
master-key, -s 'mɑːstəkiː, -z
masterl|y, -iness 'mɑːstəl|ɪ, -mɪs [-ɪnəs]
Masterman 'mɑːstəmən
masterpiece, -s 'mɑːstəpiːs, -ɪz
mastership, -s 'mɑːstəʃɪp, -s
master-stroke, -s 'mɑːstəstrəʊk, -s
mastery 'mɑːstərɪ
mast-head, -s 'mɑːsthed, -z
mastic 'mæstɪk
masticat|e, -es, -ing, -ed, -or/s 'mæstɪ-
  keɪt, -s, -ɪŋ, -ɪd, -ə*/z
mastication ˌmæstɪ'keɪʃn
mastiff, -s 'mæstɪf ['mɑː-s-], -s
mastitis mæ'staɪtɪs
mastodon, -s 'mæstədɒn [-dən], -z
mastoid, -s 'mæstɔɪd, -z
mastoidal mæ'stɔɪdl
Masurian mə'sjʊərɪən
mat (*s. v.*), **-s, -ting, -ted** mæt, -s, -ɪŋ,
  -ɪd
Matabele, -land ˌmætə'biːlɪ, -lænd
matador, -s 'mætədɔː*, -z
match (*s. v.*), **-es, -ing, -ed** mætʃ, -ɪz,
  -ɪŋ, -t
match-board 'mætʃbɔːd [-bɔəd]
match-box, -es 'mætʃbɒks, -ɪz
matchless, -ly, -ness 'mætʃlɪs [-ləs], -lɪ,
  -nɪs [-nəs]
match-maker, -s 'mætʃˌmeɪkə*, -z
matchwood 'mætʃwʊd
mat|e (*s. v.*), **-es, -ing, -ed** meɪt, -s, -ɪŋ,
  -ɪd
mater, -s 'meɪtə*, -z
material (*s. adj.*), **-s, -ly** mə'tɪərɪəl, -z, -ɪ
materiali|sm, -st/s mə'tɪərɪəlɪ|zəm, -st/s
materialistic məˌtɪərɪə'lɪstɪk
materialization [-isa-], -s məˌtɪərɪəlaɪ-
  'zeɪʃn [-lɪ'z-], -z
materializ|e [-is|e], -es, -ing, -ed
  mə'tɪərɪəlaɪz, -ɪz, -ɪŋ, -d
materiel məˌtɪərɪ'el [mæ,t-]
matern|al, -ally mə'tɜːn|l, -əlɪ
maternity mə'tɜːnɪtɪ [-rɪtɪ]
mathematician, -s ˌmæθəmə'tɪʃn
  [-θɪm-], -z
mathematic|s, -al, -ally ˌmæθə'mætɪk|s
  [-θɪ'm-], -l, -əlɪ
Mather, -s 'meɪðə*, 'mæðə*, -z
Matheson 'mæθɪsn [-θəs-]
Mathew, -s 'mæθjuː, 'meɪθ-, -z
Mathias mə'θaɪəs
Mat(h)ilda mə'tɪldə
maths mæθs

matin, -s 'mætɪn, -z
matinée, -s 'mætɪneɪ, -z
Matlock 'mætlɒk
Maton 'meɪtn
Matravers mə'trævəz
matriarch, -y 'meɪtrɪɑːk, -ɪ
matriarchal ˌmeɪtrɪ'ɑːkl
matric mə'trɪk
matricide, -s 'meɪtrɪsaɪd, -z
matriculat|e, -es, -ing, -ed mə'trɪkjʊ-
  leɪt [-kjə-], -s, -ɪŋ, -ɪd
matriculation, -s məˌtrɪkjʊ'leɪʃn
  [-kjə-], -z
matrimonial, -ly ˌmætrɪ'məʊnjəl [-nɪəl],
  -ɪ
matrimony 'mætrɪmənɪ
matri|x, -xes, -ces 'meɪtrɪ|ks ['mæt-],
  -ksɪz, -siːz
  Note.—Doctors generally pronounce
  'meɪt-. *Those connected with the
  printing trade pronounce* 'mæt-. *In
  sound recording usage varies.*
matron, -s; -hood, -ly 'meɪtrən, -z;
  -hʊd, -lɪ
matt mæt
matter (*s. v.*), **-s, -ing, -ed** 'mætə* ,-z
  -rɪŋ, -d
Matterhorn 'mætəhɔːn
matter-of-fact ˌmætərəv'fækt
Matthes 'mæθəs
Matthew, -s 'mæθjuː, -z
Matthias mə'θaɪəs
Matthiessen 'mæθɪsn
matting (*s.*) 'mætɪŋ
mattins 'mætɪnz
mattock, -s 'mætək, -s
mattress, -es 'mætrɪs [-trəs], -ɪz
maturat|e, -es, -ing, -ed 'mætjʊreɪt
  [-tjə-, -tʃʊ-, -tʃə-], -s, -ɪŋ, -ɪd
maturation ˌmætjʊ'reɪʃn [-tjə-, -tʃʊ-,
  -tʃə-]
matur|e (*adj. v.*), -ely, -eness; -es, -ing,
  -ed; -ity mə'tjʊə* [-'tʃʊə*, -'tjɔː*,
  -'tʃɔː*, -'tʃʊə*, -'tʃɔː*, -'tʃɔː:*], -lɪ, -nɪs
  [-nəs]; -z, -rɪŋ, -d; -rətɪ [-rɪtɪ]
Maturin (*surname*) 'mætjʊrɪn [-tʃʊr-,
  -tʃər-]
matutinal ˌmætjuː'taɪnl [-tjʊ-, mə'tjuː-
  tɪnl]
matzos 'mɒtsəz ['mæt-, -əʊz]
maud (M.), -s mɔːd, -z
Maude mɔːd
maudlin 'mɔːdlɪn
Mauger 'meɪdʒə*
Maugha|m, -n mɔː|m, -n
maugre 'mɔːgə*
maul (*s. v.*), -s, -ing, -ed mɔːl, -z, -ɪŋ, -d
Mauleverer mɔː'levərə*

maulstick, -s 'mɔːlstɪk, -s
Mau-Mau 'maʊmaʊ [ˌ-'-]
maunder, -s, -ing, -ed 'mɔːndə*, -z, -rɪŋ, -d
maundy (M.) 'mɔːndɪ
Maunsell 'mænsl
Maureen 'mɔːriːn [mɔːˈriːn]
Mauretania ˌmɒrɪˈteɪnjə [ˌmɔːr-, -nɪə]
Maurice 'mɒrɪs
Mauritius məˈrɪʃəs [muˈr-, mɔːˈr-, mɒˈr-, -ʃjəs]
Mauser, -s 'maʊzə*, -z
mausoleum, -s ˌmɔːsəˈlɪəm [-ˈliːəm], -z
mauve, -s məʊv, -z
maverick 'mævərɪk
mavis (M.) 'meɪvɪs
Mavourneen məˈvʊəniːn [-ˈvɔːn-, -ˈvɔːn-]
maw, -s mɔː, -z
Mawer 'mɔːə* [mɔə*]
Mawhinny məˈwɪnɪ [-ˈhw-]
mawkish, -ly, -ness 'mɔːkɪʃ, -lɪ, -nɪs [-nəs]
Max mæks
maxi, -s 'mæksɪ, -z
maxill|a, -ae, -as, -ary mækˈsɪl|ə, -iː, -əz, -ərɪ
maxim (M.), -s 'mæksɪm, -z
maximal 'mæksɪml
Maximilian ˌmæksɪˈmɪljən [-lɪən]
maxim|um, -a 'mæksɪm|əm, -ə
Maximus 'mæksɪməs
Maxse 'mæksɪ
Maxwell 'mækswəl [-wel]
may (auxil. v.) meɪ (normal form), me (occasional strong form before vowels)
May meɪ
Mayall 'meɪɔːl
maybe 'meɪbɪ [-bɪ]
may-bug, -s 'meɪbʌg, -z
may-day (M.), -s 'meɪdeɪ, -z
Mayfair 'meɪfeə*
may-flower (M.), -s 'meɪˌflaʊə*, -z
may-fl|y, -ies 'meɪfl|aɪ, -aɪz
mayhap 'meɪhæp
mayhem 'meɪhem
Mayhew 'meɪhjuː
maying 'meɪɪŋ
Maynard 'meɪnəd [-nɑːd]
Maynooth məˈnuːθ
mayn't meɪnt [meɪnt, meənt]
Maynwaring 'mænərɪŋ
Mayo, -s (in Ireland, surname) 'meɪəʊ, (American Indian) 'maɪəʊ, -z
mayonnaise, -s ˌmeɪəˈneɪz [rarely ˌmaɪəˈn, also '— when followed by a stress], -ɪz

mayor (M.), -s; -ess/es meə*, -z; -rɪs/ɪz [-res/ɪz, ˌ-'-]
mayoral, -ty 'meərəl, -tɪ
Mayou 'meɪu
maypole, -s 'meɪpəʊl, -z
may-queen, -s ˌmeɪˈkwiːn ['meɪkwiːn], -z
mazda (M.), -s 'mæzdə, -z
maze, -s meɪz, -ɪz
Mazenod 'meɪznɒd
Mazin (surname) 'meɪzɪn
Mazo de la Roche ˌmeɪzəʊ dəlɑːˈrɒʃ
mazurka, -s məˈzɜːkə, -z
maz|y, -ier, -iest, -ily, -iness 'meɪz|ɪ, -ɪə* [-jə], -ɪɪst [-jɪst], -ɪlɪ [-əlɪ], -ɪnɪs [-nəs]
me (note in Tonic Sol-fa), -s miː, -z
me (pron.) miː (normal form), mɪ (freq. weak form)
mead (M.), -s miːd, -z
Meaden 'miːdn
meadow, -s, -y 'medəʊ, -z, -ɪ
meadow-grass 'medəʊɡrɑːs
meadowsweet 'medəʊswiːt
Meagher mɑː*
meagre, -r, -st, -ly, -ness 'miːgə*, -rə*, -rɪst, -lɪ, -nɪs [-nəs]
Meaker 'miːkə*
meal, -s miːl, -z
mealie, -s 'miːlɪ, -z
mealtime, -s 'miːltaɪm, -z
meal|y, -ier, -iest, -iness 'miːl|ɪ, -ɪə* [-jə*], -ɪɪst [-jɪst], -ɪnɪs [-nəs]
mealy-bug 'miːlɪbʌg
mealy-mouthed 'miːlɪmaʊðd [ˌ-'-]
mean (s. adj. v.), -s; -er, -est, -ly, -ness; -ing, meant miːn, -z; -ə*, -ɪst, -lɪ, -nɪs [-nəs]; -ɪŋ, ment
meander (s. v.) (M.), -s, -ing, -ed mɪˈændə* [miːˈæ-], -z, -rɪŋ, -d
meaning (s. adj.), -s, -ly 'miːnɪŋ, -z, -lɪ
meaningless 'miːnɪŋlɪs [-ləs]
means (s.) miːnz
meant (from mean) ment
meantime ˌmiːnˈtaɪm ['--]
meanwhile ˌmiːnˈwaɪl [-ˈhw-, '--]
Mearns mɜːnz, meənz [mɪənz]
Mears mɪəz
meas|les, -ly 'miːz|lz, -lɪ
measurab|le, -ly, -leness 'meʒərəb|l, -lɪ, -lnɪs [-nəs]
measur|e (s. v.), -es, -ing, -ed, -er/s; -ement/s; -eless 'meʒə*, -z, -rɪŋ, -d, -rə*/z; -mənt/s; -lɪs [-ləs]
meat, -s miːt, -s
Meates miːts
Meath (Irish county) miːð [often pronounced miːθ by English people]

meatless 'mi:tlɪs [-ləs]
meat-offering, -s 'mi:t,ɒfərɪŋ, -z
meat-pie, -s ‚mi:t'paɪ, -z
meat-safe, -s 'mi:tseɪf, -s
meatus, -es mɪ'eɪtəs [mi:'eɪ-], -ɪz
meat|y, -ier, -iest, -iness 'mi:t|ɪ, -ɪə*, -ɪɪst, -ɪɪs [-nəs]
Mecca 'mekə
meccano (M.), -s mɪ'kɑ:nəʊ [me-, mə-], -z
mechanic, -s, -al, -ally mɪ'kænɪk [mə-], -s, -l, -əlɪ
mechanician, -s ‚mekə'nɪʃn, -z
mechanism, -s 'mekənɪzəm [-kn̩-], -z
mechanization [-isa-] ‚mekənaɪ'zeɪʃn [-nɪ'z-]
mechaniz|e [-is|e], -es, -ing, -ed 'mekənaɪz, -ɪz, -ɪŋ, -d
Mechlin 'meklɪn
Mecklenburg 'meklɪnbɜ:g [-lən-]
medal, -s 'medl, -z
medallion, -s mɪ'dæljən [me'd-, mə'd-], -z
medallist, -s 'medlɪst [-dəl-], -s
medd|le, -les, -ling, -led, -ler/s 'medl|l, -lz, -lɪŋ [-lɪŋ], -ld, -lə*/z [-lə*/z]
meddlesome, -ness 'medlsəm, -nɪs [-nəs]
Mede, -s mi:d, -z
Medea mɪ'dɪə [mə'd, -'di:ə]
me|dia (phonetic term), -diae 'me|dɪə, -dɪɪ: [-dɪaɪ]
media (plur. of medium) 'mi:djə [-dɪə]
mediaeval = medieval
medial 'mi:djəl [-dɪəl]
median, -s 'mi:djən [-dɪən], -z
mediant, -s 'mi:djənt [-dɪənt], -s
mediate (adj.), -ly, -ness 'mi:dɪət [-djət, -dɪt, -dɪt], -lɪ, -nɪs [-nəs]
mediat|e (v.), -es, -ing, -ed 'mi:dɪeɪt, -s, -ɪŋ, -ɪd
mediation, -s ‚mi:dɪ'eɪʃn, -z
mediator (M.), -s 'mi:dɪeɪtə*, -z
mediatorial ‚mi:dɪə'tɔ:rɪəl [-djə-]
medic|al (s. adj.), -als, -ally 'medɪk|l, -lz, -əlɪ
medicament, -s me'dɪkəmənt [mɪ'd-, mə'd-, 'medɪk-], -s
medicat|e, -es, -ing, -ed 'medɪkeɪt, -s, -ɪŋ, -ɪd
medication ‚medɪ'keɪʃn
Medicean ‚medɪ'tʃi:ən [-'tʃɪən, -'si:ən, -'sɪən]
Medici 'medɪtʃi: [-tʃɪ, me'di:tʃi:] ('me:ditʃi)
medicin|al, -ally me'dɪsɪn|l [mɪ'd-, mə'd-, -sn̩|l̩], -əlɪ [-l̩ɪ]

medicine, -s; -chest/s; -man, -men 'medsɪn [-dɪsɪn, -dsən], -z; -tʃest/s; -mæn, -men
medico, -s 'medɪkəʊ, -z
mediev|al, -alism ‚medɪ'i:v|l [‚mi:d-, me'di:v|l], -əlɪzəm [-l̩ɪzəm]
Medill mə'dɪl
Medina (in Arabia) me'di:nə [mɪ'd-], (in U.S.A.) me'daɪnə [mɪ'd-]
medinal 'medɪnl
mediocre ‚mi:dɪ'əʊkə* [‚med-, '—]
mediocrity ‚mi:dɪ'ɒkrətɪ [‚med-, -ɪtɪ]
meditat|e, -es, -ing, -ed 'medɪteɪt, -s, -ɪŋ, -ɪd
meditation, -s ‚medɪ'teɪʃn, -z
meditative, -ly, -ness 'medɪtətɪv [-teɪt-], -lɪ, -nɪs [-nəs]
Mediterranean ‚medɪtə'reɪnjən [-nɪən]
medi|um (s. adj.), -a, -ums 'mi:dj|əm [-dɪ|-], -ə, -əmz
mediumistic ‚mi:djə'mɪstɪk [-dɪə-]
medlar, -s 'medlə*, -z
medley (M.), -s 'medlɪ, -z
Medlock 'medlɒk
Médoc, -s 'meɪdɒk ['med-, me'dɒk], -s
medulla, -s me'dʌlə [mɪ'd-], -z
Medusa mɪ'dju:zə [me'd-, mə'd-, -'dju:sə]
Medway 'medweɪ
Mee mi:
meed, -s mi:d, -z
meek (M.), -er, -est, -ly, -ness mi:k, -ə*, -ɪst, -lɪ, -nɪs [-nəs]
meerschaum, -s 'mɪəʃəm [-ʃaʊm], -z
Meerut 'mɪərət (Hindi meraθh)
meet (s. adj. v.), -s, -ly, -ness; -ing/s, met mi:t, -s, -lɪ, -nɪs [-nəs]; -ɪŋ/z, met
meeting-hou|se, -ses 'mi:tɪŋhaʊ|s, -zɪz
meeting-place, -s 'mi:tɪŋpleɪs, -ɪz
Meg meg
mega- 'megə- [or ‚megə- when main stress follows]
megacycle, -s 'megə,saɪkl, -z
megahertz 'megəhɜ:ts [-heəts]
megalithic ‚megə'lɪθɪk
megalomania ‚megələʊ'meɪnjə [-nɪə]
megalomaniac, -s ‚megələʊ'meɪnɪæk [-njæk], -s
Megan 'megən
megaphone, -s 'megəfəʊn, -z
megatheri|um, -a ‚megə'θɪərɪ|əm, -ə
megaton, -s 'megətʌn, -z
megawatt, -s 'megəwɒt, -s
megilp mə'gɪlp
megrim, -s 'mi:grɪm, -z
Meier 'maɪə*
Meighen (Canadian name) 'mi:ən

Meigs megz
Meikle 'miːkl
Meiklejohn 'mɪkldʒɒn
meiosis maɪ'əʊsɪs
Meistersinger, -s 'maɪstə,sɪŋə*, -z
melancholia ,melən'kəʊljə [-lɪə]'k-, -lɪə]
melancholic ,melən'kɒlɪk [-lən]'k-]
melancholy (s. adj.) 'melənkəlɪ [-ləŋk-, -kɒlɪ]
Melanchthon me'læŋkθɒn [mɪ'l-, -θən]
Melane|sia, -sian/s ,melə'niː|zjə [-zɪə, -ʒjə, -ʒɪə, -ʒə, -sjə, -sɪə, -ʃjə, -ʃɪə, -ʃə], -zjən/z [-zɪən/z, -ʒjən/z, -ʒɪən/z, -ʒn/z, -sjən/z, -sɪən/z, -ʃjən/z, -ʃɪən/z, -ʃn/z]
mélange, -s meɪ'lɑ̃ːnʒ [-'lɔ̃ːnʒ] (melɑ̃ːʒ), -ɪz
Melanie 'melənɪ
melanism 'melənɪzəm
Melanthios me'lænθɪəs [-θɪɒs]
Melba 'melbə
Melbourne 'melbən [-bɔːn]
Note.—In Australia always 'melbən.
Melchett 'meltʃɪt
Melchizedek mel'kɪzədek
Melcombe 'melkəm
Meleager ,melɪ'eɪgə*
mêlée, -s meleɪ ['meɪl-] (mɛle), -z
Melhuish 'melɪʃ, 'meljʊɪʃ [-lhjʊɪʃ]
melinite 'melɪnaɪt
Melita 'melɪtə
mellifluous me'lɪflʊəs [-flwəs]
Mellin 'melɪn
Mellor 'melə* [-lɔː*]
mellow (adj. v.), -er, -est, -ness; -s, -ing, -ed 'meləʊ, -ə*, -ɪst, -nɪs [-nəs]; -z, -ɪŋ, -d
melodic mɪ'lɒdɪk [me'l-, mə'l-]
melodious, -ly, -ness mɪ'ləʊdjəs [me'l-, mə'l-, -dɪəs], -lɪ, -nɪs [-nəs]
melodrama, -s 'meləʊ,drɑːmə [,--'--], -z
melodramatic ,meləʊdrə'mætɪk
melodramatist, -s ,meləʊ'dræmətɪst, -s
melod|y, -ies 'meləd|ɪ [-lʊd-], -ɪz
melon, -s 'melən, -z
Melos (island) 'miːlɒs ['mel-]
Melpomene mel'pɒmɪnɪ: [-mən-, -nɪ]
Melrose 'melrəʊz
melt, -s, -ing/ly, -ed melt, -s, -ɪŋ/lɪ, -ɪd
Mel|ton, -ville 'mel|tən, -vɪl*
member, -s; -ship/s 'membə, -z; -ʃɪp/s
membrane, -s 'membreɪn, -z
membran|eous, -ous mem'breɪn|jəs [-ɪəs], -əs
Memel 'meɪml
memento, -s mɪ'mentəʊ [me'm-, mə'm-], -z
Memnon 'memnɒn

memo, -s 'meməʊ ['miːməʊ], -z
memoir, -s 'memwɑː* [-wɔː*], -z
memorabilia ,memərə'bɪlɪə [-ljə]
memorab|le, -ly 'memərəb|l, -lɪ
memorand|um, -a, -ums ,memə'rænd|əm [-mʊ'r-, -mɽ'æ-], -ə, -əmz
memorial (s. adj.), -s mɪ'mɔːrɪəl [me'm-, mə'm-], -z
memorializ|e [-is|e], -es, -ing, -ed mɪ'mɔːrɪəlaɪz [me'm-, mə'm-], -ɪz, -ɪŋ, -d
memoriter mɪ'mɒrɪtə* [me'm-, mə'm-]
memoriz|e [-is|e], -es, -ing, -ed 'meməraɪz [-mʊr-, -mɽ-], -ɪz, -ɪŋ, -d
memor|y, -ies 'memər|ɪ [-mʊr-, -mɽ-, -mrɪ], -ɪz
Memphis 'memfɪs
memsahib, -s 'mem,sɑːhɪb [-sɑːb], -z
men (plur. of man) men
menac|e (s. v.), -es -ing/ly, -ed 'menəs [-nɪs], -ɪz, -ɪŋ/lɪ, -t
ménage, -s me'nɑːʒ [meɪ'n-] (mena:ʒ), -ɪz
menagerie, -s mɪ'nædʒərɪ [me'n-, mə'n-, -'nɑːdʒərɪ], -z
Menai (strait) 'menaɪ (Welsh 'menai)
Menander mɪ'nændə* [me'n-, mə'n-]
mend, -s, -ing, -ed, -er/s mend, -z, -ɪŋ, -ɪd, -ə*/z
mendacious, -ly men'deɪʃəs, -lɪ
mendacity men'dæsətɪ [-ɪtɪ]
Mendel 'mendl
Mendeli men'diːlɪ
Mendelian men'diːljən [-lɪən]
Mendelssohn (English surname) 'mendlsn, (German composer) 'mendlsn [-səʊn]
mendican|cy, -t/s 'mendɪkən|sɪ, -t/s
mendicity men'dɪsətɪ [-ɪtɪ]
Mendip, -s 'mendɪp, -s
Mendoza men'dəʊzə
mene 'miːnɪ
Menelaus ,menɪ'leɪəs
menhir, -s 'men,hɪə*, -z
menial (s. adj.), -s, -ly 'miːnjəl [-nɪəl], -z, -ɪ
meningitis ,menɪn'dʒaɪtɪs
Meno 'miːnəʊ
men-of-war (plur. of man-of-war) ,menəʊ'wɔː*
menopause 'menəʊpɔːz ['miːn-]
Menpes 'mempɪs ['menp-, -ɪz]
menses 'mensiːz
Menshevik, -s 'menʃəvɪk [-ʃɪv-], -s
menstrual 'menstrʊəl [-trwəl]
menstruat|e, -es, -ing, -ed 'menstrʊeɪt, -s, -ɪŋ, -ɪd
menstruation ,menstrʊ'eɪʃn

319

mensurability ˌmenʃʊrəˈbɪlətɪ [-ʃər-, -nsjʊr-, -lɪt-]

mensurable ˈmenʃʊrəbl [-ʃər-]

mensuration ˌmensjʊəˈreɪʃn [-sjʊˈr-]

ment|al, -ally ˈment|l, -əlɪ [-lɪ]

mentalistic, -ally ˌmentəˈlɪstɪk [-tl̩ˈɪs-], -əlɪ [-lɪ]

mentalit|y, -ies menˈtælət|ɪ [-ɪt|ɪ], -ɪz

Menteith menˈtiːθ

menthol ˈmenθɒl [-θl]

menti|on (s. v.), -ons, -oning, -oned; -onable ˈmenʃ|n, -nz, -nɪŋ [-nɪŋ, -ənɪŋ], -nd; -nəbl [-nəbl, -ənəbl]

Mentone menˈtəʊnɪ

mentor, -s ˈmentɔː*, -z

menu, -s ˈmenjuː, -z

Menuhin (American violinist) ˈmenjʊɪn [-nʊhɪn, -nʊm]

Menzies ˈmenzɪz, ˈmenjɪs, ˈmɪnjɪs.
Note.—The former Prime Minister of Australia is ˈmenzɪz.

Meolse mels

Meopham ˈmepəm

Mepham ˈmefəm

Mephibosheth meˈfɪbəʃeθ [mɪˈf-, -bʊʃ-, among Jews also ˌmefɪˈbəʊʃeθ, -ˈbɒʃeθ]

Mephistophelean [-lian] ˌmefɪstəˈfiːljən [-tɒˈf-, -lɪən]

Mephistopheles ˌmefɪˈstɒfɪliːz [-fəl-, -fl-]

mephitic meˈfɪtɪk

mephitis meˈfaɪtɪs

Mercadi mɜːˈkɑːdɪ

mercantile ˈmɜːkəntaɪl

mercantilism ˈmɜːkəntɪlɪzəm [-taɪl-]

Mercator mɜːˈkeɪtə:* [-tə*]

Mercedes (English fem. name) ˈmɜːsɪdiːz, (car) məˈseɪdiːz [mɜːˈs-]

mercenar|y (s. adj.), -ies ˈmɜːsɪnər|ɪ [-snə-, -snə-], -ɪz

mercer (M.), -s ˈmɜːsə*, -z

merceriz|e [-is|e], -es, -ing, -ed ˈmɜːsəraɪz, -ɪz, -ɪŋ, -d

merchandise ˈmɜːtʃəndaɪz

merchant, -s; -man, -men ˈmɜːtʃənt, -s; -mən, -mən [-men]

merchant-ship, -s ˈmɜːtʃənt-ʃɪp, -s

Merchison ˈmɜːkɪsn

Merchiston ˈmɜːkɪstən

Mercia, -n ˈmɜːsjə [-sɪə, -ʃjə, -ʃɪə], -n

merci|ful, -fully, -fulness ˈmɜːsɪ|fʊl, -fʊlɪ [-fəlɪ], -fʊlnɪs [-nəs]

merciless, -ly, -ness ˈmɜːsɪlɪs [-ləs], -lɪ, -nɪs [-nəs]

mercurial, -ly mɜːˈkjʊərɪəl [-ˈkjɔər-, -ˈkjɔːr-], -ɪ

mercuric mɜːˈkjʊərɪk

mercurous ˈmɜːkjʊrəs

mercury (M.) ˈmɜːkjʊrɪ [-kjər-]

Mercutio mɜːˈkjuːʃjəʊ [-ʃɪəʊ]

merc|y (M.), -ies ˈmɜːs|ɪ, -ɪz

mercy-seat, -s ˈmɜːsɪsiːt, -s

mere (s. adj.), -s, -st, -ly mɪə*, -z, -rɪst, -lɪ

Meredith ˈmerədɪθ [-rɪd-], in Wales meˈredɪθ

meretricious, -ly, -ness ˌmerɪˈtrɪʃəs, -lɪ, -nɪs [-nəs]

merganser, -s mɜːˈgænsə* [-zə*], -z

merg|e, -es, -ing, -ed mɜːdʒ, -ɪz, -ɪŋ, -d

merger, -s ˈmɜːdʒə*, -z

meridian, -s məˈrɪdɪən [mɪˈr-, -djən], -z

meridional məˈrɪdɪənl [mɪˈr-, -djən-]

meringue, -s məˈræŋ, -z

merino məˈriːnəʊ

Merioneth, -shire ˌmerɪˈɒnɪθ [-neθ, -nəθ] (Welsh meriˈoneθ), -ʃə* [-ˌʃɪə*]

merit (s. v.), -s, -ing, -ed ˈmerɪt, -s, -ɪŋ, -ɪd

meritocrac|y, -ies ˌmerɪˈtɒkrəs|ɪ, -ɪz

meritorious, -ly, -ness ˌmerɪˈtɔːrɪəs, -lɪ, -nɪs [-nəs]

Merivale ˈmerɪveɪl

merlin (M.), -s ˈmɜːlɪn, -z

mermaid, -s ˈmɜːmeɪd, -z

mer|man, -men ˈmɜː|mæn, -men

Meroe ˈmerəʊɪ

Merope ˈmerəpɪ [-piː]

Merovingian ˌmerəʊˈvɪndʒɪən [-dʒjən]

Merrilies ˈmerɪlɪz

Merrimac ˈmerɪmæk

Merriman ˈmerɪmən

merriment ˈmerɪmənt

Merrivale ˈmerrveɪl

merr|y (M.), -ier, -iest, -ily, -iness ˈmer|ɪ, -ɪə*, -ɪɪst, -əlɪ [-ɪlɪ], -ɪnɪs [-nəs]

merry-andrew, -s ˌmerɪˈændruː, -z

merry-go-round, -s ˈmerɪɡəʊˌraʊnd, -z

merrymak|er/s, -ing ˈmerɪˌmeɪk|ə*/z, -ɪŋ

merrythought, -s ˈmerɪθɔːt, -s

Merryweather ˈmerɪˌweðə*

Mersey, -side ˈmɜːzɪ, -saɪd

Merthyr ˈmɜːθə* (Welsh ˈmerθɪr)

Merthyr Tydfil ˌmɜːθəˈtɪdvɪl (Welsh ˌmerθɪrˈtɪdvɪl)

Merton ˈmɜːtn

mésalliance, -s meˈzælɪəns [meɪˈz-, -ljəns, -lɑ̃:ns, -lɔ̃:ns, -lɪɑːns] (mezaljɑ̃:s), -ɪz

mesdames ˈmeɪdæm (medam)

meseems mɪˈsiːmz

mesembryanthemum, -s mɪˌzembrɪˈænθɪməm [mə،z-, -θəm-], -z

mesh (s. v.), -es, -ing, -ed meʃ, -ɪz, -ɪŋ, -t

Meshach [-ak] 'miːʃæk

Meshed 'meʃed

mesial 'miːzjəl [-zɪəl]

Mesmer 'mezmə*

mesmeric mez'merɪk

mesmeri|sm, -st/s 'mezmərɪ|zəm [-mɹ̩-], -st/s

mesmeriz|e [-is|e], -es, -ing, -ed, -er/s 'mezməraɪz [-mɹ̩aɪz], -ɪz, -ɪŋ, -d, -ə*/z

mesne miːn

meson, -s 'miːzɒn ['mesɒn, 'miːsɒn], -z

Mesopotamia ˌmesəpə'teɪmjə [-mɪə]

mesotron, -s 'mesəʊtrɒn, -z

mesozoic ˌmesəʊ'zəʊɪk

mess (s. v.), -es, -ing, -ed mes, -ɪz, -ɪŋ, -t

message, -s 'mesɪdʒ, -ɪz

Messala me'sɑːlə

messenger, -s 'mesɪndʒə* [-sɹ̩-], -z

Messiah, -s mɪ'saɪə [me's-, mə's-], -z

messianic ˌmesɪ'ænɪk

Messina me'siːnə [mə's-, mɪ's-]

messmate, -s 'mesmeɪt, -s

Messrs. 'mesəz

messuage, -s 'meswɪdʒ [-sjʊɪdʒ], -ɪz

mess|y, -ier, -iest, -ily, -iness 'mes|ɪ, -ɪə*, -ɪɪst, -ɪlɪ [-əlɪ], -ɪnɪs [-məs]

Mestre 'mestrɪ

met (from meet) met

meta (solidified spirit) 'miːtə

met|a, -ae (column in Roman circus) 'miːt|ə, -iː ['meɪt|ə, -aɪ]

meta- (Greek prefix) 'metə-, ˌmetə-

Meta (Christian name) 'miːtə

metabolic ˌmetə'bɒlɪk

metabolism me'tæbəlɪzəm [mɪ-, mə-, -bʊl-]

metacentre, -s 'metəˌsentə*, -z

metagalax|y, -ies 'metəˌgæləks|ɪ, -ɪz

met|al (s. v.), -als, -alling, -alled 'met|l, -lz, -lɪŋ, -ld

metallic mɪ'tælɪk [me't-, mə't-]

metalliferous ˌmetə'lɪfərəs

metallography ˌmetə'lɒgrəfɪ

metalloid 'metəlɔɪd

metallurg|ist/s, -y me'tælədʒ|ɪst/s [mɪ't-, 'metələ:dʒ-, 'metlə:dʒ-], -ɪ

metamorphos|e, -es, -ing, -ed ˌmetə-'mɔːfəʊz, -ɪz, -ɪŋ, -d

metamorphos|is, -es (plur.) ˌmetə'mɔː-fəs|ɪs [ˌmetəmɔː'fəʊs-], -iːz

metaphor, -s 'metəfə*, -z

metaphoric, -al, -ally ˌmetə'fɒrɪk, -l, -əlɪ

metaphysician, -s ˌmetəfɪ'zɪʃn, -z

metaphysic|s, -al, -ally ˌmetə'fɪzɪk|s, -l, -əlɪ

metaplasm 'metəplæzəm

metathes|is, -es me'tæθəs|ɪs [mɪ't-, mə't-, -θɪs-], -iːz

Metayers mɪ'teɪəz [mə't-]

Metcalfe (surname) 'metkɑːf [-kəf]

met|e, -es, -ing, -ed miːt, -s, -ɪŋ, -ɪd

Metellus mɪ'teləs [me't-]

metempsychosis ˌmetempsɪ'kəʊsɪs [meˌtem-, -psaɪ'k-]

meteor, -s 'miːtjə* [-tɪə*, -tɔː*], -z

meteoric ˌmiːtɪ'ɒrɪk

meteorite, -s 'miːtjəraɪt [-tɪə-], -s

meteorologic, -al ˌmiːtjərə'lɒdʒɪk [-tɪə-], -l

meteorolog|ist/s, -y ˌmiːtjə'rɒlədʒ|ɪst/s [-tɪə-], -ɪ

meter, -s 'miːtə*, -z

meth, -s meθ, -s

methane 'miːθeɪn

metheglin me'θeglɪn [mɪ'θ-, mə'θ-]

methinks mɪ'θɪŋks

method, -s 'meθəd, -z

methodic, -al, -ally mɪ'θɒdɪk [me'θ-, mə'θ-], -l, -əlɪ

methodi|sm, -st/s 'meθədɪ|zəm, -st/s

methodological ˌmeθədə'lɒdʒɪkl

methodolog|y, -ies ˌmeθə'dɒlədʒ|ɪ, -ɪz

methought mɪ'θɔːt

Methuen (surname) 'meθjʊm [-θjʊən, -θjwən], (American town) mɪ'θjʊm [mə'θ-]

Methuselah mɪ'θjuːzələ [mə'θ-, -'θuː-]

Methven 'meθvən [-ven]

methyl (commercial and general pronunciation) 'meθɪl, (chemists' pronunciation) 'miːθaɪl

methylated 'meθɪleɪtɪd [-θ|eɪ-]

meticulous, -ly mɪ'tɪkjʊləs [me't-, mə-, -kjə-], -lɪ

métier, -s 'meɪtɪeɪ ['met-, -tjeɪ], -z (metje)

metonymy mɪ'tɒnɪmɪ [me't-, mə-, -nəmɪ]

metope, -s 'metəʊp, -s

metre, -s 'miːtə*, -z

metric, -al, ally 'metrɪk, -l, -əlɪ

metrication ˌmetrɪ'keɪʃn

metrics 'metrɪks

metrist, -s 'metrɪst, -s

Metroland 'metrəʊlænd

metronome, -s 'metrənəʊm [-trŋəʊm], -z

metronomic ˌmetrə'nɒmɪk

Metropole 'metrəpəʊl

metropolis, -es mɪ'trɒpəlɪs [me't-, mə't-, -plɪs], -ɪz

metropolitan (s. adj.), -s ˌmetrə'pɒlɪtən [-lət-], -z

321

mettle 'metl
Metz mets
meuse (*track of hare*), -s mju:z, -ız
Meux mju:z, mju:ks, mju:
Mevagissey ˌmevə'gısı
mew (*s. v.*), -s, -ing, -ed mju:, -z, -ıŋ
['mjuıŋ], -d
mewl, -s, -ing, -ed mju:l, -z, -ıŋ, -d
mews (*s.*) mju:z
Mexborough 'meksbərə
Mexic|an/s, -o 'meksık|ən/z, -əʊ
Meyer 'maıə*
Meyerbeer (*composer*) 'maıəˌbıə*
Meynell 'menl, 'meml
Meyrick 'merık, 'meırık
mezzanine, -s 'metsəni:n ['mez-], -z
mezzo-soprano, -s ˌmedzəʊsə'prɑ:nəʊ
[ˌmetsəʊ-], -z
mezzotint, -s 'medzəʊtınt ['metsəʊ-], -s
Mgr., Mgrs. mɒn'si:njə*, -z
mi (*musical note*), -s mi:, -z
Miami maı'æmı
miaow, -s, -ing, -ed mi:'aʊ [mı'aʊ,
mjaʊ], -z, -ıŋ, -d
miasm|a, -as, -ata, -al mı'æzm|ə
[maı'æ-], -əz, -ətə, -l
miasmatic ˌmıæz'mætık [ˌmaıæz-,
ˌmaıəz-]
mica 'maıkə
micaceous maı'keıʃəs
Micah 'maıkə
Micaiah maı'kaıə [mı'k-]
Micawber mı'kɔ:bə*
mice (*plur. of* mouse) maıs
Michael 'maıkl
Michaelmas, -es 'mıklməs, -ız
Michelangelo ˌmaıkəl'ændʒələʊ [-k]-,
-dʒıl-]
Micheldever 'mıtʃəldevə*
Michelin, -s 'mıʃlın ['mıtʃəlın], -z
Michelle mi:'ʃel [mı'ʃ-]
Michelmore 'mıtʃəlmɔ:*
Michelson 'mıtʃəlsn, 'mıklsn
Michie 'mıkı, *in Scotland also* 'mıxı
Michigan 'mıʃıgən
Michmash 'mıkmæʃ
microbe, -s 'maıkrəʊb, -z
microcephalic ˌmaıkrəʊke'fælık
[-əʊkı'f-, -əʊse'f-, -əʊsı'f-]
microcephalous ˌmaıkrəʊ'kefələs
[-əʊ'sef-]
microcop|y, -ies 'maıkrəʊˌkɒp|ı, -ız
microcosm, -s 'maıkrəʊkɒzəm [-krʊk-],
-z
microfilm, -s 'maıkrəʊfılm, -z
micro-groove, -s 'maıkrəʊgru:v, -z
micrometer, -s maı'krɒmıtə* [-mətə*],
-z

micron, -s 'maıkrɒn [-rən], -z
micro-organism, -s ˌmaıkrəʊ'ɔ:gənızəm
[-gn̩-], -z
microphone, -s 'maıkrəfəʊn, -z
microphonic ˌmaıkrə'fɒnık
microscope, -s 'maıkrəskəʊp [-krʊs-], -s
microscopic, -al, -ally ˌmaıkrə'skɒpık
[-krʊ's-], -l, -əlı
microscop|ist/s, -y maı'krɒskəp|ıst/s,
-ı
microwatt, -s 'maıkrəʊwɒt, -s
micturat|e, -es, -ing, -ed 'mıktjʊəreıt,
-s, -ıŋ, -ıd
micturition ˌmıktjʊə'rıʃn
mid mıd
Midas 'maıdæs [-dəs]
midday, -s 'mıddeı [*also* ˌmıd'd- *when
not attributive*], -z
midden, -s 'mıdn, -z
middle, -s 'mıdl, -z
middle-aged ˌmıdl'eıdʒd [*also* '---, *esp.
when attributive*]
middlebrow 'mıdlbraʊ
middle-class ˌmıdl'klɑ:s [*also* '---, *esp.
when attributive*]
middle|man, -men 'mıdl|mæn, -men
Middlemarch 'mıdlmɑ:tʃ
Middlemast 'mıdlmɑ:st, -mæst
middlemost 'mıdlməʊst
Middlesbrough 'mıdlzbrə
Middlesex 'mıdlseks
Middleton 'mıdltən
middling 'mıdlıŋ [-dlıŋ]
midd|y, -ies 'mıd|ı, ız
midge, -s mıdʒ, -ız
midget, -s 'mıdʒıt, -s
Midhurst 'mıdhə:st
midi, -s 'mıdı, -z
Midian, -ite/s 'mıdıən [-djən], -aıt/s
midland (M.), -s 'mıdlənd, -z
Midlothian mıd'ləʊðjən [-ðıən]
midnight 'mıdnaıt
mid-off, -s ˌmıd'ɒf [*old-fashioned* -'ɔ:f],
-s
mid-on, -s ˌmıd'ɒn, -z
midriff, -s 'mıdrıf, -s
midship|man, -men 'mıdʃıp|mən, -mən
midst mıdst [mıtst]
midsummer (M.) 'mıdˌsʌmə* [-'--]
midway ˌmıd'weı ['--]
Midway (*Island*) 'mıdweı
midwi|fe, -ves 'mıdwaı|f, -vz
midwifery 'mıdwıfərı [-'---]
midwinter ˌmıd'wıntə*
mien, -s mi:n, -z
Miers 'maıəz
might (*s. v.*) maıt
mightn't 'maıtnt

might|y, -ier, -iest, -ily, -iness 'maɪt|ɪ,
-ɪə* [-jə*], -ɪst [-jɪst], -ɪlɪ [-əlɪ], -ɪnɪs
[-məs]
mignonette ,mɪnjə'net ['---]
migraine, -s 'miːɡreɪn ['mɪɡ-, 'maɪ-], -z
migrant (s. adj.), -s 'maɪɡrənt, -s
migrat|e, -es, -ing, -ed, -or/s maɪ'ɡreɪt
['--], -s, -ɪŋ, -ɪd, -ə*/z
migration, -s maɪ'ɡreɪʃn, -z
migratory 'maɪɡrətərɪ [maɪ'ɡreɪtərɪ]
Mikado, -s mɪ'kɑːdəʊ, -z
Mikardo mɪ'kɑːdəʊ
mike (M.), -s maɪk, -s
milady mɪ'leɪdɪ
Milan (in Italy) mɪ'læn [old-fashioned
'mɪlən]
Note.—'mɪlən is necessary for rhythm
in Shakespeare's 'The Tempest'.
Milan (in U.S.A.) 'maɪlən, (Serbian
king) 'miːlən
Milanese ,mɪlə'niːz
milch mɪltʃ [mɪlʃ]
mild, -er, -est, -ly, -ness maɪld, -ə*,
-ɪst, -lɪ, -nɪs [-nəs]
Mildenhall 'mɪldənhɔːl
mild|ew (s. v.), -ews, -ewing, -ewed
'mɪld|juː, -juːz, -juːɪŋ [-jʊɪŋ], -juːd
Mildmay 'maɪldmeɪ
Mildred 'mɪldrɪd [-red]
mile (M.), -s maɪl, -z
mileage, -s 'maɪlɪdʒ, -ɪz
mileometer, -s maɪ'lɒmɪtə* [-mətə*], -z
Miles maɪlz
Milesian, -s maɪ'liːzjən [mɪ'l-, -zɪən,
-ʒjən, -ʒɪən, -ʒn], -z
milestone, -s 'maɪlstəʊn, -z
Miletus mɪ'liːtəs [maɪ'l-]
milfoil, -s 'mɪlfɔɪl, -z
Milford 'mɪlfəd
Milhaud 'miːjəʊ (mijo)
milieu, -s 'miːljɜː (miljø), -z
militan|cy, -t/ly 'mɪlɪtən|sɪ [-lət-], -t/lɪ
militari|sm, -st/s 'mɪlɪtərɪ|zəm [-lət-],
-st/s
militarization [-isa-] ,mɪlɪtəraɪ'zeɪʃn
[-lət-, -rɪ'z-]
militariz|e [-is|e], -es, -ing, -ed 'mɪlɪ-
təraɪz [-lət-], -ɪz, -ɪŋ, -d
military 'mɪlɪtərɪ [-lət-]
militat|e, -es, -ing, -ed 'mɪlɪteɪt [-lət-],
-s, -ɪŋ, -ɪd
militia, -man, -men mɪ'lɪʃə [mə'l-],
-mən, -mən [-men]
milk (s. v.), -s, -ing, -ed, -er/s mɪlk, -s,
-ɪŋ, -t, -ə*/z
milkmaid, -s 'mɪlkmeɪd, -z
milk|man, -men 'mɪlk|mən, -mən
[-men]

milk-shake, -s 'mɪlkʃeɪk, -s
milksop, -s 'mɪlksɒp, -s
milk-|tooth, -teeth 'mɪlk|tuːθ, -tiːθ
milk-white 'mɪlkwaɪt [-khw-]
milkwort, -s 'mɪlkwɜːt, -s
milk|y, -ier, -iest, -ily, -iness 'mɪlk|ɪ,
-ɪə* [-jə*], -ɪst [-jɪst], -ɪlɪ [-əlɪ], -ɪnɪs
[-məs]
mill (s. v.) (M.), -s, -ing, -ed mɪl, -z, -ɪŋ, -d
Millais (sing.) 'mɪleɪ, (plur.) -z
Millard 'mɪləd, -lɑːd
Millbank 'mɪlbæŋk
mill-board 'mɪlbɔːd [-bɔəd]
millenary mɪ'lenərɪ ['mɪlmərɪ]
millenni|um, -ums, -a mɪ'lenɪ|əm
[-nj|əm], -əmz, -ə
millepede, -s 'mɪlɪpiːd, -z
miller (M.), -s 'mɪlə*, -z
millesimal mɪ'lesɪml
millet 'mɪlɪt
mill-hand, -s 'mɪlhænd, -z
milliard, -s 'mɪljɑːd [-lɪɑːd], -z
millibar, -s 'mɪlɪbɑː*, -z
Millicent 'mɪlɪsnt
milligram(me), -s 'mɪlɪɡræm, -z
millimeter, -s 'mɪlɪ,miːtə*, -z
milliner, -s 'mɪlɪnə*, -z
millinery 'mɪlɪnərɪ
million, -s 'mɪljən, -z
millionaire, -s ,mɪljə'neə*, -z
millionairess, -es ,mɪljə'neərɪs [-res,
,mɪljəneə'res], -ɪz
millionfold 'mɪljənfəʊld
millionth, -s 'mɪljənθ, -s
Millom 'mɪləm
mill-pond, -s 'mɪlpɒnd, -z
Mills mɪlz
mill-stone, -s 'mɪlstəʊn, -z
Milltimber 'mɪl,tɪmbə*
Millwall 'mɪlwɔːl ['-'-]
mill-wheel, -s 'mɪlwiːl ['mɪlhw-], -z
Miln mɪl
Milne mɪln, mɪl
Milne-Home ,mɪln'hjuːm
Milner 'mɪlnə*
Milnes mɪlz, mɪlnz
Milngavie mɪl'ɡaɪ
Milo 'maɪləʊ ['miː-]
milord, -s mɪ'lɔːd ['-lɔː*], -z
milreis (sing.) 'mɪlreɪs, (plur.) 'mɪlreɪs
[-reɪz]
Milton 'mɪltən
Miltonic mɪl'tɒnɪk
Milwaukee mɪl'wɔːkiː [-kɪ]
mime, -s maɪm, -s
mimeograph (s. v.), -s, -ing, -ed
'mɪmɪəɡrɑːf [-mɪəʊɡ-, -ɡræf], -s, -ɪŋ,
-t

mimetic mɪˈmetɪk
mimic (s. adj. v.), -s, -king, -ked
  ˈmɪmɪk, -s, -ɪŋ, -t
mimicry ˈmɪmɪkrɪ
mimosa, -s mɪˈməʊzə, -z
mimulus, -es ˈmɪmjʊləs, -ɪz
mina, -s ˈmaɪnə, -z
minaret, -s ˈmɪnəret [ˌ--ˈ-], -s
minatory ˈmɪnətərɪ [ˈmaɪn-]
minc|e (s. v.), -s, -ing/ly, -ed mɪns, -ɪz,
  -ɪŋ/lɪ, -t
mincemeat ˈmɪnsmiːt
mince-pie, -s ˌmɪnsˈpaɪ, -z
Minch, -es, -in mɪntʃ, -ɪz, -ɪn
mind (s. v.), -s, -ing, -ed maɪnd, -z, -ɪŋ,
  -ɪd
mind|ful, -fully, -fulness ˈmaɪnd|fʊl,
  -fʊlɪ [-fəlɪ], -fʊlnɪs [-nəs]
min|e (s. v.), -es, -ing, -ed, -er/s maɪn,
  -z, -ɪŋ, -d, -ə*/z
mine (pron.) maɪn
minefield, -s ˈmaɪnfiːld, -z
Minehead ˈmaɪnhed [ˌmaɪnˈhed]
mine-layer, -s ˈmaɪnˌleɪə*, -z
mine-laying ˈmaɪnˌleɪɪŋ
mineral (s. adj.), -s ˈmɪnərəl, -z
mineraliz|e [-is|e], -es, -ing, -ed
  ˈmɪnərəlaɪz, -ɪz, -ɪŋ, -d
mineralogic|al, -ally ˌmɪnərəˈlɒdʒɪk|l,
  -əlɪ
mineralog|ist/s, -y ˌmɪnəˈrælədʒ|ɪst/s,
  -ɪ
Minerva mɪˈnɜːvə
minestrone ˌmɪnɪˈstrəʊnɪ [-nə-]
mine-sweep|er/s, -ing ˈmaɪnˌswiːp|ə*/z,
  -ɪŋ
Minety ˈmaɪntɪ
minever ˈmɪnɪvə*
Ming mɪŋ
mingl|e, -les, -ling, -led ˈmɪŋg|l, -lz,
  -lɪŋ [-l̩ɪŋ], -ld
mingogram, -s ˈmɪŋgəʊgræm [ˈmɪŋəʊ-],
  -z
mingograph, -s ˈmɪŋgəʊgrɑːf [ˈmɪŋəʊ-,
  -græf], -s
ming|y, -ier, -iest ˈmɪndʒ|ɪ, -ɪə* [-jə*],
  -ɪɪst [-jɪst]
miniature, -s ˈmɪnətʃə* [-njətʃ-, -nɪtʃ-],
  -z
miniaturist, -s ˈmɪnəˌtjʊərɪst [-njət-,
  -tʃər-, ˈmɪnɪtʃərɪst], -s
mini-bus, -es ˈmɪnɪbʌs, -ɪz
mini-car, -s ˈmɪnɪkɑː*, -z
minikin (s. adj.), -s ˈmɪnɪkɪn, -z
minim (M.), -s ˈmɪnɪm, -z
minimal ˈmɪnɪml [-məl]
minimiz|e [-is|e], -es, -ing, -ed ˈmɪnɪ-
  maɪz, -ɪz, -ɪŋ, -d

minim|um, -a ˈmɪnɪm|əm, -ə
mining ˈmaɪnɪŋ
minion, -s ˈmɪnjən [-nɪən], -z
minish, -es, -ing, -ed ˈmɪnɪʃ, -ɪz, -ɪŋ, -t
mini-skirt, -s ˈmɪnɪskɜːt, -s
minist|er (s. v.), -ers, -ering, -ered
  ˈmɪnɪst|ə* [-nəs-], -əz, -ərɪŋ, -əd
ministerial, -ly, -ist/s ˌmɪnɪˈstɪərɪəl
  [-nəˈs-], -ɪ, -ɪst/s
ministration, -s ˌmɪnɪˈstreɪʃn [-nəˈs-], -z
ministr|y, -ies ˈmɪnɪstr|ɪ [-nəs-], -ɪz
miniver (M.) ˈmɪnɪvə*
mink mɪŋk
Minneapolis ˌmɪnɪˈæpəlɪs
Minne|haha, -sota ˌmɪnɪˈhɑːhɑː,
  -ˈsəʊtə
Minnesinger, -s ˈmɪnɪˌsɪŋə*, -z
Minnie ˈmɪnɪ
minnow, -s ˈmɪnəʊ, -z
Minoan mɪˈnəʊən
minol ˈmaɪnɒl
minor (s. adj.), -s ˈmaɪnə*, -z
Minorca mɪˈnɔːkə
Minories ˈmɪnərɪz
minorit|y, -ies maɪˈnɒrət|ɪ [mɪˈn-,
  məˈn-, -ɪt|ɪ], -ɪz
Minos ˈmaɪnɒs
Minotaur, -s ˈmaɪnətɔː*, -z
minster (M.), -s ˈmɪnstə*, -z
minstrel, -s; -sy ˈmɪnstrəl, -z; -sɪ
mint (s. v.), -s, -ing, -ed; -age mɪnt, -s,
  -ɪŋ, -ɪd; -ɪdʒ
Minto ˈmɪntəʊ
mint-sauce ˌmɪntˈsɔːs
minuet, -s ˌmɪnjʊˈet, -s
minus (s. adj. prep.), -es ˈmaɪnəs, -ɪz
minuscule, -s ˈmɪnəskjuːl [-nɪs-,
  mɪˈnʌskjuːl], -z
minute (very small), -st, -ly, -ness
  maɪˈnjuːt [mɪˈn-], -ɪst, -lɪ, -nɪs [-nəs]
minute (s.) (division of time, angle), -s
  ˈmɪnɪt, -s
minute (s.) (memorandum), -s ˈmɪnɪt, -s
minut|e (v.), -es, -ing, -ed ˈmɪnɪt, -s
  -ɪŋ, -ɪd
minute-book, -s ˈmɪnɪtbʊk, -s
minute-glass, -es ˈmɪnɪtglɑːs, -ɪz
minute-gun, -s ˈmɪnɪtgʌn, -z
minute-hand, -s ˈmɪnɪthænd, -z
minutiae maɪˈnjuːʃiː [mɪˈn-, -ʃjiː]
minx, -es mɪŋks, -ɪz
miocene ˈmaɪəʊsiːn
miracle, -s ˈmɪrəkl [-rɪkl], -z
miraculous, -ly, -ness mɪˈrækjʊləs
  [məˈr-, -kjəl-], -lɪ, -nɪs [-nəs]
mirage, -s ˈmɪrɑːʒ [-ˈ-], -ɪz
Miranda mɪˈrændə
mire ˈmaɪə*

Miriam ˈmɪrɪəm
mirror, -s, -ed ˈmɪrə*, -z, -d
mirth mɜ:θ
mirth|ful, -fully, -fulness ˈmɜ:θ|fʊl,
-fʊlɪ [-fəlɪ], -fʊlnɪs [-nəs]
mir|y, -ier, -iest, -iness ˈmaɪər|ɪ, -ɪə*,
-ɪɪst, -ɪnɪs [-ɪnəs]
Mirza ˈmɜ:zə
misadventure, -s ˌmɪsəd'ventʃə*, -z
misalliance, -s ˌmɪsə'laɪəns, -ɪz
misanthrope, -s ˈmɪzənθrəʊp [ˈmɪsən-],
-s
misanthropic, -al, -ally ˌmɪzən'θrɒpɪk
[ˌmɪsən-], -l, -əlɪ
misanthrop|ist/s, -y mɪ'zænθrəp|ɪst/s
[mɪ'sæ-, -θrʊp-], -ɪ
misapplication, -s ˈmɪsˌæplɪ'keɪʃn, -z
misappl|y, -ies, -ying, -ied ˌmɪsə'pl|aɪ,
-aɪz, -aɪɪŋ, -aɪd
misapprehend, -s, -ing, -ed ˈmɪsˌæprɪ-
'hend, -z, -ɪŋ, -ɪd
misapprehension, -s ˈmɪsˌæprɪ'henʃn,
-z
misappropriat|e, -es, -ing, -ed ˌmɪsə-
'prəʊprɪeɪt, -s, -ɪŋ, -ɪd
misappropriation, -s ˈmɪsəˌprəʊprɪ'eɪʃn,
-z
misbecoming ˌmɪsbɪ'kʌmɪŋ [-bə'k-]
misbegotten ˈmɪsbɪˌgɒtn [ˌ--'--]
misbehav|e, -es, -ing, -ed; -iour ˌmɪs-
bɪ'heɪv [-bə'h-], -z, -ɪŋ, -d; -jə*
misbelief ˌmɪsbɪ'li:f [-bə'l-, '---]
misbeliev|e, -es, -ing, -ed, -er/s ˌmɪs-
bɪ'li:v [-bə'l-, '---], -z, -ɪŋ, -d, -ə*/z
miscalculat|e, -es, -ing, -ed ˌmɪs'kæl-
kjʊleɪt [-kjəl-], -s, -ɪŋ, -ɪd
miscalculation, -s ˈmɪsˌkælkjʊ'leɪʃn
[-kjə'l-], -z
miscall, -s, -ing, -ed ˌmɪs'kɔ:l, -z, -ɪŋ,
-d
miscarr|y, -ies, -ying, -ied; -iage/s
ˌmɪs'kær|ɪ, -ɪz, -ɪɪŋ, -ɪd; -ɪdʒ/ɪz
miscegenation ˌmɪsɪdʒɪ'neɪʃn
miscellanea ˌmɪsə'leɪnɪə [-njə]
miscellaneous, -ly, -ness ˌmɪsɪ'leɪnjəs
[-sə'l-, -nɪəs], -lɪ, -nɪs [-nəs]
miscellan|y, -ies mɪ'selən|ɪ [ˈmɪsɪl-], -ɪz
mischance, -s ˌmɪs'tʃɑ:ns [ˈmɪstʃɑ:ns],
-ɪz
mischief, -s ˈmɪstʃɪf, -s
mischief-mak|er/s, -ing ˈmɪstʃɪfˌmeɪk|-
ə*/z, -ɪŋ
mischievous, -ly, -ness ˈmɪstʃɪvəs, -lɪ,
-nɪs [-nəs]
misconception, -s ˌmɪskən'sepʃn, -z
misconduct (s.) ˌmɪs'kɒndʌkt [-dəkt]
misconduct (v.), -s, -ing, -ed ˌmɪskən-
'dʌkt, -s, -ɪŋ, -ɪd

misconstruction, -s ˌmɪskən'strʌkʃn,
-z
misconstr|ue, -ues, -uing, -ued ˌmɪs-
kən'str|u: [-'kɒnst-], -u:z, -u:ɪŋ [-ʊɪŋ],
-u:d
miscount (s. v.), -s, -ing, -ed ˌmɪs'kaʊnt,
-s, -ɪŋ, -ɪd
miscreant, -s ˈmɪskrɪənt, -s
miscu|e (s. v.), -es, -ing, -ed ˌmɪs'kju:,
-z, -ɪŋ [-'kjʊɪŋ], -d
misdeal (s. v.), -s, -ing, misdealt ˌmɪs-
'di:l, -z, -ɪŋ, ˌmɪs'delt
misdeed, -s ˌmɪs'di:d, -z
misdemean|ant/s, -our/s ˌmɪsdɪ'mi:n|-
ənt/s [-də'm-], -ə*/z
misdirect, -s, -ing, -ed ˌmɪsdɪ'rekt
[-də'r-, -daɪ'r-], -s, -ɪŋ, -ɪd
misdirection ˌmɪsdɪ'rekʃn [-də'r-,
-daɪ'r-]
misdoing, -s ˌmɪs'du:ɪŋ [-ʊɪŋ], -z
mise-en-scène ˌmi:zɑ̃:n'seɪn [-zɔ̃:n's-,
-zɒn's-] (mizɑ̃sɛ:n)
miser, -s maɪzə*, -z
miserab|le, -ly, -leness ˈmɪzərəb|l, -lɪ,
lnɪs [-nəs]
miserere, -s ˌmɪzə'rɪərɪ [-'reərɪ], -z
misericord, -s mɪ'zerɪkɔ:d [ˈmɪzərɪ-],
-z
miserl|y, -iness ˈmaɪzəl|ɪ, -ɪnɪs [-ɪnəs]
miser|y, -ies ˈmɪzər|ɪ [-zɪ̯-], -ɪz
misfeasance mɪs'fi:zəns
misfir|e (s. v.), -es, -ing, -ed ˌmɪs'faɪə*,
-z, -ɪŋ, -d
misfit, -s ˈmɪsfɪt [ˌmɪs'f-], -s
misfortune, -s mɪs'fɔ:tʃu:n [-tʃən,
-tju:n], -z
misgiving, -s mɪs'gɪvɪŋ, -z
misgovern, -s, -ing, -ed, -ment ˌmɪs-
'gʌvən, -z, -ɪŋ, -d, -mənt
misguided, -ly ˌmɪs'gaɪdɪd, -lɪ
mishand|le, -les, -ling, -led ˌmɪs'hænd|l
-lz, -lɪŋ [-lɪŋ], -ld
mishap, -s ˈmɪshæp [mɪs'h-], -s
misinform, -s, -ing, -ed ˌmɪsɪn'fɔ:m, -z,
-ɪŋ, -d
misinterpret, -s, -ing, -ed ˌmɪsɪn'tɜ:prɪt,
-s, -ɪŋ, -ɪd
misinterpretation, -s ˈmɪsɪnˌtɜ:prɪ'teɪʃn
[-prə't-], -z
misjudg|e, -es, -ing, -ed ˌmɪs'dʒʌdʒ,
-ɪz, -ɪŋ, -d
mis|lay, -lays, -laying, -laid ˌmɪs|'leɪ,
-'leɪz, -'leɪɪŋ, -'leɪd
mis|lead, -leads, -leading, -led ˌmɪs|-
'li:d, -'li:dz, -'li:dɪŋ, -'led
mismanag|e, -es, -ing, -ed, -ement
ˌmɪs'mænɪdʒ, -ɪz, -ɪŋ, -d, -mənt
misnomer, -s ˌmɪs'nəʊmə*, -z

325

misogam|ist/s, -y mɪ'sɒgəm|ɪst/s [maɪ's-], -ɪ

misogyn|ist/s, -y mɪ'sɒdʒɪn|ɪst/s [maɪ's-, -ɒgɪ-, -ən|ɪst], -ɪ

misplac|e, -es, -ing, -ed, -ement ˌmɪs-'pleɪs, -ɪz, -ɪŋ, -t [also 'mɪspleɪst when attributive], -mənt

misprint (s.), -s 'mɪsprɪnt [also mɪs'p- when preceded by a stress], -s

misprint (v.), -s, -ing, -ed ˌmɪs'prɪnt, -s, -ɪŋ, -ɪd

misprision ˌmɪs'prɪʒn

mispronounc|e, -es, -ing, -ed ˌmɪs-prə'naʊns [-prʊ'n-, -prŋ'aʊns], -ɪz, -ɪŋ, -t

mispronunciation, -s 'mɪsprəˌnʌnsɪ-'eɪʃn [-prʊˌn-, -prŋˌʌn-], -z

misquotation, -s ˌmɪskwəʊ'teɪʃn, -z

misquot|e, -es, -ing, -ed ˌmɪs'kwəʊt, -s, -ɪŋ, -ɪd

mis|read (pres.), -reads, -reading, -read (past) ˌmɪs|'riːd, -'riːdz, -'riːdɪŋ, -'red

misreport, -s, -ing, -ed ˌmɪsrɪ'pɔːt, -s, -ɪŋ, -ɪd

misrepresent, -s, -ing, -ed 'mɪsˌreprɪ-'zent, -s, -ɪŋ, -ɪd

misrepresentation, -s 'mɪsˌreprɪzen-'teɪʃn [-zən-], -z

misrule ˌmɪs'ruːl

miss (s. v.) (M.), -es, -ing, -ed mɪs, -ɪz, -ɪŋ, -t

missal, -s 'mɪsl, -z

missel 'mɪzl ['mɪsl]

Missenden 'mɪsndən

misshapen ˌmɪs'ʃeɪpən [ˌmɪʃ'ʃ-]

missile, -s 'mɪsaɪl, -z

missing (adj.) 'mɪsɪŋ

mission, -s 'mɪʃn, -z

missionar|y, -ies 'mɪʃŋər|ɪ [-ʃnər-, -ʃŋr-, -ʃənər-], -ɪz

missioner, -s 'mɪʃŋə* [-ʃənə*], -z

missis 'mɪsɪz

Mississippi ˌmɪsɪ'sɪpɪ

missive (s. adj.), -s 'mɪsɪv, -z

Missouri mɪ'zʊərɪ [mɪ's-]

Note.—American pronunciation has -z-.

misspel|l, -ls, -ling/s, -led, -t ˌmɪs'spel, -z, -ɪŋ/z, -t [-d], -t

misspen|d, -ds, -ding, -t ˌmɪs'spen|d, -dz, -dɪŋ, -t ['-- when attributive]

misstat|e, -es, -ing, -ed, -ement/s ˌmɪs'steɪt, -s, -ɪŋ, -ɪd, -mənt/s

missuit, -s, -ing, -ed ˌmɪs'suːt [-'sjuːt], -s, -ɪŋ, -ɪd

miss|y, -ies 'mɪs|ɪ, -ɪz

mist, -s mɪst, -s

mistakable mɪ'steɪkəbl

mis|take (s. v.), -takes, -taking, -took, -taken/ly mɪs|'teɪk, -'teɪks, -'teɪkɪŋ, -tʊk, -teɪkən/lɪ

mister 'mɪstə*

mistim|e, -es, -ing, -ed ˌmɪs'taɪm, -z, -ɪŋ, -d

mistletoe 'mɪsltəʊ ['mɪzl-]

mistral, -s 'mɪstrəl [mɪs'trɑːl] (mistral), -z

mistranslat|e, -es, -ing, -ed ˌmɪstræns-'leɪt [-trɑːns-, -trænz-, -trɑːnz-, -trɑns-, -trɒnz-], -s, -ɪŋ, -ɪd

mistranslation, -s ˌmɪstræns'leɪʃn [-trɑːns-, -trænz-, -trɑːnz-, -trɒns-, -trɒnz-], -z

mistress, -es 'mɪstrɪs [-əs], -ɪz

mistrust (s. v.), -s, -ing, -ed ˌmɪs'trʌst, -s, -ɪŋ, -ɪd

mist|y, -ier, -iest, -ily, -iness 'mɪst|ɪ, -ɪə* [-jə*], -ɪɪst [-jɪst], -ɪlɪ [-əlɪ], -ɪnɪs [-məs]

misunderst|and, -ands, -anding/s, -ood ˌmɪsʌndə'st|ænd, -ændz, -ændɪŋ/z, -ʊd

misuse (s.) ˌmɪs'juːs [also 'mɪsjuːs when followed by a stress]

misus|e (v.), -es, -ing, -ed ˌmɪs'juːz, -ɪz, -ɪŋ, -d

Mitch|am, -ell 'mɪtʃ|əm, -l

mite, -s maɪt, -s

Mitford 'mɪtfəd

Mithr|a, -as 'mɪθr|ə, -æs

Mithridates ˌmɪθrɪ'deɪtiːz [-θrə-]

mitigable 'mɪtɪgəbl

mitigat|e, -es, -ing, -ed 'mɪtɪgeɪt, -s, -ɪŋ, -ɪd

mitigation ˌmɪtɪ'geɪʃn

mitrailleuse, -s ˌmɪtraɪ'ɜːz (mitrajøːz), -ɪz

mit|re (s. v.), -res, -ring, -red 'maɪt|ə*, -əz, -ərɪŋ, -əd

mitten, -s 'mɪtn, -z

mity 'maɪtɪ

Mitylene ˌmɪtɪ'liːnɪ

Mivart 'maɪvət [-vɑːt]

mix (s. v.), -es, -ing, -ed, -er/s mɪks, -ɪz, -ɪŋ, -t, -ə*/z

mixture, -s 'mɪkst|ə*, -z

mix-up, -s 'mɪksʌp, -s

Mizar (star) 'maɪzɑː* [-zə*]

Mizen 'mɪzn

Mizpah 'mɪzpə

mizzen, -s 'mɪzn, -z

mizzen-mast, -s 'mɪznmɑːst [nautical pronunciation -məst], -s

mizz|le, -les, -ling, -led 'mɪz|l, -lz, -l̩ɪŋ [-lɪŋ], -ld

326

mnemonic (s. adj.), -s niː'mɒnɪk [nɪ-, mn-], -s

Mnemosyne niː'mɒzɪniː [mniː'm-, mnɪ'm-, -ɒsɪ-]

Moab 'məʊæb

Moabite, -s 'məʊəbaɪt, -s

moan (s. v.), -s, -ing/s, -ed məʊn, -z, -ɪŋ/z, -d

Moase məʊz

moat (s. v.) (M.), -s, -ing, -ed məʊt, -s, -ɪŋ, -ɪd

mob (s. v.), -s, -bing, -bed mɒb, -z, -ɪŋ, -d

Moberly 'məʊbəlɪ

mobile 'məʊbaɪl [-biːl, -bɪl]

mobility məʊ'bɪlətɪ [-lɪt-]

mobilization [-isa-], -s ˌməʊbɪlaɪ'zeɪʃn [-bḷaɪ'z-, -bɪlɪ'z-, -bḷɪ'z-], -z

mobiliz|e [-is|e], -es, -ing, -ed 'məʊbɪlaɪz [-bḷaɪz], -ɪz, -ɪŋ, -d

moccasin, -s 'mɒkəsɪn, -z

mocha (coffee, leather, etc., from Mocha) 'mɒkə ['məʊkə]

Mocha (Arabian seaport) 'məʊkə ['mɒkə]

mock (adj. v.), -s, -ing/ly, -ed, -er/s mɒk, -s, -ɪŋ/lɪ, -t, -ə*/z

mocker|y, -ies 'mɒkər|ɪ, -ɪz

Mockett 'mɒkɪt

mocking-bird, -s 'mɒkɪŋbɜːd, -z

mock-turtle ˌmɒk'tɜːtl

mod|al, -ally 'məʊd|l, -əlɪ

modality məʊ'dælətɪ [-ɪtɪ]

mode, -s məʊd, -z

mod|el (s. v.), -els, -elling, -elled, -eller/s 'mɒd|l, -lz, -lɪŋ, -ld, -lə*/z

modena (colour) 'mɒdɪnə

Modena 'mɒdɪnə [mɒ'deɪnə, mə'd-, old-fashioned -'diːnə] ('mɔːdena)

moderate (s. adj.), -s, -ly, -ness 'mɒdərət [-rɪt], -s, -lɪ, -nɪs [-nəs]

moderat|e (v.), -es, -ing, -ed, -or/s 'mɒdəreɪt, -s, -ɪŋ, -ɪd, -ə*/z

moderation, -s ˌmɒdə'reɪʃn, -z

moderato, -s ˌmɒdə'rɑːtəʊ, -z

modern (s. adj.), -s, -ly, -ness 'mɒdən, -z, -lɪ, -nɪs [-nəs]

moderni|sm, -st/s 'mɒdənɪ|zəm, -st/s

modernity mɒ'dɜːnətɪ [məʊ'd-, -ɪtɪ]

modernization [-isa-] ˌmɒdənaɪ'zeɪʃn [-nɪ'z-]

moderniz|e [-is|e], -es, -ing, -ed 'mɒdənaɪz, -ɪz, -ɪŋ, -d

modest, -ly, -y 'mɒdɪst, -lɪ, -ɪ

modicum, -s 'mɒdɪkəm, -z

modification, -s ˌmɒdɪfɪ'keɪʃn, -z

modi|fy, -fies, -fying, -fied, -fier/s; -fiable 'mɒdɪ|faɪ, -faɪz, -faɪɪŋ, -faɪd, -faɪə*/z; -faɪəbl

modish, -ly, -ness 'məʊdɪʃ, -lɪ, -nɪs [-nəs]

modiste, -s məʊ'diːst, -s

modulat|e, -es, -ing, -ed, -or/s 'mɒdjʊleɪt [-dʒʊ-], -s, -ɪŋ, -ɪd, -ə*/z

modulation, -s ˌmɒdjʊ'leɪʃn [-dʒʊ-], -z

module, -s 'mɒdjuːl, -z

modul|us, -uses, -i 'mɒdjʊl|əs, -əsɪz, -aɪ

modus 'məʊdəs

modus operandi 'mɒdəsˌɒpə'rændiː ['məʊdəsˌɒpə'rændaɪ]

modus vivendi ˌmɒdəsviː'vendiː [-vɪ'v-, ˌməʊdəsvɪ'vendaɪ]

Moeran 'mɔːrən

Moesia 'miːsjə [-sɪə, -ʃjə, -ʃɪə, -zjə, -zɪə, -ʒjə, -ʒɪə]

Moeso-gothic ˌmiːsəʊ'gɒθɪk [ˌmiːzəʊ-]

Moffat 'mɒfət

Mogador ˌmɒgə'dɔː*

Moggach 'mɒgək [-əx]

Mogul, -s 'məʊgʌl [-'-, 'məʊgəl, -gʊl], -z

mohair 'məʊheə*

Mohammed məʊ'hæmed [-mɪd]

Mohammedan, -s məʊ'hæmɪdən, -z

Mohave məʊ'hɑːvɪ

Mohawk, -s 'məʊhɔːk, -s

Mohican, -s 'məʊɪkən, -z

Mohun 'məʊən ['məʊhən], muːn, mə'hʌn

moidore, -s 'mɔɪdɔː* ['məʊɪd-, -dɔə*, mɔɪ'd-], -z

Note.—The stressing -'- has to be used in John Masefield's poem 'Cargoes'.

moiet|y, -ies 'mɔɪət|ɪ ['mɔɪɪt-], -ɪz

moil (s. v.), -s, -ing, -ed mɔɪl, -z, -ɪŋ, -d

Moir 'mɔɪə*

Moira 'mɔɪərə

moire, -s mwɑː* [mwɔː*] (mwa:r), -z

moiré 'mwɑːreɪ ['mwɔːr-] (mware)

moist, -er, -est, -ness mɔɪst, -ə*, -ɪst, -nɪs [-nəs]

moist|en, -ens, -ening, -ened 'mɔɪs|n, -nz, -n̩ɪŋ [-nɪŋ], -nd

moisture 'mɔɪstʃə*

Moivre 'mɔɪvə*

Mojave (=Mohave) məʊ'hɑːvɪ

moke, -s məʊk, -s

molar (s. adj.), -s 'məʊlə*, -z

molasses məʊ'læsɪz

molassine 'mɒləsiːn ['məʊl-]

mold=mould

Mold məʊld

Moldavia, -n mɒl'deɪvjə [-vɪə], -n

molder, moldy=mould-

mole, -s məʊl, -z

molecular məʊ'lekjʊlə* [mɒ'l-, -kjə-]

molecule, -s 'mɒlɪkjuːl ['məʊl-], -z
mole-hill, -s 'məʊlhɪl, -z
Molesey 'məʊlzɪ
mole-skin, -s 'məʊlskɪn, -z
molest, -s, -ing, -ed məʊ'lest, -s, -ɪŋ, dɪ-
molestation, -s ˌməʊle'steɪʃn, -z
Molesworth 'məʊlzwɜːθ [-wəθ]
Moleyns 'mʌlɪnz
Molière 'mɒlɪeə* ['məʊl-, -ljeə*] (mɔljɛ:r)
mollification ˌmɒlɪfɪ'keɪʃn
molli|fy, -fies, -fying, -fied; -fiable 'mɒlɪ|faɪ, -faɪz, -faɪŋ, -faɪd; -faɪəbl
mollusc, -s 'mɒləsk [-lʌsk], -s
mollusc|an, -oid, -ous mɒ'lʌsk|ən [mə'l-], -ɔɪd, -əs
moll|y (M.), -ies 'mɒl|ɪ, -ɪz
mollycodd|le, -les, -ling, -led 'mɒlɪˌkɒd|l, -lz, -lɪŋ [-lɪŋ], -ld
Moloch 'məʊlɒk
Molony mə'ləʊnɪ
Molotov 'mɒlətɒf
molten 'məʊltən
molto 'mɒltəʊ ('molto)
Molton 'məʊltən
moly 'məʊlɪ
molybdenum mɒ'lɪbdɪnəm [məʊ'l-, ˌmɒlɪb'diːnəm]
Molyneux 'mɒlɪnjuːks, 'mʌlɪnjuːks, 'mɒlɪnjuː:, 'mʌlɪnjuː:
Mombasa mɒm'bæsə [-'bɑːsə]
moment, -s 'məʊmənt, -s
momentar|y, -ily, -iness 'məʊməntər|ɪ, -əlɪ [-ɪlɪ], -ɪnɪs [-ɪnəs]
momentous, -ly, -ness məʊ'mentəs, -lɪ, -nɪs [-nəs]
moment|um, -ums, -a məʊ'ment|əm, -əmz, -ə
Momerie 'mʌmərɪ
Mon (language) məʊn
Mon. (abbrev. of Monmouthshire) mɒn
mona (M.), -s 'məʊnə, -z. (See also Monna Lisa)
Monaco 'mɒnəkəʊ [-nɪk-]
monad, -s 'mɒnæd ['məʊn-], -z
monadic mɒ'nædɪk [məʊ'n-]
Monaghan 'mɒnəhən [-nəxən, -nəkən]
monarch, -s 'mɒnək, -s
monarch|al, -ic, -ical mɒ'nɑːk|l [mə'n-], -ɪk, -ɪkl
monarchi|sm, -st/s 'mɒnəkɪ|zəm, -st/s
monarchiz|e [-is|e], -es, -ing, -ed 'mɒnəkaɪz, -ɪz, -ɪŋ, -d
monarch|y, -ies 'mɒnək|ɪ, -ɪz
monaster|y, -ies 'mɒnəstər|ɪ, -ɪz
monastic, -al, -ally mə'næstɪk [mɒ'n-], -l, -əlɪ
monasticism mə'næstɪsɪzəm [mɒ'n-]

monaural ˌmɒn'ɔːrəl
Monck mʌnk
Monckton 'mʌnktən
Moncrieff mən'kriːf [mɒn-]
Mond (English name) mɒnd
Monday, -s 'mʌndɪ [-deɪ], -z
Monegasque ˌmɒnɪ'gæsk
monetary 'mʌnɪtərɪ
monetiz|e [-is|e], -es, -ing, -ed 'mʌnɪtaɪz, -ɪz, -ɪŋ, -d
money (M.), -s, -ed 'mʌnɪ, -z, -d
money-box, -es 'mʌnɪbɒks, -ɪz
money-changer, -s 'mʌnɪˌtʃeɪndʒə*, -z
money-grubb|er/s, -ing 'mʌnɪˌgrʌb|ə*/z, -ɪŋ
money-lend|er/s, -ing 'mʌnɪˌlend|ə*/z, -ɪŋ
money-market, -s 'mʌnɪˌmɑːkɪt, -s
money-order, -s 'mʌnɪˌɔːdə*, -z
Moneypenny 'mʌnɪˌpenɪ
money-spinner, -s 'mʌnɪˌspɪnə*, -z
monger, -s 'mʌŋgə*, -z
mongol (M.), -s, -oid 'mɒŋgɒl [-gəl], -z, -ɔɪd
Mongolia, -n/s mɒŋ'gəʊljə [-lɪə], -n/z
mongoose, -s 'mɒŋguːs ['mʌŋ-], -ɪz
mongrel, -s 'mʌŋgrəl, -z
Monica 'mɒnɪkə
Monier 'mʌnɪə* ['mɒn-, -njə*]
moni|sm, -st/s 'mɒnɪ|zəm, -st/s
monistic mɒ'nɪstɪk
monition, -s məʊ'nɪʃn [mɒ'n-], -z
monitor, -s; -ship/s 'mɒnɪtə*, -z; -ʃɪp/s
monitorial ˌmɒnɪ'tɔːrɪəl
monitory 'mɒnɪtərɪ
monk (M.), -s, -ish mʌŋk, -s, -ɪʃ
monkey, -s 'mʌŋkɪ, -z
monkey-engine, -s 'mʌŋkɪˌendʒɪn, -z
monkey-puzzle, -s 'mʌŋkɪˌpʌzl, -z
Monkhouse 'mʌŋkhaʊs
Monkton 'mʌŋktən
Monkwearmouth mʌŋk'wɪəmaʊθ
Monmouth, -shire 'mɒnməθ [rarely 'mʌn-], -ʃə* [-ˌʃɪə*]
Monna Lisa ˌmɒnə'liːzə (sometimes spelt Mona and pronounced 'məʊnə)
mono (monotype), -s 'məʊnəʊ ['mɒnəʊ], (in sound recording, opp. stereo) 'mɒnəʊ, -z
Monoceros mə'nɒsərɒs [mɒ'n-]
monochord, -s 'mɒnəʊkɔːd, -z
monochrome, -s 'mɒnəkrəʊm, -z
monocle, -s 'mɒnəkl [-nɒk-], -z
monocotyledon, -s 'mɒnəʊˌkɒtɪ'liːdən [-ˌkɒtə-], -z
monod|y, -ies 'mɒnəd|ɪ, -ɪz
monogam|ist/s, -ous, -y mɒ'nɒgəm|ɪst/s [mə'n-], -əs, -ɪ

monoglot 'mɒnəglɒt
monogram, -s 'mɒnəgræm, -z
monograph, -s 'mɒnəgrɑːf [-græf], -s
monolingual ˌmɒnəʊ'lɪŋgwəl
monolith, -s 'mɒnəʊlɪθ, -s
monolithic ˌmɒnəʊ'lɪθɪk
monologist, -s mɒ'nɒlədʒɪst, -s
monologiz|e [-is|e], -es, -ing, -ed, -er/s mɒ'nɒlədʒaɪz, -ɪz, -ɪŋ, -d, -ə*/z
monologue, -s 'mɒnəlɒg [rarely -ləʊg], -z
monoma|nia, -niac/s ˌmɒnəʊ'meɪ|njə [-nɪə], -nɪæk/s
monophthong, -s 'mɒnəfθɒŋ, -z
monophthong|al, -ic, mɒnəf'θɒŋg|l, -ɪk
monophthongiz|e [-is|e], -es, -ing, -ed 'mɒnəfθɒŋgaɪz, -ɪz, -ɪŋ, -d
monoplane, -s 'mɒnəʊpleɪn, -z
Monopole 'mɒnəpəʊl
monopolism mə'nɒpəlɪzəm [-plɪzəm]
monopolist, -s mə'nɒpəlɪst [-plɪst], -s
monopolistic mə,nɒpə'lɪstɪk [-pl'ɪstɪk]
monopoliz|e [-is|e], -es, -ing, -ed, -er/s mə'nɒpəlaɪz [-plaɪz], -ɪz, -ɪŋ, -d, -ə*/z
monopol|y, -ies mə'nɒpəl|ɪ [-pl|ɪ], -ɪz
monorail, -s 'mɒnəʊreɪl, -z
monosyllabic ˌmɒnəʊsɪ'læbɪk
monosyllable, -s 'mɒnə,sɪləbl, -z
monothei|sm, -st/s 'mɒnəʊθiː,ɪ|zəm ['mɒnəʊ,θiː-], -st/s
monoton|e (s. v.), -es, -ing, -ed 'mɒnətəʊn, -z, -ɪŋ, -d
monotonic ˌmɒnə'tɒnɪk
monotonous, -ly mə'nɒtnəs [-tənəs], -lɪ
monotony mə'nɒtnɪ [-tənɪ]
monotype, -s 'mɒnəʊtaɪp, -s
monovalen|ce, -t 'mɒnəʊ,veɪlən|s [,--'--], -t
monoxide, -s mɒ'nɒksaɪd [mə'n-], -z
Monro(e) mən'rəʊ [mʌn'rəʊ], 'mʌnrəʊ
Mons mɒnz [mɔ̃ːns] (mɔ̃ːs)
Monsarrat (surname) ˌmɒnsə'ræt
monseigneur, -s ˌmɒnsen'jɜː* (mɔ̃sɛɲœːr), -z
Monserrat (Spanish general) ˌmɒnse'rɑːt [-sə'r-]
monsieur (M.) mə'sjɜː* (strong form) (məsjø), məsjə* (weak form)
Monsignor mɒn'siːnjə*
Monson 'mʌnsn
monsoon, -s mɒn'suːn [mən-], -z
monster, -s 'mɒnstə*, -z
monstrance, -s 'mɒnstrəns, -ɪz
monstrosit|y, -ies mɒn'strɒsət|ɪ [mən-, -ɪt|ɪ], -ɪz

monstrous, -ly, -ness 'mɒnstrəs, -lɪ, -nɪs [-nəs]
montage, -s mɒn'tɑːʒ ['mɒntɑːʒ, 'mɒntɪdʒ], -ɪz
Montagu(e) 'mɒntəgjuː [-tɪg-], 'mʌn-
Montaigne mɒn'teɪn
Montana (state of U.S.A.) mɒn'tænə [-'tɑː-]
Mont Blanc ˌmɔ̃ː'blɑ̃ː:ŋ [-'blɔ̃ːŋ, ˌmɒm'blɒŋ, ˌmɒn'blɒŋ] (mɔ̃blɑ̃)
montbretia, -s mɒn'briːʃjə [mɒm'b-, -ʃɪə, -ʃə], -z
Mont Cenis ˌmɔ̃ːnsə'niː [ˌmɒnt-] (mɔ̃sni)
monte (M.) 'mɒntɪ
Monte Carlo ˌmɒntɪ'kɑːləʊ
Montefiore ˌmɒntɪfɪ'ɔːrɪ [-'fjɔːrɪ]
monteith, -s mɒn'tiːθ, -s
Monteith mən'tiːθ [mɒn-]
Montenegr|o, -ian/s, -in/s ˌmɒntɪ'niː-gr|əʊ [-'neɪg-], -ɪən/z, -ɪn/z
Monte Rosa ˌmɒntɪ'rəʊzə
Montesquieu ˌmɒnte'skjuː [-'skjə:, '---] (mɔ̃teskjø)
Montessori ˌmɒnte'sɔːrɪ [-tɪ's-]
Montevideo ˌmɒntɪvɪ'deɪəʊ [old-fashioned -'vɪdɪəʊ]
Montezuma ˌmɒntɪ'zuːmə
Montfort (Simon de Montfort) 'mɒntfət [-fɔːt]
Montgomerie mənt'gʌmərɪ [mɒnt-'gɒm-, mənt'gɒm-]
Montgomery, -shire mənt'gʌmərɪ [mɒnt'gɒm-, mənt'gɒm-] (Welsh mont'gəmri), -ʃə* [-,ʃɪə*]
month, -s, -ly mʌnθ, -s, -lɪ
Montmorency ˌmɒntmə'rensɪ
Montpelier (in U.S.A., London Street) mɒnt'piːljə* [-lɪə*]
Montpellier (in France) mɔ̃ː'm'pelɪeɪ [mɒnt'p-] (mɔ̃pəlje, -pelje), (in names of streets, etc.) mɒnt'pelɪə* [mənt-, -ljə*]
Montreal ˌmɒntrɪ'ɔːl
Montreux mɒn'trɜː (mɔ̃trø)
Montrose mɒn'trəʊz
Montserrat (island in West Indies) ˌmɒntse'ræt [-sə'r-], (monastery in Spain) -'rɑːt
Monty 'mɒntɪ
monument, -s 'mɒnjʊmənt [-jəm-], -s
monument|al, -ally ˌmɒnjʊ'ment|l [-jə'm-], -əlɪ [-lɪ]
Monzie (in Tayside) mə'niː
moo, -s, -ing, -ed muː, -z, -ɪŋ, -d
mooch, -es, -ing, -ed muːtʃ, -ɪz, -ɪŋ, -t
moo-cow, -s 'muːkaʊ, -z
mood, -s muːd, -z

mood|y (M.), -ier, -iest, -ily, -iness
'mu:d|ɪ, -ɪə* [-jə*], -ɪɪst [-jɪst], -ɪlɪ
[-əlɪ], -ɪnɪs [-ɪnəs]

moon (s. v.) (M.), -s, -ing, -ed; -beam/s
mu:n, -z, -ɪŋ, -d; -bi:m/z

moon-cal|f, -ves 'mu:nkɑ:|f, -vz

moon|less, -light, -lit 'mu:n|lɪs [-ləs],
-laɪt, -lɪt

moonshine 'mu:nʃaɪn

moonstruck 'mu:nstrʌk

moonstone, -s 'mu:nstəʊn, -z

moony 'mu:nɪ

moor (s. v.) (M.), -s, -ing/s, -ed mʊə*
[mɔə*, mɔ:*], -z, -rɪŋ/z, -d

moor-cock, -s 'mʊəkɒk ['mɔə-, 'mɔ:-],
-z

Moore mʊə*

Moorgate 'mʊəgeɪt ['mɔə-, 'mɔ:-, -gɪt]

moorhen, -s 'mʊəhen ['mɔə-, 'mɔ:-], -z

mooring-mast, -s 'mʊərɪŋmɑ:st ['mɔə-,
'mɔ:r-], -s

Moorish 'mʊərɪʃ ['mɔə-, 'mɔ:r-]

moorland, -s 'mʊələnd ['mɔəl-, 'mɔ:l-,
-lænd], -z

*Note.—The variant -lænd is not used
when the word is attributive.*

moose, -s mu:s, -ɪz

moot (s. adj. v.), -s, -ing, -ed mu:t, -s
-ɪŋ, -ɪd

mop (s. v.), -s, -ping, -ped mɒp, -s, -ɪŋ,
-t

mop|e, -es, -ing/ly, -ed məʊp, -s, -ɪŋ/lɪ,
-t

moped (s.), -s 'məʊped, -z

mopish, -ly, -ness 'məʊpɪʃ, -lɪ, -nɪs
[-nəs]

moquette mɒ'ket [məʊ-]

mor|a, -ae, -as 'mɔ:r|ə, -i: [-aɪ], -əz

Morag 'mɔ:ræg

moraine, -s mɒ'reɪn [mə'r-], -z

mor|al (s. adj.), -als, -ally 'mɒr|əl, -əlz,
-əlɪ [-lɪ]

morale mɒ'rɑ:l [mə'r-]

moralist, -s 'mɒrəlɪst [-rlɪst], -s

morality mə'rælətɪ [mɒ'r-, -ɪtɪ]

moraliz|e [-is|e], -es, -ing, -ed, -er/s
'mɒrəlaɪz [-rlaɪz], -ɪz, -ɪŋ, -d, -ə*/z

Moran 'mɔ:rən, 'mɒrən, mə'ræn
[mɒ'ræn]

Morant mə'rænt [mɒ'r-]

morass, -es mə'ræs [mɒ'r-], -ɪz

moratorium, -s ˌmɒrə'tɔ:rɪəm [ˌmɔ:r-],
-z

Moravia, -n/s mə'reɪvjə [mɒ'r-, -vɪə],
-n/z

Moray, -shire 'mʌrɪ, -ʃə* [-ˌʃɪə*]

morbid, -est, -ly, -ness 'mɔ:bɪd, -ɪst, -lɪ,
-nɪs [-nəs]

morbidity mɔ:'bɪdətɪ [-ɪtɪ]

mordant (s. adj.), -s 'mɔ:dənt, -s

Mordecai ˌmɔ:dɪ'keɪaɪ

mordent, -s 'mɔ:dənt, -s

more (M.) mɔ:* [mɔə*]

Morea mɒ'rɪə [mə'r-, mɔ:'r-]

Morecambe 'mɔ:kəm

Moreen mɔ:'ri:n ['—]

morel (M.) mɒ'rel [mə'r-]

morello, -s mə'reləʊ [mɒ'r-], -z

moreover mɔ:'rəʊvə* [mə'r-]

mores 'mɔ:ri:z [-reɪz]

Moreton 'mɔ:tn

Morgan 'mɔ:gən

morganatic, -ally ˌmɔ:gə'nætɪk, -əlɪ

morgue, -s mɔ:g, -z

Moriah mɒ'raɪə [mɔ:'r-, mə'r-]

Moriarty ˌmɒrɪ'ɑ:tɪ

moribund 'mɒrɪbʌnd ['mɔ:r-, -bənd]

Morison 'mɒrɪsn

Morley 'mɔ:lɪ

Mormon, -s, -ism 'mɔ:mən, -z, -ɪzəm

morn, -s mɔ:n, -z

morning, -s 'mɔ:nɪŋ, -z

morning-coat, -s ˌmɔ:nɪŋ'kəʊt ['—-], -s

morning-dress ˌmɔ:nɪŋ'dres

morning-room, -s 'mɔ:nɪŋrʊm [-ru:m],
-z

morning-star, -s ˌmɔ:nɪŋ'stɑ:* ['—-], -z

Mornington 'mɔ:nɪŋtən

morning-watch, -es ˌmɔ:nɪŋ'wɒtʃ, -ɪz

Moroccan, -s mə'rɒkən, -z

morocco (M.), -s mə'rɒkəʊ, -z

moron, -s 'mɔ:rɒn [-rən], -z

morose, -ly, -ness mə'rəʊs [mɒ'r-], -lɪ,
-nɪs [-nəs]

Morpeth 'mɔ:peθ [-pəθ]

morpheme, -s 'mɔ:fi:m, -z

morphemic mɔ:'fi:mɪk

Morpheus 'mɔ:fju:s [-fjəs, -fɪəs]

morph|ia, -ine 'mɔ:f|jə [-ɪə], -i:n

morphologic, -al, -ally ˌmɔ:fə'lɒdʒɪk, -l,
-əlɪ

morpholog|ist/s, -y mɔ:'fɒlədʒ|ɪst/s, -ɪ

morphophonemic ˌmɔ:fəʊfəʊ'ni:mɪk

morphophonology ˌmɔ:fəʊfəʊ'nɒlədʒɪ

Morphy 'mɔ:fɪ

Morrell 'mʌrəl, mə'rel

morris (M.), -es 'mɒrɪs, -ɪz

morris-dance, -s ˌmɒrɪs'dɑ:ns ['—-], -ɪz

Morrison 'mɒrɪsn

morrow (M.), -s 'mɒrəʊ, -z

morse (M.), -s mɔ:s, -ɪz

morsel, -s 'mɔ:sl, -z

Morshead 'mɔ:zhed

mort, -s mɔ:t, -s

mort|al, -als, -ally 'mɔ:t|l, -lz, -əlɪ [-lɪ]

mortalit|y (M.), -ies mɔ:'tælət|ɪ [-ɪt|ɪ], -ɪz

mortar, -s 'mɔːtə*, -z
mortarboard, -s 'mɔːtəbɔːd [-bɔəd],
-z
mortgag|e (s. v.), -es, -ing, -ed
'mɔːgɪdʒ, -ɪz, -ɪŋ, -d
mortgagee, -s ˌmɔːgəˈdʒiː, -z
mortgagor, -s ˌmɔːgəˈdʒɔː*, -z
mortice, -s 'mɔːtɪs, -ɪz
mortification, ˌmɔːtɪfɪˈkeɪʃn
morti|fy, -fies, -fying, -fied 'mɔːtɪ|faɪ,
-faɪz, -faɪŋ, -faɪd
Mortimer 'mɔːtɪmə*
mortis|e (s. v.), -es, -ing, -ed 'mɔːtɪs, -ɪz,
-ɪŋ, -t
Mort|lake, -lock 'mɔːt|leɪk, -lɒk
mortmain 'mɔːtmeɪn
Morton 'mɔːtn
mortuar|y, -ies 'mɔːtjʊər|ɪ [-tjwər-,
-tjʊr-, -tʃʃərɪ, -tʃərɪ], -ɪz
mosaic (s. adj.) (M.), -s məʊˈzeɪɪk, -s
Mosby 'mɒzbɪ
Moscow 'mɒskəʊ
Moseley 'məʊzlɪ
moselle (M.), -s məʊˈzel, -z
Moses 'məʊzɪz
Moslem, -s 'mɒzlem [-ləm, 'mʊzlɪm],
-z
Mosley 'mɒzlɪ, 'məʊzlɪ
mosque, -s mɒsk, -s
mosquit|o (M.), -oes, -oey; -o-net/s
məˈskiː|təʊ [mɒ's-], -əʊz, -əʊɪ;
-əʊnet/s
moss (M.), -es mɒs, -ɪz
moss-grown 'mɒsgrəʊn
moss-rose, -s ˌmɒsˈrəʊz ['--], -ɪz
moss|y, -ier, -iest, -iness 'mɒs|ɪ, -ɪə*,
-ɪɪst, -ɪnɪs [-məs]
mos|t, -tly məʊs|t, -tlɪ
Mostyn 'mɒstɪn
Mosul 'məʊsəl
mot, -s məʊ, -z
mote, -s məʊt, -s
motel, -s məʊˈtel ['--], -z
motet, -s məʊˈtet, -s
moth, -s mɒθ, -s
moth-eaten 'mɒθˌiːtn
mother (s. v.), -s, -ing, -ed; -hood,
-less 'mʌðə*, -z, -rɪŋ, -d; -hʊd, -lɪs
[-ləs, -les]
mother-countr|y, -ies 'mʌðəˌkʌntr|ɪ
[ˌ--'--], -ɪz
mother-in-law, -s 'mʌðərɪnlɔː, -z
motherl|y, -iness 'mʌðəl|ɪ, ˈ-ɪnɪs [-məs]
mother-of-pearl ˌmʌðərəvˈpɜːl
mothersill 'mʌðəsɪl
mothers-in-law (alternative plur. of
mother-in-law) 'mʌðəzɪnlɔː
motif, -s məʊˈtiːf ['--], -s

moti|on (s. v.), -ons, -oning, -oned;
-onless 'məʊʃ|n, -nz, -ŋɪŋ [-ənɪŋ],
-nd; -nlɪs [-ləs, -les]
motivat|e, -es, -ing, -ed 'məʊtɪveɪt, -s
-ɪŋ, -ɪd
motivation ˌməʊtɪˈveɪʃn
motive (s. adj.), -s 'məʊtɪv, -z
mot juste ˌməʊˈʒuːst (mɔʒyst)
motley (M.), 'mɒtlɪ
Motopo məʊˈtəʊpəʊ
motor (s. adj. v.), -s, -ing, -ed 'məʊtə*,
-z, -rɪŋ, -d
motor-bicycle, -s 'məʊtəˌbaɪsɪkl [-səkl],
-z
motor-bike, -s 'məʊtəbaɪk, -s
motor-boat, -s 'məʊtəbəʊt, -s
motorcade, -s 'məʊtəkeɪd, -z
motor-car, -s 'məʊtəkɑː*, -z
motor-cycle, -s 'məʊtəˌsaɪkl [ˌ--'--], -z
motor-cyclist, -s 'məʊtəsaɪklɪst, -s
motorist, -s 'məʊtərɪst, -s
motor-scooter, -s 'məʊtəˌskuːtə*, -z
motor-ship, -s 'məʊtəʃɪp, -s
motor-spirit 'məʊtəˌspɪrɪt [ˌ--'--]
motorway, -s 'məʊtəweɪ, -z
motory 'məʊtərɪ
Mott mɒt
Mottistone 'mɒtɪstən [-stəʊn]
mottle, -s, -d 'mɒtl, -z, -d
motto, -s 'mɒtəʊ, -z
Mottram 'mɒtrəm
Mouat 'məʊət
mouch, -es, -ing, -ed muːtʃ, -ɪz, -ɪŋ,
-t
mouf(f)lon, -s 'muːflɒn, -z
Moughton 'məʊtn
moujik, -s 'muːʒɪk [-dʒɪk], -s
Mouland (surname) muːˈlænd [mʊ-]
mould (s. v.), -s, -ing/s, -ed məʊld, -z,
-ɪŋ/z, -ɪd
mould|er, -ers, -ering, -ered 'məʊld|ə*,
-əz, -ərɪŋ, -əd
mould|y, -ier, -iest, -iness 'məʊld|ɪ, -ɪə*
[-jə*], -ɪɪst [-jɪst], -ɪnɪs [-ɪnəs]
Moule məʊl, muːl
Moulmein maʊlˈmeɪn
moulsford 'məʊlsfəd [-lzf-]
moult (s. v.), -s, -ing, -ed məʊlt, -s, -ɪŋ,
-ɪd
Moulton 'məʊltən
Moultrie 'mɔːltrɪ, 'muːtrɪ
mound (M.), -s maʊnd, -z
Mounsey 'maʊnzɪ
mount (s. v.) (M.), -s, -ing, -ed maʊnt,
-s, -ɪŋ, -ɪd
mountain, -s 'maʊntɪn [-tən], -z
mountain-ash, -es ˌmaʊntɪnˈæʃ [-tən-],
-ɪz

331

mountaineer, -s, -ing ˌmaʊntɪˈnɪə*
[-təˈn-], -z, -rɪŋ
mountainous ˈmaʊntɪnəs [-tən-]
mountant, -s ˈmaʊntənt, -s
Mountbatten maʊntˈbætn
mountebank, -s ˈmaʊntɪbæŋk, -s
Mountjoy maʊntˈdʒɔɪ, ˈmaʊntdʒɔɪ
Moura ˈmʊərə
mourn, -s, -ing, -ed, -er/s mɔːn [mɔən,
rarely mʊən], -z, -ɪŋ, -d, -ə*/z
mourn|ful, -fully, -fulness ˈmɔːn|fʊl
[ˈmɔən-, rarely ˈmʊən-], -fʊlɪ [-fəlɪ],
-fʊlnɪs [-nəs]
mouse (s.), mice maʊs, maɪs
mous|e (v.), -es, -ing, -ed maʊz, -ɪz, -ɪŋ,
-d [maʊs, -ɪz, -ɪŋ, -t]
mouse-hole, -s ˈmaʊshəʊl, -z
Mousehole (near Penzance) ˈmaʊzl
mouser, -s ˈmaʊzə* [ˈmaʊsə*], -z
mouse-trap, -s ˈmaʊstræp, -s
Mousir muːˈsɪə*
mousse muːs
mousseline ˈmuːslɪn [muːsˈliːn]
moustache, -s məˈstɑːʃ [mʊˈs-], -ɪz
mousy ˈmaʊsɪ
mou|th (s.), -ths maʊ|θ, -ðz
mouth (v.), -s, -ing, -ed maʊð, -z, -ɪŋ, -d
mouthful, -s ˈmaʊθfʊl, -z
mouth-organ, -s ˈmaʊθˌɔːgən, -z
mouthpiece, -s ˈmaʊθpiːs, -ɪz
mouth|y, -ier, -iest ˈmaʊð|ɪ, -ɪə* [-jə*],
-ɪɪst [-jɪst]
movability ˌmuːvəˈbɪlɪtɪ [-lɪt-]
movable, -s, -ness ˈmuːvəbl, -z, -nɪs
[-nəs]
mov|e (s. v.), -es, -ing/ly, -ed, -er/s,
-ement/s muːv, -z, -ɪŋ/lɪ, -d, -ə*/z,
-mənt/s
movie, -s; -tone ˈmuːvɪ, -z; -təʊn
mow (s.) (stack), -s məʊ, -z
mow (s.) (grimace), -s maʊ, -z
mow (v.) (cut down), -s, -ing, -ed, -n,
-er/s məʊ, -z, -ɪŋ, -d, -n, -ə*/z
Mowatt ˈmaʊət, ˈməʊət
Mowbray ˈməʊbreɪ, -brɪ
Mowgli ˈmaʊglɪ
mowing-machine, -s ˈməʊɪŋməˌʃiːn, -z
Mowll məʊl, muːl
Moxon ˈmɒksn
moya (M.), -s ˈmɔɪə, -z
Moyes mɔɪz
Moygashel (place) mɔɪˈgæʃl, (linen)
ˈmɔɪgəʃl
Moynihan ˈmɔɪnjən [-nɪən]
Mozambique ˌməʊzəmˈbiːk [-zæm-]
Mozart ˈməʊtsɑːt [old-fashioned
ˈməʊˈzɑːt]
M.P. (member of Parliament) ˌemˈpiː

Mr. ˈmɪstə*
Mrs. ˈmɪsɪz
MS ˌemˈes [emˈes, ˈmænjʊskrɪpt, -jəs-]
Ms. (used by some women to avoid
indicating marital status; rarely said,
the pronunciation is unstable) mɪz,
məz
MSS ˌemesˈes [ˈmænjʊskrɪpts, -jəs-]
mu mjuː
much, -ly, -ness mʌtʃ, -lɪ, -nɪs [-nəs]
Muchalls ˈmʌkəlz [ˈmʌxəlz]
mucilage, -s ˈmjuːˈsɪlɪdʒ, -ɪz
mucilaginous ˌmjuːsɪˈlædʒɪnəs [-dʒənəs]
muck (s. v.), -s, -ing, -ed mʌk, -s, -ɪŋ,
-t
mucker (s. v.), -s, -ing, -ed ˈmʌkə*, -z,
-rɪŋ, -d
muckrake, -s ˈmʌkreɪk, -s
muck|y, -ier, -iest, -iness ˈmʌk|ɪ, -ɪə*,
-ɪɪst, -ɪnɪs [-nə]
muc|ous, -us ˈmjuːk|əs, -əs
mud, -s mʌd, -z
mud-ba|th, -ths ˈmʌdbɑː|θ [ˌmʌdˈb-],
-ðz
mudd|le (s. v.), -les, -ling, -led, -ler/s
ˈmʌd|l, -lz, -lɪŋ [-lɪŋ], -ld, -lə*/z
[-lə*/z]
muddleheaded ˈmʌdlˌhedɪd [ˌ--ˈ--]
mudd|y (adj. v.), -ier, -iest, -ily, -iness;
-ies, -ying, -ied ˈmʌd|ɪ, -ɪə*, -ɪɪst, -ɪlɪ
[-əlɪ], -ɪnɪs [-nəs]; -ɪz, -ɪɪŋ, -ɪd
Mud(d)eford ˈmʌdɪfəd
mud-guard, -s ˈmʌdgɑːd, -z
Mudie ˈmjuːdɪ
mudlark, -s ˈmʌdlɑːk, -s
muezzin, -s muːˈezɪn [mʊˈe-], -z
muff (s. v.), -s, -ing, -ed mʌf, -s, -ɪŋ, -t
muffin, -s ˈmʌfɪn, -z
muffineer, -s ˌmʌfɪˈnɪə*, -z
muff|le, -les, -ling, -led ˈmʌf|l, -lz, -lɪŋ
[-lɪŋ], -ld
muffler, -s ˈmʌflə*, -z
mufti ˈmʌftɪ
mug (s. v.), -s, -ging, -ged mʌg, -z, -ɪŋ,
-d
mugger, -s ˈmʌgə*, -z
muggins, -es ˈmʌgɪnz, -ɪz
Muggins ˈmʌgɪnz, ˈmjuːgɪnz
Muggleton ˈmʌgltən
mugg|y, -ier, -iest, -iness ˈmʌg|ɪ, -ɪə*,
-ɪɪst, -ɪnɪs [-nəs]
mugwump, -s ˈmʌgwʌmp, -s
Muir, -head mjʊə* [mjɔə*, mjɔː*], -hed
Mukden ˈmʊkdən
Mukle ˈmjuːklɪ
mulatto, -s mjuːˈlætəʊ [mjʊˈl-], -z
mulberr|y, -ies ˈmʌlbər|ɪ, -ɪz
Mulcaster ˈmʌlkæstə*

mulch (s. v.), -es, -ing, -ed mʌltʃ, -ɪz, -ɪŋ, -t

mulct (s. v.), -s, -ing, -ed mʌlkt, -s, -ɪŋ, -ɪd

mule, -s mjuːl, -z

muleteer, -s ˌmjuːlɪˈtɪə* [-ləˈt-], -z

Mulgrave ˈmʌlgreɪv

mulish, -ly, -ness ˈmjuːlɪʃ, -lɪ, -nɪs [-nəs]

mull (s. v.) (M.), -s, -ing, -ed mʌl, -z, -ɪŋ, -d

Mullah, -s ˈmʌlə, -z

mullein, ˈmʌlɪn

mullet (M.), -s ˈmʌlɪt [-lət], -s

mulligatawny ˌmʌlɪgəˈtɔːnɪ

Mullin|ar, -er ˈmʌlɪn|ə*, -ə*

Mullinger ˈmʌlɪndʒə*

mullion (M.), -s, -ed ˈmʌlɪən [-ljən], -z, -d

mullock ˈmʌlək

Mulready mʌlˈredɪ

multifarious, -ly, -ness ˌmʌltɪˈfeərɪəs, -lɪ, -nɪs [-nəs]

multiform ˈmʌltɪfɔːm

multilateral ˌmʌltɪˈlætərəl

multiliter|al, -ally ˌmʌltɪˈlɪtər|əl, -əlɪ

multi-millionaire, -s ˌmʌltɪmɪljəˈneə*, -z

multiple (s. adj.), -s ˈmʌltɪpl, -z

multiplex ˈmʌltɪpleks

multiplicand, -s ˌmʌltɪplɪˈkænd, -z

multiplication, -s ˌmʌltɪplɪˈkeɪʃn, -z

multiplicative ˌmʌltɪˈplɪkətɪv [ˈmʌltɪplɪkeɪtɪv]

multiplicator, -s ˈmʌltɪplɪkeɪtə*, -z

multiplicity ˌmʌltɪˈplɪsɪtɪ [-ɪtɪ]

multipl|y, -ies, -ying, -ied, -ier/s ˈmʌltɪpl|aɪ, -aɪz, -aɪɪŋ, -aɪd, -aɪə*/z

multi-purpose ˌmʌltɪˈpɜːpəs

multitude, -s ˈmʌltɪtjuːd, -z

multitudinous, -ly, -ness ˌmʌltɪˈtjuːdɪnəs [-dŋəs], -lɪ, -nɪs [-nəs]

multum in parvo ˌmʊltəmɪnˈpɑːvəʊ [ˌmʌl-]

mum mʌm

mumb|le, -les, -ling/ly, -led, -ler/s ˈmʌmb|l, -lz, -lɪŋ/lɪ, -ld, -lə*/z

Mumbles ˈmʌmblz

mumbo-jumbo ˌmʌmbəʊˈdʒʌmbəʊ

Mumm mʌm

mummer, -s, -y ˈmʌmə*, -z, -rɪ

mummification ˌmʌmɪfɪˈkeɪʃn

mummi|fy, -fies, -fying, -fied ˈmʌmɪ|faɪ, -faɪz, -faɪɪŋ, -faɪd

mumm|y, ies ˈmʌm|ɪ, -ɪz

mump, -s, -ing, -ed mʌmp, -s, -ɪŋ, -t [mʌmt]

mumpish, -ly, -ness ˈmʌmpɪʃ, -lɪ, -nɪs [-nəs]

mumps (s.) mʌmps

munch, -es, -ing, -ed mʌntʃ, -ɪz, -ɪŋ, -t

Munchausen mʌnˈtʃɔːzn [mʊnˈtʃaʊzn] (also as German Münchhausen ˈmynç,hauzən)

mundane, -ly ˌmʌnˈdeɪn [ˈ--], -lɪ

Munich ˈmjuːnɪk

municipal mjuːˈnɪsɪpl [mjʊˈn-]

municipalit|y, -ies mjuːˌnɪsɪˈpælət|ɪ [mjʊˌn-, ˌmjuːnɪsɪˈp-, -ɪt|ɪ], -ɪz

municipaliz|e [-is|e], -es, -ing, -ed mjuːˈnɪsɪpəlaɪz [mjʊˈn-], -ɪz, -ɪŋ, -d

munificen|ce, -t/ly mjuːˈnɪfɪsn|s [mjʊˈn-], -t/lɪ

muniment, -s ˈmjuːnɪmənt, -s

munition, -s mjuːˈnɪʃn [mjʊˈn-], -z

Munro mʌnˈrəʊ [mən-], ˈmʌnrəʊ

Munsey ˈmʌnzɪ

Munster ˈmʌnstə*

muntjak, -s ˈmʌntdʒæk, -s

mural, -s ˈmjʊərəl [ˈmjɔːr-, ˈmjɔːr-], -z

Murchie ˈmɜːkɪ, in S. England also ˈmɜːtʃɪ

Murchison ˈmɜːtʃɪsn, ˈmɜːkɪsn

Murcott ˈmɜːkət

murd|er (s. v.), -ers, -ering, -ered, -erer/s ˈmɜːd|ə*, -əz, -ərɪŋ, -əd, -ərə*/z

murderess, -es ˈmɜːdərɪs [-res], -ɪz

murderous, -ly ˈmɜːdərəs, -lɪ

Murdoch ˈmɜːdɒk

Mure mjʊə* [mjɔə*, mjɔː*]

muriate ˈmjʊərɪət [ˈmjɔər-, ˈmjɔːr-, -rɪt, -rɪeɪt]

muriatic ˌmjʊərɪˈætɪk [ˌmjɔər-, ˌmjɔːr-, ˈ----]

Muriel ˈmjʊərɪəl [ˈmjɔər-, ˈmjɔːr-]

Murillo, -s mjʊəˈrɪləʊ [mjʊˈr-, -ljəʊ], -z

Murison ˈmjʊərɪsn [ˈmjɔər-, ˈmjɔːr-]

murk|y, -ier, -iest, -ily, -iness ˈmɜːk|ɪ, -ɪə* [-jə*], -ɪɪst [-jɪst], -ɪlɪ [-əlɪ], -ɪnɪs [-nəs]

murm|ur (s. v.), -urs, -uring/ly, -ured, -urer/s ˈmɜːm|ə*, -əz, -ərɪŋ/lɪ, -əd, -ərə*/z

murph|y (M.), -ies ˈmɜːf|ɪ, -ɪz

murrain ˈmʌrɪn [-reɪn]

Murray ˈmʌrɪ

Murree ˈmʌrɪ

Murrell ˈmʌrəl, mʌˈrel [məˈrel]

Murrie (surname) ˈmjʊərɪ

Murry ˈmʌrɪ

Murtagh ˈmɜːtə

Murtle ˈmɜːtl

Mus. Bac., -'s ˌmʌzˈbæk, -s

muscat (M.), -s ˈmʌskət, -s

muscatel, -s ˌmʌskəˈtel, -z

Muschamp ˈmʌskəm

muscle, -s 'mʌsl, -z
muscle-bound 'mʌslbaʊnd
Muscovite, -s 'mʌskəʊvaɪt, -s
Muscovy 'mʌskəʊvɪ
muscular, -ly 'mʌskjʊlə* [-jəl-], -lɪ
muscularity ˌmʌskjʊ'lærətɪ [-jə'l-, -ɪtɪ]
Mus.D., -'s ˌmʌz'diː, -z
mus|e (s. v.) (M.), -es, -ing/ly, -ed
mjuːz, -ɪz, -ɪŋ/lɪ, -d
musette, -s mjuː'zet [mjʊ'z-], -s
museum, -s mjuː'zɪəm [mjʊ'z-], -z
Musgrave 'mʌzgreɪv
mush (s. v.), -es, -ing, -ed mʌʃ, -ɪz, -ɪŋ, -t
mushroom, -s 'mʌʃrʊm [-ruːm], -z
mush|y -ier, -iest, -iness 'mʌʃ|ɪ, -ɪə*, -ɪist, -ɪnɪs [-məs]
music 'mjuːzɪk
musical (s.), -s 'mjuːzɪkl [ˌmjuːzɪ'kæl, -'kɑːl], -z
music|al (adj.), -ally, -alness 'mjuːzɪk|l, -əlɪ, -lnɪs [-nəs]
musical-box, -es 'mjuːzɪklbɒks, -ɪz
musicale, -s ˌmjuːzɪ'kæl [-'kɑːl], -z
music-hall, -s 'mjuːzɪkhɔːl, -z
musician, -s -ly mjuː'zɪʃn [mjʊ'z-], -z, -lɪ
musicolog|ist/s, -y ˌmjuːzɪ'kɒlədʒ|ɪst/s, -ɪ
music-stand, -s 'mjuːzɪkstænd, -z
music-stool, -s 'mjuːzɪkstuːl, -z
Musidor|a, -us ˌmjuːsɪ'dɔːr|ə, -əs
musk, -y mʌsk, -ɪ
musk-deer ˌmʌsk'dɪə* ['-ˌ-]
musket, -s; -ry 'mʌskɪt, -s; -rɪ
musketeer, -s ˌmʌskɪ'tɪə* [-kə't-], -z
Muskett 'mʌskɪt
musk-ox, -en 'mʌskɒks [ˌmʌsk'ɒks], -ən
musk-rat, -s 'mʌskræt [ˌmʌsk'ræt], -s
musk-rose, -s 'mʌskrəʊz [ˌ-'-], -ɪz
Muslim, -s 'mʊslɪm ['mʊzlɪm, 'mʌzlɪm], -z
muslin, -s 'mʌzlɪn, -z
musquash 'mʌskwɒʃ
mussel, -s 'mʌsl, -z
Musselburgh 'mʌslbərə [-bʌrə]
Mussolini ˌmʊsə'liːnɪ
Mussorgsky mʊ'sɔːgskɪ (mu'sorkskij, 'musərkskij)
Mussulman, -s 'mʌslmən, -z
must (s, adj.) mʌst
must (v.) mʌst (strong form), məst, məs, mst, ms (weak forms)
mustang, -s 'mʌstæŋ, -z
Mustapha (Turkish) 'mʊstəfə, (Egyptian) mʊ'stɑːfə

Mustapha Kemal ˌmʊstəfəke'mɑːl [-kɪ'm-]
mustard (M.) 'mʌstəd
mustard seed 'mʌstədsiːd
Mustel 'mʌstəl [-tl]
must|er (s. v.), -ers, -ering, -ered 'mʌst|ə*, -əz, -ərɪŋ, -əd
mustn't 'mʌsnt [also occasionally 'mʌsn when not final]
must|y, -ier, -iest, -ily, -iness 'mʌst|ɪ, -ɪə* [-jə*], -ɪist [-jɪst], -ɪlɪ [-əlɪ], -ɪnɪs [-məs]
mutability ˌmjuːtə'bɪlətɪ [-lɪt-]
mutable 'mjuːtəbl
mutat|e, -es, -ing, -ed mjuː'teɪt, -s, -ɪŋ, -ɪd
mutation, -s mjuː'teɪʃn [mjʊ't-], -z
mutatis mutandis muːˌtɑːtɪsmuː'tændɪs [mjuː-, tertɪsmjuː'tændɪs, mjʊ't-]
mut|e (s. adj. v.), -es; -ely, -eness; -ing, -ed mjuːt, -s; -lɪ, -nɪs [-nəs]; -ɪŋ, -ɪd
mutilat|e, -es, -ing, -ed, -or/s 'mjuːtɪ-leɪt, -s, -ɪŋ, -ɪd, -ə*/z
mutilation, -s ˌmjuːtɪ'leɪʃn, -z
mutineer, -s ˌmjuːtɪ'nɪə* [-tə'n-], -z
mutinous, -ly, -ness 'mjuːtɪnəs [-tənəs, -tnəs], -lɪ, -nɪs [-nəs]
mutin|y (s. v.), -ies, -ying, -ied 'mjuː-tɪn|ɪ [-tə|n-, -tn̩-], -ɪz, -ɪŋ, -ɪd
mutism 'mjuːtɪzəm
mutt|er (s. v.), -ers, -ering/ly, -ered, -erer/s 'mʌt|ə*, -əz, -ərɪŋ/lɪ, -əd, -ərə*/z
mutton (M.); -chop/s 'mʌtn, -'tʃɒp/s
muttony 'mʌtnɪ
mutual, -ly 'mjuːtʃʊəl [-tʃwəl, -tʃʊl, -tjʊəl, -tjwəl, -tjʊl] -ɪ
mutuality ˌmjuːtjʊ'ælətɪ [-tʃʊ-, -ɪtɪ]
muzz|le (s. v.), -les, -ling, -led 'mʌz|l, -lz, -lɪŋ [-lɪŋ], -ld
muzzle-load|er/s, -ing 'mʌzlˌləʊd|ə*/z, -ɪŋ
muzz|y, -ier, -iest, -iness 'mʌz|ɪ, -ɪə*, -ɪist, -ɪnɪs [-məs]
my maɪ (normal form), mɪ (freq. weak form)
   Note.—Many people confine the use of mɪ to the special expression my lord (see lord) and (at Eton College) to the expressions my tutor and my dame. Some use mɪ in common idioms, such as never in my life, but not elsewhere.
Mycenae maɪ'siːniː [-nɪ]
Mycenaean ˌmaɪsə'niːən [-sɪ-, -si:-, -'nɪən]
mycolog|ist/s, -y maɪ'kɒlədʒ|ɪst/s, -ɪ
Myers 'maɪəz

Myerscough (in Lancashire) 'maɪəskəʊ
Myfanwy mə'vænwɪ (Welsh mə'vanwɨ)
mynheer, -s maɪn'hɪə* [-heə*], -z
Mynheer (form of address in South
 Africa) mə'nɪə* (Afrikaans mə'neːr)
Mynott 'maɪnət
myope, -s 'maɪəʊp, -s
myopia maɪ'əʊpjə [-pɪə]
myopic maɪ'ɒpɪk
myosis maɪ'əʊsɪs
myosotis ˌmaɪəʊ'səʊtɪs
Myra 'maɪərə
myriad, -s 'mɪrɪəd, -z
myrmidon (M.), -s 'məːmɪdən [-dn,
 -dɒn], -z
myrrh məː*
Myrrha 'mɪrə
myrrhic 'məːrɪk ['mɪr-]
myrrhine 'məːraɪn ['mɪr-]
myrrhite 'məːraɪt ['mɪr-]
myrrhy 'məːrɪ
myrtle (M.), -s 'məːtl, -z
myself maɪ'self [mɪ's-, mə's-]
Mysia 'mɪsɪə [-sjə, -ʃɪə, -ʃjə]

Mysore maɪ'sɔː* [-'sɔə*]
mysterious, -ly, -ness mɪ'stɪərɪəs, -lɪ,
 -nɪs [-nəs]
myster|y, -ies 'mɪstər|ɪ, -ɪz
mystic (s. adj.), -s 'mɪstɪk, -s
mystic|al, -ally, -alness 'mɪstɪk|l, -əlɪ,
 -lnɪs [-nəs]
mysticism 'mɪstɪsɪzəm
mystification ˌmɪstɪfɪ'keɪʃn
mysti|fy, -fies, -fying, -fied 'mɪstɪ|faɪ,
 -faɪz, -faɪɪŋ, -faɪd
mystique mɪ'stiːk
myth, -s mɪθ, -s
mythic, -al, -ally 'mɪθɪk, -l, -əlɪ
Mytholmroyd (in West Yorkshire)
 'mɪðəmrɔɪd
mythologic, -al, -ally ˌmɪθə'lɒdʒɪk
 [ˌmaɪθ-], -l, -əlɪ
mytholog|ist/s, -y, -ies mɪ'θɒlədʒ|ɪst/s
 [maɪ'θ-], -ɪ, -ɪz
mythologiz|e [-is|e], -es, -ing, -ed
 mɪ'θɒlədʒaɪz [maɪ'θ-], -ɪz, -ɪŋ, -d
Mytilene ˌmɪtɪ'liːni [-nɪ]
myxomatosis ˌmɪksəʊmə'təʊsɪs

N

N (*the letter*), -'s en, -z
N.A.A.F.I. 'næfɪ
Naaman 'neɪəmən
Naas (*in Ireland*) neɪs
nab (*s. v.*), -s, -bing, -bed næb, -z, -ɪŋ, -d
Nabarro (*English surname*) nə'bɑːrəʊ
Nablus 'nɑːbləs
nabob, -s 'neɪbɒb, -z
Nabokov nə'bəʊkɒf [næ-, nɑː-, 'næb-]
Naboth 'neɪbɒθ
nacelle, -s næ'sel, -z
nacre 'neɪkə*
nacreous 'neɪkrɪəs
nacrite 'neɪkraɪt
nacrous 'neɪkrəs
nadir, -s 'neɪˌdɪə* [-də*, 'næˌdɪə*], -z
nag (*s. v.*) (N.), -s, -ging, -ged, -ger/s næg, -z, -ɪŋ, -d, -ə*/z
Naga, -s; -land 'nɑːgə, -z; -lænd
Nagaina nə'gaɪnə
Nagari 'nɑːgərɪ
Nagasaki ˌnægə'sɑːkɪ [-'sæ-]
Nahum (*prophet*) 'neɪhəm [-hʌm], (*modern surname*) 'neɪəm
naiad, -s 'naɪæd, -z
nail (*s. v.*), -s, -ing, -ed neɪl, -z, -ɪŋ, -d
nail-brush, -es 'neɪlbrʌʃ, -ɪz
nail-scissors 'neɪlˌsɪzəz
Nain 'neɪɪn [neɪn]
Nairn(e) neən
Nairnshire 'neənʃə* [-ˌʃɪə*]
Nairobi naɪ'rəʊbɪ
Naish næʃ
naïve, -ly, -ty nɑː'iːv [naɪ'iːv], -lɪ, -tɪ
naive, -ly neɪv, -lɪ
naïveté, nɑː'iːvteɪ [naɪ'iːv-] (naifte)
naked, -ly, -ness 'neɪkɪd, -lɪ, -nɪs [-nəs]
naker, -s 'neɪkə* ['næ-], -z
namby-pamby ˌnæmbɪ'pæmbɪ
nam|e (*s. v.*), -es, -ing, -ed; -eless neɪm, -z, -ɪŋ, -d; -lɪs [-ləs]
namely 'neɪmlɪ
name-plate, -s 'neɪmpleɪt, -s
namesake, -s 'neɪmseɪk, -s
Namier 'neɪˌmɪə* [-mjə*, -mɪə*]
Nanaimo næ'naɪməʊ [nə'n-]
Nancy 'nænsɪ
nankeen næŋ'kiːn [næn'k-]

Nanki|n, -ng ˌnæn'kɪ|n [ˌnæŋ'k-, *also* '-- *when followed by a stress*], -ŋ
Nannie 'nænɪ
nann|y (N.), -ies 'næn|ɪ, -ɪz
Nansen 'nænsən
Nantucket næn'tʌkɪt
Nantwich (*in Cheshire*) 'næntwɪtʃ [*locally also* -waɪtʃ]
Naomi 'neɪəmɪ ['neɪəʊm-]
nap (*s. v.*), -s, -ping, -ped næp, -s, -ɪŋ, -t
napalm 'neɪpɑːm ['næp-]
nape, -s neɪp, -s
napery 'neɪpərɪ
Naphtali 'næftəlaɪ
naphtha, -lene, -line 'næfθə ['næpθ-], -liːn, -liːn
naphthol 'næfθɒl ['næpθ-]
Napier 'neɪpɪə* [-pjə*], nə'pɪə*
napierian nə'pɪərɪən [neɪ'p-]
napkin, -s; -ring/s 'næpkɪn, -z; -rɪŋ/z
Naples 'neɪplz
napoleon (N.), -s nə'pəʊljən [-lɪən], -z
napoleonic nəˌpəʊlɪ'ɒnɪk
napp|y, -ies 'næp|ɪ, -ɪz
Narbonne nɑː'bɒn (narbɔn)
narcissism nɑː'sɪsɪzəm ['----]
narcissistic ˌnɑːsɪ'sɪstɪk
narciss|us (N.), -uses, -i nɑː'sɪs|əs, -əsɪz, -aɪ
narcosis nɑː'kəʊsɪs
narcotic (*s. adj.*), -s nɑː'kɒtɪk, -s
narcoti|sm, -st/s 'nɑːkətɪ|zəm, -st/s
nard nɑːd
Nares neəz
narghile, -s 'nɑːgɪlɪ, -z
Narkunda nɑː'kʌndə (*Hindi* nərkwnɖə)
narrat|e, -es, -ing, -ed, -or/s nə'reɪt [næ'r-], -s, -ɪŋ, -ɪd, -ə*/z
narration, -s nə'reɪʃn [næ'r-], -z
narrative (*s. adj.*), -s 'nærətɪv, -z
narr|ow (*s. adj. v.*), -ows, -ower, -owest, -owly, -owness; -owing, -owed 'nær|əʊ, -əʊz, -əʊə*, -əʊɪst, -əʊlɪ, -əʊnɪs [-nəs]; -əʊɪŋ, -əʊd
narrow-gauge 'nærəʊgeɪdʒ
narrow-minded, -ly, -ness ˌnærəʊ'maɪndɪd ['--,--], -lɪ, -nɪs [-nəs]
narwhal, -s 'nɑːwəl, -z
nas|al (*s. adj.*), -als, -ally 'neɪz|l, -lz, -əlɪ

nasalism 'neɪzəlɪzəm [-zἱɪ-]
nasality neɪ'zælətɪ [nə'z-, -ɪtɪ]
nasalization [-isa-], -s ˌneɪzəlaɪ'zeɪʃn
[-zἱaɪ'z-, -zəlɪ'z-, -zἱɪ'z-], -z
nasaliz|e [-is|e], -es, -ing, -ed 'neɪzəlaɪz
[-zἱ-], -ɪz, -ɪŋ, -d
nascent 'næsnt
Naseby 'neɪzbɪ
Nash, -ville næʃ, -vɪl
Nasmyth 'neɪzmɪθ [-eɪsm-], 'næzmɪθ
Nassau (German province) 'næsaʊ
('nasau), (princely family) 'næsɔː
[-saʊ], (in Bahamas and U.S.A.)
'næsɔː
nasturtium, -s nə'stɜːʃəm, -z
nast|y, -ier, -iest, -ily, -iness 'nɑːstɪr,
-ɪə* [-jə*], -ɪɪst [-jɪst], -ɪlɪ [-əlɪ], -ɪnɪs
[-məs]
natal (adj.) 'neɪtl
Natal nə'tæl
natation nə'teɪʃn [neɪ-]
Nathan 'neɪθən [-θæn]
Nathaniel nə'θænjəl
nation, -s 'neɪʃn, -z
na|tional, -tionally 'næʃ|ənl [-ʃnəl, -ʃṇl,
-ʃṇl, -ʃənəl], -ʃṇəlɪ [-ʃnəlɪ, -ʃṇlɪ, -ʃnlɪ,
-ʃənəlɪ]
nationali|sm, -st/s 'næʃṇəlɪ|zəm [-ʃnəl-,
-ʃṇl-, -ʃnl-, -ʃənəl-], -st/s
nationalistic ˌnæʃṇə'lɪstɪk [-ʃnə'lɪ-,
-ʃṇl'ɪ-, -ʃnl'ɪ-, -ʃənə'lɪ-]
nationalit|y, -ies ˌnæʃə'nælətɪ [-ʃṇ'æ-,
-ɪtɪ], -ɪz
nationalization [-isa-] ˌnæʃṇəlaɪ'zeɪʃn
[-ʃnəl-, -ʃṇl-, -ʃnl-, -ʃənəl-, -lɪ'z-]
nationaliz|e [-is|e], -es, -ing, -ed
'næʃṇəlaɪz [-ʃnəl-, -ʃṇl-, -ʃnl-,
-ʃənəl-], -ɪz, -ɪŋ, -d
native (s. adj.), -s, -ly 'neɪtɪv, -z, -lɪ
nativit|y (N.), -ies nə'tɪvət|ɪ [-ɪt|ɪ],
-ɪz
N.A.T.O. 'neɪtəʊ
natron 'neɪtrən [-rɒn]
natter (s. v.), -s, -ing, -ed 'nætə*, -z,
-rɪŋ, -d
natt|y, -ier, -iest, -ily, -iness 'nætɪr,
-ɪə*, -ɪɪst, -ɪlɪ [-əlɪ], -ɪnɪs [-məs]
natur|al (s. adj.), -als, -ally, -alness
'nætʃr|əl [-tʃʊr-, -tʃər-], -əlz, -əlɪ,
-əlnɪs [-nəs]
naturali|sm, -st/s 'nætʃrəlɪ|zəm [-tʃʊr-,
-tʃər-], -st/s
naturalistic ˌnætʃrə'lɪstɪk [-tʃʊr-, -tʃər-]
naturalization [-isa-] ˌnætʃrəlaɪ'zeɪʃn
[-tʃʊr-, -tʃər-, -lɪ'z-]
naturaliz|e [-is|e], -es, -ing, -ed
'nætʃrəlaɪz [-tʃʊr-, -tʃər-], -ɪz, -ɪŋ, -d
nature, -s, -d 'neɪtʃə*, -z, -d

naturi|sm, -st/s 'neɪtʃərɪ|zəm, -st/s
naught, -s nɔːt, -s
naught|y, -ier, -iest, -ily, -iness 'nɔːtɪr,
-ɪə* [-jə*], -ɪɪst [-jɪst], -ɪlɪ [-əlɪ], -ɪnɪs
[-məs]
nausea 'nɔːsjə [-sɪə, -ʃjə, -ʃɪə, -zjə, -zɪə,
-ʒjə, -ʒɪə]
nauseat|e, -es, -ing, -ed 'nɔːsɪeɪt [-sjeɪt,
-ʃɪeɪt, -ʃjeɪt, -zɪeɪt, -zjeɪt, -ʒɪeɪt,
-ʒjeɪt], -s, -ɪŋ, -ɪd
nauseous, -ly, -ness 'nɔːsjəs [-sɪəs, -ʃjəs,
-ʃɪəs, -zjəs, -zɪəs, -ʒɪəs, -ʒjəs], -lɪ, -nɪs
[-nəs]
Nausicaa nɔː'sɪkɪə [-keɪə]
nautch, -es nɔːtʃ, -ɪz
nautic|al, -ally 'nɔːtɪk|l, -əlɪ
nautilus, -es 'nɔːtɪləs, -ɪz
naval 'neɪvl
Navarino ˌnævə'riːnəʊ
Navarre nə'vɑː* (nava:r)
nave, -s neɪv, -z
navel, -s 'neɪvl, -z
navicert, -s 'nævɪsɜːt, -s
navigability ˌnævɪgə'bɪlətɪ [-lɪt-]
navigable, -ness 'nævɪgəbl, -nɪs [-nəs]
navigat|e, -es, -ing, -ed, -or/s 'nævɪ-
geɪt, -s, -ɪŋ, -ɪd, -ə*/z
navigation, -al ˌnævɪ'geɪʃn, -l [-ʃənl,
-ʃnəl]
navv|y, -ies 'næv|ɪ, -ɪz
nav|y, -ies 'neɪv|ɪ, -ɪz
nawab, -s nə'wɑːb, -z
Nawanagar nə'wɑːnəgə* (Hindi
nəvanəgər)
nay neɪ
Naylor 'neɪlə*
Nazarene, -s ˌnæzə'riːn, -z
Nazareth 'næzərəθ [-rɪθ]
Nazarite, -s 'næzəraɪt, -s
naze (N.), -s neɪz, -ɪz
Nazeing 'neɪzɪŋ
Nazi, -s 'nɑːtsɪ ['nɑːzɪ], -z
nazism 'nɑːtsɪzəm ['nɑːzɪ-]
N.B. ˌen'biː [ˌnəʊtə'biːnɪ, -'benɪ]
N.E. ˌen'iː [ˌnɔː'θiːst]
ne (in ne plus ultra) neɪ [niː]
Neaera niː'ɪərə
Neagh neɪ
Neal(e) niːl
Neanderthal nɪ'ændətɑːl
neap (s. adj.), -s niːp, -s
Neapolis nɪ'æpəlɪs
Neapolitan, -s nɪə'pɒlɪtən [ˌniː-ə-, ˌnɪə-],
-z
near (adj. v. adv. prep.), -er, -est, -ly,
-ness; -s, -ing, -ed nɪə*, -rə*, -rɪst,
-lɪ, -nɪs [-nəs]; -z, -rɪŋ, -d
nearby (adj.) 'nɪəbaɪ [ˌ-'-]

337

nearside 'nɪəsaɪd

near-sighted, -ness ˌnɪə'saɪtɪd, -nɪs [-nəs]

Neasden 'niːzdən

neat, -er, -est, -ly, -ness niːt, -ə*, -ɪst, -lɪ, -nɪs [-nəs]

'neath niːθ

Neath niːθ

Neb|at, -o 'niːb|æt, -əʊ

Nebraska nɪ'bræskə [ne'b-, nə'b-]

Nebuchadnezzar ˌnebjʊkəd'nezə*

nebul|a, -ae, -as, -ar, -ous 'nebjʊl|ə, -iː, -əz, -ə*, -əs

nebulosity ˌnebjʊ'lɒsɪtɪ [-ɪtɪ]

necessarily 'nesəsərəlɪ [-sɪs-, -ser-, ˌnesə'serəlɪ, ˌnesɪ's-, -ɪlɪ]

necessar|y (s. adj.), -ies; -iness 'nesəsər|ɪ [-sɪs-, -ser-, -ɪz; -mɪs [-məs]

necessitat|e, -es, -ing, -ed nɪ'sesɪteɪt [ne's-, nə's-], -s, -ɪŋ, -ɪd

necessitous, -ly, -ness nɪ'sesɪtəs [ne's-, nə's-], -lɪ, -nɪs [-nəs]

necessit|y, -ies nɪ'sesət|ɪ [ne's-, nə's-, -ɪt|ɪ], -ɪz

neck, -s nek, -s

neckband, -s 'nekbænd, -z

neck|-cloth, -cloths 'nek|klɒθ [old-fashioned -klɔːθ], -klɒθs [-klɔːðz, -klɔːθs]

neckerchief, -s 'nekətʃɪf [-tʃiːf], -s

necklace, -s 'neklɪs [-ləs], -ɪz

necklet, -s 'neklɪt [-lət], -s

neck-line, -s 'neklaɪn, -z

neck-tie, -s 'nektaɪ, -z

neckwear 'nekweə*

necrolog|ist/s, -y, -ies ne'krɒlədʒ|ɪst/s [nɪ'k-], -ɪ, -ɪz

necromanc|er/s, -y 'nekrəʊmæns|ə*/z, -ɪ

necropolis, -es ne'krɒpəlɪs [nɪ'k-], -ɪz

necrosis ne'krəʊsɪs [nɪ'k-]

nectar 'nektə* [-tɑː*]

nectarine, -s 'nektərɪn, -z

Nedd|y, -ies 'ned|ɪ, -ɪz

Neden 'niːdn

née neɪ

need (s. v.), -s, -ing, -ed niːd, -z, -ɪŋ, -ɪd

need|ful, -fully, -fulness 'niːd|fʊl, -fʊlɪ [-fəlɪ], -fʊlnɪs [-nəs]

Needham 'niːdəm

needle (N.), -s; -case/s, -ful/s, -shaped 'niːdl, -z; -keɪs/ɪz, -fʊl/z, -ʃeɪpt

needless, -ly, -ness 'niːdlɪs [-ləs], -lɪ, -nɪs [-nəs]

needle|woman, -women 'niːdl|ˌwʊmən, -ˌwɪmɪn

needlework 'niːdlwɜːk

needn't 'niːdnt [also occasionally 'niːdn when not final]

needs (adv.) niːdz

need|y, -ier, -iest, -ily, -iness 'niːd|ɪ, -ɪə* [-jə*], -ɪɪst [-jɪst], -ɪlɪ [-əlɪ], -ɪnɪs [-məs]

ne'er neə*

ne'er-do-well, -s 'neəduːˌwel [-dʊ-], -z

nefarious, -ly, -ness nɪ'feərɪəs [ne'f-, nə'f-], -lɪ, -nɪs [-nəs]

negation, -s nɪ'geɪʃn [ne'g-], -z

negativ|e (s. adj. v.), -es; -ely, -eness, -ing, -ed 'negətɪv, -z; -lɪ, -nɪs [-nəs]; -ɪŋ, -d

neglect (s. v.), -s, -ing, -ed, -er/s nɪ'glekt, -s, -ɪŋ, -ɪd, -ə*/z

neglect|ful, -fully, -fulness nɪ'glekt|fʊl, -fʊlɪ [-fəlɪ], -fʊlnɪs [-nəs]

négligé 'neglɪːʒeɪ [-lɪʒ-] (neglɪʒe)

negligen|ce, -ces, -t/ly 'neglɪdʒən|s, -sɪz, -t/lɪ

negligible 'neglɪdʒəbl [-dʒɪbl]

negotiability nɪˌgəʊʃjə'bɪlətɪ [-ʃɪə-, -ʃə-, -lɪt-]

negotiable nɪ'gəʊʃjəbl [-ʃɪə-, -ʃə-]

negotiat|e, -es, -ing, -ed, -or/s nɪ'gəʊʃɪ-eɪt [-ʃjeɪt, -sɪeɪt, -sjeɪt], -s, -ɪŋ, -ɪd, -ə*/z

negotiation, -s nɪˌgəʊʃɪ'eɪʃn [-əʊsɪ-], -z

negress (N.), -es 'niːgrɪs [-gres], -ɪz

negrillo, -s ne'grɪləʊ [nɪ'g-], -z

Negri Sembilan ˌnegrɪsem'biːlən [-səm-]

negrito, -s ne'griːtəʊ [nɪ'g-], -z

negro (N.), -es 'niːgrəʊ, -z

negroid 'niːgrɔɪd

negus (N.) 'niːgəs

Nehemiah ˌniːɪ'maɪə [ˌniːhɪ'm-, ˌniːhə'm-, nɪə'm-]

Nehru 'neəruː (Hindi nehru)

neigh (s. v.), -s, -ing, -ed neɪ, -z, -ɪŋ, -d

neighb|our, -ours, -ouring, -ourly, -ourliness 'neɪb|ə*, -əz, -ərɪŋ, -əlɪ, -əlmɪs [-məs]

neighbourhood, -s 'neɪbəhʊd [old-fashioned -bərʊd], -z

Neil(l) niːl

Neilson 'niːlsn

neither 'naɪðə* ['niːðə*]

Nellie [-ly] 'nelɪ

Nelson 'nelsn

nem. con. ˌnem'kɒn

Nemesis 'nemɪsɪs [-məs-]

Nemo 'niːməʊ

nemophila, -s nɪ'mɒfɪlə*, -z

Nen (river) nen

Nene (river) nen [niːn], (name of ship) niːn, (aero-engine) niːn

nenuphar, -s 'nenjʊfɑː*, -z

338

neocolonialism ˌnɪəʊkəˈləʊnɪəlɪzəm [ˌniːəʊ-, -njəl-]
neo-latin ˌniːəʊˈlætɪn [ˌnɪəʊ-]
neolithic ˌniːəʊˈlɪθɪk [ˌnɪəʊ-]
neologˌism/s, -ist/s, -y niːˈɒlədʒ|-ɪzəm/z [nɪˈɒ-], -ɪst/s, -ɪ
neologizˌe [-is|e], -es, -ing, -ed niː-ˈɒlədʒaɪz [nɪˈɒ-], -ɪz, -ɪŋ, -d
neon ˈniːən [ˈniːɒn, nɪən]
neophyte, -s ˈniːəʊfaɪt [ˈnɪəʊ-], -s
Nepal nɪˈpɔːl [neˈp-, -ˈpɑːl]
Nepalese ˌnepɔːˈliːz [-pəˈl-]
nepenthe neˈpenθɪ [nɪˈp-]
neper, -s ˈniːpə*, -z
nephew, -s ˈnevjuː [ˈnefj-, -jʊ], -z
nephritis neˈfraɪtɪs [nɪ-, nə-]
ne plus ultra ˌneɪplʊsˈʊltrɑ: [-trə, ˌniːplʌsˈʌltrə]
Nepos ˈniːpɒs [ˈnep-]
nepotism ˈnepətɪzəm [-pɒt-]
Neptune ˈneptjuːn [-tʃuːn]
neptunian (N.) nepˈtjuːnjən [-nɪən]
neptunium nepˈtjuːnjəm [-nɪəm]
Nereid, -s ˈnɪərɪid, -z
Nereus ˈnɪərjuːs [-rɪuːs, -rɪəs]
Neri ˈnɪərɪ
Nerissa nɪˈrɪsə [neˈr-, nəˈr-]
Nero ˈnɪərəʊ
nervˌe (s. v.), -es, -ing, -ed; -eless nɜːv, -z, -ɪŋ, -d; -lɪs [-ləs]
nerve-cell, -s ˈnɜːvsel, -z
nerve-centre, -s ˈnɜːvˌsentə*, -z
nerve-racking ˈnɜːvˌrækɪŋ
nervine ˈnɜːviːn
nervous, -ly, -ness ˈnɜːvəs, -lɪ, -nɪs [-nəs]
nervˌy, -ier, -iest, -ily, -iness ˈnɜːv|ɪ, -ɪə* [-jə*], -ɪɪst [-jɪst], -ɪlɪ [-əlɪ], -ɪnɪs [-məs]
Nesbit(t) ˈnezbɪt
nescience ˈnesɪəns [-sjəns]
Nesfield ˈnesfiːld
ness (N.), -es nes, -ɪz
nest (s. v.), -s, -ing, -ed nest, -s, -ɪŋ, -ɪd
Nesta ˈnestə
nest-egg, -s ˈnesteg, -z
nestˌle, -les, -ling, -led ˈnes|l, -lz, -lɪŋ [-lɪŋ], -ld
Nestlé ˈnesl [ˈneslɪ]
nestling (s.) (young bird), -s ˈnestlɪŋ, -z
Nestor ˈnestɔ:* [-tə*]
Nestorian, -s neˈstɔːrɪən, -z
net (s. v.), -s -ting, -ted net, -s, -ɪŋ, -ɪd
netball ˈnetbɔːl
nether, -most ˈneðə*, -məʊst [-məst]
Netherland, -s, -er/s ˈneðələnd [-ð|ənd], -z, -ə*/z

Netley ˈnetlɪ
Nettie ˈnetɪ
nettˌle (s. v.), -les, -ling, -led ˈnet|l, -lz, -lɪŋ [-lɪŋ], -ld
Nettleˌfold, -ship ˈnetl|fəʊld, -ʃɪp
nettlerash ˈnetlræʃ
net-work, -s ˈnetwɜːk, -s
Neuchâtel ˌnɜ:ʃæˈtel [-ʃə't-, ˈnɜ:ʃətel] (nœʃatel)
neume, -s njuːm, -z
neural ˈnjʊərəl
neuralgˌia, -ic ˌnjʊəˈrældʒ|ə [njəˈr-, njʊˈr-, njuːˈr-], -ɪk
neurasthenia ˌnjʊərəsˈθiːnjə [ˌnjuːr-, -nɪə]
neurasthenic (s. adj.), -s ˌnjʊərəs-ˈθenɪk [ˌnjuːr-], -s
neuritis ˌnjʊəˈraɪtɪs [njəˈr-, njʊˈr-, njuːˈr-]
neurological ˌnjʊərəˈlɒdʒɪkl [ˌnjuːr-]
neurologˌist/s, -y ˌnjʊəˈrɒlədʒ|ɪst/s [njəˈr-, njʊˈr-, njuːˈr-], -ɪ
neuron, -s ˈnjʊərɒn, -z
neurone, -s ˈnjʊərəʊn, -z
neurosˌis, -es ˌnjʊəˈrəʊs|ɪs [njəˈr-, njʊˈr-, njuːˈr-], -iːz
neurotic (s. adj.), -s ˌnjʊəˈrɒtɪk [njəˈr-, njʊˈr-, njuːˈr-], -s
neuter (s. adj.), -s ˈnjuːtə*, -z
neutrˌal (s. adj.), -als, -ally ˈnjuːtr|əl, -əlz, -əlɪ
neutrality njuːˈtrælətɪ [njʊ-, -ɪtɪ]
neutralization [-isa-] ˌnjuːtrəlaɪˈzeɪʃn [-trʃlaɪˈz-, -trəlɪˈz-, -trʃlɪˈz-]
neutralizˌe [-is|e], -es, -ing, -ed ˈnjuː-trəlaɪz [-trʃlaɪz], -ɪŋ, -ɪz, -d
neutron, -s ˈnjuːtrɒn [-trən], -z
Neva ˈneɪvə [old-fashioned ˈniːvə] (nji'va)
Nevada neˈvɑːdə [nɪˈv-, nəˈv-]
Neve niːv
névé ˈneveɪ
never, -more ˈnevə*, -ˈmɔ:* [-ˈmɔə*]
nevertheless ˌnevəðəˈles
Nevey ˈnevɪ
Nevil ˈnevɪl
Nevill(e) ˈnevɪl
Nevin, -son ˈnevɪn, -sn
Nevis (in Scotland) ˈnevɪs, (in West Indies) ˈniːvɪs
new, -er, -est, -ly, -ness njuː, -ə* [njʊə*], -ɪst [ˈnjʊɪst], -lɪ, -nɪs [-nəs]
Newark (in Nottinghamshire) ˈnjuːək [njʊək]
Newbiggin (place) ˈnjuːˌbɪgɪn, (surname) ˈnjuːˌbɪgɪn, njuːˈbɪgɪn
Newbolˌd, -t ˈnjuːbəʊl|d, -t
newborn ˈnjuːbɔːn

New|burgh, -bury 'nju:|bərə, -bərɪ
Newcastle 'nju:,kɑ:sl
   Note.—**Newcastle** *in Tyne and Wear
   is locally* nju'kæsl.
Newcome, -s 'nju:kəm, -z
newcomer, -s 'nju:,kʌmə*, -z
Newdigate 'nju:dɪgɪt [-geɪt]
Newe nju:
newel, -s 'nju:əl [nju:l], -z
new-fangled 'nju:,fæŋgld [,-'--]
new-fashioned ,nju:'fæʃnd [*also* '-,--
   when attributive]
Newfoundland (*place*), er/s 'nju:fənd-
   lənd [-lænd, nju:'faʊndlənd, njʊ'f-,
   ,nju:fənd'lænd], -ə*/z
   Note.—,nju:fənd'lænd *is the local
   form; it is also the nautical pronunciation in England.*
Newfoundland (*dog*), -s nju:'faʊndlənd [njʊ'f-], -z
Newgate 'nju:gɪt [-geɪt]
Newham (*London borough*) 'nju:əm
   [njʊəm, *sometimes* 'nju:hæm, ,nju:-
   'hæm]
Newhaven   nju:'heɪvn   [njʊ'h-,
   'nju:,h-]
Newington 'nju:ɪŋtən ['njʊɪ-]
new-laid (*when attributive*) 'nju:leɪd,
   (*otherwise*) ,nju:'leɪd
New|man, -market 'nju:|mən, -,mɑ:kɪt
Newn|es, -ham nju:n|z, -əm
New Orleans ,nju:'ɔ:lɪənz [-ljənz, ,nju:-
   ɔ:'li:nz]
New|port, -quay 'nju:|pɔ:t, -ki:
New Quay ,nju:'ki:
Newry 'njʊərɪ
news nju:z
newsagent, -s 'nju:z,eɪdʒənt, -s
news-boy, -s 'nju:zbɔɪ, -z
newscast|er/s, -ing 'nju:z,kɑ:st|ə*/z,
   -ɪŋ
news-letter, -s 'nju:z,letə*, -z
newsmonger, -s 'nju:z,mʌŋgə*, -z
New South Wales ,nju:saʊθ'weɪlz
newspaper, -s 'nju:s,peɪpə* ['nju:z,p-],
   -z
newsprint 'nju:zprɪnt
newsreel, -s 'nju:zri:l, -z
news-sheet, -s 'nju:zʃi:t [-u:ʒʃ-], -z
Newstead 'nju:stɪd [-sted]
newsvendor, -s 'nju:z,vendə* [-dɔ:*], -z
newsy 'nju:zɪ
newt, -s nju:t, -s
Newton 'nju:tn
Newtonian nju:'təʊnjən [-nɪən]
Newtown 'nju:taʊn
New York, -er/s ,nju:'jɔ:k [njʊ'j-],
   -ə*/z

New Zealand, -er/s ,nju:'zi:lənd[njʊ'z-],
   -ə*/z
next nekst [*often also* neks *when followed
   by a word beginning with a consonant*]
next of kin ,nekstəv'kɪn
nexus, -es 'neksəs, -ɪz
Ngaio (*authoress, suburb of Wellington,
   New Zealand*) 'naɪəʊ
Ngami ŋ'gɑ:mɪ ['ŋɑ:mɪ]
Niagara naɪ'ægərə [-grə]
nib, -s nɪb, -z
nibb|le (*s. v.*), -les, -ling, -led 'nɪb|l, -lz,
   -|ɪŋ [-lɪŋ], -ld
Nibelung, -s, -en 'ni:bəlʊŋ [-bɪl-], -z, -ən
niblick, -s 'nɪblɪk, -s
Nicaea naɪ'si:ə [-'sɪə]
Nicaragua, -n/s ,nɪkə'rægjʊə [-'rægjwə,
   -'rɑ:gwə], -n/z
nice, -r, -st, -ly, -ness naɪs, -ə*, -ɪst, -lɪ,
   -nɪs [-nəs]
Nice (*in France*) ni:s (nis)
Nicene ,naɪ'si:n [*sometimes also* 'naɪs-
   when attributive]
nicet|y, -ies 'naɪsət|ɪ [-sɪt-], -ɪz
niche, -s, -d nɪtʃ [ni:ʃ], -ɪz, -t
Nichol, -(l)s, -son 'nɪkl, -z, -sn
Nicholas 'nɪkələs [-k|əs]
nick (*s.v.*) (**N.**), -s, -ing, -ed nɪk, -s, -ɪŋ, -t
nick|el (*s. v.*), -els, -elling, -elled 'nɪk|l,
   -lz, -|ɪŋ [-əlɪŋ], -ld
Nickleby 'nɪklbɪ
nick-nack, -s 'nɪknæk, -s
nicknam|e (*s. v.*), -es, -ing, -ed 'nɪk-
   neɪm, -z, -ɪŋ, -d
Nicobar 'nɪkəʊbɑ:*
Nicodemus ,nɪkəʊ'di:məs
Nicolas 'nɪkələs [-kləs]
Nicol(l), -s 'nɪkl, -z
Nicomachean ,naɪkɒmə'ki:ən [naɪ-
   ,kɒm-, -'kɪən]
Nicomachus naɪ'kɒməkəs
Nicosia ,nɪkəʊ'si:ə [-'sɪə]
nicotine 'nɪkəti:n [,--'-]
nicotinism 'nɪkəti:nɪzəm [-tɪn-]
niece, -s ni:s, -ɪz
Niersteiner 'nɪəstaɪnə*
Nietzsche 'ni:tʃə ('ni:tʃə)
Nigel 'naɪdʒəl
Niger (*river*) 'naɪdʒə*
Niger (*formerly French West Africa*)
   ni:'ʒeə*
Nigeria, -n naɪ'dʒɪərɪə, -n
niggard, -s 'nɪgəd, -z
niggardl|y, -iness 'nɪgədl|ɪ, -mɪs [-məs]
nigger, -s 'nɪgə*, -z
nigg|le, -les, -ling, -led 'nɪg|l, -lz, -lɪŋ
   [-lɪŋ], -ld
niggl|y, -iness 'nɪgl|ɪ, -mɪs [-məs]

nigh naɪ

night, -s naɪt, -s

night-bell, -s 'naɪtbel, -z

night-bird, -s 'naɪtbɜːd, -z

nightcap, -s 'naɪtkæp, -s

nightdress, -es 'naɪtdres, -ɪz

nightfall 'naɪtfɔːl

nightgown, -s 'naɪtgaʊn, -z

nightie, -s 'naɪtɪ, -z

nightingale (N.), -s 'naɪtɪŋgeɪl, -z

nightjar, -s 'naɪtdʒɑː*, -z

night|-light/s, -long 'naɪt|laɪt/s, -lɒŋ

nightly 'naɪtlɪ

nightmar|e, -es, -ish 'naɪtmeə*, -z, -rɪʃ

night-porter, -s 'naɪt,pɔːtə* [,-'--], -z

night-school, -s 'naɪtskuːl, -z

nightshade 'naɪt-ʃeɪd

nightshirt, -s 'naɪt-ʃɜːt, -s

night-time 'naɪttaɪm

night-walk|er/s, -ing 'naɪt,wɔːk|ə*/z, -ɪŋ

nightwatch, -es ,naɪt'wɒtʃ ['--], -ɪz

night-watch|man, -men ,naɪt'wɒtʃ|mən, -mən

night-work 'naɪtwɜːk

nihili|sm, -st/s 'naɪɪlɪ|zəm ['naɪhɪl-, 'naɪəl-], -st/s

Nijmegen 'naɪmeɪgən [-'--]

Nike 'naɪkiː

nil nɪl

nil desperandum ,nɪldespə'rændəm

Nile naɪl

Nilgiri, -s 'nɪlgɪrɪ, -z

nilometer, -s naɪ'lɒmɪtə* [-mətə*], -z

Nilotic naɪ'lɒtɪk

nimb|le -ler, -lest, -ly, -leness 'nɪmb|l, -lə*, -lɪst, -lɪ, -lnɪs [-nəs]

nimb|us, -uses, -i 'nɪmb|əs, -əsɪz, -aɪ

Nimeguen 'naɪmeɪgən [-'--]

nimini-piminy ,nɪmɪnɪ'pɪmɪnɪ

Nimrod 'nɪmrɒd

Nina (Christian name) 'niːnə, 'naɪnə, (goddess) 'niːnə

nincompoop, -s 'nɪnkəmpuːp ['nɪŋk-], -s

nine, -s, -fold naɪn, -z, -fəʊld

ninepence, -s 'naɪnpəns ['naɪmp-] (see note under penny), -ɪz

ninepenny 'naɪnpənɪ ['naɪmp-]

ninepin, -s 'naɪnpɪn, -z

nineteen, -s, -th/s ,naɪn'tiːn [also '-- according to sentence-stress], -z, -θ/s

ninetieth, -s 'naɪntɪɪθ [-tjɪθ, -tɪəθ, -tjəθ], -s

ninet|y -ies 'naɪnt|ɪ, -ɪz

Nineveh 'nɪnɪvə [-nə-, -vɪ]

ninish 'naɪnɪʃ

ninn|y, -ies 'nɪn|ɪ, -ɪz

ninth, -s, -ly naɪnθ, -s, -lɪ

Ninus 'naɪnəs

Niobe 'naɪəʊbɪ

nip (s. v.), -s, -ping, -ped nɪp, -s, -ɪŋ, -t

nipper, -s 'nɪpə*, -z

nipple, -s 'nɪpl, -z

Nippon 'nɪpɒn

nipp|y, -ier, -iest, -iness 'nɪp|ɪ, -ɪə*, -ɪɪst, -mɪs [-məs]

Nirvana ,nɪə'vɑːnə [nɜː'v-] (Hindi nyrvaṇa)

Nisan 'naɪsæn [Jewish pronunciation 'nɪsɑːn]

Nisbet 'nɪzbɪt

Nish nɪʃ

nisi 'naɪsaɪ [-sɪ]

Nissen, -hut/s 'nɪsn, -hʌt/s

nitrate, -s 'naɪtreɪt [-trɪt], -s

nitre 'naɪtə*

nitr|ic, -ite/s 'naɪtr|ɪk, -aɪt/s

nitrogen 'naɪtrədʒən [-trɪdʒ-]

nitrogenous naɪ'trɒdʒɪnəs [-dʒən-, -dʒn̩-]

nitro-glycerine ,naɪtrəʊ'glɪsəriːn [-'glɪsərɪn, -glɪsə'riːn]

nitrous 'naɪtrəs

nitwit, -s 'nɪtwɪt, -s

Niven 'nɪvən

nix, -es nɪks, -ɪz

Nixey 'nɪksɪ

nixie, -s 'nɪksɪ, -z

Nixon 'nɪksən

Nizam, -s naɪ'zæm [naɪ'zɑːm, nɪ'zɑːm], -z

Nkrumah n'kruːmə,əŋ'kruː-mə [-'krʊ-]

no (s. interj.), -es nəʊ, -z

no (adj.) nəʊ (normal form), nə (in the expression no more do I (we, etc.))

no. (N.), nos. (N.) 'nʌmbə*, -z

Noah 'nəʊə [nɔə, nɔː]

Noakes nəʊks

nob, -s nɒb, -z

no-ball (s. v.), -s, -ing, -ed ,nəʊ'bɔːl, -z, -ɪŋ, -d

nobb|le, -les, -ling, -led 'nɒb|l, -lz, -lɪŋ [-lɪŋ], -ld

nobb|y, -ier, -iest, -ily, -iness 'nɒb|ɪ, -ɪə*, -ɪɪst, -ɪlɪ [-əlɪ], -ɪnɪs [-ɪnəs]

Nobel (Swedish chemist) nəʊ'bel [also 'nəʊbel in Nobel prize]

nobilit|y, -ies nəʊ'bɪlət|ɪ [-lɪt-], -ɪz

nob|le (s. adj.) (N.), -les, -ler, -lest, -ly, -leness 'nəʊb|l, -z, -lə*, -lɪst, -lɪ, -lnɪs [-nəs]

noble|man, -men 'nəʊbl|mən, -mən

noble-minded, -ness ,nəʊbl'maɪndɪd [also '--,-- when attributive], -nɪs [-nəs]

341

noblesse nəʊˈbles

nobod|y, -ies ˈnəʊbəd|ɪ [-ˌbɒd|ɪ], -ɪz

noctambul|ant, -ism, -ist/s nɒkˈtæmbjʊl|ənt, -ɪzəm, -ɪst/s

nocturn|al, -ally nɒkˈtɜ:n|l, -əlɪ

nocturn(e), -s ˈnɒktɜ:n [ˌnɒkˈt-], -z

nod (s. v.) (N.), -s, -ding, -ded nɒd, -z, -ɪŋ, -ɪd

nodal ˈnəʊdl

noddle, -s ˈnɒdl, -z

nodd|y, -ies ˈnɒd|ɪ, -ɪz

node, -s nəʊd, -z

nodul|ar, -ous ˈnɒdjʊl|ə*, -əs

nodule, -s ˈnɒdju:l, -z

Noel (personal name) ˈnəʊəl [-el, -ɪl], (Christmas) nəʊˈel

noggin, -s ˈnɒgɪn, -z

nohow ˈnəʊhaʊ

nois|e (s. v.), -es, -ing, -ed nɔɪz, -ɪz, -ɪŋ, -d

noiseless, -ly, -ness ˈnɔɪzlɪs [-ləs], -lɪ, -nɪs [-nəs]

noisette, -s nwɑ:ˈzet, -s

noisome, -ly, -ness ˈnɔɪsəm, -lɪ, -nɪs [-nəs]

nois|y, -ier, -iest, -ily, -iness ˈnɔɪz|ɪ, -ɪə* [-jə*], -ɪɪst [-jɪst], -ɪlɪ [-əlɪ], -ɪnɪs [-məs]

Nokes nəʊks

Nokomis nəʊˈkəʊmɪs

nolens volens ˌnəʊlenzˈvəʊlenz

Noll nɒl

nomad, -s ˈnəʊmæd [-məd, ˈnɒmæd], -z

nomadic, -ally nəʊˈmædɪk [nɒˈm-], -əlɪ

no-man's-land ˈnəʊmænzlænd

nom de plume, -s ˌnɔ̃:mdəˈplu:m [ˌnɒm-] (nɔ̃dplym), -z

nomenclature, -s nəʊˈmenklətʃə* [ˈnəʊmenkleɪtʃə*, ˈnəʊmənkleɪ-], -z

nomic ˈnəʊmɪk [ˈnɒmɪk]

nomin|al, -ally ˈnɒmɪn|l, -əlɪ

nominat|e, -es, -ing, -ed, -or/s ˈnɒmɪneɪt, -s, -ɪŋ, -ɪd, -ə*/z

nomination, -s ˌnɒmɪˈneɪʃn, -z

nominative (s. adj.), -s ˈnɒmɪnətɪv [-mən-], -z

nominee, -s ˌnɒmɪˈni:, -z

non nɒn

non-acceptance ˌnɒnəkˈseptəns [-næk-]

nonage ˈnəʊnɪdʒ [ˈnɒn-]

nonagenarian, -s ˌnəʊnədʒɪˈneərɪən [ˌnɒn-, -dʒə'n-], -z

non-appearance ˌnɒnəˈpɪərəns

nonary ˈnəʊnərɪ

non-attendance ˌnɒnəˈtendəns

non-belligeren|cy, -t/s ˌnɒnbəˈlɪdʒərən|sɪ [-beˈl-, -bɪˈl-, -dʒrən-], -t/s

nonce, -word/s nɒns, -wɜ:d/z

non-certifiable ˌnɒnˈsɜ:tɪfaɪəbl [ˈnɒnˌsɜ:tɪˈfaɪ-]

nonchalan|ce, -t/ly ˈnɒnʃələn|s, -t/lɪ

non-collegiate, -s ˌnɒnkəˈli:dʒɪət [-kɒˈl-, -dʒjət, -dʒɪt-, -dʒɪt], -s

non-combatant, -s ˌnɒnˈkɒmbətənt [-ˈkʌm-], -s

non-commissioned ˌnɒnkəˈmɪʃnd [also ˈ--ˌ-- when attributive]

non-committal ˌnɒnkəˈmɪtl

non-compliance ˌnɒnkəmˈplaɪəns

non-conducting ˌnɒnkənˈdʌktɪŋ [ˈ--ˌ--]

non-conductor, -s ˈnɒnkənˌdʌktə* [ˌ-ˈ-ˈ--], -z

nonconformist, -s ˌnɒnkənˈfɔ:mɪst [ˌnɒnŋk-], -s

nonconformity ˌnɒnkənˈfɔ:mətɪ [ˌnɒnŋk-, -ɪtɪ]

non-contentious ˌnɒnkənˈtenʃəs

non-delivery ˌnɒndɪˈlɪvərɪ

nondescript (s. adj.), -s ˈnɒndɪskrɪpt, -s

none (s.) (church service), -s nəʊn, -z

none (adj. pron. adv.) nʌn

nonentit|y, -ies nɒˈnentət|ɪ [nəˈn-, -ɪt|ɪ], -ɪz

nones nəʊnz

non-essential, -s ˌnɒnɪˈsenʃl, -z

nonetheless ˌnʌnðəˈles [ˈ---]

non-existen|ce, -t ˌnɒnɪgˈzɪstən|s [-eg-], -t

non-feasance ˌnɒnˈfi:zəns

nonillion, -s nəʊˈnɪljən, -z

non-intervention ˈnɒnˌɪntəˈvenʃn

nonjuror, -s ˌnɒnˈdʒʊərə* [ˈ-ˌ--], -z

non-member, -s ˈnɒnˌmembə* [ˌ-ˈ--], -z

non-observance ˌnɒnəbˈzɜ:vəns

nonpareil ˈnɒnpərəl [ˌnɒnpəˈreɪl, ˈnɒmprəl]

non-payment ˌnɒnˈpeɪmənt

non-performance ˌnɒnpəˈfɔ:məns

nonplus, -ses, -sing, -sed ˌnɒnˈplʌs, -ɪz, -ɪŋ, -t

non-resident, -s ˌnɒnˈrezɪdənt, -s

nonsense ˈnɒnsəns

nonsensic|al, -ally, -alness nɒnˈsensɪk|l, -əlɪ, -lnɪs [-nəs]

non sequitur, -s ˌnɒnˈsekwɪtə*, -z

non-stop, -s, -ping ˌnɒnˈstɒp, -s, -ɪŋ

non(e)such, -es ˈnʌnsʌtʃ, -ɪz

nonsuit (s. v.), -s, -ing, -ed ˌnɒnˈsu:t [-ˈsju:t], -s, -ɪŋ, -ɪd

non-user ˌnɒnˈju:zə*

non-violen|t, -ce ˌnɒnˈvaɪələn|t, -s

noodle, -s ˈnu:dl, -z

nook, -s nʊk, -s

noon, -s nu:n, -z

Noonan ˈnu:nən

noonday ˈnu:ndeɪ

no one 'nəʊvʌn
noontide 'nu:ntaɪd
noo|se (s. v.), -ses, -sing, -sed nu:|s [nu:|z], -sɪz [-zɪz], -sɪŋ [-zɪŋ], -st [-zd]
nor nɔ:* (normal form), nə* (occasional weak form)
Nora(h) 'nɔ:rə
Nordenfelt 'nɔ:dnfelt
Nordic 'nɔ:dɪk
Nore nɔ:* [nɔə*]
Norfolk 'nɔ:fək
Norgate 'nɔ:geɪt [-gɪt]
Norham 'nɒrəm ['nɔ:r-]
Norland 'nɔ:lənd
norm, -s nɔ:m, -z
norm|al, -ally 'nɔ:m|l, -əlɪ [-|ɪ]
normalcy 'nɔ:mlsɪ
normality nɔ:'mælətɪ [-ɪtɪ]
normalization [-isa-] ˌnɔ:məlaɪ'zeɪʃn [-m|aɪ'z-, -məlɪ'z-, -m|ɪ'z-]
normaliz|e [-is|e], -es, -ing, -ed 'nɔ:mə-laɪz [-m|aɪz], -ɪz, -ɪŋ, -d
Norman, -s 'nɔ:mən, -z
Normanby 'nɔ:mənbɪ
Normandy (in France) 'nɔ:məndɪ, (in Surrey) 'nɔ:məndɪ [also locally nɔ:'mændɪ]
Normanton 'nɔ:məntən
Norn, -s nɔ:n, -z
Norris 'nɒrɪs
Norroy, -s 'nɒrɔɪ, -z
Norse, -man, -men nɔ:s, -mən, -mən [-men]
north (N.) nɔ:θ
Northallerton nɔ:'θælətən
Northampton, -shire nɔ:'θæmptən [nɔ:θ'hæm-, locally nə'θæm-], -ʃə* [-,ʃɪə*]
Northanger nɔ:'θæŋgə*
Northants. nɔ:'θænts
North|brook, -cliffe, -cote 'nɔ:θ|brʊk, -klɪf, -kət [-kəʊt]
north-east ˌnɔ:θ'i:st [nautical pronunciation nɔ:r'i:st, also '-- according to sentence-stress]
north-easter, -s ˌnɔ:θ'i:stə* [in nautical usage also nɔ:r'i:stə*], -z
north-easterly ˌnɔ:θ'i:stəlɪ [in nautical usage also nɔ:r'i:stəlɪ]
north-eastern ˌnɔ:θ'i:stən
north-eastward, -s ˌnɔ:θ'i:stwəd, -z
Northen 'nɔ:ðən
northerly 'nɔ:ðəlɪ
northern, -most 'nɔ:ðn, -məʊst [-məst]
northerner, -s 'nɔ:ðənə*, -z
North|field, -fleet 'nɔ:θ|fi:ld, -fli:t
northing 'nɔ:θɪŋ
Northland 'nɔ:θlənd

North|man, -men 'nɔ:θ|mən, -mən [-men]
north-north-east ˌnɔ:θnɔ:θ'i:st [nautical pronunciation ˌnɔ:nɔ:r'i:st]
north-north-west ˌnɔ:θnɔ:θ'west [nautical pronunciation ˌnɔ:nɔ:'west]
north-polar ˌnɔ:θ'pəʊlə*
Northumberland nɔ:'θʌmbələnd [nə'θ-, -blənd]
Northumbria, -n/s nɔ:'θʌmbrɪə, -n/z
northward, -s, -ly 'nɔ:θwəd, -z, -lɪ
north-west, -er/s, -erly ˌnɔ:θ'west [nautical pronunciation nɔ:'west, also '-- according to sentence-stress], -ə*/z, -əlɪ
north-west|ern, -ward ˌnɔ:θ'west|ən, -wəd
North|wich, -wood 'nɔ:θ|wɪtʃ, -wʊd
Norton 'nɔ:tn
Norway 'nɔ:weɪ
Norwegian, -s nɔ:'wi:dʒən, -z
Norwich (in England) 'nɒrɪdʒ [-ɪtʃ], (in U.S.A.) 'nɔ:wɪtʃ
Norwood 'nɔ:wʊd
nos. (N.) 'nʌmbəz
nos|e (s. v.), -es, -ing, -ed nəʊz, -ɪz, -ɪŋ, -d
nose-bag, -s 'nəʊzbæg, -z
nose-div|e (s. v.), -es, -ing, -ed 'nəʊz-daɪv, -z, -ɪŋ, -d
nosegay, -s 'nəʊzgeɪ, -z
nose-ring, -s 'nəʊzrɪŋ, -z
nosey 'nəʊzɪ
nostalg|ia, -ic, -ically nɒ'stældʒ|ɪə [-|ə], -ɪk, -ɪkəlɪ
Nostradamus ˌnɒstrə'deɪməs
nostril, -s 'nɒstrəl [-ɪl], -z
nostrum, -s 'nɒstrəm, -z
nosy 'nəʊzɪ
not nɒt (normal form), nt, n (weak forms used after auxil. verbs only)
nota bene ˌnəʊtə'bi:nɪ [-'benɪ]
notabilit|y, -ies ˌnəʊtə'bɪlət|ɪ [-ɪt-], -ɪz
notab|le, -ly, -leness 'nəʊtəb|l, -lɪ, -lnɪs [-nəs]
notarial, -ly nəʊ'teərɪəl, -ɪ
notar|y, -ies 'nəʊtər|ɪ, -ɪz
notation, -s nəʊ'teɪʃn, -z
notch (s. v.), -es, -ing, -ed nɒtʃ, -ɪz, -ɪŋ, -t
not|e (s. v.), -es, -ing, -ed nəʊt, -s, -ɪŋ, -ɪd
note|-book/s, -paper, -worthy 'nəʊt|-bʊk/s, -,peɪpə*, -,wɜ:ðɪ
nothing, -ness 'nʌθɪŋ, -z, -nɪs [-nəs]
notic|e (s. v.), -es, -ing, -ed 'nəʊtɪs, -ɪz, -ɪŋ, -t
noticeab|le, -ly 'nəʊtɪsəb|l, -lɪ

notice-board, -s 'nəʊtɪsbɔːd [-bɔəd], -z
notifiable 'nəʊtɪfaɪəbl [ˌnəʊtɪ'faɪ-]
notification, -s ˌnəʊtɪfɪ'keɪʃn, -z
noti|fy, -fies, -fying, -fied 'nəʊtɪ|faɪ,
-faɪz, -faɪɪŋ, -faɪd
notion, -s 'nəʊʃn, -z
notional 'nəʊʊənl [-ʃnəl, -ʃn̩l, -ʃn̩l,
-ʃənəl]
notoriety ˌnəʊtə'raɪətɪ
notorious, -ly, -ness nəʊ'tɔːrɪəs, -lɪ, -nɪs
[-nəs]
Notre Dame (English Catholic pronunciation) ˌnəʊtrə'dɑːm [ˌnɒt-]
(notrədam) (American ˌnoʊtɪ'deɪm)
Nottingham, -shire 'nɒtɪŋəm, -ʃə*
[-ˌʃɪə*]
Notting Hill ˌnɒtɪŋ'hɪl
Notts. nɒts
notwithstanding ˌnɒtwɪθ'stændɪŋ
[-wɪð's-]
nougat, -s 'nuːgɑː ['nʌgət], 'nuːgɑːz
['nʌgəts]
nought, -s nɔːt, -s
noun, -s naʊn, -z
nourish, -es, -ing, -ed; -ment 'nʌrɪʃ, -ɪz,
-ɪŋ, -t; -mənt
nous naʊs
nouveau riche ˌnuːvəʊ'riːʃ
Nova Scotia ˌnəʊvə'skəʊʃə
novel (s. adj.), -s 'nɒvl, -z
novelette, -s ˌnɒvə'let [-vɪ'let, -vl̩'et], -s
novelist, -s 'nɒvəlɪst [-vl̩ɪst], -s
Novello nə'veləʊ
novelt|y, -ies 'nɒvlt|ɪ, -ɪz
November, -s nəʊ'vembə*, -z
Novial (language) 'nəʊvjəl [-vɪəl]
novice, -s 'nɒvɪs, -ɪz
noviciate [-itiate], -s nəʊ'vɪʃɪət [nɒ'v-,
-ʃɪeɪt, -ʃɪɪt]
novocaine 'nəʊvəʊkeɪn ['nɒv-]
now, -adays naʊ, -ədeɪz
Nowell (personal name) 'nəʊəl [-el],
(Christmas) nəʊ'el
nowhere 'nəʊweə* ['nəʊhw-]
nowise 'nəʊwaɪz
Nox nɒks
noxious, -ly, -ness 'nɒkʃəs, -lɪ, -nɪs
[-nəs]
noyau, -s 'nwaɪəʊ ['nwɔɪəʊ, 'nɔɪəʊ]
(nwajo), -z
Noyes nɔɪz
nozzle, -s 'nɒzl, -z
-n't (= not) -nt
nu njuː
nuance, -s njuː'ɑ̃ːns [njʊ-, -'ɔ̃ːns, -'ɑːns,
'--] (nɥɑ̃ːs), -ɪz
nubble, -s 'nʌbl, -z
nubbly 'nʌblɪ

Nubia, -n/s 'njuːbjə [-bɪə], -n/z
nubile 'njuːbaɪl
nucl|eus, -ei, -eal, -ear, -eic 'njuːkl|ɪəs
[-jəs], -ɪaɪ, -ɪəl [-jəl], -ɪə* [-jə*],
-ɪɪk
nude (s. adj.), -s njuːd, -z
nudg|e (s. v.), -es, -ing, -ed nʌdʒ, -ɪz,
-ɪŋ, -d
nudi|sm, -st/s 'njuːdɪ|zəm, -st/s
nudit|y, -ies 'njuːdət|ɪ [-ɪt|ɪ], -ɪz
Nuffield 'nʌfiːld
nugatory 'njuːgətərɪ [njuː'geɪtərɪ]
Nugent 'njuːdʒənt
nugget, -s 'nʌgɪt, -s
nuisance, -s 'njuːsns, -ɪz
null nʌl
nullah, -s 'nʌlə, -z
nullification ˌnʌlɪfɪ'keɪʃn
nulli|fy, -fies, -fying, -fied 'nʌlɪ|faɪ,
-faɪz, -faɪɪŋ, -faɪd
nullit|y, -ies 'nʌlət|ɪ [-ɪt|ɪ], -ɪz
Numa Pompilius ˌnjuːməpɒm'pɪlɪəs
[-ljəs]
numb (adj. v.), -ly, -ness; -s, -ing, -ed
nʌm, -lɪ, -nɪs [-nəs]; -z, -ɪŋ, -d
numb|er (s. v.), -ers (N.), -ering, -ered;
-erless 'nʌmb|ə*, -əz, -ərɪŋ, -əd; -əlɪs
[-ləs]
numerable 'njuːmərəbl
numeral (s. adj.), -s 'njuːmərəl, -z
numerate 'njuːmərət [-rɪt]
numeration ˌnjuːmə'reɪʃn
numerative, -s 'njuːmərətɪv, -z
numerator, -s 'njuːməreɪtə*, -z
numeric|al, -ally njuː'merɪk|l [njʊ'm-],
-əlɪ
numerous, -ly, -ness 'njuːmərəs, -lɪ,
-nɪs [-nəs]
Numidia, -n/s njuː'mɪdɪə [njʊ'm-, -djə],
-n/z
numismatic, -s, -ally ˌnjuːmɪz'mætɪk,
-s, -əlɪ
numismatist, -s njuː'mɪzmətɪst
[njʊ'm-], -s
numskull, -s 'nʌmskʌl, -z
nun (N.), -s nʌn, -z
Nunc Dimittis, -es ˌnʌŋkdɪ'mɪtɪs
[-daɪ'm-], -ɪz
nuncio, -s 'nʌnʃɪəʊ [-ʃjəʊ, -sɪəʊ, -sjəʊ],
-z
Nuneaton nʌn'iːtn
Nuneham 'njuːnəm
nunkey, -s 'nʌŋkɪ, -z
Nunn nʌn
nunner|y, -ies 'nʌnər|ɪ, -ɪz
nuptial, -s 'nʌpʃl ['nʌptʃəl], -z
Nuremberg 'njʊərəmbɜːg ['njɔər-,
'njɔːr-]

nurs|e (*s. v.*), **-es, -ing, -ed** nɜːs, -ɪz, -ɪŋ, -t

nurs(e)ling, -s 'nɜːslɪŋ, -z

nurse-maid, -s 'nɜːsmeɪd, -z

nurser|y, -ies 'nɜːsər|ɪ, -ɪz

nursery-maid, -s 'nɜːsrɪmeɪd, -z

nursery|man, -men 'nɜːsrɪ|mən, -mən

nurtur|e (*s. v.*), **-es, -ing, -ed** 'nɜːtʃə*, -z, -rɪŋ, -d

nut, -s nʌt, -s

nutat|e, -es, -ing, -ed njuː'teɪt, -s, -ɪŋ, -ɪd

nutation, -s njuː'teɪʃn, -z

nut-brown 'nʌtbraʊn [ˌ-'-]

nutcracker, -s 'nʌtˌkrækə*, -z

nuthat|ch, -es 'nʌthætʃ, -ɪz

nutmeg, -s 'nʌtmeg, -z

nutria 'njuːtrɪə

nutrient 'njuːtrɪənt

nutriment 'njuːtrɪmənt

nutrition, -al njuː'trɪʃn [njuˈtr-], -l

nutritious, -ly, -ness njuː'trɪʃəs[njuˈtr-], -lɪ, -nɪs [-nəs]

nutritive 'njuːtrətɪv [-trɪt-]

nutshell, -s 'nʌt-ʃel, -z

Nuttall 'nʌtɔːl

Nutter 'nʌtə*

nutty 'nʌtɪ

nux vomica ˌnʌksˈvɒmɪkə

nuzz|le, -es, -ing, -ed 'nʌz|l, -lz, -lɪŋ [-lɪŋ], -ld

N.W. ˌenˈdʌb|juː: [ˌnɔːθ'west]

Nyanja (*people, language*) 'njændʒə [nɪ'æn-]

Nyanza (*lake*) 'njænzə [nɪ'æn-, naɪ'æn-]

Nyasa (*lake*) naɪ'æsə [nɪ'æsə, 'njæsə]

Nyasaland naɪ'æsəlænd [nɪ'æs-, 'njæsəlænd]

Nyerere nje'reərɪ [njɪ-, njə-, nɪə-, -'rerɪ]

nylon 'naɪlɒn [-lən]

nymph, -s, -al nɪmf, -s, -l

nymphet nɪm'fet

nymph-like 'nɪmflaɪk

nympho, -s 'nɪmfəʊ, -z

nymphoman|ia, -iac/s ˌnɪmfəʊ'meɪm|ɪə [-jə], -ɪæk [-jæk]/s

nystagmus nɪ'stægməs

O

O (*the letter*), **-'s** [**-es**] əʊ, -z
O (*interj.*) əʊ
o' (*abbrev. of* of) ə (*weak form only*)
oaf, **-s ; -ish** əʊf, -s; -ɪʃ
oak, **-s** əʊk, -s
oak-apple, **-s** 'əʊk,æpl, -z
oak-bark 'əʊkbɑːk
Oakeley 'əʊklɪ
oaken 'əʊkən
Oak|es, **-ey** əʊk|s, -ɪ
oak-gall, **-s** 'əʊkgɔːl, -z
Oakham 'əʊkəm
Oakhampton ,əʊk'hæmptən
Oakland, **-s** 'əʊklənd, -z
Oak|leigh, **-ley** 'əʊk|lɪ, -lɪ
oakling, **-s** 'əʊklɪŋ, -z
Oaks əʊks
oakum, **-picking** 'əʊkəm, -,pɪkɪŋ
Oakworth 'əʊkwəθ [-wɜːθ]
oar (*s. v.*), **-s, -ing, -ed** ɔː* [əə*], -z, -rɪŋ, -d
oars|man, **-men** 'ɔːz|mən ['ɔəz-], -mən
oas|is, **-es** əʊ'eɪs|ɪs, -iːz
oast, **-s** əʊst, -s
oast-hou|se, **-ses** 'əʊsthaʊ|s, -zɪz
oat, **-s** əʊt, -s
oatcake, **-s** 'əʊtkeɪk, -s
oaten 'əʊtn
Oates əʊts
oa|th, **-ths** əʊ|θ, -ðz [-θs]
oath-break|er/s, **-ing** 'əʊθ,breɪk|ə*/z, -ɪŋ
Oatlands 'əʊtləndz
oatmeal 'əʊtmiːl
Ob (*river in Siberia*) ɒb (opj)
Obadiah ,əʊbə'daɪə
Oban 'əʊbən
obbligato, **-s** ,ɒblɪ'gɑːtəʊ, -z
obduracy 'ɒbdjʊərəsɪ [-djə-]
obdurate, **-ly, -ness** 'ɒbdjʊərət [-djə-, -rɪt, -reɪt, ɒb'djʊərət, -rɪt], -lɪ, -nɪs [-nəs]
obduration ,ɒbdjʊə'reɪʃn [-djə'r-, -djəə'r-, -djɔː'r-]
obeah 'əʊ,bɪə [-bɪə]
Obed 'əʊbed
Obededom ,əʊbed'iːdəm
obedien|ce, **-t/ly** ə'biːdjən|s [əʊ'b-, -dɪən-], -t/lɪ

O'Beirne əʊ'beən
obeisance, **-s** əʊ'beɪsəns, -ɪz
obelisk, **-s** 'ɒbəlɪsk [-bɪl-], -s
obelus, **-es** 'ɒbɪləs, -ɪz
Ober - Ammergau ,əʊbər'æməgaʊ [-bə'æm-] (,ɔːbər'amərgaʊ)
Oberland 'əʊbələnd
Oberlin (*in U.S.A.*) 'əʊbəlɪn
Oberon 'əʊbərən [-rɒn]
obes|e, **-eness, -ity** əʊ'biːs, -nɪs [-nəs], -ətɪ [-ɪtɪ]
obey, **-s, -ing, -ed, -er/s** ə'beɪ [əʊ'b-], -z, -ɪŋ, -d, -ə*/z ['beə*/z]
obfuscat|e, **-es, -ing, -ed** 'ɒbfʌskeɪt [-fəs-], -s, -ɪŋ, -ɪd
obfuscation, **-s** ,ɒbfʌ'skeɪʃn [-fə's-], -z
obi, **-s** 'əʊbɪ, -z
Obi (*river in Siberia*) 'əʊbɪ (opj)
Obion əʊ'baɪən
obit, **-s** 'ɒbɪt ['əʊbɪt], -s
obiter 'ɒbɪtə*
obituarist, **-s** ə'bɪtjʊərɪst [ɒ'b-, -tjwər-, -tjər-, -tjʊr-], -s
obituar|y, **-ies** ə'bɪtjʊər|ɪ [ɒ'b-, -tjwər-, -tjər-, -tjʊr-], -ɪz
object (*s.*), **-s** 'ɒbdʒɪkt [-dʒekt], -s
object (*v.*), **-s, -ing, -ed, -or/s** əb'dʒekt, -s, -ɪŋ, -ɪd, -ə*/z
object-glass, **-es** 'ɒbdʒɪktglɑːs [-dʒekt-], -ɪz
objecti|fy, **-fies, -fying, -fied** ɒb'dʒektɪ|faɪ [əb-], -faɪz, -faɪɪŋ, -faɪd
objection, **-s** əb'dʒekʃn, -z
objectionab|le, **-ly** əb'dʒekʃnəb|l [-ʃnəb-, -ʃənəb-], -lɪ
objective (*s.*), **-s** əb'dʒektɪv [ɒb-], -z
objective (*adj.*), **-ly, -ness** əb'dʒektɪv [ɒb'dʒ-], -lɪ, -nɪs [-nəs]
objectivism əb'dʒektɪvɪzəm [ɒb-]
objectivity ,ɒbdʒek'tɪvətɪ [-ɪtɪ]
objectless 'ɒbdʒɪktlɪs [-dʒekt-, -ləs]
object-lesson, **-s** 'ɒbdʒɪkt,lesn [-dʒekt-], -z
objet(s) d'art ,ɒbʒeɪ'dɑː* (ɔbʒɛdaːr)
objurgat|e, **-es, -ing, -ed** 'ɒbdʒɜː'geɪt, -s, -ɪŋ, -ɪd
objurgation, **-s** ,ɒbdʒɜː'geɪʃn, -z
objurgatory ɒb'dʒɜː'gətərɪ [əb'dʒ-, 'ɒbdʒɜː'geɪtərɪ]

346

oblate (s.), -s 'ɒbleɪt, -s
oblate (adj.) 'ɒbleɪt [ɒ'bleɪt, əʊ'b-]
oblation, -s əʊ'bleɪʃn [ɒ'b-], -z
obligant, -s 'ɒblɪgənt, -s
obligation, -s ˌɒblɪ'geɪʃn, -z
obligato (s. adj.), -s ˌɒblɪ'gɑːtəʊ, -z
obligator|y, -ily, -iness ə'blɪgətər|ɪ
  [ɒ'b-, 'ɒblɪgətər-, 'ɒblɪgertər-], -əlɪ
  [-ɪlɪ], -mɪs [-məs]
oblig|e, -es, -ing/ly, -ingness, -ed
  ə'blaɪdʒ, -ɪz, -ɪŋ/lɪ, -ɪŋnɪs [-nəs], -d
obligee, -s ˌɒblɪ'dʒiː, -z
obligor, -s ˌɒblɪ'gɔ:*, -z
oblique, -ly, -ness ə'bliːk [ɒ'b-, əʊ'b-],
  -lɪ, -nɪs [-nəs]
obliquit|y, -ies ə'blɪkwət|ɪ [ɒ'b-, əʊ'b-,
  -ɪt|ɪ], -ɪz
obliterat|e, -es, -ing, -ed ə'blɪtəreɪt
  [ɒ'b-], -s, -ɪŋ, -ɪd
obliteration, -s ə,blɪtə'reɪʃn [ɒ,b-], -z
oblivion ə'blɪvɪən [ɒ'b-, -vjən]
oblivious, -ly, -ness ə'blɪvɪəs [ɒ'b-,
  -vjəs], -lɪ, -nɪs [-nəs]
oblong (s. adj.), -s 'ɒblɒŋ, -z
obloquy 'ɒbləkwɪ
obnoxious, -ly, -ness əb'nɒkʃəs [ɒb-],
  -lɪ, -nɪs [-nəs]
Obock əʊ'bɒk ['əʊbɒk]
oboe, -s 'əʊbəʊ, -z
oboist, -s 'əʊbəʊɪst, -s
obol, -s 'ɒbɒl [-bəl], -z
obole, -s 'ɒbəʊl, -z
O'Brady əʊ'brɔːdɪ [-'breɪ-]
O'Br|ien, -yan əʊ'br|aɪən, -aɪən
obscene, -ly, -ness əb'siːn [ɒb-], -lɪ, -nɪs
  [-nəs]
obscenit|y, -ies əb'senət|ɪ [ɒb-, -'siːn-,
  -ɪt|ɪ], -ɪz
obscurant (s. adj.) ɒb'skjʊərənt [əb-,
  -bz'k-]
obscurant|ism, -ist/s ˌɒbskjʊə'rænt|-
  ɪzəm [-bzk-, -kjʊ'r-, ɒb'skjʊərənt-,
  əb'skjʊərənt-, -bz'k-], -ɪst/s
obscuration, -s ˌɒbskjʊə'reɪʃn [-bzk-,
  -kjʊ'r-, -kjə'r-], -z
obscur|e (adj. v.), -er, -est, -ely,
  -eness; -es, -ing, -ed əb'skjʊə* [ɒb-,
  -bz'k-, -jəə*, -jɔ:*], -rə*, -rɪst, -lɪ,
  -nɪs [-nəs]; -z, -rɪŋ, -d
obscurit|y, -ies əb'skjʊərət|ɪ [ɒb-, -bz'k-,
  -jəər-, -jɔ:r-, -ɪt|ɪ], -ɪz
obsecration, -s ˌɒbsɪ'kreɪʃn [-se'k-], -z
obsequial ɒb'siːkwɪəl [əb-, -kwjəl]
obsequies 'ɒbsɪkwɪz [-sə-]
obsequious, -ly, -ness əb'siːkwɪəs [ɒb-,
  -kwjəs], -lɪ, -nɪs [-nəs]
observab|le, -ly, -leness əb'zɜːvəb|l, -lɪ,
  -lnɪs [-nəs]

observan|ce, -ces, -cy əb'zɜːvn|s, -sɪz,
  -sɪ
observant, -ly əb'zɜːvnt, -lɪ
observation, -s ˌɒbzə'veɪʃn, -z
observa|tional, -tionally ˌɒbzə'veɪʃənl
  [-ʃnəl, -ʃn̩, -ʃn̩, -ʃənəl], -ʃn̩əlɪ [-ʃnəlɪ,
  -ʃn̩ɪ, -ʃn̩ɪ, -ʃənəlɪ]
observator|y, -ies əb'zɜːvətr|ɪ [-tər-],
  -ɪz
observ|e, -es, -ing/ly, -ed, -er/s əb'zɜːv,
  -z, -ɪŋ/lɪ, -d, -ə*/z
obsess, -es, -ing, -ed əb'ses [ɒb-], -ɪz,
  -ɪŋ, -t
obsession, -s, -al əb'seʃn [ɒb-], -z, -l
  [-əl, -ʃənəl]
obsessive əb'sesɪv [ɒb-]
obsidian ɒb'sɪdɪən [-djən]
obsolescen|ce, -t ˌɒbsəʊ'lesn|s, -t
obsolete, -ly, -ness 'ɒbsəliːt [-s|iːt,
  -sliːt], -lɪ, -nɪs [-nəs]
obstacle, -s 'ɒbstəkl [-bzt-, -tɪkl], -z
obstetric, -al, -s ɒb'stetrɪk [əb-, -bz't-],
  -l, -s
obstetrician, -s ˌɒbste'trɪʃn [-bzt-,
  -tə't-, -tɪ't-], -z
obstinac|y, -ies 'ɒbstɪnəs|ɪ [-bzt-,
  -tənə-], -ɪz
obstinate, -ly, -ness 'ɒbstənət [-bzt-,
  -tɪn-, -nɪt], -lɪ, -nɪs [-nəs]
obstreperous, -ly, -ness əb'strepərəs
  [ɒb-, -bz't-], -lɪ, -nɪs [-nəs]
obstruct, -s, -ing, -ed, -or/s əb'strʌkt
  [-bz't-], -s, -ɪŋ, -ɪd, -ə*/z
obstruction, -s əb'strʌkʃn [-bz't-], -z
obstructionism əb'strʌkʃənɪzəm [-bz't-,
  -ʃn̩-]
obstructionist, -s əb'strʌkʃənɪst [-bz't-,
  -ʃn̩], -s
obstructive, -ly, -ness əb'strʌktɪv
  [-bz't-], -lɪ, -nɪs [-nəs]
obstruent (s. adj.), -s 'ɒbstrʊənt, -s
obtain, -s, -ing, -ed, -er/s; -able
  əb'teɪn, -z, -ɪŋ, -d, -ə*/z; -əbl
obtrud|e, -es, -ing, -ed, -er/s əb'truːd
  [ɒb-], -z, -ɪŋ, -ɪd, -ə*/z
obtrusion, -s əb'truːʒn [ɒb-], -z
obtrusive, -ly, -ness əb'truːsɪv [ɒb-], -lɪ,
  -nɪs [-nəs]
obturat|e, -es, -ing, -ed, -or/s 'ɒbtjʊə-
  reɪt [-tjʊr-], -s, -ɪŋ, -ɪd, -ə*/z
obturation, -s ˌɒbtjʊə'reɪʃn [-tjʊ'r-], -z
obtuse, -ly, -ness əb'tjuːs [ɒb-], -lɪ, -nɪs
  [-nəs]
obverse (s. adj.), -s 'ɒbvɜːs, -ɪz
obversely ɒb'vɜːslɪ
obvert, -s, -ing, -ed ɒb'vɜːt, -s, -ɪŋ, -ɪd
obviat|e, -es, -ing, -ed 'ɒbvɪeɪt [-vjeɪt],
  -s, -ɪŋ, -ɪd

347

obvious, -ly, -ness 'ɒbvɪəs [-vjəs], -lɪ, -nɪs [-nəs]
O'Byrne əʊ'bɜːn
O'Callaghan əʊ'kæləhən [-gən]
ocarina, -s ˌɒkə'riːnə, -z
O'Casey əʊ'keɪsɪ
Occam 'ɒkəm
occasi|on (s. v.), -ons, -oning, -oned ə'keɪʒ|n, -nz, -n̩ɪŋ [-ənɪŋ, -nɪŋ], -nd
occa|sional, -sionally ə'keɪ|ʒənl [-ʒnəl, -ʒn̩l, -ʒn̩l, -ʒənəl], -ʒn̩əlɪ [-ʒnəlɪ, -ʒn̩lɪ, -ʒn̩lɪ, -ʒənəlɪ]
occasionali|sm -st/s ə'keɪʒnəlɪ|zəm [-ʒnəl-, -ʒn̩l-, -ʒnl-, -ʒənəl-], -st/s
occident (O.) 'ɒksɪdənt
occidental (s. adj.) (O.), -s ˌɒksɪ'dentl, -z
occidentali|sm, -st/s ˌɒksɪ'dentəlɪ|zəm [-tlɪ-], -st/s
occidentaliz|e [-is|e), -es, -ing, -ed ˌɒksɪ'dentəlaɪz [-tlaɪz], -ɪz, -ɪŋ, -d
occipit|al, -ally ɒk'sɪpɪt|l, -əlɪ
occiput, -s 'ɒksɪpʌt [-pət], -s
Occleve 'ɒkliːv
occlud|e, -es, -ing, -ed ɒ'kluːd [ə'k-], -z, -ɪŋ, -ɪd
occlusion, -s ɒ'kluːʒn [ə'k-], -z
occlusive (s. adj.), -s ɒ'kluːsɪv [ə'k-], -z
occult (adj.), -ly, -ness ɒ'kʌlt [ə'k-, 'ɒkʌlt], -lɪ, -nɪs [-nəs]
occult (v.), -s, -ing, -ed ɒ'kʌlt [ə'k-], -s, -ɪŋ, -ɪd
occultation, -s ˌɒkəl'teɪʃn [-kʌl-], -z
occulti|sm, -st/s 'ɒkəltɪ|zəm ['ɒkʌl-, ɒ'kʌl-], -st/s
occupan|cy, -t/s 'ɒkjʊpən|sɪ [-kjə-], -t/s
occupation, -s ˌɒkjʊ'peɪʃn [-kjə-], -z
occupational ˌɒkjuː'peɪʃənl [-kjʊ-, -kjə-, -ʃnəl, -ʃn̩l, -ʃn̩l, -ʃənəl]
occup|y, -ies, -ying, -ied, -ier/s 'ɒkjʊp|aɪ, -aɪz, -aɪɪŋ, -aɪd, -aɪə*/z
occur, -s, -ring, -red ə'kɜː*, -z, -rɪŋ, -d
occurrence, -s ə'kʌrəns, -ɪz
ocean, -s 'əʊʃn, -z
Oceania, -n/s ˌəʊʃɪ'eɪmjə [-nɪə], -n/z
oceanic (O.) ˌəʊʃɪ'ænɪk [ˌəʊsɪ-]
Oceanica ˌəʊʃɪ'ænɪkə
oceanograph|er/s, -y ˌəʊʃjə'nɒɡrəf|ə*/z [-ʃɪə-], -ɪ
oceanographic ˌəʊʃjənəʊ'ɡræfɪk [-ʃɪə-]
Oceanus əʊ'sɪənəs [əʊ'ʃɪə-]
ocell|us, -i əʊ'sel|əs, -aɪ [-iː]
ocelot, -s 'əʊsɪlɒt ['ɒs-, -sə-, -lət], -s
ochery 'əʊkərɪ
Ochill 'əʊkɪl ['əʊxɪl]
Ochiltree (in Scott's 'Antiquary') 'əʊkɪltri: ['əʊxɪl-], (in U.S.A.) 'əʊkɪltri:

och|re (s. v.), -res, -reing, -red 'əʊk|ə*, -əz, -ərɪŋ, -əd
ochreous 'əʊkrɪəs ['əʊkərəs]
ochry 'əʊkərɪ ['əʊkrɪ]
Ochterlony ˌɒktə'ləʊnɪ [ˌɒxt-]
Ock|ham, -ley 'ɒk|əm, -lɪ
Ocklynge 'ɒklɪndʒ
O'Clery əʊ'klɪərɪ
o'clock ə'klɒk
Ocmulgee əʊk'mʌlɡɪ
O'Con|nell, -(n)or əʊ'kɒn|l, -ə*
Ocracoke 'əʊkrəkəʊk
octagon, -s 'ɒktəɡən, -z
octagonal ɒk'tæɡənl
octahedr|on, -ons, -a; -al ˌɒktə'hedr|ən [-'hiːd-, 'ɒktə,h-], -ənz, -ə; -əl
octane 'ɒkteɪn
octant, -s 'ɒktənt, -s
Octateuch 'ɒktətjuːk
octave (musical term), -s 'ɒktɪv [rarely -teɪv], -z
octave (ecclesiastical term), -s 'ɒkteɪv [-tɪv], -z
Octavia, -n ɒk'teɪvjə [-vɪə], -n
Octavius ɒk'teɪvjəs [-vɪəs]
octavo, -s ɒk'teɪvəʊ, -z
octennial ɒk'tenjəl [-nɪəl]
octet(te), -s ɒk'tet, -s
octillion, -s ɒk'tɪljən, -z
October, -s ɒk'təʊbə*, -z
octodecimo, -s ˌɒktəʊ'desɪməʊ, -z
octogenarian, -s ˌɒktəʊdʒɪ'neərɪən [-dʒə'n-], -z
octopus, -es 'ɒktəpəs, -ɪz
octoroon, -s ˌɒktə'ruːn, -z
octosyllabic ˌɒktəʊsɪ'læbɪk [-təs-]
octosyllable, -s 'ɒktəʊ,sɪləbl [-tə,s-], -z
octroi, -s 'ɒktrwɑː (ɔktrwɑ), -z
octuple 'ɒktjuːpl [-tjʊpl]
ocular, -ly 'ɒkjʊlə* [-kjə-], -lɪ
oculist, -s 'ɒkjʊlɪst [-kjə-], -s
O'Curry əʊ'kʌrɪ
od (O.), -s ɒd, -z
odalisque, -s 'əʊdəlɪsk ['ɒd-], -s
O'Daly əʊ'deɪlɪ
Odam 'əʊdəm
odd, -er, -est, -ly, -ness ɒd, -ə*, -ɪst, -lɪ, -nɪs [-nəs]
Oddfellow, -s 'ɒd,feləʊ, -z
Oddie 'ɒdɪ
oddish 'ɒdɪʃ
oddit|y, -ies 'ɒdɪt|ɪ [-ət|ɪ], -ɪz
odd-looking 'ɒd,lʊkɪŋ
oddment, -s 'ɒdmənt, -s
odds ɒdz
Oddy 'ɒdɪ
ode, -s əʊd, -z
O'Dea əʊ'deɪ

Odell əʊ'del
Odeon 'əʊdjən [-drən]
Oder 'əʊdə* ('o:dər)
Odessa əʊ'desə
Ode|um, -a, -ums əʊ'di:|əm [-'drəm,
  'əʊdj|əm, 'əʊdɪ|əm], -ə, -əmz
Odgers 'ɒdʒəz
Odham 'ɒdəm
Odiham 'əʊdɪhəm
Odin 'əʊdɪn
odious, -ly, -ness 'əʊdjəs [-drəs], -lɪ,
  -nɪs [-nəs]
odium 'əʊdjəm [-drəm]
Odling 'ɒdlɪŋ
Odlum 'ɒdləm
Odo 'əʊdəʊ
Odoacer ˌɒdəʊ'eɪsə* [ˌəʊd-]
O'Doherty əʊ'dəʊətɪ, -'dɒhətɪ [-'dɒxə-]
odol 'əʊdɒl
odometer, -s əʊ'dɒmɪtə* [ɒ'd-, -mətə*],
  -z
O'Donnell əʊ'dɒnl
odontolog|ist/s, -y ˌɒdɒn'tɒlədʒ|ɪst/s, -ɪ
odoriferous, -ly, -ness ˌəʊdə'rɪfərəs
  [ˌɒd-], -lɪ, -nɪs [-nəs]
odorous, -ly, -ness 'əʊdərəs, -lɪ, -nɪs
  [-nəs]
odour, -s, -ed, -less 'əʊdə*, -z, -d, -lɪs
  [-ləs, -les]
O'Dowd əʊ'daʊd
odsbodikins ˌɒdz'bɒdɪkɪnz
O'Dwyer əʊ'dwaɪə*
Ody 'əʊdɪ
Odysseus ə'dɪsju:s [ɒ'd-, əʊ'd-, -sɪəs,
  -sjəs]
Odyssey 'ɒdɪsɪ
oecumenic, -al ˌi:kju:'menɪk [-kjʊ'm-],
  -l
oedema i:'di:mə [ɪ'd-]
oedematous i:'demətəs [ɪ'd-]
Oedipus 'i:dɪpəs
œillade, -s ɜ:'jɑːd (œjad), -z
Oeneus 'i:nju:s [-njəs, -nɪəs]
Oenomaus ˌi:nəʊ'meɪəs
Oenone i:'nəʊni: [ɪ'n-, -nɪ]
o'er (contracted form of over) 'əʊə* [ɔə*,
  ɔː*]
oes (plur. of O) əʊz
oesophageal i:ˌsɒfə'dʒi:əl [ɪ,s-, -'dʒɪəl]
oesopha|gus, -gi, -guses i:'sɒfə|gəs
  [ɪ's-], -gaɪ [-dʒaɪ], -gəsɪz
oestrogen 'i:strəʊdʒən [-dʒen]
oestrus, -es 'i:strəs, -ɪz
Oettle 'ɜ:tlɪ
Oetzmann 'ɜʊtsmən
of ɒv (strong form), əv, v, f (weak forms)
  Note.—The form f occurs only before
  voiceless consonants.

off ɒf [old-fashioned ɔ:f, and in com-
  pounds]
Offa 'ɒfə
offal 'ɒfl
Offaly 'ɒfəlɪ
off-bail, -s ˌɒf'beɪl [ˌɔ:f-, '--, when in
  contrast with leg-bail], -z
off-bye, -s ˌɒf'baɪ [ˌɔ:f-, '--, when in
  contrast with leg-bye], -z
off-drive, -s 'ɒfdraɪv ['ɔ:f-], -z
Offenbach 'ɒfənbɑ:k
offence, -s, -less ə'fens, -ɪz, -lɪs [-ləs]
offend, -s, -ing, -ed -er/s ə'fend, -z, -ɪŋ,
  -ɪd, -ə*/z
offensive (s. adj.), -s, -ly, -ness ə'fensɪv
  [ɒ'f-], -z, -lɪ, -nɪs [-nəs]
off|er (s. v.), -ers, -ering/s, -ered,
  -erer/s; -erable 'ɒf|ə*, -əz, -ərɪŋ/z,
  -əd, -ərə*/z; -ərəbl
offertor|y, -ies 'ɒfətər|ɪ, -ɪz
off-hand ˌɒf'hænd [ˌɔ:f'h-, also '--
  according to sentence-stress]
off-handed ˌɒf'hændɪd [ˌɔ:f-]
office, -s 'ɒfɪs, -ɪz
office-bearer, -s 'ɒfɪsˌbeərə*, -z
office-boy, -s 'ɒfɪsbɔɪ, -z
officer, -s 'ɒfɪsə*, -z
offici|al (s. adj.), -als, -ally, -alism
  ə'fɪʃ|l, -lz, -əlɪ [-lɪ], -əlɪzəm [-lɪzəm]
officialdom ə'fɪʃldəm
officialese ə,fɪʃə'li:z [ə,fɪʃl'i:z, ə'fɪʃəli:z,
  ə'fɪʃli:z]
officiat|e, -es, -ing, -ed ə'fɪʃɪeɪt, -s, -ɪŋ,
  -ɪd
officinal ˌɒfɪ'saɪnl [ɒ'fɪsɪnl]
officious, -ly, -ness ə'fɪʃəs, -lɪ, -nɪs [-nəs]
offing, -s 'ɒfɪŋ ['ɔ:f-], -z
offish 'ɒfɪʃ ['ɔ:f-]
off-licenc|e, -s 'ɒfˌlaɪsns ['ɔ:f-], -ɪz
Offor 'ɒfə*
off-print, -s 'ɒfprɪnt ['ɔ:f-], -s
offset (s. v.), -s, -ting 'ɒfset ['ɔ:f-], -s, -ɪŋ
offshoot, -s 'ɒfʃu:t ['ɔ:f-], -s
offside ˌɒf'saɪd [ˌɔ:f's-, '--, when in contrast with on side]
offspring, -s 'ɒfsprɪŋ ['ɔ:f-], -z
off-the-record ˌɒfðə'rekɔ:d [ˌɔ:f-]
off-time 'ɒftaɪm ['ɔ:f-, ˌ-'-]
O'Flaherty əʊ'fleətɪ [-'flæhətɪ, -'flɑ:ət-,
  -'flɑ:t-]
O'Flynn əʊ'flɪn
oft ɒft [old-fashioned ɔ:ft]
often, -times 'ɒfn [old-fashioned 'ɔ:f-,
  -fən, -ftən], -taɪmz
often|er, -est 'ɒfn|ə* ['ɔ:f-, -fn|ə*,
  -fən|ə*, -ftən|ə*, -ftn|ə*, -ftn|ə*], -ɪst
ofttimes 'ɒfttaɪmz ['ɔ:f-]
Og, -den ɒg, -dən

349

ogee, -s 'əʊdʒi: [əʊ'dʒi:], -z
Ogemaw 'əʊgɪmɔ:
og(h)am, -s 'ɒgəm, -z
og(h)amic ɒ'gæmɪk
Ogil|by, -vie, -vy 'əʊgl|bɪ, -vɪ, -vɪ
ogival əʊ'dʒaɪvl
ogive, -s 'əʊdʒaɪv [əʊ'dʒ-], -z
og|le (O.), -les, -ling, -led, -ler/s 'əʊg|l,
 -lz, -lɪŋ [-lɪŋ], -ld, -lə*/z [-lə*/z]
Ogle|by, -thorpe 'əʊgl|bɪ, -θɔːp
Ogpu 'ɒgpu:
O'Grady əʊ'greɪdɪ
ogr|e, -es, -ish 'əʊgə*, -z, -rɪʃ
ogress, -es 'əʊgrɪs [-res], -ɪz
o'Groat ə'grəʊt
oh əʊ
O'Hagan əʊ'heɪgən
O'Halloran əʊ'hælərən
O'Hara əʊ'hɑːrə
O'Hare əʊ'heə*
O'Hea əʊ'heɪ
Ohio əʊ'haɪəʊ
ohm (O.), -s əʊm, -z
oho əʊ'həʊ
oil (s. v.), -s, -ing, -ed, -er/s ɔɪl, -z, -ɪŋ,
 -d, -ə*/z
oil-box, -es 'ɔɪlbɒks, -ɪz
oil-burner, -s 'ɔɪl‚bɜːnə*, -z
oil-cake, -s 'ɔɪlkeɪk, -s
oil-can, -s 'ɔɪlkæn, -z
oil|cloth, -cloths 'ɔɪl|klɒθ [old-fashioned
 -klɔːθ], -klɒθs [-klɔːðz, -klɔːθs]
oil-colour, -s 'ɔɪl‚kʌlə*, -z
oil-field, -s 'ɔɪlfiːld, -z
oil-fuel 'ɔɪlfjʊəl [-‚fjuːəl, -fjuːl]
oil|man, -men 'ɔɪl|mən [-mæn], -mən
 [-men]
oil-paint, -s; -ing/s ‚ɔɪl'peɪnt ['— when
 in contrast with other kinds of paint],
 -s; -ɪŋ/z
oil-rig, -s 'ɔɪlrɪg, -z
oil-silk 'ɔɪlsɪlk [‚'-'-]
oil-skin 'ɔɪlskɪn, -z
oil-stone, -s 'ɔɪlstəʊn, -z
oil-stove, -s 'ɔɪlstəʊv, -z
oil-well, -s 'ɔɪlwel, -z
oil|y, -ier, -iest, -iness 'ɔɪl|ɪ, -ɪə*
 [-jə*], -ɪɪst [-ɪɪst], -ɪnɪs [-nəs]
ointment, -s 'ɔɪntmənt, -s
Oisin 'ɔɪʃɪn
Oistrakh 'ɔɪstrɑːk [-ɑːx]
Ojai (in California) 'əʊhaɪ
Ojibway, -s əʊ'dʒɪbweɪ [ɒ'dʒ-], -z
O.K. ‚əʊ'keɪ [əʊ'keɪ]
okapi, -s əʊ'kɑːpɪ, -z
okay, -s, -ing, -ed ‚əʊ'keɪ, -z, -ɪŋ, -d
O'Keef(f)e əʊ'kiːf
Okehampton ‚əʊk'hæmptən

O'Kelly əʊ'kelɪ
Okhotsk əʊ'kɒtsk [ɒ'k-] (a'xotsk)
Okinawa ‚ɒkɪ'nɑːwə
Oklahoma ‚əʊklə'həʊmə
Olav (Norwegian name) 'əʊləv [-læv]
Olave 'ɒlɪv‖[-ləv, -leɪv]
Olcott 'ɒlkət
old, -er, -est, -ness əʊld, -ə*, -ɪst, -nɪs
 [-nəs]
Oldbuck 'əʊldbʌk
Oldbury 'əʊldbərɪ
Oldcastle 'əʊld‚kɑːsl
old-clothes|man, -men ‚əʊld'kləʊðz|-
 mæn [əʊld'k-, -mən, old-fashioned
 -'kləʊz-], -men [-mən]
olden 'əʊldən
Oldenburg 'əʊldənbɜːg ('ɔldənburk,
 -burç)
old-fashioned ‚əʊld'fæʃnd [also '-‚—
 according to sentence-stress]
Oldfield 'əʊldfiːld
old-fog(e)yish ‚əʊld'fəʊgɪɪʃ [-gjɪʃ]
old-gentlemanly ‚əʊld'dʒentlmənlɪ
Oldham 'əʊldəm
oldish 'əʊldɪʃ
old-maidish ‚əʊld'meɪdɪʃ
Oldrey 'əʊldrɪ
old-time 'əʊldtaɪm
old-womanish ‚əʊld'wʊmənɪʃ
old-world ‚əʊld'wɜːld ['— when attribu-
 tive]
oleaginous, -ness ‚əʊlɪ'ædʒɪnəs, -nɪs
 [-nəs]
oleander (O.), -s ‚əʊlɪ'ændə*, -z
O'Leary əʊ'lɪərɪ
oleaster, -s ‚əʊlɪ'æstə*, -z
olefiant 'əʊlɪfaɪənt [əʊ'liːfɪənt, -'lef-]
oleograph, -s 'əʊlɪəʊgrɑːf [-lɪəg-,
 -ljəʊg-, -græf], -s
oleography ‚əʊlɪ'ɒgrəfɪ
oleomargarine 'əʊlɪəʊ‚mɑːdʒə'riːn
 [-‚mɑːgə'r-, -'mɑːdʒər-, -'mɑːgər-]
O-level, -s 'əʊ‚levl, -z
olfactory ɒl'fæktərɪ
Olga 'ɒlgə
olibanum ɒ'lɪbənəm [əʊ'l-]
Olifa(u)nt 'ɒlɪfənt
Oliffe 'ɒlɪf
oligarch, -s 'ɒlɪgɑːk, -s
oligarchal 'ɒlɪgɑːkl [‚ɒlɪ'g-]
oligarchic ‚ɒlɪ'gɑːkɪk
oligarch|y, -ies 'ɒlɪgɑːk|ɪ, -ɪz
oligocene ɒ'lɪgəʊsiːn ['——]
olio, -s 'əʊlɪəʊ [-ljəʊ], -z
Oliphant 'ɒlɪfənt
olivaceous ‚ɒlɪ'veɪʃəs
olive (O.), -s; -branch/es, -coloured
 'ɒlɪv, -z; -brɑːntʃ/ɪz, -‚kʌləd

olive oil ˌɒlɪvˈɔɪl
oliver (O.), -s ˈɒlɪvə*, -z
Oliverian ˌɒlɪˈvɪərɪən
Olivet ˈɒlɪvet [-vɪt]
olive|-tree/s, -wood ˈɒlɪvˈtriː/z, -wʊd
Olivia ɒˈlɪvɪə [əˈl-, əʊˈl-, -vjə]
Olivier (Lord) əˈlɪvɪeɪ [ɒˈl-]
olivine, -s ˌɒlɪˈviːn [ˈɒlɪv-], -z
olla podrida, -s ˌɒləpɒˈdriːdə [ˌˌɒljə-, -pəˈd-], -z
Ollendorf ˈɒləndɔːf [-nɪ-] (ˈɔlɛndɔrf)
Ollerton ˈɒlətən
Olley ˈɒlɪ
Olliffe ˈɒlɪf
Ollivant ˈɒlɪvənt
Olmstead ˈɒmsted
Olney (in Buckinghamshire) ˈəʊlnɪ [ˈəʊnɪ]
-olog|y, -ies -ˈɒlədʒ|ɪ, -ɪz
oloroso ˌɒləˈrəʊsəʊ [ˌˌəʊl-, -zəʊ]
Olver ˈɒlvə*
Olymp|ia, -iad/s, -ian, -ic/s, -us əʊˈlɪmp|ɪə [-jə], -ɪæd/z [-jæd/z], -ɪən [-jən], -ɪk/s, -əs
Olynth|iac/s, -us əʊˈlɪnθ|ɪæk/s [-jæk/s], -əs
Omagh ˈəʊmə
Omaha ˈəʊməhɑː
O'Malley əʊˈmælɪ, -ˈmeɪlɪ
Oman əʊˈmɑːn
Omar ˈəʊmɑː*
ombre ˈɒmbə*
ombudsman ˈɒmbʊdzmən [-mæn]
Omdurman ˌɒmdɜːˈmɑːn [ˈɒmdəmən]
O'Meara əʊˈmɑːrə, -ˈmɪərə
omega (O.), -s ˈəʊmɪgə [-meg-], -z
omelet(te), -s ˈɒmlɪt [-lət, -let], -s
omen, -s, -ed ˈəʊmen [-mən], -z, -d
omer (O.), -s ˈəʊmə*, -z
omicron, -s əʊˈmaɪkrən, -z
ominous, -ly, -ness ˈɒmɪnəs [ˈəʊm-], -lɪ, -nɪs [-nəs]
omissible əʊˈmɪsɪbl [-səb-]
omission, -s əˈmɪʃn [əʊˈm-], -z
omit, -s, -ting, -ted əˈmɪt [əʊˈm-], -s, -ɪŋ, -ɪd
Ommaney ˈɒmənɪ
omnibus, -es ˈɒmnɪbəs, -ɪz
omnifarious ˌɒmnɪˈfeərɪəs
omnipoten|ce, -t/ly ɒmˈnɪpətən|s, -t/lɪ
omnipresen|ce, -t ˌɒmnɪˈprezn|s, -t
omniscien|ce, -t/ly ɒmˈnɪsɪən|s [-sjən-, -ʃɪən-, -ʃjən-, -ʃn-], -t/lɪ
omnium, -s ˈɒmnɪəm [-njəm], -z
omnium gatherum, -s ˌɒmnɪəmˈgæðərəm [-njəm-], -z
omnivore, -s ˈɒmnɪvɔː*, -z
omnivorous, -ly ɒmˈnɪvərəs, -lɪ

Omond ˈəʊmənd
O'Morchoe əʊˈmʌrəʊ
omphalos ˈɒmfəlɒs
Omri ˈɒmraɪ
Omsk ɒmsk
on (s. adj. adv. prep.) ɒn (normal form, strong and weak), ən, n (rare weak forms).
onager, -s ˈɒnəgə*, -z
Onan ˈəʊnæn [-nən]
Onassis əʊˈnæsɪs [ɒˈn-]
once wʌns
once-over ˌwʌnsˈəʊvə*
oncer, -s ˈwʌnsə*, -z
oncoming (s. adj.), -s ˈɒnˌkʌmɪŋ, -z
on-drive, -s ˈɒndraɪv, -z
one, -s wʌn, -z
O'Neal əʊˈniːl
one-eyed ˌwʌnˈaɪd [also ˈ-- when attributive]
Onega ɒˈnjegə [ɒˈnegə, əʊˈneɪgə, old-fashioned ˈəʊnɪgə] (ɐˈnjegə)
one-horse (adj.) ˌwʌnˈhɔːs [ˈ--]
O'Neil(l) əʊˈniːl
oneiromancy əʊˈnaɪərəʊmænsɪ
one-ish ˈwʌnɪʃ
one-legged ˌwʌnˈlegd [-ˈlegɪd, ˈwʌn-legd, ˈwʌnˌlegɪd]
oneness ˈwʌnnɪs [-nəs]
oner, -s ˈwʌnə*, -z
onerous, -ly, -ness ˈɒnərəs [ˈəʊn-], -lɪ, -nɪs [-nəs]
oneself wʌnˈself
onesided, -ly, -ness ˌwʌnˈsaɪdɪd, -lɪ, -nɪs [-nəs]
Onesimus əʊˈnesɪməs
ongoing, -s ˈɒnˌgəʊɪŋ, -z
Onians əˈnaɪənz [əʊˈn-]
Onich (near Fort William) ˈəʊnɪk [-nɪx]
onion, -s, -y ˈʌnjən, -z, -ɪ
Onions ˈʌnjənz, əʊˈnaɪənz
on-licence, -s ˈɒnˌlaɪsns, -ɪz
onlook|er/s, -ing ˈɒnˌlʊk|ə*/z, -ɪŋ
only ˈəʊnlɪ
onomastic ˌɒnəʊˈmæstɪk
onomasticon, -s ˌɒnəʊˈmæstɪkən [-kɒn], -z
onomatolog|ist/s, -y ˌɒnəʊməˈtɒlədʒ|-ɪst/s, -ɪ
onomato|poeia, -poeias, -poeic ˌɒnəʊmætəʊˈpiːə [ɒˌnɒmət-, əˌnɒmət-, -ˈpɪə], -ˈpiːəz [-ˈpɪəz], -ˈpiːɪk
Onoto, -s əʊˈnəʊtəʊ [ɒˈn-], -z
on|rush/es, -set/s, -slaught/s ˈɒn|ˌrʌʃ/ɪz, -set/s, -slɔːt/s
Onslow ˈɒnzləʊ
Ontario ɒnˈteərɪəʊ

onto 'ɒntʊ, 'ɒntə
   Note.—The form 'ɒntə is used only
   before words beginning with a
   consonant.
ontogenesis ˌɒntəʊ'dʒenɪsɪs [-nəs-]
ontogenetic, -ally ˌɒntəʊdʒɪ'netɪk
   [-dʒə'n-], -əlɪ
ontogeny ɒn'tɒdʒɪnɪ [-dʒənɪ]
ontologic, -al, -ally ˌɒntəʊ'lɒdʒɪk, -l,
   -əlɪ
ontolog|ist/s, -y ɒn'tɒlədʒ|ɪst/s, -ɪ
onus 'əʊnəs
onward, -s 'ɒnwəd, -z
onyx, -es 'ɒnɪks ['əʊn-], -ɪz
oof uːf
oolite, -s 'əʊəlaɪt ['əʊeʊl-], -s
oolitic ˌəʊə'lɪtɪk [ˌəʊeʊl-]
oolog|ist/s, -y əʊ'ɒlədʒ|ɪst/s, -ɪ
Oolong 'uːlɒŋ [ˌuː'lɒŋ]
ooz|e (s. v.), -es, -ing, -ed uːz, -ɪz, -ɪŋ,
   -d
ooz|y, -ier, -iest, -ily, -iness 'uːz|ɪ, -ɪə*
   [-jə*], -ɪɪst [-jɪst], -ɪlɪ [-əlɪ], -ɪnɪs
   [-ɪnəs]
opacity əʊ'pæsətɪ [-ɪtɪ]
opal, -s 'əʊpl, -z
opalescen|ce, -t ˌəʊpə'lesn|s, -t
opaline (s.), -s 'əʊpəliːn [-laɪn], -z
opaline (adj.) 'əʊpəlaɪn [-ləm]
opaque, -ly, -ness əʊ'peɪk, -lɪ, -nɪs
   [-nəs]
op. cit. ˌɒp'sɪt
op|e, -es, -ing, -ed əʊp, -s, -ɪŋ, -t
Opel 'əʊpl
op|en (adj. v.), -ener, -enest, -enly,
   -enness; -ens, -ening, -ened, -ener/s
   'əʊp|ən ['əʊp|m], -ənə* [-ənə*, -ɪnə*],
   -ənɪst [-ənɪst, -ɪnɪst], -ɪnlɪ [-ənlɪ, -ɪlɪ],
   -ɪnɪs [-ənnɪs,-ɪnnɪs, -nəs];-ənz [-mz],
   -nɪŋ [-ŋɪŋ], -ənd [-md], -nə*/z
   [-ŋə*/z]
open-air ˌəʊpn̩'eə* [ˌəʊpən'eə*, '---]
opencast 'əʊpənkɑːst [-pn-]
open-eyed ˌəʊpn̩'aɪd [ˌəʊpən'aɪd, '---]
open-handed ˌəʊpn̩'hændɪd [-pən-,
   '-ˌ-]
open-handedness ˌəʊpn̩'hændɪdnɪs
   [-pən-, -nəs]
open-hearted, -ly, -ness ˌəʊpən'hɑːtɪd
   ['--ˌ--], -lɪ, -nɪs [-nəs]
opening (s.), -s 'əʊpnɪŋ, -z
open-minded, -ly, -ness ˌəʊpn̩'maɪndɪd
   [ˌəʊpən'm-, ˌəʊpn̩'m-, '--ˌ--], -lɪ, -nɪs
   [-nəs]
open-mouthed ˌəʊpn̩'maʊðd [-pən'm-,
   -pm̩'m-, '--]
Openshaw 'əʊpənʃɔː
open-work 'əʊpn̩wɜːk [-pənw-, -pm̩w-]

352

opera, -s; -bouffe, -cloak/s, -glass/es,
   -hat/s, -house, -houses 'ɒpərə, -z;
   -'buːf, -kləʊk/s, -glɑːs/ɪz, -hæt/s,
   -haʊs, -ˌhaʊzɪz
operant (s. adj.), -s 'ɒpərənt, -s
operat|e, -es, -ing, -ed, -or/s 'ɒpəreɪt,
   -s, -ɪŋ, -ɪd, -ə*/z
operatic, -s ˌɒpə'rætɪk, -s
operation, -s ˌɒpə'reɪʃn, -z
operational ˌɒpə'reɪʃənl [-ʃnəl, -ʃn̩l,
   -ʃn̩l, -ʃənəl]
operative (s.), -s 'ɒpərətɪv, -z
operative (adj.), -ly, -ness 'ɒpərətɪv
   ['ɒpəreɪtɪv], -lɪ, -nɪs [-nəs]
operetta, -s ˌɒpə'retə, -z
Ophelia ɒ'fiːljə [əʊ'f-, -lɪə]
ophicleide, -s 'ɒfɪklaɪd, -z
ophidia, -n ɒ'fɪdɪə [əʊ'f-], -n
Ophir 'əʊfə* [rarely -ˌfɪə*]
Ophiuchus ɒ'fjuːkəs
ophthalm|ia, -ic ɒf'θælm|ɪə [ɒp'θ-,
   -m|jə], -ɪk
ophthalmolog|ist/s, -y ˌɒfθæl'mɒlədʒ|-
   ɪst/s [ˌɒpθ-], -ɪ
ophthalmoscope, -s ɒf'θælməskəʊp
   [ɒp'θ-], -s
ophthalmoscopy ˌɒfθæl'mɒskəpɪ [ˌɒp-]
opiate, -s 'əʊpɪət [-pjət, -pɪɪt, -pjɪt,
   -pɪeɪt, -pjeɪt], -s
opiated 'əʊpɪeɪtɪd
Opie 'əʊpɪ
opin|e, -es, -ing, -ed əʊ'paɪn, -z, -ɪŋ,
   -d
opinion, -s; -ated ə'pɪnjən, -z; -eɪtɪd
opium; -den/s 'əʊpjəm [-pɪəm]; -den/z
opium-eater, -s 'əʊpjəmˌiːtə* [-pɪəm-],
   -z
opodeldoc ˌɒpəʊ'deldɒk [-dək]
opopanax əʊ'pɒpənæks
Oporto əʊ'pɔːtəʊ (Port. u'portu)
opossum, -s ə'pɒsəm, -z
Oppenheim, -er 'ɒpənhaɪm, -ə*
oppidan (s. adj.), -s 'ɒpɪdən, -z
opponent, -s ə'pəʊnənt, -s
opportune, -ly, -ness 'ɒpətjuːn [-tʃuːn,
   ˌɒpə'tjuːn], -lɪ, -nɪs [-nəs]
opportuni|sm, -st/s 'ɒpətjuːnɪ|zəm
   [-tjʊn-, -tʃuːn-, ˌɒpə'tjuːn-], -st/s
opportunit|y, -ies ˌɒpə'tjuːnət|ɪ [-'tjʊn-,
   -nɪt-, -'tjuːŋt|ɪ], -ɪz
oppos|e, -es, -ing, -ed, -er/s; -able
   ə'pəʊz, -ɪz, -ɪŋ, -d, -ə*/z; -əbl
opposite, -ly, -ness 'ɒpəzɪt [-əsɪt], -lɪ,
   -nɪs [-nəs]
opposition, -s ˌɒpə'zɪʃn [-pəʊ'z-], -z
oppress, -es, -ing, -ed, -or/s ə'pres, -ɪz,
   -ɪŋ, -t, -ə*/z
oppression, -s ə'preʃn, -z

oppressive, -ly, -ness ə'presɪv, -lɪ, -nɪs [-nəs]

opprobrious, -ly, -ness ə'prəʊbrɪəs [ɒ'p-], -lɪ, -nɪs [-nəs]

opprobrium ə'prəʊbrɪəm [ɒ'p-]

oppugn, -s, -ing, -ed, -er/s ɒ'pjuːn, -z -ɪŋ, -d, -ə*/z

oppugnan|cy, -s ɒ'pʌgnən|sɪ, -t

opt, -s, -ing, -ed ɒpt, -s, -ɪŋ, -ɪd

optative (s. adj.), -s 'ɒptətɪv [ɒp'teɪtɪv], -z

optic (s. v.), -s, -al, -ally 'ɒptɪk, -s, -l, -əlɪ

optician, -s ɒp'tɪʃn, -z

optimal 'ɒptɪml

optimate 'ɒptɪmət [-mɪt, -meɪt]

optimates ˌɒptɪ'meɪtiːz

optime, -s 'ɒptɪmɪ, -z

optimi|sm, -st/s 'ɒptɪmɪ|zəm [-təm-], -st/s

optimistic, -al, -ally ˌɒptɪ'mɪstɪk [-tə'm-], -l, -əlɪ

optimum 'ɒptɪməm

option, -s 'ɒpʃn, -z

op|tional, -tionally 'ɒp|ʃənl [-ʃnəl, -ʃnḷ, -ʃnḷ, -ʃənəl], -ʃnəlɪ [-ʃnəlɪ, -ʃnḷɪ, -ʃnḷɪ, -ʃənəlɪ]

opulen|ce, -t 'ɒpjʊlən|s [-pjə-], -t

opus 'əʊpəs ['ɒpəs]

opuscule, -s ɒ'pʌskjuːl [əʊ'p-], -z

or (s.) ɔː*

or (conj.) ɔː* (normal form), ə* (occasional weak form)
   Note.—The weak form is chiefly used in common phrases, such as two or three minutes.

orach|(e), -es 'ɒrɪtʃ, -ɪz

oracle, -s 'ɒrəkl [-rɪk-], -z

oracular, -ly, -ness ɒ'rækjʊlə* [ɔː'r-, ə'r-, -kjə-], -lɪ, -nɪs [-nəs]

or|al (s. adj.), -als, -ally 'ɔːr|əl, -əlz, -əlɪ [-ḷɪ]

Oran ɔː'rɑːn [ɒ'r-, -'ræn]

orang, -s 'ɔːræŋ [-ræŋ, ɔː'ræŋ, ɒ'ræŋ, ə'ræŋ], -z

orange (s. adj.) (O.), -s 'ɒrɪndʒ [-əndʒ], -ɪz

orangeade ˌɒrɪndʒ'eɪd [-əndʒ-]

orange-blossom, -s 'ɒrɪndʒˌblɒsəm [-əndʒ-], -z

orange-coloured 'ɒrɪndʒˌkʌləd [-əndʒ-]

orange-juice 'ɒrɪndʒdʒuːs [-əndʒ-]

Orange|man, -men 'ɒrɪndʒ|mən [-əndʒ-, -mæn], -mən [-men]

orange-peel 'ɒrɪndʒpiːl [-əndʒ-]

oranger|y, -ies 'ɒrɪndʒər|ɪ [-əndʒ-], -ɪz

orange-tree, -s 'ɒrɪndʒtriː [-əndʒ-], -z

orange-yellow ˌɒrɪndʒ'jeləʊ [-əndʒ-]

orang-outa|n/s, -ng/s ɔːˌræŋuː'tæ|n/z [ɒˌræŋ-, əˌræŋ-, -ʊ'tæ|n, -'tɑː|n, ˌɔː'rəŋ'uːtɑː|n, -tæ|n], -ŋ/z

orat|e, -es, -ing, -ed ɔː'reɪt [ɒ'r-, ə'r-], -s, -ɪŋ, -ɪd

oration, -s ɔː'reɪʃn [ɒ'r-, ə'r-], -z

oratio obliqua ɒˌrɑːtɪəʊ ɒ'bliːkwə [ɔːˌr-, əˌr-, ə'b-, old-fashioned əˌreɪʃɪəʊ ə'blaɪkwə]

orator, -s 'ɒrətə* [-rɪt-], -z

oratoric|al, -ally ˌɒrə'tɒrɪk|l, -əlɪ

oratorio, -s ˌɒrə'tɔːrɪəʊ, -z

orator|y (O.), -ies 'ɒrətər|ɪ, -ɪz

orb (s. v.), -s, -ing, -ed ɔːb, -z, -ɪŋ, -d

orbed (adj.) ɔːbd [in poetry generally 'ɔːbɪd]

orbicular, -ness ɔː'bɪkjʊlə* [-kjə-], -nɪs [-nəs]

orbit, -s, -al 'ɔːbɪt, -s, -l

orc, -s ɔːk, -s

Orcadian, -s ɔː'keɪdjən [-dɪən], -z

orchard (O.), -s 'ɔːtʃəd, -z

Orchardson 'ɔːtʃədsən

Orchehill 'ɔːtʃɪl

orchestra, -s 'ɔːkɪstrə [-kes-, -kəs-], -z

orchestral ɔː'kestrəl

orchestrat|e, -es, -ing, -ed 'ɔːkɪstreɪt [-kes-, -kəs-], -s, -ɪŋ, -ɪd

orchestration, -s ˌɔːke'streɪʃn [-kɪ's-, -kə's-], -z

orchestrion, -s ɔː'kestrɪən, -z

orchid, -s 'ɔːkɪd, -z

orchidaceous ˌɔːkɪ'deɪʃəs

orchideous ɔː'kɪdɪəs

orchil 'ɔːtʃɪl

orchis, -es 'ɔːkɪs, -ɪz

Orchy 'ɔːkɪ ['ɔːxɪ] (Scottish 'ɔrxɪ)

Orczy 'ɔːksɪ ['ɔːtsɪ]

Ord ɔːd

ordain, -s, -ing, -ed, -er/s ɔː'deɪn, -z, -ɪŋ, -d, -ə*/z

Orde ɔːd

ordeal, -s ɔː'diːl [-'diːəl, -'dɪəl], -z

ord|er (s. v.), -ers, -ering, -ered; -erless 'ɔːd|ə* [-əz, -ərɪŋ, -əd; -əlɪs [-ləs]

orderl|y (s. adj.), -ies, -iness 'ɔːdəl|ɪ, -ɪz, -ɪnɪs [-ɪnəs]

ordinaire ˌɔːdɪ'neə* ['ɔːdɪneə*] (ordinɛːr)

ordinal (s. adj.), -s 'ɔːdɪnl, -z

ordinance, -s 'ɔːdɪnəns [-dnəns], -ɪz

ordinand, -s ˌɔːdɪ'nænd ['---], -z

ordinar|y (s. adj.), -ies, -ily 'ɔːdn̩r|ɪ [-dɪnər-, -dənər-, -dnər-], -ɪz, -əlɪ [-ɪlɪ]

ordinate, -s 'ɔːdnət [-dɪnət, -dɪnɪt], -s

ordination, -s ˌɔːdɪ'neɪʃn, -z

ordnance 'ɔːdnəns

ordure 'ɔːˌdjʊə* [-djwə*]

353

ore (O.), -s ɔ:* [ɔə*], -z
oread, -s 'ɔ:rɪæd, -z
Oreb 'ɔ:reb
O'Regan əʊ'ri:gən
Oregon 'ɒrɪgən [-gɒn]
O'|Reilly, -Rell əʊ|'raɪlɪ, -'rel
Orellana ˌɒre'lɑ:nə [-rɪ'l-]
Orestes ɒ'resti:z [ɔ:'r-, ə'r-]
Orford 'ɔ:fəd
organ, -s; -blower/s, -builder/s, -case/s
'ɔ:gən, -z; -ˌbləʊə*/z, -ˌbɪldə*/z,
-keɪs/ɪz
organd|y [-ie], -ies 'ɔ:gənd|ɪ [ɔ:'gæn-],
-ɪz
organ-grinder, -s 'ɔ:gənˌgraɪndə*
['ɔ:gŋˌg-], -z
organic, -al, -ally ɔ:'gænɪk, -l, -əlɪ
organism, -s 'ɔ:gənɪzəm [-gn̩ɪzəm], -z
organist, -s 'ɔ:gənɪst [-gn̩ɪst], -s
organizability [-isa-] 'ɔ:gəˌnaɪzə'bɪlətɪ
[-gn̩ˌaɪ-, -lɪt-]
organization [-isa-], -s ˌɔ:gənaɪ'zeɪʃn
[-gn̩aɪ'z-, -gənɪ'z-, -gn̩ɪ'z-], -z
organiz|e [-is|e], -es, -ing, -ed, -er/s;
-able 'ɔ:gənaɪz [-gn̩aɪz], -ɪz, -ɪŋ, -d,
-ə*/z; -əbl
organ-loft, -s 'ɔ:gənlɒft, -s
organon, -s 'ɔ:gənɒn, -z
organ-pipe, -s 'ɔ:gənpaɪp, -s
organ-screen, -s 'ɔ:gənskri:n, -z
organum, -s 'ɔ:gənəm, -z
orgasm, -s 'ɔ:gæzəm, -z
org|y, -ies 'ɔ:dʒ|ɪ, -ɪz
Oriana ˌɒrɪ'ɑ:nə [ˌɔ:rɪ-]
oriel (O.), -s 'ɔ:rɪəl, -z
orient (s. adj.) (O.) 'ɔ:rɪənt ['ɒr-]
orient (v.), -s, -ing, -ed 'ɔ:rɪent ['ɒr-], -s,
-ɪŋ, -ɪd
oriental (s. adj.) (O.), -s ˌɔ:rɪ'entl [ˌɒr-],
-z
orientali|sm, -st/s ˌɔ:rɪ'entəlɪ|zəm
[ˌɒr-, -tlɪ-], -st/s
orientaliz|e [-is|e], -es, -ing, -ed ˌɔ:rɪ'en-
təlaɪz [ˌɒr-, -tlaɪz], -ɪz, -ɪŋ, -d
orientat|e, -es, -ing, -ed 'ɔ:rɪenteɪt
['ɒr-, -rɪən-, ˌɔ:rɪ'enteɪt, ˌɒrɪ'en-], -s,
-ɪŋ, -ɪd
orientation, -s ˌɔ:rɪen'teɪʃn [ˌɒr-, -rɪən-],
-z
orifice, -s 'ɒrɪfɪs, -ɪz
oriflamme, -s 'ɒrɪflæm, -z
Origen 'ɒrɪdʒen
origin, -s 'ɒrɪdʒɪn, -z
original (s. adj.), -s; -ness ə'rɪdʒənl
[ɒ'r-, -dʒɪnl, -dʒŋ̩l, -dʒn̩l, -dʒənəl], -z;
-nɪs [-nəs]
originalit|y, -ies əˌrɪdʒə'nælət|ɪ [ɒˌr-,
-dʒɪ'n-, -ɪt|ɪ], -ɪz

originally ə'rɪdʒənəlɪ [ɒ'r-, -dʒɪnəlɪ,
-dʒnəlɪ, -dʒŋ̩lɪ, -dʒŋ̩lɪ, -dʒn̩əlɪ]
originat|e, -es, -ing, -ed, -or/s; -ive
ə'rɪdʒəneɪt [ɒ'r-, -dʒɪn-], -s, -ɪŋ, -ɪd,
-ə*/z; -ɪv
origination əˌrɪdʒə'neɪʃn [ɒˌr- -dʒɪ'n-]
Orinoco ˌɒrɪ'nəʊkəʊ
oriole, -s 'ɔ:rɪəʊl, -z
Orion ə'raɪən [ɒ'r-, ɔ:'r-]
O'Riordan əʊ'rɪədən, -'raɪəd-
orison, -s 'ɒrɪzən, -z
Orissa ɒ'rɪsə [ɔ:'r-, ə'r-]
Orkney, -s 'ɔ:knɪ, -z
Orlando ɔ:'lændəʊ
Orleanist, -s ɔ:'lɪənɪst, -s
Orleans (in France) ɔ:'lɪənz ['ɔ:lɪənz,
'ɔ:ljənz] (ɔrleɑ̃), (in U.S.A.) 'ɔ:lɪənz
[-ljənz, ɔ:'li:nz]
Orlon 'ɔ:lɒn
Orly 'ɔ:lɪ (ɔrli)
Orm(e) ɔ:m
Ormelie 'ɔ:mɪlɪ
ormer, -s 'ɔ:mə*, -z
Ormes, -by ɔ:mz, -bɪ
Ormiston 'ɔ:mɪstən
ormolu 'ɔ:məʊlu: [-lju:] (ɔrmɔly,
pronounced as if French)
Ormond(e) 'ɔ:mənd
Orms|by, -kirk 'ɔ:mz|bɪ, -kɜ:k
Ormulum 'ɔ:mjʊləm
Ormuz 'ɔ:mʌz
ornament (s.), -s 'ɔ:nəmənt, -s
ornament (v.), -s, -ing, -ed 'ɔ:nəment,
-s, -ɪŋ, -ɪd
ornament|al, -ally ˌɔ:nə'ment|l, -əlɪ [-l̩ɪ]
ornamentation, -s ˌɔ:nəmen'teɪʃn, -z
Ornan 'ɔ:næn
ornate, -ly, -ness ɔ:'neɪt ['ɔ:neɪt], -lɪ,
-nɪs [-nəs]
ornithologic|al, -ally ˌɔ:nɪθə'lɒdʒɪk|l|l,
-əlɪ
ornitholog|ist/s, -y ˌɔ:nɪ'θɒlədʒ|ɪst/s, -ɪ
orographic, -al ˌɒrəʊ'græfɪk [ˌɔ:r-], -l
orography ɒ'rɒgrəfɪ [ɔ:'r-]
orological ˌɒrə'lɒdʒɪkl [ˌɔ:r-]
orology ɒ'rɒlədʒɪ [ɔ:'r-]
Oronsay 'ɒrənseɪ [-nzeɪ]
Orontes ɒ'rɒnti:z [ə'r-]
Oroonoko ˌɒru:'nəʊkəʊ
Orosius ə'rəʊsjəs [ɒ'r-, -sɪəs]
orotund 'ɒrəʊtʌnd ['ɔ:r-]
O'Rourke əʊ'rɔ:k
Orpah 'ɔ:pə
orphan, -s 'ɔ:fn, -z
orphanage, -s 'ɔ:fənɪdʒ [-fn̩ɪ-], -ɪz
Orphean ɔ:'fi:ən [-'fɪən]
Orpheus 'ɔ:fju:s
orpiment 'ɔ:pɪmənt

Orpington, -s 'ɔ:pɪŋtən, -z
Orr ɔ:*
Orrell 'ɒrəl
orrer|y (O.), -ies 'ɒrər|ɪ, -ɪz
orris 'ɒrɪs
Orrm, -in ɔ:m, -ɪn
Orrock 'ɒrək
Orsino ɔ:'si:nəʊ
Orson 'ɔ:sn
Orth ɔ:θ
orthochromatic ,ɔ:θəʊkrəʊ'mætɪk
orthodonti|cs, -st/s ,ɔ:θəʊ'dɒntɪ|ks,
  -st/s
orthodox, -ly 'ɔ:θədɒks, -lɪ
orthodox|y, -ies 'ɔ:θədɒks|ɪ, -ɪz
orthoepical ,ɔ:θəʊ'epɪkl
orthoep|ist/s, -y 'ɔ:θəʊep|ɪst/s
  [ɔ:'θəʊep-, ,ɔ:θəʊ'ep-], -ɪ
orthogonal ɔ:'θɒgənl
orthographer, -s ɔ:'θɒgrəfə*, -z
orthographic, -al, -ally ,ɔ:θəʊ'græfɪk,
  -l, -əlɪ
orthograph|ist/s, -y ɔ:'θɒgrəf|ɪst/s, -ɪ
orthopaedic [-ped-], -s ,ɔ:θəʊ'pi:dɪk,
  -s
orthopaedy [-ped-] 'ɔ:θəʊpi:dɪ
orthophonic, -s ,ɔ:θəʊ'fɒnɪk [-'fəʊ-], -s
orthophony ɔ:'θɒfənɪ
Ortler 'ɔ:tlə*
ortolan, -s 'ɔ:tələn, -z
Orton 'ɔ:tn
Orville 'ɔ:vɪl
Orwell 'ɔ:wəl [-wel]
oryx, -es 'ɒrɪks, -ɪz
Osage əʊ'seɪdʒ ['əʊseɪdʒ]
Osaka ɔ:'səkə [əʊ'sɑ:kə]
Osbaldiston(e) ,ɒzbəl'dɪstən
Osbert 'ɒzbət [-bɜ:t]
Osborn(e) 'ɒzbən [-bɔ:n]
Osbourne 'ɒzbən [-bɔ:n]
Oscan, -s 'ɒskən, -z
Oscar, -s 'ɒskə*, -z
oscillat|e, -es, -ing, -ed, -or/s 'ɒsɪleɪt
  [-səl-], -s, -ɪŋ, -ɪd, -ə*/z
oscillation, -s ,ɒsɪ'leɪʃn [-sə'l-], -z
oscillatory 'ɒsɪlətərɪ [-leɪtərɪ]
oscillogram, -s ə'sɪləʊgræm [ɒ's-], -z
oscillograph, -s ə'sɪləʊgrɑ:f [ɒ's-, -græf],
  -s
osculant 'ɒskjʊlənt
osculat|e, -es, -ing, -ed 'ɒskjʊleɪt, -s, -ɪŋ,
  -ɪd
osculation, -s ,ɒskjʊ'leɪʃn, -z
osculator|y (s.), -ies 'ɒskjʊlətər|ɪ, -ɪz
osculatory (adj.) 'ɒskjʊlətərɪ [-leɪtərɪ]
Osgood 'ɒzgʊd
O'Shaughnessy əʊ'ʃɔ:nɪsɪ [-nəsɪ]
O'Shea əʊ'ʃeɪ

osier, -s 'əʊʒə* ['əʊʒjə*, -ʒɪə*, 'əʊzjə*
  -zɪə*], -z
Osirian, -s əʊ'saɪərɪən [ɒ's-], -z
Osiris əʊ'saɪərɪs [ɒ's-]
Osler 'əʊzlə*, 'əʊslə*
Oslo 'ɒzləʊ ['ɒsləʊ]
Osman ɒz'mɑ:n [ɒs'mɑ:n]
Osmanli, -s ɒz'mænlɪ [ɒs'm-, -'mɑ:n-],
  -z
osmium 'ɒzmɪəm [-mjəm]
Osmond 'ɒzmənd
osmosis ɒz'məʊsɪs
osmotic ɒz'mɒtɪk
osmund (O.), -s 'ɒzmənd, -z
osmunda, -s ɒz'mʌndə, -z
Osnaburg(h) 'ɒznəbɜ:g
osprey, -s 'ɒsprɪ ['ɒspreɪ], -z
Ospringe 'ɒsprɪndʒ
Ossa 'ɒsə
osseous 'ɒsɪəs [-sjəs]
Ossett 'ɒsɪt
Ossian 'ɒsɪən [-sjən]
Ossianic ,ɒsɪ'ænɪk
ossicle, -s 'ɒsɪkl, -z
ossification ,ɒsɪfɪ'keɪʃn
ossifrage, -s 'ɒsɪfrɪdʒ, -ɪz
ossi|fy, -fies, -fying, -fied 'ɒsɪ|faɪ, -faɪz,
  -faɪɪŋ, -faɪd
Ossory 'ɒsərɪ
ossuar|y, -ies 'ɒsjʊər|ɪ [-sjwə-], -ɪz
Ostend ɒ'stend
ostensibility ɒ,stensɪ'bɪlətɪ [-sə'b-, -lɪt-]
ostensib|le, -ly ɒ'stensəb|l [-sɪb-], -lɪ
ostentation, -s ,ɒsten'teɪʃn [-tən-]
ostentatious, -ly, -ness ,ɒsten'teɪʃəs
  [-tən-], -lɪ, -nɪs [-nəs]
osteologic|al, -ally ,ɒstɪə'lɒdʒɪk|l
  [-tjə'l-, -tɪəʊ'l-], -əlɪ
osteolog|ist/s, -y ,ɒstɪ'ɒlədʒ|ɪst/s, -ɪ
osteopath, -s 'ɒstɪəpæθ [-tjəʊp-,
  -tɪəʊp-], -s
osteopathic ,ɒstɪə'pæθɪk [-tjəʊ'p-,
  -tɪəʊ'p-]
osteopath|ist/s, -y ,ɒstɪ'ɒpəθ|ɪst/s, -ɪ
Osterley 'ɒstəlɪ
Ostia 'ɒstɪə [-tjə]
ostiar|y, -ies 'ɒstɪər|ɪ [-tjə-], -ɪz
osti|um (O.), -a 'ɒstɪ|əm [-tj|əm], -ə
ostler, -s 'ɒslə*, -z
ostracism 'ɒstrəsɪzəm
ostraciz|e [-is|e], -es, -ing, -ed 'ɒstrə-
  saɪz, -ɪz, -ɪŋ, -d
ostrich, -es; -feather/s 'ɒstrɪtʃ [-ɪdʒ],
  -ɪz; -,feðə*/z
Ostrogoth, -s 'ɒstrəʊgɒθ, -s
O'Sullivan əʊ'sʌlɪvən
Oswald 'ɒzwəld
Oswaldtwistle 'ɒzwəldtwɪsl

355

Oswego, -s ɒz'wi:gəʊ, -z
Oswestry 'ɒzwɛstrɪ [-wɪs-, -wes-]
Otago (in New Zealand) əʊ'tɑ:gəʊ [ɒ't-]
Otaheite ˌɒʊtɑ:'heɪtɪ [-tə'h-]
otar|y, -ies 'əʊtər|ɪ, -ɪz
Ot|ford, -fried 'ɒt|fəd, -fri:d
Othello əʊ'θeləʊ [ɒ'θ-]
other, -s; -wise 'ʌðə*, -z; -waɪz
Othman ɒθ'mɑ:n
Othniel 'ɒθnɪəl [-njəl]
Otho 'əʊθəʊ
otiose, -ly, -ness 'əʊʃɪəʊs [-ʃjəʊs, 'əʊtɪəʊs, -tjəʊs], -lɪ, -nɪs [-nəs]
otiosity ˌəʊʃɪ'ɒsɪtɪ [-ɪtɪ]
Otis 'əʊtɪs
otitis əʊ'taɪtɪs
Otley 'ɒtlɪ
otolaryngolog|y, -ist/s ˌəʊtəʊˌlærɪŋ-'gɒlədʒ|ɪ [-ˌleər-], -ɪst/s
otolog|ist/s, -y əʊ'tɒlədʒ|ɪst/s, -ɪ
otoscope, -s 'əʊtəskəʊp, -s
Otranto ɒ'træntəʊ ['ɒtrəntəʊ] ('ɔ:tranto)
Otsego ɒt'si:gəʊ
Ottaw|a, -ay 'ɒtəw|ə, -eɪ
otter, -s 'ɒtə*, -z
Otterburn 'ɒtəbɜ:n
otter-hound, -s 'ɒtəhaʊnd, -z
Ott|ery, -ley 'ɒt|ərɪ, -lɪ
otto (O.) 'ɒtəʊ
ottoman (O.), -s 'ɒtəʊmən, -z
Ottoway 'ɒtəweɪ
Otway 'ɒtweɪ
oubliette, -s ˌu:blɪ'et, -s
Oubridge 'u:brɪdʒ
Oude aʊd
Oudenarde 'u:dənɑ:d [-dɪn-]
Oudh aʊd
Ough əʊ
Ougham 'əʊkəm
ought, -n't ɔ:t, -nt [occasionally also 'ɔ:tn when not final]
Oughter (Lough) 'u:ktə*
Oughterard ˌu:tə'rɑ:d
Oughton 'aʊtn, 'ɔ:tn
Oughtred 'ɔ:tred [-rɪd], 'u:t-, 'aʊt-
Ouida 'wi:də
ouija 'wi:dʒɑ: [-dʒə]
Ouin (surname) 'əʊɪn
Ould əʊld
Ouless 'u:lɪs [-les]
ounce, -s aʊns, -ɪz
Oundle 'aʊndl
our, -s 'aʊə* [ɑ:*], -z
oursel|f, -ves ˌaʊə'sel|f [ɑ:-], -vz
Oury 'aʊərɪ
Ouse u:z
ousel, -s 'u:zl, -z

Ouseley 'u:zlɪ
Ousey 'u:zɪ
Ousley (in U.S.A.) 'aʊslɪ
oust, -s, -ing, -ed, -er/s aʊst, -s, -ɪŋ, -ɪd, -ə*/z
Ouston 'aʊstən
out aʊt
out-and-out ˌaʊtnd'aʊt [ˌaʊtn̩'aʊt]
outback 'aʊtbæk
outbalanc|e, -es, -ing, -ed ˌaʊt'bæləns, -ɪz, -ɪŋ, -t
outbid, -s, -ding ˌaʊt'bɪd, -z, -ɪŋ
outboard 'aʊtbɔ:d [-bəd]
outbound 'aʊtbaʊnd
outbrav|e, -es, -ing, -ed ˌaʊt'breɪv, -z, -ɪŋ, -d
out|break/s, -building/s, -burst/s 'aʊt|breɪk/s, -ˌbɪldɪŋ/z, -bɜ:st/s
outcast, -s 'aʊtkɑ:st, -s
outcast|e (s. adj. v.), -es, -ing, -ed 'aʊt-kɑ:st, -s, -ɪŋ, -ɪd
outclass, -es, -ing, -ed ˌaʊt'klɑ:s, -ɪz, -ɪŋ, -t
out|come/s, -crop/s, -cry, -cries 'aʊt|-kʌm/z, -krɒp/s, -kraɪ, -kraɪz
outdar|e, -es, -ing, -ed ˌaʊt'deə*, -z, -rɪŋ, -d
outdistanc|e, -es, -ing, -ed ˌaʊt'dɪstəns, -ɪz, -ɪŋ, -t
out|do, -does, -doing, -did, -done ˌaʊt|'du:, -'dʌz, -'du:ɪŋ [-'dʊɪŋ], -'dɪd, -'dʌn
outdoor 'aʊtdɔ:* [-dɔə*]
outdoors ˌaʊt'dɔ:z [-'dɔəz]
outer, -most 'aʊtə*, -məʊst [-məst]
outerwear 'aʊtəweə*
outfac|e, -s, -ing, -ed ˌaʊt'feɪs, -ɪz, -ɪŋ, -t
outfall, -s 'aʊtfɔ:l, -z
outfield, -s, -er/s 'aʊtfi:ld, -z, -ə*/z
outfit (s. v.), -s, -ting, -ted, -ter/s 'aʊt-fɪt, -s, -ɪŋ, -ɪd, -ə*/z
outflank, -s, -ing, -ed ˌaʊt'flæŋk, -s, -ɪŋ, -t [-'flæŋt]
outflow (s.), -s 'aʊtfləʊ, -z
outfl|ow (v.), -ows, -owing, -owed ˌaʊt-'fl|əʊ, -əʊz, -əʊɪŋ, -əʊd
outgener|al, -als, -alling, -alled ˌaʊt-'dʒenər|əl, -əlz, -əlɪŋ, -əld
outgo (s.), -es 'aʊtgəʊ, -z
out|go (v.), -goes, -going, -went, -gone ˌaʊt|'gəʊ, -'gəʊz, -'gəʊɪŋ, -'went, -'gɒn
outgoer, -s 'aʊtˌgəʊə*, -z
outgoing (s. adj.), -s 'aʊtˌgəʊɪŋ, -z
outgrow (s.), -s 'aʊtgrəʊ, -z
out|grow (v.), -grows, -growing, -grew, -grown ˌaʊt|'grəʊ, -'grəʊz, -'grəʊɪŋ, -'gru:, -'grəʊn

356

outgrowth, -s 'aʊtgrəʊθ, -s
outguard, -s 'aʊtgɑːd, -z
out-herod, -s, -ing, -ed ˌaʊt'herəd, -z,
 -ɪŋ, -ɪd
outhou|se, -ses 'aʊthaʊ|s, -zɪz
Outhwaite 'uːθweɪt, 'əʊθweɪt, 'aʊθweɪt
 Note.—More commonly 'uːθ-.
outing, -s 'aʊtɪŋ, -z
Outis 'aʊtɪs
Outlander, -s 'aʊtˌlændə*, -z
outlandish, -ly, -ness aʊt'lændɪʃ, -lɪ,
 -nɪs [-nəs]
outlast, -s, -ing, -ed ˌaʊt'lɑːst, -s, -ɪŋ,
 -ɪd
outlaw (s. v.), -s, -ing, -ed; -ry 'aʊtlɔː,
 -z, -ɪŋ, -d; -rɪ
outlay (s.), -s 'aʊtleɪ, -z
outlay (v.), -s, -ing, outlaid aʊt'leɪ, -z,
 -ɪŋ, aʊt'leɪd
outlet, -s 'aʊtlet [-lɪt], -s
outlier, -s 'aʊtˌlaɪə*, -z
outlin|e (s. v.), -es, -ing, -ed 'aʊtlaɪn,
 -z, -ɪŋ, -d
outliv|e, -es, -ing, -ed ˌaʊt'lɪv, -z, -ɪŋ,
 -d
outlook, -s 'aʊtlʊk, -s
outlying 'aʊtˌlaɪɪŋ
outmanœuv|re, -res, -ring, -red ˌaʊt-
 mə'nuːv|ə*, -əz, -ərɪŋ, -əd
outmarch, -es, -ing, -ed ˌaʊt'mɑːtʃ, -ɪz,
 -ɪŋ, -t
outmatch, -es, -ing, -ed ˌaʊt'mætʃ, -ɪz,
 -ɪŋ, -t
outmoded ˌaʊt'məʊdɪd
outmost 'aʊtməʊst
outnumb|er, -ers, -ering, -ered ˌaʊt-
 'nʌmb|ə*, -əz, -ərɪŋ, -əd
out-of-doors ˌaʊtəv'dɔːz [-'dɔəz]
out-of-the-way ˌaʊtəvðə'weɪ [-təð-]
outpac|e, -es, -ing, -ed ˌaʊt'peɪs, -ɪz,
 -ɪŋ, -t
outpatient, -s 'aʊtˌpeɪʃnt, -s
out-pensioner, -s 'aʊtˌpenʃənə* [-ʃnə*,
 -ʃnə*], -z
outplay, -s, -ing, -ed ˌaʊt'pleɪ, -z, -ɪŋ, -d
outport, -s 'aʊtpɔːt, -s
outpost, -s 'aʊtpəʊst, -s
outpour (s.), -s 'aʊtpɔː* [-pɔə*], -z
outpour (v.), -s, -ing, -ed ˌaʊt'pɔː*
 [-'pɔə*], -z, -rɪŋ, -d
outpouring (s.), -s 'aʊtˌpɔːrɪŋ [-ˌpɔər-],
 -z
output, -s 'aʊtpʊt, -s
outrag|e (s. v.), -es, -ing, -ed 'aʊtreɪdʒ
 [-rɪdʒ], -ɪz, -ɪŋ, -d
outrageous, -ly, -ness aʊt'reɪdʒəs, -lɪ,
 -nɪs [-nəs]
Outram 'uːtrəm

outrang|le, -es, -ing, -ed ˌaʊt'reɪndʒ, -ɪz,
 -ɪŋ, -d
outré 'uːtreɪ (utre)
outreach, -es, -ing, -ed ˌaʊt'riːtʃ, -ɪz,
 -ɪŋ, -t
Outred 'uːtrɪd [-red]
out|ride, -rides, -riding, -rode, -ridden
 ˌaʊt|'raɪd, -'raɪdz, -'raɪdɪŋ, -'rəʊd,
 -'rɪdn
outrider, -s 'aʊtˌraɪdə*, -z
outrigger, -s 'aʊtˌrɪgə*, -z
outright (adj.) 'aʊtraɪt, (adv.) aʊt'raɪt
outriv|al, -als, -alling, -alled ˌaʊt-
 'raɪv|l, -lz, -lɪŋ [-əlɪŋ], -ld
out|run, -runs, -running, -ran ˌaʊt|'rʌn,
 -'rʌnz, -'rʌnɪŋ, -'ræn
outrush, -es 'aʊtrʌʃ, -ɪz
out|sell, -sells, -selling, -sold ˌaʊt|'sel,
 -'selz, -'selɪŋ, -'səʊld
outset, -s 'aʊtset, -s
out|shine, -shines, -shining, -shined,
 -shone ˌaʊt|'ʃaɪn, -'ʃaɪnz, -'ʃaɪnɪŋ,
 -'ʃaɪnd, -'ʃɒn
outside (s. adj. adv. prep.), -s ˌaʊt'saɪd
 ['-- according to sentence-stress], -z
outsider, -s ˌaʊt'saɪdə*, -z
outsize, -s, -d 'aʊtsaɪz, -ɪz, -d
outskirt, -s 'aʊtskəːt, -s
Outspan, -s 'aʊtspæn, -z
outspan (v.), -s, -ning, -ned ˌaʊt'spæn,
 -z, -ɪŋ, -d
outspok|en, -enly, -enness ˌaʊt-
 'spəʊk|ən, -ənlɪ [-n̩lɪ], -ənnɪs [-n̩nɪs,
 -nəs]
outspread ˌaʊt'spred ['-- according to
 sentence-stress]
outstanding (conspicuous, undone, remaining due) ˌaʊt'stændɪŋ, (sticking
 out (ears)) 'aʊtˌstændɪŋ
outstar|e, -es, -ing, -ed ˌaʊt'steə*, -z,
 -rɪŋ, -d
outstay, -s, -ing, -ed ˌaʊt'steɪ, -z, -ɪŋ, -d
outstretch, -es, -ing, -ed ˌaʊt'stretʃ, -ɪz,
 -ɪŋ, -t ['aʊtstretʃt when attributive]
outstrip, -s, -ping, -ped ˌaʊt'strɪp, -s,
 -ɪŋ, -t
outtop, -s, -ping, -ped ˌaʊt'tɒp, -s, -ɪŋ,
 -t
outv|ie, -ies, -ying, -ied ˌaʊt'v|aɪ, -aɪz,
 -aɪɪŋ, -aɪd
outvot|e, -es, -ing, -ed ˌaʊt'vəʊt, -s, -ɪŋ,
 -ɪd
out-voter (non-resident voter), -s 'aʊt-
 ˌvəʊtə*, -z
outwalk, -s, -ing, -ed ˌaʊt'wɔːk, -s, -ɪŋ,
 -t
outward, -s, -ly, -ness 'aʊtwəd, -z, -lɪ,
 -nɪs [-nəs]

357

outwear, -s, -ing, outworn ˌaʊt'weə*, -z, -rɪŋ, ˌaʊt'wɔːn ['aʊtwɔːn *when attributive*]

outweigh, -s, -ing, -ed ˌaʊt'weɪ, -z, -ɪŋ, -d

outwent (*from* outgo) ˌaʊt'went

outwit, -s, -ting, -ted ˌaʊt'wɪt, -s, -ɪŋ, -ɪd

outwork (s.), -s 'aʊtwɜːk, -s

outwork (v.), -s, -ing, -ed ˌaʊt'wɜːk, -s, -ɪŋ, -t

out-worker, -s 'aʊtˌwɜːkə*, -z

outworn (*when attributive*) 'aʊtwɔːn, (*when not attributive*) ˌaʊt'wɔːn

ouzel, -s 'uːzl, -z

ova (*plur. of* ovum) 'əʊvə

ov|al (s. adj.), -als, -ally 'əʊv|l, -lz, -əlɪ

ovaria|l, -n əʊ'veərɪə|l, -n

ovariotomy əʊˌveərɪ'ɒtəmɪ [ˌəʊveə-]

ovar|y, -ies 'əʊvər|ɪ, -ɪz

ovate (s.) (*Welsh title*), -s 'ɒvɪt, -s

ovate (adj.) (*egg-shaped*) 'əʊveɪt [-vɪt]

ovation, -s əʊ'veɪʃn, -z

oven, -s; -bird/s; -ware 'ʌvn, -z; -bɜːd/z; -weə*

over (s. adj. prep.), -s 'əʊvə*, -z
Note.—*Compounds with* over- *not entered below have double stress, and their pronunciation may be ascertained by referring to the simple words. Thus* over-cautious, over-peopled *are pronounced* ˌəʊvə-'kɔːʃəs, ˌəʊvə'piːpld.

over-abundan|ce, -t ˌəʊvərə'bʌndən|s, -t

overact, -s, -ing, -ed ˌəʊvər'ækt [ˌəʊvə'ækt], -s, -ɪŋ, -ɪd

overall (s. adj.) (O.), -s 'əʊvərɔːl, -z

overall (adv.) ˌəʊvər'ɔːl

over-anxiety ˌəʊvərænˈzaɪətɪ [ˌəʊvəæŋ-]

over-anxious, -ly ˌəʊvər'æŋkʃəs [ˌəʊvə'æ-], -lɪ

overarm 'əʊvərɑːm

overaw|e, -es, -ing, -ed ˌəʊvər'ɔː [ˌəʊvə'ɔː], -z, -ɪŋ, -d

overbalanc|e, -es, -ing, -ed ˌəʊvə-'bæləns, -ɪz, -ɪŋ, -t

overbear, -s, -ing, overbore, overborne ˌəʊvə'beə*, -z, -rɪŋ, ˌəʊvə'bɔː* [-'bɔə*], ˌəʊvə'bɔːn

overbearing (adj.), -ly, -ness ˌəʊvə-'beərɪŋ, -lɪ, -nɪs [-nəs]

over|blow, -blows, -blowing, -blew, -blown ˌəʊvə|'bləʊ, -'bləʊz, -'bləʊɪŋ, -'bluː, -'bləʊn

overboard 'əʊvəbɔːd [ˌəʊvə'bɔːd, -bəd]

overboil, -s, -ing, -ed ˌəʊvə'bɔɪl, -z, -ɪŋ, -d

overbold, -ly ˌəʊvə'bəʊld, -lɪ

overbrim, -s, -ming, -med ˌəʊvə'brɪm, -z, -ɪŋ, -d

overbuil|d, -ds, -ding, -t ˌəʊvə'bɪl|d, -dz, -dɪŋ, -t

overburd|en, -ens, -ening, -ened ˌəʊvə-'bɜːd|n, -nz, -nɪŋ [-nɪŋ], -nd

Overbury 'əʊvəbərɪ

over-busy ˌəʊvə'bɪzɪ

over-care|ful, -fully, -fulness ˌəʊvə-'keə|fʊl, -fʊlɪ [-fəlɪ], -fʊlnɪs [-nəs]

overcast 'əʊvəkɑːst [ˌ-'-]

overcharge (s.), -s ˌəʊvə'tʃɑːdʒ ['---], -ɪz

overcharg|e (v.), -es, -ing, -ed ˌəʊvə-'tʃɑːdʒ, -ɪz, -ɪŋ, -d

overcloud, -s, -ing, -ed ˌəʊvə'klaʊd, -z, -ɪŋ, -ɪd

overcoat, -s 'əʊvəkəʊt, -s

over-colour (s.), -s 'əʊvəˌkʌlə*, -z

over-colour (v.), -s, -ing, -ed ˌəʊvə-'kʌlə*, -z, -rɪŋ, -d

over|come, -comes, -coming, -came ˌəʊvə|'kʌm, -'kʌmz, -'kʌmɪŋ, -'keɪm
Note.—*The stress* '--- *is occasionally used by some when a stress follows, e.g. in the expression* to vanquish and overcome all her enemies *occurring in the Church service.*

over-confiden|ce, -t/ly ˌəʊvə'kɒn-fɪdən|s, -t/lɪ

over-cooked ˌəʊvə'kʊkt [*also* '--- *according to sentence-stress*]

over-credulous ˌəʊvə'kredjʊləs

overcrowd, -s, -ing, -ed ˌəʊvə'kraʊd, -z, -ɪŋ, -ɪd

over-develop, -s, -ing, -ed, -ment ˌəʊvədɪ'veləp, -s, -ɪŋ, -t, -mənt

over|do, -does, -doing, -did, -done ˌəʊvə|'duː, -'dʌz, -'duːɪŋ [-'dʊɪŋ], -'dɪd, -'dʌn

overdone (*over-cooked*) ˌəʊvə'dʌn ['---]
Overdone 'əʊvədʌn

overdose (s.), -s 'əʊvədəʊs [ˌ-'-], -ɪz

overdos|e (v.), -es, -ing, -ed ˌəʊvə'dəʊs, -ɪz, -ɪŋ, -t

overdraft, -s 'əʊvədrɑːft, -s

overdraught, -s 'əʊvədrɑːft, -s

over|draw, -draws, -drawing, -drew, -drawn ˌəʊvə|'drɔː, -'drɔːz, -'drɔːɪŋ, -'druː, -'drɔːn

overdress (v.), -es, -ing, -ed ˌəʊvə'dres, -ɪz, -ɪŋ, -t

overdress (s.), -es 'əʊvədres, -ɪz

overdrive (s.) 'əʊvədraɪv

over|drive (v.), -drives, -driving, -drove, -driven ˌəʊvə|'draɪv, -'draɪvz, -'draɪvɪŋ, -'drəʊv, -'drɪvn

358

overdue ˌəʊvə'dju: [also '— according to sentence-stress]

overeat, -s, -ing, -en, overate ˌəʊvər'i:t [-və'i:t], -s, -ɪŋ, -n, ˌəʊvər'et [-və'et, -vər'eɪt, -və'eɪt]

overestimate (s.), -s ˌəʊvər'estɪmət [ˌəʊvə'es-, -ɪt], -s

overestimat|e (v.), -es, -ing, -ed ˌəʊvər'estɪmeɪt [-və'es-], -s, -ɪŋ, -ɪd

over-estimation 'əʊvərˌestɪ'meɪʃn [-və,es-]

overexcit|e, -es, -ing, -ed, -ement ˌəʊvərɪk'saɪt [-vəɪk-, -ek-], -s, -ɪŋ, -ɪd, -mənt

overexert, -s, -ing, -ed ˌəʊvərɪg'zз:t [-vɪg-, -eg-], -s, -ɪŋ, -ɪd

overexertion ˌəʊvərɪg'zз:ʃn [-vəɪg-, -eg-]

overexpos|e, -es, -ing, -ed ˌəʊvərɪk-'spəʊz [-vəɪk-, -ek-], -ɪz, -ɪŋ, -d

over-exposure ˌəʊvərɪk'spəʊʒə* [-vəɪk-, -ek-]

overfatigu|e (s. v.), -es, -ing, -ed ˌəʊvəfə'ti:g, -z, -ɪŋ, -d

overfeed, -s, -ing, overfed ˌəʊvə'fi:d, -z, -ɪŋ, ˌəʊvə'fed

overflow (s.), -s 'əʊvəfləʊ, -z

overfl|ow (v.), -ows, -owing, -owed ˌəʊvə'fl|əʊ, -əʊz, -əʊɪŋ, -əʊd

over|-fond, -full ˌəʊvə|'fɒnd, -'fʊl

over|go, -goes, -going, -went, -gone ˌəʊvə|'gəʊ, -'gəʊz, -'gəʊɪŋ, -'went, -'gɒn

overground 'əʊvəgraʊnd [ˌ--'-]

over|grow, -grows, -growing, -grew, -grown ˌəʊvə|'grəʊ, -'grəʊz, -'grəʊɪŋ, -'gru:, -'grəʊn ['əʊvəgrəʊn when attributive]

overgrowth, -s 'əʊvəgrəʊθ, -s

overhand (s. adj.), -s 'əʊvəhænd, -z

overhang (s.), -s 'əʊvəhæŋ, -z

over|hang (v.), -hangs, -hanging, -hung ˌəʊvə|'hæŋ, -'hæŋz, -'hæŋɪŋ [also 'əʊvəˌh- when attributive], -'hʌŋ [also 'əʊvəhʌŋ when attributive]

over-happy ˌəʊvə'hæpɪ

over-hasty ˌəʊvə'heɪstɪ

overhaul (s.), -s 'əʊvəhɔ:l [ˌ--'-], -z

overhaul (v.), -s, -ing, -ed ˌəʊvə'hɔ:l, -z, -ɪŋ, -d

overhead (s. adj.), -s 'əʊvəhed, -z

overhead (adv.) ˌəʊvə'hed

overhear, -s, -ing, overheard ˌəʊvə'hɪə*, -z, -rɪŋ, ˌəʊvə'hз:d

overheat, -s, -ing, -ed ˌəʊvə'hi:t, -s, -ɪŋ, -ɪd

over-indulg|e, -es, -ing, -ed; -ence ˌəʊvərɪn'dʌldʒ [-vəɪn-], -ɪz, -ɪŋ, -d; -əns

overjoy, -s, -ing, -ed ˌəʊvə'dʒɔɪ, -z, -ɪŋ, -d

over-kind ˌəʊvə'kaɪnd

overlad|e, -es, -ing, -ed, -en ˌəʊvə'leɪd, -z, -ɪŋ, -ɪd, -n

overlaid ˌəʊvə'leɪd [also 'əʊvəl- when attributive]

overland (adj.) 'əʊvəlænd

overland (adv.) ˌəʊvə'lænd ['---]

overlap (s.), -s 'əʊvəlæp, -s

overlap (v.), -s, -ping, -ped ˌəʊvə'læp, -s, -ɪŋ, -t

overlay (s.), -s 'əʊvəleɪ, -z

overlay (v.), -s, -ing, overlaid ˌəʊvə'leɪ, -z, -ɪŋ, ˌəʊvə'leɪd [also 'əʊvəl- when attributive]

overleaf ˌəʊvə'li:f

over|leap (leap over, leap too far), -leaps, -leaping, -leaped, -leapt ˌəʊvə|'li:p, -'li:ps, -'li:pɪŋ, -'lept [-'li:pt], -'lept

overload (s.), -s 'əʊvələʊd, -z

overload (v.), -s, -ing, -ed ˌəʊvə'ləʊd, -z, -ɪŋ, -ɪd

overlook, -s, -ing, -ed ˌəʊvə'lʊk, -s, -ɪŋ, -t

overlord, -s 'əʊvəlɔ:d, -z

overlying ˌəʊvə'laɪɪŋ

over|man, -men 'əʊvə|mæn, -men

overmantel, -s 'əʊvəˌmæntl, -z

overmast|er, -ers, -ering, -ered ˌəʊvə-'mɑ:st|ə*, -əz, -ərɪŋ, -əd

overmatch, -es, -ing, -ed ˌəʊvə'mætʃ, -ɪz, -ɪŋ, -t

overmuch ˌəʊvə'mʌtʃ ['---]

over-nice ˌəʊvə'naɪs

overnight ˌəʊvə'naɪt [also '--- according to sentence-stress]

overpass (s.), -es 'əʊvəpɑ:s, -ɪz

overpass (v.), -es, -ing, -ed ˌəʊvə'pɑ:s, -ɪz, -ɪŋ, -t

overpast (adj.) ˌəʊvə'pɑ:st

over|pay, -pays, -paying, -paid, -payment/s ˌəʊvə|'peɪ, -'peɪz, -'peɪɪŋ, -'peɪd, -'peɪmənt/s

overplus, -es 'əʊvəplʌs, -ɪz

overpopulat|e, -es, -ing, -ed ˌəʊvə-'pɒpjʊleɪt [-pjə-], -s, -ɪŋ, -ɪd

overpopulation 'əʊvəˌpɒpjʊ'leɪʃn [-pjə-]

overpower, -s, -ing/ly, -ed ˌəʊvə'paʊə*, -z, -rɪŋ/lɪ, -d

overprint (s.), -s 'əʊvəprɪnt, -s

overprint (v.), -s, -ing, -ed ˌəʊvə'prɪnt ['---], -s, -ɪŋ, -ɪd

overproduc|e, -es, -ing, -ed ˌəʊvə-prə'dju:s [-prʊ'd-], -ɪz, -ɪŋ, -t

overproduction ˌəʊvəprə'dʌkʃn [-prʊ'd-]

overproud ˌəʊvə'praʊd

359

overrat|e, -es, -ing, -ed ˌəʊvəˈreɪt, -s,
  -ɪŋ, -ɪd
overreach (s.), -es ˈəʊvəriːtʃ, -ɪz
overreach (v.), -es, -ing, -ed ˌəʊvəˈriːtʃ,
  -ɪz, -ɪŋ, -t
overread (pres. tense), -s, -ing, overread (p.) ˌəʊvəˈriːd, -z, -ɪŋ, ˌəʊvəˈred
overrefin|e, -es, -ing, -ed, -ement/s
  ˌəʊvərɪˈfaɪn, -z, -ɪŋ, -d, -mənt/s
over|ride, -rides, -riding, -rode, -ridden
  ˌəʊvəˈraɪd, -ˈraɪdz, -ˈraɪdɪŋ, -ˈrəʊd,
  -ˈrɪdn
overripe, -ness ˌəʊvəˈraɪp, -nɪs [-nəs]
overrip|en, -ens, -ening, -ened ˌəʊvə-
  ˈraɪp|n, -nz, -nɪŋ [-n̩ɪŋ], -nd
overrul|e, -es, -ing, -ed, -er/s ˌəʊvə-
  ˈruːl, -z, -ɪŋ, -d, -ə*/z
overrun, -s, -ning, overran ˌəʊvəˈrʌn,
  -z, -ɪŋ, ˌəʊvəˈræn
over-scrupulous, -ly, -ness ˌəʊvəˈskruː-
  pjʊləs [-pjəl-], -lɪ, -nɪs [-nəs]
oversea, -s ˌəʊvəˈsiː [also ˈ— according
  to sentence-stress], -z
over|see, -sees, -seeing, -saw, -seen
  ˌəʊvəˈsiː, -ˈsiːz, -ˈsiːɪŋ, -ˈsɔː, -ˈsiːn
overseer, -s ˈəʊvəˌsɪə* [-ˌsiːə*], -z
overshad|ow, -ows, -owing, -owed
  ˌəʊvəˈʃæd|əʊ, -əʊz, -əʊɪŋ, -əʊd
over-shoot, -shoots, -shooting, -shot
  ˌəʊvəˈʃuːt, -ˈʃuːts, -ˈʃuːtɪŋ, -ˈʃɒt
oversight, -s ˈəʊvəsaɪt, -s
oversize (s.), -s, -d ˈəʊvəsaɪz, -ɪz, -d
overslaugh, -s ˈəʊvəslɔː, -z
over|sleep, -sleeps, -sleeping, -slept
  ˌəʊvəˈsliːp, -ˈsliːps, -ˈsliːpɪŋ, -ˈslept
oversoon ˌəʊvəˈsuːn
overspen|d, -ds, -ding, -t ˌəʊvəˈspen|d,
  -dz, -dɪŋ, -t
overspread, -s, -ing ˌəʊvəˈspred, -z, -ɪŋ
overstat|e, -es, -ing, -ed ˌəʊvəˈsteɪt,
  [ˈ—-], -s, -ɪŋ, -ɪd
overstatement, -s ˌəʊvəˈsteɪtmənt,
  [ˈ—ˌ—], -s
overstay, -s, -ing, -ed ˌəʊvəˈsteɪ [ˈ—-],
  -z, -ɪŋ, -d
overstep, -s, -ping, -ped ˌəʊvəˈstep, -s,
  -ɪŋ, -t
overstock, -s, -ing, -ed ˌəʊvəˈstɒk, -s,
  -ɪŋ, -t
overstrain (s.) ˈəʊvəstreɪn [ˌ—ˈ-]
overstrain (v.), -s, -ing, -ed ˌəʊvəˈstreɪn,
  -z, -ɪŋ, -d
Overstrand ˈəʊvəstrænd
overstretch, -es, -ing, -ed ˌəʊvəˈstretʃ,
  -ɪz, -ɪŋ, -t
overstrung (in state of nervous tension)
  ˌəʊvəˈstrʌŋ
overstrung (piano) ˈəʊvəstrʌŋ

oversubscrib|e, -es, -ing, -ed ˌəʊvəsəb-
  ˈskraɪb [-bzˈk-], -z, -ɪŋ, -d
oversupp|ly, -ies ˌəʊvəsəˈpl|aɪ, -aɪz
overt, -ly ˈəʊvɜːt [əʊˈvɜːt], -lɪ
over|take, -takes, -taking, -took, -taken
  ˌəʊvəˈteɪk, -ˈteɪks, -ˈteɪkɪŋ, -ˈtʊk,
  -ˈteɪkən [-ˈteɪkn̩]
overtask, -s, -ing, -ed ˌəʊvəˈtɑːsk, -s,
  -ɪŋ, -t
overtax, -es, -ing, -ed ˌəʊvəˈtæks, -ɪz,
  -ɪŋ, -t
overthrow (s.), -s ˈəʊvəθrəʊ, -z
over|throw (v.), -throws, -throwing,
  -threw, -thrown ˌəʊvəˈθrəʊ, -ˈθrəʊz,
  -ˈθruː, -ˈθruːɪŋ, -ˈθruː, -ˈθrəʊn
overthrust, -s ˈəʊvəθrʌst, -s
overtilt, -s, -ing, -ed ˌəʊvəˈtɪlt, -s, -ɪŋ, -ɪd
overtime ˈəʊvətaɪm
overtir|e, -es, -ing, -ed ˌəʊvəˈtaɪə*, -z,
  -ɪŋ, -d
Overton ˈəʊvətən
overtone, -s ˈəʊvətəʊn, -z
overtop, -s, -ping, -ped ˌəʊvəˈtɒp, -s,
  -ɪŋ, -t
Overtoun ˈəʊvətən
over-trump, -s, -ing, -ed ˈəʊvətrʌmp
  [ˌ—ˈ-], -s, -ɪŋ, -t [-ʌmt]
overture, -s ˈəʊvəˌtjʊə* [-tjə*, -ˌtʃʊə*,
  -tʃə*], -z
overturn (s.), -s ˈəʊvətɜːn, -z
overturn (v.), -s, -ing, -ed ˌəʊvəˈtɜːn,
  -z, -ɪŋ, -d
overval|ue, -ues, -uing, -ued ˌəʊvə-
  ˈvæl|juː [-jʊ], -juːz [-jʊz], -juːɪŋ
  [-jwɪŋ], -juːd [-jʊd]
overview, -s ˈəʊvəvjuː, -z
overweening ˌəʊvəˈwiːnɪŋ
overweight (s.), -s ˈəʊvəweɪt, -s
over-weight (adj.) ˌəʊvəˈweɪt [ˈ—-]
overweight (v.), -s, -ing, -ed ˌəʊvəˈweɪt,
  -s, -ɪŋ, -ɪd
overwhelm, -s, -ing/ly, -ed ˌəʊvəˈwelm
  [-ˈhwelm], -z, -ɪŋ/lɪ, -d
overwork (s.) (extra work) ˈəʊvəwɜːk
overwork (s.) (excessive work) ˌəʊvə-
  ˈwɜːk
overwork (v.), -s, -ing, -ed, -er/s
  ˌəʊvəˈwɜːk, -s, -ɪŋ, -t, -ə*/z
overwrought ˌəʊvəˈrɔːt
Ovid (Latin poet) ˈɒvɪd, (American
  surname) ˈəʊvɪd
Ovidian ɒˈvɪdɪən [əʊˈv-, -djən]
Oviedo ˌɒvɪˈeɪdəʊ (oˈbjeðo)
oviform ˈəʊvɪfɔːm
ovine ˈəʊvaɪn
Ovingdean ˈɒvɪŋdiːn
Ovingham (in Northumberland)
  ˈɒvɪndʒəm

Ovington (in North Yorkshire, street in London) 'ɒvɪŋtən, (in Norfolk, surname) 'əʊvɪŋtən
oviparous əʊ'vɪpərəs
Ovoca əʊ'vəʊkə
ovoid (s. adj.), -s 'əʊvɔɪd, -z
ovular 'əʊvjʊlə*
ovulation ˌɒvjʊ'leɪʃn [ˌəʊv-]
ovule, -s 'əʊvju:l, -z
ov|um, -a 'əʊv|əm, -ə
Owbridge 'əʊbrɪdʒ
ow|e, -es, -ing, -ed əʊ, -z, -ɪŋ, -d
Owego əʊ'wi:gəʊ
Owen, -s; -ite/s 'əʊɪn, -z; -aɪt/s
Ower 'aʊə*, 'əʊə*
Owers 'aʊəz
owing (from owe) 'əʊɪŋ
owl, -s aʊl, -z
owler|y, -ies 'aʊlər|ɪ, -ɪz
Owles əʊlz
owlet, -s 'aʊlɪt [-let, -lət], -s
Owlett 'aʊlɪt [-let]
owlish, -ly, -ness 'aʊlɪʃ, -lɪ, -nɪs [-nəs]
own, -s, -ing, -ed, -er/s əʊn, -z, -ɪŋ, -d, -ə*/z
ownership 'əʊnəʃɪp
Owsley 'aʊzlɪ
Owyhe əʊ'waɪhi:
ox, -en ɒks, -ən
oxalate, -s 'ɒksəleɪt [-lɪt, -lət], -s
oxalic ɒk'sælɪk
oxalis 'ɒksəlɪs
Oxbridge 'ɒksbrɪdʒ
oxbow, -s 'ɒksbəʊ, -z
Oxbrow 'ɒksbraʊ
oxen (plur. of ox) 'ɒksn
Oxen|den, -ford 'ɒksn|dən, -fəd [-fɔ:d]
Oxenham 'ɒksnəm [-snəm]
Oxenhope 'ɒksnhəʊp
oxer, -s 'ɒksə*, -z
ox-eye, -s, -d 'ɒksaɪ, -z, -d
Oxfam 'ɒksfæm
Oxford, -shire 'ɒksfəd, -ʃə* [-ˌʃɪə*]
ox-hide, -s 'ɒkshaɪd, -z
oxidat|e, -es, -ing, -ed 'ɒksɪdeɪt, -s, -ɪŋ, -ɪd

oxidation ˌɒksɪ'deɪʃn
oxide, -s 'ɒksaɪd, -z
oxidization [-isa-] ˌɒksɪdaɪ'zeɪʃn [-dɪ'z-]
oxidiz|e [-is|e], -es, -ing, -ed, -er/s; -able 'ɒksɪdaɪz, -ɪz, -ɪŋ, -d, -ə*/z; -əbl
Oxley 'ɒkslɪ
oxlip, -s 'ɒkslɪp, -s
oxo 'ɒksəʊ
Oxon. 'ɒksən [-sɒn]
Oxonian, -s ɒk'səʊnjən [-nɪən], -z
Oxshott 'ɒkʃɒt
ox-tail, -s 'ɒksteɪl, -z
ox-tongue, -s 'ɒkstʌŋ, -z
Oxus 'ɒksəs
oxy-acetylene ˌɒksɪə'setɪli:n [-sɪæ's, -lɪn]
oxychloride, -s ˌɒksɪ'klɔ:raɪd, -z
oxygen 'ɒksɪdʒən
oxygenat|e, -es, -ing, -ed ɒk'sɪdʒəneɪt ['ɒksɪ-, -dʒɪn-], -s, -ɪŋ, -ɪd
oxygenation ˌɒksɪdʒə'neɪʃn [ɒkˌsɪdʒ-, -dʒɪ'n-]
oxygenous ɒk'sɪdʒənəs [-dʒɪn-]
oxyhydrogen ˌɒksɪ'haɪdrədʒən [-drɪdʒ-]
oxymel 'ɒksɪmel
oxymoron, -s ˌɒksɪ'mɔ:rɒn [-'mɔər-, -rən], -z
oxytone (s. adj.), -s 'ɒksɪtəʊn, -z
oyer 'ɔɪə*
oyes əʊ'jes
oyez əʊ'jes ['əʊjes, 'əʊjez, əʊ'jez]
oyster (O.), -s; -bed/s, -bar/s 'ɔɪstə*, -z; -bed/z, -ba:*/z
oyster-catcher, -s 'ɔɪstəˌkætʃə*, -z
oyster-fisher|y, -ies 'ɔɪstəˌfɪʃər|ɪ, -ɪz
Oystermouth 'ɔɪstəmaʊθ
oyster-patt|y, -ies ˌɔɪstə'pætɪ, -ɪz
oyster-shell, -s 'ɔɪstəʃel, -z
oz., ozs. aʊns, 'aʊnsɪz
Ozanne əʊ'zæn
ozokerit(e) əʊ'zəʊkərɪt [ɒ'z-, ə'z-]
ozone 'əʊzəʊn [əʊ'zəʊn]
ozonic əʊ'zɒnɪk
ozoniferous ˌəʊzəʊ'nɪfərəs

P

P (*the letter*), -'s piː, -z
pa, -s pɑː, -z
pabulum 'pæbjʊləm
pac|e (*s. v.*), -es, -ing, -ed, -er/s peɪs,
  -ɪz, -ɪŋ, -t, -ə*/z
pace (*prep.*) 'peɪsɪ
pace-maker, -s 'peɪs,meɪkə*, -z
pace-setter, -s 'peɪs,setə*, -z
Pachmann (*famous pianist*) 'pɑːkmən
  [-mɑːn]
pachyderm, -s 'pækɪdəːm, -z
pachydermat|a, -ous ,pækɪ'dəːmət|ə,
  -əs
pacific (P.), -ally pə'sɪfɪk, -əlɪ
pacification, -s ,pæsɪfɪ'keɪʃn, -z
pacificatory pə'sɪfɪkətərɪ [pæ's-, -keɪtərɪ,
  'pæsɪfɪkeɪtərɪ, ,pæsɪfɪ'keɪtərɪ]
pacificist, -s pə'sɪfɪsɪst, -s
pacifism 'pæsɪfɪzəm
pacifist, -s 'pæsɪfɪst, -s
paci|fy, -fies, -fying, -fied, -fier/s
  'pæsɪ|faɪ, -faɪz, -faɪɪŋ, -faɪd, -faɪə*/z
pack, -s, -ing, -ed, -er/s pæk, -s, -ɪŋ, -t,
  -ə*/z
package, -s 'pækɪdʒ, -ɪz
pack-animal, -s 'pæk,ænɪml [-nəml], -z
Packard 'pækɑːd
Packer 'pækə*
packet, -s 'pækɪt, -s
packet-boat, -s 'pækɪtbəʊt, -s
packhorse, -s 'pækhɔːs, -ɪz
pack-ice 'pækaɪs
packing|-case/s, -needle/s, -paper,
  -sheet/s 'pækɪŋ|keɪs/ɪz, -,niːdl/z,
  -,peɪpə*, -ʃiːt/s
pack|man, -men 'pæk|mən, -mən
pack|-saddle/s, -thread 'pæk|,sædl/z,
  -θred
pact, -s pækt, -s
pad (*s. v.*), -s, -ding, -ded pæd, -z, -ɪŋ,
  -ɪd
Paddington 'pædɪŋtən
padd|le (*s. v.*), -les, -ling, -led, -ler/s
  'pæd|l, -lz, -lɪŋ [-lɪŋ], -ld, -lə*/z
  [-lə*/z]
paddle-board, -s 'pædlbɔːd [-bɔəd], -z
paddle-box, -es 'pædlbɒks, -ɪz
paddle-wheel, -s 'pædlwiːl [-hwiːl], -z
paddock (P.), -s 'pædək, -s

padd|y (P.), -ies 'pæd|ɪ, -ɪz
Padella pə'delə
Paderewski (*famous pianist*) ,pædə'rev-
  skɪ [-'refskɪ]
padlock (*s. v.*), -s, -ing, -ed 'pædlɒk, -s,
  -ɪŋ, -t
Padraic Colum ,pɑːdrɪk'kɒləm
padre, -s 'pɑːdrɪ, -z
padrone, -s pə'drəʊnɪ [pæ'd-], -z
Padstow 'pædstəʊ
Padua, -n/s 'pædjʊə ['pɑːdʊə], -n/z
paean, -s 'piːən, -z
paediatri- *see* pediatri-
paeon, -s 'piːən, -z
paeonic piː'ɒnɪk
paeony = peony
Paflagonia, -n/s ,pæflə'gəʊnjə [-nɪə],
  -n/z
pagan (*s. adj.*), -s 'peɪgən, -z
Pagani pə'gɑːnɪ
Paganini ,pægə'niːnɪ [-nɪ]
paganism 'peɪgənɪzəm [-gɳɪzəm]
paganiz|e [-is|e], -es, -ing, -ed 'peɪgən-
  aɪz, -ɪz, -ɪŋ, -d
pag|e (*s. v.*) (P.), -es, -ing, -ed peɪdʒ,
  -ɪz, -ɪŋ, -d
pageant, -s 'pædʒənt, -s
pageantry 'pædʒəntrɪ
Paget 'pædʒɪt
paginal 'pædʒɪnl ['peɪdʒ-]
paginat|e, -es, -ing, -ed 'pædʒɪneɪt
  ['peɪdʒ-], -s, -ɪŋ, -ɪd
pagination ,pædʒɪ'neɪʃn [,peɪdʒ-],
  -z
paging (*s.*) 'peɪdʒɪŋ
Pagliacci ,pælɪ'ɑːtʃɪ [-'ætʃɪ]
pagoda, -s pə'gəʊdə, -z
pah pɑː [pɑːh, pɸ]
Pahang pə'hʌŋ [-'hæŋ]
  Note.—Usually pronounced pə'hʌŋ
  in Malaya.
paid (*from* pay) peɪd
Paignton 'peɪntən
pail, -s; -ful/s peɪl, -z; -fʊl/z
paillasse, -s 'pælɪæs ['pæljæs, ,pælɪ'æs,
  pæl'jæs], -ɪz
paillette, -s pæl'jet [,pælɪ'et] (pajet), -s
pain (*s. v.*), -s, -ing, -ed peɪn, -z, -ɪŋ, -d
Pain(e) peɪn

362

pain|ful, -fully, -fulness 'peɪn|fʊl, -fʊlɪ [-fəlɪ], -fʊlnɪs [-nəs]

painless, -ly, -ness 'peɪnlɪs [-ləs], -lɪ, -nɪs [-nəs]

painstak|er/s, -ing 'peɪnz,teɪk|ə*/z, -ɪŋ

Painswick 'peɪnzwɪk

paint (s. v.), -s, -ing/s, -ed, -er/s; -able peɪnt, -s, -ɪŋ/z, -ɪd, -ə*/z; -əbl

paint|-box/es, -brush/es 'peɪnt|bɒks/ɪz, -brʌʃ/ɪz

Painter 'peɪntə*

paint|y, -ier, -iest 'peɪnt|ɪ, -ɪə*, -ɪɪst

pair (s. v.), -s, -ing, -ed peə*, -z, -rɪŋ, -d

pair-horse 'peəhɔ:s

pairing-time, -s 'peərɪŋtaɪm, -z

Paisley 'peɪzlɪ

pajamas pə'dʒɑ:məz

Pakeman 'peɪkmən

Pakenham 'pæknəm [-kənəm]

Pakistan ,pɑ:kɪ'stɑ:n [,pæk-, -'stæn]

Pakistani, -s ,pɑ:kɪ'stɑ:nɪ [,pæk-], -z

pal, -s pæl, -z

palace, -s 'pælɪs [-ləs], -ɪz

paladin, -s 'pælədɪn, -z

palaeobotany ,pælɪəʊ'bɒtənɪ [,peɪl-, -tɲɪ]

palaeograph|er/s, -y ,pælɪ'ɒgrəf|ə*/z [,peɪl-], -ɪ

palaeographic ,pælɪəʊ'græfɪk [,peɪl-]

palaeolithic ,pælɪəʊ'lɪθɪk [,peɪl-]

palaeontological ,pælɪɒntə'lɒdʒɪkl [,peɪl-]

palaeontolog|ist/s, -y ,pælɪɒn'tɒlədʒ|-ɪst/s [,peɪl-], -ɪ

palaeotype 'pælɪəʊtaɪp

Palaeozoic ,pælɪəʊ'zəʊɪk [,peɪl-]

palairet 'pælɪrɪt [-ret]

Palamedes ,pælə'mi:di:z

Palamon 'pæləmən [-mɒn]

palanquin [-nkeen], -s ,pælən'ki:n [-əŋ'k-], -z

palatab|le, -ly, -leness 'pælətəb|l [-lɪt-], -lɪ, -lnɪs [-nəs]

palatal (s. adj.), -s 'pælətl [pə'leɪtl], -z

palatalization [-isa-], -s ,pælətəlaɪ'zeɪʃn [pə,læt-, pə,leɪt-, -tʃaɪ'z-, -təlɪ'z-, -tʃɪ'z-], -z

palataliz|e [-is|e], -es, -ing, -ed 'pælə-təlaɪz [pə'læt-, pə'leɪt-, -tʃaɪz], -ɪz, -ɪŋ, -d

palate, -s 'pælət [-lɪt], -s

palatial pə'leɪʃl [-ʃjəl, -ʃɪəl]

palatinate (P.), -s pə'lætɪnət [-tŋət, -ɪt], -s

palatine (P.) 'pælətaɪn

palatogram, -s 'pælətəʊgræm [pə'læt-], -z

palatography ,pælə'tɒgrəfɪ

palav|er (s. v.), -ers, -ering, -ered, -erer/s pə'lɑ:v|ə*, -əz, -ərɪŋ, -əd, -ərə*/z

pal|e (s. adj. v.), -er, -est, -ely, -eness; -es, -ing, -ed peɪl, -ə*, -ɪst, -lɪ, -nɪs [-nəs]; -z, -ɪŋ, -d

pale-face, -s 'peɪlfeɪs, -ɪz

paleo- see palaeo-

Palermo pə'lɜ:məʊ [-leəm-] (pa'lɛrmo)

Palestine 'pæləstaɪn [-lɪs-, -les-]

Palestinian,-s ,pælə'stɪnɪən [-lɪ's-, -le's-, -njən], -z

Palestrina ,pæle'stri:nə [-lɪs-, -ləs-]

paletot, -s 'pæltəʊ, -z

palette, -s; -knife, -knives 'pælət [-lɪt, -let], -s; -naɪf, -naɪvz

Paley 'peɪlɪ

Palfery 'pɔ:lfərɪ ['pɒl-]

palfrey (P.), -s 'pɔ:lfrɪ ['pɒl-], -z

Palgrave 'pɔ:lgreɪv, 'pæl-

Pali 'pɑ:lɪ

palimpsest, -s 'pælɪmpsest, -s

Palin 'peɪlɪn

palindrome, -s 'pælɪndrəʊm, -z

paling (s.), -s 'peɪlɪŋ, -z

palingenesis ,pælɪn'dʒenɪsɪs [-nəsɪs]

palinode, -s 'pælɪnəʊd, -z

palisad|e (s. v.), -es, -ing, -ed ,pælɪ'seɪd, -z, -ɪŋ, -ɪd

palish 'peɪlɪʃ

Palk pɔ:lk [pɒlk]

pall (s. v.), -s, -ing, -ed pɔ:l, -z, -ɪŋ, -d

palladi|an (P.), -um/s pə'leɪdj|ən [-dɪ|ən], -əm/z

Pallas 'pæləs [-læs]

pall-bearer, -s 'pɔ:l,beərə*, -z

pallet, -s 'pælɪt [-lət], -s

palliasse, -s 'pælɪæs ['pæljæs, ,pælɪ'æs, pæl'jæs], -ɪz

palliat|e, -es, -ing, -ed 'pælɪeɪt, -s, -ɪŋ, -ɪd

palliation ,pælɪ'eɪʃn

palliative (s. adj.), -s 'pælɪətɪv [-ljət-], -z

pallid, -est, -ly, -ness 'pælɪd, -ɪst, -lɪ, -nɪs [-nəs]

Palliser 'pælɪsə*

pallium, -s 'pælɪəm, -z

Pall Mall ,pæl'mæl [,pel'mel, also '— according to sentence-stress]

pallor 'pælə*

palm (s. v.), -s, -ing, -ed pɑ:m, -z, -ɪŋ, -d

palm|a (P.), -ar 'pɑːlm|ə, -ə*

palmaceous pæl'meɪʃəs [-ʃjəs, -ʃɪəs]

palmate 'pælmɪt [-meɪt]

palmer (P.), -s 'pɑ:mə*, -z

Palmerston 'pɑ:məstən

palmhou|se, -ses 'pɑ:mhaʊ|s, -zɪz

palmist, -s 'pɑ:mɪst, -s

palmistry 'pɑːmɪstrɪ
palmitine, -s 'pælmɪtiːn [ˌpælmɪˈt-], -z
palm-oil 'pɑːmɔɪl [ˌ-ˈ-]
Palm Sunday, -s ˌpɑːmˈsʌndɪ [-deɪ], -z
palm|y, -ier, -iest 'pɑːm|ɪ, -ɪə* [-jə*], -ɪst [-jɪst]
palmyra (P.), -s pæl'maɪərə, -z
Palomar 'pæləʊmɑː*
palpability ˌpælpəˈbɪlətɪ [-lɪt-]
palpab|le, -ly, -leness 'pælpəb|l, -lɪ, -lnɪs [-nəs]
palpat|e, -es, -ing, -ed 'pælpeɪt, -s, -ɪŋ, -ɪd
palpation pæl'peɪʃn
palpitat|e, -es, -ing, -ed 'pælpɪteɪt, -s, -ɪŋ, -ɪd
palpitation, -s ˌpælpɪˈteɪʃn, -z
palsgrave, -s 'pɔːlzgreɪv, -z
Palsgrave 'pɔːlzgreɪv, 'pælzgreɪv
pals|y, -ies, -ied 'pɔːlz|ɪ ['pɒl-], -ɪz, -ɪd
palt|er, -ers, -ering, -ered, -erer/s 'pɔːlt|ə* ['pɒl-], -əz, -ərɪŋ, -əd, -ərə*/z
paltr|y, -ier, -iest, -ily, -iness 'pɔːltr|ɪ ['pɒl-], -ɪə*, -ɪɪst, -əlɪ [-ɪlɪ], -ɪnɪs [-ɪnəs]
pam (P.), -s pæm, -z
Pamela 'pæmələ [-mɪl-]
Pamir, -s pə'mɪə*, -z
Pampa (territory in South America), -s 'pæmpə, -z
pampas (grass) 'pæmpəs
pamp|er, -ers, -ering, -ered, -erer/s 'pæmp|ə*, -əz, -ərɪŋ, -əd, -ərə*/z
pamphlet, -s 'pæmflɪt [-lət], -s
pamphleteer, -s, -ing ˌpæmfləˈtɪə* [-lɪ-], -z, -rɪŋ
Pamphylia, -n/s pæm'fɪlɪə [-ljə], -n/z
pan (P.), -s, -ning, -ned pæn, -z, -ɪŋ, -d
panacea, -s ˌpænə'sɪə [-'siːə], -z
panache, -s pə'næʃ [pæ'n-, -'nɑː.ʃ], -ɪz
panama (P.), -s ˌpænə'mɑː [also 'pænəm- when followed by a stress], -z
Panamanian, -s ˌpænəˈmeɪnjən [-nɪən], -z
pan-american ˌpænəˈmerɪkən
pan-anglican ˌpæn'æŋglɪkən
pancake, -s 'pænkeɪk ['pæŋkeɪk], -s
panchayat, -s pʌn'tʃaɪət [pæn-, pən-, -'tʃɑːjət], -s
panchromatic ˌpænkrəʊ'mætɪk [ˌpæŋk-]
Pancras 'pæŋkrəs
pancreas, -es 'pæŋkrɪəs [-krɪæs], -ɪz
pancreatic ˌpæŋkrɪ'ætɪk
panda, -s 'pændə, -z
Pandean pæn'diːən [-'dɪən]
pandect, -s 'pændekt, -s
pandemic (s. adj.), -s pæn'demɪk, -s

pandemonium, -s ˌpændɪˈməʊnjəm [-dəm-, -nɪəm], -z
pander (s. v.), -s, -ing, -ed 'pændə*, -z, -rɪŋ, -d
pandora (P.), -s pæn'dɔːrə, -z
pan|e (s. v), -es, -ing, -ed peɪn, -z, -ɪŋ, -d
panegyric (s. adj.), -s, -al ˌpænɪˈdʒɪrɪk [-nəˈdʒ-], -s, -l
panegyrist, -s ˌpænɪˈdʒɪrɪst [-nə-, '--,--], -s
panegyriz|e [-is|e], -es, -ing, -ed 'pænɪdʒɪraɪz [-nə-], -ɪz, -ɪŋ, -d
pan|el, -els, -elling/s, -elled 'pæn|l, -lz, -lɪŋ/z [-əlɪŋ/z], -ld
panful, -s 'pænfʊl, -z
pang, -s pæŋ, -z
Pangbourne 'pæŋbɔːn [-ˌbʊən, -bɔən, -bən]
pan-german ˌpæn'dʒɜː.mən
pan-germanic ˌpændʒə'mænɪk
Pangloss 'pæŋglɒs
panic, -s, -ky; -monger/s, -stricken 'pænɪk, -s, -ɪ; -ˌmʌŋgə*/z, -ˌstrɪkən
pan-indian ˌpæn'ɪndjən [-dɪən]
Panini 'pɑːnɪnɪ: [-nɪ] (Hindi paɳyni)
panjandrum, -s pæn'dʒændrəm [pən-], -z
Pankhurst 'pæŋkhɜː.st
pannage 'pænɪdʒ
pannier, -s 'pænɪə* [-njə*], -z
pannikin, -s 'pænɪkɪn, -z
Pannill 'pænɪl
panopl|y, -ies, -ied 'pænəpl|ɪ, -ɪz, -ɪd
panorama, -s ˌpænə'rɑːmə, -z
panoramic ˌpænə'ræmɪk [-'rɑː.m-]
pan-pipe, -s 'pænpaɪp, -s
pan-slavism ˌpæn'slɑː.vɪzəm [-'slæv-]
pans|y (s. v.), -ies, -ying, -ied 'pænz|ɪ, -ɪz, -ɪŋ, -ɪd
pant (s. v.), -s, -ing/ly, -ed pænt, -s, -ɪŋ/lɪ, -ɪd
pantagraph, -s 'pæntəgrɑːf [-græf], -s
pantaloon, -s ˌpæntə'luːn, -z
pantechnicon, -s pæn'teknɪkən, -z
panthei|sm, -st/s 'pænθiː.ɪ|zəm [-θiɪzəm], -st/s
pantheistic, -al ˌpænθiː'ɪstɪk [-θɪ'ɪst-], -l
pantheon (P.), -s 'pænθɪən [pæn'θiː.ən, -'θɪən], -z
panther, -s 'pænθə*, -z
panties 'pæntɪz
pantile, -s 'pæntaɪl, -z
pantisocrac|y, -ies ˌpæntɪ'sɒkrəs|ɪ, -ɪz
pantograph, -s 'pæntəʊgrɑːf [-græf], -s
pantographic, -al ˌpæntəʊ'græfɪk, -l
pantomime, -s; -ist/s 'pæntəmaɪm, -z; -ɪst/s

pantomimic, -al, -ally ˌpæntəʊ'mɪmɪk, -l, -əlɪ
pantr|y, -ies 'pæntr|ɪ, -ɪz
pants (s.) pænts
Panza 'pænzə
panzer, -s 'pæntzə* ['pænzə*], -z
pap, -s pæp, -s
papa, -s pə'pɑ:, -z
papac|y, -ies 'peɪpəs|ɪ, -ɪz
papal 'peɪpl
papali|sm, -st/s 'peɪpəlɪ|zəm [-p|ɪ-], -st/s
papaliz|e [-is|e], -es, -ing, -ed 'peɪpəlaɪz [-p|aɪz], -ɪz, -ɪŋ, -d
papaverous pə'peɪvərəs
papaw, -s pə'pɔ:, -z
papaya, -s pə'paɪə, -z
pap|er (s. v.), -ers, -ering, -ered, -erer/s 'peɪp|ə*, -əz, -ərɪŋ, -əd, -ərə*/z
paper-back, -s 'peɪpəbæk, -s
paper-case, -s 'peɪpəkeɪs, -ɪz
paper-chase, -s 'peɪpətʃeɪs, -ɪz
paper-clip, -s 'peɪpəklɪp, -s
paper-cutter, -s 'peɪpəˌkʌtə*, -z
paper-file, -s 'peɪpəfaɪl, -z
paper-hang|er/s, -ing 'peɪpəˌhæŋ|ə*/z, -ɪŋ
paper-kni|fe, -ves 'peɪpənaɪ|f, -vz
paper-maker, -s 'peɪpəˌmeɪkə*, -z
paper-mill, -s 'peɪpəmɪl, -z
paper-money 'peɪpəˌmʌnɪ
paper-nautilus, -es ˌpeɪpə'nɔːtɪləs, -ɪz
paper-office, -s 'peɪpərˌɒfɪs [-pə,ɒf-], -ɪz
paper-weight, -s 'peɪpəweɪt, -s
Paphlagonia, -n/s ˌpæflə'gəʊnjə [-nɪə], -n/z
Paphos (in Cyprus) (ancient city) 'peɪfɒs, (modern town) 'pæfɒs
papier-mâché ˌpæpjeɪ'mæʃeɪ [-pɪeɪ-, -'mɑːʃeɪ] (papjemɑʃe)
papill|a, -ae, -ar, -ary pə'pɪl|ə, -iː, -ə*, -ərɪ
papist, -s 'peɪpɪst, -s
papistic, -al, -ally pə'pɪstɪk [peɪ'p-], -l, -əlɪ
papistry 'peɪpɪstrɪ
papoose, -s pə'puːs, -ɪz
pappus (P.), -es 'pæpəs, -ɪz
paprika 'pæprɪkə
Papua, -n/s 'pɑːpʊə [pɑː'pʊə, 'pæpjʊə], -n/z
papyr|us, -i, -uses pə'paɪər|əs, -aɪ, -əsɪz
Papyrus (as name of a horse) 'pæpɪrəs
par (P.) pɑː*
para (P.), -s 'pɑːrə, -z
parabas|is, -es pə'ræbəs|ɪs, -iːz
parable, -s 'pærəbl, -z
parabola, -s pə'ræbələ, -z

parabolic, -al, -ally ˌpærə'bɒlɪk, -l, -əlɪ
paraboloid, -s pə'ræbəlɔɪd, -z
Paracelsus ˌpærə'selsəs
parachut|e (s. v.), -es, -ing, -ed, -er/s 'pærəʃuːt [ˌ--'--], -s, -ɪŋ, -ɪd, -ə*/z
parachutist, -s 'pærəʃuːtɪst [ˌ--'--], -s
Paraclete 'pærəkliːt
parad|e (s. v.), -es, -ing, -ed pə'reɪd, -z, -ɪŋ, -ɪd
parade-ground, -s pə'reɪdgraʊnd, -z
paradigm, -s 'pærədaɪm, -z
paradigmatic, -al, -ally ˌpærədɪg'mætɪk, -l, -əlɪ
paradise (P.), -s 'pærədaɪs, -ɪz
paradisiac, ˌpærə'dɪsɪæk [-'dɪzɪ-]
paradisiacal, ˌpærədɪ'saɪəkl [-dɪ'zaɪ-]
paradisic, -al ˌpærə'dɪzɪk, -l
parados, -es 'pærədɒs, -ɪz
paradox, -es 'pærədɒks, -ɪz
paradoxic|al, -ally, -alness ˌpærə'dɒksɪk|l, -əlɪ, -lnɪs [-nəs]
paraffin 'pærəfɪn [-fiːn, ˌ--'-]
paraffine 'pærəfiːn
paragoge, -s ˌpærə'gəʊdʒɪ, -z
paragogic ˌpærə'gɒdʒɪk
paragon, -s 'pærəgən, -z
paragraph (s. v.), -s, -ing, -ed 'pærəgrɑːf [-græf], -s, -ɪŋ, -t
Paraguay 'pærəgwaɪ [-gweɪ, ˌpærə-'gwaɪ]
Paraguayan ˌpærə'gwaɪən [-'gweɪən]
parakeet, -s 'pærəkiːt [ˌ--'--], -s
paraldehyde pə'rældɪhaɪd [-dəh-]
paralexia ˌpærə'leksɪə [-sjə]
parallax, -es 'pærəlæks [-r|æks], -ɪz
parallel (s. v.), -s, -ing, -ed; -ism 'pærəlel [-r|el, -rələl, -r|əl], -z, -ɪŋ, -d; -ɪzəm
parallelepiped, -s ˌpærəle'lepɪped [-r|e'l-, -rələ'l-, -r|ə'l-], 'pærəˌlelə'paɪped, 'pær|ˌelə'paɪp-], -z
parallelogram, -s ˌpærə'leləʊgræm [-r|'el-], -z
paralysant, -s 'pærəlaɪznt [-r|aɪ-, pə'rælɪznt], -s
paralys|e, -es, -ing, -ed 'pærəlaɪz [-r|aɪz], -ɪz, -ɪŋ, -d
paralys|is, -es pə'rælɪs|ɪs [-ləs-], -iːz
paralytic (s. adj.), -s ˌpærə'lɪtɪk [-r|'ɪt-], -s
parameter, -s pə'ræmɪtə* [-mətə*], -z
paramount, -ly 'pærəmaʊnt, -lɪ
paramour, -s 'pærəˌmʊə* [-mɔə*, -mɔː*], -z
paranoi|a, -ac ˌpærə'nɔɪ|ə, -æk
paranoid 'pærənɔɪd
parapet, -s, -ed 'pærəpɪt [-pet], -s, -ɪd
paraphernalia ˌpærəfə'neɪljə [-lɪə]

365

paraphras|e (s. v.), -es, -ing, -ed
'pærəfreiz, -iz, -iŋ, -d

paraphrastic, -ally ˌpærə'fræstik, -əli

parapleg|ia, -ic ˌpærə'pli:dʒ|ə, -ik

parapsychologic, -al, -ally 'pærəˌsaikə-
'lɒdʒik ['pærəˌpsai-], -l, -əli

parapsycholog|ist/s, -y ˌpærəsai-
'kɒlədʒ|ist/s [ˌpærəpsai-], -i

parasang, -s 'pærəsæŋ, -z

parasite, -s 'pærəsait, -s

parasitic, -al, -ally, -alness ˌpærə'sitik,
-l, -əli, -lnis [-nəs]

parasol, -s 'pærəsɒl [ˌ--'-], -z

parataxis ˌpærə'tæksis

paratroop, -s, -er/s 'pærətru:p, -s, -ə*/z

paratyphoid ˌpærə'taifɔid ['--ˌ--]

paravane, -s 'pærəvein, -z

parboil, -s, -ing, -ed 'pɑ:bɔil, -z, -iŋ, -d

parc|el (s. v. adv.), -els, -elling, -elled
'pɑ:s|l, -lz, -liŋ [-əliŋ], -ld

parch, -es, -ing, -ed, -edness pɑ:tʃ, -iz,
-iŋ, -t, -idnis [-tnis, -nəs]

parchment (P.), -s 'pɑ:tʃmənt, -s

pard, -s pɑ:d, -z

Pardoe 'pɑ:dəʊ

pard|on (s. v.), -ons, -oning, -oned,
-oner/s 'pɑ:d|n, -nz, -ŋiŋ [-niŋ], -nd,
-nə*/z [-nə*/z]

pardonab|le, -ly, -leness 'pɑ:dŋəb|l
[-dnə-], -li, -lnis [-nəs]

par|e, -es, -ing, -ed peə*, -z, -riŋ, -d

paregoric ˌpærə'gɒrik [-ri'g-]

parent, -s; -age 'peərənt, -s; -idʒ

parent|al, -ally pə'rent|l, -əli

parenthes|is, -es pə'renθis|is [-θəs-], -i:z

parenthetic, -al, -ally ˌpærən'θetik, -l,
-əli

parenthood 'peərənthʊd

parentless 'peərəntlis [-ləs]

parerg|on, -a pæ'rɜ:g|ɒn, -ə

par excellence ˌpɑ:r'eksəlɑ:ns [-sel-,
-lɔ̃:ns, -lɑ:ns] (parɛksəlɑ̃:s)

parget (s. v.), -s, -ing, -ed 'pɑ:dʒit, -s,
-iŋ, -id

Pargiter 'pɑ:dʒitə*

parhe|lion, -lia pɑ:'hi:|ljən [-ljɒn, -liən,
-liɒn], -ljə [-liə]

pariah, -s 'pæriə [pə'raiə], -z

Parian, -s 'peəriən, -z

parietal pə'raitl [-'raiətl]

paring (s.), -s 'peəriŋ, -z

Paris (French capital, Trojan prince)
'pæris

parish (P.), -es 'pæriʃ, -iz

parishioner, -s pə'riʃənə* [-ʃŋə*, -ʃnə*],
-z

Parisian, -s pə'rizjən [-ziən, -ʒjən,
-ʒiən, -ʒn], -z

parisyllabic ˌpærisi'læbik

parity 'pæriti [-iti]

park (s. v.) (P.), -s, -ing, -ed pɑ:k, -s,
-iŋ, -t

Parke, -r pɑ:k, -ə*

Parkestone 'pɑ:kstən

Parkinson, -ism 'pɑ:kinsn, -izəm

Parkstone 'pɑ:kstən

parlance 'pɑ:ləns

parley (s. v.) (P.), -s, -ing, -ed 'pɑ:li, -z,
-iŋ, -d

parliament, -s 'pɑ:ləmənt[-lim-, -ljə-], -s

parliamentarian, -s ˌpɑ:ləmen'teəriən
[-lim-, -ljə-, -mən-], -z

parliamentary ˌpɑ:lə'mentəri [-li'm-,
-ljə-]

parlour, -s 'pɑ:lə*, -z

parlour-car, -s 'pɑ:ləkɑ:*, -z

parlour-maid, -s 'pɑ:ləmeid, -z

parlous, -ly 'pɑ:ləs, -li

Parma 'pɑ:mə

Parmenter 'pɑ:mintə* [-məntə*]

Parmesan ˌpɑ:mi'zæn ['--- when attri-
butive]

Parminter 'pɑ:mintə*

Parmiter 'pɑ:mitə*

Parnassian, -s pɑ:'næsiən [-sjən]

Parnassus pɑ:'næsəs

Parnell pɑ:'nel, 'pɑ:nəl

parnellism 'pɑ:nelizəm [-nəl-]

parnellite, -s 'pɑ:nelait [-nəl-], -s

parochial, -ly; -ism pə'rəʊkjəl [-kiəl],
-i; -izəm

parodist, -s 'pærədist, -s

parod|y (s. v.), -ies, -ying, -ied 'pærəd|i,
-iz, -iiŋ, -id

parole pə'rəʊl

Parolles (Shakespearian character)
pə'rɒliz [-lis, -li:z, -les, -lez]

Paros 'peərɒs

parotid, -s pə'rɒtid, -z

paroxysm, -s 'pærəksizəm, -z

paroxysmal ˌpærək'sizml

paroxytone, -s pə'rɒksitəʊn [pæ'r-], -z

parozone 'pærəzəʊn

parquet, -s 'pɑ:kei [-ki], -z ['pɑ:kit, -s]

parquetry 'pɑ:kitri

parr (P.) pɑ:*

Parratt 'pærət

parricidal ˌpæri'saidl

parricide, -s 'pærisaid, -z

Parrish 'pæriʃ

parrot (P.), -s 'pærət, -s

parr|y (s. v.) (P.), -ies, -ying, -ied
'pær|i, -iz, -iiŋ, -id

pars|e, -es, -ing, -ed pɑ:z, -iz, -iŋ, -d

Parsee, -s ˌpɑ:'si:, -z

Parsifal 'pɑ:sifəl [-fɑ:l, -fæl]

parsimonious, -ly, -ness ˌpɑːsɪˈməʊnjəs [-nɪəs], -lɪ, -nɪs [-nəs]
parsimony ˈpɑːsɪmənɪ
parsley ˈpɑːslɪ
parsnip, -s ˈpɑːsnɪp, -z
parson, -s ˈpɑːsn, -z
parsonage, -s ˈpɑːsn̩ɪdʒ [-snɪ-], -ɪz
Parsons ˈpɑːsnz
part (s. v.), -s, -ing, -ed pɑːt, -s, -ɪŋ, -ɪd
partak|e, -es, -ing, partook, partak|en, -er/s pɑːˈteɪk, -s, -ɪŋ, pɑːˈtʊk, pɑːˈteɪk|ən, -ə*/z
parterre, -s pɑːˈteə* (partɛːr), -z
Parthenia pɑːˈθiːnjə [-nɪə]
parthenogenesis ˌpɑːθɪnəʊˈdʒenɪsɪs [-ˈdʒenəsɪs]
Parthenon, -s ˈpɑːθɪnən [-θən-, -θn̩-, -nɒn], -z
Parthenope pɑːˈθenəpɪ
Parthia, -n/s ˈpɑːθjə [-θɪə], -n/z
parti|al, -ally ˈpɑːʃ|l, -əlɪ
partiality ˌpɑːʃɪˈælətɪ [-ɪtɪ]
participant, -s pɑːˈtɪsɪpənt [-səp-], -s
participat|e, -es, -ing, -ed, -or/s pɑːˈtɪsɪpeɪt [-səp-], -s, -ɪŋ, -ɪd, -ə*/z
participation, -s pɑːˌtɪsɪˈpeɪʃn [ˌpɑːtɪs-, -sə'p-], -z
participial, -ly ˌpɑːtɪˈsɪpɪəl [-pjəl], -ɪ
participle, -s ˈpɑːtɪsɪpl, -z
particle, -s ˈpɑːtɪkl, -z
particoloured ˈpɑːtɪˌkʌləd
particular (s. adj.), -s, -ly pəˈtɪkjʊlə* [-kjəl-], -z, -lɪ
particularit|y, -ies pəˌtɪkjʊˈlærət|ɪ [-kjə-, -ɪt|ɪ], -ɪz
particulariz|e [-is|e], -es, -ing, -ed pəˈtɪkjʊləraɪz [-kjəl-], -ɪz, -ɪŋ, -d
parting (s.), -s ˈpɑːtɪŋ, -z
Partington ˈpɑːtɪŋtən
partisan, -s; -ship/s ˌpɑːtɪˈzæn [ˈ---], -z; -ʃɪp/s
partite ˈpɑːtaɪt
partiti|on (s. v.), -ons, -oning, -oned pɑːˈtɪʃ|n [pəˈt-], -nz, -n̩ɪŋ [-ənɪŋ], -nd
partitive, -ly ˈpɑːtɪtɪv, -lɪ
partly ˈpɑːtlɪ
partner (s. v.), -s, -ing, -ed; -ship/s ˈpɑːtnə*, -z, -rɪŋ, -d; -ʃɪp/s
Parton ˈpɑːtn
partook (from partake) pɑːˈtʊk
partridge (P.), -s ˈpɑːtrɪdʒ, -ɪz
part-singing ˈpɑːtˌsɪŋɪŋ
part-song, -s ˈpɑːtsɒŋ, -z
parturition, -s ˌpɑːtjʊəˈrɪʃn [-tjə'r-], -z
part|y, -ies ˈpɑːt|ɪ, -ɪz
party|-man, -men ˈpɑːtɪ|mæn, -men
party-spirit ˌpɑːtɪˈspɪrɪt
party-wall, -s ˈpɑːtɪwɔːl [ˌ-ˈ-], -z

parvenu, -s ˈpɑːvənjuː (parvəny), -z
pas (sing.) pɑː, (plur.) -z
Pasadena ˌpæsəˈdiːnə
paschal ˈpɑːskəl [ˈpæs-]
pasha (P.), -s ˈpɑːʃə [ˈpæʃə, pəˈʃɑː], -z
pasquinade, -s ˌpæskwɪˈneɪd, -z
pass (s. v.), -es, -ing, -ed, -er/s pɑːs, -ɪz, -ɪŋ, -t, -ə*/z
passab|le, -ly, -leness ˈpɑːsəb|l, -lɪ, -lnɪs [-nəs]
passacaglia, -s ˌpæsəˈkɑːljə [-lɪə], -z
passag|e (s. v.), -es, -ing, -ed ˈpæsɪdʒ, -ɪz, -ɪŋ, -d
passant (in heraldry) ˈpæsənt, (in chess) ˈpæsɑ̃ːŋ [ˈpɑːs-, -sɔ̃ːŋ, -sɑːŋ, -sɒŋ] (pasɑ̃)
pass-book, -s ˈpɑːsbʊk, -s
Passe (surname) pæs
passé(e) ˈpɑːseɪ [ˈpæs-] (pɑse)
passenger, -s ˈpæsɪndʒə* [-sən-], -z
passe-partout, -s ˈpæspɑːtuː [ˈpɑːs-, -pətuː:, ˌ-ˈ-] (pɑspartu), -z
passer (one who passes), -s ˈpɑːsə*, -z
passer (sparrow), -es ˈpæsə*, -riːz
passer-by, passers-by ˌpɑːsəˈbaɪ, ˌpɑːsəzˈbaɪ
passerine ˈpæsəraɪn
Passfield ˈpæsfiːld [ˈpɑːs-]
passibility ˌpæsɪˈbɪlətɪ [-lɪt-]
passible ˈpæsɪbl
passim ˈpæsɪm
passing-note, -s ˈpɑːsɪŋnəʊt, -s
passion (P.), -s ˈpæʃn, -z
passionate, -ly, -ness ˈpæʃənət [-ʃnət, -ʃnət, -nɪt], -lɪ, -nɪs [-nəs]
passion-flower, -s ˈpæʃn̩ˌflaʊə*, -z
passive, -ly, -ness ˈpæsɪv, -lɪ, -nɪs [-nəs]
passivity pæˈsɪvətɪ [pəˈs-, -ɪtɪ]
pass-key, -s ˈpɑːskiː, -z
pass|man, -men ˈpɑːs|mæn [-mən], -men [-mən]
Passmore ˈpɑːsmɔː* [ˈpæs-, -mɔə*]
Passover, -s ˈpɑːsˌəʊvə*, -z
passport, -s ˈpɑːspɔːt, -s
pass-word, -s ˈpɑːswɜːd, -z
past pɑːst
pasta ˈpæstə [ˈpɑː-]
past|e (s. v.), -es, -ing, -ed peɪst, -s, -ɪŋ, -ɪd
paste-board ˈpeɪstbɔːd [-bɔəd]
pastel (coloured crayon, drawing made with this), -s pæˈstel [ˈpæstel, -təl, -tl], -z
pastel (attributive, as in pastel shade) ˈpæstl [-təl, -tel, rarely pæsˈtel]
pastelist, -s ˈpæstəlɪst, -s
pastellist, -s pæˈstelɪst [ˈpæstəlɪst], -s
pastern, -s ˈpæstɜːn, -z

Pasteur pæsˈtɜː* [pɑːs-] (pastœːr)
pasteurization [-isa-] ˌpæstəraɪˈzeɪʃn
[ˌpɑːs-, -stjʊə-, -stjə-, -stʃə-]
pasteuriz|e [-is|e], -es, -ing, -ed 'pæs-
təraɪz ['pɑːs-, -stjʊə-, -stjə-, -stʃə-],
-ɪz, -ɪŋ, -d
pastiche, -s pæˈstiːʃ [ˈpæstiːʃ], -ɪz
pastille, -s 'pæstəl [-stɪl, -stiːl, pæˈstiːl],
-z
pastime, -s 'pɑːstaɪm, -z
past-master, -s ˌpɑːstˈmɑːstə* ['-ˌ--], -z
Paston 'pæstən
pastor, -s 'pɑːstə*, -z
pastoral (s. adj.), -s 'pɑːstərəl ['pæs-],
-z
pastorale, -s ˌpæstəˈrɑːlɪ, -z
pastoralism 'pɑːstərəlɪzəm ['pæs-]
pastorate, -s 'pɑːstərət [-ɪt], -s
pastr|y, -ies 'peɪstr|ɪ, -ɪz
pastrycook, -s 'peɪstrɪkʊk, -s
pasturage 'pɑːstjʊrɪdʒ [-tjər-, -tʃər-]
pastur|e (s. v.), -es, -ing, -ed 'pɑːstʃə*
[-ˌtjʊə*, -tjə*], -z, -ɪŋ [-tjʊrɪŋ], -d
past|y (s.), -ies 'pæst|ɪ [for the Cornish
kind also 'pɑːs-], -ɪz
past|y (adj.), -ier, -iest, -ily, -iness
'peɪst|ɪ, -ɪə* [-jə*], -ɪɪst [-jɪst], -ɪlɪ
[-əlɪ], -mɪs [-ɪnəs]
pat (s. v. adv.) (P.), -s, -ting, -ted pæt,
-s, -ɪŋ, -ɪd
pat-a-cake, -s 'pætəkeɪk, -s
Patagonia, -n/s ˌpætəˈgəʊnjə [-nɪə],
-n/z
Patara 'pætərə
patch, -es, -ing, -ed; -able, -work pætʃ,
-ɪz, -ɪŋ, -t; -əbl, -wɜːk
patchouli 'pætʃʊlɪ [-liː]
patch|y, -ier, -iest, -ily, -iness 'pætʃ|ɪ,
-ɪə*, -ɪɪst, -ɪlɪ [-əlɪ], -mɪs [-ɪnəs]
pate, -s peɪt, -s
pâté 'pæteɪ ['pɑː-, -tɪ] (pɑte)
Pateley 'peɪtlɪ
patell|a, -as, -ae, -ar pəˈtel|ə, -əz, -iː, -ə*
paten, -s 'pætən, -z
patent (s. adj. v.), -s, -ing, -ed; -able
'peɪtənt ['pæt-], -s, -ɪŋ, -ɪd; -əbl
Note.—'pætənt seems the more usual
in letters patent and Patent Office.
In patent leather, boots, etc.,
'peɪtənt is practically universal;
'peɪtənt seems the more usual,
though by no means universal, in
all other connections.
patentee, -s ˌpeɪtənˈtiː [ˌpæt-], -z
patent leather ˌpeɪtəntˈleðə* [also
'peɪtənt͵l- when attributive]
patently 'peɪtəntlɪ
pater (P.), -s 'peɪtə*, -z

paterfamilias, -es ˌpeɪtəfəˈmɪlɪæs [-ljæs,
-lɪəs, -ljəs], -ɪz
patern|al, -ally, -alism pəˈtɜːn|l, -əlɪ,
-lɪzəm
paternity pəˈtɜːnɪtɪ [-ɪtɪ]
Paternoster (Lord's Prayer), -s ˌpætə-
ˈnɒstə*, -z
Paternoster (Row) 'pætəˌnɒstə*
Paterson 'pætəsn
Pateshall 'pætəʃl [-tɪʃ-]
Patey 'peɪtɪ
pa|th, -ths pɑː|θ, -ðz
Pathan, -s pəˈtɑːn (Hindi pəʈhan), -z
pathetic, -ally pəˈθetɪk, -əlɪ
pathfinder (P.), -s 'pɑːθˌfaɪndə*, -z
pathless 'pɑːθlɪs [-ləs]
pathologic, -al, -ally ˌpæθəˈlɒdʒɪk, -l,
-əlɪ
patholog|ist/s, -y pəˈθɒlədʒ|ɪst/s
[pæ'θ-], -ɪ
pathos 'peɪθɒs
pathway, -s 'pɑːθweɪ, -z
patience (P.), -s 'peɪʃns, -ɪz
patient (adj.), -s, -ly 'peɪʃnt, -s, -lɪ
patina 'pætɪnə
patio, -s 'pætɪəʊ ['pɑːtɪəʊ, 'peɪʃɪəʊ], -z
pâtisserie, -s pəˈtiːsərɪ [pæ-], -z (pɑtisri)
Pat|man, -mos 'pæt|mən, -mɒs
Patmore 'pætmɔː* [-mɔə*]
Patna 'pætnə (Hindi pəʈna)
patois (sing.) 'pætwɑː [-wɔː] (patwa),
(plur.) -z
Paton 'peɪtn
Patras pəˈtræs
patriarch, -s 'peɪtrɪɑːk
patriarchal ˌpeɪtrɪˈɑːkl
patriarchate, -s 'peɪtrɪɑːkɪt [-keɪt, -kət],
-s
Patricia pəˈtrɪʃə [-ʃɪə, -ʃjə]
patrician, -s pəˈtrɪʃn, -z
patriciate pəˈtrɪʃɪət [-ʃjət, -ɪt, -ʃɪeɪt,
-ʃjeɪt]
patricide 'pætrɪsaɪd ['peɪ-]
Patrick 'pætrɪk
patrimonial, -ly ˌpætrɪˈməʊnjəl [-nɪəl],
-ɪ
patrimon|y, -ies 'pætrɪmən|ɪ, -ɪz
patriot, -s 'pætrɪət ['peɪt-], -s
patriotic, -ally ˌpætrɪˈɒtɪk [ˌpeɪt-], -əlɪ
patriotism 'pætrɪətɪzəm ['peɪt-]
patristic pəˈtrɪstɪk
Patroclus pəˈtrɒkləs
patrol (s. v.), -s, -ling, -led; -man, -men
pəˈtrəʊl, -z, -ɪŋ, -d; -mæn, -men
patron, -s 'peɪtrən ['pæt-], -z
patronage 'pætrənɪdʒ [-trʊnɪdʒ, rarely
'peɪt-]
patronal pəˈtrəʊnl [pæˈt-]

patroness, -s 'peɪtrənɪs ['pæt-, -nes, -trn̩-], -ɪz
patroniz|e [-is|e], -es, -ing/ly, -ed, -er/s 'pætrənaɪz [-trn̩aɪz], -ɪz, -ɪŋ/lɪ, -d, -ə*/z
patronymic (s. adj.), -s ˌpætrə'nɪmɪk [-trn̩'ɪm-], -s
patroon, -s pə'truːn, -z
patten, -s 'pætn, -z
patter (s. v.), -s, -ing, -ed, -er/s 'pætə*, -z, -rɪŋ, -d, -rə*/z
Patterdale 'pætədeɪl
pattern, -s 'pætən [-tn̩], -z
Patterson 'pætəsn
Patteson 'pætɪsn [-təsn]
Pattison 'pætɪsn
Pattreiouex 'pætrɪəʊ
patt|y, -ies 'pæt|ɪ, -ɪz
paucity 'pɔːsətɪ [-rtɪ]
Paul, -'s pɔːl, -z
Pauline (scholar of St. Paul's school), -s 'pɔːlaɪn, -z
Pauline (fem. name) pɔː'liːn, 'pɔːliːn
Pauline (adj.) (of St. Paul) 'pɔːlaɪn
Paulinus pɔː'laɪnəs
Paulus 'pɔːləs
Pauncefote 'pɔːnsfʊt [-fət]
paunch, -es pɔːntʃ, -ɪz
pauper, -s 'pɔːpə*, -z
pauperism 'pɔːpərɪzəm
pauperization [-isa-] ˌpɔːpəraɪ'zeɪʃn [-rɪ'z-]
pauperiz|e [-is|e], -es, -ing, -ed 'pɔːpəraɪz, -ɪz, -ɪŋ, -d
Pausanias pɔː'seɪnɪæs [-njæs, -njəs, -nɪəs]
paus|e (s.v.), -es, -ing, -ed pɔːz, -ɪz, -ɪŋ, -d
pavan(e), -s 'pævən [pə'væn, -'vɑːn], -z
pav|e, -es, -ing, -ed, -er/s peɪv, -z, -ɪŋ, -d, -ə*/z
pavé, -s 'pæveɪ (pave), -z
pavement, -s 'peɪvmənt, -s
Pavia pə'viːə [pɑː'v-, -'vɪə] (pa'vi:a)
pavilion (s. v.), -s, -ing, -ed pə'vɪljən [-lɪən], -z, -ɪŋ, -d
paving-stone, -s 'peɪvɪŋstəʊn, -z
paviour, -s 'peɪvjə* [-vɪə*], -s
Pavitt 'pævɪt
Pavlov 'pævlɒv [-lɒf] ('pavləf)
Pavlova 'pævləvə ['pɑːv-, pæv'ləʊvə] ('pavləvə)
paw (s. v.), -s, -ing, -ed pɔː, -z, -ɪŋ, -d
pawk|y, -ier, -iest, -ily, -iness 'pɔːk|ɪ, -ɪə* [-jə*], -ɪɪst [-jɪst], -ɪlɪ [-əlɪ], -ɪnɪs [-ɪnəs]
pawl (s. v.), -s, -ing, -ed pɔːl, -z, -ɪŋ, -d
pawn (s. v.), -s, -ing, -ed, -er/s pɔːn, -z, -ɪŋ, -d, -ə*/z

pawnbrok|er/s, -ing 'pɔːnˌbrəʊk|ə*/z, -ɪŋ
pawnee, -s ˌpɔː'niː, -z
pawnshop, -s 'pɔːnʃɒp, -s
pawn-ticket, -s 'pɔːnˌtɪkɪt, -s
pax (s. interj.), -es pæks, -ɪz
Paxton 'pækstən
pay (s. v.), -s, -ing, paid, payer/s, payment/s peɪ, -z, -ɪŋ, peɪd, 'peɪə*/z, 'peɪmənt/s
payable 'peɪəbl
P.A.Y.E. ˌpiːeɪwaɪ'iː
payee, -s peɪ'iː, -z
Payen-Payne ˌpeɪn'peɪn
paymaster, -s 'peɪˌmɑːstə*, -z
paynim 'peɪnɪm
Paynter 'peɪntə*
pay-roll, -s 'peɪrəʊl, -z
pay-sheet, -s 'peɪʃiːt, -s
pea, -s piː, -z
Peabody 'piːˌbɒdɪ
peace (P.), -s piːs, -ɪz
peaceab|le, -ly, -leness 'piːsəb|l, -lɪ, -lnɪs [-nəs]
peace|ful, -fully, -fulness 'piːs|fʊl, -fʊlɪ [-fəlɪ], -fʊlnɪs [-nəs]
peacemaker, -s 'piːsˌmeɪkə*, -z
peace-offering, -s 'piːsˌɒfərɪŋ, -z
Peacey 'piːsɪ
peach (s. v.), -es, -ing, -ed, -er/s piːtʃ, -ɪz, -ɪŋ, -t, -ə*/z
peach-colour, -ed 'piːtʃˌkʌlə*, -d
Peachey 'piːtʃɪ
pea-chick, -s 'piːtʃɪk, -s
peachy 'piːtʃɪ
peacock (P.), -s 'piːkɒk, -s
pea-fowl 'piːfaʊl
pea-green ˌpiː'griːn ['--, esp. when attributive]
peahen, -s ˌpiː'hen ['--], -z
pea-jacket, -s 'piːˌdʒækɪt, -s
peak (s. v.) (P.), -s, -ing, -ed piːk, -s, -ɪŋ, -t
peal (s. v.), -s, -ing, -ed piːl, -z, -ɪŋ, -d
Peall piːl
pean (fur) piːn
pean (=paean), -s 'piːən, -z
peanut, -s 'piːnʌt, -s
pear, -s peə*, -z
Pear (surname) pɪə*
Pearce pɪəs
Peard pɪəd
pearl (s. v.) (P.), -s, -ing, -ed; -barley, -button/s pɜːl, -z, -ɪŋ, -d; -'bɑːlɪ, -'bʌtn/z
pearl-diver, -s 'pɜːlˌdaɪvə*, -z
pearl-fisher|y, -ies 'pɜːlˌfɪʃər|ɪ, -ɪz
pearlies 'pɜːlɪz

pearly 'pɜːlɪ
pearmain 'pɜːmeɪn, 'peəmeɪn [-'-]
Pearman 'pɪəmən
Pears pɪəz, peəz
Note.—peəz in Pears' soap; pɪəz for
singer.
Pearsall 'pɪəsɔːl [-səl]
pear-shaped 'peəʃeɪpt
Pearson 'pɪəsn
Peart pɪət
Peary 'pɪərɪ
peasant, -s 'peznt, -s
peasantry 'pezntrɪ
peas(e)cod, -s 'piːzkɒd, -z
Peascod (road at Windsor) 'peskəd
pease (P.) piːz
Peaseblossom 'piːz,blɒsəm
pease-pudding ,piːz'pʊdɪŋ
pea-shooter, -s 'piː,ʃuːtə*, -z
pea-soup, -y ,piː'suːp, -ɪ
peat, -bog/s piːt, -bɒg/z
peat-moss 'piːtmɒs [,-'-]
peat|y, -ier, -iest, -iness 'piːt|ɪ, -ɪə*
[-jə*], -ɪɪst [-jɪst], -ɪnɪs [-məs]
pebble, -s 'pebl, -z
pebbly 'peblɪ [-blɪ]
pecan, -s pɪ'kæn, -z
peccability ,pekə'bɪlətɪ [-lɪt-]
peccable 'pekəbl
peccadillo, -(e)s ,pekə'dɪləʊ, -z
peccant, -ly 'pekənt, -lɪ
peccar|y, -ies 'pekər|ɪ, -ɪz
peccavi pe'kɑːviː: [old-fashioned
-'keɪvaɪ]
Pechey 'piːtʃɪ
Pechili 'petʃɪlɪ
peck (s. v.) (P.), -s, -ing, -ed, -er/s pek,
-s, -ɪŋ, -t, -ə*/z
Peckham 'pekəm
peckish, -ly, -ness 'pekɪʃ, -lɪ, -nɪs [-nəs]
Peckitt 'pekɪt
Pecksniff 'peksnɪf
pectoral (s. adj.), -s 'pektərəl, -z
peculat|e, -es, -ing, -ed, -or/s 'pekjʊ-
leɪt [-kjə-], -s, -ɪŋ, -ɪd, -ə*/z
peculation, -s ,pekjʊ'leɪʃn [-kjə-], -z
peculiar (s. adj.), -s, -ly pɪ'kjuːljə*
[pə-, -lɪə*], -z, -lɪ
peculiarit|y, -ies pɪ,kjuːlɪ'ærət|ɪ [pə-,
-ɪt|ɪ], -ɪz
peculium, -s pɪ'kjuːljəm [pə'k-, -lɪəm],
-z
pecuniar|y, -ily pɪ'kjuːnjər|ɪ [-nɪə-],
-əlɪ [-ɪlɪ]
pedagogic, -al ,pedə'gɒdʒɪk [-'gɒgɪk,
-'gəʊdʒɪk], -l
pedagogue, -s 'pedəgɒg, -z
pedagogy 'pedəgɒgɪ [-gɒgɪ, -gəʊdʒɪ]

ped|al (s. v.), -als, -alling, -alled 'ped|l,
-lz, -lɪŋ [-lɪŋ], -ld
pedal (adj.) (pertaining to the foot) 'pedl
['piːdl], (in geometry) 'pedl
pedant, -s 'pedənt, -s
pedantic, -al, -ally pɪ'dæntɪk [pe'd-], -l,
-əlɪ
pedantism 'pedəntɪzəm [-dn-, pɪ'dænt-,
pe'dænt-]
pedantr|y, -ies 'pedəntr|ɪ, -ɪz
pedd|le, -les, -ling, -led 'ped|l, -lz, -lɪŋ
[-lɪŋ], -ld
pederast, -s, -y 'pedəræst ['piː-], -s, -ɪ
pedestal, -s 'pedɪstl, -z
pedestrian (s. adj.), -s, -ism pɪ'destrɪən
[pə'd-], -z, -ɪzəm
pedestrianiz|e [-is|e], -es, -ing, -ed
pɪ'destrɪənaɪz [pə'd-], -ɪz, -ɪŋ, -d
pediatric, -s ,piːdɪ'ætrɪk, -s
pediatrician, -s ,piːdɪə'trɪʃn, -z
pedicle, -s 'pedɪkl, -z
pedicure, -s 'pedɪ,kjʊə* [-kjɔə*, -kjɔː*],
-z
pedigree, -s, -d 'pedɪgriː, -z, -d
pediment, -s 'pedɪmənt, -s
pedimental ,pedɪ'mentl
pedimented 'pedɪmentɪd [-mənt-]
pedlar, -s 'pedlə*, -z
pedometer, -s pɪ'dɒmɪtə* [pe'd-,
-mətə*], -z
Pedro 'peɪdrəʊ ['ped-, 'piːd-]
Note.—The pronunciation 'piːdrəʊ is
generally used in Shakespeare's
'Much Ado.'
peduncle, -s pɪ'dʌŋkl, -z
Peeb|les, -lesshire 'piːb|lz, -lzʃə* [-lʒʃə*,
-lʃə*, -,ʃɪə*]
Peek piːk
peek|y, -ier, -iest 'piːk|ɪ, -ɪə*, -ɪɪst
peel (s. v.) (P.), -s, -ing/s, -ed piːl, -z,
-ɪŋ/z, -d
peeler, -s 'piːlə*, -z
peep (s. v.) (P.), -s, -ing, -ed, -er/s piːp,
-s, -ɪŋ, -t, -ə*/z
peep-bo 'piːpbəʊ
peep-hole, -s 'piːphəʊl, -z
peepshow, -s 'piːpʃəʊ, -z
peer (s. v.), -s, -ing, -ed pɪə*, -z, -rɪŋ, -d
peerage, -s 'pɪərɪdʒ, -ɪz
peeress, -es 'pɪərɪs [-res], -ɪz
peerless (P.), -ly, -ness 'pɪəlɪs [-ləs], -lɪ,
-nɪs [-nəs]
peeved piːvd
peevish, -ly, -ness 'piːvɪʃ, -lɪ, -nɪs [-nəs]
peewit, -s 'piːwɪt, -s
peg (s. v.) (P.), -s, -ging, -ged peg, -z,
-ɪŋ, -d
pegamoid 'pegəmɔɪd

Pegasus 'pegəsəs
Pegeen pe'giːn
Pegge peg
Peggotty 'pegətɪ
Peggy 'pegɪ
Pegr|am, -um 'piːgr|əm, -əm
peg-top, -s 'pegtɒp [ˌ-'-], -s
peignoir, -s 'peɪnwɑː* [-wɔː*] (peɲwaːr),
-z
Peile piːl
Peiping ˌpeɪ'pɪŋ
Peirse pɪəz
pejorative 'piːdʒərətɪv, pɪ'dʒɒrətɪv [pə-]
Pek|in, -ing ˌpiː'k|ɪn, -ɪŋ
Pekinese ˌpiːkɪ'niːz
Pekingese ˌpiːkɪŋ'iːz
pekoe 'piːkəʊ
pelagic pe'lædʒɪk [pɪ'l-]
pelargonium, -s ˌpelɑ'gəʊnjəm [-nɪəm],
-z
Pelasgian, -s pe'læzgɪən [pɪ'l-, -gjən], -z
pelasgic pe'læzgɪk [pɪ'l-, -zdʒɪk]
Peleg 'piːleg [rarely 'pel-]
pelerine, -s 'peləriːn, -z
Peleus 'piːljuːs [-ljəs, -lɪəs]
pelf pelf
Pelham 'peləm
Pelias 'piːlɪæs [-lɪəs, 'pelɪæs]
pelican, -s 'pelɪkən, -z
pelisse, -s pe'liːs [pɪ'l-, pə'l-], -ɪz
pellet, -s 'pelɪt [-lət], -s
Pelley 'pelɪ
pellicle, -s 'pelɪkl, -z
Pellisier pə'lɪsɪeɪ [pe'l-, -sɪə*, -sjə*]
pell-mell ˌpel'mel
pellucid, -ly, -ness pe'ljuːsɪd [pɪ'l-,
-'luː-], -lɪ, -nɪs [-nəs]
Pelly 'pelɪ
Pelman, -ism 'pelmən, -ɪzəm
pelmet, -s 'pelmɪt, -s
Peloponnese 'peləpəniːs [ˌ---'-]
Peloponnesian, -s ˌpeləpə'niːʃn [-ʃjən,
-ʃɪən], -z
Peloponnesus ˌpeləpə'niːsəs
Pelops 'piːlɒps
pelt (s. v.), -s, -ing, -ed pelt, -s, -ɪŋ, -ɪd
pelure pə'ljʊə* [pɪ'l-]
pelv|is, -ises, -es, -ic 'pelv|ɪs, -ɪsɪz, -iːz, -ɪk
Pemberton 'pembətən
Pembridge 'pembrɪdʒ
Pembroke, -shire 'pembrʊk, -ʃə* [-ˌʃɪə*]
Pemigewasset ˌpemɪgə'wɒsɪt
pemmican 'pemɪkən
pen (s. v.) (P.), -s, -ning, -ned pen, -z,
-ɪŋ, -d
pen|al, -ally 'piːn|l, -əlɪ
penaliz|e [-is|e], -es, -ing, -ed 'piːnəlaɪz
[-nļaɪz], -ɪz, -ɪŋ, -d

penalt|y, -ies 'penlt|ɪ, -ɪz
penance, -s 'penəns, -ɪz
pen-and-ink ˌpenəndʹɪŋk
Penang pɪ'næŋ [pə'n-]
Penarth pe'nɑːθ [pə'n-] (Welsh pen'arθ)
penates pe'nɑːteɪz [pe'neɪti:z, pɪ'n-,
pə'n-]
Penberthy 'penbəθɪ, 'penˌbɜːθɪ, 'pen-
ˌbɜːðɪ
pence (plur. of penny; see note under
penny) pens
penchant, -s 'pɑ̃ːŋʃɑ̃ːŋ ['pɔ̃ːŋʃɔ̃ːŋ,
'pɑːŋʃɑːŋ, 'pɒŋʃɒŋ] (pɑ̃ʃɑ̃), -z
penc|il (s. v.), -ils, -illing, -illed 'pens|l,
-lz, -lɪŋ [-əlɪŋ], -ld
pencil-case, -s 'penslkeɪs, -ɪz
pendant, -s 'pendənt, -s
Pendeen pen'diːn
penden|cy, -t 'pendən|sɪ, -t
Pendennis pen'denɪs
Pender 'pendə*
Pendine (in Wales) pen'daɪn (Welsh
pen'dəin)
pending 'pendɪŋ
Pendle|bury, -ton 'pendl|bərɪ, -tən
pendragon (P.), -s pen'drægən, -z
pendulous, -ly, -ness 'pendjʊləs, -lɪ,
-nɪs [-nəs]
pendulum, -s 'pendjʊləm [-djəl-], -z
Pendyce pen'daɪs
Penelope pɪ'neləpɪ [pə'n-]
penetrability ˌpenɪtrə'bɪlətɪ [-lɪt-]
penetrab|le, -ly, -leness 'penɪtrəb|l, -lɪ,
-lnɪs [-nəs]
penetralia ˌpenɪ'treɪljə [-lɪə]
penetrat|e, -es, -ing/ly, -ed 'penɪtreɪt,
-s, -ɪŋ/lɪ, -ɪd
penetration, -s ˌpenɪ'treɪʃn, -z
penetrative, -ly, -ness 'penɪtrətɪv
[-treɪt-], -lɪ, -nɪs [-nəs]
Penfold 'penfəʊld
penful, -s 'penfʊl, -z
Penge pendʒ
penguin, -s 'peŋgwɪn, -z
pen-holder, -s 'penˌhəʊldə*, -z
penicillin ˌpenɪ'sɪlɪn
Penicuik 'penɪkʊk
peninsul|a (P.), -as, -ar pə'nɪnsjʊl|ə
[pɪ'n-, pe'n-, ɪnʃʊl-], əz, ə-*
penis, -es 'piːnɪs, -ɪz
penitence 'penɪtəns
penitent (s. adj.), -s, -ly 'penɪtənt, -s, -lɪ
peniten|tial, -ally ˌpenɪ'ten|ʃl, -əlɪ
penitentiar|y, -ies ˌpenɪ'tenʃər|ɪ, -ɪz
penkni|fe, -ves 'pennaɪ|f, -vz
Penmaenmaur ˌpenmən'maʊə* [-'mɔː*,
-'mɔə*] (Welsh penmaen'maur,
-mən-)

pen|man, -men 'pen|mən, -mən
penmanship 'penmənʃɪp
Penn pen
pen-name, -s 'penneɪm, -z
pennant (P.), -s 'penənt, -s
Pennefather 'penɪ,fɑːðə*, -,feðə*
penniless 'penɪlɪs [-ləs, -les]
Pennine, -s 'penaɪn, -z
Pennington 'penɪŋtən
pennon, -s 'penən, -z
Pennsylvania ,pensɪl'veɪnjə [-s̩-, -nɪə]
penn|y (P.), -ies, pence 'pen|ɪ, -ɪz, pens
   Note.—Since decimilization of the
   currency, the pronunciation of compounds with penny, pence (now
   abbreviated to p) has been uncertain. Formerly, compounds from
   ½d to 11d invariably had -pənɪ,
   -pəns, e.g. see entries under halfpenny, fourpence, etc. With the
   extension of -pence compounds
   beyond 11p, e.g. 12p, the reduced
   forms are falling out of use. Instead,
   the full forms 'penɪ and pens, or
   commonly piː, tend to be used, e.g.
   ½p (formerly 'heɪpənɪ) is ,hɑːfə-
   'penɪ, or ,-'piː, ə,hɑːf'piː or ə'hɑːf
   (plur. hɑːfs); 4p ('fɔːpəns) is ,fɔː-
   'pens or ,-'piː; 5½p (,faɪfpəns'heɪpənɪ) is 'faɪvəndə,hɑːf'pens or
   '---,-'piː; 12p is ,twelv'pens or
   ,-'piː. The plur. pens is also to be
   heard even in ½p and 1p.
penny-a-liner, -s ,penɪə'laɪnə* [-njə-], -z
penny-royal ,penɪ'rɔɪəl
pennyweight, -s 'penɪweɪt, -s
pennyworth, -s 'penəθ ['penɪwəθ, -wɜːθ], -s
Penobscot pe'nɒbskɒt [pə'n-]
penological ,piːnə'lɒdʒɪkl
penology piː'nɒlədʒɪ
Penrhyn 'penrɪn (Welsh 'penhrɪn, 'pen-drɪn)
Penrith (town in Cumbria) 'penrɪθ [pen'r-], (surname) 'penrɪθ
Penrose (surname) 'penrəʊz, pen'r-, (place in Cornwall) pen'rəʊz
Pensarn pen'sɑːn
penseroso ,pensə'rəʊzəʊ
Penshurst 'penzhɜːst
pensi|on (s. v.) (monetary allowance, etc.), -ons, -oning, -oned 'penʃ|n, -nz, -ənɪŋ [-ŋɪŋ], -nd
pension (s.) (boarding-house, board), -s 'pãːŋsiɔ̃ːŋ ['põː-, 'pɑːŋsɪɔ̃ːŋ, 'pɑːns-, -pɒns-, -sjɔ̃ːŋ] (pãsjɔ̃), -z
pensioner, -s 'penʃənə* [-ʃnə*, -ʃnə*], -z

pensionnaire, -s ,pãː-ŋsɪə'neə* [,põː-ŋs-, ,pɑː-ns-, ,pɒns-, -sjə-] (pãsjɔ-neːr), -z
pensive, -ly, -ness 'pensɪv, -lɪ, -nɪs [-nəs]
pent pent
pentad, -s 'pentæd, -z
pentagon (P.), -s 'pentəgən, -z
pentagon|al, -ally pen'tægən|l, -əlɪ
pentagram, -s 'pentəgræm, -z
pentahedr|on, -al ,pentə'hiːdr|ɒn [-ən], -əl
pentamerous pen'tæmərəs
pentameter, -s pen'tæmɪtə* [-mətə*], -z
Pentateuch 'pentətjuːk
pentathlon pen'tæθlɒn [-lən]
pentatol 'pentətɒl
Pentecost, -s 'pentɪkɒst, -s
pentecostal ,pentɪ'kɒstl
Penthesilea ,penθesɪ'liːə [-'lɪə]
penthou|se, -ses 'penthaʊ|s, -zɪz
Pentland, -s 'pentlənd, -z
Pentonville 'pentənvɪl
pentstemon, -s pent'stemən [-'stiːm-, 'pentstɪmən], -z
penult, -s pe'nʌlt [pɪ'n-, pə'n-], -s
penultimate (s. adj.), -s pe'nʌltɪmət [pɪ'n-, pə'n-, -ɪt], -s
penumbr|a, -as, -ae, -al pɪ'nʌmbr|ə [pe'n-, pə'n-], -əz, -iː, -əl
penurious, -ly, -ness pɪ'njʊərɪəs [pe'n-, pə'n-], -lɪ, -nɪs [-nəs]
penury 'penjʊrɪ [-jʊərɪ]
pen-wiper, -s 'pen,waɪpə*, -z
Penzance pen'zæns [pən-, locally pən'zɑːns]
peon, -s (Indian servant) pjuːn ['piːən], (in U.S.A.) 'piːən, -z
peon|y, -ies 'pɪən|ɪ, -ɪz
peop|le (s. v.), -les, -ling, -led 'piːp|l, -lz, -lɪŋ [-lɪŋ], -ld
Peover 'piːvə*
pep, -talk pep, -tɔːk
Pepin 'pepɪn
pepper (s. v.) (P.), -s, -ing, -ed, -er/s 'pepə*, -z, -rɪŋ, -d, -rə*/z
pepper-box, -es 'pepəbɒks, -ɪz
pepper-caster [-tor], -s 'pepə,kɑːstə*, -z
pepper-corn, -s 'pepəkɔːn, -z
peppermint, -s 'pepəmɪnt [-mənt, 'pepmɪnt, 'pepmənt], -s
pepper-pot, -s 'pepəpɒt, -s
pepper|y, -ily, -iness 'pepər|ɪ, -əlɪ [-ɪlɪ], -ɪnɪs [-məs]
pep|sin, -tic 'pep|sɪn, -tɪk
peptone, -s 'peptəʊn, -z
peptoniz|e [-is|e], -es, -ing, -ed 'peptənaɪz, -ɪz, -ɪŋ, -d

Pepys 'pepɪs, piːps, peps
  Note.—The pronunciation in the family of the present Lord Cottenham is 'pepɪs. *Samuel Pepys is generally referred to as* piːps.
per pɜː:* (*strong form*), pə* (*weak form*)
Pera 'pɪərə
peradventure pərəd'ventʃə* [ˌpɜː:rəd'v-, ˌperə-]
Perak 'peərə ['pɪərə, pə'ræk, pɪ'r-, pe'r-]
  Note.—Those who have lived in Malaya pronounce 'peərə *or* 'pɪərə.
perambulat|e, -es, -ing, -ed pə'ræmbjuleɪt, -s, -ɪŋ, -ɪd
perambulation, -s pəˌræmbju'leɪʃn, -z
perambulator, -s pə'ræmbjuleɪtə* ['præm-], -z
per annum pər'ænəm
per capita pə'kæpɪtə [ˌpɜː:-]
perceivab|le, -ly pə'siːvəb|l [pɜː:'s-], -lɪ
perceiv|e, -es, -ing, -ed, -er/s pə'siːv, -z, -ɪŋ, -d, -ə*/z
per cent pə'sent
percentage, -s pə'sentɪdʒ, -ɪz
percept, -s 'pɜː:sept, -s
perceptibility pəˌseptə'bɪlətɪ [-tɪ'b-, -lɪt-]
perceptib|le, -ly -leness pə'septəb|l [-tɪb-], -lɪ, -lnɪs [-nəs]
perception, -s pə'sepʃn, -z
perceptive, -ly, -ness pə'septɪv, -lɪ, -nɪs [-nəs]
Perceval 'pɜː:sɪvl
perch (*s. v.*), **-es, -ing, -ed, -er/s** pɜː:tʃ, -ɪz, -ɪŋ, -t, -ə*/z
perchance pə'tʃɑːns [ˌpɜː:'tʃ-]
Percheron, -s 'pɜː:ʃərɒn (perʃərɔ̃), -z
percipien|ce, -t/s pə'sɪpɪən|s [-pjən-], -t/s
Percival 'pɜː:sɪvl
percolat|e, -es, -ing, -ed, -or/s 'pɜː:kəleɪt, -s, -ɪŋ, -ɪd, -ə*/z
percolation, -s ˌpɜː:kə'leɪʃn, -z
per contra ˌpɜː:'kɒntrə
percuss, -es, -ing, -ed pə'kʌs, -ɪz, -ɪŋ, -t
percussion, -s; -cap/s pə'kʌʃn, -z; -kæp/s
percussive pə'kʌsɪv
percutaneous, -ly ˌpɜː:kju'teɪnjəs [-kjʊ't-, -nɪəs], -lɪ
Percy 'pɜː:sɪ
per diem ˌpɜː:'daɪem [-'diːem]
Perdita 'pɜː:dɪtə
perdition pə'dɪʃn
perdu(e) pɜː:'dju:
peregrin (*s. adj.*), **-s** 'perɪgrɪn [-rəg-], -z
peregrinat|e, -es, -ing, -ed, -or/s 'perɪgrɪneɪt [-rəg-], -s, -ɪŋ, -ɪd, -ə*/z
peregrination, -s ˌperɪgrɪ'neɪʃn [-rəg-], -z

peregrine (*s. adj.*), **-s** 'perɪgrɪn [-rəg-, -griːn], -z
Peregrine (*personal name*) 'perɪgrɪn [-rəg-]
peremptor|y, -ily, -iness pə'remptər|ɪ [pɪ'rem-, 'perəm-], -əlɪ [-ɪlɪ], -ɪnɪs [-məs]
  Note.—'perəm- *is more usual when the word is used as a legal term. Otherwise* pə'rem- *and* pɪ'rem- *are probably commoner.*
perennial (*s. adj.*), **-s, -ly** pə'renjəl [pɪ'r-, -nɪəl], -z, -ɪ
perfec|t (*s. adj.*), **-ts, -tly, -tness** 'pɜː:fɪk|t, -ts, -tlɪ, -tnɪs [-nəs]
perfect (*v.*), **-s, -ing, -ed** pə'fekt [pɜː:'f-, 'pɜː:fɪkt], -s, -ɪŋ, -ɪd
perfectibility pəˌfektɪ'bɪlətɪ [pɜː:ˌf-, -tə'b-, -lɪt-]
perfectible pə'fektəbl [pɜː:'f-, -tɪb-]
perfection, -s, -ist/s pə'fekʃn, -z, -ɪst/s
perfervid pɜː:'fɜː:vɪd
perfidious, -ly, -ness pə'fɪdɪəs [pɜː:'f-, -djəs], -lɪ, -nɪs [-nəs]
perfid|y, -ies 'pɜː:fɪd|ɪ, -ɪz
perforable 'pɜː:fərəbl
perforate (*adj.*) 'pɜː:fərɪt [-rət]
perforat|e (*v.*), **-es, -ing, -ed, -or/s** 'pɜː:fəreɪt, -s, -ɪŋ, -ɪd, -ə*/z
perforation, -s ˌpɜː:fə'reɪʃn, -z
perforce pə'fɔː:s [pɜː:'f-]
perform, -s, -ing, -ed, -er/s; -able, -ance/s pə'fɔː:m, -z, -ɪŋ, -d, -ə*/z; -əbl, -əns/ɪz
perfume (*s.*), **-s** 'pɜː:fju:m, -z
perfum|e (*v.*), **-es, -ing, -ed** pə'fju:m [pɜː:'f-, 'pɜː:f-], -z, -ɪŋ, -d
perfumed (*adj.*) 'pɜː:fju:md
perfum|er, -ers; -ery pə'fju:m|ə* [pɜː:'f-], -əz; -ərɪ
perfunctor|y, -ily, -iness pə'fʌŋktər|ɪ [pɜː:'f-], -əlɪ [-ɪlɪ], -ɪnɪs [-ɪnəs]
Perga, -mos 'pɜː:gə, -mɒs
Pergam|um, -us 'pɜː:gəm|əm, -əs
pergola, -s 'pɜː:gələ, -z
Pergolese ˌpɜː:gəʊ'leɪzɪ [ˌpeəg-]
Perham 'perəm
perhaps pə'hæps, præps
  *Note.—*pə'hæps *is more usual in formal speech, and in colloquial when the word is said in isolation or used parenhetically (as˘ in* **You know, perhaps**, *. . .*). *præps is common in other situations, esp. initially (e.g. in* **Perhaps we shall, Perhaps it is a mistake**).
peri, -s 'pɪərɪ, -z
pericarditis ˌperɪkɑ:'daɪtɪs

373

pericardium, -s ˌperɪˈkɑːdjəm [-dɪəm], -z
pericarp, -s ˈperɪkɑːp, -s
Pericles ˈperɪkliːz
pericope pəˈrɪkəpɪ [pɪˈr-, peˈr-]
peridot, -s ˈperɪdɒt, -s
perigee, -s ˈperɪdʒiː, -z
periheli|on, -a ˌperɪˈhiːljən [-lɪ|ən], -ə
peril, -s ˈperəl [-rɪl], -z
perilous, -ly, -ness ˈperələs [-rɪləs, -r|əs], -lɪ, -nɪs [-nəs]
Perim ˈperɪm
perimeter, -s pəˈrɪmɪtə* [pɪˈr-, peˈr-, -mətə*], -z
period, -s ˈpɪərɪəd, -z
periodic ˌpɪərɪˈɒdɪk
periodic|al (s. adj.), -als, -ally ˌpɪərɪˈɒd-ɪk|l, -lz, -əlɪ
periodicit|y, -ies ˌpɪərɪəˈdɪsət|ɪ [-rɪɒˈd-, -rt|ɪ], -ɪz
peripatetic, -ally ˌperɪpəˈtetɪk, -əlɪ
peripher|y, -ies, -al pəˈrɪfər|ɪ [pɪˈr-, peˈr-], -ɪz, -əl
periphras|is, -es pəˈrɪfrəs|ɪs [pɪˈr-, peˈr-], -iːz
periphrastic, -al, -ally ˌperɪˈfræstɪk, -l, -əlɪ
periscope, -s ˈperɪskəup, -s
perish, -es, -ing/ly, -ed ˈperɪʃ, -ɪz, -ɪŋ/lɪ, -t
perishability ˌperɪʃəˈbɪlətɪ [-lɪt-]
perishab|le, -ly, -leness ˈperɪʃəb|l, -lɪ, -lnɪs [-nəs]
perispomenon ˌperɪˈspəumɪnən [-nɒn]
peristalsis ˌperɪˈstælsɪs
peristaltic ˌperɪˈstæltɪk
peristyle, -s ˈperɪstaɪl, -z
peritoneum, -s ˌperɪtəʊˈniːəm [-ˈnɪəm], -z
peritonitis ˌperɪtəʊˈnaɪtɪs
Perivale ˈperɪveɪl
periwig, -s ˈperɪwɪg, -z
periwinkle, -s ˈperɪˌwɪŋkl, -z
Perizzite, -s ˈperɪzaɪt, -s
perj|ure, -ures, -uring, -ured, -urer/s ˈpɜːdʒ|ə*, -əz, -ərɪŋ, -əd, -ərə*/z
perjur|y, -ies ˈpɜːdʒər|ɪ, -ɪz
perk, -s, -ing, -ed pɜːk, -s, -ɪŋ, -t
Perkin, -s ˈpɜːkɪn, -z
perk|y, -ier, -iest, -ily, -iness ˈpɜːk|ɪ, -ɪə* [-jə*], -ɪɪst [-jɪst], -ɪlɪ [-əlɪ], -ɪnɪs [-ɪnəs]
Perlis ˈpɜːlɪs
perm, -s pɜːm, -z
permanenc|e, -es, -y, -ies ˈpɜːmənəns, -ɪz, -ɪ, -ɪz
permanent, -ly ˈpɜːmənənt, -lɪ
permanganate pɜːˈmæŋɡəneɪt [pəˈm-, -nɪt, -nət]

permeability ˌpɜːmjəˈbɪlətɪ [-mɪə-, -lɪt-]
permeable ˈpɜːmjəbl [-mɪə-]
permeat|e, -es, -ing, -ed ˈpɜːmɪeɪt [-mjert], -s, -ɪŋ, -ɪd
permeation ˌpɜːmɪˈeɪʃn
permissib|le, -ly, -leness pəˈmɪsəb|l [-sɪb-], -lɪ, -lnɪs [-nəs]
permission, -s pəˈmɪʃn, -z
permissive, -ly, -ness pəˈmɪsɪv, -lɪ, -nɪs [-nəs]
permit (s.), -s ˈpɜːmɪt, -s
permit (v.), -s, -ting, -ted pəˈmɪt, -s, -ɪŋ, -ɪd
permutation, -s ˌpɜːmjuːˈteɪʃn [-mjʊˈt-], -z
permut|e, -es, -ing, -ed; -able pəˈmjuːt, -s, -ɪŋ, -ɪd; -əbl
Pernambuco ˌpɜːnæmˈbuːkəʊ [-nəm-]
pernicious, -ly, -ness pəˈnɪʃəs [pɜːˈn-], -lɪ, -nɪs [-nəs]
pernicket|y, -iness pəˈnɪkət|ɪ [-ɪt|ɪ], -mɪs [-ɪnəs]
perorat|e, -es, -ing, -ed ˈperəreɪt [-rɒr-], -s, -ɪŋ, -ɪd
peroration, -s ˌperəˈreɪʃn [-rɒˈr-], -z
Perouse pəˈruːz [pɪˈr-, peˈr-]
Perowne pəˈrəʊn [pɪˈr-, peˈr-]
peroxide, -s pəˈrɒksaɪd, -z
perpend, -s, -ing, -ed pəˈpend, -z, -ɪŋ, -ɪd
perpendicular (s. adj.), -s, -ly ˌpɜːpənˈdɪkjʊlə* [ˌpɜːpmˈd-, -kjəl-], -z, -lɪ
perpendicularity ˈpɜːpənˌdɪkjʊˈlærətɪ [ˈpɜːpmˌd-, -kjəˈl-, -rɪt]
perpetrat|e, -es, -ing, -ed, -or/s ˈpɜːpɪtreɪt [-pətr-], -s, -ɪŋ, -ɪd, -ə*/z
perpetration, -s ˌpɜːpɪˈtreɪʃn [-pəˈtr-], -z
perpetual, -ly pəˈpetjʊəl [-tʃwəl, -tʃʊl, -tjʊəl, -tjwəl, -tjʊl], -ɪ
perpetuat|e, -es, -ing, -ed pəˈpetjʊeɪt [pɜː-ˈp-, -ˈpetjʊ-], -s, -ɪŋ, -ɪd
perpetuation, -s pəˌpetjʊˈeɪʃn [pɜːˌp-, -ˌpetjʊ-], -z
perpetuit|y, -ies ˌpɜːpɪˈtjuːət|ɪ [-pəˈt-, -tjʊ-, -rt|ɪ], -ɪz
perpetuum mobile pəˌpetjʊʊmˈməʊbɪleɪ [pɜːˌp-, -ˌpetjʊ-, -lɪ]
perplex, -es, -ing/ly, -ed, -edly, -edness pəˈpleks, -ɪz, -ɪŋ/lɪ, -t, -ɪdlɪ [-tlɪ], -ɪdnɪs [-tnɪs, -nəs]
perplexit|y, -ies pəˈpleksət|ɪ [-ɪt|ɪ], -ɪz
perquisite, -s ˈpɜːkwɪzɪt, -s
Perrault ˈperəʊ (pεro)
Perrett ˈperɪt
Perrier ˈperɪeɪ [-rɪə*] (pεrje)
Perrin ˈperɪn
perr|y (P.), -ies ˈper|ɪ, -ɪz
Perse pɜːs

per se ˌpɜː'seɪ [-'siː]
persecut|e, -es, -ing, -ed, -or/s 'pɜːsɪ-
kjuːt, -s, -ɪŋ, -ɪd, -ə*/z
persecution, -s ˌpɜːsɪ'kjuːʃn, -z
Persephone pɜː'sefənɪ [-fn̩ɪ]
Persepolis pɜː'sepəlɪs
Perseus 'pɜːsjuːs [-sjəs, -sɪəs]
perseveration pəˌsevə'reɪʃn [pɜːˌs-]
persever|e, -es, -ing/ly, -ed; -ance
ˌpɜːsɪ'vɪə*, -z, -rɪŋ/lɪ, -d; -rəns
Pershing 'pɜːʃɪŋ
Persi|a, -an/s 'pɜːʃ|ə [rarely 'pɜːʒ|ə],
-n/z
persiflage ˌpɜːsɪ'flɑːʒ [ˌpeəs-, '---] (persi-
flaːʒ)
persimmon (P.), -s pɜː'sɪmən, -z
persist, -s, -ing/ly, -ed pə'sɪst, -s, -ɪŋ/lɪ,
-ɪd
persisten|ce, -cy pə'sɪstən|s, -sɪ
persistent, -ly pə'sɪstənt, -lɪ
person, -s 'pɜːsn, -z
person|a, -ae pɜː'səʊn|ə, -iː [-aɪ]
persona (non) grata pɜːˌsəʊnə (nɒn)
'grɑːtə [pəˌs-, -'greɪtə]
personable 'pɜːsn̩əbl [-sənə-, -snə-]
personage, -s 'pɜːsn̩ɪdʒ [-sənɪdʒ, -snɪdʒ],
-ɪz
pers|onal, -onally 'pɜːs|n̩| [-n̩l, -ənl],
-nəlɪ [-n̩əlɪ, -n̩lɪ, -nlɪ, -ənlɪ]
personalit|y, -ies ˌpɜːsə'nælət|ɪ [-sn̩'æ-,
-ɪt|ɪ], -ɪz
personaliz|e [is|e], -es, -ing, -ed
'pɜːsn̩əlaɪz [-snəl-, -sn̩l-, -snl-,
-sənəl-], -ɪz, -ɪŋ, -d
personalt|y, -ies 'pɜːsn̩lt|ɪ [-snəl-, -sənl-,
-sn̩l-], -ɪz
personat|e, -es, -ing, -ed, -or/s 'pɜːsən-
eɪt [-sn̩eɪt], -s, -ɪŋ, -ɪd, -ə*/z
personation, -s ˌpɜːsə'neɪʃn [-sn̩'eɪ-], -s
personification, -s pɜːˌsɒnɪfɪ'keɪʃn
[pəˌs-], -z
personi|fy, -fies, -fying, -fied pɜː'sɒnɪ|-
faɪ [pə's-], -faɪz, -faɪɪŋ, -faɪd
personnel, -s ˌpɜːsə'nel [-sn̩'el], -z
perspective (s. adj.), -s, -ly pə'spektɪv
[pɜː's-], -z, -lɪ
perspex 'pɜːspeks
perspicacious, -ly, -ness ˌpɜːspɪ'keɪʃəs,
-lɪ, -nɪs [-nəs]
perspicacity ˌpɜːspɪ'kæsətɪ [-ɪtɪ]
perspicuity ˌpɜːspɪ'kjuːətɪ [-kjʊ-, -ɪtɪ]
perspicuous, -ly, -ness pə'spɪkjʊəs
[pɜː's-, -kjwəs], -lɪ, -nɪs [-nəs]
perspiration ˌpɜːspə'reɪʃn
perspir|e, -es, -ing, -ed pə'spaɪə*, -z,
-rɪŋ, -d
persuad|e, -es, -ing, -ed, -er/s pə'sweɪd,
-z, -ɪŋ, -ɪd, -ə*/z

persuasion, -s pə'sweɪʒn, -z
persuasive, -ly, -ness pə'sweɪsɪv [-eɪzɪv],
-lɪ, -nɪs [-nəs]
pert, -est, -ly, -ness pɜːt, -ɪst, -lɪ, -nɪs
[-nəs]
pertain, -s, -ing, -ed pɜː'teɪn [pə't-], -z,
-ɪŋ, -d
Perth, -shire pɜːθ, -ʃə* [-,ʃɪə*]
pertinacious, -ly, -ness ˌpɜːtɪ'neɪʃəs, -lɪ,
-nɪs [-nəs]
pertinacity ˌpɜːtɪ'næsətɪ [-ɪtɪ]
pertinen|ce, -cy, -t/ly 'pɜːtɪnən|s, -sɪ,
-t/lɪ
perturb, -s, -ing, -ed, -er/s; -able
pə'tɜːb [pɜː't-], -z, -ɪŋ, -d, -ə*/z; -əbl
perturbation, -s ˌpɜːtə'beɪʃn [-tɜː'b-], -z
Pertwee 'pɜːtwiː
Peru pə'ruː [pɪ'r-]
Perugia pə'ruːdʒə [pɪ'r-, pe'r-, -dʒɪə,
-dʒə] (pe'ruːdʒa)
Perugino ˌperuː'dʒiːnəʊ [-rʊ'dʒ-] (peru-
'dʒiːno)
peruke, -s pə'ruːk [pɪ'r-, pe'r-], -s
perusal, -s pə'ruːzl [pɪ'r-, pe'r-], -z
perus|e, -es, -ing, -ed, -er/s pə'ruːz
[pɪ'r-, pe'r-], -ɪz, -ɪŋ, -d, -ə*/z
Peruvian, -s pə'ruːvjən [pɪ'r-, pe'r-,
-vɪən], -z
pervad|e, -es, -ing, -ed pə'veɪd [pɜː'v-],
-z, -ɪŋ, -ɪd
pervasion pə'veɪʒn [pɜː'v-]
pervasive pə'veɪsɪv [pɜː'v-]
perverse, -ly, -ness pə'vɜːs [pɜː'v-], -lɪ,
-nɪs [-nəs]
perversion, -s pə'vɜːʃn [pɜː'v-], -z
perversity pə'vɜːsətɪ [pɜː'v-, -ɪtɪ]
pervert (s.), -s 'pɜːvɜːt, -s
pervert (v.), -s, -ing, -ed, -er/s pə'vɜːt
[pɜː'v-], -s, -ɪŋ, -ɪd, -ə*/z
pervious, -ly, -ness 'pɜːvjəs [-vɪəs], -lɪ,
-nɪs [-nəs]
Pescadores ˌpeskə'dɔːrɪz
peseta, -s pə'seɪtə [pɪ's-, -'setə] (pe'seta),
-z
Peshawar pə'ʃɔːə* [pe'ʃ-, -'ʃaʊə*]
pesk|y, -ier, -iest, -ily, -iness 'peskɪ,
ɪə* [-jə*], -ɪɪst [-jɪst], -ɪlɪ [-əlɪ], -ɪnɪs
[-nəs]
peso, -s 'peɪsəʊ, -z
pessar|y, -ies 'pesər|ɪ, -ɪz
pessimi|sm, -st/s 'pesɪmɪ|zəm [-səm-],
-st/s
pessimistic, -al, -ally ˌpesɪ'mɪstɪk
[-sə'm-], -l, -əlɪ
pest (P.), -s pest, -s
Pestalozzi ˌpestə'lɒtsɪ (pesta'lɔttsi)
pest|er, -ers, -ering/ly, -ered, -erer/s
'pest|ə*, -əz, -ərɪŋ/lɪ, -əd, -ərə*/z

Pest(h) pest
pesticide, -s 'pestısaıd, -z
pestiferous, -ly pe'stıfərəs, -lı
pestilence, -s 'pestıləns, -ız
pestilent, -ly 'pestılənt, -lı
pestilenti|al, -ally ˌpestı'lenʃ|l, -əlı
pe|stle (s. v.), -stles, -stling, -stled 'pe|sl
  [-stl], -slz [-stlz], -slıŋ [-slıŋ, -stlıŋ,
  -stlıŋ], -sld [-stld]
pestolog|ist/s, -y pe'stɒlədʒ|ıst/s, -ı
pet (s. v.), -s, -ting, -ted pet, -s, -ıŋ, -ıd
petal, -s, -(l)ed 'petl, -z, -d
petaline 'petəlaın
petard, -s pe'tɑːd [pı't-], -z
Pete piːt
Peter 'piːtə*
Peterborough [-boro'] 'piːtəbrə [-bərə,
  -bʌrə]
Peterculter 'piːtəkuːtə*
Peterhead ˌpiːtə'hed
Peters 'piːtəz
Petersburg 'piːtəzbɜːg
Petersfield 'piːtəzfiːld
petersham (P.), -s 'piːtəʃəm, -z
Pethick 'peθık
petite pə'tiːt
petiti|on (s. v.), -ons, -oning, -oned,
  -oner/s pı'tıʃ|n [pə't-], -nz, -nıŋ
  [-ənıŋ, -nıŋ], -nd, -nə*/z [-ənə*/z,
  -nə*/z]
Peto 'piːtəu
Petrarch 'petrɑːk [old-fashioned 'piːt-]
Petre 'piːtə*
petrel, -s 'petrəl, -z
Petrie 'piːtrı
petrifaction ˌpetrı'fækʃn
petri|fy, -fies, -fying, -fied 'petrı|faı,
  -faız, -faıŋ, -faıd
Petrograd 'petrəugræd [-grɑːd]
petr|ol (s. v.), -ols, -oling, -oled 'petr|əl
  [-r|ɒl], -əlz [-ɒlz], -əlıŋ [-|ıŋ, -ɒlıŋ],
  -əld [-ɒld]
petroleum pı'trəuljəm [pə't-, -lıəm]
Petruchio pı'truːkıəu [pə't-, pe't-,
  -kjəu, -tʃıəu, -tʃjəu]
Pett pet
petticoat, -s, -ed 'petıkəut, -s, -ıd
pettifogg|er/s, -ery, -ing 'petıfɒg|ə*/z,
  -ərı, -ıŋ
Pettigrew 'petıgruː
pettish, -ly, -ness 'petıʃ, -lı, -nıs [-nəs]
Pettit 'petıt
pettitoes 'petıtəuz
pett|y, -ier, -iest, -ily, -iness/es 'petı|ı,
  -ıə*, -ııst, -ılı [-əlı], -ı:nıs [-ınəs]/ız
Petula pə'tjuːlə [pı't-, pe't-]
petulan|ce, -cy 'petjulən|s, -sı
petulant, -ly 'petjulənt, -lı

Petulengro ˌpetju'leŋgrəu [-tə'l-]
petunia, -s pı'tjuːnjə [pə't-, -nıə], -z
Peugeot (car), -s 'pɜːʒəu (pøʒo), -z
Pevensey 'pevənzı
Peveril 'pevərıl
pew, -s pjuː, -z
pew-holder, -s 'pjuːˌhəuldə*, -z
pewit, -s 'piːwıt, -s
pew|-opener/s, -rent/s 'pjuːˌ|ˌəupnə*/z,
  -rent/s
pewter, -s 'pjuːtə*, -z
Peynell 'peınl [-nel]
Peyton 'peıtn
pfennig, -s 'pfenıg ('pfeniç), -z
Phaedo 'fiːdəu
Phaedr|a, -us 'fiːdr|ə, -əs
Phaer 'feıə*
Phaethon 'feıəθən ['fenθ-]
phaeton, -s 'feıtn, -z
phagocyte, -s 'fægəusaıt, -s
phalange, -s 'fælændʒ, -ız
phalanges (alternative plur. of phalanx)
  fæ'lændʒiːz [fə'l-]
phalangist (F.), -s fæ'lændʒıst [fə-], -s
phalanster|y, -ies 'fælənstər|ı, -ız
phalanx, -es 'fælæŋks [rarely 'feıl-], -ız
Phalaris 'fælərıs
phalarope, -s 'fælərəup, -s
phallic 'fælık
phallicism 'fælısızəm
phallus, -es 'fæləs, -ız
phanerogam, -s 'fænərəugæm, -z
phanerogamic ˌfænərəu'gæmık
phanerogamous ˌfænə'rɒgəməs
phantasm, -s 'fæntæzəm, -z
phantasmagoria ˌfæntæzmə'gɒrıə [-təz-,
  -'gɔːr-]
phantasmagoric ˌfæntæzmə'gɒrık
  [-təz-]
phantasm|al, -ally, -ic fæn'tæzm|l, -əlı,
  -ık
phantom, -s 'fæntəm, -z
Pharamond 'færəmənd [-mɒnd]
Pharaoh, -s 'feərəu, -z
pharisaic, -al, -ally, -alness ˌfærı'seıık
  [-'zeıık], -l, -əlı, -lnıs [-nəs]
pharisaism 'færıseıızəm
pharisee (P.), -s 'færısiː, -z
pharmaceutic, -al, -ally, -s ˌfɑːmə-
  'sjuːtık [-'suː-, -'kjuː-], -l, -əlı, -s
pharmac|ist/s, -y, -ies 'fɑːməs|ıst/s, -ı,
  -ız
pharmacolog|ist/s, -y ˌfɑːmə'kɒlədʒ|-
  ıst/s, -ı
pharmacopoeia, -s, -l ˌfɑːməkə'piːə
  [-kəu'p-, -'pıə], -z, -l
Pharos 'feərɒs
Pharsalia fɑː'seıljə [-lıə]

pharyngal fəˈrɪŋgl [fæˈr-, feəˈr-]
pharyngeal ˌfærɪnˈdʒiːəl [ˌfeər-, -ˈdʒɪəl, fəˈrɪndʒɪəl, fæˈrɪndʒ-, feəˈrɪndʒ-, -ˈrɪndʒjəl]
pharyngitis ˌfærɪnˈdʒaɪtɪs [ˌfeər-]
pharynx, -es ˈfærɪŋks [ˈfeər-], -ɪz
phase, -s feɪz, -ɪz
phas|is, -es ˈfeɪs|ɪs, -iːz
phatic ˈfætɪk
Phayre (fem. Christian name) feə*
Ph.D., -'s ˌpiːeɪtʃˈdiː-, -z
Phear feə*
pheasant, -s ˈfeznt, -s
Phebe ˈfiːbɪ
Phelps felps
phenacetin frˈnæsɪtɪn [feˈn-, fəˈn-, -sət-]
Phenice frˈnaɪsɪ [fiːˈn-, -siː]
Pheni|cia, -cian/s frˈnɪ|ʃɪə [fiːˈn-, -ʃjə, -ʃə, -sɪə, -sjə], -ʃɪən/z [-ʃjən/z, -ʃn/z, -sɪən/z, -sjən/z]
phenobarbitone ˌfiːnəʊˈbɑːbɪtəʊn
phenol ˈfiːnɒl
phenolphthalein ˌfiːnɒlˈfθælɪn
phenomen|on, -a, -al, -ally fəˈnɒmɪn|ən [fɪ-], -ə, -l, -əlɪ
phew φːˌ ẙ ːˌ pẙ ːˌ ẙ uːˌ ẙ ụ ː [fjuː]
phi, -s faɪ, -z
phial, -s ˈfaɪəl, -z
Phidias ˈfɪdɪæs [ˈfaɪd-]
Philadelphia, -n/s ˌfɪləˈdelfjə [-frə], -n/z
philander, -s, -ing, -ed, -er/s frˈlændə*, -z, -rɪŋ, -d, -rə*/z
philanthrope, -s ˈfɪlənθrəʊp, -s
philanthropic, -al, -ally ˌfɪlənˈθrɒpɪk, -l, -əlɪ
philanthrop|ist/s, -y frˈlænθrəp|ɪst/s, -ɪ
philatelic ˌfɪləˈtelɪk [ˌfaɪl-]
philatel|ist, -y frˈlætəl|ɪst/s, -ɪ
Philbrick ˈfɪlbrɪk
Philemon frˈliːmɒn [faɪˈl-, -mən]
philharmonic (s. adj.), -s ˌfɪlɑːˈmɒnɪk [-ləˈm-, -lhɑːˈm-], -s
philhellene, -s ˈfɪlˌheliːn [ˌˈ-ˈ-], -z
philhellenic ˌfɪlheˈliːnɪk
philhellenism fɪlˈhelɪnɪzəm
philibeg, -s ˈfɪlɪbeg, -z
Philip, -pa ˈfɪlɪp, -ə
Philippi frˈlɪpaɪ [ˈ---]
Philippian, -s frˈlɪpɪən [-pjən], -z
Philippic, -s frˈlɪpɪk, -s
Philippine, -s ˈfɪlɪpiːn [old-fashioned -paɪn], -z
Philip(p)s ˈfɪlɪps
Philistia frˈlɪstjə [-tɪə]
philistine (P.), -s ˈfɪlɪstaɪn [rarely -tɪn], -z
philistinism ˈfɪlɪstɪnɪzəm
Phillimore ˈfɪlɪmɔː* [-mɔə*]

Phillip(p)s ˈfɪlɪps
Phillpot, -s ˈfɪlpɒt, -s
Philoctetes ˌfɪləkˈtiːtiːz [-lɒk-]
philologic, -al, -ally ˌfɪləˈlɒdʒɪk, -l, -əlɪ
philolog|ist/s, -y frˈlɒlədʒ|ɪst/s, -ɪ
Philomel, -s ˈfɪləmel [-ləʊm-], -z
Philomela ˌfɪləʊˈmiːlə
Philonous ˈfɪləʊnaʊs
philosopher, -s frˈlɒsəfə* [fə-, -pzə-], -z
philosophic, -al, -ally ˌfɪləˈsɒfɪk [-əˈzɒ-], -l, -əlɪ
philosophi|sm, -st/s frˈlɒsəfɪ|zəm [fə-, -pzə-], -st/s
philosophiz|e [-is|e], -es, -ing, -ed frˈlɒsəfaɪz [fə-, -pzə-], -ɪz, -ɪŋ, -d
philosoph|y, -ies frˈlɒsəf|ɪ [fə-, -pzə-], -ɪz
Philostratus frˈlɒstrətəs
Philpot, -ts ˈfɪlpɒt, -s
philtre [-ter], -s ˈfɪltə*, -z
Phineas ˈfɪnɪæs [-nɪəs]
Phinees ˈfɪnɪəs [-nɪes]
Phinehas ˈfɪnɪæs [-nɪəs]
Phip|ps, -son ˈfɪp|s, -sn
phiz (P.) fɪz
Phizackerley frˈzækəlɪ
phlebitic flrˈbɪtɪk [fliːˈb-, fleˈb-]
phlebitis flrˈbaɪtɪs [fliːˈb-, fleˈb-]
phlebotomy flrˈbɒtəmɪ [fliːˈb-, fleˈb-]
Phlegethon ˈflegɪθɒn [-θən]
phlegm, -s flem, -z
phlegmatic, -al, -ally flegˈmætɪk, -l, -əlɪ
phlogistic flɒˈdʒɪstɪk [-ɒˈgɪ-]
phlogiston flɒˈdʒɪstən [-ɒˈgɪ-, -tɒn]
phlox, -es flɒks, -ɪz
phob|ia, -ias, -ic ˈfəʊb|jə [-b|ɪə], -jəz [-ɪəz], -ɪk
Phocian, -s ˈfəʊʃjən [-ʃɪən, -sjən, -sɪən], -z
Phocion ˈfəʊsjən [-sɪən, -sɪɒn, -sjɒn]
Phocis ˈfəʊsɪs
Phoeb|e, -us ˈfiːb|ɪ, -əs
Phoeni|cia, -cian/s frˈnɪ|ʃɪə [fiːˈn-, -ʃjə, -ʃə, -sɪə, -sjə], -ʃɪən/z [-ʃjən/z, -ʃn/z, -sɪən/z, -sjən/z]
phoenix (P.), -es ˈfiːnɪks, -ɪz
phon, -s fɒn, -z
phonat|e, -es, -ing, -ed fəʊˈneɪt, -s, -ɪŋ, -ɪd
phonation fəʊˈneɪʃn
phonatory ˈfəʊnətərɪ [fəʊˈneɪtərɪ]
phonautograph, -s fəʊˈnɔːtəgrɑːf [-græf], -s
phon|e (s. v.), -es, -ing, -ed fəʊn, -z, -ɪŋ, -d
phonematic, -s ˌfəʊnɪˈmætɪk [-niː-], -s
phoneme, -s ˈfəʊniːm, -z
phonemic, -s fəʊˈniːmɪk, -s
phonemicist, -s fəʊˈniːmɪsɪst, -s

phonetic, -al, -ally, -s fəʊˈnetɪk, -l, -əlɪ, -s

phonetician, -s ˌfəʊnɪˈtɪʃn [ˌfɒn-, -nəˈt-, -neˈt-], -z

phoneticist, -s fəʊˈnetɪsɪst, -s

phoneticiz|e [-is|e], -es, -ing, -ed fəʊˈnetɪsaɪz, -ɪz, -ɪŋ, -d

phonetist, -s ˈfəʊnɪtɪst [-net-], -s

phoney ˈfəʊnɪ

phonic, -s ˈfəʊnɪk [ˈfɒn-], -s

phonogram, -s ˈfəʊnəgræm, -z

phonograph, -s ˈfəʊnəgrɑːf [-græf], -s

phonographer, -s fəʊˈnɒgrəfə*, -z

phonographist, -s fəʊˈnɒgrəfɪst, -s

phonography fəʊˈnɒgrəfɪ

phonographic, -al, -ally ˌfəʊnəˈgræfɪk, -l, -əlɪ

phonologic|al, -ally ˌfəʊnəˈlɒdʒɪk|l, -əlɪ

phonologist, -s fəʊˈnɒlədʒɪst, -s

phonolog|y, -ies fəʊˈnɒlədʒ|ɪ, -ɪz

phonotype, -s ˈfəʊnəʊtaɪp, -s

phonotypy ˈfəʊnəʊtaɪpɪ

phosgene ˈfɒzdʒiːn [ˈfɒs-]

phosphate, -s ˈfɒsfeɪt [-fɪt, -fət], -s

phosphite, -s ˈfɒsfaɪt, -s

phosphoresc|e, -es, -ing, -ed; -ence, -ent ˌfɒsfəˈres, -ɪz, -ɪŋ, -t; -ns, -nt

phosphoric fɒsˈfɒrɪk

phosphor|ous, -us ˈfɒsfər|əs, -əs

phossy ˈfɒsɪ

photo, -s ˈfəʊtəʊ, -z

photochrome, -s ˈfəʊtəkrəʊm, -z

photo-cop|y, -ies ˈfəʊtəʊˌkɒp|ɪ, -ɪz

photoelectric ˌfəʊtəʊɪˈlektrɪk (also '—,— when attributive, e.g. cell)

photogenic ˌfəʊtəʊˈdʒenɪk [-ˈdʒiːn-]

photograph (s. v.), -s, -ing, -ed ˈfəʊtəgrɑːf [-græf], -s, -ɪŋ, -t

photographer, -s fəˈtɒgrəfə*, -z

photographic, -al, -ally ˌfəʊtəˈgræfɪk, -l, -əlɪ

photography fəˈtɒgrəfɪ

photogravure, -s ˌfəʊtəgrəˈvjʊə*, [-təʊg-, -ˈvjɒə*, -ˈvjʊː*], -z

photosphere, -s ˈfəʊtəʊˌsfɪə*, -z

photostat (s. v.), -s, -ting, -ted ˈfəʊtəʊstæt, -s, -ɪŋ, -ɪd

photostatic ˌfəʊtəʊˈstætɪk

phrasal ˈfreɪzl

phras|e (s. v.), -es, -ing, -ed freɪz, -ɪz, -ɪŋ, -d

phrase-book, -s ˈfreɪzbʊk, -s

phrase-monger, -s ˈfreɪzˌmʌŋgə*, -z

phraseologic, -al, -ally ˌfreɪzɪəˈlɒdʒɪk [-zjə-], -l, -əlɪ

phraseolog|y, -ies ˌfreɪzɪˈɒlədʒ|ɪ, -ɪz

phrenetic, -al frɪˈnetɪk [freˈn-, frə-], -l

phrenic ˈfrenɪk

phrenologic|al, -ally ˌfrenəˈlɒdʒɪk|l, -əlɪ

phrenolog|ist/s, -y frɪˈnɒlədʒ|ɪst/s [freˈn-, frə-], -ɪ

Phrygia, -n/s ˈfrɪdʒɪə [-dʒjə], -n/z

Phryne ˈfraɪnɪ

phthisic ˈθaɪsɪk [ˈfθaɪ-, ˈtaɪ-]

phthisis ˈθaɪsɪs [ˈfθaɪ-, ˈtaɪ-]

phut fʌt

phylacter|y, -ies frɪˈlæktər|ɪ, -ɪz

Phyllis ˈfɪlɪs

phylloxer|a, -ae, -as ˌfɪlɒkˈsɪər|ə [frɪˈlɒksər|ə], -iː, -əz

physic (s. v.), -s, -king, -ked ˈfɪzɪk, -s, -ɪŋ, -t

physic|al, -ally ˈfɪzɪk|l, -əlɪ

physician, -s fɪˈzɪʃn, -z

physicist, -s ˈfɪzɪsɪst, -s

physiognomic, -al, -ally ˌfɪzɪəˈnɒmɪk [-zjə-], -l, -əlɪ

physiognomist, -s ˌfɪzɪˈɒnəmɪst, -s

physiognom|y, -ies ˌfɪzɪˈɒnəm|ɪ, -ɪz

physiography ˌfɪzɪˈɒgrəfɪ

physiologic, -al, -ally ˌfɪzɪəˈlɒdʒɪk [-zjə-], -l, -əlɪ

physiolog|ist/s, -y ˌfɪzɪˈɒlədʒ|ɪst/s, -ɪ

physiophonic ˌfɪzɪəʊˈfəʊnɪk [-ˈfɒn-]

physiotherap|y, -ist/s ˌfɪzɪəʊˈθerəp|ɪ [-zjəʊ-], -ɪst/s

physique frɪˈziːk [fiːˈz-]

pi (s. adj.), -s paɪ, -z

piacere pɪəˈtʃɪerɪ [ˌpiːə-]

piacular paɪˈækjʊlə*

piaff|e (s. v.), -es, -ing, -ed pɪˈæf [pjæf], -s, -ɪŋ, -t

pianissimo, -s pjæˈnɪsɪməʊ [ˌpɪæ'n-, pjɑːˈn-, ˌpɪɑːˈn-, pɪəˈn-, pjəˈn-], -z
Note.—Among professional musicians pjɑːˈn-, ˌpɪɑːˈn-, pɪəˈn- appear to be the most freq. used forms.

pianist, -s ˈpɪənɪst [ˈpjænɪst, pɪˈæn-], -s
Note.—Professional musicians generally pronounce ˈpɪənɪst.

piano (instrument), -s pɪˈænəʊ [ˈpjæn-, ˈpjɑːn-, pɪˈɑːn-], -z
Note.—The forms ˈpjɑːn-, pɪˈɑːn-, are freq. among professional musicians.

piano (softly), -s ˈpjɑːnəʊ [pɪˈɑː-], -z

pianoforte, -s ˌpjænəʊˈfɔːtɪ [ˌpjɑːn-, pɪˌɑːn-, ˈ—,—], -z

pianola, -s pɪəˈnəʊlə [pjæˈn-, ˌpɪəˈn-, ˌpɪæˈn-], -z

piano-organ, -s pɪˈænəʊˌɔːgən [ˈpjæn-, ˈpjɑːn-, pɪˈɑːn-], -z

piano-player, -s pɪˈænəʊˌpleɪə* [ˈpjæn-, ˈpjɑːn-, pɪˈɑːn-], -z

piano-school, -s pɪˈænəʊskuːl [ˈpjæn-, ˈpjɑːn-, pɪˈɑːn-], -z

piastre, -s pɪˈæstə* [pɪˈɑːs-], -z

piazza, -s pɪˈætsə [pɪˈɑːtsə] (ˈpjattsa), -z

pibroch, -s ˈpiːbrɒk [-ɒx], -s

pica ˈpaɪkə

picaninn|y, -ies ˈpɪkənɪn|ɪ [ˌ--ˈ--], -ɪz

Picardy ˈpɪkədɪ [-kɑːdɪ]

picaresque ˌpɪkəˈresk

picaroon (s. v.), -s, -ing, -ed ˌpɪkəˈruːn, -z, -ɪŋ, -d

Picasso pɪˈkæsəʊ

Piccadilly ˌpɪkəˈdɪlɪ [also ˈ--ˌ-- when followed by a stress]

piccalilli ˈpɪkəlɪlɪ [ˌ--ˈ--]

piccaninn|y, -ies ˈpɪkənɪn|ɪ [ˌ--ˈ--], -ɪz

piccolo, -s ˈpɪkələʊ, -z

pice paɪs

pick (s. v.), -s, -ing, -ed, -er/s pɪk, -s, -ɪŋ, -t, -ə*/z

pickaback ˈpɪkəbæk

pickaxe, -s ˈpɪkæks, -ɪz

pickerel, -s ˈpɪkərəl, -z

Pickering ˈpɪkərɪŋ

picket (s. v.), -s, -ing, -ed ˈpɪkɪt, -s, -ɪŋ, -ɪd

Pickford ˈpɪkfəd

picking (s.), -s ˈpɪkɪŋ, -z

pick|le (s. v.), -les (P.), -ling, -led ˈpɪk|l, -lz, -lɪŋ [-lɪŋ], -ld

picklock, -s ˈpɪklɒk, -s

pick-me-up, -s ˈpɪkmiːˈʌp [-mɪʌp], -s

pickpocket, -s ˈpɪkˌpɒkɪt, -s

pick-up (electric), -s ˈpɪkʌp, -s

Pickwick ˈpɪkwɪk

Pickwickian pɪkˈwɪkɪən [-kjən]

picnic (s. v.), -s, -king, -ked, -ker/s ˈpɪknɪk, -s, -ɪŋ, -t, -ə*/z

picot, -s ˈpiːkəʊ [-ˈ-, pɪˈkəʊ]

picotee, -s ˌpɪkəˈtiː, -z

picquet (military term), -s ˈpɪkɪt, -s

picric ˈpɪkrɪk

Pict, -s pɪkt, -s

Pictish ˈpɪktɪʃ

pictograph, -s ˈpɪktəʊɡrɑːf [-ɡræf], -s

Picton ˈpɪktən

pictorial, -ly pɪkˈtɔːrɪəl, -ɪ

pict|ure (s. v.), -ures, -uring, -ured ˈpɪktʃ|ə*, -əz, -ərɪŋ, -əd

picture|-book/s, -card/s ˈpɪktʃə|bʊk/s, -kɑːd/z

picture-galler|y, -ies ˈpɪktʃəˌɡælər|ɪ, -ɪz

picture-hat, -s ˈpɪktʃəhæt, -s

picturesque, -ly, -ness ˌpɪktʃəˈresk, -lɪ, -nɪs [-nəs]

picture-writing ˈpɪktʃəˌraɪtɪŋ

pidgin ˈpɪdʒɪn

Pidsley ˈpɪdzlɪ

pie, -s paɪ, -z

Piears pɪəz

piebald ˈpaɪbɔːld

piec|e (s. v.), -es, -ing, -ed, -er/s piːs, -ɪz, -ɪŋ, -t, -ə*/z

piece-goods ˈpiːsɡʊdz

piecemeal ˈpiːsmiːl

piece-work ˈpiːswɜːk

pie-crust, -s ˈpaɪkrʌst, -s

pied, -ness paɪd, -nɪs [-nəs]

pied-à-terre ˌpjeɪtɑːˈteə* (pjetatɛːr)

Piedmont ˈpiːdmənt [-mɒnt]

Piedmontese ˌpiːdmənˈtiːz [-mɒn-]

pie|man, -men ˈpaɪ|mən, -mən [-men]

pier, -s pɪə*, -z

pierc|e (P.), -es, -ing, -ed, -er/s; -eable pɪəs, -ɪz, -ɪŋ, -t, -ə*/z; -əbl

pierglass, -es ˈpɪəɡlɑːs, -ɪz

Pierian paɪˈerɪən [paɪˈɪər-, pɪ-]

Pier|point, -pont ˈpɪə|pɔɪnt, -pɒnt [-pənt]

Pierrepont (English surname) ˈpɪəpɒnt [-pənt]

pierrot, -s ˈpɪərəʊ [ˈpjer-, ˈpjɪər-], -z

Pier|s, -son pɪə|z, -sn

pietà, -s ˌpɪeˈtɑː, -z

Pietermaritzburg ˌpiːtəˈmærɪtsbɜːɡ

pieti|sm, -st/s ˈpaɪɪtɪ|zəm [ˈpaɪt-], -st/s

piety ˈpaɪətɪ [ˈpaɪɪtɪ]

piff|le (s. v.), -les, -ling, -led, -ler/s ˈpɪf|l, -lz, -lɪŋ [-lɪŋ], -ld, -lə*/z [-lə*/z]

pig (s. v.), -s, -ging, -ged pɪɡ, -z, -ɪŋ, -d

pigeon, -s ˈpɪdʒɪn [-dʒən], -z

pigeon-hol|e (s. v.), -es, -ing, -ed ˈpɪdʒɪnhəʊl [-dʒən-], -z, -ɪŋ, -d

pigger|y, -ies ˈpɪɡər|ɪ, -ɪz

piggish, -ly, -ness ˈpɪɡɪʃ, -lɪ, -nɪs [-nəs]

Piggott ˈpɪɡət

piggyback ˈpɪɡɪbæk

piggywig, -s ˈpɪɡɪwɪɡ, -z

pigheaded, -ly, -ness ˌpɪɡˈhedɪd [also ˈ-ˌ-- when attributive], -lɪ, -nɪs [-nəs]

pig-iron ˈpɪɡˌaɪən

piglet, -s ˈpɪɡlɪt [-lət], -s

pigment, -s ˈpɪɡmənt, -s

pigm|y, -ies ˈpɪɡm|ɪ, -ɪz

pignut, -s ˈpɪɡnʌt, -s

Pig|ott, -ou ˈpɪɡ|ət, -uː

pigskin, -s ˈpɪɡskɪn, -z

pig-sticking ˈpɪɡˌstɪkɪŋ

pigst|y, -ies ˈpɪɡst|aɪ, -aɪz

pigtail, -s ˈpɪɡteɪl, -z

pigwash ˈpɪɡwɒʃ

pik|e (s. v.) (P.), -es, -ing, -ed paɪk, -s, -ɪŋ, -t

pike-keeper, -s ˈpaɪkˌkiːpə*, -z

pikestaff, -s ˈpaɪkstɑːf, -s

pilaf(f), -s ˈpɪlæf [-ˈ-], -s

pilaster, -s pɪˈlæstə*, -z

Pilate ˈpaɪlət

379

Pilatus pɪˈlɑːtəs
pilau, -s pɪˈlaʊ, -z
Pilbrow ˈpɪlbrəʊ
pilch (P.), -es pɪltʃ, -ɪz
pilchard, -s ˈpɪltʃəd, -z
pil|e (s. v.), -es, -ing, -ed paɪl, -z, -ɪŋ, -d
pileated ˈpaɪlɪeɪtɪd
pile-driv|er/s, -ing ˈpaɪlˌdraɪv|ə*/z, -ɪŋ
pil|eus, -ei ˈpaɪl|iəs, -ɪaɪ
pilf|er, -ers, -ering, -ered, -erer/s
   ˈpɪlf|ə*, -əz, -ərɪŋ, -əd, -ərə*/z
pilferage ˈpɪlfərɪdʒ
pilgrim, -s; -age/s ˈpɪlgrɪm, -z; -ɪdʒ/ɪz
piling (s.), -s ˈpaɪlɪŋ, -z
pill (s. v.), -s, -ing, -ed; -box/es pɪl, -z, -ɪŋ, -d; -bɒks/ɪz
pillag|e (s. v.), -es, -ing, -ed, -er/s
   ˈpɪlɪdʒ, -ɪz, -ɪŋ, -d, -ə*/z
pillar, -s, -ed ˈpɪlə*, -z, -d
pillar-box, -es ˈpɪləbɒks, -ɪz
pillion, -s ˈpɪljən [-lɪən], -z
pillor|y (s. v.), -ies, -ying, -ied ˈpɪlər|ɪ, -ɪz, -ɪŋ, -ɪd
pillow, -s, -y ˈpɪləʊ, -z, -ɪ
pillow-case, -s ˈpɪləʊkeɪs, -ɪz
pillow-slip, -s ˈpɪləʊslɪp, -s
Pillsbury ˈpɪlzbərɪ
pilocarpine ˌpaɪləʊˈkɑːpɪn [-pam]
pilot (s. v.), -s, -ing, -ed; -age ˈpaɪlət, -s, -ɪŋ, -ɪd; -ɪdʒ
pilot|-boat/s, -engine/s ˈpaɪlət|bəʊt/s, -ˌendʒɪn/z
Pilsener ˈpɪlznə* [-lsn-]
Piltdown ˈpɪltdaʊn
pilule, -s ˈpɪlju:l, -z
pimento pɪˈmentəʊ
Pimlico ˈpɪmlɪkəʊ
pimp (s. v.), -s, -ing, -ed pɪmp, -s, -ɪŋ, -t [pɪmt]
pimpernel, -s ˈpɪmpənel [-nl], -z
pimple, -s, -d ˈpɪmpl, -z, -d
pimpl|y, -iness ˈpɪmpl|ɪ, -ɪnɪs [-məs]
Pimpo ˈpɪmpəʊ
pin (s. v.), -s, -ning, -ned pɪn, -z, -ɪŋ, -d
pinafore (P.), -s ˈpɪnəfɔː* [-fɔə*], -z
pince-nez (sing.) ˈpæ̃:nsneɪ [ˈpæns-, ˈpɪns-, ˌ-ˈ-] (pɛ̃sne), (plur.) -z
pincers ˈpɪnsəz
pinch (s. v.), -es, -ing, -ed, -er/s pɪntʃ, -ɪz, -ɪŋ, -t, -ə*/z
pinchbeck, -s ˈpɪntʃbek, -s
Pinches ˈpɪntʃɪz
Pinckney ˈpɪŋknɪ
pincushion, -s ˈpɪnˌkʊʃn [ˈpɪŋˌk-, -ʃm], -z
Pindar ˈpɪndə*
Pindaric (s. adj.), -s pɪnˈdærɪk, -s
Pindus ˈpɪndəs

pin|e (s. v.), -es, -ing, -ed paɪn, -z, -ɪŋ, -d
pineapple, -s ˈpaɪnˌæpl, -z
pine-clad ˈpaɪnklæd
Pinel pɪˈnel
Pinero pɪˈnɪərəʊ
piner|y, -ies ˈpaɪnər|ɪ, -ɪz
ping (s. v. interj.), -s, -ing, -ed pɪŋ, -z, -ɪŋ, -d
pingpong ˈpɪŋpɒŋ
pinguid ˈpɪŋgwɪd
pinhole, -s ˈpɪnhəʊl, -z
pinion (s. v.), -s, -ing, -ed ˈpɪnjən [-nɪən], -z, -ɪŋ, -d
pink (s. adj. v.) (P.), -s, -ing, -ed pɪŋk, -s, -ɪŋ, -t [pɪŋt]
Pinkerton ˈpɪŋkətən
pink-eye, -d ˈpɪŋkaɪ, -d
pinkish ˈpɪŋkɪʃ
pink|y, -iness ˈpɪŋk|ɪ, -ɪnɪs [-məs]
pin-money ˈpɪnˌmʌnɪ
pinnace, -s ˈpɪnɪs [-nəs], -ɪz
pinnac|le (s. v.), -les, -ling, -led ˈpɪnək|l, -lz, -lɪŋ [-lɪŋ], -ld
pinnate ˈpɪnɪt [-neɪt]
pinner (P.), -s ˈpɪnə*, -z
Pinocchio pɪˈnɒkɪəʊ [-ˈnəʊ-, -kjəʊ] (piˈnɔkkjo)
pin-point, -s, -ing, -ed ˈpɪnpɔɪnt, -s, -ɪŋ, -ɪd
pin-prick, -s ˈpɪnprɪk, -s
pint, -s paɪnt, -s
pintado, -s pɪnˈtɑːdəʊ, -z
pintail, -s ˈpɪnteɪl, -z
Pinter ˈpɪntə*
pint-pot, -s ˌpaɪntˈpɒt [ˈ--], -s
pin-up, -s ˈpɪnʌp, -s
pinxit ˈpɪŋksɪt
pioneer (s. v.) (P.), -s, -ing, -ed ˌpaɪəˈnɪə*, -z, -rɪŋ, -d
pious, -ly, -ness ˈpaɪəs, -lɪ, -nɪs [-nəs]
pip (s. v.) (P.), -s, -ping, -ped pɪp, -s, -ɪŋ, -t
pip|e (s. v.) (P.), -es, -ing, -ed, -er/s paɪp, -s, -ɪŋ, -t, -ə*/z
pipeclay ˈpaɪpkleɪ
pipe-line, -s ˈpaɪplaɪn, -z
Piper ˈpaɪpə*
pipette, -s pɪˈpet, -s
piping (s. adj.) ˈpaɪpɪŋ
pipit, -s ˈpɪpɪt, -s
pipkin, -s ˈpɪpkɪn, -z
Pippa ˈpɪpə
pippin, -s ˈpɪpɪn, -z
pip-pip ˌpɪpˈpɪp
pipp|y, -iness ˈpɪp|ɪ, -ɪnɪs [-məs]
pipsqueak, -s ˈpɪpskwiːk, -s
piquancy ˈpiːkənsɪ

piquant, -ly 'pi:kənt [-kɑ:nt], -lı

piqu|e (s. v.), -es, -ing, -ed pi:k, -s, -ıŋ, -t

piqué (s. v.), -s, -ing, -d 'pi:keı (pike), -z, -ıŋ, -d

piquet (group of men), -s 'pıkıt, -s

piquet (card game) pı'ket

pirac|y, -ies 'paıərəs|ı ['pır-], -ız

Piraeus paı'rıəs [-'ri:əs]

pirat|e (s. v.), -es, -ing, -ed 'paıərət [-rıt], -s, -ıŋ, -ıd

piratic|al, -ally paı'rætık|l [ˌpaıə'r-], -əlı

Piratin pı'rætın

Pirbright 'pə:braıt

Pirie 'pırı

pirouett|e (s. v.), -es, -ing, -ed ˌpıru'et, -s, -ıŋ, -ıd

Pisa 'pi:zə

pis aller, -s ˌpi:z'æleı (pizale), -z

piscatorial ˌpıskə'tɔ:rıəl

piscatory 'pıskətərı

piscean pı'si:ən ['pısıən, 'pısjən, 'pıskıən, 'pıskjən, by astrologers 'paıs-]

Pisces (constellation) 'pısi:z ['pıski:z, by astrologers 'paısi:z]

pisciculture 'pısıkʌltʃə*

piscina, -s pı'si:nə [-'saın-], -z

piscine (s., bathing pool), -s 'pısi:n [-'-], -z

piscine (adj., of fish) 'pısaın

Piscis Austrinus ˌpısısɒ'straınəs [ˌpıskıs-, -ɔ:'s-]

Pisgah 'pızgə [-gɑ:]

pish pıʃ [pʃ]

Pisidia paı'sıdıə [-djə]

Pisistratus paı'sıstrətəs [pı's-]

pismire, -s 'pısmaıə*, -z

pistachio, -s pı'stɑ:ʃıəu [-'stɑ:ʃjəu, -'stæʃ-, -'stætʃ-], -z

pistil, -s 'pıstıl, -z

pistol, -s 'pıstl, -z

pistole, -s pı'stəul ['--], -z

piston, -s; -rod/s 'pıstən [-tn, -tın], -z; -rɒd/z

pit (s. v.), -s, -ting, -ted pıt, -s, -ıŋ, -ıd

pitapat ˌpıtə'pæt ['pıtəp-]

Pitcairn (surname) pıt'keən, (island) pıt'keən ['pıtk-]

pitch (s. v.), -es, -ing, -ed pıtʃ, -ız, -ıŋ, -t

pitch-black ˌpıtʃ'blæk

pitchblende 'pıtʃblend

pitch-dark ˌpıtʃ'dɑ:k

pitcher (P.), -s 'pıtʃə*, -z

pitchfork (s. v.), -s, -ing, -ed 'pıtʃfɔ:k, -s, -ıŋ, -t

pitchpine, -s 'pıtʃpaın, -z

pitch-pipe, -s 'pıtʃpaıp, -s

pitchy 'pıtʃı

piteous, -ly, -ness 'pıtıəs [-tjəs], -lı, -nıs [-nəs]

pitfall, -s 'pıtfɔ:l, -z

Pitfodels pıt'fɒdəlz

pith, -s -less pıθ, -s, -lıs [-ləs]

pithecanthrop|us, -i ˌpıθıkæn'θrəup|əs [ˌ--'---], -aı

Pither 'paıθə*, 'paıðə*

pith|y, -ier, -iest, -ily, -iness 'pıθ|ı, -ıə*, -ııst, -ılı [-əlı], -ınıs [-ınəs]

pitiab|le, -ly, -leness 'pıtıəb|l [-tjə-], -lı, -lnıs [-nəs]

piti|ful, -fully, -fulness 'pıtı|fʊl, -fʊlı [-fəlı], -fʊlnıs [-nəs]

pitiless, -ly, -ness 'pıtılıs [-ləs], -lı, -nıs [-nəs]

Pitlochry pıt'lɒkrı [-'lɒxrı]

pit|man (P.), -men 'pıt|mən, -mən [-men]

piton, -s 'pi:tɔ̃:ŋ [-tɒn], -z

Pitt pıt

pittance, -s 'pıtəns, -ız

Pitts, -burg(h) pıts, -bə:g

pituitary pı'tjuıtərı [-'tju:-, -ətərı]

pit|y (s. v.), -ies, -ying/ly, -ied 'pıt|ı, -ız, -ıŋ/lı, -ıd

pityriasis ˌpıtı'raıəsıs

Pius 'paıəs

pivot (s. v.), -s, -ing, -ed 'pıvət, -s, -ıŋ, -ıd

pivotal 'pıvətl

pix|ie [-|y], -ies 'pıks|ı, -ız

pizza, -s 'pi:tsə ['pıtsə], -z

pizzicato, -s ˌpıtsı'kɑ:təʊ, -z

placability ˌplækə'bılətı [ˌpleık-, -lıt-]

placab|le, -ly, -leness 'plækəb|l ['pleık-], -lı, -lnıs [-nəs]

placard (s. v.), -s, -ing, -ed 'plækɑ:d, -z, -ıŋ, -ıd

placat|e, -es, -ing, -ed plə'keıt [pleı'k-], -s, -ıŋ, -ıd

placatory plə'keıtərı [pleı'k-]

plac|e (s. v.), -es, -ing, -ed, -er/s pleıs, -ız, -ıŋ, -t, -ə*/z

placebo, -s plə'si:bəʊ [plæ's-], -z

place-kick, -s 'pleıskık, -s

place|man, -men 'pleıs|mən, -mən

placement 'pleısmənt

placenta plə'sentə

placet, -s 'pleıset [-sıt], -s

placid, -est, -ly, -ness 'plæsıd, -ıst, -lı, -nıs [-nəs]

placidity plæ'sıdətı [plə's-, -ıtı]

placket, -s; -hole/s 'plækıt, -s; -həʊl/z

plagal 'pleıgəl

plage, -s plɑ:ʒ, -ız

plagiari|sm/s, -st/s 'pleıdʒjərı|zəm/z [-dʒıə-, -dʒə-], -st/s

381

plagiariz|e [-is|e], -es, -ing, -ed 'pleɪ-
    dʒjəraɪz [-dʒɪə-, -dʒə-], -ɪz, -ɪŋ, -d
plagiar|y, -ies 'pleɪdʒjər|ɪ [-dʒɪə-, -dʒə-],
    -ɪz
plagu|e (s. v.), -es, -ing, -ed, -er/s pleɪg,
    -z, -ɪŋ, -d, -ə*/z
plague-spot, -s 'pleɪgspɒt, -s
plagu|y, -ily, -iness 'pleɪg|ɪ, -ɪlɪ [-əlɪ],
    -ɪnɪs [-məs]
plaice pleɪs
plaid, -s, -ed plæd, -z, -ɪd
Plaid Cymru ˌplaɪd 'kʌmrɪ
plain (s. adj.), -s, -er, -est, -ly, -ness
    pleɪn, -z, -ə*, -ɪst, -lɪ, -nɪs [-nəs]
plainsong 'pleɪnsɒŋ
plain-spoken ˌpleɪn'spəʊkən ['-ˌ--]
plaint, -s pleɪnt, -s
plaintiff, -s 'pleɪntɪf, -s
plaintive, -ly, -ness 'pleɪntɪv, -lɪ, -nɪs
    [-nəs]
plaister, -s 'pleɪstə*, -z
Plaistow (in E. London) 'plæstəʊ
    ['pleɪs-]
    Note.—The local pronunciation is
    'pleɪstəʊ.
plait (s. v.), -s, -ing, -ed plæt, -s, -ɪŋ, -ɪd
plan (s. v.), -s, -ning, -ned, -ner/s plæn,
    -z, -ɪŋ, -d, -ə*/z
planch, -es pleɪnʃ, -ɪz
planchette, -s plɑː'nʃet [plɑː:n-, plɔ̃:n-,
    plɒn-] [plɑ̃ʃet], -s
plan|e (s. v.), -es, -ing, -ed pleɪn, -z, -ɪŋ,
    -d
planet, -s 'plænɪt, -s
planetari|um, -ums, -a ˌplænɪ'teərɪ|əm,
    -əmz, -ə
planetary 'plænɪtərɪ
plane-tree, -s 'pleɪntriː, -z
plangent 'plændʒənt
planimeter, -s plæ'nɪmɪtə* [plə'n-,
    -mətə*], -z
plank (s. v.), -s, -ing, -ed plæŋk, -s, -ɪŋ,
    -t [plæŋt]
plankton 'plæŋtən [-tɒn]
plant (s. v.), -s, -ing, -ed, -er/s plɑːnt,
    -s, -ɪŋ, -ɪd, -ə*/z
Plant (surname) plɑːnt
Plantagenet plæn'tædʒənɪt [-dʒɪn-,
    -nət, -net]
plantain, -s 'plæntɪn ['plɑː:n-], -z
plantation, -s plæn'teɪʃn [plɑː:n-], -z
Plantin (type face) 'plæntɪn ['plɑː:nt-]
plaque, -s plɑːk [plæk], -s
plaquette, -s plæ'ket [plɑː:'k-], -s
plash (s. v.), -es, -ing, -ed; -y plæʃ, -ɪz,
    -ɪŋ, -t; -ɪ
plasm 'plæzəm
plasm|a, -ic 'plæzm|ə, -ɪk

Plassey 'plæsɪ
plast|er (s. v.), -ers, -ering, -ered, -erer/s
    'plɑː:st|ə*, -əz, -ərɪŋ, -əd, -ərə*/z
plastic, -s 'plæstɪk ['plɑː:s-], -s
plasticine 'plæstɪsiːn ['plɑː:s-]
plasticity plæ'stɪsətɪ [plɑː:'s-, -ɪtɪ]
plastographic ˌplæstəʊ'græfɪk [ˌplɑː:st-]
plat, -s plɑː: (plɑ), -z
Plata 'plɑː:tə
Plataea plə'tiːə [-'tɪə]
platan, -s 'plætən, -z
plat|e (s. v.), -es, -ing, -ed pleɪt, -s, -ɪŋ,
    -ɪd
Plate (river in South America) pleɪt
plateau, -s [-x] 'plætəʊ [plæ'təʊ], -z
plate-basket, -s 'pleɪtˌbɑː:skɪt, -s
plateful, -s 'pleɪtfʊl, -z
plate-glass ˌpleɪt'glɑː:s ['--]
plate-layer, -s 'pleɪtˌleɪə*, -z
platen, -s 'plætən, -z
plate-powder 'pleɪtˌpaʊdə*
plate-rack, -s 'pleɪtræk, -s
platform (s. v.), -s, -ing, -ed 'plætfɔ:m,
    -z, -ɪŋ, -d
platiniz|e [-is|e], -es, -ing, -ed 'plætɪ-
    naɪz [-tn̩aɪz], -ɪz, -ɪŋ, -d
platinotype, -s 'plætɪnəʊtaɪp [-tn̩əʊt-],
    -s
platinum 'plætɪnəm [-tn̩əm]
platitude, -s 'plætɪtjuːd, -z
platitudinarian, -s 'plætɪˌtjuːdɪ'neərɪən,
    -z
platitudinous ˌplætɪ'tjuːdɪnəs
Plato 'pleɪtəʊ
platonic, -al, -ally plə'tɒnɪk [pleɪ't-], -l,
    -əlɪ
platoni|sm/s, -st/s 'pleɪtəʊnɪ|zəm/z,
    -st/s
platoon, -s plə'tuːn, -z
Platt, -s plæt, -s
platter, -s 'plætə*, -z
platypus, -es 'plætɪpəs, -ɪz
plaudit, -s 'plɔːdɪt, -s
plausibility ˌplɔːzə'bɪlətɪ [-zɪ'b-, -lɪt-]
plausib|le, -ly, -leness 'plɔːzəb|l [-zɪb-],
    -lɪ, -lnɪs [-nəs]
Plautus 'plɔːtəs
play (s. v.), -s, -ing, -ed, -er/s pleɪ, -z,
    -ɪŋ, -d, -ə*/z [pleə*/z]
playable 'pleɪəbl
play-actor, -s 'pleɪˌæktə*, -z
play-bill, -s 'pleɪbɪl, -z
play-box, -es 'pleɪbɒks, -ɪz
Player, -'s 'pleɪə*, -z
Playfair 'pleɪfeə*
playfellow, -s 'pleɪˌfeləʊ, -z
play|ful, -fully, -fulness 'pleɪ|fʊl, -fʊlɪ
    [-fəlɪ], -fʊlnɪs [-nəs]

playgoer, -s 'pleɪˌɡəʊə*, -z
playground, -s 'pleɪɡraʊnd, -z
playhou|se, -ses 'pleɪhaʊ|s, -zɪz
playing-field, -s 'pleɪŋfiːld, -z
playmate, -s 'pleɪmeɪt, -s
plaything, -s 'pleɪθɪŋ, -z
playtime, -s 'pleɪtaɪm, -z
play-track, -s 'pleɪtræk, -s
playwright, -s 'pleɪraɪt, -s
plaza (P.), -s 'plɑːzə ['plæzə], -z
plea, -s pliː, -z
plead, -s, -ing/ly, -ed, -er/s pliːd, -z,
  -ɪŋ/lɪ, -ɪd, -ə*/z
pleading (s.), -s 'pliːdɪŋ, -z
pleasa(u)nce 'plezəns
pleasant, -er, -est, -ly, -ness 'pleznt,
  -ə*, -ɪst, -lɪ, -nɪs [-nəs]
pleasantr|y, -ies 'plezntr|ɪ, -ɪz
pleas|e, -es, -ing/ly, -ed pliːz, -ɪz,
  -ɪŋ/lɪ, -d
pleasurab|le, -ly, -leness 'pleʒərəb|l, -lɪ,
  -lnɪs [-nəs]
pleasure, -s 'pleʒə*, -z
pleasure-boat, -s 'pleʒəbəʊt, -s
pleasure-ground, -s 'pleʒəɡraʊnd, -z
pleat (s. v.), -s, -ing, -ed pliːt, -s, -ɪŋ, -ɪd
plebeian (s. adj.), -s plɪˈbiːən [-ˈbɪən], -z
plebiscite, -s 'plebɪsɪt [-bə-, -saɪt], -s
plebs plebz
plectrum, -s 'plektrəm, -z
pledg|e (s. v.), -es, -ing, -ed, -er/s
  pledʒ, -ɪz, -ɪŋ, -d, -ə*/z
Pleiad, -s, -es 'plaɪəd [old-fashioned
  'pliːəd, plɪəd, 'pleɪæd], -z, -iːz
pleistocene 'plaɪstəʊsiːn
plenar|y, -ily 'pliːnər|ɪ, -əlɪ [-ɪlɪ]
plenipotentiar|y (s. adj.), -ies ˌplenɪ-
  pəʊˈtenʃər|ɪ [-ʃɪər-, -ʃjər-], -ɪz
plenitude 'plenɪtjuːd
plenteous, -ly, -ness 'plentjəs [-tɪəs],
  -lɪ, -nɪs [-nəs]
plenti|ful, -fully, -fulness 'plentɪ|fʊl,
  -fʊlɪ [-fəlɪ], -fʊlnɪs [-nəs]
plenty 'plentɪ
plenum, -s 'pliːnəm, -z
pleonasm, -s 'plɪəʊnæzəm ['pliːəʊ-], -z
pleonastic, -al, -ally plɪəʊˈnæstɪk
  [ˌpliːəʊˈn-], -l, -əlɪ
plesiosaur|us, -i, -uses ˌpliːsɪəˈsɔːr|əs
  [-sjə-, -sɪəʊ-s-, '—-], -aɪ, -əsɪz
plethora 'pleθərə
plethoric pleˈθɒrɪk [plɪˈθ-]
pleur|a, -ae, -as, -al 'plʊər|ə, -iː, -əz, -əl
pleurisy 'plʊərəsɪ [-rɪs-]
pleuritic ˌplʊəˈrɪtɪk
pleuro - pneumonia ˌplʊərəʊnjuː-
  'məʊnjə [-njuː-, -nɪə]
plexus, -es 'pleksəs, -ɪz

Pleyel, -s 'pleɪəl [-el], -z
pliability ˌplaɪəˈbɪlətɪ [-lɪt-]
pliab|le, -ly, -leness 'plaɪəb|l, -lɪ, -lnɪs
  [-nəs]
pliancy 'plaɪənsɪ
pliant, -ly, -ness 'plaɪənt, -lɪ, -nɪs [-nəs]
pliers 'plaɪəz
plight (s. v.), -s, -ing, -ed plaɪt, -s, -ɪŋ,
  -ɪd
plimsoll (P.), -s 'plɪmsəl [-sɒl], -z
Plinlimmon plɪn'lɪmən
plinth, -s plɪnθ, -s
Pliny 'plɪnɪ
pliocene 'plaɪəʊsiːn
plod (s. v.), -s, -ding, -ded, -der/s plɒd,
  -z, -ɪŋ, -ɪd, -ə*/z
Plomer (surname) 'pluːmə* ['plʌmə*]
Plomley 'plʌmlɪ
plop (s. v. interj.), -s, -ping, -ped plɒp,
  -s, -ɪŋ, -t
plosion, -s 'pləʊʒn, -z
plosive (s. adj.), -s 'pləʊsɪv [-əʊzɪ-], -z
plot (s. v.), -s, -ting, -ted, -ter/s plɒt, -s,
  -ɪŋ, -ɪd, -ə*/z
plough (s. v.), -s, -ing, -ed, -er/s; -able;
  -boy/s, -man, -men plaʊ, -z, -ɪŋ, -d,
  'plaʊə*/z, 'plaʊəbl; -bɔɪ/z, -mən,
  -mən [-men]
ploughshare, -s 'plaʊʃeə*, -z
plover, -s 'plʌvə*, -z
Plow|den, -man 'plaʊ|dn, -mən
Plowright 'plaʊraɪt
ploy, -s 'plɔɪ, -z
pluck (s. v.), -s, -ing, -ed plʌk, -s, -ɪŋ, -t
Pluckley 'plʌklɪ
pluck|y, -ier, -iest, -ily, -iness 'plʌk|ɪ,
  -ɪə*, -ɪst, -ɪlɪ [-əlɪ], -ɪnɪs [-nəs]
plug (s. v.), -s, -ging, -ged plʌg, -z, -ɪŋ,
  -d
plum, -s plʌm, -z
plumage, -s 'pluːmɪdʒ, -ɪz
plumb (s. v.), -s, -ing, -ed, -er/s plʌm,
  -z, -ɪŋ, -d, -ə*/z
plumbago, -s plʌm'beɪɡəʊ, -z
Plumbe plʌm
plumb-line, -s 'plʌmlaɪn, -z
plum|e (s. v.), -es, -ing, -ed pluːm, -z,
  -ɪŋ, -d
Plummer 'plʌmə*
plummet, -s 'plʌmɪt, -s
plummy 'plʌmɪ
plump (s. adj. v. adv. interj.), -s; -er,
  -est, -ly, -ness; -ing, -ed plʌmp, -s;
  -ə*, -ɪst, -lɪ, -nɪs [-nəs]; -ɪŋ, -t [plʌmt]
Plump|ton, -tre 'plʌmp|tən, -trɪ
plum-pudding, -s ˌplʌm'pʊdɪŋ, -z
Plumridge 'plʌmrɪdʒ
Plumstead 'plʌmstɪd [-ted]

383

plumy 'plu:mɪ

plund|er (s. v.), -ers, -ering, -ered,
-erer/s; -erous 'plʌnd|ə*, -əz, -ərɪŋ,
-əd, -ərə*/z, -ərəs

plung|e (s. v.), -es, -ing, -ed, -er/s
plʌndʒ, -ɪz, -ɪŋ, -d, -ə*/z

Plunket(t) 'plʌŋkɪt

pluperfect, -s ˌplu:'pə:fɪkt ['-,--], -s

plural (s. adj.), -s, -ly 'pluərəl ['plɔər-,
'plɔ:r-], -z, -ɪ

plurali|sm, -ist/s 'pluərəlɪ|zəm ['plɔər-,
'plɔ:r-, -r̩ɪ-], -st/s

pluralit|y, -ies ˌpluə'rælət|ɪ [-ɪt|ɪ], -ɪz

pluraliz|e [-is|e], -es, -ing, -ed 'pluərəlaɪz
['plɔər-, 'plɔ:r-, -r̩aɪz], -ɪz, -ɪŋ, -d

plus, -(s)es plʌs, -ɪz

plus-fours ˌplʌs'fɔ:z [-'fɔəz]

plush, -es, -y plʌʃ, -ɪz, -ɪ

Plutarch 'plu:tɑ:k

Pluto 'plu:təʊ

plutocracy plu:'tɒkrəsɪ

plutocrat, -s 'plu:təʊkræt, -s

plutocratic ˌplu:təʊ'krætɪk

Plutonian plu:'təʊnjən [-nɪən]

Plutonic plu:'tɒnɪk

plutonium plu:'təʊnjəm [-nɪəm]

pluvi|al, -ous 'plu:vj|əl [-vɪ|əl], -əs

pl|y (s. v.), -ies, -ying, -ied pl|aɪ, -aɪz,
-aɪɪŋ, -aɪd

Plymouth 'plɪməθ

plywood 'plaɪwʊd

p.m. ˌpi:'em

pneumatic, -s, -al, -ally nju:'mætɪk
[njʊ'm-], -s, -l, -əlɪ

pneumatolog|ist/s, -y ˌnju:mə'tɒlədʒ|-
ɪst/s, -ɪ

pneumoconiosis ˌnju:məʊkəʊnɪ'əʊsɪs
[-kɒn-]

pneumonia nju:'məʊnjə [njʊ'm-, -nɪə]

pneumonic nju:'mɒnɪk [njʊ'm-]

Pnompenh ˌnɒm'pen

Pnyx p̌nɪks

po, -es pəʊ, -z

Po (Italian river) pəʊ

poach, -es, -ing, -ed, -er/s pəʊtʃ, -ɪz,
-ɪŋ, -t, -ə*/z

pochard, -s 'pəʊtʃəd ['pɒtʃ-], -z

pock, -s, -ed pɒk, -s, -t

pocket (s. v.), -s, -ing, -ed; -able, -ful/s
'pɒkɪt, -s, -ɪŋ, -ɪd; -əbl, -fʊl/z

pocket-book, -s 'pɒkɪtbʊk, -s

pocket - handkerchief, -s ˌpɒkɪt-
'hæŋkətʃɪf, -s (see note to handkerchief)

pocket-knif|e, -ves 'pɒkɪtnaɪ|f, -vz

pocket-money 'pɒkɪtˌmʌnɪ

Pocklington 'pɒklɪŋtən

pockmark, -s, -ed 'pɒkmɑ:k, -s, -t

poco 'pəʊkəʊ

Pocock 'pəʊkɒk

pococurante, -s ˌpəʊkəʊkjʊə'ræntɪ, -z

pod (s. v.), -s, -ding, -ded pɒd, -z, -ɪŋ, -ɪd

podagra pəʊ'dægrə [pɒ'd-, 'pɒdəgrə]

podg|ly, -ier, -iest, -ily, -iness 'pɒdʒ|ɪ,
-ɪə*, -ɪɪst, -ɪlɪ [-əlɪ], -ɪnɪs [-məs]

podi|um, -ums, -a 'pəʊdɪ|əm [-djəm],
-əmz, -ə

Poe pəʊ

Poel 'pəʊel [-ɪl, -əl]

poem, -s 'pəʊɪm [-əm, -em], -z

poesy 'pəʊɪzɪ ['pəʊezɪ]

poet, -s 'pəʊɪt [-et], -s

poetaster, -s ˌpəʊɪ'tæstə* [ˌpəʊə't-], -z

poetess, -es 'pəʊɪtɪs ['pəʊet-, -tes], -ɪz

poetic, -al, -ally pəʊ'etɪk, -l, -əlɪ

poetiz|e [-is|e], -es, -ing, -ed, -er/s
'pəʊɪtaɪz ['pəʊet-], -ɪz, -ɪŋ, -d, -ə*/z

poetry 'pəʊɪtrɪ ['pəʊət-, rarely 'pɒɪt-]

Pogner (in Wagner's 'Die Meistersinger') 'pəʊgnə* ('po:gnər)

pogrom, -s 'pɒgrəm [-grɒm, pə'grɒm],
-z

poignan|cy, -t/ly 'pɔɪnən|sɪ ['pɔɪnjə-,
'pɔɪgnə-], -t/lɪ

poinsettia pɔɪn'setɪə [-tjə]

point (s. v.), -s, -ing, -ed, -er/s pɔɪnt, -s,
-ɪŋ, -ɪd, -ə*/z

point-blank ˌpɔɪnt'blæŋk [also '-- when
attributive]

point-duty 'pɔɪntˌdju:tɪ

pointed (adj.), -ly, -ness 'pɔɪntɪd, -lɪ,
-nɪs [-nəs]

pointillism 'pwæ̃nti:jɪzəm ['pwænt-,
'pɔɪntɪlɪzəm]

point-lace ˌpɔɪnt'leɪs ['--]

pointless, -ness 'pɔɪntlɪs [-ləs], -nɪs [-nəs]

points|man, -men 'pɔɪnts|mən, -mən
[-men]

pois|e (s. v.), -es, -ing, -ed pɔɪz, -ɪz, -ɪŋ,
-d

pois|on (s. v.), -ons, -oning, -oned,
-oner/s 'pɔɪz|n, -nz, -n̩ɪŋ [-nɪŋ], -nd,
-n̩ə*/z [-nə*/z]

poisonous, -ly, -ness 'pɔɪznəs [-zn̩əs], -lɪ,
-nɪs [-nəs]

Poitiers 'pwɑ:tjeɪ [pwɑ:'tjeɪ, old-
fashioned pɔɪ'tɪəz] (pwatje)

pok|e (s. v.), -es, -ing, -ed pəʊk, -s, -ɪŋ,
-t

poker, -s 'pəʊkə*, -z

pok|y, -ier, -iest, -ily, -iness 'pəʊk|ɪ,
-ɪə* [-jə*], -ɪɪst [-jɪst], -ɪlɪ [-əlɪ], -ɪnɪs
[-nəs]

polacca, -s pəʊ'lækə, -z

Poland 'pəʊlənd

polar (s. adj.), -s 'pəʊlə*, -z

Polaris (*star*) pəʊˈlærɪs [-ˈlɑːr-, -ˈleər-; *the rocket and submarine are usually pronounced with* -ˈlɑːr-]
polariscope, -s pəʊˈlærɪskəʊp, -s
polarity pəʊˈlærətɪ [-ɪtɪ]
polarization [-isa-] ˌpəʊləraɪˈzeɪʃn [-ɪˈz-]
polariz|e [-is|e], **-es, -ing, -ed, -er/s** ˈpəʊləraɪz, -ɪz, -ɪŋ, -d, -ə*/z
polder, -s ˈpɒldə*, -z
Poldhu ˈpɒldjuː
pole, -s pəʊl, -z
Pole (*inhabitant of Poland*), **-s** pəʊl, -z
Pole (*surname*) pəʊl, puːl
  Note.—puːl *in* **Pole Carew** (*q.v.*) *and* **Chandos Pole** (ˌʃændɒsˈpuːl).
pole|axe/s, -cat/s ˈpəʊl|æks/ɪz, -kæt/s
Pole Carew ˌpuːlˈkeərɪ
polemic (*s. adj.*), **-s, -al, -ally** pəʊˌlemɪk [pɒˈl-], -s, -l, -əlɪ
pole-star, -s ˈpəʊlstɑː*, -z
Polhill ˈpəʊlhɪl
polic|e (*s. v.*), **-es, -ing, -ed** pəˈliːs [pʊˈl-], -ɪz, -ɪŋ, -t
police|man, -men pəˈliːsmən [plˈiːs-, ˈpliːs-, pʊˈl-], -mən
polic|y, -ies ˈpɒləs|ɪ [-lɪs-], -ɪz
policy-holder, -s ˈpɒləsɪˌhəʊldə* [-lɪs-], -z
polio ˈpəʊlɪəʊ [-ljəʊ]
poliomyelitis ˌpəʊlɪəʊmaɪəˈlaɪtɪs [-ljəʊ-, -maɪˈl-, -maɪeˈl-]
polish (*s. v.*), **-es, -ing, -ed, -er/s** ˈpɒlɪʃ, -ɪz, -ɪŋ, -t, -ə*/z
Polish (*adj.*) (*of Poland*) ˈpəʊlɪʃ
politburo ˈpɒlɪtˌbjʊərəʊ
polite, -st, -ly, -ness pəˈlaɪt [pʊˈl-], -ɪst, -lɪ, -nɪs [-nəs]
politic, -s ˈpɒlɪtɪk [-lət-], -s
politic|al, -ally pəˈlɪtɪk|l [pʊˈl-, -tək-], -əlɪ
politician, -s ˌpɒlɪˈtɪʃn [-ləˈt-], -z
politiciz|e [-cis|e], **-es, -ing, -ed** pəˈlɪtɪsaɪz, -ɪz, -ɪŋ, -d
polity ˈpɒlətɪ [-ɪtɪ]
Polixenes pɒˈlɪksənɪːz [pəˈl-, -sɪn-]
Polk pəʊk
polka, -s ˈpɒlkə [ˈpəʊl-], -z
poll (*s. v.*) (*at elections*), **-s, -ing, -ed** pəʊl, -z, -ɪŋ, -d
poll (*s.*) (*parrot, student taking pass degree at Cambridge*) (**P.**), **-s** pɒl, -z
poll (*adj.*) (*hornless, cut, executed by one party*) pəʊl
pollard (*s. v.*) (**P.**), **-s, -ing, -ed** ˈpɒləd, -z, -ɪŋ, -ɪd
pollen (**P.**), **-s, -ing, -ed** ˈpɒlən [-lɪn], -z, -ɪŋ, -d

pollinat|e, -es, -ing, -ed ˈpɒləneɪt [-lɪn-], -s, -ɪŋ, -ɪd
pollination ˌpɒlɪˈneɪʃn [-ləˈn-]
poll|-man, -men ˈpɒl|mæn, -men
Pollock ˈpɒlək
pollster, -s ˈpəʊlstə*, -z
poll-tax, -es ˈpəʊltæks, -ɪz
pollutant, -s pəˈluːtənt [-ˈljuː-], -s
pollut|e, -es, -ing, -ed, -er/s pəˈluːt [-ˈljuːt], -s, -ɪŋ, -ɪd, -ə*/z
pollution, -s pəˈluːʃn [-ˈljuː-], -z
Pollux ˈpɒləks
Polly ˈpɒlɪ
Polmont ˈpəʊlmənt
polo ˈpəʊləʊ
polonaise, -s ˌpɒləˈneɪz, -ɪz
Polonius pəˈləʊnjəs [pɒˈl-, -nɪəs]
polon|y, -ies pəˈləʊn|ɪ, -ɪz
Polson ˈpəʊlsn
poltergeist, -s ˈpɒltəgaɪst, -s
poltroon, -s; -ery pɒlˈtruːn, -z; -ərɪ
Polwarth (*in Borders Region*) ˈpəʊlwəθ, (*surname*) ˈpɒlwəθ
polyandrous ˌpɒlɪˈændrəs
polyandry ˈpɒlɪændrɪ [ˌpɒlɪˈæ-]
polyanthus, -es ˌpɒlɪˈænθəs, -ɪz
Polybius pɒˈlɪbɪəs [pəˈl-, -bjəs]
Polycarp ˈpɒlɪkɑːp
Polycrates pɒˈlɪkrətiːz [pəˈl-]
polyester ˌpɒlɪˈestə*
polyethylene ˌpɒlɪˈeθɪliːn [-θəl-]
polygam|ist/s, -y, -ous pəˈlɪgəm|ɪst/s [pɒˈl-], -ɪ, -əs
polyglot (*s. adj.*), **-s** ˈpɒlɪglɒt, -s
polygon, -s ˈpɒlɪgən, -z
polygonal pɒˈlɪgənl [pəˈl-]
polyhedr|on, -ons, -a, -al ˌpɒlɪˈhedr|ən [-ˈhiːd-, ˈpɒlɪˌh-], -ənz, -ə, -l
polylogue, -s ˈpɒlɪlɒg, -z
Polyne|sia, -sian/s ˌpɒlɪˈniː|zjə [-zɪə, -ʒə, -ʒɪə, -ʒə, -sjə, -sɪə, -ʃjə, -ʃɪə, -ʃə], -zjən/z [-zɪən/z, -ʒjən/z, -ʒɪən/z, -ʒn/z, -sjən/z, -sɪən/z, -ʃjən/z, -ʃɪən/z, -ʃn/z]
polynomial (*s. adj.*), **-s** ˌpɒlɪˈnəʊmjəl [-mɪəl], -z
polyp, -s, -ous ˈpɒlɪp, -s, -əs
Polyphemus ˌpɒlɪˈfiːməs
polyphonic ˌpɒlɪˈfɒnɪk
polyphony pəˈlɪfənɪ [pɒˈl-]
polypodium, -s ˌpɒlɪˈpəʊdjəm [-dɪəm], -z
polypody ˈpɒlɪpədɪ
polyp|us, -uses, -i ˈpɒlɪp|əs, -əsɪz, -aɪ
polysemous ˌpɒlɪˈsiːməs [pəˈlɪsɪməs, pɒˈl-]
polysemy ˌpɒlɪˈsiːmɪ [ˈ----]
polystyrene ˌpɒlɪˈstaɪriːn

polysyllabic, -ally ˌpɒlɪsɪ'læbɪk, -əlɪ
polysyllable, -s 'pɒlɪˌsɪləbl, -z
polysynthesis ˌpɒlɪ'sɪnθəsɪs [-θɪs-]
polysynthetic ˌpɒlɪsɪn'θetɪk
polytechnic (s. adj.), -s ˌpɒlɪ'teknɪk, -s
polythei|sm, -st/s 'pɒlɪθiːɪ|zəm
  [-θɪɪ|zəm], -st/s
polytheistic ˌpɒlɪθiː'ɪstɪk [-θɪ'ɪstɪk]
polythene 'pɒlɪθiːn
polyurethane ˌpɒlɪ'jʊərɪθeɪn [-rəθ-]
polyvinyl ˌpɒlɪ'vaɪnɪl [-nl]
Polyxen|a, -us pɒ'lɪksɪn|ə [pə'l-, -sən-],
  -əs
Polzeath pɒl'zeθ [-'ziːθ]
  Note.—The local pronunciation is
  pɒl'zɛːθ.
pomace 'pʌmɪs
pomade, -s pə'mɑːd [pɒ'm-], -z
pomander, -s pəʊ'mændə*, -z
pomatum, -s pəʊ'meɪtəm, -z
pome, -s pəʊm, -z
pomegranate,   -s   'pɒmɪˌɡrænɪt
  ['pɒmə-g-, 'pɒm-g-], -s
pomelo, -s 'pɒmɪləʊ, -z
Pomerania, -n/s ˌpɒmə'reɪmjə [-nɪə],
  -n/z
Pomeroy 'pəʊmrɔɪ, 'pɒmərɔɪ
pomfret (fish), -s 'pɒmfrɪt, -s
Pomfret 'pʌmfrɪt ['pɒm-]
pomfret cake, -s 'pʌmfrɪtkeɪk ['pɒm-], -s
pomm|el (s. v.), -els, -elling, -elled
  'pʌm|l ['pɒml, esp. as noun], -lz, -lɪŋ
  [-əlɪŋ], -ld
Pomona pəʊ'məʊnə
pomp, -s pɒmp, -s
pompadour (P.), -s 'pɒmpəˌdʊə*
  ['pɔ̃:mp-, 'pɔːmp-, -dɔə*, -dɔː*]
  (pɔ̃paduːr), -z
Pompeian pɒm'piːən [-'pɪən]
Pompeii pɒm'peiɪ: ['pɒmpɪaɪ, pɒm-
  'piːaɪ, -'peɪɪ]
Pompey 'pɒmpɪ
pompom, -s 'pɒmpɒm, -z
pompon, -s 'pɔ̃:mpɔ̃:ŋ ['pɔːmpɔːŋ,
  'pɒmpɒn] (pɔ̃pɔ̃)
pomposity pɒm'pɒsətɪ [-ɪtɪ]
pompous, -ly, -ness 'pɒmpəs, -lɪ, -nɪs
  [-nəs]
ponce, -s pɒns, -ɪz
poncho, -s 'pɒntʃəʊ, -z
pond (s. v.) (P.), -s, -ing, -ed pɒnd, -z,
  -ɪŋ, -ɪd
pond|er, -ers, -ering/ly, -ered 'pɒnd|ə*,
  -əz, -ərɪŋ/lɪ, -əd
ponderability ˌpɒndərə'bɪlətɪ [-lɪt-]
ponderable, -ness 'pɒndərəbl, -nɪs [-nəs]
ponderous, -ly, -ness 'pɒndərəs, -lɪ, -nɪs
  [-nəs]

Ponders 'pɒndəz
Pondicherry ˌpɒndɪ'tʃerɪ [-ɪ'ʃe-]
pongee pɒn'dʒiː [pʌn-]
poniard (s. v.), -s, -ing, -ed 'pɒnjəd
  [-jɑːd], -z, -ɪŋ, -ɪd
Pons asinorum ˌpɒnzæsɪ'nɔːrəm
Ponsonby 'pʌnsnbɪ
Pontefract (in West Yorkshire) 'pɒntɪ-
  frækt
  Note.—An old local pronunciation
  'pʌmfrɪt is now obsolete. The pronunciation survives in pomfret
  cake (q.v.).
pontifex (P.), pontifices 'pɒntɪfeks,
  pɒn'tɪfɪsiːz
pontiff, -s 'pɒntɪf, -s
pontific, -al/s, -ally; -ate/s pɒn'tɪfɪk,
  -l/z, -əlɪ; -ɪt/s [-eɪt/s, -ət/s]
pontificat|e (v.), -es, -ing, -ed pɒn-
  'tɪfɪkeɪt, -s, -ɪŋ, -ɪd
Pontine 'pɒntaɪn
Pontius 'pɒntjəs [-ntɪəs, -ntʃjəs, -ntʃəs,
  -nʃjəs, -nʃəs]
pontoon, -s pɒn'tuːn, -z
Pontresina ˌpɒntrɪ'siːnə [-trə's-]
Pontus 'pɒntəs
Pontypool ˌpɒntɪ'puːl (Welsh ˌpontə-
  'puːl)
Pontypridd ˌpɒntɪ'priːð (Welsh ˌpontə-
  'priːð)
pon|y, -ies 'pəʊn|ɪ, -ɪz
pood, -s puːd, -z
poodle, -s 'puːdl, -z
pooh pu̯ [phuː, puː]
Pooh-Bah ˌpuː'bɑ
pooh-pooh, -s, -ing, -ed ˌpuː'puː, -z, -ɪŋ
  [-'pʊɪŋ], -d
pool (s. v.), -s, -ing, -ed puːl, -z, -ɪŋ, -d
Poole puːl
Pooley 'puːlɪ
poon, -s puːn, -z
Poona 'puːnə [-nɑː] (Hindi puna; new
  designation Pune pune)
poop (s. v.), -s, -ing, -ed puːp, -s, -ɪŋ, -t
poor, -er, -est, -ly, -ness pʊə* [pɔə*,
  pɔː*], -rə*, -rɪst, -lɪ, -nɪs [-nəs]
poor-box, -es 'pʊəbɒks ['pɔə-, 'pɔː-], -ɪz
Poore pʊə*
poor-hou|se, -ses 'pʊəhaʊ|s ['pɔə-,
  'pɔː-], -zɪz
poor-law 'pʊəlɔː ['pɔə-, 'pɔː-]
poorly 'pʊəlɪ ['pɔə-, 'pɔː-]
pop (s. v. interj.), -s, -ping, -ped, -per/s
  pɒp, -s, -ɪŋ, -t, -ə*/z
pop-corn 'pɒpkɔːn
pope (P.), -s; -dom/s pəʊp, -s; -dəm/z
popery 'pəʊpərɪ
pop-gun, -s 'pɒpɡʌn, -z

Popham 'pɒpəm
popinjay, -s 'pɒpɪndʒeɪ, -z
popish, -ly, -ness 'pəʊpɪʃ, -lɪ, -nɪs [-nəs]
poplar (P.), -s 'pɒplə*, -z
poplin, -s 'pɒplɪn, -z
Popocatepetl 'pɒpəʊˌkætɪ'petl ['pəʊp-, -təˈp-] (Aztec po,poka'tepetl̩)
popp|le, -les, -ling, -led 'pɒp|l̩, -lz, -l̩ɪŋ [-lɪŋ], -l̩d
popp|y (P.), -ies 'pɒp|ɪ, -ɪz
poppycock 'pɒpɪkɒk
poppy-head, -s 'pɒpɪhed, -z
pop-shop, -s 'pɒpʃɒp, -s
populace 'pɒpjʊləs [-pjəl-, -lɪs]
popular, -ly 'pɒpjʊlə* [-pjəl-], -lɪ
popularity ˌpɒpjʊ'lærətɪ [-pjə'l-, -ɪtɪ]
popularization ˌpɒpjʊləraɪ'zeɪʃn [-pjəl-, -rɪ'z-]
populariz|e [-is|e], -es, -ing, -ed 'pɒpjʊləraɪz [-pjəl-], -ɪz, -ɪŋ, -d
populat|e, -es, -ing, -ed 'pɒpjʊleɪt [-pjəl-], -s, -ɪŋ, -ɪd
population, -s ˌpɒpjʊ'leɪʃn [-pjə'l-], -z
populous, -ly, -ness 'pɒpjʊləs [-pjəl-], -lɪ, -nɪs [-nəs]
porage 'pɒrɪdʒ
porcelain, -s 'pɔːsəlɪn [-leɪn], -z
porch, -es pɔːtʃ, -ɪz
Porchester 'pɔːtʃɪstə* [-tʃəs-]
porcine 'pɔːsaɪn
porcupine, -s 'pɔːkjʊpaɪn, -z
por|e (s. v.), -es, -ing, -ed pɔː* [pɒə*], -z, -rɪŋ, -d
porgy (fish) 'pɔːdʒɪ
Porgy (name) 'pɔːgɪ
pork, -er/s, -y pɔːk, -ə*/z, -ɪ
pornographic ˌpɔːnəʊ'græfɪk
pornography pɔː'nɒgrəfɪ
porosity pɔː'rɒsətɪ [-ɪtɪ]
porous, -ly, -ness 'pɔːrəs, -lɪ, -nɪs [-nəs]
porphyry (P.) 'pɔːfɪrɪ [-fərɪ]
porpoise, -s 'pɔːpəs, -ɪz
porridge 'pɒrɪdʒ
porringer, -s 'pɒrɪndʒə*, -z
Porsche pɔːʃ
Porsena 'pɔːsɪnə [-sən-]
Porson 'pɔːsn
port (s. v.), -s, -ing, -ed pɔːt, -s, -ɪŋ, -ɪd
portability ˌpɔːtə'bɪlətɪ [-lɪt-]
portable, -ness 'pɔːtəbl, -nɪs [-nəs]
Portadown ˌpɔːtə'daʊn
portage 'pɔːtɪdʒ
portal (P.), -s 'pɔːtl, -z
portamento, -s ˌpɔːtə'mentəʊ, -z
portcullis, -es ˌpɔːt'kʌlɪs, -ɪz
Porte pɔːt
portend, -s, -ing, -ed pɔː'tend, -z, -ɪŋ, -ɪd
portent, -s 'pɔːtent [-tənt], -s

portentous, -ly pɔː'tentəs, -lɪ
porter (P.), -s; -age 'pɔːtə*, -z; -rɪdʒ
Porteus 'pɔːtjəs [-tɪəs]
portfolio, -s ˌpɔːt'fəʊljəʊ [-lɪəʊ], -z
porthole, -s 'pɔːthəʊl, -z
Portia 'pɔːʃjə [-ʃɪə, -ʃə]
portico, -s 'pɔːtɪkəʊ, -z
porti|on (s. v.), -ons, -oning, -oned 'pɔːʃ|n, -nz, -n̩ɪŋ [-ənɪŋ], -nd
Portishead 'pɔːtɪshed
Portland 'pɔːtlənd
Portlaw ˌpɔːt'lɔː
portl|y, -ier, -iest, -iness 'pɔːtl|ɪ, -ɪə* [-jə*], -ɪɪst [-jɪst], -ɪnɪs [-ɪnəs]
Portmadoc ˌpɔːt'mædək (Welsh port-'madok)
Portman 'pɔːtmən
portmanteau, -s ˌpɔːt'mæntəʊ, -z
Portobello ˌpɔːtəʊ'beləʊ
Porto Rico ˌpɔːtəʊ'riːkəʊ
portrait, -s; -ist/s 'pɔːtrɪt [-treɪt, -trət], -s; -ɪst/s
portraiture 'pɔːtrɪtʃə [-trətʃ-, -ˌtjʊə*]
portray, -s, -ing, -ed, -er/s pɔː'treɪ, -z, -ɪŋ, -d, -ə*/z [pɔː'treə*/z]
portrayal, -s pɔː'treɪəl [-'treɪl], -z
portreeve, -s 'pɔːtriːv, -z
Portrush ˌpɔːt'rʌʃ
Port Said ˌpɔːt'saɪd [old-fashioned -'seɪd]
Port Salut ˌpɔːtsə'luː [-sæ-] (pɔrsaly)
Portsea 'pɔːtsɪ [-siː]
Portsmouth 'pɔːtsməθ
Portsoy ˌpɔːt'sɔɪ
Portugal 'pɔːtʃʊgl [-tjʊ-]
Portuguese ˌpɔːtʃʊ'giːz [-tjʊ-]
posaune, -s pə'zɔːn, -z
pos|e (s. v.), -es, -ing, -ed, -er/s pəʊz, -ɪz, -ɪŋ, -d, -ə*/z
Poseidon pɒ'saɪdən [pə's-]
poser (problem), -s 'pəʊzə*, -z
poseur, -s pəʊ'zɜː* (pozœːr), -z
posh pɒʃ
posit, -s, -ing, -ed 'pɒzɪt, -s, -ɪŋ, -ɪd
position, -s pə'zɪʃn [pʊ'z-], -z
positional pə'zɪʃənl [pʊ'z-, -ʃnəl, -ʃn̩l, -ʃn̩l, -ʃnəl, -ʃənəl]
positive (s. adj.), -s, -ly, -ness 'pɒzətɪv [-zɪt-], -z, -lɪ, -nɪs [-nəs]
positivi|sm, -st/s 'pɒzɪtɪvɪ|zəm [-zət-], -st/s
positron, -s 'pɒzɪtrɒn [-trən], -z
posse, -s 'pɒsɪ, -z
possess, -es, -ing, -ed, -or/s pə'zes [pʊ'z-], -ɪz, -ɪŋ, -t, -ə*/z
possession, -s pə'zeʃn [pʊ'z-], -z
possessive (s. adj.), -s, -ly, -ness pə'zesɪv [pʊ'z-], -z, -lɪ, -nɪs [-nəs]

387

possessory pə'zesərı [pʊ'z-]

posset 'pɒsɪt

possibilit|y, -ies ˌpɒsə'bɪlət|ı [-sı'b-], -lıt-], -ız

possib|le, -ly 'pɒsəb|l [-sıb-], -lı

possum, -s 'pɒsəm, -z

post (s. v.), -s, -ing, -ed pəʊst, -s, -ıŋ, -ıd

postage, -s 'pəʊstıdʒ, -ız

postal 'pəʊstəl

postal-order (P.O.), -s 'pəʊstl̩ˌɔːdə* (ˌpiː'əʊ), -z

post-bag, -s 'pəʊstbæg, -z

postcard, -s 'pəʊstkɑːd, -z

post-chaise, -s 'pəʊst-ʃeız [ˌ-'-], -ız

postdat|e, -es, -ing, -ed ˌpəʊst'deıt ['--], -s, -ıŋ, -ıd

post-diluvian ˌpəʊstdaı'luːvjən [-dı'l-, -'ljuː-, -vıən]

poster, -s 'pəʊstə*, -z

poste restante ˌpəʊst'restãːnt [-tɔ̃ːnt, -tɑːnt, -tɒnt] (postrestã:t)

posterior, -ly pɒ'stıərıə*, -lı

posteriority pɒˌstıərı'ɒrətı [ˌpɒstıər-, -rtı]

posterit|y, -ies pɒ'sterət|ı [-rt|ı], -ız

postern, -s 'pəʊstəːn [-tən], -z

post-free ˌpəʊst'friː

Postgate 'pəʊstgeıt [-gıt]

post|horn/s, -horse/s 'pəʊst|hɔːn/z, -hɔːs/ız

posthumous, -ly 'pɒstjʊməs, -lı

postiche, -s pɒ'stiːʃ [ˈ--], -ız

postil, -s 'pɒstıl, -z

postillion, -s pə'stıljən [pɒ's-, -lıən], -z

post-impressioni|sm, -st/s ˌpəʊstım-'preʃn̩|ızəm [-ʃənı-], -st/s

Postlethwaite 'pɒslθweıt

post|man, -men 'pəʊst|mən, -mən

postmark (s. v.), -s, -ing, -ed 'pəʊst-mɑːk, -s, -ıŋ, -t

postmaster, -s 'pəʊstˌmɑːstə*, -z

post-meridian ˌpəʊstmə'rıdıən [-djən]

post-mistress, -es 'pəʊstˌmıstrıs [-trəs], -ız

post-mortem, -s ˌpəʊst'mɔːtem [-təm], -z

post-natal ˌpəʊst'neıtl

post-office, -s 'pəʊstˌɒfıs, -ız

postpon|e (s. v.), -es, -ing, -ed, -ement/s ˌpəʊst'pəʊn [pəs'p-], -z, -ıŋ, -d, -mənt/s

postposition, -s ˌpəʊstpə'zıʃn [-pʊ'z-, ˈ--ˌ--], -z

postscript, -s 'pəʊsskrıpt ['pəʊstskrıpt], -s

post-tonic ˌpəʊst'tɒnık

post-town, -s 'pəʊsttaʊn, -z

postulant, -s 'pɒstjʊlənt, -s

postulate (s.), -s 'pɒstjʊlət [-lıt, -leıt], -s

postulat|e (v.), -es, -ing, -ed 'pɒstjʊ-leıt, -s, -ıŋ, -ıd

postulation, -s ˌpɒstjʊ'leıʃn, -z

postum 'pəʊstəm

postur|e (s. v.), -es, -ing, -ed 'pɒstʃə* [-ˌtjʊə*], -z, -rıŋ, -d

post-war ˌpəʊst'wɔː* [also '-- when attributive]

pos|y -ies 'pəʊz|ı, -ız

pot (s. v.), -s, -ting, -ted, -er/s pɒt, -s, -ıŋ, -ıd, -ə*/z

potable, -ness, -s 'pəʊtəbl, -nıs [-nəs], -z

potage, -s pɒ'tɑːʒ ['pɒtɑːʒ] (pɔtaːʒ), -ız

potash, -water 'pɒtæʃ, -ˌwɔːtə*

potassium pə'tæsjəm [-sıəm]

potation, -s pəʊ'teıʃn, -z

potato, -es pə'teıtəʊ, -z

pot-bellied 'pɒtˌbelıd [ˌ-'--]

pot-boiler, -s 'pɒtˌbɔılə*, -z

poteen pɒ'tiːn [pəʊ-, -'tʃiːn]

Potemkin pə'temkın [pə'tjɒmkın]

poten|cy, -t/ly 'pəʊtən|sı, -t/lı

potentate, -s 'pəʊtənteıt [-tıt], -s

potenti|al (s. adj.), -als, -ally pəʊ'tenʃ|l [pʊ't-], -lz, -əlı

potentialit|y, -ies pəʊˌtenʃı'ælət|ı [pʊˌt-, -rt|ı], -ız

potentilla, -s ˌpəʊtən'tılə, -z

pother (s. v.), -s, -ing, -ed 'pɒðə*, -z, -rıŋ, -d

pot-herb, -s 'pɒthɜːb, -z

pot-hole, -s, -er/s 'pɒthəʊl, -z, -ə*/z

pothook, -s 'pɒthʊk, -s

pothou|se, -ses 'pɒthaʊ|s, -zız

pot-hunter, -s 'pɒtˌhʌntə*, -z

potion, -s 'pəʊʃn, -z

Potiphar 'pɒtıfə* [-fɑː*]

pot-luck ˌpɒt'lʌk

Potomac pə'təʊmək

Potosi (in Bolivia) ˌpɒtəʊ'siː, (in U.S.A.) pə'təʊsı

pot-pourri, -s ˌpəʊ'pʊri: [ˌ--'-] (popuri), -z

Potsdam 'pɒtsdæm

potsherd, -s 'pɒt-ʃɜːd, -z

pot-shot, -s 'pɒt-ʃɒt [ˌ-'-], -s

Pott pɒt

pottage 'pɒtıdʒ

pott|er (s. v.) (P.), -ers, -ering, -ered, -erer/s 'pɒt|ə*, -əz, -ərıŋ, -əd, -ərə*/z

potter|y, -ies (P.) 'pɒtər|ı, -ız

pottle, -s 'pɒtl, -z

pott|y, -ier, -iest, -iness 'pɒt|ɪ, -ɪə*,
-ɪst, -ɪnɪs [-məs]
Pou (*French-Canadian name*) pju:
pouch (*s.*), -es paʊtʃ [*in the army also*
puːtʃ], -ɪz
pouch (*v.*), -es, -ing, -ed paʊtʃ, -ɪz, -ɪŋ, -t
pouf(fe), -s puːf, -s
Poughill 'pɒfɪl
Poulett 'poːlɪt [-let]
poulpe, -s puːlp, -s
Poulson 'pəʊlsən ['puːl-]
poult (*chicken*), -s pəʊlt, -s
poult (*silk material*) puːlt
poulter, -s 'pəʊltə*, -z
poulterer, -s 'pəʊltərə*, -z
poultic|e (*s. v.*), -es, -ing, -ed 'pəʊltɪs,
-ɪz, -ɪŋ, -t
Poultney 'pəʊltnɪ
Poulton 'pəʊltən
poultry 'pəʊltrɪ
poultry-farm, -s, -ing, -er/s 'pəʊltrɪ-
faːm, -z, -ɪŋ, -ə*/z
poultry-yard, -s 'pəʊltrɪjaːd, -z
pounc|e (*s. v.*), -es, -ing, -ed paʊns, -ɪz,
-ɪŋ, -t
Pouncefoot 'paʊnsfʊt
pound (*s. v.*) (P.), -s, -ing, -ed, -er/s
paʊnd, -z, -ɪŋ, -ɪd, -ə*/z
poundage, -s 'paʊndɪdʒ, -ɪz
Pounds paʊndz
Pount(e)ney 'paʊntnɪ
Poupart (*surname*) 'pəʊpaːt, 'puːpaːt
Pouparts (*junction near Clapham Junction*) 'puːpaːts
pour (*s. v.*), -s, -ing, -ed, -er/s pɔː*
[pɔə*], -z, -ɪŋ, -d, -rə*/z
pourboire, -s 'pʊəbwaː* (purbwaːr), -z
pourparler, -s ˌpʊə'paːleɪ (purparle), -z
pout (*s. v.*), -s, -ing, -ed, -er/s paʊt, -s,
-ɪŋ, -ɪd, -ə*/z
poverty 'pɒvətɪ
poverty-stricken 'pɒvətɪˌstrɪkən
Pow paʊ
P.O.W., -'s ˌpiː:əʊ'dʌbljuː:, -z
powd|er (*s. v.*), -ers, -ering, -ered
'paʊd|ə*, -əz, -ərɪŋ, -əd
powder-magazine, -s 'paʊdəmægəˌziːn,
-z
powder-puff, -s 'paʊdəpʌf, -s
powder|y, -iness 'paʊdər|ɪ, -ɪnɪs [-məs]
Powell 'pəʊəl [-ɪl, -əl], 'paʊ-
power (P.), -s 'paʊə*, -z
power-cut, -s 'paʊəkʌt, -s
power|ful, -fully, -fulness 'paʊə|fʊl,
-fʊlɪ [-fəlɪ, -flɪ], -fʊlnɪs [-nəs]
power-hou|se, -ses 'paʊəhaʊ|s, -zɪz
powerless, -ly, -ness 'paʊəlɪs [-ləs], -lɪ,
-nɪs [-nəs]

Powerscourt (*family name*) 'pɔːzkəːt
power-station, -s 'paʊəˌsteɪʃn, -z
Powicke 'pəʊɪk
Powis (*in Scotland*) 'paʊɪs, (*surname*)
'pəʊɪs, 'paʊɪs, (*square in London*)
'paʊɪs
Powles pəʊlz
Powlett 'pɔːlɪt
Pownall 'paʊnl
Pownceby 'paʊnsbɪ
pow-wow (*s. v.*), -s, -ing, -ed 'paʊwaʊ,
-z, -ɪŋ, -d
Powyke 'pəʊɪk
Powys (*county in Wales, family name
of Viscount Lilford*) 'pəʊɪs, 'paʊɪs
pox pɒks
Poynings 'pɔɪnɪŋz
Poynt|er, -on 'pɔɪnt|ə*, -ən
practicability ˌpræktɪkə'bɪlətɪ [-lɪt-]
practicab|le, -ly, -leness 'præktɪkəb|l,
-lɪ, -lnɪs [-nəs]
practic|al, -alness 'præktɪk|l, -lnɪs [-nəs]
practicality ˌpræktɪ'kælətɪ [-rtɪ]
practically (*in a practical manner*)
'præktɪkəlɪ [-klɪ], (*very nearly*) 'præk-
tɪklɪ [-kəlɪ]
practice, -s 'præktɪs, -ɪz
practician, -s præk'tɪʃn, -z
practis|e, -es, -ing, -ed, -er/s 'præktɪs,
-ɪz, -ɪŋ, -t, -ə*/z
practitioner, -s præk'tɪʃnə* [prək-,
-ʃənə*], -z
Praed preɪd
praenomen, -s ˌpriː'nəʊmen, -z
praepostor, -s ˌpriː'pɒstə*, -z
praesidium, -s prɪ'sɪdɪəm [prɪ'zɪd-,
-djəm], -z
praetor, -s; -ship/s 'priːtə* [-tɔː*], -z;
-ʃɪp/s
praetori|al, -an, -um/s, -a priː'tɔːrɪ|əl
[prɪ-], -ən, -əm/z, -ə
pragmatic, -al, -ally præg'mætɪk, -l, -əlɪ
pragmati|sm, -st/s 'prægmətɪ|zəm, -st/s
Prague praːg
prairie (P.), -s; -land 'preərɪ, -z; -lænd
prais|e (*s. v.*), -es, -ing, -ed, -er/s
preɪz, -ɪz, -ɪŋ, -d, -ə*/z
praiseworth|y, -iness 'preɪzˌwəː:ð|ɪ, -ɪnɪs
[-məs]
Prakrit 'praːkrɪt
praline, -s 'praːliːn, -z
Prall prɔːl
pram (*perambulator*), -s præm, -z
pram (*flat-bottomed boat*), -s praːm, -z
pranc|e (P.), -es, -ing, -ed, -er/s praːns,
-ɪz, -ɪŋ, -t, -ə*/z
prandial 'prændɪəl [-djəl]
prang (*s. v.*), -s, -ing, -ed præŋ, -z, -ɪŋ, -d

prank (s. v.), **-s, -ing, -ed** præŋk, -s, -ıŋ, -t [præŋt]

prank|ish, -some 'præŋk|ıʃ, -səm

prat|e (s. v.), **-es, -ing, -ed, -er/s** preıt, -s, -ıŋ, -ıd, -ə*/z

pratincole, **-s** 'prætıŋkəʊl, -z

pratique, **-s** 'præti:k [-tık, præ'ti:k], **-s**

Pratt præt

pratt|le (s. v.), **-les, -ling, -led, -ler/s** 'præt|l, -lz, -lıŋ [-lıŋ], -ld, -lə*/z [-lə*/z]

prawn, **-s** prɔːn, -z

prax|is, **-es** 'præks|ıs, -iːz

Praxiteles præk'sıtəliːz [-tıl-]

pray (P.), **-s, -ing, -ed** preı, -z, -ıŋ, -d

prayer (one who prays), **-s** 'preıə*, -z

prayer (supplication), **-s** preə*, -z

prayer-book, **-s** 'preəbʊk, -s

prayer|ful, -fully, -fulness 'preə|fʊl, -fʊlı [-fəlı], -fʊlnıs [-nəs]

prayerless, -ly, -ness 'preəlıs [-ləs], -lı, -nıs [-nəs]

prayer-meeting, **-s** 'preə,miːtıŋ, -z

prayer-rug, **-s** 'preərʌg, -z

prayer-wheel, **-s** 'preəwiːl ['preəhw-], -z

preach (s. v.), **-es, -ing, -ed, -er/s** priːtʃ, -ız, -ıŋ, -t, -ə*/z

preachi|fy, -fies, -fying, -fied 'priːtʃı|faı, -faız, -faıŋ, -faıd

pre-adamite ,prıː'ædəmaıt

Preager 'preıgə*

preamble, **-s** priː'æmbl [prı'æ-], -z

prearrang|e, -es, -ing, -ed ,priːə'reımdʒ, -ız, -ıŋ, -d

Prebble 'prebl

prebend, **-s** 'prebənd, -z

prebendar|y, -ies 'prebəndər|ı [-bnd-], -ız

precarious, -ly, -ness prı'keərıəs [prə'k-], -lı, -nıs [-nəs]

precatory 'prekətərı

precaution, **-s** prı'kɔːʃn [prə'k-], -z

precautionary prı'kɔːʃnərı [prə'k-, -ʃnə-, -ʃənə-]

preced|e, -es, -ing, -ed ,priː'siːd [prı-], -z, -ıŋ, -ıd

preceden|ce, -cy ,priː'siːdən|s [prı-, 'presıd-, 'priː-], -sı

precedent (s.), **-s, -ed** 'presıdənt ['priːs-], -s, -ıd

precedent (adj.), **-ly** prı'siːdənt ['presıd-], -lı

precentor, **-s** ,priː'sentə* [prı-], -z

precept, **-s** 'priːsept, -s

preceptor, **-s** prı'septə*, -z

preceptor|y, -ies prı'septər|ı, -ız

preces 'priːsiːz

precession, **-s** prı'seʃn, -z

precinct, **-s** 'priːsıŋkt, -s

preciosity ,preʃı'ɒsətı [-esı-, -ıtı]

precious, -ly, -ness 'preʃəs, -lı, -nıs [-nəs]

precipice, **-s** 'presıpıs [-səp-], -ız

precipitan|ce, -cy prı'sıpıtən|s, -sı

precipitate (s.), **-s** prı'sıpıteıt [prə's-, -tət, -tıt], -s

precipitate (adj.), **-ly** prı'sıpıtət [prə's-, -tıt], -lı

precipitat|e (v.), -es, -ing, -ed prı'sıpıteıt [prə's-], -s, -ıŋ, -ıd

precipitation prı,sıpı'teıʃn [prə,s-]

precipitous, -ly, -ness prı'sıpıtəs [prə's-], -lı, -nıs [-nəs]

précis (sing.) 'preısı: ['pres-], (plur.) -z

precise, -ly, -ness prı'saıs [prə's-], -lı, -nıs [-nəs]

precisian, **-s** prı'sıʒn [prə's-], -z

precision prı'sıʒn [prə's-]

preclud|e, -es, -ing, -ed prı'kluːd, -z, -ıŋ, -ıd

preclu|sion, -sive prı'kluː|ʒn, -sıv

precocious, -ly, -ness prı'kəʊʃəs [prə'k-], -lı, -nıs [-nəs]

precocity prı'kɒsətı [prə'k-, -ıtı]

preconceiv|e, -es, -ing, -ed ,priːkən'siːv, -z, -ıŋ, -d [also 'priːkənsiːvd when attributive]

preconception, **-s** ,priːkən'sepʃn, -z

preconcert, **-s, -ing, -ed** ,priːkən'sɜːt, **-s**, -ıŋ, -ıd

precursor, **-s; -y** ,priː'kɜːsə* [prı-], -z; -rı

predation, **-s** prı'deıʃn [pre'd-], -z

predator|y, -ily, -iness 'predətər|ı, -əlı [-ılı], -ınıs [-nəs]

predeceas|e, -es, -ing, -ed ,priːdı'siːs, -ız, -ıŋ, -t

predecessor, **-s** 'priːdısesə* [,priːdı's-], -z

predestinat|e, -es, -ing, -ed ,priː-'destıneıt [prı-], -s, -ıŋ, -ıd

predestination priː,destı'neıʃn [prı'd-, 'priː,destı'neıʃn]

predestin|e, -es, -ing, -ed ,priː'destın [prı'd-], -z, -ıŋ, -d

predetermination 'priːdıˌtɜː'mı'neıʃn

predetermin|e, -es, -ing, -ed ,priːdı-'tɜːmın, -z, -ıŋ, -d

predicability ,predıkə'bılətı [-lıt-]

predicable 'predıkəbl

predicament, **-s** prı'dıkəmənt [prə'd-], -s

predicate (s.), **-s** 'predıkət [-kıt, -keıt, 'priːdıkıt, -kət], -s

predicat|e (v.), -es, -ing, -ed 'predıkeıt, -s, -ıŋ, -ıd

predication, **-s** ,predı'keıʃn, -z

predicative, -ly prɪ'dɪkətɪv [prə'd-], -lɪ
predict, -s, -ing, -ed, -or/s; -able prɪ'dɪkt [prə'd-], -s, -ɪŋ, -ɪd, -ə*/z; -əbl
prediction, -s prɪ'dɪkʃn [prə'd-], -z
predilection, -s ˌpri:dɪ'lekʃn, -z
predispos|e, -es, -ing, -ed ˌpri:dɪ'spəʊz -ɪz, -ɪŋ, -d
predisposition, -s 'pri:ˌdɪspə'zɪʃn [ˌpri:dɪs-], -z
predominan|ce, -t/ly prɪ'dɒmɪnən|s [prə'd-], -t/lɪ
predominat|e, -es, -ing, -ed prɪ'dɒmɪneɪt [prə'd-], -s, -ɪŋ, -ɪd
predomination prɪˌdɒmɪ'neɪʃn [prə,d-]
predorsal ˌpri:'dɔ:sl
Preece pri:s
pre-eminen|ce, -t/ly ˌpri:'emɪnən|s [prɪ'em-], -t/lɪ
pre-empt, -s, -ing, -ed ˌpri:'empt [prɪ'em-], -s, -ɪŋ, -ɪd
pre-emption ˌpri:'empʃn [prɪ'em-]
pre-emptive ˌpri:'emptɪv [prɪ'em-]
preen, -s, -ing, -ed pri:n, -z, -ɪŋ, -d
pre-exist, -s, -ing, -ed; -ence, -ent ˌpri:ɪg'zɪst, -s, -ɪŋ, -ɪd; -əns, -ənt
prefab, -s 'pri:fæb, -z
prefabricat|e, -es, -ing, -ed ˌpri:'fæbrɪkeɪt, -s, -ɪŋ, -ɪd
pre-fabrication 'pri:ˌfæbrɪ'keɪʃn [ˌ—'—, -ˌ—'—]
prefac|e (s. v.), -es, -ing, -ed 'prefɪs [-fəs], -ɪz, -ɪŋ, -t
prefatorial ˌprefə'tɔ:rɪəl
prefatory 'prefətərɪ
prefect, -s 'pri:fekt, -s
prefecture, -s 'pri:fekˌtjʊə* [-ˌtʃʊə*, -tʃə*], -z
prefer, -s, -ring, -red prɪ'fɜ:* [prə'f-], -z, -rɪŋ, -d
preferability ˌprefərə'bɪlətɪ [-lɪt-]
preferab|le, -ly, -leness 'prefərəb|l [rarely prɪ'fɜ:r-, prə'fɜ:r-], -lɪ, -lnɪs [-nəs]
preference, -s 'prefərəns, -ɪz
preferential ˌprefə'renʃl
preferment, -s prɪ'fɜ:mənt [prə'f-], -s
prefix (s.), -es 'pri:fɪks, -ɪz
prefix (v.), -es, -ing, -ed ˌpri:'fɪks ['pri:fɪks], -ɪz, -ɪŋ, -t
pregnable 'pregnəbl
pregnan|cy, -t/ly 'pregnən|sɪ, -t/lɪ
prehensible prɪ'hensəbl [-sɪb-]
prehensile prɪ'hensaɪl [ˌpri:'h-]
prehistoric, -ally ˌpri:hɪ'stɒrɪk, -əlɪ [-lɪ]
pre-history ˌpri:'hɪstərɪ
prejudg|e, -es, -ing, -ed ˌpri:'dʒʌdʒ, -ɪz, -ɪŋ, -d

prejudic|e (s. v.), -es, -ing, -ed 'predʒʊdɪs [-dʒəd-], -ɪz, -ɪŋ, -t
prejudici|al, -ally ˌpredʒʊ'dɪʃ|l [-dʒə'd-], -əlɪ [-lɪ]
prelac|y, -ies 'preləs|ɪ, -ɪz
prelate, -s 'prelɪt [-lət], -s
preliminar|y, -ies, -ily prɪ'lɪmɪnər|ɪ [prə'l-, -'lɪmɪnr-, -mən-], -ɪz, -əlɪ [-ɪlɪ]
prelims (preliminary examination; introductory pages in book) 'pri:lɪmz [ˌ-'-]
prelud|e (s. v.), -es, -ing, -ed 'prelju:d, -z, -ɪŋ ['preljʊdɪŋ], -ɪd ['preljudɪd]
premature, -ly, -ness ˌpremə'tjʊə* [ˌpri:m-, -'tjɔə*, -'tjɔ:*, -'tʃʊə*, 'premə,tjʊə*, 'pri:m-, -tjɔə*, -tjɔ:, -ˌtʃʊə], -lɪ, -nɪs [-nəs]
premeditate, -es, -ing, -ed/ly ˌpri:'medɪteɪt [prɪ'm-], -s, -ɪŋ, -ɪd/lɪ
premeditation pri:ˌmedɪ'teɪʃn [prɪˌm-]
premier (s. adj.), -s; -ship/s 'premjə* [-mɪə*], -z; -ʃɪp/s
première, -s 'premɪeə*, -z
premise (s.), -s 'premɪs, -ɪz
premis|e (v.), -es, -ing, -ed prɪ'maɪz ['premɪs], -ɪz, -ɪŋ, prɪ'maɪzd ['premɪst]
premium, -s 'pri:mjəm [-mɪəm], -z
premonition, -s ˌpri:mə'nɪʃn [ˌprem-], -z
premonitor|y, -ily prɪ'mɒnɪtər|ɪ, -əlɪ [-ɪlɪ]
pre-natal ˌpri:'neɪtl
Prendergast 'prendəgæst [-gɑ:st]
prentice, -s 'prentɪs, -ɪz
Prenti|ce, -ss 'prentɪ|s, -s
preoccupation, -s pri:ˌɒkjʊ'peɪʃn [prɪˌɒk-, ˌpri:ɒk-], -z
preoccup|y, -ies, -ying, -ied ˌpri:'ɒkjʊp|aɪ [prɪ'ɒk-], -aɪz, -aɪɪŋ, -aɪd
preordain, -s, -ing, -ed ˌpri:ɔ:'deɪn, -z, -ɪŋ, -d
prep (s. adj.), -s prep, -s
prepaid (from prepay) ˌpri:'peɪd [also '— when attributive]
preparation, -s ˌprepə'reɪʃn, -z
preparative, -ly prɪ'pærətɪv [prə'p-], -lɪ
preparator|y, -ily prɪ'pærətər|ɪ [prə'p-], -əlɪ [-ɪlɪ]
prepar|e, -es, -ing, -ed, -edly, -edness, -er/s prɪ'peə* [prə'p-], -z, -rɪŋ, -d, -dlɪ [-rɪdlɪ], -dnɪs [-rɪdnɪs, -nəs], -rə*/z
prepay, -s, -ing, prepaid, prepayment/s ˌpri:'peɪ, -z, -ɪŋ, ˌpri:'peɪd [also '— when attributive], ˌpri:'peɪmənt/s
prepense, -ly prɪ'pens, -lɪ
preponderan|ce, -t/ly prɪ'pɒndərən|s [prə'p-], -t/lɪ

391

preponderat|e, -es, -ing/ly, -ed prɪ-
'pɒndərert [prə'p-], -s, -ɪŋ/lɪ, -ɪd
preponderation prɪ,pɒndə'reɪʃn [prə,p-]
prepos|e, -es, -ing, -ed ,pri:'pəʊz, -ɪz,
-ɪŋ, -d
preposition, -s ,prepə'zɪʃn, -z
preposi|tional, -tionally ,prepə'zɪ|ʃənl
[-pʊ'z-, -ʃnəl, -ʃn̩l, -ʃn̩l, -ʃənəl], -ʃŋəlɪ
[-ʃnəlɪ, -ʃŋlɪ, -ʃn̩lɪ, -ʃənəlɪ]
prepositive prɪ'pɒzətɪv [-ɪtɪv]
prepossess, -es, -ing/ly, -ed ,pri:pə'zes,
-ɪz, -ɪŋ/lɪ, -t
prepossession, -s ,pri:pə'zeʃn, -z
preposterous, -ly, -ness prɪ'pɒstərəs
[prə'p-], -lɪ, -nɪs [-nəs]
prepuce, -s 'pri:pju:s, -ɪz
Pre-Raphaelite (s. adj.), -s ,pri:'ræfəlaɪt
[-fɪl-, -fʃ-, -frəl-, -ferəl-], -s
prerequisite, -s ,pri:'rekwɪzɪt, -s
prerogative (s. adj.), -s prɪ'rɒgətɪv
[prə'r-], -z
presage (s.), -s 'presɪdʒ, -ɪz
presag|e (v.), -es, -ing, -ed 'presɪdʒ
[prɪ'seɪdʒ], -ɪz, -ɪŋ, -d
presbyopia ,prezbɪ'əʊpjə [-pɪə]
presbyter, -s 'prezbɪtə*, -z
presbyterian, -s, -ism ,prezbɪ'tɪərɪən
[-bə't-], -z, -ɪzəm
presbyter|y, -ies 'prezbɪtər|ɪ, -ɪz
prescien|ce, -t/ly 'presɪən|s [-sjə-, -ʃɪə-,
-ʃjə-], -t/lɪ
Prescot(t) 'preskət
prescrib|e, -es, -ing, -ed, -er/s prɪ-
'skraɪb [prə's-], -z, -ɪŋ, -d, -ə*/z
prescript, -s 'pri:skrɪpt, -s
prescription, -s prɪ'skrɪpʃn [prə's-], -z
prescriptive prɪ'skrɪptɪv [prə's-]
presence, -s 'prezns, -ɪz
present (s.) (ordinary senses), -s 'preznt
[-zənt], -s
present (s.) (military term), -s prɪ'zent
[prə'z-], -s
present (adj.), -ly 'preznt [-zənt], -lɪ
present (v.), -s, -ing, -ed, -ment prɪ'zent
[prə'z-], -s, -ɪŋ, -ɪd, -mənt
presentable, -ness prɪ'zentəbl [prə'z-],
-nɪs [-nəs]
presentation, -s ,prezən'teɪʃn [-zen-, -]
presentient prɪ'senʃɪənt [-ʃjənt, -ʃənt]
presentiment, -s prɪ'zentɪmənt [-ɪ'se-],
-s
presently 'prezntlɪ [-zənt-]
preservation, -s ,prezə'veɪʃn, -z
preservative (s. adj.), -s prɪ'zɜ:vətɪv, -z
preserv|e (s. v.), -es, -ing, -ed, -er/s;
-able prɪ'zɜ:v, -z, -ɪŋ, -d, -ə*/z; -əbl
presid|e, -es, -ing, -ed prɪ'zaɪd, -z, -ɪŋ,
-ɪd

presidenc|y, -ies 'prezɪdəns|ɪ, -ɪz
president, -s 'prezɪdənt, -s
presidential ,prezɪ'denʃl
presidium, -s prɪ'sɪdɪəm [prɪ'zɪd-,
-djəm], -z
press (s. v.), -es, -ing/ly, -ed, -er/s pres,
-ɪz, -ɪŋ/lɪ, -t, -ə*/z
press-agent, -s 'pres,eɪdʒənt, -s
press-conference, -s 'pres,kɒnfərəns, -ɪz
press-cutting, -s 'pres,kʌtɪŋ, -z
pressgang, -s 'presgæŋ, -z
pression 'preʃn
press|man, -men 'pres|mæn [-mən],
-mən [-men]
pressure, -s 'preʃə*, -z
pressure-cooker, -s 'preʃə,kʊkə*, -z
pressuriz|e [-is|e], -es, -ing, -ed
'preʃəraɪz, -ɪz, -ɪŋ, -d
Prestage 'prestɪdʒ
Prestatyn pre'stætɪn (Welsh pres'tatin)
Presteign pre'sti:n
prestidigitation 'prestɪ,dɪdʒɪ'teɪʃn
prestidigitator, -s ,prestɪ'dɪdʒɪteɪtə*, -z
prestige pre'sti:ʒ
Prestige (surname) 'prestɪdʒ
prestigious pre'stɪdʒəs [prɪ-, prə-, -dʒɪəs]
prestissimo pre'stɪsɪməʊ
presto (P.), -s 'prestəʊ, -z
Preston 'prestən
Prestonpans ,prestən'pænz
Prestwich 'prestwɪtʃ
presum|e, -es, -ing/ly, -ed; -able, -ably
prɪ'zju:m [prə'z-, -'zu:m], -z, -ɪŋ/lɪ,
-d; -əbl, -əblɪ
presumption, -s prɪ'zʌmpʃn [prə'z-], -z
presumptive, -ly prɪ'zʌmptɪv [prə'z-],
-lɪ
presumptuous, -ly, -ness prɪ'zʌmptjʊəs
[prə'z-, -tjwəs, -tʃʊəs, -tʃwəs], -lɪ,
-nɪs [-nəs]
presuppos|e, -es, -ing, -ed ,pri:sə'pəʊz,
-ɪz, -ɪŋ, -d
presupposition, -s ,pri:sʌpə'zɪʃn, -z
pretence, -s prɪ'tens [prə't-], -ɪz
pretend, -s, -ing, -ed, -er/s prɪ'tend
[prə't-], -z, -ɪŋ, -ɪd, -ə*/z
pretension, -s prɪ'tenʃn [prə't-], -z
pretentious, -ly, -ness prɪ'tenʃəs [prə't-],
-lɪ, -nɪs [-nəs]
preterite, -s 'pretərɪt, -s
preterito-present, -s pri:,terɪtəʊ'preznt
[prɪ,t-, -zənt], -s
pretermission ,pri:tə'mɪʃn
pretermit, -s, -ting, -ted ,pri:tə'mɪt, -s,
-ɪŋ, -ɪd
preternatur|al, -ally, -alness ,pri:tə-
'nætʃr|əl [-tʃʊr-, -tʃər-], -əlɪ, -əlnɪs
[-nəs]

pretext, -s 'pri:tekst, -s
pre-tonic ˌpri:'tɒnɪk
Pretori|a, -us prɪ'tɔ:rɪ|ə [prə't-], -əs
prett|y (adj. adv.), -ier, -iest, -ily, -iness
'prɪt|ɪ, -ɪə*, -ɪɪst, -ɪlɪ [-əlɪ], -ɪnɪs [-nəs]
Pretty (surname) 'prɪtɪ, 'pretɪ
Pret(t)yman 'prɪtɪmən
pretty-pretty 'prɪtɪˌprɪtɪ
prevail, -s, -ing, -ed prɪ'veɪl [prə'v-], -z,
-ɪŋ, -d
prevalen|ce, -t/ly 'prevələn|s [-vl̩-], -t/lɪ
prevaricat|e, -es, -ing, -ed, -or/s prɪ-
'værɪkeɪt, -s, -ɪŋ, -ɪd, -ə*/z
prevarication, -s prɪˌværɪ'keɪʃn, -z
prevent (hinder), -s, -ing, -ed, -er/s;
-able prɪ'vent [prə'v-], -s, -ɪŋ, -ɪd,
-ə*/z; -əbl
prevent (go before), -s, -ing, -ed ˌpri:-
'vent [prɪ'v-], -s, -ɪŋ, -ɪd
preventability prɪˌventə'bɪlətɪ [prəˌv-,
-lɪt-]
preventative (s. adj.), -s prɪ'ventətɪv
[prə'v-], -z
prevention prɪ'venʃn [prə'v-]
preventive, -ly, -ness prɪ'ventɪv [prə'v-],
-lɪ, -nɪs [-nəs]
pre-view, -s 'pri:vju: [ˌ-'-], -z
previous, -ly, -ness 'pri:vjəs [-vɪəs], -lɪ,
-nɪs [-nəs]
prevision ˌpri:'vɪʒr [prɪ'v-]
Prevost (English surname) 'prevəʊ,
'prevəʊst, pre'vəʊ
pre-war ˌpri:'wɔ:* ['-- when attributive]
prey (s. v.), -s, -ing, -ed preɪ, -z, -ɪŋ, -d
Priam 'praɪəm [-æm]
priapism 'praɪəpɪzəm
priapus (P.), -es praɪ'eɪpəs, -ɪz
pric|e (s. v.) (P.), -es, -ing, -ed praɪs, -ɪz,
-ɪŋ, -t
priceless, -ness 'praɪslɪs [-ləs], -nɪs [-nəs]
prick (s. v.), -s, -ing/s, -ed, -er/s prɪk,
-s, -ɪŋ/z, -t, -ə*/z
prick|le (s. v.), -les, -ling, -led 'prɪk|l,
-lz, -lɪŋ [-lɪŋ], -ld
prickl|y, -iest, -iness 'prɪkl|ɪ [-k|l|ɪ], -ɪɪst,
-ɪnɪs [-nəs]
pride (P.) praɪd
Prideaux 'prɪdəʊ, 'pri:d-
Pridham 'prɪdəm
prie-Dieu, -s 'pri:djə: (pridjø), -z
priest (P.), -s; -craft, -hood, -like
pri:st, -s; -krɑːft, -hʊd, -laɪk
priestess, -es 'pri:stɪs [-tes], -ɪz
Priestley 'pri:stlɪ
priestl|y, -iness 'pri:stl|ɪ, -ɪnɪs [-nəs]
priest-ridden 'pri:st,rɪdn
prig (s. v.), -s, -ging, -ged, -ger/s; -gery
prɪg, -z, -ɪŋ, -d, -ə*/z; -ərɪ

priggish, -ly, -ness 'prɪgɪʃ, -lɪ, -nɪs [-nəs]
prim (adj. v.) (P.), -mer, -mest, -ly,
-ness; -s, -ming, -med prɪm, -ə*, -ɪst,
-lɪ, -nɪs [-nəs]; -z, -ɪŋ, -d
primac|y, -ies 'praɪməs|ɪ, -ɪz
prima-donna, -s ˌpri:mə'dɒnə, -z
primaeval = primeval
prima facie ˌpraɪmə'feɪʃi: [-ʃɪ, -si:, -sɪ,
ʃiː:, -sɪi:]
primage 'praɪmɪdʒ
primal 'praɪml
prim|ary (s. adj.), -aries, -arily,
-ariness 'praɪm|ərɪ, -ərɪz, -ərəlɪ [-ɪlɪ,
also praɪ'merəlɪ], -ərɪnɪs [-nəs]
primate (archbishop), -s 'praɪmət [-mɪt,
-meɪt], -s
primate (higher mammal), -s 'praɪmeɪt,
praɪ'meɪti:z ['praɪmeɪts]
primateship, -s 'praɪmət-ʃɪp [-mɪt-,
-meɪt-], -s
prim|e (s. adj. v.), -es, -ing, -ed praɪm,
-z, -ɪŋ, -d
primer (he who or that which primes), -s
'praɪmə*, -z
primer (elementary book), -s 'praɪmə*
['prɪm-], -z
primer (printing type) 'prɪmə*
primeval praɪ'mi:vl
primitive, -ly, -ness 'prɪmɪtɪv [-mət-],
-lɪ, -nɪs [-nəs]
primogeniture ˌpraɪməʊ'dʒenɪtʃə*
[-,tʃʊə*, -,tjʊə*]
primordial praɪ'mɔ:djəl [-dɪəl]
primrose (P.), -s 'prɪmrəʊz, -ɪz
primula, -s 'prɪmjʊlə [-jələ], -z
primus, -es 'praɪməs, -ɪz
prince (P.), -s; -dom/s, -like prɪns, -ɪz;
-dəm/z, -laɪk
prince|ly, -ier, -iest, -iness 'prɪnsl|ɪ,
-ɪə* [-jə*], -ɪɪst [-jɪst], -ɪnɪs [-nəs]
princess, princesses prɪn'ses [but '--
when used attributively, also ˌ-'-],
prɪn'sesɪz
Prince|ton, -town 'prɪns|tən, -taʊn
princip|al (s. adj.), -als, -ally, -alness
'prɪnsəp|l [-sɪp-], -lz, -lɪ [-əlɪ], -lnɪs
[-nəs]
principalit|y, -ies ˌprɪnsɪ'pælət|ɪ [-ɪt|ɪ],
-ɪz
principalship, -s 'prɪnsəplˌʃɪp [-sɪp-],
-s
principate (s.), -s 'prɪnsɪpət [-pɪt, -peɪt],
-s
Principia prɪn'sɪpɪə [-pjə]
principle, -s, -d 'prɪnsəpl [-sɪp-], -z, -d
Pring prɪŋ
Pringle 'prɪŋgl
Prinsep 'prɪnsep

393

print (s. v.), -s, -ing/s, -ed, -er/s prɪnt,
-s, -ɪŋ/z, -ɪd, -ə*/z
printable 'prɪntəbl
printing-machine, -s 'prɪntɪŋməˌʃiːn, -z
printing-office, -s 'prɪntɪŋˌɒfɪs, -ɪz
printing-press, -es 'prɪntɪŋˌpres, -ɪz
print-out 'prɪntaʊt
print-seller, -s 'prɪntˌselə*, -z
print-shop, -s 'prɪnt-ʃɒp, -s
prior (s. adj.) (P.), -s 'praɪə*, -z
prioress, -es 'praɪərɪs [-res], -ɪz
priorit|y, -ies praɪ'ɒrət|ɪ [-ɪt|ɪ], -ɪz
prior|y, -ies 'praɪər|ɪ, -ɪz
Priscian 'prɪʃɪən [-ʃjən]
Priscilla prɪ'sɪlə
pris|e (s. v.), -es, -ing, -ed praɪz, -ɪz, -ɪŋ,
-d
prism, -s 'prɪzəm, -z
prismatic, -al, -ally prɪz'mætɪk, -l, -əlɪ
prison, -s 'prɪzn, -z
prisoner, -s 'prɪznə* [-znə*], -z
prison-hou|se, -ses 'prɪznhaʊ|s, -zɪz
pristine 'prɪstaɪn [-tiːn]
Pritchard 'prɪtʃəd, -tʃɑːd
prithee 'prɪðɪ [-ðiː]
privacy 'prɪvəsɪ ['praɪv-]
private (s. adj.), -s, -ly, -ness 'praɪvɪt
[-vət], -s, -lɪ, -nɪs [-nəs]
privateer, -s ˌpraɪvə'tɪə* [-vɪ't-], -z
privation, -s praɪ'veɪʃn, -z
privative, -ly 'prɪvətɪv, -lɪ
privet, -s 'prɪvɪt, -s
privilege, -s, -d 'prɪvɪlɪdʒ [-vəl-], -ɪz,
-d
privity 'prɪvətɪ [-ɪtɪ]
priv|y (s. adj.), -ies, -ily 'prɪv|ɪ, -ɪz, -ɪlɪ
[-əlɪ]
priz|e (s. v.), -es, -ing, -ed praɪz, -ɪz, -ɪŋ,
-d
prize-fight, -s, -er/s 'praɪzfaɪt, -s, -ə*/z
prize|man, -men 'praɪz|mən, -mən
[-men]
P.R.O. (public relations officer) ˌpiː:ɑː'əʊ
pro (s. prep.), -s prəʊ, -z
probabilit|y, -ies ˌprɒbə'bɪlət|ɪ [-lɪt-], -ɪz
probab|le, -ly 'prɒbəb|l, -lɪ
probate, -s 'prəʊbeɪt [-bɪt], -s
probation, -s prə'beɪʃn [prəʊ'b-, prʊ'b-],
-z
probationary prə'beɪʃn̩ərɪ [prəʊ'b-,
prʊ'b-, -ʃnə-, -ʃənə-]
probationer, -s prə'beɪʃnə* [prəʊ'b-,
prʊ'b-, -ʃn̩ə*, -ʃənə*], -z
probative 'prəʊbətɪv
prob|e (s. v.), -es, -ing, -ed prəʊb, -z,
-ɪŋ, -d
probity 'prəʊbətɪ ['prɒb-, -ɪtɪ]
problem, -s 'prɒbləm [-lem, -lɪm], -z

problematic, -al, -ally ˌprɒblə'mætɪk
[-blɪ'm-, -ble'm-], -l, -əlɪ
proboscis, -es prəʊ'bɒsɪs [prʊ'b-], -iːz
Prob|us, -yn 'prəʊb|əs, -ɪn
procedural prə'siːdʒərəl [prəʊ's-, prʊ's-,
-djʊr-, -djər-]
procedure, -s prə'siːdʒə* [prəʊ's-, prʊ's-,
-djə*], -z
proceed (v.), -s, -ing/s, -ed prə'siːd
[prəʊ's-, prʊ's-], -z, -ɪŋ/z, -ɪd
proceeds (s.) 'prəʊsiːdz
proc|ess (s.), -esses 'prəʊs|es [rarely
'prɒs-, also sometimes -|ɪs, esp. when
followed by of], -esɪz [-ɪsɪz]
process (v.) (go in a procession), -es,
-ing, -ed prə'ses [prəʊ's-, prʊ's-], -ɪz,
-ɪŋ, -t
process (v.) (treat by a process), -es, -ing,
-ed 'prəʊses, -ɪz ['prəʊsɪsɪz], -ɪŋ
['prəʊsɪsɪŋ], -t
process-block, -s 'prəʊsesblɒk [-sɪs-], -s
procession, -s prə'seʃn [prʊ's-], -z
processional (s. adj.), -s prə'seʃənl
[prʊ's-, -ʃnəl, -ʃn̩l, -ʃn̩l, -ʃənəl], -z
proclaim, -s, -ing, -ed, -er/s prə'kleɪm
[prəʊ'k-, prʊ'k-], -z, -ɪŋ, -d, -ə*/z
proclamation, -s ˌprɒklə'meɪʃn, -z
proclitic (s. adj.), -s prəʊ'klɪtɪk, -s
proclivit|y, -ies prə'klɪvət|ɪ [prəʊ'k-,
prʊ'k-, -ɪt|ɪ], -ɪz
proconsul, -s ˌprəʊ'kɒnsəl, -z
proconsul|ar, -ate/s ˌprəʊ'kɒnsjʊl|ə*
[-sjəl-], -ət/s [-ɪt/s, -eɪt/s]
proconsulship, -s ˌprəʊ'kɒnsəlʃɪp, -s
procrastinat|e, -es, -ing, -ed, -or/s
prəʊ'kræstɪneɪt [prʊ'k-], -s, -ɪŋ, -ɪd,
-ə*/z
procrastination, -s prəʊˌkræstɪ'neɪʃn
[prʊˌk-], -z
procreant 'prəʊkrɪənt
procreat|e, -es, -ing, -ed 'prəʊkrɪeɪt, -s,
-ɪŋ, -ɪd
procreation ˌprəʊkrɪ'eɪʃn
procreative 'prəʊkrɪeɪtɪv
Procrust|es, -ean prəʊ'krʌst|iːz, -ɪən
[-jən]
Procter 'prɒktə*
proctor (P.), -s 'prɒktə*, -z
proctorial prɒk'tɔːrɪəl
procumbent prəʊ'kʌmbənt
procuration, -s ˌprɒkjʊə'reɪʃn, -z
procurator, -s 'prɒkjʊəreɪtə*, -z
procur|e, -es, -ing, -ed, -er/s, -ess/es;
-able prə'kjʊə* [prʊ'k-, -'kjɔə*,
-'kjɔː*], -z, -rɪŋ, -d, -rə*/z, -rɪs/ɪz
[-res/ɪz]; -rəbl
procurement prə'kjʊəmənt [prʊ-,
-'kjɔə-, -'kjɔː-]

Procyon (*star*) 'prəʊsjən [-sɪən]
prod (*s. v.*), **-s, -ding, -ded** prɒd, -z, -ɪŋ, -ɪd
prodig|al (*s. adj.*), **-als, -ally, -alness** 'prɒdɪg|l, -lz, -əlɪ, -lnɪs [-nəs]
prodigality ,prɒdɪ'gælətɪ [-ɪtɪ]
prodigaliz|e [-ɪs|e], **-es, -ing, -ed** 'prɒdɪgəlaɪz, -ɪz, -ɪŋ, -d
prodigious, -ly, -ness prə'dɪdʒəs [prʊ'd-], -lɪ, -nɪs [-nəs]
prodig|y, -ies 'prɒdɪdʒ|ɪ [-dədʒ|ɪ], -ɪz
produce (*s.*) 'prɒdju:s
produc|e (*v.*), **-es, -ing, -ed, -er/s** prə'dju:s [prʊ'd-], -ɪz, -ɪŋ, -t, -ə*/z
producible prə'dju:səbl [prʊ'd-, -sɪb-]
product, -s 'prɒdʌkt [-dəkt], -s
production, -s prə'dʌkʃn [prʊ'd-], -z
productional prə'dʌkʃənl [prʊ'd-, -ʃnəl, -ʃn̩l, -ʃn̩l, -ʃənəl]
productive, -ly, -ness prə'dʌktɪv [prʊ'd-], -lɪ, -nɪs [-nəs]
productivity ,prɒdʌk'tɪvətɪ [,prəʊd-, -dək-, -ɪtɪ]
proem, -s 'prəʊem, -z
profanation, -s ,prɒfə'neɪʃn, -z
profan|e (*adj. v.*), **-er, -est, -ely, -eness; -es, -ing, -ed, -er/s** prə'feɪn [prʊ'f-], -ə*, -ɪst, -lɪ, -nɪs [-nəs]; -z, -ɪŋ, -d, -ə*/z
profanit|y, -ies prə'fænət|ɪ [prʊ'f-, -ɪt|ɪ], -ɪz
profess, -es, -ing, -ed, -edly, -er/s, -or/s prə'fes [prʊ'f-], -ɪz, -ɪŋ, -t, -ɪdlɪ, -ə*/z, -ə*/z
profession, -s prə'feʃn [prʊ'f-], -z
professional (*s. adj.*), **-s** prə'feʃənl [prʊ'f-, -ʃnəl, -ʃn̩l, -ʃn̩l, -ʃənəl], -z
professionalism prə'feʃnəlɪzəm [prʊ'f-, -ʃnəl-, -ʃn̩l-, -ʃn̩l-, -ʃənəl-]
professionally prə'feʃnəlɪ [prʊ'f-, -ʃnəlɪ, -ʃn̩lɪ, -ʃn̩lɪ, -ʃənəlɪ]
professor, -s; -ate/s, -ship/s prə'fesə* [prʊ'f-], -z; -ɪt/s [-rət/s], -ʃɪp/s
professorial, -ly ,prɒfɪ'sɔ:rɪəl [-fe's-, -fə's-], -ɪ
professoriate ,prɒfɪ'sɔ:rɪət [-fe's-, -fə's-, -rɪɪt]
proffer, -s, -ing, -ed, -er/s 'prɒfə*, -z, -rɪŋ, -d, -rə*/z
proficien|cy, -t/ly prə'fɪʃn|sɪ [prʊ'f-], -t/lɪ
profil|e (*s. v.*), **-es, -ing, -ed** 'prəʊfaɪl [*old-fashioned* -fi:l], -z, -ɪŋ, -d
profit (*s. v.*), **-s, -ing, -ed, -er/s** 'prɒfɪt, -s, -ɪŋ, -ɪd, -ə*/z
profitab|le, -ly, -leness 'prɒfɪtəb|l, -lɪ, -lnɪs [-nəs]

profiteer (*s. v.*), **-s, -ing, -ed** ,prɒfɪ'tɪə* [-fə't-], -z, -rɪŋ, -d
profitless 'prɒfɪtlɪs [-ləs]
profit-sharing 'prɒfɪt,ʃeərɪŋ
profligacy 'prɒflɪgəsɪ
profligate (*s. adj.*), **-s, -ly, -ness** 'prɒflɪgət [-gɪt], -s, -lɪ, -nɪs [-nəs]
pro forma ,prəʊ'fɔ:mə
profoun|d, -der, -dest, -dly, -dness prə'faʊn|d [prʊ'f-], -də*, -dɪst, -dlɪ, -dnɪs [-nəs]
profundit|y, -ies prə'fʌndət|ɪ [prʊ'f-, -ɪt|ɪ], -ɪz
profuse, -st, -ly, -ness prə'fju:s [prʊ'f-], -ɪst, -lɪ, -nɪs [-nəs]
profusion, -s prə'fju:ʒn [prʊ'f-], -z
prog (*s. v.*), **-s, -ging, -ged** prɒg, -z, -ɪŋ, -d
progenitor, -s prəʊ'dʒenɪtə*, -z
progeniture prəʊ'dʒenɪtʃə* [-,tjʊə*, -tjə*]
progen|y, -ies 'prɒdʒən|ɪ [-dʒɪn-], -ɪz
prognathic prɒg'næθɪk
prognathism 'prɒgnəθɪzəm [prɒg-'næθ-]
prognathous prɒg'neɪθəs ['prɒgnəθəs]
prognos|is, -es prɒg'nəʊs|ɪs, -i:z
prognostic prɒg'nɒstɪk [prə'g-]
prognosticat|e, -es, -ing, -ed, -or/s prɒg'nɒstɪkeɪt [prəg-], -s, -ɪŋ, -ɪd, -ə*/z
prognostication, -s prəg,nɒstɪ'keɪʃn [prɒg-], -z
program(**me**) (*s. v.*), **-s, -ing, -(e)d, -er/s** 'prəʊgræm, -z, -ɪŋ, -d, -ə*/z
progress (*s.*), **-es** 'prəʊgres [*rarely* 'prɒg-], -ɪz
progress (*v.*), **-es, -ing, -ed** prəʊ'gres [prʊ'g-], -ɪz, -ɪŋ, -t
progression, -s prəʊ'greʃn [prʊ'g-], -z
progressional prəʊ'greʃənl [prʊ'g-, -ʃnəl, -ʃn̩l, -ʃn̩l, -ʃənəl]
progressionist, -s prəʊ'greʃn̩ɪst [prʊ'g-, -ʃənɪst], -s
progressist, -s prəʊ'gresɪst [prʊ'g-], -s
progressive (*s. adj.*), **-s, -ly, -ness** prəʊ'gresɪv [prʊ'g-], -z, -lɪ, -nɪs [-nəs]
prohibit, -s, -ing, -ed, -or/s prə'hɪbɪt [prəʊ'h-, prʊ'h-], -s, -ɪŋ, -ɪd, -ə*/z
prohibition, -s ,prəʊɪ'bɪʃn [,prəʊhɪ-], -z
prohibitioni|sm, -st/s ,prəʊɪ'bɪʃn̩|ɪzəm [,prəʊhɪ-, -ʃənɪ-], -st/s
prohibitive, -ly prə'hɪbɪtɪv [prəʊ'h-, prʊ'h-], -lɪ
prohibitory prə'hɪbɪtərɪ [prəʊ'h-, prʊ'h-]
project (*s.*), **-s** 'prɒdʒekt [-dʒɪkt], -s
project (*v.*), **-s, -ing, -ed, -or/s** prə'dʒekt [prəʊ'dʒ-, prʊ'dʒ-], -s, -ɪŋ, -ɪd, -ə*/z

projectile (s.), -s prəʊ'dʒektaɪl [prʊ-, 'prɒdʒektaɪl, -dʒɪk-], -z

projectile (adj.) prəʊ'dʒektaɪl [prʊ'dʒ-]

projection, -s prə'dʒekʃn [prəʊ'dʒ-, prʊ'dʒ-], -z

projective, -ly prə'dʒektɪv [prəʊ'dʒ-, prʊ'dʒ-], -lɪ

Prokofiev prə'kɒfief

prolapse, -s 'prəʊlæps, -ɪz

prolate 'prəʊleɪt [prəʊ'leɪt]

prolegomen|on, -a ˌprəʊle'gɒmɪn|ən [-lɪ'g-, -mən-, -ɒn], -ə

proleps|is, -es prəʊ'leps|ɪs [-'li:p-], -i:z

proleptic, -ally prəʊ'leptɪk [-'li:p-], -əlɪ

proletarian (s. adj.), -s, -ism ˌprəʊlɪ-'teərɪən [-le't-, -lə't-], -z, -ɪzəm

proletariat ˌprəʊlɪ'teərɪət [-le't-, -lə't-, -ɪæt]

proliferat|e, -es, -ing, -ed prəʊ'lɪfəreɪt, -s, -ɪŋ, -ɪd

proliferation prəʊˌlɪfə'reɪʃn

prolific, -ness prəʊ'lɪfɪk [prʊ'l-], -nɪs [-nəs]

prolix 'prəʊlɪks [prəʊ'lɪks]

prolixity prəʊ'lɪksətɪ [-ɪtɪ]

prolix|ly, -ness prəʊ'lɪks|lɪ ['prəʊlɪks-], -nɪs [-nəs]

prolocutor, -s prəʊ'lɒkjʊtə*, -z

prologu|e (s. v.), -es, -ing, -ed 'prəʊlɒg [rarely -ləʊg], -z, -ɪŋ, -d

prolong, -s, -ing, -ed prəʊ'lɒŋ [prʊ'l-], -z, -ɪŋ, -d

prolongation, -s ˌprəʊlɒŋ'geɪʃn [ˌprɒl-], -z

promenad|e (s. v.), -es, -ing, -ed, -er/s ˌprɒmə'nɑːd [-mɪ'n-], -z, -ɪŋ, -ɪd, -ə*/z

Note.—Also '--- when attributive, as in promenade concert. There exists also a pronunciation ˌprɒmə'neɪd [-mɪ'n-] used chiefly in square dancing.

Promethean prə'mi:θjən [prəʊ'm-, prʊ'm-, -θɪən]

Prometheus prə'mi:θju:s [prəʊ'm-, prʊ'm-, -θjəs, -θɪəs]

prominence, -s 'prɒmɪnəns [-mən-], -ɪz

prominent, -ly 'prɒmɪnənt [-mən-], -lɪ

promiscuity ˌprɒmɪ'skju:ətɪ [-kjʊətɪ, -ɪtɪ]

promiscuous, -ly, -ness prə'mɪskjʊəs [prʊ'm-, -kjwəs], -lɪ, -nɪs [-nəs]

promis|e (s. v.), -es, -ing/ly, -ed, -er/s 'prɒmɪs, -ɪz, -ɪŋ/lɪ, -t, -ə*/z

promissory 'prɒmɪsərɪ [prə'mɪs-, prʊ'mɪs-]

promontor|y, -ies 'prɒməntr|ɪ [-tər-], -ɪz

promot|e, -es, -ing, -ed, -er/s prə'məʊt [prʊ'm-], -s, -ɪŋ, -ɪd, -ə*/z

promotion, -s prə'məʊʃn [prʊ'm-], -z

promotive prə'məʊtɪv [prʊ'm-]

prompt (s. adj. v.), -s; -er, -est, -ly, -ness; -ing/s, -ed, -er/s prɒmpt, -s; -ə*, -ɪst, -lɪ, -nɪs [-nəs]; -ɪŋ/z, -ɪd, -ə*/z

promptitude 'prɒmptɪtju:d

promulgat|e, -es, -ing, -ed, -or/s 'prɒmlgeɪt [-mʌl-], -s, -ɪŋ, -ɪd, -ə*/z

promulgation, -s ˌprɒml'geɪʃn [-mʌl-], -z

prone, -r, -st, -ly, -ness prəʊn, -ə*, -ɪst, -lɪ, -nɪs [-nəs]

prong (s. v.), -s, -ing, -ed prɒŋ, -z, -ɪŋ, -d

pronomin|al, -ally prəʊ'nɒmɪn|l [prʊ'n-], -əlɪ [-lɪ]

pronoun, -s 'prəʊnaʊn, -z

pronounc|e, -es, -ing, -ed, -edly, -er/s, -ement/s; -eable/ness prə'naʊns [prʊ'n-, prn̩'aʊns], -ɪz, -ɪŋ, -t, -tlɪ [-ɪdlɪ], -ə*/z, -mənt/s; -əbl/nɪs [-nəs]

pronunciamento, -s prəˌnʌnsɪə'mentəʊ [prəʊˌn-, prʊˌn-, -sjə-, -ʃɪə-, -ʃjə-], -z

pronunciation, -s prəˌnʌnsɪ'eɪʃn [prʊˌn-, prn̩ˌʌn-], -z

proof, -s; -less pru:f, -s; -lɪs [-ləs]

proof-read|er/s, -ing 'pru:f,ri:d|ə*/z, -ɪŋ

prop (s. v.), -s, -ping, -ped prɒp, -s, -ɪŋ, -t

propaedeutic, -al, -s ˌprəʊpi:'dju:tɪk, -l, -s

propagand|a, -ist/s ˌprɒpə'gænd|ə, -ɪst/s

propagandism ˌprɒpə'gændɪzəm

propagat|e, -es, -ing, -ed, -or/s 'prɒpəgeɪt, -s, -ɪŋ, -ɪd, -ə*/z

propagation ˌprɒpə'geɪʃn

propane 'prəʊpeɪn

proparoxytone (s. adj.), -s ˌprəʊpə-'rɒksɪtəʊn [-tn], -z

propel, -s, -ling, -led, -ler/s; -lent/s prə'pel [prʊ'p-], -z, -ɪŋ, -d, -ə*/z; -ənt/s

propensit|y, -ies prə'pensət|ɪ [prəʊ'p-, prʊ'p-, -ɪt|ɪ], -ɪz

proper, -ly 'prɒpə*, -lɪ ['prɒp|ɪ]

properispomen|on, -a 'prəʊˌperɪ'spəʊ-mɪn|ən [-ɒn], -ə

Propertius prəʊ'pɜ:ʃjəs [prʊ'p-, -ʃɪəs, -ʃəs]

propert|y, -ies, -ied 'prɒpət|ɪ, -ɪz, -ɪd

prophec|y, -ies 'prɒfɪs|ɪ [-fəs|ɪ, -s|aɪ], -ɪz [-aɪz]

prophes|y, -ies, -ying, -ied, -ier/s 'prɒfɪs|aɪ [-fəs-], -aɪz, -aɪɪŋ, -aɪd, -aɪə*/z

prophet, -s 'prɒfɪt, -s

prophetess, -es 'prɒfɪtɪs [-tes], -ɪz

prophetic, -al, -ally prə'fetɪk [prɒ'f-, prʊ'f-], -l, -əlɪ

Prophit 'prɒfɪt

prophylactic (s. adj.), -s ˌprɒfɪ'læktɪk, -s

prophylaxis ˌprɒfɪ'læksɪs

propinquity prə'pɪŋkwətɪ [prəʊ'p-, prʊ'p-, prɒ'p-, -ɪtɪ]

propitiat|e, -es, -ing, -ed, -or/s prə-'pɪʃɪeɪt [prʊ'p-], -s, -ɪŋ, -ɪd, -ə*/z

propitiation, -s prəˌpɪʃɪ'eɪʃn [prʊˌp-], -z

propitiatory prə'pɪʃɪətərɪ [prʊ'p-, -ʃjə-tərɪ, -ʃətərɪ, -ʃɪeɪtərɪ]

propitious, -ly, -ness prə'pɪʃəs [prʊ'p-], -lɪ, -nɪs [-nəs]

proporti|on (s. v.), -ons, -oning, -oned prə'pɔːʃ|n [prʊ'p-], -nz, -ŋɪŋ [-nɪŋ, -ənɪŋ], -nd

proportionab|le, -ly prə'pɔːʃnəb|l [prʊ'p-, -ʃnə-, -ʃənə-], -lɪ

propor|tional, -tionally prə'pɔːʃnl [prʊ'p-, -ʃnəl, -ʃn̩l, -ʃn̩l, -ʃənəl], -ʃnəlɪ [-ʃnəlɪ, -ʃn̩lɪ, -ʃn̩lɪ, -ʃənəlɪ]

proportionality prəˌpɔːʃə'nælətɪ [prʊˌp-, -ʃn̩'æ-, -ɪtɪ]

proportionate, -ly, -ness prə'pɔːʃnət [prʊ'p-, -ʃnət, -ʃənət, -nɪt], -lɪ, -nɪs [-nəs]

propos|e, -es, -ing, -ed, -er/s; -al/s prə'pəʊz [prʊ'p-], -ɪz, -ɪŋ, -d, -ə*/z; -l/z

proposition, -s ˌprɒpə'zɪʃn, -z

propound, -s, -ing, -ed, -er/s prə'paʊnd [prʊ'p-], -z, -ɪŋ, -ɪd, -ə*/z

proprietary prə'praɪətərɪ [prʊ'p-]

proprietor, -s; -ship/s prə'praɪətə* [prʊ'p-], -z; -ʃɪp/s

proprietress, -es prə'praɪətrɪs [prʊ'p-, -tres], -ɪz

propriet|y, -ies prə'praɪət|ɪ [prʊ'p-], -ɪz

propriocep|tion, -tive ˌprəʊprɪəʊ'sep|ʃn, -tɪv

propul|sion, -sive prə'pʌl|ʃn [prʊ'p-], -sɪv

propylae|um (P.), -a ˌprɒpɪ'liː|əm [-'lɪ|əm], -ə

pro rata ˌprəʊ'rɑːtə [-'reɪtə]

prorogation, -s ˌprəʊrə'geɪʃn [ˌprɒr-, -rəʊ'g-], -z

prorogu|e, -es, -ing, -ed prə'rəʊg [prəʊ'r-, prʊ'r-], -z, -ɪŋ, -d

prosaic, -al, -ally, -ness prəʊ'zeɪɪk, -l, -əlɪ, -nɪs [-nəs]

prosceni|um, -ums, -a prəʊ'siː:nj|əm [-nɪ|əm], -əmz, -ə

proscrib|e, -es, -ing, -ed, -er/s prəʊ-'skraɪb, -z, -ɪŋ, -d, -ə*/z

proscription, -s prəʊ'skrɪpʃn, -z

proscriptive prəʊ'skrɪptɪv

pros|e (s. v.), -es, -ing, -ed, -er/s prəʊz, -ɪz, -ɪŋ, -d, -ə*/z

prosecut|e, -es, -ing, -ed, -or/s 'prɒsɪ-kjuːt, -s, -ɪŋ, -ɪd, -ə*/z

prosecution, -s ˌprɒsɪ'kjuːʃn, -z

prosecutrix, -es 'prɒsɪˌkjuːtrɪks [ˌ--'--], -ɪz

proselyte, -s 'prɒsɪlaɪt [-səl-], -s

proselytism 'prɒsɪlɪtɪzəm [-səl-]

proselytiz|e [-is|e], -es, -ing, -ed 'prɒsɪlɪtaɪz [-səl-], -ɪz, -ɪŋ, -d

Proserpina prɒ'sɜː:pɪnə [prɒ's-]

Proserpine 'prɒsəpaɪn

prosit 'prəʊzɪt ['prəʊsɪt, prəʊst]

prosodic, -al prə'sɒdɪk [prəʊ's-], -l

prosodist, -s 'prɒsədɪst, -s

prosod|y, -ies 'prɒsəd|ɪ, -ɪz

prospect (s.) (P.), -s 'prɒspekt, -s

prospect (v.), -s, -ing, -ed prə'spekt [prʊ's-, prɒ's-, 'prɒspekt], -s, -ɪŋ, -ɪd

prospective, -ly, -ness prə'spektɪv [prʊ's-, prɒ's-], -lɪ, -nɪs [-nəs]

prospector, -s prə'spektə* [prʊ's-, prɒ's-], -z

prospectus, -es prə'spektəs [prʊ's-], -ɪz

prosp|er, -ers, -ering, -ered 'prɒsp|ə*, -əz, -ərɪŋ, -əd

prosperity prɒ'sperɪtɪ [prəs-, -ɪtɪ]

Prospero 'prɒspərəʊ

prosperous, -ly, -ness 'prɒspərəs, -lɪ, -nɪs [-nəs]

prostate, -s 'prɒsteɪt [-tɪt], -s

prostatic prɒ'stætɪk

prosthesis 'prɒsθɪsɪs [-θəs-, prɒs'θiː:sɪs]

prosthetic, -s prɒs'θetɪk, -s

prosthetist, -s prɒs'θiː:tɪst [prəs-], -s

prostitut|e (s. v.), -es, -ing, -ed 'prɒstɪ-tjuːt, -s, -ɪŋ, -ɪd

prostitution, -s ˌprɒstɪ'tjuːʃn, -z

prostrate (adj.) 'prɒstreɪt [-rɪt]

prostrat|e (v.), -es, -ing, -ed prɒ'streɪt [prəs-], -s, -ɪŋ, -ɪd

prostration, -s prɒ'streɪʃn [prəs-], -z

pros|y, -ier, -iest, -ily, -iness 'prəʊz|ɪ, -ɪə* [-jə*], -ɪɪst [-jɪst], -ɪlɪ [-əlɪ], -ɪnɪs [-ɪnəs]

protagonist, -s prəʊ'tægənɪst, -s

Protagoras prəʊ'tægəræs [-gɒr-, -rəs]

protas|is, -es 'prɒtəs|ɪs, -iː:z

protean prəʊ'tiː:ən ['prəʊtjən, 'prəʊ-tɪən]

protect, -s, -ing/ly, -ed, -or/s prə'tekt [pro't-], -s, -ɪŋ/lɪ, -ɪd, -ə*/z

protection, -s prə'tekʃn [proˈt-], -z

protectioni|sm, -st/s prə'tekʃənɪ|zəm [proˈt-, -ʃɪ-], -st/s

protective, -ly, -ness prə'tektɪv [proˈt-], -lɪ, -nɪs [-nəs]

protectorate, -s prə'tektərət [proˈt-, -rɪt], -s

protectress, -es prə'tektrɪs [proˈt-, -trəs], -ɪz

protégé(e), -s 'prəʊteʒeɪ ['prɒt-, -teɪʒ-] (prɔteʒe), -z

proteid, -s 'prəʊtiːd [-tiːɪd, -tɪɪd], -z

protein 'prəʊtiːn [-tiːɪn, -tɪɪn]

pro tem ˌprəʊ'tem

protest (s.), -s 'prəʊtest, -s

protest (v.), -s, -ing/ly, -ed, -er/s prə'test [prəʊ't-, proˈt-, rarely 'prəʊtest], -s, -ɪŋ/lɪ, -ɪd, -ə*/z

protestant (P.), -s, -ism 'prɒtɪstənt [-təs-], -s, -ɪzəm

protestantiz|e [-is|e], -es, -ing, -ed 'prɒtɪstəntaɪz [-təs-], -ɪz, -ɪŋ, -d

protestation, -s ˌprɒte'steɪʃn [ˌprəʊt-, -tɪ's-, -tə's-], -z

Proteus 'prəʊtjuːs [-tjəs, -tɪəs]

prothalami|on, -um ˌprəʊθə'leɪmɪ|ən [-mjən], -əm [-mjəm]

Protheroe 'prɒðərəʊ

prothes|is, -es 'prɒθɪs|ɪs [-θəs-], -iːz

protium 'prəʊtjəm [-tɪəm]

protocol, -s 'prəʊtəkɒl [-təʊk-], -z

proton, -s 'prəʊtɒn, -z

protoplasm 'prəʊtəʊplæzəm

prototype, -s 'prəʊtəʊtaɪp, -s

protozo|ic, -on, -a ˌprəʊtəʊ'zəʊ|ɪk, -ən [-ɒn], -ə

protract, -s, -ing, -ed/ly; -ile prə'trækt [proˈt-], -s, -ɪŋ, -ɪd/lɪ; -aɪl

protraction, -s prə'trækʃn [proˈt-], -z

protractor, -s prə'træktə* [proˈt-], -z

protrud|e, -es, -ing, -ed prə'truːd [proˈt-], -z, -ɪŋ, -ɪd

protrusion, -s prə'truːʒn [proˈt-], -z

protrusive, -ly, -ness prə'truːsɪv [proˈt-], -lɪ, -nɪs [-nəs]

protuberan|ce/s, -t/ly prə'tjuːbərən|s/ɪz [proˈt-], -t/lɪ

proud, -er, -est, -ly, -ness praʊd, -ə*, -ɪst, -lɪ, -nɪs [-nəs]

Proust (French author) pruːst (prust)

proustian 'pruːstjən [-tɪən]

Prout praʊt

provab|le, -ly, -leness 'pruːvəb|l, -lɪ, -lnɪs [-nəs]

prov|e, -es, -ing, -ed, -en, -er/s pruːv, -z, -ɪŋ, -d, -ən, -ə*/z

provenance 'prɒvənəns [-vɪn-]

Provençal ˌprɒvɑ̃ː'sɑːl [-vɔ̃ːnˈs-, -vɑːns-, -vən's-] (prɔvɑ̃sal)

Provence prɒ'vɑ̃ːns [prəʊ'v-, -ˈvɔ̃ːns, -ˈvɑːns] (prɔvɑ̃ːs)

provender 'prɒvɪndə* [-vəndə*]

proverb, -s (P.) 'prɒvɜːb, -z

proverbial, -ly prə'vɜːbjəl [proˈv-, -bɪəl], -ɪ

provid|e, -es, -ing, -ed, -er/s prə'vaɪd [proˈv-], -z, -ɪŋ, -ɪd, -ə*/z

providen|ce (P.), -t/ly 'prɒvɪdən|s, -t/lɪ

providenti|al, -ally ˌprɒvɪ'denʃ|l, -əlɪ

province, -s 'prɒvɪns, -ɪz

provinci|al (s. adj.), -als, -ally prə'vɪnʃ|l [proˈv-], -lz, -əlɪ

provincialism, -s prə'vɪnʃəlɪzəm [proˈv-, -ʃɪ-], -z

provinciality prə,vɪnʃɪ'ælətɪ [proˈv-, -ɪtɪ]

provincializ|e [-is|e], -es, -ing, -ed prə'vɪnʃəlaɪz [proˈv-, -ʃlaɪz], -ɪz, -ɪŋ, -d

provisi|on, -ons, -oning, -oned prə'vɪʒ|n [proˈv-], -nz, -nɪŋ [-ənɪŋ], -nd

provi|sional, -sionally prə'vɪʒ|ənl [proˈv-, -ʒnəl, -ʒnl̩, -ʒnl, -ʒənəl], -ʒnəlɪ [-ʒnəlɪ, -ʒnl̩ɪ, -ʒnlɪ, -ʒənəlɪ]

proviso, -(e)s prə'vaɪzəʊ [prəʊ'v-, proˈv-], -z

provisor, -s prə'vaɪzə* [proˈv-], -z

provisor|y, -ily prə'vaɪzər|ɪ [proˈv-], -əlɪ [-ɪlɪ]

provocation, -s ˌprɒvə'keɪʃn [-vəʊˈk-], -z

provocative prə'vɒkətɪv [prəʊ'v-, proˈv-]

provok|e, -es, -ing/ly, -ed, -er/s prə'vəʊk [proˈv-], -s, -ɪŋ/lɪ, -t, -ə*/z

provost (civil and academic), -s 'prɒvəst, -s

provost-marshal (military), -s prə,vəʊ-'mɑːʃl, -z

provostship, -s 'prɒvəst-ʃɪp, -s

prow, -s praʊ, -z

prowess 'praʊɪs [-es]

prowl (s. v.), -s, -ing, -ed, -er/s praʊl, -z, -ɪŋ, -d, -ə*/z

Prowse praʊs, praʊz

prox. prɒks ['prɒksɪməʊ]

proxim|al, -ally 'prɒksɪm|l, -əlɪ

proximate, -ly 'prɒksɪmət [-ɪt], -lɪ

proxime accessit, -s ˌprɒksɪmɪæk'sesɪt [-mɪək-], -s

proximit|y, -ies prɒk'sɪmət|ɪ [-ɪt|ɪ], -ɪz

proximo 'prɒksɪməʊ

prox|y, -ies 'prɒks|ɪ, -ɪz

prude, -s; -ry pruːd, -z; -ərɪ

pruden|ce (P.), -t/ly 'pru:dn|s, -t/lɪ
prudenti|al, -ally prʊ'denʃ|l [pru:'d-], -əlɪ
prudish, -ly 'pru:dɪʃ, -lɪ
prun|e (s. v.), -es, -ing, -ed pru:n, -z, -ɪŋ, -d
prunella (P.), -s prʊ'nelə [pru:'n-], -z
pruning-kni|fe, -ves 'pru:nɪŋnaɪ|f, -vz
prurien|ce, -t/ly 'prʊərɪən|s, -t/lɪ
Prussi|a, -an/s 'prʌʃ|ə, -n/z
prussiate, -s 'prʌʃɪət [-ʃjət, -ʃət, -ɪt], -s
prussic 'prʌsɪk
Prust prʌst
Pruth (tributary of the Danube) pru:t
pr|y, -ies, -ying/ly, -ied, -yer/s pr|aɪ, -aɪz, -aɪŋ/lɪ, -aɪd, 'praɪə*/z
Prynne prɪn
Przemysl 'pʃemɪsl
psalm (P.), -s; -ist/s sɑ:m, -z; -ɪst/s
psalmodic sæl'mɒdɪk
psalmod|ist/s, -y 'sælməd|ɪst/s ['sɑ:m-, -mʊd-], -ɪ
psalter, -s 'sɔ:ltə* ['sɒl-], -z
psalter|y, -ies 'sɔ:ltər|ɪ ['sɒl-], -ɪz
Note.—In the following words beginning with ps-, the form with p is rare.
psepholog|ist/s, -y pse'fɒlədʒ|ɪst/s [psɪ-, psə-], -ɪ
pseudo, -s 'psju:dəʊ, -z ['psu:dəʊ-]
Note.—Compounds with pseudo- have double stress. Their pronunciation may be ascertained by referring to the simple words. Thus pseudo-classic is pronounced ˌpsju:dəʊ-'klæsɪk [ˌpsu:-].
pseudonym, -s 'psju:dənɪm ['psu:-], -z
pseudonymity ˌpsju:də'nɪmətɪ [ˌpsu:-, -ɪtɪ]
pseudonymous psju:'dɒnɪməs [psu:-]
pshaw (v.), -s, -ing, -ed pʃɔ: [ʃɔ:], -z, -ɪŋ, -d
pshaw (interj.) pϕ: [pʃɔ:]
psi psaɪ
psittacosis ˌpsɪtə'kəʊsɪs
psoriasis psɒ'raɪəsɪs [psɔ:'r-, psʊ'r-, psə'r-]
Psyche 'saɪkɪ [-ki:]
psychedelic ˌsaɪkɪ'delɪk [-kə'd-]
psychiatric, -al ˌsaɪkɪ'ætrɪk, -l
psychiatr|ist/s, -y saɪ'kaɪətr|ɪst/s [sɪ'k-, sə'k-], -ɪ
psychic, -al, -ally 'saɪkɪk ['psaɪk-], -l, -əlɪ [-lɪ]
psychoanalys|e, -es, -ing, -ed ˌsaɪkəʊ-'ænəlaɪz [ˌpsaɪ-], -ɪz, -ɪŋ, -d
psychoanalysis ˌsaɪkəʊə'næləsɪs [ˌpsaɪ-, -lɪs-]

psychoanalyst, -s ˌsaɪkəʊ'ænəlɪst [ˌpsaɪ-], -s
psychologic, -al, -ally ˌsaɪkə'lɒdʒɪk [ˌpsaɪ-], -l, -əlɪ
psycholog|ist/s, -y saɪ'kɒlədʒ|ɪst/s [psaɪ-], -ɪ
psychologiz|e [-is|e], -es, -ing, -ed saɪ'kɒlədʒaɪz [psaɪ-], -ɪz, -ɪŋ, -d
psychometric ˌsaɪkəʊ'metrɪk [ˌpsaɪ-]
psychometr|ist/s, -y saɪ'kɒmɪtr|ɪst/s [psaɪ-, -mət-], -ɪ
psychopath, -s 'saɪkəʊpæθ ['psaɪ-], -s
psychopathic ˌsaɪkəʊ'pæθɪk [ˌpsaɪ-]
psychophonic ˌsaɪkəʊ'fəʊnɪk [ˌpsaɪ-, -'fɒn-]
psychophysical ˌsaɪkəʊ'fɪzɪkl [ˌpsaɪ-]
psychos|is, -es saɪ'kəʊs|ɪs [psaɪ-], -i:z
psychosomatic ˌsaɪkəʊsəʊ'mætɪk [ˌpsaɪ-]
psychotherap|y, -ist/s ˌsaɪkəʊ'θerəp|ɪ [ˌpsaɪ-], -ɪst/s
psychotic saɪ'kɒtɪk [psaɪ-]
ptarmigan 'tɑ:mɪgən [-məg-]
pterodactyl, -s ˌpterəʊ'dæktɪl, -z
pterosaur, -s ˌpterəʊsɔ:*, -z
ptisan, -s tɪ'zæn ['tɪzn], -z
P.T.O. ˌpi:ti:'əʊ
Ptolemai|c, -s ˌtɒlɪ'meɪ|k [-lə'm-], -s
Ptolem|y, -ies 'tɒlɪm|ɪ [-ləm-], -ɪz
ptomaine 'təʊmeɪn [təʊ'meɪn]
pub, -s; -by pʌb, -z; -ɪ
puberty 'pju:bətɪ
pubescen|ce, -t pju:'besn|s [pjʊ'b-], -t
pubic 'pju:bɪk
public, -ly 'pʌblɪk, -lɪ
publican, -s 'pʌblɪkən, -z
publication, -s ˌpʌblɪ'keɪʃn, -z
public-hou|se, -ses ˌpʌblɪk'haʊ|s, -zɪz
publicist, -s 'pʌblɪsɪst, -s
publicity pʌb'lɪsətɪ [pə'blɪs-, -ɪtɪ]
publiciz|e, -es, -ing, -ed 'pʌblɪsaɪz, -ɪz, -ɪŋ, -d
public-relations ˌpʌblɪkrɪ'leɪʃnz
public-spirited ˌpʌblɪk'spɪrɪtɪd
publish, -es, -ing, -ed, -er/s 'pʌblɪʃ, -ɪz, -ɪŋ, -t, -ə*/z
Publius 'pʌblɪəs [-ljəs]
Puccini pu:'tʃi:nɪ [pʊ'tʃ-]
puce pju:s
puck (P.), -s pʌk, -s
pucker (s. v.), -s, -ing, -ed 'pʌkə*, -z, -rɪŋ, -d
pudding, -s 'pʊdɪŋ, -z
pudd|le (s. v.), -les, -ling, -led, -ler/s 'pʌd|l, -lz, -lɪŋ [-lɪŋ], -ld, -lə*/z [-lə*/z]
pudend|um, -a pju:'dend|əm, -ə
pudg|y, -ier, -iest 'pʌdʒ|ɪ, -ɪə*, -ɪɪst
Pudsey 'pʌdzɪ [locally 'pʌdsɪ]

pueblo, -s puˈebləʊ [ˈpwe-], -z
puerile, -ly ˈpjʊəraɪl [ˈpjɔːr-, ˈpjɔːɪr-], -lɪ
puerilit|y, -ies pjʊəˈrɪlət|ɪ [ˌpjʊəˈr-, pjɔəˈr-, pjɔːˈr-, -ɪt|ɪ], -ɪz
puerperal pjuːˈɜːpərəl [pjʊˈɜː-]
Puerto Ric|o, -an/s ˌpwɜːtəʊˈriːk|əʊ [ˌpweə-], -ən/z
puff (s. v.), -s, -ing, -ed, -er/s pʌf, -s, -ɪŋ, -t, -ə*/z
puff-ball, -s ˈpʌfbɔːl, -z
puffin, -s ˈpʌfɪn, -z
puff|y, -ier, -iest, -ily, -iness ˈpʌf|ɪ, -ɪə*, -ɪɪst, -ɪlɪ [-əlɪ], -ɪnɪs [-məs]
pug, -s pʌg, -z
puggaree, -s ˈpʌgərɪ, -z
Pugh pjuː
pugili|sm, -st/s ˈpjuːdʒɪlɪ|zəm, -st/s
pugilistic, -ally ˌpjuːdʒɪˈlɪstɪk, -əlɪ
Pugin ˈpjuːdʒɪn
pugnacious, -ly pʌgˈneɪʃəs, -lɪ
pugnacity pʌgˈnæsətɪ [-ɪtɪ]
pug-nose, -s, -d ˈpʌgnəʊz, -ɪz, -d
puisne ˈpjuːnɪ
puissan|ce, -t ˈpjuːɪsn|s [ˈpjʊɪ-, ˈpwɪs-, sometimes in poetry pjuːˈɪs-, pjʊˈɪ-, in show-jumping ˈpwiːsãːns, -sɑːns, -sɔ̃ːns, -ˈ-], -t
puk|e, -es, -ing, -ed pjuːk, -s, -ɪŋ, -t
pukka ˈpʌkə
pulchritude ˈpʌlkrɪtjuːd
pul|e, -es, -ing, -ed pjuːl, -z, -ɪŋ, -d
Puleston (in Salop) ˈpʊlɪstən [locally also ˈpɪlsn]
Pulitzer (American publisher) ˈpʊlɪtsə*, (prize at Columbia University) ˈpjuːlɪtsə*
pull (s. v.), -s, -ing, -ed, -er/s pʊl, -z, -ɪŋ, -d, -ə*/z
pullet, -s ˈpʊlɪt [-lət], -s
pulley, -s ˈpʊlɪ, -z
pullman (P.), -s; -car/s ˈpʊlmən, -z; -kɑː*/z
pull-over, -s ˈpʊlˌəʊvə*, -z
pullulat|e, -es, -ing, -ed ˈpʌljʊleɪt, -s, -ɪŋ, -ɪd
pullulation ˌpʌljʊˈleɪʃn
pull-up, -s ˈpʊlʌp [ˌpʊlˈʌp], -s
pulmonary ˈpʌlmənərɪ
pulmonic pʌlˈmɒnɪk
pulp (s. v.), -s, -ing, -ed pʌlp, -s, -ɪŋ, -t
pulpi|fy, -fies, -fying, -fied ˈpʌlpɪ|faɪ, -faɪz, -faɪɪŋ, -faɪd
pulpit, -s ˈpʊlpɪt, -s
pulp|y, -ier, -iest, -iness ˈpʌlp|ɪ, -ɪə* [-jə*], -ɪɪst [-jɪst], -ɪnɪs [-məs]
pulsar, -s ˈpʌlsə* [-sɑː*], -z
pulsat|e, -es, -ing, -ed pʌlˈseɪt [ˈpʌlseɪt], -s, -ɪŋ, -ɪd

pulsatile ˈpʌlsətaɪl
pulsation, -s pʌlˈseɪʃn, -z
pulsative ˈpʌlsətɪv
pulsatory ˈpʌlsətərɪ
puls|e (s. v.), -es, -ing, -ed pʌls, -ɪz, -ɪŋ, -t
Pulteney ˈpʌltnɪ, ˈpəʊltnɪ
pulverization [-isa-], -s ˌpʌlvəraɪˈzeɪʃn [-rɪˈz-], -z
pulveriz|e [-is|e], -es, -ing, -ed ˈpʌlvər- aɪz, -ɪz, -ɪŋ, -d
puma, -s ˈpjuːmə, -z
Pumblechook ˈpʌmbltʃʊk
pumic|e (s. v.), -es, -ing, -ed ˈpʌmɪs, -ɪz, -ɪŋ, -t
pumice-ston|e (s. v.), -es, -ing, -ed ˈpʌmɪsstəʊn [ˈpʌmɪstəʊn], -z, -ɪŋ, -d
pumm|el, -els, -elling, -elled ˈpʌm|l, -lz, -lɪŋ [-əlɪŋ], -ld
pump (s. v.), -s, -ing, -ed, -er/s pʌmp, -s, -ɪŋ, -t [pʌmt], -ə*/z
pumpernickel ˈpʊmpənɪkl
pumpkin, -s ˈpʌmpkɪn, -z
pun (s. v.), -s, -ning, -ned, -ner/s pʌn, -z, -ɪŋ, -d, -ə*/z
punch (s. v.) (P.), -es, -ing, -ed, -er/s pʌntʃ, -ɪz, -ɪŋ, -t, -ə*/z
punchbowl, -s ˈpʌntʃbəʊl, -z
punch-drunk ˌpʌntʃˈdrʌŋk [ˈ--]
puncheon, -s ˈpʌntʃən, -z
Punchinello ˌpʌntʃɪˈneləʊ
punch-ladle, -s ˈpʌntʃˌleɪdl, -z
punctilio, -s pʌŋkˈtɪlɪəʊ, -z
punctilious, -ly, -ness pʌŋkˈtɪlɪəs [-ljəs], -lɪ, -nɪs [-nəs]
punctual, -ly ˈpʌŋktjʊəl [-tjwəl, -tjʊl, -tʃʊəl, -tʃwəl, -tʃʊl], -ɪ
punctuality ˌpʌŋktjʊˈælətɪ [-tʃʊ-, -ɪtɪ]
punctuat|e, -es, -ing, -ed, -or/s ˈpʌŋk- tjʊeɪt [-tʃʊ-], -s, -ɪŋ, -ɪd, -ə*/z
punctuation, -s ˌpʌŋktjʊˈeɪʃn [-tʃʊ-], -z
punct|ure (s. v.), -ures, -uring, -ured ˈpʌŋktʃ|ə*, -əz, -ərɪŋ, -əd
pundit, -s ˈpʌndɪt (Hindi pəɳɖyt), -s
pungen|cy, -t/ly ˈpʌndʒən|sɪ, -t/lɪ
Punic ˈpjuːnɪk
puniness ˈpjuːnɪnɪs [-nəs]
punish, -es, -ing, -ed, -er/s, -ment/s; -able/ness ˈpʌnɪʃ, -ɪz, -ɪŋ, -t, -ə*/z, -mənt/s; -əbl/nɪs [-nəs]
punit|ive, -ory ˈpjuːnətɪv [-nɪt|ɪv], -ərɪ
Punjab, -i ˌpʌnˈdʒɑːb [ˈ--], -iː [-ɪ]
punka(h), -s ˈpʌŋkə, -z
punnet, -s ˈpʌnɪt, -s
Punshon ˈpʌnʃən
punster, -s ˈpʌnstə*, -z
punt (s. v.), -s, -ing, -ed, -er/s pʌnt, -s, -ɪŋ, -ɪd, -ə*/z

pun|y, -ier, -iest, -iness 'pju:n|ɪ, -ɪə*
[-jə*], -ɪɪst [-jɪst], -mɪs [-mɪnəs]
pup (s. v.), -s, -ping, -ped pʌp, -s, -ɪŋ, -t
pup|a, -ae, -al 'pju:p|ə, -i:, -l
pupil, -s 'pju:pl [-pɪl], -z
pupil(l)age, -ary 'pju:pɪl|ɪdʒ, -ərɪ
puppet, -s 'pʌpɪt, -s
pupp|y, -ies 'pʌp|ɪ, -ɪz
Purbeck 'pɜ:bek
purblin|d, -dness 'pɜ:blaɪn|d, -dnɪs [-nəs]
Purcell 'pɜ:sl [-sel, -səl, pɜ:'sel]
purchas|e (s. v.), -es, -ing, -ed, -er/s;
-able 'pɜ:tʃəs [-tʃɪs], -ɪz, -ɪŋ, -t, -ə*/z;
-əbl
purdah 'pɜ:dɑ: [-də] (Hindi pərda)
Purd|ie, -ye 'pɜ:d|ɪ, -ɪ
pure, -r, -st, -ly, -ness pjʊə* [pjɔə*,
pjɔ:*], -rə*, -rɪst, -lɪ, -nɪs [-nəs]
purée, -s 'pjʊəreɪ ['pjɔə*, 'pjɔ:r-,
'pʊər-] (pyre), -z
purf|le, -les, -ling, -led 'pɜ:f|l, -lz, -lɪŋ
[-lɪŋ], -ld
purfling (s.), -s 'pɜ:flɪŋ, -z
purgation, -s pɜ:'ɡeɪʃn, -z
purgative (s. adj.), -s 'pɜ:ɡətɪv, -z
purgatorial ,pɜ:ɡə'tɔ:rɪəl
purgator|y (P.), -ies 'pɜ:ɡətər|ɪ, -ɪz
purg|e (s. v.), -es, -ing, -ed pɜ:dʒ, -ɪz,
-ɪŋ, -d
purification (P.), -s ,pjʊərɪfɪ'keɪʃn
[,pjɔər-, ,pjɔ:r-], -z
purificatory 'pjʊərɪfɪkeɪtərɪ ['pjɔər-,
'pjɔ:r-, -kət-, ,pjʊərɪfɪ'keɪtərɪ, ,pjɔər-,
,pjɔ:r-]
puri|fy, -fies, -fying, -fied, -fier/s
'pjʊərɪ|faɪ ['pjɔər-, 'pjɔ:r-], -faɪz,
-faɪɪŋ, -faɪd, -faɪə*/z
Purim 'pjʊərɪm ['pʊə-]
puri|sm, -st/s 'pjʊərɪ|zəm ['pjɔər-,
'pjɔ:r-], -st/s
puristic, -al ,pjʊə'rɪstɪk [pjɔə'r-,
pjɔ:'r-], -l
purit|an (P.), -ans, -anism 'pjʊərɪt|ən
['pjɔər-, 'pjɔ:r-], -ənz, -ənɪzəm
[-nɪzəm]
puritanic, -al, -ally ,pjʊərɪ'tænɪk
[,pjɔər-, ,pjɔ:r-], -l, -əlɪ
purity 'pjʊərətɪ ['pjɔər-, 'pjɔ:r-, -ɪtɪ]
purl (s. v.), -s, -ing, -ed pɜ:l, -z, -ɪŋ, -d
Purley 'pɜ:lɪ
purlieu, -s 'pɜ:lju:, -z
purloin, -s, -ing, -ed pɜ:'lɔɪn ['pɜ:lɔɪn],
-z, -ɪŋ, -d
purloiner, -s pɜ:'lɔɪnə*, -z
purp|le (s. adj. v.), -ler, -lest; -les, -ling,
-led 'pɜ:p|l, -lə* [-lə*], -lɪst [-lɪst];
-lz, -lɪŋ [-lɪŋ], -ld
purplish 'pɜ:plɪʃ [-plɪʃ]

purport (s. v.), -s, -ing, -ed 'pɜ:pət
['pɜ:pɔ:t, pɜ:'pɔ:t, pə'pɔ:t], -s, -ɪŋ, -ɪd
purp|ose (s. v.), -oses, -osing, -osed
'pɜ:p|əs, -əsɪz, -əsɪŋ, -əst
purpose|ful, -fully, -fulness 'pɜ:pəs|fʊl,
-fʊlɪ [-fəlɪ], -fʊlnɪs [-nəs]
purposeless, -ly, -ness 'pɜ:pəslɪs [-ləs],
-lɪ, -nɪs [-nəs]
purposely 'pɜ:pəslɪ
purposive 'pɜ:pəsɪv
purr, -s, -ing, -ed pɜ:*, -z, -rɪŋ, -d
purs|e (s. v.), -es, -ing, -ed pɜ:s, -ɪz, -ɪŋ,
-t
purseful, -s 'pɜ:sfʊl, -z
purse-proud 'pɜ:spraʊd
purser, -s 'pɜ:sə*, -z
purse-string, -s 'pɜ:sstrɪŋ, -z
purslane 'pɜ:slɪn
pursuan|ce, -t/ly pə'sjʊən|s [-'sju:əns,
-'sʊ-, -'su:əns], -t/lɪ
purs|ue, -ues, -uing, -ued, -uer/s
pə'sju: [-'s|u:], -u:z, -u:ɪŋ [-ʊɪŋ],
-u:d, -u:ə*/z [-ʊə*/z]
pursuit, -s pə'sju:t [-'su:t], -s
pursuivant, -s 'pɜ:sɪvənt [old-fashioned
'pɜ:swɪ-], -s
purs|y, -iness 'pɜ:s|ɪ, -mɪs [-mɪnəs]
Purton 'pɜ:tn
purulen|cy, -t/ly 'pjʊərʊlən|sɪ [-rjʊ-],
-t/lɪ
Purv|er, -es 'pɜ:v|ə*, -ɪs
purvey, -s, -ing, -ed pə'veɪ [pɜ:'v-], -z,
-ɪŋ, -d
purvey|ance, -or/s pə'veɪ|əns [pɜ:'v-],
-ə*/z
purview, -s 'pɜ:vju:, -z
pus, -es pʌs, -ɪz
Pusey, -ite/s 'pju:zɪ, -aɪt/s
push (s. v.), -es, -ing/ly, -ed, -er/s pʊʃ,
-ɪz, -ɪŋ/lɪ, -t, -ə*/z
pushball 'pʊʃbɔ:l
push-bike, -s 'pʊʃbaɪk, -s
push-button, -s 'pʊʃ,bʌtn, -z
push-car, -s 'pʊʃkɑ:*, -s
push-cart, -s 'pʊʃkɑ:t, -s
pushful, -ness 'pʊʃfʊl [-fl], -nɪs [-nəs]
Pushkin 'pʊʃkɪn
Pushtu 'pʌʃtu: [,pʌʃ'tu:]
pusillanimity ,pju:sɪlə'nɪmətɪ [-ju:zɪ-,
-læ'n-, -ɪtɪ]
pusillanimous, -ly, -ness ,pju:sɪ'lænɪ-
məs [-ju:zɪ-, -nəməs], -lɪ, -nɪs [-nəs]
puss, -es pʊs, -ɪz
puss|y (cat), -ies 'pʊs|ɪ, -ɪz
pussyfoot, -s 'pʊsɪfʊt, -s
pustular 'pʌstjʊlə*
pustulat|e, -es, -ing, -ed 'pʌstjʊleɪt, -s,
-ɪŋ, -ɪd

pustulation, -s ˌpʌstjuˈleɪʃn, -z
pustule, -s ˈpʌstjuːl, -z
pustulous ˈpʌstjuləs
put (s.), (act of throwing a weight), -s
    pʊt, -s
put (v.) (place, move, throw), -s, -ting
    pʊt, -s, -ɪŋ
put(t) (s. v.) (at golf), -s, -ting, -ted
    -ter/s pʌt, -s, -ɪŋ, -ɪd, -ə*/z
putative ˈpjuːtətɪv
Puteoli pjuːˈtɪəlɪ [-ˈtɪəʊlɪ]
Putn|am, -ey ˈpʌtn|əm [-ˈæm], -ɪ
putrefaction ˌpjuːtrɪˈfækʃn
putre|fy, -fies, -fying, -fied ˈpjuːtrɪ|faɪ,
    -faɪz, -faɪɪŋ, -faɪd
putrescenc|e, -t pjuːˈtresn|s, -t
putrid, -ly, -ness ˈpjuːtrɪd, -lɪ, -nɪs [-nəs]
putridity pjuːˈtrɪdətɪ [-ɪtɪ]
putsch, -es pʊtʃ, -ɪz
putt (s. v.) (P.), -s, -ing, -ed, -er/s pʌt,
    -s, -ɪŋ, -ɪd, -ə*/z
puttee, -s ˈpʌtɪ, -z
Puttenham ˈpʌtnəm
putter, -s ˈpʌtə*, -z
Puttick ˈpʌtɪk
putting-green, -s ˈpʌtɪŋgriːn, -z
putt|y (s. v.), -ies, -ying, -ied ˈpʌt|ɪ, -ɪz,
    -ɪɪŋ, -ɪd
puzz|le, -les, -ling/ly, -led ˈpʌz|l, -lz,
    -lɪŋ/lɪ [-lɪŋ/lɪ], -ld
puzzler, -s ˈpʌzlə* [-zlə*], -z
Pwllheli pʊθˈlelɪ [pʊlˈhelɪ] (Welsh
    puːɬˈheli)
pyaemia paɪˈiːmjə [-mɪə]
Pybus ˈpaɪbəs
Pyddoke ˈpɪdək
Pye paɪ
pygmaean pɪgˈmiːən [-ˈmɪən]
Pygmalion pɪgˈmeɪljən [-lɪən]

pygm|y, -ies ˈpɪgm|ɪ, -ɪz
pyjama, -s pəˈdʒɑːmə [pɪˈdʒ-, old-
    fashioned paɪˈdʒ-], -z
Pyke paɪk
Pylades ˈpɪlədiːz
pylon, -s ˈpaɪlən, -z
pyorrhoea ˌpaɪəˈrɪə
pyramid (P.), -s ˈpɪrəmɪd, -z
pyramid|al, -ally pɪˈræmɪd|l, -əlɪ [-ļɪ]
Pyramus ˈpɪrəməs
pyre, -s ˈpaɪə*, -z
Pyrene paɪˈriːnɪ [ˌpaɪəˈr-]
Pyren|ean, -ees ˌpɪrəˈn|iːən [-rɪˈn-], -iːz
pyrethrum, -s paɪˈriːθrəm [ˌpaɪəˈr-], -z
pyretic paɪˈretɪk [ˌpaɪəˈr-, pɪˈr-]
pyriform (pear-shaped) ˈpɪrɪfɔːm
pyrites paɪˈraɪtiːz [ˌpaɪəˈr-, pɪˈr-, pəˈr-]
pyritic paɪˈrɪtɪk [ˌpaɪəˈr-]
pyro ˈpaɪərəʊ [ˈpaɪrəʊ]
pyrogallic ˌpaɪrəʊˈgælɪk [ˌpaɪər-]
pyromani|a, -ac ˌpaɪrəʊˈmeɪnɪ|ə [ˌpaɪər-,
    -njə], -æk [-njæk]
pyromet|er/s,   -ry   paɪˈrɒmɪt|ə*/z
    [ˌpaɪəˈr-, -mət|ə*], -rɪ
pyrometric, -al ˌpaɪrəʊˈmetrɪk [ˌpaɪər-],
    -l
pyrotechnic, -al, -ally, -s ˌpaɪrəʊˈteknɪk
    [ˌpaɪər-], -l, -əlɪ, -s
Pyrrh|a, -ic/s, -us ˈpɪr|ə, -ɪk/s, -əs
Pytchley ˈpaɪtʃlɪ
Pythagoras paɪˈθægəræs [-gɒr-, -rəs]
Pythagorean (s. adj.), -s paɪˌθægəˈrɪən
    [ˌpaɪθæg-, -gɒˈr-, -ˈriːən], -z
Pythian ˈpɪθɪən [-θjən]
Pythias ˈpɪθɪæs
python, -s ˈpaɪθn, -z
pythoness, -es ˈpaɪθənes [-nɪs], -ɪz
pythonic paɪˈθɒnɪk
pyx, -es pɪks, -ɪz

Q

Q (*the letter*) -'s kju:, -z
Qantas 'kwɒntæs [-təs]
Q.C., -'s ˌkju:'si:, -z
q.e.d. ˌkju:i:'di:
q.e.f. ˌkju:i:'ef
q.t. ˌkju:'ti:
qua kweɪ
quack (*s. v.*), -s, -ing, -ed; -ery, -ish
  kwæk, -s, -ɪŋ, -t; -ərɪ, -ıʃ
quad, -s kwɒd, -z
Quadragesima ˌkwɒdrə'dʒesɪmə
quadragesimal ˌkwɒdrə'dʒesɪml
quadrangle, -s 'kwɒdræŋgl [kwɒ'dræŋ-,
  kwə'dræŋ-], -z
quadrangular kwɒ'dræŋgjʊlə* [kwə'd-,
  -gjələ*]
quadrant, -s 'kwɒdrənt, -s
quadraphonic ˌkwɒdrə'fɒnɪk
quadrate (*s. adj.*), -s 'kwɒdrət [-rɪt,
  -reɪt], -s
quadrat|e (*v.*), -es, -ing, -ed kwɒ'dreɪt
  [kwə'd-], -s, -ɪŋ, -ɪd
quadratic (*s. adj.*), -s kwɒ'drætɪk
  [kwə'd-], -s
quadrature 'kwɒdrətʃə* [-rɪtʃ-, -ˌtjʊə*]
quadric (*s. adj.*), -s 'kwɒdrɪk, -s
quadriga, -s kwə'dri:gə [kwɒ'd-,
  -'draɪgə], -z
quadrilateral (*s. adj.*), -s ˌkwɒdrɪ-
  'lætərəl, -z
quadrilingual ˌkwɒdrɪ'lɪŋgwəl
quadrille, -s kwə'drɪl [*rarely* kə-], -z
quadrillion, -s kwɒ'drɪljən [kwə'd-],
  -z
quadrisyllabic ˌkwɒdrɪsɪ'læbɪk ['—ˌ—]
quadroon, -s kwɒ'dru:n [kwə'd-], -z
quadrumanous kwɒ'dru:mənəs [kwə'd-]
quadruped, -s 'kwɒdruped [-pɪd], -z
quadrup|le (*s. adj. v.*), -les, -ly; -ling,
  -led 'kwɒdrʊp|l [-dru:p-, kwɒ'dru:pl,
  kwə-], -lz, -lɪ; -lɪŋ, -ld
quadruplet, -s 'kwɒdrʊplɪt [-plet, -plət,
  kwɒ'dru:plɪt, -plət], -s
quadruplicate (*s. adj.*), -s kwɒ'dru:-
  plɪkət [kwə'd-, -kɪt, -keɪt], -s
quadruplicat|e (*v.*), -es, -ing, -ed kwɒ-
  'dru:plɪkeɪt [kwə'd-], -s, -ɪŋ, -ɪd
quaere 'kwɪərɪ
quaestor, -s 'kwi:stə* [-tɔ:*], -z

quaff, -s, -ing, -ed, -er/s kwɒf [kwɑ:f],
  -s, -ɪŋ, -t, -ə*/z
quag, -s kwæg [kwɒg], -z
quagga, -s 'kwægə, -z
Quaglino kwæg'li:nəʊ
quagmire, -s 'kwægmaɪə* ['kwɒg-], -z
quail (*s. v.*) (Q.), -s, -ing, -ed kweɪl, -z,
  -ɪŋ, -d
Quaile kweɪl
Quain kweɪn
quaint, -er, -est, -ly, -ness kweɪnt, -ə*,
  -ıst, -lɪ, -nɪs [-nəs]
quak|e (*s. v.*), -es, -ing, -ed kweɪk, -s,
  -ɪŋ, -t
Quaker, -s 'kweɪkə*, -z
qualification, -s ˌkwɒlɪfɪ'keɪʃn, -z
qualificative (*s. adj.*), -s 'kwɒlɪfɪkətɪv,
  -z
qualificatory 'kwɒlɪfɪkətərɪ [-keɪtərɪ,
  ˌ—'—'—]
quali|fy, -fies, -fying, -fied, -fier/s
  'kwɒlɪ|faɪ, -faɪz, -faɪɪŋ, -faɪd, -faɪə*/z
qualitative, -ly 'kwɒlɪtətɪv [-teɪt-], -lɪ
qualit|y, -ies 'kwɒlət|ɪ [-ɪt|ɪ], -ɪz
qualm, -s kwɑ:m [kwɔ:m], -z
qualmish, -ly, -ness 'kwɑ:mɪʃ ['kwɔ:m-],
  -lɪ, -nɪs [-nəs]
Qualtrough 'kwɒltrəʊ
quandar|y, -ies 'kwɒndər|ɪ [*rarely*
  kwɒn'deər-], -ɪz
Quandary (*Peak*) 'kwɒndərɪ
Quant kwɒnt
quantic, -s 'kwɒntɪk, -s
quanti|fy, -fies, -fying, -fied, -fier/s,
  -fiable 'kwɒntɪ|faɪ, -faɪz, -faɪɪŋ, -faɪd,
  -faɪə*/z, -faɪəbl
quantitative, -ly 'kwɒntɪtətɪv [-teɪt-], -lɪ
quantit|y, -ies 'kwɒntət|ɪ [-ɪt|ɪ], -ɪz
Quantock (*in Somerset*) 'kwɒntək, (*in
  names of streets, etc., in London*)
  'kwɒntək [-tɒk]
quantum (*amount*) 'kwɒntəm, (*in Latin
  phrases*) 'kwæntəm ['kwɒn-]
quarantin|e (*s. v.*), -es, -ing, -ed
  'kwɒrənti:n [-taɪn, ˌ—'-'], -z, -ɪŋ, -d
Quaritch 'kwɒrɪtʃ
Quarles kwɔ:lz
Quarmby 'kwɔ:mbɪ
Quarr kwɔ:*

403

quarr|el (s. v.), -els, -elling, -elled, -eller/s ˈkwɒr|əl, -əlz, -əlɪŋ [-lɪŋ], -əld, -ələ*/z [-lə*/z]

quarrelsome, -ly, -ness ˈkwɒrəlsəm, -lɪ, -nɪs [-nəs]

quarr|y (s. v.), -ies, -ying, -ied ˈkwɒr|ɪ, -ɪz, -ɪɪŋ, -ɪd

quarry|man, -men ˈkwɒrɪ|mən [-mæn], -mən [-men]

quart (measure of capacity), -s kwɔːt, -s

quart (s. v.) (in card games, fencing), -s, -ing, -ed kɑːt, -s, -ɪŋ, -ɪd

quartan ˈkwɔːtn [-tən]

quarter (s. v.), -s, -ing/s, -ed; -age ˈkwɔːtə*, -z, -rɪŋ/z, -d; -rɪdʒ

quarter-day, -s ˈkwɔːtədeɪ, -z

quarter-deck, -s ˈkwɔːtədek, -s

quarterl|y (s. adv.), -ies ˈkwɔːtəl|ɪ, -ɪz

Quartermaine ˈkwɔːtəmeɪn

quartermaster, -s ˈkwɔːtəˌmɑːstə*, -z

quartern, -s ˈkwɔːtən [-tn], -z

quarter-plate, -s ˈkwɔːtəpleɪt, -s

quarter-tone, -s ˈkwɔːtətəʊn, -z

quartet(te), -s kwɔːˈtet, -s

quartic (s. adj.), -s ˈkwɔːtɪk, -s

quartile, -s ˈkwɔːtaɪl, -z

quarto, -s ˈkwɔːtəʊ, -z

quartus (Q.) ˈkwɔːtəs

quartz kwɔːts

quasar ˈkweɪzɑː*

quash, -es, -ing, -ed kwɒʃ, -ɪz, -ɪŋ, -t

quashee (Q.), -s ˈkwɒʃɪ, -z

quasi ˈkweɪzaɪ [-saɪ, ˈkwɑːzɪ, -ziː]

quassia ˈkwɒʃə

quatercentenar|y, -ies ˌkwætəsenˈtiːnər|ɪ [ˌkwɔːt-, ˌkwɒt-, ˌkweɪt-, -ˈten-, -ˈsentɪn-], -ɪz

Quatermain ˈkwɔːtəmeɪn

quaternar|y (s. adj.), -ies kwəˈtɜːnər|ɪ, -ɪz

quaternion, -s kwəˈtɜːnjən [-nɪən], -z

quatorzain, -s kəˈtɔːzeɪn [kæˈtɔː-, ˈkætəzeɪn], -z

quatorze, -s kəˈtɔːz, -ɪz

quatrain, -s ˈkwɒtreɪn, -z

quatre-foil, -s ˈkætrəfɔɪl [-təf-], -z

quatrillion, -s kwɒˈtrɪljən [kwəˈt-], -z

quav|er (s. v.), -ers, -ering/ly, -ered ˈkweɪv|ə*, -əz, -ərɪŋ/lɪ, -əd

quay, -s; -age kiː, -z; -ɪdʒ

Quay (place-name) kiː, (surname) kweɪ

Quayle kweɪl

quean, -s kwiːn, -z

queas|y, -iness ˈkwiːz|ɪ, -ə*, -ɪst, -lɪ, -nɪs [-nəs]

Quebec kwɪˈbek [kwəˈb-]

queen (s. v.), -s, -ing, -ed kwiːn, -z, -ɪŋ, -d

Queenborough ˈkwiːnbərə

Queenie ˈkwiːnɪ

queenlike ˈkwiːnlaɪk

queenl|y, -ier, -iest, -iness ˈkwiːnl|ɪ, -ɪə* [-jə*], -ɪɪst [-jɪst], -ɪnɪs [-nəs]

Queens|berry, -bury, -ferry, -land, -town ˈkwiːnz|bərɪ, -bərɪ, -ˌferɪ, -lənd [-lænd], -taʊn

queer, -er, -est, -ly, -ness; -ish kwɪə*, -rə*, -rɪst, -lɪ, -nɪs [-nəs]; -rɪʃ

queerit|y, -ies ˈkwɪərət|ɪ [-ɪt|ɪ], -ɪz

quell, -s, -ing, -ed, -er/s kwel, -z, -ɪŋ, -d, -ə*/z

quench, -es, -ing, -ed, -er/s; -able kwentʃ, -ɪz, -ɪŋ, -t, -ə*/z; -əbl

Quen(n)ell kwɪˈnel [kwəˈn-], ˈkwenl

quenelle, -s kəˈnel [kɪˈn-], -z

Quentin ˈkwentɪn

querist, -s ˈkwɪərɪst, -s

quern, -s kwɜːn, -z

querulous, -ly, -ness ˈkwerʊləs [-rjʊl-, -rəl-], -lɪ, -nɪs [-nəs]

quer|y (s. v.), -ies, -ying, -ied ˈkwɪər|ɪ, -ɪz, -ɪɪŋ, -ɪd

Quesnel ˈkeɪnl

quest (s. v.), -s, -ing, -ed kwest, -s, -ɪŋ, -ɪd

questi|on (s. v.), -ons, -oning/ly, -oned, -oner/s ˈkwestʃ|ən [-eʃtʃ-], -ənz, -ənɪŋ/lɪ [-ɪɪŋ/lɪ, -nɪŋ/lɪ], -ənd, -ənə*/z [-ɪɪŋ-ə*/z, -nə*/z]

questionab|le, -ly, -leness ˈkwestʃənəb|l [-eʃtʃ-, -tʃnə-, -tʃnə-], -lɪ, -lnɪs [-nəs]

questionar|y (s. adj.), -ies ˈkwestʃənər|ɪ [-tʃnər-], ɪz

question-mark, -s ˈkwestʃənmɑːk [-eʃtʃ-], -s

questionnaire, -s ˌkwestɪəˈneə* [ˌkwestʃə-, ˌkwestʃə-, ˌkweʃtʃə-, kes-, ˈ---], -z

Quetta ˈkwetə

quetzal ˈkwetsl

queue (s. v.), -s, -ing, -d kjuː, -z, -ɪŋ [ˈkjʊɪŋ], -d

queue-minded ˈkjuːˌmaɪndɪd [ˌ-ˈ--]

Queux kjuː

Quex kweks

quibbl|e (s. v.), -les, -ling, -led, -ler/s ˈkwɪb|l, -lz, -lɪŋ [-lɪŋ], -ld, -lə*/z [-lə*/z]

Quibell ˈkwaɪbəl, ˈkwɪbəl, kwɪˈbel
Note.—Baron Quibell of Scunthorpe pronounced ˈkwaɪ-.

quick (s. adj.) (Q.), -s, -er, -est, -ly, -ness kwɪk, -s, -ə*, -ɪst, -lɪ, -nɪs [-nəs]

quick-change (adj.) ˈkwɪktʃeɪndʒ [ˌ-ˈ-]

Quicke kwɪk

quick|en, -ens, -ening, -ened ˈkwɪk|ən, -ənz, -ənɪŋ [-ənɪŋ], -ənd

quick-fir|er/s, -ing 'kwɪkˌfaɪər|ə*/z,
-ɪŋ
quick|-freeze, -freezes, -freezing, -froze,
-frozen, -freezer/s 'kwɪk|friːz [ˌ-'-,
and in derived forms], -ˌfriːzɪz,
-ˌfriːzɪŋ, -frəʊz, -ˌfrəʊzn, -ˌfriːzə*/z
quicklime 'kwɪklaɪm
Quickly 'kwɪklɪ
quickmarch ˌkwɪk'mɑːtʃ
quick|sand/s, -set 'kwɪk|sænd/z, -set
quicksilv|er (s. v.), -ers, -ering, -ered
'kwɪkˌsɪlv|ə*, -əz, -ərɪŋ, -əd
quick-tempered ˌkwɪk'tempəd ['-ˌ--]
quick-witted, -ness ˌkwɪk'wɪtɪd, -nɪs
[-nəs]
quid, -s kwɪd, -z
quidnunc, -s 'kwɪdnʌŋk, -s
quid pro quo, -s ˌkwɪdprəʊ'kwəʊ, -z
quiescen|ce, -t/ly kwaɪ'esn|s, -t/lɪ
quiet (s. adj. v.), -er, -est, -ly, -ness;
-s, -ing, -ed 'kwaɪət, -ə*, -ɪst, -lɪ,
-nɪs [-nəs]; -s, -ɪŋ, -ɪd
quiet|en, -ens, -ening, -ened 'kwaɪət|n,
-nz, -ṇɪŋ [-nɪŋ], -nd
quieti|sm, -st/s 'kwaɪtɪ|zəm [-aɪət-],
-st/s
quietude 'kwaɪtjuːd [-aɪət-]
quietus kwaɪ'iːtəs [-'eɪtəs]
Quiggin 'kwɪgɪn
quill (s. v.), -s, -ing, -ed kwɪl, -z, -ɪŋ,
-d
Quilleash 'kwɪliːʃ
Quiller-Couch ˌkwɪlə'kuːtʃ
Quilliam 'kwɪljəm [-lɪəm]
Quilp kwɪlp
quilt (s. v.), -s, -ing, -ed kwɪlt, -s, -ɪŋ,
-ɪd
Quilter 'kwɪltə*
quin (Q.), -s kwɪn, -z
Quinault (surname) 'kwɪnlt [-nəlt,
-nɔːlt]
quince (Q.), -s kwɪns, -ɪz
quincentenar|y, -ies ˌkwɪnsen'tiːnər|ɪ
[-'ten-, kwɪn'sentɪn-], -ɪz
Quinc(e)y 'kwɪnsɪ
quincunx, -es 'kwɪnkʌŋks ['kwɪŋk-],
-ɪz
quindecagon, -s kwɪn'dekəgən, -z
quingentenar|y, -ies ˌkwɪndʒen'tiːnər|ɪ
[-'ten-], -ɪz
quinine kwɪ'niːn ['kwɪniːn]
Quinney 'kwɪnɪ
quinquagenarian, -s ˌkwɪŋkwədʒɪ-
'neərɪən, -z
Quinquagesima ˌkwɪŋkwə'dʒesɪmə
quinquennial kwɪŋ'kwenɪəl [-njəl]
quinquennium, -s kwɪŋ'kwenɪəm
[-njəm], -z

quinquereme, -s 'kwɪŋkwɪriːm [-kwər-],
-z
quinquina kwɪŋ'kwaɪnə
quinsy 'kwɪnzɪ
quint, -s (organ stop) kwɪnt, (in piquet)
kɪnt [kwɪnt, old-fashioned kent],
-s
quintain, -s 'kwɪntɪn, -z
quintal, -s 'kwɪntl, -z
quintessence kwɪn'tesns
quintet(te), -s kwɪn'tet, -s
quintic (s. adj.), -s 'kwɪntɪk, -s
Quintilian kwɪn'tɪljən [-lɪən]
quintillion, -s kwɪn'tɪljən, -z
Quintin 'kwɪntɪn
Quinton 'kwɪntən
quintup|le, -les, -ling, -led 'kwɪntjʊp|l
[-tjuːp-, kwɪn'tjuːpl], -lz, -lɪŋ, -ld
quintuplet, -s 'kwɪntjʊplɪt [-plet, -plət,
kwɪn'tjuːplɪt, -plət], -s
quintus (Q.) 'kwɪntəs
quip, -s kwɪp, -s
quire, -s 'kwaɪə*, -z
Quirey (surname) (in England) 'kwaɪərɪ,
(in Ireland) 'kwɪərɪ
Quirinal 'kwɪrɪnəl
Quirinus kwɪ'raɪnəs
quirk (Q.), -s kwɜːk, -s
quisling, -s 'kwɪzlɪŋ, -z
quit (adj. v.), -s, -ting, -ted kwɪt, -s, -ɪŋ,
-ɪd
quite kwaɪt
Quito 'kiːtəʊ
quit-rent, -s 'kwɪtrent, -s
quits kwɪts
quittance, -s 'kwɪtəns, -ɪz
quiv|er (s. v.), -ers, -ering/ly, -ered
'kwɪv|ə*, -əz, -ərɪŋ/lɪ, -əd
qui vive ˌkiː'viːv
Quixote 'kwɪksət [-səʊt, kɪ'həʊtɪ]
(kiˈxote)
quixotic, -ally kwɪk'sɒtɪk, -əlɪ
quiz (s. v.), -zes, -zing, -zed kwɪz, -ɪz,
-ɪŋ, -d
quizmaster, -s 'kwɪzˌmɑːstə*, -z
quizzic|al, -ally 'kwɪzɪk|l, -əlɪ
quoad 'kwəʊæd
quod (s. v.), -s, -ding, -ded kwɒd, -z,
-ɪŋ, -ɪd
quodlibet, -s 'kwɒdlɪbet, -s
quoin (s. v.), -s, -ing, -ed kɔɪn [kwɔɪn],
-z, -ɪŋ, -d
quoit, -s kɔɪt [kwɔɪt], -s
quondam 'kwɒndæm [-dəm]
Quorn kwɔːn
quorum, -s 'kwɔːrəm, -z
quota (s. v.), -s, -ing, -ed 'kwəʊtə, -z,
-ɪŋ [-ərɪŋ], -d

405

quotable 'kwəʊtəbl
quotation, -s kwəʊ'teɪʃn, -z
quot|e (s. v.), -es, -ing, -ed kwəʊt, -s,
    -ɪŋ, -ɪd
quoth, -a kwəʊθ, -ə
quotidian kwɒ'tɪdɪən [kwəʊ't-, -djən]

quotient, -s 'kwəʊʃnt, -s
quousque tandem kwəʊ,ʊskwɪ'tændem
    [-,ʌs-, -dəm]
Quy (in Cambridgeshire, surname) kwaɪ
q.v. ,kjuː'viː [,wɪtʃ'siː, ,kwɒd'vɪdeɪ,
    old-fashioned ,kwɒd'vaɪdɪ]

R

R (*the letter*), -'s ɑ:*, -z
ra (*note in Tonic Sol-fa*), -s rɔ:, -z
Rabat (*in Morocco*) rə'bɑ:t
rabbet, -s 'ræbɪt, -s
rabbi, -s 'ræbaɪ, -z
rabbinic, -al, -ally ræ'bɪnɪk [rə'b-], -l, -əlɪ
rabbit, -s; -hole/s, -hutch/es 'ræbɪt, -s; -həʊl/z, -hʌtʃ/ɪz
rabbit-warren, -s 'ræbɪt,wɒrən, -z
rabble, -s 'ræbl, -z
Rabelais 'ræbəleɪ (rablɛ)
Rabelaisian ,ræbə'leɪzɪən [-zjən]
rabid, -est, -ly, -ness 'ræbɪd, -ɪst, -lɪ, -nɪs [-nəs]
rabies 'reɪbi:z [-bɪz, -bri:z, 'ræb-]
Rabin (*surname*) 'reɪbɪn
Rabindranath Tagore rə,bɪndrənɑ:ttə'gɔ:* [-'gɔə*] (*Bengali* robindrɔnath ʈhakur, *Hindi* rəbindrənath ʈhakwr)
Rabshakeh 'ræbʃɑ:kɪ [-ʃəkɪ, -ʃəkə]
Raby 'reɪbɪ
raca 'rɑ:kə
rac|e, -es, -ing, -ed, -er/s reɪs, -ɪz, -ɪŋ, -t, -ə*/z
race-course, -s 'reɪskɔ:s [-kɔəs], -ɪz
race-horse, -s 'reɪshɔ:s, -ɪz
race-meeting, -s 'reɪs,mi:tɪŋ, -z
Racheil 'reɪʃl
Rachel 'reɪtʃəl
rachitis ræ'kaɪtɪs [rə'k-]
Rachmaninoff ræk'mænɪnɒf (rax'manjinəf)
raci|al, -ally 'reɪʃ|l [-ʃɪ|əl, -ʃj|əl], -əlɪ
racialism 'reɪʃəlɪzəm [-ʃɪəl-, -ʃjəl-, -ʃlɪ-]
Racine (*English personal name*) rə'si:n, (*French author*) ræ'si:n (rasin)
racism 'reɪsɪzəm
rack (*s. v.*), -s, -ing, -ed ræk, -s, -ɪŋ, -t
racket (*s. v.*), -s, -ing, -ed; -y 'rækɪt, -s, -ɪŋ, -ɪd; -ɪ
racketeer, -s ,rækə'tɪə* [-kɪ't-], -z
rack-rail, -s 'rækreɪl [ˌ-'-], -z
rack-rent, -s 'rækrent, -s
raconteur, -s ,rækɒn'tɜ:* [-kɔ̃:n-] (rakɔ̃tœ:r), -z
racoon, -s rə'ku:n, -z
racquet, -s 'rækɪt, -s

rac|y, -ier, -iest, -ily, -iness 'reɪs|ɪ, -ɪə* [-jə*], -ɪɪst [-jɪst], -ɪlɪ [-əlɪ], -ɪnɪs [-məs]
rad (R.), -s ræd, -z
radar 'reɪdɑ:* [-də*]
Rad|cliffe, -ford 'ræd|klɪf, -fəd
radial, -ly 'reɪdjəl [-dɪəl], -ɪ
radian, -s 'reɪdjən [-dɪən], -z
radiance, -s 'reɪdjəns [-dɪəns], -ɪz
radiant (*s. adj.*), -s, -ly 'reɪdjənt [-dɪənt], -s, -lɪ
radiat|e (*v.*), -es, -ing, -ed 'reɪdɪeɪt [-djert], -s, -ɪŋ, -ɪd
radiation, -s ,reɪdɪ'eɪʃn, -z
radiator, -s 'reɪdɪeɪtə* [-djertə*], -z
radic|al (*s. adj.*), -als, -ally, -alness; -alism 'rædɪk|l, -lz, -əlɪ [-ḷɪ], -lnɪs [-nəs]; -əlɪzəm [-ḷɪzəm]
radio (*s.*), -s 'reɪdɪəʊ [-djəʊ], -z
radi|o (*v.*), -o(e)s, -oing, -oed 'reɪdɪ|əʊ [-dj|əʊ], -əʊz, -əʊɪŋ, -əʊd
radio-active ,reɪdɪəʊ'æktɪv [-djəʊ-]
radioactivity ,reɪdɪəʊæk'tɪvətɪ [-djəʊ-, -ɪtɪ]
radiogenic ,reɪdɪəʊ'dʒenɪk [-djəʊ-]
radiogram, -s 'reɪdɪəʊgræm [-djəʊg-], -z
radiograph, -s 'reɪdɪəʊgrɑ:f [-djəʊg-, -græf], -s
radiograph|y, -er/s ,reɪdɪ'ɒgrəf|ɪ, -ə*/z
radiolocat|e, -es, -ing, -ed ,reɪdɪəʊləʊ'keɪt [-djəʊ-], -s, -ɪŋ, -ɪd
radio-location ,reɪdɪəʊləʊ'keɪʃn [-djəʊ-]
radiolog|ist/s, -y ,reɪdɪ'ɒlədʒ|ɪst/s, -ɪ
radiometer, -s ,reɪdɪ'ɒmɪtə* [-mətə*], -z
radiotelegram, -s ,reɪdɪəʊ'telɪgræm [-djəʊ-], -z
radiotelephone, -s ,reɪdɪəʊ'telɪfəʊn [-djəʊ-], -z
radiotherap|y, -ist/s ,reɪdɪəʊ'θerəp|ɪ [-djəʊ-], -ɪst/s
radish, -es 'rædɪʃ, -ɪz
radium 'reɪdjəm [-dɪəm]
ra|dius, -dii 'reɪ|djəs [-dɪəs], -dɪaɪ
radix, -es, radices 'reɪdɪks, -ɪz, 'reɪdɪsi:z
Radleian, -s ræd'li:ən [-'lɪən], -z
Radley 'rædlɪ
Radmall 'rædmɔ:l
Radnor, -shire 'rædnə* [-nɔ:*], -ʃə* [-ˌʃɪə*]

407

Rae reɪ
Raeburn, -s 'reɪbə:n, -z
Raemakers 'rɑːmɑːkəz
Raf ræf
R.A.F. ˌɑːreɪ'ef
raffia 'ræfɪə [-fjə]
raffish 'ræfɪʃ
raff|le (s. v.), -les (R.), -ling, -led 'ræf|l,
  -lz, -lɪŋ [-lɪŋ], -ld
raft (s. v.), -s, -ing, -ed rɑːft, -s, -ɪŋ, -ɪd
rafter, -s, -ed 'rɑːftə*, -z, -d
rag (s. v.), -s, -ging, -ged ræg, -z, -ɪŋ, -d
ragamuffin, -s 'rægə,mʌfɪn, -z
rag-and-bone|-man,   -men   ˌrægən-
  'bəʊn|-mæn, -men
rag|e (s. v.), -es, -ing/ly, -ed reɪdʒ, -ɪz,
  -ɪŋ/lɪ, -d
ragged (adj.), -er, -est, -ly, -ness 'rægɪd,
  -ə*, -ɪst, -lɪ, -nɪs [-nəs]
Raglan 'ræglən
ragout, -s 'ræguː, -z
ragtag 'rægtæg
ragtime 'rægtaɪm
Rahab 'reɪhæb
Rahere rə'hɪə*
raid (s. v.), -s, -ing, -ed, -er/s reɪd, -z,
  -ɪŋ, -ɪd, -ə*/z
Raikes reɪks
rail (s. v.), -s, -ing, -ed reɪl, -z, -ɪŋ, -d
railhead, -s 'reɪlhed, -z
railing, -s 'reɪlɪŋ, -z
railler|y, -ies 'reɪlər|ɪ, -ɪz
rail|road/s, -way/s 'reɪl|rəʊd/z, -weɪ/z
railway|man,   -men   'reɪlweɪ|mən
  [-mæn], -mən [-men]
raiment 'reɪmənt
rain (s. v.), -s, -ing, -ed; -less reɪn, -z,
  -ɪŋ, -d; -lɪs [-ləs]
rainbow, -s 'reɪnbəʊ, -z
raincoat, -s 'reɪnkəʊt ['reɪŋk-], -s
raindrop, -s 'reɪndrɒp, -s
rainfall 'reɪnfɔːl
rain-gauge, -s 'reɪngeɪdʒ ['reɪŋg-], -ɪz
rainless 'reɪnlɪs [-ləs]
rainmak|er/s, -ing 'reɪn,meɪk|ə*/z, -ɪŋ
rainproof 'reɪnpruːf
rainstorm, -s 'reɪnstɔːm, -z
rainwater 'reɪn,wɔːtə*
rain|y, -ier, -iest, -iness 'reɪn|ɪ, -ɪə*
  [-jə*], -ɪɪst [-jɪst], -ɪnɪs [-ɪnəs]
rais|e, -es, -ing, -ed reɪz, -ɪz, -ɪŋ, -d
raisin, -s 'reɪzn, -z
raison d'être ˌreɪzɔ̃:n'deɪtrə [-'detrə,
  -zɒn'd-, -'deɪtə*] (rɛzɔ̃dɛːtr)
raj rɑːdʒ
rajah (R.), -s 'rɑːdʒə, -z
Rajasthani ˌrɑːdʒə'stɑːnɪ (Hindi raɪəs-
  thani)

Rajput 'rɑːdʒpʊt (Hindi raɪpwt)
Rajputana ˌrɑːdʒpʊ'tɑːnə (Hindi raɪ-
  pwtana)
rak|e (s. v.), -es, -ing, -ed reɪk, -s, -ɪŋ,
  -t
rakish, -ly, -ness 'reɪkɪʃ, -lɪ, -nɪs [-nəs]
rale, -s rɑːl, -z
Rale(i)gh 'rɔːlɪ, 'rɑːlɪ, 'rælɪ
  Note.—The family of the late Sir
    Walter Raleigh pronounced 'rɔːlɪ.
    Raleigh bicycles are generally called
    'rælɪ. When used as the name of a
    ship, the pronunciation is 'rælɪ.
rallentando, -s ˌrælen'tændəʊ [-lən-,
  -lɪn-], -z
rall|y (s. v.), -ies, -ying, -ied 'ræl|ɪ, -ɪz,
  -ɪɪŋ, -ɪd
Ralph (Christian name) reɪf, rælf
Ralph Cross (in North Yorkshire)
  ˌrɑːlf'krɒs [ˌrælf-,   old-fashioned
  -'krɔːs]
Ralston 'rɔːlstən
ram (s. v.), -s, -ming, -med, -mer/s
  ræm, -z, -ɪŋ, -d, -ə*/z
Ramadan ˌræmə'dæn [ˌrɑː-, -'dɑːn]
Ramah 'rɑːmə
Ramayana rɑː'maɪənə [-'mɑːjənə]
  (Hindi ramajənə)
ramb|le (s. v.), -les, -ling, -led 'ræmb|l,
  -lz, -lɪŋ [-lɪŋ], -ld
rambler (R.), -s 'ræmblə*, -z
rambling (adj.), -ly 'ræmblɪŋ, -lɪ
ramekin [-quin], -s 'ræmkɪn, -z
Rameses 'ræmɪsiːz [-məs-]
ramification, -s ˌræmɪfɪ'keɪʃn, -z
rami|fy, -fies, -fying, -fied 'ræmɪ|faɪ,
  -faɪz, -faɪɪŋ, -faɪd
Ramillies 'ræmɪlɪz
Ramoth-Gilead ˌreɪmɒθ'gɪlɪæd [-məθ-,
  -ljæd]
ramp (s. v.), -s, -ing, -ed ræmp, -s, -ɪŋ,
  -t [ræmt]
rampag|e (s. v.), -es, -ing, -ed ræm-
  'peɪdʒ, -ɪz, -ɪŋ, -d
rampageous, -ly, -ness ræm'peɪdʒəs, -lɪ,
  -nɪs [-nəs]
rampan|cy, -t/ly 'ræmpən|sɪ, -t/lɪ
rampart, -s 'ræmpɑːt [-pət], -s
rampion, -s 'ræmpjən [-pɪən], -z
ramrod, -s 'ræmrɒd, -z
Ramsay 'ræmzɪ
Ramsden 'ræmzdən
Ramsey 'ræmzɪ
Ramsgate 'ræmzgɪt [locally -geɪt]
ramshackle 'ræm,ʃækl [ˌ-'--]
ran (from run) ræn
rance ræns
Rance (surname) rɑːns

ranch (*s. v.*), **-es, -ing, -ed, -er/s** rɑːntʃ [ræntʃ], -ɪz, -ɪŋ, -t, -ə*/z

rancid, -ness 'rænsɪd, -nɪs [-nəs]

rancidity ræn'sɪdətɪ [-ɪtɪ]

rancorous, -ly 'ræŋkərəs, -lɪ

rancour 'ræŋkə*

rand, -s rænd, -z

Rand (*usual pronunciation in England*) rænd, (*pronunciation of English-speaking South Africans*) rɑːnd, rɑːnt, rɒnt (*Afrikaans* rɑnt)

Rand|all, -ell 'rændl, -l

Randolph 'rændɒlf [-dəlf]

random 'rændəm

randomization [-isa-] ˌrændəmaɪ'zeɪʃn [-mɪ'z-]

randomiz|e [-is|e], -es, -ing, -ed 'rændəmaɪz, -ɪz, -ɪŋ, -d

randy 'rændɪ

Ranee, -s ˌrɑː'niː ['--], -z

Ranelagh 'rænɪlə, 'rænələ

rang (*from* ring) ræŋ

rang|e (*s. v.*), **-es, -ing, -ed** reɪndʒ, -ɪz, -ɪŋ, -d

range-finder, -s 'reɪndʒˌfaɪndə*, -z

ranger (R.), -s 'reɪndʒə*, -z

Rangoon ræŋ'guːn

rank (*s. adj. v.*) (R.), **-s; -er, -est, -ly, -ness; -ing, -ed** ræŋk, -s; -ə*, -ɪst, -lɪ, -nɪs [-nəs]; -ɪŋ, -t [ræŋt]

Rankeillour ræŋ'kiːlə*

Rankin(e) 'ræŋkɪn

rank|le, -les, -ling, -led 'ræŋk|l, -lz, -lɪŋ, [-lɪŋ], -ld

Rannoch 'rænək [-əx]

Rann of Cutch ˌrʌnəv'kʌtʃ [ˌræn-]

Ranoe 'rɑːnəʊ

ransack, -s, -ing, -ed, -er/s 'rænsæk, -s, -ɪŋ, -t, -ə*/z

ransom (*s. v.*) (R.), **-s, -ing, -ed, -er/s** 'rænsəm, -z, -ɪŋ, -d, -ə*/z

Ransome 'rænsəm

rant (*s. v.*), **-s, -ing/ly, -ed, -er/s** rænt, -s, -ɪŋ/lɪ, -ɪd, -ə*/z

ranuncul|us, -uses, -i rə'nʌŋkjʊl|əs [-kjəl-], -əsɪz, -aɪ

Ranworth 'rænwɜːθ

rap (*s. v.*), **-s, -ping, -ped** ræp, -s, -ɪŋ, -t

rapacious, -ly, -ness rə'peɪʃəs, -lɪ, -nɪs [-nəs]

rapacity rə'pæsətɪ [-ɪtɪ]

rap|e (*s. v.*), **-es, -ing, -ed** reɪp, -s, -ɪŋ, -t

Raphael (*angel*) 'ræferəl ['ræfɑːel, 'ræfeɪl, 'reɪfɪəl, *and in Jewish usage* 'reɪfl, 'ræfəel], (*modern surname*) 'reɪfl, 'ræfeɪl, (*Italian artist*) 'ræferəl [-fɪəl, -feɪl]

rapid, -est, -ly, -ness 'ræpɪd, -ɪst, -lɪ, -nɪs [-nəs]

rapidity rə'pɪdətɪ [ræ'p-, -ɪtɪ]

rapier, -s 'reɪpjə* [-pɪə*], -z

rapine 'ræpaɪn [-pɪn]

rapparee, -s ˌræpə'riː, -z

rapping, -s 'ræpɪŋ, -z

rapport ræ'pɔː* (rapoːr)

rapporteur, -s ˌræpɔː'tɜː* (raportœːr), -z

rapprochement, -s ræ'prɒʃmɑ̃ːŋ [-mɔ̃ːŋ, -mɑːŋ, -mɒŋ] (raprɔʃmɑ̃), -z

rapscallion, -s ræp'skæljən [-lɪən], -z

rapt ræpt

rapture, -s, -d 'ræptʃə*, -z, -d

rapturous, -ly 'ræptʃərəs, -lɪ

rara avis ˌrɑːrə'ævɪs [ˌreərə'eɪvɪs]

rare, -r, -st, -ly, -ness reə*, -rə*, -rɪst, -lɪ, -nɪs [-nəs]

rarebit, -s 'reəbɪt ['ræbɪt], -s

rarefaction ˌreərɪ'fækʃn

rarefication ˌreərɪfɪ'keɪʃn

rare|fy, -fies, -fying, -fied 'reərɪ|faɪ, -faɪz, -faɪɪŋ, -faɪd

rarit|y, -ies 'reərət|ɪ [-ɪt|ɪ], -ɪz

rascal, -s 'rɑːskəl, -z

rascalit|y, -ies rɑː'skælət|ɪ [-ɪt|ɪ], -ɪz

rascally 'rɑːskəlɪ [-klɪ]

ras|e, -es, -ing, -ed reɪz, -ɪz, -ɪŋ, -d

rash (*s. adj.*), **-es; -er, -est, -ly, -ness** ræʃ, -ɪz; -ə*, -ɪst, -lɪ, -nɪs [-nəs]

rasher (*s.*), -s 'ræʃə*, -z

rasp (*s. v.*), **-s, -ing, -ed** rɑːsp, -s, -ɪŋ, -t

raspberr|y, -ies 'rɑːzbər|ɪ ['rɑːsb-], -ɪz

Rasputin ræ'spjuːtɪn [-'spuː-]

rasp|ly, -iness 'rɑːsp|ɪ, -ɪnɪs [-ɪnəs]

Rasselas 'ræsɪləs [-læs]

rat, -s, -ting, -ted ræt, -s, -ɪŋ, -ɪd

rata (*tree*), -s 'reɪtə, -z

rata (*in* pro rata) 'rɑːtə ['reɪtə]

ratability ˌreɪtə'bɪlətɪ [-lɪt-]

ratab|le, -ly 'reɪtəb|l, -lɪ

ratafia, -s ˌrætə'fɪə, -z

ratan, -s rə'tæn [ræ't-], -z

rataplan ˌrætə'plæn

ratatat ˌrætə'tæt

rat-catcher, -s 'rætˌkætʃə*, -z

ratchet, -s 'rætʃɪt, -s

Ratcliff(e) 'rætklɪf

rat|e (*s. v.*), **-es, -ing, -ed** reɪt, -s, -ɪŋ, -ɪd

rateab|le, -ly 'reɪtəb|l, -lɪ

ratel, -s 'reɪtel [-təl, -tl], -z

rate-payer, -s 'reɪtˌpeɪə*, -z

Rath ræθ

Rathbone 'ræθbəʊn [-bən]

rather 'rɑːðə* [*as interj. also* ˌrɑː'ðɜː*]

Rathfarnham ræθ'fɑːnəm

rat-hole, -s 'ræthəʊl, -z

ratification, -s ˌrætɪfɪ'keɪʃn, -z

409

rati|fy, -fies, -fying, -fied, -fier/s 'ræti|fai, -faiz, -faiiŋ, -faid, -faiə*/z

rating, -s 'reitiŋ, -z

ratio, -s 'reiʃəʊ [-ʃjəʊ], -z

ratiocinat|e, -es, -ing, -ed ˌrætɪ'ɒsmeit, -s, -iŋ, -id

ratiocination, -s ˌrætɪɒsɪ'neiʃn [-tɪəʊs-], -z

rati|on (s. v.), -ons, -oning, -oned 'ræʃ|n, -nz, -n̩iŋ [-əniŋ, -niŋ], -nd

ra|tional, -tionally 'ræ|ʃənl [-ʃnəl, -ʃņl, -ʃn̩l, -ʃənəl], -ʃņəlɪ [-ʃnəlɪ -ʃņ̩lɪ, -ʃn̩lɪ, -ʃənəlɪ]

rationale, -s ˌræʃə'nɑːl [-ʃiəʊ'n-, -ʃjə'n-, -'nɑːlɪ], -z

rationali|sm, -st/s 'ræʃņəlɪ|zəm [-ʃnəl-, -ʃņ̩l-, -ʃn̩l-, -ʃənəl-], -st/s

rationalistic ˌræʃņə'lɪstɪk [-ʃnə'lɪ-, -ʃņ̩l'ɪ-, -ʃn̩l'ɪ-, -ʃənə'lɪ-]

rationality ˌræʃə'næləti [-ʃņ'æ-, -ɪtɪ]

rationalization [-isa-] ˌræʃņəlai'zeiʃn [-ʃnəl-, -ʃņ̩l-, -ʃn̩l-, -ʃənəl-, -lɪ'z-]

rationaliz|e [-is|e], -es, -ing, -ed 'ræʃņəlaiz [-ʃnəl-, -ʃņ̩l-, -ʃn̩l-, -ʃənəl-], -iz, -iŋ, -d

Ratisbon 'rætizbɒn [-ɪsb-]

ratlin(e), -s 'rætlɪn, -z

rat-race 'rætreis

rat-tail, -ed 'rætteil, -d

rattan, -s rə'tæn [ræ't-], -z

ratt|le (s. v.), -les, -ling, -led, -ler/s 'ræt|l, -lz, -lɪŋ [-lɪŋ], -ld, -lə*/z [-lə*/z]

rattlesnake, -s 'rætlsneik, -s

rat-trap, -s 'rættræp, -s

raucous, -ly 'rɔːkəs, -lɪ

ravag|e (s. v.), -es, -ing, -ed, -er/s 'rævidʒ, -iz, -iŋ, -d, -ə*/z

rav|e, -es, -ing/s, -ed reiv, -z, -iŋ/z, -d

rav|el, -els, -elling, -elled 'ræv|l, -lz, -lɪŋ [-əliŋ], -ld

Ravel (French composer) ræ'vel (ravɛl)

ravelin, -s 'rævlɪn [-vəlɪn], -z

raven (s.) (R.), -s 'reivn [-vən], -z

raven (v.), -s, -ing, -ed 'rævn, -nz, -n̩iŋ [-əniŋ], -nd

Ravening 'reivniŋ

Ravenna rə'venə

ravenous, -ly, -ness 'rævənəs [-vnəs, -vņəs], -lɪ, -nɪs [-nəs]

Ravensbourne 'reivnzbɔːn [-bɔən]

ravin(e) (plunder) 'rævin

ravine (deep valley), -s rə'viːn, -z

raving (s. adj. adv.), -s 'reiviŋ, -z

ravish, -es, -ing/ly, -ed, -er/s, -ment 'rævɪʃ, -iz, -iŋ/lɪ, -t, -ə*/z, -mənt

raw, -er, -est, -ly, -ness rɔː, -ə*, -ist, 'rɔːlɪ, 'rɔːnɪs [-nəs]

Rawalpindi ˌrɑːwəl'pindi

Raw|don, -lings, -lins, -linson 'rɔː|dn, -lɪŋz, -lɪnz, -lɪnsn

ray (R.), -s; -less rei, -z; -lɪs [-ləs]

Ray|leigh, -ment, -mond, -ner, -nes 'rei|lɪ, -mənt, -mənd, -nə*, -nz

rayon 'reiɒn ['reiən]

raz|e, -es, -ing, -ed reiz, -iz, -iŋ, -d

razor, -s 'reizə*, -z

razorbill, -s 'reizəbil, -z

razor-blade, -s 'reizəbleid, -z

razor-edge, -s 'reizəredʒ [-zəedʒ, ˌ—'-], -iz

razor-shell, -s 'reizəʃel, -z

Razzell rə'zel

razzia, -s 'ræziə [-zjə], -z

razzle-dazzle 'ræzlˌdæzl [ˌ—'—]

re (note in Tonic Sol-fa), -s rei [riː], -z

re (prep.) riː

re- (prefix denoting repetition) ˌriː-
Note.—Compounds with this prefix not entered below have double stress. Thus restamp is ˌriː'stæmp.

Rea rei, riə, riː
Note.—Baron Rea pronounces riː.

reach (s. v.), -es, -ing, -ed riːtʃ, -iz, -iŋ, -t

react, -s, -ing, -ed rɪ'ækt [riː-], -s, -iŋ, -id

reaction, -s rɪ'ækʃn [riː-], -z

reactionar|y (s. adj.), -ies rɪ'ækʃņər|ɪ [riː-, -ʃənə-, -ʃnə-], -iz

reactive, -ly rɪ'æktɪv [riː-], -lɪ

reactor, -s rɪ'æktə* [riː-], -z

read (pres. tense) (R.), -s, -ing riːd, -z, -iŋ

read (p. tense) red

readability ˌriːdə'bɪləti [-lɪt-]

readab|le, -ly, -leness 'riːdəb|l, -lɪ, -lnɪs [-nəs]

re-address, -es, -ing, -ed ˌriːə'dres, -iz, -iŋ, -t

Reade riːd

reader, -s; -ship/s 'riːdə*, -z; -ʃɪp/s

reading (s.), -s 'riːdiŋ, -z

Reading 'rediŋ

reading-desk, -s 'riːdiŋdesk, -s

reading-glass, -es 'riːdiŋglɑːs, -iz

reading-lamp, -s 'riːdiŋlæmp, -s

reading-room, -s 'riːdiŋrʊm [-ruːm], -z

readjus|t, -ts, -ting, -ted, -tment/s ˌriːə'dʒʌs|t, -ts, -tiŋ, -tid, -tmənt/s

readmission, -s ˌriːəd'mɪʃn, -z

readmit, -s, -ting, -ted; -tance ˌriːəd'mɪt, -s, -iŋ, -id; -əns

read|y, -ier, -iest, -ily, -iness 'red|ɪ, -ɪə* [-jə*], -ɪɪst [-jɪst], -ɪlɪ [-əlɪ], -ɪnɪs [-ɪnəs] ready-made ˌredɪ'meɪd ['--- *when attributive*]

reaffirm, -s, -ing, -ed ˌriːə'fɜːm, -z, -ɪŋ, -d

reagent, -s riː'eɪdʒənt [rɪ'eɪ-], -s

real (*monetary unit*), -s reɪ'aːl, -z

real (*adj.*), really rɪəl ['riːəl], 'rɪəlɪ

reali|sm, -st/s 'rɪəlɪ|zəm ['riːəl-], -st/s

realistic, -ally ˌrɪə'lɪstɪk [ˌriːə'l-, rɪə'l-], -əlɪ [-lɪ]

realit|y, -ies rɪ'ælət|ɪ [riː-, -ɪt|ɪ], -ɪz

realization [-isa-], -s ˌrɪəlaɪ'zeɪʃn [-lɪ'z-], -z

realiz|e [-is|e], -es, -ing, -ed; -able 'rɪəlaɪz, -ɪz, -ɪŋ, -d; -əbl

really 'rɪəlɪ

realm, -s relm, -z

realty 'rɪəltɪ ['riːəl-]

ream (*s. v.*), -s, -ing, -ed riːm, -z, -ɪŋ, -d

reamer, -s 'riːmə*, -z

Rean 'riːən

reap, -s, -ing, -ed, -er/s riːp, -s, -ɪŋ, -t, -ə*/z

reappear, -s, -ing, -ed; -ance/s ˌriːə'pɪə* [ˌrɪə'p-, rɪə'p-], -z, -rɪŋ, -d; -rəns/ɪz

reapplication, -s 'riːˌæplɪ'keɪʃn, -z

reappl|y, -ies, -ying, -ied ˌriːə'pl|aɪ, -aɪz, -aɪɪŋ, -aɪd

reappoint, -s, -ing, -ed, -ment/s ˌriːə'pɔɪnt [ˌrɪə'p-, rɪə'p-], -s, -ɪŋ, -ɪd, -mənt/s

rear (*s. v.*), -s, -ing, -ed rɪə*, -z, -rɪŋ, -d

rear-admiral, -s ˌrɪə'ædmərəl [ˌrɪər'æd-], -z

rear-guard, -s 'rɪəgaːd, -z

rearm, -s, -ing, -ed ˌriː'aːm, -z, -ɪŋ, -d

rearmament rɪ'aːməmənt [riː'aː-]

rearrang|e, -es, -ing, -ed, -ement/s ˌriːə'reɪndʒ [ˌrɪə'r-, rɪə'r-], -ɪz, -ɪŋ, -d, -mənt/s

reas|on, -ons, -oning/s, -oned, -oner/s 'riːz|n, -nz, -nɪŋ/z [-ənɪŋ/z], -nd, -nə*/z [-ənə*/z]

reasonab|le, -ly, -leness 'riːznəb|l [-znə-], -lɪ, -lnɪs [-nəs]

reassemb|le, -les, -ling, -led ˌriːə'semb|l [ˌrɪə's-, rɪə's-], -lz, -lɪŋ, -ld

reassert, -s, -ing, -ed ˌriːə'sɜːt [ˌrɪə's-], -s, -ɪŋ, -ɪd

reassur|e, -es, -ing/ly, -ed; -ance ˌriːə'ʃʊə* [ˌrɪə-, rɪə-, -'ʃɔə*, -'ʃɔː*], -z, -rɪŋ/lɪ, -d; -rəns

Réaumur 'reɪəˌmjʊə* [-mə*] (reomyːr)

Reay reɪ

rebarbative rɪ'baːbətɪv [rə'b-]

rebate (*s.*) (*discount*), -s 'riːbeɪt [rɪ'beɪt], -s

rebat|e (*v.*) (*heraldic term*), -es, -ing, -ed 'ræbɪt, -s, -ɪŋ, -ɪd

Rebecca rɪ'bekə [rə'b-]

rebec(k), -s 'riːbek ['re-], -s

rebel (*s.*), -s 'rebl, -z

rebel (*v.*), -s, -ling, -led rɪ'bel [rə'b-], -z, -ɪŋ, -d

rebellion, -s rɪ'beljən [rə'b-], -z

rebellious, -ly, -ness rɪ'beljəs [rə'b-], -lɪ, -nɪs [-nəs]

re-bind, -s, -ing, re-bound ˌriː'baɪnd, -z, -ɪŋ, ˌriː'baʊnd

rebirth, -s ˌriː'bɜːθ, -s

reborn ˌriː'bɔːn

rebound (*s.*), -s 'riːbaʊnd [rɪ'baʊnd, ˌriː'baʊnd], -z

rebound (*adj.*) ˌriː'baʊnd

rebound (*v.*), -s, -ing, -ed rɪ'baʊnd [ˌriː'b-], -z, -ɪŋ, -ɪd

rebuff (*s. v.*), -s, -ing, -ed rɪ'bʌf, -s, -ɪŋ, -t

rebuil|d, -ds, -ding, -t ˌriː'bɪl|d, -dz, -dɪŋ, -t

rebuk|e (*s. v.*), -es, -ing/ly, -ed rɪ'bjuːk [rə'b-], -s, -ɪŋ/lɪ, -t

rebus, -es 'riːbəs, -ɪz

rebut, -s, -ting, -ted rɪ'bʌt, -s, -ɪŋ, -ɪd

rebutt|able, -al/s, -er/s rɪ'bʌt|əbl, -l/z, -ə*/z

recalcitrant (*s. adj.*), -s rɪ'kælsɪtrənt [rə'k-], -s

recall (*s. v.*), -s, -ing, -ed rɪ'kɔːl [rə'k-, *also* 'riːkɔːl *as noun*], -z, -ɪŋ, -d

recant, -s, -ing, -ed rɪ'kænt, -s, -ɪŋ, -ɪd

recantation, -s ˌriːkæn'teɪʃn, -z

recapitulat|e, -es, -ing, -ed ˌriːkə'pɪtjʊleɪt, -s, -ɪŋ, -ɪd

recapitulation, -s 'riːkəˌpɪtjʊ'leɪʃn, -z

recapitulatory ˌriːkə'pɪtjʊlətərɪ [-leɪtərɪ]

recapt|ure (*s. v.*), -ures, -uring, -ured ˌriː'kæptʃ|ə*, -əz, -ərɪŋ, -əd

recast, -s, -ing ˌriː'kaːst, -s, -ɪŋ

recce (R.) 'rekɪ

reced|e, -es, -ing, -ed rɪ'siːd [riː-], -z, -ɪŋ, -ɪd

receipt (*s. v.*), -s, -ing, -ed rɪ'siːt [rə's-], -s, -ɪŋ, -ɪd

receiv|e, -es, -ing, -ed, -er/s; -able rɪ'siːv [rə's-], -z, -ɪŋ, -d, -ə*/z; -əbl

recency 'riːsnsɪ

recension, -s rɪ'senʃn [rə's-], -z

recent, -ly 'riːsnt, -lɪ

receptacle, -s rɪ'septəkl [rə's-], -z

reception, -s rɪ'sepʃn [rə's-], -z

receptionist, -s rɪ'sepʃənɪst [rə's-, -ʃɪst, -ʃnɪst], -s

receptive, -ness rɪ'septɪv [rə's-], -nɪs [-nəs]

411

receptivity ‚resep'trvətɪ [‚ri:s-, ‚rɪs-, -ɪtɪ]

recess, -es rɪ'ses [rə's-, 'ri:ses], -ɪz

recession, -s rɪ'seʃn [rə's-], -z

recessional, -s rɪ'seʃənl [rə's-, -ʃn̩l, -ʃn̩l, -ʃənəl], -z

Rechab 'ri:kæb

recherché rə'ʃeəʃeɪ (rəʃɛrʃe)

re-christ|en, -ens, -ening, -ened ‚ri:'krɪs|n, -nz, -n̩ɪŋ [-nɪŋ], -nd

recidivist, -s rɪ'sɪdɪvɪst, -s

recipe, -s 'resɪpɪ [-sə-, -pi:], -z

recipient, -s rɪ'sɪpɪənt [rə's-, -pjənt], -s

reciproc|al (s. adj.), -als, -ally, -alness rɪ'sɪprək|l [rə's-, -prʊk-], -lz, -əlɪ, -lnɪs [-nəs]

reciprocat|e, -es, -ing, -ed rɪ'sɪprəkeɪt [rə's-, -prʊk-], -s, -ɪŋ, -ɪd

reciprocation rɪ‚sɪprə'keɪʃn [rə‚s-, -prʊ'k-]

reciprocity ‚resɪ'prɒsətɪ [-ɪtɪ]

recital, -s rɪ'saɪtl [rə's-], -z

recitation, -s ‚resɪ'teɪʃn, -z

recitative, -s ‚resɪtə'ti:v, -z

recit|e, -es, -ing, -ed, -er/s rɪ'saɪt [rə's-], -s, -ɪŋ, -ɪd, -ə*/z

reck, -s, -ing, -ed rek, -s, -ɪŋ, -t

reckless, -ly, -ness 'reklɪs [-ləs], -lɪ, -nɪs [-nəs]

reck|on, -ons, -oning/s, -oned, -oner/s 'rek|ən, -ənz, -n̩ɪŋ/z [-nɪŋ/z, -ənɪŋ/z], -ənd, -nə*/z [-ənə*/z]

reclaim, -s, -ing, -ed rɪ'kleɪm [‚ri:-], -z, -ɪŋ, -d

reclaimable rɪ'kleɪməbl [‚ri:-]

reclamation, -s ‚reklə'meɪʃn, -z

reclin|e, -es, -ing, -ed rɪ'klaɪn [rə'k-], -z, -ɪŋ, -d

recluse, -s rɪ'klu:s, -ɪz

recognition, -s ‚rekəg'nɪʃn, -z

recognizab|le [-isa-], -ly 'rekəgnaɪzəb|l [‚rekəg'n-], -lɪ

recognizance [-isa-], -s rɪ'kɒgnɪzəns [rə'k-, -'kɒnɪ-], -ɪz

recogniz|e [-is|e], -es, -ing, -ed 'rekəgnaɪz, -ɪz, -ɪŋ, -d

recoil (s.), -s 'ri:kɔɪl [rɪ'kɔɪl], -z

recoil (v.), -s, -ing, -ed rɪ'kɔɪl [rə'k-], -z, -ɪŋ, -d

recollect (remember), -s, -ing, -ed ‚rekə'lekt [-kl̩'ekt, '——], -s, -ɪŋ, -ɪd

recollect (regain (one's composure, etc.)), -s, -ing, -ed ‚rekə'lekt [-kl̩'ekt, ‚ri:kə'lekt], -s, -ɪŋ, -ɪd

re-collect (collect over again), -s, -ing, -ed ‚ri:kə'lekt, -s, -ɪŋ, -ɪd

recollection, -s ‚rekə'lekʃn [-kl̩'ek-], -z

recommenc|e, -es, -ing, -ed ‚ri:kə'mens [‚rekə'm-], -ɪz, -ɪŋ, -t

recommend, -s, -ing, -ed; -able ‚rekə'mend, -z, -ɪŋ, -ɪd; -əbl

recommendation, -s ‚rekəmen'deɪʃn [-km-, -mən-], -z

recompens|e (s. v.), -es, -ing, -ed 'rekəmpens [-km-], -ɪz, -ɪŋ, -t

recompos|e, -es, -ing, -ed ‚ri:kəm'pəʊz, -ɪz, -ɪŋ, -d

reconcilab|le, -ly 'rekənsaɪləb|l [‚rekən's-, -kn-], -lɪ

reconcil|e, -es, -ing, -ed, -er/s 'rekənsaɪl [-kn-], -z, -ɪŋ, -d, -ə*/z

reconciliation, -s ‚rekənsɪlɪ'eɪʃn [-kn-], -z

recondite rɪ'kɒndaɪt [rə'k-, 'rekənd-]

reconduct, -s, -ing, -ed ‚ri:kən'dʌkt, -s, -ɪŋ, -ɪd

reconnaissance, -s rɪ'kɒnɪsəns [rə'k-, -'kɒnəs-], -ɪz

reconnoit|re, -res, -ring, -red ‚rekə'nɔɪt|ə*, -əz, -ərɪŋ, -əd

reconqu|er, -ers, -ering, -ered ‚ri:'kɒŋk|ə*, -əz, -ərɪŋ, -əd

reconquest, -s ‚ri:'kɒŋkwest, -s

reconsid|er, -ers, -ering, -ered ‚ri:kən'sɪd|ə* [-kn-], -əz, -ərɪŋ, -əd

reconsideration 'ri:kən‚sɪdə'reɪʃn [-kn-]

reconstitut|e, -es, -ing, -ed ‚ri:'kɒnstɪtju:t, -s, -ɪŋ, -ɪd

reconstitution, -s 'ri:‚kɒnstɪ'tju:ʃn, -z

reconstruct, -s, -ing, -ed ‚ri:kən'strʌkt [-kn-], -s, -ɪŋ, -ɪd

reconstruction, -s ‚ri:kən'strʌkʃn [-kn-], -z

reconversion, -s ‚ri:kən'vɜ:ʃn [-kn-], -z

reconvey, -s, -ing, -ed ‚ri:kən'veɪ, -z, -ɪŋ, -d

record (s.), -s 'rekɔ:d, -z

record (v.), -s, -ing, -ed, -er/s; -able rɪ'kɔ:d [rə'k-], -z, -ɪŋ, -ɪd, -ə*/z; -əbl

recorder (musical instrument), -s rɪ'kɔ:də* [rə'k-], -z

record-player, -s 'rekɔ:d‚pleɪə*, -z

recount (s.), -s 'ri:kaʊnt [‚ri:'kaʊnt], -s

recount (v.) (count again), -s, -ing, -ed ‚ri:'kaʊnt, -s, -ɪŋ, -ɪd

recount (v.) (narrate), -s, -ing, -ed rɪ'kaʊnt, -s, -ɪŋ, -ɪd

recoup, -s, -ing, -ed, -ment rɪ'ku:p, -s, -ɪŋ, -t, -mənt

recourse rɪ'kɔ:s [rə'k-, -'kɔəs]

recov|er (get back, come back to health, etc.), -ers, -ering, -ered; -erable rɪ'kʌv|ə* [rə'k-], -əz, -ərɪŋ, -əd; -ərəbl

recover (cover again), -s, -ing, -ed ‚ri:'kʌvə*, -z, -rɪŋ, -d

recover|y, -ies rɪ'kʌvər|ɪ [rə'k-], -ɪz

recreant (s. adj.), -s, -ly 'rekrɪənt, -s, -lɪ

recreat|e (*refresh*), -es, -ing, -ed; -ive
'rekrɪeɪt, -s, -ɪŋ, -ɪd; -ɪv

re-creat|e (*create anew*), -es, -ing, -ed
ˌriːkrɪ'eɪt, -s, -ɪŋ, -ɪd

recreation (*refreshment, amusement*), -s;
-al ˌrekrɪ'eɪʃn, -z; -əl

re-creation (*creating anew*), -s ˌriːkrɪ-
'eɪʃn, -z

recriminat|e, -es, -ing, -ed, -or/s
rɪ'krɪmɪneɪt [rə'k-, -mən-], -s, -ɪŋ, -ɪd,
-ə*/z

recrimination, -s rɪˌkrɪmɪ'neɪʃn [rəˌk-,
-mə'n-], -z

recriminatory rɪ'krɪmɪnətərɪ [rə'k-,
-mən-]

recross, -es, -ing, -ed ˌriː'krɒs [*old-
fashioned* -'krɔːs, *also* 'riːk- *when
contrasted with* cross], -ɪz, -ɪŋ, -t

recrudesc|e, -es, -ing, -ed ˌriːkruː'des
[ˌrek-], -ɪz, -ɪŋ, -t

recrudescen|ce, -t ˌriːkruː'desn|s [ˌrek-],
-t

recruit (*s. v.*), -s, -ing, -ed, -er/s, -ment
rɪ'kruːt [rə'k-], -s, -ɪŋ, -ɪd, -ə*/z,
-mənt

rectal 'rektəl [-tl]

rectangle, -s 'rek,tæŋgl ['rekt,æŋ-], -z

rectangular, -ly rek'tæŋgjʊlə* [rekt-
'æŋ-, -gjəl-], -lɪ

rectification, -s ˌrektɪfɪ'keɪʃn, -z

recti|fy, -fies, -fying, -fied, -fier/s;
-fiable 'rektɪ|faɪ, -faɪz, -faɪɪŋ, -faɪd,
-faɪə*/z; -faɪəbl

rectiline|al, -ar ˌrektɪ'lɪnɪ|əl [-nj|əl], -ə*

rectitude 'rektɪtjuːd

recto 'rektəʊ

rector, -s; -ate/s, -ship/s 'rektə*, -z;
-rət/s [-rɪt/s], -ʃɪp/s

rectorial rek'tɔːrɪəl

rector|y, -ies 'rektər|ɪ, -ɪz

rect|um, -ums, -a 'rekt|əm, -əmz, -ə

Reculver, -s rɪ'kʌlvə* [rə'k-], -z

recumben|ce, -cy, -t/ly rɪ'kʌmbən|s
[rə'k-], -sɪ, -t/lɪ

recuperat|e, -es, -ing, -ed rɪ'kjuːpəreɪt
[rə'k-, -'kuː-], -s, -ɪŋ, -ɪd

recuperation rɪˌkjuːpə'reɪʃn [rəˌk-,
-ˌkuː-]

recur, -s, -ring, -red rɪ'kɜː* [rə'k-], -z,
-rɪŋ [rɪ'kʌrɪŋ], -d

recurren|ce, -ces, -t/ly rɪ'kʌrən|s [rə'k-],
-sɪz, -t/lɪ

recursive (*s. adj.*), -s rɪ'kɜːsɪv [ˌriː'k-],
-z

recurv|e, -es, -ing, -ed ˌriː'kɜːv, -z, -ɪŋ,
-d

recusancy 'rekjʊzənsɪ [rɪ'kjuːz-, rə-
'kjuːz-]

recusant, -s 'rekjʊzənt [rɪ'kjuːz-, rə-
'kjuːz-], -s

re-cycl|e, -es, -ing, -ed ˌriː'saɪkl, -z, -ɪŋ,
-d

red (*s. adj.*), -s; -der, -dest, -ness red,
-z; -ə*, -ɪst, -nɪs [-nəs]

redact, -s, -ing, -ed, -or/s rɪ'dækt, -s,
-ɪŋ, -ɪd, -ə*/z

redaction, -s rɪ'dækʃn, -z

redbreast, -s 'redbrest, -s

redcap, -s 'redkæp, -s

Redcliffe 'redklɪf

redcoat, -s 'redkəʊt, -s

Reddaway 'redəweɪ

redd|en, -ens, -ening, -ened 'red|n, -nz,
-nɪŋ [-nɪŋ], -nd

Redding 'redɪŋ

reddish, -ness 'redɪʃ, -nɪs [-nəs]

Redditch 'redɪtʃ

reddle 'redl

redecorat|e, -es, -ing, -ed ˌriː'dekəreɪt,
-s, -ɪŋ, -ɪd

redeem, -s, -ing, -ed; -able rɪ'diːm
[rə'd-], -z, -ɪŋ, -d; -əbl

redeemer (R.), -s rɪ'diːmə* [rə'd-], -z

redeliver, -s, -ing, -ed; -y ˌriːdɪ'lɪvə*,
-z, -rɪŋ, -d; -rɪ

redemption (R.), -s rɪ'dempʃn [rə'd-],
-z

redemptive rɪ'demptɪv [rə'd-]

re-deploy, -s, -ing, -ed, -ment/s ˌriːdɪ-
'plɔɪ, -z, -ɪŋ, -d, -mənt/s

Red|fern, -field 'red|fɜːn, -fiːld

Redgauntlet ˌred'gɔːntlɪt [-lət]

Redgrave 'redgreɪv

red-handed ˌred'hændɪd

Redheugh (*bridge in Newcastle upon
Tyne*) 'redjəf

Redhill ˌred'hɪl ['--]

red-hot ˌred'hɒt ['-- *according to
sentence-stress*]

re|-dial, -dials, -dialling, -dialled ˌriː|-
'daɪəl, -'daɪəlz, -'daɪəlɪŋ, -'daɪəld

rediffus|e, -es, -ing, -ed ˌriːdɪ'fjuːz, -ɪz,
-ɪŋ, -d

rediffusion ˌriːdɪ'fjuːʒn

redintegrat|e, -es, -ing, -ed re'dɪntɪgreɪt
[rɪ'd-], -s, -ɪŋ, -ɪd

redirect, -s, -ing, -ed ˌriːdɪ'rekt [-də'r-,
-daɪ'r-], -s, -ɪŋ, -ɪd

rediscover, -s, -ing, -ed; -y ˌriːdɪ'skʌvə*,
-z, -rɪŋ, -d; -rɪ

re|distribute, -distributes, -distribut-
ing, -distributed ˌriː|dɪ'strɪbjuːt
[-'dɪstrɪbjuːt], -dɪ'strɪbjuːts [-'dɪstrɪ-
bjuːts], -dɪ'strɪbjʊtɪŋ [-'dɪstrɪbjuːtɪŋ],
-dɪ'strɪbjʊtɪd [-'dɪstrɪbjuːtɪd]

redistribution, -s 'riːˌdɪstrɪ'bjuːʃn, -z

413

redivid|e, -es, -ing, -ed ˌriːdɪˈvaɪd, -z,
-ɪŋ, -ɪd
redivivus ˌredɪˈvaɪvəs
red-letter ˌredˈletə*
Redmond ˈredmənd
re|-do, -does, -doing, -did, -done
ˌriːˈduː, -ˈdʌz, -ˈduːɪŋ [-ˈduɪŋ], -ˈdɪd,
-ˈdʌn
redolen|ce, -t ˈredəʊlən|s, -t
redoub|le, -les, -ling, -led ˌriːˈdʌb|l
[rɪˈd-], -lz, -lɪŋ [-lɪŋ], -ld
redoubt, -s; -able rɪˈdaʊt [rəˈd-], -s;
-əbl
redound, -s, -ing, -ed rɪˈdaʊnd [rəˈd-],
-z, -ɪŋ, -ɪd
redpole, -s ˈredpəʊl [-pɒl], -z
redraft, -s, -ing, -ed ˌriːˈdrɑːft, -s, -ɪŋ,
-ɪd
re-draw, -s, -ing, redrew, redrawn
ˌriːˈdrɔː, -z, -ɪŋ, ˌriːˈdruː, ˌriːˈdrɔːn
redress (s. v.) (amends, make amends
for), -es, -ing, -ed rɪˈdres [rəˈd-], -ɪz,
-ɪŋ, -t
redress (dress again), -es, -ing, -ed
ˌriːˈdres, -ɪz, -ɪŋ, -t
Redriff ˈredrɪf
Redruth ˈredruːθ
redshank, -s ˈredʃæŋk, -s
redskin (R.), -s ˈredskɪn, -z
redstart, -s ˈredstɑːt, -s
red-tape ˌredˈteɪp
red-tapism ˌredˈteɪpɪzəm
reduc|e, -es, -ing, -ed, -er/s rɪˈdjuːs
[rəˈd-], -ɪz, -ɪŋ, -t, -ə*/z
reducibility rɪˌdjuːsəˈbɪlətɪ [rəˈd-, -sɪˈb-,
-lɪt-]
reducible rɪˈdjuːsəbl [rəˈd-, -sɪb-]
reduction, -s rɪˈdʌkʃn [rəˈd-], -z
redundan|ce, -cy, -cies, -t/ly rɪˈdʌnd-
ən|s [rəˈd-], -sɪ, -sɪz, -t/lɪ
redundantiz|e [-is|e], -es, -ing, -ed
rɪˈdʌndəntaɪz [rəˈd-], -ɪz, -ɪŋ, -d
reduplicat|e, -es, -ing, -ed rɪˈdjuːplɪkeɪt
[rəˈd-, ˌriː-], -s, -ɪŋ, -ɪd
reduplication, -s rɪˌdjuːplɪˈkeɪʃn [rəˌd-],
-z
reduplicative rɪˈdjuːplɪkətɪv [rəˈd-,
-keɪt-]
redwing, -s ˈredwɪŋ, -z
redwood (R.) ˈredwʊd
Reece riːs
re-ech|o, -oes, -oing, -oed riːˈek|əʊ
[rɪˈe-], -əʊz, -əʊɪŋ, -əʊd
reed (s. v.) (R.), -s, -ing, -ed riːd, -z, -ɪŋ,
-ɪd
re-edit, -s, -ing, -ed ˌriːˈedɪt, -s, -ɪŋ, -ɪd
re-edition, -s ˌriːɪˈdɪʃn, -z
reed-pipe, -s ˈriːdpaɪp, -s

re-educat|e, -es, -ing, -ed ˌriːˈedjʊkeɪt
[riːˈed-, -djuː-, -dʒʊ-, -dʒuː-], -s, -ɪŋ,
-ɪd
re-education ˈriːˌedjʊˈkeɪʃn [-dʒʊ-,
-dju:-, -dʒuː-]
reed-warbler, -s ˈriːdˌwɔːblə* [ˌ-ˈ--], -z
reed|y, -ier, -iest, -iness ˈriːd|ɪ, -ɪə*,
-ɪɪst, -ɪnɪs [-nəs]
reef (s. v.), -s, -ing, -ed riːf, -s, -ɪŋ, -t
reefer, -s ˈriːfə*, -z
reek (s. v.), -s (R.), -ing, -ed riːk, -s, -ɪŋ,
-t
Reekie ˈriːkɪ
reel (s. v.), -s, -ing, -ed riːl, -z, -ɪŋ, -d
re-elect, -s, -ing, -ed ˌriːɪˈlekt, -s, -ɪŋ, -ɪd
re-election, -s ˌriːɪˈlekʃn, -z
re-eligible ˌriːˈelɪdʒəbl [-dʒɪb-]
re-embark, -s, -ing, -ed ˌriːɪmˈbɑːk
[ˌriːem-], -s, -ɪŋ, -t
re-embarkation, -s ˈriːˌembɑːˈkeɪʃn, -z
re-enact, -s, -ing, -ed, -ment/s ˌriː-
ɪˈnækt [ˌriːeˈn-], -s, -ɪŋ, -ɪd, -mənt/s
re-engag|e, -es, -ing, -ed, -ement/s
ˌriːɪnˈgeɪdʒ [ˌriːen-], -ɪz, -ɪŋ, -d,
-mənt/s
re-enlist, -s, -ing, -ed ˌriːɪnˈlɪst [ˌriːen-],
-s, -ɪŋ, -ɪd
re-ent|er, -ers, -ering, -ered ˌriːˈent|ə*
[rɪˈen-], -əz, -ərɪŋ, -əd
re-entrant riːˈentrənt [rɪˈen-]
re-entr|y, -ies riːˈentr|ɪ [rɪˈen-], -ɪz
Rees riːs
Reese riːs
re-establish, -es, -ing, -ed, -ment
ˌriːɪˈstæblɪʃ [ˌriːeˈs-], -ɪz, -ɪŋ, -t, -mənt
reeve (R.), -s riːv, -z
re-examination, -s ˈriːɪgˌzæmɪˈneɪʃn
[ˈriːeg-, -məˈn-], -z
re-examin|e, -es, -ing, -ed ˌriːɪgˈzæmɪn
[ˌriːeg-], -z, -ɪŋ, -d
re-export (s.), -s ˌriːˈekspɔːt, -s
re-export (v.), -s, -ing, -ed ˌriːekˈspɔːt
[ˌriːɪkˈsp-], -s, -ɪŋ, -ɪd
re-fac|e, -es, -ing, -ed ˌriːˈfeɪs, -ɪz, -ɪŋ, -t
refashi|on, -ons, -oning, -oned ˌriː-
ˈfæʃ|n, -nz, -nɪŋ [-ənɪŋ], -nd
refection rɪˈfekʃn
refector|y, -ies rɪˈfektər|ɪ [rəˈf-, also
ˈrefɪkt-, esp. in monasteries], -ɪz
refer, -s, -ring, -red rɪˈfɜː* [rəˈf-], -z,
-rɪŋ, -d
referable rɪˈfɜːrəbl [rəˈf-, ˈrefərəbl]
referee, -s ˌrefəˈriː, -z
reference, -s ˈrefrəns [-fər-], -ɪz
referend|um, -ums, -a ˌrefəˈrend|əm,
-əmz, -ə
referential ˌrefəˈrenʃl
refill (s.), -s ˈriːfɪl [ˌriːˈfɪl], -z

414

refill (v.), -s, -ing, -ed ˌriːˈfɪl, -z, -ɪŋ, -d

refin|e, -es, -ing, -ed, -er/s, -ement/s rɪˈfaɪn [rəˈf-], -z, -ɪŋ, -d, -ə*/z, -mənt/s

refiner|y, -ies rɪˈfaɪnər|ɪ [rəˈf-], -ɪz

refit (s. v.), -s, -ting, -ted ˌriːˈfɪt (often '-- as noun), -s, -ɪŋ, -ɪd

reflat|e, -es, -ing, -ed ˌriːˈfleɪt, -s, -ɪŋ, -ɪd

reflation riːˈfleɪʃn

reflect, -s, -ing/ly, -ed, -or/s rɪˈflekt [rəˈf-], -s, -ɪŋ/lɪ, -ɪd, -ə*/z

reflection, -s rɪˈflekʃn [rəˈf-], -z

reflective, -ly, -ness rɪˈflektɪv [rəˈf-], -lɪ, -nɪs [-nəs]

reflex (s. adj.), -es ˈriːfleks, -ɪz

reflexed rɪˈflekst [riːˈf-, ˈriːflekst]

reflexive rɪˈfleksɪv [rəˈf-]

refloat, -s, -ing, -ed ˌriːˈfləʊt, -s, -ɪŋ, -ɪd

refluent ˈrefluənt [-flwənt]

reflux, -es ˈriːflʌks, -ɪz

re-foot, -s, -ing, -ed ˌriːˈfʊt, -s, -ɪŋ, -ɪd

reform (s. v.) (make better, become better, etc.), -s, -ing, -ed, -er/s; -able rɪˈfɔːm [rəˈf-], -z, -ɪŋ, -d, -ə*/z; -əbl

reform (v.) (form again), -s, -ing, -ed ˌriːˈfɔːm, -z, -ɪŋ, -d

reformation (R.), -s ˌrefəˈmeɪʃn [-fɔːˈm-], -z

reformative rɪˈfɔːmətɪv [rəˈf-]

reformator|y (s. adj.), -ies rɪˈfɔːmətər|ɪ [rəˈf-], -ɪz

reformist rɪˈfɔːmɪst [rəˈf-]

refract, -s, -ing, -ed, -or/s; -ive rɪˈfrækt [rəˈf-], -s, -ɪŋ, -ɪd, -ə*/z; -ɪv

refraction, -s rɪˈfrækʃn [rəˈf-], -z

refractor|y, -ily, -iness rɪˈfræktər|ɪ [rəˈf-], -əlɪ [-ɪlɪ], -mɪs [-nəs]

refrain (s. v.), -s, -ing, -ed rɪˈfreɪn [rəˈf-], -z, -ɪŋ, -d

refresh, -es, -ing/ly, -ingness, -ed, -er/s, -ment/s rɪˈfreʃ [rəˈf-], -ɪz, -ɪŋ/lɪ, -ɪŋnɪs [-nəs], -t, -ə*/z, -mənt/s

refrigerat|e, -es, -ing, -ed, -or/s rɪˈfrɪdʒəreɪt [rəˈf-], -s, -ɪŋ, -ɪd, -ə*/z

refrigeration rɪˌfrɪdʒəˈreɪʃn [rəˌf-]

reft reft

re-fuel, -s, -ling, -led ˌriːˈfjʊəl [-ˈfjuːəl, -ˈfjuːl], -z, -ɪŋ, -d

refuge, -s ˈrefjuːdʒ, -ɪz

refugee, -s ˌrefjʊˈdʒiː [-fjuː-], -z

refulgen|ce, -t/ly rɪˈfʌldʒən|s [rəˈf-], -t/lɪ

refund (s.), -s ˈriːfʌnd, -z

refund (v.), -s, -ing, -ed riːˈfʌnd [ˌriːˈf-, rɪˈf-], -z, -ɪŋ, -ɪd

refurbish, -es, -ing, -ed ˌriːˈfɜːbɪʃ, -ɪz, -ɪŋ, -t

refurnish, -es, -ing, -ed ˌriːˈfɜːnɪʃ, -ɪz, -ɪŋ, -t

refusal, -s rɪˈfjuːzl [rəˈf-], -z

refuse (s. adj.) ˈrefjuːs

refus|e (v.), -es, -ing, -ed; -able rɪˈfjuːz [rəˈf-], -ɪz, -ɪŋ, -d; -əbl

refutability ˌrefjʊtəˈbɪlətɪ [rɪˌfjuːt-, rəˌfjuːt-, -lɪt-]

refutable ˈrefjʊtəbl [rɪˈfjuːt-, rəˈfjuːt-]

refutation, -s ˌrefjuːˈteɪʃn [-fjʊ-], -z

refut|e, -es, -ing, -ed rɪˈfjuːt [rəˈf-], -s, -ɪŋ, -ɪd

Reg (short for Reginald) redʒ

regain, -s, -ing, -ed rɪˈgeɪn [ˌriːˈg-], -z, -ɪŋ, -d

regal, -ally ˈriːg|l, -əlɪ

regal|e, -es, -ing, -ed rɪˈgeɪl, -z, -ɪŋ, -d

regalia rɪˈgeɪljə [rəˈg-, -lɪə]

Regan ˈriːgən

regard (s. v.), -s, -ing, -ed rɪˈgɑːd [rəˈg-], -z, -ɪŋ, -ɪd

regardful rɪˈgɑːdfʊl [rəˈg-]

regardless, -ly, -ness rɪˈgɑːdlɪs [rəˈg-, -ləs], -lɪ, -nɪs [-nəs]

regatta, -s rɪˈgætə [rəˈg-], -z

regenc|y, -ies ˈriːdʒəns|ɪ, -ɪz

regenerate (adj.) rɪˈdʒenərət [rəˈdʒ-, -rɪt, -reɪt]

regenerat|e (v.), -es, -ing, -ed rɪˈdʒenəreɪt [rəˈdʒ-, ˌriːˈdʒ-], -s, -ɪŋ, -ɪd

regeneration, -s rɪˌdʒenəˈreɪʃn [rəˌdʒ-, ˌriːdʒen-], -z

regent (R.), -s ˈriːdʒənt, -s

regentship, -s ˈriːdʒənt-ʃɪp, -s

Reggie ˈredʒɪ

Reggio ˈredʒɪəʊ (ˈreddʒo)

regicidal ˌredʒɪˈsaɪdl

regicide, -s ˈredʒɪsaɪd, -z

régie reɪˈʒiː [ˈreɪʒiː]

regil|d, -ds, -ding, -t ˌriːˈgɪl|d, -dz, -dɪŋ, -t

régime, -s reɪˈʒiːm [reˈʒ-, ˈ—] (reʒim), -z

regimen, -s ˈredʒɪmen, -z

regiment (s.), -s ˈredʒɪmənt, -s

regiment (v.), -s, -ing, -ed ˈredʒɪment [ˌ--ˈ-], -s, -ɪŋ, -ɪd

regimental (s. adj.), -s ˌredʒɪˈmentl [-dʒəˈm-], -z

regimentation ˌredʒɪmenˈteɪʃn [-mən-]

Regina rɪˈdʒaɪnə [rəˈdʒ-]

Reginald ˈredʒɪnld

region, -s ˈriːdʒən, -z

re|gional, -gionally ˈriː|dʒənl [-dʒənəl, -dʒn̩l, -dʒn̩ḷ, -dʒənəl], -dʒn̩əlɪ [-dʒn̩lɪ, -dʒn̩lɪ, -dʒənəlɪ]

Regis ˈriːdʒɪs

regist|er (s. v.), -ers, -ering, -ered ˈredʒɪst|ə*, -əz, -ərɪŋ, -əd

415

registrant, -s 'redʒɪstrənt, -s
registrar, -s ˌredʒɪ'strɑ:* ['---], -z
registrar|y, -ies 'redʒɪstrər|ɪ, -ɪz
registration, -s ˌredʒɪ'streɪʃn, -z
registr|y, -ies 'redʒɪstr|ɪ, -ɪz
Regius 'ri:dʒəs [-dʒɪəs, -dʒəs]
regnant 'regnənt
regress (s.) 'ri:gres
regress (v.), **-es, -ing, -ed** rɪ'gres [ˌri:'g-],
  -ɪz, -ɪŋ, -t
regression, -s rɪ'greʃn [ri:'g-], -z
regressive, -ly rɪ'gresɪv [ri:'g-, ˌri:'g-],
  -lɪ
regret (s. v.), **-s, -ting, -ted** rɪ'gret
  [rə'g-], -s, -ɪŋ, -ɪd
regret|ful, -fully rɪ'gret|fʊl [rə'g-], -fʊlɪ
  [-fəlɪ]
regrettab|le, -ly rɪ'gretəb|l [rə'g-], -lɪ
re-group, -s, -ing, -ed ˌri:'gru:p, -s, -ɪŋ,
  -t
regular (s. adj.), **-s, -ly** 'regjʊlə* [-gjəl-],
  -z, -lɪ
regularity ˌregjʊ'lærətɪ [-gjə'l-, -ɪtɪ]
regularization [-isa-] ˌregjʊlərɑɪ'zeɪʃn
  [-gjəl-, -ɪ'z-]
regulariz|e [-is|e], -es, -ing, -ed 'regjʊ-
  lərɑɪz [-gjəl-], -ɪz, -ɪŋ, -d
regulat|e, -es, -ing, -ed, -or/s 'regjʊleɪt
  [-gjəl-], -s, -ɪŋ, -ɪd, -ə*/z
regulation, -s ˌregjʊ'leɪʃn [-gjə'l-], -z
regulative 'regjʊlətɪv [-gjəl-, -leɪt-]
regul|us (R.), -i 'regjʊl|əs [-gjəl-], -ɑɪ
regurgitat|e, -es, -ing, -ed rɪ'gɜ:dʒɪteɪt
  [ˌri:'g-], -s, -ɪŋ, -ɪd
rehabilitat|e, -es, -ing, -ed ˌri:ə'bɪlɪteɪt
  [ˌri:hə-, ˌrɪə-], -s, -ɪŋ, -ɪd
rehabilitation, -s 'ri:əˌbɪlɪ'teɪʃn ['ri:hə-,
  'rɪə-], -z
Rehan 'ri:ən, 'reɪən
re-hash (v.), **-es, -ing, -ed** ˌri:'hæʃ, -ɪz,
  -ɪŋ, -t
re-hash (s.), **-es** 'ri:hæʃ [ˌ-'-], -ɪz
rehear, -s, -ing, reheard ˌri:'hɪə*, -z,
  -rɪŋ, ˌri:'hɜ:d
rehears|e, -es, -ing, -ed; -al/s rɪ'hɜ:s
  [rə'h-], -ɪz, -ɪŋ, -t; -l/z
Rehoboam ˌri:ə'bəʊəm [ˌri:hə-, rɪə-]
re-hous|e, -es, -ing, -ed ˌri:'haʊz, -ɪz,
  -ɪŋ, -d
Reich rɑɪk [rɑɪx] (raiç)
Reichstag 'rɑɪkstɑ:g [-tɑ:k] ('raiçstɑ:k,
  -tɑ:x)
Reid ri:d
Reigate 'rɑɪgɪt [-geɪt]
reign (s. v.), **-s, -ing, -ed** reɪn, -z, -ɪŋ, -d
Reigny (in Cumbria) 'reɪnɪ
Reikjavik 'reɪkjəvɪ:k ['rek-, -vɪk]
Reilly 'rɑɪlɪ

reimburs|e, -es, -ing, -ed; -ement/s
  ˌri:ɪm'bɜ:s, -ɪz, -ɪŋ, -t; -mənt/s
reimport, -s, -ing, -ed ˌri:ɪm'pɔ:t, -s, -ɪŋ,
  -ɪd
reimpos|e, -es, -ing, -ed ˌri:ɪm'pəʊz, -ɪz,
  -ɪŋ, -d
reimpression, -s ˌri:ɪm'preʃn, -z
R(h)eims ri:mz
rein (s. v.), **-s, -ing, -ed** reɪn, -z, -ɪŋ, -d
reincarnate (adj.) ˌri:ɪn'kɑ:nɪt [-neɪt,
  -nət]
reincarnat|e (v.), **-es, -ing, -ed** ri:'ɪnkɑ:-
  neɪt [ˌri:ɪn'kɑ:n-], -s, -ɪŋ, -ɪd
reincarnation, -s ˌri:ɪnkɑ:'neɪʃn, -z
reindeer 'reɪnˌdɪə*
reinforc|e, -es, -ing, -ed, -ement/s
  ˌri:ɪn'fɔ:s, -ɪz, -ɪŋ, -t, -mənt/s
reinstal|l, -ls, -ling, -led, -ment ˌri:-
  ɪn'stɔ:l, -z, -ɪŋ, -d, -mənt
reinstat|e, -es, -ing, -ed, -ement ˌri:ɪn-
  'steɪt, -s, -ɪŋ, -ɪd, -mənt
reinsur|e, -es, -ing, -ed; -ance/s ˌri:-
  ɪn'ʃʊə* [-'ʃɔə*, -'ʃɔ:*], -z, -rɪŋ, -d;
  -rəns/ɪz
reintroduc|e, -es, -ing, -ed 'ri:ˌɪntrə-
  'dju:s [-trʊ'd-], -ɪz, -ɪŋ, -t
reintroduction 'ri:ˌɪntrə'dʌkʃn [-trʊ'd-]
reinvest, -s, -ing, -ed ˌri:ɪn'vest, -s, -ɪŋ,
  -ɪd
reis (monetary unit) (sing.) reɪs, (plur.)
  reɪs [reɪz]
reiss|ue (s. v.), **-ues, -uing, -ued**
  ˌri:'ɪʃ|u: [-'ɪʃj|u:, -'ɪsj|u:], -u:z, -u:ɪŋ
  [-ʊɪŋ], -u:d
reiterat|e, -es, -ing, -ed ri:'ɪtəreɪt [rɪ'ɪt-],
  -s, -ɪŋ, -ɪd
reiteration ri:ˌɪtə'reɪʃn [rɪˌɪ-]
reiterative ri:'ɪtərətɪv [rɪ'ɪt-, -təreɪt-]
Reith ri:θ
reject (s.) **-s** 'ri:dʒekt, -s
reject (v.), **-s, -ing, -ed, -or/s** rɪ'dʒekt
  [rə'dʒ-], -s, -ɪŋ, -ɪd, -ə*/z
rejection, -s rɪ'dʒekʃn [rə'dʒ-], -z
rejoic|e, -es, -ing/ly, -ings, -ed rɪ'dʒɔɪs
  [rə'dʒ-], -ɪz, -ɪŋ/lɪ, -ɪŋz, -t
rejoin (answer), **-s, -ing, -ed** rɪ'dʒɔɪn
  [rə'dʒ-], -z, -ɪŋ, -d
rejoin (join again), **-s, -ing, -ed** ˌri:'dʒɔɪn
  [ri:'dʒ-, rɪ'dʒ-], -z, -ɪŋ, -d
rejoinder, -s rɪ'dʒɔɪndə* [rə'dʒ-], -z
rejuvenat|e, -es, -ing, -ed rɪ'dʒu:vɪneɪt
  [-vən-], -s, -ɪŋ, -ɪd
rejuvenation rɪˌdʒu:vɪ'neɪʃn [rə'dʒ-,
  -və'n-]
rejuvenesc|e, -es, -ing, -ed ˌri:dʒu:vɪ'nes
  [rɪˌdʒu:-, -və'n-], -ɪz, -ɪŋ, -t
rejuvenescen|ce, -t ˌri:dʒu:vɪ'nesn|s
  [rɪˌdʒu:-, -və'n-], -t

rekind|le, -les, -ling, -led ˌriːˈkɪnd|l, -lz, -lɪŋ [-lɪŋ], -ld

re-lab|el, -els, -elling, -elled ˌriːˈleɪb|l, -lz, -lɪŋ [-lɪŋ], -ld

relaps|e (s. v.), -es, -ing, -ed rɪˈlæps [rə'l-, also 'riːlæps as noun], -ɪz, -ɪŋ, -t

relat|e, -es, -ing, -ed, -er/s rɪˈleɪt [rə'l-], -s, -ɪŋ, -ɪd, -ə*/z

relation, -s; -ship/s rɪˈleɪʃn [rə'l-], -z; -ʃɪp/s

relatival ˌreləˈtaɪvl

relative (s. adj.), -s, -ly 'relətɪv, -z, -lɪ

relativity ˌreləˈtɪvətɪ [-ɪtɪ]

relax, -es, -ing, -ed; -able rɪˈlæks [rə'l-], -ɪz, -ɪŋ, -t; -əbl

relaxation, -s ˌriːlækˈseɪʃn, -z

relay (s.) (fresh set of horses, relief gang), -s 'riːleɪ [rɪ'leɪ], -z
   Note.—Always 'riːleɪ in relay race, and in broadcasting.

relay (s.) (electrical apparatus), -s ˌriːˈleɪ ['--], -z

relay (v.) (lay again), -s, -ing, relaid ˌriːˈleɪ, -z, -ɪŋ, ˌriːˈleɪd

relay (v.) (in broadcasting), -s, -ing, -ed riːˈleɪ ['riːleɪ], -z, -ɪŋ, -d

release (s.) (liberation, discharge), -s rɪˈliːs [rə'l-], -ɪz

release (s.) (new lease), -s ˌriːˈliːs ['riːliːs], -ɪz

releas|e (v.), -es, -ing, -ed rɪˈliːs [rə'l-], -ɪz, -ɪŋ, -t

relegat|e, -es, -ing, -ed 'relɪgeɪt [-ləg-], -s, -ɪŋ, -ɪd

relegation ˌrelɪˈgeɪʃn [-ləˈg-]

relent, -s, -ing, -ed rɪˈlent [rə'l-], -s, -ɪŋ, -ɪd

relentless, -ly, -ness rɪˈlentlɪs [rə'l-, -ləs], -lɪ, -nɪs

re-let (s. v.), -s, -ting ˌriːˈlet, -s, -ɪŋ

relevan|ce, -cy, -t/ly 'reləvən|s [-lɪv-], -sɪ, -t/lɪ

reliability rɪˌlaɪəˈbɪlətɪ [rəˌlaɪ-, -lɪt-]

reliab|le, -ly, -leness rɪˈlaɪəb|l [rə'l-], -lɪ, -lnɪs [-nəs]

relian|ce, -t rɪˈlaɪən|s [rə'l-], -t

relic, -s 'relɪk, -s

relict, -s 'relɪkt, -s

relief, -s rɪˈliːf [rə'l-], -s

reliev|e, -es, -ing, -ed; -able rɪˈliːv [rə'l-], -z, -ɪŋ, -d; -əbl

relievo rɪˈliːvəʊ

re|light, -lights, -lighting, -lighted, -lit ˌriː|ˈlaɪt, -'laɪts, -'laɪtɪŋ, -'laɪtɪd, -'lɪt

religion, -s rɪˈlɪdʒən [rə'l-], -z

religioni|sm, -st/s rɪˈlɪdʒənɪ|zəm [rə'l-, -dʒnɪ-], -st/s

religiosity rɪˌlɪdʒɪˈɒsətɪ [rəˌl-, -ɪtɪ]

religioso rɪˌlɪdʒɪˈəʊsəʊ [reˌl-, rəˌl-, -'əʊzəʊ]

religious, -ly, -ness rɪˈlɪdʒəs [rə'l-], -lɪ, -nɪs [-nəs]

relin|e, -es, -ing, -ed ˌriːˈlaɪn, -z, -ɪŋ, -d

relinquish, -es, -ing, -ed, -ment rɪˈlɪŋkwɪʃ [rə'l-], -ɪz, -ɪŋ, -t, -mənt

reliquar|y, -ies 'relɪkwər|ɪ, -ɪz

reliques (in Percy's Reliques) 'relɪks, (otherwise) rɪˈliːks [rə'l-]

relish (s. v.), -es, -ing, -ed 'relɪʃ, -ɪz, -ɪŋ, -t

re-liv|e, -es, -ing, -ed ˌriːˈlɪv, -z, -ɪŋ, -d

reload, -s, -ing, -ed ˌriːˈləʊd, -z, -ɪŋ, -ɪd

reluctanc|e, -t/ly rɪˈlʌktən|s [rə'l-], -t/lɪ

rel|y, -ies, -ying, -ied rɪˈl|aɪ [rə'l-], -aɪz, -aɪɪŋ, -aɪd

remain, -s, -ing, -ed rɪˈmeɪn [rə'm-], -z, -ɪŋ, -d

remainder, -s rɪˈmeɪndə* [rə'm-], -z

re-make (s.), -s 'riːmeɪk, -s

remak|e (v.), -es, -ing, remade ˌriːˈmeɪk, -s, -ɪŋ, ˌriːˈmeɪd

remand (s.), -s rɪˈmɑːnd [rə'm-], -z

remand (v.), -s, -ing, -ed rɪˈmɑːnd [rə'm-], -z, -ɪŋ, -ɪd

remark (s. v.) (notice, comment), -s, -ing, -ed rɪˈmɑːk [rə'm-], -s, -ɪŋ, -t

re-mark (v.) (mark again), -s, -ing, -ed ˌriːˈmɑːk, -s, -ɪŋ, -t

remarkab|le, -ly, -leness rɪˈmɑːkəb|l [rə'm-], -lɪ, -lnɪs [-nəs]

remarr|y, -ies, -ying, -ied; -iage/s ˌriːˈmær|ɪ, -ɪz, -ɪɪŋ, -ɪd; -ɪdʒ/ɪz

Rembrandt, -s 'rembrænt [-rənt], -s

R.E.M.E. 'riːmɪ

remediable rɪˈmiːdjəbl [rə'm-, -dɪəb-]

remedial rɪˈmiːdjəl [rə'm-, -dɪəl]

remed|y (s. v.), -ies, -ying, -ied; -yless 'remɪd|ɪ [-məd|ɪ], -ɪz, -ɪɪŋ, -ɪd; -ɪlɪs [-ləs]

rememb|er, -ers, -ering, -ered rɪˈmemb|ə* [rə'm-], -əz, -ərɪŋ, -əd

remembrance, -s; -r/s rɪˈmembrəns [rə'm-], -ɪz; -ə*/z

re-militariz|e, -es, -ing, -ed ˌriːˈmɪlɪtəraɪz [-lət-], -ɪz, -ɪŋ, -d

remind, -s, -ing, -ed, -er/s rɪˈmaɪnd [rə'm-], -z, -ɪŋ, -ɪd, -ə*/z

Remington, -s 'remɪŋtən, -z

reminisc|e, -es, -ing, -ed ˌremɪˈnɪs [-mə'n-], -ɪz, -ɪŋ, -t

reminiscen|ce, -ces, -t ˌremɪˈnɪsn|s [-mə'n-], -sɪz, -t

remis|e (s. v.) (thrust in fencing; carriage, coach-house, etc.), -es, -ing, -ed rə'miːz [rɪ'm-], -ɪz, -ɪŋ, -d

417

remise|e (s. v.) (surrender), -es, -ing, -ed
rɪˈmaɪz [rəˈm-], -ɪz, -ɪŋ, -d
remiss, -ly, -ness rɪˈmɪs [rəˈm-], -lɪ, -nɪs
[-nəs]
remission, -s rɪˈmɪʃn [rəˈm-], -z
remit (s.), -s ˈriːmɪt, -s
remit (v.), -s, -ting, -ted, -ter/s rɪˈmɪt
[rəˈm-], -s, -ɪŋ, -ɪd, -ə*/z
remittal, -s rɪˈmɪtl [rəˈm-], -z
remittance, -s rɪˈmɪtəns [rəˈm-], -ɪz
remnant, -s ˈremnənt, -s
remod|el, -els, -elling, -elled ˌriːˈmɒd|l,
-lz, -lɪŋ, -ld
remonetiz|e [-is|e], -es, -ing, -ed
riːˈmʌnɪtaɪz, -ɪz, -ɪŋ, -d
remonstran|ce, -ces, -t/ly rɪˈmɒnstrən|s
[rəˈm-], -sɪz, -t/lɪ
remonstrat|e, -es, -ing, -ed ˈremənstreɪt
[rɪˈmɒns-, rəˈm-], -s, -ɪŋ, -ɪd
remorse rɪˈmɔːs [rəˈm-]
remorse|ful, -fully rɪˈmɔːs|fʊl [rəˈm-],
-fʊlɪ [-fəlɪ]
remorseless, -ly, -ness rɪˈmɔːslɪs [rəˈm-,
-ləs], -lɪ, -nɪs [-nəs]
remote, -ly, -ness rɪˈməʊt [rəˈm-], -lɪ,
-nɪs [-nəs]
remould, -s, -ing, -ed ˌriːˈməʊld, -z, -ɪŋ,
-ɪd
re-mould (s.), -s ˈriːməʊld, -z
remount (s.), -s ˈriːmaʊnt [ˌ-ˈ-], -s
remount (v.), -s, -ing, -ed ˌriːˈmaʊnt, -s,
-ɪŋ, -ɪd
removability rɪˌmuːvəˈbɪlətɪ [rəˌm-, -lɪt-]
removal, -s rɪˈmuːvl [rəˈm-], -z
remov|e (s. v.), -es, -ing, -ed, -er/s;
-able rɪˈmuːv [rəˈm-], -z, -ɪŋ, -d,
-ə*/z; -əbl
Remploy, -s ˈremplɔɪ, -z
remunerat|e, -es, -ing, -ed rɪˈmjuːnəreɪt
[rəˈm-, -ˈmjʊn-], -s, -ɪŋ, -ɪd
remuneration rɪˌmjuːnəˈreɪʃn [rəˌm-,
-ˌmjʊn-]
remunerative rɪˈmjuːnərətɪv [rəˈm-,
-ˈmjʊn-]
Remus ˈriːməs
Renaissance rəˈneɪsəns [rɪˈn-, ˈrene-,
-sɑ̃:ns, -sɔ̃:ns, -sɑːns] (rənɛsɑ̃:s)
renal ˈriːnl
renam|e, -es, -ing, -ed ˌriːˈneɪm, -z, -ɪŋ,
-d
renascen|ce, -t rɪˈnæsn|s [rəˈn-], -t
Renault (car), -s ˈrenəʊ (rəno), -z
rend, -s, -ing, rent rend, -z, -ɪŋ, rent
rend|er, -ers, -ering/s, -ered ˈrend|ə*,
-əz, -ərɪŋ/z, -əd
rendezvous (sing.) ˈrɒndɪvuː: [ˈrɑ̃:nd-,
ˈrɔ̃:nd-, ˈrɑːnd-, -deɪv-] (rɑ̃devu),
(plur.), -z

rendition, -s renˈdɪʃn, -z
renegade, -s ˈrenɪgeɪd, -z
reneg(u)|e (s. v.), -es, -ing, -ed rɪˈniːg
[rəˈn-, -ˈneɪg], -z, -ɪŋ, -d
ren|ew, -ews, -ewing, -ewed; -ewable
rɪˈnj|uː: [rəˈn-], -uːz, -uːɪŋ [-ʊɪŋ],
-uːd; -uːəbl [-ʊəbl]
renewal, -s rɪˈnjuːəl [rəˈn-, -ˈnjʊəl,
-ˈnjuːl], -z
Renfrew, -shire ˈrenfruː:, -ʃə* [-ˌʃɪə*]
renin ˈriːnɪn
rennet ˈrenɪt
Rennie ˈrenɪ
Reno ˈriːnəʊ
Renoir rəˈnwɑ:* [ˈ--, ˈre-] (rənwaːr)
renounc|e, -es, -ing, -ed, -ement
rɪˈnaʊns [rəˈn-], -ɪz, -ɪŋ, -t, -mənt
renovat|e, -es, -ing, -ed, -or/s
ˈrenəʊveɪt, -s, -ɪŋ, -ɪd, -ə*/z
renovation, -s ˌrenəʊˈveɪʃn, -z
renown, -ed rɪˈnaʊn [rəˈn-], -d
Renshaw ˈrenʃɔ:
rent (s. v.), -s, -ing, -ed, -er/s rent, -s,
-ɪŋ, -ɪd, -ə*/z
rent (from rend) rent
rental, -s ˈrentl, -z
rent-free ˌrentˈfriː: [also ˈ-- when attribu-
tive]
rentier, -s ˈrɒntɪeɪ (rɑ̃tje), -z
Rentoul rənˈtuːl [ren-]
rent-roll, -s ˈrentrəʊl, -z
renunciation, -s rɪˌnʌnsɪˈeɪʃn [rə,n-], -z
Renwick ˈrenwɪk, ˈrenɪk
reoccupation, -s ˈriːˌɒkjʊˈpeɪʃn [ˌrɪɒk-],
-z
reoccup|y, -ies, -ying, -ied ˌriːˈɒkjʊp|aɪ
[riːˈɒk-, rɪˈɒk-], -aɪz, -aɪɪŋ, -aɪd
reop|en, -ens, -ening, -ened ˌriːˈəʊp|ən
[riːˈəʊ-, rɪˈəʊ-, -p|m], -ənz [-mz], -nɪŋ
[-pnɪŋ], -ənd [-md]
reorganization [-isa-], -s ˈriːˌɔːgənaɪ-
ˈzeɪʃn [riːˌɔː-, rɪˌɔː-, -gŋaɪˈz-, -gənɪˈz-,
gŋɪˈz-], -z
reorganiz|e [-is|e], -es, -ing, -ed
ˌriːˈɔːgənaɪz [riːˈɔː-, rɪˈɔː-, -gŋaɪz], -ɪz,
-ɪŋ, -d
re-orientat|e, -es, -ing, -ed ˌriːˈɔːrɪenteɪt
[-ˈɒr-, -rɪən-], -s, -ɪŋ, -ɪd
re-orientation ˈriːˌɔːrɪenˈteɪʃn [-ˌɒr-,
-rɪən-]
rep rep
repaid (from repay, pay back) riːˈpeɪd
[rɪˈp-, ˌriːˈp-], (from repay, pay a
second time) ˌriːˈpeɪd
repair (s. v.), -s, -ing, -ed, -er/s rɪˈpeə*
[rəˈp-], -z, -ɪŋ, -d, -rə*/z
repairable rɪˈpeərəbl [rəˈp-]
reparability ˌrepərəˈbɪlətɪ [-lɪt-]

reparable 'repərəbl

reparation, -s ˌrepə'reɪʃn, -z

repartee ˌrepɑ:'ti:

repass, -es, -ing, -ed ˌri:'pɑ:s [*also* 'ri:pɑ:s *when contrasted with* pass], -ɪz, -ɪŋ, -t

repast, -s rɪ'pɑ:st [rə'p-], -s

repatriat|e, -es, -ing, -ed ri:'pætrɪeɪt [rɪ'p-, *rarely* -'pert-], -s, -ɪŋ, -ɪd

repatriation ˌri:pætrɪ'eɪʃn [rɪˌpætrɪ'eɪʃn]

re|pay (*pay back*), -pays, -paying, -paid ri:|'peɪ [rɪ|'peɪ, ˌri:|'peɪ], -'peɪz, -'peɪɪŋ, -'peɪd

re|pay (*pay a second time*), -pays, -paying, -paid ˌri:|'peɪ, -'peɪz, -'peɪɪŋ, -'peɪd

repayable ri:'peɪəbl [rɪ'p-, ˌri:'p-]

repayment, -s ri:'peɪmənt [rɪ'p-, ˌri:'p-], -s

repeal (*s. v.*), -s, -ing, -ed rɪ'pi:l [rə'p-], -z, -ɪŋ, -d

repeat (*s. v.*), -s, -ing, -ed/ly, -er/s rɪ'pi:t [rə'p-], -s, -ɪŋ, -ɪd/lɪ, -ə*/z

repêchage 'repəʃɑ:ʒ, ˌrepə'ʃɑ:ʒ

repel, -s, -ling, -led; -lent rɪ'pel [rə'p-], -z, -ɪŋ, -d; -ənt

repent, -s, -ing/ly, -ed rɪ'pent [rə'p-], -s, -ɪŋ/lɪ, -ɪd

repentan|ce, -ces, -t/ly rɪ'pentən|s [rə'p-], -sɪz, -t/lɪ

repeop|le, -les, -ling, -led ˌri:'pi:p|l, -lz, -lɪŋ [-lɪŋ], -ld

repercussion, -s ˌri:pə'kʌʃn [-pɜ:'k-], -z

repertoire, -s 'repətwɑ:* [-twɔ:*], -z

repertor|y, -ies 'repətər|ɪ, -ɪz

repetition, -s ˌrepɪ'tɪʃn [-pə't-], -z

repetitive rɪ'petətɪv [rə'p-, -tɪt-]

repin|e, -es, -ing, -ed rɪ'paɪn [rə'p-], -z, -ɪŋ, -d

repiqu|e (*s. v.*), -es, -ing, -ed ˌri:'pi:k [rɪ'p-, *also in contrast* 'ri:pi:k], -s, -ɪŋ, -t

replac|e, -es, -ing, -ed, -ement/s rɪ'pleɪs [ri:'p-], -ɪz, -ɪŋ, -t, -mənt/s

replaceable rɪ'pleɪsəbl [ri:'p-]

replant, -s, -ing, -ed ˌri:'plɑ:nt, -s, -ɪŋ, -ɪd

replay (*s.*), -s 'ri:pleɪ, -z

replay (*v.*), -s, -ing, -ed ˌri:'pleɪ, -z, -ɪŋ, -d

re-pleat, -s, -ing, -ed ˌri:'pli:t, -s, -ɪŋ, -ɪd

replenish, -es, -ing, -ed, -ment rɪ'plenɪʃ [rə'p-], -ɪz, -ɪŋ, -t, -mənt

replete, -ness rɪ'pli:t, -nɪs [-nəs]

repletion rɪ'pli:ʃn

replevin rɪ'plevɪn [rə'p-]

replica, -s 'replɪkə [rɪ'pli:kə, rə'pli:kə], -z

repl|y (*s. v.*), -ies, -ying, -ied rɪ'pl|aɪ [rə'p-], -aɪz, -aɪɪŋ, -aɪd

repoint, -s, -ing, -ed ˌri:'pɔɪnt, -s, -ɪŋ, -ɪd

repolish, -es, -ing, -ed ˌri:'pɒlɪʃ, -ɪz, -ɪŋ, -t

repopulat|e, -es, -ing, -ed ˌri:'pɒpjʊleɪt [ri:'p-, -pjəl-], -s, -ɪŋ, -ɪd

report (*s. v.*), -s, -ing, -ed, -er/s rɪ'pɔ:t [rə'p-], -s, -ɪŋ, -ɪd, -ə*/z

reportage ˌrepɔ:'tɑ:ʒ

repos|e (*s. v.*), -es, -ing, -ed rɪ'pəʊz [rə'p-], -ɪz, -ɪŋ, -d

repose|ful, -fully rɪ'pəʊz|fʊl [rə'p-], -fʊlɪ [-fəlɪ]

repositor|y, -ies rɪ'pɒzɪtər|ɪ [rə'p-], -ɪz

repoussé rə'pu:seɪ [rɪ'p-] (rəpuse)

reprehend, -s, -ing, -ed ˌreprɪ'hend [-prə'h-], -z, -ɪŋ, -ɪd

reprehensible ˌreprɪ'hensəbl [-prə'h-, -sɪb-]

reprehension ˌreprɪ'henʃn [-prə'h-]

represent, -s, -ing, -ed ˌreprɪ'zent [-prə'z-], -s, -ɪŋ, -ɪd

representation, -s ˌreprɪzen'teɪʃn [-prəz-, -zən-], -z

representative (*s. adj.*), -s, -ly ˌreprɪ'zentətɪv [-prə'z-], -z, -lɪ

repress, -es, -ing, -ed; -ible rɪ'pres [rə'p-], -ɪz, -ɪŋ, -t; -əbl [-ɪbl]

repression, -s rɪ'preʃn [rə'p-], -z

repressive rɪ'presɪv [rə'p-]

repriev|e (*s. v.*), -es, -ing, -ed rɪ'pri:v [rə'p-], -z, -ɪŋ, -d

reprimand (*s.*), -s 'reprɪmɑ:nd, -z

reprimand (*v.*), -s, -ing, -ed 'reprɪmɑ:nd [ˌreprɪ'm-], -z, -ɪŋ, -ɪd

reprint (*s.*), -s 'ri:prɪnt [ˌri:'prɪnt], -s

reprint (*v.*), -s, -ing, -ed ˌri:'prɪnt, -s, -ɪŋ, -ɪd

reprisal, -s rɪ'praɪzl [rə'p-], -z

reproach (*s. v.*), -es, -ing, -ed; -able rɪ'prəʊtʃ [rə'p-], -ɪz, -ɪŋ, -t; -əbl

reproach|ful, -fully, -fulness rɪ'prəʊtʃ|-fʊl [rə'p-], -fʊlɪ [-fəlɪ], -fʊlnɪs [-nəs]

reprobate (*s. adj.*), -s 'reprəʊbeɪt [-prʊb-, -bɪt], -s

reprobat|e (*v.*), -es, -ing, -ed 'reprəʊbeɪt [-prʊb-], -s, -ɪŋ, -ɪd

reprobation ˌreprəʊ'beɪʃn [-prʊ'b-]

reproduc|e, -es, -ing, -ed, -er/s ˌri:-prə'dju:s [-prʊ'd-], -ɪz, -ɪŋ, -t, -ə*/z

reproduction, -s ˌri:prə'dʌkʃn [-prʊ'd-], -z

reproductive, -ness ˌri:prə'dʌktɪv [-prʊ'd-], -nɪs [-nəs]

reproof (*s.*), -s rɪ'pru:f [rə'p-], -s

re-proof (*v.*), -s, -ing, -ed ˌri:'pru:f, -s, -ɪŋ, -t

reproval, -s rɪˈpruːvl [rəˈp-], -z

reprov|e, -es, -ing/ly, -ed, -er/s rɪˈpruːv [rəˈp-], -z, -ɪŋ/lɪ, -d, -ə*/z

reptile, -s ˈreptaɪl, -z

reptilian (s. adj.), -s repˈtɪlɪən [-ljən], -z

Repton ˈreptən

republic, -s rɪˈpʌblɪk [rəˈp-], -s

republican, -s; -ism rɪˈpʌblɪkən [rəˈp-], -z; -ɪzəm

republication, -s ˈriːˌpʌblɪˈkeɪʃn, -z

republish, -es, -ing, -ed ˌriːˈpʌblɪʃ, -ɪz, -ɪŋ, -t

repudiat|e, -es, -ing, -ed, -er/s rɪˈpjuːdɪeɪt [rəˈp-], -s, -ɪŋ, -ɪd, -ə*/z

repudiation rɪˌpjuːdɪˈeɪʃn [rəˌp-]

repugnan|ce, -t/ly rɪˈpʌgnən|s [rəˈp-], -t/lɪ

repuls|e (s. v.), -es, -ing, -ed rɪˈpʌls [rəˈp-], -ɪz, -ɪŋ, -t

repulsion rɪˈpʌlʃn [rəˈp-]

repulsive, -ly, -ness rɪˈpʌlsɪv [rəˈp-], -lɪ, -nɪs [-nəs]

reputability ˌrepjʊtəˈbɪlətɪ [-lɪt-]

reputable ˈrepjʊtəbl

reputation, -s ˌrepjʊˈteɪʃn [-pjuːˈt-], -z

repute, -d, -dly rɪˈpjuːt [rəˈp-], -ɪd, -ɪdlɪ

request (s. v.), -s, -ing, -ed rɪˈkwest [rəˈk-], -s, -ɪŋ, -ɪd

requiem, -s ˈrekwɪəm [-kwjəm, -kwɪem], -z

requir|e, -es, -ing, -ed, -ement/s rɪˈkwaɪə* [rəˈk-], -z, -rɪŋ, -d, -mənt/s

requisite (s. adj.), -s, -ly, -ness ˈrekwɪzɪt, -s, -lɪ, -nɪs [-nəs]

requisiti|on (s. v.), -ons, -oning, -oned ˌrekwɪˈzɪʃ|n, -nz, -ənɪŋ [-ənɪŋ], -nd

requit|e, -es, -ing, -ed; -al rɪˈkwaɪt [rəˈk-], -s, -ɪŋ, -ɪd; -l

re-read (pres. tense), -s, -ing, re-read (p.) ˌriːˈriːd, -z, -ɪŋ, ˌriːˈred

reredos, -es ˈrɪədɒs, -ɪz

res riːz

resartus riːˈsɑːtəs [rɪˈs-]

rescind, -s, -ing, -ed rɪˈsɪnd [rəˈs-], -z, -ɪŋ, -ɪd

rescission rɪˈsɪʒn [rəˈs-]

rescript, -s ˈriːskrɪpt, -s

resc|ue (s. v.), -ues, -uing, -ued, -uer/s ˈresk|juː, -juːz, -jʊɪŋ [-juːɪŋ, -jwɪŋ], -juːd, -jʊə*/z [-jwə*/z]

research (s.), -es rɪˈsɜːtʃ [rəˈs-, ˈriːsɜːtʃ], -ɪz

research (v.), -es, -ing, -ed, -er/s rɪˈsɜːtʃ [rəˈs-], -ɪz, -ɪŋ, -t, -ə*/z

reseat, -s, -ing, -ed ˌriːˈsiːt, -s, -ɪŋ, -ɪd

resection, -s riːˈsekʃn [rɪˈs-], -z

reseda, -s (plant) ˈresɪdə [ˈrezɪdə, rɪˈsiːdə], (colour) ˈresɪdə [ˈrezɪdə], -z

resell, -s, -ing, resold ˌriːˈsel, -z, -ɪŋ, ˌriːˈsəʊld

resemblance, -s rɪˈzembləns [rəˈz-], -ɪz

resemb|le, -les, -ling, -led rɪˈzemb|l [rəˈz-], -lz, -lɪŋ [-lɪŋ], -ld

resent, -s, -ing, -ed, -ment; -ful, -fully rɪˈzent, -s, -ɪŋ, -ɪd, -mənt; -fʊl, -fʊlɪ [-fəlɪ]

reservation, -s ˌrezəˈveɪʃn, -z

reserv|e (s. v.), -es, -ing, -ed rɪˈzɜːv [rəˈz-], -z, -ɪŋ, -d

reservedly rɪˈzɜːvɪdlɪ [rəˈz-]

reservist, -s rɪˈzɜːvɪst [rəˈz-], -s

reservoir, -s ˈrezəvwɑː* [-vwɔː*], -z

reset, -s, -ting/s ˌriːˈset, -s, -ɪŋ/z

reshap|e, -es, -ing, -ed ˌriːˈʃeɪp, -s, -ɪŋ, -t

reship, -s, -ping, -ped, -ment/s ˌriːˈʃɪp, -s, -ɪŋ, -t, -mənt/s

reshuff|le (s. v.), -les, -ling, -led ˌriːˈʃʌf|l, -lz, -lɪŋ [-lɪŋ], -ld

resid|e, -es, -ing, -ed rɪˈzaɪd [rəˈz-], -z, -ɪŋ, -ɪd

residence, -s ˈrezɪdəns, -ɪz

residenc|y, -ies ˈrezɪdəns|ɪ, -ɪz

resident, -s ˈrezɪdənt, -s

residential ˌrezɪˈdenʃl

residual rɪˈzɪdjʊəl [rəˈz-, -djwəl, -djʊl]

residuary rɪˈzɪdjʊərɪ [rəˈz-, -djwərɪ, -djʊrɪ]

residue, -s ˈrezɪdjuː, -z

residu|um, -a rɪˈzɪdjʊ|əm [rəˈz-, -djw|əm], -ə

resign (give up), -s, -ing, -ed, -edly rɪˈzaɪn [rəˈz-], -z, -ɪŋ, -d, -ɪdlɪ

re-sign (sign again), -s, -ing, -ed ˌriːˈsaɪn, -z, -ɪŋ, -d

resignation, -s ˌrezɪgˈneɪʃn, -z

resilien|ce, -cy, -t rɪˈzɪlɪən|s [rəˈzɪl-, rɪˈsɪl-, rəˈsɪl-, -ljə-], -sɪ, -t

resin, -s; -ous ˈrezɪn, -z; -əs

resist, -s, -ing, -ed rɪˈzɪst [rəˈz-], -s, -ɪŋ, -ɪd

resistan|ce, -ces, -t rɪˈzɪstən|s [rəˈz-], -sɪz, -t

resistless rɪˈzɪstlɪs [rəˈz-, -ləs]

resol|e, -es, -ing, -ed ˌriːˈsəʊl, -z, -ɪŋ, -d

resoluble rɪˈzɒljʊbl [rəˈz-, ˈrezəljʊbl]

resolute, -ly, -ness ˈrezəluːt [-zḷuːt, -zəljuːt], -lɪ, -nɪs [-nəs]

resolution, -s ˌrezəˈluːʃn [-zḷˈuː-, -zəˈljuː-], -z

resolvability rɪˌzɒlvəˈbɪlətɪ [rəˌz-, -lɪt-]

resolv|e (s. v.), -es, -ing, -ed; -able rɪˈzɒlv [rəˈz-], -z, -ɪŋ, -d; -əbl

resonan|ce, -ces, -t/ly ˈrezənən|s [-zṇə-], -sɪz, -t/lɪ

resonator, -s 'rezəneɪtə* [-zɲeɪ-], -z

resort (s. v.), -s, -ing, -ed rɪ'zɔːt [rə'z-], -s, -ɪŋ, -ɪd

re-sort (sort out again), -s, -ing, -ed ˌriː'sɔːt, -s, -ɪŋ, -ɪd

resound, -s, -ing, -ed rɪ'zaʊnd [rə'z-], -z, -ɪŋ, -ɪd

resource, -s; -ful, -fully, -fulness rɪ'sɔːs [rə's-, -'zɔːs, -ɔəs], -ɪz; -fʊl, -fʊlɪ [-fəlɪ], -fʊlnɪs [-nəs]

respect (s. v.), -s, -ing, -ed, -er/s rɪ'spekt [rə's-], -s, -ɪŋ, -ɪd, -ə*/z

respectability rɪˌspektə'bɪlətɪ [rə,s-, -lɪt-]

respectab|le, -ly, -leness rɪ'spektəb|l [rə's-], -lɪ, -lnɪs [-nəs]

respect|ful, -fully rɪ'spekt|fʊl [rə's-], -fʊlɪ [-fəlɪ]

respecting (prep.) rɪ'spektɪŋ [rə's-]

respective, -ly rɪ'spektɪv [rə's-], -lɪ

Respighi re'spiːgɪ (re'spiːgi)

respirable 'respɪrəbl [rɪ'spaɪərəbl, rə'spaɪər-]

respiration, -s ˌrespə'reɪʃn [-pɪ'r-], -z

respirator, -s 'respəreɪtə* [-pɪr-], -z

respiratory rɪ'spaɪərətərɪ [re'sp-, rə'sp-, -'spɪr-, 'respɪrətərɪ, 'respɪreɪtərɪ]

respir|e, -es, -ing, -ed rɪ'spaɪə* [rə's-], -z, -ɪŋ, -d

respit|e (s. v.), -es, -ing, -ed 'respaɪt [-pɪt], -s, -ɪŋ, -ɪd

resplenden|ce, -cy, -t/ly rɪ'splendən|s [rə's-], -sɪ, -t/lɪ

respond, -s, -ing, -ed; -ent/s rɪ'spɒnd [rə's-], -z, -ɪŋ, -ɪd; -ənt/s

response, -s rɪ'spɒns [rə's-], -ɪz

responsibilit|y, -ies rɪˌspɒnsə'bɪlət|ɪ [rə,s-, -sɪ'b-, -lɪt-], -ɪz

responsib|le, -ly, -leness rɪ'spɒnsəb|l [rə's-, -sɪb-], -lɪ, -lnɪs [-nəs]

responsions rɪ'spɒnʃnz [rə's-]

responsive, -ly, -ness rɪ'spɒnsɪv [rə's-], -lɪ, -nɪs [-nəs]

rest (s. v.), -s, -ing, -ed rest, -s, -ɪŋ, -ɪd

restart, -s, -ing, -ed ˌriː'stɑːt, -s, -ɪŋ, -ɪd

restat|e, -es, -ing, -ed ˌriː'steɪt, -s, -ɪŋ, -ɪd

re-statement, -s ˌriː'steɪtmənt, -s

restaurant, -s 'restərɔ̃ːŋ [-rɑ̃ː, -rɑːŋ, -rɒŋ], -z, 'restərɒnt [-rənt], -s

restaurateur, -s ˌrestərə'tɜː* [-tər-, -tɔː'r-] (restɔratœːr), -z

rest-cure, -s 'restˌkjʊə* [-kjɔə*, -kjɔː*], -z

rest|ful, -fully, -fulness 'rest|fʊl, -fʊlɪ [-fəlɪ], -fʊlnɪs [-nəs]

rest-hou|se, -ses 'resthaʊ|s, -zɪz

resting-place, -s 'restɪŋpleɪs, -ɪz

restitution ˌrestɪ'tjuːʃn

restive, -ly, -ness 'restɪv, -lɪ, -nɪs [-nəs]

restless, -ly, -ness 'restlɪs [-ləs], -lɪ, -nɪs [-nəs]

restock, -s, -ing, -ed ˌriː'stɒk, -s, -ɪŋ, -t

restoration, -s ˌrestə'reɪʃn [-tɔː'r-, -tʊ'r-], -z

restorative (s. adj.), -s rɪ'stɒrətɪv [re's-, rə's-, -'stɔː-r-], -z

restor|e, -es, -ing, -ed, -er/s; -able rɪ'stɔː* [rə's-, -'stɔə*], -z, -rɪŋ, -d, -rə*/z; -rəbl

restrain (hold back), -s, -ing, -ed, -er/s rɪ'streɪn [rə's-], -z, -ɪŋ, -d, -ə*/z

re-strain (strain again), -s, -ing, -ed ˌriː'streɪn, -z, -ɪŋ, -d

restraint, -s rɪ'streɪnt [rə's-], -s

restrict, -s, -ing, -ed; -ive rɪ'strɪkt [rə's-], -s, -ɪŋ, -ɪd; -ɪv

restriction, -s rɪ'strɪkʃn [rə's-], -z

restrictionism rɪ'strɪkʃənɪzəm [rə's-, -ʃɲɪ-]

result (s. v.), -s, -ing, -ed; -ant/s rɪ'zʌlt [rə'z-], -s, -ɪŋ, -ɪd; -ənt/s

resultative rɪ'zʌltətɪv [rə'z-]

resum|e, -es, -ing, -ed rɪ'zjuːm [rə'z-, -'zuːm], -z, -ɪŋ, -d

résumé, -s 'rezjuːmeɪ ['reɪz-, -zjʊm-, -zuː-, -zʊm-] (rezyme), -z

resumption, -s rɪ'zʌmpʃn [rə'z-], -z

re-surfac|e, -es, -ing, -ed ˌriː'sɜːfɪs [-fəs], -ɪz, -ɪŋ, -t

resurrect, -s, -ing, -ed ˌrezə'rekt, -s, -ɪŋ, -ɪd

resurrection (R.), -s ˌrezə'rekʃn, -z

resuscitat|e, -es, -ing, -ed rɪ'sʌsɪteɪt [rə's-], -s, -ɪŋ, -ɪd

resuscitation, -s rɪˌsʌsɪ'teɪʃn [rə,s-], -z

retail (s. adj.) 'riːteɪl [riː't-]

retail (v.), -s, -ing, -ed, -er/s riː'teɪl [rɪ't-], -z, -ɪŋ, -d, -ə*/z

retain, -s, -ing, -ed, -er/s rɪ'teɪn [rə't-], -z, -ɪŋ, -d, -ə*/z

retak|e (s.), -s 'riːteɪk, -s

retak|e (v.), -es, -ing, retook, retaken ˌriː'teɪk [-'-], -s, -ɪŋ, ˌriː'tʊk [-'-], ˌriː'teɪkən [-'--]

retaliat|e, -es, -ing, -ed rɪ'tælɪeɪt [rə't-], -s, -ɪŋ, -ɪd

retaliation rɪˌtælɪ'eɪʃn [rə,t-]

retaliatory rɪ'tælɪətərɪ [rə't-, -ljətərɪ, -lɪeɪtərɪ, rɪˌtælɪ'eɪtərɪ, rə,t-]

Retallack rɪ'tælək [rə't-]

retard, -s, -ing, -ed rɪ'tɑːd [rə't-], -z, -ɪŋ, -ɪd

retardation, -s ˌriːtɑː'deɪʃn, -z

retch, -es, -ing, -ed retʃ [riːtʃ], -ɪz, -ɪŋ, -t

retell, -s, -ing, retold ˌriː'tel, -z, -ɪŋ, ˌriː'təʊld

retention rɪ'tenʃn [rə't-]

retentive, -ly, -ness rɪ'tentɪv [rə't-], -lɪ, -nɪs [-nəs]

Retford 'retfəd

reticen|ce, -t/ly 'retɪsən|s, -t/lɪ

reticle, -s 'retɪkl, -z

reticulate (adj.) rɪ'tɪkjʊlət [re't-, rə't-, -kjəl-, -lɪt, -leɪt]

reticulat|e (v.), -es, -ing, -ed rɪ'tɪkjʊleɪt [re't-, rə't-, -kjəl-], -s, -ɪŋ, -ɪd

reticulation, -s rɪ,tɪkjʊ'leɪʃn [re,t-, rə,t-, -kjə'l-], -z

reticule, -s 'retɪkjuːl, -z

retin|a, -as, -ae 'retɪn|ə, -əz, -iː

retinue, -s 'retɪnjuː, -z

retir|e, -es, -ing, -ed; -ement/s rɪ'taɪə* [rə't-], -z, -rɪŋ, -d; -mənt/s

retold (from retell) ,riː'təʊld

retort (s. v.), -s, -ing, -ed rɪ'tɔːt [rə't-], -s, -ɪŋ, -ɪd

retouch (s. v.), -es, -ing, -ed ,riː'tʌtʃ, -ɪz, -ɪŋ, -t

retrac|e, -es, -ing, -ed rɪ'treɪs [,riː't-], -ɪz, -ɪŋ, -t

retract, -s, -ing, -ed rɪ'trækt [rə't-], -s, -ɪŋ, -ɪd

retractable rɪ'træktəbl [rə't-]

retractation ,riː'træk'teɪʃn

retraction, -s rɪ'trækʃn [rə't-], -z

retranslat|e, -es, -ing, -ed ,riː'trænslert [-trɑːns-, -trænz-, -trɑːnz-, -trəns-, -trənz-], -s, -ɪŋ, -ɪd

retranslation, -s ,riː'trænslerʃn [-trɑːns-, -trænz-, -trɑːnz-, -trəns-, -trənz-], -z

re-tread (tyres), -s 'riːtred, -z

re|tread (v.), -treads, -treading, -trod ,riː'tred, -'tredz, -'tredɪŋ, -'trɒd

retreat (s. v.), -s, -ing, -ed rɪ'triːt [rə't-], -s, -ɪŋ, -ɪd

retrench, -es, -ing, -ed, -ment/s rɪ'trentʃ [rə't-], -ɪz, -ɪŋ, -t, -mənt/s

retrial, -s ,riː'traɪəl, -z

retribution ,retrɪ'bjuːʃn

retribut|ive, -ory rɪ'trɪbjʊt|ɪv [rə't-], -ərɪ

retrievab|le, -ly, -leness rɪ'triːvəb|l [rə't-], -lɪ, -lnɪs [-nəs]

retrieval rɪ'triːvl

retriev|e, -es, -ing, -ed, -er/s rɪ'triːv [rə't-], -z, -ɪŋ, -d, -ə*/z

retrim, -s, -ming, -med ,riː'trɪm, -z, -ɪŋ, -d

retroact, -s, -ing, -ed; -ive/ly ,retrəʊ-'ækt [,riː't-], -s, -ɪŋ, -ɪd; -ɪv/lɪ

retroced|e, -es, -ing, -ed ,retrəʊ'siːd [,riː't-], -z, -ɪŋ, -ɪd

retrocession, -s ,retrəʊ'seʃn [,riː't-], -z

retroflex, -ed 'retrəʊfleks, -t

retroflexion ,retrəʊ'flekʃn

retrograde 'retrəʊgreɪd

retrogression ,retrəʊ'greʃn [,riː't-]

retrogressive, -ly ,retrəʊ'gresɪv [,riː't-], -lɪ

retro-rocket, -s 'retrəʊ,rɒkɪt, -s

retrospect, -s 'retrəʊspekt ['riː't-], -s

retrospection, -s ,retrəʊ'spekʃn [,riː't-], -z

retrospective, -ly ,retrəʊ'spektɪv [,riː't-], -lɪ

retroussé rə'truːseɪ [rɪ't-] (rətruse)

retroversion, -s ,retrəʊ'vɜːʃn [,riː't-], -z

retrovert (s.), -s 'retrəʊvɜːt ['riː't-], -s

retrovert (v.), -s, -ing, -ed ,retrəʊ'vɜːt [,riː't-], -s, -ɪŋ, -ɪd

retr|y, -ies, -ying, -ied ,riː'tr|aɪ, -aɪz, -aɪɪŋ, -aɪd

returf, -s, -ing, -ed ,riː'tɜːf, -s, -ɪŋ, -t

return (s. v.), -s, -ing, -ed; -able rɪ'tɜːn [rə't-], -z, -ɪŋ, -d; -əbl

Reuben 'ruːbɪn [-bən]

reunification, -s ,riːjuːnɪfɪ'keɪʃn [,riːjʊn-, rɪ,juː-], -z

reunion, -s ,riː'juːnjən [riː'j-, -nɪən], -z

reunit|e, -es, -ing, -ed ,riːjuː'naɪt [-jʊ'n-], -s, -ɪŋ, -ɪd

re-use (s.) ,riː'juːs ['riːjuːs]

re-us|e (v.), -es, -ing, -ed ,riː'juːz, -ɪz, -ɪŋ, -d ['riːjuːzd when attributive]

Reuter 'rɔɪtə*

Rev. 'revərənd

rev (s. v.), -s, -ving, -ved rev, -z, -ɪŋ, -d

reveal, -s, -ing, -ed, -er/s; -able rɪ'viːl [rə'v-], -z, -ɪŋ, -d, -ə*/z; -əbl

reveille, -s rɪ'vælɪ [rə'v-, -'vel-], -z

rev|el (s. v.), -els, -elling, -elled, -eller/s 'rev|l, -lz, -lɪŋ, -ld, -lə*/z

revelation (R.), -s ,revə'leɪʃn [-vl̩'eɪ-, -vɪ'l-], -z

revelr|y, -ies 'revlr|ɪ, -ɪz

Revelstoke 'revəlstəʊk

revendication, -s rɪ,vendɪ'keɪʃn [rə,v-], -z

reveng|e (s. v.), -es, -ing, -ed rɪ'vendʒ [rə'v-], -ɪz, -ɪŋ, -d

revenge|ful, -fully, -fulness rɪ'vendʒ|fʊl [rə'v-], -fʊlɪ [-fəlɪ], -fʊlnɪs [-nəs]

revenue, -s 'revənjuː [-vm-, in old-fashioned legal usage rɪ'venjuː, rə'venjuː], -z

Note.—In Shakespeare both stressings occur, e.g. '--- in 'Richard II', II. i. 226, and -'--- in 'The Tempest', I. ii. 98.

reverberat|e, -es, -ing, -ed, -or/s rɪ'vɜːbəreɪt [rə'v-], -s, -ɪŋ, -ɪd, -ə*/z reverberation, -s rɪ,vɜːbəˈreɪʃn [rəˌv-], -z

reverberatory rɪˈvɜːbərətəri [rəˈv-, -reɪtəri]

rever|e (R.), -es, -ing, -ed rɪˈvɪə* [rəˈv-], -z, -rɪŋ, -d

reverenc|e (s. v.), -es, -ing, -ed ˈrevər-əns, -ɪz, -ɪŋ, -t

reverend (R.), -s ˈrevərənd, -z

reverent, -ly ˈrevərənt, -lɪ

reverential ˌrevəˈrenʃl

reverie, -s ˈrevərɪ, -z

revers (sing.) rɪˈvɪə* [rəˈv-, -ˈveə*], (plur.) -z

reversal, -s rɪˈvɜːsl [rəˈv-], -z

reverse (s.), -s rɪˈvɜːs [rəˈv-, ˈriːvɜːs], -ɪz

revers|e (v.), -es, -ing, -ed; -ely rɪˈvɜːs [rəˈv-], -ɪz, -ɪŋ, -t; -lɪ

reversibility rɪˌvɜːsəˈbɪlətɪ [rəˌv-, -sɪˈb-, -lɪt-]

reversible rɪˈvɜːsəbl [rəˈv-, -sɪb-]

reversion, -s rɪˈvɜːʃn [rəˈv-], -z

reversionary rɪˈvɜːʃnərɪ [rəˈv-, -ʃnə-, -ʃənə-]

revert, -s, -ing, -ed rɪˈvɜːt [rəˈv-], -s, -ɪŋ, -ɪd

revet, -s, -ting, -ted, -ment/s rɪˈvet [rəˈv-], -s, -ɪŋ, -ɪd, -mənt/s

revictu|al, -als, -alling, -alled ˌriːˈvɪtl|l, -lz, -lɪŋ, -ld

revi|ew (s. v.), -ews, -ewing, -ewed, -ewer/s rɪˈvjuː [rəˈv-], -uːz, -uːɪŋ [-ʊɪŋ], -uːd, -uːə*/z [-ʊə*/z]

revill|e, -es, -ing, -ed, -er/s rɪˈvaɪl [rəˈv-], -z, -ɪŋ, -d, -ə*/z

Revillon (English surname) rəˈvɪljən

revis|e (s. v.), -es, -ing, -ed, -er/s rɪˈvaɪz [rəˈv-], -ɪz, -ɪŋ, -d, -ə*/z

revision, -s, -ist/s rɪˈvɪʒn [rəˈv-], -z, -ɪst/s

revisit, -s, -ing, -ed ˌriːˈvɪzɪt, -s, -ɪŋ, -ɪd

revisualiz|e [-is|e], -es, -ing, -ed ˌriːˈvɪzjʊəlaɪz [-zjwəl-, -zjʊl-, -zjʊəl-, -ʒjwəl-, -ʒʊəl-, -ʒwəl-, -ʒʊl-], -ɪz, -ɪŋ, -d

revitaliz|e [is|e], -es, -ing, -ed ˌriːˈvaɪtə-laɪz [-tʃaɪz], -ɪz, -ɪŋ, -d

revival, -s rɪˈvaɪvl [rəˈv-], -z

revivali|sm, -st/s rɪˈvaɪvəlɪ|zəm [rəˈv-, -vlɪ-], -st/s

reviv|e, -es, -ing, -ed rɪˈvaɪv [rəˈv-], -z, -ɪŋ, -d

revivi|fy, -fies, -fying, -fied riːˈvɪvɪ|faɪ [ˌriːˈv-, rɪˈv-], -faɪz, -faɪɪŋ, -faɪd

reviviscence ˌrevɪˈvɪsns [ˌriːvaɪˈv-, -səns]

revocability ˌrevəkəˈbɪlətɪ [-vʊk-, -lɪt-]

revocable ˈrevəkəbl [-vʊk-], (when applied to letters of credit) rɪˈvəʊkəbl [rəˈv-]

revocation, -s ˌrevəˈkeɪʃn [-vʊˈk-, -vəʊˈk-], -z

revok|e (s. v.), -es, -ing, -ed rɪˈvəʊk [rəˈv-], -s, -ɪŋ, -t

revolt (s. v.), -s, -ing, -ed rɪˈvəʊlt [rəˈv-], -s, -ɪŋ, -ɪd

revolution, -s ˌrevəˈluːʃn [-vʊˈluː-, -vlˈuː-, -vəˈljuː-], -z

revolutionar|y (s. adj.), -ies ˌrevəˈluː-ʃnər|ɪ [-vʊˈluː-, -vlˈuː-, -vəˈljuː-, -ʃnər-, -ʃnr-, -ʃənər-], -ɪz

revolutionist, -s ˌrevəˈluːʃnɪst [-vʊˈluː-, -vlˈuː-, -vəˈljuː-, -ʃənɪst, -ʃnɪst], -s

revolutioniz|e [-is|e], -es, -ing, -ed ˌrevəˈluːʃnaɪz [-vʊˈluː-, -vlˈuː-, -vəˈljuː-, -ʃənaɪz, -ʃnaɪz], -ɪz, -ɪŋ, -d

revolv|e, -es, -ing, -ed rɪˈvɒlv [rəˈv-], -z, -ɪŋ, -d

revolver, -s rɪˈvɒlvə* [rəˈv-], -z

revue, -s rɪˈvjuː [rəˈv-], -z

revulsion, -s rɪˈvʌlʃn [rəˈv-], -z

reward (s. v.), -s, -ing, -ed rɪˈwɔːd [rəˈw-], -z, -ɪŋ, -ɪd

reword, -s, -ing, -ed ˌriːˈwɜːd, -z, -ɪŋ, -ɪd

rewrit|e, -es, -ing, rewrote, rewritten ˌriːˈraɪt, -s, -ɪŋ, ˌriːˈrəʊt, ˌriːˈrɪtn

Rex reks

Reykjavik ˈreɪkjəviːk [ˈrek-, -vɪk]

Reynaldo reɪˈnældəʊ

reynard, -s ˈrenəd [ˈreɪ-, -nɑːd], -z

Reynard ˈrenəd, ˈrenɑːd, ˈreɪnɑːd

Reynold, -s ˈrenld [-nəld], -z

Rhadamanthus ˌrædəˈmænθəs

Rhae|tia, -tian ˈriːˌʃjə [-ʃɪə, -ʃə], -ʃjən [-ʃən, -ʃn]

Rhaetic ˈriːtɪk

Rhaeto-Roman|ce, -ic ˌriːtəʊrəʊˈmæn|s [-rʊˈm-, -ɪk]

rhapsodic, -al, -ally ræpˈsɒdɪk, -l, -əlɪ

rhapsodiz|e [-is|e], -es, -ing, -ed ˈræpsədaɪz, -ɪz, -ɪŋ, -d

rhapsod|y, -ies ˈræpsəd|ɪ, -ɪz

rhea (R.), -s rɪə [ˈriːə], -z

Rheims riːmz

Rheinallt ˈraɪnælt (Welsh ˈhrəmaɬt)

Rhenish ˈriːnɪʃ [ˈren-]

rheostat, -s ˈrɪəʊstæt, -s

rhesus, -es ˈriːsəs, -ɪz

rhetoric (s.) ˈretərɪk

rhetoric|al, -ally rɪˈtɒrɪk|l [rəˈt-], -əlɪ

rhetorician, -s ˌretəˈrɪʃn [-tɒˈr-], -z

rheum ruːm

rheumatic, -s, -ky ruːˈmætɪk [rʊˈm-], -s, -ɪ

rheumatism ˈruːmətɪzəm [ˈrʊm-]

rheumatoid 'ru:mətɔɪd ['rʊm-]

rheumatolog|y, -ist/s ˌruːmə'tɒlədʒ|ɪ [ˌrʊm-], -ɪst/s

Rhine, -land raɪn, -lænd [-lənd]

rhino, -s 'raɪnəʊ, -z

rhinoceros, -es raɪ'nɒsərəs, -ɪz

rhinolog|ist/s, -y raɪ'nɒlədʒ|ɪst/s, -ɪ

rhinoscope, -s 'raɪnəskəʊp, -s

rhizome, -s 'raɪzəʊm, -z

rho rəʊ

Rhoda 'rəʊdə

Rhode (biblical name) 'rəʊdɪ

Rhode (breed of fowls), -s rəʊd, -z

Rhode Island (state in U.S.A.) ˌrəʊd-'aɪlənd [rəʊ'daɪ-, 'rəʊdˌaɪlənd]
Note.—In U.S.A. the stress is ˌ-'--.

Rhode Island (breed of fowls), -s 'rəʊd-ˌaɪlənd, -z

Rhodes (Greek island, surname) rəʊdz

Rhode|sia, -sian rəʊ'di:|zjə [-zɪə, -ʒə, -ʒɪə, -ʒə, -sjə, -sɪə, -ʃjə, -ʃɪə, -ʃə], -zjən [-zɪən, -ʒjən, -ʒɪən, -ʒn, -sjən, -sɪən, -ʃjən, -ʃɪən, -ʃn]

Rhodian, -s 'rəʊdjən [-dɪən], -z

rhodium 'rəʊdjəm [-dɪəm]

rhododendron, -s ˌrəʊdə'dendrən [ˌrɒd-, -dɪ'd-], -z

rhodomontade = rodomontade

rhomb, -s rɒm, -z

rhomboid, -s 'rɒmbɔɪd, -z

rhombus, -es 'rɒmbəs, -ɪz

Rhondda 'rɒndə ['rɒnðə] (Welsh 'hrɔnða)

Rhone rəʊn

rhotacism 'rəʊtəsɪzəm

rhubarb 'ru:bɑ:b [old-fashioned -bəb]

Rhuddlan 'rɪðlən [-læn] (Welsh 'hrɪðlan)

rhumb, -s rʌm, -z

Rhyl rɪl (Welsh hrɪl)

rhym|e (s. v.), -es, -ing, -ed, -er/s raɪm, -z, -ɪŋ, -d, -ə*/z

rhymester, -s 'raɪmstə*, -z

Rhys (Welsh name) ri:s (Welsh hri:s), (family name of Baron Dynevor) raɪs

rhythm, -s 'rɪðəm ['rɪθəm], -z

rhythmic, -al, -ally 'rɪðmɪk ['rɪθm-], -l, -əlɪ

Riach rɪək ['ri:ək, -əx]

Rialto rɪ'æltəʊ

rib (s. v.), -s, -bing, -bed rɪb, -z, -ɪŋ, -d

ribald (s. adj.), -s; -ry 'rɪbəld, -z; -rɪ
Note.—A special pronunciation 'raɪbɔ:ld has to be used in Browning's 'Pied Piper' (to rhyme with piebald).

riband, -s 'rɪbənd, -z

ribbon, -s 'rɪbən, -z

Ribston, -s 'rɪbstən, -z

Rica 'ri:kə

Riccio 'rɪtʃɪəʊ

rice raɪs

Rice raɪs, ri:s

ricercata, -s ˌrɪtʃɜ:'kɑ:tə [-tʃeə'k-], -z

rich, -es, -er, -est, -ly, -ness rɪtʃ, -ɪz, -ə*, -ɪst, -lɪ, -nɪs [-nəs]

Richard, -s, -son 'rɪtʃəd, -z, -sn

Richelieu 'ri:ʃəljə: ['rɪ-, -lju:] (riʃəljø)

Riches 'rɪtʃɪz

Richey 'rɪtʃɪ

Richmond 'rɪtʃmənd

rick, -s rɪk, -s

Rickard, -s 'rɪkɑ:d, -z

rickets 'rɪkɪts

Rickett 'rɪkɪt

ricket|y, -ier, -iest, -ily, -iness 'rɪkət|ɪ [-ɪt|ɪ], -ɪə*, -ɪɪst, -ɪlɪ [-əlɪ], -ɪnɪs [-ɪnəs]

Rickmansworth 'rɪkmənzwɜ:θ [-wəθ]

rickshaw, -s 'rɪkʃɔ:, -z

Rico 'ri:kəʊ

ricoch|et, -ets, -eting, -eted 'rɪkəʃ|eɪ [-kɒʃ-, -ʃ|et, ˌ--'-], -eɪz [-ets], -eɪɪŋ [-etɪŋ], -eɪd [-etɪd]

rictus 'rɪktəs

rid, -s, -ding rɪd, -z, -ɪŋ

riddance 'rɪdəns

Riddell 'rɪdl, rɪ'del

Ridding 'rɪdɪŋ

ridd|le (s. v.), -les, -ling, -led 'rɪd|l, -lz, -lɪŋ [-lɪŋ], -ld

rid|e, -es, -ing, rode, ridden raɪd, -z, -ɪŋ, rəʊd, 'rɪdn

Rideal rɪ'di:l

Ridealgh 'raɪdældʒ, 'rɪdɪælʃ

Ridehalgh 'raɪdhælʃ, 'rɪdɪhælʃ

rider (R.), -s; -less 'raɪdə*, -z; -lɪs [-ləs, -les]

ridge (R.), -s, -d rɪdʒ, -ɪz, -d

Ridg(e)way 'rɪdʒweɪ

ridicul|e (s. v.), -es, -ing, -ed 'rɪdɪkju:l, -z, -ɪŋ, -d

ridiculous, -ly, -ness rɪ'dɪkjʊləs [rə'd-, -kjəl-], -lɪ, -nɪs [-nəs]

Riding, -s, -hood 'raɪdɪŋ, -z, -hʊd

riding-habit, -s 'raɪdɪŋˌhæbɪt, -s

riding-master, -s 'raɪdɪŋˌmɑːstə*, -z

riding-mistress, -es 'raɪdɪŋˌmɪstrɪs [-trəs], -ɪz

Rid|ley, -path 'rɪd|lɪ, -pɑ:θ

Ridout 'rɪdaʊt

Rienzi rɪ'entsɪ

Rievaulx (abbey in North Yorkshire) 'ri:vəʊ ['ri:vəʊz, 'rɪvəz]
Note.—'ri:vəʊ is the usual local pronunciation.

rife raɪf

riff-raff 'rɪfræf

424

rif|le (*s. v.*), -les, -ling, -led 'raɪf|l, -lz, -lɪŋ [-|ɪŋ], -ld

rifle|man, -men 'raɪfl|mən [-mæn], -mən [-men]

rifle-range, -s 'raɪflreɪndʒ, -ɪz

rifle-shot, -s 'raɪflʃɒt, -s

rift (*s. v.*), -s, -ing, -ed rɪft, -s, -ɪŋ, -ɪd

rig (*s. v.*), -s, -ging, -ged rɪg, -z, -ɪŋ, -d

Riga 'riːgə [*old-fashioned* 'raɪgə]

Rigby 'rɪgbɪ

Rigel (*star*) 'raɪgəl [*rarely* 'raɪdʒəl]

rigger, -s 'rɪgə*, -z

rigging (*s.*), -s 'rɪgɪŋ, -z

right (*s. adj. v. adv.*), -s, -ly, -ness; -ing, -ed raɪt, -s, -lɪ, -nɪs [-nəs]; -ɪŋ, -ɪd

rightabout 'raɪtəbaʊt

righteous, -ly, -ness 'raɪtʃəs [-tjəs], -lɪ, -nɪs [-nəs]

right|ful, -fully, -fulness 'raɪt|fʊl, -fʊlɪ [-fəlɪ], -fʊlnɪs [-nəs]

right-hand (*attributive adj.*) 'raɪthænd

right-handed ,raɪt'hændɪd ['-,--]

rightist, -s 'raɪtɪst, -s

right(h)o ,raɪt'əʊ

Rigi 'riːgɪ

rigid, -ly, -ness 'rɪdʒɪd, -lɪ, -nɪs [-nəs]

rigidity rɪ'dʒɪdɪtɪ [-ɪtɪ]

rigmarole, -s 'rɪgmərəʊl, -z

Rigoletto ,rɪgə'letəʊ [-gəʊ'l-] (rigo-'letto)

rigor (*mortis*) 'raɪgɔː* ['rɪgə*]

rigorous, -ly, -ness 'rɪgərəs, -lɪ, -nɪs [-nəs]

rigour, -s 'rɪgə*, -z

rig-out 'rɪgaʊt [,-'-]

Rigveda ,rɪg'veɪdə

Rikki-Tiki-Tavi 'rɪkɪ,tɪkɪ'tɑːvɪ

ril|le, -es, -ing, -ed raɪl, -z, -ɪŋ, -d

Riley 'raɪlɪ

rilievo ,rɪlɪ'eɪvəʊ

rill, -s rɪl, -z

rim, -s, -less rɪm, -z, -lɪs [-ləs]

Rimbault 'rɪmbəʊlt [*French poet* 'ræmbəʊ] (rɛ̃bo)

rime, -s raɪm, -z

Rimmon 'rɪmən

Rimsky-Korsakov ,rɪmskɪ'kɔːsəkɒv [-ɒf] (,rjimskij'korsəkəf)

Rinaldo rɪ'nældəʊ

rind, -s raɪnd, -z

Rind rɪnd

rinderpest 'rɪndəpest

ring (*s. v.*) (*encircle, put a ring on, etc.*), -s, -ing, -ed rɪŋ, -z, -ɪŋ, -d

ring (*s. v.*) (*sound, etc.*), -s, -ing, rang, rung, ringer/s rɪŋ, -z, -ɪŋ, ræŋ, rʌŋ, 'rɪŋə*/z

ring-dove, -s 'rɪŋdʌv, -z

ring|leader/s, -let/s, -worm 'rɪŋ|-,liːdə*/z, -lɪt/s [-lət/s], -wɜːm

ring-road, -s 'rɪŋrəʊd, -z

Ringshall 'rɪŋʃəl

rink (*s. v.*), -s, -ing, -ed rɪŋk, -s, -ɪŋ, -t [rɪŋt]

rins|e, -es, -ing, -ed rɪns, -ɪz, -ɪŋ, -t

Rio 'riːəʊ ['rɪəʊ]

Rio de Janeiro ,riːəʊdədʒə'nɪərəʊ [,rɪəʊ-, -deɪ-]

Rio Grande (*in North America*) ,riːəʊ-'grændɪ [,rɪəʊ-, -'grænd]

riot (*s. v.*), -s, -ing, -ed, -er/s 'raɪət, -s, -ɪŋ, -ɪd, -ə*/z

riotous, -ly, -ness 'raɪətəs, -lɪ, -nɪs [-nəs]

Riou ['riːuː]

rip, -s, -ping, -ped, -per/s rɪp, -s, -ɪŋ, -t, -ə*/z

riparian raɪ'peərɪən [rɪ'p-]

ripe, -r, -st, -ly, -ness raɪp, -ə*, -ɪst, -lɪ, -nɪs [-nəs]

rip|en, -ens, -ening, -ened 'raɪp|ən, -ənz, -ᵊnɪŋ [-nɪŋ], -ənd

ripieno ,rɪpɪ'eməʊ

Ripley 'rɪplɪ

Ripman 'rɪpmən

Ripon 'rɪpən

ripost(e), -s rɪ'pɒst [-'pəʊst], -s

ripper, -s 'rɪpə*, -z

ripping (*adj.*), -est, -ly 'rɪpɪŋ, -ɪst, -lɪ

ripp|le, -les, -ling, -led 'rɪp|l, -lz, -lɪŋ [-lɪŋ], -ld

ripple-mark, -s 'rɪplmɑːk, -s

ripply 'rɪplɪ [-plɪ]

ripuarian ,rɪpjuː'eərɪən [-pjʊ'eə-]

Rip van Winkle ,rɪpvæn'wɪŋkl

Risboro' [-borough] 'rɪzbərə

ris|e (*s. v.*), -es, -ing, rose, risen raɪz, -ɪz, -ɪŋ, rəʊz, 'rɪzn

riser, -s 'raɪzə*, -z

risibility ,rɪzɪ'bɪlɪtɪ [,raɪz-, -zə-, -lɪt-]

risible 'rɪzɪbl ['raɪz-, -əbl]

rising (*s.*), -s 'raɪzɪŋ, -z

risk (*s. v.*), -s, -ing, -ed rɪsk, -s, -ɪŋ, -t

risk|y, -ier, -iest, -iness 'rɪsk|ɪ, -ɪə* [-jə*], -ɪɪst [-jɪst], -ɪnɪs [-nəs]

risotto, -s rɪ'zɒtəʊ [-'sɒ-], -z

risqué 'riːskeɪ ['rɪs-] (riske)

rissole, -s 'rɪsəʊl [*old-fashioned* 'riːs-], -z

Rita 'riːtə

ritardando, -s ,rɪtɑː'dændəʊ, -z

Ritchie 'rɪtʃɪ

rite, -s raɪt, -s

Ritson 'rɪtsn

ritual, -s 'rɪtʃʊəl [-tʃwəl, -tʃʊl, -tjʊəl, -tjwəl, -tjʊl], -z

rituali|sm, -st/s 'rɪtʃʊəlɪ|zəm [tʃwəl-, -tʃʊl-, -tjʊəl-, -tjwəl-, -tjʊl], -st/s

425

ritualistic ˌrɪtʃʊəˈlɪstɪk [-tʃwəˈl-, -tjʊəˈl-, -tjwəˈl-]

riv|al (s. v.), -als, -alling, -alled ˈraɪv|l, -lz, -lɪŋ [-əlɪŋ], -ld

rivalr|y, -ies ˈraɪvlr|ɪ, -ɪz

riv|e, -es, -ing, -ed, riven raɪv, -z, -ɪŋ, -d, ˈrɪvən

river, -s (R.) ˈrɪvə*, -z

river-bank, -s ˈrɪvəbæŋk [ˌ--ˈ-], -s

river-basin, -s ˈrɪvəˌbeɪsn, -z

river-bed, -s ˈrɪvəbed [ˌ--ˈ-], -z

riverside (R.) ˈrɪvəsaɪd

rivet, -s, -(t)ing, -(t)ed, -(t)er/s ˈrɪvɪt [-vət], -s, -ɪŋ, -ɪd, -ə*/z

Riviera ˌrɪvɪˈeərə

Rivington, -s ˈrɪvɪŋtən, -z

rivulet, -s ˈrɪvjʊlɪt [-let, -lət], -s

rix-dollar, -s ˌrɪksˈdɒlə* [ˈrɪksˌd-], -z

Rizzio ˈrɪtsɪəʊ

roach (R.) rəʊtʃ

road, -s rəʊd, -z

road-block, -s ˈrəʊdblɒk, -s

road-book, -s ˈrəʊdbʊk, -s

road-hog, -s ˈrəʊdhɒg, -z

road-hou|se, -ses ˈrəʊdhaʊ|s, -zɪz

roadmanship ˈrəʊdmənʃɪp

road-mender, -s ˈrəʊdˌmendə*, -z

road-sense ˈrəʊdsens

roadside ˈrəʊdsaɪd

roadstead, -s ˈrəʊdsted, -z

roadster, -s ˈrəʊdstə*, -z

road-test, -s ˈrəʊdtest, -s

roadway, -s ˈrəʊdweɪ, -z

roadworth|y, -iness ˈrəʊdˌwɜːð|ɪ, -ɪnɪs [-ɪnəs]

roam, -s, -ing, -ed rəʊm, -z, -ɪŋ, -d

roan (s. adj.) (R.), -s rəʊn, -z

Roanoke ˌrəʊəˈnəʊk

roar (s. v.), -s, -ing, -ed, -er/s rɔː* [rɔə*], -z, -rɪŋ, -d, -rə*/z

roast (s. v.), -s, -ing, -ed, -er/s rəʊst, -s, -ɪŋ, -ɪd, -ə*/z

roasting-jack, -s ˈrəʊstɪŋdʒæk, -s

rob (R.), -s, -bing, -bed, -ber/s rɒb, -z, -ɪŋ, -d, -ə*/z

Robb rɒb

robber|y, -ies ˈrɒbər|ɪ, -ɪz

Robbins ˈrɒbɪnz

rob|e (s. v.), -es, -ing, -ed rəʊb, -z, -ɪŋ, -d

Robens ˈrəʊbɪnz

Roberson ˈrəʊbəsn, ˈrɒbəsn

Note.—In Roberson's medium the usual pronunciation is ˈrɒb-.

Robert, -s, -son ˈrɒbət, -s, -sn

Roberta rəˈbɜːtə [rɒˈb-, rəʊˈb-]

Robeson ˈrəʊbsn

Robespierre ˈrəʊbzpjeə* [-spjeə*] (robespje:r)

robin, -s ˈrɒbɪn, -z

Robin, -son ˈrɒbɪn, -sn

Robina rɒˈbiːnə [rəʊˈb-]

Robins ˈrəʊbɪnz, ˈrɒbɪnz

Robinson ˈrɒbɪnsən

Roboam rəʊˈbəʊəm

robot, -s ˈrəʊbɒt [ˈrɒb-, -bət], -s

Robotham ˈrəʊbəθəm

robotic rəʊˈbɒtɪk [rɒˈb-]

Rob Roy ˌrɒbˈrɔɪ

Robsart ˈrɒbsɑːt

Robson ˈrɒbsn

robust, -ly, -ness rəʊˈbʌst, -lɪ, -nɪs [-nəs]

Rochdale ˈrɒtʃdeɪl

Roche rəʊtʃ, rəʊʃ, rɒʃ

Rochester ˈrɒtʃɪstə* [-tʃəstə*]

rochet, -s ˈrɒtʃɪt, -s

rock (s. v.) (R.), -s, -ing, -ed, -er/s rɒk, -s, -ɪŋ, -t, -ə*/z

rock-bottom ˌrɒkˈbɒtəm

rock-bound ˈrɒkbaʊnd

Rockefeller ˈrɒkɪfelə* [-kə-]

rocker|y, -ies ˈrɒkər|ɪ, -ɪz

rocket (s. v.), -s, -ing, -ed ˈrɒkɪt, -s, -ɪŋ, -ɪd

rocketry ˈrɒkɪtrɪ

rock-garden, -s ˈrɒkˌgɑːdn, -z

Rockies ˈrɒkɪz

rocking-chair, -s ˈrɒkɪŋtʃeə*, -z

Rockingham ˈrɒkɪŋəm

rocking-horse, -s ˈrɒkɪŋhɔːs, -ɪz

rocking-stone, -s ˈrɒkɪŋstəʊn, -z

rock 'n roll ˌrɒkənˈrəʊl

rock-plant, -s ˈrɒkplɑːnt, -s

rock-rose, -s ˈrɒkrəʊz, -ɪz

rock-salt ˌrɒkˈsɔːlt [-ˈsɒlt, in contrast ˈrɒks-]

rock-salmon ˌrɒkˈsæmən

Rockstro ˈrɒkstrəʊ

rockwork, -s ˈrɒkwɜːk, -s

rock|y, -ier, -iest, -iness ˈrɒk|ɪ, -ɪə*, -ɪɪst, -ɪnɪs [-ɪnəs]

rococo rəʊˈkəʊkəʊ

rod (R.), -s rɒd, -z

rode (from ride) rəʊd

rodent (s. adj.), -s ˈrəʊdənt, -s

rodeo, -s rəʊˈdeɪəʊ [ˈrəʊdɪəʊ], -z

Roderic(k) ˈrɒdərɪk

Rodgers ˈrɒdʒəz

Roding (several places in Essex) ˈrəʊdɪŋ [locally sometimes ˈruːdɪŋ, ˈruːðɪŋ]

Rod|ney, -way ˈrɒd|nɪ, -weɪ

rodomontad|e (s. v.), -es, -ing, -ed ˌrɒdəmɒnˈteɪd [-ˈtɑːd], -z, -ɪŋ, -ɪd

roe (R.), -s rəʊ, -z

roebuck (R.), -s ˈrəʊbʌk, -s

Roedean ˈrəʊdiːn

Roehampton rəʊˈhæmptən

Roentgen, see Röntgen
rogation (R.), -s rəʊˈɡeɪʃn, -z
Roger, -s ˈrɒdʒə* [ˈrəʊdʒə*, esp. Scottish], -z
Roget ˈrɒʒeɪ
Rogozin rəˈɡəʊzɪn [rɒˈg-]
rogue, -s rəʊɡ, -z
roguer|y, -ies ˈrəʊɡər|ɪ, -ɪz
roguish, -ly, -ness ˈrəʊɡɪʃ, -lɪ, -nɪs [-nəs]
roil, -s, -ing, -ed rɔɪl, -z, -ɪŋ, -d
roist|er, -ers, -ering, -ered, -erer/s ˈrɔɪst|ə*, -əz, -ərɪŋ, -əd, -ərə*/z
rok|e, -es, -ing, -ed rəʊk, -s, -ɪŋ, -t
Rokeby ˈrəʊkbɪ
Roker ˈrəʊkə*
Roland ˈrəʊlənd
role, -s rəʊl, -z
Rolf(e) rɒlf, rəʊf
roll, -s, -ing, -ed, -er/s rəʊl, -z, -ɪŋ, -d, -ə*/z
roll-back, -s ˈrəʊlbæk, -s
roll-call, -s ˈrəʊlkɔːl, -z
roller-skat|e (s. v.), -es, -ing, -ed ˈrəʊlə-skeɪt [ˌ-ˈ-], -s, -ɪŋ, -ɪd
roller-towel, -s ˈrəʊlə͵taʊəl [ˌ-ˈ-], -z
Rolleston ˈrəʊlstən
rollick, -s, -ing, -ed ˈrɒlɪk, -s, -ɪŋ, -t
rolling-pin, -s ˈrəʊlɪŋpɪn, -z
rolling-stock, -s ˈrəʊlɪŋstɒk, -s
Rollo ˈrɒləʊ
Rolls rəʊlz
Rolls-Royce, -s ͵rəʊlzˈrɔɪs, -ɪz
roll-top (s.), -s ͵rəʊlˈtɒp, -s
roll-top (attributive adj.) ˈrəʊltɒp
roly-pol|y, -ies ͵rəʊlɪˈpəʊl|ɪ, -ɪz
Romagna rəʊˈmɑːnjə (roˈmaɲɲa)
Romaic rəʊˈmeɪɪk
Roman, -s ˈrəʊmən, -z
romanc|e (s. v.) (R.), -es, -ing, -ed, -er/s rəʊˈmæns [rʊˈm-], -ɪz, -ɪŋ, -t -ə*/z
Romanes (surname) rəʊˈmɑːnɪz (gipsy language) ˈrɒmənes
romanesque ͵rəʊməˈnesk
Romania (Ru-), -n/s ruːˈmeɪnjə [rʊˈm-, -nɪə], -n/z
Romanic rəʊˈmænɪk
romani|sm, -st/s ˈrəʊmənɪ|zəm, -st/s
romanization [-isa-], -s ͵rəʊmənaɪˈzeɪʃn, -z
romaniz|e [-is|e], -es, -ing, -ed ˈrəʊ-mənaɪz, -ɪz, -ɪŋ, -d
Romansch rəʊˈmænʃ
romantic, -ally rəʊˈmæntɪk, -əlɪ
romantici|sm, -st/s rəʊˈmæntɪsɪ|zəm, -st/s
Roman|y, -ies ˈrɒmən|ɪ [ˈrəʊm-], -ɪz
romaunt, -s rəʊˈmɔːnt, -s

Rome rəʊm
Romeike rəʊˈmiːkɪ
Romeo ˈrəʊmɪəʊ [-mjəʊ]
Romford ˈrɒmfəd [old-fashioned ˈrʌm-]
romic (R.) ˈrəʊmɪk
Romish ˈrəʊmɪʃ
Romney, -s ˈrɒmnɪ [ˈrʌm-], -z
Romola ˈrɒmələ
romp (s. v.), -s, -ing, -ed rɒmp, -s, -ɪŋ, -t [rɒmt]
romper, -s ˈrɒmpə*, -z
Romsey ˈrʌmzɪ
Romulus ˈrɒmjʊləs
Ronald, -shay ˈrɒnld, -ʃeɪ
Ronan ˈrəʊnən
rondeau, -s ˈrɒndəʊ, -z
rondel, -s ˈrɒndl, -z
rondo, -s ˈrɒndəʊ, -z
roneo (s. v.), -s, -ing, -ed ˈrəʊnɪəʊ [-njəʊ], -z, -ɪŋ, -d
Roney ˈrəʊnɪ
Rongbuk ˈrɒŋbʊk
Ronson ˈrɒnsən
Rontgen ˈrɒntjən [-tɡən]
Röntgen ˈrɒntjən [ˈrʌnt-, ˈrɜːnt-, -tɡən]
röntgenogram, -s rɒntˈɡenəɡræm [rʌnt-, rɜːnt-, ˈrɒntjənəɡ-, ˈrʌnt-jənəɡ-, ˈrɜːntjənəɡ-], -z
Ronuk ˈrɒnək
rood, -s ruːd, -z
rood-loft, -s ˈruːdlɒft, -s
rood-screen, -s ˈruːdskriːn, -z
roo|f (s.), -fs, -ves ruː|f, -fs, -vz
roof (v.), -s, -ing, -ed ruːf, -s, -ɪŋ, -t
roof-garden, -s ˈruːf͵ɡɑːdn, -z
rook (s. v.), -s, -ing, -ed rʊk, -s, -ɪŋ, -t
rooker|y, -ies ˈrʊkər|ɪ, -ɪz
rookie, -s ˈrʊkɪ, -z
room, -s ruːm [rʊm], -z
Room ruːm
-roomed -ruːmd [-rʊmd]
roomful, -s ˈruːmfʊl [ˈrʊm-], -z
Rooms ruːmz
room|y, -ier, -iest, -ily, -iness ˈruːm|ɪ [ˈrʊm-], -ɪə*, -ɪɪst, -ɪlɪ [-əlɪ], -ɪnɪs [-ɪnəs]
Roosevelt (American surname) ˈrəʊzə-velt [ˈruːsvelt]
  Note.—ˈrəʊzəvelt is the pronunciation used in the families of the late presidents of the U.S.A. In England this name is often pronounced ˈruːsvelt.
roost (s. v.), -s, -ing, -ed, -er/s ruːst, -s -ɪŋ, -ɪd, -ə*/z
root (s. v.) (R.), -s, -ing, -ed; -y ruːt, -s, -ɪŋ, -ɪd; -ɪ
Rootham ˈruːtəm

rop|e (*s. v.*), -es, -ing, -ed rəʊp, -s, -ıŋ, -t
rope-dancer, -s 'rəʊp‚dɑːnsə*, -z
Roper 'rəʊpə*
rope-trick, -s 'rəʊptrık, -s
rope-walker, -s 'rəʊp‚wɔːkə*, -z
Ropner 'rɒpnə*
Roquefort, -s 'rɒkfɔː* (rɔkfɔːr), -z
roquet (*s. v.*), -s, -ing, -ed 'rəʊkı [-keı],
    -z, -ıŋ, -d
Rorke rɔːk
Rosa 'rəʊzə
rosace, -s 'rəʊzeıs, -ız
rosaceous rəʊ'zeıʃəs
Rosalba rəʊ'zælbə
Rosalie 'rəʊzəlı, 'rɒzəlı
Rosalind 'rɒzəlınd
Rosaline (*Shakespearian character*)
    'rɒzəlaın
Rosamond 'rɒzəmənd
rosarium, -s rəʊ'zreərıəm, -z
rosar|y, -ies 'rəʊzər|ı, -ız
Roscius 'rɒʃıəs [-'ʃjəs]
Roscoe 'rɒskəʊ
Roscommon rɒs'kɒmən
rose (R.), -s rəʊz, -ız
rose (*from* rise) rəʊz
roseate 'rəʊzıət [-zjət, -zıt, -zjıt]
Rosebery 'rəʊzbərı
rose-bud, -s 'rəʊzbʌd, -z
rose-bush, -es 'rəʊzbʊʃ, -ız
rose-colour 'rəʊz‚kʌlə*
rose-garden, -s 'rəʊz‚gɑːdn, -z
Rosehaugh 'rəʊzhɔː
rose-lea|f, -ves 'rəʊzliː|f, -vz
rosemar|y (R.), -ies 'rəʊzmər|ı, -ız
Rosencrantz 'rəʊzənkrænts
roseola rəʊ'zıːələ [-'zıə-]
rose-pink ‚rəʊz'pıŋk
rose-red ‚rəʊz'red
rose-tree, -s 'rəʊztriː, -z
Rosetta rəʊ'zetə
rosette, -s rəʊ'zet, -s
rose-water 'rəʊz‚wɔːtə*
rosewood 'rəʊzwʊd
Rosherville 'rɒʃəvıl
Rosicrucian, -s ‚rəʊzı'kruːʃjən [‚rɒz-,
    -ʃıən, -ʃn], -z
Rosier 'rəʊ‚zıə* [-zıə*, -zjə*]
rosin 'rɒzın
Rosina rəʊ'zıːnə
Roslin 'rɒzlın
Ross rɒs
Rossall 'rɒsəl
Rosse, -r rɒs, -ə*
Rossetti (*English surname*) rɒ'setı [rə's-]
Rossini rɒ'sıːnı [rə's-, -niː] (ros'si:ni)
Rosslare 'rɒsleə*, rɒs'leə*
Rosslyn 'rɒslın

Ross-shire 'rɒsʃə* ['rɒʃʃə*, -‚ʃıə*]
roster, -s 'rəʊstə* ['rɒs-], -z
Rostrevor rɒs'trevə*
rostrum, -s 'rɒstrəm, -z
ros|y (R.), -ier, -iest, -ily, -iness 'rəʊz|ı,
    -ıə* [-jə*], -ııst [-jıst], -ılı [-əlı], -ınıs
    [-nəs]
Rosyth rɒ'saıθ [rə's-]
rot (*s. v.*), -s, -ting, -ted, -ter/s rɒt, -s,
    -ıŋ, -ıd, -ə*/z
rota, -s 'rəʊtə, -z
rotar|y (*s. adj.*), -ies 'rəʊtər|ı, -ız
rotatable rəʊ'teıtəbl
rotat|e, -es, -ing, -ed, -or/s rəʊ'teıt, -s,
    -ıŋ, -ıd, -ə*/z
rotation, -s rəʊ'teıʃn, -z
rotatory 'rəʊtətərı [rəʊ'teıtərı]
rote rəʊt
Rothamsted 'rɒθəmsted
Rothenstein (*English surname*) 'rəʊθən-
    staın, 'rəʊtən-, 'rɒθən-
Rothera 'rɒθərə
Rother|ham, -hithe 'rɒðə|rəm, -haıð
Rothermere 'rɒðə‚mıə*
Rotherston 'rɒðəstən
Rotherwick 'rɒðərık, -ðəwık
Rothes 'rɒθıs
Rothesay 'rɒθsı [-seı]
Rothschild (*English surname*) 'rɒθtʃaıld,
    'rɒstʃ-, 'rɒθstʃ-
rotor, -s 'rəʊtə*, -z
rott|en, -enest, -enly, -enness 'rɒt|n,
    -nıst, -nlı, -nnıs [-nnəs]
rottenstone 'rɒtnstəʊn
rotter, -s 'rɒtə*, -z
Rotterdam 'rɒtədæm [‚--'-]
Rottingdean 'rɒtıŋdiːn
rotund, -ity, -ness rəʊ'tʌnd, -ətı [-ıtı],
    -nıs [-nəs]
rotunda (R.), -s rəʊ'tʌndə, -z
rouble, -s 'ruːbl, -z
roué, -s 'ruːeı ['rʊeı], -z
Rouen 'ruːɑ̃ːŋ [-ɔ̃ːŋ, -ɑːŋ, -ɒŋ] (rwɑ̃)
roug|e (*s. v.*), -es, -ing, -ed ruːʒ, -ız, -ıŋ,
    -d
rough (*s. adj. v.*), -s; -er, -est, -ly, -ness;
    -ing, -ed rʌf, -s; -ə*, -ıst, -lı, -nıs
    [-nəs], -ıŋ, -t
roughage 'rʌfıdʒ
rough-cast 'rʌfkɑːst
rough-hew, -s, -ing, -ed, -n ‚rʌf'hjuː,
    -z, -ıŋ [-'hjʊıŋ], -d, -n
roughish 'rʌfıʃ
rough-rider, -s 'rʌf‚raıdə*, -z
rough-shod 'rʌfʃɒd
rough-spoken ‚rʌf'spəʊkən [*also* '-‚--
    when attributive]
Rough Tor (*in Cornwall*) ‚rəʊ'tɔː*

428

roulade, -s ruːˈlɑːd, -z
roulette ruːˈlet [rʊˈl-]
Ro(u)mania, -n/s ruːˈmeɪnjə [rʊˈm-, -nɪə], -n/z
Roumelia ruːˈmiːljə [rʊˈm-, -lɪə]
rounceval, -s ˈraʊnsɪvl, -z
round (s. adj. v. adv. prep.), -s; -er, -est, -ly, -ness, -ish; -ing, -ed raʊnd, -z; -ə*, -ɪst, -lɪ, -nɪs [-aʊnnɪs, -nəs], -ɪʃ; -ɪŋ, -ɪd
roundabout (s. adj.), -s ˈraʊndəbaʊt, -s
roundel, -s ˈraʊndl, -z
roundelay, -s ˈraʊndɪleɪ, -z
rounders ˈraʊndəz
roundhand ˈraʊndhænd
Roundhead, -s ˈraʊndhed, -z
roundish ˈraʊndɪʃ
round-shouldered ˌraʊndˈʃəʊldəd [ˈ-ˌ--]
round-the-clock ˈraʊndðəklɒk [ˌ--ˈ-]
round-up, -s ˈraʊndʌp [ˌ-ˈ-], -s
Rourke rɔːk
Rous raʊs
rous|e, -es, -ing/ly, -ed raʊz, -ɪz, -ɪŋ/lɪ, -d
Rouse raʊs, ruːs
Rousseau ˈruːsəʊ (rusọ)
Roussin ˈrʊsɪn
rout (s. v.), -s, -ing, -ed raʊt, -s, -ɪŋ, -ɪd
route, -s ruːt [in the army also raʊt], -s
route-march, -es ˈruːtmɑːtʃ [ˈraʊt-], -ɪz
Routh raʊθ
routine, -s ruːˈtiːn [rʊˈt-], -z
Routledge ˈraʊtlɪdʒ [-ledʒ], ˈrʌt-
Routley ˈraʊtlɪ
rov|e, -es, -ing, -ed, -er/s rəʊv, -z, -ɪŋ, -d, -ə*/z
Rover, -s ˈrəʊvə*, -z
row (s.) (number of persons or things in a line), -s rəʊ, -z
row (s.) (excursion in a rowing-boat), -s rəʊ, -z
row (s.) (disturbance), -s raʊ, -z
row (s.) (propel boat with oars), -s, -ing, -ed rəʊ, -z, -ɪŋ, -d
row (v.) (quarrel), -s, -ing, -ed raʊ, -z, -ɪŋ, -d
Rowallan rəʊˈælən
rowan (tree), -s ˈraʊən [ˈrəʊən], -z
   Note.—More commonly ˈraʊən in Scotland.
Rowan (surname) ˈrəʊən, ˈraʊən
Rowant (in Oxfordshire) ˈraʊənt
row-boat, -s ˈrəʊbəʊt, -s
row-de-dow [rowdydow], -s ˌraʊdɪˈdaʊ, -z
Rowden ˈraʊdn

rowd|y (s. adj.), -ies, -ier, -iest, -ily, -iness, -yism ˈraʊd|ɪ, -ɪz, -ɪə* [-jə*], -ɪɪst [-jɪst], -ɪlɪ [-əlɪ], -ɪnɪs [-məs], -ɪɪzəm
Rowe rəʊ
Rowed ˈrəʊɪd
rowel, -s ˈraʊəl, -z
Rowell ˈraʊəl, ˈrəʊəl
Rowena rəʊˈiːnə
rower (one who rows a boat), -s ˈrəʊə*, -z
rowing-boat, -s ˈrəʊɪŋbəʊt, -s
Rowland, -s ˈrəʊlənd, -z
Rowles rəʊlz
Rowley ˈrəʊlɪ
rowlock, -s ˈrɒlək [ˈrəʊlɒk, ˈrʌlək], -s
Rowney ˈrəʊnɪ, ˈraʊnɪ
Rowntree ˈraʊntriː
Rowridge ˈraʊrɪdʒ
Rowse raʊs
Rowton ˈraʊtn, ˈrɔːtn
Roxburgh(e) ˈrɒksbərə
Roy rɔɪ
roy|al, -ally ˈrɔɪ|əl, -əlɪ
royali|sm, -st/s ˈrɔɪəlɪ|zəm, -st/s
royalt|y, -ies ˈrɔɪəlt|ɪ, -ɪz
Royce rɔɪs
Royston ˈrɔɪstən
Ruabon ruːˈæbən [rʊˈæ-] (Welsh riuˈabon)
rub (s. v.), -s, -bing, -bed rʌb, -z, -ɪŋ, -d
Rubáiyát ˈruːbaɪjæt [ˌ--ˈ-, -jɑːt]
rubato, -s rʊˈbɑːtəʊ [ruːˈb-], -z
rubber, -s ˈrʌbə*, -z
rubbish, -y ˈrʌbɪʃ, -ɪ
rubb|le, -ly ˈrʌb|l, -lɪ
Rubbra ˈrʌbrə
rubefacient ˌruːbɪˈfeɪʃjənt [-ʃɪənt]
rubella rʊˈbelə [ruːˈb-]
Rubens ˈruːbɪnz [-bənz, -benz]
rubeola rʊˈbiːəʊlə [ruːˈb-, -ˈbɪələ]
Rubicon ˈruːbɪkən [-kɒn]
rubicund ˈruːbɪkənd
rubidium ruːˈbɪdɪəm [rʊˈb-, -djəm]
Rubinstein (pianist) ˈruːbɪnstaɪn
rubric, -s ˈruːbrɪk, -s
rub|y (R.), -ies ˈruːb|ɪ, -ɪz
ruche, -s ruːʃ, -ɪz
ruck rʌk
rucksack, -s ˈrʌksæk [ˈrʊk-], -s
ruction, -s ˈrʌkʃn, -z
rudd (R.), -s rʌd, -z
rudder, -s, -less ˈrʌdə*, -z, -lɪs [-ləs]
Ruddigore ˈrʌdɪgɔː* [-gəʊ*]
rudd|le (s. v.), -les, -ling, -led ˈrʌd|l, -lz, -lɪŋ, -ld
rudd|y, -ier, -iest, -ily, -iness ˈrʌd|ɪ, -ɪə* [-jə*], -ɪɪst [-jɪst], -ɪlɪ [-əlɪ], -ɪnɪs [-məs]

rude, -r, -st, -ly, -ness ruːd, -ə*, -ɪst, -lɪ, -nɪs [-nəs]

Rudge, -s rʌdʒ, -ɪz

rudiment, -s 'ruːdɪmənt, -s

rudiment|al, -ary ˌruːdɪ'ment|l, -ərɪ

Rudmose 'rʌdməʊz

Rudol|f, -ph 'ruːdɒl|f, -f

Rudyard 'rʌdjəd

rue (s. v.), -s, -ing, -d ruː, -z, -ɪŋ ['rʊɪŋ], -d

rue|ful, -fully, -fulness 'ruː|fʊl, -fʊlɪ [-fəlɪ], -fʊlnɪs [-nəs]

ruff (s. v.), -s, -ing, -ed rʌf, -s, -ɪŋ, -t

ruffian, -s, -ly; -ism 'rʌfjən [-fɪən], -z, -lɪ; -ɪzəm

ruff|le (s. v.), -les, -ling, -led 'rʌf|l, -lz, -lɪŋ [-lɪŋ], -ld

Rufus 'ruːfəs

rug, -s rʌg, -z

Rugbeian, -s rʌg'biːən [-'bɪən], -z

Rugby 'rʌgbɪ

Rugeley 'ruːdʒlɪ ['ruːʒlɪ]

rugged, -ly, -ness 'rʌgɪd, -lɪ, -nɪs [-nəs]

rugger 'rʌgə*

Ruhmkorff 'ruːmkɔːf

ruin (s. v.), -s, -ing, -ed 'rʊɪn ['ruːɪn], -z, -ɪŋ, -d

ruination rʊɪ'neɪʃn [ˌruːɪ'n-]

ruinous, -ly, -ness 'rʊɪnəs ['ruːɪn-], -lɪ, -nɪs

Ruislip (in Greater London) 'raɪslɪp ['raɪzl-]

Ruiz ruː'iːθ [rʊ'iːθ]

rul|e (s. v.), -es, -ing, -ed, -er/s ruːl, -z, -ɪŋ, -d, -ə*/z

ruling (s.), -s 'ruːlɪŋ, -z

rum (s. adj.), -mer, -mest rʌm, -ə*, -ɪst

Rumania (Ro-), -n/s ruː'meɪnjə [rʊ'm-, -nɪə], -n/z

rumba, -s 'rʌmbə, -z

rumb|le (s. v.), -les, -ling/s, -led 'rʌmb|l, -lz, -lɪŋ/z, -ld

Rumbold 'rʌmbəʊld

rumbustious rʌm'bʌstɪəs [-tjəs, -tʃəs]

Rumelia ruː'miːljə [rʊ'm-, -lɪə]

Rumford 'rʌmfəd

ruminant (s. adj.), -s 'ruːmɪnənt, -s

ruminat|e, -es, -ing, -ed 'ruːmɪneɪt, -s, -ɪŋ, -ɪd

rumination, -s ˌruːmɪ'neɪʃn, -z

ruminative 'ruːmɪnətɪv [-neɪt-]

rummag|e (s. v.), -es, -ing, -ed 'rʌmɪdʒ, -ɪz, -ɪŋ, -d

rumm|y (s. adj.), -ier, -iest, -ily, -iness 'rʌm|ɪ, -ɪə*, -ɪst, -ɪlɪ [-əlɪ], -ɪnɪs [-ɪnəs]

rumour, -s, -ed 'ruːmə*, -z, -d

rumour-mong|er, -ers, -ering 'ruːmə-ˌmʌŋg|ə*, -əz, -ərɪŋ

rump, -s rʌmp, -s

rump|le, -les, -ling, -led 'rʌmp|l, -lz, -lɪŋ [-lɪŋ], -ld

rumptitum ˌrʌmptɪ'tʌm

rumpus, -es 'rʌmpəs, -ɪz

rum-runner, -s 'rʌmˌrʌnə*, -z

run (s. v.), -s, -ning, ran rʌn, -z, -ɪŋ, ræn

runabout, -s 'rʌnəbaʊt, -s

runagate, -s 'rʌnəgeɪt, -s

runaway (s. adj.), -s 'rʌnəweɪ, -z

Runciman 'rʌnsɪmən

Runcorn 'rʌŋkɔːn

run-down, -s 'rʌnˌdaʊn, -z

rune (R.), -s ruːn, -z

rung (s.), -s rʌŋ, -z

rung (from ring) rʌŋ

runic (R.) 'ruːnɪk

runnel, -s 'rʌnl, -z

runner, -s 'rʌnə*, -z

runner-up, runners-up ˌrʌnər'ʌp, ˌrʌnəz'ʌp

running-board, -s 'rʌnɪŋbɔːd [-bɔəd], -z

Runnymede 'rʌnɪmiːd

runt, -s rʌnt, -s

Runton 'rʌntən

runway, -s 'rʌnweɪ, -z

Runyon 'rʌnjən

rupee, -s ruː'piː [rʊ'p-], -z

Rupert 'ruːpət

rupt|ure (s. v.), -ures, -uring, -ured 'rʌptʃ|ə*, -əz, -ərɪŋ, -əd

rur|al, -ally 'rʊər|əl, -əlɪ

ruridecanal ˌrʊərɪdɪ'keɪnl [-'dekənl]

Ruritania ˌrʊərɪ'teɪnjə [-nɪə]

ruse, -s ruːz, -ɪz

rusé 'ruːzeɪ (ryze)

rush (s. v.), -es, -ing, -ed, -er/s rʌʃ, -ɪz, -ɪŋ, -t, -ə*/z

Rushforth 'rʌʃfɔːθ

rush-hour, -s 'rʌʃˌaʊə*, -z

rush|light/s, -like 'rʌʃ|laɪt/s, -laɪk

Rushmere 'rʌʃˌmɪə*

Rusholme (near Manchester) 'rʌʃəm ['rʌʃhəʊm]

Rushton 'rʌʃtən

Rushworth 'rʌʃwɜːθ

rushy 'rʌʃɪ

rusk (R.), -s rʌsk, -s

Ruskin 'rʌskɪn

Rusper 'rʌspə*

Russell 'rʌsl

russet (s. adj.), -s, -y 'rʌsɪt, -s, -ɪ

Russi|a, -an/s 'rʌʃ|ə, -n/z

russianism, -s 'rʌʃənɪzəm [-ʃn̩-], -z

russianiz|e [-is|e], -es, -ing, -ed 'rʌʃənaɪz [-ʃn̩aɪz], -ɪz, -ɪŋ, -d

430

rust (s. v.), -s, -ing, -ed rʌst, -s, -ɪŋ, -ɪd
rustic (s. adj.), -s, -ally 'rʌstɪk, -s, -əlɪ
rusticat|e, -es, -ing, -ed 'rʌstɪkeɪt, -s, -ɪŋ, -ɪd
rustication ˌrʌstɪ'keɪʃn
rusticity rʌ'stɪsətɪ [-ɪtɪ]
rust|le (s. v.), -les, -ling, -led 'rʌs|l, -lz, -lɪŋ [-lɪŋ], -ld
Rustum 'rʌstəm
rust|y, -ier, -iest, -iness 'rʌst|ɪ, -ɪə* [-jə*], -ɪɪst [-jɪst], -ɪnɪs [-məs]
Ruswarp (near Whitby) 'rʌsəp [-zəp, -zwɔːp]
rut, -s, -ted rʌt, -s, -ɪd
Rutgers 'rʌtgəz
ruth (R.) ruːθ
Ruthenian, -s ruːˈθiːnjən [ruˈθ-, -nɪən], -z
Ruther|ford, -glen 'rʌðə|fəd, -glen
Ruthin 'rɪðɪn ['ruːθɪn] (Welsh 'hrɪθɪn)
ruthless, -ly, -ness 'ruːθlɪs [-ləs], -lɪ, -nɪs [-nəs]
Ruthrieston 'rʌðrɪstən

Ruthven (personal name) 'ruːθvən, 'rɪvən, (place in Tayside Region) 'rɪvən, (place in Grampian Region, loch in Highland Region) 'rʌθvən
Note.—Baron Ruthven is 'rɪvən.
Ruthwell 'rʌθwəl [locally 'rɪðl]
Rutland, -shire 'rʌtlənd, -ʃə* [-ˌʃɪə*]
Rutter 'rʌtə*
rutt|y, -ier, -iest, -iness 'rʌt|ɪ, -ɪə*, -ɪɪst, -ɪnɪs [-məs]
Ruy Lopez ˌruːɪ'ləʊpez
Ruysdael 'raɪzdɑːl
Ruyter 'raɪtə*
Rwanda rʊ'ændə [ruː'æ-, 'rwændə]
Ryan 'raɪən
Ryde raɪd
rye (R.), -grass raɪ, -grɑːs
Ryle raɪl
Rylstone 'rɪlstən [-stəʊn]
Ryman 'raɪmən
ryot, -s 'raɪət, -s
Ryswick 'rɪzwɪk
Ryvita raɪ'viːtə

S

S (*the letter*), **-'s** es, -ız
Saab (*car*) sɑːb
Saba (*in Arabia*) 'sɑːbə, (*in West Indies*) 'sæbə
Sabaean sə'biːən [sæ'b-, -'bıən]
Sabaoth sæ'beɪɑθ [sə'b-, 'sæbeɪɑθ, -əθ]
sabbatarian, -s, -ism ˌsæbə'teərɪən, -z, -ızəm
Sabbath, -s 'sæbəθ, -s
sabbatical sə'bætɪkl
Sabin (*surname*) 'seɪbɪn, 'sæbɪn
Sabine (*Italian people*), **-s** 'sæbaɪn, -z
Sabine (*surname*) 'sæbaɪn, 'sæbɪn, 'seɪbɪn
Sabine (*river, lake, pass*) sə'biːn [sæ'b-]
sable (*s. adj.*), **-s** 'seɪbl, -z
sabot, -s 'sæbəʊ, -z
sabotag|e (*s. v.*), **-es, -ing, -ed** 'sæbətɑːʒ [-tɑːdʒ], -ız, -ıŋ, -d
saboteur, -s ˌsæbə'tɜː* ['---], -z
sab|re (*s. v.*), **-res, -ring, -red** 'seɪb|ə*, -əz, -ərıŋ, -əd
sabretache, -s 'sæbətæʃ, -ız
sabre-toothed 'seɪbətuːθt [-tuːðd]
sabulous 'sæbjʊləs
sac, -s sæk, -s
saccade, -s sæ'kɑːd, -z
saccharine (*s.*) 'sækərın [-riːn, -raɪn]
saccharine (*adj.*) 'sækəraɪn [-riːn]
sacerdot|al, -ally ˌsæsə'dəʊt|l, -əlı
sachem, -s 'seɪtʃəm [-tʃem], -z
sachet, -s 'sæʃeɪ, -z
Sacheverell sə'ʃevərəl
sack (*s. v.*), **-s, -ing, -ed, -er/s** sæk, -s, -ıŋ, -t, -ə*/z
sackbut, -s 'sækbʌt [-bət], -s
sackful, -s 'sækfʊl, -z
sacking (*s.*) 'sækıŋ
Sackville 'sækvıl
sacral 'seɪkrəl
sacrament, -s 'sækrəmənt [-krım-], -s
sacramental ˌsækrə'mentl [-krı'm-]
Sacramento ˌsækrə'mentəʊ
sacred, -ly, -ness 'seɪkrıd, -lı, -nıs [-nəs]
sacrific|e (*s. v.*), **-es, -ing, -ed** 'sækrıfaɪs, -ız, -ıŋ, -t
sacrifici|al, -ally ˌsækrı'fıʃ|l, -əlı
sacrilege 'sækrılıdʒ [-krə-]

sacrilegious ˌsækrı'lıdʒəs [-krə-, -'lıdʒɪəs, -'lıdʒəs, *rarely* -'liːdʒ-]
sacristan, -s 'sækrıstən, -z
sacrist|y, -ies 'sækrıst|ı, -ız
sacrosanct 'sækrəʊsæŋkt
sad, -der, -dest, -ly, -ness sæd, -ə*, -ıst, -lı, -nıs [-nəs]
sadd|en, -ens, -ening, -ened 'sæd|n, -nz, -nıŋ [-nıŋ], -nd
sadd|le, -les, -ling, -led 'sæd|l, -lz, -lıŋ [-lıŋ], -ld
saddleback (**S.**) 'sædlbæk
saddlebag, -s 'sædlbæg, -z
saddle-horse, -s 'sædlhɔːs, -ız
saddler, -s; -y 'sædlə*, -z; -rı
Sadducee, -s 'sædjʊsiː, -z
Sade sɑːd
Sadie 'seɪdı
sadi|sm, -st/s 'seɪdı|zəm ['sæd-, 'sɑːd-], -st/s
sadistic sə'dıstık [sæ'd-]
Sadleir 'sædlə*
Sadler 'sædlə*
Sadowa 'sɑːdəʊə*
safari, -s sə'fɑːrı, -z
safe (*s. adj.*), **-s; -r, -st, -ly, -ness** seɪf, -s; -ə*, -ıst, -lı, -nıs [-nəs]
safe-conduct, -s ˌseɪf'kɒndʌkt [-dəkt], -s
safe-deposit, -s 'seɪfdı,pɒzıt, -s
safeguard (*s. v.*), **-s, -ing, -ed** 'seɪfgɑːd, -z, -ıŋ, -ıd
safe-keeping ˌseɪf'kiːpıŋ
safety 'seɪftı
safety-bolt, -s 'seɪftıbəʊlt, -s
safety-catch, -es 'seɪftıkætʃ, -ız
safety-curtain, -s 'seɪftı,kɜːtn [-tən, -tın], -z
safety-lamp, -s 'seɪftılæmp, -s
safety-lock, -s 'seɪftılɒk, -s
safety-match, -es 'seɪftımætʃ, -ız
safety-pin, -s 'seɪftıpın, -z
safety-razor, -s 'seɪftı,reɪzə*, -z
safety-valve, -s 'seɪftıvælv, -z
Saffell sə'fel
saffron (**S.**) 'sæfrən
sag (*s. v.*), **-s, -ging, -ged** sæg, -z, -ıŋ, -d
saga, -s 'sɑːgə, -z

432

sagacious, -ly, -ness sə'geɪʃəs, -lɪ, -nɪs [-nəs]

sagacity sə'gæsətɪ [-ɪtɪ]

sage (s. adj.) (S.), -s, -ly, -ness seɪdʒ, -ɪz, -lɪ, -nɪs [-nəs]

sagitt|a, -ae sə'dʒɪt|ə, -iː [-aɪ]

Sagitta (constellation) sə'gɪtə [sə'dʒɪ-]

sagittal 'sædʒɪtl

Sagittarian, -s ‚sædʒɪ'teərɪən, -z

Sagittarius (constellation) ‚sædʒɪ'teərɪəs [‚sægɪ-, -'tɑːrɪəs]

sago 'seɪgəu

Sahara sə'hɑːrə

sahib (S.), -s sɑːb ['sɑːhɪb], -z

said (from say) sed (normal form), səd (occasional weak form)

Said (in Port Said) saɪd [old-fashioned seɪd]

sail (s. v.), -s, -ing/s, -ed, -er/s, -or/s seɪl, -z, -ɪŋ/z, -d, -ə*/z, -ə*/z

sailor|man, -men 'seɪlə|mæn, -men

sailplane, -s 'seɪlpleɪn, -z

sainfoin 'sænfɔɪn ['sem-]

Sainsbury 'seɪnzbərɪ

saint (S.), -s seɪnt (strong form), -s, sənt, sɪnt, snt (weak forms)

St. Abb's snt'æbz [sənt-, sɪnt-]

St. Agnes snt'ægnɪs [sənt-, sɪnt-]

St. Alban, -'s snt'ɔːlbən [sənt-, sɪnt-, -'ɒl-], -z

St. Aldate's (street in Oxford) snt'ɔːl-dɜːts [sənt-, sɪnt-, -'ɒl-, -dɪts, old-fashioned -'əuldz]

St. Ambrose snt'æmbrəuz [sənt-, sɪnt-, -əus]

St. Andrew, -s snt'ændruː [sənt-, sɪnt-, -z

St. Anne snt'æn [sənt-, sɪnt-]

St. Anthony snt'æntənɪ [sənt-, sɪnt-]

St. Asaph snt'æsəf [sənt-, sɪnt-]

St. Augustine sənt ɔː'gʌstɪn [sɪnt-, ‚sent-, ‚seɪnt-, -tə'g-, rarely sənt-'ɔːgəstɪn, snt'ɔːgəstɪn]

St. Austell snt'ɔːstl [sənt-, sɪnt-, locally -'ɔːsl]

St. Bartholomew, -'s sənt bɑː'θɒləmjuː [sɪnt-, -bə'θ-], -z

St. Bees snt'biːz [sənt-, sɪnt-]

St. Bernard, -s snt'bɜːnəd [sənt-, sɪnt-], -z

St. Blaize snt'bleɪz [sənt-, sɪnt-]

St. Blazey snt'bleɪzɪ [sənt-, sɪnt-]

St. Bride's snt'braɪdz [sənt-, sɪnt-]

St. Catherine [-thar-], -'s snt'kæθərɪn [sənt-, sɪnt-, sn̩'k-], -z

St. Cecilia səntsɪ'sɪljə [sɪnt-, -lɪə]

St. Christopher snt'krɪstəfə* [sənt-, sɪnt-, sn̩'k-]

St. Clair (surname) 'sɪŋkleə* ['sɪnk-], (place in U.S.A.) snt'kleə* [sənt-, sɪnt-]

St. Columb snt'kɒləm [sənt-, sɪnt-]

St. David, -'s snt'deɪvɪd [sənt-, sɪnt-], -z

St. Edmunds snt'edməndz [sənt-, sɪnt-]

St. Elian snt'iːljən [sənt-, sɪnt-, -lɪən]

St. Elias səntɪ'laɪəs [sɪnt-, -'laɪæs]

St. Elmo snt'elməu [sənt-, sɪnt-]

St. Francis snt'frɑːnsɪs [sənt-, sɪnt-]

St. Gall snt'gæl [sənt-, sɪnt-, -'gɑːl, -'gɔːl]

St. Galmier sn'gælmɪeɪ [sŋ'g-, sənt'g-, sɪnt'g-, -mjeɪ] (sẽgalmje)

St. George, -'s snt'dʒɔːdʒ [sənt-, sɪnt-], -ɪz

St. Giles, -'s snt'dʒaɪlz [sənt-, sɪnt-], -ɪz

St. Gotthard snt'gɒtəd [sənt-, sɪnt-]

St. Helena (Saint) snt'helɪnə [sənt-, sɪnt-], (island) ‚sentɪ'liːnə [sɪnt-, sənt-, -ə'l-]

St. Helen's snt'helɪnz [sənt-, sɪnt-, -lənz]

St. Helier, -'s snt'heljə* [sənt-, sɪnt-, -lɪə*], -z

St. Ives snt'aɪvz [sənt-, sɪnt-]

St. James, -'s snt'dʒeɪmz [sənt-, sɪnt-], -ɪz

St. Joan snt'dʒəun [sənt-, sɪnt-]

St. John, -'s (Saint, place) snt'dʒɒn [sənt-, sɪnt-], -z, (surname) 'sɪndʒən

St. Joseph snt'dʒəuzɪf [sənt-, sɪnt-, -zəf]

St. Kilda snt'kɪldə [sənt-, sɪnt-]

St. Kitts snt'kɪts [sənt-, sɪnt-]

St. Lawrence snt'lɒrəns [sənt-, sɪnt-]

St. Leger (surname) snt'ledʒə* [sənt-, sɪnt-], 'selɪndʒə*, (race) snt'ledʒə* [sənt-, sɪnt-]

Note.—Most people bearing this name (including the Irish families) pronounce snt'ledʒə* [sənt-, sɪnt-]. But there are members of the Doncaster family who pronounce 'selɪndʒə*.

St. Legers snt'ledʒəz [sənt-, sɪnt-]

St. Leonards snt'lenədz [sənt-, sɪnt-]

St. Levan snt'levən [sənt-, sɪnt-]

saintlike 'seɪntlaɪk

St. Louis (city in U.S.A.) snt'luɪs [sənt-, sɪnt-, -'luːɪs], (places in Canada) -'luɪ [-'luːɪ, -ɪs]

St. Lucia snt'luːʃə [sənt-, sɪnt-, rarely -ʃjə, -ʃɪə, -sjə, -sɪə]

St. Ludger snt'luːdʒə* [sənt-, sɪnt-]

St. Luke snt'luːk [sənt-, sɪnt-]

saintl|y, -ier, -iest, -iness 'seɪntl|ɪ, -ɪə* [-jə*], -ɪɪst [-jɪst], -ɪnɪs [-ɪnəs]

433

St. **Malo** snt'mɑ:ləu [sənt-, sɪnt-]
(sẽmalo)

St. **Margaret, -'s** snt'mɑ:gərɪt [sənt-,
sɪnt-], -s

St. **Mark** snt'mɑ:k [sənt-, sɪnt-]

St. **Martin, -'s** snt'mɑ:tɪn [sənt-, sɪnt-],
-z

St. **Martin's le Grand** snt,mɑ:tɪnzlə-
'grænd [sənt-, sɪnt-]

St. **Mary, -'s** snt'meərɪ [sənt-, sɪnt-], -z

St. **Mary Axe** snt,meərɪ'æks [sənt-, sɪnt-,
old-fashioned ,sɪmərɪ'æks]
Note.—The old form ,sɪmərɪ'æks has
to be used in Gilbert and Sullivan's
opera 'The Sorcerer'.

St. **Marylebone** snt'mærələbən [sənt-,
sɪnt-]
Note.—See also **Marylebone**.

St. **Mary-le-Bow** snt,meərɪlə'bəu [sənt-,
sɪnt-]

St. **Matthew** snt'mæθju: [sənt-, sɪnt-]

St. **Maur** (surname) 'si:mɔ:* [-mɔə*]

St. **Mawes** snt'mɔ:z [sənt-, sɪnt-]

St. **Michael, -'s** snt'maɪkl [sənt-, sɪnt-],
-z

St. **Moritz** snt'mɒrɪts [sənt-, sɪnt-,
,sænmə'rɪts]

St. **Neots** (in Cambridgeshire) snt'ni:ts
[sənt-, sɪnt-, -'ni:əts]

St. **Nicholas** snt'nɪkələs [sənt-, sɪnt-,
-kləs]

St. **Olaves** (in Suffolk) snt'ɒlɪvz [sənt-,
sɪnt-, -ləvz]

St. **Olave's** (hospital in London) snt-
'ɒlɪvz [sənt-, sɪnt-, -ləvz]

St. **Osyth** (in Essex) snt'əuzɪθ [sənt-,
sɪnt-, -'əusɪθ]

St. **Pancras** snt'pæŋkrəs [sənt-, sɪnt-,
sm'pæŋkrəs]

St. **Patrick** snt'pætrɪk [sənt-, sɪnt-]

St. **Paul, -'s** snt'pɔ:l [sənt-, sɪnt-], -z

St. **Peter, -'s, -sburg** snt'pi:tə* [sənt-,
sɪnt-], -z, -zbɜ:g

St. **Regis** snt'ri:dʒɪs [sənt-, sɪnt-]

St. **Ronan** snt'rəunən [sənt-, sɪnt-]

Saint-Saëns sæŋ'sɑ:ŋs [sæŋ-, -'sɑ:ns,
-'sɔ̃:ŋs] (sẽsɑ̃:s)

St. **Salvator's** (college) sntsæl'veɪtəz
[sənt-, sɪnt-]

Saintsbury 'seɪntsbərɪ

St. **Simon** snt'saɪmən [sənt-, sɪnt-]

St. **Thomas, -'s** snt'tɒməs [sənt-, sɪnt-],
-ɪz

St. **Vincent** snt'vɪnsənt [sənt-, sɪnt-]

St. **Vitus, -'s** snt'vaɪtəs [sənt-, sɪnt-], -ɪz

saith (from **say**) seθ [seɪθ]

sake, -s seɪk, -s

saké (Japanese wine) 'sɑ:kɪ

Saki 'sɑ:kɪ

salaam (s. v.), **-s, -ing, -ed** sə'lɑ:m, -z,
-ɪŋ, -d

salacious, -ly, -ness sə'leɪʃəs, -lɪ, -nɪs
[-nəs]

salacity sə'læsətɪ [-ɪtɪ]

salad, -s 'sæləd, -z

Saladin 'sælədɪn

Salamanca ,sælə'mæŋkə

salamander, -s 'sælə,mændə* [-,mɑ:n-],
-z

salami sə'lɑ:mɪ [-mi:]

Salamis 'sæləmɪs

sal-ammoniac ,sælə'məunɪæk [-njæk]

salar|y, -ies, -ied 'sælər|ɪ, -ɪz, -ɪd

Salcombe (in Devon) 'sɔ:lkəm ['sɒl-]

sale (S.), **-s** seɪl, -z

sal(e)ability ,seɪlə'bɪlətɪ [-ɪtɪ]

sal(e)able 'seɪləbl

Salem 'seɪlem [-ləm]

Salesbury 'seɪlzbərɪ

sales|man, -men 'seɪlz|mən, -mən
[-men]

salesmanship 'seɪlzmənʃɪp

salesroom, -s 'seɪlzrum [-ru:m], -z

Salford 'sɔ:lfəd ['sɒl-]

Salian, -s 'seɪlɪən [-lɪən], -z

Salic 'sælɪk

salicional, -s sə'lɪʃənl [-ʃn̩l, -ʃnl, -ʃənəl],
-z

salicylate sæ'lɪsɪleɪt [sə'l-]

salicylic ,sælɪ'sɪlɪk

salient (s. adj.), **-s** 'seɪljənt [-lɪənt], -s

saline (s.), **-s** sə'laɪn, -z

saline (adj.) 'seɪlaɪn ['sæl-, sə'laɪn]

Saline (in Fife) 'sælɪn, (in U.S.A.)
sə'li:n

Salinger 'sælɪndʒə* [-'seɪ-]

salinity sə'lɪnətɪ [-ɪtɪ]

Salisbury 'sɔ:lzbərɪ ['sɒlz-]

saliva sə'laɪvə [sl̩'aɪ-]

salivary 'sælɪvərɪ [sə'laɪvərɪ, sl̩'aɪv-]

sallet, -s 'sælɪt [-lət], -s

sallow (s. adj.), **-s, -y, -ness** 'sæləu, -z,
-ɪ, -nɪs [-nəs]

Sallust 'sæləst

sall|y (s. v.) (S.), **-ies, -ying, -ied** 'sæl|ɪ,
-ɪz, -ɪŋ, -ɪd

sally-lunn, -s ,sælɪ'lʌn, -z

salmi, -s 'sælmɪ [-mi:], -z

salmon 'sæmən

Salmon (surname) 'sæmən, 'sælmən,
'sɑ:mən, (river, etc., in Canada and
U.S.A.) 'sæmən, (biblical name)
'sælmɒn [-mən]

salmonella ,sælmə'nelə

Salome sə'ləumɪ [sl̩'əu-]

salon, -s 'sælɔ̃:ŋ [-lɒn] (salɔ̃), -z

Salonica (*modern town*) sə'lɒnɪkə [*old-fashioned* ˌsælə'niːkə], (*in Greek history*) ˌsælə'naɪkə

saloon, -s sə'luːn [sl̩'uːn], -z

Salop 'sæləp

Salopian, -s sə'ləʊpjən [sl̩'əʊ-, -prən], -z

Salpeter (*English name*) 'sælpiːtə*

salpiglossis ˌsælpɪ'glɒsɪs

Salsette sɔː'l̩set [sɒl-]

salsify 'sælsɪfɪ

salt (*s. adj. v.*) (**S.**), -s; -er, -est, -ly, -ness, -ish; -ing, -ed, -er/s sɔːlt [sɒlt], -s; -ə*, -ɪst, -lɪ, -nɪs [-nəs], -ɪʃ; -ɪŋ, -ɪd, -ə*/z

saltant 'sæltənt ['sɔːl-, -sɒl-]

Saltash 'sɔːltæʃ ['sɒlt-]

saltation sæl'teɪʃn

salt-cellar, -s 'sɔːlt.selə* ['sɒlt-], -z

Salter, -ton 'sɔːltə* ['sɒl-], -tən

Saltfleetby 'sɔːlt.fliːtbɪ ['sɒlt-, *locally also* 'sɒləbɪ]

Salting 'sɔːltɪŋ ['sɒl-]

saltire, -s 'sɔːltaɪə* ['sæl-], -z

Saltmarsh 'sɔːltmɑːʃ ['sɒlt-]

Saltoun 'sɔːltən ['sɒlt-]

saltpetre 'sɔːlt.piːtə* ['sɒlt-, -'--]

saltspoon, -s 'sɔːltspuːn ['sɒlt-], -z

salt|y, -ier, -iest, -iness 'sɔːlt|ɪ ['sɒl-], -ɪə* [-jə*], -ɪɪst [-jɪst], -ɪnɪs [-ɪnəs]

salubrious, -ly, -ness sə'luːbrɪəs [sl̩'u-:, sə'ljuː-], -lɪ, -nɪs [-nəs]

salubrity sə'luːbrətɪ [sl̩'u-:, sə'ljuː-, -ɪtɪ]

Salusbury (*surname*) 'sɔːlzbərɪ

Salut (*in Port Salut*) sə'luː (saly)

Salutaris ˌsælju:'teərɪs [-ljʊ't-, -'tɑːr-]

salutary 'sæljʊtərɪ

salutation, -s ˌsælju:'teɪʃn [-ljʊ't-], -z

salut|e (*s. v.*), -es, -ing, -ed sə'luːt [sl̩'uːt, sə'ljuːt], -s, -ɪŋ, -ɪd

salvable 'sælvəbl

Salvador 'sælvədɔː* [ˌsælvə'dɔː*]

salvag|e (*s. v.*), -es, -ing, -ed 'sælvɪdʒ, -ɪz, -ɪŋ, -d

salvarsan 'sælvəsən [-sæn]

salvation, -s sæl'veɪʃn -z

salvationi|sm, -st/s sæl'veɪʃnɪ|zəm [-ʃənɪ-], -st/s

salv|e (*s. v.*) (*anoint, soothe, etc.*), -es, -ing, -ed sælv [sɑːv], -z, -ɪŋ, -d

salv|e (*save ship, cargo*), -es, -ing, -ed sælv, -z, -ɪŋ, -d

Salve (*Catholic antiphon*), -s 'sælvɪ, -z

salver, -s 'sælvə*, -z

salvia, -s 'sælvɪə [-vjə], -z

Salviati ˌsælvɪ'ɑːtɪ

salvo, -es 'sælvəʊ, -z

sal volatile ˌsælvə'lætəlɪ [-vəʊ'l-, -vʊ'l-, -tlɪ]

Salyut sə'ljuːt ['sæljuːt]

Salzburg 'sæltsbɔːg ['sɑː-l-] ('zaltsburk, -burç)

Sam sæm

Samantha sə'mænθə

Samaria sə'meərɪə [sm̩'eə-]

Samaritan, -s sə'mærɪtən [sm̩'æ-], -z

Samarkand ˌsæmɑː'kænd [-mə'k-]

same, -ness seɪm, -nɪs [-nəs]

samite 'sæmaɪt ['seɪm-]

Sammy 'sæmɪ

samnite, -s 'sæmnaɪt, -s

Samoa, -n/s sə'məʊə [sɑː'm-], -n/z

Samos 'seɪmɒs

Samothrace 'sæməʊθreɪs

Samothracian, -s ˌsæməʊ'θreɪʃjən [-rɪən, -ʃn], -z

samovar, -s ˌsæməʊ'vɑː* ['---] (səma'var), -z

Samoyed, -s (*people*) ˌsæmɔɪ'ed, (*dog*) sə'mɔɪed, -z

sampan, -s 'sæmpæn, -z

samphire 'sæmfaɪə*

samp|le (*s. v.*), -les, -ling, -led 'sɑːmp|l, -lz, -lɪŋ [-l̩ɪŋ], -ld

sampler, -s 'sɑːmplə*, -z

Sampson 'sæmpsn

Samson 'sæmsn [-mps-]

Samuda sə'mjuːdə

Samuel, -s 'sæmjʊəl [-mjwəl, -mjʊl], -z

samurai, -s 'sæmʊraɪ [-mjʊ-], -z

sanatorium, -s ˌsænə'tɔːrɪəm, -z

sanatory 'sænətərɪ

Sancho Panza ˌsæntʃəʊ'pænzə [-kəʊ-]

sanctification ˌsæŋktɪfɪ'keɪʃn

sancti|fy, -fies, -fying, -fied 'sæŋktɪ|faɪ, -faɪz, -faɪɪŋ, -faɪd

sanctimonious, -ly, -ness ˌsæŋktɪ'məʊnjəs [-nɪəs], -lɪ, -nɪs [-nəs]

sancti|on (*s. v.*), -ons, -oning, -oned 'sæŋkʃ|n, -nz, -ṇɪŋ [-ənɪŋ], -nd

sanctity 'sæŋktətɪ [-ɪtɪ]

sanctuar|y, -ies 'sæŋktjʊər|ɪ [-tjwər-, -tjʊr-, -tʃʊərɪ, -tʃwərɪ, -tʃərɪ], -ɪz

sanctum, -s 'sæŋktəm, -z

Sanctus, -es 'sæŋktəs, -ɪz

sand sænd

sandal, -s; -wood 'sændl, -z; -wʊd

Sandbach 'sændbætʃ

sandbag, -s 'sændbæg, -z

sandbank, -s 'sændbæŋk, -s

sandboy, -s 'sændbɔɪ, -z

sanderling, -s 'sændəlɪŋ, -z

Sander|s, -son 'sɑːndə|z, -sn

Sanderstead 'sɑːndəsted [-stɪd]

sandfl|y, -ies 'sændfl|aɪ, -aɪz

Sand|ford, -gate 'sæn|fəd, -gɪt [-geɪt]

435

sandhi 'sændhi: ['sʌn-, -di:] (*Hindi* səndhi)
sandhopper, -s 'sænd,hɒpə*, -z
Sandhurst 'sændhə:st
Sandling 'sændlɪŋ
sand|man, -men 'sænd|mæn, -men
San Domingo ,sændə'mɪŋgəʊ [-dəʊ'm-, -dɒ'm-]
Sandown 'sændaʊn
sand-pap|er (*s. v.*), -ers, -ering, -ered 'sænd,peɪp|ə*, -əz, -ərɪŋ, -əd
sandpiper, -s 'sænd,paɪpə*, -z
Sandra 'sændrə ['sɑ:n-]
Sandringham 'sændrɪŋəm
sandstone 'sændstəʊn
sandstorm, -s 'sændstɔ:m, -z
sandwi|ch (*s. v.*), -ches, -ching, -ched 'sænwɪ|dʒ [-tʃ], -dʒɪz [-tʃɪz], -dʒɪŋ [-tʃɪŋ], -dʒd [-tʃt]
  Note.—Some people use -tʃ *in the uninflected form and* -dʒ- *in the inflected forms of this word.*
Sandwich (*in Kent*) 'sænwɪtʃ [-ndw-, -wɪdʒ, *old-fashioned* 'sænɪdʒ]
sandwich|man, -men 'sænwɪdʒ|mæn [-ɪtʃ-], -men
sand|y (S.), -ier, -iest, -iness 'sænd|ɪ, -ɪə* [-jə*], -ɪɪst [-jɪst], -ɪnɪs [-məs]
Sandys sændz
sane, -r, -st, -ly, -ness seɪn, -ə*, -ɪst, -lɪ, -nɪs [-nəs]
Sanford 'sænfəd
sanforiz|e [-is|e], -es, -ing, -ed 'sænfəraɪz, -ɪz, -ɪŋ, -d
San Francisco ,sænfrən'sɪskəʊ
sang (*from* sing) sæŋ
Sanger 'sæŋgə*, 'sæŋə*
sang-froid ,sɑ̃:ŋ'frwɑ: [,sɔ̃:ŋ-, ,sɑ:ŋ-, ,sɒŋ-, ,sæŋ-, -'frwɔ:] (sɑ̃frwɑ)
sanguinar|y, -ily, -iness 'sæŋgwɪnər|ɪ, -əlɪ [-ɪlɪ], -ɪnɪs [-məs]
sanguine, -ly, -ness 'sæŋgwɪn, -lɪ, -rɪs [-nəs]
sanguineous sæŋ'gwɪnɪəs [-njəs]
Sanhedri|m, -n 'sænɪdrɪ|m [-ned-, -nəd-, *Jewish pronunciation* sæn'hed-], -n
sanitar|y, -ily, -iness 'sænɪtər|ɪ, -əlɪ [-ɪlɪ], -ɪnɪs [-məs]
sanitation ,sænɪ'teɪʃn
sanity 'sænɪtɪ [-ɪtɪ]
sank (*from* sink) sæŋk
Sankey 'sæŋkɪ
San Marino ,sænmə'ri:nəʊ
Sanquhar 'sæŋkə*
San Remo ,sæn'reɪməʊ [-'ri:m-]
sans (*English word*) sænz, (*in French phrases*) sɑ̃:ŋ [sɔ̃:ŋ] (sɑ̃)
Sanscrit, *see* Sanskrit

sanserif ,sæn'serɪf
Sanskrit 'sænskrɪt
sanskritic sæn'skrɪtɪk
sanskritiz|e [-is|e], -es, -ing, -ed 'sænskrɪtaɪz, -ɪz, -ɪŋ, -d
Santa Claus ,sæntə'klɔ:z ['---]
Santa Cruz ,sæntə'kru:z
Santa Fé ,sæntə'feɪ
Santander ,sæntən'deə* [,sæntæn'deə*, sæn'tændə*] (santan'der)
Santayana ,sæntə'jɑ:nə
Santiago ,sæntɪ'ɑ:gəʊ
Santley 'sæntlɪ
Saône səʊn (so:n)
sap (*s. v.*), -s, -ping, -ped, -per/s sæp, -s, -ɪŋ, -t, -ə*/z
Sapele (*place in Nigeria*) 'sæpɪlɪ, (*mahogany from that district*) sə'pi:lɪ
sapien|ce, -t/ly 'seɪpjən|s [-pɪən-], -t/lɪ
Sapir (*American linguist*) sə'pɪə*
sapless 'sæplɪs [-ləs]
sapling, -s 'sæplɪŋ, -z
saponaceous ,sæpəʊ'neɪʃəs
sapper, -s 'sæpə*, -z
Sapphic, -s 'sæfɪk, -s
Sapphira sə'faɪərə [sæ'f-]
sapphire, -s 'sæfaɪə*, -z
Sappho 'sæfəʊ
sapp|y, -iness 'sæp|ɪ, -ɪnɪs [-məs]
Sapt sæpt
saraband, -s 'særəbænd, -z
Saracen, -s 'særəsn [-sɪn, -sen], -z
Saracenic ,særə'senɪk
Saragossa ,særə'gɒsə
Sarah 'seərə
sarai (*palace*), -s sə'raɪ [sɑ:'raɪ], -z
Sarai (*wife of Abram*) 'seəreɪaɪ [-raɪ]
Sarajevo ,særə'jeɪvəʊ
Sarasate ,særə'sɑ:tɪ
Saratoga ,særə'təʊgə
Sarawak sə'rɑ:wək [-wæk, -wə, ,særə'wæk]
  Note.—Those who have lived in Sarawak pronounce sə'rɑ:wək *or* sə'rɑ:wə.
sarcasm, -s 'sɑ:kæzəm, -z
sarcastic, -ally sɑ:'kæstɪk, -əlɪ
sarcoma, -s, -ta sɑ:'kəʊmə, -z, -tə
sarcopha|gus, -guses, -gi sɑ:'kɒfə|gəs, -gəsɪz, -gaɪ [-dʒaɪ]
Sardanapalus ,sɑ:də'næpələs [-nə-'pɑ:ləs]
sardine (*fish*), -s sɑ:'di:n ['--], -z
sardine (*stone*) 'sɑ:daɪn
Sardinia, -n/s sɑ:'dɪnjə [-nɪə], -n/z
Sardis 'sɑ:dɪs
sardius, -es 'sɑ:dɪəs [-djəs], -ɪz
sardonic, -ally sɑ:'dɒnɪk, -əlɪ

sardonyx, -es 'sɑːdənɪks ['sɑːdˌɒn-, -ˈ--], -ɪz

Sarepta səˈreptə

Sargant 'sɑːdʒənt

sargasso (S.), -(e)s sɑːˈgæsəʊ, -z

Sargeant 'sɑːdʒənt

Sargent, -s 'sɑːdʒənt, -s

sari, -s 'sɑːrɪ [-riː] (Hindi saɽi), -z

Sark sɑːk

Sarma|tia, -tian-s sɑːˈmeɪ|ʃjə [-ʃɪə, -ʃə], -ʃjən/z [-ʃɪən/z, -ʃn/z]

sarong, -s səˈrɒŋ ['sɑːr-, 'sær-], -z

Saroyan səˈrɔɪən

sarsaparilla ˌsɑːsəpəˈrɪlə

sarsenet 'sɑːsnɪt [-net]

Sartor 'sɑːtɔː*

sartorial sɑːˈtɔːrɪəl

Sarum 'seərəm

sash, -es sæʃ, -ɪz

Saskatchewan səsˈkætʃɪwən [sæs-, -wɒn]

sassafras, -es 'sæsəfræs, -ɪz

Sassanian sæˈseɪnjən [-nɪən]

Sassenach, -s 'sæsənæk [-nək, -nəx], -s

Sassoon səˈsuːn

sat (from sit) sæt

Satan 'seɪtən [old-fashioned 'sæt-]

satanic, -ally səˈtænɪk [seɪˈt-], -əlɪ

satchel, -s 'sætʃəl, -z

sat|e, -es, -ing, -ed seɪt, -s, -ɪŋ, -ɪd

sateen, -s sæˈtiːn [səˈt-], -z

satellite, -s 'sætəlaɪt [-tɪl-, -tl-], -s

satiable 'seɪʃjəbl [-ʃɪə-, -ʃə-]

satiat|e, -es, -ing, -ed 'seɪʃɪeɪt [-ʃjeɪt], -s, -ɪŋ, -ɪd

satiation ˌseɪʃɪˈeɪʃn

satiety səˈtaɪətɪ [-aɪtɪ, 'seɪʃjətɪ, 'seɪʃɪətɪ]

satin, -s, -y 'sætɪn, -z, -ɪ

satinette ˌsætɪˈnet

satin-wood 'sætɪnwʊd

satire, -s 'sætaɪə*, -z

satiric|al, -ally, -alness səˈtɪrək|l [-rɪ-], -əlɪ, -lnɪs [-nəs]

satirist, -s 'sætərɪst [-tɪr-], -s

satiriz|e [-is|e], -es, -ing, -ed 'sætəraɪz [-tɪr-], -ɪz, -ɪŋ, -d

satisfaction ˌsætɪsˈfækʃn

satisfactor|y, -ily, -iness ˌsætɪsˈfæktər|ɪ, -əlɪ [-ɪlɪ], -ɪnɪs [-nəs]

satis|fy, -fies, -fying, -fied 'sætɪs|faɪ, -faɪz, -faɪɪŋ, -faɪd

Satow 'sɑːtəʊ

satrap, -s; -y, -ies 'sætrəp [-træp], -s; -ɪ, -ɪz

Satsuma ˈsætˈsuːmə ['sætsʊmə]

saturat|e, -es, -ing, -ed 'sætʃəreɪt [-tʃʊr-, -tjʊr-], -s, -ɪŋ, -ɪd

saturation ˌsætʃəˈreɪʃn [-tʃʊˈr-, -tjʊˈr-]

Saturday, -s 'sætədɪ [-deɪ], -z

Saturn 'sætən [-tɜːn]

saturnalia (S.) ˌsætəˈneɪljə [-tɜːˈn-, -lɪə]

saturnian sæˈtɜːnjən [səˈt-, -nɪən]

saturnine 'sætənaɪn

satyr, -s 'sætə*, -z

satyric səˈtɪrɪk

sauce, -s sɔːs, -ɪz

sauce-boat, -s 'sɔːsbəʊt, -s

saucepan, -s 'sɔːspən, -z

saucer, -s 'sɔːsə*, -z

sauce-tureen, -s 'sɔːstəˌriːn [-tʊˌr-, -tjʊˌr-], -z

Sauchiehall ˌsɔːkɪˈhɔːl [ˌsɒk-, 'ˈ---] (Scottish ˌsɒxiˈhɔl)

sauc|y, -ier, -iest, -ily, -iness 'sɔːs|ɪ, -ɪə* [-jə*], -ɪɪst [-jɪst], -ɪlɪ [-əlɪ], -ɪnɪs [-nəs]

Saudi Arabia ˌsaʊdɪəˈreɪbɪə [ˌsɔː-, -bjə]

sauerkraut 'saʊəkraʊt ('zauərkraut)

Saul sɔːl

Sault St. Marie (in Ontario) ˌsuːseɪntməˈriː

sauna 'sɔːnə ['saʊnə]

Saunder|s, -son 'sɔːndə|z, 'sɑːndə|z, -sn

saunt|er, -ers, -ering, -ered 'sɔːnt|ə*, -əz, -ərɪŋ, -əd

saurian, -s 'sɔːrɪən, -z

sausage, -s 'sɒsɪdʒ, -ɪz

Sausmarez 'sɒmərɪz [-rez]

sauté, -s 'səʊteɪ, -z

Sauterne, -s səʊˈtɜːn [-ˈteən], -z

Sauvage (English surname) 'sævɪdʒ, səʊˈvaːʒ

savage (s. adj.) (S.), -s, -st, -ly, -ness -ry 'sævɪdʒ, -ɪz, -ɪst, -lɪ, -nɪs [-nəs]; -ərɪ

savanna(h) (S.), -s səˈvænə, -z

savant, -s 'sævənt, -s

sav|e (s. v. prep. conj.), -es, -ing, -ed seɪv, -z, -ɪŋ, -d

saveloy, -s ˌsævəˈlɔɪ ['sævəlɔɪ, -vɪ-], -z

Savels (surname) 'sævəlz

Savernake 'sævənæk

Savile 'sævɪl [-vl]

saving (s. adj. prep.), -s 'seɪvɪŋ, -z

saviour (S.), -s 'seɪvjə*, -z

savoir faire ˌsævwaːˈfeə* [-vwɔː-] (savwarfeːr)

Savonarola ˌsævənəˈrəʊlə [-vnə-]

savory (S.) 'seɪvərɪ

sav|our (s. v.), -ours, -ouring, -oured; -ourless 'seɪv|ə*, -əz, -ərɪŋ, -əd; -əlɪs [-ləs]

savour|y (s. adj.), -ies, -ily, -iness 'seɪvər|ɪ, -ɪz, -əlɪ [-ɪlɪ], -ɪnɪs [-nəs]

savoy (S.), -s səˈvɔɪ, -z

Savoyard, -s səˈvɔɪɑːd [ˌsævɔɪˈɑːd], -z

437

savvy 'sævɪ

saw (s. v.), -s, -ing, -ed, -n sɔː, -z, -ɪŋ, -d, -n

saw (from see) sɔː

sawbones, -es 'sɔːbəʊnz, -ɪz

Sawbridgeworth 'sɔːbrɪdʒwɜːθ

sawder 'sɔːdə*

sawdust 'sɔːdʌst

sawfish 'sɔːfɪʃ

Sawney, -s 'sɔːnɪ, -z

sawyer (S.), -s 'sɔːjə*, -z

Saxe - Coburg - Gotha (')sæks,kəʊbɜːg-'gəʊθə [-'gəʊtə]

saxhorn, -s 'sækshɔːn, -z

saxifrage, -s 'sæksɪfrɪdʒ [-freɪdʒ, -freɪʒ], -ɪz

Saxon, -s 'sæksn, -z

Saxone (shoe company) sæk'səʊn [also 'sæksəʊn when attributive]

Saxony 'sæksnɪ [-sənɪ, -snɪ]

saxophone, -s 'sæksəfəʊn, -z

saxophonist, -s sæk'sɒfənɪst ['sæksəfəʊnɪst], -s

Note.—Professional saxophone players use the first pronunciation.

say (s. v.); says; saying/s; said seɪ; sez (normal form), səz (occasional weak form); 'seɪɪŋ/z; sed (normal form), səd (occasional weak form)

Sayce seɪs

Saye and Sele ,seɪən'siːl

Sayer, -s 'seɪə*, -z

'sblood zblʌd

scab, -s, -by, -biness skæb, -z, -ɪ, -ɪnɪs [-məs]

scabbard, -s 'skæbəd, -z

scabies 'skeɪbɪːz [-bjiːz, -biːz]

scabious, -es 'skeɪbjəs [-brəs], -ɪz

scabrous 'skeɪbrəs

Scafell ,skɔː'fel [also 'skɔːfel, according to sentence-stress]

scaffold, -s 'skæfəld [-fəʊld], -z

scaffolding, -s 'skæfəldɪŋ, -z

Scala 'skɑːlə

scalable 'skeɪləbl

scald (s. v.), -s, -ing, ed skɔːld, -z, -ɪŋ, -ɪd

scal|e (s. v.), -es, -ing, -ed skeɪl, -z, -ɪŋ, -d

scalene 'skeɪliːn [skeɪ'liːn, skæ'liːn]

Scaliger 'skælɪdʒə*

scallion, -s 'skæljən [-lɪən], -z

scallop (s. v.), -s, -ing, -ed 'skɒləp, -s, -ɪŋ, -t

scallop-shell, -s 'skɒləpʃel, -z

scallywag, -s 'skælɪwæg, -z

scalp (s. v.), -s, -ing, -ed skælp, -s, -ɪŋ, -t

scalpel, -s 'skælpəl, -z

scal|y, -ier, -iest, -iness 'skeɪl|ɪ, -ɪə* [-jə*], -ɪɪst [-jɪst], -ɪnɪs [-məs]

Scammell 'skæməl

scamp (s. v.), -s, -ing, -ed skæmp, -s, -ɪŋ, -t [skæmt]

scamp|er (s. v.), -ers, -ering, -ered 'skæmp|ə*, -əz, -ərɪŋ, -əd

scampi 'skæmpɪ

scan, -s, -ning, -ned skæn, -z, -ɪŋ, -d

scandal, -s 'skændl, -z

scandalization [-isa-] ,skændəlaɪ'zeɪʃn [-dʃaɪ-]

scandaliz|e [-is|e], -es, -ing, -ed 'skændəlaɪz [-dʃaɪz], -ɪz, -ɪŋ, -d

scandalmong|er, -ers, -ering 'skændl-,mʌŋg|ə*, -əz, -ərɪŋ

scandalous, -ly, -ness 'skændələs [-dʃəs], -lɪ, -nɪs [-nəs]

scandent 'skændənt

Scandinavia, -n/s ,skændɪ'neɪvjə [-vɪə], -n/z

Scan|lan, -lon 'skæn|lən, -lən

scansion, -s 'skænʃn, -z

scant, -ly skænt, -lɪ

scant|y, -ier, -iest, -ily, -iness 'skænt|ɪ, -ɪə* [-jə*], -ɪɪst [-jɪst], -ɪlɪ [-əlɪ], -ɪnɪs [-məs]

Scapa Flow ,skæpə'fləʊ

scape, -s; -goat/s, -grace/s skeɪp, -s; -gəʊt/s, -greɪs/ɪz

scapul|a, -as, -ae, -ar 'skæpjʊl|ə, -əz, -iː, -ə*

scar (s. v.) (S.), -s, -ring, -red skɑː*, -z, -rɪŋ, -d

scarab, -s 'skærəb, -z

scarab|aeus, -aeuses, -aei ,skærə'b|iːəs [-'brəs], -iːəsɪz [-ɪəsɪz], -iːaɪ

scaramouch, -es 'skærəmuːtʃ [-muːʃ, -maʊtʃ], -ɪz

Scarborough [-boro'] 'skɑːbrə [-bərə]

Scarbrough 'skɑːbrə

scarc|e, -er, -est, -ely, -eness; -ity skeəs, -ə*, -ɪst, -lɪ, -nɪs [-nəs]; -ətɪ [-ɪtɪ]

scar|e (s. v.), -es, -ing, -ed skeə*, -z, -rɪŋ, -d

scarecrow, -s 'skeəkrəʊ, -z

scaremong|er, -ers, -ering 'skeə-,mʌŋg|ə*, -əz, -ərɪŋ

scar|f (s.), -ves, -fs skɑː|f, -vz, -fs

scarf (v.), -s, -ing, -ed skɑːf, -s, -ɪŋ, -t

scarf-pin, -s 'skɑːfpɪn, -z

scarification ,skeərɪfɪ'keɪʃn [,skær-]

scari|fy, -fies, -fying, -fied 'skeərɪ|faɪ ['skær-], -faɪz, -faɪɪŋ, -faɪd

scarlatina ,skɑːlə'tiːnə [-lɪ't-]

Scarlatti skɑː'lætɪ (skar'latti)

scarlet 'skɑːlət [-lɪt]

scarp (s. v.), **-s, -ing, -ed** skɑːp, -s, -ɪŋ, -t
scarves (plur. of scarf) skɑːvz
Scase skeɪs
scath|e, **-es, -ing/ly, -ed; -eless** skeɪð,
-z, -ɪŋ/lɪ, -d; -lɪs [-ləs]
scatt|er (s. v.), **-ers, -ering, -ered, -erer/s**
'skætə*, -əz, -ərɪŋ, -əd, -ərə*/z
scatterbrain, **-s, -ed** 'skætəbreɪn, -z, -d
scaup, **-s** skɔːp, -s
scaveng|e, **-es, -ing, -ed, -er/s** 'skæv-
ɪndʒ [-vəndʒ], -ɪz, -ɪŋ, -d, -ə*/z
Scawen 'skɔːɪn ['skɔːən]
Scawfell ˌskɔːˈfel [also 'skɔːfel according
to sentence-stress]
scean dhu, **-s** ˌskiːənˈduː [ˌskɪə-], -z
Sceats skiːts
scena, **-s** 'ʃeɪnə, -z
scenario, **-s** sɪˈnɑːrɪəʊ [seˈn-, səˈn-], -z
scenarist, **-s** 'siːnərɪst, -s
scene, **-s** siːn, -z
scene-paint|er/s, **-ing** 'siːnˌpeɪntə*/z,
-ɪŋ
scenery 'siːnərɪ
scene-shifter, **-s** 'siːnˌʃɪftə*, -z
scenic, **-ally** 'siːnɪk ['sen-], -əlɪ
scent (s. v.), **-s, -ing, -ed** sent, -s, -ɪŋ,
-ɪd
scent-bag, **-s** 'sentbæg, -z
scent-bottle, **-s** 'sentˌbɒtl, -z
sceptic (s. adj.), **-s, -al, -ally** 'skeptɪk, -s,
-l, -əlɪ
scepticism 'skeptɪsɪzəm
sceptre, **-s, -d** 'septə*, -z, -d
schedul|e (s. v.), **-es, -ing, -ed** 'ʃedjuːl,
-z, -ɪŋ, -d
Scheherazade ʃɪˌhɪərəˈzɑːdə [ʃəˌh-,
-ˌher-, -dɪ]
Scheldt skelt [ʃelt]
schema, **-s, -ta** 'skiːmə, -z, -tə
schematic, **-ally** skɪˈmætɪk [skiːˈm-], -əlɪ
schem|e (s. v.), **-es, -ing/ly, -ed, -er/s**
skiːm, -z, -ɪŋ/lɪ, -d, -ə*/z
Schenectady skɪˈnektədɪ
scherzando skeətˈsændəʊ [skɑːt-]
scherzo, **-s** 'skeətsəʊ ['skɑːt-], -z
Schiedam skɪˈdæm ['--]
Schiehallion ʃɪˈhæljən [-lɪən]
Schiller 'ʃɪlə* (ʃilər)
Schipperke, **-s** 'ʃɪpəkɪ ['skɪ-], -z ['ʃɪpək,
-s]
schism, **-s** 'sɪzəm ['skɪ-], -z
schismatic, **-al** sɪzˈmætɪk [skɪ-], -l
schist, **-s, -ose** ʃɪst, -s, -əʊs
schizoid 'skɪtsɔɪd
schizophrenia ˌskɪtsəʊˈfriːnjə [ˌskɪdzəʊ-,
-nɪə]
schizophrenic, **-s** ˌskɪtsəʊˈfrenɪk
[ˌskɪdzəʊ-], -s

Schleswig 'ʃlezwɪg [-zvɪg] ('ʃleːsviç)
schnap(p)s ʃnæps
Schofield 'skəʊfiːld
scholar, **-s, -ly** 'skɒlə*, -z, -lɪ
scholarship, **-s** 'skɒləʃɪp, -s
scholastic, **-ally** skəˈlæstɪk [skɒˈl-], -əlɪ
scholasticism skəˈlæstɪsɪzəm [skɒˈl-]
Scholes skəʊlz
scholiast, **-s** 'skəʊlɪæst, -s
scho|lium, **-lia** 'skəʊ|ljəm [-lɪəm], -ljə
[-lɪə]
Scholl (surname) ʃɒl, ʃəʊl
school (s. v.), **-s, -ing, -ed** skuːl, -z, -ɪŋ,
-d
school-book, **-s** 'skuːlbʊk, -s
schoolboy, **-s** 'skuːlbɔɪ, -z
schoolfellow, **-s** 'skuːlˌfeləʊ, -z
schoolgirl, **-s** 'skuːlgɜːl, -z
schoolhous|e, **-ses** 'skuːlhaʊ|s, -zɪz
school|man, **-men** 'skuːl|mən [-mæn],
-mən [-men]
school-marm, **-s** 'skuːlmɑːm, -z
schoolmaster, **-s** 'skuːlˌmɑːstə*, -z
schoolmate, **-s** 'skuːlmeɪt, -s
schoolmistress, **-es** 'skuːlˌmɪstrɪs [-trəs],
-ɪz
schoolroom, **-s** 'skuːlrʊm [-ruːm], -z
school-teacher, **-s** 'skuːlˌtiːtʃə*, -z
school-time 'skuːltaɪm
schooner, **-s** 'skuːnə*, -z
Schopenhauer 'ʃəʊpənhaʊə* ['ʃɒp-]
('ʃoːpənhauər)
schottische, **-s** ʃɒˈtiːʃ [ʃəˈt-], -ɪz
Schreiner 'ʃraɪnə*
Schubert 'ʃuːbət [-bɜːt]
Schumann 'ʃuːmən [-mæn, -mɑːn]
schwa, **-s** ʃwɑː, -z
Schwabe (English surname) ʃwɑːb
Schwann (English surname) ʃwɒn
Schweppe, **-s** ʃwep, -s
sciagram, **-s** 'skaɪəgræm ['saɪə-], -z
sciagraph, **-s** 'skaɪəgrɑːf ['saɪə-, -græf],
-s
sciatic, **-a** saɪˈætɪk, -ə
science, **-s** 'saɪəns, -ɪz
scientific, **-ally** ˌsaɪənˈtɪfɪk, -əlɪ
scientist, **-s** 'saɪəntɪst, -s
scilicet 'saɪlɪset
Scillonian, **-s** sɪˈləʊnjən [-nɪən], -z
Scill|y, **-ies** 'sɪl|ɪ, -ɪz
scimitar, **-s** 'sɪmɪtə* [-mətə*], -z
scintilla sɪnˈtɪlə
scintillat|e, **-es, -ing, -ed** 'sɪntɪleɪt, -s,
-ɪŋ, -ɪd
scintillation, **-s** ˌsɪntɪˈleɪʃn, -z
scioli|sm, **-st/s** 'saɪəʊlɪ|zəm, -st/s
scion, **-s** 'saɪən, -z
Scipio 'skɪpɪəʊ ['sɪ-]

439

scire facias ˌsaɪərɪˈfeɪʃɪæs [-ʃjæs, -ʃjəs, -ʃɪəs]

scirrhous 'sɪrəs

scirrh|us, -i 'sɪr|əs, -aɪ

scission, -s 'sɪʒn ['sɪʃn], -z

scissors 'sɪzəz

scleros|is, -es ˌsklɪəˈrəʊs|ɪs [sklɪˈr-, skleˈr-, sklɪˈr-], -iːz

sclerotic ˌsklɪəˈrɒtɪk [sklɪˈr-, skleˈr-, sklɪˈr-]

scoff, -s, -ing/ly, -ed, -er/s skɒf, -s, -ɪŋ/lɪ, -t, -ə*/z

Scofield 'skəʊfiːld

scold, -s, -ing/s, -ed skəʊld, -z, -ɪŋ/z, -ɪd

scoliosis ˌskɒlɪˈəʊsɪs

scollop (s. v.), -s, -ing, -ed 'skɒləp, -s, -ɪŋ, -t

sconc|e (s. v.), -es, -ing, -ed skɒns, -ɪz, -ɪŋ, -t

scone, -s skɒn [skəʊn], -z

Scone (in Scotland) skuːn

scoop (s. v.), -s, -ing, -ed, -er/s skuːp, -s, -ɪŋ, -t, -ə*/z

scoot (s. v.), -s, -ing, -ed skuːt, -s, -ɪŋ, -ɪd

scooter, -s 'skuːtə*, -z

scope, -s skəʊp, -s

scorbutic skɔːˈbjuːtɪk

scorch (s. v.), -es, -ing/ly, -ed, -er/s skɔːtʃ, -ɪz, -ɪŋ/lɪ, -t, -ə*/z

scor|e (s. v.), -es, -ing, -ed, -er/s skɔː* [skɔə*], -z, -rɪŋ, -d, -rə*/z

scoria 'skɔːrɪə ['skɒr-]

scoriaceous ˌskɔːrɪˈeɪʃəs [ˌskɒr-]

scorn (s. v.), -s, -ing, -ed skɔːn, -z, -ɪŋ, -d

scorn|ful, -fully, -fulness 'skɔːn|fʊl, -fʊlɪ [-fəlɪ], -fʊlnɪs [-nəs]

Scorpio (constellation) 'skɔːpɪəʊ [-pjəʊ]

scorpion, -s 'skɔːpjən [-pɪən], -z

scot (S.), -s skɒt, -s

scotch (s. v.) (S.), -es, -ing, -ed skɒtʃ, -ɪz, -ɪŋ, -t

Scotch|man, -men 'skɒtʃ|mən, -mən

Scotch|woman, -women 'skɒtʃ|ˌwʊmən, -ˌwɪmɪn

scoter, -s 'skəʊtə*, -z

scot-free ˌskɒtˈfriː

Scotia 'skəʊʃə

Scotland 'skɒtlənd

Scots (adj.) skɒts

Scots|man, -men 'skɒts|mən, -mən

Scots|woman, -women 'skɒts|ˌwʊmən, -ˌwɪmɪn

Scott skɒt

scottice 'skɒtɪsɪ [-siː]

scotticism, -s 'skɒtɪsɪzəm, -z

scotticiz|e [-is|e], -es, -ing, -ed 'skɒtɪsaɪz, -ɪz, -ɪŋ, -d

Scottish 'skɒtɪʃ

scoundr|el, -els, -elly 'skaʊndr|əl, -əlz, -əlɪ [-lɪ]

scour (s. v.), -s, -ing, -ed 'skaʊə*, -z, -rɪŋ, -d

scourg|e (s. v.), -es, -ing, -ed skɜːdʒ, -ɪz, -ɪŋ, -d

scout (s. v.), -s, -ing, -ed skaʊt, -s, -ɪŋ, -ɪd

scoutmaster, -s 'skaʊtˌmɑːstə*, -z

scow, -s skaʊ, -z

Scowen 'skaʊən [-ɪn]

scowl (s. v.), -s, -ing/ly, -ed skaʊl, -z, -ɪŋ/lɪ, -d

scrabb|le, -les, -ling, -led 'skræb|l, -lz, -lɪŋ [-l̩ɪŋ], -ld

scrag (s. v.), -s, -ging, -ged; -gy, -gier, -giest, -gily, -giness skræg, -z, -ɪŋ, -d; -ɪ, -ɪə*, -ɪɪst, -ɪlɪ [-əlɪ], -ɪnɪs [-məs]

scrag-end ˌskrægˈend

scramb|le (s. v.), -les, -ling, -led 'skræmb|l, -lz, -lɪŋ, [-l̩ɪŋ], -ld

scrap (s. v.), -s, -ping, -ped; -py, -pier, -piest, -pily, -piness skræp, -s, -ɪŋ, -t; -ɪ, -ɪə*, -ɪɪst, -ɪlɪ [-əlɪ], -ɪnɪs [-məs]

scrap|e (s. v.), -es, -ing/s, -ed, -er/s skreɪp, -s, -ɪŋ/z, -t, -ə*/z

scrap|y, -ier, -iest, -ily, -iness 'skreɪp|ɪ, -ɪə* [-jə*], -ɪɪst [-jɪst], -ɪlɪ [-əlɪ], -ɪnɪs [-məs]

scratch (s. v.), -es, -ing, -ed; -y, -ier, -iest, -ily, -iness skrætʃ, -ɪz, -ɪŋ, -t; -ɪ, -ɪə*, -ɪɪst, -ɪlɪ [-əlɪ], -ɪnɪs [-məs]

scrawl (s. v.), -s, -ing, -ed; -y, -ier, -iest, -iness skrɔːl, -z, -ɪŋ, -d; -ɪ, -ɪə* [-jə*], -ɪɪst [-jɪst], -ɪnɪs [-məs]

scray, -s skreɪ, -z

scream (s. v.), -s, -ing, -ed, -er/s; -y, -ier, -iest, -ily, -iness skriːm, -z, -ɪŋ, -d, -ə*/z; -ɪ, -ɪə* [-jə*], -ɪɪst [-jɪst], -ɪlɪ [-əlɪ], -ɪnɪs [-məs]

scree, -s skriː, -z

screech (s. v.), -es, -ing, -ed, -er/s skriːtʃ, -ɪz, -ɪŋ, -t, -ə*/z

screech-owl, -s 'skriːtʃaʊl, -z

screed, -s skriːd, -z

screen (s. v.), -s, -ing, -ed skriːn, -z, -ɪŋ, -d

screen-play, -s 'skriːnpleɪ, -z

screen-writer, -s 'skriːnˌraɪtə*, -z

screw (s. v.), -s, -ing, -ed skruː, -z, -ɪŋ ['skruɪŋ], -d

screw-cap, -s 'skruːkæp, -s

screwdriver, -s 'skruːˌdraɪvə*, -z

screw-steamer, -s 'skruːˌstiːmə*, -z

screw-top, -s 'skruːtɒp, -s

Scriabin 'skrɪəbɪn [skrɪ'æbɪn] ('skrjabjin)

scribal 'skraɪbl

scribb|le (s. v.), -les, -ling, -led, -ler/s 'skrɪb|l, -lz, -lɪŋ [-lɪŋ], -ld, -lə*/z [-lə*/z]

scribbling-paper 'skrɪb|ɪŋ,peɪpə* [-blɪŋ-]

scribe, -s skraɪb, -z

Scriblerus skrɪb'lɪərəs

Scribner ,skrɪbnə*

scrim skrɪm

scrimmage, -s 'skrɪmɪdʒ, -ɪz

scrimp, -s, -ing, -ed skrɪmp, -s, -ɪŋ, -t [skrɪmt]

scrimshaw (s. v.), -s, -ing, -ed 'skrɪmʃɔ:, -z, -ɪŋ, -d

scrip, -s skrɪp, -s

scripsit 'skrɪpsɪt

script (s. v.), -s, -ing, -ed, -er/s skrɪpt, -s, -ɪŋ, -ɪd, -ə*/z

scriptor|ium, -iums, -ia skrɪp'tɔ:r|ɪəm, -ɪəmz, -ɪə

scriptur|al, -ally 'skrɪptʃər|əl [-tʃur-], -əlɪ

scripture (S.), -s 'skrɪptʃə*, -z

script-writer, -s 'skrɪpt,raɪtə*, -z

Scriven 'skrɪvən

scrivener (S.), -s 'skrɪvnə*, -z

scrofula 'skrɒfjʊlə

scrofulous, -ly, -ness 'skrɒfjʊləs, -lɪ, -nɪs [-nəs]

scroll, -s skrəʊl, -z

Scrooge skru:dʒ

Scroope skru:p

Scrope skru:p, skrəʊp

scrotum, -s 'skrəʊtəm, -z

scroung|e, -es, -ing, -ed skraʊndʒ, -ɪz, -ɪŋ, -d

scrub (s. v.), -s, -bing, -bed; -by, -bier, -biest, -bily, -biness skrʌb, -z, -ɪŋ, -d; -ɪ, -ɪə*, -ɪɪst, -ɪlɪ [-əlɪ], -ɪnɪs [-ɪnəs]

scruff, -s skrʌf, -s

scruff|y, -ily 'skrʌf|ɪ, -ɪlɪ [-əlɪ]

scrum, -s skrʌm, -z

scrummage, -s 'skrʌmɪdʒ, -ɪz

scrumptious 'skrʌmpʃəs [-mptʃəs]

scrunch, -es, -ing, -ed skrʌntʃ, -ɪz, -ɪŋ, -t

scrup|le (s. v.), -les, -ling, -led 'skru:p|l, -lz, -lɪŋ [-lɪŋ], -ld

scrupulosity ,skru:pjʊ'lɒsətɪ [-rtɪ]

scrupulous, -ly, -ness 'skru:pjʊləs [-pjəl-], -lɪ, -nɪs [-nəs]

scrutator, -s skru:'teɪtə*, -z

scrutineer, -s ,skru:tɪ'nɪə* [-tə'n-], -z

scrutiniz|e [-is|e], -es, -ing, -ed 'skru:tɪnaɪz [-tənaɪz, -tŋaɪz], -ɪz, -ɪŋ, -d

scrutin|y, -ies 'skru:tɪn|ɪ [-tən|ɪ, -tŋ|ɪ], -ɪz

scr|y, -ies, -ying, -ied skr|aɪ, -aɪz, -aɪɪŋ, -aɪd

Scrymgeour 'skrɪmdʒə*

Scrymsour 'skrɪmsə*

scud (s. v.), -s, -ding, -ded skʌd, -z, -ɪŋ, -ɪd

Scudamore 'skju:dəmɔ:* [-mɔə*]

scudo, -s 'sku:dəʊ, -z

scuff, -s, -ing, -ed skʌf, -s, -ɪŋ, -t

scuff|le (s. v.), -les, -ling, -led 'skʌf|l, -lz, -lɪŋ [-lɪŋ], -ld

scull (s. v.), -s, -ing, -ed, -er/s skʌl, -z, -ɪŋ, -d, -ə*/z

sculler|y, -ies 'skʌlər|ɪ [-lr|ɪ], -ɪz

scullery-maid, -s 'skʌlərɪmeɪd [-lrɪ-], -z

scullion, -s 'skʌljən [-lɪən], -z

sculpsit 'skʌlpsɪt

sculpt, -s, -ing, -ed skʌlpt, -s, -ɪŋ, -ɪd

sculptor, -s 'skʌlptə*, -z

sculptur|e (s. v.), -es, -ing, -ed 'skʌlptʃə*, -z, -rɪŋ ['skʌlptʃrɪŋ], -d

scum (s. v.), -s, -ming, -med; -my skʌm, -z, -ɪŋ, -d; -ɪ

Scunthorpe 'skʌnθɔ:p

scupper, -s 'skʌpə*, -z

scurf, -y, -iness skɜ:f, -ɪ, -ɪnɪs [-nəs]

scurrility skʌ'rɪlətɪ [skə'r-, -rtɪ]

scurrilous, -ly, -ness 'skʌrɪləs [-rəl-], -lɪ, -nɪs [-nəs]

scurr|y (s. v.), -ies, -ying, -ied 'skʌr|ɪ, -ɪz, -ɪɪŋ, -ɪd

scurv|y (s. adj.), -ier, -iest, -ily, -iness 'skɜ:v|ɪ, -ɪə* [-jə*], -ɪɪst [-jɪst], -ɪlɪ [-əlɪ], -ɪnɪs [-nəs]

Scutari 'sku:tərɪ [sku:'tɑ:rɪ, skʊ't-]

scutcheon, -s 'skʌtʃən, -z

scutt|le (s. v.), -les, -ling, -led 'skʌt|l, -lz, -lɪŋ [-lɪŋ], -ld

scut|um, -ums, -a 'skju:t|əm, -əmz, -ə

Scylla 'sɪlə

scyth|e (s. v.), -es, -ing, -ed saɪð, -z, -ɪŋ, -d

Scythia, -n/s 'sɪðɪə ['sɪθ-, -jə], -n/z

'sdeath zdeθ

se (note in Tonic Sol-fa), -s si:, -z

sea, -s si:, -z

sea-bird, -s 'si:bɜ:d, -z

seaboard 'si:bɔ:d [-bɔəd]

sea-borne 'si:bɔ:n [-bɔən]

sea-breeze, -s ,si:'bri:z ['si:bri:z], -ɪz

Seabright 'si:braɪt

sea-captain, -s 'si:,kæptɪn [-tən], -z

sea-coast, -s ,si:'kəʊst ['--], -s

sea-cow, -s 'si:kaʊ, -z

sea-dog, -s 'si:dɒg, -z

sea-elephant, -s 'si:,elɪfənt [-ləf-, ,-'---], -s

seafar|er/s, -ing 'si:,feər|ə*/z, -ɪŋ

sea-fog, -s 'si:fɒg, -z
Seaford (*in East Sussex*) 'si:fəd [-fɔ:d]
Seaforth, -s 'si:fɔ:θ, -s
Seager 'si:gə*
Seago 'si:gəʊ
sea-going 'si:ˌgəʊɪŋ
sea-green ˌsi:'gri:n ['--]
sea-gull, -s 'si:gʌl, -z
seakale 'si:keɪl [ˌsi:'keɪl]
seal (*s. v.*), -s, -ing, -ed, -er/s si:l, -z, -ɪŋ, -d, -ə*/z
sealing-wax 'si:lɪŋwæks
sea-lion, -s 'si:ˌlaɪən, -z
sealskin, -s 'si:lskɪn, -z
Sealyham, -s 'si:lɪəm, -z
seam (*s. v.*), -s, -ing, -ed; -less si:m, -z, -ɪŋ, -d; -lɪs [-ləs]
sea|man (S.), -men, -manship 'si:|mən, -mən [-men], -mənʃɪp
Seamas 'ʃeɪməs
sea-mew, -s 'si:mju:, -z
sea-monster, -s 'si:ˌmɒnstə*, -z
seamstress, -es 'semstrɪs [-mps-, -strəs], -ɪz
Seamus 'ʃeɪməs
seamy 'si:mɪ
Sean ʃɔ:n
seance, -s 'seɪɑ̃:ns [-ɔ̃:ns, -ɑ:ns] (seɑ̃:s), -ɪz
sea-pink ˌsi:'pɪŋk
seaplane, -s 'si:pleɪn, -z
seaport, -s 'si:pɔ:t, -s
sea-power 'si:ˌpaʊə*
sear, -s, -ing, -ed sɪə*, -z, -rɪŋ, -d
search (*s. v.*), -es, -ing/ly, -ed, -er/s sɜ:tʃ, -ɪz, -ɪŋ/lɪ, -t, -ə*/z
searchlight, -s 'sɜ:tʃlaɪt, -s
search-part|y, -ies 'sɜ:tʃˌpɑ:t|ɪ, -ɪz
search-warrant, -s 'sɜ:tʃˌwɒrənt, -s
Searle sɜ:l
seascape, -s 'si:skeɪp, -s
sea-serpent, -s 'si:ˌsɜ:pənt, -s
seashore(s) 'si:ʃɔ:* [-ʃɔə*, ˌ-'-]
seasick, -ness 'si:sɪk, -nɪs [-nəs]
seaside 'si:saɪd [ˌ-'-]
seas|on (*s. v.*), -ons, -oning, -oned 'si:z|n, -nz, -nɪŋ [-nɪŋ], -nd
seasonab|le, -ly, -leness 'si:zŋəb|l [-znə-], -lɪ, -lnɪs [-nəs]
seasonal 'si:zənl [-zŋl, -znl]
seasoning (*s.*), -s 'si:zŋɪŋ [-znɪŋ], -z
season-ticket, -s 'si:zn,tɪkɪt [ˌ-'--], -s
seat (*s. v.*), -s, -ing, -ed si:t, -s, -ɪŋ, -ɪd
seat-belt, -s 'si:tbelt, -s
S.E.A.T.O. 'si:təʊ
Seaton 'si:tn
sea-trout 'si:traʊt
Seattle sɪ'ætl

sea-urchin, -s 'si:ˌɜ:tʃɪn [ˌ-'--], -z
sea-wall, -s ˌsi:'wɔ:l ['--], -z
seaward 'si:wəd
sea-water 'si:ˌwɔ:tə*
seaweed 'si:wi:d
seaworth|y, -iness 'si:ˌwɜ:ð|ɪ, -ɪnɪs [-nəs]
sebaceous sɪ'beɪʃəs [se'b-]
Sebastian sɪ'bæstjən [se'b-, sə'b-, -tɪən]
Sebastopol sɪ'bæstəpl [se'b-, sə'b-, -pɒl]
seborrhea ˌsebə'ri:ə [-'rɪə]
sec sek
secant, -s 'si:kənt, -s
secateurs ˌsekə'tɜ:z ['sekətɜ:z]
seced|e, -es, -ing, -ed, -er/s sɪ'si:d [si:'s-], -z, -ɪŋ, -ɪd, -ə*/z
secession, -s sɪ'seʃn, -z
secessionist, -s sɪ'seʃrɪst [-ʃənɪst], -s
seclud|e, -es, -ing, -ed sɪ'klu:d, -z, -ɪŋ, -ɪd
seclusion sɪ'klu:ʒn
second (*s. adj. v.*) (*ordinary senses*), -s; -ly; -ing, -ed, -er/s 'sekənd, -z; -lɪ; -ɪŋ, -ɪd, -ə*/z
second (*to release for temporary service*), -s, -ing, -ed sɪ'kɒnd [sə'k-], -z, -ɪŋ, -ɪd
secondar|y (*s. adj.*), -ies, -ily 'sekəndər|ɪ, -ɪz, -əlɪ [-ɪlɪ]
second-class ˌsekənd'klɑ:s [*also* '-- *when attributive*]
second hand (*of clock or watch*), -s 'sekəndhænd, -z
second-hand (*adj.*) ˌsekənd'hænd [*when attributive* '---]
Secondi (*town in Ghana*) ˌsekən'di:, (*surname*) sɪ'kɒndɪ [sə'k-]
secondment sɪ'kɒndmənt [sə'k-]
secondo, -s se'kɒndəʊ [sɪ'k-], -z
second-rate ˌsekənd'reɪt [*also* '-- *when attributive*]
second-rater, -s ˌsekənd'reɪtə*, -z
secrecy 'si:krəsɪ [-krɪs-]
secret (*s. adj.*), -s, -ly 'si:krɪt [-krət], -s, -lɪ
secretarial ˌsekrə'teərɪəl [-krɪ't-]
secretariat, -s ˌsekrə'teərɪət [-krɪ't-, -ɪæt], -s
secretar|y, -ies; -yship/s 'sekrətr|ɪ, [-krɪt-, -ter|ɪ], -ɪz; -ɪʃɪp/s
secret|e, -es, -ing, -ed sɪ'kri:t [si:'k-], -s, -ɪŋ, -ɪd
secretion, -s sɪ'kri:ʃn [si:'k-], -z
secretive, -ly, -ness 'si:krətɪv [-krɪ-, sɪ'kri:tɪv], -lɪ, -nɪs [-nəs]
Secrett 'si:krɪt
sect, -s sekt, -s
sectarian (*s. adj.*), -s, -ism sek'teərɪən, -z, -ɪzəm

sectar|y, -ies 'sektər|ɪ, -ɪz
section, -s 'sekʃn, -z
sec|tional, -tionally 'sek|ʃənl [-ʃnəl, -ʃn̩l, -ʃnl, -ʃənəl], -ʃŋəlɪ [-ʃnəlɪ, -ʃn̩lɪ, -ʃn̩lɪ, -ʃənəlɪ]
sector, -s 'sektə*, -z
secular, -ly 'sekjʊlə* [-kjəl-], -lɪ
seculari|sm, -st/s 'sekjʊlərɪ|zəm [-kjəl-], -st/s
secularity ˌsekjʊ'lærətɪ [-kjə'l-, -ɪtɪ]
secularization [-isa-] ˌsekjʊləraɪ'zeɪʃn [-kjəl-, -rɪ'z-]
seculariz|e [-is|e], -es, -ing, -ed 'sekjʊləraɪz [-kjəl-], -ɪz, -ɪŋ, -d
secur|e (adj. v.), -er, -est, -ely; -es, -ing, -ed; -able sɪ'kjʊə* [sə'k-, -'kjɔə*, -'kjɔ:*], -rə*, -rɪst, -lɪ; -z, -rɪŋ, -d; -rəbl
securit|y, -ies sɪ'kjʊərət|ɪ [sə'k-, -'kjɔər-, 'kjɔ:r-, -ɪt|ɪ], -ɪz
Sedan sɪ'dæn [sə'd-]
sedan-chair, -s sɪ'dæntʃeə* [sə'd-, -ˌ-'-], -z
sedate, -ly, -ness sɪ'deɪt, -lɪ, -nɪs [-nəs]
sedative (s. adj.), -s 'sedətɪv, -z
Sedbergh (public school) 'sedbə* [-bɜ:g], (name of town) 'sedbə*
Sedd|ing, -on 'sed|ɪŋ, -n
sedentar|y, -ily, -iness 'sedntər|ɪ, -əlɪ [-ɪlɪ], -ɪnɪs [-məs]
sedge, -s sedʒ, -ɪz
Sedge|field, -moor 'sedʒ|fi:ld, -ˌmʊə* [-mɔə*, -mɔ:*]
sedge-warbler, -s 'sedʒˌwɔ:blə* [ˌ-'--], -z
Sedgley 'sedʒlɪ
Sedgwick 'sedʒwɪk
sedil|e, -ia sɪ'daɪl|ɪ [sɪ'd-], -jə [-ɪə, -'dɪljə, -'dɪlɪə]
sediment, -s 'sedɪmənt, -s
sedimentary ˌsedɪ'mentərɪ
sedition, -s sɪ'dɪʃn [sə'd-], -z
seditious, -ly, -ness sɪ'dɪʃəs [sə'd-], -lɪ, -nɪs [-nəs]
Sedlescombe 'sedlskəm
Sedley 'sedlɪ
seduc|e, -es, -ing, -ed, -er/s, -ement/s sɪ'dju:s, -ɪz, -ɪŋ, -t, -ə*/z, -mənt/s
seduction, -s sɪ'dʌkʃn, -z
seductive, -ly, -ness sɪ'dʌktɪv, -lɪ, -nɪs [-nəs]
sedulous, -ly, -ness 'sedjʊləs, -lɪ, -nɪs [-nəs]
sedum, -s 'si:dəm, -z
see (s. v.) (S.), -s, -ing, saw, seen si:, -z, -ɪŋ, sɔ:, si:n
seed (s. v.), -s, -ing, -ed si:d, -z, -ɪŋ, -ɪd
seed-cake 'si:dkeɪk
seedless 'si:dlɪs [-ləs]

seedling, -s 'si:dlɪŋ, -z
seed-pearl, -s ˌsi:d'pɜ:l ['--], -z
seed-potato, -es 'si:dpəˌteɪtəʊ [ˌ--'--], -z
seeds|man, -men 'si:dz|mən, -mən [-men]
seed-time, -s 'si:dtaɪm, -z
seed|y, -ier, -iest, -ily, -iness 'si:d|ɪ, -ɪə* [-jə*], -ɪɪst [-jɪst], -ɪlɪ [-əlɪ], -ɪnɪs [-məs]
seek, -s, -ing, sought, seeker/s si:k, -s, -ɪŋ, sɔ:t, 'si:kə*/z
Seel(e)y 'si:lɪ
seem, -s, -ing/ly, -ed si:m, -z, -ɪŋ/lɪ, -d
seeml|y, -ier, -iest, -iness 'si:ml|ɪ, -ɪə* [-jə*], -ɪɪst [-jɪst], -ɪnɪs [-məs]
seen (from see) si:n
seep, -s, -ing, -ed si:p, -s, -ɪŋ, -t
seepage 'si:pɪdʒ
seer (one who sees), -s 'si:ə* [sɪə*], -z
seer (Indian weight), -s sɪə*, -z
seersucker 'sɪəˌsʌkə*
seesaw (s. v.), -s, -ing, -ed 'si:sɔ: [ˌsi:'sɔ:], -z, -ɪŋ, -d
seeth|e, -es, -ing, -ed si:ð, -z, -ɪŋ, -d
segment (s.), -s 'segmənt, -s
segment (v.), -s, -ing, -ed seg'ment ['--, səg'm-], -s, -ɪŋ, -ɪd
segmental seg'mentl [səg'm-]
segregate (adj.) 'segrɪgɪt [-geɪt, -gət]
segregat|e (v.), -es, -ing, -ed 'segrɪgeɪt, -s, -ɪŋ, -ɪd
segregation ˌsegrɪ'geɪʃn
Seidlitz 'sedlɪts
Seigel 'si:gəl
seignior, -s 'seɪnjə* [-nɪə*, rarely 'si:n-], -z
Seignior (surname) 'si:njə*
seignior|y, -ies 'seɪnjər|ɪ [-nɪər-, rarely 'si:n-], -ɪz
seine (net), -s seɪn, -z
Seine (river in France) seɪn (sɛn, sɛ:n)
seis|ed, -in/s si:z|d, -ɪn/z
seismic 'saɪzmɪk
seismograph, -s 'saɪzməgrɑ:f [-məʊg-, -græf], -s
seismograph|er/s, -y saɪz'mɒgrəf|ə*/z, -ɪ
seismographic ˌsaɪzmə'græfɪk [-məʊ'g-]
seismologic|al, -ally ˌsaɪzmə'lɒdʒɪk|l [-məʊ'l-], -əlɪ
seismolog|ist/s, -y saɪz'mɒlədʒ|ɪst/s, -ɪ
seismometer, -s saɪz'mɒmɪtə* [-mətə*], -z
seizable 'si:zəbl
seiz|e, -es, -ing, -ed si:z, -ɪz, -ɪŋ, -d
seizin, -s 'si:zɪn, -z
seizure, -s 'si:ʒə*, -z
sejant 'si:dʒənt

443

Sejanus sɪ'dʒeməs [se'dʒ-]
selah, -s 'siːlə, -z
Selangor sə'læŋə* [-ŋɔː*]
Sel|borne, -by 'sel|bɔːn [-bən], -bɪ
Selden 'seldən
seldom 'seldəm
select (adj. v.), -ness; -s, -ing, -ed, -or/s; -ive/ly sɪ'lekt [sə'l-], -nɪs [-nəs]; -s, -ɪŋ, -ɪd, -ə*/z; -ɪv/lɪ
selection, -s sɪ'lekʃn [sə'l-], -z
selective sɪ'lektɪv [sə'l-]
selectivity ,sɪlek'tɪvətɪ [,sel-, -ɪtɪ]
Selena sɪ'liːnə [sə'l-]
selenite (substance) 'selɪnaɪt
Selenite (inhabitant of moon), -s sɪ'liːnaɪt [sə'l-], -s
selenium sɪ'liːnjəm [sə'l-, -nɪəm]
Seleucia, -n/s sɪ'ljuːʃjə [sə'l-, -'luː-, -ʃɪə, -sjə, -sɪə], -n/z
Seleucid, -s sɪ'ljuːsɪd [se'l-, -'luː-], -z
Seleucus sɪ'ljuːkəs [se'l-, -'luː-]
sel|f, -ves sel|f, -vz
Note.—Most compounds with self-
have double stress, e.g. self-com-
placent ,selfkəm'pleɪsənt, self-con-
fidence ,self'kɒnfɪdəns, self-sup-
porting ,selfsə'pɔːtɪŋ. Only a few of
the most important are given below.
self-centred ,self'sentəd
self-command ,selfkə'mɑːnd
self-conscious, -ness ,self'kɒnʃəs, -nɪs [-nəs]
self-contained ,selfkən'teɪnd
self-control, -led ,selfkən'trəʊl, -d
self-deception ,selfdɪ'sepʃn
self-defence ,selfdɪ'fens
self-denial ,selfdɪ'naɪəl
self-denying ,selfdɪ'naɪɪŋ
self-determination 'selfdɪ,tɜːmɪ'neɪʃn
self-employed ,selfɪm'plɔɪd [-em-]
self-esteem ,selfɪ'stiːm [-ə's-]
self-evident ,self'evɪdənt
self-explanatory ,selfɪk'splænətərɪ [-ek's-, -nɪt-]
self-governing ,self'gʌvənɪŋ [-vnɪŋ]
self-government ,self'gʌvnmənt [-vɪmmənt, -vənmənt, -vəmənt]
self-importan|ce, -t ,selfɪm'pɔːtən|s, -t
self-indulgen|ce, -t ,selfɪn'dʌldʒən|s, -t
self-interest ,self'ɪntrɪst [-tərest, -trəst]
selfish, -ly, -ness 'selfɪʃ, -lɪ, -nɪs [-nəs]
selfless 'selflɪs [-ləs]
self-made ,self'meɪd [also '-- when attributive]
self-pity ,self'pɪtɪ
self-possessed ,selfpə'zest [-pʊ'z-]
self-possession ,selfpə'zeʃn
self-preservation 'self,prezə'veɪʃn

self-relian|ce, -t ,selfrɪ'laɪən|s [-rə'l-], -t
self-respect ,selfrɪ'spekt [-rə's-]
self-respecting ,selfrɪ'spektɪŋ [-rə's-]
self-restraint ,selfrɪ'streɪnt
Selfridge 'selfrɪdʒ
self-righteous ,self'raɪtʃəs [-tjəs]
self-rule ,self'ruːl
self-sacrifice ,self'sækrɪfaɪs
selfsame 'selfseɪm
self-satisfaction 'self,sætɪs'fækʃn
self-satisfied ,self'sætɪsfaɪd
self-service ,self'sɜːvɪs
self-starter, -s ,self'stɑːtə*, -z
self-styled ,self'staɪld ['selfstaɪld]
self-sufficien|cy, -t ,selfsə'fɪʃn|sɪ, -t
self-taught ,self'tɔːt
self-will, -ed ,self'wɪl, -d
self-winding ,self'waɪndɪŋ ['self-,waɪndɪŋ]
Selim (Sultan of Turkey) 'siːlɪm ['sel-]
Selkirk 'selkəːk
sell (s. v.) (S.), -s, -ing, sold, seller/s sel, -z, -ɪŋ, səʊld, 'selə*/z
Sellar 'selə*
Sellers 'seləz
Selous sə'luː
Selsey 'selsɪ
Seltzer, -s 'seltsə*, -z
selvage, -s 'selvɪdʒ, -ɪz
selvedge, -s 'selvɪdʒ, -ɪz
selves (plur. of self) selvz
Selwyn 'selwɪn
semantic, -s, -ally sɪ'mæntɪk [se'm-, sə'm-, si'm-], -s, -əlɪ
semanticism sɪ'mæntɪsɪzəm [se'm-, sə'm-, si'm-]
semanticiz|e [-is|e], -es, -ing, -ed sɪ'mæntɪsaɪz [se'm-, sə'm-, si'm-], -ɪz, -ɪŋ, -d
semaphore, -s 'seməfɔː* [-fɒə*], -z
semaphoric, -ally ,semə'fɒrɪk, -əlɪ
semasiology sɪ,meɪsɪ'ɒlədʒɪ [se,m-, sə,m-, -eɪzɪ-]
sematology ,semə'tɒlədʒɪ [,siːm-]
semblance, -s 'sembləns, -ɪz
semé 'semeɪ
Semele 'semɪlɪ
semen 'siːmen [-mən]
semester, -s sɪ'mestə* [sə'm-], -z
semi- 'semɪ-
Note.—Numerous compounds may be
formed by prefixing semi- to other
words. Compounds not entered below
have double stress, i.e. a stress on
semi- and the stress of the simple
word. Examples: semi-detached
,semɪdɪ'tætʃt, semi-official ,semɪə-
'fɪʃl, semi-tropical ,semɪ'trɒpɪkl.

semibreve, -s 'semɪbriːv, -z
semicircle, -s 'semɪˌsɜːkl, -z
semicircular ˌsemɪ'sɜːkjʊlə* [-kjəl-]
semicolon, -s ˌsemɪ'kəʊlən ['semɪˌk-, -lɒn], -z
semi-final, -s ˌsemɪ'faɪnl, -z
seminal 'semɪnl ['siːm-]
seminar, -s 'semɪnɑː* [ˌ-'-], -z
seminar|y, -ies, -ist/s 'semɪnər|ɪ, -ɪz, -ɪst/s
Seminole, -s 'semɪnəʊl, -z
semiology ˌsemɪ'ɒlədʒɪ [ˌsiːm-]
semiotic, -s ˌsemɪ'ɒtɪk [ˌsiːm-], -s
semi-precious ˌsemɪˌpreʃəs [ˌ-'--]
semiquaver, -s 'semɪˌkweɪvə*, -z
Semiramide ˌsemɪ'rɑːmɪdɪ
Semiramis se'mɪrəmɪs [sɪ'm-]
Semite, -s 'siːmaɪt ['sem-], -s
Semitic sɪ'mɪtɪk [se'm-, sə'm-]
semitism 'semɪtɪzəm
semitone, -s 'semɪtəʊn, -z
semivowel, -s 'semɪˌvaʊəl [ˌsemɪ'v-, -el], -z
semmit, -s 'semɪt, -s
semolina ˌsemə'liːnə [-mʊ'l-]
Semon (surname) 'siːmən
Sempill 'sempl
sempiternal ˌsempɪ'tɜːnl
semplice 'semplɪtʃɪ
sempre 'semprɪ
sempstress, -es 'sempstrɪs [-strəs], -ɪz
sen sen
senary 'siːnərɪ
senate (S.), -s 'senɪt [-nət], -s
senator, -s 'senətə* [-nɪt-], -z
senatorial, -ly ˌsenə'tɔːrɪəl, -ɪ
senatus se'neɪtəs [sɪ'n-, -'nɑː-]
send, -s, -ing, sent, sender/s send, -z, -ɪŋ, sent, 'sendə*/z
send-off, -s 'sendɒf [old-fashioned -ɔːf, ˌ-'- when preceded by a stress], -s
Seneca 'senɪkə
Senegal ˌsenɪ'gɔːl
Senegalese ˌsenɪgə'liːz [-gə:'l-]
Senegambia ˌsenɪ'gæmbɪə [-bjə]
senescen|ce, -t sɪ'nesn|s [se'n-, sə'n-], -t
seneschal, -s 'senɪʃl, -z
senile 'siːnaɪl
senility sɪ'nɪlɪtɪ [se'n-, -rtɪ]
senior (s. adj.) (S.), -s 'siːnjə* [-nɪə*], -z
seniorit|y, -ies ˌsiːnɪ'ɒrət|ɪ [-ɪt|ɪ], -ɪz
Senlac 'senlæk
senna 'senə
Sennacherib se'nækərɪb [sɪ'n-, sə'n-]
sennet, -s 'senɪt [-nət]
sennight, -s 'senaɪt, -s
señor se'njɔː*
sensation, -s sen'seɪʃn [sən-, sn-], -z

sensa|tional, -tionally sen'seɪ|ʃənl [sən-, -ʃnəl, -ʃn̩l, -ʃnl, -ʃənl], -ʃnəlɪ [-ʃnəlɪ, -ʃn̩lɪ, -ʃnlɪ, -ʃənəlɪ]
sensationali|sm, -st/s sen'seɪʃnəlɪ|zəm [sən-, -ʃnəl-, -ʃn̩l-, -ʃnl-, -ʃənəl-], -st/s
sense, -s sens, -ɪz
senseless, -ly, -ness 'senslɪs [-ləs], -lɪ, -nɪs [-nəs]
sensibility ˌsensɪ'bɪlɪtɪ [-sə'b-, -lɪt-]
sensib|le, -ly 'sensəb|l [-sɪb-], -lɪ
sensitive (s. adj.), -s, -ly, -ness 'sensɪtɪv [-sət-], -z, -lɪ, -nɪs [-nəs]
sensitivity ˌsensɪ'tɪvətɪ [-sə't-, -ɪtɪ]
sensitization [-isa-] ˌsensɪtaɪ'zeɪʃn [-sət-]
sensitiz|e [-is|e], -es, -ing, -ed 'sensɪtaɪz [-sət-], -ɪz, -ɪŋ, -d
sensorial sen'sɔːrɪəl
sensor|y, -ily 'sensər|ɪ, -əlɪ [-ɪlɪ]
sensual, -ly, -ness, -ism, -ist/s 'sensjʊəl [-sjwəl, -sjʊl, -ʃʊəl, -ʃwəl, -ʃʊl], -ɪ, -nɪs [-nəs], -ɪzəm, -ɪst/s
sensuality ˌsensjʊ'ælətɪ [ˌsenʃʊ-, -ɪtɪ]
sensuous, -ly, -ness 'sensjʊəs [-sjwəs, -ʃʊəs, -ʃwəs], -lɪ, -nɪs [-nəs]
sent (from send) sent
sentenc|e (s. v.), -es, -ing, -ed 'sentəns, -ɪz, -ɪŋ, -t
sententious, -ly, -ness sen'tenʃəs [sən-], -lɪ, -nɪs [-nəs]
sentience 'senʃəns [-ʃɪəns, -ʃjəns]
sentient, -ly 'senʃnt [-ʃɪənt, -ʃjənt], -lɪ
sentiment, -s 'sentɪmənt, -s
sentiment|al, -ally, -alism ˌsentɪ'ment|l, -əlɪ [-l̩ɪ], -əlɪzəm [-l̩ɪzəm]
sentimentality ˌsentɪmen'tælətɪ [-mən-, -ɪtɪ]
sentimentalization [-isa-] ˌsentɪmentl̩aɪ'zeɪʃn [-təl-, -tl̩ɪ'z-, sentɪˌment-]
sentimentaliz|e [-is|e], -es, -ing, -ed ˌsentɪ'mentl̩aɪz [-təl-] -ɪz, -ɪŋ, -d
sentinel, -s 'sentɪnl, -z
sentr|y, -ies 'sentr|ɪ, -ɪz
sentry-box, -es 'sentrɪbɒks, -ɪz
sentry-go 'sentrɪgəʊ
senza 'sentsə
Seoul səʊl
sepal, -s 'sepəl ['siːp-], -z
separability ˌsepərə'bɪlətɪ [-lɪt-]
separab|le, -ly, -leness 'sepərəb|l, -lɪ -lnɪs [-lnəs]
separ|ate (adj.), -ately, -ateness 'sepr|ət [-pər-, -rɪt], -ətlɪ [-ɪtlɪ], -ətnɪs [-ɪtnɪs, -nəs]
separat|e (v.), -es, -ing, -ed, -or/s 'sepəreɪt, -s, -ɪŋ, -ɪd, -ə*/z
separation, -s ˌsepə'reɪʃn, -z
separati|sm, -st/s 'sepərətɪ|zəm, -st/s

445

Sephardi|c, -m se'fɑːdɪ|k, -m
sepia 'siːpjə
sepoy, -s 'siːpɔɪ, -z
sepsis 'sepsɪs
September, -s sep'tembə* [səp-, sɪp-],
 -z
septennial sep'tenjəl [-nɪəl]
septet(te), -s sep'tet, -s
septic 'septɪk
septicaemia ,septɪ'siːmɪə [-mjə]
septillion, -s sep'tɪljən, -z
septime, -s 'septiːm, -z
septuagenarian, -s ,septjʊədʒɪ'neərɪən
 [-tjwə-, -dʒə'n-], -z
Septuagesima ,septjʊə'dʒesɪmə [-tjwə-]
Septuagint 'septjʊədʒɪnt [-tjwə-]
sept|um, -ums, -a 'sept|əm, -əmz, -ə
septuple 'septjʊpl
sepulchral sɪ'pʌlkrəl [se'p-, sə'p-]
sepulchre, -s 'sepəlkə*, -z
sepulture 'sepəltʃə* [-,tjʊə*]
sequacious sɪ'kweɪʃəs [se'k-, sə'k-]
sequel, -s 'siːkwəl, -z
sequel|a, -ae sɪ'kwiːl|ə, -iː
sequence, -s 'siːkwəns, -ɪz
sequenti|al, -ally sɪ'kwenʃ|l, -əlɪ
sequest|er, -ers, -ering, -ered sɪ'kwest|ə*
 [sə'k-], -əz, -ərɪŋ, -əd
sequestrat|e, -es, -ing, -ed sɪ'kwestreɪt
 ['siːkw-], -s, -ɪŋ, -ɪd
sequestration, -s ,siːkwe'streɪʃn [,sek-],
 -z
sequin, -s 'siːkwɪn, -z
sequoia, -s sɪ'kwɔɪə [se'k-], -z
serac, -s 'seræk, -s
seraglio, -s se'rɑːlɪəʊ [sɪ'r-, sə'r-, -ljəʊ],
 -z
serai, -s se'raɪ [sə'r-], -z
seraph (S.), -s, -im 'serəf, -s, -ɪm
seraphic, -al, -ally se'ræfɪk [sɪ'r-, sə'r-],
 -l, -əlɪ
Serapis 'serəpɪs
Serb, -s, -ia, -ian/s sɜːb, -z, -jə [-ɪə],
 -jən/z [-ɪən/z]
Serbo-Croat, -s ,sɜːbəʊ'krəʊæt, -s
Serbo-Croatian ,sɜːbəʊkrəʊ'eɪʃn
Serbonian sɜː'bəʊnjən [-nɪən]
sere (s. adj.), -s sɪə*, -z
Seremban sə'rembən
serenad|e (s. v.), -es, -ing, -ed ,serə'neɪd
 [-rɪ'n-], -z, -ɪŋ, -ɪd
serenata, -s ,serə'nɑːtə [-rɪ'n-], -z
serendipity ,serən'dɪpətɪ [-ren-, -ɪtɪ]
serene, -st, -ly sɪ'riːn [sə'r-], -ɪst, -lɪ
serenity sɪ'renətɪ [sə'r-, -ɪtɪ]
serf, -s, -dom sɜːf, -s, -dəm
serge (S.), -s sɜːdʒ, -ɪz
sergeant (S.), -s 'sɑːdʒənt, -s

sergeant-major, -s ,sɑːdʒənt'meɪdʒə*,
 -z
serial (s. adj.), -s 'sɪərɪəl, -z
seriatim ,sɪərɪ'eɪtɪm [,ser-, -'ɑːtɪm]
series 'sɪəriːz [-rɪz, rarely -riːz]
serif [cer-], -s 'serɪf, -s
serin, -s 'serɪn, -z
seringa, -s sɪ'rɪŋgə [sə'r-], -z
Seringapatam sə,rɪŋgəpə'tɑːm [sɪ,r-,
 -'tæm]
serio-comic ,sɪərɪəʊ'kɒmɪk
serious, -ly, -ness 'sɪərɪəs, -lɪ, -nɪs [-nəs]
serjeant (S.), -s 'sɑːdʒənt, -s
Serjeantson 'sɑːdʒəntsn
sermon, -s 'sɜːmən, -z
sermonette, -s ,sɜːmə'net, -s
sermoniz|e [-is|e], -es, -ing, -ed
 'sɜːmənaɪz, -ɪz, -ɪŋ, -d
serous 'sɪərəs
Serpell 'sɜːpl
Serpens (constellation) 'sɜːpenz
serpent, -s 'sɜːpənt, -s
serpentine (s. adj.) (S.) 'sɜːpəntaɪn
serrate (adj.) 'serɪt [-reɪt, -rət]
serrated se'reɪtɪd [sə'r-, sɪ'r-]
serration, -s se'reɪʃn [sə'r-, sɪ'r-], -z
serried 'serɪd
serum, -s 'sɪərəm, -z
servant, -s 'sɜːvənt, -s
servant-girl, -s 'sɜːvəntgɜːl, -z
serv|e (s. v.), -es, -ing/s, -ed, -er/s sɜːv,
 -z, -ɪŋ/z, -d, -ə*/z
servic|e (s. v.) (S.), -es, -ing, -ed 'sɜːvɪs,
 -ɪz, -ɪŋ, -t
serviceability ,sɜːvɪsə'bɪlətɪ [-lɪt-]
serviceab|le, -ly, -leness 'sɜːvɪsəb|l, -lɪ,
 -lnɪs [-nəs]
serviette ,sɜːvɪ'et, -s
servile, -ly 'sɜːvaɪl, -lɪ
servility sɜː'vɪlətɪ [-ɪtɪ]
serving-spoon, -s 'sɜːvɪŋspuːn, -z
servitor, -s 'sɜːvɪtə*, -z
servitude 'sɜːvɪtjuːd
sesame (S.), -s 'sesəmɪ, -z
sesquialtera, -s ,seskwɪ'æltərə, -z
sesquicentennial ,seskwɪsen'tenɪəl
 [-sən-, -njəl]
sesquipedalian ,seskwɪpɪ'deɪljən [-pe'd-,
 -lɪən]
session, -s 'seʃn, -z
sessional (s. adj.), -s 'seʃənl [-ʃnəl, -ʃnl̩,
 -ʃn̩l, -ʃənəl], -z
sesterce, -s 'sestɜːs, -ɪz ['sestəsɪz]
sester|tium, -tia se'stɜː|tjəm [-trəm,
 -ʃjəm, -ʃɪəm], -tjə [-trə, -ʃjə, -ʃɪə]
sestet, -s ses'tet, -s
set (s. v.), -s, -ting set, -s, -ɪŋ
set-back, -s 'setbæk, -s

Setebos 'setɪbɒs
Seth seθ
set-off, -s ˌset'ɒf [old-fashioned -'ɔːf],
  -s
seton (S.), -s 'siːtn, -z
set-out, -s set'aʊt ['--], -s
set-square, -s 'setskweə*, -z
settee, -s se'tiː, -z
setter, -s 'setə*, -z
setting (s.), -s 'setɪŋ, -z
sett|le (s. v.), -les, -ling, -led, -ler/s,
  -lement/s 'set|l, -lz, -lɪŋ [-lɪŋ], -ld,
  -lə*/z [-lə*/z], -lmənt/s
set-to ˌset'tuː: ['--]
set-up, -s 'setʌp, -s
Seurat 'sɜːrɑː: (sœra)
seven, -s, -th/s, -thly; -fold 'sevn, -z,
  -θ/s, -θlɪ; -fəʊld
sevenish 'sevnɪʃ ['sevənɪʃ]
Sevenoaks 'sevn̩əʊks [-vnəʊ-]
seven|pence,   -penny   'sevn|pəns
  [-vm|p-], -pənɪ (see note under penny)
seventeen, -s, -th/s, -thly ˌsevn'tiːn
  ['-- according to sentence-stress], -z,
  -θ/s, -θlɪ
sevent|y, -ies, -ieth/s 'sevnt|ɪ, -ɪz, -ɪɪθ/s
  [-jɪθ/s, -ɪɪθ/s, -jəθ/s]
sever, -s, -ing, -ed; -able, -ance 'sevə*,
  -z, -rɪŋ, -d; -rəbl, -rəns
sever|al, -ally 'sevr|əl, -əlɪ
severe, -r, -st, -ly, -ness sɪ'vɪə* [sə'v-],
  -rə*, -rɪst, -lɪ, -nɪs [-nəs]
severit|y, -ies sɪ'verət|ɪ [sə'v-, -ɪt|ɪ], -ɪz
Severn 'sevən [-vn]
Severus sɪ'vɪərəs [sə'v-]
Sevier 'seviə* [-vjə*]
Seville sə'vɪl [se'v-, sɪ'v-, 'sevɪl, 'sevl]
Sèvres 'seɪvrə [-və*] (sɛːvr)
sew, -s, -ing, -ed, -n səʊ, -z, -ɪŋ, -d,
  -n
sewage 'sjuːɪdʒ ['sjʊɪdʒ, 'suː-, 'suɪ-]
Sewanee sə'wɒnɪ
Seward 'siːwəd
Sewell 'sjuːəl [sjʊəl]
sewer (one who sews), -s 'səʊə*, -z
sewer (drain), -s sjʊə*, -z
sewerage 'sjʊərɪdʒ
sewer-gas 'sjʊəgæs
sewing-machine, -s 'səʊɪŋməˌʃiːn, -z
sewing|-woman,   -women   'səʊɪŋ|-
  ˌwʊmən, -ˌwɪmɪn
sex, -es, -less seks, -ɪz, -lɪs [-ləs]
sexagenarian,   -s   ˌseksədʒɪ'neərɪən
  [-dʒə'n-], -z
Sexagesi|ma, -mal ˌseksə'dʒesɪ|mə, -ml
sex-appeal 'seksəˌpiːl
sext(e) sekst
sextan 'sekstən

sextant, -s 'sekstənt, -s
sextet(te), -s seks'tet, -s
sextillion, -s seks'tɪljən, -z
sexto, -s 'sekstəʊ, -z
sextodecimo, -s ˌsekstəʊ'desɪməʊ, -z
sexton, -s 'sekstən, -z
sextuple 'sekstjʊpl
sexual, -ly 'seksjʊəl [-ksjwəl, -ksjʊl,
  -kʃʊəl, -kʃwəl, -kʃʊl], -ɪ-
sexuality ˌseksjʊ'ælətɪ [-kʃʊ-, -ɪtɪ]
Seychelle, -s seɪ'ʃel, -z
Seymour 'siːmɔː* [-mɔə*, -mə*], 'seɪm-
  Note.—'seɪm- chiefly in families of
    Scottish origin.
Seys seɪs
sforzando sfɔːt'sændəʊ
sgeandhu ˌskiːən'duː: [ˌskɪən-]
shabb|y, -ier, -iest, -ily, -iness 'ʃæb|ɪ,
  -ɪə*, -ɪɪst, -ɪlɪ [-əlɪ], -ɪnɪs [-ɪnəs]
shack|le (s. v.) (S.), -les, -ling, -led
  'ʃæk|l, -lz, -lɪŋ [-lɪŋ], -ld
Shackleton 'ʃækltən
Shadbolt 'ʃædbəʊlt
shaddock (S.) 'ʃædək
shad|e (s. v.), -es, -ing, -ed; -eless ʃeɪd,
  -z, -ɪŋ, -ɪd; -lɪs [-ləs]
shadoof, -s ʃə'duːf [ʃæ'd-], -s
shad|ow (s. v.), -ows, -owing, -owed;
  -owy, -owiness 'ʃæd|əʊ, -əʊz, -əʊɪŋ,
  -əʊd; -əʊɪ, -əʊɪnɪs [-ɪnəs]
shadowless 'ʃædəʊlɪs [-ləs]
Shadrach [-ak] 'ʃeɪdræk ['ʃæd-]
  Note.—Some Jews pronounce 'ʃædrɑːx.
Shadwell 'ʃædwəl [-wel]
shad|y, -ier, -iest, -ily, -iness 'ʃeɪd|ɪ, -ɪə*
  [-jə*], -ɪɪst [-jɪst], -ɪlɪ [-əlɪ], -ɪnɪs
  [-ɪnəs]
shaft, -s ʃɑːft, -s
Shaftesbury 'ʃɑːftsbərɪ
shag, -s ʃæg, -z
shagg|y, -ier, -iest, -ily, -iness 'ʃæg|ɪ,
  -ɪə*, -ɪɪst, -ɪlɪ [-əlɪ], -ɪnɪs [-ɪnəs]
shagreen ʃæ'griːn [ʃə'g-]
shah (S.), -s ʃɑː, -z
shaikh, -s ʃaɪk, -s
Shairp ʃeəp, ʃɑːp
shak|e (s. v.), -es, -ing, shook, shak|en,
  -er/s ʃeɪk, -s, -ɪŋ, ʃʊk, 'ʃeɪk|ən, -ə*/z
shakedown, -s 'ʃeɪkdaʊn [also -'- when
  preceded by a stress], -z
Shak(e)spear(e) 'ʃeɪkˌspɪə*
Shak(e)spearian ʃeɪk'spɪərɪən
Shak(e)speariana 'ʃeɪkˌspɪərɪ'ɑːnə [ʃeɪk-
  ˌspɪər-]
shake-up, -s 'ʃeɪkʌp [also -'- when
  preceded by a stress], -s
shako, -s 'ʃækəʊ, -z

447

shak|y, -ier, -iest, -ily, -iness 'ʃeɪk|ɪ, -ɪə* [-jə*], -ɪɪst [-jɪst], -ɪlɪ [-əlɪ], -ɪnɪs [-məs]

Shalders 'ʃɔ:ldəz

shale ʃeɪl

shall ʃæl (strong form), ʃəl, ʃl, ʃə, ʃ (weak forms)
Note.—The forms ʃə, ʃ, are chiefly used when we or be follows.

shallop, -s 'ʃæləp, -s

shallot (S.), -s ʃə'lɒt, -s

shall|ow (s. adj. v.) (S.), -ows, -ower, -owest, -owness, -owly 'ʃæl|əʊ, -əʊz, -əʊə*, -əʊɪst, -əʊnɪs [-nəs], -əʊlɪ

shalt (from shall) ʃælt (strong form), ʃəlt, ʃlt (weak forms)

shall|y, -iness 'ʃeɪl|ɪ, -ɪnɪs [-məs]

sham (s. v.), -s, -ming, -med, -mer/s ʃæm, -z, -ɪŋ, -d, -ə*/z

shaman, -s, -ism 'ʃæmən, -z, -ɪzəm

shamb|le, -les, -ling, -led 'ʃæmb|l, -lz, -lɪŋ, -ld

shambles (s.) 'ʃæmblz

sham|e (s. v.), -es, -ing, -ed ʃeɪm, -z, -ɪŋ, -d

shamefaced ‚ʃeɪm'feɪst ['-- when attributive]

shamefacedly ‚ʃeɪm'feɪstlɪ [-sɪdlɪ, '-‚--]

shamefacedness 'ʃeɪm‚feɪstnɪs [-sɪdnɪs, -nəs, ‚-'---]

shame|ful, -fully, -fulness 'ʃeɪm|fʊl, -fʊlɪ [-fəlɪ], -fʊlnɪs [-nəs]

shameless, -ly, -ness 'ʃeɪmlɪs [-ləs], -lɪ, -nɪs [-nəs]

shammy 'ʃæmɪ

shampoo (s.), -s ʃæm'pu: [‚ʃæm-], -z

shampoo (v.), -(e)s, -ing, -ed ʃæm'pu: [‚ʃæm-], -z, -ɪŋ [-'pʊɪŋ], -d

shamrock (S.) 'ʃæmrɒk

Shan (state, language) ʃɑ:n

shandy (S.) 'ʃændɪ

shandygaff, -s 'ʃændɪgæf, -s

Shane ʃɑ:n, ʃɔ:n, ʃeɪn

Shanghai ‚ʃæŋ'haɪ

shank, -s ʃæŋk, -s

Shanklin 'ʃæŋklɪn

Shanks ʃæŋks

Shannon 'ʃænən

shan't ʃɑ:nt

shantung (silk material) ‚ʃæn'tʌŋ

Shantung ‚ʃæn'dʌŋ [-'tʌŋ, -'dʊŋ, -'tʊŋ]

shant|y, -ies 'ʃænt|ɪ, -ɪz

shanty-town, -s 'ʃæntɪtaʊn, -z

shap|e (s. v.), -es, -ing, -ed ʃeɪp, -s, -ɪŋ, -t

S.H.A.P.E. ʃeɪp

shapeless, -ness 'ʃeɪplɪs [-ləs], -nɪs [-nəs]

shapel|y, -ier, -iest, -iness 'ʃeɪpl|ɪ, -ɪə*, -ɪɪst, -ɪnɪs [-məs]

Shapiro ʃə'pɪərəʊ

shard, -s ʃɑ:d, -z

shar|e (s. v.), -es, -ing, -ed ʃeə*, -z, -rɪŋ, -d

shareholder, -s 'ʃeə‚həʊldə*, -z

share-out, -s 'ʃeəraʊt [‚-'-], -s

shark, -s ʃɑ:k, -s

sharkskin 'ʃɑ:kskɪn

Sharon 'ʃeərɒn ['ʃæ-, 'ʃɑ:-, -rən]

sharp (s. adj. adv.) (S.), -s; -er, -est, -ly, -ness ʃɑ:p, -s; -ə*, -ɪst, -lɪ, -nɪs [-nəs]

Sharpe ʃɑ:p

sharp|en, -ens, -ening, -ened 'ʃɑ:p|ən, -ənz; -nɪŋ [-pnɪŋ], -ənd

sharpener, -s 'ʃɑ:pnə*, -z

sharper (s.), -s 'ʃɑ:pə*, -z

Sharples 'ʃɑ:plz

sharp-set ‚ʃɑ:p'set

sharpshooter, -s 'ʃɑ:p‚ʃu:tə*, -z

sharp-sighted ‚ʃɑ:p'saɪtɪd

sharp-witted ‚ʃɑ:p'wɪtɪd

Shasta (in California) 'ʃæstə

shatter, -s, -ing, -ed 'ʃætə*, -z, -rɪŋ, -d

Shaughnessy 'ʃɔ:nəsɪ

Shaula (star) 'ʃəʊlə

Shaun ʃɔ:n

shav|e (s. v.), -es, -ing/s, -ed ʃeɪv, -z, -ɪŋ/z, -d

shaven 'ʃeɪvn

shaver, -s 'ʃeɪvə*, -z

Shavian 'ʃeɪvjən [-vɪən]

shaving-brush, -es 'ʃeɪvɪŋbrʌʃ, -ɪz

shaving-stick, -s 'ʃeɪvɪŋstɪk, -s

shaw (S.), -s ʃɔ:, -z

shawl, -s ʃɔ:l, -z

shawm, -s ʃɔ:m, -z

shay, -s ʃeɪ, -z

she ʃi: (normal form), ʃɪ (freq. weak form)

shea, -s ʃɪə ['ʃi:ə, ʃi:], -z

Shea ʃeɪ

shea|f, -ves ʃi:|f, -vz

Sheaffer 'ʃeɪfə*

shear (s. v.), -s, -ing, -ed, shorn ʃɪə*, -z, -rɪŋ, -d, ʃɔ:n

Sheard ʃeəd, ʃɪəd, ʃɜ:d

shearer (S.), -s 'ʃɪərə*, -z

Shearman 'ʃɪəmən, 'ʃɜ:mən

Shearme ʃɜ:m

Shearn ʃɪən, ʃɜ:n

shears (S.) ʃɪəz

Shearson 'ʃɪəsn

shearwater, -s 'ʃɪə‚wɔ:tə*, -z

shea|th, -ths ʃi:|θ, -ðz [-θs]

sheath|e, -es, -ing, -ed ʃi:ð, -z, -ɪŋ, -d

sheaves (plur. of sheaf) ʃi:vz

Sheba 'ʃiːbə
she-bear, -s 'ʃiːbeə*, -z
shebeen, -s ʃɪ'biːn [ʃe'b-], -z
she-cat, -s 'ʃiːkæt, -s
Shechem 'ʃiːkem [*among Jews also* 'ʃekem, ʃə'xem]
shed (*s. v.*), -s, -ding ʃed, -z, -ɪŋ
she-devil, -s 'ʃiːˌdevl [ˌ-'---], -z
Shee ʃiː
sheen (S.) ʃiːn
sheen|y (*s. adj.*), -ies 'ʃiːn|ɪ, -ɪz
sheep ʃiːp
sheep-dip 'ʃiːpdɪp
sheep-dog, -s 'ʃiːpdɒg, -z
sheep-fold, -s 'ʃiːpfəʊld, -z
sheepish, -ly, -ness 'ʃiːpɪʃ, -lɪ, -nɪs [-nəs]
sheep-pen, -s 'ʃiːppen, -z
sheep-run, -s 'ʃiːprʌn, -z
Sheepshanks 'ʃiːpʃæŋks
sheep-shearing 'ʃiːpˌʃɪərɪŋ
sheepskin, -s 'ʃiːpskɪn, -z
sheer (*s. adj. v. adv.*), -s, -ing, -ed ʃɪə*, -z, -rɪŋ, -d
Sheerness ˌʃɪə'nes [*also* '-- *according to sentence-stress*]
sheet, -s, -ing ʃiːt, -s, -ɪŋ
sheet-anchor, -s 'ʃiːtˌæŋkə*, -z
sheet-iron 'ʃiːtˌaɪən
sheet-lightning 'ʃiːtˌlaɪtnɪŋ
Sheffield 'ʃefiːld [*locally* -fɪld]
she-goat, -s 'ʃiːgəʊt [*also* ˌʃiː'g- *when preceded by a stress*], -s
sheik(h), -s ʃeɪk [ʃiːk, ʃek, ʃex], -s
Sheila 'ʃiːlə
shekel, -s 'ʃekl, -z
Shekinah ʃe'kaɪnə [ʃɪ'k-]
Shelagh 'ʃiːlə
Sheldon 'ʃeldən
Sheldonian ʃel'dəʊnjən [-nɪən]
sheldrake, -s 'ʃeldreɪk, -s
shelduck, -s 'ʃeldʌk, -s
shel|f, -ves ʃel|f, -vz
shell (*s. v.*), -s, -ing, -ed ʃel, -z, -ɪŋ, -d
shellac (*s. v.*), -s, -king, -ked ʃə'læk [ʃe'l-, 'ʃelæk], -s, -ɪŋ, -t
Shelley 'ʃelɪ
shell-fish 'ʃelfɪʃ
shell-proof 'ʃelpruːf
Shelmerdine 'ʃelmədiːn
shelt|er (*s. v.*), -ers, -ering, -ered; -erless 'ʃelt|ə*, -əz, -ərɪŋ, -əd; -əlɪs [-ləs]
shelv|e, -es, -ing, -ed ʃelv, -z, -ɪŋ, -d
shelves (*plur. of* shelf, *3rd sing. pres. of* shelve) ʃelvz
Shem ʃem
Shemeld 'ʃeməld
shemozzle, -s ʃɪ'mɒzl, -z
Shenandoah ˌʃenən'dəʊə

Shennan 'ʃenən
Shenstone 'ʃenstən
she-oak, -s 'ʃiːəʊk [ˌ-'-], -s
shepherd (*s. v.*) (S.), -s, -ing, -ed 'ʃepəd, -z, -ɪŋ, -ɪd
shepherdess, -es 'ʃepədɪs [-des, ˌʃepə-'des], -ɪz
Shepp|ard, -ey 'ʃep|əd, -ɪ
Sheraton 'ʃerətən
sherbet 'ʃɜːbət
Sherborne 'ʃɜːbən [-bɔːn]
Sherbrooke 'ʃɜːbrʊk
sherd, -s ʃɜːd, -z
Shere ʃɪə*
Sheridan 'ʃerɪdn
sheriff, -s 'ʃerɪf, -s
Sherlock 'ʃɜːlɒk
Sherman 'ʃɜːmən
Sherriff 'ʃerɪf
sherr|y, -ies 'ʃer|ɪ, -ɪz
Sherwood 'ʃɜːwʊd
she's (=she is *or* she has) ʃiːz (*normal form*), ʃɪz (*occasional weak form*)
Shetland, -s, -er/s 'ʃetlənd, -z, -ə*/z
shew, -s, -ing, -ed, -n ʃəʊ, -z, -ɪŋ, -d, -n
shewbread 'ʃəʊbred
Shewell ʃʊəl ['ʃuːəl]
shewn (*from* shew) ʃəʊn
she-wol|f, -ves 'ʃiːwʊl|f [ˌ-'-], -vz
Shewry 'ʃʊərɪ
shibboleth (S.), -s 'ʃɪbəleθ [-bəʊl-], -s
shield (*s. v.*) (S.), -s, -ing, -ed ʃiːld, -z, -ɪŋ, -ɪd
shieling, -s 'ʃiːlɪŋ, -z
shift (*s. v.*), -s, -ing, -ed ʃɪft, -s, -ɪŋ, -ɪd
shiftless 'ʃɪftlɪs [-ləs]
shift|y, -ier, -iest, -ily, -iness 'ʃɪft|ɪ, -ɪə* [-ɪə*], -ɪɪst [-ɪɪst], -ɪlɪ [-əlɪ], -ɪnɪs [-məs]
shikaree, -s ʃɪ'kærɪ [-'kɑː-], -z
Shillan ʃɪ'læn
shillela(g)h (S.), -s ʃɪ'leɪlə [-lɪ], -z
Shilleto [-lito] 'ʃɪlɪtəʊ
shilling, -s; -sworth 'ʃɪlɪŋ, -z; -zwɜːθ [-wəθ]
shilly-shall|y (*s. v.*), -ies, -ying, -ied 'ʃɪlɪˌʃælɪ, -ɪz, -ɪŋ [-jɪŋ], -ɪd
Shiloh 'ʃaɪləʊ
shimmer (*s. v.*), -s, -ing, -ed 'ʃɪmə*, -z, -rɪŋ, -d
shin (*s. v.*), -ning, -ned ʃɪn, -z, -ɪŋ, -d
shin-bone, -s 'ʃɪnbəʊn, -z
shind|y, -ies 'ʃɪnd|ɪ, -ɪz
shin|e (*s. v.*), -es, -ing, -ed, shone ʃaɪn, -z, -ɪŋ, -d, ʃɒn
shingle, -s 'ʃɪŋgl, -z
shingly 'ʃɪŋglɪ

449

Shint|o, -oism, -oist/s 'ʃɪnt|əʊ, -əʊɪzəm, -əʊɪst/s

shin|y, -ier, -iest, -iness 'ʃaɪn|ɪ, -ɪə* [-jə*], -ɪɪst [-jɪst], -ɪnɪs [-məs]

ship (s. v.), -s, -ping, -ped, -per/s ʃɪp, -s, -ɪŋ, -t, -ə*/z

shipboard 'ʃɪpbɔːd [-bəd]

ship-build|er/s, -ing 'ʃɪp,bɪld|ə*/z, -ɪŋ

Shiplake 'ʃɪpleɪk

Shipley 'ʃɪplɪ

shipload, -s 'ʃɪpləʊd, -z

ship-master, -s 'ʃɪp,mɑːstə*, -z

shipmate, -s 'ʃɪpmeɪt, -s

shipment, -s 'ʃɪpmənt, -s

ship-money 'ʃɪp,mʌnɪ

ship-owner, -s 'ʃɪp,əʊnə*, -z

shipshape 'ʃɪpʃeɪp

Shipton 'ʃɪptən

ship-way, -s 'ʃɪpweɪ, -z

shipwreck (s. v.), -s, -ing, -ed 'ʃɪprek, -s, -ɪŋ, -t

shipwright (S.), -s 'ʃɪpraɪt, -s

shipyard, -s 'ʃɪpjɑːd, -z

Shiraz ,ʃɪə'rɑːz

shire, -s 'ʃaɪə*, -z

-shire (suffix) -ʃə* [-,ʃɪə*]

shirk (s. v.), -s, -ing, -ed, -er/s ʃɜːk, -s, -ɪŋ, -t, -ə*/z

Shirley 'ʃɜːlɪ

shirt, -s, -ing/s; -collar/s ʃɜːt, -s, -ɪŋ/z; -,kɒlə*/z

shirt-front, -s 'ʃɜːtfrʌnt, -s

shirty 'ʃɜːtɪ

Shishak 'ʃaɪʃæk [-ʃək, rarely 'ʃɪʃ-]

Shiva 'ʃiːvə ['ʃɪvə] (Hindi ʃyva)

shiv|er, -ers, -ering/ly, -ered 'ʃɪv|ə*, -əz, -ərɪŋ/lɪ, -əd

shiver|y, -iness 'ʃɪvər|ɪ, -ɪnɪs [-məs]

shoal, -s ʃəʊl, -z

shock (s. v.), -s, -ing/ly, -ed, -er/s ʃɒk, -s, -ɪŋ/lɪ, -t, -ə*/z

shockhead, -s, -ed 'ʃɒkhed, -z, -ɪd

shod (from shoe v.) ʃɒd

shodd|y, -ier, -iest, -ily, -iness 'ʃɒd|ɪ, -ɪə*, -ɪɪst, -ɪlɪ [-əlɪ], -ɪnɪs [-məs]

shoe (s. v.), -s, -ing, shod ʃuː, -z, -ɪŋ ['ʃʊɪŋ], ʃɒd

shoeblack, -s 'ʃuːblæk, -s

Shoeburyness ,ʃuːbərɪ'nes

shoehorn, -s 'ʃuːhɔːn, -z

shoe-lace, -s 'ʃuːleɪs, -ɪz

shoe-leather 'ʃuː,leðə*

shoeless 'ʃuːlɪs [-ləs]

shoe-maker, -s 'ʃuː,meɪkə*, -z

Shona (language) 'ʃɒnə ['ʃəʊnə]

shone (from shine) ʃɒn

shoo (v. interj.), -s, -ing, -ed ʃuː, -z, -ɪŋ, -d

shook (from shake) ʃʊk

Shoolbred 'ʃuːlbred

shoot (s. v.), -s, -ing, shot ʃuːt, -s, -ɪŋ, ʃɒt

shooter (S.), -s 'ʃuːtə*, -z

shooting-box, -es 'ʃuːtɪŋbɒks, -ɪz

shooting-galler|y, -ies 'ʃuːtɪŋ,gælər|ɪ, -ɪz

shop (s. v.), -s, -ping, -ped ʃɒp, -s, -ɪŋ, -t

shop-assistant, -s 'ʃɒpə,sɪstənt, -s

shop-floor ,ʃɒp'flɔː* [-'flɔə*]

shop-girl, -s 'ʃɒpgɜːl, -z

shopkeeper, -s 'ʃɒp,kiːpə*, -z

shop-lift|er/s, -ing 'ʃɒp,lɪft|ə*/z, -ɪŋ

shop|man, -men 'ʃɒp|mən, -mən [-men]

shoppy 'ʃɒpɪ

shop-soiled ,ʃɒp'sɔɪld ['--]

shop-steward, -s ,ʃɒp'stjʊəd [-'stjuːəd, '-,-(-)], -z

shop-walker, -s 'ʃɒp,wɔːkə*, -z

shop-window, -s ,ʃɒp'wɪndəʊ, -z

shore, -s ʃɔː* [ʃɔə*], -z

Shore|ditch, -ham 'ʃɔː|dɪtʃ ['ʃɔə-], -rəm

shoreward 'ʃɔːwəd ['ʃɔə-]

shorn (from shear) ʃɔːn

Shorncliffe 'ʃɔːnklɪf

short (s. adj.) (S.), -s; -er, -est, -ly, -ness ʃɔːt, -s; -ə*, -ɪst, -lɪ, -nɪs [-nəs]

shortage, -s 'ʃɔːtɪdʒ, -ɪz

shortbread, -s 'ʃɔːtbred, -z

shortcake, -s 'ʃɔːtkeɪk, -s

short-circuit (s. v.), -s, -ing, -ed ,ʃɔːt-'sɜːkɪt, -s, -ɪŋ, -ɪd

shortcoming, -s ,ʃɔːt'kʌmɪŋ ['-,--], -z

short-dated ,ʃɔːt'deɪtɪd

short-eared 'ʃɔːt,ɪəd

short|en, -ens, -ening, -ened 'ʃɔːt|n, -nz, -nɪŋ [-ŋɪŋ], -nd

shortfall, -s 'ʃɔːtfɔːl, -z

shorthand 'ʃɔːthænd

short-handed ,ʃɔːt'hændɪd

shorthorn, -s 'ʃɔːthɔːn, -z

short-lived ,ʃɔːt'lɪvd [also '-- when attributive]

short-sighted, -ly, -ness ,ʃɔːt'saɪtɪd, -lɪ, -nɪs [-nəs]

short-tempered ,ʃɔːt'tempəd [also '-,-- when attributive]

short-term 'ʃɔːtɜːm [,-'-]

short-winded ,ʃɔːt'wɪndɪd

Shostakovich ,ʃɒstə'kəʊvɪtʃ

shot, -s ʃɒt, -s

shot-gun, -s 'ʃɒtgʌn, -z

shough, -s ʃʌf, -s

should ʃʊd (strong form), ʃəd, ʃd, ʃt (weak forms)

) Note.—The form ʃt occurs only before voiceless consonants.

450

should|er (*s. v.*), **-ers, -ering, -ered**
'ʃəʊld|ə*, -əz, -ərɪŋ, -əd
shoulder-blade, -s 'ʃəʊldəbleɪd, -z
shoulder-strap, -s 'ʃəʊldəstræp, -s
shouldn't 'ʃʊdnt
shout (*s. v.*), **-s, -ing, -ed** ʃaʊt, -s, -ɪŋ, -ɪd
shov|e (*s. v.*), **-es, -ing, -ed** ʃʌv, -z, -ɪŋ, -d
Shove (*surname*) ʃəʊv
shov|el (*s. v.*) (**S.**), **-els, -elling, -elled, -eller/s;** -elful/s 'ʃʌv|l, -lz, -lɪŋ [-lɪŋ], -ld, -lə*/z [-lə*/z]; -lfʊl/z
show (*s. v.*), **-s, -ing, -ed, -n** ʃəʊ, -z, -ɪŋ, -d, -n
show-business 'ʃəʊˌbɪznɪs
show-case, -s 'ʃəʊkeɪs, -ɪz
show-down, -s 'ʃəʊdaʊn, -z
shower (*one who shows*), -s 'ʃəʊə*, -z
shower (*s. v.*) (*fall of rain, etc.*), **-s, -ing, -ed;** -y 'ʃaʊə*, -z, -rɪŋ, -d; -rɪ
shower-ba|th, -ths 'ʃaʊəba:|θ, -ðz
show|man, -men 'ʃəʊ|mən, -mən [-men]
showmanship 'ʃəʊmənʃɪp
shown (*from* show) ʃəʊn
showpiece, -s 'ʃəʊpiːs, -ɪz
show-place, -s 'ʃəʊpleɪs, -ɪz
show-room, -s 'ʃəʊrʊm [-ruːm], -z
show|y, -ier, -iest, -ily, -iness 'ʃəʊ|ɪ, -ɪə*, -ɪɪst, -ɪlɪ [-əlɪ], -ɪnɪs [-ɪnəs]
shrank (*from* shrink) ʃræŋk
shrapnel 'ʃræpnl [-nəl]
shred (*s. v.*), **-s, -ding, -ded** ʃred, -z, -ɪŋ, -ɪd
shrew, -s ʃruː, -z
shrewd, -er, -est, -ly, -ness ʃruːd, -ə*, -ɪst, -lɪ, -nɪs [-nəs]
shrewish, -ly, -ness 'ʃruːɪʃ, -lɪ, -nɪs [-nəs]
Shrewsbury 'ʃrəʊzbərɪ ['ʃruːz-]
  Note.—'ʃrəʊ- is the pronunciation used by those connected with Shrewsbury School and by many residents in the neighbourhood. The form 'ʃruː- is used by outsiders, and is commonly heard in the town.
shriek (*s. v.*), **-s, -ing, -ed** ʃriːk, -s, -ɪŋ, -t
shrieval|t|y, -ies 'ʃriːvlt|ɪ, -ɪz
shrift ʃrɪft
shrike, -s ʃraɪk, -s
shrill, -er, -est, -y, -ness ʃrɪl, -ə*, -ɪst, -ɪ, -nɪs [-nəs]
shrimp, -s, -ing, -er/s ʃrɪmp, -s, -ɪŋ, -ə*/z
shrine, -s ʃraɪn, -z
shrink, -s, -ing/ly, shrank, shrunk, shrunken ʃrɪŋk, -s, -ɪŋ/lɪ, ʃræŋk, ʃrʌŋk, 'ʃrʌŋkən
shrinkage 'ʃrɪŋkɪdʒ

shriv|e (**S.**), **-es, -ing, shrove, shriven** ʃraɪv, -z, -ɪŋ, ʃrəʊv, 'ʃrɪvn
shriv|el, -els, -elling, -elled 'ʃrɪv|l, -lz, -lɪŋ [-lɪŋ], -ld
Shropshire 'ʃrɒpʃə* [-ˌʃɪə*]
shroud (*s. v.*), **-s, -ing, -ed; -less** ʃraʊd, -z, -ɪŋ, -ɪd; -lɪs [-ləs]
Shrove ʃrəʊv
shrub, -s ʃrʌb, -z
shrubber|y, -ies 'ʃrʌbər|ɪ, -ɪz
shrubby 'ʃrʌbɪ
shrug (*s. v.*), **-s, -ging, -ged** ʃrʌg, -z, -ɪŋ, -d
shrunk (*from* shrink), -en ʃrʌŋk, -ən
Shubrook 'ʃuːbrʊk
shuck, -s ʃʌk, -s
Shuckburgh 'ʃʌkbrə
shudder, -s, -ing, -ed 'ʃʌdə*, -z, -rɪŋ, -d
shuff|le, -les, -ling, -led, -ler/s 'ʃʌf|l, -lz, -lɪŋ [-lɪŋ], -ld, -lə*/z [-lə*/z]
shuffle-board, -s 'ʃʌflbɔːd [-bəʊd], -z
shun, -s, -ning, -ned ʃʌn, -z, -ɪŋ, -d
shunt (*s. v.*), **-s, -ing, -ed, -er/s** ʃʌnt, -s, -ɪŋ, -ɪd, -ə*/z
shut, -s, -ting ʃʌt, -s, -ɪŋ
Shute ʃuːt
Shutte ʃuːt
shutter, -s, -ed 'ʃʌtə*, -z, -d
shuttle, -s; -cock/s 'ʃʌtl, -z; -kɒk/s
sh|y (*s. adj. v.*), -ies, -yer, -yest, -yly, -yness; -ying, -ied ʃ|aɪ, -aɪz; -aɪə*, -aɪɪst, -aɪlɪ, -aɪnɪs [-nəs]; -aɪɪŋ, -aɪd
Shylock 'ʃaɪlɒk
si (*musical note*) siː
Siam ˌsaɪ'æm ['saɪæm]
Siamese ˌsaɪə'miːz
Sibelius sɪ'beɪlɪəs [-ljəs]
Siberia, -n/s saɪ'bɪərɪə, -n/z
sibilant (*s. adj.*), -s 'sɪbɪlənt, -s
sibilation, -s ˌsɪbɪ'leɪʃn, -z
Sible (*in Essex*) 'sɪbl
Sibley 'sɪblɪ
sibling, -s 'sɪblɪŋ, -z
Sibun 'saɪbən
sibyl (**S.**), -s 'sɪbɪl [-bəl], -z
sibylline sɪ'bɪlaɪn ['sɪbɪl-]
sic sɪk
sice, -s saɪs, -ɪz
Sichel 'sɪtʃəl
Sichem 'saɪkem
Sicilian, -s sɪ'sɪljən [-lɪən], -z
siciliano, -s sɪˌsɪlɪ'ɑːnəʊ [sɪˌtʃɪ-, ˌ——'—], -z
Sicill|y, -ies 'sɪsɪl|ɪ [-səl|ɪ], -ɪz
sick, -er, -est, -ness sɪk, -ə*, -ɪst, -nɪs [-nəs]
sick-bed, -s 'sɪkbed, -z

sick|en, -ens, -ening (adj. v.), -ened, -ener/s 'sık|ən, -ənz, -nıŋ [-ənıŋ], -nd, -nə*/z [-nə*/z]
sickish 'sıkıʃ
sickle, -s 'sıkl, -z
sick-list, -s 'sıklıst, -s
sickl|y, -ier, -iest, -iness 'sıkl|ı, -ıə*, -ııst, -mıs [-nəs]
sickness 'sıknıs [-nəs]
sick-nurse, -s 'sıknə:s, -ız
sick-room, -s 'sıkrʊm [-ru:m], -z
Siddeley 'sıdəlı
Siddons 'sıdnz
sid|e (s. v.), -es, -ing, -ed saıd, -z, -ıŋ, -ıd
sideboard, -s 'saıdbɔ:d [-bɔəd], -z
Sidebotham 'saıd,bɒtəm
side-car, -s 'saıdkɑ:*, -z
sidelight, -s 'saıdlaıt, -s
side-line, -s 'saıdlaın, -z
sidelong 'saıdlɒŋ
sidereal saı'dıərıəl
siderite 'saıdəraıt
Sidery 'saıdərı
side-saddle, -s 'saıd,sædl, -z
side-show, -s 'saıdʃəʊ, -z
side-slip (s. v.), -s, -ping, -ped 'saıdslıp, -s, -ıŋ, -t
sides|man, -men 'saıdz|mən, -mən [-men]
side-stroke 'saıdstrəʊk
side-track (s. v.), -s, -ing, -ed 'saıdtræk, -s, -ıŋ, -t
side-walk, -s 'saıdwɔ:k, -s
sideways 'saıdweız
Sidgwick 'sıdʒwık
siding (s.), -s 'saıdıŋ, -z
sid|le, -les, -ling, -led 'saıd|l, -lz, -lıŋ [-lɪŋ], -ld
Sid|mouth, -ney 'sıd|məθ, -nı
Sidon 'saıdn [-dɒn]
Sidonian, -s saı'dəʊnjən [-nıən], -z
Sidonie sı'dəʊnı
siege, -s si:dʒ, -ız
Siegfried 'si:gfri:d ('zi:kfri:t)
Sieglinde sı:g'lındə (zi:k'lındə)
Siegmund 'si:gmʊnd [-mənd] ('zi:k-munt)
Siemens 'si:mənz
sienna sı'enə
Sien(n)a sı'enə
Sien(n)ese ,sıe'ni:z [,sıə'n-]
sierra (S.), -s 'sıərə [sı'erə], -z
Sierra Leone sı,erəlı'əʊn [,sıər-, -'əʊnı]
siesta, -s sı'estə, -z
siev|e (s. v.), -es, -ing, -ed sıv, -z, -ıŋ, -d
sift, -s. -ing, -ed, -er/s sıft, -s, -ıŋ, -ıd, -ə*/z
sigh (s. v.), -s, -ing, -ed saı, -z, -ıŋ, -d

sight (s. v.), -s, -ing, -ed; -less saıt, -s, -ıŋ, -ıd; -lıs [-ləs]
sightl|y, -iness 'saıtl|ı, -ınıs [-ınəs]
sight-read|er/s, -ing 'saıt,ri:d|ə*/z, -ıŋ
sight-seeing 'saıt,si:ıŋ
sightseer, -s 'saıt,si:ə* ['saıt,sıə*], -z
Sigismond [-mund] 'sıgısmənd
sigma, -s 'sıgmə, -z
sign (s. v.), -s, -ing, -ed saın, -z, -ıŋ, -d
sign|al (s. adj. v.), -als; -ally; -alling, -alled, -aller/s 'sıgn|l [-əl], -l̩z [-əlz]; -əlı; -l̩ıŋ [-əlıŋ], -l̩d [-əld], -ələ*/z
signal-box, -es 'sıgnlbɒks [-nəl-], -ız
signaliz|e [-is|e), -es, -ing, -ed 'sıgnəl-aız, -ız, -ıŋ, -d
signal|man, -men 'sıgnl̩|mən [-nəl|-, -mæn], -mən [-men]
signator|y, -ies 'sıgnətər|ı, -ız
signature, -s 'sıgnətʃə* [-nɪtʃ-], -z
signboard, -s 'saınbɔ:d [-bɔəd], -z
signeme, -s 'sıgni:m, -z
signet, -s 'sıgnıt, -s
signet-ring, -s 'sıgnıtrıŋ, -z
significan|ce, -t/ly sıg'nıfıkən|s, -t/lı
signification ,sıgnıfı'keıʃn
significative sıg'nıfıkətıv [-keıt-]
signi|fy, -fies, -fying, -fied 'sıgnı|faı, -faız, -faııŋ, -faıd
Signior 'si:njɔ:*
signor (S.), -s 'si:njɔ:* (siɲ'ɲor), -z
sign-paint|er/s, -ing 'saın,peınt|ə*/z, -ıŋ
sign-post, -s 'saınpəʊst, -s
Sigurd (English Christian name) 'si:gə:d, (Scandinavian name) 'sı,gʊəd [-gə:d]
Sikes saıks
Sikh, -s si:k (Hindi sikh), -s
Sikkim 'sıkım
silage 'saılıdʒ
Silas 'saıləs [-læs]
Silchester 'sıltʃıstə*
silenc|e (s. v.), -es, -ing, -ed 'saıləns, -ız, -ıŋ, -t
silencer, -s 'saılənsə*, -z
silent, -ly 'saılənt, -lı
Silenus saı'li:nəs
Silesia saı'li:zjə [sı'l-, -zıə, -ʒjə, -ʒıə, -ʒə, -sjə, -sıə, -ʃjə, -ʃıə, -ʃə]
Silesian, -s saı'li:zjən [sı'l-, -zıən, -ʒjən, -ʒıən, -ʒn, -sjən, -sıən, -ʃjən, -ʃıən, -ʃn], -z
silex 'saıleks
silhouette, -s ,sılu:'et [-lʊ'et, '---], -s
silic|a, -ate, -ated 'sılık|ə, -ıt [-eıt, -ət], -eıtıd
silicon 'sılıkən
silicone 'sılıkəʊn
silicosis ,sılı'kəʊsıs

silicotic (s. adj.), -s ,sɪlɪ'kɒtɪk, -s
silk, -s, -en sɪlk, -s, -ən
silkworm, -s 'sɪlkwəːm, -z
silk|y, -ier, -iest, -iness 'sɪlk|ɪ, -ɪə*
[-jə*], -ɪɪst [-jɪst], -ɪnɪs [-ɪnəs]
sill, -s (S.) sɪl, -z
sillabub 'sɪləbʌb [-bəb]
Sillence 'saɪləns
Sillery 'sɪlərɪ
Sillitoe 'sɪlɪtəʊ
sill|y (s. adj.), -ies; -ier, -iest, -ily, -iness
'sɪl|ɪ, -ɪz; -ɪə*, -ɪɪst, -ɪlɪ [-əlɪ], -ɪnɪs
[-ɪnəs]
silo, -s 'saɪləʊ, -z
Siloam saɪ'ləʊəm [-'ləʊæm]
silt (s. v.), -s, -ing, -ed; -y sɪlt, -s, -ɪŋ,
-ɪd; -ɪ
Silurian saɪ'ljʊərɪən [sɪ'l-, -'lʊə-, -'ljɔər-,
-'ljɔːr-]
Silva 'sɪlvə
silvan 'sɪlvən
Silvanus sɪl'veɪnəs
silv|er (s. v.), -ers, -ering, -ered; -ery,
-eriness 'sɪlv|ə*, -əz, -ərɪŋ, -əd; -ərɪ,
-ərɪnɪs [-ɪnəs]
silver-gilt ,sɪlvə'gɪlt [also '--- when
attributive]
silver-grey ,sɪlvə'greɪ
silver-plate ,sɪlvə'pleɪt
silverside, -s 'sɪlvəsaɪd, -z
silversmith, -s 'sɪlvəsmɪθ, -s
Silvertown, -s 'sɪlvətaʊn, -z
Silvester sɪl'vestə*
Silvia 'sɪlvɪə [-vjə]
Simca 'sɪmkə
Simenon 'siːmənɔ̃ːŋ [-nɒn] (simnɔ̃)
Simeon 'sɪmɪən [-mjən]
simian (s. adj.), -s 'sɪmɪən [-mjən], -z
similar, -ly 'sɪmɪlə* [-mələ*], -lɪ
similarit|y, -ies ,sɪmɪ'lærət|ɪ [-məˈl-,
-ɪt|ɪ], -ɪz
simile, -s 'sɪmɪlɪ, -z
similitude, -s sɪ'mɪlɪtjuːd, -z
Simla 'sɪmlə
simmer, -s, -ing, -ed 'sɪmə*, -z, -rɪŋ, -d
Simmon(d)s 'sɪmənz
simnel (S.), -s 'sɪmnl̩ [-nəl], -z
Simon 'saɪmən, as surname also sɪ'məʊn
Simond 'saɪmənd, 'sɪmənd
Simonds (Lord) 'sɪmənd z
simoniacal ,saɪmə'naɪəkl [-məʊ'n-]
simony 'saɪmənɪ
simoom, -s sɪ'muːm, -z
simper (s. v.), -s, -ing, -ed 'sɪmpə*, -z,
-rɪŋ, -d
Simpkin, -s, -son 'sɪmpkɪn, -z, -sn
simp|le, -ler, -lest, -ly, -leness 'sɪmp|l̩,
-lə*, -lɪst, -lɪ, -lnɪs [-nəs]

simplehearted ,sɪmpl'hɑːtɪd ['--,--]
simple-minded ,sɪmpl'maɪndɪd [also
'--,-- when attributive]
simpleton, -s 'sɪmpltən, -z
simplicity sɪm'plɪsətɪ [-ɪtɪ]
simplification, -s ,sɪmplɪfɪ'keɪʃn, -z
simpli|fy, -fies, -fying, -fied 'sɪmplɪ|faɪ,
-faɪz, -faɪɪŋ, -faɪd
Simplon 'sæmplɔ̃ːŋ ['sæmp-, 'sɪmplən]
(sɛ̃plɔ̃)
simply 'sɪmplɪ
Simpson 'sɪmpsn
Sims sɪmz
Simson 'sɪmsn [-mps-]
simulacr|um, -a ,sɪmjʊ'leɪkr|əm, -ə
simulat|e, -es, -ing, -ed 'sɪmjʊleɪt, -s,
-ɪŋ, -ɪd
simulation, -s ,sɪmjʊ'leɪʃn, -z
simultaneity ,sɪməltə'niːɪtɪ [,saɪm-,
-mʊl-, -'niːɪtɪ, -'niːətɪ, -'neɪtɪ, -neɪətɪ]
simultaneous, -ly, -ness ,sɪməl'teɪnjəs
[,saɪm-, -mʊl-, -nɪəs], -lɪ, -nɪs [-nəs]
sin (s. v.), -s, -ning, -ned, -ner/s sɪn, -z,
-ɪŋ, -d, -ə*/z
sin (in trigonometry) saɪn
Sinai 'saɪnɪaɪ [-neɪaɪ, -naɪ]
sinapism, -s 'sɪnəpɪzəm, -z
Sinatra sɪ'nɑːtrə
Sinbad 'sɪnbæd
since sɪns
sincere, -r, -st, -ly, -ness sɪn'sɪə* [sn-],
-rə*, -rɪst, -lɪ, -nɪs [-nəs]
sincerity sɪn'serətɪ [sn-, -rɪtɪ]
sinciput, -s 'sɪnsɪpʌt [-pət], -s
Sinclair 'sɪŋkleə* ['sɪnk-], 'sɪŋklə*
Sind sɪnd
Sindbad 'sɪnbæd [-ndb-]
Sindh sɪnd (Hindi syndh)
Sindhi 'sɪndiː [-dɪ] (Hindi syndhi)
Sindlesham 'sɪndlʃəm
sine, -s saɪn, -z
sinecure, -s 'saɪnɪˌkjʊə* ['sɪn-, -kjɔə*,
-kjɔː*], -z
sine die ,saɪnɪ'daɪiː [-daɪ, ,sɪnɪ'diːeɪ]
Sinel 'sɪnəl
sine qua non, -s ,saɪnɪkweɪ'nɒn [,sɪnɪ-
kwɑː'nəʊn], -z
sinew, -s 'sɪnjuː:, -z
sinewy 'sɪnjuːɪ [-njʊɪ]
sin|ful, -fully, -fulness 'sɪn|fʊl, -fʊlɪ
[-fəlɪ], -fʊlnɪs [-nəs]
sing, -s, -ing, sang, sung, singer/s sɪŋ,
-z, -ɪŋ, sæŋ, sʌŋ, 'sɪŋə*/z
singable 'sɪŋəbl
Singapore ,sɪŋə'pɔː:* [,sɪŋgə-,-'pɔə*]
singe, -s, -ing, -d sɪndʒ, -ɪz, -ɪŋ, -d
Singer 'sɪŋə*, 'sɪŋgə*
Singhalese ,sɪŋhə'liːz [,sɪŋgə'l-]

singing-master, -s 'sɪŋɪŋ,mɑːstə*, -z
sing|le, -ly, -leness 'sɪŋg|l, -lɪ, -lnɪs [-nəs]
single-handed ,sɪŋgl'hændɪd
singlehearted, -ly, -ness ,sɪŋgl'hɑːtɪd ['--,--], -lɪ, -nɪs [-nəs]
single-minded ,sɪŋgl'maɪndɪd ['--,--]
singlestick, -s 'sɪŋglstɪk, -s
singlet, -s 'sɪŋglɪt [-lət], -s
singleton (S.), -s 'sɪŋgltən, -z
singly 'sɪŋglɪ
singsong (s. adj.), -s 'sɪŋsɒŋ, -z
singular (s. adj.), -s, -ly 'sɪŋgjʊlə* [-gjəl-], -z, -lɪ
singularit|y, -ies ,sɪŋgjʊ'lærət|ɪ [-gjə'l-, -ɪt|ɪ], -ɪz
sinh (in trigonometry) ʃaɪn
Sinhalese ,sɪŋhə'liːz [,sɪnhə'l-, ,sɪnə'l-]
Sinim 'sɪnɪm ['saɪn-]
sinister 'sɪnɪstə*
sinistr|al, -ally 'sɪnɪstr|əl, -əlɪ
sink (s. v.), -s, -ing, sank, sunk, sunken, sink|er/s; -able sɪŋk, -s, -ɪŋ, sæŋk, sʌŋk, 'sʌŋkən, 'sɪŋk|ə*/z; -əbl
sinless, -ly, -ness 'sɪnlɪs [-ləs], -lɪ, -nɪs [-nəs]
sinner, -s 'sɪnə*, -z
Sinnett 'sɪnɪt, sɪ'net
Sinn Fein, -er/s ,ʃɪn'feɪn [,sɪn-], -ə*/z
sinologue, -s 'sɪnəlɒg ['saɪ-, -ləʊg], -z
sinolog|y, -ist sɪ'nɒlədʒ|ɪ [saɪ'n-], -ɪst
sinuosit|y, -ies ,sɪnjʊ'ɒsət|ɪ [-ɪt|ɪ], -ɪz
sinuous 'sɪnjʊəs [-njwəs]
sinus, -es 'saɪnəs, -ɪz
sinusitis ,saɪnə'saɪtɪs
sinusoid, -s 'saɪnəsɔɪd, -z
Siobhan ʃɪ'vɔːn [ʃə'v-]
Sion 'saɪən ['zaɪən]
Sioux (sing.) suː, (plur.) suːz
sip (s. v.), -s, -ping, -ped sɪp, -s, -ɪŋ, -t
siph|on (s. v.), -ons, -oning, -oned 'saɪf|n, -nz, -ənɪŋ [-nɪŋ], -nd
sir, -s sɜː*, -z (strong form), sə* (weak form)
Sirach 'sɪəræk
sirdar (S.), -s 'sɜːdɑː*, -z
sir|e (s. v.), -es, -ing, -ed 'saɪə*, -z, -rɪŋ, -d
siren, -s 'saɪərən [-rɪn], -z
Sirion 'sɪrɪən
Sirius (star) 'sɪrɪəs [rarely 'saɪər-]
sirloin, -s 'sɜːlɔɪn, -z
sirocco, -s sɪ'rɒkəʊ, -z
sirrah 'sɪrə
sisal 'saɪsl [old-fashioned 'sɪsl]
Sisal (Mexican port) sɪ'sɑːl (si'sal)
Sisam 'saɪsəm
Sisera 'sɪsərə

siskin (S.), -s 'sɪskɪn, -z
sisson (S.) 'sɪsn
siss|y, -ies 'sɪs|ɪ, -ɪz
sister, -s; -ly 'sɪstə*, -z; -lɪ
sisterhood, -s 'sɪstəhʊd, -z
sister-in-law, sisters-in-law 'sɪstərɪnlɔː, 'sɪstəzɪnlɔː
Sistine 'sɪstiːn [-taɪn]
sistrum, -s 'sɪstrəm, -z
Sisum 'saɪsəm
Sisyphean ,sɪsɪ'fiːən [-'frən]
Sisyphus 'sɪsɪfəs
sit, -s, -ting/s, sat, sitter/s sɪt, -s, -ɪŋ/z, sæt, 'sɪtə*/z
sitar sɪ'tɑː
sit-down (s.) 'sɪtdaʊn
site, -s saɪt, -s
sit-in, -s 'sɪtɪn, -z
sitter-in, sitters-in ,sɪtər'ɪn, ,sɪtəz'ɪn
Sittingbourne 'sɪtɪŋbɔːn [-bɔən]
situate (adj.) 'sɪtjʊeɪt [-tʃʊeɪt, -tjʊɪt, -tʃʊɪt, -ʊət]
situat|e (v.), -es, -ing, -ed 'sɪtjʊeɪt [-tʃʊ-], -s, -ɪŋ, -ɪd
situation, -s ,sɪtjʊ'eɪʃn [-tʃʊ-], -z
Sitwell 'sɪtwəl [-wel]
Siva 'siːvə ['ʃiːv-, 'sɪv-, 'ʃɪv-] (Hindi ʃɪva)
Sivyer (surname) 'sɪvɪə* [-vjə*]
Siward 'sjuːəd [sjʊəd]
six, -es; -fold sɪks, -ɪz; -fəʊld
sixain, -s 'sɪkseɪn, -z
sixer, -s 'sɪksə*, -z
six-foot (adj.) 'sɪksfʊt
six-footer, -s ,sɪks'fʊtə*, -z
sixish 'sɪksɪʃ
six|pence, -pences, -penny 'sɪks|pəns, -pənsɪz, -pənɪ (see note under penny)
six-shooter, -s ,sɪks'ʃuːtə* [,sɪkʃ'ʃ-], -z
sixte sɪkst
sixteen, -s, -th/s, -thly ,sɪks'tiːn ['-- according to sentence-stress], -z, -θ/s, -θlɪ
sixteenmo [16mo] sɪks'tiːnməʊ
sixth, -s, -ly sɪksθ [-kstθ], -s, -lɪ
Sixtus 'sɪkstəs
sixt|y, -ies, -ieth/s 'sɪkst|ɪ, -ɪz, -nθ/s [-jɪθ/s, -ɪəθ/s, -jəθ/s]
sizar, -s; -ship/s 'saɪzə*, -z; -ʃɪp/s
siz|e (s. v.), -es, -ing, -ed saɪz, -ɪz, -ɪŋ, -d
siz(e)able 'saɪzəbl
sizz|le, -les, -ling, -led 'sɪz|l, -lz, -lɪŋ [-lɪŋ], -ld
sjambok (s. v.), -s, -ing, -ed 'ʃæmbɒk, -s, -ɪŋ, -t
Skagerrak 'skægəræk
skat|e (s. v.), -es, -ing, -ed, -er/s skeɪt, -s, -ɪŋ, -ɪd, -ə*/z

skating-rink, -s 'skeɪtɪŋrɪŋk, -s
skean dhu, -s ˌskiːənˈduː [ˌskiən-], -z
Skeat skiːt
skedadd|le, -les, -ling, -led skɪˈdæd|l,
-lz, -l̩ŋ [-lɪŋ], -ld
Skeggs skegz
Skegness ˌskegˈnes ['-- according to
sentence-stress]
skein, -s skeɪn, -z
skeletal 'skelɪtl [skəˈliːtl]
skeleton, -s 'skelɪtn, -z
skelter 'skeltə*
Skelton 'skeltən
sketch (s. v.), -es, -ing, -ed; -able sketʃ,
-ɪz, -ɪŋ, -t; -əbl
sketch-book, -s 'sketʃbʊk, -s
Sketchley 'sketʃlɪ
sketch|y, -ier, -iest, -ily, -iness 'sketʃ|ɪ,
-ɪə*, -ɪɪst, -ɪlɪ [-əlɪ], -ɪnɪs [-ɪnəs]
skew (s. adj.), -s skjuː, -z
skewer (s. v.), -s, -ing, -ed skjʊə*, -z,
-rɪŋ, -d
Skey skiː
ski (s. v.), -s, -ing, -'d [ski-ed] skiː, -z,
-ɪŋ, -d
skiagram, -s 'skaɪəgræm, -z
skiagraph, -s 'skaɪəgrɑːf [-græf], -s
Skibo 'skiːbəʊ
ski-borne 'skiːbɔːn [-bɔən]
skid, -s, -ding, -ded skɪd, -z, -ɪŋ, -ɪd
Skiddaw 'skɪdɔː [locally also -də]
skier (one who skis), -s 'skiːə*, -z
skiff, -s skɪf, -s
skiffle 'skɪfl
ski-jump, -s 'skiːdʒʌmp, -s
skil|ful, -fully, -fulness 'skɪl|fʊl, -fʊlɪ
[-fəlɪ], -fʊlnɪs [-nəs]
skill, -s, -ed skɪl, -z, -d
skilly 'skɪlɪ
skim, -s, -ming, -med, -mer/s skɪm, -z,
-ɪŋ, -d, -ə*/z
skim-milk ˌskɪm'mɪlk ['--]
skimp, -s, -ing/ly, -ed; -y, -ier, -iest,
-iness skɪmp, -s, -ɪŋ/lɪ, -t [skɪmt]; -ɪ,
-ɪə* [-jə*], -ɪɪst [-jɪst], -ɪnɪs [-ɪnəs]
skin (s. v.), -s, -ning, -ned skɪn, -z, -ɪŋ,
-d
skin-deep ˌskɪn'diːp ['--]
skin-div|e, -es, -ing, -ed, -er/s 'skɪn-
daɪv, -z, -ɪŋ, -d, -ə*/z
skinflint, -s 'skɪnflɪnt, -s
skinhead, -s 'skɪnhed, -s
skinner (S.), -s 'skɪnə*, -z
skinn|y, -ier, -iest, -iness 'skɪn|ɪ, -ɪə*,
-ɪɪst, -ɪnɪs [-ɪnəs]
skip (s. v.), -s, -ping, -ped skɪp, -s, -ɪŋ, -t
skipper, -s 'skɪpə*, -z
skipping-rope, -s 'skɪpɪŋrəʊp, -s

Skipton 'skɪptən
skirmish (s. v.), -es, -ing, -ed, -er/s
'skɜːmɪʃ, -ɪz, -ɪŋ, -t, -ə*/z
skirt (s. v.), -s, -ing/s, -ed skɜːt, -s,
-ɪŋ/z, -ɪd
skirt-danc|er/s, -ing 'skɜːtˌdɑːns|ə*/z,
-ɪŋ
skirting-board, -s 'skɜːtɪŋbɔːd [-bɔəd],
-z
skit, -s skɪt, -s
ski-troops 'skiːtruːps
skittish, -ly, -ness 'skɪtɪʃ, -lɪ, -nɪs
[-nəs]
skittle, -s 'skɪtl, -z
skiv|e, -es, -ing, -ed, -er/s skaɪv, -z, -ɪŋ,
-d, -ə*/z
skivv|y, -ies 'skɪv|ɪ, -ɪz
Skrimshire 'skrɪmʃə*
Skrine skriːn
skua, -s 'skjuːə [skjʊə], -z
skulduggery skʌl'dʌgərɪ
skulk, -s, -ing, -ed skʌlk, -s, -ɪŋ, -t
skull, -s skʌl, -z
skull-cap, -s 'skʌlkæp, -s
skunk, -s skʌŋk, -s
sk|y (s. v.), -ies, -ying, -ied, -ier/s sk|aɪ,
-aɪz, -aɪɪŋ, -aɪd, -aɪə*/z
sky-blue ˌskaɪ'bluː [also '-- when attri-
butive]
Skye skaɪ
sky-high ˌskaɪ'haɪ
skyjack (s. v.), -s, -ing, -ed, -er/s
'skaɪdʒæk, -s, -ɪŋ, -t, -ə*/z
skylark (s. v.), -s, -ing, -ed 'skaɪlɑːk, -s,
-ɪŋ, -t
skylight, -s 'skaɪlaɪt, -s
sky-line, -s 'skaɪlaɪn, -z
skymaster, -s 'skaɪˌmɑːstə*, -z
sky-rocket (s. v.), -s, -ing, -ed 'skaɪ-
ˌrɒkɪt, -s, -ɪŋ, -ɪd
skyscape, -s 'skaɪskeɪp, -s
skyscraper, -s 'skaɪˌskreɪpə*, -z
skyward, -s 'skaɪwəd, -z
sky-writing 'skaɪˌraɪtɪŋ
slab (s. v.), -s, -bing, -bed slæb, -z, -ɪŋ,
-d
slack (s. adj. v.), -s; -er, -est, -ly, -ness;
-ing, -ed, -er/s slæk, -s; -ə*, -ɪst, -lɪ,
-nɪs [-nəs]; -ɪŋ, -t, -ə*/z
slack|en, -ens, -ening, -ened 'slæk|ən,
-ənz, -ənɪŋ [-nɪŋ, -ənɪŋ], -ənd
Slade sleɪd
slag, -gy slæg, -ɪ
slain (from slay) sleɪn
Slaithwaite 'slæθwət [-weɪt, locally also
'slaʊt]
slak|e, -es, -ing, -ed sleɪk, -s, -ɪŋ, -t
slalom, -s 'slɑːləm ['sleɪl-], -z

455

slam (*s. v.*), **-s, -ming, -med** slæm, -z, -ıŋ, -d

sland|er (*s. v.*), **-ers, -ering, -ered, -erer/s** 'slɑːnd|ə*, -əz, -ərıŋ, -əd, -ərə*/z

slanderous, **-ly, -ness** 'slɑːndərəs, -lı, -nıs [-nəs]

slang (*s. v.*), **-s, -ing, -ed; -y, -ier, -iest, -ily, -iness** slæŋ, -z, -ıŋ, -d; -ı, -ıə*, -ııst, -ılı [-əlı], -ınıs [-ınəs]

slant (*s. adj. v.*), **-s, -ing/ly, -ed** slɑːnt, -s, -ıŋ/lı, -ıd

slantwise 'slɑːntwaız

slap (*s. v. adv.*), **-s, -ping, -ped** slæp, -s, -ıŋ, -t

slap-bang ˌslæp'bæŋ

slapdash 'slæpdæʃ

slap-stick, **-s** 'slæpstık, -s

slap-up (*adj.*) 'slæpʌp [ˌ-'-]

slash (*s. v.*), **-es, -ing, -ed** slæʃ, -ız, -ıŋ, -t

slat, **-s** slæt, -s

slat|e (*s. v.*), **-es, -ing, -ed, -er/s** sleıt, -s, -ıŋ, -ıd, -ə*/z

slate-coloured 'sleıtˌkʌləd

slate-grey ˌsleıt'greı

slate-pencil, **-s** ˌsleıt'pensl, -z

Slater 'sleıtə*

slattern, **-s, -ly, -liness** 'slætən [-tɜːn], -z, -lı, -lınıs [-nəs]

slaty 'sleıtı

slaught|er (*s. v.*) (**S.**), **-ers, -ering, -ered, -erer/s; -erous/ly** 'slɔːt|ə*, -əz, -ərıŋ, -əd, -ərə*/z, -ərəs/lı

slaughterhou|se, **-ses** 'slɔːtəhaʊ|s, -zız

Slav, **-s** slɑːv [*rarely* slæv], -z

slav|e (*s. v.*), **-es, -ing, -ed, -er/s** sleıv, -z, -ıŋ, -d, -ə*/z

slave-driv|er/s, **-ing** 'sleıvˌdraıv|ə*/z, -ıŋ

slave-owner, **-s** 'sleıvˌəʊnə*, -z

slaver (*slave-trader*), **-s** 'sleıvə*, -z

slaver (*s. v.*) (*slobber*), **-s, -ing, -ed** 'slævə* ['sleıvə*], -z, -rıŋ, -d

slavery 'sleıvərı

slave-ship, **-s** 'sleıvʃıp, -s

slave-trade, **-r/s** 'sleıvtreıd, -ə*/z

slavey, **-s** 'sleıvı ['slævı], -z

Slavic 'slɑːvık ['slæv-]

slavish, **-ly, -ness** 'sleıvıʃ, -lı, -nıs [-nəs]

Slavonic slə'vɒnık [slæ'v-, slɑː'v-]

slay, **-s, -ing, slew, slain, slayer/s** sleı, -z, -ıŋ, slu:, sleın, 'sleıə*/z

Slazenger 'slæzəndʒə*

sledg|e (*s. v.*), **-es, -ing, -ed** sledʒ, -ız, -ıŋ, -d

sledge-hammer, **-s** 'sledʒˌhæmə*, -z

sleek, **-er, -est, -ly, -ness** sli:k, -ə*, -ıst, -lı, -nıs [-nəs]

sleep (*s. v.*), **-s, -ing, slept** sli:p, -s, -ıŋ, slept

sleeper, **-s** 'sli:pə*, -z

sleeping-car, **-s** 'sli:pıŋkɑ:*, -z

sleeping-draught, **-s** 'sli:pıŋdrɑ:ft, -s

sleepless, **-ly, -ness** 'sli:plıs [-ləs], -lı, -nıs [-nəs]

sleepwalk|er/s, **-ing** 'sli:pˌwɔ:k|ə*/z, -ıŋ

sleep|y, **-ier, -iest, -ily, -iness** 'sli:p|ı, -ıə* [-jə*], -ııst [-jıst], -ılı [-əlı], -ınıs [-nəs]

sleepyhead, **-s** 'sli:pıhed, -z

sleet (*s. v.*), **-s, -ing, -ed; -y, -iness** sli:t, -s, -ıŋ, -ıd; -ı, -ınıs [-ınəs]

sleeve, **-s, -d; -less** sli:v, -z, -d; -lıs [-ləs]

sleigh (*s. v.*), **-s, -ing, -ed** sleı, -z, -ıŋ, -d

sleight (**S.**) slaıt

Sleights (*in North Yorkshire*) slaıts

slender, **-er, -est, -ly, -ness** 'slendə*, -rə*, -rıst, -lı, -nıs [-nəs]

slept (*from* sleep) slept

sleuth (*s. v.*), **-s, -ing, -ed** slu:θ [slju:θ], -s, -ıŋ, -t

sleuth-hound, **-s** 'slu:θhaʊnd ['slju:θ-], -z

slew (*from* slay) slu:

slic|e (*s. v.*), **-es, -ing, -ed, -er/s** slaıs, -ız, -ıŋ, -t, -ə*/z

slick, **-er, -est, -ly, -ness** slık, -ə*, -ıst, -lı, -nıs [-nəs]

slid (*from* slide) slıd

slid|e (*s. v.*), **-es, -ing, slid** slaıd, -z, -ıŋ, slıd

slide-rule, **-s** 'slaıdru:l, -z

slide-valve, **-s** 'slaıdvælv, -z

slight (*s. adj. v.*), **-s; -er, -est, -ly, -ness; -ing/ly, -ed** slaıt, -s; -ə*, -ıst, -lı, -nıs [-nəs]; -ıŋ/lı, -ıd

slightish 'slaıtıʃ

Sligo 'slaıgəʊ

slim (*adj. v.*) (**S.**), **-mer, -mest, -ly, -ness; -s, -ming, -med** slım, -ə*, -ıst, -lı, -nıs [-nəs]; -z, -ıŋ, -d

slim|e (*s. v.*), **-es, -ing, -ed** slaım, -z, -ıŋ, -d

slim|y, **-ier, -iest, -ily, -iness** 'slaım|ı, -ıə* [-jə*], -ııst [-jıst], -ılı [-əlı], -ınıs [-nəs]

sling (*s. v.*), **-s, -ing, slung** slıŋ, -z, -ıŋ, slʌŋ

slink, **-s, -ing, slunk** slıŋk, -s, -ıŋ, slʌŋk

slip (*s. v.*), **-s, -ping, -ped** slıp, -s, -ıŋ, -t

slip-carriage, **-s** 'slıpˌkærıdʒ, -ız

slip-coach, **-es** 'slıpkəʊtʃ, -ız

slip-knot, **-s** 'slıpnɒt, -s

slipover, **-s** 'slıpˌəʊvə*, -z

slipper, **-s, -ed** 'slıpə*, -z, -d

slipper|y, -ier, -iest, -ily, -iness 'slɪpər|ɪ,
-ɪə*, -ɪɪst, -əlɪ [-ɪlɪ], -ɪnɪs [-məs]

slipp|y, -ier, -iest, -iness 'slɪp|ɪ, -ɪə*,
-ɪɪst, -ɪnɪs [-məs]

slipshod 'slɪpʃɒd

slipstream, -s 'slɪpstriːm, -z

slipway, -s 'slɪpweɪ, -z

slit (s. v.), -s, -ting slɪt, -s, -ɪŋ

slith|er, -ers, -ering, -ered; -ery 'slɪð|ə*,
-əz, -ərɪŋ, -əd; -ərɪ

sliver (s. v.), -s, -ing, -ed 'slɪvə* ['slaɪv-],
-z, -rɪŋ, -d

Sloan(e) sləʊn

slobber (s. v.), -s, -ing, -ed 'slɒbə*, -z,
-rɪŋ, -d

slobber|y, -iness 'slɒbər|ɪ, -ɪnɪs [-məs]

Slocombe 'sləʊkəm

Slocum 'sləʊkəm

sloe, -s sləʊ, -z

slog (s. v.), -s, -ging, -ged, -ger/s slɒg,
-z, -ɪŋ, -d, -ə*/z

slogan, -s 'sləʊgən, -z

sloid slɔɪd

sloop, -s sluːp, -s

slop (s. v.), -s, -ping, -ped slɒp, -s, -ɪŋ,
-t

slop-basin, -s 'slɒp,beɪsn, -z

slop|e (s. v.), -es, -ing/ly, -ed, -er/s
sləʊp, -s, -ɪŋ/lɪ, -t, -ə*/z

Sloper 'sləʊpə*

slop-pail, -s 'slɒppeɪl, -z

slopp|y, -ier, -iest, -ily, -iness 'slɒp|ɪ,
-ɪə*, -ɪɪst, -ɪlɪ [-əlɪ], -ɪnɪs [-məs]

slops (s.) slɒps

slosh (s. v.), -es, -ing, -ed; -y, -ier, -iest,
-iness slɒʃ, -ɪz, -ɪŋ, -t; -ɪ, -ɪə*, -ɪɪst,
-ɪnɪs [-məs]

slot (s. v.), -s, -ting, -ted slɒt, -s, -ɪŋ,
-ɪd

sloth, -s sləʊθ, -s

sloth|ful, -fully, -fulness 'sləʊθ|fʊl,
-fʊlɪ [-fəlɪ], -fʊlnɪs [-məs]

slot-machine, -s 'slɒtmə,ʃiːn, -z

slouch (s. v.), -es, -ing/ly, -ed slaʊtʃ,
-ɪz, -ɪŋ/lɪ, -t

slouch-hat, -s ,slaʊtʃ'hæt, -s

slough (bog), -s, -y slaʊ, -z, -ɪ

slough (skin of snake), -s slʌf, -s

slough (v.) (cast off skin), -s, -ing, -ed
slʌf, -s, -ɪŋ, -t

Slough slaʊ

Slovak, -s 'sləʊvæk, -s

Slovakia sləʊ'vækɪə [-'vækjə, -'vɑːkɪə,
-'vɑːkjə, rarely -'veɪkɪə, -'veɪkjə]

sloven, -s 'slʌvn, -z

Slovene, -s 'sləʊviːn [sləʊ'viːn], -z

Slovenian, -s sləʊ'viːnjən [-nɪən], -z

slovenl|y, -iness 'slʌvnl|ɪ, -ɪnɪs [-məs]

slow (adj. v.), -er, -est, -ly, -ness; -s,
-ing, -ed sləʊ, -ə*, -ɪst, 'sləʊlɪ,
'sləʊnɪs [-nəs], -z, -ɪŋ, -d

slow-coach, -es 'sləʊkəʊtʃ, -ɪz

slow-motion ,sləʊ'məʊʃn [also '-,-- when
attributive]

slow-worm, -s 'sləʊwɜːm, -z

slug, -s slʌg, -z

sluggard, -s 'slʌgəd, -z

sluggish, -ly, -ness 'slʌgɪʃ, -lɪ, -nɪs
[-nəs]

sluic|e (s. v.), -es, -ing, -ed sluːs, -ɪz,
-ɪŋ, -t

sluice-gate, -s 'sluːsgeɪt [,-'-], -s

slum (s. v.), -s, -ming, -med, -mer/s
slʌm, -z, -ɪŋ, -d, -ə*/z

slumb|er (s. v.), -ers, -ering, -ered,
-erer/s; -erless 'slʌmb|ə*, -əz, -ərɪŋ,
-əd, -ərə*/z; -əlɪs [-ləs]

slumland 'slʌmlænd

slumm|y, -ier, -iest, -iness 'slʌm|ɪ, -ɪə*,
-ɪɪst, -ɪnɪs [-məs]

slump (s. v.), -s, -ing, -ed slʌmp, -s, -ɪŋ,
-t [slʌmt]

slung (from sling) slʌŋ

slunk (from slink) slʌŋk

slur (s. v.), -s, -ring, -red slɜː*, -z, -rɪŋ,
-d

slush, -y, -ier, -iest, -iness slʌʃ, -ɪ, -ɪə*,
-ɪɪst, -ɪnɪs [-məs]

slut, -s slʌt, -s

sluttish, -ly, -ness 'slʌtɪʃ, -lɪ, -nɪs [-nəs]

Sluys slɔɪs

sly, -er, -est, -ly, -ness slaɪ, 'slaɪə*,
'slaɪɪst, 'slaɪlɪ, 'slaɪnɪs [-nəs]

slyboots 'slaɪbuːts

smack (s. v.), -s, -ing/s, -ed smæk, -s,
-ɪŋ/z, -t

Smale smeɪl

small (s. adj. adv.) (S.), -s; -er, -est,
-ness; -ish smɔːl, -z; -ə*, -ɪst, -nɪs
[-nəs]; -ɪʃ

smallage 'smɔːlɪdʒ

Smalley 'smɔːlɪ

smallfry 'smɔːlfraɪ

small-hold|er/s, -ing/s 'smɔːl,həʊld|-
ə*/z [,-'---], -ɪŋ/z

smallpox 'smɔːlpɒks

small-talk 'smɔːltɔːk

Smallwood 'smɔːlwʊd

smalt smɔːlt [smɒlt]

smarm (s. v.), -s, -ing, -ed; -y, -iness
smɑːm, -z, -ɪŋ, -d; -ɪ, -ɪnɪs [-məs]

smart (s. adj. v.) (S.), -s; -er, -est, -ly,
-ness; -ing, -ed smɑːt, -s; -ə*, -ɪst,
-lɪ, -nɪs [-nəs]; -ɪŋ, -ɪd

smart|en, -ens, -ening, -ened 'smɑːt|n,
-nz, -ɳɪŋ [-nɪŋ], -nd

457

smartish 'smɑ:tɪʃ

smash (s. v.), -es, -ing, -ed, -er/s smæʃ, -ɪz, -ɪŋ, -t, -ə*/z

smash-and-grab ˌsmæʃn'græb ['---]

smatterer, -s 'smætərə*, -z

smattering, -s 'smætərɪŋ, -z

smear (s. v.), -s, -ing, -ed; -y, -iness smɪə*, -z, -rɪŋ, -d; -rɪ, -rɪnɪs [-nəs]

Smeaton 'smi:tn

smel|l (s. v.), -ls, -ling, -t smel, -z, -ɪŋ, -t

smelling-bottle, -s 'smelɪŋˌbɒtl, -z

smelling-salts 'smelɪŋsɔ:lts [-sɒlts]

smell|y, -ier, -iest, -iness 'smel|ɪ, -ɪə*, -ɪɪst, -ɪnɪs [-nəs]

smelt (s. v.), -s, -ing, -ed smelt, -s, -ɪŋ, -ɪd

Smetana 'smetənə

Smethwick 'smeðɪk

smew, -s smju:, -z

Smieton 'smi:tn

Smike smaɪk

smilax, -es 'smaɪlæks, -ɪz

smil|e (s. v.), -es (S.), -ing/ly, -ed smaɪl, -z, -ɪŋ/lɪ, -d

Smiley 'smaɪlɪ

Smillie 'smaɪlɪ

smirch (s. v.), -es, -ing, -ed smɜ:tʃ, -ɪz, -ɪŋ, -t

smirk (s. v.), -s, -ing, -ed, -er/s; -y smɜ:k, -s, -ɪŋ, -t, -ə*/z; -ɪ

Smirke smɜ:k

smit (from smite) smɪt

smit|e, -es, -ing, smote, smit, smitten, smiter/s smaɪt, -s, -ɪŋ, sməʊt, smɪt, 'smɪtn, 'smaɪtə*/z

smith (S.), -s smɪθ, -s

Smith|ells, -er/s 'smɪð|əlz, -ə*/z

smithereens ˌsmɪðə'ri:nz

Smithfield 'smɪθfi:ld

Smithson 'smɪθsn

Smithsonian smɪθ'səʊnjən [-nɪən]

smith|y, -ies 'smɪð|ɪ ['smɪθ|ɪ], -ɪz

smitten (from smite) 'smɪtn

smock (s. v.), -s, -ing, -ed smɒk, -s, -ɪŋ, -t

smock-frock, -s 'smɒkfrɒk, -s

smog smɒg

smokable, -s 'sməʊkəbl, -z

smok|e (s. v.), -es, -ing, -ed, -er/s sməʊk, -s, -ɪŋ, -t, -ə*/z

smoke-ball, -s 'sməʊkbɔ:l, -z

smoke-bomb, -s 'sməʊkbɒm, -z

smoke-box, -es 'sməʊkbɒks, -ɪz

smokeless 'sməʊklɪs [-ləs]

smoke-room, -s 'sməʊkrʊm [-ru:m], -z

smoke-screen, -s 'sməʊkskri:n, -z

smoke-stack, -s 'sməʊkstæk, -s

Smokies 'sməʊkɪz

smoking-carriage, -s 'sməʊkɪŋˌkærɪdʒ, -ɪz

smoking-compartment, -s 'sməʊkɪŋkəmˌpɑ:tmənt, -s

smoking-concert, -s 'sməʊkɪŋˌkɒnsət, -s

smoking-jacket, -s 'sməʊkɪŋˌdʒækɪt, -s

smoking-room, -s 'sməʊkɪŋˌrʊm [-ˌru:m], -z

smok|y, -ier, -iest, -ily, -iness 'sməʊk|ɪ, -ɪə* [-jə*], -ɪɪst [-jɪst], -ɪlɪ [-əlɪ], -ɪnɪs [-nəs]

Smollett 'smɒlɪt

smolt sməʊlt

smooth (adj.), -er, -est, -ly, -ness smu:ð, -ə*, -ɪst, -lɪ, -nɪs [-nəs]

smooth|(e) (v.), -(e)s, -ing, -ed smu:ð, -z, -ɪŋ, -d

smooth-faced 'smu:ðfeɪst [ˌ-'-]

smorgasbord 'smɔ:gəsbɔ:d [-bɔəd]

smote (from smite) sməʊt

smoth|er, -ers, -ering, -ered 'smʌð|ə*, -əz, -ərɪŋ, -əd

smould|er, -ers, -ering, -ered 'sməʊld|ə*, -əz, -ərɪŋ, -əd

smudg|e (s. v.), -es, -ing, -ed; -y, -ier, -iest, -ily, -iness smʌdʒ, -ɪz, -ɪŋ, -d; -ɪ, -ɪə*, -ɪɪst, -ɪlɪ [-əlɪ], -ɪnɪs [-nəs]

smug (s. adj.), -s, -ly, -ness smʌg, -z, -lɪ, -nɪs [-nəs]

smugg|le, -les, -ling, -led 'smʌg|l, -lz, -lɪŋ [-lɪŋ], -ld

smuggler, -s 'smʌglə*, -z

smut, -s; -ty, -tier, -tiest, -tily, -tiness smʌt, -s; -ɪ, -ɪə*, -ɪɪst, -ɪlɪ [-əlɪ], -ɪnɪs [-nəs]

Smyrna 'smɜ:nə

Smyth smɪθ, smaɪθ

Smythe smaɪð, smaɪθ

snack, -s snæk, -s

snack-bar, -s 'snækbɑ:*, -z

Snaefell ˌsneɪ'fel

snaff|le (s. v.), -les, -ling, -led 'snæf|l, -lz, -lɪŋ [-lɪŋ], -ld

snag, -s snæg, -z

Snagge snæg

snail, -s; -like sneɪl, -z; -laɪk

snake, -s sneɪk, -s

snake-charmer, -s 'sneɪkˌtʃɑ:mə*, -z

snak|y, -iness 'sneɪk|ɪ, -ɪnɪs [-nəs]

snap (s. v.), -s, -ping, -ped snæp, -s, -ɪŋ, -t

snapdragon, -s 'snæpˌdrægən, -z

snappish, -ly, -ness 'snæpɪʃ, -lɪ, -nɪs [-nəs]

snapp|y, -ier, -iest, -ily, -iness 'snæp|ɪ, -ɪə*, -ɪɪst, -ɪlɪ [-əlɪ], -ɪnɪs [-nəs]

snapshot (s. v.), -s, -ting, -ted 'snæpʃɒt, -s, -ɪŋ, -ɪd

snar|e (*s. v.*), **-es, -ing, -ed** sneə*, -z, -rɪŋ, -d

snark, **-s** snɑːk, -s

snarl (*s. v.*), **-s, -ing, -ed** snɑːl, -z, -ɪŋ, -d

snatch (*s. v.*), **-es, -ing, -ed, -er/s** snætʃ, -ɪz, -ɪŋ, -t, -ə*/z

snatch|y, **-ier, -iest, -ily** 'snætʃ|ɪ, -ɪə*, -ɪɪst, -ɪlɪ [-əlɪ]

sneak (*s. v.*), **-s, -ing/ly, -ed; -y, -ier, -iest, -ily, -iness** sniːk, -s, -ɪŋ/lɪ, -t; -ɪ, -ɪə* [-jə*], -ɪɪst [-jɪst], -ɪlɪ [-əlɪ], -ɪnɪs [-məs]

sneakers 'sniːkəz

sneak-raid, **-s, -ing, -er/s** 'sniːkreɪd, -z, -ɪŋ, -ə*/z

sneer (*s. v.*), **-s, -ing/ly, -ed** snɪə*, -z, -rɪŋ/lɪ, -d

sneez|e (*s. v.*), **-es, -ing, -ed** sniːz, -ɪz, -ɪŋ, -d

Sneffels 'snefəlz

Snelgrove 'snelgrəʊv

snell (S.), **-s** snel, -z

Snewin 'snjuːɪn ['snjʊm]

Sneyd (*in Staffordshire*) sniːd

Sneyd-Kinnersley ˌsniːd'kɪnəslɪ

snick (*s. v.*), **-s, -ing, -ed** snɪk, -s, -ɪŋ, -t

snickersnee, **-s** ˌsnɪkə'sniː, -z

snide snaɪd

sniff (*s. v.*), **-s, -ing, -ed; -y, -ier, -iest, -ily, -iness** snɪf, -s, -ɪŋ, -t; -ɪ, -ɪə*, -ɪɪst, -ɪlɪ [-əlɪ], -ɪnɪs [-məs]

snigger (*s. v.*), **-s, -ing, -ed** 'snɪgə*, -z, -rɪŋ, -d

snip, **-s, -ping, -ped, -per/s** snɪp, -s, -ɪŋ, -t, -ə*/z

snip|e (*s. v.*), **-es, -ing, -ed, -er/s** snaɪp, -s, -ɪŋ, -t, -ə*/z

snippet, **-s; -y** 'snɪpɪt, -s; -ɪ

sniv|el, **-els, -elling, -elled, -eller/s** 'snɪv|l, -lz, -lɪŋ, -ld, -lə*/z

snob, **-s; -bery, -bism** snɒb, -z; -ərɪ, -ɪzəm

snobbish, **-ly, -ness** 'snɒbɪʃ, -lɪ, -nɪs [-nəs]

Snodgrass 'snɒdgrɑːs

snood, **-s, -ed** snuːd [snʊd], -z, -ɪd

snook [snoek] (*fish*), **-s** snuːk, -s

snook (*gesture*), **-s** snuːk [snʊk], -s

snooker 'snuːkə*

snoop, **-s, -ing, -ed, -er/s** snuːp, -s, -ɪŋ, -t, -ə*/z

snoot|y, **-ily, -iness** 'snuːt|ɪ, -ɪlɪ [-əlɪ], -ɪnɪs [-məs]

snooz|e (*s. v.*), **-es, -ing, -ed** snuːz, -ɪz, -ɪŋ, -d

snor|e (*s. v.*), **-es, -ing, -ed, -er/s** snɔː* [snɔə*], -z, -rɪŋ, -d, -rə*/z

snorkel, **-s** 'snɔːkl, -z

snort (*s. v.*), **-s, -ing, -ed** snɔːt, -s, -ɪŋ, -ɪd

snorter, **-s** 'snɔːtə*, -z

snort|y, **-ier, -iest, -ily, -iness** 'snɔːt|ɪ, -ɪə*, -ɪɪst, -ɪlɪ [-əlɪ], -ɪnɪs [-məs]

snot, **-ty** snɒt, -ɪ

snout (S.), **-s** snaʊt, -s

snow (*s. v.*) (S.), **-s, -ing, -ed** snəʊ, -z, -ɪŋ, -d

snowball, **-s, -ing** 'snəʊbɔːl, -z, -ɪŋ

snow-blindness 'snəʊˌblaɪndnɪs [-nəs]

snow-boot, **-s** 'snəʊbuːt, -s

snow-bound 'snəʊbaʊnd

snow-cap, **-s, -ped** 'snəʊkæp, -s, -t

snowcat, **-s** 'snəʊkæt, -s

Snow|den, **-don** 'snəʊ|dn, -dn

Snowdonia snəʊ'dəʊnjə [-nɪə]

snow-drift, **-s** 'snəʊdrɪft, -s

snowdrop, **-s** 'snəʊdrɒp, -s

snowfall, **-s** 'snəʊfɔːl, -z

snow-field, **-s** 'snəʊfiːld, -z

snowflake, **-s** 'snəʊfleɪk, -s

snow-line, **-s** 'snəʊlaɪn, -z

snow|-man, **-men** 'snəʊ|mæn, -men

snow-plough, **-s** 'snəʊplaʊ, -z

snow-shoe, **-s** 'snəʊʃuː, -z

snowstorm, **-s** 'snəʊstɔːm, -z

snow-white ˌsnəʊ'waɪt [-'hwaɪt, '--]

snow|y, **-ily, -iness** 'snəʊ|ɪ, -ɪlɪ [-əlɪ], -ɪnɪs [-məs]

snub (*s. adj. v.*), **-s, -bing, -bed** snʌb, -z, -ɪŋ, -d

snub-nosed 'snʌbnəʊzd [ˌ-'-]

snuff (*s. v.*), **-s, -ing, -ed, -er/s** snʌf, -s, -ɪŋ, -t, -ə*/z

snuff-box, **-es** 'snʌfbɒks, -ɪz

snuff-coloured 'snʌfˌkʌləd

snuff|le, **-les, -ling, -led, -ler/s** 'snʌf|l, -lz, -lɪŋ [-lɪŋ], -ld, -lə*/z [-lə*/z]

snug, **-ger, -gest, -ly, -ness** snʌg, -ə*, -ɪst, -lɪ, -nɪs [-nəs]

snugger|y, **-ies** 'snʌgər|ɪ, -ɪz

snugg|le, **-les, -ling, -led** 'snʌg|l, -lz, -lɪŋ [-lɪŋ], -ld

so səʊ (*normal form*), sə (*occasional weak form*)

Soak (*s. v.*), **-s, -ing, -ed** səʊk, -s, -ɪŋ, -t

Soames səʊmz

so-and-so 'səʊənsəʊ

Soane, **-s** səʊn, -z

soap (*s. v.*), **-s, -ing, -ed; -y, -ier, -iest, -ily, -iness** səʊp, -s, -ɪŋ, -t; -ɪ, -ɪə* [-jə*], -ɪɪst [-jɪst], -ɪlɪ [-əlɪ], -ɪnɪs [-məs]

soap-bubble, **-s** 'səʊpˌbʌbl, -z

soapstone 'səʊpstəʊn

soapsuds 'səʊpsʌdz

soar, **-s, -ing, -ed** sɔː* [sɔə*], -z, -rɪŋ, -d

Soares səʊ'ɑːrɪz

459

sob (s. v.), -s, -bing, -bed sɒb, -z, -ɪŋ, -d
sober, -er, -est, -ly, -ness 'səʊbə*, -rə*, -rɪst, -lɪ, -nɪs [-nəs]
sobriety səʊ'braɪətɪ
sobriquet, -s 'səʊbrɪkeɪ, -z
sob-stuff 'sɒbstʌf
socage 'sɒkɪdʒ
so-called ˌsəʊ'kɔːld ['-- according to sentence-stress]
soccer 'sɒkə*
sociability ˌsəʊʃə'bɪlətɪ [-lɪt-]
sociab|le, -ly, -leness 'səʊʃəb|l, -lɪ, -lnɪs [-nəs]
soci|al, -ally 'səʊʃ|l, -əlɪ [-l̩ɪ]
sociali|sm, -st/s 'səʊʃəlɪ|zəm [-ʃlɪ-], -st/s
socialistic ˌsəʊʃə'lɪstɪk [-ʃl̩'ɪ-]
socialite, -s 'səʊʃəlaɪt [-ʃlaɪt], -s
socialization [-isa-] ˌsəʊʃəlaɪ'zeɪʃn [-ʃlaɪ-]
socializ|e [-is|e], -es, -ing, -ed 'səʊʃəlaɪz [-ʃlaɪz], -ɪz, -ɪŋ, -d
societ|y (S.), -ies sə'saɪət|ɪ, -ɪz
Socinian, -s səʊ'sɪnɪən [-njən], -z
socinianism səʊ'sɪnɪənɪzəm [-njən-]
Socinus səʊ'saɪnəs
sociologic|al, -ally ˌsəʊsjə'lɒdʒɪk|l [-sɪə-, -fjə-, -fɪə-], -əlɪ
sociolog|ist/s, -y ˌsəʊsɪ'ɒlədʒ|ɪst/s, -ɪ
sock, -s sɒk, -s
socket, -s, -ed 'sɒkɪt, -s, -ɪd
Socotra səʊ'kəʊtrə [sɒ'k-]
Socrates 'sɒkrəti:z ['səʊk-]
socratic, -ally sɒ'krætɪk [səʊ'k-], -əlɪ
sod, -s sɒd, -z
soda, -s 'səʊdə, -z
soda-fountain, -s 'səʊdəˌfaʊntɪn [-tən], -z
sodalit|y, -ies səʊ'dælət|ɪ [-ɪt|ɪ], -ɪz
soda-water 'səʊdəˌwɔːtə*
soda-water-bottle, -s 'səʊdəˌwɔːtəˌbɒtl, -z
sodd|en (adj. v.), -enness; -ens, -ening, -ened 'sɒd|n, -nnɪs [-nnəs]; -nz, -n̩ɪŋ, -nd
sodium 'səʊdjəm [-dɪəm]
Sodom 'sɒdəm
sodom|y, -ite/s 'sɒdəm|ɪ, -aɪt/s
Sodor 'səʊdə*
soever səʊ'evə*
sofa, -s 'səʊfə, -z
Sofala səʊ'fɑːlə
Soffe (surname) səʊf
soffit, -s 'sɒfɪt, -s
Sofia (in Bulgaria) 'səʊfjə ['səʊfɪə, 'sɒfɪə, səʊ'fi:ə, old-fashioned sə'faɪə]
soft (s. adj.), -s; -er, -est, -ly, -ness sɒft [old-fashioned sɔːft, and in compounds], -s; -ə*, -ɪst, -lɪ, -nɪs [-nəs]

soft|en, -ens, -ening, -ened 'sɒf|n ['sɔːf-], -nz, -nɪŋ [-n̩ɪŋ], -nd
softener, -s 'sɒfnə* ['sɔːf-, -fnə*], -z
soft-headed 'sɒft,hedɪd ['sɔːft-]
soft-hearted ˌsɒft'hɑːtɪd [ˌsɔːft-, also '-,--, when attributive]
softish 'sɒftɪʃ ['sɔːft-]
soft-ped|al (v.), -als, -alling, -alled ˌsɒft'ped|l [ˌsɔːft-], -lz, -l̩ɪŋ, -ld
soft-spoken 'sɒft,spəʊkən ['sɔːft-, ˌ-'--]
sogg|y, -ier, -iest, -iness 'sɒg|ɪ, -ɪə*, -ɪɪst, -ɪnɪs [-məs]
soh (note in Tonic Sol-fa), -s səʊ, -z
Soho 'səʊhəʊ [səʊ'həʊ]
Sohrab 'sɔːræb
soi-disant ˌswɑːdi:'zɑ̃:ŋ [-'zɒŋ, ˌ-'--] (swadizã)
soil (s. v.), -s, -ing, -ed sɔɪl, -z, -ɪŋ, -d
soil-pipe, -s 'sɔɪlpaɪp, -s
soirée, -s 'swɑːreɪ ['swɒr-] (sware), -z
sojourn (s. v.), -s, -ing, -ed, -er/s 'sɒdʒɜːn ['sʌdʒ-, -dʒən], -z, -ɪŋ, -d, -ə*/z
sol (S.), -s sɒl, -z
sola 'səʊlə
solac|e (s. v.), -es, -ing, -ed 'sɒləs [-lɪs], -ɪz, -ɪŋ, -t
solamen, -s səʊ'leɪmen, -z
solanum səʊ'leɪməm [-'lɑːnəm]
solar 'səʊlə*
solarium, -s səʊ'leərɪəm, -z
solati|um, -ums, -a səʊ'leɪʃj|əm [-ʃɪ|-], -əmz, -ə
sold (from sell) səʊld
sold|er (s. v.), -ers, -ering, -ered 'sɒld|ə* ['sɔːd-, 'sɒd-, 'səʊld-], -əz, -ərɪŋ, -əd
soldier, -s, -ing; -y 'səʊldʒə* [rarely -djə*], -z, -ɪŋ; -rɪ
soldierly 'səʊldʒəlɪ [rarely -djə-]
sold|o, -i 'sɒld|əʊ, -i:
sol|e (s. adj. v.) (S.), -es; -ely; -ing, -ed səʊl, -z; -lɪ; -ɪŋ, -d
solecism, -s 'sɒlɪsɪzəm [-les-, -ləs-], -z
solemn, -ly 'sɒləm, -lɪ
solemnity sə'lemnətɪ [sɒ'l-, -ɪtɪ]
solemnization [-isa-], -s ˌsɒləmnaɪ'zeɪʃn [-nɪ'z-], -z
solemniz|e [-is|e], -es, -ing, -ed 'sɒləmnaɪz, -ɪz, -ɪŋ, -d
solenoid, -s 'səʊlənɔɪd ['sɒlɪ-, -lɪn-], -z
Solent 'səʊlənt
sol-fa (S.) ˌsɒl'fɑː
solfegg|io, -i sɒl'fedʒ|ɪəʊ, -i:
solferino (S.) ˌsɒlfə'ri:nəʊ
solicit, -s, -ing, -ed sə'lɪsɪt, -s, -ɪŋ, -ɪd
solicitation, -s səˌlɪsɪ'teɪʃn, -z
solicitor, -s sə'lɪsɪtə* [s]'ɪs-, -sətə*], -z
solicitous, -ly sə'lɪsɪtəs, -lɪ

solicitude səˈlɪsɪtjuːd

solid (s. adj.), -s; -est, -ly, -ness ˈsɒlɪd, -z; -ɪst, -lɪ, -nɪs [-nəs]

solidarity ˌsɒlɪˈdærətɪ [-ɪtɪ]

solidifiable səˈlɪdɪfaɪəbl [sɒˈl-]

solidification səˌlɪdɪfɪˈkeɪʃn [sɒˌl-]

solidi|fy, -fies, -fying, -fied səˈlɪdɪ|faɪ [sɒˈl-], -faɪz, -faɪɪŋ, -faɪd

solidity səˈlɪdətɪ [sɒˈl-, -ɪtɪ]

solid|us, -i ˈsɒlɪd|əs, -aɪ [-iː]

Solihull ˌsəʊlɪˈhʌl

soliloquiz|e [-is|e], -es, -ing, -ed səˈlɪlə-kwaɪz [sɒˈl-], -ɪz, -ɪŋ, -d

soliloqu|y, -ies səˈlɪləkw|ɪ [sɒˈl-], -ɪz

solipsism ˈsɒlɪpsɪzəm [ˈsəʊ-]

solitaire, -s ˌsɒlɪˈteə* [ˈ---], -z

solitar|y (s. adj.), -ies; -ily, -iness ˈsɒlɪtər|ɪ [-lət-], -ɪz; -əlɪ [-ɪlɪ], -ɪnɪs [-nəs]

solitude, -s ˈsɒlɪtjuːd, -z

Sollas ˈsɒləs

Solloway ˈsɒləweɪ [-lʊw-]

solo, -s ˈsəʊləʊ, -z

soloist, -s ˈsəʊləʊɪst, -s

Solomon ˈsɒləmən

Solon ˈsəʊlɒn [-lən]

so-long ˌsəʊˈlɒŋ [səˈl-]

solstice, -s ˈsɒlstɪs, -ɪz

solubility ˌsɒljʊˈbɪlətɪ [-lɪt-]

soluble ˈsɒljʊbl

solus ˈsəʊləs

solution, -s səˈluːʃn [s|ˈuː-, səˈljuː-], -z

solvability ˌsɒlvəˈbɪlətɪ [-lɪt-]

solv|e, -es, -ing, -ed; -able sɒlv, -z, -ɪŋ, -d; -əbl

solven|cy, -t ˈsɒlvən|sɪ, -t

Solway ˈsɒlweɪ

Solzhenitsyn ˌsɒlʒəˈnɪtsɪn

Somal|i, -ia, -is, -iland səʊˈmɑːl|ɪ, -ɪə [-jə], -ɪz, -ɪlænd

somatic səʊˈmætɪk

sombre, -st, -ly, -ness ˈsɒmbə*, -rɪst, -lɪ, -nɪs [-nəs]

sombrero, -s sɒmˈbreərəʊ [-ˈbreɪr-], -z

some sʌm (strong form), səm, sm (weak forms)

somebody ˈsʌmbədɪ [-ˌbɒdɪ, -bdɪ]

somehow ˈsʌmhaʊ [occasionally ˈsʌmaʊ in quick speech]

someone ˈsʌmwʌn

Somers ˈsʌməz

somersault, -s ˈsʌməsɔːlt [-sɒlt], -s

Somerset, -shire ˈsʌməsɪt [-set], -ʃə* [-ˌʃɪə*]

Somerton ˈsʌmətn

Somervell ˈsʌməvɪl [-vel]

Somerville ˈsʌməvɪl

something ˈsʌmθɪŋ [-mpθ-]

sometime ˈsʌmtaɪm

sometimes ˈsʌmtaɪmz

somewhat ˈsʌmwɒt [-mhw-]

somewhere ˈsʌmweə* [-mhw-]

Somme sɒm

somnambuli|sm, -st/s sɒmˈnæmbjʊ-lɪ|zəm, -st/s

somniferous sɒmˈnɪfərəs

somnolen|ce, -t/ly ˈsɒmnələn|s [-nʊl-, -nəʊl-], -t/lɪ

son (S.), -s sʌn, -z

sonagram, -s ˈsəʊnəgræm, -z

sonagraph, -s ˈsəʊnəgrɑːf [-græf], -s

sonalator, -s ˈsəʊnəleɪtə*, -z

sonant (s. adj.), -s ˈsəʊnənt, -s

sonar ˈsəʊnɑː*

sonata, -s səˈnɑːtə [sɲˈɑːtə], -z

sonatina, -s ˌsɒnəˈtiːnə, -z

song, -s sɒŋ, -z

song-bird, -s ˈsɒŋbɜːd, -z

song-book, -s ˈsɒŋbʊk, -s

songster, -s ˈsɒŋstə*, -z

songstress, -es ˈsɒŋstrɪs [-trəs], -ɪz

song-thrush, -es ˈsɒŋθrʌʃ, -ɪz

Sonia ˈsɒnɪə [-njə, ˈsəʊ-]

sonic ˈsɒnɪk

son-in-law, sons-in-law ˈsʌnɪnlɔː, ˈsʌnzɪnlɔː

sonnet, -s ˈsɒnɪt, -s

sonneteer (s. v.), -s, -ing, -ed ˌsɒnɪˈtɪə* [-nəˈt-], -z, -rɪŋ, -d

Sonning (near Reading) ˈsɒnɪŋ [ˈsʌn-]

sonn|y, -ies ˈsʌn|ɪ, -ɪz

sonometer, -s səʊˈnɒmɪtə* [-mətə*], -z

sonorant, -s ˈsɒnərənt [ˈsəʊ-], -s

sonorit|y, -ies səˈnɒrət|ɪ [səʊˈn-, -ɪt|ɪ], -ɪz

sonorous, -ly səˈnɔːrəs [səʊˈn-, ˈsɒn-ərəs], -lɪ

sonship ˈsʌnʃɪp

soon suːn [rarely sʊn]

soot, -y, -ier, -iest, -iness sʊt; -ɪ, -ɪə*, -ɪɪst, -ɪnɪs [-nəs]

sooth suːθ

sooth|e, -es, -ing/ly, -ed suːð, -z, -ɪŋ/lɪ, -d

soothsayer, -s ˈsuːθˌseɪə* [ˈsuːð-], -z

sop (s. v.), -s, -ping, -ped sɒp, -s, -ɪŋ, -t

soph, -s sɒf, -s

Sophia səʊˈfaɪə

Sophie ˈsəʊfɪ

sophi|sm/s, -st/s ˈsɒfɪ|zəm/z, -st/s

sophister, -s ˈsɒfɪstə*, -z

sophistic, -al, -ally səˈfɪstɪk [səʊˈf-], -l, -əlɪ

sophisticat|e, -es, -ing, -ed səˈfɪstɪkeɪt, -s, -ɪŋ, -ɪd

sophistication səˌfɪstɪˈkeɪʃn

sophistr|y, -ies 'sɒfɪstr|ɪ, -ɪz
Sophoclean ˌsɒfə'kliːən [-'kliən]
Sophocles 'sɒfəkliːz
sophomore, -s 'sɒfəmɔː* [-mɔə*], -z
Sophy 'səʊfɪ
soporific ˌsɒpə'rɪfɪk [ˌsəʊp-]
sopp|y, -ier, -iest, -iness 'sɒp|ɪ, -ɪə*,
-ɪɪst, -ɪnɪs [-məs]
sopran|o, -os, -i sə'prɑːn|əʊ, -əʊz, -iː
Sopwith, -s 'sɒpwɪθ, -s
sorbet 'sɔːbət [-bɪt]
Sorbonne sɔː'bɒn (sɔrbɔn)
sorcer|y, -ies; -er/s; -ess/es 'sɔːsər|ɪ,
-ɪz; -ə*/z; -ɪs/ɪz [-es/ɪz]
sordid, -ly, -ness 'sɔːdɪd, -lɪ, -nɪs [-nəs]
sordin|o, -i sɔː'diːn|əʊ, -iː
sore (s. adj. adv.), -s; -r, -st, -ly, -ness
sɔː* [sɔə*], -z; -rə*, -rɪst, -lɪ, -nɪs
[-nəs]
soroptimist, -s sɔː'rɒptɪmɪst [-təm-], -s
sororit|y, -ies sə'rɒrət|ɪ [sɒ'r-, sɔː'r-,
-ɪt|ɪ], -ɪz
sorosis (S.) sə'rəʊsɪs [sɒ'r-, sɔː'r-]
sorrel 'sɒrəl
sorr|ow (s. v.), -ows, -owing/ly, -owed,
-ower/s 'sɒr|əʊ, -əʊz, -əʊɪŋ/lɪ, -əʊd,
-əʊə*/z
sorrow|ful, -fully, -fulness 'sɒrəʊ|fʊl
[-rʊ|f-], -flɪ [-fəlɪ, -fʊlɪ], -fʊlnɪs [-nəs]
sorr|y, -ier, -iest, -ily, -iness 'sɒr|ɪ, -ɪə*,
-ɪɪst, -əlɪ [-ɪlɪ], -ɪnɪs [-nəs]
sort (s. v.), -s, -ing, -ed, -er/s sɔːt, -s,
-ɪŋ, -ɪd, -ə*/z
sortie, -s 'sɔːtiː [-tɪ], -z
sortilege 'sɔːtɪlɪdʒ
so-so 'səʊsəʊ
sostenuto ˌsɒstə'nuːtəʊ [-tɪ'n-, -'njuː-]
Sosthenes 'sɒsθəniːz [-θɪn-]
sot, -s sɒt, -s
Sotheby 'sʌðəbɪ ['sɒð-]
Sothern 'sʌðən
sottish, -ly, -ness 'sɒtɪʃ, -lɪ, -nɪs [-nəs]
sotto voce ˌsɒtəʊ'vəʊtʃɪ (ˌsotto'voːtʃe)
sou, -s suː, -z
soubrette, -s suː'bret [sʊ'b-], -s
souchong ˌsuː'tʃɒŋ [-'ʃɒŋ, also '—
according to sentence-stress]
souffle (murmur), -s 'suːfl, -z
soufflé, -s 'suːfleɪ, -z
sough (s. v.), -s, -ing, -ed saʊ, -z, -ɪŋ, -d
[sʌf, -s, -ɪŋ, -t]
sought (from seek) sɔːt
soul, -s səʊl, -z
Soulbury 'səʊlbərɪ
soul|ful, -fully, -fulness 'səʊl|fʊl [-fl],
-fʊlɪ [-fəlɪ, -flɪ], -fʊlnɪs [-flnɪs, -nəs]
soulless, -ly, -ness 'səʊllɪs [-ləs], -lɪ,
-nɪs [-nəs]

sound (s. adj. v. adv.), -s; -er, -est, -ly,
-ness; -ing/s, -ed saʊnd, -z; -ə*, -ɪst,
-lɪ, -nɪs ['saʊnnɪs, -nəs]; -ɪŋ/z, -ɪd
sound-board, -s 'saʊndbɔːd [-bɔəd],
-z
sound-box, -es 'saʊndbɒks, -ɪz
sound-film, -s 'saʊndfɪlm, -z
soundless 'saʊndlɪs [-ləs]
sound-track, -s 'saʊndtræk, -s
sound-wave, -s 'saʊndweɪv, -z
soup, -s; -y suːp, -s; -ɪ
soupçon, -s 'suːpsɔ̃ːŋ [-sɒŋ] (supsɔ̃),
-z
soup-kitchen, -s 'suːpˌkɪtʃɪn, -z
soup-plate, -s 'suːppleɪt, -s
soup-ticket, -s 'suːpˌtɪkɪt, -s
soup-tureen, -s 'suːptəˌriːn [-tʊˌr-,
-tjʊˌr-], -z
sour (adj. v.), -er, -est, -ly, -ness; -s,
-ing, -ed 'saʊə*, -rə*, -rɪst, -lɪ, -nɪs
[-nəs], -z, -rɪŋ, -d
source, -s sɔːs [sɔəs], -ɪz
sourdine, -s ˌsʊə'diːn, -z
Sousa (American conductor and composer) 'suːzə
sous|e, -es, -ing, -ed saʊs, -ɪz, -ɪŋ, -t
Souter 'suːtə*
south (s. adj. adv.) (S.) saʊθ
sou|th (v.), -ths, -thing, -thed saʊ|ð
[-θ], -ðz [-θs], -ðɪŋ [-θɪŋ], -ðd [-θt]
Southall 'saʊðɔːl ['saʊðɔːl]
Southampton saʊθ'æmptən [saʊθ'hæ-,
saʊ'θ-, sə'θæ-]
Southdown 'saʊθdaʊn
south-east ˌsaʊθ'iːst [in nautical usage
also saʊ'iːst, also '— according to
sentence-stress]
south-easter, -s ˌsaʊθ'iːstə*, -z
south-easterly ˌsaʊθ'iːstəlɪ
south-eastern ˌsaʊθ'iːstən
south-eastward, -s ˌsaʊθ'iːstwəd, -z
Southend ˌsaʊθ'end [also '— according
to sentence-stress]
souther|ly, -n, -ner/s, -nmost 'sʌðə|lɪ,
-n, -nə*/z, -nməʊst [-nməst]
southernwood 'sʌðənwʊd
Southey 'saʊðɪ, 'sʌðɪ
Southon 'saʊðən
south-paw, -s 'saʊθpɔː, -z
Southport 'saʊθpɔːt
southron, -s 'sʌðrən, -z
Southsea 'saʊθsiː [-sɪ]
south-south-east ˌsaʊθsaʊθ'iːst [in
nautical usage also ˌsaʊsaʊ'iːst]
south-south-west ˌsaʊθsaʊθ'west [nau-
tical pronunciation ˌsaʊsaʊ'west]
southward, -s, -ly 'saʊθwəd, -z, -lɪ
Southwark 'sʌðək, 'saʊθwək

Southwell (surname) 'saʊθwəl, 'sʌðl,
(cathedral town in Nottinghamshire)
'saʊθwəl [locally 'sʌðl]
Note.—Viscount Southwell is 'sʌðl.

south-west ,saʊθ'west [nautical pronunciation saʊ'west, also '-- according
to sentence-stress]

south-wester (wind), -s ,saʊθ'westə* [in
nautical usage also saʊ'westə*], -z

south-westerly ,saʊθ'westəlɪ [nautical
pronunciation saʊ'w-]

south-western ,saʊθ'westən

south-westward, -s ,saʊθ'westwəd, -z

South|wick, -wold 'saʊθ|wɪk, -wəʊld

Soutter 'suːtə*

souvenir, -s ,suːvə'nɪə* [-vɪn-, '-ˌ-], -z

sou'wester (hat), -s saʊ'westə*, -z

Souza 'suːzə

sovereign (s. adj.), -s 'sɒvrɪn, -z

sovereignty 'sɒvrəntɪ [-rɪn-]

soviet (S.), -s; -ism 'səʊvɪət ['sɒv-,
-vjət, -vjet, səʊ'vjet, sɒ'vjet], -s;
-ɪzəm

sovran 'sɒvrən

sow (s.) (fem. pig, block of iron, trough
for molten iron), -s saʊ, -z

sow (v.) (plant seed), -s, -ing, -ed, -n,
-er/s səʊ, -z, -ɪŋ, -d, -n, -ə*/z

Sowerby (in North Yorkshire) 'saʊəbɪ,
(in West Yorkshire) 'səʊəbɪ ['saʊəbɪ],
(surname) 'səʊəbɪ, 'saʊəbɪ

Sowry 'saʊərɪ

soy sɔɪ

soya 'sɔɪə

Soyuz 'sɔːjʊz [sə'juːz]

spa, -s spɑː, -z

Spa spɑː

spac|e (s. v.), -es, -ing, -ed speɪs, -ɪz,
-ɪŋ, -t

space-bar, -s 'speɪsbɑː*, -z

space-craft, -s 'speɪskrɑːft, -s

space|-ship/s, -shot/s 'speɪʃ|ʃɪp/s,
-ʃɒt/s

space-suit, -s 'speɪssuːt [-sjuːt], -s

space-time ,speɪs'taɪm

space-walk 'speɪswɔːk

spacious, -ly, -ness 'speɪʃəs, -lɪ, -nɪs
[-nəs]

spade, -s; -ful/s speɪd, -z; -fʊl/z

spade-work 'speɪdwɜːk

spaghetti spə'getɪ [spɑː'g-]

spahi, -s 'spɑːhiː ['spɑːiː], -z

Spain speɪn

spake (archaic p. tense of speak) speɪk

Spalding 'spɔːldɪŋ ['spɒl-]

spall (s. v.), -s, -ing, -ed spɔːl, -z, -ɪŋ,
-d

spam spæm

span (s. v.), -s, -ning, -ned spæn, -z, -ɪŋ,
-d

spandrel, -s 'spændrəl, -z

spang|le (s. v.), -les, -ling, -led 'spæŋg|l,
-lz, -lɪŋ [-lɪŋ], -ld

Spaniard, -s 'spænjəd, -z

spaniel, -s 'spænjəl, -z

Spanish 'spænɪʃ

spank (s. v.), -s, -ing, -ed, -er/s spæŋk,
-s, -ɪŋ, -t [spæŋt], -ə*/z

spanking (s. adj.), -s 'spæŋkɪŋ, -z

spanner, -s 'spænə*, -z

spar (s. v.), -s, -ring, -red spɑː*, -z, -rɪŋ,
-d

spar|e (adj. v.), -ely, -eness; -es, -ing/ly,
-ed speə*, -lɪ, -nɪs [-nəs]; -z, -rɪŋ/lɪ, -d

spark (s. v.) (S.), -s, -ing, -ed spɑːk, -s,
-ɪŋ, -t

sparking-plug, -s 'spɑːkɪŋplʌg, -z

spark|le (s. v.), -les, -ling, -led 'spɑːk|l,
-lz, -lɪŋ, -ld

sparklet, -s 'spɑːklɪt [-lət], -s

spark-plug, -s 'spɑːkplʌg, -z

sparring-match, -es 'spɑːrɪŋmætʃ, -ɪz

sparrow, -s 'spærəʊ, -z

sparrowhawk, -s 'spærəʊhɔːk, -s

sparse, -ly, -ness spɑːs, -lɪ, -nɪs [-nəs]

Spart|a, -an/s 'spɑːt|ə, -ən/z

spasm, -s 'spæzəm, -z

spasmodic, -ally spæz'mɒdɪk, -əlɪ

spastic (s. adj.), -s 'spæstɪk, -s

spat (s.), -s spæt, -s

spat (from spit) spæt

spatchcock (s. v.), -s, -ing, -ed 'spætʃ-
kɒk, -s, -ɪŋ, -t

spate, -s speɪt, -s

spati|al, -ally 'speɪʃ|l [-ʃjəl, -ʃɪ|əl], -əlɪ

spatter (s. v.), -s, -ing, -ed 'spætə*, -z,
-rɪŋ, -d

spatul|a, -ae, -as 'spætjʊl|ə, -iː, -əz

spatulate (adj.) 'spætjʊlət [-lɪt, -leɪt]

spavin 'spævɪn

spawn (s. v.), -s, -ing, -ed spɔːn, -z, -ɪŋ,
-d

Speaight speɪt

speak, -s, -ing, spoke, spoken, speaker/s
spiːk, -s, -ɪŋ, spəʊk, 'spəʊkən,
'spiːkə*/z

speak-eas|y, -ies 'spiːkˌiːz|ɪ, -ɪz

speaking-trumpet, -s 'spiːkɪŋˌtrʌmpɪt,
-s

speaking-tube, -s 'spiːkɪŋtjuːb, -z

Spean spɪən ['spiːən]

spear (s. v.), -s, -ing, -ed spɪə*, -z, -rɪŋ,
-d

spear-head, -s 'spɪəhed, -z

spear|man (S.), -men 'spɪə|mən, -mən
[-men]

463

spearmint 'spɪəmɪnt
spec spek
speci|al (s. adj.), -als, -ally 'speʃ|l, -lz, -əlɪ [-lɪ, -lɪ]
speciali|sm, -st/s 'speʃəlɪ|zəm [-ʃlɪ-, -ʃlɪ-], -st/s
specialit|y, -ies ˌspeʃɪ'ælət|ɪ [-ɪt|ɪ], -ɪz
specialization [-isa-] ˌspeʃəlaɪ'zeɪʃn [-ʃlaɪ'z-, -ʃəlɪ'z-, -ʃlɪ'z-]
specializ|e [-is|e], -es, -ing, -ed 'speʃəl-aɪz [-ʃlaɪz], -ɪz, -ɪŋ, -d
specialt|y, -ies 'speʃlt|ɪ, -ɪz
specie 'spi:ʃi: [-ʃɪ]
species 'spi:ʃi:z [-ʃɪz]
specific (s. adj.), -s; -ally spɪ'sɪfɪk [spə's-], -s; -əlɪ
specification, -s ˌspesɪfɪ'keɪʃn, -z
specificity ˌspesɪ'fɪsətɪ [-ɪtɪ]
speci|fy, -fies, -fying, -fied; -fiable 'spesɪ|faɪ, -faɪz, -faɪɪŋ, -faɪd; -faɪəbl
specimen, -s 'spesɪmən [-mɪn], -z
specious, -ly, -ness 'spi:ʃəs, -lɪ, -nɪs [-nəs]
speck, -s, -ed spek, -s, -t
speckle, -s, -d 'spekl, -z, -d
speckless 'speklɪs [-ləs]
spectacle, -s, -d 'spektəkl [-tɪk-], -z, -d
spectacular, -ly spek'tækjʊlə* [-kjələ*], -lɪ
spectator (S.), -s spek'teɪtə*, -z
spectral 'spektrəl
spectre, -s 'spektə*, -z
spectrogram, -s 'spektrəʊgræm, -z
spectrograph, -s 'spektrəʊgrɑːf [-græf], -s
spectrographic ˌspektrəʊ'græfɪk
spectrography spek'trɒgrəfɪ
spectrometer, -s spek'trɒmɪtə* [-mətə*], -z
spectroscope, -s 'spektrəskəʊp, -s
spectroscopic, -al, -ally ˌspektrə'skɒpɪk, -l, -əlɪ
spectroscop|ist/s, -y spek'trɒskəp|ɪst/s, -ɪ
spectr|um, -a, -ums 'spektr|əm, -ə, -əmz
speculat|e, -es, -ing, -ed, -or/s 'spekjʊ-leɪt [-kjəl-], -s, -ɪŋ, -ɪd, -ə*/z
speculation, -s ˌspekjʊ'leɪʃn [-kjə'l-], -z
speculative, -ly, -ness 'spekjʊlətɪv [-kjəl-, -leɪt-], -lɪ, -nɪs [-nəs]
specul|um, -a, -ar 'spekjʊl|əm, -ə, -ə*
sped (from speed) sped
speech, -es spi:tʃ, -ɪz
speech-day, -s 'spi:tʃdeɪ, -z
speechification, -s ˌspi:tʃɪfɪ'keɪʃn, -z
speechi|fy, -fies, -fying, -fied, -fier/s 'spi:tʃɪ|faɪ, -faɪz, -faɪɪŋ, -faɪd, -faɪə*/z

speechless, -ly, -ness 'spi:tʃlɪs [-ləs], -lɪ, -nɪs [-nəs]
speech-sound, -s 'spi:tʃsaʊnd, -s
speed (s. v.) (S.), -s, -ing, -ed, sped; -y, -ier, -iest, -ily, -iness spi:d, -z, -ɪŋ, -ɪd, sped; -ɪ, -ɪə* [-jə*], -ɪɪst [-jɪst], -ɪlɪ [-əlɪ], -ɪnɪs [-nəs]
speed-cop, -s 'spi:dkɒp, -s
speed-limit, -s 'spi:d,lɪmɪt, -s
speed-merchant, -s 'spi:d,mɜ:tʃənt, -s
speedometer, -s spɪ'dɒmɪtə* [spi:'d-, -mətə*], -z
speedway, -s 'spi:dweɪ, -z
speedwell (S.), -s 'spi:dwel [-wəl], -z
Speen spi:n
Speigal 'spi:gəl
Speight speɪt
Speirs spɪəz
speiss spaɪs
speleolog|y, -ist/s ˌspi:lɪ'ɒlədʒ|ɪ, [ˌspe-], -ɪst/s
spel|l (s. v.), -ls, -ling/s, -led, -t, -ler/s spel, -z, -ɪŋ/z, -t [-d], -t, -ə*/z
spellbound 'spelbaʊnd
spelt (from spell) spelt
spelt|er (s. v.), -ers, -ering, -ered 'spelt|ə*, -əz, -ərɪŋ, -əd
spence (S.), -s spens, -ɪz
spencer (S.), -s 'spensə*, -z
spen|d, -ds, -ding, -t, -der/s spen|d, -dz, -dɪŋ, -t, -də*/z
Spender 'spendə*
spendthrift, -s 'spendθrɪft, -s
Spens spenz
Spenser 'spensə*
Spenserian spen'sɪərɪən
spent (from spend) spent
sperm, -s spɜːm, -z
spermaceti ˌspɜːmə'setɪ [-'si:t-]
spermatoz|oon, -oa ˌspɜːmətəʊ'z|əʊɒn [-əʊən], -əʊə
sperm-whale, -s 'spɜːmweɪl [-hw-], -z
spew, -s, -ing, -ed spju:, -z, -ɪŋ ['spjuɪŋ], -d
Spey speɪ
Spezia (Italian port) 'spetsɪə [-tsjə, -dzɪə, -dzjə]
Spezzia (Greek island) 'spetsɪə [-tsjə]
sphagnum 'sfægnəm
sphene (jewel), -s spi:n [sf-], -z
sphere, -s sfɪə*, -z
spheric, -s, -al, -ally 'sferɪk, -s, -l, -əlɪ
spheroid, -s 'sfɪərɔɪd, -z
spheroidal ˌsfɪə'rɔɪdl [sfe'r-]
spherometer, -s ˌsfɪə'rɒmɪtə* [-mətə*], -z
spherule, -s 'sferju:l [-ru:l], -z
sphincter, -s 'sfɪŋktə*, -z
sphinx, -es; -like sfɪŋks, -ɪz; -laɪk

Spica (*star*) 'spaɪkə

spic|e (*s. v.*) (S.), -es, -ing, -ed; -y, -ier, -iest, -ily, -iness spaɪs, -ɪz, -ɪŋ, -t; -ɪ, -ɪə* [-jə*], -ɪɪst [-jɪst], -ɪlɪ [-əlɪ], -ɪɪs [-ɪnəs]

spick spɪk

spicule, -s 'spaɪkjuːl ['spɪk-], -z

spider, -s; -y 'spaɪdə*, -z; -rɪ

Spiers spɪəz, 'spaɪəz

spiff|ing/ly, -y 'spɪf|ɪŋ/lɪ, -ɪ

spigot, -s 'spɪgət, -s

spik|e (*s. v.*), -es, -ing, -ed spaɪk, -s, -ɪŋ, -t

spikenard 'spaɪknɑːd

Spikins 'spaɪkɪnz

spik|y, -ier, -iest, -iness 'spaɪk|ɪ, -ɪə*, -ɪɪst, -ɪnɪs [-ɪnəs]

spil|l (*s. v.*), -ls, -ling, -led, -t spɪl, -z, -ɪŋ, -d, -t

spiller (S.), -s 'spɪlə*, -z

spillikins 'spɪlɪkɪnz

Spilling 'spɪlɪŋ

spilt (*from* spill) spɪlt

spin (*s. v.*), -s, -ning, span, spun, spinner/s spɪn, -z, -ɪŋ, spæn, spʌn, 'spɪnə*/z

spina bifida ˌspaɪnə'bɪfɪdə

spinach 'spɪnɪdʒ [-ɪtʃ]

spinal 'spaɪnl

spind|le, -les, -ly 'spɪndl|l, -lz, -lɪ

spindle|-legged, -shaped 'spɪndl|legd, -ʃeɪpt

spindrift 'spɪndrɪft

spin-dr|y (*s. v.*), -ies, -ying, -ied, -ier/s ˌspɪn'dr|aɪ ['--], -aɪz, -aɪɪŋ, -aɪd, -aɪə*/z

spine, -s, -d; -less spaɪn, -z, -d; -lɪs [-ləs]

spinel spɪ'nel

spinet, -s spɪ'net ['spɪnet, 'spɪnɪt], -s

Spink spɪŋk

spinney, -s 'spɪnɪ, -z

spinning-wheel, -s 'spɪnɪŋwiːl [-hwiːl], -z

spin|ose, -ous 'spaɪn|əʊs, -əs

Spinoza spɪ'nəʊzə

spinster, -s; -hood 'spɪnstə*, -z; -hʊd

spiny 'spaɪnɪ

Spion Kop ˌspaɪən'kɒp

spiraea, -s spaɪ'rɪə [-'riːə], -z

spir|al (*s. adj.*), -als, -ally 'spaɪər|əl, -əlz, -əlɪ

spirant (*s. adj.*), -s 'spaɪərənt, -s

spire, -s, -d 'spaɪə*, -z, -d

spirit, -s, -ed, -edly, -edness 'spɪrɪt, -s, -ɪd, -ɪdlɪ, -ɪdnɪs [-nəs]

spirit-gum 'spɪrɪtgʌm

spiritism 'spɪrɪtɪzəm

spirit-lamp, -s 'spɪrɪtlæmp, -s

spiritless, -ly, -ness 'spɪrɪtlɪs [-ləs], -lɪ, -nɪs [-nəs]

spirit-level, -s 'spɪrɪtˌlevl, -z

spirit-rapping, -s 'spɪrɪtˌræpɪŋ, -z

spirit-stove, -s 'spɪrɪtstəʊv, -z

spiritual, -ly 'spɪrɪtjʊəl [-tjwəl, -tjʊl, -tʃʊəl, -tʃwəl, -tʃʊl], -ɪ

spirituali|sm, -st/s 'spɪrɪtjʊəlɪ|zəm [-tjwəl-, -tjʊl-, -tʃʊəl-, -tʃwəl-, -tʃʊl-], -st/s

spiritualistic ˌspɪrɪtjʊə'lɪstɪk [-tjwə'l-, -tjʊ'l-, -tʃʊə'l-, -tʃwə'l-, -tʃʊ'l-]

spiritualit|y, -ies ˌspɪrɪtjʊ'ælət|ɪ [-tʃʊ-, -ɪt|ɪ], -ɪz

spirituous 'spɪrɪtjʊəs [-tjwəs, -tʃʊəs, -tʃwəs]

spiritus 'spɪrɪtəs ['spaɪər-]

spirometer, -s ˌspaɪə'rɒmɪtə* [-mətə*], -z

spirt (*s. v.*), -s, -ing, -ed spɜːt; -s, -ɪŋ, -ɪd

spit (*s. v.*) (*eject saliva, etc.*), -s, -ting, spat spɪt, -s, -ɪŋ, spæt

spit (*s. v.*) (*for roasting, etc.*), -s, -ting, -ted spɪt, -s, -ɪŋ, -ɪd

Spitalfields 'spɪtlfiːldz

spit|e (*s. v.*), -es, -ing, -ed; -eful, -efully, -efulness spaɪt, -s, -ɪŋ, -ɪd; -fʊl, -fʊlɪ [-fəlɪ], -fʊlnɪs [-nəs]

spitfire (S.), -s 'spɪtˌfaɪə*, -z

Spithead ˌspɪt'hed ['-- *according to sentence-stress*]

Spitsbergen 'spɪtsˌbɜːgən [ˌ-'--]

spittle 'spɪtl

spittoon, -s spɪ'tuːn, -z

spiv, -s; -vy spɪv, -z; -ɪ

splash (*s. v.*), -es, -ing, -ed, -er/s splæʃ, -ɪz, -ɪŋ, -t, -ə*/z

splash-board, -s 'splæʃbɔːd [-bəəd], -z

splash|y, -iness 'splæʃ|ɪ, -ɪnɪs [-ɪnəs]

splatter, -s, -ing, -ed 'splætə*, -z, -rɪŋ, -d

splay (*s. v.*), -s, -ing, -ed spleɪ, -z, -ɪŋ, -d

spleen, -s; -ful, -fully, -ish, -ishly; -y spliːn, -z; -fʊl, -fʊlɪ [-fəlɪ], -ɪʃ, -ɪʃlɪ; -ɪ

splendid, -ly, -ness 'splendɪd, -lɪ, -nɪs [-nəs]

splendiferous splen'dɪfərəs

splendour, -s 'splendə*, -z

splenetic (*s. adj.*), -s, -ally splɪ'netɪk, -s, -əlɪ

splic|e (*s. v.*), -es, -ing, -ed splaɪs, -ɪz, -ɪŋ, -t

splint (*s. v.*), -s, -ing, -ed splɪnt, -s, -ɪŋ, -ɪd

splinter, -s; -y 'splɪntə*, -z; -rɪ

split (*s. v.*), -s, -ting splɪt, -s, -ɪŋ

465

splodd|y, -ier, -iest, -iness 'splɒd|ɪ, -ɪə*, -ɪst, -ɪnɪs [-məs]

splodg|e, -es splɒdʒ, -ɪz

splodg|y, -ier, -iest, -iness 'splɒdʒ|ɪ, -ɪə* [-jə*], -ɪst [-jɪst], -ɪnɪs [-məs]

splotch, -es, -y splɒtʃ, -ɪz, -ɪ

splutter (s. v.), -s; -ing, -ed 'splʌtə*, -z, -rɪŋ, -d

Spode spəʊd

Spofforth 'spɒfəθ [-fɔ:θ]

Spohr spɔ:* [spəʊ*] (ʃpo:r)

spoil (s. v.), -s, -ing, -ed, -t, -er/s spɔɪl, -z, -ɪŋ, -t [-d], -t, -ə*/z

spoil-sport, -s 'spɔɪlspɔ:t, -s

spoke (s.), -s spəʊk, -s

spoke, -n (from speak) spəʊk, -ən

spokes|man, -men 'spəʊks|mən, -mən

spokes|woman, -women 'spəʊks|-ˌwʊmən, -ˌwɪmɪn

spoliation ˌspəʊlɪ'eɪʃn

spoliator, -s 'spəʊlɪeɪtə*, -z

spondaic spɒn'deɪk

spondee, -s 'spɒndi: [-dɪ], -z

spong|e (s. v.), -es, -(e)ing, -ed, -er/s spʌndʒ, -ɪz, -ɪŋ, -d, -ə*/z

sponge|-cake/s, -finger/s 'spʌndʒ|-keɪk/s, -ˌfɪŋgə*/z

spong|y, -ier, -iest, -iness 'spʌndʒ|ɪ, -ɪə* [-jə*], -ɪst [-jɪst], -ɪnɪs [-məs]

sponson, -s 'spɒnsn, -z

sponsor (s.v.), -s, -ing, -ed 'spɒnsə*, -z, -rɪŋ, -d

spontaneity ˌspɒntə'neɪətɪ [-'nɪətɪ, -'ni:ətɪ, -'ni:ɪtɪ]

spontaneous, -ly, -ness spɒn'teɪnjəs [spən-, -nɪəs], -lɪ, -nɪs [-nəs]

spoof (s.v.), -s, -ing, -ed spu:f, -s, -ɪŋ, -t

spook, -s; -ish, -y, -iness spu:k, -s; -ɪʃ, -ɪ, -ɪnɪs [-məs]

spool (s.v.), -s, -ing, -ed spu:l, -z, -ɪŋ, -d

spoon (s.v.), -s, -ing, -ed spu:n, -z, -ɪŋ, -d

spoonbill, -s 'spu:nbɪl, -z

Spooner 'spu:nə*

spoonerism, -s 'spu:nərɪzəm, -z

spoon|-feed, -feeds, -feeding, -fed 'spu:n|fi:d, -fi:dz, -ˌfi:dɪŋ, -fed

spoonful, -s 'spu:nfʊl, -z

spoon|y, -ier, -iest, -ily, -iness 'spu:n|ɪ, -ɪə*, -ɪst, -ɪlɪ [-əlɪ], -ɪnɪs [-məs]

spoor, -s spʊə* [spɔə*, spɔ:*], -z

Sporades 'spɒrədi:z

sporadic, -ally spə'rædɪk [spɒ'r-], -əlɪ

spore, -s spɔ:* [spɔə*], -z

sporran, -s 'spɒrən, -z

sport (s.v.), -s, -ing, -ed spɔ:t, -s, -ɪŋ, -ɪd

sportive, -ly, -ness 'spɔ:tɪv, -lɪ, -nɪs [-nəs]

sports|man, -men 'spɔ:ts|mən, -mən

sportsman|like, -ship 'spɔ:tsmən|laɪk, -ʃɪp

spot (s.v.), -s, -ting, -ted spɒt, -s, -ɪŋ, -ɪd

spotless, -ly, -ness 'spɒtlɪs [-ləs], -lɪ, -nɪs [-nəs]

spotlight, -s 'spɒtlaɪt, -s

Spottiswoode 'spɒtɪzwʊd ['spɒtɪswʊd], 'spɒtswʊd

spott|y, -ier, -iest, -iness 'spɒt|ɪ, -ɪə*, -ɪst, -ɪnɪs [-məs]

spouse, -s spaʊz [spaʊs], -ɪz

spout (s.v.), -s, -ing, -ed, -er/s spaʊt, -s, -ɪŋ, -ɪd, -ə*/z

Spragge spræg

Sprague spreɪg

sprain (s.v.), -s, -ing, -ed spreɪn, -z, -ɪŋ, -d

sprang (from spring) spræŋ

Sprange spreɪndʒ

Sprangle 'spræŋgl

sprat (S.), -s spræt, -s

Spratt spræt

sprawl (s.v.), -s, -ing, -ed, -er/s sprɔ:l, -z, -ɪŋ, -d, -ə*/z

sprawl|y, -ier, -iest, -iness 'sprɔ:l|ɪ, -ɪə* [-jə*], -ɪst [-jɪst], -ɪnɪs [-məs]

spray (s.v.), -s, -ing, -ed; -ey spreɪ, -z, -ɪŋ, -d; -ɪ

spread (s.v.), -s, -ing, -er/s spred, -z, -ɪŋ, -ə*/z

spread-eagl|e, -es, -ing, -ed ˌspred'i:gl, -z, -ˌlɪŋ [-lɪŋ], -d

spree, -s spri:, -z

sprig, -s sprɪg, -z

Sprigg sprɪg

sprightl|y, -ier, -iest, -iness 'spraɪtl|ɪ, -ɪə* [-jə*], -ɪst [-jɪst], -ɪnɪs [-məs]

Sprigings 'sprɪgɪŋz

spring (s. v.), -s, -ing, sprang, sprung, springer/s sprɪŋ, -z, -ɪŋ, spræŋ, sprʌŋ, 'sprɪŋə*/z

spring-balance, -s ˌsprɪŋ'bæləns ['-ˌ--], -ɪz

spring-bed, -s ˌsprɪŋ'bed ['--], -z

spring-board, -s 'sprɪŋbɔ:d [-bɔəd], -z

springbok, -s 'sprɪŋbɒk, -s

springe, -s sprɪndʒ, -ɪz

Springell 'sprɪŋəl, 'sprɪŋgəl

Springfield 'sprɪŋfi:ld

spring-gun, -s 'sprɪŋgʌn, -z

springlike 'sprɪŋlaɪk

Springpark 'sprɪŋpɑ:k

springtime 'sprɪŋtaɪm

spring|y, -ier, -iest, -ily, -iness 'sprɪŋ|ɪ, -ɪə*, -ɪst, -ɪlɪ [-əlɪ], -ɪnɪs [-məs]

sprink|le (s. v.), -les, -ling, -led, -ler/s 'sprɪŋk|l, -lz, -lɪŋ [-ˌlɪŋ], -ld, -lə*/z [-ˌlə*/z]

sprinkling (s.), -s 'sprɪŋklɪŋ, -z
sprint (s. v.), -s, -ing, -ed, -er/s sprɪnt, -s, -ɪŋ, -ɪd, -ə*/z
sprit, -s sprɪt, -s
sprite, -s spraɪt, -s
spritsail, -s 'sprɪtsl [-seɪl], -z
sprocket, -s 'sprɒkɪt, -s
Sproule sprəʊl
sprout (s. v.), -s, -ing, -ed spraʊt, -s, -ɪŋ, -ɪd
spruce (s. adj.), -s; -r, -st, -ly, -ness spruːs, -ɪz; -ə*, -ɪst, -lɪ, -nɪs [-nəs]
sprue, -s spruː, -z
sprung (from spring) sprʌŋ
Sprunt sprʌnt
spry (S.), -er, -est, -ness spraɪ, 'spraɪə*, 'spraɪɪst, 'spraɪnɪs [-nəs]
spud, -s spʌd, -z
spu|e, -es, -ing, -ed spjuː, -z, -ɪŋ ['spjʊɪŋ], -d
spum|e, -es, -ing, -ed spjuːm, -z, -ɪŋ, -d
spun (from spin) spʌn
spunk; -y, -ier, -iest spʌŋk; -ɪ, -ɪə*, -ɪɪst
spur (s. v.), -s, -ring, -red spɜː*, -z, -rɪŋ, -d
Spurgeon 'spɜːdʒən
spurious, -ly, -ness 'spjʊərɪəs [-jɔər-, -jɔːr-], -lɪ, -nɪs [-nəs]
spurn (S.), -s, -ing, -ed spɜːn, -z, -ɪŋ, -d
Spurr spɜː*
Spurrier (surname) 'spʌrɪə*
spurt (s. v.), -s, -ing, -ed spɜːt, -s, -ɪŋ, -ɪd
sputnik, -s 'spʊtnɪk ['spʌt-], -s
sputter (s. v.), -s, -ing, -ed, -er/s 'spʌtə*, -z, -rɪŋ, -d, -rə*/z
sputum 'spjuːtəm
sp|y (s. v.), -ies, -ying, -ied sp|aɪ, -aɪz, -aɪɪŋ, -aɪd
spy-glass, -es 'spaɪɡlɑːs, -ɪz
squab (s. adj.), -s skwɒb, -z
squabb|le (s. v.), -les, -ling, -led, -ler/s 'skwɒb|l, -lz, -lɪŋ [-lɪŋ], -ld, -lə*/z [-lə*/z]
squad, -s skwɒd, -z
squadron, -s 'skwɒdrən, -z
squalid, -est, -ly, -ness 'skwɒlɪd, -ɪst, -lɪ, -nɪs [-nəs]
squall (s. v.), -s, -ing, -ed; -y skwɔːl, -z, -ɪŋ, -d; -ɪ
squaloid 'skweɪlɔɪd
squalor 'skwɒlə*
squam|a, -ae 'skweɪm|ə, -iː
squam|ose, -ous 'skweɪm|əʊs, -əs
squand|er, -ers, -ering, -ered, -erer/s 'skwɒnd|ə*, -əz, -ərɪŋ, -əd, -ərə*/z
squandermania ˌskwɒndə'meɪnjə [-nɪə]

squar|e (s. adj. v. adv.), -es; -er, -est, -ely, -eness; -ing, -ed skweə*, -z; -rə*, -rɪst, -lɪ, -nɪs [-nəs]; -rɪŋ, -d
square-jawed ˌskweə'dʒɔːd ['-- when attributive]
square-toed ˌskweə'təʊd ['-- when attributive]
squarish 'skweərɪʃ
squash (s. v.), -es, -ing, -ed skwɒʃ, -ɪz, -ɪŋ, -t
squash-hat, -s ˌskwɒʃ'hæt, -s
squash|y, -ier, -iest, -iness 'skwɒʃ|ɪ, -ɪə*, -ɪɪst, -ɪnɪs [-ɪnəs]
squat (s. adj. v.), -s, -ting, -ted, -ter/s skwɒt, -s, -ɪŋ, -ɪd, -ə*/z
squaw, -s skwɔː, -z
squawk (s. v.), -s, -ing, -ed skwɔːk, -s, -ɪŋ, -t
squeak (s. v.), -s, -ing, -ed, -er/s skwiːk, -s, -ɪŋ, -t, -ə*/z
squeak|y, -ier, -iest, -ily, -ness 'skwiːk|ɪ, -ɪə* [-jə*], -ɪɪst [-jɪst], -ɪlɪ [-əlɪ], -ɪnɪs [-ɪnəs]
squeal (s. v.), -s, -ing, -ed, -er/s skwiːl, -z, -ɪŋ, -d, -ə*/z
squeamish, -ly, -ness 'skwiːmɪʃ, -lɪ, -nɪs [-nəs]
squeegee (s. v.), -s, -ing, -d ˌskwiː'dʒiː, -z, -ɪŋ, -d
Squeers skwɪəz
squeez|e (s. v.), -es, -ing, -ed, -er/s; -able skwiːz, -ɪz, -ɪŋ, -d, -ə*/z; -əbl
squegger, -s 'skwegə*, -z
squelch (s. v.), -es, -ing, -ed skweltʃ, -ɪz, -ɪŋ, -t
squib, -s skwɪb, -z
squid, -s skwɪd, -z
squiff|y, -ier, -iest 'skwɪf|ɪ, -ɪə*, -ɪɪst
squigg|le (s. v.), -les, -ling, -led 'skwɪɡ|l, -lz, -lɪŋ [-lɪŋ], -ld
squilgee (s. v.), -s, -ing, -d ˌskwɪl'dʒiː, -z, -ɪŋ, -d
squill, -s skwɪl, -z
squint (s. v.), -s, -ing, -ed skwɪnt, -s, -ɪŋ, -ɪd
squint-eyed 'skwɪntaɪd
squire (S.), -s 'skwaɪə*, -z
squirearchy 'skwaɪərɑːkɪ
squireen, -s ˌskwaɪə'riːn, -z
squirm, -s, -ing, -ed skwɜːm, -z, -ɪŋ, -d
squirrel, -s 'skwɪrəl, -z
squirt (s. v.), -s, -ing, -ed skwɜːt, -s, -ɪŋ, -ɪd
squish (s. v.), -es, -ing, -ed skwɪʃ, -ɪz, -ɪŋ, -t
Sri Lanka ˌsriː'læŋkə
Srinagar sriː'nʌɡə* [srɪ'n-, -'nɑːɡ-, 'sriːnəɡə*] (Hindi syrinəɡər)

s.s. ˌes'es ['eses, 'sti:mʃɪp]

St. (=**Saint**) sənt, sɪnt, snt [*rarely* sent, semt]
Note.—Names beginning with **St.** *are entered after* **saint**.

stab (*s. v.*), **-s, -bing, -bed** stæb, -z, -ɪŋ, -d

Stabat Mater, -s ˌstɑː'bæt'mɑːtə* [-bət-], -z

stability stə'bɪlətɪ [-lɪt-]

stabilization [-isa-] ˌsteɪbəlaɪ'zeɪʃn [ˌstæb-, -bɪl-, -bl̩-, -lɪ'z-]

stabiliz|e [-is|e], **-es, -ing, -ed, -er/s** 'steɪbəlaɪz ['stæb-, -bɪl-, -bl̩-], -ɪz, -ɪŋ, -d, -ə*/z

stab|le (*s. adj. v.*), **-les; -ly, -leness; -ling, -led** 'steɪb|l, -lz; -lɪ, -lnɪs [-nəs]; -lɪŋ [-l̩ɪŋ], -ld

stable-boy, -s 'steɪblbɔɪ, -z

stable|man, -men 'steɪbl|mən [-mæn], -mən [-men]

stabling (*s.*) 'steɪblɪŋ

stablish, -es, -ing, -ed 'stæblɪʃ, -ɪz, -ɪŋ, -t

staccato, -s stə'kɑːtəʊ, -z

Stac(e)y 'steɪsɪ

stack (*s. v.*), **-s, -ing, -ed** stæk, -s, -ɪŋ, -t

stadi|um, -ums, -a 'steɪdj|əm [-dɪ|-], -əmz, -ə

staff (*s. v.*), **-s, -ing, -ed** stɑːf, -s, -ɪŋ, -t

Staffa 'stæfə

Stafford, -shire 'stæfəd, -ʃə* [-ˌʃɪə*]

Staffs. stæfs

stag, -s stæg, -z

stag|e (*s. v.*), **-es, -ing, -ed** steɪdʒ, -ɪz, -ɪŋ, -d

stage-craft 'steɪdʒkrɑːft

stage-effect, -s 'steɪdʒɪˌfekt, -s

stage-manag|e, -es, -ing, -ed, -er/s ˌsteɪdʒ'mænɪdʒ ['-ˌ--], -ɪz, -ɪŋ, -d, -ə*/z [-nədʒə*/z]

stager, -s 'steɪdʒə, -z

stage-struck 'steɪdʒstrʌk

stagger (*s. v.*), **-s, -ing, -ed, -er/s** 'stægə*, -z, -rɪŋ, -d, -rə*/z

staghound, -s 'stæghaʊnd, -z

stag-hunting 'stægˌhʌntɪŋ

Stagirite, -s 'stædʒɪraɪt, -s

stagnan|cy, -t/ly 'stægnən|sɪ, -t/lɪ

stagnat|e, -es, -ing, -ed stæg'neɪt ['--], -s, -ɪŋ, -ɪd

stagnation stæg'neɪʃn

stag|y, -ier, -iest, -ily, -iness 'steɪdʒ|ɪ, -ɪə* [-jə*], -ɪɪst [-jɪst], -ɪlɪ [-əlɪ], -ɪnɪs [-ɪnəs]

staid, -ly, -ness steɪd, -lɪ, -nɪs [-nəs]

stain (*s. v.*), **-s, -ing, -ed, -er/s** steɪn, -z, -ɪŋ, -d, -ə*/z

Stainer (*English name*) 'steɪnə*, (*German name*) 'staɪnə* ('ʃtaɪnər)

Staines steɪnz

stainless, -ly, -ness 'steɪnlɪs [-ləs], -lɪ, -nɪs [-nəs]

stair, -s steə*, -z

stair-carpet, -s 'steəˌkɑːpɪt, -s

staircase, -s 'steəkeɪs, -ɪz

stair-rod, -s 'steərɒd, -z

stairway, -s 'steəweɪ, -z

Staithes steɪðz

stak|e (*s. v.*), **-es, -ing, -ed** steɪk, -s, -ɪŋ, -t

stake-holder, -s 'steɪkˌhəʊldə*, -z

stalactite, -s 'stæləktaɪt, -s

stalagmite, -s 'stæləgmaɪt, -s

Stalbridge 'stɔːlbrɪdʒ ['stɒl-]

stale, -r, -st, -ly, -ness steɪl, -ə*, -ɪst, -lɪ, -nɪs [-nəs]

stalemat|e (*s. v.*), **-es, -ing, -ed** 'steɪlmeɪt [ˌ-'-], -s, -ɪŋ, -ɪd

Stalin 'stɑːlɪn ['stæl-] ('staljin)

Stalingrad 'stɑːlɪngræd ['stæl-, -grɑːd] (stəljin'grat)

stalinism 'stɑːlɪnɪzəm ['stæl-]

stalk (*s. v.*), **-s, -ing, -ed, -er/s; -y** stɔːk, -s, -ɪŋ, -t, -ə*/z; -ɪ

stalking-horse, -s 'stɔːkɪŋhɔːs, -ɪz

Stalky 'stɔːkɪ

stall (*s. v.*), **-s, -ing, -ed; -age** stɔːl, -z, -ɪŋ, -d; -ɪdʒ

stallion, -s 'stæljən, -z

stalwart (*s. adj.*), **-s, -ly, -ness** 'stɔːlwət ['stɒl-, -wɜːt], -s, -lɪ, -nɪs [-nəs]

Stalybridge 'steɪlɪbrɪdʒ

Stamboul stæm'buːl

stamen, -s 'steɪmen [-mən], -z

Stamford, -ham 'stæmfəd, -əm

stamina 'stæmɪnə [-mənə]

stammer (*s. v.*), **-s, -ing, -ed, -er/s** 'stæmə*, -z, -rɪŋ, -d, -rə*/z

stamp (*s. v.*) (**S.**), **-s, -ing, -ed, -er/s** stæmp, -s, -ɪŋ, -t [stæmt], -ə*/z

stamp-album, -s 'stæmpˌælbəm, -z

stamp-collection, -s 'stæmpkəˌlekʃn, -z

stamp-collector, -s 'stæmpkəˌlektə*, -z

stamp-dut|y, -ies 'stæmpˌdjuːt|ɪ, -ɪz

stamped|e (*s. v.*), **-es, -ing, -ed** stæm'piːd, -z, -ɪŋ, -ɪd

stamp-machine, -s 'stæmpməˌʃiːn, -z

stance, -s stæns [stɑːns], -ɪz

stanch, -es, -ing, -ed stɑːntʃ, -ɪz, -ɪŋ, -t

stanchion, -s 'stɑːnʃn, -z

stand (*s. v.*), **-s, -ing, stood** stænd, -z, -ɪŋ, stʊd

standard, -s 'stændəd, -z

standardization [-isa-] ˌstændədaɪ'zeɪʃn [-dɪ'z-]

standardiz|e [-is|e], -es, -ing, -ed
'stændədaɪz, -ɪz, -ɪŋ, -d
standard-lamp, -s 'stændədlæmp [ˌ-'-],
-s
stand-by, -s 'stændbaɪ ['stæmbaɪ], -z
stand-in, -s 'stændɪn [ˌ-'-], -z
standing (s.), -s 'stændɪŋ, -z
standish (S.), -es 'stændɪʃ, -ɪz
standoffish ˌstænd'ɒfɪʃ [old-fashioned
-'ɔːf-]
standpoint, -s 'stændpɔɪnt ['stæm-
pɔɪnt], -s
standstill, -s 'stændstɪl, -z
stand-to 'stændtu: [ˌ-'-]
stand-up (adj.) 'stændʌp
Stan|field, -ford 'stæn|fiːld, -fəd
stanhope (S.), -s 'stænəp, -s
staniel, -s 'stænjəl [-nɪəl], -z
Stanis|las, -aus 'stænɪsl|əs [-ɑːs], -ɔːs
stank (from stink) stæŋk
Stanley 'stænlɪ
stannar|y, -ies 'stænər|ɪ, -ɪz
stann|ic, -ous 'stæn|ɪk, -əs
Stansfield 'stænzfiːld [-nsf-]
Stanton 'stæntən, 'stɑːn-
stanza, -s 'stænzə, -z
stapl|e (S.) (s. v.), -es, -ing, -ed, -er/s
'steɪpl, -z, -ɪŋ, -d, -ə*/z
Stapleton 'steɪpltən
Stapley 'stæplɪ, 'steɪplɪ
star (s. v.), -s, -ring, -red stɑː*, -z, -rɪŋ,
-d
starboard 'stɑːbəd [-bɔːd, -bɔəd]
Note.—The nautical pronunciation is
'stɑːbəd.
starch (s. v.), -es, -ing, -ed; -y, -ier,
-iest, -iness stɑːtʃ, -ɪz, -ɪŋ, -t; -ɪ, -ɪə*,
-ɪɪst, -ɪnɪs [-məs]
stardom 'stɑːdəm
star|e (s. v.), -es, -ing/ly, -ed, -er/s
steə*, -z, -rɪŋ/lɪ, -d, -rə*/z
starfish, -es 'stɑːfɪʃ, -ɪz
star-gaz|er/s, -ing 'stɑːˌgeɪz|ə*/z, -ɪŋ
stark (S.), -ly, -ness stɑːk, -lɪ, -nɪs [-nəs]
starland 'stɑːlænd
star|less, -light, -lit 'stɑː|lɪs [-ləs], -laɪt,
-lɪt
starlet, -s 'stɑːlɪt [-lət], -s
starling (S.), -s 'stɑːlɪŋ, -z
Starr stɑː*
starr|y, -iness 'stɑːr|ɪ, -ɪnɪs [-məs]
starry-eyed ˌstɑːrɪ'aɪd ['--- when attri-
butive]
start (s. v.) (S.), -s, -ing, -ed, -er/s
stɑːt, -s, -ɪŋ, -ɪd, -ə*/z
starting-point, -s 'stɑːtɪŋpɔɪnt, -s
start|le, -les, -ling, -led, -ler/s 'stɑːt|l,
-lz, -lɪŋ, -ld, -lə*/z

starvation stɑː'veɪʃn
starv|e, -es, -ing, -ed; -eling/s stɑːv, -z,
-ɪŋ, -d; -lɪŋ/z
stat|e (s. v.), -es, -ing, -ed, -ement/s
steɪt, -s, -ɪŋ, -ɪd, -mənt/s
statecraft 'steɪtkrɑːft
statel|y, -ier, -iest, -iness 'steɪtl|ɪ, -ɪə*
[-jə*], -ɪɪst [-jɪst], -ɪnɪs [-məs]
stateroom, -s 'steɪtrʊm [-ruːm], -z
states|man, -men 'steɪts|mən, -mən
statesman|like, -ly, -ship 'steɪtsmən|-
laɪk, -lɪ, -ʃɪp
Statham 'steɪθəm, 'steɪðəm
static, -s, -al, -ally 'stætɪk, -s, -l, -əlɪ
statice (plant), -s 'stætɪsɪ, -z ['stætɪs,
-ɪz]
stati|on (s. v.), -ons, -oning, -oned
'steɪʃ|n, -nz, -ŋɪŋ [-nɪŋ], -nd
stationar|y, -ily, -iness 'steɪʃŋər|ɪ
[-ʃnər-, -ʃŋr-, -ʃənər-], -əlɪ [-ɪlɪ], -ɪnɪs
[-məs]
stationer, -s 'steɪʃnə* [-ʃŋə*], -z
stationery 'steɪʃŋərɪ [-ʃnər-, -ʃŋr-,
-ʃənər-]
station-master, -s 'steɪʃnˌmɑːstə*, -z
station-wag(g)on, -s 'steɪʃnˌwægən, -z
statism 'steɪtɪzəm
statist, -s 'steɪtɪst, -s
statistic, -s, -al, -ally stə'tɪstɪk [stæ't-],
-s, -l, -əlɪ
statistician, -s ˌstætɪ'stɪʃn, -z
statuary 'stætjʊərɪ [-tjwərɪ, -ˌtjʊərɪ]
statue, -s 'stætʃuː [-tjuː], -z
statuesque ˌstætjʊ'esk [-tʃʊ'e-]
statuette, -s ˌstætjʊ'et [-tʃʊ'e-], -s
stature, -s 'stætʃə*, -z
status, -es 'steɪtəs, -ɪz
status quo ˌsteɪtəs'kwəʊ [ˌstæt-]
statute, -s 'stætjuːt [-tʃuːt], -s
statute-book, -s 'stætjuːtbʊk [-tʃuːt-], -s
statutory 'stætjʊtərɪ [-tʃʊt-]
staunch, -er, -est, -ly, -ness stɔːnʃ
[stɑːn-], -ə*, -ɪst, -lɪ, -nɪs [-nəs]
Staunton (English surname) 'stɔːntən,
'stɑːn-, (towns in U.S.A.) 'stæntən
Stavanger stə'væŋə*
stav|e (s. v.), -es, -ing, -ed, stove steɪv,
-z, -ɪŋ, -d, stəʊv
stay (s. v.), -s, -ing, -ed, -er/s steɪ, -z,
-ɪŋ, -d, -ə*/z [steə*/z]
stay-at-home 'steɪəthəʊm
stay-in 'steɪɪn [ˌ-'-]
staysail, -s 'steɪseɪl [nautical pronunciation 'steɪsl], -z
Steabben 'stebən
stead (S.) sted
steadfast, -ly, -ness 'stedfəst [-fɑːst],
-lɪ, -nɪs [-nəs]

469

stead|y, -ier, -iest, -ily, -iness; -ies, -ying, -ied 'sted|ɪ, -ɪə*, -ɪst, -ɪlɪ [-əlɪ], -mɪs [-məs]; -ɪz, -ɪŋ, -ɪd

steak, -s steɪk, -s

steal (s. v.), -s, -ing, stole, stolen, stealer/s stiːl, -z, -ɪŋ, stəʊl, 'stəʊlən, 'stiːlə*/z

stealth, -y, -ier, -iest, -ily, -iness stelθ, -ɪ, -ɪə* [-jə*], -ɪst [-jɪst], -ɪlɪ [-əlɪ], -mɪs [-məs]

steam (s. v.), -s, -ing, -ed, -er/s; -y, -iness stiːm, -z, -ɪŋ, -d, -ə*/z; -ɪ, -mɪs [-məs]

steamboat, -s 'stiːmbəʊt, -s

steam-engine, -s 'stiːm,endʒɪn, -z

steam-hammer, -s 'stiːm,hæmə*, -z

steam-launch, -es 'stiːmlɔːntʃ [-lɑːntʃ], -ɪz

steam-power 'stiːm,paʊə*

steam-roller, -s 'stiːm,rəʊlə* [ˌ-'--], -z

steamship, -s 'stiːmʃɪp, -s

stearic stɪˈærɪk

stearin 'stɪərɪn

Stearn(e), -s stɜːn, -z

steatite 'stɪətaɪt

steatopy|gia, -gous ˌstɪətəʊ'paɪ|dʒɪə [-dʒɪə], -gəs

Stedman 'stedmən

steed, -s stiːd, -z

steel (s. v.), -s, -ing, -ed; -y, -ier, -iest, -iness stiːl, -z, -ɪŋ, -d; -ɪ, -ɪə* [-jə*], -ɪst [-jɪst], -mɪs [-məs]

Steele stiːl

steel-plated ˌstiːl'pleɪtɪd ['-,--]

steelyard, -s 'stiːljɑːd ['stɪljɑːd, 'stɪljəd], -z

steenbok, -s 'stiːnbɒk ['steɪn-], -s

steep (s. adj. v.), -s; -er, -est, -ly, -ness; -ing, -ed stiːp, -s; -ə*, -ɪst, -lɪ, -nɪs [-nəs]; -ɪŋ, -t

steep|en, -ens, -ening, -ened 'stiːp|ən, -ənz, -nɪŋ [-nɪŋ], -ənd

steeple, -s, -d; -chase/s, -jack/s 'stiːpl, -z, -d; -tʃeɪs/ɪz, -dʒæk/s

steer (s. v.), -s, -ing, -ed, -er/s; -age; -sman, -smen stɪə*, -z, -rɪŋ, -d, -rə*/z; -rɪdʒ; -zmən, -zmən [-zmen]

steering-gear 'stɪərɪŋ,gɪə*

steering-wheel, -s 'stɪərɪŋwiːl[-ŋhw-], -z

steev|e (s. v.), -es, -ing, -ed stiːv, -z, -ɪŋ, -d

Steevens 'stiːvnz

Stein (English name), -itz staɪn, -ɪts

Steinbeck 'staɪnbek

steinbock, -s 'staɪnbɒk, -s

Steinway, -s 'staɪnweɪ, -z

stel|e, -ae 'stiːl|ɪ [-iː], -iː

Stella, -land 'stelə, -lænd

stellar 'stelə*

stem (s. v.), -s, -ming, -med stem, -z, -ɪŋ, -d

stemma, -ta 'stemə, -tə

stemple, -s 'stempl, -z

Sten sten

stench, -es stentʃ, -ɪz

stenc|il, -ils, -illing, -illed 'stens|l [-ɪl], -lz [-ɪlz], -lɪŋ [-ɪlɪŋ], -ld [-ɪld]

sten-gun, -s 'stengʌn, -z

stenograph, -s 'stenəgrɑːf [-nəʊg-, -græf], -s

stenograph|er/s, -y stə'nɒgrəf|ə*/z [ste'n-], -ɪ

stenotyp|e, -ing 'stenəʊtaɪp, -ɪŋ

Stent stent

stentorian sten'tɔːrɪən

step (s. v.), -s, -ping, -ped, -per/s step, -s, -ɪŋ, -t, -ə*/z

step-aunt, -s 'stepɑːnt, -s

step-brother, -s 'step,brʌðə*, -z

step|-child, -children 'step|tʃaɪld, -,tʃɪldrən [-,tʃʊldrən]

step-dance, -s 'stepdɑːns, -ɪz

step-daughter, -s 'step,dɔːtə*, -z

step-father, -s 'step,fɑːðə*, -z

Stephano 'stefənəʊ

stephanotis ˌstefə'nəʊtɪs

Stephany (-ie) 'stefənɪ

Stephen, -s, -son 'stiːvn, -z, -sn

step-ladder, -s 'step,lædə*, -z

step-mother, -s 'step,mʌðə*, -z

Stepney 'stepnɪ

steppe, -s step, -s

stepping-stone, -s 'stepɪŋstəʊn, -z

step-sister, -s 'step,sɪstə*, -z

step-son, -s 'stepsʌn, -z

step-uncle, -s 'step,ʌŋkl, -z

stereo, -s 'sterɪəʊ ['stɪər-], -z

stereophonic ˌsterɪəʊ'fɒnɪk [ˌstɪə-]

stereophony ˌsterɪ'ɒfənɪ [ˌstɪə-]

stereopticon, -s ˌsterɪ'ɒptɪkən [ˌstɪər-], -z

stereoscope, -s 'sterɪəskəʊp ['stɪər-], -s

stereoscopic, -al, -ally ˌsterɪə'skɒpɪk [ˌstɪər-], -l, -əlɪ

stereoscopy ˌsterɪ'ɒskəpɪ [ˌstɪər-]

stereotyp|e (s. v.), -es, -ing, -ed, -er/s; -y 'sterɪətaɪp ['ster-, -rɪəʊt-], -s, -ɪŋ, -t, -ə*/z; -ɪ

sterile 'steraɪl

sterility ste'rɪlətɪ [stə'r-, -ɪtɪ]

sterilization [-isa-], -s ˌsterəlaɪ'zeɪʃn [-rɪl-, -lɪ'z-]

steriliz|e [-is|e], -es, -ing, -ed, -er/s 'sterəlaɪz [-rɪl-], -ɪz, -ɪŋ, -d, -ə*/z

sterling 'stɜːlɪŋ

stern (s.) (of ship), -s; -most stɜ:n, -z;
-məʊst [-məst]
stern (adj.), -er, -est, -ly, -ness stɜ:n,
-ə*, -ɪst, -lɪ, -nɪs [-nəs]
Sterne stɜ:n
stern|um, -ums, -a 'stɜ:n|əm, -əmz, -ə
steroid, -s 'stɪərɔɪd ['ste-], -z
stertorous, -ly, -ness 'stɜ:tərəs, -lɪ, -nɪs
[-nəs]
stet stet
stethoscope, -s 'steθəskəʊp, -s
stethoscopic, -al, -ally ‚steθə'skɒpɪk, -l,
-əlɪ
stethoscopy ste'θɒskəpɪ
stetson (S.) 'stetsn
Steve sti:v
stevedore, -s 'sti:vədɔ:* [-vɪd-], -z
Stevenage 'sti:vnɪdʒ [-vənɪdʒ]
Steven|s, -son 'sti:vn|z, -sn
stew (s. v.), -s, -ing, -ed stju:, -z, -ɪŋ
['stjʊɪŋ], -d
steward (S.), -s; -ess/es; -ship/s stjʊəd
['stju:əd], -z; -ɪs/ɪz [‚stjʊə'des/ɪz];
-ʃɪp/s
Stewart stjʊət ['stju:ət]
stew-pan, -s 'stju:pæn, -z
Steyne sti:n
Steyning 'stenɪŋ
stg. 'stɜ:lɪŋ
stichomythia, -s ‚stɪkəʊ'mɪθɪə [-θjə], -z
stick (s. v.), -s, -ing, stuck, sticker/s
stɪk, -s, -ɪŋ, stʌk, 'stɪkə*/z
stick-in-the-mud, -s 'stɪkɪnðəmʌd, -z
stickjaw, -s 'stɪkdʒɔ:, -z
stickleback, -s 'stɪklbæk, -s
stickler, -s 'stɪklə*, -z
stick-up (s. adj.), -s 'stɪkʌp, -s
stick|y, -ier, -iest, -ily, -iness 'stɪk|ɪ,
-ɪə*, -ɪɪst, -ɪlɪ [-əlɪ], -ɪnɪs [-məs]
stiff, -er, -est, -ly, -ness stɪf, -ə*, -ɪst,
-lɪ, -nɪs [-nəs]
stiff|en, -ens, -ening, -ened 'stɪf|n, -nz,
-nɪŋ [-nɪŋ], -nd
Stiffkey (in Norfolk) 'stɪfki: [-kɪ, old-
fashioned local pronunciation 'stju:kɪ]
stiff-necked ‚stɪf'nekt [also '--, esp.
when attributive]
stif|le, -les, -ling/ly, -led 'staɪf|l, -lz,
-lɪŋ/lɪ, -ld
Stiggins 'stɪgɪnz
stigma, -s, -ta 'stɪgmə, -z, -tə
stigmatic stɪg'mætɪk
stigmatization [-isa-] ‚stɪgmətaɪ'zeɪʃn
[-tɪ'z-]
stigmatiz|e [-is|e], -es, -ing, -ed 'stɪg-
mətaɪz, -ɪz, -ɪŋ, -d
stile, -s staɪl, -z
stiletto (s.), -(e)s stɪ'letəʊ, -z

stilett|o (v.), -oes, -oing, -oed stɪ'let|əʊ,
-əʊz, -əʊɪŋ, -əʊd
still (s. adj. v. adv.) (S.), -s; -er, -est,
-ness; -ing, -ed stɪl, -z; -ə*, -ɪst, -nɪs
[-nəs]; -ɪŋ, -d
still-born 'stɪlbɔ:n
still-life ‚stɪl'laɪf ['--]
still-room, -s 'stɪlrʊm [-ru:m], -z
stilly (adj.) 'stɪlɪ
stilt, -s, -ed/ly, -edness stɪlt, -s, -ɪd/lɪ,
-ɪdnɪs [-nəs]
Stilton, -s 'stɪltən, -z
stimie = stimy
stimulant, -s 'stɪmjʊlənt [-mjəl-], -s
stimulat|e, -es, -ing, -ed, -or/s 'stɪmjʊ-
leɪt [-mjəl-], -s, -ɪŋ, -ɪd, -ə*/z
stimulation, -s ‚stɪmjʊ'leɪʃn [-mjə'l-], -z
stimulative 'stɪmjʊlətɪv [-mjəl-, -leɪt-]
stimul|us, -i 'stɪmjʊl|əs [-mjəl-], -aɪ [-i:]
stim|y (s. v.), -ies, -ying, -ied 'staɪm|ɪ,
-ɪz, -ɪɪŋ, -ɪd
sting (s. v.), -s, -ing, stung, stinger/s
stɪŋ, -z, -ɪŋ, stʌŋ, 'stɪŋə*/z
stinging-nettle, -s 'stɪŋɪŋ‚netl, -z
stingo 'stɪŋgəʊ
sting|y, -ier, -iest, -ily, -iness 'stɪndʒ|ɪ,
-ɪə* [-jə*], -ɪɪst [-jɪst], -ɪlɪ [-əlɪ], -ɪnɪs
[-məs]
stink (s. v.), -s, -ing, stank, stunk stɪŋk,
-s, -ɪŋ, stæŋk, stʌŋk
stinker, -s 'stɪŋkə*, -z
stink-pot, -s 'stɪŋkpɒt, -s
stint (s. v.), -s, -ing, -ed stɪnt, -s, -ɪŋ, -ɪd
stipend, -s 'staɪpend [-pənd], -z
stipendiar|y (s. adj.), -ies staɪ'pendjər|ɪ
[stɪ'p-, -dɪə-], -ɪz
stipp|le, -les, -ling, -led 'stɪp|l, -lz, -lɪŋ
[-lɪŋ], -ld
stipulat|e, -es, -ing, -ed, -or/s 'stɪpjʊ-
leɪt [-pjəl-], -s, -ɪŋ, -ɪd, -ə*/z
stipulation, -s ‚stɪpjʊ'leɪʃn [-pjə'l-], -z
stipule, -s 'stɪpju:l, -z
stir (s. v.), -s, -ring, -red, -rer/s stɜ:*, -z,
-rɪŋ, -d, -rə*/z
Stirling 'stɜ:lɪŋ
stirp|s, -es stɜ:p|s, -i:z [-eɪz]
stirrup, -s 'stɪrəp, -s
stirrup-pump, -s 'stɪrəppʌmp, -s
stitch (s. v.), -es, -ing, -ed stɪtʃ, -ɪz, -ɪŋ,
-t
stith|y, -ies 'stɪð|ɪ, -ɪz
stiver, -s 'staɪvə*, -z
stoat, -s stəʊt, -s
Stobart 'stəʊbɑ:t
stochastic stɒ'kæstɪk [stə-]
stock (s. v.), -s, -ing, -ed stɒk, -s, -ɪŋ, -t
stockad|e (s. v.), -es, -ing, -ed stɒ'keɪd,
-z, -ɪŋ, -ɪd

stock-book, -s 'stɒkbʊk, -s
stock-breeder, -s 'stɒk,briːdə*, -z
stockbrok|er/s, -ing 'stɒk,brəʊk|ə*/z,
-ɪŋ
Stock Exchange 'stɒkɪks,tʃeɪndʒ
stock-farm, -s 'stɒkfɑːm, -z
stockfish 'stɒkfɪʃ
stockholder, -s 'stɒk,həʊldə*, -z
Stockholm 'stɒkhəʊm
stockinet ,stɒkɪ'net
stocking (s.), -s, -ed 'stɒkɪŋ, -z, -d
stock-in-trade ,stɒkɪn'treɪd
stockjobber, -s 'stɒk,dʒɒbə*, -z
stock-market, -s 'stɒk,mɑːkɪt, -s
stockpil|e (s. v.), -es, -ing, -ed 'stɒkpaɪl,
-z, -ɪŋ, -d
Stockport 'stɒkpɔːt
stock-pot, -s 'stɒkpɒt, -s
stock-raising 'stɒk,reɪzɪŋ
stock-still ,stɒk'stɪl
stock-taking 'stɒk,teɪkɪŋ
Stock|ton, -well 'stɒk|tən, -wəl [-wel]
stock|y, -ier, -iest, -iness 'stɒk|ɪ, -ɪə*,
-ɪɪst, -ɪnɪs [-məs]
Stoddar|d, -t 'stɒdə|d, -t
stodg|e (s. v.), -es, -ing, -ed; -y, -ier,
-iest, -iness stɒdʒ, -ɪz, -ɪŋ, -d; -ɪ, -ɪə*,
-ɪɪst, -ɪnɪs [-məs]
stoep, -s stuːp, -s
Stogumber (in Somerset) stəʊ'ɡʌmbə*,
(character in Shaw's 'Saint Joan')
'stɒɡəmbə*
stoic (S.), -s, -al, -ally 'stəʊɪk, -s, -l, -əlɪ
stoicism (S.) 'stəʊɪsɪzəm
stok|e (S.), -es, -ing, -ed, -er/s stəʊk, -s,
-ɪŋ, -t, -ə*/z
Stoke Courcy [Stogursey] stəʊ'ɡəːzɪ
Stoke d'Abernon ,stəʊk'dæbənən
stokehold, -s 'stəʊkhəʊld, -z
stokehole, -s 'stəʊkhəʊl, -z
Stoke Poges ,stəʊk'pəʊdʒɪz
stole (S.), -s stəʊl, -z
stole (from steal), -n stəʊl, -ən
stolid, -est, -ly 'stɒlɪd, -ɪst, -lɪ
stolidity stɒ'lɪdətɪ [stə'l-, -ɪtɪ]
Stoll (surname) stəʊl, stɒl
stomach (s. v.), -s, -ing, -ed 'stʌmək, -s,
-ɪŋ, -t
stomach-ache, -s 'stʌməkeɪk, -s
stomacher, -s 'stʌməkə* [old-fashioned
-ətʃə*, -ədʒə*], -z
stomachic stəʊ'mækɪk [stɒ-]
stomatitis ,stəʊmə'taɪtɪs [,stɒ-]
stomatoscope, -s stəʊ'mætəskəʊp [stɒ-],
-s
ston|e (s. v.) (S.), -es, -ing, -ed stəʊn, -z,
-ɪŋ, -d
stone-blind ,stəʊn'blaɪnd

stone-breaker, -s 'stəʊn,breɪkə*, -z
stone-cast, -s 'stəʊnkɑːst, -s
stonechat, -s 'stəʊntʃæt, -s
stone-cold ,stəʊn'kəʊld
stonecrop, -s 'stəʊnkrɒp, -s
stone-cutter, -s 'stəʊn,kʌtə*, -z
stone-dead ,stəʊn'ded
stone-deaf ,stəʊn'def
stone-fruit 'stəʊnfruːt
Stonehaven stəʊn'heɪvn
Stonehenge ,stəʊn'hendʒ [also '--
according to sentence-stress]
Stonehouse 'stəʊnhaʊs
stonemason, -s 'stəʊn,meɪsn, -z
stonewall, -s, -ing, -ed, -er/s ,stəʊn-
'wɔːl, -z, -ɪŋ, -d, -ə*/z
stone-ware 'stəʊnweə*
stone-work 'stəʊnwəːk
Stoney 'stəʊnɪ
ston|y (adj. adv.), -ier, -iest, -ily, -iness
'stəʊn|ɪ, -ɪə* [-jə*], -ɪɪst [-jɪst], -ɪlɪ
[-əlɪ], -ɪnɪs [-məs]
stony-hearted 'stəʊnɪ,hɑːtɪd [,--'--]
stood (from stand) stʊd
stoog|e (s. v.), -es, -ing, -ed stuːdʒ, -ɪz,
-ɪŋ, -d
stook, -s stʊk [stuːk], -s
stool, -s stuːl, -z
stoop (s. v.), -s, -ing, -ed, -er/s stuːp, -s,
-ɪŋ, -t, -ə*/z
stop (s. v.), -s, -ping, -ped, -per/s stɒp,
-s, -ɪŋ, -t, -ə*/z
stop|-cock/s, -gap/s 'stɒp|kɒk/s,
-ɡæp/s
Stopford 'stɒpfəd
stop-go ,stɒp'ɡəʊ
Stopher 'stəʊfə*
stoppage, -s 'stɒpɪdʒ, -ɪz
stopper, -s 'stɒpə*, -z
stop-watch, -es 'stɒpwɒtʃ, -ɪz
storage 'stɔːrɪdʒ ['stɒə-]
storage-heater, -s 'stɔːrɪdʒ,hiːtə*
['stɒə-], -z
stor|e (s. v.), -es, -ing, -ed; -able stɔː*
[stɒə*], -z, -rɪŋ, -d; -rəbl
store-hou|se, -ses 'stɔːhaʊ|s ['stɒə-], -zɪz
store-keeper, -s 'stɔː,kiːpə* ['stɒə-],
-z
store-room, -s 'stɔːrʊm ['stɒərʊm,
-ruːm], -z
storey (S.), -s, -ed 'stɔːrɪ, -z, -d
storiated 'stɔːrɪeɪtɪd
storiette, -s ,stɔːrɪ'et, -s
stork, -s stɔːk, -s
storm (s. v.) (S.), -s, -ing, -ed stɔːm, -z,
-ɪŋ, -d
storm-bound 'stɔːmbaʊnd
storm-centre, -s 'stɔːm,sentə*, -z

storm-cloud, -s 'stɔːmklaʊd, -z
Stormont 'stɔːmənt [-mɒnt]
Stormonth (surname) 'stɔːmʌnθ [-mənθ]
storm-tossed 'stɔːmtɒst [old-fashioned -tɔːst]
storm-trooper, -s 'stɔːm,truːpə*, -z
storm|y, -ier, -iest, -ily, -iness 'stɔːm|ɪ, -ɪə* [-jə*], -ɪɪst [-jɪst], -ɪlɪ [-əlɪ], -ɪnɪs [-məs]
Stornoway 'stɔːnəweɪ [-nʊw-]
Storr, -s stɔː*, -z
Stortford (in Hertfordshire) 'stɔːfəd [-ɔːtf-]
Storthing 'stɔːtɪŋ
stor|y (S.), -ies 'stɔːr|ɪ, -ɪz
story-book, -s 'stɔːrɪbʊk, -s
story-tell|er/s, -ing 'stɔːrɪ,tel|ə*/z, -ɪŋ
Stothard 'stɒðəd
Stoughton (in West Sussex, Leicestershire) 'stəʊtn, (in Somerset) 'stɔːtn, (in Surrey) 'staʊtn, (surname) 'stɔːtn, 'staʊtn, 'stəʊtn
    Note.—'stəʊtn in Hodder & Stoughton, the publishers.
stoup, -s stuːp, -s
Stour (in Suffolk, Essex) stʊə*, (in Kent) stʊə* [rarely 'staʊə*], (in Hampshire) 'staʊə*, stʊə*, (in Warwickshire) 'staʊə*, 'stəʊə*, (in Dorset) 'staʊə*
Stourbridge 'staʊəbrɪdʒ
Stourmouth (in Kent) 'staʊəmaʊθ [rarely 'stʊəmaʊθ]
Stourton (in Wiltshire, surname) 'stɜːtn
stout (s. adj.), -s; -er, -est, -ly, -ness staʊt, -s; -ə*, -ɪst, -lɪ, -nɪs [-nəs]
stout-hearted, -ly, -ness staʊt'hɑːtɪd ['-,-- when attributive], -lɪ, -nɪs [-nəs]
stoutish 'staʊtɪʃ
stove (s.), -s stəʊv, -z
stove (from stave) stəʊv
stove-pipe, -s 'stəʊvpaɪp, -s
Stovold 'stɒvəʊld
stow (S.), -s, -ing, -ed; -age stəʊ, -z, -ɪŋ, -d; -ɪdʒ
stowaway, -s 'stəʊəweɪ [-əʊʊweɪ], -z
Stowe stəʊ
Stowers 'stəʊəz
Stowey (in Somerset) 'stəʊɪ
Strabane strə'bæn
strabismus strə'bɪzməs [stræ'b-]
Strabo 'streɪbəʊ
Strabolgi strə'bəʊgɪ
Strachan strɔːn, 'strækən
Strachey 'streɪtʃɪ
Strad, -s stræd, -z
stradd|le (s. v.), -les, -ling, -led 'stræd|l, -lz, -lɪŋ [-lɪŋ], -ld

Stradivarius, -es ,strædɪ'veərɪəs [-'vɑːr-], -ɪz
straf|(e) (s. v.), -(e)s, -ing/s, -ed strɑːf, -s, -ɪŋ/z, -t
Strafford 'stræfəd
stragg|le, -les, -ling, -led, -ler/s; -ly, -liness 'stræg|l, -lz, -lɪŋ [-lɪŋ], -ld, -lə*/z [-lə*/z]; -lɪ [-lɪ], -lɪnɪs [-lɪnɪs, -nəs]
Strahan strɔːn, strɑːn
straight (adj. adv.), -er, -est, -ness streɪt, -ə*, -ɪst, -nɪs [-nəs]
straight-edge, -s 'streɪtedʒ, 'streɪt,edʒɪz
straight|en, -ens, -ening, -ened 'streɪt|n, -nz, -nɪŋ [-n̩ɪŋ], -nd
straightforward, -ly, -ness ,streɪt'fɔːwəd, -lɪ, -nɪs [-nəs]
straightway 'streɪtweɪ
strain (s. v.) (S.), -s, -ing, -ed, -er/s streɪn, -z, -ɪŋ, -d, -ə*/z
strait, -s (S.), -ened streɪt, -s, -nd
strait-jacket, -s 'streɪt,dʒækɪt, -s
strait-laced ,streɪt'leɪst
strait-waistcoat, -s ,streɪt'weɪskəʊt [-stk-, old-fashioned -'weskət, '-,--], -s
Straker 'streɪkə*
strand (s. v.) (S.), -s; -ing, -ed strænd, -z; -ɪŋ, -ɪd
strange (S.), -r (adj.), -st, -ly, -ness streɪndʒ, -ə*, -ɪst, -lɪ, -nɪs [-nəs]
stranger (s.), -s 'streɪndʒə*, -z
Strangeways 'streɪndʒweɪz
strang|le, -les, -ling, -led 'stræŋg|l, -lz, -lɪŋ, -ld
strangle-hold, -s 'stræŋglhəʊld, -z
strangulat|e, -es, -ing, -ed 'stræŋgjʊleɪt [-gjəl-], -s, -ɪŋ, -ɪd
strangulation, -s ,stræŋgjʊ'leɪʃn [-gjə'l-], -z
Strangways 'stræŋweɪz
Stranraer stræn'rɑː* [-'rɑː*ə*]
strap (s. v.), -s, -ping, -ped, -per/s stræp, -s, -ɪŋ, -t, -ə*/z
strap|hang, -hangs, -hanging, -hung, -hanger/s 'stræp|hæŋ, -hæŋz, -,hæŋɪŋ, -hʌŋ, -,hæŋə*/z
strapless 'stræplɪs [-ləs]
Stras(s)b(o)urg 'stræzbɜːg
strata (plur. of stratum) 'strɑːtə [-reɪt-]
stratagem, -s 'strætədʒəm [-tɪdʒ-, -dʒɪm, -dʒem], -z
strategic, -al, -ally strə'tiːdʒɪk [stræ't-, -'tedʒ-], -l, -əlɪ
strateg|ist/s, -y 'strætɪdʒ|ɪst/s [-tədʒ-], -ɪ
Stratford 'strætfəd

473

Stratford-atte-Bowe 'strætfəd,ætɪ'bəʊɪ [-ætə'bəʊə]

Stratford-on-Avon ˌstrætfədɒn'eɪvn

strath, -s stræθ, -s

Strathaven 'streɪvən

Strathavon stræθ'ɑːn

Strathclyde stræθ'klaɪd

Strathcona stræθ'kəʊnə

Strathearn stræθ'ɜːn

Strathmore stræθ'mɔː* [-'mɔə*]

Strathpeffer stræθ'pefə*

strathspey (S.), -s stræθ'speɪ, -z

stratification ˌstrætɪfɪ'keɪʃn

strati|fy, -fies, -fying, -fied 'strætɪ|faɪ, -faɪz, -faɪɪŋ, -faɪd

stratocruiser, -s 'strætəʊ,kruːzə* ['strɑː-t-, rarely 'streɪt-], -z

Straton 'strætn

stratosphere, -s 'strætəʊ,sfɪə* ['strɑː-t-, old-fashioned 'streɪt-], -z

stratospheric ˌstrætəʊ'sferɪk [ˌstrɑː-t-, old-fashioned ˌstreɪt-]

Stratton 'strætn

strat|um, -a 'strɑː-t|əm [-reɪt-], -ə

stratus 'streɪtəs [-rɑː-t-]

Straus(s) straʊs

Stravinsky strə'vɪnskɪ (stra'vjinskij)

straw, -s, -y strɔː, -z, -ɪ

strawberr|y (S.), -ies 'strɔː'bər|ɪ, -ɪz

stray (s. adj. v.) (S.), -s, -ing, -ed streɪ, -z, -ɪŋ, -d

streak (s. v.), -s, -ing, -ed; -y, -ier, -iest, -iness 'striː:k, -s, -ɪŋ, -t; -ɪ, -ɪə* [-jə*], -ɪst [-jɪst], -ɪnɪs [-məs]

stream (s. v.), -s, -ing, -ed, -er/s striː:m, -z, -ɪŋ, -d, -ə*/z

streamlet, -s 'striː:mlɪt [-lət], -s

streamlin|e (s. v.), -es, -ing, -ed 'striː:m-laɪn, -z, -ɪŋ, -d

Streatfeild 'stretfiː:ld

Streatfield 'stretfiː:ld

Streatham 'stretəm

Streatley 'striː:tlɪ

street (S.), -s striː:t, -s

strength, -s streŋθ [-ŋkθ], -s

strength|en, -ens, -ening, -ened, -ener/s 'streŋθ|n [-ŋkθ-], -nz, -ənɪŋ [-ɪŋ, -nɪŋ], -nd, -ənə*/z [-ŋə*/z, -nə*/z]

strenuous, -ly, -ness 'strenjʊəs [-njwəs], -lɪ, -nɪs [-nəs]

streptococc|us, -i ˌstreptəʊ'kɒk|əs, -aɪ

streptomycin ˌstreptəʊ'maɪsɪn

stress (s. v.), -es, -ing, -ed stres, -ɪz, -ɪŋ, -t

stress-group, -s 'stresgruː:p, -s

stressless 'streslɪs [-ləs]

stretch (s. v.), -es, -ing, -ed, -er/s stretʃ, -ɪz, -ɪŋ, -t, -ə*/z

Strevens 'strevənz

strew, -s, -ing, -ed, -n struː:, -z, -ɪŋ ['strʊɪŋ], -d, -n

stri|a, -ae 'straɪ|ə, -iː:

striate (adj.) 'straɪɪt [-aɪeɪt]

striated straɪ'eɪtɪd

striation, -s straɪ'eɪʃn, -z

stricken (from strike) 'strɪkən

Strickland 'strɪklənd

strict, -er, -est, -ly, -ness strɪkt, -ə*, -ɪst, -lɪ ['strɪklɪ], -nɪs ['strɪknɪs, -nəs]

stricture, -s 'strɪktʃə*, -z

strid|e (s. v.), -es, -ing, strode, stridden straɪd, -z, -ɪŋ, strəʊd, 'strɪdn

strident, -ly 'straɪdnt, -lɪ

strife straɪf

strigil, -s 'strɪdʒɪl, -z

strik|e (s. v.), -es, -ing/ly, struck, stricken, striker/s straɪk, -s, -ɪŋ/lɪ, strʌk, 'strɪkən, 'straɪkə*/z

strike-break|er/s, -ing 'straɪk,breɪk|-ə*/z, -ɪŋ

strike-pay 'straɪkpeɪ

Strindberg 'strɪndbɑ:g (strind,berj)

string (s. v.), -s, -ing, -ed, strung, stringer/s strɪŋ, -z, -ɪŋ, -d, strʌŋ, 'strɪŋə*/z

stringen|cy, -t/ly 'strɪndʒən|sɪ, -t/lɪ

stringendo strɪn'dʒendəʊ

Stringer 'strɪŋə*

string|y, -ier, -iest, -iness 'strɪŋ|ɪ, -ɪə*, -ɪst, -ɪnɪs [-məs]

strip (s. v.), -s, -ping, -ped, -per/s strɪp, -s, -ɪŋ, -t, -ə*/z

strip|e (s. v.), -es, -ing, -ed; -y, -iness straɪp, -s, -ɪŋ, -t; -ɪ, -ɪnɪs [-məs]

stripling, -s 'strɪplɪŋ, -z

striptease 'strɪptiː:z

striv|e, -es, -ing/s, strove, striven, striver/s straɪv, -z, -ɪŋ/z, strəʊv, 'strɪvn, 'straɪvə*/z

strobilion, -s strəʊ'bɪlɪən [-ljən], -z

strobolion, -s strəʊ'bəʊljən [-lɪən], -z

stroboscope, -s 'strəʊbəskəʊp ['strɒb-], -s

stroboscopic ˌstrəʊbəʊ'skɒpɪk [ˌstrɒb-]

stroboscopy strəʊ'bɒskəpɪ [strɒ'b-]

strode (from stride) strəʊd

strok|e (s. v.), -es, -ing, -ed strəʊk, -s, -ɪŋ, -t

stroll (s. v.), -s, -ing, -ed, -er/s strəʊl, -z, -ɪŋ, -d, -ə*/z

Stromboli 'strɒmbəlɪ [-bʊl-, -bəʊl-, strɒm'bəʊlɪ] ('stromboli)

strong (S.), -er, -est, -ly, -ish strɒŋ, -gə*, -gɪst, -lɪ, -ɪʃ

strong-box, -es 'strɒŋbɒks, -ɪz

stronghold, -s 'strɒŋhəʊld, -z

strong-minded ˌstrɒŋ'maɪndɪd [*also* '-ˌ-- *when attributive*]

strong-mindedness ˌstrɒŋ'maɪndɪdnɪs [-nəs]

strong-room, -s 'strɒŋrʊm [-ru:m], -z

stron|tia, -tian, -tium 'strɒn|ʃɪə [-ʃjə, -ʃə, -tɪə, -tjə], -ʃɪən [-ʃjən, -ʃn, -tɪən, -tjən], -tɪəm [-tjəm, *rarely* -ʃɪəm, -ʃjəm, -ʃəm]

Strood stru:d

strop (*s. v.*), -s, -ping, -ped strɒp, -s, -ɪŋ, -t

strophe, -s 'strəʊfɪ ['strɒf-], -z

strophic 'strɒfɪk

Stroud straʊd (*sometimes* stru:d *as a surname*)

strove (*from* strive) strəʊv

strow, -s, -ing, -ed, -n strəʊ, -z, -ɪŋ, -d, -n

struck (*from* strike) strʌk

structur|al, -ally 'strʌktʃər|əl [-tʃʊr-], -əlɪ

structural|ism, -ist/s 'strʌktʃərəl|ɪzm [-tʃʊr-], -ɪst/s

structure, -s 'strʌktʃə*, -z

strugg|le (*s. v.*), -les, -ling, -led, -ler/s 'strʌg|l, -lz, -lɪŋ [-lɪŋ], -ld, -lə*/z [-lə*/z]

strum (*s. v.*), -s, -ming, -med, -mer/s strʌm, -z, -ɪŋ, -d, -ə*/z

strumpet, -s 'strʌmpɪt, -s

strung (*from* string) strʌŋ

strut (*s. v.*), -s, -ting, -ted strʌt, -s, -ɪŋ, -ɪd

Struthers 'strʌðəz

Strutt strʌt

Struwwelpeter (*English*) 'stru:əlˌpi:tə*

strychnine 'strɪkni:n

Stuart, -s stjʊət ['stju:ət], -s

stub, -s; -by, -bier, -biest, -biness stʌb, -z; -ɪ, -ɪə*, -ɪɪst, -ɪnɪs [-ɪnəs]

stubb|le, -ly 'stʌb|l, -lɪ [-lɪ]

stubborn, -er, -est, -ly, -ness 'stʌbən, -ə*, -ɪst, -lɪ, -nɪs [-nəs]

Stubbs stʌbz

stucco (*s.*), -(e)s 'stʌkəʊ, -z

stucco (*v.*), -es, -ing, -ed 'stʌkəʊ, -z, -ɪŋ, -d

stuck (*from* stick) stʌk

stuck-up ˌstʌk'ʌp [*also* '-- *according to sentence-stress*]

Stucley 'stju:klɪ

stud (*s. v.*), -s, -ding, -ded stʌd, -z, -ɪŋ, -ɪd

studding-sail, -s 'stʌdɪŋseɪl [*nautical pronunciation* 'stʌnsl], -z

Studebaker 'stu:dəbeɪkə*

student, -s 'stju:dnt, -s

studentship, -s 'stju:dnt-ʃɪp, -s

studio, -s 'stju:dɪəʊ [-djəʊ], -z

studious, -ly, -ness 'stju:djəs [-dɪəs], -lɪ, -nɪs [-nəs]

stud|y (*s. v.*), -ies, -ying, -ied 'stʌd|ɪ, -ɪz, -ɪɪŋ, -ɪd

stuff (*s. v.*), -s, -ing, -ed; -y, -ier, -iest, -iness stʌf, -s, -ɪŋ, -t; -ɪ, -ɪə*, -ɪɪst, -ɪnɪs [-ɪnəs]

stuffing (*s.*), -s 'stʌfɪŋ, -z

stultification ˌstʌltɪfɪ'keɪʃn

stulti|fy, -fies, -fying, -fied 'stʌltɪ|faɪ, -faɪz, -faɪɪŋ, -faɪd

stum stʌm

stumb|le (*s. v.*), -les, -ling, -led, -ler/s 'stʌmb|l, -lz, -lɪŋ, -ld, -lə*/z

stumbling-block, -s 'stʌmblɪŋblɒk, -s

stump (*s. v.*), -s, -ing, -ed; -y, -ier, -iest, -iness stʌmp, -s, -ɪŋ, -t [stʌmt]; -ɪ, -ɪə* [-jə*], -ɪɪst [-jɪst], -ɪnɪs [-ɪnəs]

stun, -s, -ning/ly, -ned stʌn, -z, -ɪŋ/lɪ, -d

stung (*from* sting) stʌŋ

stunk (*from* stink) stʌŋk

stunner, -s 'stʌnə*, -z

stunt (*s. v.*), -s, -ing, -ed stʌnt, -s, -ɪŋ, -ɪd

stupe, -s stju:p, -s

stupefaction ˌstju:pɪ'fækʃn [ˌstjʊpɪ'f-]

stupe|fy, -fies, -fying, -fied 'stju:pɪ|faɪ ['stjʊp-], -faɪz, -faɪɪŋ, -faɪd

stupendous, -ly, -ness stju:'pendəs [stjʊ'p-], -lɪ, -nɪs [-nəs]

stupid (*s. adj.*), -s, -er, -est, -ly, -ness 'stju:pɪd ['stjʊp-, *rarely* 'stʊp-], -z, -ə*, -ɪst, -lɪ, -nɪs [-nəs]

stupidit|y, -ies stju:'pɪdət|ɪ [stjʊ'p-, -ɪt|ɪ], -ɪz

stupor 'stju:pə*

Sturdee 'stɜ:dɪ

sturd|y, -ier, -iest, -ily, -iness 'stɜ:d|ɪ, -ɪə* [-jə*], -ɪɪst [-jɪst], -ɪlɪ [-əlɪ], -ɪnɪs [-ɪnəs]

sturgeon, -s 'stɜ:dʒən, -z

Sturtevant 'stɜ:tɪvənt [-vænt]

stutter (*s. v.*), -s, -ing, -ed, -er/s 'stʌtə*, -z, -rɪŋ, -d, -rə*/z

Stuttgart 'stʊtgɑ:t ('ʃtutgart)

Stuyvesant 'staɪvəsənt

st|y, -ies st|aɪ, -aɪz

Styche staɪtʃ

stye, -s staɪ, -z

Stygian 'stɪdʒɪən [-dʒən]

styl|e (*s. v.*), -es, -ing, -ed staɪl, -z, -ɪŋ, -d

stylet, -s 'staɪlɪt [-lət], -s

stylish, -ly, -ness 'staɪlɪʃ, -lɪ, -nɪs [-nəs]

stylist, -s 'staɪlɪst, -s

stylistic, -s staɪ'lɪstɪk, -s

stylite, -s 'staɪlaɪt, -s
Stylites (*Simeon S.*) staɪ'laɪtiːz
stylization [-isa-] ˌstaɪlaɪ'zeɪʃn [-lɪ'z-]
stylize [-ise], -d 'staɪlaɪz, -d
stylograph, -s 'staɪləʊgrɑːf [-græf], -s
stylographic ˌstaɪləʊ'græfɪk
styl|us, -uses, -i 'staɪl|əs, -əsɪz, -aɪ
stymie = stimy
styptic 'stɪptɪk
styrax, -es 'staɪəræks ['staɪr-], -ɪz
Styria, -n/s 'stɪrɪə, -n/z
Styx stɪks
suable 'sjuːəbl ['sjʊəbl]
Suaki|m, -n suː'ɑːkɪ|m [sʊ'ɑː-], -n
suasion 'sweɪʒn
suave, -r, -st, -ly, -ness swɑːv [*old-fashioned* sweɪv], -ə*, -ɪst, -lɪ, -nɪs [-nəs]
suavity 'swɑːvətɪ ['sweɪv-, 'swæv-, -ɪtɪ]
sub (*s. prep.*), -s sʌb, -z
subacid ˌsʌb'æsɪd
subalpine ˌsʌb'ælpaɪn
subaltern, -s 'sʌbltən, -z
sub-bass, -es ˌsʌb'beɪs, -ɪz
subclass, -es 'sʌbklɑːs, -ɪz
subclassification, -s 'sʌbˌklæsɪfɪ'keɪʃn ['-ˌ---ˌ--], -z
subclassi|fy, -fies, -fying, -fied ˌsʌb'klæsɪ|faɪ, -faɪz, -faɪɪŋ, -faɪd
subcommittee, -s 'sʌbkəˌmɪtɪ, -z
subconscious, -ly, -ness ˌsʌb'kɒnʃəs, -lɪ, -nɪs [-nəs]
subcutaneous ˌsʌbkjuː'teɪnjəs [-kjʊ't-, -nɪəs]
subdean, -s ˌsʌb'diːn, -z
subdivid|e, -es, -ing, -ed ˌsʌbdɪ'vaɪd ['--ˌ-], -z, -ɪŋ, -ɪd
subdivision, -s 'sʌbdɪˌvɪʒn [ˌ--'--], -z
subdominant, -s ˌsʌb'dɒmɪnənt, -s
subdual, -s səb'djuːəl [-'djʊəl], -z
subd|ue, -ues, -uing, -ued, -uer/s, -uable səb'd|juː, -juːz, -juːɪŋ [-jʊɪŋ], -juːd, -juːə*/z [-jʊə*/z]; -juːəbl [-jʊəbl]
sub-edit, -s, -ing, -ed ˌsʌb'edɪt, -s, -ɪŋ, -ɪd
sub-editor, -s; -ship/s ˌsʌb'edɪtə* ['-ˌ---], -z; -ʃɪp/s
sub-famil|y, -ies ˌsʌbˌfæməl|ɪ [-mɪl-], -ɪz
subfusc 'sʌbfʌsk
subgroup, -s 'sʌbgruːp, -s
sub-heading, -s ˌsʌb'hedɪŋ [ˌ-'--], -z
sub-human (*s. adj.*), -s ˌsʌb'hjuːmən, -z
subjacent sʌb'dʒeɪsənt [səb-]
subject (*s. adj.*), -s 'sʌbdʒɪkt [-dʒekt], -s
subject (*v.*), -s, -ing, -ed səb'dʒekt [sʌb'dʒekt, *less commonly* 'sʌbdʒɪkt, 'sʌbdʒekt], -s, -ɪŋ, -ɪd

subjection səb'dʒekʃn
subjective, -ly, -ness səb'dʒektɪv [sʌb'dʒ-, ˌsʌb'dʒ-], -lɪ, -nɪs [-nəs]
subjectivism səb'dʒektɪvɪzəm [sʌb-]
subjectivity ˌsʌbdʒek'tɪvətɪ [-ɪtɪ]
subject-matter 'sʌbdʒɪktˌmætə*
subjoin, -s, -ing, -ed ˌsʌb'dʒɔɪn, -z, -ɪŋ, -d
sub judice ˌsʌb'dʒuːdɪsɪ [ˌsʊb'juːdɪkɪ]
subjugat|e, -es, -ing, -ed, -or/s 'sʌbdʒʊgeɪt [-dʒəg-], -s, -ɪŋ, -ɪd, -ə*/z
subjugation ˌsʌbdʒʊ'geɪʃn [-dʒə'g-]
subjunctive (*s. adj.*), -s səb'dʒʌŋktɪv, -z
sublease, -s ˌsʌb'liːs ['sʌbliːs], -ɪz
subless|ee/s, -or/s ˌsʌble's|iː/z, -ɔː*/z
sublet, -s, -ting ˌsʌb'let, -s, -ɪŋ
sub-librarian, -s ˌsʌblaɪ'breərɪən, -z
sub-lieutenan|t/s; -cy, -cies ˌsʌblef'tenən|t/s [-ləf't-], -sɪ, -sɪz (*see note under* lieutenancy)
sublimate (*s.*), -s 'sʌblɪmət [-mɪt, -meɪt], -s
sublimat|e (*v.*), -es, -ing, -ed 'sʌblɪmeɪt, -s, -ɪŋ, -ɪd
sublimation ˌsʌblɪ'meɪʃn
sublim|e (*s. adj. v.*), -er, -est, -ely, -eness; -es, -ing, -ed sə'blaɪm, -ə*, -ɪst, -lɪ, -nɪs [-nəs]; -z, -ɪŋ, -d
subliminal ˌsʌb'lɪmɪnl [səb-, -mən-]
sublimity sə'blɪmətɪ [-ɪtɪ]
submachine-gun, -s ˌsʌbmə'ʃiːngʌn [-'ʃiːŋgʌn], -z
submarin|e (*s. adj. v.*), -es, -ing, -ed ˌsʌbmə'riːn ['sʌbməriːn], -z, -ɪŋ, -d
submerg|e, -es, -ing, -ed; -ence səb'mɜːdʒ [sʌb-], -ɪz, -ɪŋ, -d; -əns
submersible (*s. adj.*), -s səb'mɜːsəbl [sʌb-, -sɪbl], -z
submersion, -s səb'mɜːʃn [sʌb-], -z
submission, -s səb'mɪʃn, -z
submissive, -ly, -ness səb'mɪsɪv, -lɪ, -nɪs [-nəs]
submit, -s, -ting, -ted səb'mɪt, -s, -ɪŋ, -ɪd
submultiple, -s ˌsʌb'mʌltɪpl, -z
sub-normal ˌsʌb'nɔːml [*in contrast* '-ˌ--]
suboctave, -s 'sʌbˌɒktɪv, -z
subordinate (*s. adj.*), -s; -ly sə'bɔːdnət [-dənət, -dɪnət, -dnət, -ɪt], -s; -lɪ
subordinat|e (*v.*), -es, -ing, -ed sə'bɔːdɪneɪt, -s, -ɪŋ, -ɪd
subordination səˌbɔːdɪ'neɪʃn
subordinative sə'bɔːdɪnətɪv [-dn-, -dən-]
suborn, -s, -ing, -ed, -er/s sʌ'bɔːn [sə'b-], -z, -ɪŋ, -d, -ə*/z
subornation ˌsʌbɔː'neɪʃn
subpoena (*s. v.*), -s, -ing, -ed səb'piːnə [ˌsʌb'p-, sə'p-], -z, -ɪŋ [-nərɪŋ], -d

sub-prefect, -s ˌsʌb'priːfekt [*in contrast*
'-ˌ--], -s

subrogation ˌsʌbrəʊ'geɪʃn

sub rosa ˌsʌb'rəʊzə

subscrib|e, -es, -ing, -ed, -er/s səb-
'skraɪb [-bzˈk-], -z, -ɪŋ, -d, -ə*/z

subscript 'sʌbskrɪpt [-bzk-]

subscription, -s səb'skrɪpʃn [-bzˈk-], -z

sub-section, -s 'sʌbˌsekʃn, -z

subsensible ˌsʌb'sensəbl [-sɪb-]

subsequent, -ly 'sʌbsɪkwənt, -lɪ

subserv|e, -es, -ing, -ed səb'sɜːv [sʌb-],
-z, -ɪŋ, -d

subservien|ce, -cy, -t/ly səb'sɜːvjən|s
[sʌb-, -vɪən-], -sɪ, -t/lɪ

subsid|e, -es, -ing, -ed səb'saɪd, -z, -ɪŋ,
-ɪd

subsidence, -s səb'saɪdns ['sʌbsɪd-], -ɪz

subsidiar|y (*s. adj.*), -ies, -ily səb'sɪdjər|ɪ
[-dɪə-], -ɪz, -əlɪ [-ɪlɪ]

subsidiz|e [-is|e], -es, -ing, -ed 'sʌb-
sɪdaɪz [-səd-], -ɪz, -ɪŋ, -d

subsid|y, -ies 'sʌbsɪd|ɪ [-səd|ɪ], -ɪz

subsist, -s, -ing, -ed; -ence səb'sɪst, -s,
-ɪŋ, -ɪd; -əns

subsoil, -s 'sʌbsɔɪl, -z

sub-species 'sʌbˌspiːʃiːz [-ʃɪz]

substance, -s 'sʌbstəns [-bzt-], -ɪz

substanti|al, -ally, -alness səb'stænʃ|l
[-bzˈt-], -əlɪ [-ḷɪ, -lɪ], -lnɪs [-nəs]

substantiality səbˌstænʃɪ'ælətɪ [-bzˌt-,
-ɪtɪ]

substantiat|e, -es, -ing, -ed səb'stæn-
ʃɪeɪt [-bzˈt-, -ʃjert, -nsɪ-], -s, -ɪŋ, -ɪd

substantiation səbˌstænʃɪ'eɪʃn [-bzˌt-,
-nsɪ-]

substantival ˌsʌbstən'taɪvl [-bzt-]

substantive (*s.*), -s 'sʌbstəntɪv [-bzt-], -z

substantive (*adj.*), -ly, -ness 'sʌbstəntɪv
[-bzt-, səb'stæn-], -lɪ, -nɪs [-nəs]
Note.—*Generally* səb'stæntɪv *when
applied to rank, pay, etc.*

substitut|e (*s. v.*), -es, -ing, -ed 'sʌb-
stɪtjuːt [-bzt-], -s, -ɪŋ, -ɪd

substitution, -s ˌsʌbstɪ'tjuːʃn [-bzt-], -z

substitu|tional, -tionally ˌsʌbstɪ'tjuː|ʃənl
[-bzt-, -ʃnəl, -ʃn̩l, -ʃn̩l, -ʃənəl], -ʃn̩əlɪ
[-nəlɪ, -ʃn̩lɪ, -ʃn̩lɪ, -ʃənəlɪ]

substitutive 'sʌbstɪtjuːtɪv [-bzt-]

substratosphere, -s ˌsʌb'strætəˌsfɪə*
[-'strɑːt-, *rarely* -'streɪt-, -təʊs-], -z

substrat|um, -a ˌsʌb'strɑːt|əm [-reɪt-,
'-ˌ--], -ə

substructure, -s 'sʌbˌstrʌktʃə*, -z

subsum|e, -es, -ing, -ed səb'sjuːm, -z,
-ɪŋ, -d

subtangent, -s ˌsʌb'tændʒənt, -s

subtenan|cy, -t/s ˌsʌb'tenən|sɪ, -t/s

subtend, -s, -ing, -ed səb'tend, -z, -ɪŋ, -ɪd

subterfuge, -s 'sʌbtəfjuːdʒ, -ɪz

subterranean ˌsʌbtə'reɪnjən [-nɪən]

subterraneous ˌsʌbtə'reɪnjəs [-nɪəs]

subtil(e) 'sʌtl

subtility sʌb'tɪlətɪ [-ɪtɪ]

subtiliz|e [-is|e], -es, -ing, -ed 'sʌtɪlaɪz
[-tḷaɪz], -ɪz, -ɪŋ, -d

subtilty 'sʌtltɪ [-tɪltɪ]

sub-title, -s 'sʌbˌtaɪtl [ˌ-'--], -z

subt|le, -ler, -lest, -ly, -leness 'sʌt|l,
-ḷə* [-lə*], -ḷɪst [-lɪst], -lɪ, -lnɪs [-nəs]

subtlet|y, -ies 'sʌtlt|ɪ, -ɪz

subtopia sʌb'təʊpɪə [-pjə]

subtract, -s, -ing, -ed səb'trækt, -s, -ɪŋ,
-ɪd

subtraction, -s səb'trækʃn, -z

subtrahend, -s 'sʌbtrəhend, -z

subtropical ˌsʌb'trɒpɪkl

suburb, -s 'sʌbɜːb [-bəb], -z

suburban 'sʌbɜːbən

suburbaniz|e [-is|e], -es, -ing, -ed
sə'bɜːbənaɪz, -ɪz, -ɪŋ, -d

suburbia sə'bɜːbɪə [-bjə]

subvariet|y, -ies 'sʌbvəˌraɪət|ɪ, -ɪz

subvention, -s səb'venʃn [sʌb-], -z

subver|sion, -sive səb'vɜː|ʃn [sʌb-], -sɪv

subvert, -s, -ing, -ed sʌb'vɜːt [səb-], -s,
-ɪŋ, -ɪd

subway, -s 'sʌbweɪ, -z

succeed, -s, -ing, -ed sək'siːd, -z, -ɪŋ,
-ɪd

succentor, -s sək'sentə* [sʌk-], -z

success, -es; -ful, -fully sək'ses, -ɪz;
-fʊl, -fʊlɪ [-fəlɪ]

succession, -s sək'seʃn, -z

successive, -ly sək'sesɪv, -lɪ

successor, -s sək'sesə*, -z

succinct, -ly, -ness sək'sɪŋkt [sʌk-], -lɪ,
-nɪs [-nəs]

succory 'sʌkərɪ

succotash 'sʌkətæʃ

Succoth 'sʌkəθ

succour (*s. v.*), -s, -ing, -ed 'sʌkə*, -z,
-rɪŋ, -d

succub|a, -ae, -us, -i 'sʌkjʊb|ə, -iː, -əs,
-aɪ

succulen|ce, -t/ly 'sʌkjʊlən|s [-kjəl-],
-t/lɪ

succumb, -s, -ing, -ed sə'kʌm, -z, -ɪŋ, -d

succursal, -s sʌ'kɜːsl, -z

such sʌtʃ (*normal form*), sətʃ (*occasional
weak form*)

such-and-such 'sʌtʃənsʌtʃ

suchlike 'sʌtʃlaɪk

suck (*s. v.*), -s, -ing, -ed, -er/s sʌk, -s,
-ɪŋ, -t, -ə*/z

sucking-pig, -s 'sʌkɪŋpɪg, -z

suck|le (s. v.), -les, -ling, -led 'sʌk|l, -lz, -lɪŋ [-lɪŋ], -ld
suckling (s.), -s 'sʌklɪŋ, -z
suction 'sʌkʃn
Suda 'suːdə
Sudan suː'dɑːn [sʊ'd-, -'dæn]
Sudanese ˌsuːdə'niːz [also '— when attributive]
Sudanic suː'dænɪk [sʊ'd-]
sudarium, -s sjuː'deərɪəm [sjʊ-, suː-, sʊ-], -z
sudatory 'sjuːdətərɪ ['suː-]
Sudbury 'sʌdbərɪ
sudd sʌd
sudd|en, -enest, -enly, -enness 'sʌd|n, -nɪst, -nlɪ, -nnɪs [-nnəs]
Sudeley 'sjuːdlɪ
sudorific (s. adj.), -s ˌsjuːdə'rɪfɪk [ˌsuː-, -dɒ'r-], -s
suds sʌdz
sue (S.), sues, suing, sued sjuː [suː], sjuːz [suːz], 'sjuːɪŋ ['sjʊɪŋ, 'suːɪŋ, 'sʊɪŋ], sjuːd [suːd]
suède sweɪd (sɥɛːd)
suet, -y 'sjʊɪt ['sʊɪt, 'sjuːɪt, 'suːɪt], -ɪ
Suetonius swiː'təʊnjəs [swɪ't-, -nɪəs]
Suez 'suɪz ['sjuɪz, 'suːɪz, 'sjuːɪz]
suff|er, -ers, -ering/s, -ered, -erer/s; -erable, -erance 'sʌf|ə*, -əz, -ərɪŋ/z, -əd, -ərə*/z; -ərəbl, -ərəns
suffic|e, -es, -ing, -ed sə'faɪs, -ɪz, -ɪŋ, -t
sufficien|cy, -t/ly sə'fɪʃn|sɪ, -t/lɪ
suffix (s.), -es 'sʌfɪks, -ɪz
suffix (v.), -es, -ing, -ed 'sʌfɪks [-'-], -ɪz, -ɪŋ, -t
suffocat|e, -es, -ing/ly, -ed 'sʌfəkeɪt, -s, -ɪŋ/lɪ, -ɪd
suffocation ˌsʌfə'keɪʃn
Suffolk 'sʌfək
suffragan (s. adj.), -s 'sʌfrəgən, -z
suffrage, -s 'sʌfrɪdʒ, -ɪz
suffragette, -s ˌsʌfrə'dʒet, -s
suffragist, -s 'sʌfrədʒɪst, -s
suffus|e, -es, -ing, -ed sə'fjuːz [sʌ'f-], -ɪz, -ɪŋ, -d
suffusion, -s sə'fjuːʒn [sʌ'f-], -z
sufi, -s; -sm 'suːfɪ, -z; -zəm
sugar (s. v.), -s, -ing, -ed 'ʃʊgə*, -z, -rɪŋ, -d
sugar-basin, -s 'ʃʊgəˌbeɪsn, -z
sugar-cane, -s 'ʃʊgəkeɪn, -z
sugarloa|f, -ves 'ʃʊgələʊ|f, -vz
sugar-plum, -s 'ʃʊgəplʌm, -z
sugar-refiner, -s 'ʃʊgərɪˌfaɪnə*, -z
sugar-refiner|y, -ies 'ʃʊgərɪˌfaɪnər|ɪ, -ɪz
sugar-tongs 'ʃʊgətɒŋz
sugar|y, -iest, -iness 'ʃʊgər|ɪ, -ɪɪst, -ɪnɪs [-ɪnəs]

suggest, -s, -ing, -ed sə'dʒest, -s, -ɪŋ, -ɪd
suggestion, -s sə'dʒestʃən [-eʃtʃ-], -z
suggestive, -ly, -ness sə'dʒestɪv, -lɪ, -nɪs [-nəs]
suicidal sjʊɪ'saɪdl [ˌsjuː-, sʊɪ-, ˌsuː-, '----]
suicide, -s 'sjʊɪsaɪd ['sjuː-, 'sʊɪ-, 'suː-], -z
sui generis ˌsjʊaɪ'dʒenərɪs [ˌsʊ-, ˌsjuː-, ˌsuː-, -i:'gen-]
sui juris ˌsjʊaɪ'dʒʊərɪs [ˌsʊ-, ˌsju:-, ˌsuː-, -'dʒɔːr-, -'dʒɔːr-, -i:'jʊərɪs]
Suirdale 'ʃɜːdl [-dəl]
suit (s. v.), -s, -ing/s, -ed, -or/s suːt [sjuːt], -s, -ɪŋ/z, -ɪd, -ə*/z
    Note.—The word in isolation and in compounds increasingly has the form suːt.
suitability ˌsuːtə'bɪlətɪ [ˌsjuː-, -lɪt-]
suitab|le, -ly, -leness 'suːtəb|l ['sjuː-], -lɪ, -lnɪs [-nəs]
suit-case, -s 'suːtkeɪs ['sjuːt-], -ɪz
suite, -s swiːt, -s
sulcal 'sʌlkəl [-kl]
sulcalization [-isa-] ˌsʌlkəlaɪ'zeɪʃn
sulcaliz|e [-is|e], -es, -ing, -ed 'sʌlkəlaɪz, -ɪz, -ɪŋ, -d
Suleiman ˌsʊleɪ'mɑːn ['---]
Suliman ˌsʊlɪ'mɑːn ['---]
sulk (s. v.), -s, -ing, -ed; -y, -ier, -iest, -ily, -iness sʌlk, -s, -ɪŋ, -t; -ɪ, -ɪə*[-jə*], -ɪɪst [-jɪst], -ɪlɪ [-əlɪ], -ɪnɪs [-nəs]
Sulla 'sʌlə ['sʊlə]
sullen, -est, -ly, -ness 'sʌlən, -ɪst, -lɪ, -nɪs [-nəs]
Sullivan 'sʌlɪvən
sull|y (S.), -ies, -ying, -ied 'sʌl|ɪ, -ɪz, -ɪŋ, -ɪd
sulphanilamide ˌsʌlfə'nɪləmaɪd
sulphate, -s 'sʌlfeɪt [-frt, -fət], -s
sulphi|de/s, -te/s 'sʌlfaɪ|d/z, -t/s
sulphur 'sʌlfə*
sulphureous sʌl'fjʊərɪəs [-'fjɔər-, -'fjɔːr-]
sulphuretted 'sʌlfjʊretɪd [-fər-]
sulphuric sʌl'fjʊərɪk [-'fjɔər-, -'fjɔːr-]
sulphurous 'sʌlfərəs [-fjʊr-]
sulphury 'sʌlfərɪ
sultan (S.), -s 'sʌltən, -z
sultana (kind of raisin), -s səl'tɑːnə [sʌl-], -z
Sultana (Sultan's wife, mother, etc.), -s sʌl'tɑːnə, -z
sultanate, -s 'sʌltənət [-neɪt, -nɪt], -s
sultr|y, -ier, -iest, -ily, -iness 'sʌltr|ɪ, -ɪə*, -ɪɪst, -əlɪ [-ɪlɪ], -ɪnɪs [-ɪnəs]
sum (s. v.), -s, -ming, -med sʌm, -z, -ɪŋ, -d

sumach, -s 'ʃuːmæk ['sjuː-, 'suː-], -s
Sumatra sʊ'mɑːtrə [sjʊ-, suː-, sjuː-]
Sumerian sjuː'mɪərɪən [suː-, sjʊ'm-, sʊ'm-]
summariz|e [ise|e], -es, -ing, -ed 'sʌməraɪz, -ɪz, -ɪŋ, -d
summar|y (s. adj.), -ies, -ily, -iness 'sʌmər|ɪ, -ɪz, -əlɪ [-ɪlɪ], -ɪnɪs [-məs]
summation, -s sʌ'meɪʃn, -z
summer, -s; -like 'sʌmə*, -z; -laɪk
Summerfield, -s 'sʌməfiːld, -z
summerhou|se, -ses 'sʌməhaʊ|s, -zɪz
summertime 'sʌmətaɪm
Summerville 'sʌməvɪl
summery 'sʌmərɪ
summing-up, summings-up ˌsʌmɪŋ'ʌp, ˌsʌmɪŋz'ʌp
summit, -s 'sʌmɪt, -s
summon, -s, -ing, -ed, -er/s 'sʌmən, -z, -ɪŋ, -d, -ə*/z
summons (s. v.), -es, -ing, -ed 'sʌmənz, -ɪz, -ɪŋ, -d
Sumner 'sʌmnə*
sump, -s sʌmp, -s
sumpter (S.), -s 'sʌmptə*, -z
sumptuary 'sʌmptjʊərɪ [-tjwərɪ, -tjʊrɪ, -tʃʊərɪ, -tʃwərɪ, -tʃʊrɪ]
sumptuous, -ly, -ness 'sʌmptjʊəs [-tjwəs, -tʃʊəs, -tʃwəs], -lɪ, -nɪs [-nəs]
Sumsion 'sʌmʃn
Sumurun ˌsʊmʊ'ruːn
sun (s. v.), -s, -ning, -ned sʌn, -z, -ɪŋ, -d
sun-ba|th, -ths 'sʌnbɑː|θ, -ðz
sun-bath|e, -es, -ing, -ed, -er/s 'sʌnbeɪð, -z, -ɪŋ, -d, -ə*/z
sunbeam (S.), -s 'sʌnbiːm, -z
sunblind, -s 'sʌnblaɪnd, -z
sun-bonnet, -s 'sʌn,bɒnɪt, -s
sunburn, -s, -t 'sʌnbɜːn, -z, -t
Sunbury 'sʌnbərɪ
Sunda 'sʌndə
sundae, -s 'sʌndeɪ, -z
Sundanese ˌsʌndə'niːz
Sunday, -s 'sʌndɪ [-deɪ], -z
sunder, -s, -ing, -ed 'sʌndə*, -z, -rɪŋ, -d
Sunderland 'sʌndələnd
sundial, -s 'sʌndaɪəl, -z
sundown 'sʌndaʊn
sun-dried 'sʌndraɪd
sundry 'sʌndrɪ
sun-fish 'sʌnfɪʃ
sunflower, -s 'sʌn,flaʊə*, -z
sung (from sing) sʌŋ
Sung (Chinese dynasty) sʊŋ [sʌŋ]
sun-hat, -s 'sʌnhæt, -s
sun-helmet, -s 'sʌn,helmɪt [ˌ-'--], -s
sunk (from sink) sʌŋk
sunken (from sink) 'sʌŋkən

sun|less, -light, -like 'sʌn|lɪs [-ləs], -laɪt, -laɪk
Sunningdale 'sʌnɪŋdeɪl
sunn|y, -ier, -iest, -iness 'sʌn|ɪ, -ɪə*, -ɪɪst, -ɪnɪs [-ɪnəs]
Sunnyside 'sʌnɪsaɪd
sunproof 'sʌnpruːf
sunrise, -s 'sʌnraɪz, -ɪz
sunset, -s 'sʌnset, -s
sunshade, -s 'sʌnʃeɪd, -z
sunshin|e, -y 'sʌnʃaɪn, -ɪ
sun-spot, -s 'sʌnspɒt, -s
sunstroke, -s 'sʌnstrəʊk, -s
sun-trap, -s 'sʌntræp, -s
sun-worship, -per/s 'sʌn,wɜːʃɪp, -ə*/z
sup (s. v.), -s, -ping, -ped sʌp, -s, -ɪŋ, -t
super (s. adj.), -s 'suːpə* ['sjuː-], -z
Note.—super in isolation and in compounds is increasingly 'suːpə.
superab|le, -ly, -leness 'suːpərəb|l ['sjuː-], -lɪ, -lnɪs [-nəs]
superabundan|ce, -t/ly ˌsuːpərə'bʌndən|s [ˌsjuː-], -t/lɪ
superadd, -s, -ing, -ed ˌsuːpər'æd [ˌsjuː-], -z, -ɪŋ, -ɪd
superannuat|e, -es, -ing, -ed ˌsuːpə'rænjʊet [ˌsjuː-pə'r-, sjʊpə'r-, sʊpə'r-], -s, -ɪŋ, -ɪd
superannuation, -s 'suːpə,rænjʊ'eɪʃn ['sjuː-], -z
superb, -ly, -ness sjuː'pɜːb [suː-, sjʊ-, sʊ-], -lɪ, -nɪs [-nəs]
superbus (extra large bus), -es 'suːpəbʌs ['sjuː-], -ɪz
Superbus sjuː'pɜːbəs [suː-, sjʊ-, sʊ-]
supercargo, -es 'suːpə,kɑː|gəʊ ['sjuː-], -z
supercharg|e (s. v.), -es, -ing, -ed 'suːpətʃɑːdʒ ['sjuː-], -ɪz, -ɪŋ, -d
supercilious, -ly, -ness ˌsuːpə'sɪlɪəs [ˌsjuː-pə's-, sjʊpə's-, sʊpə's-, -ljəs], -lɪ, -nɪs [-nəs]
supererogation 'suːpər,erə'geɪʃn ['sjuː-, -rəʊ'g-]
supererogatory ˌsuːpəre'rɒgətərɪ [ˌsjuː-, -rɪ'r-]
superfici|al, -ally, -alness ˌsuːpə'fɪʃ|l [ˌsjuː-pə'f-, sjʊpə'f-, sʊpə'f-], -əlɪ [-l̩ɪ], -lnɪs [-nəs]
superficialit|y, -ies 'suːpə,fɪʃɪ'ælət|ɪ ['sjuː-, -ɪt|ɪ], -ɪz
superficies ˌsuːpə'fɪʃiːz [ˌsjuː-pə'f-, sjʊpə'f-, sʊpə'f-, -ʃɪiːz]
superfine ˌsuːpə'faɪn [ˌsjuː-, '---]
superfluit|y, -ies ˌsuːpə'flʊət|ɪ [ˌsjuː-pə'f-, sjʊpə'f-, sʊpə'f-, -ɪt|ɪ], -ɪz
superfluous, -ly, -ness suː'pɜːflʊəs [sjuː-, sʊ-, sjʊ-, -flwəs], -lɪ, -nɪs [-nəs]
superglottal ˌsuːpə'glɒtl [ˌsjuː-, '--,--]

superhet, -s 'suːpəhet ['sjuː-], -s
superheterodyne, -s ˌsuːpə'hetərədaɪn [ˌsju:-, -rəʊd-], -z
superhuman, -ly ˌsuːpə'hjuːmən [ˌsju:-], -lɪ
superimpos|e, -es, -ing, -ed ˌsuːpər'ɪm'pəʊz [ˌsju:-], -ɪz, -ɪŋ, -d
superintend, -s, -ing, -ed; -ence, -ent/s ˌsuːpərɪm'tend [ˌsju:-], -z, -ɪŋ, -ɪd; -əns, -ənt/s
superior (s. adj.), -s suː'pɪərɪə* [sjuː'p-, sʊ'p-, sjʊ'p-, sə'p-], -z
superiorit|y, -ies suːˌpɪərɪ'ɒrət|ɪ [sjuː-, sʊˌp-, sjʊˌp-, səˌp-, -ɪt|ɪ], -ɪz
superlative (s. adj.), -s, -ly, -ness suː'pəːlətɪv [sjuː-, sʊ'p-, sjʊ'p-, -'pəːˌtɪv], -z, -lɪ, -nɪs [-nəs]
super|man, -men 'suːpə|mæn ['sjuː-], -men
supermarket, -s 'suːpəˌmɑːkɪt ['sjuː-], -s
supernal suː'pəːnl [sjuː-, sʊ'p-, sjʊ'p-]
supernatur|al, -ally ˌsuːpə'nætʃr|əl [ˌsjuːpə'n-, sjʊpə'n-, sʊpə'n-, -tʃʊr-, -tʃər-], -əlɪ
supernormal ˌsuːpə'nɔːml [ˌsju:-]
supernumerar|y (s. adj.), -ies ˌsuːpə'njuːmərər|ɪ [ˌsju:-], -ɪz
superoctave, -s 'suːpərˌɒktɪv ['sjuː-], -z
superpos|e, -es, -ing, -ed ˌsuːpə'pəʊz [ˌsju:-], -ɪz, -ɪŋ, -d
superposition, -s ˌsuːpəpə'zɪʃn [ˌsju:-, -pʊ'z-], -z
superpriorit|y, -ies ˌsuːpəpraɪ'ɒrət|ɪ [ˌsju:-, -ɪt|ɪ], -ɪz
superscrib|e, -es, -ing, -ed ˌsuːpə'skraɪb [ˌsju:-, '---], -z, -ɪŋ, -d
superscript 'suːpəskrɪpt ['sjuː-]
superscription, -s ˌsuːpə'skrɪpʃn [ˌsjuːpə's-, sjʊpə's-, sʊpə's-], -z
supersed|e, -es, -ing, -ed ˌsuːpə'siːd [ˌsjuːpə's-, sjʊpə's-, sʊpə's-], -z, -ɪŋ, -ɪd
supersession ˌsuːpə'seʃn [ˌsjuːpə's-, sjʊpə's-, sʊpə's-]
supersonic ˌsuːpə'sɒnɪk [ˌsju:-, also '--,-- when attributive]
superstition, -s ˌsuːpə'stɪʃn [ˌsjuːpə's-, sjʊpə's-, sʊpə's-], -z
superstitious, -ly, -ness ˌsuːpə'stɪʃəs [ˌsjuːpə's-, sjʊpə's-, sʊpə's-], -lɪ, -nɪs [-nəs]
superstructure, -s 'suːpəˌstrʌktʃə* ['sjuː-], -z
super-submarine, -s ˌsuːpə'sʌbməriːn [ˌsju:-], -z
supertax, -es 'suːpətæks ['sjuː-], -ɪz
supertonic, -s ˌsuːpə'tɒnɪk [ˌsju:-, in contrast '--,-], -s

superven|e, -es, -ing, -ed ˌsuːpə'viːn [ˌsjuːpə'v-, sjʊpə'v-, sʊpə'v-], -z, -ɪŋ, -d
supervis|e, -es, -ing, -ed, -or/s 'suːpəvaɪz ['sjuː-, ˌsjuːpə'v-, ˌsuːpə'v-, sjʊpə'v-, sʊpə'v-], -ɪz, -ɪŋ, -d, -ə*/z
supervision, -s ˌsuːpə'vɪʒn [ˌsjuːpə'v-, sjʊpə'v-, sʊpə'v-], -z
supervisory 'suːpəvaɪzərɪ ['sjuː-, ˌsjuːpə'v-, ˌsuːpə'v-, sjʊpə'v-, sʊpə'v-]
supine (s.), -s 'sjuːpaɪn ['suː-], -z
supine (adj.), -ly, -ness sjuː'paɪn [suː'p-, '--], -lɪ, -nɪs [-nəs]
supper, -s, -less 'sʌpə*, -z, -lɪs [-ləs]
supplant, -s, -ing, -ed, -er/s sə'plɑːnt, -s, -ɪŋ, -ɪd, -ə*/z
supp|le, -leness, -ly 'sʌp|l, -lnɪs [-nəs], -lɪ [-l̩ɪ]
supplement (s.), -s 'sʌplɪmənt, -s
supplement (v.), -s, -ing, -ed 'sʌplɪment [ˌ--'-], -s, -ɪŋ, -ɪd
supplement|al, -ary ˌsʌplɪ'ment|l, -ərɪ
supplementation ˌsʌplɪmen'teɪʃn
suppliant (s. adj.), -s, -ly 'sʌplɪənt [-pljənt], -s, -lɪ
supplicant, -s 'sʌplɪkənt, -s
supplicat|e, -es, -ing/ly, -ed 'sʌplɪkeɪt, -s, -ɪŋ/lɪ, -ɪd
supplication, -s ˌsʌplɪ'keɪʃn, -z
supplicatory 'sʌplɪkətərɪ [-keɪtərɪ]
suppl|y (s. v.), -ies, -ying, -ied, -ier/s sə'pl|aɪ, -aɪz, -aɪɪŋ, -aɪd, -aɪə*/z
support (s. v.), -s, -ing, -ed, -er/s; -able, -ably sə'pɔːt, -s, -ɪŋ, -ɪd, -ə*/z; -əbl, -əblɪ
supportive sə'pɔːtɪv
suppos|e, -es, -ing, -ed sə'pəʊz [spəʊz], -ɪz, -ɪŋ, -d
supposedly sə'pəʊzɪdlɪ
supposition, -s ˌsʌpə'zɪʃn [-pʊ'z-], -z
supposi|tional, -tionally ˌsʌpə'zɪ|ʃənl [-pʊ'z-, -ʃnəl, -ʃn̩l, -ʃnl̩, -ʃənəl], -ʃn̩əlɪ [-ʃnəlɪ, -ʃn̩l̩ɪ, -ʃnl̩ɪ, -ʃənəlɪ]
supposititious, -ly, -ness səˌpɒzɪ'tɪʃəs, -lɪ, -nɪs [-nəs]
suppositor|y, -ies sə'pɒzɪtər|ɪ, -ɪz
suppress, -es, -ing, -ed, -or/s; -ible sə'pres, -ɪz, -ɪŋ, -t, -ə*/z; -əbl [-ɪbl]
suppression, -s sə'preʃn, -z
suppurat|e, -es, -ing, -ed 'sʌpjʊəreɪt, -s, -ɪŋ, -ɪd
suppuration, -s ˌsʌpjʊə'reɪʃn, -z
supra (in vide s.) 'suːprə ['sjuː-]
supradental ˌsuːprə'dentl [ˌsju:-]
supra-national ˌsuːprə'næʃənl [ˌsju:-, -ʃnəl, -ʃn̩l̩, -ʃn̩l, -ʃənəl]
suprarenal ˌsuːprə'riːnl [ˌsju:-, '--,--]

suprasegmental ˌsuːprəsegˈmentl [ˌsjuː-]

supremac|y, -ies suˈpreməsɪ [sjʊˈp-, sjuːˈp-, suːˈp-], -ɪz

supreme, -ly, -ness suˈpriːm [suːˈp-, sjʊˈp-, sjuːˈp-], -lɪ, -nɪs [-nəs]

sura, -s ˈsʊərə, -z

surah ˈsjʊərə

surat (cotton fabric) sʊˈræt

Surat ˈsʊərət [ˈsuːrət, sʊˈrɑːt, sʊˈræt] (Hindi surət)

Surbiton ˈsɜːbɪtn

surceas|e (s. v.), -es, -ing, -ed sɜːˈsiːs, -ɪz, -ɪŋ, -t

surcharge (s.), -s ˈsɜːtʃɑːdʒ [ˌsɜːˈtʃ-], -ɪz

surcharg|e (v.), -es, -ing, -ed sɜːˈtʃɑːdʒ, -ɪz, -ɪŋ, -d

surcoat, -s ˈsɜːkəʊt, -s

surd (s. adj.), -s sɜːd, -z; -ətɪ [-ɪtɪ]

sure (adj. adv.), -r, -st, -ly, -ness; -footed ʃʊə* [ʃɔə*, ʃɔː*], -rə*, -rɪst, -lɪ [ˈʃɔːlɪ, ˈʃɔəlɪ], -nɪs [ˈʃɔːnɪs, ˈʃɔənɪs, -nəs]; -ˈfʊtɪd. (The middle and younger generations increasingly use the form ʃɔː* in the isolate word and in compounds.)

suret|y, -ies; -yship/s ˈʃʊərətɪ|ɪ [ˈʃʊət-, ˈʃɔə-, ˈʃɔː-], -ɪz; -ɪʃɪp/s

surf sɜːf

surfac|e (s. v.), -es, -ing, -ed ˈsɜːfɪs [-fəs], -ɪz, -ɪŋ, -t

surf-bathing ˈsɜːfˌbeɪðɪŋ

surf-boat, -s ˈsɜːfbəʊt, -s

surfeit (s. v.), -s, -ing, -ed ˈsɜːfɪt, -s, -ɪŋ, -ɪd

surf-riding ˈsɜːfˌraɪdɪŋ

surg|e (s. v.), -es, -ing, -ed sɜːdʒ, -ɪz, -ɪŋ, -d

surgeon, -s ˈsɜːdʒən, -z

surger|y, -ies ˈsɜːdʒərɪ, -ɪz

surgic|al, -ally ˈsɜːdʒɪk|l, -əlɪ

Surinam ˌsʊərɪˈnæm

surl|y, -ier, -iest, -ily, -iness ˈsɜːl|ɪ, -ɪə* [-jə*], -ɪɪst [-jɪst], -ɪlɪ [-əlɪ], -ɪnɪs [-nəs]

surmise (s.), -s ˈsɜːmaɪz [sɜːˈmaɪz, səˈm-], -ɪz

surmis|e (v.), -es, -ing, -ed sɜːˈmaɪz [ˈ--, səˈm-], -ɪz, -ɪŋ, -d

surmount, -s, -ing, -ed; -able sɜːˈmaʊnt [səˈm-], -s, -ɪŋ, -ɪd; -əbl

surnam|e (s. v.), -es, -ing, -ed ˈsɜːneɪm, -z, -ɪŋ, -d

surpass, -es, -ing/ly, -ed; -able səˈpɑːs [sɜːˈp-], -ɪz, -ɪŋ/lɪ, -t; -əbl

surplice, -s, -d ˈsɜːplɪs [-pləs], -ɪz, -t

surplus, -es; -age ˈsɜːpləs, -ɪz; -ɪdʒ

surpris|e (s. v.), -es, -ing/ly, -ed, -edly səˈpraɪz, -ɪz, -ɪŋ/lɪ, -d, -ɪdlɪ

surreali|sm, -st/s səˈrɪəlɪ|zəm [sjʊ-, sʊ-], -st/s

surrend|er (s. v.), -ers, -ering, -ered səˈrend|ə*, -əz, -ərɪŋ, -əd

surreptitious, -ly ˌsʌrəpˈtɪʃəs [-rɪp-, -rep-], -lɪ

Surrey ˈsʌrɪ

surrogate, -s ˈsʌrəgɪt [-rʊg-, -geɪt, -gət], -s

surround (s. v.), -s, -ing/s, -ed səˈraʊnd, -z, -ɪŋ/z, -ɪd

surtax, -es ˈsɜːtæks, -ɪz

Surtees ˈsɜːtiːz

surtout, -s ˈsɜːtuː [ˌ-ˈ-], -z

surveillance sɜːˈveɪləns [səˈv-]

survey (s.), -s ˈsɜːveɪ [ˌ-ˈ-], -z

survey (v.), -s, -ing, -ed səˈveɪ [sɜːˈveɪ], -z, -ɪŋ, -d

surveyor, -s səˈveɪə*, -z

surviv|e, -es, -ing, -ed, -or/s; -al/s səˈvaɪv, -z, -ɪŋ, -d, -ə*/z; -l/z

Susan ˈsuːzn

Susanna suːˈzænə [sʊˈz-]

susceptibilit|y, -ies səˌseptəˈbɪlətɪ [-tɪˈb-, -lɪt-], -ɪz

susceptib|le, -ly səˈseptəb|l [-tɪb-], -lɪ

susceptive səˈseptɪv

suspect (s. adj.), -s ˈsʌspekt, -s

suspect (v.), -s, -ing, -ed səˈspekt, -s, -ɪŋ, -ɪd

suspend, -s, -ing, -ed, -er/s səˈspend, -z, -ɪŋ, -ɪd, -ə*/z

suspens|e, -ible səˈspens, -əbl [-ɪbl]

suspensibility səˌspensɪˈbɪlətɪ [-sə'b-, -lɪt-]

suspension, -s səˈspenʃn, -z

suspens|ive, -ory səˈspens|ɪv, -ərɪ

suspicion, -s səˈspɪʃn, -z

suspicious, -ly, -ness səˈspɪʃəs, -lɪ, -nɪs [-nəs]

Sussams ˈsʌsəmz

Sussex ˈsʌsɪks

sustain, -s, -ing, -ed, -er/s; -able səˈsteɪn, -z, -ɪŋ, -d, -ə*/z; -əbl

sustenance ˈsʌstɪnəns [-tnəns]

sustentation ˌsʌstenˈteɪʃn [-tən-]

susurration, -s ˌsjuːsəˈreɪʃn [ˌsuː-], -z

Sutherland ˈsʌðələnd

Sutlej ˈsʌtlɪdʒ [-ledʒ] (Hindi sətlwɟ)

sutler, -s ˈsʌtlə*, -z

Sutro ˈsuːtrəʊ

suttee, -s ˈsʌtiː [sʌˈtiː] (Hindi səti), -z

Sutton ˈsʌtn

suture, -s ˈsuːtʃə* [-tjə*], -z

suzerain, -s ˈsuːzəreɪn [ˈsjuː-], -z

481

suzeraint|y, -ies 'su:zəreɪnt|ɪ ['sju:-, -rən-], -ɪz

svarabhakti ˌsvʌrə'bʌktɪ [ˌsvɑːr-, -'bæk-, -tiː] (*Hindi* svərəbhəkti)

svelte svelt

Svengali sven'gɑːlɪ

Sverdlov 'sveədlɒv [-lɒf, -ləf] ('svjerdləf)

Sverdlovsk 'sveədlɒvsk [-ləvsk, -ləfsk] ('svjerdləfsk)

swab (*s. v.*), -s, -bing, -bed, -ber/s swɒb, -z, -ɪŋ, -d, -ə*/z

Swabia, -n/s 'sweɪbjə [-bɪə], -n/z

swadd|le, -les, -ling, -led 'swɒd|l, -lz, -lɪŋ [-lɪŋ], -ld

swaddling-clothes 'swɒdlɪŋkləʊðz [-dļ-, *old-fashioned* -kləʊz]

Swadling 'swɒdlɪŋ

Swaffer 'swɒfə*

swag swæg

swag|e (*s. v.*), -es, -ing, -ed sweɪdʒ, -ɪz, -ɪŋ, -d

swagg|er (*s. v.*), -ers, -ering/ly, -ered, -erer/s 'swæg|ə*, -əz, -ərɪŋ/lɪ, -əd, -ərə*/z

Swahili, -s swɑː'hiːlɪ [swə'h-], -z

swain (S.), -s sweɪn, -z

swall|ow (*s. v.*), -ows, -owing, -owed 'swɒl|əʊ, -əʊz, -əʊɪŋ, -əʊd

swallow-tail, -s, -ed 'swɒləʊteɪl, -z, -d

swam (*from* swim) swæm

Swami, -s 'swɑːmɪ (*Hindi* svami), -z

swamp (*s. v.*), -s, -ing, -ed; -y, -ier, -iest, -iness swɒmp, -s, -ɪŋ, -t [swɒmt]; -ɪ, -ɪə* [-jə*], -ɪɪst [-jɪst], -ɪnɪs [-məs]

swan, -s swɒn, -z

Swanage 'swɒnɪdʒ

Swanee 'swɒnɪ

swank; -y, -ier, -iest, -ily, -iness swæŋk; -ɪ, -ɪə* [-jə*], -ɪɪst [-jɪst], -ɪlɪ [-əlɪ], -ɪnɪs [-məs]

swan-like 'swɒnlaɪk

swanner|y, -ies 'swɒnər|ɪ, -ɪz

swan's-down 'swɒnzdaʊn

Swansea (*in Wales*) 'swɒnzɪ, (*in Tasmania*) 'swɒnsɪ [-siː]

swan-shot 'swɒnʃɒt

swan-song, -s 'swɒnsɒŋ, -z

Swanwick 'swɒnɪk

swap (*s. v.*), -s, -ping, -ped swɒp, -s, -ɪŋ, -t

swaraj, -ist/s swə'rɑːdʒ [swɑː'r-] (*Hindi* svərɑj), -ɪst/s

sward, -s swɔːd, -z

swarf swɔːf

swarm (*s. v.*), -s, -ing, -ed swɔːm, -z, -ɪŋ, -d

swart swɔːt

swarth|y, -ier, -iest, -ily, -iness 'swɔː:ð|ɪ [-ɔː:θ|ɪ], -ɪə* [-jə*], -ɪɪst [-jɪst], -ɪlɪ [-əlɪ], -ɪnɪs [-məs]

swash, -es, -ing, -ed; -buckler/s swɒʃ, -ɪz, -ɪŋ, -t; -ˌbʌklə*/z

swastika, -s 'swɒstɪkə, -z

swat, -s, -ting, -ted, -ter/s swɒt, -s, -ɪŋ, -ɪd, -ə*/z

swath, -s swɒːθ, -s [swɒːðz]

swath|e, -es, -ing, -ed sweɪð, -z, -ɪŋ, -d

Swatow 'swɒtaʊ

sway (*s. v.*), -s, -ing, -ed sweɪ, -z, -ɪŋ, -d

Swaziland 'swɑːzɪlænd

swear (*s. v.*), -s, -ing, swore, sworn, swearer/s sweə*, -z, -rɪŋ, swɔː:* [swɔə*], swɔːn, 'sweərə*/z

swear-word, -s 'sweəwɜːd, -z

sweat (*s. v.*), -s, -ing, -ed, -er/s; -y, -iness swet, -s, -ɪŋ, -ɪd, -ə*/z; -ɪ, -ɪnɪs [-məs]

swede (S.), -s swiːd, -z

Sweden, -borg 'swiːdn, -bɔːg

Swedenborgian, -s ˌswiːdn'bɔːdʒjən [-dʒɪən], -z

Swedish 'swiːdɪʃ

Sweeney 'swiːnɪ

sweep (*s. v.*), -s, -ing, swept, sweeper/s swiːp, -s, -ɪŋ, swept, 'swiːpə*/z

sweeping (*s. adj.*), -s 'swiːpɪŋ, -z

sweepstake, -s 'swiːpsteɪk, -s

sweet (*s. adj.*) (S.), -s; -er, -est, -ly, -ness swiːt, -s; -ə*, -ɪst, -lɪ, -nɪs [-nəs]

sweetbread, -s 'swiːtbred, -z

sweet-brier [-briar], -s ˌswiːt'braɪə*, -z

sweet|en, -ens, -ening, -ened, -ener/s 'swiːt|n, -nz, -nɪŋ [-n̩ɪŋ], -nd, -nə*/z [-nə*/z]

sweetheart, -s 'swiːthɑːt, -s

sweeting (S.), -s 'swiːtɪŋ, -z

sweetish 'swiːtɪʃ

sweetmeat, -s 'swiːtmiːt, -s

sweet-scented ˌswiːt'sentɪd ['-ˌ--]

sweet-tempered ˌswiːt'tempəd ['-ˌ--]

sweet-william, -s ˌswiːt'wɪljəm, -z

sweet|y, -ies 'swiːt|ɪ, -ɪz

swell (*s. v.*), -s, -ing/s, -ed, swollen swel, -z, -ɪŋ/z, -d, 'swəʊlən

swell-box, -es 'swelbɒks, -ɪz

swelt|er, -ers, -ering/ly, -ered 'swelt|ə*, -əz, -ərɪŋ/lɪ, -əd

swept (*from* sweep) swept

swerv|e (*s. v.*), -es, -ing, -ed swɜːv, -z, -ɪŋ, -d

Swete swiːt

Swettenham 'swetnəm

swift (*s. adj. adv.*) (S.), -s; -er, -est, -ly, -ness swɪft, -s; -ə*, -ɪst, -lɪ, -nɪs [-nəs]

swift-footed ˌswɪft'fʊtɪd ['-ˌ--]

Swiftsure 'swɪft͵ʃuə* [-ʃee*, -ʃɔ:*]

swig (s. v.), -s, -ging, -ged swɪg, -z, -ɪŋ, -d

swill (s. v.), -s, -ing, -ed swɪl, -z, -ɪŋ, -d

swim (s. v.), -s, -ming/ly, swam, swum, swimmer/s swɪm, -z, -ɪŋ/lɪ, swæm, swʌm, 'swɪmə*/z

swimming-ba|th, -ths 'swɪmɪŋbɑ:|θ, -ðz

swimming-pool, -s 'swɪmɪŋpu:l, -z

swim-suit, -s 'swɪmsu:t [-sju:t], -s

Swinburne 'swɪnbə:n [-bən]

swind|le, -les, -ling, -led, -ler/s 'swɪnd|l, -lz, -lɪŋ, -ld, -lə*/z

Swindon 'swɪndən

swine, -herd/s swaɪn, -hə:d/z

swing (s. v.), -s, -ing, swung swɪŋ, -z, -ɪŋ, swʌŋ

swing-boat, -s 'swɪŋbəut, -s

swinge, -s, -ing, -d swɪndʒ, -ɪz, -ɪŋ, -d

swingeing (adj.) 'swɪndʒɪŋ

swing|le (s. v.), -les, -ling, -led 'swɪŋg|l, -lz, -lɪŋ, -ld

swinish, -ness 'swaɪnɪʃ, -nɪs [-nəs]

swip|e (s. v.), -es, -ing, -ed, -er/s swaɪp, -s, -ɪŋ, -t, -ə*/z

swirl (s. v.), -s, -ing, -ed swə:l, -z, -ɪŋ, -d

swish (s. v.), -es, -ing, -ed swɪʃ, -ɪz, -ɪŋ, -t

Swiss swɪs

switch (s. v.), -es, -ing, -ed swɪtʃ, -ɪz, -ɪŋ, -t

switchback, -s 'swɪtʃbæk, -s

switch-board, -s 'swɪtʃbɔ:d [-bɔəd], -z

Swithin 'swɪðɪn [-ɪθɪn]

Switzerland 'swɪtsələnd

swiv|el (s. v.), -els, -elling, -elled 'swɪv|l, -lz, -lɪŋ [-lɪŋ], -ld

swizz|le (s. v.), -les, -ling, -led, -ler/s 'swɪz|l, -lz, -lɪŋ [-lɪŋ], -ld, -lə*/z [-lə*/z]

swollen (from swell) 'swəulən

swoon (s. v.), -s, -ing, -ed swu:n, -z, -ɪŋ, -d

swoop (s. v.), -s, -ing, -ed swu:p, -s, -ɪŋ, -t

swop (s. v.), -s, -ping, -ped swɒp, -s, -ɪŋ, -t

sword, -s sɔ:d [sɔəd], -z

sword-bearer, -s 'sɔ:d͵beərə* ['sɔəd-], -z

sword-belt, -s 'sɔ:dbelt ['sɔəd-], -s

sword-dance, -s 'sɔ:dɑ:ns ['sɔəd-], -ɪz

Sworder 'sɔ:də*

swordfish 'sɔ:dfɪʃ ['sɔəd-]

swords|man, -men 'sɔ:dz|mən ['sɔədz-], -mən

swore (from swear) swɔ:* [swɔə*]

sworn (from swear) swɔ:n

swot (s. v.), -s, -ting, -ted, -ter/s swɒt, -s, -ɪŋ, -ɪd, -ə*/z

swum (from swim) swʌm

swung (from swing) swʌŋ

Sybaris 'sɪbərɪs

sybarite, -s 'sɪbəraɪt, -s

Sybil 'sɪbɪl [-bəl]

sycamine, -s 'sɪkəmaɪn [-mɪn], -z

sycamore (S.), -s 'sɪkəmɔ:* [-mɔə*], -z

syce, -s saɪs, -ɪz

sycophancy 'sɪkəfənsɪ [-kʊf-, -fænsɪ]

sycophant, -s 'sɪkəfænt [-kʊf-, -fənt], -s

sycophantic ͵sɪkəʊ'fæntɪk

Sycorax 'sɪkəræks

Sydenham 'sɪdnəm [-dnəm]

Sydney 'sɪdnɪ

Syed 'saɪed ['saɪəd]

syenite 'saɪnaɪt ['saɪən-]

Sygrove 'saɪgrəʊv

Sykes saɪks

syllabar|y, -ies 'sɪləbər|ɪ, -ɪz

syllabic, -ally sɪ'læbɪk, -əlɪ

syllabicat|e, -es, -ing, -ed sɪ'læbɪkeɪt, -s, -ɪŋ, -ɪd

syllabication sɪ͵læbɪ'keɪʃn

syllabicity ͵sɪlə'bɪsɪtɪ [-ɪtɪ]

syllabification sɪ͵læbɪfɪ'keɪʃn

syllabi|fy, -fies, -fying, -fied sɪ'læbɪ|faɪ, -faɪz, -faɪɪŋ, -faɪd

syllable, -s 'sɪləbl, -z

syllabub 'sɪləbʌb

syllabus, -es 'sɪləbəs, -ɪz

syllogism, -s 'sɪlədʒɪzəm [-ləʊdʒ-], -z

syllogistic, -ally ͵sɪlə'dʒɪstɪk [-ləʊ'dʒ-], -əlɪ

syllogiz|e [-is|e], -es, -ing, -ed 'sɪlədʒaɪz [-ləʊdʒ-], -ɪz, -ɪŋ, -d

sylph, -s sɪlf, -s

Sylva 'sɪlvə

sylvan 'sɪlvən

Sylvester sɪl'vestə*

Sylvia 'sɪlvɪə [-vjə]

symbiosis ͵sɪmbɪ'əʊsɪs

symbol, -s 'sɪmbl, -z

symbolic, -al, -ally sɪm'bɒlɪk, -l, -əlɪ

symbolism 'sɪmbəlɪzəm [-bʊl-, -bl-]

symbolization [-isa-] ͵sɪmbəlaɪ'zeɪʃn [-bʊl-, -bl͵aɪ'z-, -bəlɪ'z-, -blɪ'z-]

symboliz|e [-is|e], -es, -ing, -ed 'sɪmbəlaɪz [-bʊl-, -bl-], -ɪz, -ɪŋ, -d

Syme saɪm

Symington 'saɪmɪŋtən, 'sɪm-

symmetric, -al, -ally, -alness sɪ'metrɪk, -l, -əlɪ, -lnɪs [-nəs]

symmetry 'sɪmɪtrɪ [-mətrɪ]

Symond 'saɪmənd

Symonds (surname) 'saɪməndz, 'sɪm-

Symonds Yat ͵sɪməndz'jæt

483

Symons 'saɪmənz, 'sɪm-
sympathetic, -al, -ally ˌsɪmpə'θetɪk, -l, -əlɪ
sympathiz|e [-is|e], -es, -ing, -ed 'sɪmpəθaɪz, -ɪz, -ɪŋ, -d
sympath|y, -ies 'sɪmpəθ|ɪ, -ɪz
symphonic sɪm'fɒnɪk
symphon|y, -ies 'sɪmfən|ɪ, -ɪz
symposi|um, -ums, -a sɪm'pəʊzj|əm [-'pɒz-, -zɪ|əm], -əmz, -ə
symptom, -s 'sɪmptəm [-tm], -z
symptomatic ˌsɪmptə'mætɪk [-tɪ'm-]
synaer = syner-
synagogue, -s 'sɪnəgɒg, -z
synaloepha ˌsɪnə'li:fə
synapse 'saɪnæps [sɪ'næps]
synchromesh, -es ˌsɪŋkrəʊ'meʃ ['---], -ɪz
synchronic sɪŋ'krɒnɪk [sɪn'k-]
synchronism 'sɪŋkrənɪzəm [-krʊn-]
synchronistic ˌsɪŋkrə'nɪstɪk [-krʊ'n-]·
synchronization [-isa-], -s ˌsɪŋkrənaɪ'zeɪʃn [-krʊn-, -nɪ'z-], -z
synchroniz|e [-is|e], -es, -ing, -ed 'sɪŋkrənaɪz [-krʊn-], -ɪz, -ɪŋ, -d
synchronous, -ly, -ness 'sɪŋkrənəs [-krʊn-], -lɪ, -nɪs [-nəs]
synchrony 'sɪŋkrənɪ [-krʊn-]
synchrotron, -s 'sɪŋkrəʊtrɒn, -z
syncopat|e, -es, -ing, -ed 'sɪŋkəpeɪt [-kəʊp-, -kʊp-], -s, -ɪŋ, -ɪd
syncopation, -s ˌsɪŋkə'peɪʃn [-kəʊ'p-, -kʊ'p-], -z
syncope 'sɪŋkəpɪ [-kʊp-]
syncretic sɪŋ'kri:tɪk [sɪn'k-]
syncretism 'sɪŋkrɪtɪzəm
syndic, -s 'sɪndɪk, -s
syndicali|sm, -st/s 'sɪndɪkəlɪ|zəm [-klɪ-], -st/s
syndicate (s.), -s 'sɪndɪkət [-kɪt], -s
syndicat|e (v.), -es, -ing, -ed 'sɪndɪkeɪt, -s, -ɪŋ, -ɪd
syndication ˌsɪndɪ'keɪʃn
syndrome, -s 'sɪndrəʊm [-drəmɪ, -drəʊmɪ], -z
syne saɪn
synecdoche sɪ'nekdəkɪ
syneres|is, -es sɪ'nɪərəs|ɪs [-rɪs-], -i:z
Synge sɪŋ
synod, -s, -al 'sɪnəd [-nɒd], -z, -l

synodic, -al, -ally sɪ'nɒdɪk, -l, -əlɪ
synonym, -s 'sɪnənɪm [-nɒn-, -nʊn-], -z
synonymous, -ly sɪ'nɒnɪməs [-nəm-], -lɪ
synonymy sɪ'nɒnɪmɪ [-nəmɪ]
synops|is, -es sɪ'nɒps|ɪs, -i:z
synoptic, -s, -al, -ally sɪ'nɒptɪk, -s, -l, -əlɪ
syntactic, -al, -ally sɪn'tæktɪk, -l, -əlɪ
syntagm, -s 'sɪntægəm, -z
syntax, -es 'sɪntæks, -ɪz
synthes|is, -es 'sɪnθəs|ɪs [-θɪs-], -i:z
synthesiz|e [-is|e], -es, -ing, -ed 'sɪnθəsaɪz [-θɪs-], -ɪz, -ɪŋ, -d
synthetic, -s, -al, -ally sɪn'θetɪk, -s, -l, -əlɪ
synthetist, -s 'sɪnθrtɪst [-θət-], -s
synthetiz|e [-is|e], -es, -ing, -ed 'sɪnθrtaɪz [-θət-], -ɪz, -ɪŋ, -d
syphilis 'sɪfɪlɪs [-fəl-]
syphilitic ˌsɪfɪ'lɪtɪk [-fə'l-]
syph|on (s. v.), -ons, -oning, -oned 'saɪf|n, -nz, -ənɪŋ [-ņɪŋ], -nd
Syracusan ˌsaɪərə'kju:zən
Syracuse (in classical history) 'saɪərəkju:z, (modern town in Sicily) 'saɪərəkju:z ['sɪr-], (town in U.S.A.) 'sɪrəkju:s
syren, -s 'saɪərən [-rɪn], -z
Syria, -n/s 'sɪrɪə, -n/z
Syriac 'sɪrɪæk
syringa, -s sɪ'rɪŋgə, -z
syring|e (s. v.), -es, -ing, -ed 'sɪrɪndʒ [-'-], -ɪz, -ɪŋ, -d
syrinx (all senses), -es 'sɪrɪŋks, -ɪz
syrophoenician ˌsaɪərəʊfɪ'nɪʃɪən [-fi:'n-, -ʃjən, -ʃn, -sɪən, -sjən]
syrt|is (S.), -es 'sɜ:t|ɪs, -i:z
syrup, -s; -y 'sɪrəp, -s; -ɪ
system, -s 'sɪstəm [-tɪm], -z
systematic, -ally ˌsɪstɪ'mætɪk [-tə'm-], -əlɪ
systematization [-isa-] ˌsɪstɪmətaɪ'zeɪʃn [-təm-, -tɪ'z-]
systematiz|e [-is|e], -es, -ing, -ed, -er/s 'sɪstɪmətaɪz [-təm-], -ɪz, -ɪŋ, -d, -ə*/z
systemic sɪ'stemɪk [-'sti:mɪk]
systole 'sɪstəlɪ
systolic sɪ'stɒlɪk
syzyg|y, -ies 'sɪzɪdʒ|ɪ, -ɪz

T

T (*the letter*), **-'s** tiː, -z

ta (*Tonic Sol-fa name for diminished seventh from the tonic*), **-s** tɔː, -z

ta (*syllable used in Tonic Sol-fa for counting time*) *generally* tɑː, *but* tæ *in the sequence* **ta fe tay fe**, *q.v.*

ta (*thank you*) tɑː

Taal tɑːl

tab, -s tæb, -z

tabard (T.), -s 'tæbəd [-bɑːd], -z

tabb|y, -ies 'tæb|ɪ, -ɪz

taberdar, -s 'tæbədɑː* [-də*], -z

tabernacle, -s 'tæbənækl, -z

Taberner tə'bɜːnə*

tabes 'teɪbiːz

Tabitha 'tæbɪθə

tablature, -s 'tæblətʃə* [-blɪtʃ-, -ˌtjʊə*], -z

tab|le (*s. v.*) **(T.), -les, -ling, -led** 'teɪb|l, -lz, -lɪŋ [-lɪŋ], -ld

tableau, -s 'tæbləʊ, -z

table-|cloth, -cloths 'teɪbl|klɒθ [*old-fashioned* -klɔːθ], -klɒθs [-klɔːðz, -klɔːθs]

table d'hôte ˌtɑːblˈdəʊt

table-kni|fe, -ves 'teɪblnaɪ|f, -vz

table-land, -s 'teɪbllænd, -z

table-leg, -s 'teɪblleg, -z

table-linen 'teɪblˌlɪnɪn

tablespoon, -s 'teɪblspuːn, -z

tablespoonful, -s 'teɪblˌspuːnfʊl ['---ˌ-], -z

tablet, -s 'tæblɪt [-lət], -s

table-tennis 'teɪblˌtenɪs

table-turning 'teɪblˌtɜːnɪŋ

tabloid, -s 'tæblɔɪd, -z

taboo (*s.*), **-s** tə'buː, -z

taboo (*v.*), **-(e)s, -ing, -ed** tə'buː, -z, -ɪŋ [tə'bʊɪŋ], -d

tabor, -s 'teɪbə* [-bɔː*], -z

Tabor (*Mount*) 'teɪbɔː* [-bə*]

tabouret, -s 'tæbərɪt [-bʊr-, -ret], -s

tabul|a, -ae 'tæbjʊl|ə, -iː

tabular 'tæbjʊlə* [-bjəl-]

tabulat|e, -es, -ing, -ed, -or/s 'tæbjʊleɪt [-bjəl-], -s, -ɪŋ, -ɪd, -ə*/z

tabulation, -s ˌtæbjʊ'leɪʃn [-bjə'l-], -z

tacet 'teɪset ['tæs-]

tache, -s tɑːʃ [tæʃ], -ɪz

tachism 'tæʃɪzəm

tachograph, -s 'tækəʊɡrɑːf [-ɡræf], -s

tachometer, -s tæ'kɒmɪtə* [-mətə*], -z

tachycardia ˌtækɪ'kɑːdɪə [-djə]

tachygraph|er/s, -y tæ'kɪɡrəf|ə*/z, -ɪ

tacit, -ly, -ness 'tæsɪt, -lɪ, -nɪs [-nəs]

taciturn, -ly 'tæsɪtɜːn, -lɪ

taciturnity ˌtæsɪ'tɜːnətɪ [-ɪtɪ]

Tacitus 'tæsɪtəs

tack (*s. v.*), **-s, -ing, -ed** tæk, -s, -ɪŋ, -t

tack|le (*s. v.*), **-les, -ling, -led, -ler/s** 'tæk|l [*nautical often* 'teɪkl], -lz, -lɪŋ [-lɪŋ], -ld, -lə*/z [-lə*/z]

tacky 'tækɪ

Tacon 'teɪkən

tact tækt

tact|ful, -fully, -fulness 'tækt|fʊl, -fʊlɪ [-fəlɪ], -fʊlnɪs [-nəs]

tactic, -s, -al, -ally 'tæktɪk, -s, -l, -əlɪ

tactician, -s tæk'tɪʃn, -z

tactile 'tæktaɪl

tactless, -ly, -ness 'tæktlɪs [-ləs], -lɪ, -nɪs [-nəs]

tactual, -ly 'tæktjʊəl [-tjwəl, -tjʊl, -tʃʊəl, -tʃʊl], -ɪ

Tadcaster 'tædkæstə* [-kəs-]

Tadema 'tædɪmə

Tadhg taɪɡ

tadpole, -s 'tædpəʊl, -z

tael, -s teɪl ['teɪəl], -z

ta'en (*dialectal for* **taken**) teɪn

ta fe tay fe (*syllables used in Tonic Sol-fa for counting four in a bar*) 'tæfɪˌtefɪ [-fəˌt-]

Taff tæf

taffeta 'tæfɪtə [-fətə]

taffrail, -s 'tæfreɪl [-frɪl, -frəl], -z

Taff|y, -ies 'tæf|ɪ, -ɪz

taft, -s, -ing, -ed tɑːft [tæft], -s, -ɪŋ, -ɪd

Taft (*surname*) tæft, tɑːft, (*town in Iran*) tɑːft

tag (*s. v.*), **-s, -ging, -ged** tæg, -z, -ɪŋ, -d

Tagalog tə'ɡɑːlɒɡ [-ləɡ]

tagetes tæ'dʒiːtiːz

Tagore tə'ɡɔː* [-'ɡɔə*] (*Bengali* ʈhakur)

tagrag 'tæɡræɡ

Tagus 'teɪɡəs

Tahi|ti, -tian tɑː'hiː|tɪ [tə'h-], -ʃn

485

tail (s. v.), -s, -ing, -ed; -less teɪl, -z, -ɪŋ, -d; -lɪs [-ləs]

tail-back, -s 'teɪlbæk, -s

tail-coat, -s ˌteɪl'kəʊt [in contrast '--], -s

tail-end, -s ˌteɪl'end ['teɪlend], -z

tailor (s. v.), -s, -ing, -ed 'teɪlə*, -z, -rɪŋ, -d

tailoress, -es ˌteɪlə'res ['teɪləres], -ɪz

tailor-made (s. adj.), -s 'teɪləmeɪd [often ˌ--'- for predicative adj.], -z

tailpiece, -s 'teɪlpi:s, -ɪz

tail-spin, -s 'teɪlspɪn, -z

Taine teɪn (tɛːn)

taint (s. v.), -s, -ing, -ed; -less teɪnt, -s, -ɪŋ, -ɪd; -lɪs [-ləs]

Taiping (in Malaysia) ˌtaɪ'pɪŋ

Tait teɪt

Taiwan ˌtaɪ'wɑːn [-'wæn]

Taj Mahal ˌtɑːdʒmə'hɑːl [-'hʌl] (Hindi taɪˈməhəl)

tak|e, -es, -ing, took, tak|en, -er/s teɪk, -s, -ɪŋ, tʊk, 'teɪk|ən [-ŋ], -ə*/z

take-in, -s 'teɪkɪn [ˌ-'-], -z

take-off, -s 'teɪkɒf [old-fashioned -ɔːf, ˌ-'-], -s

take-over, -s 'teɪkˌəʊvə*, -z

take-up, -s 'teɪkʌp, -s

taking (s. adj.), -s, -ly, -ness 'teɪkɪŋ, -z, -lɪ, -nɪs [-nəs]

talbot, -s 'tɔːlbət ['tɒl-], -s

Talbot (surname) 'tɔːlbət ['tɒl-], (place) 'tɔːlbət ['tɒl-], -tælbət

Note.—Both pronunciations are current at Port Talbot in Wales.

talc tælk

talcum, -powder 'tælkəm, -ˌpaʊdə*

tale, -s teɪl, -z

tale-bearer, -s 'teɪlˌbeərə*, -z

talent, -s, -ed, -less 'tælənt, -s, -ɪd, -lɪs [-ləs]

tales (for completing a jury) 'teɪliːz

tales|man (person summoned to complete a jury), -men 'teɪliːz|mən [-lz-, -mæn], -mən [-men]

tale-teller, -s 'teɪlˌtelə*, -z

Talfourd 'tælfəd

Taliesin ˌtælɪ'esɪn (Welsh tal'jesin)

talisman, -s 'tælɪzmən [-ɪsm-], -z

talk (s. v.), -s, -ing, -ed, -er/s tɔːk, -s, -ɪŋ, -t, -ə*/z

talkative, -ly, -ness 'tɔːkətɪv, -lɪ, -nɪs [-nəs]

talkie, -s 'tɔːkɪ, -z

talking-to, -s 'tɔːkɪŋtuː, -z

tall, -er, -est, -ness tɔːl, -ə*, -ɪst, -nɪs [-nəs]

tallage 'tælɪdʒ

tallboy, -s 'tɔːlbɔɪ, -z

Tallis 'tælɪs

tall|ow, -owy 'tæl|əʊ, -əʊɪ

tall|y (s. v.), -ies, -ying, -ied 'tæl|ɪ, -ɪz, -ɪŋ, -ɪd

tally-ho (T.), -s ˌtælɪ'həʊ, -z

tally|man, -men 'tælɪ|mən, -mən [-men]

Talman 'tɔːlmən

Talmud 'tælmʊd [-məd, -mʌd]

talmudic, -al tæl'mʊdɪk [-'mʌd-, -'mjuːd-], -l

talon, -s 'tælən, -z

tam(e)ability ˌteɪmə'bɪlɪtɪ [-ltɪ-]

tam(e)able 'teɪməbl

Tamaqua tə'mɑːkwə

Tamar (river in W. of England) 'teɪmə*, (biblical name) 'teɪmɑː* [-mə*]

tamarind, -s 'tæmərɪnd, -z

tamarisk, -s 'tæmərɪsk, -s

tamber, -s 'tæmbə*, -z

tambour, -s 'tæmˌbʊə* [-bɔə*, -bɔː*, -bə*], -z

tambourine, -s ˌtæmbə'riːn, -z

Tamburlaine 'tæmbəleɪn

tam|e (adj. v.), -er, -est, -ely, -eness; -es, -ing, -ed, -er/s teɪm, -ə*, -ɪst, -lɪ, -nɪs [-nəs]; -z, -ɪŋ, -d, -ə*/z

Tamerlane 'tæmələɪn

Tamil, -s 'tæmɪl [-ml], -z

Tammany 'tæmənɪ

Tammerfors 'tæməfɔːz

Tamora 'tæmərə

tam-o'-shanter (T.), -s ˌtæmə'ʃæntə*, -z

tamp, -s, -ing, -ed tæmp, -s, -ɪŋ, -t [tæmt]

tamp|er, -ers, -ering, -ered 'tæmp|ə*, -əz, -ərɪŋ, -əd

tampon, -s 'tæmpən [-pɒn], -z

Tamworth 'tæmwəθ [-wɜːθ]

tan (s. adj. v.), -s, -ning, -ned, -ner/s tæn, -z, -ɪŋ, -d, -ə*/z

Tancred 'tæŋkred [-rɪd]

tandem, -s 'tændəm [-dem], -z

Tanfield 'tænfiːld

tang, -s tæŋ, -z

Tang (Chinese dynasty) tæŋ

Tanganyika ˌtæŋgə'njiːkə [-gæn-]

tangent, -s 'tændʒənt, -s

tangenti|al, -ally tæn'dʒenʃ|l [-entʃ-], -əlɪ

tangerine, -s ˌtændʒə'riːn ['---], -z

tangibility ˌtændʒə'bɪlɪtɪ [-dʒɪ'b-, -ltɪ-]

tangib|le, -ly, -leness 'tændʒəb|l [-dʒɪb-], -lɪ, -lnɪs [-nəs]

Tangier tæn'dʒɪə* ['--]

tang|le (s. v.), -les, -ling, -led 'tæŋg|l, -lz, -lɪŋ [-lŋ], -ld

Tanglewood 'tæŋglwʊd

tangly 'tæŋglɪ

tango, -s ˈtæŋɡəʊ, -z
Tangye ˈtæŋɡɪ
tanh (*mathematical term*) θæn
tank, -s; -age, -er/s tæŋk, -s; -ɪdʒ, -ə*/z
tankard, -s ˈtæŋkəd, -z
tank-buster, -s ˈtæŋkˌbʌstə*, -z
tanner (T.), -s ˈtænə*, -z
tanner|y, -ies ˈtænər|ɪ, -ɪz
Tannhäuser ˈtænˌhɔɪzə* (ˈtanˌhɔyzər)
tanni|c, -n ˈtænɪ|k, -n
Tannoy ˈtænɔɪ
Tanqueray ˈtæŋkərɪ
tansy ˈtænzɪ
tantalization [-isa-], -s ˌtæntəlaɪˈzeɪʃn,
 -z
tantaliz|e [-is|e], -es, -ing/ly, -ed, -er/s
 ˈtæntəlaɪz, -ɪz, -ɪŋ/lɪ, -d, -ə*/z
tantalum, -s ˈtæntələm, -z
tantalus (T.), -es ˈtæntələs, -ɪz
tantamount ˈtæntəmaʊnt
tantiv|y, -ies tænˈtɪv|ɪ, -ɪz
tanto ˈtæntəʊ
tantrum, -s ˈtæntrəm, -z
Tanzania, -n/s ˌtænzəˈnɪə [tænˈzeɪnɪə,
 -njə], -n/z
Taoi|sm, -st/s ˈtɑːəʊɪ|zm ['taʊ-], -st/s
tap (s. v.), -s, -ping, -ped tæp, -s, -ɪŋ, -t
tap-danc|e, -es, -ing, -ed, -er/s ˈtæp-
 dɑːns, -ɪz, -ɪŋ, -t, -ə*/z
tap|e (s. v.) (T.), -es, -ing, -ed teɪp, -s,
 -ɪŋ, -t
tape-machine, -s ˈteɪpməˌʃiːn, -z
tape-measure, -s ˈteɪpˌmeʒə*, -z
taper (s. v.), -s, -ing, -ed ˈteɪpə*, -z,
 -rɪŋ, -d
tape-recorder, -s ˈteɪprɪˌkɔːdə*, -z
tapestr|y, -ies ˈtæpɪstr|ɪ [-pəs-], -ɪz
tapeworm, -s ˈteɪpwɜːm, -z
tapioca ˌtæpɪˈəʊkə
tapir, -s ˈteɪpə* [-ˌpɪə*, *rarely* ˈtæp-],
 -z
tapis ˈtæpiː [-pɪ] (tapi)
tapist, -s ˈteɪpɪst, -s
Tapling ˈtæplɪŋ
Tappertit ˈtæpətɪt
tapping (s.), -s ˈtæpɪŋ, -z
tap-room, -s ˈtæprʊm [-ruːm], -z
tap-root, -s ˈtæpruːt, -s
tapster, -s ˈtæpstə*, -z
tar (s. v.), -s, -ring, -red tɑː*, -z, -rɪŋ,
 -d
taradiddle, -s ˈtærədɪdl, -z
tarantella, -s ˌtærənˈtelə, -z
Taranto təˈræntəʊ [ˈtɑːrəntəʊ]
 (ˈtaːranto)
tarantula, -s təˈræntjʊlə [-tjələ], -z
taraxacum təˈræksəkəm
tar-brush, -es ˈtɑːbrʌʃ, -ɪz

tard|y, -ier, -iest, -ily, -iness ˈtɑːd|ɪ,
 -ɪə* [-jə*], -ɪɪst [-jɪst], -ɪlɪ [-əlɪ], -ɪnɪs
 [-məs]
tare, -s teə*, -z
Tarentaise ˌtærənˈteɪz (tarɑ̃tɛːz)
Tarentum təˈrentəm
target, -s, -ed ˈtɑːɡɪt, -s, -ɪd
targeteer, -s ˌtɑːɡɪˈtɪə* [-ɡə't-], -z
tariff, -s ˈtærɪf, -s
Tarkington ˈtɑːkɪŋtən
Tarleton ˈtɑːltən
tarmac, -s ˈtɑːmæk, -s
tarn, -s tɑːn, -z
tarnish, -es, -ing, -ed ˈtɑːnɪʃ, -ɪz, -ɪŋ,
 -t
tarot, -s ˈtærəʊ, -z
tarpaulin, -s tɑːˈpɔːlɪn, -z
Tarpeian tɑːˈpiːən [-ˈpɪən]
tarpon, -s ˈtɑːpɒn, -z
Tarquin, -s ˈtɑːkwɪn, -z
Tarquin|ius, -ii tɑːˈkwɪn|ɪəs [-jəs], -ɪaɪ
 [-iː]
tarradiddle, -s ˈtærədɪdl, -z
tarragon ˈtærəɡən
Tarragona ˌtærəˈɡəʊnə
Tarring (*surname*) ˈtærɪŋ
tarrock, -s ˈtærək, -s
tarry (*adj.*) (*tarred, like tar*) ˈtɑːrɪ
tarr|y (v.) (*wait*), -ies, -ying, -ied, -ier/s
 ˈtær|ɪ, -ɪz, -ɪɪŋ, -ɪd, -ɪə*/z
Tarshish ˈtɑːʃɪʃ
Tarsus ˈtɑːsəs
tart (s. adj.), -s, -ly, -ness tɑːt, -s, -lɪ,
 -nɪs [-nəs]
tartan, -s ˈtɑːtən, -z
tartar (T.), -s ˈtɑːtə*, -z
tartaric tɑːˈtærɪk
Tartar|us, -y ˈtɑːtər|əs, -ɪ
tartlet, -s ˈtɑːtlɪt [-lət], -s
Tarzan ˈtɑːzæn [-zn]
Tashken|d, -t tæʃˈken|d, -t
task (s. v.), -s, -ing, -ed tɑːsk, -s, -ɪŋ,
 -t
Tasker ˈtæskə*
taskmaster, -s ˈtɑːskˌmɑːstə*, -z
task-mistress, -es ˈtɑːskˌmɪstrɪs [-trəs],
 -ɪz
Tasman ˈtæzmən
Tasmania, -n/s tæzˈmeɪnjə [-nɪə], -n/z
Tass tæs
tassel, -s, -led ˈtæsl, -z, -d
Tasso ˈtæsəʊ
tast|e (s. v.), -es, -ing, -ed, -er/s teɪst,
 -s, -ɪŋ, -ɪd, -ə*/z
taste|ful, -fully, -fulness ˈteɪst|fʊl, -fʊlɪ
 [-fəlɪ], -fʊlnɪs [-nəs]
tasteless, -ly, -ness ˈteɪstlɪs [-ləs], -lɪ,
 -nɪs [-nəs]

tast|y, -ier, -iest, -ily, -iness 'teɪst|ɪ, -ɪə*
[-jə*], -ɪɪst [-jɪst], -ɪlɪ [-əlɪ], -ɪnɪs
[-ɪnəs]

tat (s. v.), -s, -ting, -ted tæt, -s, -ɪŋ, -ɪd

ta-ta ˌtæˈtɑː

Tatar, -s 'tɑːtə*, -z

ta tay fe (syllables used in Tonic Sol-fa
for counting time) 'tɑːtefɪ

Tate teɪt

Tatham 'teɪθəm

Tatiana ˌtætɪˈɑːnə

tatler (T.), -s 'tætlə*, -z

tatter, -s, -ed 'tætə*, -z, -d

tatterdemalion ˌtætədəˈmeɪljən [-dɪˈm-,
-lɪən]

Tattersall, -s 'tætəsɔːl [-sl], -z

tatt|le (s. v.), -les, -ling, -led, -ler/s
'tæt|l, -lz, -lɪŋ [-lɪŋ], -ld, -lə*/z
[-lə*/z]

tatt|oo (s. v.) (all senses), -oo(e)s, -ooing,
-ooed, -ooer/s tə'tu: [tæ't-], -u:z,
-u:ɪŋ [-ʊɪŋ], -u:d, -u:ə*/z [-ʊə*/z]

tau taʊ

Tauchnitz 'taʊknɪts ('tauxnits)

taught (from teach) tɔːt

taunt, -s, -ing/ly, -ed, -er/s tɔːnt, -s,
-ɪŋ/lɪ, -ɪd, -ə*/z

Taunton (in Somerset) 'tɔːntən [locally
'tɑːn-]

Taurus (constellation) 'tɔːrəs

taut, -ness tɔːt, -nɪs [-nəs]

tautologic, -al, -ally ˌtɔːtə'lɒdʒɪk, -l, -əlɪ

tautologism, -s tɔː'tɒlədʒɪzəm, -z

tautologiz|e [-is|e], -es, -ing, -ed
tɔː'tɒlədʒaɪz, -ɪz, -ɪŋ, -d

tautologous tɔː'tɒləgəs

tautolog|y, -ies tɔː'tɒlədʒ|ɪ, -ɪz

Tautpheus tɔː'tfiːəs

tavern, -s 'tævən, -z

Tavistock 'tævɪstɒk

taw (s. v.), -s, -ing, -ed tɔː, -z, -ɪŋ, -d

tawdr|y, -ier, -iest, -ily, -iness 'tɔːdr|ɪ,
-ɪə*, -ɪɪst, -əlɪ [-ɪlɪ], -ɪnɪs [-ɪnəs]

Tawell 'tɔːəl

tawn|y, -ier, -iest, -iness 'tɔːn|ɪ, -ɪə*
[-jə*], -ɪɪst [-jɪst], -ɪnɪs [-ɪnəs]

tax (s. v.), -es, -ing, -ed tæks, -ɪz, -ɪŋ, -t

taxability ˌtæksə'bɪlɪtɪ [-lɪt-]

taxable, -ness 'tæksəbl, -nɪs [-nəs]

taxation, -s tæk'seɪʃn, -z

tax-collector, -s 'tækskəˌlektə*, -z

tax-free ˌtæks'friː ['--]

tax-gatherer, -s 'tæksˌgæðərə*, -z

taxi (s.), -s 'tæksɪ, -z

tax|i (v.), -ies, -ying, -ied 'tæks|ɪ, -ɪz,
-ɪɪŋ, -ɪd

taxi-cab, -s 'tæksɪkæb, -z

taxiderm|al, -ic ˌtæksɪ'dɜːm|l, -ɪk

taxidermist, -s 'tæksɪdɜːmɪst [ˌ--'--,
tæk'sɪdəmɪst], -s

taxidermy 'tæksɪdɜːmɪ

taximeter, -s 'tæksɪˌmiːtə*, -z

taxis (T.) 'tæksɪs

taxonomic, -ally ˌtæksəʊ'nɒmɪk, -əlɪ

taxonomy tæk'sɒnəmɪ

tax-payer, -s 'tæksˌpeɪə*, -z

tay (syllable used in Tonic Sol-fa in
counting time) generally teɪ, but te in
the sequence tay fe, q.v.

Tay, -side teɪ, -saɪd

tay fe (syllables used in Tonic Sol-fa in
counting time) 'tefɪ, ˌtefɪ, see ta fe
tay fe

Taylor 'teɪlə*

Taylorian teɪ'lɔːrɪən

Taymouth 'teɪmaʊθ [-məθ]

T.B. ˌtiː'biː

Tchad tʃæd

Tchaikovsky (Russian composer)
tʃaɪ'kɒfskɪ [-'kɒvskɪ] (tʃij'kofskij)

Tcherkasy tʃɜː'kæsɪ

Tcherkessian, -s tʃɜː'kesɪən [-sjən], -z

tchick (s. v.), -s, -ing, -ed tʃɪk, -s, -ɪŋ,
-t

tchick (interj.) ʖ [tʃɪk]

te (Tonic sol-fa name for leading-note),
-s tiː, -z

tea, -s tiː, -z

tea-cadd|y, -ies 'tiːˌkæd|ɪ, -ɪz

tea-cake, -s 'tiːkeɪk, -s

teach, -es, -ing/s, taught, teacher/s
tiːtʃ, -ɪz, -ɪŋ/z, tɔːt, 'tiːtʃə*/z

teachability ˌtiːtʃə'bɪlətɪ [-lɪt-]

teachable, -ness 'tiːtʃəbl, -nɪs [-nəs]

tea-chest, -s 'tiːtʃest, -s

teach-in, -s 'tiːtʃɪn, -z

tea-|cloth, -cloths 'tiː|klɒθ [old-
fashioned -klɔːθ], -klɒθs [-klɔːðz,
-klɔːθs]

tea-cup, -s; -ful/s 'tiːkʌp, -s; -ˌfʊl/z

tea-fight, -s 'tiːfaɪt, -s

tea-garden, -s 'tiːˌgɑːdn, -z

tea-gown, -s 'tiːgaʊn, -z

Teague, -s tiːg, -z

tea-hou|se, -ses 'tiːhaʊ|s, -zɪz

teak tiːk

tea-kettle, -s 'tiːˌketl, -z

teal tiːl

tea-lea|f, -ves 'tiːliː|f, -vz

team (s. v.), -s, -ing, -ed tiːm, -z, -ɪŋ, -d

teamster, -s 'tiːmstə*, -z

team-work 'tiːmwɜːk

tea-part|y, -ies 'tiːˌpɑːt|ɪ, -ɪz

tea-pot, -s 'tiːpɒt, -s

teapoy, -s 'tiːpɔɪ, -z

tear (s.) (fluid from the eye), -s tɪə*, -z

tear (s. v.) (pull apart, rend, rush, a rent, etc.), -s, -ing, tore, torn teə*, -z, -rɪŋ, tɔ:* [teə*], tɔːn

tear-drop, -s 'tɪədrɒp, -s

tear|ful, -fully, -fulness 'tɪə|fʊl, -fʊlɪ [-fəlɪ], -fʊlnɪs [-nəs]

tear-gas 'tɪəgæs

tearless 'tɪəlɪs [-ləs]

tea-room, -s 'tiːrʊm [-ruːm], -z

tea-rose, -s 'tiːrəʊz, -ɪz

tear-shell, -s 'tɪəʃel, -z

tear-stained 'tɪəsteɪnd

teas|e (s. v.), -es, -ing/ly, -ed, -er/s tiːz, -ɪz, -ɪŋ/lɪ, -d, -ə*/z

teas|el (s. v.), -els, -eling, -eled 'tiːz|l, -lz, -əlɪŋ [-lɪŋ], -ld

tea-service, -s 'tiː,sɜːvɪs, -ɪz

tea-set, -s 'tiːset, -s

tea-shop, -s 'tiːʃɒp, -s

teaspoon, -s 'tiːspuːn, -z

teaspoonful, -s 'tiːspuːnfʊl [-spʊn-], -z

tea-strainer, -s 'tiː,streɪnə*, -z

teat, -s tiːt, -s

tea-table, -s 'tiː,teɪbl, -z

tea-things 'tiːθɪŋz

tea-time 'tiːtaɪm

tea-tray, -s 'tiːtreɪ, -z

tea-urn, -s 'tiːɜːn, -z

Teazle 'tiːzl

Tebay 'tiːbeɪ

tec, -s tek, -s

technic, -s 'teknɪk, -s

technic|al, -ally, -alness 'teknɪk|l, -əlɪ [-ḷɪ], -lnɪs [-nəs]

technicalit|y, -ies ,teknɪ'kælət|ɪ [-ɪt|ɪ], -ɪz

technician, -s tek'nɪʃn, -z

technicolor 'teknɪ,kʌlə*

technique, -s tek'niːk [-'--], -s

technocrat, -s 'teknəʊkræt, -s

technologic, -al ,teknə'lɒdʒɪk, -l

technolog|ist/s, -y tek'nɒlədʒ|ɪst/s, -ɪ

tech|y, -ier, -iest, -ily, -iness 'tetʃ|ɪ, -ɪə*, -ɪɪst, -ɪlɪ [-əlɪ], -ɪnɪs [-ɪnəs]

Teck tek

ted (T.), -s, -ding, -ded, -der/s ted, -z, -ɪŋ, -ɪd, -ə*/z

Teddington 'tedɪŋtən

Teddy 'tedɪ

Te Deum, -s ,tiː'diːəm [-'dɪəm, ,teɪ'deɪʊm], -z

tedious, -ly, -ness 'tiːdjəs [-dɪəs], -lɪ, -nɪs [-nəs]

tedium 'tiːdjəm [-dɪəm]

tee (s. v.), -s, -ing, -d tiː, -z, -ɪŋ, -d

Teed tiːd

teem, -s, -ing, -ed tiːm, -z, -ɪŋ, -d

teen, -s tiːn, -z

teenager, -s 'tiːn,eɪdʒə*, -z

teen|y, -iest 'tiːn|ɪ, -ɪɪst [-jɪst]

Tees, -dale tiːz, -deɪl

teeshirt, -s 'tiːʃɜːt, -s

tee-square, -s 'tiːskweə* [,tiː's-], -z

teeter, -s, -ing, -ed 'tiːtə*, -z, -rɪŋ, -d

Teetgen 'tiːdʒən

teeth (pl. of tooth) tiːθ

teeth|e, -es, -ing, -ed tiːð, -z, -ɪŋ, -d

teetot|al, -alism tiː'təʊt|l, -ḷɪzəm [-əlɪzəm]

teetotaller, -s tiː'təʊtlə* [-tḷə*], -z

teetotum, -s ,tiː'təʊtʌm ['tiː:təʊtʌm, tiː'təʊtəm], -z

tegument, -s 'tegjʊmənt, -s

Teheran ,teə'rɑːn [,tehə'r-, ,terə'r-]

Teign (in Devon) tɪn [tiːn]

Teignbridge 'tɪnbrɪdʒ

Teignmouth 'tɪnməθ [locally also 'tɪŋməθ]

Teignton 'teɪntən

tekel 'tiːkel [-kəl]

telamon (T.), -s 'teləmən [-mɒn], -z

telautograph, -s te'lɔːtəgrɑːf [-græf], -s

tele, -s 'telɪ, -z

telecast (s. v.), -s, -ing, -ed, -er/s 'telɪkɑːst, -s, -ɪŋ, -ɪd, -ə*/z

tele-cine ,telɪsɪnɪ

telecommunication, -s 'telɪkə,mjuːnɪ'keɪʃn, -z

telefilm, -s 'telɪfɪlm, -z

telegenic ,telɪ'dʒenɪk

telegram, -s 'telɪgræm, -z

telegraph (s. v.), -s, -ing, -ed 'telɪgrɑːf [-græf], -s, -ɪŋ, -t

telegrapher, -s tɪ'legrəfə* [te'l-, tə'l-], -z

telegraphese ,telɪgrɑː'fiːz [-græ'f-, -grə'f-]

telegraphic, -ally ,telɪ'græfɪk, -əlɪ

telegraphist, -s tɪ'legrəfɪst [te'l-, tə'l-], -s

telegraph-|line/s, -pole/s, -post/s, -wire/s 'telɪgrɑːf|laɪn/z [-græf-], -pəʊl/z, -pəʊst/s, -waɪə*/z

telegraphy tɪ'legrəfɪ [te'l-, tə'l-]

Telemachus tɪ'leməkəs [te'l-, tə'l-]

telemark (s. v.), -s, -ing, -ed 'telɪmɑːk [-ləm-], -s, -ɪŋ, -t

telemeter (s. v.), -s, -ing, -ed 'telɪmiːtə*, -z, -rɪŋ, -d

telemetric ,telɪ'metrɪk [-'miːt-]

telemetry tɪ'lemɪtrɪ [-mətrɪ]

teleological ,telɪə'lɒdʒɪkl [,tiːlɪ-, -ljə-]

teleology ,telɪ'ɒlədʒɪ [,tiːlɪ-]

telepathic, -ally ,telɪ'pæθɪk, -əlɪ

telepath|ist/s, -y tɪ'lepəθ|ɪst/s [te'l-, tə'l-], -ɪ

telepathiz|e [-is|e], -es, -ing, -ed tɪ'lepəθaɪz [te'l-, tə'l-], -ɪz, -ɪŋ, -d

489

telephon|e (s. v.), -es, -ing, -ed, -er/s 'telɪfəʊn, -z, -ɪŋ, -d, -ə*/z
telephonee, -s ˌtelɪfəʊˈni:, -z
telephonic, -ally ˌtelɪˈfɒnɪk, -əlɪ
telephonist, -s tɪˈlefənɪst [teˈl-, təˈl-], -s
telephony tɪˈlefənɪ [teˈl-, təˈl-]
telephoto, -s ˌtelɪˈfəʊtəʊ [ˈ-ˌ-- when attributive], -z
telephotograph, -s ˌtelɪˈfəʊtəgrɑːf [-græf], -s
telephotography ˌtelɪfəˈtɒgrəfɪ
teleprinter, -s 'telɪˌprɪntə*, -z
teleprompter, -s 'telɪˌprɒmptə*, -z
telerecord (s.), -s 'telɪˌrekɔːd, -z
telerecord (v.), -s, -ing/s, -ed 'telɪrɪˌkɔːd [-rə-ˌk-, ˌ---ˈ-], -z, -ɪŋ/z, -ɪd
telescop|e (s. v.), -es, -ing, -ed 'telɪskəʊp, -s, -ɪŋ, -t
telescopic, -ally ˌtelɪˈskɒpɪk, -əlɪ
telescop|ist/s, -y tɪˈleskəp|ɪst/s [teˈl-, təˈl-], -ɪ
telescreen, -s 'telɪskriːn, -z
teletype, -s 'telɪtaɪp, -s
teletypesetter, -s ˌtelɪˈtaɪpˌsetə*, -z
teleview, -s, -ing, -ed, -er/s 'telɪvjuː, -z, -ɪŋ [-ˌvjuːɪŋ], -d, -ə*/z [-ˌvjuːə*/z]
televis|e, -es, -ing, -ed 'telɪvaɪz, -ɪz, -ɪŋ, -d
television 'telɪˌvɪʒn [ˌ--ˈ--]
televisor, -s 'telɪvaɪzə*, -z
telex 'teleks
tell (T.), -s, -ing, told, teller/s tel, -z, -ɪŋ, təʊld, 'telə*/z
telling (adj.), -ly 'telɪŋ, -lɪ
telltale, -s 'telteɪl, -z
tellurium teˈljʊərɪəm [-jɔər-, -jɔːr-]
tell|y, -ies 'tel|ɪ, -ɪz
Telstar 'telstɑː*
Telugu 'teləguː [-lʊg-, ˌ--ˈ-]
Teme tiːm
Téméraire ˌteməˈreə* (temereːr)
temerity tɪˈmerətɪ [teˈm-, təˈm-, -ɪtɪ]
Tempe 'tempɪ
temp|er (s. v.), -ers, -ering, -ered, -erer/s 'temp|ə*, -əz, -ərɪŋ, -əd, -ərə*/z
tempera 'tempərə
temperable 'tempərəbl
temperament, -s 'tempərəmənt, -s
temperament|al, -ally ˌtempərəˈment|l, -əlɪ [-lɪ]
temperance 'tempərəns
temperate, -ly, -ness 'tempərət [-rɪt], -lɪ, -nɪs [-nəs]
temperature, -s 'temprətʃə* [-pər-, -rɪtʃ-], -z
temperedly 'tempədlɪ
Temperley 'tempəlɪ

tempest (T.), -s 'tempɪst, -s
tempestuous, -ly, -ness temˈpestjʊəs [təm-, -tjwəs], -lɪ, -nɪs [-nəs]
Templar, -s 'templə*, -z
temple (T.), -s 'templ, -z
templet, -s 'templɪt [-lət], -s
Templeton 'templtən
temp|o, -os, -i 'temp|əʊ, -əʊz, -iː
tempor|al, -ally 'tempər|əl, -əlɪ
temporality ˌtempəˈrælətɪ [-ɪtɪ]
temporar|y (s. adj.), -ies, -ily, -iness 'tempərər|ɪ [-prər-], -ɪz, -əlɪ [-ɪlɪ], -ɪnɪs [-nəs]
temporization [-isa-] ˌtempəraɪˈzeɪʃn
temporiz|e [-is|e], -es, -ing/ly, -ed, -er/s 'tempəraɪz, -ɪz, -ɪŋ/lɪ, -d, -ə*/z
tempt, -s, -ing, -ed, -er/s tempt, -s, -ɪŋ, -ɪd, -ə*/z
temptation, -s tempˈteɪʃn, -z
tempting (adj.), -ly, -ness 'temptɪŋ, -lɪ, -nɪs [-nəs]
ten, -s, -th, -ths, -thly ten, -z, -θ, -θs, -θlɪ
tenability ˌtenəˈbɪlətɪ [ˌtiːn-, -lɪt-]
tenable, -ness 'tenəbl [ˈtiːn-], -nɪs [-nəs]
tenacious, -ly, -ness tɪˈneɪʃəs [teˈn-, təˈn-], -lɪ, -nɪs [-nəs]
tenacity tɪˈnæsətɪ [teˈn-, təˈn-, -ɪtɪ]
tenanc|y, -ies 'tenəns|ɪ, -ɪz
tenant, -s 'tenənt, -s
tenant|able, -less, -ry 'tenənt|əbl, -lɪs [-ləs], -rɪ
Ten|bury, -by 'ten|bərɪ, -bɪ
tench tenʃ [-ntʃ]
tend, -s, -ing, -ed tend, -z, -ɪŋ, -ɪd
tendencious [-ntious] tenˈdenʃəs
tendenc|y, -ies 'tendəns|ɪ, -ɪz
tend|er (s. adj. v.), -ers, -erer, -erest, -erly, -erness; -ering, -ered 'tend|ə*, -əz, -ərə*, -ərɪst, -əlɪ, -ənɪs [-nəs]; -ərɪŋ, -əd
tenderfoot, -s 'tendəfʊt, -s
tender-hearted, -ly, -ness ˌtendəˈhɑːtɪd ['tendəˌh-], -lɪ, -nɪs [-nəs]
tenderloin, -s 'tendəlɔɪn, -z
tendon, -s 'tendən, -z
tendril, -s 'tendrɪl [-drəl], -z
tenebrae 'tenɪbriː
tenebrous 'tenɪbrəs
tenement, -s 'tenɪmənt [-nəm-], -s
Tenerif(f)e ˌtenəˈriːf
tenet, -s 'tiːnet ['ten-, -nɪt], -s
tenfold 'tenfəʊld
Teniers 'tenɪəz [-njəz]
tenish 'tenɪʃ
Tenison 'tenɪsn
Tennant 'tenənt
tenner, -s 'tenə*, -z

Tennessee ˌtenəˈsiː [-nɪˈs-]
Tenniel ˈtenjəl [-nɪəl]
tennis, -ball/s ˈtenɪs, -bɔːl/z
tennis-court, -s ˈtenɪskɔːt [-kɔət], -s
tennis-racket, -s ˈtenɪsˌrækɪt, -s
Tennyson ˈtenɪsn
tenon, -s ˈtenən, -z
tenor, -s ˈtenə*, -z
tenour ˈtenə*
ten|pence, -penny ˈten|pəns, -pənɪ (see note under penny)
tense (s. adj.), -s, -r, -st, -ly, -ness tens, -ɪz, -ə*, -ɪst, -lɪ, -nɪs [-nəs]
tensile ˈtensaɪl
tension, -s ˈtenʃn, -z
tensity ˈtensɪtɪ [-ɪtɪ]
tensor, -s ˈtensə*, -z
tent (s. v.), -s, -ing, -ed tent, -s, -ɪŋ, -ɪd
tentacle, -s ˈtentəkl [-tɪk-], -z
tentacular tenˈtækjʊlə* [-kjələ*]
tentative (s. adj.), -s, -ly ˈtentətɪv, -z, -lɪ
tent-bed, -s ˈtentbed, -z
tenter, -s ˈtentə*, -z
Tenterden ˈtentədən
tenter-hook, -s ˈtentəhʊk, -s
tenth, -s, -ly tenθ, -s, -lɪ
tent-pegging ˈtentˌpegɪŋ
tenu|is, -es ˈtenjʊ|ɪs, -iːz [-eɪz]
tenuity teˈnjuːɪtɪ [tə'n-, tɪ'n-, -ˈnjʊ-, -ɪtɪ]
tenuous ˈtenjʊəs [-njwəs]
tenure, -s ˈte̞ˌnjʊə* [-njə*], -z
tepee, -s ˈtiːpiː, -z
tepid, -est, -ly, -ness ˈtepɪd, -ɪst, -lɪ, -nɪs [-nəs]
tepidity teˈpɪdɪtɪ [-ɪtɪ]
ter (three times) tɜː*
Ter (river in Essex) tɑː*
Terah ˈtɪərə [rarely ˈterə]
teraph, -im ˈterəf, -ɪm
tercel, -s ˈtɜːsl, -z
tercentenar|y (s. adj.), -ies ˌtɜːsenˈtiːnər|ɪ [-ˈten-, tɜːˈsentɪn-], -ɪz
tercentennial ˌtɜːsenˈtenjəl [-nɪəl]
tercet, -s ˈtɜːsɪt [-set], -s
terebene ˈterəbiːn [-rɪb-]
terebinth, -s ˈterəbɪnθ [-rɪb-], -s
terebinthine ˌterəˈbɪnθaɪn [-rɪ'b-]
Terence ˈterəns
Teresa təˈriːzə [tɪ'r-, te'r-]
tergiversat|e, -es, -ing, -ed ˈtɜːdʒɪvɜː:-ˌseɪt, -s, -ɪŋ, -ɪd
tergiversation ˌtɜːdʒɪvɜːˈseɪʃn
Terling (in Essex) ˈtɑːlɪŋ [ˈtɜːl-]
term, -s tɜːm, -z
termagant (s. adj.), -s ˈtɜːməgənt, -s
terminable, -ness ˈtɜːmɪnəbl, -nɪs [-nəs]
terminal (s. adj.), -s ˈtɜːmɪnl, -z

terminat|e, -es, -ing, -ed, -or/s ˈtɜː-mɪnert, -s, -ɪŋ, -ɪd, -ə*/z
termination, -s ˌtɜːmɪˈneɪʃn, -z
terminative, -ly ˈtɜːmɪnətɪv [-neɪt-], -lɪ
terminer ˈtɜːmɪnə*
terminologic|al, -ally ˌtɜːmɪnəˈlɒdʒɪk|l, -əlɪ
terminolog|y, -ies ˌtɜːmɪˈnɒlədʒ|ɪ, -ɪz
termin|us, -i, -uses ˈtɜːmɪn|əs, -aɪ, -əsɪz
termite, -s ˈtɜːmaɪt, -s
tern, -s tɜːn, -z
ternary ˈtɜːnərɪ
Ternate (island) tɜːˈnɑːtɪ
terner|y, -ies ˈtɜːnər|ɪ, -ɪz
Terpsichore tɜːpˈsɪkərɪ
Terpsichorean ˌtɜːpsɪkəˈriːən [-kɒ'r-, -ˈrɪən]
terra ˈterə
terrac|e (s. v.), -es, -ing, -ed ˈterəs [-rɪs], -ɪz, -ɪŋ, -t
terra-cotta ˌterəˈkɒtə
Terra del Fuegian, -s ˌterədelfʊˈiːdʒən [-dʒɪən, -dʒən], -z
Terra del Fuego ˌterədelfʊˈeɪgəʊ [-ˈfweɪ-]
terra firma ˌterəˈfɜːmə
terrain, -s teˈreɪn [ˈ--], -z
terra incognita ˌterəɪnˈkɒgnɪtə
terramycin ˌterəˈmaɪsɪn
terrapin, -s ˈterəpɪn, -z
terrestrial, -ly, -ness tɪˈrestrɪəl [te'r-, tə'r-], -ɪ, -nɪs [-nəs]
terret, -s ˈterɪt, -s
terrib|le, -ly, -leness ˈterəb|l [-rɪb-], -lɪ, -lnɪs [-nəs]
terrier, -s ˈterɪə*, -z
terrific, -ally təˈrɪfɪk [tɪ'r-], -əlɪ
terri|fy, -fies, -fying, -fied ˈterɪ|faɪ, -faɪz, -faɪɪŋ, -faɪd
territorial (s. adj.), -s, -ly ˌterɪˈtɔːrɪəl, -z, -ɪ
territorializ|e [-is|e], -es, -ing, -ed ˌterɪˈtɔːrɪəlaɪz, -ɪz, -ɪŋ, -d
territor|y, -ies ˈterɪtər|ɪ, -ɪz
terror, -s ˈterə*, -z
terrori|sm, -st/s ˈterərɪ|zəm, -st/s
terrorization [-isa-] ˌterəraɪˈzeɪʃn [-rɪ'z-]
terroriz|e [-is|e], -es, -ing, -ed, -er/s ˈterəraɪz, -ɪz, -ɪŋ, -d, -ə*/z
Terry ˈterɪ
terse, -r, -st, -ly, -ness tɜːs, -ə*, -ɪst, -lɪ, -nɪs [-nəs]
tertian ˈtɜːʃn [-ʃjən, -ʃɪən]
tertiary ˈtɜːʃərɪ [-ʃjə-, -ʃɪə-]
Tertis ˈtɜːtɪs
tertium quid ˌtɜːtjəmˈkwɪd [ˌtɜːtɪəm-, ˌtɜːˈʃjəm-, ˌtɜːˈʃɪəm-]
Tertius (as English name) ˈtɜːʃjəs [-ʃɪəs]

491

Tertullian tə:'tʌliən [-ljən]
terylene 'terəli:n [-rɪ-]
terzetto, -s tɜ:t'setəʊ [teət-], -z
Tesla 'teslə
tessaract, -s 'tesərækt, -s
tessellat|e, -es, -ing, -ed 'tesɪleɪt [-səl-], -s, -ɪŋ, -ɪd
tessellation ˌtesɪ'leɪʃn [-sə'l-]
tessitura ˌtesɪ'tu:rə
test (s. v.) (T.), -s, -ing, -ed; -able test, -s, -ɪŋ, -ɪd; -əbl
testac|ean, -eous te'steɪʃ|n [-jən, -ɪən], -əs [-jəs, -ɪəs]
testament (T.), -s 'testəmənt, -s
testament|al, -ary, -arily ˌtestə'ment|l, -ərɪ, -ərəlɪ [-ɪlɪ]
testamur, -s te'steɪmə*, -z
testate, -s 'testeɪt [-tɪt], -s
testation, -s te'steɪʃn, -z
testator, -s te'steɪtə*, -z
testatri|x, -ces, -xes te'steɪtrɪ|ks, -si:z, -ksɪz
tester, -s 'testə*, -z
testicle, -s 'testɪkl, -z
testicular te'stɪkjʊlə* [-kjələ*]
testification, -s ˌtestɪfɪ'keɪʃn, -z
testi|fy, -fies, -fying, -fied, -fier/s 'testɪ|faɪ, -faɪz, -faɪɪŋ, -faɪd, -faɪə*/z
testimonial, -s ˌtestɪ'məʊnjəl [-nɪəl], -z
testimonializ|e [-is|e], -es, -ing, -ed ˌtestɪ'məʊnjəlaɪz [-nɪəl-], -ɪz, -ɪŋ, -d
testimon|y, -ies 'testɪmən|ɪ, -ɪz
Teston (Kent) 'ti:sən
testosterone te'stɒstərəʊn
test-tube, -s 'testtju:b, -z
testud|o, -os, -ines te'stju:d|əʊ [-'stu:-], -əʊz, te'stju:dɪni:z [te'stu:dɪneɪz]
test|y, -ier, -iest, -ily, -iness 'test|ɪ, -ɪə* [-jə*], -ɪɪst [-jɪst], -ɪlɪ [-əlɪ], -ɪnɪs [-məs]
tetan|us, -y 'tetən|əs [-tŋ-], -ɪ
tetch|y, -ier, -iest, -ily, -iness 'tetʃ|ɪ, -ɪə*, -ɪɪst, -ɪlɪ [-əlɪ], -ɪnɪs [-məs]
tête-à-tête, -s ˌteɪtɑ:'teɪt, -s
tether (s. v.), -s, -ing, -ed 'teðə*, -z, -rɪŋ, -d
tetrachord, -s 'tetrəkɔ:d, -z
tetrad, -s 'tetræd [-rəd], -z
tetragon, -s 'tetrəgən, -z
tetrahedr|on, -ons, -a; -al ˌtetrə'hedr|ən [-'hi:d-, 'tetrə,h-], -ənz, -ə; -əl
tetralog|y, -ies tə'trælədʒ|ɪ, -ɪz
tetrameter, -s te'træmɪtə* [-mətə*], -z
tetrarch, -s; -y, -ies 'tetrɑ:k ['ti:t-], -s; -ɪ, -ɪz
tetrasyllabic ˌtetrəsɪ'læbɪk
tetrasyllable, -s 'tetrə,sɪləbl [ˌ-'---], -z
tetter 'tetə*

Teucer 'tju:sə*
Teutoburgian ˌtju:təʊ'bɜ:gjən [-gɪən]
Teuton, -s 'tju:tən, -z
Teutonic tju:'tɒnɪk [tjʊ't-]
teutonization [-isa-] ˌtju:tənar'zeɪʃn [-tnaɪ'z-, -tənɪ'z-, -tnɪ'z-]
teutoniz|e [-is|e], -es, -ing, -ed 'tju:tən-aɪz [-tnaɪz], -ɪz, -ɪŋ, -d
Teviot (river) 'ti:vjət [-vɪət], (Lord) 'tevɪət [-vjət]
Teviotdale 'ti:vjətdeɪl [-vɪət-]
Tewfik 'tju:fɪk
Tewin 'tju:ɪn ['tjʊɪn]
Tewkesbury 'tju:ksbərɪ
Texan 'teksən
Texas 'teksəs [-sæs]
Texel 'teksl
text, -s tekst, -s
text-book, -s 'tekstbʊk, -s
textile, -s 'tekstaɪl, -z
textual, -ly 'tekstjʊəl [-tjwəl, -tjʊl], -ɪ
texture, -s 'tekstʃə*, -z
Teynham (Baron, place in Kent) 'tenəm
Thackeray 'θækərɪ
Thackley 'θæklɪ
Thaddeus θæ'di:əs [-'dɪəs]
Thai, -s, -land taɪ, -z, -lænd [-lənd]
thalamus 'θæləməs
Thalben 'θælbən, 'θɔ:lbən
thaler, -s 'tɑ:lə*, -z
Thales 'θeɪli:z
Thalia, -n θə'laɪə, -n
thalidomide θə'lɪdəmaɪd [θæ'l-]
thallium 'θælɪəm [-ljəm]
Thame (in Oxfordshire) teɪm
Thames (in England, Canada, New Zealand) temz, (in Connecticut) θeɪmz [temz]
than ðæn (strong form), ðən, ðn (weak forms)
    Note.—The strong form is normally used only when the word is said in isolation.
thane (T.), -s θeɪn, -z
Thanet 'θænɪt
thank (s. v.), -s, -ing, -ed, -er/s θæŋk, -s, -ɪŋ, -t [θæŋt], -ə*/z
    Note.—The interjection Thank you (normally 'θæŋkjʊ) has several other forms, the chief of which are 'hæŋkjʊ, 'ŋkjʊ, 'kkjʊ. The first k of 'kkjʊ has no sound, but the speaker feels the stress to be there.
thank|ful, -fully, -fulness 'θæŋk|fʊl, -fʊlɪ [-fəlɪ], -fʊlnɪs [-nəs]
thankless, -ly, -ness 'θæŋklɪs [-ləs], -lɪ, -nɪs [-nəs]
thank-offering, -s 'θæŋk,ɒfərɪŋ, -z

thanksgiving, -s 'θæŋks,gɪvɪŋ [,-'--], -z
thankworth|y, -iness 'θæŋk,wɜ:ð|ɪ, -ɪnɪs [-məs]
that (adj., demonstr. pron., adv.) ðæt
that (relative pron.) ðæt (strong form), ðət, ðt (weak forms)
  Note.—The strong form is seldom used, except in very deliberate speech or when the word is said in isolation.
that (conj.) ðæt (strong form), ðət (weak form)
  Note.—The strong form is rarely used.
thatch (s. v.), -es, -ing, -ed, -er/s θætʃ, -ɪz, -ɪŋ, -t, -ə*/z
Thatcher 'θætʃə*
thaumaturge, -s 'θɔ:mətɜ:dʒ, -ɪz
thaumaturgic ,θɔ:mə'tɜ:dʒɪk
thaumaturg|ist/s, -y 'θɔ:mətɜ:dʒ|ɪst/s, -ɪ
thaw (s. v.), -s, -ing, -ed θɔ:, -z, -ɪŋ, -d
thaw|y, -ily, -iness 'θɔ:|ɪ, -ɪlɪ [-əlɪ], -ɪnɪs [-məs]
the ði: (strong form, also sometimes used as a weak form before vowels), ðɪ (weak form before vowels), ðə, ð (weak forms before consonants)
Thea θɪə, 'θi:ə
theatre, -s 'θɪətə* [θɪ'etə*], -z
theatre-land 'θɪətəlænd [θɪ'et-]
theatric|al, -als, -ally, -alness θɪ'ætrɪk|l ['θjæ-], -lz, -əlɪ, -lnɪs [-nəs]
theatricality θɪ,ætrɪ'kælətɪ [-ɪtɪ]
Thebaid 'θi:beɪɪd
Theban, -s 'θi:bən, -z
Thebes θi:bz
thee (accus. of thou) ði: (normal form), ðɪ (occasional weak form)
theft, -s θeft, -s
their ðeə* (normal form), ðər (occasional weak form when a vowel follows)
theirs ðeəz
thei|sm, -st/s 'θi:ɪ|zəm, -st/s
theistic, -al θi:'ɪstɪk, -l
Thelma 'θelmə
Thelusson (surname) 'teləsn
them ðem (strong form), ðəm, ðm (weak forms), əm, m (occasional weak forms)
thematic θɪ'mætɪk
theme, -s θi:m, -z
Themistocles θɪ'mɪstəkli:z [θe'm-, θə'm-]
themselves ðəm'selvz
then ðen
thence ðens
thenceforth ,ðens'fɔ:θ
thenceforward ,ðens'fɔ:wəd
Theo 'θi:əʊ, 'θɪəʊ

Theobald 'θɪəbɔ:ld [old-fashioned 'θɪbəld, 'tɪbəld]
Theobalds (in Hertfordshire) 'tɪbldz ['θɪəbɔ:ldz], (road in London) 'θɪəbɔ:ldz [formerly 'tɪbldz]
theocrac|y, -ies θɪ'ɒkrəs|ɪ, -ɪz
theocratic, -al θɪə'krætɪk [,θɪəʊ'k-], -l
Theocritus θɪ'ɒkrɪtəs
theodicy θɪ'ɒdɪsɪ
theodolite, -s θɪ'ɒdəlaɪt, -s
Theodora ,θɪə'dɔ:rə [,θi:ə-]
Theodore 'θɪədɔ:* [-dɔə*]
Theodoric θɪ'ɒdərɪk
Theodosi|a, -us θɪə'dəʊsj|ə [,θɪə'd-, -sɪ|ə], -əs
theologian, -s θɪə'ləʊdʒən [,θɪə'l-, -dʒɪən, -dʒən], -z
theologic, -al, -ally θɪə'lɒdʒɪk [,θɪə'l-], -l, -əlɪ
theolog|ist/s, -y θɪ'ɒlədʒ|ɪst/s, -ɪ
theologiz|e [-is|e], -es, -ing, -ed θɪ'ɒlədʒaɪz, -ɪz, -ɪŋ, -d
Theophilus θɪ'ɒfɪləs
Theophrastus θɪə'fræstəs [,θɪəʊ'f-]
theorem, -s 'θɪərəm [-rem, -rɪm], -z
theoretic, -al, -ally θɪə'retɪk [,θɪə'r-], -l, -əlɪ
theoretician, -s ,θɪərə'tɪʃn [-rɪ't-, -re't-], -z
theorist, -s 'θɪərɪst, -s
theoriz|e [-is|e], -es, -ing, -ed, -er/s 'θɪəraɪz, -ɪz, -ɪŋ, -d, -ə*/z
theor|y, -ies 'θɪər|ɪ, -ɪz
theosophic, -al, -ally θɪə'sɒfɪk [,θɪə's-, ,θi:ə's-], -l, -əlɪ
theosoph|ism, -ist/s, -y θɪ'ɒsəf|ɪzəm [θi:'ɒ-], -ɪst/s, -ɪ
theosophiz|e [-is|e], -es, -ing, -ed θɪ'ɒsəfaɪz [θi:'ɒ-], -ɪz, -ɪŋ, -d
Thera 'θɪərə
therapeutic, -s, -ally ,θerə'pju:tɪk, -s, -əlɪ
therapeutist, -s ,θerə'pju:tɪst, -s
therap|ist/s, -y 'θerəp|ɪst/s, -ɪ
there ðeə* (normal form), ðə* (weak form), ðər (alternative weak form before vowels)
  Note.—The weak forms occur only when the word is used expletively, as in there is, there are, there was, there won't be, etc. The form ðeə* is also used in such expressions.
thereabouts 'ðeərəbaʊts [,ðeərə'b-]
  Note.—The form ,ðeərə'bauts is always used in the expression there or thereabouts.
thereafter ,ðeər'ɑ:ftə*
thereat ,ðeər'æt

thereby ˌðeə'baɪ ['— *according to sentence-stress*]
therefor ˌðeə'fɔ:*
therefore 'ðeəfɔ:* [-fɔə*]
therefrom ˌðeə'frɒm
therein ˌðeər'ɪn [*occasionally* '—]
thereinafter ˌðeərɪn'ɑ:ftə*
thereof ˌðeər'ɒv
thereon ˌðeər'ɒn
there's (=there is, there has) ðeəz (*strong form*), ðəz (*weak form*)
Theresa tɪ'ri:zə [tə'r-]
thereto ˌðeə'tu:
thereunto ˌðeər'ʌntu: [-tʊ, ˌðeərʌn'tu:]
thereupon ˌðeərə'pɒn ['—]
therewith ˌðeə'wɪð [-'wɪθ]
therewithal ˌðeəwɪ'ðɔ:l ['— *when used as noun*]
therm, -s θɜ:m, -z
therm|al, -ally 'θɜ:m|l, -əlɪ
thermic, -ally 'θɜ:mɪk, -əlɪ
Thermidor 'θɜ:mɪdɔ:*
thermionic, -s ˌθɜ:mɪ'ɒnɪk, -s
thermit 'θɜ:mɪt
thermodynamic, -s ˌθɜ:məʊdaɪ'næmɪk [-dɪ'n-], -s
thermogene 'θɜ:məʊdʒi:n
thermograph, -s 'θɜ:məʊgrɑ:f [-græf], -s
thermometer, -s θə'mɒmɪtə* [-mətə*], -z
thermometric, -al, -ally ˌθɜ:məʊ'metrɪk [-mʊ'm-], -l, -əlɪ
thermopile, -s 'θɜ:məʊpaɪl, -z
thermoplastic (*s. adj.*), -s ˌθɜ:məʊ-'plæstɪk, -s
Thermopylae θɜ:'mɒpɪli: [θə'm-]
thermos, -es 'θɜ:mɒs [-məs], -ɪz
thermostat, -s 'θɜ:məʊstæt, -s
thermostatic ˌθɜ:məʊ'stætɪk
Thersites θɜ:'saɪti:z
thesaur|us, -i, -uses θɪ'sɔ:r|əs [θi:'s-, θə's-], -aɪ, -əsɪz
these (*plur. of* this) ði:z
Theseus (*in Greek legend*) 'θi:sju:s [-sjəs, -sɪəs], (*Shakespearian character, and as name of ship*) 'θi:sjəs [-sɪəs]
Thesiger 'θesɪdʒə*
thes|is (*dissertation*), -es 'θi:s|ɪs, -i:z
thesis (*metrical term*) 'θesɪs ['θi:s-]
Thespian 'θespɪən [-pjən]
Thespis 'θespɪs
Thessalian, -s θe'seɪljən [-lɪən], -z
Thessalonian, -s ˌθesə'ləʊnjən [-nɪən], -z
Thessalonica ˌθesələ'naɪkə [-'ni:kə]
Thessaly 'θesəlɪ
Thetis (*Greek*) 'θetɪs, (*asteroid, name of ship*) 'θi:tɪs
theurgic, -al θi:'ɜ:dʒɪk [θɪ'ɜ:-], -l

theurg|ist/s, -y 'θi:ɜ:dʒ|ɪst/s, -ɪ
thews θju:z
they ðeɪ (*normal form*), ðe (*not infrequent as weak form, esp. before vowels*)
Note.—ðe *occurs as a strong form in the single expression* they are, *when* are *has its weak form* ə*. They are *in this case is also written* they're.
Theydon Bois ˌθeɪdn'bɔɪz
thias|us, -i 'θaɪəs|əs, -aɪ
thick (*s. adj. adv.*), -er, -est, -ly, -ness/es θɪk, -ə*, -ɪst, -lɪ, -nɪs [-nəs]/ɪz
thick|en, -ens, -ening, -ened 'θɪk|ən, -ənz, -ənɪŋ, ˌpn] -ənd
thicket, -s 'θɪkɪt, -s
thick-headed ˌθɪk'hedɪd [*also* '-ˌ-- *when attributive*]
thickish 'θɪkɪʃ
thick-set ˌθɪk'set ['-- *when attributive*]
thick-skinned ˌθɪk'skɪnd ['-- *when attributive*]
thick-skulled ˌθɪk'skʌld ['-- *when attributive*]
thick-witted ˌθɪk'wɪtɪd [*also* '-ˌ-- *when attributive*]
thie|f, -ves θi:|f, -vz
thiev|e, -es, -ing, -ed; -ery θi:v, -z, -ɪŋ, -d; -ərɪ
thievish, -ly, -ness 'θi:vɪʃ, -lɪ, -nɪs [-nəs]
thigh, -s; -bone/s θaɪ, -z; -bəʊn/z
thill, -s θɪl, -z
thimble, -s; -ful/s 'θɪmbl, -z; -fʊl/z
thimblerig (*s. v.*), -s, -ging, -ged 'θɪmblrɪg, -z, -ɪŋ, -d
thin (*adj. v.*), -ner, -nest, -ly, -ness; -s, -ning, -ned θɪn, -ə*, -ɪst, -lɪ, -nɪs [-nəs]; -z, -ɪŋ, -d
thine ðaɪn
thing, -s θɪŋ, -z
thingam|y, -ies 'θɪŋəm|ɪ, -ɪz
thingumabob, -s 'θɪŋəmɪbɒb [-məb-], -z
thingumajig, -s 'θɪŋəmɪdʒɪg [-mədʒ-], -z
thingumbob, -s 'θɪŋəmbɒb, -z
thingumm|y, -ies 'θɪŋəm|ɪ, -ɪz
think, -s, -ing, thought, thinker/s θɪŋk, -s, -ɪŋ, θɔ:t, 'θɪŋkə*/z
thinkable 'θɪŋkəbl
Thinn θɪn
thinnish 'θɪnɪʃ
thin-skinned ˌθɪn'skɪnd ['-- *when attributive*]
third (*s. adj.*), -s, -ly θɜ:d, -z, -lɪ
third-rate ˌθɜ:d'reɪt [*also* '-- *when attributive*]
Thirsk θɜ:sk
thirst (*s. v.*), -s, -ing, -ed θɜ:st, -s, -ɪŋ, -ɪd

thirst|y, -ier, -iest, -ily, -iness 'θɜːst|ɪ,
 -ɪə* [-jə*], -ɪɪst [-jɪst], -ɪlɪ [-əlɪ], -ɪnɪs
 [-məs]
thirteen, -s, -th/s, -thly ˌθɜːˈtiːn ['--
 according to sentence-stress], -z, -θ/s,
 -θlɪ
thirt|y, -ies, -ieth/s, -iethly, -yfold
 'θɜːt|ɪ, -ɪz, -ɪɪθ/s [-jɪθ/s, -ɪəθ/s,
 -jəθ/s], -ɪɪθlɪ [-jɪθlɪ, -ɪəθlɪ, -jəθlɪ],
 -ɪfəʊld
this ðɪs
 Note.—Some use a weak form ðəs in
 this morning (afternoon, evening).
Thisbe 'θɪzbɪ
Thiselton 'θɪslt*n
thistle, -s 'θɪsl, -z
thistle-down 'θɪsldaʊn
thistly 'θɪslɪ [-slɪ]
thither, -ward 'ðɪðə*, -wəd [-wɔːd]
tho' ðəʊ
thole, -s θəʊl, -z
Thom tɒm
Thomas 'tɒməs
Thomond (in Ireland) 'θəʊmənd
Thompson 'tɒmpsn
Thompstone 'tɒmpstəʊn
Thomson 'tɒmsn [-mpsn]
thong, -s θɒŋ, -z
Thor θɔː*
thoracic θɔːˈræsɪk [θɒˈr-, θəˈr-]
thorax, -es 'θɔːræks, -ɪz
Thoreau (American writer) 'θɔːrəʊ
thorium 'θɔːrɪəm
thorn, -s θɔːn, -z
Thornaby 'θɔːnəbɪ
thornbush, -es 'θɔːnbʊʃ, -ɪz
Thorne θɔːn
Thorneycroft 'θɔːnɪkrɒft
Thornhill 'θɔːnhɪl
thornless 'θɔːnlɪs [-ləs]
Thornton 'θɔːntən
thorn|y, -ier, -iest, -ily, -iness 'θɔːn|ɪ,
 -ɪə* [-jə*], -ɪɪst [-jɪst], -ɪlɪ [-əlɪ], -ɪnɪs
 [-məs]
Thorold 'θɒrəld, 'θʌrəld
thorough, -ly, -ness 'θʌrə, -lɪ, -nɪs [-nəs]
thorough-bass ˌθʌrəˈbeɪs
thorough-bred, -s 'θʌrəbred, -z
thoroughfare, -s 'θʌrəfeə*, -z
thoroughgoing 'θʌrəˌɡəʊɪŋ [ˌ--'--]
thorough-paced 'θʌrəpeɪst
thorp(e) (T.), -s θɔːp, -s
Thor(r)owgood 'θʌrəɡʊd
those (plur. of that) ðəʊz
thou ðaʊ
though ðəʊ
thought (s.), -s θɔːt, -s
thought (from think) θɔːt

thought|ful, -fully, -fulness 'θɔːt|fʊl,
 -fʊlɪ [-fəlɪ], -fʊlnɪs [-nəs]
thoughtless, -ly, -ness 'θɔːtlɪs [-ləs], -lɪ,
 -nɪs [-nəs]
thought-read|er/s, -ing 'θɔːtˌriːd|ə*/z,
 -ɪŋ
thought-wave, -s 'θɔːtweɪv, -z
Thouless 'θaʊlɪs [-lɪs]
thousan|d, -ds, -dth/s, -dfold 'θaʊzn|d,
 -dz, -tθ/s, -dfəʊld
Thrace θreɪs
Thracian, -s 'θreɪʃjən [-ʃɪən, -ʃn], -z
thraldom 'θrɔːldəm
thrall (s. v.), -s, -ing, -ed θrɔːl, -z, -ɪŋ, -d
thrash, -es, -ing, -ed, -er/s θræʃ, -ɪz, -ɪŋ,
 -t, -ə*/z
thread (s. v.), -s, -ing, -ed; -bare θred,
 -z, -ɪŋ, -ɪd; -beə*
Threadneedle (street) ˌθredˈniːdl ['-,--]
thread|y, -iness 'θred|ɪ, -ɪnɪs [-məs]
threat, -s θret, -s
threat|en, -ens, -ening/ly, -ened 'θret|n,
 -nz, -nɪŋ/lɪ [-nɪŋ/lɪ], -nd
three, -s θriː, -z
three-cornered ˌθriːˈkɔːnəd ['-,-- when
 attributive]
three-decker, -s ˌθriːˈdekə*, -z
three-dimensional ˌθriːdɪˈmenʃənl
 [-daɪˈm-, -ʃnəl, -ʃn̩l, -ʃn̩l, -ʃənəl]
threefold 'θriːfəʊld
threeish 'θriːɪʃ
three-legged ˌθriːˈleɡd ['-- when attributive, ˌθriːˈleɡɪd]
three|pence, -pences, -penny 'θre|pəns
 ['θrɪ|p-, 'θrʌ|p-, 'θrʊ|p-], -pənsɪz,
 -pənɪ [-pn̩ɪ, -pnɪ] (see note under
 penny)
three-ply 'θriːplaɪ [ˌ-'-]
three-quarter, -s ˌθriːˈkwɔːtə* ['-,--
 according to sentence-stress], -z
threescore ˌθriːˈskɔː* [-kɔə*, '-- when
 followed by a stress]
threesome, -s 'θriːsəm, -z
threnod|y, -ies 'θrenəd|ɪ ['θriːn-,
 -nəʊd-], -ɪz
thresh, -es, -ing, -ed, -er/s θreʃ, -ɪz, -ɪŋ,
 -t, -ə*/z
threshing-floor, -s 'θreʃɪŋflɔː* [-flɔə*],
 -z
threshold, -s 'θreʃhəʊld, -z
threw (from throw) θruː
thrice θraɪs
thrift θrɪft
thriftless, -ly, -ness 'θrɪftlɪs [-ləs], -lɪ,
 -nɪs [-nəs]
thrift|y, -ier, -iest, -ily, -iness 'θrɪft|ɪ,
 -ɪə* [-jə*], -ɪɪst [-jɪst], -ɪlɪ [-əlɪ], -ɪnɪs
 [-məs]

thrill (s. v.), -s, -ing/ly, -ed θrɪl, -z, -ɪŋ/lɪ, -d

thriller, -s 'θrɪlə*, -z

Thring θrɪŋ

thriv|e, -es, -ing/ly, -ed, throve, thriven θraɪv, -z, -ɪŋ/lɪ, -d, θrəʊv, 'θrɪvn

thro' θru:

throat, -s, -ed θrəʊt, -s, -ɪd

throat|y, -ier, -iest, -ily, -iness 'θrəʊt|ɪ, -ɪə* [-jə*], -ɪɪst [-jɪst], -ɪlɪ [-əlɪ], -ɪnɪs [-ɪnəs]

throb (s. v.), -s, -bing/ly, -bed θrɒb, -z, -ɪŋ/lɪ, -d

throe, -s θrəʊ, -z

Throgmorton θrɒg'mɔ:tn ['-,--]

thrombosis θrɒm'bəʊsɪs

thrombus 'θrɒmbəs

thron|e (s. v.), -es, -ing, -ed θrəʊn, -z, -ɪŋ, -d

throneless 'θrəʊnlɪs [-ləs]

throng (s. v.), -s, -ing, -ed θrɒŋ, -z, -ɪŋ, -d

throstle, -s 'θrɒsl, -z

thrott|le (s. v.), -les, -ling, -led 'θrɒt|l, -lz, -lɪŋ [-lɪŋ], -ld

through, -ly, -ness θru:, -lɪ, -nɪs [-nəs]

Througham (place) 'θrʌfəm

throughout θru:'aʊt [θrʊ'aʊt]

throughput, -s 'θru:pʊt, -s

throve (from thrive) θrəʊv

throw (s. v.), -s, -ing, threw, throw|n, -er/s θrəʊ, -z, -ɪŋ, θru:, 'θrəʊ|n, -ə*/z

throw-back, -s 'θrəʊbæk, -s

thrum (s. v.), -s, -ming, -med θrʌm, -z, -ɪŋ, -d

thrush, -es θrʌʃ, -ɪz

thrust (s. v.), -s, -ing θrʌst, -s, -ɪŋ

Thucydides θju:'sɪdɪdi:z [θjʊ's-, -dəd-]

thud (s. v.), -s, -ding, -ded θʌd, -z, -ɪŋ, -ɪd

thug, -s θʌg [rarely tʌg] (Hindi ṭhəg), -z

thuggery 'θʌgərɪ

Thuillier 'twɪljə* [-lɪə*]

Thule 'θju:li: [-lɪ]

thumb (s. v.), -s, -ing, -ed θʌm, -z, -ɪŋ, -d

thumb-mark, -s 'θʌmmɑ:k, -s

thumbscrew, -s 'θʌmskru:, -z

thumbstall, -s 'θʌmstɔ:l, -z

thummim 'θʌmɪm [in Jewish usage also 'θʊm- and 'tʊm-]

thump (s. v.), -s, -ing, -ed, -er/s θʌmp, -s, -ɪŋ, -t [θʌmt], -ə*/z

thumping (adj.) 'θʌmpɪŋ

Thun tu:n

thund|er, -ers, -ering/ly, -ered, -erer/s 'θʌnd|ə*, -əz, -ərɪŋ/lɪ, -əd, -ərə*/z

thunderbolt, -s 'θʌndəbəʊlt, -s

thunder-clap, -s 'θʌndəklæp, -s

thunderous, -ly 'θʌndərəs, -lɪ

thunder-storm, -s 'θʌndəstɔ:m, -z

thunderstruck 'θʌndəstrʌk

thund|ery, -eriness 'θʌnd|ərɪ, -ərɪnɪs [-nəs]

thurible, -s 'θjʊərɪbl, -z

Thuringia, -n/s θjʊə'rɪndʒɪə [tʊə'r-, -dʒjə, -ɪŋgjə], -n/z

Thurloe 'θɜ:ləʊ

Thurlow 'θɜ:ləʊ

Thurn tɜ:n

Thuron (English surname) tʊ'rɒn [,tʊə'r-, tə'r-]

Thursday, -s 'θɜ:zdɪ [-deɪ], -z

Thurso 'θɜ:səʊ ['θɜ:zəʊ] (Scottish 'θʌrzo)

Thurston 'θɜ:stən

thus, -ness ðʌs, -nɪs [-nəs]

thwack (s. v.), -s, -ing, -ed θwæk, -s, -ɪŋ, -t

thwaite (T.), -s θweɪt, -s

thwart (of a boat), -s θwɔ:t [in nautical usage also θɔ:t], -s

thwart (v.), -s, -ing, -ed θwɔ:t, -s, -ɪŋ, -ɪd

thy ðaɪ

Thyatira ,θaɪə'taɪərə

thyme, -s taɪm, -z

thymol 'θaɪmɒl ['taɪmɒl]

thymus, -es 'θaɪməs, -ɪz

thymy 'taɪmɪ

Thynne θɪn

thyroid (s. adj.), -s 'θaɪrɔɪd ['θaɪər-], -z

Thyrsis 'θɜ:sɪs

thyself ðaɪ'self

tiara, -s, -ed tɪ'ɑ:rə, -z, -d

Tibbitts 'tɪbɪts

Tibbs tɪbz

Tiber 'taɪbə*

Tiberias taɪ'bɪərɪæs [-rɪəs]

Tiberius taɪ'bɪərɪəs

Tibet tɪ'bet

Tibetan, -s tɪ'betən, -s

tib|ia, -iae, -ias 'tɪb|ɪə ['taɪb-, -bjə], -ɪi:, -ɪəz

Tibullus tɪ'bʌləs [-'bʊl-]

tic tɪk

tic douloureux ,tɪkdu:lə'rɜ: (tik dulurø)

tic|e (s. v.), -es, -ing, -ed taɪs, -ɪz, -ɪŋ, -t

Ticehurst 'taɪshɜ:st

Tichborne 'tɪtʃbɔ:n [-bɔən, -bən]

Ticino tɪ'tʃi:nəʊ (ti'tʃi:no)

tick (s. v.), -s, -ing, -ed, -er/s tɪk, -s, -ɪŋ, -t, -ə*/z

ticket (s. v.), -s, -ing, -ed 'tɪkɪt, -s, -ɪŋ, -ed

ticket-of-leave ,tɪkɪtəv'li:v

ticking (s.), -s 'tɪkɪŋ, -z

tick|le, -les, -ling, -led, -ler/s 'tɪk|l, -lz, -lɪŋ [-lɪŋ], -ld, -lə*/z [-lə*/z]

Tickler 'tɪklə*

ticklish, -ly, -ness 'tɪklɪʃ [-lɪʃ], -lɪ, -nɪs [-nəs]

tickly 'tɪklɪ [-klɪ]

tick-tack, -s 'tɪktæk, -s

tidal 'taɪdl

tidbit, -s 'tɪdbɪt, -s

tiddledywinks 'tɪdldɪwɪŋks

tiddlywinks 'tɪdlɪwɪŋks [-dlɪ-]

tid|e (s. v.), -es, -ing, -ed taɪd, -z, -ɪŋ, -ɪd

tide-waiter, -s 'taɪd,wertə*, -z

tidewater 'taɪd,wɔːtə*

tidings 'taɪdɪŋz

tid|y (s. adj. v.), -ies; -ier, -iest, -ily, -iness; -ying, -ied 'taɪd|ɪ, -ɪz; -ɪə* [-jə*], -ɪɪst [-jɪst], -ɪlɪ [-əlɪ], -ɪnɪs [-məs]; -ɪŋ [-jɪŋ], -ɪd

tie (s. v.), ties, tying, tied taɪ, taɪz, 'taɪɪŋ, taɪd

tie-break, -s, -er/s 'taɪbreɪk, -s, -ə*/z

Tien-tsin ˌtjen'tsɪn

tier (one who ties), -s 'taɪə*, -z

tier (set of seats in theatre, etc.), -s tə*, -z

tierce (in music, in fencing, cash), -s tɪəs, -ɪz

tierce (in cards), -s tɜːs [tɪəs], -ɪz

tiercel, -s 'tɜːsl, -z

Tierra del Fuego tɪˌerədel'fweɪɡəʊ [ˌtjerə-, -fʊ'eɪ-]

tiff (s. v.), -s, -ing, -ed tɪf, -s, -ɪŋ, -t

tiffany 'tɪfənɪ

tiffin, -s 'tɪfɪn, -z

Tiflis 'tɪflɪs

tig, -s tɪg, -z

tige, -s tiːʒ, -ɪz

tiger, -s 'taɪɡə*, -z

tiger-cat, -s 'taɪɡəkæt, -s

tigerish 'taɪɡərɪʃ

tiger-lil|y, -ies 'taɪɡə,lɪl|ɪ, -ɪz

tiger-moth, -s 'taɪɡəmɒθ, -s

Tighe taɪ

tight, -er, -est, -ly, -ness taɪt, -ə*, -ɪst, -lɪ, -nɪs [-nəs]

tight|en, -ens, -ening, -ened, -ener/s 'taɪt|n, -nz, -ṇɪŋ [-nɪŋ], -nd, -nə*/z [-nə*/z]

tight-fisted ˌtaɪt'fɪstɪd ['-ˌ-- when attributive]

tights taɪts

Tiglath-pileser ˌtɪɡlæθpaɪ'liːzə* [-pɪ'l-]

tigon, -s 'taɪɡən, -z

tigress, -es 'taɪɡrɪs [-ɡres], -ɪz

Tigris 'taɪɡrɪs

tike, -s taɪk, -s

tilbur|y (T.), -ies 'tɪlbər|ɪ, -ɪz

tilde, -s 'tɪldə ['tɪldɪ, -d], -z

till|e (s. v.), -es, -ing, -ed taɪl, -z, -ɪŋ, -d

Tilehurst 'taɪlhɜːst

tiler, -s 'taɪlə*, -z

tiler|y, -ies 'taɪlər|ɪ, -ɪz

till (s. v. prep. conj.), -s, -ing, -ed, -er/s; -able, -age tɪl, -z, -ɪŋ, -d, -ə*/z; -əbl, -ɪdʒ

tiller (of rudder), -s 'tɪlə*, -z

Tilley 'tɪlɪ

Tilling, -s 'tɪlɪŋ, -z

Tillotson 'tɪlətsn

Tilly 'tɪlɪ

tilt (s. v.), -s, -ing, -ed, -er/s tɪlt, -s, -ɪŋ, -ɪd, -ə*/z

tilth tɪlθ

tilt-yard, -s 'tɪltjɑːd, -z

Timaeus taɪ'miːəs [tɪ'm-, -'mɪəs]

timbal, -s 'tɪmbl, -z

timbale, -s tæm'bɑːl ['tɪmbl] (tɛ̃bal), -z

timber, -s, -ing, -ed 'tɪmbə*, -z, -rɪŋ, -d

timbre, -s 'tæmbrə ['tæm-, -bə*, 'tɪmbə*] (tɛ̃ːbr), -z

timbrel, -s 'tɪmbrəl, -z

Timbuctoo ˌtɪmbʌk'tuː [-bək-]

tim|e (s. v.), -es, -ing, -ed, -er/s taɪm, -z, -ɪŋ, -d, -ə*/z

time-base, -s 'taɪmbeɪs, -ɪz

time-bomb, -s 'taɪmbɒm, -z

time-expired 'taɪmɪkˌspaɪəd [-mek-]

time-honoured 'taɪmˌɒnəd [ˌ-'--]

timekeeper, -s 'taɪmˌkiːpə*, -z

timeless 'taɪmlɪs [-ləs]

time-lock, -s 'taɪmlɒk, -s

timel|y, -ier, -iest, -iness 'taɪml|ɪ, -ɪə*, -ɪɪst, -mɪs [-məs]

timeous 'taɪməs

timepiece, -s 'taɪmpiːs, -ɪz

Times taɪmz

time-saving 'taɪmˌseɪvɪŋ

time-serv|er/s, -ing 'taɪmˌsɜːv|ə*/z, -ɪŋ

time-sheet, -s 'taɪmʃiːt, -s

time-table, -s 'taɪmˌteɪbl, -z

time-work 'taɪmwɜːk

timid, -est, -ly, -ness 'tɪmɪd, -ɪst, -lɪ, -nɪs [-nəs]

timidity tɪ'mɪdɪtɪ [-ɪtɪ]

Timon 'taɪmən [-mɒn]

Timor 'tiːmɔː*

timorous, -ly, -ness 'tɪmərəs, -lɪ, -nɪs [-nəs]

Timotheus tɪ'məʊθjəs [-θɪəs]

timothy (T.), -grass 'tɪməθɪ, -grɑːs

timous 'taɪməs

timpan|o, -i 'tɪmpən|əʊ, -ɪ [-iː]

Timpson 'tɪmpsn

tin (s. v.), -s, -ning, -ned tɪn, -z, -ɪŋ, -d

tinctorial tɪŋk'tɔːrɪəl

497

tinctur|e (s. v.), -es, -ing, -ed 'tɪŋktʃə*, -z, -rɪŋ, -d

Tindal(e) 'tɪndl

Tindall 'tɪndl

tinder; -box/es 'tɪndə*; -bɒks/ɪz

tine, -s taɪn, -z

tinfoil ˌtɪn'fɔɪl ['--]

ting|e (s. v.), -es, -(e)ing, -ed tɪndʒ, -ɪz, -ɪŋ, -d

Tingey 'tɪŋgɪ

ting|le (s. v.), -les, -ling, -led 'tɪŋg|l, -lz, -lɪŋ [-lɪŋ], -ld

tink|er (s. v.), -ers, -ering, -ered 'tɪŋk|ə*, -əz, -ərɪŋ, -əd

tink|le (s. v.), -les, -ling/s, -led, -ler/s 'tɪŋk|l, -lz, -lɪŋ/z, -ld, -lə*/z

Tinnevelly tɪ'nevəlɪ [ˌtɪnɪ'velɪ]

   Note.—Both pronunciations were formerly in use by Anglo-Indians.

tinnitus tɪ'naɪtəs ['tɪnɪtəs]

tinny 'tɪnɪ

Tin Pan Alley ˌtɪnpæn'ælɪ

tin-plate 'tɪnpleɪt [ˌ-'-]

tinsel 'tɪnsl

tint (s. v.), -s, -ing, -ed, -er/s tɪnt, -s, -ɪŋ, -ɪd, -ə*/z

Tintagel tɪn'tædʒəl

Tintern 'tɪntən [-tɜːn]

tintinnabulation, -s 'tɪntɪˌnæbjʊ'leɪʃn, -z

tintinnabul|um, -a, -ar, -ary, -ous ˌtɪntɪ'næbjʊl|əm, -ə, -ə*, -ərɪ, -əs

Tintoretto, -s ˌtɪntə'retəʊ [-tɒ'r-], -z

tin|y, -ier, -iest, -iness 'taɪn|ɪ, -ɪə* [-jə*], -ɪɪst [-jɪst], -ɪnɪs [-ɪnəs]

tip (s. v.), -s, -ping, -ped tɪp, -s, -ɪŋ, -t

tipcat 'tɪpkæt

Tippell 'tɪpəl

Tipperary ˌtɪpə'reərɪ

tippet, -s 'tɪpɪt, -s

Tippett 'tɪpɪt

tipp|le, -les, -ling, -led, -ler/s 'tɪp|l, -lz, -lɪŋ [-lɪŋ], -ld, -lə*/z [-lə*/z]

tipstaff, -s 'tɪpstɑːf, -s

tipster, -s 'tɪpstə*, -z

tips|y, -ier, -iest, -ily, -iness 'tɪps|ɪ, -ɪə* [-jə*], -ɪɪst [-jɪst], -ɪlɪ [-əlɪ], -ɪnɪs [-ɪnəs]

tipsy-cake 'tɪpsɪkeɪk

tiptoe 'tɪptəʊ [ˌ-'-]

tiptop (s. adj.), ˌtɪp'tɒp ['--]

tirade, -s taɪ'reɪd [tɪ'reɪd, tɪ'rɑːd], -z

tirailleur, -s ˌtɪraɪ'ɜː* [-aɪ'jɜː*, -aɪ'lɜː*] (tirɑjœːr), -z

tirasse, -s tɪ'ræs, -ɪz

tir|e (s. v.), -es, -ing, -ed/ly, -edness 'taɪə*, -z, -rɪŋ, -d/lɪ, -dnɪs [-nəs]

tireless, -ly, -ness 'taɪəlɪs [-ləs], -lɪ, -nɪs [-nəs]

Tiresias taɪ'riːsɪæs [ˌtaɪə'r-, -'res-, -sɪəs, -sjəs]

tiresome, -ly, -ness 'taɪəsəm, -lɪ, -nɪs [-nəs]

tiro, -s 'taɪərəʊ, -z

Tirzah 'tɜːzə

'tis tɪz

tisane, -s ti:'zæn [tɪ'z-], -z

Tishbite, -s 'tɪʃbaɪt, -s

Tissaphernes ˌtɪsə'fɜːniːz

tissue, -s 'tɪʃuː ['tɪsjuː, 'tɪʃjuː], -z

tit, -s tɪt, -s

Titan, -s 'taɪtən, -z

Titania tɪ'tɑːnjə [tɪ'tem-, taɪ'tem-, -nɪə]

titanic (T.) taɪ'tænɪk [tɪ't-]

titanium taɪ'teɪnjəm [tɪ't-, -nɪəm]

titbit, -s 'tɪtbɪt, -s

tith|e (s. v.), -es, -ing, -ed taɪð, -z, -ɪŋ, -d

tithing (s.), -s 'taɪðɪŋ, -z

Titian, -s 'tɪʃn [-ʃjən, -ʃɪən], -z

titillat|e, -es, -ing, -ed 'tɪtɪleɪt, -s, -ɪŋ, -ɪd

titillation, -s ˌtɪtɪ'leɪʃn, -z

titivat|e, -es, -ing, -ed 'tɪtɪveɪt, -s, -ɪŋ, -ɪd

titivation, -s ˌtɪtɪ'veɪʃn, -z

title, -s, -d; -less 'taɪtl, -z, -d; -lɪs [-ləs]

titling (stamping a title), -s 'taɪtlɪŋ, -z

Titlis 'tɪtlɪs

Titmarsh 'tɪtmɑːʃ

tit|mouse, -mice 'tɪt|maʊs, -maɪs

Tito 'tiːtəʊ

titter (s. v.), -s, -ing, -ed, -er/s 'tɪtə*, -z, -rɪŋ, -d, -rə*/z

tittle, -s 'tɪtl, -z

tittle-tattle 'tɪtlˌtætl

titular (s. adj.), -s, -ly 'tɪtjʊlə* [-jəl-], -z, -lɪ

titular|y (s. adj.), -ies 'tɪtjʊlər|ɪ [-jəl-], -ɪz

Titus 'taɪtəs

Tiverton 'tɪvətən

Tivoli 'tɪvəlɪ

Tivy (surname) 'taɪvɪ

Tizard 'tɪzəd

tmesis 'tmiːsɪs

T.N.T. ˌtiːen'tiː

to (adv.) tuː

to (prep.) tuː (strong form, also occasionally used as weak form, esp. in final position), tʊ (weak form, also used as strong form before vowels), tə (weak form used before consonants only), t (occasional weak form before consonants)

toad, -s təʊd, -z

toad-flax 'təʊdflæks

toad-in-the-hole ˌtəʊdɪnðə'həʊl

toadstool, -s 'təʊdstuːl, -z

toad|y (s. v.), -ies, -ying, -ied 'təʊd|ɪ, -ɪz, -ɪɪŋ [-jɪŋ], -ɪd

to-and-fro ˌtuːənˈfrəʊ [ˌtʊən-]

toast (s. v.), -s, -ing, -ed, -er/s təʊst, -s, -ɪŋ, -ɪd, -ə*/z

toasting-fork, -s 'təʊstɪŋfɔːk, -s

toast-master, -s 'təʊstˌmɑːstə*, -z

toast-rack, -s 'təʊstræk, -s

tobacco, -s təˈbækəʊ, -z

tobacconist, -s təˈbækənɪst [-kn̩ɪ-], -s

tobacco-pouch, -es təˈbækəʊpaʊtʃ, -ɪz

Tobago təʊˈbeɪgəʊ

Tobias təˈbaɪəs [təʊˈb-]

Tobi|n, -t 'təʊbɪ|n, -t

tobogg|an (s. v.), -ans, -aning, -aned, -aner/s təˈbɒg|ən, -ənz, -ənɪŋ [-n̩ɪŋ], -ənd, -ənə*/z [-n̩ə*/z]

tob|y (T.), -ies 'təʊb|ɪ, -ɪz

tobyman, -men 'təʊbɪmæn, -men

toccata, -s təˈkɑːtə [tɒˈk-], -z

Tocharian tɒˈkeərɪən [təʊ-, -ˈkɑː-]

toco 'təʊkəʊ

tocsin, -s 'tɒksɪn, -z

tod (T.), -s tɒd, -z

today təˈdeɪ [tʊˈd-]

Todd tɒd

todd|le, -les, -ling, -led, -ler/s 'tɒd|l, -lz, -lɪŋ [-lɪŋ], -ld, -lə*/z [-lə*/z]

toddy 'tɒdɪ

Todhunter 'tɒdˌhʌntə* ['tɒdʌˈəntə*]

Todmorden 'tɒdmədən ['tɒdˌmɔːdn̩]

to-do, -s təˈduː [tʊˈd-], -z

toe (s. v.), -s, -ing, -d təʊ, -z, -ɪŋ, -d

toe-cap, -s 'təʊkæp, -s

toe-nail, -s 'təʊneɪl, -z

toe-strap, -s 'təʊstræp, -s

toff, -s tɒf, -s

toffee 'tɒfɪ

tog (s. v.), -s, -ging, -ged tɒg, -z, -ɪŋ, -d

toga, -s, -ed 'təʊgə, -z, -d

together, -ness təˈgeðə* [tʊˈg-], -nɪs [-nəs]

toggery 'tɒgərɪ

toggle, -s, -d 'tɒgl, -z, -d

Togo, -land 'təʊgəʊ, -lænd

toil (s. v.), -s, -ing, -ed, -er/s tɔɪl, -z, -ɪŋ, -d, -ə*/z

toile, -s twɑːl [twɔːl] (twal), -z

toilet, -s 'tɔɪlɪt [-lət], -s

toilet-cover, -s 'tɔɪlɪtˌkʌvə* [-lət-], -z

toilet-paper 'tɔɪlɪtˌpeɪpə* [-lət-]

toilet-powder, -s 'tɔɪlɪtˌpaʊdə* [-lət-], -z

toiletr|y, -ies 'tɔɪlɪtr|ɪ [-lətr|ɪ], -ɪz

toilet-set, -s 'tɔɪlɪtset [-lət-], -s

toilet-table, -s 'tɔɪlɪtˌteɪbl [-lət-], -z

toilette, -s twɑːˈlet (twalɛt), -s

toilsome, -ly, -ness 'tɔɪlsəm, -lɪ, -nɪs [-nəs]

toilworn 'tɔɪlwɔːn

tokay (T.) təʊˈkeɪ [təʊˈkaɪ, 'təʊkaɪ, tɒˈkaɪ] (Hung. 'toːkɒj)

token, -s 'təʊkən, -z

Tokharian tɒˈkeərɪən [təʊˈk-, -ˈkɑː-]

Tokley 'təʊklɪ

Tokyo [-kio] 'təʊkjəʊ [-kɪəʊ]

Toland 'təʊlənd

tolbooth, -s 'tɒlbuːθ, -s ['tɒlbuːð, -z]

told (from tell) təʊld

toledo (blade), -s təˈliːdəʊ [tɒˈl-], -z

Toledo (in Spain) tɒˈleɪdəʊ [təˈl-, -ˈliːd-] (toˈledo), (in U.S.A.) təˈliːdəʊ

tolerability ˌtɒlərəˈbɪlətɪ [-lɪt-]

tolerab|le, -ly, -leness 'tɒlərəb|l, -lɪ, -lnɪs [-nəs]

toleran|ce, -t/ly 'tɒlərən|s, -t/lɪ

tolerat|e, -es, -ing, -ed 'tɒləreɪt, -s, -ɪŋ, -ɪd

toleration ˌtɒləˈreɪʃn

Tolkien 'tɒlkiːn [tɒlˈkiːn]

toll (s. v.), -s, -ing, -ed, -er/s təʊl, -z, -ɪŋ, -d, -ə*/z

toll-booth, -s 'tɒlbuːθ, -s ['tɒlbuːð, -z]

Tollemache 'tɒlmæʃ, -mɑːʃ

Tollesbury 'təʊlzbərɪ

Tolleshunt (in Essex) 'təʊlzhʌnt

toll-gate, -s 'təʊlgeɪt, -s

toll-hou|se, -ses 'təʊlhaʊ|s, -zɪz

Tolstoy 'tɒlstɔɪ (talˈstoj)

Toltec, -s 'tɒltek, -s

tolu (T.) təʊˈluː [təˈlju:]

tom (T.), -s tɒm, -z

tomahawk (s. v.), -s, -ing, -ed 'tɒmə-hɔːk, -s, -ɪŋ, -t

toman, -s təʊˈmɑːn, -z

tomato, -es təˈmɑːtəʊ, -z

tomb, -s tuːm, -z

tombola, -s tɒmˈbəʊlə ['tɒmbələ, -bʊlə], -z

tomboy, -s 'tɒmbɔɪ, -z

tombstone, -s 'tuːmstəʊn, -z

tomcat, -s ˌtɒmˈkæt ['--], -s

tome, -s təʊm, -z

Tomelty 'tʌməltɪ

tomfool, -s ˌtɒmˈfuːl, -z

tomfoolery tɒmˈfuːlərɪ

Tomintoul ˌtɒmɪnˈtaʊl

tomm|y (T.), -ies 'tɒm|ɪ, -ɪz

tommy-gun, -s 'tɒmɪgʌn, -z

tommy-rot ˌtɒmɪˈrɒt

tomogram, -s 'təʊməgræm ['tɒm-], -z

tomorrow təˈmɒrəʊ [tʊˈm-]

Note.—Variants with final -rə or -rʊ are often used in the expressions tomorrow morning, tomorrow night, and with -rʊ in tomorrow afternoon, tomorrow evening.

499

Tompion 'tɒmpjən [-pɪən]
Tompkins 'tɒmpkɪnz
Tomsk tɒmsk (tomsk)
tomtit, -s 'tɒmtɪt [,tɒm't-], -s
tom-tom, -s 'tɒmtɒm, -z
ton (weight), -s tʌn, -z
ton (fashion) tɔ̃:ŋ (tɔ̃)
tonal 'təʊnl
tonalit|y, -ies təʊ'nælət|ɪ [-ɪt|ɪ], -ɪz
Tonbridge 'tʌnbrɪdʒ ['tʌmb-]
ton|e (s. v.), -es, -ing, -ed təʊn, -z, -ɪŋ, -d
toneless 'təʊnlɪs [-ləs]
tonematic, -s ,təʊnɪ'mætɪk, -s
toneme, -s 'təʊni:m, -z
tonemic, -s təʊ'ni:mɪk, -s
tonetic, -s təʊ'netɪk, -s
tonga (cart, medicinal bark), -s 'tɒŋgə, -z
Tonga (Friendly Islands), -n/s 'tɒŋə [-ŋgə], -n/z
Tonga (East Africa), -s, -n 'tɒŋgə, -z, -n
Tongking ,tɒŋ'kɪŋ
tongs tɒŋz
tongue, -s, -d; -less tʌŋ, -z, -d; -lɪs [-ləs]
tongue-tied 'tʌŋtaɪd
tongue-twister, -s 'tʌŋ,twɪstə*, -z
tonic (s. adj.), -s 'tɒnɪk, -s
tonicity təʊ'nɪsɪtɪ [-ɪtɪ]
tonic-solfa [Tonic Sol-fa] ,tɒnɪksɒl'fɑː
tonight tə'naɪt [tʊ'n-]
tonnage, -s 'tʌnɪdʒ, -ɪz
tonological ,təʊnə'lɒdʒɪkl
tonology təʊ'nɒlədʒɪ
tonsil, -s 'tɒnsl [-sɪl], -z
tonsillectom|y, -ies ,tɒnsɪ'lektəm|ɪ [-sə'l-, -sɪl'e-], -ɪz
tonsil(l)itis ,tɒnsɪ'laɪtɪs [-sl'aɪ-]
tonsorial tɒn'sɔːrɪəl
tonsure, -s, -d 'tɒnʃə* [-,ʃʊə*, -,sjʊə*], -z, -d
tontine tɒn'ti:n ['tɒnti:n]
tony (T.) 'təʊnɪ
Tonypandy ,tɒnɪ'pændɪ (Welsh tonə-'pandi)
too tu:
toodle-oo ,tu:dl'u:
took (from take) tʊk
Tooke tʊk
tool (s. v.), -s, -ing, -ed tu:l, -z, -ɪŋ, -d
tool-box, -es 'tu:lbɒks, -ɪz
tool-chest, -s 'tu:ltʃest, -s
Toole tu:l
Tooley 'tu:lɪ
toot (s. v.), -s, -ing, -ed, -er/s tu:t, -s, -ɪŋ, -ɪd, -ə*/z
tooth (s.), teeth tu:θ, ti:θ
tooth (v.), -s, -ing, -ed tu:θ, -s, -ɪŋ, -t
toothache 'tu:θeɪk
toothbrush, -es 'tu:θbrʌʃ, -ɪz

toothcomb (s. v.), -s, -ing, -ed 'tu:θ-kəʊm, -z, -ɪŋ, -d
toothed (having teeth) tu:θt [tu:ðd]
toothless 'tu:θlɪs [-ləs]
toothpaste, -s 'tu:θpeɪst, -s
toothpick, -s 'tu:θpɪk, -s
tooth-powder, -s 'tu:θ,paʊdə*, -z
toothsome, -ly, -ness 'tu:θsəm, -lɪ, -nɪs [-nəs]
toot|le, -les, -ling, -led 'tu:t|l, -lz, -lɪŋ [-lɪŋ], -ld
top (s. v.), -s, -ping, -ped tɒp, -s, -ɪŋ, -t
topaz, -es 'təʊpæz, -ɪz
top-boot, -s ,tɒp'bu:t, -s
top-coat, -s ,tɒpkəʊt, -s
top-dressing ,tɒp'dresɪŋ ['-,--]
top|e (s. v.), -es, -ing, -ed, -er/s təʊp, -s, -ɪŋ, -t, -ə*/z
Topeka təʊ'pi:kə
topflight 'tɒpflaɪt
top-gallant ,tɒp'gælənt [nautical pronunciation tə'gælənt]
Topham 'tɒpəm
top-hat, -s ,tɒp'hæt, -s
top-heav|y, -iness ,tɒp'hev|ɪ, -ɪnɪs [-nəs]
Tophet 'təʊfet
top-hole ,tɒp'həʊl
topi (topee), -s 'təʊpɪ, -z
topiary 'təʊpjərɪ [-pɪə-]
topic, -s, -al, -ally 'tɒpɪk, -s, -l, -əlɪ
topicalit|y, -ies ,tɒpɪ'kælət|ɪ [-ɪt|ɪ], -ɪz
topknot, -s 'tɒpnɒt, -s
Toplady 'tɒp,leɪdɪ
topless 'tɒplɪs [-ləs]
topmast, -s 'tɒpmɑːst [-məst], -s
topmost 'tɒpməʊst [-məst]
topnotch ,tɒp'nɒtʃ
topograph|er/s, -y tə'pɒgrəf|ə*/z [tɒ'p-, təʊ'p-], -ɪ
topographic, -al, -ally ,tɒpə'græfɪk [,təʊp-, -pəʊ'g-], -l, -əlɪ
toponymy tɒ'pɒnɪmɪ [tə'p-, -nəmɪ]
topper, -s 'tɒpə*, -z
topping (s. adj.), -s, -ly 'tɒpɪŋ, -z, -lɪ
topp|le, -les, -ling, -led 'tɒp|l, -lz, -lɪŋ [-lɪŋ], -ld
topsail, -s 'tɒpsl [-seɪl], -z
Topsham (near Exeter) 'tɒpsəm
topsyturv|y, -ily, -yness, -ydom ,tɒpsɪ-'tɜ:v|ɪ, -ɪlɪ [-əlɪ], -ɪnɪs [-nəs], -ɪdəm
toque, -s təʊk, -s
tor, -s tɔ:*, -z
Torah 'tɔ:rə [with some Jews 'təʊrɑ:, təʊ'rɑ:]
Torbay ,tɔ:'beɪ [also '-- when attributive]
torch, -es tɔ:tʃ, -ɪz
torchlight, -s 'tɔ:tʃlaɪt, -s

torchon 'tɔːʃn [-ʃɒn] (tɔrʃɔ̃)
tore (*from* tear) tɔː* [tɔə*]
toreador, -s 'tɒrɪədɔː:*, -z
toric 'tɒrɪk
torment (*s.*), -s 'tɔːment [-mənt], -s
torment (*v.*), -s, -ing/ly, -ed, -or/s
 tɔː'ment, -s, -ɪŋ/lɪ, -ɪd, -ə*/z
torn (*from* tear) tɔːn
tornado, -es tɔː'neɪdəʊ, -z
Toronto tə'rɒntəʊ
torped|o (*s. v.*), -oes, -oing, -oed
 tɔː'piːd|əʊ, -əʊz, -əʊɪŋ, -əʊd
torpedo|-boat/s, -net/s, -tube/s tɔː:-
 'piːdəʊ|bəʊt/s, -net/s, -tjuːb/z
Torpenhow (*in Cumbria*) 'tɔːpənhaʊ
 [*also very commonly* trə'penə *locally,*
 and sometimes tɔː'penəʊ]
Torphichen tɔː'fɪkən [-'fɪxən]
Torphins tɔː'fɪnz
torpid, -s, -ly, -ness 'tɔːpɪd, -z, -lɪ, -nɪs
 [-nəs]
torpidity tɔː'pɪdətɪ [-ɪtɪ]
torpor, -s 'tɔːpə*, -z
Torquay ˌtɔː'kiː
torque, -s tɔːk, -s
Torquemada (*Spanish inquisitor*)
 ˌtɔːkɪ'mɑːdə [-ke'm-, -kwɪ'm-,
 -kwe'm-] (torkə'mada)
torrefaction ˌtɒrɪ'fækʃn
torre|fy, -fies, -fying, -fied 'tɒrɪ|faɪ,
 -faɪz, -faɪɪŋ, -faɪd
torrent, -s 'tɒrənt, -s
torrenti|al, -ally tə'renʃ|l [tɒ'r-], -əlɪ
torrentiality tɒˌrenʃɪ'ælətɪ [tɒˌr-, -ɪtɪ]
Torres 'tɒrɪs [-ɪz]
Torricell|i, -ian ˌtɒrɪ'tʃel|ɪ, -ɪən [-jən]
torrid, -ness 'tɒrɪd, -nɪs [-nəs]
Torrington 'tɒrɪŋtən
torsion 'tɔːʃn
torso, -s 'tɔːsəʊ, -z
tort, -s tɔːt, -s
tortilla tɔː'tɪlə
tortious 'tɔːʃəs
tortoise, -s 'tɔːtəs, -ɪz
tortoiseshell 'tɔːtəʃel [-ʃʃel]
tortuosity ˌtɔːtjʊ'ɒsətɪ [-ɪtɪ]
tortuous, -ly, -ness 'tɔːtjʊəs [-tjwəs,
 -tʃʊəs, -tʃwəs], -lɪ, -nɪs [-nəs]
tor|ture (*s. v.*), -tures, -turing/ly,
 -tured, -turer/s 'tɔː|tʃə*, -tʃəz,
 -tʃərɪŋ/lɪ, -tʃəd, -tʃərə*/z
torturous 'tɔːtʃərəs
tor|y (T.), -ies, -yism 'tɔːr|ɪ, -ɪz, -ɪɪzəm
Tosberry 'tɒsbərɪ
Toscanini ˌtɒskə'niːnɪ (toska'niːni)
tosh tɒʃ
toss (*s. v.*), -es, -ing, -ed tɒs [*old-
fashioned* tɔːs], -ɪz, -ɪŋ, -t

toss-up, -s 'tɒsʌp [ˌ-'-], -s
tot (*s. v.*), -s, -ting, -ted tɒt, -s, -ɪŋ, -ɪd
tot|al (*s. adj. v.*) (T.), -als, -ally; -alling,
 -alled 'təʊt|l, -lz, -lɪ [-əlɪ]; -lɪŋ [-əlɪŋ],
 -ld
totalizator [-isa-], -s 'təʊtəlaɪzeɪtə*
 [-tʃaɪ-], -z
totalitarian, -ism ˌtəʊtælɪ'teərɪən
 [təʊˌt-], -ɪzəm
totality təʊ'tælətɪ [-ɪtɪ]
totaliz|e [-is|e], -es, -ing, -ed, -er/s
 'təʊtəlaɪz [-tʃaɪz], -ɪz, -ɪŋ, -d, -ə*/z
tote, -s təʊt, -s
totem, -s; -ism 'təʊtəm, -z; -ɪzəm
t'other 'tʌðə*
Tothill 'tɒthɪl ['tɒtɪl]
Totland 'tɒtlənd
Totnes 'tɒtnɪs [-nes]
Tottenham 'tɒtnəm [-tnəm]
totter, -s, -ing/ly, -ed, -er/s 'tɒtə*, -z,
 -rɪŋ/lɪ, -d, -rə*/z
Totteridge 'tɒtərɪdʒ
tottery 'tɒtərɪ
toucan, -s 'tuːkən [-kæn, -kɑːn], -z
touch (*s. v.*), -es, -ing, -ed tʌtʃ, -ɪz, -ɪŋ, -t
touchable 'tʌtʃəbl
touch-and-go ˌtʌtʃən'gəʊ [-əŋ'gəʊ]
touch-down 'tʌtʃdaʊn
touching (*adj. prep.*), -ly, -ness 'tʌtʃɪŋ,
 -lɪ, -nɪs [-nəs]
touch-line, -s 'tʌtʃlaɪn, -z
touch-paper 'tʌtʃˌpeɪpə*
touchstone (T.), -s 'tʌtʃstəʊn, -z
touchwood 'tʌtʃwʊd
touch|y, -ier, -iest, -ily, -iness 'tʌtʃ|ɪ,
 -ɪə*, -ɪɪst, -ɪlɪ [-əlɪ], -ɪnɪs [-nəs]
tough (*s. adj.*), -s, -er, -est, -ly, -ness
 tʌf, -s, -ə*, -ɪst, -lɪ, -nɪs [-nəs]
tough|en, -ens, -ening, -ened 'tʌf|n, -nz,
 -nɪŋ [-nɪŋ], -nd
toughish 'tʌfɪʃ
Toulmin 'tuːlmɪn
Toulon tuː'lɔ̃ːŋ [-'lɒn, -'lɒŋ] (tulɔ̃)
Toulouse tuː'luːz (tuluːz)
toupée, -s 'tuːpeɪ, -z
tour (*s. v.*), -s, -ing, -ed tʊə* [tɔə*,
 tɔː*], -z, -rɪŋ, -d
Touraine tʊ'reɪn
tourbillon, -s ˌtʊə'brɪljən [tɜː'b-,
 'tʊəbɪlən, 'tɜːbɪlən], -z
tour de force, -s ˌtʊədə'fɔːs, -ɪz
tourist, -s 'tʊərɪst ['tɔər-, 'tɔːr-], -s
Tourle tɜːl
tourmal|in/s, -ine/s 'tʊəməl|ɪn/z
 ['tɜːm-], -iːn/z
tournament, -s 'tʊənəmənt ['tɔən-,
 'tɔːn-, 'tɜːn-], -s
tournedos 'tʊənədəʊ ['tɜː-] (turnədo)

Tourneur (*English surname*) 'tɜ:nə*
tourney, -s 'tʊənɪ ['tɔən-, 'tɔ:n-], -z
tourniquet, -s 'tʊənɪkeɪ ['tɔən-, 'tɔ:n-, 'tɜ:n-], -z [*rarely* -ket, -kets]
tournure, -s 'tʊə͵njʊə* ['tɜ:n-, *also* -'-] (turny:r), -z
Tours (*French town*) tʊə* (tu:r), (*English musical composer*) tʊəz
tous|le, -les, -ling, -led 'taʊz|l, -lz, -lɪŋ, -ld
tout (*s. v.*), **-s, -ing, -ed** taʊt, -s, -ɪŋ, -ɪd
Tout (*in* Belle Tout *in East Sussex*) tu:t, (*surname*) taʊt
Tovey 'təʊvɪ, 'tʌvɪ
tow (*s. v.*), **-s, -ing, -ed** təʊ, -z, -ɪŋ, -d
toward (*adj.*), **-ly, -ness** 'təʊəd, -lɪ, -nɪs [-nəs]
toward (*prep.*), **-s** tə'wɔ:d [tʊ'wɔ:d, twɔ:d, tɔ:d, təd], -z
Towcester 'təʊstə*
towel, -s 'taʊəl [taʊl], -z
towel-horse, -s 'taʊəlhɔ:s, -ɪz
towelling, -s 'taʊəlɪŋ, -z
tower (*one who tows*), **-s** 'təʊə*, -z
tower (*s. v.*) (*tall building, etc.*), **-s, -ing, -ed** 'taʊə*, -z, -rɪŋ, -d
Towle təʊl
Towler 'taʊlə*
town, -s taʊn, -z
Towne taʊn
townee, -s taʊ'ni:, -z
town|ish, -y 'taʊn|ɪʃ, -ɪ
townscape, -s 'taʊnskeɪp, -s
Townsend 'taʊnzend
townsfolk 'taʊnzfəʊk
Townshend 'taʊnzend
township, -s 'taʊnʃɪp, -s
towns|man, -men 'taʊnz|mən, -mən [-men]
townspeople 'taʊnz͵pi:pl
tow-pa|th, -ths 'təʊpɑ:|θ, -ðz
tow-rope, -s 'təʊrəʊp, -z
Towton 'taʊtn
Towyn 'taʊɪn (*Welsh* 'təʊɪn)
toxaemia tɒk'si:mɪə [-mjə]
toxic, -al, -ally 'tɒksɪk, -l, -əlɪ
toxicity tɒk'sɪsətɪ [-ɪtɪ]
toxicolog|ist/s, -y ͵tɒksɪ'kɒlədʒ|ɪst/s, -ɪ
toxin, -s 'tɒksɪn, -z
toxophilite, -s tɒk'sɒfɪlaɪt [-fəl-], -s
Toxteth 'tɒkstəθ [-təθ]
toy (*s. v.*), **-s, -ing, -ed** tɔɪ, -z, -ɪŋ, -d
Toye tɔɪ
toyes, -es tɔɪz, -ɪz
Toynbee 'tɔɪnbɪ
Toyota tɔɪ'jəʊtə [tɔ:'j-]
toy-shop, -s 'tɔɪʃɒp, -s
Tozer 'təʊzə*

trac|e (*s. v.*), **-es, -ing, -ed, -er/s** treɪs, -ɪz, -ɪŋ, -t, -ə*/z
traceab|le, -ly, -leness 'treɪsəb|l, -lɪ, -lnɪs [-nəs]
tracer-bullet, -s 'treɪsə͵bʊlɪt, -s
tracer-element, -s 'treɪsər͵elɪmənt [-sə͵el-, -͵eləm-], -s
tracer|y, -ies 'treɪsər|ɪ, -ɪz
trachea, -s, -l, -n trə'ki:ə [-'kɪə], -z, -l, -n
tracheae (*alternative plur. of* **trachea**) trə'ki:i: [-'ki:aɪ]
tracheotomy ͵trækɪ'ɒtəmɪ
trachoma trə'kəʊmə [træ'k-]
tracing (*s.*), **-s** 'treɪsɪŋ, -z
tracing-paper 'treɪsɪŋ͵peɪpə*
track (*s. v.*), **-s, -ing, -ed, -er/s** træk, -s, -ɪŋ, -t, -ə*/z
trackless, -ly, -ness 'træklɪs [-ləs], -lɪ, -nɪs [-nəs]
tract, -s trækt, -s
tractability ͵træktə'bɪlətɪ [-ɪtɪ-]
tractab|le, -ly, -leness 'træktəb|l, -lɪ, -lnɪs [-nəs]
tractarian, -s, -ism træk'teərɪən, -z, -ɪzəm
tractate, -s 'trækteɪt, -s
tractile 'træktaɪl
traction 'trækʃn
traction-engine, -s 'trækʃn͵endʒɪn, -z
tractor, -s 'træktə*, -z
Tracy 'treɪsɪ
trad|e (*s. v.*), **-es, -ing, -ed, -er/s** treɪd, -z, -ɪŋ, -ɪd, -ə*/z
trade-mark, -s 'treɪdmɑ:k, -s
trade-name, -s 'treɪdneɪm, -z
tradesfolk 'treɪdzfəʊk
trades|man, -men 'treɪdz|mən, -mən
tradespeople 'treɪdz͵pi:pl
trade(s)-union, -s ͵treɪd(z)'ju:njən [-nɪən], -z
trade-wind, -s 'treɪdwɪnd, -z
tradition, -s trə'dɪʃn, -z
tradi|tional, -tionally trə'dɪʃ|ənl [-ʃnəl, -ʃn̩l, -ʃnl, -ʃənəl], -ʃnəlɪ [-ʃnəlɪ, -ʃn̩lɪ, -ʃn̩lɪ, -ʃənəlɪ]
traditionalism trə'dɪʃnəlɪzəm [-ʃn̩l-, -ʃn̩l-, -ʃənəl-]
traduc|e, -es, -ing, -ed, -er/s, -ement trə'dju:s, -ɪz, -ɪŋ, -t, -ə*/z, -mənt
Trafalgar (*in Spain*) trə'fælgə* [*archaic and poetical* ͵træfl'gɑ:*], (*Square*) trə'fælgə*, (*Viscount*) trə'fælgə* [͵træfl'gɑ:*], (*House near Salisbury*) ͵træfl'gɑ:*
Note.—The present Lord Nelson pronounces the family name as trə'fælgə*. *Previous holders of the title pronounced* ͵træfl'gɑ:*.

traffic (*s. v.*), **-s, -king, -ked, -ker/s**
'træfık, -s, -ıŋ, -t, -ə*/z
trafficator, -s 'træfıkertə*, -z
traffic-jam, -s 'træfıkdʒæm, -z
traffic-warden, -s 'træfık,wɔːdn, -z
tragacanth 'trægəkænθ
tragedian, -s trə'dʒiːdjən [-dıən], -z
traged|y, -ies 'trædʒıd|ı [-dʒəd|ı], -ız
Trager 'treıgə*
tragic, -al, -ally, -alness 'trædʒık, -l,
-əlı, -lnıs [-nəs]
tragi-comed|y, -ies ,trædʒı'kɒmıd|ı
[-məd|ı], -ız
tragi-comic, -al, -ally ,trædʒı'kɒmık, -l,
-əlı
tragus, -es 'treıgəs, -ız
Traherne trə'hɜːn
trail (*s. v.*), **-s, -ing, -ed, -er/s** treıl, -z,
-ıŋ, -d, -ə*/z
train (*s. v.*), **-s, -ing/s, -ed, -er/s** treın,
-z, -ıŋ/z, -d, -ə*/z
train-band, -s 'treınbænd, -z
train-bearer, -s 'treın,beərə*, -z
trainee, -s treı'niː, -z
train-ferr|y, -ies 'treın,fer|ı, -ız
training-ship, -s 'treınıŋʃıp, -s
train-oil 'treınɔıl
train-sick 'treınsık
traips|e, -es, -ing, -ed treıps, -ız, -ıŋ, -t
trait, -s treı, -z [treıt, -s]
traitor, -s 'treıtə*, -z
traitorous, -ly, -ness 'treıtərəs, -lı, -nıs
[-nəs]
traitress, -es 'treıtrıs [-trəs, -tres], -ız
Trajan 'treıdʒən
trajector|y, -ies 'trædʒıktər|ı [-dʒək-,
trə'dʒektər|ı], -ız
Tralee trə'liː
tram, -s træm, -z
tramcar, -s 'træmkɑː*, -z
tram-line, -s 'træmlaın, -z
tramm|el (*s. v.*), **-els, -elling, -elled**
'træm|l, -lz, -əlıŋ [-lıŋ], -ld
tramp (*s. v.*), **-s, -ing, -ed, -er/s** træmp,
-s, -ıŋ, -t [træmt], -ə*/z
tramp|le, -les, -ling, -led, -ler/s
'træmp|l, -lz, -lıŋ [-lıŋ], -ld, -lə*/z
[-lə*/z]
trampolin(e), -s 'træmpəlın [-liːn], -z
tramway, -s 'træmweı, -z
trance, -s trɑːns, -ız
tranquil, -ly, -ness 'træŋkwıl, -ı, -nıs
[-nəs]
tranquillity træŋ'kwılətı [-ıtı]
tranquillization [-isa-] ,træŋkwılaı'zeıʃn
tranquilliz|e [-is|e], -es, -ing/ly, -ed,
-er/s 'træŋkwılaız, -ız, -ıŋ/lı, -d,
-ə*/z

transact, -s, -ing, -ed, -or/s træn'zækt
[trɑː-, trən-, -n'sækt], -s, -ıŋ, -ıd,
-ə*/z
transaction, -s træn'zækʃn [trɑː-,
trən- -n'sæk-], -z
transalpine ,trænz'ælpaın [,trɑː-]
transatlantic ,trænzət'læntık [,trɑː-,
-zə'tlæn-, -zæt'læn-, -zæ'tlæn-]
Transbaikalia ,trænzbaı'kɑːljə [,trɑː-,
-lıə]
Transcaspian ,trænz'kæspjən [,trɑː-,
-pıən]
transcend, -s, -ing, -ed træn'send
[trɑː-], -z, -ıŋ, -ıd
transcenden|ce, -cy, -t/ly træn'sendən|s
[trɑː-, -sı, -t/lı]
transcendent|al, -ally ,trænsen'dent|l
[,trɑː-, -sən-], -əlı [-lı]
transcendentali|sm, -st/s ,trænsen-
'dentəlı|zəm [,trɑː-, -sən-, -tļı-],
-st/s
transcontinental 'trænz,kɒntrı'nentl
['trɑː:nz-]
transcrib|e, -es, -ing, -ed, -er/s træn-
'skraıb [trɑː-], -z, -ıŋ, -d, -ə*/z
transcript, -s 'trænskrıpt ['trɑː-], -s
transcription, -s træn'skrıpʃn [trɑː-],
-z
transducer, -s trænz'djuːsə* [trɑː-,
-ns-], -z
transept, -s 'trænsept ['trɑː-], -s
transfer (*s.*), -s 'trænsfɜː* ['trɑː-], -z
transfer (*v.*), **-s, -ring, -red, -rer/s**
træns'fɜː* [trɑː-], -z, -rıŋ, -d, -rə*/z
transferability træns,fɜːrə'bılətı [trɑːns-,
,trænsfərə'b-, ,trɑː:nsfərə'b-, -lıt-]
transferable træns'fɜːrəbl [trɑːns'fɜːrə-,
'trænsfərə-, 'trɑːnsfərə-]
transferee, -s ,trænsfɜː'riː [,trɑː-], -z
transference, -s 'trænsfɜrəns ['trɑːns-
fər-, træns'fɜːr-, trɑːns'fɜːr-], -ız
transfiguration (T.), -s ,trænsfıgjʊ'reıʃn
[,trɑː:nsf-, træns,f-, trɑː:ns,f-, -gjʊə'r-,
-gjə'r-, -gə'r-], -z
transfigur|e, -es, -ing, -ed, -ement/s
træns'fıgə* [trɑː-], -z, -rıŋ, -d,
-mənt/s
transfix, -es, -ing, -ed træns'fıks
[trɑː-], -ız, -ıŋ, -t
transfixion, -s træns'fıkʃn [trɑː-], -z
transform, -s, -ing, -ed, -er/s; -able
træns'fɔːm [trɑː-], -z, -ıŋ, -d, -ə*/z;
-əbl
transformation, -s ,trænsfə'meıʃn
[,trɑː:n-, -fɔː'm-], -z
transfus|e, -es, -ing, -ed, -er/s træns-
'fjuːz [trɑː-], -ız, -ıŋ, -d, -ə*/z
transfusible træns'fjuːzəbl [trɑː-, -zıb-]

503

transfusion, -s træns'fju:ʒn [trɑ:n-],
-z

transgress, -es, -ing, -ed, -or/s træns-
'gres [trɑ:n-, -nz'g-], -ɪz, -ɪŋ, -t, -ə*/z

transgression, -s træns'greʃn [trɑ:n-,
-nz'g-], -z

transien|ce, -cy, -t/ly, -tness 'trænzɪən|s
['trɑ:n-, -nzjən-, -nʒɪən-, -nʒjən-,
-nsɪən-, -nsjən-, -nʃɪən-, -nʃjən-], -sɪ,
-t/lɪ, -tnɪs [-nəs]

transilient træn'sɪlɪənt [trɑ:n-, -ljənt]

transistor, -s, -ized [-ised] træn'sɪstə*
[trɑ:n-, -n'z-], -z, -raɪzd

transit, -s 'trænsɪt ['trɑ:nsɪt, 'trænzɪt,
'trɑ:nzɪt], -s

transition, -s træn'sɪʒn [trɑ:n-, trən-,
-n'zɪʃn], -z

tran|sitional, -sitionally træn|'sɪʒənl
[trɑ:n-, trən-, -'sɪʒnəl, -'sɪʒn̩l, -'sɪʒn̩l,
-'sɪʒənəl, -'zɪʃənl, -'zɪʃnəl, -'zɪʃn̩l,
-'zɪʃn̩l, -'zɪʃənəl], -'sɪʒəlɪ [-'sɪʒnəlɪ,
-'sɪʒn̩lɪ, -'sɪʒn̩lɪ, -'sɪʒənəlɪ, -'zɪʃn̩əlɪ,
-'zɪʃnəlɪ, -'zɪʃn̩lɪ, -'zɪʃn̩lɪ, -'zɪʃənəlɪ]

transitive, -ly, -ness 'trænsɪtɪv ['trɑ:n-,
-nzɪ-, -nsə-, -nzə-], -lɪ, -nɪs [-nəs]

transitor|y, -ily, -iness 'trænsɪtər|ɪ
['trɑ:n-, -nzɪ-, -sət-, -zət-], -əlɪ [-ɪlɪ],
-ɪnɪs [-məs]

Transjordan ,trænz'dʒɔːdn [,trɑ:n-]

Transjordania, -n/s ,trænzdʒɔː'demjə
[,trɑ:n-, -nɪə], -n/z

Transkei ,træns'kaɪ [,trɑ:ns-, ,trænz-,
,trɑ:nz-]

translat|e, -es, -ing, -ed, -or/s; -able
træns'leɪt [trɑ:ns-, trænz-, trɑ:nz-,
trəns-, trənz-], -s, -ɪŋ, -ɪd, -ə*/z; -əbl

translation, -s træns'leɪʃn [trɑ:ns-,
trænz-, trɑ:nz-, trəns-, trənz-], -z

transliterat|e, -es, -ing, -ed, -or/s
trænz'lɪtərert [trɑ:n-, -ns'l-], -s, -ɪŋ,
-ɪd, -ə*/z

transliteration, -s ,trænzlɪtə'reɪʃn
[,trɑ:n-, -nsl-, -,--'--], -z

translucen|ce, -cy, -t/ly trænz'lu:sn|s
[trɑ:n-, -ns'l-, -'lju:-], -sɪ, -t/lɪ

transmigrat|e, -es, -ing, -ed, -or/s
,trænzmaɪ'greɪt [,trɑ:n-, -nsm-, -'--],
-s, -ɪŋ, -ɪd, -ə*/z

transmigration, -s ,trænzmaɪ'greɪʃn
[,trɑ:n-, -nsm-], -z

transmissibility trænz,mɪsə'bɪlɪtɪ
[trɑ:n-, -ns,m-, -sɪ'b-, -lɪt-, ,--'--]

transmissible trænz'mɪsəbl [trɑ:n-,
-ns'm-, -sɪb-]

transmission, -s trænz'mɪʃn [trɑ:n-,
-ns'm-], -z

transmit, -s, -ting, -ted, -ter/s trænz-
'mɪt [trɑ:n-, -ns'm-], -s, -ɪŋ, -ɪd, -ə*/z

transmittal, -s trænz'mɪtl [trɑ:n-,
-ns'm-], -z

transmittance, -s trænz'mɪtəns [trɑ:n-,
-ns'm-], -ɪz

transmogrification ,trænzmɒgrɪfɪ'keɪʃn
[,trɑ:n-, -nsm-, -,---'--]

transmogri|fy, -fies, -fying, -fied trænz-
'mɒgrɪ|faɪ [trɑ:n-, -ns'm-], -faɪz,
-faɪɪŋ, -faɪd

transmutability trænz,mju:tə'bɪlɪtɪ
[trɑ:nz,m-, -ns,m-, -lɪt-, ,--'--]

transmutation, -s ,trænzmju:'teɪʃn
[,trɑ:n-, -nsm-, -mju't-], -z

transmut|e, -es, -ing, -ed, -er/s; -able
trænz'mju:t [trɑ:n-, -ns'm-], -s, -ɪŋ,
-ɪd, -ə*/z; -əbl

transoceanic 'trænz,əʊʃɪ'ænɪk [-,əʊsɪ-]

transom, -s 'trænsəm, -z

transparenc|y, -ies træns'pærəns|ɪ
[trɑ:n-, trən-, -nz'p-, -'peər-], -ɪz

transparent, -ly, -ness træns'pærənt
[trɑ:n-, trən-, -nz'p-, -'peər-], -lɪ, -nɪs
[-nəs]

transpir|e, -es, -ing, -ed træn'spaɪə*
[trɑ:n-], -z, -rɪŋ, -d

transplant, -s, -ing, -ed; -able træns-
'plɑ:nt [trɑ:n-], -s, -ɪŋ, -ɪd; -əbl

transplant (s.), -s 'trænsplɑ:nt ['trɑ:n-],
-s

transplantation, -s ,trænsplɑ:n'teɪʃn
[,trɑ:n-], -z

transpontine ,trænz'pɒntaɪn

transport (s.), -s 'trænspɔ:t ['trɑ:n-],
-s

transport (v.), -s, -ing, -ed; -able
træn'spɔ:t [trɑ:n-], -s, -ɪŋ, -ɪd; -əbl

transportability træn,spɔ:tə'bɪlɪtɪ
[trɑ:n-, -lɪt-, ,--'--]

transportation, -s ,trænspɔ:'teɪʃn
[,trɑ:n-], -z

transporter, -s træn'spɔ:tə* [trɑ:n-], -z

transpos|e, -es, -ing, -ed, -er/s; -able,
-al/s træns'pəʊz [trɑ:n-], -ɪz, -ɪŋ, -d,
-ə*/z; -əbl, -l/z

transposition, -s ,trænspə'zɪʃn [,trɑ:n-,
-pʊ'z-], -z

trans-ship, -s, -ping, -ped, -ment/s
træns'ʃɪp [trɑ:n-, -nʃ'ʃ-, -nz'ʃ-, -nʒ'ʃ-,
træn'ʃ-, trɑ:n'ʃ-], -s, -ɪŋ, -t, -mənt/s

Trans - Siberian ,trænzsaɪ'bɪərɪən
[,trɑ:n-]

transubstantiat|e, -es, -ing, -ed ,træn-
səb'stænʃɪert [,trɑ:n-, -bz't-, -ʃjert,
-sɪert], -s, -ɪŋ, -ɪd

transubstantiation, -s 'trænsəb,stæn-
ʃɪ'eɪʃn ['trɑ:n-, -bz,t-, -nsɪ-], -z

Transvaal 'trænzvɑ:l ['trɑ:n-, -nsv-,
,-'-]

504

Transvaaler, -s 'trænz,vɑ:lə* ['trɑ:n-, -nsv-, ,-'-'--], -z
transversal, -s trænz'vɜ:sl [trɑ:n-], -z
transverse 'trænzvɜ:s ['trɑ:n-, *also* ,-'-, *esp. when not attributive*]
transversely ,trænz'vɜ:slɪ [,trɑ:n-, '-,--]
transvesticism trænz'vestɪsɪzəm [trɑ:n-]
transvestite, -s trænz'vestaɪt [trɑ:n-], -s
Transylvania, -n ,trænsɪl'veɪnjə [,trɑ:n-, -nɪə], -n
tranter, -s 'træntə*, -z
trap (*s. v.*), **-s, -ping/s, -ped, -per/s** træp, -s, -ɪŋ/z, -t, -ə*/z
trap-door, -s ,træp'dɔ:* [-'dɔə*], -z
trapes (*v.*), **-es, -ing, -ed** treɪps, -ɪz, -ɪŋ, -t
trapeze, -s trə'pi:z, -ɪz
trapezium, -s trə'pi:zjəm [-zɪəm], -z
trapezoid, -s 'træpɪzɔɪd, -z
Trappist, -s 'træpɪst, -s
trapp|y, -iness 'træp|ɪ, -ɪnɪs [-məs]
Traprain trə'preɪn
trapse, *see* **traipse, trapes**
Traquair trə'kweə*
trash (*s. v.*), **-es, -ing, -ed** træʃ, -ɪz, -ɪŋ, -t
trash|y, -ier, -iest, -iness 'træʃ|ɪ, -ɪə*, -ɪɪst, -mɪs [-məs]
Trasimene 'træzɪmi:n
trauma, -s 'trɔ:mə ['traʊ-], -z
traumatic trɔ:'mætɪk [traʊ'm-]
trav|ail (*s. v.*), **-ails, -ailing, -ailed** 'træv|eɪl, -eɪlz, -eɪlɪŋ [-elɪŋ, -ɪlɪŋ], -eɪld
Travancore ,trævəŋ'kɔ:* [-'kɔə*]
trav|el (*s. v.*), **-els, -elling, -elled, -eller/s** 'træv|l, -lz, -lɪŋ [-lɪŋ], -ld, -lə*/z [-lə*/z]
travelator, -s 'trævəleɪtə*, -z
travelogue, -s 'trævəlɒg [-ləʊg], -z
Travers 'trævəz
travers|e (*s. adj. v.*), **-es, -ing, -ed** 'trævəs [trə'vɜ:s], -ɪz, -ɪŋ, -t
travest|y (*s. v.*), **-ies, -ying, -ied** 'trævɪst|ɪ [-vəs-], -ɪz, -ɪŋ, -ɪd
Traviata ,trævɪ'ɑ:tə
Travis 'trævɪs
trawl (*s. v.*), **-s, -ing, -ed** trɔ:l, -z, -ɪŋ, -d
trawler, -s 'trɔ:lə*, -z
tray, -s treɪ, -z
Traylee, -s treɪ'li:, -z
treacherous, -ly, -ness 'tretʃərəs, -lɪ, -nɪs [-nəs]
treacher|y, -ies 'tretʃər|ɪ, -ɪz
treacle, -s 'tri:kl, -z
treac|ly, -liness 'tri:k|lɪ [-lɪ], -lmɪs [-lnɪs, -məs]
tread (*s. v.*), **-s, -ing, trod, trodden, treader/s** tred, -z, -ɪŋ, trɒd, 'trɒdn, 'tredə*/z

treadle, -s 'tredl, -z
treadmill, -s 'tredmɪl, -z
Treanor 'tremə*
treason, -s 'tri:zn, -z
treasonab|le, -ly, -leness 'tri:zŋəb|l [-znə-, -zənə-], -lɪ, -lnɪs [-nəs]
treasonous 'tri:zŋəs [-znəs, -zənəs]
treas|ure (*s. v.*), **-ures, -uring, -ured** 'treʒ|ə*, -əz, -ərɪŋ, -əd
treasure-hou|se, -ses 'treʒəhaʊ|s, -zɪz
treasurer, -s 'treʒərə*, -z
treasurership, -s 'treʒərəʃɪp, -s
treasure-trove 'treʒətrəʊv
treasur|y, -ies 'treʒər|ɪ, -ɪz
treat (*s. v.*), **-s, -ing, -ed, -ment/s** tri:t, -s, -ɪŋ, -ɪd, -mənt/s
treatise, -s 'tri:tɪz [-tɪs], -ɪz
treat|y, -ies 'tri:t|ɪ, -ɪz
Trebarwith trɪ'bɑ:wɪθ [trə'b-]
Trebizond 'trebɪzɒnd
treb|le (*s. adj. v.*), **-les, -ly; -ling, -led** 'treb|l, -lz, -lɪ, -lɪŋ [-lɪŋ], -ld
Tredegar trɪ'di:gə* [trə'd-] (*Welsh* tre'degar)
Tredennick trɪ'denɪk [trə'd-]
tree (*s. v.*) (**T.**), **-s, -ing, -d** tri:, -z, -ɪŋ, -d
tree-creeper, -s 'tri:,kri:pə*, -z
tree-fern, -s 'tri:fɜ:n, -z
treeless 'tri:lɪs [-ləs]
trefoil, -s 'trefɔɪl ['tri:f-, trɪ'f-], -z
Trefor 'trevə* (*Welsh* 'trevor)
Trefriw 'trevrɪu: (*Welsh* 'trevriu)
Trefusis trɪ'fju:sɪs [trə'f-]
Tregaskis trɪ'gæskɪs [trə'g-]
Tregear (*surname, place in Cornwall*) trɪ'gɪə* [trə'g-]
Tregoning trɪ'gɒnɪŋ [trə'g-]
Treherne trɪ'hɜ:n [trə'h-]
trek (*s. v.*), **-s, -king, -ked, -ker/s** trek, -s, -ɪŋ, -t, -ə*/z
Trelawn(e)y trɪ'lɔ:nɪ [trə'l-]
Treleaven trɪ'levən [trə'l-]
trellis, -es, -ed 'trelɪs, -ɪz, -t
trellis-work 'trelɪswɜ:k
Treloar trɪ'ləʊə* [trə'l-], -'lɔə*
Tremadoc trɪ'mædək [trə'm-]
Tremayne trɪ'meɪn [trə'm-]
Trembath trem'bɑ:θ, 'trembɑ:θ
tremb|le, -les, -ling/ly, -led, -ler/s 'tremb|l, -lz, -lɪŋ/lɪ, -ld, -lə*/z
trembly 'trembler
tremendous, -ly, -ness trɪ'mendəs [trə'm-], -lɪ, -nɪs [-nəs]
Tremills 'tremlz
tremolo, -s 'tremələʊ, -z
Tremont trɪ'mɒnt [trə'm-]
tremor, -s 'tremə*, -z
Tremoutha trɪ'maʊðə [trə'm-]

505

tremulant, -s 'tremjʊlənt [-mjə-], -s
tremulous, -ly, -ness 'tremjʊləs [-mjə-],
-lɪ, -nɪs [-nəs]
trench (s. v.) (T.), -es, -ing, -ed, -er/s
trentʃ, -ɪz, -ɪŋ, -t, -ə*/z
trenchan|cy, -t/ly 'trentʃən|sɪ, -t/lɪ
Trenchard 'trentʃɑːd [-tʃəd]
trencher, -s 'trentʃə*, -z
trend (s. v.), -s, -ing, -ed trend, -z, -ɪŋ,
-ɪd
trend|y, -ies 'trend|ɪ, -ɪz
Trent trent
Trentham 'trentəm
trepan (s. v.), -s, -ning, -ned trɪ'pæn
[trə'p-], -z, -ɪŋ, -d
trephin|e (s. v.), -es, -ing, -ed trɪ'fiːn
[tre'f-, trə'f-, -'fam], -z, -ɪŋ, -d
trepidation ˌtrepɪ'deɪʃn
Treshinish trɪ'ʃɪnɪʃ [trə'ʃ-]
Tresilian trɪ'sɪlɪən [trə's-, -ljən]
Tresmeer 'trez.mɪə*
trespass (s. v.), -es, -ing, -ed, -er/s
'trespəs, -ɪz, -ɪŋ, -t, -ə*/z
tress, -es, -ed; -y tres, -ɪz, -t; -ɪ
trestle, -s 'tresl, -z
Trethewy trɪ'θjuːɪ [trə'θ-, -'θjʊɪ]
Trethowan trɪ'θəʊən [trə'θ-, -'θaʊən],
-'θəːən
Trevaldwyn trɪ'vɔːldwɪn [trə'v-]
Trevaskis trɪ'væskɪs [trə'v-]
Trevelga trɪ'velgə [trə'v-]
Trevelyan trɪ'vɪljən [trə'v-], -'veljən
Treves triːvz
Trevethick trɪ'veθɪk [trə'v-]
Trevigue trɪ'viːg [trə'v-]
Trevisa (John of) trɪ'viːsə [trə'v-]
Trevithick 'trevɪθɪk
Trevor 'trevə* (Welsh 'trevor)
Trew truː
Trewavas trɪ'wɒvəs [trə'w-]
Trewin trɪ'wɪn [trə'w-]
trews truːz
trey, -s treɪ, -z
triable 'traɪəbl
triad, -s 'traɪəd ['traɪæd], -z
trial, -s 'traɪəl, -z
trialogue, -s 'traɪəlɒg, -z
triangle, -s, -d 'traɪæŋgl, -z, -d
triangular, -ly traɪ'æŋgjʊlə* [trɪ-,
-gjəl-], -lɪ
triangularity traɪˌæŋgjʊ'lærətɪ [trɪ-,
ˌtraɪæŋ-, -gjə'l-, -ɪtɪ]
triangulat|e, -es, -ing, -ed traɪ'æŋg-
jʊleɪt [trɪ-, -gjəl-], -s, -ɪŋ, -ɪd
triangulation traɪˌæŋgjʊ'leɪʃn [trɪ-,
ˌtraɪæŋ-, -gjə'l-]
Triangulum traɪ'æŋgjʊləm [-gjəl-]
triassic traɪ'æsɪk

trib|al, -ally, -alism 'traɪb|l, -əlɪ, -əlɪzəm
[-lɪzəm]
tribe, -s traɪb, -z
tribes|man, -men 'traɪbz|mən, -mən
[-men]
tribrach, -s 'trɪbræk, -s
tribrachic trɪ'brækɪk
tribulation, -s ˌtrɪbjʊ'leɪʃn, -z
tribunal, -s traɪ'bjuːnl [trɪ'b-], -z
tribunate, -s 'trɪbjʊnɪt [-neɪt, -nət], -s
tribune, -s 'trɪbjuːn, -z
tributar|y (s. adj.), -ies 'trɪbjʊtər|ɪ, -ɪz
tribute, -s 'trɪbjuːt, -s
tricar, -s 'traɪkɑː*, -z
trice traɪs
tricel 'traɪsel
triceps, -es 'traɪseps, -ɪz
trichin|a, -ae, -as trɪ'kaɪn|ə, -iː, -əz
Trichinopoli [-ly] ˌtrɪtʃɪ'nɒpəlɪ
trichinosis ˌtrɪkɪ'nəʊsɪs [-kə'n-]
trichord (s. adj.), -s 'traɪkɔːd, -z
trichosis trɪ'kəʊsɪs
trichotomy trɪ'kɒtəmɪ
trick (s. v.), -s, -ing, -ed, -er/s trɪk, -s,
-ɪŋ, -t, -ə*/z
tricker|y, -ies 'trɪkər|ɪ, -ɪz
trickish, -ly, -ness 'trɪkɪʃ, -lɪ, -nɪs [-nəs]
trick|le (s. v.), -les, -ling, -led 'trɪk|l, -lz,
-lɪŋ [-lɪŋ], -ld
trickle-charger, -s 'trɪkl.tʃɑːdʒə*, -z
trickly 'trɪklɪ [-klɪ]
trickster, -s 'trɪkstə*, -z
trick|y, -ier, -iest, -ily, -iness 'trɪk|ɪ,
-ɪə*, -ɪɪst, -ɪlɪ [-əlɪ], -ɪnɪs [-məs]
tricolo(u)r, -s 'trɪkələ* ['traɪ.kʌlə*], -z
tricoloured 'traɪ.kʌləd
tricot, -s 'triːkəʊ ['trɪk-] (triko), -z
tricyc|le (s. v.), -les, -ling, -led 'traɪsɪk|l
[-səkl], -lz, -lɪŋ, -ld
trident, -s 'traɪdnt, -s
Tridentine trɪ'dentaɪn [traɪ-, -tiːn]
tried (from try) traɪd
triennial, -ly traɪ'enjəl [-nɪəl], -ɪ
trier, -s 'traɪə*, -z
trierarch, -s; -y, -ies 'traɪərɑːk, -s; -ɪ,
-ɪz
tries (from try) traɪz
Trieste triː'est [trɪ'e-, -'estɪ] (trɪ'ɛste)
trifid 'traɪfɪd
trif|le (s. v.), -les, -ling, -led, -ler/s
'traɪf|l, -lz, -lɪŋ [-lɪŋ], -ld, -lə*/z
[-lə*/z]
trifling (adj.), -ly, -ness 'traɪflɪŋ, -lɪ, -nɪs
[-nəs]
trifolium, -s traɪ'fəʊljəm [-lɪəm], -z
trifori|um, -a, -ums traɪ'fɔːrɪ|əm, -ə,
-əmz
trig (s. v.), -s, -ging, -ged trɪg, -z, -ɪŋ, -d

trigam|ist/s, -ous, -y 'trɪgəm|ɪst/s, -əs, -ɪ

trigger, -s 'trɪgə*, -z

triglyph, -s 'traɪglɪf ['trɪg-], -s

trigon, -s 'traɪgən, -z

trigonometric, -al, -ally ˌtrɪgənə'metrɪk [-nəʊ'm-], -l, -əlɪ

trigonometr|y, -ies ˌtrɪgə'nɒmɪtr|ɪ [-mət-], -ɪz

trigraph, -s 'traɪgrɑːf [-græf], -s

trilater|al, -ally, -alness ˌtraɪ'lætər|əl, -əlɪ, -əlnɪs [-nəs]

trilb|y (T.), -ies 'trɪlb|ɪ, -ɪz

trilingual ˌtraɪ'lɪŋgwəl

triliteral ˌtraɪ'lɪtərəl

trill (s. v.), -s, -ing, -ed trɪl, -z, -ɪŋ, -d

trillion, -s, -th/s 'trɪljən, -z, -θ/s

trilobite, -s 'traɪləʊbaɪt, -s

trilog|y, -ies 'trɪlədʒ|ɪ, -ɪz

trim (s. adj. v.) (T.), -mer, -mest, -ly, -ness; -s, -ming/s, -med, -mer/s trɪm, -ə*, -ɪst, -lɪ, -nɪs [-nəs]; -z, -ɪŋ/z, -d, -ə*/z

trimaran, -s 'traɪməræn [ˌ—'-], -z

Trimble 'trɪmbl

trimeter, -s 'trɪmɪtə [-mətə*], -z

Trincomalee ˌtrɪŋkəʊmə'liː

Trinculo 'trɪŋkjʊləʊ

Trinder 'trɪndə*

trine (T.) traɪn

Tring trɪŋ

tringle, -s 'trɪŋgl, -z

Trinidad 'trɪnɪdæd [ˌ—'-]

Trinidadian, -s ˌtrɪnɪ'dædɪən [-'deɪ-, -djən], -z

trinitarian (T.), -s, -ism ˌtrɪnɪ'teərɪən, -z, -ɪzəm

trinitrotoluene traɪˌnaɪtrəʊ'tɒljuːiːn ['traɪˌnaɪ-]

trinit|y (T.), -ies 'trɪnɪt|ɪ [-ət|ɪ], -ɪz

trinket, -s 'trɪŋkɪt, -s

trinomial traɪ'nəʊmjəl [-mɪəl]

trio, -s 'triːəʊ ['trɪəʊ], -z

triode, -s 'traɪəʊd, -z

triolet, -s 'triːəʊlet ['trɪəʊ-, 'traɪəʊ-, -lɪt, -lət], -s

trip (s. v.), -s, -ping/ly, -ped, -per/s trɪp, -s, -ɪŋ/lɪ, -t, -ə*/z

tripartite, -ly ˌtraɪ'pɑːtaɪt ['-ˌ—], -lɪ

tripe, -s traɪp, -s

triphibious traɪ'fɪbɪəs [-bjəs]

triphthong, -s 'trɪfθɒŋ [-ɪpθ-], -z

triphthongal trɪf'θɒŋgl [-ɪp'θ-]

triplane, -s 'traɪpleɪn, -z

trip|le (adj. v.), -ly; -les, -ling, -led 'trɪp|l, -lɪ; -lz, -lɪŋ [-lɪŋ], -ld

triplet, -s 'trɪplɪt [-lət], -s

triplex 'trɪpleks

triplicate (adj.) 'trɪplɪkət [-kɪt]

triplicat|e (v.), -es, -ing, -ed 'trɪplɪkeɪt, -s, -ɪŋ, -ɪd

tripod, -s 'traɪpɒd, -z

tripoli (T.) 'trɪpəlɪ [-pʊl-]

Tripolis 'trɪpəlɪs [-pʊl-]

Tripolitania ˌtrɪpɒlɪ'teɪnjə [-ˌ—'—-, -pəl-, -nɪə]

tripos, -es 'traɪpɒs, -ɪz

triptych, -s 'trɪptɪk, -s

trireme, -s 'traɪriːm ['traɪər-], -z

Trisagion trɪ'sægɪɒn [-gɪən]

trisect, -s, -ing, -ed, -or/s traɪ'sekt, -s, -ɪŋ, -ɪd, -ə*/z

trisection, -s traɪ'sekʃn, -z

Tristan (personal name) 'trɪstən [-tæn]

Tristan da Cunha ˌtrɪstəndə'kuːnə [-njə]

Tristram 'trɪstrəm [-ræm]

trisyllabic, -al, -ally ˌtraɪsɪ'læbɪk [ˌtrɪsɪ-], -l, -əlɪ

trisyllable, -s ˌtraɪ'sɪləbl [ˌtrɪ's-, '-ˌ—], -z

trite, -r, -st, -ly, -ness traɪt, -ə*, -ɪst, -lɪ, -nɪs [-nəs]

tritium 'trɪtɪəm [-tjəm]

Triton, -s 'traɪtn, -z

tritone, -s 'traɪtəʊn, -z

Tritonia traɪ'təʊnjə [-nɪə]

triumph (s. v.), -s, -ing, -ed, -er/s 'traɪəmf [-ʌmf], -s, -ɪŋ, -t, -ə*/z

triumphal traɪ'ʌmfl

triumphant, -ly traɪ'ʌmfənt, -lɪ

triumvir, -s trɪ'ʌmvə* [trɪ'ʊm-, traɪ'ʌm-, 'traɪəm-, -vɜː*], -z

triumvirate, -s traɪ'ʌmvɪrət [-vər-, -ɪt], -s

triumviri (alternative plur. of triumvir) trɪ'ʊmvɪraɪ: [traɪ'ʌmvɪraɪ, -vər-]

triune 'traɪjuːn

trivet, -s 'trɪvɪt, -s

trivia 'trɪvɪə [-vjə]

trivial, -ly, -ness 'trɪvɪəl [-vjəl], -ɪ, -nɪs [-nəs]

trivialit|y, -ies ˌtrɪvɪ'ælət|ɪ [-ɪt|ɪ], -ɪz

trivializ|e [-is|e], -es, -ing, -ed 'trɪvɪəlaɪz [-vjəl-], -ɪz, -ɪŋ, -d

trivium 'trɪvɪəm

Trixie 'trɪksɪ

trizonal ˌtraɪ'zəʊnl [-nəl]

Trizone 'traɪzəʊn

Troa|d, -s 'trəʊæ|d, -z

Trocadero ˌtrɒkə'dɪərəʊ

trochaic trəʊ'keɪɪk [trɒ-]

troche (lozenge), -s trəʊʃ, -ɪz [rarely trəʊk, -s, 'trəʊkɪ, -z]

trochee, -s 'trəʊkiː [-kɪ], -z

trod, -den (from tread) trɒd, -n

troglodyte, -s 'trɒglədaɪt [-ləʊd-], -s

507

troika, -s 'trɔɪkə, -z
Troilus 'trəʊɪləs ['trɔɪl-]
Trojan, -s 'trəʊdʒən, -z
troll (s.), -s trəʊl [trɒl], -z
troll (v.), -s, -ing, -ed trəʊl, -z, -ɪŋ, -d
trolley, -s 'trɒlɪ, -z
trolley-bus, -es 'trɒlɪbʌs, -ɪz
trollop, -s 'trɒləp, -s
Trollope 'trɒləp
tromba, -s 'trɒmbə, -z
trombone, -s trɒm'bəʊn, -z
trombonist, -s trɒm'bəʊnɪst, -s
Trondheim 'trɒnhaɪm [-ndh-]
Trondhjem (old name of Trondheim)
   'trɒnjəm
troop (s. v.), -s, -ing, -ed tru:p, -s, -ɪŋ, -t
troop-carrier, -s 'tru:p͵kærɪə*, -z
trooper, -s 'tru:pə*, -z
troop-ship, -s 'tru:pʃɪp, -s
troop-train, -s 'tru:ptreɪn, -z
trope, -s trəʊp, -s
trophic 'trɒfɪk
trophy, -ies 'trəʊfɪ, -ɪz
tropic, -s, -al, -ally 'trɒpɪk, -s, -l, -əlɪ
troppo 'trɒpəʊ [trɒppo]
Trossachs 'trɒsəks [-sæks, -səxs]
trot (s. v.), -s, -ting, -ted, -ter/s trɒt, -s,
   -ɪŋ, -ɪd, -ə*/z
troth trəʊθ [trɒθ]
Trott, -er trɒt, -ə*
Trottiscliffe (Kent) 'trɒslɪ
trottoir, -s 'trɒtwɑ:* (trɔtwa:r), -z
troubadour, -s 'tru:bə͵dʊə* [-dɔə*,
   -dɔ:*], -z
troub|le (s. v.), -les, -ling, -led, -ler/s
   'trʌb|l, -lz, -lɪŋ [-lɪŋ], -ld, -lə*/z
   [-lə*/z]
troublesome, -ly, -ness 'trʌblsəm, -lɪ,
   -nɪs [-nəs]
troublous 'trʌbləs
Troubridge 'tru:brɪdʒ
trough, -s trɒf [old-fashioned trɔ:f, and
   in compounds], -s
   Note.—Some bakers pronounce trəʊ,
   -z.
Troughton 'trəʊtn
trounc|e, -es, -ing/s, -ed traʊns, -ɪz,
   -ɪŋ/z, -t
Troup tru:p
troupe, -s tru:p, -s
Trousdell 'tru:zdel [-dəl, -dl]
trousering, -s 'traʊzərɪŋ, -z
trousers 'traʊzəz
trousse, -s tru:s, -ɪz
trousseau, -s 'tru:səʊ, -z
trout traʊt
trout|let/s, -ling/s 'traʊt|lɪt/s [-lət/s],
   -lɪŋ/z

Trouton 'traʊtn
trove trəʊv
trover 'trəʊvə*
trow trəʊ [traʊ]
Trowbridge (in Wiltshire) 'trəʊbrɪdʒ
trow|el (s. v.), -els, -elling, -elled
   'traʊ|əl [-el], -əlz [-elz], -əlɪŋ [-elɪŋ],
   -əld [-eld]
Trowell 'trəʊəl, 'traʊəl
trowsers 'traʊzəz
troy (T.) trɔɪ
truancy 'tru:ənsɪ ['trʊənsɪ]
truant, -s 'tru:ənt [trʊənt], -s
trubeniz|e [-is|e], -es, -ing, -ed 'tru:-
   bənaɪz [-bɪn-], -ɪz, -ɪŋ, -d
Trübner 'tru:bnə* ('try:bnər)
truce, -s tru:s, -ɪz
trucial 'tru:sjəl [-sɪəl]
truck (s. v.), -s, -ing, -ed; -age trʌk, -s,
   -ɪŋ, -t; -ɪdʒ
truck|le, -les, -ling, -led 'trʌk|l, -lz, -lɪŋ
   [-lɪŋ], -ld
truckler, -s 'trʌklə*, -z
truculen|ce, -cy, -t/ly 'trʌkjʊlən|s
   [-kjəl-], -sɪ, -t/lɪ
trudg|e (s. v.), -es, -ing, -ed trʌdʒ, -ɪz,
   -ɪŋ, -d
trudg|en (s. v.) (T.), -ens, -ening, -ened
   'trʌdʒ|ən, -ənz, -ənɪŋ [-ŋɪŋ], -ənd
Trudgian 'trʌdʒɪən [-dʒən]
Trudy 'tru:dɪ
tr|ue (T.), -uer, -uest, -uly, -ueness
   tr|u:, -u:ə* [-ʊə*], -u:ɪst [-ʊɪst],
   'tru:lɪ, 'tru:nɪs [-nəs]
Truefitt 'tru:fɪt
true-hearted ͵tru:'hɑ:tɪd ['-͵--]
truffle, -s, -d 'trʌfl, -z, -d
trug, -s trʌg, -z
truism, -s 'tru:ɪzəm ['trʊɪ-], -z
truly 'tru:lɪ
Tru(e)man 'tru:mən
trump (s. v.), -s, -ing, -ed trʌmp, -s, -ɪŋ,
   -t [trʌmt]
trump-card, -s ͵trʌmp'kɑ:d [in contrast
   '-͵-], -z
Trumper 'trʌmpə*
trumpery 'trʌmpərɪ
trumpet (s. v.), -s, -ing/s, -ed, -er/s
   'trʌmpɪt, -s, -ɪŋ/z, -ɪd, -ə*/z
trumpet-call, -s 'trʌmpɪtkɔ:l, -z
trumpet-shaped 'trʌmpɪt-ʃeɪpt
truncat|e, -es, -ing, -ed trʌŋ'keɪt
   ['trʌŋk-], -s, -ɪŋ, -ɪd
truncation, -s trʌŋ'keɪʃn, -z
truncheon, -s, -ed 'trʌntʃən, -z, -d
trund|le (s. v.), -les, -ling, -led 'trʌnd|l,
   -lz, -lɪŋ [-lɪŋ], -ld
trunk, -s; -ful/s trʌŋk, -s; -fʊl/z

trunk-hose ˌtrʌŋkˈhəʊz
trunk-line, -s ˈtrʌŋklaɪn, -z
trunnion, -s, -ed ˈtrʌnjən [-nɪən], -z, -d
Truro ˈtrʊərəʊ
Truscott ˈtrʌskət
Truslove ˈtrʌslʌv
truss (s. v.), -es, -ing, -ed trʌs, -ɪz, -ɪŋ, -t
trust (s. v.), -s, -ing/ly, -ed, -er/s trʌst, -s, -ɪŋ/lɪ, -ɪd, -ə*/z
trustee, -s ˌtrʌsˈtiː, -z
trusteeship, -s ˌtrʌsˈtiːʃɪp, -s
trust|ful, -fully, -fulness ˈtrʌst|fʊl, -fʊlɪ [-fəlɪ], -fʊlnɪs [-nəs]
trustworth|y, -iness ˈtrʌst,wɜːð|ɪ, -ɪnɪs [-məs]
trust|y, -ier, -iest, -ily, -iness ˈtrʌst|ɪ, -ɪə* [-jə*], -ɪɪst [-jɪst], -ɪlɪ [-əlɪ], -ɪnɪs [-məs]
tru|th, -ths truː|θ, -ðz [-θs]
truth|ful, -fully, -fulness ˈtruːθfʊl, -fʊlɪ [-fəlɪ], -fʊlnɪs [-nəs]
tr|y (s. v.), -ies, -ying, -ied, -ier/s tr|aɪ, -aɪz, -aɪɪŋ, -aɪd, -aɪə*/z
Tryon ˈtraɪən
try-on, -s ˈtraɪɒn, -z
try-out, -s ˈtraɪaʊt, -s
trypanosome, -s ˈtrɪpənəsəʊm, -z
trypanosomiasis ˌtrɪpənəʊsəʊˈmaɪəsɪs
tryst (s. v.), -s, -ing, -ed trɪst [traɪst], -s, -ɪŋ, -ɪd
Trystan ˈtrɪstæn [-tən]
Tsar, -s zɑː* [tsɑː*], -z
Tsarevitch, -es ˈzɑːrəvɪtʃ [ˈtsɑː-, -rɪv-], -ɪz
Tsarina, -s zɑːˈriːnə [tsɑː-], -z
tsarist, -s ˈzɑːrɪst [ˈtsɑː-], -s
tsetse ˈtsetsɪ [ˈtetsɪ]
T-square, -s ˈtiːskweə*, -z
T.T. ˌtiːˈtiː [ˈ--, esp. when attributive]
tub (s. v.), -s, -bing, -bed tʌb, -z, -ɪŋ, -d
tuba, -s ˈtjuːbə, -z
Tubal ˈtjuːbəl [rarely -bæl]
tubb|y, -ier, -iest, -iness ˈtʌb|ɪ, -ɪə*, -ɪɪst, -ɪnɪs [-məs]
tube, -s tjuːb, -z
tubeless ˈtjuːblɪs [-ləs]
tuber, -s ˈtjuːbə*, -z
tubercle, -s ˈtjuːbəkl [-bəːkl], -z
tubercular tjuːˈbɜːkjʊlə* [tjʊˈb-, -kjəl-]
tuberculariz|e [-is|e], -es, -ing, -ed tjuːˈbɜːkjʊləraɪz [tjʊˈb-, -kjəl-], -ɪz, -ɪŋ, -d
tuberculization [-isa-] tjuːˌbɜːkjʊlaɪˈzeɪʃn [tjʊˌb-, -kjəl-, -lɪˈz-]
tuberculiz|e [-is|e], -es, -ing, -ed tjuːˈbɜːkjʊlaɪz [tjʊˈb-, -kjəl-], -ɪz, -ɪŋ, -d

tuberculosis tjuːˌbɜːkjuˈləʊsɪs [tjʊˌb-, -kjəˈl-]
tuberculous tjuːˈbɜːkjʊləs [tjʊˈb-, -kjəl-]
tuberose (s.) ˈtjuːbərəʊz
tuberose (adj.) ˈtjuːbərəʊs
tuberous ˈtjuːbərəs
tubful, -s ˈtʌbfʊl, -z
tubiform ˈtjuːbɪfɔːm
tubing, -s ˈtjuːbɪŋ, -z
tubular ˈtjuːbjʊlə* [-bjəl-]
tubule, -s ˈtjuːbjuːl, -z
tuck (s. v.) (T.), -s, -ing, -ed tʌk, -s, -ɪŋ, -t
tucker (T.), -s ˈtʌkə*, -z
tuck-shop, -s ˈtʌkʃɒp, -s
Tucson (in U.S.A.) tuːˈsɒn [ˈtuːsɒn]
Tudor, -s ˈtjuːdə*, -z
Tuesday, -s ˈtjuːzdɪ [-deɪ], -z
tufa ˈtjuːfə
Tufnell ˈtʌfnl [-nəl]
tuft (s. v.), -s, -ing, -ed tʌft, -s, -ɪŋ, -ɪd
tuft|y, -ier, -iest, -iness ˈtʌft|ɪ, -ɪə* [-jə*], -ɪɪst [-jɪst], -ɪnɪs [-məs]
tug (s. v.), -s, -ging, -ged, -ger/s tʌg, -z, -ɪŋ, -d, -ə*/z
tug-of-war, -s ˌtʌgəvˈwɔː*, -z
tugs-of-war (alternative plur. of tug-of-war) ˌtʌgzəvˈwɔː*
Tuileries ˈtwiːlərɪ [-rɪ] (tɥilri)
tuition, -s tjuːˈɪʃn [tjʊˈɪ-], -z
tuitionary tjuːˈɪʃnərɪ [tjʊˈɪ-, -ʃnərɪ, -ʃɲɪ, -ʃənərɪ]
Tuke tjuːk
tulip, -s ˈtjuːlɪp, -s
tulle, -s tjuːl (tyl), -z
Tullibardine ˌtʌlɪˈbɑːdɪn
Tullichewan ˌtʌlɪˈkjuːən [-ɪˈxj-, -juːən]
Tulloch ˈtʌlək [-əx]
Tulloh ˈtʌləʊ
Tulse tʌls
tumb|le (s. v.), -les, -ling, -led ˈtʌmb|l, -lz, -lɪŋ, -ld
tumble-down (adj.) ˈtʌmbldaʊn
tumbler, -s; -ful/s ˈtʌmblə*, -z; -fʊl/z
tumbl|y, -iness ˈtʌmbl|ɪ, -ɪnɪs [-məs]
tumbrel, -s ˈtʌmbrəl, -z
tumbril, -s ˈtʌmbrɪl, -z
tumefaction ˌtjuːmɪˈfækʃn
tume|fy, -fies, -fying, -fied ˈtjuːmɪ|faɪ, -faɪz, -faɪɪŋ, -faɪd
tumescen|ce, -t tjuːˈmesn|s [tjʊˈm-], -t
tumid, -ly, -ness ˈtjuːmɪd, -lɪ, -nɪs [-nəs]
tumidity tjuːˈmɪdɪtɪ [tjʊˈm-, -ɪtɪ]
tumm|y, -ies ˈtʌm|ɪ, -ɪz
tumour, -s ˈtjuːmə*, -z
tum-tum, -s ˈtʌmtʌm, -z
tumular, -y ˈtjuːmjʊlə*, -rɪ
tumult, -s ˈtjuːmʌlt [-məlt], -s

509

tumultuous, -ly, -ness tju:'mʌltjʊəs [tjʊ'm-, -tjwəs], -lɪ, -nɪs [-nəs]

tumul|us, -i, -uses 'tju:mjʊl|əs, -aɪ, -əsɪz

tun (s. v.), -s, -ning, -ned tʌn, -z, -ɪŋ, -d

tuna, -s 'tu:nə ['tju:-], -z

Tunbridge 'tʌnbrɪdʒ ['tʌmb-]

tundra, -s 'tʌndrə, -z

tun|e (s. v.), -es, -ing, -ed, -er/s tju:n, -z, -ɪŋ, -d, -ə*/z

tune|ful, -fullest, -fully, -fulness 'tju:n|fʊl, -fʊlɪst [-fəlɪst], -fʊlɪ [-fəlɪ], -fʊlnɪs [-nəs]

tuneless 'tju:nlɪs [-ləs]

Tun(g)ku, -s 'tʊŋku:, -z

tungsten 'tʌŋstən [-ten, -tɪn]

tunic, -s 'tju:nɪk, -s

tunicle, -s 'tju:nɪkl, -z

tuning-fork, -s 'tju:nɪŋfɔ:k, -s

Tunis 'tju:nɪs

Tunisia, -n/s tju:'nɪzɪə [tjʊ'n-, -zjə, -sɪə, -sjə], -n/z

Tunnard 'tʌnəd

tunn|el, -els, -elling, -elled 'tʌn|l, -lz, -lɪŋ [-əlɪŋ], -ld

tunny 'tʌnɪ

Tuohy 'tu:ɪ, 'tu:hɪ

Tupman 'tʌpmən

tuppence, -s 'tʌpəns [-pns, -pms], -ɪz (see note under penny)

tuppeny 'tʌpnɪ [-pnɪ, -pənɪ]

tu quoque, -s ,tju:'kwəʊkwɪ, -s

Turandot (operas by Puccini and Busoni) 'tʊərəndəʊ ['tjʊə-, -dɒt]

Turania, -n/s ,tjʊə'reɪnjə [tjʊ'r-, -nɪə], -n/z

turban, -s, -ed 'tɜ:bən, -z, -d

turbid, -ly, -ness 'tɜ:bɪd, -lɪ, -nɪs [-nəs]

turbidity tɜ:'bɪdɪtɪ [-ɪtɪ]

turbine, -s 'tɜ:baɪn [-bɪn, rarely -bi:n], -z

turbo-jet, -s ,tɜ:bəʊ'dʒet ['---], -s

turbo-prop, -s ,tɜ:bəʊ'prɒp ['---], -s

turbot, -s 'tɜ:bət, -s

turbulen|ce, -cy, -t/ly 'tɜ:bjʊlən|s [-bjəl-], -sɪ, -t/lɪ

Turcoman, -s 'tɜ:kəmən [-mæn, -mɑ:n], -z

tureen, -s tə'ri:n [tʊ'r-, tjʊ'r-, tjə'r-], -z

tur|f (s.), -fs, -ves tɜ:|f, -fs, -vz

turf (v.), -s, -ing, -ed tɜ:f, -s, -ɪŋ, -t

turf|y, -ier, -iest, -iness 'tɜ:f|ɪ, -ɪə*, -ɪɪst, -ɪnɪs [-ɪnəs]

Turgenev tɜ:'gemjev [,tʊə'g-, -njef, -njɪf, -nev, -nəv] (tur'genjif)

turgescen|ce, -t tɜ:'dʒesn|s, -t

turgid, -ly, -ness 'tɜ:dʒɪd, -lɪ, -nɪs [-nəs]

turgidity tɜ:'dʒɪdətɪ [-ɪtɪ]

Turin tjʊ'rɪn [,tjʊə'r-]

Turk, -s tɜ:k, -s

Turkestan ,tɜ:kɪ'stɑ:n [-'stæn]

turkey (T.), -s 'tɜ:kɪ, -z

turkey-cock, -s 'tɜ:kɪkɒk, -s

Turki 'tɜ:ki:

Turkish 'tɜ:kɪʃ

Turkoman, -s 'tɜ:kəmən [-mæn, -mɑ:n], -z

turmeric 'tɜ:mərɪk

turmoil, -s 'tɜ:mɔɪl, -z

turn (s. v.), -s, -ing, -ed tɜ:n, -z, -ɪŋ, -d

Turnbull 'tɜ:nbʊl

turn|coat/s, -cock/s 'tɜ:n|kəʊts ['tɜ:ŋk-], -kɒk/s

turner (T.), -s 'tɜ:nə*, -z

turnery 'tɜ:nərɪ

Turnham 'tɜ:nəm

Turnhouse 'tɜ:nhaʊs

turning (s.), -s 'tɜ:nɪŋ, -z

turning-point, -s 'tɜ:nɪŋpɔɪnt; -s

turnip, -s 'tɜ:nɪp, -s

turnip-tops 'tɜ:nɪptɒps

turnkey, -s 'tɜ:nki: ['tɜ:ŋk-], -z

Turnour 'tɜ:nə*

turn-out (assembly, equipage), -s 'tɜ:n-aʊt [also ,-'- when preceded by a stress], -s

turnover, -s 'tɜ:n,əʊvə*, -z

turnpike, -s 'tɜ:npaɪk, -s

turn-round, -s 'tɜ:nraʊnd, -z

turnstile, -s 'tɜ:nstaɪl, -z

turnstone, -s 'tɜ:nstəʊn [-stən], -z

turntable, -s 'tɜ:n,teɪbl, -z

turn-up, -s 'tɜ:nʌp, -s

turpentine 'tɜ:pəntaɪn [-pnt-]

Turpin 'tɜ:pɪn

turpitude 'tɜ:pɪtju:d

turps tɜ:ps

turquoise, -s 'tɜ:kwɔɪz [-kwɑ:z, -kwɔ:z], -ɪz

turret, -s, -ed 'tʌrɪt [-rət], -s, -ɪd

turtle, -s 'tɜ:tl, -z

turtle-dove, -s 'tɜ:tldʌv, -z

turves (plur. of turf) tɜ:vz

Tuscan, -s, -y 'tʌskən, -z, -ɪ

tush (s. interj.), -es tʌʃ, -ɪz

Tusitala ,tu:sɪ'tɑ:lə

tusk, -s, -ed, -y tʌsk, -s, -t, -ɪ

tusker, -s 'tʌskə*, -z

Tussaud (surname) 'tu:səʊ

Tussaud's (exhibition) tə'sɔ:dz [tʊ's-, -'səʊz]

tuss|le (s. v.), -les, -ling, -led 'tʌs|l, -lz, -lɪŋ [-lɪŋ], -ld

tussock, -s, -y 'tʌsək, -s, -ɪ

tussore 'tʌsə* [-sɔ:*, -sɔə*]

tut (s. v.), -s, -ting, -ted tʌt, -s, -ɪŋ, -ɪd

tut (*interj.*) ʇ [tʌt]
Tutankhamen ˌtuːtəŋˈkɑːmen [-tæŋ-,
  -mən] (*also, with* -mun, ˌtuːtəŋkɑː-
  ˈmuːn)
tutel|age, -ar, -ary ˈtjuːtɪl|ɪdʒ [-təl-],
  -ə*, -ərɪ
Tuthill ˈtʌthɪl
tutor (*s. v.*), -s, -ing, -ed; -age ˈtjuːtə*,
  -z, -rɪŋ, -d; -rɪdʒ
tutorial, -ly tjuːˈtɔːrɪəl [tjʊˈt-], -ɪ
tutorship, -s ˈtjuːtəʃɪp, -s
tutti, -s ˈtuti: [-tɪ], -z
tutti-frutti ˌtutɪˈfrutɪ [ˌtuː-, ˈfruː-]
Tuttle ˈtʌtl
tu-whit tʊˈwɪt [tʊˈhwɪt, tə-]
tu-whoo tʊˈwuː [tʊˈhwuː, tə-]
tuxedo (T.), -s tʌkˈsiːdəʊ, -z
TV ˌtiːˈviː
Twaddell ˈtwɒdl, twɒˈdel
twadd|le (*s. v.*), -les, -ling, -led, -ler/s
  ˈtwɒd|l, -lz, -lɪŋ [-lɪŋ], -ld, -lə*/z
  [-lə*/z]
twaddly ˈtwɒdlɪ
twain (T.) tweɪn
twang (*s. v.*), -s, -ing, -ed twæŋ, -z, -ɪŋ,
  -d
twang|le, -les, -ling, -led ˈtwæŋg|l, -lz,
  -lɪŋ, -ld
'twas twɒz (*strong form*), twəz (*weak
  form*)
tweak, -s, -ing, -ed twiːk, -s, -ɪŋ, -t
tweed (T.), -s twiːd, -z
Tweeddale ˈtwiːddeɪl
Tweedie ˈtwiːdɪ
tweed|le (*s. v.*), -les, -ling, -led ˈtwiːd|l,
  -lz, -lɪŋ [-lɪŋ], -ld
Tweedle|dee, -dum ˌtwiːdl|ˈdiː, -ˈdʌm
Tweedmouth ˈtwiːdməθ [-maʊθ]
Tweedsmuir ˈtwiːdzˌmjʊə* [-mjɔə*,
  -mjɔː*]
'tween twiːn
tween|y, -ies ˈtwiːn|ɪ, -ɪz
tweeny-maid, -s ˈtwiːnɪmeɪd, -z
tweet, -s, -ing, -ed, -er/s twiːt, -s, -ɪŋ,
  -ɪd, -ə*/z
tweezers ˈtwiːzəz
twelfth, -s, -ly twelfθ [-elθ], -s, -lɪ
twelve, -s twelv, -z
twelvemo [12mo] ˈtwelvməʊ
twelvemonth, -s ˈtwelvmʌnθ, -s
twelvish ˈtwelvɪʃ
twent|y, -ies, -ieth/s, -iethly, -yfold
  ˈtwent|ɪ, -ɪz, -ɪnθ/s [-jɪθ/s, -ɪəθ/s,
  -jəθ/s], -ɪnθlɪ [-jɪθlɪ, -ɪəθlɪ, -jəθlɪ],
  -ɪfəʊld
Twentyman ˈtwentɪmən
'twere twɜː* (*strong form*), twə* (*weak
  form*)

twerp, -s twɜːp, -s
Twi twiː
twice twaɪs
Twickenham ˈtwɪkŋəm [-knəm, -kənəm]
twidd|le, -les, -ling, -led ˈtwɪd|l, -lz, -lɪŋ
  [-lɪŋ], -ld
twig (*s. v.*), -s, -ging, -ged twɪg, -z, -ɪŋ,
  -d
Twigg twɪg
twiggy ˈtwɪgɪ
twilight, -s ˈtwaɪlaɪt, -s
twill (*s. v.*), -s, -ing, -ed; -y twɪl, -z, -ɪŋ,
  -d; -ɪ
'twill twɪl (*normal form*), twəl, twl
  (*occasional weak forms*)
twin (*s. v.*), -s, -ning, -ned twɪn, -z, -ɪŋ,
  -d
twin|e, -es, -ing/ly, -ed, -er/s twaɪn, -z,
  -ɪŋ/lɪ, -d, -ə*/z
twing|e (*s. v.*), -es, -(e)ing, -ed twɪndʒ,
  -ɪz, -ɪŋ, -d
Twining ˈtwaɪnɪŋ
twink|le (*s. v.*), -les, -ling, -led, -ler/s
  ˈtwɪŋk|l, -lz, -lɪŋ [-lɪŋ], -ld, -lə*/z
  [-lə*/z]
twirl, -s, -ing, -ed twɜːl, -z, -ɪŋ, -d
twirp, -s twɜːp, -s
twist (*s. v.*) (T.), -s, -ing, -ed, -er/s
  twɪst, -s, -ɪŋ, -ɪd, -ə*/z
Twistington ˈtwɪstɪŋtən
twist|y, -ier, -iest, -iness ˈtwɪst|ɪ, -ɪə*
  [-jə*], -ɪɪst [-jɪst], -ɪnɪs [-ɪnəs]
twit, -s, -ting/ly, -ted twɪt, -s, -ɪŋ/lɪ, -ɪd
twitch (*s. v.*), -es, -ing/s, -ed twɪtʃ, -ɪz,
  -ɪŋ/z, -t
twite, -s twaɪt, -s
twitt|er (*s. v.*), -ers, -ering, -ered
  ˈtwɪt|ə*, -əz, -ərɪŋ, -əd
'twixt twɪkst
two, twos tuː [*also* tʊ *when the following
  word begins with* ə], tuːz
two-dimensional ˌtuːdɪˈmenʃənl
  [-daɪˈm-, -ʃnəl, -ʃn̩l, -ʃn̩l, -ʃənəl]
two-edged ˌtuːˈedʒd [ˈ-- *when attributive*]
twofold ˈtuːfəʊld
two-ish ˈtuːɪʃ
two-legged ˌtuːˈlegd [ˈ-- *when attributive*, ˌtuːˈlegɪd]
twopence, -s ˈtʌpəns [-pms], -ɪz (*see
  note under* penny)
twopenny ˈtʌpn̩ɪ [-pnɪ, -pənɪ]
twopenny-halfpenny ˌtʌpn̩ɪˈheɪpnɪ
  [ˌtʌpnɪˈheɪpnɪ, ˌtʌpənɪˈheɪpənɪ]
twopennyworth, -s ˌtuːˈpenɪwɜːθ [ˌtuː-
  ˈpenəθ, ˈtʌpn̩ɪwɜːθ, ˈtʌpnɪ-, ˈtʌpənɪ-,
  -wəθ], -s
two-ply ˈtuːˌplaɪ [ˌ-ˈ-]

two-seater, -s ˌtuːˈsiːtə*, -z
two-step, -s ˈtuːstep, -s
two-year-old, -s ˈtuːˌjɜːʊld, -z
Twyford ˈtwaɪfəd
Tyacke ˈtaɪək
Tyana ˈtaɪənə
Tybalt ˈtɪbəlt [-blt]
Tyburn ˈtaɪbɜːn
Tychicus ˈtɪkɪkəs
Tycho ˈtaɪkəʊ
tycoon, -s taɪˈkuːn, -z
Tydeus ˈtaɪdjuːs [-djəs, -dɪəs]
Tydfil ˈtɪdvɪl (Welsh ˈtidvil)
tying (from tie) ˈtaɪɪŋ
Tyldesley ˈtɪldzlɪ
Tyler ˈtaɪlə*
tympan|i, -ist/s ˈtɪmpən|ɪ, -ɪst/s
tympanic tɪmˈpænɪk
tympan|um, -ums, -a ˈtɪmpən|əm, -əmz, -ə
Tynan ˈtaɪnən
Tynd|ale, -all ˈtɪnd|l, -l
Tyndrum taɪnˈdrʌm
Tyne, -and Wear taɪn, -ənd ˈwɪə*
Tynemouth ˈtaɪnmaʊθ [-məθ, old-fashioned ˈtɪnməθ]
typ|e (s. v.), -es, -ing, -ed taɪp, -s, -ɪŋ, -t
type-bar, -s ˈtaɪpbɑː*, -z
type-cutter, -s ˈtaɪpˌkʌtə*, -z
type-founder, -s ˈtaɪpˌfaʊndə*, -z
type-foundr|y, -ies ˈtaɪpˌfaʊndr|ɪ, -ɪz
typescript, -s ˈtaɪpskrɪpt, -s
type-set ˈtaɪpset
type-setter, -s ˈtaɪpˌsetə*, -z
typewrit|e, -es, -ing, typewrote, type-written, typewriter/s ˈtaɪpraɪt, -s, -ɪŋ, ˈtaɪprəʊt, ˈtaɪpˌrɪtn, ˈtaɪpˌraɪtə*/z
typhoid ˈtaɪfɔɪd
typhonic taɪˈfɒnɪk

typhoon, -s taɪˈfuːn, -z
typh|ous, -us ˈtaɪf|əs, -əs
typic|al, -ally, -alness ˈtɪpɪk|l, -əlɪ, -lnɪs [-nəs]
typi|fy, -fies, -fying, -fied ˈtɪpɪ|faɪ, -faɪz, -faɪɪŋ, -faɪd
typist, -s ˈtaɪpɪst, -s
typo, -s ˈtaɪpəʊ, -z
typograph|er/s, -y taɪˈpɒgrəf|ə*/z, -ɪ
typographic, -al, -ally ˌtaɪpəˈgræfɪk [-pəʊˈg-], -l, -əlɪ
typology taɪˈpɒlədʒɪ
typtolog|ist/s, -y tɪpˈtɒlədʒ|ɪst/s, -ɪ
tyrannic|al, -ally, -alness tɪˈrænɪk|l [taɪˈr-], -əlɪ, -lnɪs [-nəs]
tyrannicide, -s tɪˈrænɪsaɪd [taɪˈr-], -z
tyranniz|e [-is|e], -es, -ing, -ed ˈtɪrənaɪz [ˈtɪrɪnaɪz], -ɪz, -ɪŋ, -d
tyrannosaurus, -i tɪˌrænəˈsɔːr|əs, -aɪ
tyrannous, -ly ˈtɪrənəs [ˈtɪrŋəs], -lɪ
tyrann|y, -ies ˈtɪrən|ɪ [ˈtɪrŋ|ɪ], -ɪz
tyrant, -s ˈtaɪərənt, -s
tyre (T.), -s ˈtaɪə*, -z
Tyrian, -s ˈtɪrɪən, -z
tyro, -s ˈtaɪərəʊ, -z
Tyrol ˈtɪrəl [tɪˈrəʊl]
Tyrolean tɪˈrəʊlɪən [ˌtɪrəˈliːən, -ˈlɪən]
Tyrolese ˌtɪrəˈliːz [-rəʊˈl-]
Tyrolienne, -s tɪˌrəʊliˈen [ˌtɪrəʊliˈen], -z
Tyrone tɪˈrəʊn
Tyrrell ˈtɪrəl
Tyrrhenian, -s tɪˈriːnjən [-nɪən], -z
Tyrtaeus tɜːˈtiːəs
Tyrwhitt ˈtɪrɪt
Tyser ˈtaɪzə*
Tyson ˈtaɪsn
Tytler ˈtaɪtlə*
Tyzack ˈtaɪzæk [-zək], ˈtɪzæk [-zək]
tzigane, -s tsɪˈgɑːn, -z

U

U (*the letter*), -'s juː, -z
Ubbelohde (*surname*) ˈʌbələud
ubiquitarian (U.), -s juːˌbɪkwɪˈteəriən
[juˌb-], -z
ubiquitous juːˈbɪkwɪtəs [juˈb-]
ubiquity juːˈbɪkwɪtɪ [juˈb-, -ɪtɪ]
U-boat, -s ˈjuːbəut, -s
Uckfield ˈʌkfiːld
udal (U.) ˈjuːdl
Udall ˈjuːdəl
udder, -s ˈʌdə*, -z
U.D.I. ˌjuːdiːˈaɪ
Udolpho uːˈdɒlfəu [juː-]
udometer, -s juːˈdɒmɪtə* [-mətə*], -z
U.F.O. (*unidentified flying object*)
ˌjuːefˈəu
Uganda juːˈgændə [juˈg-]
ugh ɯːx, ɯh, ʌx, uφ, ʊh, ɜːh
Ughtred ˈuːtrɪd [-red]
uglification ˌʌglɪfɪˈkeɪʃn
ugli|fy, -fies, -fying, -fied ˈʌglɪ|faɪ, -faɪz,
-faɪɪŋ, -faɪd
ugl|y, -ier, -iest, -iness ˈʌgl|ɪ, -ɪə*
[-jə*], -ɪɪst [-jɪst], -ɪnɪs [-məs]
Ugrian, -s ˈuːgrɪən [ˈjuːg-], -z
u(h)lan, -s ʊˈlɑːn, -z
Uhland ˈuːlənd [-lænd, -lɑːnd] (ˈuːlant)
Uig ˈuːɪg [ˈjuːɪg]
Uist ˈjuːɪst
Uitlander, -s ˈeɪtlændə*, -z
ukase, -s juːˈkeɪz [-eɪs], -ɪz
ukelele, -s ˌjuːkəˈleɪlɪ, -z
Ukraine juːˈkreɪn [juˈk-, -ˈkraɪn]
Ukrainian, -s juːˈkreɪnjən [juˈk-, -nɪən,
rarely -ˈkraɪn-]
ulcer, -s, -ed ˈʌlsə*, -z, -d
ulcerat|e, -es, -ing, -ed ˈʌlsəreɪt, -s, -ɪŋ,
-ɪd
ulceration, -s ˌʌlsəˈreɪʃn, -z
ulcerous ˈʌlsərəs
ulema, -s ˈuːlɪmə, -z
ulex ˈjuːleks
Ulfilas ˈulfɪlæs
Ulgham (*in Lincolnshire and Northumberland*) ˈʌfəm
Ulick ˈjuːlɪk
ullage ˈʌlɪdʒ
Ullswater ˈʌlzˌwɔːtə*
ulmus ˈʌlməs

uln|a, -ae, -ar ˈʌln|ə, -iː, -ə*
Ulrica (*English name*) ˈʌlrɪkə
Ulrich ˈulrɪk (ˈulriç)
ulster (U.), -s, -ed ˈʌlstə*, -z, -d
ulterior, -ly ʌlˈtɪərɪə*, -lɪ
ultim|ate, -ately ˈʌltɪm|ət [-mɪt], -ətlɪ
[-ɪtlɪ]
ultimatum, -s ˌʌltɪˈmeɪtəm, -z
ultimo ˈʌltɪməu
ultra (*s. adj.*), -s ˈʌltrə, -z
ultra (*in* ne plus ultra), *see* ne plus ultra
ultra- ˈʌltrə-
Note.—*Numerous compound adjectives may be formed by prefixing
*ultra- *to adjectives. These com-
pounds have double stress, e.g.*
ultra-fashionable ˌʌltrəˈfæʃənəbl
[-ʃnə-]; *the pronunciation of all
such words may therefore be ascertained by reference to the simple
words. When such adjectives are
used as substantives they keep the
double stress. (The words* ultramarine, ultramontane *given below
do not count as compounds.*)
ultraism ˈʌltrəɪzəm
ultramarine ˌʌltrəməˈriːn
ultramontane ˌʌltrəˈmɒnteɪn
ultramontanism ˌʌltrəˈmɒntɪnɪzəm
[-tən-, -teɪn-]
ultrasonic ˌʌltrəˈsɒnɪk
ultra vires ˌʌltrəˈvaɪəriːz [ˌultrɑː-
ˈvɪəreɪz]
ululant ˈjuːljʊlənt
ululat|e, -es, -ing, -ed ˈjuːljʊlert, -s, -ɪŋ,
-ɪd
ululation, -s ˌjuːljʊˈleɪʃn, -z
Ulverston ˈʌlvəstən
Ulysses juːˈlɪsiːz [jʊˈl-, ˈjuːlɪsiːz]
umbel, -s ˈʌmbəl [-bel], -z
umbellifer|ae, -ous ˌʌmbeˈlɪfər|iː
[-bəˈl-], -əs
umber, -s, -y ˈʌmbə*, -z, -rɪ
umbilic, -s ʌmˈbɪlɪk, -s
umbilical (*mathematical term*) ʌmˈbɪlɪkl
[-lək-], (*medical term*) ˌʌmbɪˈlaɪkl
[-bəˈl-, ʌmˈbɪlɪkl, -lək-]
umbilicus, -es ʌmˈbɪlɪkəs [-lək-, ˌʌmbɪ-
ˈlaɪkəs, -bəˈl-], -ɪz

513

umble, -s ˈʌmbl, -z
umbo, -s, -nes ˈʌmbəʊ, -z, ʌmˈbəʊniːz
umbr|a, -as, -al ˈʌmbr|ə, -əz, -əl
umbrage ˈʌmbrɪdʒ
umbrageous, -ly, -ness ʌmˈbreɪdʒəs, -lɪ, -nɪs [-nəs]
umbrated ˈʌmbreɪtɪd
umbration, -s ʌmˈbreɪʃn, -z
umbrella, -s ʌmˈbrelə, -z
Umbria, -n/s ˈʌmbrɪə, -n/z
umbriferous ʌmˈbrɪfərəs
umbril, -s ˈʌmbrɪl, -z
Umfreville ˈʌmfrəvɪl
umiak, -s ˈuːmɪæk [-mjæk], -s
umlaut, -s ˈʊmlaʊt, -s
umph m̩m̩m̩ [ʌmf]
umpir|e (s. v.), -es, -ing, -ed ˈʌmpaɪə*, -z, -rɪŋ, -d
umpteen, -th ˌʌmpˈtiːn [ˈ--], -θ
umpty ˈʌmptɪ
un- ʌn-

> Notes.—1. The stressing of un- com-
> pounds depends on the meaning of
> the prefix, the commonness of the
> word, and other factors. Those not
> included in the following list are to
> be taken to have double stress. Thus
> undetachable is ˌʌndɪˈtætʃəbl, un-
> countenanced is ˌʌnˈkaʊntmənst.
> 2. ʌn- freq. assimilates before p, b
> to ʌm- (e.g. in unpopular, un-
> broken) and before k, g to ʌŋ- (e.g.
> in unkind, ungrateful).

Una ˈjuːnə
unabashed ˌʌnəˈbæʃt
unabated ˌʌnəˈbeɪtɪd
unable ʌnˈeɪbl [ˌʌn-]
unabridged ˌʌnəˈbrɪdʒd
unaccented ˌʌnækˈsentɪd [-nək-, also ˈ--ˌ-- when attributive]
unacceptable ˌʌnəkˈseptəbl [-næk-]
unaccompanied ˌʌnəˈkʌmpənɪd [also ˈ--ˌ--- when attributive]
unaccountable ˌʌnəˈkaʊntəbl
unaccountab|ly, -leness ˌʌnəˈkaʊntəb|lɪ, -lnɪs [-nəs]
unaccustomed ˌʌnəˈkʌstəmd
unacknowledged ˌʌnəkˈnɒlɪdʒd
unacquainted ˌʌnəˈkweɪntɪd
unacted ʌnˈæktɪd
unadaptable ˌʌnəˈdæptəbl
unaddressed ˌʌnəˈdrest
unadorned ˌʌnəˈdɔːnd
unadulterated ˌʌnəˈdʌltəreɪtɪd
unadvisability ˈʌnədˌvaɪzəˈbɪlətɪ [-lɪt-]
unadvisable ˌʌnədˈvaɪzəbl
unadvisableness ˌʌnədˈvaɪzəblnɪs [-nəs]
unadvised ˌʌnədˈvaɪzd

unadvisedly ˌʌnədˈvaɪzɪdlɪ
unaffected (not influenced) ˌʌnəˈfektɪd
unaffected (without affectation), -ly, -ness ˌʌnəˈfektɪd, -lɪ, -nɪs [-nəs]
unafraid ˌʌnəˈfreɪd
unaided ˌʌnˈeɪdɪd [ˌʌn-]
unalienable ˌʌnˈeɪljənəbl [ˌʌn-, -lɪən-]
unalienably ʌnˈeɪljənəblɪ [-lɪən-]
unallotted ˌʌnəˈlɒtɪd
unallowable ˌʌnəˈlaʊəbl
unalloyed ˌʌnəˈlɔɪd
unalterability ʌnˌɔːltərəˈbɪlətɪ [ˈʌnˌɔːl-, -ˌɒl-, -lɪt-]
unalterab|le, -ly, -leness ʌnˈɔːltərəb|l [ˌʌnˈɔː-, -ˈɒl-], -lɪ, -nɪs [-nəs]
unaltered ˌʌnˈɔːltəd [ˌʌn-, -ˈɒl-]
unambiguous, -ly ˌʌnæmˈbɪgjʊəs [-gjwəs], -lɪ
unanalysable ˌʌnˈænəlaɪzəbl
unanimity ˌjuːnəˈnɪmətɪ [jʊn-, -næˈn-, -ɪtɪ]
unanimous, -ly, -ness juːˈnænɪməs [jʊˈn-, -nən-], -lɪ, -nɪs [-nəs]
unannounced ˌʌnəˈnaʊnst
unanswerable ˌʌnˈɑːnsərəbl [ʌnˈɑː-]
unanswered ˌʌnˈɑːnsəd [ʌnˈɑː-]
unappeas|able, -ed ˌʌnəˈpiːz|əbl, -d
unappetizing ʌnˈæpɪtaɪzɪŋ [ˌʌn-, -pət-]
unapplied ˌʌnəˈplaɪd
unappreciable ˌʌnəˈpriːʃəbl [-ʃjə-, -ʃɪə-]
unappreciated ˌʌnəˈpriːʃɪeɪtɪd
unapproachab|le, -ly, -leness ˌʌnəˈprəʊtʃəb|l, -lɪ, -lnɪs [-nəs]
unapproached ˌʌnəˈprəʊtʃt
unappropriate (adj.) ˌʌnəˈprəʊprɪət [-prɪt]
unappropriated ˌʌnəˈprəʊprɪeɪtɪd
unapproved ˌʌnəˈpruːvd
unarm, -s, -ing, -ed ˌʌnˈɑːm [ʌn-], -z, -ɪŋ, -d
unascertain|able, -ed ˌʌnæsəˈteɪn|əbl, -d
unashamed ˌʌnəˈʃeɪmd
unasked ˌʌnˈɑːskt [ʌn-]
unaspirated ʌnˈæspəreɪtɪd [ˌʌn-, -pɪr-]
unassailable ˌʌnəˈseɪləbl
unassignable ˌʌnəˈsaɪnəbl
unassimilated ˌʌnəˈsɪmɪleɪtɪd [-mɪl-]
unassisted ˌʌnəˈsɪstɪd
unassuming ˌʌnəˈsjuːmɪŋ [-ˈsuː-]
unattached ˌʌnəˈtætʃt
unattainable ˌʌnəˈteɪnəbl
unattempted ˌʌnəˈtemptɪd
unattended ˌʌnəˈtendɪd
unattested ˌʌnəˈtestɪd
unattractive, -ly, -ness ˌʌnəˈtræktɪv, -lɪ, -nɪs [-nəs]
unauthenticated ˌʌnɔːˈθentɪkeɪtɪd
unauthorized [-ised] ˌʌnˈɔːθəraɪzd [ʌn-]

unavailing ˌʌnəˈveɪlɪŋ [*also* '—ˌ— *when attributive*]

unavailingly ˌʌnəˈveɪlɪŋlɪ

unavenged ˌʌnəˈvendʒd

unavoidab|le, -ly, -leness ˌʌnəˈvɔɪdəb|l, -lɪ, -lnɪs [-nəs]

unaware, -s ˌʌnəˈweə*, -z

unbalanc|e, -es, -ing, -ed ˌʌnˈbæləns [ʌn-], -ɪz, -ɪŋ, -t

unbaptized ˌʌnbæpˈtaɪzd

unbar, -s, -ring, -red ˌʌnˈbɑː*, -z, -rɪŋ, -d

unbearab|le, -ly, -leness ʌnˈbeərəb|l [ˌʌn-], -lɪ, -lnɪs [-nəs]

unbeatable ʌnˈbiːtəbl

unbeaten ʌnˈbiːtn [ʌn-]

unbecoming, -ly, -ness ˌʌnbɪˈkʌmɪŋ [-bəˈk-], -lɪ, -nɪs [-nəs]

unbefitting ˌʌnbɪˈfɪtɪŋ [-bəˈf-]

unbegotten ˌʌnbɪˈgɒtn [-bəˈg-]

unbeknown ˌʌnbɪˈnəʊn [-bəˈn-]

unbelief ˌʌnbɪˈliːf [-bəˈl-, '——]

unbelievable ˌʌnbɪˈliːvəbl [-bəˈl-]

unbeliever, -s ˌʌnbɪˈliːvə* [-bəˈl-, '—ˌ—], -z

unbelieving ˌʌnbɪˈliːvɪŋ [-bəˈl-, '—ˌ—]

unben|d, -ds, -ding, -ded, -t ʌnˈben|d, -dz, -dɪŋ, -dɪd, -t

unbeneficed ʌnˈbenɪfɪst

unbias(s)ed ʌnˈbaɪəst

unbidden ˌʌnˈbɪdn

un|bind (*undo binding*), **-binds, -binding, -bound** ʌnˈbaɪnd, -ˈbaɪndz, -ˈbaɪndɪŋ, -ˈbaʊnd

unbleached ʌnˈbliːtʃt [*also* '— *when attributive*]

unblemished ʌnˈblemɪʃt [ʌnˈb-]

unblushing, -ly ʌnˈblʌʃɪŋ, -lɪ

unboiled ʌnˈbɔɪld [*also* '— *when attributive*]

unbolt, -s, -ing, -ed ʌnˈbəʊlt, -s, -ɪŋ, -ɪd

unborn ˌʌnˈbɔːn ['ʌnb- *according to sentence-stress*]

unbosom, -s, -ing, -ed ʌnˈbʊzəm, -z, -ɪŋ, -d

unbought ʌnˈbɔːt [*also* 'ʌnb- *when attributive*]

unbound (*not bound*) ʌnˈbaʊnd [*also* 'ʌnb- *when attributive*]

unbounded ʌnˈbaʊndɪd [ʌn-]

unbridled ʌnˈbraɪdld [ʌn-]

unbroken ʌnˈbrəʊkən [ʌn-]

unbuck|le, -les, -ling, -led ʌnˈbʌk|l [ʌn-], -lz, -lɪŋ [lɪŋ], -ld

unburd|en, -ens, -ening, -ened ˌʌnˈbɜːd|n [ʌn-], -nz, -ŋɪŋ [-nɪŋ], -nd

unburied ʌnˈberɪd [ʌn-]

unbusiness-like ˌʌnˈbɪznɪslaɪk [ʌnˈb-]

unbutt|on, -ons, -oning, -oned ˌʌnˈbʌt|n [ʌn-], -nz, -ŋɪŋ [-nɪŋ], -nd

uncalled for ˌʌnˈkɔːldfɔ:* [ʌnˈk-]

uncandid, -ly, -ness ʌnˈkændɪd, -lɪ, -nɪs [-nəs]

uncann|y, -ier, -iest, -ily, -iness ʌnˈkæn|ɪ, -ɪə*, -ɪst, -ɪlɪ [-əlɪ], -ɪnɪs [-nəs]

uncanonical ˌʌnkəˈnɒnɪkl

uncared for ˌʌnˈkeədfɔ:* [ʌn-]

uncatalogued ʌnˈkætələɡd

unceasing, -ly ʌnˈsiːsɪŋ [ˌʌn-], -lɪ

uncensored ˌʌnˈsensəd [ʌnˈs-]

unceremonious, -ly, -ness 'ʌnˌserɪ-ˈməʊnjəs [-nɪəs], -lɪ, -nɪs [-nəs]

uncertain ʌnˈsɜːtn [ˌʌn-ˈs-, -tən, -tn̩]

uncertaint|y, -ies ʌnˈsɜːtnt|ɪ [-tən-, -tn̩-], -ɪz

unchain, -s, -ing, -ed ʌnˈtʃem, -z, -ɪŋ, -d

unchallenged ʌnˈtʃæləndʒd [-lm-]

unchangeability 'ʌnˌtʃeɪndʒəˈbɪlətɪ [ʌnˌtʃ-, -lɪt-]

unchangeable ˌʌnˈtʃeɪndʒəbl [ʌnˈtʃ-]

unchangeab|ly, -leness ˌʌnˈtʃeɪndʒəb|lɪ [ʌnˈtʃ-], -lnɪs [-nəs]

unchanged ˌʌnˈtʃeɪndʒd [ʌn-]

unchanging ʌnˈtʃeɪndʒɪŋ [ʌnˈtʃ-]

uncharged ʌnˈtʃɑːdʒd

uncharitab|le, -ly, -leness ʌnˈtʃærɪtəb|l [ʌnˈtʃ-], -lɪ, -lnɪs [-nəs]

uncharted ʌnˈtʃɑːtɪd

unchartered ʌnˈtʃɑːtəd

unchaste, -ly ʌnˈtʃeɪst [ʌn-], -lɪ

unchastened ʌnˈtʃeɪsnd [ʌnˈtʃ-]

unchastity ʌnˈtʃæstətɪ [-ɪtɪ]

uncheck|able, -ed ʌnˈtʃek|əbl [ʌn-], -t

unchristian, -ly ʌnˈkrɪstjən [ʌn-, -tʃən], -lɪ

uncial (*s. adj.*), **-s** 'ʌnsɪəl [-nsjəl, -nʃɪəl, -nʃjəl, -nʃl], -z

unciform 'ʌnsɪfɔːm

uncinate 'ʌnsɪnɪt [-neɪt]

uncircumcised ˌʌnˈsɜːkəmsaɪzd

uncircumcision 'ʌnˌsɜːkəmˈsɪʒn

unciv|il, -illy ʌnˈsɪv|l [ʌn-, -ɪl], -əlɪ [-ɪlɪ]

unciviliz|ed [-is|ed], -able ʌnˈsɪv|aɪz|d [ʌn-, -vəl-, -vɪlaɪ-], -əbl

unclaimed ˌʌnˈkleɪmd [*also* '— *when attributive*]

unclasp, -s, -ing, -ed ʌnˈklɑːsp, -s, -ɪŋ, -t

unclassifiable ˌʌnˈklæsɪfaɪəbl [-ˌ—'——]

unclassified ˌʌnˈklæsɪfaɪd [ʌn-]

uncle, -s 'ʌŋkl, -z

unclean, -ness ʌnˈkliːn [ʌn-, *also* '— *when attributive*], -nɪs [-nəs]

unclean|ly, -iness ʌnˈklenl|ɪ [ʌn-], -ɪnɪs [-nəs]

unclear ˌʌnˈklɪə*

unclos|e, -es, -ing, -ed ˌʌnˈkləʊz, -ɪz, -ɪŋ, -d

unclothed ˌʌnˈkləʊðd [*also '— when attributive*]

unclouded ˌʌnˈklaʊdɪd

uncluttered ˌʌnˈklʌtəd

uncoffined ˌʌnˈkɒfɪnd

uncoil, -s, -ing, -ed ˌʌnˈkɔɪl, -z, -ɪŋ, -d

uncollected ˌʌnkəˈlektɪd

uncoloured ˌʌnˈkʌləd

un-come-at-able ˌʌnkʌmˈætəbl

uncomely ˌʌnˈkʌmlɪ

uncomfortab|le, -ly, -leness ʌnˈkʌm-fətəb|l, -lɪ, -lnɪs [-nəs]

uncommercial ˌʌnkəˈmɜːʃl [*also 'ʌnkə,m- when attributive*]

uncommitted ˌʌnkəˈmɪtɪd

uncommon ʌnˈkɒmən [ˌʌnˈk-]

uncommon|ly, -ness ʌnˈkɒmən|lɪ, -nɪs [-nəs]

uncommunic|able, -ated ˌʌnkəˈmjuː-nɪk|əbl [-ˈmjʊn-], -eɪtɪd

uncommunicative, -ness ˌʌnkəˈmjuːnɪ-kətɪv [-ˈmjʊn-, -keɪt-], -nɪs [-nəs]

uncomplaining, -ly ˌʌnkəmˈpleɪnɪŋ [*also 'ʌnkəm,p- when attributive*], -lɪ

uncompleted ˌʌnkəmˈpliːtɪd

uncomplimentary 'ʌn,kɒmplɪˈmentərɪ

uncompounded ˌʌnkəmˈpaʊndɪd

uncompromising, -ly, -ness ʌnˈkɒm-prəmaɪzɪŋ [ˌʌn-, -prʊm-], -lɪ, -nɪs [-nəs]

unconcealed ˌʌnkənˈsiːld

unconcern, -ed, -edly, -edness ˌʌn-kənˈsɜːn, -d, -ɪdlɪ, -ɪdnɪs [-nəs]

uncondi|tional, -tionally ˌʌnkənˈdɪʃ|ənl [-ˈʃnəl, -ˈʃnl, -ˈʃnl, -ˈʃənəl], -ˈʃnəlɪ [-ˈʃnəlɪ, -ˈʃnlɪ, -ˈʃnlɪ, -ˈʃənəlɪ]

unconditioned ˌʌnkənˈdɪʃnd

unconfined ˌʌnkənˈfaɪnd

unconfirmed ˌʌnkənˈfɜːmd

uncongenial ˌʌnkənˈdʒiːnjəl [-nɪəl]

unconnected ˌʌnkəˈnektɪd

unconquerable ʌnˈkɒŋkərəbl

unconquered ʌnˈkɒŋkəd [ʌn-]

unconscionab|le, -ly, -leness ʌnˈkɒn-ʃnəb|l [-ˈʃnə-, -ˈʃənə-], -lɪ, -lnɪs [-nəs]

unconscious, -ly, -ness ʌnˈkɒnʃəs [ˌʌnˈk-], -lɪ, -nɪs [-nəs]

unconsecrated ʌnˈkɒnsɪkreɪtɪd [ʌn-]

unconsidered ˌʌnkənˈsɪdəd [*also '—,— when attributive*]

unconstitu|tional, -tionally 'ʌn,kɒnstɪ-ˈtjuː|ʃənl [ˌʌn-, -ʃnəl, -ʃnl, -ʃnl, -ʃənəl], -ʃnəlɪ [-ʃnəlɪ, -ʃnlɪ, -ʃnlɪ, -ʃənəlɪ]

unconstrain|ed, -edly ˌʌnkənˈstreɪn|d, -ɪdlɪ

unconsumed ˌʌnkənˈsjuːmd [-ˈsuːmd]

uncontaminated ˌʌnkənˈtæmɪneɪtɪd

uncontestable ˌʌnkənˈtestəbl

uncontested ˌʌnkənˈtestɪd [*also 'ʌnkən,t- when attributive*]

uncontradicted 'ʌn,kɒntrəˈdɪktɪd

uncontrollable ˌʌnkənˈtrəʊləb|l

uncontrollab|ly, -leness ˌʌnkənˈtrəʊl-əb|lɪ, -lnɪs [-nəs]

uncontrolled ˌʌnkənˈtrəʊld

unconventional ˌʌnkənˈvenʃənl [-ˈʃnəl, -ˈʃnl, -ˈʃnl, -ˈʃənəl]

unconventionalit|y, -ies 'ʌnkən,ven-ʃəˈnælət|ɪ [-ˈʃnˈæ-, -rt|ɪ], -ɪz

unconverted ˌʌnkənˈvɜːtɪd [*also 'ʌn-kən,v- when attributive*]

unconvertible ˌʌnkənˈvɜːtəbl [-tɪb-]

unconvinced ˌʌnkənˈvɪnst

unconvincing ˌʌnkənˈvɪnsɪŋ

uncooked ˌʌnˈkʊkt ['ʌnk- *according to sentence-stress*]

uncooperative ˌʌnkəʊˈɒpərətɪv [-kʊˈɒ-]

uncord, -s, -ing, -ed ˌʌnˈkɔːd, -z, -ɪŋ, -ɪd

uncork, -s, -ing, -ed ˌʌnˈkɔːk, -s, -ɪŋ, -t

uncorrected ˌʌnkəˈrektɪd ['ʌnkə,r- *when attributive*]

uncorroborated ˌʌnkəˈrɒbəreɪtɪd

uncorrupt, -ly, -ness ˌʌnkəˈrʌpt, -lɪ, -nɪs [-nəs]

uncountable ˌʌnˈkaʊntəbl

uncounted ˌʌnˈkaʊntɪd

uncoup|le, -les, -ling, -led ˌʌnˈkʌp|l, -lz, -lɪŋ [-lɪŋ], -ld

uncouth, -ly, -ness ʌnˈkuːθ, -lɪ, -nɪs [-nəs]

uncov|er, -ers, -ering, -ered ʌnˈkʌv|ə* [ˌʌnˈk-], -əz, -ərɪŋ, -əd

uncritical, -ally ˌʌnˈkrɪtɪk|l [ʌn-], -əlɪ

uncrossed ˌʌnˈkrɒst [*old-fashioned* -ˈkrɔːst, *also* 'ʌnkr- *when attributive*]

uncrowned ˌʌnˈkraʊnd [*also* 'ʌnkraʊnd *when attributive*]

unction, -s 'ʌŋkʃn, -z

unctuosity ˌʌŋktjʊˈɒsətɪ [-ɪtɪ]

unctuous, -ly, -ness 'ʌŋktjʊəs [-tjwəs, -tʃʊəs, -tʃwəs], -lɪ, -nɪs [-nəs]

uncultivated ˌʌnˈkʌltɪveɪtɪd

uncultured ˌʌnˈkʌltʃəd

uncurbed ˌʌnˈkɜːbd

uncurl, -s, -ing, -ed ˌʌnˈkɜːl, -z, -ɪŋ, -d

uncut ˌʌnˈkʌt [*also* 'ʌnkʌt *according to sentence-stress*]

undamaged ˌʌnˈdæmɪdʒd

undate 'ʌndeɪt

undated (*wavy*) 'ʌndeɪtɪd

undated (*not dated*) ˌʌnˈdeɪtɪd

undaunted, -ly, -ness ˌʌnˈdɔːntɪd
[ʌnˈd-], -lɪ, -nɪs [-nəs]

undebated ˌʌndɪˈbeɪtɪd

undeceiv|e, -es, -ing, -ed ˌʌndɪˈsiːv, -z,
-ɪŋ, -d

undecennial ˌʌndɪˈsenjəl

undecided, -ly, -ness ˌʌndɪˈsaɪdɪd [also
'--ˌ-- when attributive], -lɪ, -nɪs [-nəs]

undecipherable ˌʌndɪˈsaɪfərəbl

undecisive ˌʌndɪˈsaɪsɪv

undefended ˌʌndɪˈfendɪd [also '--ˌ--
when attributive]

undefiled ˌʌndɪˈfaɪld

undefin|able, -ed ˌʌndɪˈfaɪn|əbl, -d

undelivered ˌʌndɪˈlɪvəd

undemonstrative ˌʌndɪˈmɒnstrətɪv

undeniable ˌʌndɪˈnaɪəbl

undeniably ˌʌndɪˈnaɪəblɪ

undenomina|tional, -tionalism 'ʌndɪ-
ˌnɒmɪˈneɪ|ʃənl [-ʃnəl, -ʃn̩l, -ʃnl̩,
-ʃənəl], -ʃn̩əlɪzəm [-ʃnəl-, -ʃn̩l-, -ʃnl̩-,
-ʃənəl-]

under (s. adj. adv. prep.), -s 'ʌndə*,
-z

Note.—Compounds with under- not
included in the following list are to
be taken to have double stress. Thus
under-masticate is ˌʌndəˈmæstɪkeɪt

underact, -s, -ing, -ed ˌʌndərˈækt
[-dəˈækt], -s, -ɪŋ, -ɪd

under-age ˌʌndərˈeɪdʒ [-dəˈeɪ-]

underbid, -s, -ding ˌʌndəˈbɪd, -z, -ɪŋ

underbred ˌʌndəˈbred

underbrush 'ʌndəbrʌʃ

under|buy, -buys, -buying, -bought
ˌʌndə|ˈbaɪ, -ˈbaɪz, -ˈbaɪɪŋ, -ˈbɔːt

undercarriage, -s 'ʌndəˌkærɪdʒ, -ɪz

undercast, -s 'ʌndəkɑːst, -s

undercharge (s.), -s ˌʌndəˈtʃɑːdʒ
['ʌndətʃ-], -ɪz

undercharg|e (v.), -es, -ing, -ed ˌʌndə-
ˈtʃɑːdʒ, -ɪz, -ɪŋ, -d

underclay 'ʌndəkleɪ

under-clerk, -s 'ʌndəklɑːk, -s

undercliff, -s 'ʌndəklɪf, -s

underclothed ˌʌndəˈkləʊðd

underclothes 'ʌndəkləʊðz [old-fashioned
-kləʊz]

underclothing 'ʌndəˌkləʊðɪŋ

undercoat, -s 'ʌndəkəʊt, -s

under-colour, -s 'ʌndəˌkʌlə*, -z

under-cover 'ʌndəˌkʌvə*

undercroft, -s 'ʌndəkrɒft, -s

undercurrent, -s 'ʌndəˌkʌrənt, -s

undercut (s.), -s 'ʌndəkʌt, -s

undercut (adj. v.), -s, -ting ˌʌndəˈkʌt,
-s, -ɪŋ

under-developed ˌʌndədɪˈveləpt

under|do, -does, -doing, -did, -done
ˌʌndə|ˈduː, -ˈdʌz, -ˈduːɪŋ [-ˈdʊɪŋ],
-ˈdɪd, -ˈdʌn ['ʌndədʌn when attribu-
tive]

underdog, -s 'ʌndədɒg [ˌ--ˈ-], -z

underdose, -s 'ʌndədəʊs, -ɪz

under|draw, -draws, -drawing, -drew,
-drawn ˌʌndə|ˈdrɔː, -ˈdrɔːz, -ˈdrɔːɪŋ
-ˈdruː, -ˈdrɔːn

under-dressed ˌʌndəˈdrest

underestimate (s.), -s ˌʌndərˈestɪmət
[-dəˈes-, -mɪt, -meɪt], -s

underestimat|e (v.), -es, -ing, -ed
ˌʌndərˈestɪmeɪt [-dəˈes-], -s, -ɪŋ, -ɪd

under-expo|se, -ses, -sing, -sed; -sure/s
ˌʌndərɪkˈspəʊ|z [-dəɪkˈs-, -dərekˈs-,
-dəekˈs-], -zɪz, -zɪŋ, -zd; -ʒə*/z

under|feed, -feeds, -feeding, -fed ˌʌndə|-
ˈfiːd, -ˈfiːdz, -ˈfiːdɪŋ, -ˈfed

under-felt, -s 'ʌndəfelt, -s

underfoot ˌʌndəˈfʊt

undergarment, -s 'ʌndəˌgɑːmənt, -s

under|go, -goes, -going, -went, -gone
ˌʌndə|ˈgəʊ, -ˈgəʊz, -ˈgəʊɪŋ, -ˈwent,
-ˈgɒn

undergraduate, -s ˌʌndəˈgrædjuət
[-ˈgrædʒuət, -djʊɪt, -dʒʊɪt], -s

underground (s. adj.) (U.) 'ʌndəgraʊnd

underground (adv.) ˌʌndəˈgraʊnd

undergrown ˌʌndəˈgrəʊn ['ʌndəgrəʊn]

undergrowth 'ʌndəgrəʊθ

underhand ˌʌndəˈhænd [---]

underhanded, -ly, -ness ˌʌndəˈhændɪd
['ʌndəˌh-], -lɪ, -nɪs [-nəs]

Underhill 'ʌndəhɪl

underhung ˌʌndəˈhʌŋ [also 'ʌndəh-
when attributive]

underlay (s.), -s 'ʌndəleɪ, -z

under|lay (v.), -lays, -laying, -laid
ˌʌndə|ˈleɪ, -ˈleɪz, -ˈleɪɪŋ, -ˈleɪd

underlease, -s 'ʌndəliːs, -ɪz

underlet, -s, -ting ˌʌndəˈlet ['ʌndəl-], -s,
-ɪŋ

under|lie, -lies, -lying, -lay, -lain
ˌʌndə|ˈlaɪ, -ˈlaɪz, -ˈlaɪɪŋ, -ˈleɪ, -ˈleɪn

underline (s.), -s 'ʌndəlaɪn [ˌ--ˈ-], -z

underlin|e (v.), -es, -ing, -ed ˌʌndəˈlaɪn,
-z, -ɪŋ, -d

underlinen 'ʌndəˌlɪnɪn

underling, -s 'ʌndəlɪŋ, -z

under|man (s.), -men 'ʌndə|mæn, -men

underman (v.), -s, -ning, -ned ˌʌndə-
ˈmæn, -z, -ɪŋ, -d

undermentioned ˌʌndəˈmenʃnd
['ʌndəˌm-]

undermin|e, -es, -ing, -ed, -er/s ˌʌndə-
ˈmaɪn, -z, -ɪŋ, -d, -ə*/z

undermost 'ʌndəməʊst

517

underneath ˌʌndə'ni:θ
underpants 'ʌndəpænts
underpass, -es 'ʌndəpɑ:s, -ɪz
under|pay, -pays, -paying, -paid ˌʌndə|-
'peɪ, -'peɪz, -'peɪɪŋ, -'peɪd [also
'ʌndəpeɪd when attributive]
underpayment, -s ˌʌndə'peɪmənt, -s
underpeopled ˌʌndə'pi:pld
underpin, -s, -ning, -ned ˌʌndə'pɪn, -z,
-ɪŋ, -d
underplay (s.) 'ʌndəpleɪ
underplay (v.), -s, -ing, -ed ˌʌndə'pleɪ,
-z, -ɪŋ, -d
underplot, -s 'ʌndəplɒt, -s
underpopulated ˌʌndə'pɒpjʊleɪtɪd
[-pjəl-]
underprais|e, -es, -ing, -ed ˌʌndə'preɪz,
-ɪz, -ɪŋ, -d
underprivileged ˌʌndə'prɪvɪlɪdʒd [-vəl-]
underpriz|e, -es, -ing, -ed ˌʌndə'praɪz,
-ɪz, -ɪŋ, -d
underproduction ˌʌndəprə'dʌkʃn
[-prʊ'd-, '---,--]
underprop, -s, -ping, -ped ˌʌndə'prɒp,
-s, -ɪŋ, -t
underrat|e, -es, -ing, -ed ˌʌndə'reɪt, -s,
-ɪŋ, -ɪd
under-ripe ˌʌndə'raɪp [also 'ʌndər-
according to sentence-stress]
under-roof, -s 'ʌndəru:f, -s
under|run, -runs, -running, -ran ˌʌndə|-
'rʌn, -'rʌnz, -'rʌnɪŋ, -'ræn
underscor|e, -es, -ing, -ed ˌʌndə'skɔ:*
[-'skɔə*], -z, -rɪŋ, -d
undersea (adj.) 'ʌndəsi:
underseal (s. v.), -s, -ing, -ed 'ʌndəsi:l
[,--'-], -z, -ɪŋ, -d
under-secretar|y, -ies; -yship/s ˌʌndə-
'sekrətər|ɪ, -ɪz; -ɪʃɪp/s
under|sell, -sells, -selling, -sold ˌʌndə|-
'sel, -'selz, -'selɪŋ, -'səʊld
undersheriff, -s 'ʌndəˌʃerɪf [,--'--], -s
undershirt, -s 'ʌndəʃɜ:t, -s
undershot 'ʌndəʃɒt
underside, -s 'ʌndəsaɪd, -z
undersign, -s, -ing, -ed ˌʌndə'saɪn, -z,
-ɪŋ, -d
undersigned (s.) 'ʌndəsaɪnd [,--'-]
undersized ˌʌndə'saɪzd ['---]
underskirt, -s 'ʌndəskɜ:t, -s
understaffed ˌʌndə'stɑ:ft
under|stand, -stands, -standing, -stood,
-standed; -standable, -standably
ˌʌndə|'stænd, -'stændz, -'stændɪŋ,
-'stʊd, -'stændɪd; -'stændəbl,
-'stændəblɪ
understat|e, -es, -ing, -ed ˌʌndə'steɪt, -s,
-ɪŋ, -ɪd

understatement, -s ˌʌndə'steɪtmənt
['ʌndəˌs-], -s
understocked ˌʌndə'stɒkt
understood (from understand) ˌʌndə-
'stʊd
understrapp|er/s, -ing 'ʌndəˌstræp|ə*/z,
-ɪŋ
understrat|um, -a ˌʌndə'strɑ:t|əm
['ʌndəˌs-, -streɪt-], -ə
understud|y (s. v.), -ies, -ying, -ied
'ʌndəˌstʌd|ɪ, -ɪz, -ɪŋ [-jɪŋ], -ɪd
under|take (take upon oneself), -takes,
-taking, -took, -taken ˌʌndə|'teɪk,
-'teɪks, -'teɪkɪŋ, -'tʊk, -'teɪkən
[-'teɪkɪŋ]
undertaker (one who agrees to perform),
-s ˌʌndə'teɪkə*, -z
undertaker (one who arranges funerals),
-s 'ʌndəˌteɪkə*, -z
Undertaker (special historical sense), -s
'ʌndəˌteɪkə*, -z
undertaking (s.) (enterprise, promise), -s
ˌʌndə'teɪkɪŋ ['-,--], -z
undertaking (s.) (arranging funerals)
'ʌndəˌteɪkɪŋ
undertenan|cy, -cies, -t/s ˌʌndə-
'tenən|sɪ ['ʌndə,t-], -sɪz, -t/s
under-the-counter ˌʌndəðə'kaʊntə*
undertime 'ʌndətaɪm
under-timed ˌʌndə'taɪmd
undertint, -s 'ʌndətɪnt, -s
undertone, -s 'ʌndətəʊn, -z
undertook (from undertake) ˌʌndə'tʊk
undertow, -s 'ʌndətəʊ, -z
undervaluation, -s ˌʌndəˌvæljʊ'eɪʃn,
-z
underval|ue, -ues, -uing, -ued ˌʌndə-
'væl|ju: [-jʊ], -ju:z [-jʊz], -jʊɪŋ
[-jwɪŋ], -ju:d [-jʊd]
under|vest/s, -wear 'ʌndə|vest/s, -weə*
underwent (from undergo) ˌʌndə'went
underwing, -s 'ʌndəwɪŋ, -z
underwood (U.), -s 'ʌndəwʊd, -z
underwork (s.) 'ʌndəwɜ:k
underwork (v.), -s, -ing, -ed ˌʌndə-
'wɜ:k, -s, -ɪŋ, -t
underworker (subordinate worker), -s
'ʌndəˌwɜ:kə*, -z
underworld (U.) 'ʌndəwɜ:ld
underwrit|e, -es, -ing, underwrote,
underwritten 'ʌndəraɪt [,ʌndə'r-], -s,
-ɪŋ, 'ʌndərəʊt [,ʌndə'r-], 'ʌndəˌrɪtn
[,ʌndə'r-]
underwriter, -s 'ʌndəˌraɪtə*, -z
undescribable ˌʌndɪ'skraɪbəbl
undeserv|ed, -edly, -edness ˌʌndɪ'zɜ:v|d,
-ɪdlɪ, -ɪdnɪs [-nəs]
undeserving, -ly ˌʌndɪ'zɜ:vɪŋ, -lɪ

undesign|ed, -edly, -edness ˌʌndɪˈzaɪn|d, -ɪdlɪ, -ɪdnɪs [-nəs]
undesirability ˈʌndɪˌzaɪərəˈbɪlətɪ [-lɪt-]
undesirab|le, -ly, -leness ˌʌndɪˈzaɪərəb|l, -lɪ, -lnɪs [-nəs]
undesirous ˌʌndɪˈzaɪərəs
undetected ˌʌndɪˈtektɪd
undeterminable ˌʌndɪˈtɜːmɪnəbl
undeterminate, -ly, -ness ˌʌndɪˈtɜː-mɪnət [-nɪt], -lɪ, -nɪs [-nəs]
undetermination ˈʌndɪˌtɜːmɪˈneɪʃn
undetermined ˌʌndɪˈtɜːmɪnd
undeterred ˌʌndɪˈtɜːd
undeveloped ˌʌndɪˈveləpt
undeviating ʌnˈdiːvɪeɪtɪŋ [ˌʌnˈd-, -vjeɪt-]
undeviatingly ʌnˈdiːvɪeɪtɪŋlɪ [-vjeɪt-]
undid (from undo) ˌʌnˈdɪd [ʌn-]
undies ˈʌndɪz
undigested ˌʌndɪˈdʒestɪd [-daɪˈdʒ-]
undignified ʌnˈdɪgnɪfaɪd [ˌʌnˈd-]
undiluted ˌʌndəˈljuːtɪd [-dɪˈl-, -ˈluːt-]
undiminished ˌʌndɪˈmɪnɪʃt [also ˈ-ˌ- when attributive]
undimmed ˌʌnˈdɪmd [ʌn-]
undine (U.), -s ˈʌndiːn [ʌnˈd-, ʊnˈd-], -z
undiplomatic ˌʌndɪpləˈmætɪk [-pləʊˈm-, -pluˈm-]
undiscerning ˌʌndɪˈsɜːnɪŋ [-ɪˈzɜː-]
undischarged ˌʌndɪsˈtʃɑːdʒd [also ˈ--ˌ- when attributive]
undisciplined ʌnˈdɪsɪplɪnd [ˌʌnˈd-, -səp-]
undisclosed ˌʌndɪsˈkləʊzd
undiscouraged ˌʌndɪsˈkʌrɪdʒd
undiscoverab|le, -ly ˌʌndɪsˈkʌvərəb|l, -lɪ
undiscovered ˌʌndɪsˈkʌvəd [also ˈʌndɪˌsk- when attributive]
undiscussed ˌʌndɪsˈkʌst
undisguised ˌʌndɪsˈgaɪzd
undismayed ˌʌndɪsˈmeɪd
undisposed ˌʌndɪsˈpəʊzd
undisputed ˌʌndɪsˈpjuːtɪd
undissolved ˌʌndɪsˈzɒlvd
undistinctive ˌʌndɪsˈtɪŋktɪv
undistinguishab|le, -ly, -leness ˌʌndɪsˈtɪŋgwɪʃəb|l, -lɪ, -lnɪs [-nəs]
undistinguished ˌʌndɪsˈtɪŋgwɪʃt
undistracted ˌʌndɪsˈtræktɪd
undisturbed ˌʌndɪsˈtɜːbd
undivided, -ly, -ness ˌʌndɪˈvaɪdɪd, -lɪ, -nɪs [-nəs]
un|do, -does, -doing, -did, -done, -doer/s ˌʌn|ˈduː [ʌn-], -ˈdʌz, -ˈduːɪŋ [-ˈdʊɪŋ], -ˈdɪd, -ˈdʌn, -ˈduːə*/z [-ˈdʊə*/z]
undock, -s, -ing, -ed ˌʌnˈdɒk, -s, -ɪŋ, -t
undomesticated ˌʌndəˈmestɪkeɪtɪd [-dəʊˈm-]

undoubted, -ly ʌnˈdaʊtɪd, -lɪ
undraped ˌʌnˈdreɪpt [also ˈʌndreɪpt when attributive]
undreamed of ʌnˈdremtɒv [ˌʌnˈd-, -ˈdrempt-, -ˈdriːmd-]
undreamt of ʌnˈdremtɒv [ˌʌnˈd-, -ˈdrempt-]
undress (s.) ˌʌnˈdres
undress (adj.) ˈʌndres
undress (v.), -es, -ing, -ed ˌʌnˈdres [ʌn-], -ɪz, -ɪŋ, -t
undrinkable ˌʌnˈdrɪŋkəbl [ʌn-]
undue ˌʌnˈdjuː [ˈʌnd-, ʌnˈd-, according to sentence-stress]
undulat|e, -es, -ing/ly, -ed ˈʌndjʊleɪt, -s, -ɪŋ/lɪ, -ɪd
undulation, -s ˌʌndjʊˈleɪʃn, -z
undulatory ˈʌndjʊlətrɪ [-leɪt-, ˌʌndjʊˈleɪtərɪ]
unduly ˌʌnˈdjuːlɪ [ʌn-]
unduti|ful, -fully, -fulness ˌʌnˈdjuːtɪ|fʊl [ʌn-], -fʊlɪ [-fəlɪ], -fʊlnɪs [-nəs]
undying, -ly ʌnˈdaɪɪŋ [ˌʌn-], -lɪ
unearned ˌʌnˈɜːnd [ˈʌnɜː-, ʌnˈɜː-, according to sentence-stress]
unearth, -s, -ing, -ed ˌʌnˈɜːθ [ʌnˈɜːθ], -s, -ɪŋ, -t
unearthl|y, -iness ʌnˈɜːθl|ɪ, -ɪnɪs [-məs]
uneas|y, -ier, -iest, -ily, -iness ʌnˈiːz|ɪ [ˌʌnˈiː-], -ɪə* [-jə*], -ɪɪst [-jɪst], -ɪlɪ [-əlɪ], -ɪnɪs [-nəs]
uneatable, -ness ˌʌnˈiːtəbl [ʌn-], -nɪs [-nəs]
uneaten ˌʌnˈiːtn [ʌn-]
uneconomic, -al ˈʌnˌiːkəˈnɒmɪk [ˌʌniːk-, ˈʌnˌek-, ˌʌnek-], -l
unedifying ˌʌnˈedɪfaɪɪŋ [ʌn-]
uneducated ˌʌnˈedjʊkeɪtɪd [ʌn-, -dʒʊ-]
unelected ˌʌnɪˈlektɪd
unembarrassed ˌʌnɪmˈbærəst [-nem-]
unemo|tional, -tionally ˌʌnɪˈməʊ|ʃənl [-ʃnəl, -ʃn̩l, -ʃənəl], -ʃn̩əlɪ [-ʃnəlɪ, -ʃn̩lɪ, -ʃn̩lɪ, -ʃənəlɪ]
unemphatic ˌʌnɪmˈfætɪk
unemployable ˌʌnɪmˈplɔɪəbl [-nem-]
unemployed ˌʌnɪmˈplɔɪd [-nem-]
unemployment ˌʌnɪmˈplɔɪmənt [-nem-]
unenclosed ˌʌnɪnˈkləʊzd [-nɪŋˈkl-, -nenˈkl-]
unencumbered ˌʌnɪnˈkʌmbəd [-nɪŋˈk-, -nenˈk-]
unending ʌnˈendɪŋ [ˌʌnˈen-]
unendowed ˌʌnɪnˈdaʊd [-nen-]
unendurable ˌʌnɪnˈdjʊərəbl [-nen-, -ˈdjɔər-, -ˈdjɔːr]
unengaged ˌʌnɪŋˈgeɪdʒd
un-English ˌʌnˈɪŋglɪʃ [rarely -ˈeŋ-]
unenlightened ˌʌnɪnˈlaɪtnd [-nen-]

519

unenterprising ˌʌn'entəpraɪzɪŋ [ʌn-]
unenviable ˌʌn'envɪəbl [ʌn-, -vjə-]
unequ|al/s, -ally, -alness, -alled ˌʌn'i:-
kwǀəl/z [ʌn-], -əlɪ, -əlnɪs [-nəs], -əld
unequitab|le, -ly ˌʌn'ekwɪtəbǀl [ʌn-], -lɪ
unequivoc|al, -ally, -alness ˌʌnɪ'kwɪ-
vəkǀl [-vʊk-], -əlɪ, -lnɪs [-nəs]
unerring, -ly, -ness ˌʌn'ɜːrɪŋ [ʌn-], -lɪ,
-nɪs [-nəs]
unescapable ˌʌnɪ'skeɪpəbl
U.N.E.S.C.O. ju:'neskəʊ [jʊ'n-]
unessential ˌʌnɪ'senʃl
uneven, -ly, -ness ˌʌn'i:vn [ʌn-], -lɪ,
-nɪs [-nəs]
unevent|ful, -fully, -fulness ˌʌnɪ'ventǀ-
fʊl, -fʊlɪ [-fəlɪ], -fʊlnɪs [-nəs]
unexampled ˌʌnɪg'zɑ:mpld [-neg-]
unexceptionab|le, -ly, -leness ˌʌnɪk'sep-
ʃnəbǀl [-nek-, -ʃɲə-, -ʃənə-], -lɪ, -lnɪs
[-nəs]
unexcep|tional, -tionally ˌʌnɪk'sepǀʃənl
[-nek-, -ʃnəl, -ʃn̩l, -ʃn̩l, -ʃənəl], -ʃɲəlɪ
[ʃnəlɪ, -ʃn̩lɪ, -ʃn̩lɪ, -ʃənəlɪ]
unexhausted ˌʌnɪg'zɔ:stɪd [-neg-]
unexpected, -ly, -ness ˌʌnɪk'spektɪd
[-nek-], -lɪ, -nɪs [-nəs]
unexpired ˌʌnɪk'spaɪəd [-nek-]
unexplained ˌʌnɪk'spleɪnd [-nek-]
unexplored ˌʌnɪk'splɔ:d [-nek-, -'splɔəd]
unexposed ˌʌnɪk'spəʊzd [-nek-]
unexpressib|le, -ly ˌʌnɪk'spresəbǀl
[-nek-, -srb-], -lɪ
unexpressive ˌʌnɪk'spresɪv [-nek-]
unexpurgated ˌʌn'ekspəgeɪtɪd [ʌn-]
unfading ʌn'feɪdɪŋ
unfailing, -ly, -ness ʌn'feɪlɪŋ, -lɪ, -nɪs
[-nəs]
unfair, -ly, -ness ˌʌn'feə* [ʌn-], -lɪ, -nɪs
[-nəs]
unfaith|ful, -fully, -fulness ʌn'feɪθǀfʊl
[ʌn-], -fʊlɪ [-fəlɪ], -fʊlnɪs [-nəs]
unfaltering, -ly ʌn'fɔ:ltərɪŋ [ˌʌn-, -'fɒl-],
-lɪ
unfamiliar, -ly ˌʌnfə'mɪljə* [-fɪŋ'ɪ-], -lɪ
unfamiliarity 'ʌnfəˌmɪlɪ'ærətɪ [-fɪŋˌɪ-,
-ɪtɪ]
unfashionable ʌn'fæʃnəbl [ʌn-, -ʃɲə-]
unfast|en, -ens, -ening, -ened ˌʌn-
'fɑ:sǀn [ʌn-], -nz, -nɪŋ [-ɳɪŋ], -nd
unfathomab|le, -ly, -leness ʌn'fæðəm-
əbǀl, -lɪ, -lnɪs [-nəs]
unfathomed ˌʌn'fæðəmd [ʌn-]
unfavourab|le, -ly, -leness ˌʌn'feɪvərəbǀl
[ʌn-], -lɪ, -lnɪs [-nəs]
unfed ˌʌn'fed
unfeeling, -ly, -ness ʌn'fi:lɪŋ, -lɪ, -nɪs
[-nəs]
unfeigned ʌn'feɪnd [ˌʌn'f-]

unfeigned|ly, -ness ʌn'feɪnɪdǀlɪ, -nɪs
[-nəs]
unfelt ˌʌn'felt
unfermented ˌʌnfə'mentɪd [-fɜ:'m-, also
'--,-- when attributive]
unfertilized [-ised] ˌʌn'fɜ:tɪlaɪzd [-təl-]
unfetter, -s, -ing, -ed ˌʌn'fetə*, -z, -rɪŋ,
-d
unfilial, -ly ˌʌn'fɪljəl [-lɪəl], -ɪ
unfinished ˌʌn'fɪnɪʃt [ʌn-, also '-,-- when
attributive]
unfit (adj.), -ly, -ness ˌʌn'fɪt [ʌn-], -lɪ,
-nɪs [-nəs]
unfit (v.), -s, -ting, -ted ˌʌn'fɪt [ʌn'f-],
-s, -ɪŋ, -ɪd
unfitting (adj.) ˌʌn'fɪtɪŋ [ʌn-]
unfittingly ʌn'fɪtɪŋlɪ
unfix, -es, -ing, -ed ˌʌn'fɪks, -ɪz, -ɪŋ, -t
unflagging ˌʌn'flægɪŋ [ʌn'f-]
unflappable ˌʌn'flæpəbl
unflattering, -ly ˌʌn'flætərɪŋ [ʌn-], -lɪ
unfledged ˌʌn'fledʒd [ʌn-, also '-- when
attributive]
unflinching ʌn'flɪntʃɪŋ [ˌʌn'f-]
unflinching|ly, -ness ʌn'flɪntʃɪŋǀlɪ, -nɪs
[-nəs]
unfold (open out folds, release sheep
from fold), -s, -ing, -ed ˌʌn'fəʊld
[ʌn-], -z, -ɪŋ, -ɪd
unfold (reveal), -s, -ing, -ed ʌn'fəʊld
[ˌʌn'f-], -z, -ɪŋ, -ɪd
unforeseeable ˌʌnfɔ:'si:əbl
unforesee|ing, -n ˌʌnfɔ:'si:ǀɪŋ, -n
unforgettable ˌʌnfə'getəbl
unforgiv|able, -en, -ing ˌʌnfə'gɪvǀəbl,
-n, -ɪŋ
unforgotten ˌʌnfə'gɒtn
unformed ˌʌn'fɔ:md ['ʌnfɔ:md when
attributive]
unfortified ˌʌn'fɔ:tɪfaɪd [ʌn-]
unfortun|ate, -ately, -ateness ʌn'fɔ:-
tʃnǀət [-tʃɳ|ət, -tʃən|ət, -nɪt], -ətlɪ
[-tlɪ], -ətnɪs [-nɪt-, -nəs]
unfounded ˌʌn'faʊndɪd [ʌn-]
unframed ˌʌn'freɪmd [also '-- when
attributive]
un|freeze, -freezes, -froze, -frozen
ˌʌnǀ'fri:z, -'fri:zɪz, -'frəʊz, -'frəʊzn
unfrequent, -ly ʌn'fri:kwənt, -lɪ
unfrequented ˌʌnfrɪ'kwentɪd
unfriend|ly, -liness ˌʌn'frendǀlɪ [ʌn-],
-lnɪs [-nəs]
unfrock, -s, -ing, -ed ˌʌn'frɒk [ʌn-], -s,
-ɪŋ, -t
unfruit|ful, -fully, -fulness ˌʌn'fru:tǀfʊl
[ʌn-], -fʊlɪ [-fəlɪ], -fʊlnɪs [-nəs]
unfulfilled ˌʌnfʊl'fɪld
unfurl, -s, -ing, -ed ˌʌn'fɜ:l, -z, -ɪŋ, -d

unfurnished ˌʌnˈfɜːnɪʃt [ʌn-, *also* ˈʌnˌf- *when attributive*]

ungainl|y, -iest, -iness ʌnˈgeɪnl|ɪ [ˌʌn-], -ɪɪst [-ɪɪst], -ɪnɪs [-ɪnəs]

ungarbled ˌʌnˈgɑːbld [ʌn-]

ungenerous, -ly ˌʌnˈdʒenərəs [ʌn-], -lɪ

ungenial ˌʌnˈdʒiːnjəl [ʌn-, -nɪəl]

ungent|le, -ly, -leness ˌʌnˈdʒent|l [ʌn-], -lɪ, -lnɪs [-nəs]

ungentleman|ly, -liness ʌnˈdʒentl-mən|lɪ [ˌʌn-], -lɪnɪs [-nəs]

un-get-at-able ˌʌngetˈætəbl

ungird, -s, -ing, -ed ˌʌnˈgɜːd, -z, -ɪŋ, -ɪd

unglazed ˌʌnˈgleɪzd [*also* ˈ-- *when attributive*]

unglorious ˌʌnˈglɔːrɪəs [ʌn-]

ungloved ˌʌnˈglʌvd [*also* ˈʌng- *when attributive*]

ungl|ue, -ues, -uing, -ued ˌʌnˈgl|uː, -uːz, -uːɪŋ [-ʊɪŋ], -uːd

ungodl|y, -ier, -iest, -iness ˌʌnˈgɒdl|ɪ [ʌn-], -ɪə* [-jə*], -ɪɪst [-jɪst], -ɪnɪs [-ɪnəs]

Ungoed ˈʌŋɡɔɪd

ungotten ˌʌnˈgɒtn

ungovernab|le, -ly, -leness ˌʌnˈgʌvən-əb|l [ʌn-, -vn̩ə-], -lɪ, -lnɪs [-nəs]

ungoverned ˌʌnˈgʌvənd

ungrace|ful, -fully, -fulness ˌʌnˈgreɪs|-fʊl [ʌn-], -fʊlɪ [-fəlɪ], -fʊlnɪs [-nəs]

ungracious, -ly, -ness ʌnˈgreɪʃəs [ʌn-], -lɪ, -nɪs [-nəs]

ungrammatic|al, -ally ˌʌngrəˈmætɪk|l, -əlɪ

ungrateful ʌnˈgreɪtfʊl [ˌʌn'g-]

ungrate|fully, -fulness ʌnˈgreɪt|fʊlɪ [-fəlɪ], -fʊlnɪs [-nəs]

ungrounded ˌʌnˈgraʊndɪd [ʌn'g-]

ungrudging ˌʌnˈgrʌdʒɪŋ [ʌn-]

ungrudgingly ʌnˈgrʌdʒɪŋlɪ

unguarded ˌʌnˈgɑːdɪd [ʌn-]

unguarded|ly, -ness ʌnˈgɑːdɪd|lɪ, -nɪs [-nəs]

unguent, -s ˈʌŋgwənt [-gjʊənt], -s

unguided ˌʌnˈgaɪdɪd [ʌn-]

ungul|a, -ae ˈʌŋgjʊl|ə, -iː

ungulate (*s. adj.*), -s ˈʌŋgjʊleɪt [-lət, -lɪt], -s

unhallowed ˌʌnˈhæləʊd [ʌn'h-]

unhampered ˌʌnˈhæmpəd [ʌn-]

unhand, -s, -ing, -ed ˌʌnˈhænd, -z, -ɪŋ, -ɪd

unhapp|y, -ier, -iest, -ily, -iness ʌn-ˈhæp|ɪ [ˌʌn'h-], -ɪə*, -ɪɪst, -ɪlɪ [-əlɪ], -ɪnɪs [-ɪnəs]

unharmed ˌʌnˈhɑːmd [ʌn-]

unharness, -es, -ing, -ed ˌʌnˈhɑːnɪs, -ɪz, -ɪŋ, -t

unhatched ˌʌnˈhætʃt

unhealth|y, -ier, -iest, -ily, -iness ʌnˈhelθ|ɪ [ˌʌn'h-], -ɪə* [-jə*], -ɪɪst [-jɪst], -ɪlɪ [-əlɪ], -ɪnɪs [-ɪnəs]

unheard (*not granted a hearing, etc.*) ˌʌnˈhɜːd

unheard of ˌʌnˈhɜːdɒv [ʌn-]

unheed|ed, -ing ˌʌnˈhiːd|ɪd [ʌn-], -ɪŋ

unhesitating, -ly ʌnˈhezɪteɪtɪŋ, -lɪ

unhing|e, -es, -ing, -ed ˌʌnˈhɪndʒ [ʌn'h-], -ɪz, -ɪŋ, -d

unhistoric, -al ˌʌnhɪˈstɒrɪk [*occasionally* ˌʌnɪˈs-], -l

unhitch, -es, -ing, -ed ˌʌnˈhɪtʃ [ʌn-], -ɪz, -ɪŋ, -t

unhol|y, -iness ˌʌnˈhəʊl|ɪ [ʌn-], -ɪnɪs [-ɪnəs]

unhook, -s, -ing, -ed ˌʌnˈhʊk [ʌn-], -s, -ɪŋ, -t

unhoped for ʌnˈhəʊptfɔː* [ˌʌn-]

unhors|e, -es, -ing, -ed ˌʌnˈhɔːs [ʌn-], -ɪz, -ɪŋ, -t

unhospitable ˌʌnˈhɒspɪtəbl [ʌn-, ˌʌnhɒˈsp-]

unhous|e, -es, -ing, -ed ˌʌnˈhaʊz, -ɪz, -ɪŋ, -d

unhuman ˌʌnˈhjuːmən [ʌn-]

unhung (*not hung*) ˌʌnˈhʌŋ

unhurt ˌʌnˈhɜːt

Uniat, -s ˈjuːnɪæt, -s

uniaxial, -ly ˌjuːnɪˈæksɪəl [-sjəl], -ɪ

U.N.I.C.E.F. ˈjuːnɪsef

unicorn, -s ˈjuːnɪkɔːn, -z

unicycle, -s ˈjuːnɪsaɪkl [ˌjuːnɪˈs-], -z

unideal ˌʌnaɪˈdɪəl [-ˈdiːəl, -ˈdiːl]

unidentified ˌʌnaɪˈdentɪfaɪd

unidiomatic ˈʌnˌɪdɪəˈmætɪk [-djəˈm-, -dɪʊˈm-, -djʊˈm-, -dɪəʊˈm-, -djəʊˈm-]

unifiable ˈjuːnɪfaɪəbl

unification, -s ˌjuːnɪfɪˈkeɪʃn [jʊn-], -z

uniform (*s. adj.*), -s, -ed, -ly, -ness ˈjuːnɪfɔːm, -z, -d, -lɪ, -nɪs [-nəs]

uniformity ˌjuːnɪˈfɔːmətɪ [jʊn-, -ɪtɪ]

uni|fy, -fies, -fying, -fied ˈjuːnɪ|faɪ, -faɪz, -faɪɪŋ, -faɪd

unilater|al, -ally ˌjuːnɪˈlætər|əl, -əlɪ

Unilever ˈjuːnɪliːvə*

uniliter|al, -ally ˌjuːnɪˈlɪtər|əl, -əlɪ

unimaginab|le, -ly, -leness ˌʌnɪˈmædʒɪ-nəb|l, -lɪ, -lnɪs [-nəs]

unimaginative, -ness ˌʌnɪˈmædʒɪnətɪv, -nɪs [-nəs]

unimagined ˌʌnɪˈmædʒɪnd

unimpaired ˌʌnɪmˈpeəd

unimpeachable ˌʌnɪmˈpiːtʃəbl

unimpeachab|ly, -leness ˌʌnɪmˈpiːtʃ-əb|lɪ, -lnɪs [-nəs]

unimpeded ˌʌnɪmˈpiːdɪd

unimportan|ce, -t ˌʌnɪm'pɔ:tən|s, -t
unimpress|ive, -ed ˌʌnɪm'pres|ɪv, -t
uninflated ˌʌnɪn'fleɪtɪd
uninflected ˌʌnɪn'flektɪd
uninfluenced ˌʌn'ɪnflʊənst [ʌn-, -flwənst]
uninformed ˌʌnɪn'fɔ:md
uninhabitable, -ness ˌʌnɪn'hæbɪtəbl, -nɪs [-nəs]
uninhabited ˌʌnɪn'hæbɪtɪd
uninhibited ˌʌnɪn'hɪbɪtɪd
uninitiated ˌʌnɪ'nɪʃɪeɪtɪd [-ʃjeɪt-]
uninjured ˌʌn'ɪndʒəd [ʌn-]
uninspired ˌʌnɪn'spaɪəd
uninstructed ˌʌnɪn'strʌktɪd
uninsured ˌʌnɪn'ʃʊəd [-'ʃɔəd, -'ʃɔ:d]
unintelligent, -ly ˌʌnɪn'telɪdʒənt, -lɪ
unintelligibility 'ʌnɪnˌtelɪdʒə'bɪlətɪ [-dʒɪ'b-, -ɪtɪ-]
unintelligib|le, -ly ˌʌnɪn'telɪdʒəb|l [-ledʒ-, -dʒɪb-], -lɪ
uninten|tional, -tionally ˌʌnɪn'ten|ʃənl [-ʃnəl, -ʃn̩l, -ʃnl, -ʃənəl], -ʃnəlɪ [-ʃnəlɪ, -ʃn̩lɪ, -ʃnlɪ, -ʃənəlɪ]
uninterest|ed, -ing ˌʌn'ɪntrəst|ɪd [ʌn-, -trɪs-, -tərəs-], -ɪŋ
unintermitting, -ly 'ʌnˌɪntə'mɪtɪŋ [ˌʌnɪ-], -lɪ
uninterrupted, -ly 'ʌnˌɪntə'rʌptɪd [ˌʌnɪ-], -lɪ
uninvit|ed, -ing ˌʌnɪn'vaɪt|ɪd, -ɪŋ
union (U.), -s 'ju:njən [-nɪən], -z
unioni|sm, -st/s 'ju:njənɪ|zəm [-nɪən-], -st/s
unipartite ˌju:nɪ'pɑ:taɪt ['ju:nɪˌp-]
unique, -ly, -ness ju:'ni:k [jʊ'n-], -lɪ, -nɪs [-nəs]
unisex 'ju:nɪseks
unisexual ˌju:nɪ'seksjʊəl [-ksjwəl, -ksjʊl, -kʃʊəl, -kʃwəl, -kʃʊl, -kʃl]
unison, -s 'ju:nɪzn [-ɪsn], -z
unissued ˌʌn'ɪʃu:d [-'ɪʃju:d, -'ɪsju:d]
unit, -s 'ju:nɪt, -s
unitable ju:'naɪtəbl [jʊ'n-]
unitarian (U.), -s, -ism ˌju:nɪ'teərɪən [jʊn-], -z, -ɪzəm
unitary 'ju:nɪtərɪ
unit|e, -es, -ing, -ed/ly, -er/s ju:'naɪt [jʊ'n-], -s, -ɪŋ, -ɪd/lɪ, -ə*/z
unit|y (U.), -ies 'ju:nət|ɪ [-ɪt|ɪ], -ɪz
univalve, -s 'ju:nɪvælv, -z
univers|al, -als, -ally, -alness, -alism, -alist/s ˌju:nɪ'vɜ:s|l [jʊn-], -lz, -əlɪ [-l̩ɪ], -lnɪs [-nəs], -əlɪzəm [-ɪzəm], -əlɪst/s [-l̩ɪst/s]
universality ˌju:nɪvɜ:'sælətɪ [-ɪtɪ]
universaliz|e [-is|e], -es, -ing, -ed ˌju:nɪ'vɜ:səlaɪz [jʊn-, -s|aɪz], -ɪz, -ɪŋ, -d

universe (U.), -s 'ju:nɪvɜ:s, -ɪz
universit|y, -ies ˌju:nɪ'vɜ:sət|ɪ [jʊn-, -sɪt|ɪ, -st|ɪ], -ɪz
univocal (s. adj.), -s ˌju:nɪ'vəʊkl, -z
unjust, -ly, -ness ʌn'dʒʌst [ʌn-, also '-- when attributive], -lɪ, -nɪs [-nəs]
unjustifiab|le, -ly, -leness ʌn'dʒʌstɪfaɪəb|l [ˌʌn'dʒ-, ʌn,dʒʌstɪ'f-, 'ʌn-,dʒʌstɪ'f-], -lɪ, -lnɪs [-nəs]
unkempt ˌʌn'kempt [ʌn-, also 'ʌnk- when attributive]
unkept ˌʌn'kept
unkin|d, -der, -dest, -dly, -dness ʌn'kaɪn|d [ˌʌn'k-], -də*, -dɪst, -dlɪ, -dnɪs [-nəs]
unknot, -s, -ting, -ted ˌʌn'nɒt, -s, -ɪŋ, -ɪd
unknowable ˌʌn'nəʊəbl [ʌn-]
unknowing, -ly, -ness ˌʌn'nəʊɪŋ [ʌn-], -lɪ, -nɪs [-nəs]
unknown ˌʌn'nəʊn [also 'ʌnn-, ʌn'n-, according to sentence-stress]
unlac|e, -es, -ing, -ed ˌʌn'leɪs, -ɪz, -ɪŋ, -t
unlad|e, -es, -ing, -ed ˌʌn'leɪd, -z, -ɪŋ, -ɪd
unladylike ˌʌn'leɪdɪlaɪk [ʌn-]
unlamented ˌʌnlə'mentɪd [also '--,-- when attributive]
unlash, -es, -ing, -ed ˌʌn'læʃ, -ɪz, -ɪŋ, -t
unlatch, -es, -ing, -ed ˌʌn'lætʃ, -ɪz, -ɪŋ, -t
unlaw|ful, -fully, -fulness ˌʌn'lɔ:|fʊl [ʌn-], -fʊlɪ [-fəlɪ], -fʊlnɪs [-nəs]
unleaded (without lead) ˌʌn'ledɪd [also '-,-- when attributive]
unlearn, -s, -ing, -ed (p. tense, p. partic.), -t ˌʌn'lɜ:n, -z, -ɪŋ, -t [-d], -t
unlearned (adj.), -ly, -ness ˌʌn'lɜ:nɪd, -lɪ, -nɪs [-nəs]
unleavened ˌʌn'levnd [also 'ʌn,l- when attributive]
unled ˌʌn'led
unless ən'les, [ʌn'les, n̩'les, also ˌʌn'les for special emphasis]
unlettered ˌʌn'letəd
Unley 'ʌnlɪ
unlicensed ˌʌn'laɪsənst [ʌn-]
unlike ˌʌn'laɪk ['ʌnl-, ʌn'l-]
unlikel|y, -ihood, -iness ʌn'laɪkl|ɪ [ˌʌn'l-], -ɪhʊd, -ɪnɪs [-məs]
unlikeness ˌʌn'laɪknɪs [ʌn-, -nəs]
unlimber, -s, -ing, -ed ˌʌn'lɪmbə*, -z, -rɪŋ, -d
unlimited ʌn'lɪmɪtɪd [ˌʌn'l-]
unlink, -s, -ing, -ed ˌʌn'lɪŋk, -s, -ɪŋ, -t [-'lɪŋt]
unliquidated ˌʌn'lɪkwɪdeɪtɪd [also 'ʌn-ˌlɪkwɪdeɪtɪd when attributive]

522

unlit ˌʌnˈlɪt [also ˈʌnlɪt when attributive]

unload, -s, -ing, -ed, -er/s ˌʌnˈləʊd [ʌn-], -z, -ɪŋ, -ɪd, -ə*/z

unlock, -s, -ing, -ed ˌʌnˈlɒk [ʌn-], -s, -ɪŋ, -t

unlooked for ʌnˈlʊktfɔː* [ˌʌn-]

unloos|e, -es, -ing, -ed ˌʌnˈluːs [ʌn-], -ɪz, -ɪŋ, -t

unloos|en, -ens, -ening, -ened ʌnˈluːs|n [ˌʌnˈl-], -nz, -nɪŋ [-nɪŋ], -nd

unlovel|y, -iness ˌʌnˈlʌvl|ɪ, -ɪnɪs [-nəs]

unloving ˌʌnˈlʌvɪŋ

unluck|y, -ier, -iest, -ily, -iness ʌnˈlʌk|ɪ [ˌʌnˈl-], -ɪə*, -ɪɪst, -ɪlɪ [-əlɪ], -ɪnɪs [-ɪnəs]

un|make, -makes, -making, -made ˌʌnˈ|meɪk, -ˈmeɪks, -ˈmeɪkɪŋ, -ˈmeɪd

unman, -s, -ning, -ned ˌʌnˈmæn, -z, -ɪŋ, -d

unmanageable ʌnˈmænɪdʒəbl [ˌʌnˈm-]

unmanageab|ly, -leness ʌnˈmænɪdʒ-əb|lɪ, -lnɪs [-nəs]

unman|ly, -ier, -iest, -iness ˌʌnˈmænl|ɪ [ʌn-], -ɪə* [-jə*], -ɪɪst [-jɪst], -ɪnɪs [-ɪnəs]

unmanner|ly, -liness ʌnˈmænə|lɪ, -lɪnɪs [-nəs]

unmarked ˌʌnˈmɑːkt [also ˈ- according to sentence-stress]

unmarriageable ˌʌnˈmærɪdʒəbl

unmarried ˌʌnˈmærɪd [also ˈʌnˌm-according to sentence-stress]

unmask, -s, -ing, -ed ˌʌnˈmɑːsk, -s, -ɪŋ, -t

unmatched ˌʌnˈmætʃt

unmeaning ˌʌnˈmiːnɪŋ

unmeaning|ly, -ness ʌnˈmiːnɪŋ|lɪ, -nɪs [-nəs]

unmeasurable ˌʌnˈmeʒərəbl

unmeasured ˌʌnˈmeʒəd

unmentionable, -s, -ness ʌnˈmenʃnəbl [-ʃnə-, -ʃənə-], -z, -nɪs [-nəs]

unmentioned ˌʌnˈmenʃnd

unmerci|ful, -fully, -fulness ʌnˈmɜːsɪ|-fʊl [ˌʌn-], -fʊlɪ [-fəlɪ], -fʊlnɪs [-nəs]

unmerited ˌʌnˈmerɪtɪd [ʌn-]

unmethodical ˌʌnmɪˈθɒdɪkl [-meˈθ-, -məˈθ-]

unmind|ful, -fully, -fulness ʌnˈmaɪnd|-fʊl [ˌʌn-], -fʊlɪ [-fəlɪ], -fʊlnɪs [-nəs]

unmingled ˌʌnˈmɪŋgld

unmistak(e)ab|le, -ly, -leness ˌʌnmɪˈs-teɪkəb|l, -lɪ, -lnɪs [-nəs]

unmitigated ʌnˈmɪtɪgeɪtɪd

unmixed ˌʌnˈmɪkst [also ˈʌnm- when attributive]

unmodifiable ˌʌnˈmɒdɪfaɪəbl [ʌn-]

unmodified ˌʌnˈmɒdɪfaɪd [ʌn-]

unmolested ˌʌnməʊˈlestɪd

unmoor, -s, -ing, -ed ˌʌnˈmʊə* [-ˈmɔə*, -ˈmɔː*], -z, -rɪŋ, -d

unmounted ˌʌnˈmaʊntɪd [also ˈʌnˌm-when attributive]

unmourned ˌʌnˈmɔːnd [-ˈmɔənd, rarely -ˈmʊənd]

unmov(e)able ˌʌnˈmuːvəbl [ʌn-]

unmoved ˌʌnˈmuːvd [ʌn-]

unmuff|le, -les, -ling, -led ˌʌnˈmʌf|l, -lz, -lɪŋ [-lɪŋ], -ld

unmusic|al, -ally ʌnˈmjuːzɪk|l, -əlɪ

unmuzz|le, -les, -ling, -led ˌʌnˈmʌz|l, -lz, -lɪŋ [-lɪŋ], -ld

unnamed ˌʌnˈneɪmd [also ˈʌnn- when attributive]

unnatur|al, -ally, -alness ʌnˈnætʃr|əl [ˌʌnˈn-, -tʃʊr-, -tʃər-], -əlɪ, -əlnɪs [-nəs]

unnavigable ˌʌnˈnævɪgəbl

unnecessarily ʌnˈnesəsərəlɪ [-sɪs-, -ser-, ˌʌnˌnesɪˈser-, ˌʌnˌnesəˈser-, -ɪlɪ]

unnecessar|y, -iness ʌnˈnesəsər|ɪ [ˌʌnˈn-, -sɪs-, -ser-], -ɪnɪs [-ɪnəs]

unneighbourly ˌʌnˈneɪbəlɪ

unnerv|e, -es, -ing, -ed ˌʌnˈnɜːv, -z, -ɪŋ, -d

unnotice|able, -d ˌʌnˈnəʊtɪs|əbl [ʌn-], -t

U.N.N.R.A. ˈʌnrə

unnumbered ˌʌnˈnʌmbəd [in contrast ˈ-ˌ-]

U.N.O. ˈjuːnəʊ

unobjectionab|le, -ly ˌʌnəbˈdʒəkʃnəb|l [-ʃnə-, -ʃənə-], -lɪ

unobliging ˌʌnəˈblaɪdʒɪŋ

unobliterated ˌʌnəˈblɪtəreɪtɪd [ˌʌnɒˈb-]

unobservan|ce, -t ˌʌnəbˈzɜːvən|s, -t

unobserv|ed, -edly ˌʌnəbˈzɜːv|d, -ɪdlɪ

unobstructed ˌʌnəbˈstrʌktɪd [also ˈʌnəbˌs- when attributive]

unobtainable ˌʌnəbˈteɪnəbl

unobtrusive, -ly, -ness ˌʌnəbˈtruːsɪv, -lɪ, -nɪs [-nəs]

unoccupied ˌʌnˈɒkjʊpaɪd [ʌn-]

unoffending ˌʌnəˈfendɪŋ [also ˈʌnəˌf-when attributive]

unoffensive ˌʌnəˈfensɪv

unofficial ˌʌnəˈfɪʃl [also ˈʌnəˌf- when attributive]

unopened ˌʌnˈəʊpənd [-pmd]

unopposed ˌʌnəˈpəʊzd

unordained ˌʌnɔːˈdeɪnd

unordered ˌʌnˈɔːdəd

unorganized ˌʌnˈɔːgənaɪzd [ʌn-, -gŋaɪ-]

unorthodox ˌʌnˈɔːθədɒks [ʌn-]

unorthodoxy ʌnˈɔːθədɒksɪ [ˌʌnˈɔː-]

unostentatious, -ly, -ness ˈʌnˌɒsten-ˈteɪʃəs [-tən-], -lɪ, -nɪs [-nəs]

523

unowned ˌʌnˈəʊnd
unpack, -s, -ing, -ed, -er/s ˌʌnˈpæk, -s,
-ɪŋ, -t, -ə*/z
unpaid ˌʌnˈpeɪd [also ˈʌnp- according to
sentence-stress]
unpaired ˌʌnˈpeəd
unpalatable ʌnˈpælətəbl [ˌʌnˈp-, -lɪt-]
unpalatableness ʌnˈpælətəblnɪs [-lɪt-,
-nəs]
unparalleled ʌnˈpærəleld [ˌʌn-, -rˌleld,
-rələld, -rˌləld]
unpardonable ʌnˈpɑːdn̩əbl [ˌʌnˈp-,
-dnə-]
unpardonab|ly, -leness ʌnˈpɑːdn̩əb|lɪ
[-dnə-], -lnɪs [-nəs]
unparliamentary ˈʌnˌpɑːləˈmentərɪ
[-lɪˈm-, -ljə-]
unpatriotic ˈʌnˌpætrɪˈɒtɪk [-ˌpeɪt-]
unpaved ˌʌnˈpeɪvd [also ˈʌnp- when
attributive]
unpeeled ˌʌnˈpiːld [also ˈʌnp- when
attributive]
unperceiv|able, -ed ˌʌnpəˈsiːv|əbl, -d
unperforated ˌʌnˈpɜːfəreɪtɪd [ʌn-]
unperformed ˌʌnpəˈfɔːmd
unpersua|dable, -sive ˌʌnpəˈsweɪ|dəbl,
-sɪv [-zɪv]
unperturbed ˌʌnpəˈtɜːbd
unperverted ˌʌnpəˈvɜːtɪd
unphilosophic|al, -ally, -alness ʌn-
ˌfɪləˈsɒfɪk|l [-əˈzɒ-], -əlɪ, -lnɪs [-nəs]
unpick, -s, -ing, -ed ˌʌnˈpɪk, -s, -ɪŋ, -t
unpierced ˌʌnˈpɪəst
unpiloted ˌʌnˈpaɪlətɪd
unpin, -s, -ning, -ned ˌʌnˈpɪn, -z, -ɪŋ,
-d
unpitied ˌʌnˈpɪtɪd
unpitying ˌʌnˈpɪtɪɪŋ [ʌnˈp-]
unpityingly ʌnˈpɪtɪɪŋlɪ
unplaced ˌʌnˈpleɪst
unplait, -s, -ing, -ed ˌʌnˈplæt, -s, -ɪŋ, -ɪd
unplayable ˌʌnˈpleɪəbl
unpleasant ˌʌnˈpleznt
unpleasant|ly, -ness ʌnˈpleznt|lɪ, -nɪs
[-nəs]
unpleasing ˌʌnˈpliːzɪŋ
unpleasing|ly, -ness ˌʌnˈpliːzɪŋ|lɪ, -nɪs
[-nəs]
unpliable ˌʌnˈplaɪəbl
unpoetic|al, -ally, -alness ˌʌnpəʊˈetɪk|l,
-əlɪ, -lnɪs [-nəs]
unpolished ˌʌnˈpɒlɪʃt [also ˈʌnˌp-
according to sentence-stress]
unpolitic ˌʌnˈpɒlɪtɪk [-lət-]
unpolluted ˌʌnpəˈluːtɪd [-ˈljuː-]
unpopular ˌʌnˈpɒpjʊlə* [ʌn-, -pjəl-]
unpopularity ˈʌnˌpɒpjʊˈlærətɪ [-pjəˈl-,
-ɪtɪ]

unpractic|al, -ally ˌʌnˈpræktɪk|l [ʌn-],
-əlɪ
unpracticality ˈʌnˌpræktɪˈkælətɪ [-ɪtɪ]
unpractised ʌnˈpræktɪst [ˌʌnˈp-]
unprecedented ʌnˈpresɪdəntɪd [ˌʌn-,
rarely -ˈpriːs-, -den-]
unpredictable ˌʌnprɪˈdɪktəbl [-prəˈd-]
unprejudiced ˌʌnˈpredʒʊdɪst [ʌnˈp-]
unpremeditated ˌʌnprɪˈmedɪteɪtɪd
unpreparation ˈʌnˌprepəˈreɪʃn
unprepar|ed, -edly, -edness ˌʌnprɪˈpeə|d
[-prəˈp-], -rɪdlɪ [-dlɪ], -rɪdnɪs [-dnɪs,
-nəs]
unprepossessing ˈʌnˌpriːpəˈzesɪŋ
unpresentable ˌʌnprɪˈzentəbl [-prəˈz-]
unpresuming ˌʌnprɪˈzjuːmɪŋ [-prəˈz-,
-ˈzuː-]
unpretending, -ly ˌʌnprɪˈtendɪŋ [also
ˈʌnprɪˌt- when attributive], -lɪ
unpretentious ˌʌnprɪˈtenʃəs [also ˈ--ˌ--
when attributive]
unpretentious|ly, -ness ˌʌnprɪˈtenʃəs|lɪ,
-nɪs [-nəs]
unpreventable ˌʌnprɪˈventəbl [-prəˈv-]
unpriced ˌʌnˈpraɪst
unprincipled ʌnˈprɪnsəpld [ˌʌnˈp-, -sɪp-]
unprintable ˌʌnˈprɪntəbl [ʌn-]
unprinted ˌʌnˈprɪntɪd
unproclaimed ˌʌnprəˈkleɪmd [-prəʊˈk-,
-prʊˈk-]
unprocurable ˌʌnprəˈkjʊərəbl [-prʊˈk-,
-ˈkjɔər-, -ˈkjɔːr-]
unproductive, -ly, -ness ˌʌnprəˈdʌktɪv
[-prʊˈd-], -lɪ, -nɪs [-nəs]
unprofes|sional, -sionally ˌʌnprəˈfe|ʃənl
[-prʊˈf-, -ʃnəl, -ʃn̩l, -ʃnl, -ʃənəl],
-ʃn̩əlɪ [-ʃnəlɪ, -ʃn̩lɪ, -ʃn̩lɪ, -ʃənəlɪ]
unprofitab|le, -ly, -leness ˌʌnˈprɒfɪtəb|l
[ʌnˈp-], -lɪ, -lnɪs [-nəs]
unprohibited ˌʌnprəʊˈhɪbɪtɪd [-prʊˈh-]
unpromising ˌʌnˈprɒmɪsɪŋ [ʌn-]
unpronounceable ˌʌnprəˈnaʊnsəbl
[-prʊˈn-, -prn̩ˈaʊ-]
unprop, -s, -ping, -ped ˌʌnˈprɒp, -s, -ɪŋ, -t
unpropitious, -ly, -ness ˌʌnprəˈpɪʃəs
[-prʊˈp-], -lɪ, -nɪs [-nəs]
unprotected ˌʌnprəˈtektɪd [-prʊˈt-]
unproved ˌʌnˈpruːvd
unprovided ˌʌnprəˈvaɪdɪd [-prʊˈv-]
unprovok|ed, -edly ˌʌnprəˈvəʊk|t
[-prʊˈv-], -ɪdlɪ [-tlɪ]
unpublished ˌʌnˈpʌblɪʃt [ˈʌnˌp- according to sentence-stress]
unpunctual, -ly ˌʌnˈpʌŋktjʊəl [ʌn-,
-tjwəl, -tjʊl, -tʃʊəl, -tʃwəl, -tʃʊl], -ɪ
unpunctuality ˈʌnˌpʌŋktjʊˈælətɪ [-tʃʊ-,
-ɪtɪ]
unpunished ˌʌnˈpʌnɪʃt

unqualified (*without qualifications*) ˌʌn-ˈkwɒlɪfaɪd [ʌn-], (*without reservation, downright*) ʌnˈkwɒlɪfaɪd
unquenchable ˌʌnˈkwenʃəbl
unquestionab|le, -ly, -leness ʌnˈkwestʃənəb|l [ˌʌn-, -eʃtʃ-, -tʃn̩ə-, -tʃnə-, -lɪ, -lnɪs [-nəs]
unquesti|oned, -oning/ly ʌnˈkwestʃ|ənd [ˌʌn-, -eʃtʃ-, -ənɪŋ/lɪ [-n̩ɪŋ/lɪ]
unrav|el, -els, -elling, -elled, -eller/s ʌnˈræv|l [ˌʌn-], -əlz, -lɪŋ [-əlɪŋ], -ld, -lə*/z [-ələ*/z]
unread ˌʌnˈred
unreadable, -ness ˌʌnˈriːdəbl [ʌn-], -nɪs [-nəs]
unread|y, -ily, -iness ˌʌnˈred|ɪ [ʌn-], -ɪlɪ [-əlɪ], -mɪs [-ɪnəs]
unreal ˌʌnˈrɪəl [ʌn-, -ˈriːəl]
unrealit|y, -ies ˌʌnrɪˈælət|ɪ [-riːˈæ-, -ɪt|ɪ], -ɪz
unreason ˌʌnˈriːzn [*in contrast* ˈʌnˌr-]
unreasonable ʌnˈriːzn̩əbl [ˌʌnˈr-, -znə-]
unreasonab|ly, -leness ʌnˈriːzn̩əb|lɪ [ˌʌn-, -znə-], -lnɪs [-nəs]
unreasoning ʌnˈriːzn̩ɪŋ [ˌʌnˈr-, -znɪŋ]
unreceipted ˌʌnrɪˈsiːtɪd [-rə's-, *also* '--ˌ-- *when attributive*]
unreceived ˌʌnrɪˈsiːvd [-rə's-]
unreciprocated ˌʌnrɪˈsɪprəkeɪtɪd [-rə's-, -prʊk-]
unreckoned ˌʌnˈrekənd
unreclaimed ˌʌnrɪˈkleɪmd [*also* '--ˌ-- *when attributive*]
unrecognizable [-isa-] ˌʌnˈrekəgnaɪzəbl [ʌnˈr-, ˈʌnˌrekəgˈn-, -kɪg-]
unrecognized [-ised] ˌʌnˈrekəgnaɪzd [ʌn-, -kɪg-]
unreconcilable ʌnˈrekənsaɪləbl [ʌnˈr-, ˈʌnˌrekən's-, -kn-]
unreconciled ʌnˈrekənsaɪld [ʌn-, -kn-]
unrecorded ˌʌnrɪˈkɔːdɪd [-rə'k-]
unrecounted ˌʌnrɪˈkaʊntɪd [-rə'k-]
unredeemable ˌʌnrɪˈdiːməbl [-rə'd-]
unredeemed ˌʌnrɪˈdiːmd [-rə'd-, *also* '--- *when attributive*]
unrefined ˌʌnrɪˈfaɪnd [-rə'f-]
unreflecting ˌʌnrɪˈflektɪŋ [-rə'f-]
unreformed ˌʌnrɪˈfɔːmd [-rə'f-]
unrefuted ˌʌnrɪˈfjuːtɪd [-rə'f-]
unregenerate ˌʌnrɪˈdʒenərət [-rə'dʒ-, -rɪt]
unregistered ˌʌnˈredʒɪstəd [ʌn-]
unrehearsed ˌʌnrɪˈhɜːst [-rə'h-]
unrelated ˌʌnrɪˈleɪtɪd [-rə'l-]
unrelaxed ˌʌnrɪˈlækst [-rə'l-]
unrelenting ˌʌnrɪˈlentɪŋ [-rə'l-]
unrelenting|ly, -ness ˌʌnrɪˈlentɪŋ|lɪ [-rə'l-], -nɪs [-nəs]

unreliability ˈʌnrɪˌlaɪəˈbɪlətɪ [-rə,l-, -lɪt-]
unreliable, -ness ˌʌnrɪˈlaɪəbl [-rə'l-], -nɪs [-nəs]
unrelieved ˌʌnrɪˈliːvd [-rə'l-]
unremembered ˌʌnrɪˈmembəd [-rə'm-]
unremitting ˌʌnrɪˈmɪtɪŋ [-rə'm-]
unremitting|ly, -ness ˌʌnrɪˈmɪtɪŋ|lɪ [-rə'm-], -nɪs [-nəs]
unremonstrative ˌʌnrɪˈmɒnstrətɪv [-rə'm-]
unremovable ˌʌnrɪˈmuːvəbl [-rə'm-]
unremunerative ˌʌnrɪˈmjuːnərətɪv [-rə'm-]
unrepaid ˌʌnrɪˈpeɪd
unrepair, -able ˌʌnrɪˈpeə* [-rə'p-], -rəbl
unrepealed ˌʌnrɪˈpiːld [-rə'p-]
unrepeatable ˌʌnrɪˈpiːtəbl [-rə'p-]
unrepentant ˌʌnrɪˈpentənt [-rə'p-]
unreported ˌʌnrɪˈpɔːtɪd [-rə'p-]
unrepresented ˌʌnreprɪˈzentɪd
unrequested ˌʌnrɪˈkwestɪd [-rə'k-]
unrequited ˌʌnrɪˈkwaɪtɪd [-rə'k-]
unreserved ˌʌnrɪˈzɜːvd [-rə'z-, *also* '--- *when attributive*]
unreservedly ˌʌnrɪˈzɜːvɪdlɪ [-rə'z-]
unresisting, -ly ˌʌnrɪˈzɪstɪŋ [-rə'z-], -lɪ
unresolved ˌʌnrɪˈzɒlvd [-rə'z-]
unresponsive ˌʌnrɪˈspɒnsɪv [-rə's-]
unrest ˌʌnˈrest [ʌn-]
unrest|ful, -fully, -fulness ˌʌnˈrest|fʊl [ʌn-], -fʊlɪ [-fəlɪ], -fʊlnɪs [-nəs]
unresting ˌʌnˈrestɪŋ [ʌn-]
unrestored ˌʌnrɪˈstɔːd [-rə's-, -'stɔəd]
unrestrain|ed, -edly ˌʌnrɪˈstreɪn|d [-rə's-], -ɪdlɪ
unrestricted ˌʌnrɪˈstrɪktɪd [-rə's-]
unretentive ˌʌnrɪˈtentɪv [-rə't-]
unrevealed ˌʌnrɪˈviːld [-rə'v-]
unrevoked ˌʌnrɪˈvəʊkt [-rə'v-]
unrewarded ˌʌnrɪˈwɔːdɪd [-rə'w-]
unrighteous, -ly, -ness ʌnˈraɪtʃəs [*rarely* -tjəs], -lɪ, -nɪs [-nəs]
unright|ful, -fully, -fulness ˌʌnˈraɪt|fʊl [ʌn-], -fʊlɪ [-fəlɪ], -fʊlnɪs [-nəs]
unripe ˌʌnˈraɪp [*also* ˈʌnr-, ʌnˈr-, *according to sentence-stress*]
unripeness ˌʌnˈraɪpnɪs [ʌn-, -nəs]
unrivalled ʌnˈraɪvld [ˌʌn-]
unrob|e, -es, -ing, -ed ˌʌnˈrəʊb [ʌn-], -z, -ɪŋ, -d
unroll, -s, -ing, -ed ˌʌnˈrəʊl [ʌn-], -z, -ɪŋ, -d
unromantic, -ally ˌʌnrəˈmæntɪk [-rəʊ'm-], -əlɪ
unrop|e, -es, -ing, -ed ˌʌnˈrəʊp, -s, -ɪŋ, -t
unruffled ˌʌnˈrʌfld [ʌn-]
unrul|y, -ier, -iest, -iness ʌnˈruːl|ɪ, -ɪə* [-jə*], -ɪɪst [-jɪst], -ɪnɪs [-nəs]

525

unsadd|le, -les, -ling, -led ˌʌn'sæd|l
[ʌn-], -lz, -lɪŋ [-lɪŋ], -ld

unsafe, -ly, -ness ˌʌn'seɪf [ʌn-], -lɪ, -nɪs
[-nəs]

unsaid ˌʌn'sed [ʌn-]

unsal(e)able, -ness ˌʌn'seɪləbl [ʌn-], -nɪs
[-nəs]

unsalted ˌʌn'sɔːltɪd [-'sɒl-]

unsanctified ˌʌn'sæŋktɪfaɪd

unsanitary ˌʌn'sænɪtərɪ [ʌn-, -ətərɪ]

unsatisfactor|y, -ily, -iness 'ʌnˌsætɪs-
'fæktər|ɪ [ˌ---'---], -əlɪ [-ɪlɪ], -ɪnɪs
[-məs]

unsatisf|ied, -y¦ing ˌʌn'sætɪsf|aɪd, -aɪɪŋ

unsavour|y, -ily, -iness ˌʌn'seɪvər|ɪ
[ʌn-], -əlɪ [-ɪlɪ], -mɪs [-məs]

uns|ay, -ays, -aying, -aid ˌʌn's|eɪ
['ʌns|eɪ], -ez, -eɪɪŋ, -ed

unscalable ˌʌn'skeɪləbl

unscathed ˌʌn'skeɪðd [ʌn-]

unscented ˌʌn'sentɪd [in contrast 'ʌnˌs-]

unscheduled ˌʌn'ʃedjuːld

unscholarly ˌʌn'skɒləlɪ

unschooled ˌʌn'skuːld

unscientific 'ʌnˌsaɪən'tɪfɪk [ˌ---'--]

unscr|ew, -ews, -ewing, -ewed ˌʌn-
'skr|uː [ʌn-], -uːz, -uːɪŋ [-uɪŋ], -uːd

unscriptur|al, -ally ˌʌn'skrɪptʃər|əl
[-tʃʊr-], -əlɪ

unscrupulous ʌn'skruːpjʊləs [ˌʌn's-,
-pjəl-]

unscrupulous|ly, -ness ʌn'skruːpjʊləs|lɪ
[-pjəl-], -nɪs [-nəs]

unseal, -s, -ing, -ed ˌʌn'siːl, -z, -ɪŋ, -d

unseasonab|le, -ly, -leness ʌn'siːznəb|l
[ˌʌn's-, -znə-], -lɪ, -lnɪs [-nəs]

unseasoned ˌʌn'siːznd [also '-ˌ-- when
attributive]

unseat, -s, -ing, -ed ˌʌn'siːt, -s, -ɪŋ, -ɪd

unseaworth|y, -iness ˌʌn'siːˌwɜːð|ɪ
[ʌn-], -mɪs [-məs]

unsectarian, -ism ˌʌnsek'teərɪən, -ɪzəm

unsecured ˌʌnsɪ'kjʊəd [-sə'k-, -'kjɔəd,
-'kjɔːd]

unseeing ˌʌn'siːɪŋ

unseeml|y, -iness ˌʌn'siːml|ɪ, -mɪs [-məs]

unseen ˌʌn'siːn [also 'ʌns-, ʌn's-,
according to sentence-stress]

unselfish, -ly, -ness ˌʌn'selfɪʃ, -lɪ, -nɪs
[-nəs]

unsensational ˌʌnsen'seɪʃənl [-sən-,
-ʃnəl, -ʃn̩l, -ʃn̩l, -ʃənəl]

unsensitive ˌʌn'sensətɪv [ʌn's-, -sɪt-]

unsentimental ˌʌnˌsentɪ'mentl

unserviceable ˌʌn'sɜːvɪsəbl [ʌn-]

unsett|le, -les, -ling, -led ˌʌn'set|l [ʌn-],
-lz, -lɪŋ [-lɪŋ], -ld

unsevered ˌʌn'sevəd [ʌn-]

unshack|le, -les, -ling, -led ˌʌn'ʃæk|l
[ʌn-], -lz, -lɪŋ [-lɪŋ], -ld

unshakable ʌn'ʃeɪkəbl

unshaken ˌʌn'ʃeɪkən [ʌn-]

unshapely ˌʌn'ʃeɪplɪ [ʌn-]

unshaven ˌʌn'ʃeɪvn

unsheath|e, -es, -ing, -ed ˌʌn'ʃiːð [ʌn-],
-z, -ɪŋ, -d

unship, -s, -ping, -ped ˌʌn'ʃɪp, -s, -ɪŋ, -t

un|shod, -shorn ˌʌn|'ʃɒd, -'ʃɔːn

unshrinkable ˌʌn'ʃrɪŋkəbl [ʌn-]

unshrinking, -ly ʌn'ʃrɪŋkɪŋ, -lɪ

unsighted ˌʌn'saɪtɪd [ʌn-]

unsightl|y, -ier, -iest, -iness ʌn'saɪtl|ɪ,
-ɪə* [-jə*], -ɪɪst [-jɪst], -ɪnɪs [-məs]

unsigned ˌʌn'saɪnd [also 'ʌnsaɪnd when
attributive]

unskil|ful, -fully, -fulness ˌʌn'skɪl|fʊl
[ʌn-], -fʊlɪ [-fəlɪ], -fʊlnɪs [-nəs]

unskilled ˌʌn'skɪld [also 'ʌnskɪld when
attributive]

unslaked ˌʌn'sleɪkt

unsociability 'ʌnˌsəʊʃə'bɪlətɪ [-lɪt-]

unsociab|le, -ly, -leness ʌn'səʊʃəb|l
[ˌʌn's-], -lɪ, -lnɪs [-nəs]

unsold ˌʌn'səʊld [also 'ʌnsəʊld when
attributive]

unsolder, -s, -ing, -ed ˌʌn'sɒldə*
[-'sɔːd-, -'sɒd-, -'səʊld-], -z, -rɪŋ, -d

unsolicited ˌʌnsə'lɪsɪtɪd

unsolved ˌʌn'sɒlvd [also 'ʌns- according
to sentence-stress]

unsophisticated, -ly, -ness ˌʌnsə'fɪs-
tɪkeɪtɪd [-tək-], -lɪ, -nɪs

unsophistication 'ʌnsəˌfɪstɪ'keɪʃn

unsorted ˌʌn'sɔːtɪd

unsought ˌʌn'sɔːt [ʌn's- in unsought for]

unsoun|d, -dly, -dness ˌʌn'saʊn|d, -dlɪ,
-dnɪs [-nəs]

unsparing, -ly, -ness ʌn'speərɪŋ, -lɪ, -nɪs
[-nəs]

unspeakab|le, -ly ʌn'spiːkəb|l, -lɪ

unspecified ˌʌn'spesɪfaɪd [ʌn-]

unspent ˌʌn'spent [also 'ʌnspent when
attributive]

unspoiled ˌʌn'spɔɪlt [-ld]

unspoilt ˌʌn'spɔɪlt

unspoken ˌʌn'spəʊkən [ʌn-]

unsporting ˌʌn'spɔːtɪŋ

unsportsmanlike ˌʌn'spɔːtsmənlaɪk
[ʌn-]

unspotted ˌʌn'spɒtɪd

unstable, -ness ˌʌn'steɪbl [ʌn-], -nɪs
[-nəs]

unstack, -s, -ing, -ed ˌʌn'stæk, -s, -ɪŋ, -t

unstamped ˌʌn'stæmpt ['ʌnstæmpt
when attributive]

unstarched ˌʌn'stɑːtʃt

unstatesmanlike ˌʌn'steɪtsmənlaɪk [ʌn-]
unsteadfast, -ly, -ness ˌʌn'stedfəst [ʌn-],
-fɑ:st], -lɪ, -nɪs [-nəs]
unstead|y, -ier, -iest, -ily, -iness ˌʌn-
'sted|ɪ [ʌn-], -ɪə*, -ɪɪst, -ɪlɪ [-əlɪ], -ɪnɪs
[-ɪnəs]
un|stick, -sticks, -sticking, -stuck ˌʌn|-
'stɪk, -'stɪks, -'stɪkɪŋ, -'stʌk
unstinted ʌn'stɪntɪd
unstitch, -es, -ing, -ed ˌʌn'stɪtʃ, -ɪz, -ɪŋ,
-t
unstop, -s, -ping, -ped ˌʌn'stɒp, -s, -ɪŋ, -t
unstrap, -s, -ping, -ped ˌʌn'stræp, -s,
-ɪŋ, -t
unstressed ˌʌn'strest [also 'ʌnstrest
when attributive]
unstrung ˌʌn'strʌŋ
unstudied ˌʌn'stʌdɪd [ʌn-]
unsub|duable, -dued ˌʌnsəb|'djuːəbl
[-'djʊəbl], -'djuːd
unsubmissive, -ly, -ness ˌʌnsəb'mɪsɪv,
-lɪ, -nɪs [-nəs]
unsubstantial ˌʌnsəb'stænʃl [-bz't-]
unsubstantiality 'ʌnsəbˌstænʃɪ'ælətɪ
[-bzˌt-, -ɪtɪ]
unsuccess ˌʌnsək'ses ['ʌnsəkˌses]
unsuccess|ful, -fully, -fulness ˌʌnsək-
'ses|fʊl, -fʊlɪ [-fəlɪ], -fʊlnɪs [-nəs]
unsuitability 'ʌnˌsuːtə'bɪlətɪ ['ʌnˌsjuː-,
ˌʌnsuː-, ˌʌnsjuː-, -lɪt-]
unsuitab|le, -ly, -leness ˌʌn'suːtəb|l
[ʌn-, -'sjuː-], -lɪ, -lnɪs [-nəs]
unsuited ˌʌn'suːtɪd [ʌn-, -'sjuː-]
unsullied ˌʌn'sʌlɪd
unsung ˌʌn'sʌŋ
unsupportab|le, -ly, -leness ˌʌnsə'pɔːt-
əb|l, -lɪ, -lnɪs [-nəs]
unsupported ˌʌnsə'pɔːtɪd
unsure ˌʌn'ʃɔː* [ʌn-, -'ʃʊə*, -'ʃɔə*]
unsurmountable ˌʌnsə'maʊntəbl
unsurpass|able, -ed ˌʌnsə'pɑːs|əbl, -t
unsusceptibility 'ʌnsəˌseptə'bɪlətɪ
[-tɪ'b-, -lɪt-]
unsusceptible ˌʌnsə'septəbl [-tɪb-]
unsuspected, -ly, -ness ˌʌnsə'spektɪd,
-lɪ, -nɪs [-nəs]
unsuspecting, -ly, -ness ˌʌnsə'spektɪŋ,
-lɪ, -nɪs [-nəs]
unsuspicious, -ly, -ness ˌʌnsə'spɪʃəs, -lɪ,
-nɪs [-nəs]
unsweetened ˌʌn'swiːtnd [also 'ʌnˌs-
when attributive]
unswerving, -ly ʌn'swɜːvɪŋ, -lɪ
unsymmetric, -al, -ally ˌʌnsɪ'metrɪk, -l,
-əlɪ
unsymmetry ˌʌn'sɪmətrɪ [-ɪtrɪ]
unsympathetic, -ally 'ʌnˌsɪmpə'θetɪk,
-əlɪ

unsystematic, -al, -ally ˌʌnsɪstɪ'mætɪk
['-ˌ--'--, -təm-], -l, -əlɪ
untainted ˌʌn'teɪntɪd [ʌn-]
untamable ˌʌn'teɪməbl
untang|le, -les, -ling, -led ˌʌn'tæŋg|l
[ʌn-], -lz, -lɪŋ [-lɪŋ], -ld
untapped ˌʌn'tæpt
untarnished ˌʌn'tɑːnɪʃt [ʌn-]
untasted ˌʌn'teɪstɪd
untaught ˌʌn'tɔːt [also 'ʌntɔːt when
attributive]
untaxed ˌʌn'tækst [also 'ʌntækst when
attributive]
unteachable ˌʌn'tiːtʃəbl [ʌn-]
untempered ˌʌn'tempəd [also 'ʌnˌt-
when attributive]
untenable ˌʌn'tenəbl [ʌn-, -'tiːn-]
untenanted ˌʌn'tenəntɪd
unthank|ful, -fully, -fulness ˌʌn'θæŋk|-
fʊl [ʌn-], -fʊlɪ [-fəlɪ], -fʊlnɪs [-nəs]
unthinkable ʌn'θɪŋkəbl
unthinking, -ly ˌʌn'θɪŋkɪŋ [ʌn-]
unthinkingly ʌn'θɪŋkɪŋlɪ
unthought|ful, -fully, -fulness ˌʌn-
'θɔːt|fʊl [ʌn-], -fʊlɪ [-fəlɪ], -fʊlnɪs
[-nəs]
unthought of ʌn'θɔːtɒv
unthread, -s, -ing, -ed ʌn'θred, -z, -ɪŋ,
-ɪd
unthrift|y, -ily, -iness ʌn'θrɪft|ɪ [ʌn-],
-ɪlɪ [-əlɪ], -ɪnɪs [-nəs]
untid|y (adj. v.), -ier, -iest, -ily, -iness;
-ies, -ying, -ied ʌn'taɪd|ɪ [ˌʌn't-], -ɪə*
[-jə*], -ɪɪst [-jɪst], -ɪlɪ [-əlɪ], -ɪnɪs
[-ɪnəs]; -ɪz, -ɪŋ [-jɪŋ], -ɪd
un|tie, -ties, -tying, -tied ˌʌn|'taɪ, -'taɪz,
-'taɪɪŋ, -'taɪd
until ən'tɪl [ʌn'tɪl, n'tɪl, also occasionally 'ʌntɪl, 'ʌntl when followed by a
stress]
untimel|y, -iness ʌn'taɪml|ɪ [ˌʌn-], -ɪnɪs
[-ɪnəs]
untinged ˌʌn'tɪndʒd
untiring, -ly ʌn'taɪərɪŋ, -lɪ
unto 'ʌntʊ [-tuː, -tə]
Note.—The form 'ʌntu: occurs chiefly
in final position; the form 'ʌntə
occurs only before consonants.
untold ˌʌn'təʊld [ʌn't-, also occasionally
'ʌntəʊld when attributive]
untouchable, -s ʌn'tʌtʃəbl [ˌʌn't-], -z
untouched ˌʌn'tʌtʃt [ʌn-]
untoward, -ly, -ness ˌʌntə'wɔːd [-tʊ'w-,
ʌn'təʊəd, ˌʌn't-], -lɪ, -nɪs [-nəs]
untraceable ˌʌn'treɪsəbl
untrained ˌʌn'treɪnd [also 'ʌnt-, ʌn't-,
according to sentence-stress]
untrammelled ʌn'træməld [ˌʌn-]

527

untransferable ˌʌntrænsˈfɜːrəbl [-trɑːns-]

untranslat|able, -ed ˌʌntrænsˈleɪt|əbl [-trɑːns-, -trænz-, -trɑːnz-, -trəns-, -trənz-], -ɪd

untried ˌʌnˈtraɪd [also ˈʌntraɪd when attributive]

untrimmed ˌʌnˈtrɪmd [also ˈʌntrɪmd when attributive]

untrodden ˌʌnˈtrɒdn [also ˈʌnˌt- when attributive]

untroubled ˌʌnˈtrʌbld [ʌn-]

un|true, -trueness ˌʌn|ˈtruː [ʌn-], -ˈtruː-nɪs [-nəs]

untruly ˌʌnˈtruːlɪ [ʌn-]

untrustworth|y, -ily, -iness ˌʌnˈtrʌst-ˌwɜːðɪ [ʌn-], -ɪlɪ [-əlɪ], -ɪnɪs [-ɪnəs]

untru|th, -ths ˌʌnˈtruː|θ [ʌn-], -ðz [-θs]

untruth|ful, -fully, -fulness ˌʌnˈtruːθ|-fʊl [ʌn-], -fʊlɪ [-fəlɪ], -fʊlnɪs [-nəs]

untuck, -s, -ing, -ed ˌʌnˈtʌk, -s, -ɪŋ, -t

unturned ˌʌnˈtɜːnd

untutored ˌʌnˈtjuːtəd

untwist, -s, -ing, -ed ˌʌnˈtwɪst [ʌn-], -s, -ɪŋ, -ɪd

unused (not made use of) ˌʌnˈjuːzd [ʌn-]

unused (not accustomed) ˌʌnˈjuːst [ʌn-, rarely -ˈjuːzd]

unu|sual, -sually, -sualness ʌnˈjuː|ʒʊəl [ˌʌn|j-, -ʒwəl, -ʒʊl, -ʒl], -ʒʊəlɪ [-ʒwəlɪ, -ʒʊlɪ, -ʒəlɪ, -ʒlɪ], -ʒʊəlnɪs [-ʒwəlnɪs, -ʒʊlnɪs, -ʒlnɪs, -nəs]

unutterab|le, -ly, -leness ʌnˈʌtərəb|l, -lɪ, -lnɪs [-nəs]

unuttered ˌʌnˈʌtəd

unvaccinated ˌʌnˈvæksɪneɪtɪd

unvariable ʌnˈveərɪəbl [ˌʌnˈv-]

unvaried ˌʌnˈveərɪd

unvarnished (not varnished) ˌʌnˈvɑːnɪʃt [ʌn-], (simple) ʌnˈvɑːnɪʃt

unvarying ʌnˈveərɪɪŋ

unveil, -s, -ing, -ed, -er/s ˌʌnˈveɪl [ʌnˈv-], -z, -ɪŋ, -d, -ə*/z

unventilated ˌʌnˈventɪleɪtɪd [ʌn-, -təl-]

unversed ˌʌnˈvɜːst [ʌn-]

unvoic|e, -es, -ing, -ed ˌʌnˈvɔɪs, -ɪz, -ɪŋ, -t [also ˈʌnvɔɪst when attributive]

unwanted ˌʌnˈwɒntɪd [also ˈʌnˌw- when attributive]

unwar|ily, -iness ʌnˈweər|əlɪ [-ɪlɪ], -ɪnɪs [-nəs]

unwarlike ˌʌnˈwɔːlaɪk [ʌn-]

unwarmed ˌʌnˈwɔːmd [also ˈʌnw- when attributive]

unwarned ˌʌnˈwɔːnd

unwarrantab|le, -ly, -leness ʌnˈwɒrənt-əb|l, -lɪ, -lnɪs [-nəs]

unwarranted (not guaranteed) ˌʌn-ˈwɒrəntɪd

unwarranted (unjustified) ʌnˈwɒrəntɪd

unwary ʌnˈweərɪ [ˌʌnˈw-]

unwashed ˌʌnˈwɒʃt [also ˈʌnw- when attributive]

unwavering, -ly ʌnˈweɪvərɪŋ, -lɪ

unwearable ˌʌnˈweərəbl [ʌn-]

unwearied ʌnˈwɪərɪd

unwearying ʌnˈwɪərɪɪŋ

unwed ˌʌnˈwed

unwelcome ʌnˈwelkəm [ˌʌnˈw-]

unwell ˌʌnˈwel [ʌn-]

unwholesome, -ly, -ness ʌnˈhəʊlsəm [ʌn-], -lɪ, -nɪs [-nəs]

unwield|y, -ier, -iest, -ily, -iness ʌn-ˈwiːld|ɪ, -ɪə* [-jə*], -ɪɪst [-jɪst], -ɪlɪ [-əlɪ], -ɪnɪs [-nəs]

unwilling ˌʌnˈwɪlɪŋ [ʌn-]

unwilling|ly, -ness ʌnˈwɪlɪŋ|lɪ, -nɪs [-nəs]

Unwin ˈʌnwɪn

un|wind, -winds, -winding, -wound ˌʌn|ˈwaɪnd [ʌn-], -ˈwaɪndz, -ˈwaɪndɪŋ, -ˈwaʊnd

unwiped ˌʌnˈwaɪpt

unwisdom ˌʌnˈwɪzdəm

unwise ˌʌnˈwaɪz [also ˈʌnw-, ʌnˈw-, according to sentence-stress]

unwisely ˌʌnˈwaɪzlɪ [ʌn-]

unwished for ʌnˈwɪʃtɔː* [ˌʌnˈw-]

unwitting, -ly ʌnˈwɪtɪŋ, -lɪ

unwoman|ly, -liness ʌnˈwʊmən|lɪ [ˌʌnˈw-], -lɪnɪs [-nəs]

unwonted, -ly, -ness ʌnˈwəʊntɪd, -lɪ, -nɪs [-nəs]

unworkable ˌʌnˈwɜːkəbl [ʌn-]

unworkmanlike ˌʌnˈwɜːkmənlaɪk [ʌn-]

unworld|ly, -liness ˌʌnˈwɜːld|lɪ [ʌn-], -lnɪs [-nəs]

unworn ˌʌnˈwɔːn [ˈʌnw- when attributive]

unworth|y, -ily, -iness ʌnˈwɜːð|ɪ [ˌʌnˈw-], -ɪlɪ [-əlɪ], -ɪnɪs [-nəs]

unwound (from unwind) ˌʌnˈwaʊnd [ʌn-]

unwounded ˌʌnˈwuːndɪd

unwrap, -s, -ping, -ped ˌʌnˈræp [ʌn-], -s, -ɪŋ, -t

unwritten ˌʌnˈrɪtn [also ˈʌnˌr- when attributive]

unwrought ˌʌnˈrɔːt

unyielding, -ly, -ness ʌnˈjiːldɪŋ [ˌʌnˈj-], -lɪ, -nɪs [-nəs]

unyok|e, -es, -ing, -ed ˌʌnˈjəʊk [ʌn-], -s, -ɪŋ, -t

up ʌp

up-and-down ˌʌpənˈdaʊn

528

upas, -es 'juːpəs, -ɪz
upbraid, -s, -ing, -ed ʌp'breɪd, -z, -ɪŋ, -ɪd
upbringing 'ʌp,brɪŋɪŋ
upcast, -s 'ʌpkɑːst, -s
Upcott 'ʌpkət [-kɒt]
upcountry (s. adj.) ,ʌp'kʌntrɪ, (adv.) ʌp'kʌntrɪ
Updike 'ʌpdaɪk
Upham 'ʌpəm
upharsin juː'fɑːsɪn [uː-]
upheav|e, -es, -ing, -ed; -al/s ʌp'hiːv, -z, -ɪŋ, -d; -l/z
upheld (from uphold) ʌp'held
uphill ,ʌp'hɪl ['ʌph-, ʌp'h-, according to sentence-stress]
up|hold, -holds, -holding, -held, -holder/s ʌp|'həʊld, -'həʊldz, -'həʊldɪŋ, -'held, -'həʊldə*/z
upholst|er, -ers, -ering, -ered, -erer/s; -ery ʌp'həʊlst|ə* [əp-], -əz, -ərɪŋ, -əd, -ərə*/z; -ərɪ
Upjohn 'ʌpdʒɒn
upkeep 'ʌpkiːp
upland, -s; -er/s 'ʌplənd, -z; -ə*/z
uplift (s.) 'ʌplɪft
uplift (v.), -s, -ing, -ed ʌp'lɪft, -s, -ɪŋ, -ɪd
Upminster 'ʌp,mɪnstə*
upmost 'ʌpməʊst
upon ə'pɒn (strong form), əpən (occasional weak form)
upper (s. adj.), -s; -most 'ʌpə*, -z; -məʊst [-məst]
uppercut, -s 'ʌpəkʌt, -s
Uppingham 'ʌpɪŋəm
uppish, -ly, -ness 'ʌpɪʃ, -lɪ, -nɪs [-nəs]
Uppsala 'ʌpsɑːlə ['ʊp-, ʌp's-, ʊp's-]
uprais|e, -es, -ing, -ed ʌp'reɪz, -ɪz, -ɪŋ, -d ['ʌpreɪzd when attributive]
uprear, -s, -ing, -ed ʌp'rɪə*, -z, -rɪŋ, -d
Uprichard juː'prɪtʃɑːd [-tʃəd], ʌp'rɪtʃəd
upright (s.), -s 'ʌpraɪt, -s
upright (adj.) (honest) 'ʌpraɪt [,ʌp'r-]
upright (adj. adv.) (erect) ,ʌp'raɪt [also 'ʌpr-, ʌp'r-, according to sentence-stress]
upright|ly, -ness 'ʌp,raɪt|lɪ [ʌp'r-], -nɪs [-nəs]
uprising, -s 'ʌp,raɪzɪŋ [,-'--], -z
uproar, -s 'ʌprɔː* [-rɔə*], -z
uproarious, -ly, -ness ʌp'rɔːrɪəs [-'rɔər-], -lɪ, -nɪs [-nəs]
uproot, -s, -ing, -ed ʌp'ruːt, -s, -ɪŋ, -ɪd
Upsala 'ʌpsɑːlə ['ʊp-, ʌp's-, ʊp's-]
upset (s.), -s ʌp'set ['ʌpset], -s
upset (adj.) ʌp'set ['-- when attributive]
upset (v.), -s, -ting, -ter/s ʌp'set, -s, -ɪŋ, -ə*/z

Upsher 'ʌpʃə*
upshot 'ʌpʃɒt
upside, -s 'ʌpsaɪd, -z
upside-down ,ʌpsaɪd'daʊn
upsilon, -s juːp'saɪlən [ʊp's-, 'juːpsɪlən], -z
up-stag|e, -es, -ing, -ed ,ʌp'steɪdʒ, -ɪz, -ɪŋ, -d
upstairs ,ʌp'steəz ['ʌps-, ʌp's-, according to sentence-stress]
upstart, -s 'ʌpstɑːt, -s
upstream ,ʌp'striːm ['ʌpstriːm]
upstroke, -s 'ʌpstrəʊk, -s
upsurge (s.), -s 'ʌpsɜːdʒ, -ɪz
upsurg|e (v.), -es, -ing, -ed ʌp'sɜːdʒ, -ɪz, -ɪŋ, -d
uptake, -s 'ʌpteɪk, -s
upthrust, -s 'ʌpθrʌst [,ʌp'θrʌst], -s
uptight 'ʌptaɪt [,-'-]
uptilt, -s, -ing, -ed ʌp'tɪlt, -s, -ɪŋ, -ɪd
Upton 'ʌptən
uptown ,ʌp'taʊn [ʌp't- when preceded by a stress]
upturn, -s, -ing, -ed ʌp'tɜːn, -z, -ɪŋ, -d
upturned (adj.) ,ʌp'tɜːnd ['ʌpt-, ʌp't-, according to sentence-stress]
upward, -ly, -s 'ʌpwəd, -lɪ, -z
Upwey 'ʌpweɪ
ur (interj.), ʌː, ɜː
Ur ɜː* [ʊə*]
uraemia ,jʊə'riːmjə [jʊ'r-, jə'r-, jɔə'r-, jɔː'r-, -mɪə]
Ural 'jʊərəl ['jɔər-, 'jɔːr-]
uralite 'jʊərəlaɪt ['jɔər-, 'jɔːr-]
Urania, -n ,jʊə'reɪnjə [jʊ'r-, jə'r-, jɔə'r-, jɔː'r-, -nɪə], -n
uranium jʊ'reɪnjəm [,jʊə'r-, jə'r-, jɔə'r-, jɔː'r-, -nɪəm]
Uranus 'jʊərənəs ['jɔər-, 'jɔːr-, jʊə'reɪnəs]
urate, -s 'jʊəreɪt ['jɔər-, 'jɔːr-, -rɪt], -s
urban (U.) 'ɜːbən
Urbana ɜː'bænə [-'bɑːn-]
urbane (U.), -ly ɜː'beɪn, -lɪ
urbanity ɜː'bænətɪ [-ɪtɪ]
urbanization ,ɜːbənaɪ'zeɪʃn
urbaniz|e, -es, -ing, -ed 'ɜːbənaɪz, -ɪz, -ɪŋ, -d
Urbevilles 'ɜːbəvɪlz
urchin, -s 'ɜːtʃɪn, -z
Urdu 'ʊəduː ['ɜːd-, ,-'-, -'-) (Hindi wrdu)
Ure jʊə*
urea, -l 'jʊərɪə ['jɔər-, 'jɔːr-, jʊə'rɪə], -l
ureter, -s ,jʊə'riːtə*, -z
urethra, -s ,jʊə'riːθrə [jʊ'r-], -z
uretic (s. adj.), -s jʊə'retɪk [jʊ'r-, jə'r-], -s

urg|e (s. v.), -es, -ing, -ed, -er/s ɜːdʒ,
-ɪz, -ɪŋ, -d, -ə*/z
urgen|cy, -t/ly 'ɜːdʒən|sɪ, -t/lɪ
Uriah ˌjʊə'raɪə [jʊ'r-, jə'r-]
uric 'jʊərɪk ['jɔər-, 'jɔːr-]
Uriel 'jʊərɪəl ['jɔər-, 'jɔːr-]
Urim 'jʊərɪm ['jɔər-, 'jɔːr-, 'ʊər-]
urin|al, -als, -ary 'jʊərɪn|l ['jɔər-, 'jɔːr-,
jʊə'raɪnl, jə'r-], -lz, -ərɪ
urinat|e, -es, -ing, -ed 'jʊərɪneɪt ['jɔər-,
'jɔːr-, -rən-], -s, -ɪŋ, -ɪd
urination ˌjʊərɪ'neɪʃn [ˌjɔər-, ˌjɔːr-]
urine, -s 'jʊərɪn ['jɔər-, 'jɔːr-], -z
Urmia 'ɜːmjə ['ʊəm-, -mɪə]
urn, -s ɜːn, -z
Urquhart 'ɜːkət
Ursa (constellation) 'ɜːsə
ursine 'ɜːsaɪn
Ursula 'ɜːsjʊlə [rarely 'ɜːʃjʊ-, 'ɜːʃʊ-]
Ursuline 'ɜːsjʊlaɪn ['ɜːʃ-, -lɪn]
urtica 'ɜːtɪkə
urticaria ˌɜːtɪ'keərɪə
Uruguay 'jʊərʊgwaɪ ['jʊr-, 'ʊr-, -rəg-,
ˌ-ʼ-, old-fashioned 'ʊrʊgweɪ, 'jʊrʊ-
gweɪ, 'jʊərʊgweɪ, -rəg-]
Uruguayan, -s ˌjʊərʊ'gwaɪən [ˌjʊr-,
ˌʊr-, -rəʼg, old-fashioned -'gweɪən],
-z
Urumiah ʊ'ruːmjə [-mɪə]
urus 'jʊərəs ['jɔər-, 'jɔːr-]
us ʌs (strong form), əs, s (weak forms)
U.S.A. ˌjuːeˈseɪ
usable 'juːzəbl
usage, -s 'juːzɪdʒ ['juːsɪ-], -ɪz
usance, -s 'juːzns, -ɪz
use (s.), -s juːs, -ɪz
us|e (v.) (make use of), -es, -ing, -ed,
-er/s juːz, -ɪz, -ɪŋ, -d, -ə*/z
used (adj.) (accustomed) juːst [rarely
juːzd]
used (from use v.) juːzd
used (v.) (was or were accustomed) juːst
(when followed by to), juːst (when not
followed by to) [rarely juːzd]
use(d)n't 'juːsnt (when followed by to),
'juːsnt (when not followed by to)
use|ful, -fully, -fulness 'juːs|fʊl, -fʊlɪ
[-fəlɪ], -fʊlnɪs [-nəs]
useless, -ly, -ness 'juːslɪs [-ləs], -lɪ, -nɪs
[-nəs]
usen't 'juːsnt (when followed by to),
'juːsnt (when not followed by to)
user, -s 'juːzə*, -z
uses (plur. of use s.) 'juːsɪz
uses (from use v.) 'juːzɪz
Ushant 'ʌʃənt
usher (s. v.) (U.), -s, -ing, -ed 'ʌʃə*, -z,
-rɪŋ, -d

usherette, -s ˌʌʃə'ret, -s
usquebaugh, -s 'ʌskwɪbɔː, -z
U.S.S.R. ˌjuːeses'ɑː*
Ustinov 'juːstɪnɒf [-ɒv]
u|sual, -sually, -sualness 'juː|ʒʊəl [ʒwəl,
-ʒʊl, -ʒl], -ʒʊəlɪ [-ʒwəlɪ, -ʒʊlɪ, -ʒəlɪ,
-ʒlɪ], -ʒʊəlnɪs [-ʒwəlnɪs, -ʒʊlnɪs,
-ʒlnɪs, -nəs]
usufruct, -s 'juːsjuːfrʌkt [-sjʊ-, 'juːzj-],
-s
usurer, -s 'juːʒərə*, -z
usurious, -ly, -ness juː'zjʊərɪəs [jʊ'z-,
-'zjɔər-, -'zjɔːr-, juː'ʒʊə-, jʊ'ʒ-], -lɪ,
-nɪs [-nəs]
usurp, -s, -ing, -ed, -er/s juː'zɜːp
[jʊ'z-], -s, -ɪŋ, -t, -ə*/z
usurpation, -s ˌjuːzɜː'peɪʃn, -z
usury 'juːʒʊrɪ [-ʒərɪ, -ʒʊərɪ]
Utah 'juːtɑː [or -tɔ: as in U.S.A.]
utensil, -s juː'tensl [jʊ't-, -sɪl], -z
uterine 'juːtəraɪn
uter|us, -i, -uses 'juːtər|əs, -aɪ, -əsɪz
Uther 'juːθə*
Uthwatt 'ʌθwɒt
Utica 'juːtɪkə
utilitarian (s. adj.), -s, -ism ˌjuːtɪlɪ-
'teərɪən [juːˌtɪlɪ't-, jʊˌt-, -lə't-], -z,
-ɪzəm
utility juː'tɪlətɪ [jʊ't-, -ɪtɪ]
utilization [-isa-] ˌjuːtɪlaɪ'zeɪʃn [-təl-,
-lɪ'z-]
utiliz|e [-is|e], -es, -ing, -ed, -er/s; -able
'juːtɪlaɪz [-təl-], -ɪz, -ɪŋ, -d, -ə*/z;
-əbl
utmost 'ʌtməʊst [-məst]
Utopia, -n/s juː'təʊpjə [jʊ't-, -pɪə], -n/z
Utrecht 'juːtrekt [-trext, -'-]
utricle, -s 'juːtrɪkl, -z
utter (adj. v.), -ly, -ness; -s, -ing, -ed,
-er/s; -able 'ʌtə*, -lɪ, -nɪs [-nəs]; -z,
-rɪŋ, -d, -rə*/z; -rəbl
utterance, -s 'ʌtərəns, -ɪz
uttermost 'ʌtəməʊst [-məst]
Uttoxeter juː'tɒksɪtə* [ʌ'tɒksɪtə*,
'ʌksɪtə*]
 Note.—The common pronunciation is
 juː'tɒksɪtə* or ʌ'tɒksɪtə*. The
 former is more freq., and is the
 pronunciation of most outsiders.
U-turn, -s 'juːtɜːn, -z
uvula, -s 'juːvjʊlə [-jəl-], -z
uvular 'juːvjʊlə* [-jəl-]
Uxbridge 'ʌksbrɪdʒ
uxorious ʌk'sɔːrɪəs
Uzbekistan ʊzˌbekɪ'stɑːn [ʌz-]
Uzzah 'ʌzə
Uzzell 'ʌzl
Uzziah ʌ'zaɪə

V

V (*the letter*), **-'s** viː, -z

v. (*versus*) viː: ['vɜːsəs], (*vide*) viː: [siː, 'vɪdeɪ, 'vaɪdɪ]

vac, -s væk, -s

vacanc|y, -ies 'veɪkəns|ɪ, -ɪz

vacant, -ly 'veɪkənt, -lɪ

vacat|e, -es, -ing, -ed vəˈkeɪt [veɪˈk-], -s, -ɪŋ, -ɪd

vacation, -s vəˈkeɪʃn, -z

vaccinat|e, -es, -ing, -ed, -or/s 'væksɪn-ert [-ksŋeɪt], -s, -ɪŋ, -ɪd, -ə*/z

vaccination, -s ˌvæksɪ'neɪʃn [-ksŋ'eɪ-], -z

vaccine 'væksiːn [-sɪn]

Vachel(l) 'veɪtʃəl

Vacher 'væʃə*, 'veɪtʃə*

vacillat|e, -es, -ing/ly, -ed, -or/s 'væsɪleɪt [-səl-, -s|-], -s, -ɪŋ/lɪ, -ɪd, -ə*/z

vacillation ˌvæsɪ'leɪʃn [-sə'l-]

vacuity væ'kjuːətɪ [və'k-, -'kjʊətɪ, -ɪtɪ]

vacuo (*in* in vacuo) 'vækjʊəʊ

vacuous, -ness 'vækjʊəs [-kjwəs], -nɪs [-nəs]

vacuum, -s 'vækjʊəm [-kjwəm, -kjʊm], -z

vacuum-cleaner, -s 'vækjʊəmˌkliːnə* [-kjwəm-, -kjʊm-], -z

vade-mecum, -s ˌveɪdɪ'miːkəm [-kʌm, ˌvɑːdɪ'meɪkʊm], -z

vagabond (*s. adj.*), **-s** 'vægəbɒnd [-bənd], -z

vagabondage 'vægəbɒndɪdʒ

vagar|y, -ies 'veɪgər|ɪ [və'geər-], -ɪz

vagin|a/s, -al və'dʒaɪn|ə/z, -l

vagrancy 'veɪgrənsɪ

vagrant (*s. adj.*), **-s, -ly** 'veɪgrənt, -s, -lɪ

vague, -r, -st, -ly, -ness veɪg, -ə*, -ɪst, -lɪ, -nɪs [-nəs]

vail (**V.**), **-s, -ing, -ed** veɪl, -z, -ɪŋ, -d

Vaile veɪl

vain, -er, -est, -ly, -ness veɪn, -ə*, -ɪst, -lɪ, -nɪs [-nəs]

vainglorious, -ly, -ness ˌveɪn'glɔːrɪəs, -lɪ, -nɪs [-nəs]

vainglory ˌveɪn'glɔːrɪ

Valais 'væleɪ (vale)

valance, -s, -d 'væləns, -ɪz, -t

vale (*s.*) (**V.**), **-s** veɪl, -z

vale (*goodbye*) 'veɪlɪ ['væleɪ, 'vɑː-]

valediction, -s ˌvælɪ'dɪkʃn, -z

valedictory ˌvælɪ'dɪk'ərɪ

valence (*damask, short curtain*), **-s, -d** 'væl*ə*ns, -ɪz, -t

valence (*in chemistry*) 'veɪləns

Valencia, -s və'lenjɪə [-fjə, -ʃə, -sɪə, -sjə], -z

Valenciennes ˌvælənsɪ'en [-lɑ̃ːns-, -lɑːns-, -sɪ'enz, -'sjen, -'sjenz] (valɑ̃sjɛn)

Note.—There was formerly a pronunciation ˌvælən'siːnz.

valenc|y, -ies 'veɪləns|ɪ, -ɪz

valentine, -s 'væləntaɪn, -z

Valentine (*Christian name*) 'væləntaɪn, -tɪn, (*surname*) 'væləntɪn, -taɪn

Valentinian ˌvælən'tɪnɪən [-njən]

Valera və'leərə

valerian (**V.**), **-s** və'lɪərɪən, -z

Valerius və'lɪərɪəs

Valery(-rie) 'vælərɪ

valet (*s.*), **-s** 'vælɪt, -s ['vælɪ, 'væleɪ, -z]

valet (*v.*), **-s, -ing, -ed** 'vælɪt, -s, -ɪŋ, -ɪd

valetudinarian, -s, -ism ˌvælɪtjuːdɪ-'neərɪən, -z, -ɪzəm

Valhalla væl'hælə

valiant, -ly, -ness 'væljənt, -lɪ, -nɪs [-nəs]

valid, -ly, -ness 'vælɪd, -lɪ, -nɪs [-nəs]

validat|e, -es, -ing, -ed 'vælɪdeɪt, -s, -ɪŋ, -ɪd

validation ˌvælɪ'deɪʃn

validit|y, -ies və'lɪdət|ɪ [væ'l-, -ɪt|ɪ], -ɪz

valise, -s və'liːz [væ'l-, -iːsː, -ɪz

Valium 'væləm ['veɪ-, -ljəm]

Valkyrie, -s væl'kɪərɪ ['vælkɪrɪ], -z

Valladolid ˌvælədəʊ'lɪd [-dɒ'l-] (baʎaðo'li)

Valletta və'letə

valley, -s 'vælɪ, -z

Valois 'vælwɑː [-lwɔː] (valwa)

valorous, -ly 'vælərəs, -lɪ

valour 'vælə*

Valparaiso ˌvælpə'raɪzəʊ [-'reɪzəʊ] (balpara'iso)

Valpy 'vælpɪ

valse, -s vɑːls [vɔːls], -ɪz

valuable, -s, -ness 'væljʊəbl [-ljwəb-, -ljʊb-], -z, -nɪs [-nəs]

valuation, -s ˌvæljʊ'eɪʃn, -z

val|ue (s. v.), -ues, -uing, -ued, -uer/s
'væl|juː: [-jʊ], -juːz [-jʊz], -jʊŋ
[-jwɪŋ], -juːd [-jʊd], -jʊə*/z [-jwə*/z]
valueless 'væljʊlɪs [-ləs]
valve, -s vælv, -z
valvular 'vælvjʊlə*
vamoos|e, -es, -ing, -ed və'muːs [-uːz],
-ɪz, -ɪŋ, və'muːst [-uːzd]
vamp (s. v.), -s, -ing, -ed, -er/s væmp,
-s, -ɪŋ, -t [væmt], -ə*/z
vampire, -s 'væmpaɪə*, -z
van (s. v.), -s, -ning, -ned væn, -z, -ɪŋ, -d
vanadium və'neɪdjəm [-dɪəm]
Vanbrugh 'vænbrə
    Note.—Sir John Vanbrugh, the seven-
    teenth-century dramatist and archi-
    tect, is sometimes referred to as
    væn'bruː:.
Vancouver væn'kuːvə* [væŋ'k-]
vandal (V.), -s 'vændl, -z
vandalism 'vændəlɪzəm
Vanderb|ilt, -yl 'vændəb|ɪlt, -aɪl
Van Diemen ˌvæn'diːmən
Vandyke [Van Dyck] (name of artist,
    picture by him), -s ˌvæn'daɪk, -s
vandyke (adj.) (brown, etc.) 'vændaɪk
vane (V.), -s, -d veɪn, -z, -d
Vanessa və'nesə
Van Eyck, -s ˌvæn'aɪk, -s
Vange vændʒ
van Gogh ˌvæn'gɒf [-'gɒk, -'gɒx]
vanguard, -s 'vænɡɑːd ['væŋg-], -z
van Homrigh ˌvæn'hɒmrɪg
vanilla və'nɪlə [vɲ'ɪlə]
vanish, -es, -ing, -ed 'vænɪʃ, -ɪz, -ɪŋ, -t
vanit|y, -ies 'vænət|ɪ [-ɪt|ɪ], -ɪz
vanquish, -es, -ing, -ed, -er/s; -able
    'væŋkwɪʃ, -ɪz, -ɪŋ, -t, -ə*/z; -əbl
Vansittart væn'sɪtət [-tɑːt]
van Straubenzee (English surname)
    ˌvænstrɔː'benzɪ
vantage, -s 'vɑːntɪdʒ, -ɪz
vapid, -ly, -ness 'væpɪd, -lɪ, -nɪs [-nəs]
vapidity væ'pɪdətɪ [və'p-, -ɪtɪ]
vaporization [-isa-], -s ˌveɪpəraɪ'zeɪʃn
    [-rɪ'z-], -z
vaporiz|e [-is|e], -es, -ing, -ed, -er/s
    'veɪpəraɪz, -ɪz, -ɪŋ, -d, -ə*/z
vaporosity ˌveɪpə'rɒseɪtɪ [-ɪtɪ]
vaporous, -ly, -ness 'veɪpərəs, -lɪ, -nɪs
    [-nəs]
vapour (s. v.), -s, -ing/s, -ed; -y 'veɪpə*,
    -z, -rɪŋ/z, -d; -rɪ
vapour-ba|th, -ths 'veɪpəbɑː|θ, -ðz
varec 'værek [-rɪk]
variability ˌveərɪə'bɪlətɪ [-ɪtɪ]
variab|le, -ly, -leness 'veərɪəb|l, -lɪ,
    -lnɪs [-nəs]

varian|ce, -t/s 'veərɪən|s, -t/s
variation, -s ˌveərɪ'eɪʃn [rarely ˌvær-], -z
varicella ˌværɪ'selə
varices (plur. of varix) 'værɪsiːz ['veər-]
varicose 'værɪkəʊs
varied 'veərɪd
variegat|e, -es, -ing, -ed 'veərɪɡeɪt
    [rarely -rɪəg-, -rɪɡ-], -s, -ɪŋ, -ɪd
variegation, -s ˌveərɪ'geɪʃn [rarely
    -rɪə'g-, -rɪ'g-], -z
variet|y, -ies və'raɪət|ɪ, -ɪz
variform 'veərɪfɔːm
variola və'raɪələ
variole, -s 'veərɪəʊl, -z
varioloid 'veərɪəlɔɪd
variorum ˌveərɪ'ɔːrəm [ˌvær-]
various, -ly, -ness 'veərɪəs, -lɪ, -nɪs
    [-nəs]
variphone, -s 'veərɪfəʊn, -z
varix, varices 'veərɪks, 'værɪsiːz ['veər-]
varlet, -s 'vɑːlɪt, -s
Varley 'vɑːlɪ
varmint, -s 'vɑːmɪnt, -s
Varney 'vɑːnɪ
varnish (s. v.), -es, -ing, -ed, -er/s
    'vɑːnɪʃ, -ɪz, -ɪŋ, -t, -ə*/z
Varro 'værəʊ
varsit|y, -ies 'vɑːsət|ɪ [-ɪt|ɪ], -ɪz
varsovienne, -s ˌvɑːsəʊvɪ'en, -z
var|y, -ies, -ying, -ied 'veər|ɪ, -ɪz, -ɪɪŋ,
    -ɪd
Vasco da Gama ˌvæskəʊdə'gɑːmə
    [-dɑː'g-]
vascular 'væskjʊlə* [-kjə-]
vascularity ˌvæskjʊ'lærətɪ [-kjə-, -ɪtɪ]
vascul|um, -a 'væskjʊl|əm, -ə
vase, -s vɑːz [old-fashioned vɔːz], -ɪz
vasectom|y, -ies væ'sektəm|ɪ, -ɪz
vaseline 'væsɪliːn [-æsl-, -æsəl-, -æzɪl-,
    -æzl-, ˌvæsə'liːn]
vaso-motor ˌveɪzəʊ'məʊtə* [ˌveɪsəʊ-]
vassal, -s 'væsl, -z
vassalage 'væsəlɪdʒ [-slɪ-]
vast, -er, -est, -ly, -ness vɑːst, -ə*, -ɪst,
    -lɪ, -nɪs [-nəs]
vasty 'vɑːstɪ
vat (s. v.), -s, -ting, -ted væt, -s, -ɪŋ, -ɪd
V.A.T. ˌviːeɪ'tiː:
vatful, -s 'vætfʊl, -z
Vathek 'væθek
Vatican 'vætɪkən
vaticinat|e, -es, -ing, -ed væ'tɪsɪneɪt, -s,
    -ɪŋ, -ɪd
vaticination, -s ˌvætɪsɪ'neɪʃn [væˌt-], -z
Vaud vəʊ (vo)
vaudeville (V.), -s 'vəʊdəvɪl ['vɔːd-,
    -viːl], -z
Vaudin (surname) 'vəʊdɪn

Vaudois (*sing.*) 'vəʊdwɑː [-dwɔː] (vodwa), (*plur.*) -z

Vaughan vɔːn

vault (*s. v.*), **-s, -ing/s, -ed, -er/s** vɔːlt [vɒlt], -s, -ɪŋ/z, -ɪd, -ə*/z

vaunt (*s. v.*), **-s, -ing/ly, -ed, -er/s** vɔːnt, -s, -ɪŋ/lɪ, -ɪd, -ə*/z

Vaux (*English surname*) vɔːz, vɒks, vɔːks, vəʊks, (*in de Vaux*) vəʊ *Note.*—**Brougham and Vaux** *is* ˌbruːmən'vɔːks

Vauxhall ˌvɒks'hɔːl [ˌvɒk'sɔːl, *also* '— *according to sentence-stress*]

vavasour (V.), -s 'vævəˌsʊə*, -z

V.C., -'s ˌviː'siː, -z

V-day 'viːdeɪ

veal (V.), -y viːl, -ɪ

vector (*s.*), **-s** 'vektə* [-tɔː*], -z

vector (*v.*), **-s, -ing, -ed** 'vektə*, -z, -rɪŋ, -d

vectorial vek'tɔːrɪəl

Veda, -s 'veɪdə ['viːd-], -z

Vedanta ve'dɑːntə [vɪ'd-, və'd-, -'dæn-] (*Hindi* vedanta)

vedette, -s vɪ'det [və'd-], -s

Vedic 'veɪdɪk ['viːd-]

veer, -s, -ing/ly, -ed vɪə*, -z, -rɪŋ/lɪ, -d

Vega (*star*) 'viːgə, (*foreign surname*) 'veɪgə

vegetable (*s. adj.*), **-s** 'vedʒtəbl [-dʒə-, -dʒɪ-], -z

vegetal 'vedʒɪtl

vegetarian (*s. adj.*), **-s, -ism** ˌvedʒɪ-'teərɪən [-dʒə't-], -z, -ɪzəm

vegetat|e, -es, -ing, -ed 'vedʒɪteɪt [-dʒə-], -s, -ɪŋ, -ɪd

vegetation, -s ˌvedʒɪ'teɪʃn [-dʒə't-], -z

vegetative, -ly 'vedʒɪtətɪv [-dʒə-, -teɪt-], -lɪ

vehemen|ce, -t/ly 'viːɪmən|s ['vɪ:əm-, 'vɪəm-, 'vi:hɪm-, 'vi:həm-], -t/lɪ

vehicle, -s 'viːɪkl ['vɪək-], -z

vehicular vɪ'hɪkjʊlə* [və'h-, -kjəl-]

veil (*s. v.*), **-s, -ing/s, -ed** veɪl, -z, -ɪŋ/z, -d

vein, -s, -ed; -less, -like veɪn, -z, -d; -lɪs [-ləs], -laɪk

vein|y, -ier, -iest 'veɪn|ɪ, -ɪə*, -ɪɪst

Veitch viːtʃ

velar (*s. adj.*), **-s** 'viːlə*, **-z**

velaric viː'lærɪk [vɪ'l-]

velarization [-isa-], -s ˌviːləraɪ'zeɪʃn [-rɪ'z-], -z

velariz|e [-is|e], -es, -ing, -ed 'viːləraɪz, -ɪz, -ɪŋ, -d

Velasquez (*artist*) vɪ'læskwɪz [ve'l-, -kɪz, -kez, -kwɪθ]

veldt (V.) velt

velic 'viːlɪk

velleity ve'liːətɪ [-ɪtɪ]

vellum, -s 'veləm, -z

veloce vɪ'ləʊtʃɪ [ve'l-, və'l-]

velocipede, -s vɪ'lɒsɪpiːd [və'l-, -səp-], -z

velocit|y, -ies vɪ'lɒsətɪ [və'l-, -ɪt|ɪ], -ɪz

velours və'lʊə*

velum, -s 'viːləm, -z

velvet, -s, -ed 'velvɪt, -s, -ɪd

velveteen, -s ˌvelvɪ'tiːn [-və't-, '---],-z

velvety 'velvɪtɪ [-vətɪ]

Venables 'venəblz

ven|al, -ally 'viːn|l, -əlɪ

venality viː'nælətɪ [vɪ'n-, -ɪtɪ]

vend, -s, -ing, -ed vend, -z, -ɪŋ, -ɪd

vendee, -s ˌven'diː, -z

vendetta, -s ven'detə, -z

vendible 'vendəbl [-dɪb-]

vendor, -s 'vendɔː* [-də*], -z

veneer (*s. v.*), **-s, -ing, -ed** və'nɪə* [vɪ'n-], -z, -rɪŋ, -d

venerab|le, -ly, -ness 'venərəb|l, -lɪ, -lnɪs [-nəs]

venerat|e, -es, -ing, -ed, -or/s 'venəreɪt, -s, -ɪŋ, -ɪd, -ə*/z

veneration ˌvenə'reɪʃn

venereal və'nɪərɪəl [vɪ'n-, vi:'n-]

venery 'venərɪ

Venetian (*s. adj.*), **-s** və'ni:ʃn [vɪ'n-, -ʃjən, -ʃɪən], -z

Venezuela, -n/s ˌvene'zweɪlə [ˌvenɪ'z-, ˌvenə'z-], -n/z

veng|e, -es, -ing, -ed vendʒ, -ɪz, -ɪŋ, -d

vengeance 'vendʒəns

venge|ful, -fully, -fulness 'vendʒ|fʊl, -fʊlɪ [-fəlɪ], -fʊlnɪs [-nəs]

venial, -ly, -ness 'viːnjəl [-nɪəl], -ɪ, -nɪs [-nəs]

veniality ˌveniˈælɪtɪ

veniality 'venɪzn [-nɪsn, -nzn]

Venice 'venɪs

venison 'venɪzn [-nɪsn, -nzn]

Venite, -s vɪ'naɪtɪ [ve'n-, -'niːtɪ], -z

veni, vidi, vici 'veɪniː,viːdiː'viːkiː [*also with* w *for* v]

Venn, -er ven, -ə*

venom, -s, -ed 'venəm, -z, -d

venomous, -ly, -ness 'venəməs, -lɪ, -nɪs [-nəs]

venous 'viːnəs

vent (*s. v.*), **-s, -ing, -ed** vent, -s, -ɪŋ, -ɪd

ventilat|e, -es, -ing, -ed 'ventɪleɪt [-təl-], -s, -ɪŋ, -ɪd

ventilation ˌventɪ'leɪʃn [-tə'l-]

ventilator, -s 'ventɪleɪtə* [-təl-], -z

Ventnor 'ventnə*

ventricle, -s 'ventrɪkl, -z

ventricular ven'trɪkjʊlə* [-kjə-]

ventriloquial, -ly ˌventrɪ'ləʊkwɪəl [-kwjəl], -ɪ

533

ventriloqui|sm, -st/s ven'trɪləkwɪ|zəm, -st/s

ventriloquiz|e [-is|e], -es, -ing, -ed ven'trɪləkwaɪz, -ɪz, -ɪŋ, -d

ventriloquy ven'trɪləkwɪ

vent|ure (s. v.), -ures, -uring, -ured, -urer/s 'ventʃ|ə*, -əz, -ərɪŋ, -əd, -ərə*/z

venturesome, -ly, -ness 'ventʃəsəm, -lɪ, -nɪs [-nəs]

venturous, -ly, -ness 'ventʃərəs, -lɪ, -nɪs [-nəs]

venue, -s 'venju:, -z

Venue (in Ben Venue) və'nju: [vɪ'n-]

Venus, -es 'vi:nəs, -ɪz

Venusian, -s vɪ'nju:sɪən [və'n-, -sjən, -zɪən, -zjən], -z

Vera 'vɪərə

Vera Cruz ˌvɪərə'kru:z [ˌve-, ˌveə-]

veracious, -ly və'reɪʃəs [vɪ'r-, ve'r-], -lɪ

veracity və'ræsɪtɪ [vɪ'r-, ve'r-, -ɪtɪ]

veranda(h), -s və'rændə, -z

verb, -s vɜ:b, -z

verb|al, -ally 'vɜ:b|l, -əlɪ

verbali|sm, -st/s 'vɜ:bəlɪ|zəm [-bļɪ-], -st/s

verbaliz|e [is|e], -es, -ing, -ed 'vɜ:bəlaɪz [-bḷaɪz], -ɪz, -ɪŋ, -d

verbatim vɜ:'beɪtɪm [-'bɑ:t-]

verbena, -s vɜ:'bi:nə [və'b-], -z

verbiage 'vɜ:bɪɪdʒ [-bjɪdʒ]

verbose, -ly, -ness vɜ:'bəʊs, -lɪ, -nɪs [-nəs]

verbosity vɜ:'bɒsətɪ [-ɪtɪ]

Vercingetorix ˌvɜ:sɪn'dʒetərɪks

verdan|cy, -t/ly 'vɜ:dən|sɪ, -t/lɪ

verd-antique ˌvɜ:dæn'ti:k

Verde vɜ:d

Verdi 'veədi: [-dɪ] ('verdi)

verdict, -s 'vɜ:dɪkt, -s

verdigris 'vɜ:dɪgrɪs [-gri:s]

verditer 'vɜ:dɪtə*

Verdun (in France and Canada) vɜ:'dʌn ['--] (verdœ̃)

verdure 'vɜ:dʒə* [-djə*, -ˌdjʊə*]

Vere vɪə*

verg|e (s. v.), -es, -ing, -ed vɜ:dʒ, -ɪz, -ɪŋ, -d

verger, -s 'vɜ:dʒə*, -z

Vergil, -s 'vɜ:dʒɪl, -z

veridical ve'rɪdɪkl [vɪ'r-, və'r-]

verifiable 'verɪfaɪəbl [ˌ--'---]

verification, -s ˌverɪfɪ'keɪʃn, -z

veri|fy, -fies, -fying, -fied, -fier/s 'verɪ|faɪ, -faɪz, -faɪɪŋ, -faɪd, -faɪə*/z

verily 'verəlɪ [-ɪlɪ]

verisimilitude ˌverɪsɪ'mɪlɪtju:d

veritab|le, -ly 'verɪtəb|l, -lɪ

verit|y (V.), -ies 'verət|ɪ [-ɪt|ɪ], -ɪz

verjuice 'vɜ:dʒu:s

Vermeer, -s veə'mɪə*[vɜ:'m-, -'meə*], -z

vermeil 'vɜ:meɪl [-mɪl]

vermicelli ˌvɜ:mɪ'selɪ [-'tʃelɪ]

vermicide, -s 'vɜ:mɪsaɪd, -z

vermicular vɜ:'mɪkjʊlə* [-kjə-]

vermiform 'vɜ:mɪfɔ:m

vermilion, -s və'mɪljən [vɜ:'m-], -z

vermin, -ous 'vɜ:mɪn, -əs

Vermont vɜ:'mɒnt

vermouth, -s 'vɜ:məθ [-mu:θ, vɜ:'mu:θ, və'mu:θ], -s

vernacular (s. adj.), -s, -ly və'nækjʊlə* [-kjələ*], -z, -lɪ

vern|al, -ally 'vɜ:n|l, -əlɪ

Verne (French author) veən [vɜ:n] (vɛrn)

Verner (English surname) 'vɜ:nə*, (Danish grammarian) 'vɜ:nə* ['veənə*] ('vɛrnər)

Verney 'vɜ:nɪ

vernier, -s 'vɜ:njə* [-nɪə*], -z

Vernon 'vɜ:nən

Verona vɪ'rəʊnə [və'r-, ve'r-]

veronal 'verənl

Veronese (artist) ˌverəʊ'neɪzɪ (vero-'ne:ze)

veronese (adj.) ˌverə'ni:z [-rəʊ'n-, '---]

veronica (V.), -s vɪ'rɒnɪkə [və'r-, ve'r-], -z

Verrall 'verɔ:l, 'verəl

Verrey 'verɪ

verruca, -s və'ru:kə [vɪ'r-, ve'r-], -z

verrucose ve'ru:kəʊs [vɪ'r-, və'r-]

Versailles veə'saɪ [vɜ:'s-] (vɛrsɑ:j)

versant, -s 'vɜ:sənt, -s

versatile, -ly, -ness 'vɜ:sətaɪl, -lɪ, -nɪs [-nəs]

versatility ˌvɜ:sə'tɪlətɪ [-ɪtɪ]

Verschoyle 'vɜ:skɔɪl

verse, -s vɜ:s, -ɪz

versed vɜ:st

verset, -s 'vɜ:set [-sɪt], -s

versicle, -s 'vɜ:sɪkl, -z

versification ˌvɜ:sɪfɪ'keɪʃn

versificator, -s 'vɜ:sɪfɪˌkeɪtə*, -z

versi|fy, -fies, -fying, -fied, -fier/s 'vɜ:sɪ|faɪ, -faɪz, -faɪɪŋ, -faɪd, -faɪə*/z

version, -s 'vɜ:ʃn [-ʒn], -z

verso 'vɜ:səʊ

verst, -s vɜ:st, -s

Verstegan vɜ:'sti:gən

Verstone 'vɜ:stən

versus 'vɜ:səs

vert (s. adj.) (V.), -s vɜ:t, -s

vertebr|a, -ae 'vɜ:tɪbr|ə, -i: [-aɪ, -eɪ]

vertebr|al, -ally 'vɜ:tɪbr|əl, -əlɪ

vertebrata ˌvɜːtɪˈbrɑːtə [-ˈbreɪtə]
vertebrate (s. adj.), -s ˈvɜːtɪbrət [-brɪt, -breɪt], -s
vertebrated ˈvɜːtɪbreɪtɪd
vertebration ˌvɜːtɪˈbreɪʃn
vert|ex, -ices, -exes ˈvɜːt|eks, -ɪsiːz, -eksɪz
vertic|al, -ally, -alness ˈvɜːtɪk|l, -əlɪ, -lnɪs [-nəs]
vertiginous vɜːˈtɪdʒɪnəs
vertigo ˈvɜːtɪgəʊ [vɜːˈtaɪg-, less commonly vɜːˈtiːg-]
vertu vɜːˈtuː
Verulam ˈveruləm
Verulami|an, -um ˌveruˈleɪmj|ən [-mɪ|ən], -əm
vervain ˈvɜːveɪn
verve vɜːv [veəv]
very ˈverɪ
Very ˈvɪərɪ, ˈverɪ
Vesey ˈviːzɪ
Vesian ˈveziən [-zjən]
vesica, -s ˈvesɪkə [vɪˈsaɪkə, ˈviːsɪkə], -z
vesicle, -s ˈvesɪkl, -z
Vespa ˈvespə
Vespasian veˈspeɪʒjən [-ʒɪən, -ʒn, -zjən, -zɪən]
vesper, -s ˈvespə*, -z
vespertine ˈvespətaɪn [-pɜːt-]
vespiar|y, -ies ˈvespɪər|ɪ [-pjə-], -ɪz
vessel, -s ˈvesl, -z
vest (s. v.), -s, -ing, -ed vest, -s, -ɪŋ, -ɪd
vesta (V.), -s ˈvestə, -z
vestal (s. adj.), -s ˈvestl, -z
vestibular veˈstɪbjʊlə*
vestibule, -s, -d ˈvestɪbjuːl, -z, -d
vestige, -s ˈvestɪdʒ, -ɪz
vestigial veˈstɪdʒɪəl [-dʒəl]
vestiture ˈvestɪtʃə*
vestment, -s ˈvestmənt, -s
vest-pocket, -s ˌvestˈpɒkɪt [ˈ-ˌ--], -s
Vestris ˈvestrɪs
vestr|y, -ies ˈvestr|ɪ, -ɪz
vesture, -s ˈvestʃə*, -z
vesuvian (V.), -s; -ite vɪˈsuːvjən [vəˈs-, -ˈsjuː-, -vɪən], -z; -aɪt
Vesuvius vɪˈsuːvjəs [vəˈs-, -ˈsjuː-, -vɪəs]
vet (s. v.), -s, -ting, -ted vet, -s, -ɪŋ, -ɪd
vetch, -es vetʃ, -ɪz
veteran (s. adj.), -s ˈvetərən, -z
veterinar|y (s. adj.), -ies ˈvetərɪnər|ɪ [ˈvetrɪnɪ, ˈvetnr|ɪ], -ɪz
veto (s.), -(e)s ˈviːtəʊ, -z
veto (v.), -es, -ing, -ed ˈviːtəʊ, -z, -ɪŋ, -d
Vevey ˈveveɪ [ˈvevɪ] (in Switzerland vəˈve)
vex, -es, -ing, -ed veks, -ɪz, -ɪŋ, -t
vexation, -s vekˈseɪʃn, -z

vexatious, -ly, -ness vekˈseɪʃəs, -lɪ, -nɪs [-nəs]
Vezian ˈveziən [-zjən]
V.H.F. ˌviːeɪtʃˈef
via ˈvaɪə
viability ˌvaɪəˈbɪlətɪ [-lɪt-]
viable ˈvaɪəbl
viaduct, -s ˈvaɪədʌkt [-dəkt], -s
vial, -s ˈvaɪəl [vaɪl], -z
Vialls ˈvaɪəlz, ˈvaɪɔːlz
Via Mala ˌvɪəˈmɑːlə [ˌviːə-]
viand, -s ˈvaɪənd, -z
viaticum, -s vaɪˈætɪkəm [vɪˈæ-], -z
vibes vaɪbz
vibrant (s. adj.), -s ˈvaɪbrənt, -s
vibraphone, -s ˈvaɪbrəfəʊn, -z
vibrat|e, -es, -ing, -ed vaɪˈbreɪt, -s, -ɪŋ, -ɪd
vibration, -s vaɪˈbreɪʃn, -z
vibrational vaɪˈbreɪʃənl [-ʃnəl, -ʃn̩l, -ʃənəl]
vibrative vaɪˈbreɪtɪv
vibrato, -s vɪˈbrɑːtəʊ, -z
vibrator, -s vaɪˈbreɪtə*, -z
vibratory ˈvaɪbrətərɪ [vaɪˈbreɪtərɪ]
viburnum, -s vaɪˈbɜːnəm, -z
vic (V.), -s vɪk, -s
vicar, -s; -age/s ˈvɪkə*, -z; -rɪdʒ/ɪz
vicarial vɪˈkeərɪəl [vaɪˈk-]
vicarious, -ly, -ness vɪˈkeərɪəs [vaɪˈk-], -lɪ, -nɪs [-nəs]
Vicary ˈvɪkərɪ
vice (s.), -s vaɪs, -ɪz
vice (prep.) ˈvaɪsɪ
vice- (prefix) ˌvaɪs-
Note.—Compounds with **vice-** have, as a rule, double stress, and the pronunciation of those not entered below may be ascertained by referring to the simple words.
vice-admiral, -s ˌvaɪsˈædmərəl, -z
vice-chair|man, -men ˌvaɪsˈtʃeə|mən, -mən
vice-chancellor, -s ˌvaɪsˈtʃɑːnsələ* [-slə*], -z
vice-consul, -s ˌvaɪsˈkɒnsl, -z
vice-consulate, -s ˌvaɪsˈkɒnsjʊlət [-sjə-, -səl-, -sʊl-, -lɪt], -s
vicegerent, -s ˌvaɪsˈdʒerənt [-ˈdʒɪər-], -s
vice-president, -s ˌvaɪsˈprezɪdənt, -s
vice-principal, -s ˌvaɪsˈprɪnsəpl [-sɪp-], -z
viceregal ˌvaɪsˈriːgl [also ˈ-ˌ-- when attributive]
vicereine, -s ˌvaɪsˈreɪn [ˈ--], -z
viceroy, -s ˈvaɪsrɔɪ, -z
viceroyship, -s ˈvaɪsrɔɪʃɪp, -s
vice versa ˌvaɪsɪˈvɜːsə

Vichy 'vi:ʃi: ['vi:ʃɪ, 'vɪ-] (viʃi)
vicinage 'vɪsɪnɪdʒ
vicinity vɪ'sɪnətɪ [və-, vaɪ's-, -ɪtɪ]
vicious, -ly, -ness 'vɪʃəs, -lɪ, -nɪs [-nəs]
vicissitude, -s vɪ'sɪsɪtju:d [vaɪ's-], -z
Vicker|s, -y 'vɪkə|z, -rɪ
Vicky 'vɪkɪ
victim, -s 'vɪktɪm, -z
victimization [-isa-] ,vɪktɪmaɪ'zeɪʃn
victimiz|e [-is|e], -es, -ing, -ed 'vɪktɪm-
    aɪz, -ɪz, -ɪŋ, -d
victor, -s 'vɪktə*, -z
Victor 'vɪktə*
victoria (V.), -s, -n/s vɪk'tɔ:rɪə, -z,
    -n/z
victorine, -s 'vɪktəri:n [,vɪktə'ri:n], -z
Victorine 'vɪktəri:n
victorious, -ly, -ness vɪk'tɔ:rɪəs, -lɪ, -nɪs
    [-nəs]
victor|y (V.), -ies 'vɪktər|ɪ, -ɪz
victu|al (s. v.), -als, -alling, -alled,
    -aller/s 'vɪt|l, -lz, -lɪŋ, -ld, -lə*/z
vicuna vɪ'kju:nə [vaɪ'k-]
vide 'vaɪdi: [-dɪ, 'vɪdeɪ]
videlicet vɪ'di:lɪset [vaɪ'd-, vɪ'deɪlɪket]
video, -tape/s 'vɪdɪəʊ, -teɪp/s
video-cassette, -s ,vɪdɪəʊkə'set [-kæ's-],
    -s
video-recording, -s 'vɪdɪəʊrɪ,kɔ:dɪŋ
    [-rə,k-], -z
vie, vies, vying, vied vaɪ, vaɪz, 'vaɪɪŋ,
    vaɪd
Vienna vɪ'enə
Viennese ,vɪə'ni:z [vɪə'n-]
Viet-cong ,vjet'kɒŋ
Viet-minh ,vjet'mɪn
Viet-nam ,vjet'næm [-'nɑ:m]
Vietnamese ,vjetnə'mi:z
view (s. v.), -s, -ing, -ed, -er/s; -able
    vju:, -z, -ɪŋ ['vjʊɪŋ], -d, -ə*/z
    [vjʊə*/z]; -əbl
Vieweg 'fi:veg
view-finder, -s 'vju:,faɪndə*, -z
viewless 'vju:lɪs [-ləs]
Vigar 'vaɪgə*
Vigers 'vaɪgəz
vigil, -s 'vɪdʒɪl [-dʒəl], -z
vigilan|ce, -t/ly 'vɪdʒɪlən|s [-dʒəl-,
    -dʒl̩ən-], -t/lɪ
vigilante, -s ,vɪdʒɪ'læntɪ, -z
vignett|e (s. v.), -es, -ing, -ed vɪ'njet
    [-'net], -s, -ɪŋ, -ɪd
Vignoles 'vɪnjəʊlz ['vi:-, -jəʊl, -jɒlz],
    vɪn'jɒlz [-'jəʊlz]
Vigo (in Spain) 'vi:gəʊ [old-fashioned
    'vaɪgəʊ] ('bigo), (as name of ship)
    'vi:gəʊ, (street in London) 'vaɪgəʊ,
    (in Indiana) 'vaɪgəʊ ['vi:gəʊ]

vigorous, -ly, -ness 'vɪgərəs, -lɪ, -nɪs
    [-nəs]
vigour 'vɪgə*
viking (V.), -s 'vaɪkɪŋ ['vi:k-], -z
vilayet, -s vɪ'lɑ:jet [vɪ'lɑ:jət, vɪ'laɪet,
    ,vɪlɑ:'jet], -s
vile, -r, -st, -ly, -ness vaɪl, -ə*, -ɪst, -lɪ,
    -nɪs [-nəs]
vilification ,vɪlɪfɪ'keɪʃn
vili|fy, -fies, -fying, -fied, -fier/s 'vɪlɪ|faɪ,
    -faɪz, -faɪɪŋ, -faɪd, -faɪə*/z
villa (V.), -s 'vɪlə, -z
village, -s 'vɪlɪdʒ, -ɪz
villager, -s 'vɪlɪdʒə*, -z
villain, -s 'vɪlən [in historical sense also
    -lɪn, -leɪn], -z
villainage 'vɪlɪnɪdʒ [-lən-]
villainous, -ly, -ness 'vɪlənəs, -lɪ, -nɪs
    [-nəs]
villain|y, -ies 'vɪlən|ɪ, -ɪz
villeg(g)iatura vɪ,ledʒɪə'tʊərə [-dʒjə't-,
    -dʒɔ't-, -'tjʊər-, -'tjɔər-, -'tjɔ:r-]
villein, -s; -age 'vɪlɪn [-leɪn], -z; -ɪdʒ
Villette vɪ'let
Villiers 'vɪləz, 'vɪljəz [-lɪəz]
Vilna 'vɪlnə
vim vɪm
vinaigrette, -s ,vɪneɪ'gret [-nɪ'g-], -s
Vincennes væn'sen [væn's-] (vɛ̃sen)
Vincent 'vɪnsənt
Vinci 'vɪntʃi: [-tʃɪ]
vincul|um, -a, -ums 'vɪŋkjʊl|əm, -ə,
    -əmz
vindicability ,vɪndɪkə'bɪlətɪ [-lɪt-]
vindicable 'vɪndɪkəbl
vindicat|e, -es, -ing, -ed, -or/s 'vɪndɪ-
    keɪt, -s, -ɪŋ, -ɪd, -ə*/z
vindication ,vɪndɪ'keɪʃn
vindicative 'vɪndɪkətɪv ['vɪndɪkeɪtɪv,
    ,vɪn'dɪkətɪv]
vindictive, -ly, -ness vɪn'dɪktɪv, -lɪ, -nɪs
    [-nəs]
vine, -s vaɪn, -z
vine-dresser, -s 'vaɪn,dresə*, -z
vinegar, -s, -y 'vɪnɪgə* [-nəg-], -z, -rɪ
viner|y, -ies 'vaɪnər|ɪ, -ɪz
Viney 'vaɪnɪ
vineyard, -s 'vɪnjəd [-jɑ:d], -z
vingt-et-un ,vænteɪ'ɜ:ŋ [,vænt-, -'ɜ:n,
    -'u:n] (vɛ̃tœ̃)
viniculture 'vɪnɪkʌltʃə* [,--'--]
viniculturist, -s ,vɪnɪ'kʌltʃərɪst ['----],
    -s
vinous 'vaɪnəs
vint, -s, -ing, -ed vɪnt, -s, -ɪŋ, -ɪd
vintage, -s 'vɪntɪdʒ, -ɪz
Vinter 'vɪntə*
vintner, -s 'vɪntnə*, -z

viny 'vaɪnɪ

vinyl 'vaɪnɪl

viol, -s 'vaɪəl [vaɪl, vɪəl], -z

viola (flower), -s 'vaɪələ ['vɪələ, 'vaɪəʊlə, 'vɪəʊlə, vaɪ'əʊlə, vɪ'əʊlə], -z

viola (musical instrument), -s vɪ'əʊlə ['vɪəʊlə], -z

Viola (Christian name) 'vaɪələ ['vaɪəʊlə], 'vɪəʊlə

violable 'vaɪələbl

violat|e, -es, -ing, -ed, -or/s 'vaɪəleɪt ['vaɪəʊl-], -s, -ɪŋ, -ɪd, -ə*/z

violation, -s ‚vaɪə'leɪʃn [‚vaɪəʊ'l-], -z

violen|ce, -t/ly 'vaɪələn|s, -t/lɪ

violet (V.), -s 'vaɪələt [-lɪt], -s

violin (musical instrument), -s ‚vaɪə'lɪn, -z

violin (chemical substance) 'vaɪəlɪn

violinist, -s 'vaɪəlɪnɪst [‚--'--], -s

violin-string, -s ‚vaɪə'lɪnstrɪŋ, -z

violist, -s (viola player) vɪ'əʊlɪst [viol player) 'vaɪəlɪst, -s

violoncell|ist/s, -o/s ‚vaɪələn'tʃel|ɪst/s [rarely ‚vɪəl-, -lɪn-], -əʊ/z

violone, -s 'vaɪələʊn ['vɪəl-], -z

V.I.P., -'s ‚viː'aɪ'piː, -z

Vipan 'vaɪpæn

viper, -s; -ish, -ous 'vaɪpə*, -z; -rɪʃ, -rəs

virago, -(e)s vɪ'rɑːgəʊ [-'reɪg-], -z

vires 'vaɪəriːz

Virgil, -s 'vɜːdʒɪl, -z

Virgili|an, -us vɜː'dʒɪlɪ|ən [və'dʒ-, -lj|ən], -əs

virgin, -s 'vɜːdʒɪn, -z

virginal (s. adj.), -s 'vɜːdʒɪnl, -z

Virginia, -s, -n/s və'dʒɪnjə [vɜː'dʒ-, -nɪə], -z, -n/z

virginibus puerisque vɜː‚gɪnɪbəs-pʊə'rɪskwɪ [vɜː‚dʒɪn-, -pjʊə-]

virginity və'dʒɪnətɪ [vɜː'dʒ-, -ɪtɪ]

Virgo (constellation) 'vɜːgəʊ ['vɪəg-]

virgule, -s 'vɜːgjuːl, -z

viridescen|ce, -t ‚vɪrɪ'desn|s, -t

viridity vɪ'rɪdətɪ [-ɪtɪ]

virile 'vɪraɪl

virility vɪ'rɪlətɪ [və'r-, -ɪtɪ]

virology ‚vaɪə'rɒlədʒɪ

virtu vɜː'tuː

virtual, -ly 'vɜːtʃʊəl [-tʃwəl, -tʃʊl, -tjʊəl, -tjwəl, -tjʊl], -ɪ

virtue, -s 'vɜːtjuː, 'vɜːtʃuː, -z

virtuosity ‚vɜːtjʊ'ɒsətɪ [-tʃʊ-, -ɪtɪ]

virtuoso, -s ‚vɜːtjʊ'əʊzəʊ [-tʃʊ-, -'əʊsəʊ], -z

virtuous, -ly, -ness 'vɜːtʃʊəs [-tʃwəs, -tjʊəs, -tjwəs], -lɪ, -nɪs [-nəs]

virulen|ce, -t/ly 'vɪrʊlən|s [-rjʊ-], -t/lɪ

virus, -es 'vaɪərəs, -ɪz

ris vɪs

visa (s. v.), -s, -ing, -ed 'viːzə, -z, -ɪŋ ['viːzərɪŋ], -d

visage, -s 'vɪzɪdʒ, -ɪz

vis-à-vis 'viːzɑːviː ['vɪz-, -zəv-, -zæv-, ‚-- -] (vizavi)

viscer|a, -al 'vɪsər|ə, -əl

viscid 'vɪsɪd

viscidity vɪ'sɪdətɪ [-ɪtɪ]

viscosity vɪ'skɒsətɪ [-ɪtɪ]

viscount, -s; -ess/es, -y, -ies 'vaɪkaʊnt, -s; -ɪs/ɪz, -ɪ, -ɪz

viscountc|y, -ies 'vaɪkaʊnts|ɪ, -ɪz

viscous, -ness 'vɪskəs, -nɪs [-nəs]

visé (s. v.), -s, -ing, -d 'viːzeɪ, -z, -ɪŋ, -d

visibility ‚vɪzɪ'bɪlətɪ [-zə'b-, -lɪt-]

visib|le, -ly, -leness 'vɪzəb|l [-zɪb-], -lɪ, -lnɪs [-nəs]

Visigoth, -s 'vɪzɪgɒθ ['vɪsɪ-], -s

vision, -s 'vɪʒn, -z

vi|sional, -sionally 'vɪ|ʒnl [-ʒnəl, -ʒŋ̩l, -ʒɲ̩l, -ʒənəl], -ʒŋ̩əlɪ [-ʒnəlɪ, -ʒŋ̩lɪ, -ʒɲ̩lɪ, -ʒənəlɪ]

visionar|y (s. adj.), -ies 'vɪʒŋ̩ər|ɪ [-ʒənə-], -ɪz

visit (s. v.), -s, -ing, -ed, -or/s 'vɪzɪt, -s, -ɪŋ, -ɪd, -ə*/z

visitant (s. adj.), -s 'vɪzɪtənt, -s

visitation, -s ‚vɪzɪ'teɪʃn, -z

visite, -s vɪ'ziːt [viː'z-], -s

visor, -s 'vaɪzə*, -z

vista, -s 'vɪstə, -z

Vistula 'vɪstjʊlə

visual, -ly 'vɪzjʊəl [-zjwəl, -zjʊl, -ʒjʊəl, -ʒjwəl, -ʒʊəl, -ʒwəl, -ʒʊl], -ɪ

visualization [-isa-] ‚vɪzjʊəlaɪ'zeɪʃn [-zjwəl-, -zjʊl-, -ʒjʊəl-, -ʒjwəl-, -ʒʊl-, -lɪ'z-]

visualiz|e [-is|e], -es, -ing, -ed, -er/s 'vɪzjʊəlaɪz [-zjwəl-, -zjʊl-, -ʒjʊəl-, -ʒjwəl-, -ʒʊəl-, -ʒwəl-, -ʒʊl-], -ɪz, -ɪŋ, -d, -ə*/z

vita (glass) 'vaɪtə, (aqua) 'viːtə

vitae (curriculum) 'viːtaɪ ['vaɪtiː]

vit|al, -ally 'vaɪt|l, -əlɪ [-l̩ɪ]

vitality vaɪ'tælətɪ [-ɪtɪ]

vitalization [-isa-] ‚vaɪtəlaɪ'zeɪʃn [-tl̩aɪ-]

vitaliz|e [-is|e], -es, -ing, -ed 'vaɪtəlaɪz [-tl̩aɪz], -ɪz, -ɪŋ, -d

vitals 'vaɪtlz

vitamin, -s 'vɪtəmɪn ['vaɪt-], -z

vitamine, -s 'vɪtəmɪn ['vaɪt-, -miːn], -z

vitiat|e, -es, -ing, -ed, -or/s 'vɪʃɪeɪt, -s, -ɪŋ, -ɪd, -ə*/z

vitiation ‚vɪʃɪ'eɪʃn

viticulture 'vɪtɪkʌltʃə* ['vaɪt-]

vitreosity ‚vɪtrɪ'ɒsətɪ [-ɪtɪ]

vitreous, -ness 'vɪtrɪəs, -nɪs [-nəs]

vitrescen|ce, -t vɪ'tresn|s, -t
vitrifaction ,vɪtrɪ'fækʃn
vitrification ,vɪtrɪfɪ'keɪʃn
vitri|fy, -fies, -fying, -fied; -fiable
'vɪtrɪ|faɪ, -faɪz, -faɪŋ, -faɪd; -faɪəbl
vitriol 'vɪtrɪəl
vitriolic ,vɪtrɪ'ɒlɪk
Vitruvi|an, -us vɪ'truːvj|ən [-vɪ|ən], -əs
vituperat|e, -es, -ing, -ed, -or/s
vɪ'tjuːpəreɪt [vaɪ't-], -s, -ɪŋ, -ɪd, -ə*/z
vituperation, -s vɪ,tjuːpə'reɪʃn [vaɪ,t-],
-z
vituperative, -ly vɪ'tjuːpərətɪv [vaɪ't-,
-pəreɪt-], -lɪ
viva (s. interj.) (long live, car), -s 'viːvə,
-z
viva (viva voce), -s 'vaɪvə, -z
vivace, -s vɪ'vɑːtʃɪ, -z
vivacious, -ly, -ness vɪ'veɪʃəs [vaɪ'v-],
-lɪ, -nɪs [-nəs]
vivacity vɪ'væsətɪ [vaɪ'v-, -rtɪ]
vivarium, -s vaɪ'veərɪəm [vɪ'v-], -z
vivat (s.), -s 'vaɪvæt ['viː-v-], -s
viva voce ,vaɪvə'vəʊsɪ [-'vəʊtʃɪ]
vive viːv
Vivian 'vɪvɪən [-vjən]
vivid, -est, -ly, -ness 'vɪvɪd, -ɪst, -lɪ, -nɪs
[-nəs]
Vivien 'vɪvɪən [-vjən]
Vivienne 'vɪvɪən [-vjən], ,vɪvɪ'en
vivification ,vɪvɪfɪ'keɪʃn
vivi|fy, -fies, -fying, -fied 'vɪvɪ|faɪ, -faɪz,
-faɪŋ, -faɪd
viviparity ,vɪvɪ'pærətɪ [-rtɪ]
viviparous, -ly, -ness vɪ'vɪpərəs [vaɪ'v-],
-lɪ, -nɪs [-nəs]
vivisect, -s, -ing, -ed, -or/s ,vɪvɪ'sekt
['---], -s, -ɪŋ, -ɪd, -ə*/z
vivisection ,vɪvɪ'sekʃn
vivisectionist, -s ,vɪvɪ'sekʃnɪst [-ʃənɪ-],
-s
vixen, -s 'vɪksn, -z
vixenish 'vɪksnɪʃ [-sənɪʃ]
Viyella vaɪ'elə
viz. vɪ'diːlɪset [vaɪ'd-, vɪ'deɪlɪket, vɪz]
Note.—Most people in reading aloud
substitute namely 'neɪmlɪ for this
word.
Vizard 'vɪzɑːd
Vizetelly ,vɪzɪ'telɪ
vizier, -s vɪ'zɪə* ['vɪ,zɪə*], -z
Vladimir 'vlædɪ,mɪə* [-mə*], (Russian
vla'djimjir, Czech 'vladimir)
Vladivostok ,vlædɪ'vɒstɒk (vladjivas-
'tok)
vocable, -s 'vəʊkəbl, -z
vocabular|y, -ies vəʊ'kæbjʊlər|ɪ [vʊ'k-,
-bjəl-], -ɪz

voc|al, -ally 'vəʊk|l, -əlɪ
vocalic vəʊ'kælɪk
vocalism 'vəʊkəlɪzəm [-kl̩ɪ-]
vocalist, -s 'vəʊkəlɪst [-kl̩ɪ-], -s
vocality vəʊ'kælətɪ [-rtɪ]
vocalization [-isa-], -s ,vəʊkəlaɪ'zeɪʃn
[-kl̩aɪ'z-, -kəlɪ'z-, -kl̩ɪ'z-], -z
vocaliz|e [-is|e], -es, -ing, -ed 'vəʊkəlaɪz
[-kl̩aɪz], -ɪz, -ɪŋ, -d
vocation, -s vəʊ'keɪʃn [vʊ'k-], -z
voca|tional, -tionally vəʊ'keɪʃ|ənl
[vʊ'k-, -ʃnəl, -ʃn̩l, -ʃnl, -ʃənəl], -ʃnəlɪ
[-ʃnəlɪ, -ʃn̩lɪ, -ʃnlɪ, -ʃənəlɪ]
vocative (s. adj.), -s 'vɒkətɪv, -z
voce (in viva voce) 'vəʊsɪ [-tʃɪ], (in
sotto voce) 'vəʊtʃɪ
vociferat|e, -es, -ing, -ed, -or/s vəʊ'sɪ-
fəreɪt, -s, -ɪŋ, -ɪd, -ə*/z
vociferation, -s vəʊ,sɪfə'reɪʃn, -z
vociferous, -ly, -ness vəʊ'sɪfərəs, -lɪ,
-nɪs [-nəs]
vocoid, -s 'vəʊkɔɪd, -z
vodka, -s 'vɒdkə, -z
Vogt (English surname) vəʊkt
vogue vəʊg
voic|e (s. v.), -es, -ing, -ed vɔɪs, -ɪz, -ɪŋ,
-t
voiceless, -ly, -ness 'vɔɪslɪs [-ləs], -lɪ,
-nɪs [-nəs]
void (s. adj. v.), -ness; -s, -ing, -ed;
-able, -ance vɔɪd, -nɪs [-nəs]; -z, -ɪŋ,
-ɪd; -əbl, -əns
voile vɔɪl
vol vɒl
volant 'vəʊlənt
Volapuk 'vɒləpʊk ['vəʊl-]
volatile (adj.), -ness 'vɒlətaɪl, -nɪs [-nəs]
volatile (in sal volatile) və'lætəlɪ [vəʊ'l-,
vʊ'l-, -tl̩ɪ]
volatility ,vɒlə'tɪlətɪ [-rtɪ]
volatilization [-isa-] vɒ,lætɪlaɪ'zeɪʃn
[vəʊ,læt-, və,læt-, ,vɒlət-, -təl-, -lɪ'z-]
volatiliz|e [-is|e], -es, -ing, -ed
vɒ'lætɪlaɪz [vəʊ'læt-, və'læt-, 'vɒlət-,
-təl-], -ɪz, -ɪŋ, -d
vol-au-vent, -s 'vɒləʊvɑ̃ːŋ [-vɔ̃ːŋ,
-vɑːŋ, -vɒŋ, ,--'-] (volovã), -z
volcanic, -ally vɒl'kænɪk, -əlɪ
volcanist, -s 'vɒlkənɪst, -s
volcano, -(e)s vɒl'keɪnəʊ, -z
vol|e (s. v.), -es, -ing, -ed vəʊl, -z, -ɪŋ, -d
volet, -s 'vɒleɪ (vɔlɛ), -z
Volga 'vɒlgə
Volhynia vɒl'hɪnɪə [-njə]
volition vəʊ'lɪʃn
volitive 'vɒlɪtɪv
volks|lied, -lieder 'fɔlks|liːd ['vɒl-]
('fɔlksliːt), -,liːdə* ('fɔlks,liːdər)

Volkswagen (*car*), -s 'fɒlks,vɑ:gən ['vɒlks-], -z

voll|ey (*s. v.*), -eys, -eying, -eyed, -eyer/s 'vɒl|ɪ, -ɪz, -ɪŋ, -ɪd, -ɪə*/z

volley-ball 'vɒlibɔ:l

volplan|e (*s. v.*), -es, -ing, -ed 'vɒlpleɪn, -z, -ɪŋ, -d

Volpone vɒl'pəʊnɪ

Volsci 'vɒlskɪ: ['vɒlsaɪ]

Vol|scian, -s 'vɒl|skɪən [-skjən, -ʃɪən, -ʃjən, -sɪən, -sjən], -z

Volstead 'vɒlsted

volt (*electric unit*), -s vəʊlt [vɒlt], -s

volt (*movement of horse, movement in fencing*), -s vɒlt, -s

volta (V.) 'vɒltə

voltage, -s 'vəʊltɪdʒ ['vɒl-], -ɪz

voltaic vɒl'teɪɪk

Voltaire 'vɒlteə* [-'-] (vɔltɛ:r)

voltameter, -s vɒl'tæmɪtə* [-mətə*], -z

volte 'vɒltɪ

volte-face, -s ˌvɒlt'fɑ:s [-'fæs] (vɔltəfas), -ɪz

voltmeter, -s 'vəʊlt,mi:tə* ['vɒlt-], -z

volubility ˌvɒljʊ'bɪlətɪ [-lɪt-]

volub|le, -ly, -leness 'vɒljʊb|l, -lɪ, -lnɪs [-nəs]

volume, -s 'vɒlju:m [-ljʊm, -ljəm], -z

volumeter, -s vɒ'lju:mɪtə* [və'l-, -'lu:-, -mətə*], -z [-əlɪ

volumetric, -al, -ally ˌvɒljʊ'metrɪk, -l, -əlɪ

voluminous, -ly, -ness və'lju:mɪnəs [vɒ'l-, -'lu:-], -lɪ, -nɪs [-nəs]

voluntar|y (*s. adj.*), -ies, -ily, -iness 'vɒləntər|ɪ [-lɪt-], -ɪz, -əlɪ [-ɪlɪ], -ɪnɪs [-ɪnəs]

volunteer (*s. v.*), -s, -ing, -ed ˌvɒlən'tɪə* [-lɪ't-], -z, -rɪŋ, -d

voluptuar|y (*s. adj.*), -ies və'lʌptjʊər|ɪ [-tjwər-, -tjʊr-, -tʃʊər-, -tʃwər-, -tʃər-], -ɪz

voluptuous, -ly, -ness və'lʌptʃʊəs [-tʃwəs, -tjʊəs, -tjwəs], -lɪ, -nɪs [-nəs]

volute, -s, -d və'lju:t [vɒ'l-, vəʊ'l-, -'lu:t], -s, -ɪd

volution, -s və'lju:ʃn [vɒ'l-, vəʊ'l-, -'lu:-], -z

Volvo (*car*), -s 'vɒlvəʊ, -z

Volze vəʊlz

vomit (*s. v.*), -s, -ing, -ed 'vɒmɪt, -s, -ɪŋ, -ɪd

vomitor|y (*s. adj.*), -ies 'vɒmɪtər|ɪ, -ɪz

Vondy 'vɒndɪ

voodoo 'vu:du:

Vooght (*surname*) vu:t

voracious, -ly, -ness və'reɪʃəs [vɔ:'r-, vɒ'r-], -lɪ, -nɪs [-nəs]

voracity vɒ'ræsətɪ [vɔ:'r-, və'r-, -ɪtɪ]

vort|ex, -ices, -exes 'vɔ:t|eks, -ɪsi:z, -eksɪz

vortic|al, -ally 'vɔ:tɪk|l, -əlɪ

vortices (*plur. of* vortex) 'vɔ:tɪsi:z

Vosges vəʊʒ

votaress, -es 'vəʊtərɪs [-res], -ɪz

votar|y, -ies 'vəʊtər|ɪ, -ɪz

vot|e (*s. v.*), -es, -ing, -ed, -er/s vəʊt, -s, -ɪŋ, -ɪd, -ə*/z

voteless 'vəʊtlɪs [-ləs]

votive 'vəʊtɪv

vouch, -es, -ing, -ed vaʊtʃ, -ɪz, -ɪŋ, -t

voucher, -s 'vaʊtʃə*, -z

vouchsaf|e, -es, -ing, -ed vaʊtʃ'seɪf, -s, -ɪŋ, -t

Voules vəʊlz

vow (*s. v.*), -s, -ing, -ed vaʊ, -z, -ɪŋ, -d

vow|el (*s. v.*), -els, -elling, -elled 'vaʊ|əl, -əlz, -əlɪŋ, -əld

vowel-like 'vaʊəllaɪk

Vowles vəʊlz, vaʊlz

vox (V.) vɒks

vox celeste, -s ˌvɒkssɪ'lest, -s

vox humana, -s ˌvɒkshju:'mɑ:nə [-hjʊ'm-], -z

voyag|e (*s. v.*), -es, -ing, -ed 'vɔɪɪdʒ [vɔɪdʒ], -ɪz, -ɪŋ, -d

voyager, -s 'vɔɪədʒə* ['vɔɪɪdʒ-], -z

voyeur, -s vwɑ:'jɜ:*, -z

Voynich 'vɔɪnɪk

vraisemblance ˌvreɪsɑ̃:m'blɑ̃:ns [-sɔ̃:m-'blɔ̃:ns, -sɑ:m'blɑ:ns, -sɒm'blɒns, '---] (vrɛsɑ̃blɑ̃:s)

Vryburg 'vraɪbɜ:g

vulcan (V.) 'vʌlkən

vulcanite 'vʌlkənaɪt [-knaɪt]

vulcanization [-isa-] ˌvʌlkənaɪ'zeɪʃn [-knaɪ'z-, -kənɪ'z-, -knɪ'z-]

vulcaniz|e [-is|e], -es, -ing, -ed 'vʌlkən-aɪz [-knaɪz], -ɪz, -ɪŋ, -d [-lɪ

vulgar, -er, -est, -ly 'vʌlgə*, -rə*, -rɪst, -lɪ

vulgarism, -s 'vʌlgərɪzəm, -z

vulgarit|y, -ies vʌl'gærət|ɪ [-ɪt|ɪ], -ɪz

vulgarization [-isa-] ˌvʌlgəraɪ'zeɪʃn [-rɪ'z-]

vulgariz|e [-is|e], -es, -ing, -ed, -er/s 'vʌlgəraɪz, -ɪz, -ɪŋ, -d, -ə*/z

Vulgate 'vʌlgeɪt [-gɪt, -gət]

Vulliamy 'vʌljəmɪ

vulnerability ˌvʌlnərə'bɪlətɪ [-lɪt-]

vulnerable, -ness 'vʌlnərəbl, -nɪs [-nəs]

Vulpecula vʌl'pekjʊlə

vulpine 'vʌlpaɪn

vulture, -s 'vʌltʃə*, -z

vultur|ine, -ous 'vʌltʃʊr|aɪn [-tʃər-, -tjʊr-], -əs

vulva 'vʌlvə

vying (*from* vie) 'vaɪɪŋ

539

W

W (*the letter*), **-'s** ˈdʌbļjuː [-jʊ], **-z**

Waaf, -s wæf, -s

Wabash ˈwɔːbæʃ

wabble, *etc.* = **wobble**, *etc.*

Wace weɪs

Wacey ˈweɪsɪ

wad (*s. v.*), **-s, -ding, -ded** wɒd, -z, -ɪŋ, -ɪd

Waddell wɒˈdel, ˈwɒdl̩

wadding ˈwɒdɪŋ

Waddington ˈwɒdɪŋtən

wadd|le, -les, -ling, -led, -ler/s ˈwɒd|l̩, -lz, -lɪŋ [-lɪŋ], -ld, -lə*/z [lə*/z]

wadd|y (*water-course*), **-ies** ˈwɒd|ɪ, [ˈwæd-], -ɪz

wadd|y (*war-club*), **-ies** ˈwɒd|ɪ, -ɪz

Waddy ˈwɒdɪ

wad|e (*s. v.*) (**W.**), **-es, -ing, -ed** weɪd, -z, -ɪŋ, -ɪd

wader, -s ˈweɪdə*, -z

Wadey ˈweɪdɪ

Wadham ˈwɒdəm

Wadhurst ˈwɒdhɜːst

wadi, -s ˈwɒdɪ [ˈwæd-, ˈwɑːd-], -z

Wadi Halfa ˌwɒdɪˈhælfə [ˌwæd-, ˌwɑːd-]

Wadman ˈwɒdmən

Wadsworth ˈwɒdzwɜːθ [-wəθ]

Wady ˈweɪdɪ

W.A.F., -'s wæf, -s

Wafd wɒft [wæft, wɑːft]

Wafdist, -s ˈwɒfdɪst [ˈwæf-, ˈwɑːf-], -s

wafer, -s; -y ˈweɪfə*, -z; -rɪ

waffle, -s ˈwɒfl̩, -z

waffle-iron, -s ˈwɒfl̩ˌaɪən, -z

waft (*s. v.*), **-s, -ing, -ed** wɑːft [wɒft, wɔːft], -s, -ɪŋ, -ɪd

wag (*s. v.*), **-s, -ging, -ged** wæg, -z, -ɪŋ, -d

wag|e (*s. v.*), **-es, -ing, -ed** weɪdʒ, -ɪz, -ɪŋ, -d

wage-earner, -s ˈweɪdʒˌɜːnə*, -z

wag|er (*s. v.*), **-ers, -ering, -ered, -erer/s** ˈweɪdʒ|ə*, -əz, -ərɪŋ, -əd, -ərə*/z

wagger|y, -ies ˈwægər|ɪ, -ɪz

waggish, -ly, -ness ˈwægɪʃ, -lɪ, -nɪs [-nəs]

wagg|le, -les, -ling, -led ˈwæg|l̩, -lz, -lɪŋ [-lɪŋ], -ld

waggon, -s ˈwægən, -z

waggoner, -s ˈwægənə*, -z

waggonette, -s ˌwægəˈnet, -s

Waghorn ˈwæghɔːn

Wagnall ˈwægnl̩ [-nəl]

Wagner (*English name*) ˈwægnə*, (*German composer*) ˈvɑːgnə* (ˈvaːgnɐr)

Wagnerian, -s vɑːgˈnɪərɪən, -z

Wagneriana ˌvɑːgnɪˈɑːnə [vɑːgˌnɪə-]

wagon, -s ˈwægən, -z

wagoner, -s ˈwægənə*, -z

wagonette, -s ˌwægəˈnet, -s

wagon-lit, -s ˌvægɔ̃ːnˈliː [ˌvɑːg-, -gɒn-, ˈ---] (vagɔ̃li), -z

Wagstaff ˈwægstɑːf

wagtail, -s ˈwægteɪl, -z

Wahabi, -s wəˈhɑːbɪ [wɑːˈh-], -z

waif, -s weɪf, -s

wail (*s. v.*), **-s, -ing/ly, -ed** weɪl, -z, -ɪŋ/lɪ, -d

wain, -s weɪn, -z

wainscot, -s, -ing, -ed ˈweɪnskət [ˈwen-, -skɒt], -s, -ɪŋ, -ɪd

Wainwright ˈweɪnraɪt

waist, -s weɪst, -s

waistband, -s ˈweɪstbænd, -z

waistcoat, -s ˈweɪskət [-stk-, *old-fashioned* ˈweskət, -kɪt], -s

waist-deep ˌweɪstˈdiːp [ˈ--]

waist-high ˌweɪstˈhaɪ [ˈ--]

waistline ˈweɪstlaɪn

wait (*s. v.*), **-s, -ing, -ed, -er/s** weɪt, -s, -ɪŋ, -ɪd, -ə*/z

waiting-maid, -s ˈweɪtɪŋmeɪd, -z

waiting-room, -s ˈweɪtɪŋrʊm [-ruːm], -z

waitress, -es ˈweɪtrɪs [-trəs], -ɪz

Waitrose ˈweɪtrəʊz

waiv|e, -es, -ing, -ed weɪv, -z, -ɪŋ, -d

waiver, -s ˈweɪvə*, -z

wak|e (*s. v.*), **-es, -ing, -ed, woke, woken** weɪk, -s, -ɪŋ, -t, wəʊk, ˈwəʊkən

Wakefield ˈweɪkfiːld

wake|ful, -fully, -fulness ˈweɪk|fʊl, -fʊlɪ [-fəlɪ], -fʊlnɪs [-nəs]

wak|en, -ens, -ening, -ened ˈweɪk|ən, -ənz, -ənɪŋ [-ənɪŋ, -nɪŋ], -ənd

Wal (*personal name*) wɒl [wɔːl]

Walachia, -n/s wɒˈleɪkjə [wə-, -kɪə], -n/z

Walbrook ˈwɔːlbrʊk [ˈwɒl-]

540

Walcheren 'vɑːlkərən ['vɑːlxə-, 'wɔːl-kərən, *old-fashioned* 'wɔːlʃərən, 'wɒl-ʃərən]

Walcott 'wɔːlkət ['wɒl-, -kɒt]

Waldeck 'wɔːldek ['wɒl-] ('valdɛk)

Waldegrave 'wɔːlgreɪv ['wɒl-], 'wɔːldə-greɪv ['wɒl-]
Note.—Earl Waldegrave is 'wɔːlgreɪv ['wɒl-].

Waldemar 'vældəmɑː* ['vɑːl-, 'wɔːl-, -dɪm-]

Walden 'wɔːldən ['wɒl-]

Waldo 'wɔːldəʊ ['wɒl-]

Waldorf 'wɔːldɔːf ['wɒl-]

Waldstein (*American name*) 'wɔːldstaɪn ['wɒl-], (*German name*) 'vældstaɪn ['vɑːl-, 'vɔːl-, 'vɒl-, 'wɔːl-, 'wɒl-, -dʃtaɪn] ('valtʃtain)

wale, -s weɪl, -z

Waler, -s 'weɪlə*, -z

Waleran (*Baron*) 'wɔːlrən ['wɒl-], (*Buildings in Borough High Street, London*) 'wɒlərən

Wales weɪlz

Waley 'weɪlɪ

Walfish 'wɔːlfɪʃ ['wɒl-]

Walford 'wɔːlfəd ['wɒl-]

Walhalla væl'hælə

Walham 'wɒləm

walk (*s. v.*), **-s, -ing, -ed, -er/s** wɔːk, -s, -ɪŋ, -t, -ə*/z

Walker 'wɔːkə*

Walkern 'wɔːlkɜːn [-kən]

Walkiden 'wɔːkɪdn

walkie-talkie, -s ˌwɔːkɪ'tɔːkɪ, -z

walking-stick, -s 'wɔːkɪŋstɪk, -s

walking-tour, -s 'wɔːkɪŋˌtʊə* [-tɔː*, -tɔː*], -z

walk-out, -s 'wɔːkaʊt, -s

walk-over, -s 'wɔːkˌəʊvə*, -z

Walkyrie, -s væl'kɪərɪ ['vælkɪrɪ], -z

wall (*s. v.*) (**W.**), **-s, -ing, -ed** wɔːl, -z, -ɪŋ, -d

wallab|y (**W.**), **-ies** 'wɒləb|ɪ, -ɪz

Wallace 'wɒlɪs [-ləs]

Wallach, -s 'wɒlək, -s

Wallachia, -n/s wɒ'leɪkjə [wə'l-, -kɪə], -n/z

walla(h), -s 'wɒlə, -z

Wallasey 'wɒləsɪ

Waller 'wɒlə*

wallet, -s 'wɒlɪt, -s

wall-eye, -s, -d 'wɔːlaɪ, -z, -d

wallflower, -s 'wɔːlˌflaʊə*, -z

wall-fruit 'wɔːlfruːt

Wallingford 'wɒlɪŋfəd

Wallis 'wɒlɪs

Walloon, -s wɒ'luːn [wə'l-], -z

wallop, -s, -ing/s, -ed 'wɒləp, -s, -ɪŋ/z, -t

wall|ow (*s. v.*), **-ows, -owing, -owed, -ower/s** 'wɒl|əʊ, -əʊz, -əʊɪŋ, -əʊd, -əʊə*/z

wall-paper, -s 'wɔːlˌpeɪpə*, -z

Wallsend 'wɔːlzend

Wallwork 'wɔːlwɜːk ['wɒl-]

Walmer 'wɔːlmə* ['wɒl-]

Walm(e)sley 'wɔːmzlɪ

Walmisley 'wɔːmzlɪ

Walney 'wɔːlnɪ ['wɒl-]

walnut, -s 'wɔːlnʌt [-nət], -s

Walpole 'wɔːlpəʊl ['wɒl-]

Walpurgis væl'pʊəgɪs [vɑːl-, -'pɜːg-] (val'purgis)

walrus, -es 'wɔːlrəs ['wɒl-, -rʌs], -ɪz

Walsall 'wɔːlsɔːl ['wɒl-, -sl]

Walsh wɔːlʃ [wɒlʃ]

Walsham 'wɔːlʃəm [*locally* 'wɔːlsəm]

Walsingham (*surname*) 'wɔːlsɪŋəm ['wɒl-], (*place*) 'wɔːlzɪŋəm ['wɒl-, -lsɪŋ-]

Walt wɔːlt [wɒlt]

Walter (*English name*) 'wɔːltə* ['wɒl-], (*German name*) 'vɑːltə* ('valtər)

Walters 'wɔːltəz ['wɒl-]

Waltham 'wɔːltəm, 'wɔːlθəm ['wɒl-]
Note.—The traditional local pronunciation at Great Waltham and Little Waltham in Essex is 'wɔːltəm, *and this is the pronunciation used by those who have lived there for a long time. Some new residents pronounce* -lθəm. *In the case of Waltham Abbey and other places, the more common form is* 'wɔːlθəm.

Walthamstow 'wɔːlθəmstəʊ ['wɒl-, *old-fashioned* -ltəm-]

Walther (*German name*) 'vɑːltə* ('valtər)

Walthew 'wɔːlθjuː ['wɒl-]

Walton 'wɔːltən ['wɒl-]

waltz (*s. v.*), **-es, -ing, -ed, -er/s** wɔːls [wɒls, wɔːlts, wɒlts], -ɪz, -ɪŋ, -t, -ə*/z

Walworth 'wɔːlwəθ ['wɒl-, -wɜːθ]

wampum, -s 'wɒmpəm, -z

wan, -ner, -nest, -ly, -ness wɒn, -ə*, -ɪst, -lɪ, -nɪs [-nəs]

Wanamaker 'wɒnəmeɪkə*

wand (**W.**), **-s** wɒnd, -z

wand|er, -ers, -ering, -ered, -erer/s 'wɒnd|ə*, -əz, -ərɪŋ, -əd, -ərə*/z

wanderlust 'wɒndəlʌst ['vɑːndəlʊst]

Wandle 'wɒndl

Wandsworth 'wɒndzwəθ [-wɜːθ]

wan|e (*s. v.*), **-es, -ing, -ed** weɪn, -z, -ɪŋ, -d

Wanganui (*in New Zealand*) ˌwɒŋəˈnʊɪ
[-ˈŋgə-]
*Note.—The first is the form always
used by those of Polynesian descent.*
wang|le (*s. v.*), -les, -ling, -led ˈwæŋg|l,
-lz, -lɪŋ, -ld
Wann wɒn
Wanstall ˈwɒnstɔːl
Wanstead ˈwɒnstɪd [-sted]
want (*s. v.*), -s, -ing, -ed wɒnt, -s, -ɪŋ,
-ɪd
Wantage ˈwɒntɪdʒ
wanting ˈwɒntɪŋ
wanton, -ly, -ness ˈwɒntən, -lɪ, -nɪs
[-nəs-]
wapentake, -s ˈwæpənteɪk [ˈwɒp-], -s
wapiti, -s ˈwɒpɪtɪ, -z
Wapping ˈwɒpɪŋ
Wappinger ˈwɒpɪndʒə*
war (*s. v.*), -s, -ring, -red wɔː*, -z, -rɪŋ,
-d
Warbeck ˈwɔːbek
warb|le, -les, -ling, -led ˈwɔːb|l, -lz, -lɪŋ
[-lɪŋ], -ld
warbler, -s ˈwɔːblə*, -z
Warburg (*Institute*) ˈwɔːbɜːg
Warburton ˈwɔːbətn [-bɜːtn]
war-cloud, -s ˈwɔːklaʊd, -z
war-club, -s ˈwɔːklʌb, -z
war-cr|y, -ies ˈwɔːkr|aɪ, -aɪz
ward (*s. v.*) (W.), -s, -ing, -ed wɔːd, -z,
-ɪŋ, -ɪd
war-dance, -s ˈwɔːdɑːns, -ɪz
warden (W.), -s ˈwɔːdn, -z
warder (W.), -s ˈwɔːdə*, -z
Wardlaw ˈwɔːdlɔː
Wardle ˈwɔːdl
Wardour (*street in London*) ˈwɔːdə*
wardress (*fem. warder*), -es ˈwɔːdrɪs
[-dres], -ɪz
war-dress (*war costume*), -es ˈwɔːdres,
-ɪz
wardrobe, -s ˈwɔːdrəʊb, -z
wardroom, -s ˈwɔːdrʊm [-ruːm], -z
wardship ˈwɔːdʃɪp
ware (*s. interj.*) (W.), -s weə*, -z
Wareham ˈweərəm
warehou|se (*s.*), -ses ˈweəhaʊ|s, -zɪz
warehou|se (*v.*), -ses, -sing, -sed ˈweə-
haʊ|z [-s], -zɪz [-sɪz], -zɪŋ [-sɪŋ], -zd
[-st]
warehouse|man, -men ˈweəhaʊs|mən,
-mən
warfare ˈwɔːfeə*
war-god, -s ˈwɔːgɒd, -z
war-grave, -s ˈwɔːgreɪv, -z
Wargrave ˈwɔːgreɪv
Warham ˈwɔːrəm

warhead, -s ˈwɔːhed, -z
war-horse, -s ˈwɔːhɔːs, -ɪz
war|ily, -iness ˈweər|əlɪ [-ɪlɪ], -ɪnɪs
[-nəs]
Waring ˈweərɪŋ
warlike ˈwɔːlaɪk
warlock (W.), -s ˈwɔːlɒk, -s
war-lord, -s ˈwɔːlɔːd, -z
warm (*s. adj. v.*), -er, -est, -ly, -ness;
-s, -ing, -ed wɔːm, -ə*, -ɪst, -lɪ, -nɪs
[-nəs]; -z, -ɪŋ, -d
war-maker, -s ˈwɔːˌmeɪkə*, -z
warm-blooded ˌwɔːmˈblʌdɪd [*also* ˈ-ˌ--
when attributive]
warmer (*s.*), -s ˈwɔːmə*, -z
warm-hearted ˌwɔːmˈhɑːtɪd [*also* ˈ-ˌ--
when attributive]
warming-pan, -s ˈwɔːmɪŋpæn, -z
Warmington ˈwɔːmɪŋtən
Warminster ˈwɔːmɪnstə*
warmish ˈwɔːmɪʃ
war-monger, -s ˈwɔːˌmʌŋgə*, -z
warmth wɔːmθ [-mpθ]
warn, -s, -ing/ly, -ed wɔːn, -z, -ɪŋ/lɪ, -d
Warn|e, -er wɔːn, -ə*
warning, -s ˈwɔːnɪŋ, -z
warp (*s. v.*), -s, -ing, -ed wɔːp, -s, -ɪŋ, -t
war|-paint, -path ˈwɔːpeɪnt, -pɑːθ
warrant (*s. v.*), -s, -ing, -ed, -er/s
ˈwɒrənt, -s, -ɪŋ, -ɪd, -ə*/z
warrantab|le, -ly, -leness ˈwɒrəntəb|l,
-lɪ, -lnɪs [-nəs]
warrantee, -s ˌwɒrənˈtiː, -z
warrantor, -s ˈwɒrəntɔː* [-tə*, ˌwɒrən-
ˈtɔː*], -z
warrant|y, -ies ˈwɒrənt|ɪ, -ɪz
Warre wɔː*
warren (W.), -s ˈwɒrən [-rɪn], -z
Warrender ˈwɒrəndə* [-rɪn-]
Warrington ˈwɒrɪŋtən
warrior (W.), -s ˈwɒrɪə*, -z
Warsaw ˈwɔːsɔː
warship, -s ˈwɔːʃɪp, -s
Warsop ˈwɔːsəp
Warspite ˈwɔːspaɪt
wart, -s; -y wɔːt, -s; -ɪ
wart-hog, -s ˈwɔːthɒg, -z
Warton ˈwɔːtn
war-wearied ˈwɔːˌwɪərɪd
Warwick, -shire ˈwɒrɪk, -ʃə* [-ˌʃɪə*]
war-worn ˈwɔːwɔːn
war|y, -ier, -iest, -ily, -iness ˈweər|ɪ,
-ɪə*, -ɪɪst, -əlɪ [-ɪlɪ], -ɪnɪs [-nəs]
was (*from* be) wɒz (*strong form*), wəz,
wz (*weak forms*)
Wasbrough ˈwɒzbrə
wash (*s. v.*) (W.), -es, -ing, -ed, -er/s;
-able wɒʃ, -ɪz, -ɪŋ, -t, -ə*/z; -əbl

wash-basin, -s 'wɒʃˌbeɪsn, -z
washday, -s 'wɒʃdeɪ, -z
washer, -s 'wɒʃə*, -z
washer|woman, -women 'wɒʃə|ˌwʊmən,
    -ˌwɪmɪn
wash-hou|se, -ses 'wɒʃhaʊ|s, -zɪz
washing 'wɒʃɪŋ
washing-day, -s 'wɒʃɪŋdeɪ, -z
washing-machine, -s 'wɒʃɪŋməˌʃiːn, -z
washing-stand, -s 'wɒʃɪŋstænd, -z
Washington 'wɒʃɪŋtən
washing-up 'wɒʃɪŋˈʌp
wash-out, -s 'wɒʃaʊt, [ˌ-ˈ-], -s
wash-pot, -s 'wɒʃpɒt, -s
wash-stand, -s 'wɒʃstænd, -z
wash-tub, -s 'wɒʃtʌb, -z
wash|y, -ier, -iest, -iness 'wɒʃ|ɪ, -ɪə*,
    -ɪɪst, -ɪnɪs [-nəs]
wasn't 'wɒznt [also occasionally 'wɒzn
    when not final]
wasp, -s wɒsp, -s
waspish, -ly, -ness 'wɒspɪʃ, -lɪ, -nɪs [-nəs]
wasplike 'wɒsplaɪk
wassail, -s 'wɒseɪl ['wæs-, -sl], -z
wassailing 'wɒsəlɪŋ ['wæs-, -slɪŋ, -seɪlɪŋ]
Wassell 'wæsl
Wasson 'wɒsn
wast (from be) wɒst (strong form), wəst
    (weak form)
Wast, -water wɒst, -ˌwɔːtə*
wast|e (s. adj. v.), -es, -ing, -ed, -er/s;
    -age weɪst, -s, -ɪŋ, -ɪd, -ə*/z; -ɪdʒ
waste|ful, -fully, -fulness 'weɪst|fʊl,
    -fʊlɪ [-fəlɪ], -fʊlnɪs [-nəs]
waste-paper-basket, -s ˌweɪstˈpeɪpə-
    ˌbɑːskɪt, -s
waste-pipe, -s 'weɪstpaɪp, -s
wastrel, -s 'weɪstrəl, -z
Wat wɒt
watch (s. v.), -es, -ing, -ed, -er/s wɒtʃ,
    -ɪz, -ɪŋ, -t, -ə*/z
watch-case, -s 'wɒtʃkeɪs, -ɪz
watch-chain, -s 'wɒtʃtʃeɪn, -z
watch-dog, -s 'wɒtʃdɒg, -z
watch|ful, -fully, -fulness 'wɒtʃ|fʊl,
    -fʊlɪ [-fəlɪ], -fʊlnɪs [-nəs]
watch-glass, -es 'wɒtʃglɑːs, -ɪz
watch-key, -s 'wɒtʃkiː, -z
watch-maker, -s 'wɒtʃˌmeɪkə*, -z
watch|man, -men 'wɒtʃ|mən, -mən
    [-men]
watch-pocket, -s 'wɒtʃˌpɒkɪt, -s
watch-spring, -s 'wɒtʃsprɪŋ, -z
watch-stand, -s 'wɒtʃstænd, -z
watch-tower, -s 'wɒtʃˌtaʊə*, -z
watchword, -s 'wɒtʃwɜːd, -z
wat|er (s. v.), -ers, -ering, -ered 'wɔːt|ə*,
    -əz, -ərɪŋ, -əd

water-bed, -s 'wɔːtəbed, -z
water-borne 'wɔːtəbɔːn
water-bottle, -s 'wɔːtəˌbɒtl, -z
water-buck 'wɔːtəbʌk
Waterbur|y, -ies 'wɔːtəbər|ɪ, -ɪz
water-butt, -s 'wɔːtəbʌt, -s
water-carrier, -s 'wɔːtəˌkærɪə*, -z
watercart, -s 'wɔːtəkɑːt, -s
water-chute, -s 'wɔːtəʃuːt, -s
water-closet, -s 'wɔːtəˌklɒzɪt, -s
water-colour, -s 'wɔːtəˌkʌlə*, -z
water-cooled 'wɔːtəkuːld [ˌ-ˈ-]
watercourse, -s 'wɔːtəkɔːs [-kɔːs], -ɪz
watercress, -es 'wɔːtəkres, -ɪz
water-diviner/s 'wɔːtədɪˌvaɪnə*/z
water-divining 'wɔːtədɪˌvaɪnɪŋ
water-drinker, -s 'wɔːtəˌdrɪŋkə*, -z
waterfall, -s 'wɔːtəfɔːl, -z
water-finder, -s 'wɔːtəˌfaɪndə*, -z
Waterford 'wɔːtəfəd
waterfowl 'wɔːtəfaʊl
waterfront, -s 'wɔːtəfrʌnt, -s
water-gas 'wɔːtəgæs [ˌ-ˈ-]
water-gate, -s 'wɔːtəgeɪt, -s
Watergate 'wɔːtəgeɪt
water-gauge, -s 'wɔːtəgeɪdʒ, -ɪz
waterglass 'wɔːtəglɑːs
water-glass, -es 'wɔːtəglɑːs, -ɪz
Waterhouse 'wɔːtəhaʊs
wateriness 'wɔːtərɪnɪs [-nəs]
watering-can, -s 'wɔːtərɪŋkæn, -z
watering-cart, -s 'wɔːtərɪŋkɑːt, -s
watering-place, -s 'wɔːtərɪŋpleɪs, -ɪz
waterless 'wɔːtəlɪs [-ləs]
water-level, -s 'wɔːtəˌlevl, -z
water-lil|y, -ies 'wɔːtəˌlɪl|ɪ, -ɪz
water-line, -s 'wɔːtəlaɪn, -z
waterlogged 'wɔːtəlɒgd
Waterloo ˌwɔːtəˈluː [ˈ----]
    Note.—The stressing '--- is that
    regularly used when the word is
    attributive (as in Waterloo Road).
water-main, -s 'wɔːtəmeɪn, -z
water|man (W.), -men 'wɔːtə|mən,
    -mən [-men]
watermark (s. v.), -s, -ing, -ed 'wɔːtə-
    mɑːk, -s, -ɪŋ, -t
water-nymph, -s 'wɔːtənɪmf, -s
water-pipe, -s 'wɔːtəpaɪp, -s
water-power 'wɔːtəˌpaʊə*
waterproof (s. v.), -s, -ing, -ed 'wɔːtə-
    pruːf, -s, -ɪŋ, -t
Waters 'wɔːtəz
watershed, -s 'wɔːtəʃed, -z
water-ski (s. v.), -s, -ing, -ed, -er/s
    'wɔːtəskiː, -z, -ɪŋ, -d, -ˌskiːə*/z
    [-ˌskɪə*/z]
waterspout, -s 'wɔːtəspaʊt, -s

water-sprite, -s 'wɔːtəspraɪt, -s
water-suppl|y, -ies 'wɔːtəsəˌpl|aɪ, -aɪz
watertight 'wɔːtətaɪt
water-wav|e (s. v.), -es, -ing, -ed
'wɔːtəweɪv, -z, -ɪŋ, -d
waterway, -s 'wɔːtəweɪ, -z
water-wheel, -s 'wɔːtəwiːl [-təhw-], -z
water-wings 'wɔːtəwɪŋz
waterworks 'wɔːtəwɜːks
water-worn 'wɔːtəwɔːn
watery 'wɔːtərɪ
Wat|ford, -kin/s, -son 'wɒt|fəd, -kɪn/z, -sn
Wathen 'wɒθən
Watling (Street) 'wɒtlɪŋ
watt (W.), -s wɒt, -s
wattage 'wɒtɪdʒ
Watteau, -s 'wɒtəʊ, -z
wattle, -s, -d 'wɒtl, -z, -d
wattmeter, -s 'wɒtˌmiːtə*, -z
Watton 'wɒtn
Wauchope (surname, place in Scotland)
'wɔːkəp [in Scotland 'wɔxəp]
Waugh wɔː [in Scotland wɔx]
waught, -s wɔːt [in Scotland wɔxt], -s
waul, -s wɔːl, -z
wav|e (s. v.), -es, -ing, -ed; -eless,
-elet/s weɪv, -z, -ɪŋ, -d; -lɪs [-ləs],
-lɪt/s [-lət/s]
wave-length, -s 'weɪvleŋkθ, -s
Wavell 'weɪvl
wav|er, -ers, -ering/ly, -ered, -erer/s
'weɪv|ə*, -əz, -ərɪŋ/lɪ, -əd, -ərə*/z
Waverley 'weɪvəlɪ
wav|y, -ier, -iest, -ily, -iness 'weɪv|ɪ,
-ɪə* [-jə*], -ɪɪst [-jɪst], -ɪlɪ [-əlɪ], -ɪnɪs
[-nəs]
wax (s. v.), -es, -ing, -ed; -en wæks, -ɪz,
-ɪŋ, -t; -ən
waxwing, -s 'wækswɪŋ, -z
waxwork, -s 'wækswɜːk, -s
wax|y, -ier, -iest, -iness 'wæks|ɪ, -ɪə*
[-jə*], -ɪɪst [-jɪst], -ɪnɪs [-nəs]
way (W.), -s weɪ, -z
wayfar|er/s, -ing 'weɪˌfeər|ə*/z, -ɪŋ
Wayland 'weɪlənd
way|lay, -lays, -laying, -laid, -layer/s
ˌweɪ|'leɪ, -'leɪz, -'leɪɪŋ, -'leɪd, -'leɪə*/z
Wayn|e, -flete weɪn, -fliːt
wayside 'weɪsaɪd
wayward, -ly, -ness 'weɪwəd, -lɪ, -nɪs
[-nəs]
W.C., -'s ˌdʌblju:'siː [-jʊ-], -z
Note.—When used as an abbrev. for
the West Central District of London,
some people pronounce in full
ˌwest'sentrəl.

we wiː (normal form), wɪ (freq. weak
form)
Note.—wɪ also occurs as a strong form
in the single expression we are
when are has its weak form ə*. We
are in this case is also written we're.
weak, -er, -est, -ly, -ness wiːk, -ə*, -ɪst,
-lɪ, -nɪs [-nəs]
weak|en, -ens, -ening, -ened 'wiːk|ən,
-ənz, -nɪŋ [-nɪŋ, -ənɪŋ], -ənd
weakening (s. adj.), -s 'wiːknɪŋ, -z
weakish 'wiːkɪʃ
weak-kneed ˌwiːk'niːd ['--]
weakling, -s 'wiːklɪŋ, -z
weak-minded ˌwiːk'maɪndɪd [also '-,--
when attributive]
weal, -s wiːl, -z
weald (W.), -s wiːld, -z
wealden (W.) 'wiːldən
wealth, -s welθ, -s
wealth|y, -ier, -iest, -ily, -iness 'welθ|ɪ,
-ɪə* [-jə*], -ɪɪst [-jɪst], -ɪlɪ [-əlɪ], -ɪnɪs
[-nəs]
wean, -s, -ing, -ed wiːn, -z, -ɪŋ, -d
weanling, -s 'wiːnlɪŋ, -z
weapon, -s; -less 'wepən, -z; -lɪs [-ləs]
wear (s.) (corresponding to wear v.)
weə*
wear (s.) (=weir), -s wɪə*, -z
Wear (river) wɪə*
wear (v.), -s, -ing, wore, worn, wearer/s
weə*, -z, -rɪŋ, wɔː* [wɔə*], wɔːn,
'weərə*/z
wearable 'weərəbl
Wearing 'weərɪŋ
wearisome, -ly, -ness 'wɪərɪsəm, -lɪ, -nɪs
[-nəs]
Wearmouth 'wɪəməθ [-maʊθ]
Wearn wɜːn
wear|y (adj. v.), -ier, -iest, -ily, -iness;
-ies, -ying, -ied 'wɪər|ɪ, -ɪə*, -ɪɪst,
-əlɪ [-ɪlɪ], -ɪnɪs [-nəs]; -ɪz, -ɪŋ, -ɪd
weasand, -s 'wiːzənd ['wɪz-, -znd], -z
weasel, -s 'wiːzl, -z
weather (s. v.), -s, -ing, -ed; -beaten
'weðə*, -z, -rɪŋ, -d; -ˌbiːtn
weatherboard, -s, -ing 'weðəbɔːd
[-bəəd], -z, -ɪŋ
weather-bound 'weðəbaʊnd
weathercock, -s 'weðəkɒk, -s
weather-eye, -s 'weðəraɪ, -z
weather-glass, -es 'weðəɡlɑːs, -ɪz
Weatherhead 'weðəhed
weatherly (W.) 'weðəlɪ
weatherproof 'weðəpruːf
weathership, -s 'weðəʃɪp, -s
weather-tanned 'weðətænd
weatherwear 'weðəweə*

weather-wise 'weðəwaɪz
weather-worn 'weðəwɔːn
weav|e, -es, -ing, wove, woven
    weaver/s wiːv, -z, -ɪŋ, wəʊv, 'wəʊvən,
    'wiːvə*/z
weazened 'wiːznd
web, -s, -bed web, -z, -d
Webb(e) web
webb|ing, -y 'web|ɪŋ, -ɪ
Weber (English name) 'wiːbə*, (German
    composer) 'veɪbə* ('veːbər)
webfooted 'web‚fʊtɪd [‚-'--]
Webster, -s 'webstə*, -z
wed, -s, -ding/s, -ded wed, -z, -ɪŋ/z, -ɪd
Weddell (surname) wə'del, 'wedl, (Sea)
    'wedl
Wedderburn 'wedəbɜːn
wedding-cake, -s 'wedɪŋkeɪk, -s
wedding-day, -s 'wedɪŋdeɪ, -z
wedding-ring, -s 'wedɪŋrɪŋ, -z
wedg|e (s. v.), -es, -ing, -ed; -ewise
    wedʒ, -ɪz, -ɪŋ, -d; -waɪz
wedge-shaped 'wedʒʃeɪpt
Wedgwood 'wedʒwʊd
wedlock 'wedlɒk
Wednesbury 'wenzbərɪ [locally also
    'wedʒbərɪ]
Wednesday, -s 'wenzdɪ ['wedn-, -deɪ],
    -z
wee wiː
weed (s. v.), -s, -ing, -ed wiːd, -z, -ɪŋ, -ɪd
Weedon 'wiːdn
weed|y, -ier, -iest, -iness 'wiːd|ɪ, -ɪə*
    [-jə*], -ɪɪst [-jɪst], -ɪnɪs [-məs]
week, -s wiːk, -s
weekday, -s 'wiːkdeɪ, -z
week-end, -s ‚wiːk'end ['--], -z
week-ender, -s ‚wiːk'endə*, -z
Weekes wiːks
Weekl(e)y 'wiːklɪ
weekl|y (s. adv.), -ies 'wiːkl|ɪ, -ɪz
Weeks wiːks
Weelkes wiːlks
Weems wiːmz
ween, -s, -ing, -ed wiːn, -z, -ɪŋ, -d
weep, -s, -ing/ly, wept wiːp, -s, -ɪŋ/lɪ,
    wept
weeper, -s 'wiːpə*, -z
weever, -s 'wiːvə*, -z
weevil, -s 'wiːvɪl [-vl], -z
weewee, -s, -ing, -d 'wiːwiː, -z, -ɪŋ, -d
weft weft
Weguelin 'wegəlɪn
Weigall 'waɪgɔːl
weigh, -s, -ing, -ed; -able weɪ, -z, -ɪŋ,
    -d; -əbl ['weəbl]
weight (s. v.), -s, -ing, -ed weɪt, -s, -ɪŋ,
    -ɪd

weightless, -ness 'weɪtlɪs [-ləs], -nɪs
    [-nəs]
Weighton (in Market Weighton, Hum-
    berside) 'wiːtn
weight|y, -ier, -iest, -ily, -iness 'weɪt|ɪ,
    -ɪə* [-jə*], -ɪɪst [-jɪst], -ɪlɪ [-əlɪ], -ɪnɪs
    [-məs]
Wei-hai-wei ‚weɪhaɪ'weɪ
Weimar 'vaɪmɑː* ('vaɪmar)
weir (W.), -s wɪə*, -z
weird, -er, -est, -ly, -ness wɪəd, -ə*, -ɪst,
    -lɪ, -nɪs [-nəs]
Weisshorn 'vaɪshɔːn
Weland 'weɪlənd, 'wiːlənd
Welbeck 'welbek
Welch welʃ
Welcombe 'welkəm
welcom|e (s. adj. v. interj.), -es, -ing, -ed
    'welkəm, -z, -ɪŋ, -d
weld (s. v.), -s, -ing, -ed, -er/s weld, -z,
    -ɪŋ, -ɪd, -ə*/z
weldment 'weldmənt
Weldon 'weldən
welfare 'welfeə*
Welford 'welfəd
welkin 'welkɪn
well (s. adj. v. interj.), -s, -ing, -ed wel,
    -z, -ɪŋ, -d
welladay ‚welə'deɪ ['---]
well-advised ‚weləd'vaɪzd
Welland 'welənd
well-appointed ‚welə'pɔɪntɪd
well-balanced ‚wel'bælənst [also '-‚--
    when attributive]
well-behaved ‚welbɪ'heɪvd [also '--‚-
    when attributive]
well-being ‚wel'biːɪŋ ['-‚--]
well-born ‚wel'bɔːn
well-bred ‚wel'bred [also '-- according
    to sentence-stress]
Wellby 'welbɪ
well-chosen ‚wel'tʃəʊzn [also '-‚-- when
    attributive]
Wellcome 'welkəm
well-conducted ‚welkən'dʌktɪd [also
    '--‚-- when attributive]
well-connected ‚welkə'nektɪd [also '--‚--
    when attributive]
well-cooked ‚wel'kʊkt [also '-- when
    attributive]
well-directed ‚weldɪ'rektɪd [-də'r-,
    -daɪ'r-, also '--‚-- when attributive]
well-disposed ‚weldɪ'spəʊzd
well-do|er/s, -ing 'wel‚duː|ə*/z
    [-‚duə*/z, ‚-'- - -], -ɪŋ
Welldon 'weldən
well-done ‚wel'dʌn ['-- when attributive]
Weller 'welə*

545

Wellesley 'welzlɪ
well-found ˌwel'faʊnd [also '-- when attributive]
well-groomed ˌwel'gruːmd ['-- when attributive]
well-grounded ˌwel'graʊndɪd
well-informed ˌwelɪn'fɔːmd
Wellingborough 'welɪŋbərə
Wellington, -s 'welɪŋtən, -z
wellingtonia, -s ˌwelɪŋ'təʊnjə [-nɪə], -z
well-intentioned ˌwelɪn'tenʃnd [also '--,-- when attributive]
well-judged ˌwel'dʒʌdʒd [also '-- when attributive]
well-known ˌwel'nəʊn [also '-- according to sentence-stress]
well-made ˌwel'meɪd [also '-- according to sentence-stress]
well-marked ˌwel'mɑːkt [also '-- when attributive]
well-meaning ˌwel'miːnɪŋ
well-meant ˌwel'ment [also '-- according to sentence-stress]
well-nigh 'welnaɪ
well-off ˌwel'ɒf [old-fashioned -'ɔːf, also '-- according to sentence-stress]
well-ordered ˌwel'ɔːdəd [also '--,-- when attributive]
well-proportioned ˌwelprə'pɔːʃnd [-prʊ'p-, also '--,-- when attributive]
well-read ˌwel'red [also '-- according to sentence-stress]
well-rounded ˌwel'raʊndɪd
Wells welz
well-spoken ˌwel'spəʊkən [also '-,-- when attributive]
well-timed ˌwel'taɪmd [also '-- when attributive]
well-to-do ˌweltə'duː [also '--- when attributive]
well-wisher, -s 'welˌwɪʃə* [ˌ-'--], -z
welsh, -es, -ing, -ed, -er/s welʃ, -ɪz, -ɪŋ, -t, -ə*/z
Welsh, -man, -men welʃ, -mən, -mən [-men]
Welshpool 'welʃpuːl (Welsh ˌwelʃ'puːl)
welt (s. v.), -s, -ing, -ed welt, -s, -ɪŋ, -ɪd
welt|er, -ers, -ering, -ered 'welt|ə*, -əz, -ərɪŋ, -əd
welterweight, -s 'weltəweɪt, -s
Welwyn 'welɪn
Wembley 'wemblɪ
Wemyss wiːmz
wen, -s wen, -z
Wenceslas 'wensɪsləs [-səs-, -læs]
wench, -es wenʃ, -ɪz
wend, -s, -ing, -ed wend, -z, -ɪŋ, -ɪd

Wend, -s, -ic, -ish wend [vend], -z, -ɪk, -ɪʃ
Wendell 'wendl
Wendover 'wendəʊvə*
Wengen 'veŋən
Wengern Alp ˌveŋən'ælp
Wenham 'wenəm
Wenish 'wenɪʃ
Wenlock 'wenlɒk
Wensleydale 'wenzlɪdeɪl
went (from go) went
Wentworth 'wentwəθ [-wɜː'θ]
wept (from weep) wept
we're (=we are) wɪə*
were (from be) wɜː* (strong form; rarely weə*), wə* (weak form)
weren't wɜːnt (rarely weənt)
werewol|f, -ves 'wɪəwʊl|f ['wɜː:-], -vz
Wernher 'wɜːnə*
wert (from be) wɜːt (strong form), wət (weak form)
Weser (German river) 'veɪzə* ('veːzər)
   Note.—'wiːzə* is necessary for rhyme in Browning's 'Pied Piper', but this pronunciation is exceptional.
Wesley 'wezlɪ, 'weslɪ
   Note.—Most people bearing the name Wesley pronounce 'weslɪ, but they are commonly called 'wezlɪ by others.
Wesleyan, -s; -ism 'wezlɪən ['wesl-, -ljən], -z; -ɪzəm
   Note.—'wesl- appears to be the more usual pronunciation among Wesleyans; with those who are not Wesleyans 'wezl- is probably the commoner form. There exists also an old-fashioned pronunciation wes'liːən.
Wessex 'wesɪks
west (s. adj. v.) (W.) west
Westbourne 'westbɔːn [-bɔən, -bən, esp. when attributive, as in W. Terrace]
West|brook, -bury 'west|brʊk, -bərɪ
Westcott 'westkət
Westenra 'westənrə
Westerham 'westərəm
westering 'westərɪŋ
wester|ly, -n, -ner/s 'westə|lɪ, -n, -nə*/z
westerniz|e [-is|e], -es, -ing, -ed 'westənaɪz, -ɪz, -ɪŋ, -d
westernmost 'westənməʊst
Westfield 'westfiːld
Westgate 'westgɪt [-geɪt]
Westlake 'westleɪk
Westmeath west'miːð
Westminster 'westmɪnstə* [-'--]
Westmor(e)land 'westmələnd ['wes-mḷənd]

west-north-west ˌwestnɔ:θ'west [*nautical pronunciation* -nɔ:'west]

Weston 'westən

Weston - super - Mare 'westən,su:pə-'meə* [-n,sju:pə-, -nsjʊpə-, ˌ--'---, *rarely* -'meərɪ]

Westphalia, -n/s west'feɪljə [-lɪə], -n/z

west-south-west ˌwestsaʊθ'west [*nautical pronunciation* -saʊ'west]

westward, -s, -ly 'westwəd, -z, -lɪ

Westward Ho ˌwestwəd'həʊ

wet, -ter, -test, -ness wet, -ə*, -ɪst, -nɪs [-nəs]

wether, -s 'weðə*, -z

Wetherby 'weðəbɪ

wet-nurse, -s 'wetnɜ:s, -ɪz

Wetterhorn 'vetəhɔ:n

wettish 'wetɪʃ

Wexford 'weksfəd

wey (W.), -s weɪ, -z

Wey|bridge, -man, -mouth 'weɪ|brɪdʒ, -mən, -məθ

whack (*s. v.*), -s, -ing/s, -ed, -er/s wæk [hw-], -s, -ɪŋ/z, -t, -ə*/z

Whait weɪt [hw-]

whal|e, -es, -ing, -er/s weɪl [hw-], -z, -ɪŋ, -ə*/z

whalebone 'weɪlbəʊn ['hw-]

whale-fisher|y, -ies 'weɪl,fɪʃər|ɪ ['hw-], -ɪz

whale-oil 'weɪlɔɪl ['hw-]

Whaley (*place near Buxton*) 'weɪlɪ ['hw-]

Whalley (*surname*) ' veɪlɪ ['hw-], 'wɔ:lɪ ['hw-], (*abbey near Blackburn*) 'wɔ:lɪ ['hw-]

whang (*s. v.*), -s, -in ʒ, -ed wæŋ [hw-], -z, -ɪŋ, -d

whangee wæŋ'gi: [hw-]

Wharam 'weərəm ['hw-]

whar|f, -ves, -fs wɔ:|f [hw-], -vz, -fs

wharfage 'wɔ:fɪdʒ ['hw-]

wharfinger, -s 'wɔ: ɪndʒə* ['hw-], -z

Wharton 'wɔ:tn ['ʌw-]

what wɒt [hw-]

what-d'you-call-it 'wɒtdjʊˌkɔ:lɪt ['hw-, -dʒʊ-]

whate'er wɒt'eə* [hw-]

Whateley 'weɪtlɪ ['hw-]

whatever wɒt'evə* [hw-, *rarely* wət-, hwət-]

What|ley, -man 'wɒt|lɪ ['hw-], -mən

Whatmough 'wɒtməʊ ['hw-]

whatnot, -s 'wɒtnɒt ['hw-], -s

what's-her-name 'wɒtsəneɪm ['hw-, -sn̩eɪm]

what's-his-name 'wɒtsɪzneɪm ['hw-]

whatsoe'er ˌwɒtsəʊ'eə* [ˌhw-]

whatsoever ˌwɒtsəʊ'evə* [ˌhw-]

what-you-may-call-it 'wɒtʃəməˌkɔ:lɪt ['hw-]

wheat, -en wi:t [hw-], -n

wheat-ear, -s 'wi:t,ɪə* ['hw-], -z

Wheathampstead (*in Hertfordshire*) 'wi:təmpsted ['wet-, 'hw-]

Wheat|ley, -on 'wi:t|lɪ ['hw-], -n

Wheatstone 'wi:tstən ['hw-, -stəʊn]

wheed|le, -les, -ling, -led, -ler/s 'wi:d|l ['hw-], -lz, -lɪŋ [-l̩ɪŋ], -ld, -lə*/z [-l̩ə*/z]

wheel (*s. v.*), -s, -ing, -ed wi:l [hw-], -z, -ɪŋ, -d

wheelbarrow, -s 'wi:l,bærəʊ ['hw-], -z

wheel-chair, -s ˌwi:l'tʃeə* [ˌhw-, '--], -z

wheeler (W.), -s 'wi:lə* ['hw-], -z

wheelwright (W.), -s 'wi:lraɪt ['hw-], -s

Wheen wi:n [hw-]

wheez|e (*s. v.*), -es, -ing, -ed; -y, -ier, -iest, -iness wi:z [hw-], -ɪz, -ɪŋ, -d; -ɪ, -ɪə* [-jə*], -ɪɪst [-jɪst], -ɪnɪs [-ɪnəs]

Whelan 'wi:lən ['hw-]

whelk, -s welk, -s

Note.—Not hwelk.

whelm, -s, -ing, -ed welm [hw-], -z, -ɪŋ, -d

whelp (*s. v.*), -s, -ing, -ed welp [hw-], -s, -ɪŋ, -t

when wen [hw-]

whence wens [hw-]

whene'er wen'eə* [hw-]

whenever wen'evə* [wən-, hw-]

whensoever ˌwensəʊ'evə* [ˌhw-]

where weə* [hw-]

whereabouts (*s.*) 'weərəbaʊts ['hw-]

whereabouts (*interrogation*) ˌweərə'baʊts [ˌhw-, *occasionally* '--- *when followed by a stress*]

whereas weər'æz [wər-, hw-]

whereat weər'æt [wər-, hw-]

whereby weə'baɪ [hw-]

where'er weər'eə* [wər-, hw-]

wherefore 'weəfɔ:* ['hw-, -fɔə*]

where|in, -of, -on weər|'ɪn [hw-], -'ɒv [-'ɒf], -'ɒn

whereso|e'er, -ever ˌweəsəʊ'eə* [ˌhw-, -'evə*]

whereto weə'tu: [hw-]

whereunder weər'ʌndə* [hw-]

whereunto ˌweərʌn'tu: [ˌhw-]

whereupon ˌweərə'pɒn [ˌhw-, '---]

wherever weər'evə* [wə'r-, hw-]

wherewith weə'wɪθ [hw-, -'wɪð]

wherewithal (*s.*) 'weəwɪðɔ:l ['hw-]

wherewithal (*adv.*) ˌweəwɪ'ðɔ:l [ˌhw-, '---]

wherr|y, -ies 'wer|ɪ ['hw-], -ɪz

whet (*s. v.*), **-s, -ting, -ted** wet [hw-], -s,
-ıŋ, -ıd
whether 'weðə* ['hw-]
whetstone (**W.**), **-s** 'wetstəʊn ['hw-],
-z
whew ŷ: [ŷ̃:, ŷ̃:u:, hwu:]
Whewell 'hju:əl [-ʋəl, -el, -ıl]
whey weı [hw-]
Whibley 'wıblı ['hw-]
which wıtʃ [hw-]
whichever wıtʃ'evə* [hw-]
Whickham 'wıkəm ['hw-]
whiff (*s. v.*), **-s, -ing, -ed** wıf [hw-], -s,
-ıŋ, -t
Whiffen 'wıfın ['hw-]
whig (**W.**), **-s** wıg [hw-], -z
whigg|ery, **-ism** 'wıg|ərı ['hw-], -ızəm
whiggish, **-ly, -ness** 'wıgıʃ ['hw-], -lı,
-nıs [-nəs]
Whigham 'wıgəm ['hw-]
while (*s. v. conj.*), **-es, -ing, -ed** waıl
[hw-], -z, -ıŋ, -d
whilom 'waıləm ['hw-]
whilst waılst [hw-]
whim, **-s** wım [hw-], -z
whimbrel, **-s** 'wımbrəl ['hw-], -z
whimper, **-s, -ing/ly, -ed, -er/s** 'wı npə*
['hw-], -z, -rıŋ/lı, -d, -rə*/z
whimsic|al, **-ally, -alness** 'wımzıkl
['hw-, -msı-], -əlı, -lnıs [-nəs]
whimsicality ˌwımzı'kælətı [ˌhw-, -msı-,
-ıtı]
whims|y, **-ies** 'wımz|ı ['hw-], -ız
whin, **-s** wın [hw-], -z
whinchat, **-s** 'wıntʃæt ['hw-], -s
whin|e (*s. v.*), **-es, -ing/ly, -ed** waın
[hw-], -z, -ıŋ/lı, -d
whinger, **-s** 'wıŋə* [hw-], -z
whinn|y (*s. v.*), **-ies, -ying, -ied** 'wın|ı
['hw-], -ız, -ıŋ, -ıd
whin|y, **-ier, -iest, -iness** 'waın|ı ['hw-],
-ıə*, -ııst, -ınıs [-nəs]
whip (*s. v.*), **-s, -ping/s, -ped** wıp [hw-],
-s, -ıŋ/z, -t
whip-cord 'wıpkɔ:d ['hw-]
whip-hand ˌwıp'hænd [ˌhw-, '--]
whipp|er-in, **-ers-in** ˌwıp|ər'ın [ˌhw-,
-əz'ın
whippersnapper, **-s** 'wıpəˌsnæpə* ['hw-],
-z
whippet, **-s** 'wıpıt ['hw-], -s
whipping-boy, **-s** 'wıpıŋbɔı ['hw-], -z
Whippingham 'wıpıŋəm ['hw-]
whipping-top, **-s** 'wıpıŋtɒp ['hw-], -s
Whipple 'wıpl ['hw-]
whippoorwill, **-s** 'wıpˌpʊəˌwıl ['hw-,
-pɔə,w-, -pɔːˌw-], -z
Whipsnade 'wıpsneıd ['hw-]

whir (*s. v.*), **-s, -ring/s, -red** wɜ:* [hw-],
-z, -rıŋ/z, -d
whirl (*s. v.*), **-s, -ing, -ed** wɜ:l [hw-], -z,
-ıŋ, -d
whirligig, **-s** 'wɜ:lıgıg ['hw-], -z
whirlpool, **-s** 'wɜ:lpu:l ['hw-], -z
whirlwind, **-s** 'wɜ:lwınd ['hw-], -z
whirr (*s. v.*), **-s, -ing/s, -ed** wɜ:* [hw-],
-z, -rıŋ/z, -d
whisk (*s. v.*), **-s, -ing, -ed** wısk [hw-], -s,
-ıŋ, -t
whisker, **-s, -ed** 'wıskə* ['hw-], -z, -d
whiskey, **-s** 'wıskı ['hw-], -z
whisk|y, **-ies** 'wısk|ı ['hw-], -ız
whisp|er (*s. v.*), **-ers, -ering/s, -ered,
-erer/s** 'wısp|ə* ['hw-], -əz, -ərıŋ/z,
-əd, -ərə*/z
whist wıst [hw-]
whist-drive, **-s** 'wıstdraıv ['hw-], -z
whist|le (*s. v.*), **-les, -ling, -led** 'wıs|l
['hw-], -lz, -lıŋ [-l̩ıŋ], -ld
whistler (**W.**), **-s** 'wıslə* ['hw-], -z
whit (**W.**) wıt [hw-]
Whitaker 'wıtəkə* ['hw-, -tık-]
Whit|bread, **-by, -church** 'wıt|bred
['hw-], -bı, -tʃɜ:tʃ
whit|e (*s. adj. v.*) (**W.**), **-es; -er, -est,
-ely, -eness; -ing, -ed** waıt [hw-], -s;
-ə*, -ıst, -lı, -nıs [-nəs]; -ıŋ, -ıd
whitebait 'waıtbeıt ['hw-]
whitebeard, **-s, -ed** 'waıtˌbıəd ['hw-], -z,
-ıd
whitecap, **-s** 'waıtkæp ['hw-], -s
Whitechapel 'waıtˌtʃæpl ['hw-]
Whitefield 'waıtfi:ld ['hw-], 'wıt- ['hw-]
Whitefriars 'waıtˌfraıəz ['hw-, ˌ-'--]
Whitehall ˌwaıt'hɔ:l ['hw-, *also* '--
according to sentence-stress]
Whitehaven 'waıtˌheıvn ['hw-]
whitehead (**W.**), **-s** 'waıthed ['hw-], -z
white-heat ˌwaıt'hi:t [ˌhw-]
white-hot ˌwaıt'hɒt [ˌhw-, *also* '-- *when
attributive*]
Whiteley 'waıtlı ['hw-]
white-livered 'waıtˌlıvəd ['hw-]
whit|en, **-ens, -ening, -ened** 'waıt|n
['hw-], -nz, -nıŋ [-n̩ıŋ], -nd
whitening (*s.*) 'waıtnıŋ ['hw-]
whitethorn, **-s** 'waıtθɔ:n ['hw-], -z
whitethroat, **-s** 'waıtθrəʊt ['hw-], -s
whitewash (*s. v.*), **-es, -ing, -ed, -er/s**
'waıtwɒʃ ['hw-], -ız, -ıŋ, -t, -ə*/z
whitewood 'waıtwʊd ['hw-]
Whit|field, **-gift** 'wıt|fi:ld ['hw-], -gıft
whither 'wıðə* ['hw-]
whithersoever ˌwıðəsəʊ'evə* [ˌhw-]
whiting (**W.**), **-s** 'waıtıŋ ['hw-], -z
whitish, **-ness** 'waıtıʃ ['hw-], -nıs [-nəs]

whitleather 'wɪt‚leðə* ['hw-]
Whitley 'wɪtlɪ ['hw-]
whitlow, -s 'wɪtləʊ ['hw-], -z
Whit|man, -marsh, -ney, -stable, -stone 'wɪt|mən ['hw-], -mɑːʃ, -nɪ, -stəbl, -stəʊn
Whitsun 'wɪtsn ['hw-]
Whitsunday, -s ‚wɪt'sʌndɪ [‚hw-, -'sʌndeɪ, -sn'deɪ], -z
Whitsuntide, -s 'wɪtsntaɪd ['hw-], -z
Whittaker 'wɪtəkə* ['hw-, -tɪk-]
Whittier 'wɪtɪə* ['hw-]
Whittingeham(e) 'wɪtɪndʒəm ['hw-]
Whittington 'wɪtɪŋtən ['hw-]
whitt|le (W.), -les, -ling, -led 'wɪt|l ['hw-], -lz, -lɪŋ [-lɪŋ], -ld
Whitworth 'wɪtwɜːθ ['hw-, -wəθ]
whit|y, -iness 'waɪt|ɪ ['hw-], -ɪnɪs [-nəs]
whiz, -zes, -zing, -zed wɪz [hw-], -ɪz, -ɪŋ, -d
whizz (s. v.), -es, -ing, -ed wɪz [hw-], -ɪz, -ɪŋ, -d
who (interrogative) huː [also hʊ when followed by a word beginning with ə or unstressed ɪ]
who (relative) huː (normal form), hʊ (freq. weak form), uː, ʊ (occasional weak forms)
whoa wəʊ
who-dun-it, -s ‚huː'dʌnɪt, -s
whoe'er huː'eə* [hʊ'eə*]
whoever huː'evə* [hʊ'e-, occasionally uː-, ʊ- when closely connected to preceding word in the sentence]
whole, -ness həʊl, -nɪs [-nəs]
whole-hearted ‚həʊl'hɑːtɪd
whole-hog, -ger/s ‚həʊl'hɒg, -ə*/z
whole-meal 'həʊlmiːl
wholesale 'həʊlseɪl
wholesaler, -s 'həʊl‚seɪlə*, -z
wholesome, -st, -ly, -ness 'həʊlsəm, -ɪst, -lɪ, -nɪs [-nəs]
wholly 'həʊllɪ ['həʊlɪ]
whom huːm (normal form), hʊm (occasional weak form)
whomsoever ‚huːmsəʊ'evə*
whoop (s. v.), -s, -ing, -ed huːp, -s, -ɪŋ, -t
whoopee (s.) 'wʊpiː [-pɪ], (interj.) wʊ'piː
whooping-cough 'huːpɪŋkɒf [old-fashioned -kɔːf]
whop, -s, -ping/s, -ped wɒp [hw-], -s, -ɪŋ/z, -t
whopper, -s 'wɒpə* ['hw-], -z
whor|e (s. v.), -es, -ing, -ed; -edom/s hɔː* [hɒə*], -z, -rɪŋ, -d; -dəm/z
whoreson, -s 'hɔːsn ['hɔəsn], -z
whorl, -s, -ed wɜːl [hw-], -z, -d

whortle, -s 'wɜːtl ['hw-], -z
whortleberr|y, -ies 'wɜːtl‚ber|ɪ ['hw-, -bər|ɪ], -ɪz
whose (interrogative) huːz
whose (relative) huːz (normal form), uːz (occasional weak form)
whoso 'huːsəʊ
whosoever ‚huːsəʊ'evə*
why waɪ [hw-]
Whyle (surname) 'waɪlɪ ['hw-]
Whymper 'wɪmpə* ['hw-]
Whyte waɪt [hw-]
Whytt waɪt [hw-]
wick (W.), -s wɪk, -s
wicked, -est, -ly, -ness/es 'wɪkɪd, -ɪst, -lɪ, -nɪs/ɪz [-nəs/ɪz]
Wickens 'wɪkɪnz
wicker, -work 'wɪkə*, -wɜːk
wicket, -s 'wɪkɪt, -s
wicket-gate, -s 'wɪkɪtgeɪt, -s
wicket-keeper, -s 'wɪkɪt‚kiːpə*, -z
Wickham 'wɪkəm
Wickliffe 'wɪklɪf
Wicklow 'wɪkləʊ
wide (s. adj.), -s, -r, -st, -ly, -ness waɪd, -z, -ə*, -ɪst, -lɪ, -nɪs [-nəs]
wide-awake (s.), -s 'waɪdəweɪk, -s
wide-awake (adj.) ‚waɪdə'weɪk
Widecombe 'wɪdɪkəm
Widemouth 'wɪdməθ
wid|en, -ens, -ening, -ened 'waɪd|n, -nz, -nɪŋ [-nɪŋ], -nd
widespread 'waɪdspred [‚-'-]
widgeon, -s 'wɪdʒən [-dʒɪn], -z
widish 'waɪdɪʃ
Widnes 'wɪdnɪs
widow, -s, -ed 'wɪdəʊ, -z, -d
widower, -s 'wɪdəʊə*, -z
widowhood 'wɪdəʊhʊd
width, -s wɪdθ [wɪtθ], -s
wield, -s, -ing, -ed wiːld, -z, -ɪŋ, -ɪd
Wiesbaden 'viːs‚bɑːdn ['viːz‚b-, viːs'b-, viːz'b-] ('viːs‚bɑːdən, locally vis-'bɑːdən)
wi|fe, -ves waɪ|f, -vz
wife|hood, -less 'waɪf|hʊd, -lɪs [-ləs]
wife|like, -ly 'waɪf|laɪk, -lɪ
Wiffen 'wɪfɪn
wig (s. v.), -s, -ging, -ged wɪg, -z, -ɪŋ, -d
Wigan 'wɪgən
wigging (s.), -s 'wɪgɪŋ, -z
Wiggins 'wɪgɪnz
wigg|le (s. v.), -les, -ling, -led 'wɪg|l, -lz, -lɪŋ [-lɪŋ], -ld
wiggle-waggle 'wɪgl‚wægl
wiggly 'wɪglɪ [-glɪ]
wight (W.), -s waɪt, -s
wig-maker, -s 'wɪg‚meɪkə*, -z

Wigmore 'wɪgmɔː* [-mɔə*]
Wigram 'wɪgrəm
Wig|ton, -town 'wɪg|tən, -tən
wigwam, -s 'wɪgwæm, -z
Wilberforce 'wɪlbəfɔːs
Wilbraham 'wɪlbrəhæm [-brəm, -brɪəm]
Wil|bur, -bye 'wɪl|bə*, -bɪ
Wilcox 'wɪlkɒks
wild (s. adj. adv.) (W.), -s, -er, -est, -ly, -ness waɪld, -z, -ə*, -ɪst, -lɪ, -nɪs [-nəs]
Wilde waɪld
wildebeest, -s 'wɪldɪbiːst ['vɪldə-], -s
Wilder 'waɪldə*
wilderness, -es 'wɪldənɪs [-nəs], -ɪz
wildfire 'waɪld,faɪə*
wilding (W.), -s 'waɪldɪŋ, -z
wildish 'waɪldɪʃ
wil|e (s. v.) (W.), -es, -ing, -ed waɪl, -z, -ɪŋ, -d
Wilfred [-rid] 'wɪlfrɪd ['wʊl-]
wil|ful, -fullest, -fully, -fulness 'wɪl|fʊl, -fʊlɪst [-fəlɪst], -fʊlɪ [-fəlɪ], -fʊlnɪs [-nəs]
Wilhelmina (English name) ˌwɪlhel-'miːnə, ˌwɪləˈmiːnə
Wilk|es, -ie, -ins wɪlk|s, -ɪ, -ɪnz
Wilkinson 'wɪlkɪnsn
Wilks wɪlks
will (s.) (W.), -s wɪl, -z
will (transitive v.), -s, -ing, -ed wɪl, -z, -ɪŋ, -d
will (auxil. v.) wɪl (strong form), l (normal weak form), wəl, əl (occasional weak forms)
Willard 'wɪlɑːd [-ləd]
Willcocks [-cox] 'wɪlkɒks
Willes wɪlz
Willesden 'wɪlzdən
William, -s, -son 'wɪljəm, -z, -sn
Willie 'wɪlɪ
willing (adj.) (W.), -ly, -ness 'wɪlɪŋ, -lɪ, -nɪs [-nəs]
Willing|don, -ton 'wɪlɪŋ|dən, -tən
Willis 'wɪlɪs
will-o'-the-wisp, -s ˌwɪləðəˈwɪsp [-əðˈw-, ˈ----], -s
Willoughby 'wɪləbɪ
will|ow (s. v.), -ows, -owing, -owed; -owy 'wɪl|əʊ, -əʊz, -əʊɪŋ, -əʊd; -əʊɪ
willowherb 'wɪləʊhɜːb
willow-pattern 'wɪləʊˌpætən [-tn]
willow-wren, -s 'wɪləʊren, -z
will-power, -s 'wɪl,paʊə*, -z
Wills wɪlz
Will|steed, -y 'wɪl|stiːd, -ɪ
willy-nilly ˌwɪlɪˈnɪlɪ
Wilma 'wɪlmə
Wilmcote 'wɪlmkəʊt

Wilmington 'wɪlmɪŋtən
Wilmot(t) 'wɪlmət [-mɒt]
Wilmslow 'wɪlmzləʊ [locally 'wɪmzləʊ]
Wilna 'vɪlnə
Wilno (in Ontario) 'wɪlnəʊ
Wilsden 'wɪlzdən
Wilshire 'wɪlʃə* [-ˌʃɪə*]
Wilson 'wɪlsn
wilt (from will, auxil. v.) wɪlt (normal form), əlt, lt (occasional weak forms)
wilt (v.), -s, -ing, -ed wɪlt, -s, -ɪŋ, -ɪd
Wilton, -s 'wɪltən, -z
Wilts. wɪlts
Wiltshire 'wɪlt-ʃə* [-ˌʃɪə*]
wil|y, -ier, -iest, -iness 'waɪl|ɪ, -ɪə*, -ɪɪst, -ɪnɪs [-nəs]
Wimble, -don 'wɪmbl, -dən
Wimborne 'wɪmbɔːn [-bəən]
Wimms wɪmz
Wimperis 'wɪmpərɪs
wimple, -s 'wɪmpl, -z
Wimpole 'wɪmpəʊl
win (s. v.), -s, -ning, won, winner/s wɪn, -z, -ɪŋ, wʌn, 'wɪnə*/z
winc|e, -es, -ing, -ed wɪns, -ɪz, -ɪŋ, -t
wincey 'wɪnsɪ
winceyette ˌwɪnsɪˈet
winch, -es wɪntʃ, -ɪz
Win|chelsea, -chester 'wɪn|tʃlsɪ [-siː], -tʃɪstə*
Winch|field, -ilsea, -more 'wɪntʃ|fiːld, -lsɪ [-siː], -mɔː* [-mɔə*]
wind (s.) (air blowing), -s wɪnd [in poetry sometimes waɪnd], -z
wind (v.) (go round, roll round), -s, -ing, wound waɪnd, -z, -ɪŋ, waʊnd
wind (v.) (blow horn), -s, -ing, -ed waɪnd, -z, -ɪŋ, -ɪd
wind (v.) (detect by scent, exhaust breath), -s, -ing, -ed wɪnd, -z, -ɪŋ, -ɪd
windage 'wɪndɪdʒ
windbag, -s 'wɪndbæg, -z
windbreak, -s, -er/s 'wɪndbreɪk, -s, -ə*/z
windcheater, -s 'wɪndˌtʃiːtə*, -z
wind-chest, -s 'wɪndtʃest, -s
wind-cone, -s 'wɪndkəʊn, -z
Winder, -mere 'wɪndə*, -ˌmɪə*
windfall, -s 'wɪndfɔːl, -z
Windham 'wɪndəm
Note.—The place in Vermont, U.S.A., is called locally 'wɪndhæm.
windhover, -s 'wɪnd,hɒvə*, -z
winding (in furnaces) 'wɪndɪŋ
winding (s. adj.), -s, -ly 'waɪndɪŋ, -z, -lɪ
winding-sheet, -s 'waɪndɪŋʃiːt, -s
winding-up ˌwaɪndɪŋˈʌp

wind-instrument, -s 'wɪnd,ɪnstrʊmənt
[-trəm-], -s
wind-jammer, -s 'wɪnd,dʒæmə*, -z
windlass, -es 'wɪndləs, -ɪz
Windley 'wɪndlɪ
windmill, -s 'wɪnmɪl [-ndm-], -z
window, -s 'wɪndəʊ, -z
window-box, -es 'wɪndəʊbɒks, -ɪz
window-cleaner, -s 'wɪndəʊ,kliːnə*, -z
window-dressing 'wɪndəʊ,dresɪŋ
window-pane, -s 'wɪndəʊpeɪn, -z
window-seat, -s 'wɪndəʊsiːt, -s
windpipe, -s 'wɪndpaɪp, -s
windrow, -s 'wɪndrəʊ, -z
wind-screen, -s, -wiper/s 'wɪndskriːn,
-z, -,waɪpə*/z
Windsor 'wɪnzə*
wind-swept 'wɪndswept
Windus 'wɪndəs
windward (W.) 'wɪndwəd
wind|y, -ier, -iest, -ily, -iness 'wɪnd|ɪ,
-ɪə* [-jə*], -ɪst [-jɪst], -ɪlɪ [-əlɪ], -ɪnɪs
[-məs]
wine, -s waɪn, -z
wine-bibber, -s 'waɪn,bɪbə*, -z
wine-bottle, -s 'waɪn,bɒtl, -z
wine-cellar, -s 'waɪn,selə*, -z
wineglass, -es 'waɪnglɑːs, -ɪz
wineglassful, -s 'waɪnglɑːs,fʊl, -z
wine-press, -es 'waɪnpres, -ɪz
wine-skin, -s 'waɪnskɪn, -z
wing (s. v.) (W.), -s, -ing, -ed, -er/s
wɪŋ, -z, -ɪŋ, -d, -ə*/z
wing-commander, -s 'wɪŋkə,mɑːndə*,-z
wing-covert, -s ,wɪŋ'kʌvət, -s
winged (adj.) wɪŋd
-winged -wɪŋd
Wingfield 'wɪŋfiːld
wingspan 'wɪŋspæn
Winifred 'wɪnɪfrɪd
wink (s. v.) (W.), -s, -ing, -ed, -er/s
wɪŋk, -s, -ɪŋ, -t [wɪŋt], -ə*/z
Winkfield 'wɪŋkfiːld
Winkie 'wɪŋkɪ
winkle (W.), -s 'wɪŋkl, -z
Winnepesaukee ,wɪnəpə'sɔːkɪ
winner, -s 'wɪnə*, -z
Winnie 'wɪnɪ
winning (s. adj.) (W.), -s, -ly 'wɪnɪŋ, -z,
-lɪ
winning-post, -s 'wɪnɪŋpəʊst, -s
Winnipeg 'wɪnɪpeg
winn|ow, -ows, -owing, -owed, -ower/s
'wɪn|əʊ, -əʊz, -əʊɪŋ, -əʊd, -əʊə*/z
winnowing-fan, -s 'wɪnəʊɪŋfæn, -z
Winslow 'wɪnzləʊ
winsome, -ly, -ness 'wɪnsəm, -lɪ, -nɪs
[-nəs]

Winstanley (in Greater Manchester)
'wɪnstənlɪ [wɪn'stænlɪ, esp. by new-
comers], (surname) 'wɪnstənlɪ, wɪn-
'stænlɪ
Winston 'wɪnstən
wint|er (s. v.) (W.), -ers, -ering, -ered
'wɪnt|ə*, -əz, -ərɪŋ, -əd
Winterbourne 'wɪntəbɔːn [-bɔən,
-,bʊən]
wintertime 'wɪntətaɪm
Winterton 'wɪntətən
Winton 'wɪntən
Wintour 'wɪntə*
wintr|y, -iness 'wɪntr|ɪ, -ɪnɪs [-məs]
winy 'waɪnɪ
wip|e (s. v.), -es, -ing, -ed, -er/s waɪp,
-s, -ɪŋ, -t, -ə*/z
wir|e (s. v.), -es, -ing, -ed 'waɪə*, -z,
-rɪŋ, -d
wire-cutter, -s 'waɪə,kʌtə*, -z
wire|draw, -draws, -drawing, -drew,
-drawn, -drawer/s 'waɪədrɔː, -drɔːz,
-,drɔːɪŋ, -dru:, -drɔːn, -,drɔːə*/z
wire-haired 'waɪəheəd
wireless (s. adj.), -es 'waɪəlɪs [-ləs], -ɪz
wire-pull|er/s, -ing 'waɪə,pʊl|ə*/z, -ɪŋ
wire-worm, -s 'waɪəwɜːm, -z
wiring 'waɪərɪŋ
wir|y, -ier, -iest, -iness 'waɪər|ɪ, -ɪə*,
-ɪst, -ɪnɪs [-məs]
wis wɪs
Wisbech 'wɪzbiːtʃ
Wisconsin wɪs'kɒnsɪn
wisdom 'wɪzdəm
wise (s. adj.) (W.), -r, -st, -ly, -ness
waɪz, -ə*, -ɪst, -lɪ, -nɪs [-nəs]
wiseacre, -s 'waɪz,eɪkə*, -z
wisecrack, -s 'waɪzkræk, -s
Wiseman 'waɪzmən
wish (s. v.), -es, -ing, -ed, -er/s wɪʃ, -ɪz,
-ɪŋ, -t, -ə*/z
wishbone, -s 'wɪʃbəʊn, -z
wish|ful, -fully, -fulness 'wɪʃ|fʊl, -fʊlɪ
[-fəlɪ], -fʊlnɪs [-nəs]
wishing-bone, -s 'wɪʃɪŋbəʊn, -z
wish-wash 'wɪʃwɒʃ
wishy-washy 'wɪʃɪ,wɒʃɪ [,--'--]
wisp, -s wɪsp, -s
wist wɪst
Wist|ar, -er 'wɪst|ə*, -ə*
wistaria, -s wɪ'steərɪə, -z
wisteria, -s wɪ'stɪərɪə, -z
wist|ful, -fully, -fulness 'wɪst|fʊl, -fʊlɪ
[-fəlɪ], -fʊlnɪs [-nəs]
wit (s. v.), -s wɪt, -s
witch (s. v.), -es, -ing/ly, -ed wɪtʃ, -ɪz,
-ɪŋ/lɪ, -t
witchcraft 'wɪtʃkrɑːft

551

witch-doctor, -s 'wɪtʃˌdɒktə*, -z
witch-elm, -s 'wɪtʃelm [ˌ-'-'-], -z
witcher|y, -ies 'wɪtʃər|ɪ, -ɪz
witch-hazel, -s 'wɪtʃˌheɪzl [ˌ-'--], -z
witch-hunt, -s 'wɪtʃhʌnt, -s
witching 'wɪtʃɪŋ
witena gemot, -s ˌwɪtɪnəgɪ'məʊt
[-tən-, -gəˈm-], -s
with wɪð [occasionally also wɪθ, esp.
before words beginning with voiceless
consonants]
Note.—In the N. of England the word
is generally pronounced wɪθ in all
positions.
withal wɪ'ðɔ:l
Witham (surname) 'wɪðəm, (river in
Lincolnshire) 'wɪðəm, (town in Essex)
'wɪtəm
with|draw, -draws, -drawing, -drew,
-drawn wɪð|'drɔ: [wɪθ|'d-], -'drɔ:z,
-'drɔ:ɪŋ, -'dru:, -'drɔ:n
withdrawal, -s wɪð'drɔ:əl [wɪθ'd-], -z
withe, -s wɪθ, -s [wɪð, waɪð, -z]
with|er (W.), -ers, -ering/ly, -ered
'wɪð|ə*, -əz, -ərɪŋ/lɪ, -əd
withers (s.) (W.) 'wɪðəz
with|hold, -holds, -holding, -held,
-holden, -holder/s wɪð|'həʊld
[wɪθ|'h-], -'həʊldz, -'həʊldɪŋ, -'held,
-'həʊldən, -'həʊldə*/z
within wɪ'ðɪn [wɪð'ɪn]
without wɪ'ðaʊt [wɪð'aʊt]
with|-stand, -stands, -standing, -stood
wɪð|'stænd [wɪθ|'s-], -'stændz,
-'stændɪŋ, -'stʊd
with|y, -ies 'wɪð|ɪ, -ɪz
witless, -ly, -ness 'wɪtlɪs [-ləs], -lɪ, -nɪs
[-nəs]
Witley 'wɪtlɪ
witness (s. v.), -es, -ing, -ed 'wɪtnɪs
[-nəs], -ɪz, -ɪŋ, -t
witney (W.) 'wɪtnɪ
-witted -'wɪtɪd [-ˌwɪtɪd]
Wittenberg 'vɪtnbɜ:g [-beəg, old-
fashioned 'wɪtnbɜ:g] ('vɪtənberk)
witticism, -s 'wɪtɪsɪzəm, -z
wittingly 'wɪtɪŋlɪ
witt|y, -ier, -iest, -ily, -iness 'wɪt|ɪ, -ɪə*,
-ɪɪst, -ɪlɪ [-əlɪ], -ɪnɪs [-ɪnəs]
Witwatersrand (usual pronunciation in
England) wɪt'wɔ:təzrænd ['wɪt,w-],
(pronunciations of English-speaking
South Africans) 'wɪt,wɑ:təz'rɑ:nd
[-'rɑ:nt, 'vɪt,vɑ:təz'rɒnt, '-ˌ-ˌ-]
(Afrikaans 'vɪt,vɑtərs'rɑnt)
wiv|e, -es, -ing, -ed waɪv, -z, -ɪŋ, -d
Wiveliscombe 'wɪvəlɪskəm [locally also
'wɪlskəm]

Wivelsfield 'wɪvəlzfi:ld
wivern, -s 'waɪvɜ:n, -z
wives (plur. of wife, and from v. wive)
waɪvz
wizard (s. adj.), -s, -ry 'wɪzəd, -z, -rɪ
wizen, -ed 'wɪzn, -d
w-ness 'dʌblju:nɪs [-jʊ-, -nəs]
wo wəʊ
woad wəʊd
wo-back ˌwəʊ'bæk
wobb|le (s. v.), -les, -ling, -led, -ler/s
'wɒb|l, -lz, -l̩ɪŋ [-lɪŋ], -ld, -l̩ə*/z
[-lə*/z]
wobb|ly, -liness 'wɒb|l̩ɪ [-lɪ], -l̩ɪnɪs
[-lɪnɪs, -nəs]
Woburn (place in Bedfordshire)
'wu:bɜ:n [-bən], (street and square in
London) 'wəʊbən [-bɜ:n]
Wodehouse 'wʊdhaʊs
Woden 'wəʊdn
woe, -s wəʊ, -z
woebegone 'wəʊbɪˌgɒn
woe|ful, -fully, -fulness 'wəʊ|fʊl, -fʊlɪ
[-fəlɪ], -fʊlnɪs [-nəs]
woke, -n (from wake) wəʊk, -ən
Woking, -ham 'wəʊkɪŋ, -əm
Wolborough 'wɒlbərə
Wolcot(t) 'wʊlkət
wold, -s wəʊld, -z
Woldingham 'wəʊldɪŋəm
Woledge 'wʊlɪdʒ
wol|f (s.) (W.), -ves wʊl|f, -vz
wolf (v.), -s, -ing, -ed wʊlf, -s, -ɪŋ, -t
wolf-cub, -s 'wʊlfkʌb, -z
Wolfe wʊlf
Wolfenden 'wʊlfəndən
Wolff wʊlf, vɒlf
wolf-hound, -s 'wʊlfhaʊnd, -z
wolfish, -ly, -ness 'wʊlfɪʃ, -lɪ, -nɪs [-nəs]
wolfram (W.), -ite 'wʊlfrəm, -aɪt
wolf-skin, -s 'wʊlfskɪn, -z
Wollaston 'wʊləstən
Wollaton (Nottinghamshire) 'wʊlətn
Wollstonecraft 'wʊlstənkrɑ:ft
Wolmer 'wʊlmə*
Wolseley, -s 'wʊlzlɪ, -z
Wolsey 'wʊlzɪ
Wolsingham 'wɒlsɪŋəm
Wolstanton 'wʊlstæntən [locally 'wʊl-
stən]
Wolstenholme 'wʊlstənhəʊm
Wolverhampton 'wʊlvəˌhæmptən
[ˌwʊlvə'h-]
wolverine, -s 'wʊlvəri:n, -z
Wolverton 'wʊlvətn [-tən]
wolves (plur. of wolf) wʊlvz
woman, women 'wʊmən, 'wɪmɪn
woman-hater, -s 'wʊmənˌheɪtə*, -z

womanhood 'wʊmənhʊd

womanish, -ly, -ness 'wʊmənɪʃ, -lɪ, -nɪs [-nəs]

womaniz|e [-is|e], -es, -ing, -ed, -er/s 'wʊmənaɪz, -ɪz, -ɪŋ, -d, -ə*/z

womankind ‚wʊmən'kaɪnd ['---]

womanlike 'wʊmənlaɪk

womanl|y, -iness 'wʊmənl|ɪ, -ɪnɪs [-nəs]

womb, -s wuːm, -z

wombat, -s 'wɒmbət [-bæt], -s

Wombwell (*place in South Yorkshire*) 'wʊmwel [-wəl], (*surname*) 'wʊmwəl, 'wʌm-, 'wɒm-

women (*plur. of* woman) 'wɪmɪn

womenfolk 'wɪmɪnfəʊk

won (*from* win) wʌn

wond|er, -ers, -ering|ly, -ered, -erer/s 'wʌnd|ə*, -əz, -ərɪŋ/lɪ, -əd, -ərə*/z

wonder|ful, -fully, -fulness 'wʌndə|fʊl, -flɪ [-fʊlɪ, -fəlɪ], -fʊlnɪs [-nəs]

Wonderland 'wʌndələænd

wonderment 'wʌndəmənt

wonder-worker, -s 'wʌndə‚wɜːkə*, -z

wondrous, -ly, -ness 'wʌndrəs, -lɪ, -nɪs [-nəs]

wonk|y, -ier, -iest, -ily, -iness 'wɒŋk|ɪ, -ɪə*, -ɪɪst, -ɪlɪ [-əlɪ], -ɪnɪs [-nəs]

wont (*s. adj.*), -ed wəʊnt, -ɪd

won't wəʊnt [*also* wəʊn *when not final, also* wəʊmp *before the sounds* p, b, m, *and* wəʊŋk *before* k, g]

woo, -s, -ing, -ed, -er/s wuː, -z, -ɪŋ ['wʊɪŋ], -d, -ə*/z [wʊə*/z]

Wooburn 'wuːbɜːn

wood (W.), -s, -ed wʊd, -z, -ɪd

woodbind 'wʊdbaɪnd

woodbine (W.), -s 'wʊdbaɪn, -z

woodblock, -s 'wʊdblɒk, -s

Woodbridge 'wʊdbrɪdʒ

Woodbury 'wʊdbərɪ

wood-carv|er/s, -ing 'wʊd‚kɑːv|ə*/z, -ɪŋ

woodchuck, -s 'wʊdtʃʌk, -s

woodcock (W.), -s 'wʊdkɒk, -s

woodcut, -s 'wʊdkʌt, -s

wood-cutter, -s 'wʊd‚kʌtə*, -z

wooden, -ly, -ness 'wʊdn, -lɪ, -nɪs [-nəs]

wooden-headed 'wʊdn‚hedɪd [‚--'--]

Wood|ford, -house 'wʊd|fəd, -haʊs

woodland, -s 'wʊdlənd, -z

wood-|louse, -lice 'wʊd|laʊs, -laɪs

wood|man (W.), -men 'wʊd|mən, -mən

wood-nymph, -s 'wʊdnɪmf, -s

wood-pavement ‚wʊd'peɪvmənt ['-‚--]

woodpecker, -s 'wʊd‚pekə*, -z

wood-pigeon, -s 'wʊd‚pɪdʒɪn [-dʒən], -z

Woodroffe 'wʊdrɒf, -rʌf

Woodrow 'wʊdrəʊ

woodruff (W.), -s 'wʊdrʌf, -s

Woods wʊdz

Woodside ‚wʊd'saɪd ['--]

Wood|stock, -ward 'wʊd|stɒk, -wəd

wood-wind, -s 'wʊdwɪnd, -z

woodwork 'wʊdwɜːk

wood|y, -ier, -iest, -iness 'wʊd|ɪ, -ɪə*, -ɪɪst, -ɪnɪs [-nəs]

woof, -s (*weaving*) wuːf, -s (*dog's bark*) wʊf

Woof (*surname*) wʊf

Wookey 'wʊkɪ

wool, -s wʊl, -z

Wooldridge 'wʊldrɪdʒ

Woolf wʊlf

Woolfardisworthy (*near Bideford, Devon*) 'wʊlzərɪ [wʊl'fɑːdɪs‚wɜːðɪ], (*near Crediton, Devon*) wʊl'fɑːdɪs‚wɜːðɪ

wool-gathering 'wʊl‚gæðərɪŋ

Woollard 'wʊlɑːd

woollen 'wʊlən [-lɪn]

Woolley 'wʊlɪ

Woolliams 'wʊljəmz

wooll|y (*s. adj.*), -ies, -ier, -iest, -iness 'wʊl|ɪ, -ɪz, -ɪə*, -ɪɪst, -ɪnɪs [-nəs]

woolly-headed 'wʊlɪ‚hedɪd [‚--'--]

Wooln|er, -ough 'wʊln|ə*, -əʊ

woolsack 'wʊlsæk

woolsey (W.) 'wʊlzɪ

Woolwich 'wʊlɪdʒ [-ɪtʃ]

woolwork 'wʊlwɜːk

Woolworth 'wʊlwəθ [-wɜːθ]

Woomera 'wʊmərə ['wuː-]

Woorstead 'wʊstɪd [-təd]

Woosley 'wuːzlɪ

Wooster 'wʊstə*

Wootton 'wʊtn

Worcester, -shire 'wʊstə*, -ʃə* [-‚ʃɪə*]

Worcs. wɜːks

word (*s. v.*), -s, -ing/s, -ed; -less wɜːd, -z, -ɪŋ/z, -ɪd; -lɪs [-ləs]

word-book, -s 'wɜːdbʊk, -s

word-formation 'wɜːdfɔː‚meɪʃn

word-painting 'wɜːd‚peɪntɪŋ

word-perfect ‚wɜːd'pɜːfɪkt

word-picture, -s 'wɜːd‚pɪktʃə*, -z

word-splitting 'wɜːd‚splɪtɪŋ

Wordsworth 'wɜːdzwəθ [-wɜːθ]

Wordsworthian wɜːdz'wɜːðjən [-ðɪən]

word|ly, -ier, -iest, -ily, -iness 'wɜːd|ɪ, -ɪə* [-jə*], -ɪɪst [-jɪst], -ɪlɪ [-əlɪ], -ɪnɪs [-nəs]

wore (*from* wear) wɔː* [wɔə*]

work, -s, -ing/s, -ed, -er/s; -able/ness wɜːk, -s, -ɪŋ/z, -t, -ə*/z; -əbl/nɪs [-nəs]

work-bag, -s ˈwɜːkbæg, -z
work-basket, -s ˈwɜːkˌbɑːskɪt, -s
workbook, -s ˈwɜːkbʊk, -s
work-box, -es ˈwɜːkbɒks, -ɪz
work-day, -s ˈwɜːkdeɪ, -z
workhou|se, -ses ˈwɜːkhaʊ|s, -zɪz
Workington ˈwɜːkɪŋtən
workless ˈwɜːklɪs [-ləs]
work|man (W.), -men; -manlike
 ˈwɜːk|mən, -mən; -mənlaɪk
workman|ly, -ship ˈwɜːkmən|lɪ, -ʃɪp
work-people ˈwɜːkˌpiːpl
work-room, -s ˈwɜːkrʊm [-ruːm], -z
workshop, -s ˈwɜːkʃɒp, -s
work-shy ˈwɜːkʃaɪ
Worksop ˈwɜːksɒp [-səp]
work-table, -s ˈwɜːkˌteɪbl, -z
world, -s wɜːld, -z
worldling, -s ˈwɜːldlɪŋ, -z
worldl|y, -ier, -iest, -iness ˈwɜːldl|ɪ, -ɪə*
 [-jə*], -ɪɪst [-jɪst], -ɪnɪs [-nəs]
worldly-minded ˌwɜːldlɪˈmaɪndɪd [ˈ--ˌ--]
worldly-wise ˌwɜːldlɪˈwaɪz
world-wide ˈwɜːldwaɪd [also ˌ-ˈ- when
 not attributive]
worm (s. v.), -s, -ing, -ed wɜːm, -z, -ɪŋ,
 -d
Worman ˈwɔːmən
worm-cast, -s ˈwɜːmkɑːst, -s
worm-eaten ˈwɜːmˌiːtn
worm-gear, -s ˈwɜːmˌgɪə*, -z
worm-hole, -s ˈwɜːmhəʊl, -z
Worms (German city) vɔːmz [wɜːmz]
 (vɔrms)
wormwood (W.) ˈwɜːmwʊd
worm|y, -iness ˈwɜːm|ɪ, -ɪnɪs [-məs]
worn (from wear) wɔːn
worn-out ˌwɔːnˈaʊt [ˈ-- when attribu-
 tive]
Worple, -sdon ˈwɔːpl, -zdən
Worrall ˈwʌrəl, wɒrəl
worr|y (s. v.), -ies, -ying/ly, -ied, -ier/s
 ˈwʌr|ɪ, -ɪz, -ɪŋ/lɪ, -ɪd, -ɪə*/z
Worsborough ˈwɜːzbərə
worse wɜːs
wors|en, -ens, -ening, -ened ˈwɜːs|n,
 -nz, -nɪŋ [-ṇɪŋ], -nd
Worsfold ˈwɜːsfəʊld, ˈwɔːzfəʊld
worship (s. v.) (W.), -s, -ping, -ped,
 -per/s ˈwɜːʃɪp, -s, -ɪŋ, -t, -ə*/z
worship|ful, -fully, -fulness ˈwɜːʃɪp|fʊl,
 -fʊlɪ [-fəlɪ], -fʊlnɪs [-nəs]
Worsley (surname) ˈwɜːslɪ, ˈwɜːzlɪ,
 (place near Manchester) ˈwɜːslɪ
Worsnop ˈwɜːznəp
worst (s. adj. v.), -s, -ing, -ed wɜːst, -s,
 -ɪŋ, -ɪd
Worstead ˈwʊstɪd [-təd]

worsted (s.) (yarn, cloth) ˈwʊstɪd [-təd]
worsted (v.) (from worst) ˈwɜːstɪd
Worswick (surname) ˈwɜːsɪk
wort, -s wɜːt, -s
worth (W.), -s wɜːθ, -s
Worthing, -ton ˈwɜːðɪŋ, -tən
worthless, -ly, -ness ˈwɜːθlɪs [-ləs], -lɪ,
 -nɪs [-nəs]
worthwhile ˌwɜːθˈwaɪl [-ˈhwaɪl]
worth|y (s. adj.), -ies, -ier, -iest, -ily,
 -iness ˈwɜːð|ɪ, -ɪz, -ɪə* [-jə*], -ɪɪst
 [-jɪst], -ɪlɪ [-əlɪ], -ɪnɪs [-nəs]
Wortley ˈwɜːtlɪ
wot wɒt
Wotherspoon ˈwɒðəspuːn
Wotton ˈwɒtn, ˈwʊtn
 Note.—The place in Buckinghamshire is called ˈwʊtn.
would (from will) wʊd (strong form),
 wəd, əd, d (weak forms)
would-be ˈwʊdbiː [-bɪ]
wouldn't ˈwʊdnt
wound (s. v.), -s, -ing, -ed wuːnd, -z, -ɪŋ,
 -ɪd
wound (from wind, v.) waʊnd
wove (from weave), -n wəʊv, -ən
wow, -s waʊ, -z
wrack, -s ræk, -s
wraith, -s reɪθ, -s
wrang|le, -les, -ling, -led, -ler/s ˈræŋg|l,
 -lz, -lɪŋ [-l̩ŋ], -ld, -lə*/z [-l̩ə*/z]
wrangler (candidate obtaining first class
 in mathematical tripos), -s ˈræŋglə*,
 -z
wrap (s. v.), -s, -ping/s, -ped ræp, -s,
 -ɪŋ/z, -t
wrapper, -s ˈræpə*, -z
wrasse, -s ræs, -ɪz
wrath rɒθ [rɔː]
Wrath (Cape) rɔːθ [in Scotland raθ, also
 rɑːθ, ræθ]
wrath|ful, -fully, -fulness ˈrɒθ|fʊl
 [ˈrɔːθ-], -fʊlɪ [-fəlɪ], -fʊlnɪs [-nəs]
Wratislaw (English surname) ˈrætɪslɔː
Wraxall ˈræksɔːl
Wray reɪ
wreak, -s, -ing, -ed, -er/s riːk, -s, -ɪŋ, -t,
 -ə*/z
wrea|th, -ths riː|θ, -ðz [-θs]
wreath|e, -es, -ing, -ed riːð, -z, -ɪŋ, -d
Wreay (in Cumbria) reɪ [locally rɪə]
wreck (s. v.), -s, -ing, -ed, -er/s; -age/s
 rek, -s, -ɪŋ, -t, -ə*/z; -ɪdʒ/ɪz
Wrekin ˈriːkɪn
wren (W.), -s ren, -z
wrench (s. v.), -es, -ing, -ed rentʃ, -ɪz,
 -ɪŋ, -t
Wrenn ren

wrest, -s, -ing, -ed rest, -s, -ɪŋ, -ɪd
wrest|le, -les, -ling, -led, -ler/s 'res|l,
  -lz, -lɪŋ [-lɪŋ], -ld, -lə*/z [-lə*/z]
wretch, -es retʃ, -ɪz
wretched, -ly, -ness 'retʃɪd, -lɪ, -nɪs
  [-nəs]
Wrexham 'reksəm
wrigg|le, -les, -ling, -led, -ler/s 'rɪg|l,
  -lz, -lɪŋ [-lɪŋ], -ld, -lə*/z [-lə*/z]
wright (W.), -s raɪt, -s
Wrigley 'rɪglɪ
wring, -s, -ing, wrung rɪŋ, -z, -ɪŋ, rʌŋ
wrink|le, -les, -ling, -led 'rɪŋk|l, -lz, -lɪŋ
  [-lɪŋ], -ld
wrinkly 'rɪŋklɪ
Wriothesley 'raɪəθslɪ
wrist, -s rɪst, -s
wristband, -s 'rɪstbænd, -z
wristlet, -s 'rɪstlɪt [-lət], -s
wrist-watch, -es 'rɪstwɒtʃ, -ɪz
writ (s.), -s rɪt, -s
writ (=written) rɪt
writ|e, -es, -ing/s, wrote, written,
  writer/s raɪt, -s, -ɪŋ/z, rəʊt, 'rɪtn,
  'raɪtə*/z
writh|e, -es, -ing, -ed raɪð, -z, -ɪŋ, -d
writing (s.), -s 'raɪtɪŋ, -z
writing-case, -s 'raɪtɪŋkeɪs, -ɪz
writing-desk, -s 'raɪtɪŋdesk, -s
writing-paper 'raɪtɪŋˌpeɪpə*
writing-table, -s 'raɪtɪŋˌteɪbl, -z
written-off ˌrɪtn'ɒf [old-fashioned -'ɔːf]
Wroclaw (formerly Breslau) 'vrɒtslɑːf
  [-æf, -tswɑːf]
wrong (s. adj. v.) (W.), -s; -ly, -ness;
  -ing, -ed rɒŋ, -z; -lɪ, -nɪs [-nəs]; -ɪŋ, -d
wrong-doer, -s ˌrɒŋ'dʊə* [-'duː*,
  'rɒŋˌdʊə*, 'rɒŋˌduː*], -z
wrong-doing ˌrɒŋ'duːɪŋ [-'dʊɪŋ, 'rɒŋ-
  ˌduːɪŋ, -ˌdʊɪŋ]
wrong|ful, -fully, -fulness 'rɒŋ|fʊl, -fʊlɪ
  [-fəlɪ], -fʊlnɪs [-nəs]
wrongheaded, -ly, -ness ˌrɒŋ'hedɪd, -lɪ,
  -nɪs [-nəs]
Wrose rəʊz, rəʊs
wrote (from write) rəʊt
wroth rəʊθ [rɔːθ, rɒθ]

Wrotham (in Kent) 'ruːtəm
Wrottesley 'rɒtslɪ
wrought rɔːt
wrought-|iron, -up ˌrɔːt|'aɪən, -'ʌp
Wroxham 'rɒksəm
wrung (from wring) rʌŋ
W.R.V.S. ˌdʌblju:ɑːvi:'es [-jʊɑː-]
wry|y, -ier [-yer], -iest [-yest], -yly,
  -yness r|aɪ, -aɪə*, -aɪɪst, -aɪlɪ, -aɪnɪs
  [-aɪnəs]
wryneck, -s 'raɪnek, -s
Wrythe raɪð
Wulf wʊlf
Wulfila 'wʊlfɪlə
Wulfstan 'wʊlfstən
Wurlitzer, -* 'wɜːlɪtsə*, -z
Württemberg 'vɜːtəmbeəg ['wɜːtəm-
  bɜːg] ('vyrtəmberk)
Wuthering 'wʌðərɪŋ
W.V.S. ˌdʌblju:vi:'es [-jʊ-]
Wyandotte, -s 'waɪəndɒt, -s
Wyat(t) 'waɪət
Wych waɪtʃ, wɪtʃ
wych-elm, -s ˌwɪtʃ'elm ['--], -z
Wycherley 'wɪtʃəlɪ
wych-hazel, -s 'wɪtʃheɪzl [ˌ-'--], -z
Wyclif(fe) 'wɪklɪf
Wyclif(f)ite, -s 'wɪklɪfaɪt, -s
Wycombe 'wɪkəm
Wye waɪ
Wygram 'waɪgrəm
Wykeham, -ist/s 'wɪkəm, -ɪst/s
Wyld(e) waɪld
Wyl(l)ie 'waɪlɪ
Wylly 'waɪlɪ
Wyman 'waɪmən
Wymondham (in Norfolk) 'wɪməndəm
  [locally 'wɪndəm], (in Leicestershire)
  'waɪməndəm
Wyndham 'wɪndəm
Wynn(e) wɪn
Wynyard 'wɪnjəd [-jɑːd]
Wyoming waɪ'əʊmɪŋ
Wysard 'waɪzɑːd
Wytham 'waɪtəm
Wythenshawe 'wɪðənʃɔː
wyvern (W.), -s 'waɪvən [-vɜːn], -z

X

X (*the letter*), **-'s** eks, -ɪz
Xanadu 'zænədu:
Xanthipp|e, -us zæn'θɪp|ɪ [gz-, -n'tɪ-], -əs
Xanthus 'zænθəs ['gz-]
Xavier 'zævɪə* ['zeɪv-, -vjə*] (xaˈbjer)
xebec, -s 'ziːbek, -s
Xenia 'zenɪə [gz-, ks-, -eɪn-, -njə]
xenogamy ziːˈnɒgəmɪ [gz-, zɪ-]
xenon 'zenɒn ['gz-]
xenophobe, -s 'zenəfəʊb ['gz-, -nəʊf-], -z
xenophobia ˌzenəˈfəʊbjə [ˌgz-, -nəʊˈf-, -bɪə]
Xenophon 'zenəfən ['gz-]

xerography ˌzɪəˈrɒgrəfɪ [ze'r-]
xerox (*s. v.*), **-es, -ing, -ed** 'zɪərɒks, -ɪz, -ɪŋ, -t
Xerxes 'zɜːksiːz ['gz-]
Xhosa 'kɔːsə ['kəʊsə, kl-] (ǁhɔːsa)
xi (*Greek letter*), **-'s** saɪ [gzaɪ, zaɪ], -z
Xmas 'krɪsməs [-stm-]
X-ray (*s. v.*), **-s, -ing, -ed** ˌeksˈreɪ ['--], -z, -ɪŋ, -d
xylograph, -s 'zaɪləgrɑːf ['gz-, -ləʊg-, -græf], -s
xylograph|er/s, -y zaɪˈlɒgrəf|ə*/z [gz-], -ɪ
xylonite 'zaɪlənaɪt ['gz-, -ləʊn-]
xylophone, -s 'zaɪləfəʊn ['gz-, 'zɪl-], -z

556

Y

Y (*the letter*), **-'s** waɪ, -z
yacht (*s. v.*), **-s, -ing, -ed** jɒt, -s, -ɪŋ, -bɪ-
yachts|man, -men 'jɒts|mən, -mən
yah jɑː
yahoo, -s jə'huː [jɑː'h-], -z
Yahveh 'jɑːveɪ [jɑː'veɪ, 'jɑːvə]
yak, -s jæk, -s
Yakutsk jæ'kʊtsk [jɑː'k-, jə'k-]
(ji'kutsk)
Yalding (*surname*) 'jældɪŋ, (*place name*)
'jɔːldɪŋ
Yale jeɪl
Yalta 'jæltə
yam, -s jæm, -z
Yangtse-Kiang ˌjæŋtsɪ'kjæŋ [-kɪ'æŋ]
yank (**Y.**), **-s, -ing, -ed** jæŋk, -s, -ɪŋ, -t
[-jæŋt]
Yankee, -s 'jæŋkɪ, -z
yap, -s, -ping, -ped jæp, -s, -ɪŋ, -t
yappy 'jæpɪ
yard, -s jɑːd, -z
yardarm, -s 'jɑːdɑːm, -z
Yardley 'jɑːdlɪ
yard-stick, -s 'jɑːdstɪk, -s
Yare (*in Norfolk*) jeə*, (*in the Isle of
Wight*) jɑː:*
Yarico 'jærɪkəʊ
Yarmouth 'jɑːməθ
yarn (*s. v.*), **-s, -ing, -ed** jɑːn, -z, -ɪŋ, -d
yarrow (**Y.**) 'jærəʊ
yashmak, -s 'jæʃmæk, -s
yataghan, -s 'jætəgən, -z
Yate, -s jeɪt, -s
Yatman 'jætmən
yaw (*s. v.*), **-s, -ing, -ed** jɔː, -z, -ɪŋ, -d
yawl, -s jɔːl, -z
yawn (*s. v.*), **-s, -ing/ly, -ed** jɔːn, -z,
-ɪŋ/lɪ, -d
yaws jɔːz
yclept ɪ'klept
ye (*you*) jiː: (*normal form*), jɪ (*occasional
weak form*)
ye (*the*) jiː: [*or as* **the**, *q.v.*]
yea jeɪ
Yeading 'jedɪŋ
yeah jeə
Yealm jæm
Yealmpton 'jæmptən
Yeames jiːmz

yean, -s, -ing, -ed jiːn, -z, -ɪŋ, -d
yeanling, -s 'jiːnlɪŋ, -z
year, -s, -ly jɜ:* [jɪə*], -z, -lɪ
year-book, -s 'jɜːbʊk ['jɪəb-], -s
yearling, -s 'jɜːlɪŋ ['jɪəl-], -z
yearn, -s, -ing/s, -ed jɜːn, -z, -ɪŋ/z, -d
yeast, -y, -iness jiːst, -ɪ, -ɪnɪs [-məs]
Yeat(e)s jeɪts
Yeatman 'jiːtmən, 'jeɪtmən, 'jetmən
Yeddo (*old name of Tokyo*) 'jedəʊ
Yehudi je'huːdɪ [jɪ'h-, jə'h-]
yelk jelk
yell (*s. v.*) (**Y.**), **-s, -ing, -ed** jel, -z, -ɪŋ,
-d
yellow, -s, -ed 'jeləʊ, -z, -d
yellow-ammer, -s 'jeləʊˌæmə*, -z
yellow-band 'jeləʊbænd
yellow-hammer, -s 'jeləʊˌhæmə*, -z
yellowish, -ness 'jeləʊɪʃ, -nɪs [-nəs]
yellowness 'jeləʊnɪs [-nəs]
yellowplush 'jeləʊplʌʃ
Yellowstone 'jeləʊstəʊn [-stən]
yellowy 'jeləʊɪ
yelp (*s. v.*), **-s, -ing, -ed** jelp, -s, -ɪŋ, -t
Yemen, -i, -is 'jemən, -ɪ, -ɪz
yen, -s jen, -z
Yeo jəʊ
Yeoburgh 'jɑːbərə
yeo|man, -men 'jəʊ|mən, -mən
yeoman|ly, -ry 'jəʊmən|lɪ, -rɪ
Yeomans 'jəʊmənz
Yeovil 'jəʊvɪl
Yerkes (*American name*) 'jɜːkiːz
yes jes [jeə]
yes|-man, -men 'jes|mæn, -men
yesterday 'jestədɪ [-deɪ, 'jestdɪ, ˌjestə-
'deɪ]
yet jet
Yetholm 'jetəm
yeti, -s 'jetɪ, -z
yew, -s juː, -z
Yg(g)drasil 'ɪgdræsl ['ɪgdrəsɪl]
Y-gun, -s 'waɪgʌn, -z
Yiddish 'jɪdɪʃ
yield (*s. v.*), **-s, -ing/ly, -ed** jiːld, -z,
-ɪŋ/lɪ, -ɪd
y-ness 'waɪnɪs [-nəs]
yobo, -s 'jɒbəʊ, -z
yod, -s jɒd, -z

557

yod|el (*s. v.*), **-els, -el(l)ing, -el(l)ed** 'jəʊd|l ['jɒd-], -lz, -lɪŋ [-əlɪŋ], -ld

yog, -a, -i/s, -ism 'jəʊg, -ə, -ɪ/z, -ɪzəm

yogh(o)urt 'jɒgət ['jəʊg-, -gɜːt, -gʊət]

yo-ho jəʊ'həʊ

yoick, -s, -ing, -ed jɔɪk, -s, -ɪŋ, -t

yoicks (*interj.*) jɔɪks

yok|e (*s. v.*), **-es, -ing, -ed** jəʊk, -s, -ɪŋ, -t

yokel, -s 'jəʊkl, -z

Yokohama ˌjəʊkəʊ'hɑːmə

yolk, -s, -y jəʊk, -s, -ɪ

Yom Kippur ˌjɒm'kɪpə* [-kɪ'pʊə*]

yon(d) jɒn(d)

yonder 'jɒndə*

Yonge jʌŋ

yore jɔː* [jɔə*]

Yorick 'jɒrɪk

York, -shire jɔːk, -ʃə* [-ˌʃɪə*]

Yorke jɔːk

yorker, -s 'jɔːkə*, -z

Yorkist, -s 'jɔːkɪst, -s

Yorks. jɔːks

Yorkshire|man, -men 'jɔːkʃə|mən, -mən [-men]

Yoruba 'jɒrʊbə ['jəʊ-]

Yosemite jəʊ'semɪtɪ

Yost, -s jəʊst, -s

yotization [-isa-], -s ˌjəʊtaɪ'zeɪʃn [ˌjɒt-, -tɪ'z-], -z

yotiz|e [-is|e], **-es, -ing, -ed** 'jəʊtaɪz ['jɒt-], -ɪz, -ɪŋ, -d

you juː (*normal form*), jʊ (*freq. weak form*), jə (*occasional weak form*)

> Note 1.—Sometimes when **you** *is weakly stressed and is preceded by a word normally ending in* d, *the two words are joined closely together as if they formed a single word with the 'affricate' sound* dʒ *linking the two parts. Thus* **did you** *is often pronounced* 'dɪdʒuː (*or* 'dɪdʒʊ), *and* **behind you** *by* bɪ'haɪndʒu: [-dʒʊ].
>
> Similarly *when the preceding word normally ends in* t; *i.e.* **hurt you** *is sometimes pronounced* 'hɜːtʃuː *or* 'hɜːtʃʊ, *and* **don't you know** *as* ˌdəʊntʃuː'nəʊ [-tʃʊ-] *or* ˌdəʊntʃə'nəʊ. *See also* **what-you-may-call-it.**
>
> Note 2.—jʊ *occurs as a strong form in the expression* **you are** *when* **are** *has its weak form* ə*.* **You are** *in this*

case is also written **you're.** *For other variants used in this case see* **you're.**

Youghal (*near Cork*) jɔːl, (*on Lake Derg*) 'jɒkəl ['jɒxəl]

Youmans 'juːmənz

young (*s. adj.*) (**Y.**), **-er, -est** jʌŋ, -gə*, -gɪst

Younger 'jʌŋə*, 'jʌŋgə*

Younghusband 'jʌŋˌhʌzbənd

youngish 'jʌŋɪʃ [-ŋgɪ-]

Youngman 'jʌŋmən

youngster, -s 'jʌŋstə* [-ŋks-], -z

younker, -s 'jʌŋkə*, -z

your jɔː* [jɔə*, *rarely* jʊə*] (*normal forms*), jə* (*occasional weak form*)

you're (=you are) jʊə* [jɔə*, jɔː*]

yours jɔːz [jɔəz, *rarely* jʊəz]

yoursel|f, -ves jɔː'sel|f, [jɔə's-, *rarely* ˌjʊə's-, jɔ's-], -vz

you|th, -ths juː|θ, -ðz

youth|ful, -fully, -fulness 'juːθ|fʊl, -fʊlɪ [-fəlɪ], -fʊlnɪs [-nəs]

you've (=you have) juːv (*normal form*), jʊv, jəv (*occasional weak forms*)

yo-yo, -s 'jəʊjəʊ, -z

Ypres (*in Belgium*) 'iːprə ['iːpəz, *sometimes facetiously* 'aɪpəz, 'waɪpəz] (ipr)

Ypres (*tower at Rye*) 'iːprə ['iːpreɪ, 'waɪpəz]

> Note.—*The* '*Ypres Castle*', *a public house near by, is called locally the* 'waɪpəz.

Ysaye ɪ'zaɪ [ɪ'zaɪ]

Yser (*in Belgium*) 'iːzə* (izɛːr)

Ysolde ɪ'zɒldə

Ystradgynlais ˌɪstræd'gɪnlaɪs [ˌʌstræd-'gʌnlaɪs] (*Welsh* əstrad'gənlais)

Ythan 'aɪθən

ytterbium ɪ'tɜːbjəm [-bɪəm]

yttrium 'ɪtrɪəm

Y-tube, -s 'waɪtjuːb, -z

Yucatan ˌjuːkə'tɑːn [jʊk-, -'tæn]

yucca, -s 'jʌkə, -z

Yugoslav, -s ˌjuːgəʊ'slɑːv ['---], -z

Yugoslavia, -n ˌjuːgəʊ'slɑːvjə [-vɪə], -n

Yuill 'juːɪl ['jʊɪl]

Yukon 'juːkɒn

Yule juːl

yulery 'juːlərɪ

Yuletide 'juːltaɪd

Yum-Yum ˌjʌm'jʌm

Yussuf 'jʊsʊf [-səf]

Z

Z (*the letter*), -'s zed, -z
Zabulon 'zæbjʊlən [zəˈbjuːlən, zæˈbjuː-]
Zacchaeus zæˈkiːəs [zəˈk-, -ˈkɪəs]
Zachariah ˌzækəˈraɪə
Zacharias ˌzækəˈraɪəs [-ˈraɪæs]
Zachary 'zækərɪ
Zadok 'zeɪdɒk
Zagreb 'zɑːgreb ['zæ-]
Zaïr|e, -ean zɑːˈɪə* [-ˈiːə*], -rɪən
Zalmunna zælˈmʌnə
Zama 'zɑːmə
Zambez|i, -ia zæmˈbiːz|ɪ, -jə [-ɪə]
Zambia, -n 'zæmbɪə [-bjə], -n
Zambra 'zæmbrə
Zangwill 'zæŋgwɪl
zan|y, -ies 'zeɪn|ɪ, -ɪz
Zanzibar ˌzænzɪˈbɑː*
Zarathustra ˌzærəˈθuːstrə [ˌzɑː-r-]
zareba, -s zəˈriːbə, -z
Zarephath 'zærɪfæθ [-ref-, -rəf-]
Zaria 'zɑːrɪə
zeal ziːl
Zealand, -er/s 'ziːlənd, -ə*/z
zealot, -s, -ry 'zelət, -s, -rɪ
zealous, -ly, -ness 'zeləs, -lɪ, -nɪs [-nəs]
Zebah 'ziːbə
Zebedee 'zebɪdiː
zebra, -s 'zebrə ['ziːb-], -z
zebu, -s 'ziːbuː, -z
Zebub 'ziːbʌb [-bəb, *rarely* zɪˈbʌb]
Zebulon 'zebjʊlən [zeˈbjuːlən]
Zechariah ˌzekəˈraɪə
zed, -s zed, -z
Zedekiah ˌzedɪˈkaɪə
Zeeb 'ziːeb [ziːb]
Zeeland 'zeɪlənd ['ziːl-]
Zeiss, -es zaɪs, -ɪz
Zeitgeist 'tsaɪtgaɪst ['zaɪt-] ('tsaitgaist)
Zeller (*wine*) 'zelə*
Zelotes ziːˈləʊtiːz [zɪˈl-]
zemindar, -s 'zemɪndɑː*, -z
zemstvo, -s 'zemstvəʊ ('zjemstvə), -z
Zen zen
Zena 'ziːnə
zenana, -s zeˈnɑːnə [zɪˈn-], -z
Zend zend
zenith, -s 'zenɪθ ['ziːn-], -s
Zeno 'ziːnəʊ

Zenobia zɪˈnəʊbjə [zeˈn-, -bɪə]
Zephaniah ˌzefəˈnaɪə
zephyr (Z.), -s 'zefə*, -z
zeppelin (Z.), -s 'zepəlɪn [-pḷɪn], -z
Zermatt 'zɜːmæt
zero, -s 'zɪərəʊ, -z
zerography ˌzɪəˈrɒgrəfɪ [zeˈr-]
Zerubbabel zɪˈrʌbəbl [zəˈr-, *in Jewish
    usage also* zɪˈruːˌbɑː-, zəˈruːˌbɑː-]
Zeruiah ˌzerʊˈaɪə [-rjʊ-]
zest zest
zeta, -s 'ziːtə, -z
Zetland 'zetlənd
zeugma, -s 'zjuːgmə ['zuː-], -z
Zeus zjuːs
Zidon 'zaɪdn [-dɒn]
zigzag (*s. v.*), -s, -ging, -ged 'zɪgzæg, -z,
    -ɪŋ, -d
Ziklag 'zɪklæg
Zilliacus ˌzɪlɪˈɑːkəs, -'eɪkəs
Zimbabwe zɪmˈbɑːbwɪ [-'bæ-, -bweɪ]
Zimri 'zɪmraɪ
zinc (*s. v.*), -s, -king, -ked zɪŋk, -s, -ɪŋ, -t
zin(c)ky 'zɪŋkɪ
zinco, -s 'zɪŋkəʊ, -z
zincograph, -s 'zɪŋkəʊgrɑːf [-græf], -s
zingar|o, -i 'zɪŋgər|əʊ, -iː
zinnia, -s 'zɪnjə [-nɪə], -z
Zion, -ism, -ist/s, -ward/s 'zaɪən, -ɪzəm,
    -ɪst/s, -wəd/z
zip, -s zɪp, -s
zip-fastener, -s 'zɪpˌfɑːsnə* [ˌ-ˈ--], -z
zipper, -s 'zɪpə*, -z
Zippor 'zɪpɔː* [zɪˈpɔː*]
Zipporah zɪˈpɔːrə [*rarely* 'zɪpərə]
zirconium zɜːˈkəʊnjəm [-nɪəm]
zither, -s 'zɪðə* ['zɪθə*], -z
zloty, -s 'zlɒtɪ, -z
Zoar 'zəʊɑː* ['zəʊə*]
zodiac 'zəʊdɪæk [-djæk]
zodiacal zəʊˈdaɪəkl
Zoe 'zəʊɪ
zoetrope, -s 'zəʊɪtrəʊp, -s
zoic 'zəʊɪk
Zola 'zəʊlə
zollverein, -s 'tsɒlfəraɪn ['zɒlvəraɪn]
    ('tsɔlfərʔain), -z
zombie, -s 'zɒmbɪ, -z
zon|al, -ally 'zəʊn|l [-əl], -əlɪ

zon|e (*s. v.*), **-es, -ing, -ed; -eless** zəʊn,
-z, -ɪŋ, -d; -lɪs [-əl]

Zoo, -s zuː, -z

zoograph|er/s, -y zəʊˈɒgrəf|ə*/z, -ɪ

zooks zuːks

zoolite, -s ˈzəʊəlaɪt [ˈzəʊəʊl-], -s

zoologic|al, -ally ˌzəʊəˈlɒdʒɪk|l [zʊəˈl-,
zʊˈl-], -əlɪ

Zoological Garden, -s zʊˌlɒdʒɪklˈgɑːdn
[zəʊˌl-, zʊə,l-, zə,l-, zlˌɒdʒ-, ˌzlɒdʒ-,
-ɒdʒk-], -z

zoolog|ist/s, -y zəʊˈɒlədʒ|ɪst/s [zʊˈɒl-], -ɪ

zoom, -s, -ing, -ed zuːm, -z, -ɪŋ, -d

zoomorphic ˌzəʊəˈmɔːfɪk

zo|on, -a ˈzəʊ|ɒn, -ə

zoophyte, -s ˈzəʊəfaɪt, -s

zoot, -s zuːt, -s

zootom|ist/s, -y zəʊˈɒtəm|ɪst/s, -ɪ

Zophar ˈzəʊfɑː* [-fə*]

zoril, -s ˈzɒrɪl, -z

Zoroaster ˌzɒrəʊˈæstə*

Zoroastrian, -s, -ism ˌzɒrəʊˈæstrɪən, -z,
-ɪzəm

zouave (Z.), -s zuːˈɑːv [zʊˈɑːv, zwɑːv,
ˈzuːɑːv], -z

Zouch(e) zuːʃ

zounds zaʊndz [zuːndz]

Zuleika (*Persian name*) zuːˈleɪkə [zʊˈl-,
-ˈlaɪkə], (*as English personal name*)
zuːˈleɪkə [zʊˈl-]

Zulu, -s ˈzuːluː, -z

Zululand ˈzuːluːlænd

Zürich ˈzjʊərɪk [ˈzʊə-] (ˈtsyːriç)

Zutphen ˈzʌtfən

Zuyder Zee ˌzaɪdəˈzeɪ [-ˈziː]

zwieback, -s ˈzwiːbæk [-bɑːk]
(ˈtsviːbak), -s

zygoma, -ta zaɪˈgəʊmə [zɪˈg-], -tə

zymosis zaɪˈməʊsɪs [zɪˈm-]

zymotic zaɪˈmɒtɪk [zɪˈm-]